EYEWITNESS HISTORY

# The 1980s

Elin Woodger
and
David F. Burg

☑ Facts On File
*An imprint of Infobase Publishing*

**The 1980s**

Facts On File, Inc.
An imprint of Infobase Publishing
132 West 31st Street
New York NY 10001

**Library of Congress Cataloging-in-Publication Data**
Woodger, Elin.
  The 1980s / Elin Woodger and David F. Burg.
    p.   cm.—(Eyewitness history)
  Includes bibliographical references and index.
  ISBN 0-8160-5809-1
    1. United States—History—1969–   —Juvenile literature. 2. United States—History—1969–   —Juvenile literature. 3. United States—Politics and government—1981–1989—Juvenile literature. 4. Nineteen eighties—Juvenile literature. I. Burg, David F. II. Title. III. Series.
  E876.W666 2006
973.92—dc22                                            2005018732

Facts On File books are available at special discounts when purchased in bulk quantities for businesses, associations, institutions, or sales promotions. Please call our Special Sales Department in New York at (212) 967-8800 or (800) 322-8755.

You can find Facts On File on the World Wide Web at http://www.factsonfile.com

Text design by Joan M. McEvoy
Cover design by Cathy Rincon
Maps and graphs by Sholto Ainslie

Printed in the United States of America

VB JM 10 9 8 7 6 5 4 3 2 1

This book is printed on acid-free paper.

*For my sisters Laura, Susan, and Elizabeth,*
*without whom I never would have made it through the 1980s—*
*and for Barbara and Mom.*

—Elin Woodger

# CONTENTS

# ACKNOWLEDGMENTS

Thanks are due first of all to Nicole Bowen and Laura Shauger of Facts On File. Their advice, encouragement, and patience in answering all sorts of questions, from the intelligent ones to the very feeble, are appreciated more than words can say. Thanks also to Gene Brissie of James Peters Associates, who brought the authors together and made this fascinating project possible.

Eyewitness History: *The 1980s* is a book about the United States and Canada in the 1980s, but it was primarily written in England. The authors are extremely grateful to the staff of the British Library (BL) at St. Pancras, London, and to Brian Huff and his staff at the BL's Colindale extension; this book simply could not have been written without the BL's excellent resources.

Of course, the Internet proved another primary source of information. We would like to acknowledge particularly the Web site for The Eighties Club (http://eightiesclub.tripod.com/id4.htm), which is filled to the brim with tremendously helpful information and articles about the 1980s. Among other things, it provided much of the data used for the chronologies in this book, as did the 10th edition (1997) of *Encyclopedia of American Facts and Dates* by Gorton Carruth.

The authors wish to acknowledge with gratitude those helpful individuals who assisted in our search for photos: Karen Anson, Franklin D. Roosevelt Presidential Library and Museum; Bonnie Burlbaw, George Bush Presidential Library; Nancy Mirshah, Gerald R. Ford Library; David Stanhope, Jimmy Carter Library and Museum; and Josh Tenenbaum, Ronald Reagan Presidential Library. Particular thanks to Emma Perry of AP/Wide World Photos, Cora Bauer of Landov LLC, and Ron Mandelbaum of Photofest; extraspecial thanks to Photofest's Brent N. Earle, who gave new meaning to the phrase "above and beyond the call of duty."

Several people were good enough to read sections of this book and provide expert feedback that ensured accuracy and readability. For their invaluable assistance, sincerest thanks and gratitude are extended to Dr. Kurt J. Isselbacher of the Massachusetts General Hospital and to Elizabeth Adkins, director of global information management for Ford Motor Company. Thanks for their advice and contributions also go to William D. Caughlin, corporate archivist for SBC Communications, Inc; John Keess for a wealth of information on Canadian history; Susan Keess; Walter G. Korntheuer, former president of Dime Savings Bank of New York; Paul Lasewicz, IBM corporate archivist; and Phil Mooney, director of the Archives Department, The Coca-Cola Company. Our deepest gratitude goes to Daniel and Susan Cohen for their willingness to review the account of the Pan Am 103 tragedy; and to Laura Loehr, who patiently read the entire manuscript and provided a tremendous amount of helpful feedback. Thanks also to Paul Korntheuer for providing some useful material on the Iran-contra affair; and to Fred D. Adkins, Alan Keess, Paul Loehr, Rachael Murphy, Tim Murphy, Anne Quigley, and Herbert Woodger for their on-site and long-distance cheer-leading and input.

A note from Elin Woodger: In the last-but-definitely-not-least department, there is my husband, Lieutenant Colonel Norman Murphy, who not only endured without complaint (which had to be difficult) everything involved in the writing of this book but also came to my rescue time and again. Most of the biographies in Appendix B and the maps in Appendix C are his, but even more important was his help in shaping the book. Nobody could have had a more patient or thorough editor; his suggestions vastly improved the manuscript. Norman, words are inadequate to express my appreciation, but at least two are essential: Thank you.

# INTRODUCTION

What made the 1980s different? Supply-side economics? Greed and material acquisitions? Breakthroughs in technology and communications? The personal computer revolution? The emergence and frightening spread of AIDS? The triumphs and disasters of the space-shuttle program? High-profile political scandals, from Abscam to Iran-contra? The near-collapse of the savings-and-loan industry? Terrorist attacks against the United States overseas? The intensification of the cold war—or its sudden end?

The self-centered, self-absorbed 1970s had been known as the Me Decade, but pundits struggle to apply a label to the 1980s, when the United States experienced social and economic change even more strongly "me"-oriented. The 1970s had ended with a "malaise," a defeatist attitude, but by 1990 things had completely changed. The national feeling was euphoric as the United States, despite disasters and scandals, recovered the global dominance it had seemed in danger of losing, and millions of Americans enjoyed luxuries once the prerogative of a privileged few. With the fall of the Soviet Union in 1991, the United States became the major world power, leading in business, communications, scientific and medical knowledge, social advances—and human failings.

Many attribute the dramatic change to the "Reagan revolution"—the conservative juggernaut led by Republican president Ronald Reagan—and unquestionably the policies of his administration strongly influenced personal lifestyles and societal attitudes. Reagan symbolized a decade in which Americans repudiated the do-unto-others philosophy of the New Deal of the 1930s, the rise to world leadership of the 1940s, the desegregation efforts of the 1950s, and the Civil Rights movement and social legislation of the 1960s. Now they embraced a more materialistic outlook. It was a radical shift driven by such technological advances as personal computers, cable television, and fiber optics and by a growing determination to attain wealth and financial security faster than ever before. Capitalism ruled in the 1980s, and its virtues were confirmed for many when the Berlin Wall fell in 1989 and communist governments collapsed throughout Eastern Europe. From a U.S. perspective, this was the natural result of the rise in material acquisition that characterized the decade.

The 1980s were the years when Americans rejected the tenets of the past and focused on hopes for the future. To understand how this happened requires understanding the events that preceded a most remarkable decade in the nation's history.

## REJECTING THE NEW DEAL

A key factor in the malaise of the late 1970s was the lingering legacy of President Franklin Delano Roosevelt. Elected in 1932, when the country was suffering the

Franklin Delano Roosevelt, president from 1931 to 1945, initiated the New Deal policies that affected American society for most of the 20th century. *(Courtesy Franklin D. Roosevelt Library)*

worst of the Great Depression, Roosevelt believed that a government should care for its citizens. He therefore implemented programs that provided jobs and hope— a "New Deal" for Americans that included Social Security (1935), a form of insurance that provided guaranteed income for citizens in their old age. This was supplemented by further social legislation over the years, culminating in the measures championed by Lyndon Johnson in the 1960s.

Johnson was a natural successor to Roosevelt. Assuming the presidency in late 1963, he declared war on poverty and proposed programs to fight illiteracy and unemployment as well as to strengthen public services. To achieve his "Great Society," with legislation in the Roosevelt tradition, he pushed through Congress such measures as the Economic Opportunity Act and Civil Rights Act (1964), revisions to the Social Security Act that created Medicare and Medicaid (1965), the Voting Rights Act (1965), and the Civil Rights Acts of 1968. Yet even as Johnson earned praise for improving lives at home, he was criticized for his actions abroad and specifically for involving the country in the Vietnam War.

World War II had seen the United States take a triumphant place at the head of the world order, but it sometimes paid a heavy price. As the Vietnam War escalated in the 1960s, the loss of American lives was too heavy a price for many. Resistance to the war grew, and Washington came under increasing scrutiny; even as Congress passed laws guaranteeing social and medical security as well as civil rights for citizens, those same citizens were questioning the role of government in their lives. Demonstrations to protest federal policy became common, while the major social advances achieved by the Civil Rights movement led to a conservative backlash from those who opposed big government and the huge cost of Johnson's Great Society legislation. The more programs were enacted for the well-being of Americans, the more opponents attacked the wastefulness of a "welfare state" funded by reluctant American taxpayers.

Conservatives attacked government regulations as interference in private enterprise, while liberals complained that there were not enough controls. Accusations and denunciations were standard in the late 1960s and early 1970s: Business leaders were accused of failing labor, men were accused of hindering the political and economic advancement of women, white Americans were held responsible for race riots, and so on. It seemed one was either a guilty member of the Establishment, a protester against Establishment injustice, or a victim of it.

In the 1970s many Americans tired of expensive social legislation that not only affected their pocketbooks but created a sense of guilt that went against the grain. They were weary, too, of the war in Vietnam, which had exposed the myth of American military supremacy. Even former supporters of the war began to regard Vietnam as an appalling blunder. It became apparent that the government had deliberately misled the nation on the progress of the conflict, and such grue-

President Lyndon Baines Johnson signs the Civil Rights Act of 1964 as Martin Luther King, Jr., and others look on, July 2, 1964. *(Courtesy LBJ Library)*

some events as the My Lai massacre in 1969 had tarnished America's image as South Vietnam's savior. Most now wanted to quit a war initiated by one Democratic president, John F. Kennedy, and escalated by another, Lyndon Johnson. The task of ending the conflict was therefore entrusted to a Republican, Richard Nixon, who was elected in 1968 and reelected in 1972.

In 1973 the United States withdrew its remaining 23,000 troops from South Vietnam, ending the country's involvement. But any satisfaction that Americans might have felt in this was quickly offset by the Watergate scandal.

Richard Milhous Nixon, 37th president, took the country out of Vietnam and into the mire of the Watergate scandal. *(National Archives Nixon Presidential Materials Staff [NLNP-WHPO-MPF-C4538(1A2)])*

## LOSS OF FAITH

The story of the June 1972 break-in at the Watergate complex in Washington, D.C., needs no repeating here. Its significance, however, deserves examination. Americans had always felt free to criticize their political leaders and government policy, but there was a mystique associated with the presidency. A chief executive might be flawed, but he was entrusted with the country's leadership and expected to use his power properly. Although he was not above the law, it was tacitly accepted by the public that sometimes that principle had to be breached—for instance, when national security was threatened. If a president engaged in illicit or illegal activities, the country usually did not know or want to know about it—until Watergate.

The Watergate scandal broke the mold in many ways. In addition to unmasking corruption, lies, and deceit in the White House, it exposed a sitting president to scorn, diminishing the presidency itself. Richard Nixon was revealed as a paranoid individual whose many statesmanlike achievements were completely overshadowed by "dirty tricks," flagrant abuses of

President Gerald R. Ford's decent character and attempts to move the country beyond Watergate were not enough to win him the president's office in the 1976 election. *(Courtesy Gerald R. Ford Library)*

campaign-finance regulations, secret tapings of conversations, and the Watergate break-in and cover-up. With impeachment a certainty, in August 1974 Nixon became the first president to resign from office.

The scandal opened a deep wound in American society. Hoping to put Watergate to rest and allow the country to get back to normalcy and deal with other problems, the new president, Gerald Ford, granted Nixon an unconditional pardon in September 1974. Instead, he raised more controversy as critics claimed that his protection of Nixon was the price for his appointment to the vice presidency late in 1973 (following Spiro Agnew's resignation). The charge was never proven, but suspicions about the pardon scarred Ford's short presidency irretrievably.

Watergate spawned distrust in the probity of politicians in general, and government secrecy was severely criticized, leading to the Freedom of Information Act in November 1974. This law liberalized the 1966 act of the same name by imposing deadlines for federal agencies to meet requests for documents and requiring the government to justify its classification of secret information. Consequently, more records were made public, and what Americans read did little to inspire confidence in their leaders or in agencies such as the FBI and the CIA. Further, journalists sought to emulate Bob Woodward and Carl Bernstein, the *Washington Post* reporters who had exposed Watergate, and a wave of investigative political reporting produced scandalous stories of campaign-finance abuses, legislative manipulations, and unsavory private peccadilloes.

The more people learned about their political leaders, the more cynicism permeated the country. In addition, the fall of South Vietnam to communist rule in 1975 reminded them of the trauma that had taken the lives of countless Americans. The United States' global standing had become seriously weakened by Vietnam, Watergate, mounting economic problems, and the apparent ineptitude of the country's leaders. President Ford himself became a target for satirists when newscasts showed him falling down stairs, making him appear clumsy and further emphasizing the presidency's poor public image.

In July 1976 the country celebrated its 200th birthday, with Ford presiding over the festivities, hoping to be elected to the office he had attained by appointment and accession. He managed to secure the Republican nomination despite a strong challenge from Ronald Reagan, but he was still contending with a weakening economy and the Watergate aftermath. Generally accepted as an honest man, Ford tried to restore public trust in government by fighting Congress's lavish spending and supporting laws to prevent further abuses of power. But his association with Richard Nixon told against him, and despite all his efforts, the electorate still had little faith in their president.

## ENTER JIMMY CARTER

Public mistrust was not confined to the presidency. By the mid-1970s, voters felt cynical about most of their elected leaders in Washington. Many believed the nation's bureaucracy needed overhauling and that Gerald Ford was not the man to do it. His many years in Congress, along with his pardon of Nixon, made him suspect. It was felt that an outsider was needed to clean up government and renew the democratic principles on which the country had been founded. It needed, perhaps, a man like Jimmy Carter.

Carter was as much "outside" Washington as anyone could be. He had entered politics in 1962, when he was elected to the Georgia state senate, and six years later he was elected state governor. When, in 1974, he announced his intention to run for president, his chances of succeeding seemed nonexistent: He was almost completely unknown outside Georgia, and he was up against such formidable opponents as Alabama governor George Wallace, Idaho senator Frank Church, and California governor Jerry Brown. But Carter appealed to voters, particularly to farmers, blue-collar workers, and urban African Americans, while many liked his unabashed spiritual faith and devotion to his wife, Rosalynn.

To many, Jimmy Carter seemed a refreshing change: a trustworthy man of strong religious beliefs who promised never to lie to them. Unlike most politicians, Carter had openly incorporated his faith into his approach to governing, and his sincerity struck a chord. His lack of political experience was overlooked; that he was not part of the Washington establishment was in his favor, and he promised to make government more efficient and more responsive to the populace. This was what they wanted to hear.

It was nonetheless a close election: Carter won 50.1 percent of the popular vote and 297 electoral votes to Ford's 48 percent and 240 electoral votes. In what can be regarded as a return to liberal attitudes of the past, voters chose Jimmy

Gerald Ford visits Jimmy Carter at the White House in December 1978. *(Courtesy Jimmy Carter Library)*

Carter to "rescue" them from what they saw as the corruption and entrenched bureaucracy in Washington. And he set the tone of his administration at once when he wore a simple business suit on his inauguration day, taking the oath of office not as James Earl Carter, Jr., but as Jimmy Carter, man of the people. Following the ceremony, he rejected the customary limousine and walked the mile and a half from the Capitol to the White House, hand-in-hand with Rosalynn and their nine-year-old daughter Amy. Thereafter, he maintained an informal image that appealed to voters—for example, by wearing cardigan sweaters in televised addresses to the nation, stressing that he was simply an ordinary man in an extraordinary job, nothing more.

Carter's presidency got off to a good start as the Democratic majority in Congress cooperated with him on such legislation as a revision of the Social Security system—shades of Roosevelt—that raised both the wage base and the rate of taxation, measures that would bring in more revenue to fund the program. He pardoned draft resisters from the Vietnam era; eliminated funding for the B-1 bomber airplane; deregulated the airline, trucking, and railroad industries; and reorganized the federal civil service. A foreign policy that stressed human rights produced mixed reactions, but Carter achieved some major successes, including the Panama Canal treaties. He also oversaw the completion of full diplomatic relations with the People's Republic of China, formalized on January 1, 1979. March 26, 1979, saw the historic peace agreement between President Anwar Sadat of Egypt and Prime Minister Menachim Begin of Israel. The treaty became known as the Camp David accords after the presidential retreat where Carter had brought Begin and Sadat together to resolve conflicts between Israel and Egypt and to settle issues of Palestinian sovereignty. It was unquestionably the greatest moment of his presidency.

Jimmy Carter, Egyptian president Anwar Sadat, left, and Israeli prime minister Menachim Begin, right, shake hands upon the signing of the Camp David Accords on March 26, 1979. *(AP Photo/Bob Daughtery)*

Yet these achievements were offset by the president's mounting problems in Washington. Elected to "clean up" government, he soon learned that he was unable to overturn bureaucratic practices that had become the accepted method of working in the nation's capital. The system may have been flawed, but it was deeply rooted and worked well for the senators and representatives who controlled the legislative strings of government. Unlike Lyndon Johnson, whose years in Congress had given him expertise in working it, Carter was reluctant to play the you-scratch-my-back-and-I'll-scratch-yours game that prevailed in Washington. His idealism and desire for reform were out of place in a world where practical politics meant the formation of alliances and legislative bargaining. It was a shock to Carter to find that, instead of automatic approval for his programs from the Senate and the House, he had to court votes and make concessions—adapting to the very system he wanted to reform.

He did not adapt willingly, and as the legislature rejected many of his proposals, he countered by vetoing legislation that he considered wasteful. Repeatedly, the battles between president and Congress resulted in the latter overruling him. Only when the interests of president and legislature merged did they agree and pass bills without lengthy argument.

Carter did succeed in achieving some of his goals. Concerned about the energy crisis, he pushed hard for the Emergency Natural Gas Act and Energy Security Act and the creation of the Department of Energy. His first energy package, signed into law on November 9, 1978, led to initiatives that brought about an increase in the supply of energy and the subsequent lowering of prices. However, the full effects of his work here and in nuclear-energy reform would not be felt until after he left office. His success might have been enjoyed sooner had not the Organization of Petroleum Exporting Countries (OPEC) more than doubled oil prices (from $13 to more than $34 a barrel), an increase with frightening repercussions.

In the first half of Carter's administration, the economy showed strong signs of recovery, growing by a 4 percent annual rate. Unemployment dropped to 6.1 percent in 1978 (from 7.7 percent in 1976), while inflation was slightly more than 6 percent, an improvement on the rate during Ford's administration. But all this was undone by the OPEC actions, which worsened inflation. By late 1978 this had risen to 8 percent, while productivity had gone up by less than a half of 1 percent. These factors affected all Americans, and as the economy worsened, their resentment grew.

The irony of Jimmy Carter's presidency is that despite his common depiction as an ineffectual president, he was far more successful in pushing his initiatives through Congress than were his predecessors, Ford and Nixon, or his successors, Reagan and Bush. He did not like the system, but he learned to work it successfully. Nevertheless, the OPEC energy crisis and the resultant economic problems weakened public confidence. Hoping to restore that confidence, the president decided to address the nation—but only made matters worse.

## THE "MALAISE" SPEECH

To President Carter, leadership meant persuading the nation's citizens to act in concert to overcome the problems besetting them. He believed that only by pulling together could the American people triumph, as they had done during

World War II. But circumstances were different now: The country was not at war, and the current American self-perception had little to do with neighborly cooperation and everything to do with "What's in it for me?" Personal sacrifice might be fine for some, but people felt they had already played their part with high taxes and the costs incurred by pork-barrel legislation.

Carter recognized that the country was despondent but failed to perceive that Americans had had enough of sacrifice, and he continued to push his message that *everybody* needed to do his or her part. In a televised address on July 15, 1979, he admonished the nation, "The erosion of our confidence in the future is threatening to destroy the social and the political fabric of America." He spoke of a loss of faith, "not only in government but in the ability as citizens to serve as the ultimate rulers and shapers of our democracy." Noting that "piling up material goods cannot fill the emptiness of lives which have no confidence or purpose," he urged the country to avoid the path "that leads to fragmentation and self-interest" but instead to pursue "the path of common purpose and the restoration of American values." He spoke of the effect that the energy crisis was having on the nation, but he believed that "we can and we must rebuild our confidence." He concluded:

> In closing, let me say this: I will do my best, but I will not do it alone. Let your voice be heard. Whenever you have a chance, say something good about our country. With God's help and for the sake of our Nation, it is time for us to join hands in America. Let us commit ourselves together to a rebirth of the American spirit. Working together with our common faith we cannot fail.[1]

It was meant to be an inspiring speech, one that would draw Americans together. Instead, it seemed that the president was blaming the people for the current crisis and laying responsibility on their shoulders rather than his own. This message did not appeal to voters who felt the nation's problems stemmed from poor leadership rather than anything they had done or not done. Moreover, the idealistic attitudes of the 1960s in the president's words no longer struck a chord. The address backfired, contributing to both the general depression and to the president's plummeting popularity.[2]

Carter followed the "malaise" speech (as it became known, although he never used the word *malaise*) by purging his staff, firing four cabinet secretaries, transferring others, and forcing out numerous lower-level officials. Once again, however, this attempt to show leadership only confirmed the growing opinion of him as inept. His perceived failings were examined and reexamined: He did not know how to delegate and took too much on himself; he was obsessed with details; he relied too much on his wife's advice rather than that of qualified government advisers; he was too informal and did not set a true presidential tone in either appearance or personality; and so on. His management style often led to conflict among his staff, the most serious being major differences of opinion between Secretary of State Cyrus Vance and National Security Advisor Zbigniew Brzezinski. In the post-Watergate world of the late 1970s, every crisis of the Carter administration was exposed to public view and ruthlessly analyzed. It did not help that he did not like the press, nor they him, which meant that every opportunity to show him in a bad light was eagerly pursued.

There was indeed a malaise in the country—and many thought Carter had caused it. He seemed to be an idealist out of step with the times; he had said as much in his inaugural address: "I have no new dream to set forth today, but rather urge a fresh faith in the old dream."[3] Unfortunately, Americans wanted not the old dream but a fresh vision; they wanted to move forward, not back. Voters were beginning to think they did not want someone, even of undoubted moral probity, blaming them for the country's problems, but someone who would provide strong, confident leadership and restore American power and prestige.

## THE RISE OF RONALD REAGAN

In the years between the presidencies of Franklin Roosevelt and Richard Nixon, the word *conservative* had the same negative connotation as the word *liberal* would come to have in the 1980s. Irrespective of party, the New Deal philosophy of social improvement largely held good from 1932 to 1980. Even Nixon, a Republican, oversaw such programs as the National Environmental Policy Act of 1969, the Occupational Safety and Health Act of 1970, and the new Supplementary Security Income system implemented in 1972.

But by Jimmy Carter's time, the pendulum was starting to swing the other way. Expensive social legislation, high taxes, regulations controlling and restricting private enterprise and economic growth—all were anathema to the conservative New Right. Paradoxically, the prosperity of the 1960s and early 1970s played a part; as people became better off, their attitude changed from "love thy neighbor" to "look out for number one"—hence the "Me Decade." Douglas Fraser, former president of the United Auto Workers, summed up this trend: "The most disturbing thing about it, and I wish it weren't true, is that when people become affluent, their values change. They don't think they should be paying taxes to support people who are less well off."[4]

The social consciousness of the 1960s was fading; Carter had recognized and attacked this in his "malaise" speech when he said, "In a nation that was proud of hard work, strong families, close-knit communities, and our faith in God, too many of us now tend to worship self-indulgence and consumption. Human identity is no longer defined by what one does, but by what one owns."[5]

He was right, but only the most idealistic Americans agreed when he said, "[W]e've discovered that owning things and consuming things does not satisfy our longing for meaning."[6] On the contrary, the acquisition of material goods had come to be what people longed for most in a country that had experienced tremendous growth since the days of the Great Depression. Contributing factors to this attitude included technological developments, which were beginning to exert an important effect on lifestyles and personal outlooks, and the progression toward globalized competition, emphasizing new opportunities for big business.

The New Right was on the rise, crying out against high taxes, government regulations, the escalating crime rate, and the loss of family values that the free-wheeling 1960s had engendered. Evangelists of the New Religious Right were becoming "televangelists," reaching increasing audiences through televised sermons with politically conservative messages. Carter's faith had played an important part in his 1976 campaign and gained the support of such religious leaders as the Reverend Marion "Pat" Robertson. But by 1980 Robertson, the Moral Majority's Jerry Falwell, and others supported a candidate who espoused many

Ronald Wilson Reagan, here seen in an official 1981 portrait, had charisma and an optimistic outlook that resonated with voters. *(Courtesy Ronald Reagan Library)*

of the values of the New Religious Right: Ronald Reagan.

Reagan—formerly an actor, Democrat, and governor of California—had first run for president in 1976 and was only barely beaten for the Republican nomination by Gerald Ford. Undaunted, he began his 1980 campaign almost at once, criticizing the Carter administration repeatedly in newspaper columns, radio interviews, and public speeches. He finally announced his candidacy on November 13, 1979, from the ballroom of the Hilton Hotel in New York City.

Reagan's opponents included Gerald Ford (although he ultimately decided not to run); John Connolly, the former governor of Texas; George H.W. Bush, a man with many years of government experience; and Senator Howard Baker of Tennessee. Reagan got off to a rocky start, losing the Iowa caucuses to Bush, but things changed on the night of February 26, 1980, before the New Hampshire primary. There was to be a debate between Reagan and Bush alone, and the other candidates protested their omission. Reagan agreed they should be included; Bush's campaign team and the newspaper sponsoring the debate did not. As Reagan attempted to explain to the audience what was happening, the newspaper's editor ordered the sound man to turn off his microphone, and an angry Reagan cried out, "I'm paying for this microphone, Mr. Breen!"

Former speechwriter Peggy Noonan writes: "Reagan's words electrified the audience, which roared its approval. Bush looked weak, Reagan strong. He thought afterward he might have won the primary, and the nomination, at that moment."[7]

Such was the case: Reagan became the untouchable front-runner. He was 69 years old—the oldest man ever to run for president—but he was in good health and had a youthful, energetic way about him. He had humor and charm in abundance, and if he made gaffes, he more than compensated for them with witty remarks and stirring speeches. From New Hampshire onward, he fairly sailed through to the nomination, and he had the sense to choose Bush as his running mate.[8] The combination of Reagan's charisma, Bush's experience, and a conservative message was to prove unbeatable.

Reagan had many factors in his favor, including the support of business leaders who welcomed his promises of corporate tax cuts. But it was the economy that provided his most effective weapon against Carter. In 1980 the nation was experiencing its second year of double-digit inflation (it was now up to 12.4 percent), the average per capita income had dropped, unemployment was at 7.1 percent for the year, and sales of automobiles were at a 19-year low. The press reminded readers how consumer prices had nearly doubled; how the dollar had dropped drastically; how huge trade deficits had resulted from the soaring prices of foreign crude oil; how productivity had risen at only half the pace of the 1960s; how the Dow Jones industrial average had dropped some 20 percent from its high of 1,051 in early 1973.[9] The final straw was the decision by Federal Reserve Board chairman Paul Volcker to raise interest rates in an attempt to stop further inflation. Taken against Carter's wishes, the decision was made just weeks before the election, and the immediate economic downturn helped to seal the president's fate.[10]

Taking advantage of Carter's weaknesses and problems, Reagan swept into office on a tide of public opinion in close harmony with his own slogan that "government is not the solution to our problems; government is the problem."[11] He was a conservative, the nation's first divorced president, and its oldest ever. But he was the right man at the right time, and he would make the ensuing eight years his own as few other presidents have done.

# 1 The Fall of Jimmy Carter
## November 1979–
## January 1981

November 1979 did not start well. On November 3 in Greensboro, North Carolina, a protest march against the Ku Klux Klan turned violent when Klansmen opened fire on the demonstrators, killing five and wounding 10. The event underscored a high level of tension in the kjavikcountry. Americans were unhappy and discouraged—an attitude that President Jimmy Carter had described as a "crisis of the spirit in our country."[1]

To many, Carter was to blame for that crisis. He had been elected to lift America out of its post-Watergate gloom; instead, the country seemed even gloomier as he neared the end of his third year in office. As well as racial tensions, the economy was faltering: Inflation and unemployment rates were outrageously high, and oil prices had more than doubled. Carter had asked for sacrifices to overcome an "erosion of our confidence in the future."[2] But the nation believed the fault lay not with them but with their president.

Such was Carter's unpopularity that even before the 1980 presidential race had begun, it seemed possible he would lose the Democratic nomination to Massachusetts senator Ted Kennedy. Current events, however, were about to play a far more important part in Jimmy Carter's career than Kennedy, as less than 24 hours after the Greensboro shootout, the most fateful day of his presidency dawned.

## BACKGROUND TO DISASTER

The United States had enjoyed a comfortable relationship with Iran and its shah, Reza Mohammed Pahlavi, since his accession to the throne in 1941. The country's location on the Persian Gulf and the Arabian Sea, bordering the Soviet Union and serving as a conduit

President Jimmy Carter would face innumerable problems during his last 14 months in office. *(National Archives Still Picture Records LICON [NWDNA-428-KN-26854])*

between the Middle East and Asia, made it strategically important, as did its rich oil fields. When Pahlavi was ousted by an uprising in 1953, he quickly regained control with U.S. assistance. His subsequent modernization of Iran, which included improvements in housing, education, and health care, earned him Western approval, but Muslim fundamentalists were enraged as he seized clerical lands and granted greater freedoms and rights to women, defying centuries of Islamic traditions. He also exercised brutal control through his secret police force, SAVAK. By the late 1970s anti-shah and anti-American feelings were running high in Iran, especially after the shah declared martial law in September 1978.

The revolution, when it came, was quick; on January 16, 1979, Pahlavi was overthrown and escaped to Egypt with his family. His departure was followed by the return to Iran of the Shiite ayatollah Ruhollah Khomeini after 15 years' exile in France. Khomeini quickly took control and in early February appointed a secular prime minister, Mehdi Bazargan. Trouble ensued almost immediately when, on February 14, an armed mob attacked the U.S. embassy in Tehran, taking approximately 70 Americans captive, but the politically experienced Bazargan convinced Khomeini to order the hostages' release, resolving the crisis quickly.

By early April Iran had become a fundamentalist Islamic republic, and Khomeini's control was absolute. The country was nonetheless important to the Carter administration, especially since the revolution had severely reduced oil production and also made Iran vulnerable to Soviet influence or even invasion. A small group of U.S. officials therefore remained in Tehran, the capital, to establish diplomatic relations with the new regime.

The shah, meanwhile, had moved to Morocco, expecting to travel from there to the United States. Secretary of State Cyrus Vance and President Carter, how-

Reza Mohammed Pahlavi, shah of Iran, and his wife, Empress Farah Pahlavi, are seen here with the Carters during a state dinner in Washington in November 1977. *(Courtesy Jimmy Carter Library)*

ever, conscious of how this would be viewed by the Iranians, felt U.S. interests would be better served if Pahlavi found another place to live. Consequently, he went to the Bahamas and from there to Cuernavaca, Mexico. In October, though, the administration learned the shah was ill with cancer and needed treatment best obtained in the States. Consequently, Vance changed his mind, feeling Pahlavi should be admitted on humanitarian grounds; Carter reluctantly agreed.

On October 22 Reza Mohammed Pahlavi entered New York Hospital–Cornell Medical Center. Almost two weeks later, disaster struck.

## AMERICANS HELD HOSTAGE

On November 4, 1979, responding to calls from Ayatollah Khomeini to demonstrate against the United States, a mob of Iranian students broke into the U.S. embassy in Tehran, seizing its 90 occupants. Six Americans managed to escape and took refuge in the Canadian embassy. Of those seized at the U.S. embassy and at the Iran-America Society and the Iranian Foreign Ministry,[3] 66 were made prisoners, while most non-Americans were released. November 19 and 20 saw the release, on Khomeini's orders, of almost all the women and the black hostages, except three who had not been cleared of spying. On November 22, five more non-Americans were let go, leaving 53 Americans still in captivity.

The attack highlighted the hostility felt for the United States within many Middle East countries as Islamic militants increasingly responded violently to what they regarded as American imperialism and interference. In late November a mob broke into the U.S. embassy in Islamabad, Pakistan, trapping approximately 90 embassy employees in a vault room for about five hours and setting the building afire; the employees later escaped. Elsewhere in Pakistan, demonstrations resulted in two American cultural centers being burned and gutted. There were further attacks on U.S. consulates and embassies in Turkey and Libya.

These events horrified Americans, but it was Iran that gained the greatest attention. Khomeini publicly condoned the militants' actions and, except for ordering the release of a few hostages, refused to intervene, leading Bazargan to resign as prime minister. Some captives, accused of spying for the CIA, were beaten, tortured, and threatened with death. But fear of American reprisals—President Carter had privately relayed a message that if any captives were killed, the United States would take immediate military action—probably prevented the students from carrying out their threats. Instead, they continually iterated their demands: that the United States return the deposed shah to Iran to stand trial; that his assets be turned over to the Islamic Republic of Iran; and that the United States apologize for its crimes against the Iranian people. President Carter refused, declared an embargo on oil imports from Iran, ordered a review of the visas of Iranian students in the United States, and froze all Iranian assets in U.S. banks and their overseas branches. On November 20 he ordered a naval task force into the Indian Ocean, and on December 12 he expelled 183 Iranian diplomats from the country.

On December 4 all members of the United Nations Security Council condemned the Iranians' actions and demanded the hostages' immediate release. The International Court of Justice also upheld the U.S. call for a speedy release, and Iran found itself isolated by economic sanctions and universal condemnation. Within the United States, there were calls for military action; Carter immediately ruled this out, convinced the hostages would be killed before a rescue team could reach them. There was too much at stake for both the hostages and the United States for him to consider anything but a diplomatic solution.

Initially it seemed the simplest solution was for the United States to divest itself of its greatest liability: Pahlavi. The argument was that once the shah left U.S. protection, the Iranian students would give up their hostages. Consequently, the Carter administration began to seek a refuge for him elsewhere. But only Anwar Sadat was willing to take Pahlavi, and Carter believed that would be politically and personally dangerous for the Egyptian leader. Finally, Panamanian leader General Omar Torrijos was persuaded to give the shah asylum.

After six weeks of treatment, including surgery, Pahlavi left Cornell Medical Center on December 2. On December 15 he and his family flew to Contadora Island, 35 miles off the coast of Panama, but the students only reiterated their demands. UN secretary general Kurt Waldheim flew to Tehran to negotiate a solution, but after three days—during which he was humiliated, berated, and threatened—Waldheim returned, convinced, as Jimmy Carter put it, that "the Iranians had no government at all; the terrorists were making all the decisions."[4]

Americans followed every step of the crisis, led by the press, which was increasingly influencing public opinion—sometimes even manipulating it. *Time* magazine aroused much antagonism when it named Ayatollah Khomeini its Man of the Year for 1979. On CBS, veteran reporter Walter Cronkite signed off his newscast each night by intoning the number of days the hostages had been held captive. ABC News began to air a nightly program entitled *The Iran Crisis: America Held Hostage;* presided over by anchorman Ted Koppel, it proved so successful that it was turned into *Nightline,* which premiered on March 24, 1980.

Another outcome was the victimization of many innocent Iranians living in the United States. Employers fired Iranian workers; schools expelled or refused to admit Iranian students; homes and other Islamic-owned properties were vandalized and sometimes burned. The federal government deported Iranian students who were found not to be complying with immigration rules. Many compared the experience to the internment of Japanese Americans during World War II.

In late January the country rejoiced as the six Americans who had been hidden by Canadian embassy personnel in Tehran finally escaped Iran, using Canadian passports. But the celebration was brief, and support for the president gradually waned as Americans came to feel that Carter was weak and indecisive. When he did finally use American military power to attempt a rescue, it would prove disastrous.

## REACTION TO AN INVASION

Earlier in 1979, the Soviet government had begun to send military aid to Afghanistan's communist leaders, who had seized control in April 1978 but were increasingly troubled by tribal resistance and a power struggle within their own ranks. Although Afghanistan was not in the Warsaw Pact, the USSR regarded it as a "member of the socialist community" and therefore requiring Soviet protection. The danger of an Islamic revolution in Afghanistan, similar to that in Iran, seemed very strong, and the Soviets saw this as a threat to the communist regime there as well as to other socialist republics in the area. Thus, on December 24 Soviet forces took control of the airfields of Kabul, Afghanistan's capital. More troops followed, and by December 29 more than 50,000 were occupying the country.

Western countries were quick to condemn the invasion. Carter immediately ordered embargoes on the sale of high-technology equipment to the Soviet Union and on all grain deliveries beyond the 8 million tons allowed under a 1976 trade agreement; curtailed Soviet fishing rights; and called a halt to economic and cultural exchanges between the United States and the Soviet Union. He also asked the Senate to delay ratification of the SALT II (Strategic Arms Limitation Talks) treaty.

In his State of the Union address on January 21, 1980, Carter called the invasion "the most serious threat to the peace since the Second World War." He also announced a new doctrine that would acquire his name: "Any attempt by any outside force to gain control of the Persian Gulf region will be regarded as an assault on the vital interests of the United States and such an assault will be repelled by any means necessary, including military force." Within weeks, National Security Advisor Zbigniew Brzezinski and Colonel William Odom formed a Rapid Deployment Joint Task Force (RDJTF)—"to give some muscle to the Carter Doctrine," as Brzezinski put it. Within a year the RDJTF consisted of more than 150,000 troops from the army and the marines, plus navy and air force personnel. In 1983 it became the U.S. Central Command.[5]

"Military readiness" included, Carter felt, reinstating draft registration, which had been suspended in 1975. (The draft itself had ended in 1972.) He therefore supported a bill to restore draft registration for 19- and 20-year-olds; it was passed on June 27 and became effective on January 5, 1981. The move was controversial, and Carter's political opponents, including Ronald Reagan, attacked him for it. But subsequent presidents agreed that while draft registration was not desirable, it was necessary, and it remains in place today, as does the Carter Doctrine—two surprising legacies of a president known for his pacifist views.

Carter's reactions to the Soviet invasion were to have widespread repercussions. The SALT II treaty, then due to be put to a vote in the Senate, proved a particularly delicate matter. Carter felt it "was patently of advantage to the United States and vital to the maintenance of world peace."[6] But if it were to be voted on so soon after the Soviet invasion, it would surely be defeated. The president therefore asked Senator Robert Byrd to put off the vote on the treaty, leaving it for a later date.

Many members of Congress opposed the grain embargo, feeling that it would harm American farmers—as well as Carter's own career, with the Iowa caucuses just six weeks away. Refusing to be influenced by political considerations, the president promised to maintain grain prices and compensate farmers for losses they might incur. Fortunately, allies such as Canada and Australia supported the embargo, making its effect more damaging to the Soviet Union. After an initial dip in prices, the market gained such strength that grain exports actually enjoyed their strongest year to date.

The grain embargo was not the only action that threatened Carter's popularity. On January 20, 1980, while appearing on the NBC news program *Meet the Press,* he announced what was to be one of the most controversial decisions of his presidency:

> I've sent a message today to the United States Olympic Committee spelling out my own position: that unless the Soviets withdraw their troops within a month from

Afghanistan, that the Olympic games be moved from Moscow to an alternate site or multiple sites or postponed or canceled. If the Soviets do not withdraw their troops immediately from Afghanistan within a month, I would not support the sending of an American team to the Olympics.[7]

The statement aroused bitter controversy. Athletes were indignant, but polls indicated the majority of Americans supported the president and saw the boycott as a major blow against the Soviets.

Carter made an unsuccessful attempt to persuade the International Olympic Committee to move the games to Greece, after which, in late April, the U.S. Olympic Committee (USOC) voted to implement the boycott. Unfortunately, some important allies who had initially expressed support for the U.S. action—Great Britain, France, Italy, and Sweden—later announced that they would send athletes to Moscow, weakening the boycott's effect. Meanwhile, the Supreme Court rejected a lawsuit filed against the USOC by 25 athletes.

The Soviet Union condemned the U.S. action, which turned the Summer Games in Moscow later that year into the most one-sided Olympics since 1904:[8] Soviet athletes won 195 medals, 80 of them gold.

## THE ABSCAM SCANDAL

American faith in the government was already shaky when, on February 3, 1980, newspapers published reports of an undercover FBI "sting" operation, code-named Abscam, that revealed widespread government corruption. Since September 1978, FBI agents posing as Middle Eastern businessmen had met officials and offered them bribes in exchange for specific favors. Each meeting was videotaped, and when the sting was concluded, 31 federal, state, and local officials, including several members of Congress, were arrested for abusing their office.

The FBI's Abscam operation was a major attempt to ferret out corruption in government, but public reaction was mixed: While many applauded the bureau's actions, many others questioned the sting's legality. Politicians who might have been caught themselves were especially quick to speak of "entrapment." The FBI agents' pose as Arabs also attracted criticism; as one irate citizen wrote to FBI director William Webster, "Since a scam is a crime, the word 'ABSCAM' associates 'Arab' with 'crime.' But the only Arabs involved in this scandal are fictitious. The guilty parties are Americans."[9]

Replays of the videotaped meetings demonstrated a frightening level of corruption. Most notoriously, Florida representative Richard Kelly (R) was seen stuffing $25,000 into his pockets and then asking one of the undercover agents, "Does it show?" In the following months, several bureaucrats were indicted and brought to trial. Despite his humiliating videotape, Kelly was lucky: His January 1981 conviction was overturned in 1982 by a judge who agreed that the FBI had entrapped him unlawfully. Others, however, were not so fortunate: In separate trials in 1980–81, a senator and six representatives, among others, were found guilty of bribery and conspiracy, resulting in fines, imprisonment, and public disgrace.[10]

The FBI would never again conduct such a large-scale probe into government corruption. Despite public praise for the operation, the charges of entrapment generated bad publicity for the bureau, and it seemed U.S. citizens had come to accept that some corruption in high places was part of political life.

## OLYMPIC TRIUMPH

February 1980 brought some welcome news with the winter Olympics at Lake Placid, New York. Because of the U.S. boycott of the Summer Games in Moscow, the Winter Games attracted special attention. More than 1,000 athletes from 37 nations—including, for the first time, the People's Republic of China—attended, and, as expected, the Soviet Union and East Germany dominated as they had done for years. When the competition ended on February 24, the USSR had 10 gold medals and 22 overall, while East Germany had nine golds and 23 overall; the United States finished third, with six gold medals, four silver, and two bronze.

But there were some happy surprises. American skier Phil Mahre won a silver medal despite four screws and a metal plate in an ankle that had been shattered just a year before. Eric Heiden won the gold medal in all five speed-skating events, with Olympic-record speeds in the 500-meter, 1,000-meter, 1,500-meter, and 5,000-meter races and a world record in the 10,000-meter race. Heiden's sister Elizabeth won the bronze in the women's 3,000-meter speed-skating event. But most exciting was the American triumph in ice hockey. The U.S. team of college students had been cobbled together by coach Herb Brooks; the favored Soviet team were professional players who had previously won four successive Olympic gold medals. The Americans prevailed in game after game, and the semifinals saw them pitted against the Soviet Union—the odds-on favorite. The Americans played brilliantly, and in the third period team captain Mike Eruzione shot the goal that gave them a dramatic 4-3 victory. In the ensuing pandemonium, sportscaster Al Michaels expressed the nation's emotion, crying, "Do you believe in miracles? Yes-s-s-s!"[11]

The United States went on to win the gold medal against Finland, capping a cheering interlude in an otherwise bleak period.

Pierre Elliott Trudeau, seen here in a 1988 photo, was a force in Canadian politics even after he stepped down as prime minister in 1984. *(Peter Jones/Reuters/Landov)*

## CANADA: THE RETURN OF TRUDEAU

By 1980 the United States' northern neighbor was experiencing massive social change. The 1970s had been dominated by one man, the Liberal Party's Pierre Elliott Trudeau, who had held office as prime minister from April 20, 1968, to June 4, 1979. During that time he had drawn the nation away from its association with Great Britain and into a new Canadian nationalism. Canada was still a young nation: Created by an act of Parliament in 1867, it was not until 1931 that the Statute of Westminster gave it control over its own external affairs, and it did not have an official flag until 1965. Although Canada had its own parliament, it still could not amend its constitution without British approval. Further, there was a strong movement in French-speaking Quebec to secede and form a separate nation. The country was thus neither fully independent nor fully unified.

A charismatic man, Trudeau had generated a phenomenon called Trudeaumania as mobs of supporters followed him everywhere, but by the late 1970s his popularity had dropped. After 11 years in power, Trudeau's Liberals were defeated on May 11, 1979, by the Progressive Conservatives, led by 39-year-old Joe Clark. Trudeau became leader of the opposition and, in November, decided to resign, seeing his political career coming to a close. No replacement for him had yet been named when, just four weeks later, Clark suffered a parliamentary defeat over a budget proposal. Failing to win a vote of confidence, Clark dissolved Parliament and set February 18, 1980, as the date for a new election. Seeing his opportunity, Trudeau reassumed the Liberal Party leadership.

Clark's prospects improved just three weeks before the voting: On January 28, 1980, six Americans who had evaded capture during the Tehran embassy attack the previous November managed to leave Iran using false passports supplied by Canadian embassy personnel who had risked their lives to hide the Americans in their homes. When the news broke, both countries celebrated what proud Canadians dubbed "the Canada caper." But despite the positive publicity, Clark lost the election.

On March 3, 1980, Trudeau became prime minister for the second time. He set himself a major goal: a unified Canada with control over its own constitution. His work was hindered by divisive language issues—on December 13, 1979, the Supreme Court of Canada had ruled the unilingual legislatures of Manitoba (English) and Quebec (French) to be unconstitutional—and by the separatist movement in Trudeau's native Quebec. The province's premier, René Lévesque, had fought for 13 years to make Quebec independent of Canada, and it seemed that victory might at last be in his grasp. On May 20, 1980, Quebec held a referendum on separation; 59.5 percent of the province's voters said "No." A devastated Lévesque vowed to carry on the fight, saying, *A la prochaine fois* ("Till the next time").

For Trudeau the victory was a relief. He hoped his main objective—bringing the constitution under full Canadian control—would appease Quebec separatists and bring about the united, bilingual nation he envisioned. A symbolic move in that direction occurred on July 1, 1980, when "O Canada!"—with lyrics in French and English—was proclaimed Canada's national anthem. But full independence was still to come.

## CARTER AND THE ECONOMY

In the months leading up to the 1980 U.S. election, inflation, interest rates, the foreign trade deficit, the Consumer Price Index, and unemployment were all at frighteningly high levels. The previous year Carter had appointed Paul Volcker as chairman of the Federal Reserve Board. Believing that a fall in real income was the way to fight inflation, Volcker had raised interest rates and intentionally brought on a recession, sparking more massive unemployment. In October 1979, with the inflation rate at 13.3 percent, Volcker announced a further increase in the discount rate to 12 percent and the imposition of new reserve requirements on bank deposits. By mid-November the prime rate had risen to 15.75 percent, and in some states it had become impossible to obtain mortgages, thus putting pressure on savings-and-loan institutions. To make matters worse, housing costs had skyrocketed.

The public mood was not improved by a November 1979 report that the Chrysler Corporation had applied for a bailout loan from the federal government.

Congress agreed to guarantees of $1.5 billion with certain conditions that included Chrysler reducing employee wages. The automaker negotiated concessions from the United Auto Workers (UAW), which Chrysler chairman Lee Iacocca managed to achieve after appointing UAW president Douglas Fraser to the company's board of directors. Congress then passed the Loan Guarantee Act in late December, which saved the company. Chrysler eventually repaid the loan ahead of schedule, but thousands of workers were laid off. In the view of many Americans, big business was surviving, but their jobs were not.

Late in January 1980 Carter presented a budget that included both major cuts and increases in defense spending. Many viewed it as insufficient to revive the economy, and inflation continued to rise as the Volcker measures failed to bring the right results. The president therefore produced a revised budget with an anti-inflation program that included plans for keeping wages and prices down, higher taxes on oil, and a 3 percent surcharge on the discount rate. Carter also suggested the Federal Reserve impose credit controls. He consulted with congressional leaders on large budget cuts, and on March 31 he signed and sent to Congress a revised, balanced budget that projected a $16.5 billion surplus, the first in 12 years. Critics, however, attacked his proposals as too little too late, especially when it was announced that inflation had reached a staggering 18.2 percent by the end of the first quarter of 1980.

On April 2 Carter signed the Crude Oil Windfall Profits Tax, a tax on the country's oil industry designed to produce $227 billion within the next 10 years. The president had previously attempted to address the energy crisis when he established the Department of Energy (in 1977) and proposed tax penalties and conservation. Congress had rejected this, and Americans had rejected his calls for energy conservation. Reaction to Carter's anti-inflation program was initially positive as interest rates began to drop. Congress, however, hacked away at his budget proposal and threw out the proposed oil-import fee, nullifying his attempts to curb inflation and conserve energy. Carter had resisted income-tax cuts, which cemented his general unpopularity and gave Ronald Reagan, the likely Republican presidential nominee, political ammunition. Reagan persistently championed tax cuts that would, he said, lead Americans to spend more, which would in turn boost tax revenues, stimulating the economy and lowering inflation. The popularity of this view led Democrats in Congress to echo the call for tax cuts, although Carter felt the timing was not right.

The combination of taxes and inflation meant that, though wages had almost doubled in 10 years, there had been a 6 percent drop in buying power. An article in *U.S. News & World Report* noted: "If the past decade's average inflation rate of 7.8 percent a year continues and tax laws aren't changed, the family earning $15,000 in 1980 will need $87,708 to stay even in 1990."[12] While Carter had inherited, not created, the country's economic problems, his failure to solve them made him appear culpable and vulnerable.

## APRIL: A FAILED RESCUE

When the hostages were seized in Iran, President Carter had ruled out military intervention, believing it too dangerous, but by April 1980 he was reconsidering this. There had been hope for a breakthrough in late March when two French intermediaries cabled the White House that President Abolhassan Bani-Sadr had apparently convinced the students holding the hostages to turn them over to the government. On April 1 Bani-Sadr affirmed that the government would take charge of the hostages, provided that "the American authorities make an official announcement that they will not spread propaganda or say anything provocative about the hostages until the formation of Parliament." Doubtful but still hopeful, Carter responded with the announcement that he considered this development a "positive step" and would therefore delay imposing sanctions against Iran. Just two days later, though, the Iranian Revolutionary Council declared that the United States had failed to meet certain conditions to ensure the transfer; decisions clearly still rested with Ayatollah Khomeini, not Bani-Sadr.

Negotiations were thus at a standstill. Iran was in disarray; no parliament had yet been elected, and it was possible the hostages would become pawns in the struggle between political factions. Americans were becoming impatient, as was the president, who had been criticized for his April 1 announcement and accused of using the hostage situation for personal gain. As the need for action became apparent, he began to consider a rescue mission.

One of Carter's problems was the growing conflict between Secretary of State Cyrus Vance and National Security Advisor Zbigniew Brzezinski. Vance was a seasoned diplomat who believed in caution, negotiation, and mutually beneficial solutions to problems. Brzezinski, an expert on foreign affairs who had advised the Kennedy and Johnson administrations, was abrasive, favoring confrontation when U.S. interests were threatened. Carter had chosen them for the balance they could bring to his team, and they often agreed on major issues. But they were not friends, and Brzezinski frequently acted as foreign-policy spokesman for the administration, technically the secretary of state's responsibility, which caused confusion about where authority lay.

Differences of opinion between Zbigniew Brzezinski (left) and Cyrus Vance, seen here in a 1977 photo, became even more pronounced during the Iran hostage crisis. *(Courtesy Jimmy Carter Library)*

When his presidency began, Carter had listened to both men and weighed their advice before making a decision. But Brzezinski's influence on the president had grown, and Vance found himself increasingly overruled. He saw any attempt to rescue the hostages as a recipe for disaster. The dangers were frighteningly apparent: getting into Iran undetected, getting into the embassy compound in the middle of Tehran, and removing the hostages before they could be harmed.

Nevertheless, Carter's military advisers felt confident that a rescue was possible, as did Brzezinski. On April 11, while Vance was on vacation, Brzezinski made compelling arguments for the mission to the president. A dismayed Vance argued forcefully against it on his return to Washington on April 15, pointing out that the operation would endanger not only the hostages but also world opinion if Iranians were killed in what would be perceived as a military strike against a Muslim country. Carter rejected this view, however, and on April 16 he met army colonel Charlie Beckwith. From Beckwith he learned that the elite Delta Force had repeatedly rehearsed a scenario that involved sending a number of helicopters—which could fly low and escape radar detection—into Iran to land at designated sites near the embassy in Tehran, break into the compound, and fly the hostages out.

A few days after this meeting, Carter gave the go-ahead for the mission, code-named Operation Eagle Claw and scheduled for the nights of April 24–25. During the first part of the operation, eight helicopters and several C-130 transporter planes were to rendezvous at an airstrip in the Great Salt Desert in southeastern Iran. Two helicopters, however, were delayed by weather and mechanical problems, and a third was damaged on landing, leaving only five useable; Beckwith had previously determined that at least six helicopters were needed. Word was sent back to Carter, who reluctantly decided the mission should be aborted. But as the withdrawal was beginning, another of the helicopters clipped a C-130 and burst into flames. Eight crewmen were killed, and five more were injured.

As *Time* magazine noted:

> For Carter in particular, and for the U.S. in general, the desert debacle was a military, diplomatic and political fiasco. A once dominant military machine, first humbled in its agonizing standoff in Viet Nam, now looked incapable of keeping its aircraft aloft even when no enemy knew they were there, and even incapable of keeping them from crashing into each other despite four months of practice for their mission.[13]

Carter took full responsibility for the failure, addressing the nation early on the morning of April 25 on what had happened and why he had taken the action when he did. Most Americans were glad an attempt had been made, and expressions of sympathy poured in from around the world. Nevertheless, Carter was criticized for putting the hostages at risk in an operation that had resulted in the loss of eight American lives and also heightened tensions in the Middle East. The Soviet Union accused him of endangering the hostages for the sake of his own political interests—a charge echoed by many of his Republican opponents.

The failed mission had another unfortunate consequence: Cyrus Vance's resignation as secretary of state. Though proven right about the operation, he felt he could no longer function effectively when his opinions were disregarded and in perpetual conflict with those of Brzezinski. The president accepted his resignation and nominated Maine senator Edmund Muskie to replace him.

Meanwhile, in Iran the hostages were split up and moved around the country, making any further rescue attempt impossible. Negotiation was now going to be the only way to get the Americans home.

## MOMENTOUS MAY

On May 9, 1980, as the Liberian freighter *Summit Venture* made its way into Tampa Bay, a sudden storm blew up, bringing strong winds and rain that drove the ship into the Sunshine Skyway bridge, near Tampa. The bridge support collapsed, sending the southbound span into the bay, and several vehicles, including a bus, plunged into the waters below. Thirty-five people were killed in the tragedy.

The Skyway bridge calamity was the beginning of a disaster-filled month—much of it dominated by events in Florida, which was already troubled by a vast tide of Cuban refugees. Further trouble erupted in Miami, where four policemen—all white—were on trial for the December 1979 fatal beating of Arthur McDuffie, a black insurance executive who died four days after he was arrested for a traffic violation. Many leading African Americans were already convinced that Miami police officers and prosecutors (including Dade County state attorney Janet Reno) were deliberately targeting blacks, so the McDuffie case was under close scrutiny, especially because of an all-white jury.

On May 17 the verdict was announced: not guilty. A racially mixed crowd gathered at the Justice Building, but what was meant to be a prayer meeting quickly became an angry demonstration. The whites soon left, and a group of about 500 blacks broke into the building and vandalized the county court office. Nearby, the State Office Building was set afire, and cars were smashed or burned. Before long, the violence had moved into other parts of the city. Hardest hit was the section called Liberty City, which suffered three days of looting, arson, stonings, beatings, and shootings. By the time the National Guard restored order to the area, 14 people had been killed. Three of those were white teenagers; the remainder were all black. More than 300 people had been injured, close to 1,000 were arrested, and the damages amounted to some $100 million.

On May 20 U.S. Attorney General Benjamin Civiletti announced an immediate investigation into the McDuffie case, plus alleged civil rights abuses by Miami law-enforcement officers. But the damage had been done. The three days of racial violence—the worst in more than 10 years—were a dramatic reminder that there was still much to be done to improve American race relations.

The day after the Miami riots began, May 18, an eruption of a different sort took place in Washington State. Mount St. Helens, a volcanic mountain that had been dormant since 1857 but had been experiencing

The awesome intensity of the Mount St. Helens eruption can be viewed in this photo taken May 18, 1980. *(AP/Wide World Photos)*

seismic shocks since March, finally reacted to an earthquake below it, and at 8:32 A.M. PDT, its north flank collapsed. A plume of hot ash, pumice, and dust shot 12 to 15 miles into the air, showering the area with volcanic debris and darkening the skies over an area of more than 160 square miles, while fallout from the ash drifted 500 miles downwind. The explosion's tremors were felt in Vancouver, British Columbia, more than 200 miles north.

Approximately 57 people were killed; the number could have been much higher, but geologists had warned of impending volcanic activity, and thousands had already evacuated residential and resort areas. One who had stubbornly refused to leave was 84-year-old Harry Truman, who had lived for 50 years by Spirit Lake—a region completely devastated by the explosion. Truman was never seen again.

The eruption—which took 1,314 feet off the mountain's peak—ended by the early morning of May 19; two days later President Carter declared Washington State a disaster area, with damage later estimated at approximately $1.1 billion. Tourism was expected to suffer, but visitor centers soon opened for people to view the devastated area and witness the gradual but impressive ecological recovery.

## WOMEN IN THE MILITARY

A month marked by disaster ended on a positive note as May 28 saw 215 women graduate from the American military academies at West Point, Annapolis, and Colorado Springs—a first in U.S. history.

By 1980 nearly 20,000 women held commissions, gained primarily through the Reserve Officers' Training Corps or officer-candidate schools, and there were now two female army generals, two air force generals, a marine corps general, and two navy admirals.[14] But it was a major step for women to enter the previously all-male military academies. The graduations also highlighted the change in the U.S. military. In the last year of the draft, 1972, there had been 45,000 women in the armed forces, just 1.6 percent of total troops. By 1980 the 2-million-strong, all-volunteer services had some 150,000 women in uniform—nearly 8 percent of the total—and the Pentagon was estimating that the figure would surpass 250,000, or 12.5 percent, by 1985.

Women were also doing jobs once considered male preserves, including operating and repairing trucks and heavy equipment, working on helicopters, and engaging in military intelligence. Though barred from combat duty, they often operated in roles that exposed them to enemy fire. Though occasionally subjected to sexual discrimination and harassment, it was becoming clear that women were just as capable as their male colleagues. Indeed, as President Carter prepared to reinstate draft registration (passed by Congress in late June), he briefly considered expanding it to include women.[15]

The May 28 graduations heralded changes for women in the decade ahead as they progressed up through the structures of command—not only in the military but also in the business world.

## FIGHTING FOR JUSTICE

The U.S. Census of 1980 recorded 1.37 million Native Americans, of whom approximately 332,000 were living on 250 reservations across the United States.

For more than a century, the country's indigenous peoples had struggled to overcome the injustice of broken treaties, lands taken from them illegally, loss of much of their old ways of life, and forced dependence on government assistance. Not until 1924 were they all granted U.S. citizenship, and even then many states imposed suffrage requirements that restricted their ability to vote as late as 1956. By that time, House Concurrent Resolution No. 108, terminating the existence of certain tribes as legal entities as well as ending federal support to many American Indian tribes and communities, had been in effect for two years and would continue to be policy until 1962.

The resolution inflicted enormous damage on those tribes unable to survive without assistance, and throughout the 1960s and 1970s, suits were filed to reverse the termination. One of these groups was the Cow Creek Band of Umpqua (southwestern Oregon), who also sought to recover lands that had been taken from them in the 1850s. On May 26, 1980, Congress passed legislation allowing the Cow Creek to file suit against the federal government; this was later followed by legislation overturning their termination, which became effective in 1982. In 1984 the tribe settled with the U.S. Justice Department for $1.5 million for the lost land.

Increasingly, Native Americans were winning suits filed with the Indian Claims Commission, although the actual return of land to tribes remained a distant goal. Instead, the most likely result was an offer of financial compensation. In March 1980 the Passamaquoddy, Penobscot, and Maliseet settled a land claim of 12.5 million acres (approximately two-thirds of northern Maine) by accepting $81.5 million. Throughout the 1980s, other Indian nations reached similar settlements, and the money was either invested by tribal governments or paid in royalties to tribal members. However, other nations refused to accept anything but the return of their land.

June 1980 saw a Supreme Court decision that was considered a semivictory for the Sioux (Dakota, Lakota, Nakota). The case, *United States v. Sioux Nation of Indians,* concerned the Black Hills, a large swathe of mountainous land stretching across western South Dakota, northeast Wyoming, and southeast Montana. This area had long been sacred to the Omaha, the Northern Cheyenne, and especially the Lakota, Dakota, and Nakota. In 1851 the Treaty of Fort Laramie guaranteed 60 million acres of the Black Hills "for the absolute and undisturbed use and occupancy of the Sioux." Under pressure from white settlers, a second treaty, reducing the Lakota, Dakota, and Nakota holdings to 20 million acres, was signed in 1868. After gold was discovered in the Black Hills in 1874, attempts to force the Lakota Sioux into selling their remaining land led to the War for the Black Hills (1876–77). In 1877 a new treaty, signed by only 10 percent of adult male Sioux, turned all the land over to the federal government, an action described by a federal judge a century later as a "ripe and rank case of dishonorable dealing." Following this, the sacred Black Hills were extensively mined and logged; insult was added to injury when Mount Rushmore was carved in the late 1920s.

In the 20th century the Sioux began filing lawsuits to reclaim their land. On June 30, 1980, the Supreme Court upheld decisions by the Indian Claims Commission and the Court of Claims that the eight Sioux nations held rights to the 20 million acres specified in the 1868 treaty. However, the Court also upheld the Claims Commission's decision to not return the land but to award financial compensation based on the land's value in 1877 plus interest. Although some of the Sioux groups, such as those of Standing Rock Reservation, voted to accept the award, the majority refused it; only the return of Paha Sapa (their name for the Black Hills) would satisfy them, and in July the Oglala Lakota Sioux filed a new suit in federal court, beginning another extended series of legal actions that have been largely unsuccessful. As of 2005 the money awarded remained in an interest-bearing account and totaled more than $700 million—as opposed to the more than $4 billion that has been extracted from the area's natural resources. Meanwhile, congressional efforts to return even a small portion of the land have failed because of overriding outside business interests.

A week after the Supreme Court decision in the Black Hills case, Congress passed an amendment to the Hopi-Navajo Relocation Act of 1974. In an attempt to resolve a long-standing and bitter dispute, land claimed by both the Hopi and the Navajo (Dineh) nations was partitioned, tribal members were relocated, and any Navajo living on Hopi land were to be subject to Hopi rule. This solution failed to satisfy either the Hopi, who saw themselves as victims of both the Navajo and the U.S. government, or the Navajo, many of whom refused to be relocated. Their resistance to the act would continue throughout the 1980s. For these and other Native Americans fighting similar battles, justice still seemed to be a long way off.

## THE MARIEL BOATLIFT

The United States traditionally welcomes immigrants and political refugees from other countries, but the arrival of potential new citizens frequently poses problems of integration into American society. Although laws have been passed to limit the numbers admitted, special cases always arise, especially with those seeking asylum, and for years debate has raged on what constitutes a refugee. Prior to 1980, the federal government had overseen an orderly arrival of refugees from Indochina and a less-orderly influx of "boat people" from Haiti; many Haitians, however, were turned back because they were considered to be entering the country for economic rather than political reasons.

On March 17, 1980, President Carter signed the Refugee Act, which increased the number of refugees allowed into the country from 290,000 to 320,000 annually. The act also broadened the definition of *refugee* to include people from any part of the world with a legitimate claim for asylum, established new criteria for admitting refugees to the United States, and created the Office of Refugee Resettlement.

Less than a month later, Cubans began to arrive. Since 1973 Cuba's dictator, Fidel Castro, had forbidden emigration.[16] But a poor economy and rising discontent had caused Castro to change his mind, and early in April 1980 he ordered the removal of an armed guard around the Peruvian embassy in Havana. At once, some 10,800 Cubans besieged the embassy, all seeking asylum. Peru appealed for help from other countries, and eight nations agreed to take 6,250 émigrés, with 3,500 going to the United States alone. Twice-daily airlifts began between Havana and San José, Costa Rica, but after three days Castro halted them; he would only allow émigrés to leave on flights going directly to the countries of their final destination.

In Miami, Florida, some Cuban Americans awaiting the arrival of family members from Cuba decided to send two boats to retrieve their relatives on April

19. The vessels arrived back in Key West with 48 refugees, and the following day Cuban authorities announced that boats from America would be allowed into the port of Mariel. A flotilla set off, and by week's end Mariel's harbor was jammed. As quickly as the vessels—many of them chartered at high cost—could retrieve refugees and deliver them to Key West, they went back for more, and soon the number of new arrivals had gone well beyond the 3,500 the United States had agreed to take.

Concerned by the numbers arriving, federal officials initially attempted to stop the sealifts, warning boat owners that bringing undocumented aliens into the country was a felony. But Castro refused to stop the emigration or take people back, so several processing centers were set up and the refugees were admitted conditionally for 60 days, allowing them time to file for political asylum. There seemed little doubt, though, that the outcome would be positive for the Cubans; President Carter himself set the tone when he announced on May 5, "We will continue to provide an open heart and open arms to refugees seeking freedom from communist domination and economic deprivation. . . ."[17] Many Americans, nervous about the effects the refugees would have on jobs and the economy, criticized what they saw as a lax federal attitude and demanded more immigration controls. Rumors also arose that Castro was sending criminals to America, although these rumors proved largely baseless.

The refugees kept coming—more than 88,800 arrived in May alone—and U.S. authorities found it increasingly difficult to deal with them. Additional processing centers were established, but before long they began to overflow. As the crowding in the centers worsened and processing time lengthened, tempers and violence flared. In early June, refugees who were being detained at Fort Chaffee, Arkansas, rioted, burning two buildings. Fights and riots subsequently broke out at other detention centers around the country. The United States offered to send ships and airplanes to Cuba to collect refugees if the government would allow them to be screened there first, but Castro refused, apparently enjoying what had now become a debacle for the Americans and a big relief to him: He had rid himself of thousands of dissidents and eased the demands for food and other goods that were strapping his country's economy.

On September 26 Castro closed the port of Mariel and ordered all remaining boats to leave the harbor. By then 125,262 Cubans had entered the United States via Key West.[18] President Carter, already under fire for his handling of the economy and the Iran hostage crisis, was also castigated for allowing the refugee question to get out of hand, and it became a major blow to his presidential campaign. But things were worse for thousands of Cubans kept in detention camps for months and, in some cases, years, turning their American dream into a nightmare.

## THE LONG, HOT SUMMER—AND FALL

In late June 1980 the nation was hit by a heat wave that ravaged large areas of the country, causing the highest heat-related fatalities since 1926. Hardest hit were Texas and Oklahoma, but almost half of the country was affected by temperatures that consistently exceeded 100°F. By the fourth week, more than 1,000 deaths in 20 states had been recorded, an average of 100 deaths a day.[19] For much of the country the heat wave lasted into September, and in some areas the drought lasted for months.

President Carter was also feeling the heat. As the economy continued to deteriorate, fingers pointed at him as the primary cause, and the Iran hostage crisis made him an easy target for media attacks on his apparent lack of leadership. Ronald Reagan was about to win the Republican nomination for president, and Carter was already trailing in the polls. He needed a miracle if he were to win a second term in office. Instead, he was beset by more problems, which included his brother Billy.

On July 14, as the Republican National Convention was getting underway in Detroit, Billy Carter registered with the Justice Department as an agent of the Libyan government. This had been a long time coming. Though Libya had paid him $220,000 for services performed since 1978, he had refused to register as an agent, claiming that the money had been a loan only, even though no formal loan agreement had been drawn up. Not until he was threatened with legal action did he finally comply with Justice Department regulations; then further details regarding his transactions with Libya started to come out.

Although the Justice Department claimed to be satisfied with Billy's registration and said there was no need for a criminal prosecution, questions persisted on what he was doing for Libya and why; consequently, on July 24 the Senate authorized a panel to investigate the matter. The primary concern was whether Libya had attempted to use Billy to influence his brother and therefore U.S. foreign policy. Both brothers vigorously denied this, but when it was revealed that First Lady Rosalynn Carter had suggested that Billy use his Libyan connections to try to help the American hostages in Iran, their veracity was called into question.

Irregularities began to appear in Billy's story. He reported that he had helped to arrange increased supplies from Libya for a Florida oil company, and he had made two trips to Libya and hosted the visit of a Libyan delegation to the United States, for which he had received travel expenses and personal gifts. He claimed that Libya had sought his aid in 1978 "to expand contacts in the U.S. . . . . Through a people-to-people program."[20] But intelligence reports revealed that Libya had wanted to use Billy and other prominent Americans in an attempt to purchase U.S. military aircraft and equipment, which was against U.S. policy. Billy, however, denied ever discussing aircraft purchases with Libyan representatives.

On August 4 President Carter sent a 13,000-word statement to the Senate in which he refuted any wrongdoing on the part of either himself or his brother. On August 21–22, Billy Carter testified before the Senate panel investigating him and strongly defended his previous statements. The panel's October 2 report stated it had found no evidence of illegal or obvious unethical activities by federal officials. It concluded, however, that what Billy Carter had done "was contrary to the interests of the President and the U.S. and merits severe criticism."[21] President Carter was also criticized for allowing his brother to be cultivated by the Libyan government without making it clear to the Libyans that there was nothing to be gained by it; worse, he was cited for using Billy to contact Libyan diplomats regarding the hostage crisis, which the panel dryly noted was "ill-advised."

During the "Billygate" investigation, Carter won the Democratic presidential nomination at the party's convention in New York City, but the hostage crisis continued to focus attention on his weaknesses. One hostage was released on July 11 due to illness, but 52 were still captive. When the exiled shah of Iran died in Egypt on July 27, there was a fleeting hope that the Iranians would finally give up their prisoners. By this time, however, their grievances with the United States had changed to straightforward financial demands. On September 12 Ayatollah Khomeini announced the latest conditions for the hostages' release: First, all financial claims against Iran must be canceled; second, the shah's wealth must be returned to Iran; third, the freeze on Iranian assets must be lifted; and, finally, the United States must agree not to interfere in Iranian affairs, either militarily or politically.

There was a significant omission: No longer was the United States required to apologize for its crimes against the Iranian people. With this and with the outbreak of war between Iran and Iraq on September 22—a development that made Iran's need for money all the more important—Carter finally saw a chance to obtain the hostages' freedom. If he could do it before the November 4 presidential election, so much the better.

## ELECTION TRIALS AND THE OCTOBER SURPRISE

For Jimmy Carter, the 1980 election would prove very different from his 1976 triumph. When the hostage crisis struck, he had immediately canceled a state visit to Canada as well as several political engagements. He had also pledged not to campaign or take part in any partisan activity until the hostages came home. This effectively insulated him in the White House, and his critics claimed he was using the hostage crisis as a way of appearing more presidential as well as an excuse to

Massachusetts senator Edward Kennedy and President Jimmy Carter shake hands in June 1978; a year and a half later, they were rivals for the Democratic nomination. *(Courtesy Jimmy Carter Library)*

avoid facing both his political opponents and the voters. His self-imposed isolation was derisively called "the Rose Garden strategy."

At first the biggest threat to Carter was Massachusetts senator Edward Kennedy, but following the hostage seizure in Tehran, popular support for Carter rose quickly, and his opponent's candidacy was soon in trouble. When the president withdrew from a debate with the senator in Iowa, Kennedy immediately went on the attack, and Carter's advisers questioned the wisdom of his self-imposed isolation. Nevertheless, Carter won Iowa, and he went on to score more wins. Kennedy, meanwhile, had the occasional victory but otherwise ran a listless and directionless campaign. He won some important primaries, but he also made some gaffes, and he remained haunted by the infamous 1969 accident at Chappaquiddick Island, Massachusetts, when he drove his car off a bridge and a passenger, Mary Jo Kopechne, drowned.

By April 1980 Carter still did not have enough delegates to win the Democratic nomination and therefore announced that the nation's problems were "manageable enough for me to leave the White House for a limited travel schedule, including some campaigning if I choose." His job-approval rating had been fluctuating for months. It rose again after the failed hostage-rescue attempt, and thereafter he steadily accumulated delegates. By the end of "Super Tuesday" (June 3, 1980), he had more than enough to ensure the nomination, even though Kennedy had won five of the eight primaries that day.

Yet not until the second night of the Democratic National Convention, August 12, did Kennedy formally withdraw from the race. The speech he gave that night was one of the best of his career, and he dominated the convention, using his own delegates and position within the Democratic Party to shape the campaign platform. Although Carter won the nomination, he came away from the convention looking insubstantial, an image that would continue in his encounters with his Republican opponent.

Despite being 13 years older, Ronald Reagan seemed younger and more vigorous than the tired, careworn president. By midsummer the Republican candidate had a 20-point advantage in the polls, but in the subsequent campaigning he made blunders that put him in a bad light. He unashamedly espoused such controversial issues as banning abortions and permitting prayer in schools, and his support for a military buildup, combined with his fervid anticommunism, led to growing public concern over his nuclear policy. It soon became a tight campaign, though the main issue was undoubtedly the economy, a downside for Carter that provided Reagan with his best openings for attack.

The race was made more interesting by the candidacy of John Anderson, a Republican running as an independent and the first third-party presidential aspirant to seriously challenge the two-party system since George Wallace in 1968. As Anderson's support gradually declined, plans for a three-way debate were scrapped, and Reagan and Carter faced each other alone in a televised confrontation on October 28. The difference in their demeanors was marked: Carter was tense and on guard; Reagan was relaxed and exuded confidence. The former actor was quick with comeback lines: "There you go again," he said in response to Carter's attack on his Medicare position, implying that the president was exaggerating and eliciting laughter from the audience. Responding to Carter's comment that the American people had done "very well" in making sacrifices, Reagan riposted, "We do not have to go on sharing in sacrifice." As the debate concluded, the Republican challenger summed up the nation's mood when he looked into the camera and asked, "Are you better off than you were four years ago?" The answer, he implied, was obvious: It was time for a change.

Subsequent polls had the two candidates running neck-and-neck in the few days remaining before the election. Then it all collapsed for Carter.

Since the summer, the Reagan camp had been preparing for an "October Surprise" from Carter—a dramatic resolution to the hostage crisis, the timing of which would make electoral victory certain for the president. Rumors to this effect were abetted by newspaper columnist John Anderson, who on August 18 published allegations, later proved false, that the Carter administration was preparing an invasion of Iran to take place in mid-October. Two days later, Ronald Reagan expressed publicly his concern that the president might be "tempted to take reckless actions designed to reassure Americans that our power is undiminished."[22] Yet although Carter was aware of the advantages for him in finding a solution before the election, his primary concern was always the hostages' safety, and as the interminable negotiations dragged on, his frustration grew.

In the end, there was no October Surprise, and less than 24 hours before the election, polls showed that voters had turned away from the president, ensuring a landslide victory for Reagan. The deciding factors had been the economy and Carter's failure to get the hostages home, something voters had been forcefully reminded of during the preceding weekend when Iran suddenly began to raise the situation with the media and news programs rebroadcast tapes of the seizure from nearly a year before.

Several years later, speculation spread that the so-called October Surprise was merely a ruse invented by Reagan's staff to cover up secret meetings with representatives of the Iranian government. Reportedly, they had agreed to delay the hostage negotiations until after the presidential election, thus denying Carter any opportunity to capitalize on the prisoners' release. This theory of underhanded Republican dealings was originally published by author Barbara Honegger (*October Surprise*, 1989). But it gained credence when Gary Sick—an expert on the Middle East who had served on the National Security Council under Presidents Ford, Carter, and Reagan—published his own book on the subject (*October Surprise: America's Hostages in Iran and the Election of Ronald Reagan*, 1991).[23]

According to Sick, Reagan's campaign manager, William Casey, a former CIA spymaster, had brokered a deal whereby Iran would turn the hostages over to the Republicans after the election; in exchange, Iran would receive arms from Israel at once and acquire more arms and other political benefits once Reagan took office. In making his case, Sick pointed out that Israel began to supply arms to Iran before the election and that the flow intensified after Reagan took office. With their country at war with Iraq, the Iranians needed arms badly. Although Carter had been willing to deliver military equipment for which Iran had previously paid, he was unwilling to authorize any new deal for arms. It was therefore to the Iranians' advantage to work with Reagan rather than with Carter, and thus the plot was hatched to intercede covertly in the hostage negotiations.[24]

There are numerous flaws in Sick's arguments: While he presents some convincing documentation, he fails to provide conclusive proof of the conspiracy, and the credibility of some of his sources has been questioned. Both Republicans and Democrats (including Carter) have vigorously attacked Sick's charges as baseless, although much of his evidence remains persuasive and hard to explain outside the context of a conspiracy. The timing of some events also seems suspicious—for instance, Iran's decision to talk to the media the weekend before the election and the replaying of images of the hostage seizure to Americans who were bound to be influenced by these reminders of an unhappy situation.

On January 3, 1993, a House of Representatives task force issued a report stating that there was "no credible evidence supporting any attempt by the Reagan Presidential Campaign—or persons representing or associated with the campaign—to delay the release of the American hostages in Iran."[25] Nevertheless, conspiracy theorists have clung to their arguments, and for many the affair, if true, presaged the Iran-contra scandal of 1986–87. Thus, the term *October Surprise* has taken its place in the American lexicon to mean not the preelection release of the hostages that would have benefited Carter but rather the alleged covert negotiations to delay the release that definitely benefited Reagan.

In any event, Ronald Reagan and George H. W. Bush won the November 4 election overwhelmingly, securing 489 electoral votes in 43 states, although taking only 50.9 percent of the popular vote. Carter and Walter Mondale managed only 49 electoral votes in seven states and the District of Columbia, coming away with 41.1 percent of the popular vote, while John Anderson and his running mate, Patrick Lucey, took 6.6 percent of the popular vote. It was the first time since Herbert Hoover lost in 1932 that an elected incumbent president had been defeated.[26] In addition, the Republicans won control of the Senate for the first time since 1954.

The Carter presidency was over, and the Reagan era was about to begin. But the lame-duck president still had work to do; the hostages were not home yet.

## ASSASSINATION

Around 5:00 on the afternoon of December 8, 1980, John Lennon, onetime Beatle and peace activist, left his home in the Dakota building on West 72nd Street in New York City with his wife, Yoko Ono. As they exited the building, a fan stopped Lennon and asked him to sign a copy of his most recent album, *Double Fantasy.* Lennon obliged and then went off to a recording session. When the couple returned nearly six hours later, the same fan, Mark David Chapman, was waiting for them. As Lennon and Ono passed him, Chapman pulled out a .38 revolver and fired five bullets into Lennon's back and shoulder. As Ono screamed, Lennon stumbled and collapsed into the sentry box by the building's entrance. The security guard knocked the gun out of Chapman's hand, shouting at him, "Do you know what you've done?"

Chapman knew. "I just shot John Lennon," he replied. Taking a copy of *The Catcher in the Rye,* by J. D. Salinger, from his pocket, he began to read, waiting calmly until the police took him into custody.

Lennon's injuries were fatal; he died in the emergency room at Roosevelt Hospital. As soon as the news got out, tearful fans appeared by the gate at the Dakota, burning candles, playing cassettes of Lennon songs, and waving posters expressing their grief. The outpouring of emotion continued for days, and on December 14, at 2:00 P.M., Yoko Oko led a silent vigil that lasted 10 minutes.

Mark David Chapman was later revealed to be a former mental patient who had believed himself to be John Lennon and was driven by inner voices to kill

John Lennon and Yoko Ono are shown in an undated photo. *(Library of Congress, Prints and Photographs Division [LC-USZ62-123100])*

his bad "alter ego." A public defender worked for six months to prepare his case, but shortly before the trial was to begin, Chapman changed his plea to guilty, apparently on the orders of a "small male voice" that spoke to him, which he interpreted to be God; he has been incarcerated ever since. In subsequent years it was suggested that he was a pawn in a plot to kill Lennon, but no conspiracy has ever been proven. Mark David Chapman remains simply "the deranged fan who shot John Lennon."

## THE HOSTAGES COME HOME

In the final weeks of Jimmy Carter's presidency, apart from the Lennon assassination, the biggest headlines revolved around the "Who Shot J.R.?" episode of the nighttime soap *Dallas* on November 21, 1980, which attracted the largest viewing audience to that date in television history. On January 14, 1981, President Carter delivered his farewell address to the nation, in which he said, "I will continue as I have the last 14 months to work hard and to pray for the lives and the well-being of the American hostages held in Iran. I can't predict yet what will happen, but I hope you will join me in my constant prayer for their freedom."[27] His words gave no indication of the sleepless nights and endless hours he had devoted to making the freeing of the hostages the last great task of his administration.

Obsessed with resolving the crisis, Carter spent the weeks before Reagan's inauguration cloistered in the White House, conferring with Secretary of State Muskie and Assistant Secretary of State Warren Christopher regarding the financial transactions that would, he hoped, win the hostages' freedom at last. By this time the negotiations revolved almost solely around money.

The Iranians renewed discussions after Iraq invaded their country on September 22—an invasion that meant a need for arms and the financial resources with which to buy them. It was now in Iran's interests to negotiate, and President Carter opened the way on October 20 when he announced in a campaign speech that if the hostages were released, the United States would unfreeze assets, lift sanctions, and seek normal diplomatic relations with Iran. On November 2 the Iranian parliament replied by restating the four conditions of September 12: Cancel financial claims against Iran, return all of the shah's wealth, release Iran's assets, and guarantee that the United States would not interfere in Iran's affairs.

On November 5 the Iranians indicated that Reagan's election had changed things and would probably result in delays. A desperate Carter appealed for help, which came when a team of Farsi-speaking Algerians entered the negotiations, becoming messengers between the two sides. The resulting improvement in communications sped up talks and helped to resolve problems in the complicated business of sorting out the money.

The chief negotiator on the American side was Warren Christopher, whose team included John E. Hoffman, Jr., the chief legal counsel for Citibank, and representatives from the State Department, the National Security Council, and the Treasury Department. It took weeks to untangle the finances and determine how the transactions would be handled. The Iranian assets were currently controlled by the Federal Reserve Bank and overseas branches of 12 major American banks. Their cooperation was needed to implement complicated financial exchanges; some heads of government also became involved in the process, including British prime minister Margaret Thatcher and German chancellor Helmut Schmidt.

On November 20 Secretary of State Muskie announced that the United States had accepted Iran's four conditions for the hostages' release "on principle." A week later the Iranian government took custody of 49 of the hostages, giving Americans hope that a resolution was near. Even then the Iranians continued to change their minds, sometimes raising their demands, sometimes lowering them. Remarkably, they agreed to leave a third of the impounded assets in escrow to settle claims on both sides through the American legal system. By January 16, 1981, it seemed that agreement had finally been reached. Transfers between banks began to take place, and on January 18 the Iranians signed the Declaration of Algiers in Tehran; Christopher and Algerian foreign minister Mohammede Benyahia signed it the next day. President Carter had already signed 15 documents authorizing the complicated transfer of funds to the Iranian government. In Iran the hostages were prepared for their release.

Carter had originally hoped to fly to West Germany to greet the hostages before the inauguration, but as that chance vanished he wanted only to be able to announce the hostages' freedom before handing the reins of government over to Reagan. The hours ticked away, and the financial transactions were completed by the early morning of January 20, but by the time Carter had to leave for the inauguration, the hostages had still not left Iran. It was therefore President Reagan who, at an inaugural luncheon, shared the news with the nation that the hostages had been freed and were on their way to West Germany. They had left Iran within minutes of Reagan's taking the oath of office.

Even Carter's opponents admitted that the timing of the hostages' release was a cruel twist that seemed to have been deliberately planned by the Iranians as a slap in the face to the president. October Surprise theorists claim William Casey had insisted that Iran delay the release until Reagan's inauguration day, but Reagan himself seemed sympathetic to Carter's plight. He immediately offered Air Force One to the former president to fly to Wiesbaden, West Germany, to greet the 52 former hostages. Carter accepted gratefully and the following day met most of the people for whose release he had worked for 14 months. Several refused to talk to him, angry at what they perceived as his lack of action during the 444 days they had been in captivity. Others forgave him, realizing that he too had been a victim.

It was an unhappy end to an unhappy affair—but Jimmy Carter had done all he could.

## CHRONICLE OF EVENTS

### 1979

*November 1:* Mamie Eisenhower, widow of former president Dwight D. Eisenhower, dies at the age of 82.

*November 3:* In Greensboro, North Carolina, a group of Klu Klux Klansmen and neo-Nazis attack a "Death to the Klan" rally. Five people are shot dead, and 10 are wounded in the attack.

*November 4:* In Tehran, Iran, the U.S. embassy is overrun by revolutionary Iranian students who take some 90 hostages, including 66 Americans. Most of the non-Americans will be released in the days to follow.

*November 10:* President Jimmy Carter orders the deportation of Iranian students who are in the United States illegally.

*November 12:* The president declares an embargo on Iranian oil imports.

*November 14:* President Carter issues Executive Order 12170, freezing all Iranian assets in the United States.

*November 15:* George Meany retires as head of the AFL-CIO; he is succeeded by Lane Kirkland on November 19. Meany had headed the organization since the two labor unions merged in 1955.

*November 19–20:* In Tehran, Iranian students release five women and eight African Americans; two women and one African American are among the 53 Americans who remain in captivity.

*November 21:* Four people, including two American soldiers, are killed when a mob attacks the U.S. embassy in Islamabad, Pakistan.

*November 22:* Islamic students attack the U.S. consulate in Izmir, Turkey.

*December 2:* A mob attacks the U.S. embassy in Tripoli, Libya, damaging two floors in the building; the 21 occupants escape unhurt.

*December 3:* Eleven youths are trampled to death during a scramble to get seats at a concert by The Who at Riverfront Coliseum in Cincinnati, Ohio.

*December 4:* President Carter announces that he will run for reelection in 1980.

*December 6:* Shirley Hufstedler is sworn in as the first Secretary of Education. She has six months to get the new Department of Education (created on October 17) up and running.

*December 12:* The United States expels most of the Iranian diplomats within its borders.

*December 13:* Canadian prime minister Joe Clark loses a confidence vote. Within 10 hours he dissolves Parliament and calls for a new national election to take place on February 18, 1980.

*December 24:* Soviet troops begin an invasion of Afghanistan; by December 29 more than 50,000 Soviet troops will occupy the country. The invasion provokes international condemnation.

### 1980

*January 4:* In reaction to the Soviet invasion of Afghanistan, President Jimmy Carter announces an embargo on grain deliveries to the Soviet Union.

*January 5:* Hewlett-Packard announces the release of its first personal computer.

*January 7:* President Carter signs a bailout bill authorizing loan guarantees of $1.5 billion for the financially troubled Chrysler Corporation.

*January 10:* Longtime labor leader George Meany, head of the AFL-CIO for 24 years until his retirement in November 1979, dies at the age of 85.

*January 14:* According to a report from the Office of the Surgeon General, cases of lung cancer in women are increasingly rapidly, and the disease could overtake breast cancer as the leading cause of cancer deaths in women within three years.

*January 16:* Boston scientists announce the successful synthesis of human interferon, a possible agent to treat certain types of cancer.

*January 20:* President Carter announces that the United States will probably boycott the 1980 summer Olympics in Moscow as a protest against the Soviet invasion of Afghanistan.

*January 20:* The Pittsburgh Steelers defeat the Los Angeles Rams, 31-19, to win Super Bowl XIV.

*January 28:* Six Americans posing as Canadians escape from Iran with the help of Canadian embassy personnel.

*January 29:* Entertainer Jimmy Durante dies at age 86. Known for his large nose, raspy voice, and comic skills, Durante, who started his career in vaudeville, was also a singer, an actor, and a songwriter ("Inka Dinka Doo").

*February 3:* The FBI's Abscam operation to expose official corruption is revealed to the American public.

*February 12–24:* The winter Olympics are held in Lake Placid, New York. The United States wins six gold medals—five won by speed-skater Eric Heiden—finishing third behind the Soviet Union and East

Germany. The U.S. hockey team scores a major upset over the Soviet team and goes on to win the gold medal in the final against Finland.

*February 15:* Walter Cronkite, veteran television news reporter, announces his intention to retire in 1981. He has anchored the *CBS Evening News* since 1950.

*February 18:* Pierre Trudeau is elected prime minister of Canada, defeating Joe Clark. He will take office on March 3. (Trudeau had already served as prime minister from April 20, 1968, to June 4, 1979.)

*February 27:* At the Grammy Awards, Billy Joel wins best album of 1979 and best male pop vocalist for *52nd Street.* The Doobie Brothers win for best record and best pop group, while Dionne Warwick is named best female pop vocalist.

*March 10:* Dr. Herman Tarnower, author of a bestselling diet book, is shot dead by Jean Harris, headmistress of a Virginia girls' school.

*March 12:* In Chicago, John Wayne Gacy, Jr., is found guilty of the murders of 33 men and boys. He will be sentenced to death the next day and executed in 1994.

*March 14:* An airliner crashes while making an emergency landing near Warsaw, Poland, killing 95, including 22 members of a U.S. amateur boxing team.

*March 14:* President Carter unveils an anti-inflation program that he hopes will cure the ailing economy.

*March 17:* President Carter signs the Refugee Act.

*March 31:* Famed African-American athlete Jesse Owens dies at age 66. Owens had shattered Adolf Hitler's belief in Aryan supremacy with his wins at the 1936 Olympics in Munich, Germany.

*April 2:* President Carter signs the Crude Oil Windfall Profits Tax.

*April 7:* As the hostage crisis continues, the United States breaks off diplomatic relations with Iran and expels all remaining Iranian diplomats. Economic sanctions are also imposed as all exports to Iran are banned.

*April 14:* Pulitzer Prizes are awarded to Norman Mailer (fiction), Edmund Morris (biography), Leon F. Litwack (history), Douglas R. Hofstadter (general nonfiction), Donald R. Justice (poetry), and Lanford Wilson (drama).

*April 14: Kramer vs. Kramer* wins the Academy Award as the best motion picture of 1979. Its star, Dustin Hoffman, wins as best actor, and Sally Field wins the best actress award for *Norma Rae.* Melvyn Douglas and Meryl Streep win as best supporting actor and actress, respectively.

*April 21:* Rosie Ruiz wins the women's race at the Boston Marathon but is subsequently disqualified when it is discovered that she jumped into the race about a mile from the finish line.

*April 24:* An attempt to rescue the U.S. hostages being held in Iran is aborted, and a collision between aircraft results in the deaths of eight members of the rescue team and injuries to five others.

*April 26:* In the wake of the failed rescue attempt on April 24, Secretary of State Cyrus Vance resigns from office. He will be succeeded by Senator Edmund Muskie (D, Maine).

*April 28:* The American Cancer Society issues a report projecting that 8.5 million Americans will die from cancer in the 1980s, 2 million more than in the 1970s.

*April 29:* Noted film director Alfred Hitchcock dies at the age of 80. A master of suspense, his films included such classics as *North by Northwest, Vertigo, Psycho,* and *The Birds.*

*April–September:* More than 125,000 Cuban refugees arrive in the United States, with the Cuban government's approval. Although the refugees are initially welcomed, by mid-May fears that many are criminals and deadbeats result in measures to screen the refugees and control their admittance into the country.

*May 1:* The first American Book Awards (previously the National Book Awards) are presented to William Styron (fiction), Tom Wolfe (general nonfiction), Edmund Morris (biography), Henry Kissinger (history), and Philip Levine (poetry). Eudora Welty is given the National Medal for Literature.

*May 4:* The Department of Health, Education, and Welfare (HEW) officially goes out of existence, replaced by the Department of Education and the Department of Health and Human Services (HHS). HEW programs were transferred from HHS to Education beginning October 17, 1979.

*May 5:* In its annual report on U.S. corporations, *Forbes* magazine announces that Exxon was the country's largest corporation in 1979, with sales of $79,106,471,000. General Motors takes second place in the report.

*May 9:* In Tampa, Florida, the Liberian freighter *Summit Venture* rams the Sunshine Skyway bridge, collapsing one of its spans and killing 35 people, most of them trapped in a bus that plummets into the waters below.

*May 17–19:* Race riots break out in Miami, Florida, after an all-white jury acquits four white former Miami police officers of the fatal beating of a black man; 14 are killed, almost all of them African American.

*May 18:* Mount St. Helens in southwestern Washington State erupts, killing at least 57 people. The explosion blows the top off the mountain and sets off fires, floods, and mudslides.

*May 20:* Voters in a referendum in Quebec, Canada, reject a call for the province to separate from the rest of the country.

*May 28:* For the first time, women graduate from the U.S. military academies at West Point, Annapolis, and Colorado Springs.

*May 29:* Vernon Jordan, civil rights leader and president of the National Urban League, is shot and critically wounded by a sniper in Fort Wayne, Indiana. His recovery will take months.

*June 7:* Controversial author Henry Miller dies, age 88. Miller's books were noted for their sexuality and surrealism and were frequently banned; *Tropic of Cancer* (1934) and *Tropic of Capricorn* (1939) were not published in the United States until the 1960s.

*June 8:* Tony Awards are presented for the 1979–80 Broadway theater season. Winners include *Children of a Lesser God* (best play), *Evita* (best musical), and John Rubinstein and Phyllis Frelich as best dramatic actor and actress.

*June 16:* In *Diamond v. Chakrabarty,* the U.S. Supreme Court approves the patenting of living organisms.

*June 23–September:* The worst drought since the 1930s hits the country, devastating large parts of the South, Southwest, and mid-Mississippi River Valley, killing thousands and destroying crops and livestock.

*June 27:* Draft registration for 19- and 20-year-old men is reinstated after being suspended in 1975, despite no plans for implementing a draft.

Ronald Reagan accepts the nomination for president at the Republican National Convention in Detroit on July 17, 1980. *(Courtesy Ronald Reagan Library)*

*June 30:* The U.S. Supreme Court upholds an award of financial compensation to the Lakota, Dakota, Nakota (Sioux) for the government's illegal seizure of the Black Hills in the 1800s but refuses to authorize the return of the land itself.

*July 8:* An amendment to the Hopi-Navajo Relocation Act is passed, requiring some 10,000 Navajo (Dineh) to move off land designated for the Hopi.

*July 11:* Richard Queen, one of the 53 American hostages in Iran, is released due to illness.

*July 14–17:* The Republican National Convention in Detroit, Michigan, nominates Ronald W. Reagan as president and George H. W. Bush as vice president.

*July 27:* Mohammed Reza Pahlavi, shah of Iran, age 60, dies in exile in Cairo, Egypt. His death has little effect on the negotiations to secure the release of U.S. hostages in Tehran, Iran.

*August 10:* Golf great Jack Nicklaus wins the PGA (Professional Golfers Association) championship for the fifth time.

*August 11–14:* The Democratic National Convention is held in New York City, where President Jimmy Carter and Vice President Walter F. Mondale are nominated for reelection.

*August 31:* U.S. Representative Michael J. Myers (D, Pa.) is convicted on charges of bribery and conspiracy related to the Abscam investigation. He is sentenced to three years in prison and fined $20,000.

*September 16–25:* The United States successfully defends the America's Cup when the yacht *Freedom* beats the *Australia* by four races to one.

*September 22:* Iraq invades Iran, beginning what will become a 10-year war. This will impact on the negotiations for the release of the American hostages in Iran.

*September 22:* Procter and Gamble recalls its Rely-brand tampons after federal studies showed a link between tampon use and toxic shock syndrome, which had been responsible for the deaths of 25 women.

*October 2:* U.S. Representative Michael J. Myers (D, Pa.) is expelled from the House of Representatives, having been convicted of bribery and conspiracy charges related to the Abscam scandal.

*October 21:* In baseball, the National League's Philadelphia Phillies defeat the American League's Kansas City Royals, four games to two, to win the World Series.

*October 27:* Opera diva Beverly Sills gives her final performance at the New York City Opera, singing Rosalinda in *Die Fledermaus.*

*November 4:* Ronald Reagan takes 43 states in the presidential election to defeat Jimmy Carter. The Republicans win the majority in the Senate, but the Democrats retain their majority in the House of Representatives.

*November 12: Voyager I,* which had been launched in 1977, flies within 77,000 miles of the planet Saturn, finding more rings around the planet and three new moons.

*November 21:* In the second-worst hotel fire in U.S. history, 84 people are killed in a blaze at the MGM Grand Hotel in Las Vegas, Nevada.

*November 21:* The television evening soap *Dallas* broadcasts its "Who Shot J.R.?" episode, which attracts the largest viewing audience in TV history to that time: 88.6 million.

*December 2:* President Carter signs the Alaska Lands Bill, legalizing the Alaska National Interest Lands Conservation Act after nine years of discussions between the government and native Alaskans about the conservation of land and use of natural resources in the state.

*December 2:* In El Savador, four American women—three nuns and a Catholic churchwoman—are kidnapped, raped, and murdered. The killings cause an international outcry. Five Salvadoran National Guardsmen will later be accused of the murder.

*December 3:* U.S. representatives Frank Thompson, Jr. (D, N.J.) and John M. Murphy (D, N.Y.) are convicted on bribery and conspiracy charges related to the Abscam investigation. Both are sentenced to three years in prison, and Murphy is fined $20,000.

*December 8:* Former Beatle and rock icon John Lennon is shot dead by Mark David Chapman, a former mental patient, outside Lennon's apartment building in New York City.

*December 11:* President Carter signs the Comprehensive Environmental Response, Compensation, and Liability Act, or Superfund Bill, which was created to clean up toxic waste dumps in the United States.

*December 15:* In *United States v. Will,* the Supreme Court rules that Congress can only cut cost-of-living increases for life-tenured judges before scheduled increases are to go into effect; to do so afterward would be unconstitutional.

*December 16:* Colonel Harland Sanders, founder of Kentucky Fried Chicken, dies at age 90.

*December 31:* Author Marshall McLuhan dies at age 69. Born in Canada, McLuhan shot to fame with his observations on the media, becoming best known for his catchphrases "the medium is the message" and "the global village."

**1981**

*January 7:* A forecaster's advice to "sell everything" results in a run on the stock market, causing the Dow Jones average to fall 23.8 points. The stock market will stabilize by January 19.

*January 8:* A report in the *New England Journal of Medicine* on a 20-year study of 1,900 men links the consumption of high amounts of cholesterol to increased risk of coronary death.

*January 9:* U.S. Representative Raymond Lederer (D, Pa.) is found guilty of bribery and conspiracy charges relating to the Abscam investigation. He is sentenced to three years in prison and fined $20,000.

*January 14:* The Federal Communications Commission (FCC) eases broadcasting regulations, allowing stations to increase the number of commercials aired and canceling the obligation to allocate time for news or public-affairs programming.

*January 14:* President Carter broadcasts his farewell address, in which he emphasizes the "threat of nuclear destruction, our stewardship of the physical resources of the planet, and the preeminence of the basic rights of human beings."

*January 20:* Minutes after Ronald Reagan is inaugurated as president, Iran releases the 52 American hostages it had held since November 1979. The next day, former president Jimmy Carter flies to West Germany to greet them.

## Eyewitness Testimony

### Jimmy Carter's Travails

One does not have to be very astute to recognize the fact that a malaise permeates the atmosphere. . . . The important thing is to recognize the cause, and there can be no doubt that it has been brought about by a lack of leadership in the White House and Congress. Our President makes a determined speech, pounds on the dais, promises action and then does nothing constructive. He has failed to give us leadership in fighting inflation, meeting the energy crisis or in foreign policy. Yes, one can feel a malaise sweeping the country, and it hurts every one of us.

*Letter to the editor commenting on the national mood,*
*in* U.S. News & World Report,
*November 26, 1979, p. 4.*

There is . . . a nationwide, perhaps worldwide, predisposition to criticize Carter for softness if his response is restrained and cautious. Never mind that restraint and caution are precisely what is called for. Overreaction would exacerbate the turmoil in Iran and the instability of the region, which in turn could escalate into a conflict with the Soviet Union. That is the essence of Carter's dilemma: how to behave responsibly without looking weak.

*Essayist Strobe Talbott commenting on Carter's problems*
*following the seizure of American hostages in Iran,*
*in Talbott, "The Symbolism of the Siege,"*
Time, *November 26, 1979,*
*pp. 44–45.*

To friend and enemy alike, America seems to be slipping. "For the first time, the U.S. appears to have lost faith in the future," says Thierry de Montbrial, director of the French Institute of International Relations. "There is a recognition that the American way of life isn't so superior." Makoto Momoi, a professor at Japan's National Defense College, says that not so long ago, "We admired the United States because of its self-confidence. I used to look forward eagerly to my visits; but I don't even want to go again this year. When you meet Americans nowadays, somehow their behavior has changed; they are always grumbling, becoming increasingly self-critical."

*Critical comments from abroad, in "Has the U.S. Lost Its*
*Clout?"* Newsweek, *November 26, 1979, p. 46.*

This past week, we ended a third year of the Carter administration. . . . At the start of his first year, we—and our country—were much better off. On the home front, inflation was under 5 percent and getting better; now it's over 13 percent and not getting better. . . .

And inflation's not the worst of it. The combination of inflation and unemployment under Mr. Carter has been greater than for any other President in more than 50 years. Measured by what Mr. Carter himself used to be fond of calling the "misery index"—the unemployment rate added to the inflation rate—our economy is 50 percent worse off then it was at the start of 1977 when he became President. . . .

*Republican national chairman Bill Brock, responding to*
*President Carter's State of the Union address, in*
*"Republicans' Reply to Carter Message,"* U.S. News &
World Report, *February 4, 1980, p. 77.*

In retrospect, you can pick out some things that might have been done if you had known ahead of time that events that are unpredictable would have occurred. Had we known ahead of time that the Iranians would have seized our hostages, we may—could have taken some different step. It's hard to know what could have been done. Had we known ahead of time that the Soviets would have invaded Afghanistan, we may have taken some additional measures. But not being able to know those things ahead of time, you can't say what could have been done.

*Jimmy Carter responding to Dan Rather's question,*
*"What do you consider your major mistake to be*
*this year?" in an interview on* 60 Minutes,
*broadcast August 10, 1980, quoted in Richardson,*
Conversations with Carter *(1998), pp. 202–203.*

1980 was pure hell—the Kennedy challenge, Afghanistan, having to put the SALT Treaty on the shelf, the recession, Ronald Reagan, and the hostages . . . always the hostages! It was one crisis after another.

*Jimmy Carter to Hamilton Jordan on January 22, 1981,*
*quoted in Jordan,* Crisis *(1982), p. 7.*

### Terrorism Abroad

"The bastards are inside the Chancellery building!" screams a marine guard shrilly as he Paul Reveres through the second-floor hallway. People are sitting along both sides of the wide hallway as they've been instructed to do by the security chief, Al Golacinski. It's like the final moments on the deck of the *Titanic* must have been. Disbelief and terror highlight the facial expressions of everyone, including the local Iranian employees who have been herded to the second floor for their protection. I stop a young Marine, Billy Gallegos, who's running down the hall. He is excited and scared, but he's more incredulous than anything else. "How'd they manage to get inside the Chancellery so damned fast?" I ask him. He's breathing hard and his huge chest is expanding and contracting rapidly. His eyes are dancing with fear as he pushes me, almost carefully, out of his way. "Sir, I've got to go. They came in through the only window in the basement that didn't have steel bars."

> *Colonel Charles W. Scott, describing the moment when Iranian student revolutionaries broke into the American embassy in Tehran on November 4, 1979, in Scott,* Pieces of the Game *(1984), p. 18.*

Americans reacted with a wave of anger against a foreign country that was almost without precedent in the postwar era. Some Americans burned the Iranian flag. In Washington, Los Angeles, Houston and other cities, there were fights as Iranian students living in the U.S. marched in support of Khomeini. . . . Workers refused to unload Iranian ships or service Iranian airliners. As an emotional week neared its end, Jimmy Carter wearily confessed that "the last two days have been the worst ever" of his Presidency.

> *U.S. reaction to the embassy seizure in Tehran, in* "A Helpless Giant in Iran," Newsweek, *November 19, 1979, p. 61.*

Cpl. Steve Crowley, 19, a Long Islander who served in Pakistan about three months, had been assigned to roof duty, and a rioter had shot him in the side of the head. They got him down and brought him to the anteroom of the vault. A nurse hovered over him, fitting an oxygen mark. He lay in a pool of blood. I hadn't been scared at first, but now I was as I stood there looking at this young dying Marine.

> *Marcia Gauger, then* Time *magazine's New Delhi Bureau Chief, who was among the group trapped in the U.S. embassy in Islamabad, Pakistan, when a large mob stormed it on November 21, 1979, in* "'You Could Die Here,'" Time, *December 3, 1979, p. 26.*

They are awakened each morning at 6:30, and spend their day reading, smoking, writing letters and—despite themselves—listening to the chants of the crowds outside. Conversation isn't permitted. Except for brief exercise periods, they remain seated in armchairs, their hands bound lightly though firmly in front of them, their feet bare. They must ask permission to go to the bathroom. Twice a week, they are allowed to take showers, though not to change their clothing. They are fed simply but adequately three times a day. At 10 p.m., they are bedded down on mattresses to get what sleep they can. For the 50 American hostages being held in the U.S. Embassy compound in Tehran, this is what life has been like for this past five weeks.

> *A description of the American hostages' living conditions in Tehran, in* "Boredom—and Terror," Newsweek, *December 17, 1979, p. 32.*

Following the seizure of the embassy in Tehran, Americans were distressed to see images such as this one of a hostage being led by militants outside the embassy on November 8, 1979. *(AP/Wide World Photos)*

There is always a crowd in front of the chained gates of the American Embassy here. The chanting goes on night and day, with loudspeakers issuing a slogan and the crowd then repeating it over and over and over.

Westerners quickly tire of hearing, *"Marg bar Carter"*—Death to Carter—and "Down with the Satan U.S." We wonder how the nerves of hostages inside can possibly hold up after hearing such chants 24 hours a day.

*Reporter William D. Hartley depicting the scene in Tehran, in "On the Scene: A Look at Ranting in Iran,"* U.S. News & World Report, *December 17, 1979, p. 30.*

*Tuesday, February 26, 1980 (23:00) Day 115*
I really can't believe this is all happening just over one man. A man accused of murder, stealing and many other things but still our government keeps him under protection. . . . I'm not a person to judge if the Shah is innocent or guilty but what I do know is that there were a lot of people killed/misled and the person responsible should pay! I guess I'll never learn the truth about all this until I return home and see our point of view, too! The students are so determined that the Shah's going to return. We wish we were as determined, but we're not! Still each day and night we sit and pray, hoping that each next day will bring good news. There's still that sad feeling inside me hinting to be prepared for a long stay. How I hope that feeling is wrong!

*U.S. Sergeant Rodney (Rocky) V. Sickmann, a security guard at the U.S. embassy in Tehran, from his diary in* Sickmann, Iranian Hostage *(1982), p. 36.*

## Action and Reaction

I told the President, "Mr. President, if you embargo this grain there's going to be political pandemonium in Iowa." This was the end of December and the Iowa Democratic precinct caucuses were on the 16th of February. The President rejected our counsel flat out. He said he was not interested in the political implications of his actions. He said it was a very serious matter with the security of the United States at stake and that if it caused him to lose the election, so be it. He approached the situation very philosophically. He didn't allow me or anybody in his Cabinet to bring up the politics of the issues at stake.

*Bob S. Bergland, secretary of agriculture during the Carter administration, describing the late-December 1979 discussions that preceded the president's decision to embargo the sale and export of grain to the Soviet Union, quoted in Thompson,* The Carter Presidency *(1990), p. 126.*

"It's the toughest question of all for me," Carter said. "I don't want the onus for the failure of the Olympics to fall exclusively on the United States. . . . It must be seen as a legitimate worldwide political reaction to what the Russians are doing in Afghanistan. After the grain embargo, the farmers raised hell." He smiled slyly. "But after I announce our Olympics boycott, we'll have to face the wrath of an even more powerful force— Howard Cosell, telling the sports fans that Jimmy Carter killed the Olympics."

*Jimmy Carter on January 18, 1980, reflecting on his decision to have the United States boycott the 1980 Olympics in Moscow, quoted in Jordan,* Crisis *(1982), pp. 112–113.*

The vast majority of nations on Earth have condemned this latest Soviet attempt to extend its colonial domination of others and have demanded the immediate withdrawal of Soviet troops. The Moslem world is especially and justifiably outraged by this aggression against an Islamic people. No actions of a world power has ever been so quickly and so overwhelmingly condemned. But verbal condemnation is not enough. The Soviet Union must pay a concrete price for their aggression.

*President Jimmy Carter criticizing the Soviet Union for its December 1979 invasion of Afghanistan, in his televised State of the Union address, January 21, 1980. Available online. URL: http://jimmycarterlibrary.org/ documents/speeches/su80jec.phtml.*

It is becoming increasingly apparent that one thing can be expected consistently of American foreign policy: it will always be too little, too late. While Washington deliberates over the recent invasion of Afghanistan . . . and considers such countermeasures as boycotting the Moscow Olympics, the Russians complete their military action. Perhaps the hope in Washington is that if we dally long enough, the whole crisis will simply disappear of itself. The British, in the 1930s, approached Hitler with similar expectations. The ultimate result, of course, was not precisely what they intended. Afghanistan will probably fade from the headlines in a few weeks, accompanied by pious sighs of relief. So did Munich in 1938.

*Letter to the editor criticizing U.S. policy, in* Newsweek, *January 28, 1980, p. 6.*

Ever since he was a boy, Franklin Jacobs has "dreamed of being a superstar." Now 22 and a top-rated high jumper, Jacobs could have his chance at stardom in Moscow this summer—if he is allowed to compete in the Olympic Games. But Jacobs is no longer sure he wants to. "I was never thrilled about going to Moscow," he says, "and the recent invasion of Afghanistan bothers me. I don't like talking politics, but there seems no way around it. I still want to be a superstar, but I have faith in my government and if they believe it would be best to boycott the Olympics, then I'm all for it."

*An American Olympic athlete commenting on the proposed U.S. boycott of the Moscow Olympics, in "An Olympic Boycott?"* Newsweek, *January 28, 1980, p. 20.*

When I first heard about it, I was pretty reactionary: "Why me?" But I thought about it and when I was on a run the next day, I decided that if everybody feels that's the right thing to do, we should do it. The Olympic spirit has been lost anyway.

· · · · ·

I'm going to write to my congressman and ask to be compensated in some way, like the farmers in the grain embargo.

*Olympians Dean Matthews and Herb Lindsay expressing their reactions to President Carter's announcement that the United States would be boycotting the 1980 Olympics in Moscow, in* Running Times *(April 1980). Available online. URL: http://www.runningtimes.com/issues/80/boycotts1980.htm.*

## The Economy

Imagine the possibilities had the Government given Chrysler $10 billion to provide a vehicle that runs on alternative fuels or solar power. Instead, it gives $1.5 billion for an obsolete product.

*From a letter to the editor commenting on the proposed federal bailout of Chrysler Corporation, in* Time, *November 26, 1979, p. 12.*

It was one of the gloomiest economic messages ever delivered by a U.S. President. According to Jimmy Carter, the nation faces an imminent recession that will push up unemployment but provide little relief from the inflationary spiral. "There are no economic miracles waiting to be performed," the President admitted last week. The best the Administration can do is to try "to prevent the spread of double-digit price increases from oil and other problem sectors to the rest of the economy."

. . . Republicans complained about the lack of business tax cuts, Democrats feared that social programs were being slighted in favor of a Pentagon buildup— and nearly everyone denounced Carter's $15.8 billion deficit. "This budget is not balanced even with the highest level of taxation since World War II," thundered Republican Sen. Henry Bellmon of Oklahoma.

*Reaction to the federal budget for the next fiscal year, presented by President Carter to Congress in January 1980, reported in " 'No Economic Miracles,' "* Newsweek, *February 11, 1980, p. 75.*

While Washington swarmed with interest groups protesting against the budget cuts, Congressional leaders hoped that they had enough support to overcome such pressures and give the President the balanced budget he is calling for. But even if they do, many private economists will have little to cheer about. "This program would have been adequate had it been part of the original budget in January," says Alan Greenspan, who served as Chairman of the CEA during the Ford Administration. "But having made the mistake of introducing an inflationary budget and creating chaos in the financial markets, Carter will now need a much larger package to get back to where he would have been had he done it in the first place."

*Early reaction to President Carter's revised budget proposal, which includes an anti-inflation program, in "Carter's Attack on Inflation,"* Newsweek, *March 24, 1980, p. 30.*

This is likely to be the second worst recession of the postwar period. Although it is already too late for a tax cut to go into effect in calendar year 1980, the recession had killed all hope of a balanced budget. So, in view of the bad news about the current decline, don't be surprised when President Carter tears up his old game plan and speaks out for a 1981 tax cut.

*Nobel prize winner Paul A. Samuelson commenting on the economic downturn, in Samuelson, "How Deep the Recession?" Newsweek, June 30, 1980, p. 56.*

Almost every change in policy has been in the same direction—fighting inflation. We've been consistent on that score. . . . [T]his is the only government in the world where you have to submit to Congress in January a budget for a fiscal year that begins nine months later. Other countries, including Japan, have frequent re-evaluations. Everybody congratulates the Japanese on their marvelous flexibility, and we catch hell when we change course.

In many ways we have had a fairly reasonable record, trying for a soft landing for the economy after a good recovery from the last recession. But we got hit in 1979 by a doubling of oil prices and by the very sharp slowdown in productivity growth. Together, they gave us a significant increase in inflation, and they're importantly responsible for the recession.

*Charles L. Schultze, chairman of the Council of Economic Advisers under Jimmy Carter, rationalizing administration policies in "Tax-Cut Targets: Productivity and Investment," U.S. News & World Report, July 7, 1980, p. 24.*

Though they have ostensibly similar goals, the programs of Carter and Reagan are actually quite different. Of the two, Carter is far more cautious about how far he is willing to go in cutting taxes to stimulate growth. Some critics charge that, in the current inflationary climate, the Reagan tax cuts would push prices up even faster. Warns Economist Jagdish Bhagwati of Columbia University: "If one argues that budget deficits are a major source of inflation, then, paradoxically, I would be much more worried about inflation if the Republicans came to power rather than the Democrats."

*A comparison of the economic policies of Jimmy Carter and Ronald Reagan, in "The Great 1980 Non-Debate," Time, October 20, 1980, p. 71.*

## Scandals

This smacks of a setup. A lot of guys feel that the FBI has got it in for this place.

*A leading congressional Democrat commenting after news breaks on February 3, 1980, of the FBI's Abscam operation, quoted in "The FBI Stings Congress," Time, February 18, 1980, p. 10.*

4 Feb 80

Dear Sir:
A wonderful job—Hang them all.

. . . .

February 4, 1980

Dear Mr. Director:
It is most reassuring to read and view the efforts of your Bureau as reported on media communications. I speak of operation ABSCAM. To know that these operations are designed to remove or ethically sanction weak members of our representative government through trial and House debate is truly comforting. It underscored my faith in *The United States of America* as a progressive society dedicated to responsible freedom and decision. . . .

Thank you for your dedication toward supporting the backbone of our representative government, ethics. I personally hope that more operations are planned for the future, an effective program must continue.

. . . .

14 Feb. 1980

For years it has been disheartening to view government corruption, great and small, occur, attracting only momentary media interest, then fading into the background of succeeding events.

We had, it seems to me, become so inured to that pattern (many refer to such an attitude as sophisticated) that the notion of public office being a public trust can be safely disregarded.

Too, the discrediting of the F.B.I. during the recent past for activities which I found distasteful, did little to lend confidence to the citizen. He knew, of course, that elected office was one over which he had no control, excepting one based on good faith—that the elected official would discharge his responsibilities according to the oath he took.

The almost epedemic [sic] violation of the compact between office holder and citizen, much of which, but not all, has been written about routinely has been not just sickening, but frightening.

. .... .

[postmarked 2/16/80]

I am deeply troubled by the lack of ethics shown by F.B.I. personnel at the highest level in pulling off Abscam. You deliberately created a trap that appealed to some of the most basic of human desires, and in so doing caught and politically ruined individuals who may never, until that moment, have committed any crime.

What you people did scares the hell out of me in that it points out so clearly your total lack of any sense of right or wrong. The whole scheme, from conception to execution, smacks of college hijinks with about the same level of maturity behind it. This is not how I want to see my tax money spent.

. .... .

February 16, 1980

Dear Sir,

Now that the Country has finally recovered from Watergate, and it is no longer a topic of daily conversation, the F.B.I. has created Abscam for us!

I was certainly amazed that there were so few crimes for the Bureau to investigate that it had to create one of its own. I also resent my tax dollars going to support such a scheme. This investigation lasted for 23 months and involved 100 agents. If there were not crimes to be investigated, then I believe the FBI should be reduced in force to save tax dollars. . . .

There will always be someone who will take a bribe, but I think we should use our time and efforts to reveal crimes created by someone other than our own F.B.I.

. .... .

19 February 1980

Congratulations!! It is a rare and real pleasure as a tax payer to see that my Federal dollars are going to efforts to keep the Congressmen honest. Your Abscam investigation should have been done years ago and *should be continued*. If we can not create an honest Congress or

judicial system there is no hope that anyone else will be honest. If it takes "entrapment" "so be it" as Carl Rowan and all the other columnists are saying. No one is entrapped who has not been transgressing the line.

*Extracts from letters written to FBI director William Webster regarding the Abscam "sting" operation, published online under the Freedom of Information Act. URL: http://foia.fbi.gov/abscam.htm.*

I don't see where him being the President should have any damn thing to do with what I do, and I'm not going to argue with him about it. He might not like what I do. There are a hell of a lot of things that he does that I don't like. . . . I can see him getting rid of me now because of my political liabilities . . . but frankly I don't think it's any of his damn business.

*Presidential brother Billy Carter in an interview broadcast on national television, July 24, 1980, concerning his dealings with the Libyan government; reported in "Carter Brothers 'Close but So Far Apart It's Pathetic,' " U.S. News & World Report, August 4, 1980, p. 19.*

I do not approve of the fact that my brother has gotten involved in a controversial relationship with an extremely unpopular government. He has, still, certain legal and Constitutional rights. If he is found to have violated the law, my belief is—and my hope is—that he will be treated properly, in accordance with the law: punished if he's guilty, exonerated if he's innocent. But I have seen these things sweep across this nation every now and then, with highly publicized allegations that prove *not* to be true, and you and others have participated in the raising of these questions.

*President Carter defending his brother Billy and also attacking the media at an August 4, 1980, press conference. Available online. URL: http://www.rotten. com/library/bio/black-sheep/billy-carter/.*

## Native Rights and Redress

You do not see us as people. Now, as always, you are taking our land and killing our people. You are committing our culture to your museums, to your Disneylands and Knott's Berry Farms. And you are destroying us.

You say that we are a part of your culture, but it is not so. Our death, *that* is a part of your culture.

. . . .

When, at last, you have taken the Indian's land, desecrated the bones of his ancestors and destroyed him, you will begin to destroy yourself, if you have not already. Those of you who remain after the destruction of the Indian will turn, eventually, against one another, for you have bred an entire race of people whose motivation is greed, avarice and self-assertion.

*Alexander Mott, a Mohawk and radio host, attacking non-Indians' attitudes toward Native Americans and their plunder of natural resources, in Mott, "When the Indian is No More, America Will Have Destroyed Its Own Dreams," Los Angeles Times, March 4, 1980, Part II, p. 5.*

Unquestionably, the arrogant, unconscionable treatment of this country's only true native, the American Indian, is a black mark on our nation's history. There is also no question, as Mott eloquently elucidates, that the land, its natural resources, wildlife and wildlife habitat—all the intricate, irreplaceable ecosystem—is being raped and ruthlessly destroyed, with no concern for the inevitable, detrimental consequences.

*From a letter to the editor commenting on Alexander Mott's column of March 4, in Los Angeles Times, March 15, 1980, Part II, p. 4.*

That they [the Hopi Tribal Council] have rejected the traditional Hopi relationship to the land—and departed from the Way of the kikmongwis and the elders in the process—is, to them, a reflection of the Way's limitations, and of the realities of the age. They believe the tribe had to seize the opportunities available to it in the white man's world, and the land that Massau'u left them was the fundamental resource of the Hopis. Motioning at the surrounding expanse of badlands, they say that they have made much out of what the white men themselves once considered to be worthless. And they will do more. That, they say, is what America is all about.

*Journalist David Harris reporting on the Hopi's move away from traditional practices, in Harris, "Last Stand for an Ancient Indian Way," New York Times Magazine, March 16, 1980, pp. 41, 63.*

Writing for the majority, Associate Justice Harry Blackmun agreed with the Court of Claims that "the Government's uncertain and indefinite obligation to provide the Sioux with rations until they became self-sufficient did not constitute adequate consideration for the Black Hills." The absence of compensation meant that the seizure did violate the First Amendment, and that the Government was thus liable for back interest.

*Examining the Supreme Court's decision in* United States v. Sioux Nation of Indians, *in "$105 Million Award to 8 Tribes Is Upheld," New York Times, July 1, 1980, p. B-9.*

Since 1946 the Government has paid out more than $2 billion to tribes that were victimized long ago by the white man's territorial takeovers. It is admittedly conscience money, but in most cases conscience money is the only practicable form of redress.

Even conscience money doesn't always flow easily. It took generations of lawyering. Congress had to be reminded how General Custer lured the gold miners to the Black Hills and double-crossed Sitting Bull. And how the Government rode roughshod over treaty pledges, seized the land and issued food rations in return. Finally, a bill was passed giving the courts another look at the sorry record. Justice delayed may be justice denied but July 4 is a fine day to feel good about making at least some amends.

*The* New York Times *applauding the Supreme Court decision approving financial compensation to the Lakota for their loss of the Black Hills, in its editorial "Paying for America," New York Times, July 4, 1980, p. A-16.*

A lot of the older people still don't understand that there is such a thing as a dollar-for-acre claim. They don't realize that one precludes the other. It would just not occur to them because their concepts are Indian concepts and the court simply is not understood.

*Suzan Harjo of the Native American Rights Fund explaining the differences between generations in the Lakota's attitude toward the Black Hills, quoted in Bruske, "Black Hills Suit—A Will of Its Own," Washington Post, August 19, 1980, p. A-9.*

In short, disposition of Indian claims is in a state of flux, caught up in conflicting demands for land and natural resources or for cash, tribal integrity and justice for the descendants of those who were wronged. Underlying all such disputes is the truth that whatever shape the settlements take, nothing can really right those wrongs.

"We're not going back to 1492 or 1789 in the land settlements," said Robert Pennington of the Bureau of Indian Affairs. "If we gave them what it is worth today, we wouldn't have a U.S. Treasury. So, dissatisfaction is built in."

*Reporter Ann Crittenden describing the land-versus-cash conflict of Native American claims for redress, in Crittenden, "In the Braves' New World, Indians Like Land, Not Cash,"* New York Times, *November 2, 1980, Sect. 4, p. 8-E.*

## The Refugees Arrive

In 1962 the Soviet missiles that eventually touched off the Cuban missile crisis between the U.S. and the Soviet Union were delivered through this port, but now the harbor resembled a circus of the seas. The curious watched in wonder from apartments as an overeager skipper ran his 16-footer into one of Castro's launches, snapping its flagpole. At nightfall the flotilla twinkled like a floating city, with boats lashed together and crews exchanging festive visits. Castro's searchlights swept the surrounding waters, guarding against Cubans who might try to swim out to the boats.

*Reporter Richard Woodbury describing the scene in Mariel, Cuba, at the start of the boatlift of Cuban refugees to the United States, April 1980, in "Voyage from Cuba,"* Time, *May 5, 1980, p. 43.*

It is a dream so pretty. It is the thing we have dreamed about and prayed for but never thought would happen.

*Hugo Landa, 27, an interpreter from Havana, Cuba, expressing his feelings after arriving in the United States, quoted in "Voyage from Cuba,"* Time, *May 5, 1980, p. 44.*

As the hours ticked into days, life in Mariel harbor grew monotonous, strangely communal. On one shrimper, a woman gave birth; on another boat, a man suffered a heart attack. There was a mini-mutiny aboard one boat; the captain, impatient after five days, decided to return home, although he had a $38,000 charter to pick up refugees. An angry exile pulled out a pistol and held him in his cabin a full day. The Cuban military presence also became more visible. Soldiers patrolled the banks of the harbor with automatic rifles. Jumbo choppers whipped across the bay by day, and

searchlights swept the waters by night. Suddenly, the rescuers had become captives.

*Reporter Richard Woodbury, depicting life for those on the boats in Mariel harbor, Cuba, as they wait to leave for the United States, in "Escape from Bedlam and Boredom,"* Time, *May 12, 1980, p. 38.*

By the weekend, the once-manageable stream of Cubans seeking reunion with their families in America had become a deluge of more than 30,000 refugees in helter-skelter flight to the Promised Land. In a single day last week, 4,500 Cubans arrived, surpassing the total in any one month during the peak of the "freedom flights" from Cuba in the mid-1960s and early '70s. The three-week total was also more than double the number of Indochinese "boat people" admitted during last year's far more orderly refugee-relief effort. Nobody knew just how many more would come; estimates ranged as high as 250,000, a remarkable defection from a country of 10 million. "It's just a constant barrage of people," sighed Dade County official Danny Ivarez. "There's no end to it. Nobody thought it was going to be like this."

*Report on the spiraling numbers of refugees arriving from Cuba, in "The Cuban Tide Is a Flood,"* Newsweek, *May 19, 1980, p. 28.*

Just where the Cubans can go and how they will fare once they get there remains the ultimate problem for the U.S., and the answer will depend on the human reactions of many Americans. . . . In Key West, one 75-year-old man slowly climbed off a shrimp boat, and somebody asked him, "You've come to live in freedom?" As a volunteer took his arm to help him onto the dock, the man quietly replied: "No, I've come to die in freedom."

*Conclusion of a report on the problems caused by the Cuban refugees crisis, in "Open Heart, Open Arms,"* Time, *May 19, 1980, p. 18.*

## Women in the Military

At Fort Jackson, S.C., a young Army recruit falls out of line, too tired and fed up to march another 10 miles. When drill sergeant Linda Taylor orders him to keep pace, he refuses and calls her "bitch." Calmly, Taylor removes the recruit's 20-pound field pack and 8.4 pound M-16 rifle and slings them over her shoulder.

"Let me show you how it's done, soldier," she says—and totes his gear for the rest of the hike. That night, in the barracks, the recruit's buddies chew him out for being rude.

*An example of the changing roles of women in the military, in "The True Adventures of GI Jane,"* Newsweek, *February 18, 1980, p. 39.*

We are brought up with a myth that women are nicer than men, that they are the keepers of the hearth and the mothers. Yet American women have had a long-standing frontier tradition, and many of those women had shotguns by their sides.

*Nora Scott Kinzer, a military personnel expert, defending women joining the military, in "No 'Special Stresses' for Women in Battle,"* U.S. News & World Report, *March 3, 1980, p. 34.*

They will be expected to go further and faster than others. They will be part of a new elite. And, with their qualifications, they will be testing the military's commitment to sexual equality.

*A West Point instructor commenting on the first crop of women to graduate from all three major U.S. military academies, in "Academy Women: Ready to Take Command,"* U.S. News & World Report, *May 26, 1980, p. 32.*

## The Presidential Race and Ronald Reagan

Reagan seems to have attained his position simply by running in place. His once lonely demands for a balanced budget and limits on government spending now echo throughout the corridors of Washington. His once hawkish-sounding call for high defense spending looks positively mainstream these days. And his talk-tough foreign policy doesn't seem so terrible with Americans held hostage in Iran and Russian troops in Afghanistan. In effect, Reagan is playing the same old tune, but the audience seems more ready to harmonize.

*Newsweek's San Francisco bureau chief Gerald C. Lubenow commenting on Ronald Reagan's front-runner position, in Lubenow, "Reagan: Secret of Success,"* Newsweek, *April 7, 1980, p. 26.*

There is little dispute that Reagan has a talent for campaigning and communicating his views. His experience as an actor comes through in the rhythm of his speeches, his sense of timing and platform presence. Face to face with voters, he exhibits a humble sincerity that often wins over skeptics.

A frequent critic concedes: "You have to hand it to him. He is able to rouse the masses, to reflect what the majority of the people are thinking."

A Los Angeles Democrat offers a harsher judgment: "I think Reagan is a shallow and superficial man. He'd rely too heavily on others. But I will say he's cunning smart."

*Reasons why Ronald Reagan is leading the race for the Republican presidential nomination, in "Reagan: What He Stands For,"* U.S. News & World Report, *May 5, 1980, p. 29.*

The President looked irritated when I asked, "What happened?"

"Nothing good," he snapped. "He was nervous and kept rambling on about wanting to debate me, and that I should change my policies and stimulate the economy, and that he felt a special responsibility to his voters and the party. Finally I said, 'Ted, are you going to get out or not?' He said that he wouldn't and that was that." The President paused. The frustration that he had undoubtedly disguised during his meeting with Kennedy was all coming out now. "I think he's going to fight us right through the convention, and I wouldn't bet on his support for the ticket in the general election. I don't think he cares about the party or who wins in November. Deep down, I think he'd rather see Reagan elected than me."

*Jimmy Carter reporting to Hamilton Jordan on a June 5, 1980, meeting with Senator Edward Kennedy, quoted in Jordan,* Crisis *(1982), p. 299.*

In preparing my own acceptance speech notes, it's become more and more obvious that Reagan and I have perhaps the sharpest divisions between us of any two presidential candidates in my lifetime—and also that his policies are a radical departure from those pursued by Ford and Nixon. I am also convinced that on the major issues—concerning the farmers, women, minorities, labor, educators, the elderly, and other groups—we're on the right side, and if we can present our case clearly to the American people, we will win overwhelmingly in November.

*Jimmy Carter's diary entry for July 31, 1980, noting his preparations for the Democratic National Convention, in Carter,* Keeping Faith *(1982), p. 549.*

For me, a few hours ago, this campaign came to an end. For all those whose cares have been our concern, the work goes on, the cause endures, the hope still lives, and the dream shall never die.

*Conclusion of Senator Edward Kennedy's campaign-withdrawal speech at the Democratic National Convention in New York City on August 12, 1980. Available online. URL: http://www.jfklibrary.org/ e081280.htm.*

The Carter Administration lives in the world of make-believe. Every day, drawing up a response to that day's problems, troubles, regardless of what happened yesterday and what'll happen tomorrow.

But you and I live in a real world, where disasters are overtaking our nation without any real response from Washington.

. . . .

The administration which has brought us to this state is seeking your endorsement for four more years of weakness, indecision, mediocrity and incompetence. No. No. No American should vote until he or she has asked: Is the United States stronger and more respected now than it was three-and-a-half years ago? Is the world today a safer place in which to live?

*Ronald Reagan drawing the battle lines in his speech accepting the nomination for president at the Republican National Convention in Detroit, Michigan, July 17, 1980. Available online. URL: http://www. nationalcenter.org/ReaganConvention1980.html.*

Reagan is different from me in almost every basic element of commitment and experience and promise to the American people, and the Republican party now is sharply different from what the Democratic party is. And I might add parenthetically that the Republican party is sharply different under Reagan from what it was under Gerald Ford and Presidents all the way back to Eisenhower.

*Jimmy Carter in a September 2, 1980, speech at a town hall meeting in Independence, Missouri, quoted in Carter,* Keeping Faith *(1982), p. 554.*

. . . doubts that substitution of one leader for another will make much difference are widespread in Snow Hill [North Carolina]. "A President's just a showpiece," says Wilbur MacArthur, 51, a retired farmer. "They

could put you and me up there in Washington and there won't be any difference. The ones who control are Congress, the Supreme Court and labor unions. Them three scoundrels running for President ain't going to give you nothing."

*An apathetic voter expressing his feelings about the presidential election, quoted in " 'None of the Above': Nation's Political Mood,"* U.S. News & World Report, *September 29, 1980, p. 21.*

The old joke still applies. Someone chases a voter down the alley, points a gun to his head and demands an answer: "Carter or Reagan?" After thinking for a moment, the voter replies, "Shoot." Since we recalled the joke during the primary season last March, it has traveled around the world and onto television, for it turns out to be not merely a joke but the story of the 1980 campaign.

. . . What a choice, says Johnny Carson: between fear of the unknown and fear of the known. Neither man personifies our ideal candidate. But that does not mean there is no difference; it is important; and we choose Jimmy Carter. Ronald Reagan is the better sales man; Jimmy Carter keeps dropping his sample case on his own foot. But it contains better goods.

*Beginning and ending of "At the End of the Alley," an editorial endorsing Jimmy Carter for president (the majority of American newspapers endorsed Ronald Reagan), in* New York Times, *October 26, 1980, sec. 4, p. 18.*

Are you better off than you were four years ago? Is it easier for you to go and buy things in the store than it was four years ago? Is there less unemployment than there was four years ago? Is America as respected throughout the world as it was? Do you feel that our security is as safe, that we're as strong as we were four years ago?

If you answer all of those questions yes, why, then, I think your choice is very obvious. If you *don't* agree, if you *don't* think that this course we've been on for the last four years is what you would like to see us follow for the next four, then I could suggest another choice that you have.

*Ronald Reagan's closing statement in his televised debate against Jimmy Carter on October 28, 1980, quoted in Jordan,* Crisis *(1982), pp. 356–357.*

Despite pre-election polls that had forecast a fairly close election, the rout was so pervasive and so quickly apparent that Mr. Carter made the earliest concession statement of a major Presidential candidate since 1904 when Alton B. Parker bowed to Theodore Roosevelt.

At 9:50 P.M., Mr. Carter appeared with his wife, Rosalynn, before supporters at the ballroom of the Sheraton Washington Hotel and disclosed that an hour earlier he had telephoned Mr. Reagan to concede and to pledge cooperation for the transition to new leadership.

"The people of the United States have made their choice and, of course, I accept that decision," he said. "I can't stand here tonight and say it doesn't hurt."

At a celebration in the Century Plaza Hotel in Los Angeles, Mr. Reagan claimed his victory and said: "There's never been a more humbling moment in my life. I give you my sacred oath that I will do my utmost to justify your faith."

*Hedrick Smith reporting the November 4, 1980, election results, in Smith, "Reagan Easily Beats Carter; . . . ,"* New York Times, *November 5, 1980, p. 1.*

I had to find a silver lining in the cloud of defeat. At least it was a relief that the political campaign was over. A lot of work remained to be done during the next two and a half months, and I could perform these duties as a President, and not as a candidate. I was thankful for this small blessing.

*Jimmy Carter reflecting on his loss to Ronald Reagan, November 4, 1980, in Carter,* Keeping Faith *(1982), p. 571.*

But the Reagan "mandate" was clouded by the suspicion that the difference people most wanted was to be rid of Jimmy Carter. Three-quarters of adult Americans stayed home on Election Day or voted for someone other than Reagan; only one-fourth voted for him—and their principal reason by far, according to CBS/New York Times exit polling, was that it was time for a change. What brought Reagan to power was thus not so much love for him or a sudden shift in American politics as what Carter polltaker Pat Caddell called "a referendum on unhappiness"—a range of discontents ranging from inflation to Iran. "The people are looking for generals who can win," said George Shipley, a Democratic strategist. Carter could not. It is now Reagan's chancy lot to try.

*Assessing the postelection mood in "Mr. Reagan Goes to Washington,"* Newsweek, *November 24, 1980, pp. 38–39.*

## Natural Disasters and Human Tragedies

It was just like a war movie, with everybody shooting all over the place and people screaming. I saw two people go down, a man and a woman.

*Truck driver Jeff Reckley describing the scene in Greensboro, North Carolina, on November 3, 1979, when members of the Ku Klux Klan began to shoot anti-Klan protesters, quoted in "Shootout in Greensboro,"* Time, *November 12, 1979, p. 31.*

"It was crazy," said one woman who had waited on line for hours. "Some guy reached out and grabbed my wrist and pulled me into the middle. Then I fell down. Then somebody grabbed me and pulled me up again. By then, my shoes and purse were gone. Then I fell down again. I fell over some guy and people were just walking over him. It felt like a lot of people stepped on me, but somebody grabbed me again. When I got up, I just ran."

. . . "I didn't even move my feet," said Nancy Tyler, 19, of Covington, Ky. "One moment I was maybe 200 feet from the door and the next thing I was stacked up like kindling. I don't know, but I'd bet there were six or eight people under me."

*Two people caught in the scramble for seats at the Riverfront Coliseum in Cincinnati, where The Who were performing on December 3, 1979, describing their experiences in "Cincinnati Stampede,"* Newsweek, *December 17, 1979, p. 52.*

Get emergency . . . all the emergency equipment out to the Skyway bridge. Vessel has just hit the Skyway bridge. The Skyway bridge is down! Get all emergency equipment out to the Skyway bridge. The Skyway bridge is down. Emergency situation! [Nearly screaming] Stop the traffic on that Skyway bridge!

*Distress call to the Coast Guard by John Lerro, who was piloting the freighter* Summit Venture *when it crashed into the Sunshine Skyway bridge near Tampa, Florida, on May 9, 1980, reported in an online obituary following his death in September 2002. URL: http://www.mult-sclerosis.org/news/Sep2002/ShipsPilotwMS.html.*

The police had put up a roadblock. I couldn't get around it. I went into a U-turn, but my car stalled and they came running at me. I heard them scream, "Honky!" I got the car into gear and knocked them out of the way. I heard gunfire. I saw a police officer and I screamed, "What should I do?" He said, "I've been shot at all night. Do what you have to do to get out."

*Jim Davis, a white motorist caught in the midst of racial rioting that shook Miami, May 17–19, 1980, quoted in "Fire and Fury in Miami," Time, June 2, 1980, p. 11.*

But as usual in such rioting, blacks probably suffered the most and will surely be the most affected. A crudely lettered sign outside the Ability Tire Co. read BLACK-OWNED AND OPERATED. But the store was ransacked, and James Price, who worked there, was puzzled. "I was under the impression that this was a rebellion against the white man," he said. "So why did they break in here?"

*Time magazine reporting on the effects of three days of racial rioting in Miami, May 17–19, 1980, in "Fire and Fury in Miami," Time, June 2, 1980, p. 12.*

I am walking toward the only light I can see. I can hear the mountain rumble. At this very moment I have to say, "Honest to God, I believe I am dead." The ash in my eyes burns my eyes, burns my eyes! Oh dear God, this is hell! It's very, very hard to breathe and very dark. God, just give me a breath! I will try the radio. Mayday! Ash is coming down on me heavily. It's either dark or I am dead. God, I want to live!

*David Crockett, a photographer for KOMO-TV, Seattle, recording his impressions of the Mount St. Helens eruption into a sound camera, May 18, 1980; reported in "'God, I Want to Live!'" Time, June 2, 1980, p. 26.*

It was a little puff, at the top of the mountain. Then, within two or three seconds, it appeared that the north side of the mountain just blew out. The whole top of the mountain was engulfed in the column of smoke. It rose like an atomic explosion . . . With sort of a shock wave that went to the north. It reminded me of the pictures you see on late-night TV of the world blowing up.

*Fred Grimm, one of 12 climbers who had been ascending Mount Adams when Mount St. Helens (30 miles to the east) erupted on May 18, 1980, reporting what he saw, in "The Convulsion of St. Helens," Newsweek, June 2, 1980, p. 22.*

In Ritzville, Wash., more than 150 miles from Mount St. Helens, the high-flying cloud of ash brought darkness at noon. There was no light until the next morning, when residents awoke to an eerily quiet world coated in snowlike powder up to 4 inches deep. "You look out your window and you want to put on your coat," said local newspaper editor Terri Thompson-Crone. "But it's hot, over 70 degrees."

*Newsweek magazine reporting on the far-reaching effects of the May 18, 1980, Mount St. Helens eruption, in "The Convulsion of St. Helens," Newsweek, June 2, 1980, p. 22.*

Although the hottest weather gripped Texas and Oklahoma, the highest death toll—more than 250—was in Missouri. In St. Louis, where nearly 100 heat-related deaths were recorded, the morgue was full and the ambulance drivers were working double shifts.

In most areas, at least 9 of every 10 deaths appeared to be among the aged. Health officials reported only partial success in efforts to ease the suffering of the elderly. An average of 18 persons a day accepted offers of free food and shelter in Nashville's air-conditioned community centers.

. . . .

In Kansas City, a man gave his 80-year-old mother a fan and told her to stop worrying about using electricity. The next day he found her dead. The fan was on a table, still unplugged.

*Description of the devastating heat wave that gripped more than half of the country in the summer of 1980, in "Heat Wave: 100-a-Day Killer," U.S. News & World Report, July 28, 1980, p. 7.*

He walked past me and I heard in my head, "Do it, do it, do it," over and over again, saying, "Do it, do it, do it," like that. . . . I don't remember aiming. I must have done, but I don't remember drawing a bead or whatever you call it. And I just pulled the trigger steady five times.

*Mark David Chapman describing the moment when he shot John Lennon on December 8, 1980, in a statement to police after the shooting, reported on Court TV's Crime Library. Available online. URL: http://www.crimelibrary.com/terrorists_spies/assassins/chapman/8.html?sect=24.*

Some reaction was tragic. A teen-age girl in Florida and a man of 30 in Utah killed themselves over Lennon's death. On Thursday, [Yoko] Ono said, "This is not the end of an era. The '80s are still going to be a beautiful time, and John believed in it."

*The tragedy of John Lennon's assassination on December 8, 1980, begetting more tragedy, as reported in "The Last Day in the Life,"* Time, *December 22, 1980, p. 18.*

I told Sean what happened. I showed him the picture of his father on the cover of the paper and explained the situation. I took Sean to the spot where John lay after he was shot. Sean wanted to know why the person shot John if he liked John. I explained that he was probably a confused person. Sean said we should find out if he was really confused or if he really had meant to kill John. I said that was up to the court. He asked what court—a tennis court or a basketball court? That's how Sean used to talk with his father. They were buddies. John would have been proud of Sean if he had heard this. Sean cried later. He also said "Now Daddy is part of God. I guess when you die you become more bigger because you're part of everything."

*From a statement issued by Yoko Ono on December 10, 1980, two days following the assassination of her husband, John Lennon, by Mark David Chapman, telling how she explained his father's death to her five-year-old son, reprinted in* Newsweek, *December 22, 1980, p. 36.*

## Freeing the Hostages

We've always had a few basic principles to guide me since I've been involved in meeting this absolutely illegal and abhorrent act. One is to protect the long-range interests of our country; secondly, to protect the lives and well-being of the hostages; third, to seek their release; fourth, to avoid bloodshed if possible, but still to protect our interests if necessary; and lastly, to make sure that a strong majority of the nations of the world understand that Iran is a criminal actor in this process and that we are the aggrieved party, and to keep world support for our position.

*Jimmy Carter in a televised interview with John Chancellor on January 7, 1980, explaining why no military action would be taken to free the hostages; quoted in Richardson,* Conversations with Carter *(1998), p. 179.*

The U.S. reacted with an outpouring of gratitude. Congress swiftly passed what officials termed the first congressional resolution ever expressing appreciation to another government. President Carter made a "Thank you, Joe" phone call to Canadian prime minister Joe Clark.

On a more personal basis, Americans flooded the Canadian Embassy in Washington with phone calls, telegrams, letters, flowers—even a cake. Several state legislatures adopted resolutions of thanks. In Lansing, Mich., the Canadian flag was ordered flown alongside the American emblem at the State Capitol.

*Reactions to the news that six Americans managed to escape Iran on January 28, 1980, with the help of Canadian embassy personnel, in "Canada: A Good Neighbor Proves Itself,"* U.S. News & World Report, *February 11, 1980, p. 5.*

I ordered this rescue mission prepared in order to safeguard American lives, to protect America's national interests, and to reduce the tensions in the world that have been caused among many nations as this crisis has continued.

It was my decision to attempt the rescue operation. It was my decision to cancel it when problems developed in the placement of our rescue team for a future rescue operation. The responsibility is fully my own.

In the aftermath of the attempt, we continue to hold the government of Iran responsible for the safety and for the early release of the American hostages who have been held for so long. The United States remains determined to bring about their safe release at the earliest date possible.

*President Carter addressing the nation by television on April 25, 1980, the morning after the failed rescue mission in Iran, quoted in "This Rescue Attempt 'Became a Necessity and a Duty,'"* Washington Post, *April 26, 1980, p. A-11.*

I'm not about to be party to a half-assed loading of a bunch of aircraft and going up and murdering a bunch of the finest soldiers in the world. I wouldn't do that and I've been accused of that. It burns me up because I'm not that kind of man.

*Colonel Charlie Beckwith, Delta Force commander, responding to speculation that he wanted to continue the hostage rescue mission with only five helicopters, quoted in Halloran, "Hostage Rescue Commander Denies He Favored Pushing on to Tehran,"* New York Times, *May 2, 1980, p. A-12.*

What did ordinary citizens think about the aborted rescue attempt?

Most voiced satisfaction that at least the U.S. had tried direct action to end the long crisis. "I'm proud to be an American," said a woman in Chicago, "I can lift up my head once more."

But equally widespread was chagrin that Americans were unable to succeed in the type of daring actions that Israelis and West Germans have performed with spectacular success.

"I am disappointed that the U.S. can't seem to be competent in international affairs," said a Dallas businessman. "I feel a sense of despair, shame and disappointment."

*Domestic reaction to the failed mission to rescue the hostages in Iran, in "Big Setback for U.S.," U.S. News & World Report, May 5, 1980, p. 23.*

One by one, the lost men were eulogized. Said Lieut. Colonel Calvin Chasteen about his comrade, Captain Richard L. Bakke, a 33-year-old navigator: "He looked forward with enthusiasm and anticipation to this last opportunity to serve, not for the glory it offered but for the deep satisfaction of defending that which is good and decent."

*Description of the memorial service held on May 9, 1980, for the eight men killed during the aborted rescue mission, in "Raging Debate over the Desert Raid," Time, May 12, 1980, p. 32.*

May 21, 1980

Dear Katherine,

How are you? My name is——. I'm ten and in the fourth grade and I'm writing this letter to cheer you up.

I'm sorry that the rescue didn't succeed. But I hope they try again.

I have no pets so I will talk about you. Do you have any children? What do you look like? Do you have any hobbys? What are they?

My hobby is rollerskating.

Please write back. I'll be waiting for your letter back.

Your friend,

*A typical letter among hundreds sent by American schoolchildren to the hostages in Iran. This one was unusual in that mention of the rescue attempt managed to get by the Iranian censors. Reproduced in Koob,* Guest of the Revolution *(1982), photographs section.*

August 4, 1980: Today we begin the 10th month of our captivity—nine months from November 4, 1979 when we were kidnapped; and still there is absolutely nothing doing that makes me feel that we will get out of here soon. Just can't understand what our Gov't is doing to obtain our release. It is very, very, discouraging!

*From the diary of Robert C. Ode, one of the 52 Americans held hostage in Iran. Available online on the Jimmy Carter Library Web site. URL: http:// jimmycarterlibrary.org/documents/r_ode/ ode_ aug80.phtml.*

As I looked at myself in the mirror, I wondered if I had aged so much as President or whether I was just exhausted. As I rode to the Capitol and sat through the inaugural ceremonies, the hostages were always on my mind. I still had no assurance that all my recent efforts would be successful, and no way to know that this would soon become one of my happiest days— even happier than that day exactly four years earlier when President Gerald Ford had greeted me on the way to my own inauguration.

*Jimmy Carter on the moments before he turned the presidency over to Ronald Reagan, January 20, 1981, still not knowing whether the American hostages in Iran had been released yet, in Carter,* Keeping Faith *(1982), p. 13.*

The voice came over the Algerian plane's speaker: "You are now leaving Iranian air space!" What a cheer went up from the American hostages on the plane! This was the moment for which we had waited 444 days. Now we knew we were really free! Even though we had been told by the Iranian terrorists that we were being set free, I'm sure all of the hostages didn't really feel that we were on our way to freedom until we actually were out of Iran. So much still could go wrong in the process of obtaining our freedom . . . but the confirmation that we were actually out of Iran and the Ayatollah Khomeini's jurisdiction made us finally realize that our ordeal was over! What a magnificent feeling! We were on our way at last! We were going home!

*Former hostage Robert C. Ode, expressing his feelings on his January 20, 1981, release. Diary excerpts available online on the Jimmy Carter Library Web site. URL: http://jimmycarterlibrary.org/documents/ r_ode/ode_aug80.phtml.*

While a waiting throng of newsmen sent up a few thin cheers and American personnel from the embassy called out "Welcome" and "We love you," the hostages filed into the airport's VIP lounge. For a moment there was confused milling. "How do I look, have I changed?" one anxious returnee asked [Warren] Christopher, adding a bit disjointedly: "They allowed us to take one suitcase, but they even stole that from us at the airport." Another hostage grabbed a startled Algerian protocol officer and yelled: "Are you press? Are you press? We had one lousy magazine to read and they took that away—they're rats." A third hostage said more softly, "I Hope Allah *never* answers their prayers." In embarrassment, Algerian officials quickly turned off the microphones in the room.

*The released hostages unwinding after their arrival at the airport in Athens, Greece, January 20, 1981, in "The Hostages Return,"* Newsweek, *February 2, 1981, p. 25.*

I wonder how we'll react to the presence of our former Commander-in-Chief—the man who admitted the Shah to the United States, thereby setting the stage for the outpouring of Iranian hostility that led to our imprisonment. Many of the embassy staff blamed Carter for the whole thing. I did, too, at first, but time heals many wounds. I have sensed President Carter's dilemma this past year from my prison cell, and I know, realistically, that there was little he could do to achieve our release once the embassy fell. I think he has demonstrated great courage and patience in working for our eventual freedom. It may have even cost him his political career. As a professional soldier, I must show proper respect to my Commander-in-Chief. But I wonder how the others will act, and what he'll say to us at this awkward moment.

*Colonel Charles W. Scott, reflecting on his feelings as the newly freed hostages prepare to meet former president Jimmy Carter in West Germany on January 21, 1981, the day after their release, in Scott,* Pieces of the Game *(1984), p. 397.*

## The Final Days

Nuclear weapons are an expression of one side of our human character. But there is another side. The same rocket technology that delivers nuclear warheads has also taken us peacefully into space. From that perspec-

tive, we see our Earth as it really is—a small and fragile and beautiful blue globe, the only home we have. We see no barriers of race or religion or country. We see the essential unity of our species and our planet; and with faith and common sense, that bright vision will ultimately prevail.

*President Carter expressing his concerns about the world's future in his televised farewell address to the nation on January 14, 1981. Available online. URL: http://www.jimmycarterlibrary.gov/documents/ speeches/farewell.phtml.*

Max Cleland came to tell me good-bye. He brought me a plaque with a quote from Thomas Jefferson:

I HAVE THE CONSOLATION TO REFLECT
THAT DURING THE PERIOD OF MY
ADMINISTRATION NOT A DROP
OF THE BLOOD OF A SINGLE CITIZEN
WAS SHED BY THE SWORD OF WAR.

This is something I shall always cherish.

*Jimmy Carter's diary entry on the last day of his presidency, January 20, 1981, in Carter,* Keeping Faith *(1982), p. 596.*

As we drove up Pennsylvania Avenue, the limousine was very quiet. The president and I were seated side by side. Although he was polite, he said hardly a word to me as we moved slowly toward the Capitol, and I think he hesitated to look me in the face.

. . . [T]he atmosphere in the limousine was as chilly as it had been at the White House a few days before when Nancy and I had gone there to see for the first time the rooms where we would be living. We'd expected the Carters to give us a tour of the family quarters, but they had made a quick exit and turned us over to the White House staff.

At the time, Nancy and I took this as an affront. It seemed rude. But eight years later I think we could sense a little of how President Carter must have felt that day—to have served as president, to have been through the intense highs and lows of the job, to have tried to do what he thought was right, to have had all the farewells and good-bye parties, and then to be forced out of the White House by a vote of the people. . . . It must have been very hard on him.

*Ronald Reagan looking back at his interaction with Jimmy Carter on his inauguration day, January 20, 1981, in Reagan,* An American Life *(1990), pp. 225–226.*

Shortly after 11 A.M.: Word just received from the Swiss that the Swiss Ambassador has been summoned by the Iranians to the airport to witness the takeoff of the hostages. I increasingly suspect that the timing is deliberately contrived so that it will coincide with the swearing-in.

1:18 P.M.: Airborne in Air Force One to Atlanta. Until the very last minute the transfer of power and departure of the President dominated by the Iranian affair. I went down to the Sit. Room before leaving my office to monitor the latest developments from Iran. The plane as of 11:30 was still on the ground. It became clear that the Iranians were deliberately holding it up so that the transfer of hostages would not occur while Jimmy Carter is President of the United States.

*National Security Advisor Zbigniew Brzezinski's journal entry for January 20, 1981, describing the delay in the hostage transfer during the last moments of the Carter presidency, in Brzezinski,* Power and Principle *(1983), p. 508.*

# 2

# The Great Communicator Takes Over
## January 1981–October 1982

On January 20, 1981, Ronald Reagan was inaugurated the 40th president of the United States. Four years earlier Jimmy Carter had come to Washington as an outsider whom the country hoped would pull them out of an economic crisis. Now they had transferred that hope to Reagan—also an outsider. Like Carter, he was a religious man, he was devoted to his wife, and he had a vision for America. There the similarities ended.

The Reagan vision was very different from that of the modest and low-key Carter, a difference symbolized in the inauguration ceremony and celebrations. To begin, Reagan changed the location of the swearing-in ceremony to the west side of the Capitol, facing the country. Then, as he took his position before Chief Justice Warren E. Burger, the Sun broke through the clouds, casting "an explo-

Ronald Reagan is sworn in by Chief Justice Warren Burger at the U.S. Capitol on January 20, 1981.
*(Courtesy Ronald Reagan Library)*

sion of warmth and light"[1] on the ceremony. Nobody missed the implication: A new day was dawning.

Reagan's inaugural address emphasized the need to change the way government worked. "To paraphrase Winston Churchill," he said, "I did not take the oath I've just taken with the intention of presiding over the dissolution of the world's strongest economy." He concluded that the current crisis required "our best effort and our willingness to believe in ourselves and to believe in our capacity to perform great deeds, to believe that together with God's help we can and will resolve the problems which now confront us. And after all, why shouldn't we believe that? We are Americans."[2]

The speech was not the most stirring of Reagan's career, but it contained one of his best-known lines ("government is not the solution to our problem; government is the problem"), and his promise to remove "the roadblocks that have slowed our economy and reduced productivity" was what many Americans wanted to hear. It was speeches like this that earned him the label "The Great Communicator."

That night there were nine lavish inaugural balls in Washington, and the new president and first lady attended them all. The exultant Reagan had no reservations in displaying pride in his new position—and despite the huge expense of the celebrations, much of the country approved.

The following morning he got to work. In the Cabinet Room at the White House, a portrait of Harry S. Truman had been replaced with one of Reagan's personal heroes, Calvin Coolidge, the president who had said, "The business of America is business." The new president wanted to prove him right.

## PUTTING SUPPLY-SIDE ECONOMICS TO WORK

Ronald Reagan's immediate problem was the economy. His proposed solution was based on a theory called supply-side economics, eventually dubbed *Reaganomics.* For decades presidents and economists had followed the theories of John Milton Keynes (1883–1946). Keynesianism was essentially "demand-side" economics, manipulating fiscal policy to increase demand and thus develop the economy to satisfy it. Supply-side economics was born in 1974 when, at a lunch with friends, Californian economist Arthur Laffer drew a graph on a napkin demonstrating the effect of levels of taxation on the economy. From that informal discussion grew a new economic theory: A low rate, near 0 percent, meant inadequate tax revenues no matter how well business was doing; a high rate, near 100 percent, was equally counterproductive since business activity was stifled and tax revenues were reduced. The Laffer Curve set theoretical taxation levels to meet changing economic needs but made no allowance for such external influences as the cold war, adverse trading conditions, or the national deficit. Although the Laffer theory could not specify the ideal tax rate, it was strongly supported by *Wall Street Journal* editorialist Jude Wanniski and by Representative Jack Kemp (R, N.Y.) and Senator William Roth (R, Del.), leading them to advocate reducing federal income taxes by 30 percent.

Supply-side economics was a variation of the "trickle-down" theory that held economic stimulation would occur when taxes for business and the wealthy were reduced. Ideally, the Laffer theory would benefit everybody, not just the wealthy, and therein lay its appeal for Reagan, who had long called for tax reductions (although as California governor he had been forced by circumstances to raise them). In 1980 he met with Kemp, Laffer, and Wanniski, who convinced him that supply-side economics could create prosperity for businesses and individual Americans. Later analysts claimed that Reagan never fully understood the Laffer theory, which required severe reductions in spending in addition to tax cuts to work. But Reagan's determination to make major budget cuts was offset by his equal determination to increase military spending. Laffer supported this, maintaining that tax cuts would eventually produce a revenue increase to offset any deficit.

Pushing ahead quickly, President Reagan presented "America's New Beginning: A Program for Economic Recovery" to a joint session of Congress on February 18. He called for "reducing the growth in government spending and taxing, reforming and eliminating regulations which are unnecessary and unproductive or counterproductive, and encouraging a consistent monetary policy aimed at maintaining the value of the currency."[3] He proposed federal income-tax and business-tax cuts of 10 percent in each of the next three years (a total of a 30 percent reduction); eliminating allowances for inflation that placed taxpayers in certain tax brackets; reducing estate, gift, and capital-gains taxes; and allowing faster depreciation on business investments. He also proposed budget cuts of $41 billion except in defense spending, which would be increased substantially.

Ronald Reagan explains his plan to reduce income taxes in a televised address to the nation on July 27, 1981. *(Courtesy Ronald Reagan Library)*

While retaining vital welfare programs, he wanted to eliminate some, reduce others, and trim Social Security. Further, he proposed cuts to federal agencies that regulated business, the environment, and public health. In early March, he submitted to Congress a budget proposal for fiscal year 1982 that called for cuts to 200 programs, with total expenditures of $695.3 billion.

Implementation of Reagan's fiscal policies fell to David Stockman, director of the Office of Management and Budget (OMB). Publicly, Stockman, a former Republican congressman from Michigan, was a fervent supply-side supporter; privately, he fretted about the resulting deficits he foresaw. (Reagan's budget proposal already projected a deficit of $45 billion.) Initially Stockman kept his doubts to himself, countering objections with statistics that impressed—and confused—his listeners while hoping that tax cutting would force Congress to reduce welfare programs to compensate for the loss of revenue.

Reagan worked tirelessly for his program, meeting with congressmen and senators and selling it to the public in televised addresses. His efforts were interrupted by an attempt on his life in late March, an event that boosted both his popularity and support for his economic solutions; by early summer more than two to one Americans favored Reagan's tax-cutting proposals. Finally, on July 29, 1981, the House of Representatives passed a modified version, reducing taxes by 5 percent in the first year and 10 percent in each of the following two years. The Senate approved the bill on August 4, and on August 13 Reagan signed the Economic Recovery Act—also known as the Kemp–Roth tax cut—into law.

Reagan and Stockman also attacked many Great Society programs through the Omnibus Budget and Reconciliation Act. Though partially successful, they failed to cut entitlement programs such as Medicare and Social Security. These were a political minefield; drastic reductions would lose votes from working-class and middle-class Americans who benefited from them as much as the poor did. When Congress resisted slashing such welfare spending, Reagan yielded, knowing that he needed public goodwill. But he still looked for solutions to the welfare problem. In his January 1982 State of the Union address, he introduced what he called a "new federalism," whereby the federal government retained responsibility for Medicaid while turning over other welfare and social care programs to the states, which would be compensated by gradually diminishing federal grants. This plan attracted little enthusiasm and was never implemented to the extent Reagan envisioned, though it did bring about some changes.

While compromising on social programs, Reagan was persuaded by Secretary of Defense Caspar Weinberger to request even more money for defense. Consequently, a frustrated Stockman, who had expected the president to take a firmer stand with both Weinberger and Congress, made his concerns public in an *Atlantic Monthly* (December 1981) article by William Grieder. Stockman's forecast of a massive rise in the federal deficit aroused such controversy that he offered to resign, but Reagan refused. Within a year, Stockman's prediction proved correct.

*Voodoo economics* was the term George Bush had applied to Reagan's supply-side proposal during the 1980 presidential campaign. As vice president he supported the program, but there was some justification in his description. When Jimmy Carter left office in 1981, the national debt was $908 billion; eight years later, when Reagan left, it had ballooned to almost $2.7 trillion. Not until the Clinton administration were federal deficits reduced significantly and the budget

Margaret Thatcher, seen here with Ronald Reagan on February 26, 1981, was the first world leader to visit the new president in Washington. *(Courtesy Ronald Reagan Library)*

brought back under control (albeit temporarily). Yet this, Reagan supporters maintained, was the result of a decrease in defense spending in the 1990s made possible by the end of the cold war, which was achieved by the *increase* in U.S. military expenditures during the 1980s.

Though supply-side economics increased the national debt, it eventually produced positive effects that many felt offset the negative side of Reaganomics. These included business growth, millions of new jobs, and an unprecedented increase in personal wealth. But in 1981, Americans and their president still had a rocky road ahead of them.

## "Honey, I Forgot to Duck"

After Reagan's inauguration, the United States settled down to business as usual. In late January, the 52 former hostages returned home to parades and celebrations. February 6 saw the nation's oldest president reach his 70th birthday. Later that month, British prime minister Margaret Thatcher arrived in the United States for talks. She and Reagan already knew and respected each other, and their politics were well attuned as they discussed a wide range of concerns, including a potential Soviet nuclear weapons buildup. In early March, President Reagan made his first trip out of the country, conducting two days of talks with Prime Minister Elliott Trudeau of Canada. Shortly after the president's return, Secretary of State Al Haig accused the Soviet Union of promoting terrorism and trying to exert undue influence on governments in Central America. This generated much excitement in an otherwise quiet month—until March 30.

That afternoon the president gave a speech to the Construction Trades Council at the Washington Hilton Hotel. He left by a side entrance, surrounded by aides and Secret Service agents, and headed for his limousine. At 2:27 P.M., as the group passed a line of reporters, a question was shouted at Reagan, who paused—and several shots rang out. At once, two Secret Service agents thrust Reagan into his car while another, Tim McCarthy, placed himself between the president and the shooter; a bullet hit McCarthy in the stomach. Nearby, Press Secretary James Brady and a Washington policeman, Thomas Delahanty, lay on the ground; Brady had been shot in the head, Delahanty in the neck. The would-be assassin, a 25-year-old drifter named John Hinckley, Jr., was quickly overpowered and arrested.

Six shots had been fired. In later reconstructions it was determined that the fifth had ricocheted off the car, flattened, and sped through a gap in the closing door, hitting Reagan under his left armpit. In the limousine, the president showed no visible sign of having been shot, thinking only that he had broken a rib, but when he began to spit blood and turn gray, the driver, who had been heading to the White House, changed direction and rushed to George Washington University Hospital. At the emergency room entrance, Reagan refused assistance and got out of the car to walk into the building. Just after he passed through the doors, though, he had trouble breathing and began to fall; he was caught and carried the rest of the way in.

It was some time before doctors found the entry wound under his left arm; the bullet had entered so cleanly there had been no blood. Surgery was performed, and a .22 caliber bullet was found lodged in his left lung, having missed his heart by less than an inch. It was later discovered to be a Devastator bullet, designed to explode within its target when shot from a rifle—but Hinckley had used a short-barreled Röhm RG-14 handgun (a "Saturday night special"). The error saved the president's life, as well as those of Jim Brady, Tim McCarthy, and Thomas Delahanty, although all would suffer long-term effects—Brady especially, who was permanently disabled.[4]

The country learned of the attack almost immediately, but reports were conflicting. Nobody seemed to know whether the president had been hit or what his condition was, and it was during this period of confusion that Secretary of State Al Haig made the statement that haunted him thereafter.

When the news reached Vice President Bush at Fort Worth, Texas, he immediately flew back to Washington. With Reagan undergoing surgery and Bush in the air, the country appeared leaderless, and at a press conference White House spokesman Larry Speakes was asked who was acting president. When Speakes admitted he did not know, Haig, who had been listening from the Situation Room, ran into the press room and answered himself. "Constitutionally, gentlemen," he said in a voice trembling from haste, "you have the president, the vice president, and the secretary of state in that order, and should the president decide he wants to transfer the helm, he will do so. He has not done that. As of now, I am in control here, in the White House, pending return of the vice president and in close touch with him. If something came up, I would check with him, of course."[5]

Haig's intention had been to emphasize that the government was not in a state of disarray, but his statement created a furor: He was in fact fourth in line, after the vice president, the Speaker of the House, and the President Pro Tempore

President Reagan waves to the crowd at the Washington Hilton Hotel moments before being shot by John Hinckley, Jr. *(Courtesy Ronald Reagan Library)*

of the Senate. Many interpreted his words as an inappropriate grab for power, a view enhanced when numerous reporters quoted only the "I'm in control" part of his statement. (Haig had always wanted more control over foreign affairs than the president would give him, and this aspect of his character, along with his verbal gaffe, led finally to his resignation as secretary of state in June 1982.[6])

The question of responsibility was short-lived: The day after the shooting, President Reagan was conducting business from his hospital bed. Stories were already emerging of his fortitude and sense of humor. "Honey, I forgot to duck," he quipped to his wife, Nancy, before going into surgery. The line was not original—it was what heavyweight boxing champion Jack Dempsey had said to his wife on the night he was beaten by Gene Tunney in 1926—but the quotation has since become indelibly associated with Reagan.

Reassured by staff members that the government was doing fine, Reagan retorted, "What makes you think that would make me feel better?" Before his surgery, he looked up at the medical staff surrounding him and said, "I just hope you're all Republicans." One of the doctors produced a reply Hollywood would be proud of: "Today, Mr. President, we're all Republicans." Later, when intubated and unable to speak, Reagan communicated by means of notes, asking about his condition and that of the others who had been shot. Even then he could not resist a joke. "Send me to LA, where I can see the air I'm breathing," he wrote to one nurse. Another note showed a more reflective side: "Winston Churchill said that there is no more exhilarating feeling than being shot at without result."

President Reagan, with his wife Nancy, at the hospital on April 4, 1981, impressed Americans with his resilience and humor after the assassination attempt. *(Courtesy Ronald Reagan Library)*

John Hinckley, Jr., turned out to be a troubled loner from a wealthy Republican Texan family and sometime member of the National Socialist Party of America. Hinckley was obsessed with the actress Jodie Foster, who had portrayed a teenage prostitute in Martin Scorsese's *Taxi Driver* (1976). In that film, Robert De Niro plays a crazed cab driver who plots to kill a U.S. senator. Having failed to attract Foster's notice through letters and telephone calls, Hinckley decided to imitate De Niro's character and go after Reagan as a way of impressing her. Investigators learned he may have previously considered killing Jimmy Carter or Edward Kennedy before settling on Reagan.

Judged competent to stand trial, Hinckley was charged with the attempted murders of Reagan, Brady, McCarthy, and Delahanty. On June 21, 1982, he was found not guilty by reason of insanity and committed to a mental institution. The verdict outraged many who felt Hinckley had benefited from well-paid legal maneuvering on his behalf.[7]

Reagan did not emerge from the shooting entirely unscathed. His strong constitution helped his recovery, but he was 70 years old, and many years later analysts contended he had been more seriously affected than generally thought. Nevertheless, he survived, and his calm and humor raised his approval rating across America and increased support for his economic program. Because of Reagan's dignity and courage in an emergency, the assassination attempt became a public-relations triumph.

## A NEW ERA IN SPACE EXPLORATION

The day after President Reagan left the hospital, April 12, saw the successful liftoff of the space shuttle *Columbia*.[8] For the first time, a U.S. spacecraft would fly into orbit around the Earth, return—and be used again for future missions. It was the dawn of a new space age.

Nine years earlier, President Richard Nixon had authorized developing a rocket-assisted craft that could land like an ordinary airplane. Though the *Mercury* and *Apollo* programs had taken men into space and to the Moon, they had drawbacks that could no longer be ignored. Chief among these were the costs of rocket-propelled capsules that could not be reused and the expense of retrieving astronauts from their splashdown point in the ocean. The National Space and Aeronautics Administration (NASA) was therefore tasked with developing a space-shuttle program, called the National Space Transportation System (NSTS). Research, development, and tests took much longer than expected, and costs escalated by billions of dollars. An experimental shuttle, named *Enterprise,* was tested in 1977, but it was another four years before the program was ready to launch.

After an initial postponement, the first shuttle, *Columbia,* lifted smoothly into space from Cape Canaveral in Florida at 7:00 A.M. EST on April 12—coincidentally, the 20th anniversary of the first manned space flight by Soviet cosmonaut Yuri Gagarin. The task of the two astronauts, veteran John Young and first-timer Robert Crippen, was to test the orbiter (as NASA termed it) and its systems. They returned two days later, making a textbook landing at Edwards Air Force Base in California on April 14 at 10:20 A.M. PST.

The flight had not been without problems: On liftoff, the shuttle lost 16 of its ceramic insulating tiles, designed to absorb the heat of reentry, and 148 were damaged as a result of a pressurized "shock wave" from the solid rocket boosters. Nevertheless, its safe return was cause for celebration. Modifications took care of the problem with the heat tiles, and NASA confidently moved ahead with the shuttle program.

*Columbia* went on to fly the next three NASA missions, all for test purposes with two-man crews. The flight of November 12–14, 1981, tested instrumentation and mapping radar as well as the Remote Manipulator System (RMS), developed by a Canadian firm and dubbed the Canadarm. On the third flight, lifting off March 22, 1982, three of the four communication links to Earth failed, but the mission continued, and the shuttle landed at White Sands, New Mexico, on March 30. Despite another communications failure, the fourth flight was carried out successfully from June 27 to July 4, 1982, upon which President Reagan declared NSTS to be operational. Although some felt the tests were insufficient, *Columbia* began operational flights in November 1982. It was eventually followed by the shuttles *Discovery, Atlantis,* and *Challenger,* and both the crew size and the mission length expanded to meet increasingly ambitious goals in space.

The NSTS program restored NASA's supremacy in space exploration and aroused much public excitement. In time, however, Americans simply came to regard shuttle flights as an everyday event, a complacency shared by NASA, whose overconfidence would lead to disaster a few years later.[9]

## THE NATIONAL PASTIME IN TROUBLE

In 1965, the average salary for a baseball player was $6,000—just $1,000 more than it had been in 1947. Club owners still wielded almost absolute control, and apart from the game's stars, players had few rights. In 1966, things changed when the Major League Baseball Players Association (MLBPA) hired longtime labor organizer Marvin Miller as its first executive director. Before long the MLBPA began to file complaints with the National Labor Relations Board, and players began to hire agents and to demand higher salaries.

The first strike in the history of baseball, over players' pensions, occurred in April 1972, causing the cancellation of 86 games. This was followed by two 17-day-long preseason lockouts in 1973 and 1976. The first was about salary arbitration; the second centered on free agency. Since the 1880s, a reserve clause had given owners the right to renew contracts every year, allowing them to keep their top stars indefinitely and preventing players from signing with other clubs. In 1975 two pitchers refused to sign their contracts and took their case to arbitration, which found in their favor. They were allowed to become free agents, signing with any team they liked after fulfilling their initial contract for a specified number of years. Other players immediately followed their example.

The consequent salary explosion led to wealthier clubs signing players to expensive, long-term contracts to retain their services. This affected poorer clubs that could not compete and feared going out of business: Baseball Commissioner Bowie Kuhn claimed that 21 of 26 teams had lost money in the 1979 season. However, owners would not allow their books to be examined, and Marvin Miller filed complaints that they were refusing to bargain.

For owners the issue was not just soaring salaries—by 1981 the average player's salary was $185,651—but compensation for losing players in whom they had invested heavily. Specifically, they felt that if one club lost a player to another team, the acquiring club should be forced to give the losing club a replacement. Since this negated the right to free agency, Miller rejected the idea, leading to a preseason players' strike in 1980. This was quickly settled by an agreement that a joint committee of players and owners examine compensation during the next 12 months.

No settlement had been reached when the 1981 season got under way. Finally, on June 12, players walked out on strike; the action lasted until July 31, when both sides made concessions. Although they did not receive compensation for the loss of free agents, owners won the right to retain players for six years and to be compensated with players who were not free agents as well as amateurs from the draft. Meanwhile, players who were ineligible for free agency would have their salaries decided by an arbitrator.

Both sides suffered financially during the 50-day strike: The players lost $28 million and the owners some $72 million (although $44 million was regained through strike insurance). The season resumed on August 10, having been divided into two, and it was agreed the first-place teams from each half in each division would meet in a best-of-five divisional playoff series. One result was that teams that seemed to be on a winning course prior to the strike fell out of the picture afterward. The Cincinnati Reds had the best overall record in 1981, but because they finished a close second in each half of the season, they failed to make the playoffs.

The real losers were the fans, who saw 712 games canceled, resulting in only a 65-game season. Nevertheless, once the strike was over, attendance at games rose steadily as players began to break old records and set new ones.[10]

Between the strike of 1981 and the end of 1983, when Marvin Miller resigned as executive director of the MLBPA, players' salaries increased by 46 percent. By 1984 the average player's salary was $330,000—a far cry from the 1965 $6,000 average when Miller took over—and 36 players each earned more than $1 million. Revenues from television and rising ticket prices brought the clubs more money, and players demanded a larger share of it. August 1985 saw a strike for salary arbitration that lasted only two days, but the arguments would continue, setting the stage for the massive 232-day strike of 1994.

## A MEDICAL PUZZLE—THE EMERGENCE OF AIDS

The summer of 1981 saw the publication of several articles on the mysterious increase of a rare cancer called Kaposi's sarcoma among gay patients in New York and California. On July 3, 1981, the *New York Times* noted: "The cause of the outbreak is unknown, and there is as yet no evidence of contagion. But the doctors who have made the diagnoses, mostly in New York City and the San Francisco Bay area, are alerting other physicians who treat large numbers of homosexual men to the problem in an effort to help identify more cases and to reduce the delay in offering chemotherapy treatment."[11] After describing the symptoms of Kaposi's sarcoma, the reporter emphasized the common factor: The victims were all male homosexuals. One physician quoted in the article said, "The best evidence against contagion is that no cases have been reported to date outside the homosexual community or in women."[12]

Kaposi's sarcoma (KS) normally occurred in older people, but the new patients were younger and had a more aggressive form of KS. Further, homosexuals were also suffering an increase in cases of *Pneumocystis carinii* pneumonia (PCP), a rare lung infection. In June 1981 the Centers for Disease Control (CDC) in Atlanta issued a report on the PCP development and formed a Task Force on Kaposi's Syndrome and Opportunistic Infections (KSOI). These actions are now considered the harbinger of the AIDS (acquired immune deficiency syndrome) epidemic.

AIDS did not just "appear" in 1981. The basic cause of the syndrome, infection by the human immunodeficiency virus (HIV), has been traced to before 1970, and it is now believed that by 1980, 100,000–300,000 persons worldwide had been infected by HIV. Little, however, was known of the cause. It seemed clear that the symptoms were not stand-alone conditions but signs of something affecting the immune system, breaking it down and leaving the body vulnerable to infections and cancers. Other symptoms ranged from swollen glands to viral and parasitic infections to non-Hodgkin's lymphoma, and because of this the disease did not acquire a permanent name—AIDS—until 1982. Until then it had various labels, including KSOI (from the CDC task force name), gay-related immunodeficiency (GRID), and gay compromise syndrome.

The syndrome's initial manifestation in homosexual men led to its being referred to as the "gay disease." Although AIDS eventually came to affect men and women from all conditions of life, its association with homosexuals would never quite disappear. This had dire consequences as the pandemic spread and heterosexuals believed they were safe from it, resulting in fatal carelessness. But in 1981 scientists were still groping in the dark. Later that year the first cases were reported in the United Kingdom, and Canada revealed outbreaks in February 1982. In the United States the disease began to spread outside New York and California, and instances of PCP among intravenous drug users were reported.

In May 1982 the CDC reported that at least 335 cases of AIDS had been recorded—136 of them fatalities. Furthermore, cases had been noted among heterosexual and bisexual men and women; only homosexual women had escaped infection thus far. It seemed that sexual intercourse was somehow responsible for the transmission of an as-yet unidentified infectious agent, but what it was and how it was transmitted still eluded doctors and scientists. By this time symptoms included lupus, different types of anemia, Burkitt's lymphoma, eye damage, thrush, and lymphadenopathy. The chief identifying symptom, though, continued to be Kaposi's sarcoma.

By July 1982, 452 cases had been reported to the CDC; by August the numbers had risen to 505, with 202 fatalities—a 40 percent death rate. Almost half of the cases were from New York City.[13] *AIDS* (*SIDA* in French and Spanish) had now become the accepted name of the disease—which was not actually a disease but a syndrome: a number of illnesses caused by a deficiency in the immune system that was acquired rather than inherited; hence "acquired immune deficiency syndrome."

Yet despite evidence to the contrary, public opinion still held AIDS to be a gay disease, and only the gay community responded with any level of anxiety. Guidelines for safer sex practices started to appear; the knowledge that sexual relations could lead to the disease's transmission resulted in a more puritanical attitude toward sex that would eventually affect American culture for the rest of the 1980s and into the early 1990s, as AIDS hysteria gripped the world.

That hysteria would not erupt until 1983. Until then, the only hint of what was to come lay in the increasing spread of a syndrome that baffled the medical community.

## A HISTORIC APPOINTMENT

During his election campaign, Ronald Reagan promised voters that he would name a woman to "one of the first" vacancies on the nation's Supreme Court. In June 1981 Associate Justice Potter Stewart announced his retirement at the end of the court term;[14] Reagan immediately asked Attorney General William French Smith to focus on qualified female candidates. The list was soon pared down to five; the standout was Sandra Day O'Connor.[15]

O'Connor, 51, had experienced the classic female struggle in a predominantly male profession, overcoming many obstacles to reach her position as a judge on the Arizona Court of Appeals. A moderate conservative who supported the Equal Rights Amendment, she was widely admired for her intellect and dedication to work; her supporters included her fellow Arizonan, Republican senator Barry Goldwater. O'Connor was the first candidate to meet President Reagan, on July 1, 1981; after 45 minutes, Reagan had made up his mind. On July 7 he announced his decision in a televised press conference, describing O'Connor as

"truly a 'person for all seasons,' possessing those unique qualities of temperament, fairness, intellectual capacity and devotion to the public good which have characterized the 101 'brethren' [Supreme Court justices] who have preceded her."

O'Connor's nomination was applauded by both major political parties and hailed by feminist groups. Even Chief Justice Warren Burger, who in 1971 had threatened to quit the Court if a woman were appointed to it, seemed to approve. Yet O'Connor had her detractors, particularly those from the New Right. The Moral Majority's Jerry Falwell criticized her views on abortion, O'Connor having supported family-planning legislation and voted to decriminalize abortion when she was a state senator. Falwell called on all "good Christians" to oppose her; Barry Goldwater responded that "every good Christian ought to kick Jerry Falwell right in the ass."[16]

During the confirmation hearings before the Senate Judiciary Committee, O'Connor refused to predict how she would vote as a Supreme Court justice. She expressed conservative views on capital punishment and school busing, but the hot topic was abortion. Liberals feared that a conservative president would make

President Reagan and his Supreme Court nominee, Sandra Day O'Connor, talk at the White House on July 15, 1981. *(Courtesy Ronald Reagan Library)*

changes to the Court that would affect the right to abortion currently protected under *Roe v. Wade* (1973). In her July meeting with Reagan, O'Connor admitted that she found abortion to be repugnant but would not allow that to affect her judicial decisions. Before the Senate committee, she said her state senatorial vote to decriminalize abortion had been a mistake; otherwise she would not commit herself on abortion or any other matter that might come before the Court, saying, "As a judge, it is not my function to develop public policy." The Judiciary Committee approved her nomination, and on September 22 the Senate voted 99–0 for her confirmation as the 102nd—and first female—justice of the U.S. Supreme Court.

President Reagan subsequently appointed two more justices (both male) and elevated William Rehnquist to chief justice in June 1986. O'Connor—the lone female voice on the Court for 12 years, until President Bill Clinton appointed Ruth Bader Ginsburg in 1993—proved to be a cautious interpreter of the Constitution. Because of her open-mindedness, attention to detail, and commitment to moderation, she became the swing vote on many decisions, leading one observer to comment in 1990, "As O'Connor goes, so goes the Court."[17]

Reagan was proud of his choice: "She was forthright and convincing, and I had no doubt she was the right woman for the job. I appointed her and she turned out to be everything I hoped for."[18]

## REAGAN STANDS FIRM

As a conservative Republican, Ronald Reagan attracted little support from labor during his 1980 presidential campaign; however, the Professional Air Traffic Controllers Organization (PATCO) had strongly endorsed him. PATCO's members were acknowledged to have extremely stressful occupations; they were also employees of the Federal Aviation Authority (FAA) and therefore forbidden by law to strike. Nonetheless, in July 1981, when contract negotiations with PATCO reached an impasse, its members threatened to walk out.

There were three areas of dispute. The union, led by Robert Poli, wanted a four-day, 32-hour workweek (down from 40 hours), a better retirement package—and an astonishing across-the-board pay increase of $10,000 annually. (Base pay for controllers was then $20,462; the average was $31,000.) Reagan, negotiating budget cuts with Congress, could not possibly authorize such an increase, although he agreed that the controllers deserved more money. He therefore offered an 11 percent increase, well above average and considered generous at a time of cost cutting.

A strike would cause chaos for air travelers and severely affect the nation's economy; in addition, air-traffic controllers needed specialized skills, making them difficult to replace. For these reasons Poli felt that the union held the upper hand, and when talks broke down in early August, he and other PATCO leaders called on their members to strike. On August 3 approximately 13,000 of the nation's 17,000 controllers walked out, causing the cancellation of some 7,000 flights.

Reagan, a onetime president of the Screen Actors Guild and the first U.S. president to be a lifetime member of the AFL-CIO, was sympathetic to the strikers' position, but he was also infuriated that they had broken the law. He announced that if they did not return to work within 48 hours, he would fire them, and they would not be rehired. He also approved measures to ensure the nation's air traffic continued as smoothly as possible. Supervisory personnel were called in to augment the nonstriking controllers, and the FAA, the Defense Department, and the private sector assisted in the transition to a non–PATCO workforce.

The PATCO strike was no ordinary labor dispute: It affected the nation's security. Without air-traffic control, the emergency launch of military jets would be hampered, and the United States would be vulnerable to attack. Because of this, PATCO thought Reagan would accept their claims. The president's 48-hour deadline came and went, and only 1,650 controllers returned to work. Reagan thereupon fired the remaining 11,350, reducing the workforce by 70 percent. To compensate, military personnel were brought in to help direct commercial flights, along with the managers who had already been pressed into service.

Inevitably, the salary increase generated the most publicity, overshadowing the other demands, which PATCO considered even more important. Flight controllers were acknowledged to be grossly overworked, a potentially dangerous factor in a high-stress job. As *Time* magazine noted, the 32-hour week was "a reduction that the controllers seem to want more than the pay increases. . . . [M]ost PATCO members see this issue as the key to lowering their on-the-job anxieties and enhancing safety."[19] Nevertheless, the salary issue became the most-cited reason for the strike; consequently, the strikers received little support from either congressional Democrats or the public.

On August 17 the FAA began to accept applications for new personnel to be hired and trained.[20] Reagan instituted a lifetime ban on rehiring strikers and barred them from other federal jobs. Fortunately, no major accidents occurred as overworked personnel staffing air-control towers and radar centers coped with the situation. As the president stood firm in his determination not to rehire the controllers, other union leaders began to fear that the PATCO situation signaled new antilabor initiatives. Consequently, on September 19 the AFL–CIO, in conjunction with civil rights organizations, organized a massive demonstration against Reagan's policies, with more than 250,000 protesters descending on Washington.

On October 22 the Labor Relations Authority decertified PATCO, a move that ended any chance of a settlement; within a year the union would go bankrupt and collapse. On December 9 President Reagan canceled his ban on federal jobs for those who had been fired, although they still could not return to work as controllers. No other concessions were made to the strikers, and as the once-depleted workforce filled up again, flight schedules gradually returned to normal.

Reagan's handling of the strike had two important consequences. First, the clear message it sent to government unions kept wage negotiations at a reasonable level and prevented other strikes from occurring. This, in turn, helped keep inflation down and was an important factor in the economic turnaround that lay ahead. Second, Reagan's response sent a message to foreign powers that he was capable of acting decisively to protect national security. He made the United States and its leader appear strong again, earning the country renewed respect (and subsequent investment) from abroad. George Shultz, later secretary of state in Reagan's administration, noted that the president's response to the PATCO strike was the most important foreign-policy decision he ever made.

The strike was a major test of Reagan's presidency, which many felt he passed with flying colors. A heavy price was paid by the strikers, however, who were unable to return to their profession until President Bill Clinton signed an executive order on August 12, 1993, lifting the ban on their being hired.

## THE COMPUTER REVOLUTION

Until 1981, stand-alone desktop computers had limited uses in the business world and were almost nonexistent in the home. Most companies used large mainframe computers for data-processing purposes, while functions such as correspondence were still handled by typewriters. Then, on August 12, 1981, IBM introduced its first personal computer: the IBM PC. Apple Computers, which had blazed the trail with its Apple II model in 1977, already had many competitors, but the entry of IBM into the market made business analysts take notice. Apple's founders, Steve Jobs and Steve Wozniak, welcomed the business giant to the field, foreseeing it would bring innovations that could only make computers better. They were right—and the computer revolution began.

In the 1950s, the invention of the transistor and integrated circuit drastically reduced the size of computers and improved their efficiency. Throughout the 1960s and 1970s, improvements continued with the development of integrated-circuit technology and the creation of the microprocessor chip, making it possible to build smaller computers for relatively little cost. Yet by the mid-1970s, these machines still generally had no keyboard, video display, or storage capability, and they required specialized knowledge to build (from kits supplied by the manufacturer) and operate. Jobs and Wozniak set out to make a computer that could be purchased already assembled and operated by anybody, regardless of technical expertise. Apple I (1976) included a video display and keyboard but failed to arouse much interest. Apple II, however, proved a vast improvement, incorporating the BASIC (Beginner's All-purpose Symbolic Instruction Code) programming language, displaying text and graphics in color, and holding up to 64 kilobytes (kb) of memory. Its built-in keyboard and power supply gave it a major advantage, and expansion slots allowed manufacturers to design plug-in cards that made it adaptable for many purposes. Most important, Apple II required no special expertise; the most inexperienced user could set it up and start to use it. In 1978 Apple sold 25,000 units—and 100,000 units in 1979, making it the market leader. (It was replaced by the Apple IIe in 1983; Apple III was introduced in 1980.)

When IBM entered the field in 1981, innumerable companies, including Xerox, Texas Instruments, Commodore, and Hewlett Packard, were trying to emulate Apple's success with a bewildering choice of models. Apple II had its own specialized operating system, but most of its competitors relied on Digital's CP/M system, which allowed only limited compatibility among different manufacturers' computers. Realizing the importance of compatibility, IBM set up a secret development team, Project Acorn, to create a more usable and reliable personal computer. The result was the IBM PC, based on the Intel 8088 microprocessor, with revolutionary innovations. Like Apple, IBM published its technical specifications so that other manufacturers could design additional hardware and software for it. A thriving industry soon grew up around the PC that benefited not only IBM but firms producing successful add-on products.

The crucial factor was the computer's operating system. Buyers could obtain the PC with either Digital's CP/M-86, priced at $180, or IBM's own PC-DOS, which became an instant success at only $40. PC-DOS was produced by a software developer named Microsoft—headed by a young Harvard dropout named Bill Gates and his friend Paul Allen. Gates and Allen had already developed a version of BASIC that allowed software applications for a variety of purposes and licensed it to Apple computers. Microsoft's spectacular rise, however, really began in 1980, when Gates persuaded IBM to use his MS-DOS (Microsoft disk/operating system). Gates retained the rights to it, and his perspicacity helped Microsoft become a formidable competitor in the industry.

IBM priced its first PC model at $2,495, competitive with Apple, and sold 65,000 units in 1981. Within a few months of the original PC's release, the company introduced its Personal Computer/XT with an improved keyboard and optional hard disk (as opposed to the one or two floppy drives of the original machine).

But IBM was not the only computer maker introducing innovations and challenging Apple in 1981. Commodore, which ultimately went out of business under the weight of IBM's success, introduced the first color computer to cost under $300: the VIC-20, which at one point sold 9,000 units per day. In 1982 Commodore produced the first color portable computer, although this was not the very first portable; that distinction belonged to the Osborne I, introduced by Adam Osborne on April 3, 1981. Like other computer makers, Osborne would not survive after IBM came out with its PC—his company folded in 1983—and one of the reasons was that his machine could not run IBM programs. Once again, someone perceived a niche, and Compaq Computer Corporation of Houston, Texas, would go on to make the first IBM-compatible portable computers with spectacular success.

The most important innovation of 1981 did not come into its own at once. In April Xerox Corporation had unveiled its Xerox Star, remarkable for the means by which the user "interacted" with the machine and gave it its commands. At that time, computer operators used combinations of strokes on their keyboards to convey instructions. The Xerox Star had a new component: a little box on wheels that allowed the user to move an arrow on the screen, point it to a certain location, and then press a button that would effect the desired command. Xerox called this innovation a "graphical user interface" (GUI)—otherwise known as a mouse.[21]

The Xerox Star was not successful because the machine itself was too slow, but both Microsoft and Apple saw its possibilities and launched GUI-based projects, which were initially unsuccessful. Then Apple produced the Macintosh in 1984—and the computer revolution entered an exciting new phase.

## A CHANGING CULTURE

Computer breakthroughs were only part of the 1980s economic and cultural revolution. The early years of the decade comprised an exciting period of fads, trends, and technological developments. Sometimes even the simplest inventions made a huge impact on American life, as Spencer Sylver of the 3M Corporation proved in 1981 when he invented the now-indispensable Post-it Notes. The Rubik's Cube craze was more short-lived: Between 1979 and the end of 1982, it sold more than 100 million of the three-dimensional geometrical puzzles sold;[22] then the Cube went the way of most fads, disappearing until the late 1990s.

Video games had been around since the 1960s, but their popularity exploded in 1981 with personal computers and the introduction of Pac-Man, which toppled Pong as the king of arcade games. It would go on to become the most popular video game of all time, spawning Ms. Pac-Man, Super Pac-Man, and hundreds of imitators and successors such as Donkey Kong. A saturation of these games combined with the poor economy led to a crash in 1983, but the industry eventually recovered, and as technology improved over time, so did the games. The development of videodiscs and laser discs in the early 1980s allowed people not only to play games but also to access information simply by touching parts of a video screen, making them valuable as teaching tools.

The use of videocassette recorders (VCRs, introduced in 1975) was also expanding, as was cable television: By 1980 almost 7.5 million American households were subscribers to pay-TV systems via cable, satellite dishes, or subscription channels that entailed decoding devices.[23] Their numbers would increase dramatically after the cable industry was deregulated in 1984. In the meantime, many leading corporations, such as CBS, ABC, and PBS, had seen the writing on the wall and begun to explore the possibilities of expanding to cable, particularly in the area of cultural programming. Yet the long-established broadcasters did not do as well as the upstarts, as 1981 saw the launch of new channels such as Bravo (originally Bravo!) and MTV, which have become staples of modern-day cable menus. CNN, the first all-news network, had already been launched in 1980.

Pay TV and subscription TV initially involved limited programming; Bravo!, for example, started out broadcasting only two nights a week, with its offerings confined to theater, dance, and concerts. But as channels such as the all-music MTV succeeded, others entered the market, offering increasing variety to the American viewing public: 24-hour news, sports, and movie channels; innovative children's programming; pay-per-view programming; and shows specifically targeted at African Americans, Hispanics, and others. Furthermore, public-access channels allowed anybody to air his or her own show, leading to an assortment of programs that ranged from the informative to the bizarre.

On the regular airwaves, television reflected the diverse and sometimes extravagant tastes of the times. The most popular shows included *Dallas* (premiered 1978), *Knots Landing* (1979), and *Dynasty* (1981), all of which revolved around the self-centered lives of the rich and pampered. *Hill Street Blues* (1981) presented a realistic, gritty view of a city police force, while *St. Elsewhere* (1982) did the same for the staff of a Boston hospital. Several long-popular shows premiered in 1982, including *Cheers, Family Ties, Newhart,* and *Late Night with David Letterman.* These and other programs reflected an increasing trend toward sharp writing and situations that reflected the modern world. In contrast were programs that catered to the American fascination with celebrity, such as *Entertainment Tonight,* which debuted in September 1981 and spawned the term *infotainment.* However, the number-one ratings winner in 1982 was the more intelligent and reliable newsmagazine *60 Minutes.*

Offerings on the big screen ranged from the thrills of *Raiders of the Lost Ark* to the poignancy of *On Golden Pond* and the inanity of *Porky's* in 1981; and from the imagination and wonder of *E.T.*—which became one of the greatest box-office hits—to the heartbreak and triumph of *An Officer and a Gentleman* in 1982. Moreover, in movies as in so many areas, new technology was making a profound impact. In summer 1982 the Disney company released *TRON,* an innovative film whose extensive use of computer animation brought new dimensions to filmmaking: Of 350 backgrounds used in the movie, 286 were drawn by computer, and some 15 minutes of the film were produced by high-speed data processing. Appropriately, the plot centered on video games.

Among the more exciting technological advances of the 1980s were developments in the medical field. The decade's early years saw vast improvements in microsurgery, allowing surgeons to replace and reattach parts of the body they were once unable to repair at all. Biotechnology also made major advances, and companies such as Genentech went public with stock offerings based not on tangible products but merely on the future promise of new techniques such as gene splicing.

When Kodak introduced the disc camera in 1982, it seemed that 35-mm film was about to be replaced by a revolutionary concept: a disc that stored the images taken by the camera. But the cameras often lacked good-quality lenses and were complicated to use; worse, the images they produced were extremely small, and when enlarged, the quality was very poor. As a result, the disc camera never really caught on, though it was seven years before Kodak finally pulled it from the shelves.

Another notable product of the 1980s had an even shorter run. Named after its creator, the De Lorean, with its stainless-steel body and doors hinging upwards, seemed to be the car of the future. Manufactured in Northern Ireland, the first shipment reached the United States in early spring 1981—but a year later the De Lorean company was bankrupt and John De Lorean was arrested for dealing cocaine. Having failed to generate any public interest, the car went the way of Ford's Edsel. Its later appearance in the movie *Back to the Future* (1985) epitomized the De Lorean as a 1980s icon, a symbol of both affluence and failure.

## CANADA ACHIEVES INDEPENDENCE

On November 13, 1981, Canada made a significant contribution to space exploration with the deployment of the Canadian-designed Remote Manipulator System (RMS) during the second flight of the U.S. space shuttle *Challenger. A* robotic "arm" that could be operated remotely from the aft flight deck, the RMS became affectionately known as the Canadarm after images of it, emblazoned with a giant red maple leaf and the word *Canada,* were transmitted from space. The Canadarm would go on to perform almost flawlessly on more than 50 space missions, demonstrating the growing importance of Canadian technology throughout the world.

The Canadarm came out when the country was about to achieve a historic goal. When Pierre Trudeau resumed leadership of Canada in March 1980, he was determined to accomplish the country's full, legal independence from Great Britain. This meant repatriating the constitution—that is, "bringing it home." The constitution had been under the control of the British parliament since the British North America Act of 1867 had granted self-government to Canada. While that act had allowed Canada to set up a confederation and allotted various powers and authorities (legislating, taxing, etc.) among federal and provincial governments, the constitution could not be

The repatriation of the Canadian constitution was one of Pierre Trudeau's greatest triumphs. He is seen here being applauded by members in the House of Commons after a vote on the constitution on December 1, 1981. *(Andy Clark/Reuters/Landov)*

amended without Britain's authority. Therefore, even though the Balfour Report of 1926 recognized Canada's independence and the Statute of Westminster in 1931 officially ended its status as a British colony, Canada was still not fully autonomous.

Negotiations to repatriate the Canadian constitution had been going on for decades. The constitution itself was (and still is) not a single document with amendments, as in the United States, but an accumulation of measures comprising the "acts of the British and Canadian Parliaments, as well as legislation, judicial decisions and agreements between the federal and provincial governments."[24] There was also a very complex framework of numerous unwritten elements. British and Canadian representatives had been unable to agree on amendment procedures, and this had delayed the constitution's repatriation. In 1949 the Canadian parliament gained some amending authority on questions of federal jurisdiction, but that was the sole progress up to 1980.

In April 1981, a year after Trudeau resumed office, a new federal constitution was presented, supported by eight provincial premiers. Trudeau rejected it, convinced that it did not provide for a strong central government; it also lacked the support of all 10 provinces, a condition crucial to the Canadian Supreme Court's approval. A few months later the premiers approved a revised version that essentially protected the distribution of powers established under the British North America Act of 1867 while creating a formula for making further constitutional amendments. It also incorporated a Canadian Charter of Rights and Freedoms and strengthened the provinces' control over natural resources. Although this version was supported by Trudeau and nine provinces, Quebec objected to the Charter of Rights and Freedoms. The 1867 act allowed Quebec to maintain its own civil code and protected its French-language charter and public funding for religious schools. Quebec's leaders believed that the charter not only impinged on fundamental Quebecois rights but also limited the province's legislative powers.

Nonetheless, the proposed constitution was passed over the Quebec National Assembly objections since, as the Supreme Court of Canada later ruled, Canada's laws under the 1867 act had been respected throughout the repatriation process and the constitution therefore applied to the entire country. On March 8, 1982, the British House of Commons passed the Canada Act, granting Canada the right to amend its constitution. On April 17, at a ceremony in Ottawa, Queen Elizabeth II formally signed the Canada Act into law and proclaimed the Canadian constitution. She would remain the country's head of state, and Canada would still be a member of the British Commonwealth, but it was now free to make its own constitutional amendments, the final step in its 115-year transition to autonomy. The British North America Act was renamed the Constitution Act, 1867, and to it was added the Constitution Act, 1982—the two foundations of modern Canada.

Having achieved his goal of Canadian sovereignty, Trudeau turned his attention to the economy. Like its southern neighbor, Canada was in a major recession, leading Parliament to reorganize several federal agencies and to create a Ministry of State for Economic Development in January 1982. In June of that year, Finance Minister Allan MacEachen proposed a federal budget of increased taxes, wage restraints, and investment incentives. In late August, the country's 10 provincial premiers called on Prime Minister Trudeau to put together a plan for economic recovery.

As in the United States, Canada would emerge from the recession, but the hard times were, for many, offset by pride in the constitutional repatriation. July 1 had always been a national holiday called Dominion Day, marking the creation of the Canadian confederation. On October 27, 1982, it was officially renamed Canada Day, commemorating the full independence the country had finally achieved.

## A BATTLE IS LOST

On June 30, 1982, the Equal Rights Amendment (ERA) "died." The failure of the proposed 27th amendment to the Constitution was a serious setback in a long-fought campaign that has persisted into the 2000s.

The campaign began in 1923, when the feminist Alice Paul introduced the Lucretia Mott Amendment (later to be called the Alice Paul Amendment) at a celebration in Seneca Falls, New York, marking the 75th anniversary of the 1848 Women's Rights Convention. The proposed amendment was short and simple: "Men and women shall have equal rights throughout the United States and every place subject to its jurisdiction." It was soon modified, but its intent remained straightforward:

> Section 1. Equality of rights under the law shall not be denied or abridged by the United States or by any state on account of sex.
> Section 2. The Congress shall have the power to enforce, by appropriate legislation, the provisions of this article.
> Section 3. This amendment shall take effect two years after the date of ratification.

At the time, many women believed the proposed amendment to be the natural successor of the Nineteenth Amendment to the Constitution (1920).

American women had won the right to vote, but legal equality of the sexes remained a dream, and only by amending the Constitution could equal justice for all citizens, regardless of sex, be achieved. This, at least, was what feminists believed.

The ERA was proposed at every session of Congress from 1923 to 1972, when it was finally passed and sent to the states. To become law, it needed ratification by at least 38 states within seven years; 30 ratified after only one year. However, by 1979 only 35 states had given their approval. Under pressure from powerful women's rights groups, Congress extended the deadline three more years, to June 30, 1982. But no more states ratified the amendment, and, in fact, five states that had approved it later rescinded their ratification. Consequently, the amendment died.

The proposed amendment seemed so simple and its aim so basic—equal rights for all—that its failure mystified its supporters. Yet there were many arguments against it, primarily the belief that constitutional equality of the sexes would create numerous legal pitfalls when distinctions between men and women that many considered sensible were called into question. For example, women would be required to go into combat where previously they had been excused, and many other protections afforded them (such as exemption from heavy labor) would be removed. For many feminists, this was not a problem, but for many others it would be an abhorrent outcome.

Other arguments raised by ERA opponents included claims that the amendment would remove a woman's right to be supported by her husband, adversely affect family values, encourage abortions and homosexual marriages, and infringe on the right to privacy. Religious groups were vocal anti-ERA voices, but the leading opponent was Phyllis Schlafly, the conservative organizer of the "Stop ERA" movement, whose massive lobbying was a significant factor in the amendment's defeat.

The ERA has been reintroduced into every session of Congress since July 14, 1982, but has still to be passed. Many supporters hold that the original amendment remains valid and still needs only three more states to achieve ratification, citing other amendments that were ratified without a deadline imposed on them.[25] But others believe it is no longer needed, as existing legislation has done more for women's rights than a controversial amendment to the Constitution could have accomplished. It may also be significant that the ERA, support for which peaked when the women's movement was strong in the 1970s, failed during the conservative revolution of the 1980s.

## A RECESSION, BUT . . .

The 1980s would be a decade of economic highs and lows—and the lows came first. By November 1981 it was clear that the country had entered a recession. Year-end figures showed an inflation rate of 14 percent, up from 12.4 percent at the end of 1980, and by December 1981, an unemployment rate of 8.5 percent and rising. The cost of living was soaring; medical care costs had risen by 12.5 percent and were at their most expensive level since 1935. Industry was also suffering; automobile production was at its lowest point in 20 years, and in 1981 the 10 major airlines had a combined operating loss of $577 billion—more than double their 1980 losses.

Reagan was slow to acknowledge the difficulties, then called it a "light recession" and blamed former president Jimmy Carter. Yet he clearly shared some of the responsibility as David Stockman's fears regarding federal deficits were proving well founded. On December 7, 1981, the Reagan administration officially forecast a record deficit of $109 billion for 1982—although that, too, was blamed on Jimmy Carter.

The bad news carried into 1982, which saw the gross national product (GNP) fall by 1.8 percent, the largest drop since 1946, as well as the failure of more than 30 banks and thousands of businesses, foreclosures on hundreds of farm mortgages, and a dramatic increase in homelessness. Unemployment also continued to climb, reaching a staggering 10.8 percent by the end of the year—the highest rate since 1940. More than 11.5 million Americans lost their jobs in 1982; millions more had to take lower-paying work. The only good news was the slow reduction of the inflation rate.

The president remained convinced that the new tax cuts and industrial deregulation would eventually achieve the results he hoped for. Furthermore, the consequences of the PATCO strike were reaching the private sector: As wage settlements and labor costs came down and as strikes dropped to the lowest level since 1945, businesses benefited from lower operating expenses. In theory, this meant that American firms would become more competitive and boost the economy.

Deregulation was key to Reagan's optimism and a major goal for his administration. Jimmy Carter had already deregulated the airline, trucking, railroad, and oil industries, but Reagan wanted to go further and free companies from unnecessary governmental restrictions. He did so by reducing the thousands of regulations on businesses; decreasing the budgets of key regulatory agencies, such as the Occupational Safety and Health Administration and the Environmental Protection Agency; and appointing to other agencies, such as the Federal Trade Commission (FTC) and the Federal Communications Commission, people who he believed would carry out his agenda.

The public largely supported the president; consequently, Congress was cooperative, passing legislation that put more controls on the FTC. Greater freedom was afforded savings-and-loan (S&L) institutions (also called thrifts), allowing them to lend to more types of businesses than previously and allowing developers to own S&Ls. This and later deregulation of the S&L industry meant the thrifts could move into commercial banking, with devastating consequences in the late 1980s.

Deregulation in other industries would have both positive and negative effects on American commerce, as would changes in previously monopolistic industries. A typical example was American Telephone and Telegraph's (AT&T) loss of its monopoly in telecommunications. On January 8, 1982, after a lawsuit that lasted nearly eight years, the government and AT&T agreed that the communications giant would divest itself of 22 of its 24 Bell Operating Systems as of January 1, 1984. The suit allowed others to challenge AT&T's supremacy in the industry, leading to major changes in telecommunications after the divestiture.

Meanwhile, high-powered takeovers, which would become a hallmark of the 1980s, were already taking place. On August 4, 1981, the largest industrial merger in U.S. history (to that time) took place when E. I. du Pont de Nemours acquired

Conoco, the ninth-largest oil company, for more than $7.5 billion. Just a few months later, in March 1982, the country's second-largest merger occurred as Marathon Oil Company joined United States Steel Corporation in a deal worth $6 billion. Such transactions would make their mark on the American economy. On October 7, 1982, the New York Stock Exchange set a record with 147,070,000 shares traded in one day. On October 15 it established a weekly trading record of 592,460,000 shares. Although unemployment was still appallingly high, the recession was showing signs of lifting. Before long, American business would be booming.

## CHRONICLE OF EVENTS

**1981**

*January 20:* Ronald Reagan is inaugurated as president.

*January 23:* The Labor Department reports the 1980 inflation rate was 12.4 percent, its second double-digit increase in two years.

*January 23:* Samuel Barber, composer of *Adagio for Strings* and other well-known classics, dies at age 70.

*January 25:* The Oakland Raiders defeat the Philadelphia Eagles, 27-10, to win Super Bowl XV.

*January 26:* U.S. Representative Richard Kelly (R, Fla.) is convicted on Abscam-related charges; the conviction will be overturned on May 14.

*February 2:* General Motors announces losses in all four quarters of 1980, its first full-year loss since 1921.

*February 9:* Rock-and-roll pioneer Bill Haley dies, age 55. He and his group The Comets were best known for "Rock Around the Clock."

*February 24:* Former schoolmistress Jean Harris is convicted of murdering Scarsdale Diet creator Dr. Herman Tarnower in March 1980; she will be sentenced to 15 years to life.

*March 6:* Veteran reporter Walter Cronkite makes his final broadcast as anchor of *CBS Evening News.*

*March 10:* The U.S. Postal Service announces that the price of a first-class stamp will be raised from 15 to 18 cents.

*March 30:* President Reagan and three others survive an assassination attempt by John W. Hinckley, Jr.

*March 30:* Dewitt Wallace, publisher who founded the *Reader's Digest* in 1922, dies at age 91.

*March 31:* At the Academy Awards, *Ordinary People* wins as best picture; Robert De Niro (*Raging Bull*) and

President and Mrs. Reagan wave to the crowd at an inaugural ball at the Air and Space Museum, one of nine held the night of January 20, 1981. *(Courtesy Ronald Reagan Library)*

Robert De Niro won his only Oscar for his role as the boxer Jake LaMotta in *Raging Bull* (1980). *(Photofest)*

Sissy Spacek (*Coal Miner's Daughter*) win the top acting awards.

*April 4:* In San Antonio, Texas, Henry Cisneros becomes the first Mexican American to be elected mayor of a major U.S. city.

*April 8:* Five-star general Omar Bradley, known as the "GI's General" because of his care and concern for American soldiers, dies at age 88.

*April 9:* In the East China Sea, the American submarine *George Washington* strikes a small Japanese freighter, the *Nissho Maru,* and then leaves without offering assistance. The freighter sinks; its captain and first mate die. The U.S. Navy will not acknowledge responsibility for the tragedy until April 20.

*April 12:* Boxing champion Joe Louis, who held the world heavyweight title from 1937 to 1949, dies at the age of 66.

*April 12–14:* The *Columbia* makes its maiden flight, launching the space-shuttle program.

*April 13:* Pulitzer Prize winners include John Kennedy Toole (*A Confederacy of Dunces*) for fiction,

James Schuyler (*The Morning of the Poem*) for poetry, and Beth Henley (*Crimes of the Heart*) for drama.

*April 23:* In Boston, doctors at the Massachusetts General Hospital announce the successful grafting of artificial skin on human burn patients.

*April 24:* President Reagan lifts the embargo on grain shipments to the Soviet Union that President Carter had imposed following the Soviet invasion of Afghanistan in December 1979.

*April 24:* Horse racing's Willie Shoemaker wins his 8,000th race. To date he has won 2,000 more races than any other jockey.

*April 29:* U.S. Representative Raymond F. Lederer (D, N.J.) resigns his seat, having been convicted in January on charges related to the Abscam scandal.

*May 4:* In an effort to curb inflation, the Federal Reserve Board raises the discount rate to 14 percent.

*May 6:* The United States closes Libya's mission in Washington, D.C., and expels Libyan diplomats.

*May 11:* Reggae musician Bob Marley, 36, dies of brain and lung cancer in Miami, Florida.

*May 13:* Pope John Paul II is shot and wounded in St. Peter's Square in the Vatican; two American women tourists are also wounded in the attack. The pope survives; his would-be assassin, 23-year-old Turkish terrorist Mehmet Ali Agca, is arrested.

*June 6:* Maya Yang Lin, a 21-year-old Yale undergraduate, wins a national competition to design a Vietnam War memorial to be situated in Washington, D.C. Her design consists of two long granite slabs, meeting in a V point, on which are inscribed all the names of the war dead.

*June 6:* The United Mine Workers vote to end a 10-week-old strike that has closed hundreds of coal mines in the East and Midwest.

*June 8:* In *County of Washington v. Gunther,* the U.S. Supreme Court rules that women can sue for equal pay even if their work is not equivalent to that of male employees.

*June 12:* In midseason, professional baseball players walk out on a strike that will last until July 31.

*June 16:* Secretary of State Alexander Haig announces the United States will sell arms to the People's Republic of China.

*June 25:* In *Rostker v. Goldberg,* the Supreme Court rules it is constitutional to exclude women from the military draft.

*June 28:* Terry Fox, a Canadian marathoner, dies of cancer at age 22. Fox had attracted worldwide attention in 1980, when he attempted to run across Canada on a prosthetic leg. His marathon was cut short when his cancer recurred; he nonetheless raised C$25 million for cancer research.

*July 9:* A *New England Journal of Medicine* report reveals that acyclovir, an experimental drug, has successfully suppressed the herpes simplex virus (responsible for genital herpes, the most rapidly spreading sexually transmitted disease in the United States).

*July 22:* Chrysler Corporation, which had received a federal bailout loan in January 1980, announces its first profit since 1978: $11.6 million in the second quarter of 1981.

*August 1:* MTV, the first 24-hour music television station, begins broadcasting. The first song it airs is the Buggles' "Video Killed the Radio Star."

*August 3:* The air-traffic controllers' union, PATCO, initiates a nationwide strike that will ultimately result in the firing of 11,350 controllers.

*August 4:* The U.S. Senate passes a modified version of President Reagan's income-tax reduction plan; the House of Representatives had approved the bill on July 29. Reagan will sign the Economic Recovery Act into law on August 13.

*August 19:* Sixty miles off the coast of Libya, two U.S. Navy jets shoot down two Libyan fighter planes that had attacked an American aircraft carrier.

*August 23:* In New York City, John Lennon's assassin, Mark David Chapman, is sentenced to 20 years to life.

*August 25:* *Voyager 2* passes within 63,000 miles of Saturn; photographs transmitted from the spacecraft reveal that the planet has thousands of rings. The spacecraft is expected to reach Uranus in 1986.

*August 29:* Author and news commentator Lowell Thomas, best known for his book *Lawrence of Arabia,* dies at age 89.

*September 8:* Roy Wilkins, who led the NAACP from 1931 to 1977, dies at age 80.

*September 13:* *Hill Street Blues* dominates the Emmy Awards, winning best dramatic series; its stars, Daniel J. Travanti and Barbara Babcock, win as best actor and actress in a dramatic series.

*September 19:* In Washington, D.C., a rally to protest Reagan administration policies attracts 250,000 participants from labor and civil rights organizations.

*September 19:* In New York City, the musical duo Simon and Garfunkel reunite for a historic concert in Central Park.

*September 25:* Sandra Day O'Connor is sworn in as a justice of the U.S. Supreme Court, replacing retired justice Potter Stewart. She had been nominated by President Reagan in July and approved unanimously by the Senate on September 22.

*October 2:* President Reagan announces the United States Strategic Weapons Initiative, a $180 billion defense program that includes a plan to build 100 MX missiles to be placed in existing Titan II or Minuteman silos in Arizona, Arkansas, and Kansas.

*October 2:* The body of Lee Harvey Oswald is exhumed and positively identified. The action was taken after a British author claimed the coffin of John F. Kennedy's accused assassin actually contained the body of a Soviet spy.

*October 6:* Egyptian president Anwar Sadat is assassinated in Cairo.

*October 25:* Alberto Salazar sets a world record in the New York City Marathon, winning in 2 hours, 8 minutes, 13 seconds. The women's winner, Allison Roe, finishes in 2:25:28, setting a women's record for the marathon.

*October 28:* The U.S. Senate votes to retain an $8.5 billion deal made in April to sell AWACS (Airborne Warning and Control System) radar planes as well as other military equipment to Saudi Arabia. Earlier in the month, the House of Representatives had voted to reject the deal, which Israel had strongly protested.

*October 28:* The Los Angeles Dodgers defeat the New York Yankees to win the World Series in six games.

New Supreme Court Justice Sandra Day O'Connor is sworn into office on September 25, 1981. *(Courtesy Ronald Reagan Library)*

*November 1:* The price of a first-class stamp is raised to 20 cents, the second increase this year.

*November 11:* The first Trident submarine, USS *Ohio,* is commissioned at a ceremony in Groton, Connecticut; Vice President George Bush is the principal speaker.

*November 14:* The space shuttle *Columbia* returns to Earth after a successful two-day test flight.

*November 16:* Film actor William Holden, noted for his roles in *Stalag 17* and *The Bridge on the River Kwai,* dies at age 63.

*November 30:* The United States and Soviet Union begin arms-control talks in Geneva, Switzerland.

*November 30:* Because of deteriorating relations between Libya and the United States, President Reagan instructs Americans in Libya to leave that country.

*December 4:* The U.S. Department of Labor announces that the unemployment rate in November was 8.5 percent.

*December 11:* In Nassau, the Bahamas, Muhammed Ali loses a heavyweight boxing fight against Trevor Berbick after 10 rounds. The 39-year-old former champion had come out of retirement for the bout, which earned him $3 million.

*December 28:* The United States' first test-tube baby, Elizabeth Carr, is born to Judith and Roger Carr.

*December 29:* President Reagan announces heavy sanctions against the Soviet Union after it declares martial law in Poland and outlaws the Solidarity movement. The sanctions include stopping U.S.-bound flights of Aeroflot and suspending negotiations on long-term grain purchases.

## 1982

*January 4:* Richard Allen resigns as National Security Advisor after being accused of taking a bribe from Japanese journalists to arrange an interview with Nancy Reagan. Allen, who is replaced by William Clark, is later cleared of the charges.

*January 5:* A federal judge invalidates an Arkansas law that requires the teaching of creationism whenever evolution is taught.

*January 8:* AT&T's monopoly of American telephone services comes to an end when the company agrees to divest itself of its 22 Bell Telephone operating systems.

*January 13:* An Air Florida jetliner taking off from Washington National Airport crashes into the Fourteenth Street Bridge in Washington, D.C., killing 78 (of whom seven were on the bridge). Lenny Skutnik becomes a hero when he plunges into the Potomac River and rescues one of five survivors.

*January 13:* Legendary batter and outfielder Hank Aaron is elected to the Baseball Hall of Fame.

*January 24:* The San Francisco 49ers beat the Cincinnati Bengals, 26–21, in Super Bowl XVI.

*January 26:* President Reagan delivers his first State of the Union address, in which he announces his plan for a "new federalism."

*January 30:* At the Golden Globe Awards, *On Golden Pond* wins Best Motion Picture–Drama, and *Arthur* wins Best Motion Picture–Comedy. Their stars, Henry Fonda and Dudley Moore, respectively, take the top film acting awards, along with Meryl Streep and Bernadette Peters.

*February 1: Late Night with David Letterman* makes its debut on NBC.

*February 17:* Two notable deaths occur: Thelonius Monk, 64, innovative jazz pianist and composer; and Lee Strasburg, 80, actor and coach famed for introducing the Method style of acting.

*February 24:* At the Grammy Awards, John Lennon and Yoko Ono's *Double Fantasy* wins Album of the Year. Kim Carnes's "Bette Davis Eyes" is named Record of the Year and Song of the Year.

*February 27:* In Atlanta, 23-year-old freelance photographer Wayne Williams is found guilty of the murders of two black children. He is suspected of 26 other deaths in a murder spree that had terrified Atlantans.

*March 4:* As imports of crude oil reach a seven-year low, the American Petroleum Institute announces that U.S. refineries are operating at 63.9 percent of capacity.

*March 5:* Comedian and actor John Belushi dies of a drug overdose at age 33.

*March 6:* Ayn Rand, author noted for her advocacy of individualism in such books as *The Fountainhead* and *Atlas Shrugged,* dies at age 77.

*March 10:* The government announces sanctions against Libya for its involvement with international terrorist organizations. These include embargoes on Libyan oil and on the export of certain advanced technology to Libya.

*March 11:* Harrison Williams (D, N.J.) resigns his U.S. Senate seat when it becomes clear that he will be expelled because of his May 1981 conviction for bribery and conspiracy relating to the Abscam scandal.

*March 11–13:* At the World Figure Skating Championships in Copenhagen, Denmark, the United States'

Scott Hamilton and Elaine Zayak win the men's and women's singles titles, respectively.

*March 22–30:* The space shuttle *Columbia* carries out its third mission.

*March 29:* At the 54th Academy Awards, the British film *Chariots of Fire* wins Best Picture. Henry Fonda and Katharine Hepburn win the major acting prizes for their work in *On Golden Pond.*

*April 2–3:* The Falkland Islands War begins when Argentina seizes the British-owned Falkland Islands in the South Atlantic Ocean, as well as the nearby South Georgia Islands and South Sandwich Islands. The seizure prompts Great Britain to send troops to the islands and to freeze Argentinian assets. Secretary of State Alexander Haig will try but fail to negotiate a peace between the two countries.

*April 5:* Former Supreme Court justice Abe Fortas dies, age 71.

*April 17:* Queen Elizabeth II proclaims the first formal Canadian constitution as Canada becomes legally independent of Great Britain.

*April 20:* Poet and playwright Archibald MacLeish dies at age 90.

*April 23:* Inflation drops by 0.3 percent, its first decline in a year.

*April 30:* The United States declares its support for Great Britain in the Falkland Islands War.

*May 1:* The 1982 World's Fair opens in Knoxville, Tennessee.

*May 7:* The unemployment rate for April is announced: 9.4 percent, the worst since World War II.

*May 13:* Braniff International Corporation, the nation's eighth-largest air carrier, announces the termination of 8,000 employees as it files for Chapter 11 bankruptcy protection. Braniff is the largest U.S. airline to seek reorganization under federal law.

*May 22:* George Wallace, disabled by a sniper's bullet in 1972, announces his intention to run for a fourth term as governor of Alabama.

*June 6:* At the 36th annual Tony Awards, *The Life and Adventures of Nicholas Nickleby* wins Play of the Year; *Nine* wins as Musical of the Year. Roger Rees, Ben Harney, Zoe Caldwell, and Jennifer Holliday win the top acting awards.

*June 8:* Baseball pitcher Leroy "Satchel" Paige, one of the Negro Leagues' greatest players, whose career lasted from 1924 to 1965, dies at the age of 75.

*June 12:* More than 700,000 demonstrators gather in New York's Central Park to call for an end to the production and deployment of nuclear weapons.

*June 14:* The Falkland Islands War effectively ends when Argentine forces surrender to Britain, which will formally declare the conclusion of hostilities on June 20.

*June 18:* Pulitzer Prize–winning author John Cheever dies at age 70.

*June 21:* John W. Hinckley, Jr., is found not guilty by reason of insanity in the March 1981 shootings of President Reagan and three others. He will be committed to a mental institution in Washington, D.C., on August 9, after a federal judge rules that there is "clear and convincing evidence" that he is dangerous.

*June 24:* On a 5-4 vote, the U.S. Supreme Court rules that no president or former president can be sued for actions taken while in office.

*June 25:* Secretary of State Alexander M. Haig, Jr., resigns from the cabinet; he will be succeeded by George P. Shultz.

*June 29:* The first session of the Strategic Arms Reduction Talks (START) between the United States and the Soviet Union opens in Geneva, Switzerland.

*June 30:* The Equal Rights Amendment fails to achieve ratification and therefore dies.

*July 1:* At Madison Square Garden in New York City, the Reverend Sun Myung Moon of the Unification Church officiates at a mass wedding ceremony uniting more than 2,000 couples.

*July 4: Columbia* returns from its fourth test mission, upon which the space-shuttle program is declared operational.

*July 19:* The poverty rate rises to 14 percent, the highest since 1967.

*July 23:* Actor Vic Morrow and two children are killed in a tragic helicopter accident during the filming of *Twilight Zone: The Movie.*

*August 5:* After preliminary reports link its antiarthritic drug Oroflex to 72 deaths in the United States and Great Britain, Eli Lilly & Company withdraws the drug from the market.

*August 12:* Actor Henry Fonda dies in Los Angeles at age 77. His best-known films include *The Grapes of Wrath, My Darling Clementine, Mister Roberts, 12 Angry Men,* and *On Golden Pond.*

*August 13:* The prime interest rate is lowered to 13.5 percent, from 15 percent.

*August 14:* Baseball star Pete Rose of the Philadelphia Phillies surpasses Hank Aaron's old record with 12,365 at-bats.

*August 17:* The U.S. Senate passes a new immigration bill granting permanent resident status to illegal aliens who arrived in the United States before 1977. Those who arrived after December 31, 1979, may be deported.

*August 20:* U.S. Marines land in Beirut, Lebanon, to help a multinational force oversee the withdrawal of PLO fighters.

*August 20:* U.S. officials announce a plan to help Mexico through a financial crisis with a multibillion-dollar loan.

*August 29:* Swedish-born actress Ingrid Bergman, renowned for her roles in such films as *Casablanca, Gaslight, Anastasia,* and *Murder on the Orient Express,* dies at age 67.

*September 10:* U.S. Marines withdraw from Beirut, but they will return on September 29, following a Lebanese request for assistance.

*September 14:* Princess Grace of Monaco, formerly American film actress Grace Kelly, dies at age 52 as a result of injuries sustained in a car crash.

*September 15:* The Gannett newspaper group begins publication of *Today,* a new national newspaper. Its initial publication is restricted to the Baltimore-Washington area, but eventually it will be sold throughout the country.

*September 19: Hill Street Blues* wins as outstanding television drama series, and *Barney Miller* wins outstanding comedy series at the 34th annual Emmy Awards.

*September 21:* Players for the 28 teams in the National Football League (NFL) call the first in-season strike in NFL history.

*September 29–October 1:* Seven people in Chicago die after ingesting Tylenol capsules laced with cyanide. This results in a nationwide alert and the company's recall of 264,000 bottles of Tylenol. The killer will never be found.

*October 1:* A balanced-budget amendment to the Constitution is defeated in the House of Representatives.

*October 2:* The Andrew Lloyd Webber musical *Cats* opens on Broadway and becomes an instant smash. It will go on to enjoy an eight-year run.

*October 4:* Canadian pianist Glenn Gould, renowned for his interpretations of Johann Sebastian Bach, dies at age 50 after a stroke.

Terence Mann played Rum Tum Tigger in the long-running Broadway hit *Cats. (Photofest)*

*October 6:* In Geneva, the United States and the Soviet Union commence the second round of strategic arms reductions talks (START).

*October 7:* The New York Stock Exchange (NYSE) reaches a one-day trading high of 147,070,000 shares.

*October 8:* The U.S. Department of Labor announces that the national unemployment rate reached 10.1 percent in September, the highest monthly rate since 1940.

*October 15:* The United States announces an agreement to sell grain to the Soviet Union.

*October 15:* President Reagan signs the Garth–St. Germain Depository Institutions Act, a new law lifting restraints on federally insured savings-and-loan companies.

*October 18:* Bess Truman, widow of President Harry Truman, dies at age 97.

*October 20:* The National League's St. Louis Cardinals win game 7 of baseball's World Series, defeating the American League's Milwaukee Brewers, 6-3.

*October 29:* The U.S. Food and Drug Administration approves the sale of synthetic human insulin for use by diabetics. It is the first time that a drug created by gene-splicing techniques has been approved by the FDA.

## EYEWITNESS TESTIMONY

### The Reagan Style

So, as we begin, let us take inventory. We are a nation that has a government—not the other way around. And this makes us special among the nations of the Earth. Our government has no power except that granted it by the people. It is time to check and reverse the growth of government, which shows signs of having grown beyond the consent of the governed.

It is my intention to curb the size and influence of the Federal establishment and to demand recognition of the distinction between the powers granted to the Federal Government and those reserved to the States or to the people. All of us need to be reminded that the Federal Government did not create the States; the States created the Federal Government.

Now, so there will be no misunderstanding, it's not my intention to do away with government. It is rather to make it work—work with us, not over us; to stand by our side, not ride on our back. Government can and must provide opportunity, not smother it; foster productivity, not stifle it.

*Ronald Reagan making clear what he will do as president, in his inaugural address, January 20, 1981. Available online. URL: http://www.reagan.utexas.edu/resource/speeches/1981/12081a.htm.*

Ronald Reagan moved into 1600 Pennsylvania Avenue last week "bouncy and eager," in one aide's phrase, to try his hand at operating the most powerful office in the land. He flipped switches, poked into closets and startled the White House mess with a cheery "Hi! I'm taking a tour." The Oval Office, he concluded, "seems comfortable," and he was plainly delighted with a brassy revival of "Hail to the Chief," a bit of pomp once mothballed by his predecessor as overly imperial. . . . "He's impressed with the history of it all, but he's not overwhelmed," said an aide. A close friend found him "very relaxed—and tickled with himself."

*Ronald Reagan settling into office, reported in "Hail to the New Chief," Newsweek, February 2, 1981, p. 47.*

Reagan's ability to win over an audience with his affable manner and homespun sincerity came through clearly in his televised economic speech on February 5. To gain public support for his view of the nation's eco-

President Reagan poses with his first cabinet on February 2, 1981. *(Courtesy Ronald Reagan Library)*

nomic problems, he went back to the basic lessons taught in Economics I, even pulling a dollar bill and 36 cents in change from his pocket to illustrate inflation's impact. The White House reported that public reaction to the speech was overwhelmingly favorable.

*Describing how President Reagan connects with Americans, in "The Reagan Style Starts to Pay Off," U.S. News & World Report, February 16, 1981, p. 9.*

Why is it that we think of Ronald Reagan as "a nice guy"? And is it "we" who think it? In fact, it is not the growing numbers of the unemployed, the desperate single mothers, the students and teachers forced to leave school, or the farmers, or the union members, or the old, or the young, or the poor, or the middle class, who keep babbling about how "nice" the president is. Those who find him "nice" are in a dwindling group, comprised of some defense contractors, a few lunatics in Orange County, and most of our TV newsmen, who persist as Reagan's biggest boosters. . . .

*Writer Mark Crispin Miller criticizing the president in his article "Virtù, Inc.," New Republic, April 7, 1982, quoted in Boyer, Reagan as President (1990), p. 80.*

Reagan has demonstrated, in a way that Jimmy Carter never did, that he understands how to be President. He knows that a president can deal only with a relatively small number of issues at a time. He also understands that his principal task is public leadership. Therefore, he has concentrated primarily upon economic policy and in particular on forming public opinion and working relationships with Congress.

From that point of view, I would give him an A.

*Erwin C. Hargrove, director of the Institute for Public Policy Studies, rating Ronald Reagan's first three months as president, quoted in "'Reagan Understands How to Be President,'" U.S. News & World Report, April 27, 1981, p. 23.*

Not since the days of John and Jacqueline Kennedy 20 years ago has there been such a turnabout in style at the Executive Mansion. The Nancy Reagan imprint is everywhere—from the newly redecorated family quarters upstairs to the pageantry that again reigns at official events downstairs.

After four years during which the Jimmy Carters often cut pomp to a minimum, a color guard has returned to precede the Reagans and their guests of

President Ronald Reagan and Vice President George H. W. Bush pose for an official portrait taken in July 1981. *(Courtesy Ronald Reagan Library)*

honor. Trumpeters on the White House balcony welcome foreign visitors. Ruffles and flourishes are heard when the President and official guests arrive. At state dinners, military social aides escort each member of the official party throughout the evening.

*The return of the imperial presidency, recorded in "Reagan White House—Glitter and Grace," U.S. News & World Report, June 1, 1981, p. 43.*

The reasons he [President Reagan] has stunned so many people are, first, that once in office he set out to do exactly what he promised on the budget and taxes. And, second, that he takes seriously his oath to execute the laws duly passed under the Constitution. We are little accustomed to Presidents who do both.

In doing this effectively Ronald Reagan has reminded us that the presidency is indeed a "bully pulpit." The actual powers of the President, contrary to the general view, are quite limited. He cannot order the government's budget, command the level of taxes or himself pass or repeal laws. His chief power is that of persuasion. A President who recognizes that, is skilled at it and will be resolute in the face of opposition can do much.

Mr. Reagan is all three. . . .

*Columnist Vermont Royster commenting on aspects of President Reagan's success, in Royster, "Thinking Things Over: A Warrior President," Wall Street Journal, August 11, 1981, p. 22.*

Reagan rang his secretary and asked her to get Menachim Begin on the phone. In the meantime, George Shultz had joined us and added his endorsement of the president's intervention. When the call came through he told the Israeli prime minister, in the plainest of language, that the shelling had to stop, that Israel was in danger of losing the moral support of the American people. His final words were: "It has gone too far. You must stop it."

Twenty minutes later, Begin called him back and said he had just issued orders to Ariel Sharon. The bombings had ceased. There were no planes over Beirut. When he hung up the phone, Ronald Reagan looked up and said, seriously, "I didn't know I had that kind of power."

*Michael Deaver relating the moment when President Reagan, at the insistence of Deaver and other staff members, intervened in the Israeli bombing of Beirut, Lebanon, August 12, 1982, in Deaver, Behind the Scenes (1987), p. 165.*

## The Highs and Lows of Reaganomics

If the Reagan administration can keep in mind the reason why it wants to cut taxes, it may have a fighting chance of keeping its tax policy from being held hostage by budget considerations. Otherwise it may lose its nerve in the face of the budget deficits projected by static revenue estimates. Delaying the tax cuts "because the deficit is too large" is a way of sending a signal that the administration doesn't have confidence in its own policy. Once that signal is sent, Congress and the Fed will have the administration on the run.

Remember, the reason for the tax cuts is to cause real output to grow faster than government spending. That's the way to keep the budget from hemorrhaging.

*Paul Craig Roberts, political columnist and nominee for assistant secretary of the Treasury for economic affairs, offering words of caution regarding Reaganomics, in Roberts, "Supply-Side Economics: A Fiscal Revolution?" Wall Street Journal, January 22, 1981, p. 24.*

If the 1982 election comes, and we are bringing interest rates and inflation down, and employment and output are going up, and Reagan reaches out to blacks and Hispanics and demonstrates that our Republican civil-rights strategy for the '80s is restoring social justice and economic opportunities, we could have a realignment in '82 the likes of which the Democrats had in '34. If we do it right, Republicans could be in power for 20 years as the party of Mr. Lincoln, prosperity and peace.

*Congressman Jack Kemp (R, N.Y.) predicting the future, quoted in "Inside the GOP's Economic 'Revolution,'" U.S. News & World Report, February 16, 1981, p. 22.*

We can no longer procrastinate and hope that things will get better. They will not. Unless we act forcefully, and now, the economy will get worse.

*President Reagan's opening remarks to Congress prior to presenting his "Program for Economic Recovery," February 18, 1981. Available online. URL: http://www.reagan.utexas.edu/resource/ speeches/1981/21881a.htm.*

On the day the President signed his budget message, 8,000 jeering coal miners marched three blocks from their union headquarters to the White House to denounce a proposed $378 million cut in federal pay-

ments for victims of black-lung disease. United Mine Workers President Sam Church Jr. asserted that 4,000 miners a year die of black lung, and cried: "That translates to eleven people a day who, after agonizing years of gasping and wheezing, finally breathe their last." The Administration says that mining companies should pay for black-lung treatment but has not yet proposed a specific way for them to do it.

*Reaction to President Reagan's proposed budget cuts, submitted to Congress in early March 1981, in "When the Cheering Died," Time, March 23, 1981, p. 9.*

The good news is that a great many upper-income Americans promise to save and invest much of the extra money they will have if taxes fall—just what Reagan wants.

The bad news: A large number of middle and lower-income taxpayers plan to spend the cash on themselves just as soon as they get it. Critics of the Reagan policy warn that if consumers use their tax bonus for a buying spree, inflation could soar even higher.

*Examining the pros and cons of President Reagan's proposed tax cuts in "Save? Spend? What People Would Do with a Tax Cut," U.S. News & World Report, March 23, 1981, p. 22.*

…But what could be more degrading than struggling to move to a nicer home, a better neighborhood, trying to "keep up with the Joneses" who just happen to be setting the pace with your tax money?

And where is the incentive for the Joneses to get off welfare, to "live the good life"? They already live it.

Sure, he's employed. So is she. They are not married, but it seems that one or the other of them qualifies for section 8 housing, medicaid, low-interest farmers' loans, free college tuition—plus expenses—free child care, as well as food stamps.

Another neighbor summed it up for many of us when she said: "Why should my husband and I have to work 70-odd hours a week to earn $30,000 a year, to live equal to, or substandard to, a welfare family? Ridiculous!"

*Kathleen Kroll, a mother and newspaper columnist, complaining about the welfare state, in Kroll, "A Worker: 'I Begrudge Living Less Well than the Poor Do,'" U.S. News & World Report, March 30, 1981, p. 46.*

For the less affluent, confidence in the future is more limited. Waitress Darla Chilcott of Aurora [Colorado], a single parent struggling to make ends meet, says: "I don't look too far in the future because it's too scary. For me, the future is next week."

Criticisms of Reagan's economic-austerity policies permeate the general mood of support for the new President. "Reagan is taking from minorities and the poor," says Carolyn White, a Denver manicurist whose husband works two jobs. "He is a President strictly for the rich. Carter didn't make things better, but he didn't take things away, either."

*A sampling of public opinion about the president and the economy, in "America's Springtime Mood: 'We're Rallying,'" U.S. News & World Report, June 8, 1981, p. 23.*

The heart of Reagan's argument to the NAACP was that Washington was precisely the problem—that blacks ought to break the habit of looking there for help and seek their "economic emancipation" instead in the revitalization of the private sector. "Government is no longer the strong draft horse of minority progress," he said; the Great Society programs of the 1960s were in fact mainly sustaining the bureaucrats who run them, with minimal impact on poverty and none whatever on black unemployment. The time has come now, he said, to move beyond the special relationship of the blacks to the government of the past twenty years and act on John F. Kennedy's formulation that a rising economic tide lifts *all* ships. "The economic package we've put forth will move us toward black economic freedom," he said, "because it's aimed at lifting an entire country and not just parts of it."

*A report examining President Reagan's appearance at the July 1981 convention of the NAACP in Denver, Colorado, where he presented a new outlook for African Americans, in "Reagan and the Blacks," Newsweek, July 13, 1981, p. 20.*

Stockman himself had been a late convert to supply-side theology, and now he was beginning to leave the church. . . .

"The hard part of the supply-side tax cut is dropping the top rate from 70 to 50 percent—the rest of it is a secondary matter," Stockman explained. "The original argument was that the top bracket was too high, and that's having the most devastating effect on the economy. Then, the general argument was that, in order to make this palatable as a political matter, you

had to bring down all the brackets. But, I mean, Kemp–Roth was always a Trojan horse to bring down the top rate."

. . . Yes, Stockman conceded, when one stripped away the new rhetoric emphasizing across-the-board cuts, the supply-side theory was really new clothes for the unpopular doctrine of the old Republican orthodoxy. "It's kind of hard to sell 'trickle down,'" he explained, "so the supply-side formula was the only way to get a tax policy that was really 'trickle down.' Supply-side is 'trickle-down' theory."

*Author-editor William Greider exposing David Stockman's doubts about supply-side economics, surfacing in about September 1981, in Greider, "The Education of David Stockman," Atlantic Monthly, December 1981. Available online. URL: http://www.theatlantic.com/unbound/flashbks/classics/stockman.htm.*

In one year, the Reagan Administration and a compliant Congress have legislated the most significant income redistribution since the 1930s. This time, however, the shift was from the poor and the working class to the rich. The redistribution has been accomplished by transferring resources from the public to the private sector. Thus, Reaganomics does not really mean getting the government off people's backs; it means repealing the hard-won social gains of the past fifty years and using the government to transfer money to large corporations, high-income earners and military contractors.

*Writers Martin Carnoy and Derek Shearer assessing "Reaganomics: The Supply Side of the Street" in Nation, November 7, 1981, quoted in Boyer, Reagan as President (1990), p. 112.*

One thing we are very unhappy about is the increase in unemployment, and we won't relax as long as anybody who wants to work can't get a job. I'm not suggesting everything is rosy, because it isn't. A lot of industries and small businesses are hurting.

But the president's program has only been in effect for 60 days. I believe it will work, and the markets are saying it will work. They weren't saying that 30 days ago.

*Vice President George H. W. Bush, previously a critic of supply-side economics, demonstrating his loyalty to President Reagan, in "White House Leaks: 'We Have Been Undisciplined,'" U.S. News & World Report, December 14, 1981, p. 20.*

You see, the naïve definition of "supply side" economics—the idea that a big tax cut would produce a balanced budget without spending cuts and an economic boon without recession—never was a credible theory. The promise of supply side, properly defined, is that the better way to achieve a healthier economy, with higher incomes for everyone, is by encouraging savings and investment rather than by stimulating consumer purchasing power.

*Martin Feldstein, president of the National Bureau of Economic Research, criticizing supply-side economics, quoted in "Will Reaganomics Work? Five Views," U.S. News & World Report, December 28, 1981, p. 71.*

Deficits aren't the cause of bad economics; deficits are the consequences of bad economics. You never balance the budget when you have slow growth, high unemployment, high inflation, and high interest rates, as we do now.

*Economist Arthur Laffer explaining "What Went Wrong with 'Supply-Side' Economics," U.S. News & World Report, January 18, 1982, p. 36.*

There are no quick fixes. The major deterrent to economic growth is the adverse long-term expectation caused by large budget deficits. It's feared that, sooner or later, the Federal Reserve will turn on the printing press and expand the money supply to pay for the deficit, which would be inflationary. So, the sooner we get the deficits down, the quicker those fears will abate. Then, interest rates will come down and the economy will take off.

*David Stockman defending President Reagan's economic policy, in Stockman, "When Reaganomics Will Start Working," U.S. News & World Report, July 19, 1982, p. 33.*

The 530-page study [by the Urban Institute] concludes that Mr. Reagan is achieving the biggest change in U.S. domestic policies since the New Deal, as he promised voters in 1980 he would.

But the consequences promise to be painful for poorer regions and poorer people, the study suggests. It finds, for example, that Reaganomics "will aggravate the imbalance in regional growths," favoring more prosperous states of the Sun Belt and Pacific and New England regions while slighting the less affluent East South Central region and the "stagnant" Midwest.

Similarly, Reagan-backed tax cuts for middle-income and wealthy individuals, combined with cuts in social programs for the poor, such as food stamps, mean that "even if the administration's policy changes result in a healthy economy by 1984, many low-income households will be worse off than in 1980," the study says.

*From a report on an Urban Institute study examining the effects of supply-side economics, in "Reaganomics Widens Gap between the Rich and Poor, Study Says," Wall Street Journal, September 14, 1982, p. 21.*

## Notable Events

America's joy pealed from church belfries, rippled from flag staffs and wrapped itself in a million miles of yellow ribbon, tied around trees, car antennas and even the 32-story Foshay Tower in Minneapolis. Barbara Deffley, wife of the Methodist minister in Holmer, Ill., rang the church bell 444 times, once for each day of captivity. . . . In Mountain Home, Idaho, some 200 townspeople staged an impromptu parade, driving their cars three abreast, headlights on and horns blaring. Patrolman Joseph McDermott coasted his cruiser to the side of a street in Rochester, N.H., fighting back the tears. Said he: "I am overjoyed. I feel proud again."

*U.S. citizens reacting to the news—announced shortly after President Reagan's inauguration on January 20, 1981—that the American hostages in Iran have finally been released, reported in "An End to the Long Ordeal," Time, February 2, 1981, p. 24.*

And that's the way it is, Friday, March 6th, 1981. I'll be away on assignment and Dan Rather will be sitting here for the next few years. Good night.

*Walter Cronkite's closing words in his final broadcast as anchor of CBS Evening News, March 6, 1981.*

Cronkite's awesome stature as a national icon is bound up with television's pervasiveness, intimacy and power to confer authority. But it also reflects Cronkite himself. The man and the medium are ideally suited to each other—in no small part because of his physical attributes. Even the Soviet weekly Literaturnaya Gazeta, commenting on Cronkite's leave-taking, took note of his "kind, open face." Old hands at CBS refer to his soothing basso profundo as "The Magic." Cronkite's on-air stamina has inspired a more earthy appellation: "Old Iron Pants."

*Saluting TV news icon Walter Cronkite upon his retirement, in "A Man Who Cares,"* Newsweek, *March 9, 1981, p. 57.*

Today, at long last, Canada is acquiring full and complete national sovereignty. The Constitution of Canada has come home. . . .

. . . . .

I know that many Quebecers feel themselves pulled in two directions. . . . But one need look only at the results of the referendum in May, 1980, to realize how strong is the attachment to Canada among the people of Quebec. By definition, the silent majority does not make a lot of noise; it is content to make history.

*Prime Minister Pierre Elliott Trudeau, speaking at the proclamation ceremony for the repatriated Canadian constitution in Ottawa, April 17, 1982. Available online. URL: http://www.canadahistory. com/sections/documents/trudeau_ _patriation_of_constitution.htm.*

Perhaps the most significant step in Canada's history was the decision of the communities to take pride in their several languages and cultures rather than to deplore the differences. Quebec was both the inspiration and the principal agent of the profound transformation that has resulted from that decision. Although we regret the absence of the Premier of Quebec, it is right to associate the people of Quebec with this celebration because, without them, Canada would not be what it is today.

*Queen Elizabeth II, speaking at the proclamation ceremony for the repatriated Canadian constitution in Ottawa, April 17, 1982, quoted in "Leaders' Tolerance Praised by Queen,"* Globe and Mail *(Montreal), April 19, 1981, p. 12.*

## Assassination Averted

Jodie, I would abandon this idea of getting Reagan in a second if I could only win your heart and live out the rest of my life with you, whether it be in total obscurity or whatever. I will admit to you that the reason I'm going ahead with this attempt now is

because I cannot wait any longer to impress you. I've got to do something now to make you understand in no uncertain terms that I am doing all of this for your sake. By sacrificing my freedom and possibly my life I hope to change your mind about me. This letter is being written an hour before I leave for the Hilton Hotel.

Jodie, I'm asking you to please look into your heart and at least give me the chance with this historical deed to gain your respect and love.

I love you forever.

*Would-be presidential assassin John Hinckley's letter to actress Jodie Foster, written on March 30, 1981, just hours before shooting President Reagan. Published in* Newsweek, *April 13, 1981, p. 35.*

I walked around Jim [Brady] on my way to the other side of the car. I had reached the right rear fender when a reporter called out to the president. He did exactly what I had seen him do times beyond counting . . . he smiled and raised his left arm in a friendly wave, at once acknowledging the voice and rejecting the question.

Then I heard the first pop. Later, everyone would say what people often say of gunfire: It sounded like firecrackers going off. I knew differently. I got a quick whiff of sulfur and my reflexes took over. I ducked, the only one who did, and then, as more shots went off, I hit the pavement and stayed there.

*Michael Deaver, President Reagan's assistant chief of staff, describing his view of the attempt on Reagan's life, March 30, 1981, in Deaver,* Behind the Scenes *(1987), pp. 16–17.*

I knew I'd been hurt, but I thought that I'd been hurt by the Secret Service man landing on me in the car, and it was, I must say, it was the most paralyzing pain. I've described it as if someone had hit you with a hammer.

But that sensation, it seemed to me, came after I was in the car, and so I thought that maybe his gun or something, when he had come down on me, had broken a rib.

But when I sat up on the seat and the pain wouldn't go away, and suddenly I found that I was coughing up blood, we both decided that maybe I'd broken a rib and punctured a lung.

So that's when we headed for the hospital, and I walked in and gave them my own diagnosis, and the next thing I knew I was on a cart, and it was then, I

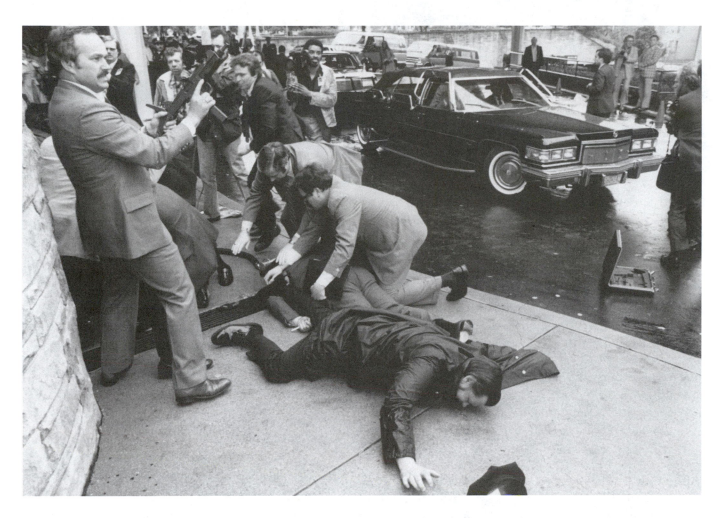

In the chaos following the attempt on President Reagan's life, police officer Thomas Delahanty lies wounded. *(Courtesy Ronald Reagan Library)*

guess, that they found the wound and that I'd—actually been shot.

> *Ronald Reagan, in an interview with the Associated Press and United Press International, describing his thoughts in the moments immediately after he was shot on March 30, 1981, in "Transcript of an Interview With the President on His Wounding and Recovery,"* New York Times, *April 23, 1981, p. B-12.*

The official White House spokesman was being asked who was running the government at a time of national crisis, and he was responding that he did not know. He was being asked if the country was being defended, and he was saying that he did not know. This was no fault of [Larry] Speakes's. . . . He had no current information. "This is very bad," [National Security Advisor Richard] Allen said. "We have to do something."

"We've got to get him off," I said. Allen agreed. It was essential to reassure the country and the world that we had an effective government. I asked Allen to join me, and, together, Allen and I dashed out of the situation room and ran headlong up the narrow stairs. Then we hurried along the jigsaw passageways and into the press room.

> *Alexander Haig, secretary of state, recounting the circumstances that led him to take over a White House press conference following the assassination attempt on March 30, 1981, in Haig,* Caveat *(1984), p. 159.*

White House officials also went to extraordinary lengths today [March 31, 1981] to praise Mr. Haig for acting as the coordination point immediately after yesterday's shooting. They were concerned that at the moment the Reagan Administration should show a united front and that, as one official put it, Mr. Haig be presented to the world as "a vital player" enjoying White House confidence rather than an over-eager Cabinet member sometimes at odds with the White House and Pentagon.

*Reporter Hedrick Smith describing the damage control following Secretary of State Al Haig's "I'm in control" statement, in Smith, "Reagan, Making Good Recovery, Signs a Bill; White House Working, Bush Assures Senate,"* New York Times, *April 1, 1981, p. 1.*

Early Tuesday morning, Reagan asked about the man who had shot him, phrasing the question in his usual casual manner: "Does anybody know what that guy's beef was?" Later in the day, Dr. Ruge told Reagan for the first time that three others had been wounded. Said Reagan: "That means four bullets hit, good Lord." He wondered if the gunman had fired deliberately at the others or whether they had been struck by shots aimed at him. "I didn't want a supporting cast," he said. His eyes filled with tears as he talked about the others. "I guess it goes with the territory," he said sadly.

*President Reagan reacting to bad news the day after the shooting, March 31, 1981, in "Six Shots at a Nation's Heart,"* Time, *April 13, 1981, p. 37.*

Almost always, however, as happened again when the first bulletin about President Reagan was announced, what instinctively emerged was "My God." These were the words—"My God"—that the co-pilot of the Enola Gay entered in his diary when he looked back on the first atomic bomb exploding on Hiroshima.

What the words express, I suppose, is a sense of something happening that is too horrible for a man to grasp. In the case of our increasing commonplace American shootings, this horror transcends the violence committed upon the dead and wounded. It is the destruction of the fragile civility of American society that causes the shudders.

*Columnist Russell Baker reflecting on the effects of violence, in Baker, "Once Again,"* New York Times, *April 1, 1981, p. 31.*

Yet these shootings leave scars, and they ought to. Why *are* all these handguns still around? Why *can't* creatures like Hinckley be reached before they reach others? When the President entered the hospital, he told his friend, Nevada Senator Paul Laxalt: "Don't worry about me. I'll make it." By the weekend the

country was thinking the same thing, with the same uncertain bravery.

*Reporter Roger Rosenblatt assessing the nation's mood in the wake of the attempt on President Reagan's life, in Rosenblatt, "A Sense of Where We Are,"* Time, *April 13, 1981, p. 21.*

What did she feel? Fear? Anger? "There's an unreal kind of feeling . . . It's hard to describe. There's an unrealness to it . . ." Nancy Reagan gropes for words. Something rare for her. Usually she dismisses an unwelcome question politely, as if it were a boring suitor. This time she seems as interested in finding the answer as the reporter is.

"You're frightened, sure," she says finally. "Of course you're frightened, especially because he was having trouble breathing. But it just seemed so unreal. And I guess you . . . must go into a sort of a . . ."

The thought trails off. She sighs. She hugs herself with both arms as if she feels the image before she speaks it. "Then all you're thinking is you've got to hold yourself together and not be a bother to anybody so that they can do whatever has to be done."

*First Lady Nancy Reagan struggling to describe her feelings after learning that her husband was shot, quoted in "An Interview with Nancy Reagan,"* Time, *April 13, 1981, p. 39.*

He seems to be a very disturbed young man. I hope he'll get well too.

*President Reagan commenting on John Hinckley in a postshooting interview, quoted in "Now Comes the Hard Part,"* Time, *May 4, 1981, p. 17.*

## A Year for Strikes

It was almost noon. On any normal home date, the Cubs would have been taking batting practice, and the Bleacher Bums would have been daubing the first handfuls of suntan lotion on their pale Middle West bodies and pouring the first cupful of beer down their parched last-place gullets. But Mark Didtler was the only Bum in the park.

"I can't imagine a summer without baseball," he said. "I go to most of the games here and lot of the games at Comiskey Park, too. It's my way of relaxing between semesters at college. It's one of the last things you could count on. What will people do this summer?"

*A baseball fan bemoaning the players' strike that began June 12, 1981, in Vecsey, "Bleakly Looms the Summer," New York Times, June 13, 1981, p. 17.*

Oh, somewhere in this favored land the sun is shining bright,

The band is playing somewhere, and somewhere hearts are light;

And somewhere men are laughing, and the kids have what they like,

But there is no joy for most of us—when Casey's out on strike.

*The Washington Post editorializing on the baseball strike à la "Casey at the Bat," in "Casey on Strike," Washington Post, June 15, 1981, p. 20.*

O, Sovereign Owners and Princely Players, masters of amortization, tax shelters, bonuses and deferred compensation, go back to work. You have been entrusted with the serious work of play, and your season of responsibility has come. Be at it. There is no general sympathy for either of your sides. Nor will there be.

The people of America care about baseball, not about your squalid little squabbles. Reassume your dignity and remember that you are the temporary custodians of an enduring public trust. . . .

*A. Bartlett Giametti, president of Yale University and a devoted Boston Red Sox fan, issuing an appeal to baseball club owners and striking players, in Giametti, "Men of Baseball, Lend an Ear," New York Times, June 16, 1981, p. 19.*

I jumped up in the middle of my bed and grabbed my wife and hugged her. I told her now I'm going to be making money again so she doesn't have to divorce me. I drove my wife crazy. She wanted to watch the soap operas and I wanted to watch the news. I didn't realize how important the game was to my life. I didn't know what to do with myself. The biggest thing was waiting.

*Yankee outfielder Bobby Brown describing his reaction on learning that the baseball strike had ended, July 31, 1981, quoted in "Players' Happiness Has Limit," New York Times, August 1, 1981, p. 17.*

Whatever the merits of their case—and they appear to be dubious—the air controllers have no right to hold up

the nation. President Reagan's tough threat to fire workers who are not back at work by Wednesday is appropriate. A settlement that rewards them for illegally withholding vital services would be a serious mistake.

*The New York Times supporting President Reagan's position on the striking air-traffic controllers, in its editorial "Holding Up America," New York Times, August 4, 1981, p. 14.*

A Parkersburg, W.Va., man showed the kind of pluck that determined travelers were using to defeat the strike. Domhnail Obroin, a glass-making consultant, got up early and drove to the Parkersburg airport for his scheduled 6:30 flight to New York, from which he intended to catch a plane to Lima, Peru. But no one was at the Parkersburg airport. So Mr. Obroin drove 150 miles to Pittsburgh, where he was booked on a U.S. Air flight to New York.

That flight, too, was canceled, as was a second one on which he got a reservation. Mr. Obroin's next idea was to drive to New York from Pittsburgh, but he finally was able to catch a 1:50 flight on U.S. Air out of Pittsburgh. "When you have commitments to keep," he explained, in Pittsburgh before boarding the New York flight, "you keep them."

*An American traveler coping with the PATCO strike, reported in "Travelers Find Skies Aren't So Friendly As Controllers Strike," Wall Street Journal, August 4, 1981, p. 1.*

At Dallas–Fort Worth Regional Airport, William E. Crosby of American Airlines said that 91 percent of his line's flights operated on time. In Los Angeles, another American Airline executive said that 84 percent of the flights were within five minutes of their scheduled time and that 91 percent were no more than 10 minutes off schedule. A spokesman for the airline said these figures reflected general conditions at those airports.

All the airline officials interviewed said that cancellations had diminished and that their planes were flying with fewer empty seats.

*Reporter Joseph B. Treaster noting some of the good news in the midst of PATCO's ongoing strike, in Treaster, "Airlines Increase Number of Flights; Losses Linked to Strike Are on Rise," New York Times, August 6, 1981, p. D-20.*

The Canadian Air Traffic Controllers announced last night that its members would no longer handle air traffic to and from the United States, except in emergencies. The union said it had acted because of what it regards as unsafe conditions created by the six-day-old strike of the American controllers.

At a meeting in Ottawa, the union announced that beginning at 7 A.M. Today scores of flights to or from the United States "would not be processed."

*Josh Barbanel reporting on the support of Canadian air-traffic controllers for the U.S. strike, in Barbanel, "Air Controllers in Canada Refuse Most U.S. Flights," New York Times, August 7, 1981, p. 1. The Canadian action ended quickly after the U.S. government issued threats that if it continued, American planes would never land in Canada again.*

While forceful, the President was not vindictive. "Dammit," he said privately to his aides, including Chief of Staff James Baker and Counsellor Ed Meese, "the law is the law, and the law says they can't strike. By striking they've quit their jobs." Later, Reagan noted publicly that the air controllers were "fine people," and added: "I do feel badly. I take no joy in this. There is just no other choice."

*President Reagan grappling with his decision to fire striking air-traffic controllers, quoted in "Turbulence in the Tower," Time, August 17, 1981, p. 16.*

Controllers concede that their chief complaint is not money but hours, working conditions and a lack of recognition for the pressure they face. Still, most insist that they love their jobs. "It's a tremendous ego trip when you've done it well," says one Chicago controller. John DeVane of Atlanta agrees and argues that shorter working hours will prolong his career. But striking controllers already are beginning to discover another work-related pressure: their hard-earned skills and experience are not marketable anywhere in the private sector.

*Examining the lot of air-traffic controllers in "What Air Controllers Do," Newsweek, August 17, 1981, p. 23.*

## Gains and Setbacks for Women

Gone from the daily headlines are Betty Friedan, Gloria Steinem, Bella Abzug and other leaders who carried the fight in those years [the 1970s]. Replacing them is a cadre of little-known individuals laboring intensively on specific issues ranging from abortion rights to jobs to Social Security. Foremost in their minds: Preserving the gains of the '70s in the face of the growing "new right."

Meanwhile, a woman whom most observers view as a foe of the movement—Phyllis Schlafly, an outspoken critic of the equal-rights amendment—seems to garner more attention than anyone.

*Describing changes in the women's rights movement, in "As Women's Leaders Remap Their Strategy—," U.S. News & World Report, July 6, 1981, p. 54.*

Now, this is not to say I would appoint a woman merely to do so. That would not be fair to women nor to future generations of all Americans whose lives are so deeply affected by decisions of the Court. Rather, I pledged to appoint a woman who meets the very high standards I demand of all court appointees. I have identified such a person.

*President Ronald Reagan remarking about his campaign promise to appoint a woman to the Supreme Court prior to announcing his nominee, Sandra Day O'Connor, to the press on July 7, 1981. Available online. URL: http://www.reagan.utexas.edu/resource/speeches/ 1981/70781.a.htm.*

Good morning. This is a momentous day in my life and the life of my family and I'm extremely happy and honored to have been nominated by President Reagan for a position on the United States Supreme Court. If I am confirmed in the United States Senate I will do my best to serve the Court and this nation in a manner that will bring credit to the President, to my family and to all the people of this great nation.

*Sandra Day O'Connor introducing herself at a press conference in Phoenix, Arizona, on the day President Reagan announced that he had nominated her to serve on the Supreme Court, July 7, 1981; quoted in "Transcript of Remarks by Reagan and Nominee to High Court," New York Times, July 8, 1981, p. A-12.*

Until last week, Sandra O'Connor was an obscure judge who has served a mere eighteen months on an intermediate appeals court. She has never decided weighty constitutional issues and her *curriculum vitae* does not include a bibliography of scholarly law-review articles. What then are her qualifications for a seat on the U.S. Supreme Court? One of her mentors in Phoenix offers an answer. O'Connor brings two key qualities to the job, says Arizona Gov. Bruce Babbitt: "raw intellectual ability and a great sense of judgment."

*An evaluation of Sandra Day O'Connor, the first woman to be nominated to the U.S. Supreme Court, in "A Keen Mind, Fine Judgment," Newsweek, July 20, 1981, p. 18.*

Begin at the top. Scarcely a hundred years ago the U.S. Supreme Court held that women had no constitutional right to be lawyers, noting in what now seems such quaint language that "the natural and proper timidity and delicacy which belongs to the female sex evidently unfits them for many of the occupations of civil life."

Now Madam Justice Sandra O'Connor sits upon that selfsame court, and if she perchance retains some of that delicacy of the female sex, she certainly has none of the timidity of which her antecedent colleagues spoke.

So it is also in other parts of public and political life. I have no exact statistics but it's been estimated that from 12% to 15% of our elected officials, from local aldermen to state governors to congressmen (pardon me, congresswomen) belong to that no longer gentler sex.

*Columnist Vermont Royster offering some solace and perspective to feminists disappointed by the Equal Rights Amendment's defeat, in Royster, "Thinking Things Over: Weep Not, Dear Ladies," Wall Street Journal, June 23, 1982, p. 26.*

Women are even more tired of the hypocrisy of ERA opponents who fully participate in all the rights our foremothers won for us—voting, owning property, access to higher education and the professions, etc.—yet oppose the ERA. Phyllis Schlafly, the leader of the STOP-ERA movement, is a lawyer, author, congressional candidate and opponent of equal rights for women—contradictions aplenty for a hilarious Lily Tomlin skit. But how can Lily Tomlin be funnier than the real thing?

*Representative Pat Schroeder (D, Colo.) expressing the frustration of feminists at the imminent demise of the Equal Rights Amendment (ERA), in Schroeder, "ERA: The Fight Isn't Over . . .," Washington Post, June 28, 1982, p. A-13.*

There are more women working now than ever before, more women in politics, more teaching, more learning. And yet.

Most of the women hold down-scale jobs and draw salaries smaller than a man's for the same work; many live below the poverty line. The majority of American college students now are women, and yet the faculties instructing them are still mostly male. There are, all together, more women in state legislatures, more in the House and senate than at any time in history. And yet. Neither these increasing numbers of women politicians, nor their male colleagues could manage to get women something that once looked elementary, something that should have been so simple: a constitutional guarantee of equal rights under the law.

*Examining the current status of women in the wake of the Equal Rights Amendment's defeat, in "How Long till Equality?" Time, July 12, 1982, p. 20.*

## A Medical Mystery

Dr. Friedman-Kien said he had tested nine of the victims and found severe defects in their immunological systems. The patients had serious malfunctions of two types of cells called T and B cell lymphocytes, which have important roles in fighting infections and cancer. But Dr. Friedman-Kien emphasized that the researchers did not know whether the immunological defects were the underlying problem or had developed secondarily in the infections or drug use.

*Lawrence K. Altman reporting on the conundrums posed by a number of mysterious deaths among gay men, in Altman, "Rare Cancer Seen in 41 Homosexuals," New York Times, July 3, 1981, p. 20.*

Jim Groundwater wasn't surprised when he learned Ken Horne had died. The autopsy on his battered body that day, however, revealed that Ken had withstood infections far beyond what his doctors had imagined.

The primary cause of death was listed as cryptococcal pneumonia, which was a consequence of his Kaposi's sarcoma and *Pneumocystis carinii* pneumonia. Those, however, were only the obvious diseases. The KS lesions, it turned out, covered not only his skin but also his lungs, bronchi, spleen, bladder, lymph nodes, mouth, and adrenal glands. His eyes were infected not only with cytomegalovirus but also with cryptococcus and the *Pneumocystis* protozoa. It was the first time the pathologist could recall seeing the protozoa infect a person's eye.

*The gruesome death of an early AIDS patient, November 30, 1981, described in Shilts,* And the Band Played On *(1987), p. 100.*

The fact that the disease first surfaced in California and New York and is now being seen in other cities may be an important clue to finding the causes. In her study, Dr. Dritz has established a "whole bunch of connections which we haven't unscrambled yet." For example, she has three sets of roommates on her list in which one of the roommates suffers from either Kaposi's or pneumocystitis. One of these roommates has contacts with other people in the Bay Area who have developed Kaposi's, and one roommate has a gay nephew in New York whose lover died of Kaposi's. "While we can't yet say how, it begins to look like a transmissible agent," says Dritz.

*Reporter Nikki Meredith reporting a study by epidemiologist Selma Dritz, San Francisco Office of Disease Control, on the increasing incidence of Kaposi's Syndrome, in Meredith, "Search for the Cause and Treatment of a Rare Cancer That Has Reached Epidemic Proportions among Homosexuals,"* San Francisco Chronicle, *June 6, 1982, Cal. sec., pp. 13–14.*

Reports of the disease have not abated. About two new cases a day are recorded at the disease control center. Officials there attribute the increase both to improved reporting and to a real rise in cases. The disease has already killed more people than reported cases of toxic shock syndrome and the original outbreak of Legionnaire's disease, and it has engendered as much fear. . . .

The disease has been recorded in 27 states; New York State's 259 cases is the largest concentration.

*Reporter Robin Herman hinting at the rising panic as AIDS proliferates, in Herman, "A Disease's Spread Provokes Anxiety,"* New York Times, *August 8, 1982, p. 31.*

## Science and Technology Make an Impact

The fraternity of personal-computer users grows less exclusive by the day. The number of computers in individual hands has risen above 500,000. At the same time, the far-flung army of electronic enthusiasts is drawing closer together through telephone-connected networks known as computer bulletin boards, electronically tacking up messages and reading them with keyboard terminals.

Some 200 or so home-computer owners around the country have started bulletin boards to store and receive information and messages for thousands of other home-computer owners. The conversation, which appears on users' video screens or is printed out by machine, still reflects the fascination with technology that is characteristic of ham and citizens'-band radio. But old hands in micro-computing detect a serious potential in the now amateurish home networks. Bulletin board technology has business applications, in mail order, for example, and could distribute electronic mail, bypassing central computers as well as the U.S. Postal Service.

*Reporter John Henderson describing trends in PC use and the implications, in Henderson, "Home Users of Computers Form Network,"* Wall Street Journal, *April 1, 1981, p. 31.*

"Yeeeow!" they screamed as the ship left the ground. "All riight!" they yelled as it rose. "Please, God, don't let it fall," some of them prayed out loud.

The power of the ship's rockets made the viewing stands tremble and sent waves of noises rolling across the cape.

When viewers could finally hear themselves speak, the reaction reflected a presumption gained from earlier space flights that today's mission would succeed. There also seemed to be a collective feeling that Americans had again joined in a new space achievement.

"Great, great, absolutely great!" said Mabel Pierce of Melbourne, Fla., who witnessed Alan Shepherd's suborbital flight 20 years ago. "There isn't another country in the world that's going to do this—you've got to say America's first."

*Viewers gathered at Cape Canaveral reacting to the space shuttle* Columbia's *inaugural launch on April 12, 1981, in " 'Yeeeow!' and 'Doggone!' Are Shouted on Beaches as Crowds Watch Liftoff,"* New York Times, *April 13, 1981, p. 13.*

First came the sonic boom announcing that it was near: two loud shocks that reverberated like cannon blasts across the desert floor.

Over the public address system, the voice of Mission Control read out the orbiter's speed and altitude, now rapidly declining: "Columbia, you're right on the money, right on the money."

"Where is it? Where is it?" perhaps 10,000 voices asked at once from the edges of Rogers Dry Lake.

Then, the sharpest eyes on the ground, squinting upwards, saw it: a tiny, moving speck high over the horizon, dropping fast through a dusty, luminescent haze that rose from the surface of the parched dry lake like a cloudy mist. Suddenly, the tension broke.

"There it is!" the first voice said, and then others. . . .

*Reporter Robert Lindsey describing the scene at Andrews Air Force Base as spectators wait for the space shuttle* Columbia *to make its historic landing on April 14, 1981, in Lindsey, "A Speck Pierces the Horizon,"* New York Times, *April 15, 1981, p. 1.*

"Gear down," reported a chase jet, buzzing alongside and counting off the altitude: "50 feet . . . 40 . . . 5—4—3—2—1—Touchdown!" As its rear wheels made contact, the flight director in far-off Houston told his tense crew: "Prepare for exhilaration." Nine seconds later, the nose wheels were down too. *Columbia* settled softly onto the lake bed. [John] Young had floated the shuttle along 3,000 ft. beyond the planned landing spot, able to use its surprising lift to make a notably smooth touchdown. As it rolled to a stop through the shimmering desert air, *The Star-Spangled Banner* rattled forth from hundreds of portable radios tuned to a local station. From Mission Control in Houston's Johnson Space Center came an exuberant "Welcome home, *Columbia*. Beautiful. Beautiful."

*Describing the successful conclusion of the historic first flight of the first space shuttle on April 14, 1981, in "Touchdown,* Columbia*!" Time, April 27, 1981, p. 16.*

I'd been at it for only five hours, but already my side of the dialogue had escalated from "Aw, com'on" through a whiny "That's not fair" to "Dammit, I did exactly what you said." Finally, unable to contain my outrage, I shouted a command that Apple III is anatomically unable to obey and then, remembering that computers have no ears, took to the keyboard. "____ you," I typed furiously, slamming the return button to provoke a reply. What I got is probably what I deserved. "SYNTAX ERROR," replied Apple III, haughtily.

*Reporter Elizabeth Peer describing her experiences as a neophyte PC owner, in Peer, "How to Work the Thing,"* Newsweek, *February 22, 1982, p. 53.*

More so than adults, the young know the computer for what it is. Says a ten-year-old at Manhattan's Bank Street School: "It's dumb. I have to tell it everything." They also know something important is afoot. Says Shawn Whitfield: "When I grow up, it's going to be the Computer Age. It won't affect parents. They're out of the Computer Age. They had their own age."

*Examining the impact of PCs on the young, in "Here Come the Microkids,"* Time, *May 3, 1982, p. 56.*

We are at a turning point in the development of the species. Man is producing technology so complex that human minds cannot imagine all of its possibilities. In order to use it, to move on, man must accept that machines which can be wrong will make judgments about his life and property.

*Lee M. Hecht, chairman and chief executive of Teknowledge, Inc. (Palo Alto, California), commenting on the ramifications of artificial intelligence, quoted in Shaffer, "Judgment Day: The Thinking Computer Arrives,"* Wall Street Journal, *September 3, 1982, p. 14.*

## The American Scene

In the ramshackle housing projects near Atlanta's Memorial Drive, kids whisper his name in fear: "The Man." Going down to the store for a quart of milk, they carry sticks to defend themselves against The Man. When a strange car pulls up at the school-bus stop, they drop their books and run—in case it's The Man. When they awaken in the middle of the night and slink into their parents' bedroom to sleep, it's because they dreamed of The Man. For half of Atlanta—the black half—day and night are in the shadow of a phantom killer who lures children off the street with frightful ease.

*Describing the state of fear caused by a rash of killings of black children in Atlanta, Georgia, in "Terror in Atlanta,"* Newsweek, *March 2, 1981, p. 34.*

The baby boom has come of age. That bumper crop of 64 million infants born between 1946 and 1961 is now 20 to 35 years old—and just as they crowded the maternity wards, the elementary schools, the high schools and the colleges, they are now jostling one another for jobs, housing and the adult Good Life. They are by far the largest generation in American history—nearly one-third of the U.S. population today. By the sheer force of their numbers, they have set the nation's tone at every stage of their lives. . . . Now, with more than 45 million Americans set to turn 30 in the next decade, the country is inevitably concerned with the problems of young adulthood—finding work, settling down, balancing family and career.

*Description of a generation growing up, in "The Baby Boomers Come of Age," Newsweek, March 30, 1981, p. 34.*

I can't say if there is any single innovation taking form right now that will exert as great and direct an impact on our economy as the tractor or the Model T. On the other hand, I can see a host of advances in knowledge that will almost certainly lead to much the same kind of enhancement of our well-being. . . .

The clear implication of these trends is that yet another generation of far more sophisticated devices will soon be touching all of our lives in much deeper ways than anything we have yet experienced.

*John B. Slaughter, director of the National Science Foundation, sharing his thoughts about the future with graduates at the University of Southern California, May 1981, quoted in "College Grads Hear Words of Wisdom," U.S. News & World Report, June 15, 1981, p. 35.*

Wealth is back in style. Poverty is déclassé. . . .

The old less-is-more, down-with-materialism atmosphere that achieved a high-art patina during the Carter years has been brushed aside by the new ruling class. A flaunt-it-if-you-have-it style is rippling in concentric circles across the land.

. . . . .

"We are all living and entertaining more lavishly now," says San Francisco socialite Pat Montandon. "The Reagans are setting a lifestyle so different from the hide-it-under-a-bushel attitude of the Carters. The feeling now is that if you have it, why not enjoy it? There is almost a sense of desperation, that if you don't do it now, you won't have the chance again."

. . . . .

Show-off wealth is not yet accepted everywhere. "It's regarded in some places, like Boston, as vulgar,"

asserts sociologist David Riesman of Harvard. "In many places, culture and breeding still matter, but wealth is waging a very powerful fight to legitimize itself" as the key determinant of social standing.

*Examining changing societal attitudes, in "Flaunting Wealth: It's Back in Style," U.S. News & World Report, September 21, 1981, p. 61.*

People do not take kindly to seeing their children bused halfway across town for no advantage. I hear a lot of people asking why busing for integration is so terrible when children are bused for other reasons. My response is that if a child is bused just because someone else wants that done and the child pays the price and gets no benefit, then any decent, responsible parent is going to be mad as hell. And a lot of people who don't think the thing through are not simply mad at the courts, they become mad at blacks.

*African-American economist and conservative writer Thomas Sowell considering the current state of civil rights, in Sowell, "Culture—Not Discrimination—Decides Who Gets Ahead," U.S. News & World Report, October 12, 1981, p. 75.*

To most devoted vidkids, the play's the thing. "It's a challenge to myself, and when I get a high score, I feel *happy*," exults Chris Edwards, a 10-year old Spectar expert from New York's Bronx, who grew so addicted to his game that he filched quarters from his mother's handbag. Other regulars praise the emotional rescue. "It can take the anger out of you," says Steve Marmel, 15, of Lincolnwood, Ill., who practices his spacecraft every day and is a Midwest video-tournament champ. "Rather than blowing up at my history teacher, I can take it out on Asteroids." Still other players cite the chance for nonathletes to show off—or to assuage loneliness. "This is my world—it stinks, don't it?" says Jacky Hughes, 17, a self-described Times Square drifter who can shine in the Broadway arcades. "When you start to think you're a loser, you come here and get 4,000 at Space Invaders, and you ain't a loser anymore."

*Reporting on the proliferation of video games and how they are taking over young lives, in "Invasion of the Video Creatures," Newsweek, November 16, 1981, pp. 90–91.*

Our household has changed dramatically. At first, meals went uneaten and homework undone as cries of "just let me finish this game" echoed through the house. I finally convinced my husband to stop. But the kids still have trouble wrestling the joystick away once he starts on video football. Now we have developed a "code of the console" to control the technological marvel in our midst. Rule Number One: No Atari before breakfast.

Atari also has become our ultimate parental weapon. Bad behavior is punishable by banishment from the video arena. Good behavior—bedmaking, dishwashing and the like—is rewarded by the purchase of a new cartridge. I know it is reprehensible to buy your kids this way—but it works, oh how it works!

*Leslie Berg Milk, a freelance writer and public-affairs consultant, describing the effects of video games on her family and home life, in Milk, "The Age of Atari: Bleeping into Oblivion,"* Washington Post, *January 28, 1982, p. MD2.*

I didn't realize I was a lesbian until I came to Mills [College]. When I looked back, I was never with a man I really liked. I didn't know what to call the crushes I had on women. I didn't know what a lesbian was until I was with a woman who was one. We were spending a lot of time together, and one night she said to me, "I really like you. May I kiss you?" I knew right then what I wanted, and I came out pretty quickly on campus. I cut my hair in a butch. I told one roommate, and she gave me a hug and told me that her younger sister was gay. My other roommate was not quite so overjoyed. She did not talk to me for three days.

*A lesbian student revealing her coming out, in "Gays and Lesbians on Campus,"* Newsweek, *April 5, 1982, p. 75.*

"TRON," a $20-million cinematic journey through the mind of a computer, frequently looks like the ultimate video game, played by—and with—human beings on a screen 70 feet wide and 30 feet high. The film has over 800 shots in which such actors as Jeff Bridges, David Warner and Cindy Morgan are put into computer-generated environments. Disney is the first to tell a story with the computer-generated imagery that Hollywood is looking at as the herald of a major change in its way of making movies.

*Reporter John Culhane on the effects of computers in moviemaking, in Culhane, "Special Effects Are Revolutionizing Film,"* New York Times, *July 4, 1982, sec. 2, p. 13.*

Even when today's recession finally ends, America's blue-collar workers and the industries they serve will face more and deeper troubles.

From now on, old-line manufacturing industries such as steel, autos, rubber and textiles—once the economy's backbone—will provide a smaller share of the nation's employment. In those and related blue-collar industries, more than 1 million jobs have vanished permanently since 1978.

Instead, employment will grow in the high-technology, service and information sectors as the nation travels further down the road toward what some experts describe as a "postindustrial society."

*Discussing the permanency of some unemployment, in "Jobs: A Million That Will Never Come Back,"* U.S. News & World Report, *September 13, 1982, p. 53.*

# 3

# Highs, Lows, and Frightening Times
## November 1982–
## December 1983

By the midterm elections of November 2, 1982, Ronald Reagan's popularity was approaching the lowest point of his eight-year presidency, primarily because of the economy. Although the recession was starting to lift, public opinion of Reaganomics ranged from deep pessimism to cautious optimism. Polls revealed that many thought the supply-side approach would make their personal financial situations worse rather than better, yet there was also a feeling that it would eventually help the nation as a whole.[1] Despite widespread doubts, many Americans still retained faith in their president.

The doubts, however, were enough to spoil Republican hopes in the November elections. Although they retained their 54-46 majority in the Senate, they lost 26 seats in the House to the Democrats, who now had a 269-166 advantage there. In addition, Democrats won seven governorships, giving them 34 states to the Republicans' 16.

This was a setback for Reagan, but he was nothing if not resilient. Realizing that the budget deficits that he had created would limit social spending, he made repeated calls for a constitutional amendment to balance the budget and therefore limit future excessive expenditure by the liberals. Furthermore, the Democratic electoral gains had mainly been in regions that had yet to experience economic improvement, such as the industrial and agricultural areas of the Midwest. Reagan believed that as inflation rates came down and the economy revived, the entire nation would profit from his supply-side program—and that would reap political benefits for him in 1984.

Therefore, with characteristic self-confidence and optimism, the president focused on the second important element of his agenda: the nation's defense.

## MX MISSILES AND "STAR WARS"

For years, the common basis of U.S. and Soviet defense policy had been that of mutual assured destruction (MAD; also called mutually assured destruction). The theory was that a nuclear strike by one side would result in a nuclear response by the other—and thus catastrophic destruction for both. Each country, therefore, needed sufficient nuclear weapons to assure such retaliation, enough to deter any thought of a hostile preemptive first strike. While this philosophy of mutual deterrence had been successful, it had resulted in an exorbitantly expensive race to produce ever-larger nuclear arsenals.

President Reagan called MAD "the craziest thing I ever heard of. . . . We were a button push away from oblivion."[2] He decided one solution was to strengthen America's conventional forces to convince the Soviets that the United States was not dependent solely on its nuclear capability. He therefore initiated the biggest and costliest peacetime military buildup in U.S. history. Not surprisingly, his actions aroused widespread criticism of Reagan as a trigger-happy cowboy, a view intensified by his championing of the MX missile.

The long-range MX ("missile experimental"), an advanced, land-based intercontinental ballistic missile (ICBM), was originally proposed in the 1960s because of fears that future Soviet missiles would be accurate enough to target and destroy the concrete ("hardened") underground silos in which American ICBMs, such as the Minuteman and Titan II, were based. The MX would be mobile, enabling it to be moved around among "soft" silos, which reduced the likelihood of its destruction by Soviet missiles. But years of debate over the MX's funding and deployment meant that it was not until 1979 that President Carter authorized it and the U.S. Air Force brought out a "horizontal shelter" plan whereby 200 MX missiles would be moved around among 4,600 soft shelters using a specially designed railway system.

On October 2, 1981, President Reagan had announced the United States Strategic Weapons Initiative, which included development of the Trident submarine, B1 bomber plane, and MX missile. However, he had scrapped the proposed horizontal-shelter plan in favor of deploying 100 MX missiles in hard shelters. As critics pointed out, deploying the MX in hardened sites completely negated the missile's initial purpose, but Secretary of Defense Caspar Weinberger responded that the planned silos would be more blast resistant, forcing the Soviets to develop even more accurate missiles.

Secretary of Defense Caspar Weinberger, seen with President Reagan in a 1983 photo, was a vigorous proponent of the U.S. military buildup. *(Courtesy Ronald Reagan Library)*

Weinberger and Reagan pursued the MX plan vigorously, and in a televised address on November 22, the president presented his plan to construct 100 multiple-warhead MX missiles (now dubbed *Peacekeepers*) to be based in a cluster of "superhard" silos near Cheyenne, Wyoming. According to Reagan, this would require "fewer silos, much less land, and in fact fewer missiles. . . . Closely Spaced Basing is a reasonable way to deter attack—which is our objective."[3]

Objections to the plan were vociferous. Two weeks after Reagan's address, the House of Representatives rejected, 245-176, his request for $988 million to build and deploy the first five Peacekeeper missiles. The president then appointed Brent Scowcroft—once head of the National Security Council—to lead the bipartisan Commission on Strategic Forces to evaluate the MX missile system. The Scowcroft Commission recommended both the development of single-warhead

ICBMs (dubbed *Midgetmen*) and the immediate deployment of 100 Peacekeepers in existing Minuteman silos in Wyoming and Nebraska. These would replace aging Titan II ICBMs and slow down the trend toward multiple-warhead weaponry.

The commission report won more congressional backing for the Peacekeeper, and after Reagan pledged more flexibility in arms-control negotiations, Congress authorized an initial $625 million for MX missile development on May 24. A further $2.6 billion for missile production was approved in July, and funds for the first 21 Peacekeepers were approved in September.

The MX missile battle was won—for the time being.[4] But another battle had begun for a program even more controversial than the Peacekeepers—and dearer to President Reagan's heart.

Reagan wanted to ensure that the United States would never suffer the devastation of a nuclear attack and believed that the key lay in its defensive, not offensive, capability. In February 1983, after a two-year study, the Joint Chiefs of Staff recommended that the United States construct a defense system that would destroy incoming missiles before they reached their targets—exactly what Reagan already wanted to do. On March 23, he addressed the nation on national security and defense, and, after noting the differences between the U.S. and Soviet military capabilities and stressing the need to build up American strength, he said:

> Let me share with you a vision of the future which offers hope. It is that we embark on a program to counter the awesome Soviet missile threat with measures that are defensive. Let us turn to the very strengths in technology that spawned our great industrial base and that have given us the quality of life we enjoy today.
>
> What if free people could live secure in the knowledge that their security did not rest upon the threat of instant U.S. retaliation to deter a Soviet attack, that we could intercept and destroy strategic ballistic missiles before they reached our own soil or that of our allies?[5]

The president went on to state his purpose of making nuclear weapons "impotent and obsolete," to which end he was "directing a comprehensive and intensive effort to define a long-term research and development program to begin to achieve our ultimate goal of eliminating the threat posed by strategic nuclear missiles. This could pave the way for arms control measures to eliminate the weapons themselves."[6]

This address became known as Reagan's "Star Wars" speech as details of the Strategic Defense Initiative (SDI)—as it was later called officially—became available. In essence, the idea was to construct a space-based shield that used satellites to intercept and destroy Soviet missiles. It was not yet known how this would work nor how long it would take to develop the technology; even Reagan admitted that it "may not be accomplished before the end of this century."

Some critics saw SDI as further evidence that Reagan was leading the country into a nuclear holocaust. Others maintained that the program was a bargaining chip in negotiations with the Soviet Union. Less than a week later, on March 29, the president announced that he would willingly share the program's technology with the USSR since it would benefit both countries, an offer he would reiterate later. Nevertheless, the SDI aroused heated criticism: It was technologically impossible; it would destabilize the current balance of nuclear power; its costs would be astronomically high; it could never provide complete protection; it violated the terms of the 1972 Anti–Ballistic Missile (ABM) treaty.

Yet Reagan eventually got his way as Congress approved a five-year, $26 billion funding package, and the Strategic Defense Initiative Organization was established in April 1984. Over subsequent years the program would undergo several changes in name and scope, with almost $17 billion spent on research and experiments by 1989, but it never came to full fruition as Reagan envisioned it. All the same, his determination on SDI played a significant role in arms-reduction talks with the Soviet Union later in the decade. Good or bad, "Star Wars" would have an impact, just as Reagan hoped.

## HEALING AN OLD WOUND

As President Reagan prepared to do battle over the MX missile, the nation was struggling to come to terms with a previous, more painful conflict. Nearly a decade had passed since the United States had withdrawn its troops from Vietnam, but the wounds left by that war were still very deep for many Americans. Most affected were the veterans who felt they had not received recognition or appreciation for what they had gone through. Unlike those who had fought in other wars, for the Vietnam vets there had been no parades, no welcome-home ceremonies. If anything, they were almost pariahs—reminders of a traumatic experience that most wanted to forget.

But the veterans themselves and the families and friends of the nearly 58,000 men and women who had perished in the conflict could not forget what they had sacrificed to fight for their country. In April 1979 Jan Scruggs, who had served as a corporal with the 199th Light Infantry Brigade (1969–70), founded the Vietnam Veterans Memorial Fund (VVMF) with a number of other veterans. Their purpose was to "begin a healing process, a reconciliation of the grievous divisions wrought by the war."[7] Conflicting emotions about Vietnam meant initial support for the VVMF was minimal at best. Then the veterans gained two important patrons: Senator John W. Warner (R, Va.), who helped launch a national fund-raising campaign, and Senator Charles M. Mathias, Jr. (R, Md.), who in November 1979 introduced legislation authorizing the federal donation of a site for a Vietnam War memorial. For the VVMF, this had to be in Washington, D.C., to ensure it had appropriate national prominence. Further, the group refused to accept federal funds for the project. With $12 million recently cut from the Veterans Administration budget, Scruggs and his colleagues distrusted the government and preferred to build their memorial with private contributions; they ultimately raised nearly $9 million.

On July 1, 1980, Congress approved a site in the Constitution Gardens near the Lincoln Memorial. In October of that year, the VVMF launched a national competition inviting designs for the new memorial, to be judged by an independent panel that consisted largely of architects and sculptors. Instructions to the entrants were simple but bold: The memorial had to invite reflection and contemplation, be in harmony with its surroundings, list the names of those who had died in the war or were still missing, and make no political statement about the war.

The jury received 1,421 entries, and on May 1, 1981, they unanimously selected the proposal submitted by 21-year-old Maya Ying Lin, a student at Yale University School of Architecture. Lin's design comprised two long black slabs of stone, meeting at a 125-degree angle, on which would be inscribed the names of those who had died or were missing in the Vietnam War. Its stark simplicity met the VVMF's original vision admirably, and around the country, the majority of veterans cautiously approved. Thousands, however, were outraged by the design, especially as it failed to include the statues that Americans had come to expect in war monuments. Conservatives led the charge that it was too intellectual and not heroic enough; even its V shape came under attack for evoking the antiwar peace symbol of the 1960s and 1970s. That the designer was a young, female Chinese American with no connection to the war also gave offense to some.

During the following months, Lin made minor changes in her original proposal to satisfy her critics, but the furor did not die down until it was agreed that a U.S. flag and a statue depicting Vietnam War service members would also be installed at the site. Even then there were calls to scrap Lin's design, a "black gash of shame" that was widely seen as an insult to the memory of all vets, living and dead. Such accusations threatened to make the memorial a divisive issue.

On March 26, 1982, the ground was formally broken for the memorial, which was already being called "the Wall." Construction was swift, and in late October work was completed on the two 247-foot stone walls set into a small hill, meeting at a six-foot high point in the center and tapering away on either side; one end pointed toward the Lincoln Memorial, the other toward the Washington Monument. It suggested an open book, an image enhanced by 70 panels of names—listed in order of date lost—on black granite so highly polished that visitors could see themselves and their surroundings in it.

Overnight, criticism turned to approval as veterans descended on Washington for a week of reunions, symposia, and parades prior to the memorial's dedication on November 13. As visitors poured into the Constitution Gardens, it immediately became apparent that Lin had successfully created a restful place for personal contemplation and reflection. Her design invited people to touch the names and make rubbings to take away with them. For veterans, for families and friends of the war dead and missing, and even for those who had no direct connection to the war, the long, tapering slabs of granite with their seemingly endless rows of names induced a sense of reconciliation with the loss and grief the Vietnam War had created.

Prior to the dedication, the 57,939 names on the memorial were read out in the National Cathedral during an extended service that included a visit from President Reagan, who gave speech. The reading of the names took 58 hours and was as emotional as the dedication itself, which was attended by more than 15,000 veterans. Maya Lin—who received only a B for the project in her funerary architecture course—did not attend, and her name was not mentioned. Nevertheless, she had achieved what both she and the VVMF had wanted, and the memorial itself became (and remains) one of the most visited sites in Washington. In 1984—the same year it became a national monument and the National Park Service (NPS) took it over—the obligatory U.S. flag and a statue of three service members, sculpted by Frederick Hart, were installed at the site. The Vietnam Women's Memorial, the first national memorial to women veterans, was erected and dedicated in 1993. But for most visitors, it is Lin's granite Wall that has provided solace and healing, so much so that in 1996 a half-scale replica of the memorial began to travel throughout the country, along with a museum and an information center. (Names continue to be added to the Wall, and by the end of 2004, the total had risen to 58,245, of which 1,200 are considered missing.)

The Vietnam Veterans Memorial had one other moving outcome. Even before it was dedicated, visitors began to leave objects by the Wall. From letters, poems, photographs, and books to rings, military medals, teddy bears, and even human remains, these offerings constitute intensely individual memorials. So diverse and personal are they that in 1984 the Vietnam Veterans Memorial Collection was created to store and catalog the objects with the aim of establishing a national museum. Since then, all items have been collected on a weekly basis by NPS volunteers, carefully labeled, and stored at a warehouse in Maryland. In October 1992 the first exhibition of representative articles was opened at the Smithsonian's National Museum of American History. By 1993 the warehoused collection had grown to 250,000 objects; today about 50,000 form the core of the NPS museum. Offerings continue to be left on a daily basis, emphasizing the changed emotions toward a war of which the country was once ashamed but has now come to accept.

*Since November 1982, "the Wall" in Washington, D.C., has been a poignant and dramatic reminder of the men and women who died in the Vietnam War. (National Park Service)*

## A MEDICAL BREAKTHROUGH

By the early 1980s major technological advances in science and medicine were giving new hope to millions. One such advance was in the treatment of heart disease. Transplantation, first performed in 1967, had become the only option for those with an inoperable condition, but many died while waiting for a donor heart to become available. The solution was an artificial heart to keep the patient alive until a real heart could be transplanted—serving a similar function to that of the kidney dialysis machine. There were even hopes that an artificial heart could be implanted permanently.

Attempts to create an artificial heart began in 1957, and in 1969 Denton Cooley at the Texas Heart Institute kept a patient alive for more than 36 hours on a device made of Dacron and plastic. By 1982 Dr. Robert Jarvik had developed a plastic-and-aluminum heart composed of two polyurethane pumps (ventricles) with air chambers and six titanium valves. Slightly larger than its human counterpart but weighing the same, the Jarvik-7 functioned like a natural heart as the ventricles pushed blood from the inlet valve to the outlet valve. Modified versions had already been implanted in calves and sheep; now Jarvik needed a human volunteer.

Dr. Barney Clark was a 61-year-old retired dentist from Seattle whose heart had become irreparably damaged by a viral infection. Too old for a normal transplant, he was facing certain death when his cardiologist introduced him to Jarvik and Dr. William DeVries, chief thoracic surgeon at the University of Utah Medical Center, who discussed the possibilities of an artificial-heart implant with him. In his case, due to his age and condition, the implant would have to be permanent. Although Clark knew the Jarvik-7 might allow him only a short remission and that he could die on the operating table, he decided it was worth the chance, both for himself and for medical research.

Clark was admitted to the medical center in Utah on December 2, 1982—coincidentally the 15th anniversary of the world's first live human heart transplant. Although his operation was scheduled for the next day, his heart began to fail, and he was rushed into surgery at 10:30 P.M. That night. Seven and a half hours later, he was in the intensive care unit with the Jarvik-7 pumping in his chest. Complications returned him to the operating table several times during the following weeks. Nevertheless, he made progress, and on January 11, 1983, it was announced that he might soon be able to leave the hospital. This prediction proved to be overly optimistic: Not until February 14 was he moved out of intensive care and into a private room.

The story hit the headlines with detailed reports of the operation and pictures of the still-ailing Clark. On March 2, along with Dr. DeVries, he gave his first public interview, in which he said that whatever happened, his role as a guinea pig had been worth all he had experienced. Yet he was essentially a prisoner, immobilized because of the massive, 375-pound compressor needed to power his heart and the tubes and hoses involved. He also suffered infections and blood clots, resulting in a number of strokes as well as pneumonia and vomiting.

Clark finally died on March 23, 1983, 112 days after the implant. The cause of death was given as circulatory collapse, shock, and multiorgan collapse; everything had failed, except for the artificial heart.

Clark's courage paved the way for others as the Food and Drug Administration (FDA) approved another six Jarvik-7 transplants. The longest to survive was William J. Schroeder, who received his implant on November 25, 1984, and died 620 days later. As it became increasingly clear that the human body could not accommodate an artificial heart on a permanent basis, the FDA ruled that one should be used only as a temporary measure until a natural heart could be transplanted. The first such operation occurred in August 1985, when a Jarvik-7 was implanted in a patient who was kept alive for a week before receiving a live donor heart. By the late 1980s more than 70 Jarvik-7 hearts had been successfully implanted in patients at 16 medical centers around the nation—all as a means of support prior to live-tissue transplantation.

There was much controversy over the artificial heart, centering around its effectiveness; the bulky, cumbersome equipment involved; and its exorbitant costs, money that many felt should be applied toward treatment of patients with a better chance of survival. Despite the Jarvik-7's success as a bridge to transplantation, other ways of combating heart disease still needed to be found.[8]

## EPIDEMIC OF FEAR

While national attention focused on Barney Clark and his artificial heart, there were ominous portents from another quarter. Throughout 1982, the number of cases of AIDS (acquired immune deficiency syndrome) had been rising steadily, but any sense of panic was confined to the gay community, which had been hit hardest by the disease. In the third quarter of 1982, only 15 AIDS stories appeared in the nation's leading newspapers and newsmagazines.[9] The number jumped to 30 in December, following two reports from the Centers for Disease Control (CDC) in Atlanta. On December 9, the CDC announced that a child diagnosed with AIDS had received a blood transfusion from an adult victim, and on December 17, its *Morbidity and Mortality Weekly Report* detailed several instances of "Unexplained Immunodeficiency and Opportunistic Infections in Infants—New York, New Jersey, California"; the babies had all been born to IV (intravenous) drug users. This dramatic development—children afflicted with the "gay disease"—resulted in wide media coverage, yet even then most reporters took a cautiously relaxed view owing to the presumed selectivity of the disease.

On January 4, 1983, the CDC held a national conference to discuss AIDS infections through blood transfusions and the institution of blood-screening measures. No decisions were reached due to continued ignorance of the syndrome's cause, even though it was now known that the disease could be transmitted between heterosexual men and women. Yet despite CDC efforts to warn of the growing epidemic, it was still several months before the full significance of their reports penetrated the national consciousness—and panic finally set in. Soon the airwaves and print media were flooded with AIDS "epidemic of fear" stories, and as gruesome details about the disease's deadliness emerged, anxieties about the means and risks of infection spread across the country.

On May 24 the Department of Health and Human Services announced that AIDS had become the federal government's top medical priority. Given the syndrome's virulence in breaking down the body's immune system, most doctors believed their work would not be easy and finding a treatment could take years. Nonetheless, there was a glimmer of hope. Just a few days earlier, on May 20, the Pasteur Institute in Paris announced that one of their scientists, Luc Montagnier, had isolated a virus believed to be related to AIDS. This was significant: If the virus could be identified, work could begin on establishing how it worked and therefore on finding a cure—if there was one.

The general public, though, knew nothing of the science and only saw that the number of cases was growing rapidly—as was the panic, fueled by fear and ignorance. The appearance of the disease in children led many to believe it could be transmitted by everyday casual contact, a belief that only worsened the stigma for AIDS victims. Increasingly, to have the syndrome was to become a pariah. AIDS patients were fired from jobs, evicted from apartments, and shunned by friends and even by family. Homosexuals especially were vilified by bigots who believed God was punishing them for their sinful behavior.

The lack of any palliative treatment, much less a cure, meant a diagnosis of AIDS had come to be considered a death sentence, not just in the United States but around the world. Two World Health Organization meetings in October and November 1983 confirmed the presence of AIDS in the United States, Canada, Haiti, Zaire, seven Latin American countries, and 15 European countries, as well as possible cases in Australia and Japan. By the end of the year the number of U.S. AIDS cases had risen to 3,064; of these, 1,292 had died.[10]

The epidemic had finally arrived, but for many the fear was almost as bad as the disease itself.

## ECONOMIC RECOVERY, SOCIAL SECURITY REFORM

As 1983 began, so did the economic recovery that President Reagan had predicted: Interest rates were declining, trading was booming on Wall Street, and there was an increase in the money supply. In early February the unemployment rate finally started to drop, to 10.4 percent from a high of 10.8 percent in the previous three months. On February 9 Reagan reported some positive figures: At the end of 1982, the inflation rate was 3.9 percent, a dramatic improvement on the double-digit numbers of the previous two years; in the last quarter of 1982, there had been a significant rise in production, increasing wages and employment; and the index of leading economic indicators had risen 6.2 percent.

This good news was not entirely attributable to Reaganomics. The president had benefited from the collapse of the high oil prices set by OPEC during the Carter administration, which had caused inflation to soar and President Carter's approval rating to plummet. Equally advantageous had been the Federal Reserve's high interest rates of 1981 and 1982, which had worsened unemployment and contributed to the recession but had also checked inflation—just as Chairman Paul Volcker had planned. Consequently, in June 1983 an approving Reagan reappointed Volcker to a second term.

With federal deregulation and tax cuts, clever entrepreneurs were able to exploit high-technology developments and the rise in consumer confidence. The after-effects of the recession would still doom some 31,000 businesses to failure in 1983, but many more would thrive in the new economic climate, and production grew dramatically during the year. Yet while economic growth created hundreds of thousands of new jobs, it also resulted in the loss of others as technological advances mechanized many semiskilled or unskilled occupations. Even as the national unemployment rate dropped—by November it would reach a two-year low of 8.4 percent—it stayed high in certain fields: 14.2 percent for the construction trades, for example, and 15.4 percent for machine operators, assemblers, and inspectors. Furthermore, many states remained depressed, leading Congress to pass a $9.6 billion bill in March to underwrite unemployment benefits and provide jobs for 400,000 people.

The president's approval rating rose steadily with the nation's economic rebound. On May 13 the Federal Reserve Board announced that industrial production had increased by 2.1 percent in April, the largest one-month gain in more than seven years. As the gross national product (GNP) increased—in the second quarter of 1983 alone it grew an impressive 9.7 percent—Wall Street responded by setting new trading records.

The bad news, of course, was the federal debt: For the 1983 fiscal year ending on September 30, the government reported a deficit of $195.4 billion. Reagan blithely ignored it, confident the supply-side approach was setting the economy aright. Ironically, the deficit actually helped wealthier Americans who were able to purchase Treasury notes that guaranteed a high rate of return. It was clear to many that Reaganomics was—as its critics had always contended—going to make the rich even richer.

Meanwhile, the president and Congress turned their attention to the most revered program of the New Deal. Reagan had long criticized Social Security for a major drawback: As workers lived longer, they took more out of the system than they put into it. Reagan's objections were basic: Rather than Social Security being an insurance fund for citizens' retirement years, he said, "it had become a compulsory tax producing revenues Congress could—and did—use for any purpose it wanted, while letting the reserves needed for future benefits fall . . . in the hole."[11] This, of course, endangered the program's future solvency. In his original budget proposal in 1981, David Stockman, director of the Office of Management and Budget, had slashed Social Security benefits, but Congress firmly rejected this politically dangerous move. Reagan therefore appointed a bipartisan commission to make recommendations for reforming Social Security, a compromise solution that dismayed Stockman.

In January 1983 the National Commission on Social Security Reform issued its recommendations, which included increases in payroll tax deductions, a reduction in the growth rate of benefits, and raising the retirement age over a period of time. These proposals were well received, and on March 25 Congress passed the Social Security Reform Act, implementing the majority of the commission's recommendations. Signed into law on April 20, the act increased the retirement age from 65 to 66 by the year 2009 and to 67 by the year 2027. In addition, a cost-of-living increase scheduled to take effect on July 1, 1983, was delayed for a half year. As of January 1, 1984, all previously exempted employees of government and nonprofit organizations were required to enroll in the Social Security program, and some benefits became taxable, while other reforms impacted the benefits of early retirees, divorcees, and widowed people. To help maintain solvency, Congress added a "stabilizer" provision that would ensure the program's reserves never fell below 20 percent.

Despite these measures, the public still lacked confidence in Social Security's stability. The memory of President Reagan's early determination to make major cuts in the program lingered, and though he later pledged he would never reduce benefits, this did not help him politically. The problems of Social Security that he had cited all along—more monies going out than coming in—still existed despite the 1983 act, and younger voters saw their benefits threatened as they continued paying into a program that could yet become insolvent. Clearly more extensive reform was needed —but it would not come during the Reagan administration.

## VARYING TEMPERATURES IN THE COLD WAR

In December 1982 in Manchester, Maine, a 10-year-old schoolgirl named Samantha Smith wrote a letter to Yuri Andropov, leader of the Soviet Union, expressing her worries about nuclear war and Soviet intentions "to conquer the world or at least our country." To her astonishment, she received a reply from Andropov the following April, assuring her that the Soviet Union wanted "very much to live in peace" and that his country had "solemnly declared throughout the entire world that never—never—will it use nuclear weapons first against any country." Andropov concluded his letter by inviting Samantha to visit the Soviet Union in the coming summer.[12]

Samantha immediately became the focus of media attention around the world, and she willingly took on her role of goodwill ambassador. In July 1983 she and her parents were flown to the USSR at Soviet expense for a two-week visit that was followed closely by the press of both countries. After her return she became a celebrated peace activist who continued to speak out against nuclear war.

The Reagan administration ignored the publicity surrounding Samantha, taking the view that she was merely a pawn in a Soviet propaganda war. But many lauded the girl for one simple reason: They shared her fears. Reagan's military buildup had conjured up visions of a nuclear holocaust in the public mind, and current relations with the Soviet Union did little to reassure them. The president eschewed the policy of détente practiced by his predecessors, making his views clear in a March 8, 1983, speech in which he referred to the USSR as an "evil empire." The phrase resounded around the world, and Reagan was criticized for what was seen as a deliberate attempt to provoke the Soviets. Yet such statements were commonplace for him. Almost a year earlier, in a speech to the British House of Commons, he had asked, "Must freedom wither in a quiet, deadening accommodation with totalitarian evil?" and described his intention to "leave Marxism–Leninism on the ash-heap of history as it has left other tyrannies which stifle the freedom and muzzle the self-expression of the people."[13]

Several members of Reagan's administration took an even stronger view. The day after the president took office in 1981, Secretary of State Al Haig had accused the Soviet Union of being linked to terrorism throughout the world, a charge supported by William Casey, director of the Central Intelligence Agency (CIA). Two months later, Haig had accused the Soviets of interfering in Central American politics. Reagan's foreign policy regarding Central America and developing countries was based on his belief that the Soviets were infiltrating and pressuring smaller countries. He condemned the presence of Soviet troops in Afghanistan, and when in December 1981 the USSR declared martial law in Poland to clamp down on the Solidarity labor movement, he had further cause to accuse the communist regime of tyranny.

The recent accession of Andropov to the Soviet leadership did little to change Reagan's mind. Although Andropov was reportedly willing to institute reforms in his country, the Soviet Union, in Reagan's view, was still governed by a tough (if aging) hard-line oligarchy who had expanded its nuclear arsenal and deployed missiles in locations that threatened Western democracies, hence his commitment to an unprecedented peacetime U.S. military and arms buildup and his belief that eliminating all atomic weapons was unrealistic. As he put it, "If you were going to approach the Russians with a dove of peace in one hand, you had to have a sword in the other."[14]

This was the situation as the United States and the Soviet Union prepared to resume the Strategic Arms Reduction Talks (START), which had begun in Geneva in June 1982. Reagan, in cooperation with NATO allies, was pursuing Jimmy Carter's plan to deploy medium-range Pershing II and cruise missiles in Western Europe as a counter to Soviet missiles already deployed there. On December 21, 1982, Andropov proposed that both sides reduce the number of medium-range missiles in Europe, but France, the United Kingdom, and the United States rejected this as insufficient. On January 5, 1983, another Soviet proposal suggested a nonaggression pact with NATO members that included a commitment not to carry out a first-strike attack with either nuclear or conventional weapons. In response, the United States offered to cancel the deployment of its missiles in Europe if the Soviet Union would dismantle all of its missiles that were currently deployed there—a plan that Reagan called the "zero option." But by early June no progress had been made, and NATO defense ministers confirmed their support of U.S. missile deployment unless an agreement with the Soviet Union was reached by December.

Despite President Reagan's hard line on arms controls, he was willing to reach accommodation with communist countries in nonmilitary matters. Relations with China had improved as Secretary of State George Shultz worked on expanding U.S. Trade and cultural exchanges with that country. But on April 4 the American government's grant of asylum to Hu Na, China's top female tennis player, led the Chinese to cancel sports and cultural exchanges with the United States in 1983. Nevertheless, by late May the United States was preparing to sell high-technology equipment to China, and in late September Defense Secretary Caspar Weinberger went to Beijing to discuss military cooperation between the two countries.

Commercial agreements were also being made with the USSR. President Reagan had already lifted the grain embargo that President Carter had imposed following the Soviet invasion of Afghanistan in 1979, and by August 1983 a new five-year pact on the Soviet purchase of U.S. grain had been signed. In addition, Reagan suspended controls on the export of certain pipe-laying equipment to the Soviet Union.

These positive developments, though, were hampered by a tragic incident on September 1. When Korean Airlines (KAL) flight 007 strayed into Soviet space near Sakhalin Island in the North Pacific, a Soviet fighter jet shot it down, killing all 269 onboard (including Georgia congressman Larry McDonald). The Soviets initially denied the incident, but the release of radio tapes led them to claim instead that KAL 007 was an American spy plane that had refused to obey the Soviet pilot's instructions to alter its flight route. An outraged President Reagan responded on September 5 by announcing sanctions against the Soviet Union, and both the House of Representatives and the Senate passed resolutions condemning the shooting. Reagan's sanctions, however—closing Aeroflot offices in the United States and suspending negotiations on cultural and scientific exchanges—were largely token measures that did little to hurt the Soviets and angered old supporters from the New Right who believed that Reagan was becoming soft.

The following month the Reagan administration protested the transfer of MiG-23 aircraft to Cuba, in apparent violation of the 1962 agreement reached by President Kennedy and Soviet premier Khruschev following the Cuban missile crisis. This and other events resulted in the START negotiations stalling. Consequently, on November 14 the first U.S. cruise missiles for deployment in Europe arrived in the United Kingdom, and on November 22 the West German parliament approved the installation of U.S. missiles in that country. The following day, in protest, the Soviet Union pulled out of the START talks in Geneva. With no date set to resume discussions, the two major world powers had reached an impasse.

## TERROR IN THE MIDDLE EAST

Although the United States and its allies believed democratic government was the ideal, many cultures did not welcome Western values in their countries. In the Middle East and Eastern Europe especially, Islamic militants resented U.S. support for Israel and attempts to apply American solutions to their problems. Terrorist attacks against U.S. citizens and property increased throughout the 1970s, culminating in the November 1979 seizure of American hostages in Tehran, Iran.

Ronald Reagan had criticized President Carter's handling of the hostage crisis and other Middle East disputes, but he was to experience far more troublesome problems himself almost from the start of his administration. In May 1981 he had expelled Libyan diplomats from the United States after receiving intelligence reports that Muammar al-Gadhafi, Libya's dictator and a known supporter of terrorists, was planning to assassinate American diplomats in Rome and Paris; there were also rumors of Libyan hit squads in the United States. Three months later Reagan had ordered U.S. Navy fighter planes to shoot down any Libyan jets flying outside the internationally agreed 12-mile limit that constituted Libya's territorial waters in the Gulf of Sidra. (Gadhafi had claimed a 100-mile demarcation right across the gulf, which he called the "line of death.") On August 19, 1981, after Libya attacked an American aircraft carrier, U.S. fighters shot down the two warplanes approximately 60 miles off the Libyan coast. Critics claimed this was excessive as Reagan's order had provoked the attack from Libya. Administration officials defended the shooting, however, and insisted that Libya's links to terrorism made it a real threat to U.S. security.

Terrorism was not confined to the Middle East, but increasingly that volatile region became the center of attacks against the United States. Much of this stemmed from U.S. support for Israel and the Reagan administration's actions in the area, which included attempts to forge an alliance against the Soviet Union involving Israel and such Arab states as Saudi Arabia, Jordan, and Egypt.[15] In June 1982 the United States was unable to prevent Israel from invading Lebanon to eradicate forces of the Palestine Liberation Organization (PLO) based there, although Reagan was later able to stop Israel's intensive bombing of Beirut, which had aroused international protest. Subsequently, U.S. Marines were sent to oversee the withdrawal of PLO forces from Lebanon. After they had left, Lebanon requested additional assistance for UN multinational peacekeeping forces; the marines therefore returned in late September 1982.

By then a new wave of terrorism had begun. In July 1982 members of Hezbollah—a fundamentalist Shiite group with ties to Iran—had kidnapped David Dodge, acting president of the American University in Beirut, Lebanon. He was released a year later, and two U.S. Marines, kidnapped in September 1983, were freed soon afterward. But later kidnapping victims would endure years of captivity, forcing Reagan officials to take desperate—and controversial—measures to free them (resulting in the Iran-contra scandal of 1986–87).

In addition to the kidnappings, there was an increase in bombings, especially by Syrian factions who objected to U.S. Troops in Lebanon. On April 18, 1983, a van loaded with explosives killed 63 staff at the U.S. embassy in Beirut. Seventeen Americans died, including Robert C. Ames, U.S. chief CIA analyst of Middle East affairs, and seven other CIA personnel—a serious blow that destroyed key U.S. intelligence resources in the area. The Hezbollah operatives blamed for the attack had reportedly received funding from Syria and Iran.

Worse was to come. Following the embassy bombing, the USS *New Jersey* retaliated by shelling Shiite and Druze positions, arousing much local antagonism. On August 29, 1983, two U.S. Marines were killed in a skirmish, and three days later President Reagan ordered 2,000 marines into position off the Lebanese coast to reinforce the 1,370 then stationed there. Following further attacks on the peacekeeping troops, on September 8 U.S. warships offshore fired on sites near Beirut and on September 17 began to bombard positions inside Syrian-controlled territory. Three days later, Congress passed a resolution to keep the marines in Lebanon for another 18 months. What was not then known was that top military officials had been urging the White House to withdraw U.S. Troops who, they felt, had become far too vulnerable.

These fears proved correct. On October 23, 1983, a suicide bomber drove a truck full of explosives into a U.S. Marines barracks at Beirut International Airport. The blast destroyed the building, killing 241 marine and navy service members and wounding more than 100 others. Two miles away, a similar blast ripped into a French paratroop barracks, killing dozens of soldiers. Though Hezbollah denied any involvement in the attacks, they were nonetheless believed to be the perpetrators. The USS *New Jersey* was put on alert, but no retaliatory military

A U.S. Marine stands before the marine operations center in Beirut on October 24, 1983, the day after it was destroyed by a suicide bomb. (*AP/Wide World Photos*)

action was taken for fear that any major response would affect the United States' already difficult position in the Middle East.

On December 4, in response to an attack by Syrian forces on U.S. planes, American warplanes attacked Syrian positions near Beirut, Lebanon. In the engagement, two American planes were shot down, killing one of the pilots; an airman, Lieutenant Robert Goodman, Jr., was captured. Eight days later, terrorists in Kuwait bombed several embassies, including that of the United States, killing six and injuring 63.

The worsening violence was a lesson for Reagan, who admitted later he had not fully appreciated the complex Middle East situation and the strength of anti-American hatred. On December 22 a Pentagon commission reported that lapses in security had made the Beirut marine barracks an easy target. Five days later, the president publicly absolved military staff from blame and took responsibility on himself for the October 23 bombing. In his State of the Union address on January 25, 1984, he stressed the need to keep the marines in Lebanon to maintain U.S. credibility. Nevertheless, two weeks later, on February 7, he ordered the marines' withdrawal.

This did not end the violence against American personnel: Bombings and kidnappings would continue to characterize U.S relationships in the Middle East for a long time to come, and in 1983 alone more than 200 attacks against the United States were carried out around the world.

## ENVIRONMENTAL TURMOIL

"Trees cause more pollution than automobiles do," Ronald Reagan famously asserted in 1981. This statement typified his attitude toward—and apparent ignorance about—the environment. Though he was a lover of the outdoors and professed support for land conservation, he was also strongly influenced by friends like the Colorado brewer Joseph Coors who felt environmental regulations were too restrictive and favored increased exploitation of natural resources. Consequently, as President Reagan carried out his commitment to deregulate industry, there was a concurrent rise in environmental abuses that aroused the indignation of groups such as the Sierra Club and Audubon Society.

Despite the public outcry against his policies, the president held to his views with a stubbornness and apparent indifference to environmental issues that offended many. This mystified Reagan, who believed that his "common-sense" approach to the environment was that of most Americans. However, three disastrous appointments added strength to environmentalists' complaints: Anne Gorsuch Burford and Rita Lavelle of the Environmental Protection Agency (EPA) and James G. Watt, secretary of the interior.

The EPA had been established in 1970 to oversee compliance with government regulations, formulate new criteria for protecting the environment, and set national standards for environmental programs. In 1980 the Comprehensive Environmental Response, Compensation and Liability Act (CERCLA) established the Superfund Program to investigate and clean up hazardous-waste sites, based on an EPA priority list, using monies from taxes on the chemical and petroleum industries. From its inception, the Superfund was sharply criticized for its high costs and inefficient organization, while the EPA itself was increasingly attacked for laxness in enforcing the regulations it was meant to implement.

In 1981 Reagan appointed attorney Anne Gorsuch (later Burford) as the EPA's administrator and Rita Lavelle, a former corporate executive, as assistant administrator overseeing the Superfund program. Burford shared Reagan's views regarding federal deregulation and strongly favored transferring environmental problems to states and local governments. She slashed the EPA's budget to dangerously low levels and supported reduced environmental restrictions on industry. Under her control, the EPA lost much of its influence in environmental matters.

In autumn 1982 several House committees began to investigate the EPA's management and finances. In October John Dingell (D, Mich.), chairman of the House Commerce and Energy Investigations Subcommittee, issued a subpoena to obtain Superfund records from Rita Lavelle. Under orders from Burford, Lavelle refused to comply, and she was subsequently cited for contempt of Congress. In defying the subpoena herself, Burford claimed executive privilege—apparently under instructions from the White House Office of Legal Counsel. House attorneys, however, claimed executive privilege did not protect her, and, like Lavelle, she was cited for contempt—the most senior official in the executive branch to be so cited in U.S. history.

Meanwhile, Lavelle and the Superfund had come under Justice Department scrutiny due to allegations that she had made deals with industry, manipulated funds, and perjured herself in testimony before Congress. President Reagan dismissed Lavelle and several of her aides on February 7, 1983; approximately two weeks later, the White House instructed Burford to turn over all of the subpoenaed EPA documents to the investigating committee, except those designated "enforcement sensitive." Dingell and others objected, and though Reagan announced his support for her on March 5, Burford resigned on March 9; all relevant EPA documents were turned over to Congress the same day.

Lavelle's offenses—more serious than Burford's since there was clear evidence of conflict of interest—earned her three month's imprisonment. Burford, who was not prosecuted, was replaced by William D. Ruckelshaus, a respected official who had headed the EPA during the Nixon administration. Although he subsequently managed to restore some of the agency's reputation and improve its efficiency, his work was seriously hindered by Reagan's refusal to increase EPA funding or take an interest in environmental matters. He was particularly frustrated by the president's failure to take action on acid rain, which was seriously harming not only the environment but also relations with Canada, where U.S.-created pollution was taking a heavy toll. Although the United States entered into an agreement with Canada in August 1983 to study the causes of acid rain, Reagan stubbornly refused to accept the scientific evidence on the effects of industrial emissions. Ruckelshaus felt impelled to resign in November 1984, by which time the General Accounting Office had identified more than 378,000 toxic-waste sites needing corrective action. However, only 850 were on the EPA's priority list, and only six had been cleaned up.

Things were no better at the Department of the Interior. Reagan usually allowed others to propose "minor" cabinet secretaries, and Senator Paul Laxalt (R, Nev.) had selected James G. Watt for Interior. Laxalt had wanted a secretary who respected prodevelopment interests but could reach compromises with Congress on environmental matters. By these criteria, though, Watt was, in the view of many, the wrong man for the job. A public-interest attorney whose strong conservative views did not favor environmentalists, Watt saw his role at Interior as one in which the United States "will mine more, drill more, cut more timber to use our resources rather than simply keep them locked up."[16] He proposed increased offshore oil drilling, a moratorium on acquiring national park lands, and opening up wilderness lands to mining, drilling, and private development. Once in office, he opened U.S. coastal waters to drilling and some previously protected lands to mining and timber-cutting interests. But his confrontational approach aroused such public criticism that Congress repeatedly blocked many of his proposals.

Though polls indicated that not just environmentalists but the majority of the nation disagreed strongly with Watt's views, Reagan supported him even when Watt made comments seemingly designed to antagonize public opinion. Testifying before Congress on February 5, 1981, he agreed that natural resources should be preserved for future generations but added, "I do not know how many future generations we can count on before the Lord returns." By midterm the media could barely keep up with Watt's increasingly offensive remarks. In an interview with *Business Week* (January 24, 1983), he compared environmentalists to Nazis: "Look what happened to Germany in the 1930s. The dignity of man was subordinated to the powers of Nazism. . . . Those are the forces that this can evolve into." He was equally forthright on other issues. On August 13, 1983, he told a church group in Anaheim, California, that people who failed to speak out against abortion were equivalent to those who had offered no resistance to Hitler and had therefore brought about the Holocaust.

Watt finally went too far when, on September 21, he described the members of his coal-leasing commission to a group of lobbyists: "We have every kind of mix you can have. I have a black, I have a woman, two Jews and a cripple. And we have talent." The uproar that followed sealed Watt's fate. Though officials fought to excuse his remarks, and President Reagan stated that he did not believe Watt to be prejudiced or bigoted, the calls for the secretary's resignation became impossible to ignore.

On October 9 Watt finally stepped down, and Reagan named National Security Advisor William Clark to succeed him. Even then the president defended his former secretary in a radio address that applauded Watt for improving the national parks system and for increasing protection of conservation lands. But he carefully avoided any mention of those controversial actions that emphasized his administration's poor record on the environment. Watt had done exactly what Reagan had wanted him to do, and even under Clark the administration's environmental policy remained essentially unchanged.

## GRENADA

From the beginning of his administration, President Reagan kept a watchful eye on events in Central America. The Reagan Doctrine—though never made official—sought to contain communism and support the efforts of other nations to resist or eradicate Marxist- or Soviet-backed regimes. The president's speeches reflected this stance, particularly concerning the Soviet presence in Cuba and Central America. In his Star Wars speech of March 23, 1983, he noted:

> On the small island of Grenada, at the southern end of the Caribbean chain, the
> Cubans, with Soviet financing and backing, are in the process of building an airfield

with a 10,000-foot runway. Grenada doesn't even have an air force. Who is it intended for?[17]

From Reagan's point of view, events on Grenada, a former British colony and still a member of the British Commonwealth, were indeed disturbing. The current government had come to power in a March 1979 coup led by Maurice Bishop, a Marxist closely allied to the Cuban leader Fidel Castro. The U.S. government had suspended aid to the island in 1981, but there was still a small tourist industry, and about 600–800 American students were enrolled in the St. George's University School of Medicine.[18] According to Bishop, who visited the United States in late May and early June 1983, the airfield that Reagan had questioned in his speech was intended to boost the tourist industry. This and other indications of Bishop's willingness to encourage private enterprise resulted in increasing opposition from his own New Jewel Movement. Finally, on October 13 Deputy Prime Minister Bernard Coard and a militant New Jewel faction under the command of General Hudson Austin overthrew Bishop in a coup and placed him under house arrest. Six days later, Bishop was executed along with four of his supporters.

Martial law was imposed on the island's residents, which included the medical students and approximately 200–300 other Americans. President Reagan's initial response was to send navy ships to the Caribbean to stand by in the event an evacuation was needed. Then the Organization of Eastern Caribbean States (OECS) appealed to the United States and other governments for help in ousting Coard and Austin. British prime minister Margaret Thatcher shared President Reagan's anticommunist views but nonetheless felt strongly that there was insufficient justification to interfere in the island's affairs. Reagan and his advisers took a different view; the memory of the Iran hostage crisis was still fresh, and anything that threatened U.S. citizens abroad was considered to threaten U.S. security as well. The president therefore welcomed the OECS appeal and ordered an invasion force to be prepared, ignoring Thatcher's objections and those of the Caribbean Community (CARICOM), which, unlike the OECS, did not want the United States to intervene.

On October 23 the U.S. Marines barracks in Beirut, Lebanon, was bombed, killing 241 service members. The tragedy made Reagan pause briefly, but he finally gave the order to proceed with Operation Urgent Fury. On October 25 a combined force of 2,200 U.S. and OECS troops landed on Grenada, where they met minimal resistance from New Jewel soldiers, though the Cuban forces around the airport fought back strongly. After two days, during which the number of invading troops rose to more than 5,000, the Cubans surrendered, and the American students were evacuated. Though the campaign was over quickly, failures in communication and preparation—for example, the invaders had no accurate maps and relied on tourist brochures—had resulted in some unfortunate incidents. The most serious was the accidental bombing of an insane asylum, killing most of the 35 Grenadians who had died during the invasion. Another 335 islanders had been wounded.

Nineteen American soldiers were killed in the fighting, and 115 were injured, while the 800-strong Cuban force suffered 59 killed and 25 wounded. Despite international criticism—on November 2 the UN General Assembly condemned the invasion by a vote of 108-9, an even larger majority than that condemning the 1979 Soviet invasion of Afghanistan—most Grenadians welcomed the U.S. action, seeing it as a return to democracy and therefore prosperity for their island. In the United States, the public rejoiced in the news, and the students returning home were shown on television tearfully kissing U.S. soil.

In the postvictory glow, President Reagan announced that Cuba had been using Grenada as a base for stockpiling weapons—enough for a force of 10,000—and that evidence had also been uncovered of Soviet support for the former Marxist regime. In his mind, this was as good a reason for the operation as the rescue of the American students. This news, along with overwhelming public support of the president, led Congress to rescind its previous disapproval of the invasion. Yet certain unpalatable details were brushed to one side, including the statement by the medical school's director and others that the students had never been in danger and could have been evacuated without recourse to invasion. It was also reported, however, that Governor General Sir Paul Scoon, Grenada's head of state, had sent Reagan a secret request for help. Opinion on the merits of the American action was therefore decidedly mixed.

By December 15 most U.S. Troops had left Grenada, although some support personnel remained. Eventually elections were held, and a pro-American democratic government was put in place, but the United States soon lost interest in the island that it had liberated. Washington had promised financial aid for development programs, but this never fully materialized. In the end the invasion proved more beneficial to the American projection of strength and power than to the Grenadians themselves.

## CIVIL RIGHTS IN THE EARLY 1980S

On November 2, 1983, President Reagan signed a bill designating January 15, the birthday of slain civil rights leader Dr. Martin Luther King, Jr., a national holiday commencing in 1986. Dr. King thus became the first American since George Washington to be honored with a federal holiday. Congress, however, had passed the bill over Reagan's objections, adding to the criticism of his administration's record on civil rights.

The conservative Reagan viewed the social legislation and liberal policies of the 1960s and 1970s with a jaundiced eye. During the 1980 presidential campaign, he had made no secret of his opposition to affirmative action, school busing, and the Equal Rights Amendment. As former speechwriter Peggy Noonan has written, "He did not believe in racial preferences, did not believe in quotas or what has come to be institutionalized as affirmative action and thought it necessary that no one be given special treatment on account of his race or religion."[19] Consequently, civil rights activists greeted his election with alarm.

In attacking some cherished institutions of civil rights, Reagan was perceived as racist and antifeminist. He was also criticized for the small number of minority representatives in his administration, although his overall record was similar to that of other presidents, and he made some notable appointments, particularly that of Sandra Day O'Connor to the Supreme Court.[20] Nevertheless, he provided his opponents with more ammunition when, in June 1981, he mistook his only African-American cabinet member, Housing Secretary Samuel Pierce, for one of the big-city mayors he was greeting at a White House reception. ("How are things in your city?" he asked Pierce, whom he had not recognized.)

Reagan's appointment of William Bradford Reynolds to head the Justice Department's civil rights division seemed to confirm activists' fears. Reynolds, who proclaimed that he believed in a color-blind society, made it clear that he, too, opposed affirmative action and would do what he could to either limit or eliminate it. He was hampered in his efforts, however, as the Supreme Court consistently upheld the legality of affirmative action to protect victims of discrimination in hiring and education.

Civil rights activists—but not Reagan—applauded the Court for its decisions on *Bob Jones University v. United States* and *Goldsboro Christian Schools Inc. V. United States,* both decided in May 1983. These cases revolved around a 1970 change in Internal Revenue Service (IRS) policy that refused tax-exempt status to private schools found to engage in racial discrimination. On this basis, the IRS had revoked the tax-exempt status of Bob Jones University and Goldsboro Christian Schools, the former for its policy prohibiting interracial dating and marriage, the latter for an admissions policy accepting primarily white students based on its own interpretation of the Bible. The schools sued, claiming that their rights under the First Amendment to the U.S. Constitution had been violated; President Reagan supported the plaintiffs, maintaining that Congress had not given the IRS the power to decide questions of tax-exempt status. However, the Supreme Court upheld both IRS decisions since the schools had exercised racially discriminatory policies that violated a "fundamental national public policy." The public interest in eliminating racial discrimination was thus held to outweigh individual religious beliefs.

Until he could appoint Supreme Court justices more in sympathy with his views, Reagan was frustrated by such decisions. But he was still able to manipulate other relevant bodies. On May 25, 1983, he dismissed three Democrats on the U.S. Civil Rights Commission and replaced them with Republicans. The popular outcry abated somewhat a month later when the commission criticized the administration for its lax enforcement of civil rights legislation in schools. Reagan nevertheless felt such laws placed unfair restrictions on individual liberties.

Despite the Reagan administration's opposition, the Civil Rights movement made important advances, such as the 1982 bill extending the Voting Rights Act of 1965. There was further encouragement in the August 27, 1983, march on Washington by some 250,000 people, reenacting the landmark march led by Martin Luther King, Jr., 20 years earlier. The year 1983 also saw the election of Harold Washington as Chicago's first black mayor on April 12; the first American woman in space, physicist Sally K. Ride aboard the space shuttle *Challenger* (June 18–24); the election of Frederico Peña as the first Hispanic mayor of Denver, Colorado, on June 21; the country's first black astronaut, Lieutenant Colonel Guion S. Bluford of the U.S. Air Force, and the oldest person to fly in space to that time, 54-year-old Dr. William Thornton, both aboard *Challenger* (August 30–September 5); the first African-American winner of the Miss America pageant, Vanessa Williams of Millwood, New York, on September 17;[21] and the election of Martha Layne Collins as the first woman governor of Kentucky and Wilson Goode as the first black mayor of Philadelphia on November 8.

These and other events, such as the advent of Reverend Jesse Jackson on the national political stage in 1984, would ensure that minorities and women continued to break down racial and sexual barriers to equality.

Sally K. Ride, the first American woman in space, communicates with ground controllers from the flight deck of the *Challenger* during its six-day mission in June 1983. *(National Archives Still Picture Records LICON [NWDNS-306-PS-E83(2274C(A)])*

## ALSO IN THE NEWS

Like other decades, the 1980s had its fads, such as the engaging (and still-popular) Trivial Pursuit, a simple board game invented by two Canadians. But there were bizarre fads as well, most notably the Cabbage Patch Kids, soft and cuddly dolls that made Christmas 1983 a nightmare for parents. Created by designer Xavier Roberts and distributed by Coleco, the Kids were wide-eyed, chubby-cheeked babies, each of unique appearance and personality. They were "born" at Babyland General Hospital, then dispatched to stores to be adopted; upon purchasing a Kid, the new "parent" received a birth certificate and adoption papers. Such a success was this marketing ploy that it seemed every child in the United States had to have a Cabbage Patch Kid. As Christmas approached, parents went to extraordinary lengths to obtain Kids for their children, getting into toy store fights with other parents, offering huge sums of money, sometimes traveling outrageous distances—just to buy a doll. Failure resulted in unhappy "deprived" children.

The Cabbage Patch craze ended a year of emotional highs, such as the February 28 broadcast of the final episode of *M*A*S*H,* which attracted 125 million viewers;[22] and devastating lows, such as the summer-autumn drought that ravaged large parts of the country, killing more than 220 people and causing billions of dollars of crop damage. The year also saw milestone advances in technology typified by the increase in speed of fax transmissions to 9,600 bits per second (bps), sparking a communications revolution: By the end of the decade, few offices would be without a facsimile machine. Meanwhile, Chicago became the birthplace of cellular phones when, in October 1983, Ameritech, Inc., launched Advanced Mobile Phone Service.

The impact of the computer revolution was highlighted when *Time* magazine's issue of January 3, 1983, named the computer "Machine of the Year" for 1982. In addition to other major developments, 1983 witnessed what was soon to become a common pastime when, in August, a group of 17–22-year-olds in Milwaukee hacked into approximately 60 computers nationwide, including machines at New York's Memorial Sloan Kettering Cancer Center and New Mexico's Los Alamos National Laboratory. This trend was spotlighted in the year's hit movie *War Games,* in which a teenager hacks into U.S. military computers.

On April 4 the second shuttle in NASA's fleet, *Challenger,* took off on its maiden flight, a mission that saw the first shuttle space walk on April 7. The shuttle program was to provide news throughout the year, with the first nighttime shuttle landing (September 5) and crews that included minority representatives and Europeans for the first time. Meanwhile, in June *Pioneer 10,* which had been launched back in 1972, became the first human-made object to cross Neptune's orbit and travel beyond the solar system.

Sports was marked by highs and lows. In March the newly formed United States Football League (USFL), comprising 12 teams, began its first season of 18 spring games, as an alternative to the National Football League's autumn season. On July 17 the Michigan Panthers won the first USFL championship game, defeating the Philadelphia Stars 24-22.[23] In August the United States was triumphant in the Pan American Games in Caracas, Venezuela, winning 137 gold medals. But on September 26 the country was shaken when the U.S. yacht *Liberty* lost the America's Cup trophy to the Australian-crewed *Australia II.* It was the United States' first defeat in the historic yachting race since 1851.

Michael Jackson topped the charts in 1983 with "Thriller," "Billie Jean," and "Beat It." *(Photofest)*

The years 1982–83 also saw the advent of the empty-headed Valley Girl, another 1980s icon. Named after California's San Fernando Valley, where the type originated, Valley Girls were teenagers known mainly for haunting shopping malls and speaking in, like, a totally cool lingo that only other Vals (as they referred to themselves) could understand or even want to speak. The Vals became famous in 1982 when Moon Unit Zappa, daughter of rocker Frank, wrote and recorded a song that satirized their lifestyle and vocabulary. ("It's like so bitchin'," "grody to the max," etc.) The following year, Hollywood depicted them in *Valley Girl,* starring Julie Richman and Nicholas Cage, a comedy that helped spread the Valley Girl culture across the nation—to the despair of millions of parents.

In entertainment, the headliner of the year was Michael Jackson, whose album *Thriller* came out in 1982 and, on February 26, 1983, became *Billboard*'s number-one album. It remained on *Billboard*'s Top Ten list for 78 weeks, becoming one of the best-selling albums of all time. The video of the title song "Thriller," a John Landis-directed, 15-minute-long piece featuring break-dancing zombies, set a new standard for music videos that other artists struggled to emulate. Jackson's other big hits of 1983 were "Beat It" and "Billie Jean," which, together with "Thriller," earned him seven Grammies in February 1984. Despite some noteworthy competition from the Police ("Every Breath You Take"), Men at Work ("Down Under"), and Hall and Oates ("Maneater"), among others, Jackson dominated pop music in 1983—and entered 1984 without an equal.

## CHRONICLE OF EVENTS

### 1982

*November 2:* In the midterm elections, the Democrats gain 26 seats in the House of Representatives, while the Republicans retain a majority in the Senate.

*November 10:* Soviet leader Leonid Brezhnev dies; he is succeeded by Yuri Andropov, former head of the KGB.

*November 11–16:* The space shuttle *Columbia* carries out its first operational flight, launching two satellites into orbit, but a planned space walk is canceled due to malfunctioning spacesuits.

*November 13:* The Vietnam Veterans Memorial in Washington, D.C., is dedicated at a service attended by approximately 15,000 Vietnam veterans. The controversially stark memorial quickly becomes a national landmark.

*November 16:* An agreement ends the strike by the National Football League Players Association that began on September 21. Regular season games resume on November 21, but the playoff schedule is radically altered.

*November 23:* The Federal Communications Commission abandons limitations on the length and frequency of television ads.

*November 26:* Heavyweight boxing champion Larry Holmes defeats Randy Cobb to win his 13th straight defense of the WBC championship.

*December 2:* The world's first successful transplant of an artificial heart is carried out on Barney C. Clark, 61, at the University of Utah Medical Center.

*December 2–9:* The Midwest is devastated by floods that kill 22 and force the evacuation of 35,000. Estimated damage is $600 million.

*December 3:* The U.S. Department of Labor reports the November unemployment rate to be 10.8 percent, the highest since 1940.

*December 7:* In Huntsville, Texas, convicted murderer Charles Brooks, Jr., is executed by lethal injection, the first time in U.S. history this means of execution has been used.

*December 9:* The Centers for Disease Control report the first known case of AIDS in a child who had received a blood transfusion from an adult victim.

*December 12:* Thieves in New York City rob an armored truck company and make off with the largest cash heist in U.S. history to this time: $9.8 million.

*December 16:* Anne Gorsuch (later Burford), head of the Environmental Protection Agency (EPA), is cited for contempt of Congress for her refusal to hand over documents relating to a House investigation.

*December 23:* Virtuoso pianist Arthur Rubinstein dies at age 95.

*December 26:* The current issue of *Time* magazine (dated January 3, 1983) names "The Computer" as Machine of the Year for 1982.

### 1983

*January 1:* The Internet is created when the Department of Defense's ARPANET (Advanced Research Projects Agency Network, established in 1969) changes to the Internet Protocol.

*January 5:* President Reagan nominates Elizabeth Dole for Secretary of Transportation. Sworn in on February 7, she becomes the first woman in his cabinet.

*January 6:* Apple unveils the Lisa, a computer with a graphical user interface (GUI), or mouse. However, it is not very successful due to its slowness.

*January 14:* Congress passes the Indian Tribal Governmental Tax Status Act.

*January 15:* Organized crime boss Meyer Lansky, 80, dies.

*January 18:* More than 70 years after Jim Thorpe's 1912 Olympic wins in the decathlon and pentathlon, his gold medals are returned to his family. Thorpe, an American Indian who was considered to be the greatest athlete of his time, had been stripped of his medals after it was learned that he had played semiprofessional basketball in 1909.

*January 19:* Apple introduces the Apple IIe, which quickly becomes the most popular computer for businesses, schools, and homes.

*January 21:* The inflation rate decreases to 3.9 percent; it had been as high as 8.9 percent in 1982.

*January 24:* Noted film director George Cukor, whose career lasted more than 50 years, dies at age 83.

*January 25:* In his State of the Union address, President Reagan calls for continued increases in military spending along with a freeze in domestic spending.

*January 26:* Paul "Bear" Bryant, University of Alabama football coach who logged the most wins in college football history (323, with only 85 defeats and 17 ties), dies at age 69, less than a month after his retirement.

*January 26:* The computer spreadsheet software program Lotus 1-2-3 is released and quickly becomes a runaway success.

*January 29:* At the Golden Globe Awards, *E.T., the Extraterrestrial* wins as best motion picture–drama, *Tootsie* wins as best comedy or musical, and *Gandhi* is named best foreign film. Ben Kingsley, Dustin Hoffman, Meryl Streep, and Julie Andrews take top acting honors.

*January 30:* The Washington Redskins defeat the Miami Dolphins, 27-17, to win Super Bowl XVII.

*January 31:* President Reagan presents his 1984 budget proposal to Congress; it projects a federal deficit of $188.8 billion.

*January 31–February 10:* In protest against higher truck registration fees and fuel taxes, the Independent Truckers Association institutes a nationwide strike.

*February 4:* Unemployment declines to 10.4 percent (from 10.8 percent in January), signaling an end to the recession.

*February 4:* Pop singer Karen Carpenter, 32, dies of heart failure caused by anorexia.

*February 10:* The United States and Canada sign an agreement allowing Americans to test unarmed cruise missiles in northern Alberta.

*February 12:* Eubie Blake, famed pianist and composer of ragtime and popular music, including 315 songs, dies at age 100.

*February 14:* The United American Bank of Knoxville, Tennessee, is declared insolvent and is shut down. With deposits of $760 million, it is the fourth-largest U.S. bank failure during the last 50 years. The bank will reopen on February 15 as a unit of First Tennessee National Corporation.

*February 22:* Anne Burford, head of the Environmental Protection Agency (EPA), announces the federal government will purchase all homes and businesses in Times Beach, Missouri, which requires evacuation due to high levels of dioxin contamination. The costs of purchasing and demolishing the town are estimated at $33 million.

*February 23:* The 1984 presidential race begins when Senator Alan Cranston (D, Calif.) announces his intention to run.

*February 23:* At the Grammy Awards, the pop group Toto wins for best album of 1982 (*Toto IV*) and best record ("Rosanna"). The song of the year is "Always on My Mind."

*February 24:* A special commission appointed by Congress releases a report criticizing the internment of Japanese Americans during World War II.

*February 25:* Tennessee Williams, author of *Cat on a Hot Tin Roof* and *A Streetcar Named Desire,* dies at age 71 after swallowing a plastic bottle cap.

*February 26:* Michael Jackson's *Thriller* becomes the number one U.S. album; it will remain on *Billboard's* Top-Ten list for 78 weeks.

*February 28:* The largest television viewing audience for a nonsports program—125 million—tunes in for the final episode of *M★A★S★H,* the long-running series about a mobile army hospital in the Korean War.

*March 6:* The newly formed United States Football League begins its first season, with the Michigan Panthers winning the USFL's first championship game on July 17.

*March 9:* Anne Burford resigns as the head of the Environmental Protection Agency amid charges of gross mismanagement and conflict of interest.

*March 10–11:* At the world figure-skating championships in Helsinki, Finland, the United States' Scott Hamilton wins the men's singles title for the third straight year, while Rosalynn Sumners wins the women's singles title.

*March 16:* Radio and television personality Arthur Godfrey dies, age 79.

*March 23:* Barney Clark, 62, dies 112 days after receiving an artificial heart.

*March 23:* In a televised address, President Reagan announces his plan for an antiballistic missile defense program, which quickly becomes known as Star Wars.

*April 4:* Screen legend Gloria Swanson dies at 84.

*April 4–9:* The second spacecraft in NASA's shuttle fleet, *Challenger,* carries out its first mission with four astronauts; Story Musgrave and Don Peterson perform the first shuttle space walk on April 7.

*April 11:* At the Academy Awards, *Gandhi* is voted best picture of 1982; its star, Ben Kingsley, wins as best actor. Meryl Streep (*Sophie's Choice*) wins as best actress; Louis Gossett, Jr., and Jessica Lange take the supporting acting awards.

*April 12:* Harold Washington (D) is elected Chicago's first black mayor.

*April 18:* A truck-bomb explosion in Beirut nearly destroys the U.S. embassy there and kills 63 people, including 17 Americans. Pro-Iranian terrorists are blamed.

*April 18:* Pulitzer Prize winners include Alice Walker for fiction (*The Color Purple*), Galway Kinnell for poetry (*Selected Poems*), Marsha Norman for drama (*'Night, Mother*), and Russell Baker for biography (*Growing Up*).

*April 22:* Earl "Fatha" Hines, considered to be the father of the modern jazz piano, dies at age 77.

*April 26:* In a 36-page report, the National Commission on Excellence in Education, established in 1981, warns that "a rising tide of mediocrity" in U.S. schools "threatens our very future as a nation and a people."

*April 30:* Russian-born choreographer George Balanchine, age 79, dies, as does blues singer and guitarist Muddy Waters (McKinley Morganfield), age 68.

*May 4:* The artist Christo completes a massive $3 million installation, surrounding 11 islets in Biscayne Bay, Florida, with 6 million feet of pink tarpaulin. The work remains in place for two weeks.

*May 17:* The New York Islanders defeat the Edmonton Oilers in four straight games to win the National Hockey League's Stanley Cup.

*May 24:* The federal government announces that AIDS has become its top medical priority.

*May 24:* An estimated 2.1 million people celebrate the 100th anniversary of the Brooklyn Bridge; the festivities are capped by a dazzling fireworks display.

*May 25:* The movie *Return of the Jedi* sets an opening-day record with gross receipts of $6,219,629.

*May 28–30:* In Williamsburg, Virginia, President Reagan joins six other world leaders at the College of William and Mary for an annual review of the world's economies; they issue the "Williamsburg Declaration on Economic Recovery."

*May 31:* Jack Dempsey, world heavyweight boxing champion from 1919 to 1926, dies at age 86.

President and Mrs. Reagan honor the victims of the bombing of the U.S. embassy in Beirut, at Andrews Air Force Base, Maryland, on April 23, 1983. *(Courtesy Ronald Reagan Library)*

*May 31:* In the fourth game of their series, the Philadelphia 76ers beat the Los Angeles Lakers to win the National Basketball Association championship.

*June 5:* At the Tony Awards for the 1982–83 season, *Torch Song Trilogy* by Harvey Fierstein wins as best play, while Andrew Lloyd Webber's *Cats* is named best musical. Fierstein, Tommy Tune, Jessica Tandy, and Natalia Makarova take the top acting awards.

*June 7:* In response to the expulsion of U.S. diplomats from Nicaragua, the United States orders 21 Nicaraguan officials to leave the country.

*June 11:* In Canada, Brian Mulroney replaces Joe Clark as leader of the Progressive Conservative Party.

*June 13:* *Pioneer 10* becomes the first spacecraft to travel beyond the solar system when it crosses Neptune's orbit.

*June 15:* A Supreme Court ruling prevents states from limiting access to legal abortions, thus upholding women's right to abortions during the first three months of pregnancy.

*June 18–24:* Physicist Sally K. Ride becomes the first American woman in space as a crew member on the shuttle *Challenger's* second flight, during which the shuttle successfully releases and retrieves a satellite.

*June 21:* Federico Peña is elected the first Hispanic mayor of Denver, Colorado.

*June 28:* The Senate fails to get a two-thirds majority for an amendment allowing legislation to ban or curb abortions.

*June 28:* At a news conference, President Reagan is questioned about a Jimmy Carter briefing book for the 1980 presidential debate that had been obtained by Reagan campaign workers.

*July 1:* Architect R. Buckminster Fuller, celebrated for his invention of the geodesic dome, dies at age 87; his wife dies two days later.

*July 2:* Larry Walters flies as high as 16,000 feet in a lawn chair to which 42 weather balloons are tied; he then starts to shoot the balloons with a pellet gun. He lands about 90 minutes after taking off. The FAA will fine him $1,500 for the stunt.

*July 6:* Famed trumpeter and band leader Harry James dies, age 67.

*July 7:* Maine schoolgirl Samantha Smith flies to the Soviet Union for a two-week visit at the invitation of Soviet leader Yuri Andropov.

*July 13:* The Chrysler Corporation announces that it will pay off the remaining $800 million owed in federally guaranteed loans by the end of September, well ahead of its 1990 deadline.

*July 15:* The U.S. Supreme Court rules that Native American disputes over water rights can be heard in state courts.

*July 18:* President Reagan announces that former Secretary of State Henry Kissinger will head a bipartisan commission to make recommendations on U.S. policy in Central America.

*July 28:* A new five-year agreement on grain purchases is reached with the Soviet Union, which will buy a minimum of 9 million metric tons a year.

*July 29:* Canadian-born actor Raymond Massey dies at age 86.

*August 2:* The U.S. Census Bureau reports 15 percent of Americans lived below the poverty level in 1982, the highest rate since the War on Poverty began in 1964.

*August 14–18:* The United States wins 137 gold medals at the Pan American Games in Caracas, Venezuela, finishing first in unofficial team standings.

*August 17:* Ira Gershwin, lyricist who wrote the words to many of his brother George's songs, dies at age 86.

*August 18:* Twenty-two people are killed when Hurricane Alicia strikes the Texas coast; damage estimates exceed $1 billion.

*August 23:* The United States and Canada sign an agreement for a joint study of the causes of acid rain, particularly air pollutants.

*August 27:* The 1963 civil rights march on Washington is commemorated with a similar march; 250,000 people take part in the event, whose theme is "Jobs, Peace, and Freedom."

*August 30:* The space shuttle *Challenger* is launched on its third mission. On board is Lieutenant Colonel Guion S. Bluford of the U.S. Air Force, the country's first black astronaut, and Dr. William Thornton, a physician who, at 54, is the oldest person to fly in space to date. When *Challenger* returns on September 5, it makes the first nighttime shuttle landing.

*September 1:* Senator Henry M. ("Scoop") Jackson (D, Wash.), a leading supporter of a strong national defense, dies at age 71.

*September 2:* Secretary of Agriculture John Block begins to declare disaster areas after a two-month drought that has devastated parts of the country.

*September 10–11:* At tennis's U.S. Open in Queens, New York, Martina Navratilova defeats Chris Evert Lloyd to take her first singles championship, and Jimmy Connors defeats Ivan Lendi to capture his fifth men's singles title.

*September 17:* The Miss America beauty pageant is won for the first time by a black woman: Vanessa Williams of Millwood, New York.

*September 20:* U.S. Marines will stay in Lebanon as a peacekeeping force as a result of a resolution reaffirming the 1973 War Powers Act.

*September 21:* The economy continues to recover as it is announced that the GNP grew by 9.7 percent in the second quarter of 1983.

*September 24:* The nation's eighth-largest air carrier, Continental Airlines, lays off all its employees and files for Chapter 11 bankruptcy protection. Two days later the president of fourth-largest Eastern Airlines, Frank Borman, asks employees to take a 15 percent pay cut to help avert the same consequence.

*September 25:* At the Emmy Awards, Ed Flanders (*St. Elsewhere*) and Tyne Daly (*Cagney and Lacey*) take the top dramatic acting awards, while *Hill Street Blues* wins as best dramatic series.

*September 26:* For the first time in 132 years, the United States loses the America's Cup when, after seven races, the U.S. yacht *Liberty* yields to the Australian-crewed *Australia II.*

*September 27: A Chorus Line,* which opened on October 25, 1975, stages its 3,389th performance, overtaking *Grease* as the longest-running Broadway show of all time.

*September 30:* A record heat wave in the U.S. Midwest—the worst in 50 years—comes to an end after nine weeks in which at least 220 people died and billions of dollars of crops were ruined.

*October 6:* Terence Cardinal Cooke, archbishop of New York, dies at age 62.

*October 12:* In Chicago, Illinois, Ameritech, Inc., establishes Advanced Mobile Phone Service, launching the first commercial cellular phone service.

*October 14:* The National Council of Churches announces plans for a new translation of the Bible that would eliminate references to God as a male entity.

*October 16:* In the fifth game of the World Series, the American League's Baltimore Orioles defeat the National League's Philadelphia Phillies to win the championship.

*October 23:* Terrorists bomb a U.S. Marine barracks in Beirut, Lebanon, killing 241 marine and navy personnel.

*October 25:* U.S. Troops invade the Caribbean island of Grenada.

*October 26:* The federal government reports a deficit of $195.4 billion in the 1983 fiscal year, which ended September 30.

*October 28:* An earthquake measuring 6.9 on the Richter Scale—the strongest in the contiguous 48 states since 1959—hits eight northwestern states.

*October 31:* Famed football coach George Halas, who guided the Chicago Bears for many years, dies at age 88.

*November 2:* President Reagan signs a bill making January 15, the birthday of Dr. Martin Luther King, Jr., a federal holiday, beginning in 1986.

*November 7:* Late in the evening a bomb explodes outside the U.S. Senate chamber; there are no injuries.

*November 8:* In elections, Martha Layne Collins becomes the first woman governor of Kentucky, and W. Wilson Goode becomes the first black mayor of Philadelphia.

*November 10:* Microsoft Corporation launches its Windows operating system, version 1.0.

*November 14:* The United States begins to deploy cruise missiles in the United Kingdom.

*November 18:* Congress authorizes aid to the contra rebels in Nicaragua.

*November 20:* An ABC television movie about nuclear war, *The Day After,* becomes, to date, the second-most-watched dramatic program in TV history, with a viewing audience of about 100 million.

*November 28–December 8:* The space shuttle *Columbia* lifts off with a crew of six—including West German physicist Ulf Merbold, the first non-American to fly in the shuttle—and the European-built Spacelab in its cargo bay. The shuttle's 10 days in space are the longest for the program thus far.

*November 29:* At an international meeting on AIDS in Geneva, it is announced that 3,000 cases of AIDS have been positively identified worldwide; most are in the United States.

*December 2:* The unemployment rate continues to drop as the U.S. Department of Labor announces a two-year low of 8.4 percent in November.

*December 4:* An American pilot is killed and another airman is captured during an attack by U.S. warplanes on Syrian positions near Beirut, Lebanon.

*December 8:* In Geneva the strategic arms reductions talks (START) between the United States and Soviet Union come to an end without any date for further discussions being set.

*December 12:* In Kuwait terrorists bomb several embassies, including that of the United States; six are killed and 63 injured.

*December 22:* General Motors and Japan's Toyota announce plans for a joint U.S.-Japanese auto venture, opposed by Ford and Chrysler, that will produce 200,000–250,000 cars a year at a new plant in Fremont, California.

*December 28:* Dennis Wilson of The Beach Boys drowns in Marina del Rey, California, at the age of 39.

# EYEWITNESS TESTIMONY

## The Nation's Defense

Continuity of effort in national security affairs is essential. Turbulence is wasteful beyond words. These programs to increase the stability and security of our strategic nuclear forces are urgently needed. The planning by my predecessors made them possible, but it is for my successor that I make these decisions. With every effort, the Peacekeeper missile still will not be fully deployed until the late 1980s, when yet another President shoulders these burdens.

*President Reagan presenting his arguments in support of constructing and deploying 100 MX missiles, in a televised address to the nation, November 22, 1982. Available online. URL: http://www.reagan. utexas.edu/resource/speeches/1982/112282b.htm.*

The administration's present and prospective MX difficulties are to a considerable extent its own creation. From the first it has inordinately tied the case for the MX to a survivable basing mode. Yet U.S. ICBM vulnerability is determined primarily by the trend in weapons technology and by Soviet actions. Nonetheless, silo vulnerability has been blamed on U.S. decisions, especially on arms control (that, one presumes, was SALT II's "fatal flaw"). Much of the rhetoric about "closing the window of vulnerability" presupposed some easy U.S. solution to ICBM vulnerability. Thus, the administration has now become entangled in its own rhetoric, for in the years ahead the window of vulnerability will gradually and inevitably open more widely.

*James R. Schlesinger, secretary of defense in the Nixon and Ford administrations, criticizing Reagan's actions on the MX missile, in Schlesinger, "Strategic Deterrence—or Strategic Confusion?" Washington Post, November 28, 1982, p. C-8.*

You may have noticed that the new name for the MX missile is "The Peacekeeper." As much thought went into what to call the missile as into where to put it. You can say what you want about our military planners, but when it comes to naming mega-death weapons, they know their business.

An entire military establishment is involved in thinking up new names for weapons. It is one of the most important divisions in the Pentagon, because when Defense is acquiring new hardware, it doesn't want to tip off the taxpayer that it is buying a weapon that can obliterate millions of people.

*Columnist Art Buchwald commenting satirically on the MX missile, in Buchwald, "That Which We Call MX by Any Other Name," Washington Post, December 5, 1982, p. G-1.*

If the Soviet Union will join with us in our effort to achieve major arms reduction, we will have succeeded in stabilizing the nuclear balance. Nevertheless, it will still be necessary to rely on the specter of retaliation, on mutual threat. And that's a sad commentary on the human condition. Wouldn't it be better to save lives than to avenge them? Are we not capable of demonstrating our peaceful intentions by applying all our abilities and our ingenuity to achieving a truly lasting stability? I think we are. Indeed, we must.

*President Reagan in a televised address to the nation on March 23, 1983, prior to describing plans for an antimissile defense system. Available online. URL: http://www.reagan.utexas.edu/resource/speeches/1983/32383d.htm.*

Make no mistake about it: Mr. Reagan is proposing to embark on a major escalation of the arms race in the only environment that is now relatively free of military activity. We can fight wars on land, in the air, on the sea and under the sea. Space remains the only arena in which the superpowers cannot now do combat. Mr. Reagan would change that by developing and deploying an antimissile system that, through exotic technologies, would ostensibly render the nation immune from atomic attack.

It would, of course, do no such thing. The Reagan plan would cost untold billions, involve a research and development effort that would rival the scope of the Manhattan project (and provide less assurance of success) and, in the end, leave America no more secure than it is now. . . .

*The St. Louis Post Post-Dispatch assessing the Reagan proposal for an antimissile defense system in its editorial "A Star Wars Defense," March 23, 1983, quoted in Boyer, Reagan as President (1990), pp. 210–211.*

We need to be in a situation where we are not subject to nuclear blackmail, where no matter how other conflicts come out we can at least be safe at home, without

President Reagan addresses the nation from the Oval Office on national security—known as his Star Wars speech—on March 23, 1983. *(Courtesy Ronald Reagan Library)*

allies. I don't believe that the United States can maintain its happy position in the world—I don't think we can even survive—without high technology.

*Nuclear physicist Dr. Edward Teller giving his support to a space-based antimissile system, quoted in "The Old Lion Still Roars,"* Time, *April 4, 1983, p. 12.*

Though no one today can guarantee the development of a viable defense against missiles, and although it would lie some years in the future in any case, a variety of approaches have been under study for some time. They include non-nuclear air/ground systems using a kind of shrapnel, as in High Frontier; nuclear-armed anti-missiles; and laser beams, perhaps bounced off mirrors orbiting in space. It would take a bold prophet to guarantee that *no* such defense is feasible.

Politically, the President scored psychologically against the freeze advocates and their apocalyptic backers, and placed himself visibly on the side of saving lives and cities. It was no doubt this political aspect that infuriated his critics, that and their instinctive suspicion of any proposal that would enhance American power and security.

*The* National Review *applauding the president's defense proposal in its editorial "Star Wars," April 15, 1983, quoted in Boyer,* Reagan as President *(1990), p. 212.*

We are looking at a new departure both in our strategic forces and in arms control. We are advocating integrating our strategic forces with arms control and moving both of them in the direction of stability. In order to get there, it is important to have the kind of negotiation with the Soviet Union that would at least permit us to go in that direction and would encourage the Soviets to go that way, too.

In addition, we think that it is very important to demonstrate U.S. national will and cohesiveness. Four American Presidents have said that the MX Missile is important, if not essential, to our national security. If we back away from it now, it will underscore our paralysis for both our opponents and for our friends and allies. That would have a damaging effect on deterrence, which depends on national will in a critical sense.

*Brent Scowcroft, chairman of the Commission on Strategic Forces, making his case for the MX missile, quoted in "MX 'Important to Demonstrate National Will,'"* U.S. News & World Report, *April 25, 1983, p. 25.*

I think the time has come to say the common sense way, that we're as safe as we can be—that we have all the deterrence that we need. We will modernize our airborne and submarine systems when the time comes, but we should no longer insist on a full-blown triad, when it won't work, it won't solve our problems and it will only increase likelihood of a nuclear conflict.

This latest MX silo plan does not meet the test of common sense. All it does is create a bullseye in middle America for Soviet defense planners. We've had a nuclear triad not because of the number three, but for one reason only. We have better odds in deterring a nuclear war.

*Morris Udall (D, Ariz.), arguing against funding for 100 MX missiles in a House debate, May 23, 1983. Available online. URL: http://dizzy.library. arizona.edu/branches/spc/udall/missiles.rtf.*

Finally, the MX is a step toward nuclear war. Because its power and vulnerability provide compelling reasons for the Soviets to strike it first, the MX, from a military point of view, is useful only as a first-strike weapon, or as a weapon to be fired the moment *we think* the Soviet missiles are on their way. In fact, the Joint Chiefs of Staff testified in April that we must have the MX so we can threaten Soviet missile silos and command posts. We have truly arrived at 1984 and "Newspeak" a year early when a missile can be called "Peacekeeper."

*Senator Gary Hart (D, Colo.) opposing the MX missile, in Hart, "The MX: Bad for Security, Bad for Survival," Washington Post, May 25, 1983, p. A-25.*

## Reconciliation

The starkness so affronted some of its patrons that they demanded the addition of a statue and a flag. To others, that is a touch of Norman Rockwell in the middle of a Dante-like statement, one which quarrels with the dark majesty of a wall constructed to bear the unbearable grief and pain of the only war in our history where the men who fled it were honored more than those who fought it.

*Columnist Mary McGrory commenting on some of the controversy surrounding the Vietnam Veterans Memorial, in McGrory, "Vietnam Memorial Seen as 'First Step in a Healing Process,' " Washington Post, November 9, 1982, p. A-3.*

[T]he names also memorialize the historic crisis of authority that Vietnam brought on American society. Conflicts between generations, classes and races took shape around the war. The mounting death toll added tragic force to the debate, and brought it directly home to 58,000 American families.

Their questions would not be ignored: Could the policies and the officials sending young Americans to their deaths be trusted? Did the best and the brightest in Washington understand Vietnam? Or were they clinging too stubbornly to anti-Communist ideology and to military tactics that didn't work? Did the investment of lives, the list of names that grew each week, only drive them, ever more isolated, to see vindication?

Promoters of the memorial, which was built with private contributions, hope this week's ceremonies will heal some of the lingering divisions and finally give all Vietnam veterans a rightful sign of national gratitude. Let it stand for that gratitude; let it also stand for the promise that America will not again so unquestioningly send its young to war.

*From the editorial "The Vietnam Names," New York Times, November 11, 1982, p. A-30.*

"I don't know what it is," said Kenneth Young, a Vietnam veteran who stood for two hours, staring at the wall, stepping away to think, stepping back to touch the names he knew. "You have to touch it. There's something about touching it."

. . . . .

"Tonight, I'm sure we'll all get drunk," Ken Young said as word spread of numerous barroom reunions around town.

"Well, not drunk," said Niles Delfosse. "We'll have a toast to these gentlemen. We'll definitely drink to these gentlemen."

*Describing the gathering and reactions of veterans at the new Vietnam Veterans Memorial, in Clines, "Salute Opening for Vietnam Veterans," New York Times, November 11, 1982, p. B-15.*

When your country called, you came. When your country refused you honor, you remained silent. With time, our nation's wounds have healed. We have finally come to appreciate your sacrifices and to pay you your tribute you so richly deserve.

*Extract from a letter written by Defense Secretary Caspar Weinberger to memorial organizer Jan Scruggs and read at the dedication on November 13, 1982, quoted in McCombs, "Veterans Honor Fallen, Mark Reconciliation," Washington Post, November 14, 1982, p. A-18.*

From across the country, a wave of veterans swept into Washington, D.C., for reunions, a candlelight vigil, a parade and the dedication of a monument that belatedly admits them to a place of honor.

It was a haunting commemoration that called forth memories of what had divided the nation even as it drew countrymen together.

The monument is a stone's throw from where young people massed on the Mall to chant, in that angry time of war, "Hell, no, we won't go!"

The gleaming, black-granite wall that pays tribute to their service bears the names of the 57,939 Americans killed or missing in Vietnam—names that were shouted through the White House gates during the demonstrations of the war years.

*Evoking painful memories in "A Thank You That Was 7 Years Late," U.S. News & World Report, November 22, 1982, p. 66.*

They died in an unpopular war, fought for uncertain ends and prolonged far beyond hope of success. But that was not their fault. When their country called, they answered, and they fought bravely and well. They gave no less than those Americans who died at Valley Forge, Gettysburg or Normandy. But their memorial is not a monument to the abstract ideal of war, to glory and victories or even to a cause. It is a reminder of the cost of war. It is a bill of sale.

*Vietnam veteran and* Newsweek *editor in chief William Broyles, Jr., putting the Vietnam memorial into perspective, in Broyles, "Remembering a War We Wanted to Forget,"* Newsweek, *November 22, 1982, p. 82.*

The people of the U.S. have finally taken their heads from under the eagle's wing and acknowledged that those who fought, died and were wounded in Viet Nam are heroes and not bums.

*From a letter to the editor commenting on the Vietnam Veterans Memorial,* Time, *December 13, 1982, p. 3.*

[The monument] is a place in which we and our fellow citizens at long last find reconciliation. One need only go and stand quietly at the apex of the walls to see it happen. Gentle volunteers help the confused find the name they seek. The young, with grace and tenderness, assist the old. Adolescents find the father they never knew. Widows find tangible connection with the best of fading memories. Strangers spontaneously share tearful and bittersweet embraces. Flowers, flags, mementos, even photographs, are left in undisputed tribute. Universally, the hands reach out and the fingertips stroke the wall where at every point names merge with reflections of national pride, the Washington Monument and the Lincoln Memorial.

In this place there is no rancor, no debate; not even bygones are raised. There is only reconciliation on basic human terms.

*Veteran R. Christian Berg giving an eloquent description of the memorial's effect, in a letter to the editor,* Washington Post, *January 15, 1983, p. A-20.*

## Federal Foibles and Fanfare

Ottawa admits that Canada may be responsible for as much as 25% of the acid rain in the U.S., but adds that it is on the deficit side of this unhappy balance of trade. It contends that about 70% of the acidic sulfates that fall on Canada come from the U.S., wafted by winds from areas like the industrialized Ohio Valley. Says Environ-

ment Minister [John] Roberts: "We are at the end of a gigantic geographical exhaust pipe."

*A description of the strained relations with Canada over the issue of acid rain, in "Storm over a Deadly Downpour,"* Time, *December 6, 1982, p. 85.*

The new numbers—representing 12 million Americans without jobs—stunned the experts, who had expected no more than a .1 percentage-point rise over October's 10.4 percent jobless rate. And the figures enraged labor leaders, who blamed the worsening unemployment directly on the economic policies of Ronald Reagan's administration. "A dramatic example of what staying the course means to American workers," declared United Steelworkers president Lloyd McBride, "a first-order calamity to the American economy." . . . Reagan himself called the figures "a continuous tragedy," but insisted that the worst would soon be over. "As the recovery comes onstream," he said, "we can expect to make progress on the unemployment front."

*Gloomy reaction in the wake of news that the unemployment rate for November 1982 was 10.8 percent, the highest in 42 years, in "Twelve Million Out of Work,"* Newsweek, *December 13, 1982, p. 30.*

Despite conventional wisdom and political demagoguery, the social-security mess is a problem not so much for older people as it is for younger people. They are the ones who will pay increasingly higher taxes and find, in the autumn of their lives, a bankrupted, politically unacceptable system. Recent surveys demonstrate pessimism among our young. A 1982 Washington Post-ABC News poll found that 66 percent of those under 45 and 74 percent of those under 30 believe that social security won't be in existence when they retire. A 1981 New York Times-CBS News poll found that 75 percent between ages 25 and 34 doubted that they would receive the social-security benefits they have been promised. The same poll found that 75 percent of all Americans had lost confidence in social security.

*Walter E. Williams, professor of economics at George Mason University, commenting on the problems inherent in the Social Security system, in Williams, "A Skeptic's Challenge,"* Newsweek, *January 24, 1983, p. 26.*

White House officials quickly put to rest any speculation that Burford's March 8 resignation might signal a major change in EPA policies, painted by critics as "soft" on polluters. "There will be no vast departure," declared an aide.

Reagan made clear in a news conference March 11 that he would not retreat from his goals in the face of what he called "environmental extremism." Said the President, "I don't think they'll be happy until the White House looks like a bird's nest."

*Reporting the administration's reaction following Anne Burford's resignation as director of the Environmental Protection Agency on March 9, 1983, in "After Burford—What Next for EPA?"* U.S. News & World Report, *March 21, 1983, p. 25.*

If Congress had not acted, benefit checks would have been delayed, starting in July, then halted altogether. So precarious was the situation that the Old Age and Survivors Insurance Trust Fund, largest of Social Security's three funds, had to borrow 17.5 billion dollars in late 1982 to keep benefit checks flowing on schedule through June.

Now, the outlook is much brighter. Surpluses in Social Security's combined old-age and disability trust funds are scheduled to build up rapidly, reaching 88 billion dollars by the end of the decade. Prior to the rescue campaign, the system was facing a 56-billion-dollar deficit over the same period.

*Noting the hoped-for benefits of the Social Security Reform Act, passed by Congress on March 25, 1983, in "Social Security Rescue—What It Means to You,"* U.S. News & World Report, *April 4, 1983, p. 23.*

"The changes in this legislation will allow Social Security to age as gracefully as all of us hope to do ourselves, without becoming an overwhelming burden on generations still to come," the President declared.

Nearby stood the Speaker of the House, Thomas P. O'Neill Jr., who was enjoying one of his rare invitations from Mr. Reagan to a White House bill-signing ceremony.

"It shows, as the President said, the system does work," Mr. O'Neill said. "This is a happy day for America."

*President Reagan and House Speaker Tip O'Neill in rare agreement upon the signing of the Social Security Reform Act, April 20, 1983, reported in Clines, "Pension Changes Signed into Law,"* New York Times, *April 21, 1983, p. A-17.*

The reason I'm so controversial is that I stand for change. I had to confront those who wanted to let our parks deteriorate, who wanted us to be subject to blackmail by OPEC nations and who didn't believe in a strategic-minerals policy. It took confrontation to turn Congress around to change the direction of our resource program

When I was in college, it was the liberals who were bringing change, and we conservatives were branded as being the sticks-in-the-mud. Now I want change, and the liberals can't stand change.

*Secretary of the Interior James G. Watt defending his controversial actions, quoted in "When James Watt Speaks Out,"* U.S. News & World Report, *June 6, 1983, p. 55.*

The most somber note in this generally improving picture is that one group—black workers—has not shared at all in the recovery. Black unemployment exceeded 20 percent in June, just as it did last December, and fewer than half of black teen-agers seeking work could find it. General recovery will enable most Americans to adjust in some measure to the changing shape of the economy. But government intervention may be needed to make sure that no group of Americans is left behind.

*The* Washington Post *noting the failure of the economic recovery to improve lives in certain areas, in its editorial "Ten Percent, But Improving,"* Washington Post, *July 9, 1983, p. A-20.*

At my confirmation hearings in January 1981, I outlined the major changes we knew were needed in management of our natural resources if we were to restore America's greatness.

With your undaunted support, those changes have been put in place. We confronted the neglect and the problems. We gave purpose and direction to management of our nation's natural resources. The restoration of our national parks, refuges and public lands is well under way.

In fact, the Department of Interior lands are better managed under our stewardship than they were when we inherited the responsibility. Our actions to reduce the nation's dependency on foreign sources of energy and strategic materials are working. The balance is being restored.

. . . It is my view that my usefulness to you in this Administration has come to an end. A different type of leadership will best serve you and the nation.

*From James G. Watt's letter to President Reagan, October 9, 1983, resigning as secretary of the interior, reproduced in "Text of Resignation by Watt and Its Acceptance by Reagan," New York Times, October 10, 1983, p. D-10.*

Sometimes when we shop we don't realize how much inflation has dropped, because prices are still going up. But they're going up much more slowly than before. If food prices had kept rising as fast the last 2 years as the 2 years before we took office, a loaf of bread would cost 7 cents more than it does today, a half gallon of milk 18 cents more, a pound of hamburger 60 cents more, and a gallon of gas 97 cents more.

The prime interest rate has been cut nearly in half, so costs of business, mortgage, education, and car loans have dropped. The Federal income tax on a typical working family is $700 less than if our tax program had not been passed. With parents, students, entrepreneurs, workers, and consumers feeling more secure, opportunities for jobs are expanding. Our work force in September rose by nearly 400,000 to 101.9 million—the highest level in American history. And the trend will continue.

*President Reagan in a radio address, October 14, 1983, citing statistics that prove the improvement in U.S. quality of life. Available online. URL: http://www.reagan. utexas.edu/resource/speeches/1983/101583b.htm.*

## Terror and Trouble in the Middle East

The explosion was over in a flash, but the horror of it all deepened through the week. Day and night, rescue workers picked through the rubble, desperately looking for survivors. Cranes gingerly hoisted slabs of broken concrete up and away from the site, while bulldozers scraped away debris. A searcher somewhere inside the wreckage kept yelling through a bullhorn: "If anybody can hear me, please call for help." No one did. By Saturday, members of the rescue teams were still uncovering corpses buried under the avalanche of what was once the U.S. embassy. At one point, the rescuers pulled the body of a Marine out of the ruins and wrapped it in an American flag. As the figure was placed in a wait-

ing ambulance, a squad of Marines snapped to attention and saluted.

*Describing the carnage after a truck bomb destroyed the U.S. embassy in Beirut, Lebanon, on April 18, 1983, killing 63, in "The Horror, the Horror!" Time, May 2, 1983, p. 28.*

This tragedy, however awful, must not distract us from our search for peace in Lebanon and elsewhere. Your devotion to duty is known to all of us. Please let everyone know we will never give in to this cowardly type of incident. I am determined now more than ever that we do everything that is necessary to make Lebanon a free and safe country again.

*President Reagan in a telephone call to Ambassador Robert S. Dillon in Beirut, Lebanon, on April 20, 1983, following the embassy bombing there, quoted in "Reagan Says Blast Won't Deter Peace Efforts," New York Times, April 21, 1983, p. A-14.*

The president struck exactly the right note Saturday when he admitted that he could not joke at the White House correspondents' dinner, having come so recently from Andrews Air Force Base, where the bodies of those killed were brought home. His emotion was that of the leader of a nation that has suffered an outrage. But it was also the very personal anguish of a man who had touched and consoled the grieving survivors.

*From "Memorial," an editorial eulogizing those who were killed in the bombing of the U.S. embassy in Beirut, in Washington Post, April 26, 1983, p. A-18.*

It is not the United States' job to prevent a war in that part of the world. We have watched Israel, Lebanon and the Palestine Liberation Organization bring this mess about. As long as we haven't settled the question of where the PLO should live, we're going to have trouble.

If there is going to be a Middle East war in spite of every dollar we've spent and every effort that we've made, then let them have a war. I don't see it growing at this point to the extent that the Soviets could move in.

*Senator Barry Goldwater (R, Ariz.) arguing for withdrawing the U.S. Marines from peacekeeping forces in Lebanon, quoted in "Pull U.S. Marines Out of Lebanon?" U.S. News & World Report, September 19, 1983, p. 29.*

I know there are no words that can express our sorrow and grief for the loss of those splendid young men and the injury to so many others. I know there are no words also that can ease the burden of grief for the families of those young men.

Likewise, there are no words to properly express our outrage and I think the outrage of all Americans at the despicable act following as it does on the one perpetrated several months ago in the spring that took the lives of scores of people at our Embassy in that same city, Beirut.

But I think we should all recognize that these deeds make so evident the bestial nature of those who would assume power if they could have their way and drive us out of that area; that we must be more determined than ever that they cannot take over that vital and strategic area of the earth, or for that matter, any part of the earth.

*President Reagan's remarks to the Associated Press, October 23, 1983, on the destruction of a U.S. Marines barracks in Beirut that day, reproduced in "Reagan's Remarks on Attack,"* New York Times, *October 24, 1983, p. A-8.*

All across the nation on Sunday night, Marine Corps officers walked up to homes and apartments to inform Americans that their sons or brothers or fathers or husbands had died under the twisted, smoking debris in Beirut. It was the Marine way: personal notification, not an anonymous telegram or faceless phone call. Some of the bodies were already headed home; others still lay under tons of metal and concrete as the search team worked around the clock. It would be days before America could fully count its dead and wounded.

*Reporting the devastation caused by the suicide bombing that destroyed a U.S. Marines barracks in Beirut on October 23, 1983, in "Carnage in Lebanon,"* Time, *October 31, 1983, p. 14.*

The hard fact of the matter is that what happens in the Middle East is of vital importance to the United States. What happened in Lebanon, therefore, is vital to us. Withdrawing our Marines and turning our back on Lebanon would be an easy and quick solution for the problems and dangers that now face us. But it will accomplish nothing if it leads us into more difficulty with even more severe dangers in the future.

*Senator Nancy Landon Kassebaum (R, Kans.) supporting the Reagan administration policy of keeping U.S. Marine troops in Lebanon, in Kassebaum, "Hold Firm on Lebanon,"* New York Times, *October 26, 1983, p. A-27.*

## Fighting the Cold War

There are indeed new opportunities for peace. The 1980s may well give us a chance to make major progress with the Soviets on arms control, economic relations and, ultimately, even on developing some ground rules for international conduct. But Yuri Andropov's fondness for American novels and Western fantasies about intrigues between hawks and doves in the Kremlin are not the sources of these opportunities. The arms race imposes dangerous uncertainties and staggering financial burdens on both parties, but especially on the Soviet Union. The recession in the east and economic stagnation in the communist world may compel both of us to re-evaluate our high levels of military spending as well as to seek mutually beneficial economic cooperation. And the increasing complexity of a world filled with regional tensions reminds both sides of the necessity of cooperation, lest a minor crisis explode into a major one.

*Henry Kissinger, former National Security Advisor and secretary of state, assessing the future of cold war relations following the succession of Yuri Andropov to the Soviet leadership, quoted in "How to Deal with Moscow,"* Newsweek, *November 29, 1982, p. 30.*

Dear Mr. Andropov,

My name is Samantha Smith. I am ten years old.

Congratulations on your new job. I have been worrying about Russia and the United States getting into a nuclear war. Are you going to vote to have a war or not? If you aren't please tell me how you are going to help to not have a war. This question you do not have to answer, but I would like to know why you want to conquer the world or at least our country. God made the world for us to live together in peace and not to fight.

Sincerely,
Samantha Smith
*Full text of the letter written by Maine schoolgirl Samantha Smith to Soviet leader Yuri Andropov in December 1982. Available online, in Carkin, "Looking Back: Samantha Smith, the Girl Who Went to the Soviet Union." URL: http://www.smilkwash. wednet.edu/Samantha_Smith.htm.*

As so often in Soviet-American relations, the superpowers are playing a form of poker. The U.S. is trying to use the threat of new missiles in Europe as a bargaining chip to force the Soviets to discard the most powerful and modern of their intermediate-range missiles already in place. The prospective U.S. arsenal includes 108 Pershing IIs, all bound for West Germany, to replace the shorter-range Pershing Is that have been there since 1969, plus 464 Tomahawk ground-launched cruise missiles (GLCMs) that are earmarked for Britain, Belgium, Italy and The Netherlands as well as West Germany. The Pershing IIs would arc up to the edge of space and unleash earth-penetrating warheads that can destroy concrete-reinforced bunkers 100 ft. underground; the slow but elusive cruise missiles home in on their targets with pinpoint accuracy.

*A special report analyzing the stakes in nuclear arms talks with the Soviet Union, in "Playing Nuclear Poker," Time, January 31, 1983, p. 11.*

So, in your discussions of the nuclear freeze proposals, I urge you to beware the temptation of pride—the temptation of blithely declaring yourselves above it all and label both sides equally at fault, to ignore the facts of history and the aggressive impulses of an evil empire, to simply call the arms race a giant misunderstanding and thereby remove yourself from the struggle between right and wrong and good and evil.

I ask you to resist the attempts of those who would have you withhold your support for our efforts, this administration's efforts, to keep America strong and free, while we negotiate real and verifiable reductions in the world's nuclear arsenals and one day, with God's help, their total elimination.

*President Reagan addressing the National Association of Evangelicals on March 8, 1983, on the need to take a strong stance against the Soviet Union; referred to as his "evil empire" speech. Available online. URL: http://www.reagan.utexas.edu/resource/speeches/1982/112282b.htm.*

Dear Samantha,

I received your letter, which is like many others that have reached me recently from your country and from other countries around the world.

It seems to me—I can tell by your letter—that you are a courageous and honest girl, resembling Becky, the friend of Tom Sawyer in the famous book of your compatriot Mark Twain. This book is well known and loved in our country by all boys and girls.

. . . . .

We want peace—there is something that we are occupied with: growing wheat, building and invent-

ing, writing books and flying into space. We want peace for ourselves and for all peoples of the planet. For our children and for you, Samantha.

I invite you, if your parents will let you, to come to our country, the best time being this summer. You will find out about our country, meet with your contemporaries, visit an international children's camp—"Artek"—on the sea. And see for yourself: in the Soviet Union—everyone is for peace and friendship among peoples.

*From the April 1983 response of Yuri Andropov to Samantha Smith. Available online, in Carkin, "Looking Back: Samantha Smith, the Girl Who Went to the Soviet Union." URL: http://www.smilkwash. wednet.edu/Samantha_Smith.htm.*

Why Samantha and not any of the other Americans who have written letters to Andropov? The answer: Letters are carefully screened, and her opposition to nuclear war fitted into the Kremlin's war of words with the Reagan administration.

*Examining why Maine schoolgirl Samantha Smith was invited by Soviet leader Yuri Andropov to visit the USSR, in "Samantha Smith—Pawn in Propaganda War," U.S. News & World Report, July 18, 1983, p. 27.*

The Soviet deed has been the subject of a U.N. debate. For the Kremlin that was an ordeal akin to being bombarded with marshmallows. Thank God it is not December or some dunce would suggest dimming the national Christmas tree. The state of Ohio, which has a better foreign policy than the United States, has removed Russian vodka from state-run liquor stores. Perhaps the 269 murders will complicate the process of subordinating foreign policy to presidential politics. Perhaps it will now be harder for the president to sally off to an election-year summit and sign an arms-control agreement ruined by American eagerness. But summits and agreements have no noticeable influence on the behavior of the Soviet rainmakers—the "yellow rain" rainmakers.

*Columnist George Will expressing his sardonic view of the Soviet downing of KAL 007 on September 1, 1983, in Will, "Needed: A Policy of Punishment," Newsweek, September 12, 1983, p. 32.*

Obviously you are tempted to think about vengeance, but there is no way you can avenge such a thing. It is very difficult to find anything you can do that matches the enormity of what they have done . . . you can find that there is a great limit on what you can do. You can do some things for short-term public relations advantage and show your own feelings about this. But what you have to look for is what you can do, first of all, to get restitution for the families of the victims, and what you can do to see that this never happens again.

*Ronald Reagan describing his reaction to the Soviet shooting of KAL 007, in "An Interview with President Reagan,"* Time, *September 19, 1983, p. 21.*

First: Since by its actions the United States has torpedoed the possibility of reaching a mutually acceptable accord at the talks on questions of limiting nuclear arms in Europe and their continuation in these conditions would only serve as a cover for the actions of the United States and a number of other NATO countries directed at undermining European and international security, the Soviet Union considers its further participation in these talks impossible.

*From Soviet leader Yuri Andropov's November 24, 1983, announcement regarding the deployment of missiles in Europe and the USSR's decision to pull out of the START talks, quoted in "Text of Andropov's Statement on Missile Dispute,"* New York Times, *November 25, 1983, p. A-18.*

## Fear and Rage

Tom Biscotto seemed to have it all. He owned an apartment building and lived in a beautifully restored Victorian home. He loved his job as a stage manager for the prestigious Goodman Theatre and had many friends in Chicago's gay community. His life was full, his future bright. Today Biscotto, 35, doesn't know if he has a future at all. Seven months ago he developed AIDS-related Kaposi's sarcoma. The chemotherapy has caused most of his thick, brown hair to fall out; chronic infections have so weakened him that at times stairs have been as difficult to climb as mountains. But the tall, soft-spoken Biscotto is not giving up. From the moment he was diagnosed, he recalls, "I got mad. I made plans, contacted my lawyer and arranged for a will. Then I got on with fighting this thing."

*Looking at the fading life of an AIDS victim, in "The AIDS Epidemic: The Search for a Cure,"* Newsweek, *April 18, 1983, p. 76.*

The staggering increase in AIDS cases comes at a time when the stereotypes about who gets the disease have broken down. Early research found that AIDS patients tended to come from fast-lane gays who engaged in heavy drug use and esoteric sexual practices. It appears now, however, that AIDS probably was just striking the most debilitated first. The series of lethal infections associated with AIDS now is striking randomly within the gay population, and it appears that just one contact with an infected person could transmit the disease.

"It's not retribution for a profligate lifestyle—it's more like a lottery," said one prominent gay doctor privately. "The more tickets you buy, the more chances you have to get the prize, which in this case is death."

*Reporter Randy Shilts describing the increase in public information about AIDS and its effects on homosexuals, in Shilts, "How AIDS Is Changing Gay Lifestyles,"* San Francisco Chronicle, *May 2, 1983, p. 5.*

Fighting the fear of AIDS, it seems, is as important as fighting the disease itself. . . . It is a delicate balancing act, raising the level of concern for the disease on the one hand, while reducing the level of panic on the other.

*From a June 20, 1983, ABC news broadcast, quoted by Timothy E. Cook and David Colby, "The Mass-Mediated Epidemic: The Politics of AIDS on the Nightly Network News," in Fee,* AIDS: The Making of a Chronic Disease *(1992), p. 99.*

In Manhattan last week a WABC-TV crew refused to enter the Gay Men's Health Crisis office to cover a story on AIDS. Two back-up crews also balked at going in. Said one of the technicians: "Look, nobody knows anything about AIDS. What makes them so cocksure I'm not going to get it from a sweaty palm?" One of the homosexuals in the office had a question of his own: "Do you understand now that we're treated like lepers?"

*Confronting the fears and prejudices of the AIDS crisis, in "The Real Epidemic: Fear and Despair,"* Time, *July 4, 1983, p. 56.*

If the Reagan administration does not put its full weight against this, what is now a gay plague in this country, I feel that a year from now, President Ronald Reagan, personally, will be blamed for allowing this awful disease to break out among the innocent American public.

*Reverend Jerry Falwell of the Moral Majority offering his viewpoint of the AIDS crisis on an ABC television program, "AIDS: The Anatomy of a Crisis," broadcast in early July 1983, quoted in Shilts,* And the Band Played On *(1987), p. 347.*

As the alarm over AIDS spreads, blood banks are screening potential donors more rigorously. At Red Cross centers, volunteers are given a card that explains the disease and asks them to leave if they might be at high risk of developing AIDS or other blood-borne diseases such as hepatitis, malaria and syphilis. Nurses are also encouraged to question donors and turn down any who seem risky. In New York, 2 to 4 percent of donors are being rejected.

*Reporting the precautions being taken in blood donations as the AIDS epidemic worsens, in "As AIDS Scare Hits Nation's Blood Supply,"* U.S. News & World Report, *July 25, 1983, p. 72.*

Despair is what I hear in Gary's voice tonight. . . . He has just reason for despair. He fell down three times today when his legs simply gave out on him. He had an infection in one eye and now the same infection in the other eye.

He went to the dentist for a routine checkup and learned he has an infection and may well need a root canal. And he has a new infection of the prostate for which his doctor told him beating off may alleviate the pressure and pain. Masturbation is a distant memory for him and holds no appeal.

. . . Horribly, I recognize that dark corner in my mind that wishes it were all over and I could talk about Gary and his illnesses in the past tense.

My mind plays that game. Sometimes I think it is all over. Gary is dead. Back in the eighties, I had a best friend and former lover, a wonderful man whom I loved very deeply, and he suffered and he died in that terrible epidemic that hit the gay community nationally, the disease we hardly remember now. It was called AIDS.

*Matt Krieger, a San Francisco homosexual, writing in his diary on September 22, 1983, about a friend dying of AIDS, quoted in Shilts,* And the Band Played On *(1987), p. 373. (Gary Walsh died on February 21, 1984.)*

On the last working day of 1983, the statistician gave Lawrence the results. Lawrence was horrified. According to the analysis, the mean incubation period for the disease was 5.5 years. It appeared that some cases would take more than 11 years to incubate, based on the mathematical projections, although some people would come down with AIDS in as little as six months.

. . . He had believed that tens of thousands would die in the AIDS epidemic. This long incubation period, however, meant that the genetic machinations of the still-unknown virus had permitted it to sleep for years before anyone knew it existed, before anyone knew it was spreading. It just hadn't shown up yet in a dramatic way because of the long incubation. The 3,000 AIDS cases now reported marked the barest beginning of the havoc the epidemic would bring. The future these projections promised was going to be worse, far worse, then anyone had ever imagined.

*Dr. Dale Lawrence of the Centers for Disease Control receiving some data with frightening implications on December 30, 1983, in Shilts,* And the Band Played On *(1987), p. 402.*

## Equal and Unequal Rights

Cutbacks in federal aid have renewed complaints that the government isn't giving the nation's black, Hispanic and other minority businesses enough help. Such claims may soon be muted by a new White House plan to do 22 billion dollars' worth of federal business with minorities over the next three years.

That will be welcome news because minority businesses in general are a "depressed industry," says James H. Lowry, a Chicago consultant who studied such firms for the Commerce Department. Others note that minority-owned companies have had a tougher time than most small businesses in getting funds and that management skills often are sorely lacking. By one estimate, 85 percent of black firms eventually fail.

*Examining the problems faced by African-American business owners in "Blacks' Growing Toehold in Business,"* U.S. News & World Report, *November 22, 1982, p. 84.*

Sally's ride—the word play is irresistible—is, however, only one sign of a major change in what can no longer properly be called the U.S. manned space program. In fact, the elite circle has become all but a melting pot.

Among its 78 members, there are now four blacks, two Jews and one naturalized American who happens to be part Chinese. Two Europeans, a German and a Dutchman, are training for a shuttle flight later this year. But NASA seems to feel no particular guilt about its past neglect.

*Looking at the integration of NASA's astronaut corps as Sally K. Ride prepares to become the first American woman in space, in "Sally's Joy Ride into the Sky,"* Time, *June 13, 1983, p. 56.*

The Commission on Civil Rights was established as the only independent and bipartisan agency monitoring civil rights in this country. In its 26-year history, almost without exception, both Republican and Democratic presidents have respected the independence of the commission. Thus, this president is in a unique position of being the only president in the history of the commission to attempt to replace five of the six commissioners.

… What we will not abide is the taking of an independent and respected voice for civil rights and strapping it down to mold the preferences of any single administration.

*Julian C. Dixon, chairman of the Congressional Black Caucus, criticizing President Reagan's firing of three members of the Civil Rights Commission, in a letter to the editor,* Washington Post, *June 19, 1983, p. B-6.*

… Equal political rights and abortion are only two issues on which Mr. Reagan's stands have cost him support among women—and women are scarcely united on those. His economic program that discriminates against the working poor and the elderly, his unrelenting emphasis on expanding the military and building up nuclear weaponry and his dangerous Cold War approach to the Soviet Union also are costing him with women. He cannot easily change policy on so broad a front.

*From "President and Gender Gap," an editorial in the* St. Louis Post-Dispatch, *July 13, 1983, quoted in Boyer,* Reagan as President *(1990), p. 158.*

It is critical for those who have been historical victims of negative action to have protection under the law—affirmative action to offset racial and sexual denials.

Workers, black and white, need some kind of international affirmative action to protect them from unfair competition with unorganized or slave labor abroad and unfair competition with robots at home. It is really unfortunate for them to be fighting against each other in the schoolyard when they should be fighting *with* each other at the shipyard.

*Reverend Jesse Jackson positing the need to make affirmative action a presidential campaign issue, quoted in "Is the U.S. Ready for a Black President?"* U.S. News & World Report, *July 25, 1983, p. 21.*

King's legacy hangs over Jackson, as it does over the rest of the nation. The dream that he spoke of 20 years ago, a century after the Emancipation Proclamation, is still a dream deferred. What was then a civil rights movement has become a political movement, but the goal is still the same: an equal place for black Americans. First as a King lieutenant, now as leader in his own right, Jesse Jackson has been part of both movements. His continued presence on the public stage is a reminder that the nation's racial dilemma is far from solved. And the stark fact that he, or any other black, cannot be elected President in 1984 is, understandably to Jackson, perhaps the most compelling reason for him to run.

*Analyzing the likely reasons that Jesse Jackson will run for president in 1984, in "Seeking Votes and Clout,"* Time, *August 22, 1983, p. 31.*

Observers say many Americans have grown tired of hearing about troubles of the underprivileged—"compassion fatigue," some call it—and are preoccupied with their own economic problems.

"If you're helping a guy with a broken leg and you break your own arm, you start concentrating on your arm," says Dennis Dickerson, an Afro-American-history professor at Williams College in Massachusetts.

In the '60s, discrimination meant police dogs and cattle prods. Now, civil-rights leaders note, it is far more subtle. In politics, for example, they say blacks are discriminated against through gerrymandering, multi-member districts and other tactics that dilute minority voting strength.

*Examining changes in the fight for civil rights, in "King's Dream: How It Stands 20 Years Later,"* U.S. News & World Report, *August 29, 1983, p. 48.*

As charges and denials flew between the Reagan and feminist camps, the president installed his daughter Maureen as his adviser on women's issues.

"My father came to me and said, 'I seem to have this problem, and I don't think I'm such a bad guy,' "

Maureen Reagan explained. She added, however, that it would take a speedup in action to convince many women that the President really is trying to help them.

*Commenting on Ronald Reagan's problems with women's rights groups, in Kittle and Avery, "Women's Issues—And the Reagan Record,"* U.S. News & World Report, *September 5, 1983, p. 34.*

## Fads and Phenomena

There are now more than 100,000 computers in U.S. schools, compared with 52,000 only 18 months ago. This is roughly one for every 400 pupils. The richer and more progressive states do better. Minnesota leads with one computer for every 50 children and a locally produced collection of 700 software programs. To spread this development more evenly and open new doors for business, Apple has offered to donate one computer to every public school in the U.S.—a total of 80,000 computers worth $200 million retail—if Washington will authorize a 25% tax write-off (as is done for donations of scientific equipment to colleges). Congress has so far failed to approve the idea, but California has agreed to a similar proposal.

Many Americans concerned about the erosion of the schools put faith in the computer as a possible savior of their children's education, at school and at home. . . .

*Time magazine explaining one of the reasons its editors named the computer "Machine of the Year" for 1982, in "The Computer Moves In,"* Time, *January 3, 1983, p. 23.*

Jackson's appeal is so wide, however, that white publications and radio stations that normally avoid "black music" seem willing to pretend he isn't black after all. On one level, that's admirable, in that color distinctions are often best avoided altogether. But Jackson *is* black, and while he sings a duet here with Paul McCartney, enlists Eddie Van Halen for a guitar solo and observes no color exclusivity in his choice of backup musicians, he still works honorably within the context of contemporary black popular music at its fervent, eclectic best.

*Journalist John Rockwell reviewing Michael Jackson's album* Thriller *and also extolling Jackson himself, in Rockwell, "A 'Thriller' from Jackson,"* San Francisco Chronicle, *January 16, 1983, Review sect., p. 15.*

No work of popular art can tap the money machine so deftly without touching a national pulse or nerve. *M★A★S★H,* a Viet Nam parable that hit the airwaves three months before the Christmas bombing of Hanoi, surely did so. Like the surgeons whose no-sweat heroism it celebrated, the series began by operating on the wounded American body politic with skill and daring good humor. For half an hour each week, hawk and dove could sit together in front of the TV set and agree war is an existential hell to which some pretty fine people had been unfairly assigned; now they were doing their best to do good and get out. As the Viet Nam War staggered to a close and *M★A★S★H* generated the momentum any TV series needs to sustain its quality after the first few seasons, the show revealed itself as a gritty romance about the finest American instincts. Here were gruff pragmatism, technical ingenuity, grace under pressure, the saving perspective of wit. The men and women of 4077 MASH could be seen as us at our worst hour, finding the best part of ourselves.

*Paying tribute to the long-running series* M★A★S★H, *which broadcast its final episode on February 28, 1983, in "M★A★S★H, You Were a Smash,"* Time, *February 28, 1983, p. 65.*

The game's appeal is far less obscure than most of the questions. It derives from the pleasure of playing against people armed not with joysticks but with arsenals of minutiae. Notes John Nason, vice president of marketing at Selchow & Righter: "The pendulum's swinging back from video games. With a video game you sit alone in a corner. Playing a board game there is interaction—moaning, groaning, laughter."

*Looking at the latest popular craze, the board game* Trivial Pursuit, *in "Let's Get Trivial,"* Time, *October 24, 1983, p. 88.*

No one went farther for a Cabbage Patch doll than Kansas City postman Edward Pennington who, despairing of finding one in the Western Hemisphere, flew to London to get one for his five-year-old daughter. His mission made eminent sense compared with that of a dozen or so Wisconsites who drove through the cold to Milwaukee County Stadium in the expectation that 2,000 dolls would drop out of the sky: a local announcer had reported, as a lark, that a B-29 bomber would be making the airborne delivery and that customers should bring catcher's mitts and credit cards to be photographed from the air.

*Describing some of the insanity suffered by parents trying to acquire Cabbage Patch Kids, in "Oh, You Beautiful Dolls!" Newsweek, December 12, 1983, p. 78.*

A San Francisco psychologist—a specialist in counseling adopted children—told The Chronicle the Cabbage Patch adoptees create "a lot of confusion among young children." The psychologist, Stefan Greene, cautioned, "It's important that adopted children not feel they were born in a cabbage patch or that they are for sale."

And the executive director of the JACKIE adoption agency is worried that the fake adoption papers "might tell a child, You come out of the cabbage patch; your parents bought you in a store.' "

As the adoptive father of two daughters, I wonder whether these experts aren't simply creating an issue where none existed and furthering the already bloated commercial hype. What, after all, is a fad without "worried psychologists"?

*Columnist Peter Y. Sussman reflecting on the psychological aspects of the Cabbage Patch Kids craze, in Sussman, "Where I Bought My Kids," San Francisco Chronicle, Sunday Punch, December 18, 1983, p. 2.*

At its core, rock video is the kind of cultural shotgun wedding that delights the heart of any aging McLuhanist: rock, radio, movies, music, video, new technologies and new marketing tilting the popular culture onto an angle so it can, if so ordained, slip off onto a whole new course. "The musician in me really resents having to interpret my music into something visual," says Billy Joel. "But the thing that outweighs all of that is that video is a form of communication. Why not use every means of communication available?"

*Examining the explosion of rock videos, in "Sing a Song of Seeing," Time, December 26, 1983, p. 56.*

## The Pioneer Spirit

What Clark will never escape is the attention that comes from being part of medical history. The day-to-day variations in his cardiac output are recorded on a small computer, which staff members can consult at any time. Clark's control unit monitors the action of the Jarvik-7, which can then be adjusted by

twirling a dial. The mechanical heart has actually played a major role in Clark's progress. The higher output of blood it provided right after it was installed cleared away the fluid that had accumulated in Clark's lungs. And unlike a natural heart, the new one doesn't require an oxygen supply of its own, which has helped Clark through the crises that have occurred during his recovery period.

*Charting the progress and courage of Barney Clark, in "Taking Heart from Dr. Clark," Newsweek, February 28, 1983, pp. 73–74.*

Well, I would tell them that it's worth it if the alternative is they either die or they have it done.

*Dr. Barney Clark, first recipient of an artificial heart, in an interview televised on March 2, 1983, responding to a question about what advice he would give to other potential artificial-heart recipients; quoted in Mathews, "Barney Clark in TV Debut, Taped, but Live," Washington Post, March 3, 1983, p. A-2.*

No one could doubt the wisdom of the choice. The dentist from Des Moines, Washington, may have been in failing health, but it was clear from the moment he set foot in the University of Utah Medical Center that Barney Clark was a dauntless spirit. "A rugged old Rocky Mountain sagebrush. Tough. Eager for life." That was how Dr. Chase Peterson, a university vice president, described the man who was to make medical history. . . . Those same traits enabled Clark to endure the arduous operation on Dec. 1 and to struggle for 112 days through the perilous and uncharted territory of life with a plastic heart.

*Eulogizing artificial-heart pioneer Barney Clark, in "Death of a Gallant Pioneer," Time, April 4, 1983, p. 62.*

Dr. Musgrave, the first out, all but swung himself over the side of the spaceship, doing a handstand on the rail, restrained by his tether. At times, television showed the Earth spinning 176 miles below them.

"It's so bright out here," Dr. Musgrave said.

"Mr. Peterson followed a minute later. Each was tethered to slide wires running the length of the cargo bay. . . .

At one point, as Dr. Musgrave was looking around in the front of the bay, Mission Control joked, "While you're looking under the hood, Story, why don't you check the oil?"

Dr. Musgrave replied: "I don't see any."

"That's good," said Mission Control.

*Astronauts Story Musgrave and Don Peterson carrying out the first shuttle space walk from* Challenger, *April 7, 1983, reported in John Noble Wilford, "Astronauts Walk Outside Shuttle,"* New York Times, *April 8, 1983, p. A-20.*

I did not come to NASA to make history. It's important to me that people don't think I was picked for the flight because I am a woman and it's time for NASA to send one.

*Sally K. Ride on her role as the first American woman in space, quoted in "Sally Ride: Ready for Liftoff,"* Newsweek, *June 13, 1983, p. 36.*

The epochal departure, determined by faint signals from Pioneer 10 picked up by NASA's tracking antennas, occurred early this week when Pioneer crossed the orbit of Neptune, currently the outermost planet. At that moment, it was 2,813,685,909 miles from the sun and moving at a brisk 30,558 m.p.h.

The event, said Astronomer Carl Sagan, "is filled with symbolism. Lots of things have entered the solar system during its 5 billion-year history—comets, asteroids, every sort of cosmic debris. This is the first time, however, that something associated with life and intelligence has left it."

*Reporting a major event in U.S. space exploration,* Pioneer 10*'s departure from the solar system on June 13, 1983, in "Hurtling through the Void,"* Time, *June 20, 1983, p. 68.*

Married and the father of two teenage sons, Bluford is one of four blacks in the astronaut program. Says he: "The four of us never talk about my going first. We all recognize that somebody's going to play this role, just like one of the women had to be first. I'm just looking forward to flying."

*Looking at Lieutenant Colonel Guion (Guy) Bluford, Jr., the first African-American astronaut to fly in space on* Challenger*'s third mission (August 30–September 5, 1983), in "NASA Readies a Nighttime Dazzler,"* Time, *August 29, 1983, p. 62.*

## The Grenada Invasion

Today at about 5:00 A.M. Eastern Daylight Time, approximately 1,900 United States Army and United States Marine Corps personnel began landing in Grenada. They were supported by elements of the United States Navy and the United States Air Force. Member States of the OECS along with Jamaica and Barbados are providing approximately 300 personnel. This deployment of United States Armed Forces is being undertaken pursuant to my constitutional authority with respect to the conduct of foreign relations and as Commander-in-Chief of the United States Armed Forces.

*President Reagan in a letter to the Speaker of the House and president pro tempore of the Senate, October 25, 1983, advising Congress of his decision to invade Grenada that day. Available online. URL: http://www.reagan.utexas.edu/resource/speeches/1983/102583e.htm.*

Awakened by the explosions, the American students at the True Blue campus of St. George's University School of Medicine did not know who was shooting at whom. "There was antiaircraft fire coming from the Cubans around the airport," said Harold Harvey, 22, of Beckley, W. Va. "Then I saw the paratroopers jumping. It was really thrilling to see, kind of like an old John Wayne movie, but I knew people were going to get killed." Student Stephen Renae of Point Pleasant, N.J., saw "planes diving and strafing at ground targets we couldn't see. The worst thing was not knowing where the planes were from."

*American medical students on Grenada describing the confusion of the U.S. invasion of the island on October 25, 1983, in "D-Day in Grenada,"* Time, *November 7, 1983, p. 23.*

. . . [T]he medical students were grateful for the rescue. In fact, they were almost delirious with joy. When that first planeload returned to the air force base at Charleston, South Carolina, on October 26 and the first student off the plane knelt and kissed the ground and they all cheered their country and thanked the U.S. military for rescuing them from a dangerous and chaotic situation, the public relations problem was solved right there. There was no way that all the negative reporting and complaining by the press about being kept off the island could overcome the power of that television picture. My staff and I were watching when the first students arrived in Charleston, and when we saw how happy they were to be home, we started cheering and pounding the table. "That's it! We won!" I shouted.

*Presidential spokesman Larry Speakes commenting on the public relations triumph as American students rescued from Grenada returned home on October 26, 1983, in Speakes,* Speaking Out *(1988), pp. 159–160.*

Two hours ago we released the first photos from Grenada. They included pictures of a warehouse of military equipment—one of three we've uncovered so far. This warehouse contained weapons and ammunition stacked almost to the ceiling, enough to supply thousands of terrorists. Grenada, we were told, was a friendly island paradise for tourism. Well, it wasn't. It was a Soviet-Cuban colony, being readied as a major military bastion to export terror and undermine democracy. We got there just in time.

*President Reagan in a televised address to the nation, October 27, 1983, justifying the U.S. invasion of Grenada two days earlier. Available online. URL: http://www.reagan.utexas.edu/resource/speeches/ 1983/102783b.htm.*

The Reagan formulation has placed America in the immoral position of taking it upon itself to define democracy abroad—and to act on it if we wish. This is uncomfortably reminiscent of the Breshnev Doctrine in Czechoslovakia, where the Soviet-led Warsaw Pact forces struck to impose "internal order," as it is of the Soviet invasion of Afghanistan and the crackdown in Poland.

Obviously, the United States has strategic interests to defend. But, just as importantly, it must defend its moral high ground. We cannot pretend that we sacrificed lives to defend democracy in Grenada . . . if we remain untroubled, for example, by the Chilean military regime's rejection of democracy and elections after a decade of dictatorship. Then, too, we maintain a double standard toward South Korea and the Philippines.

Our nation should instantly proscribe the new "Reagan Doctrine."

*Foreign-affairs expert Tad Szulc criticizing the military intervention in Grenada, in Szulc, "Making the World 'Safe' for Hypocrisy,"* New York Times, *October 28, 1983, p. A-27.*

President and Mrs. Reagan attend a November 4 memorial service in Camp Lejeune, North Carolina, for servicemen killed in the Beirut marine barracks bombing and in the Grenada military operation. *(Courtesy Ronald Reagan Library)*

If you are going to pronounce a new law that "wherever there is communism imposed against the will of the people then the U.S. shall enter," then we are going to have really terrible wars in the world.

*British prime minister Margaret Thatcher expressing her displeasure with the U.S. invasion of Grenada during a phone-in radio program on the BBC World Service, October 30, 1983, quoted in Beck,* The Grenada Invasion *(1993), p. 2.*

We believe that the use of force by the task force was lawful under international law and the UN Charter, because it was undertaken to protect American nationals from a clear and present danger, because it was a legitimate exercise of regional collective security, because it was carried out with concern for lawful procedures and carried out in the service of values of the charter, including the restoration of the rule of law, self-determination, sovereignty, democracy, respect for human rights of the people of Grenada.

*U.S. ambassador to the United Nations Jeane Kirkpatrick justifying the U.S. invasion of Grenada in a statement to the UN General Assembly on November 2, 1983, quoted in Beck,* The Grenada Invasion *(1993), p. 61.*

# 4

# "Morning in America"
## January–December 1984

When, on November 3, 1983, the Reverend Jesse Jackson formally announced his candidacy for the 1984 Democratic presidential nomination, he entered a crowded field. President Reagan's approval rating had waned steadily over that year, and many Democrats had boarded the campaign bandwagon early. The first to announce his intention to run was California senator Alan Cranston on February 2, 1983. He was followed by Colorado senator Gary Hart (February 17); Walter "Fritz" Mondale, the former vice president (February 21); Reubin Askew, the former governor of Florida (February 23); South Carolina senator Ernest "Fritz" Hollings (April 18); Ohio senator John Glenn (April 21); and former senator George McGovern of South Dakota (September 13). Then came Jackson—the first African American to be a serious contender for the nomination of a major political party.[1]

Just a month after Jackson announced his candidacy, two American planes were shot down near Beirut, Lebanon. An airman on one of them, Lieutenant Robert O. Goodman, Jr., was captured by Syrian troops, and by late December no progress had been made in freeing him. On his own initiative, Jackson contacted Syrian officials to request the release of Goodman, an African American; in response, he was invited to Syria to negotiate in person. The Reagan administration disapproved of the trip, but Jackson flew to Syria anyway and met President Hafez al-Assad. On January 3, al-Assad ordered Goodman's release, and the airman was turned over to Jackson.

When Jackson and Goodman arrived back in the United States on January 4, the nation was jubilant. President Reagan joined in the celebration, meeting the two men at a White House ceremony—"You can't quarrel with success," he said of Jackson—and sending a letter to al-Assad, thanking him. Unsurprisingly, Jackson joined the front-runners for the Democratic presidential nomination, although also unsurprisingly, critics were quick to accuse him of using Goodman for his own political gain.

Whatever his motives, Jackson's successful mission had provided an exhilarating start to the election year.

## INTERESTING TIMES FOR AMERICAN BUSINESS

Another important event took place a few days before Jesse Jackson's triumphant return from Syria. On January 1 AT&T's monopoly on telecommunications ended with the formal divestiture of 22 of its 24 Bell operating companies (that is, Illinois Bell Telephone Co., Northwestern Bell, and so on), which provided local exchange services throughout the country. Other companies were now free to break into the industry that AT&T (American Telephone & Telegraph Co.) had dominated for most of the century.

The divestiture had been a long time coming. The federal government had attempted to check AT&T's monopolistic practices several times since 1913, but matters started to come to a head in 1968, when the Federal Communications Commission (FCC) authorized other businesses to attach their telephones and equipment to the Bell network. The following year the fledgling Microwave Communications Inc. (later MCI) won FCC approval to build a microwave long-distance telephone system between St. Louis and Chicago. MCI and other carriers, however, were limited to providing private-line services, still using Bell network lines. In 1974 the Justice Department filed a lawsuit charging AT&T with anticompetitive behavior, which the company denied, and sought divestiture of its Western Electric division as well as "some or all of the Bell Operating Companies."

Legal haggling resulted in numerous delays in the suit against AT&T, and it was not until January 15, 1981, that the trial finally began. The presentations of evidence, filing of motions, and out-of-court negotiating took almost a year before the Justice Department reached an agreement with AT&T. On January 8, 1982, the communications giant formally agreed to relinquish its 22 wholly owned Bell operating companies as of January 1, 1984; in return, the Justice Department would lift a 1956 ruling that had forbidden AT&T from entering the computer market.

On the eve of divestiture, seven regional holding companies (affectionately known as Baby Bells) were incorporated. These companies, such as Bell Atlantic Corp. (later Verizon Communications Inc.) and Southwestern Bell Corp. (renamed SBC Communications Inc. in 1995), became the new parents of the 22 Bell operating companies that provided local services, while AT&T continued to provide long-distance services as well as equipment manufacture and sales. As soon as the divestiture took place, MCI introduced a virtual private-line service. Later in the year, Bell Atlantic Corp. began to provide equal-access service that allowed telephone subscribers to dial up MCI and other long-distance service providers using its lines. Other equal-access services soon followed around the country.

With competition in telecommunications now established, the way was clear for MCI, Sprint Corp., and other competitors to grab shares of the market from AT&T. The divested Baby Bells proved formidable competitors themselves, in some cases merging to form larger, more powerful companies after the signing of the Telecommunications Act of 1996. The financial effect of the breakup on AT&T was devastating, and only 373,000 employees remained of the 1 million plus that it had once employed. As a monopolist, the company had to work within government-imposed regulations; with open, customer-driven competition, there were adjustments to make. Inevitably, AT&T's market share fell, from more than 90 percent in 1984 to about 50 percent by 1996, and its incursion into the personal computer market was short-lived. Nevertheless, the corporation remained a force in telecommunications for almost two decades.

While AT&T failed to avoid federal antitrust litigation, another business giant did. In 1969 the Department of Justice had filed suit against IBM, claiming it was attempting to monopolize the market for business computers by blocking other companies from making software and peripherals for its System/360. These same charges were being pursued by the European Economic Commission (EEC). Although the Reagan administration dropped the Justice Department's suit in 1982, the EEC pursued its case, and in 1984 IBM agreed to open its system to other companies. IBM had spent millions in litigation and, despite its strong start in the PC market in 1981, became more cautious and missed key opportunities for fear of appearing monopolistic. Consequently, the company's market position fell over the decade as its competitors developed new products.

The Reagan administration's feelings about antitrust actions were made clear when the Justice Department's suit against IBM was dropped. Determined from the start to encourage growth and profitability in American business, Reagan had wasted no time in removing many of the shackles that had confined industries in the past. Deregulation, of course, was a crucial element in his economic plans, but though it was proving highly successful in some respects, it was having mixed results in others, including dire consequences for the environment. In service industries, increased competition brought prices down, which was fine for consumers but devastating for many businesses. The airline industry, deregulated in 1978, was hit particularly hard as new carriers slashed prices, and competition for routes resulted in major carriers losing money and becoming vulnerable to takeovers. In May 1982 Braniff International Corporation filed for Chapter 11 bankruptcy protection; Continental Airlines went the same route in September 1983, while Eastern Airlines cut wages to avoid bankruptcy. Deregulation would continue to wreak havoc in the industry into the 1990s: Both Eastern and Pan Am went under in 1991, and TWA declared bankruptcy in 1992.[2]

Yet another outcome of deregulation and the cessation of antitrust actions was an increased number of large mergers and acquisitions, which the Reagan administration encouraged as a way of boosting economic efficiency. On January 8, 1984, Texaco, Inc., paid $10 billion for Getty Oil Company, the largest corporate merger to date. The deal was eclipsed on June 15, however, when Standard Oil Company of California (SOCAL) acquired Gulf Corporation for $13.4 billion, becoming the country's third-largest oil company in the process. Weeks earlier, Beatrice Foods Company had become the world's second-largest food and consumer products company when it bought Esmark, Inc., for $2.8 billion on May 24. Later in the year, Ziff-Davis Publishing Company made headlines when it sold 12 of its magazines to CBS for $362.5 million on November 20 and, the following day two more to Australian publisher Rupert Murdoch for $350 million. Larger amounts would be involved as such deals became an "art form" in the 1980s, profoundly affecting American business.

But of all the industrial changes taking place, the most exciting was the computer revolution—for which 1984 was a banner year.

## MAC, THE MOUSE, AND MICROSOFT

January 22, 1984: It was the third quarter of Super Bowl XVIII, the Los Angeles Raiders were beating the Washington Redskins easily, and television viewers had already been bombarded with dozens of commercials. Then came the one that everyone remembers.

In a scene evoking George Orwell's *1984,* cowed, gray, automaton workers are shown marching into an auditorium as a Big Brother figure on a huge screen lectures them. Suddenly a blonde woman dressed in bright red shorts and shoes, her white top bearing an Apple logo, runs in, pursued by storm troopers. She launches a hammer at the giant screen, which explodes with a blinding flash. A white light illuminates the awed faces of the workers, and a voice is heard saying: "On January 24th, Apple Computer will introduce Macintosh. And you will see why 1984 won't be like *1984.*"

Although the 60-second commercial, directed by Ridley Scott, was only aired once, it was analyzed for years afterward. It had atmosphere, impact—and a complete lack of concrete information about the product. Yet it dramatically conveyed the impression that something revolutionary was about to happen in the computer industry—which was certainly the case. Two days later, Apple Computer released the Macintosh, the first machine to employ a graphical user interface (GUI) successfully. No longer would users rely solely on the keyboard to implement commands; using a "mouse," they could simply point to commands on the screen and click.

The Macintosh was not the first computer to have a mouse; that distinction belonged to the failed Xerox Star, introduced in 1981. In January 1983 Apple brought out the Lisa, with a mouse and the first pull-down menus, but it was expensive ($9,995 for the base model), complicated, and beset with quality-control problems. In fact, none of the early GUI models were entirely successful in integrating the desirable components of affordability, speed, and ease of use—until the Macintosh. A hit with consumers and small businesses, the Mac (as it came to be called) set new standards in computer manufacturing and selling.

Though Apple was the first personal computer company to reach $1 billion in annual sales (in 1982), its dominance had been threatened by numerous competitors. But with the release of the Apple IIe in 1983 and now the Mac in 1984, it temporarily resumed its position as the company to beat. Its chief competitor remained IBM, whose much-heralded PCjr, released the previous fall, was not doing as well as expected. IBM's operating system, MS-DOS, had been designed by Microsoft, which was beginning its own climb toward the top, releasing its first versions of Word and Windows, both MS-DOS based, in 1983. Both, however, were a long way from perfection, and Windows especially was prone to bugs and slow speeds. Not until 1990 would Windows version 3.0 finally make IBM PCs as easy to use as Apple computers.

Meanwhile, another company was making the news. With Apple and IBM dominating the field, success came to those who found a profitable niche, and Compaq Computer Corporation (founded 1982) did this in sensational fashion. The Osborne portable computer, introduced in 1981, had failed, but IBM had not yet brought out a portable version of its successful PC. Compaq engineers therefore developed one.

The first Compaq had a built-in video and a detachable keyboard and weighed 28 pounds, but it was also faster than the Osborne and more efficient than current IBM desktop models. Introduced in 1983, it was an instant hit, and in January 1984 Compaq announced first-year revenues of $111.2 million, a U.S. business record. That April it introduced Compaq portable computers to Europe; in June the company brought out its first desktop model, the Compaq Deskpro. In its second year of business, 1984, Compaq set another record when it reported revenues of $329 million.

Software development was another ingredient of success. Since Apple and IBM had different operating systems, there was a need to create software for both systems, something that was beyond most developers—except Microsoft, which eventually became the largest provider of software for Apple computers. Its involvement with both companies helped boost Microsoft to its later dominance of the industry.

In January 1983 the Lotus Corporation released Lotus 1–2–3, which became the most popular spreadsheet program ever developed. The following year, Satellite Software International introduced a word processing program called Word-Perfect. Since Microsoft's Word did not really come into its own until the end of the decade, WordPerfect became the word processing program of choice in the business world throughout the 1980s, especially once a GUI version became available.

The personal computer industry had come a long way in a short time, and there were more spectacular developments to come, as precursors of the Internet and World Wide Web would prove from the mid-1980s and onward.

## SCIENTIFIC MARVELS

Technological advances were also benefiting other areas, especially the space-shuttle program. By the beginning of 1984, two shuttles, *Columbia* and *Challenger,* were operational and had carried out nine missions to deploy satellites and conduct experiments. *Columbia*'s flight of November 28–December 8, 1983, was the longest shuttle mission to date as well as the first to include a non-American among its crew members, West German physicist Ulf Merbold. With Byron Lichtenburg, Merbold was also the first payload specialist, a new category of astronaut.[3] *Columbia*'s cargo bay carried Spacelab, a reusable research laboratory that had been built by the European Space Agency for scientific experiments. The mission was a milestone in the growing scientific cooperation between the United States and other countries, highlighting NASA's growing role as an international space agency.

The shuttle program's 10th mission, February 3–11, 1984, was a disappointment in some respects as two communications satellites were sent into incorrect orbits (they were later recovered and returned to Earth), and *Challenger*'s vaunted mechanical Canadarm failed to operate properly. But a precedent was set on February 7, when astronauts Bruce McCandless II and Robert Stewart left *Challenger* and flew in space wearing jet packs—without being attached to the spacecraft by a lifeline.

*Challenger* was also used for a successful mission in April, during which the crew deployed the Long Duration Exposure Facility, a laboratory satellite containing 57 experiments to be retrieved on a later mission; the crew also retrieved and repaired "Solar Max," a satellite designed to carry out observations of the sun that had suffered a number of failures not long after its February 1980 launch.

Despite initial difficulties in retrieving Solar Max—solved thanks to technicians on Earth who sent computerized instructions that adjusted its position—the astronauts' success in fixing and redeploying the satellite led them to dub themselves the "Ace Satellite Repair Co."

On August 30 a third shuttle, *Discovery,* lifted off into space with a crew of six, one of whom was Judith Resnick, the United States' second female astronaut. *Challenger*'s flight of October 5–13 included Marc Garneau, NASA's first Canadian astronaut, and, for the first time, two women: Sally Ride, the nation's first female astronaut making her second flight, and Dr. Kathryn D. Sullivan, who became the first female American astronaut to walk in space on October 11. A month later on November 12 and November 14, during *Discovery*'s second flight, astronauts Joseph Allen and Dale Gardner carried out NASA's first salvage operation when they retrieved two nonfunctioning satellites.

While space-based scientific advances were important, advances in biological knowledge affected society far more closely. What had been impossible 10 years earlier became commonplace during the 1980s; this was especially true in the area of human fertility. The United States had seen the birth of its first test-tube baby, Elizabeth Carr, in December 1981. On February 3, 1984, doctors in California announced that for the first time a baby conceived by one woman had been transferred to another woman's womb and brought to term. This opened the way to a new form of surrogacy, whereby women could bear children for those who could not; while women who could not conceive could have embryos derived from donor ova and donor sperm implanted in them.[4]

More was also being learned about the mysteries of DNA (deoxyribonucleic acid), as scientists increasingly developed the extraction and study of DNA, not just from living matter but from the fossilized tissue of long-dead animals. In June 1984 University of California scientists announced they had successfully cloned the DNA of an extinct equine species. Six months later, researchers in Florida reported they had extracted and analyzed DNA from the still-intact brains of 7,000-year-old human skulls found there. Advances in DNA research were also making it possible to identify inherited predispositions to certain diseases.

The most momentous discovery, though, was made in the summer of 1984, when Alec Jeffreys, an English scientist, showed that "markers" in DNA made it possible to identify an individual's unique genetic characteristics as well as closely related traits in family members. The implications of such "DNA fingerprinting" were boundless, and research laboratories in the United States and around the world quickly expanded on Jeffreys's findings. Within a few years DNA was revolutionizing medicine as well as police investigations and forensics. Such was the power of the new DNA technology that it would be used on its own to prove or disprove an individual's involvement in a crime, in addition to solving long-standing mysteries. Such progress in biological knowledge was to have a profound impact on society.

## MEDICAL MILESTONES

The year also saw significant advances in medical knowledge. Eleven months after artificial-heart recipient Barney Clark died (March 23, 1983), a six-year-old Texas girl underwent an operation to replace both her heart and her liver—the first such operation in medical history. Stormie Jones had suffered from a rare genetic condition, hypercholesterolemia, in which the blood cholesterol levels are dangerously high; Stormie's were so high that her liver and heart were irreparably damaged.

Scientists believed the liver controlled the body's cholesterol; if this was correct, ways of altering cholesterol levels could be developed. Stormie's case provided important research opportunities for doctors and scientists at the University of Texas Health Science Center (UTHSC) in Dallas, where she was being treated. She had already undergone a double bypass operation when she was five, but the damage to her liver was so great that a transplant was urgently needed, something her heart could not survive. She was therefore sent east to Children's Hospital in Pittsburgh, and on February 13–14, 1984, a 16-hour operation, replacing first her heart and then her liver, was carried out by two transplant teams.

Back at UTHSC, research continued as Stormie's successful recovery confirmed scientists' hypotheses on cholesterol and its buildup in the body. The following year, in October 1985, UTHSC scientists Michael S. Brown and Joseph L. Goldstein won the Nobel Prize in medicine for their work, which led to improved treatments for high cholesterol levels. Stormie, meanwhile, lived for more than six years before her body finally rejected the transplanted heart; she died on November 11, 1990, at the age of 13.

As Stormie's case demonstrated, organ transplantation had come a long way since the 1960s, largely because the drug cyclosporine, introduced in 1979, helped to keep the body from rejecting organs that had been implanted in it. As live-tissue transplants became increasingly common, though, a lack of donors remained a problem; many died as they waited for hearts, livers, lungs, or kidneys to become available. A possible solution was cross-species transplants—taking an organ from one animal species and implanting it in another, also known as xenotransplantation. Valves from pig hearts were already used regularly to replace failing human heart valves, and as early as 1964 a chimpanzee's heart had been transplanted in a 68-year-old man. Prior to November 1984, in fact, five hearts and 20 kidneys from simians had been implanted into human patients (none of whom survived long).[5]

Xenotransplantation was controversial, but for the Seventh Day Adventist Church, the answer was clear: Animals could and should be sacrificed for the sake of preserving human life. The church ran the Loma Linda University Medical Center in California, and it was there that Dr. Leonard Bailey was working on the problem of hypoplastic heart, in which the left side of the heart is underdeveloped at birth. This condition was generally considered fatal, although some surgical success had been achieved at Children's Hospital in Boston. Infant-to-infant transplantation was technically possible, but this was still a new field, and no infant heart recipient had yet survived a transplant. Bailey felt xenotransplantation was the solution, and he had spent seven years at Loma Linda performing cross-species transplants on animals. Then a week-old infant girl with hypoplastic heart, born three weeks prematurely, was brought to his attention.

Baby Fae—the name by which she was known publicly—was in such serious condition that a review board quickly approved Bailey's proposal to replace her heart with one from a young female baboon; her original heart failed just before the operation. The four-hour surgery on October 26, 1984, left the 12-day-old Baby Fae with a baboon's heart beating in her chest. Yet her chance of survival was still slight. Antirejection drugs were no guarantee in one so young, and a major difference between human and baboon hearts—humans have three major arteries leaving the aortic arch, baboons only two—meant that two of Baby Fae's heart apertures had to be sewn together to be connected to one of the arterial openings in the new heart. The risks were huge.

Newspapers and news programs carried daily bulletins on Baby Fae's condition, and the entire country watched her struggle for survival. But not everybody was thrilled with Baby Fae's story. Animal rights activists demonstrated at Loma Linda University Medical Center, protesting the sacrifice of an animal to save a baby who was probably going to die anyway. Conservative religious groups spoke out against the contamination of a human body, made in God's image, by the organ of a brute beast. More liberal voices supported such experimental surgery as necessary for extending medical knowledge. So the debate between morality and science continued.

Baby Fae fought bravely for her life, eventually becoming the longest-living human recipient of an animal heart. She lasted 20 days until her organs failed on November 15 because her red cells had coagulated, a result of blood mismatching. Remarkably, the heart had not been rejected, although it was clear that rejection was imminent.

Baby Fae's death did not resolve the debate on xenotransplantation, which most scientists contend is hazardous due to the biological differences between species. Even though her condition had been dire, many felt Bailey had been both precipitous in operating without pursuing other options and unethical in that he knew before surgery that her blood was not a match with the baboon's. Nevertheless, her case brought the issue of organ transplants to national attention and taught physicians much about such surgery. A year later, in November 1985, a four-day-old infant named Baby Moses became the youngest person to survive a human heart transplant. He remains alive today, and the current survival rate for infant heart transplants is 80 percent—a legacy of Baby Fae.

## Morass in Central America

From the start of his administration, Ronald Reagan had been concerned about Central America, as had previous presidents. But there was good reason for this.

With the Monroe Doctrine of 1823, the United States had made it clear that it would resist attempts by European powers to colonize or interfere with any nation in the Western Hemisphere. American interference in Central America and the Caribbean, however, had become a common occurrence. In Nicaragua alone, the United States had intervened 11 times since 1853—to protect Americans, restore order, or supervise elections—and U.S. Marines were stationed there continuously from 1912 to 1933. When Fidel Castro installed a Soviet-friendly regime in Cuba in the late 1950s, American fears of Soviet influence in the region intensified.

Central American countries have a long history of conflict between right-wing and left-wing groups, resulting in a recurring cycle of dictatorship, revolution, and more dictatorship. By 1979 Guatemala, El Salvador, and Honduras were under right-wing control, while Costa Rica was enjoying a peaceful democratic regime. In Nicaragua that year, the reviled dictator Anastasio Somoza was overthrown by the Sandinistas, a Marxist coalition. President Carter, who had opposed the harsh Somoza regime, welcomed them with $125 million in economic aid, setting off Republican charges that he was encouraging Cuban and Soviet influence. These charges appeared justified when, in January 1981, word came that the Sandinistas were supporting guerrillas who were rebelling against El Salvador's pro-American government. Carter immediately suspended aid to Nicaragua and sent arms and equipment to El Salvador, but the incoming Reagan administration saw trouble ahead.

Less than two months after Reagan took office, Secretary of State Al Haig publicly accused the Soviet Union of abetting antidemocratic activities in Central America. To combat the Soviet threat, he advocated financial assistance, arms, equipment, and, if necessary, military aid to the Salvadoran government. Eventually, government forces achieved some success against the rebels, but the problem of the Sandinistas remained. Since overthrowing the Nicaraguan government was morally and politically out of the question, Haig and CIA director William Casey proposed covert assistance to the guerrillas who were resisting the Sandinistas. On December 1, 1981, President Reagan authorized $19 million in funding for Argentine military experts to train a 500-man anti-Sandinista force in Honduras. However, when the Falkland Islands War between Argentina and Great Britain broke out in April 1982, the United States supported the British, causing Argentina to cease its assistance to the contras, as the anti-Sandinista rebels were called. The United States nonetheless continued its secret campaign against the Sandinistas. One ally was Manuel Noriega, a colonel in the Panamanian army who would become Panama's dictator in 1983. From 1981 Noriega, a dealer in drugs and weapons, became a conduit for the CIA, transferring U.S. money and arms to contras in Honduras and Costa Rica.

Gradually the contra forces increased, and controversy arose over the apparent U.S. attempt to bring down the Nicaraguan government, which Reagan officials denied. Nonetheless, news of increasing civilian deaths caused by fighting between the Sandinistas and contras led Congress to take action. In 1982 Representative Edward P. Boland (D, Mass.) sponsored a resolution attached to that

CIA director William Casey, seen here with President Reagan in a January 1983 photo, strongly advocated providing covert assistance to the contra rebels in Nicaragua; his plans would unravel when the Iran-contra affair was exposed in late 1986. *(Courtesy Ronald Reagan Library)*

year's House Appropriations Bill. Known as the Boland Amendment, it forbade the government to provide any military support "for the purpose of overthrowing the Government of Nicaragua." The following year the amendment became part of the Defense Appropriations Act (DAA) of December 1983. The Democratic House had voted against financial aid to the contras, but the Republican Senate had approved funding. As a compromise, the DAA put a cap of $24 million on aid to the contras—but only to assist anti-Sandinista activities in El Salvador.

Angered by these congressional attempts to stop him, Reagan directed subordinates to find other ways of continuing the CIA's covert activities and maintaining assistance to the contras. In the meantime, in July 1983 he established the National Bipartisan Commission on Central America, subsequently called the Kissinger Commission after its chairman, Henry Kissinger. The 12-member group[6] was to report "on the elements of a long-term United States policy that will best respond to the challengers of social, economic and democratic developments in the region, and to internal and external threats to its security and stability."[7] The commission reported on January 11, 1984, and essentially endorsed Reagan's policies, noting that the region was in crisis and that the United States must "act boldly" to protect it against "the intrusion of aggressive outside powers." The report recommended increased economic aid for the entire region and significantly increased military assistance to El Salvador, although there was criticism about that government's right-wing death squads and a suggestion that aid be linked to improving human rights. It also expressed the view that the use of force against the Nicaraguan government be a last resort if the Sandinistas continued to support guerrillas in other countries.

Overall, the Kissinger Commission favored Reagan's approach, but he did not take advantage of this because 1984 was an election year, and Central America had become a politically sensitive issue. In any event, the covert activities continued, including the mining of Nicaragua's harbors, which was carried out in January and February by CIA agents. The mining was originally attributed to the contras, but in early April the *Wall Street Journal* revealed the CIA's involvement, resulting in an explosion of outrage from Democrats, Republicans, and the general public. The Sandinistas subsequently went to the International Court of Justice in The Hague and won their case against the United States for using force while illegally intervening in Nicaragua's affairs. The U.S. government rejected the court's ruling.

Though Reagan remained convinced that the communist presence in Central America was threatening U.S. security, the mining incident destroyed any chance of obtaining further monies for the contras from Congress. Reagan officials therefore began to look for other sources of funding, and in May discreet approaches were made to Saudi Arabia, which in July began to send installments of $1 million a month; the arrangements were handled by a staff member of the National Security Council (NSC), Lieutenant Colonel Oliver North. By this time Secretary of State George Shultz had traveled to Managua in a failed attempt to persuade Nicaraguan president Daniel Ortega to cease helping the rebels in El Salvador, and both the House and the Senate had voted to cut off all aid to the contras. In addition, William Casey had apologized to the Senate Select Intelligence Committee for failing to inform them of covert operations in Central America and pledged full disclosure of all such activities in the future.

On October 12, 1984, a second Boland Amendment was passed, this time specifically forbidding the CIA, the Department of Defense, "or any other agency or entity involved in intelligence activities" to support operations in Nicaragua "directly or indirectly." This should have put the matter to rest, but, unfortunately, it merely forced the administration's secret activities to become even more secret under the aegis of the NSC, which was technically not an intelligence agency. This resulted in a complex web of operations that led to the 1986–87 Iran-contra scandal, which was to prove far more damaging than the mining of the harbors.

## OTHER HOT TOPICS

Central America was not the only political hotbed for Ronald Reagan. Arguably the nation's most conservative president, Reagan held rigid views on certain topics that fueled heated debate; among the most contentious were abortion and school prayer. His opposition to the one and support of the other were so strong that he was not afraid to speak publicly on these divisive issues in an election year, despite the possible political damage.

On his election as president, one of Reagan's hopes—and abortion-rights activists' fears—was that he would place more conservative justices on the Supreme Court and possibly overturn *Roe v. Wade,* the 1973 decision that protected a woman's right to abort a fetus during the first three months of pregnancy. By 1983 he had only been able to appoint one justice, Sandra Day O'Connor, and on June 15 of that year, the Court issued two rulings—*City of Akron v. Akron Center for the Reproductive Health* and *Planned Parenthood Association of Kansas City, Mo. v. Ashcroft*—which, to Reagan's disappointment, upheld the *Roe* decision. He was further dismayed when, later that month, the Republican Senate voted down an amendment that would have allowed legislation to ban or curb abortions. Reagan had already written an essay, "Abortion and the Conscience of the Nation," for the spring 1983 issue of *Human Life Review.* In 1984 the essay was published in book form, giving wider publicity to his views: "It is not for us to decide who is worthy to live and who is not," he wrote. "Even the Supreme Court's opinion in *Roe v. Wade* did not explicitly reject the traditional American idea of intrinsic worth and value in all human life; it simply dodged this issue."[8]

Reagan—who wanted to limit access to abortion by restricting federal funding—believed that abortion should be an option only when the mother's life was in danger. Yet polls showed the majority of Americans disagreed with him and supported *Roe v. Wade.* Similarly, he represented a minority view on such matters of public concern as handgun controls, national speed limits, and nuclear power-plant construction. The debate concerning school prayer, though, had been extremely divisive ever since the Supreme Court's 1962 and 1963 rulings that nondenominational prayers, recitation of the Lord's Prayer, and daily Bible readings in public schools were unconstitutional. Over the next two decades, these rulings produced a spate of proposed amendments to the Constitution to allow voluntary prayers in schools as well as a failed 1979 attempt to prevent the Supreme Court from hearing cases related to such matters.

The 1962 (*Engel v. Vitale*) ruling had led to 23 states passing laws that allowed silent meditation as a substitute for prayer. By 1984 even these were coming under attack as a violation of the constitutional separation of church and state. On March 1 the board of education in Hicksville, New York, instituted a ban on the

30 seconds of silent meditation that students had been observing since 1962. Although the majority of parents and teachers favored retaining the meditation—generally acknowledged not to be prayer per se—the school board feared being taken to court.

Acting on a campaign promise, in 1982 President Reagan had submitted his own amendment authorizing school prayers. Like the New Religious Right, he sincerely believed that American schools had gone into a moral decline since 1962, that students should be free to observe their chosen faiths in their schools, and that prayer was an allowable form of such observance. In March 1984 the Senate debated his amendment—and then voted against it. Not even the concerted lobbying efforts of such powerful groups as the Moral Majority, who aimed to "put God back in the classroom," could overcome the fundamental problem facing the legislators and politicians: Prayer—even voluntary prayer—implied religion, and though the free exercise of religion was permitted under the constitution, there must be no official sanctioning of any faith, real or perceived, in any public institution.[9]

Sensitivity over religious practices had reached such a pitch by the early 1980s that student-driven religious groups were suffering discrimination. Bible-study groups, for example, were forbidden to meet in public high school facilities, which the religious right claimed was unconstitutional. Congress agreed and, on August 11, 1984, passed the Equal Access Act (EAA), which required federally funded public schools to allow student groups with a religious basis to have the same right to use school facilities as other groups so long as their activities were initiated by students, not held during school hours, and not connected with the school curriculum. The Supreme Court subsequently upheld the EAA's constitutionality, and it has since been invoked in gay rights cases as well.

Another 1984 Supreme Court case examined the separation of church and state from a different angle. In *Lynch v. Donnelly,* the city of Pawtucket, Rhode Island, had come under fire for maintaining a public crèche, a Christmas tradition for 40 years. The American Civil Liberties Union (ACLU) and National Council of Churches believed this violated the Constitution; the Supreme Court disagreed, ruling on March 5 that a city may display a Nativity scene on private land, as Pawtucket had done, without violating the establishment clause. Similar cases would continue to come before the Court as the ACLU and others challenged any form of officially authorized religious expression.

Reagan and the religious right drew some comfort from occasional victories, such as the EAA and *Lynch v. Donnelly,* but the failure to ban abortion or reinstate prayers in public schools rankled. Their fight would continue as televangelists such as Pat Robertson and Jerry Falwell did their best to influence public opinion—as well as elections.

## CHANGING THE GUARD IN CANADA

For almost 16 years Prime Minister Pierre Elliott Trudeau had dominated Canadian politics, but by early 1984 both he and the country were feeling that his time was coming to an end. He had some major achievements to his credit, the most recent and perhaps most important being the repatriation of the constitution in 1982. Since then, he had sought greater economic growth for Canada and worked to increase aid to developing nations. In July 1983 his government authorized the

United States to test cruise-missile guidance systems in Canada's northern regions, provoking angry protests from peace activists and environmentalists. Later in the year, as if to compensate, he went on a global tour to promote peace and nuclear disarmament. However, he seemed to be neglecting domestic problems—inflation, unemployment, and a growing federal deficit—giving more ammunition to his political opponents. He was tired, he had lost much of the flair of his Trudeaumania days, and he was looking after his three sons. (He and his estranged wife Margaret would divorce in 1984.)

Trudeau also faced a strong challenge from Brian Mulroney, who had defeated Joe Clark to win the leadership of the Progressive Conservative Party in June 1983. On February 28, 1984, a blizzard hit Ottawa, and Trudeau went for "a long walk in the snow." By the time he returned home, he had made up his mind, as he related in a subsequent interview:

> I walked till midnight in the storm, just singing. And then I went home and took a sauna for an hour-and-a-half. It was all clear I was going to leave. And I went to sleep, just in case I'd change my mind overnight. And I didn't. I woke up and felt great. To use the old cliché, this is the first day of the rest of my life.[10]

On February 29 he announced his decision in a letter to Iona Campagnola, president of the Liberal Party, who read it to reporters at a news conference that same day. Trudeau pledged to remain in office until his successor as Liberal Party leader was elected. This was John Napier Turner, who defeated Jean Chrétien at the party's leadership convention in June. Turner had been Trudeau's minister of justice and then minister of finance until 1975, when he left government and became a corporate lawyer. He returned to politics after Trudeau's retirement announcement, and on June 30, 1984, he became the country's 17th prime minister.

Turner immediately attracted unfavorable comment by failing to revoke the large number of controversial patronage appointments that Trudeau had made during his final days in office. In confirming the appointments, Turner fulfilled a promise made to Trudeau during the Liberal leadership elections, but there was uproar when the news broke, and the new prime minister was excoriated by both the press and the public.

This was one of several errors Turner made; another was to call an early election, giving Brian Mulroney and the Progressive Conservatives the opportunity to take advantage of the nation's discontent with Liberal Party leadership. In a televised debate less than two weeks before the election, Turner was asked to explain why he had retained the Trudeau appointments, to which he weakly replied, "I had no option." Mulroney immediately attacked: "You had an option, sir. You could have said I'm not going to do that, it's wrong for Canada.'. . . You chose to say 'yes' to the old attitudes and ways of the Liberal Party. . . ."[11]

Mulroney virtually won the election that night. On September 4 he swept into office as the Progressive Conservatives gained 211 of the 282 seats in the House of Commons. He also broke the Liberal Party's decades-long dominance of his native Quebec, where the Progressive Conservatives took 54 of its 75 seats.

Mulroney was sworn into office on September 17 and at once set about smoothing relations between the federal government and the 10 provinces, in addition to addressing the country's economic problems. In November it was announced that private and foreign investment would be encouraged to reduce the national debt and that crown corporations would be privatized. Like Ronald Reagan, Mulroney disliked the social legislation that had depleted the federal treasury, and he intended to cut those programs as much as he could. It remained to be seen, though, how far to the right the country could move after its long era of liberalism.

Canada had seen three prime ministers in one year—and also the installation of its first female governor general, Jeanne Sauvé. In August the country enjoyed its best showing yet at a summer Olympics, and in October everybody celebrated as the first Canadian astronaut, Marc Garneau, went into space aboard the shuttle *Challenger*. It had been an eventful year in the nation's history.

## OLYMPIC PRIDE

In 1980 the United States had hosted one Olympic Games and boycotted another. In 1984 it was time for the world's athletes to meet again: in Sarajevo, Yugoslavia, for the winter Olympics (February 8–19), and in Los Angeles, California, for the summer Olympics (July 28–August 12). As anticipation mounted, so did speculation about whether the Soviet Union would pull out of the Summer Games in retaliation for the U.S. boycott of 1980.

The Sarajevo games began with 1,590 athletes from 49 nations participating, a record number, and the hope that the U.S. hockey team would repeat its gold medal triumph of four years earlier. But the Americans suffered early defeats and were soon knocked out of the competition. This was bad news for ABC, which had won the rights to broadcast the games, only to see audiences dwindling due partly to the time difference between Sarajevo and the United States but mainly to a lack of U.S. medals in the early days of competition. Americans wanted to see Americans winning; failing that, they turned off their televisions or switched to another channel.

By February 18 the United States had won only six medals. Then, on the final day, twin brothers Phil and Steve Mahre won the gold and silver medals in the men's slalom, giving people at home some final consolation. For many, though, the highlight of the games was Britain's Jayne Torvill and Christopher Dean ice dancing to Ravel's *Bolero* and scoring an unprecedented nine scores of 6.0 for artistic impression to win the gold medal.

When the games ended, East Germany (24 medals, nine of them gold) and the Soviet Union (25 medals, six gold) were tied for first place, followed by Finland, Norway—and, in fifth place, the United States, with four gold and four silver medals. This compared badly to Lake Placid in 1980 (12 medals) and Innsbruck, Austria, in 1976 (11), and it worried ABC, which was planning 187.5 hours of coverage for Los Angeles's Summer Games. The Los Angeles Olympic Organizing Committee (LAOOC) was also worried that the poor U.S. showing in Sarajevo and a possible Soviet boycott would adversely affect its games.

The Los Angeles Olympics were to redefine how the games were organized. By May 1978 the city had become the sole candidate for the 1984 games, making it possible to amend certain conditions normally imposed by the International Olympic Committee (IOC). The major problem was that although the host country normally financed the games, the citizens of Los Angeles refused to contribute any funds and amended the city charter to prevent any federal subsidy. Consequently, the IOC agreed to allow an independent group, the LAOOC, to organize the games (sharing responsibility with the United States Olympic Committee) and also permitted financial support from industry.

The result was the first "private enterprise" Olympic Games, managed by the LAOOC's president, businessman Peter Ueberroth. It was Ueberroth who conceived the idea of corporate sponsorships, whereby major companies paid the expenses of the games, gaining worldwide publicity as "official sponsors." Ueberroth limited the primary sponsors to 30, each making a minimum subscription of $4 million. Coca-Cola was the first to sign, pledging $30 million in addition to sponsoring more than 30 countries' teams. Ueberroth quickly signed up his remaining 29 sponsors, raising $126.7 million in all. There were also secondary sponsors who had their names attached to particular events. When Kodak delayed becoming a primary sponsor, Ueberroth gave the deal to Kodak's competitor Fuji instead. Fuji's share of the U.S. camera-film market subsequently rose from 3 percent to 9 percent. Kodak had to settle for sponsoring the American track-and-field team—and several of its top executives were replaced.

U.S. Television rights were sold to ABC for $225 million;[12] another $33 million came from networks outside the United States. Forty-three companies were licensed to sell "official" Olympic products, and other corporations paid for athletic venues or donated equipment, from cars to copiers. Meanwhile, the LAOOC recruited thousands of volunteers who represented the majority of the 72,000-strong workforce in the final weeks.

Ueberroth and the LAOOC also raised $30 million for local youth programs through the Olympic torch relay, zigzagging across the nation through 33 states from New York to Los Angeles. Each kilometer cost $3,000, paid either by the torch carrier or by someone sponsoring the carrier. The Greek National Olympic Committee objected to this commercialization of a sacred tradition and refused to allow the torch's flame to be kindled in Olympia, as customary. Only when two Swiss students kindled a flame at the Temple of Hera and smuggled it out of Greece did the Greeks finally relent and allow an "official" flame to be kindled and sent to New York. Beginning on May 8, the relay became an emotional event for the nation as thousands of people—celebrities, athletes, disabled people, and children—proudly carried the torch over a 9,100-mile route.

The day the relay began, the USSR announced its intention "not to participate" in the summer Olympics. Among the reasons cited were security concerns and the cost of staying in the Olympic villages, although these rang hollow given previous apparent Soviet approval of the arrangements. For most it seemed clear that the Soviet Union was simply getting its own back for the U.S. boycott of the 1980 Moscow games. At that time, some 60 American allies joined the boycott; in 1984 only 16 other countries supported the Soviet boycott, but these included East Germany, Poland, Bulgaria, Cuba, and Hungary, who, along with the USSR, were among the top 10 medal winners in Montreal (1976).

The United States was already in anti-Soviet mood following the downing of KAL flight 007 the previous

Gina Hemphill, granddaughter of the legendary runner Jesse Owens, passes the Olympic torch to Rafer Johnson, 1960 Olympics decathlon champion, who lit the Olympic flame to open the XXIII Olympiad in Los Angeles on July 28, 1984. *(AP/Wide World Photos)*

September. Now the boycott created a swell of patriotism throughout the country and enthusiastic support for the games. Stories of Ueberroth's organizing genius, the positive publicity generated by the torch relay, and extensive previews in the press all helped to guarantee the games' success.

The Summer Games opened on July 28 with a spectacular opening ceremony and some 6,800 athletes from 140 nations. These included the People's Republic of China, participating in its first Summer Games since 1952; Taiwan, which had boycotted the 1980 Lake Placid games because of Communist China's participation; and Romania, whose athletes received rousing cheers from the spectators because they had defied the Soviet boycott.

The presence of the Romanians, who won 53 medals, went some way to compensate for the boycott's most obvious effect: The United States won 174 medals in all, 83 of them gold. This was inevitable given the lack of competition the Soviets and their allies would have provided, but the crowds filling the Los Angeles Coliseum and other sites were overwhelmingly partisan, with constant chants of "USA! USA!" and television broadcasts unashamedly centered on American athletes. When the favored American Mary Decker fell as she was gaining on Britain's Zola Budd in the 3,000-meter race, spectators were quick to blame Budd for the mishap, loudly and incorrectly accusing her of having intentionally tripped Decker; rattled, Budd lost the race.

If these sorts of unsportsmanlike displays marred the games, they were offset by the performances of such great athletes as Carl Lewis and Mary Lou Retton—and by the news that Ueberroth and the LAOOC had made a profit of $215 million, all of which would be donated to youth and sports programs. It was the first time that an Olympics had made a profit since 1932—which were also held in Los Angeles. Deservedly, Ueberroth was named *Time* magazine's Person of the Year for 1984.

## A PRESIDENTIAL RACE MAKES HISTORY

By early 1984, Ronald Reagan's unpopularity of a year before had largely vanished. The country's economic improvement, a feeling of patriotism following the Grenada invasion, a welcome sense of confidence far removed from the malaise of 1980—all were attributed to Reagan. Further, despite innumerable verbal gaffes and a management style criticized both inside and outside the administration, people simply liked Reagan. His charm, humor, well-written and well-delivered speeches, and resolution when firm action was required combined to make him the most popular president in years.

This was what Democrats were up against as the election year began, and they were not helped by divisions within their party. It had been assumed that Massachusetts senator Edward Kennedy would run, but he surprised everybody by pulling out in December 1982. This left the field wide open, and by January 1984, there were eight contenders for the Democratic nomination. The early front-runner was Walter Mondale, vice president under Jimmy Carter, but he faced strong challenges from Ohio senator (and former astronaut) John Glenn and Colorado senator Gary Hart, who described himself as "an independent Western Jeffersonian Democrat," eschewing the legacy of Franklin Roosevelt that so many Democrats still revered.

Then there was Jesse Jackson. Most civil rights and black political leaders felt the time was not right for an African-American presidential candidate. In their view, not only was it impossible for an African American to win, but a black candidate would hinder a close working relationship with a successful white nominee. Jackson knew he could not win but felt that by running, he would stimulate a voter registration drive that would increase the numbers of black voters—and thus perhaps defeat Reagan, whose economic program he blamed for a downturn in African-American fortunes. He also hoped to form a "Rainbow Coalition" to include those outside the political mainstream—black, Hispanic, Native American, impoverished, and disabled.

Jackson had never run for political office before, his campaign was disorganized, and he entered the race late, all of which prevented his establishing a strong political base. However, he had determination—and a stroke of luck when he negotiated the release of Lieutenant Robert Goodman from Syria in early January 1984. Unfortunately, during a January 25 breakfast with *Washington Post* reporter Milton Coleman, he referred to New York City as "Hymietown." The remark was off the record, but Coleman mentioned it to a colleague who subsequently published it on February 13, resulting in tremendous public reaction against Jackson.

Jackson was also weakened by his association with Louis Farrakhan, the fiercely anti-Semitic leader of the Nation of Islam. After the "Hymietown" uproar, Farrakhan publicly accused Coleman, an African American, of betrayal and threatened to have him killed. This attracted even more negative publicity, but despite pressure to disassociate himself from Farrakhan, Jackson merely denied the threat, and Farrakhan continued to speak at his rallies. A few months later, when Farrakhan called Judaism a "gutter religion," Jackson finally distanced himself from the Black Muslim leader, but the damage had been done.

The battle for delegates was mostly between Mondale and Hart, although Glenn hung on until Super Tuesday, March 13. Mondale finally secured the nomination in early June, but it had not been easy. Though Hart had won the western states plus Alaska, Florida, and most of the Northeast, Mondale had taken the Midwest and most of the eastern seaboard and South. Jackson, meanwhile, had won four states—Virginia, South Carolina, Mississippi, and Louisiana—due primarily to his voter registration drives that increased the numbers of black voters considerably and gave him 90 percent of the black vote nationwide. He had hoped this might give him some clout—perhaps even the vice presidential nomination—but he was soon disappointed. In late June he took another foreign-policy trip, this time to Cuba to hold discussions with Fidel Castro. However, unlike his earlier trip to Syria, Jackson's success in securing the release of 49 American and Cuban political prisoners was largely met with indifference or regarded as a political ploy.

By July Reagan led strongly in the polls, and Mondale knew he needed a bold stroke if he were to win. Many applauded, therefore, when he selected as his running mate Representative Geraldine Ferraro of New York, the first woman to be nominated on a major party ticket. The choice seemed ideal: Not only would Ferraro, an intelligent and articulate woman, help to close the "gender gap" in American politics, but as a Catholic and Italian American, she would also appeal to other voting blocs.

The convention opened on July 16, and Jackson addressed the assembly two days later, endorsing the Mondale-Ferraro ticket, extolling his Rainbow Coalition, and repeating the refrain "Our time has come." On the 20th the two run-

Walter Mondale announced his choice of Geraldine Ferraro as his running mate on July 12, 1984, in the chamber of the Minneapolis House of Representatives, St. Paul, Minnesota. *(AP/Wide World Photos)*

ning mates accepted their nominations, and Mondale unleashed a bombshell: To reduce the federal deficit, he would raise taxes. Reagan would take the same action, he said, but only he, Mondale, would admit it. The pledge was a calculated risk. Taxes had been reduced under Reagan, which Americans liked, but the national debt had risen enormously, a major cause for concern. Mondale's honesty was lauded but not necessarily welcomed.

Reagan was quick to link Mondale's statement to the inadequacies of the Carter-Mondale administration, and throughout the fall his team contrasted the malaise-ridden years of 1976–80 with the sunnier times now being enjoyed by Americans:

> It's morning again in America. . . . Three years ago, even the smallest house seemed completely out of reach. Right down the street, one of the neighbors has just bought himself a new car, with all the options. The factory is working again. Not long ago, people were saying it would probably be closed forever. . . . Life is better, America is back. . . . Now that our country is turning around, why would we ever turn back?[13]

The "Morning in America" ads were a vital factor in Reagan's success. With no plans or priorities for his second term, the president had little of substance to say, so his team repeatedly stressed how things had improved since the Carter-Mondale years. This effectively countered Mondale's forebodings on issues such as the federal deficit, while his own ads, which essentially showed him saying "I want to help you," provided no explanation of how he would do so. Reagan was resoundingly optimistic; Mondale appeared pessimistic and never came close to matching his opponent's ability to win over an audience.

Moreover, Mondale's choice of running mate did not bring him the advantage he had sought. Controversy arose over Ferraro's financial statement for her 1978 congressional campaign, which had failed to disclose the money her husband, John Zaccaro, had given her, in violation of federal regulations governing campaign financing. This turned into a witch hunt as the press investigated Zaccaro's business dealings, even trying to find connections to the Mafia. Not until Ferraro held a forthright press conference was the issue put to rest, but it had been an unfortunate distraction for the Democrats. Furthermore, the campaign had failed to capitalize on Ferraro's appeal to her own sex, and she did not begin to talk about women's issues until late in the race—too late to make an effective impression on that crucial voting bloc.

Mondale gained some advantage from the first presidential debate on October 7, which he won handily. Reagan was weak, tired, and seemingly confused, which raised questions about his age and capability. At once, his campaign ads began to portray him as healthy and confident, emphasizing his role as the United States' chief defender and attacking Mondale vigorously. The Democratic candidate, however, failed to capitalize on his own strong performance. By the second debate on October 21, Reagan had recovered his usual form and talked his way out of questions regarding the recent discovery of a CIA training manual for the Nicaraguan contras that seemed to advocate political assassinations. The manual not only violated federal policy but also indicated clearly that his administration was continuing its covert activities in Central America. Mondale, however, did not press the matter sufficiently and then lost the debate on a point of humor. When a question was put to Reagan about his age, he quipped: "I want you to know that also I will not make age an issue of this campaign. I am not going to exploit, for political purposes, my opponent's youth and inexperience." The audience laughed, as did Mondale. Once again, the president's charm had won the day; it was the joke voters remembered, not the disquieting issue of Central America.

The November 6 election was never in doubt. Reagan won in a landslide, taking 49 states, a record 525 electoral votes, and 59 percent of the popular vote. Mondale, at 41 percent, carried only his home state of Minnesota and the District of Columbia. It was not, however, an overwhelming victory: Although they maintained their majority in the Senate, Republicans lost two seats; and though they gained 14 seats in the House of Representatives, the Democrats remained in control there. Furthermore, Reagan, having accomplished many of his goals in his first term, was entering his second with little idea of what he wanted to do next.

## THE YUPPIES EMERGE

One of the interesting side effects of the presidential race was the entry of *yuppie*—"young urban professional"*—into the American vocabulary. The word had existed since the late 1970s and first appeared in newsprint in 1983, which also saw the publication of *The Yuppie Handbook*. But it was 1984 when the word *yuppie* came into its own, mainly from its association with Gary Hart. Only eight years younger than Walter Mondale, he was nonetheless popularly associated with the baby boom generation, which eschewed traditional Democratic philosophy and embraced the new values of the 1980s. Old-time Democrats such as Mondale felt that this brought him too close in spirit to the current Republican

---

*Sometimes also rendered as "young, upwardly mobile, urban professional." Another version is yumpie, for "young, upwardly mobile person."

regime, but Hart was adamant that the New Deal was long past and that it was time to look forward. Consequently, Democratic yuppies supported him in large numbers.

By 1984 the yuppies—members of the 1946–64 baby boom—had emerged in force. Qualifications for yuppiedom ranged from salary to type of job (usually professional or managerial) to place of residence (mostly metropolitan areas). Primarily, though, what defined the yuppies was a lifestyle in which particular clothes, cars, homes, and other possessions (especially the latest gadgets) were considered essentials rather than luxuries.

Yuppies were products of the Reagan era, enjoying the economic boom that the nation's oldest president had brought about. More conservative and materialistic than the preceding generation, they were epitomized in such books as *Bright Lights, Big City* (1984) by Jay McInerney and *From Rockaway* (1987) by Jill Eisenstadt; and in the popular television series *Family Ties* (1982–89), in which former hippies Steve and Elyse Keaton attempted unsuccessfully to impose their idealistic 1960s viewpoint on their three very 1980s children. The most conservative of the three was Alex, played by Michael J. Fox (who shot to stardom in the role). Invariably wearing a suit and tie, Alex idolized the conservative columnist and commentator William F. Buckley. Not surprisingly, *Family Ties* was President Reagan's favorite show.

Shown here is the cast of President Reagan's favorite TV series, *Family Ties.* From left to right are: Tina Yothers, Justine Bateman, Michael Gross, Meredith Baxter-Birney, and Michael J. Fox. *(Photofest)*

Yet not all yuppies were Reagan supporters, as Gary Hart's popularity demonstrated. Their primary attribute was that regardless of politics, yuppies—direct successors of the late 1970s' preppies—pursued upwardly mobile careers and, for many, represented the greed and conspicuous consumption that defined the Reagan years. Though young, they had become the Establishment, in contrast to their predecessors the hippies and yippies (from the 1960s Youth International Party). Exemplifying this change in attitude was the former yippie Jerry Rubin, who by 1983 had become a member of the business community, promoting "networking" parties for Wall Street denizens. Equally representative was the 1983 movie *The Big Chill,* featuring characters who have turned their backs on their idealistic past for a materialistic present.

Yuppies were scorned by many; yet many more aspired to join them. Such was their impact that *Newsweek* named 1984 "The Year of the Yuppie" in its December 31 issue. The yuppie era is generally considered to have run its course by 1987, but they have not entirely disappeared: Their influence is still to be seen in American attitudes toward wealth and material goods.[14]

## CHRONICLE OF EVENTS

**1984**

*January 1:* AT&T divests its 22 "Baby Bells," which become seven independent regional telephone companies.

*January 3:* After Reverend Jesse Jackson makes a personal appeal to Syrian president al-Assad, Syria releases captured U.S. Navy pilot Robert Goodman.

*January 8:* Texaco, Inc., takes over the Getty Oil Company in a $10 billion deal, the largest corporate merger to date.

*January 10:* The U.S. government announces restoration of diplomatic relations with the Vatican after 117 years.

*January 11:* The Kissinger Commission, established in July 1983, recommends the United States provide $8 billion in economic aid to Central America and increased military aid to El Salvador.

*January 13:* Influential drama critic Brooks Atkinson, who won a Pulitzer Prize in 1947, dies at 89.

*January 17:* In a 5-4 decision, the U.S. Supreme Court rules that it is legal to record television broadcasts with a videocassette recorder and that retailers have the right to sell such equipment.

*January 20:* Johnny Weismuller, Olympic star and the cinema's most famous Tarzan, dies at age 79.

*January 22:* The Los Angeles Raiders defeat the Washington Redskins, 38-9, to win Super Bowl XVIII, a game that also sees the broadcast of Apple's famous commercial introducing the Macintosh.

*January 23:* President Reagan nominates Edwin Meese as attorney general. The confirmation process will take more than a year.

*January 25:* President Reagan delivers his State of the Union address, in which he praises the nation's "renewed energy and optimism."

*January 27:* Singer Michael Jackson suffers second-degree burns to his scalp when his hair catches fire during the filming of a Pepsi-Cola commercial.

*February 3:* California physicians announce the first case of surrogate conception, in which a baby is conceived in one woman's womb and brought to term by another woman.

*February 3–11: Challenger* carries out the shuttle program's 10th mission, during which jet packs are used without a lifeline for the first time.

*February 7:* President Reagan announces that U.S. Marines will be withdrawn from Beirut, Lebanon. The withdrawal is completed by February 29.

*February 8–19:* The United States finishes fifth at the winter Olympics in Sarajevo, Yugoslavia, winning four gold medals (Debbie Armstrong in women's giant slalom, Scott Hamilton in men's singles figure skating, Bill Johnson in men's downhill skiing, and Phil Mahre in men's slalom skiing) and four silver.

*February 9:* Soviet leader Yuri Andropov dies of kidney failure only 15 months after becoming general secretary. He is succeeded by Konstantin Chernenko.

*February 13:* A report in the *Washington Post* reveals that Jesse Jackson had privately referred to Jews as "Hymies" and New York City as "Hymietown" in a conversation with *Post* reporter Milton Coleman on January 25.

*February 13:* The world's first heart and liver transplant is performed on Stormie Jones, a six-year-old Texan girl.

*February 15:* Ethel Merman, whose clarion voice wowed Broadway audiences for years, dies at age 76.

*February 28:* In *Grove City College v. Bell,* the Supreme Court rules that Title IX of the 1964 Civil Rights Act applies only to specific programs administered by academic organizations receiving federal funds. This opens a loophole for some institutions to legally engage in discriminatory practices.

*February 28:* At the Grammy Awards, Michael Jackson's *Thriller* wins best album of 1983, and "Beat It" wins as best record. Jackson himself is named best male pop vocalist, while Irene Cara is best female pop vocalist for "Flashdance."

*February 29:* Pierre Elliott Trudeau announces his decision to resign as prime minister of Canada.

*March 1:* Jackie Coogan, the film industry's first major child star and Uncle Fester on *The Addams Family,* dies at age 69.

*March 3:* Peter V. Ueberroth, president of the Los Angeles Olympic Organizing Committee, is named the new baseball commissioner, succeeding Bowie Kuhn.

*March 4:* Lucille Ball, Milton Berle, Paddy Chayefsky, Norman Lear, Edward R. Murrow, William S. Paley, and David Sarnoff become the first inductees into the newly established Television Academy Hall of Fame.

*March 5:* Longtime movie star William Powell dies, age 91.

*March 11:* On a radio broadcast, Louis Farrakhan threatens *Washington Post* reporter Milton Coleman with death for telling colleagues about Jesse Jackson's "Hymietown" comment.

*March 15:* The Senate votes down a Reagan-supported amendment to the Constitution that would have permitted silent prayer in public schools. On March 20 organized spoken prayer is also voted down.

*March 16:* In Beirut, Lebanon, William Buckley, CIA station chief, is kidnapped by Islamic fundamentalists. He will subsequently die in captivity.

*March 20:* A Soviet tanker detonates a mine off the coast of Nicaragua, apparently placed there by Nicaraguan contras.

*March 23:* At the world figure-skating championships in Ottawa, Canada, the United States' Scott Hamilton wins the men's singles title.

*April 1:* Soul singer Marvin Gaye is shot to death by his father during an argument, one day before his 45th birthday.

*April 6:* The *Wall Street Journal* publishes a report revealing that the mines laid in Nicaraguan harbors were actually placed there by CIA agents.

*April 6–13:* The space shuttle *Challenger* completes a successful mission that included the deployment of one satellite and retrieval, repair, and redeployment of the Solar Max satellite.

*April 7:* Senator Frank Church (D, Ohio), who served from 1957 to 1981, dies at age 59.

*April 9:* Nicaragua files a suit in the World Court, accusing the United States of placing mines in its harbor and supporting guerrillas.

*April 9:* At the Academy Awards, *Terms of Endearment* wins as best motion picture of 1983, and its star, Shirley MacLaine, wins best actress honors. Robert Duvall (*Tender Mercies*) wins as best actor.

*April 15:* Ben Crenshaw defeats Tom Watson by two strokes to win the Masters golf tournament in Augusta, Georgia.

*April 16:* William Kennedy wins the Pulitzer Prize for fiction for his novel *Ironweed*. Other Pulitzers are awarded to Mary Oliver (*American Primitive*) for poetry, David Mamet (*Glengarry Glen Ross*) for drama, Louis R. Harlan (*Booker T. Washington*) for biography, and Paul Starr (*Social Transformation of American Medicine*) for nonfiction.

*April 20:* Singer Mabel Mercer, whose style strongly influenced modern popular music, dies at age 84.

*April 22:* Renowned photographer Ansel Adams dies, age 82.

*April 23:* The U.S. government announces Dr. Robert Gallo's identification of a virus thought to cause AIDS (acquired immune deficiency syndrome). To date the fatal disease has afflicted some 4,000 Americans.

*April 26:* The body of Robert F. Kennedy's son David, dead from a drug overdose, is found in a Palm Beach, Florida, hotel.

*April 26:* William "Count" Basie, popular band leader and jazz pianist, dies at age 79.

*April 26–May 1:* President Reagan makes a state visit to China, during which he signs scientific and cultural accords.

*May 8:* On the same day the Olympic torch relay begins, the Soviet Union withdraws from the 1984 summer Olympics in Los Angeles, claiming the United States grossly flouted Olympic ideals.

*May 9:* The General Conference of the United Methodist Church prohibits the ordination of noncelibate homosexuals.

*May 16:* Controversial comedian Andy Kaufman, 35, dies of lung cancer.

The Reagans stand with terra-cotta figures in Xi'an (Sian), China, on April 29, 1984. *(Courtesy Ronald Reagan Library)*

*May 19:* In the fifth game of the National Hockey League finals, the Edmonton Oilers defeat the New York Islanders, winning the Stanley Cup.

*May 22:* The Supreme Court rules that law firms may not discriminate on the basis of sex, race, religion, or national origin when promoting associates to partnership.

*May 23:* For the first time, a woman, Kristine Holderied, graduates at the top of the class at the U.S. Naval Academy, Annapolis, Maryland.

*May 24:* In El Salvador, five former national guardsmen are found guilty of the murder of U.S. churchwomen in 1980.

*May 24:* Beatrice Foods Company becomes the world's second-largest food and consumer products company when it purchases Esmark, Inc., for $2.8 billion.

*May 30:* Scientists announce the development of an effective chicken-pox vaccine.

*June 3:* At the Tony Awards for the 1983–84 season, *The Real Thing* by Tom Stoppard wins as best play, and the gender-bending *La Cage Aux Folles* by Jerry Herman and Harvey Fierstein wins as best musical. *The Real Thing*'s Jeremy Irons and Glenn Close take the top dramatic acting awards.

*June 4:* Scientists at the University of California report they have successfully cloned DNA from an extinct animal species related to the zebra and the horse.

*June 6:* The Senate establishes a permanent Committee on Indian Affairs, replacing the temporary one that had been in place since 1977.

*June 9:* The cartoon character Donald Duck celebrates his 50th birthday at Disneyland in California. His career began with a bit part in 1934's *Wee Little Men*.

*June 11:* The U.S. Supreme Court rules that illegally obtained evidence may be admitted at trial if it can be proved that the evidence would have been found lawfully by other means anyway. This ruling is followed by another on July 5 stating that certain evidence found with defective search warrants could still be used in trials.

*June 12:* The Supreme Court rules that lower courts cannot overturn corporate seniority programs to prevent companies from laying off employees who were hired on an affirmative action basis. This allows businesses to maintain a traditional policy of "last hired, first fired."

*June 12:* In the seventh game of the final series, the Boston Celtics defeat the Los Angeles Lakers to win the National Basketball Association championship.

*June 14:* The Southern Baptist Convention passes a resolution opposing the ordination of women, but this does not apply to women already ordained as Baptist ministers.

*June 15:* Standard Oil Company of California (SOCAL) becomes the third-largest U.S. oil company when it takes over Gulf Corporation for $13.4 billion.

*June 16:* The nation's first roller coaster, at Coney Island, New York, celebrates its centennial.

*June 18:* Bruce Springsteen's album *Born in the U.S.A.* hits the Top Ten, where it will stay for 84 weeks.

*June 19:* Abstract expressionist painter Lee Krasner Pollock, the widow of Jackson Pollock, dies at age 75.

*June 25:* Following on a similar resolution by the House of Representatives, the U.S. Senate votes to cut off all aid to the contras in Nicaragua.

*June 30:* Pierre Elliott Trudeau officially resigns as prime minister of Canada after 16 years in office (excepting a 10-month gap). John Turner succeeds him to become the country's 17th prime minister.

*June 30:* Distinguished playwright Lillian Hellman dies at age 79.

*July 2:* President Reagan nominates former EPA head Anne Burford to chair the National Advisory Committee on Oceans and Atmosphere; she withdraws on July 27.

*July 14:* Al Schacht, player and coach known as the Clown Prince of Baseball, dies at age 91.

*July 15:* The Philadelphia Stars win the second United States Football League championship, defeating the Arizona Wranglers, 23-3. In August the league decides to move its season from spring to autumn, which will put it into competition with the National Football League.

*July 16–19:* At the Democratic National Convention in San Francisco, Minnesota's Walter F. Mondale is nominated for the presidency. Representative Geraldine Ferraro of New York is nominated for vice president, becoming the first woman to run for national office on a major party ticket.

*July 17:* President Reagan signs a bill giving states until October 1, 1986, to raise their legal drinking age to 21 or suffer cuts in federal highway funding.

*July 18:* President Reagan signs the Deficit Reduction Act, which raises taxes by approximately $50 billion and cuts spending by $13 billion through 1987.

*July 20:* Jim Fixx, runner whose books inspired an American passion for jogging, dies of a heart attack at age 52.

*July 22:* The Federal Deposit Insurance Corporation (FDIC) decides to invest $4.5 billion in the struggling Continental Illinois National Bank and Trust Company, with the assistance of a $3.5 billion loan from the Federal Reserve Bank.

*July 23:* Vanessa Williams, the first African-American Miss America, resigns after nude photos of her are published in *Penthouse.* Runner-up Suzette Charles is named to succeed her.

*July 28–August 12:* The United States wins 83 gold medals, finishing first in unofficial team standings at the summer Olympics in Los Angeles, which were marked by the absence of athletes from the Soviet Union.

*August 3:* The New York Stock Exchange sets a new daily volume record with 236.6 million shares, the first time the volume has exceeded 200 million shares.

*August 3:* The National Dance Hall of Fame, which will include a National Museum of Dance at Saratoga, New York, is established.

*August 11:* Congress passes the Equal Access Act, which requires public schools to provide to religious student groups the same access to their facilities as other groups.

*August 11:* Alfred A. Knopf, founder of the publishing company, dies at age 91.

*August 16:* John De Lorean, creator of the defunct car that bears his name, is acquitted of charges of using and distributing cocaine.

*August 20–23:* At the Republican National Convention in Dallas, Texas, President Ronald Reagan and Vice President George Bush are nominated to run for reelection.

*August 21:* Geraldine Ferraro holds a 90-minute news conference on the controversy surrounding the finances of herself and her husband. With clear and confident explanations, she manages to put the affair to rest.

*August 25:* Author Truman Capote, known for such works as *In Cold Blood* and *Breakfast at Tiffany's,* dies at age 59.

*August 30–September 5:* The third of NASA's fleet of shuttles, *Discovery,* makes its maiden flight with a crew of six, including Judith Resnick, the second U.S. Woman astronaut.

*September 4:* Brian Mulroney, 45, leads the Progressive Conservatives to a landslide victory in Canadian national elections, defeating John Turner to become the 18th prime minister of Canada. Sworn in on September 17, he will lead the nation for the next nine years.

*September 8–9:* John McEnroe wins the men's singles title, and Martina Navratilova wins the women's title in the U.S. Open tennis championships.

*The Cosby Show* became the biggest hit of the 1980s. Shown in the front row from left to right are Keshia Knight Pulliam, Bill Cosby, and Phylicia Ayers Rashad; in the back row from left to right are Tempest Bledsoe, Malcolm Jamal Warner, and Lisa Bonet. *(Eve Goldsmith/DPA/Landov)*

*September 14:* Janet Gaynor, who won the first Academy Award for best actress, dies at age 77.

*September 14–18:* Joe W. Kittinger becomes the first man to make a transatlantic solo balloon flight when he travels 3,535 miles from Caribou, Maine, to Savona, Italy, in a 10-story-tall, helium-filled craft named *Rosie O'Grady's Balloon of Peace.*

*September 17:* The American Kennel Club celebrates its centennial.

*September 20:* A suicide car bomb explodes outside the U.S. embassy in Beirut, killing two Americans and 21 others.

*September 20: The Cosby Show,* destined to become one of the most popular television shows of the 1980s, debuts on NBC.

*September 23:* At the Emmy Awards, Tom Selleck (*Magnum, P.I.*) and Tyne Daly take the top dramatic acting awards, while *Hill Street Blues* wins again as best dramatic series.

*September 30:* Diplomat Ellsworth Bunker, who had served under six presidents, dies at age 90.

*October 3:* Richard W. Miller, the first FBI agent to be accused of espionage, is arrested for passing a classified document to Soviet agents.

*October 5–13:* The space shuttle *Challenger* carries out its sixth mission. Its crew includes Marc Garneau, the first Canadian astronaut, and Dr. Kathryn D. Sullivan, the first female American astronaut to walk in space.

*October 7:* Walter Mondale wins the first presidential debate against President Reagan.

*October 12:* President Reagan signs the second Boland Amendment into law. The amendment forbids intelligence agencies to provide any military support to the contras in Nicaragua.

*October 14:* The Detroit Tigers of the American League win the World Series, four games to one, defeating the National League's San Diego Padres.

*October 15:* The Associated Press reveals the discovery of a CIA manual that provides guidelines for the Nicaraguan contras, including how to "neutralize" government officials. The Reagan administration will later claim the manual violates no laws.

*October 18:* The *New York Post* reports on a high-class prostitution ring run by Sydney Biddle Barrows, a *Mayflower* descendant. In the ensuing accounts of Barrows's operation, she becomes known as the Mayflower Madam.

*October 21:* President Reagan appears to win the second presidential debate against Walter Mondale.

*October 26:* For the first time, a baboon's heart is transplanted in a human, a 12-day-old girl who is identified only as Baby Fae. Although initially her condition will improve after the operation, she will die on November 15.

*November 1:* Willem de Kooning's 1953 work *Two Women* is sold at auction for $1,980,000, the highest price paid for a post–World War II artwork to date.

*November 2:* Margie Velma Barfield, a convicted murderer, is put to death in North Carolina; it is the first execution of a woman in 22 years.

*November 6:* Ronald Reagan is reelected president of the United States in a landslide victory over Walter F. Mondale. The Republicans retain their majority in the Senate, and the Democrats retain theirs in the House of Representatives.

*November 9:* In Las Vegas, Nevada, Larry Holmes knocks out James "Bonecrusher" Smith in the 12th round to win the first world heavyweight boxing match conducted by the International Boxing Federation (IBF).

*November 11:* The Reverend Martin Luther King, Sr., father of the assassinated civil rights leader, dies at age 84.

*November 12:* On the fourth day of the space shuttle *Discovery's* second flight (November 8–16), astronauts Joseph Allen and Dale Gardner retrieve a nonfunctioning satellite and bring it into the spacecraft's cargo bay. A second satellite will be retrieved on November 14.

*November 20:* CBS, Inc., pays $362.5 million for 12 publications owned by Ziff-Davis Publishing Company, the largest magazine acquisition in history at that time. On November 21 Australian publisher Rupert Murdoch will buy two more publications from Ziff-Davis for $350 million.

*November 22:* Secretary of State George Shultz and Soviet foreign minister Andrei Gromyko announce that arms talks will resume in Geneva, Switzerland, in January 1985.

*November 25:* The world's second artificial-heart transplant is carried out on William J. Schroeder, 52, in Louisville, Kentucky; he will survive 620 days.

*November 30:* Nine major Protestant denominations, consisting largely of Methodists, Presbyterians, and Episcopalians, reach an agreement on merging as the result of a 22-year effort by the Consultation on Church Union.

*December 4:* John Rock, one of the developers of the birth-control pill, dies at age 94.

*December 11–12:* Archaeologists announce the discovery in Florida of 7,000-year-old human skulls with their brains virtually intact, making it possible to extract and analyze DNA.

*December 20:* Bell Laboratories announces the development of a megabit memory chip, which is able to store more than 1 million bits of electronic data, making it the most powerful chip to date.

*December 22:* In New York City, vigilante Bernie Goetz shoots four youths in a subway train. He flees in a rented car but is later tracked down and arrested in New Hampshire.

*December 31:* The United States withdraws from UNESCO (United Nations Educational, Scientific, and Cultural Organization) due to the organization's financial mismanagement and political bias as well as its failure to make policy changes.

## Eyewitness Testimony

### *Jesse Jackson in the Headlines*

Jesse Jackson is not going to be president. But he must decide what he will be. He can be serious, or merely a dash of ginger in American politics—a spice, not a nutrient. His exploitation of Robert Goodman, the Navy flier held by Syria, suggests that he is bent on being merely, and unpleasantly, spicy.

*Columnist George F. Will commenting negatively on Jesse Jackson's mission to Syria to free Lieutenant Robert Goodman, Jr., in Will, "Jesse Jackson in Syria," Washington Post, January 1, 1984, p. H-7.*

Answering the human appeal of the Rev. Jesse Jackson to President Hafez al-Assad during their meeting Mon-

Reverend Jesse Jackson is shown in a 1983 photo. *(Library of Congress, Prints and Photographs Division [LC-U9-41583-29])*

day and also the demands of the U.S. Government to release the American pilot Lieutenant Goodman and in a contribution of the Syrian Government to creating circumstances that would facilitate the withdrawal of American troops from Lebanon, the Syrian Government has decided to release the American pilot.

The Syrian Government hopes that the U.S. Government will take measures to end its military involvement in Lebanon, which has contributed pain and suffering to Lebanon, to the area and to the American people and which also has increased the complications of the situation in Lebanon and in the entire area.

At the same time, the Syrian Government stresses that Syrian armed forces will confront very firmly all provocative and aggressive acts that it may be subject to.

*Statement issued by the Syrian government upon the January 3, 1984, release of Navy flyer Lieutenant Robert O. Goodman, Jr., following negotiations with Rev. Jesse Jackson, reproduced in "Text of Statement By Syria on Flier," New York Times, January 4, 1984, p. A-8.*

What it was, Washington wits quickly realized, was the invention of "the Syria primary"—a political coup composed of one part divine inspiration, one part pure chutzpah and a truckload of plain old-fashioned luck. In almost three weeks of ceaseless maneuver and nearly continuous press conferences, Jackson had: (1) initially put Ronald Reagan on the defensive and underscored the diplomatic impasse over his policy in Lebanon; (2) eclipsed his seven rivals for the Democratic presidential nomination, most notably Walter Mondale; (3) rallied—indeed, positively galvanized—his core constituency in black America; (4) reopened communication between the United States and the government of Syrian leader Hafez Assad . . . , and, almost in passing, rescued a Navy aviator from captivity. "He knocked one out of four ballparks at the same time," sighed one presidential aide.

*Describing the impact of Jesse Jackson's success in achieving the freedom of Lieutenant Robert Goodman from Syria on January 3, 1984, in "Jesse Wins a 'Syria Primary,' " Newsweek, January 16, 1984, p. 14.*

Jackson was, in fact, quizzed about the "Hymie" reference on Sunday, according to The New York Times. Here is the answer he gave: "It's not my standard operating procedure to refer to Jewish people like that." Then he added: "It's a lingo; I don't engage in it. I don't even realize it, frankly, I really don't." This sounds an awful lot like that old defense that goes: I have never in my life held a gun; besides it wasn't loaded and it went off by accident. Jackson, easily the most eloquent of the 1984 candidates, cannot avail himself of the excuse of lack of verbal agility.

> *Columnist Mark Shields attacking Jesse Jackson for his "Hymietown" comments, in Shields, ". . . Or Not Hard Enough?"* Washington Post, *February 24, 1984, p. A-19.*

There is the Jesse Jackson that blacks revere. He is the embodiment of black pride, an incandescent force glowing beside dull white politicians, demanding respect and "our fair share." He is the powerbroker who is ignored or patronized at great risk.

There is the Jesse Jackson that many whites distrust and some even fear. He is the former black radical, the civil rights leader who threatened white businessmen with economic boycotts, the presidential candidate who called Jews "Hymie" and New York City "Hymietown." In his shadow, neither embraced nor disavowed, stands Minister Louis Farrakhan, leader of the Nation of Islam, a Black Muslim sect, who has praised Hitler and seemed to threaten a black reporter with death.

In recent weeks, these conflicting perceptions of Jesse Jackson have come to overshadow his remarkable achievements in the Democratic primaries. . . .

> *Examining the impact of Jesse Jackson on the American political scene in "Pride and Prejudice,"* Time, *May 7, 1984, p. 30.*

Although most of the press has chosen not to note it, Minister Farrakhan has not participated in my campaign in recent months because I discouraged his participation. He is not part of our campaign. That was a conscious policy which I intend to continue because our campaign is structured and disciplined and cannot have others perceived as spokespersons for the Rainbow Coalition.

I will not permit Minister Farrakhan's words, wittingly or unwittingly, to divide the Democratic Party. Neither anti-Semitism nor anti-black statements have any place in our party. Having expressed my views on this matter as clearly as I can, I would observe that those who continue to use those statements to make an issue in the Democratic Party are not working for the good of the party.

> *Jesse Jackson in a June 28, 1984, statement distancing himself from the controversial Black Muslim Louis Farrakhan, quoted in "Jesse Jackson's Statement,"* Washington Post, *June 29, 1984, p. A-4.*

## The Business of Business

It is the dumbest thing that has ever been done. You don't have to break up the only functioning organization in the country to spur innovation.

> *Charles Wohlstetter, chairman of Continental Telecom Inc., decrying the AT&T divestiture; quoted in Pollack, "Bell System Breakup Opens Era of Great Expectations and Great Concern,"* New York Times, *January 1, 1984, p. 12.*

So why do huge corporate giants engage in this merger mania? The conventional wisdom, backed by the multinational banks that have vested interest in keeping the price of oil high (because they have financed so many oil expansion projects), is that the cheapest way to acquire additional oil reserves is to buy them from somebody else.

"More people are spending more money finding less oil than ever before," [Dillard] Spriggs [of Petroleum Analysts Ltd.] told me. Texaco, especially, was having big troubles in stemming a decline in its oil and gas reserves.

So the takeovers are aimed at picking up cheap, highly valued proved reserves. To be sure, no one is going to know for a number of years whether these deals are brilliant, or the "millstone around their necks" predicted by [oil broker Harry] Neustein in the cases of DuPont and U.S. Steel.

> *Columnist Hobart Rowan speculating on the impact of high-profile oil industry mergers, in Rowan, "Doubts about Texaco's Takeover,"* Washington Post, *January 12, 1984, p. A-19.*

Corporate America's merger fever was escalating last week. Standard Oil of California offered a record $13.2 billion for Gulf Corp. stealing the price from once favored Atlantic Richfield. Texaco seemed to have wiggled out of takeover range for the moment—buying up the Bass brothers' 10 percent stake in the company for $1.3 billion—but American Express awoke to find that Financial Corp. of America, a big savings-and-loan outfit, had bought 5 percent of its stock.

> *Tracking the growing number of mergers, in "Why All the Mega-Mergers?"* Newsweek, *March 19, 1984, p. 70.*

This Reagan-corporatist revolution, whereby business regulates government in pursuit of private profit at the expense of the legitimate interests of Americans as taxpayers, consumers and citizens, has little to do with being conservative. It has everything to do with building a government of the Exxons, by the General Motors, and for the DuPonts.

*Consumer advocate Ralph Nader in a speech to the National Press Club on June 6, 1984, commenting satirically on the Reagan administration's preferential treatment of big business interests, quoted in Nader, "The Megacorporate World of Ronald Reagan,"* The Ralph Nader Reader *(2000), p. 80.*

A. T. & T. prudently planned and implemented a telecommunications network second to no other. Its long-distance network provides high-quality and readily available service to all Americans at a reasonable price. Its revenues support a research-and-development effort which has not only driven the worldwide technological revolution but also led to rapid obsolescence in switching and transmission equipment.

In a society which rewards institutions and industries that fail to plan adequately for the future, I believe that A. T. & T. should be applauded for its foresight.

*Bell Laboratories employee Richard B. Wolf defending AT&T practices in a letter to the editor,* New York Times, *August 4, 1984, p. 22.*

The telephone industry has undergone sweeping changes since last Jan. 1, when the American Telephone and Telegraph Company divested itself of its 22 Bell operating companies. But as the first year comes to a close, Americans cannot agree whether the breakup of the Bell System was a good idea.

Supporters of the breakup say that it has already produced lower long-distance rates, a telephone industry teeming with competitors and a rush of new communications technologies that will give American companies an important edge in competition with foreign rivals.

. . . . .

Opponents, however, do not see the benefits of the divestiture, at least not yet. They contend that so far the lower long-distance rates mainly benefit industry and big business and are already requiring households to pay higher local rates.

*Reporter Eric N. Berg weighing the pros and cons of the AT&T divestiture in Berg, "One Year Later, the Debate over Bell Breakup Contin ues,"* New York Times, *December 27, 1984, p. A-1.*

## Computers and Consumers

People will like it, because it is a cuddly machine. The question is whether the simplicity will prove compelling to someone deciding whether to buy a computer.

*David Lawrence, an industry analyst for Montgomery Securities, San Francisco, assessing the potential for the Macintosh computer's success, quoted in Sanger, "For Apple, a Risky Assault on I.B.M.,"* New York Times, *January 23, 1984, p. D-5.*

The cause of all the hullabaloo is a jaunty, cream-colored computer that will sell for $2,495. From the side, Macintosh looks like an offspring of E.T. and R2–D2 that might start walking. But the fuss is also about Apple, the company that likes to say it invented the personal computer. If Apple is to beat back IBM and continue the whirlwind progress that has taken it on a seven-year tide from manufacturing in a California garage to annual sales of $1 billion, Macintosh must be a triumph.

. . . The early verdict of those who have used Mac is generally good. Says William Gates, chairman of Microsoft, the largest personal-computer software firm, "Macintosh is the only personal computer worth writing software for apart from the IBM PC." Says William Cranz, a Huntington Station, N.Y., computer dealer, "Mac is light years ahead of the IBM PC." . . .

*A report describing the excitement preceding the January 24, 1984, release of Apple Computer's new Macintosh, in "Apple Launches a Mac Attack,"* Time, *January 30, 1984, pp. 68–69.*

But the real excitement in the industry is software for personal computers. While only $260 million worth was sold as recently as 1980, sales this year are expected to reach $1.5 billion. And by 1989 revenues could exceed $6 billion. At least 1,000 companies are making programs. Microsoft, located in Bellevue, Wash. (pop. 75,000), near Seattle, is the largest. In 1980 it sold $4 million worth of software; projected 1984 revenues are $100 million. William Gates, 28, Microsoft's chairman and co-founder, has amassed a personal fortune estimated at $100 million.

*Reporting the growing explosion of computer software programs and the rise of Microsoft, in "The Wizard inside the Machines,"* Time, *April 16, 1984, p. 56.*

I hear that computers are indispensable household management tools. I must run a very simple household, because all my important documents, checks and receipts of the past five years are filed in three-quarters of a shoe box. At that rate, I should need about five shoe boxes in my lifetime. Five shoe boxes take up less space than the average computer. Shoe boxes also cost less and don't use electricity. In case of fire, flood or theft, either system is useless, so, all things considered, I don't see the advantage of having a computer when it comes to organizing receipts, warranties and records of payment.

*Publisher Katherine Gale DeCosta making the case against computers in DeCosta, "Anticomputerism,"* New York Times, *August 27, 1984, p. A-19.*

## Central American Troubles

Perhaps the United States should have paid more attention to Central America sooner. Perhaps, over the years, we should have intervened less, or intervened more, or intervened differently. But all these are questions of what might have been. What confronts us now is a question of what might become. Whatever its roots in the past, the crisis in Central America exists urgently in the present, and its successful resolution is vital to the future.

*From the introduction to the Kissinger Commission report on U.S. policy in Central America, reproduced in "Key Sections from Study of Latin Region by Kissinger Panel,"* New York Times, *January 12, 1984, p. A-14.*

The report makes a powerful and intelligent case that what happens in Central America is important to the United States—something that many Americans have been slow to recognize. And from this it proceeds with flawless logic to the proposition that Americans should be prepared to expend substantially more in aid and in political energy than they are spending now. It is a tribute to the seriousness of the commission members and the efficiency of the Kissinger operation that many all-too-familiar commission pitfalls were avoided and that consensus was reached on a number of important points. There was something less than consensus, however, on how the commission's agreed-on goals were to be achieved, and this in a way goes to the heart of the matter.

The Washington Post *editorializing on the ramifications of the Kissinger Commission's report on U.S. policy in Central America, in "The Central American Debate,"* Washington Post, *January 12, 1984, p. A-18.*

The President has asked us to back his foreign policy. Bill, how can we back his foreign policy when we don't know what the hell he is doing? Lebanon, yes, we all knew that he sent troops over there. But mine the harbors in Nicaragua? This is an act violating international law. It is an act of war. For the life of me, I don't see how we are going to explain it.

*Senator Barry Goldwater (R, Ariz.), in a letter written on April 9, 1984, scolding CIA director William Casey for the illicit mining of Nicaraguan harbors, quoted in Johnson,* Sleepwalking Through History *(2003), p. 277.*

I have announced today that I will resign as vice chairman of the Senate Select Committee on Intelligence.

This appears to me the most emphatic way I can express my view that the Senate committee was not properly briefed on the mining of Nicaraguan harbors with American mines from an American ship under American command.

*Beginning of April 15, 1984, statement by senator Daniel Patrick Moynihan (R, N.Y.), announcing his resignation from the Senate Intelligence Committee, reproduced in "Text of Moynihan Statement,"* New York Times, *April 16, 1984, p. A-8. Moynihan rescinded his resignation on April 26 after CIA director Willliam Casey apologized for the agency's lapses in keeping the committee informed on its activities in Nicaragua.*

And what is the world to think when the White House spokesman, announcing a new anti-terrorism policy, says with a straight face that "the states that practice terrorism or actively support it cannot be allowed to do so without consequence"? What is it if not terrorism when the C.I.A., as Congressional sources belatedly learned, directed last Oct. 10 a sabotage raid against the Nicaraguan port of Corinto in which 3.2 million gallons of fuel were destroyed and the town's 25,000 people had to be evacuated?

*Columnist Tom Wicker pointing out the inconsistencies of U.S. policy in Central America in Wicker, "Escalating the Rhetoric,"* New York Times, *April 20, 1984, p. A-27.*

I think that people in the long run are less concerned about reports of mining Nicaraguan harbors than they are about creating a wave of immigration into the country if Central America or any part of it should fall under Soviet-Cuban domination. If we have another Cuba in Central America, Mexico will have a big problem and we're going to have a massive wave of immigration. The effort to prevent this from happening is not going to excite Americans as much as the threat they would face if things go wrong.

*CIA director William Casey, downplaying the CIA's mining of Nicaragua harbors, quoted in "What's Behind Reagan Strategy in Nicaragua,"* U.S. News & World Report, *April 23, 1984, p. 28.*

Only one American in three supports President Reagan's policies in Central America, and nearly half the people say they are afraid that those policies might lead the United States into a war there, according to the latest New York Times/CBS News Poll.

Asked about a specific element of American activity in the region, the mining of Nicaraguan harbors, the public responds even more negatively. By 67 percent to 13 percent, the respondents disapproved of American involvement in the mining.

Those findings of the poll of 1,367 Americans reflect a general unease that Americans were found to feel toward Mr. Reagan's conduct of foreign affairs.

*Reporter David Shribman summarizing the results of a poll on American attitudes toward U.S. policy in Central America, in Shribman, "Poll Finds a Lack of Public Support for Latin Policy,"* New York Times, *April 29, 1984, p. A-1.*

In law school, we were taught to believe that the rule of law should govern international relations if the human race is to be spared the horrors of war. Now the United States has declared that it will not accept the jurisdiction of the International Court of Justice at The Hague, either over the CIA's mining of Nicaraguan ports or, for the next two years, over any disputes involving Central America. What has this nation come to when it formally repudiates the rule of law in international relations? And what kind of hypocrisy is it that enables President Reagan to participate on the very next day in a ceremony proclaiming "Law Day, U.S.A." and telling us that "without law, there can be no freedom, only chaos and disorder"?

*From a letter to the editor about the United States' repudiation of a World Court decision regarding the CIA's mining of Nicaraguan harbors, in* Newsweek, *May 7, 1984, p. 6.*

The administration's "secret" war against the Sandinistas is wrong, unfocused and counterproductive, and has been from the start. Congress, having approved of it when it was small and quiet, seems intent on dropping it now that it has become hot and public. Something is owed, however, to Nicaraguans who took up arms expecting American support. If they are not to be sustained further in battle, they must be sustained in retreat and in readjusting their lives.

*The* Washington Post *arguing for some form of support for the Nicaraguan contras in its editorial "Central American Moment,"* Washington Post, *June 28, 1984, p. A-14.*

It is possible to neutralize carefully selected and planned targets, such as court judges, police and state security officials, etc. For psychological purposes, it is necessary to take extreme precautions, and it is absolutely necessary to gather together the population affected, so that they will be present, take part in the act, and formulate accusations against the oppressor.

. . . . .

If the majority of the people give their support or backing to the target or subject, do not try to change these sentiments through provocation.

*From "Psychological Operations in Guerilla Warefare," a CIA-written manual for Nicaraguan rebels, reproduced in "Excerpts from Primer for Insurgents,"* New York Times, *October 17, 1984, p. A-12.*

## Medical and Scientific Wonders

A 6-year-old Texas girl who received the first simultaneous heart and liver transplant is "responsive and alert" and may be breathing on her own within a day, hospital officials said Wednesday.

Stormie Jones of Cumbie, Tex., who suffers from a rare liver disease and weak heart, was in critical but stable condition at Children's Hospital [in Pittsburgh, Pa.].

She received the new organs in a 16-hour operation that ended Tuesday morning.

"She got a new heart for Valentine's Day," said Stormie's mother, Lois Jones, 27.

*A February 16, 1984, UPI report on the condition of double-transplant patient Stormie Jones, in "Girl 'Responsive, Alert' after Double Transplant,"* Chicago Tribune, *February 16, 1984, p. 8.*

The image could have come from a once and future fantasy, yet it aired on the evening news. A U.S. astronaut, looking like a modern knight-errant in shining space suit, sallies forth into the darkness, powered by a Buck Rogers backpack called an MMU (manned maneuvering unit). Armed with a space-age lance nicknamed the stinger, he spears a stray satellite and rockets back to the mother ship. There, silhouetted against the shimmering earth, some 225 miles below, he spins along at 17,500 m.p.h., shouldering his prize like a sci-fi Atlas.

*Eloquently describing an astronaut's tether-free space walk to retrieve a satellite during* Discovery's *November 8–16, 1984, mission, in "Roaming the High Frontier,"* Time, *November 26, 1984, p. 16.*

Inspired by such cosmic wanderlust, Reagan is ready to move on from the space shuttle to what NASA calls the "next logical step": a permanent manned space station. . . .

The space station had many detractors, even within the inner councils of the White House. Budget Director David Stockman bitterly opposed the idea early this year as a waste of money. Reagan finally turned on him and quipped, "If you had been at the court of Isabella and Ferdinand, Columbus never would have made it to the New World."

*Considering the future of the space exploration program in "Roaming the High Frontier,"* Time, *November 26, 1984, p. 19.*

The dying heart was an ugly yellowish color when Dr. William DeVries finally cut it loose, tore it out of the Merchurochrome-stained chest cavity, and put it to one side. For the next three hours, while a nearby heart-lung bypass machine kept the unconscious patient alive—and while a tape in the background eerily played Mendelssohn and Vivaldi—DeVries' sure hands carefully stitched into place a grapefruit-size gadget made of aluminum and polyurethane. At 12:50 p.m. last Monday, the Jarvik-7 artificial heart newly sewn inside William J. Shroeder began beating steadily, 70 beats to the minute. When Shroeder opened his eyes 3 1/2 hours later in the intensive-care unit, DeVries bent over his patient and whispered assurances, "The operation is all through. You did really well. Everything is perfect."

*Describing the implantation of an artificial heart into patient William J. Schroeder on November 25, 1984, in "One Miracle, Many Doubts,"* Time, *December 10, 1984, p. 70.*

It's different, but at least it's beating and I can feel it. . . . It was very weak before and now it's a thump, thump sort of feeling.

*Margaret Schroeder, wife of artificial-heart patient William J. Schroeder, describing the sensation of feeling her husband's new heart beating, quoted in Altman, "Heart Patient Briefly Leaves Bed,"* New York Times, *November 30, 1984, p. A-1.*

## The Baby Fae Controversy

We're not in the business of uselessly sacrificing animals. But we're forced here to make a choice. We can either decide to continue to let these otherwise healthy human babies die, because they are born with only half of their heart, or we can intervene and, in so doing, sacrifice some lesser form than our own human species.

*Dr. Leonard Bailey in a news release, October 27, 1984, explaining his rationale for implanting a baboon's heart into 12-day-old Baby Fae, quoted in Altman, "Baboon's Heart Implanted in Infant on Coast,"* New York Times, *October 28, 1984, sec. I, p. 38.*

This child was drafted in the name of science. These scientists were geared up for a very important piece of experimental research, and that's all that seemed important to them.

*Ronald Bayer, a bioethicist at the Hastings Center, Hastings-on-Hudson, New York, commenting critically on the motives and methods of doctors who transplanted a baboon's heart into Baby Fae, quoted in Altman, "Confusion Surrounds the Case of Baby Fae,"* New York Times, *November 6, 1984, p. C-11.*

When the operation was announced, Bailey had faced accusations of callous experimentation on a dying baby; but subsequent weeks had shown him to be deeply caught up in the drama of her struggle. He had been at her bedside almost round the clock. Friday morning he appeared shaken and ashen-faced at a news conference where he read an often emotional, at times sentimental, tribute. "Baby Fae will live in our memories," he said, his voice cracking, ". . . for a lifetime."

*Describing the emotional aftermath of Baby Fae's death on November 15, 1984, in "Baby Fae's Heart Gives Out,"* Newsweek, *November 26, 1984, p. 94.*

A single trial is not enough to prove a technique. If the experiment on Baby Fae was justified, so too is a second in the series Dr. Bailey plans. But both the animal data and those on Baby Fae should be published and criticized before the next experiment. Optimism is never bad, but it was overhopeful for Dr. Bailey to tell the American Medical Association in an interview published yesterday, "I really believe that [Baby Fae] will celebrate more than one birthday with her new heart."

> *The* New York Times *assessing the importance and inherent problems in the Baby Fae case in its editorial "The Life and Death of Baby Fae,"* New York Times, *November 17, 1984, p. 22.*

Baby Fae brought out defenders of man, beast and press. But who was defending Baby Fae? There *was* something disturbing—subtly, but profoundly disturbing—about the baboon implant. It has nothing to do with animal rights or the Frankenstein factor or full disclosure. It has to do with means and ends.

It turns out that before placing a baboon heart into the chest of Baby Fae, doctors at Loma Linda had not sought a human heart for transplant. That fact betrays their primary aim: to advance a certain line of research. As much as her life became dear to them, Baby Fae was to be their means.

> *Essayist Charles Krauthammer reflecting on the ethics of the Baby Fae case, in Krauthammer, "The Using of Baby Fae,"* Time, *December 3, 1984, p. 87.*

## The Presidential Race

People are realistic. They know Jesse can go so far and that's why they're supporting Mondale. But I think this trip to Syria suggests that Jesse can produce, and it's going to help him here. Jesse injects emotionalism into the campaign, excitement. Listen to Mondale and Glenn. They're dull. Jesse's sure not dull.

> *E. C. Foster, a history teacher at Jackson State College in Jackson, Mississippi, commenting on Jesse Jackson's effect on the presidential campaign, quoted in Weinraub, "Mondale, Campaigning in the South, Appeals for Support of Blacks,"* New York Times, *January 5, 1984, p. B-10.*

... [A]t times President Reagan glides along altogether too smoothly, virtually unaware of the gritty, often bumpy policymaking processes of his Administration.

His lapses are more than a forgivable matter of mixing up history at a press conference or misrepresenting a trivial budget figure now and again. Reagan is remarkably disengaged from the substance of his job. His aides no longer dismiss as glib the theory that Reagan has a movie-star approach to governing. "In Reagan's mind," says a White House adviser, "somebody does the lighting, somebody else does the set, and Reagan takes care of his role, which is the public role."

> *Analyzing Ronald Reagan following his January 29, 1984, announcement that he will run for reelection, in "A View Without Hills or Valleys,"* Time, *February 6, 1984, p. 23.*

When I hear your new ideas, I'm reminded of that ad, "Where's the beef?"

> *Walter Mondale to Gary Hart, using the tag line from a popular commercial for the fast-food chain Wendy's during a televised Democratic primary debate in Atlanta, Georgia, on March 11, 1984.*

And then there were two—one for each kind of Democrat.

On one side are voters who tend to be younger, more intellectual, more sophisticated, more affluent, more tolerant but not necessarily more liberal. They are typified by the Yuppies, Young Urban Professionals who once supported Eugene McCarthy, then Mr. [George] McGovern, then John Anderson—and now Gary Hart. Mr. Hart has established his popularity among Yuppies without tainting himself as unduly liberal. The good news for him is that McGovern and Glenn supporters both are apt to turn to him.

On the other side are traditional Democrats—older, more conservative, more blue-collar and much closer to the hard edges of unemployment and poverty. They too may care about acid rain and a nuclear freeze, but are likely to think first about bread and butter. They are the party of Hubert Humphrey and Scoop Jackson—and Walter Mondale. . . .

> *From a* New York Times *editorial examining the divisions in the Democratic Party, in "The Democrats—and the Democrats,"* New York Times, *March 15, 1984, p. A-30.*

People say Gary Hart took support, energy, the spotlight away from Fritz Mondale. It seems to us more likely that when Jesse Jackson lost steam, the damage had been done to John Glenn and his much-needed momentum. Gary Hart inherited what was the real Jackson legacy, the curiosity and the excitement and the sense that there actually was an alternative to Walter Mondale. Meanwhile, Mr. Jackson was taking in the South, a lot of what otherwise might have been Mondale votes.

*The* Washington Post *examining the impact of the Jackson candidacy on the Democratic presidential nomination race, in its editorial "The Man Who Made Super Tuesday,"* Washington Post, *March 15, 1984, p. A-20.*

I intend to pick the best person I can find who's compatible, whose selection speaks for my vision of our future, and there are sufficient differences between Reverend Jackson and myself that I can't do that.

*Walter Mondale in a July 11, 1984, interview citing reasons why he would not select Jesse Jackson as a running mate, quoted in Raines, "Mondale Says He Won't Run with Jackson,"* New York Times, *July 12, 1984, p. A-1.*

I was in the sitting room putting the finishing touches on my speech to the council when the phone rang again. This time it was Mondale. I took the call in the privacy of the bedroom. "Hi," he said. "Hi," I replied. "How are you doing?" he said. "Fine," I replied. Here it comes, I thought. And no matter what he was going to say, I had my reply ready: I will work as hard as I can for the ticket. I want you to win and you have my total support. I think you will be a tremendous President.

"Will you be my running mate?" he asked. I didn't pause for a minute. "That would be terrific," I answered, and then added the extra phrase I'd been saving for my planned response. "I want you to know, Fritz, that I am deeply honored." And I still am.

*Geraldine Ferraro recounting the moment on July 11, 1984, when Walter Mondale asked her to join the Democratic ticket as the vice presidential nominee in Ferraro,* Ferraro: My Story *(1986), p. 110.*

Feminism has scored no more spectacular triumph since women won the right to vote. Even with universal suffrage, American women had enjoyed, until last Thursday, nothing more than the right to elect a man to the White House. With one swift stroke, however, the Democrats have made it possible for women to enter the final phase of their enfranchisement. Win or lose in November, Geraldine Ferraro is now emblematic of the truest, purest facet of the American dream: that every child can grow up to be President. . . .

*Examining the impact of Geraldine Ferraro's selection as Walter Mondale's running mate on July 11, 1984, in "Ripples Throughout Society,"* Time, *July 23, 1984, p. 34.*

There's another city, another part of the city, the part where some people can't pay their mortgages and most young people can't afford one, where students can't afford the education they need and middleclass parents watch the dream they hold for their children evaporate. In this part of the city, there are more poor than ever, more families in trouble. There is despair, Mr. President, in places that you don't visit in your shining city.

*New York governor Mario Cuomo in his keynote speech to the Democratic National Convention, July 16, 1984, responding to President Reagan's recent description of the United States as "a shining city on a hill," quoted in "Transcript of Keynote Address by Cuomo to the Convention,"* New York Times, *July 17, 1984, p. A-16.*

My constituency is the desperate, the damned, the disinherited, the disrespected, and the despised. They've voted in record numbers. They have invested faith, hope and trust that they have in us. The Democratic Party must send them a signal that we care. I pledge my best not to let them down.

*Reverend Jesse Jackson in his speech to the Democratic National Convention, July 18, 1984. Available online. URL: http://www.pbs.org/wgbh/pages/frontline/ jesse/speeches/jesse84speech.html.*

Whoever is inaugurated in January, the American people will pay Mr. Reagan's bills. The budget will be squeezed. Taxes will go up. And anyone who says they won't is not telling the truth. I mean business. By the end of my first term I will cut the deficit by two thirds. Let's tell the truth. Mr. Reagan will raise taxes, and so will I. He won't tell you. I just did.

*Walter Mondale in his speech accepting the Democratic nomination for president, July 19, 1984. Available online. URL: http://www.cnn.com/ALLPOLITICS/ 1996/conventions/chicago/facts/famous.speeches/ mondale.84.shtml.*

What I have done since I got elected to Congress was to keep our finances totally separate. I did that in 1979 as soon as I entered Congress. We filed separate returns. We used to file jointly up until I got elected. You saw our returns. By '78 was a joint return. After that they were separate. I had the accountants check recently—I knew I suffered a penalty by filing separately. We have suffered over the last several years $6,000 or $7,000 that we could have pocketed had we filed jointly. But I deliberately wanted to keep our finances separate. We live two separate professional lives.

> *Representative Geraldine Ferraro, Democratic candidate for vice president, at an August 21, 1984, news conference regarding her finances and those of her husband, John Zaccaro; quoted in "Excerpts from Ferraro's News Conference About Finances," New York Times, August 22, 1984, p. B-6.*

In 1980 we asked the people of America, "Are you better off than you were 4 years ago?" Well, the people answered then by choosing us to bring about a change. We have every reason now, 4 years later, to ask that same question again, for we have made a change.

The American people joined us and helped us. Let us ask for their help again to renew the mandate of 1980, to move us further forward on the road we presently travel, the road of common sense, of people in control of their own destiny; the road leading to prosperity and economic expansion in a world at peace.

> *Ronald Reagan in his speech accepting the Republican nomination for president, August 23, 1984. Available online. URL: http://www.reagan.utexas.edu/resource/speeches/1984/82384f.htm.*

Reagan appeals to this hunger for self-respect through both his programs and his personality. Despite all the charges of unfairness, Reagan retains a populist look—especially as compared to Walter Mondale or Geraldine Ferraro. He is seen as a power-to-the-people, shrink-big-government President who wants to slash taxes, cut spending, and redirect money outward and downward (federalism). Mr. Reagan has "a democratic personality," as Richard Wirthlin has appositely noted, with his geniality, wit, and obvious enjoyment of the job; he is more reminiscent of FDR or JFK than of Herbert Hoover or Calvin Coolidge.

> *Conservative commentator John McLaughlin drawing some unusual comparisons in McLaughlin, "The New Nationalism," National Review, September 21, 1984, quoted in Boyer, Reagan as President (1990), p. 90.*

. . . [T]he fact of it is every estimate by this Administration about the size of the deficit has been off by billions and billions of dollars. As a matter of fact, over four years, they've missed the mark by nearly $600 billion. We were told we would have a balanced budget in 1983. It was a $200 billion deficit instead. And now we have a major question facing the American people as to whether we'll deal with this deficit and get it down for the sake of a healthy recovery. Virtually every economic analysis I've heard of, including the distinguished Congressional Budget Office, . . . says that even with historically high levels of economic growth, we will suffer a $263 billion deficit. In other words, it doesn't converge, as the President suggests. It gets larger, even with growth.

> *Walter Mondale making a strong point about the economy in his first debate with Ronald Reagan, October 7, 1984, quoted in "Transcript of Louisville Debate Between Reagan and Mondale," New York Times, October 8, 1984, p. B-4.*

The question comes down to this: do you want to see America return to the policies of weakness of the last four years, or do we want to go forward marching together as a nation of strength and that's going to continue to be strong?

We shouldn't be dwelling on the past or even the present. The meaning of this election is the future, and whether we're going to grow and provide the jobs and the opportunities for all Americans that they need. . . .

> *Ronald Reagan stressing a favorite theme during his closing statement at his second debate with Walter Mondale, October 21, 1984, quoted in "Transcript of the Reagan-Mondale Debate on Foreign Policy," New York Times, October 22, 1984, p. B-6.*

Now consider Mr. Mondale's strengths. His election would mean franker, fairer decisions on the hard economic choices that the President has concealed during the campaign. Mr. Mondale would offer an enlightened and human conception of what Government should, and should not, do. Most of all, he would bring to the White House the will to control nuclear weapons.

So give Ronald Reagan due credit for what he has done, 1981 to 1984. The decision now should turn on who offers brighter promise for 1985 to 1988. In all

President Reagan and Walter Mondale face each other in their second debate in Kansas City, Missouri, on October 21, 1984. *(Courtesy Ronald Reagan Library)*

three Presidential categories, our choice is Walter Mondale.

> *The* New York Times *endorsing Walter Mondale for president in its editorial "Mondale for President,"* New York Times, *October 28, 1984, sec. 4, p. 22.*

I know how you feel because I've been there myself. Do not despair. The fight didn't end tonight. It began tonight. I have been around for a while, and I have noticed in the seeds of most every victory are to be found the seeds of defeat, and in every defeat are to be found the seeds of victory. Let us fight on. Let us fight on.

> *Walter Mondale to his supporters during his statement conceding defeat in the presidential election, November 6, 1984, quoted in "Statement of Concession by Mondale,"* New York Times, *November 7, 1984, p. A-21.*

More than his predecessors, they say, Mr. Reagan has been able to articulate a sweeping sense of the direction in which he wants to take the country. Democratic aides say Walter F. Mondale, the Democratic candidate, never succeeded in giving similar coherence to his own collection of policies. Among the other factors adding to Mr. Reagan's popularity has been the simplicity and consistency of his message, his practice of speaking in the broadest of terms about values rather than issues, his identification with America's myths and the apparent sincerity of his beliefs.

> *Reporter Steve R. Weisman analyzing the reasons for Ronald Reagan's success in Weisman, "The Politics of Popularity,"* New York Times, *November 8, 1984, p. A-19.*

Growth and change have always been major goals of the Democratic Party, but in recent years protection of the status quo has become an increasingly dominant preoccupation. Instead of inventing ways to create new jobs, the party has been trying to maintain existing jobs in out-of-date industries. It has been fighting to keep old bureaucracies alive, and it has been using quotas to dictate equality of results rather then deregulating and encouraging minorities to use the market to advance economically. It has been defending middle-class entitlement programs such as Social Security without heed to the changes that everyone agrees privately are going to have to be made. In the damning phrase of the Republican political analyst Kevin Phillips, the Democratic Party has become dedicated to "reactionary liberalism." It's little wonder that the party did so poorly among young voters. A 73-year-old man told them that the best days of America were yet to come, and the once-dynamic Democratic Party seemed to say it wasn't so. The Democrats need to find leaders who believe it is so—and can make it so in reality, not just in television ads.

> *A postelection editorial in the* New Republic, *November 26, 1984, commenting on the need for the Democrats to change if they want to win, reproduced in Sewall,* The Eighties *(1997), pp. 86–87.*

## Olympic Ups and Downs

Day after day, the word drifts back here from the United States about the low television ratings for the XIV Olympic Winter Games. With the American hockey team skating uphill, with other American athletes unable to win even a bronze medal in the first seven events, not much has happened to arouse American patriotism, which translates into American viewers. But the low ratings also represent how the TV generation has come to look at sports.

Because of the networks' theatrical buildup at the start of sports shows, some viewers think they have been shortchanged if that hype doesn't materialize into a drama. . . .

> *Columnist Dave Anderson reporting from Sarajevo, Yugoslavia, on one of the reasons for the lack of U.S. interest in the winter Olympics there, in Anderson, "'Sarajevo' as a TV Sitcom,"* New York Times, *February 12, 1984, sec. 4, p. 1.*

Washington has made assurances of late of the readiness to observe the rules of the Olympic charter. The practical deeds by the American side, however, show that it does not intend to ensure the security of all athletes, respect their rights and human dignity and create normal conditions for holding the games. . . . In these conditions, the National Olympic Committee of the USSR is compelled to declare that participation of Soviet sportsmen in the Games is impossible.

*From the statement issued by the Soviet Union on May 8, 1984, announcing its decision to boycott the summer Olympic Games in Los Angeles, quoted in Guttman,* The Olympics *(1992), p. 157.*

For their part, Soviet sports officials deny that the decision is related in any way to the fact that Soviet Olympic teams are weak this year in track and field, swimming and gymnastics. And they claim that it has nothing to do with retaliation for the Western boycott of the 1980 summer games in Moscow, an action led by the U.S.

There is no doubt, however, that the Kremlin has been laying the groundwork for the withdrawal for at least six weeks with a steady barrage of public charges that the U.S. is violating Olympic principles and that Los Angeles is an unsafe city riddled with dangerous anti–Communists.

*Journalist Nicholas Daniloff examining the reasons behind the Soviet withdrawal from the summer Olympics, in Daniloff, "What Kremlin Seeks By Boycotting Games,"* U.S. News & World Report, *May 21, 1984, p. 25.*

As a runner enters town, church bells sound, fire sirens blare, trucks blast air horns. Some people throw roses, offer beers or run alongside to touch someone, anyone, involved with the torch. "Look at that runner, honey," one mother urged her daughter. "Look at that runner and always remember him!"

It is heady stuff for runners.

"The people are making heroes out of people who aren't," said Richard Boehner, the relay manager. But out there on the road, running with the crowd cheering, it's hard to separate the torch-bearer from the torch.

*Reporter Andrew H. Malcolm describing the wave of patriotic emotion being generated by the Olympic torch relay, in Malcolm, "Something More than Olympic Torch Is Crossing the Country,"* New York Times, *June 10, 1984, sec. 1, p. 26.*

[I]t was one of the most moving experiences of my life. This little boy could barely walk. He had a specially designed walker with wheels and a socket to hold the torch and he pushed it along real slow. You could see the determination in his face. O.J. [Simpson] walked along with him, offering encouragement. People in the crowd were cheering and crying. It took him fifteen minutes and I don't think anybody will ever forget it.

I was beside myself. I was crying—like everybody else. I didn't want to let go of the moment, so I jumped the press truck and followed it for a few more miles. The whole thing is really something else. People are on a high and it's going to carry over into the Games.

*Summer Olympics general manager Harry Usher to Los Angeles Olympic Organizing Committee president Peter Ueberroth, describing an emotional moment in the Olympic torch relay in Los Angeles, July 21, 1984, quoted in Ueberroth,* Made in America *(1986), p. 286.*

It is titled "Rebirth of a Nation" and stars America with a supporting cast of thousands.

The subtitle was "The Games of the XXIII Olympiad," but it has proved to be wanting in marquee value.

Out in Los Angeles, where "dreams come true," as we have been told by ABC, which is televising this epic, United States athletes are either winning gold medals, are close to winning them, or have just missed winning them and there will be a next time.

In the most hallowed tradition of Hollywood, ABC is bringing us from out of the Old West the dusty tale of the good guys against the bad guys. The good guys is "Us," the bad guys is "Them."

*Columnist Ira Berkow commenting on the Americanization of the Olympics in the games' television coverage, in Berkow, "Commentators of Patriots?",* New York Times, *August 3, 1984, p. B-13.*

Nationalism at the Olympics is essentially unavoidable because of the flags and anthems and the money for the badges. So the home court must be acknowledged as a powerful advantage, though at least it did not extend to ragging the Chinese gymnasts (whom Mitch Gaylord reassuringly called "very human human beings") or to begrudging the Rumanians their corresponding triumph over the U.S. Women gymnasts. News that the Rumanians' traveling expenses were defrayed by the Olympic organizers had no noticeable effect on their popularity since it did not change the fact that they had stood up to the Soviet Union.

*Describing the nationalistic spirit of the Los Angeles Olympics in "Glory Hallelujah!" Time, August 13, 1984, p. 37.*

## Debating Sensitive Issues

We cannot pretend that America is preserving her first and highest ideal, the belief that each life is sacred, when we've permitted the deaths of 15 million helpless innocents since the Roe versus Wade decision—15 million children who will never laugh, never sing, never know the joy of human love, will never strive to heal the sick, feed the poor, or make peace among nations. Abortion has denied them the first and most basic of human rights. We are all infinitely poorer for their loss.

*President Reagan offering an emotional argument against abortion in an address to the Annual Convention of the National Religious Broadcasters, January 30, 1984. Available online. URL: http://www.reagan.utexas.edu/resource/speeches/1984/13084b.htm.*

Why has Reagan espoused policies that threw 700,000 children off AFDC and Medicaid in fiscal 1982, leaving only 52 poor children out of 100 getting AFDC and 73 out of 100 receiving Medicaid?

Why has a president who professes to care so much about saving children taken compensatory education opportunities away from 440,000 disadvantaged children and taken child care agencies out of the reach of many thousands more?

*Columnist Carl T. Rowan commenting critically on President Reagan's public statements against abortion in light of a report by the Children's Defense Fund about the plight of children in poverty, in Rowan, "Do Only the Unborn Matter?" Washington Post, February 1, 1984, p. A-15.*

It [silent meditation] is simply an attempt to promote prayer. I don't object to prayer or any individual student's thinking or meditating. I object to the school board orchestrating a specific time of day. I think it violates my constitutional rights.

*Sharon Rubin, a mother who filed a complaint against the Hicksville, New York, Board of Education, explaining her objections to the moment of silent meditation in Hicksville's schools, quoted in Gruson, "Hicksville Divided by Moment of Silence," New York Times, February 29, 1984, p. B-4.*

We are being separated into two camps, one camp of the faithful and the other camp of the unbelievers. Does God stay in Hicksville or does God go?

*Harry Smith, a sixth-grade teacher at Hicksville (New York) Junior High School, commenting on the recent banning of a moment of silent meditation at his school; quoted in "Silent Meditation Time Banned at School on L.I.," New York Times, March 2, 1984, p. B-2.*

I hear it repeated time and again—"Well, 80 percent of the nation wants prayer." My answer to that is very simple. Eighty percent of the nation supported racial discrimination, 80 percent of the nation went ahead and discriminated against the retarded and disabled at one time. Shall we have followed 80 percent of the nation in what it felt on either of those issues?

Let me turn the coin over. Eighty percent of the nation wants abortion as defined by the Supreme Court decision. Yet, are we not trying to contest that? Eighty percent of the nation wants E.R.A., the Equal Rights Amendment. Are we following that popular opinion?

*Senator Lowell P. Weicker, Jr. (R, Conn.), explaining why he voted against the constitutional amendment to allow silent prayer in public schools, quoted in Perlez, "5 Senators Oppose School Prayer Measure," New York Times, March 16, 1984, pp. B-1, B-5.*

The important distinction is not between public policy and private religious beliefs. You can't have politicians who are schizophrenic. I think the line that must be drawn is between what one believes are moral and human values that should be protected by law, given the social realities of our society. On abortion, for example, one must consider the fact that there are many people who will try to have abortions even if they are declared illegal, that the matter is seen by different groups as an extremely important exercise of their personal rights. The judgment about what is the right law is a judgment on which good people, who share opposition to abortion, can disagree.

*Father Joseph O'Hare, Jesuit priest and president of Fordham University, offering his viewpoint on the issue of separation of church and state, quoted in "Voices of Reason, Voices of Faith," Time, September 17, 1984, p. 28.*

## Canada Moves Forward

Mr. Trudeau has had a long and often happy tenure, but he has run his course. The Liberal Party is dying under him, lacking drive and direction. He has tested Parliament as a petty annoyance, something to be endured rather than respected, and the institution, and the people it answers to, have been diminished in the process. His Government has trafficked in patronage to a disgraceful degree, . . . Worse, in portfolio after portfolio, his ministers lack energy and ideas.

*From an editorial calling for Prime Minister Trudeau to step down, published the day he announced he would do just that, in "The Long Goodbye,"* Globe and Mail *(Montreal), February 29, 1984, p. 6.*

I had a good day yesterday, worked on aboriginal rights, and it seemed like a good day to have a last day. . . . I had a good day. It was a great walk in the snow. I went to judo, felt very combative, and here I am.

*Pierre Trudeau to reporters following the February 29, 1984, announcement of his retirement, quoted in Montgomery and Walkom, "Pierre Trudeau Steps Down,"* Globe and Mail *(Montreal), March 1, 1984, p. 1.*

The great achievement of Pierre Trudeau's long tenure in office was an event that never happened. Quebec never seceded from the country, and Canada never broke into two—or perhaps it would have been three or four—independent fragments. It could have happened very easily at any of several points in the 1970s, when Quebec nationalism was strongly on the rise. If Canada had had a less skillful and determined prime minister, perhaps it would have happened.

The Washington Post *pays tribute to retiring Canadian prime minister Pierre Trudeau, in its editorial "Mr. Trudeau Resigns,"* Washington Post, *March 2, 1984, p. A-26.*

North America's attic is also where an abundance of riches is stored. We own one-third of the world's freshwater supply, enough oil and gas to be self-sufficient; there are wheat and timber and iron ore. But we have never been able to put it together. After all these years we remain a loose-knit, quarrelsome federation. Put California into a typewriter and the third carbon will yield British Columbia. Out there, beyond the Rockies, they look upon Ottawa as distant and uncaring. The fulminating west feels, with some justice, that it

remains an internal colony, the National Energy Policy's sacrificial goal.

What we are being offered in this election is not a leader of vision but choice of managers. Interchangeable political parts. For too long this country, like the Expos, has looked good only on paper. Canadians are weary of being told we will inherit a golden tomorrow. We need something more right now.

*Author Mordechai Richler commenting on Canada's status and the upcoming federal election, in Richler, "Reverberations in America's Attic,"* Time, *August 27, 1984, p. 28.*

The new Prime Minister will face a substantial challenge in living up to the expectations aroused by his sweep. There are no magic cures for the weak economy he inherits. And Canada's peculiar psychological discontents will persist. Given sharp regional differences and an expansive giant southern neighbor, Canada can never be sure of its national identity.

Few nations anywhere, however, can boast of such a healthy democratic process, capable of healing regional wounds and clearly transmitting a popular mandate for change. Canadians have given themselves new reason for national pride. And as Mr. Mulroney's campaign emphasized, they've given Americans a good reminder to appreciate having Canada for a neighbor.

The *New York Times appraising Canada's new prime minister Brian Mulroney with approval in i ts editorial "Canada Turns Right,"* New York Times, *September 6, 1984, p. A-22.*

## Year of the Yuppie

Depression and Munich and Holocaust burned lifelong scars into the sensibility of people a few years older. Never again, they said, in one way or another. Just so did Vietnam and the arrogant dispatch of American troops abroad sear the boom babies, the yuppies. They have their own never again. It could become a campaign issue in this Year of the Yuppies. They will make it a political reality for a lot longer.

The *New York Times editorializing on the impact of yuppies, in "The Year of the Yuppies,"* New York Times, *March 25, 1984, sec. 4, p. 20.*

. . . It was a year in which the aging hippies of *Doonesbury* returned to the comic pages after a two-year absence with $20 haircuts and a new set of middle-class values. It was a year, also, in which Carrie Cook, a 25-year-old associate producer for a Boston ad agency, saw the value of her condominium go from $65,000 to $95,000, which means she made more money going to sleep each night than she did at work each day; . . .

. . . . .

But if Yuppies change the world, it will be through force of example, not weight of numbers. Their strength is as the strength of 10, because they want it all so badly, a quality that doesn't show up in the statistics. The science of marketing has a long way to go to understand someone like Laurie Gilbert, a 28-year-old lawyer at the Disney Channel, who says she "would be comfortable with $200,000 a year," and more if she has children.

*Looking at the impact of the yuppie culture, in "The Year of the Yuppie," Newsweek, December 31, 1984, pp. 14, 17.*

. . . What enhances the importance of being Yuppie is that they sit on top of the largest, richest, best-educated generation ever born. The heart of that group, 25- to 35-year-olds, constitutes 23 percent of the population, yet, even at this early stage in their earnings curve, controls a remarkable 23 percent of after-tax income. That enormous economic muscle will get stronger. In a generation that has been a focus of media attention since its infancy, and is accustomed to taking its cues from television, fads have a way of feeding on themselves. "Yuppies are definitely trend setters," says Cindy Hale, advertising manager for Nike, the running-shoe company. "All that media attention . . . caused more people in the marketplace to gravitate toward Yuppie identity, [bringing] them into target market." In short, even those who don't meet all the statistical criteria may find their lives and spending habits to a large degree falling into patterns set by the Yuppies.

*Describing the impact of yuppies on advertising, in "They Live to Buy," Newsweek, December 31, 1984, p. 28.*

# 5

# Terrorism and Disaster
## January 1985–April 1986

Ronald Reagan's "troika"—James Baker, Ed Meese, and Michael Deaver (left to right)—are shown in a 1981 photo. *(Courtesy Ronald Reagan Library)*

On January 20, 1985, a day so cold that the ceremony had to be moved indoors and the parade canceled, Ronald Reagan was inaugurated for his second term. On the surface, things looked good for the next four years. A majority of Americans felt Reagan had brought prosperity and international prestige back to the United States, and if he occasionally displayed ignorance or seemed too much an actor playing a role, what of it? The role was president of the United States, and he played it exceptionally well.

Yet there were signs of trouble ahead. The president had managed to circumvent the negative reaction to his administration's actions in Central America—at least temporarily—but difficult questions remained. Reaganomics had given the country a boost but created a deficit spiraling out of control. Another important factor that boded ill for Reagan's second term was the lack of clear policy direction. An indication of the problem was demonstrated toward the end of the 1984 reelection campaign when National Security Advisor Robert "Bud" McFarlane presented Reagan with a list of foreign-policy initiatives that he and Secretary of State George Shultz had drawn up. McFarlane asked the president to choose "two or three at most," but when the list came back, he found Reagan had enthusiastically written, "Let's do them all!"—an impossibility, given the complexity of the proposals.[1]

This, however, was typical. Unlike the micromanager Jimmy Carter, Reagan followed a hands-off approach, making his wishes known and leaving those responsible to carry them out. This worked well during his first term when the "troika" of James Baker (chief of staff), Michael Deaver (assistant chief of staff), and Edwin Meese III (special counsel) restricted access to him, controlled his agenda, and implemented his policies. It was an unusual arrangement, marked by jealousy and infighting among the three strong-willed men, but it was successful, due mainly to Baker's political acumen.

However, the efficient organization the troika had provided for Reagan during his first years in office was coming to an end. Deaver, disappointed in his hope of taking over from Baker as chief of staff, had decided to leave the White House to return to public-relations work (which he finally did in May 1985). Meese was undergoing an exhaustive examination of his finances and ethics after his January 1984 nomination as attorney general, an appointment finally confirmed on February 28, 1985. But it was Baker's change of role that would have the greatest impact. Eager for a different position in the administration, Baker decided to exchange jobs with Treasury Secretary Donald Regan, who was also looking for a change; the president assented to the switch, which was announced on January 8, 1985.

Later analysts considered the Baker-Regan exchange one of the key factors in the president's troubled second term. Both men had excelled in their original posts; both were no more than competent in their new positions, and Regan especially did not possess the skills of conciliation and politics that the job of chief of staff required. Partly because of this, and partly because of Reagan's tendency to turn a blind eye to what his staff was doing, the control and effectiveness that had marked his first term were almost completely lacking in his second, leading—perhaps inevitably—to the Iran-contra scandal of 1986–87.

## MOUNTING TERRORS

Terrorism continued to plague the administration in 1985. Despite the withdrawal of U.S. Marines from Beirut in February 1984, the Shiite group Hezbollah, the Islamic Jihad, and other Muslim militants increasingly engaged in kidnappings, bombings, and hijackings—anything to achieve their avowed goal of driving all Americans out of Lebanon. In 1984, six Americans were kidnapped in Beirut and one assassinated (Malcolm H. Kerr, head of the American University of Beirut, gunned down on January 18). Two of the six were soon freed, two were released in 1985, and two were killed—CIA station chief William Buckley in October 1985 and American University librarian Peter Kilburn in April 1986.

The year 1985 saw four abductions, including journalist Terry Anderson, seized on March 16. Three more followed in 1986, four in 1987, and one in 1988. Anderson would suffer the longest captivity, not being released until December 4, 1991, though his ordeal was nearly matched by American University professor Thomas Sutherland, kidnapped on June 9, 1985, and released on November 18, 1991. Nor were just Americans being targeted: Nationals from Great Britain, West Germany, France, India, Ireland, Italy, and South Korea were also taken by the militants.

As the abductions increased, so did other acts of violence. On April 3, 1984, President Reagan signed National Security Decision Directive 138 (NSDD 138), approving counterterrorism measures including diplomacy, economic sanctions, improved intelligence gathering, and military force. As if in response, on April 12 the Islamic Jihad bombed a restaurant near a joint U.S.-Spanish air force base in Torrejon, Spain; 18 Spaniards were killed and 82 people were injured, including 15 Americans. Later in the year, on September 20, a car-bomb explosion outside the U.S. embassy in Beirut killed two Americans and 21 others.

Two major terrorist attacks came in 1985. On June 14 Islamic Jihad militants hijacked TWA Flight 847 from Athens to Rome, diverting the jet to Beirut, to Algiers, and finally back to Beirut. Forty-one of the 153 passengers and crew (of whom 104 were Americans) were released almost at once, but on June 15 a passenger, U.S. Navy diver Robert Dean Stetham, was murdered after authorities delayed in meeting the hijackers' demand that an official from the extremist group Amal come talk to them. In addition, seven passengers with Jewish-sounding surnames were removed from the plane and secreted in unknown locations in Beirut. By this time Amal militants had taken over the situation, and they forced the plane to again fly to Algiers, where more hostages were released. Finally they returned to Beirut, where the remaining 33 Americans, like the other seven hostages already removed from the plane, were dispersed throughout the city. Eventually one hostage was released due to ill health, leaving 39 in captivity.

As the drama dragged on, two images were burned into the minds of Americans back home: Stetham's body dumped ruthlessly on the airport tarmac and pilot John Testrake talking to reporters from the cockpit window with a terrorist's gun to his head. The primary condition for the hostages' freedom was that Israel release more than 700 Shiite prisoners, which the United States would not formally request Israel to do and Israel would not do until requested by the United States. At last, after extensive secret negotiations, the Israeli army began to free its prisoners, and on June 30 all 39 hostages were bused to Damascus, Syria, and freedom. Israel continued to release Shiite prisoners but denied that this was related to the hijacking. Meanwhile, Americans were reminded that while this hostage crisis had been resolved, seven of their countrymen were still captives.

On July 1 the U.S. government banned Americans from traveling to Lebanon—a measure, ironically, in line with the terrorists' aim of ridding the country of Americans. The United States also issued arrest warrants for three of the hijackers. One, Mohammed Ali Hamadei, was arrested and tried in West Germany in 1987 and sentenced to life imprisonment. The others remain at large, as does Imad Mughniyah, another hijacker indicted in 1987 who was placed on the FBI's list of Most Wanted Terrorists.

In October 1985, four Palestinian gunmen seized an Italian cruise ship, the *Achille Lauro,* off the Egyptian coast, taking hostage more than 400 passengers, including 19 Americans. The terrorists sought the release of 50 members of the Palestinian Liberation Front (PLF) who were currently being held by Israel. The United States urged Israel not to agree, while American, British, and Italian special forces mobilized to attempt a rescue mission. Before this could be implemented, however, the hijackers arrived at Port Said, Egypt (October 9), where they offered to surrender if promised immunity from prosecution and put in the care of the Palestinian Liberation Organization (PLO). Against U.S. and Italian wishes, Egypt agreed to the deal, which had been brokered secretly with the PLO's leader, Yasser Arafat. Understandably, the arrangement was regarded with suspicion; Arafat's right-hand man, Muhammed Abul Abbas (also known as Mohammed Ahmed Abbas, or Abu Abbas), was one of the world's most wanted terrorists as well as a cofounder of the PLF, and many believed he had masterminded the hijacking.

Further, U.S. authorities learned that before the ship's arrival in Port Said, a passenger had been murdered. Leon Klinghoffer, 69, a wheelchair-bound retired appliance manufacturer from New York City, had been shot in the head and chest and his body dumped overboard. There was outrage throughout the United States over both the murder and the prospect that the perpetrators would escape as the TWA hijackers had done. When President Reagan learned that Abul Abbas had joined the hijackers as they boarded an EgyptAir 737 flight for Tunis (headquarters of the PLO) on October 10, he ordered American fighter jets from USS *Saratoga* to divert the plane to a NATO base at Sigonella, Sicily. The fighters carried out their mission, but by the time the EgyptAir jet landed, Italy's Prime Minister, Bettino Craxi, had decided the hijackers should be tried in Italy rather than the United States. U.S. troops surrounding the plane found themselves encircled by Italian troops, who took the terrorists into custody.

The United States wanted Abbas, but Arafat threatened "uncontrollable reactions" if the Italians turned him over to the Americans. They did not, and soon Abbas was set free, while Arafat publicly—and ironically—accused Reagan of air piracy for his interception of the EgyptAir jet. Egyptians were also outraged by the act, and President Hosni Mubarak demanded an apology from the United States, which was not forthcoming. The Italian courts sentenced the hijackers to long prison terms in 1986.[2] However, by turning Abbas loose, Craxi caused the collapse of his own coalition government as colleagues abandoned him because of his apparent pro-PLO—and therefore anti-Israel—action.

## 1980s PHILANTHROPY

The American people are noted for responding charitably to the disasters of others, and celebrities have led the way in encouraging such public responses. In November 1984 in Great Britain, musicians Bob Geldof and Midge Ure assembled an international group of rock and pop artists named Band Aid to record a single they had written, "Do They Know It's Christmas?" to raise money for famine relief in Ethiopia. Released on December 15, 1984, the song immediately

Shown here is a "We Are the World" recording session that was held on January 28, 1985. In the front row from left to right are Cyndi Lauper, Bruce Springsteen, James Ingram, Smoky Robinson, Ray Charles, Sheila E, June Pointer, and Randy Jackson. In the second row from left to right are Al Jarreau, Dionne Warwick, Lionel Richie, Kenny Rogers, Huey Lewis, Bob Dylan, John Oates, and Ruth Pointer. In the back row from left to right are Daryl Hall, Steve Perry, Kenny Loggins, Jeffrey Osborne, Lindsey Buckingham, and Anita Pointer. *(Photofest)*

became the number-one single in the United Kingdom, and by Christmas 1985, when it was reissued, it had raised more than £8 million in that country alone.[3]

In the United States, singer Harry Belafonte and his manager, Ken Kragen, discussed the idea of a concert featuring black musicians for the benefit of starving and disease-ridden peoples in Africa. Believing something similar to Band Aid would be more successful, Kragen enlisted another client, Lionel Richie, to cowrite a song with Michael Jackson, and Quincy Jones to produce it. The result was a 45-strong group called USA for Africa, who recorded "We Are the World" at a Hollywood sound studio on January 28, 1985, the night they assembled for the American Music Awards.

In addition to Richie and Jackson, USA for Africa included some of the biggest names in pop and rock music, among them Belafonte, Stevie Wonder, Billy Joel, Bette Midler, Diana Ross, Bruce Springsteen, Bob Dylan, Tina Turner, Paul Simon, Kenny Rogers, Dionne Warwick—and, fittingly, Bob Geldof. While all took part in the chorus ("We are the world, we are the children / We are the ones who make a brighter day / so let's start giving"), 21 of the performers also sang solos or duets.

Released on March 7, the record sold out almost at once, and by April 13 it had reached the top of the charts, where it stayed for four weeks. It was subsequently included on the album *USA for Africa: We Are the World,* which featured another famine-relief song, "Tears Are Not Enough," by the Canadian group Northern Lights, as well as songs by Springsteen, Turner, and Prince. Total sales of the single were some 7.5 million in the United States, while more than 3 million copies of the album were sold. Revenues from these as well as from the video and related merchandise raised approximately $50 million for the USA for Africa Foundation. To nobody's surprise, "We Are the World" won Grammy awards for Song of the Year, Record of the Year, and Best Pop Performance by a Duo or Group.

Geldof capped the success of Band Aid and USA for Africa with his organization of Live Aid, a global charity "jukebox" involving sites and performing artists in London and Philadelphia as well as New York, Sydney, and Moscow. A complicated satellite linkup and the cooperative efforts of the BBC, ABC, and MTV culminated in what became the largest international television broadcast to that date, a 16-hour marathon on July 13, 1985. While some singers performed live in the selected venues, others provided video clips or did both; Mick Jagger and David Bowie, for instance, did a taped duet of "Dancing In the Street" when it proved impossible to do it live, with Bowie in London and Jagger in Philadelphia.

The cream of the pop-rock world—almost 50 individual artists and groups as well as Band Aid in London and USA for Africa in Philadelphia—took part in Live Aid, which succeeded beyond even Geldof's wildest hopes. When planning began in 1981, organizers hoped to raise about $1–2 million; in fact, Live Aid brought in close to $100 million for famine relief in Ethiopia. In Britain, Geldof, who had put his career on hold to organize the event, was awarded an honorary knighthood.

Other charity concerts followed Live Aid, notably Farm Aid, which was inspired by Bob Dylan's comment during the Live Aid concert, "It would be nice if some of this money went to the American farmers." Almost at once, Willie Nelson, John Mellencamp, and Neil Young began to organize another star-studded event, which took place on September 22, 1985, in Champaign, Illinois. With numerous artists participating from pop, rock, and country & western music, it was yet another success, raising more than $7 million to aid family farmers in the United States. Willie Nelson subsequently became a leading spokesman as well as president of Farm Aid, which still holds concerts and provides assistance to farmers.

In 2005 Bob Geldof marked the 20th anniversary of Live Aid by organizing Live 8, a megaevent of seven all-star concerts on July 2 at 10 locations in the United States, United Kingdom, Europe, Africa, and Asia. With hundreds of rock and pop stars taking part and broadcasts by 140 television networks, 200 radio stations, and live feeds online, it was justifiably billed as the biggest event in rock history. Though it eclipsed Live Aid in its financial success, earning millions more for the relief of poverty in Africa, memories of the 1985 concert were revived by the participation of many of the stars of that milestone event.

## MONEY AND MERGERS

In contrast to the charity of "We Are the World" and Live Aid was the glorification of wealth that became a symbol of the 1980s. By 1985 there had been a complete turnaround in American commerce. From the malaise and soaring inflation of the Carter years, the nation was now experiencing an economic boom, and as the era's yuppies blatantly demonstrated, personal wealth had become the standard by which success was judged. For many this was achieved through high-powered deals or stock market manipulation; for others it was an elusive goal as technology and business methods changed so rapidly that they were left behind.

Important factors in the new economic climate were the Reagan administration's cessation of antitrust lawsuits and increased industrial deregulation. With the removal of government restrictions came increasing freedom to pursue mergers, acquisitions, and takeovers that created "megacompanies." There had been an escalation in high-value mergers and acquisitions up to 1985, but that year saw an explosion in such buyout transactions, with some $180 billion exchanged by year's end; 36 of the mergers each involved sums of $1 billion or more. Numbers became almost meaningless as record after record was set in different industries. In broadcasting, ABC was bought by Capital Cities Communications, Inc., for $3.5 billion on March 18, 1985. It was the largest acquisition to date (outside of the oil industry) as well as the first time a major broadcasting corporation had been sold. It would not be the last, as later in the year General Electric acquired RCA for $6.3 billion, a purchase that included NBC. Other major buyouts included Procter & Gamble's acquisition of Richardson-Vicks for $1.24 billion and R.J. Reynolds's purchase of Nabisco Brands for $4.9 billion. But it was Philip Morris that set new levels when it bought General Foods for $5.7 billion, thus becoming the country's largest consumer-products company.

In the oil industry, Texaco's January 1984 purchase of Getty Oil for $10 billion attracted headlines in 1985 due to questionable aspects of the sale. Although Texaco had a signed contract with Getty, its rival Pennzoil had a prior agreement to acquire Getty that was unsigned but still binding. Pennzoil sued Texaco, and on November 19, 1985, a Texas jury found in Pennzoil's favor, ordering Texaco to pay $10.53 billion in damages, the largest civil-case award in U.S. history. (Texaco appealed, and as the case dragged on, the oil giant took the unusual step in April 1987 of filing for Chapter 11 bankruptcy protection to renegotiate the award. In December that year, Texaco finally agreed to pay Pennzoil $3 billion, then a record cash settlement.)

Adding to this activity was an increased number of hostile takeovers, whereby corporate raiders accumulated stock to take control of companies that were unwilling to be bought outright. There were many advantages to large-scale mergers, whether friendly or hostile, among them the fact that acquisition of a competitor meant an immediate increase in market share, bringing in more revenue. Wall Street led the finance frenzy that Reaganomics had introduced: Between 1982 and 1988, one out of four new jobs in New York City's private sector was in the financial-services industry.[4] To succeed there became the dream of business school graduates who made quick money as financiers, arbitrageurs, stocks and securities speculators, and investment bankers. Most paid the price with 80-hour workweeks, little home life, and failed personal relationships—but they had the wealth and possessions to signal their financial success. Some thrived in the global marketplace that the boom had helped produce; others fell victim to their own greed or that of others.

The new race for profit and growth was having other effects on American society as well. In the past, people had sought security in a job with a company that cared for its employees and rewarded their loyalty. By 1985, such security was becoming a thing of the past as American commerce threw itself into a takeover frenzy that killed job stability and made employer-employee loyalty an outmoded concept. People with talent and determination looked for firms that paid top salaries and bonuses, pushing aside anybody who got in their way. Business and industry became more cutthroat than ever before, and in this overheated atmosphere some entrepreneurs became both admired and emulated for their unabashed pursuit of wealth. The nation was heading for a fall, but while the boom lasted, dealmakers such as Donald Trump, Carl Icahn, and Boone Pickens and stock speculators such as Ivan Boesky and Michael Milken exemplified the excesses of the money culture.

The Reagans and the Mulroneys enjoy the final night of the Shamrock Summit in Quebec City on March 18, 1985. *(Courtesy Ronald Reagan Library)*

## WHEN IRISH EYES WEREN'T SMILING

The election of Brian Mulroney as Canada's prime minister in September 1984 did much to transform that country's relations with the United States, which over the years had swung between warm cooperation and cold antagonism. Now the two nations were led by like-minded conservative ideologues, and when Mulroney and Ronald Reagan met in Quebec City on March 17–18, 1985, they hit it off at once. Because of their shared Irish background, the meeting was dubbed the "Shamrock Summit," the harmony of which was symbolized on St. Patrick's Day when the two leaders and their spouses appeared on television singing "When Irish Eyes Are Smiling."

The summit was important to Reagan, who wanted concessions on a free-trade agreement between the United States and Canada. Mulroney's willingness to consider it as well as his commitment to strengthening Canada's military and defenses met with American approval, but his anxiety not to appear a Reagan puppet, as well as significant opposition to free trade in Canada, prevented him from publicly embracing an open-market economy. Nevertheless, a trade cooperation accord was agreed on, and the Shamrock Summit laid the groundwork for the U.S.–Canada Free Trade Agreement of 1989 and, five years later, the North American Free Trade Agreement (NAFTA).

Not all was sweetness and light, however. The issue of acid rain had been added to the agenda to mollify the Canadians, for whom it was a major concern. Reagan considered it unimportant because, as he had said prior to the summit, "We haven't had air as clean as we have now for decades."[5] However, he recognized the Canadians' sensitivity on the matter, and special envoys from both sides were appointed to study a problem that many Canadians felt was caused by U.S. industrial emissions.

While the Shamrock Summit was undoubtedly a success for Mulroney, there were also mistakes and scandals. A spring trip to London and Bonn for the G7* economic summit went wrong when aides' gaffes attracted bad publicity and made the visiting Canadians appear arrogant to their hosts. Such problems abroad, though, were nothing compared to those at home. Having inherited a huge national debt—by 1984 it was nearly 50 percent of all the goods and services that Canada produced—Mulroney set out to cut spending and to raise taxes, which made only a small dent in the problem. Many of his budget cuts involved social welfare programs, which Mulroney disliked as much as Reagan did. Although he had made a campaign promise not to cut Old Age Security indexing, which raised pensions to the elderly in line with the cost-of-living index, he finally decided that it was economically necessary to do so.

The de-indexation proposal outraged Canadians. In his book *So, What Are the Boys Saying?* Mulroney press aide Michel Gratton described a famous scene on television when an elderly woman confronted Mulroney:

> "You lied to us! You made us vote for you, and then goodbye Charlie Brown. If you do anything [on pension de-indexing] you won't be back in three years."
>
> . . . If Brian Mulroney didn't know how serious the situation was before, he certainly understood now. Sure enough, at the Press Club they were talking about nothing else. "Goodbye Charlie Brown" became the rallying cry of a media pack that smelled blood.[6]

On June 27, to nobody's surprise, the government withdrew its de-indexation proposals.

In August Mulroney faced more public fury when the United States sent a Coast Guard icebreaker through the Northwest Passage without requesting Canadian permission. Canada had always claimed sovereignty over the passage, but the United States countered that the area constituted international waters. As a result, in September Canada laid formal claim to jurisdiction over the passage between the mainland and the Arctic islands. The dispute, which still continues, upset the harmony established by the Shamrock Summit.

On September 17 Mulroney was hit by the first of several scandals that would rock his administration. The CBC program *The Fifth Estate* revealed that

---

*The G7 nations were Canada, France, Great Britain, Italy, Japan, West Germany, and the United States.

fisheries inspectors had discovered cans of StarKist tuna that had become so spoiled they were unfit for human consumption. The order to destroy millions of cans shook StarKist executives, who appealed to Minister of Fisheries and Oceans John Fraser. In the mistaken belief that his inspectors had erred in their judgment, Fraser decided to allow the tainted tuna on the store shelves. It was later reported that Fraser had ordered independent testing of the tuna, but the two labs had not completed their tests when he made his decision.

Within two days the tuna was recalled (although none of the cans that were sold had made people sick), and in less than a week Fraser had resigned his post. Speculation mounted as to how much Mulroney knew, and inconsistencies in his public statements were highlighted. Consequently, his approval rating fell badly, and by early January 1986 polls were showing the Liberals ahead for the first time since July 1984. StarKist was eventually forced to close its New Brunswick plant and pull out of Canada; 400 Canadians lost their jobs.

Other bad news included the March 1985 collision of two military planes over New Brunswick, killing 10, followed by the June explosion of Air India flight 182 en route from Toronto to London; it was later revealed that the plane had been bombed, probably by Sikh terrorists. On December 12, an Arrow Airlines jet crashed soon after taking off from Gander, Newfoundland, killing 256, while two train crashes in February 1986 completed a year of transport disasters.

The public mood was reflected in the Canadian dollar hitting an all-time low of 70.2 U.S. cents on international money markets by the end of January 1986. Overall, Brian Mulroney's first 18 months in office had not been happy ones.

## CONTINUING BATTLES

By the mid-1980s North American Indians were making progress in their efforts to regain lands taken from them in the 1800s, preserve their cultural and religious traditions, and overcome bigotry and greed. Time, new attitudes, and the courts helped them to an extent, and public opinion increasingly supported their claims for redress of injustices. In Canada, just seven months after the United Nations had condemned the government for its repressive Indian status laws, the Constitution Act of 1982 made a point of affirming "existing aboriginal and treaty rights." Two years later, the Inuvialuit of northern Canada were granted 35,000 square miles of mineral-rich territory; they went on to establish the Inuvialuit Petroleum Corporation.

Despite the general recognition that American Indians had been ill treated, negative perceptions of them persisted, often due to the very way of life to which the federal government had consigned them a century earlier. In 1983 Secretary of the Interior James Watt remarked, "If you want an example of the failures of socialism, don't go to Russia. Come to America, and see the American Indian reservations."[7] Sadly, it was a viewpoint with which many agreed.

In the early 1980s, President Reagan's determination to cut federal spending extended to the Bureau of Indian Affairs (BIA) and to numerous programs supporting Native Americans, resulting in increased poverty and homelessness among many tribes. In November 1984 the president's Commission on Indian Reservation Economies called for the "dismantling of the BIA, abrogation of tribal sovereign immunity, greater exploitation of Indian natural resources, subordination of tribal courts to the federal courts and a host of other controversial rec-ommendations."[8] Yet the report was largely ignored, and despite his spending cuts and perceptions that he was insensitive to the needs of Native Americans,[9] Rea-gan supported self-determination and tribal autonomy. The Indian Tribal Gov-ernmental Tax Status Act, passed in 1982 and amended in 1984 and 1987, gave nations tax status equivalent to state and local governments and certain federal tax exemptions. The president also transferred White House management of Amer-ican Indian affairs from the Office of Liaison to the Office of Intergovernmen-tal Affairs (1983), an action that put tribal governments on an equal footing with federal and state agencies.

Meanwhile, disputes over land and the destruction of sacred sites continued. In 1983 court decisions in *Wilson v. Block* and *Fools Crow v. Gullet* allowed recre-ational development in Arizona's San Francisco peaks and South Dakota's Bear Butte, respectively. This affected the private religious practices of the Hopi, Navajo, Lakota, and Tsistsistas (Cheyenne), who held those areas sacred, and for Native Americans such decisions made a mockery of the American Indian Reli-gious Freedom Act (1978).

Also in 1983 the Ninth Court of Appeals ruled in favor of Mary and Carrie Dann, who had claimed that the Shoshone still owned a large area in the Great Basin, which was taken from them illegally. However, in *United States v. Dann,* decided on February 20, 1985, the U.S. Supreme Court overturned the ruling on the grounds that a 1979 Indian Claims Commission decision paying $26 million to the Shoshone had adequately compensated them for their loss. Like the Sioux in the 1980 Black Hills case, the Western Shoshone Sacred Lands Association rejected this money (which today totals more than $136 million), even though many Shoshone believed it should be accepted.

On March 4, 1985, a month after the Dann case, the Supreme Court ruled in support of the Oneida's land claims against New York State. Unlike other nations, the Oneida had chosen not to pursue their case through the Indian Claims Commission, since that body was not empowered to return land. In *County of Oneida v. Oneida Indian Nation,* the Court ruled that a 1795 transaction purchasing tribal land had been illegal, and, therefore, the Oneida had the right to sue the state. Consequently, the tribe began negotiations, and eventually some 18,000 acres of their land were returned. In March 2005, however, another Supreme Court decision held against the tribe's claimed sovereignty and refused to exempt the Oneida from paying government taxes.

In Arizona, many Navajo were still resisting the relocation of 10,000–12,000 tribe members from Hopi territory to the "New Lands" (near Sanders, Arizona) as a result of the 1980 amendment to the Hopi-Navajo Relocation Act of 1974; it was the largest forced civilian relocation since the World War II internment of Japanese Americans. Although the 1980 amendment had given the tribe 150,000 more acres, the act was disputed by those forced to move to unfamiliar territory that also contained chilling dangers: The New Lands happened to be at the site of a dam burst that had released radioactive water into the local waters. Conse-quently, one-quarter of the first group of Navajo to move there in 1980 were dead from cancer by 1986. This was yet another reason for many Navajo to defy the July 1986 deadline to vacate partitioned Hopi lands. Further aggravating matters were Hopi plans to lease the land for coal mining as well as their refusal to rent land to older Navajo who had lived there for decades. In 1988 the Navajo filed suit against the Relocation Act, but *Manybeads v. United States* was dismissed in 1989. Nevertheless, legal actions continued through the 1990s.

Land and religious practices were not the only points of contention for Native Americans; water, fishing, and hunting rights also were (and remain) major concerns. Significantly, Native Americans were included on the U.S. panels negotiating the Pacific Salmon Treaty with Canada, passed by Congress in March 1985. This treaty improved regulations governing the propagation and harvesting of salmon between the two countries, an area of special concern for American Indians in the Pacific Northwest. Tribal representatives from both countries were also appointed to the Pacific Salmon Commission.

In principle, the U.S. government had recognized American Indians' right to self-determination for decades, but within federally imposed restrictions. The jurisdiction of tribal courts became a major issue in the 1980s as non-Indians complained of Native Americans' insistence on following their own legal system rather than employing normal due-process and trial-by-jury procedures. In 1985 and 1987, the Supreme Court upheld the sovereignty of tribal courts over non-Indians to adjudicate personal-injury cases. But criminal cases were mostly confined to minor issues such as hunting and fishing rights; more serious felonies were tried in non-Indian courts. This upset Native Americans who cited the 1968 Indian Civil Rights Act (ICRA) as the basis for claiming that all crimes committed on reservations, whether by Indians or non-Indians, should be adjudicated in tribal courts.

Beginning in 1986, the U.S. Civil Rights Commission investigated tribal court systems and complaints that tribal councils interfered in judges' decisions, thus violating Indians' civil rights. As a consequence, some legislators proposed giving federal courts the power to review questionable cases, but this was considered a blatant violation of both the ICRA and a 1978 Supreme Court decision that protected the sovereignty of tribal courts. Instead, legislation was introduced to provide funding for staffing and training that would improve tribal court procedures.

For years, Native American activists labored to improve the lives of their people, although non-Indians usually knew only of headline-earning extremists. This changed in December 1985, when Wilma Mankiller became the first woman to head a major American tribe, succeeding Ross Swimmer as principal chief of the 140,000-member Cherokee Nation. Elected to the position in 1987 and 1991, Mankiller won praise and national respect for her work, improving the negative perceptions of American Indians typified in James Watt's 1983 remarks. Yet though Mankiller and other tribal leaders achieved much, statistics showed that the country's highest rates of alcoholism and suicide were to be found within Native American reservations. Until such internal problems could be solved, tribal communities would continue to be vulnerable to the outside world.

## CHANGES IN THE MARKETPLACE

As the U.S. economic recovery continued, so did the recovery of business. The auto industry, for example, was beginning a comeback from the 1970s crisis that had brought the Big Three—in particular, Ford and Chrysler—to the edge of disaster. Soaring inflation, high oil prices, and new regulations on safety and emissions had contributed to their problems, made worse when consumers who had turned to smaller foreign automobiles found that Japanese-made vehicles offered better quality. In 1982, Honda became the first Japanese firm to assemble its cars in the United States, while Toyota joined forces with General Motors two years later to produce Toyota vehicles.

By the mid-1980s, the Big Three had forged better relationships with the unions that allowed them to negotiate favorable contracts, close plants, and reduce employee numbers.[10] Equally important to their turnaround were the quality improvements this new management-labor relationship produced. The style and fuel economy of the new Ford Taurus and the success of Chrysler's minivan brought customers back, and the Big Three gradually returned to prosperity. The improving efficiency and profitability came at a price, however, as jobs continued to be lost throughout the 1980s.

Technological advances led to similar profitability in other fields. In 1985 sales of videocassette recorders (VCRs) began to skyrocket, partly stemming from the January 1984 Supreme Court decision that allowed users to record television broadcasts using VCRs and retailers to sell the equipment. Another factor was the growing popularity of the VHS (video home system) format of videocassette, produced by Japan Victor Company (JVC). Although Betamax, manufactured by Sony, was generally deemed to be better, JVC's marketing of VHS proved effective, and by 1985 it was clear that VHS was going to prevail. Ballooning VCR sales meant that the movie industry suffered a 7 percent drop in ticket sales, while 1986 saw 13 million VCRs sold in the United States.

Another product to take the country by storm in 1985 was the compact disc (CD) and its adjunct, the CD player. Engineers had been working on a small disc to hold photographic and video images since 1969, and Philips developed ways of recording and playing back sound digitally, eliminating many of the drawbacks of standard records. In 1979 Sony and Philips entered into a collaborative effort that in 1980 led to agreement on a standard CD format. The collaboration ended in 1981, but both companies began to market their products in Europe and Japan the following year.

In 1983 Sony and Philips sold 800,000 CDs and 30,000 CD players in the United States, which saw the building of its first CD mass-production plant in 1984; another soon followed. But it was 1985 when the full impact of CDs was felt as customers realized the discs' advantages over LPs (long-playing records) in terms of sound quality and storage space. With only two CD-producing factories in the United States, demand soon exceeded supply. Further, the complicated processes involved in remastering meant that many had to wait months for their old favorites to be reissued on CD. Nevertheless, it was evident that the day of the LP—and possibly also its successor, the audiotape—was coming to an end. Also in 1985, the CD explosion produced the first personal computers equipped with CD-ROM drives.

New technologies provided excitement in 1985, but the biggest business story of the year involved an old, familiar, and distinctly untechnological product. Invented in 1886, Coca-Cola and its closely guarded secret formula were U.S. institutions, while its position as the soft-drinks market leader had been unassailable for decades. But by the early 1980s, Pepsi-Cola was steadily gaining ground, and with Pepsi's sales in supermarkets now overtaking them, Coke's executives were uneasy.

Diet Coke, introduced in 1982, had been an instant hit, with flavor a key factor in its popularity; its success led to the introduction of Cherry Coke in early

1985. In the intervening years the Coca-Cola Company spent $4 million in market research and interviewed almost 200,000 consumers in blind taste tests comparing Coca-Cola and the sweeter-tasting Pepsi-Cola. Pepsi won with such consistency that the answer seemed clear: Make Coke sweeter. After a year of juggling with the formula, the company came up with a beverage that consistently beat Pepsi in blind tests. However, the project's secrecy was such that Coca-Cola felt no reason to test public opinion on abandoning the famous Coke formula, ignoring earlier research that had shown consumers would not favor any such change. The omission was to have shattering consequences.

On April 23, 1985, just before the company's 99th anniversary, Coca-Cola executives proudly announced the production of what the press called New Coke, replacing the old formula as of May 8. To their astonishment, the public responded with outrage. Negative reaction was so overwhelming that despite the clear superiority of New Coke's taste in blind tests, customers rejected it outright, comparing it to sewer water, furniture polish, "or worse, *two-day-old Pepsi*."[11] Before long, Americans were reverting to Prohibition practices, stockpiling cases of the old Coca-Cola and ordering supplies from Canada. Black marketeers sold the old beverage for more than $30 a case; boycotts of Coca-Cola products were called for; and a support group, the Old Coke Drinkers of America, was formed (taking more than 60,000 calls before the crisis ended). By June, Coca-Cola's consumer hotline was fielding 1,500 calls a day.

Critics emphasized the irony. Coca-Cola had always prided itself on a beverage that had remained unchanged. Now it had become "just one of the gang," producing a drink much like its rival Pepsi's and joining the legions of products that were "new and improved." Many called it the marketing blunder of the century. As consumers snubbed New Coke and sales plummeted, Coca-Cola executives acknowledged reality, and on July 11, the company's chairman, Robert Goizueta, and president, Donald Keough, announced that the old formula was returning under a new name: Coca-Cola Classic (also referred to as Classic Coke).

Such was the psychological importance of Coca-Cola that the announcement was headline news; on ABC the popular soap opera *General Hospital* was interrupted by a special bulletin about the old Coke's return. Consumers greeted the news with cheers, although it took some time before sales reflected forgiveness for what Coca-Cola had done. At the end of 1985, Pepsi was ahead of Classic Coke and New Coke combined, but sales of the original formula were such that Coca-Cola was back as market leader by early 1986. The dramatic recovery led some to accuse the company of engineering the New Coke disaster, both as a marketing ploy and as a way of masking a change in the original formula from cane sugar to high-fructose corn syrup. Most agree, however, that the Coca-Cola Company had simply blundered in a big way, having failed to appreciate the truth of the axiom: If it ain't broke, don't fix it.[12]

## PRESIDENTIAL FAUX PAS

Coca-Cola did not have the prerogative on bad public relations in 1985. Ronald Reagan suffered similarly when a visit to West Germany went wrong due to poor planning and political sensitivities.

On May 8, 1985, Europe would celebrate the 40th anniversary of V-E (Victory in Europe) Day, following the G7 economic summit in Bonn. West German chancellor Helmut Kohl thought this would be an ideal time to emphasize the growing friendship between Germany and the United States since World War II. In November 1984, therefore, he invited President Reagan to join him in laying wreaths at a military cemetery in Bitburg, near a joint U.S.-German air base. Reagan accepted out of a sense of obligation to Kohl, who had previously supported the deployment of U.S. missiles in Europe. The chancellor also suggested visiting a concentration camp site, but the president turned this down, saying he did not want to risk "reawakening the passions of the time."[13]

Michael Deaver made the preliminary arrangements, and in February 1985 he visited the snow-covered Kolmeshohe Cemetery in Bitburg, where approximately 2,000 German servicemen were buried. What neither Deaver nor his staff realized—or were told by West German aides—was that the dead soldiers included 49 members of the Waffen SS (elite Nazi troops). Not until April, after White House spokesman Larry Speakes announced the planned visit to the press, was this discovered by reporters investigating Speakes's incorrect statement that American servicemen may have been buried in the cemetery. A public outcry ensued, especially when it was revealed that a Waffen SS division had been responsible for the massacre of 71 American prisoners of war during the Battle of the Bulge. It was not known whether the Kolmeshohe graves included members of that division, and Bitburg's mayor pointed out that SS graves could probably be found in all German military cemeteries. Nevertheless, American public opinion was that Reagan should cancel his Bitburg visit on moral grounds.

Protests came from many quarters, including Holocaust survivors, veterans, and members of Congress, but neither Reagan nor Kohl would change their plans, believing that to do so would offend the West German people. The president then aroused more controversy when he stated that the soldiers buried in Kolmeshohe were "victims of Nazism also . . . drafted into service to carry out the hateful wishes of the Nazis."[14] Reagan also said that most of the SS troopers in Kolmeshohe had been teenagers drafted into service against their will. This turned out to be correct but failed to appease Jews incensed by his remarks and by his stubborn refusal to cancel the visit.

As the European trip approached, White House staff members and even First Lady Nancy Reagan urged the president to withdraw Bitburg from his schedule. Reagan realized the possible damage to his reputation but held firm to his decision since there was more than his own self-interest at stake: "I owe him," he said upon learning that Kohl would suffer political damage if the visit were canceled. But he made one concession by including a stop at the notorious Bergen-Belsen concentration camp on his itinerary. Adding to the controversy was Nancy Reagan's insistence on consulting her astrologer to determine the best timing for the two visits, causing Deaver intense embarrassment as he tried to finalize the schedule.

On May 5 Reagan and Kohl went first to Bergen-Belsen, where the president gave a speech that *Time* magazine described as a "skillful exercise in both the art of eulogy and political damage control."[15] The two leaders then went to Kolmeshohe Cemetery, where, along with U.S. general Matthew Ridgway and Luftwaffe general Johannes Steinhoff, they laid wreaths at a wall of remembrance but made no speeches. The visit was short, only eight minutes, and there were remarkably few protesters. Then, finally, Reagan and Kohl went to the nearby American air base, where they found some relief in the enthusiastic reception from a crowd of 7,500.

President Reagan walks with General Matthew Ridgway at Kolmeshohe Cemetery, Bitburg, on May 5, 1985. *(Courtesy Ronald Reagan Library)*

Though Reagan had managed to salvage something with his speech at Bergen-Belsen, the Bitburg incident did him no good. The timing was especially unfortunate, since he had hoped to use the economic summit in Bonn to persuade other G7 nations to agree to a reduction in trade barriers. Further, it occurred at a time when he was trying to convince Congress to reverse its position and authorize more aid to the contras in Nicaragua. As fallout from the controversy continued, his opponents gleefully wondered whether the fabled Reagan star was finally losing some of its luster.

## ESPIONAGE SCANDALS

On May 28, 1985, John Anthony Walker, Jr., a retired navy warrant officer, and his son, Michael Lance Walker, were indicted by a federal grand jury in Baltimore on six counts of espionage. Such cases were not new in U.S. history, but 1985 spawned an epidemic, with 13 Americans being indicted during the course of the year. This followed 13 arrests of U.S. and foreign nationals in 1984 and preceded 10 more in 1986–87. The American public was deeply disturbed to learn that the majority of those indicted in 1984–85 were CIA or U.S. Navy personnel; others included an FBI agent and army and air force personnel. Equally worrying was that most of the accused had spied not from principle or political ideology but simply for money.

Most of the espionage cases involved the Soviet Union, although some spies brokered deals with China, East Germany, Poland, and, surprisingly, Israel. Some of the more high-profile cases included that of Richard W. Miller, an FBI agent caught passing a classified document to two Soviet agents, who were also arrested. The first FBI agent ever indicted for espionage, he was convicted in July 1986 and then, following appeals and another trial, convicted again in 1990 and released from prison in 1994.

On December 18, 1984, Thomas Patrick Cavanagh, an engineering specialist for Northrop Corporation, had been arrested for attempting to sell classified documents on Stealth-bomber technology to the Soviet Union. Cavanagh pleaded guilty and was sentenced to two life terms on May 23, 1985. A few months later, on November 21, 1985, Jonathan J. Pollard, an intelligence analyst with the Naval Investigative Service, was arrested for selling classified documents to an Israeli intelligence unit. The case embarrassed Israel, an American ally; four Israeli nationals later named as coconspirators were not indicted. Pollard pleaded guilty to espionage in June 1986 and was sentenced to life imprisonment in March 1987.

Another case involved Ronald William Pelton, a onetime communications specialist with the National Security Agency (NSA), whose sale of secret documents to the Soviet Union after leaving the NSA in 1980 was revealed by a Soviet defector. Pelton was indicted on December 20, 1985, and pleaded not guilty. Convicted in June 1986, he was sentenced to three concurrent life terms on December 6, 1986.

Of all the 1984–87 espionage cases, though, none attracted more attention than that of John Walker and his accomplices, dubbed the "Walker Spy Ring"—though carelessness almost resulted in the ring not being caught. Walker's ex-wife, Barbara, had contacted the FBI at their Hyannis, Massachusetts, office to report her former husband as a spy and had been interviewed in late November 1984, but her information was regarded as unimportant and filed away. A subsequent phone call to the FBI from her daughter Laura was also ignored. Not until a counterintelligence agent, Joseph Wolfinger, came across a memo regarding Barbara Walker's interview and realized its importance was an investigation of John Walker finally undertaken.

Learning that Walker, who had held Top Secret Crypto clearance during his navy career, had frequently—and mysteriously—come into large sums of money over the years, Wolfinger quickly began to build the FBI's case against him. Barbara Walker also implicated her former brother-in-law, Arthur Walker, a retired naval lieutenant commander, as well as another naval officer who she knew only as "Wentworth." This later proved to be Jerry Alfred Whitworth, a retired communications specialist who had held Top Secret clearance.

The FBI learned that John Walker had begun to spy for the Soviets in 1962 while based in Norfolk, Virginia, and had supplied confidential information through subsequent postings for years; he was paid from $2,000 to $4,000 a month, based on the value of the material he passed on. After 20 years with the navy, Walker retired in 1975, but by that time he had recruited Jerry Whitworth to funnel secrets to him. What Whitworth provided was so valuable that Walker convinced his KGB contacts to pay a lump sum of $200,000 to get Whitworth, who had wanted to retire, to reenlist and continue supplying classified documents and photographs. When, in December 1981, Whitworth was finally transferred to areas where he no longer had access to secret information, Walker attempted to recruit his daughter Laura, an army officer, but she refused. He had already conscripted his brother Arthur, however, who in 1981–82 provided him with confidential documents relating to ship construction and design that were passed on to the Soviets.

Finally, Walker turned to his son Michael, who had joined the navy in 1982, becoming a petty officer aboard the USS *Nimitz*. In 1983 Michael began to steal and photograph classified documents that were obtained through his work in the *Nimitz*'s operations office, passing them on to his father whenever the ship docked. In 1984 Whitworth attempted to sell more information to Walker, who turned him down. Consequently Whitworth began to send anonymous letters to the FBI warning of a spy ring that had been selling navy secrets to the Soviets. His letters, in combination with secretly taped conversations between Walker and his daughter Laura (working in cooperation with the FBI), finally led to the arrests of John, Michael, and Arthur Walker in late May 1985 and Jerry Whitworth on June 3.

On October 28, 1985, John and Michael Walker pleaded guilty to all six espionage charges against them. In November the following year, John Walker—who had received a total of approximately $1 million selling naval secrets to the Soviets—was sentenced to two concurrent life terms plus an additional 10 years. In exchange for his testimony against Whitworth, he negotiated a lighter prison term for Michael, who was sentenced to 25 years. Arthur Walker, the recipient of $12,000 (most of which was returned to his brother to repay a debt), was tried and convicted in August 1985 for his role in the spy ring; on November 12 he was given three concurrent life sentences and fined $250,000.

The heaviest sentence, however, was passed on Jerry Whitworth, who had reportedly received a total of $332,000 for passing naval communications material to John Walker between 1975 and 1982. Because so much of what he had stolen related to U.S. security—information about cryptographic equipment and lists that would enable the Soviets to decode naval communications—Whitworth was indicted on 13 counts of espionage, to which he pleaded not guilty. After a highly publicized trial that lasted three months, he was found guilty on 12 counts of espionage and tax evasion, and on August 28, 1986, he was sentenced to a prison term of 365 years and a fine of $410,000.

The implications of the Walker Spy Ring and other major espionage cases were evident, particularly the security weaknesses they highlighted. Inevitably, there was a tightening of security procedures and clearances for personnel with access to classified information. Whether this clampdown proved efficacious in preventing further espionage is a matter of debate.

## AIDS IN THE OPEN

Although the AIDS crisis continued to attract attention, to many it remained a faceless disease associated with a "different" element of U.S. society. The numbers were rising at an alarming rate: By the end of 1984, the United States had logged 7,699 known cases and 3,665 deaths; the following year, 15,948 cases were reported in the country, out of 20,303 worldwide. But the recitation of statistics only added to the detachment that a large number of Americans felt about AIDS. The subject was so frightening—and so intimate, due to its association with sex— that most people simply did not want to talk about it. President Reagan in particular had scrupulously avoided mentioning the word *AIDS* in public.

Yet 1985 saw public attitudes begin to change as the cause of the disease, a virus, was confirmed, and a blood-test kit was patented. The kit's inventor was Dr. Robert Gallo of the National Cancer Institute, who in 1984 linked a retrovirus, HTLV-III, to AIDS. The previous year, Luc Montagnier of the Pasteur Institute had also isolated an AIDS virus, T-cell lymphotrophic retrovirus (later lymphadenopathy-associated virus, or LAV). It was some time before LAV and HTLV-III were found to be the same virus, finally named human immunodeficiency virus (HIV) by an international committee of scientists in 1986. Meanwhile, there was much controversy when Gallo was, temporarily, given sole credit for the discovery and then patented his HIV test kit. The Pasteur Institute sued and subsequently won rights to half of the royalties from the kit.[16]

While the scientific argument was going on backstage, Americans were slowly becoming better informed on how the virus was transmitted and instituting safeguards against infection. Nevertheless, physicians and AIDS activists continued to fight misunderstandings and widely held prejudice. Because AIDS was still thought of as a "gay disease," even unaffected homosexuals were treated like lepers. The new blood test was welcome news, but it raised concerns about confidentiality and the impact of positive results on people unaware they had the virus.

AIDS finally gained "acceptance" in 1985 thanks to two very different victims. The first, Ryan White, was a 13-year-old hemophiliac in Kokomo, Indiana, who had contracted HIV from a blood transfusion. Learning of Ryan's infection, officials barred him from school, forcing him and his mother to go to court in a highly publicized battle. Although they won their case in November, the town turned against them, and the injustice of the discrimination made Ryan known across the nation.

But it was a better-known name that grabbed most of the headlines in 1985. Rock Hudson, the macho star of such classic films as *Giant* and a series of romantic comedies with Doris Day, had always kept his homosexuality secret. During the year, however, his increasing gauntness and frailty in public appearances sparked rumors about his condition. Finally, after months of denial, on July 25 Hudson allowed a Parisian publicist to announce what reporters and friends already suspected: He had contracted AIDS. On July 30 his doctor at the UCLA Medical Center confirmed that Hudson's condition was very serious.

The country exploded with the news, and suddenly the AIDS crisis had real currency and meaning. The general public had paid little attention to the warnings of the Centers for Disease Control, Mobilization Against AIDS, and other organizations; now they were listening. AIDS was the story of the year, and Hudson's courage in acknowledging his illness and establishing a research foundation highlighted the epidemic's significance. This brought little consolation to those who had already lost loved ones to the disease, their deaths unnoticed and unmarked by the American public. Nonetheless, all joined in mourning Rock Hudson when he died on October 2.

Hudson's illness had several positive effects, one of which was to stir his friend, President Reagan, into acknowledging the crisis. At a news conference on September 17, Reagan talked of AIDS publicly for the first time, and he included the topic in his Message to the Congress on America's Agenda for the Future on February 6, 1986 (although he continued to largely ignore it for the remainder of his presidency). In time, as other HIV-positive celebrities acknowledged their condition, some of the stigma of the disease began to lessen, though many continued to disguise their illnesses under other names.

In the year 1985, 6,972 people died of AIDS in the United States. The rising numbers and particularly Hudson's death highlighted the urgent need for further research, the money to fund it, and better public education if the war against AIDS was to be won.

Rock Hudson is seen here in a 1984 TV movie, *The Vegas Strip Wars.* Though he had not yet revealed that he had AIDS, the effects of the illness were already becoming apparent. *(Photofest)*

## DISASTER IN THE SKY

Repetition dulls the most stirring of events, as NASA's space-shuttle program proved. By 1985 the United States, though proud of its lead in space travel, had come to take it for granted. NASA's program had been cautious—three flights in 1982, four in 1983, and five in 1984—and there had been occasional delays, cancellations, and systems failures. Nevertheless, increasing confidence in the space shuttles meant an impressive nine missions were flown in 1985.

In April Senator Jake Garn (R, Utah) became the first civilian observer to join a shuttle mission; *Discovery*'s June 17–24 mission included in its crew Prince Sultan Salman Abdul Aziz al-Saud of Saudi Arabia as a payload specialist, and *Atlantis*, the latest addition to NASA's fleet, made its maiden flight in October. Although these and other flights marked increasing and impressive scientific progress, they had become everyday events to the American public. However, the program received a significant public-relations boost on July 19, 1985, when Vice President George H. W. Bush announced that Christa McAuliffe of Concord, New Hampshire, would be the first schoolteacher to fly aboard a space shuttle.

NASA had begun to consider taking private citizens into space in 1982. Sending a teacher aloft would not only publicize the shuttle program but also encourage children into the sciences. The Teacher in Space Project, announced by President Reagan on August 27, 1984, produced more than 11,000 applicants, and by June 1985 NASA had selected 114, with at least two teachers from each state. Finally, on July 18 the agency picked Christa McAuliffe as its flight candidate, with Barbara Morgan of McCall, Idaho, as her backup.

In September McAuliffe and Morgan began their training for a *Challenger* mission that would take place in early 1986.[17] McAuliffe's primary tasks would be to conduct at least two lessons from the shuttle, to be simulcast to students around the world, and, after her return from space, to spend nine months lecturing to students across the country. Intelligent, enthusiastic, and charismatic, McAuliffe made an immediate hit with the press and the public, reviving interest in the shuttle program, as NASA had hoped. Plans were made to broadcast the *Challenger*'s launch live so that students could watch the nation's first astronaut-teacher go into space.

Nevertheless, there were some forebodings as *Challenger*'s launch date was put back, due to constant rescheduling of the mission immediately preceding it. *Columbia*'s seventh flight was originally due to lift off in December 1985, but when computers detected problems in a hydraulic assembly, the launch was stopped. Subsequent problems meant the flight was postponed a record seven times until its January 12, 1986, liftoff. Further difficulties caused two postponements in its landing, which took place on January 18.

Consequently, *Challenger*'s launch date was moved from January 22 to the 25th, 26th, 27th, and finally the 28th. The main worry was the weather in Florida, which had turned cold, rainy, and windy; in addition, like *Columbia*, *Challenger* was having its share of computer-detected mechanical difficulties that threatened a safe launch. On January 27 the astronauts spent several hours strapped into their seats as engineers worked to resolve one problem after the next, including a jammed hatch. Finally, the launch was postponed to the next day.

The flight was crucial to NASA, not just because of McAuliffe's high-profile involvement but because *Challenger* carried two satellites that had to be deployed as soon as possible; one of these was to study Halley's comet, due to pass close to the sun on February 8. Further, additional delay would affect the launch of subsequent important missions. Yet as NASA management fretted, engineers at Morton

Thiokol, Inc., the builder of the shuttle's solid-fuel boosters, became concerned about Florida's increasingly cold weather and its potentially damaging effect on the O-ring seals used in the joints between fuel segments of the booster rockets. With overnight temperatures expected to go below freezing and uncertainty that the sensitive O-rings would be able to withstand the cold, they recommended the January 28 launch be postponed. Similarly, engineers from Rockwell International, makers of the shuttle's engines, felt strongly that ice could hazard a safe launch. NASA's engineers, however, disputed these conclusions, and managers at Morton Thiokol and Rockwell ultimately approved the liftoff in spite of their employees' misgivings.

Overnight the weather worsened as the wind-chill temperature plummeted to −10°F, creating concerns about ice on the launchpad. Fueling problems caused a further postponement of the liftoff time. As the crew boarded the shuttle shortly before 8:30 A.M., technicians presented a nervous McAuliffe with a shiny red apple. The liftoff was again delayed, to 11:08 and then to 11:38, while a thorough inspection of the launchpad was carried out to remove ice, which nonetheless kept accumulating.

Finally, after engineers had given their approval, the countdown proceeded. At 11:38 *Challenger* lifted off to the cheers of spectators in the viewing stands—who included the astronauts' families—and students watching on television sets around the country. Commander Dick Scobee was heard to say, "Roger. Go at throttle up." Then came pilot Mike Smith's voice: "Uh-oh."

Only 73 seconds after launch, as horrified observers watched, the shuttle disappeared in an explosion that sent ribbons of smoke spiraling through the sky. With unintentional understatement, a NASA announcer was heard saying, "Obviously a major malfunction." For an hour afterward, showers of debris rained down into the Atlantic.

That night President Reagan postponed his State of the Union message to address a stunned nation by television. His speech, ranked among his finest, ended with an eloquent—and fitting—quote from "High Flight," a sonnet by John Magee:

> The crew of the space shuttle Challenger honored us by the manner in which they lived their lives. We will never forget them, nor the last time we saw them, this morning, as they prepared for their journey and waved goodbye and "slipped the surly bonds of earth" to "touch the face of God."[18]

On February 3, 1986, by executive order, Reagan created the Presidential Commission on the Space Shuttle to investigate the tragedy and its causes. Chaired by former U.S. attorney general William Rogers, the commission included several noted astronauts and Nobel Prize–winning physicist Richard Feynman. More than a month later, on March 9, U.S. Navy divers found *Challenger*'s crew

Mike Smith, Christa McAuliffe, Ellison Onizuka, and Gregory Jarvis walk toward the launchpad on January 28, 1986. *(AP/Wide World Photos)*

President Reagan addresses the nation following the *Challenger* explosion. *(Courtesy Ronald Reagan Library)*

compartment on the ocean floor. Though heavily damaged, it was still intact, and the bodies of all seven astronauts were inside.

By the time the commission's report was issued on June 6, the controversy over the O-ring seals had been widely reported in the press, so there was no surprise when the group determined the cause had been "a failure in the joint between the two lower segments of the Right Rocket Motor" and specifically the seals in that location.[19] Ice, too, had played a part in the disaster; several large chunks had struck and were sucked into the left-hand solid rocket booster. The commission identified flawed decision making as a contributory cause, and an infuriated press and public attacked management at NASA, Morton Thiokol, and Rockwell for critical errors in judgment caused by haste and complacency.

No one doubted that the disaster had been preventable, and NASA was forced to change its procedures and decision-making processes. The shuttle program was put on hold, and new safety systems were installed in *Columbia, Discovery,* and *Atlantis.* Flights finally resumed in 1988, but questions persisted about the shuttles' safety and whether NASA was risking astronauts' lives by cutting costs (resulting, for example, in there being no escape vehicle should a similar disaster occur).

Nevertheless, as successful space missions resumed, NASA slowly regained its earlier prestige. In 1998 the agency reactivated its Teacher in Space program with Barbara Morgan, McAuliffe's original alternate, as its teacher-astronaut. After extensive training, Morgan was scheduled to fly a mission in 2004, but this was aborted by the February 1, 2003, tragedy in which *Columbia,* the oldest shuttle in NASA's fleet, disintegrated on its landing approach. All seven astronauts aboard were killed—once again bringing the space-shuttle program to a halt.

## COMBATING THE "MAD DOG"

In the ongoing fight against terrorism, circumstances had not allowed President Reagan to use the military force approved by NSDD 138, but a chain of events beginning late in 1985 finally gave him the opportunity. On December 27, seven men with hand grenades and automatic rifles attacked Israel's El Al check-in counters at airports in Rome and Vienna. Of the 18 people killed, five were Americans, and four were terrorists; 111 were wounded.[20] The attackers were subsequently identified as members of the pro-Palestinian Abu Nidal Organization (ANO). Abu Nidal himself was known to have strong links to Libya and its leader, Muammar al-Gadhafi, who Reagan described as "the mad dog of the Middle East."

In January 1986 Italy issued an international warrant for Nidal's arrest, charging him with masterminding the airport attacks, and President Reagan ordered economic sanctions against Libya for its support not only of Nidal but of other terrorist groups as well. U.S. citizens in Libya were ordered to return home, and naval forces were sent to patrol the international waters claimed by Libya in the Gulf of Sidra. As he had done in 1981, Reagan warned Gadhafi the United States would attack any Libyan forces venturing outside the internationally agreed 12-mile limit off Libya's coast. At the same time, aircraft from three U.S. carriers (*Saratoga, Coral Sea*, and *America*) began to fly across Gadhafi's "line of death," which bounded the expanse of sea, 100 miles from the coast, that Gadhafi arbitrarily claimed as Libyan territory.

Finally, the three carriers, supported by airplanes and a submarine, crossed the line of death, leading to a missile attack by the Libyans on March 24, 1986. U.S. jamming technology prevented the missiles from hitting their targets, and during the next four days American air forces attacked Libyan boats and missile batteries, leaving 56 Libyans dead. Gadhafi responded by declaring the United States to be at war with Libya and ordering retaliatory terrorist attacks.

Two bombings followed. On April 2, as TWA flight 840 from Rome was making its landing approach into Athens, an explosion ripped a hole in the plane's side. Four Greek Americans, including a woman and her baby, were sucked out of the aircraft; nine other passengers, including five Americans, were injured. The plane managed to land safely, and subsequent investigation linked the bombing to Abu Nidal.

Then La Belle, a discotheque in West Berlin, was bombed on April 5. Two were killed—a Turkish woman and U.S. Army sergeant Kenneth Ford—and 230 were injured, including more than 60 Americans. Intelligence confirmed Libya's involvement in the bombing, and Reagan officials began to plan retaliation. Prime Minister Margaret Thatcher pledged her support and the use of British bases, but other European leaders refused to permit American warplanes to fly over their countries. This would mean refueling in the air five times along the circuitous route from Britain to Libya, but Reagan was determined to carry out the raid, codenamed Operation El Dorado Canyon.

On April 14, 24 F-111s, 28 refueling tankers, and five EF-111 Ravens with jamming equipment took off from British bases and flew to Libya, where they joined 12 A-6 aircraft from the *Coral Sea* and *America* to carry out strikes on targets in Tripoli and Benghazi, including Gadhafi's barracks compound. The raid lasted 11 minutes, destroying much Libyan aircraft and equipment and killing 15 Libyans, including Gadhafi's 18-month-old adopted daughter; subsequent news footage showed him carrying her body out of a wrecked building.

Although Americans overwhelmingly approved of the attack, much of the world did not, and both Reagan and Thatcher were widely criticized for their actions. Reagan announced on television, "Today we

President Reagan and Prime Minister Margaret Thatcher were good friends as well as political allies. Here, they confer informally at Camp David on November 6, 1986. *(Courtesy Ronald Reagan Library)*

have done what we had to do. If necessary, we shall do it again." Thatcher was subjected to a scolding in the House of Commons but withstood it like a "lioness in a den of Daniels," according to the London *Times*.[21] European leaders critical of the attack forecast reprisals from terrorists, and they came: On April 15, U.S. embassy official William Cokals was shot dead in Khartoum, Sudan, and two days later the bodies of American hostage Peter Kilburn and Britons John Douglas and Paul Padfield were discovered near Beirut. All had been executed by Arab Revolutionary Cells, a group affiliated with Abu Nidal.

Nevertheless, the raid on Libya produced the result Reagan wanted, as Gadhafi—now convinced that the United States *would* resort to force, despite international criticism—began to show more restraint. Yet bombings and other attacks against the United States continued around the world, and the Libyan leader would become heavily involved in the worst terrorist attack of the time: the December 1988 bombing of Pan Am 103 over Lockerbie, Scotland.

# CHRONICLE OF EVENTS

## 1985

*January 6:* Robert H. W. Welch, Jr., founder of the John Birch Society (in 1958), dies at age 85.

*January 18:* Claiming the World Court had gone outside its jurisdiction, the United States withdraws from a case brought against it by Nicaragua, which accused it of carrying out a secret war against the Nicaraguan government.

*January 20:* President Ronald Reagan and Vice President George Bush are inaugurated for their second terms.

*January 20:* The San Francisco 49ers defeat the Miami Dolphins, 38-16, to win football's Super Bowl XIX.

*January 20–21:* A record cold wave hits the United States, killing at least 40 people in 15 states.

*January 24:* The space shuttle *Discovery* takes off on a secret, military-related, three-day mission.

*January 30:* Jeane Kirkpatrick announces her resignation as U.S. ambassador to the United Nations.

*February 4:* A controversy over Pentagon expenditures erupts when it is revealed that (for example) the U.S. Navy has been paying $640 each for toilet seats worth only $25.

*February 6:* In his State of the Union address, President Reagan calls for Congress to implement major tax reforms.

*February 6–8:* At the U.S. Figure Skating Championships, Debi Thomas becomes the first African-American skater to win a singles championship; Brian Boitano wins the men's singles title.

*February 17:* The price of a first-class postage stamp increases to 22 cents.

*February 17:* General William Westmoreland drops a $120 million libel suit against CBS over a 1982 documentary that claimed that Westmoreland had withheld vital information on the strength of enemy troops during the Vietnam War.

*February 19:* William J. Schroeder, implanted with a permanent artificial heart on November 25, 1984, becomes the first such patient to be released from the hospital.

*February 20:* Disney actor Clarence Nash, famous for being the voice of Donald Duck, dies at 81.

*February 26:* At the Grammy Awards, *Can't Slow Down* by Lionel Richie wins best album of 1984; Tina Turner's "What's Love Got to Do with It" is named best record. Turner also wins as best female pop vocalist, and Phil Collins is named best male pop vocalist.

*February 27:* Former diplomat and senator Henry Cabot Lodge (R, Mass.) dies, age 82.

*March 3:* Winning the Santa Anita Handicap in Arcadia, California, Willie Shoemaker becomes the first jockey to achieve $100 million in career earnings.

*March 4:* The Environmental Protection Agency orders the removal of 90 percent of lead in gasoline by the end of 1985.

*March 4:* The Food and Drug Administration (FDA) approves a blood test to detect the virus that causes AIDS; the test will eventually be used for all blood donations.

*March 11:* Mikhail Gorbachev becomes the new leader of the Soviet Union.

*March 12:* U.S.-USSR arms-control negotiations resume in Geneva.

*March 15:* Raymond Donovan resigns as secretary of labor amid charges of fraud and larceny prior to his cabinet appointment.

*March 16:* Journalist Terry A. Anderson is abducted in Beirut; of Americans kidnapped in Lebanon, he will endure the longest captivity.

*March 17–18:* President Reagan and Prime Minister Brian Mulroney meet in Quebec City, Canada, for the Shamrock Summit.

*March 20:* In Alaska, Libby Riddles becomes the first woman to win the grueling, 1,135-mile Iditarod dog-sledding race.

*March 25:* At the Academy Awards, *Amadeus* wins as best film of 1984, while F. Murray Abraham (*Amadeus*)

President Reagan is sworn in for his second term in the rotunda at the U.S. Capitol on January 20, 1985. *(Courtesy Ronald Reagan Library)*

and Sally Field (*Places in the Heart*) win as best actor and actress. Haing S. Ngor (*The Killing Fields*) and Peggy Ashcroft (*A Passage to India*) take the supporting acting awards.

*March 27:* In a decision invalidating laws in many states, the Supreme Court rules that police may not shoot fleeing suspects who are unarmed and not considered dangerous.

*April 8:* The government of India files suit against the Union Carbide Corporation for a 1984 plant disaster in Bhopal, India, that killed approximately 1,700 and injured up to 200,000 Indian citizens.

*April 12–19:* The space shuttle *Discovery* completes its fourth mission, the 16th of the entire shuttle program to date.

*April 23:* The Coca-Cola Company announces the scrapping of its famous 99-year-old secret recipe and introduces a sweeter cola nicknamed New Coke.

*April 23:* Former senator Sam J. Ervin, Jr. (D, N.C.), who had headed the Senate committee investigating the Watergate affair, dies at 88.

*April 24:* Alison Lurie's *Foreign Affairs* wins the Pulitzer Prize for fiction; Studs Terkel wins the nonfiction prize for *The Good War: An Oral History of World War II.* Other winners include Thomas K. McCraw (history), Kenneth Silverman (biography), Carolyn Kizer (poetry), and Stephen Sondheim (drama).

*May 1:* The Reagan administration announces a trade embargo against Nicaragua.

*May 10:* Chester Gould, the cartoonist who brought detective Dick Tracy to life, dies at 84.

*May 12:* Amy Eilberg, 30, is ordained as the first woman Conservative rabbi at the Jewish Theological Seminary in New York City.

*May 13:* In Philadelphia, police raid the headquarters of MOVE, a radical black cult, setting off an explosive device that kills 11 MOVE members. The resulting fire spreads out of control, destroying 61 buildings and leaving some 250 residents homeless.

*May 15:* The skeleton of the earliest known dinosaur to date—225 million years old—is uncovered in Arizona's Painted Desert.

*May 21:* In California, Patricia Frustaci gives birth to seven children, the largest multiple birth in the United States to date; one is stillborn, and three die a short time later. On December 3 Frustaci and her husband will file a $3.2 million malpractice suit against the clinic that had given her fertility drugs.

*May 28:* President Reagan announces a plan to raise taxes on corporations while increasing personal exemptions and lowering individual tax bills.

*May 30:* The Edmonton Oilers win the National Hockey League's Stanley Cup for the second consecutive year, defeating the Philadelphia Flyers in the fifth game of the championship series.

*May 31:* Forty-one tornadoes kill 93 people and destroy a number of towns in Ohio, Pennsylvania, New York, and Ontario.

*June 2:* At the Tony Awards, *Biloxi Blues* wins as best play and *Big River* wins as best musical. Derek Jacobi and Stockard Channing take the dramatic acting awards.

*June 9:* The Los Angeles Lakers defeat the Boston Celtics, four games to two, to win the National Basketball Association championship.

*June 11:* Longtime comatose patient Karen Ann Quinlan, the subject of a famous right-to-die case, dies of pneumonia nearly 10 years after her parents won permission to remove their daughter from the respirator keeping her alive. Against all expectations, Quinlan had continued to breathe on her own.

*June 12:* The House of Representatives approves $27 million in humanitarian aid for the Nicaraguan contras, reversing its previous position.

*June 14–30:* Shiite Muslim terrorists hijack a TWA jet to Beirut and subsequently kill an American hostage. After prolonged negotiations, 39 Americans are released, but the hijackers escape.

*July 10:* In Auckland, New Zealand, a Greenpeace vessel, the *Rainbow Warrior,* is bombed and sunk by agents of the French Direction Générale de la Sécurité Extérieure (DGSE).

*July 11:* As New Coke proves a disaster, the Coca-Cola Company announces the return of its old formula as Classic Coke.

*July 11:* The Houston Astros' Nolan Ryan becomes the first pitcher in Major League Baseball history to strike out 4,000 batters.

*July 13:* President Reagan undergoes surgery to remove a cancerous tumor from his colon; doctors announce that the cancer had not spread.

*July 13:* Live Aid, a 16-hour marathon of rock concerts broadcast worldwide from Philadelphia and London, raises almost $100 million for famine relief in Ethiopia.

*July 19:* Vice President George Bush announces that Christa McAuliffe of Concord, New Hampshire, will be the first schoolteacher to fly aboard a space shuttle.

*July 23:* In Washington, D.C., President Reagan and Chinese president Li Xiannian sign an accord allowing the sale of nonmilitary technology to China.

*July 29–August 6: Challenger* makes its eighth flight, the 19th of the shuttle program.

*July 31:* David Stockman announces his resignation as director of the Office of Management and Budget, effective August 1.

*July 31:* In Kokomo, Indiana, 13-year-old hemophiliac Ryan White, who had contracted the AIDS virus through a blood transfusion, is barred from returning to school.

*August 1:* Congress passes a budget for the 1986 fiscal year with a spending level of $967.6 billion and a federal deficit of $171.9 billion.

*August 2:* Montgomery Ward & Company discontinues the publication of its famous catalog. Published since 1872, the catalog was long an essential item in rural communities.

*August 5:* The Rock and Roll Hall of Fame is established.

*August 6–7:* Baseball players strike over salary arbitration, but a settlement is quickly reached.

*August 8:* At the Rhein-Main air base in Frankfurt, West Germany, a car bomb kills two Americans. Two terrorist groups, a faction of the West German Red Army and the French Direct Action, claim responsibility.

*August 14:* The Social Security system celebrates its 50th anniversary. Since 1935 it has paid $1.8 billion in benefits and carried 36.7 million people on its rolls.

*August 25:* Samantha Smith, 13, who became famous in 1983 when she visited the Soviet Union at the invitation of then-Soviet leader Yuri Andropov, dies with her father in a plane crash.

*August 25:* The New York Mets' Dwight Gooden, 20, called Dr. K by his fans, becomes the youngest major league pitcher to win 20 games in a season.

*August 28:* Renowned stage and screen actress Ruth Gordon dies at age 88.

*September 1:* A U.S.-French team discovers the wreck of the *Titanic,* the liner that sank after hitting an iceberg during its maiden voyage in 1912. The location, some 500 miles south of Newfoundland, is kept secret to discourage looters.

*September 9:* President Reagan announces sanctions against South Africa in protest of its apartheid policy. Many consider the sanctions insufficient.

*September 11:* The Cincinnati Reds' Pete Rose beats Ty Cobb's longstanding baseball record of 4,191 hits when he notches his 4,192nd in a 2-0 win over the San Diego Padres.

*September 22:* At the Emmy Awards, *Cagney and Lacey* wins as best dramatic series. Its star, Tyne Daly, is named best actress in a dramatic series; William Daniels (*St. Elewhere*) wins as best dramatic actor.

*September 27–28:* Hurricane Gloria hits the North Carolina coast and moves north to the New York City area, killing three people and causing the evacuation of 280,000 coastal residents. Damage is estimated at $900 million.

*September 30:* At the end of the fiscal year, the federal deficit hits a record $211.9 billion. For the first time since World War I, the United States is a debtor nation.

*September 30:* Charles F. Richter, after whom the Richter scale for measuring earthquakes is named, dies at 85.

*October 1:* Author E. B. White dies at 86.

*October 2:* Actor Rock Hudson, 59, becomes the first major public figure to die of AIDS.

*October 3–7:* The latest addition to the space-shuttle fleet, *Atlantis,* makes its maiden flight.

*October 7:* The United States announces that it will no longer comply automatically with World Court decisions, claiming the court's procedures were "abused for political ends."

*October 7–10:* Four members of the Palestinian Liberation Front hijack the Italian cruise liner *Achille Lauro,* taking it to Port Said, Egypt, and killing an American passenger, Leon Klinghoffer. After surrendering to Egyptian authorities on October 9, they are arrested by Italian authorities on October 10.

*October 10:* Yul Brynner, actor best known for his stage and screen role of the king in *The King and I,* dies of lung cancer at 65.

*October 10:* Orson Welles, actor and director famed for his seminal film *Citizen Kane* (1941), dies at 70.

*October 18:* The Defense Department announces that it will test all military personnel for the HIV virus.

*October 27:* The Kansas City Royals defeat the St. Louis Cardinals, winning the World Series in the seventh game.

*October 27–November 7:* Hurricane Juan hits the Gulf Coast, where it kills seven people and causes some $1 billion in damage in Louisiana alone. Moving to the Middle Atlantic coast, Juan's heavy rains cause enormous damage and kill 42 people.

*October 30–November 6:* The space shuttle *Challenger* completes its ninth flight, the 22nd mission of the shuttle program.

*November 19:* Lincoln Theodore Perry, better known as the actor Stepin Fetchit, dies at 83. Hollywood's first well-known African-American actor, his roles usually reinforced black stereotypes.

*November 19–20:* President Reagan and Soviet secretary Mikhail Gorbachev meet in Geneva, Switzerland.

*November 26–December 3:* The space shuttle *Atlantis* makes its second flight.

*December 11:* Congress passes the Gramm-Rudman bill with the aim of eliminating the federal deficit by 1991; President Reagan signs it the next day.

*December 14:* Wilma Mankiller succeeds Ross Swimmer as principal chief of the Cherokee Nation, the first woman to become chief of a major Native American tribe.

*December 14:* Yankees batting champion Roger Maris, who in 1961 broke Babe Ruth's single-season home-run record, dies at 51.

*December 19:* In Minneapolis, Mary Lund of Kensington, Minnesota, becomes the first woman to receive an artificial heart, intended only to keep her alive until a human donor can be found.

*December 23:* President Reagan signs the biggest farm bill in history, estimated to cost some $169 billion over five years. Nevertheless, the inclusion of new ancillary programs means that income and price supports to farmers are reduced for the first time since 1933.

President Reagan met Soviet leader Mikhail Gorbachev for the first time at their summit in Geneva, Switzerland. *(Courtesy Ronald Reagan Library)*

*December 27:* Terrorist attacks at the Rome and Vienna airports result in 18 deaths, among them five U.S. citizens.

*December 27:* American naturalist Dian Fossey, who had been studying mountain gorillas, is found murdered in Rwanda.

*December 31:* Pop singer Ricky Nelson, 45, dies in a plane crash.

## 1986

*January 1:* Bill Veeck, the "Barnum of Baseball" who had owned the Cleveland Indians, St. Louis Browns, and Chicago White Sox, dies at 71.

*January 12–18:* The space shuttle *Columbia* completes its seventh mission after its liftoff had been postponed a record seven times and its landing postponed twice.

*January 20:* Americans mark the first observance of the new federal holiday honoring Dr. Martin Luther King, Jr.

*January 24:* *Voyager 2* flies within 50,679 miles of Uranus and finds evidence of a magnetic field around the planet, along with new moons and rings.

*January 24:* L. Ron Hubbard, founder of Scientology as well as a science-fiction author, dies at 71.

*January 24:* Singer-actor Gordon McRae, best known for his role in the movie version of *Oklahoma!,* dies at 64.

*January 26:* The Chicago Bears trounce the New England Patriots, 46-10, to win Super Bowl XX.

*January 28:* Seventy-three seconds after liftoff from Cape Canaveral, Florida, the space shuttle *Challenger* explodes, killing all seven aboard, including schoolteacher Christa McAuliffe.

*February 4:* In his seventh State of the Union address, President Reagan discusses the need to cut the budget deficit and strengthen family values.

*February 19:* After 38 years, the Senate finally ratifies a United Nations treaty outlawing genocide; the United States had signed the treaty in 1948.

*February 25:* At the Grammy Awards, "We Are the World" wins as best record of 1985. Best album is *No Jacket Required* by Phil Collins, also named best male pop vocalist. Whitney Houston ("Saving All My Love for You") is named best female pop vocalist.

*February 26:* Robert Penn Warren becomes the United States' first official poet laureate.

*March 6:* Artist Georgia O'Keeffe, known for her paintings of the desert and close-range views of colorful, exotic flowers, dies at 98.

President Reagan and his staff watch a televised replay of the space shuttle *Challenger* explosion on January 28, 1986. *(Courtesy Ronald Reagan Library)*

*March 10:* Actor Ray Milland, who won an Oscar for his role in *The Lost Weekend* (1945), dies at 81.

*March 14:* The government issues a policy statement that commits the United States to "democratic revolution" around the world.

*March 18:* Famed short-story writer, novelist, and Pulitzer Prize winner Bernard Malamud dies, age 71.

*March 24:* At the Academy Awards, *Out of Africa* is named best film of 1985. William Hurt and Geraldine Page win the top acting awards, while Don Ameche and Angelica Huston win the supporting acting honors.

*March 25:* Congress approves $20 million in military aid to Honduras after learning of Nicaraguan efforts to destroy contra rebels' bases.

*March 30:* Actor James Cagney dies at 86.

*April 2:* A bomb explodes aboard a TWA plane approaching Athens; though it lands safely, four Americans, including a baby, are killed.

*April 3:* IBM releases the PC Convertible, the first laptop computer.

*April 3:* The U.S. national debt exceeds $2 trillion; it has doubled in five years.

*April 5:* La Belle, a discotheque in West Berlin, is bombed by terrorists, killing a U.S. soldier and a Turkish woman.

*April 8:* Popular movie actor and Republican Clint Eastwood is elected mayor of Carmel, California.

*April 11:* Dodge Morgan, 54, sets a new record for a solo, nonstop circumnavigation of the globe when he arrives in St. George, Bermuda, aboard his 60-foot sloop *American Promise,* having sailed 27,000 miles in 150 days, beating the old record of 292 days.

*April 13:* Jack Nicklaus, 46, becomes the oldest golfer to win the Masters and the first to win it for the sixth time.

*April 14:* In retaliation for the April 5 bombing in West Berlin and other terrorist acts, the United States launches an air strike on five military bases and terrorist centers near Tripoli and Benghazi, Libya.

*April 16:* Mount Sinai Hospital in Cleveland, Ohio, announces the first test-tube baby born to a surrogate mother.

*April 17:* IBM introduces computers that use a megabit memory chip and are able to store more than 1 million bits of electronic data.

*April 17:* Pulitzer Prize winners include Larry McMurty for *Lonesome Dove* (fiction), Henry Taylor for *The Flying Change* (poetry), and Elizabeth Frank for *Louise Bogan: A Portrait* (biography). The nonfiction award goes to two authors: Joseph Lelyveld for *Move Your Shadow: South Africa, Black and White* and J. Anthony Lukas for *Common Ground: A Turbulent Decade in the Lives of Three American Families.*

*April 23:* Harold Arlen, composer whose innumerable popular songs include "Over the Rainbow," dies at age 81.

*April 26:* Noted tough-guy actor Broderick Crawford dies at 74.

*April 27:* Advertising agencies BBDO International, Doyle Dane Bernbach Group, and Needham Harper Worldwide merge to form the largest ad agency in the world.

# EYEWITNESS TESTIMONY

## *Mergers and Takeovers*

Of course, everyone, to some degree, fears change. But the ability to face and accommodate change has been one of the pillars on which American prosperity has been built. Many European countries, and others before them, have attempted to restrict freedom and to refuse change. The results are available for evaluation: loss of prosperity and loss of freedom.

The solution to the problems posed by hostile takeovers and the panoply of consequent "shark repellants" is relatively straightforward. First it must be remembered that the shareholders are the owners, and that management is employed by them. If management feels that it is in the best interest of shareholders to introduce "shark repellants" into the company's articles of association, then it should explain its reasoning to the owners of the company, namely the shareholders. It is then up to the shareholders to vote on the resolutions.

*Sir James Goldsmith, chairman of General Oriental Investments Ltd., advising how to react to hostile takeovers, in Goldsmith, "Hostile Takeovers Easier to Swallow Than Poison Pills,"* Wall Street Journal, *February 11, 1985, p. 22.*

Arbitrageurs employ secrecy, subterfuge and sleuthing. To throw competitors and bidders off the scent [Ivan] Boesky is said to buy and sell securities through third parties or shell corporations. He denies that. Another arbitrage firm reportedly hired a photographer to take photos of people entering a big merger law firm on Park Avenue. If a corporate chieftain enters, the traders are the first outsiders to know.

Hard work and expensive on-the-spot research and analysis are a necessity for arbitrageurs. Their challenge: Immediately calculate the odds on whether a proposed merger will go through—and at what final price—then jump in to buy, or stay out.

*Examining the inside tricks of arbitrage, in "Wall Street's Risk Takers Roll the Dice Again,"* U.S. News & World Report, *February 18, 1985, p. 60.*

Jonah swallowed more than the whale last week. He also gulped down *Dynasty, Hotel, Good Morning America, Monday Night Football,* the 1988 Winter Olympics and Ted Koppel. It was as simple as, well, ABC. In the first purchase ever of a major television network, small and scrappy Capital Cities Communications (1984 revenues: less than $1 billion) of New York City agreed to buy the American Broadcasting Co., which is almost four times its size. . . .

*Reporting one of the biggest acquisitions in U.S. corporate history, in "A Network Blockbuster,"* Time, *April 1, 1985, p. 60.*

Takeover abuses have become a pressing national problem. During the past three years instances of "greenmail"—where shareholders threaten to buy up a company and so force management to buy out their shares at a premium price—have risen. So have cases of highly leveraged takeovers, of bust-up liquidations, and of forced "white knight" transactions. All these financial transfers benefit takeover entrepreneurs. They don't add to the national wealth. They merely rearrange ownership interests by substituting lenders for shareholders and shift risk from equity owners to creditors. They both place our banking system and credit markets in jeopardy and keep businesses from growing and increased productivity.

*Martin Lipton, an attorney specializing in takeover law, commenting harshly on the current takeover mania, in Lipton, "Takeover Abuses Mortgage the Future,"* Wall Street Journal, *April 5, 1985, p. 16.*

Coming one after another in a frenzy that suggests financial roulette, the raids raise questions about the way investors look at companies whose shares they own, and how managements run their companies.

. . . . .

A backlash clearly is under way. Hundreds of companies are enacting antitakeover defenses this year. Measures that make raids more difficult to carry off, however, also tend to depress stock prices. Further, say critics, the effect of many of these "shark repellents" is to weaken the control that shareholders possess.

Lawmakers and regulators are beginning to look more closely at the rising number of raids and hostile takeovers and the widening impact of those actions. Federal Reserve Board Chairman Paul Volcker recently warned banks to "be mindful of the potential risks" in financing takeovers. But there is no consensus in Washington for altering the rules of the game. Like the public, the makers of government policy are either divided or bewildered.

> *Examining the pros and cons of corporate raiding and hostile takeovers, in "The Raider Barons: Boon or Bane for Business?"* U.S. News & World Report, *April 8, 1985, p. 51.*

. . . When the so-called raiders move in on a target company, they immediately are involved in a battle with existing management. Both the "raiders" and management fight the battle in many areas, most notably in the newspapers.

The stockholders of the target company ultimately are going to decide the winner, so it's in the interest of current management to call the outsiders raiders, whether they are or not. Management wants to sell the stockholders on the idea that they'll be hurt by a takeover, while the "raiders" want to convince stockholders they will gain.

> *Columnist Lindley H. Clark, Jr., explaining one of the aspects of corporate raiding, in Clark, "Are the Corporate Raiders Really White Knights?"* Wall Street Journal, *July 16, 1985, p. 33.*

These mergers involve thousands of companies and millions of workers. The 100 biggest mergers of 1984 involved firms employing 4.5 million people, or 4.3 percent of the nation's work force. If one tenth of those people were affected in some manner, just 100 mergers altered the lives of 450,000—some for the better, some for the worse. As the boom continues, it will touch the lives of many more. Concludes Wesley Cann, Jr., a law professor at the University of Connecticut: "There is no such thing as a neutral merger. Everyone is affected in one way or another."

> *Examining the impact of megamergers in "What Are Mergers Doing to America?"* U.S. News & World Report, *July 22, 1985, p. 48.*

Merger specialists and businessmen in general are trying to deal with the new uncertainty introduced by both the Texaco decision and the size of the judgment. The $11 billion figure may yet prove decisive, with the need for ordinary business credit forcing Texaco to settle regardless of its chances of success in the courts. We already have too much litigation, even without bizarre happenings in Texas. Merger decisions shouldn't depend on the vagaries of Judge Caseb's instructions to jurors.

They ought to be fought out not in the courts but in the marketplace.

> *The* Wall Street Journal *commenting critically on the $11 billion legal judgment against Texaco for buying Getty Oil out from under Pennzoil, in its editorial "Texas C.L. Massacre II,"* Wall Street Journal, *December 20, 1985, p. 24.*

## Terrorist Perils

The front-seat passenger leaned over the back of his seat. "Don't worry. It's political," he said in a normal tone as the car lurched back and forth, the driver cutting in and out of traffic.

The strange comment, apparently meant to be reassuring, wasn't. As my mind began to function again, it made me think of the other Americans kidnapped in Beirut for political reasons. William Buckley, missing twelve months. The Reverend Benjamin Weir, missing ten months. Father Lawrence Jenco, missing two months.

There wasn't any real fear yet—it was drowned by adrenaline. Just a loud, repeating mental refrain: Anderson, you stupid shit, you're in deep, deep trouble.

> *Journalist Terry Anderson writing of his thoughts as he was being abducted in Beirut on March 16, 1985, in Anderson,* Den of Lions *(1993), p. 7.*

Tower: "You have no permission to land at Beirut."

Pilot: "Beirut, the hijacker has pulled the pin on his hand grenade. We will land in Beirut. He is desperate. He has pulled a hand-grenade pin, and he is ready to blow up the aircraft. We must—I repeat must—land at Beirut. No alternative."

Tower: "You must fly on. You must. The airport is closed. I cannot give you permission to land. . . . Can you hold for 10 minutes?"

Pilot: "Understand we must land at Beirut. We must. Be advised we must land."

Tower: "Land quietly. Please land quietly."

> *June 14, 1985, conversation between the pilot of the hijacked TWA flight 847 and the control tower at Beirut airport, reproduced in "'He is Ready to Blow Up the Aircraft,'"* U.S. News & World Report, *June 24, 1985, p. 11.*

You are asking Shiites to release our hostages without any guarantees. They don't trust the American government. . . . It's more important to bend your strong policy than jeopardize 40 Americans, who are more important than your foreign policy, which has created hate for America.

*Bob Peel, Sr., father of one of the hostages aboard TWA flight 847, in a telegram to President Reagan, quoted in Reid, "3 Ex-Hostages Are Still Captives of Concern," Washington Post, June 28, 1985, p. A-28.*

We cannot and will not abstain from forcible action to prevent, preempt or respond to terrorist acts where conditions merit the use of force.

*National Security Advisor Robert McFarlane commenting on the possibility of retaliating against terrorists, quoted in "The Reagan Team on Terrorism," U.S. News & World Report, July 1, 1985, p. 21.*

I don't argue that all these attacks should go unanswered. I'm not saying, "Never retaliate." In some instances, we may have to do it. What I'm saying is: The U.S. shouldn't lash out in blind emotion but should be a little bit more cold-blooded. We ought to do some thinking for a change. What we are seeing now, to my mind, is nothing but raw emotion and the tip of the iceberg.

*Robert Kupperman of the Georgetown University Center for Strategic and International Studies, arguing against taking retaliatory measures, in "Should U.S. Strike Back at Terrorists?" U.S. News & World Report, July 1, 1985, p. 22.*

No, we didn't get "even"! We simply apprehended the criminals. To get even we would have had to shoot one of the Palestinian Liberation Front pirates and brutalize the others. I am thankful that President Reagan was strong enough to make the correct decision to be strong—but not brutal. We don't always have to get even, but we do have to be strong—no matter what the price.

*From a letter to the editor commenting on a* Newsweek *article about the capture of the* Achille Lauro *terrorists, in* Newsweek, *November 11, 1985, p. 4.*

Suddenly we heard what was like a sonic boom, the kind you hear a plane make. We realized this isn't a movie, this is really happening. I put my arms around my son and said, "We're not going to die, we still have things to do." One of the rows had disappeared and we did not know if people had actually blown out of the

plane . . . I was just looking up in daylight because the hole had been in the section where there had been a row of seats.

*Tom Kojis, a passenger on TWA flight 840, describing the moments after a bomb exploded on April 2, 1986, quoted in "TWA Passengers Recall Vanishing Row of Seats," Washington Post, April 3, 1986, p. A-32.*

We didn't plan this and we didn't do this, and we think it was wrong. We are against terrorism. The Americans cannot accuse us this time.

*A Libyan official denying responsibility for the April 2, 1985, bombing of TWA flight 840, quoted in Fish, "Libya Ducks Bomb Blame," Times (London), April 4, 1986, p. 7.*

We will not allow Americans to be bombed out of our country.

*West German foreign minister Hans-Dietrich Genscher in a statement to reporters on April 6, 1986, a day after La Belle discotheque was bombed, killing an American serviceman, quoted in "West Berlin Police Seek Suspects in Discotheque Blast That Killed 2," Washington Post, April 7, 1986, p. A-9.*

I have no illusion that these actions will eliminate entirely the terrorist threat. But it will show that officially sponsored terrorist actions by a government—such as Libya has repeatedly perpetrated—will not be without cost. The loss of such state sponsorship will inevitably weaken the ability of terrorist organizations to carry out their criminal attacks even as we work through diplomatic, political, and economic channels to alleviate the more fundamental causes of such terrorism.

*Ronald Reagan, in an April 10, 1986, message to British prime minister Margaret Thatcher, explaining why he wanted to carry out a military raid against Libya, quoted in Thatcher, The Downing Street Years (1993), p. 444.*

We Americans are slow to anger. We always seek peaceful avenues before resorting to the use of force, and we did. We tried quiet diplomacy, public condemnation, economic sanctions and demonstrations of military force—none succeeded. Despite our repeated warnings, Qaddafi continued his reckless policy of intimidation, his relentless pursuit of terror.

He counted on America to be passive. He counted wrong. I warned that there should be no place on earth where terrorists can rest and train and practice their deadly skills. I meant it. I said that we would act with others if possible and alone if necessary to insure that terrorists have no sanctuary anywhere.

Tonight we have. Thank you, and God bless you.
*President Reagan in a televised address to the nation, April 14, 1986, explaining the reasons he authorized a raid against Libya that day, quoted in "Transcript of Address by Reagan on Libya," New York Times, April 15, 1986, p. A-10.*

As so often before, however, she proved to be a lioness in a den of Daniels. Every criticism from the Opposition benches was turned away with remorseless logic; every hint of nervousness on the Tory benches was soothed away with painstaking explanation....
*Reporter John O'Sullivan describing the scene in the House of Commons on April 15, 1985, as Prime Minister Margaret Thatcher defended her decision to support the U.S. raid on Libya, in O'Sullivan, "Lioness in a Den of Daniels," Times (London), April 16, 1985, p. 20.*

## Oh, Canada

What does Mr. Reagan have to offer in return? Despite a steady stream of scientific reports documenting the dangers of acid rain, he has for five years insisted that it merits only more study, not action. Yet even an acid rain panel picked by the White House confirmed the message of the previous studies, and specifically warned against further delay: "If we . . . wait until the scientific knowledge is definitive, the accumulated deposition [of acid rain] and damaged environment may reach the point of 'irreversibility,'" the panel concluded.

. . . . .

By having the E.P.A. crack down on tall stacks, Mr. Reagan could at the stroke of a pen substantially diminish the United States' export of acid rain to its neighbor. Instead the White House is said to be planning yet another study, this time jointly with Canada.

The man who is Mr. Reagan's host this weekend deserves better.
*The New York Times admonishing President Reagan for his failure to respond to Canada's concerns about acid rain, in its editorial "Acid Rain and the Shamrock Summit," New York Times, March 16, 1985, p. 22.*

The appointment of two "special envoys" to break the four-year-old Canadian-U.S. deadlock on acid rain has brought a mixture of pragmatic optimism and critical cynicism.

Allan Gotlieb, Canada's Ambassador to the United States, called the agreement a "very important" step in dealing with the problem.

However, William Davis, the former Ontario premier named as Canada's special envoy on the issue, acknowledged that the Canadian-U.S. study is not likely to produce dramatic results.

"I don't think anyone is promising miracles," Mr. Davis told reporters.
*Reporting Canadian cynicism regarding the appointment of special envoys to study acid rain, agreed at the Shamrock Summit, in Michael Keating, "Environmentalists Skeptical about Acid-Rain Talks," Globe and Mail (Montreal), March 19, 1985, p. 5.*

At the recent "summit" meeting in Quebec—amid all the protestations of mutual devotion—President Reagan smilingly delivered a slap in the face to Canada that his admirer, Prime Minister Brian Mulroney, had no choice but smilingly to accept. The Canadians had desperately tried to get Mr. Reagan to agree to specific control goals or, at minimum, to persuade the Environmental Protection Agency to tighten and to enforce its own regulations, which it has been scandalously deficient in doing.

Instead, Mr. Reagan appointed a political pal, Drew Lewis, with no known expertise on acid rain, as "special envoy" to examine this much-examined question with a Canadian counterpart and to report back sometime in the future. Only last year, Mr. Reagan quietly shelved his own science adviser's recommendations for action, based on previous joint United States–Canadian study groups. The new arrangement with Mr. Mulroney is not a compromise as advertised but a farce that, the White House hopes, will keep the Canadians tranquil for at least another year.
*Editorialist John B. Oakes criticizing the Reagan administration's attitude on acid rain and Canada, in Oakes, "Acid Rain's Political Poison," New York Times, April 8, 1985, p. A-17.*

British decorum is giving way to exasperation under what many officials consider the aggressive tactics of advance men planning tomorrow's visit [to London] by Prime Minister Brian Mulroney.

Usually unflappable British officials, speaking privately, are annoyed and frustrated over efforts by Bill Fox, Mulroney's press secretary, to orchestrate the four-day visit to the advantage of the TV cameras.

In fact, several British officials have unfavorably compared Fox's style to that of demanding White House advance men.

*Reporting negative reaction in England to a forthcoming visit by Prime Minister Brian Mulroney, in " 'Pushy' Mulroney Aides Ruffle British Feathers," Saturday Star (Toronto), April 27, 1985, p. A-1.*

One official was quoted as saying Mr Fox "wanted to turn the meeting with the Queen into a rolling cinema verité which, of course, is not our style."

…"We were surprised that a country like Canada, a leading Commonwealth country which had been going through this for a hundred years, would act like it didn't know the rules."

*Presenting British reaction to the Canadian press secretary's request to have television cameras present at a meeting between Prime Minister Brian Mulroney and Queen Elizabeth II, reported in John Best, "Mulroney's Man in Royal Row," Times (London), April 29, 1985, p. 7.*

… When questioned whether his company distributed tuna "unfit for human consumption," he replied, "That term is incorrect."

We wonder which term *is* correct. "Rancid and decomposed," the words used by the federal inspectors, are fairly descriptive. Defence Department officials noted "a strong smell, tuna oozing out of the cans and fish that was not recognizable as tuna." That, too, seems clear enough.

Mr. Fraser, after deliberately ignoring the advice of federal health officials, would have us believe the tuna poses no serious health hazard. Sorry, Mr. Fraser, but Canadians won't eat just anything. Simply put, this isn't an area for ministerial discretion.

*The Globe and Mail criticizing Fisheries Minister John Fraser at the outbreak of "Tunagate" in its editorial "The Nature of Tuna," Globe and Mail (Montreal), September 19, 1985, p. 10.*

No, the Tories have to do something dramatic to prove they are right, that the nation is safe, and that you can feed the controversial tuna to puss without her spitting up all over the carpet or, worse, rolling over and playing dead, very convincingly.

The solution, dear friends, is for Prime Minister Brian Mulroney and wife Mila to make a gigantic tuna casserole of the now-it's-banned, now-it's-not tuna.

And then they should invite the Tory caucus to dinner.

*Journalist Gary Lautens offering a satiric suggestion for what to do with tainted tuna, in Lautens, "Make Tuna Surprise a Compulsory Dish at Tory Caucus Dinner," Toronto Star, September 20, 1985, p. A-2.*

## Native American Troubles

The panel said the current tribal practices had made the nation's Indians dependent on more than $2.5 billion in Federal aid annually without bringing them closer to economic self-sufficiency.

"Economic development, without subsidy, can be successfully put together only within a new social and economic setting which entails a radical break with the past dependency on the Federal Government," the panel said.

Elmer Savilla, executive director of the [National Tribal Chairmen's Association], said this approach misinterpreted Indian values.

"The non-Indian approach is, you go into business with one motive," he said in an interview. "The Indian way is to go into business to provide income for tribal members, to provide employment for as many tribal members as you can. So we may put more people on the payroll than non-Indians would, because the business has a different purpose for us."

*Analyzing the controversial November 1984 report of the presidential Commission on Indian Reservation Economies, in Peterson, "Indians Resisting Shift in Economics," New York Times, January 13, 1985, p. A-16.*

No one owns the land. We were born here and we just use the land; it is our Earth mother, a part of our religion.

*Shoshone Carrie Dann explaining why she and her sister Mary refuse to consider themselves trespassers on federal land, quoted in Ronald B. Taylor, "Indians Sisters Spur Land Rights Battle," Los Angeles Times, March 24, 1985, Part I, p. 3.*

As Roberta Blackgoat's children were born, their umbilical cords were buried in a corner of her sheep corral. It is a tradition that ties each Navajo to the land and to the animals that provide the food and clothing necessary for survival.

So it is too late now to ask her to move off the land where she was born, where her great-grandmother is buried, Mrs. Blackgoat said. Congress may have given the land to the Hopis, but God gave it to her and the Navajo people.

"No, no matter what they are going to do, we are going to stay," she said. "No matter what they do, we are going to stay."

*Journalist Iver Peterson describing the typical reaction of many Navajo to their forced relocation, in Peterson, "Navajos Refuse to Bow to Relocation by U.S.," New York Times, May 9, 1985, p. A-1.*

For more than a century now, two Indian tribes have shared the area: the mesa-dwelling Hopis and the Navajos who lived everywhere else. Over time, the Navajos were fruitful and multiplied; they surrounded the Hopis and, with their ubiquitous sheep, came to dominate the land. The Hopis complained, and 11 years ago the U.S. Congress imposed a settlement: divide the land, move a few Hopis and, more dramatically, evict 10,000 Navajos from what is called Hopi Partition Land . . . in the largest forced civilian relocation since the World War II internment of Japanese Americans.

Now, with 10 months left before a congressional deadline, the relocation has reached an impasse. Hundreds of Navajos have refused to leave the land they call "our mother." And the Hopi leaders insist on forcing their rights. . . .

*Examining the emotional issues involved in the Hopi-Navajo dispute, in "Two Tribes, One Land," Newsweek, September 23, 1985, p. 78.*

Some tribespeople view the suicide epidemic as a reason to re-examine the reservation's social and economic ills. About 70% of the Wind River work force is unemployed, and jobs for the young are especially scarce. At the same time, the reservation's oil and gas wealth provides royalty payments of up to $300 a month per person, thus fostering a debilitating welfare culture. Howard Smith, fiscal officer for the Arapaho tribe, which shares the 2 million-acre reservation with the Shoshones, says, "Too many of our young people have

time on their hands, so they drink and watch TV and get depressed."

*Looking at a sad rash of suicides on the Wind River Reservation, in "Wind River's Lost Generation," Time, October 21, 1985, p. 40.*

Although the weapons have changed, American Indians are fighting much the same battles over tribal sovereignty and the ownership of land and natural resources that they waged in the 19th century. The difference is that this time—from tribal courthouses to the United States Supreme Court—they are winning.

"The Indians who started going through law school in the 1960's realized for the first time that we had a lot of legal rights that had not been enforced and that could make a difference," said John Echohawk, director of the Native American Rights Foundation in Boulder, Colo.

. . . . .

Since 1959, the Native American Rights Foundation says, the Supreme Court has handed down about 75 opinions on Indian law, all but a few in the tribes' favor. Some Indian lawyers argue that as long as the special status of Indians is upheld, there will be forces seeking to take away their rights.

*Journalist Iver Peterson describing the changes in Native Americans' approach to legal action, in Peterson, "Rights Reserved for the Reservation," New York Times, February 2, 1986, sec. 4, p. 7.*

I bore my first child here. I've been here as long as memory can serve me. There are pure trees here with the blessing of the Great Spirit. We pray to our maker through those trees. The same is true with the hulls, when we give sacred stones and talk to the Maker. There are so many pure places to go to for strength and to talk to the Great Spirit. If we were put elsewhere, we will not know those pure places. How could we talk to the Great Spirit?

*Ruth Benally, a Navajo being evicted from her land, quoted in Curry, "Hundreds of Navajos Being Forced Off Lands," Los Angeles Times, February 16, 1986, part 1, p. 1.*

Our resistance is not mainly on restoring Hopi lands, but a fight for our survival that we are not wiped off this land. The Hopi are the victims. If we do not speak up, the Hopi will be the victims. We have won every [court] case. The Supreme Court has stood by the decision. Something is wrong that we are still not using the land. We have been the victims of broken promises.

*Tribal chairman Ivan Sidney explaining the Hopi side of their land dispute with the Navajo, quoted in Curry, "Hundreds of Navajos Being Forced Off Lands,"* Los Angeles Times, *February 16, 1986, part 1, pp. 1, 30.*

## Products, Old and New

Here's a VCR development that is as daring as it is obvious: Borrowing a feature found in some of the fancier audio-cassette players, Sharp Electronics Corp. is manufacturing a double-cassette VCR.

. . . . .

. . . Jack Valenti, president of the Motion Picture Association of America, said selling a machine such as Sharp's is "like selling a skeleton key that can open the front door to any home in America."

. . . The movie studios already have demonstrated antagonism toward VCRs, despite their eagerness to put movies on cassettes. It took no less than the Supreme Court, in last year's landmark Betamax case, to establish the legality of recording TV off the air for one's own enjoyment.

But a single-unit home copying machine is a new wrinkle. Looming like a green light for home tapers and a red flag to the film industry, it would almost certainly provoke fresh legal skirmishes. Yet it's a battle that seems ultimately unavoidable.

*Journalist Andy Wickstrom reporting concerns over new developments in VCR technology, in Wickstrom, "Double-decker VCR a Dream Machine for Tape Copiers,"* Chicago Tribune, *March 15, 1985, sec. 7, p. 57.*

Home computers are in the doldrums, telephone makers are still in the throes of a shakeout and color-television sales are stagnant. Amid this wreckage, the consumer-electronics industry and gadget lovers have a new darling: The compact disc.

Using digital technology to create sound far superior to that of traditional phonograph records, the compact disc, or CD, is rejuvenating the audio business and producing a generation of born-again music lovers.

. . . . .

Esoteric and futuristic? There's nothing obscure about the compact-disc phenomenon. which already is being touted as the most revolutionary audio breakthrough since Thomas Edison's first crude phonograph.

*Highlighting the rise of compact discs, in "Compact Discs Now the Hottest Sound in Town,"* U.S. News & World Report, *June 17, 1985, pp. 62–63.*

## New Coke, Old Coke

As I drive home, my mood goes like a roller coaster. At the bottom, bleak despair: We're getting a new product to compete with, maybe a product that will taste great. At the top, elation: We've just been paid a great compliment; Coke is admitting defeat by changing its formula. . . .

Unfortunately, I think, no one outside of Pepsi will see it that way. A new product as a *defeat* for Coke? People will shake their heads and wonder what we've been smoking if we try that gambit. No, the next week's going to be grim. Coke will tell its story in a slick, positive way. And if we try to attack, we'll look like sore losers.

*Roger Enrico, president of Pepsi-Cola USA, describing his mixed reactions on April 19, 1985, on learning that Coca-Cola was changing its formula, in Enrico,* The Other Guy Blinked *(1986), p. 196. Pepsi-Cola's advertising subsequently took full advantage of Coca-Cola's faux pas.*

For many, much more is on the line here than just a soda that tastes different. For Southerners especially, many of whom were weaned on the stuff and still drink more Coke per capita than people in any other region in the nation, the very notion of tampering with the formula for Coke—something so sacred it has been locked in an Atlanta bank vault since the turn of the century—seems as unthinkable as putting sugar in cornbread.

Lewis Grizzard, an Atlanta writer and columnist, was among those shaken by the announcement. "The only way that I could figure they could improve upon Coca-Cola, one of life's most delightful elixirs, which studies prove will heal the sick and occasionally raise the dead, is to put rum or bourbon in it," he said today.

> *Reporting the reaction to New Coke in Coca-Cola Company's home base of Atlanta, in William E. Schmidt, "Home of Coke Laments Change in Winning Formula," New York Times, April 26, 1985, p. A-15.*

. . . San Francisco Examiner columnist Bill Mandel calls it "Coke for wimps" and laments the disappearance of that "battery acid" tang. "It just doesn't have that zing," says John Thomas Grisham, 30, a Santa Clara, Calif., locksmith who started drinking Coke at 18 months. "For years, Coke *was* it," he says disconsolately. "Now it's gone."

> *Examining ongoing negative reaction several weeks after the introduction of New Coke, in "Saying 'No' to New Coke," Newsweek, June 24, 1985, p. 33.*

There is a twist to this story which will please every humanist and will probably keep Harvard professors puzzled for years. The simple fact is that all the time and money and skill poured into consumer research on the new Coca-Cola could not measure or reveal the deep and abiding emotional attachment to the original Coca-Cola felt by so many people. . . .

> *Donald Keough, president and chief operating officer of Coca-Cola, rationalizing during the July 11, 1985, press conference in which the company announced the return of Classic Coke, quoted in Wikipedia, "New Coke." Available online. URL: http://en.wikipedia.org/wiki/New_Coke.*

In the beginning, there was the Edsel.

Today, there is the Coca-Cola Co.'s New Coke, apparently destined to join AT&T's Picturephone, Pringle's potato chips, Schlitz Beer and IBM's PCjr in the marketing hall of flops.

In the long run, Coca-Cola may ultimately succeed in turning its marketing misstep into a promotional prize—by convincing its customers that it is a caring company, listening to them after all. But marketing experts said yesterday that Coke's decision to abandon and then bring back its age-old formula is, at the very least, a major marketing blunder that will be discussed for years to come.

> *One of many comparisons of the New Coke mistake to Ford Motor Company's Edsel, in Mayer, "New Coke Joins Marketing Hall of Flops," Washington Post, July 12, 1985, p. B-1.*

Clearly this is the Edsel of the '80s. This was a terrible mistake. Coke's got a lemon on its hands, and now they're trying to make lemonade.

> *Roger Enrico, president of Pepsi-Cola USA, commenting cynically on Coca Cola's decision to bring back its old formula, quoted in "Coca-Cola's Big Fizzle," Time, July 22, 1985, p. 48.*

We all owe the folks at Coca-Cola Co. a debt of gratitude. They've provided us with free summertime entertainment and, just coincidentally, an elementary lesson in the mechanics of modern capitalism. They have infused new meaning into an old concept: consumer sovereignty. They have shown that the most successful corporations, for all their elaborate marketing surveys and lavish advertising, remain hostage to often unpredictable consumer habits, life styles and desires.

. . . Indeed, the Coke furor fed on our victim mentality. It was less a flavor crusade than an anticorporate rebellion. It was that rare issue simple and symbolic enough to concentrate our vague anticorporate hostilities against a single target. It was satisfying (even if you don't drink Coke) precisely because it relieved a mass urge to yell "Up the organization!"—and get some results.

> *Columnist Robert J. Samuelson commenting on another aspect of the Coca-Cola brouhaha, in Samuelson, "Consumer Sovereignty," Washington Post, July 24, 1985, p. D-1.*

## Presidential Problems

Taken together, the sudden flurry of shifts and departures creates unexpected leadership gaps only two months after Reagan declared he saw no need "to break up a winning team." Ahead lies an uneasy transition period, during which new aides must learn the delicate business of running the White House. Because the modern presidency has increasingly drawn power to the keepers of the Oval Office, and because Reagan leaves so much of the detail work to underlings, the changes and uncertainty among his advisers are no small matter to the nation.

> *Commenting on the ramifications of the early January 1985 decision by Chief of Staff James Baker and Treasury Secretary Donald Regan to swap jobs, in "Shake-Up at the White House," Time, January 21, 1985, p. 10.*

And today, after 40 years of peace, here we are, our staunchest allies in that summit are the countries that were our enemies in World War II. Now, their leaders have come here and visited Arlington. They have—leaders from Germany, from Italy, from Japan. And this cemetery, we only found out later, someone dug up the fact, that there are about 30 graves of SS troops. These were the villains, as we know, that conducted the persecutions and all. But there are 2,000 graves there. And most of these, the average age is about 18. These were those young teenagers that were conscripted, forced into military service in the closing days of the Third Reich, when they were short of manpower, and we're the victor and they're there.

*President Reagan in a press conference on April 18, 1985, defending his decision to visit a military cemetery in Bitburg, West Germany, quoted in "Responses of the President to Queries on German Visit,"* New York Times, *April 19, 1985, p. A-13.*

May I, Mr. President, if it's possible at all, implore you to do something else, to find a way, to find another way, another site? That place, Mr. President, is not your place. Your place is with the victims of the SS.

*Elie Wiesel, chairman of the United States Holocaust Memorial Council, to President Reagan during an April 19, 1985, White House ceremony at which he received the Congressional Gold Medal of Achievement, quoted in "Transcript of Remarks by Reagan and Wiesel at White House Ceremony,"* New York Times, *April 20, 1985, p. 4.*

It is surely not the intention of President Reagan to encourage those unrepentant Germans, but undoubtedly, his visit to the Bitburg cemetery will have such an effect. Furthermore, his comparison of Nazi war dead to concentration-camp victims constitutes an erosion of the fundamental difference between those who were murdered because they were Jewish and those who served Hitler as soldiers.

Comparisons like this one not only reveal a regrettable lack of sensitivity, but also serve as an embarrassment for the majority of the Germans of 1985, who know that the Nazi period was the abyss of German history. No one should try to obscure this.

*Jens Drews, a German student in State College, Pennsylvania, adding to the criticism regarding President Reagan's upcoming trip to a military cemetery in West Germany, in a letter to the editor,* New York Times, *April 28, 1985, sec. 4, p. 22.*

Everywhere here are memories—pulling us, touching us, making us understand that they can never be erased. Such memories take us where God intended His children to go—toward learning, toward healing, and, above all, toward redemption. They beckon us through the endless stretches of our heart to the knowing commitment that the life of each individual can change the world and make it better.

We're all witnesses; we share the glistening hope that rests in every human soul. Hope leads us, if we're prepared to trust it, toward what our President Lincoln called the better angels of our nature. And then, rising above all this cruelty, out of this tragic and nightmarish time, beyond the anguish, the pain and the suffering for all time, we can and must pledge: Never again.

*From President Reagan's speech at Bergen-Belsen concentration camp on May 5, 1985. Available online. URL: http://www.reagan.utexas.edu/resource/speeches/1985/50585a.htm.*

Ronald Reagan stood at last in the cemetery at Bitburg yesterday.

"Never again," he said later, in his speech at the U.S. military base nearby, referring to Nazism. "Never again," he had said earlier, in his speech at the site of the former concentration camp at Belsen.

He could be forgiven for investing the phrase with more than one meaning. Never again must a combination of an ignoramus of a White House public relations expert, a jovial, but wily German politician and his own

President Reagan lays a wreath at Kolmeshohe Cemetery, Bitburg, on May 5, 1985. *(Courtesy Ronald Reagan Library)*

endlessly genial nature land him among the remains of 49 SS men—at least, not with him laying a wreath.

*Reporter Frank Johnson commenting on President Reagan's controversial visit to Bergen-Belsen and Bitburg, in Johnson, "Belsen and Bitburg: Sorrow and Slapstick," Times (London), May 6, 1985, p. 10.*

## Espionage Trauma

The sordid profession of betraying one's country has lost its ideological appeal. No longer do American traitors sell out to the enemy, it seems, because of misguided idealism.

Now it's strictly cash on the barrelhead. The "Me" generation of traitors has arrived. The Soviets must pay for what they get. This is no problem for the cynics in the Kremlin.

In fact, the Soviets abandoned communist commitment as their chief recruiting device long ago. The KGB laid other traps: money for the greedy, blackmail for the vulnerable.

*Jack Anderson and Dale Van Atta commenting on the latest motivations for spying, in Anderson and Van Atta, "Traitors of the 'Me' Generation," Washington Post, June 2, 1985, p. C-7.*

The F.B.I. faces another potentially large problem in that about 1,000 Soviet émigrés, many naturalized American citizens, work in military industries and have access to classified information. The F.B.I. assumes these people are loyal Americans, but because most of them still have families in the Soviet Union the bureau believes they are vulnerable targets for the K.G.B.

Soviet officers place special emphasis on trying to recruit American agents, but most Americans who spy for the Soviet Union are volunteers, not recruits, bureau officials say. Soviet officers also use Americans who can be unknowingly tricked into revealing secrets.

*Reporting some unsettling facts about Soviet espionage, in "U.S. Frustrated in Effort to Counter Soviet Spying," New York Times, June 16, 1985, p. 22.*

As authorities tried to pinpoint the losses and pursue other leads, the nation struggled with the disturbing implications of the Walker case and other recent spy arrests. Suddenly, ordinary Americans seemed all too willing to betray their country, not for ideology, as in Stalin's early days, but for money, prestige and thrills.

The Walker fiasco also made the U.S. acutely aware of its growing vulnerability to spies. More Soviet agents are operating in the U.S. than ever before, and the number of military and technological secrets is growing exponentially. Says Retired Admiral Bobby Inman, former director of the National Security Agency and deputy director of the CIA: "We must be one of the world's easiest targets."

*Assessing the impact of the espionage scandal following the arrest of the Walker spy ring, in "Very Serious Losses,'" Time, June 17, 1985, p. 19.*

It . . . confirms what we have known right along—that the Soviet KGB has a very large and well-organized program operating on a worldwide basis. They get a lot of intelligence.

We have had success in thwarting the KGB ranks, and over the last couple of years, they've had a lot of failures. But they have had their success, too—and this particular case seems to be a big success.

*CIA director William Casey admitting that the Walker spy ring did a lot of damage to the United States, quoted in "Soviet Espionage: 'A Big Effort—and It Pays Off Big,'" U.S. News & World Report, June 17, 1985, p. 23.*

Caspar Weinberger's opinion was blunt and harsh. Asked how the four suspects in the Walker spy scandal should be punished if found guilty, the Defense Secretary replied, "They should be shot," adding that he supposed "hanging is the preferred method." Republican Senator Ted Stevens of Alaska, who introduced a bill to make spying for money punishable by death, was even more draconian. "If there is an execution, it should be public and on television," he said. "I want the widest possible visibility of this kind of crime [to] deter people who may be starting down this road."

*Describing official reaction to the Walker spy scandal, in "Operation Damage Control," Time, June 24, 1985, p. 31.*

Among other things, . . . critics want to see more use of lie detectors, fewer Americans granted access to top secrets and fewer East-bloc citizens of all kinds—diplomats, businessmen, students and tourists—entering the United States, where about a third are judged to be on intelligence missions. Some critics are pressing hard for a reduction in the number of Soviets who work for the U.S. Embassy in Moscow—about 200, more than half the number of U.S. citizens on staff. Other ideas include upgrading CI [counterintelligence] by making it a separate career service within the CIA, insulated so that CI specialists need not fear retribution from agency officers whose security or loyalty they question.

*Examining some of the ideas for tightening U.S. security against espionage, in "CIA Spy Hunt," Newsweek, November 4, 1985, p. 23.*

So many Federal employees are now selling American secrets to foreigners that the country faces an acute secrets shortage.

Within the past two weeks authorities struggling to stop the secrets drain have arrested Government workers, both active and retired, on charges of peddling the stuff to China, Israel and the Soviet Union. Does anyone doubt that dozens of other foreign powers are even now in touch with financially desperate federal workers eager to cash in while there are still secrets left for selling?

. . . .

As this goes to press I am informed that Federal employees, alarmed by the secrets drain, plan to band together and set sharply reduced quotas on sales, thereby driving up the price of secrets. More on this later as soon as I can raise the cash to pay for the complete details.

*Columnist Russell Baker commenting sardonically on the high number of espionage cases, in Baker, "The Secrets Boom," New York Times, November 30, 1985, p. 23.*

The Government of Israel assures the Government of the United States that in the wake of the inquiry, if the allegations are confirmed, those responsible will be brought to account, the unit involved in this activity will be completely and permanently dismantled, and necessary organizational steps will be taken to ensure that such activities are not repeated.

*Israeli prime minister Shimon Peres in a statement issued on December 1, 1985, apologizing to the United States following the arrest of Jonathan Jay Pollard on charges of spying for Israel, quoted in "Israel Apologizes to U.S. in Spy Case," New York Times, December 2, 1985, p. A-4.*

What's going on here? Not only does the Government seem to be infested with spies, but they aren't even the kind of subversives good Americans have been taught to fear and loathe.

Four mostly ordinary persons were arrested within five days last week and charged with spying for China, Israel and the Soviet Union. Together with last summer's Walker family spy case and other recent espionage scandals, all this must have given a rude shock to those who've bought the idea that it's the press and undetected Communists who "give away" vital U.S. secrets.

. . . .

The direct passage of real security secrets to foreign governments, by professionals or by coerced victims, is the problem. The Espionage Act provides all the prosecutorial power the Government needs; what's lacking is an effective counterespionage program, not just to lock the barn after the horse has been stolen, but to deter the potential thief.

*Columnist Tom Wicker commenting on the United States' espionage problems, in Wicker, "Spies Real and Unreal," New York Times, December 2, 1985, p. A-15.*

### Aid to the Needy, 1980s-style

We are using television as a tool, as a catalyst to get the world, on one given day, to focus their attention on a problem of world-wide importance.

*Michael C. Mitchell, president of Worldwide Sports and Entertainment, hyping the upcoming Live Aid concert, quoted in Fein, "'Live Aid' Concert Is Aiming for the Sky," New York Times, July 12, 1985, p. C-5.*

It's not just the greatest show on earth, it's the greatest gig in the galaxy.

*Bob Geldof, chief organizer of the Live Aid concert on July 13, 1985, quoted in Harrington, "Live Aid Concerts Raise Millions for African Relief," Washington Post, July 14, 1985, p. A-16.*

Good morning, children of the 80s. This is your Woodstock, and it's long overdue.

*Folk singer Joan Baez, opening the Philadelphia concert for Live Aid on July 13, 1985, quoted in Fein, "Reports of Concert Aid Range up to $50 Million," New York Times, July 15, 1985, p. C-18.*

Bob Geldof gestures onstage at London's Wembley Stadium during the Live Aid concert on July 13, 1985. *(Photofest)*

Between then and now, rock-and-roll has moved from the turbulent, youthful fringe into the vast middle ground of American culture and commerce. Its audience—and in many cases, performers—has turned from social rebels to solid citizens. Woodstock was on the surface an apolitical event, promising merely "three days of music and peace," which took on enormous resonance more by what it represented than by what it said outright. Live Aid was a political event—in that it was created solely to raise money for African famine relief—that largely appealed to fans as a mega-concert.

*Reporter Samuel G. Freedman analyzing the differences between the 1980s' Live Aid and the 1960s' Woodstock, in Freedman, "Live Aid and the Woodstock Nation,"* New York Times, *July 18, 1985, p. C-19.*

From the moment of its conception . . . the Live Aid concert and telethon was a long march of superlatives: the most complicated live broadcast ever mounted (aired live throughout on MTV and ABC Radio and for 11 hours on an ad hoc network of 107 broadcast stations; ABC-TV carried it for three hours). The most satellites used on one global broadcast (14, to link JFK with Wembley and the world; last summer's Olympics used only four). The most pizzas ever delivered backstage per hour (50). Inevitably, frenzy set in. . . .

Miraculously, Live Aid was reined in, and came off without a hitch. The only chore left was to remind people what the event was really about: not rock and roll or technology, but hunger—the devastating hunger that has swept Africa in the wake of searing droughts. . . .

*Noting some Live Aid statistics, in "Rock Around the World,"* Newsweek, *July 22, 1985, p. 56.*

I think this is just the beginning of a resurgence of caring for others. It says something about getting back to the basic human family. It's a dream, a positive dream.

*Mary Travers of Peter, Paul, and Mary, expressing thoughts shared by many following the Live Aid concert, quoted in Fein, "Reports of Concert Aid Range up to $50 Million,"* New York Times, *July 15, 1985, p. C-18.*

But if Woodstock was the obvious point of reference for the mammoth Live Aid concert in Philadelphia and London—seen by 162,000 fans in Kennedy and Wembley stadiums and an estimated 1.5 billion on a worldwide television broadcast—it was not necessarily the right one. If anything, the distance from a rain-soaked dairy farm in Bethel, N.Y., to a state-of-the-art stage in Philadelphia is measured in much more than 16 years and a few hundred miles.

The dreams all ran together. Feed the world. Make a joyful noise, raise a ruckus and millions of dollars. Lift a voice. Lend a hand. Come to Wembley Stadium in London. Go down to John F. Kennedy Stadium in Philadelphia. Turn on the television. Be a part of it all.

Ninety thousand came to JFK, 72,000 to Wembley. More than a billion people, including those in the Soviet Union, could have tuned in on live satellite broadcasts to watch over 60 of the world's most prominent rock acts. All together, this dream was called Live Aid. The breadth and heart of it were great.

*A postconcert depiction of Live Aid in "Rocking the Global Village,"* Time, *July 22, 1985, p. 66.*

What made Farm Aid an extraordinary event, in addition to its all-star line-up, was the feeling of community among performers and audience. At many benefits, the music is mere entertainment—a trade-off for contributions. At Farm Aid, however, the performers were eager to speak up for farmers. Even with its overtones of chauvinism—Farm Aid's subtitle was "the concert for America"—and confusion over what to do for farmers in both the long and short run, Farm Aid showed how much performers can do when they feel a connection with their audience.

> *Reporter Jon Pareles giving a positive review to the September 22, 1985, Farm Aid concert, in Pareles, "Concert: A Daylong Mix of Country with Rock," New York Times, September 23, 1985, p. A-16.*

## The Reality of AIDS

You have to remember that in the gay community, people have had friends dying for two years from a disease that's been considered to be of epidemic proportions and we've never been able to get this media. But it takes one movie star to let the public know it's not going to be just your local pansy or hairdresser.

> *Kent Fordyce, buyer for a gay bookstore in Washington, D.C., expressing a viewpoint shared by many homosexuals, following the revelation that Rock Hudson was ill with AIDS, quoted in Hall, "Sympathy in the Gay Community," Washington Post, July 27, 1985, p. G-1.*

Two years ago Secretary of Health and Human Services Margaret Heckler declared AIDS her department's "No. 1 priority." Recently the Reagan administration asked for an additional $43 million for 1985 and 1986 to bring the budget request for AIDS research to $126.3 million. But from the outset the government has been accused of not taking AIDS seriously enough. "The fact that it hit primarily gay men, as opposed to other groups such as the chamber of commerce, means that they didn't react with the sense of urgency that otherwise would have been the case," says Rep. Henry Waxman, whose constituency includes heavily gay West Hollywood. "If anything comes out of this Rock Hudson business," says [Dr. William] Haseltine, "it may be the impetus to focus on the problem."

> *Looking at official reaction to the AIDS crisis, in "AIDS," Newsweek, August 12, 1985, p. 21.*

In West Hollywood, Calif., a city heavily populated by homosexuals, a network-TV executive recently quit his health club because, he confessed, he was afraid of coming into contact with the perspiration of some of the gay clientele. In New York City, a business executive fired an employee who has AIDS, then phoned a doctor to find out if he had to throw out the employee's telephone and "spray Lysol in the bathrooms." In Kokomo, Ind., Ryan White, a 13-year-old hemophiliac who contracted AIDS while receiving injections of a clotting agent, was barred from resuming seventh-grade classes by a school superintendent who said two dentist friends had helped him decide whether it would be safe to let classmates associate with the boy.

> *Examining the continuing prejudicial attitudes toward AIDS victims, in "The Social Fallout from an Epidemic," Newsweek, August 12, 1985, p. 28.*

French medical researchers have accused the United States of stealing their research for a blood test used to screen patients for AIDS, the frightening virus that has killed more than 6000 people since it was first detected in 1981.

The dispute about who should get credit for the blood test has been simmering beneath the surface, apparently bringing to a standstill cooperation between French and American scientists searching for a cure for acquired immune deficiency syndrome.

The feud has pitted the Pasteur Institute against the Department of Health and Human Services, and now Pasteur officials are threatening to take the United States to court.

> *Columnist Jack Anderson reporting on the problems caused by the conflict between French researcher Luc Montagnier and American Dr. Robert Gallo, in Anderson, "Feud Hampers AIDS Progress," San Francisco Chronicle, August 19, 1985, p. 47.*

I don't think we understand enough about the disease and all the potential ways that it can be spread. It seems that each day, we're getting reassessments on how transmissible it is. We can operate only on the basis of what we know now. My basic approach is until we get a handle on this illness, we'd better be cautious.

> *Neurologist and bioethicist Dr. Richard Restak, arguing in favor of separating AIDS patients from others, quoted in "Should AIDS Victims Be Isolated?" U.S. News & World Report, September 30, 1985, p. 50.*

What kind of society would we be if we tried to separate a million people this year and 2 million next year? That would be practically impossible, and we would be a society that I would find inhumane and uncompassionate.

*Carol Levine, codirector of the Hastings Center Project, arguing against the idea of separating AIDS victims, quoted in "Should AIDS Victims Be Isolated?" U.S. News & World Report, September 30, 1985, p. 50.*

Rock Hudson's final role was one he never sought, and it followed a script that Hollywood would never have written.

But the dramatic disclosure 10 weeks ago that Rock Hudson had AIDS has had a bigger effect than any part he played on the screen, completely transforming the public perception of the AIDS epidemic.

After four years of being viewed as a curious affliction affecting a handful of outcast groups, AIDS has leaped to the forefront of the public consciousness and grasped the attention of everyone, from National Enquirer readers to the president of the United States.

*Reporter Randy Shilts commenting on the public's reaction to Rock Hudson's battle with AIDS following the star's October 2, 1985, death, in Shilts, "Hudson's Contribution to AIDS Battle," San Francisco Chronicle, October 3, 1985, p. 16.*

The House voted yesterday to increase federal spending for AIDS research by 90 percent over the next 12 months, but a small knot of conservatives used the debate on the deadly disease to launch an attack on homosexual behavior.

Leading the assault were two California Republicans, William E. Dannemeyer and Robert K. Dornan, who said that incidence of the disease, which often is transmitted through male homosexual acts, would abate significantly if gay men would abstain from intimate contact.

Dannemeyer created a stir when he declared: "God's plan for man was Adam and Eve, not Adam and Steve." His graphic speech on the House floor was laced with anatomical detail of how homosexuals transmit AIDS.

*Reporting a rise in funding for AIDS research concurrent with continued prejudice, in "House OKs Boost in AIDS Spending," San Francisco Chronicle, October 3, 1985, p. 16.*

Everyone detected with AIDS should be tattooed in the upper forearm, to protect common-needle users, and on the buttocks, to prevent the victimization of other homosexuals.

*You have got to be kidding! That's exactly what we suspected all along! You are calling for the return of the Scarlet Letter, but only for homosexuals!*

Answer: The Scarlet Letter was designed to stimulate public obloquy. The AIDS tattoo is designed for private protection. And the whole point of this is that we are not talking about a kidding matter. Our society is generally threatened, and in order to fight AIDS, we need the civil equivalent of universal military training.

*Conservative columnist William F. Buckley, Jr., taking a controversial stand following reports that the U.S. military will discharge any soldiers found to have the AIDS virus, in Buckley, "Identify All the Carriers," New York Times, March 18, 1986, p. A-27.*

## The Challenger *Tragedy*

In the Orbiter, the crew was feeling the effects of the long wait. They fully expected the Mission Management Team to terminate the countdown because of the hazard on the launchpad. Judy Resnick commented on the long, frustrating process. "I hope we don't drive this down to the bitter end again today," she said.

From the lefthand flight deck seat, Commander Dick Scobee agreed. "Yeah," he sighed.

. . . . .

A few moments later, Scobee was contacted on the air-to-ground loop and told that the countdown would proceed. The Mission Management Team had reviewed the ice situation and found no constraints to launch. "All right!" he shouted, then added with his habitual optimism, "That's great."

Behind him on the flight deck, Judy Resnick quickly calculated the new lift-off time: 11:38.

*Depicting conversation on the flight deck of the Challenger less than a half-hour before liftoff on January 28, 1986, in McConnell, A Major Malfunction (1987), pp. 230–231.*

The space shuttle *Challenger* explodes moments after launching on January 28, 1986.  *(NASA)*

We were rejoicing in the liftoff. We were exalting in it. We were celebrating with her. Then it stopped. That's all. It stopped.

> *Charles Foley, principal of Concord High School, where Christa McAuliffe had been a teacher, in a news conference on January 28, 1986, describing the school's reaction upon witnessing the* Challenger *explosion that day; quoted in "Suddenly, the Celebration Stopped,"* Washington Post, *January 29, 1986, p. A-1.*

At 11:40 A.M. this morning, the space program experienced a national tragedy with the explosion of the space shuttle Challenger approximately a minute and a half after launch from here at the Kennedy Space Center.

I regret that I have to report that, based on very preliminary searches of the ocean where the Challenger impacted this morning, these searches have not revealed any evidence that the crew of Challenger survived.

. . . .

I am aware, and have seen, the media showing footage of the launch today from the NASA select system. We will not speculate on the specific cause of the explosion based on that footage. It will take all the data, careful review of that data, before we can draw any conclusions on this national tragedy.

> *From a statement by Jesse W. Moore, associate administrator of NASA, on January 28, 1986, in "NASA Official's Statement,"* Washington Post, *January 29, 1986, p. A-6.*

Seeing the Challenger, with its crew of seven on board, blow up in the sky in the full view of everyone at Cape Canaveral and all the others watching on television will leave an indelible impression in the national memory, like the assassination of President Kennedy or the attack on Pearl Harbor.

Americans will again put their trust in this bold new technology. Astronauts will fly the shuttles again because it is their calling, and they believe in what they are doing. Others, including journalists, will probably venture into space, too, no doubt approaching the adventure with a new respect, and some dread, with the image of the Challenger fireball in mind forever.

*Journalist John Noble Wilford looking to the future, in Wilford, "Faith in Technology Is Jolted, but There Is No Going Back,"* New York Times, *January 29, 1986, p. A-7.*

The president of the United States was able to convey a precise sense of mood and occasion in response to the destruction of Challenger. Speaking as if simultaneously to bereaved relatives and the nation at large, his words fitted. He referred to Drake who once explored the California coast. He read a piece of verse. In other circumstances and in other deliveries these would have seemed hackneyed. But Ronald Reagan has an ability his detractors never seem to fathom. He can reach deep into the American sense of self and articulate otherwise inchoate emotion.

The *Times (London) conveying British reaction to President Reagan's speech following the* Challenger *disaster, in its editorial "Symbol in the Skies,"* Times, *January 30, 1986, p. 13.*

The test pilot in me was not surprised when Challenger blew up. I have been expecting something like this for more than 20 years, but knowing it's going to happen doesn't make the moment any less painful. On the contrary, I feel I am part of a family that has lost seven children and will lose more.

·····

What perspective would our pioneering ancestors bring to this business of space flight, this new form of exploration? Would they load the space wagons with women and children? Would they expect losses? Whole families? Would they bury the dead and press on? I don't know, but I think I do know what my friend,

astronaut Judy Resnick would say: fix the problem, and then let's get on with it.

*Former astronaut Michael Collins offering his perspective on the* Challenger *tragedy, in Collins, "Riding the Beat,"* Washington Post, *January 30, 1986, p. A-25.*

What we say today is only an inadequate expression of what we carry in our hearts. Words pale in the shadow of grief; they seem insufficient even to measure the brave sacrifice of those you loved and we so admired. Their truest testimony will not be in the words we speak, but in the way they led their lives and in the way they lost their lives—with dedication, honor and an unquenchable desire to explore this mysterious and beautiful universe.

*From President Reagan's eulogy to the seven astronauts at a memorial service at the Johnson Space Center, Houston, on January 31, 1986, quoted in "Transcript of the President's Eulogy for the Seven Challenger Astronauts,"* New York Times, *February 1, 1986, p. 11.*

No longer, now, will we look at the rise of rockets as being as routine as elevators going up and down. Now we will know, when we reach for stars, the fears of Old World explorers who sailed for the unknown with maps of empty spaces warning, "Here be dragons."

The horror came home like the assassination of President John F. Kennedy, for, just as then, television captured clearly the 73-second ride to catastrophe. The world witnessed, over and over and over, astronauts die.

*Depicting the horror of the* Challenger *tragedy, in " 'We Will Not Disappoint Them,' "* U.S. News & World Report, *February 10, 1986, p. 14.*

I thought at first that Christa's death would be hardest on the children. They had learned all about the shuttle, and in an age without heroes, they had found one in her. Most had witnessed the dreadful moment. Yet times like these remind us that children are resilient. Age robs us of the instinct to go forward without a backward glance. I even suspect now that we have tried too hard to make our children feel what we want them to feel. It is the adults in Concord who still have swollen eyes and stricken looks. They comprehend what was lost, and what was lost was a part of them. . . .

*Mike Pride, editor of the Concord, New Hampshire, Monitor, describing reaction in Concord to Christa McAuliffe's death aboard* Challenger, *in Pride, " 'There Had Been a Death in the Family,' "* Newsweek, *February 10, 1986, p. 42.*

# 6 Arms and the President
## May 1986–December 1987

As president, Ronald Reagan aroused emotions ranging from approbation to derision, admiration to contempt. While his public persona was that of an easygoing "ordinary guy," privately he could be obtuse, disengaged, and unfathomable. Even those closest to him admitted he was not the most intellectual of leaders: "Poor dear, there's nothing between his ears,"[1] his friend Margaret Thatcher once said of him. While brilliant with a script, he was otherwise so prone to verbal gaffes that his wife and staff had to "stage-manage" his public appearances. Though he was nicknamed the Great Communicator, his opponents delighted in publicizing Reagan pronouncements that showed him at his worst.

Nevertheless, he was one of America's most popular presidents. Even Speaker of the House Tip O'Neill (D, Mass.), a staunch opponent who persistently derided him, admitted to admiring the man if not his policies. Charismatic and personable, Reagan radiated an aura of "What you see is what you get," and people liked him for it. Though his scripts were written by others, they were Reagan's ideas. What he believed in, he believed in fervently, and he held to his principles regardless of what others thought; this too earned public approval.

So successful was Reagan's public-relations team, headed by assistant chief of staff Michael Deaver, that by 1984, the term *spin doctor* had entered the American vocabulary. It seemed Reagan could do no wrong, and Democrats were frustrated by the president's ability to weather the worst publicity. One day in 1983, while scrambling eggs for her children, Representative Patricia Schroeder (D, Colo.) had the thought that Reagan was "just like a Teflon frying pan. Nothing sticks to him."[2] The description was publicized by reporter Michael Kenney in the *Boston Globe* of October 24, 1984—and the term *Teflon president* stuck.

But from the Bitburg debacle in May 1985, followed by Deaver's departure from the White House, Reagan's public image began to deteriorate. Now, a year later, he was on the verge of enjoying a major triumph—and would have to weather a major scandal. The Teflon coating was about to wear thin.

# IRAN-CONTRA: A FAILED ENTERPRISE

When Reagan assumed the presidency in January 1981, he could have repudiated the deal that Jimmy Carter had struck for the release of the 52 American hostages in Iran. That he did not do so was partly out of sympathy for Carter and partly because, as biographer Lou Cannon writes, "release of the hostages while Carter was still president would free Reagan from an immense burden at the onset of his presidency . . ."[3] Nevertheless, he had been highly critical of Carter's decisions, making his position clear with a State Department press release on February 18, 1981: "The present Administration would not have negotiated with Iran for the release of the hostages."[4]

Bargaining with terrorists may have been anathema to Reagan, but by 1985 Americans abroad were increasingly being kidnapped, hijacked, and murdered. With no opportunity to employ military force against an unseen and elusive enemy, desperate administration officials looked for other options. On July 3, 1985, Reagan and his staff discussed acquiring better intelligence in the Middle East and means of freeing the seven Americans then being held hostage in Lebanon. That same day National Security Advisor Robert "Bud" McFarlane met with David Kimche, an Israeli official and former Mossad spy, who offered to put him in touch with Iranian moderates seeking a better relationship with the United States. They proposed to help free the hostages in Lebanon if the United States supplied antitank missiles for Iran in its war against Iraq; Israel would provide the missiles and have them replaced from America.

Reagan subsequently approved an initial shipment of 100 U.S. TOW* missiles, which Israel delivered to Iran on August 20. Iranian intermediary Manucher Ghorbanifar then reported that his country required 400 more TOWs before a hostage would be released; the shipment was made on September 14, and the Reverend Benjamin Weir was freed the next day.[5] This encouraged the Americans to continue arms negotiations to free more hostages.

In November 1985, after Israel withdrew from the operation for fear of exposure, Lieutenant Colonel Oliver North of the National Security Council (NSC) became involved. North had already established a secret operation, dubbed Enterprise, securing funds from Saudi Arabia (and eventually from other countries) to provide weapons and money for the contra rebels in Nicaragua. Now he set about securing the hostages' release through the sale of arms.

Enterprise had been conceived by CIA director William Casey as a way of circumventing the 1984 Boland amendment, which forbade unauthorized military assistance to the contras. While North raised at least $10 million from private foundations, organizations, and individual Reagan supporters, the administration also sought congressional aid. Packages of $174 million (February 1985) and $20 million (March 1986) were approved for contra-supporting Honduras, and $27 million in humanitarian aid was voted to the contras themselves (June 1985). Eventually, on June 25, 1986, Congress approved $100 million for the contras—including military aid—though the funding would not begin until October.

Despite this, Reagan officials continued to defy the Boland amendment by illicitly providing weapons and military assistance to the contras and soliciting

---

*TOW = Tube-launched, optically-tracked, wire-guided missile, a widely used antitank missile.

money from others. Saudi Arabia's King Fahd was persuaded to contribute $24 million (later upped to $32 million), funds that were funneled through Enterprise. Yet Reagan, Casey, McFarlane, and others publicly denied any illegal activity, maintaining that since congressionally authorized monies were not being used for the covert activities, they were acting within the law.

An important Enterprise figure, former air force general Richard V. Secord, worked with Albert A. Hakim, an Iranian-American arms dealer, to purchase arms for the contras and, in November 1985, to ship 18 Hawk antiaircraft missiles to Iran. When CIA lawyers questioned the legality of this, Reagan signed an intelligence finding that retroactively approved the three shipments (by Israel and Secord). Congress, however, was never told of the document.

On December 5, 1985, Robert McFarlane resigned as National Security Advisor—he was succeeded by Vice Admiral John Poindexter—but continued as a personal envoy for Reagan. By now the Americans were increasing both the amount of arms they sold to Iran and the prices charged, with an average markup of 38 percent. The monies raised were used for arms for the contras, for other covert and unspecified operations—and for enriching the Enterprise operators' personal bank accounts.

In late May 1986 McFarlane and North went to Iran to negotiate with Ghorbanifar and his associates. Only one hostage, Weir, had been freed, but the Iranians wanted more weapons and better intelligence on Iraq. Although McFarlane and North promised a planeload of weapons for the release of all the American hostages in Beirut, the Iranians wanted the weapons first, as well as the release of Shiite terrorists imprisoned in Kuwait. Unable to agree, the Americans abandoned their mission.

When another hostage, Reverend Martin Lawrence Jenco, was finally set free in July, North persuaded Poindexter and Reagan to authorize a shipment of Hawk missile components to Iran and a promise of more weapons to secure the other hostages' freedom. Late in October 1986, on instructions from Reagan officials, Israel shipped 500 TOW missiles to Iran, leading to hostage David Jacobsen's release on November 2. But by then three more Americans had been kidnapped (in September and October)—and the supply of arms to the contras in Central America was no longer a secret.

One month before, on October 5, Sandinista soldiers in Nicaragua had shot down a plane carrying ammunition, uniforms, and medicine to the contras. The sole survivor of the American crew, an ex-marine named Eugene Hasenfus, revealed that he was working for the CIA to drop arms to the contras. Documents recovered from the plane also indicated CIA involvement.

The Sandinistas wasted no time in broadcasting the news, which was at once countered by White House denials of any U.S. government connection. Secretary of State George Shultz and President Reagan both insisted the plane had been hired by private individuals who were trying to help the contras. Meanwhile, Oliver North diverted a U.S. Customs investigation of the crash, delaying the detection of secret bank accounts. But it was clear that Enterprise was falling apart. William Casey—now also under pressure from two Canadian businessmen involved in the Iran arms sales who wanted $10 million to keep silent—instructed North to "clean up" the Enterprise files. North immediately began to shred documents and destroy evidence of the contra supply operation. Even while doing so, he continued to pursue his arms-for-hostages mission, but that aspect of Enterprise was also about to be exposed.

## America, America

Following the successes of the previous year, the headline charity event of 1986 was Hands Across America, conceived by USA for Africa's Ken Kragen. The aim was to raise money for the homeless by forming a human chain from coast to coast, with millions of Americans linking hands for 15 minutes, each paying $10–$35 for the privilege of standing in the line. On the afternoon of May 25, 1986, more than 5 million people formed a chain that stretched 4,152 miles, from New York City to Long Beach, California, and through dozens of cities, including Washington, D.C.; St. Louis, Missouri; Amarillo, Texas; and Phoenix, Arizona. Inevitably, breaks occurred and gaps were often filled with miles of red and blue ribbon. Smaller chains were formed where linkage to the main chain was not feasible. Thus joined together, the participants sang songs: "America the Beautiful," "We Are the World," and "Hands Across America," written especially for the occasion.

Despite the enthusiasm for Hands Across America—even President Reagan participated—it did not generate the $50 million hoped for, and corporate donations accounted for much of the $20 million that was raised in the end. Following so soon after other charity events, Americans were tiring of reaching into their pockets, especially when they learned their donations were not all reaching the intended cause. Nevertheless, Hands Across America brought millions of people together and highlighted the needs of the homeless and hungry.

In early July 1986 the nation celebrated the centenary of its symbol of immigration, the Statue of Liberty. The four-day series of events capped three years of restoration on "Lady Liberty," including structural reinforcements and a torch redone in gold leaf. On July 4, more than 6 million people squeezed into New York to watch the day's ceremonies, which included a parade of tall ships, concerts, fireworks, and numerous speeches from President Reagan throughout the day, concluding with his "lighting" the torch that night. A few months later the statue's true birthday, October 28, was observed in a much smaller ceremony.

Appropriately, perhaps, on November 6 President Reagan signed the Immigration and Control Act of 1986, also known as the Simpson-Mazzoli Act. The new legislation—the culmination of years of heated congressional debate over unlawful immigration, particularly from Latin America—made it a federal crime to hire illegal aliens knowingly and imposed fines on violators that ranged up to $10,000 per alien. To placate western farmers who relied on illegal labor, however, the law granted temporary resident status to as many as 350,000 aliens who could show they had worked in U.S. agriculture for at least 90 days between May 1985 and May 1986. Despite this, illegal immigration continued to be a major problem.

President Reagan speaks on Governor's Island, New York, during the celebrations for the Statue of Liberty's 100th birthday on July 4, 1986. *(Courtesy Ronald Reagan Library)*

AIDS still dominated the headlines. Celebrities like Elizabeth Taylor raised money for research and education; "That's What Friends Are For," by Dionne Warwick, Elton John, and Stevie Wonder became the number-one song of the year in 1986, raising both awareness of and funds for pediatric AIDS research. Meanwhile, the government was criticized for being slow to act and for focusing on testing to identify HIV-positive individuals, something that only emphasized the pariah status of afflicted victims. Although President Reagan had called AIDS a top priority, he made only one major speech about it (in May 1987) and seemed reluctant to commit more federal monies to research. In 1986 he established a panel headed by Surgeon General C. Everett Koop to make recommendations, which were published in October. These included increased sex education starting "at the lowest grade possible" and emphasizing abstinence, monogamy, and condoms as ways to prevent the disease's spread. One result was attacks on Koop from ultraconservatives and the religious right.

Koop became a hero of the AIDS awareness movement for his forthright stand and criticism of the Reagan administration. His report was immediately followed by one from the National Academy of Sciences predicting a national catastrophe if the spread of AIDS continued at its present rate. It was left to the states to act if the federal government would not, and in 1987, 30 states appropriated money to fight the disease, up from only five in 1983. *Safe sex* was becoming the watchword of the time, and on January 16, 1987, the first commercial for condoms as a protection against AIDS was aired on KRON in San Francisco. Two months later the Food and Drug Administration approved the use of azidothymidine (AZT), the first drug found to decelerate the deadly AIDS virus. Progress was slow, but it was progress.

In 1987–88 the religious right's attacks on Koop and AIDS campaigners were weakened as the televangelists' own scandals came to light. The 1980s had seen religious broadcasting flourish, and fund-raising programs such as Pat Robertson's *700 Club* and Jim and Tammy Faye Bakker's *PTL* (Praise the Lord) show, which reached wide audiences with their fundamentalist messages, enabled their presenters to enjoy luxurious lifestyles. But their "saintly" image began a harsh downslide in January 1987 when Oral Roberts made the startling claim that God would "call him home" in March if his followers did not donate several millions dollars within weeks. He was saved by a gambler who made a large contribution, but he became the subject of public derision.

Then, in March 1987, Jim Bakker was indicted for fraud, conspiracy, and theft of ministry funds. It was also reported that Bakker had forced Jessica Hahn, a PTL church member, to have sex with him and then paid her hush money of some $200,000, using church funds. Bakker resigned from PTL on March 19, and in October he was convicted on 24 counts. The scandal shook televangelism to its core.

In February 1988 Bakker's rival televangelist Jimmy Swaggart became the subject of ridicule when it was revealed that he had enjoyed the services of prostitutes. Unable to refute the allegation, Swaggart's tearful appearance on television asking for forgiveness had little effect other than a reduction in donations to his ministry; he was subsequently defrocked by the Assemblies of God after rejecting church-ordered punishment, although he continued preaching. Adding to televangelists' problems that year was the collapse of Pat Robertson's presidential campaign after he claimed his prayers had diverted a hurricane from Virginia Beach to New York City. Only Jerry Falwell—who took over Bakker's PTL ministry—seemed to escape censure, and in 1988 he quit to focus on his church. The influence of televangelists was weakening.

Crime became another major topic when the Unabomber reemerged to carry out a series of bombings between 1985 and 1987. Then, on April 27, 1987, the trial of the controversial "Subway Vigilante" began. The case dated back to December 22, 1984, when Bernhard Hugo Goetz, a 37-year-old electrical engineer, shot four young African-American men on a New York City subway train after one of them, 19-year-old Darrell Cabey, asked him for $5. By the time he turned himself in to police nine days later, Goetz had become a national hero, someone who had successfully defended himself against muggers—or so it seemed.

Support for Goetz was so strong that when Manhattan District Attorney Robert Morgenthau convened a grand jury on January 25, 1985, he was able to obtain only one indictment, for illegal possession of a handgun. But then further details about the shooting came out, with witnesses disputing that Goetz had ever been in danger. Most significantly, he had shot two of the teenagers in the back as they tried to flee and, by his own account, leaned over Cabey and said, "You seem to be doing all right. Here's another," before firing a shot that severed Cabey's spinal cord. It became evident that the Subway Vigilante had been just that, rather than somebody who had acted in self-defense.

In March 1985, with new evidence, Morgenthau convened a second grand jury. This time Goetz was indicted on 10 counts, including attempted murder, assault, reckless endangerment of other passengers, and criminal possession of a weapon; seven more counts were added later. Nevertheless, outraged by a rising crime rate and recent legislation that increased suspects' rights, many Americans continued to support Goetz. By taking the law into his own hands he had, for many, emulated the Charles Bronson character in the *Death Wish* series of films, making him a dubious hero.

Debate on Goetz's case raged on through 1985 and 1986. Finally, at his 1987 trial the jury concluded that Goetz (who had been mugged previously) had genuine reason to have felt threatened and had acted in self-defense. He was found guilty only on the illegal handgun possession charge. When verdicts of not guilty on the other counts were announced, the courtroom broke into applause, and some jurors asked for Goetz's autograph. But many were horrified by his acquittal.

In later years, the three men who recovered from the shooting all went on to commit serious crimes, justifying Goetz's supporters. Cabey, meanwhile, filed a civil suit that did not come to trial until 1996, when the verdict went against the Subway Vigilante. Goetz was ordered to pay Cabey $43 million in damages—money that he was unable to pay and that his paralyzed victim would never see.

## COLD WAR ADVANCES AND WITHDRAWALS

Many historians consider Ronald Reagan's greatest achievement to be the transformation of the United States' relationship with the Soviet Union. The president had never hidden his hatred of communism, and his determination to strengthen the U.S. military and nuclear arsenal—even while the Strategic Arms Reduction Talks (START) were taking place—had the effect of making the Soviets appear not as aggressors but as unwilling targets of American hostility.

Further, Reagan's persistent championing of the Strategic Defense Initiative (SDI) led the Soviets—as well as political opponents at home—to depict him as a reckless warmonger leading the world into nuclear annihilation.

In any event, Reagan was able to justify his refusal to meet his Russian counterparts with the comment, "They keep dying on me."[6] And indeed, since the death of Leonid Brezhnev in November 1982, the leadership had passed to Yuri Andropov, who died in February 1984, and then to the old and ill Konstantin Chernenko, who died on March 10, 1985. However, the following day it was announced that the new general secretary of the Communist Party would be 54-year-old Mikhail Gorbachev—a succession that would ultimately bring an end to the 40-year-old cold war.

Several factors made administration officials feel they could work with Gorbachev. Much younger than his predecessors, he was no sooner in office than he accused Brezhnev, Andropov, and Chernenko of leading the USSR into "stagnation." But more important to Western nations, he sought reforms in the Soviet Union. Faced with a failing economy, Gorbachev began a program of perestroika (restructuring) to improve Russian living standards and worker productivity. Further, recognizing the appalling cost of the arms race and eager for better relations with Western nations, he instituted a policy of glasnost (openness). To emphasize his intentions, on April 7, 1985, less than a month after taking office, he announced a moratorium on the Soviet deployment of medium-range missiles.

The West reacted favorably, and Reagan met Gorbachev for a summit in Geneva on November 19–20, 1985. No firm agreements resulted, apart from a mutually expressed willingness to work toward reductions in strategic arms and the decision to meet again in 1986. Yet it was a crucial encounter. As Reagan described it years later, "There was warmth in [Gorbachev's] face and his style, not the coldness bordering on hatred I'd seen in most senior Soviet officials I'd met until then."[7] Though the two leaders accused each other of imperialism and arms treaty violations, they nonetheless developed a mutual personal regard that inspired a willingness to carry their talks forward.

On January 1, 1986, Reagan and Gorbachev each appeared on television in the other's country to express his New Year's greetings and desire for world peace. That same month, Gorbachev wrote to Reagan, proposing the complete elimination of nuclear weapons in three stages over 15 years—a "zero option" package that was certain to appeal to the president. Nevertheless, Reagan and several of his cabinet remained suspicious of Soviet intentions.

Determined to bargain from a position of strength, Reagan announced on May 27 that the United States would no longer be bound by the terms of the SALT II arms treaty (which the Senate had never ratified). He also announced the construction of a new Trident submarine, even as two Poseidon submarines were being dismantled, and he remained committed to his cherished SDI program, even though it had been responsible for numerous setbacks during the START negotiations. By May 29, the Soviets were no longer insisting on the cancellation of SDI as a prerequisite to agreement on reductions in strategic forces. However, it was clear that "Star Wars" still rankled, and U.S. assurances that SDI deployment would be delayed did little to reassure them.

In addition to the continuing impasse in arms talks, other events in 1986 aggravated cold war tensions. In early April the U.S. raid on Libya, a Soviet client state, was strongly condemned by Gorbachev, who in turn was criticized the following month when he delayed almost three weeks before announcing the explosion at a nuclear power plant in Chernobyl on April 26 and then made no apology for it. On August 23 the FBI arrested Soviet spy recruiter Gennadi Zakharov in New York City; exactly a week later, in Moscow, the KGB arrested Nicholas Daniloff, a *U.S. News & World Report* correspondent, charging him with espionage. (On September 30 Zakharov was expelled from the United States in exchange for Daniloff and several Russian dissidents.)

Anxious for a better relationship and an agreement on arms, Gorbachev proposed another two-day summit, which took place on October 11–12, 1986, in Reykjavík, Iceland. The meetings went well as Gorbachev offered what was, according to American negotiator Paul Nitze, "the best Soviet proposal we have received in 25 years."[8] The Soviets agreed to many of the American terms, including on-site verification of missile destruction by both countries and agreement that France and Britain should not be bound by any U.S.-Soviet treaties on arms reductions in Europe. A Soviet offer of a 50 percent reduction in all strategic weapons was countered, to avoid disparities, by an American one limiting the numbers of warheads and delivery vehicles. As further accords were reached, including one that linked human rights considerations to future negotiations, it seemed a historic agreement was possible.

Then, at the final meeting, Gorbachev dropped a bombshell: In exchange for all the concessions made by the Soviets, the United States must cancel deployment of SDI (still in research and development). Surprised and angered, Reagan refused. Although the United States was willing to restrict SDI to the laboratory for 10 years—by which time all ballistic missiles would be destroyed, according to the planned agreement—it would not abandon the program entirely. As he had done before, Reagan offered to share SDI technology with the Soviet Union, his aim being a defense system that would protect the world, not just the United States.

But Gorbachev stood firm. He would not, he said, go home and announce that while the Soviet Union was giving up its ballistic missiles, the United States

President Reagan and Soviet general secretary Gorbachev meet at Hofdi House on October 11, 1986, during their summit in Reykjavík, Iceland. *(Courtesy Ronald Reagan Library)*

would continue SDI development and possible deployment. The meeting ended with no agreement and both Reagan and Gorbachev furious. In the eyes of many, the summit had been a failure, and Reagan was attacked by the press, Congress, and American allies for his intransigence on SDI, which had apparently destroyed the best chance of ending the nuclear arms race.

## TAXING TIMES

Whatever advantages Reaganomics might have had for the country's economic recovery, the negative effects were equally apparent. The federal budget for 1987, passed on June 27, 1986, was based on expenditures of $995 billion and a deficit of $142.6 billion, while estimates of the rising national debt ranged into the trillions. Some blamed Reagan's first-term income-tax cuts for the appalling figures, and these had certainly resulted in decreasing government revenues. But the real cause was defense spending, which had risen, uncontrolled, year by year,[9] and in 1986 Congress finally defied the president and reduced defense expenditures by $28 billion. (His situation would worsen after the November midterm elections, when the Democrats won back control of the Senate and increased their majority in the House of Representatives.)

The president's public stand on taxes was clear: He would not raise them. Yet it became clear early in his administration that he would have to do so, as results showed his post tax-cut budget projections were naively optimistic. Consequently, from 1982 to 1987 he signed bills that increased taxes—measures he called revenue enhancements—in different areas. These included, in 1982, the Highway Revenue Act, which raised the gasoline tax by $3.3 billion, and the Tax Equity and Fiscal Responsibility Act (TEFRA), a law that scaled back recently enacted tax breaks for businesses and raised other rates, resulting in increased revenues of $37.5 billion. The Social Security Reform Act of 1983 initiated automatic, annual increases in payroll taxes that were still in effect as of 2004, while the Deficit Reduction Act of 1984 raised $18 billion per year by closing tax loopholes.

Despite these measures, the government's continued inability to bring the deficit under control resulted in the Balanced Budget and Emergency Deficit Control Act of 1985—better known as the Gramm-Rudman Act after two of its sponsors, Republican senators Phil Gramm (Tex.) and Warren Rudman (N.H.). This bill, whose other sponsor was Senator Ernest Hollings (D, S.C.), sought to balance the federal budget by October 1990 through cuts implemented automatically should Congress fail to meet certain budgetary targets. Reagan approved the bill and signed it into law on December 12, 1985, but on July 7, 1986, the Supreme Court ruled, 7–2, that Gramm-Rudman violated the constitutional separation of powers by giving budget-cutting authority to the controller general, an agent of Congress, rather than the executive branch. Consequently, in 1987 Congress passed another version of the bill, although it ultimately failed to meet its budget-balancing objectives.[10]

While Congress sought to bring the deficit under control, the president turned his attention to a related matter. Building on the popular success of his 1981 income-tax cuts, Reagan set out to change the government's taxation system to lessen Americans' individual tax burdens and make taxation simpler and fairer. In May 1985 he proposed a sweeping reform of the tax code that included reducing the number of tax brackets from 14 to three, raising the personal exemption, ending deductions for state and local taxes, and limiting deductions on interest payments. Initially pessimistic, Congress eventually warmed to the theory and began work on a compromise package that differed in detail from Reagan's proposal—for example, reducing the number of tax brackets to two instead of three—but retained his original intent of simplifying the tax code.

On October 22, 1986, President Reagan signed into law the Tax Reform Act, which lowered the top tax rate from 50 to 28 percent and raised the lowest one from 11 to 15 percent. It also eliminated many tax shelters, preferences, and deductions; increased the personal exemption and standard deduction; increased incentives for home-ownership investments while decreasing those for rental housing; restricted tax deductions for individual retirement accounts; imposed restrictions on corporations regarding payroll deductions and pension plans; and restored full capital-gains tax rates in addition to imposing new taxes on businesses.

Analysts still argue over the results of the Tax Reform Act, which went into effect on January 1, 1987, and did not change the total amount of taxes collected. Some cite figures to show the tax burden was distributed more fairly among the different levels of taxpayers. According to Reagan, writing in 1990, "More than eighty percent of the increased personal income tax revenues since 1981 have come from taxpayers with incomes of over $100,000 a year, while the amount paid by those earning less than $50,000 dropped by billions of dollars."[11] However, others note that middle-class Americans were hit harder through raises in payroll taxes (among other causes) and that wealthier citizens still found loopholes that allowed them to pay less. In any event, the actual increase in overall taxation produced by the act, along with the "revenue enhancements" in other bills (including the Omnibus Budget Reconciliation Act, signed December 22, 1987), essentially canceled out the personal income-tax cuts that had been one of his proudest achievements.

A case could be made for either argument. Nothing, however, could alter the fact that most Americans still found filing tax returns a daunting task—and, often, an expensive one.

## THE GRAPES OF GREED

On May 18, 1986, Ivan Boesky told the graduating class of the University of California at Berkeley, "I think greed is healthy. You can be greedy and still feel good about yourself."[12] These words—echoed a year later in the film *Wall Street* when Gordon Gekko, played by Michael Douglas, coolly announced, "Greed is good"—made Boesky a symbol of the wealth-driven 1980s. An arbitrageur, Boesky's specialty was trading in the stock of companies targeted for takeover, a practice at which he so excelled that he had become a legend in financial circles; his fame increased in 1985 when he published *Merger Mania,* a book on the art of arbitrage. But what his enthusiastic audience at Berkeley did not know was that in a few months he would hit the headlines for another reason.

Six days earlier, on May 12, Dennis Levine—an employee of the investment firm Drexel Burnham Lambert—had been arrested by the Securities and Exchange Commission (SEC) on charges of illegal insider trading.[13] A mergers-and-acquisitions specialist, he implicated Boesky, who had made huge profits

Michael Douglas starred as Gordon Gekko in *Wall Street* (1987); Gekko—who makes the pronouncement "greed is good"— was based in part on Ivan Boesky. *(Photofest)*

using information obtained from Levine. Boesky sought to save his own skin by implicating others and cooperating with the SEC in revealing what he knew about inside trading deals, secretly recording conversations with those he had named as tipsters.

Not until November 14, 1986, when the SEC announced Boesky's arrest, did the public learn of his activities. Boesky had plea-bargained a deal for himself: In addition to paying $100 million to the federal government and serving a three-year prison sentence,[14] he was also banned from participating in the securities business for the rest of his life. This news was bad enough for a financial community already shaken by the revelations regarding Levine's activities, but far worse was the report of Boesky's covert activities on behalf of the SEC. When the stock exchange opened on Monday, traders immediately sold stocks of companies involved in takeover bids, sending prices into a steep dive.

Worse was to come as the SEC pursued its investigations. One indictment followed another as employees of such firms as Shearson Lehman; Kidder, Peabody; Goldman, Sachs; E. F. Hutton; and others were revealed to be involved in an extensive ring of insider trading. Even the venerable *Wall Street Journal* became involved as one of its reporters, R. Foster Winans, was convicted of securities fraud for having passed on *Journal* tips prior to publication.

One major figure implicated by Boesky was Michael Milken, a Drexel Burnham Lambert employee known as the "junk bond king," who was finally arrested in 1989. Milken's case would rivet the nation even more than Boesky's had done, particularly because it was largely his junk bonds that were financing the era's mania for mergers and acquisitions. The year 1986 alone witnessed nearly 3,000 transactions worth more than $130 billion.[15] The Tax Reform Act that year fueled the craze even further as businesses sought to complete deals before the new law went into effect. Few companies— not even giants such as Gulf, Conoco, and Walt Disney—were immune to takeover attacks by corporate raiders who were reshaping the country's industrial and financial landscape. Major businesses were bought and sold in more leveraged buyouts and merger deals than ever before (or since) in U.S. history.

When it was possible to make $1 million or more annually within three to five years of graduation, it was not surprising that investment banking had become the career of choice for newly graduated MBAs. And with financial success came a conspicuously opulent lifestyle, with New York—a magnet for fortune hunters and social climbers—at the epicenter. For good or bad, Wall Street established the nation's contemporary societal ideals and excesses, famously satirized in Tom Wolfe's novel *Bonfire of the Vanities* (1987). People worked hard and partied harder, and drug-taking was an accepted part of the scene—truly a "best of times, worst of times" environment.

Despite the SEC's efforts to rein in the speculators, the takeover craze continued, and after the initial hiccup caused by Boesky's arrest, the stock market recovered to set new records. Wall Street had been in a bull market since 1982, but the high-value mergers and leveraged buyouts were pushing it off balance. By early 1987 other factors had come into play as well. The ever-growing federal deficit generated fears of a declining dollar resulting in the loss of foreign capital. Further, inflation had begun to rise, leading the Federal Reserve to raise short-term interest rates. As this affected stock prices, many trading firms began to buy precautionary portfolio insurance (which uses futures contracts for insuring against losses). Gradually, this began to overload the futures market in addition to devaluing stocks. Meanwhile, in summer 1987 the yield of a 30-year U.S. bond rose to almost 10 percent, leading many investors to buy stocks less and bonds more.

Some analysts also consider the computerization of Wall Street to be a key factor in its mounting problems. Program trading—using computers to buy and sell stocks automatically based on preset, programmed prices—meant a loss of independent human judgment in trading decisions. How significant this was is a matter of conjecture. In any event, the stock market crashed on October 19, 1987—"Black Monday," as it came to be called.

The Dow Jones Index fell 508 points (22.6 percent) that day, the largest one-day drop in stock market history (and almost double the 12.82 percent fall that initiated the Great Crash of 1929). Phone lines jammed as people tried to reach their brokers to issue sell orders that never got through, resulting in personal fortunes being wiped out. As in 1929, some people killed themselves, and a few mentally unstable individuals went on shooting sprees that left several brokers dead. Around the world, other markets followed Wall Street: By the end of the month, Canada had seen a drop of 22.5 percent, the United Kingdom 26.4 percent, Australia 41.8 percent, and Hong Kong an appalling 45.8 percent.

The Federal Reserve immediately pumped money into the country's banks, lowering interest rates, and this, along with federal deposit insurance, helped to avoid the nationwide crisis that had followed the 1929 crash. In addition, companies began to buy back their own now-undervalued stock, triggering a slow but steady recovery: Within a week, the Dow average was up 42.77 points, and after a period of volatility, trading eventually returned to steady, record-breaking levels. Ironically, the crash proved advantageous for the "Wall Street wolves" as raiders grabbed stocks at bargain-basement prices, increasing the number of hostile takeovers.

In January 1988 the stock market dropped 140 points. Following this scare, controls were installed in the trading system: "circuit breakers," automated methods of monitoring and restraining abnormally sharp levels of activity and thus, theoretically, preventing extreme variations in the stock market. Circuit breakers were controversial and remain so; it is still not known whether they will prevent another devastating crash. But their installation, along with improved communications technology, has helped the SEC, Federal Reserve Board, and other regulatory agencies to lessen the chances of another Black Monday recurring.[16]

## CONNECTING TO THE WORLD

By the mid-1980s computer technology was entering a critical phase as equipment became smaller and more powerful; in December 1984, for example, Bell

Laboratories introduced a memory chip able to store more than 1 million bits of electronic data. Operating systems were also improving, and UNIX, first conceived in the late 1960s, was now making possible the Internet's growth.

Computers were changing in many ways. Commodore's Amiga (1985), the first multimedia computer, demonstrated the machines' expanding possibilities, while portable computers, increasingly smaller and lighter, were becoming truly portable. April 3, 1986, saw the release of IBM's PC Convertible, its first laptop computer as well as the first IBM model to use a 3.5" floppy disk (soon to become the industry standard). The machine did not do well against its more efficient and less expensive competitors, but it was still a significant step forward, and IBM remained the market leader.

Software development was also making great strides. In 1985 Aldus (later Adobe) introduced PageMaker for the Macintosh computer, inaugurating desktop publishing. In 1987 a spate of desktop-publishing programs from Aldus, Interleaf, and Ventura, among others, were introduced for both the Mac and IBM-based computers. However, throughout the rest of the 1980s and into the early 1990s—when Microsoft perfected the Windows operating system—Apple's Macintosh was the computer of choice for users working in graphics and word processing.

Computer companies were changing as well, and inevitably some joined forces. In 1986 Sperry Rand and Burroughs merged to form Unisys Corporation, which immediately began to rival IBM in computer sales. That same year Compaq shipped its 500,000th personal computer, introduced its first PC based on the Intel 80386 processor, and joined the Fortune 500 faster than any company in history.

As personal computers became cheaper and simpler to operate, they became essential in business and more numerous in homes. Moreover, by connecting computers to telephone lines, users increasingly communicated with others through bulletin boards on which they could read and post messages and from which they could download software. This usually involved a local or regional telephone network, since long-distance charges and slow modems restricted access for many. However, with the introduction of faster modems around 1985, bulletin-board systems became more popular and extensive—the precursors, though not the only ones, of today's Internet.

Theoretically, the Internet began in 1957 when the Department of Defense established the Advanced Research Projects Agency (ARPA) as a technological think tank. The development of linking technology led in 1969 to a network system called ARPANET, connecting four host computers in California and Utah to each other. Two years later ARPANET linked 23 host computers, and in 1973 machines in England and Norway were added to its system.

Throughout the 1970s, technology improved, and more networks were created. TELENET, a commercial version of ARPANET, debuted in 1974, and in 1976 THEORYNET began to provide e-mail services to computer scientists. In 1979 USENET—still active today—was born; in 1984 this became the first network to host moderated news groups. In 1981 BITNET ("Because It's Time NETwork") began to link the City University of New York and Yale, and CSNET (Computer Science NETwork) provided a network for university scientists who had no access to ARPANET.

Until 1983, such networks could only be accessed through mainframe computers, but the explosion in personal computers meant that better ways of linking from desktops were needed. The previous year had seen the establishment of the Transmission Control Protocol (TCP) and Internet Protocol (IP), more commonly called TCP/IP and an early use of the term *Internet* to describe a connected set of computer networks; ARPANET adopted the protocol on January 1, 1983. The Domain Name Server (DNS) was created in 1984 and officially established on January 1, 1985. The DNS not only provided an easier way of identifying the host (for example, yale.edu) but also stored information about host names and domain names, with Symbolics.com becoming the first registered domain on March 15, 1985. Also in 1985, the National Science Foundation awarded supercomputer contracts to five centers to create a new network, NSFNET, specifically for research and education. As a result, the number of hosts worldwide jumped from 5,000 in 1986 to 28,000 in 1987; by 1989, the number surpassed 100,000.

As more networks were established, more protocols were designed to simplify Internet navigation (a daunting experience for ordinary computer users). Further, although the government and academic centers still ran the networks, commercial users were starting to link up. Not until the birth of the World Wide Web in 1991 would it become the Internet we know today—but it was already transforming the lives of millions making contact with each other through their computers.

## THE MEECH LAKE ACCORD

Brian Mulroney's initial problems as prime minister were not only a failing economy but a Canada still beset by regional dissent despite Pierre Trudeau's efforts to unify it. Mulroney did not help matters during his first two years in office. Severe economic problems meant he was forced to reduce social program funding, going back on campaign promises to the Atlantic provinces (New Brunswick, Newfoundland and Labrador, Nova Scotia, and Prince Edward Island) that they would be spared such cuts. His popularity plummeted overnight.

In addition, Mulroney faced discontent from the four western provinces (Alberta, British Columbia, Manitoba, and Saskatchewan), which had helped to oust the Liberal Party because voters there felt the Trudeau government had given preferential treatment to Quebec and ignored their concerns. The new prime minister had initially found favor when he ended the Liberals' National Energy Program, which oil and gas interests in the western provinces had opposed. But his 1986 decision to move the maintenance contract for Canada's CF-18 fighter aircraft from Manitoba to Quebec aroused much western hostility.

Quebec itself remained at odds with the national government, and the fact that the province had never approved the Canada Act of 1982 rankled with many. Most French-speaking Quebecois felt betrayed by the English-speaking provinces, and until Quebec could be persuaded to sign the constitution, Canada would remain a nation divided.

One of Mulroney's 1984 campaign promises had been to negotiate an agreement that would "bring Quebec into the Constitution." This, however, required the province's cooperation, something not possible until the Liberal Party's Robert Bourassa became its premier in December 1985. Unlike his separatist predecessor, René Lévesque of the Parti Québecois, Bourassa favored Quebec autonomy within a sovereign Canada and was willing to entertain constitutional negotiations.

In May 1986 Quebec established five conditions for its approval of the Canada Act: (1) recognition of the province as a distinct, bilingual society; (2) increased authority over the selection and settlement of immigrants; (3) provincial participation in appointing judges to Canada's Supreme Court; (4) limits on federal spending power, allowing the province to withdraw from a national program and create its own with federal funds; and (5) the right to veto constitutional amendments. Though the first condition applied exclusively to Quebec, the remainder were applicable to all provinces and were thus acceptable to other premiers. The "distinct society" provision was potentially divisive but was ultimately agreed by the nine English-speaking provinces.

A year later the 10 premiers and the prime minister gathered at Meech Lake in Hull, Quebec, where, on April 30, they unanimously approved the 1987 Constitutional Accord—better known as the Meech Lake Accord. The following day Mulroney proudly addressed the House of Commons: "I am honored to inform the House that at about 10 P.M. last night the Premiers and I reached unanimous agreement in principle on a Constitutional package which will allow Quebec to rejoin the Canadian constitutional family."[17] Bourassa called it "a historic breakthrough for Quebec as a Canada partner."[18]

In addition to Quebec's original five conditions, the accord also approved a new relationship between the federal and provincial governments that required at least one annual meeting of the first ministers (premiers) at which issues regarding Senate reform, the fisheries, and other matters would be discussed. Because this involved changing the constitution's amending formula, the accord needed the unanimous consent of Parliament and all provincial legislatures before it could become law. Quebec, which ratified the agreement on June 23, 1987, insisted on a deadline of three years from that date.

In the intervening period, however, new governments opposed to the Meech Lake Accord were elected in Manitoba, Newfoundland, and New Brunswick. This led to heated public debate on Meech Lake, resulting in modifications to the agreement that finally brought New Brunswick into the fold but not the other two provinces. Significantly, polls showed that many English-speaking Canadians opposed the accord and especially the special recognition given to Quebec. On June 9, 1990, Mulroney and the first ministers met in Ottawa, and all agreed to work to ensure full ratification by the June 23 deadline. However, procedural problems in Manitoba's and Newfoundland's legislatures produced delays, preventing them from voting in time. The Meech Lake Accord was dead—and Canada was still a nation divided.

## SUPREME CHOICES

On June 17, 1986, Chief Justice Warren Burger, 78, announced his retirement from the U.S. Supreme Court to devote himself to work on celebrations for the Constitution's 1987 bicentennial. This gave Ronald Reagan his first major opportunity to fulfill a 1980 campaign promise. Unhappy with the liberal slant the Court had followed since the days of Earl Warren, the president wanted more conservative justices but thus far had only been able to appoint Sandra Day O'Connor in 1981. Now, with Burger retiring, three other justices (Thurgood Marshall, Harry Blackmun, Lewis Powell) in their late 70s, and one (William Brennan) just turned 80, it seemed he would finally get his chance.

Burger, nominated as chief justice by Richard Nixon in 1969, was more conservative than his predecessor, Warren, but not enough for many critics, including Reagan. It was the Burger Court that had handed down two landmark decisions hated by ultraconservatives: *Roe v. Wade* (1973), which decriminalized abortion, and *University of California Regents v. Bakke* (1978), which narrowly upheld affirmative action. Reagan was especially opposed to the *Roe* decision and determined to overturn it if he could. His choice of a new chief justice was therefore crucial.

He did not look far, making his selection from the associate justices. William Hubbs Rehnquist, a 1971 Nixon appointee and dissenter in the *Roe* decision, was the Court's most right-wing jurist. To fill the associate justice vacancy, Reagan chose Antonin Scalia, a U.S. Court of Appeals judge whose conservative views were even more pronounced than Rehnquist's. Known to be a fierce opponent of abortion and affirmative action as well as someone likely to favor the executive branch in cases of conflict with the legislature, Scalia nonetheless sailed through his confirmation hearing and won the Senate's unanimous approval.

Normally, Scalia would have met opposition, but attention had focused on the conflict over Reagan's nominee for chief justice. Liberals attacked Rehnquist's right-wing views and, in particular, his record on race relations, going back to his years as a law clerk. Unable to find any serious fault in Rehnquist's 15 years as an associate justice, however, the Senate finally confirmed his appointment on September 17, 1986, though 33 senators voted against him (the largest negative vote ever on a confirmed appointee). On September 26 Rehnquist was sworn in as the Supreme Court's 16th chief justice, and Scalia became its 103rd associate justice.

The problems over Rehnquist's confirmation were minor compared to what was to come. On June 26, 1987, Justice Lewis Powell announced his retirement, and Democrats (who now controlled the Senate) prepared for a struggle. Powell was a moderate justice whose views were generally left of center, especially on such critical issues as abortion and affirmative action. With four conservatives currently on the Court—Rehnquist, Scalia, O'Connor, and Byron White—replacing Powell meant that Reagan could at last engineer a right-wing majority.

On July 1 the president announced his nominee: Robert Bork, a federal appeals judge for the District of Columbia. At once the Democrats voiced their vehement opposition. Though acknowledged to be a brilliant jurist, Bork was also a controversial conservative who had been openly critical of many Court decisions, especially *Roe v. Wade.* Furthermore, he supported the death penalty and favored a very narrow interpretation of the Constitution based on his view of the founding fathers' original intent, with little to no allowance made for privacy, free speech, and civil liberties. Many were also concerned about his role in the Watergate scandal: It was Bork who, as solicitor general, carried out Richard Nixon's orders and fired Special Prosecutor Archibald Cox during the "Saturday Night Massacre" of October 20, 1973.

But it was his conservative views and abrasive personality that aroused most enmity. Senator Edward Kennedy expressed the feelings of many when he said, "Robert Bork's America is a land in which women would be forced into back-alley abortions, blacks would sit at segregated lunch counters, rogue policemen could break down citizens' doors in midnight raids, schoolchildren could not be taught about evolution, writers and artists could be censured at the whim of government."[19] In the weeks prior to his confirmation hearing in September, campaigns against Bork were mounted by labor unions, civil rights organizations, and women's groups, among others. The nominee surprised many during his five days of testimony before the Senate Judiciary Committee (the longest for any Supreme Court nominee), claiming that he had modified his more controversial views, but opponents regarded this turnaround with suspicion.

After another week of testimony involving some 100 witnesses, the Senate Judiciary Committee voted on October 6 not to recommend Bork's appointment. However, both Bork and Reagan refused to withdraw, which forced the battle onto the Senate floor. After considerable debate, on October 23 the Senate voted against confirmation, 58–42; the anti-Bork ranks included six moderate Republicans who had broken party lines. Disgusted by the outcome, Bork left the Court of Appeals within months to work for the American Enterprise Institute, a conservative think tank.

On October 29 Reagan, angered and determined to have his way, named Douglas Ginsburg, a colleague of Bork's on the D.C. Court of Appeals, as his replacement nominee. However, this also proved ill-fated when it was revealed that Ginsburg had smoked marijuana while teaching at Harvard during the 1970s. This, combined with his lack of trial experience, caused Ginsburg to withdraw his nomination on November 7. Four days later Reagan nominated Anthony Kennedy, a respected and more politically acceptable 12-year veteran of California's Ninth Circuit Court of Appeals. Only the National Organization of Women opposed Kennedy, and after winning confirmation relatively easily, he was sworn in on February 18, 1988.

Kennedy was the last Reagan-nominated Supreme Court justice, but his appointment brought about the conservative majority the president had wanted (augmented by two subsequent appointments made by George H. W. Bush). In the years to come, Rehnquist Court decisions increasingly favored states' rights, redefined laws affecting civil liberties and criminal procedure, and exercised more judicial restraint than the previous Warren and Burger courts. Though Reagan never saw *Roe v. Wade* overturned, his influence on the highest court is still being felt today.

## THE THAW BEGINS

The Reykjavík summit of October 1986 had ended badly, but arms-control negotiations between the United States and the USSR continued, and 1987 would finally see a significant thaw in the cold war. One contributing factor was the changes in President Reagan's staff as the Iran-contra scandal threatened his administration; the November 1987 resignation of his hard-line defense secretary, Caspar Weinberger, would be particularly significant. Weinberger was succeeded by Frank Carlucci, who was himself succeeded as National Security Advisor by Lieutenant General Colin Powell. These and other changes produced a more moderate administration and a consequent warmer relationship with the Soviet Union.

Meanwhile, overriding both the hawks who distrusted the Soviets and the doves who urged more conciliation, Reagan had his own plan for a new relationship with the Soviet Union. He believed that Mikhail Gorbachev was sincere in his efforts for reform and should be encouraged—even pressured—to institute democratic measures. On June 12, 1987, in a speech at Berlin's Brandenburg Gate (the major crossing point in the Berlin Wall, which the Soviets had erected in

Ronald Reagan leads a cabinet meeting on March 13, 1987; he is flanked on the left by Secretary of State George Shultz and on the right by Secretary of Defense Caspar Weinberger, who would resign in November. *(Courtesy Ronald Reagan Library)*

1961 to separate the eastern and western sections of the city), Reagan sent Gorbachev a dramatic and unequivocal message:

> There is one sign the Soviets can make that would be unmistakable, that would advance dramatically the cause of freedom and peace. General Secretary Gorbachev, if you seek peace, if you seek prosperity for the Soviet Union and Eastern Europe, if you seek liberalization: Come here to this gate! Mr. Gorbachev, open this gate! Mr. Gorbachev, tear down this wall![20]

Reagan's foreign-policy advisers had wanted him to delete this section, arguing that it was too provocative. But as with SDI, Reagan held firm. The call to Gorbachev stayed in the speech—and made headlines the world over.

By autumn 1987 Soviet and American negotiators had agreed to remove all intermediate-range nuclear forces (INF) missiles from Europe. While this was not as far-reaching as the treaty that had almost been agreed to in Reykjavík—the INF missiles represented only a small percentage of the nuclear arsenal—it was nonetheless important because for the first time the two superpowers had agreed to destroy an entire class of nuclear weapons. Further, the Soviets had finally given up demanding that the Americans drop SDI and also concurred that both countries would verify, on-site, the destruction of 2,611 U.S. and Soviet medium- and short-range missiles located in Europe.

Reagan supporters maintain that it was the president's firm line and refusal to stand down on SDI that eventually caused the Soviets to give way. But other factors should not be overlooked. The antinuclear protest movement, for instance, had influenced public opinion—in both the United States and Europe—to a degree that was impossible for Reagan officials to ignore. This, along with staff changes, Reagan's personal respect for Gorbachev, and a softening of his anticommunist rhetoric enabled the administration to consider compromise. (Such was this policy reversal that Reagan came under attack from ultraconservatives who accused him of selling out the United States.)

However, historians now largely agree that the critical factor in the USSR's treaty concessions was the state of the Soviet economy: Gorbachev simply could

Mikhail Gorbachev and Ronald Reagan sign the INF Treaty in Washington, D.C., on December 8, 1987. *(Courtesy Ronald Reagan Library)*

not afford a seemingly unending arms race. He wanted to modernize his country, and that would require help from Western nations. In addition, unlike his Stalinist predecessors, Gorbachev believed that Russian security depended on peaceful coexistence and cooperation with its neighbors rather than on domination and forced imposition of communist values.

Whatever the reasons, Gorbachev flew to Washington, where, on December 8, 1987, he and Reagan signed the INF Treaty, the first firm agreement on nuclear arsenal reductions. Both men, however, knew it was only a beginning, and during their three-day summit they defined the principles for the START agreement that would be transmitted to that treaty's writers in Geneva. These included ceilings on the numbers of warheads allowed by each country and further arsenal reductions. It was also agreed that Reagan would go to Moscow in spring 1988 to continue discussions.

The INF Treaty, which the Senate ratified on May 27, 1988, saw the beginning of the end of the nuclear-arms race and the cold war. The president claimed it as a major personal triumph—but it was as much a victory for Gorbachev as it was for Reagan.

## IRAN-CONTRA: DAMAGE CONTROL

On November 3, 1986, the day that President Reagan announced the release of David Jacobsen from captivity, the Lebanese magazine *Al-Shiraa* revealed that the United States had secretly shipped arms to Iran to obtain the release of American hostages in Lebanon. The White House immediately began to issue denials, but as new charges appeared in the press, there was a gradual, partial admission of culpability.

Ten days after the *Al-Shiraa* article, President Reagan told the nation on television that the United States and Iran had engaged in talks for the previous 18 months to forge a new diplomatic relationship, find a way to end the Iran-Iraq

War, and halt state-sponsored Iranian terrorism. By these means he had also hoped to seek Iran's assistance in freeing American hostages in Lebanon, and thus there had been "modest deliveries" of "defensive weapons and spare parts" to Iran. He stated emphatically, "We did not—repeat—did not trade weapons or anything else for hostages, nor will we."[21]

Even as the press pounced on the story, Oliver North continued negotiations with Iranian representatives, but now, knowing they had been overcharged for the weapons, the Iranians insisted that no more hostages would be released until the Shiite terrorists in Kuwait were freed. Frustrated, North concentrated on cover-up tactics with John Poindexter and William Casey. These tactics included passing false information to the media, such as claims that they had believed the Iran shipments were oil-drilling equipment, and trying to blame Secretary of State George Shultz (who had opposed the operation). They also held a "shredding party" in which some 5,000 pages of documents on the Iran deals were destroyed. When the shredder broke down, North's secretary, Fawn Hall, concealed papers in her clothing and smuggled them out.

At Reagan's request, Attorney General Edwin Meese began an unhurried investigation during which more shredding occurred until, finally, a Justice Department employee found a document that clearly linked the Iran arms sales to funds for the contras. On November 24 Meese informed Reagan of this discovery, and the following day the two held a press conference to admit that funds from sales of arms to Iran had been diverted to support the contras in Nicaragua. Attempts to deny any advance knowledge of the arms sales failed when Israel flatly refused to take the blame for initiating the scheme, upon which Reagan had no choice but to fire North and ask for Poindexter's resignation on November 25.

On November 26 Reagan appointed a three-member Special Review Board that was headed by former Texas senator John Tower.[22] Two days later, under pressure from Congress, Meese reluctantly requested an independent counsel (special prosecutor) to conduct an inquiry, and Lawrence Walsh was appointed on December 19. Meanwhile, Casey and Poindexter had already testified secretly before the House and Senate Intelligence Committees on November 20–21, both stating they had no prior knowledge of the Israeli shipments to Iran and believed that later shipments contained oil-drilling equipment, not arms. Oliver North, called before the committee on December 9, took the Fifth Amendment.

The president persistently denied knowledge of the arms deals or the diversion of funds—assertions that the majority of Americans did not believe. At the beginning of November his approval rating was 67 percent; by December 2 it had plunged to 46 percent, the biggest one-month drop ever recorded by the Gallup organization. On December 6 Reagan admitted that the decision to sell arms to Iran in exchange for hostages had been "a mistake"; on January 22, 1987, a *Washington Post*–ABC News poll showed that 62 percent of Americans believed that the president was lying. As revelation followed revelation, the country remembered Watergate and pondered the possibility of impeachment.

William Casey resigned as CIA director on February 2, 1987, and a week later Robert McFarlane attempted suicide. On February 26 the Tower Commission report placed responsibility for the affair firmly on the president for having allowed his staff to carry out illegal acts, apparently without his knowledge.

Exonerating Reagan from breaking any laws himself, the panel nonetheless found him at fault for a negligent management style that allowed others to deceive and manipulate him. Chief of Staff Donald Regan was also blamed for failing to restrain out-of-control personnel.

On March 4 the president appeared on television to acknowledge his mistakes and some of his lies. "I take full responsibility for my own actions and for those of my administration," he said, but also claimed he could not remember specific orders related to his staff's activities, which he described as "personally distasteful." It was a claim he would repeat time and again in the months to follow.

During this address, Reagan also confirmed a number of staff changes: Frank Carlucci had become the new National Security Advisor in December 1986; former FBI director William Webster had replaced Casey as CIA director; and former senator Howard Baker had become chief of staff after Donald Regan was fired on February 27.[23] These changes and Reagan's apparent contrition helped to boost the president's approval rating by 10 percentage points.

Meanwhile, on January 6–7 the two houses of Congress had formed special committees chaired by Senator Daniel Inouye (D, Hawaii) and Representative Lee Hamilton (D, Ind.) to carry out a joint inquiry. Despite the notorious shredding party, much material had been retrieved from back-up tapes on the NSC's master computer. Reagan officials refused to release many documents, however, limiting the congressional investigation mostly to public hearings that began May 5. The most crucial witnesses were to be Casey, Poindexter, and North—but on May 6 Casey succumbed to a brain tumor.

With the "ringleader" of the operation dead, public attention focused on Poindexter and North, who were given grants of immunity in exchange for their congressional testimony. In July the nation became gripped by "Olliemania" as North testified before the television cameras. In a vigorous defense, he criticized Congress for doing nothing about the communist threat in Central America and caring little for the hostages in Lebanon. Across the country, Americans were riveted by North's articulate and unapologetic justification of his actions; many saw him as a selfless patriot whose superiors had made him a fall guy. Even the news that some of the funds had ended up in the personal accounts of Enterprise members did little to detract from the public's approval of North. Many applauded his efforts, illegal or not, to free the hostages, while others blamed the orders from the White House.

North implied that the president had approved all of Enterprise's activities but unequivocally asserted that he was right to do so. Poindexter was more circumspect, denying that the president had known about or authorized the diversion of funds. (He later recanted this statement when he was tried in 1990.)

In the end, North's public impact, Poindexter's statements, inconclusive evidence from other witnesses, and lack of access to key documents all hampered the congressional investigation, which was concluded

Donald Regan, seen here with President Reagan during the Geneva summit in November 1985, had numerous difficulties as chief of staff, including clashes with First Lady Nancy Reagan. *(Library of Congress, Prints and Photographs Division [LC-USZ62-117700])*

quickly so as not to affect the 1988 election. Their report, issued on November 18, managed to account for nearly $48 million raised by the Iranian arms sales, and, like the Tower Commission, it placed "ultimate responsibility" on Reagan, who had failed to oversee his subordinates' actions and did not "take care that the laws be faithfully executed." In fact, very little was made public about Reagan's direct role in Iran-contra, thanks to the protection given him by his aides (several of whom later asserted he had known about and authorized everything). Congress did not want to see another president impeached, and the public was already forgiving Reagan for his administrative failings; his Teflon coating was holding, after all. Significantly, on December 22, 1987, the president signed an appropriations bill authorizing $14 million in nonlethal aid to the contras.[24]

Lieutenant Colonel Oliver North testifies before the joint congressional committee investigating the Iran-contra affair on July 10, 1987. *(AP/Wide World Photos)*

Lawrence Walsh's investigation went on and resulted in 14 indictments. Oliver North stood trial in 1989; acquitted on nine counts, he was convicted of three charges (obstructing Congress, destroying documents, and accepting an illegal gratuity); his convictions were set aside in July 1990. In March 1988 McFarlane pleaded guilty to withholding information from Congress; Secord and Hakim both pleaded guilty to charges against them in November 1989. Poindexter's trial took place in 1990; convicted on five counts, he was sentenced to six months in prison, although his conviction was overturned in 1991. Lesser figures were also tried. In June 1992 former defense secretary Caspar Weinberger (who had opposed Iran-contra) was indicted on perjury charges, but on December 24, 1992—over Walsh's objections—President George H. W. Bush pardoned Weinberger, McFarlane, and four others.

Altogether Walsh achieved 11 convictions of participants in the Iran-contra debacle, although many were later overturned. His report was finally issued on January 18, 1994, but by then America had seen Reagan's successor win the Persian Gulf War (1991), and Enterprise was only an unhappy memory.

## CHRONICLE OF EVENTS

### 1986

*May 2:* A team of six U.S and Canadian explorers become the first expedition since 1909 to reach the North Pole using only dogs.

*May 2:* Expo '86—officially the World Exposition on Transportation and Communication—opens in Vancouver, British Columbia.

*May 6:* Pepsi Cola pays Michael Jackson $15 million to become its product sponsor, the biggest deal of its kind to date.

*May 6:* Donald E. Pelotte, a 41-year-old Abenaki from Maine, becomes the first Native American to be ordained a Roman Catholic bishop.

*May 15:* Pulitzer Prize winner Theodore H. White dies at 71.

*May 16–24:* In an all-Canadian Stanley Cup ice-hockey series, the Montreal Canadiens beat the Calgary Flames four games to one.

*May 19:* President Reagan signs a new gun-control law, significantly weaker than the 1968 law. The bill allows retail sales of rifles among states, along with other provisions.

*May 23:* Actor Sterling Hayden, known for his role as the crazed general in *Dr. Strangelove,* dies at age 70.

*May 25:* Hands Across America, a fund-raising event to aid the homeless and hungry, links nearly 6 million people in a chain extending through most of the country.

*June 1:* At the Tony Awards for the 1985–86 season, *I'm Not Rappaport* is named best play, while *The Mystery of Edwin Drood* wins as best musical. Judd Hirsch and Lily Tomlin win the top dramatic acting awards.

*June 8:* At Yankee Stadium in New York, the longest nine-inning game in American League baseball history is played as the Baltimore Orioles beat the New York Yankees, 18-9, in four hours and 16 minutes.

*June 8:* In the sixth game of the National Basketball Association championship series, the Boston Celtics beat the Houston Rockets to win their 16th NBA title.

*June 11:* The Supreme Court narrowly reaffirms women's right to abortions, overriding a Pennsylvania law that had put restrictions on abortions in that state.

*June 12:* Federal health officials predict that the number of deaths from AIDS will increase more than 10-fold in five years.

*June 13:* Bandleader Benny Goodman, known as the King of Swing, dies at age 77.

*June 17:* Chief Justice Warren E. Burger announces his resignation from the U.S. Supreme Court as of July 10. President Reagan nominates Associate Justice William H. Rehnquist to succeed Burger and appeals court judge Antonin Scalia for associate justice.

*June 17:* Kate Smith, the powerful singer who popularized "God Bless America" as an unofficial U.S. anthem, dies at age 79.

*June 19:* The Supreme Court decides that sexual harassment on the job constitutes sex discrimination and violates Title VII of the 1964 Civil Rights Act.

*June 27:* The International Court of Justice rules that U.S. actions against Nicaragua are a violation of international law. The United States is ordered to pay damages to Nicaragua and to stop arming and training rebels.

*June 30:* In a 5-4 ruling, the U.S. Supreme Court declares that the right of consenting adults to engage in homosexual activity in the privacy of the home is not protected under the Constitution.

*July 3:* Singer and bandleader Rudy Vallee dies at 84.

*July 3–6:* Ceremonies and celebrations marking the 100th anniversary of the Statue of Liberty are held in New York City.

*July 8:* Admiral Hyman G. Rickover, famed as the "father of the nuclear navy," dies at age 86.

*July 25:* Vincente Minnelli, notable Hollywood director and producer, dies at 76.

*July 27:* Bicyclist Greg LeMond becomes the first American to win the prestigious Tour de France, which began July 4.

*August 6:* William J. Schroeder, 59, the last survivor of five persons to have had permanent artificial hearts implanted, dies after a series of strokes, having lived 620 days.

*August 20:* In Edmond, Oklahoma, Patrick Henry Sherrill shoots 14 of his coworkers at the U.S. Post Office and then kills himself. Six more are wounded in what is then the third-worst mass murder in U.S. history.

*September 4:* Baseball Hall of Famer Hank Greenberg, who played first base for the Detroit Tigers, dies at age 75.

*September 5:* In Karachi, Pakistan, terrorists from the Abu Nidal Organization seize Pan Am Flight 73, holding its 379 passengers and crew hostage for some

16 hours before attacking them with gunfire. More than 20 are killed, including two Americans.

*September 21:* At the Emmy Awards, *Cagney and Lacey* wins again as best dramatic series, while the best comedy series is *The Golden Girls*. William Daniels (*St. Elsewhere*), Sharon Gless (*Cagney and Lacey*), Michael J. Fox (*Family Ties*), and Betty White (*The Golden Girls*) take the top acting awards.

*September 23:* After almost 100 years of debate, Congress finally votes to make the rose the United States' official national flower.

*October 11–12:* President Reagan meets Soviet leader Mikhail Gorbachev at a summit in Reykjavík, Iceland.

*October 20:* General Motors announces that it is selling its operations in South Africa in protest of South Africa's apartheid policy; other companies will follow suit.

*October 22:* President Reagan signs the Tax Reform Act, the most complete revision of the tax code in 40 years.

*October 23:* The Office of Management and Budget announces that for the fiscal year that ended September 30, the federal deficit was $220.7 billion, the fourth record figure in five years.

*October 27:* In the seventh game of the World Series, which began October 18, the National League's New York Mets beat the American League's Boston Red Sox to win the championship.

*November 3:* A Lebanese magazine, *Al-Shiraa*, reports that the United States had secretly sold arms to Iran in an attempt to obtain the release of hostages held in Lebanon. More revelations will follow in what becomes known as the Iran-contra affair.

*November 4:* Following midterm elections, the Democratic Party wins back control of the Senate and increases its majority in the House of Representatives.

*November 22:* At age 20, boxing's Mike Tyson defeats Trevor Berbick to become the youngest heavyweight champion in history.

*November 22:* Actor, musician, and songwriter Scatman Crothers dies, age 76.

*November 25:* The president admits that arms had been sold to Iran but insists that he had not been fully informed. National Security Advisor John M. Poindexter resigns, and his assistant, Marine lieutenant colonel Oliver L. North, is dismissed.

*November 26:* Reagan appoints a three-member commission, headed by former senator John G. Tower,

to investigate the National Security Council and its staff. Congress also plans to investigate.

*November 29:* Debonair actor Cary Grant dies in Davenport, Iowa, at the age of 80.

*December 2:* Frank Carlucci is appointed the new National Security Advisor.

*December 2:* Desi Arnaz, Cuban-born singer and actor best known for the classic 1950s TV series *I Love Lucy* with his then-wife Lucille Ball, dies at 69.

*December 19:* An independent counsel, Lawrence Walsh, is named to lead an inquiry into the Iran-contra affair.

*December 23:* Piloted by Richard G. Rutan and Jeana Yeager, the experimental airplane *Voyager,* made of plastic and stiffened paper, lands at Edwards Air Force Base, California, completing the first nonstop flight around the world without refueling in nine days, three minutes, and 44 seconds.

## 1987

*January 5:* Concerns about President Reagan's health are sparked when he undergoes prostate surgery.

*January 15:* Actor and dancer Ray Bolger, best known for his role as Scarecrow in *The Wizard of Oz,* dies at 83.

*January 21:* British envoy Terry Waite, who had been negotiating for the release of hostages in Lebanon, is himself kidnapped. His captivity will last more than four years.

*January 22:* The entire East Coast, from Maine to Florida, is hit by a blizzard that causes at least 37 deaths.

*January 25:* The New York Giants defeat the Denver Broncos, 39-20, to win Super Bowl XXI.

*January 31–February 4:* In four straight races, Dennis Connor of San Diego, California, and his crew aboard the yacht *Stars & Stripes* win back the America's Cup from Australia's *Kookaburra III*.

*February 2:* William Casey resigns as director of the Central Intelligence Agency.

*February 4:* Congress overrides President Reagan's veto and passes the Clean Water Act, which allocates $20 billion through 1994 to construct sewers and clean up estuaries and toxic "hot spots," among other things.

*February 4:* Flamboyant entertainer Liberace, 67, dies of AIDS.

*February 9:* Former National Security Advisor Robert McFarlane, implicated in the Iran-contra affair, attempts suicide.

*February 20:* The Unabomber, whose reign of terror has continued in intermittent cycles since 1978, strikes again when a bomb explodes at a computer store in Salt Lake City, Utah.

*February 22:* Modern pop artist Andy Warhol, whose works were considered icons of the 1960s and 1970s, dies at 58.

*February 24:* At the Grammy Awards, Paul Simon's *Graceland* wins best album of 1986. Steve Winwood wins for best record ("Higher Love") and best male pop vocalist, while Barbra Streisand is named best female pop vocalist for *The Broadway Album.*

*February 25:* In *California v. Cabazon Band,* the U.S. Supreme Court authorizes unregulated American Indian gaming houses.

*February 26:* The Tower Commission issues its report on the Iran-contra affair.

*February 27:* White House Chief of Staff Donald T. Regan resigns; he is replaced by Senator Howard H. Baker, Jr.

*March 2:* Chrysler Corporation purchases Renault's interest in American Motors Corporation (AMC); the cost of the acquisition is estimated at as much as $1.2 billion.

*March 4:* In a televised address, President Reagan says he takes "full responsibility" for his administration's actions in the Iran-contra scandal, although he does not admit those actions were wrong.

*March 12:* Famed college football coach Wayne "Woody" Hayes dies at 74.

*March 20:* The Food and Drug Administration (FDA) approves the first drug to benefit AIDS patients: azidothymidine (AZT). While the drug cannot cure AIDS, it will help victims of the disease to live longer. It is estimated that it will cost as much as $10,000 per patient per year.

*March 22:* Apple Computers announces the release of its Macintosh II and Macintosh SE models.

*March 25:* The Supreme Court upholds a voluntary affirmative action plan that allows gender and race to be considered when recruiting to fill positions where women and minorities are severely underrepresented.

*March 30:* *Platoon* is named the outstanding film of 1986 at the Academy Awards. Paul Newman (*The Color of Money*) and Marlee Matlin (*Children of a Lesser God*) win as best actor and actress, respectively, while Michael Caine and Dianne Wiest win the supporting acting awards for their performances in *Hannah and Her Sisters.*

*March 31:* The House of Representatives overrides President Reagan's veto of a public-works bill. The Senate will override the veto two days later.

*March 31:* In a controversial case, custody of the infant girl known only as Baby M, born in March 1986, is awarded to her father, William Stern, and his wife, Elizabeth, rather than to her natural mother, Mary Beth Whitehead, who had agreed to carry the baby for the Sterns and then reneged on the deal.

*April 2:* Drummer par excellence Buddy Rich dies, age 69.

*April 7:* The first museum devoted to women in the arts, the National Museum of Women, opens in Washington, D.C.

*April 11:* Erskine Caldwell, whose novels set in the South included *Tobacco Road,* dies at 83.

*April 16:* The federal government announces that new forms of life created through gene splicing and reproductive technologies such as genetic engineering may be patented. Patenting of new genetic characteristics in human beings, however, is banned.

*April 27:* Kurt Waldheim—former secretary general of the United Nations and currently president of Austria—is refused entry to the United States because of his anti-Jewish activities during World War II. He is the first head of state to be banned from the United States.

*May 4:* The Supreme Court rules that women must be admitted to Rotary Clubs, previously accessible only to men. By early July the Lions Club International and Kiwanis International will vote to admit women.

*May 6:* Former CIA director William J. Casey, 74, dies of a brain tumor prior to giving testimony in the Iran-contra affair.

*May 8:* Senator Gary Hart (D, Colo.) withdraws from the 1988 presidential race after reports are published of his affair with model Donna Rice.

*May 12:* In a medical first carried out in Baltimore, Maryland, a healthy heart is taken from a living person and transplanted to another person; the heart donor then receives the heart and lungs of a dead accident victim. Two days later a British spokesperson says that similar operations had been performed in the United Kingdom in late April and early May.

*May 14:* Hollywood siren Rita Hayworth, 68, dies of Alzheimer's disease.

*May 17:* An Iraqi war plane mistakenly fires two missiles that damage the American frigate USS *Stark,* killing 37 sailors and wounding 21 more. Iraq later apologizes for the attack.

*May 19:* Former FBI director William Webster becomes the CIA's new director.

*May 25:* Delegates from the 13 original states gather on Independence Mall in Philadelphia to commemorate the 200th anniversary of the U.S. Constitution.

*June 2:* President Reagan names Alan Greenspan to succeed Paul Volcker as chairman of the Federal Reserve Board.

*June 5:* On a special four-hour live broadcast of *Nightline,* anchor Ted Koppel hosts a "National Town Meeting on AIDS."

*June 13:* Stage and screen actress Geraldine Page dies at 62.

*June 14:* The Los Angeles Lakers win the National Basketball Association championship, beating the Boston Celtics in the sixth game of the series.

*June 16:* In New York City, subway vigilante Bernie Goetz is found guilty of illegal gun possession but is otherwise acquitted of all charges related to his shooting of four youths on December 22, 1984.

*June 19:* In a 7-2 vote, the Supreme Court overturns a 1984 Louisiana law, ruling that the creationist theory of human origin cannot be taught alongside the theory of evolution when the motivation is to enforce religious beliefs.

*June 22:* Actor-dancer-singer Fred Astaire dies at age 88.

*June 24:* Jackie Gleason, comedian famed for his 1950s cult TV series, *The Honeymooners,* dies at age 71.

*July 1:* President Reagan nominates the conservative U.S. Circuit Court judge Robert Bork to the Supreme Court, replacing retiring justice Lewis Powell.

*July 2:* Tony Award–winning choreographer Michael Bennett dies of AIDS at age 44.

*July 7:* Oliver North, a key figure in the Iran-contra scandal, begins to testify before the congressional inquiry committee. His week-long televised testimony makes him a hero in the eyes of many.

*July 16–17:* In Philadelphia, 200 members of Congress commemorate the signing of the Constitution. Ceremonies include a ringing of a replica of the Liberty Bell.

*August 1:* Mike Tyson becomes the first boxer since Leon Spinks in 1978 to hold the title to all heavyweight boxing crowns when he defeats Tony Rucker, the International Boxing Federation's champion, in a 12-round decision in Las Vegas, Nevada.

*August 8–23:* The 10th Pan-American Games are held in Indianapolis, Indiana, where the United States wins 369 medals, 168 of them gold. Cuba is second with 175 medals (75 gold), and Canada is third with 162 medals (30 gold).

*August 16:* Approximately 20,000 fans make a pilgrimage to the home of rock-and-roll legend Elvis Presley to mark the 10th anniversary of his death.

*August 16:* Northwest Airlines Flight 255 crashes after taking off from Detroit Metropolitan Airport. All on board are killed (153 people) except for one passenger, four-year-old Cecelia Cichan.

*August 18:* The Food and Drug Administration approves the trial use of a possible AIDS vaccine using CD4, a protein that prevents the AIDS virus from entering nearby body cells.

*August 25:* As the Dow Jones industrial average hits 2,722.42, the stock market enjoys a record high in trading.

*August 28:* Famed movie director John Huston dies, age 81.

*August 30:* Canadian runner Ben Johnson sets a new world record in the 100-meter dash.

*September 20:* At the Emmy Awards, *L.A. Law* is named best drama series and *The Golden Girls* is the best comedy series. Bruce Willis (*Moonlighting*) and Sharon Gless (*Cagney and Lacey*) take the dramatic acting awards; Michael J. Fox (*Family Ties*) and Rue McClanahan (*The Golden Girls*) win Emmies for comedy acting.

*September 21:* In the Persian Gulf, U.S. helicopters fire on Iranian ships that are laying mines.

*September 23:* Dancer, choreographer, and director Bob Fosse dies at age 60.

*September 29:* Don Mattingly of the New York Yankees hits his sixth grand-slam home run of the year, setting a new major league record for grand-slam home runs in a single season.

*September 29:* Henry Ford II, who had brought his grandfather's automobile company back from near-bankruptcy, dies at age 70.

*October 1:* An earthquake registering 6.1 on the Richter scale hits Los Angeles, killing eight people and injuring 111.

*October 9:* Playwright, politician, and ambassador Clare Boothe Luce dies at 84.

*October 12:* Alfred M. Landon, unsuccessful Republican candidate for president in 1936, dies at age 100.

*October 14–16:* The entire country becomes gripped by efforts to free 18-month-old Jessica McClure from an oil pipe in Midland, Texas. After 58.5 hours, she is finally rescued.

*October 16:* A three-hour-old baby at the Loma Linda (California) Medical Center becomes the youngest person to undergo a heart transplant, receiving the heart of an infant declared legally dead a few days previously.

*October 17:* First Lady Nancy Reagan undergoes surgery for breast cancer; the tumor is benign.

*October 19:* The New York Stock Exchange suffers the worst stock crash in its history as the Dow Jones industrial average falls 508 points.

*October 25:* The American League's Minnesota Twins defeat the National League's St. Louis Cardinals in the seventh game to win baseball's World Series.

*October 29:* Big-band leader Woody Herman dies at 74.

*October 31:* Author Joseph Campbell, renowned for his works on mythology, dies at age 83.

*November 1:* In San Antonio, Texas, Tom Watson wins $384,000 in the Nabisco Championship, the richest prize in golf history to date.

*November 5:* Caspar Weinberger resigns as secretary of defense; President Reagan nominates National Security Advisor Frank Carlucci to succeed him.

*November 9:* Larry Heinemann (*Paco's Story*) and Richard Rhodes (*The Making of the Atomic Bomb*) win the National Book Awards (formerly the American Book Awards) for fiction and nonfiction, respectively.

*November 18:* The report of congressional committees regarding the Iran-contra affair assigns blame to President Reagan.

*November 21:* News that some 2,600 Cubans who had arrived in the United States during the 1980 Mariel boatlift will be returned to Cuba starts a riot involving some 1,000 detainees at a federal detention center in Louisiana.

*November 28:* In Wappingers Fall, New York, a black teenager named Tawana Brawley claims she was kidnapped and raped by six white men, including a policeman. Later, after much controversial publicity and a grand jury investigation, it will be determined that she manufactured the story.

*December 1:* James Baldwin, award-winning African-American author, dies at age 63.

*December 8:* At a summit in Washington, D.C., President Reagan and Soviet general secretary Mikhail Gorbachev sign the INF Treaty.

*December 10:* Although the Roman Catholic Church remains opposed to birth control, U.S. bishops give qualified support to promoting the use of condoms in the battle against AIDS.

*December 15:* Colorado senator Gary Hart reenters the race for the Democratic presidential nomination.

*December 16:* Michael Deaver, President Reagan's former deputy chief of staff, is found guilty of three counts of perjury, resulting from investigations into his activities as a lobbyist after he left the White House.

*December 18:* Financier Ivan Boesky, found guilty of insider trading, is given a three-year prison sentence, which he will begin serving on March 24, 1988.

*December 22:* President Reagan signs a compromise appropriation bill authorizing nonlethal aid to Nicaraguan contras in the amount of $14 million.

*December 27:* The FDA approves the antidepressant drug Prozac for sale in the United States. It will be released in early 1988.

## EYEWITNESS TESTIMONY

### *The Iran-Contra Affair*

I have been briefed on the efforts being made by private parties to obtain the release of Americans held hostage in the Middle East, and hereby find that the following operations in foreign countries (including all support necessary to such operations) are important to the national security of the United States. Because of the extreme sensitivity of these operations, in the exercise of the President's constitutional authorities, I direct the Director of Central Intelligence not to brief the Congress of the United States, as provided for in Section 501 of the National Security Act of 1947, as amended, until such time as I may direct otherwise.

> *Ronald Reagan's intelligence finding, dated December 5, 1985, retroactively approving the shipment of arms to Iran (in exchange for hostages); quoted in Johnson,* Sleepwalking Through History *(2003), p. 291.*

To Ronald Reagan, the House vote on military aid to the contras was "a step forward in bipartisan consensus in American foreign policy." But Reagan was being diplomatic. His 12-vote margin of victory had cost him six years, 10 separate votes and all the presidential lobbying clout he could muster. In the end, only 51 Democrats supported his Nicaragua policy.

> *Looking at President Reagan's position following Congress's June 25, 1986, vote to approve military aid to the Nicaraguan contras, in "Is This Any Way to Make Foreign Policy?"* Newsweek, *July 7, 1986, p. 22.*

. . . "It was a benefactor flight," said Elliott Abrams, assistant secretary of state for inter-American affairs. "[They] happen all the time." Others saw something more shadowy at work. "It's not a violation of our law for people to go down there on their own," said Sen. Patrick Leahy, vice chairman of the Intelligence Committee. "But I think it is a violation of our law if the administration is allowing it . . . with a wink and a shrug."

> *Questioning U.S. involvement in Nicaragua following the downing of a cargo plane carrying supplies to the contras, in "The Contras' Proxy War,"* Newsweek, *October 20, 1986, p. 31.*

In the wee hours of the morning, John Adams, our State Department liaison, called. "Peggy . . ." he said.

Already, I didn't like the sound of his voice. "Now, don't be upset. It's not Terry who's out, it's David Jacobsen."

I was devastated and angry. "Don't be upset, John? How the hell am I supposed to feel!" I was crying, out of control.

It was so unfair. It was Terry's turn. He had been in there longer than Jacobsen. We had done everything they'd asked.

I was overwhelmed with guilt. Maybe I had done something wrong. I had already been criticized and it hurt: "If you just keep your big mouth shut, he would get out of there." All of these cruel things.

> *Peggy Say, sister of abducted journalist Terry Anderson, describing her unhappiness on learning that David Jacobsen, and not her brother, had been released from captivity on November 2, 1986, in* Say, Forgotten *(1991), pp. 169–170. Say had been fervently working for her brother's release.*

For the United States, preventing Islamic fanaticism from sweeping through the Persian Gulf is a crucial national interest. And yet, as a ransom for hostages and protection money against future terrorism, we are considering altering our policy, tilting toward Iran and thus jeopardizing that interest. . . . Such a capitulation would constitute an appalling act of dereliction.

Easy for me to say. What if I had a loved one being held hostage in Beirut? Wouldn't I be screaming for the government to do anything necessary to get the hostages back? Of course, I would. Families are right to use every instrument they can to force government to capitulate.

Which is why hostage families should not make foreign policy. . . .

> *Columnist Charles Krauthammer decrying the Reagan administration's making deals with Iran, in Krauthammer, "Government as Rescue Squad,"* Washington Post, *November 7, 1986, p. A-27.*

About an hour into the meeting, Meese said, "Is there anything else that can jump up and bite the president on the ass?"

"Not that I can think of," I replied.

"How about this?" he said, handing me a nine-page document. It was an April 1986 memorandum from me to Admiral Poindexter, which detailed a planned arms shipment to Iran and included a specific mention of twelve million dollars in residuals from the arms sale that would go to the Nicaraguan resistance.

*Oh, shit,* I thought.

This was precisely the kind of document I had shredded. Or so I thought.

*Oliver North describing a tense meeting with Attorney General Edwin Meese on November 23, 1986, in North,* Under Fire *(1991), p. 327.*

There is that old line about you can't fire me, I quit . . . I am prepared to depart at the time you and the President decide. . . . We nearly succeeded. Semper fidelis. Oliver North.

*Computer message from Oliver North to National Security Advisor John Poindexter, November 24, 1986, quoted in Woodward,* Veil *(1987), p. 497.*

No transfer of money went through anyone. Bank accounts were established, as best we know, by representatives of the forces in Central America. And this information was provided to representatives of the Israeli government and the funds—or representatives of Israel, I should say—and then these funds were put into the accounts. So far as we know at this stage, no American person actually handled any of the funds that went to the forces in Central America.

*Attorney General Edwin Meese on November 25, 1986, giving an inaccurate account of money transactions in the Iran-contra operation, quoted in "Transcript of Attorney General Meese's News Conference,"* Washington Post, *November 26, 1986, p. A-8.*

If he did know about it, then he has willfully broken the law. If he didn't know about it, then he is failing to do his job.

*Senator John Glenn (D, Ohio) on November 25, 1986, summing up the paradox of President Reagan's role in the Iran-contra affair, quoted in "Under Siege,"* Newsweek, *December 8, 1986, p. 33.*

President Reagan gestures toward Attorney General Ed Meese during a White House press briefing on the Iran-contra affair on November 25, 1986. *(Courtesy Ronald Reagan Library)*

President Reagan receives the Tower Commission's bad news in the Cabinet Room on February 26, 1987; he is flanked by John Tower on the left and Edmund Muskie on the right. *(Courtesy Ronald Reagan Library)*

We do not regard him as a mental patient. But we regard him as a President who didn't do his job.

*Tower Commission member Edmund Muskie on President Reagan, March 1, 1987, quoted in Slansky,* The Clothes Have No Emperor *(1989), p. 190.*

. . . First, let me say I take full responsibility for my own actions and for those of my administration. As angry as I may be about activities undertaken without my knowledge, I am still accountable for those activities. As disappointed as I may be in some who served me, I'm still the one who must answer to the American people for this behavior. And as personally distasteful as I find secret bank accounts and diverted funds—well, as the Navy would say, this happened on my watch.

*Ronald Reagan taking the blame for the Iran-contra affair in a televised address to the nation on March 4, 1987. Available online. URL: http://www.reagan. utexas.edu/resource/speeches/1987/030487h.htm.*

Despite the omissions and circumlocutions that abounded in the president's Wednesday night speech, his acceptance of responsibility for what happened on his watch was assuring. We are heartened by his pledge to put the recommendations of the Tower Commission into practice and his appointment of Howard Baker as White House chief of staff. Iran-contra has changed everything, much of it for the better, and Mr. Reagan's task is to prove he can really change with it.

*From an otherwise critical editorial, "Reagan's Limited Hang-Out," in the* Baltimore Sun, *March 6, 1987, quoted in Boyer,* Reagan as President *(1990), p. 226.*

In answer to the question that began as a joke and grew to be the focal point of the Tower Commission's questions—What did the president forget and when did he forget it?—Reagan finally claimed, "I don't remember—period." How could a president forget authorizing a violation of his own oft-stated anti-terrorism policy? Coming after a yes-no-maybe answer, Reagan's disclaimer is hard to believe. Hard, that is, for the rest of us. What may be really involved here, however, is not a memory lapse, not a legal denial, but psychological denial. Reagan apparently cannot remember what he cannot admit to himself.

*Journalist Gail Sheehy psychoanalyzing President Reagan and Iran-contra, in Sheehy, "Reality? Just Say No,"* New Republic, *March 30, 1987, quoted in Boyer,* Reagan as President *(1990), p. 226.*

I think it is very important for the American people to understand that this is a dangerous world, that we live at risk and that this nation is at risk in a dangerous world. And that they ought not to be led to believe, as a consequence of these hearings, that this nation cannot or should not conduct covert operations. . . . The effort to conduct these covert operations was made in such a way that our adversaries would not have knowledge of them, or we could deny American association with it, or the association of this government with those activities. And that is not wrong.

*Lieutenant Colonel Oliver North testifying before the joint congressional committees investigating the Iran-contra affair on July 7, 1987, quoted in Meyer,* The Life and Exploits of Lt. Colonel Oliver L. North *(1987), p. 15.*

Once I realized I hadn't been fully informed, I sought to find the answers. Some of the answers I don't like. As the Tower board reported, and as I said last March, our original initiative rapidly got all tangled up in the sale of arms, and the sale of arms got tangled up with hostages. Secretary Shultz and Secretary Weinberger both predicted that the American people would immediately assume this whole plan was an arms-for-hostages deal and nothing more. Well, unfortunately, their predictions were right. As

I said to you in March, I let my preoccupation with the hostages intrude into areas where it didn't belong. The image—the reality—of Americans in chains, deprived of their freedom and families so far from home, burdened my thoughts. And this was a mistake.

My fellow Americans, I've thought long and often about how to explain to you what I intended to accomplish, but I respect you too much to make excuses. The fact of the matter is that there's nothing I can say that will make the situation right. I was stubborn in my pursuit of a policy that went astray.

*Ronald Reagan in a televised address to the nation on August 12, 1987, following the congressional investigations into Iran-contra. Available online. URL: http://www.reagan.utexas.edu/resource/ speeches/1987/081287d.htm.*

## Corporate Raiding and Insider Trading

. . . The Street is hardly awash in illicit activity. But in the overheated atmosphere, where personal fortunes can be made with one deal, the temptation to cheat has apparently become irresistible to a few of the players. Mounting a merger or acquisition campaign demands careful, secret plans of battle, but the rules of engagement are clear: the securities markets are supposed to operate openly, with all investors having equal access to important information about companies. At an investment banking house, which both arranges mergers and trades stock, using "material non-public information" as Levine is alleged to have done is a double violation of trust.

*Examining the situation on Wall Street in the wake of Dennis Levine's arrest for insider trading, in "Greed on Wall Street,"* Newsweek, *May 26, 1986, p. 45.*

We have created two big myths in the 1980s. One is that you need to be smart to be an investment banker. That's wrong. Finance is easy. Myth number two is that investment bankers somehow create value. They don't. They shuffle around value other people have created. It's a parasitical industry. The flight to Wall Street now is a brain drain from the rest of American industry.

*A recent Harvard MBA commenting on the growth of investment banking, quoted in "The New Dealmakers,"* Newsweek, *May 26, 1986, p. 49.*

I do it to make money. I'm not saying I don't. I'm a competitive guy and I do it with a profit motive. That's how you score in this game and those are the points. I'm not saying I'm an altruist.

. . . . .

It's almost like a tiger hunter. Alright, it might be fun to hunt tigers but after a while, unless you hunt the tigers because you're saving the village it's sort of just bloody and messy. So if you want to be saving the village and if the village is paying you very handsomely and it has a lot of poor babies in it, there is a great deal of satisfaction in taking on the risk of fighting the tigers. And I think that's why I do it.

*Corporate raider Carl Icahn using an unusual analogy to explain why he takes over companies, quoted in "Confessions of a Raider,"* Newsweek, *October 20, 1986, p. 55.*

What we have here is a form of theft. Mr. Boesky has admitted to offering a commission to Dennis Levine, the former Drexel Burnham Lambert merger specialist, for passing on confidential information. Mr. Levine noted the names of companies that were about to be put into takeover play by Drexel clients. Mr. Boesky then bought stock, often in the hundreds of thousands of shares, in the target companies and watched the prices rise on confirmation of the takeover bid. Think of Mr. Boesky as the fence for stolen property, in this case information of impending bids.

The SEC is not in the business of punishing theft, only what it calls insider trading. . . .

*The* Wall Street Journal *providing background to the Boesky scandal prior to contending that the Securities and Exchange Commission (SEC) made the right arrest for the wrong reasons, in its editorial "Boesky the Terrible,"* Wall Street Journal, *November 18, 1986, p. 32.*

Far more is at stake than a few ruined careers and pilfered millions. The question hanging over Wall Street is whether the case involves more than isolated instances of insider trading—whether raiders, arbitrageurs and investment bankers conspired to manipulate stock prices. Roger Blanc, a former SEC attorney, says the issue is "whether the SEC can establish its own Bermuda Triangle—the void into which corporations disappear. If they can show that the people who are the movers and the shakers are going to the bond people and the arbs and tying them all together," says Blanc, "there will be criminal convictions at the highest levels . . . there will be hell to pay."

*Reporting the possible impact of the Securities and Exchange Commission's investigations into insider trading, in "The Secret World of Ivan Boesky," Newsweek, December 1, 1986, p. 51.*

Perhaps it was inevitable. John Maynard Keynes, who originated the casino metaphor for stock markets, wrote: "The game of professional investment is intolerably boring . . . to anyone who is entirely exempt from the gambling instinct." Boesky surely affirms that. His need was not simply to be rich, but to be seen as richer and smarter than anyone else. He gambled less on stocks than on his ability to beat the cops. He lost and, despite his huge fine, deserves the fate of caught crooks: jail.

*Essayist Robert J. Samuelson commenting on Ivan Boesky, in Samuelson, "The Super Bowl of Scandal," Newsweek, December 1, 1986, p. 64.*

Despite the notoriety of the Boesky and Dennis Levine insider-trading cases, recruiting at business schools this year is business as usual. Investment bankers say they plan to hire as many graduates from the top business schools as they did in 1986, if not more. And students are eager to accept their offers.

"I don't know of one single student who because of the scandal has decided not to go into" investment banking, says Sally Lannin, acting director of the M.B.A. career center at Stanford University.

If anything, students seem to regard the Boesky affair as an aberration. And that attitude worries some business educators. Although the current scandals seem to provide vivid enough examples of the consequences of excess and unethical behavior, it is unclear what lessons—if any—business students have learned.

*Reporter Janice Simpson discussing college graduates and investment banking, in Simpson, "Wall Street's Courting of M.B.A.s Proceeds Apace Despite Scandals," Wall Street Journal, January 28, 1987, p. 31.*

## Tax Reform

This bill went from immovable to unstoppable in 24 hours. Something came together, some chemistry.

*Senator Robert Packwood (R, Oreg.), chairman of the Senate Finance Committee, commenting on the sudden, dramatic drafting of a tax reform bill, quoted in "Wow! Real Reform!" Time, May 19, 1986, p. 14.*

Indeed, the prospects for tax reform looked so good that partisans were already battling over who should share the credit. [Senator Robert] Packwood certainly had beaten back the swarm of lobbyists. Fellow committee members also praised Democrat Bill Bradley [N.J.], who has preached tax reform for four years. Bradley played purist on the panel, holding out for substantive reform and quietly finding ways to achieve it. "It wouldn't have happened without Bill," said [David] Durenberger [R, Minn.]. "He was the only one who knew what we were doing." But Ronald Reagan probably deserved the lion's share—for making tax reform an issue and for pressing it when most advisers thought he was wasting his time and popularity. . . .

*Assessing how Congress managed to craft a tax reform package, in "A Radical Plan for Tax Reform," Newsweek, May 19, 1986, p. 23.*

Analysis of the bill's economic effects, though, should not dwell too long on the immediate winners and losers. In a macroeconomic sense, we're all in the same boat, and it is nearly impossible to sort out the dynamic effects. If the bill comes to pass as advertised, we have little doubt that when the dynamic effects are seen, it will be evident that there are very few losers indeed.

*The Wall Street Journal examining the beneficial aspects of the new tax reform bill in its editorial "Winners and Losers," Wall Street Journal, August 20, 1986, p. 14.*

It is not reform in any dignified meaning of the word to say that a system already favoring the rich should be rendered all the more unsympathetic to the rest. Recent economic history has demonstrated with startling clarity that the vaunted free market is miserably incompetent at turning capital, supposedly freed up for productive investment, to socially beneficial ends. The only long-term alternative to economic stagnation would be a profound redistribution and broadening of the wealth now clotted at the top of the system. But as the Journal delightedly recognized, redistribution now has yet another stake driven through its heart. In sum, what we have with the ending of progressive taxation is a counterrevolution: that is, a return to a past that was long ago found wanting.

*Essayist Alexander Cockburn finding nothing to cheer about in the new tax reform bill, in Cockburn, "Tax Revision Is Social Regression," Wall Street Journal, August 21, 1986, p. 23.*

The bill's overarching attitude is very much in line with the recent trend toward deregulation. Rather than using the tax code to push certain social and economic goals, the new law lets people decide what to do with their money.

*Economist A. Gary Shilling applauding the new tax reform act, quoted in "Changing Course," U.S. News & World Report, October 6, 1986, p. 46.*

. . . [T]his tax bill is less a freedom—or a reform, I should say—than a revolution. . . . I'm certain that the bill I'm signing today is not only an historic overhaul of our tax code and a sweeping victory for fairness, it's also the best antipoverty bill, the best profamily measure, and the best job-creation program ever to come out of the Congress of the United States.

*From President Reagan's remarks prior to signing the Tax Reform Act on October 22, 1986. Available online. URL: http://www.reagan.utexas.edu/resource/ speeches/1986/102286a.htm.*

## America the Beautiful

Within a week the event will be forgotten, but there will still be homeless and hungry people.

*Ernest Miller of the Salvation Army, being cynical about the forthcoming Hands Across America event, quoted in "A $50 Million Handshake," Newsweek, May 19, 1986, p. 25.*

Ken Kragen, the Harvard Business School–educated mastermind of USA for Africa and Hands Across America, has heard all the arguments—and he's still bullish on Awareness. "The money is really secondary," he says. "What an event like this does is create tremendous momentum"—by keeping media attention focused on the issues, influencing legislation and encouraging participants to make long-term commitments. In New York, for example, organizers listed facilities where hand holders could volunteer afterward. "We may not get 6 million people to sign up—but we may get 25,000," says Kragen. "You swing the pendulum back to the individual making a contribution in his community."

*Examining whether a fund-raising megaevent like Hands Across America is effective, in "A New Spirit of Giving," Newsweek, June 2, 1986, p. 19.*

From Amy [Sherwood, 6, a homeless girl who began the chain], 200,000 New Yorkers, nine deep in some places, wound up Manhattan's West Side and over the George Washington Bridge to New Jersey. A 50-yd. stretch near Newark threatened to be the first gap, but at the last minute people in the line stopped a commuter bus; the 40-plus passengers all cheerfully piled out to fill the hole. The first breaks developed in Pennsylvania, but the line wound south to Washington, where it was routed through the White House. Persuaded at the last minute by his daughter Maureen to take part, President Reagan stood somewhat stiffly among staff members' children and friends, using a crib sheet for some lyrics but needing no help for a flawless rendition of *America the Beautiful*—both verses. (Across from the White House, protestors demonstrated against the President's policies toward the homeless.)

*Describing the human chain of "Hands Across America" on May 25, 1986, in "People," Time, June 9, 1986, pp. 66–67.*

It has been much more than a simple restoration. It's also been a remembrance, and a renewal. We've restored a statue, we've remembered our forefathers, but most important of all, we've renewed our commitment to an ideal. Without that renewal, the restoration and the remembrance don't mean very much.

*Lee Iacocca, chairman of the Statue of Liberty and Ellis Island Foundation, commenting on the Statue of Liberty's restoration, in Iacocca, "What Liberty Means to Me," Newsweek, July 7, 1986, p. 19.*

. . . Americans do some things pretty well, like playing games and making machines and movies, but what they do best is gettin' free. Of course freedom gits folks into a mess of trouble too, 'cause when everybody's free, they're free to fall on their faces, and if no one cares to pick 'em up, they're free to drown. . . . Americans also git into trouble by being too free of the past. They never really did feel part of the world anyway, I guess, but it's too late for hiding out now. Sometimes I can feel the whole world rockin' on the raft with Jim and me, pretendin' that there ain't no shore, and that the river flowed from nowhere.

Millions of people were linked in the Hands Across America chain on May 25, 1986. This group is joined on Santa Monica Beach in California.  *(AP/Wide World Photos)*

Not that I'm down on Americans, you understand. They're mostly good and almost normal once you git to know 'em. . . .

*"Hucklebery Finn"—essayist Roger Rosenblatt, writing in the style of Mark Twain—reflecting on the meaning of freedom prior to the Statue of Liberty's 100th birthday, in Rosenblatt, "Huck and Miss Liberty,"* Time, *July 7, 1986, p. 25.*

For four golden days and gaudy nights, she was the still point of a turning, kaleidoscopic world. Immovable, she gazed upon the revelry with her forthright, rather stern expression. While not exactly a wallflower at her own birthday party, she appeared slightly aloof, distant. What's the big fuss? She might have been thinking. The question is understandable:

after 100 years there is little the old girl has not seen before. But as an immigrant herself, she is perhaps even more sensitive to the curious ways of her adopted country, silently indulgent of good old American exuberance, excess and, yes, glitz. Let them cavort, she seemed to say with an imperceptible smile. Liberty may be proud, but she isn't haughty. Look again. Was that—could it have been—a wink?

*Describing the Statue of Liberty's viewpoint during celebrations for her 100th birthday, in "The Lady's Party,"* Time, *July 14, 1986, p. 10.*

Immigration officials say they expect a huge market in bogus documents to emerge soon to help those living illegally in the United States take advantage of or circumvent the immigration measure that Congress passed Friday.

Already, the officials say, fake rent receipts, utility bills, income tax forms, driver's licenses, birth certificates and the like are being tailored to the requirements in the legislation.

*Forecasting one result of the recently passed immigration legislation, in Robert Reinhold, "Surge in Bogus Papers predicted In Wake of Change in Alien Law," New York Times, October 20, 1986, p. A-1.*

It doesn't matter what the law says, we will cross. There are jobs on the other side, and we can make more money than here. There will always be jobs that no American wants that a Mexican will perform with much happiness.

*Ismael Medina, a Mexican laborer, explaining why illegal immigration will continue despite the new law, quoted in Stockton, "Mexicans Expecting No Good of Immigration Law," New York Times, November 6, 1986, p. A-22.*

[The Immigration and Control Act] will go far to improve the lives of a class of individuals who now must hide in the shadows, without access to any of the benefits of a free and open society. Very soon many of these men and women will be able to step into the sunlight and ultimately, if they choose, they may become Americans.

*President Reagan commenting on a positive aspect of the Immigration and Control Act, which he signed on November 6, 1986, quoted in Thornton, "Immigration Changes Are Signed into Law," Washington Post, November 7, 1986, p. A-3.*

## Confronting Arms Control

The administration has taken its foot off the brakes of nuclear-arms deployment and is about to press down on the accelerator of nuclear-arms production.

*Speaker of the House Tip O'Neill speaking in reaction to President Reagan's announcement that the United States was abandoning the SALT II agreement, quoted in "The SALT Backlash," Newsweek, June 16, 1986, p. 23.*

At the moment, the Strategic Defense Initiative is a starry vision rather than an actual weapons program. It exists only in the mind's eye of Ronald Reagan and on the blinking computer screens and slide projectors of an array of purposeful scientists. Yet the president's concept of a space-based shield against nuclear weapons—the most radical plan put forward by any Administration since the dawn of the nuclear age—has become the single most powerful force affecting Soviet-American relations. It is also becoming the chief element in an intensifying showdown, within the Administration as well as at the bargaining table in Geneva, over the future of arms control.

*Examining the impact and future of the Strategic Defense Initiative, in "Star Wars at the Crossroads," Time, June 23, 1986, p. 16.*

. . . Since there are reasons to question whether SDI is scientifically feasible or strategically wise, restricting the program to research in exchange for significant reductions in the most threatening Soviet weapons could be the deal of the century.

Because of his awesome political strength, Reagan is in a unique position to cut that deal with the Kremlin and win the approval of Congress. But to do so, he will require not only the luck and acumen he has already demonstrated in such abundance but also a clearer understanding than he has shown to date of both the risks and opportunities he faces as a result of SDI. He will also need a firmer ability to control the unruly, ideologically divided bureaucracy over which he presides.

*Essayist Strobe Talbott assessing President Reagan's position in arms talks, in Talbott, "Grand Compromise," Time, June 23, 1986, p. 22.*

"Why is he [Gorbachev] so against SDI?" the President asked to no one in particular as he settled into a big armchair in the corner.

"For two reasons." I spoke before anyone else could respond. "First, they have vested massive resources in their own SDI program over the past fifteen years, far more than we have. They've found there's something to it. The 'something' there is [that] it can be done better by us than by them, since SDI plays into our strength, high-tech, rather than their strength, brute military force. Second, SDI represents a strategic end run. Rather than matching their new missiles with our new missiles—their SS-24 with our MX, their SS-25 with our Midgetman—SDI discounts the importance of these missiles altogether."

The President still looked miffed. He thought of SDI as apple pie. Everyone should want it, it's good

Grim and tired, Ronald Reagan and Mikhail Gorbachev leave Hofdi House in Reykjavík, their summit concluded, on October 12, 1986. *(Courtesy Ronald Reagan Library)*

for everyone. It's protection. The rest of this stuff is destruction.

> *Kenneth Adelman, director of the Arms Control and Disarmament Agency (1983–88), describing an October 12, 1986, conference with President Reagan and his negotiating team in Reykjavík, Iceland, just prior to the breakdown of talks with Mikhail Gorbachev; in Adelman,* The Great Universal Embrace *(1989), p. 72.*

He wanted language that would have killed SDI. The price was high but I wouldn't sell and that's how the day ended. All our people thought I'd done exactly right. I'd pledged I wouldn't give away SDI and I didn't, but that meant no deal on any of the arms reductions. He tried to act jovial but I was mad and showed it. Well,

the ball is now in his court and I'm convinced he'll come around when he sees how the world is reacting.

> *Ronald Reagan's diary entry for October 12, 1986, expressing his frustration with Soviet leader Mikhail Gorbachev after the Reykjavík summit ended in a stalemate, in Reagan,* An American Life *(1990), p. 679.*

But there is the other side of Ronald Reagan, the believer in dreams. He attaches himself to some visions so strongly that no facts can shake him off. Mounting deficits have not shaken his belief in the miracle of drastic tax cuts. And almost alone he believes in the early perfectibility of his Strategic Defense Initiative.

It was over that dream that Reykjavík broke down. The President could not see the realistic basis of the

President Reagan speaks at the Brandenberg Gate in West Berlin on June 12, 1987. *(Courtesy Ronald Reagan Library)*

Soviet fear that a technological breakthrough on S.D.I. could turn all of space into an armory of new *offensive* weapons.

> *Columnist Anthony Lewis looking at one of the reasons for the breakdown of the Reykjavík summit, in Lewis, "Reagan's Dream,"* New York Times, *October 16, 1986, p. A-31.*

Gorbachev insisted that "it would have taken a madman" to accept Reagan's position on Star Wars. "The United States came to this meeting with empty hands," he said at a news conference. "The president of the United States did not have permission to reach agreement, and the talks collapsed."

> *Describing Mikhail Gorbachev's position on the failure of the Reykjavík summit, in "Deadlock in Iceland,"* Newsweek, *October 20, 1986, p. 20.*

While we pursue these arms reductions, I pledge to you that we will maintain the capacity to deter Soviet aggression at any level at which it might occur. And in cooperation with many of our allies, the United States is pursuing the Strategic Defense Initiative research to base deterrence not on the threat of offensive retaliation, but on defenses that truly defend; on systems, in short, that will not target populations, but shield them. By these means we seek to increase the safety of Europe and all the world. But we must remember a crucial fact: East and West do not mistrust each other because we are armed; we are armed because we mistrust each other. And our differences are not about weapons but about liberty.

> *Ronald Reagan making his position clear in his speech at the Brandenburg Gate, Berlin, on June 12, 1987. Available online. URL: http://www.reagan.utexas. edu/resource/speeches/1987/061287d.htm.*

For everyone, and, above all, for our two great powers, the treaty whose text is on this table offers a big chance at last to get onto the road leading away from the threat of catastrophe. It is our duty to take full advantage of that chance and move together toward a nuclear-free world, which holds out for our children and grandchildren the promise of a fulfilling and happy life without fear and without a senseless waste of resources on weapons of mass destruction. . . . May December 8, 1987 become a date that will be inscribed in history books, a date that will mark the watershed separating the era of a mounting risk of nuclear war from the era of a demilitarization of human life.

*Mikhail Gorbachev's remarks preceding the signing of the INF treaty on December 8, 1987, quoted in Reagan,* An American Life *(1990), p. 699.*

After the hoopla, Reagan and Gorbachev met for their private discussions which became their least interesting summit talks. Much of their time was spent congratulating one another; the rest was spent misunderstanding each other.

On SDI, Gorbachev was uncommonly calm. His sense of determination, if not desperation, on SDI had dissipated if not disappeared. Gorbachev adopted a Californian (or Siberian) laid-back posture about it all. He told American officials that his prior virulent opposition had only raised U.S. support for SDI.

He was right, even if late. Gorbachev, renowned for his quick grasp, was an appallingly slow learner on this. Years before he should have shrugged off SDI as a visionary mission bound to fail. . . .

*Kenneth Adelman, chief American arms negotiator, commenting on the aftermath of the signing of the INF Treaty on December 8, 1987, in Adelman,* The Great Universal Embrace *(1989), p. 225.*

## Reagan and the Court

He has opposed busing and the right to abortion; he has fought expanded constitutional protection for blacks, women, criminal defendants and the news media. He has voted to allow religious exercises in public schools, for state aid to parochial schools and for nativity scenes in city parks. At the same time, Rehnquist has worked to limit access to the federal courts for those who object to such practices, as well as for those challenging presidential authority or controversial actions of federal administrative agencies.

Rehnquist has done these things in the belief, voiced consistently, that the role of the Supreme Court should be extremely limited, that it should restrain itself from intervening in the business of state and federal government and that the Constitution should be interpreted narrowly, and rarely.

*Journalist Fred Barbash examining the conservative credentials of William Rehnquist, President Reagan's nominee for chief justice of the Supreme Court, in Barbash, "Utterly Consistent in Conservative Votes and Opinions,"* Washington Post, *June 18, 1986, p. A-1.*

[Antonin] Scalia is an intellectual in a way that [Warren] Burger is not: by training and inclination, Scalia has taught at several of the finest law schools. He has the theoretical turn of mind that deepens analytical powers and does not dispose a judge to try to split all differences. That disposition can make intellectuals ineffective politicians but forceful judges. With Scalia leavening the court, it may be less inclined to torture itself, and all who love logic, with ever-more-baroque criteria for distinguishing permissible from impermissible "race-conscious" state action.

*Columnist George F. Will assessing Supreme Court nominee Antonin Scalia, in Will, "The Court: These Two Will Have Impact,"* Washington Post, *June 19, 1986, p. A-25.*

You are trading a vote by Burger for a guy who has a far better brain, endless energy and a total commitment to the job. Rehnquist and Scalia write very well, are very likeable and are bright as hell. The impact will be considerable.

*Professor Gerald Gunther of Stanford University giving a positive appraisal of William Rehnquist and Antonin Scalia, quoted in "Reagan Justice,"* Newsweek, *June 30, 1986, p. 15.*

Presidents come and go regularly, but there have been only 15 Chief Justices in the past 200 years. Some have been nonentities, many mere caretakers. But a few—most notably John Marshall, Charles Evan Hughes and Earl Warren—have played a vanguard role in determining what justice and equality mean in an evolving democratic society. For better or worse, Justice Rehnquist has the vision and the sureness of purpose to redefine the Constitution radically. The question is whether, given his powers of persuasion and collegial style, he will be able, with the aid of his new associate Scalia, to win the struggle for the soul of the Court.

*Looking at the Supreme Court's future if William Rehnquist is confirmed as chief justice, in "Reagan's Mr. Right," Time, June 30, 1986, p. 33.*

At the confirmation hearings, Sen. Edward Kennedy called the likely chief justice an "extremist." Kennedy is entitled to his views, but extremism, as Barry Goldwater once maintained in a different context, is hardly a vice. Indeed, if over the years either the court or society had substantially moved Rehnquist's way, his "extremism" would be praiseworthy. After all, abolitionists were once extremists, but today there would be nothing extreme about their views—unless, of course, you happen to think slavery is a good idea.

But Rehnquist's extremism, if that is what it is, is hardly prescient. It does not foreshadow the future, but instead reiterates the past. . . .

*Columnist Richard Cohen taking issue with chief justice nominee William Rehnquist, in Cohen, "Rehnquist's 'Brilliance,'" Washington Post, August 7, 1986, p. A-23.*

Bork's occasional contrariness shouldn't mislead anyone about what kind of a justice he is likely to be. He is confident of his vision of the law, and in his view, that vision compels him to depart from established means of judging to expunge what he calls "corrupt" constitutional law.

When Bork resolves the tension between a legal principle and some political expediency, he often rejects the techniques of restrained reasoning to bring about a conservative political result. Since he has weighed in on the Reagan side in almost every social controversy whose outcome will be determined by his rise to the court, especially abortion (he regularly calls the *Roe* decision "unconstitutional"), it is easy to argue that Bork's conservative politics have dictated his expedient choices, and that the main role principle has played in his judgments is an after-the-fact rationalization.

*Author Lincoln Caplan analyzing Supreme Court nominee Robert Bork, in Caplan, "If Robert Bork Didn't Exist, Reagan Would Have to Invent Him," Washington Post, July 5, 1987, p. D-2.*

Perhaps the most striking aspect of Judge Bork's writings and speeches since the late 1960's is his vehement denunciation, repeated over many years, of Supreme Court decisions representing much of the legal evolution since the 1920's.

In a 1982 speech, he said a "large proportion" of the "most significant constitutional decisions of the past three decades" could not have been reached through legitimate means of constitutional interpretation.

Over the years, he has used epithets like "unconstitutional," "illegitimate," "utterly specious," "pernicious" and "judicial imperialism" to describe dozens of Supreme Court decisions expanding the rights of individuals and minority groups.

*Journalist Stuart Taylor, Jr., looking at the judicial philosophy of Supreme Court nominee Robert Bork, in Taylor, "Activism vs. Restraint: The Complex Philosophy of Judge Bork," New York Times, September 13, 1987, sec. 1, p. 36.*

It is, to say no more, unsatisfying to be the target of a campaign that must of necessity be one-sided, a campaign in which the "candidate," a sitting Federal judge, is prevented by the plain standards of his profession from becoming an energetic participant.

Were the fate of Robert Bork the only matter at stake, I would ask the President to withdraw my nomination.

The most serious and lasting injury in all of this, however, is not to me. Nor is it to all of those who have steadfastly supported my nomination and to whom I am deeply grateful. Rather, it is to the dignity and integrity of law and of public service in this country.

I therefore wish to end the speculation. There should be a full debate and a final Senate decision. In deciding on this course, I harbor no illusions.

*Robert Bork announcing that he will fight on even though the Senate Judiciary Committee voted not to recommend his appointment to the Supreme Court, quoted in "Bork Gives Reasons for Continuing Fight," New York Times, October 16, 1987, p. 13.*

When the President nominated him two weeks ago, Ginsburg assured his audience that he was looking forward to the confirmation process. Given the gauntlet that Bork had just run, the statement seemed gracious but a little naïve. Given what is now known about Ginsburg, it was foolhardy. In the wake of withdrawal, few were talking publicly about the long-range implications of the embarrassment. A lame-duck President who has been buffeted by scandal, a stock-market crash and the bruising defeat of his first court nominee could ill afford this latest fiasco.

*Looking at the repercussions of Douglas Ginsburg's nomination for the Supreme Court followed closely by his withdrawal from consideration, in "Sins of the Past,"* Time, *November 16, 1987, p. 20.*

Nevertheless, and in spite of what seems to be a widespread feeling of relief that this nomination is not already certain to result in conflict, it is too soon to say that confirmation is a foregone conclusion. It probably never will be anymore. The ground rules for the confirmation of a Supreme Court justice have changed. Judge Kennedy has been on the Ninth Circuit Court of Appeals for more than a decade. He has written many opinions and they will now be reread. His personal life will be examined in minute detail, and every facet of his judicial philosophy, his experience and his character will be explored. No more all-but-automatic confirmations, it seems. That's reasonable, but it is also reasonable to suggest that even a judge is entitled to due process. The marijuana question has, of course, already been asked—no, Judge Kennedy has never even had a puff.

*From a* Washington Post *editorial on the nomination of Anthony Kennedy to the Supreme Court, "Again, a Nominee for the Court,"* Washington Post, *November 12, 1987, p. A-22.*

Nobody knows what kind of Supreme Court justice Anthony Kennedy would make, but his opinions and the estimates of his colleagues give reason to believe he has an attractive openness of mind.

There's an attractive turn, also, in the spirit of this nomination. Mr. Reagan observed that everyone had learned something from the Bork fight, and he has abandoned the pugnacity of the Ginsburg nomination. His third choice vindicates the moderation of his chief of staff, Howard Baker, over the endless partisanship of Attorney General Edwin Meese.

*The* New York Times *expressing approval for the Supreme Court nomination of Anthony Kennedy, in its editorial "After the Storm over the Court,"* New York Times, *December 14, 1987, p. A-22.*

## AIDS Hitting Home

We must face sex in a realistic way. This is no longer the free-love '60s; it's the fear-of-AIDS '80s.

*Dr. Vicki Hufnagel, a Los Angeles gynecologist pointing out a new fact of life, quoted in "Women and AIDS,"* Newsweek, *July 14, 1986, p. 61.*

Talking about sex needs to be less taboo. Then safe sex may become part of life, and not so unpleasant and clinical. The whole ritual of courting needs to be reinstated. We can think about this as an opportunity to put "our" back into romance and foreplay.

*Venita Porter, director of Rhode Island Project AIDS, on the need to change sexual attitudes, quoted in Dunning, "Women and AIDS: Discussing Precautions,"* New York Times, *November 3, 1986, p. C-15.*

There is now no doubt that we need sex education in schools and that it includes information on heterosexual and homosexual relationships. The threat of AIDS should be sufficient to permit a sex education curriculum with a heavy emphasis on prevention of AIDS and other sexually transmitted diseases.

*From the 36-page report on AIDS issued by Surgeon General C. Everett Koop, quoted in "A Most Explicit Report,"* Time, *November 3, 1986, p. 76.*

[The National Academy of Sciences] study urged Ronald Reagan to make controlling AIDS "a major national goal." But the White House last week reserved comment on the panel's conclusions, and the president's aides seemed to doubt that Reagan would give AIDS the same kind of personal attention he has given to drug abuse. "Frankly, I don't have a clue what we're going to do, if anything," said one—and another, asked whether there would be direct involvement by Reagan himself, said, "I don't see that." Reagan, who has made very few public comments on the AIDS crisis, seems somehow squeamish on the issue.

*Reporting the lack of administration reaction to a major report from the National Academy of Sciences about the AIDS crisis, in "AIDS: Grim Prospects,"* Newsweek, *November 10, 1986, p. 21.*

As is often the case, the sins committed against a minority take a toll on the majority as well. That is true both in civil liberties and in public health. With AIDS the two merge. An administration that has been loathe to stand up for the civil liberties of homosexuals has been equally loath to offer the scientific community either the leadership or the money it needs to fight a disease that is killing homosexuals. Presumably, it was waiting for the infectious spread of celibacy.

*Columnist Richard Cohen commenting on the paucity of federal support for the fight against AIDS, in Cohen, "AIDS: Victims Twice Over," Washington Post, November 25, 1986, p. A-21.*

What our citizens must know is this: America faces a disease that is fatal and spreading. And this calls for urgency, not panic. It calls for compassion, not blame. And it calls for understanding, not ignorance. It's also important that America not reject those who have the disease, but care for them with dignity and kindness. Final judgment is up to God; our part is to ease the suffering and to find a cure. This is a battle against disease, not against our fellow Americans. We mustn't allow those with the AIDS virus to suffer discrimination. I agree with Secretary of Education Bennett: We must firmly oppose discrimination against those who have AIDS. We must prevent the persecution, through ignorance or malice, of our fellow citizens.

*Ronald Reagan in a speech at the American Foundation for AIDS Research Awards Dinner on May 31, 1987. Available online. URL: http://www.reagan.utexas.edu/resource/speeches/1987/053187a.htm.*

The President's remarks were one of several dramatic expressions in the capital last week of the intense national debate over a key issue involving AIDS control: mandatory testing. Reagan drew boos and hisses during a May 31 speech at a private AIDS fund-raising dinner when he urged "routine" testing of inmates in federal prisons and patients in Veterans Administration hospitals. He also asked that all foreigners seeking residence visas be screened for exposure to the virus and strongly encouraged states to test marriage-license applicants.

*Looking at the Reagan administration's unpopular policy on the AIDS crisis, in "At Last, the Battle Is Joined," Time, June 15, 1987, p. 56.*

## Televangelic Embarrassment

I'm asking you to help extend my life. We're at the point where God could call Oral Roberts home in March.

*Televangelist Oral Roberts on a January 4, 1987, broadcast in which he pleaded for more cash donations to save his ministry, quoted in "Your Money or His Life," Time, January 26, 1987, p. 63.*

Some experts on evangelism and television ministries said the week of turmoil would take its toll in the way people viewed these ministries. "It's not going to destroy individual ministries as such, but the immediate impact on all of them will be significant," said Jeffrey Hadden, a professor of sociology at University of Virginia who wrote the book "Prime Time Preachers."

Mr. Hadden said the events of recent days would feed the "Elmer Gantry image" that many people had of television evangelists, although he said the audiences of individual ministers would probably not be affected.

*Looking at the effect of the Jim Bakker and Oral Roberts controversies on television ministries, in Toner, "Preacher's Battle Transfixing the South," New York Times, March 26, 1987, p. A-16.*

The scandal has left the entire evangelical community in disarray. Some PTL contributors were understandably disillusioned to discover that part of their donations may have been used to hush up sexual shenanigans on the part of their preacher. [Jerry] Falwell thinks the damage spreads farther. "It would be dishonest for me to say this is not a blow to the cause of Christ," he said. "We've taken a broadside." Still, if anyone is to benefit from the mess, it is Falwell. The conservative minister is taking a risk by subsuming the flashy PTL, but the move also strengthens his position as televangelism's senior statesman. And the Moral Majority leader could use Bakker's TV facilities for his syndicated "Old Time Gospel Hour."

*Examining the impact of the Jim Bakker scandal on televangelism, in "Paying the Wages of Sin," Newsweek, March 30, 1987, p. 28.*

Evangelical Protestantism, America's great folk faith, is usually as plain and decent as a clapboard chapel, but on occasion it can turn as raucous and disorderly as a frontier camp meeting. Over the past two weeks sweet order has fled, seemingly overwhelmed by hot words and rackety confusion. Perhaps not since famed Pentecostal Preacher Aimee Semple McPherson was accused of faking her own kidnaping in the Roaring Twenties has the nation witnessed a spectacle to compare with the lurid adultery-and-hush-money scandal that has forced a husband-and-wife team of televangelists, Jim and Tammy Bakker, to abandon their multimillion-dollar spiritual empire and seek luxurious refuge in Palm Springs, Calif.

*From the beginning of a report on the televangelism scandals, in "TV's Unholy Row," Time, April 6, 1987, p. 60.*

No, the more serious indictment of the Bakkers is Mr. Falwell's: "The greed, the self-centeredness, the avarice that brought them down." To which might fairly be added: "The deceit of preaching the gospel while fleecing the poor."

Those are ample reasons why the Bakkers have no right whatever to be restored by Mr. Falwell or anyone else to PTL, their so-called "ministry"—which appears to have been devoted mostly to money-changing in the temple.

*Columnist Tom Wicker arguing against the idea that Jim and Tammy Bakker be allowed to resume their television ministry, in Wicker, "A Ministry of Loot," New York Times, May 30, 1987, p. 31.*

It is not difficult to discern why many contributors are becoming edgy about secretive and sensationalistic televangelism empires. Asks McKendree R. Langley in *Eternity*, a respected evangelical news monthly: "Wouldn't it be a step in the right direction for TV preachers to cut back on financial appeals, end outrageous claims of having direct pipelines to God, reaffirm by example of modest life-styles, demonstrate deeper biblical spirituality and articulate a Christian worldview?" That sound you hear is an army of embarrassed Christians shouting "Amen!"

*Examining the impact of the Bakker PTL scandal on public attitudes toward televangelists, in "Of God and Greed," Time, June 8, 1987, p. 74.*

## Vigilantism

I don't think the social issues are going to be settled by this trial, if that's what people are looking for. In New York, you're still not allowed the right to defend yourself.

*Bernhard Goetz commenting on his case, about to go to trial two years after he shot some black youths in a subway car, quoted in Johnson, "Goetz Case, Back in Court Today, Is Still Legal Puzzle After 2 Years," New York Times, March 23, 1987, p. B-7.*

To the judge, Acting Justice Stephen G. Crane, this is "one of the most difficult criminal cases of our generation." To [Defense Attorney Barry I.] Slotnick, "the four muggers got exactly what the law allowed." To [Prosecutor Gregory L.] Waples, "the right to be concerned for your safety does not necessarily imply the right to lash out in very ambiguous circumstances, or to

go further and actually take the offense, to become the aggressor, and try to kill four human beings."

And for the jurors, carefully drawn questions about the reasonable person's judgment may come down to the question: "What would I have done?"

*Journalist E. R. Shipp examining the complexities of the Bernhard Goetz case, in Shipp, "Gauging Reasonability in the Goetz Case," New York Times, May 31, 1987, sec. 4, p. 7.*

Is society safer when a jury sanctions gunfire in the confines of a subway car? What encouragement might an unhinged mind find in this case? What bloodshed might result from the belief that a gleam in the eye warrants deadly self-defense? Those fears weigh powerfully against those of potential victims. Where lies the proper balance?

*The New York Times posing some troubling questions after Bernhard Goetz is acquitted of all but gun-possession charges, in its editorial "The Other Goetz Jury," New York Times, June 17, 1987, p. A-30.*

I think he was just a scared person. Considering the point in time and the place he was at, he probably did the right thing. Like in any large city, your life is more or less, on a daily basis, in jeopardy. New York's a breeding ground for muggings, not like in a little town.

*Terry Wolfe, an African-American retired military officer from St. Roberts, Missouri, offering his viewpoint of Bernhard Goetz, quoted in Gross, "Public's Response to the Jury's Decision: Divided and Deep-Seated Opinions," New York Times, June 18, 1987, p. B-6.*

This was a jury of ordinary people, people who ride the crime-ridden subway and know how things are down there. Six of the twelve had been victims of street crime. Anyone taking a subway ride last week could hear similar views. "I can understand what Goetz did," said Eileen Dudley, a black secretary. "I was held up once. You would do anything in that situation."

*Looking at continuing support for Bernhard Goetz following his acquittal on the most serious charges against him, in " 'Not Guilty'," Time, June 29, 1987, p. 11.*

## Mulroney and Meech Lake

Mulroney deserves credit for trying to accommodate Quebec's demands. It is not healthy for the country to have one province declaring its continuing opposition to the Constitution.

But in offering to surrender its power to spend money wherever it sees fit, the Mulroney government is going too far. Before he meets [Robert] Bourassa and the other nine premiers on Thursday, Mulroney should think again.

*The* Toronto Star *criticizing Brian Mulroney's willingness to accede to a Quebec demand limiting federal spending power, in its editorial "Drawing the Line on the Constitution,"* Toronto Star, *April 28, 1987, p. A-10.*

Quebec nationalism will always exist. It could be revived in any of various forms, depending on the circumstances. . . . In five, 10 or 20 years, it could take a new turn that I can't see today.

This is why we can never take for granted that Canada will always be what it is. We could rest on our laurels and say that we've come far enough, that the problem has been settled, that we should move on to other things. No, I say! Our cultural and linguistic reality must always be borne in mind by federal and provincial legislators.

*Prime Minister Brian Mulroney commenting on Quebec nationalism prior to constitutional talks in Meech Lake, quoted in Fraser, "Outlook Unsettled for Talks on Constitution,"* Globe and Mail *(Montreal), April 30, 1987, p. A-8.*

Someone last night sold the house of Quebec, and he sold it at market value.

*Pierre Marc Johnson, leader of the Parti Québecois, criticizing Quebec premier Robert Bourassa for his role in the Meech Lake Accord, quoted in Marotte, "Bourassa Is Selling Out Quebec, Johnson Charges,"* Globe and Mail *(Montreal), May 2, 1987, p. A-5.*

Fifty-three years of constitutional wrangling had finally come to an end.

The technicalities of what the first ministers achieved this week will probably never be clear to most Canadians. They don't matter. But the pride and patriotism that enveloped the Meech Lake conference centre would have been clear to any Canadian. They do matter. They are the real ingredients of nation-building.

*National affairs correspondent Carol Goar putting a positive gloss on the Meech Lake Accord, in Goar, "Constitution: Last Piece in Place,"* Toronto Star, *May 2, 1987, p. B-1.*

Those Canadians who fought for a single Canada . . . can say goodbye to their dream: We are henceforth to have two Canadas, each defined in terms of its language.

*Former Canadian prime minister Pierre Trudeau voicing his opposition to the Meech Lake Accord, quoted in Denton, "Trudeau Emphatically Ends Silence,"* Washington Post, *May 29, 1987, p. A-28.*

Mr. Trudeau's outburst is hard to understand. It was his impassioned federalism that helped provoke a separatist reaction in Quebec, where a party pledged to pulling out of Canada won power in 1975. After bitter argument and a divisive referendum, Quebecers finally rejected separatism, and in 1984 elected a Liberal as provincial premier. But Quebec still rejected the new Canadian Constitution, whose adoption by the Federal Parliament in 1982 was Prime Minister Trudeau's finest hour.

. . . . .

Why did the former Prime Minister switch from initial congratulations to impassioned attack, aligning himself with diehard Quebec separatists? He fears that a Canada weakened at the center will impel Québécois to turn once again to separatism. Maybe so, but it's easy to believe that Mr. Trudeau misses the limelight and finds it unbearable that the caravan somehow proceeds without him.

*The* New York Times *wondering at Pierre Trudeau's motives for speaking out against the Meech Lake Accord, in its editorial "Trudeau the Spoiler,"* New York Times, *June 6, 1987, p. 26.*

Quebec has won one of the greatest victories of her history, one of the greatest political victories in the two centuries of our history. For the first time we have emerged the winners in a constitutional debate. All the provinces have accepted our conditions.

*Quebec premier Robert Bourassa on June 23, 1987, speaking euphorically following the Quebec National Assembly's ratification of the Meech Lake Accord, quoted in McKenzie, "Quebec First to Approve Accord,"* Toronto Star, *June 24, 1987, p. A-1.*

Any constitution should ensure that citizens, irrespective of culture, region or sex, are treated as equals. The Meech Lake accord fails to meet these criteria. We will have instead a Constitution that, to paraphrase the American, will say, in effect: All citizens are created equal, except for some citizens of Quebec who will be more equal than others.

That kind of agreement is the first step in legalizing the dissolution of our country and the elimination of the English language and institutions in Quebec.

*F. K. Kirkman, an English-speaking native of Quebec, offering a common argument against the Meech Lake Accord, in a letter to the editor,* Globe and Mail *(Montreal), June 24, 1987, p. A-7.*

## Black Monday

All the talk of recession and depression, while unsettling, is probably healthy. Since the biggest crashes occur as a result of surprises, nervous discussion may produce some vitally needed preventive measures. The first priority on nearly everyone's list is to halt the U.S. Government's free-spending ways. This will no doubt bring a more modest standard of living in the short run. But it may help America avoid waking up to find frightening headlines in the morning paper a year or two from now.

*Looking at the possibility of trouble on Wall Street, in "How Ripe for a Crash?"* Time, *October 5, 1987, p. 46.*

I've been down here for 30 years. I thought pandemonium set in when John F. Kennedy was assassinated. But I've never seen anything like this. I thought there would be a correction in the market. But this is shocking. There's hysteria and fear. It's absolute fear.

*Joel L. Lovett, a trader for Jaycee Securities, describing the scene on the day the stock market crashed, quoted in Cowan, "Day to Remember in Financial District,"* New York Times, *October 20, 1987, p. D-1.*

If in 1929 the market was telling us to dispel the gathering clouds of protectionism, what is it telling us today? There is of course plenty of protectionism in the air, and congressional pressures for a tax increase; these are certainly part of a worrisome horizon. But we think yesterday's warning shot is about exchange-rate insta-

bility, a possible collapse of the value of the dollar, the vehicle that carries world trade and investment.

*The* Wall Street Journal *examining some possible reasons for the stock market crash in its editorial "In Our Hands,"* Wall Street Journal, *October 20, 1987, p. 38.*

. . . I approve very much of what the exchange is going to do with regard to the next three days. That the market is—trading is going on, in quitting two hours early to give them [a] chance to catch up with their paperwork, which is the reason for that. But, this is, I think, purely a stock market thing and there are no indicators out there of recession or hard times at all.

*President Reagan responding to reporters' questions about the stock market crash in a press conference, October 22, 1987, quoted in "Reagan's News Conference on Domestic and Foreign Matters,"* New York Times, *October 23, 1987, p. A-8.*

In the space of a few days' time, the losses totaled an astonishing $385 billion—on paper. But paper losses can be just as devastating as the real thing, and the truth of the matter is that, in what seemed like just a matter of moments, tens of millions of Americans suddenly *felt* poorer, whether they were or not, and couldn't understand why. . . .

*Analyzing reaction in the wake of the stock market crash, in "Staring into the Abyss,"* U.S. News & World Report, *November 2, 1987, p. 19.*

. . . An economy that was once based on manufacturing might and inventive genius began pursing wealth through mergers and takeovers and the creation of new "financial instruments." Fortunes were conjured out of thin air by fresh-faced traders who created nothing more than paper—gilded castles in the sky held aloft by red suspenders.

So when the fall came, so did a few smirks, along with jokes about yuppie brokers losing their BMWs. But mainly the reaction was personal: What did the crash mean for me, my pension, my mortgage, my business, my job, my tuition bills? Most of the momentous events that splash their headlines for history can be viewed dispassionately from afar. Not a Wall Street panic, however, not even for those who don't play the market.

*Columnist Walter Isaacson putting the stock market crash in perspective, in Isaacson, "After the Fall,"* Time, *November 2, 1987, pp. 20–21.*

# 7

# Beginning of the End
## January 1988–January 1989

Ronald Reagan entered the final year of his presidency on the verge of achieving something not seen since Dwight D. Eisenhower: two full terms in office. He had survived an assassination attempt and, defying predictions of his downfall, was surviving the Iran–contra scandal. Reaganomics had unquestionably had a major effect on the country, but whether it was for good or ill was still being debated. The United States was more dominant in the world than ever, from its lead in science, technology, and communications; from the emergence of a global marketplace, expanding the reach of American business; and from Reagan's hard-line foreign and defense policies.

The country itself was changing. The median age of Americans was now 32.1, exceeding 32 for the first time in history. By 1987 the number living on farms had reached its lowest level since before the Civil War. The nation's Hispanic population had risen by 34 percent since 1980, reaching some 19.4 million by March 1988. Births were approaching 4 million a year, the highest rate since 1964. Yet this did not affect the increasing role and importance of working women: By June 1988 more than half of all new mothers were staying in the job market; the figure was 63 percent for those with college degrees.[1]

Even as insider-trading scandals emphasized the perils of greed, the rush to acquire wealth and possessions continued unabated. Cable television, VCRs, computers, compact discs—these and other technological wonders were becoming commonplace, and consequent consumer debt was on the rise. People no longer waited until they could afford a new home, a new car, or the latest gadget, running up credit card bills at an ever-faster pace. The desire to have more and have it now had become a worrying trend, but even more alarming was a rise in drug use, leading the government to declare a "war on drugs."

The country was abandoning the attitudes that had shaped its thinking since 1945, and as Reagan's presidency neared its end, it became clear that the cold war was ending as well. New dangers had taken its place: AIDS, drugs, and terrorism, among other major concerns. The United States had become stronger—but it had also become a more complicated and uncertain place in which to live.

## AIDS and the Nation

Throughout 1988, the struggle against AIDS took different forms. Statistics underlined the urgency for a cure or at least some way of slowing the disease's spread: 71,751 cases of AIDS had been reported to the World Health Organization by the end of 1987, of which a frightening preponderance—47,022—were in the United States.[2] According to figures from the National Centers for Disease Control, 38,897 Americans had died of AIDS between June 1981 and July 1988.

The Reagan administration, long criticized for its dilatory response, finally began to appreciate the significance of the escalating crisis. In February 1988 the president's proposed budget for fiscal 1989 included $1.3 billion for AIDS programs, a 37 percent increase over the $951 million appropriated for 1988. Not only did this exceed the original request from the Department of Health and Human Services, the proposed budget also included $700 million for AIDS-related programs outside the Public Health Service, bringing the total appropriation to $2 billion. Though this was an improvement, critics still felt it was insufficient.

Later in February, Admiral James D. Watkins, chairman of the Presidential Commission on the Human Immunodeficiency Virus Epidemic, issued a preliminary report of the commission's conclusions and—like Surgeon General C. Everett Koop the previous year—became headline news for his forthright stance. When the president created the commission in June 1987, most expected little from it, believing that Reagan was simply paying lip service to his critics. The commission itself got off to a poor start and was widely criticized for having few physicians or scientists with experience in AIDS and for including conservatives who opposed AIDS education. There was much internal dissent and lack of direction until Admiral Watkins took over from the original chairman in fall 1987 and worked tirelessly to meet the commission's aim of formulating recommendations for a federal AIDS policy. The results surprised those who were expecting little from a Reagan appointee. In addition to demonstrating a comprehensive appreciation of the medical, scientific, and social aspects of the disease, Watkins denounced the government's weak response to the emergency and recommended that billions of dollars be allotted to health care and hospice programs. AIDS activists applauded him for his emphasis on measures to counter the rampant, nationwide discrimination against HIV-positive individuals.

The Watkins Commission report—issued in its final form in June 1988—did much to counter criticism of the presidential AIDS policy. However, Reagan continued to neglect both the problem and his commission's recommendations, as did his successor, George Bush. On the positive side, millions of copies of the Koop-written booklet *Understanding AIDS* were distributed throughout the country, improving public awareness, and the U.S. government banned discrimination against HIV-positive federal workers, the result of a 1987 Supreme Court ruling, *School Board of Nassau County, Fla. v. Arline.*

Meanwhile, research was intensifying. On May 13 the government announced the results of a year-long trial of azidothymidine (AZT). With 84.5 percent of 144 people still living after receiving the drug, it seemed that AZT could prolong patients' lives, news that raised hopes of an effective treatment if not a cure. There was also a growing number of HIV-positive patients who were surviving for no apparent medical reason. Notwithstanding such reassuring news, many experts remained skeptical that AIDS could ever be conquered.

One controversial attempt to control the epidemic's spread centered on drug users, whose high rate of HIV infection was largely attributable to many addicts sharing needles and thus transferring contaminated blood. In 1986 San Francisco officials had considered but rejected providing free, clean needles to addicts. In 1988, however, New York and other cities introduced pilot needle-exchange programs in an attempt to contain the epidemic. The plan's major drawback was obvious: When drug abuse and drug-related crime were matters of major national concern, providing free needles was viewed as encouraging illegal activity. But many felt the crisis justified such action.

While doctors and scientists concentrated on treating the disease and government and public health officials bickered over how to respond to the crisis, organizations such as ACT UP (AIDS Coalition to Unleash Power, established in 1987) continued to be most effective in educating the public on the seriousness of the epidemic. These groups used marches, demonstrations, graphic posters, ads, and more to get their message across, sometimes arousing hostility and controversy. Books, plays, movies, and television programs also kept the disease in the forefront of the public consciousness. But it was an unlikely event that captured the nation's attention in 1988.

In San Francisco, gay rights activist Cleve Jones envisioned a patchwork quilt, with panels paying tribute to those who had died of AIDS. In 1986 he created the first panel in memory of his friend Marvin Feldman, and the following year he and other activists organized the NAMES Project Foundation. When word got out, people from all over the country responded, sending handmade panels commemorating a loved one lost to AIDS. Volunteers worked long hours assembling the AIDS Memorial Quilt, which was first displayed on October 11, 1987, in Washington, D.C., during the National March on Washington for Lesbian and Gay Rights. Spread out on the National Mall, the quilt included 1,920

The NAMES Project AIDS quilt hangs from the ceiling and is laid out on the floor at UCLA's Pauley Pavilion, Los Angeles, on April 7, 1988. *(AP/Wide World Photos)*

panels and was larger than a football field. More than 500,000 people viewed it that weekend, and public response was so great that a 20-city national tour was planned for 1988.

The quilt grew, and by the time it left San Francisco in April 1988, it consisted of 3,488 panels made of everything from burlap to naugahyde. When it returned to Washington in October, there were 8,288 panels covering 8 acres when laid out. Reporter George Raine noted: "It weighs 16 tons. It contains 298,366 feet, or about 57 miles, of seams. The canvas edging measures 59,052 feet. There are 37,660 grommets. Fifty states are represented, as are 12 other nations."[3]

On October 8, 1988, with the quilt laid out on the Ellipse in front of the White House, Cleve Jones began to read the names of those it commemorated. The reading was taken up by others and lasted for 10 hours; even then the participants had covered only a fraction of the total dead from AIDS.

The AIDS Memorial Quilt continued to grow, and by 1992 it included panels from 28 countries. A book on the project was first published in May 1988, and a movie, *Common Threads: Stories from the Quilt,* won the Academy Award for best feature-length documentary in 1989, the same year the quilt was nominated for a Nobel Peace Prize. Last displayed in its entirety on Washington's National Mall in October 1996, it is the largest community art project in the world. The quilt has raised millions of dollars for AIDS research and education, making it a powerful symbol of sympathy and understanding.

## HISPANIC INFLUX AND INFLUENCE

The idea of the United States as a giant melting pot has often been disparaged as a fallacy since many immigrants tend to retain their national characteristics while adapting to life in a new country. Yet the United States has absorbed and adopted many of its newer citizens' cultural traits, giving credence to the melting pot theory. This has been particularly true of the Hispanic population, which increased significantly throughout the 1980s and was, by 1988, exerting a powerful influence on U.S. culture. Latinos (Latin Americans) and Chicanos (Mexican Americans) were everywhere, it seemed, and their presence was reflected in business, politics, education, music, cinema, literature—even in food.

Hispanic influence had always been strong in the Southwest, due both to history and to legal and illegal immigration across the Mexican border. Other populations were established in urban areas: New York City became the center for migrants from Puerto Rico, and Miami attracted those from Cuba escaping Fidel Castro's totalitarian regime. In 1980, however, the pattern began to change when the Refugee Act was passed, quickly followed by Cubans fleeing their homeland and flooding American shores in the Mariel boat lift that summer. The decade's early years also saw a steep rise in the number of immigrants from Central and South America, due primarily to the establishment of Marxist regimes there (sometimes leading to U.S. intervention, as in Nicaragua).

Mexico was—and continues to be—the source of the largest numbers of U.S. immigrants, many of them illegal, making it almost impossible for the U.S. Census Bureau to count its Spanish-speaking citizens accurately. The Immigration Reform and Control Act of 1986 made some progress in stemming (although not stopping) the growing wave of illegal immigration, which in turn enabled census officials to get a clearer picture of actual numbers of Latinos and Chicanos in the country. Consequently, the recorded figure of persons of Hispanic descent in the United States rose from an estimated 14.5 million in 1980 to 19.4 million as of March 1988—a 34 percent increase, as compared to a 7 percent increase for non-Hispanics in the same period. In 1987–88 alone, the Hispanic population rose by 3 percent, due to both immigration and a rapidly growing birth rate.

In 1964 migration from the Americas had accounted for 44.3 percent of the total documented immigration to the United States; by 1989 this would rise to 61.4 percent, with Hispanic Americans forming almost 8 percent of the nation's population. More significantly, between 1980 and 1988, the number of Hispanics in the workforce increased by 48 percent, representing 30 percent of U.S. employment growth.[4]

Such statistics helped to explain why the Latino and Chicano influence was being felt in so many areas. Hit movies such as *La Bamba* (1987), *Born in East L.A.* (1987), and *Stand and Deliver* (1988) highlighted the growing role of Hispanics in American life. The arts especially provided a long roll call of talent, from actors (Edward James Olmos, Maria Conchita Alonso) to singers (Linda Ronstadt, Lisa Velez) to writers (Carlos Fuentes, Richard Rodriguez) to show-biz stars (choreographer Kenny Ortega, playwright-director Luis Valdez) to television personalities (Geraldo Rivera). Hispanic Americans were also making their mark in politics (San Antonio mayor Henry Cisneros, Denver mayor Frederico Peña), government (Secretary of Education Lauro Cavazos), education (Jaime Escalante, Linda Chavez), and business (Coca-Cola chairman Robert Goizueta). With myriad others, they were changing the American landscape of the 1980s.

Hispanic businesses were also on the rise: In 1987 they numbered approximately 340,000, with revenues of about $20 billion; the U.S. Hispanic Chamber of Commerce predicted an increase to $25 billion by 1990. Though these figures represented only a small percentage of total American business, the implications of the growth were significant, especially given the concurrent growth of the global economy. Moreover, as the fastest-growing sector of the population, Hispanics had tremendous purchasing power, exceeding $134 billion in 1987. Consequently, non-Hispanic businesses increasingly courted their Latino and Chicano customers and bought more advertising in the media and on television. Whereas Spanish-language TV networks had been largely ignored just 10 years earlier, 24 of the 25 advertisers on network television bought time in 1988 on Univisión, one of the country's two Spanish-language networks. Such was the growing power of the Hispanic market that Univisión itself was bought by Hallmark Cards for $585 million in February 1988.

Yet, that market was still largely concentrated in just four main areas. When the U.S. Census Bureau released its latest estimates in September 1988, figures showed that 33.9 percent of the country's Hispanics lived in California, and 21.3 percent were in Texas. These two regions together accounted for more than 50 percent of the nation's Hispanic population; 90 percent lived in just nine states, with New York and Florida being home to the greatest numbers after California and Texas. Significantly, these were all key states in the presidential election, so it was no surprise that candidates in 1988 spent much of their time courting the Hispanic vote.

But not all the statistics were favorable. Hispanic Americans were still a minority, and like other minorities, circumstances were often against them. Cuban

Americans in Miami, many of whom had come from middle-class backgrounds, largely fared much better than Latinos of other backgrounds elsewhere. The poorer Puerto Ricans who settled in New York City, for instance, were far more likely to remain in the barrio and far less likely to start a successful business. In 1988 the unemployment rate for Hispanic Americans was 8.5 percent, compared to 5.8 percent for non-Hispanics. The figures on poverty were equally gloomy: A report issued by the Census Bureau on August 31 revealed that although the numbers of white Americans living in poverty had declined, the proportion of poor black and Hispanic Americans had increased. Nationwide, the poverty rate was 13.5 percent, its lowest point since it peaked in 1984 at 15.2 percent; for Hispanic Americans, though, the rate had grown from 27.3 percent in 1986 to 28.2 percent in 1988. More frightening was the finding that 70 percent of Hispanic households headed by women with children were living in poverty.

The depressing implications of such figures, however, seemed to be belied by the ever-increasing Hispanic influence on American culture. By the late 1980s, Latin dances had become the rage, fashions were showing a distinctive Spanish flair, and foods such as tacos and burritos had become staples for innumerable non-Hispanics around the country. In many areas, bilingual education was the norm despite fierce arguments against it, and Spanish as the nation's second language was an increasingly accepted fact of life. In July 1988 a special issue of *Time* magazine examined the "surging new spirit" that such trends were bringing to the country: "With each fresh connection tastes are being rebuilt, new understandings concluded. The American mind is adding a new wing."[5] The melting pot theory had proved a reality.

## CIVIL RIGHTS AND WELFARE REFORM

Civil rights in the 1980s saw both progress and setbacks for other American minorities as well. The battle against injustice occasionally scored notable victories: In 1988 Congress passed a bill to apologize to Japanese Americans who were interned during World War II and pay tax-free compensation of $20,000 each to surviving internees and their families.

American Indians were also making advances in their struggle to achieve equality and win rights that were long overdue. In the 20th century the U.S. government's attitude toward its indigenous citizens had undergone several changes, one of the most drastic being Congress's passage of House Concurrent Resolution No. 108 in 1953. This had terminated federal support to 13 tribes and more than 100 Indian communities between 1954 and 1962 in an effort to "emancipate" them from dependence on government assistance. In some instances, tribes managed to thrive and became self-sufficient, but others suffered severe social and economic declines and sued to reverse the termination. Finally, on April 28, 1988, the Repeal of Termination Act was signed, making it possible to set new guidelines for federal protection of Native American tribes and communities.

Lands seized from American Indians continued to be a major area of dispute, as were sacred sites. Among the setbacks was the April 1988 Supreme Court decision in *Lyng v. Northwest Indian Cemetery Protective Association*. This case centered around the Forest Service's planned construction of a road in northwest California that went through sacred lands and thus impinged upon the freedom of

Northwest Indians to conduct religious practices. Though lower courts had ruled that the Indians' rights superseded the government's interest in building the road, the Supreme Court decided otherwise, noting that the First Amendment provided no protection against any governmental action that affected a sacred site, even if it was destroyed. The disappointment Native Americans felt in this decision was somewhat alleviated on August 27, when, in one of the biggest settlements in U.S. history, the federal government agreed to pay Washington State's Puyallup tribe $162 million in cash, land, and jobs in return for their relinquishing claims to more than $750 million worth of land and buildings in Tacoma. Another important development took place in October, when the Smithsonian returned the skeletal remains of 16 men to the Blackfeet. This was a major step in Native Americans' fight to have museums restore Indian remains and sacred objects to their origins.

On October 17, 1988, President Reagan signed the Indian Gaming Regulatory Act (IGRA) into law. This was the direct result of efforts by some states to regulate or close down American Indian gaming operations that had been established as a way of making money and helping tribal communities. In *California v. Cabazon Band* (1987), the Supreme Court upheld the right of tribes to conduct their operations free of state control as long as gaming was legal in the state. The decision led to Congress's passage of the IGRA, which recognized Indian gaming rights but also required tribes to negotiate with state governments on the gambling to be allowed.

Meanwhile, in 1986 the Mashantucket Pequot had already established a bingo operation on their reservation in Connecticut. The Foxwoods High Stakes Bingo and Resort Casino eventually became one of the state's biggest employers and the largest gaming resort in the country. The success of the Pequot and other nations running gambling concerns has resulted in financial gain for some tribal organizations and major improvements in living conditions for many Native Americans. Though some states continued to demand a more regulatory role and access to the revenues generated by Indian gaming operations, the 1980s saw the country's indigenous peoples at last beginning to participate in the American Dream.

For African Americans the decade produced mixed blessings. Those who achieved prominence included sports stars such as Carl Lewis, Magic Johnson, and Michael Jordan; television personalities such as Oprah Winfrey, Arsenio Hall, and Bill Cosby; movie luminaries such as the controversial director Spike Lee and box-office champion Eddie Murphy; and innumerable musicians and singers, led by the ubiquitous Michael Jackson. In business, politics, and government, black achievements were much slower in coming; only Jesse Jackson enjoyed national name recognition, though increasing numbers of African Americans were having important impacts on their communities.

In contrast were the many African Americans who continued to suffer poverty and discrimination. Integration was still a major concern in many areas of the country, but by the late 1980s, the civil rights movement had largely become a struggle against Reagan administration policies. Of special concern were the president's attempts to dismantle affirmative action, and an epic battle followed the 1984 Supreme Court decision in *Grove City College v. Bell*. The justices' ruling was that Title IX of the Civil Rights Act (1964)—which prohibited federally subsidized educational institutions from engaging in gender discrimination—applied not to entire academic organizations but only to specific programs administered by those institutions that received federal funds. The ruling opened a legal loophole that not only allowed such discrimination but could also encourage challenges to other antidiscriminatory legislation. Consequently, in April 1984 both houses of Congress introduced a bill requiring enforcement of existing antidiscrimination laws on an institution-wide basis, thus closing the loophole.

President Reagan opposed the bill, considering it too broad, and with the Senate then controlled by the Republicans, its defeat was assured. However, after the Democrats took control in November 1986, the bill was reintroduced, and though Reagan lobbied hard against it, the Senate finally passed it on January 28, 1988. In the House, a modified, Reagan-supported version of the bill was promptly rejected, and the original act was passed. Reagan thereupon vetoed the legislation, but both houses overrode his veto, and on March 22 the Civil Rights Restoration Act of 1987 became law.

Closely linked to the civil rights struggle was the issue of welfare. Though there had been an encouraging rise in the numbers of affluent and middle-class black families, the majority of African Americans were still classified as poor. Throughout the country, millions from all ethnic groups lived below the poverty level[6] and existed primarily on welfare. Reagan abhorred entitlement programs, feeling they discouraged people from looking for work. This attitude, along with his attempts to reduce social spending (excepting Social Security and Medicare, which were steadily increased) and turn entitlement responsibilities over to the states, contributed to the perception of Reagan as insensitive to the needs of the poor. Nevertheless, many agreed with him that the welfare system was seriously flawed and in need of reform.

In his last two years in office, Reagan worked with Congress to carry out the most significant restructuring of the welfare system since 1935. The result was the Family Support Act of 1988, signed into law on October 13. This act aimed to get single parents off the welfare rolls and into the workforce by guaranteeing child care and health benefits while they were job hunting and training. The new law also required that after 1994, for two-parent families receiving support from Aid for Families with Dependent Children (AFDC), one parent *must* either get a job or, failing that, participate in a public-works program.

The Family Support Act went some way toward meeting the welfare dilemma, but many problems still existed. Chief among them was the pressure placed on states from the financial burden of social programs once run by the federal bureaucracy, forcing many state governments to raise taxes and make budget cuts in those very programs. The working poor also suffered from generally inferior educations, the growth of high technology calling for specialized skills, and the likelihood that they would be ineligible for health insurance in low-paying jobs. They also did not qualify for such income supplements as food stamps. The incentive to look for work was thus almost nonexistent, making reform doubly difficult. Until an alternative could be found for a system that encouraged capable individuals to stay on welfare rather than find work, it would be a long time before the poor could escape the ghetto of poverty.

## CONTROVERSIAL MATTERS

Civil rights and welfare reform were just two topics sparking debate in the 1980s. Abortion was still a contentious issue, and since 1984 right-to-life movements such as Operation Rescue and Pro-Life Action League had been bombing abortion and birth control facilities. In 1988 they changed tactics and began to blockade clinics, leading to numerous arrests but much publicity. Although the militants succeeded in intimidating patients, doctors, and staff, by 1989 lawsuits filed against them by women's groups were beginning to deplete their financial resources and restrict their activities. Meanwhile, President Reagan continued his personal antiabortion battle, banning federal funding to family-planning clinics that provided abortion assistance.

The decade also saw a renewed crusade against smoking, led by Surgeon General C. Everett Koop, who in 1982 called it the "chief preventable cause of death" in the United States. Cities began to pass laws that restricted smoking in public buildings, and there was a sharp rise in lawsuits against cigarette manufacturers. In May 1988—two months after a federal law banned smoking on domestic air flights of two hours or less went into effect—Koop issued a 682-page report on the hazards of smoking. His claim that nicotine was addictive in the same way as heroin and cocaine caused a sensation. The next month a federal jury found Liggett Group, Inc., the parent company of Liggett & Myers, responsible for the death of Rose Cipollone, a heavy smoker, and awarded her husband $400,000 in damages.[7] Nevertheless, many smokers clung stubbornly to their habit and complained as more antismoking laws were passed. Ironically, 1988 also saw the debut of Camel cigarettes' "Joe Camel," a cartoon character whose appeal to teenagers caused many to accuse the company of enticing young people into smoking.

There was equal concern about education. In April 1988, five years after the Department of Education report *A Nation at Risk* had warned of a "rising tide of mediocrity" in U.S. schools, Secretary of Education William Bennett issued *American Education: Making It Work*. Rating the performance of American schools as "unacceptably low," Bennett said that although some "modest gains" had been achieved, "we are still at risk." His words aroused anger among educators who had tried to implement reforms but were often stymied by bureaucracy and tight budgets. While schools in affluent areas had largely been successful in raising standards, low-income schools, especially those in the inner cities, had neither the teachers nor the resources to make significant improvements.

There were exceptions, of course, and some inner-city educators attracted national notice. These included Jaime Escalante, a math instructor at Los Angeles's Garfield High School whose success with motivating students led to his being called a "teaching genius," and Joe Clark, the principal of Eastside High School in Paterson, New Jersey. When Clark arrived there in 1982, the school had been "crawling with pushers, muggers and just about every other species of juvenile thug."[8] The new principal restored order with a harsh regime that included a dress code, innumerable suspensions and expulsions, chaining doors against drug pushers, and carrying a baseball bat through school halls. His autocratic methods gained him commendations from some, condemnations from others. Among his admirers was William Bennett, who said, "Sometimes you need Mr. Chips, sometimes you need Dirty Harry."[9] Both Clark and Escalante became the subjects of popular movies[10] and symbols of the challenges facing modern teachers.

# BABY M

Of all the controversies attracting attention in the late 1980s, one of the most riveting was a long-running, emotional legal case that culminated in February 1988 with a Solomonic court decision. The issue was surrogacy, a practice that dated back to biblical times but had become commercialized due to recent medical advances. Since 1976, agencies had been matching infertile couples with potential birth mothers, and by 1985 the average fee paid to the surrogate mother—who by contract agreed to relinquish all rights to the child—was $10,000, with the matching agency also receiving a hefty fee.

In February 1985 Mary Beth Whitehead, a 29-year-old married mother of two, contracted with New Jersey biochemist William (Bill) Stern to be inseminated with his sperm; if she conceived, she would carry the baby to term for him and his wife, Elizabeth (Betsy), a pediatrician who claimed to be infertile due to a mild case of multiple sclerosis. The agreement was arranged by attorney Noel Keane, who ran the Infertility Center of New York. Whitehead was picked because of her seemingly genuine desire to help a childless couple. However, Keane failed to tell the Sterns of a psychologist's report questioning whether Mary Beth would be able to give up her baby to them.

The psychologist's concern was well founded: On giving birth to a baby girl on March 27, 1986, Whitehead decided she had made a mistake. After three days—during which she and her husband, Rick, a sanitation-truck driver, filed a birth certificate naming the girl Sara Elizabeth Whitehead and listing Rick as the father—she gave up the baby as agreed. Almost at once, though, she begged to have her daughter back for a little longer; the Sterns, taking pity on her, acceded in the belief that it would be temporary.

When, after two weeks, Mary Beth refused to accept payment or give the child to them, the Sterns obtained a court order and went with police to the Whitehead home to claim Melissa Elizabeth, as they had named her. But Rick fled with the baby, and the following day the family escaped to Florida, where a private detective eventually tracked them down. On July 31, 1986, while Mary Beth lay sick in a hospital, police raided their house and grabbed the baby, who subsequently returned to New Jersey with the Sterns.

Judge Harvey Sorkow, in granting custody to the Sterns, deemed Mary Beth Whitehead to be "mentally unstable" for her refusal to give up her baby. Initially, public opinion seemed to agree with him—she had, after all, entered into a contract and was morally and legally obliged to meet its terms. In addition, the wealthy Sterns were viewed by many—especially Sorkow—as being able to provide a better home for the baby than the Whiteheads. But women's groups and opponents of surrogacy rallied around Mary Beth, and soon public debate reached a fever pitch, especially as questions about the Sterns' motives and veracity were raised; for instance, it was revealed that Betsy Stern had never made any effort to conceive or be tested for fertility. Critics also attacked Judge Sorkow for clearly favoring the Sterns and ordering the baby's seizure without talking to Whitehead or holding a hearing, as required by law.

Though there were several other surrogacy cases attracting attention, it was Mary Beth Whitehead's plight that aroused the most controversy. On March 31, 1987, Judge Sorkow upheld his own earlier ruling and the surrogacy contract, granting full custody of "Baby M"—the only name used by the press—to the

Sterns. He also severed Mary Beth's parental rights, which allowed Elizabeth Stern to adopt Melissa Elizabeth. However, after an appeal was lodged, the New Jersey Supreme Court reinstated Whitehead's visiting rights on April 10.

In November 1987 Mary Beth and Rick Whitehead divorced, and she married Dean Gould, with whom she subsequently had a son. But her fight continued and finally came before the New Jersey Supreme Court. In a decision made on February 2 and announced on February 3, 1988, that court effectively overturned Judge Sorkow's ruling and declared commercial surrogacy contracts to be illegal (although unpaid surrogacy arrangements were still allowable, with reservations). In what it deemed the "best interests of the child," the court gave legal custody of Baby M to the Sterns, believing they could provide a more stable home. Yet the justices were sympathetic to Whitehead-Gould's situation and restored her parental rights, thus vacating Betsy Stern's adoption.

The case finally concluded when, on April 6, Judge Birger M. Sween ordered that Whitehead-Gould be allowed unrestricted, unsupervised visitation rights with her daughter, to be implemented gradually. The resolution was accepted by both Whitehead-Gould and the Sterns, the latter reluctantly. Even so, there were many who felt the maternal rights of a lower-middle-class woman had been rejected in favor of a wealthier, upper-class couple, while the "best interests of the child" are still a subject of heated controversy.

## THE WAR ON DRUGS

First Lady Nancy Reagan, seen here with her husband in a 1985 portrait, was a tireless campaigner to get children to "just say no" to drugs. *(Courtesy Ronald Reagan Library)*

Drug use and abuse became a paramount concern in the 1980s, when—in the minds of millions of Americans—drug traffickers replaced the Soviet Union as the greatest threat to the nation. Previously, the use of hard-core recreational drugs had seemed to be confined to specific groups—ghetto addicts, flamboyant rock stars, hippies, the occasional good-kid-gone-bad. Yet the lethal overdoses of celebrities such as John Belushi (1982) and sports stars such as basketball's Len Bias (1986) contradicted the belief of many in the middle and upper classes that they were immune from such degradation. In fact, high-profile deaths as well as a sky rocketing drug-related crime rate emphasized the growing problem, now permeating all levels of society.

By the mid-1980s, recreational drug use among young people had become an unsavory but largely accepted part of the American scene. The decade's blatant materialism had also brought with it—in some circles—a growing market for "designer drugs" such as "crack" cocaine. This state of affairs was depressingly depicted in such novels as Jay McInerney's *Bright Lights, Big City* (1984) and Bret Ellis Easton's *Less Than Zero* (1985), which contained hard-core scenes of drug abuse and sexual excesses. That the protagonists in these books represented a trend in American society was appalling to those who saw drugs as threatening the country's children and therefore its foundations.

The crusade against drugs took many forms, the most visible being First Lady Nancy Reagan's "Just Say No" campaign for young people. Since the days of Eleanor Roosevelt, first ladies have been expected to adopt a "cause," and Mrs. Reagan had made drugs the focus of her public duties. Her dedication to the Just Say No Foundation concentrated national attention on a frightening problem and also redeemed her in the eyes of those who had previously criticized her extravagant lifestyle.[11] Throughout her husband's administration, she traveled the country, making public appearances and speeches that urged children to "just say no" to drugs. The simple but effective message did have an impact, and the phrase wove itself into the public consciousness.

But a slogan did little to eradicate the root cause of the problem: the alarming growth of drug organizations in South and Central America, especially Colombia's powerful Medellin cartel, whose operations extended insidiously into the United States. Public opinion on dealing with the traffickers included the controversial idea that drugs should be legalized, which would effectively eliminate the cartels' market. The majority, however, believed the only answer lay in tougher law enforcement.

In 1982 President Reagan created the cabinet-level Vice President's Task Force on South Florida, combining the resources of the armed services and government agencies (including U.S. Customs, the FBI, and the Drug Enforcement Agency [DEA]) to battle against drug traffickers in that region. This was soon followed by other regional task forces, and American agents worked with foreign police forces to shut down the drug cartels, albeit with limited success. Nevertheless, the South Florida Drug Task Force managed to reduce trafficking in that state so well that drug traffickers were forced to move their transportation routes to the Mexican border.

When DEA agent Enrique Camerena was kidnapped and murdered in Mexico in February 1985, there was public outrage over the cartels' apparent invincibility, and efforts against them increased. In September 1986 Ronald and Nancy Reagan announced a national crusade against drug abuse; the president subsequently signed an executive order mandating that federal employees be tested for drugs. The following month he signed the Anti-Drug Abuse Act, which appropriated $1.7 billion to fight the drug war and imposed tougher, mandatory sentences for various drug offenses. The powerful drug lords, however, only increased their operations, effectively resisting U.S. attempts to stop them, which included the February 5, 1988, drug-trafficking indictment of Panama's leader, General Manuel Noriega, by a federal grand jury in Miami. Noriega, a onetime American ally, had allowed the Medellin cartel to build cocaine laboratories and launder money in his country.

On November 18, 1988, President Reagan signed another Anti-Drug Abuse Act, which established two agencies, the Office of National Drug Control Policy (whose head became known as the drug czar) and the Substance Abuse and Mental Health Services Administration. In addition to such tougher measures as imposition of the death penalty for drug traffickers, the act called for an appropriation of $2.8 billion to fight the war on drugs. Only $500 million could actually be spent in 1989 under the conditions imposed by the Gramm-Rudman Act of 1985. Nevertheless, the new law gained significant public approval, bequeathing a legacy to Reagan's successor that would result in one of the two most important initiatives of the Bush administration.

## MULRONEY'S SALVATION

In Canada, 1988 began and ended in triumph—fortunately for Brian Mulroney, whose prospects for reelection had long seemed dubious. Among the many reasons for this were his failure to fulfill certain campaign promises and numerous scandals and controversies attached to his cabinet. Repeatedly between 1985 and 1987, ministers were accused of misconduct or inappropriate use of their office, and several political careers had been damaged or destroyed. Mulroney himself was accused of granting political favors to friends and of entrusting a largely incompetent staff with powers that were abused or misdirected. So unpopular was he that victory for the Liberals in the next election seemed almost certain.

Among the factors that saved him was the Meech Lake Accord negotiated in 1987. This had strengthened support for Mulroney in his native Quebec and enhanced his reputation nationally by apparently resolving the longstanding crisis over that province's threatened secession from Canada (though it would reemerge in 1990 when the accord failed to be ratified by all 10 provinces). But just as important was the upturn in the economy that had finally begun in early 1988. As in the United States, tax reforms and deregulation played an important part; by privatizing government-owned businesses and reducing federal involvement in certain industries, Mulroney claimed, investment and innovation would be encouraged—and such certainly seemed to be the case.

Good public relations also helped in the form of the winter Olympics in Calgary, February 13–28, 1988—the first time an Olympics encompassed three weekends. The expanded Winter Games featured a record 1,423 athletes from 57 nations, 46 events, and performances that ranged from spectacular (Finland's Matti Nykänen winning three gold medals in ski jumping) to heartwarming (Canada's Elizabeth Manley unexpectedly taking the silver medal in figure skating) to heartbreaking (U.S. speed skater Dan Jansen, whose sister had just died, failing to win any medals after twice falling during his races). The novice Jamaican bobsled team so captivated the world that they were later depicted in the film *Cool Runnings* (1993), starring John Candy. The Soviet Union led with 29 medals overall (11 gold), followed by East Germany with 25 (nine gold); the United States finished a disappointing ninth with only six medals (two gold). Though Canada did not place in the top 10, the country had done itself proud with an exciting and successful games called "the best ever."

Meanwhile, since May 1986 Canadian and U.S. negotiators had been hammering out a free trade agreement, long a controversial subject since a similar agreement was turned down in 1911. Many Canadians, fearful of an American takeover, favored protectionist policies for their country's businesses, resources, and economy, even if it was to their financial disadvantage. But several factors, including the crippling recession in the early part of the decade, had strengthened the call to liberalize what was already the biggest trading relationship in the world. Further, although large in area, Canada did not have the population to sustain strong domestic growth, making the unfettered export of goods and services to the United States a commercial imperative. Although the United States' own protectionist policies were a cause for concern, economic necessity dictated removing barriers and creating a tariff-free trading zone.

In October 1987 the two governments announced a comprehensive, bilateral accord, the U.S.-Canada Free Trade Agreement (FTA), which was signed by Mulroney and Reagan in separate ceremonies on January 2, 1988. The pact aimed to eliminate most tariffs between the United States and Canada by January 1998, with numerous provisions covering access to government contracts, selling across borders, investment regulation, promotion of competition, and settlement of disputes, among other factors.

The FTA needed ratification by the U.S. Congress and Canada's Parliament, and the U.S. Senate approved the agreement on September 21 by a vote of 83-9. Canada, however, was divided. Supporting it were Mulroney and his Progressive Conservatives, who had negotiated the pact, while the Liberals and New Democratic Party felt that Canada had been sold out to the United States and would lose its sovereignty and financial independence. Many criticized the overly generous concessions they felt Mulroney had made to the Americans, and public opinion was sharply divided among the provinces and between such sectors as business groups (most of which favored the agreement) and unions (most of which did not). When the pact was presented to Parliament, the House of Commons, controlled by the Conservatives, readily ratified it, but the Senate, controlled by the Liberals, blocked it. Consequently, on October 1 Mulroney was forced to dissolve Parliament and schedule a general election. The following contentious and hard-fought race focused almost exclusively on the FTA.

On November 21 Canadians went to the polls, and though the Liberals and National Democratic Party together won more of the popular vote, the Progressive Conservatives retained their majority in the House of Commons, winning 169 of 295 seats. Consequently, when the pact was again presented to Parliament, the Senate felt obliged to ratify it on December 30, and the FTA took effect on January 1, 1989. As of January 1, 1994, it was absorbed into the North American Free Trade Agreement (NAFTA), which extended the trade zone to include Mexico. By that time the Progressive Conservative Party had all but disintegrated, and the Liberal Party, under Jean Chrétien, had come into power. Nevertheless, the Liberals allowed the pact to remain in place.

Opinion remains divided on whether the FTA, and subsequently NAFTA, has been good or bad for Canada. Although trade was liberalized in many areas, in others (such as soft wood lumber), the United States has continued to practice protectionism and retained its tariffs. However, the benefits appear to have outweighed the disadvantages. Canada's fears of being swallowed up by its powerful neighbor were never realized, and since 1990 the country's exports have accounted for 40 percent of its gross domestic product, up from a pre-FTA average of 25 percent.

Today the United States and Canada exchange more goods and services than any other two nations in the world. While some still doubt that it was the best thing for Canada, it was undoubtedly a victory for the Mulroney administration.

## ELECTION HIGHS AND LOWS

It was rough going for Vice President George H. W. Bush in the 1988 presidential race. In addition to overcoming challenges from Republican opponents, especially Kansas senator Bob Dole,[12] Bush also had to surmount frequent depictions of him in the press as a wimp. On January 25 a live interview on CBS turned sour when news anchor Dan Rather (in New York) grilled an increasingly irritated Bush (in Washington) about the Iran-contra affair, and Bush finally lashed out. His words provoked Rather, who abruptly ended the interview. Stunned, Bush—his microphone still on—snapped, "The bastard didn't lay a glove on me."[13] Public reaction backed Bush against Rather, and the interview unexpectedly helped the candidate to bury his wimp image.

Most pundits believed that Bush's association with Ronald Reagan would ultimately assure him of the Republican nomination, and public interest therefore focused on the Democratic race. In early 1987 the clear front-runner was Colorado senator Gary Hart, who had made such a strong impression in the 1984 race. Hart was young and charismatic, but he was also overconfident, challenging reporters to catch him in an indiscretion. They did. The *Miami Herald,* having received a tip that Hart was having an extramarital affair with actress-model Donna Rice, had already staked out the candidate, and within days, salacious details were being broadcast in all the tabloids. Most notoriously, a picture of Rice on Hart's lap appeared on the front page of the *National Enquirer.* On May 8, 1987—a week after the Rice story broke—Hart withdrew his candidacy, though he reentered the race on December 15.

Another candidate forced into an early withdrawal was Delaware senator Joseph Biden, brought down by reports—instigated by campaign workers for Massachusetts governor Michael Dukakis—that he had plagiarized large sections of a campaign speech by British Labour Party leader Neil Kinnock. After this early excitement, both Democrats and Republicans failed to produce little more than yawns from the public until October 10, when Jesse Jackson formally announced his candidacy.

Jackson's official entry into the race was late, but that was the only similarity to his 1984 run. This time he had assembled an efficient organization with more experienced (and white) advisers; better financing; a clear-cut plan for campaigning; and, most importantly, the support of major black leaders across the country. In 1984 Jackson had fought the system; in 1988 he used it to his advantage. Focusing on issues that resonated with the public, such as the prevalence of drug use and teenage sex, and enjoying a better relationship with the press, he made himself a surprising favorite for the Democratic nomination.

Jackson's chances seemed poor at first, but after winning five southern states on Super Tuesday (March 8) and subsequently scoring an upset win in the Michigan caucuses, he became a serious contender. Finally, there were just two candidates—Dukakis and Jackson—as others gradually dropped out of the race: former Arizona governor Bruce Babbitt on February 18, Hart (this time for good) on March 11, Missouri congressman Richard Gephardt on March 28, Illinois senator Paul Simon on April 7, and Tennessee senator Al Gore on April 21.

By late June Jackson had won 29 percent of the vote and 1,105 delegates to Dukakis's 43 percent and 2,309 delegates. His strong finish had given him credibility and an important role in shaping the Democratic platform. But it did not give him the vice presidential nomination. Shaken by the long, grueling primary process, Democratic Party leaders felt that however far Jackson had taken the country in accepting a black candidate, it would be political suicide to include him on the ticket.

At the Democratic convention in Atlanta (July 18–21), the young governor of Arkansas gave a long, rambling speech placing Dukakis's name in nomination. (In four years he would himself be nominated for president. His name was Bill Clinton.) For his running mate, Dukakis chose the respected Texas senator Lloyd Bentsen. Initially furious, Jackson nonetheless campaigned faithfully for the team.

In August, George Bush, having secured the Republican nomination, stunned many supporters by his selection of a running mate: 41-year-old Senator Dan Quayle of Indiana. Nationally unknown until then, the photogenic Quayle initially seemed an odd choice, one that was mocked by reporters, Democrats, and even fellow Republicans. But there was logic in Bush's thinking: Having stayed quietly in Ronald Reagan's shadow for eight years, he wanted somebody compliant and loyal, who would appeal to women and young voters. Further, Quayle, a dyed-in-the-wool conservative, guaranteed support for Bush from those on the far right who distrusted his moderation.

Bush hired former Reagan speechwriter Peggy Noonan, and for his acceptance speech at the Republican convention in New Orleans (August 15–18), she produced three memorable phrases. One was "a thousand points of light," describing the thousands of organizations that make America a "nation of communities"; another was "I want a kinder, gentler nation."[14] Although these two phrases won praise for Bush, the third would haunt him later: "The Congress will push me to raise taxes," he said, "and I'll say no, and they'll push, and I'll say no, and they'll push again, and I'll say to them, 'Read my lips: no new taxes.' "[15] While Americans welcomed the pledge, commentators questioned the wisdom of such a promise when the budget deficit was a matter of national concern.

Though Bush's standing rose, he was far behind Dukakis as the campaign swung into high gear. Neither candidate excited much public enthusiasm, especially when mudslinging reached unprecedented levels. "Poor George . . . He was born with a silver foot in his mouth," quipped Democratic Texas governor Ann Richards. Quayle was repeatedly criticized for his inexperience and for having served in the National Guard to avoid Vietnam. But Democratic accusations were nothing compared to those of the Bush "handlers" who stage-managed every step of his campaign.

A Greek American, Michael Dukakis had won the Democratic nomination largely because of an economic turnaround in his home state that was termed the "Massachusetts miracle." By late summer, however, Massachusetts was experiencing a slowdown, hampering Dukakis's quoting the "miracle" to show what he could do for the country. Additionally, his inexperience in national and international affairs as well as an impassive personality worked against him. Like Bush, he suffered from a "wimp" image. To counter Republican charges that he was soft on defense, Dukakis visited a General Dynamics plant in Michigan where he donned a helmet and boarded an M1 tank, which then circled around as he waved to reporters from the turret. The effect was so comical that the Bush team immediately produced a devastating ad, showing Dukakis circling around in the tank while a voiceover listed the defense systems and operations that Dukakis had opposed. "And now he wants to be our commander-in-chief," intoned the narrator. "America can't afford that risk."

Bush workers later admitted to embellishing Dukakis's record on defense, and the ad was withdrawn. This, however, was only one of several controversial ads that severely damaged Dukakis. The most notorious—by an independent group

Democratic presidential nominee Michael Dukakis arrives at his polling station in Brookline, Massachusetts, to cast his ballot on November 8, 1988. *(Kenneth Martin/Landov)*

called National Security Political Action Committee (NSPAC)—centered on Massachusetts's prison furlough program. In 1986 Willie Horton, a convicted murderer, jumped his furlough and a year later savagely attacked a Maryland couple, beating and stabbing the man and raping the woman. Though the Massachusetts legislature repealed weekend passes for prisoners in April 1988, the NSPAC ran several television ads on the furlough program that made Dukakis appear not only soft on crime but actually culpable for Horton's deeds. One claimed that 268 first-degree murderers had been furloughed, leading voters to draw their own inferences. Similar ads appeared in print and on radio.

Because Horton was an African American, the Bush campaign (which had not actually produced the ads) was accused of racism. There was much abhorrence about the ads' content and presentation, but they succeeded all the same: Once Bush took the lead, Dukakis never recovered. The Democrats' ads were often unfocused and too slow in countering the Bush charges. Dukakis's best attacks were reserved for Dan Quayle, whose weaknesses were highlighted during his one debate with the more experienced Lloyd Bentsen.

There were two presidential debates, on September 25 and October 13. Dukakis came off well in the first debate, but the effectiveness of the Willie Horton ads was already reducing his chances. Further, Bush frequently sneered at his opponent as a "liberal," a word that had become pejorative in the Reagan era. An exhausted Dukakis lost the second debate by giving a philosophical discourse on capital punishment when asked how he would react to the rape and murder of his own wife.

On November 8, in a runaway victory, Bush won 41 states, 426 electoral votes, and 54 percent of the popular vote—more than Ronald Reagan had won in 1980—while Dukakis managed 111 electoral votes and 45 percent of the popular vote.[16] One West Virginia elector cast his vote for Bentsen as a protest against the electoral college system. For many voters, though, it was the election process that needed fixing after what was regarded as the dirtiest campaign in U.S. history.

## TRAGEDY

Although the United States' 1986 raid on Libya had reduced Muammar al-Gadhafi's terrorist activities, tensions in the Middle East continued to deteriorate. In September that year, members of the Abu Nidal Organization seized Pan Am Flight 73 on the ground in Karachi, Pakistan, and held 379 passengers and crew hostage for 16 hours. The incident left 20 dead, including two Americans. Almost immediately afterward, three Americans were kidnapped in Beirut, followed by the abductions of British envoy Terry Waite and three more Americans in January

1987. A year later, on February 17, 1988, marine lieutenant colonel William Higgins was kidnapped, bringing the number of U.S. hostages in Beirut to nine.[17]

On April 18, 1988, after an Iranian mine damaged an American ship, the U.S. Navy attacked two Iranian oil platforms and six armed Iranian vessels in the Persian Gulf. Then, on July 3, shortly after a skirmish between Iranian gunboats and U.S. warships, inexperienced radar operators aboard the USS *Vincennes* identified a blip on their screens as an Iranian plane in an attack position. Captain Will Rogers immediately launched surface-to-air missiles, which destroyed the aircraft—an Iranian commercial airbus that had actually been climbing, following a prepublished flight plan. All 290 persons aboard Iran Air flight 655, including 63 children, were killed; 248 of them had been Iranians.

The incident was reminiscent of the Soviet Union's 1983 downing of Korean Air Lines flight 007. Nevertheless, most in the international community, including the Soviets and the International Civil Aviation Organization (ICAO), agreed that the *Vincennes* crew had simply made a terrible mistake in a time of stress. Enraged Iranians, though, viewed it as a deliberate attack against their country.[18] Other events that exacerbated the tension were the trial of Ali Hammedei for the June 1985 hijacking of TWA flight 847 and the death sentences imposed on five terrorists in connection with the September 1986 Pan Am attack.

Increasingly, planes had become terrorist targets. In June 1985 Air India flight 182 exploded off the coast of Ireland, killing all 329 aboard. A bomb had been transferred onto the aircraft in Toronto by a passenger who did not board the flight; a similar occurrence obliterated a Korean Air Boeing 707 two years later. Following the Air India bombing, the Federal Aviation Authority (FAA) introduced new procedures requiring airlines to match all pieces of baggage with passengers actually aboard the plane; any bags not so reconciled were to be removed. The importance of this precaution had already been demonstrated when unreconciled suitcases removed from planes were found to have bombs inside.

Nonetheless, the airlines' implementation of bag reconciliation was haphazard and not then fully supervised by the FAA. In 1988 Pan American World Airways replaced the procedure with X-ray screening in Frankfurt and London, two cities designated as high security risks. This was to prove a fatal mistake.

Earlier in the year, Israeli intelligence had revealed that a Palestine terrorist group was active in Germany. On October 26 German police raided the group's premises in Neuss and Frankfurt and seized a Toshiba radio cassette player that had been modified as a bomb. Details were circulated throughout Europe and North America; German police warned that the cassette player was modified in such a way as to make the bomb almost undetectable by X-ray screening.

On December 5 the U.S. embassy in Helsinki, Finland, received a call warning of a plot to bomb a Pan Am flight from Frankfurt to the United States sometime within the next two weeks. The informant even revealed how this was to be done (using an unwitting Finnish woman to carry the bomb in her luggage). Because of its precise details, the "Helsinki warning" was circulated to all U.S. air carriers. Passengers, however, were not made aware of the warning, which was later determined to be a hoax.

On December 21—16 days after the Helsinki warning—passengers at London's Heathrow Airport boarded Pan Am flight 103, a Boeing 747 bound for New York. They included a CIA officer, several service people stationed in West Germany, and 35 Syracuse University students heading home for the holidays.

When it lifted off just after 6:20 P.M. it held 259 people, of whom 189 were Americans and 32 were Britons; altogether, 20 nationalities were represented on the flight.

Also on board was a Samsonite suitcase that had been transferred from Air Malta flight KM180 onto Pan Am flight 103A in Frankfurt and then onto the plane at Heathrow. There was no corresponding passenger for the bag, which contained a Toshiba radio cassette player modified into a bomb.[19] Chance had placed the suitcase in the forward cargo hold, below the cockpit.

The plane proceeded north over Scotland, and shortly after 7:00 P.M., a timing device set off the explosive. Because of the bomb's placement, the plane's nose separated from the fuselage, leading to its disintegration. Pieces of flight 103 fell over a huge area of southern Scotland and as far east as the North Sea, but the largest parts descended on the Scottish town of Lockerbie. There the fuel-filled wings vaporized six houses, set fire to others, and killed 11 people. All aboard the plane perished.

The horror of the attack and the gradual emergence of details led to angry questions: Why had airlines not made passengers aware of the Helsinki warning? Why did Pan Am abandon bag reconciliation at the Frankfurt and London airports? How much did the government know? And could the tragedy have been prevented?

It soon became apparent that the answer to the last question was yes. Critics damned the federal government for being sluggish and secretive in both its response to the bombing and its attitude toward the victims' families (many of whom banded together to seek answers). President-elect Bush expressed sympathy for the families, but not until August 4, 1989, did he establish the Commission on Aviation Security and Terrorism, which reported on May 15, 1990. By then several other investigations had been published, and it was clear that Pan Am's lax security was much to blame. Victims' families sued the airline, which was forced into bankruptcy in 1991.

A deep gash in the ground shows the impact of the crash of Pan Am flight 103 in Lockerbie, Scotland, on December 21, 1988. *(AP/Wide World Photos)*

That same year the British and U.S. governments indicted two Libyans: Abdel Basset Ali al-Megrahi and Al Amin Fhimah (also known as Lamen Kalifa Fhimah). Though many still suspected Syria and Iran, the United States absolved those governments of involvement and restored diplomatic relations with both. Meanwhile Gadhafi refused to turn over the suspects for trial without guarantees that they would, if convicted, be jailed in Libya. He also objected to their being tried in either the United States or Scotland.

Finally, in 1998 the United States and Great Britain agreed that the Libyans would be tried in the Netherlands—before a Scottish court.[20] Megrahi and Fhimah were extradited and brought to trial in 2000. On January 31, 2001, Fhimah was acquitted; Megrahi was found guilty but sentenced to only 20 years in prison; the term was later increased to 27 years. The light sentence further encouraged cover-up theorists who felt the U.S. and British governments had concealed more than they had revealed and made Megrahi a solitary scapegoat.

In 2003—seven years after the families won the right to sue Libya[21]—Gadhafi agreed to a settlement of $2.7 billion ($10 million for each victim's family), payable in three parts, conditional on the lifting of, first, UN sanctions and then U.S. commercial sanctions on Libya. The third payment was to be made when the United States removed Libya from a list of state sponsors of terrorism, which had not yet occurred by the end of 2004. The relatives' reaction to the settlement was mixed; at least one family refused to accept the second payment or the third if it is ever made.

The horror of the Pan Am 103 bombing has now been eclipsed by the terrorist attack of September 11, 2001. Nevertheless, it remains a pivotal terrorist event of the 1980s.

## THE REAGAN LEGACY

With the signing of the INF Treaty in December 1987, few doubted that the cold war was nearing its end. In April 1988 an agreement was reached to withdraw Soviet troops from Afghanistan, more than eight years after the invasion that had led to the U.S. boycott of the Moscow Olympics. The withdrawal began in May, the month that Pepsi Cola became the first American company to buy commercial time on Soviet television. On May 27 the U.S. Senate ratified the INF Treaty—and two days later Reagan arrived in Moscow for his last summit with Gorbachev.

In one respect, little had changed: The president risked giving offense by entertaining a group of Soviet dissidents at the U.S. ambassador's residence and speaking on the importance of human rights and religious freedom, areas where he felt the Soviet Union still needed to make improvements. But in every other respect, the difference between the anticommunist Reagan of 1980 and the Gorbachev-embracing Reagan of 1988 was both dramatic and historic. Whether strolling along Arbat Street, talking to students at Moscow State University, or touring Red Square with Gorbachev as his guide, the president manifestly demonstrated his change in attitude toward the country he had once called an "evil empire." Asked by reporters about that famous phrase, he replied, "I was talking about another time, another era."

At their meetings, Reagan and Gorbachev agreed on cultural exchanges and nuclear testing; though no further specific accord was reached on arms reductions,

President Reagan and Soviet general secretary Gorbachev shake hands after signing the INF Treaty ratification in the Grand Kremlin Palace, Moscow, on June 1, 1988. *(Courtesy Ronald Reagan Library)*

they signed the INF treaty ratification and laid the groundwork for final negotiations on the Strategic Arms Reduction Treaty (START). On the last day, June 1, an attempt to agree on a joint communiqué became bogged down in disagreements over language. Nevertheless, the positive public impact of the summit made it every bit as important as Reykjavík had been, if only because of the unmistakable overt cordiality now existing between Moscow and Washington. As Margaret Thatcher said approvingly, the Moscow summit would "encourage the course of history for years to come."[22]

Gorbachev and Reagan met officially once more in December, when Gorbachev addressed the United Nations in New York—the first Soviet general secretary to speak there since Nikita Khrushchev had famously banged his shoe on the table in 1963. The speech, on December 7, was electrifying primarily for Gorbachev's announcement that the Soviet Union would be making major withdrawals of troops from Eastern Europe in addition to reducing its armed forces by 500,000 men. With this it became clear that Moscow would no longer intervene to protect communist governments, paving the way for the subsequent withering of totalitarian regimes.

Following the UN speech, Gorbachev lunched with Reagan and George Bush on Governor's Island. Though the president wrote positively of the meeting in his diary, others present observed that the Soviet leader, though polite, spoke cursorily to Reagan and focused principally on Bush, the president-elect. It seemed that history was already moving on without the retiring president.

But few disputed his part in that history, certainly not Gorbachev, who years later would acknowledge how Reagan's attitude toward and exchanges with the Soviet Union had affected the course of world affairs. The Berlin Wall came down the year Reagan left office, Gorbachev and Bush signed the first START treaty in July 1991, and the Soviet Union was dissolved in December 1992—historic legacies of Reagan's presidency.

Ronald Reagan left office with a 68-percent approval rating, the highest of any president since Franklin Delano Roosevelt. Yet his legacy to the nation was decidedly mixed. His domestic programs were held responsible for the federal deficit, the increased poverty, the stock market crash of 1987, and the savings-and-loan debacle of 1989. Deregulation and lax management led to crises in several areas, especially the environment. But in international affairs, his work in arms reductions and his sincere, often-stated goal of ending nuclear weaponry effaced his early image as a trigger-happy cowboy. Whether events would have turned out differently had someone else been leading the country at such a critical time is a matter for debate. But in the opinion of many, the collapse of communism in the Soviet Union and Eastern Europe would have been delayed much longer had not Reagan's firm, if expensive, line on defense caused it to crumble and bring the cold war to a surprisingly rapid end.

In his farewell address to the nation on January 11, 1989, Reagan said, "Once you begin a great movement, there's no telling where it will end. We meant to change a nation, and instead, we changed a world."[23] For some, this made him a great president, while others simply saw him as someone who happened to be in the right place at the right time. But few would deny that the world *had* changed and that the 1980s, for good or bad, would long be regarded as the Reagan era.

## CHRONICLE OF EVENTS

### 1988

*January 2:* In separate ceremonies, President Ronald Reagan and Prime Minister Brian Mulroney sign the U.S.-Canada Free Trade Agreement.

*January 2:* In one of the largest inland spills ever, an Ashland Oil Company tank collapses and spills 860,000 gallons of oil into the Monongahela River near Pittsburgh, Pennsylvania.

*January 5:* Peter Press ("Pistol Pete") Maravich, basketball star who scored a record 3,667 points in his college career, dies at age 40.

*January 8–9:* Brian Boitano and Debi Thomas win the singles titles at the U.S. figure-skating championships. It is Thomas's second win.

*January 11:* World War II flying ace Gregory "Pappy" Boyington, who won the Medal of Honor for shooting down 28 Japanese planes, dies at age 75.

*January 28:* A Canadian Supreme Court decision results in the legalization of abortion in Canada.

*January 29:* The Reagan administration bans federal funding to family-planning clinics that provide abortion assistance.

*January 31:* The Washington Redskins defeat the Denver Broncos, 42-10, to win football's Super Bowl XXII.

*February 2:* The New Jersey Supreme Court overturns a previous ruling in the Baby M case and declares commercial surrogacy contracts to be illegal.

*February 3:* The U.S. Senate confirms Anthony Kennedy's appointment to the Supreme Court; he will be sworn on February 18.

*February 3:* The House of Representatives rejects a request from President Reagan for $36.25 million in aid to the Nicaraguan contras.

*February 5:* A U.S. grand jury in Miami, Florida, indicts Panamanian leader Manuel Noriega on drug-trafficking charges.

*February 11:* Lyn Nofziger, former White House political director, is convicted of three counts of illegal lobbying under the Ethics in Government Act of 1978. The conviction stems from his involvement in a long-running scandal concerning a government contract awarded to the Wedtech Corporation.

*February 13–28:* The United States wins just six medals at the winter Olympic Games in Calgary, Canada.

*February 15:* Nobel Prize–winning physicist Richard Feynman, who had served on the presidential commission investigating the *Challenger* tragedy, dies at age 69.

*February 17:* Marine lieutenant colonel William R. Higgins becomes the ninth American to be abducted in Lebanon since Terry Anderson was seized in March 1985.

*February 21:* Evangelist Jimmy Swaggart tearfully confesses to a television audience that he had an affair with a Louisiana prostitute and says he will be leaving his pulpit temporarily.

*February 24:* The Supreme Court upholds the right to criticize public figures—protected under the free-speech clause—when it overturns a lower court's award to Reverend Jerry Falwell, who had been satirized in *Hustler* magazine.

*February 29:* Action Comics superhero Superman celebrates his 50th birthday. He made his debut in April 1938, but his birthday is traditionally considered to be February 29.

*March 2:* At the Grammy Awards, U2's *Joshua Tree* wins best album of 1987, and Paul Simon's "Graceland" is named best song. Other winners include Sting, Whitney Houston, and Bruce Springsteen.

*March 7:* Harris Glen Milsted, overweight transvestite actor better known as Divine, dies at 42.

*March 8:* In Fort Campbell, Kentucky, two U.S. Army helicopters collide, killing 17 service members.

*March 10:* Pop idol Andy Gibb dies at age 30.

*March 11:* Former National Security Advisor Robert McFarlane pleads guilty to withholding information from Congress in relation to the Iran-contra affair.

*March 14:* The Senate ratifies a treaty to protect Earth's ozone shield. The international agreement, arrived at in Montreal in September 1987, calls for a rollback in the use of chlorofluorocarbons, believed to cause damage to ozone in the upper atmosphere.

*March 15:* Pope John Paul II names the first African-American Catholic archbishop in the United States: Eugene Antonio Marino of Atlanta, Georgia.

*March 16:* After a grand jury investigation lasting 14 months, Vice Admiral John M. Poindexter, Lieutenant Colonel Oliver L. North, and two others are indicted on charges related to the Iran-contra affair. Accused of attempting to defraud the U.S. government by funding the Nicaraguan rebels with the profits from the sale of arms to Iran, the four defendants will be tried separately, according to a June 8 ruling by the judge in the case.

*March 16:* The United States sends 3,200 troops to Honduras after receiving intelligence that Sandinista forces from Nicaragua had crossed the border to attack contra bases there. The American troops do not take part in any fighting and will return to the United States by March 28.

*March 22:* Congress overrides President Reagan's veto to pass the Civil Rights Restoration Act of 1987.

*March 23:* In Nicaragua, the Sandinistas and contras sign a cease-fire agreement in hopes of ending their six-year civil war. The agreement is for a 60-day period, but it soon falls apart.

*March 25:* Robert Joffrey, who founded and ran the Joffrey Ballet Company, dies at 57.

*March 31:* Pulitzer Prize winners include Toni Morrison for *Beloved* (fiction), Richard Rhodes for *The Making of the Atomic Bomb* (nonfiction), William Meredith for *Partial Accounts: New and Selected Poems* (poetry), and Alfred Uhry for *Driving Miss Daisy* (drama).

*April 1:* President Reagan signs a bill authorizing $47.9 million in humanitarian aid to the Nicaraguan contras.

*April 1:* Champeau Corporation of Canada buys the U.S.-based Federated Department Stores, Inc., for $6.6 billion, the largest department store takeover and fifth-largest acquisition in U.S. history to date.

*April 4:* In the first impeachment trial of a governor in 60 years, Evan Mecham of Arizona is found guilty of two charges of misconduct and one of obstructing justice; a state senate vote of 21-9 removes him from office.

*April 11:* At the Academy Awards ceremony, *The Last Emperor* wins as outstanding motion picture of 1987. Michael Douglas (*Wall Street*) and Cher (*Moonstruck*) win the major acting awards, while supporting acting Oscars go to Sean Connery (*The Untouchables*) and Olympia Dukakis (*Moonstruck*).

*April 12:* Harvard University obtains the world's first patent for a "transgenic nonhuman mammal"—a mouse. The genetically altered mice were created when scientists injected a gene that causes cancer into fertilized mouse eggs.

*April 14:* The United States, Soviet Union, Afghanistan, and Pakistan sign agreements providing for the withdrawal of Soviet troops from Afghanistan, which the Soviets had invaded in December 1979, and for the understanding that the United States and Soviet Union will not interfere in the affairs of Afghanistan and Pakistan. The latter two countries also agree not interfere in each other's internal affairs.

*April 17:* Artist Louise Nevelson, creator of environmental sculpture, dies at 88.

*April 18:* The U.S. Navy attacks two Iranian oil platforms and six armed Iranian vessels in the southern part of the Persian Gulf.

*April 20:* In a 69-27 vote, the Senate approves the Civil Liberties Act of 1988, a reparations package to Japanese Americans who had been interned during World War II. It includes $20,000 each, an official apology to all survivors and their beneficiaries, and a $1.25 billion education fund. President Reagan will sign the bill on August 10; the first payment will be made on October 1, 1990.

*April 20:* The New York Yankees become the first Major League Baseball team to hit more than 10,000 home runs when Jack Clark hits his first of the season, the team's 10,001st.

*April 23:* A ban on smoking in passenger planes is instituted; it applies to flights of two hours or less, with some exceptions. Northwest Airlines decides to ban smoking on all flights, regardless of length.

*April 25:* Warner Books wins the right to publish a sequel to Margaret Mitchell's *Gone with the Wind* by bidding $4,940,000 in an auction. The new book, to be published in 1990, will be written by Alexandra Ripley.

*April 28:* Congress repeals House Concurrent Resolution No. 108 of 1953, which had terminated federal support to Native Americans.

On August 10, 1988, President Reagan signed the Civil Liberties Act, making reparations to Japanese Americans interned during World War II. *(Courtesy Ronald Reagan Library)*

*May 1:* Federal officials announce the government's intention to sell $15 billion worth of arms abroad, some $3 billion more than the previous year.

*May 4:* Near Henderson and Las Vegas, Nevada, a chemical plant that made fuel for the space shuttles is leveled by four explosions that injure some 200 people. The effects of the blast are felt for 15 miles.

*May 8:* Noted science fiction writer Robert A. Heinlein dies, age 80.

*May 11:* Celebrated songwriter Irving Berlin turns 100. His birthday is celebrated in a concert at Carnegie Hall, New York City, with Leonard Bernstein, Ray Charles, Marilyn Horne, Willie Nelson, and Frank Sinatra among the performers. Berlin himself is not present but will watch a taped telecast of the gala.

*May 11:* President Reagan officially endorses George Bush's candidacy for president.

*May 15:* The Soviet Union begins its withdrawal of troops from Afghanistan under the terms of the April 14 agreement.

*May 16:* Surgeon General C. Everett Koop declares cigarettes to be addictive drugs, similar to heroin and cocaine.

*May 16:* The Supreme Court rules that police officers do not need a search warrant when looking through discarded garbage for evidence.

*May 26:* The Edmonton Oilers beat the Boston Bruins in a four-game sweep that gives them their fourth Stanley Cup hockey triumph in five years.

*May 27:* The Senate ratifies the Intermediate-Range Nuclear Forces (INF) Treaty, the first U.S.-Soviet arms accord ratified since 1972.

*May 29–June 1:* Ronald Reagan and Mikhail Gorbachev hold their fourth summit, a public-relations triumph, in Moscow.

The Reagans and the Bushes join hands at a dinner in Washington, D.C., after the president endorsed Bush's run for the presidency on May 11, 1988. *(Courtesy George Bush Presidential Library)*

*June 5:* David Henry Hwang's *M. Butterfly* wins as best play at the Tony Awards, while Andrew Lloyd Webber's *The Phantom of the Opera* is named best musical. Ron Silver, Joan Allen, Michael Crawford, and Joanna Gleason win the major acting awards.

*June 10:* Louis L'Amour, best-selling author of western novels and stories, dies at 80.

*June 12:* An American finally wins the Tour of Italy bicycle race when Andy Hampsten, 26, defeats 198 other cyclists.

*June 13:* For the first time, a cigarette manufacturer, the Liggett Group, is found guilty of causing death by cancer. The case centered on Rose Cipollone, whose husband, Antonio, is awarded damages of $400,000. After a retrial in 1990, Cipollone will finally drop the lawsuit in November 1992.

*June 20:* The Supreme Court upholds a law to force the admission of women to private clubs that were previously men-only.

*June 21:* The Los Angeles Lakers win the National Basketball Association championship for the second year in a row, defeating the Detroit Pistons in the finals' seventh game.

*June 27:* Governor James J. Blanchard of Michigan signs a bill that effectively outlaws commerical surrogate motherhood. Other states may follow suit.

*June 27:* In Atlantic City, boxing champion Mike Tyson knocks out Michael Spinks in 91 seconds to win $20 million. It is Tyson's third successful defense of his boxing title in 1988.

*June 29:* The Supreme Court upholds a federal law providing for the investigation of high-ranking government officials by independent prosecutors when a crime is suspected.

*July 3:* In the Persian Gulf, the U.S. Navy warship *Vincennes* mistakes an Iranian passenger jet for a fighter plane and shoots it down, killing all 290 persons aboard.

*July 5:* Edwin Meese announces his resignation as U.S. attorney general after months spent dealing with allegations of tax evasion, bribery, and conflict of interest.

*July 12:* Richard L. Thornburgh is nominated for attorney general; he will be sworn in on August 12.

*July 13:* Samuel Leroy Mendel, the country's oldest veteran, dies at 104. He was 14 when he first attempted to join the army during the Spanish-American War (1898) but subsequently served for three years, 1901–04.

*July 16:* At the Olympic trials in Indianapolis, Jackie Joyner-Kersee sets a new world record for the women's heptathlon, with 7,215 points for the seven events. Her sister-in-law, Florence Griffith Joyner, also sets a new world record, running 10.49 seconds in the women's 100-meter dash.

*July 18–21:* At the Democratic Party convention in Atlanta, Massachusetts governor Michael Dukakis and Texas senator Lloyd M. Bentsen, Jr., are nominated for president and vice president.

*July 20:* Iran and Iraq agree to a cease-fire, ending eight years of warfare.

*July 31:* In Lansing, Michigan, the last Playboy Club closes its doors.

*August 7:* Rupert Murdoch pays $3 billion for Triangle Publications, publisher of *TV Guide* among other magazines.

*August 9:* To the dismay of Canadian fans, the Edmonton Oilers trade hockey great Wayne Gretzky to the Los Angeles Kings.

*August 10:* Journalist, author, and screenwriter Adela Rogers St. John dies at 94.

*August 15–18:* At the Republican Party convention in New Orleans, Vice President George H. W. Bush and Indiana senator J. Danforth (Dan) Quayle are nominated for president and vice president.

*August 17:* Teams from the United States and Soviet Union use different methods to determine the strength of a nuclear blast in Nevada. It is the first joint U.S.-Soviet nuclear test verification experiment.

*August 17:* Franklin D. Roosevelt, Jr., son of the late president and former U.S. representative from New York, dies at age 74.

*August 20:* After winning the International Golf Tournament in Castle Rock, Colorado, Jack Nicklaus brings his career earnings to $5,002,825, making him the first golfer to win more than $5 million in tournament play.

*August 23:* President Reagan signs a foreign trade bill aimed at restricting other nations' unfair trading practices and allowing the president to negotiate international marketing agreements.

*August 27:* Approximately 55,000 gather at the Lincoln Memorial to commemorate the 25th anniversary of 1963's historic March on Washington.

*August 28:* At the Emmy Awards, *thirtysomething* is named television's best dramatic series, while *The Wonder Years* wins as best comedy series. Acting awards go to Bea Arthur, Tyne Daly, Richard Kiley, and Michael J. Fox, among others.

*August 31:* By this date, the worst forest fires since 1919 have destroyed 3.4 million acres of land and trees in the United States. The number of forest fires has reached 66,895.

*September 7:* The Securities and Exchange Commission charges the finance firm Drexel Burnham Lambert with using inside information to defraud its clients.

*September 17–October 2:* At the summer Olympics in Seoul, Korea, the United States wins 36 gold medals and 94 overall, finishing third in the medal race. The Soviet Union is first with 132 medals (36 gold) and East Germany second with 102 medals (37 gold).

*September 20:* Lauro F. Cavazos, president of Texas Tech University, takes office as secretary of education, replacing William Bennett. Cavazos is the first Hispanic to join a presidential cabinet.

*September 24:* Reverend Barbara Harris, an African American, is chosen to be suffragan bishop of Massachusetts, the first woman to become a bishop of the Episcopal Church. She will be consecrated on February 11, 1989.

*September 25:* Presidential brother Billy Carter, 51, dies of pancreatic cancer.

*September 26:* After testing positive for steroids, Canadian sprinter Ben Johnson is stripped of his Olympic gold medal, and his world record is declared invalid.

*September 29:* Macabre cartoonist Charles Addams dies at age 76.

*September 29–October 3:* For the first time since the *Challenger* accident, a U.S. manned space flight takes place as the space shuttle *Discovery,* with five astronauts aboard, successfully deploys a communications satellite.

*October 13:* President Reagan signs the Family Support Act, the first welfare reform legislation in 50 years.

*October 15–20:* The National League's Los Angeles Dodgers defeat the American League's Oakland Athletics in five games to win baseball's World Series.

*October 17:* The United States pledges short-term loans to Mexico of up to $3.5 billion for assistance with a severe economic crisis.

*October 17:* President Reagan signs the Indian Gaming Regulatory Act.

*October 18:* Congress passes a bill to raise the Veterans Administration to cabinet level, the fifth addition to the cabinet since 1953. The Department of Veteran Affairs will be established officially on March 15, 1989.

*October 21:* A federal grand jury in New York City indicts former president of the Philippines Ferdinand Marcos and his wife Imelda on embezzlement charges.

*October 30:* In a record takeover transaction that forms the world's largest consumer-products company, Philip Morris Companies, Inc., acquires Kraft, Inc., for $13.1 billion.

*October 30:* Actor and producer John Houseman dies, age 86.

*November 2:* The Internet is infected by a virus called the Morris worm.

*November 4:* Military computers throughout the nation are disrupted by a virus that is later revealed to have been planted by the son of a National Security Agency expert on data security.

*November 8:* George Bush easily defeats Michael Dukakis to win the presidential election. Nevertheless, the Democrats hold majorities in both houses of Congress.

*November 18:* President Reagan signs the Anti-Drug Abuse Act into law.

*November 21:* In the Canadian election, the Progressive Conservative Party wins a majority in the House of Commons, giving Prime Minister Brian Mulroney a second term in office.

*November 22:* The B-2 stealth bomber, designed to evade radar on long-range bombing missions, is unveiled to the media and members of Congress. The U.S. Air Force plans to buy 132 bombers at $500 million each.

*November 30:* In the nation's biggest-ever corporate takeover, Kohlberg, Kravis, Roberts & Company agrees to buy RJR Nabisco for $24.88 billion. The deal will be finalized in April 1989.

*December 1:* World AIDS Day is observed.

*December 2–6:* The space shuttle *Atlantis* carries out a mission for the Department of Defense.

*December 8:* Singer Roy Orbison, best known for his hit "Pretty Woman," dies at 52.

*December 16:* In Tunisia, representatives of the U.S. government and the Palestine Liberation Organization (PLO) meet for the first time, following an American decision that talks are possible now that the PLO has renounced terrorism and accepted the existence of Israel.

*December 21:* The investment firm Drexel, Burnham Lambert, Inc., pleads guilty to charges of mail, wire, and securities fraud and agrees to a fine of $650 million. The company will declare bankruptcy in February 1990 after defaulting on loans of $100 million.

*December 21:* Pan Am flight 103 from London to New York City explodes over Lockerbie, Scotland, killing all 259 people on board and 11 on the ground.

*December 31:* The Federal Home Loan Bank Board reports it had sold or merged 222 failing savings-and-loan associations in 1988, representing $100 billion in accounts. Assistance of $38.6 billion was supplied by the Federal Savings and Loan Insurance Corp.

## 1989

*January 2:* The U.S.–Canada Free Trade Agreement officially goes into effect.

*January 4:* American warplanes shoot down two Libyan fighter planes over international waters. Libya protests that the planes were unarmed, but on the following day, the U.S. government issues a statement that there is visual evidence the fighters had been armed with missiles.

*January 8:* The second-longest-running musical in New York theater history, *42nd Street,* closes after 3,486 performances, a record exceeded only by *A Chorus Line.*

*January 11:* At a meeting in Paris, the United States and 139 other nations condemn the use of chemical weapons. The delegates also urge a treaty to ban the development and production of chemical weapons.

*January 11:* President Reagan delivers his farewell address to the nation.

*January 16:* Miami, Florida, erupts in racial rioting after a Hispanic policeman shoots dead an unarmed black man.

## EYEWITNESS TESTIMONY

### *The Turmoil of AIDS*

I don't believe a cure . . . will ever be found because of the nature of this virus. . . . I do believe that someday there will be a vaccine. Whether it will be totally effective, whether it will be readily available—that, I think, is not in this century.

> *Surgeon General C. Everett Koop being pessimistic in a BBC radio interview on January 27, 1988, quoted in "Health Official Doubts AIDS Will Be Cured,"* San Francisco Chronicle, *January 28, 1988, p. A-11.*

"I've learned a lot," said Admiral Watkins, adding that he felt much like a Southern doctor who told the commission that he had a reputation for being conservative, "but the more that I'm in this fight against AIDS, the more I become a liberal."

> *Admiral James Watkins, chairman of the Presidential Commission on the Human Immunodeficiency Virus Epidemic, noting the personal effects of his work, quoted in Boffey, "Old Critics Now Praise AIDS Panel,"* New York Times, *March 7, 1988, p. B-4.*

HIV-related discrimination is impairing this nation's ability to limit the spread of the epidemic. Crucial to this effort are epidemiological studies to track the epidemic as well as the education, testing, and counseling of those who have been exposed to the virus. However, public health officials will not be able to gain the confidence and cooperation of infected individuals or those at high risk for infection if such individuals fear they will be unable to retain their jobs and their housing, and that they will be unable to obtain the medical and support services they need because of discrimination based on a positive HIV antibody test.

> *From the draft recommendations for dealing with the AIDS crisis written by presidential commission chairman Admiral James Watkins, quoted in "Excerpts from Report by AIDS Panel Chairman,"* New York Times, *June 3, 1988, p. A-16.*

Admiral Watkins took over a bickering commission on the verge of self-destruction. He has now produced what the Administration has failed to achieve in five years: a national strategy to combat AIDS. It's not revolutionary; as he observes, he found surprising consensus on what needs to be done. But the White House has persistently ignored this consensus, preferring to emphasize testing as a means of control while ducking a Federal anti-discrimination law.

What's needed, he argues cogently, is precisely the reverse. Federal protection against discrimination is the centerpiece of his policy. He seeks firm guarantees of confidentiality for test results, and he questions the worth of indiscriminately testing groups like immigrants and prisoners.

> The New York Times *looking approvingly on Admiral James Watkins's report for the AIDS presidential commission on AIDS, in its editorial "If America Is Serious about AIDS, Then Washington Must Fight Discrimination,"* New York Times, *June 5, 1988, sec. 4, p. 30.*

Giving a needle to shoot drugs is like giving a bank robber a car for the getaway.

> *New York City prosecutor Sterling Johnson, Jr., criticizing the city's new needle exchange program, quoted in Lambert, "Needles for Addicts: Test Phase Begins,"* New York Times, *June 26, 1988, sec. 4, p. 7.*

The arguments for needle-swapping programs are compelling. AIDS is spreading fastest among IV drug users sharing needles. These drug users are a direct route into the "general" community, through the partners they have sex with and the children they conceive. The mayor of Boston, Ray Flynn, arguing for the needle-swap program, rested his case on the fact that 18 out of every 1,000 babies born in Boston inherit the virus.

The arguments against dispensing needles are compelling as well. Drugs, after all, are destructive. The messages exchanged with needles would be, at best, mixed. One arm of government abhors drugs, while another distributes sterile paraphernalia. There may even be a more subtle message delivered with the syringe: you may destroy yourself, destroy your community, as long as you don't infect "us."

> *Columnist Ellen Goodman examining the pros and cons of needles exchanges, in Goodman, "Needles for Addicts? No,"* Washington Post, *July 2, 1988, p. A-23.*

The latest casualties of the AIDS epidemic are not those newly struck down by the fatal syndrome, but the doctors, nurses, attorneys, social workers and volunteers who stand by their sides.

Battling burnout, they work long hours at a frantic pace against an incurable disease. The feeling, psychiatrists say, is like combat fatigue. But there's no coming home from this war.

"We've felt an ocean of grief," said Alison Moet, head nurse of S.F. General Hospital's inpatient AIDS ward, a five-year veteran of the unit.

"We've seen so many people die so young, watched their fine minds and talent struck down. How can it not affect us—individually and as a community?"

*Looking at yet another toll taken by the AIDS crisis, in Krieger, "AIDS Workers Battle Burnout," San Francisco Chronicle, August 27, 1988, pp. A-1, A-10.*

The bright and cheery morning sun was hoisting itself over the Department of Commerce and had just lit the National Christmas Tree on the Ellipse Saturday when Cleve Jones paid tribute to the dead.

"Bob Greenwood," he said. "Richard Anderson. Reggie Hightower. . . . and my good friend, Marvin Feldman."

For the next 10 hours, the litany went on. Hundreds of readers followed Jones to the microphone, and all recited several names of people who had died of AIDS—8,288 of them, all remembered in the quilts that were displayed on the green field just south of the White House.

There were no speeches. There were only names, and these are only 22 percent of the Americans who have died of AIDS.

*Reporter George Raine describing the scene in Washington, D.C., when the NAMES Project AIDS Memorial Quilt was displayed on The Mall, in Raine, "150,000 See AIDS Quilt," San Francisco Chronicle, October 9, 1988, p. A-1.*

## The Hispanic Surge

Based on a true story, "Stand and Deliver" tells how so many of teacher Jaime Escalante's students at gang-ridden Garfield High [East Los Angeles] passed the college advanced-placement calculus exam that the Educational Testing Service accused them of cheating. Today, Escalante's students have the highest advanced-placement-test passing percentage in the country. Teachers' organizations who previewed the movie gave it sustained ovations.

It received another when [Edward James] Olmos, who plays Escalante, screened it last month for 1,000

cheering United Farm Workers. At Cesar Chaves's request, the lights stayed down for the credits so the teen-agers present could see the number of Chicanos in the cast and crew, and they applauded still harder.

"This film about our people," Olmos told them, "will touch the nation. It shows we can achieve anything we want. Being able to do a film like this is the finest moment of my life."

*Reporting reactions to the movie based on the experiences of Jaime Escalante as a teacher in East Los Angeles, in "The Hollywood Route," Los Angeles Times Magazine, March 27, 1988, p. 16.*

"In 5 or 10 years we are going to see an incredible ascension of Cubans in positions of power in Miami," said Antonio Gonzalez, a lawyer who was six years old when he arrived unescorted from Cuba and was sent to a Roman Catholic orphanage in Montana, where he lived three years before he was reunited with his parents.

It is unclear just how much this transfer of power will change the Cuban economy here and therefore alter Miami itself in outlook and style. The evidence points to significant shifts, some already being felt in politics, relations between the sexes and other aspects of family life and the workplace.

"I still feel like I'm a Cuban born in the U.S.A.," said Margaret Pulles, born 27 years ago in Miami Beach. "But our outlook is so different from the older generation on most issues that there's no comparison."

*Reporter Jon Nordheimer looking at the Cuban-American community in Miami, in Nordheimer, "For Cuban-Americans, an Era of Change," New York Times, April 13, 1988, pp. A-1, A-19.*

The greater visibility of Hispanics in the cultural landscape is a reminder that the roots of Spanish culture go deep into American life, especially in that spawning ground of the national self-image, the West. Much of the territory of the Western states, from Texas to California, was first held by Spain, then Mexico. The Spanish names of many Western cities—Los Angeles, San Francisco, Santa Fe—bear witness to the settlements of the early Franciscan friars. The first play on American soil was performed by Spanish colonists in New Mexico in 1598. Yet in the hills of New Mexico and the old mission towns of the Pacific Coast, the descendants of Spanish settlers who greeted the Anglo pioneers are amused (and sometimes not amused) to find themselves perennially arriving in the national consciousness. As

Luis Valdez, writer and director of *La Bamba,* once put it, "We did not, in fact, come to the United States at all. The United States came to us."

> *Looking at the irony of the current fascination with all things Hispanic, in "A Surging New Spirit," Time, July 11, 1988, pp. 47–48.*

For a long time, Hispanics in the U.S. felt hostility. Perhaps because we were occupied by nostalgia, we withheld our Latin American gift. We denied the value of assimilation. But as our presence is judged less foreign in America, we will produce a more generous art, less timid, less parochial. Hispanic Americans do not have a pure Latin American art to offer. Expect bastard themes. Expect winking ironies, comic conclusions. For Hispanics live on this side of the border, where Kraft manufactures Mexican-style Velveeta, and where Jack in the Box serves Fajita Pita. Expect marriage. We will change America even as we will be changed. We will disappear with you into a new miscegenation.

> *Author and essayist Richard Rodriguez taking stock of Hispanic culture in the United States, in Rodriguez, "The Fear of Losing a Culture," Time, July 11, 1988, p. 84.*

Michael S. Dukakis has discovered the Latino vote and is pursuing it with a vengeance. No wonder. Latinos make up a large percentage of the population in some key electoral states: 21% in Texas, 19% in California, 9% in Florida. Presumably Dukakis was aiming at those voters when he broke into Spanish in the middle of his acceptance speech at the Democratic national convention.

Politicians routinely bow to the culture and heritage of specific ethnic groups during election time. But Dukakis appears to be going further, He's using Spanish so extensively on the campaign trail that one television producer quipped, "We're going to have to hire a translator. This is like El Salvador."

· . . . ·

A majority of second-generation Mexican Americans speak only one language: English. . . . Ironically, these English-speaking Latinos—the ones to whom Michael Dukakis is speaking Spanish—are the ones most likely to vote.

> *Linda Chavez, chair of the National Commission on Migrant Education, commenting on the role of language in the competition for Hispanic votes during the presidential race, in Chavez, "Is Spanish Wrong Signal to Latinos?" Los Angeles Times, August 8, 1988, part 2, p. 5.*

Separated by language and religion, school and neighborhood, it is sometimes difficult to see what blacks and Hispanics have in common. . . . Often fair-skinned, Hispanics have an easier time assimilating into white society. And generally, the Latino community is more diverse than the black; unlike blacks, for example, Hispanics do not vote as a bloc. That has carried a political price. With the notable exceptions of Miami and San Antonio, Latinos as a group have been unable to come together and form a solid power base.

> *Examining differences between two large American minorities, in "A Conflict of the Have-Nots," Newsweek, December 12, 1988, p. 28.*

Employers have come up with their own slave labor force. They work the [undocumented immigrants] for five days or two weeks, then throw them out of their truck and say, "If you call the police, we'll call the immigration service."

> *Police officer Karen McNally commenting on one of the problems facing illegal Hispanic immigrants, quoted in Zita Arocha, "Wage Complaints from Hispanic Immigrants Increase Sharply in Past Year," Washington Post, December 18, 1988, p. B-9.*

## Rights and Reform

The Administration has consistently pursued a disruptive policy on civil rights, from its attempt to give tax exemptions to racially discriminatory Bob Jones University to its efforts to weaken the U.S. Commission on Civil Rights. President Reagan's veto of the civil rights restoration bill enlarges this unhappy record and saddles Republican candidates in the 1988 campaign with the burden of having to explain this latest, stubborn insistence on fighting a lost, and ugly, cause. The mystery is why Mr. Reagan wants to leave for himself so dismal a legacy.

> *The New York Times criticizing the Reagan administration in its editorial "Dismal Legacy on Civil Rights," New York Times, March 21, 1988, p. A-18.*

Now a heavy majority in Congress—no doubt made heavier by this election season—has made it clear that the intent is to ban discrimination throughout any institution that gets federal money. The principle is fair. If you want to discriminate, don t ask for federal help. And despite the hysterical ravings of Rev. Jerry Falwell and Sen. Orrin Hatch, the bill exempts any "entity" controlled by a religious organization. Like other civil rights statutes, it says nothing about protection based on sexual preference. And alcoholics or addicts who cannot do their jobs can still be fired.

The override was never in doubt, nor was the reasonableness of this bill. The only mystery was why, in his final months in office, Mr. Reagan felt he had to continue to pander to anti–civil rights extremists.

> *The* Chicago Tribune *giving its approval to the Senate's override of President Reagan's veto of the Civil Rights Restoration Act of 1987, in its editorial "A Fair Rebuke to President Reagan,"* Chicago Tribune, *March 24, 1988, sec. 1, p. 24.*

One wonders . . . what has happened to the concept of privacy? But the only private rights anybody ever got exercised about in recent times is the right to use birth-control devices. Private clubs are gradually disappearing, under the sanction of civil rights. If I were in Congress, I would be tempted, . . . even if only on April Fool's Day, to introduce a "Civil Rights Bill for Preemptive War Against the Soviet Union." My only purpose would be to permit me in the campaign ahead to point to all those Democrats who voted against the "Civil Rights Bill of 1988" and thereby stifle 100 political careers.

Somebody, somewhere, somehow, has got to stop the civil rights thing. It is making a joke out of one after another of our Bill of Rights.

> *Conservative columnist William F. Buckley, Jr., commenting on civil rights following congressional passage of the Civil Rights Restoration Act, in Buckley, "Somebody Has Got to Stop This Civil Rights Thing,"* Washington Post, *April 12, 1988, p. A-23.*

However much we might wish it were otherwise, government simply could not operate if it were required to satisfy every citizen's religious needs and desires. The First Amendment must apply to all citizens alike and it can give to none of those a veto over public programs that do not prohibit the free exercise of religion.

> *From Justice Sandra Day O'Connor's majority opinion in a case allowing the Forest Service to carry out logging in territory used by northern California Indians for religious purposes, quoted in Savage, "U.S. Needs Outweigh Those of Religions, Court Rules,"* Los Angeles Times, *April 20, 1988, part 1, p. 1.*

But the rules work against them. A welfare recipient who tries to become self-sufficient through self-employment,

for instance, not only threatens her eligibility but, after four months, would have her self-employment income deducted, dollar for dollar, from her welfare check. Even her eligibility for day care would be jeopardized.

The fact is that this country, which claims to love free enterprise, has been ambivalent toward—even hostile to—free enterprise by the dependent poor. We have been perfectly willing to finance their consumption but not their movement toward independence.

> *Columnist William Raspberry pointing out one of the problems with the welfare system, in Raspberry, "From Unemployed to Self-Employed,"* Washington Post, *May 18, 1988, p. B-3.*

Nowhere has the shifting frontier of the civil rights struggle been more apparent than in Yonkers, a racially divided blue-collar suburb of New York City. Last week Leonard Sand, a soft-spoken, patient federal judge, got fed up with that city's refusal over three years to carry out his orders to place public housing in its white neighborhoods. Gazing down sternly from his bench in Manhattan at four Yonkers councilmen, the jurist delivered a tongue-lashing. "What we're clearly confronted with is a total breakdown of any sense of responsibility," he charged. "What we have here is a competition to see . . . who can be the biggest political martyr. There does have to come a moment of truth, a moment when the city of Yonkers seeks not to become a national symbol of defiance to civil rights."

> *Describing one aspect of the ongoing problem of integration, in "A House Divided,"* Time, *August 15, 1988, p. 14.*

All this does is say that the Indian is for sale. You put money on an Indian's head and he'll go for it. That's what is happening here.

> *Puyallop Indian Silas Cross expressing his disgust over the tribe's monetary settlement with the federal government for Puyallop land in Washington State, quoted in Egan, "Indians Agree to Drop Tacoma Claim,"* New York Times, *August 29, 1988, p. A-12.*

With this settlement, we can protect our culture and our river system. Our people should know they will always have a future.

> *Puyallop administrative manager Frank Wright, Jr., expressing his satisfaction with the tribe's monetary settlement, quoted in Egan, "Indians Agree to Drop Tacoma Claim,"* New York Times, *August 29, 1988, p. A-12.*

Education and job training, leading toward employment, are the heart of welfare reform. States must offer them, and able-bodied adults with children over age 3 must accept them to get public aid. To ease the transition to job rolls, the bill also provides for extended Medicaid coverage and child support subsidies.

"This is the moment we've been waiting for," exults Senator Daniel Patrick Moynihan, "for half a century." A slight exaggeration, perhaps. But welfare can now do what it ought to do: help the Barbara Harrises of the nation care for themselves.

*The* New York Times *applauding the newly passed welfare reform bill, in its editorial "Real Welfare Reform, At Last,"* New York Times, *October 1, 1988, p. 26.*

I favor a return of all remains where a tribe is requesting, no matter what kind of documentation is available. We need to be defined as human beings, not resources for scientists and pseudo-scientists to study.

*Suzan Shown Harjo, executive director of the National Congress of American Indians, expressing the feelings of many Native Americans following the Smithsonian's return of Blackfeet remains to the tribe, quoted in Robbins, "A Fight for Fragments of Indian Culture,"* New York Times, *October 23, 1988, sec. 4, p. 7.*

## Smoke Gets in Your Eyes

The Great Airline Smoking Revolution of 1988, a time of tense readjustment to a new social order, began in spectacular fashion—if somewhat early— Wednesday night on TWA Flight 853 from Boston to Los Angeles.

When it was all over, 11 passengers had lit cigarettes and booed loudly to protest a temporary smoking ban, a flight attendant had filed criminal charges, the captain had radioed Los Angeles for police and four protesters were led away for questioning.

*Reporter Jay Mathews relating an early attempt to limit in-flight smoking four months before a federal ban on short flights goes into effect, in Mathews, "Smoking Ban Sparks Midair Revolt,"* Washington Post, *January 1, 1988, p. A-1.*

Some people are smoking more. It's like Prohibition. You tell someone not to do this or that and they want to do it more.

*Bob Farello, manager of a smoke shop near Wall Street, commenting on the response to antismoking ordinances recently passed in New York City, quoted in Marriott, "Smokers Adjust to New York Curbs,"* New York Times, *May 2, 1988, p. B-3.*

We tend to forget, in this nonsmoking age, that for generations smoking was regarded not merely as permissible but as, in some quarters, even desirable, a sign not merely of maturity, but also of sophistication and urbanity. These certainly were false assumptions, but a great many people believed in them all the same and conducted themselves accordingly. Now all of a sudden they find themselves pariahs, scorned and rebuked by the likes of [New York mayor] Ed Koch; small wonder many of them are angry and confused.

*Columnist Jonathan Yardley sympathizing with smokers who must cope with an antismoking climate, in Yardley, "Antismokers: Lighten Up!"* Washington Post, *May 16, 1988, p. B-2.*

Perhaps it is naïve to wonder about that bland persistence in pretending that evil does not exist. When a government goes badly wrong, we hope that some officials will cry out—and some do, from time to time. Where are the voices of decency and courage in the tobacco industry?

*Columnist Anthony Lewis complaining of the tobacco industry's attitude in the smoking debate, in Lewis, "Merchants of Death,"* New York Times, *May 19, 1989, p. A-31.*

Smokers are getting more and more fed up. We're getting more and more calls from people saying: "We're tired of being made to feel like second-class citizens. We're not politicians; what can we do to at least be heard?"

*David Fishel, vice president of R. J. Reynolds Tobacco Company, offering a rationale for the tobacco industry's campaign against antismoking laws, quoted in McGill, "Cigarette Makers in a War on Bans,"* New York Times, *December 24, 1988, p. 37.*

## The Education Debate

It was more of the same—toughen up the traditional system—even though there was lots of research to indicate the system was deeply flawed.

> *Theodore B. Sizer, chairman of Brown University's Education Department, commenting on Education Secretary William Bennett's report "American Education: Making It Work," quoted in Berger, "Educators Call Bennett Too Negative," New York Times, April 26, 1988, p. A-23.*

The constant criticism is demoralizing. If the Secretary of Commerce disliked businessmen as much as Bennett dislikes teachers, the President would throw him out of the Cabinet.

> *Albert Shanker, head of the American Federation of Teachers, complaining about Secretary of Education William Bennett's recent critique of the American educational system, quoted in "A New Battle over School Reform," Time, May 9, 1988, p. 61.*

Bennett has had the temerity to suggest that our educational system should exist to serve the interests of its students rather than to feather the beds of careerist administrators and teachers. For this he has been widely if predictably vilified, but he has persisted in his conviction that teachers should be rewarded not for seniority but for quality of work and that the unchecked growth of administrative bureaucracy is choking the educational system as well as diverting it from its fundamental obligations, both to students and to society,

> *Columnist Jonathan Yardley expressing admiration for outgoing education secretary William Bennett, in Yardley, "The Report Card of William J. Bennett," Washington Post, September 5, 1988, p. D-2.*

While responsibilities and demands have multiplied, teachers have seen little increase in the financial or moral support they need to do the job. Overcrowded classes, inadequate or outdated equipment and long hours are common. At the same time, in a panicked effort to improve their schools, many states and localities have added new and often burdensome course requirements, typically without input from teachers. "Traditionally, teachers have been treated like very tall children," observed Marty Futrell, president of the National Education Association (NEA), which represents 1.6 million schoolteachers. "We are not perfect," concedes Baltimore elementary school teacher Kathryn Jacobs. "But people need to walk in our shoes before they criticize."

> *Examining the difficult situation of teachers under pressure, in "Who's Teaching Our Children?" Time, November 14, 1988, p. 59.*

## Baby M

It seems to us that given her predicament, Mrs. Whitehead was rather harshly judged—both by the trial court and by some of the experts. She was guilty of a breach of contract, and indeed, she did break a very important promise, but we think it is expecting something well beyond normal human capabilities to suggest that this mother should have parted with her newly born infant without a struggle. Other than survival, what stronger force is there?

> *From the February 2, 1988, New Jersey Supreme Court ruling awarding custody of Baby M to her biological father, William Stern, but restoring parental rights to her mother, Mary Beth Whitehead, quoted in Chesler, Sacred Bond (1990), p. 201.*

It's a bad turn for surrogacy. Without judicial sanction, it will now be necessary for the legislature to write new laws. But surrogacy is just the kind of issue politicians would rather leave to the courts. It's such a hot potato nobody wants to mess with it. Besides, without payment there will be no surrogates or very few.

> *Gary Skoloff, attorney for Bill and Betsy Stern, on February 3, 1988, expressing his disappointment with the New Jersey Supreme Court ruling declaring commercial surrogacy illegal, quoted in Whitehead, A Mother's Story (1990), p. 199.*

But the reason the seven judges deserve a poem goes beyond surrogacy. What they really did was rule that a human soul was more important than a contract, that Judge Sorkow's philosophy that a deal is a deal is wrong when the deal involves the selling of a human being. Seven to zero wrong.

> *A. M. Rosenthal lauding the New Jersey Supreme Court's decision in the Baby M case, in Rosenthal, "A Poem for Seven Judges," New York Times, February 5, 1988, p. A-31.*

Just one year ago, the media were in full cry after Ms. Whitehead. It was like a wholesale retreat to the double standards of the 1950's: clean-cut, middle-class boy versus tainted "bad girl" of the underclass.

William Stern, the sperm donor, was "the natural father." She, the birth mother, was "the surrogate." He was controlled; she was distraught. She was "contemptible" for agreeing to have a baby-for-sale, and then "irresponsible" for turning down the money and trying to keep the baby. She was publicly sneered at for everything from dyeing her hair to buying teddy bears and playing "pat-a-cake" the "wrong" way.

"A deal's a deal!" everyone said. "She signed the contract, didn't she? She knew what she was doing." There was an almost unanimous public sentiment that "breaking the contract" was a crime against society.

*Journalist Michele Landsberg highlighting the public attitude toward Mary Beth Whitehead, in Landsberg, "Judge in Baby M Case Spoke in the Language of Feminists,"* Globe and Mail *(Montreal), February 6, 1988, p. A-2.*

The New Jersey Supreme Court applied a brake on the surrogate motherhood business. With dozens of laws being presented in state legislatures, with thousands of infertile couples rifling desperately through a filing cabinet of options, this decision hasn't come a moment too soon. But a more powerful message may well come, not from the courthouse, but from the obvious human muddle, the emotional shambles we've all witnessed.

The Baby M legal case is finally over. But the families are smack dab in the middle of a lifelong Baby M story. The M that stands for Mess.

*Columnist Ellen Goodman offering another perspective on the Baby M case, in Goodman, "In the Swirl of Surrogacy,"* Washington Post, *February 6, 1988, p. A-23.*

Approaching the case of Baby M, the New Jersey Supreme Court might have wished for the sword of Solomon—not to divide the child, but to cut through the Gordian thicket of paradox, bad faith and conflicting feelings that has surrounded the matter from the start. As it turned out, in a unanimous ruling last week the court sliced the issue in a way that gave important

concessions to both the parents, but cut to the quick the practice of surrogacy for pay.

*Illustrating the complex problems faced by the New Jersey Supreme Court in deciding the Baby M case, in "Baby M Meets Solomon's Sword,"* Time, *February 15, 1988, p. 97.*

## A Hard War to Fight

A plan whereby the government would supply drugs is not intended as a panacea. It would not eliminate drugs—as it hasn't in England—and, in a way, it would admit defeat, itself a bitter pill. It would mean, though, that we recognize that the drug problem is with us to stay—a tenacious enemy that mocks our every effort. When it comes to drugs, we've been making war long enough. It's time we started making sense instead.

*Columnist Richard Cohen suggesting that drugs be legalized, in Cohen, "Just Say Yes?"* Washington Post Magazine, *February 28, 1988, p. 5.*

It doesn't make sense to me when there are thousands of troops defending our allies' borders when our own borders are being overrun by what is killing us today. We must not just focus on children and athletes. Dope is corrupting governments, overthrowing systems. We must have a war on drugs and be serious about it.

*Reverend Jesse Jackson speaking at a presidential campaign rally in College Park, Maryland, on March 5, 1988, quoted in Hill, "Jackson Calls Drugs Threat to U.S. Security,"* Washington Post, *March 6, 1988, p. A-20.*

The destructive and insidious menace of drugs has again boiled to a crisis. Once more, the First Couple and other Americans have declared themselves fed up and angry about the damage that illegal drugs are wreaking on their homes and communities. This time, however, many people were asking more insistently whether the U.S. is really serious about combatting its drug problem. How long should Washington tolerate drug-financed corruption in such allied nations as Panama, Mexico and Colombia? And how long will ordinary Americans wink at the widespread, casual drug use that underwrites the violence on the streets?

*Looking at the growing epidemic of drug use and drug-related crimes, in "Tears of Rage,"* Time, *March 14, 1988, p. 18.*

In a primary season that has lacked emotional issues, drugs is the one subject thus far that seems to touch the voters directly, viscerally. Unlike the national debt and the trade deficit, it is neither abstruse nor abstract. It is a backyard issue. It is also one with wide appeal: it allows a candidate to sound tough in both domestic and foreign affairs while arousing passions among all economic groups, from the mean streets of the South Bronx to the manicured lawns of Westchester County. A recent New York *Times/CBS* News poll showed that Americans believed, 3 to 1, that fighting the flow of drugs into the country was more important than fighting communism.

*Examining the impact of the war on drugs on the presidential race, in "Riding the Drug Issue," Time, April 25, 1988, p. 32.*

The homeboys call him Frog. But as he swaggers through the Rancho Pedro Housing Project in East Los Angeles, Frog is a cocky prince of the barrio. His mane of lustrous jeri curls, his freckled nose and innocent brown eyes belie his prodigious street smarts. Frog is happy to tell you that he rakes in $200 a week selling crack [cocaine], known as rock in Los Angeles. He proudly advertises his fledgling membership in an ultra-violent street gang, the Crips. And he brags that he has used his drug money to rent a Nissan Z on weekends. He has not yet learned how to use a stick shift, however, and at 4 ft. 10 in., he sometimes has trouble seeing over the dashboard. Frog is 13 years old.

*Describing one of the more frightening trends in the explosive growth of drug use, in "Kids Who Sell Crack," Time, May 9, 1988, p. 20.*

Have we failed to consider the lessons of the Prohibition era? Now is the time to fight on the only terms the drug underground empire respects—money. Let's take the profit out of drug trafficking.

*Baltimore mayor Kurt L. Schmoke, arguing in favor of legalizing drugs, quoted in Kerr, "The Unspeakable is Debated: Should Drugs Be Legalized?" New York Times, May 15, 1988, sec. 1, p. 24.*

The legalization debate, to some extent, pits proponents, who would accept more drug abuse as the terrible price of reducing crime, against opponents, who would accept a continued high level crime as the equally dreadful price of holding down addiction. In fact, neither side can be sure to what extent legalization would reduce crime and increase addiction, unless it is tried. But the idea is risky, exceedingly risky.

*Examining the prospect of legalizing drugs, in "Thinking the Unthinkable," Time, May 30, 1988, p. 19.*

There are no needles in the schoolyards here, no gun battles in the streets. There are no Ferraris, no gently swaying palm trees or boatloads of drugs. This, emphatically, is not Miami, Los Angeles or even Chicago, a 3-hour drive to the northeast. In Peoria, the drug problem doesn't slap you in the face, but it's here. Drugs can be found on almost any block, from the decrepit Warner Homes, a dank public-housing ghetto on the city's south side, to Grandview Drive's old-money mansions up on the bluff overlooking the Illinois River. . . .

*Illustrating the pervasiveness of the country's drug-abuse problem, in "Drugs on Main Street: The Enemy Up Close," U.S. News & World Report, June 27, 1988, p. 15.*

Why, except for show, strip a person of benefits for a drug offense and no other crimes? Why favor rape and murder and stock fraud? The final bill also creates new federal penalties for the distribution of obscene material. The adopted procedures are better than broader ones originally favored by the Senate but still take the federal government into a difficult First Amendment area where legislation ought not be hastily written in the closing hours of a session on the back of even a plain brown envelope. That is about what happened here. The legislation also imposes the death penalty for certain drug-related killings. That may be constitutional, but it remains immoral.

*The Washington Post finding little to cheer about in the recently passed Anti-Drug Abuse Act, in its editorial "The Drug Bill," Washington Post, October 25, 1988, p. A-26.*

## Canadian Pride

There are no grand expectations here about going for the gold. "Go for it!" is not an expression found in the Canadian lexicon, perhaps in part because Canadian athletes have not often excelled in Olympic events. But winning takes a back seat in Canadian life to such other ideals as compassion, generosity, playing by the rules, being polite and not being uppity.

*Reporter Herbert H. Denton looking ahead positively to the winter Olympics in Calgary, in Denton, "Canadians Basking in Olympic Glow,"* Washington Post, *February 12, 1988, p. A-1.*

Canada's athletes didn't win a gold medal at the XV Winter Olympics, but let's award one just the same— unofficially, but with lots of feeling—to the citizens of Calgary.

They put on a show that has given this nation a special place in Olympic history. The end came yesterday with none of the rancor that clings to the memory of Montreal's Summer Games in 1976. Staggering debts and political turmoil don t figure in the indelible sports story Calgarians have written.

The lasting image of the Calgary Olympics will be the friendly atmosphere these hospitable people created and the quality of the spectacle, which was superb. There were glitches, to be sure; there always are. But they're so easy to overlook amid all this warmth.

*Journalist Jim Proudfoot commenting favorably on the Calgary winter Olympics, in Proudfoot, "Give Citizens of Calgary a Gold,"* Toronto Star, *February 29, 1988, p. D-1.*

## Canadian Prejudice

There will be some convulsions in adjusting to a new trade relationship but it will be a long process and a mistake to overestimate either the benefits or the losses, as it would be to put all our eggs in one continental basket. Canada should continue to make strenuous efforts to expand its world trade, especially in the Pacific Rim. But if we can do good business with the U.S., then we should try it. If we don't like it, we know what we can do about it.

*The* Vancouver Sun *being cautiously optimistic about the U.S.-Canada Free Trade Agreement in its editorial "Try It, We Might Even Like It,"* Vancouver Sun, *January 2, 1988, p. B-6.*

If I am successful in persuading Canadians that it's not just a matter of a trade agreement, it's a matter of political and economic and cultural independence, of our uniqueness as a nation, and of our way of life, I feel that it will be accepted by Americans. If there's an election

first, and the agreement is rejected, it will have been by the democratic process. In American corporate terms, we're taking this one to the shareholders. Americans understand that.

*John N. Turner, former prime minister and Liberal Party leader, explaining his opposition to the free trade agreement with respect to the American view, quoted in "Canada's Liberals Battle the Trade Pact,"* New York Times, *August 7, 1988, sec. 4, p. 3.*

No one really doubts that, purely in terms of trade and economics, the agreement would bring very substantial benefits to both countries. As the border impediments vanish—the tariffs, the quotas and most of the other restrictions—companies on both sides would be able to reorganize more effectively to serve a common market. These benefits would be more highly visible in Canada than here, simply because the Canadian economy is smaller. But there is also a long Canadian tradition of uneasiness about being folded into the United States and losing, for everyone but the mapmakers, a separate identity. There is no specific provision in the agreement that is being attacked as unfair. Instead, the debate is over the fear that closer association will inevitably mean a loss of national independence.

*The* Washington Post *examining the conflict in Canada over the free trade agreement, in its editorial "Making Up the Canadian Mind,"* Washington Post, *September 2, 1988, p. A-20.*

Free trade promotes consumerism. Consumerism promotes acid rain. How Canada, an acid-damaged nation and a world leader in the effort to stop acid rain, can justify free trade and therefore more energy and material production and consumption in two nations that already have the highest per capita energy consumption on earth strains logic.

*John Carroll, professor of environmental conservation at the University of New Hampshire, pointing out a conundrum of the proposed U.S.-Canada Free Trade Agreement, in a letter to the editor,* Globe and Mail *(Montreal), September 23, 1988, p. A-6.*

We have built a country . . . that resisted the continental pressure of the United States. For 120 years we've done it, and with one stroke of the pen you've reversed that. . . . And that will reduce us, I'm sure, to an economic colony of the United States, because when the economic levers go, the political independence is sure to follow.

*Liberal Party leader John Turner to Prime Minister Brian Mulroney in a preelection debate, quoted in " 'You Have Sold Us Out,' "* Newsweek, *November 14, 1988, p. 38.*

Of course, the Canadian economy has been growing nicely for 125 years without the deal. And accusations of Anti-Americanism are ridiculous. The trade deal was poorly negotiated by a Canadian Government that did not have confidence in its country's social and economic model.

Washington has learned over the past decades that it is better to have strong, self-confident allies than fearful shadows. If Canadians reject Mr. Mulroney and his trade deal, then Americans should be very pleased. It will mean that their closest ally and friend is alive and well.

*John Raulston Saul, a Toronto-based economic historian and novelist, expressing his anti–free trade opinion, in Saul, "Canada Debates Its Soul,"* New York Times, *November 16, 1988, p. A-31.*

Today, Canadians have stated, with a clear sense of their identity, what they want to be and what they want to do. The margin is decisive and the mandate is clear: to implement the free trade agreement, which holds the promise of new opportunities and new prosperity.

*Prime Minister Brian Mulroney claiming a mandate following a successful election campaign, quoted in Diebel, "It's Time for Healing, PM Says,"* Toronto Star, *November 22, 1988, p. B-1.*

The people of Canada have spoken, with pretty much the same language across the country.

We have a majority Conservative government, which seemed unthinkable in mid-1987 when the Tories ran third in opinion polls, plumbing historic depths.

We have a majority of seats for free trade. That seemed unlikely as recently as two weeks ago. Canada has avoided the paralysis of international trade policy, the disarray of business and investment, that would have followed any outcome but a pro-free-trade majority.

And we have a national consensus on free trade, a social contract that will settle that historic question with the assent of all parts of the country.

*Columnist William Johnson stressing the important results of the national election, in Johnson, "A Truly National Government Just When It's Needed,"* Vancouver Sun, *November 22, 1988, p. B-3.*

## A Dirty Campaign

If I am elected I won't be the first adulterer in the White House. I may be the first one to have publicly confessed.

*Colorado senator Gary Hart offering an unusual version of the truth on January 10, 1988, quoted in Slansky,* The Clothes Have No Emperor *(1989), p. 226.*

We came on the air. There were four minutes of clips—all questioning my word. It was a mean, tough interview. Dan came on, and he and I got right with it. I tried to keep cool. In fact, I think I did. But I'd be damned if I was going to let this guy walk all over me. . . .

*From George Bush's diary entry for January 25, 1988, describing his confrontation with journalist Dan Rather, in Bush,* All the Best, George Bush *(1999), p. 376.*

Trying to ask honest questions and trying to be persistent about answers is part of a reporter's job, and however it may seem at any given time, the intention of even persistent questions in a spirited interview is to do an honest, honorable job.

*Dan Rather defending his interview techniques with George Bush on CBS Evening News, January 26, 1988. Available online. URL: http://www. ratherbiased.com/bush_attack.htm.*

The operative midget strategy is meanness. Drawn-out nominating fights are not new in American politics. What is unprecedented this year is that, in the absence of a great issue or dominating personality defining either race, several candidates have structured their campaigns around assaulting their opponents—especially with negative commercials.

*Highlighting a disturbing trend in the presidential race, in "And Now, Campaign '88's Munchkin Marathon,"* U.S. News & World Report, *February 29, 1988, p. 12.*

Suddenly, what was once unthinkable has become worth considering, and some would say almost possible. And while few think the Democrats are ready to put Jackson on their national ticket, the fact that they are even talking about it represents a quantum leap in American politics. "Six months ago, no one was talking about his winning," says political strategist Robert Beckel. "People are beginning to talk about it in whispers late at night."

> *Looking at the growing impact of Jesse Jackson in the wake of his Super Tuesday primary wins, in "The New Age of Jackson,"* U.S. News & World Report, *March 14, 1988, p. 15.*

I'm drawn to a candidate I believe in, someone who could possibly carry the goals and ideals I found in the '60s. His whole campaign has been a healing process for the party. He's talking about issues and people we've ignored for years: drugs and economic devastation, issues that transcend ethnic and religious problems. The other candidates are just politicians. I can't get excited about them.

> *Joan Scerbo, a voter from Lyndhurst, New Jersey, explaining why she supports Jesse Jackson's candidacy, quoted in "Voices for Jesse,"* Time, *April 11, 1988, p. 17.*

Wherever you are tonight, you can make it. Hold your head high; stick your chest out. You can make it. It gets dark sometimes, but the morning comes. Don't you surrender!

Suffering breeds character, character breeds faith. In the end faith will not disappoint.

You must not surrender! You may or may not get there but just know that you're qualified! And you hold on, and hold out! We must never surrender! America will get better and better.

Keep hope alive. Keep hope alive! Keep hope alive! On tomorrow night and beyond, keep hope alive!

I love you very much. I love you very much.

> *Jesse Jackson, concluding his speech to the Democratic National Convention in Atlanta, July 19, 1988. Available online. URL: http://www.americanrhetoric. com/speeches/jessejackson1988dnc.htm.*

My friends, if anyone tells you that the American dream belongs to the privileged few and not to all of us, you tell them that the Reagan era is over and a new era is about to begin.

Because it's time to raise our sights—to look beyond the cramped ideals and limited ambitions of the past eight years—to recapture the spirit of energy and of confidence and of idealism that John Kennedy and Lyndon Johnson inspired a generation ago.

It's time to meet the challenge of the next American Frontier—the challenge of building an economic future for America that will create good jobs at good wages for every citizen in this land, no matter who they are or where they come from or what the color of their skin.

It's time to rekindle the American spirit of invention and daring, to exchange voodoo economics for can-do economics, to build the best America by bringing out the best in every American.

> *Massachusetts governor Michael Dukakis in his acceptance speech at the Democratic National Convention in Atlanta, July 21, 1988. Available online. URL: http://www.geocities.com/Wellesley/ 1116/dukakis88.html.*

What a funny lull of a period. After the Dukakis triumph at the convention, we're getting all kinds of cosmetic advice: wear dark suits, stand up straighter, wear Cary Grant glasses—those are the ones with the dark frames—hold hands with Barbara more, be politer to her, didn't you see the way the Dukakises were hugging there in public; and I'm thinking, come on, this stuff about them dancing with no music in the holding room, and the press finding out about it—that's crazy; or that arm around his shoulder, looking like they're madly in love—it just doesn't seem real. And yes, I'm being advised to do that, reach out, hold Bar's hand, and she and I laugh about it and think how ridiculous it's gotten in this country; but that's the way things go, and that's probably why I'm 18 points back. . . .

> *From George H. W. Bush's diary entry for July 27, 1988, in Bush,* All the Best, George Bush *(1999), p. 394.*

And there is another tradition. And that is the idea of community—a beautiful word with a big meaning. Though liberal democrats have an odd view of it. They see "community" as a limited cluster of interest groups, locked in odd conformity. In this view, the country waits passive while Washington sets the rules.

But that's not what community means—not to me.

For we are a nation of communities, of thousands and tens of thousands of ethnic, religious, social, business, labor union, neighborhood, regional and other organizations, all of them varied, voluntary and unique.

This is America: the Knights of Columbus, the Grange, Hadassah, the Disabled American Veterans, the Order of Ahepa, the Business and Professional Women of America, the union hall, the Bible study group, LULAC, "Holy Name"—a brilliant diversity spread like stars, like a thousand points of light in a broad and peaceful sky.

Does government have a place? Yes. Government is part of the nation of communities—not the whole, just a part.

*Vice President George H. W. Bush in his acceptance speech at the Republican National Convention in New Orleans, August 18, 1988. Available online. URL: http://www.geocities.com/rickmatlick/nomahbush88.htm.*

If Bush's speech [accepting his nomination for president] can be considered a triumph, the selection of Indiana Senator Dan Quayle for the second spot has so far been a disaster. Even before the stories of Quayle's National Guard service surfaced—and the senator stumbled through conflicting accounts of the problem—his designation was met with stunned disbelief. Without prompting, most GOP leaders brushed past their on-the-record enthusiasm to express not-for-attribution shock. Some were so upset they didn't bother with distinctions. "I'm underwhelmed," said Illinois Representative Henry Hyde, an archconservative one might expect to welcome the presence of an ideological soul mate. Hyde's reaction was typical—and mild.

*Looking at the reaction to George H. W. Bush's choice of running mate, in "Can Bush Survive Quayle?" U.S. News & World Report, August 29/September 5, 1988, pp. 24–25.*

**Dan Quayle:** Three times that I've had this question—and I will try to answer it again for you, because the question you are asking is what kind of qualifications does Dan Quayle have to be president, what kind of qualifications do I have and what would I do in this kind of a situation. . . . It is not just age; it's accomplishments, it's experience. I have far more experience than many others that sought the office of vice president of this country. I have as much experience in the Congress as Jack Kennedy did when he sought the presidency.

George H. W. Bush and Dan Quayle pose in a June 1989 photo. *(Courtesy George Bush Presidential Library)*

**Judy Woodruff:** Senator Bentsen.

**Lloyd Bentsen:** Senator, I served with Jack Kennedy, I knew Jack Kennedy, Jack Kennedy was a friend of mine. Senator, you are no Jack Kennedy.

*An exchange in the vice presidential debate of October 5, 1988, with CNN moderator Judy Woodruff; Bentsen's comment caused shouts and applause from the audience. Available online. URL: http://eightiesclub.tripod.com/id346.htm.*

Such is the sour legacy of 1988, an election year that was to substance what cold pizza is to a balanced breakfast. Think of the words and phrases that 18 months of nonstop electioneering have underlined in the political lexicon: *Monkey Business,* the character issue, attack videos, plagiarism, wimp, handlers, sound bites, flag factories, tank rides, negative spots, the A.C.L.U., Willie Horton and likability. Match them with all the pressing national concerns that were never seriously discussed: from the Japanese economic challenge to the plight of the underclass. As the voters trudge off to the polls with all the enthusiasm of dental patients, one can almost hear their collective lament: "What has America done as a nation to deserve an election like this?"

*Taking a sardonic view of the 1988 election race, in "Why It Was So Sour," Time, November 14, 1988, pp. 18–19.*

The race really had turned into a referendum on what Ronald Reagan had done. That's why students at Notre Dame bellowed "Four more years" in the face of George Bush, the understudy who finally got his star's part. And that's why Michael Dukakis's final cries were about drugs and Noriega and guns and the Ayatollah and other leftover misdemeanors.

*Analyzing the outcome of the presidential election, in "An End and a Beginning," U.S. News & World Report, November 14, 1988, p. 21.*

Bush won by default, and by fouls. His "mandate" is to ignore the threats to our economy, sustain the Reagan heritage of let's-pretend, and serve as a figurehead for what America has become, a frightened empire hiding its problems from itself.

*Columnist Garry Wills taking a pessimistic view of George H. W. Bush's win, in Wills, "The Power Populist," Time, November 21, 1988, p. 72.*

## Terror Strikes

This is a burden I will carry for the rest of my life. But under the circumstances and considering all the information available to me at the moment, I took this action to defend my ship and my crew.

*Captain Will Rogers of the USS Vincennes to his commanders following the accidental shootdown of Iran Air Flight 655 on July 3 1988, quoted in "Seven Minutes to Death," Newsweek, July 18, 1988, p. 21.*

Post has been notified by the Federal Aviation Administration that on December 5, 1988, an unidentified individual telephoned a U.S. diplomatic facility in Europe and stated that sometime within the next two weeks there would be a bombing attempt against a Pan American aircraft flying from Frankfurt to the United States.

The FAA reports that the reliability of the information cannot be assessed at this point, but the appropriate police authorities have been notified and are pursuing the matter. Pan Am also has been notified.

In view of the lack of confirmation of this information, post leaves to the discretion of individual travelers any decisions on altering personal travel plans or changing to another American carrier. This does not absolve the traveler from flying an American carrier.

*Notice of the Helsinki warning, posted at the American Embassy in Moscow on December 13, 1988, quoted in Cox and Foster, Their Darkest Day (1992), p. 55.*

Everything started falling down—lumps of plane, bits of seat belts, packets of sugar, bits of bodies. There were burning bits all over the forecourt. It seemed to shower for ages, but it was only for about five minutes. We had just had a delivery of petrol that morning, and I thought the whole forecourt was going to go up.

*Lockerbie resident Ruth Jameson describing the scene at Townfoot petrol station in Lockerbie, Scotland, after Pan Am 103 exploded on December 21, 1988, quoted in Sheridan and Kenning, Survivors (1993), p. 120.*

I was sitting at my desk when Dan burst into the room and said that Clem had called, saying a plane from England had crashed. "It can't be Theo," I said, jumping up and running out of the room. "That must be the morning flight, the one she wasn't on." I rushed downstairs to the calendar next to my kitchen desk. There it was, glowing in huge numbers, "Pan Am 103." "It *is* Theo's flight," I screamed. I turned around and looked at the television facing me from the den. That horrible picture of the flaming wreckage. She was in that. My Theo was in there. Dan looked at me and said, "Susan, I don't see how anyone could have survived."

*Author Susan Cohen describing the moment on December 21, 1988, when she and her husband learned of the crash of Pan Am 103, in which their daughter Theo had been a passenger, in Cohen, Pan Am 103 (2000), pp. 7–8.*

There was an almighty bang which knocked me to the floor. I thought the whole place was going to fall in on top of us. I picked myself up, went outside and saw fires all over the place and wreckage raining down.

We started getting the old people out of the way. We were worried about the filling station nearby and whether the petrol tanks would go up.

We had to leave the house, we could do nothing about it and the whole place was burnt down, completely destroyed.

> *Archie Smith, a Lockerbie resident, describing his experience in the disaster, quoted in Gill and Faux, "Flames Light the Night Sky as Crash of Jumbo Brings Horror to A Small Town,"* Times (London), *December 22, 1988, p. 2.*

In a field close by lies a seat with its safety belt still attached. In the woods alongside lies a twisted lump of fuselage the size of a tractor. And on the steep hill rising from Lockerbie to the golf course lies the body of a man.

He is not burnt beyond recognition. He is not crushed. The clichéd descriptions which spring to mind when you hear that a 747 has disintegrated at 31,000 feet cannot distance you from him.

He is whole, strong and unmistakably human. His arms are braced against the earth and one hand grips the surface.

Around him are things which should not have survived when he did not. An unopened and unbroken quarter-bottle of Pan Am's claret. A green seat cushion with a gaudy cover.

> *Nick Cohen, a reporter for the* Independent, *graphically depicting the scene in Lockerbie in an article published December 22, 1988, quoted in Deppa,* The Media and Disasters *(1993), pp. 75–80.*

Jeffrey F. Kreindler, vice president for communications at Pan Am, said that when the bulletin was received by the airline "immediate action was taken, and the steps that were implemented at that time are still in place."

But Pan Am and the Federal Aviation Administration refused to say what security measures were adopted after the bomb threat this month.

Aviation security experts cited three reasons not to warn the public of threats. First, they said such notice would undermine security by disclosing to terrorist groups how much the authorities know. Second, they said public notice might lead to "copy cat" threats, magnifying the problem. Third, the airlines would suffer

cancellations by passengers even when the threats were not valid.

> *Examining the reasons why the Helsinki warning was not made public, in Cushman, "U.S. Was Tipped Off 2 Weeks Ago of Possible Attack on Pan Am,"* New York Times, *December 23, 1988, p. A-16.*

If a bomb was the cause, who planted it, and why? The inevitable anonymous callers only added to the uncertainty. In London, a group identifying itself as "the Guardians of the Islamic Revolution" claimed responsibility in a phone call to a wire service, saying it had exacted "revenge" for the Iranian airliner accidentally shot down by a U.S. Navy cruiser in the Persian Gulf last summer. In Rome, a caller to another news agency said the 747 had been destroyed on behalf of Libya, bombed in 1986 by U.S. warplanes in retaliation for Muammar Kaddafi's alleged sponsorship of terrorism.

> *Beginning the process of discovering who bombed Pan Am 103, in "An Explosion in the Sky,"* Newsweek, *January 2, 1989, p. 16.*

The need for tougher measures was apparent long before the metallic shower struck Lockerbie. A ten-man Israeli security team studied 25 Pan Am airport facilities for the airline in 1986. It concluded that Pan Am was "almost totally vulnerable to midair explosion through explosive charges concealed in the cargo." The team claimed, for example, that baggage could be loaded on Pan Am airliners in London and Hamburg without its owner also boarding; that Pan Am planes too often carried both passengers and general cargo; that in Europe the checked baggage of some citizens of certain nations, including the U.S., was not examined at all.

The Israelis say Pan Am officials rejected many of the suggested remedies as too expensive for such a large airline to implement. "We told them many times it was a matter of life and death," said one of the authors of the report last week. "But they seemed to know better and told us they would go their own way. What a pity."

> *Reflecting on the lapses in security that led to the Pan Am 103 bombing, in "'Diabolically Well-Planned,'"* Time, *January 9, 1989, p. 28.*

## A New World Order Emerges

The United States does not understand that we have different values. The United States values private initiative, private property. Its media, its philosophy, its politicians all protect that. That's the choice of the United States. Whereas in the Soviet Union, we're just beginning to develop new forms of cooperation and individual work. And people are asking if that means a return to private property, to capitalism, to the exploitation of the working class. We are just beginning to develop these forms, and the charges [against private initiatives] have nothing to do with reality.

*General Secretary Mikhail Gorbachev complaining to Secretary of State George Shultz about U.S. criticism of Soviet human rights during a meeting in Moscow, April 22, 1988, quoted in Shultz,* Turmoil and Triumph *(1993), pp. 1,098–1,099.*

A people free to choose will always choose peace.... Your generation is living in one of the most exciting, hopeful times in Soviet history. It is a time when the first breath of freedom stirs the air and the heart beats to the accelerated rhythm of hope, when the accumulated spiritual energies of a long silence yearn to break free.

*Ronald Reagan speaking to Moscow State University students on May 31, 1988, quoted in Shultz,* Turmoil and Triumph *(1993), p. 1104.*

Sights! Camera! Action! Reagan the actor and Reagan the campaigner took his White House road show to Moscow for his fourth summit with Mikhail Gorbachev. With the Kremlin as his almost constant backdrop, the President seemed to be out on the stump for his host, praising the man and his reforms. Although there were seven signed agreements, those treaties were merely a sideshow: the main event was Ron and Mikhail. Gorbachev later complained about "missed opportunities," but nobody could have interpreted that as "missed photo opportunities," because none were.

*Time magazine commenting on the public-relations aspect of the Moscow summit in "'Good Chemistry,'"* Time, *June 13, 1988, p. 13.*

The new U.S. shorthand for this latest turn in relations will do for now. Yet somehow "realistic engagement" falls far short of capturing what has really transpired in four telescoped summits. That odd couple, Ronald Reagan and Mikhail Gorbachev, have begun to put the cold war to rest. It won't die easily: There are simply too many ideological divisions and real-world flash points. But images of this most conservative of Presidents,

George H. W. Bush, Ronald Reagan, and Mikhail Gorbachev meet in New York City on December 7, 1988.  *(Courtesy Ronald Reagan Library)*

peaceably strolling through Red Square with the leader of the Communist empire, symbolize something new—an era of routine Soviet-American superchat that may make future summits hardly worthy of the word.

*Summarizing the implications of the Moscow summit, in "A Triumph of Symbols,"* U.S. News & World Report, *June 13, 1988, p. 41.*

The goal of Gorbachev's foreign policy is not to end the cold war and certainly not to lose it, but to continue the struggle with the subtlety and finesse that befits the modern man he is. He is cutting his losses not because he has lost the nationalist or ideological faith that underlies Soviet realpolitik, but because he knows that what the times demand is discrimination. And in an age of triage, that means concentrating on supreme geopolitical objectives and making sacrifices at the periphery.

*Essayist Charles Krauthammer examining Mikhail Gorbachev's motives, in Krauthammer, "No, the Cold War Isn't Really Over,"* Time, *September 5, 1988, p. 83.*

At the end of the luncheon, President Reagan said to Gorbachev, "This is my last meeting with you, and I raise a glass to what you have accomplished, what we have accomplished together, and to what you and George Bush will accomplish together after January 20."

"I can join in that toast, and will the vice president do so as well?" asked Gorbachev.

"Yes, I do," George Bush said.

"Good, then, that is our first agreement," Gorbachev said jovially.

> *George Shultz describing the positive atmosphere of a luncheon meeting on Governor's Island, New York, December 7, 1988, during Mikhail Gorbachev's visit to the United States, in Shultz,* Turmoil and Triumph *(1993), p. 1108.*

## *Farewell*

Reagan is the last president for whom the Depression will have been a formative experience, the last president whose foremost model was the first modern president, Franklin Roosevelt. Roosevelt's first words as president ("the only thing we have to fear is fear itself") emphasized the tone-setting role of the office, and the need for high public morale. America was far less troubled in 1983 than in 1933, but it needed reassurance. It needed to recover confidence in its health and goodness. It needed to recover what was lost in the 1960s and 1970s, the sense that it has a competence commensurate with its nobility and responsibilities. Reagan, like Roosevelt, has been a great reassurer, a steadying captain who calmed the passengers and, to some extent, the sea.

> *Columnist George F. Will examining Ronald Reagan's remarkable staying power, in Will, "How Reagan Changed America,"* Newsweek, *January 9, 1989, p. 17.*

I've spoken of the shining city all my political life, but I don't know if I've ever quite communicated what I saw when I said it. But in my mind, it was a tall proud city built on rocks stronger than oceans, wind swept, God blessed, and teeming with people of all kinds living in

A cheerful former president salutes before boarding the helicopter that will take him away from Washington on January 20, 1989. *(Courtesy Ronald Reagan Library)*

harmony and peace—a city with free ports that hummed with commerce and creativity, and if there had to be city walls, the walls had doors, and the doors were open to anyone with the will and the heart to get here.

That's how I saw it, and see it still.

And how stands the city on this winter night? More prosperous, more secure and happier than it was eight years ago. But more than that: after 200 years, two centuries, she still stands strong and true on the granite ridge, and her glow has held steady no matter what storm.

And she's still a beacon, still a magnet for all who must have freedom, for all the Pilgrims from all the lost places who are hurtling through the darkness, toward home.

*Ronald Reagan in his farewell address to the nation, January 11, 1989, invoking his favorite metaphor for the United States as a "shining city upon a hill." Available online. URL: http://www.ronaldreagan. com/sp_21.html.*

Any meaningful grand analysis of the Reagan presidency must await a longer perspective and more exhaustive analysis than the president's own goodbye speech. But it is undeniably the Reagan legacy and accomplishment that he made us feel good about ourselves as a country and about the office of the presidency. He brought us measurably closer to the ideal of a "shining city upon a hill" by his own powers of persuasion. Perhaps it is in part illusion made reality by the power of positive thinking—but it is reality nonetheless.

America really likes Ronald Reagan.

*The* Albuquerque Journal *summing up a national attitude in its editorial "Reagan's World View,"* Albuquerque Journal, *January 14, 1989, quoted in Boyer,* Reagan as President *(1990), pp. 280–281.*

# 8

# The Torch Is Passed
## January 1989–January 1990

On January 20, 1989, George Herbert Walker Bush became the United States' 41st president, the most experienced in federal government administration since Richard Nixon. In his inaugural address, he described the American people's purpose as making "kinder the face of the Nation and gentler the face of the world." Evoking another Bush catchphrase, he added: "I will go to the people and the programs that are the brighter points of light, and I'll ask every member of my government to become involved. The old ideas are new again because they're not old, they are timeless: duty, sacrifice, commitment, and a patriotism that finds its expression in taking part and pitching in."[1]

Bush's words echoed a message that Jimmy Carter had tried to convey, but history and changed circumstances gave them a new meaning. Ronald Reagan had lifted Americans out of the malaise that began the decade; now the torch was passed to George H. W. Bush, who would continue Reagan's policies while trying to put his personal stamp on the presidency after eight years in his predecessor's shadow.

Yet Bush, like Carter, would be a one-term president, a victim of circumstances. One important factor in this was his lack of what he derisively called "the vision thing." In 1980 Reagan had offered a very clear picture of what he intended to do. In 1988 Bush had no fresh proposals to make, no new vision to offer. His inaugural address foreshadowed his approach:

> Some see leadership as high drama and the sound of trumpets calling, and sometimes it is that. But I see history as a book with many pages, and each day we fill a page with acts of hopefulness and meaning. The new breeze blows, a page turns, the story unfolds.[2]

He was not a crusader like Reagan but a negotiator. As Dilys M. Hill and Phil Williams write in *The Bush*

President George H. W. Bush poses for his official portrait in February 1989. *(Courtesy George Bush Presidential Library)*

*Presidency,* "he was the ultimate pragmatist, rejecting what he dismissed as the 'vision thing' in favour of an approach which treated issues on their merits and regarded political compromise as the norm."[3]

This approach worked successfully in certain areas, particularly in foreign policy. Despite criticisms that he was too cautious, Bush was well qualified to deal with the momentous changes in world affairs that took place during his watch and were a direct result of the Reagan legacy, most especially the collapse of communism in Eastern Europe. His administration would also see major successes such as the Panama invasion in 1989 and the Persian Gulf War in 1991, following which his popularity skyrocketed. All this was on the credit side of the ledger.

On the debit side, his predecessor had left domestic affairs in disarray. With an out-of-control budget deficit, innumerable scandals, and continued heated debate over such issues as civil rights, homelessness, AIDS funding, abortion, gun control, the drug war, and the environment, Bush had his hands full. In 1990 the combined effects of supply-side economics and 1989's savings-and-loan crisis brought about a two-year recession for which Americans came to blame him. Like Carter, he had inherited rather than created the country's economic difficulties, but Bush could do little more than react to them and produce interim solutions. For obvious reasons, he could not blame his predecessor, as Reagan had done in 1981, and when he was forced to renege on his famous campaign pledge and raise taxes in 1990, his fate was sealed. In 1992 Bill Clinton would make the economy the key issue of his campaign, using it just as effectively against Bush as Reagan had done against Carter in 1980.

This, then, was what lay in front of George Bush: four years of euphoric highs thanks to overseas achievements and devastating lows due to crises at home and questions about his leadership qualities. The problems began almost at once when, because of allegations of impropriety, the Senate rejected his nominee for

As chairman of the Joint Chiefs of Staff, Colin Powell oversaw the Panama invasion in December 1989. He was also National Security Advisor for President Reagan, with him in this April 1988 photo. *(Courtesy Ronald Reagan Library)*

secretary of defense, former Texas senator John Tower.[4] Bush had better success with other appointments, most notably James Baker as secretary of state, Brent Scowcroft as National Security Advisor, and Colin Powell as chairman of the Joint Chiefs of Staff. He was a hands-on administrator with strong control over his staff—a reassuring quality after the Iran-contra affair. But many of his difficulties in 1989 were the direct result of his predecessor's laissez-faire management, making it a year when his primary task seemed to be cleaning up after Ronald Reagan.

## LINGERING SCANDALS

Controversy had become a hallmark of Reagan's administration: By the time he left office, 138 of his staff had been indicted or investigated for misconduct or wrongdoing. Even those closest to him did not escape censure. Labor Secretary Raymond Donovan was the first cabinet member to be indicted while in office, although he was acquitted in 1987 of grand larceny and fraud. Michael Deaver, whose service with Reagan dated from the California governorship days, left the White House in 1985. Two years later he was indicted for violating laws on lobbying by former senior government officials; in 1988 he was fined $100,000 for lying under oath to Congress, sentenced to community service, and given a three-year suspended prison term. That same year another former Reagan aide, Lyn Nofziger, was convicted for his involvement in a defense contract that was awarded to Wedtech Electronics, a minority-owned firm that engaged in bribes, payoffs, and fraud; his conviction was overturned in 1989.

Edwin Meese, whose appointment as attorney general in 1985 had taken more than a year for the Senate to approve, was subjected to accusations of ethical misconduct throughout his service with Reagan, including probable involvement in the Wedtech scandal. No grounds for indictment were found, nor was there sufficient evidence to charge him with taking bribes or illegal gratuities. Nevertheless, Meese was continually forced to defend himself, morale plummeted at the Justice Department, and he finally resigned on July 5, 1988.

Several scandals spilled over into the Bush years, most famously the savings-and-loan crisis (discussed separately). One scandal had erupted in June 1988 when Americans learned that since 1986 the FBI had been investigating Pentagon officials and defense contractors. Operation Ill Wind exposed a web of bribery, fraud, rigged contracts, and trading of inside information, all resulting in incredible waste. That the Pentagon was spending hundreds, sometimes thousands, of dollars on such items as toilet seats was bad enough, but the public was appalled to learn that some $160 million a day was being spent on military procurement, with contracts usually awarded to preferred firms. The investigation concluded in 1989, and seven companies, nine government officials, and 42 individuals were prosecuted.

An even lengthier investigation focused on the Department of Housing and Urban Development (HUD). At the center of the scandal were Secretary Samuel R. Pierce, Jr., and his executive assistant, Deborah Gore Dean. Pierce, a former lawyer and judge who had once defended Martin Luther King, Jr., was the highest-ranking African American in Reagan's administration. Known as Silent Sam for his unassuming ways, he was the only cabinet member to remain in office for the entire eight years, and until 1989 he was largely unknown to the public.

HUD had been created in 1965 to provide housing assistance to low-income families. Reagan saw the department as wasteful and unnecessary, and Pierce did not object when his funding was cut by more than 50 percent between 1981 and 1986 and its staff reduced from 16,000 to 11,000. The secretary's focus on civil rights was reflected in legislation to eliminate discrimination in rental housing, among several positive initiatives. But he largely neglected other HUD areas, and after promoting Dean in 1984, he increasingly left the department's management to her and other young aides, referred to as the "brat pack" by career officials.

Dean, a former bartender, reveled in the power of her position and frequently used Pierce's autopen to sign documents and contracts when the secretary was unavailable. Ironically, the severe cutback of HUD's appropriations only made her more important, as developers competed for the available monies, and members of Congress sought funding for projects in their states. Dean took full advantage, accepting gifts and kickbacks while doling out contracts based on friendship and political favoritism. Influential Republicans courted her, and former HUD employees who were Dean pals benefited by getting "most favored" status for the firms they joined after leaving government service. James G. Watt, former secretary of the interior, received more than $400,000 for "consultancy fees." Escrow agent Marilyn Louise Harrell, who received $5 million of HUD money, later claimed that she had allotted the money to the poor; federal investigators dubbed her Robin HUD.

As a result of such activities, billions of HUD dollars were spent not on renovations to low-income housing but on golf courses, swimming pools, and condominiums. More than 80 congressional committees and subcommittees had some degree of oversight for HUD activities, in addition to the Office of Management and Budget. Yet it was not until former New York congressman Jack Kemp became secretary in 1989 and the inspector general released an internal audit that the scandal became public knowledge. Kemp promptly purged the department of hundreds of employees and spent months trying to restore order.

In May 1989 the House Government Operations subcommittee, chaired by Representative Tom Lantos (D, Calif.), began hearings to investigate HUD. Pierce admitted to "lax supervision" but denied involvement in specific funding decisions and blamed Dean and her associates. Nevertheless, he was excoriated for allowing unethical practices to take place, and it transpired that he had occasionally intervened to award contracts to friends and political cronies. When the hearings resumed in the fall, Pierce took the Fifth Amendment.

Independent counsels were appointed to investigate HUD practices, but matters were so complicated that their final reports were not released until 1998. They revealed extraordinary levels of waste and a "monumental and calculated abuse of the public trust."[5] The prosecutors managed to retrieve $10 million in misappropriated funds and collected $2 million in fines. They also achieved 17 criminal convictions, including that of James Watt, who, indicted on 25 felony counts, pleaded guilty in 1996 to a single misdemeanor, for which he received five years' probation and a $5,000 fine.

Though Pierce was never charged, his reputation was severely damaged by the scandal, and his aspirations for a Supreme Court seat were shattered. In 1994 he publicly acknowledged having created an environment for corruption. Deborah Gore Dean was convicted on 12 felony counts in 1993 (five were later overturned) and sentenced to three concurrent 21-month terms in prison; by the end of 2004 she had yet to serve any time due to pending appeals.

In December 1989 the Kemp-backed Housing and Urban Development Reform Act was signed into law, establishing more than 50 measures to insure HUD's financial integrity. Kemp was nonetheless hindered by senators and representatives determined to use "discretionary" HUD funds for pork-barrel spending on projects in their states.

Congress suffered its own share of damage in 1989, when Republicans brought charges of unethical conduct against Democratic congressman Jim Wright (Tex.), who had succeeded Tip O'Neill as Speaker of the House in 1987. Questions were asked about his connections with federal bank officials in the savings-and-loan troubles, gifts that he had received from a Fort Worth developer, and royalties from his 1984 autobiography, all of which were believed to have been inflated in exchange for political favors. Although nothing was proven, the accusations and searching examinations were too much for Wright, who, on May 31, announced his intention to resign, citing his colleagues' "mindless cannibalism." Within two weeks, Democratic majority whip Tony Coelho (Calif.) resigned under similar circumstances.

Wright's chief accuser, Newt Gingrich (R, Ga.), would later become the first Republican Speaker of the House in 40 years—and would resign in 1998 amid charges of campaign funding violations. No wonder most Americans considered unethical behavior in government to be an inescapable fact of life.

## THE SAVINGS-AND-LOAN DEBACLE

Another legacy from the Reagan era that finally boiled over in 1989 concerned the savings-and-loan (S&L) industry. S&L associations (also called thrifts) had been established during the Great Depression to make home mortgages available through a reserve credit system overseen by the Federal Home Loan Bank Board (FHLBB), which had been created under the Home Loan Bank Act of 1932. The FHLBB became the primary agency regulating federally chartered S&Ls, and the National Housing Act of 1934 established the Federal Savings and Loan Insurance Corporation (FSLIC) to insure thrift deposits.

FHLBB and FSLIC regulations imposed funding and lending rates based on geographic location. Twelve regional Federal Home Loan Banks served as intermediaries between federal and district banks, the latter providing funds (at below-market rates) to member S&Ls. Individual thrifts were restricted to home loans to borrowers living within a 50-mile radius of their offices. During the 1960s some regulations were relaxed, and S&Ls gained greater lending powers but were still subject to certain restrictions. When the economic climate worsened in the late 1970s, so did the thrifts' profitability. As the authors of *Big Money Crime* write, "With inflation at 13.3 percent by 1979 and with thrifts constrained by regulation to pay no more than 5.5 percent interest on new deposits, the industry could not attract new money."[6] The raising of interest rates in 1979 only made matters worse, and by 1982 "the entire industry was insolvent by $150 billion on a market-value basis and the FSLIC had only $6 billion in reserve."[7]

Deregulation had begun prior to the Reagan era. The Depository Institutions Deregulation and Monetary Control Act of 1980 ended restrictions on the thrifts' interest rates and increased FSLIC insurance from a maximum $40,000 to

$100,000 per deposit, encouraging many S&Ls to engage in riskier loans. Further, the FHLBB eliminated its 5 percent limit on brokered deposits, which allowed brokers to combine individual investments into $100,000 certificates of deposit (CDs), setting off a boom in that area.

The 1981 Tax Reform Act led to a real estate explosion, but the S&L industry was still troubled, and Reagan determined to deregulate it even further. The Garn–St. Germain Depository Institutions Act of December 1982 phased out ceilings on interest rates and allowed the thrifts to invest in areas other than residential real estate. It also allowed S&Ls to make commercial and corporate loans and provide 100 percent financing with no down payment from borrowers. Intended to attract new business to the industry, the act also provided opportunities for fraud and insider abuses, with appraisals often exceeding the real value of properties.

The FHLBB aggravated matters by abandoning other restrictions. After 1982, S&Ls no longer needed to have at least 400 stockholders, and a stockholder was no longer restricted to owning a maximum 25 percent of a thrift. Further, not only could a single investor now own an entire institution, but an S&L could be established using noncash assets (land and real estate). Many states also relaxed regulations, giving S&Ls further freedom, although many state-regulated S&Ls rushed to become federally chartered institutions instead. Even state-chartered thrifts could be FSLIC-insured as long as they made the payments, which most did. By 1986 the FSLIC was insuring 92.6 percent of the nation's S&Ls and holding more than 98 percent of the industry's assets.[8]

Deregulation aimed to give the S&Ls access to free-market competition while protected by federal insurance. But the same competition only put the thrifts deeper into debt as they tried to attract "hot" deposits to boost their profitability—and also put depositors' funds into high-risk loans and investments. Consequently, a growing number of S&Ls went under, and the FSLIC had to merge or close insolvent thrifts. By 1986 the FSLIC itself was broke and, unable to pay off depositors, had to reduce the numbers of closures—leaving extant insolvent institutions to go deeper into debt.

Since 1983 FHLBB chairman Edwin J. Gray had been trying to control matters with new regulations, but this ran contrary to Reagan administration aims of giving free rein to the thrifts. Congress also dragged its feet in legislating reforms, severely hampering the board's efforts to reassert control and investigate cases of fraud. Meanwhile, throughout the country S&Ls were failing at an astounding rate;[9] the scale of the crisis became apparent in July 1988, when the cost of saving the Texas failures alone was estimated at $152 billion. At the end of the year, the FHLBB reported that it had sold or merged 222 S&Ls in 1988, representing $100 billion in accounts; the FSLIC paid out $38.6 billion in emergency assistance—all at taxpayers' expense.

The situation came to a head in 1989, when the Lincoln Savings and Loan Association of Irvine, California, collapsed; its liquidation would cost at least $2.5 billion. The FHLBB blamed the thrift's failure on Charles H. Keating, Jr., chairman of Lincoln's parent company, American Continental Corporation, but Keating informed the House Banking Committee that he had been victimized by Edwin Gray, who had resigned as FHLBB chairman in 1987. Gray told a different story: Prior to his resignation, five U.S. senators had approached him and asked him to ease off on the board's audit of the Lincoln S&L. Press investigations had already revealed that Keating had made campaign contributions totaling $1.3 million to those same senators: Alan Cranston (D, Calif.), Dennis DeConcini (D, Ariz.), John Glenn (D, Ohio), John McCain (R, Ariz.), and Donald Riegle, Jr. (D, Mich.). In the resulting scandal, the "Keating Five" were investigated by the Department of Justice and Senate Ethics Committee.[10]

The senators' interference in the Lincoln audit indicated another reason why Congress had been slow to act on the mounting S&L crisis. The public would later learn that hundreds of thrifts had donated money to political campaigns, approximately $11 million throughout the 1980s; some $800,000 in "soft money" (campaign contributions not regulated by federal election laws) had apparently gone to George Bush's presidential campaign. Further, it was found that up to 40 percent of the failed S&Ls had allegedly been involved in some form of criminal action.[11]

These revelations were still to come, but by early 1989 the crisis—hardly mentioned during the 1988 campaign—could no longer be ignored. On February 6, 1989, President Bush unveiled a bailout plan for the S&Ls which, after considerable debate and changes, became law on August 9. The Financial Institutions Reform Recovery and Enforcement Act (FIRREA) provided $166 billion to rescue the failed thrifts, with 75 percent of the money to be obtained from taxes over 10 years. The act replaced the Federal Home Loan Bank Board, with the Office of Thrift Supervision (OTS) to serve as the S&L industry's new regulatory agency. The bankrupt FSLIC was also abolished, and deposit insurance for the thrifts was transferred to the Federal Deposit Insurance Corporation (FDIC). To oversee the S&Ls' finances and restructuring, the Resolution Trust Corporation (RTC) was created to merge or liquidate vulnerable thrifts, with its work to be completed by the end of 1996.

In 1993 Charles Keating was convicted of fraud, racketeering, and conspiracy, and he served four and a half years in prison before his convictions were overturned. Prior to retrial, however, he entered into a plea bargain in which he admitted extracting large sums from the Lincoln Savings and Loan just before its failure. Keating came to symbolize the greed and excess that had nearly caused the collapse of the entire industry until the federal government intervened—the very thing that Ronald Reagan abhorred and George Bush had to invoke. In the end, though, it was the taxpayers who suffered, as the crisis produced high interest rates, inflated the already high budget deficit, reduced economic growth, and eventually induced a recession, all of which forced Bush to renege on his 1988 campaign promise and raise taxes in 1990. It was later estimated that, with interest, the actual total cost of the bailout could come to as much as $500 billion expended over a 30-year period—a high price to pay for deregulating an industry.

## ENVIRONMENTAL DISASTER

During the 1988 presidential campaign, George Bush claimed he would be the "environmental president." Subsequently, his administration worked with Congress to implement the Clean Air Act of 1989 as well as the Clean Water Act of 1990, a far-reaching if imperfect piece of legislation that included reducing automobile and industrial emissions. Though his presidency ended with environmentalists complaining that he had not done enough, his record was nonetheless considered to be far better than his predecessor's.

Ronald Reagan's questionable appointments, disregard of scientific evidence on industrial pollution, and consistent favoring of big business were all seen as damaging to the environment. In 1986 Congress forced him to extend the Superfund's hazardous-waste cleanup program. That same year, Reagan vetoed an $18 billion extension of the Clean Water Act, but Congress overrode him and, in early 1987, overwhelmingly passed the Water Quality Control Act. In March 1988, the Senate ratified an international treaty, reached in Montreal, reducing the use of chlorofluorocarbons that were damaging the earth's ozone layer. Only by such means were important environmental initiatives achieved during Reagan's second term.

The problems inherent in trying to take account of both the environment and business interests were emphasized by occasional human-made disasters. On January 2, 1988, a 40-year-old oil tank owned by the Ashland Oil Company collapsed, spilling 860,000 gallons into the Monongahela River near Pittsburgh, Pennsylvania. The slick flowed into the Ohio River, devastating both water supplies and wildlife in one of the world's largest inland oil spills. But a year later the other side of the continent saw an even worse accident. Just after midnight on March 24, 1989, the oil tanker *Exxon Valdez,* bound for California from Alaska, made a wrong turn and grounded on Bligh Reef in Prince William Sound, rupturing its hull and eight of its 13 tanks. Although Captain Joseph Hazelwood managed to keep the tanker from sliding off the reef, more than 11 million gallons of crude oil escaped.

In the subsequent investigation, sole blame was initially placed on Captain Hazelwood, who had been below deck when the ship ran aground and reportedly had been "reeking" of alcohol hours after the accident. An excellent seaman, Hazelwood also had a drinking problem that he had tried—and clearly failed—to overcome. He was held culpable not only for his apparent drunkenness but also because he had left the third mate in charge at the helm, a man who did not have the pilotage endorsement necessary for traversing Prince William Sound. However, it was later learned that the Coast Guard had eased its pilotage rules and, further, had been at fault for failing to track the *Exxon Valdez* through the sound, which would have allowed them to alert the tanker about the reef.

As argument over culpability raged, so did criticism of the cleanup efforts, initially begun by Alyeska, an Alaska-based oil-industry association. Though Alyeska had emergency measures in place—booms to corral the oil, mechanical skimmers to skim it out of the water, and lasers to burn it off—the organization was slow in implementing them, allowing the oil to spread outside the sound. On the third day after the accident, high winds blew up that made the booms useless—and spread the slick even farther. Chemical dispersants were then also used, but Exxon had failed to get enough supplies, slowing down the work, and as the oil turned to sludge, even dispersants proved ineffective. Accused of incompetence, Alyeska and Exxon, in turn, tried to blame the Alaskan government, while President Bush was accused of being too slow in approving both Superfund assistance and additional people for the cleanup.

Although cleaning was hindered by the spill's remote location, it was widely believed that had the government and Exxon reacted more quickly, the extent of the catastrophe would not have been as great. By the time it was finally contained, the oil had contaminated more than 1,000 miles of coastline. The effect on wildlife was devastating, with more than 400,000 birds, animals, and sea otters injured or killed. Equally devastated were the fishing industry—the 1989 fishing season was canceled, and stock was depleted for years—and American Indian groups who made their living from the waters; the Chugach went bankrupt.

The size of the catastrophe made it the worst oil spill in U.S. history.[12] Because of the delayed response and subsequent problems in the cleanup work, scientists predicted that it could be as long as 30 years before Prince William Sound would fully recover. In March 1991 Exxon initially reached agreement with the Alaskan and federal governments to pay a penalty of $100 million as well as $1 billion over 10 years for cleanup costs. Two months later both the company and the state rejected this, although in October 1991 Exxon agreed to pay an extra $25 million penalty.

A class-action lawsuit was brought against Exxon by 32,000 fishers, landowners, and Alaskan Natives, and in 1994 Exxon was found guilty and fined $5 billion, the largest punitive damage verdict in U.S. history. In 2001 the Ninth Circuit Court of Appeals overturned this as excessive, but a year later U.S. District Court judge H. Russell Holland adjusted the award to $4 billion. As interest on the award has accumulated, Exxon has continued to file appeals, and as of 2004 claimants had yet to see any money. But neither the legal judgments nor a brief consumer boycott following the spill seemed to affect the company: Ten years after the disaster, Exxon was still the nation's biggest oil company despite spending more than $2 billion on the cleanup (mostly paid for by insurance).

The *Exxon Valdez* itself was repaired and renamed the *SeaRiver Mediterranean*, resuming work as an oil tanker; it was mothballed in 2002. In March 1990 Joseph Hazelwood was acquitted of all charges except for one misdemeanor, for which he was fined $50,000 and ordered to perform 1,000 hours of community service; this conviction was overturned by an Alaskan court in July 1992. After a nine-month suspension, Hazelwood regained his captain's license, but with his reputation destroyed, he was unable to get work at sea.

A year after the accident, Congress passed the Oil Pollution Act of 1990, which banned the *Exxon Valdez* from Alaskan waters, mandated double hulls for newly built oil tankers, and required the Coast Guard to strengthen regulations on oil tankers and their operators. As cynical contemporary observers noted, it took a major disaster to force the government to act—and many felt the legislation was still insufficient.

## TROUBLING TIMES IN CANADA

Those Canadians who predicted disaster from the U.S.-Canada Free Trade Agreement (FTA) were to be disappointed in 1989. Though criticism of the FTA continued, it was now law, and most accepted that there was no turning back. Besides, Brian Mulroney gave voters new reason to be angry when, on August 8, Finance Minister Michael Wilson announced a national goods and services tax (GST), replacing the Manufacturers' Sales Tax (MST), which had been in effect since 1924. As the MST had been levied at 13.5 percent and the GST (first proposed in 1987) would be only 9 percent (eventually changed to 7 percent), it seemed superficially to be a fairer tax. But the MST had been an "invisible" tax applied to manufactured goods at the wholesale level, whereas the GST applied to *all* goods and services excepting exports, food, rent, medical services, and other essentials. Consequently, individual Canadians would be directly affected,

In May 1989, Prime Minister Brian Mulroney of Canada paid a visit to President Bush; here they are seen on the White House grounds on May 4. *(Courtesy George Bush Presidential Library)*

although low earners would be able to apply for a GST rebate in their income-tax returns.

At that time, every province except Alberta had its own sales tax. Not surprisingly, the idea of a further national sales tax was immensely unpopular, and the GST was universally attacked. Conservative arguments that the new tax would merely replace existing tax revenues were met with derision. With public opinion against him and the Liberal-controlled Senate certain to vote against the GST, Mulroney had to take the unusual—but constitutionally legal—step of temporarily increasing the upper chamber by eight senators. With Conservative majorities in both houses of Parliament, he was thus able to push through the GST, which became law on January 1, 1991.

Mulroney's steamrolling tactics aroused even more enmity in a country increasingly turning against him. His unpopularity stemmed not only from the GST and the Meech Lake Accord (support for which began to unravel in summer 1989) but from an ever-growing public perception of him as opportunistic and unprincipled. He finally resigned in 1993, and during the subsequent national election, Liberal leader Jean Chrétien promised to repeal the GST. But once elected, Chrétien realized—as Mulroney knew—that the tax was necessary to overcome a high budget deficit and bring the Canadian economy under control. As a result, the GST remained in place, and today it is an accepted—if still resented—part of Canadian life. Nevertheless, it played a major role not only in Mulroney's downfall but also in the disintegration of the entire Progressive Conservative Party, which won only two seats in the House of Commons in 1993.

In 1989, though, Mulroney was still in control, and he aroused further public resentment in June, when he announced funding cuts to Canada's passenger rail service, VIA Rail. That year was also to see the establishment of the Canadian Space Agency, the first baseball game played in Toronto's SkyDome, the debut of the cable television network CBC Newsworld, and replacement of the one-dollar bill with a one-dollar coin, immediately dubbed the "loonie" because one side featured an engraving of a loon.

Still, it was a relatively quiet year in Canada—until December 6, when Marc Lépine, 25, took a gun into an engineering class at the École Polytechnique, a branch of the University of Montreal. After separating the men from the women, he ranted about his hatred for feminists—and then opened fire on the women. Making his way through the building, he continued to gun down females he encountered, before finally turning his gun on himself, leaving 14 women dead and 13 injured (including four men). A suicide note found afterward revealed that Lépine had blamed feminists for his failure to be admitted to engineering school.

The Quebec and Montreal governments declared three days of mourning following the massacre, which spurred a massive growth in the Canadian feminist movement. In 1991 Parliament designated December 6 as the National Day of Remembrance and Action on Violence Against Women, and Montreal observes the massacre's anniversary as a memorial day when white ribbons are worn. Another consequence of the shooting was an increase in gun-control lobbying; stricter legislation was finally passed in 1998.

It had been a troubled year, but there was one sign of progress. On December 2 Audrey McLaughlin replaced Ed Broadbent as leader of the New Democratic Party—the first woman to head a federal political party. Though the Polytechnique École massacre a few days later overshadowed this feminist victory in the public mind, it was nevertheless a significant step forward for women and for Canada.

## GAINS AND SETBACKS

One of the most significant trends of the 1980s was the growing numbers of women in the workforce and the consequences of that growth. While the women's movement of the 1960s and 1970s had induced many white, middle-class women to find satisfaction by going to work, for women of lower classes and different ethnic groups, job seeking was simply a matter of economic necessity. The tradition of the man as the sole breadwinner in the family no longer held true as salaries failed to keep pace with a cost of living that was mounting ever higher each year. Further, a higher divorce rate, increasing numbers of single mothers, and greater incidence of marriage being delayed until later in life meant that the employment landscape had altered.

Statistics highlighted the changing conditions: In 1970, 43.3 percent of women made up 38.1 percent of the nation's total labor force; by 1990, 57.5 percent of women made up 45.3 percent of the labor force, and the numbers were still rising. The change is more clearly seen when it is noted that in 1900 there were approximately 5 million women working outside the home; by the mid-1990s there were more than 60 million. Further, the number of working women increased by 11 million in the 1980s alone, a rate higher than the country's overall population growth, while only 7 million men joined the workforce during the same period.[13]

With the change in numbers came changing attitudes as well. In 1980, though the new order was already becoming apparent, it was still considered atypical for mothers with young children—especially white middle-class and upper-class mothers—to join or rejoin the workforce. But at the decade's end, what was "normal" was not mothers who stayed home with their children but those who went to work: By 1990, a striking 59.4 percent of married mothers with preschool children were employed; of those with children under age one, 51.3 percent had chosen to go to work.[14] As more women joined the workforce, families became smaller, with a national average of 2.22 children per household in 1988; by then females were the breadwinners in 20 percent of American families (the majority of them single parents).

Inevitably, there were problems for women in balancing work and family life. Single mothers—of which the majority were African Americans—had the worst of it, coping with the pressures inherent in keeping a job when child care issues frequently intervened. Significantly, by 1990 more than a third of white and Asian-American single-mother families lived in poverty, while this was true for more than half of African-American, Hispanic, and American Indian single-mother households.[15]

Married women's lives were also stressful if they did not receive adequate support from their husbands. The concept of the "super woman" holding down a full-time job while looking after her husband and children, and sometimes elderly relatives as well, was belied by the realities of two shifts of work, the first at her job and the second at home. Though it was still rare, in the late 1980s the press began to notice a new trend in the form of the helpful mate. Not only were men increasingly willing to abandon their traditional sole-breadwinner roles and assist with housework and child-minding responsibilities, but many were now choosing to take lower-paying jobs or even stay home to look after the children while their wives pursued high-powered careers.

Times were changing, but they did so slowly as traditional visions of male and female roles persisted. Having two working spouses in a family often created marital problems, especially if the wife earned more than her husband. Further, there was a significant difference between the small numbers of "dual career" families—those headed by spouses, usually white, who both enjoyed well-paid professional positions and could afford child care—and the far higher numbers of working-class families needing two paychecks to get by. Almost invariably, the female spouse in such families held the lower-paying job, had the greater demands on her time, and was less likely to advance in her career if she had children, who were seen by many employers as a distraction and therefore a liability in her work.

Nevertheless, the reality of women in the workforce was inescapable, and as the 1980s progressed, many of the equal rights issues of the previous two decades were giving way to more practical concerns. Rather than aiming for equality with men, women wanted solutions that would enable them to reconcile work and family, such as reduced working hours, less-demanding jobs, extended maternity leave, and affordable day care. By 1988 employers were beginning to accommodate these concerns, recognizing, however slowly, that the workforce *was* changing. Congress, too, appreciated the new climate, passing legislation that would lead eventually to the Family and Medical Leave Act of 1993.

By the mid-1980s, though the nation's women had made significant strides, the imbalances were still painfully evident. Equal pay for equal work was a long way from being a reality—on average women earned just 66 cents to the men's dollar (although this would rise to a high of 77 cents by 1993)—and they still met resistance as they tried to break into areas considered to be male provinces, whether blue collar or white collar. In a 1986 *Wall Street Journal* article, reporters Carol Hymowitz and Timothy D. Schellhardt used the term *glass ceiling* to describe the invisible barrier that kept women from being promoted to top jobs.[16] The glass ceiling seemed to be most impregnable in the business world: By 1989 women held only 2 percent of executive positions in Fortune 500 companies. Many who were frustrated in their careers struck out on their own, creating a new breed of female entrepreneurs who would have a profound impact on the 1990s.

Those women who did succeed in business were usually well educated, white, and middle or upper class. Women of minority backgrounds were generally more likely to be poorly educated and hold menial or low-paying clerical jobs; they also suffered a higher unemployment rate than white female workers. For these women, feminism was a joke and a waste of time; success was not breaking through the glass ceiling but simply ensuring their children had enough to eat. Health care was also a major concern as many held jobs that did not provide the insurance they could not afford to pay for themselves. This was especially true of the high number of minority women who were single mothers: In 1987 only 40 percent of black children lived with two parents, whereas 66 percent of Hispanic children and 80 percent of white children lived in two-parent families.[17]

The rise in single-parent families—both minority and white, and headed by men as well as women—would continue into the 1990s, a decade that would also see increasing numbers of women shattering the glass ceiling. The 1980s marked gains for some and setbacks for others, while the lot of minorities remained frustratingly depressed. But the decade crystallized changing circumstances for American women, who faced the 1990s with both hope and trepidation.

## CRUCIAL DECISIONS

Ronald Reagan's influence on the American judiciary cannot be ignored. As well as appointing three Supreme Court justices and elevating William Rehnquist to chief justice, he made a remarkable 358 appointments to the federal bench, almost half of its 741 seats; 306 were still serving as of June 2004.[18] Reagan chose mostly young men and women—some of them controversial—whose ideologies were in tune with his own. In this way, he brought long-lasting conservative attributes into the American legal system, especially regarding judicial restraint and decisions affecting civil liberties.

Nevertheless, some decisions still reflected liberal values. In *Hustler Magazine, Inc. v. Falwell* (1988) the right of free speech—specifically the right to criticize public figures—was sustained when the high justices overturned a lower court's award to Reverend Jerry Falwell, who had sued *Hustler* and its publisher, Larry Flynt, for vilifying him in print. The women's movement won a victory in 1989 when, in *Price Waterhouse v. Hopkins,* the Court ruled that if a plaintiff presents evidence of sexual discrimination, the employer has to prove that the decision would have been the same without regard to gender.

More important to conservatives were Court decisions dealing with two of Reagan's pet targets: affirmative action and abortion. On January 23, 1989, the justices' 6-3 ruling on *City of Richmond v. J. A. Croson Co.* invalidated a Richmond, Virginia, law that had mandated 30 percent of public-works funds must go to minority-owned businesses. The Court stated that such legislation was legally binding only when it reduced "identifiable discrimination," a qualification that the Richmond city government had failed to meet. Equally significant was the June 12 decision in *Martin v. Wilks,* which allowed white workers to claim unfair treatment in cases involving affirmative action. Such decisions were victories for conservatives who saw racial quotas as reverse discrimination.

One of the most important cases to come before the Court in 1989 was *Webster v. Reproductive Health Services,* decided on July 3. The justices voted 5-4 to uphold a Missouri law that forbade public employees to perform abortions, banned the use of tax-supported public buildings for abortions not needed to save a mother's life, and required doctors to determine the possible survival of fetuses in women requesting an abortion when they were 20 weeks or more pregnant. Significantly, the preamble to the Missouri statute specifically stated that life began at conception, a statement with important legal consequences given that some contraceptives take effect after fertilization. Feminists also believed that the preamble violated the First Amendment since it endorsed a theological doctrine not held by all faiths.

*Webster* came close to overturning *Roe v. Wade*—Reagan's cherished dream—but it was Sandra Day O'Connor who prevented this from happening. Though she voted with the majority in *Webster,* she argued that it was not the time to deal with the vexatious *Roe,* which needed to be categorically contradicted by a state law restricting abortion before it could be revisited. This challenged states to draft antiabortion laws that could then be used to overturn *Roe,* and more than 40 considered such legislation, much of it so harsh that even pro-life governors vetoed it. In November 1989 Pennsylvania did enact a law in defiance of *Roe* as well as other Supreme Court decisions on abortion, and the U.S. territory of Guam passed similar legislation in March 1990. However, no direct legal challenge has yet succeeded in overturning *Roe,* which as of late 2005 remains in place and continues to provoke pro-life activists.

Another case centered on an issue evoking memories of the 1988 campaign, when George Bush visited a U.S. flag factory to prove himself more patriotic than Michael Dukakis. When, on June 12, 1989, the Supreme Court ruled (5-4) in *Texas v. Johnson* that burning the U.S. flag as a political protest was a right guaranteed under the First Amendment, Bush was outraged and demanded a constitutional amendment to ban flag burning. Congress rejected this but passed a law to ban flag burning, which Bush—determined to have his amendment—vetoed on October 12. Congress overrode him and passed the legislation without his signature, but in June 1990, in *United States v. Eichman,* the Supreme Court ruled it unconstitutional. Like abortion and affirmative action, flag burning remains a constitutional right and an example of the sometimes emotional and often highly complex issues with which the Court has to deal.

## THE PRICE OF TAKEOVERS

Appropriately, the 1980s saw a proliferation of books about corporate takeovers and their practitioners. Among the best-selling authors who shared some of their trading secrets were Ivan Boesky (*Merger Mania,* 1985), T. Boone Pickens (*Boone,* 1987), and Donald Trump (*The Art of the Deal,* 1988). All described a complex world where money reigned supreme, exemplified by a frenzy of mergers and acquisitions at the decade's end.

In April 1988 Hachette S.A., a French publisher, acquired the American companies Grolier Inc. and Diamandis Communications Inc. The two deals, totaling $1,162,000,000, made Hachette the largest magazine publisher in the world, with 74 publications in 10 countries. Four months later Australian publisher Rupert Murdoch enlarged his empire by acquiring Triangle Publications Inc. (*TV Guide, Daily Racing Form, Seventeen,* and so on) for $3 billion, the largest publishing takeover to date.

On April 1, 1988, Canada's Champeau Corporation bought Federated Department Stores Inc. for $6.6 billion, the largest department-store takeover to date. On October 30 Philip Morris Companies acquired Kraft Inc. for $13.1 billion, forming the largest consumer-products company in the world. Exactly a month later the investment firm Kohlberg, Kravis, and Roberts (KKR) announced its intention to buy RJR Nabisco for $24.88 billion, the largest leveraged buyout in history.[19] The deal was finalized in April 1989, and in combination with its 1986 acquisition of Beatrice Companies, KKR now controlled 13 percent of all U.S. food manufacturers.

The frenzy continued in 1989 when Donald Trump bought Eastern Airlines and renamed it the Trump Shuttle; Ford Motor Company bought Jaguar Motors for $2.5 billion; and Sony Corporation bought Columbia Pictures Entertainment for $3.4 billion, then the largest Japanese acquisition of an American company. A particularly noteworthy transaction took place in July, when Warner Communications Inc. and Time Inc. merged to form Time Warner Inc., the world's largest media and entertainment conglomerate, with a stock market value of $15.2 billion and annual revenues of $10 billion.

While all this was happening, the insider-trading scandals triggered by Dennis Levine and Ivan Boesky in 1986 culminated when Michael Milken, the "junk bond king," was indicted in 1989 on 98 counts of violating federal securities and tax laws. Milken had first been implicated by Boesky, a client of the investment firm Drexel Burnham Lambert, which was having its own problems. In September 1988 the Securities and Exchange Commission (SEC) charged Drexel with using inside information to defraud its clients. The company subsequently pleaded guilty to six felony counts of mail, wire, and securities fraud and agreed to pay a fine of $650 million. It also agreed to help the SEC against Milken, its star employee.

Milken's specialty was trading in junk bonds, often used to finance corporate takeovers. Bonds are classified according to their security (safety) rating; the best (investment grade) are classified AAA, and the worst are classified D (in default). Junk bonds—also referred to as speculative-grade and below-investment-grade bonds—have a low credit rating (less than BBB) and high risk, meaning they also have a high yield. Like stocks, the value of junk bonds rises as the issuer's financial condition improves. In the 1970s Milken foresaw a gold mine and began persuading clients to buy junk bonds, with spectacular results. He was particularly successful with "fallen angels," bonds that had been downgraded from investment grade. Though others tried to emulate Milken's success, he seemed to have a special gift for rating companies and knowing which bonds would provide the best yield for clients, who made huge amounts of money on his recommendations. Consequently, by the mid-1980s his department at Drexel controlled two-thirds of the junk-bond market and enjoyed an amazing 100 percent return on its investments.

The use of junk bonds to finance leveraged buyouts made even more money for Drexel—and for Milken, who in 1987 alone took home $550 million. The bubble had already burst, though, as the insider-trading scandals broke in 1986 and he was found to have been heavily involved. It took more than two years for the SEC to build its case against Milken, who attempted to improve his public image by presenting a defense that emphasized his philanthropy and charitable works. After admitting that he had cheated clients and engaged in illegal activities with Boesky, he asked to be sentenced to community service. But on April 14, 1990, he was given 10 years in prison, 1,800 hours of community service, and a fine of $600 million. He ultimately served 22 months, and upon being diagnosed with prostate cancer in 1993, he was released and returned to business. In 1998 the SEC again investigated him and fined him $47 million for having violated an order banning him from work as a broker.

Milken's conviction barely hurt him financially, and he has since gained a reputation as a philanthropist. Many supporters—including Rupert Murdoch and Ted Turner—believe that he was unjustly railroaded by the SEC, and charges that his activities contributed to the savings-and-loan debacle have never been proved. Nevertheless, he remains, like Boesky, a symbol of the money-mad 1980s, when some entrepreneurs made millions and considered themselves above the law.

One of the most notorious was Leona Helmsley, a New York hotelier known as the Queen of Mean, who was indicted for income-tax evasion along with her husband, Harry, in 1989. According to her former housekeeper, Helmsley expressed her disdain for the charges against her by sniffing, "We don't pay taxes. Only the little people pay taxes."[20] To the satisfaction of the country's little people, she was found guilty, imprisoned, and fined. On occasion, it seemed, even the wealthy had to pay their dues.

## THE COLD WAR ENDS

Despite the new warmth in the superpowers' relationship, George Bush adopted a cautious approach to U.S.-USSR dialogues. Fearful that Mikhail Gorbachev might be deposed and convinced that Reagan had moved too far too fast, on February 13, 1989, Bush ordered a "pause" in diplomacy with Moscow to review U.S. policy. This irritated Gorbachev, who, in a private meeting with Margaret Thatcher in London on April 6, denounced the president's decision as "intolerable." Many in the American press and Congress shared his opinion that the review process was too slow and plodding.

On May 12 Bush finally gave his first official speech on the Soviet Union. Noting recent historic events, he said it was time for the United States to move "beyond containment," adding that "as the Soviet Union itself moves toward greater openness and democratization, as they meet the challenge of responsible international behavior, we will match their steps with steps of our own."[21]

Moscow had already taken some substantial steps. On February 2 the last Soviet troops left Afghanistan after nine years of military occupation. On March 26 free elections were held in the USSR for the first time since the Bolshevik Revolution—and the Communist Party suffered major losses. Among those elected to the new Congress of People's Deputies that day was Boris Yeltsin, a reformer whom Gorbachev had fired in 1987 and who would succeed Gorbachev—a victim of his own reforms—as the country's leader at the end of 1991.

Equally significant was the growing democratic movement among Warsaw Pact countries. On June 4 Poland held its first parliamentary elections since World War II, producing a celebrated victory for Solidarity, the labor union headed by Lech Wałesa.[22] But it was a tragedy in China that same day that reverberated around the world.

Since 1978 China, under Deng Xiaoping, had been slowly liberalizing its policies and moving toward a market economy. Though they welcomed this, intellectuals and students felt the reforms did not go far enough. By spring 1989 antigovernment protests were occurring throughout the country, and in May students converged on Tiananmen Square in Beijing. Because of a recent Gorbachev visit, foreign journalists and photographers were also present and reported the protests in the square—and their consequences.

On May 20 the Chinese government declared martial law, but this had little effect on the demonstrations, and military force was finally employed. On June 4 (June 3 in the United States) Chinese troops entered Tiananmen Square to clear it of protestors. Scores were killed as troops approached the square and fired into crowds; many more were wounded or arrested. The shooting continued into the next day. One famous picture, of a student standing alone in front of a column of tanks, was broadcast around the world and came to symbolize protest against the Chinese military machine.

Western leaders denounced the Chinese government's actions. President Bush declared: "I deeply deplore the decision to use force against peaceful demonstrators and the consequent loss of life. We have been urging—and continue to urge—nonviolence, restraint, and dialog. Tragically, another course has been chosen."[23] He subsequently ordered the suspension of military weapons shipments to China.

Bush advocated restraint rather than confrontation because of his personal knowledge of the Chinese (having headed the U.S. Liaison Office in Beijing, 1974–76) and because of the United States' delicate relations with China. Though many Americans supported his careful response, just as many saw his moderation as weakness. So did Congress, which, on June 29 and July 14, passed a package of economic sanctions and punitive measures by such overwhelming margins that Bush was reluctantly forced to sign it.[24] Meanwhile, in early July, he sent Brent Scowcroft on a secret mission to China to begin restoring relations. When news of the mission was revealed subsequently, the president was accused of kowtowing to the repressive Chinese regime.

Meanwhile, the elections in Poland initiated a wave of reform throughout Eastern Europe, and change came with dizzying speed. On August 23 Hungary lifted its border restrictions with Austria; on September 10 it opened its western borders to refugees from East Germany; and on October 13 the government declared that Hungary was now a free republic. In Romania on December 22, the communist dictator Nicolae Ceauşescu was ousted from power, and on the 25th he and his wife, Elena, were executed. On December 29 writer and human-rights advocate Václav Havel was elected president of Czechoslovakia in what was called the velvet revolution, and in the following months all the remaining communist governments in Europe would collapse.

No event more dramatically represented this collapse than the fall of the Berlin Wall. At midnight on November 9, the East German government—prompted by Mikhail Gorbachev—opened all its borders, including the barrier between East and West Berlin that had long symbolized the division between communism and democracy. At once elated Berliners began to break down the Wall, singing and dancing as they moved freely between the two parts of the city for the first time since August 1961. The full dismantling of the Wall would take months, but on December 1 East Germany's parliament effectively abolished communist rule, and there was already talk of Germany's eventual reunification.

Berliners celebrate atop the Berlin Wall on November 12, 1989, after the border between East and West Germany was opened. *(AP/Wide World Photos)*

The USSR, meanwhile, did little to interfere as it faced more urgent internal problems. Along with Gorbachev's perestroika and glasnost had come a growing resistance to Moscow's regime. The Baltic states of Estonia, Latvia, and Lithuania became the first to demand self-rule, with a 2-million-strong human chain formed across the three countries on August 23. They were soon followed by Armenia, Azerbaijan, Byelorussia, Georgia, and Ukraine, among others, and the domino effect would culminate in the disintegration of the Soviet Union and Gorbachev's resignation in late 1991.

Wisely, Bush let events take their course. In July he visited Poland and Hungary and conveyed messages of support for the independence movements underway in Eastern Europe. Seeing how the world was changing, he sought an accommodation with the Soviet Union that would further encourage the trend toward democracy. Therefore, rejecting National Security Advisor Brent Scowcroft's advice, Bush sent a confidential message to Gorbachev suggesting they should meet. Commentators subsequently criticized him for his failure to become excited about the fall of the Berlin Wall—"I'm not going to dance on the wall," he said repeatedly—but as always his reason was caution: He did not want to aggravate hard-liners in East Germany and Moscow who might rise up against Gorbachev.

On December 2–3 the leaders met aboard two ships off Malta for a "non-summit" intended to discuss a full-scale summit the following year. The weather was so stormy that movement between the two vessels was continually disrupted and events canceled; it was later referred to as the "seasick summit." After discussions that included nuclear disarmament, the Baltic states, Central America, Soviet economic reform, and even human rights, Bush and Gorbachev ended by conducting a joint press conference, the first in such superpower meetings. Their obvious positive attitude augured well for the future.

There was still much to negotiate, still much to happen. But as the Soviet Foreign Ministry spokesman Gennadi Gerasimov said of the Malta meeting, "We buried the Cold War at the bottom of the Mediterranean Sea."[25]

## OPERATION JUST CAUSE

Late 1989 gave President Bush an opportunity to counter criticism of his cautious approach to foreign affairs. Since 1967 Panama's Manuel Noriega had worked for the Central Intelligence Agency (CIA), providing intelligence on Cuba and Nicaragua. In 1983 he seized control of the Panamanian government, and by 1985 he was working in league with Marxist nations and allowing drug cartels to trade freely. These developments worried President Reagan, who had opposed the Panama Canal treaties that had been negotiated by President Carter and feared returning the canal zone in 2000 to a country where Noriega was in charge. Corruption, electoral fraud, and human-rights abuses gave further cause for concern. Nevertheless, Reagan failed to take direct action against Noriega, chiefly because of his assistance in airlifting secret military supplies to the Nicaraguan contras.

After the Iran-contra story broke, Noriega's usefulness ceased, and thereafter he became an increasing embarrassment as his criminal activities came to light. Consequently, administration officials began looking for ways to remove the dictator from power, one of which was his February 1988 federal indictment on drug-trafficking and money-laundering charges. (This was allowable under Supreme Court–approved extraterritorial jurisdiction, compatible with international law—similar to indicting pirates.) Noriega countered by demanding that the U.S. Southern Command withdraw from its headquarters in Panama. After he successfully blocked President Eric Delvalle's attempt to dismiss him, the United States imposed economic sanctions on Panama; even more were imposed after Noriega suppressed a coup attempt in March.

On May 7, 1989, presidential elections were held, and the U.S.-backed Guillermo Endara prevailed over Noriega's candidate, Carlos Duque.[26] However, on May 10 the Panamanian government declared Duque victorious, even though independent counts and surveys showed that Endara had won by a margin of 3-1. Noriega retained power, using brutal methods to put down demonstrations against him. In response, the United States increased its military presence in the area and defied the Panama Canal treaties by carrying out military maneuvers in areas that had been returned to Panama in 1979.

On October 3 another U.S.-backed coup was attempted, but the rebels were soundly defeated by Noriega's forces, and some were summarily executed. By this time, there was public outrage against Noriega in the United States, and Bush was criticized for his apparent failure to take action. Later that month, the U.S. Treasury Department designated Noriega an agent of Cuba, and Bush approved further CIA action in assisting attempts to overthrow the dictator.

By late November invasion seemed to be inevitable, even though it was opposed by the Organization of American States (OAS). On December 15 the Panamanian legislature named Noriega head of government and declared the country to be in a "state of war" with the United States. The following day, members of the Panamanian Defense Forces (PDF) killed an American military officer dressed in civilian clothes, wounded another, and beat, harassed, and interrogated a third serviceman and his wife. Bush's reaction was swift: On December 17 he ordered more troops to Panama, and early on the morning of December 20 a force of 12,000 soldiers and paratroopers began the long-awaited invasion, called Operation Just Cause.

The invading troops were joined by 10,500 already stationed in the country, and within 72 hours the PDF had been defeated. Looting by Panamanian soldiers and civilians meant an additional 2,000 U.S. troops had to be flown in to restore order. Noriega, meanwhile, took refuge in the Vatican embassy, where American soldiers outside bombarded the building with rock music, which Noriega hated. He finally surrendered to U.S. authorities on January 3, 1990, and was flown to Miami to await trial.[27] By that time Guillermo Endara and two vice presidents had been sworn in to head the new government, and the withdrawal of U.S. troops had already begun.

In the United States, Americans heard of the invasion from President Bush via radio and television on the morning of December 20. Noting that the "goals of the United States have been to safeguard the lives of Americans, to defend democracy in Panama, to combat drug trafficking and to protect the integrity of the Panama Canal treaty," Bush explained his reasons for the invasion and noted that he had advised leaders of Congress, Latin American countries, and U.S. allies of the military action. "Tragically," he said, "some Americans have lost their lives in the defense of their fellow citizens, in defense of democracy. . . . We also regret and mourn the loss of innocent Panamanians."[28]

Though only 23 U.S. soldiers were killed, figures on Panamanian casualties ranged from 57 to more than 300 military dead and from 200 to as many as 700 civilians killed in the fighting, attributable to U.S. attacks on densely populated areas. Thousands of Panamanians were left homeless but received little support or restitution from the United States. This and the fact that the United States had no grounds in international law for invading led to condemnation from the OAS and the UN General Assembly as well as disapproval from some U.S. allies. Some of the criticism was alleviated by the quick withdrawal of U.S. troops and the concurrent restoration of democracy. However, Panama's role in drug trafficking continued to be a problem, even with Noriega removed from power.

The Panama invasion had been a better-planned and -executed operation than the 1983 invasion of Grenada. Media coverage showed the American forces in the best possible light, and initial reaction seemed to indicate that Panamanians approved of Noriega's removal. Consequently, most Americans supported the action and gave Bush high marks, especially because it was over so quickly. However, enthusiasm in both countries waned as news leaked out of the high numbers of civilian deaths as well as military errors and Noriega's CIA involvement. Some critics commented that sending 24,000 troops just to arrest one man seemed a trifle excessive.

Operation Just Cause was the biggest U.S. military action since the Vietnam War. More than a year after Noriega's arrest, Bush would authorize an even bigger operation, Desert Storm (also known as the first Persian Gulf War), and once again his approval rating would rise significantly. Though most Americans deplored war, U.S. military intervention in the affairs of other countries was seen by many as both a right and a duty.

## THE 1980s—AN AMERICAN TRANSFORMATION

Every decade brings change, but the United States of 1990 was *very* different from the United States of 1980. Bare statistics give little indication of the political, economic, and technological revolutions that 10 years had wrought. The nation's very structure had altered as more Americans chose to remain single rather than marry, the numbers of single-parent families rose, and the average size of households shrank. Life expectancy continued to improve—it was now 71.8 for men and 78.6 for women—and there were greater numbers of senior citizens making their voices heard on such issues as health care.

The decade's major distinctive health issue, AIDS, was also the most devastating: By June 1989 nearly 106,000 cases had been reported, of which 61,000 had died. As treatments improved, so did public acceptance of the disease—and, gradually, of homosexuality, although gays still suffered prejudice from their initial unwilling association with the epidemic.

As a result of Reaganomics, the prosperity of many increased, but so did poverty and homelessness, further widening the gap between rich and poor. Minorities experienced mixed fortunes, having grown in population and made a greater impact on American politics, business, and culture. Yet, paradoxically, there was also a drop in living standards for many. While millions of new jobs had brought the national unemployment rate down to a satisfactory 5.3 percent in 1989, the rate had actually risen for African Americans and other minorities, further emphasizing the economic disparities. President Reagan had battled against raising the minimum wage, convinced that it would cause an economic decline, especially among African Americans. In 1989 President Bush compromised with Congress, signing a measure on November 17 to raise the minimum wage from $3.35 to $4.25 over a two-year period, but allowing employers to pay a training wage below the minimum for up to three months.

Rural communities suffered through most of the decade due to droughts, huge drops in exports, and declining land values, among other reasons. By 1989 farming revenues were growing again, although larger concerns did considerably better than small family farmers.

With more families now consisting of single parents or two working parents, child care became a major issue of the 1980s as young children increasingly spent their days in nurseries or preschool programs. The possible consequences were highlighted when, in summer 1983, charges of child abuse were brought against the McMartin Preschool in Manhattan Beach, California. During the next seven years, school owner Peggy McMartin Buckey, her husband Ray Buckey, mother Virginia McMartin, and various employees and family members were accused of innumerable perverted acts with the children in their care. Much of the evidence came from the children themselves, who later were found to have been coaxed into describing events that never happened. The Buckeys' experience inspired a host of accusations against other schools and underscored the problems of parents in getting reliable care for their children.[29]

Meanwhile, many of the nation's children and their parents were taking for granted new technological marvels, including fax machines, cordless telephones, answering machines, television remote controls, and microwave ovens. In 1988 sales of compact discs (CDs) surpassed those of LPs for the first time. That same year saw the first transatlantic fiber-optic cable, carrying as many as 37,000 telephone transmissions. Fiber optics were to revolutionize telecommunications, and not surprisingly there was a surge of cellular telephone sales in 1989, which also saw the debut of Sony's CCD-V99 camcorder. By then 62 percent of households owned VCRs (up from 56 percent in 1988), and 56.4 percent of households had cable television.

By 1989 computers had become indispensable in business and government and were rapidly becoming as common in homes as televisions and VCRs. As modems improved, email became an increasingly popular form of communication, and more people were accessing the Internet. However, with advances in technology also came viruses and "worms" that damaged computers, sometimes irretrievably. In a nine-month period in 1988 alone, more than 250,000 machines were infected by viruses. On November 2 one of the first worms was launched into the Internet by Cornell University student Robert Tappan Morris, Jr., infecting some 6,000 Unix machines and causing up to $100 million in damage. Morris was subsequently caught and became the first individual to be prosecuted under the Computer Fraud and Abuse Act of 1986.

Cable television revolutionized the music business by broadcasting music videos, whose sales exploded in the 1980s. The trend-setting station MTV, which debuted in 1981, was available in nearly 36 million homes by 1987 and brought the word *veejay* into the American vocabulary. Thanks largely to MTV, Michael Jackson, Madonna, Bruce Springsteen, and other "megastars" enjoyed greater visibility, while rap, hip-hop, and country & western music gained wider audiences.

Michael Crawford and Sarah Brightman perform in *Phantom of the Opera* on January 26, 1988. *(Photofest)*

Other entertainment media reflected both the conservative values and the changing mores of the time. When the decade began, the wealth-flaunting *Dallas* and then its spin-off, *Dynasty,* dominated the television ratings. From 1985 to 1988, Bill Cosby's gently humorous *The Cosby Show* stole America's heart, giving way in 1989 to Roseanne Barr's working-class *Roseanne.* In the movies, Stephen Spielberg and George Lucas dominated the 1980s with such blockbusters as *The Empire Strikes Back* (1980), *Raiders of the Lost Ark* (1981) and its sequels (1984 and 1989), *E.T., the Extraterrestrial* (1982), *Back to the Future* (1985), and more. Other filmmakers, such as John Hughes and Spike Lee, were making their mark as well, as were actors such as Sally Field, Harrison Ford, Arnold Schwarzenegger, and the group of rising young stars known as the "Brat Pack" (Molly Ringwald, Emilio Estevez, et al.).

Like the movies, Broadway shows became bigger and more lavish, especially the musicals, but this was only after a severe slump in the mid-1980s that many believed signaled the end of American theater. Things changed with the opening of *Les Miserables* in 1987, followed by Andrew Lloyd Webber's *Starlight Express* and, in 1988, *The Phantom of the Opera*—blockbuster musicals that brought new life to Broadway.

Things had changed in America's spirit as well: Prosperity, new technologies, and the end of the cold war had made the malaise of 10 years before a distant memory. A new decade was about to begin—and most of the nation faced it with optimism.

# CHRONICLE OF EVENTS

## 1989

*January 20:* George H. W. Bush is inaugurated as the nation's 41st president.

*January 22:* The San Francisco 49ers defeat the Cincinnati Bengals, 20-16, to win Super Bowl XXIII.

*January 24:* Serial killer Ted Bundy, responsible for the deaths of at least 36 women, is executed in Florida.

*January 28:* At a Moscow meeting of Soviet, Cuban, and American officials who were involved in the Cuban missile crisis, the Russians reveal that, unbeknownst to the United States, there were already 20 nuclear warheads (unattached to missiles) stored in Cuba before John F. Kennedy ordered a naval blockade in October 1962.

*January 31:* The U.S. Census Bureau announces its projection that the country's population will reach about 302 million in 2038 and thereafter decline to about 292 million by 2080. The bureau also estimates that by 2030, 66 million persons (22 percent of the population) will be age 65 or older, compared to 30 million in 1989.

*January 31:* It is announced that in comparison with 13-year-old students from Great Britain, Ireland, South Korea, Spain, and four Canadian provinces, those from the United States ranked last in math and science.

*February 2:* The last Soviet troops leave Afghanistan, nine years after the invasion that instigated the U.S. boycott of the Moscow Olympics.

*February 3:* Bill White becomes the first African American to head a major sports organization when he is elected president of Major League Baseball's National League.

*February 6:* Noted historian Barbara Tuchman dies at age 77.

*February 7:* Following a vehement public protest, the U.S. Congress votes against a pay increase for its members.

*February 10:* Attorney Ron Brown is elected the first African-American chairman of the Democratic National Committee.

President George H. W. Bush is sworn into office by Chief Justice William Rehnquist on January 20, 1989. *(Library of Congress, Prints and Photographs Division [LC-USZ4-7722])*

*February 14:* The first satellite (of 24 all told) in the new Global Positioning System is sent into orbit.

*February 16:* Investigators into the crash of Pan Am flight 103 on December 21, 1988, announce that the plane had been destroyed by a bomb hidden inside a radio-cassette player.

*February 17:* Baseball Hall of Famer Vernon "Lefty" Gomez, who won six World Series games and lost none, dies at 80.

*February 22:* At the Grammy Awards, George Michael's *Faith* wins best album of 1988; Bobby McFerrin's "Don't Worry, Be Happy" is named best record. Robert Palmer and Tina Turner are best male and female rock vocalists, and Tracy Chapman ("Fast Car") is best new artist and best female pop vocalist.

*February 24:* A United Airlines 747 plane from Honolulu, Hawaii, to New Zealand rips open during its flight; nine passengers and crew are sucked through the opening and killed, but the plane manages to land safely.

*March 1:* The Canadian Space Agency is created.

*March 3:* Former National Security Advisor Robert McFarlane is sentenced to two years' probation, $20,000 in fines, and 200 hours of community service for his role in the Iran-contra affair.

*March 9:* Eastern Airlines declares bankruptcy.

*March 13–18:* The space shuttle *Discovery* completes the year's first successful mission.

*March 14:* The Bush administration announces a ban on the importation of semiautomatic assault rifles into the United States. Another 24 gun models will be added to the list on April 5.

*March 15:* The Department of Veterans Affairs is made an official part of the presidential cabinet, following a law passed by Congress in October 1988.

*March 21:* In a 7-2 ruling, the Supreme Court upholds mandatory drug testing for federal workers whose jobs involve public health and safety.

*March 23:* Chemists B. Stanley Pons and Martin Fleischmann of the University of Utah announce they have achieved nuclear fusion at room temperature. There is almost universal skepticism from the scientific community, and a federal conference in May will decide against the scientists.

*March 24:* In New York, disbarred lawyer Joel Steinberg is sentenced to 8⅓–25 years in prison for killing his illegally adopted daughter Lisa. The case had attracted headlines for Steinberg's brutal abuse of Lisa and his lover, Hedda Nussbaum.

*March 24:* In Alaska's Prince William Sound, the oil supertanker *Exxon Valdez* runs aground and releases 240,000 barrels of crude oil into the water, the worst U.S. spill to date.

*March 26:* The Soviet Union holds its first free national election since 1917.

*March 29: Rain Man* wins the Academy Award for outstanding motion picture of 1988; its star, Dustin Hoffman, wins as best actor. Jodie Foster is named best actress for her performance in *The Accused.* Kevin Kline (*A Fish Called Wanda*) and Geena Davis (*The Accidental Tourist*) win the supporting acting awards.

*March 30:* Pulitzer Prize winners include Anne Tyler (*Breathing Lessons*) for fiction; Taylor Branch (*Parting the Waters*) and James M. McPherson (*Battle Cry of Freedom*) for history; and Wendy Wasserstein (*The Heidi Chronicles*) for drama.

*April 3:* A U.S. Supreme Court decision strengthen the role of tribes in the adoption of Native American children.

*April 12:* Boxing champion Sugar Ray Robinson, who won the middleweight title five times, dies at 67.

Jodie Foster and Dustin Hoffman enjoy their Oscars at the 61st Academy Awards. *(Photofest)*

*April 17:* The Bush administration announces special aid to Poland, currently in the throes of a democracy movement.

*April 18:* President Bush signs a bill granting $50 million in humanitarian aid to the contras in Nicaragua, still fighting the Sandinista government.

*April 18:* Figures show the growing impact of cable television when it is announced all three major television networks lost viewers during the 1988–89 season for the sixth year in a row. NBC ranked first in viewership, followed by ABC and then CBS.

*April 19:* An explosion in a gun turret aboard the USS *Iowa* kills 47 sailors. The U.S. Navy initially claims the blast was caused by a sailor attempting to commit suicide but will apologize to the accused sailor's family in October 1991.

*April 26:* Legendary comedienne Lucille Ball dies, age 77.

*May 4:* Oliver North is found guilty on three charges in relation to the Iran-contra affair; he is cleared of nine other charges. On July 5 he will be sentenced to 1,200 hours of community service and a fine of $150,000.

*May 4–8:* The space shuttle *Atlantis* launches an unmanned spacecraft, *Magellan,* which is expected to reach Venus in August 1990 and send back pictures of that planet.

*May 12:* In his first major speech on the Soviet Union, President Bush pledges to move "beyond containment."

*May 22:* At the National Institutes of Health in Maryland, scientists successfully transfer cancer-fighting cells containing foreign genes into a human being's bloodstream. Although there is no direct benefit to the patient, the scientists hope to use the technique to improve cancer treatment.

*May 25:* The Calgary Flames defeat the Montreal Canadiens in six games to win hockey's Stanley Cup.

*May 30:* Longtime congressman Claude Pepper (D, Fla.), a spokesman for the elderly, dies at 88.

*May 31:* Congressman Jim Wright (D, Tex.) resigns as Speaker of the House after a long ethics investigation; he will be replaced by Thomas Foley (D, Wash.) on June 6.

*May 31:* Owen Lattimore, a noted scholar on Far Eastern affairs, dies at 88.

*June 3:* Chinese troops attack prodemocracy demonstrators in Tiananmen Square, Beijing; the scene—which takes place on June 4 in China—is viewed on televisions around the world.

*June 4:* Iran's Ayatollah Khomeini dies at age 86.

*June 4:* At the Tony Awards for the 1988–89 season, Wendy Wasserstein's *The Heidi Chronicles* wins as best play, and *Jerome Robbins' Broadway* is named best musical. Acting awards go to Philip Bosco, Pauline Collins, Jason Alexander, and Ruth Brown.

*June 5:* In response to the Tiananmen Square massacre on June 4, President Bush orders the suspension of military weapons shipments to China.

*June 10:* Reverend Jerry Falwell announces the disbanding of the Moral Majority, the conservative religious group he had founded in 1979.

*June 13:* The Detroit Pistons win the National Basketball Association championship when they defeat the Los Angeles Lakers in the sixth game of the finals.

*June 14:* Actress Zsa Zsa Gabor is arrested after slapping a police officer in Beverly Hills, California.

*June 21:* The Supreme Court rules that burning the American flag as a political protest is a right permitted under the First Amendment.

*June 27:* The U.S. Court of Appeals overturns the conviction of former White House political director Lyn Nofziger, who had been found guilty of illegal lobbying in February 1988.

*June 29:* The Supreme Court restricts the authority of Native American tribes to impose zoning regulations on non-Indians living within reservations.

*July 3:* In a controversial decision that almost overturns *Roe v. Wade,* the Supreme Court votes 5-4 to uphold a Missouri law severely restricting abortions.

*July 9:* *Forbes* magazine announces that Sam Moore Walton, founder of Wal-Mart, is the richest man in the United States, with a fortune worth $8.7 billion.

*July 10:* Mel Blanc, the voice of Bugs Bunny and innumerable other cartoon characters, dies at 81.

*July 19:* United Airlines Flight 232 crashes at Sioux City, Iowa, killing 112, but 184 on board survive, thanks to the heroism of the pilot and crew. A subsequent investigation by the National Transportation Safety Board will place blame for the accident on the airline for failing to detect an engine flaw.

*July 21:* President Bush signs the Clean Air Act of 1989.

*July 23:* Noted author Donald Barthelme dies at the age 58.

*July 23:* American bicyclist Greg LeMond repeats his 1986 triumph in the Tour de France, winning by only eight seconds, the smallest margin of victory ever.

President Bush signs the Clean Air Act in the White House Rose Garden on July 21, 1989, as Environmental Protection Agency administrator William Reilly and Secretary of Energy James Watkins look on. *(Courtesy George Bush Presidential Library)*

*July 24:* Warner Communications, Inc., announces its merger with Time, Inc., to form the world's largest media and entertainment conglomerate.

*July 25:* Charges of theft and wire fraud (relating to the Iran-contra affair) against former National Security Advisor John Poindexter are dropped. He remains charged with two counts of obstructing Congress and two counts of making false statements.

*July 26:* Robert Tappan Morris, Jr., becomes the first person prosecuted under the Computer Fraud and Abuse Act of 1986. Charged with releasing a worm into the Internet on November 2, 1988, he will be convicted on January 22, 1990, and sentenced to three years' probation and a heavy fine.

*August 8–13:* The space shuttle *Columbia* carries out a secret military mission.

*August 9:* President Bush signs a bill to rescue the nation's savings-and-loan associations.

*August 19:* In Tangier, Morocco, publisher Malcolm Forbes throws himself a 70th birthday party that includes 600 guests, fireworks, and a display by Berber horsemen. At an estimated $2 billion, it is one of the most ostentatious parties ever.

*August 22:* Playing against the Oakland Athletics, Nolan Ryan of the Texas Rangers becomes the first Major League Baseball pitcher to strike out 5,000 batters.

*August 22:* Black Panther founder Huey Newton, 47, is murdered in Oakland, California.

*August 22:* Influential fashion editor Diana Vreeland dies at 86.

*August 24:* Baseball commissioner A. Bartlett Giamatti bans Pete Rose from the sport for life following allegations that Rose had bet on games, including those of his own team, the Cincinnati Reds.

*August 24:* After 12 years of exploring the solar system and sending thousands of pictures back to Earth, *Voyager 2* completes its mission. The next day it passes Triton, the moon of Neptune, then the farthest planet from the Sun.

*August 30:* New York hotel owner Leona Helmsley is convicted on 33 counts of tax evasion, fraud, and conspiracy. On December 12 she will be sentenced to four years in prison, a fine of $7.1 million, and 750 hours of community service.

*September 1:* A. Bartlett Giamatti, baseball commissioner and former president of Yale University, dies at 51. He will be succeeded as commissioner by Francis F. "Fay" Vincent on September 13.

*September 15:* Robert Penn Warren, the United States' first poet laureate, dies at age 84.

*September 17:* Emmy Awards are presented to *L.A. Law* for best dramatic series and *Cheers* as best comedy series. Carroll O'Connor (*In the Heat of the Night*) and Dana Delaney (*China Beach*) win the dramatic acting awards, while Richard Mulligan (*Empty Nest*) and Candice Bergen (*Murphy Brown*) win in the comedy series category.

*September 17–25:* Hurricane Hugo hits the U.S. Virgin Islands, Puerto Rico, and (on September 21) South Carolina; 24 Americans are killed. Total damage comes to $9 billion—$5 billion in South Carolina alone—making it the costliest hurricane in U.S. history to date.

*September 20:* In Los Angeles, Richard Ramirez, the notorious mass murderer known as the Night Stalker, who had terrorized Southern California in 1985, is found guilty of 30 murders in addition to 30 other crimes.

*September 22:* Irving Berlin, considered the United States' greatest songwriter, dies at 101.

*September 27:* At a meeting of the nation's governors in Virginia, President Bush asserts that major reforms in the education system are needed.

*September 27:* Sony Corp. buys Columbia Pictures Entertainment for $3.4 billion, the largest Japanese acquisition of an American company to date.

*September 28:* Federal drug officials announce that they will depart from normal procedure in AIDS cases and allow the experimental drug dideoxyinosine (DDI) to be prescribed, even though it is still in its testing stages. Meanwhile, those patients using azidothymidine (AZT) are showing improvement in their conditions.

*September 29:* In the country's largest drug operation to date, law officers seize some 20 tons of cocaine worth $2 billion (wholesale) as well as $10 million in cash in a Los Angeles warehouse. Four are arrested in the raid.

*October 5:* Televangelist Jim Bakker is convicted on 24 counts of fraud and conspiracy, having misappropriated $158 million from his PTL ministry followers. On October 24 he is sentenced to 45 years in prison and a fine of $500,000.

*October 6:* Movie great Bette Davis dies at 81.

*October 9:* The Dow Jones industrial average closes at 2791.41, a new high, although four days later it will fall 190.58 points, the second-largest plunge ever.

*October 12:* President Bush refuses to sign a law passed by Congress to ban flag burning, saying he wants a constitutional amendment instead. The law is passed without his signature, but in June 1990 the Supreme Court will declare it unconstitutional.

*October 14–28:* The American League's Oakland Athletics defeat the National League's San Francisco Giants to win the World Series in four games. The final two games had been postponed due to the October 17 earthquake.

*October 15:* Hockey great Wayne Gretzky, playing for the Los Angeles Kings in his 11th season as a professional, scores his 1,850th point, breaking the old record set by Gordie Howe over 26 seasons.

*October 17:* An earthquake registering 7.1 on the Richter scale hits the San Francisco Bay area, causing widespread damage, including the collapse of a section of the San Francisco–Oakland Bay Bridge. The quake kills 62–67 people (mostly in the bridge collapse), and property damage alone is estimated at $7 billion. It is North America's most destructive trembler since the infamous 1906 earthquake in the same area.

*October 18–23:* Astronauts aboard the space shuttle *Atlantis* launch *Galileo,* an unmanned spacecraft, which will reach Venus in February 1990 and use a gravitational push from that planet to send it to Jupiter, where it is expected to arrive in December 1995. Along the way it will come to within 600 miles of Earth and take pictures of the far side of the Moon never seen before.

*October 25:* Novelist and critic Mary McCarthy dies at 77.

*October 30:* The Mitsubishi Estate Co. of Tokyo buys 51 percent of Rockefeller Center for $864 billion, giving the Japanese corporation a controlling interest in the historic skyscraper complex.

*November 5:* Famed pianist Vladimir Horowitz dies at age 85.

*November 7:* In Virginia Douglas Wilder becomes the first African American to be elected governor of a state. David Dinkins becomes New York City's first black mayor.

*November 9:* East Germany opens its borders with West Germany, and elated Berliners begin to knock down the Berlin Wall, symbolizing the end of the cold war.

*November 16:* Government forces in El Salvador murder six Jesuit priests, their housekeeper, and her teenage daughter. The U.S. Congress will subsequently suspend aid to the country.

*November 17:* President Bush signs a bill increasing the minimum wage, currently $3.35/hour. The rate will be raised to $3.80 on April 1, 1990, and then to $4.25 on April 1, 1991, although the law maintains the $3.35 rate as a "training wage" for new employees during the first three months of employment.

*November 17:* Congress votes to fund a Native American museum, to be located in Washington, D.C.

*November 19:* American astronomers claim they have detected a source of light coming from the edge of the universe—and the beginning of time.

*November 21:* President Bush signs a bill appropriating $3.18 billion to provide treatment facilities, federal prison expansion, education, and law enforcement in the fight against drug use. He also signs a bill banning smoking on most domestic flights, excepting those to Alaska and Hawaii taking more than six hours.

*November 22–27:* The space shuttle *Discovery* completes the fifth shuttle mission of the year; it is also the program's fifth mission for the Department of Defense.

*November 22–December 11:* In baseball, records for contracts signed are set and broken in a short period when Kirby Pucket signs with the Minnesota Twins on November 11 for $3 million a year over three years; pitcher Mark Langston signs, on December 1, a five-year contract with the California Angels, amounting to $3.2 million a year; and another pitcher, Mark Davis, signs with the Kansas City Royals on December 11 for $13 million over four years—$3.25 million a year.

*November 27:* At the University of Chicago Medical Center, doctors perform the United States' first successful liver transplant using a live donor, with a mother giving a third of her liver to her 21-month-old daughter. The operation has already been performed four times in other countries.

*November 29:* John Casey (*Spartina*) wins the National Book Award for fiction, and Thomas L. Friedman (*From Beirut to Jerusalem*) wins for nonfiction.

*December 1:* Alvin Ailey, founder of the American Dance Theater, dies at 58.

*December 2–3:* In Malta, President Bush and Soviet president Mikhail Gorbachev hold their first official meeting which is disrupted by fierce storms. At the summit's conclusion, they announce that the cold war is effectively at an end.

*December 6:* At the École Polytechnique in Montreal, antifeminist Marc Lépine kills 14 women and injures 13, then commits suicide in one of the worst massacres in Canadian history.

*December 20:* U.S. armed forces invade Panama to overthrow the government of General Manuel Noriega, who takes refuge in the Vatican embassy.

*December 25:* Baseball's William "Billy" Martin, the frequently hired and fired New York Yankees manager, dies at 61.

*December 31:* The Dow Jones industrial average closes at 2753.20, a total gain over the year of 584.63, or 27 percent.

## 1990

*January 3:* In Panama, Manuel Noriega surrenders to U.S. forces and is flown to the United States to await trial on drug-trafficking charges.

*January 18:* In the long-running McMartin child-abuse case, Peggy Buckey is acquitted on all counts, but there is a hung jury on Ray Buckey.

## Eyewitness Testimony

### George H. W. Bush Takes Over

A new breeze is blowing, and a nation refreshed by freedom stands ready to push on. There is new ground to be broken and new action to be taken. There are times when the future seems thick as a fog; you sit and wait, hoping the mists will lift and reveal the right path. But this is a time when the future seems a door you can walk right through into a room called tomorrow.

*From George H. W. Bush's inaugural address, January 20, 1989. Available online. URL: http://bushlibrary. tamu.edu/research/papers/1989/89012000.html.*

Where has Bush been since 1980? How was it possible for the man who now asks more money for Head Start to have sat quietly when Reagan attempted to kill the program? How could a man who now speaks movingly about the homeless have kept his trap shut when Reagan blamed them for their own plight? How could someone who now declares war on acid rain, professes love for clean beaches and sympathy for the poor, have served a president who didn't care if the homeless slept on the beaches where the acid rain fell?

*Columnist Richard Cohen expressing George H. W. Bush's dilemma in escaping Ronald Reagan's shadow, in Cohen, "Bush 'Conflicted,'" Washington Post, February 14, 1989, p. A-21.*

. . . I just want to get progress on the budget, Savings and Loan, the ethics bill, the education bill, and the re-evaluation so we can move out in front of Gorbachev. We cannot let him continue to erode our standing in Europe. Eastern Europe offers an opportunity and it's all a tremendous challenge and I'm loving every minute of it.

*From George H. W. Bush's diary entry for March 22, 1989, in Bush,* All the Best, George Bush *(1999), p. 418.*

By their own testimony, Bush's appointees are frustrated at the constraints forced on them by more than $1 trillion in budget deficits left during Reagan's reign and angry at the truckload of problems left in Bush's path, from collapsing thrift institutions and pillaged housing programs to tainted chickens and leaking nuclear plants. . . . [N]ow the White House mood is turning sour, and the real transition from the Reagan to the Bush era is finally happening.

. . . The President now knows how Donald Regan felt when the former White House chief of staff compared his job to "a shovel brigade that follows a parade down Main Street, cleaning up."

*Describing the unwanted problems handed down to President Bush from Ronald Reagan, in "Bush's Shovel Brigade,"* U.S. News & World Report, *August 7, 1989, p. 14.*

After seven months as President, Bush has emerged as a much more complex Commander in Chief than expected, a hybrid of presidential personalities served and observed. Bush possesses Lyndon Johnson's penchant for secrecy, without retributive sense of justice. He has Richard Nixon's feel for foreign policy, but so far lacks his mentor's grip on grand strategy. He shares Jimmy Carter's fascination with the fine details of government, but understands better which pieces are more important. Bush says he learned from Reagan the importance of stubborn principle in politics, but he sees more clearly than Reagan the sweet reason of expedient compromise.

*Evaluating George H. W. Bush as president, in "Mr. Consensus,"* Time, *August 21, 1989, p. 16.*

The President's disposition to let events take their course has not served him badly so far. His popularity has now soared to 70 percent, a near-record in the last decade. But his standing will not survive catastrophe, and catastrophe almost certainly will result if he forgoes the advantages of decisive U.S. action and is compelled to be merely reactive in a crisis.

The New York Times *deploring President Bush's approach to foreign policy, in its editorial "The Passive President,"* New York Times, *September 17, 1989, sec. 4, p. 22.*

If war preparations are scarcely usual in the Bush White House, they are not as stunningly out of character as they would have seemed only a few months ago. The Panama invasion marks the latest, but far from the last, stage in a monumental transformation of George Bush: from a President whose overriding imperative during his initial months in office was to avoid doing "something dumb," to a self-confident chief mapping a bold and individual—if not always prudent—foreign policy that he is quite willing to back with military force.

*Noting a major change in George H. W. Bush's foreign policy behavior, in "Showing Muscle,"* Time, *January 1, 1990, pp. 20–21.*

## Washington Scandals

Reports of rigged bids, contract awards swapped for lifetime employment and mutual back-scratching lace the Defense Department inspector general's latest report about wrongdoing. Good news, such as the Navy buying half its supply of a $54 helicopter part for $8.31 each, is offset by bad news: It paid $3,474 apiece for the other half.

*Journalist Mark Thompson reporting developments in the investigation of the Pentagon procurement scandal, in Thompson, "Record Pentagon Procurement Overcharges Cited,"* Washington Post, *January 1, 1989, p. A-12.*

Senator Tower now stands accused of being a drunk, a womanizer (a new noun for which no female equivalent has been coined) and a revolving-door sleaze; in fairness, it should be recorded that he has not been charged with pederasty, insider trading, the smoking of cornsilk, or mopery—at least not yet.

Will this hard-bitten little hard-liner (who is no drinking buddy of mine) die the death of a thousand cuts? Many in Washington now expect him to relieve the President of the public relations burden and withdraw. I think he should not and will not.

*Essayist William Safire expressing his dismay over the controversy surrounding Senator John Tower, in Safire, "Towering Inferno,"* New York Times, *February 13, 1989, p. A-21. The Senate voted against Tower's nomination for secretary of defense in March.*

I'm no Jim Wright fan. But everybody knows he's no more guilty and no less guilty of corruption than 60 percent of the people in Washington, D.C. Maybe 70 percent.

*Elementary schoolteacher Nelda Krohn, a Democrat, expressing the viewpoint of many Americans, quoted in Apple, "Outside Washington, Scandal Is Defined as Issues Ignored,"* New York Times, *May 7, 1989, sec. 1, p. 1.*

"Ethics" is a weighty term. It connotes duty and ideals and high professional standards. But in the lexicon of Washington, it rarely comes down to more than avoiding conflicts of interest—not of deed, but of interest. The idea is that you can't serve two masters, though all of us serve two and frequently more. Members of Congress serve thousands. They cast hundreds of votes a year—on issues that affect themselves, relatives and friends.

*Editor-publisher James K. Glassman, commenting on the ethics investigations in Washington, in Glassman, "The Ethics' Frenzy,"* Washington Post, *May 28, 1989, pp. B-1, B-2.*

It is intolerable that qualified members of the executive and legislative branches are resigning because of the ambiguities and the confusion surrounding the ethics laws and because of their own consequent vulnerability to personal attack. That's a shame. It is happening.

And it is grievously hurtful to our society when vilification becomes an accepted form of political debate and negative campaigning becomes a fulltime occupation. When members of each party become self-appointed vigilantes carrying out personal vendettas against members of the other party. In God's name, that's not what this institution is supposed to be about.

*Congressman Jim Wright, decrying the process that has forced him to resign as Speaker of the House, quoted in "Partial Text of Wright's Resignation Speech,"* Washington Post, *June 1, 1989, p. A-18.*

Mr. Wright spoke of his resignation as a form of propitiation. It was for him. It is not for Congress. The need is to clean up a system in which members, in behalf of both standard of living and reelection, spend too much time with their hands outstretched. The private funding of the Congress has gone too far; the new House leaders need to steer to higher ground.

*The* Washington Post, *calling on Congress to improve ethical standards, in its editorial "Jim Wright Resigns,"* Washington Post, *June 1, 1989, p. A-24.*

## The Mess at HUD

She liked power. She liked the idea that "I can call the shots, I can get this for you if I want, I can stomp on you, I can kill you"—that's the kind of thing she liked.

*Former secretary of housing and urban development Samuel Pierce describing his former executive assistant, Deborah Gore Dean, in testimony before a House of Representatives subcommittee on May 25, 1989, quoted in Shenon, "Ex-Housing Secretary Says Aides Were at Fault in Disputed Program,"* New York Times, *May 26, 1989, p. A-12.*

... Mr. Pierce's former executive assistant has stepped right up to the subject: "I would have to say we ran it in a political manner," she told The Wall Street Journal.

Hardly the first time that has happened in this town, and Mr. Pierce said he was sure a lot of Democrats benefited from the program, too. We never doubted it. Talk about cynical. As someone said a few years back when the first evidence was being brought forward of how much of the money appropriated to help out the less fortunate ended up as paychecks for those who made an "industry" of helping them, "There's money in poverty."

*The* Washington Post *offering a cynical view of the growing HUD scandal, in its editorial " 'There's Money in Poverty,' "* Washington Post, *May 30, 1989, p. A-18.*

It was kind of scary, but there were so many hurting people. . . . We bought them groceries. We paid their electric and gas bills so they could be warm. We paid their rent. . . . I figured that as long as I was going to jail anyway, I would help a few people with the time I had left.

*Marilyn Louise Harrell, also known as "Robin HUD," explaining why she had diverted millions in funds from the Department of Housing and Urban Development (HUD), quoted in Shenon, "H.U.D. Agent Details Diverting Millions,"* New York Times, *June 11, 1989, sec. 1, p. 30.*

The power and favoritism exercised by Ms. Dean and her friends have become yet another emblem of Washington's loose ethical moorings—indiscretions that were magnified by their youth and inexperience. "It was the kiddie corps," says Bart Baylor, the former Senate investigator, who did the background check on Ms. Dean after her nomination. "We're talking about millions of dollars of taxpayer money in the hands of these young adults."

It was not a place, says one member of Ms. Dean's youthful set, "where there was enough adult supervision."

*Reporters Jill Abramson and Edward T. Pound examining Deborah Gore Dean and her staff, in Abramson and Pound, "How Deborah Dean and Washington Pals Controlled HUD Cash,"* Wall Street Journal, *June 26, 1989, p. A1.*

In the mix of Washington scandals HUD ranks as historically less important than the Iran-contra and finan-cially less costly than the S&L crisis. Yet in terms of breathtaking cynicism and hypocrisy it's hard to match. Over eight years ostensibly respectable people became poverty pimps, getting rich and powerful by subverting programs intended to help the poor. Washington scandals usually involve more than money, and in this case ideology and lust for power also played a role. Big-name consultants selling influence, former government officials "cashing in" on their expertise, congressional failure to oversee agencies—all are familiar patterns of Washington behavior. The HUD scandals seem to combine the city's worst tendencies at the same time, in grossly exaggerated form.

*Newsweek expressing dismay over the blooming HUD scandal, in "The HUD Ripoff,"* Newsweek, *August 7, 1989, p. 16.*

It now appears that the taxpayers will take a loss of at least $2 billion on the cozy little, sleazy little, greedy little deals that were made. Let it be said up top: the primary responsibility for this debacle lies squarely in the lap of Ronald Reagan. The buck stopped there.

For the eight years of his administration, it now seems evident, the president paid virtually no attention to this huge, costly department. For political reasons that are understandable, if not altogether admirable, he named a token black to be HUD secretary. This was "Silent Sam" Pierce, the invisible man. What a choice!

*Conservative columnist James J. Kilpatrick, decrying the HUD scandal and the primary reason for it, in Kilpatrick, "It's Reagan's Mess at HUD,"* Washington Post, *August 11, 1989, p. A-25.*

Instead of giving the poor housing vouchers to buy their own shelter, Congress decided that it would involve itself heavily in the residential real estate business. Congress accomplished this by making sure that the housing money flowed through and to the middlemen. The middlemen, of course, included everyone connected with the wonderful world of subsidized real-estate development—Congressmen themselves, federal bureaucrats, state and local politicians, bankers, unions and the developers. Somewhere at the bottom of this long, trickle-down funnel, no doubt, would be the genuinely poor.

*The* Wall Street Journal *finding Congress accountable for the HUD scandal, in its editorial "Where Was Congress?"* Wall Street Journal, *September 6, 1989, p. A-18.*

## Saving the Thrifts

The cleanup can't be financed by the S&L industry alone. Mr. Bush candidly concedes that a lot of the money—perhaps $40 billion over the next 10 years—is going to have to come from the taxpayers. Is it fair to use general funds to clean up one industry? The answer is that it's both fair and necessary.

*The* Washington Post *approving President Bush's proposed bill to save the savings-and-loan industry, in its editorial "At Last, Action on the S&Ls,"* Washington Post, *February 7, 1989, p. 24.*

Bush deserves a heck of a lot of credit for bellying up to the bar and putting a real plan on the table. Over all, the view of Democrats in Congress is that this is a good, constructive starting point.

*Representative Charles E. Schumer (D, N.Y.), expressing approval for President Bush's proposed bailout plan for the savings-and-loan industry, quoted in Hershey, "Praise on Capitol Hill for Rescue Proposal,"* New York Times, *February 7, 1989, p. D-9.*

I think in retrospect we could—everybody could—have done a better job in ferreting out corruption and fraud, things of that nature. . . . I don't know the details of that enough to know whether—how much of the problem should be put on the regulatory system. So much of it is economics, pure economics.

*President Bush in an interview, replying to a question about whether deregulation contributed to the savings-and-loan crisis, quoted in "Excerpts from the Interview with the President,"* Wall Street Journal, *February 14, 1989, p. A-4.*

One question, among the many raised in recent weeks, had to do with whether my financial support in any way influenced several political figures to take up my cause. I want to say in the most forceful way I can: I certainly hope so.

*Charles Keating, disgraced chairman of American Continental Corporation, talking to reporters on April 17, 1989; quoted in Jefferson, "Keating of American Continental Corp. Comes Out Fighting,"* Wall Street Journal, *April 18, 1989, p. B-2.*

A gang is huddled together conspiring to steal from honest citizens to finance its costly addictions. The damage this does to the economy could easily run into the hundreds of billions of dollars. . . .

We're talking, of course, about the members of Congress now working on the savings-and-loan bailout bill. What they are doing is simply incredible. Faced with the task of trying to clean up this extraordinary mess, many of the Congressmen are instead cutting deals and pushing expensive special breaks for favored constituents. You'd think just once they could resist this crummy behavior, But no, doing deals seems to have become a form of Congressional crack.

*The* Wall Street Journal *decrying congressional alterations to the savings-and-loan bailout bill, in its editorial "Congressional Crack,"* Wall Street Journal, *May 17, 1989, p. A-18.*

Seldom in our experience as accountants have we encountered a more egregious example of the misapplication of generally accepted accounting principles. This Association was made to function as an engine designed to funnel insured deposits to its parent in tax allocation and dividends. To do this, it had to generate reported earnings, and it generated earnings by making loans or other transfers of cash or property to facilitate sham sales of land. It created profits by making loans. Many of the loans were bad. Lincoln was manufacturing profits by giving its money away.

*From a July 14, 1989, report by the accounting firm Kenneth Leventhal & Company, following their analysis of 15 real estate deals conducted by the failed Lincoln Savings and Loan Association, quoted in Adams,* The Big Fix, *(1990), pp. 252–253.*

If the savings and loan industry had invested the $100 billion in depositors' money wisely instead of squandering it on bad real estate loans and bloated salaries for executives, the money would now be earning $10 billion a year in interest. That, however, is only pennies for a nation generating $5 trillion in annual income.

"The thrift crisis was like a hurricane that destroyed a small town, with its handful of stores and jobs," said Barry Bosworth, a senior fellow at the Brookings Institution. "Even if the town is never rebuilt, the big city nearby still provides plenty of jobs and income."

*Journalist Louis Uchitelle, analyzing the outcome of the savings-and-loan bailout plan, in Uchitelle, "Ripples from a Bailout,"* New York Times, *August 13, 1989, sec. 1, p. 1.*

The Senators say their efforts on Mr. Keating's behalf were merely "constituent service." All five Senators somehow claimed him as a constituent. An Arizona resident from a prominent Ohio Republican family, Mr. Keating controlled Lincoln in California as well as a large hotel in Michigan.

Senator McCain has likened his intervention with the federal regulators examining Lincoln to "helping the little lady who didn't get her Social Security check." But Charles Keating was asking for a lot more than a lost check—and was willing to pay for it. He and his allies gave the Senators a total of $1.4 million for their campaigns and their pet political causes.

*The* Wall Street Journal *looking at Charles Keating and the "Keating Five," in its editorial "Congress's Watergate,"* Wall Street Journal, *November 15, 1989, p. A-26.*

These fellas did what Senators have been doing for a long time. There's nothing illegal about it. It's just wrong.

*Former senator William Proxmire commenting on the actions of the Keating Five, quoted in "Community Standards,"* Wall Street Journal, *December 6, 1989, p. A-14.*

## The Exxon Valdez *Spill*

Over the years, they have promised they would do everything to clean up a spill and to maintain our quality of life. I think it's quite clear right now that our area is faced with destruction of our entire way of life.

*John Devens, mayor of Valdez, Alaska, expressing his anger over Exxon's failure to react quickly to clean up the spill from the* Exxon Valdez, *quoted in Egan, "Fishermen and State Take Charge of Effort to Control Alaska Spill,"* New York Times, *March 29, 1989, p. B-5.*

Oil company officials acknowledged that they did not begin putting out cleanup booms until 10 hours after the accident—twice the amount of time called for in the cleanup plan they are required to maintain. The contingency plan also says chemical dispersants should be the chief method of breaking up the oil in such a large spill. But by Tuesday, Exxon officials said it was too late to use the chemicals.

*Journalist Timothy Egan reporting distressing developments in the* Exxon Valdez *oil spill, in Egan, "Exxon Concedes It Can't Contain Most of Oil Spill,"* New York Times, *March 30, 1989, p. A-1.*

Now, the icebergs are stained brown. Sea lions, yelping in confusion, crowd atop buoys in a sea of gunk. Oiled otters quickly lose their warmth and freeze to death. Black crude oil, six inches thick in parts, covers dozens of islands, leaving an industrial ring on places seldom visited by man.

*Reporter Timothy Egan describing the effects of the* Exxon Valdez *oil spill, in Egan, "As Oil Stain Spreads, the Delicate Balance of Resources Is Undone,"* New York Times, *April 1, 1989, p. 8.*

The energy that oil would provide—at great cost, not least in global warming—can be replaced, over time and with effort, by conservation measures that as recently as 10 years ago were pursued by Americans without complaint, and by new steps of greater severity: by a renewed emphasis on solar devices; by a heavy tax on gasoline to force faster development and great use of less harmful fuels—by a variety of means that mostly require discipline, encouragement, education and the kind of American ingenuity those responsible for the Exxon Valdez seem to have forgotten.

*Columnist Tom Wicker commenting on problems in environmental care, in Wicker, "Oil Can Be Replaced,"* New York Times, *April 4, 1989, p. A-27.*

If the image of an uncareful and uncaring industry prevails among the U.S. public, then we can kiss goodbye to domestic oil and gas exploration in the [Arctic National Wildlife Refuge], offshore, and in the public lands.

*Interior Secretary Manuel Lujan speaking to an industry group on April 3, 1989, about how the poor response to the* Exxon Valdez *spill is eroding public support for further oil exploration and drilling, quoted in "Oil and Dirty Hands,"* New York Times, *April 5, 1989, p. A-28.*

Of this tragic episode, one thing can be said without serious refutation. No one involved has come out well—not Alaskan authorities, not the consortium of oil companies of which Exxon is a member, not the federal government and not President Bush, who promised to be the environmental president and in his first true environmental test developed what Abraham Lincoln saw in his reluctant commanding general—a case of "the slows."

*Columnist Haynes Johnson criticizing many in the aftermath of the* Exxon Valdez *spill, in Johnson, "Exxon's Good Fortune,"* Washington Post, *May 5, 1989, p. A-2.*

## Taxing Times in Canada

The Conservatives have broken every single commitment they made. They promised a visible tax and have delivered in invisible one. They promised tax reform would be revenue neutral and instead have snatched billions from the pockets of Canadians.

*New Democratic Party member Nelson Riis voicing his anger over the first proposed version of the Goods and Services Tax, quoted in Sears, "MPs Vow to Fight 'Cruel, Brutal, Mean' Tax,"* Toronto Star, *August 9, 1989, p. A-17.*

The sales tax is a much tougher proposition that cannot be sold. It's a much tougher script than free trade. And the timing is a kind of political suicide—in the third year of a four-year mandate. It's a godsend to the Liberals and New Democrats.

*Pollster Angus Reid expressing his view of the proposed Goods and Services Tax, quoted in Sears, "New Tax a Tough Sell for Tories, Critics Say,"* Toronto Star, *August 10, 1989, pp. A-1, A-30.*

Liberal MPs did their bit to incite a tax revolt yesterday, launching a campaign to collect signatures of Canadians who reject the proposed goods and services tax.

There was no shortage of people willing to sign the petition as about 10 Liberal members of Parliament fanned out among lunchtime crowds on the Sparks Street mall a block from Parliament Hill.

Once passersby were told the petition called on the federal government not to proceed with its plan for a new 9 per cent levy on consumers beginning Jan. 1, 1991, their most common reaction was: "Where do I sign?"

*Journalist Madelaine Drohan reporting public reaction to the proposed Goods and Services Tax, in Drohan, "Liberal MPs Campaign against Proposed GST,"* Globe and Mail (Montreal), *August 24, 1989, p. A-10.*

We are bringing in the new goods and services tax not because it is easy but because it is right. Our opponents say that to do nothing on tax reform is an alternative. That is their usual policy: do nothing, embrace the past and evade the future.

*Prime Minister Brian Mulroney speaking to the federal Conservative convention, quoted in "Alternatives to the Tax,"* Globe and Mail (Montreal), *August 29, 1989, p. A-6.*

Finance Minister Michael Wilson's seven-per-cent solution is no solution at all to the ills that will be visited upon Canadians as a result of his goods and services tax. It is merely the figure he can be reasonably sure of getting away with.

Seven per cent is what the economists and business tycoons told Mr. Wilson is the maximum the economy can stand, and he has fallen into line after months of insisting it would be nine per cent. The rest of us are supposed to feel good because he has decided to hit us with a slightly smaller hammer.

*The* Vancouver Sun *commenting sarcastically on the reduction of the goods and services tax to 7 percent, in its editorial "A Smaller Hammer but Still a Hammer,"* Vancouver Sun, *December 20, 1989, p. A-10.*

The only other reason Mr. Wilson has given for the new tax is to raise new revenue. The GST is an inefficient, bureaucratic nightmare which can raise plenty of money. Our government is already getting too many tax dollars. Unfortunately, the money is not well spent.

*Alex Perlman, a chartered tax accountant, writing about the goods and services tax (GST) in a letter to the* Globe and Mail (Montreal), *December 21, 1989, p. A-6.*

## Massacre

I didn't see him walk in. When I saw him, he was two or three feet from the students presenting their projects. Then he asked all the men to move to one side of the room and the women on the other. Nobody moved. We thought it was a joke.

It doesn't make sense.

*Teacher Yvon Bouchard describing the moment when gunman Marc Lépine walked into his class at the École Polytechnique, quoted in "Students' Disbelief Transforms into Terror When 'Really Calm' Killer Begins Shooting,"* The Globe and Mail (Montreal), *December 7, 1989, p. A-5.*

He told them: "You're women, you're going to be engineers. You're all a bunch of feminists. I hate feminists!" My friend Nathalie said: "No, it's not true. We're not feminists." He fired into the group.

*Robert Leclerc, a witness to the massacre at Montreal's École Polytechnique on December 6, 1989, describing gunman Marc Lépine, quoted in "Killer of 14 Wanted 'Revenge,'"* Vancouver Sun, *December 7, 1989, p. A-2.*

In your town and mine, in every town in this country, violent woman-hating is a daily truth. "Marc" was insane. But his murderous rage took the path it so often takes in our society: it targetted women. Women are generally smaller, unlikely to strike back, and they're available. Right now, somewhere in Canada, women's bones are being cracked, their eyes blackened, arms twisted, minds and hearts stabbed with abusive words. When a man in a rage goes hunting for a victim, nine times out of 10 he hunts for a woman . . . any woman.

*Journalist Michele Landsberg, noting the high incidence of rage against women, in Landsberg, "Killer's Rage Too Familiar to Canadians," Toronto Star, December 8, 1989, p. A-1.*

We can't absolutely prevent incidents like the University of Montreal killings.

What we must do, for the good of our souls and our society, is to deny them the justification of finding antifeminism in society. We must become intolerant of attitudes and actions that denigrate women and block their progress to true equality.

And this, for once, isn't a job for women. It must be done by men.

*Columnist Don McGillivray, commenting on antifeminist attitudes, in McGillivray, "Were Killings Just a Random Act?" Vancouver Sun, December 8, 1989, p. A-13.*

Marc Lépine's ghastly crime is being viewed by a lot of vocal people as a political act: incited by "feminism," its victims, coldly and with calculation, women. The reason for this view is the keening belief that if only men were educated properly to respect women, Marc Lépine would not have killed 14 of them. It places him alongside Corday and John Wilkes Booth and Oswald and the Medellin gangsters and airplane bombers as a person who, if circumstances were changed to his satisfaction, would not have acted. It fails to take madness into account.

*Columnist "Slinger" offering another view of mass murderer Marc Lépine, in Slinger, "There's No Place to Hide from a Madman," Toronto Star, December 10, 1989, p. A-2.*

## Women, Work, and Children

Women end up as care givers of the elderly because it is expected of them. As part of our religious and social backgrounds, women cook, clean, and take care of people. And though women have been in the work force for years, their careers have usually taken a back seat to their husband's when a crisis situation comes up.

*Elizabeth Mullen, an official with the American Association of Retired Persons, commenting on one of the many problems facing working women, quoted in "Juggling Family, Job and Aged Dependent," New York Times, January 26, 1989, p. B-8.*

It is 7:30 on a weekday morning as I stand in the bathroom of my home ready to leave for another day at the office. There I am, the picture of the professional woman, dressed in a business suit under a tan raincoat, briefcase in hand.

Also in hand is a screaming 4-year-old who just bumped her head so hard on the sink that the pipes are still vibrating. My 5-year-old is begging, on an equivalent decibel level, that I put the toothpaste on her brush, since the tube has already been squeezed practically dry. It wouldn't be so bad, but my belly, seven months pregnant, keeps getting in the way, and my train is due to leave the station in exactly 15 minutes.

*Working mother Geri L. S. Mandorf vividly describing the situation of many women, in Mandorf, "Career and Family, An Elusive Balance," New York Times, February 26, 1989, sec. 21, p. 16.*

Working mothers are right to sense clear and imminent danger in any talk of separate tracks—and nothing illustrates this better than the fact that this was instantly given the dead-end name "mommy track." The benefit that can come out of this debate, however, is that it can set the stage for talking about a respected and rewarded career and family track that is not limited to women. That's the only way that separate can ever be equal.

*Columnist Judy Mann commenting on a controversial theory that employers should separate women into two tracks, for career women and working mothers, in Mann, "The Demeaning 'Mommy Track': Separate and Unequal," Washington Post, March 15, 1989, p. C-3.*

When it comes to management skills, what you need on your resume may not be an MBA, but a baby. Because anyone who juggles work and children learns things about management that make the Harvard Business School seem like kindergarten.

That's why today's working mothers may be among the top managers of corporate America in the 1990s. In their struggle to combine jobs and children, they are learning the crucial modern management skills—of using time efficiently, setting priorities, making decisions, developing staff and handling crises.

*Looking at a positive aspect of juggling career and family, in Trafford, "Mommy Track—Right to the Top," Washington Post, March 19, 1989, p. C-1.*

If white women are, to varying degrees, frustrated, then black women are, to a great degree, angry.

"Black women face twice the problem," said Pamela O'Brien, 39, who is starting her own construction company in Chicago. "The white men look at you and see a black. The black men look at you and see a woman."

*One result from a recent New York Times poll on work attitudes and pay equity, in Belkin, "Old Barriers to Sexual Equality Seen as Eroding, but Slowly," New York Times, August 20, 1989, sec. 1, p. 26.*

The price paid for change is high and, it seems, unequally shared. Many women affirm the proposition that "Men are willing to let women get ahead, but only if women still do all the housework at home." Nearly half the women say they have "given up too much"—time with their children, quality of their home lives—in exchange for gains in the workplace. One-third of the men agree.

But would they want to turn back the clock? Absolutely not. If anything, the majority of all women, and the majority of men between 18 and 44, want to see the clock tick faster. The United States, they say, needs a strong women's movement—one that will keep on pushing. Feminism, for all its long history, has had continually to reinvent itself. Now it has put down strong, deep roots.

*The New York Times examining the results of its recent poll on women in the workforce, in its editorial "The Women's Movement: Here to Stay," New York Times, August 26, 1989, p. 22.*

I was reared by parents who stressed the importance of getting an education and being able to support yourself. But that doesn't mean that I can't have a family, and having children doesn't mean that I can't be as dedicated to my job as much as a single woman. Black women always have been successful at balancing family and job responsibilities. In most cases we have no choice.

*Sharon Woods, a human resources supervisor and mother of two, expressing the viewpoint of many African-American women, in Norment, "The Trials and Triumphs of Working Mothers," Ebony, September 1989, pp. 40, 42.*

If past experience is any indication of future trends, . . . it will probably be some time before men start lining up for paternal leave or job sharing—largely because they are bound by the same social norms that say a woman should do the balancing act, not the man.

*Journalist Elizabeth Spayd looking at differences in attitude toward male and female workers with families, in Spayd, "Being Too Nice to Working Mothers," Washington Post, October 15, 1989, p. H-3.*

Many mid-career women blame the [feminist] movement for not knowing [how tough it would be for women in business] and for emphasizing the wrong issues. The ERA and lesbian rights, while noble causes, seemed to have garnered more attention than the pressing need for child care and more flexible work schedules. The bitterest complaints come from the growing ranks of women who have reached 40 and find themselves childless, having put their careers first. Is it fair that 90% of male executives 40 and under are fathers but only 35% of their female counterparts have children? "Our generation was the human sacrifice," says Elizabeth Mehren, 42, a feature writer for the Los Angeles *Times*. "We believed the rhetoric. We could control our biological destiny. For a lot of us the clock ran out, and we discovered we couldn't control infertility."

*Confronting the new age of women's liberation, in "Onward, Women!" Time, December 4, 1989, p. 82.*

## Judicial Judgments

While there is no doubt that the sorry history of both private and public discrimination in this country has contributed to a lack of opportunities for black entrepreneurs, this observation, standing alone, cannot justify a rigid racial quota in the awarding of public contracts in Richmond, Va. Like the claim that discrimination in primary and secondary schooling justifies a rigid racial preference in medical school admissions, an amorphous claim that there has been past discrimination in a particular industry cannot justify the use of an unyielding racial quota.

*Justice Sandra O'Connor writing the majority opinion on* City of Richmond v. J. A. Croson, *January 23, 1989, quoted in "Excerpts from Court Opinions in Voiding of Richmond's Contracting Plan," New York Times, January 24, 1989, p. A-18.*

The present Court may have a majority eager to assume that the nation is color-blind well before racial equality has become real. It is one thing to wish for that and to resist any need to classify Americans by race. But as Justice Thurgood Marshall charged in his dissent, the majority is "constitutionalizing its wishful thinking" by applying color-blind rules. The result is that Richmond's remedies receive the same suspicious scrutiny the Court once applied to Virginia's massive resistance to school desegregation.

Wishful thinking notwithstanding, the Richmond decision leaves room for affirmative action that is carefully constructed. And affirmative action thrives in the private sector; companies have told the Court that diversity is good business and good citizenship. The ground rules are tighter now but the struggle for racial equality continues.

*The* New York Times *offers its opinion on the Supreme Court's decision in* City of Richmond v. J. A. Croson, *in its editorial "Even So, Affirmative Action Lives," New York Times, January 25, 1989, p. A-22.*

Like a pebble dropped into a pond, a presidency radiates lingering ripples. Last week's Supreme Court decision sharply limiting reverse discrimination by governments is a ripple from the Reagan administration, which advocated such a ruling.

It does much to roll back the racial spoils system that exists for certain government-favored minorities.

Unfortunately, the ruling only inhibits, not proscribes, reverse discrimination. Government may still allocate shares of wealth to groups—groups, not individuals—to which government awards the lucrative status of victim.

*Columnist George Will finding the Supreme Court did not go far enough in its affirmative action ruling, in Will, "Backing Out of a Swamp," Washington Post, January 29, 1989, p. D-7.*

The Government may not prohibit the expression of an idea simply because society finds the idea itself offensive or disagreeable.

*Justice William J. Brennan, writing the majority opinion in* Texas v. Johnson, *asserting the right to burn the American flag, quoted in "Excerpts from High Court's Decision Barring Prosecution in Flag Protest," New York Times, June 22, 1989, p. B-8.*

Mr. Speaker, I'm mad as hell. What in God's name is going on? . . . America should be outraged. Are there any limitations? Are they going to allow fornication on the moon?

*Representative Douglas Applegate (D, Ohio), expressing his outrage over the Supreme Court ruling allowing flag burning, quoted in Philips and Dewar, "Flag Ruling Angers Congress; Bush Denounces Desecration," Washington Post, June 23, 1989, p. A-1.*

People say the Court is turning right, but in this case it turned wrong.

*Republican senator Robert Dole (Kans.), expressing his view of the Supreme Court's June 21 decision allowing flag burning, quoted in Apple, "The Capital," New York Times, June 23, 1989, p. A-10.*

This is not a conservative or a liberal issue. It goes to the heart of what this country and the flag stand for. When the Court upheld the First Amendment right to burn the flag as a form of political protest, the majority included conservatives, like Antonin Scalia and Anthony Kennedy, as well as liberals, like William Brennan and Thurgood Marshall. They understand, as George Bush does not, that the First Amendment is indivisible and that what the flag stands for includes the freedom to defile it.

*Ira Glasser, executive director of the American Civil Liberties Union, arguing against President Bush's proposed constitutional amendment to ban flag burning, in Glasser, "Bush Lowers the Flag," New York Times, June 28, 1989, p. A-23.*

This body ought not to go on record criticizing the Supreme Court for discharging its solemn duty to vindicate the freedoms protected by the Constitution and symbolized by our hallowed flag.

*Senator Edward M. Kennedy (D, Mass.), one of only three senators to vote against a resolution condemning the Supreme Court for its decision, quoted in Hentoff, "A Frenzy of Flag-Waving," Washington Post, July 1, 1989, p. A-17.*

I fear for the future. I fear for the liberty and quality of the millions of women who have lived and come of age in the 16 years since Roe was decided. I fear for the integrity of, and public esteem for, the Court.

*Justice Harry A. Blackmum in his dissenting opinion on*
Webster v. Reproductive Health Services of
Missouri, *quoted in Greenhouse, "Supreme Court, 5-4,
Narrowing* Roe v. Wade, *Upholds Sharp State Limits
on Abortions," New York Times, July 4, 1989, p. 1.*

Nothing in the Constitution requires States to enter or remain in the business of performing abortions. Nor, as appellees suggest, do private physicians and their patients have some kind of constitutional right of access to public facilities for the performance of abortions.

*Chief Justice William Rehnquist, writing for the majority
in the Supreme Court's decision on* Webster v.
Reproductive Health Services of Missouri, *quoted
in "Excerpts from Court Decision on the Regulation of
Abortion," New York Times, July 4, 1989, p. 12.*

I think it's unfortunate that we still have to argue about what a woman can do with her body. . . . Now the states are going to make it so the poor women who would get an abortion won't be able to get one. It makes it harder for poor women to take care of their families.

*Administrator Martha Neal, expressing her
disappointment with the Supreme Court decision on
abortion, quoted in Rosenfeld, "Across the Nation,
Reactions Divided on Court's Abortion Ruling,"
Washington Post, July 4, 1989, p. A-5.*

Yes, the pro-lifers will accept the Supreme Court's invitation to redouble efforts to restrict abortion in the 50 state legislatures. And yes, the pro-choicers will energize their silent majority to win rights in the political arena they thought had been given by the Court.

But the analogy to slavery is as distorted as the analogy to murder; the nation is not about to fight a civil war on this issue.

*Essayist William Safire, offering an objective viewpoint of
the abortion controversy, in Safire, "Option 3: 'Pro-
Comp,' " New York Times, July 6, 1989, p. A-21.*

## The American Way of Business

No bugles blared. No oaths were sworn. No teary chief executive officer showed up to clean out his desk. In a most unceremonious way, Kohlberg Kravis Roberts & Co. completed the largest corporate acquisition ever yesterday, taking control of RJR Nabisco Inc. in a leveraged buy-out totaling $25.3 billion.

"Maybe things will finally get back to normal over there," said a dentist whose offices are near RJR's headquarters in Atlanta. "A lot of my RJR patients have been very tense."

*Describing the completion of the country's biggest business
acquisition, in Waldman and Anders, "KKR Completes
Buy-Out of RJR Without Fanfare," Wall Street
Journal, February 10, 1989, p. A-3.*

There's only one Mike Milken I know. He's the guy who breathed life into the low-grade debt market.

*Mark J. Meagher, chairman of Financial World, expressing
his admiration for Michael Milken at a meeting of chief
executives, quoted in "Milken's Woes Not on Menu,"
New York Times, March 17, 1989, p. D-2.*

Views differ, of course, on the merits of what Mr. Milken and his "junk bonds" have done to American business. Captains of industry view the threat of takeovers and the extension of debt leverage as disruptive of good business. Even the most confirmed capitalist can muster doubts about the level of Mr. Milken's compensation, measured in the hundreds of millions a year. Many Wall Street competitors have been appalled by the brash tactics of Drexel Burnham Lambert in general and Mr. Milken in particular.

The same competitors have gone on to start their own high-yield bond departments, though. For Mr. Milken's success was propelled by a valid financial insight: that sleepy bond markets, with rating agencies pretending to do the market's work, discounted the prospects of smaller, often more entrepreneurial companies.

*The* Wall Street Journal *commenting on Michael
Milken's influence on bond trading, in its editorial
"The Milken Indictment," Wall Street Journal,
March 31, 1989, p. A-14.*

Given the magnitude of the charges against him and the scale of his $1 billion compensation during the 1980s, Milken will face serious challenges in convincing a jury that he is an ordinary, hard-working family man.

The jury, like the public, will be confronted with two diametrically opposed descriptions of Milken. They will have to choose whether they agree with the executives at the Waldorf Astoria who gave him a standing ovation or with the Manhattan prosecutors whose indictment suggests they want to lock Michael Milken up and throw away the key.

*Journalists David A. Vise and Steve Coll, assessing what to expect in the upcoming trial of Michael Milken, in Vise and Coll, "Trial of Milken Would Showcase the Millions He Made on Deals," Washington Post, April 2, 1989, p. H-5.*

In revitalizing the U.S. economy, another valuable Milken legacy is what a forthcoming book by economist Harvey Segal calls the corporate "makeover" movement. The misbegotten conglomerate binge of the 1970s created a huge opportunity in the 1980s. Raiders could achieve massive gains merely by liberating thousands of companies then caught up in the gummy webs of large corporate bureaucracies. The diversification movement clearly has failed, and Mr. Milken helped ring down the curtain, which many leading business executives cannot forget.

*Columnist George Gilder putting Michael Milken's role in the 1980s takeover craze into perspective, in Gilder, "The Victim of His Virtues," Wall Street Journal, April 18, 1989, p. A-24.*

I don't believe Mrs. Helmsley is charged in the indictment with being a tough bitch.

*Gerald A. Feffer, lawyer for Leona Helmsley, in his summation to the jury during her trial for tax evasion, quoted in Fried, "Jury Finds Helmsley Guilty of Evading Federal Taxes," New York Times, August 31, 1989, p. B-3.*

## Confronting China

Amazement had already turned to fear and defiance earlier in the evening as citizens saw the military convoys entering the city. Some troops from other provinces practically paraded their AK-47 rifles as they stood in their trucks, stranded by the human blockades that had formed around the trucks.

By dark, tensions had soared throughout the city. Hundreds of thousands of people were impelled outdoors by their disbelief and anger, yet brought back to their homes by fear of the violence. The sound of tanks whizzing by and reports of open firing fanned their fears.

"You beasts! You beasts!" shouted the people at the troopers.

*Reporter Sheryl WuDunn, describing the scene in Beijing as military forces entered Tiananmen Square, in WuDunn, "In the Streets, Anguish, Fury and Tears," New York Times, June 4, 1989, sec. 1, p. 1.*

We have to make it clear that the United States will not continue to conduct business as usual with a government that engages in the wanton slaughter of its own people. And I have to say that if the president doesn't take the initiative in changing American policy in this regard, the Congress will do it for him.

*Representative Stephen J. Solarz (D, N.Y.) speaking on* Face the Nation, *June 4, 1989, quoted in McAllister, "Lawmakers Ask Strong U.S. Action," Washington Post, June 5, 1989, p. A-24.*

In recent weeks, we've urged mutual restraint, nonviolence, and dialogue; instead, there has been a violent and bloody attack on the demonstrators. The United States cannot condone the violent attack and cannot ignore the consequences for our relationship with China, which had been built on a foundation of broad support by the American people. This is not the time for an emotional response, but for a reasoned, careful action that takes into account both our long-term interests and recognition of a complex internal situation in China.

*President Bush expressing a note of caution in a news conference on June 5, 1989, quoted in "Excerpts from Bush's News Session," New York Times, June 6, 1989, p. A-15.*

President Bush seems to me to have walked this tightrope with extraordinary skill and delicacy. The administration must take care not to let itself be pushed into measures or pronouncements that might cast doubt on American's vital concern for the territorial integrity and modernization of China. Such actions would place a serious strain on long-term U.S.-Chinese relations. They could also rekindle dangerous temptations by some of China's neighbors.

If ever there was an occasion for bipartisan foreign policy, it is now. Everybody should forego the temptation to score debating points and unite behind an agreed-upon definition of the national interest. Thus, in the end, the drama in Beijing is for Americans a test of our political maturity.

*Former secretary of state Henry Kissinger, endorsing the Bush approach to China, in Kissinger, "The Drama in Beijing,"* Washington Post, *June 11, 1989, p. C-7.*

As you know, the clamor for stronger action remains intense. I have resisted that clamor, making clear that I did not want to see destroyed this relationship that you and I have worked hard to build. I explained to the American people that I did not want to unfairly burden the Chinese people through economic sanctions.

*From a letter written by George H. W. Bush to Chairman Deng Xiaoping on June 20, 1989, two weeks following the Tiananmen Square tragedy, in Bush,* All the Best, George Bush *(1999), p. 430.*

Those on the far right who oppose any relations with China will demand economic and diplomatic sanctions. So will the human rights lobby, which calls for punishing every regime that does not live up to our standards regardless of our interests or of the millions living under those regimes, whom sanctions would hurt the most. . . . The Bush Administration should continue to ignore these extremist voices and stay the prudent course it has already set.

*Former President Richard Nixon, writing in support of President Bush's position on China, quoted in "Nixon Lauds Bush for China Policy,"* New York Times, *June 25, 1989, sec. 1, p. 11.*

We have been feeling since the outset of these events more than two months ago that the various aspects of US foreign policy have actually cornered China. That's the feeling of us here . . . because the aim of the counterrevolutionary rebellion was to overthrow the People's Republic of China and our socialist system. If they should succeed in achieving that aim the world would be a different one. To be frank, this could even lead to war.

*Chinese leader Deng Xiaoping to National Security Advisor Brent Scowcroft on July 2, 1989, quoted in Bush and Scowcroft,* A World Transformed *(1998), p. 106.*

## Goodbye, Cold War

We understand the need for a transition period, but enough! The Russians have pulled out of Afghanistan, they're making unilateral troop reductions in Eastern Europe and Gorbachev is popping up everywhere. Bush has to start taking some initiatives of his own, or the Soviets will gain the strategic initiative.

*An unidentified European government member expressing the frustration of many over President Bush's apparent lack of a decisive foreign policy, quoted in Apple, "Statesman Bush's Debut,"* New York Times, *February 22, 1989, p. A-1.*

The cold war of poisonous Soviet-American feelings, of domestic political hysteria, of events enlarged and distorted by East-West confrontation, of almost perpetual diplomatic deadlock is over.

The we-they world that emerged after 1945 is giving way to the more traditional struggles of great powers. That contest is more manageable. It permits serious negotiations. It created new possibilities—for cooperation in combating terrorism, the spread of chemical weapons and common threats to the environment, and for shaping a less violent world.

*The* New York Times *forecasting a positive outlook in its editorial "The Cold War Is Over,"* New York Times, *April 2, 1989, sec. 4, p. 30.*

Let me share with you my vision: I see a Western Hemisphere of democratic, prosperous nations, no longer threatened by a Cuba or a Nicaragua armed by Moscow. I see a Soviet Union as it pulls away from ties to terrorist nations like Libya that threaten the legitimate security of their neighbors. I see a Soviet Union which respects China's integrity and returns the northern territories to Japan, a prelude to the day when all the great nations of Asia will live in harmony.

*President George H. W. Bush in his address at the Texas A&M University commencement ceremonies, May 12, 1989. Available online. URL: http://bushlibrary.tamu. edu/research/papers/1989/89051201.html.*

The earthquakes in the Communist world will go on. With millions of Chinese listening daily to the Voice of America and the BBC, with Russians watching Poles and Europeans, and with all governed by Communism increasingly able to compare their misery with the richer and freer life elsewhere, there will be two profound tests: of decency in the East, and of wisdom in the West.

*The* New York Times *commenting on the developments in China and Eastern Europe, in its editorial "Earthquakes in the Communist World,"* New York Times, *June 11, 1989, sec. 4, p. 28.*

Let me get quickly to the point of this letter. I would like very much to sit down and talk to you, if you are agreeable to the idea. I want to do it without thousands of assistants hovering over our shoulders, without the ever-present briefing papers and certainly without the press yelling at us every 5 minutes about "who's winning," "what agreements have been reached" or "had our meeting succeeded or failed."

> *George H. W. Bush in a personal note to Mikhail Gorbachev on July 18, 1989, quoted in Beschloss and Talbott,* At the Highest Levels *(1993), p. 94. The result was the December summit in Malta.*

The most important aspect of Bush's visit was its symbolism. "The Iron Curtain has begun to part," the President declared in an eloquent speech at the Karl Marx University in Budapest. In front of Gdansk's Lenin shipyard, he told cheering Poles, "America stands with you."

While offering lavish praise for the courage shown by Poland and Hungary, he avoided baiting the Soviet Union, a sensible strategy for dealing with a bear that for the moment seems unusually amiable.

> *Looking at President Bush's visit to Europe in light of ongoing events, in "From Patrons to Partners,"* Time, *July 24, 1989, p. 19.*

If the Soviets are going to let the communists fall in East Germany, they've got to be really serious—more serious than I realized.

> *George H. W. Bush to his aides while watching the fall of the Berlin Wall on television, November 9, 1989, quoted in Beschloss and Talbott,* At the Highest Levels *(1993), p. 132.*

At Checkpoint Charlie, where Allied and Soviet tanks were locked in a tense face-off while the Berlin wall

U.S. president Bush and Soviet president Gorbachev talk things over at the Malta summit on December 2, 1989. *(Courtesy George Bush Presidential Library)*

was being erected in August 1961, lines of cars and people began to file across the border by late evening. Cheers, sparkling wine, flowers and applause greeted the new arrivals. On the West Berlin side of the wall, at the Brandenberg Gate, the most prominent landmark of the city's division, hundreds of people chanted, "Gate open! Gate open!"

"I can't believe I'm here," an elderly East Berliner told reporters as he crossed into the West. "This is what we have dreamed of all these years."

*Reporter Ferdinand Protzman describing the euphoria of Berliners upon the fall of the Berlin Wall, in Protzman, "East Berliners Explore Land Long Forgotten,"* New York Times, *November 10, 1989, p. A-1.*

We don't consider you an enemy anymore. Things have changed. We want you in Europe. You ought to be in Europe. It's important for the future of the continent that you're there. So don't think we want you to leave.

*Mikhail Gorbachev to George H. W. Bush in a surprising—and welcome—statement during the Malta summit, December 3, 1989, quoted in Beschloss and Talbott,* At the Highest Levels *(1993), p. 163.*

Gone was the soaring rhetoric of the Reagan-Gorbachev summits in Washington and Moscow. Instead of competing to put forward bold visions, Bush and Gorbachev appeared intent on not upstaging each other and not adding to each other's problems.

Asked anew if the Cold War was over, Gorbachev made no sweeping declaration. Instead, he said prosaically that he and Bush had "sought the answer to the question, 'Where do we stand now?'"

*Journalist Jim Hoagland analyzing the outcome of the Malta summit, in Hoagland, "Bush, Gorbachev Star in Own 'Ghostbusters,'"* Washington Post, *December 4, 1989, p. A-21.*

## The Panama Problem

The Government is taking the election by fraud. It's robbing the people of Panama of their legitimate rights.

*Former president Jimmy Carter, leader of an international delegation monitoring the Panamanian presidential elections, quoted in Gruson, "Noriega Stealing Election, Carter Says,"* New York Times, *May 9, 1989, p. A-1.*

Gen. Noriega provides the best example in recent U.S. foreign policy of how a foreign leader is able to manipulate the United States to the detriment of our own interests. Gen. Noriega recognized that, by making himself indispensable to various U.S. agencies, he could develop U.S. clients who would become dependent on him. As a result, they would be reluctant to pursue intelligence of Noriega's criminal activities and less likely to investigate what intelligence they did receive.

*From an April 1989 Senate Foreign Relations subcommittee report on terrorism, narcotics, and international operations, quoted in Johnson, "Noriega: A Specter of U.S. Policy,"* Washington Post, *May 12, 1989, p. A-2.*

There may come a time when it makes sense to use U.S. troops in Panama, as Secretary of State Baker noted yesterday. But that ought to be a deliberate American decision, not a precipitous response to a problematic opportunity. Superpower armies aren't frontier posses. Critics, disappointed at being denied instant gratification, are wrong to attack the president for understanding the value of restraint.

The New York Times *supporting President Bush's cautious response following a failed coup attempt in Panama, in its editorial "Sensible Restraint on Panama,"* New York Times, *October 5, 1989, p. A-30.*

The problem is that speeches, sanctions and votes by the Organization of American States do not interest General Noriega: Raw power does. He watches what we do, not what we or other hemispheric democracies say. He notes that we have been willing to do next to nothing to topple him. When power seemed to hang in the balance on Tuesday, we did not act.

From the facts thus far known publicly—and, judging from the reactions of the chairman of the Senate Intelligence Committee, Senator David Boren, the classified information as well—the U.S. missed an opportunity to topple General Noriega.

*Former Reagan official Elliott Abrams criticizing the Bush administration's response to a failed coup attempt in Panama, in Abrams, "Noriega Respects Power. Use It.,"* New York Times, *October 5, 1989, p. A-31.*

I want to see him out of there and I want to see him brought to justice. And that should not imply that that automatically means, no matter what the plan is or no matter what the coup attempt is or what the effort is, diplomatically and anything else, that we give carte blanche support to that.

*President Bush responding to questions about contradictory aspects of his calls for Manuel Noriega's ouster, quoted in "President's News Conference on Foreign and Domestic Issues,"* New York Times, *October 14, 1989, p. 8.*

Any course in Panama would have had costs. In the end, the most important questions are: Did President Bush test less drastic approaches? Yes. Is there a legal basis for the presence of Americans in Panama? Yes. Does the President have a responsibility to protect them? Yes.

*The* New York Times *supporting President Bush's decision to invade Panama, in its editorial "Why the Invasion Was Justified,"* New York Times, *December 21, 1989, p. A-30.*

General Noriega is no longer in power. He no longer commands the instruments of government or the forces of repression that he's used for so long to brutalize the Panamanian people. And we are continuing the efforts to apprehend him, see that he's brought to justice.

*President Bush in a press conference on December 21, one day following the U.S. invasion of Panama, quoted in "Excerpts from Bush's News Conference on Central America,"* New York Times, *December 22, 1989, p. A-10.*

The fact that George Bush's use of force was riskier than Ronald Reagan's seizure of virtually defenseless Grenada—and far more efficient than military ventures by John F. Kennedy, Gerald Ford and Jimmy Carter—should be seen as an opportunity. He has in hand the makings of an activist foreign policy.

*Columnists Rowland Evans and Robert Novak, pointing out some implications of the Panama invasion, in Evans and Novak, "Toughening Up,"* Washington Post, *December 22, 1989, p. A-19.*

Mr. Bush claimed a responsibility to save American lives. So far, at least 18 Americans have died in the inva-

President Bush discusses the Panama invasion by telephone in the Oval Office study on December 20, 1989, with National Security Advisor Brent Scowcroft and Chief of Staff John Sununu (right) standing by. *(Courtesy George Bush Presidential Library)*

sion, and blood is flowing freely in the streets of Panama.

None of the Administration's declared purposes for intervening stand up under scrutiny. It's perfectly obvious that its only real concern was the image problem of Gen. Manuel Noriega in power, thumbing his nose at the U.S. That alone was seen as sufficient provocation for intervention.

*Saul Landau, a senior fellow at the Institute for Policy Studies, speaking out against the Panama invasion, in Landau, "Imperialism, Bush Style," New York Times, December 22, 1989, p. A-39.*

Operations in Grenada, Libya and now Panama were all roundly criticized—until it was clear that they had succeeded. As Mr. Bush knows, leadership means understanding that the inevitable naysayers cannot be allowed to foreclose necessary actions that may have no guarantee of triumph. Success, however, has a way of quickly attracting well-wishers.

*The Wall Street Journal justifying U.S. actions in Panama despite international criticism, in its editorial "Regrets Only," Wall Street Journal, December 27, 1989, p. A-6.*

Thousands of Panamanians took to their cars, honking their horns and snarling traffic across the city. Thousands came out of their homes onto the lawns or verandas of their homes to bang pots and pans as soon as General Noriega's surrender to the United States was announced over national radio and television.

On street corners, youths waved Panamanian flags and sang and danced. Some lighted firecrackers and hoisted pineapple effigies of General Noriega pierced with knives.

*Journalist Larry Rohter describing the reaction in Panama following news of Manuel Noriega's surrender, in Rohter, "As Word Spreads in Panama, Thousands Turn Out to Cheer," New York Times, January 4, 1990, p. A-1.*

## Farewell, 1980s

Money fever was more normal in the '80s than it was in the '60s and '70s. Previously, there was an atmosphere among educated people that it was simply very bad form to show wealth or naked ambition. That was the period of the debutante in blue jeans.

In the '80s, that rather odd atmosphere evaporated. People think this has something to do with Ronald Reagan. They're getting it backwards. His election was made possible, in part, by the fact that this atmosphere evaporated. In the '80s people began to do what is really very normal, as in that wonderful Zero Mostel line in "The Producers": "That's right, baby; if you've got it, flaunt it."

*Author Tom Wolfe assessing the 1980s money culture, in Wolfe, "Tom Wolfe: The Years of Living Prosperously," U.S. News & World Report, December 25, 1989/January 1, 1990, p. 117.*

# APPENDIX A
## Documents

# 1. President Jimmy Carter's Address to the Nation on the Attempt to Rescue American Hostages in Iran, April 25, 1980

Late yesterday, I cancelled a carefully planned operation which was underway in Iran to position our rescue team for later withdrawal of American hostages, who have been held captive there since November 4. Equipment failure in the rescue helicopters made it necessary to end the mission.

As our team was withdrawing, after my order to do so, two of our American aircraft collided on the ground following a refueling operation in a remote desert location in Iran. Other information about this rescue mission will be made available to the American people when it is appropriate to do so.

There was no fighting; there was no combat. But to my deep regret, eight of the crewmen of the two aircraft which collided were killed, and several other Americans were hurt in the accident. Our people were immediately airlifted from Iran. Those who were injured have gotten medical treatment, and all of them are expected to recover.

No knowledge of this operation by any Iranian officials or authorities was evident to us until several hours after all Americans were withdrawn from Iran.

Our rescue team knew and I knew that the operation was certain to be difficult and it was certain to be dangerous. We were all convinced that if and when the rescue operation had been commenced that it had an excellent chance of success. They were all volunteers; they were all highly trained. I met with their leaders before they went on this operation. They knew then what hopes of mine and of all Americans they carried with them.

To the families of those who died and who were wounded, I want to express the admiration I feel for the courage of their loved ones and the sorrow that I feel personally for their sacrifice.

The mission on which they were embarked was a humanitarian mission. It was not directed against Iran; it was not directed against the people of Iran. It was not undertaken with any feeling of hostility toward Iran or its people. It has caused no Iranian casualties.

Planning for this rescue effort began shortly after our Embassy was seized, but for a number of reasons, I waited until now to put those rescue plans into effect. To be feasible, this complex operation had to be the product of intensive planning and intensive training and repeated rehearsal. However, a resolution of this crisis through negotiations and with voluntary action on the part of the Iranian officials was obviously then, has been, and will be preferable.

This rescue attempt had to await my judgment that the Iranian authorities could not or would not resolve this crisis on their own initiative. With the steady unraveling of authority in Iran and the mounting dangers that were posed to the safety of the hostages themselves and the growing realization that their early release was highly unlikely, I made a decision to commence the rescue operations plans.

This attempt became a necessity and a duty. The readiness of our team to undertake the rescue made it completely practicable. Accordingly, I made the decision to set our long-developed plans into operation. I ordered this rescue mission prepared in order to safeguard American lives, to protect America's national interests, and to reduce the tensions in the world that have been caused among many nations as this crisis has continued.

It was my decision to attempt the rescue operation. It was my decision to cancel it when problems developed in the placement of our rescue team for a future rescue operation. The responsibility is fully my own.

In the aftermath of the attempt, we continue to hold the Government of Iran responsible for the safety and for the early release of the American hostages, who have been held so long. The United States remains determined to bring about their safe release at the earliest date possible.

As President, I know that our entire Nation feels the deep gratitude I feel for the brave men who were prepared to rescue their fellow Americans from captivity. And as President, I also know that the Nation shares not only my disappointment that the rescue effort could not be mounted, because of mechanical difficulties, but also my determination to persevere and to bring all of our hostages home to freedom.

We have been disappointed before. We will not give up in our efforts. Throughout this extraordinarily difficult period, we have pursued and will continue to pursue every possible avenue to secure the release of the hostages. In these efforts, the support of the American people and of our friends throughout the world has been a most crucial element. That support of other nations is even more important now.

We will seek to continue, along with other nations and with the officials of Iran, a prompt resolution of the crisis without any loss of life and through peaceful and diplomatic means.

Thank you very much.

## 2. PRESIDENT JIMMY CARTER'S FAREWELL ADDRESS, JANUARY 14, 1981

Good evening. In a few days, I will lay down my official responsibilities in this office—to take up once more the only title in our democracy superior to that of president, the title of citizen.

Of Vice President Mondale, my Cabinet and the hundreds of others who have served with me during the last four years, I wish to say publicly what I have said in private: I thank them for the dedication and competence they have brought to the service of our country.

But I owe my deepest thanks to you, the American people, because you gave me this extraordinary opportunity to serve. We have faced great challenges together. We know that future problems will also be difficult, but I am now more convinced than ever that the United States—better than any other nation—can meet successfully whatever the future might bring.

These last four years have made me more certain than ever of the inner strength of our country—the unchanging value of our principles and ideals, the stability of our political system, the ingenuity and the decency of our people.

Tonight I would like first to say a few words about this most special office, the presidency of the United States.

This is at once the most powerful office in the world—and among the most severely constrained by law and custom. The president is given a broad responsibility to lead—but cannot do so without the support and consent of the people, expressed informally through the Congress and informally in many ways through a whole range of public and private institutions.

This is as it should be. Within our system of government every American has a right and duty to help shape the future course of the United States.

Thoughtful criticism and close scrutiny of all government officials by the press and the public are an important part of our democratic society. Now as in our past, only the understanding and involvement of the people through full and open debate can help to avoid serious mistakes and assure the continued dignity and safety of the nation.

Today we are asking our political system to do things of which the founding fathers never dreamed. The government they designed for a few hundred thousand people now serves a nation of almost 230 million people. Their small coastal republic now spans beyond a continent, and we now have the responsibility to help lead much of the world through difficult times to a secure and prosperous future.

Today, as people have become ever more doubtful of the ability of the government to deal with our problems, we are increasingly drawn to single-issue groups and special interest organizations to ensure that whatever else happens our own personal views and our own private interests are protected.

This is a disturbing factor in American political life. It tends to distort our purposes because the national interest is not always the sum of all our single or special interests. We are all Americans together—and we must not forget that the common good is our common interest and our individual responsibility.

Because of the fragmented pressures of special interests, it's very important that the office of the president be a strong one, and that its constitutional authority be preserved. The president is the only elected official charged with the primary responsibility of representing all the people. In the moments of decision, after the different and conflicting views have been aired, it is the president who then must speak to the nation and for the nation.

I understand after four years in office, as few others can, how formidable is the task the president-elect is about to undertake. To the very limits of conscience and conviction, I pledge to support him in that task. I wish him success, and Godspeed.

I know from experience that presidents have to face major issues that are controversial, broad in scope, and which do not arouse the natural support of a political majority.

For a few minutes now, I want to lay aside my role as leader of one nation, and speak to you as a fellow citizen of the world about three issues, three difficult issues: The threat of nuclear destruction, our stewardship of the physical resources of our planet, and the preeminence of the basic rights of human beings.

It's now been 35 years since the first atomic bomb fell on Hiroshima. The great majority of the world's people cannot remember a time when the nuclear shadow did not hang over the earth. Our minds have adjusted to it, as after a time our eyes adjust to the dark.

Yet the risk of a nuclear conflagration has not lessened. It has not happened yet, thank God, but that can give us little comfort—for it only has to happen once.

The danger is becoming greater. As the arsenals of the superpowers grow in size and sophistication and as other governments acquire these weapons, it may only be a matter of time before madness, desperation, greed or miscalculation lets loose this terrible force.

In an all-out nuclear war, more destructive power than in all of World War II would be unleashed every second during the long afternoon it would take for all the missiles and bombs to fall. A World War II every second—more people killed in the first few hours than all the wars of history put together. The survivors, if any, would live in despair amid the poisoned ruins of a civilization that had committed suicide.

National weakness—real or perceived—can tempt aggression and thus cause war. That's why the United States cannot neglect its military strength. We must and we will remain strong. But with equal determination, the United States and all countries must find ways to control and reduce the horrifying danger that is posed by the world's enormous stockpiles of nuclear arms.

This has been a concern of every American president since the moment we first saw what these weapons could do. Our leaders will require our understanding and our support as they grapple with this difficult but crucial challenge. There is no disagreement on the goals or the basic approach to controlling this enormous destructive force. The answer lies not just in the attitudes or actions of world leaders, but in the concern and demands of all of us as we continue our struggle to preserve the peace.

Nuclear weapons are an expression of one side of our human character. But there is another side. The same rocket technology that delivers nuclear warheads has also taken us peacefully into space. From that perspective, we see our Earth as it really is—a small and fragile and beautiful blue globe, the only home we have. We see no barriers of race or religion or country. We see the essential unity of our species and our planet; and with faith and common sense, that bright vision will ultimately prevail.

Another major challenge, therefore, is to protect the quality of this world within which we live. The shadows that fail across the future are cast not only by the kinds of weapons we have built, but by the kind of world we will either nourish or neglect.

There are real and growing dangers to our simple and most precious possessions: the air we breathe; the water we drink; and the land which sustains us. The rapid depletion of irreplaceable minerals, the erosion of topsoil, the destruction of beauty, the blight of pollution, the demands of increasing billions of people, all combine to create problems which are easy to observe and predict but difficult to resolve. If we do not act, the world of the year 2000 will be much less able to sustain life than it is now.

But there is no reason for despair. Acknowledging the physical realities of our planet does not mean a dismal future of endless sacrifice. In fact, acknowledging these realities is the first step in dealing with them. We can meet the resource problems of the world—water, food, minerals, farmlands, forests, overpopulation, pollution—if we tackle them with courage and foresight.

I have just been talking about forces of potential destruction that mankind has developed, and how we might control them. It is equally important that we remember the beneficial forces that we have evolved over the ages, and how to hold fast to them. One of those constructive forces is enhancement of individual human freedoms through the strengthening of democracy, and the fight against deprivation, torture, terrorism and the persecution of people throughout the world. The struggle for human rights overrides all differences of color, nation or language.

Those who hunger for freedom, who thirst for human dignity, and who suffer for the sake of justice—they are the patriots of this cause.

I believe with all my heart that America must always stand for these basic human rights—at home and abroad. That is both our history and our destiny.

America did not invent human rights. In a very real sense, it is the other way round. Human rights invented America.

Ours was the first nation in the history of the world to be founded explicitly on such an idea. Our social and political progress has been based on one fundamental principle—the value and importance of the individual. The fundamental force that unites us is not kinship or place of origin or religious preference. The love of liberty is a common blood that flows in our American veins.

The battle for human rights—at home and abroad—is far from over. We should never be surprised nor discouraged because the impact of our efforts has had, and will always have, varied results. Rather, we should take pride that the ideals which gave birth to our nation still inspire the hopes of oppressed people around the world. We have no cause for self-righteousness or complacency. But we have every reason to persevere, both within our own country and beyond our borders.

If we are to serve as a beacon for human rights, we must continue to perfect here at home the rights and values which we espouse around the world: A decent education for our children, adequate medical care for all Americans, an end to discrimination against minorities and women, a job for all those able to work, and freedom from injustice and religious intolerance.

We live in a time of transition, an uneasy era which is likely to endure for the rest of this century. It will be a period of tensions both within nations and between nations—of competition for scarce resources, of social political and economic stresses and strains. During this period we may be tempted to abandon some of the time-honored principles and commitments which have been proven during the difficult times of past generations.

We must never yield to this temptation. Our American values are not luxuries but necessities—not the salt in our bread but the bread itself. Our common vision of a free and just society is our greatest source of cohesion at home and strength abroad—greater even than the bounty of our material blessings.

Remember these words: "We hold these truths to be self-evident, that all men are created equal; that they are endowed by their creator with certain inalienable rights; that among these are life liberty and the pursuit of happiness."

This vision still grips the imagination of the world. But we know that democracy is always an unfinished creation. Each generation must renew its foundations. Each generation must rediscover the meaning of this hallowed vision in the light of its own modern challenges. For this generation, ours, life is nuclear survival; liberty is human rights; the pursuit of happiness is a planet whose resources are devoted to the physical and spiritual nourishment of its inhabitants.

During the next few days I will work hard to make sure that the transition from myself to the next president is a good one so that the American people are served well. And I will continue as I have the last 14 months to work hard and to pray for the lives and the well-being of the American hostages held in Iran. I can't predict yet what will happen, but I hope you will join me in my constant prayer for their freedom.

As I return home to the South where I was born and raised, I am looking forward to the opportunity to reflect and further to assess—I hope with accuracy—the circumstances of our times. I intend to give our new president my support, and I intend to work as a citizen, as I have worked in this office as president, for the values this nation was founded to secure.

Again, from the bottom of my heart, I want to express to you the gratitude I feel. Thank you, fellow citizens, and farewell.

## 3. PRESIDENT RONALD REAGAN'S INAUGURAL ADDRESS, JANUARY 20, 1981

Senator Hatfield, Mr. Chief Justice, Mr. President, Vice President Bush, Vice President Mondale, Senator Baker, Speaker O'Neill, Reverend Moomaw, and my fellow citizens:

To a few of us here today this is a solemn and most momentous occasion, and yet in the history of our nation it is a commonplace occurrence. The orderly transfer of authority as called for in the Constitution routinely takes place, as it has for almost two centuries, and few of us stop to think how unique we really are. In the eyes of many in the world, this every-4-year ceremony we accept as normal is nothing less than a miracle.

Mr. President, I want our fellow citizens to know how much you did to carry on this tradition. By your gracious cooperation in the transition process, you have shown a watching world that we are a united people pledged to maintaining a political system which guarantees individual liberty to a greater degree than any other, and I thank you and your people for all your help in maintaining the continuity which is the bulwark of our Republic.

The business of our nation goes forward. These United States are confronted with an economic affliction of great proportions. We suffer from the longest and one of the worst sustained inflations in our national history. It distorts our economic decisions, penalizes thrift, and crushes the struggling young and the fixed-income elderly alike. It threatens to shatter the lives of millions of our people.

Idle industries have cast workers into unemployment, human misery, and personal indignity. Those who do work are denied a fair return for their labor by a tax system which penalizes successful achievement and keeps us from maintaining full productivity.

But great as our tax burden is, it has not kept pace with public spending. For decades we have piled deficit upon deficit, mortgaging our future and our children's future for the temporary convenience of the present. To continue this long trend is to guarantee tremendous social, cultural, political, and economic upheavals.

You and I, as individuals, can, by borrowing, live beyond our means, but for only a limited period of time. Why, then, should we think that collectively, as a nation, we're not bound by that same limitation? We must act today in order to preserve tomorrow. And let there be no misunderstanding: We are going to begin to act, beginning today.

The economic ills we suffer have come upon us over several decades. They will not go away in days, weeks, or months, but they will go away. They will go away because we as Americans have the capacity now, as we've had in the past, to do whatever needs to be done to preserve this last and greatest bastion of freedom.

In this present crisis, government is not the solution to our problem; government is the problem. From time to time we've been tempted to believe that society has become too complex to be managed by self-rule, that government by an elite group is superior to government for, by, and of the people. Well, if no one among us is capable of governing himself, then who among us has the capacity to govern someone else? All of us together, in and out of government, must bear the burden. The solutions we seek must be equitable, with no one group singled out to pay a higher price.

We hear much of special interest groups. Well, our concern must be for a special interest group that has been too long neglected. It knows no sectional boundaries or ethnic and racial divisions, and it crosses political party lines. It is made up of men and women who raise our food, patrol our streets, man our mines and factories, teach our children, keep our homes, and heal us when we're sick—professionals, industrialists, shopkeepers, clerks, cabbies, and truckdrivers. They are, in short, "We the people," this breed called Americans.

Well, this administration's objective will be a healthy, vigorous, growing economy that provides equal opportunities for all Americans with no barriers born of bigotry or discrimination. Putting America back to work means putting all Americans back to work. Ending inflation means freeing all Americans from the terror of runaway living costs. All must share in the productive work of this "new beginning," and all must share in the bounty of a revived economy. With the idealism and fair play which are the core of our system and our strength, we can have a strong and prosperous America, at peace with itself and the world.

So, as we begin, let us take inventory. We are a nation that has a government—not the other way around. And this makes us special among the nations of the Earth. Our government has no power except that granted it by the people. It is time to check and reverse the growth of government, which shows signs of having grown beyond the consent of the governed.

It is my intention to curb the size and influence of the Federal establishment and to demand recognition of the distinction between the powers granted to the Federal Government and those reserved to the States or to the people. All of us need to be reminded that the Federal Government did not create the States; the States created the Federal Government.

Now, so there will be no misunderstanding, it's not my intention to do away with government. It is rather to make it work—work with us, not over us; to stand by our side, not ride on our back. Government can and must provide opportunity, not smother it; foster productivity, not stifle it.

If we look to the answer as to why for so many years we achieved so much, prospered as no other people on Earth, it was because here in this land we unleashed the energy and individual genius of man to a greater extent than has ever been done before. Freedom and the dignity of the individual have been more available and assured here than in any other place on Earth. The price for this freedom at times has been high, but we have never been unwilling to pay that price.

It is no coincidence that our present troubles parallel and are proportionate to the intervention and intrusion in our lives that result from unnecessary and excessive growth of government. It is time for us to realize that we're too great a nation to limit ourselves to small dreams. We're not, as some would have us believe, doomed to an inevitable decline. I do not believe in a fate that will fall on us no matter what we do. I do believe in a fate that will fall on us if we do nothing. So, with all the creative energy at our command, let us begin an era of national renewal. Let us renew our determination, our courage, and our strength. And let us renew our faith and our hope.

We have every right to dream heroic dreams. Those who say that we're in a time when there are not heroes, they just don't know where to look. You can see heroes every day going in and out of factory gates. Others, a handful in number, produce enough food to feed all of us and then the world beyond. You meet heroes across a counter, and they're on both sides of that counter. There are entrepreneurs with faith in themselves and faith in an idea who create new jobs, new wealth and opportunity. They're individuals and families whose taxes support the government and whose voluntary gifts support church, charity, culture, art, and education. Their patriotism is quiet, but deep. Their values sustain our national life.

Now, I have used the words "they" and "their" in speaking of these heroes. I could say "you" and "your," because I'm addressing the heroes of whom I speak—you, the citizens of this blessed land. Your dreams, your hopes, your goals are going to be the dreams, the hopes, and the goals of this administration, so help me God.

We shall reflect the compassion that is so much a part of your makeup. How can we love our country and not love our countrymen; and loving them, reach out a hand when they fall, heal them when they're sick, and provide opportunity to make them self-sufficient so they will be equal in fact and not just in theory?

Can we solve the problems confronting us? Well, the answer is an unequivocal and emphatic "yes." To paraphrase Winston Churchill, I did not take the oath I've just taken with the intention of presiding over the dissolution of the world's strongest economy.

In the days ahead I will propose removing the roadblocks that have slowed our economy and reduced productivity. Steps will be taken aimed at restoring the balance between the various levels of government. Progress may be slow, measured in inches and feet, not miles, but we will progress. It is time to reawaken this industrial giant, to get government back within its means, and to lighten our punitive tax burden. And these will be our first priorities, and on these principles there will be no compromise.

On the eve of our struggle for independence a man who might have been one of the greatest among the Founding Fathers, Dr. Joseph Warren, president of the Massachusetts Congress, said to his fellow Americans, "Our country is in danger, but not to be despaired of.... On you depend the fortunes of America. You are

to decide the important questions upon which rests the happiness and the liberty of millions yet unborn. Act worthy of yourselves."

Well, I believe we, the Americans of today, are ready to act worthy of ourselves, ready to do what must be done to ensure happiness and liberty for ourselves, our children, and our children's children. And as we renew ourselves here in our own land, we will be seen as having greater strength throughout the world. We will again be the exemplar of freedom and a beacon of hope for those who do not now have freedom.

To those neighbors and allies who share our freedom, we will strengthen our historic ties and assure them of our support and firm commitment. We will match loyalty with loyalty. We will strive for mutually beneficial relations. We will not use our friendship to impose on their sovereignty, for our own sovereignty is not for sale.

As for the enemies of freedom, those who are potential adversaries, they will be reminded that peace is the highest aspiration of the American people. We will negotiate for it, sacrifice for it; we will not surrender for it, now or ever.

Our forbearance should never be misunderstood. Our reluctance for conflict should not be misjudged as a failure of will. When action is required to preserve our national security, we will act. We will maintain sufficient strength to prevail if need be, knowing that if we do so we have the best chance of never having to use that strength.

Above all, we must realize that no arsenal or no weapon in the arsenals of the world is so formidable as the will and moral courage of free men and women. It is a weapon our adversaries in today's world do not have. It is a weapon that we as Americans do have. Let that be understood by those who practice terrorism and prey upon their neighbors.

I'm told that tens of thousands of prayer meetings are being held on this day, and for that I'm deeply grateful. We are a nation under God, and I believe God intended for us to be free. It would be fitting and good, I think, if on each Inaugural Day in future years it should be declared a day of prayer.

This is the first time in our history that this ceremony has been held, as you've been told, on this West Front of the Capitol. Standing here, one faces a magnificent vista, opening up on this city's special beauty and history. At the end of this open mall are those shrines to the giants on whose shoulders we stand.

Directly in front of me, the monument to a monumental man, George Washington, father of our country. A man of humility who came to greatness reluctantly. He led America out of revolutionary victory into infant nationhood. Off to one side, the stately memorial to Thomas Jefferson. The Declaration of Independence flames with his eloquence. And then, beyond the Reflecting Pool, the dignified columns of the Lincoln Memorial. Whoever would understand in his heart the meaning of America will find it in the life of Abraham Lincoln.

Beyond those monuments to heroism is the Potomac River, and on the far shore the sloping hills of Arlington National Cemetery, with its row upon row of simple white markers bearing crosses or Stars of David. They add up to only a tiny fraction of the price that has been paid for our freedom.

Each one of those markers is a monument to the kind of hero I spoke of earlier. Their lives ended in places called Belleau Wood, The Argonne, Omaha Beach, Salerno, and halfway around the world on Guadalcanal, Tarawa, Pork Chop Hill, the Chosin Reservoir, and in a hundred rice paddies and jungles of a place called Vietnam.

Under one such marker lies a young man, Martin Treptow, who left his job in a small town barbershop in 1917 to go to France with the famed Rainbow Division. There, on the western front, he was killed trying to carry a message between battalions under heavy artillery fire.

We're told that on his body was found a diary. On the flyleaf under the heading, "My Pledge," he had written these words: "America must win this war. Therefore I will work, I will save, I will sacrifice, I will endure, I will fight cheerfully and do my utmost, as if the issue of the whole struggle depended on me alone."

The crisis we are facing today does not require of us the kind of sacrifice that Martin Treptow and so many thousands of others were called upon to make. It does require, however, our best effort and our willingness to believe in ourselves and to believe in our capacity to perform great deeds, to believe that together with God's help we can and will resolve the problems which now confront us.

And after all, why shouldn't we believe that? We are Americans.

God bless you, and thank you.

## 4. United Nations Security Council Resolution on the U.S. Invasion of Grenada, October 28, 1983

THE SECURITY COUNCIL,

Having heard the statements made in connection with the situation in Grenada,

Recalling the Declaration on Principles of International Law concerning Friendly Relations and Cooperation among states,

Recalling also the principles concerning the inadmissibility of intervention and interference in the internal affairs of States,

Reaffirming the sovereign and inalienable right of Grenada freely to determine its own political, economic and social system and to develop its international relations without outside intervention, interference, subversion, coercion or threat in any form whatsoever,

Deeply deploring the events in Grenada leading to the killing of the Prime Minister, Mr. Maurice Bishop, and other prominent Grenadians,

Bearing in mind that, in accordance with Article 2, (4), of the Charter of the United Nations, all member states are obliged to refrain in their international relations from the threat or use of force against the territorial integrity of or political independence of any state or to act in any other manner inconsistent with the principles of the Charter of the United Nations,

Gravely concerned at the military intervention taking place and determined to insure a speedy return to normalcy in Grenada,

Conscious of the need for states to show consistent respect for the principles of the Charter of the United Nations,

1. Deeply deplores the armed intervention in Grenada, which constitutes a flagrant violation of international law and of the independence, sovereignty and territorial integrity of that state;

2. Deplores the deaths of innocent civilians resulting from the armed intervention;

3. Calls on all states to show strictest respect for the sovereignty, independence and territorial integrity of Grenada;

4. Calls for an immediate cessation of the armed intervention and the immediate withdrawal of the foreign troops from Grenada;

5. Requests the Secretary General to follow closely the development of the situation in Grenada and to

report to the Council within 48 hours on the implementation of this resolution.

## 5. President Ronald Reagan's Address to the Nation on the Explosion of the Space Shuttle *Challenger*, January 28, 1986

Ladies and gentlemen, I'd planned to speak to you tonight to report on the state of the Union, but the events of earlier today have led me to change those plans. Today is a day for mourning and remembering. Nancy and I are pained to the core by the tragedy of the shuttle *Challenger*. We know we share this pain with all of the people of our country. This is truly a national loss.

Nineteen years ago, almost to the day, we lost three astronauts in a terrible accident on the ground. But we've never lost an astronaut in flight; we've never had a tragedy like this. And perhaps we've forgotten the courage it took for the crew of the shuttle. But they, the *Challenger* Seven, were aware of the dangers, but overcame them and did their jobs brilliantly. We mourn seven heroes: Michael Smith, Dick Scobee, Judith Resnik, Ronald McNair, Ellison Onizuka, Gregory Jarvis, and Christa McAuliffe. We mourn their loss as a nation together.

For the families of the seven, we cannot bear, as you do, the full impact of this tragedy. But we feel the loss, and we're thinking about you so very much. Your loved ones were daring and brave, and they had that special grace, that special spirit that says, "Give me a challenge, and I'll meet it with joy." They had a hunger to explore the universe and discover its truths. They wished to serve, and they did. They served all of us. We've grown used to wonders in this century. It's hard to dazzle us. But for 25 years the United States space program has been doing just that. We've grown used to the idea of space, and perhaps we forget that we've only just begun. We're still pioneers. They, the members of the *Challenger* crew, were pioneers.

And I want to say something to the schoolchildren of America who were watching the live coverage of the shuttle's takeoff. I know it is hard to understand, but sometimes painful things like this happen. It's all part of the process of exploration and discovery. It's all part of taking a chance and expanding man's horizons. The future doesn't belong to the fainthearted; it belongs to the brave. The *Challenger* crew was pulling us into the future, and we'll continue to follow them.

I've always had great faith in and respect for our space program, and what happened today does nothing to diminish it. We don't hide our space program. We don't keep secrets and cover things up. We do it all up front and in public. That's the way freedom is, and we wouldn't change it for a minute. We'll continue our quest in space. There will be more shuttle flights and more shuttle crews and, yes, more volunteers, more civilians, more teachers in space. Nothing ends here; our hopes and our journeys continue. I want to add that I wish I could talk to every man and woman who works for NASA or who worked on this mission and tell them: "Your dedication and professionalism have moved and impressed us for decades. And we know of your anguish. We share it."

There's a coincidence today. On this day 390 years ago, the great explorer Sir Francis Drake died aboard ship off the coast of Panama. In his lifetime the great frontiers were the oceans, and an historian later said, "He lived by the sea, died on it, and was buried in it." Well, today we can say of the *Challenger* crew: Their dedication was, like Drake's, complete.

The crew of the space shuttle *Challenger* honored us by the manner in which they lived their lives. We will never forget them, nor the last time we saw them, this morning, as they prepared for their journey and waved goodbye and "slipped the surly bonds of earth" to "touch the face of God."

## 6. President Ronald Reagan's Address to the Nation on the United States Air Strike Against Libya, April 14, 1986

My fellow Americans:

At 7 o'clock this evening eastern time air and naval forces of the United States launched a series of strikes against the headquarters, terrorist facilities, and military assets that support Mu'ammar Qadhafi's subversive activities. The attacks were concentrated and carefully targeted to minimize casualties among the Libyan people with whom we have no quarrel. From initial reports, our forces have succeeded in their mission.

Several weeks ago in New Orleans, I warned Colonel Qadhafi we would hold his regime accountable for any new terrorist attacks launched against American citizens. More recently I made it clear we would respond as soon as we determined conclusively who was responsible for such attacks. On April 5th in West Berlin a terrorist bomb exploded in a nightclub frequented by American servicemen. Sergeant Kenneth Ford and a young Turkish woman were killed and 230 others were wounded, among them some 50 American military personnel. This monstrous brutality is but the latest act in Colonel Qadhafi's reign of terror. The evidence is now conclusive that the terrorist bombing of La Belle discotheque was planned and executed under the direct orders of the Libyan regime. On March 25th, more than a week before the attack, orders were sent from Tripoli to the Libyan People's Bureau in East Berlin to conduct a terrorist attack against Americans to cause maximum and indiscriminate casualties. Libya's agents then planted the bomb. On April 4th the People's Bureau alerted Tripoli that the attack would be carried out the following morning. The next day they reported back to Tripoli on the great success of their mission.

Our evidence is direct; it is precise; it is irrefutable. We have solid evidence about other attacks Qadhafi has planned against the United States installations and diplomats and even American tourists. Thanks to close cooperation with our friends, some of these have been prevented. With the help of French authorities, we recently aborted one such attack: a planned massacre, using grenades and small arms, of civilians waiting in line for visas at an American Embassy.

Colonel Qadhafi is not only an enemy of the United States. His record of subversion and aggression against the neighboring States in Africa is well documented and well known. He has ordered the murder of fellow Libyans in countless countries. He has sanctioned acts of terror in Africa, Europe, and the Middle East, as well as the Western Hemisphere. Today we have done what we had to do. If necessary, we shall do it again. It gives me no pleasure to say that, and I wish it were otherwise. Before Qadhafi seized power in 1969, the people of Libya had been friends of the United States. And I'm sure that today most Libyans are ashamed and disgusted that this man has made their country a synonym for barbarism around the world. The Libyan people are a decent people caught in the grip of a tyrant.

To our friends and allies in Europe who cooperated in today's mission, I would only say you have the permanent gratitude of the American people. Europeans who remember history understand better than most that there is no security, no safety, in the appeasement of evil. It must be the core of Western policy that there be no sanctuary for terror. And to sustain such a policy, free men and free nations must unite and work together. Sometimes it is said that by imposing sanctions against Colonel Qadhafi or by striking at his terrorist installations we only magnify the man's importance, that the proper way to deal with him is to ignore him. I do not agree.

Long before I came into this office, Colonel Qadhafi had engaged in acts of international terror, acts that put him outside the company of civilized men. For years, however, he suffered no economic or political or military sanction; and the atrocities mounted in number, as did the innocent dead and wounded. And for us to ignore by inaction the slaughter of American civilians and American soldiers, whether in nightclubs or airline terminals, is simply not in the American tradition. When our citizens are abused or attacked anywhere in the world on the direct orders of a hostile regime, we will respond so long as I'm in this Oval Office. Self-defense is not only our right, it is our duty. It is the purpose behind the mission undertaken tonight, a mission fully consistent with Article 51 of the United Nations Charter.

We believe that this preemptive action against his terrorist installations will not only diminish Colonel Qadhafi's capacity to export terror, it will provide him with incentives and reasons to alter his criminal behavior. I have no illusion that tonight's action will ring down the curtain on Qadhafi's reign of terror. But this mission, violent though it was, can bring closer a safer and more secure world for decent men and women. We will persevere. This afternoon we consulted with the leaders of Congress regarding what we were about to do and why. Tonight I salute the skill and professionalism of the men and women of our Armed Forces who carried out this mission. It's an honor to be your Commander in Chief.

We Americans are slow to anger. We always seek peaceful avenues before resorting to the use of force—and we did. We tried quiet diplomacy, public condemnation, economic sanctions, and demonstrations of military force. None succeeded. Despite our repeated warnings, Qadhafi continued his reckless policy of intimidation, his relentless pursuit of terror. He counted on America to be passive. He counted wrong. I warned that there should be no place on Earth where terrorists can rest and train and practice their deadly skills. I meant it. I said that we would act with others, if possible, and alone if necessary to ensure that terrorists have no sanctuary anywhere. Tonight, we have.

Thank you, and God bless you.

# 7. Excerpt from the Report of the Presidential Commission on the Space Shuttle *Challenger* Accident, June 6, 1986

## Chapter 4:
## *The Cause of the Accident*

The consensus of the Commission and participating investigative agencies is that the loss of the Space Shuttle *Challenger* was caused by a failure in the joint between the two lower segments of the right Solid Rocket Motor. The specific failure was the destruction of the seals that are intended to prevent hot gases from leaking through the joint during the propellant burn of the rocket motor. The evidence assembled by the Commission indicates that no other element of the Space Shuttle system contributed to this failure.

In arriving at this conclusion, the Commission reviewed in detail all available data, reports and records; directed and supervised numerous tests, analyses, and experiments by NASA, civilian contractors and various government agencies; and then developed specific scenarios and the range of most probable causative factors.

### *Findings*

1. A combustion gas leak through the right Solid Rocket Motor aft field joint initiated at or shortly after ignition eventually weakened and/or penetrated the External Tank initiating vehicle structural breakup and loss of the Space Shuttle *Challenger* during STS Mission 51-L.

2. The evidence shows that no other STS 51-L Shuttle element or the payload contributed to the causes of the right Solid Rocket Motor aft field joint combustion gas leak. Sabotage was not a factor.

3. Evidence examined in the review of Space Shuttle material, manufacturing, assembly, quality control, and processing on non-conformance reports found no flight hardware shipped to the launch site that fell outside the limits of Shuttle design specifications.

4. Launch site activities, including assembly and preparation, from receipt of the flight hardware to launch were generally in accord with established procedures and were not considered a factor in the accident.

5. Launch site records show that the right Solid Rocket Motor segments were assembled using approved procedures. However, significant out-of-round conditions existed between the two segments joined at the right Solid Rocket Motor aft field joint (the joint that failed).

a. While the assembly conditions had the potential of generating debris or damage that could cause O-ring seal failure, these were not considered factors in this accident.

b. The diameters of the two Solid Rocket Motor segments had grown as a result of prior use.

c. The growth resulted in a condition at time of launch wherein the maximum gap between the tang and clevis in the region of the joint's O-rings was no more than .008 inches and the average gap would have been .004 inches.

d. With a tang-to-clevis gap of .004 inches, the O-ring in the joint would be compressed to the extent that it pressed against all three walls of the O-ring retaining channel.

e. The lack of roundness of the segments was such that the smallest tang-to-clevis clearance occurred at the initiation of the assembly operation at positions of 120 degrees and 300 degrees around the circumference of the aft field joint. It is uncertain if this tight condition and the resultant greater compression of the O-rings at these points persisted to the time of launch.

6. The ambient temperature at time of launch was 36 degrees Fahrenheit, or 15 degrees lower than the next coldest previous launch.

a. The temperature at the 300 degree position on the right aft field joint circumference was estimated to be 28 degrees plus or minus 5 degrees Fahrenheit. This was the coldest point on the joint.

b. Temperature on the opposite side of the right Solid Rocket Booster facing the sun was estimated to be about 50 degrees Fahrenheit.

7. Other joints on the left and right Solid Rocket Boosters experienced similar combinations of tang-to-clevis gap clearance and temperature. It is not known whether these joints experienced distress during the flight of 51-L.

8. Experimental evidence indicates that due to several effects associated with the Solid Rocket Booster's ignition and combustion pressures and associated vehicle motions, the gap between the tang and the clevis will open as much as .017 and .029 inches at the secondary and primary O-rings, respectively.

a. This opening begins upon ignition, reaches its maximum rate of opening at about 200-300 milliseconds, and is essentially complete at 600 milliseconds when the Solid Rocket Booster reaches its operating pressure.

b. The External Tank and right Solid Rocket Booster are connected by several struts, including one at 310 degrees near the aft field joint that failed. This strut's effect on the joint dynamics is to enhance the opening of the gap between the tang and clevis by about 10-20 percent in the region of 300-320 degrees.

9. O-ring resiliency is directly related to its temperature.

a. A warm O-ring that has been compressed will return to its original shape much quicker than will a cold O-ring when compression is relieved. Thus, a warm O-ring will follow the opening of the tang-to-clevis gap. A cold O-ring may not.

b. A compressed O-ring at 75 degrees Fahrenheit is five times more responsive in returning to its uncompressed shape than a cold O-ring at 30 degrees Fahrenheit.

c. As a result it is probable that the O-rings in the right solid booster aft field joint were not following the opening of the gap between the tang and cleavis at time of ignition.

10. Experiments indicate that the primary mechanism that actuates O-ring sealing is the application of gas pressure to the upstream (high-pressure) side of the O-ring as it sits in its groove or channel.

a. For this pressure actuation to work most effectively, a space between the O-ring and its upstream channel wall should exist during pressurization.

b. A tang-to-clevis gap of .004 inches, as probably existed in the failed joint, would have initially compressed the O-ring to the degree that no clearance existed between the O-ring and its upstream channel wall and the other two surfaces of the channel.

c. At the cold launch temperature experienced, the O-ring would be very slow in returning to its normal rounded shape. It would not follow the opening of the tang-to-clevis gap. It would remain in its compressed position in the O-ring channel and not provide a space between itself and the upstream channel wall. Thus, it is probable the O-ring would not be pressure actuated to seal the gap in time to preclude joint failure due to blow-by and erosion from hot combustion gases.

11. The sealing characteristics of the Solid Rocket Booster O-rings are enhanced by timely application of motor pressure.

a. Ideally, motor pressure should be applied to actuate the O-ring and seal the joint prior to significant opening of the tang-to-clevis gap (100 to 200 milliseconds after motor ignition).

b. Experimental evidence indicates that temperature, humidity and other variables in the putty compound used to seal the joint can delay pressure application to the joint by 500 milliseconds or more.

c. This delay in pressure could be a factor in initial joint failure.

12. Of 21 launches with ambient temperatures of 61 degrees Fahrenheit or greater, only four showed signs of O-ring thermal distress; i.e., erosion or blow-by and soot. Each of the launches below 61 degrees Fahrenheit resulted in one or more O-rings showing signs of thermal distress.

a. Of these improper joint sealing actions, one-half occurred in the aft field joints, 20 percent in the center field joints, and 30 percent in the upper field joints. The division between left and right Solid Rocket Boosters was roughly equal.

b. Each instance of thermal O-ring distress was accompanied by a leak path in the insulating putty. The leak path connects the rocket's combustion chamber with the O-ring region of the tang and clevis. Joints that actuated without incident may also have had these leak paths.

13. There is a possibility that there was water in the clevis of the STS 51-L joints since water was found in the STS-9 joints during a destack operation after exposure to less rainfall than STS 51-L. At time of launch, it was cold enough that water present in the joint would freeze. Tests show that ice in the joint can inhibit proper secondary seal performance.

14. A series of puffs of smoke were observed emanating from the 51-L aft field joint area of the right Solid Rocket Booster between 0.678 and 2.500 seconds after ignition of the Shuttle Solid Rocket Motors.

a. The puffs appeared at a frequency of about three puffs per second. This roughly matches the natural structural frequency of the solids at lift off and is reflected in slight cyclic changes of the tang-to-clevis gap opening.

b. The puffs were seen to be moving upward along the surface of the booster above the aft field joint.

c. The smoke was estimated to originate at a circumferential position of between 270 degrees and 315 degrees on the booster aft field joint, emerging from the top of the joint.

15. This smoke from the aft field joint at Shuttle lift off was the first sign of the failure of the Solid Rocket Booster O-ring seals on STS 51-L.

16. The leak was again clearly evident as a flame at approximately 58 seconds into the flight. It is possible that the leak was continuous but unobservable or non-existent in portions of the intervening period. It is possible in either case that thrust vectoring and normal vehicle response to wind shear as well as planned maneuvers reinitiated or magnified the leakage from a degraded seal in the period preceding the observed flames. The estimated position of the flame, centered at a point 307 degrees around the circumference of the aft field joint, was confirmed by the recovery of two fragments of the right Solid Rocket Booster.

a. A small leak could have been present that may have grown to breach the joint in flame at a time on the order of 58 to 60 seconds after lift off.

b. Alternatively, the O-ring gap could have been resealed by deposition of a fragile buildup of aluminum oxide and other combustion debris. This resealed section of the joint could have been disturbed by thrust vectoring, Space Shuttle motion and flight loads inducted by changing winds aloft.

c. The winds aloft caused control actions in the time interval of 32 seconds to 62 seconds into the flight that were typical of the largest values experienced on previous missions.

## Conclusion

In view of the findings, the Commission concluded that the cause of the *Challenger* accident was the failure of the pressure seal in the aft field joint of the right Solid Rocket Booster. The failure was due to a faulty design unacceptably sensitive to a number of factors. These factors were the effects of temperature, physical dimensions, the character of materials, the effects of reusability, processing and the reaction of the joint to dynamic loading.

## 8. Excerpts from the Special Review Board (Tower Commission) Report on the Iran-contra Affair, February 26, 1987
### Part IV: What Was Wrong

The arms transfers to Iran and the activities of the N.S.C. staff in support of the contras are case studies in the perils of policy pursued outside the constraints of orderly process.

The Iran initiative ran directly counter to the Administration's own policies on terrorism, the Iran-Iraq war, and military support to Iran. This inconsistency was never resolved, nor were the consequences of this inconsistency fully considered and provided for. The result taken as a whole was a U.S. policy that worked against itself.

The Board believes that failure to deal adequately with these contradictions resulted in large part from the flaws in the manner in which decisions were made. Established procedures for making national security decisions were ignored. Reviews of the initiative by all the N.S.C. principals were too infrequent. The initiatives were not adequately vetted below the Cabinet level. Intelligence resources were underutilized. Applicable legal constraints were not adequately addressed. The whole matter was handled too informally, without adequate written records of what had been considered, discussed, and decided.

This pattern persisted in the implementation of the Iran initiative. The N.S.C. staff assumed direct operational control. The initiative fell within the traditional jurisdictions of the Departments of State, Defense, and C.I.A. Yet these agencies were largely ignored. Great reliance was placed on a network of private operators and intermediaries. How the initiative was to be carried out never received adequate attention from the N.S.C. principals or a tough working-level review. No periodic evaluation of the progress of the initiative was ever conducted. The result was an unprofessional and, in substantial part, unsatisfactory operation.

In all of this process, Congress was never notified.

\* \* \*

### A Flawed Process
#### 1. Contradictory Policies Were Pursued.

The arms sales to Iran and the N.S.C. support for the contras demonstrate the risks involved when highly controversial initiatives are pursued covertly.

#### Arms Transfer to Iran

The initiative to Iran was a covert operation directly at odds with important and well-publicized policies of the Executive Branch. But the initiative itself embodied a fundamental contradiction. Two objectives were apparent from the outset: a strategic opening to Iran, and release of the U.S. citizens held hostage in Lebanon. The sale of arms to Iran appeared to provide a means to achieve both these objectives. It also played into the hands of those who had other interests—some of them personal financial gain—in engaging the United States in an arms deal with Iran.

In fact, the sale of arms was not equally appropriate for achieving both these objectives. Arms were what Iran wanted. If all the United States sought was to free the hostages, then an arms-for-hostages deal could achieve the immediate objectives of both sides. But if the U.S. objective was a broader strategic relationship, then the sale of arms should have been contingent upon first putting into place the elements of that relationship. An arms-for-hostages deal in this context could become counter-productive to achieving this broader strategic objectives. In addition, release of the hostages would require exerting influence with Hezbollah, which could involve the most radical elements of the Iranian regime. The kind of strategic opening sought by the United States, however, involved what were regarded as more moderate elements.

* * *

While the United States was seeking the release of the hostages in this way, it was vigorously pursuing policies that were dramatically opposed to such efforts. The Reagan Administration in particular had come into office declaring a firm stand against terrorism, which it continued to maintain. In December of 1985, the Administration completed a major study under the chairmanship of the Vice President. It resulted in a vigorous reaffirmation of U.S. opposition to terrorism in all its forms and a vow of total war on terrorism whatever its source. The Administration continued to pressure U.S. allies not to sell arms to Iran and not to make concessions to terrorists.

No serious effort was made to reconcile the inconsistency between these policies and the Iran initiative. No effort was made systematically to address the consequences of this inconsistency—the effect on U.S. policy when, as it inevitably would, the Iran initiative became known.

The Board believes that a strategic opening to Iran may have been in the national interest but that the United States never should have been a party to the arms transfers. As arms-for-hostages trades, they could not help but create an incentive for further hostage-taking. As a violation of the U.S. arms embargo, they could only remove inhibitions on other nations from selling arms to Iran. This threatened to upset the military balance between Iran and Iraq, with consequent jeopardy to the Gulf States and the interests of the West in that region. The arms-for-hostages trades rewarded a regime that clearly supported terrorism and hostage-taking. They increased the risks that the United States would be perceived, especially in the Arab world, as a creature of Israel. They suggested to other U.S. allies and friends in the region that the United States had shifted its policy in favor of Iran. They raised questions as to whether U.S. policy statements could be relied upon.

N.S.C. Staff Support for the Contras

The activities of the N.S.C. staff in support of the contras sought to achieve an important objective of the Administration's foreign policy. The President had publicly and emphatically declared his support for the Nicaragua resistance. That brought his policy in direct conflict with that of the Congress, at least during the period that direct or indirect support of military operations in Nicaragua was barred.

Although the evidence before the Board is limited, no serious effort appears to have been made to come to grips with the risks to the President of direct N.S.C. support for the Contras in the face of these Congressional restrictions. . . .

## 2. The Decision-Making Process Was Flawed.

Because the arms sales to Iran and the N.S.C. support for the contras occurred in settings of such controversy, one would expect that the decisions to undertake these activities would have been made only after intense and thorough consideration. In fact, a far different picture emerges.

Arms Transfers to Iran

The Iran initiative was handled almost casually and through informal channels, always apparently with an expectation that the process would end with the next arms-for-hostages exchange. It was subjected neither to the general procedures for interagency consideration and review of policy issues nor the more restrictive procedures set out in N.S.D.D. 159 for handling covert operations. This had a number of consequences:

(i) The Opportunity for a Full Hearing Before the President Was Inadequate.

(ii) The Initiative Was Never Subjected to a Rigorous Review Below the Cabinet Level.

(iii) The Process Was Too Informal.

The whole decision process was too informal. Even when meetings among N.S.C. principals did occur, often there was no prior notice of the agenda. No formal written minutes seem to have been kept. Decisions subsequently taken by the President were not formally recorded. An exception was the January 17 Finding, but even this was apparently not circulated or shown to key U.S. officials.

\* \* \*

### 3. Implementation Was Unprofessional.

The manner in which the Iran initiative was implemented and Lt Col North undertook to support the contras are very similar. This is in large part because the same cast of characters was involved. In both cases the operations were unprofessional, although the Board has much less evidence with respect to Lt Col North's contra activities.

Arms Transfers to Iran

With the signing of the Jan. 17 Finding, the Iran initiative became a U.S. operation run by the N.S.C. staff. Lt Col North made most of the significant operational decisions. He conducted the operation through Mr. Secord and his associates, a network of private individuals already involved in the contra resupply operation. To this was added a handful of selected individuals from the C.I.A.

But the C.I.A. support was limited. Two C.I.A. officials, though often at meetings, had a relatively limited role. One served as the point man for Lt Col North in providing logistics and financial arrangements. The other (Mr. Allen) served as a contact between Lt Col North and the intelligence community. By contrast, George Cave actually played a significant and expanding role. However, Clair George, Deputy Director for Operations, at C.I.A., told the Board: "George was paid by me and on the paper was working for me. But I think in the heat of the battle, . . . George was working for Oliver North."

Because so few people from the departments and agencies were told of the initiative, Lt Col North cut himself off from resources and expertise from within the government. He relied instead on a number of private intermediaries, businessmen and other financial brokers, private operators, and Iranians hostile to the United States. Some of these were individuals with questionable credentials and potentially large personal financial interests in the transactions. This made the transactions unnecessarily complicated and invited kickbacks and payoffs. This arrangement also dramatically increased the risks that the initiative would leak. Yet no provision was made for such an eventuality. Further, the use of Mr. Secord's private network in the Iran initiative linked those operators with the resupply of the contras, threatening exposure of both operations if either became public.

The result was a very unprofessional operation.

\* \* \*

The implementation of the initiative was never subjected to a rigorous review. Lt Col North appears to have kept VADM Poindexter fully informed of his activities. In addition, VADM Poindexter, Lt Col North, and the C.I.A. officials involved apparently apprised Director Casey of many of the operational details. But Lt Col North and his operation functioned largely outside the orbit of the U.S. Government. Their activities were not subject to critical reviews of any kind.

\* \* \*

N.S.C. Staff Support for the Contras

As already noted, the N.S.C. activities in support of the Contras and its role in the Iran initiative were of a piece. In the former, there was an added element of Lt Col North's intervention in the customs investigation of the crash of the S.A.T. aircraft. Here too, selected C.I.A. officials reported directly to Lt Col North. The limited evidence before the Board suggested that the activities in support of the Contras involved unprofessionalism much like that in the Iran operation.

### 4. Congress Was Never Notified.

Congress was not apprised either of the Iran initiative or of the N.S.C. staff's activities in support of the Contras.

\* \* \*

The Board was unable to reach a conclusive judgment about whether the 1985 shipments of arms to Iran were approved in advance by the President. On balance the Board believes that it is plausible to conclude that he did approve them in advance.

\* \* \*

### *Failure of Responsibility*

The N.S.C. system will not work unless the President makes it work. After all, this system was created to serve the President of the United States in ways of his choosing. By his actions, by his leadership, the President therefore determines the quality of its performance.

By his own account, as evidenced in his diary notes, and as conveyed to the Board by his principal advisors, President Reagan was deeply committed to securing the release of the hostages. It was this intense compassion for the hostages that appeared to motivate his steadfast support of the Iran initiative, even in the face of opposition from his Secretaries of State and Defense.

In his obvious commitment, the President appears to have proceeded with a concept of the initiative that was not accurately reflected in the reality of the operation. The President did not seem to be aware of the way in which the operation was implemented and the full consequences of U.S. participation.

The President's expressed concern for the safety of both the hostages and the Iranians who could have been at risk may have been conveyed in a manner so as to inhibit the full functioning of the system.

The President's management style is to put the principal responsibility for policy review and implementation on the shoulders of his advisors. Nevertheless, with such a complex, high-risk operation and so much at stake, the President should have insured that the N.S.C. system did not fail him. He did not force his policy to undergo the most critical review of which the N.S.C. participants and the process were capable. At no time did he insist upon accountability and performance review. Had the President chosen to drive the N.S.C. system, the outcome could well have been different. As it was, the most powerful features of the N.S.C. system—providing comprehensive analysis, alternatives and follow-up—were not utilized.

The Board found a strong consensus among N.S.C. participants that the President's priority in the Iran initiative was the release of U.S. hostages. But setting priorities is not enough when it comes to sensitive and risky initiatives that directly affect U.S. national security. He must ensure that the content and tactics of an initiative match his priorities and objectives. He must insist upon accountability. For it is the President who must take responsibility for the N.S.C. system and deal with the consequences.

Beyond the President, the other N.S.C. principals and the national security adviser must share in the responsibility for the N.S.C. system.

President Reagan's personal management style places an especially heavy responsibility on his key advisors. Knowing his style, they should have been particularly mindful of the need for special attention to the manner in which this arms-sale initiative developed and proceeded. On this score, neither the national security adviser nor the other N.S.C. principals deserve high marks.

It is their obligation as members and advisors to the council to ensure that the President is adequately served. The principal subordinates to the President must not be deterred from urging the President not to proceed on a highly questionable course of action even in the face of his strong conviction to the contrary.

In the case of the Iran initiative, the N.S.C. process did not fail, it simply was largely ignored. The national security adviser and the N.S.C. principals all had a duty to raise the issue and insist that orderly process be imposed. None of them did so.

All had the opportunity. While the national security adviser had the responsibility to see that an orderly process was observed, his failure to do so does not excuse the other N.S.C. principals. It does not appear that any of the N.S.C. principals called for more frequent consideration of the Iran initiative by the N.S.C. principals in the presence of the President. None of the principals called for a serious vetting of the initiative by even a restricted group of disinterested individuals. The intelligence questions do not appear to have been raised, and legal considerations, while raised, were not pressed. No one seemed to have complained about the informality of the process. No one called for a thorough re-examination once the initiative did not meet expectations or the manner of execution changed. While one or another of the N.S.C. principals suspected that something was amiss, none vigorously pursued the issue.

Mr. Regan also shares in this responsibility. More than almost any chief of staff of recent memory, he asserted personal control over the White House staff and sought to extend this control to the national security adviser. He was personally active in national security affairs and attended almost all the relevant meetings regarding the Iran initiative. He, as much as anyone, should have insisted that an orderly process be observed. In addition, he especially should have ensured that plans were made for handling any public disclosure of the initiative. He must bear primary responsibility for the chaos that descended upon the White House when such disclosure did occur.

Mr. McFarlane appeared caught between a President who supported the initiative and the Cabinet officers who strongly opposed it. While he made efforts to keep these Cabinet officers informed, the board heard complaints from some that he was not always successful. VADM Poindexter on several occasions apparently sought to exclude N.S.C. principals other than the President from knowledge of the initiative. Indeed, on one or more occasions Secretary Shultz may have been actively misled by VADM Poindexter.

VADM Poindexter also failed grievously on the matter of contra diversion. Evidence indicates that VADM Poindexter knew that a diversion occurred, yet he did not take the steps that were required given the gravity of that prospect. He apparently failed to appreciate or ignored the serious legal and political risks presented. His clear obligation was either to investigate the matter or take it to the President—or both. He did neither. Director Casey shared a similar responsibility. Evidence suggests that he received information about the possible diversion of funds to the contras almost a month before the story broke. He, too, did not move promptly to raise the matter with the President. Yet his responsibility to do so was clear.

The N.S.C. principals other than the President may be somewhat excused by the insufficient attention on the part of the national security adviser to the need to keep all the principals fully informed. Given the importance of the issue and the sharp policy divergences involved, however, Secretary Shultz and Secretary Weinberger in particular distanced themselves from the march of events. Secretary Shultz specifically requested to be informed only as necessary to perform his job. Secretary Weinberger had access through intelligence to details about the operation. Their obligation was to give the President their full support and continued advice with respect to the program or, if they could not in conscience do that, to so inform the President. Instead, they simply distanced themselves from the program. They protected the record as to their own positions on this issue. They were not energetic in attempting to protect the President from the consequences of his personal commitment to freeing the hostages.

Director Casey appears to have been informed in considerable detail about the specifics of the Iranian operation. He appears to have acquiesced in and to have encouraged North's exercise of direct operational control over the operation. Because of the N.S.C. staff's proximity to and close identification with the President, this increased the risks to the President if the initiative became public or the operation failed.

There is no evidence, however, that Director Casey explained this risk to the President or made clear to the President that Lt Col North, rather than the C.I.A., was running the operation. The President does not recall ever being informed of this fact. Indeed, Director Casey should have gone further and pressed for operational responsibility to be transferred to the C.I.A.

Director Casey should have taken the lead in vetting the assumptions presented by the Israelis on which the program was based and in pressing for an early examination of the reliance upon Mr. Ghorbanifar and the second channel as intermediaries. He should also have assumed responsibility for checking out the other intermediaries involved in the operation. Finally, because Congressional restrictions on covert actions are both largely directed at and familiar to the C.I.A., Director Casey should have taken the lead in keeping the question of Congressional notification active.

Finally, Director Casey, and, to a lesser extent, Secretary Weinberger should have taken it upon themselves to assess the effect of the transfer of arms and intelligence to Iran on the Iran-Iraq military balance, and to transmit that information to the President.

### The Role of the Israelis

Conversations with emissaries from the Government of Israel took place prior to the commencement of the initiative. It remains unclear whether the initial proposal to open the Ghorbanifar channel was an Israeli initiative, was brought on by the avarice of arms dealers, or came as a result of an American request for assistance. There is no doubt, however, that it was Israel that pressed Mr. Ghorbanifar on the United States. U.S. officials accepted Israeli assurances that they had had for some time an extensive dialogue that involved high-level Iranians, as well as their assurances of Mr. Ghorbanifar's bona fides. Thereafter, at critical points in the initiative, when doubts were expressed by critical U.S. participants, an Israeli emissary would arrive with encouragement, often a specific proposal, and pressure to stay with the Ghorbanifar channel.

From the record available to the board, it is not possible to determine the role of key U.S. participants in prompting these Israeli interventions. There were active and ongoing consultations between Lt Col North and officials of the Israeli Government, specifically David Kimche and Amiram Nir. In addition, Mr. Schwimmer, Mr. Nimrodi, and Mr. Ledeen, also in frequent contact with Lt Col North, had close ties with the Government of Israel. It may be that the Israeli interventions were actively solicited by particular U.S. officials. Without the benefit of the views of the Israeli officials involved, it is hard to know the facts.

It is clear, however, that Israel had its own interests, some in direct conflict with those of the United States, in having the United States pursue the initiative. For this reason, it had an incentive to keep the initiative alive. It sought to do this by interventions with the N.S.C. staff, the national security adviser and the President. Although it may have received suggestions from Lt Col North, Mr. Ledeen and others, it responded affirmatively to these suggestions by reason of its own interests.

Even if the Government of Israel actively worked to begin the initiative and to keep it going, the U.S. Government is responsible for its own decisions. Key participants in U.S. deliberations made the point that Israel's objectives and interests in this initiative were different from, and in some respects in conflict with, those of the United States. Although Israel dealt with those portions of the U.S. Government that it deemed were sympathetic to the initiative, there is nothing improper per se about this fact. U.S. decision-makers made their own decisions and must bear responsibility for the consequences.

## Aftermath—The Efforts to Tell the Story

From the first hint in late October 1986 that the McFarlane trip would soon become public, information on the Iran initiative and contra activity cascaded into the press. The veiled hints of secret activities, random and indiscriminate disclosures of information from a variety of sources, both knowledgeable and otherwise, and conflicting statements by high-level officials presented a confusing picture to the American public. The board recognized that conflicts among contemporaneous documents and statements raised concern about the management of the public presentation of facts on the Iran initiative. Though the board reviewed some evidence on events after the exposure, our ability to comment on these events remains limited.

The board found evidence that immediately following the public disclosure, the President wanted to avoid providing too much specificity or detail out of concern for the hostages still held in Lebanon and those Iranians who had supported the initiative. In doing so, he did not, we believe, intend to mislead the American public or cover up unlawful conduct. By at least Nov.

20, the President took steps to insure that all the facts would come out. From the President's request to Mr. Meese to look into the history of the initiative, to his appointment of this board, to his request for an independent counsel, to his willingness to discuss this matter fully and to review his personal notes with us, the board is convinced that the President does indeed want the full story to be told.

Those who prepared the President's supporting documentation did not appear, at least initially, to share in the President's ultimate wishes. Mr. McFarlane described for the board the process used by the N.S.C. staff to create a chronology that obscured essential facts. Mr. McFarlane contributed to the creation of this chronology which did not, he said, present "a full and completely accurate account" of the events and left ambiguous the President's role. This was, according to Mr. McFarlane, done to distance the President from the timing and nature of the President's authorization. He told the board that he wrote a memorandum on Nov. 18, which tried to, in his own words, "gild the President's motives."

This version was incorporated into the chronology. Mr. McFarlane told the board that he knew the account was "misleading, at least, and wrong, at worst." Mr. McFarlane told the board that he did provide the Attorney General an accurate account of the President's role.

The board found considerable reason to question the actions of Lt Col North in the aftermath of the disclosure. The board has no evidence to either confirm or refute that Lt Col North destroyed documents on the initiative in an effort to conceal facts from threatened investigations. The board found indications that Lt Col North was involved in an effort, over time, to conceal or withhold important information. The files of Lt Col North contained much of the historical documentation that the board used to construct its narrative. Moreover, Lt Col North was the primary U.S. Government official involved in the details of the operation. The chronology he produced has many inaccuracies. These "histories" were to be the basis of the "full" story of the Iran initiative. These inaccuracies lend some evidence to the proposition that Lt Col North, either on his own or at the behest of others, actively sought to conceal important information.

Out of concern for the protection of classified material, Director Casey and VADM Poindexter were to brief only the Congressional intelligence committees on the "full" story; the D.C.I. before the committees and VADM Poindexter in private sessions with the chairmen and vice chairmen. The D.C.I. and VADM Poindexter undertook to do this on November 21, 1986. It appears from the copy of the D.C.I.'s testimony and notes of VADM Poindexter's meetings that they did not fully relate the nature of events as they had occurred. The result is an understandable perception that they were not forthcoming.

The board is also concerned about various notes that appear to be missing. VADM Poindexter was the official note taker in some key meetings, yet no notes for the meetings can be found. The reason for the lack of such notes remains unknown to the board. If they were written, they may contain very important information. We have no way of knowing if they exist.

## 9. Excerpts from the Intermediate-Range Nuclear Forces (INF) Treaty, December 8, 1987

The United States of America and the Union of Soviet Socialist Republics, hereinafter referred to as the Parties,

Conscious that nuclear war would have devastating consequences for all mankind,

Guided by the objective of strengthening strategic stability,

Convinced that the measures set forth in this Treaty will help to reduce the risk of outbreak of war and strengthen international peace and security, and

Mindful of their obligations under Article VI of the Treaty on the Non-Proliferation of Nuclear Weapons,

Have agreed as follows:

### Article I

In accordance with the provisions of this Treaty which includes the Memorandum of Understanding and Protocols which form an integral part thereof, each Party shall eliminate its intermediate-range and shorter-range missiles, not have such systems thereafter, and carry out the other obligations set forth in this Treaty.

\* \* \*

### Article IV

1. Each Party shall eliminate all its intermediate-range missiles and launchers of such missiles, and all support structures and support equipment of the categories listed in the Memorandum of Understanding associated with such missiles and launchers, so that no later than

three years after entry into force of this Treaty and thereafter no such missiles, launchers, support structures or support equipment shall be possessed by either Party.

2. To implement paragraph 1 of this Article, upon entry into force of this Treaty, both Parties shall begin and continue throughout the duration of each phase, the reduction of all types of their deployed and non-deployed intermediate-range missiles and deployed and non-deployed launchers of such missiles and support structures and support equipment associated with such missiles and launchers in accordance with the provisions of this Treaty. These reductions shall be implemented in two phases so that:

(a) by the end of the first phase, that is, no later than 29 months after entry into force of this Treaty:

(i) the number of deployed launchers of intermediate-range missiles for each Party shall not exceed the number of launchers that are capable of carrying or containing at one time missiles considered by the Parties to carry 171 warheads;

(ii) the number of deployed intermediate-range missiles for each Party shall not exceed the number of such missiles considered by the Parties to carry 180 warheads;

(iii) the aggregate number of deployed and non-deployed launchers of intermediate-range missiles for each Party shall not exceed the number of launchers that are capable of carrying or containing at one time missiles considered by the Parties to carry 200 warheads;

(iv) the aggregate number of deployed and non-deployed intermediate-range missiles for each Party shall not exceed the number of such missiles considered by the Parties to carry 200 warheads; and

(v) the ratio of the aggregate number of deployed and non-deployed intermediate-range GLBMs of existing types for each Party to the aggregate number of deployed and non-deployed intermediate-range missiles of existing types possessed by that Party shall not exceed the ratio of such intermediate-range GLBMs to such intermediate-range missiles for that Party as of November 1, 1987, as set forth in the Memorandum of Understanding; and

(b) by the end of the second phase, that is, no later than three years after entry into force of this Treaty, all intermediate-range missiles of each Party, launchers of such missiles and all support structures and support equipment of the categories listed in the Memorandum of Understanding associated with such missiles and launchers, shall be eliminated.

## Article V

1. Each Party shall eliminate all its shorter-range missiles and launchers of such missiles, and all support equipment of the categories listed in the Memorandum of Understanding associated with such missiles and launchers, so that no later than 18 months after entry into force of this Treaty and thereafter no such missiles, launchers or support equipment shall be possessed by either Party.

2. No later than 90 days after entry into force of this Treaty, each Party shall complete the removal of all its deployed shorter-range missiles and deployed and non-deployed launchers of such missiles to elimination facilities and shall retain them at those locations until they are eliminated in accordance with the procedures set forth in the Protocol on Elimination. No later than 12 months after entry into force of this Treaty, each Party shall complete the removal of all its non-deployed shorter-range missiles to elimination facilities and shall retain them at those locations until they are eliminated in accordance with the procedures set forth in the Protocol on Elimination.

3. Shorter-range missiles and launchers of such missiles shall not be located at the same elimination facility. Such facilities shall be separated by no less than 1000 kilometers.

## Article VI

1. Upon entry into force of this Treaty and thereafter, neither Party shall:

(a) produce or flight-test any intermediate-range missiles or produce any stages of such missiles or any launchers of such missiles; or

(b) produce, flight-test or launch any shorter-range missiles or produce any stages of such missiles or any launchers of such missiles.

2. Notwithstanding paragraph 1 of this Article, each Party shall have the right to produce a type of GLBM not limited by this Treaty which uses a stage which is outwardly similar to, but not interchangeable with, a stage of an existing type of intermediate-range GLBM having more than one stage, providing that that Party does not produce any other stage which is outwardly similar to, but not interchangeable with, any other stage of an existing type of intermediate-range GLBM.

* * *

## Article X

1. Each Party shall eliminate its intermediate-range and shorter-range missiles and launchers of such missiles and support structures and support equipment associated with such missiles and launchers in accordance with the procedures set forth in the Protocol on Elimination.

2. Verification by on-site inspection of the elimination of items of missile systems specified in the Protocol on Elimination shall be carried out in accordance with Article XI of this Treaty, the Protocol on Elimination and the Protocol on Inspection.

* * *

## 10. THE CIVIL LIBERTIES ACT OF 1988, AUGUST 10, 1988

The Congress recognizes that, as described in the Commission on Wartime Relocation and Internment of Civilians, a grave injustice was done to both citizens and permanent residents of Japanese ancestry by the evacuation, relocation, and internment of civilians during World War II.

As the Commission documents, these actions were carried out without adequate security reasons and without any acts of espionage or sabotage documented by the Commission, and were motivated largely by racial prejudice, wartime hysteria, and a failure of political leadership.

The excluded individuals of Japanese ancestry suffered enormous damages, both material and intangible, and there were incalculable losses in education and job training, all of which resulted in significant human suffering for which appropriate compensation has not been made.

For these fundamental violations of the basic civil liberties and constitutional rights of these individuals of Japanese ancestry, the Congress apologizes on behalf of the Nation.

## 11. PRESIDENT RONALD REAGAN'S FAREWELL ADDRESS TO THE NATION, JANUARY 11, 1989

This is the 34th time I'll speak to you from the Oval Office and the last. We've been together eight years now, and soon it'll be time for me to go. But before I do, I wanted to share some thoughts, some of which I've been saving for a long time.

It's been the honor of my life to be your President. So many of you have written the past few weeks to say thanks, but I could say as much to you. Nancy and I are grateful for the opportunity you gave us to serve.

One of the things about the Presidency is that you're always somewhat apart. You spent a lot of time going by too fast in a car someone else is driving, and seeing the people through tinted glass—the parents holding up a child, and the wave you saw too late and couldn't return. And so many times I wanted to stop and reach out from behind the glass, and connect. Well, maybe I can do a little of that tonight.

People ask how I feel about leaving. And the fact is, "parting is such sweet sorrow." The sweet part is California and the ranch and freedom. The sorrow—the goodbyes, of course, and leaving this beautiful place.

You know, down the hall and up the stairs from this office is the part of the White House where the President and his family live. There are a few favorite windows I have up there that I like to stand and look out of early in the morning. The view is over the grounds here to the Washington Monument, and then the Mall and the Jefferson Memorial. But on mornings when the humidity is low, you can see past the Jefferson to the river, the Potomac, and the Virginia shore. Someone said that's the view Lincoln had when he saw the smoke rising from the Battle of Bull Run. I see more prosaic things: the grass on the banks, the morning traffic as people make their way to work, now and then a sailboat on the river.

I've been thinking a bit at that window. I've been reflecting on what the past eight years have meant and mean. And the image that comes to mind like a refrain is a nautical one—a small story about a big ship, and a refugee, and a sailor. It was back in the early eighties, at the height of the boat people. And the sailor was hard at work on the carrier Midway, which was patrolling the South China Sea. The sailor, like most American servicemen, was young, smart, and fiercely observant. The crew spied on the horizon a leaky little boat. And crammed inside were refugees from Indochina hoping to get to America. The Midway sent a small launch to bring them to the ship and safety. As the refugees made their way through the choppy seas, one spied the sailor on deck, and stood up, and called out to him. He yelled, "Hello, American sailor. Hello, freedom man."

A small moment with a big meaning, a moment the sailor, who wrote it in a letter, couldn't get out of his mind. And, when I saw it, neither could I. Because that's what it was to be an American in the 1980's. We stood, again, for freedom. I know we always have, but in the past few years the world again—and in a way, we ourselves—rediscovered it.

It's been quite a journey this decade, and we held together through some stormy seas. And at the end, together, we are reaching our destination.

The fact is, from Grenada to the Washington and Moscow summits, from the recession of '81 to '82, to the expansion that began in late '82 and continues to this day, we've made a difference. The way I see it, there were two great triumphs, two things that I'm proudest of. One is the economic recovery, in which the people of America created—and filled—19 million new jobs. The other is the recovery of our morale. America is respected again in the world and looked to for leadership.

Something that happened to me a few years ago reflects some of this. It was back in 1981, and I was attending my first big economic summit, which was held that year in Canada. The meeting place rotates among the member countries. The opening meeting was a formal dinner of the heads of government of the seven industrialized nations. Now, I sat there like the new kid in school and listened, and it was all Francois this and Helmut that. They dropped titles and spoke to one another on a first-name basis. Well, at one point I sort of leaned in and said, "My name's Ron." Well, in that same year, we began the actions we felt would ignite an economic comeback—cut taxes and regulation, started to cut spending. And soon the recovery began.

Two years later, another economic summit with pretty much the same cast. At the big opening meeting we all got together, and all of a sudden, just for a moment, I saw that everyone was just sitting there looking at me. And then one of them broke the silence. "Tell us about the American miracle," he said.

Well, back in 1980, when I was running for President, it was all so different. Some pundits said our programs would result in catastrophe. Our views on foreign affairs would cause war. Our plans for the economy would cause inflation to soar and bring about economic collapse. I even remember one highly respected economist saying, back in 1982, that "The engines of economic growth have shut down here, and they're likely to stay that way for years to come." Well, he and the other opinion leaders were wrong. The fact is what they call "radical" was really "right." What they called "dangerous" was just "desperately needed."

And in all of that time I won a nickname, "The Great Communicator." But I never thought it was my style or the words I used that made a difference: it was the content. I wasn't a great communicator, but I communicated great things, and they didn't spring full bloom from my brow, they came from the heart of a great nation—from our experience, our wisdom, and our belief in the principles that have guided us for two centuries. They called it the Reagan revolution. Well, I'll accept that, but for me it always seemed more like the great rediscovery, a rediscovery of our values and our common sense.

Common sense told us that when you put a big tax on something, the people will produce less of it. So, we cut the people's tax rates, and the people produced more than ever before. The economy bloomed like a plant that had been cut back and could now grow quicker and stronger. Our economic program brought about the longest peacetime expansion in our history: real family income up, the poverty rate down, entrepreneurship booming, and an explosion in research and new technology. We're exporting more than ever because American industry became more competitive and at the same time, we summoned the national will to knock down protectionist walls abroad instead of erecting them at home.

Common sense also told us that to preserve the peace, we'd have to become strong again after years of weakness and confusion. So, we rebuilt our defenses, and this New Year we toasted the new peacefulness around the globe. Not only have the superpowers actually begun to reduce their stockpiles of nuclear weapons—and hope for even more progress is bright—but the regional conflicts that rack the globe are also beginning to cease. The Persian Gulf is no longer a war zone. The Soviets are leaving Afghanistan. The Vietnamese are preparing to pull out of Cambodia, and an American-mediated accord will soon send 50,000 Cuban troops home from Angola.

The lesson of all this was, of course, that because we're a great nation, our challenges seem complex. It will always be this way. But as long as we remember our first principles and believe in ourselves, the future will always be ours. And something else we learned: Once you begin a great movement, there's no telling where it will end. We meant to change a nation, and instead, we changed a world.

Countries across the globe are turning to free markets and free speech and turning away from the ideologies of the past. For them, the great rediscovery of the 1980's has been that, lo and behold, the moral way of government is the practical way of government: Democracy, the profoundly good, is also the profoundly productive.

When you've got to the point when you can celebrate the anniversaries of your 39th birthday you can sit back sometimes, review your life, and see it flowing before you. For me there was a fork in the river, and it was right in the middle of my life. I never meant to go into politics. It wasn't my intention when I was young. But I was raised to believe you had to pay your way for the blessings bestowed on you. I was happy with my career in the entertainment world, but I ultimately went into politics because I wanted to protect something precious.

Ours was the first revolution in the history of mankind that truly reversed the course of government, and with three little words: "We the People." "We the People" tell the government what to do; it doesn't tell us. "We the People" are the driver; the government is the car. And we decide where it should go, and by what route, and how fast. Almost all the world's constitutions are documents in which governments tell the people what their privileges are. Our Constitution is a document in which "We the People" tell the government what it is allowed to do. "We the People" are free. This belief has been the underlying basis for everything I've tried to do these past 8 years.

But back in the 1960's, when I began, it seemed to me that we'd begun reversing the order of things—that through more and more rules and regulations and confiscatory taxes, the government was taking more of our money, more of our options, and more of our freedom. I went into politics in part to put up my hand and say, "Stop." I was a citizen politician, and it seemed the right thing for a citizen to do.

I think we have stopped a lot of what needed stopping. And I hope we have once again reminded people that man is not free unless government is limited. There's a clear cause and effect here that is as neat and predictable as a law of physics: As government expands, liberty contracts.

Nothing is less free than pure communism—and yet we have, the past few years, forged a satisfying new closeness with the Soviet Union. I've been asked if this isn't a gamble, and my answer is no because we're basing our actions not on words but deeds. The detente of the 1970s was based not on actions but promises. They'd promise to treat their own people and the people of the world better. But the gulag was still the gulag, and the state was still expansionist, and they still waged proxy wars in Africa, Asia, and Latin America.

Well, this time, so far, it's different. President Gorbachev has brought about some internal democratic reforms and begun the withdrawal from Afghanistan. He has also freed prisoners whose names I've given him every time we've met.

But life has a way of reminding you of big things through small incidents. Once, during the heady days of the Moscow summit, Nancy and I decided to break off from the entourage one afternoon to visit the shops on Arbat Street—that's a little street just off Moscow's main shopping area. Even though our visit was a surprise, every Russian there immediately recognized us and called out our names and reached for our hands. We were just about swept away by the warmth. You could almost feel the possibilities in all that joy. But within seconds, a KGB detail pushed their way toward us and began pushing and shoving the people in the crowd. It was an interesting moment. It reminded me that while the man on the street in the Soviet Union yearns for peace, the government is Communist. And those who run it are Communists, and that means we and they view such issues as freedom and human rights very differently.

We must keep up our guard, but we must also continue to work together to lessen and eliminate tension and mistrust. My view is that President Gorbachev is different from previous Soviet leaders. I think he knows some of the things wrong with his society and is trying to fix them. We wish him well. And we'll continue to work to make sure that the Soviet Union that eventually emerges from this process is a less threatening one. What it all boils down to is this: I want the new closeness to continue. And it will, as long as we make it clear that we will continue to act in a certain way as long as they continue to act in a helpful manner. If and when they don't, at first pull your punches. If they persist, pull the plug. It's still trust by verify. It's still play, but cut the cards. It's still watch closely. And don't be afraid to see what you see.

I've been asked if I have any regrets. Well, I do. The deficit is one. I've been talking a great deal about that lately, but tonight isn't for arguments, and I'm going to hold my tongue. But an observation: I've had my share of victories in the Congress, but what few people noticed is that I never won anything you didn't win for me. They never saw my troops, they never saw Reagan's regiments, the American people. You won every battle with every call you made and letter you wrote demanding action. Well, action is still needed. If we're to finish the job, Reagan's regiments will have to become the Bush brigades. Soon he'll be the chief, and he'll need you every bit as much as I did.

Finally, there is a great tradition of warnings in Presidential farewells, and I've got one that's been on my mind for some time. But oddly enough it starts with one of the things I'm proudest of in the past eight years: the resurgence of national pride that I called the new patriotism. This national feeling is good, but it won't count for much, and it won't last unless it's grounded in thoughtfulness and knowledge.

An informed patriotism is what we want. And are we doing a good enough job teaching our children what America is and what she represents in the long history of the world? Those of us who are over 35 or so years of age grew up in a different America. We were taught, very directly, what it means to be an American. And we absorbed, almost in the air, a love of country and an appreciation of its institutions. If you didn't get these things from your family you got them from the neighborhood, from the father down the street who fought in Korea or the family who lost someone at Anzio. Or you could get a sense of patriotism from school. And if all else failed you could get a sense of patriotism from the popular culture. The movies celebrated democratic values and implicitly reinforced the idea that America was special. TV was like that, too, through the mid-sixties.

But now, we're about to enter the nineties, and some things have changed. Younger parents aren't sure that an unambivalent appreciation of America is the right thing to teach modern children. And as for those who create the popular culture, well-grounded patriotism is no longer the style. Our spirit is back, but we haven't reinstitutionalized it. We've got to do a better job of getting across that America is freedom—freedom of speech, freedom of religion, freedom of enterprise. And freedom is special and rare. It's fragile; it needs protection.

So, we've got to teach history based not on what's in fashion but what's important—why the Pilgrims came here, who Jimmy Doolittle was, and what those 30 seconds over Tokyo meant. You know, four years ago on the 40th anniversary of D-day, I read a letter from a young woman writing to her late father, who'd fought on Omaha Beach. Her name was Lisa Zanatta Henn, and she said, "We will always remember, we will never forget what the boys of Normandy did." Well, let's help her keep her word. If we forget what we did, we won't know who we are. I'm warning of an eradication of the American memory that could result, ultimately, in an erosion of the American spirit. Let's start with some basics: more attention to American history and a greater emphasis on civic ritual.

And let me offer lesson number one about America: All great change in America begins at the dinner table. So, tomorrow night in the kitchen I hope the talking begins. And children, if your parents haven't been teaching you what it means to be an American, let 'em know and nail 'em on it. That would be a very American thing to do.

And that's about all I have to say tonight, except for one thing. The past few days when I've been at that window upstairs, I've thought a bit of the "shining city upon a hill." The phrase comes from John Winthrop, who wrote it to describe the America he imagined. What he imagined was important because he was an early Pilgrim, an early freedom man. He journeyed here on what today we'd call a little wooden boat; and like the other Pilgrims, he was looking for a home that would be free. I've spoken of the shining city all my political life, but I don't know if I ever quite communicated what I saw when I said it. But in my mind it was a tall, proud city built on rocks stronger than oceans, windswept, God-blessed, and teeming with people of all kinds living in harmony and peace; a city with free ports that hummed with commerce and creativity. And if there had to be city walls, the walls had doors and the doors were open to anyone with the will and the heart to get here. That's how I saw it, and see it still.

And how stands the city on this winter night? More prosperous, more secure, and happier than it was eight years ago. But more than that: After 200 years, two centuries, she still stands strong and true on the granite ridge, and her glow has held steady no matter what storm. And she's still a beacon, still a magnet for all who must have freedom, for all the pilgrims from all the lost places who are hurtling through the darkness, toward home.

We've done our part. And as I walk off into the city streets, a final word to the men and women of the Reagan revolution, the men and women across America who for eight years did the work that brought America back. My friends: We did it. We weren't just marking time. We made a difference. We made the city stronger, we made the city freer, and we left her in good hands. All in all, not bad, not bad at all.

And so, goodbye, God bless you, and God bless the United States of America.

## 12. President George H. W. Bush's Inaugural Address, January 20, 1989

Mr. Chief Justice, Mr. President, Vice President Quayle, Senator Mitchell, Speaker Wright, Senator Dole, Congressman Michel, and fellow citizens, neighbors, and friends:

There is a man here who has earned a lasting place in our hearts and in our history. President Reagan, on behalf of our Nation, I thank you for the wonderful things that you have done for America.

I have just repeated word for word the oath taken by George Washington 200 years ago, and the Bible on which I placed my hand is the Bible on which he placed his. It is right that the memory of Washington be with us today, not only because this is our Bicentennial Inauguration, but because Washington remains the Father of our Country. And he would, I think, be gladdened by this day; for today is the concrete expression of a stunning fact: our continuity these 200 years since our government began.

We meet on democracy's front porch, a good place to talk as neighbors and as friends. For this is a day when our nation is made whole, when our differences, for a moment, are suspended.

And my first act as President is a prayer. I ask you to bow your heads:

Heavenly Father, we bow our heads and thank You for Your love. Accept our thanks for the peace that yields this day and the shared faith that makes its continuance likely. Make us strong to do Your work, willing to heed and hear Your will, and write on our hearts these words: "Use power to help people." For we are given power not to advance our own purposes, nor to make a great show in the world, nor a name. There is but one just use of power, and it is to serve people. Help us to remember it, Lord. Amen.

I come before you and assume the Presidency at a moment rich with promise. We live in a peaceful, prosperous time, but we can make it better. For a new breeze is blowing, and a world refreshed by freedom seems reborn; for in man's heart, if not in fact, the day of the dictator is over. The totalitarian era is passing, its old ideas blown away like leaves from an ancient, lifeless tree. A new breeze is blowing, and a nation refreshed by freedom stands ready to push on. There is new ground to be broken, and new action to be taken. There are times when the future seems thick as a fog; you sit and wait, hoping the mists will lift and reveal the right path. But this is a time when the future seems a door you can walk right through into a room called tomorrow.

Great nations of the world are moving toward democracy through the door to freedom. Men and women of the world move toward free markets through the door to prosperity. The people of the world agitate for free expression and free thought through the door to the moral and intellectual satisfactions that only liberty allows.

We know what works: Freedom works. We know what's right: Freedom is right. We know how to secure a more just and prosperous life for man on Earth: through free markets, free speech, free elections, and the exercise of free will unhampered by the state.

For the first time in this century, for the first time in perhaps all history, man does not have to invent a system by which to live. We don't have to talk late into the night about which form of government is better. We don't have to wrest justice from the kings. We only have to summon it from within ourselves. We must act on what we know. I take as my guide the hope of a saint: In crucial things, unity; in important things, diversity; in all things, generosity.

America today is a proud, free nation, decent and civil, a place we cannot help but love. We know in our hearts, not loudly and proudly, but as a simple fact, that this country has meaning beyond what we see, and that our strength is a force for good. But have we changed as a nation even in our time? Are we enthralled with material things, less appreciative of the nobility of work and sacrifice?

My friends, we are not the sum of our possessions. They are not the measure of our lives. In our hearts we know what matters. We cannot hope only to leave our children a bigger car, a bigger bank account. We must hope to give them a sense of what it means to be a loyal friend, a loving parent, a citizen who leaves his home, his neighborhood and town better than he found it. What do we want the men and women who work with us to say when we are no longer there? That we were more driven to succeed than anyone around us? Or that we stopped to ask if a sick child had gotten better, and stayed a moment there to trade a word of friendship?

No President, no government, can teach us to remember what is best in what we are. But if the man you have chosen to lead this government can help make a difference; if he can celebrate the quieter, deeper successes that are made not of gold and silk, but of better hearts and finer souls; if he can do these things, then he must.

America is never wholly herself unless she is engaged in high moral principle. We as a people have such a purpose today. It is to make kinder the face of the Nation and gentler the face of the world. My friends, we have work to do. There are the homeless, lost and roaming. There are the children who have nothing, no love, no normalcy. There are those who cannot free themselves of enslavement to whatever addiction—drugs, welfare, the demoralization that rules the slums. There is crime to be conquered, the rough crime of the streets. There are young women to be helped who are about to become mothers of children they can't care for and might not love. They need our care, our guidance, and our education, though we bless them for choosing life.

The old solution, the old way, was to think that public money alone could end these problems. But we have learned that is not so. And in any case, our funds are low. We have a deficit to bring down. We have more will than wallet; but will is what we need. We will make the hard choices, looking at what we have and perhaps allocating it differently, making our decisions based on honest need and prudent safety. And then we will do the wisest thing of all: We will turn to the only resource we have that in times of need always grows—the goodness and the courage of the American people.

I am speaking of a new engagement in the lives of others, a new activism, hands–on and involved, that gets the job done. We must bring in the generations, harnessing the unused talent of the elderly and the unfocused energy of the young. For not only leadership is passed from generation to generation, but so is stewardship. And the generation born after the Second World War has come of age.

I have spoken of a thousand points of light, of all the community organizations that are spread like stars throughout the Nation, doing good. We will work hand in hand, encouraging, sometimes leading, sometimes being led, rewarding. We will work on this in the White House, in the Cabinet agencies. I will go to the people and the programs that are the brighter points of light, and I will ask every member of my government to become involved. The old ideas are new again because they are not old, they are timeless: duty, sacrifice, commitment, and a patriotism that finds its expression in taking part and pitching in.

We need a new engagement, too, between the Executive and the Congress. The challenges before us will be thrashed out with the House and the Senate. We must bring the Federal budget into balance. And we must ensure that America stands before the world united, strong, at peace, and fiscally sound. But, of course, things may be difficult. We need compromise; we have had dissension. We need harmony; we have had a chorus of discordant voices.

For Congress, too, has changed in our time. There has grown a certain divisiveness. We have seen the hard looks and heard the statements in which not each other's ideas are challenged, but each other's motives. And our great parties have too often been far apart and untrusting of each other. It has been this way since Vietnam. That war cleaves us still. But, friends, that war began in earnest a quarter of a century ago; and surely the statute of limitations has been reached. This is a fact: The final lesson of Vietnam is that no great nation can long afford to be sundered by a memory. A new breeze is blowing, and the old bipartisanship must be made new again.

To my friends—and yes, I do mean friends—in the loyal opposition—and yes, I mean loyal: I put out my hand. I am putting out my hand to you, Mr. Speaker. I am putting out my hand to you Mr. Majority Leader. For this is the thing: This is the age of the offered hand. We can't turn back clocks, and I don't want to. But when our fathers were young, Mr. Speaker, our differences ended at the water's edge. And we don't wish to turn back time, but when our mothers were young, Mr. Majority Leader, the Congress and the Executive were capable of working together to produce a budget on which this nation could live. Let us negotiate soon and hard. But in the end, let us produce. The American people await action. They didn't send us here to bicker. They ask us to rise

above the merely partisan. "In crucial things, unity"—and this, my friends, is crucial.

To the world, too, we offer new engagement and a renewed vow: We will stay strong to protect the peace. The "offered hand" is a reluctant fist; but once made, strong, and can be used with great effect. There are today Americans who are held against their will in foreign lands, and Americans who are unaccounted for. Assistance can be shown here, and will be long remembered. Good will begets good will. Good faith can be a spiral that endlessly moves on.

Great nations like great men must keep their word. When America says something, America means it, whether a treaty or an agreement or a vow made on marble steps. We will always try to speak clearly, for candor is a compliment, but subtlety, too, is good and has its place. While keeping our alliances and friendships around the world strong, ever strong, we will continue the new closeness with the Soviet Union, consistent both with our security and with progress. One might say that our new relationship in part reflects the triumph of hope and strength over experience. But hope is good, and so are strength and vigilance.

Here today are tens of thousands of our citizens who feel the understandable satisfaction of those who have taken part in democracy and seen their hopes fulfilled. But my thoughts have been turning the past few days to those who would be watching at home to an older fellow who will throw a salute by himself when the flag goes by, and the women who will tell her sons the words of the battle hymns. I don't mean this to be sentimental. I mean that on days like this, we remember that we are all part of a continuum, inescapably connected by the ties that bind.

Our children are watching in schools throughout our great land. And to them I say, thank you for watching democracy's big day. For democracy belongs to us all, and freedom is like a beautiful kite that can go higher and higher with the breeze. And to all I say: No matter what your circumstances or where you are, you are part of this day, you are part of the life of our great nation.

A President is neither prince nor pope, and I don't seek a window on men's souls. In fact, I yearn for a greater tolerance, an easy-goingness about each other's attitudes and way of life.

There are few clear areas in which we as a society must rise up united and express our intolerance. The most obvious now is drugs. And when that first cocaine was smuggled in on a ship, it may as well have been a deadly bacteria, so much has it hurt the body, the soul of our country. And there is much to be done and to be said, but take my word for it: This scourge will stop.

And so, there is much to do; and tomorrow the work begins. I do not mistrust the future; I do not fear what is ahead. For our problems are large, but our heart is larger. Our challenges are great, but our will is greater. And if our flaws are endless, God's love is truly boundless.

Some see leadership as high drama, and the sound of trumpets calling, and sometimes it is that. But I see history as a book with many pages, and each day we fill a page with acts of hopefulness and meaning. The new breeze blows, a page turns, the story unfolds. And so today a chapter begins, a small and stately story of unity, diversity, and generosity—shared, and written, together.

Thank you. God bless you and God bless the United States of America.

## 13. PRESIDENT GEORGE H. W. BUSH'S REMARKS AT THE TEXAS A&M UNIVERSITY COMMENCEMENT CEREMONY IN COLLEGE STATION, MAY 12, 1989

Thank you, Governor. Thank you all very much for that welcome. Good luck, good luck to you. Thank you, ladies and gentlemen, thank you all. Chairman McKenzie and Dr. Adkisson and Dr. Mobley, thank you for having me here. And to the Singing Cadets, thank you for that very special treat. And to my Secretary of Commerce, Bob Mosbacher, I'm delighted that he's with me today.

I want to pay my special respects to our Governor, Bill Clements; to your Congressman from this district, Joe Barton; and then, of course, to Senator Phil Gramm. He said he taught economics here and in Congress. It's hard to be humble. But nevertheless—the point is the guy's telling the truth, and we are grateful to him every day for his leadership up there in Washington, as we are for Joe Barton as well. So, we've got a good combination—Phil Gramm in the Senate and today Joe Barton in the United States Congress—a wonderful combination, with these Aggie values in the forefront.

I was brought here today by an Aggie, and I brought him here to this marvelous ceremony with me. He was mentioned by Congressman Barton, but I would like to ask the pilot of Air Force One, Lieutenant Colonel Dan Barr, to stand up so you can see another Aggie all suited up, up there. And you met my day-to-day inside Aggie, Fred McClure. We work every minute of the day on matters affecting the legislative interests of this country, but I won't reintroduce Fred. But I am delighted to be back among my fellow Texans and friends. And for those of you who are Democrats, there is no truth to the rumor that Phil Gramm and I are ready to take our elephant walk.

My sincerest congratulations go to every graduate and to your parents. In this ceremony, we celebrate nothing less than the commencement of the rest, and the best, of your life. And when you look back at your days at Texas A&M, you will have a lot to be proud of: a university that is first in baseball and first in service to our nation. Many are the heroes whose names are called at muster. Many are those you remember in Silver Taps.

We are reminded that no generation can escape history. Parents, we share a fervent desire for our children and their children to know a better world, a safer world. And students, your parents and grandparents have lived through a world war and helped America to rebuild the world. They witnessed the drama of postwar nations divided by Soviet subversion and force, but sustained by an allied response most vividly seen in the Berlin airlift. And today I would like to use this joyous and solemn occasion to speak to you and to the rest of the country about our relations with the Soviet Union. It is fitting that these remarks be made here at Texas A&M University.

Wise men—Truman and Eisenhower, Vandenberg and Rayburn, Marshall, Acheson, and Kennan—crafted the strategy of containment. They believed that the Soviet Union, denied the easy course of expansion, would turn inward and address the contradictions of its inefficient, repressive, and inhumane system. And they were right—the Soviet Union is now publicly facing this hard reality. Containment worked. Containment worked because our democratic principles and institutions and values are sound and always have been. It worked because our alliances were, and are, strong and because the superiority of free societies and free markets over stagnant socialism is undeniable.

We are approaching the conclusion of an historic postwar struggle between two visions: one of tyranny and conflict and one of democracy and freedom. The review of U.S.–Soviet relations that my administration has just completed outlines a new path toward resolving this struggle. Our goal is bold, more ambitious than any of my predecessors could have thought possible. Our review indicates that 40 years of perseverance have brought us a precious opportunity, and now it is time to move beyond containment to a new policy for the 1990's—one that recognizes the full scope of change taking place around the world and in the Soviet Union itself. In sum, the United States now has as its goal much more than simply containing Soviet expansionism. We seek the integration of the Soviet Union into the community of nations. And as the Soviet Union itself moves toward greater openness and democratization, as they meet the challenge of responsible international behavior, we will match their steps with steps of our own. Ultimately, our objective is to welcome the Soviet Union back into the world order.

The Soviet Union says that it seeks to make peace with the world and criticizes its own postwar policies. These are words that we can only applaud, but a new relationship cannot simply be declared by Moscow or bestowed by others; it must be earned. It must be earned because promises are never enough. The Soviet Union has promised a more cooperative relationship before, only to reverse course and return to militarism. Soviet foreign policy has been almost seasonal: warmth before cold, thaw before freeze. We seek a friendship that knows no season of suspicion, no chill of distrust.

We hope perestroika is pointing the Soviet Union to a break with the cycles of the past—a definitive break. Who would have thought that we would see the deliberations of the Central Committee on the front page of Pravda or dissident Andrei Sakharov seated near the councils of power? Who would have imagined a Soviet leader who canvasses the sidewalks of Moscow and also Washington, DC? These are hopeful, indeed, remarkable signs. And let no one doubt our sincere desire to see perestroika, this reform, continue and succeed. But the national security of America and our allies is not predicated on hope. It must be based on deeds, and we look for enduring, ingrained economic and political change.

While we hope to move beyond containment, we are only at the beginning of our new path. Many dangers and uncertainties are ahead. We must not forget that the Soviet Union has acquired awesome military capabilities. That was a fact of life for my predecessors, and that's always been a fact of life for our allies. And that is a fact of life for me today as President of the United States.

As we seek peace, we must also remain strong. The purpose of our military might is not to pressure a weak Soviet economy or to seek military superiority. It is to deter war. It is to defend ourselves and our allies and to do something more: to convince the Soviet Union that there can be no reward in pursuing expansionism, to convince the Soviet Union that reward lies in the pursuit of peace.

Western policies must encourage the evolution of the Soviet Union toward an open society. This task will test our strength. It will tax our patience, and it will require a sweeping vision. Let me share with you my vision: I see a Western Hemisphere of democratic, prosperous nations, no longer threatened by a Cuba or a Nicaragua armed by Moscow. I see a Soviet Union as it pulls away from ties to terrorist nations like Libya that threaten the legitimate security of their neighbors. I see a Soviet Union which respects China's integrity and returns the northern territories to Japan, a prelude to the day when all the great nations of Asia will live in harmony.

But the fulfillment of this vision requires the Soviet Union to take positive steps, including: First, reduce Soviet forces. Although some small steps have already been taken, the Warsaw Pact still possesses more than 30,000 tanks, more than twice as much artillery, and hundreds of thousands more troops in Europe than NATO. They should cut their forces to less threatening levels, in proportion to their legitimate security needs. Second, adhere to the Soviet obligation, promised in the final days of World War II, to support self-determination for all the nations of Eastern Europe and central Europe. And this requires specific abandonment of the Brezhnev doctrine. One day it should be possible to drive from Moscow to Munich without seeing a single guard tower or a strand of barbed wire. In short, tear down the Iron Curtain.

And third, work with the West in positive, practical—not merely rhetorical—steps toward diplomatic solution to these regional disputes around the world. I welcome the Soviet withdrawal from Afghanistan, and the Angola agreement. But there is much more to be done around the world. We're ready. Let's roll up our sleeves and get to work.

And fourth, achieve a lasting political pluralism and respect for human rights. Dramatic events have already occurred in Moscow. We are impressed by limited, but freely contested elections. We are impressed by a greater toleration of dissent. We are impressed by a new frankness about the Stalin era. Mr. Gorbachev, don't stop now!

And fifth, join with us in addressing pressing global problems, including the international drug menace and dangers to the environment. We can build a better world for our children.

As the Soviet Union moves toward arms reduction and reform, it will find willing partners in the West. We seek verifiable, stabilizing arms control and arms reduction agreements with the Soviet Union and its allies. However, arms control is not an end in itself but a means of contributing to the security of America and the peace of the world. I directed Secretary [of State James] Baker to propose to the Soviets that we resume negotiations on strategic forces in June and, as you know, the Soviet Union has agreed.

Our basic approach is clear. In the strategic arms reductions talks, we wish to reduce the risk of nuclear war. And in the companion defense and space talks, our objective will be to preserve our options to deploy advanced defenses when they're ready. In nuclear testing, we will continue to seek the necessary verification improvements in existing treaties to permit them to be brought into force. And we're going to continue to seek a verifiable global ban on chemical weapons. We support NATO efforts to reduce the Soviet offensive threat in the negotiations on conventional forces in Europe. And as I've said, fundamental to all of these objectives is simple openness.

Make no mistake, a new breeze is blowing across the steppes and the cities of the Soviet Union. Why not, then, let this spirit of openness grow, let more barriers come down. Open emigration, open debate, open airwaves—let openness come to mean the publication and sale of banned books and newspapers in the Soviet Union. Let the 19,000 Soviet Jews who emigrated last year be followed by any number who wish to emigrate this year. And when people apply for exit visas, let there be no harassment against them. Let openness come to mean nothing less than the free exchange of people and books and ideas between East and West.

And let it come to mean one thing more. Thirty-four years ago, President Eisenhower met in Geneva with Soviet leaders who, after the death of Stalin, promised a new approach toward the West. He proposed a plan called Open Skies, which would allow unarmed aircraft from the United States and the Soviet Union to fly over the territory of the other country. This would open up military activities to regular scrutiny and, as President Eisenhower put it, "convince the world that we are lessening danger and relaxing tension." President Eisenhower's suggestion tested the Soviet readiness to open their society, and the Kremlin failed that test.

Now, let us again explore that proposal, but on a broader, more intrusive and radical basis—one which I hope would include allies on both sides. We suggest that those countries that wish to examine this proposal meet soon to work out the necessary operational details, separately from other arms control negotiations. Such surveillance flights, complementing satellites, would provide regular scrutiny for both sides. Such unprecedented territorial access would show the world the true meaning of the concept of openness. The very Soviet willingness to embrace such a concept would reveal their commitment to change.

Where there is cooperation, there can be a broader economic relationship; but economic relations have been stifled by Soviet internal policies. They've been injured by Moscow's practice of using the cloak of commerce to steal technology from the West. Ending discriminatory treatment of U.S. firms would be a helpful step. Trade and financial transactions should take place on a normal commercial basis.

And should the Soviet Union codify its emigration laws in accord with international standards and implement its new laws faithfully, I am prepared to work with Congress for a temporary waiver of the Jackson-Vanik amendment, opening the way to extending most favored nation trade status to the Soviet Union. After that last weighty point, I can just imagine what you were thinking: It had to happen. Your last day in college had to end with yet another political science lecture.

In all seriousness, the policy I have just described has everything to do with you. Today you graduate. You're going to start careers and families, and you will become the leaders of America in the next century. And what kind of world will you know? Perhaps the world order of the future will truly be a family of nations.

It's a sad truth that nothing forces us to recognize our common humanity more swiftly than a natural disaster. I'm thinking, of course, of Soviet Armenia just a few months ago, a tragedy without blame, warlike devastation without war. Our son took our 12-year-old grandson to Yerevan. At the end of the day of comforting the injured and consoling the bereaved, the father and son went to church, sat down together in the midst of the ruins, and wept. How can our two countries magnify this simple expression of caring? How can we convey the good will of our people?

Forty-three years ago, a young lieutenant by the name of Albert Kotzebue, the class of 1945 at Texas A&M, was the first American soldier to shake hands with the Soviets at the bank of the Elbe River. Once again, we are ready to extend our hand. Once again, we are ready for a hand in return. And once again, it is a time for peace.

Thank you for inviting me to Texas A&M. I wish you the very best in years to come. God bless you all. Thank you very much.

## 14. President George H. W. Bush's Address to the Nation Announcing United States Military Action in Panama, December 20, 1989

My fellow citizens, last night I ordered U.S. military forces to Panama. No President takes such action lightly. This morning I want to tell you what I did and why I did it.

For nearly 2 years, the United States, nations of Latin America and the Caribbean have worked together to resolve the crisis in Panama. The goals of the United States have been to safeguard the lives of Americans, to defend democracy in Panama, to combat drug trafficking, and to protect the integrity of the Panama Canal treaty. Many attempts have been made to resolve this crisis through diplomacy and negotiations. All were rejected by the dictator of Panama, General Manuel Noriega, an indicted drug trafficker.

Last Friday, Noriega declared his military dictatorship to be in a state of war with the United States and publicly threatened the lives of Americans in Panama. The very next day, forces under his command shot and killed an unarmed American serviceman; wounded another; arrested and brutally beat a third American serviceman; and then brutally interrogated his wife, threatening her with sexual abuse. That was enough.

General Noriega's reckless threats and attacks upon Americans in Panama created an imminent danger to the 35,000 American citizens in Panama. As President, I have no higher obligation than to safeguard the lives of American citizens. And that is why I directed our Armed Forces to protect the lives of American citizens in Panama and to bring General Noriega to justice in the United States. I contacted the bipartisan leadership of Congress last night and informed them of this decision, and after taking this action, I also talked with leaders in Latin America, the Caribbean, and those of other U.S. allies.

At this moment, U.S. forces, including forces deployed from the United States last night, are engaged in action in Panama. The United States intends to withdraw the forces newly deployed to Panama as quickly as possible. Our forces have conducted themselves courageously and selflessly. And as Commander in Chief, I salute every one of them and thank them on behalf of our country.

Tragically, some Americans have lost their lives in defense of their fellow citizens, in defense of democracy. And my heart goes out to their families. We also regret and mourn the loss of innocent Panamanians.

The brave Panamanians elected by the people of Panama in the elections last May, President Guillermo Endara and Vice Presidents Calderon and Ford, have assumed the rightful leadership of their country. You remember those horrible pictures of newly elected Vice President Ford, covered head to toe with blood, beaten mercilessly by so-called "dignity battalions." Well, the United States today recognizes the democratically elected government of President Endara. I will send our Ambassador back to Panama immediately.

Key military objectives have been achieved. Most organized resistance has been eliminated, but the operation is not over yet: General Noriega is in hiding. And nevertheless, yesterday a dictator ruled Panama, and today constitutionally elected leaders govern.

I have today directed the Secretary of the Treasury and the Secretary of State to lift the economic sanctions with respect to the democratically elected government of Panama and, in cooperation with that government, to take steps to effect an orderly unblocking of Panamanian Government assets in the United States. I'm fully committed to implement the Panama Canal treaties and turn over the Canal to Panama in the year 2000. The actions we have taken and the cooperation of a new, democratic government in Panama will permit us to honor these commitments. As soon as the new government recommends a qualified candidate—Panamanian—to be Administrator of the Canal, as called for in the treaties, I will submit this nominee to the Senate for expedited consideration.

I am committed to strengthening our relationship with the democratic nations in this hemisphere. I will continue to seek solutions to the problems of this region through dialog and multilateral diplomacy. I took this action only after reaching the conclusion that every other avenue was closed and the lives of American citizens were in grave danger. I hope that the people of Panama will put this dark chapter of dictatorship behind them and move forward together as citizens of a democratic Panama with this government that they themselves have elected.

The United States is eager to work with the Panamanian people in partnership and friendship to rebuild their economy. The Panamanian people want democracy, peace, and the chance for a better life in dignity and freedom. The people of the United States seek only to support them in pursuit of these noble goals. Thank you very much.

# APPENDIX B
# Biographies of Major Personalities

**Baker, James Addison, III** (1930–  ) *White House chief of staff, secretary of the treasury, secretary of state* Born in Houston, Texas, James Baker graduated from Princeton University (1952), served in the U.S. Marines for two years, and then earned his law degree at the University of Texas at Austin (1957). He was working as a lawyer in Houston when an old friend, George H. W. Bush, asked him to run his campaign for the U.S. Senate in 1970. Bush lost, but Baker liked the job and became committed to Republican politics. He served as undersecretary of commerce during President Gerald Ford's term of office and was Ford's campaign manager for the 1976 presidential election. He tried for political office himself in 1978 but failed to win election as Texas's attorney general.

In 1980 Baker managed Bush's campaign for the presidential nomination, which was won by Ronald Reagan. He then became a senior adviser in Reagan's successful campaign and was rewarded with the post of White House chief of staff. With Special Counsel Edwin Meese and Assistant Chief of Staff Michael Deaver, Baker became one of the "Troika" who controlled the president's schedule and strongly influenced policy formulation. His ability to work well with legislative leaders was a significant factor in Reagan's successful first term in office. At the beginning of Reagan's second term, Baker and Secretary of the Treasury Donald Regan swapped jobs. Regan was not effective as chief of staff, and Baker was no more than competent in his Treasury post. The scandals that plagued Reagan's second term are thought by many to stem in part from this move.

In 1988 Baker left the cabinet to manage Bush's campaign for president. As secretary of state under Bush, he saw the reunification of Germany in 1990, and in 1990–91 he helped form the international coalition formed to overturn Iraq's invasion of Kuwait, leading to the Persian Gulf War. He resigned in 1992 to return to his old job as chief of staff and manage Bush's reelection campaign, but he was unable to equal his success of 1988. When Bill Clinton won the presidency, Baker returned to private law practice. The recipient of numerous awards in recognition of his government service, he is highly regarded for his political astuteness and managerial skills, which many believe make him the most important staff member of the Reagan and Bush administrations.

**Bakker, Jim (James Orson Bakker)** (1939–  ) and **Bakker Messner, Tammy Faye (Tamara Faye Bakker)** (1942–  ) *televangelists* Jim Bakker was born James Orson in Muskegon, Michigan, and when he married Tammy Faye Bakker (born in International Falls, Minnesota) in April 1961, he took her last name. They had two children together. In 1964 Bakker was ordained a minister in the Assembly of God, and the couple become tent-revival preachers. In 1974 they founded the PTL (Praise The Lord) Ministry, and its evangelist television show, the *PTL Club,* which proved wildly successful. The Bakkers' appeals for funds brought in large amounts of money, much of which they used for their own purposes. Between 1984 and 1987 they drew salaries of $200,000, and Jim paid himself $4 million in bonuses. Among other extravagances, they acquired six luxurious houses, bought their dog an air-conditioned dog kennel, and spent more than $100,000 for a private jet to fly their clothing across the country.

In 1980 Jim began an affair with church secretary Jessica Hahn and later paid her $265,000 to keep it secret. As the Bakkers' extravagant spending became public, questions began to be asked, and on March 19, 1987, Jim resigned from PTL. His fellow evangelist— and rival—Jerry Falwell took over PTL and, with Jimmy Swaggart and other televangelists, publicly condemned Jim Bakker, who protested that he had been victimized.

Bakker was defrocked as a minister in May 1987 and then indicted on December 5, 1988, charged with embezzling $158 million from the PTL ministry. In October 1989 he was convicted of 23 counts of fraud and conspiracy and sentenced to 45 years' imprisonment and a fine of $500,000. He never ceased to protest that he had been "wickedly manipulated by treacherous former friends and colleagues." Tammy Faye divorced him in 1992, two years before he was paroled in July 1994; she subsequently married Roe Messner and became a gospel and inspirational singer. A movie of her life, *The Eyes of Tammy Faye,* was released in 2000; her autobiography, *Tammy: Telling It My Way,* was published in 1996. That same year Jim Bakker published his own autobiography, *I Was Wrong.* He married his second wife, Lori Graham, in 1998 and returned to broadcasting with *The New Jim Bakker Show* in January 2003.

### Bennett, William John (1943–    ) *secretary of education, drug czar*

William Bennett was born in Brooklyn, New York, and later moved with his family to Washington, D.C., where he attended Gonzaga High School. He obtained his B.A. at Williams College, his Ph.D. at the University of Texas, and his law degree at Harvard. Bennett came to public attention in 1981, when President Reagan appointed him chairman of the National Endowment for the Humanities. He served in this post until 1985, when he was named secretary of education; he subsequently caused a stir with his condemnation of what he termed *academical permissiveness.* Though he aroused the ire of many teachers, his forthright views on the need for discipline in schools made him a popular figure. He resigned from the post on September 20, 1988.

On January 12, 1989, President-elect George H. W. Bush named Bennett director of national drug control policy—the "drug czar." His mission was to prepare a report for Congress within six months, outlining an antidrugs campaign. In September 1989 Bush endorsed Bennett's findings and approved funding of $7.9 billion to implement his proposals. Bennett thereupon retired from public service. He subsequently wrote or edited a series of books on cultural, political, and social issues, advocating a strong moral approach and the encouragement of family values. His *The Book of Virtues* (1993) and *The Children's Book of Virtues* (1995) were best sellers.

In 1993 Bennett cofounded the America Awake organization. He later became chairman and cofounder of the educational organization K12 Inc. and, with former New York governor Mario Cuomo, set up Partnership for a Drug-Free America. He became a sought-after lecturer and wrote feature articles on educational and social matters. His public image was tarnished in May 2003, when it became known that he lost an alleged $8 million gambling during a 10-year period. Nevertheless, he has continued to make public appearances, and his daily "Bill Bennett's Morning in America" broadcasts, which began in April 2004, have a nationwide audience. Bennett lives in Maryland with his wife Elayne, with whom he has two sons.

### Boesky, Ivan Frederick (1937–    ) *financier*

Ivan Boesky was born in a poor area of Detroit, earned his law degree at Detroit College, and subsequently worked as a tax accountant. In the mid-1960s he began to work in the securities sector in New York City. By the early 1980s, he headed Ivan F. Boesky & Company (renamed CX Partners Limited Partnership), a financial organization specializing in arbitrage. He also ran Cambrian and General Securities, based in London, England. Boesky's skill at identifying likely takeover deals before his rivals made him a multimillionaire and a dominant figure among Wall Street traders. He played a leading part in the corporate takeovers that were the fashion in the period. Boesky made no secret of his pride in his abilities, as he demonstrated in his semiautobiographical book *Merger Mania—Arbitrage: Wall Street's Best Kept Money-Making Secret* (1985).

In 1986 Boesky was indicted and convicted on insider-trading charges to which he pleaded guilty on November 14 of that year. It was revealed that he had paid millions of dollars to Dennis Levine, an investment banker with Drexel Burnham Lambert, for private information on takeover targets; when Levine was apprehended, he named Boesky. In a plea-bargain agreement, Boesky agreed to pay $100 million to the Securities and Exchange Commission and inform on other securities fraudsters. He then implicated Michael Milken, "the junk bond king," and recorded their conversations about illicit deals.

Boesky served about 18 months and was barred for life from trading in American securities. His career inspired the 1987 Oliver Stone film *Wall Street,* in which Michael Douglas gave a speech based on

Boesky's 1986 address to business students at Berkeley. Boesky famously asserted: "You can be greedy and still feel good about yourself."

## Brzezinski, Zbigniew Kazimierz (1928– )
*National Security Advisor*

Born in Warsaw, Poland, the son of a Polish diplomat, Zbigniew Brzezinski spent his youth in France and Germany before moving to Canada, where he earned his B.A. and M.A. degrees from McGill University. He went from there to Harvard University, receiving his doctorate in political science in 1953. He taught at Harvard until 1961 and then moved to Columbia University, where he established the Research Institute on Communist Affairs (subsequently the Research Institute on International Change). In 1958 he became a U.S. citizen. During the 1960s he acted as adviser to the Kennedy and Johnson administrations. Although he took a hard line on the Soviet Union, he was influential in President Johnson's "bridge-building" in Eastern Europe. In the last years of the Johnson administration, he served as foreign-policy adviser to Vice President Hubert Humphrey.

In 1973 Brzezinski became the first director of the Trilateral Commission, a group of political and business leaders for the United States, Western Europe, and Japan who worked to strengthen links among those regions. When Jimmy Carter, who was also a member of the commission, campaigned for the presidency in 1976, Brzezinski became his foreign-affairs adviser, and in 1977 President Carter appointed him National Security Advisor. In this capacity he established a foreign-policy "architecture" very different from that taken by his predecessor, Henry Kissinger. He advocated a hard-line stance with the Soviet Union, although he did support the SALT II treaty and worked to improve relations with Communist China. His strongly held views gave him increasing sway over Carter, causing friction between him and Secretary of State Cyrus Vance and subsequent tension with Vance's successor, Edmund Muskie.

After Carter's term as president ended in 1981, Brzezinski returned to Columbia and became a senior adviser at Georgetown University's Center for Strategic and International Studies. In 1989 he was appointed a professor at Johns Hopkins University's Nitze School. His books include *Soviet Bloc—Unity and Conflict* (1960); *Between Two Ages* (1970); *The Fragile Blossom* (1971); and his memoirs, *Power and Principle* (1983).

## Bush, Barbara Pierce (1925– ) *first lady of the United States*

Barbara Bush, born Barbara Pierce, was brought up in Rye, New York; her father, Marvin Pierce, became president of McCall's Publishing. She attended school at Ashley Hall in Charleston, South Carolina, where, at age 16, she first met George Herbert Walker Bush. She became engaged to him two years later in 1943, just before he went off to serve in World War II. She then attended Smith College in Northampton, Massachusetts, but left to marry Bush on January 6, 1945. After he graduated from Yale in 1948, the couple went to Texas, where he went into the oil business.

The Bushes had six children, one of whom, a daughter named Robin, died of leukemia when she was three. Her death affected her mother deeply, and it was during the final period of her daughter's illness that Mrs. Bush's hair turned white. George Bush entered politics in 1962 and went on to occupy a series of posts that involved constant movement and change of homes. Mrs. Bush was to say later that she had moved house 29 times in her marriage. When her husband became vice president in 1981, she became a spokesperson in the cause of literacy, a cause close to her heart because her son Neil had dyslexia. In 1989 she initiated the Barbara Bush Foundation for Family Literacy.

As the vice president's wife, Mrs. Bush observed the role of first lady closely, and when she assumed the position herself, she was seen by many as a welcome contrast to the sometimes controversial Nancy Reagan. Her willing acceptance of her role as mother and homemaker was seen by some feminists to be a retrograde step, an attitude exemplified by some of the students' adverse reaction when she gave the commencement address at Wellesley College, Connecticut, in June 1990. Accompanied by Raisa Gorbachev, wife of the Soviet leader, she won her audience over with her speech and especially her comment that she hoped among the audience there was someone who would also be a support and helpmate to a future president, "and I wish him well."

Mrs. Bush has written three books. *C. Fred's Story* (1984) and *Millie's Book* (1990) raised funds for literacy causes. Her autobiography *Barbara Bush: A Memoir* was published in 1994.

## Bush, George Herbert Walker (1924– )
*vice president, 41st president of the United States*

Born in Milton, Massachusetts, George H. W. Bush was the son of Prescott Bush, an investment banker and

U.S. senator from Connecticut, and Dorothy Walker Bush. He became a student leader at the prestigious Phillips Academy in Andover, Massachusetts, and after graduation he enlisted in the armed forces on his 18th birthday (1942), becoming the youngest pilot in the U.S. Navy. He flew 58 missions during World War II and was shot down by Japanese antiaircraft fire; rescued by a U.S. submarine, he was subsequently awarded the Distinguished Flying Cross. A few months after leaving the navy, in January 1945, Bush married Barbara Pierce. He attended Yale University, and, after graduating in 1948 with a degree in economics, he set up a successful business in the Texas oil industry.

In the late 1950s Bush became interested in Republican Party politics, and in 1964 he campaigned unsuccessfully for a U.S. Senate seat. He won election to the U.S. House of Representatives in 1966 and was reelected in 1968 but left his seat in 1970 to try again for the Senate; he was defeated by Lloyd Bentsen. Shortly thereafter, President Richard Nixon appointed Bush U.S. ambassador to the United Nations, a post he filled from 1971 to 1972. He became chairman of the Republican National Committee in 1973 and initially supported Nixon in the Watergate scandal but subsequently called for the president's resignation. In 1974 he became chief of the U.S. Liaison Office in Beijing until he was named director of the Central Intelligence Agency in 1976. When Jimmy Carter became president, Bush left the CIA and returned to Texas, where he announced his candidacy for president in 1979. He lost the Republican nomination to Ronald Reagan, with whom he had many differences of opinion, but he became Reagan's loyal vice president, and the two developed a close working and personal relationship.

In 1988 Bush won the Republican nomination for president and easily defeated Massachusetts governor Michael Dukakis. He thus become the first vice president since Martin Van Buren to succeed to the presidency by election rather than through the death or resignation of the incumbent. He took office as the cold war was coming to an end but generally followed Reagan's policies. When Saddam Hussein invaded Kuwait in August 1990, Bush painstakingly formed a coalition of European and Arab states with whom the United States routed the Iraqi army and restored Kuwait's freedom in Operation Desert Storm, the first Persian Gulf War of 1991. Though he was later criticized for not invading Iraq and bringing down Hussein, he was adamant about holding to promises made to

Middle Eastern allies, thus prolonging Hussein's reign until the second gulf war was instigated by his son, President George W. Bush, in 2003.

Although Bush achieved significant successes in foreign policy, the weak economy at home joined with his apparent lack of interest in domestic problems to bring down his job approval ratings. He had famously promised during the 1988 presidential campaign that he would not raise taxes, but he did so in 1990, incurring widespread criticism. Public rancor was also aroused by the failing economy and the savings-and-loan crisis, which contributed to his image as a weak leader. These factors plus his disdain for what he called "the vision thing" led to an unfocused reelection campaign in 1992 that resulted in his loss to Bill Clinton. Bush then retired from public life. His son, George W. Bush, was elected president in 2000.

### Carter, Jimmy (James Earl Carter, Jr.)
(1924– ) *39th president of the United States*
One of the most idealistic U.S. presidents, Jimmy Carter—he has rarely used his full name—was born in Plains, Georgia, the son of a peanut farmer; his Baptist upbringing strongly affected his later political career. After graduating from the Annapolis Naval Academy in 1946, he married Rosalyn Smith, with whom he had three sons and a daughter. He served as a naval officer for seven years, upon which he returned to Plains and the family peanut business. In 1962 he was elected to the Georgia state senate, and eight years later he won the governor's office. In this capacity he reorganized many agencies and revolutionized the state government by appointing women and blacks to numerous key posts. His dedication to equality, fairness, efficiency, and ecology attracted some national attention, and even though he was still a relative unknown, he announced his candidacy for the presidency in 1974. Two years later he gained the Democratic nomination and won a narrow victory over Gerald Ford.

During his term as president, Carter achieved a number of reforms in domestic affairs, including a national energy policy and decontrolling prices to stimulate production. As he had done in Georgia, he reorganized the federal bureaucracy, improved efficiency, and brought about reforms in the civil service. He also deregulated the trucking and airline industries; expanded the National Park system; created the Departments of Energy and Education; and appointed record numbers of blacks, Hispanics, and women to government jobs. While his efforts to combat unemployment resulted in almost 8 million new jobs by the end of his term, he failed to bring down inflation and interest rates, and the country entered a short-term recession.

In foreign affairs, Carter championed peace and human rights, and his most significant achievement was to bring about accord between Israel and Egypt during the Camp David talks of 1978. He also oversaw ratification of the Panama Canal treaties, established full diplomatic relations with the People's Republic of China, and completed negotiations with the Soviet Union for the SALT II arms-limitation treaty. Ratification of SALT II never took place, though, as the Soviet invasion of Afghanistan in 1979 heightened tension between the United States and the Soviet Union. However, the greatest crisis of Carter's administration came with the seizure of American hostages by Iranian students in November 1979. Carter's failure to resolve the hostage crisis combined with a severely weakened economy to bring about his defeat by Ronald Reagan in the 1980 presidential election.

After leaving the presidency, Carter continued his efforts at peacemaking and improving human rights. In 1982 he founded the Carter Center, a think tank and activist policy center based in Atlanta. In later years he acted as mediator in local and international conflicts and monitored elections in developing countries. In 2002 he was awarded the Nobel Peace Prize "for his decades of untiring effort to find peaceful solutions to international conflicts, to advance democracy and human rights."

**Casey, William Joseph** (1913–1987) *CIA director*
Born in Elmhurst, New York, the son of a sanitation worker, William Casey graduated from Fordham University in 1934. After a brief time at Catholic University of America, he received a law degree from St. John's University in 1937 and then began to work at the Research Institute of America in Washington, D.C. In 1944, a year after he had joined the U.S. Navy, Casey met and impressed Major General William J. Donovan, the head of the Office of Strategic Services (OSS, the forerunner of the Central Intelligence Agency [CIA]). Donovan made Casey chief of intelligence in the OSS London office.

After the war, Casey spent some time serving as associate general counsel at the European headquarters of the Marshall Plan. From 1948 to 1962 he practiced

law, lectured on tax law at New York University, and wrote several legal and business books. In 1957 he joined a New York law firm in which another partner was Leonard Hall, the Republican Party leader. In 1966 Casey tried unsuccessfully for a congressional seat, and in 1968 he worked for Richard Nixon's presidential campaign.

Casey was appointed chairman of the Securities and Exchange Commission in 1971 and served there for two years before being appointed undersecretary of state for economic affairs in 1973–74. He then served as a member of the Foreign Intelligence Advisory Board and chairman of the Import–Export Bank of the United States before joining the law firm of Rogers and Wells, where he stayed from 1976 to 1981. In 1980 Casey became manager of Ronald Reagan's presidential campaign, improving both its funding and its sense of direction. He was said to have masterminded the October Surprise conspiracy that figured in Jimmy Carter's loss to Reagan.

As director of the CIA under Reagan—the first to be designated a cabinet officer—Casey reorganized the agency and restored morale, but his obsession for secrecy aroused adverse comment, and commentators have likened him to J. Edgar Hoover in abusing his authority. He involved the agency in foreign policy by increasing anticommunist activities in Afghanistan, Central America, and Angola. When conflict with Congress resulted in reduced funding, he sought other ways of financing covert operations in Nicaragua. He was known to have played a key part in the Iran-contra affair, but prior to appearing before a congressional inquiry committee, he suffered a seizure. He died of brain cancer in Glen Cove, New York, in January 1987, leaving many questions unanswered.

**Cisneros, Henry Gabriel** (1947– ) *mayor of San Antonio, secretary of housing and urban development*
Born in San Antonio, Texas, Henry Cisneros was educated in Catholic schools, graduated from high school at age 16, and earned his B.A. at Texas A&M University in 1968. In 1970, a year after marrying Mary Alice Perez, he earned a master's degree in urban planning from Texas A&M. The couple moved to Washington, D.C., where, in addition to working for the National League of Cities, Cisneros became the youngest person ever to be named a White House fellow (1971). He then went to Harvard University for his M.A. in public administration. After working at the Massachusetts

Institute of Technology and earning his doctorate in public administration from Georgetown University (1975), he and his family returned to San Antonio, where he became the youngest person ever to win a seat on the city council, serving three terms.

Elected mayor of San Antonio in 1981, Cisneros became the first Hispanic American to head a major American city. During his four terms in office, he attracted national attention for his development of San Antonio's business sector, especially high-tech companies, and for his success in promoting ethnic cooperation. A candidate for the 1984 Democratic vice-presidential nomination, he was elected president of the National League of Cities in 1985. After leaving public office in 1989, he became chairman of the Cisneros Asset Management Company, in addition to other financial positions.

For family reasons, Cisneros did not run for Texas governor in 1990 and turned down an appointment as U.S. senator from Texas in 1992. In 1993 he accepted an appointment from President Bill Clinton as secretary of Housing and Urban Development (HUD), where he transformed the scandal-ridden department and reformed the nation's public housing system. In 1995, however, it was revealed that he had lied to FBI investigators about his affair with political fund-raiser Linda Medlar while he was mayor of San Antonio, as well as about payments that he had made to her to keep their relationship quiet. In January 1997 he resigned as HUD secretary, and in December he was indicted on 18 counts of conspiracy, perjury, and obstruction of justice. Two years later he negotiated a plea agreement under which he pleaded guilty to lying to the FBI and was fined $10,000. President Clinton pardoned him in January 2001.

Following his resignation from HUD, Cisneros became president of Univisión, a Spanish-language television station. He started American City Vista, a construction company, in 2002.

## Cosby, Bill (William Henry Cosby, Jr.)
(1937–   ) *actor, comedian*
Bill Cosby was born in Germantown, Pennsylvania, and served in the U.S. Navy from 1956 to 1960. He then attended Temple University, paying his way by working as a stand-up comedian. The comedy albums produced from his stand-up acts won him five Grammys and seven gold records. Married in 1965 to Camille Hanks, with whom he had five children, he also

studied at the University of Massachusetts, earning his M.A. in 1972 and his Ed.D. in 1977.

In 1964–65 Cosby appeared on the television show *That Was the Week That Was.* From 1965 to 1968 he costarred in the TV series *I Spy* with Robert Culp. In his groundbreaking role, for which he won three Emmy awards, he portrayed an African American who paid little attention to his color and the difference it made in relations with others. In his later comedy series *The Bill Cosby Show* (1969–71), he played a warm and sympathetic character, Chet Kincaid, who was clearly proud of his blackness. His successful animated series *Fat Albert and the Cosby Kids* (1972–77) used humor to convey positive messages of social and racial importance.

Two more comedy series, *The New Bill Cosby Show* (1972–73) and *Cos* (1976), were less successful, but in 1984 Cosby struck gold with *The Cosby Show.* The show portrayed a likeable, close-knit African-American family, the Huxtables, headed by parents who were both working professionals; Cosby milked his laughs from the ordinary, everyday events of family and working life. The show was a major hit and ran until 1992.

Cosby also produced and starred in *The Cosby Mysteries* (1994–95) and *Cosby* (1996–99). While he has been less successful in films, his books have sold well, with such titles as *The Wit and Wisdom of Fat Albert* (1973), *Fatherhood* (1986), and *Love and Marriage* (1989). A frequent speaker on race relations, his forthright statements on the contrast between the work ethic of Asian children and that of African-American children have led to heated argument from some civil rights groups.

## Dean, Deborah Gore (1954–   ) *executive assistant, department of housing and urban development*
Deborah Gore Dean was born in New York City. Her father, Gordon Dean, was a prosecutor at the Nuremburg Trials and also the first chairman of the Atomic Energy Commission; he died in a plane crash five years after his daughter was born. Her mother, Mary Benton Gore, was former attorney general John Mitchell's companion for the last 14 years of his life. Dean's other family connections to politics include her aunt, Louise Gore, a Republican who ran unsuccessfully for Maryland governor against Marvin Mandel; and her second cousin, former vice president Al Gore.

Dean graduated from high school in 1972 and worked in a number of Georgetown, restaurants and bars while attending Georgetown University; she finally graduated with a B.A. degree in 1980. That year, following the national election, she used her connection with John Mitchell to obtain a low-level job at the Department of Energy, where she worked for 18 months. By November 1982 she was a special assistant at the Department of Housing and Urban Development (HUD). As cutbacks reduced the size of the department and its staff, a vacuum developed, and Dean began to assume authority. In 1984 she became HUD Secretary Samuel Pierce's executive assistant and consequently de facto head of the department, making funding decisions and exercising political clout in awarding contracts.

In 1987 Dean failed to win confirmation as HUD's assistant secretary for community development; among the objections lodged was the charge that she required subordinates to perform personal chores for her during office hours. Two years later, after George H. W. Bush became president, she achieved public notoriety when investigations into HUD practices revealed extensive corruption and misuse of funds. In 1993 she was convicted on 12 felony counts—five of which were later overturned—and she was sentenced to three concurrent 21-month terms in prison, which she has not served due to ongoing appeals. Now married to Richard Pawlik, she lives in Washington, D.C., and operates an antiques store in Georgetown.

### Deaver, Michael Keith (1938–  ) *White House deputy chief of staff*

Raised in Bakersfield, California, Michael Deaver received a B.A. in public administration from San Jose University in 1960 and then became active in Republican politics. He married Carolyn Judy, with whom he had two children. In the mid-1960s he worked as cabinet secretary when Ronald Reagan was governor of California, and he acted as political strategist and fund-raiser during Reagan's 1980 presidential campaign.

Deaver was one of the so-called Reagan Troika, the three Californians who made up Reagan's inner circle during his first presidential term. The other two were Edwin Meese III and James Baker. As deputy chief of staff in the White House, Deaver was considered a "voice for political pragmatism." He looked at everything from a public-relations aspect, with an attention to detail that undoubtedly helped maintain Reagan's popularity. For example, he ensured that morning outside press conferences were held on the eastern side of the White House and afternoon press conferences on

the western side so that the sun always shone on the president.

After James Baker and Donald Regan switched jobs in 1985, Deaver—who had hoped to become chief of staff—left the White House and set up a lobbying firm. Two years later, however, he was indicted for violating laws that limited lobbying by former senior government officials. Found guilty of lying under oath to both Congress and a federal grand jury, he received a three-year suspended jail sentence and a fine of $10,000 and was ordered to perform community service work. He subsequently resumed his Washington lobbying business. Currently vice chairman of Edelman PR, Deaver has written three books: *Behind the Scenes: In Which the Author Talks about Ronald and Nancy Reagan and Himself* (1987, written with Mickey Herskowitz), *A Different Drummer: My Thirty Years with Ronald Reagan* (2001), and *Nancy: A Portrait of My Life with Nancy Reagan* (2004).

### Dole, Elizabeth Hanford (1936–  ) *secretary of transportation, secretary of labor*

Born Elizabeth Hanford in Salisbury, North Carolina, Dole earned her B.A. at Duke University in 1958 before spending a year at Oxford and going on to Harvard, where she received her M.A. in 1960 and her J.D. in 1965. Then a Democrat (and subsequently independent), she joined the Department of Health, Education and Welfare in Washington, D.C., before starting work with a public-interest law firm in 1967. In 1968 she entered the Office of Consumer Affairs under President Lyndon Johnson, and from 1969 to 1973 she was executive director for consumer affairs under President Nixon. In 1973 Nixon appointed her to a five-year term as a member of the Federal Trade Commission.

In 1975 Elizabeth Hanford became Senator Robert Dole's (R, Kans.) second wife and joined the Republican Party. After serving as an assistant in the public liaison office under President Reagan (1981–83), she became the first woman to be named secretary of transportation (1983–87). From 1989 to 1991 she served as secretary of labor under President Bush before resigning and becoming president of the American Red Cross. Foregoing her salary for the first year, she served in that post until 2000. In 1995 she played a large part in her husband's presidential nomination campaign, and she stood herself as a Republican presidential candidate in 2000. In 2002 she was elected Republican senator for North Carolina.

Dole has been given honorary degrees by 40 universities and has received numerous awards, including the National Safety Council's Distinguished Service Award in 1989. With her husband, she is coauthor of *Unlimited Partners: Our American Story* (1996).

**Dukakis, Michael Stanley** (1933–   ) *governor of Massachusetts, Democratic presidential nominee*
The son of Greek emigrants, Michael Dukakis was born in Brookline, Massachusetts, and graduated from Brookline High School in 1951. After graduating from Swarthmore College in 1955, he served two years in the U.S. Army and then attended Harvard Law School, graduating in 1960. In 1963 he married Katherine (Kitty) Dickson, with whom he had three children.

Dukakis's political career began with his election as town meeting member for Brookline, followed by election as chairman of the town's Democratic organization in 1960. He was elected to the Massachusetts state legislature in 1962, 1964, 1966, and 1968, winning an increasing majority each time. He also moderated *The Advocate,* a popular TV show. In 1970 he ran for lieutenant governor of Massachusetts as the running mate of Boston mayor Kevin White, but they lost to Republicans Frank Sergeant and Donald Dwight. Four years later, however, Dukakis won election as governor. Although he worked hard to solve the record deficit and high unemployment, he was forced to reverse his pre-election pledge not to raise taxes. This probably led to his subsequent defeat by Edward King in the Democratic gubernatorial primary of 1978.

Dukakis taught at Harvard's Kennedy School of Government for three years and then won election as governor again in 1982. He played an important part in the economic boom called the Massachusetts Miracle, saving old industries and encouraging new ones. In 1986 Dukakis was reelected for an unprecedented third four-year term, and his colleagues in the National Governors Association voted him the most effective governor in the nation. Two years later he ran for president and won the Democratic nomination, but he lost the election to George H. W. Bush. After his defeat, Dukakis returned to his office as Massachusetts governor until his retirement in January 1991. He then spent three months as a visiting professor at the University of Hawaii, where he taught courses in political leadership and health policy. Since June 1991 he has been visiting professor at Northeastern University's political science department. He has also taught at Florida Atlantic University and at the John F. Kennedy School of Government at Harvard.

**Falwell, Jerry** (1933–   ) *evangelist, founder of the Moral Majority*
Jerry Falwell was born in Lynchburg, Virginia; his father, a businessman, was an alcoholic who died when Jerry was 15. Falwell was an excellent student, but his tendency to get into trouble barred him from presenting the valedictory address at Brookville High School. In 1950 he enrolled in Lynchburg College, but a year later he became a born-again Christian and transferred to Baptist Bible College in Springfield, Missouri, graduating in 1956. That same year he established the Thomas Road Baptist Church in Lynchburg; in 1957 he opened the Lynchburg (now Liberty) Bible College and presented his first televised religious service, "Old Time Gospel Hour." He married Macel Pate in 1958, and in 1971 he founded Liberty University, a Christian college, also in Lynchburg.

Falwell initially opposed mixing politics with religion, but as his ministry grew and his television audience increased, his views gradually changed. By the late 1970s he had become a leader of the New Religious Right, preaching against homosexuality, abortion, pornography, the Equal Rights Amendment, and the women's rights movement. In 1979 he founded the Moral Majority, whose aims were to change educational methods, lobby for conservative causes, and get fundamentalist Christians into politics. The Moral Majority's philosophy was that society should adhere to God's law as laid down in Scripture and the Ten Commandments. Its precepts were echoed in Falwell's book *Listen America* (1980), which brought him thousands of new followers. He supported Ronald Reagan in the 1980 presidential election but later attacked some of Reagan's policies, including the nomination of Sandra Day O'Connor to the Supreme Court.

By the mid-1980s the Moral Majority's membership was near 2 million. In 1987, however, scandals involving fellow televangelists Jim Bakker and Jimmy Swaggart damaged the New Religious Right's reputation. In addition, the Moral Majority had failed to achieve many of its goals, causing a severe drop in membership and a shift of influence to Pat Robertson's Christian Coalition. Falwell took over Bakker's PTL television ministry in 1988 and closed down the Moral Majority in 1989. He has continued his conservative preaching, mostly at Thomas Road

Baptist Church, which has become the biggest congregation in North America.

## Ferraro, Geraldine Anne (Geraldine Anne Zaccaro) (1935– ) *congresswoman, Democratic vice presidential nominee*

Born in Newburgh, New York, Geraldine Ferraro is the daughter of a first-generation Italian immigrant. She was eight when her father died, and the family subsequently moved to the Bronx. In 1956 Ferraro earned her B.A. degree at Marymount College, New York City, and then became a teacher for four years while earning her law degree at night. She graduated from Fordham Law School in 1960 and married John Zaccaro that same year. She was admitted to the bar in 1961 and for the next 13 years worked part-time as a lawyer and part-time for her husband's real estate business while also raising their three children. In 1974 she became an assistant district attorney at the Investigation Bureau in Queens, where she helped to create the Special Victims Bureau and handled cases of child abuse, rape, and domestic violence.

An active member of her local Democratic club, Ferraro resigned her job and ran for Congress in 1978. Elected on her first attempt, she gained the support of House Speaker Thomas (Tip) O'Neill and became a strong advocate of women's rights. She won reelection in 1980 and 1982 and in 1984 was appointed chairwoman of the Democratic platform committee. This position brought her to the attention of Walter Mondale, who chose her as his running mate in that year's presidential campaign. Unfortunately, the controversy surrounding possible election-funding irregularities involving her husband muddied the waters regarding Ferraro's suitability and abilities, although it is not known how much this was a factor in the Democrats' defeat.

Following the election, Ferraro returned to the practice of law. In 1988 she held a fellowship at the Harvard Institute of Politics, and in 1992 she made an unsuccessful bid for the U.S. Senate. She has published two memoirs: *Ferraro: My Story* (1985) and *Changing History* (1993).

## Foster, Jodie (Alicia Christian Foster) (1962– ) *actress, director*

Born Alicia Christian Foster in Los Angeles, Jodie Foster made her debut as an actress at age three when she appeared in a suntan lotion commercial. She continued making commercials until age 6, when she acted in the TV series *Mayberry R.F.D.* She made regular television appearances thereafter. In 1976 she became famous when, at the age of 13, she played the part of a prostitute in *Taxi Driver* (1976) and earned an Academy Award nomination in the Best Supporting Actress category.

Foster graduated as best of her class from the Lycée Français in Los Angeles in 1980 and went on to study English literature at Yale University, graduating in 1985. It was during this period that she once again, albeit unwillingly, hit the headlines when John Hinkley, Jr., tried to assassinate President Reagan. Hinkley was obsessed by Foster's appearance in *Taxi Driver* and sought to win her attention by replicating the film's plot, which involved an attempted assassination.

Foster has enjoyed a varied and influential career in the film business. She made her directing debut with *Little Man Tate* (1991), but she is primarily known for her acting. She has won two Oscars, for *The Accused* (1988) and *The Silence of the Lambs* (1991). She received an honorary doctorate from Yale in 1997 and was also awarded an honorary degree from Smith College. She has two sons: Charles, born 1998, and Kit, born 2001.

## Fox, Michael J. (Michael Andrew Fox) (1961– ) *actor*

Michael Andrew Fox was born in Edmonton, Alberta, Canada on June 9, 1961. Because his father was in the Canadian army, the family moved frequently but eventually settled in Burnaby, Vancouver. At 15, Fox made his debut in the TV comedy *Leo and Me* (1976) before moving to Los Angeles when he was 18. He dropped out of high school for his senior year but later returned to earn his GED in 1995.

In Los Angeles he changed his name to Michael J. Fox as a tribute to character actor Michael J. Pollard. After securing several small parts and appearing in the TV series *Palmerston, U.S.A.* (1980), Fox became well known to the public for his role as Alex P. Keaton in the TV sitcom *Family Ties* (1982–89). He also starred in TV films and the feature film *Teen Wolf* (1985) before starring as Marty McFly in the successful Steven Spielburg-produced film *Back to the Future* (1985). For six months his schedule involved attending the TV studios from 10 A.M. until 6 P.M. to film *Family Ties* and then working on *Back to the Future* at Universal Studios from 6 P.M. until 2 A.M. The film's success produced two popular sequels in 1989 and 1990.

Fox made several more well-received films before starring for four years in the TV series *Spin City*. He left the series in 2000 with the onset of Parkinson's disease, initially diagnosed in 1991. In 1988 he married Tracy Pollan, who had played his girlfriend on *Family Ties;* they have four children. In 2002 Fox published a memoir of his life since his Parkinson's diagnosis, entitled *Lucky Man.*

**Gallo, Robert C.** (1937– ) *pathologist, virologist*
Brought up in Connecticut, Robert Gallo's interest in medicine began when he was 16, triggered by the death of his sister from leukemia. He graduated as a biology major from Providence College in 1959 and continued his medical research studies at Jefferson Medical College in Philadelphia. He published his first scientific paper there in 1962 and gained his M.D. in 1963. He went on to Chicago to work on blood-cell biology and the biosynthesis of hemoglobin.

In 1965 Gallo joined the National Institutes of Health in Maryland, where he studied the development of chemotherapy for cancer patients, followed by work on the enzymes involved in the synthesis of deoxyribonucleic acid (DNA) components. In 1972 he was appointed head of the newly created research department of the Laboratory of Tumor Cell Biology at the National Cancer Institute, concentrating on cancer-causing viruses, specifically retroviruses. In 1975 Gallo and his colleague Robert E. Gallagher discovered a human leukemia virus, which led in turn to identifying HLTV, the T-cell leukemia virus, in 1981.

After he was appointed head of the AIDS Task Force of the National Cancer Institute, in 1984 Gallo and his colleagues developed a blood test for the human immunodeficiency virus (HIV), the retrovirus that causes AIDS. His earlier identification of HIV had led to some academic rivalry over the equally significant discoveries by the French scientist Luc Montagnier, although they eventually made up their differences. In 1996 Gallo founded the Institute of Human Virology, part of the University of Maryland Biotechnology Institute; in 2002 Montagnier joined the institute as an adjunct professor to speed international research into AIDS. Gallo's work has been recognized by 14 honorary doctorates and numerous scientific and medical honors from countries around the world as well as the World Health Award in 2001.

**Gates, Bill  (William Henry Gates III)**
(1955– ) *software developer, entrepreneur*
The son of a Seattle attorney, Bill Gates was enrolled in Lakeside, a private school noted for academic excellence. His interest in computers began in 1968 when General Electric and then the Computer Center Corporation (CCC) rented computer time to Lakeside for its students. Gates and his friends, including Paul Allen, broke into CCC's security system and altered the files that recorded the amount of time they had used. Realizing their security system needed improvement, CCC hired them to find the weaknesses, giving them unlimited computer time in exchange. Gates later reported that this event enabled him and Allen to develop the skills that would lead to the formation of Microsoft Corporation.

In March 1970 Gates and his friends formed the Lakeside Programmers Group and began to develop computer programs. When defense contractor TRW asked Allen and Gates to solve software problems on their computer, the two realized the business potential of their skills. After Gates entered Harvard in 1973 and, later that year, also took a job with Honeywell, Allen urged him to leave school and set up a software company. Not until 1975, however, when the two developed a version of the BASIC programming language for Micro Instrumentation and Telemetry Systems (MITS), makers of the Altair computer, did Gates finally drop out of Harvard and establish Microsoft with Allen.

Microsoft's development of IBM's original operating system and of software for both IBM-based and Apple computers, as well as Gates's astute business sense, made the company a dominant player in the computer industry by the end of the 1980s. Before long, lawsuits were being brought against Microsoft for monopolistic practices. Its success made Gates, who is also interested in biotechnology and protein-based therapeutics, one of the country's wealthiest men. In January 1994 he married Melinda French, with whom he has three children. He and his wife have endowed a foundation with more than $5 billion to support initiatives in health and learning around the world. He has published two books: *The Road Ahead* (1995) and *Speed of Thought* (1999).

**Gorbachev, Mikhail** (1931– ) *Soviet general secretary, president of the USSR*
Born in the then famine-stricken Caucasus region, Mikhail Gorbachev came from peasant stock. At 14 he began to work as an agricultural machinist and so

impressed local leaders that he was allowed to enroll at Moscow University, where he studied law and joined the Communist Party. He became a full member in 1952, took his degree in 1955, and married Raisa Maximovna Titorenko the same year. Gorbachev rose slowly through the ranks as an administrator in the Stravropol area. He took another degree in agronomics and economics in 1967. By 1978 he had become secretary of the Agriculture Central Committee, and in 1980 he became the youngest member of the Politburo.

In 1982 Premier Yuri Andropov, also from the Stavropol district, made Gorbachev a protégé. He attended foreign conferences, met Western politicians, and, on a brief visit to London in 1984, impressed Prime Minister Margaret Thatcher, who said, "I like Mr. Gorbachev. We can do business together." In March 1985, following the deaths of Andropov and Konstantin Chernenko, Gorbachev became secretary of the Communist Party and thus leader of the Soviet Union. He inherited severe domestic problems at a time when the United States took a strong anticommunist stance and was building up its armed forces. He hoped to reform the USSR by improving living standards and productivity through more democratic government; his policies of glasnost (openness) and perestroika (restructuring) received favorable international comment.

Gorbachev held four summit meetings with President Reagan between 1985 and 1988, with the last two (in Washington and Moscow) particularly noteworthy for the signing of the INF Treaty and Gorbachev's rising popularity. In March 1989 Gorbachev was elected president of the Soviet Union, though his influence was then in sharp decline since his reforms had brought about the collapse of communism throughout Eastern Europe and had little effect on the economy. That year there was revolt all over Europe, but, unlike his predecessors, Gorbachev did not send in Russian tanks; on November 9, demonstrators started to pull down the Berlin Wall.

By the time Gorbachev held his first summit with President Bush in December 1989, the cold war was considered to be over. *Time* magazine named him Man of the Year and Man of the Decade, and in 1990 he won the Nobel Peace Prize for his role in ending the cold war. This, however, did nothing to help the ever-worsening Soviet economy, and in late 1991 Gorbachev was kidnapped by hard-line communists. His rival Boris Yeltsin helped restore him to power, but his power base

had evaporated. On December 25, 1991, he resigned as president of the Soviet Union.

Gorbachev subsequently founded Green Cross International to convert military bases to civilian use, remedying the effects of nuclear contamination and destroying chemical weapons stockpiles in an environmentally friendly way. In 1996 he ran for reelection but received only 1 percent of the votes. In November 2001 he founded the Social Democratic Party of Russia, but he resigned from it in 2004 over policy differences. He published his book *Perestroika* in 1987.

**Gretzky, Wayne** (1961–   ) *ice hockey player*
Born and raised in Brantford, Ontario, Canada, Gretzky started to skate on the Nith River on his grandparents' farm when he was two years old. He began to play hockey at six, practicing on the backyard rink that his father had made with a lawn sprinkler. By the time he was eight, he had scored 378 goals in 82 games. At 17, Gretzky began to play with the Indianapolis Racers, and he was then sold to the Edmonton Oilers, where he was the youngest player to score 50 goals. In 1980–81 he notched 164 points, and the following year he scored 76 goals and received a record 212 points. He also won his first Lester B. Pearson Award, which he won again the following year after registering 196 points in the 1982–83 season. The 1983–84 season saw even more awards, including the Lord Stanley Cup.

Gretzky continued to dominate hockey in the 1980s, although he was sold by the Oilers to the Los Angeles Kings during the 1987–88 season. His transfer aroused a wave of enthusiasm for hockey on the West Coast, which he fully justified by tallying 168 points in the 1988–89 season and becoming the all-time leading scorer in NHL history in his sixth game of the 1989–90 season. In that same season, he won the Art Ross Trophy for leading goal scorer for the sixth time. In 1995–96, his free-agent year, he was traded to the St. Louis Blues, but "The Great Gretsky" then signed with the New York Rangers. In 1997–98 he played for Canada in the winter Olympics, and on April 25, 1999, he played his 1,487th and final game, recording his 2,857th point against the Pittsburgh Penguins. Gretzky was awarded an Honorary Doctorate of Laws by the University of Alberta in 2000.

**Haig, Alexander Meigs, Jr.** (1924–   ) *U.S. Army officer, secretary of state*
Alexander Haig was born in Bala-Cynwyd, Pennsylvania, attended Notre Dame University for a year, and graduated

from West Point in 1947. He served as aide to General Douglas MacArthur in Japan and Korea (1950–51), then returned to the United States, where he studied business administration at Columbia University (1954–55), graduated from the Naval War College in 1960, and obtained his M.A. degree from Georgetown University in 1961.

In 1962, as a lieutenant colonel, Haig became a staff assistant at the Pentagon, at one time serving as special assistant to Secretary of Defense Robert McNamara. In 1966 he was a battalion commander in Vietnam, for which he received a Distinguished Service Cross. Promoted to colonel, he became deputy commandant at West Point and in 1969 was appointed military adviser to National Security Advisor Henry Kissinger. Two years later he became deputy assistant in charge of national security affairs under President Nixon, in which role he participated in the Vietnam peace talks in Paris. Haig was promoted to four-star general in 1972 and became army vice chief of staff in 1973. In the final year of Nixon's presidency, he served as White House chief of staff and was lauded for keeping the government running in the midst of the Watergate scandal; it is believed that he played a crucial part in convincing Nixon to resign. When Gerald Ford became president in 1974, Haig was appointed SACEUR (Supreme Allied Commander Europe) of NATO, serving until 1979, when he retired from the army and became president of United Technologies Corporation.

When Ronald Reagan became president in January 1981, he appointed Haig secretary of state. Haig's insistence on controlling foreign policy led to frequent clashes with other members of the administration. Although he made strong efforts in opposing Soviet expansion, combating international terrorism, and mediating (unsuccessfully) in the dispute between Great Britain and Argentina over the Falkland Islands, his abrasive personality and strong disagreements with Reagan's handling of foreign policy finally led to his resignation in June 1982. He later founded an international consulting firm and tried but failed to win the Republican nomination for president in 1988. He has served on several boards and commissions and written two memoirs: *Caveat: Realism, Reagan, and Foreign Policy* (1984); and *Inner Circles: How America Changed the World* (1992).

### Hart, Gary  (Gary Warren Hartpence)

(1936–   ) *U.S. senator, Democratic presidential candidate*
Gary Hart was born Gary Warren Hartpence in Ottawa, Kansas. His parents were members of the Church of the Nazarene, which forbade smoking, dancing, and alcohol. After graduating from Bethany Nazarene College in Oklahoma City in 1959, he enrolled in the divinity school at Yale University, intending to become a preacher or teacher of philosophy. In 1960 he became involved in politics, campaigning for John F. Kennedy in the presidential election. Soon afterward, Hart left the Church of the Nazarene, changed his last name, and transferred to the law school at Yale, graduating in 1964.

Hart worked in the Department of Justice from 1964 to 1965 and the Department of the Interior from 1965 to 1967, after which he set up a private law practice in Denver, Colorado. In 1972 he managed Senator George McGovern's presidential campaign; he then returned to private practice until he was elected U.S. senator from Colorado in 1974. In Washington he served on the Senate Armed Services Committee, where he urged shifting funds from nuclear weapons to conventional armaments.

After being reelected to the Senate in 1980, Hart became a strong candidate for the 1984 Democratic presidential nomination, winning 25 primaries and caucuses, but was defeated by Walter Mondale. Although he left the Senate in January 1987, he entered the Democratic nomination contest again that year and became a leading contender until media reports revealed his extramarital affair with model Donna Rice. This caused him to withdraw his candidacy temporarily, but his attempts to reenter the race in December 1987 met with little support, and he withdrew again. Hart then returned to his private law practice in Denver until being appointed by President Bill Clinton to serve on the Commission on National Security in 1998.

### Helmsley, Leona  (Leona Mindy Rosenthal)

(1920–   ) *real estate tycoon*
Born in Ulster County, New York, Leona Rosenthal dropped out of school and, in 1938, married attorney Leo E. Panzirer, with whom she had a son, Jay, in 1942. After she and Panzirer divorced in the late 1940s, Leona worked as secretary to Joseph Lubin, a garment industry executive whom she married, divorced, and remarried before parting after another five years. She then joined a real estate firm, became a successful saleswoman, and met the real estate tycoon Harry Helmsley in 1969. He took her into his firm and soon promoted her to senior vice president. In 1971 Helmsley and his wife,

Eve, divorced, and he married Leona the following year. She immediately took over the management of his hotels, and her insistence on perfection played a large part in the success of the Helmsley Palace Hotel on Madison Avenue. However, her volatile temper made her a figure of terror to Helmsley employees, who dubbed her "the Queen of Mean."

In 1983 the Helmsleys bought a large estate in Greenwich, Connecticut, for $11 million and spent another $8 million on alterations. Because of the couple's reluctance to pay the bills for the work, the contractors filed suit and claimed the Helmsleys were writing off the costs as business expenses rather than paying the taxes due. The publicity led to an official investigation that culminated in 188 charges of tax fraud. Leona Helmsley and two members of her staff were brought to trial in 1989; Harry Helmsley was found mentally unfit to stand trial. There was intense public interest in the case as employees testified to the pressures brought on them to save money. Leona was sentenced to 16 years and a $7 million fine, although the prison sentence was reduced on appeal to 18 months. Harry Helmsley died in 1997, age 87, leaving his entire estate of $1.7 billion to Leona.

## Iacocca, Lee (Lido Anthony Iacocca) (1924– )
*business executive*

The son of Italian immigrants, Lee Iacocca was born in Allentown, Pennsylvania, and by age 16 was working 16 hours a day in a fruit market. He graduated from Lehigh University in 1945 and earned his M.A. in engineering at Princeton University in 1946. He then joined the Ford Motor Company as an engineering trainee but soon realized he was better suited to selling. In 1956 Ford sold millions more autos than expected with Iacocca's successful "56–56" program, by which a customer could buy a 1956 Ford for 20 percent down and $56 a month for three years. After Robert McNamara left the company, Iacocca took over the development of the Falcon model, eventually transforming it into the highly successful Ford Mustang.

In 1970 Iacocca became president of Ford, but a power struggle with Henry Ford II led to his dismissal in July 1978. He was immediately approached by Chrysler, where he became president in November 1978. With Chrysler nearing a financial crisis, Iacocca asked the federal government for a guaranteed loan of $1.5 billion dollars on the grounds that the depressed national economy would be unable to accept losing

such a major manufacturing organization. The application roused widespread opposition but was finally approved by Congress in 1980, the biggest federal loan made to a private firm. The guarantee saved the company, and by hard negotiations with the unions and the introduction of fuel-efficient models, Chrysler was able to report record results in three years. Iacocca's national reputation was further enhanced when the loan was fully repaid seven years ahead of schedule.

In 1984 he published his best-selling autobiography, *Iacocca,* followed by *Talking Straight* in 1988, the year he rejected an invitation to stand as a Democratic presidential candidate. After retiring from Chrysler in 1992, he worked on the North American Free Trade Agreement at President Clinton's request. He founded an investment bank in 1994, and in 1995 he joined Kirk Kerkorian in an unsuccessful takeover bid for Chrysler. In 2000 Iacocca approached Daimler-Benz, the German firm who had bought Chrysler in 1998, with a view to returning to the company, but his offer was rejected.

## Jackson, Jesse Louis (1941– ) *religious leader, civil rights activist, Democratic presidential candidate*

Jesse Jackson was born the son of Helen Burns in Greenville, South Carolina; he was formally adopted by his stepfather, Charles Henry Jackson, in 1957. He won a sports scholarship to the University of Illinois, but when he was not allowed to play quarterback, he transferred in his second year to the all-black University of North Carolina Agricultural and Technical (A&T) State College in Greensboro, where he received his B.A. degree in 1964. While at A&T, he became involved in the Civil Rights movement, joined the Congress of Racial Equality (CORE), and participated in the March on Washington in 1963. After his graduation he married Jacqueline Brown and entered a graduate program at the Chicago Theological Seminary. He left in 1966 to work for the Southern Christian Leadership Conference (SCLC) alongside his mentor, Dr. Martin Luther King, Jr.

In 1966 King asked Jackson to direct the Chicago branch of Operation Breadbasket, an SCLC jobs-opportunity program. He served as Operation Breadbasket's national director from 1967 to 1971 and was also CORE's field director in 1967. Jackson was ordained a Baptist minister in 1968, the same year he witnessed King's assassination in Memphis, Tennessee. After King's death, disputes arose between Jackson and other SCLC leaders, and in 1971 he left the organization to found Operation PUSH (People United to Save [later Serve] Humanity). This and a companion project, PUSH-EXCEL, aimed at improving the economic and academic conditions of African Americans, as well as increasing their self-esteem. Jackson's often-repeated slogan became "I am somebody."

In early January 1984, Jackson flew to Syria and negotiated the release of Lieutenant Robert O. Goodman, Jr., an American airman who had been captured by Syrian troops after his plane was shot down near Beirut. The favorable publicity Jackson received boosted his bid for the Democratic nomination for president that year. His decision to run had been triggered by his outrage over the effect of President Reagan's supply-side economic program on African Americans. Though his campaign had problems, his success in registering new voters meant that he did far better than expected in the primaries. He mounted an even stronger campaign in 1988, accumulating 1,105 delegates before losing the nomination to Massachusetts governor Michael Dukakis. Jackson's impact on the presidential race that year was impressive; particularly noteworthy was his "Keep Hope Alive" address to the Democratic National Convention.

In 1990 Jackson won election as one of the District of Columbia's then-new "shadow senators." He has often attracted headlines with his outspokenness, and his efforts in international diplomacy have been both criticized and lauded. Prior to the Persian Gulf War of 1991, he visited Iraq and helped negotiate the release of American hostages in Kuwait. In 1997 President Bill Clinton made him a special envoy and designated him Secretary of State for the Promotion of Democracy in Africa. Two years later Jackson successfully obtained the release of three captured American service members who were being held by Yugoslav forces. In 2000 he was awarded the U.S. Presidential Medal of Freedom.

**Jackson, Michael** (1958–    ) *entertainer*
Michael Jackson was born in Gary, Indiana, to Joe and Katherine Jackson; his mother was a fervent Jehovah's Witness. In 1963, at the age of five, Michael joined his four older brothers in the family music group his domineering father had formed, and his precocity and musical skill soon made him the Jackson Five's leading attraction. The group issued their debut single recording in 1969, when Michael was 11. The Jackson Five subsequently became the first group to have their first four singles top the charts. Jackson made his first solo recording, "Got to Be There," in 1971, and the following year he recorded "Ben," which earned him an Oscar nomination for best song. His popularity grew quickly, and in 1977 he starred with Diana Ross in *The Wiz,* an all-black musical film version of *The Wizard of Oz.* In 1982 and 1983 his *Thriller* became the best-selling album ever: At the top of the charts for 37 weeks, it sold 25 million copies in the United States and another 20 million overseas. More successful recordings followed, and in 1987, the year he left the Jehovah's Witnesses, Jackson released *Bad,* another great success.

Since the 1980s, plastic surgery operations have resulted in considerable alterations in Jackson's physical appearance. Long-circulating rumors about his private life culminated in 1993 with accusations that he had molested a 13-year-old boy; he denied the charge but settled it out of court. In 1994 Jackson married Lisa Marie Presley; they divorced 19 months later. Shortly afterward, in 1996, he married a nurse, Debbie Rowe, by whom he had two children within the next two years; they were divorced in 1999. In February 2002 Jackson had another son by a surrogate mother whose identity has not been revealed, and that same year he began a legal battle with his recording company, Sony.

Jackson was inducted into the Rock and Roll Hall of Fame in 2001, but he is no longer at the top of his field. In January 2004, with a total of 18 Grammys to his name and more than 200 million records sold, he was arraigned on charges of lewd and lascivious acts with a child, bringing further damage to his career. He was declared not guilty of all charges by a jury in June 2005.

**Jobs, Steven Paul** (1955–    ) *computer entrepreneur*
Steve Jobs was adopted and brought up by Paul and Clara Jobs of Mountain View, California. Graduating from Homestead High School in 1972, he enrolled in Reed College, Portland, Oregon, but dropped out after one semester and returned to California, where he and his friend Steve Wozniak designed computer games for Atari. In 1976 they founded Apple Computer Co., named after Jobs's favorite fruit, with their office in the Jobs family garage. They marketed their first personal computer, Apple I, for $666.66, but it was the Wozniak-designed Apple II, released in 1977, that proved a sensation and made their company the leader in the emerging personal computer market. Apple went public

in 1980, though the Apple III released that year did not do well. In 1982 Apple became the first personal-computer company to reach $1 billion in annual sales.

The Macintosh, the first computer to utilize a mouse successfully, was brought out in 1984, the year before Jobs left Apple over policy disagreements with John Sculley, the president he had hired. He then founded NeXT Computer, where he introduced several technical innovations. In 1986 he cofounded Pixar, a computer animation studio that made the revolutionary *Toy Story* in 1995, and he returned to Apple when it took over NeXT in 1996. Apple had lost ground during his absence, but with the introduction of the iMac in 1998, sales soon rose, and the company went from strength to strength. Its innovations include the iPod portable music player and iTunes digital music software. Jobs is notable for drawing a salary of $1 a year, earning him a listing as "Lowest Paid Chief Executive Officer" in the *Guinness Book of World Records*.

## Johnson, Magic (Earvin Johnson) (1959– ) *basketball player*

Earvin Johnson was born in Lansing, Michigan, where he attended Everett School High (1974–77) and earned the nickname Magic for his prowess on the basketball court. As a senior, Johnson averaged 28.8 points and 16.8 rebounds while leading Everett to the state title with a record of 25 wins and one loss. He went on to Michigan State University, and in 1979 his team beat Indiana State in the NCAA championship. That game was the first of many against his rival, Larry Bird, who went on to play for the Boston Celtics.

At 6 feet 9 inches, Johnson was basketball's tallest point guard. He joined the Los Angeles Lakers in 1979 and immediately justified their choice by leading them to the 1980 NBA championship (although Bird was named Rookie of the Year). In the finals against the Philadelphia 76ers, Johnson played in all five positions and scored 42 points. He took the Lakers to four more NBA championships in 1982, 1985, 1987, and 1988. During his career he set records in all-time assists and steals and was nominated for the NBA All-Star Team 12 times and the All-NBA First Team nine times. He was named the league's most valuable player in the 1986–87 season. Many, including his friend Bird, consider him the greatest player of the 1980s.

On November 7, 1991, two month after his marriage to his longtime girl friend, Earletha "Cookie" Kelly, Johnson announced he had contracted HIV, the virus that causes AIDS. He left the Lakers but played with the gold-medal-winning "Dream Team" in the 1992 Olympics. In 1993–94 he returned to coach the Lakers for a season, but this proved unsuccessful, and although he returned as a player in 1995, he retired after 32 games. Since then he has developed successful business interests and worked tirelessly for charities helping those with AIDS and in HIV educational programs. His personal popularity and sports reputation have done much to remove the stigma from HIV-afflicted individuals. He now lives in Los Angeles with his wife and three children.

## Jordan, Michael (1963– ) *basketball player*

Michael Jordan was born to James and Delores Jordan in Brooklyn, New York, and raised in Wilmington, North Carolina. He began to play basketball at an early age and led his Laney High School team to the state championship. He subsequently won a basketball scholarship to the University of North Carolina, and in 1982 he scored the winning basket in the 1982 NCAA championship final against the Georgetown Hoyas. Named college player of the year in 1983–84, he led the American team to a gold medal in the 1984 Olympics. That year he left college and began his professional career with the Chicago Bulls, scoring an average 28.2 points in his first season and making the first of nine appearances on the All-Star Team; he was named Rookie of the Year. Throughout his career he set numerous records, including the most points by a single player in a playoff game (63 points against the Boston Celtics in 1986). At the end of the 1986–87 season, Jordan became only the second player, after Wilt Chamberlain, to score more than 3,000 points in a single season.

In 1991 Jordan led the Bulls to the first of three consecutive NBA championships. After NBA players became eligible to compete in the Olympics, he led the American team to another gold medal in 1992. The following year his father was murdered by armed robbers, and the NBA investigated allegations that Jordan had bet on NBA games. Although cleared, he announced his retirement from basketball, and in 1994 he signed a minor league baseball contract with the Chicago White Sox. His statistics, however, were unimpressive, and in March 1995 he rejoined the Chicago Bulls. In the 1995–96 season he led them to another NBA championship, winning 72 games (losing only 10), the first team to win 70 games in a season. Two more NBA championships followed in 1997 and 1998. In 1996 Jordan was named one of the 50 Greatest Players in NBA History. He retired again in 1999 and became president of the Washington Wizards, returning to play with them for two seasons before retiring for good in 2003.

## Kirkpatrick, Jeane (Jeane Duane Jordan Kirkpatrick) (1926– ) *U.S. ambassador to the United Nations*

Born Jeane Duane Jordan in Duncan, Oklahoma, Jeane Kirkpatrick was educated at Stephens College in Columbia, Missouri; earned her B.A. from Barnard College in 1948; and took her master's and doctorate degrees at Columbia University in 1950 and 1968, respectively. During this period she studied under Franz Neumann, a revisionist Marxist at Columbia. After working as a research analyst in the Office of Intelligence Research in the Defense Department, she went to Europe and studied at the Institute of Political Science in Paris. She married political scientist Evron M. Kirkpatrick in 1955, served on several Democratic Party committees, and became involved with the "Communism in Government" project of the Fund for the Republic Organization. In 1962 she began to teach at Trinity College before moving to George Washington University. She joined the faculty of Georgetown University in 1967, becoming a full professor of political science there the following year, and worked for Hubert Humphrey's failed presidential campaigns of 1968 and 1972. In time she became unhappy with the Democrats and especially with President Jimmy Carter's foreign policies. Her 1979 article in *Commentary* magazine, "Dictatorships and Double Standards," attracted the attention of Ronald Reagan, who hired her to advise on foreign policy during his successful 1980 presidential campaign.

As president, Reagan appointed Kirkpatrick U.S. ambassador to the United Nations and made her a member of his cabinet. Kirkpatrick took a strong, often abrasive, anticommunist line at the United Nations, frequently criticizing the organization itself, and her single-minded support for anticommunist dictators caused many to attack her diplomacy. After Reagan's reelection, she was considered for the post of national security advisor, but her persistent unwillingness to accept other points of view went against her. She resigned in 1985 and returned to teaching at Georgetown University as the Leavey Professor of Government. She then joined the Republican Party, acted as chief foreign policy adviser to Senate Republicans, and became a fellow of the American Enterprise Institute. In 1993 she cofounded Empower America, a conservative think tank. In 2003 President George W. Bush named Kirkpatrick U.S. representative to the UN Human Rights Commission. She has written several books, including *Political Women* (1974), *Dismantling the Parties* (1978), and *The Reagan Phenomenon* (1982).

## Koop, Charles Everett (1916– ) *U.S. surgeon general*

C. Everett Koop was born in Brooklyn, New York, the only child of parents of Dutch and German descent. He went to the private Flatbush School, developed an early interest in surgery, and undertook summer jobs at hospitals while still a teenager. He received his B.A. from Dartmouth College in 1937 and his M.D. from Cornell in 1941, then completed his surgical residency at University of Pennsylvania Hospital in half the allotted nine years. In 1946 Koop became first surgeon-in-chief at the Children's Hospital of Philadelphia. Among his innovations was a device to prevent anesthesia overdoses to children; an improved method in correcting child hernias; and a technique to correct esophageal atresia, whereby the esophagus is detached from the stomach. He established the nation's first neonatal surgical intensive care unit in 1956 and became the first surgeon to separate two Siamese twins joined at the heart, saving the life of one of them in 1977.

After the 1973 *Roe v. Wade* Supreme Court decision, Koop publicized his fears that abortion devalued human life in *The Right to Live, the Right to Die* (1976). Five years later, President Reagan nominated him for U.S. surgeon general. Koop assumed the post in November 1981 and became a respected spokesperson on public health in addition to strengthening the influence of the U.S. Public Health Service. He surprised many by declaring that abortion was a moral issue, not one of public health, and calling for a larger government role in the fight against AIDS. His widely read 1986 report on AIDS emphasized better sex education and the use of condoms to prevent the spread of HIV. He also warned tirelessly against the dangers of smoking, issuing a definitive report in 1988, and championed the rights of infants born with defects to receive medical treatment and for people with disabilities to have access to public facilities and employment.

Koop resigned as surgeon general in October 1989, just before the official end of his second term of office, and became chairman of the National Safe Kids Campaign to reduce accidents among children. In 1939 he married Betty Flanagan, with whom he has three children; a fourth died in a climbing accident in 1968. He is currently a senior scholar at the C. Everett Koop Institute at Dartmouth.

## Lewis, Carl (Frederick Carlton Lewis) (1961– ) athlete

Carl Lewis was born in Birmingham, Alabama, to parents who were both athletes. His boyhood hero was his father's friend, Jesse Owens, who had won four gold medals at the 1936 Berlin Olympics. Lewis grew up in Willingboro, New Jersey, where he began to develop his skill as a long jumper. Selected for the U.S team for the 1979 Pan-American Games, he finished third with a jump equaling that of Jesse Owens back in 1936. He was selected for the 1980 Olympic Games in Moscow but did not take part because of the American boycott that year.

At the inaugural World Championships in 1983, Lewis won three gold medals in the 100-meters race, the long jump, and the 4 x 100 meter relay. The following year, at the Los Angeles Olympics, he equaled Jesse Owen's feat of winning four golds in the 100- and 200-meters races, the long jump, and the sprint relay. In the 1987 World Championships, he again won the 100 meters, the long jump, and the 4 x 100 meters relay, and he was expected to repeat his success in the 1988 Olympics. In Seoul that year, Canada's Ben Johnson beat him in the 100 meters, but Johnson was subsequently disqualified for taking drugs, giving the gold to Lewis, who also won the long jump and finished second in the 200 meters. Four years later, at the 1992 Barcelona Olympics, Lewis again won gold in the long jump and 4 x 100 meters relay. Finally, at the age of 36, he won his last gold medal in the long jump at the 1996 Atlanta Olympics.

Between 1981 and 1991, Lewis was the national 100-meters champion five times, 200-meters champion twice, and long-jump champion six times. In total he has won nine world championships and nine Olympic gold medals, and he is one of only three athletes to have won the same event at four consecutive Olympics. After running competitively for the last time in 1997, he became an actor, appearing in the film *Atomic Twister* (2002). He has written two autobiographies: *Inside Track* (1990) and *One More Victory Lap* (1996).

## Lin, Maya Yang (1959– ) architect

Maya Lin was born and raised in Athens, Ohio, the daughter of Henry Huan Lin and Julia Chang Lin; her parents had fled China before the communist takeover in 1949 and later became professors at Ohio State University. Lin studied sculpture while earning her B.A. (1981) and M.A. (1986) degrees at Yale University School of Architecture. In 1980, still a student at Yale, she entered the national competition to design a memorial for those who had died in the Vietnam War. The following year Lin's proposal—a massive, V-shaped black granite wall bearing the names of more than 58,000 war dead—was selected from among more than 1,400 entries. Her design aroused such considerable controversy that her name was not even mentioned at the memorial's dedication in November 1982. Nevertheless, it became highly popular with veterans and the general public and quickly became one of the most visited sites in Washington, D.C. The memorial has been credited with doing much to heal the nation's psychic wounds from the Vietnam War.

Lin has since become a leading sculptor and architect. Her memorial to the Civil Rights movement in Montgomery, Alabama, features words from Martin Luther King, Jr., inscribed on black granite stone underneath a thin sheet of flowing water. Her other architectural designs include the Peace Chapel at Juniata College, Pennsylvania; Yale University's "Women's Table": the Langston Hughes Library in Clinton, Tennessee; and a federal courthouse in New York City. She is also the creator of "Groundswell," a sculptural landscape at Ohio State University that is composed of a garden of crushed green glass on three levels; and "The Wave Field" at the University of Michigan, which is made entirely of soil covered with grass "billowing" in six-feet waves. These reflect her strong interest in environmental concerns, and she is an advocate for using sustainable energy.

Lin's life and work were portrayed in a 1995 Academy Award-winning documentary film, *Maya Lin: A Strong Clear Vision*. In 2000 she published *Boundaries,* a book she described as a "visual and verbal sketchbook." Like the Vietnam Memorial, her innovative works continue to move and inspire many today.

**Lucas, George** (1944–   ) *filmmaker*

Born in Modesto, California, George Lucas attended Modesto Junior College and hoped to become a racing driver. Forced by an accident to forgo this ambition, he enrolled at the University of Southern California film school, where he made several short films and took first prize at the 1967–68 National Student Film Festival with *Electronic Labyrinth THX–1138 4EB.* Awarded a scholarship to Warner Brothers, he spent the year watching Francis Ford Coppola filming *Finian's Rainbow* (1968). The following year he worked as Coppola's assistant on *The Rain People,* about which he made a short film called *The Film Maker.* In 1969 he and Coppola formed American Zoetrope and made a full-length version of *THX:1138.*

In 1971 Lucas formed his own company, Lucasfilm Ltd. Two years later he cowrote and directed—in 28 days—*American Graffiti,* which won the Golden Globe and five Academy Award nominations. In 1977 he wrote and directed *Star Wars,* which broke box office records and won seven Academy Awards. Its successors, *The Empire Strikes Back* (1980) and *Return of the Jedi* (1983), were equally successful and set new standards in film technology. Lucas's reputation was confirmed by producing *The Raiders of the Lost Ark,* directed by Steven Spielberg, in 1980 as well as its two sequels, *Indiana Jones and the Temple of Doom* (1984) and *Indiana Jones and the Last Crusade* (1989). His *Willow* (1988) and *Radioland Murders* (1994) made little impact, but another Star Wars trilogy has produced more box office successes: *The Phantom Menace* (1999), *Attack of the Clones* (2002), and *Revenge of the Sith* (2005).

During the 1980s Lucas constructed Skywalker Ranch (named after the lead character in the Star Wars films), which became home to his several enterprises, including Industrial Light & Magic (ILM), an award-winning visual-effects studio, and LucasArts Entertainment, developer and publisher of entertainment software. ILM won an Academy Award in 1994 for *Forrest Gump* and has played a key role in more than half of the top 15 all-time box office hits. Lucas thus continues to be a major force in filmmaking today.

**Madonna (Madonna Louise Veronica Ciccione)** (1958–   ) *entertainer*

Born in Rochester, Michigan, Madonna studied dance and drama at high school and attended the University of Michigan on a dance scholarship for two years. In 1977 she went to New York and took modeling jobs while studying under choreographer Alvin Ailey. After a year singing in France, she returned to New York, where she formed the band Breakfast Club with Don Gilroy and then Emmy in 1980 with drummer Steve Bray. Their dance tracks led to a contract with Sire Records in 1982, and "Holiday," written and produced with John "Jellybean" Benitez, became Madonna's first hit, reaching the U.S. Top Twenty and the Top Ten in Europe in 1984.

It was at this stage that Madonna became known for her tough, exhibitionist image. Her 1984 single "Like a Virgin" was the first of her 10 U.S. Number 1 hits. Her video of "Material Girl" (from the *Like a Virgin* album) mimicked Marilyn Monroe's "blonde bombshell" look, one of many images she has projected over the years. Another big—and controversial—hit was 1989's "Like a Prayer," which linked eroticism and religion, was condemned by the Vatican, and led Pepsi-Cola to cancel a sponsorship deal. It also helped to cement Madonna's position as one of the biggest artists of the 1980s, second only to Michael Jackson. She has won several Grammy awards—three in 1998 alone.

Madonna appeared in the Live Aid concert of 1985 and married actor Sean Penn the same year; they divorced in 1989. Her Blond Ambition world tour in 1992 played to packed audiences, and that same year her photographic book *Sex* created a sensation. As an actress she appeared on the Broadway stage in David Mamet's *Speed the Plow* in 1988, and her movies include *Desperately Seeking Susan* (1985), *Shanghai Surprise* (1986, with Penn), *Dick Tracy* (1990), and *A League of Their Own* (1992). Her portrayal of Eva Peron in the film *Evita* won her a Golden Globe award in 1996. In December 2000 she married British film director Guy Ritchie. She has a daughter (Lourdes, born 1996), and, with Ritchie, a son (Rocco, born 2000).

**Mankiller, Wilma** (1945–   ) *principal chief of the Cherokee Nation*

A member of the Cherokee Nation, the second-largest American Indian tribe in the United States, Wilma Mankiller was born in Tahlequah, Oklahoma. Her family name *Mankiller* is an ancestral title that was probably given to the person charged with protecting the tribe's village. In 1957 she and her family moved to California as part of a government relocation program, but in the mid-1970s she returned to Mankiller Flats, the Oklahoma land that had been allotted to her paternal grandfather in 1907. By this time she had worked as a social worker in San Francisco and had become heavily involved in the American Indian rights movement.

In 1977 Mankiller became an economic stimulus coordinator for the Cherokee Nation. While completing her degree in social science and taking courses in community planning at the University of Arkansas, she also initiated projects to develop the Cherokee communities in Oklahoma. In 1983, against considerable opposition, Mankiller was elected deputy principal Cherokee chief. When the principal chief, Ross Swimmer, became head of the Bureau of Indian Affairs (BIA) in December 1985, Mankiller succeeded him and thus became the first woman to serve as chief of a major Native American nation. She was subsequently elected to the position in 1987 and reelected in 1991, serving as chief of the 140,000-strong tribe until 1995.

As principal chief, Mankiller worked to reduce the high unemployment rate among the Cherokee people; improve tribal government, community health care, and education; and preserve Cherokee traditions. She also focused on women's rights, social services, and community development, as well as the creation of the Institute for Cherokee Literacy. Her awards and honors include: American Indian Women of the Year, 1986; Oklahoma Women's Hall of Fame, 1986; Woman of the Year, *Ms. Magazine,* 1987; the John W. Gardner Leadership Award, Independent Sector, 1988; the Indian Health Service Award, U.S. Public Health Service, 1989; and the OSU Henry G. Bennett Distinguished Service Award, 1990. Mankiller was inducted into the National Women's Hall of Fame in 1993, the same year she published her autobiography, *Mankiller: A Chief and Her People.*

Divorced from her first husband in 1974, Mankiller married the former director of tribal development, Charlie Soap, in 1986. Although she has suffered from numerous health problems, including a kidney transplant, her continued work for the Cherokee cause has kept her in the public eye.

### McAuliffe, Christa (Sharon Christa Corrigan)
(1948–1986) *first teacher to fly in space*
Born Sharon Christa Corrigan, Christa McAuliffe grew up in the Boston suburb of Framingham, Massachusetts, and along with the rest of the nation she watched the missions of the Mercury and Apollo space programs on television. Shortly after graduating from Framingham State College, she married Steven McAuliffe and moved with him to the Washington,

D.C., area, where he attended law school, and she became a teacher while also studying for her M.A. at Bowie State College (now University) in Maryland. In 1978 they moved to Concord, New Hampshire, where Steven McAuliffe became an assistant to the state attorney general. In 1984, two years after Christa McAuliffe became a teacher at Concord High School, she learned that NASA was looking for a teacher to become an astronaut to establish communications with students from space. She applied for the program, noting on her application form, "I watched the Space Age being born and I would like to participate." She proposed to keep a three-part journal of her experiences—describing her training, her flight in space, and her feelings after returning to Earth—as well as a video record.

Summer 1985 brought the announcement that McAuliffe had been selected from among more than 11,000 applicants to be NASA's teacher in space, and that fall she began to train for a mission that would take place in early 1986. An immediate favorite with the press and the public, she aroused renewed interest in the space program. Her death along with six other astronauts aboard the space shuttle *Challenger* on January 28, 1986, made that terrible event even more tragic for the nation. Numerous memorials were later established to her, and the Saxonville branch of the Framingham Public Library was renamed the Christa Corrigan McAuliffe Library in her honor.

### McFarlane, Robert Carl (Bud McFarlane)
(1937–    ) *National Security Advisor*
The son of a Texas Democratic congressman, Robert McFarlane, known as Bud, grew up in Texas and graduated from Annapolis at the head of his class. After nearly seven years of service in the Far East, he won an Olmsted Scholarship (for study abroad) and took his Master's Degree at the University of Geneva. After further service in Vietnam and Korea, he served as a White House Fellow (a prestigious public duties internship) in 1971. In 1973 he became military assistant to Henry Kissinger and then worked in the same position under Brent Scowcroft, National Security Advisor to President Ford. After Jimmy Carter became president, McFarlane taught at the National Defense University at Washington until 1979, when he resigned from the Marines. He then spent two years working on the professional staff of the Senate Armed Service Committee.

Following President Reagan's inauguration, McFarlane worked as counsel to the State Department under Alexander Haig until 1982, when National Security Advisor William Clark appointed him deputy assistant for national security matters. A year later, when Clark was appointed secretary of the interior, McFarlane became National Security Advisor and, almost at once, had to deal with the bomb attack on the U.S. Marines headquarters in Beirut, followed by the TWA 847 and *Achille Lauro* hijackings. He also became deeply involved in the arms-for-hostages agreement with Iran, though it is uncertain if he specifically agreed to the diversion of funds to the contras. He resigned on December 4, 1985, but continued to act as a special envoy for President Reagan. When the Iran-contra scandal became public, he attempted suicide by taking Valium on February 7, 1987, the day before he was to testify to the Tower Commission. As a result of the investigation into the affair, McFarlane was charged with withholding information from Congress. He pleaded guilty to four charges in March 1988 and was sentenced to two years' probation, 200 hours of community service, and a fine of $20,000. He was pardoned by President Bush on December 4, 1992. In 1988 he became a counselor at the Center for Strategic & International Studies, Washington, and later became cofounder and CEO of Global Investors. In 2004 he joined Vadium Technology. He is married to Jonda Riley, with whom he has three children.

## Meese, Edwin, III (1931–    ) *White House counsel, U.S. attorney general*

Edwin Meese III was born in Oakland, California, graduated with a B.A. from Yale University in 1953, and earned his law degree at the University of California, Berkeley, in 1958. After serving as Almeda County assistant district attorney from 1958 to 1967, he joined the staff of Governor Ronald Reagan as secretary of legal affairs and subsequently succeeded William Clark as Reagan's executive assistant and chief of staff, serving from 1969 to 1974. In 1975 he joined Rohr Industries as vice president for administration, but after 18 months he became a law professor at the University of San Diego as well as director of the Center for Criminal Justice Policy and Management.

Meese was a member of the California group who persuaded Reagan to stand for the presidency, and he played a large part in the successful campaign of 1980. As a member of the president's close circle of advisers known as the Troika (with James Baker and Michael Deaver), he served as White House counsel from 1981 to 1985, holding cabinet rank. Appointed the 75th attorney general in 1985 after a long confirmation process, he brought in measures to combat drugs and child pornography but resigned in 1988 amid controversy over his financial affairs and involvement in the Iran-contra scandal; no charges were ever brought against him. He was subsequently appointed to the Ronald Reagan Chair in Policy at the Heritage Foundation, a public policy research and education foundation, and became a visiting fellow at the Hoover Institution at Stanford University. Married to Ursula Herrick, with whom he has three children, he published his autobiography, *With Reagan: An Inside Story,* in 1992.

## Milken, Michael Robert (1946–    ) *financier*

Michael Milken was born in Los Angeles and grew up in Encino, California. As a student at the University of California, Berkeley, he invested money for members of his fraternity in return for 50 percent of the profits and also began to develop his theory of low-grade "junk bonds." His belief was that normal bond ratings were based too much on a firm's past performance and failed to take account of such factors as cash flow, business plans, and personnel. By his calculations, low-grade bonds with their high rate of interest could, in fact, be a very good investment.

In 1968 Milken married Lori Hackel and moved with her to Philadelphia, where he earned his M.B.A. at the Wharton School, University of Pennsylvania. In 1970 he went to work for Drexel Corporation, where he became head of bond research. Three years later Drexel merged with Burnham and Company, and Milken became head of the department dealing in non-investment-grade bonds. By 1976 his income was estimated at $5 million a year. In the early 1980s he started to develop buyouts and takeovers financed by manipulating and trading junk bonds. He began to work with arbitrageur Ivan Boesky in 1982, and the two were highly successful—Milken is said to have earned $550 million in 1987—but an investigation into illegal insider trading by the Securities and Exchange Commission (SEC) led to Boesky's conviction in November 1986. Milken resigned from Drexel Burnham Lambert in 1989 and set up his own company, but the SEC brought charges of insider trading and other offenses. Found guilty on six counts, he was given probation on one and a total of 10 years' imprisonment on five others, later reduced to two years. He received a further sentence of 1,800 hours of community service, was banned from trading in American securities, and paid $600 million to the government.

Milken was released from prison in 1993 and set up various enterprises. In 1998 he was again investigated by the SEC and fined $47 million for breaching the ban on trading as a broker. Diagnosed with cancer in 1992, he set up, among other charitable foundations, an organization to search for a cure for cancer.

### Mondale, Walter Frederick (1928– ) U.S. senator, vice president of the United States, presidential nominee

Walter Mondale was born in Ceylon, Minnesota, the son of a Methodist minister of Norwegian descent. He received his B.A. from the University of Minnesota in 1951, and after serving in the army (1951–53), he attended University of Minnesota Law School, graduating in 1956. He was admitted to the Minnesota bar the same year and spent the next four years in private practice.

Mondale began his political activities early. In 1947, as a member of the "Diaper Brigade" of volunteer students, he campaigned for Hubert Humphrey and worked for him again in his 1948 senatorial campaign. In 1949 Mondale went to Washington with Humphrey, and for a year he was executive secretary of Students for Democratic Action. The next year, he managed Orville Freeman's unsuccessful campaign for Minnesota attorney general. Freeman was subsequently elected governor, and in 1960 he appointed Mondale attorney general. When Hubert Humphrey resigned his Senate seat in December 1964 to become vice president, Mondale was appointed to fill the vacancy and then was elected in 1966. As a senator, he was a strong supporter of Great Society legislation and also favored détente with the Soviet Union. Reelected in 1972, he resigned his seat in late 1976 after winning the vice presidency as Jimmy Carter's running mate. Vice President Mondale's particular political goals were civil rights, child care, and arms limitations, and he supported Carter well in these areas.

Mondale stood against Ronald Reagan as the Democratic nominee in the 1984 presidential race and, in a bold move, selected New York congresswoman Geraldine Ferraro as his running mate. Although this political gambit was widely praised, he and Ferraro lost the election. He returned to private practice, though he was called back to public service by President Bill Clinton to be U.S. ambassador to Japan from 1993 to 1996. Mondale stood again for the Senate in 2002 but was unsuccessful and retired to private life. However, he is still active in Democratic politics and has publicly criticized the administration of George W. Bush for its military involvement in Iraq.

### Mulroney, Brian Martin (1939– ) 18th prime minister of Canada

Brian Mulroney was born in Baie-Comeau, Quebec. Bilingual in English and French, he earned his B.A. in 1959 at Saint Francis Xavier University, Antigonish, Nova Scotia, and his law degree in 1962 at Laval University, Quebec City. He served as a student adviser to Prime Minister John Diefenbaker in 1961. In 1965 he joined the firm of Howard, Cate, Ogilvy et al., specializing in labor law. His work on Laurent Picard's Commission of Inquiry on the St. Lawrence Ports gave him experience in negotiating labor relations. In 1974 he served as a member of the Cliche Commission on Industrial Violence, established by Quebec premier Robert Bourassa to look into crime in Quebec's construction industry. The commission found unprecedented corruption and violence, and the high-profile report brought Mulroney's name to public attention.

Although he had done fund-raising and written political pamphlets, Mulroney did not formally enter politics until 1976, when he ran for the leadership of the Progressive Conservative Party. He lost to Joe Clark, probably because he was not well known outside Quebec and had never been elected to Parliament. He then became executive vice president of the Iron Ore Company of Canada, succeeding to president the following year. In 1983, as the only bilingual Quebec candidate, he won the Conservative Party leadership. He secured a seat in Parliament representing Central Nova and became leader of the opposition. The following year he led the Conservatives to their greatest majority in Canadian history, winning 211 seats. He repeated his success in 1988, though with a smaller majority.

As prime minister, Mulroney deregulated key industries, reformed the tax structure, and negotiated the Canada-U.S. Free Trade Agreement of 1988 and the North American Free Trade Agreement of 1992. A sharp increase in federal tax on goods and services in 1991 brought him much unpopularity, but the Nunavut Agreement with the Inuit of the Eastern Arctic was an important step in aboriginal land settlement, and Mulroney's opposition to South Africa's apartheid system gained him international popularity. However, he was unable to secure the constitutional reforms he felt were needed. The desire to recognize Quebec's special status as a "distinct society" hampered his efforts, and the Meech Lake Accord he negotiated in 1987 failed to secure ratification from all 10 provinces. In 1992 he proposed the Charlottetown Accord, which was accepted by all the provincial premiers, but this was rejected in the subsequent national referendum.

Mulroney retired from politics in 1993 and returned to private law practice in Montreal. He was succeeded as party leader and prime minister by Kim Campbell.

### Murphy, Eddie  (Edward Regan Murphy) (1961–  ) *stand-up comedian, actor*

Eddie Murphy was born in Brooklyn, New York, and his father died soon afterward. He was brought up by his mother and stepfather, who moved to Roosevelt, Long Island, when he was 10. By the age of 15, Murphy was writing and performing his comedy routines at youth clubs and local bars. He specialized in impressions of celebrities and caustic social comment, and at 17 he appeared in Manhattan's Comic Strip club. In 1980 he appeared on the TV show *Saturday Night Live* and stayed for four years, becoming its most popular artist. In 1982, the same year he received a Grammy nomination, he made his film debut in *48 Hrs* and signed a lucrative contract with Paramount Pictures. The following year he made a successful tour and an equally successful LP, while his movie *Trading Places* became 1983's highest-grossing film. His smash-hit 1985 film *Beverly Hills Cop* cemented his reputation as the leading comedic actor of the time. This was followed by the popular pictures *The Golden Child* (1986), *Beverly Hills Cop II* (1987), and *Coming to America* (1988). However, he experienced a dip in fortunes when his first venture as a director, *Harlem Nights* (1989), did not do well. *Another 48 Hours* (1990) and *Boomerang* (1992) were also failures, but he enjoyed a comeback in 1996 with his remake of Jerry Lewis's *The Nutty Professor*. This was followed by such successful, family-oriented films as *Doctor Dolittle* (1998), *Bowfinger* (1999), and the animated smash hit *Shrek* (2001). In 1993 he married model Nicole Mitchell, with whom he has four children. The couple separated in 2005.

### Nicklaus, Jack  (1940–  ) *golfer*

Jack Nicklaus was born in Columbus, Ohio, and began to play golf at the age of 10. At 12 he won the first of six successive State Junior titles. He won the U.S. Amateur titles in 1959 and 1962 and first played in the U.S. Open in 1957 at age 17; he came second to Arnold Palmer in 1960. Nicklaus turned professional in 1962 and won the U.S. Open that year, beating Gary Player in an 18-hole playoff. With his blond hair and strong build, he became known as the Golden Bear, hitting the ball farther than any of his rivals. By age 26 he had won three Masters titles, the U.S. Open, the British Open, and the PGA Championship. He endeared himself to golfers across the Atlantic with his enthusiasm for the British Open, played on historic links courses very different from those in the United States.

Nicklaus continued to set records in the 1980s, and with his 1988 victory in the International Golf Tournament in Castle Rock, Colorado, he became the first player to earn more than $5 million in tournament play. Probably his most popular win was his victory in the 1986 Masters—his last major championship. On the last day he was in eighth place, and his son, caddying for him, told him he could win with a score of 65. He did exactly that, playing the back nine in 30 strokes to the huge delight of golfers around the world. He was then 46, the oldest golfer to win the Masters.

Altogether, Nicklaus has won the Masters six times, the U.S. Open four times, the British Open three times, and the PGA Championship five times. Winner of 73 PGA Tour events (second only to Sam Snead), he also played in the Ryder Cup six times and captained the team twice. He continued to play in occasional senior competitions until his retirement in 2005. The veteran champion Gene Sazaren said of Nicklaus: "I never thought anyone would ever put [Ben] Hogan in the shadows, but he did."

### North, Oliver Laurence  (1943–  ) *U.S. Marine officer, National Security Council staff member*

Oliver North was born in San Antonio, Texas, and raised in Philmont, New York. He joined the U.S. Marines, and after graduating from Annapolis Naval Academy in 1968, he served in Vietnam; he was awarded the Silver Star, the Bronze Star for Valor, and two Purple Hearts. After his return, he worked at the U.S. Navy Staff and Command College in Newport, Rhode Island. In 1981, as a lieutenant colonel, North was posted to the staff of the National Security Council. There he became assistant deputy director for political-military affairs, specializing in Central American affairs. In 1983 he was assigned as liaison officer to the contra revolutionaries in Nicaragua. Whether he initiated the plan to contravene the congressional ban on aid to the contras by providing them with funds and support by selling arms to Iran is still uncertain, but he certainly played a key part.

At the Iran-contra congressional hearings in 1987, North claimed his actions had been authorized by his superiors. In March 1988 he was indicted on 16 counts, including obstructing Congress, destruction of documents, and accepting illegal gratuities; he was found guilty in May on three counts. In July 1989 he was sentenced to a suspended three-year term in prison, two years' probation, 1,200 hours of community service, and a fine of $150,000. In July 1990 the U.S. Court of Appeals overturned one of the counts and suspended the other two on the grounds that his immunized testimony to the congressional hearing probably influenced his conviction. In September 1991 all charges were dropped.

During the scandal, North became a public figure who was both celebrated and denigrated, applauded mostly by conservatives who viewed him as a patriot as well as a scapegoat. He resigned from the Marine Corps (on March 18, 1988) and appeared often on radio and televisions programs, in addition to lecturing and writing newspaper columns. In 1994 he stood as the Republican candidate for the U.S. Senate from Virginia but was defeated. Married with four children, he has written several books, including his autobiography *Under Fire* (1991).

### O'Connor, Sandra Day (1930– ) *first woman justice of the U.S. Supreme Court*

A native of El Paso, Texas, Sandra Day graduated from Stanford Law School in 1952 and married her fellow student John O'Connor that same year. Although her academic credentials were excellent—she had graduated third in her class of 102—initially the only job offer she could get was as a legal secretary at a firm whose partners included the future U.S. attorney general William French Smith. She turned down the job and later moved with her husband to Phoenix, where he set up a law practice and she looked after their three sons. In 1965 she joined the Arizona attorney general's office on a part-time basis, serving as assistant attorney general until 1969, when Governor Jack Williams

appointed her to a vacancy in the Arizona Senate. She subsequently won election to the seat, and in 1972 she became the first American woman to be elected majority leader of a state senate. Two years later she was elected to a state judgeship on the Maricopa County Superior Court, and in 1979 she was appointed to the Arizona Court of Appeals.

On July 7, 1981, President Ronald Reagan nominated O'Connor to become the 102nd justice of the U.S. Supreme Court—and its first female member. Although she had never served in the federal court system and was regarded by conservatives as being too moderate (especially in the area of abortion), the Senate voted 99-0 to approve her nomination, and she took her seat in September 1981. O'Connor's voting record was generally conservative, although she occasionally demonstrated her political independence and often acted as a swing vote on the Court, providing a voice of moderation in difficult cases. In *Webster v. Reproductive Health Services* (1989), she was the deciding vote in the 5-4 decision to uphold a Missouri law restricting abortions—in essence, affirming the rights of all states to make specific decisions regarding abortions. However, she did not support repeal of the controversial *Roe v. Wade* decision, believing that the Court's responsibility is to interpret the law, not to legislate.

O'Connor retired from the Supreme Court in 2005. Respected for her diligence, integrity, and ability to find compromise solutions to complex matters, she was widely believed to be tough, cold, and humorless—as well as one of the country's most influential women. But as she said, "The power I exert on the court depends on the power of my arguments, not on my gender."

### O'Neill, Thomas Philip, Jr. (Tip O'Neill) (1912–1994) *Speaker of the House of Representatives*

Born in Cambridge, Massachusetts, Thomas P. O'Neill, Jr., was the son of the superintendent of sewers, from whom he learned the phrase he was to make famous: "All politics is local." Nicknamed Tip after the baseball player James "Tip" O'Neill, he lost his mother at an early age, and some commentators suggest the loss made him sympathetic to the needs of the poor.

O'Neill began his involvement in politics early, campaigning for Al Smith in 1928 and for Franklin D. Roosevelt in 1932. In his senior year at Boston College, he contested a seat on the Cambridge City Council and lost by only 229 votes. After graduating with a B.A.

degree in 1936, he was elected to the Massachusetts House of Representatives, retaining his seat thereafter and serving as speaker from 1949 to 1952. When John F. Kennedy left the U.S. House of Representatives to stand for the Senate in 1952, O'Neill won the vacated seat and kept it for 34 years, from January 3, 1953, to January 3, 1987. Selected to the House Rules Committee in his second term, his lifelong concern for working people and their families was widely admired. This stood him in good stead when fellow Democrats felt he was disloyal for criticizing President Johnson's Vietnam policies. In 1973 O'Neill became majority leader of the House, and he is believed to have played an important part in President Nixon's resignation the following year. In 1977 he became Speaker of the House by unanimous vote, and he supported Jimmy Carter loyally, though he resisted many of the president's attempts to solve economic difficulties with retrenchments in federal funding. He became a leading opponent of Reagan administration policies and managed to save many welfare programs that Reagan had wanted to cut or abolish.

A great wit and an old-fashioned politician, O'Neill won the respect and admiration of many outside his party and successfully shrugged off Republican attacks until his retirement in 1987. His autobiography, *Man of the House,* was published that same year. When he died in January 1994, at age 81, his funeral was attended by former presidents Carter and Ford. He was survived by his wife and five children.

**Peller, Clara** (1902–1987) *television personality*
Originally a manicurist, Clara Peller was in her 80s when she appeared in television commercials for the fast-food chain Wendy's. The diminutive (less than five feet), gray-haired woman was seen at the counters of rival establishments, peering at puny hamburger patties, and crying out querulously, "Where's the beef?" The wording and the little old lady captured the nation's imagination, and her question became a catchphrase of the time, recited by comedians and seen on T-shirts everywhere. When, during the 1984 presidential primaries, former vice president Walter Mondale used the phrase to dismiss the "new ideas" of his rival Senator Gary Hart, many believed "Where's the beef?" helped win the nomination for Mondale. The advertisements (1984–85) were so successful that a "Where's the Beef?" record was made, with Peller repeating the refrain. With her newfound fame, she made TV guest appearances and appeared in two 1985 films, *The Stuff* and *Moving Violations.* That same year she appeared in advertisements for Prego Plus spaghetti sauce with the lines "I found it!" or "I finally found it!" Wendy's fired her with the reported comment: "Clara can find the beef only in one place, and that is Wendy's." She died two years later.

**Pickens, T. Boone  (Thomas Boone Pickens, Jr.)** (1928–    ) *businessman*
T. Boone Pickens was born in Holdenville, Oklahoma, the son of a company lawyer who claimed kinship to Daniel Boone. After moving to Amarillo, Texas, he attended Texas A&M University for a year and then studied for a degree in geology at Oklahoma University, graduating in 1951. After working as a technician in the field and geologist to a petrol company, Pickens set up a small partnership with Eugene McCartt and John O'Brien called Petroleum Exploration, Incorporated (PEI). PEI began by selling oil prospects it had found, retaining a percentage of any early profits. It then went on to drill its own wells and discovered eight gas and one oil well in 1958. In 1960 Pickens acquired a Utah mining company and went on to drill 98 successful wells in 1962. Two years later he bought out McCartt by taking the company public and renaming it Mesa Petroleum.

Although Mesa produced excellent profits from its wells, Pickens decided to expand by acquiring other oil firms. By buying shares in rival companies, he was able to either take them over or, when the stock rose as a result of his bid, to sell his holdings at a profit. He merged Mesa with Hugoton Production of Kansas in 1969 and acquired Pubco Petroleum in 1970. In 1982 he made an offer for City Service Company of Tulsa, Oklahoma, more than 20 times the size of Mesa. He did not succeed, but his shareholders made $30 million when he sold Mesa's City Service holdings. He did the same thing with Gulf Oil, the sixth-biggest oil company in America, and Mesa made $760 million.

Pickens was a controversial figure in the 1980s, criticized as a corporate raider and accused of buying and then breaking up companies, but his methods are now copied by other financiers across the country. Further, his views that executives of large corporations concentrated too much on their own salaries rather than on the interests of their shareholders gained him much popular support. His autobiography, *Boone* (1988), headed the best-seller list for 15 weeks.

## Poindexter, John Marlan (1936– )  *U.S. naval officer, National Security Advisor*

John Poindexter, born in Washington, Indiana, won a place at the U.S Naval Academy after high school and graduated head of his class in 1958, the same year he married Linda Goodwin. He went on to the California Institute of Technology, where he obtained his degree in science in 1961 and his Ph.D. in 1964. He then followed a normal naval career, serving in destroyers and commanding a destroyer squadron before being appointed, in 1971, aide to the secretary of the navy and then to the chief of naval operations. From 1978 to 1981 he was deputy chief of naval education and training before being appointed to the National Security Council as assistant to the National Security Advisor. In this role he was involved in the 1983 U.S. invasion of Grenada. When Robert McFarlane resigned as National Security Advisor in December 1984, Poindexter was promoted to vice admiral and named to replace him.

Regarded as a leading figure in the Iran–contra affair, Poindexter resigned after the scandal broke in late 1986. He informed the investigating Senate committee the following July that he had conducted the operation without President Reagan's knowledge and declared he had no regrets about what he had done. He was indicted on seven felony charges, including conspiracy, lying to Congress, and defrauding the government. Though found guilty of five charges, an appeal in 1991 found him not guilty since his 1987 testimony to Congress, made under immunity, was held to have prejudiced the jury against him. Poindexter subsequently went into industry and founded TP Systems in 1990. In 1996 he became vice president of SYNTEX Technologies, and in 2002 he reentered public life as director of the Pentagon Information Awareness Office.

## Powell, Colin Luther (1937– )  *U.S. Army general, chairman of the Joint Chiefs of Staff*

The son of Jamaican immigrants Luther and Maud Powell, Colin Powell was born in the South Bronx, New York City, and studied at City College, where he joined the ROTC. He graduated with a B.S. degree in 1958 and was commissioned into the U.S. Army the same year. After serving two tours in Vietnam, he studied for a degree in business administration at George Washington University, earning his M.A. in 1969.

During the 1970s, Powell alternated between military appointments, including Korea in 1973, and staff positions in the White House, one of which was a tour in the Office of Management and Budget. In 1979 he was promoted to major general and appointed military assistant to the deputy secretary of defense. In 1981 he took command of the 4th Infantry Division and then served as military assistant to the secretary of defense from 1983 to 1986. In 1986 he was promoted to commander of V Corps in Europe, and from 1987 to 1989 he served as assistant to the president on national security affairs.

In 1989 Powell was the first African American to be named chairman of the Joint Chiefs of Staff, in which post he served until 1993. He coordinated the planning of the Panama invasion of 1989 and won widespread support for his achievement in organizing and coordinating U.S. and coalition forces in the Persian Gulf War of 1991. After leaving the army, Powell published his autobiography, *My American Journey,* in 1995, the same year that he rejected proposals to run in the presidential campaign. Two years later he became chairman of America's Promise—the Alliance for Youth, a charitable body to help needy and disadvantaged American children. In 2001 President George W. Bush appointed him secretary of state. In this post he continued to advocate what has become known as the Powell Doctrine—that U.S. military power should only be used in overwhelming strength to achieve agreed and clearly defined national interests. He resigned in 2005.

## Quayle, Dan (James Danforth Quayle) (1947– )  *U.S. senator, vice president of the United States*

Dan Quayle was born in Indianapolis, Indiana, received his B.A. in political science from DePauw University in 1969, and then joined the Indiana National Guard, serving from 1969 to 1975. In 1974 he took his law degree at Indiana University. While studying and serving in the guard, he became an investigator for the Consumer Protection Division of the Indiana attorney general's office in 1971, and after some months he became administrative assistant to Governor Edgar Whitcomb. He married Marilyn Tucker of Indianapolis in November 1972. From 1973 to 1974 he was director of the Inheritance Tax Division of the Indiana Department of Revenue. In 1976, having been awarded his law degree, he practiced law with his wife in Huntington and worked as associate publisher of the Quayle family newspaper, the *Huntington Herald-Press.*

Quayle was elected to the U.S. House of Representatives in 1976 and 1978. In 1980, at the age of 33, he became the youngest U.S. senator ever elected in Indiana; he was reelected in 1986. As a senator, Quayle, known as a spokesman of the New Right, was a member of the Armed Services Committee, the Budget Committee, and Labor and Human Resources Committee. In 1982, in conjunction with Senator Edward Kennedy (D, Mass.), he initiated the Job Training Partnership Act (JTPA). In August 1988 George H. W. Bush chose Quayle as his running mate in the presidential election, which they won by a convincing margin. As vice president, Quayle made official visits to 47 foreign countries, promoting U.S. trade interests and human rights. Distrusted by many because of his youth and relative political inexperience, he came to be remembered less for his service as vice president and more for his numerous verbal gaffes. The most famous was probably the occasion in June 1992 when he corrected a schoolboy's spelling of "potato" by adding an "e" at the end.

From 1995 to 1999 Quayle was chairman of Campaign America, a political action group. He put his name forward for the 2000 presidential campaign but withdrew after a few months. He has written two books, currently writes a nationally syndicated newspaper column, and is involved in several business ventures, including an investment firm.

## Reagan, Nancy (Anne Frances Robbins Davis Reagan) (1921– ) *first lady of the United States*

Born Anne Frances Robbins in New York City, Nancy Reagan was the daughter of Edith Robbins, an actress, and spent her early childhood with an aunt in Bethesda, Maryland. When she was six, her divorced mother married neurosurgeon Dr. Loyal Davis, and they moved to Chicago; Davis legally adopted Nancy when she was 14. After attending the Girl's Latin School in Chicago, she majored in theater at Smith College in Massachusetts, where she earned her B.A. in 1943. As Nancy Davis she toured with a road company, appeared on Broadway, and eventually got a contract with MGM in Hollywood, where she made 11 films between 1949 and 1956.

Nancy Davis met Ronald Reagan in 1951, when he was president of the Screen Actors Guild. They were married the following year in Los Angeles and had two children: Patricia Ann in 1954 and Ronald Prescott in 1958. By the 1960s her husband had become actively involved in Republican politics, and after he became governor of California in 1967, she worked with numerous charity organizations, spending much time

fund-raising and making personal appearances on their behalf. After Reagan was elected president in 1980, Nancy carried her reputation for expensive elegance and style into the White House, earning her widespread criticism for ostentation in a time of economic cutbacks. As first lady she supported the Foster Grandparent Program, which became the subject of her 1982 book, *To Love a Child,* before becoming increasingly involved on the problems of drug and alcohol abuse among young people. The theme of her antidrug campaign was "Just Say No." In 1985 she hosted a conference at the White House for the first ladies of 17 nations to bring the problem to international attention.

A steadfast advocate of family life, Reagan's support for her husband was unwavering. She monitored his schedule scrupulously, and he consulted her on every matter of importance. Her reported reliance on astrology in making major decisions led to adverse comment from political opponents, but no one could deny her devotion to her husband and care of him in his final years of illness. She published her memoir, *My Turn,* in 1989.

## Reagan, Ronald Wilson (1911–2004) *40th president of the United States*

Born in Tampico, Illinois, Ronald Reagan was a 1932 graduate of Eureka College, Illinois. His first job was as a radio sports announcer in Iowa. In 1937, however, a Hollywood talent agent persuaded him to become an actor, and he went on to make more than 50 films, which include *Brother Rat* (1938), *Knute Rockne—All American* (1940), and *Kings Row* (1941). In 1940 he married actress Jane Wyman, with whom he had two children, Maureen and Michael. They divorced in 1948, and four years later Reagan married Nancy Davis, an actress who gave up her career to devote herself to him and their two children.

When his movie career began to decline, Reagan went into television, hosting the popular *General Electric Theater* for several years, a job that also required him to go around the country visiting General Electric plants. He served as president of the Screen Actors Guild from 1947 to 1952 and from 1959 to 1960. During this time, Reagan's political outlook became increasingly conservative, and the onetime Democrat became a Republican in 1962. He came to public attention during the closing days of the 1964 presidential campaign with a nationally televised address, "A Time for

Choosing," in support of Barry Goldwater. In 1966 Reagan won election as governor of California, and two years later he tried unsuccessfully for the Republican nomination for president. After serving as California's governor for two terms, 1967–75, he tried and failed again to win the presidential nomination (1976). He succeeded in 1980, however, and won an easy victory over Jimmy Carter in that fall's election; at 69 he was the oldest man ever to be elected president. He went on to survive an assassination attempt and serve two full terms in office, the first president to do so since Dwight D. Eisenhower (1953–61).

Reagan's "supply-side" approach to economics was both effective and controversial as he reduced spending in all areas except the military and defense, which received increased funding. However, his dedication to tax cuts and building up the military produced budget deficits that doubled the national debt between 1981 and 1986. His foreign and defense policies were rooted in his hatred for communism, and he stubbornly adhered to his commitment to "peace through strength" via such programs as the Strategic Defense Initiative. Yet he also worked to reduce stockpiles of nuclear arms worldwide and established a warm personal relationship with Soviet leader Mikhail Gorbachev, resulting in the Intermediate Range Nuclear Forces (INF) Treaty of 1988 and, eventually, an end to the cold war.

Reagan's sometimes controversial actions—for example, his support of the Nicaraguan contras and the 1983 invasion of Grenada—led to a strengthening of U.S. power and prestige but also an increase in anti-U.S. feelings and terrorist activity in many areas of the world. The revelations of the Iran-contra affair, in which the proceeds of the sale of arms to Iran were used to fund the contras in Nicaragua, damaged Reagan's reputation, though the public tended to believe that staff members had carried out illicit actions without his knowledge. Regarded as one of the 20th century's greatest communicators, he was also one of the most popular presidents in the nation's history, though bitterly reviled by many leading intellectuals of the day.

After Reagan left the White House in 1989, he wrote his memoirs, *An American Life* (published 1990), and became a public speaker. In November 1994 he announced that he was suffering from Alzheimer's disease, and he spent his remaining years in seclusion at his California home, tended by his wife, Nancy. Following his death in June 2004, he was given a state funeral and buried on the grounds of his presidential library in Simi Valley, California.

**Regan, Donald Thomas** (1918–2003) *secretary of the Treasury, White House chief of staff*
Born in Cambridge, Massachusetts, the son of a railway security guard, Donald Regan excelled at school and won a partial scholarship to Harvard University. While taking a series of jobs to pay his way, he was fourth in the class of 1940 (which included John F. Kennedy) and earned a scholarship to Harvard Law School. He decided, however, to go into the armed forces and was commissioned in the U.S. Marines. He served in the Pacific theater and finished the war as a lieutenant colonel. In 1946 he joined Merrill Lynch & Co. and rose through the ranks to become president in 1968 and chief executive in 1973. From 1973 to 1975 he was also vice chairman of the New York Stock Exchange.

In 1980 President Reagan selected Regan to become the 66th secretary of the Treasury; he took office on January 22, 1981. An enthusiastic and powerful supporter of supply-side economics, he was effective in engineering tax reforms and piloting through reductions in income-tax rates. In 1985 he switched jobs with White House Chief of Staff James Baker. An autocratic man, Regan saw himself as a chief executive officer who made the tough decisions and protected the president from unnecessary worry whenever possible. His methods soon caused other members of the administration to complain that he assumed too much authority and was deciding policy matters not of his concern, essentially acting as a "prime minister." He also aroused the enmity of Nancy Reagan, whose influence and reliance on astrology, he believed, were harming the presidency.

When the Iran-contra scandal broke, Regan was blamed by many for his failure to control the president's staff, even though he had little involvement in the matter. In addition, he was held accountable for the administration's reluctance to reveal the full facts and its apparent cover-up of legally questionable activity. Because of this controversy and his differences with the first lady, Regan was forced to resign. He explained his side of the argument in his book *For the Record* (1988) but was recalled to give evidence in the follow-up independent counsel investigations of 1991–92. After his retirement from public life, Regan took up landscape painting. Married for more than 60 years to Ann

Buchanan Regan, with whom he had four children, he was 84 when he died of cancer.

**Rehnquist, William Hubbs** (1924–2005) *chief justice of the Supreme Court*

The son of a paper salesman, William Rehnquist was born in Milwaukee, Wisconsin, and served in World War II as a weather observer in North Africa. He attended Stanford University (M.A., 1948); Harvard University (M.A., 1950); and then Stanford Law School; he graduated first in his class (1952) and met Supreme Court justice Robert Jackson, who accepted him as a law clerk. In 1953, having completed his clerkship, Rehnquist married Natalie Cornell and moved to Phoenix, Arizona, where he practiced law and became active in local Republican politics. He opposed such liberal moves as busing to implement school integration, and he campaigned for Barry Goldwater in 1964. During this period he became friends with Richard Kleindienst, another Phoenix lawyer who became deputy attorney general in Richard Nixon's administration. On Kleindienst's recommendation, Rehnquist was appointed assistant attorney general for the Justice Department's Office of Legal Counsel in 1969. One of his duties was to screen candidates for the Supreme Court, but Attorney General John Mitchell decided that Rehnquist's name should go forward for the vacancy. Although Rehnquist's conservative views and lack of judicial experience made his nomination controversial, the Senate confirmed his appointment in December 1971.

As a justice, Rehnquist soon made it clear that he intended to stand by his right-wing opinions, and he dissented in *Roe v. Wade,* the famous 1973 abortion case. In 1986, when Chief Justice Warren Burger resigned, President Reagan nominated Rehnquist as his successor. Once again there was strong liberal opposition over his appointment, which was eventually approved but with 33 senators objecting. Rehnquist fully justified his appointment and often defied his reputation for conservatism, supporting a dismissed homosexual CIA agent's right to seek a judicial review and freedom-of-speech claims put forward by *Hustler* magazine. In *Morrison v. Olson* (1988) he wrote the majority verdict upholding the right of Congress to appoint independent counsels to investigate and prosecute high government officials, which had been strongly challenged by the Reagan administration. He earned the reputation of being an effective leader of the Court and of fostering good relations amongst its justices. In 1988 and 1992 he published two popular books on the Supreme Court's history. Diagnosed with thyroid cancer in 2004, he nonetheless remained on the Court until his death on September 3, 2005.

**Ride, Sally Kristen** (1951–   ) *first American woman to fly in space*

Born in Encino, California, Sally Ride left Swarthmore College for a career in professional tennis but returned to academic life after three months. She earned her B.A. in English and B.S. in physics (1973) at Stanford University, and after taking her masters degree at Stanford, she became a teaching assistant while working on her Ph.D. in astrophysics, which she obtained in 1978. That same year Ride became one of six female astronaut candidates accepted by the National Aeronautics and Space Administration (NASA). In 1979 she completed her NASA training and qualified as a pilot. She subsequently served as communications officer at mission control for the second and third flights of the space shuttle *Columbia* in 1981 and 1982.

In June 1983 Ride became the first American woman to go into space when she served as flight engineer on the space shuttle *Challenger*'s second flight. In October 1984, again aboard *Challenger,* she participated in the 13th shuttle mission, but after the *Challenger* tragedy in 1986, all training was suspended. Ride served on the presidential commission investigating the accident; then she became assistant to the NASA administrator for long-range planning. In this capacity, she set up NASA's Office of Exploration and wrote a report on the future of the space program, "Leadership and America's Future in Space." She resigned from NASA in 1987 and became a science fellow at the Center for International Security and Arms Control at Stanford University. In 1989 she was appointed director of the Space Science Institute at the University of California, San Diego. In June 1999 she became executive vice president of space.com, a space industry website, and was soon named president, a post she held for 12 months. After leaving space.com, Ride set up EarthKAM, a NASA Internet project that enables schools to download pictures of Earth taken in space. She went on to found Imaginary Lines, an organization to encourage science, mathematics, and technology among schoolgirls.

Ride has written or collaborated on five children's books about space and was awarded the Jefferson Award for Public Service and the Women's Research and Education Institute's American Woman Award. A two-time winner of the National Spaceflight Medal, she was inducted into the Astronaut Hall of Fame at the Kennedy Space Center on June 21, 2003.

## Robertson, Pat (Marion Gordon Robertson)
(1930–   ) *evangelist, Republican presidential candidate*

An ordained Southern Baptist minister, Pat Robinson was born in Lexington, Virginia, the son of A. Willis and Gladys Churchill Robertson; his father served for 34 years in the U.S. House of Representatives and Senate. Following his graduation from McCallie School, a military prep school in Chattanooga, Tennessee, Robertson attended Washington and Lee University, where he joined the U.S. Marine Corps Reserve. After receiving his B.A. in 1950, he served for two years with the marines in Korea. He then attended Yale Law School, receiving his juris doctorate in 1955, followed by a master of divinity degree from New York Theological Seminary in 1959. That year, Robertson returned to Virginia, where he raised the funds to purchase a bankrupt TV station. He founded CBN (Christian Broadcasting Network) in 1960, and it went on the air for the first time on October 1, 1961. The station's blend of Protestant evangelism and conservative politics proved popular, and it soon attracted sponsors and a strong and loyal audience across the country. By 1977 Robertson had gathered enough financial backing to found Regent University at Virginia Beach, Virginia.

Robertson campaigned unsuccessfully for the Republican presidential nomination in 1988. The following year he founded the Christian Coalition, a conservative Christian group designed to monitor and influence Republican policy; he remained its president until 2001. In 1990 he founded the American Center for Law and Justice, a public-interest law firm aimed at defending religious liberty, the sanctity of human life, and the preservation of family life. Certain of Robertson's claims have caused adverse comment in the past. One well-known example was his claim that the power of prayer had caused Hurricane Gloria to change course in 1985 and avoid his headquarters on Virginia Beach. He made a similar claim in 1989. Critics have also commented on his reported financial involvement with such African leaders as Charles Taylor of Liberia and his investments in the African mining industry. Robertson is the author of 14 books.

## Rose, Pete (Peter Edward Rose) (1941–   )
*baseball player*

Born in Cincinnati, Pete Rose grew up in Anderson Ferry, Ohio, and played both baseball and football at Western Hills High School. He signed with the Cincinnati Reds after leaving school, and by 1963 he was the Reds' regular second baseman. His hard work earned him the nickname Charlie Hustle, and his efforts earned him the title National League Rookie of the Year in 1963. In 1965 Rose batted .312, led the league with 209 hits, and made the first of 17 All-Star teams. He won the batting title in 1968, hitting .335, and again in 1969 with .349. He won it a third and last time in 1973 with a .338 average, leading the league with 230 hits. From 1965 to 1973 he consistently batted over .300 and played on four league championship teams and two World Series winners. In 1975 he was named World Series Most Valuable Player, *Sports Illustrated* Sportsman of the Year, and *The Sporting News* Man of the Year.

In 1978, as a free agent, Rose signed with the Philadelphia Phillies and helped them win the pennant in 1980 and 1983 and the World Series in 1980. In 1984, he joined the Montreal Expos, but when he was offered a chance to return to the Cincinnati Reds as the team's manager as well as a player, he took it. On September 11, 1985, he established his name in baseball history by breaking Ty Cobb's long-standing record when he made his 4,192nd hit. He went on to score a total of 4,256 hits before he retired as a player in 1986. He managed the Reds to four second-place finishes from 1985 to 1988 and then retired in 1988. In 1989 allegations were made that he had lost money betting on horse races, and he was also charged with having bet on baseball games while managing the Reds. Rose denied the charges, but in August 1989 Commissioner A. Bartlett Giametti banned him from the game. Following an investigation, Rose pleaded guilty to income-tax evasion in April 1990 and served five months' imprisonment. Denied entry to the Baseball Hall of Fame, he now lives in California and Florida with his wife and four children.

## Scowcroft, Brent (1925–   ) *National Security Advisor, head of presidential commission*

Born in Ogden, Utah, Brent Scowcroft received his B.S. at West Point in 1947. He subsequently became a fighter pilot for the U.S. Air Force, but after suffering major injuries in a plane crash, he was limited to nonflying assignments. He continued his education at Columbia University, obtaining his M.A. in 1953 and his Ph.D. in

1967. In 1953 Scowcroft began to teach, first at West Point and then at Georgetown University. After a posting to the embassy in Belgrade, Yugoslavia, he returned in 1962 and became head of the political science department at the U.S. Air Force Academy in Colorado Springs. In 1964 he was posted to air force headquarters in Washington, D.C., and in 1967 he taught at the National War College. A year later he was posted to the Department of Defense, where he worked on aspects of national security. By 1971 he was a colonel, and he accompanied President Nixon on a visit to China. Promoted to brigadier general, he visited the Soviet Union in preparation for Nixon's official visit in 1972. He was then chosen by Henry Kissinger to become deputy assistant (later assistant) for national security affairs.

In 1975 Scowcroft, now a lieutenant general, succeeded Kissinger as head of the National Security Council (NSC) and resigned from the air force. He became known as a skillful and diplomatic official involved in the interim SALT II pacts signed by President Ford in 1974 and in the evacuation of U.S. forces from South Vietnam in 1975. After Jimmy Carter was elected president, Scowcroft resigned from the NSC but continued to sit on committees on security, nuclear arms control, and weapons development. In 1983 he headed the Commission on Strategic Forces to examine the potentiality of MX missiles for strategic purposes. The Scowcroft Commission, as it was known, reported in three months, approving the MX missile's introduction and proposing a deployment that would "confound, complicate and frustrate the effects of Soviet strategic war planners."

Scowcroft was a member of the Tower Commission that investigated the Iran-contra affair, which found little at fault in the NSC but much to be criticized among administration officials. In 1989 President Bush appointed him National Security Advisor, in which role Scowcroft played a major role in talks with the Soviet Union; he is credited with coining the phrase *new world order*. Following his service in the Bush administration, he chaired the Forum for International Policy and subsequently became president of The Scowcroft Group, an international business consultancy.

**Shultz, George Pratt** (1920–   ) *secretary of state, secretary of the Treasury, secretary of labor*
George Shultz was born in New York City and grew up in Englewood, New Jersey. He attended private school in Windsor, Connecticut, and studied economics at Princeton University, receiving his B.A. in 1942. He then joined the U.S. Marine Corps, served in the Pacific, and reached the rank of captain. In 1946 he married Helena Maria O'Brien, with whom he had three daughters and two sons. The previous year he had enrolled at the Massachusetts Institute of Technology (MIT), where he earned his Ph.D. in labor relations and then stayed to teach industrial relations. He also served on arbitration panels and was appointed to President Eisenhower's Council of Economic Advisers. After leaving MIT in 1957, he went to the University of Chicago Graduate School of Business, becoming dean in 1962 and serving on several government task forces and committees on labor management and employment.

Appointed secretary of labor by President Nixon in December 1968, Shultz often found himself intervening in labor disputes, despite his view that government should not do so. After 18 months he accepted President Nixon's request to become the first director of the Office of Management and Budget, where he again had to cope with problems of wages and price freezes. In May 1972 Shultz was appointed secretary of the Treasury, but his efforts to contain rising inflation were nullified by a sharp increase in oil prices in 1973, and he resigned in March 1974 to join the Bechtel Corporation.

In July 1982, following Alexander Haig's resignation as secretary of state, President Reagan recalled Shultz to government service as the nation's 60th secretary of state. In this role he became deeply involved with the attempts to settle the problems of the Middle East and Central America as well as the growing threat of international terrorism. He supported President Reagan's Strategic Defense Initiative, and his long experience in labor negotiations helped him play an important part in the United States' improving relations with the Soviet Union and the consequent end of the cold war. Although he won respect for his integrity and inconspicuous style, some blamed Shultz for failing to oppose more strongly the covert operations that resulted in the Iran-contra affair. In 1989 he left government service and joined Stanford University's Hoover Institute and Graduate School of Business. Four years later he published *Turmoil and Triumph: My Years as Secretary of State*.

**Smith, Samantha** (1972–1985) *schoolgirl, antinuclear activist*
Born and raised in Manchester, Maine, Samantha Smith was only 10 years old when, in December 1982, she

wrote a letter to Soviet leader Yuri Andropov expressing her concern about nuclear war. She was 11 when she and her parents flew to the Soviet Union at Andropov's invitation. During her two weeks in the country, she visited Moscow and Leningrad; met Valentina Tereshkova, the first woman in space; and spent several days at the Artek Pioneer Camp, where she made friends with members of the Young Pioneers, a group equivalent to the Girl Scouts and Boy Scouts. She returned to the United States an international celebrity and a social activist. Thereafter, she wrote a book entitled *Journey to the Soviet Union* in which she described her experiences during her historic visit, and she hosted a Disney Channel special about politics during the 1984 presidential campaign. At the Children's International Symposium in Kobe, Japan, she gave a speech in which she suggested that U.S. and Soviet leaders should exchange their granddaughters for two weeks every year, since a president "wouldn't want to send a bomb to a country his granddaughter would be visiting."

In 1985 Smith became an actress on a television series called *Lime Street,* playing Robert Wagner's daughter. In August that year, while returning to Maine from filming an episode of the series, she and her father were killed in a plane crash. Her funeral was attended by a representative of the Soviet embassy in Washington—but no members of the Reagan administration. The Soviet Union subsequently honored her by issuing a stamp of her and naming a diamond, flower, mountain, and planet after her. In Maine, a life-sized statue of Smith was erected near the state capitol, Augusta; it shows Smith releasing a dove with a bear cub—a symbol of both Maine and Russia—by her side. In October 1985 her mother, Jane Smith, established the Samantha Smith Foundation, which is dedicated to teaching peace and encouraging friendship among children of all countries.

**Spielberg, Steven** (1946–   ) *film director, producer*
Born in Cincinnati, Ohio, Steven Spielberg began to make films at home at the age of 12. He enrolled in Long Beach University in California but soon dropped out to pursue a career in filmmaking, becoming an uncredited assistant editor on the classic TV western *Wagon Train.* The first film that he formally directed was *Amblin* (1969), which attracted enough notice for Universal Studios to give him a seven-year contract, an event he commemorated by naming his production

company Amblin. In the early 1970s Spielberg directed television episodes of *Columbo* and *Marcus Welby, M.D.* In 1974 he directed a made-for-TV movie, *Duel,* which, together with his first major feature film, *Sugarland Express,* earned him major acclaim. He achieved world notice with the summer 1975 release of *Jaws,* a film credited with starting the tradition of the summer blockbuster. This was followed by *Close Encounters of the Third Kind* (1977) and the less-successful *1941* (1979). He began to produce movies in 1978 with *I Wanna Hold Your Hand,* directed by Robert Zemeckis.

In 1981 Spielberg had a great success directing *Raiders of the Lost Ark,* produced by his friend George Lucas. A year later he brought out the highest-grossing movie to date, *E.T., the Extraterrestrial.* Using strong story lines, thrilling special effects, and riveting action sequences, Spielberg became the decade's leading producer-director. Among the films he produced were the *Back to the Future* sequence of films, *Young Sherlock Holmes* (1985), *An American Tail* (1986), and *Who Framed Roger Rabbit?* (1988). As a director his 1980s credits include two more films in the Indiana Jones series (1984, 1989), *The Color Purple* (1985), *Empire of the Sun* (1987), and *Always* (1989). His *Jurassic Park* (1993) grossed even more than *E.T.,* and *Schindler's List* won him his long-overdue Oscar for Best Picture and Best Director of 1993. Spielberg continued to dominate the film world through the 1990s with such releases as *Saving Private Ryan* (1998), while his more recent films include *Catch Me If You Can* (2003) and *The Terminal* (2004). In 1995 he joined forces with Jeffrey Katzenberg and David Geffen to found DreamWorks, a studio engaged in producing movies and other creative projects.

**Springsteen, Bruce** (1949–   ) *singer, songwriter*
Bruce Springsteen grew up in Freehold, New Jersey, and began to play in rock-and-roll bands as a teenager. One band was called Steel Mill, and three members would join Springsteen later in the E-Street Band. By the 1970s he was a singer-songwriter in New York, specializing in songs that celebrated the lives of blue-collar workers. In 1972 he signed a recording contract with Columbia, who hoped he would succeed Bob Dylan. The following year he released his debut album, *Greetings from Asbury Park,* which was followed by *The Wild, the Innocent & the E-Street Shuffle.* Neither album sold particularly well, though two songs, "Rosalita" and

"Incident on 57th Street," were to become famous. It was after the second album that Springsteen renamed his backing band the E-Street Band.

Springsteen proved very successful as a live performer because audiences related to his songs of everyday life. His third album, *Born to Run,* came out in 1975 and reached the top three in the album charts. He then set out on a three-year tour that culminated in *Darkness on the Edge of Town* in 1978 and *The River* in 1980. Both won him praise, but both were surpassed by his 1984 *Born in the USA,* which combined the blue-collar image he sought to portray with patriotism; it sold 14 million copies. Two-year and one-year tours followed until 1989, when he separated from the E-Street Band, breaking up a team that had been together for 15 years. In 1992 he released two popular though less-successful albums, *Human Touch* and *Lucky Town,* but he achieved enormous sales with his 1993 song "Streets of Philadelphia," part of the soundtrack for the film *Philadelphia.* It went on to become a 1994 Top Ten hit and win the Academy Award for Best Song. Springsteen then reassembled the E-Street Band and issued his *Greatest Hits* album with them in 1995. Inducted into the Rock & Roll Hall of Fame in 1999, he was still touring in 2005.

Springsteen's first marriage was to actress Julianne Phillips. They divorced in 1987, after which he married his back-up singer, Patti Sciafa.

### Stockman, David Alan (1946–    ) *U.S. congressman, director of the Office of Management and Budget*

David Stockman was born in Fort Hood, Texas, and raised in Michigan. After earning his B.A. degree at Michigan State University (MSU) in 1968, he went on to Harvard University (1968–70, 1974–75). At MSU he had changed his conservative Republican political views and become a strong opponent of the Vietnam War. However, the extreme radicalism he saw at Harvard brought about a reversion to Republicanism as well as a change of studies from divinity to social sciences. While at Harvard, he met Daniel Patrick Moynihan, the prominent Democrat politician, who recommended Stockman as special assistant for Representative John Anderson of Illinois (1970–72). He then became executive director of the U.S. House of Representatives Republican Conference (1972–75).

In 1976 Stockman was elected to the U.S. House of Representatives, representing Michigan. He was reelected in 1978 and 1980 but resigned his seat in January 1981 when President Reagan named him director of the Office of Management and Budget (OMB). The youngest cabinet member in the 20th century, Stockman, who worked up to 18 hours a day, impressed many with his firm grasp of the federal budget and its detail. A fervent supporter of tax and spending cuts, he was initially an enthusiastic supporter of Reagan's supply-side economics program, but his proposals to cut the politically sensitive Social Security budget and other welfare programs proved unsuccessful. In a series of weekly meetings with the *Washington Post*'s William Greider, whom he hoped to convert to his economic views, Stockman revealed his frustration with Reagan's slow-moving policy and his growing doubts about supply-side economics. Greider published Stockman's conversations in the December 1981 issue of *The Atlantic,* which caused an uproar. Stockman offered to resign, but Reagan asked him to remain in his post. Nevertheless, the article alienated Stockman from many of his colleagues and fellow Republicans, and he finally resigned from the OMB on July 9, 1985. He subsequently wrote *Triumph of Politics: Why the Reagan Revolution Failed* (1986), after which he joined the financial firm of Salomon Brothers, New York, and later the Blackstone Group.

### Thatcher, Margaret (Margaret Roberts) (1925–    ) *first woman British prime minister*

Born in Grantham, Lincolnshire, England, the elder daughter of a greengrocer, Margaret Roberts was educated at Kesteven & Grantham Girls School. She then attended Somerville College, Oxford University, where she obtained B.A. and B.Sc. degrees in law and science. She worked as a research chemist from 1947 until 1951, when she married businessman Denis Thatcher; the couple had two children. Mrs. Thatcher became a barrister in 1953, and six years later she was elected to Parliament. She served as secretary of state for education and science from 1970 to 1974, and in 1975 she was elected leader of the Conservative Party. When the Conservatives took power in the 1979 general election, she became the country's first woman prime minister. In this role she took a strong line on the economy, believing in less tax, less public expenditure, and the reduction of state interference in commerce. She privatized many state-owned enterprises, and although unemployment rose to record levels for a period, the long-term results reduced inflation dramatically.

In 1982, against the advice of many, Thatcher responded to the Argentinian occupation of the Falkland Islands by sending a small British force to retake the islands in a sharp and vigorous campaign. Already closely allied in spirit with President Reagan, she had his tacit support during this brief war, and in return she allowed American warplanes to use British airfields for the United States' April 1986 raid on Libya.

At home Thatcher aroused both admiration and controversy. Her firm policy toward IRA terrorists made her their target, and she narrowly escaped death when an IRA bomb exploded in a Brighton hotel during the 1984 Conservative Party conference, killing five of her colleagues. Because of a series of national strikes, she believed trade unions had become too powerful, and she fought against them, using legislative and other measures. Her opposition to the coal miners' strike of 1984–85 finally forced that union to concede defeat, although the price was the closure of many mines and long-term depression in many mining areas. Her firm stance earned her the nickname "The Iron Lady."

Thatcher won the elections of 1983 and 1987, serving as prime minister for 11 years, longer than any other in the nation's history. Concerned at the growing power of the European Union, she resisted their economic and constitutional proposals, arousing opposition among pro-European members of her party and leading to her resignation in 1990. She became Baroness Thatcher of Kesteven in 1992 and published a partial autobiography, *The Downing Street Years,* the following year. In 1995 she published *The Path To Power,* covering her life before becoming prime minister, and in 2002 she published *Statecraft: Strategies for a Changing World.*

### Trudeau, Pierre Elliott (1919–2000) *15th prime minister of Canada*

The longest-serving Western leader in the post–World War II era, Pierre Trudeau was prime minister of Canada from April 20, 1968, to June 4, 1979, and from March 3, 1980, to June 30, 1984. He was born in Montreal, Quebec, studied at Montreal's Collège Jean-de-Brébeuf, earned his law degree at the University of Montreal (1943), and then obtained his master's at Harvard University (1945). After further study abroad, he returned to Canada, taking a job at the Privy Council Office in Ottawa and setting up a law practice. In 1950 he helped found the radical monthly *Cité libre.* He was an assistant professor of law at the University of

Montreal from 1961 until 1965, when, as a Liberal, he was elected to the House of Commons. In 1967 he became a minister of justice in the cabinet of Prime Minister Lester Pearson. When Pearson announced his resignation the following year, Trudeau sought the party leadership, winning it on a split vote and thus becoming Canada's prime minister. Many considered him too radical, and his espousal of participatory democracy to make Canada a "Just Society" lost him much support until he finally abandoned the theory. He was more successful in his initiatives for universal health care and regional development. He took a strong and popular stand against the terrorist movement Front de Libération du Québec during the October Crisis of 1970, declaring martial law after the group kidnapped British High Commissioner James Cross and then kidnapped and murdered Quebec Cabinet Minister Pierre Laporte.

Trudeau had a penchant for unconventional behavior, dating celebrities such as Barbra Streisand, doing a pirouette behind Queen Elizabeth's back, and frequently using obscenities when insulting his opponents. He gained a cult following that became known as Trudeaumania, but in 1971 he seemed to settle down when he married Margaret Sinclair, a former flower child who at 22 was more than half his age. Although they had three sons, the marriage was not successful; they separated in 1977 and divorced in 1984.

Among Trudeau's many goals was a larger role for Canada in world affairs, which he accomplished through his ebullient personality and such ploys as becoming the first Western leader to visit Communist China. He also worked to make Canada less dependent on the United States and to improve the country's commercial relations with Europe. After losing the premiership in 1979 and then regaining it in 1980, Trudeau focused on the repatriation of Canada's constitution. With this accomplished in 1982, he spent his last two years in office working on economic reforms and improved trade relationships among Western and developing nations. He resigned from the Liberal Party leadership in February 1984 after his famous "long walk in the snow" in which he made his decision to retire, but he remained in office until John Turner succeeded him in June that year. In his retirement he continued to be a major voice in Canadian politics. His books include *Federalism and the French Canadians* (1968), *Approaches to Politics* (1970), and *Conversations with Canadians* (1972).

**Trump, Donald John** (1946–  ) *businessman*
Born in Queens, New York, Donald Trump, the son of a builder, attended Wharton Business School at the University of Pennsylvania. He then learned the construction and development business from his father before setting out on his own as a developer and entrepreneur. After moving to Manhattan, he began to build up social and business contacts and soon made his name as a dealmaker. By the 1970s he had begun the real estate deals that were to make his name. Using banks and city governments to finance his projects, he secured large loans on low collateral for prestige acquisitions on which, in turn, he was able to secure further loans. In 1982 he built the Trump Tower on Fifth Avenue and became involved in the New Jersey casino business. His business empire later expanded to include Trump Parc (with 24,000 rental and co-op apartments), the Trump Shuttle airline, a riverboat casino in Indiana, and the New Jersey Generals (United States Football League). In 1990 the recession forced his creditors to seek payment, and Trump, then reportedly more than $900 million in personal debt and $3.5 billion in business debt, had to relinquish much of his empire. However, he was able to restructure much of his liabilities, and by 1994 he had paid off most of his debts. In 1996 he opened a new hotel and office building in New York, and three years later he considered running for the presidency as the Reform Party candidate.

The flamboyant Trump is known as much for his self-promotion and personal life as his business deals. Married to and divorced (1977–92) from Ivana Zelnicek—who famously called him The Donald—his 1993 marriage to Marla Maples in the Trump Plaza Hotel was attended by thousands of guests; they divorced in 1999. His spectacular January 2005 wedding to Slovenian model Melania Knauss also attracted the publicity he loves, further boosted by his role in the popular NBC reality series *The Apprentice*. Trump has written an autobiography and several books on success in business, most notably *Trump: The Art of the Deal* (1988). He has three children with Ivana Trump.

**Ueberroth, Peter Victor** (1937–  ) *business executive, Olympic Games organizer, baseball commissioner*
Peter Ueberroth was born in Evanston, Illinois, the second child of Victor and Laura Ueberroth; his mother died when he was four. Victor Ueberroth remarried in 1942 and moved the family to Davenport, Iowa. By the time Peter reached high school, he held a succession of jobs and, in his sophomore year, became recreation director at an orphanage for children from broken homes. Although he received a small grant for playing water polo at San Jose State University, he paid the rest of his fees by spending 15 hours a week in the classroom and 40 hours in odd jobs. After graduating, he married Ginny Nicolaus and moved to Hawaii, where he became operations manager for a small airline owned by entrepreneur Kirk Kerkorian; he expanded the operation so quickly that Kerkorian offered him part ownership. Ueberroth then set up his own air service between Los Angeles and Seattle and created a successful nationwide travel reservation service, Transportation Consultants, which led him to expand into hotels and travel agencies. By 1978 his First Travel Corporation had become the biggest travel company in the United States after American Express.

Ueberroth came to public attention when, in 1979, he accepted the task of organizing the 1984 Olympic Games in Los Angeles. With no public funding for the games, he sought sponsorship from major corporations, supervised every detail of the planning, and worked without pay the final year. Although the Soviet Union boycotted the games, they were nevertheless a vast success, and Ueberroth proudly reported a profit of $215 million, which was passed on to support youth and sports programs. As a result, *Time* magazine named him Person of the Year for 1984. In October 1984 Ueberroth became commissioner of baseball. During his five-year term, he took strong action against drug users, although he was unable to solve the problem of club owners colluding against free-agency players. In 1992–93 he led the work on municipal recovery after the 1992 Los Angeles riots. He subsequently joined the Contrarian Group, a business management company. In 2003 he entered his name as a candidate for California governor but withdrew it in September 2003. In June 2004 he was named chairman of the United States Olympic Committee.

**Vance, Cyrus Roberts** (1917–2002) *diplomat, secretary of state*
Cyrus Vance was born in Clarksburg, West Virginia, and graduated from Yale University with a B.A. degree in 1939. After earning his law degree from Yale in 1942, he enlisted in the U.S. Navy, serving until 1946, and then went into private law practice. In 1957 he became counsel to the U.S. Senate Armed Services Committee, and three years later he was appointed general counsel

for the Department of Defense. He became secretary of the army (1961–62) under President John F. Kennedy and then deputy secretary of defense (1964–67) under Lyndon Johnson. Initially a strong advocate of the Vietnam War, he eventually changed his views and later urged Johnson to stop the bombing of North Vietnam. After Vance resigned his Pentagon post in 1967, he became special envoy to Cyprus (1967) and Korea (1968). In the latter post he negotiated the release of the USS *Pueblo,* which had been seized by the North Koreans. In May 1968 Johnson appointed him deputy chief delegate to the Vietnam peace talks in Paris, serving under Averill Harriman. After a year in this post, he returned to private law practice.

In 1977 Vance reentered public service when President Jimmy Carter appointed him secretary of state. In this role he worked to maintain the détente with the Soviet Union that was begun by Richard Nixon and Henry Kissinger, and he helped to procure the SALT II treaty of 1979 (although it was never ratified). He also worked toward U.S. recognition of China and played a significant part in the Camp David Accords of 1979. A noninterventionist, he frequently clashed with National Security Advisor Zbigniew Brzezinski on foreign policy, especially over the handling of the hostage crisis in Iran. Following the April 1980 failure to rescue the hostages, Vance resigned from the State Department and returned to private law practice. He later served on several diplomatic missions, however, including heading UN efforts to end violence in Yugoslavia (1991–92). As a UN special envoy from 1991 to 1993, he negotiated cease-fires between warring factions in Bosnia, Croatia, and Nagorno-Karabakh. Vance served on many public bodies and was chairman of the Federal Reserve Bank of New York from 1988 to 1990. His memoir, *Hard Choices,* was published in 1983.

**Volcker, Paul Adolph** (1927–   ) *economist, banker, chairman of the Federal Reserve System*
Paul Volcker was born in Cape May, New Jersey, graduated from Princeton University in 1949, and earned his M.A. at Harvard University in 1951. In 1952 he attended the London School of Economics, following which he worked for the Federal Reserve Bank of New York (1953–57) before joining the Chase Manhattan Bank. In 1963 he was appointed deputy undersecretary in the Department of the Treasury; two years later he became a vice president of Chase Manhattan Bank. From 1969 to 1974 he served as undersecretary for

monetary affairs in the Treasury and played a major part in the United States' abandonment of the gold standard in 1971. He became president of the Federal Reserve Bank of New York in 1975.

In 1979 President Jimmy Carter appointed Volcker to head the Federal Reserve System. With inflation then at almost 13 percent, the new chairman took decisive action, restricting the money supply and raising interest rates. This brought down inflation but also induced widespread unemployment and the worst recession since the Great Depression. However, Volcker's measures achieved the result the country needed as inflation was brought under control, coming down to 3.2 percent by 1983. President Reagan therefore reappointed him for a second four-year term, during which he followed the same prudent approach, but he declined a third term in 1987.

After leaving the Federal Reserve, Volcker taught politics at Princeton University and worked as a successful investment banker, retiring in 1996. In 1992, with Toyoo Gyothen, he published *Changing Fortunes: The World's Money Supply and the Threat to American Leadership.* In 1999 he led the panel that investigated how Swiss banks had handled the accounts of Holocaust victims, and he accepted the post of chairman of the International Accounting Standards Committee Foundation in 2000. In 2002 Volcker led the independent committee overseeing the audit of Enron Corporation's controversial bankruptcy.

**Weinberger, Caspar Willard** (1917–   ) *secretary of defense, secretary of health, education, and welfare*
Caspar Weinberger was born in San Francisco and studied at Harvard, earning his B.A. in 1938 and his LL.B. from Harvard Law School in 1941. He enlisted as a private in the infantry, served in the Pacific theater with the 41st Infantry Division, rose to the rank of captain, and was a member of General Douglas MacArthur's intelligence staff. Following the war, Weinberger clerked for U.S. Court of Appeals judge William E. Orr (1945–47) and then joined the San Francisco law firm of Heller, Ehrman, White and McAuliffe, becoming a partner in 1959.

Elected to the California state legislature in 1952, Weinberger was reelected in 1954 and 1956. In 1967 he became chairman of the California State Government Organization and Economy Commission, and the following year he was appointed director of finance of California by Governor Ronald Reagan. In 1970, after a short period as chairman of the Federal Trade Commission, he was named deputy director of the Office of Management and Budget, becoming director in June 1972. In February 1973 President Nixon appointed him secretary of health, education and welfare, in which role he continued under President Ford until his return to private life in 1975. He then became director on the boards of various commercial firms, including PepsiCo, Quaker Oats, and the Bechtel Company, but he returned to public service when President Reagan appointed him secretary of defense in 1980. He took a strong line as secretary, overseeing a major buildup in American military strength, although he also made clear his strong reluctance to use it in combat.

On November 28, 1984, Weinberger set out the six points that became known as the Weinberger Doctrine. This reflected Americans' widespread popular discontent and resentment regarding the Vietnam War and sought to reassure the nation that such a haphazard military involvement would not recur. Weinberger stated that the United States should not commit its forces to combat unless the vital national interests of the nation or its allies are involved and there is a clear intention of winning, with clearly defined political and military objectives and with a "reasonable assurance" of the support of American public opinion. There were significant weaknesses in the proposals—for example, who was to decide what was "a vital U.S. interest"? Nevertheless, the specific inclusion of public opinion reassured many.

In 1987 Weinberger resigned from the cabinet in the aftermath of the Iran-contra affair, but he served as a member of the President's Foreign Intelligence Advisory Board from 1988 to 1990. In 1992, along with other officials suspected of involvement in the Iran-contra affair, he was indicted on charges of obstruction and lying to Congress but was given a presidential pardon by President George H. W. Bush before the trial opened. In 1989 he became publisher of the business magazine *Forbes,* succeeding to its chairmanship in May 1993.

**White, Ryan** (1971–1990) *hemophiliac AIDS victim*
Ryan White was born on December 6, 1971, and diagnosed as a hemophiliac three days later. Hospitalized frequently during his childhood, he had an operation when he was 13, after which his mother, Jeanne White, had to inform him that he had contracted AIDS from a transfusion of infected blood. It was then believed he had only six months to live. Ryan determined to struggle on as long as he could, but the news of his condition led to his rejection by the community of Kokomo, Indiana, where he lived. When many local parents opposed his attending the local school and the educational authorities became reluctant to admit him, Ryan had to go to court to fight for his right to attend. He won, but his fellow pupils continued to treat him as a pariah. The daily discrimination became so intolerable that he and his mother moved to Cicero, Indiana, in 1987.

In Cicero Ryan attended Hamilton Heights High School, accepted by fellow students who had attended a seminar on AIDS. He testified on his experiences to the Presidential Commission on AIDS, and as his story became known, he was asked to appear on talk shows and at charity events. Celebrities such as Elton John and Michael Jackson befriended him and supported his pleas for tolerance and understanding. Such was the impression he made that a television movie, *The Ryan White Story,* aired on ABC in 1989. Inevitably, though, Ryan's condition worsened, and he died on April 8, 1990, more than five years after he had been diagnosed with AIDS. Four months later, on August 18, Congress passed the Public Law 101-381, the Ryan White Comprehensive AIDS Resources Emergency (CARE) Act to help families and communities cope with the impact of the AIDS epidemic.

**Winfrey, Oprah Gail** (1954–   ) *television talk-show host, producer, actress, philanthropist*
Born in Kosciusko, Mississippi, Oprah Winfrey spent the early part of her life with her grandmother on a farm before joining her mother in Milwaukee when she was six. Subjected to abuse and molestation, she ran away and was then put in her father's care in Nashville, Tennessee. She graduated from East Nashville High School in 1971 and began to broadcast with WVOL radio in Nashville, joining a local television station two years later and attending Tennessee State University. In 1976 she moved to Baltimore to coanchor WJZ-TV news; two years later she became cohost of their talk show *People Are Talking.* In January 1984 she moved to Chicago to host WLS-TV's *AM Chicago* talk show, and within a year it became the most popular in the region. In 1985 it was renamed *The Oprah Winfrey Show.* That same year she played Sofia in Steven Spielberg's film *The Color Purple,*

winning an Oscar nomination as Best Supporting Actress. She also appeared in the film *Native Son.*

In September 1986 *The Oprah Winfrey Show* was syndicated nationally, and it went on to win many awards. The show's formula, with discussions of popular and sometimes controversial topics involving both a panel of guests and the studio audience, inspired many imitators, but Winfrey's charm and intelligence made hers the number-one talk show in the nation. Reversing the letters of her first name, she formed Harpo Productions, which bought *The Oprah Winfrey Show* and made the miniseries *The Women of Brewster Place,* with Winfrey both starring and producing. She also produced and starred in such TV movies as *There Are No Children Here* (1993) and *Before Women Had Wings* (1997), as well as the feature film *Beloved* (1998).

In 1991 Winfrey began a campaign to establish a national database of child abusers; President Clinton signed the "Oprah Bill" into law in 1993. She was named by *Time* magazine as one of the 100 Most Influential People of the 20th Century and received a Lifetime Achievement Award from the National Academy of Television Arts and Sciences in 1998. One of the most powerful people in the entertainment industry, Winfrey is also known for her philanthropy. In 2000 her Angel Network began to present a $100,000 "Use Your Life Award" to people who are improving the lives of others. In 2003 *Forbes* magazine named her the first African-American woman to become a billionaire.

# APPENDIX C
## Graphs and Maps

1. Laffer Curve
2. U.S. Inflation Rate, 1979–1990
3. U.S. Unemployment Rate, 1979–1990
4. U.S. Federal Deficit, 1981–1990
5. Attempted Rescue of Iran Hostages, April 24–25, 1980
6. U.S. Invasion of Grenada, October 25–26, 1983
7. Hijacking of TWA 847, June 14–30, 1985
8. U.S. Raid on Libya, April 14, 1986
9. U.S. Invasion of Panama, December 20, 1989
10. Collapse of Communism in Eastern Europe, 1989–1990
11. Electoral Vote in the U.S. Presidential Election, 1980
12. Electoral Vote in the U.S. Presidential Election, 1984
13. Electoral Vote in the U.S. Presidential Election, 1988

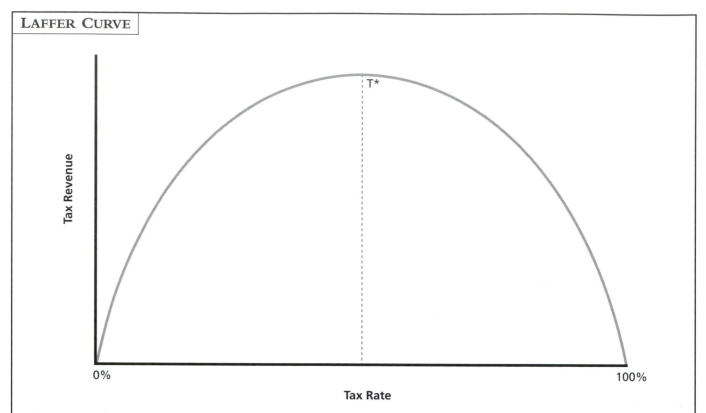

LAFFER CURVE

Tax Revenue

T*

0%                                                                    100%

Tax Rate

The creation of economist Arthur Laffer, the Laffer Curve demonstrates the effects of taxation on the economy. A low tax rate (near 0 percent) means that revenues would be insufficient no matter how well business is doing. However, a high rate (toward 100 percent) would stifle business activity and, therefore, also produce poor tax revenues. The ideal point of taxation is represented by T* on the graph. Tax increases beyond that point mean people have less incentive to work, thereby leading to reduced revenues. The Laffer Curve provided much of the basis for President Reagan's supply-side economics program (also called Reaganomics).

© Infobase Publishing

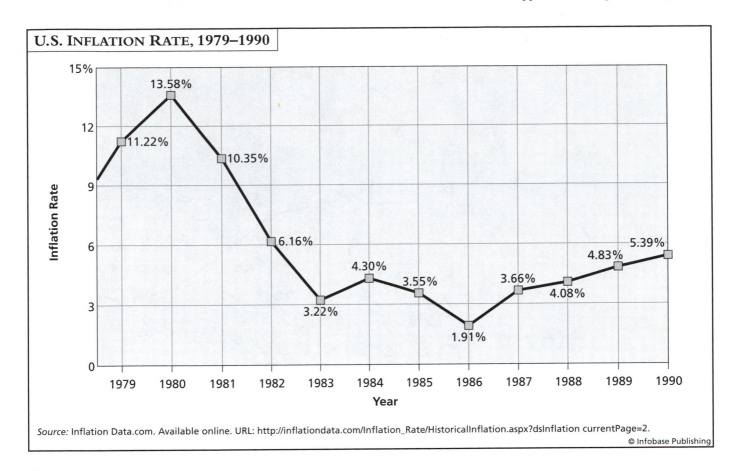

**U.S. INFLATION RATE, 1979–1990**

*Source:* Inflation Data.com. Available online. URL: http://inflationdata.com/Inflation_Rate/HistoricalInflation.aspx?dsInflation currentPage=2.

© Infobase Publishing

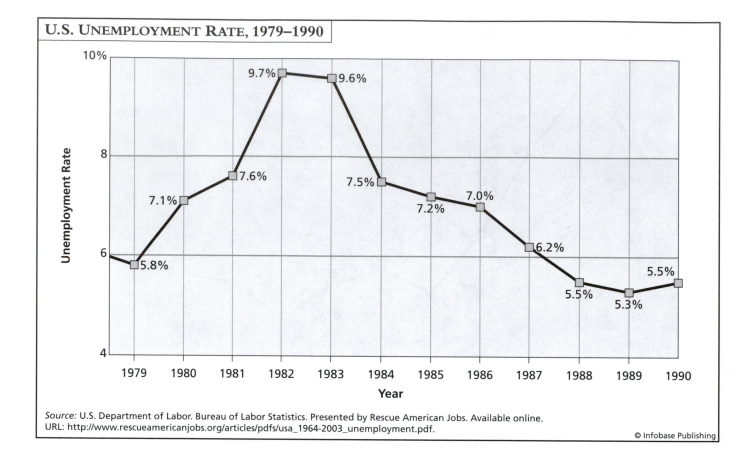

### U.S. UNEMPLOYMENT RATE, 1979–1990

*Source:* U.S. Department of Labor. Bureau of Labor Statistics. Presented by Rescue American Jobs. Available online.
URL: http://www.rescueamericanjobs.org/articles/pdfs/usa_1964-2003_unemployment.pdf.

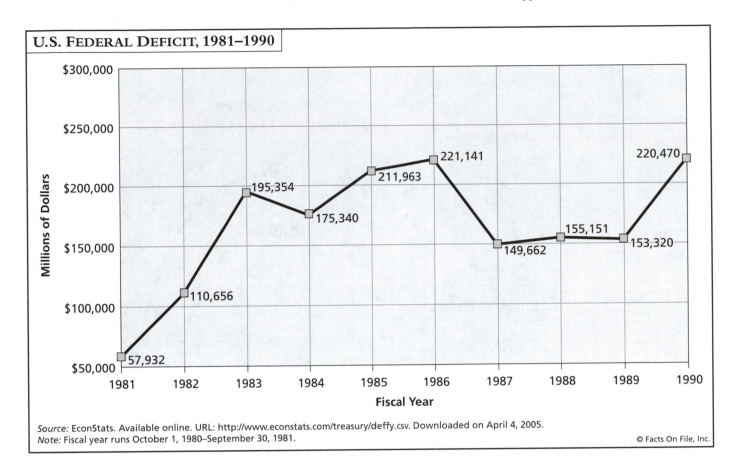

**U.S. FEDERAL DEFICIT, 1981–1990**

Millions of Dollars

- 1981: 57,932
- 1982: 110,656
- 1983: 195,354
- 1984: 175,340
- 1985: 211,963
- 1986: 221,141
- 1987: 149,662
- 1988: 155,151
- 1989: 153,320
- 1990: 220,470

Fiscal Year

*Source:* EconStats. Available online. URL: http://www.econstats.com/treasury/deffy.csv. Downloaded on April 4, 2005.
*Note:* Fiscal year runs October 1, 1980–September 30, 1981.

© Facts On File, Inc.

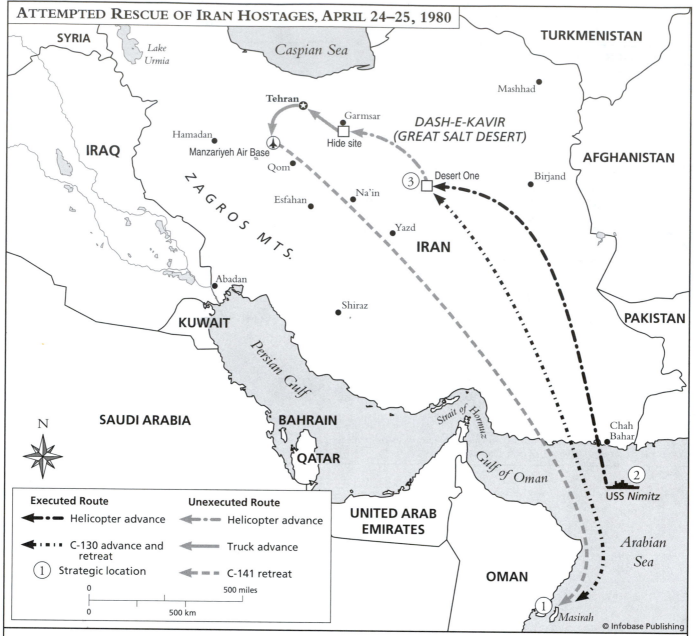

# ATTEMPTED RESCUE OF IRAN HOSTAGES, APRIL 24–25, 1980

**SYRIA**

*Lake Urmia*

*Caspian Sea*

**TURKMENISTAN**

Mashhad

**Tehran**

Garmsar

*DASH-E-KAVIR (GREAT SALT DESERT)*

Hamadan

Manzariyeh Air Base

Hide site

**AFGHANISTAN**

**IRAQ**

Qom

3 Desert One

Birjand

Esfahan

Na'in

**IRAN**

Yazd

**ZAGROS MTS.**

Abadan

Shiraz

**KUWAIT**

*Persian Gulf*

N

**SAUDI ARABIA**

**BAHRAIN**

*Strait of Hormuz*

Chah Bahar

**QATAR**

*Gulf of Oman*

**PAKISTAN**

2

USS *Nimitz*

**Executed Route** | **Unexecuted Route**

◄──·· Helicopter advance | ◄──·· Helicopter advance

◄··· C-130 advance and retreat | ◄─── Truck advance

① Strategic location | ◄--- C-141 retreat

0 — 500 miles
0 — 500 km

**UNITED ARAB EMIRATES**

*Arabian Sea*

**OMAN**

1 *Masirah*

© Infobase Publishing

Operation Eagle Claw, scheduled for April 24–26, 1980, called for eight Sea Stallion helicopters (flying from the USS *Nimitz* just south of the Persian Gulf) to rendezvous with refueling aircraft (flying from Masirah Island, Oman) at Desert One and then proceed with the Delta Force team to a hide site just southeast of Tehran to rendezvous before dawn with agents already inside the country. (A minimum of six helicopters were necessary for the mission's successful completion.) On the next night, team members would leave the hide site to enter Tehran in trucks, infiltrate the embassy, seize the hostages, and take them to a nearby stadium; then the helicopters would fly in, pick up the hostages and their rescuers, and fly them to Manzariyeh, an abandoned airfield southwest of Tehran that a force of U.S. Army Rangers were to seize the same night. The helicopters would then be destroyed, and waiting C-141 transport planes would take everyone back to Masirah Island.

**1. April 24, 6:00–7:00 P.M.:** Six C-130 aircraft carrying Delta Force team members, including mission commander Colonel Charlie Beckworth, depart from Masirah Island. They arrive at Desert One on time, 10:00–11:00 P.M.

**2. April 24, 7:30 P.M.:** Eight RH-53D Sea Stallion helicopters depart on time from the USS *Nimitz*, but because of dust storms and mechanical problems, two are forced to abort their flights and the rest are delayed.

**3. April 25, 12:20–12:45 P.M.:** Six helicopters arrive separately at Desert One, 50–85 minutes behind schedule. One helicopter is damaged on landing, leaving only five usable copters.

**April 25, 2:00 A.M.:** The mission is aborted on President Carter's orders. Disaster occurs during the withdrawal when one of the helicopters clips a C-130 and both aircraft burst into flames, killing eight crewmen. The whole team evacuates back to Masirah on the remaining C-130s but fail to destroy the other helicopters before departing, leaving top-secret plans to be discovered by the Iranians (thus risking the exposure of agents inside the country).

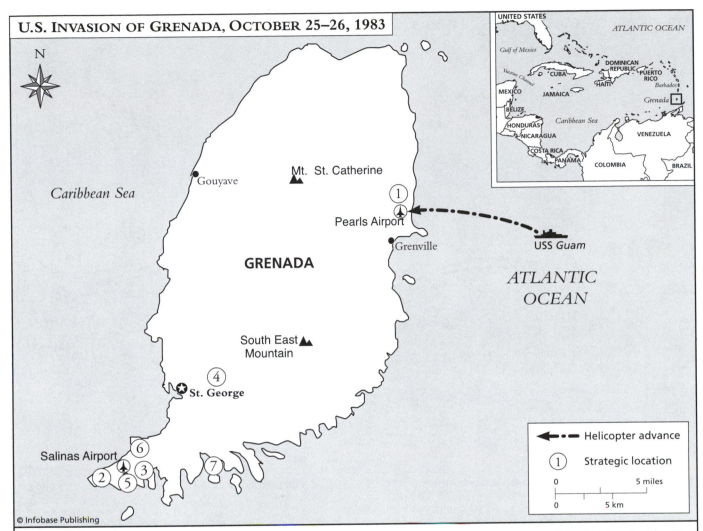

## U.S. INVASION OF GRENADA, OCTOBER 25–26, 1983

1. **October 25, 5:00 A.M.:** Helicopters with 400 U.S. Marines leave the USS *Guam* and commence an assault on Pearls Airport. They secure the airport within two hours, and the *Guam* then moves to the west coast.

2. **October 25, 5:36 A.M.:** Flying from a staging area in Barbados, hundreds of U.S. Army Rangers parachute into the Point Salines area. They meet heavy resistance, but by 7:15 A.M. the airport is secured.

3. **October 25, 8:50 A.M.:** Rangers secure the True Blue campus of St. George's University School of Medicine.

4. **October 25, 7:30 A.M.:** In the St. George's area, the Governor's House is secured after 250 U.S. Marines land with five tanks and 13 amphibious vehicles; later Richmond Hill Prison and

Fort Frederick nearby are captured. By this time the island is overrun by a combined force of 2,200 U.S. and Organization of Eastern Caribbean States troops. Pockets of resistance from some Cuban troops continue.

5. **October 26, 9:00 A.M.:** The evacuation of medical students begins from Salinas Airport. Meanwhile, additional troops arrive from Barbados; the invading force will eventually exceed 5,000.

6. **October 26, 4:00 A.M.:** Following a helicopter assault on the Grand Anse medical campus, students are evacuated.

7. **October 26, late afternoon:** U.S. planes strafe positions still occupied by Cuban soldiers. However, the fighting is effectively over, and the entire island is soon secured.

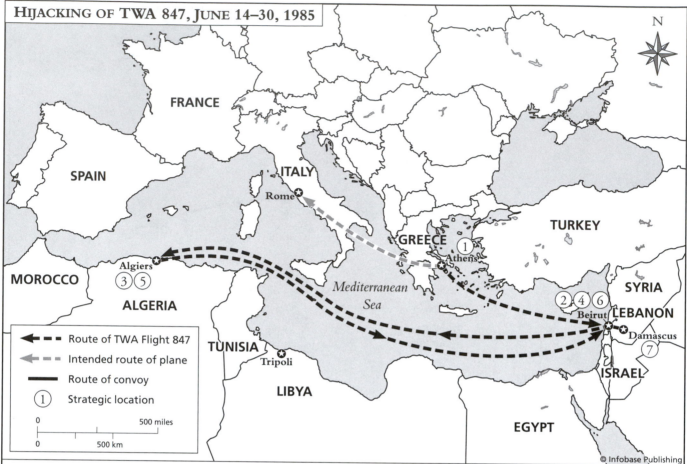

## HIJACKING OF TWA 847, JUNE 14–30, 1985

1. **June 14, 10:10 A.M.:** TWA Flight 847 departs Athens, bound for Rome, with 153 passengers and crew aboard; 104 are Americans. Shortly after takeoff, two armed militants from Islamic Jihad hijack the plane and force the pilot to fly to Beirut. An accomplice who had failed to board the plane is subsequently arrested in Athens.

2. **June 14, 11:55 A.M.:** The plane lands in Beirut, where it is refueled. The hijackers free 19 passengers and read their demands, which include the release of more than 700 Shiite prisoners being held by Israel. The plane then takes off at 1:30 P.M.

3. **June 14, 3:30 P.M.:** TWA 847 lands at Houari Boumediene International Airport, Algiers, where it is refueled. The hijackers threaten to kill all the passengers unless Israel releases its Shiite prisoners. They subsequently free 22 hostages, and the plane takes off again at 8:15 P.M.

4. **June 15, 2:20 A.M.:** The plane returns to Beirut, where the hijackers, angered by the slow response to their demands, beat and then shoot Robert Dean Stetham, a U.S. Navy diver; his body is subsequently dumped on the tarmac. The militants threaten to kill eight Greek passengers on the plane unless their accomplice in Athens is released. Subsequently, about a dozen members of the militant group Amal take over the plane. Seven male passengers with Jewish-sounding names are removed from the aircraft

and hidden in Beirut. TWA 847 is then forced to lift off again at 5:40 A.M.

5. **June 15, 7:45 A.M.:** The plane again lands in Algiers. After Greek officials release the hijackers' accomplice, the Greek passengers are freed, followed by three Americans later in the morning. At 5:00 P.M. all remaining women and non-American men are released; more than seven hours later, three more hostages are freed.

**June 16, 9:00 A.M.:** The plane takes off again. By this time a total of 33 hostages remain on the aircraft, while seven are still hidden in Beirut.

6. **June 16, 2:50 P.M.:** TWA 847 arrives in Beirut for the third and last time. The hijackers repeat their demands, stressing the release of Israel's Shiite prisoners. Most of the hostages are removed from the plane and sequestered in Beirut. One hostage is subsequently freed due to poor health.

**June 16–29:** Negotiations drag on for almost two weeks before Israel begins the gradual release of its Shiite prisoners, which will continue after the hostages are freed.

7. **June 30, 10:40 A.M.:** All 39 hostages, now freed, board a Red Cross convoy, which takes them out of Beirut and across the Syrian border. At 2:30 P.M. they arrive in Damascus, where they meet the press. None of the hijackers are captured.

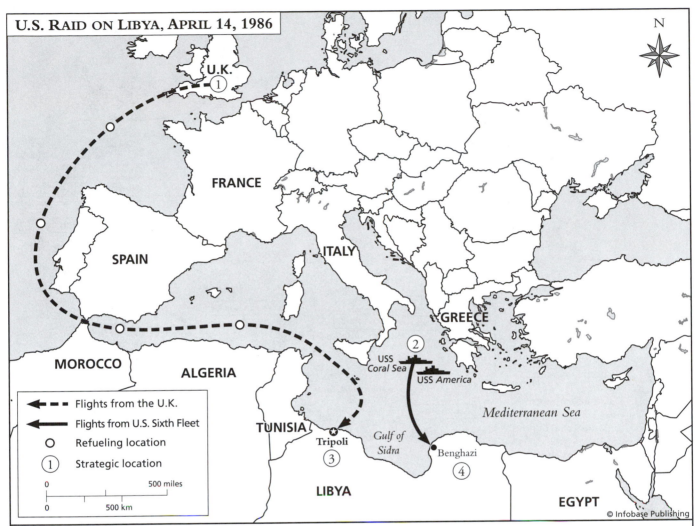

## U.S. RAID ON LIBYA, APRIL 14, 1986

Legend:
- ◄ ═ ═ Flights from the U.K.
- ◄ ── Flights from U.S. Sixth Fleet
- ○ Refueling location
- ① Strategic location

0 ————— 500 miles
0 ————— 500 km

N

Labels on map: U.K., FRANCE, SPAIN, MOROCCO, ALGERIA, TUNISIA, ITALY, GREECE, USS Coral Sea, USS America, Mediterranean Sea, Gulf of Sidra, Tripoli, Benghazi, LIBYA, EGYPT

© Infobase Publishing

1. **April 14, 12:00–1:00 P.M.:** The U.S. air strike force takes off from several sites in Great Britain to rendezvous over the English Channel. They include 24 F-111s from Lakenheath, five EF-111s from Upper Heyford, and 28 refueling tankers from Mildenhall and Fairford. Because France and Spain have refused permission to use their airspace, the aircraft must take a circuitous route of 2,800 nautical miles, entirely over water, which requires them to refuel in the air four times along the journey.

2. **April 14, 12:00–1:00 P.M.:** Nearly 100 aircraft take off from carriers USS *America* and USS *Coral Sea* of the U.S. Sixth Fleet. They include A-6 bombers, EA-6B electronic-warfare planes, A-7s and F/A-18s with radar-jamming missiles, F-14 fighters, and E-2C command-and-control aircraft.

3. **April 14, 7:00–7:11 P.M. (April 15, 2:00–2:11 A.M., Libyan time):** In two waves of attacks, 13 F-111s bomb selected targets in Tripoli, including a military airfield, the Sidi Bilal naval base, and the Bab al Azziziya barracks the location of Muammar al-Gadhafi's headquarters. Though they fail to kill Gadhafi, his 18-month-old daughter is mortally wounded. One F-111 is struck by a surface-to-air missile and plunges into the water, killing the pilot and a crew member.

4. **April 14, 7:00–7:11 P.M. (April 15, 2:00–2:11 A.M., Libyan time):** Twelve A-6 bombers attack Benghazi, hitting the Jamahiriya barracks and Benina air base, where they destroy eight Libyan aircraft. The bombers inadvertently also demolish some civilian houses during the raid. The combined attacks on Benghazi and Tripoli leave 15 Libyans dead and numerous aircraft destroyed.

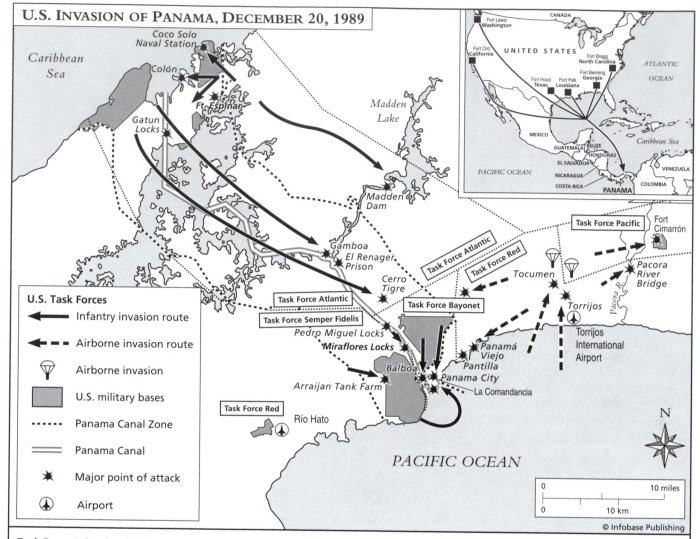

## U.S. INVASION OF PANAMA, DECEMBER 20, 1989

**U.S. Task Forces**

→ Infantry invasion route

⇢ Airborne invasion route

⛱ Airborne invasion

▨ U.S. military bases

⋯ Panama Canal Zone

═ Panama Canal

✴ Major point of attack

✈ Airport

© Infobase Publishing

**Task Force Atlantic:** This force consists of a battalion from the 7th Light Infantry Division and a battalion from the 82nd Airborne Division, backed by special units. Overcoming heavy resistance from the PDF, troops secure vital facilities near Colón; an electrical distribution center at Cerro Tigre; and Madden Dam, which stores the water used to raised and lower ships in the Panama Canal locks. They also take the prison at Gamboa and free 48 PDF prisoners.

**Task Force Semper Fidelis:** U.S. Marine rifle company and light armored infantry company as well as MPs secure the Howard Air Force base against a PDF counterattack by occupying the Bridge of the Americas, which spans the canal.

**Task Force Red:** Consisting of U.S. Army Ranger paratroopers and special troops of the Southern Command, this force lands in two areas on either side of Panama City. In the western part, rangers land near Río Hato, where they capture a PDF barracks, taking 250 prisoners. In the eastern section, commandos take control of the Torrijos International Airport and block a bridge across the Pacora River.

**Task Force Pacific:** At 1:55 A.M., after Task Force Red has secured the airport, troops from the 82nd Airborne Brigade parachute in from C-141 transports and fan out to assist rangers and the special forces in combating attacks from PDF infantry and cavalry units as well as to prevent the PDF's Battalion 2000 from coming to Manuel Noriega's aid. There are several engagements with PDF troops, but when U.S. forces reach Fort Cimarrón, they find Battalion 2000 has gone.

**Task Force Bayonet:** Troops from the 16th Mechanized Battalion, a light tank platoon, and the 5th Battalion of the 87th Infantry Mechanized Battalion attack and contain the PDF's 5th Infantry Company at Fort Armador. They also assault and destroy La Comandancia, the PDF headquarters in downtown Panama City. When they later search the building, they find it empty, indicating a breakdown in Panamanian resistance to the invasion. By 8:00 A.M. U.S. officials feel confident of success.

*Note:* The invasion began shortly before "H-hour" (1:00 A.M.) on December 20 when 12,000 U.S.-based troops joined 12,000 U.S. Southern Command troops already in the country to strike selected targets simultaneously and thus paralyze the Panamanian Defense Force (PDF). Unless otherwise noted, all actions described here occurred on or just prior to H-hour. Task force names and operations are according to contemporary press accounts.

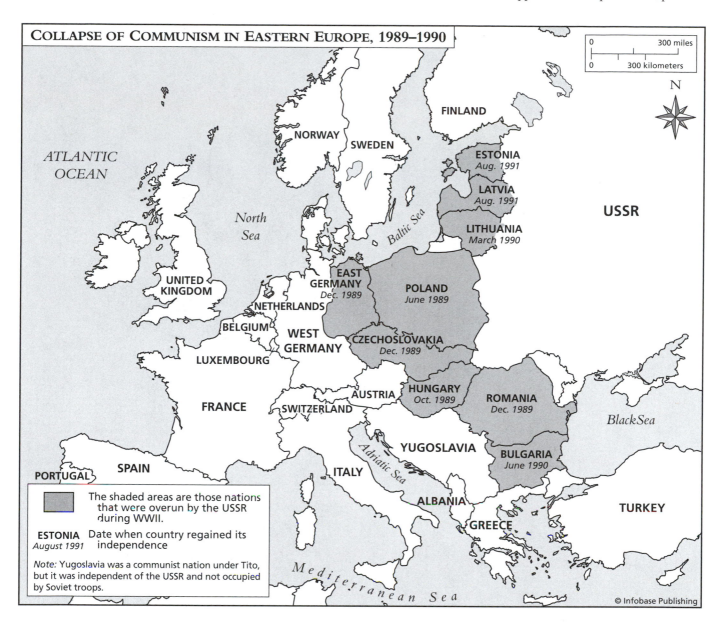

## COLLAPSE OF COMMUNISM IN EASTERN EUROPE, 1989–1990

The shaded areas are those nations that were overrun by the USSR during WWII.

**ESTONIA**
*August 1991*    Date when country regained its independence

*Note:* Yugoslavia was a communist nation under Tito, but it was independent of the USSR and not occupied by Soviet troops.

© Infobase Publishing

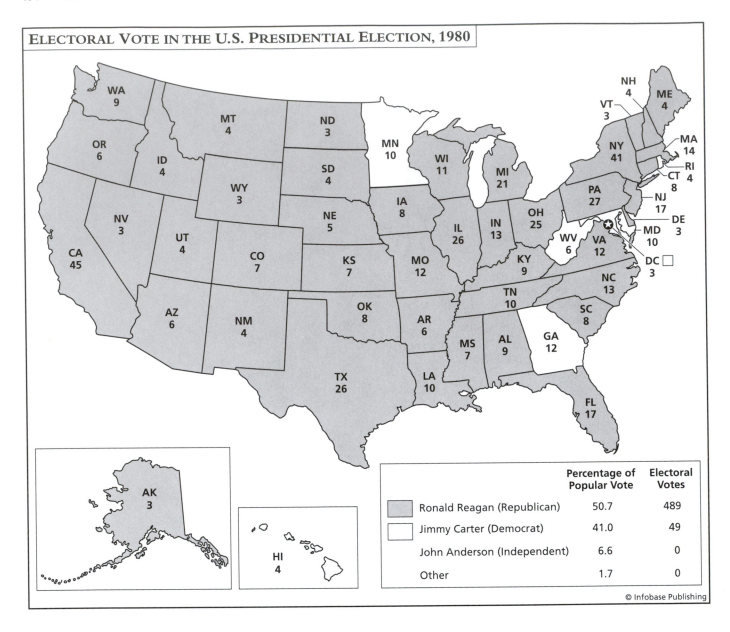

## ELECTORAL VOTE IN THE U.S. PRESIDENTIAL ELECTION, 1980

| | | Percentage of Popular Vote | Electoral Votes |
|---|---|---|---|
| | Ronald Reagan (Republican) | 50.7 | 489 |
| | Jimmy Carter (Democrat) | 41.0 | 49 |
| | John Anderson (Independent) | 6.6 | 0 |
| | Other | 1.7 | 0 |

© Infobase Publishing

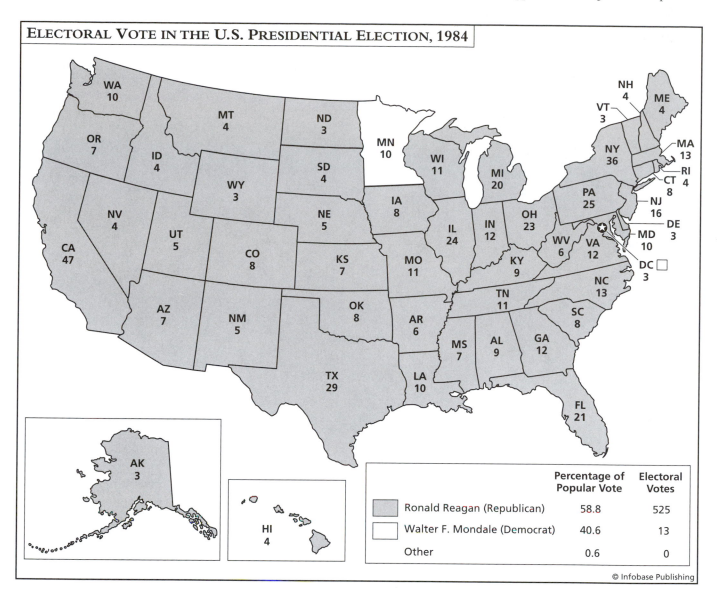

## ELECTORAL VOTE IN THE U.S. PRESIDENTIAL ELECTION, 1984

WA 10
OR 7
ID 4
MT 4
ND 3
MN 10
WI 11
MI 20
NH 4
VT 3
ME 4
NY 36
MA 13
RI 4
CT 8
NV 4
UT 5
WY 3
SD 4
NE 5
IA 8
IL 24
IN 12
OH 23
PA 25
NJ 16
DE 3
MD 10
WV 6
VA 12
DC 3
CA 47
CO 8
KS 7
MO 11
KY 9
NC 13
AZ 7
NM 5
OK 8
AR 6
TN 11
SC 8
MS 7
AL 9
GA 12
TX 29
LA 10
FL 21
AK 3
HI 4

| | Percentage of Popular Vote | Electoral Votes |
|---|---|---|
| Ronald Reagan (Republican) | 58.8 | 525 |
| Walter F. Mondale (Democrat) | 40.6 | 13 |
| Other | 0.6 | 0 |

© Infobase Publishing

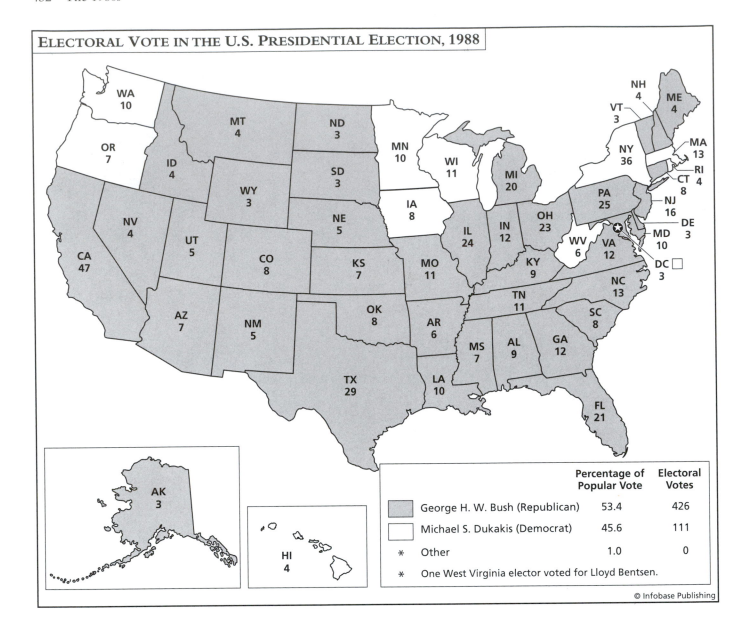

## ELECTORAL VOTE IN THE U.S. PRESIDENTIAL ELECTION, 1988

|  |  | Percentage of Popular Vote | Electoral Votes |
|---|---|---|---|
|  | George H. W. Bush (Republican) | 53.4 | 426 |
|  | Michael S. Dukakis (Democrat) | 45.6 | 111 |
| * | Other | 1.0 | 0 |
| * | One West Virginia elector voted for Lloyd Bentsen. |  |  |

© Infobase Publishing

# NOTES

## INTRODUCTION

1. Jimmy Carter, "Jimmy Carter's Malaise Speech, 1979," *Right Wing News.* URL: http://www.rightwingnews.com/speeches/carter.php.

2. By this time Carter's approval rating, according to an Associated Press/NBC Poll, was a miserable 19 percent. (Garland A. Haas, *Jimmy Carter and the Politics of Frustration* [Jefferson, N.C., and London: McFarland & Company, Inc., 1992], 116.)

3. Jimmy Carter, "Inaugural Address of President Jimmy Carter, Thursday, January 20, 1977." URL: http://www.jimmycarterlibrary.gov/documents/speeches/inaugadd.phtml.

4. Douglas Fraser, quoted in William C. Berman, *America's Right Turn: From Nixon to Bush* (Baltimore: Johns Hopkins University Press, 1994), 47.

5. Carter, "Jimmy Carter's Malaise Speech, 1979," *Right Wing News.* URL: http://www.rightwingnews.com/speeches/carter.php.

6. Ibid.

7. Peggy Noonan, *When Character Was King: A Story of Ronald Reagan* (New York: Penguin Books, 2001), 130.

8. Reagan had badly wanted Gerald Ford to be his running mate, but negotiations broke down when it became clear that Ford wanted responsibilities that would effectively make him a co-president.

9. "U.S. Economy in the 80s: Can We Meet the Challenge?" *U.S. News and World Report,* January 21, 1980, 57–58.

10. The other important factor in Carter's downfall was the Iran hostage crisis of 1979–81.

11. Ronald Reagan, "Inaugural Address, January 20, 1981." URL: http://www.Reagan.utexas.edu/resources/speeches/1981/12081a.htm.

## 1. THE FALL OF JIMMY CARTER: NOVEMBER 1979–JANUARY 1981

1. Jimmy Carter, "Jimmy Carter's Malaise Speech, 1979," *Right Wing News.* URL: http://www.rightwingnews.com/speeches/carter.php.

2. Ibid.

3. Most accounts specify only the U.S. Embassy as the students' target, but, in fact, hostage Kathryn Koob was seized at the Iran–America Society and Chargé d'Affaires Bruce Laingen and two aides at the Iranian Foreign Ministry.

4. Jimmy Carter, *Keeping Faith: Memoirs of a President* (London: Collins, 1982), 478.

5. The Carter Doctrine was later invoked by both Ronald Reagan and George H. W. Bush in carrying out U.S. military actions in the Persian Gulf arena.

6. Carter, *Keeping Faith,* 475.

7. Jimmy Carter on *Meet the Press,* January 20, 1980, quoted in Don Richardson, ed., *Conversations with Carter* (Boulder, Colo.: Lynne Riemer Publishers, 1998), 181.

8. In 1904 the United States won 211 medals; the nine other participating countries shared the remaining 43.

9. From letters to FBI director William Webster, published online. "Freedom of Information Act: Abscam." URL: http://foia.fbi.gov/foiaindex/abscam.htm.

10. These were U.S. senator Harrison Williams (D, N.J.) and representatives John Jenrette (D, S.C.), Raymond Lederer (D, Pa.), John M. Murphy (D, N.Y.), Michael Myers (D, Pa.), and Frank Thompson, Jr. (D, N.J.). Myers was expelled from the House on October 2, 1980, the first such expulsion since 1861.

11. The final moment of the game against the Soviets was replayed on television and sports highlight

videotapes for years afterward; *Sports Illustrated* selected the "Miracle on Ice" as the number-one sports moment of the century.

12. "The Double Whammy of Taxes and Inflation," *U.S. News & World Report,* July 14, 1980, 47.

13. "Debacle in the Desert," *Time,* May 5, 1980, 12.

14. "Academy Women: Ready to Take Command," *U.S. News & World Report,* May 26, 1980, 32–36.

15. The final decision to exclude women from the draft was challenged in court, but in 1981 the Supreme Court held the exclusion to be constitutional.

16. Approximately 250,000 Cubans, mostly middle-class, emigrated to the United States, with Fidel Castro's approval, between 1965 and 1973.

17 Jimmy Carter, May 5, 1980, quoted in "Open Heart, Open Arms, *Time,* May 19, 1980, 14.

18. Cuban Information Archive, Document 0038: "Mariel Chronology May 13, 1979–Dec, 11, 1981." URL: http://cuban-exile.com/doc_026-050/doc0038.html.

19. "Heat Wave: 100-a-Day Killer," *U.S. News & World Report,* July 28, 1980, 7.

20. Billy Carter, quoted in "New Headache for the President," *U.S. News & World Report,* August 4, 1980, 18.

21. Senate panel report quoted in *Facts on File Yearbook 1980* (New York: Facts On File, 1981), 647.

22. Ronald Reagan, quoted by Associated Press, August 20, 1980.

23. Sick had previously written *All Fall Down* (1985) about the Iranian hostage crisis but had not yet become a convert to the conspiracy theory.

24. Gary Sick, *October Surprise: America's Hostages in Iran and the Election of Ronald Reagan* (London, New York: I.B. Taurus & Co., 1991), 10–12.

25. *Joint Report of the Task Force to Investigate Certain Allegations Concerning the Holding of American Hostages by Iran in 1980.* 102d Congress, 2d sess., Report 102–1102, January 3, 1993.

26. While Reagan's victory was a landslide in terms of electoral votes, the popular vote was much closer. Poll data at the time indicated that "although Carter was the most unpopular president since the end of World II, Reagan was the least popular candidate to capture the White House in the same period." (Berman, *America's Right Turn,* 81.)

27. Jimmy Carter, "Farewell Address, January 14, 1981." URL: http://jimmycarterlibrary.org/documents/speeches/farewell.phtml.

## 2. THE GREAT COMMUNICATOR TAKES OVER: JANUARY 1981–OCTOBER 1982

1. Reagan's own description, as quoted in Peggy Noonan's *When Character Was King: A Story of Ronald Reagan* (New York: Penguin Books, 2001), 160. As Noonan describes on page 95, the same thing had happened at Reagan's swearing-in as governor of California in 1967.

2. Ronald Reagan, "Inaugural Address, January 20, 1981." URL: http://www.Reagan.utexas.edu/resources/speeches/1981/12081a.htm.

3. Ronald Reagan, "Address Before a Joint Session of the Congress on the Program for Economic Recovery, February 18, 1981." URL: http://www.Reagan.utexas.edu/resource/speeches/1981/21881s.htm.

4. Brady returned to work in November 1982 but played only a minimal role; the press secretary's duties were carried out by Larry Speakes (and later by Marlin Fitzwater).

5. Alexander Haig, quoted in several sources including Haig, *Caveat: Realism, Reagan, and Foreign Policy* (London: Weidenfeld and Nicolson, 1984), 160; and Larry Speakes, *Speaking Out: The Reagan Presidency from Inside the White House* (New York: Charles Scribner's Sons, 1988), xi.

6. Haig was replaced by George Shultz, an experienced public servant.

7. Since 2003, Hinckley has been allowed unsupervised day trips away from the hospital; he may someday be released.

8. The *Columbia* was named after the first American ship to circumnavigate the globe in 1792.

9. *Challenger* exploded upon liftoff on January 28, 1986. *Columbia* was destroyed on February 1, 2003, when it disintegrated during its landing approach; all seven crew were killed.

10. For example, on September 4, 1985, Pete Rose registered his 4,191st hit, breaking Ty Cobb's all-time hits record. In 1987, 28 players each hit more than 30 home runs, a once-rare occasion.

11. Lawrence K. Altman, "Rare Cancer Seen in 41 Homosexuals," *New York Times,* July 3, 1981, A-20.

12. Ibid.

13. Robin Herman, "A Disease's Spread Provokes Anxiety," *New York Times,* August 8, 1982, 31.

14. Potter Stewart, 66, had been appointed by President Eisenhower in 1959 and was the youngest justice to retire from the Court. He died in 1985.

15. Other women candidates who were considered included Cornelia Kennedy of the U.S. Court of Appeals for the Sixth Circuit, Chief Justice Mary Coleman of Michigan Supreme Court, and Amalya L. Kearse of the U.S. Court of Appeals for the Second Circuit.

16. Barry Goldwater, quoted in Michael Schaller, *Reckoning with Reagan: America and Its President in the 1980s* (New York and Oxford: Oxford University Press, 1992), 41.

17. Quoted in an online biography of Sandra Day O'Connor. URL: http://www.supremecourthistory. org/justice/o'connor.htm.

18. Ronald Reagan, *An American Life* (London: Hutchinson, 1990), 280.

19. R. Magnuson et al., "Turbulence in the Tower," *Time,* August 17, 1981, 17.

20. It would take more than two years to fully train newly hired controllers. However, the FAA trimmed the total workforce to 10,000—7,000 less than it had been prestrike.

21. The Xerox Star was an immediate descendant of the Xerox Alto, which also had a GUI but was much less sophisticated. The first mouse was developed at Stanford Research Institute in 1964.

22. Eighty–eighty-nine website, "The Rubik's Cube—history and tips for solving it." URL: http://www.eightyeightynine.com/games/rubiks-cube.html.

23. Figures taken from "TV's Big Leap Forward into Culture," *U.S. News & World Report,* February 23, 1981, 53. Other sources show as many as 15 million accessing cable or subscription TV.

24. Canadian Embassy, Washington, D.C., "Canada's Constitution." URL: http://www.canadianembassy.org/government/constitution-en.asp.

25. For example, the 27th Amendment to the Constitution, concerning changes in congressional pay—called the Madison Amendment—was passed by Congress in 1789 but not ratified until 1992.

## 3. HIGHS, LOWS, AND FRIGHTENING TIMES: NOVEMBER 1982–DECEMBER 1983

1. Frank Newport et al., "Ronald Reagan from the People's Perspective: A Gallup Poll Review." URL: http://www.gallup.com/content/default.aspx?ci=11887.

2. Ronald Reagan, *An American Life* (London: Hutchinson, 1990), 13.

3. Ronald Reagan, "Statement on Deployment of the MX Missile," November 22, 1982. URL: http://www.reagan.utexas.edu/resource/speeches/1982/112282b.htm.

4. Production on the MX missile began in February 1984, but in July 1985 Congress limited deployment to 50 missiles due to continued questions about the basing plan. The START II treaty of 1993 called for the retirement of the MX, and in October 2002 the first Peacekeeper deactivation was carried out.

5. Ronald Reagan, "Address to the Nation on Defense and National Security, March 23, 1983." URL: http://www.reagan.utexas.edu/resources/speeches/1983/32383d.htm.

6. Ibid.

7. Jan Scruggs, quoted in Kristin Hass, *Carried to the Wall: American Memory and the Vietnam Veterans Memorial* (Berkeley and Los Angeles: University of California Press, 1998), 13.

8. Research and development on artificial hearts continued over the years, and on July 2, 2001, the first self-contained, battery-powered artificial heart, the AbioCor, was implanted in a 59-year-old patient in Louisville, Kentucky; he died nearly five months later, on November 30.

9. Randy Shilts, *And the Band Played On* (New York and London: Viking Penguin, 1987), 213.

10. AIDS Activity Center for Infectious Diseases Center for Disease Control, "Acquired Immunodeficiency Syndrome (AIDS) Weekly Surveillance Report—United States," December 22, 1983.

11. Reagan, *An American Life,* 140.

12. Both Samantha's and Andropov's letters are reproduced in full in Patrick Carkin, "Looking Back: Samantha Smith, the Girl Who Went to the Soviet Union." URL: http://wwwsmi.lkwash.wednet.edu/Samantha_Smith.htm.

13. Ronald Reagan, "Address to Members of the British Parliament, June 8, 1982." URL: http://www.reagan.utexas.edu/resource/speeches/1982/60882a.htm.

14. Reagan, *An American Life,* 294.

15. In October 1981 Reagan pushed through a controversial sale to Saudi Arabia of five airborne warning and control systems (AWACS) planes and additional equipment for F-15 fighters.

16. James G. Watt, quoted in Robert Dallek, *Ronald Reagan: The Politics of Symbolism* (Cambridge, Mass.: Harvard University Press, 1999), 85.

17. Ronald Reagan, "Address to the Nation on Defense and National Security, March 23, 1983." URL: http://www.reagan.utexas.edu/resource/speeches/1983/32383d.htm.

18. The exact number of students on the island has varied in both contemporary and modern-day sources.

19. Peggy Noonan, *When Character Was King: A Story of Ronald Reagan* (New York: Penguin Books, 2001), 254.

20. Other notable female appointees in the Reagan administration included Elizabeth Dole as Secretary of Transportation (1983–87), Margaret Heckler as Secretary of Health and Human Services (1983–85), and Jeane Kirkpatrick as U.S. ambassador to the United Nations (1981–85).

21. On July 23, 1984, Vanessa Williams was forced to resign as Miss America after nude photos of her were published in *Penthouse*.

22. The audience for the last episode of M★A★S★H was the largest television viewing audience to date for a nonsports program.

23. The USFL went on to play two more seasons, in 1984 and 1985, but its attempts to switch to a fall season in 1986 met in failure, and the league disbanded.

## 4. "MORNING IN AMERICA": NOVEMBER 1983–DECEMBER 1984

1. Jesse Jackson was not the first African American to run for president. At the Republican Convention in 1888, the abolitionist Frederick Douglass won a single complimentary vote; in 1972 Representative Shirley Chisholm (N.Y.) ran for the Democratic nomination and won 152 delegates.

2. Deregulation of the banking industry would also have hugely damaging consequences, as demonstrated by the savings-and-loan crisis of 1989.

3. Payload specialists are astronauts who are not professionally employed by NASA but who join a crew to carry out specialized duties.

4. Surrogacy—bearing children for others—has been in existence for centuries. In the 1980s, however, science made it much more complex, and it took on moral and legal overtones, as demonstrated by the Baby M case of 1986–88.

5. The Eighties Club. "Baby Fae." URL: http://eightiesclub.tripod.com/id302.htm.

6. In addition to Henry Kissinger, the bipartisan commission included former New Jersey senator Nicholas Brady, San Antonio mayor Henry Cisneros, Boston University president John Silber, and retired Supreme Court justice Potter Stewart.

7. From the charter of the National Bipartisan Commission on Central America, quoted in "The Kissinger Commission," URL: http://www.uscubacommission.org/htm/kisscom.htm.

8. Ronald Reagan, *Abortion and the Conscience of the Nation* (Nashville: Thomas Nelson Publishers, 1984), 30.

9. In June 1985 an attempt to pass a revised version of the Reagan amendment again failed to pass in the Senate.

10. Pierre Trudeau in March 1984, quoted in a televised tribute following his death, PBS "Online Newshour," October 3, 2000. URL: http://www.pbs.org/newshour/bb/remember/july-dec00/trudeau_10-3html.html.

11. Brian Mulroney to John Turner, August 25, 1984, quoted in "Election Campaign Televised Leaders' Debate: Prime Minister John Turner Faces Brian Mulroney." *Historic Moments in Canadian Politics.* URL: http://www.planetcast.com/historic-moments/turner-01.shtml.

12. In the end, ABC made a profit of $435 million on the games, largely by charging inflated amounts for advertising; McDonald's alone spent $30 million.

13. From a typical "Morning in America" ad, quoted in Kathleen Hall Jamieson, *Packaging the Presidency: A History and Criticism of Presidential Campaign Advertising,* 3d ed. (New York & Oxford: Oxford University Press, 1996), 451.

14. An excellent discussion of the yuppie culture is provided by Hendrik Hertzberg, "The Short Happy Life of the American Yuppie," in Nicolaus Mills, ed., *Culture in an Age of Money: The Legacy of the 1980s in America* (Chicago: I. R. Dee, 1990), 66–82.

## 5. TERRORISM AND DISASTER: JANUARY 1985–APRIL 1986

1. This episode is reported in Jayne Mayer and Doyle McManus, *Landslide: The Unmaking of the President* (Boston: Houghton Mifflin, 1988), 19–20.

2. Two of the hijackers managed to escape, but one, Magid al-Molgi—who had confessed to the murder of Leon Klinghoffer—was caught and returned to prison.

3. Twenty years later, Geldof formed Band Aid 20 with 47 artists (and only himself and Bono of U2 from the original group) to record a new version of "Do They Know It's Christmas?"—again for famine relief. Again the record went right to the top of the charts when released in November 2004.

4. John Taylor, *Circus of Ambition: The Culture of Wealth and Power in the Eighties* (New York: Warner Books, 1989), 218.

5. Ronald Reagan, quoted in Lawrence Martin, "Mulroney Toast of Reaganites." *The Ottawa Citizen.* URL: http://squawk.ca/lbo-talk/9909/0814.html.

6. Michel Gratton, *"So, What Are the Boys Saying?": An Inside Look at Brian Mulroney in Power* (Toronto: McGraw-Hill Ryerson Ltd., 1987), 120.

7. James Watt on January 19, 1983, quoted in Paul Slansky, *The Clothes Have No Emperor* (New York: Simon and Schuster, 1989), 60.

8. Indianz.com, "Reagan's Indian Policies Recalled with Fervor" (June 11, 2004). URL: http://www.indianz.com/News/2004/002878.asp.

9. In June 1988 Reagan further complicated matters when, while addressing Soviet university students in Moscow, he said: "Maybe we made a mistake [trying to maintain Indian cultures]. Maybe we should not have humored them in that, wanting to stay in that kind of primitive life style. Maybe we should have said: 'No, come join us. Be citizens along with the rest of us.' " (" 'Humoring' Indians Bring Protest from Tribal Leaders," *New York Times,* June 1, 1988, A-13.) It took Reagan months to recover from this gaffe.

10. Another factor in Chrysler's recovery was the 1980 government loan that saved the company from bankruptcy.

11. "Saying 'No' to New Coke," *Newsweek,* June 24, 1985, 33.

12. Coca-Cola eventually changed the name of New Coke to Coke II. It is still available in some metropolitan areas.

13. Ronald Reagan, quoted in Jason Manning, "Bitburg." URL: http://eightiesclub.tripod.com/id342.htm.

14. Ronald Reagan, quoted in "Responses of the President to Queries on German Visit," *New York Times,* April 19, 1985, A-13.

15. "Paying Homage to History," *Time,* May 13, 1985, 16.

16. In time, Gallo and Montagnier—later designated codiscoverers of HIV—resolved their differences and worked together on cloning the virus's genome.

17. In addition to McAuliffe, the crew of Flight 51-L included another woman, Judith Resnick; an African American, Ronald McNair; and an Asian American, Ellison Onizuka—all mission specialists.

18. Ronald Reagan, "Address to the Nation on the Explosion of the Space Shuttle Challenger, January 28, 1986." URL: http://www.reagan.utexas.edu/resource/speeches/1986/12886b.htm. John Gillespie Magee, Jr., a 19-year-old World War II flier, was killed shortly after writing "High Flight," which ends: "With silent, lifting mind I've trod / The high, untrespassed sanctity of space, / Put out my hand, and touched the face of God."

19. *Report of the Presidential Commission on the Space Shuttle Challenger Accident,* Volume I, Chapter 4: "The Cause of the Accident." URL: http://sunnyday.mit.edu/accidents/Chapter-4.txt.

20. Of the three surviving terrorists, the two in Austria were arrested, tried in 1986, and sentenced to life in prison. The one in Italy was not tried until February 1988, when he was convicted of the massacre at the Rome airport and sentenced to 30 years in prison.

21. John O'Sullivan, "Lioness in a Den of Daniels," *Times* (London), April 16, 1985, 20.

# 6. ARMS AND THE PRESIDENT: MAY 1986–DECEMBER 1987

1. Margaret Thatcher, quoted in Howell Raines, "Thatcher Salute to Reagan Years," *New York Times,* June 2, 1988, A-9. The original source of this quote was *Mrs. Thatcher's Revolution* (1987) by British writer Peter Jenkins.

2. Patricia Schroeder, quoted in "Simpson's Contemporary Quotations," Bartleby.com. URL: http://www.bartleby.com/63/40/940.html.

3. Lou Cannon, *President Reagan: The Role of a Lifetime* (New York: Public Affairs, 1991, 2000), 81.

4. *Department of State Bulletin* 81, no. 2048 (March 1981), 17.

5. As part of their efforts to cover up the illegal arms-for-hostages deal with Iran, Reagan officials allowed Terry Waite, an envoy with the Church of England, to take credit for negotiating the release of Weir, Martin Jenco, and David Jacobsen. Waite himself was kidnapped in January 1987 and spent four years in captivity.

6. Ronald Reagan, quoted in Schaller, *Reckoning with Reagan* (New York and Oxford: Oxford University Press, 1992), 133.

7. Ronald Reagan, *An American Life* (London: Hutchinson, 1990), 635.

8. Paul Nitze, quoted in Jason Manning, "Reykjavik." URL: http://eightiesclub.tripod.com/id322.htm.

9. There was an ironic twist to this: Secretary of Defense Caspar Weinberger had been known as Cap the Knife, a notorious budget slasher during his days in Richard Nixon's cabinet. But from the start of the Reagan administration, he had fought for and won huge increases in defense spending, frequently clashing with David Stockman in the process.

10. A further revised version of Gramm-Rudman was passed in 1990, with the focus changed from deficit reduction to spending control.

11. Reagan, *An American Life,* 334.

12. Ivan Boesky, quoted in "The Columbia World of Quotations." URL: http://www.bartleby.com/66/63/7663.html.

13. Insider trading is the practice of trading shares based on information provided by someone with inside knowledge; it is usually illegal because the insider has breached a position of trust to disclose confidential information.

14. Boesky was released from a minimum-security prison in California on November 15, 1989, having served one and a half years of his sentence.

15. Jason Manning, "Wolves on Wall Street." URL: http://eightiesclub.tripod.com/id316htm.

16. On January 8, 1988, the Presidential Task Force on Market Mechanisms reported that the crash was the result of large money management programs and their automatic trading programs, generating massive sell orders. The task force recommended the Federal Reserve Board become responsible for regulation of trading.

17. Brian Mulroney, "Report on the First Ministers' Meeting at Meech Lake," May 1, 1987. URL: http://www.collectionscanada.ca/premiersministres/h4-4022-e.html.

18. Robert Bourassa, April 30, 1987, quoted in Cleroux, Fraser, and Oziewicz, "Premiers Approve Quebec Demands," *Globe and Mail* (Montreal), May 1, 1987, A1.

19. Edward Kennedy on the Senate floor, July 1, 1987, quoted in Henry J. Abraham, *Justices and Presidents: A Political History of Appointments to the Supreme Court,* 3d ed. (New York: Oxford University Press, 1992), 357.

20. Ronald Reagan, "Remarks on East-West Relations at the Brandenburg Gate in West Berlin, June 12, 1987." URL: http://www.reagan.utexas.edu/resource/speeches/1987/061287d.htm.

21. Ronald Reagan, "Address to the Nation on the Iran Arms and Contra Aid Controversy, November 13, 1986." URL: http://www.reagan.utexas.edu/resource/speeches/1986/111386c.htm.

22. The Tower Commission's other two members were former secretary of state Edmund Muskie and former National Security Advisor Brent Scowcroft.

23. The Tower Commission report was the final straw for Donald Regan, already beset by criticism of his performance as chief of staff and by ongoing clashes with First Lady Nancy Reagan, who had led the calls for his dismissal.

24. Events in Nicaragua later took an unexpected and very welcome turn for Reagan's successor, George Bush, when, in February 1990, the U.S.-backed National Opposition Union defeated the Sandinistas at the polls, and a democratic government was installed. This ended the fighting in Nicaragua—and aid for the contras.

## 7. BEGINNING OF THE END: JANUARY 1988–JANUARY 1989

1. All figures taken from Gorton Carruth, *The Encyclopedia of American Facts and Dates,* 10th ed. (New York: HarperCollins, 1997), 800, 809, 814. A further note: By October 1989 the U.S. Hispanic population had passed 20 million, making up 8.2 percent of the country's total population, compared with 6.5 percent in 1980. (Carruth, 814.)

2. Statistics from "The History of AIDS from 1987 to 1992." URL: http://www.avert.og/his87-92.htm.

3. George Raine, "Size of Project Reflects the Nation's Loss," *San Francisco Chronicle,* October 9, 1988, A-21.

4. Statistics cited in this section are taken from contemporary sources, primarily "U.S. Hispanic Population Is Up 34% since 1980," *New York Times,* September 7, 1988, A-20. An additional source was Nicolás Kanellos, ed., *The New Hispanic American Almanac,* 2d ed. (Detroit: Gale, 1997).

5. "A Surging New Spirit," *Time,* July 11, 1988, 46.

6. By 1989 the poverty line was considered to be $12,675 annually for a family of four (Harry S. Ashmore, *Civil Rights and Wrongs* [New York: Pantheon Books, 1994], 340).

7. The ruling against Liggett was overturned in 1990, and the case went before the U.S. Supreme Court in June 1992. The Court ruled that the federally required warning labels on cigarette packages protected manufacturers from most lawsuits but that tobacco companies could still be sued for withholding or falsifying information on the health risks of smoking.

8. From "Getting Tough," *Time,* February 1, 1988, 52.

9. William Bennett, quoted in "Getting Tough," *Time,* February 1, 1988, 53.

10. The movies were *Stand and Deliver* (1988), starring Edward James Olmos as Jaime Escalante, and *Lean on Me* (1989), starring Morgan Freeman as Joe Clark.

11. Nancy Reagan attracted bad publicity because of her widely criticized redecoration of the White House and acquisition of new china in 1981. Due to breakages over the years, the White House did not possess a single complete set of china, which meant mixed sets had to be used at state dinners. The first lady arranged for the Knapp Foundation to donate new china to the White House; she did not, as was frequently reported, purchase it with taxpayers' money.

12. The other Republican candidates included former Delaware governor Pierre DuPont, former secretary of state Alexander Haig, New York congressman Jack Kemp, and evangelical preacher Pat Robertson.

13. George H. W. Bush, January 25, 1988, quoted in Germond and Witcover, *Whose Broad Stars and Bright Stars?* (1989), 123.

14. "George H. Bush: Before the Republican Convention Accepting Its Nomination for President August 18, 1988." *The American Presidency.* URL: http://www.geocities.com/rickmatlick/nomahbush88.htm.

15. Ibid.

16. An interesting footnote to the 1988 election was that George Bush became the first vice president to succeed a two-term president since Martin Van Buren succeeded Andrew Jackson in 1836.

17. Higgins was the only military man to be abducted in the period 1984–91. He was murdered on July 31, 1989, in retaliation for U.S. activities in the Middle East. The remaining hostages were finally released in 1990–91.

18. On May 17, 1989, Iran brought a suit against the United States before the International Court of Justice. The case was finally dropped in February 1996 after the United States and Iran reached agreement on a settlement.

19. The bomb was technically different from the one discovered during the German raid in October, but the similarities were impossible for investigators to ignore.

20. It should be noted that Scotland has its own legal system.

21. The lawsuit did not represent all the victims' families. One widow refused to take part in it, and one victim had no next of kin.

22. Margaret Thatcher, June 3, 1988, quoted in Lou Cannon, *President Reagan: The Role of a Lifetime* (New York: Public Affairs, 1991, 2000), 709.

23. Ronald Reagan, "Farewell Address to the Nation, Oval Office, January 11, 1989." URL: http://www.ronaldreagan.com/sp_21.html.

## 8. THE TORCH IS PASSED: JANUARY 1989–JANUARY 1990

1. George Bush, "Inaugural Address, January 20, 1989." URL: http://bushlibrary.tamu.edu/research/papers/1989/89012000.html.

2. Ibid.

3. Dilys M. Hill and Phil Williams, "Introduction: The Bush Administration—An Overview," in Hill and Williams, eds., *The Bush Presidency: Triumphs and Adversities* (Houndmills, Basingstoke, Hampshire, U.K.: Macmillan, 1994), 3.

4. Bush's second nominee for defense secretary—approved by the Senate—was Richard Cheney, later to become vice president under George W. Bush.

5. Independent counsels' report quoted in John Henneberger, "Independent Counsels Release Report on Reagan Era HUD Abuses," *Better Homes and Shelters.* URL: http://www.texashousing.org/txlihis/bhs/bhsarticles/QN2AUR.html.

6. Kitty Calavita et al., *Big Money Crime: Fraud and Politics in the Savings and Loan Crisis* (Berkeley, Los Angeles, and London: University of California Press, 1997), 10.

7. Ibid., 10.

8. Ibid., 13.

9. More than 500 savings-and-loan institutions failed in the 1980s.

10. Of the Keating Five, DeConcini, Riegle, and especially Cranston were found to have interfered with the FHLBB's investigation of the Lincoln Savings and Loan. In August 1991 the Senate Ethics Committee recommended that Cranston—cited for "substantial credible evidence" of misconduct—be censured, but he had already decided not to seek reelection in 1992; DeConcini and Riegle stood down in 1994. Glenn and McCain were found to have been only marginally involved, and both continued to serve full terms in the Senate, although they were scarred by their connection to the scandal. McCain subsequently spearheaded campaign finance reform measures in Congress.

11. Peter B. Levy, "Savings and Loan Crisis," *Encyclopedia of the Reagan-Bush Years* (Westport, Conn.: Greenwood Press, 1996), 316.

12. It should be noted that an even larger spill occurred in 1978 when the *Amoco Cadiz* foundered off the coast of France and spilled six times as much oil as the *Exxon Valdez.* Since that incident occurred in open seas, however, the oil dissipated quickly and did not cause as much damage as the *Exxon Valdez* spill.

13. Statistics cited from Daphne Spain and Suzanne M. Bianchi, *Balancing Act: Motherhood, Marriage, and Employment Among American Women* (New York: Russell Sage Foundation, 1996), 79–80. Spain and Bianchi also point out that "women workers would have increased by only five million if they were simply keeping pace with population growth." (80)

14. Phyllis Moen, *Women's Two Roles: A Contemporary Dilemma* (New York: Auburn House, 1992), 4. Moen further notes: "In 1950 only 18 percent of mothers with children under 18 were in the labor force; by 1990 this had tripled to 63 percent." (14)

15. Spain and Bianchi, *Balancing Act,* 166.

16. The article was "The Glass Ceiling," *Wall Street Journal,* March 24, 1986, sec. 4, 1D–5D. Hymowitz and Schellhardt are often given credit for coining the term *glass ceiling,* although there is evidence that it existed before their article made it a catchphrase of the 1980s and 1990s.

17. Moen, *Women's Two Roles,* 29.

18. Michael McGough, "Reagan's Legal Revolution Lives through Federal Bench Appointments," *Pittsburgh Post-Gazette: post-gazette.com* (June 8, 2004). URL: http://www.post-gazette.com/pg/pp/04160/328555.stm. Besides Reagan, only Franklin Roosevelt and Dwight Eisenhower made so many federal bench appointments in the 20th century.

19. A leveraged buyout (LBO) is the takeover of a company (or controlling interest in a company) using a large amount of borrowed money, often 70 percent or more of the purchase price. Kohlberg Kravis and Roberts (founded 1976) helped perfect this acquisition method in the 1980s and still specializes in late-stage LBOs. In 1995 the company divested its remaining holdings in RJR Nabisco.

20. Leona Helmsley, quoted in "Maid Testifies Helmsley Denied Paying Taxes," *New York Times,* July 12, 1989, B-2.

21. George Bush, "Remarks at the Texas A&M University Commencement Ceremony in College Station, May 12, 1989." URL: http://bushlibrary.tamu.edu/research/papers/1989/89051201.html.

22. The Polish elections on June 4 and 18 were held as the result of an agreement reached between Solidarity and the Communist Party; Solidarity won all but one of the seats it contested. Consequently, on August 19 Solidarity activist Tadeusz Mazowiecki became the first noncommunist prime minister in 42 years.

23. George Bush, "Statement on the Chinese Government's Suppression of Student Demonstrations, June 3, 1989." URL: http://bushlibrary.tamu.edu/research/papers/1989/89060300.html.

24. The vote of the House of Representatives on June 29 was a remarkable 418-0; the Senate vote on July 14 was 81-10.

25. Gennadi Gerasimov, December 3, 1989, quoted in Michael R. Beschloss and Strobe Talbott, *At the Highest Levels: The Inside Story of the End of the Cold War* (London: Little, Brown, 1993), 165.

26. It should be noted that the Americans openly gave $10 million to Endara's campaign; it is unknown how much was provided covertly. Ironically, U.S. election laws forbid candidates to accept donations from foreign sources.

27. Manuel Noriega languished in jail for more than 18 months, his trial delayed chiefly because of his threats to implicate U.S. officials in many of his illegal activities. In April 1992 he was finally convicted on drug charges and subsequently sentenced to 40 years in a federal prison.

28. George Bush, "Address to the Nation Announcing United States Military Action in Panama, December 20, 1989." URL: http://bushlibrary. tamu.edu/research/papers/1989/89122000.html.

29. In the end, only Peggy and Ray Buckey were tried, with Peggy acquitted and Ray's case finally dropped in 1990 after two hung juries.

# BIBLIOGRAPHY

## BOOKS

Abraham, Henry J. *Justices and Presidents: A Political History of Appointments to the Supreme Court,* 3d ed. New York: Oxford University Press, 1992.

Adams, James Ring. *The Big Fix: Inside the S&L Scandal.* New York: John Wiley & Sons, 1990.

Adelman, Kenneth L. *The Great Universal Embrace: Arms Summitry—A Skeptic's Account.* New York: Simon and Schuster, 1989.

Anderson, Terry. *Den of Lions: Memoirs of Seven Years.* London: Hodder & Stoughton, 1993.

Ashmore, Harry S. *Civil Rights and Wrongs: A Memoir of Race and Politics, 1944–1994.* New York: Pantheon Books, 1994.

Ashton, John, and Ian Ferguson. *Cover-up of Convenience: The Hidden Scandal of Lockerbie.* Edinburgh and London: Mainstream Publishing, 2001.

Beck, Robert J., *The Grenada Invasion: Politics, Law, and Foreign Policy Decisionmaking.* Boulder, Colo.: Westview Press, 1993.

Berman, William C. *America's Right Turn: From Nixon to Bush.* Baltimore and London: Johns Hopkins University Press, 1994.

Beschloss, Michael R., and Strobe Talbott. *At the Highest Levels: The Inside Story of the End of the Cold War.* London: Little, Brown, 1993.

Boyer, Paul, ed. *Reagan as President: Contemporary Views of the Man, His Politics, and His Policies.* Chicago: Ivan R. Dee, 1990.

Brzezinski, Zbigniew. *Power and Principle: Memoirs of a National Security Advisor.* New York: Farrar, Strauss & Giroux, 1983.

Burns, Richard Dean, ed. *Encyclopedia of Arms Control and Disarmament.* 3 vols. New York: Charles Scribner's Sons, 1993.

Busby, Robert. *Reagan and the Iran-Contra Affair: The Politics of Recovery.* London: Macmillan Press, 1999.

Bush, George. *All the Best, George Bush: My Life in Letters and Other Writings.* New York: Touchstone, 2000.

Bush, George, and Brent Scowcroft. *A World Transformed.* New York: Alfred A. Knopf, 1998.

Calavita, Kitty, Henry N. Pontell, and Robert H. Tillman. *Big Money Crime: Fraud and Politics in the Savings and Loan Crisis.* Berkeley, Los Angeles, and London: University of California Press, 1997.

Cannon, Lou. *President Reagan: The Role of a Lifetime.* New York: Public Affairs, 1991, 2000.

Carruth, Gorton. *Encyclopedia of American Facts and Dates,* 10th ed. New York: HarperCollins, 1997.

Carter, Jimmy. *Keeping Faith: Memoirs of a President.* London: Collins, 1982.

Chesler, Phyllis. *Sacred Bond: The Legacy of Baby M.* London: Virago Press, 1990.

Christopher, Warren, et al. *American Hostages in Iran: The Conduct of a Crisis.* New Haven, Conn., and London: Yale University Press, 1985.

Cohen, Susan, and Daniel Sohen. *Pan Am 103: The Bombing, the Betrayals, and a Bereaved Family's Search for Justice.* New York: New American Library, Penguin Books, 2000.

Cox, Matthew, and Tom Foster. *Their Darkest Day: The Tragedy of Pan Am 103 and Its Legacy of Hope.* London: Arrow Books, 1992.

Dallek, Robert. *Ronald Reagan: The Politics of Symbolism.* Cambridge, Mass.: Harvard University Press, 1999.

David, Mary B., ed. *Native America in the Twentieth Century: An Encyclopedia.* New York and London: Garland Publishing, 1994.

Davis, Flora. *Moving the Mountain: The Women's Movement in America since 1960.* New York: Simon and Schuster, 1991.

Deaver, Michael K., with Mickey Hershowitz. *Behind the Scenes: In Which the Author Talks About Ronald and Nancy Reagan . . . and Himself.* New York: William Morrow and Company, 1987.

Deppa, Joan. *The Media and Disasters: Pan Am 103.* London: David Fulton Publishers, 1993.

Detlefsen, Robert R. *Civil Rights under Reagan.* San Francisco: Institute for Contemporary Studies, 1991.

D'Souza, Dinesh. *Ronald Reagan: How an Ordinary Man Became an Extraordinary Leader.* New York: The Free Press, 1997.

Ehrenreich, Barbara. *The Worst Years of Our Lives: Irreverent Notes from a Decade of Greed.* London: Octopus Publishing Group, 1991.

Enrico, Roger, and Jesse Kornbluth. *The Other Guy Blinked: How Pepsi Won the Cola Wars.* London: Bantam Books, 1986.

Epstein, Dan. *20th Century Pop Culture.* London: Carlton Books, 1999.

*Facts On File Yearbook, 1980.* New York: Facts On File, 1981.

Fee, Elizabeth, and Daniel M. Fox, eds. *AIDS: The Making of a Chronic Disease.* Berkeley, Los Angeles, and Oxford: University of California Press, 1992.

Ferraro, Geraldine A., with Linda Bird Francke. *Ferraro: My Story.* New York and London: Bantam Press, 1986.

Feuer, Jane. *Seeing Through the Eighties: Television and Reaganism.* Durham, N.C.: Duke University Press, and London: British Film Institute, 1995.

Fitzgerald, Frances. *Way Out There in the Blue: Reagan, Star Wars and the End of the Cold War.* New York: Simon and Schuster, 2000.

Foner, Eric, and John A. Garraty, eds. *The Reader's Companion to American History.* Boston: Houghton Mifflin, 1991.

Freed, Les. *The History of Computers.* Emeryville, Calif.: Ziff-Davis Press, 1995.

Garthoff, Raymond L. *The Great Transition: American-Soviet Relations and the End of the Cold War.* Washington, D.C.: The Brookings Institution, 1994.

Gates, Robert M. *From the Shadows: The Ultimate Insider's Story of Five Presidents and How They Won the Cold War.* New York: Simon and Schuster, 1986.

Germond, Jack W., and Jules Witcover. *Whose Broad Stripes and Bright Stars?: The Trivial Pursuit of the Presidency 1988.* New York: Warner Books, 1989.

Gratton, Michel. *"So, What Are the Boys Saying?": An Inside Look at Brian Mulroney in Power.* Toronto: McGraw-Hill Ryerson, 1987.

Green, Mark, and Gail MacColl. *There He Goes Again: Ronald Reagan's Reign of Error.* New York; Pantheon Books, 1983.

Guttman, Allen. *The Olympics: A History of the Modern Games.* Urbana and Chicago: University of Illinois Press, 1992.

Haas, Garland A. *Jimmy Carter and the Politics of Frustration.* Jefferson, N.C., and London: McFarland & Company, 1992.

Haig, Alexander M., Jr. *Caveat: Realism, Reagan, and Foreign Policy.* London: Weidenfeld and Nicolson, 1984.

Hampton Henry, and Steve Fayer, comp. *Voices of Freedom: An Oral History of the Civil Rights Movement from the 1950s through the 1980s.* New York: Bantam Books, 1990.

Harland, David M. *The Space Shuttle: Roles, Missions and Accomplishments.* New York: John Wiley & Sons, 1998.

Hass, Kristin Ann. *Carried to the Wall: American Memory and the Vietnam Veterans Memorial.* Berkeley and Los Angeles: University of California Press, 1998.

Hill, Dilys M., and Phil Williams, eds. *The Bush Presidency: Triumphs and Adversities.* Houndmills, Basingstoke, Hampshire, U.K.: MacMillan, 1994.

Hill, Dilys M., Raymond A. Moore, and Phil Williams, eds. *The Reagan Presidency: An Incomplete Revolution?* Houndmills, Basingstoke, Hampshire, U.K.: MacMillan, 1990.

Houghton, David Patrick. *US Foreign Policy and the Iran Hostage Crisis.* Cambridge: Cambridge University Press, 2001.

Hurst, Steven. *The Foreign Policy of the Bush Administration: In Search of a New World Order.* London and New York: Cassell, 1999.

Jamieson, Kathleen Hall. *Packaging the Presidency: A History and Criticism of Presidential Campaign Advertising,* 3d ed. New York and Oxford: Oxford University Press, 1996.

Johnson, Haynes. *Sleepwalking Through History: America in the Reagan Years.* New York: W. W. Norton, 2003.

*Joint Report of the Task Force to Investigate Certain Allegations Concerning the Holding of American Hostages by Iran in 1980.* 102d Congress, 2d sess., Report 102–1102, January 3, 1993.

Jordan, Hamilton. *Crisis: The Last Year of the Carter Presidency.* New York: Putnam, 1982; London: Michael Joseph, 1982.

Kalb, Marvin, and Hendrik Hertzberg. *Candidates '88.* Dover, Mass.: Auburn House, 1988.

Kanellos, Nicolás, ed. *The Hispanic American Almanac,* 2d ed. Detroit: Gale Research, 1997.

Koob, Kathryn. *Guest of the Revolution.* Nashville, Tenn.: T. Nelson, 1982.

Laham, Nicholas. *The Reagan Presidency and the Politics of Race: In Pursuit of Colorblind Justice and Limited Government.* Westport, Conn., and London: Praeger, 1998.

Lancaster, Tony. *Civil Rights in America 1945–89.* London: Macmillan, 1990.

Levy, Peter B. *Encyclopedia of the Reagan-Bush Years.* Westport, Conn.: Greenwood Press, 1996.

Marty, Myron A. *Daily Life in the United States, 1960–1990: Decades of Discord.* Westport, Conn.: Greenwood Press, 1997.

Mayer, Jane, and Doyle McManus. *Landslide: The Unmaking of the President, 1984–1988.* London: Collins, 1988.

McConnell, Malcolm. *Challenger: A Major Malfunction.* London: Unwin Paperbacks, 1987.

Mervin, David. *George Bush and the Guardianship Presidency.* Houndmills, Basingstoke, Hampshire, U.K.: MacMillan, 1996.

Meyer, Peter. *Defiant Patriot: The Life and Exploits of Lt. Colonel Oliver L. North.* New York: St. Martin's Press, 1987.

Mills, Nicolaus, ed. *Culture in an Age of Money: The Legacy of the 1980s in America.* Chicago: I. R. Dee, 1990.

Moen, Phyllis. *Women's Two Roles: A Contemporary Dilemma.* New York: Auburn House, 1992.

Morris, Jeffrey B., and Richard B. Morris. *Encyclopedia of American History,* 7th ed. New York: HarperCollins, 1996.

Morris, Lorenzo, ed. *The Social and Political Implications of the 1984 Jesse Jackson Presidential Campaign.* New York: Praeger, 1990.

Nader, Ralph. *The Ralph Nader Reader.* New York: Seven Stories Press, 2000.

Nies, Judith. *Native American History: A Chronology of a Culture's Vast Achievements and Their Links to World Events.* New York: Ballantine Books, 1996.

Noonan, Peggy. *What I Saw at the Revolution: A Political Life in the Reagan Era.* New York: Random House, 1990.

———. *When Character Was King: A Story of Ronald Reagan.* New York: Penguin Books, 2001.

North, Oliver, with William Novak. *Under Fire: An American Story.* New York: HarperCollins, 1991.

Payne, Anthony, Paul Sutton, and Tony Thorndyke. *Grenada: Revolution and Invasion.* London and Sydney: Croom Helm, 1984.

Pelletier, Jean, and Claude Adams. *The Canadian Caper.* Markham, Ontario: Paper Jacks, 1982.

Reagan, Nancy, with William Novak. *My Turn.* London: Weidenfeld and Nicolson, 1989.

Reagan, Ronald. *Abortion and the Conscience of the Nation.* Nashville: Thomas Nelson Publishers, 1984.

———. *An American Life.* London: Hutchinson, 1990.

Regan, Donald T. *For the Record: From Wall Street to Washington.* San Francisco and New York: Harcourt Brace Jovanovich, 1988.

Richardson, Don, ed. *Conversations with Carter.* Boulder, Colo.: Lynne Riemer Publishers, 1998.

Riddlesperger, James W., Jr., and Donald W. Jackson, eds. *Presidential Leadership and Civil Rights Policy.* Westport, Conn.: Greenwood Press, 1995.

Rose, Richard. *George Bush as a Postmodern President.* Studies in Public Policy, 191. Glasgow, U.K.: Centre for the Study of Public Policy, University of Strathclyde, 1991.

Say, Peggy, and Peter Knobler. *Forgotten: A Sister's Struggle to Save Terry Anderson, America's Longest-Held Hostage.* New York: Simon and Schuster, 1991.

Schaller, Michael. *Reckoning with Reagan: America and Its President in the 1980s.* New York and Oxford: Oxford University Press, 1992.

Schmertz, Eric J., Natalie Datlof, and Alexej Ugrinsky, eds. *President Reagan and the World.* Westport, Conn.: Greenwood Press, 1997.

——— *Ronald Reagan's America.* 2 vols. Westport, Conn.: Greenwood Press, 1997.

Scott, Charles W. *Pieces of the Game: The Human Drama of Americans Held Hostage in Iran.* Atlanta, Ga.: Peachtree Publishers, 1984.

Secord, Richard, with Jay Wurts. *Honored and Betrayed: Irangate, Covert Affairs, and the Secret War in Laos.* New York: John Wiley & Sons, 1992.

Sewall, Gilbert T., ed. *The Eighties: A Reader.* Reading, Mass.: Perseus Books, 1998.

Sheridan, Geraldine, and Thomas Kenning. *Survivors.* London: Pan Books, 1993.

Shilts, Randy. *And the Band Played On: Politics, People, and the AIDS Epidemic.* New York and London: Viking Penguin, 1987.

Shultz, George P. *Turmoil and Triumph: My Years as Secretary of State.* New York: Charles Scribner's Sons, 1993.

Sick, Gary. *All Fall Down: America's Tragic Encounter with Iran.* New York: Random House, 1985.

———. *October Surprise: America's Hostages in Iran and the Election of Ronald Reagan.* London and New York: I.B. Taurus & Co., 1991.

Sickmann, Rocky. *Iranian Hostage: A Personal Diary of 444 Days in Captivity.* Topeka, Kans.: Crawford Press, 1982.

Slansky, Paul. *The Clothes Have No Emperor: A Chronicle of the American '80s.* New York: Simon and Schuster, 1989.

Spain, Daphne, and Suzanne M. Bianchi. *Balancing Act: Motherhood, Marriage, and Employment Among American Women.* New York: Russell Sage Foundation, 1996.

Speakes, Larry, with Robert Pack. *Speaking Out: The Reagan Presidency from Inside the White House.* New York: Charles Scribner's Sons, 1988.

Stevens, Mark. *The Insiders: The Truth Behind the Scandal Rocking Wall Street.* London: Harrap, 1987.

Stewart, James B. *Den of Thieves.* New York: Touchstone, 1992.

Taylor, John. *Circus of Ambition: The Culture of Wealth and Power in the Eighties.* New York: Warner Books, 1989.

Thatcher, Margaret. *The Downing Street Years.* New York: HarperCollins, 1993.

Thomas, G. Scott. *The Pursuit of the White House: A Handbook of Presidential Election Statistics and History.* New York: Greenwood Press, 1987.

Thompson, Kenneth W., ed. *The Carter Presidency: Fourteen Intimate Perspectives of Jimmy Carter.* Lanham, Md.: University Press of America, 1990.

Toropov, Brandon. *Encyclopedia of Cold War Politics.* New York: Facts on File, 2000.

Ueberroth, Peter, with Richard Levin and Amy Quinn. *Made in America: His Own Story.* London: Kingswood Press, 1986.

Wallis, Rodney. *Lockerbie: The Story and the Lessons.* Westport, Conn., and London: Praeger, 2001.

Walsh, Lawrence E. *Firewall: The Iran-Contra Conspiracy and Cover-up.* New York and London: W. W. Norton, 1997.

———. *Iran-Contra: The Final Report.* Washington, D.C.: Office of Independent Council for Iran/contra Matters, 1993. Reprint, New York: Times Books, 1994.

Welfeld, Irving. *HUD Scandals: Howling Headlines and Silent Fiascoes.* New Brunswick, N.J.: Transaction Publishers, 1992.

Weyr, Thomas. *Hispanic U.S.A.: Breaking the Melting Pot.* New York: Harper & Row, 1988.

Whitehead, Mary Beth, with Loretta Schwartz-Nobel. *A Mother's Story: The Truth About the Baby M Case.* London: Arrow Books, 1990.

Wills, Garry. *Reagan's America: Innocents at Home.* New York: Doubleday, 1987.

Woodward, Bob. *Veil: The Secret Wars of the CIA, 1981–87.* London: Headline, 1987.

## PERIODICALS

Abrams, Elliott. "Noriega Respects Power. Use It." *New York Times,* October 5, 1989, p. A-31.

Abramson, Jill, and Edward T. Pound. "How Deborah Dean and Washington Pals Controlled HUD Cash." *Wall Street Journal,* June 26, 1989, p. A-1.

"Academy Women: Ready to Take Command." *U.S. News & World Report,* May 26, 1980, pp. 32–36.

"Acid Rain and the Shamrock Summit." *New York Times,* March 16, 1985, p. 22.

"After Burford—What Next for EPA?" *U.S. News & World Report,* March 21, 1983, pp. 25–26.

"After the Storm over the Court." *New York Times,* December 14, 1987, p. A-22.

"Again, a Nominee for the Court." *Washington Post,* November 12, 1987, p. A-22.

"AIDS." *Newsweek,* August 12, 1985, pp. 20–27.

AIDS Activity Center for Infectious Diseases Center for Disease Control. "Acquired Immunodeficiency Syndrome (AIDS) Weekly Surveillance Report—United States." December 22, 1983.

"The AIDS Epidemic: The Search for a Cure." *Newsweek,* April 18, 1983, pp. 74–79.

"AIDS: Grim Prospects." *Newsweek,* November 10, 1986, pp. 20–21.

"Alternatives to the Tax." *Globe and Mail,* August 29, 1989, p. A-6.

Altman, Lawrence K. "Baboon's Heart Implanted in Infant on Coast." *New York Times,* October 28, 1984, sec. I, p. 38.

———. "Confusion Surrounds the Case of Baby Fae." *New York Times,* November 6, 1984, p. C-11.

———. "Heart Patient Briefly Leaves Bed." *New York Times,* November 30, 1984, p. A-1.

———. "Rare Cancer Seen in 41 Homosexuals." *New York Times,* July 3, 1981, p. A-20.

"America's Springtime Mood: 'We're Rallying.' " *U.S. News & World Report,* June 8, 1981, pp. 22–26.

Anderson, Dave. " 'Sarajevo' as a TV Sitcom." *New York Times,* February 12, 1984, sec. 4, p. 1.

Anderson, Jack. "Feud Hampers AIDS Progress." *San Francisco Chronicle,* August 19, 1985, p. 47.

Anderson, Jack, and Dale Van Atta. "Traitors of the 'Me' Generation." *Washington Post,* June 2, 1985, p. C-7.

"And Now, Campaign '88's Munchkin Marathon." *U.S. News & World Report,* February 29, 1988, pp. 12–14.

"Angry Attacks on America." *Time,* December 3, 1979, pp. 24–34.

Apple, R. W., Jr. "The Capital." *New York Times,* June 23, 1989, p. A-10.

———. "Outside Washington, Scandal Is Defined as Issues Ignored." *New York Times,* May 7, 1989, sec. 1, p. 1.

———. "Statesman Bush's Debut." *New York Times,* February 22, 1989, p. A-1.

"Apple Launches a Mac Attack." *Time,* January 30, 1984, pp. 68–69.

Arocha, Zita. "Wage Complaints from Hispanic Immigrants Increase Sharply in Past Year." *Washington Post,* December 18, 1988, p. B-9.

"As AIDS Scare Hits Nation's Blood Supply." *U.S. News & World Report,* July 25, 1983, pp. 71–72.

"As Women's Leaders Remap Their Strategy—." *U.S. News & World Report,* July 6, 1981, pp. 54–55.

"At Last, Action on the S&Ls." *Washington Post,* February 7, 1989, p. 24.

"At Last, the Battle Is Joined." *Time,* June 15, 1987, pp. 56–58.

"At the End of the Alley." *New York Times,* October 26, 1980, sec. 4, p. 18.

"The Baby Boomers Come of Age." *Newsweek,* March 30, 1981, pp. 34–37.

"Baby Fae's Heart Gives Out." *Newsweek,* November 26, 1984, p. 94.

"Baby M Meets Solomon's Sword." *Time,* February 15, 1988, p. 97.

Baker, Russell. "Once Again." *New York Times,* April 1, 1981, p. 31.

———. "The Secrets Boom." *New York Times,* November 30, 1985, p. 23.

Barbanel, Josh. "Air Controllers in Canada Refuse Most U.S. Flights." *New York Times,* August 7, 1981, p. 1.

Barbash, Fred. "Utterly Consistent in Conservative Votes and Opinions." *Washington Post,* June 18, 1986, p. A-1.

Belkin, Lisa. "Old Barriers to Sexual Equality Seen as Eroding, but Slowly." *New York Times,* August 20, 1989, sec. 1, p. 26.

Berg, Eric N. "One Year Later, the Debate over Bell Breakup Continues." *New York Times,* December 27, 1984, p. A-1.

Berger, Joseph. "Educators Call Bennett Too Negative." *New York Times,* April 26, 1988, p. A-23.

Berkow, Ira. "Commentators of Patriots?" *New York Times,* August 3, 1984, p. B-13.

Best, John. "Mulroney's Man in Royal Row." *Times* (London), April 29, 1985, p. 7.

"Big Setback for U.S." *U.S. News & World Report,* May 5, 1980, pp. 21–23.

"Blacks' Growing Toehold in Business." *U.S. News & World Report,* November 22, 1982, pp. 84–85.

"Boesky the Terrible." *Wall Street Journal,* November 18, 1986, p. 32.

Boffey, Philip M. "Old Critics Now Praise AIDS Panel." *New York Times,* March 7, 1988, p. B-4.

"Boredom—and Terror." *Newsweek,* December 17, 1979, pp. 32–33.

"Bork Gives Reasons for Continuing Fight." *New York Times,* October 16, 1987, p. 13.

Broyles, William, Jr. "Remembering a War We Wanted to Forget." *Newsweek,* November 22, 1982, pp. 82–83.

Bruske, Ed. "Black Hills Suit—A Will of Its Own." *Washington Post,* August 19, 1980, p. A-9.

Buchwald, Art. "That Which We Call MX by Any Other Name." *Washington Post,* December 5, 1982, p. G-1.

Buckley, William F., Jr. "Identify All the Carriers." *New York Times,* March 18, 1986, p. A-27.

———. "Somebody Has Got to Stop This Civil Rights Thing." *Washington Post,* April 12, 1988, p. A-23.

"Bush's Shovel Brigade." *U.S. News & World Report,* August 7, 1989, pp. 14–16.

"Canada: A Good Neighbor Proves Itself." *U.S. News & World Report,* February 11, 1980, p. 5.

"Canada's Liberals Battle the Trade Pact." *New York Times,* August 7, 1988, sec. 4, p. 3.

"Canada Turns Right." *New York Times,* September 6, 1984, p. A-22.

"Can Bush Survive Quayle?" *U.S. News & World Report,* August 29/September 5, 1988, pp. 24–29.

Caplan, Lincoln. "If Robert Bork Didn't Exist, Reagan Would Have to Invent Him." *Washington Post,* July 5, 1987, p. D-2.

"Carnage in Lebanon." *Time,* October 31, 1983, pp. 14–25.

"Carter Brothers 'Close but So Far Apart It's Pathetic.' " *U.S. News & World Report,* August 4, 1980, p. 19.

"Carter's Attack on Inflation." *Newsweek,* March 24, 1980, pp. 24–30.

"Casey on Strike." *Washington Post,* June 15, 1981, p. 20.

"The Central American Debate." *Washington Post,* January 12, 1984, p. A-18.

"Central American Moment." *Washington Post,* June 28, 1984, p. A-14.

"Changing Course." *U.S. News & World Report,* October 6, 1986, pp. 46–47.

Chavez, Linda. "Is Spanish Wrong Signal to Latinos?" *Lost Angeles Times,* August 8, 1988, part 2, p. 5.

"CIA Spy Hunt." *Newsweek,* November 4, 1985, pp. 22–24.

"Cincinnati Stampede." *Newsweek,* December 17, 1979, pp. 52–54.

Clark, Lindley H., Jr. "Are the Corporate Raiders Really White Knights?" *Wall Street Journal,* July 16, 1985, p. 33.

Cleroux, Richard, Graham Fraser, and Stanley Oziewicz. "Premiers Approve Quebec Demands." *Globe and Mail* (Montreal), May 1, 1987, p. A-1.

Clines, Francis X. "Pension Changes Signed into Law." *New York Times,* April 21, 1983, p. A-17.

———. "Salute Opening for Vietnam Veterans." *New York Times,* November 11, 1982, p. B-15.

"Coca-Cola's Big Fizzle." *Time,* July 22, 1985, pp. 48–52.

Cockburn, Alexander. "Tax Revision Is Social Regression." *Wall Street Journal,* August 21, 1986, p. 23.

Cohen, Richard. "AIDS: Victims Twice Over." *Washington Post,* November 25, 1986, p. A-21.

———. "Bush 'Conflicted.' " *Washington Post,* February 14, 1989, p. A-21.

———. "Just Say Yes?" *Washington Post Magazine,* February 28, 1988, p. 5.

———. "Rehnquist's 'Brilliance.' " *Washington Post,* August 7, 1986, p. A-23.

"The Cold War Is Over." *New York Times,* April 2, 1989, sec. 4, p. 30.

"College Grads Hear Words of Wisdom." *U.S. News & World Report,* June 15, 1981, p. 35.

Collins, Michael. "Riding the Beat." *Washington Post,* January 30, 1986, p. A-25.

"Community Standards." *Wall Street Journal,* December 6, 1989, p. A-14.

"Compact Discs Now the Hottest Sound in Town." *U.S. News & World Report,* June 17, 1985, pp. 62–63.

"The Computer Moves In." *Time,* January 3, 1983, pp. 14–24.

"Confessions of a Raider." *Newsweek,* October 20, 1986, pp. 51–55.

"A Conflict of the Have-Nots." *Newsweek,* December 12, 1988, pp. 28–29.

"Congressional Crack." *Wall Street Journal,* May 17, 1989, p. A-18.

"Congress's Watergate." *Wall Street Journal,* November 15, 1989, p. A-26.

"The Contras' Proxy War." *Newsweek,* October 20, 1986, pp. 31–32.

"The Convulsion of St. Helens." *Newsweek,* June 2, 1980, pp. 22–31.

Cowan, Alison Leigh. "Day to Remember in Financial District." *New York Times,* October 20, 1987, p. D-1.

Crittenden, Ann. "In the Braves' New World, Indians Like Land, Not Cash." *New York Times,* November 2, 1980, sec. 4, p. 8-E.

"The Cuban Tide is a Flood." *Newsweek,* May 19, 1980, pp. 28–29.

Culhane, John. "Special Effects Are Revolutionizing Film." *New York Times,* July 4, 1982, sec. 2, p. 13.

Cushman, John H., Jr. "U.S. Was Tipped Off 2 Weeks Ago of Possible Attack on Pan Am." *New York Times,* December 23, 1988, p. A-16.

Daniloff, Nicholas. "What Kremlin Seeks By Boycotting Games." *U.S. News & World Report,* May 21, 1984, p. 25.

"D-Day in Grenada." *Time,* November 7, 1983, pp. 22–28.

"Deadlock in Iceland." *Newsweek,* October 20, 1986, pp. 20–26.

"Death of a Gallant Pioneer." *Time,* April 4, 1983, p. 62.

"Debacle in the Desert." *Time,* May 5, 1980, pp. 12–25.

DeCosta, Katherine Gale. "Anticomputerism." *New York Times,* August 27, 1984, p. A-19.

"The Democrats—and the Democrats." *New York Times,* March 15, 1984, p. A-30.

Denton, Herbert H. "Canadians Basking in Olympic Glow." *Washington Post,* February 12, 1988, p. A-1.

———. "Trudeau Emphatically Ends Silence." *Washington Post,* May 29, 1987, p. A-28.

*Department of State Bulletin* 81, no. 2048, March 1981, p. 17.

"'Diabolically Well-Planned.'" *Time,* January 9, 1989, pp. 26–28.

Diebel, Linda. "It's Time for Healing, PM Says." *Toronto Star,* November 22, 1988, p. B-1.

"Dismal Legacy on Civil Rights." *New York Times,* March 21, 1988, p. A-18.

"The Double Whammy of Taxes and Inflation." *U.S. News & World Report,* July 14, 1980, p. 47.

"Drawing the Line on the Constitution." *Toronto Star,* April 28, 1987, p. A-10.

Drohan, Madelaine. "Liberal MPs Campaign against Proposed GST." *Globe and Mail,* August 24, 1989, p. A-10.

"The Drug Bill." *Washington Post,* October 25, 1988, p. A-26.

"Drugs on Main Street: The Enemy Up Close." *U.S. News & World Report,* June 27, 1988, pp. 14–19.

Dunning, Jennifer. "Women and AIDS: Discussing Precautions." *New York Times,* November 3, 1986, p. C-15.

"Earthquakes in the Communist World." *New York Times,* June 11, 1989, sec. 4, p. 28.

Egan, Timothy. "As Oil Stain Spreads, the Delicate Balance of Resources Is Undone." *New York Times,* April 1, 1989, p. 8.

———. "Exxon Concedes It Can't Contain Most of Oil Spill." *New York Times,* March 30, 1989, p. A-1.

———. "Fishermen and State Take Charge of Effort to Control Alaska Spill." *New York Times,* March 29, 1989, p. B-5.

"An End and a Beginning." *U.S. News & World Report,* November 14, 1988, p. 21.

"An End to the Long Ordeal." *Time,* February 2, 1981, pp. 24–29.

"Escape from Bedlam and Boredom." *Time,* May 12, 1980, p. 38.

Evans, Rowland, and Robert Novak, "Toughening Up." *Washington Post,* December 22, 1989, p. A-19.

"Even So, Affirmative Action Lives." *New York Times,* January 25, 1989, p. A-22.

"Excerpts from Bush's News Conference on Central America." *New York Times,* December 22, 1989, p. A-10.

"Excerpts from Bush's News Session." *New York Times,* June 6, 1989, p. A-15.

"Excerpts from Court Decision on the Regulation of Abortion." *New York Times,* July 4, 1989, p. 12.

"Excerpts from Court Opinions in Voiding of Richmond's Contracting Plan." *New York Times,* January 24, 1989, p. A-18.

"Excerpts from Ferraro's News Conference About Finances." *New York Times,* August 22, 1984, p. B-6.

"Excerpts from High Court's Decision Barring Prosecution in Flag Protest." *New York Times,* June 22, 1989, p. B-8.

"Excerpts from Primer for Insurgents." *New York Times,* October 17, 1984, p. A-12.

"Excerpts from Report by AIDS Panel Chairman." *New York Times,* June 3, 1988, p. A-16.

"Excerpts from the Interview with the President." *Wall Street Journal,* February 14, 1989, p. A-4.

"An Explosion in the Sky." *Newsweek,* January 2, 1989, pp. 16–19.

"A Fair Rebuke to President Reagan" *Chicago Tribune,* March 24, 1988, sec. 1, p. 24.

"The FBI Stings Congress." *Time,* February 18, 1980, pp. 10–20.

Fein, Esther B. " 'Live Aid' Concert Is Aiming for the Sky." *New York Times,* July 12, 1985, p. C-5.

———. "Reports of Concert Aid Range up to $50 Million." *New York Times,* July 15, 1985, p. C-18.

"A $50 Million Handshake." *Newsweek,* May 19, 1986, p. 25.

"Fire and Fury in Miami." *Time,* June 2, 1980, pp. 10–19.

Fish, Robert. "Libya Ducks Bomb Blame." *Times* (London), April 4, 1986, p. 7.

"Flaunting Wealth: It's Back in Style." *U.S. News & World Report,* September 21, 1981, pp. 61–64.

Fraser, Graham. "Outlook Unsettled for Talks on Constitution." *Globe and Mail* (Montreal), April 30, 1987, p. A-8.

Freedman, Samuel G. "Live Aid and the Woodstock Nation." *New York Times,* July 18, 1985, p. C-19.

Fried, Joseph P. "Jury Finds Helmsley Guilty of Evading Federal Taxes." *New York Times,* August 31, 1989, p. B-3.

"From Patrons to Partners." *Time,* July 24, 1989, p. 19.

Gauger, Marcia. " 'You Could Die Here.' " *Time,* December 3, 1979, pp. 26–27.

"Gays and Lesbians on Campus." *Newsweek,* April 5, 1982, pp. 75–77.

"Getting Tough." *Time,* February 1, 1988, pp. 52–53.

Giametti, A. Bartlett. "Men of Baseball, Lend an Ear." *New York Times,* June 16, 1981, p. 19.

Gilder, George. "The Victim of His Virtues." *Wall Street Journal,* April 18, 1989, p. A-24.

Gill, Kerry, and Ronald Faux. "Flames Light the Night Sky as Crash of Jumbo Brings Horror to a Small Town." *Times* (London), December 22, 1988, p. 2.

"Girl 'Responsive, Alert' after Double Transplant." *Chicago Tribune,* February 16, 1984, p. 8.

Glasser, Ira. "Bush Lowers the Flag." *New York Times,* June 28, 1989, p. A-23.

Glassman, James K. "The 'Ethics' Frenzy." *Washington Post,* May 28, 1989, pp. B-1, B-2.

"Glory Hallelujah!" *Time,* August 13, 1984, pp. 36–40.

Goar, Carol. "Constitution: Last Piece in Place." *Toronto Star,* May 2, 1987, p. B-1.

" 'God, I Want to Live!' " *Time,* June 2, 1980, pp. 26–35.

Goldsmith, James. "Hostile Takeovers Easier to Swallow than Poison Pills." *Wall Street Journal,* February 11, 1985, p. 22.

" 'Good Chemistry.' " *Time,* June 13, 1988, pp. 12–18.

Goodman, Ellen. "In the Swirl of Surrogacy." *Washington Post,* February 6, 1988, p. A-23.

———. "Needles for Addicts? No." *Washington Post,* July 2, 1988, p. A-23.

"The Great 1980 Non-Debate." *Time,* October 20, 1980, pp. 70–71.

"Greed on Wall Street." *Newsweek,* May 26, 1986, pp. 45–46.

Greenhouse, Linda. "Supreme Court, 5-4, Narrowing Roe v. Wade, Upholds Sharp State Limits on Abortions." *New York Times,* July 4, 1989, p. 1.

Gross, Jane. "Public's Response to the Jury's Decision: Divided and Deep-Seated Opinions." *New York Times,* June 18, 1987, p. B-6.

Gruson, Lindsey. "Hicksville Divided by Moment of Silence." *New York Times,* February 29, 1984, p. B-4.

———. "Noriega Stealing Election, Carter Says." *New York Times,* May 9, 1989, p. A-1.

"Hail to the New Chief." *Newsweek,* February 2, 1981, pp. 47–51.

Hall, Carla. "Sympathy in the Gay Community." *Washington Post,* July 27, 1985, p. G-1.

Halloran, Richard. "Hostage Rescue Commander Denies He Favored Pushing on to Tehran." *New York Times,* May 2, 1980, p. A-12.

Harrington, Richard. "Live Aid Concerts Raise Millions for African Relief." *Washington Post,* July 14, 1985, p. A-16.

Harris, David. "Last Stand for an Ancient Indian Way." *New York Times Magazine,* March 16, 1980, pp. 41, 63.

Hart, Gary. "The MX: Bad for Security, Bad for Survival." *Washington Post,* May 25, 1983, p. A-25.

"Has the U.S. Lost Its Clout?" *Newsweek,* November 26, 1979, pp. 46–49.

"Health Official Doubts AIDS Will Be Cured." *San Francisco Chronicle,* January 28, 1988, p. A-11.

"Heat Wave: 100-a-Day Killer." *U.S. News & World Report,* July 28, 1980, p. 7.

" 'He Is Ready to Blow Up the Aircraft.' " *U.S. News & World Report,* June 24, 1985, p. 11.

"A Helpless Giant in Iran." *Newsweek,* November 19, 1979, pp. 61–75.

Henderson, John. "Home Users of Computers Form Network." *Wall Street Journal,* April 1, 1981, p. 31.

Hentoff, Nat. "A Frenzy of Flag-Waving." *Washington Post,* July 1, 1989, p. A-17.

"Here Come the Microkids." *Time,* May 3, 1982, pp. 50–56.

Herman, Robin. "A Disease's Spread Provokes Anxiety." *New York Times,* August 8, 1982, p. 31.

Hershey, Robert D., Jr. "Praise on Capitol Hill for Rescue Proposal." *New York Times,* February 7, 1989, p. D-9.

Hill, Retha. "Jackson Calls Drugs Threat to U.S. Security." *Washington Post,* March 6, 1988, p. A-20.

Hoagland, Jim. "Bush, Gorbachev Star in Own 'Ghostbusters.' " *Washington Post,* December 4, 1989, p. A-21.

"Holding Up America." *New York Times,* August 4, 1981, p. 14.

"The Hollywood Route." *Los Angeles Times Magazine,* March 27, 1988, p. 16.

"The Horror, the Horror!" *Time,* May 2, 1983, pp. 28–31.

"The Hostages Return." *Newsweek,* February 2, 1981, p. 22–32.

"A House Divided." *Time,* August 15, 1988, pp. 14–15.

"House OKs Boost in AIDS Spending." *San Francisco Chronicle,* October 3, 1985, p. 16.

"How Long till Equality?" *Time,* July 12, 1982, pp. 20–29.

"How Ripe for a Crash?" *Time,* October 5, 1987, pp. 44–46.

"How to Deal with Moscow." *Newsweek,* November 29, 1982, pp. 30–37.

"The HUD Ripoff." *Newsweek,* August 7, 1989, pp. 16–22.

" 'Humoring' Indians Bring Protests from Tribal Leaders." *New York Times,* June 1, 1988, p. A-13.

"Hurtling through the Void." *Time,* June 20, 1983, p. 68.

Hymowitz, Carol, and Timothy D. Schellhardt. "The Glass Ceiling." *Wall Street Journal,* March 24, 1986, sec. 4, pp. 1D–5D.

Iacocca, Lee. "What Liberty Means to Me." *Newsweek,* July 7, 1986, pp. 18–19.

"If America Is Serious about AIDS, Then Washington Must Fight Discrimination." *New York Times,* June 5, 1988, sec. 4, p. 30.

"In Our Hands." *Wall Street Journal,* October 20, 1987, p. 38.

"Inside the GOP's Economic 'Revolution.'" *U.S. News & World Report,* February 16, 1981, pp. 21–22.

"An Interview with Nancy Reagan." *Time,* April 13, 1981, p. 39.

"An Interview with President Reagan." *Time,* September 19, 1983, p. 21.

"Invasion of the Video Creatures." *Newsweek,* November 16, 1981, pp. 90–91.

Isaacson, Walter. "After the Fall." *Time,* November 2, 1987, pp. 20–21.

"Israel Apologizes to U.S. in Spy Case." *New York Times,* December 2, 1985, p. A-4.

"Is the U.S. Ready for a Black President?" *U.S. News & World Report,* July 25, 1983, pp. 21–22.

"Is This Any Way to Make Foreign Policy?" *Newsweek,* July 7, 1986, p. 22.

Jefferson, David J. "Keating of American Continental Corp. Comes Out Fighting." *Wall Street Journal,* April 18, 1989, p. B-2.

"Jesse Jackson's Statement." *Washington Post,* June 29, 1984, p. A-4.

"Jesse Wins a 'Syria Primary.'" *Newsweek,* January 16, 1984, pp. 14–15.

"Jim Wright Resigns." *Washington Post,* June 1, 1989, p. A-24.

"Jobs: A Million That Will Never Come Back." *U.S. News & World Report,* September 13, 1982, pp. 53–56.

Johnson, Frank. "Belsen and Bitburg: Sorrow and Slapstick." *Times* (London), May 6, 1985, p. 10.

Johnson, Haynes. "Exxon's Good Fortune." *Washington Post,* May 5, 1989, p. A-2.

———. "Noriega: A Specter of U.S. Policy." *Washington Post,* May 12, 1989, p. A-2.

Johnson, Kirk. "Goetz Case, Back in Court Today, Is Still Legal Puzzle After 2 Years." *New York Times,* March 23, 1987, p. B-7.

Johnson, William. "A Truly National Government Just When It's Needed." *Vancouver Sun,* November 22, 1988, p. B-3.

"Juggling Family, Job and Aged Dependent." *New York Times,* January 26, 1989, p. B-8.

Kassebaum, Nancy Landon. "Hold Firm on Lebanon." *New York Times,* October 26, 1983, p. A-27.

Keating, Michael. "Environmentalists Skeptical about Acid-Rain Talks." *Globe and Mail* (Montreal), March 19, 1985, p. 5.

"A Keen Mind, Fine Judgment." *Newsweek,* July 20, 1981, pp. 18–19.

Kerr, Peter. "The Unspeakable is Debated: Should Drugs Be Legalized?" *New York Times,* May 15, 1988, sec. 1, p. 24.

"Key Sections from Study of Latin Region by Kissinger Panel." *New York Times,* January 12, 1984, p. A-14.

"Kids Who Sell Crack." *Time,* May 9, 1988, pp. 20–23.

"Killer of 14 Wanted 'Revenge.'" *Vancouver Sun,* December 7, 1989, p. A-2.

Kilpatrick, James J. "It's Reagan's Mess at HUD." *Washington Post,* August 11, 1989, p. A-25.

"King's Dream: How It Stands 20 Years Later." *U.S. News & World Report,* August 29, 1983, pp. 47–48.

Kissinger, Henry. "The Drama in Beijing." *Washington Post,* June 11, 1989, p. C-7.

Kittle, Robert A., and Patricia Avery. "Women's Issues—and the Reagan Record." *U.S. News & World Report,* September 5, 1983, p. 34.

Krauthammer, Charles. "Government as Rescue Squad." *Washington Post,* November 7, 1986, p. A-27.

———. "No, the Cold War Isn't Really Over," *Time,* September 5, 1988, pp. 83–84.

———. "The Using of Baby Fae." *Time,* December 3, 1984, p. 87.

Krieger, Lisa M. "AIDS Workers Battle Burnout." *San Francisco Chronicle,* August 27, 1988, pp. A-1, A-10.

Kroll, Kathleen. "A Worker: 'I Begrudge Living Less Well than the Poor Do.' " *U.S. News & World Report,* March 30, 1981, p. 46.

"The Lady's Party." *Time,* July 14, 1986, pp. 10–20.

Laffer, Arthur. "What Went Wrong with 'Supply-Side' Economics." *U.S. News & World Report,* January 18, 1982, pp. 36–38.

Lambert, Bruce. "Needles for Addicts: Test Phase Begins." *New York Times,* June 26, 1988, sec. 4, p. 7.

Landau, Saul. "Imperialism, Bush Style." *New York Times,* December 22, 1989, p. A-39.

Landsberg, Michele. "Judge in Baby M Case Spoke in the Language of Feminists." *Globe and Mail,* February 6, 1988, p. A-2.

———. "Killer's Rage Too Familiar to Canadians." *Toronto Star,* December 8, 1989, p. A-1.

"The Last Day in the Life." *Time,* December 22, 1980, pp. 18–24.

Lautens, Gary. "Make Tuna Surprise a Compulsory Dish at Tory Caucus Dinner." *Toronto Star,* September 20, 1985, p. A-2.

"Leaders' Tolerance Praised by Queen." *Globe and Mail* (Montreal), April 19, 1981, p. 12.

"Let's Get Trivial." *Time,* October 24, 1983, p. 88.

Lewis, Anthony. "Merchants of Death." *New York Times,* May 19, 1989, p. A-31.

———. "Reagan's Dream." *New York Times,* October 16, 1986, p. A-31.

"The Life and Death of Baby Fae." *New York Times,* November 17, 1984, p. 22.

"Life on the Precipice with the Arbitrage King." *Newsweek,* December 1, 1986, p. 52.

Lindsey, Robert. "A Speck Pierces the Horizon." *New York Times,* April 15, 1981, p. 1.

Lipton, Martin. "Takeover Abuses Mortgage the Future." *Wall Street Journal,* April 5, 1985, p. 16.

"The Long Goodbye." *Globe and Mail* (Montreal), February 29, 1984, p. 6.

Lubenow, Gerald C. "Reagan: Secret of Success." *Newsweek,* April 7, 1980, pp. 26–27.

Magnuson, R., et al. "Turbulence in the Tower." *Time,* August 17, 1981, p. 17.

"Maid Testifies Helmsley Denied Paying Taxes." *New York Times,* July 12, 1989, p. B-2.

"Making Up the Canadian Mind." *Washington Post,* September 2, 1988, p. A-20.

Malcolm, Andrew H. "Something More Than Olympic Torch Is Crossing the Country." *New York Times,* June 10, 1984, sec. 1, p. 26.

Mandorf, Geri L. S. "Career and Family, An Elusive Balance." *New York Times,* February 26, 1989, sec. 21, p. 16.

Mann, Judy. "The Demeaning 'Mommy Track': Separate and Unequal." *Washington Post,* March 15, 1989, p. C-3.

"A Man Who Cares." *Newsweek,* March 9, 1981, p. 57.

"The Man Who Made Super Tuesday." *Washington Post,* March 15, 1984, p. A-20.

Marotte, Bertrand. "Bourassa Is Selling Out Quebec, Johnson Charges." *Globe and Mail* (Montreal), May 2, 1987, p. A-5.

Marriott, Michel. "Smokers Adjust to New York Curbs." *New York Times,* May 2, 1988, p. B-3.

"*M★A★S★H,* You Were a Smash." *Time,* February 28, 1983, pp. 64–66.

Mathews, Jay. "Barney Clark in TV Debut, Taped, but Live." *Washington Post,* March 3, 1983, p. A-2.

———. "Smoking Ban Sparks Midair Revolt." *Washington Post,* January 1, 1988, p. A-1.

Mayer, Caroline E. "New Coke Joins Marketing Hall of Flops." *Washington Post,* July 12, 1985, p. B-1.

McAllister, Bill. "Lawmakers Ask Strong U.S. Action." *Washington Post,* June 5, 1989, p. A-24.

McCombs, Phil. "Veterans Honor Fallen, Mark Reconciliation." *Washington Post,* November 14, 1982, p. A-18.

McGill, Douglas C. "Cigarette Makers in a War on Bans." *New York Times,* December 24, 1988, p. 37.

McGillivray, Don. "Were Killings Just a Random Act?" *Vancouver Sun,* December 8, 1989, p. A-13.

McGrory, Mary. "Vietnam Memorial Seen as 'First Step in a Healing Process.'" *Washington Post,* November 9, 1982, p. A-3.

McKenzie, Robert. "Quebec First to Approve Accord." *Toronto Star,* June 24, 1987, p. A-1.

"Memorial." *Washington Post,* April 26, 1983, p. A-18.

Meredith, Nikki. "Search for the Cause and Treatment of a Rare Cancer That Has Reached Epidemic Proportions among Homosexuals." *San Francisco Chronicle,* June 6, 1982, Cal. sec., pp. 13–14.

Milk, Leslie Berg. "The Age of Atari: Bleeping Into Oblivion." *Washington Post,* January 28, 1982, p. MD-2.

"The Milken Indictment." *Wall Street Journal,* March 31, 1989, p. A-14.

"Milken's Woes Not on Menu." *New York Times,* March 17, 1989, p. D-2.

"Mondale for President." *New York Times,* October 28, 1984, sec. 4, p. 22.

Montgomery, Charlotte, and Thomas Walkom. "Pierre Trudeau Steps Down." *Globe and Mail* (Montreal), March 1, 1984, p. 1.

"A Most Explicit Report." *Time,* November 3, 1986, pp. 76–77.

Mott, Alexander. "When the Indian is No More, America Will Have Destroyed Its Own Dreams." *Los Angeles Times,* March 4, 1980, part 2, p. 5.

"Mr. Consensus." *Time,* August 21, 1989, pp. 16–22.

"Mr. Reagan Goes to Washington." *Newsweek,* November 24, 1980, pp. 38–39.

"Mr. Trudeau Resigns." *Washington Post,* March 2, 1984, p. A-26.

"MX 'Important to Demonstrate National Will.'" *U.S. News & World Report,* April 25, 1983, pp. 24–25.

"NASA Official's Statement." *Washington Post,* January 29, 1986, p. A-6.

"NASA Readies a Nighttime Dazzler." *Time,* August 29, 1983, p. 62.

"The Nature of Tuna." *Globe and Mail* (Montreal), September 19, 1985, p. 10.

"A Network Blockbuster." *Time,* April 1, 1985, pp. 60–63.

"The New Age of Jackson." *U.S. News & World Report,* March 14, 1988, pp. 15–19.

"A New Battle over School Reform." *Time,* May 9, 1988, pp. 60–61.

"The New Dealmakers." *Newsweek,* May 26, 1986, pp. 47–52.

"New Headache for the President." *U.S. News & World Report,* August 4, 1980, pp. 17–19.

"A New Spirit of Giving." *Newsweek,* June 2, 1986, pp. 18–20.

"Nixon Lauds Bush for China Policy." *New York Times,* June 25, 1989, sec. 1, p. 11.

" 'No Economic Miracles.' " *Newsweek,* February 11, 1980, p. 75.

" 'None of the Above': Nation's Political Mood." *U.S. News & World Report,* September 29, 1980, pp. 20–22.

Nordheimer, Jon. "For Cuban-Americans, an Era of Change." *New York Times,* April 13, 1988, pp. A-1, A-19.

Norment, Lynn. "The Trials and Triumphs of Working Mothers." *Ebony,* September 1989, pp. 38–45.

"No 'Special Stresses' for Women in Battle," *U.S. News & World Report,* March 3, 1980, p. 34.

" 'Not Guilty.' " *Time,* June 29, 1987, pp. 10–11.

"Now Comes the Hard Part." *Time,* May 4, 1981, p. 17–18.

Oakes, John B. "Acid Rain's Political Poison." *New York Times,* April 8, 1985, p. A-17.

"Of God and Greed." *Time,* June 8, 1987, pp. 70–74.

"Oh, You Beautiful Dolls!" *Newsweek,* December 12, 1983, pp. 78–81.

"Oil and Dirty Hands." *New York Times,* April 5, 1989, p. A-28.

"The Old Lion Still Roars." *Time,* April 4, 1983, p. 12.

"An Olympic Boycott?" *Newsweek,* January 28, 1980, pp. 20–28.

"$105 Million Award to 8 Tribes Is Upheld." *New York Times,* July 1, 1980, p. B-9.

"One Miracle, Many Doubts." *Time,* December 10, 1984, pp. 70–77.

Ono, Yoko. Statement following the death of John Lennon, December 10, 1980. *Newsweek,* December 22, 1980, p. 36.

"On the Scene: A Look at Ranting in Iran." *U.S. News & World Report,* December 17, 1979, pp. 30–31.

"Onward, Women!" *Time,* December 4, 1989, pp. 80–89.

"Open Heart, Open Arms." *Time,* May 19, 1980, pp. 14–18.

"Operation Damage Control." *Time,* June 24, 1985, pp. 31–32.

O'Sullivan, John. "Lioness in a Den of Daniels." *Times* (London), April 16, 1985, p. 20.

"The Other Goetz Jury." *New York Times,* June 17, 1987, p. A-30.

Pareles, Jon. "Concert: A Daylong Mix of Country with Rock." *New York Times,* September 23, 1985, p. A-16.

"Partial Text of Wright's Resignation Speech." *Washington Post,* June 1, 1989, p. A-18.

"The Passive President." *New York Times,* September 17, 1989, sec. 4, p. 22.

"Paying for America." *New York Times,* July 4, 1980, p. A-16.

"Paying Homage to History." *Time,* May 13, 1985, pp. 16–24.

"Paying the Wages of Sin." *Newsweek,* March 30, 1987, p. 28.

Peer, Elizabeth. "How to Work the Thing." *Newsweek,* February 22, 1982, p. 53.

"People." *Time,* June 9, 1986, pp. 66–67.

Perlez, Jane. "5 Senators Oppose School Prayer Measure." *New York Times,* March 16, 1984, pp. B-1, B-5.

Philips, Don, and Helen Dewar. "Flag Ruling Angers Congress; Bush Denounces Desecration." *Washington Post,* June 23, 1989, p. A-1.

"Players' Happiness Has Limit." *New York Times,* August 1, 1981, p. 17.

"Playing Nuclear Poker." *Time,* January 31, 1983, pp. 10–23.

Pollack, Andrew. "Bell System Breakup Opens Era of Great Expectations and Great Concern." *New York Times,* January 1, 1984, p. 12.

"President's News Conference on Foreign and Domestic Issues." *New York Times,* October 14, 1989, p. 8.

"Pride and Prejudice." *Time,* May 7, 1984, pp. 30–40.

Protzman, Ferdinand. "East Berliners Explore Land Long Forgotten." *New York Times,* November 10, 1989, p. A-1.

Proudfoot, Jim. "Give Citizens of Calgary a Gold." *Toronto Star,* February 29, 1988, p. D-1.

"Pull U.S. Marines Out of Lebanon?" *U.S. News & World Report,* September 19, 1983, p. 29.

" 'Pushy' Mulroney Aides Ruffle British Feathers." *Saturday Star* (Toronto), April 27, 1985, p. A-1.

"A Radical Plan for Tax Reform." *Newsweek,* May 19, 1986, pp. 20–23.

"Raging Debate over the Desert Raid." *Time,* May 12, 1980, pp. 32–34.

"The Raider Barons: Boon or Bane for Business?" *U.S. News & World Report,* April 8, 1985, pp. 51–54.

Raine, George. "150,000 See AIDS Quilt." *San Francisco Chronicle,* October 9, 1988, p. A-1.

———. "Size of Project Reflects the Nation's Loss." *San Francisco Chronicle,* October 9, 1988, p. A-21.

Raines, Howell. "Mondale Says He Won't Run with Jackson." *New York Times,* July 12, 1984, p. A-1.

———. "Thatcher Salute to Reagan Years." *New York Times,* June 2, 1988, p. A-9.

Raspberry, William. "From Unemployed to Self-Employed." *Washington Post,* May 18, 1988, p. B-3.

"Reagan and the Blacks." *Newsweek,* July 13, 1981, pp. 20–21.

"Reagan Justice." *Newsweek,* June 30, 1986, pp. 14–19.

"Reagan, Mulroney Cement Friendship." *Times* (London), March 19, 1985, p. 7.

"Reaganomics Widens Gap between the Rich and Poor, Study Says." *Wall Street Journal,* September 14, 1982, p. 21.

"Reagan Says Blast Won't Deter Peace Efforts." *New York Times,* April 21, 1983, p. A-14.

"Reagan's Mr. Right." *Time,* June 30, 1986, pp. 24–33.

"Reagan's News Conference on Domestic and Foreign Matters." *New York Times,* October 23, 1987, p. A-8.

"Reagan's Remarks on Attack." *New York Times,* October 24, 1983, p. A-8.

"The Reagan Style Starts to Pay Off." *U.S. News & World Report,* February 16, 1981, p. 9.

"The Reagan Team on Terrorism." *U.S. News & World Report,* July 1, 1985, p. 21.

"'Reagan Understands How to Be President.'" *U.S. News & World Report,* April 27, 1981, pp. 23–24.

"Reagan: What He Stands For." *U.S. News & World Report,* May 5, 1980, pp. 29–32.

"Reagan White House—Glitter and Grace." *U.S. News & World Report,* June 1, 1981, pp. 43–45.

"The Real Epidemic: Fear and Despair." *Time,* July 4, 1983, pp. 56–58.

"Real Welfare Reform, At Last." *New York Times,* October 1, 1988, p. 26.

"Regrets Only." *Wall Street Journal,* December 27, 1989, p. A-6.

Reid, T. R. "3 Ex-Hostages Are Still Captives of Concern." *Washington Post,* June 28, 1985, p. A-28.

Reinhold, Robert. "Surge in Bogus Papers Predicted In Wake of Change in Alien Law." *New York Times,* October 20, 1986, p. A-1.

"Republicans' Reply to Carter Message." *U.S. News & World Report,* February 4, 1980, p. 77.

"Responses of the President to Queries on German Visit." *New York Times,* April 19, 1985, p. A-13.

Richler, Mordechai. "Reverberations in America's Attic." *Time,* August 27, 1984, p. 28.

"Riding the Drug Issue." *Time,* April 25, 1988, pp. 32–34.

"Ripples Throughout Society." *Time,* July 23, 1984, pp. 34–35.

"Roaming the High Frontier." *Time,* November 26, 1984, pp. 16–20.

Roberts, Paul Craig. "Supply-Side Economics: A Fiscal Revolution?" *Wall Street Journal,* January 22, 1981, p. 24.

"Rock Around the World." *Newsweek,* July 22, 1985, pp. 56–58.

"Rocking the Global Village." *Time,* July 22, 1985, pp. 66–67.

Rockwell, John. "A 'Thriller' from Jackson." *San Francisco Chronicle,* January 16, 1983, Review sect., p. 15.

Rodriguez, Richard. "The Fear of Losing a Culture." *Time,* July 11, 1988, p. 84.

Rohter, Larry. "As Word Spreads in Panama, Thousands Turn Out to Cheer." *New York Times,* January 4, 1990, p. A-1.

Rosenblatt, Roger. "Huck and Miss Liberty." *Time,* July 7, 1986, p. 25.

———. "A Sense of Where We Are." *Time,* April 13, 1981, p. 21.

Rosenfeld, Megan. "Across the Nation, Reactions Divided on Court's Abortion Ruling." *Washington Post,* July 4, 1989, p. A-5.

Rosenthal, A. M. "A Poem for Seven Judges." *New York Times,* February 5, 1988, p. A-31.

Rowan, Carl. "Do Only the Unborn Matter?" *Washington Post,* February 1, 1984, p. A-15.

Rowan, Hobart. "Doubts about Texaco's Takeover." *Washington Post,* January 12, 1984, p. A-19.

Royster, Vermont. "Thinking Things Over: A Warrior President." *Wall Street Journal,* August 11, 1981, p. 22.

———. "Thinking Things Over: Weep Not, Dear Ladies." *Wall Street Journal,* June 23, 1982, p. 26.

Safire, William. "Option 3: Pro-Comp.' " *New York Times,* July 6, 1989, p. A-21.

————. "Towering Inferno." *New York Times,* February 13, 1989, p. A-21.

"Sally Ride: Ready for Liftoff." *Newsweek,* June 13, 1983, pp. 36–51.

"Sally's Joy Ride into the Sky." *Time,* June 13, 1983, pp. 56–58.

"The SALT Backlash." *Newsweek,* June 16, 1986, p. 23.

"Samantha Smith—Pawn in Propaganda War." *U.S. News & World Report,* July 18, 1983, p. 27.

Samuelson, Paul A. "How Deep the Recession?" *Newsweek,* June 30, 1980, p. 56.

Samuelson, Robert J. "Consumer Sovereignty." *Washington Post,* July 24, 1985, p. D-1.

————. "The Super Bowl of Scandal." *Newsweek,* December 1, 1986, p. 64.

Sanger, David E. "For Apple, a Risky Assault on I.B.M." *New York Times,* January 23, 1984, p. D-5.

Saul, John Raulston. "Canada Debates Its Soul." *New York Times,* November 16, 1988, p. A-31.

"Save? Spend? What People Would Do with a Tax Cut." *U.S. News & World Report,* March 23, 1981, pp. 22–23.

"Saying 'No' to New Coke." *Newsweek,* June 24, 1985, pp. 32–33.

Schlesinger, James R. "Strategic Deterrence—or Strategic Confusion?" *Washington Post,* November 28, 1982, p. C-8.

Schmidt, William E. "Home of Coke Laments Change in Winning Formula." *New York Times,* April 26, 1985, p. A-15.

Schroeder, Pat. "ERA: The Fight Isn't Over . . . ." *Washington Post,* June 28, 1982, p. A-13.

Sears, Val. "MPs Vow to Fight 'Cruel, Brutal, Mean' Tax." *Toronto Star,* August 9, 1989, p. A-17.

————. "New Tax a Tough Sell for Tories, Critics Say." *Toronto Star,* August 10, 1989, pp. A-1, A-30.

"The Secret World of Ivan Boesky." *Newsweek,* December 1, 1986, pp. 50–63.

"Seeking Votes and Clout." *Time,* August 22, 1983, pp. 20–31.

"Sensible Restraint on Panama." *New York Times,* October 5, 1989, p. A-30.

"Seven Minutes to Death." *Newsweek,* July 18, 1988, pp. 18–24.

Shaffer, Richard A. "Judgment Day: The Thinking Computer Arrives." *Wall Street Journal,* September 3, 1982, p. 14.

"Shake-Up at the White House." *Time,* January 21, 1985, pp. 10–14.

Shenon, Philip. "Ex-Housing Secretary Says Aides Were at Fault in Disputed Program." *New York Times,* May 26, 1989, p. A-12.

———. "H.U.D. Agent Details Diverting Millions." *New York Times,* June 11, 1989, sec. 1, p. 30.

Shields, Mark. ". . . Or Not Hard Enough?" *Washington Post,* February 24, 1984, p. A-19.

Shilts, Randy. "How AIDS is Changing Gay Lifestyles." *San Francisco Chronicle,* May 2, 1983, p. 5.

———. "Hudson's Contribution to AIDS Battle." *San Francisco Chronicle,* October 3, 1985, p. 16.

Shipp, E. R. "Gauging Reasonability in the Goetz Case." *New York Times,* May 31, 1987, sec. 4, p. 7.

"Shootout in Greensboro." *Time,* November 12, 1979, p. 31.

"Should AIDS Victims Be Isolated?" *U.S. News & World Report,* September 30, 1985, p. 50.

"Should U.S. Strike Back at Terrorists?" *U.S. News & World Report,* July 1, 1985, p. 22.

"Showing Muscle." *Time,* January 1, 1990, pp. 20–23.

Shribman, David. "Poll Finds a Lack of Public Support for Latin Policy." *New York Times,* April 29, 1984, p. A-1.

"Silent Meditation Time Banned at School on L.I." *New York Times,* March 2, 1984, p. B-2.

Simpson, Janice. "Wall Street's Courting of M.B.A.s Proceeds Apace Despite Scandals." *Wall Street Journal,* January 28, 1987, p. 31.

"Sing a Song of Seeing." *Time,* December 26, 1983, pp. 54–64.

"Sins of the Past." *Time,* November 16, 1987, pp. 18–20.

"Six Shots at a Nation's Heart." *Time,* April 13, 1981, pp. 24–38.

Slinger. "There's No Place to Hide from a Madman." *Toronto Star,* December 10, 1989, p. A-2.

"A Smaller Hammer but Still a Hammer." *Vancouver Sun,* December 20, 1989, p. A-10.

Smith, Hedrick. "Reagan Easily Beats Carter; . . ." *New York Times,* November 5, 1980, p. 1.

———. "Reagan, Making Good Recovery, Signs a Bill; White House Working, Bush Assures Senate." *New York Times,* April 1, 1981, p. 1.

"The Social Fallout from an Epidemic." *Newsweek,* August 12, 1985, p. 28–29.

"Social Security Rescue—What It Means to You." *U.S. News & World Report,* April 4, 1983, pp. 23–25.

"Soviet Espionage: 'A Big Effort—and It Pays Off Big.'" *U.S. News & World Report,* June 17, 1985, pp. 23–25.

Sowell, Thomas. "Culture—Not Discrimination—Decides Who Gets Ahead." *U.S. News & World Report,* October 12, 1981, pp. 74–75.

Spayd, Elizabeth. "Being Too Nice to Working Mothers." *Washington Post,* October 15, 1989, p. H-3.

"Staring into the Abyss." *U.S. News & World Report,* November 2, 1987, pp. 19–23.

"Star Wars at the Crossroads." *Time,* June 23, 1986, pp. 16–17.

"Statement of Concession by Mondale." *New York Times,* November 7, 1984, p. A-21.

Stockman, David. "When Reaganomics Will Start Working." *U.S. News & World Report,* July 19, 1982, pp. 33–34.

Stockton, William. "Mexicans Expecting No Good of Immigration Law." *New York Times,* November 6, 1986, p. A-22.

"Storm over a Deadly Downpour." *Time,* December 6, 1982, pp. 84–86.

"Students' Disbelief Transforms into Terror When 'Really Calm' Killer Begins Shooting." *Globe and Mail* (Montreal), December 7, 1989, p. A-5.

"Suddenly, the Celebration Stopped." *Washington Post,* January 29, 1986, p. A-1.

"A Surging New Spirit." *Time,* July 11, 1988, pp. 46–49.

Sussman, Peter Y. "Where I Bought My Kids." *San Francisco Chronicle,* Sunday Punch, December 18, 1983, p. 2.

"Symbol in the Skies." *Times* (London), January 30, 1986, p. 13.

Szulc, Tad. "Making the World 'Safe' for Hypocrisy." *New York Times,* October 28, 1983, p. A-27.

"Taking Heart from Dr. Clark." *Newsweek,* February 28, 1983, pp. 73–74.

Talbott, Strobe. "Grand Compromise." *Time,* June 23, 1986, pp. 22–27.

———. "The Symbolism of the Siege." *Time,* November 26, 1979, pp. 44–45.

"A Tale of Urban Greed." *Time,* April 20, 1987, pp. 30–32.

"Tax-Cut Targets: Productivity and Investment." *U.S. News & World Report,* July 7, 1980, pp. 23–24.

Taylor, Stuart, Jr. "Activism vs. Restraint: The Complex Philosophy of Judge Bork." *New York Times,* September 13, 1987, sec. 1, p. 36.

"Tears of Rage." *Time,* March 14, 1988, pp. 18–20.

"Ten Percent, but Improving." *Washington Post,* July 9, 1983, p. A-20.

"Terror in Atlanta." *Newsweek,* March 2, 1981, pp. 34–37.

"Texas C.L. Massacre II." *Wall Street Journal,* December 20, 1985, p. 24.

"Text of Andropov's Statement on Missile Dispute." *New York Times,* November 25, 1983, p. A-18.

"Text of Moynihan Statement." *New York Times,* April 16, 1984, p. A-8.

"Text of Resignation by Watt and Its Acceptance by Reagan." *New York Times,* October 10, 1983, p. D-10.

"Text of Statement By Syria on Flier." *New York Times,* January 4, 1984, p. A-8.

"Text of the U.N. Resolution." *New York Times,* October 29, 1983, p. 4.

"A Thank You That Was 7 Years Late." *U.S. News & World Report,* November 22, 1982, p. 66.

" 'There Had Been a Death in the Family.' " *Newsweek,* February 10, 1986, p. 42.

" 'There's Money in Poverty.' " *Washington Post,* May 30, 1989, p. A-18.

"They Live to Buy." *Newsweek,* December 31, 1984, pp. 28–29.

"Thinking the Unthinkable." *Time,* May 30, 1988, pp. 12–19.

"This Rescue Attempt 'Became a Necessity and a Duty.' " *Washington Post,* April 26, 1980, p. A-11.

Thompson, Mark. "Record Pentagon Procurement Overcharges Cited." *Washington Post,* January 1, 1989, p. A-12.

Thornton, Mary. "Immigration Changes Are Signed into Law." *Washington Post,* November 7, 1986, p. A-3.

Toner, Robin. "Preacher's Battle Transfixing the South." *New York Times,* March 26, 1987, p. A-16.

"Touchdown, *Columbia!*" *Time,* April 27, 1981, pp. 16–23.

Trafford, Abigail. "Mommy Track—Right to the Top." *Washington Post,* March 19, 1989, p. C-1.

"Transcript of Address by Reagan on Libya." *New York Times,* April 15, 1986, p. A-10.

"Transcript of an Interview With the President on His Wounding and Recovery." *New York Times,* April 23, 1981, p. B-12.

"Transcript of Attorney General Meese's News Conference." *Washington Post,* November 26, 1986, p. A-8.

"Transcript of Keynote Address by Cuomo to the Convention." *New York Times,* July 17, 1984, p. A-16.

"Transcript of Louisville Debate Between Reagan and Mondale." *New York Times,* October 8, 1984, p. B-4.

"Transcript of Remarks by Reagan and Nominee to High Court." *New York Times,* July 8, 1981, p. A-12.

"Transcript of Remarks by Reagan and Wiesel at White House Ceremony." *New York Times,* April 20, 1985, p. 4.

"Transcript of the President's Eulogy for the Seven Challenger Astronauts." *New York Times,* February 1, 1986, p. 11.

"Transcript of the Reagan-Mondale Debate on Foreign Policy." *New York Times,* October 22, 1984, p. B-6.

"Travelers Find Skies Aren't So Friendly As Controllers Strike." *Wall Street Journal,* August 4, 1981, p. 1.

Treaster, Joseph B. "Airlines Increase Number of Flights; Losses Linked to Strike Are on Rise." *New York Times,* August 6, 1981, p. D-20.

"A Triumph of Symbols." *U.S. News & World Report,* June 13, 1988, pp. 38–41.

"Trudeau the Spoiler." *New York Times,* June 6, 1987, p. 26.

"The True Adventures of GI Jane." *Newsweek,* February 18, 1980, p. 39.

"Try It, We Might Even Like It." *Vancouver Sun,* January 2, 1988, p. B-6.

"Turbulence in the Tower." *Time,* August 17, 1981, pp. 14–20.

"TV's Big Leap Forward into Culture." *U.S. News & World Report,* February 23, 1981, pp. 53–54.

"TV's Unholy Row." *Time,* April 6, 1987, pp. 60–67.

"TWA Passengers Recall Vanishing Row of Seats." *Washington Post,* April 3, 1986, p. A-32.

"Twelve Million Out of Work." *Newsweek,* December 13, 1982, pp. 30–31.

Uchitelle, Louis. "Ripples from a Bailout." *New York Times,* August 13, 1989, sec. 1, p. 1.

"Under Siege." *Newsweek,* December 8, 1986, pp. 32–35.

"U.S. Economy in the 80s: Can We Meet the Challenge?" *U.S. News & World Report,* January 21, 1980, pp. 57–58.

"U.S. Frustrated in Effort to Counter Soviet Spying." *New York Times,* June 16, 1985, p. 22.

"The Vietnam Names." *New York Times,* November 11, 1982, p. A-30.

Vecsey, George. "Bleakly Looms the Summer." *New York Times,* June 13, 1981, p. 17.

" 'Very Serious Losses.' " *Time,* June 17, 1985, pp. 18–22.

"U.S. Hispanic Population Is Up 34% Since 1980." *New York Times,* September 7, 1988, p. A-20.

"A View Without Hills or Valleys." *Time,* February 6, 1984, pp. 23–26.

Vise, David A., and Steve Coll. "Trial of Milken Would Showcase the Millions He Made on Deals." *Washington Post,* April 2, 1989, pp. H-4–H-5.

"Voices for Jesse." *Time,* April 11, 1988, pp. 16–17.

"Voices of Reason, Voices of Faith." *Time,* September 17, 1984, pp. 28–29.

"Voyage from Cuba." *Time,* May 5, 1980, pp. 42–44.

Waldman, Peter, and George Anders. "KKR Completes Buy-Out of RJR Without Fanfare." *Wall Street Journal,* February 10, 1989, p. A-3.

"Wall Street's Risk Takers Roll the Dice Again." *U.S. News & World Report,* February 18, 1985, p. 60.

Weinraub, Bernard. "Mondale, Campaigning in the South, Appeals for Support of Blacks." *New York Times,* January 5, 1984, p. B-10.

Weisman, Steve R. "The Politics of Popularity." *New York Times,* November 8, 1984, p. A-19.

"West Berlin Police Seek Suspects in Discotheque Blast That Killed 2." *Washington Post,* April 7, 1986, p. A-9.

" 'We Will Not Disappoint Them.' " *U.S. News & World Report,* February 10, 1986, p. 14.

"What Air Controllers Do." *Newsweek,* August 17, 1981, pp. 22–23.

"What Are Mergers Doing to America?" *U.S. News & World Report,* July 22, 1985, pp. 48–50.

"What's Behind Reagan Strategy in Nicaragua." *U.S. News & World Report,* April 23, 1984, pp. 27–29.

"When James Watt Speaks Out." *U.S. News & World Report,* June 6, 1983, p. 55.

"When the Cheering Died." *Time,* March 23, 1981, pp. 8–10.

"Where Was Congress?" *Wall Street Journal,* September 6, 1989, p. A-18.

"White House Leaks: 'We Have Been Undisciplined.' " *U.S. News & World Report,* December 14, 1981, pp. 20–21.

"Who's Teaching Our Children?" *Time,* November 14, 1988, pp. 58–64.

"Why All the Mega-Mergers?" *Newsweek,* March 19, 1984, pp. 70–71.

"Why It Was So Sour." *Time,* November 14, 1988, pp. 18–21.

"Why the Invasion Was Justified." *New York Times,* December 21, 1989, p. A-30.

Wicker, Tom. "Escalating the Rhetoric," *New York Times,* April 20, 1984, p. A-27.

———. "A Ministry of Loot." *New York Times,* May 30, 1987, p. 31.

———. "Oil Can Be Replaced." *New York Times,* April 4, 1989, p. A-27.

———. "Spies Real and Unreal." *New York Times,* December 2, 1985, p. A-15.

Wilford, John Noble. "Astronauts Walk Outside Shuttle." *New York Times,* April 8, 1983, p. A-20.

———. "Faith in Technology Is Jolted, but There is No Going Back." *New York Times,* January 29, 1986, p. A-7.

Will, George F. "Backing Out of a Swamp." *Washington Post,* January 29, 1989, p. D-7.

———. "The Court: These Two Will Have Impact." *Washington Post,* June 19, 1986, p. A-25.

———. "How Reagan Changed America. *Newsweek,* January 9, 1989, pp. 12–17.

———. "Jesse Jackson in Syria." *Washington Post,* January 1, 1984, p. H-7.

———. "Needed: A Policy of Punishment." *Newsweek,* September 12, 1983, p. 32.

Williams, Walter E. "A Skeptic's Challenge." *Newsweek,* January 24, 1983, p. 26.

"Will Reaganomics Work? Five Views." *U.S. News & World Report,* December 28, 1981, pp. 71–72.

Wills, Garry. "The Power Populist." *Time,* November 21, 1989, pp. 61–72.

"Winners and Losers." *Wall Street Journal,* August 20, 1986, p. 14.

"The Wizard inside the Machines." *Time,* April 16, 1984, pp. 56–63.

Wolfe, Tom. "Tom Wolfe: The Years of Living Prosperously." U.S. *News & World Report,* December 25, 1989/January 1, 1990, p. 117.

"Women and AIDS." *Newsweek,* July 14, 1986, pp. 60–61.

"The Women's Movement: Here to Stay." *New York Times,* August 26, 1989, p. 22.

"Wow! Real Reform!" *Time,* May 19, 1986, pp. 12–14.

Wren, Christopher S. "A Very French City Gives in to Irish for a Day." *New York Times,* March 18, 1985, p. A-7.

WuDunn, Sheryl. "In the Streets, Anguish, Fury and Tears." *New York Times,* June 4, 1989, sec. 1, p. 1.

Yardley, Jonathan. "Antismokers: Lighten Up!" *Washington Post,* May 16, 1988, p. B-2.

———. "The Report Card of William J. Bennett." *Washington Post,* September 5, 1988, p. D-2.

"The Year of the Yuppie." *Newsweek,* December 31, 1984, pp. 14–24.

"The Year of the Yuppies." *New York Times,* March 25, 1984, sec. 4, p. 20.

" 'Yeeeow!' and 'Doggone!' Are Shouted on Beaches as Crowds Watch Liftoff." *New York Times,* April 13, 1981, p. 13.

" 'You Have Sold Us Out.' " *Newsweek,* November 14, 1988, p. 38.

"Your Money or His Life." *Time,* January 26, 1987, p. 63.

## INTERNET SITES
### General Web Sites

Awesome80s.com Web site. URL: http://awesome80s.com.

Canadahistory.com Web site. URL: http://www.canadahistory.com.

The Eighties Club. URL: http://eightiesclub.tripod.com/id4.htm.

Eighty–eighty-nine. Web site. URL: http://www.eightyeightynine.com.

George Bush Presidential Library and Museum. URL: http://bushlibrary.tamu.edu/.

Inthe80s Web site. URL: http://www.inthe80s.com.

Jimmy Carter Library and Museum. URL: http://jimmycarterlibrary.org/.

Ronald Reagan Presidential Library. URL: http://www.reagan.utexas.edu/.

Wikipedia, the Free Encyclopedia. URL: http://en.wikipedia.org.

## Specific Articles

"Abscam." Federal Bureau of Investigation Freedom of Information—Privacy Act. Available online. URL: http://foia.fbi.gov/foiaindex/abscam.htm. Downloaded on January 9, 2004.

American Collegians for Life. "Abortion and the Supreme Court." Available online. URL: http://www.aclife.org/education/court.html. Updated on April 4, 2002.

AT&T. "A Brief History: The Bell System." Available online. URL: http://www.att.com/history/history3.html. Downloaded on July 19, 2004.

————. "A Brief History: Post-Divestiture AT&T." Available online. URL: http://www.att.com/history/history4.html. Downloaded on July 19, 2004.

"Attack on Bush." Available online. URL http://www.ratherbiased.com/bush_attack.htm. Downloaded on October 27, 2004.

Avert.org. "The History of AIDS up to 1986." Available online. URL: http://www.avert.org/his81_86.htm. Downloaded on December 5, 2003.

————. "The History of AIDS from 1987 to 1992." Available online. URL: http://www.avert.og/his87_92.htm. Downloaded on December 5, 2003.

Bastedo, Michael, and Angela Davis. " 'God, What a Blunder': The New Coke Story." Available online. URL: http://members.lycos.co.uk/thomassheils/newcoke.htm. Downloaded on March 15, 2004.

"A Brief History of Baseball: Part III: Labor Battles in the Modern Era." Available online. URL: http://play-cash-bingo-online.com/Online-Sports-Betting/history-of-baseball-pt3.html. Downloaded on March 25, 2004.

"A Brief History of Canada: 1980–1989." Available online. URL: http://www3.sympatico.ca/goweezer/canada/can1980.htm. Downloaded on January 20, 2004.

Brink, Graham. "Pilot in Skyway Disaster Is Dead." *St. Petersburg Times* (September 3, 2002). Available online. URL: http://www.mult-sclerosis.org/news/Sep2002/ShipsPilotwMS.html. Downloaded on January 20, 2004.

Bush, George. "Address to the Nation Announcing United States Military Action in Panama, December 20, 1989." Available online. URL: http://bushlibrary.tamu.edu/research/papers/1989/89122000.html. Downloaded on December 1, 2004.

————. "George H. Bush: Before the Republican Convention Accepting Its Nomination for President, New Orleans, August 18, 1988." *The American*

*Presidency.* Available online. URL: http://www.geocities.com/rickmatlick/ nomahbush88.htm. Downloaded on November 8, 2004.

———. "Inaugural Address, January 20, 1989." Available online. URL: http://bushlibrary.tamu.edu/research/papers/1989/89012000.html. Downloaded on December 11, 2004.

———. "Remarks at the Texas A&M University Commencement Ceremony in College Station, May 12, 1989." Available online. URL: http:// bushlibrary.tamu.edu/research/papers/1989/89051201.html. Downloaded on December 12, 2004.

———. "Statement on the Chinese Government's Suppression of Student Demonstrations, June 3, 1989." Available online. URL: http://bushlibrary.tamu. edu/research/papers/1989/89060300.html. Downloaded on December 12, 2004.

Canadian Embassy, Washington, D.C. "Canada's Constitution." Available online. URL: http://www.canadianembassy.org/government/constitution-en.asp. Updated on January 17, 2003.

Carkin, Patrick. "Looking Back: Samantha Smith, the Girl Who Went to the Soviet Union." Available online. URL: http://wwwsmi.lkwash.wednet.edu/ Samantha_Smith.htm. Downloaded on July 7, 2004.

Carter, Jimmy. "Farewell Address, January 14, 1981." Available online. URL: http://jimmycarterlibrary.org/documents/speeches/farewell.phtml. Downloaded on January 2, 2004.

———. "Inaugural Address of President Jimmy Carter, Thursday, January 20, 1977." Available online. URL: http://www.jimmycarterlibrary.org/ documents/speeches/inaugadd.phtml. Downloaded on January 2, 2004.

———. "Jimmy Carter's Malaise Speech, 1979," *Right Wing News.* Available online. URL: http://www.rightwingnews.com/speeches/carter.php. Downloaded on September 30, 2003.

———. "Rescue Attempt for American Hostages in Iran Address to the Nation, April 25th, 1980." *The American Presidency Project.* Available online. URL: http://www.presidency.ucsb.edu/ws/index.php?pid=33322&st=&st1=. Downloaded on January 5, 2005.

———. "State of the Union Address, January 21, 1980." Available online. URL: http://jimmycarterlibrary.org/documents/speeches/su80jec.phtml. Downloaded on November 13, 2003.

Centre for Canadian Studies at Mount Allison University. "The Constitutional Crisis and the Meech Lake Accord." Available online. URL: http://www. mta.ca/faculty/arts/canadian_studies/english/about/study_guide/debates/ meech_lake .html. Downloaded on October 9, 2004.

Centre for Research and Information on Canada. "Meech Lake Accord Chronology." Available online. URL: http://www.cric.ca/en_html/guide/meech/meech.html. Downloaded on October 9, 2004.

"A Chronology of Computer History." Available online. URL: http://www.cyberstreet.com/hcs/museum/chron.htm. Downloaded on January 12, 2004.

"Civil Rights Restoration Act of 1987." Available online. URL: http://www.civilrights.org/library/permanent_collection/resources/1987crra.html. Downloaded on January 5, 2005.

"Columbia Contemporary Quotations." Bartleby.com. Available online. URL: http://www.bartleby.com/66/63/7663.html. Downloaded on October 20, 2004.

Court TV Crime Library. "Do It! Do It! Do It!" Available online. URL: http://www.crimelibrary.com/terrorists_spies/assassins/chapman/8.html?sect=24. Downloaded on January 24, 2004.

Cuban Information Archive, Document 0038: "Mariel Chronology May 13, 1979–Dec. 11, 1981." Available online. URL: http://cuban-exile.com/doc_026-050/doc0038.html. Downloaded on January 10, 2004.

Defense Personnel Security Research Center. "Recent Espionage Cases: 1985." Available online. URL: http://www.dss.mil/training/espionage/1985.htm. Downloaded on September 30, 2004.

Dukakis, Michael. "Michael Dukakis, 1988 Nomination Acceptance Speech (21 July 1988)." Available online. URL: http://www.geocities.com/Wellesley/1116/dukakis88.html. Downloaded on October 28, 2004.

Dumas, Ernest. "Reagan's Tax Increases." *Arkansas Times* (June 17, 2004). Available online. URL: http://www.arktimes.com/dumas/061704dumas.html. Downloaded on October 13, 2004.

Ecker, Tom. "1984—The Smuggled Flame. Olympic Facts and Fables, July 19, 1996." *The Gazette*. Available online. URL: http://www.gazetteonline.com/special/olympics/summer96/olym054.htm. Downloaded on August 2, 2004.

The Eighties Club. "Baby Fae." Available online. URL: http://eightiesclub.tripod.com/id302.htm. Downloaded on July 28, 2004.

Eighty–eighty-nine Web site. "The Rubik's Cube—history and tips for solving it." Available online. URL: http://www.eightyeightynine.com/games/rubiks-cube.html. Downloaded on January 24, 2004.

"Election Campaign Televised Leaders' Debate: Prime Minister John Turner Faces Brian Mulroney." *Historic Moments in Canadian Politics*. Available online. URL: http://www.planetcast.com/historic-moments/turner-01.shtml. Downloaded on July 15, 2004.

Equal Employment Opportunity Commission. "Supreme Court in the 1980s." Available online. URL: http://www.eeoc.gov/abouteeoc/35th/1980s/ supremecourt.html. Downloaded on September 3, 2004.

"Excerpts from the Tower Commission's Report." *The American Presidency Project.* Available online. URL: http://www.presidency.ucsb.edu/PS157/ assignment%20files%20public/TOWER%20EXCERP TS.htm#PartIV. Downloaded on January 5, 2005.

Federation of American Scientists. *Arms Control Agreements.* Available online. URL: http://www.fas.org/nuke/control/index.html. Updated on May 24, 2002.

Francis, Roberta W. "The History Behind the Equal Rights Amendment." Available online. URL: http://www.equalrightsamendment.org/era.htm. Downloaded on April 5, 2004.

Frenze, Christopher. "The Reagan Tax Cuts: Lessons for Tax Reform." *JEC Report* (April 1996). Available online. URL: http://www.house.gov/jec/fiscal/ tx-grwth/reagtxct/reagtxct.htm. Downloaded on October 13, 2004.

*Frontline: Drug Wars.* "Thirty Years of America's Drug War: A Chronology." PBS. Available online. URL: http://www.pbs.org/wgbh/pages/frontline/shows/ drugs/cron/. Downloaded on November 1, 2004.

*Frontline: Target America.* "Terrorist Attacks on Americans, 1979–1988." PBS. Available online. URL: http://www.pbs.org/wgbh/pages/frontline/shows/tar-get/etc/cron.html. Downloaded on March 5, 2004.

Greider, William. "The Education of David Stockman." *Atlantic Monthly* (December 1981). Available online. URL: http://www.theatlantic.com/ unbound/flashbks/classics/stockman.htm. Downloaded on February 4, 2004.

Griffiths, Richard T. "History of the Internet, Internet for Historians (and Just About Anybody Else)." Available online. URL: http://www.let.leidenuniv.nl/ history/ivh/frame_theorie.html. Updated on October 11, 2002.

Harwood, William. "Voyage Into History Chapter Four: Preparations." CBS News Web site. Available online. URL: http://cbsnews.cbs.com/network/ news/space/51Lchap4preparations.html. Downloaded on September 7, 2004.

Henneberger, John. "Independent Counsels Release Report on Reagan Era HUD Abuses." *Better Homes and Shelters.* Available online. URL: http:// www.texashousing.org/txlihis/bhs/bhsarticles/QN2AUR.html. Downloaded on December 6, 2004.

Historica: Peace and Conflict. "The 1989 Canada–U.S. Free Trade Agreement." Available online. URL: http://www.histori.ca/peace/page.do?pageID=346. Downloaded on September 20, 2004.

History of Quebec and Canada Resource Center. "The Constitution Act 1982." Available online. URL: http://fc.lbpsb.qc.ca/~history/m7u511a.htm. Downloaded on April 4, 2004.

Howe, Walt. "A Brief History of the Internet." Available online. URL: http://www.walthowe.com/navnet/history.html. Updated on July 1, 2004.

Indianz.com. "Reagan's Indian Policies Recalled with Fervor." (June 11, 2004) Available online. URL: http://www.indianz.com/News/2004/002878.asp. Downloaded on April 17, 2005.

"The Iran-Contra Affairs: A Chronology." Available online. URL: http://cas. memphis.edu/~sherman/chronoirancontra.htm. Downloaded on September 13, 2004.

Jackson, Jesse. "Address before the Democratic National Convention, July 18, 1984, Wednesday." *Frontline: The Pilgrimage of Jesse Jackson.* Available online. URL: http://www.pbs.org/wgbh/pages/frontline/jesse/speeches/jesse84speech.html. Downloaded on July 10, 2004.

————. "Jesse Jackson: 1988 Democratic National Convention Address." Available online. URL: http://www.americanrhetoric.com/speeches/jessejackson1988dnc.htm. Downloaded on October 28, 2004.

Kennedy, Edward M. "Address to the Democratic National Convention." New York City, August 12, 1980. Available online. URL: http://www.jfklibrary.org/e081280.htm. Downloaded on January 12, 2004.

"The Kissinger Commission." Available online. URL: http://www.uscubacommission.org/htm/kisscom.htm. Downloaded on July 28, 2004.

Lofgren, Stephen. "*Exxon Valdez* Spill 15 Years Later: Damage Lingers." *National Geographic News* (March 22, 2004). Available online. URL: http://news.nationalgeographic.com/news/2004/03/0318_040318_exxonvaldez.html. Downloaded on November 12, 2004.

Loma Linda University Medical Center. "News: December 2, 1999: Leonard Bailey, World-renowned Heart Surgeon, Remembers with Fondness a Tiny Baby Named Fae." Available online. URL: http://www.llu.edu/news/today/dec299/mc.htm. Downloaded on July 28, 2004.

Malvasi, Meg Greene. "Samantha Smith: America's Youngest Ambassador." Available online. URL: http://www.suite101.com/article.cfm/3679/17086. Downloaded on July 7, 2004.

Manning, Jason. "Baby Fae." The Eighties Club. Available online. URL: http://eightiesclub.tripod.com/id302.htm. Downloaded on June 30, 2004.

————. "Bitburg." The Eighties Club. Available online. URL: http://eightiesclub.tripod.com/id342.htm. Downloaded on August 9, 2004.

————. "The Bork Nomination." The Eighties Club. Available online. URL: http://eightiesclub.tripod.com/id320.htm. Downloaded on October 3, 2004.

————. "The Crash of '87." The Eighties Club. Available online. URL: http://eightiesclub.tripod.com/id329.htm. Downloaded on March 10, 2004.

————. "The Dirtiest Campaign." The Eighties Club. Available online. URL: http://eightiesclub.tripod.com/id346.htm. Downloaded on October 27, 2004.

————. "Donna and the Senator." The Eighties Club. Available online. URL: http://eightiesclub.tripod.com/id323.htm. Downloaded on October 13, 2004.

————. "The Exxon Valdez." The Eighties Club. Available online. URL: http://eightiesclub.tripod.com/id317.htm. Downloaded on November 5, 2004.

————. "Hands Across America." The Eighties Club. Available online. URL: http://eightiesclub.tripod.com/id312.htm. Downloaded on October 10, 2004.

————. "Raid on Libya." The Eighties Club. Available online. URL: http://eightiesclub.tripod.com/id313.htm. Downloaded on September 3, 2004.

————. "Reykjavik." The Eighties Club. Available online. URL: http://eightiesclub.tripod.com/id322.htm. Downloaded on March 10, 2004.

————. "The Subway Vigilante." The Eighties Club. Available online. URL: http://eightiesclub.tripod.com/id311.htm. Downloaded on October 17, 2004.

————. "Wolves on Wall Street." The Eighties Club. Available online. URL: http://eightiesclub.tripod.com/id316.htm. Downloaded on September 30, 2004.

Martin, Lawrence. "Mulroney Toast of Reaganites." *The Ottawa Citizen*. Available online. URL: http://squawk.ca/lbo-talk/9909/0814.html. Downloaded on August 28, 2004.

McGough, Michael. "Reagan's Legal Revolution Lives through Federal Bench Appointments." *Pittsburgh Post-Gazette: post-gazette.com* (June 8, 2004). Available online. URL: http://www.post-gazette.com/pg/pp/04160/328555.stm. Downloaded on November 17, 2004.

Micromedia ProQuest. "Canada Timeline: 1980–1989." Available online. URL: http://www.micromedia.ca/Timeline/1980–1989.htm. Downloaded on March 31, 2004.

Mikkelson, Barbara. "Knew Coke." Urban Legends Reference Pages. Available online. URL: http://www.snopes.com/cokelore/newcoke.asp. Updated on May 2, 1999.

———. "Nuclear Family (Cabbage Patch Kids)." Urban Legends Reference Pages. Available online. URL: http://www.snopes.com/business/origins/cabbage.asp. Updated on June 11, 2002.

Mondale, Walter. "Mondale's Acceptance Speech, 1984." Associated Press. Available online. URL: http://www.cnn.com/ALLPOLITICS/1996/conventions/chicago/facts/famous.speeches/mondale.84.shtml. Downloaded on July 12, 2004.

Mulroney, Brian. "Report on the First Ministers' Meeting at Meech Lake, May 1, 1987." Available online. URL: http://www.collectionscanada.ca/premiersministres/h4-4022-e.html. Downloaded on October 8, 2004.

National Aeronautics and Space Administration. "History of the Space Shuttle." Available online. URL: http://history.nasa.gov/shuttlehistory.html. Downloaded on March 20, 2004.

National Oceanographic and Atmospheric Administration. "Billion-Dollar U.S. Weather Disasters, 1980–2003." Available online. URL: http://lwf.ncdc.noaa.gov/oa/reports/billionz.html. Downloaded on January 20, 2004.

National Organization for Women. "Chronology of the Equal Rights Amendment, 1923–1996." Available online. URL: http://www.now.org/issues/economic/cea/history.html. Downloaded on April 5, 2004.

Neff, Donald. "With Release of Terry Anderson, U.S. Hostage Ordeal Ended in Lebanon." *Washington Report on Middle East Affairs* (December 1995). Available online. URL: http://www.wrmea.com/backissues/1295/9512079.html. Downloaded on June 25, 2004.

Newport, Frank, et al. "Ronald Reagan from the People's Perspective: A Gallup Poll Review." Available online. URL: http://www.gallup.com/content/default.aspx?ci=11887. Downloaded on March 18, 2004.

The New York Times on the Web. "The Iran-Contra Report: Chronology." (January 19, 1994). Available online. URL: http://www.nytimes.com/books/97/06/29/reviews/iran-chronology.html?oref=login. Downloaded on September 29, 2004.

Niskanen, William. "Reaganomics." *The Concise Encyclopedia of Economics* (Library of Economics and Liberty). Available online. URL: http://www.econlib.org/library/Enc/Reaganomics.html. Downloaded on January 28, 2004.

Ode, Robert. "Excerpts from an Iran Hostage's Diary." Jimmy Carter Library Web site. Available online. URL: http://jimmycarterlibrary.org/documents/r_ode/index.phtml. Downloaded on November 30, 2003.

PBS Online Newshour. "Case Closed, July 1, 1999." Available online. URL: http://www.pbs.org/newshour/bb/law/july-dec99/hud_7-1.html. Downloaded on December 12, 2004.

———. "Pierre Trudeau, October 3, 2000." Available online. URL: http://www.pbs.org/newshour/bb/remember/july-dec00/trudeau_10-3html.html. Downloaded on July 15, 2004.

"Reaction to the 1980 Olympic Boycott Decision." *Running Times* (April 1980). Available online. URL: http://www.runningtimes.com/issues/80/boycotts1980.htm. Downloaded on January 4, 2004.

Reagan, Ronald. "Acceptance Speech at the 1980 Republican Convention." July 17, 1980. Available online. URL: http://www.nationalcenter.org/ReaganConvention1980.html. Downloaded on January 10, 2004.

———. "Address Before a Joint Session of the Congress on the Program for Economic Recovery, February 18, 1981." Available online. URL: http://www.Reagan.utexas.edu/resource/speeches/1981/21881s.htm. Downloaded on March 14, 2004.

———. "Address to Members of the British Parliament, June 8, 1982." Available online. URL: http://www.reagan.utexas.edu/resource/speeches/1982/60882a.htm. Downloaded on July 8, 2004.

———. "Address to the Nation on Defense and National Security, March 23, 1983." Available online. URL: http://www.reagan.utexas.edu/resources/speeches/1983/32383d.htm. Downloaded on July 5, 2004.

———. "Address to the Nation on Events in Lebanon and Grenada, October 27, 1983." Available online. URL: http://www.reagan.utexas.edu/resources/speeches/1983/102783b.htm. Downloaded on July 25, 2004.

———. "Address to the Nation on the Explosion of the Space Shuttle Challenger, January 28, 1986." Available online. URL: http://www.reagan.utexas.edu/resource/speeches/1986/12886b.htm. Downloaded on August 3, 2003.

———. "Address to the Nation on the Iran Arms and Contra Aid Controversy, November 13, 1986." Available online. URL: http://www.reagan.utexas.edu/resource/speeches/1986/111386c.htm. Downloaded on September 30, 2004.

———. "Address to the Nation on the Iran Arms and Contra Aid Controversy, March 4, 1987." Available online. URL: http://www.reagan.utexas.edu/resource/speeches/1987/030487h.htm. Downloaded on November 1, 2004.

———. "Address to the Nation on the Iran Arms and Contra Aid Controversy and Administration Goals, August 12, 1987." Available online. URL: http://www.reagan.utexas.edu/resource/speeches/1987/081287d.htm. Downloaded on November 1, 2004.

———. "Address to the Nation on the United States Air Strike Against Libya, April 14, 1986." Available online. URL: http://www.reagan.utexas.edu/resource/speeches/1986/41486g.htm. Downloaded on January 5, 2005.

———. "Farewell Address to the Nation, Oval Office, January 11, 1989." Available online. URL: http://www.ronaldreagan.com/sp_21.html. Downloaded on October 23, 2004.

———. "Inaugural Address, January 20, 1981." Available online. URL: http://www.Reagan.utexas.edu/resources/speeches/1981/12081a.htm. Downloaded on August 3, 2003.

———. "Letter to the Speaker of the House and President Pro Tempore of the Senate on the Deployment of United States Forces in Grenada." Available online. URL: http://www.Reagan.utexas.edu/resources/speeches/1983/102583e.htm. Downloaded on April 1, 2003.

———. "Radio Address to the Nation on the Quality of Life in America, October 15, 1983." Available online. URL: http://www.reagan.utexas.edu/resource/speeches/1983/101583b.htm. Downloaded on April 1, 2004.

———. "Remarks Accepting the Presidential Nomination at Republican National Convention in Dallas, Texas, August 23, 1984." Available online. URL: http://www.reagan.utexas.edu/resource/speeches/1984/82384f.htm. Downloaded on July 12, 2004.

———. "Remarks Announcing the Intention to Nominate Sandra Day O'Connor to Be an Associate Justice of the Supreme Court, July 7, 1981." Available online. URL: http://www.reagan.utexas.edu/resource/speeches/1981/70781.a.htm. Downloaded on March 8, 2004.

———. "Remarks at a Commemorative Ceremony at Bergen–Belsen Concentration Camp in the Federal Republic of Germany, May 5, 1985." Available online. URL: http://www.reagan.utexas.edu/resource/speeches/1985/50585a.htm. Downloaded on September 20, 2004.

———. "Remarks at the American Foundation for AIDS Research Awards Dinner, May 31, 1987." Available online. URL: http://www.reagan.utexas.edu/resource/speeches/1987/053187a.htm. Downloaded on November 3, 2004.

———. "Remarks at the Annual Convention of the National Religious Broadcasters, January 30, 1984." Available online. URL: http://www.reagan.utexas.edu/resource/speeches/1984/13084b.htm. Downloaded on July 24, 2004.

————. "Remarks on East-West Relations at the Brandenburg Gate in West Berlin, June 12, 1987." Available online. URL: http://www.reagan.utexas.edu/resource/speeches/1987/061287d.htm. Downloaded on October 4, 2004.

————. "Remarks on Signing the Tax Reform Act of 1986, October 22, 1986." Available online. URL: http://www.reagan.utexas.edu/resource/speeches/1986/102286a.htm. Downloaded on November 1, 2004.

————. "Statement on Deployment of the MX Missile," November 22, 1982. Available online. URL: http://www.reagan.utexas.edu/resource/speeches/1982/112282b.htm. Downloaded on June 29, 2004.

*Report of the Presidential Commission on the Space Shuttle Challenger Accident,* Volume I, Chapter 4: "The Cause of the Accident." Available online. URL: http://sunnyday.mit.edu/accidents/Chapter-4.txt. Downloaded on September 22, 2004.

Robinson, Peter. "Tearing Down That Wall." *Hoover Digest* (1997, No.4). Available online. URL: http:www.hooverdigest.org/974/robinson.html. Downloaded on October 8, 2004.

Rotten dot com. "Billy Carter." Available online. URL: http://www.rotten.com/library/bio/black-sheep/billy-carter/. Downloaded on January 15, 2004.

Sacred Land Film Project. "Black Hills." Available online. URL: http://www.sacredland.org/historical_sites_pages/black_hills.html. Downloaded on April 17, 2005.

"Sandra Day O'Connor." Available online. URL: http://www.supremecourthistory.org/justice/o'connor.htm. Updated on July 3, 2001.

"Simpson's Contemporary Quotations." Bartleby.com. Available online. URL: http://www.bartleby.com/63/40/940.html. Downloaded on October 4, 2004.

Tilling, Robert I., et al. "Mount St. Helens Erupts!" Available online. URL: http://www.awesome80s.com/Awesome80s/Tech/Nature/Disasters/Volcanoes/Mount_St.Helens.asp. Downloaded on January 24, 2004.

Trudeau, Pierre Elliott. "Remarks at the Proclamation Ceremony." (Patriation of Constitution). Available online. URL: http://www.canadahistory.com/sections/documents/trudeau_-_patriation_of_constitution.htm. Downloaded on March 12, 2004.

Udall, Morris K. "The MX Missile." Available online. URL: http://dizzy.library.arizona.edu/branches/spc/udall/missiles.rtf. Downloaded on March 30, 2004.

U.S. Department of State Bulletin. "U.S.-Canada Free Trade Agreement."
Available online. URL: http://www.findarticles.com/p/articles/mi_m1079/
is_n2151_v89/ai_8139819. Downloaded on September 27, 2004.

The Washington Post Online. "World Terrorist Attacks and Organizations."
Available online. URL: http://www.washingtonpost.com/wp-dyn/
world/issues/terrordata/. Downloaded on September 3, 2004.

# INDEX

Locators in *italic* indicate illustrations. Locators in **boldface** indicate main entries/topics and biographies. Locators followed by *m* indicate maps. Locators followed by *g* indicate graphs. Locators followed by *c* indicate chronology entries.

hostages in Iran *(continued)*
    Jimmy Carter 3–4, **9–12,** 17,
        18, 22–24, 25*c,* 29*c,* 30, 42,
        43, 102, 219
    Billy Carter and 17
    William Casey and 24
    failed rescue attempt of 19,
        26*c,* 42, 352–353, 424*m*
    freeing of the 42–44
    homecoming of **22–24**
    Ayatollah Khomeini and 3, 10,
        18
    and "October surprise"
        20–21
    reaction to release of 79
    Ronald Reagan 23, 24, 29*c*
    Charles W. Scott on 31
    Strobe Talbott on 30
    Margaret Thatcher and 23
    Cyrus Vance and 10, 11
hostages in Lebanon 219, 220,
    238, 241*c,* 278–279
hostile takeovers 180, 202
Houston, Whitney 200*c*
HUD. *See* Department of
    Housing and Urban
    Development
Hudson, Rock 191, *191,* 199*c,*
    214, 215
Hufnagel, Vicki 257
Hufstedler, Shirley 25*c*
Hughes, John 328
human fertility 139
human immunodeficiency virus
    (HIV) 55, 190, 199*c,*
    263–264
human rights xiv
humor 52
Hu Na 101
Hungary 323
Hurricane Alicia 116*c*
Hurricane Gloria 199*c*
Hurricane Hugo 332*c*
Hurricane Juan 199*c*
*Hustler Magazine, Inc. v. Falwell*
    284*c,* 319
"Hymietown" remark 150, 154*c,*
    155*c,* 160–161
Hymowitz, Carol 318

## I

Iacocca, Lee 9, 250, **394**
IBM. *See* International Business
    Machines
ICBMs 92
ice hockey 7, 26*c,* 115*c,* 156*c,*
    198*c,* 240*c,* 286*c,* 287*c*
Ichan, Carl 248

ICRA (Indian Civil Rights Act)
    (1968) 184
IGRA. *See* Indian Gaming
    Regulatory Act
illegal immigration 73*c*–74*c,*
    221, 265–266, 292
illegally obtained evidence 156*c*
immigration 73*c*–74*c,* 251–252
    Hispanic 265
    illegal 73*c*–74*c,* 221, 265–266,
        292
Immigration and Control Act of
    1986 221
Immigration Reform and
    Control Act (1986) 265–266
"I'm paying for this microphone,
    Mr. Breen!" xviii
imperial presidency 76
inauguration
    of George H. W. Bush 307,
        *329,* 329*c,* 335, 374–377
    of Jimmy Carter xiv, xvii
    of Ronald Reagan 46, *46,* 47,
        *69,* 69*c,* 75, *197,* 197*c,*
        355–358
Indian Civil Rights Act (ICRA)
    (1968) 184
Indian Gaming Regulatory Act
    (IGRA) 268, 288*c*
inflation and inflation rate
    in 1979 1, 8
    in 1979–1990 421*g*
    in 1980 xviii, xix, 8
    in 1981 66, 69*c,* 70*c*
    in 1982 73*c,* 113*c*
    and Carter administration xv,
        xviii, xix, 1, 30
    and elections of 1980 xviii,
        xix, 8
    rising 229
    and Paul Volcker 8, 9
*infotainment* 62
INF Treaty 244*c,* 255, 281, 282,
    *282 See also* Intermediate-
    Range Nuclear Forces (INF)
    treaty
Inouye, Daniel 238
insider trading 227, 228,
    248–249, 262, 288*c,* 321
insulin (synthetic human) 74*c*
insurance (FSLIC) 311–312
interest rates
    in 1979 8
    in 1980 xix, 8
    in 1982 73*c*
    and elections of 1980 8
    high 98
    and savings-and-loans 311, 312
    Paul Volcker raises xix

interferon (human) 25*c*
Intermediate-Range Nuclear
    Forces (INF) treaty 235, 236,
    *236,* 369–370
Internal Revenue Service (IRS)
    109
International Business Machines
    (IBM) 201*c*
    PCjr. 137
    and personal computers 60–61
    suit against 136
Internet 113*c,* 230–231, 288*c,*
    327, 332*c*
internment of Japanese
    Americans 114*c,* 267, 285,
    *285,* 285*c,* 370
*In the Heat of the Night* (television
    series) 332*c*
Iran. *See also* hostages in Iran
    attack on oil platforms of 285*c*
    embargo on 3, 25*c*
    Israel and 20
    Ayatollah Khomeini 2–4, 10,
        18
    Reza Mohammed Pahlavi
        1–4, *2*
    and terrorism 103
    unrest in 1, 2
    war with Iraq 18, 20, 23, 28*c,*
        287*c*
Iran Air flight 655 279, 287*c,*
    302
Iran-contra 331*c,* 332*c. See also*
    Boland Amendment; North,
    Oliver Laurence
    accounts of 245–248
    William Casey and 220, 237,
        238
    damage control for **236–239**
    a failed enterprise **219–220**
    and hostages 103
    Israel and 219, 220, 237
    Charles Krauthammer on 245
    Robert McFarlane and 219,
        220, 239, 284*c,* 330*c*
    Edwin Meese and 237, 245,
        246, *246*
    Manuel Noriega and 324
    John Marlan Poindexter 237,
        238, 241*c,* 245, 284*c*–285*c,*
        332*c*
    Ronald Reagan 219, 220,
        236–239, 242*c,* 244*c,* 245,
        *246,* 247, 248
    George Shultz and 237, 247
    Tower Commission 237, 239,
        242*c,* 247, *247,* 363–369
    Caspar Weinberger and 247

Iran hostages. *See* hostages in
    Iran
Iranian Americans 4
*Iranian Hostage* (Sickmann) 32
Iran-Iraq War 18, 20, 23, 28*c,*
    287*c*
Iraq 242*c*
IRS (Internal Revenue Service)
    109
Isaacson, Walter 261
Islamic fundamentalists 2, 3
Islamic Jihad 175, 176
Israel
    Menachim Begin xiv, *xiv,* 76
    bombing of Beirut by 76, 102
    Camp David accords xiv
    El-Al check-in counter 194
    and hijacking of TWA flight
        847 176
    invades Lebanon 102
    and Iran 20
    and Iran-contra 219, 220, 237
    Ariel Sharon 76
    spying by 188, 212
    U.S. support for 102

## J

Jackson, Jesse Louis *160,* 268,
    **394–395**
    and 1984 elections 109, 134,
        149–150, 154*c,* 155*c,*
        160–161, 166, 167
    and 1988 elections 276, 277,
        300
    on affirmative action 129
    on drugs 296
    and Robert O. Goodman, Jr.
        134, 150, 154*c,* 160
    "Hymietown" remark 150,
        154*c,* 155*c,* 160–161
    trip to Cuba 150
    George Will on 160
Jackson, Michael *111,* 327, **395**
    Band Aid 178
    and MTV 268
    Pepsi commercial 240*c*
    *Thriller* 111, 112, 114*c,* 130,
        154*c*
Jacobsen, David 220, 236
Jagger, Mick 178
Jaguar Motors 321
Jamaican bobsled team 274
Jameson, Ruth 302
Jansen, Dan 274
Japanese Americans, internment
    of 114*c,* 267, 285, *285,* 285*c,*
    370
Jarvik, Robert 96

# MICROBIAL ECOLOGY

## FUNDAMENTALS AND APPLICATIONS

**fourth edition**

**RONALD M. ATLAS**
UNIVERSITY OF LOUISVILLE

**RICHARD BARTHA**
RUTGERS UNIVERSITY

An imprint of Addison Wesley Longman, Inc.

Menlo Park, California • Reading, Massachusetts • New York • Harlow, England
Don Mills, Ontario • Sydney • Mexico City • Madrid • Amsterdam

Sponsoring Editor: Daryl Fox
Project Editors: Lauren Fogel, Grace Wong
Managing Editor: Wendy Earl
Production Supervisor: Sharon Montooth
Editorial Assistant: Marcia Skelton
Cover Designer: Yvo Riezebos
Compositor: Fog Press
Senior Manufacturing Supervisor: Merry Free Osborn

**Library of Congress Cataloging-in-Publication-Data**
Atlas, Ronald M., 1946–
    Microbial ecology : fundamentals and applications / Ronald M.
Atlas, Richard Bartha. -- 4th ed.
        p.      cm.
    Includes bibliographical references and index.
    1. Microbial ecology.    I. Bartha, Richard.    II. Title.
QR100.A87    1997
579' .17--dc21                                      97-31965
                                                    CIP

ISBN 0-8053-0655-2

    2 3 4 5 6 7 8 9 10 -MA-01 00 99 98

Benjamin/Cummings Science Publishing
2725 Sand Hill Road
Menlo Park, California 94025

# PREFACE

The discipline of microbial ecology started to emerge in the early 1960s. It became firmly established as an area of specialization during the late 1970s with society's increased focus on the environment. The 1990s have seen the introduction of molecular biology into the field of microbial ecology, with the development of new techniques for applying molecular methods to environmental studies. These methods have allowed microbial ecologists to begin to explore the extent of biodiversity in the microbial world and the microorganisms inhabiting extreme habitats. Recombinant DNA technology has raised the possibility of using genetically engineered microorganisms for environmental applications, including pest control and removal of pollutants.

Many of today's environmental problems, as well as their potential solutions, are intimately interwoven with the microbial component of the global ecosystem. Numerous practical implications add relevance and excitement to the field; the volume and quality of the work performed in it is steadily increasing. We hope that the fourth edition of *Microbial Ecology: Fundamentals and Applications* will provide an overview of the current status of this dynamic field and stimulate student interest in performing the research necessary to move this exciting field forward with new discoveries.

Microbial ecology cuts across traditional academic subjects and is truly an interdisciplinary science. Students who attend courses in microbial ecology have diverse backgrounds and career goals. A challenge in writing this book has been to accommodate the varied backgrounds of students taking a course in microbial ecology and the diverse interests of instructors, many of whom are experts in specialized areas of microbial ecology. The first edition of this textbook in 1981 provided a comprehensive and flexible teaching tool designed for one-semester courses on the advanced undergraduate and graduate level. In the second edition, published in 1987, we raised the level of presentation and increased the usefulness of the book as a reference source for investigators in the field of microbial ecology with the inclusion of extensive references. We updated and expanded the references in the third edition (1993) and have added a wealth of new material to this fourth edition, including information on molecular microbial ecology, biofilms, extremophiles, and archaea.

Like previous editions, the fourth edition of *Microbial Ecology: Fundamentals and Applications* contains both basic ecological and applied environmental information. The organization of the book is from the basic to the applied. Chapter 1 contains a short historical introduction and discusses the field of microbial ecology in relation to other scientific disciplines. Chapter 2 discusses microbial evolution and the diversity of microorganisms, including the various physiological types of microorganisms. This chapter has been greatly updated to reflect the three domains of life. Chapter 3 describes the interactions between microorganisms, and Chapters 4 and 5 explore the interactions of microorganisms with plants and with animals, respectively. Chapter 6 is devoted to microbial communities and includes a discussion of successional processes. Chapter 7 discusses the quantitative measurement of numbers, biomass, and activity of microorganisms. Chapter 8 examines the influence and measurement of environmental determinants. Chapter 9 presents air, water, and soil as microbial habitats and describes the typical composition of their communities. Chapters 10 and 11 contain an expanded discussion of the biogeochemical cycling activities performed by microbial communities. Chapters 12 through 16 deal with applications of microbial ecology to biodeterioration control, sanitation, soil conservation, pollution control inclusive of bioremediation, resource recovery, and biological control of pests and pathogens. The glossary is intended to aid the reader in finding new terms that are used in the field of microbial ecology.

Throughout the textbook, we discuss not only the state of our understanding of microbial ecology but also the methodology employed in obtaining this knowledge. Boxed material highlights topics and methods of current interest in microbial ecology. Experimental approaches are emphasized because most introductory laboratory courses in microbiology stress pure culture procedures and do little to prepare the student for the investigation of the dynamic interactions of organisms and their environment. We have liberally illustrated general statements with specific figures and tables taken from journal articles; the source articles are cited in the legends and are included among the references. Along with the literature references within the text, they provide access points to the relevant literature on specific topics. End-of-chapter questions are included to help students focus on areas covered in each chapter.

We wish to acknowledge our colleagues who have assisted in the development of *Microbial Ecology: Fundamentals and Applications,* particularly Drs. J. Staley, J. C. Meeks, W. Mitsch, G. Cobbs, M. Finstein, D. Eveleigh, and D. Pramer who reviewed various sections of the first edition of this work; Drs. B. Olson, M. Klug, and C. Remsen, who reviewed the complete revised manuscript for the second edition; Drs. M. Franklin, M. H. Franklin, J. Harner, M. Sadowsky, S. Schmidt, and S. Jennett, who made valuable suggestions for the third edition; and Drs. David B. Knaebel, Brian Kinkle, Dennis D. Focht, Scott Kellogg, Ethelynda Harding, Marc Lavoie, Michael Klug, and Vivian Shanker, who reviewed drafts of this fourth edition. Also we want to thank our many colleagues who generously took the time to respond to our inquiries regarding the strengths and weaknesses of the previous editions and who have informally made suggestions to us for improvements. Their suggestions proved most helpful in improving the final product. The production of the fourth edition was greatly aided by the efforts of Grace Wong of Benjamin/Cummings. We are indebted to the many individuals, societies, and companies who generously provided permission to reprint illustrative material. We wish to thank the late Larry Parks especially for his tireless efforts in preparing the manuscript and revising the illustrations; his contributions will endure. We are again grateful to our families for their support during the writing of this book.

R. M. A.          Louisville, Kentucky
R. B.             New Brunswick, New Jersey

# CONTENTS

v

## CHAPTER 7

## Quantitative Ecology: Numbers, Biomass, and Activities   218

## CHAPTER 8

## Physiological Ecology of Microorganisms: Adaptations to Environmental Conditions   281

## CHAPTER 15

## Microorganisms in Mineral and Energy Recovery and Fuel and Biomass Production   599

## CHAPTER 16

## Microbial Control of Pests and Disease-Causing Populations   624

## Glossary   659

## Index   675

# part one

## ECOLOGY AND EVOLUTION

# 1

# MICROBIAL ECOLOGY: HISTORICAL DEVELOPMENT

*Early microbiologists observed microorganisms within their environment, but the pure culture methods fostered by Louis Pasteur and Robert Koch were not conducive to ecological observations. Only a few early microbiologists, most notably Sergei Winogradsky and Martinus Beijerinck, examined the interactions of microorganisms, soil processes, and plants. Most microbiologists focused on examining pure cultures and the roles of microorganisms in disease or fermentation processes of economic importance.*

*Pure culture methods inhibit the examination of ecological interactions. Other methods permitting interactions among microorganisms and their environments have been essential to the development of the field of microbial ecology. In response to methodological advances and an increasing environmental consciousness, the field of microbial ecology developed rapidly after the 1960s and is now an important branch of the microbiological sciences.*

## THE SCOPE OF MICROBIAL ECOLOGY

The desire of a segment of society to live in harmony with nature rather than disrupt it changed the once eso-

teric concept of ecology into a household word and stimulated a broad interest in this branch of biology. The term *ecology* is derived from the Greek words *oikos* (household or dwelling) and *logos* (law). Thus, ecology is "the law of the household" or, by its contemporary definition, the science that explores the interrelationships between organisms and their living (biotic) and nonliving (abiotic) environments. Ecology was first defined and used in this sense by the German biologist Ernst Häeckel (1866). Microbial ecology is the science that specifically examines the relationships between microorganisms and their biotic and abiotic environments. The term *microbial ecology* came into frequent use only in the early 1960s. The development of microbial ecology represented a holistic approach to environmental quality that recognized the importance of all living organisms—including microorganisms—in maintaining ecological balance. The current popularity of microbial ecology and the rapid development of this field are reflective of public interest in ecology and the scientific recognition of the essential roles of microorganisms in ecosystems.

The emergence of microbial ecology as a scientific discipline followed an unprecedented spurt of technological and economic growth in the wake of World War II. By the 1960s, the boundless expectations that followed WWII gave way to alarm over the population explosion, deterioration of the environment, and rapid depletion of nonrenewable natural resources. Humankind, having acquired almost limitless powers to subdue and exploit Earth, appeared able neither to control its own population size nor to manage the limited resources of "Spaceship Earth" in a wise and sustainable fashion.

With a sense of impending doom, groups of scientists and economists drew up grim but credible scenarios of disaster based on projection of prevailing trends in population growth, consumption, and pollution. Proposed remedies stressed population control, limits to technological and economic growth, pollution abatement, and increased reliance on renewable resources for energy and raw materials. Such ideas were presented in books understandable to large segments of society and had notable effects on societal attitudes and on legislative action. Most notable for its impact on the general public was Rachel Carson's *Silent Spring*. Changes in societal attitudes led to various forms of antipollution legislation, to conservation and consumer activism, and to the formation of the United States Environmental Protection Agency (EPA) in 1970 and other environmental regulatory bodies around the world. Various legislative actions on air pollution, water pollution, and strip mining—such as the Clean Air and Clean Water Acts in the United States—were enacted to conserve natural resources and to protect human health against deteriorating environmental quality.

Increasingly, scientists have recognized that microorganisms occupy a key position in the orderly flow of materials and energy through the global ecosystem by virtue of their metabolic abilities to transform organic and inorganic substances. The environmental persistence of various synthetic chemicals and plastics, biomagnification of pollutants, eutrophication, acid mine drainage, nitrate pollution of well water, methylation of mercury, depletion of ozone by nitrous oxide in the stratosphere, and a plethora of other environmental problems reflect unfavorable and unintended interactions of human activities with the microbial component of the global ecosystem. At the same time, microorganisms have been crucial to solving some of our pressing environmental and economic problems; they have helped us to dispose of various liquid and solid wastes in a safe and efficacious manner; to relieve nitrogen fertilizer shortage; to recover metals from low-grade ores; to biologically control pests; and to produce food, feed, and fuel from by-products and waste materials. These and many other practical implications make microbial ecology a highly relevant and exciting subject for study.

## HISTORICAL OVERVIEW

Although the widespread use of the term *microbial ecology* is rather recent, ecologically oriented research on microorganisms was performed as soon as their existence was realized. Much of that early research was identified as soil or aquatic microbiology, but general microbiology also contributed to the understanding of the microbial activities crucial to the balance of nature. The essential role of microorganisms in the global cycling of materials (biogeochemical cycles) has emerged slowly in the shadow of more glamorous investigations in medical microbiology (Table 1.1).

From its inception, advances in microbial ecology have been closely tied to methodological developments. The progress in methodology and in our understanding of the structure and function of microbial ecosystems that has taken place in the last 35 years makes up a large portion of the material covered in this book. However, some fundamental approaches to studying microorganisms, such as the isolation of pure cultures and their cultivation on synthetic media, are not conducive to ecological observations of the type that the general ecologist can readily make on plants and animals in their natural environments. Studying pure cultures of individual microorganisms eliminates the biological interactions that are the essence of ecological relationships. It is not surprising that some important observations relating to microbial ecology either predated the pure culture technique or were made later by investigators who unwittingly or out of necessity dealt with mixed microbial populations rather than with pure cultures.

**Table 1.1**
An overview of some major events in the development of microbial ecology

| Year | Milestones in microbial ecology | Contemporary historic events |
|---|---|---|
| 1676 | Leeuwenhoek describes microbes, including bacteria. | Anglo-Dutch war (1672–74). |
| 1799 | Spallanzani attempts to disprove the spontaneous generation of microbes. | The presidency of George Washington (1789–96). |
| 1837–39 | Schwann, Kützing, and Cagniard-Latour independently implicate yeasts in alcoholic fermentation. Liebig opposes this view. | Siege of the Alamo and the independence of Texas (1836). |
| 1861 | Pasteur demolishes the spontaneous generation theory of microbes. | The American Civil War (1861–65). |
| 1866 | Häeckel introduces the term *ecology*. | |
| 1867 | Cohn describes bacterial endospores and their heat resistance. | Invention of the telephone by Bell (1876). |
| 1879 | Schloesing and Müntz describe microbial nitrification. | First light bulb by Edison. |
| 1883 | Koch uses solid media for isolation and culture of bacteria. | First electric power station built by Edison (1882). |
| 1887 | Winogradsky develops the concept of chemoautotrophy. | Discovery of radio waves (1888). |
| 1905 | Beijerinck characterizes his work as "the study of microbial ecology." | Japan destroys the Russian navy in the battle of Tsusima. |
| 1929 | Discovery of penicillin by Fleming. | The U.S. stockmarket crash. |
| 1934 | Gause's competition and predation experiments using microbial cultures. | In Germany, Hitler comes to power (1933). |
| 1953 | Discovery of the double helical structure of DNA. | School desegregation ruling by the U.S. Supreme Court (1954). |
| 1957 | Symposium on microbial ecology in London. | The first satellite, *Sputnik,* is orbited by the Soviet Union. |
| 1972 | Symposium in Uppsala, Sweden, on modern methods in the study of microbial ecology. | The end of the Vietnam War (1973). |
| 1976 | The ASM journal *Applied Microbiology* becomes *Applied and Environmental Microbiology.* | Bicentennial year of the United States. *Viking* spacecraft's soft-landing on Mars. |
| 1977 | The annual review *Advances in Microbial Ecology* is started. | |
| 1978 | The first international symposium on microbial ecology is held in Dunedin, New Zealand, beginning a series of symposia that occur every three years. | Hostage crisis in Iran. |
| 1980 | Woese describes archaea (archaebacteria) as a separate domain. | The AIDS epidemic recognized (1981). |
| 1985 | Invention of the polymerase chain reaction (PCR). | In the Soviet Union, Gorbachev comes to power. |
| 1988 | First International Conference on the release of genetically modified microorganisms. | Fall of the Berlin Wall and the end of the Cold War (1989). |

## The Beginnings of Microbiology

Although microorganisms are ubiquitous and the most abundant living organisms on Earth, it was not until the mid-seventeenth century that the advent of the microscope permitted their observation. During this period, Robert Hooke, an English experimental philosopher, described his microscopic observations of fungi and protozoa (Hooke 1665) and Antonie van Leeuwenhoek in the 1680s viewed the multitude and diversity of the previously hidden world of microbes, including such small forms as yeasts and some bacteria (Dobell 1932). Leeuwenhoek, an amateur scientist and microscope maker in Delft, Holland, used simple but powerful lenses to tediously observe the otherwise invisible microbes (Figure 1.1). His observations, including detailed and recognizable drawings, were recorded in a series of letters he sent between 1674 and 1723 to the Royal Society in London. Through the *Proceedings of the Royal Society* his discoveries, which otherwise might have been lost, were rapidly disseminated. Leeuwenhoek's reports included descriptions of microbes in rainwater (microbes in their natural habitats) and of the effects of pepper on microbes (environmental influences on microbes), thus providing not only the earliest descriptions of bacteria but also the earliest studies in microbial ecology.

After Leeuwenhoek, little additional progress in microbiology took place until the end of the eighteenth century, when the Italian naturalist Lazzaro Spallanzani, debating the then-prevalent view of spontaneous generation, produced experimental evidence that putrefaction of organic substrates is caused by minute organisms that do not arise spontaneously but multiply by cell division. Spallanzani showed that heating destroys these organisms and that sealing the containers after heating prevents spoilage indefinitely.

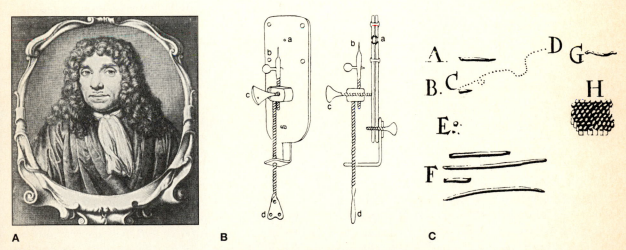

**A**          **B**          **C**

**Figure 1.1**
(A) Antonie van Leeuwenhoek (1632–1723), who developed simple but powerful microscopes and published the first sketches of microscopic observations of bacteria. (Source: National Library of Medicine.) (B) Leeuwenhoek's early microscopes were simple, consisting of (a) a spherical glass lens held by two metal plates; (b) a specimen holder; and (c) and (d) screws for positioning and focusing the specimen. (Source: C. Dobell 1932. Reprinted by permission of Russell and Russell.) (C) Drawings of microorganisms by Leeuwenhoek show several recognizable common bacterial shapes: (a) and (f) rods of varying size; (b) and (e) cocci; (c) and (d) the path of a short motile rod; (g) spiral; (h) cluster of cocci. (Courtesy of Royal Society of London.)

However, heating did not always prevent putrefaction. The heat resistance of bacterial endospores, unknown at that time, contributed to inconsistent and confusing results. Advocates of the spontaneous generation theory, who claimed that microorganisms arise spontaneously and are the result of the putrefaction of organic substances, were not convinced despite the growing experimental evidence against their views, and they tried to explain Spallanzani's results as due to the partial removal of air during the heat treatment. In retrospect the idea seems strange to us, yet in the first half of the nineteenth century even such eminent scientists as the German chemist Justus von Liebig (1839) firmly believed that yeasts and other microorganisms are the products rather than the causative agents of fermentations.

Using slightly different experimental protocols, Charles Cagniard-Latour (1838), Theodor Schwann (1837), and Friedrich Kützing (1837) sought to disprove the theory of spontaneous generation, independently reaching the conclusion that living plantlike microorganisms (yeasts) cause alcoholic fermentations. Experiments by Schwann clearly implicated airborne microorganisms as agents of subsequent spoilage in heat-sterilized media, but the controversy dragged on until the classic experiments of Louis Pasteur silenced even the most obstinate advocates of the spontaneous generation theory. Interestingly, much of the controversy was over whether the experimental procedure had changed the "environmental conditions" so as to prevent a "chemical life force" from acting to create living organisms.

Louis Pasteur, in a beautifully logical series of experiments (1860–1862), demolished the theory of spontaneous generation (Pasteur 1861), reportedly stating, "No more shall the theory of spontaneous generation ever rear its ugly head again." By direct microscopic observation, as well as by cultural methods, he demonstrated the presence of microorganisms in the air and their role in initiating fermentation or spoilage in presterilized media. Pasteur placed yeast water, sugared yeast water, urine, sugar beet juice, and pepper water into ordinary flasks. He then reshaped the necks of the flasks so that there were several curves in each neck, resembling a swan's neck. By using curved necks, Pasteur could leave the flasks open to the air, thus overcoming a major criticism of previous experiments aimed at disproving spontaneous generation where air, an "essential life force," had been partially excluded. Pasteur boiled the liquids until they steamed through the necks. Dust and microbes settled out in the curved necks of the flasks, and thus, though exposed to air, the broth did not become contaminated with microorganisms. Contrary to the opinion of those who believed in spontaneous generation, no change or alteration appeared in the liquid. These flasks, still sterile, were later sealed and may be seen at the Pasteur Institute in Paris.

In his efforts to disprove spontaneous generation, Pasteur found a powerful ally in the English physicist John Tyndall (1820–1893), who demonstrated that optically clear (particle-free) air does not cause spoilage of sterile media and solved the nagging problem of heat-resistant bacterial endospores by discontinuous heat treatments (Tyndall 1877). This technique resulted in germination of endospores and their destruction upon a subsequent heating, thus accomplishing the reliable sterilization of all media at 100°C. One year before Tyndall devised his sterilization method by intermittent heating, Ferdinand Julius Cohn (1876), professor of botany at the University of Breslau, Germany, described the endospores of *Bacillus subtilis* and their heat-resistant properties. He began efforts to establish the taxonomy of bacteria and was the first scientist to recognize and encourage the work of Robert Koch on the cause of anthrax. He recognized that microorganisms have consistent and characteristic morphologies. This view was not shared by many uncritical investigators who, observing a succession of forms in their impure cultures, believed them to be one and the same organism. The studies of Pasteur, Tyndall, and Cohn on bacterial endospores showed how bacteria could survive passage through the air and how they could be disseminated from one ecosystem to another. They also showed how bacteria could adapt to environmental stress and how they could survive for long periods in hostile environments.

## The Pure Culture Period

The mainstream of microbiology from 1880 to the middle of the twentieth century was greatly influenced by the towering figures of Louis Pasteur and Robert Koch (Figure 1.2). A large portion of Pasteur's and Koch's works were oriented toward the most pressing practical problems of their time. Pasteur was trained as a chemist and was prompted to begin his microbiological studies because of the problems of wine producers, brewers, distillers, and vinegar makers. His studies on fermentations between 1857 and 1876 clearly established microorganisms as the causative agents of the various fermentation processes. Both Pasteur and Koch also devoted much of their efforts to examining the roles of microorganisms as causative agents of infectious diseases and to the prevention of such diseases through immunization and sanitation measures. The ability to determine the etiology (cause) of disease depended on the development of appropriate techniques and methodological approaches.

Koch and his coworkers developed simple methods for the isolation and maintenance of pure microbial cultures on solid media (Koch 1883). Previous attempts to obtain pure cultures by dilution or on slices of boiled potato had been cumbersome, uncertain, and not generally applicable. Gelatin and later agar, which Koch used to solidify liquid media of any desired composition, were eminently suitable for use in the identification of disease-causing agents. The use

**A**

**B**

**Figure 1.2**
(A) Louis Pasteur (1822–1895), noted for his many accomplishments in microbiology. He demolished the theory of spontaneous generation, demonstrated the microbial origin of various fermentations and diseases, and contributed to the development of immunization by use of attenuated microorganisms. (Source: National Library of Medicine.) (B) Robert Koch (1843–1910), who made major contributions to the development of pure culture technique and the field of medical microbiology. (Source: National Library of Medicine.)

of solidified agar media allowed microbiologists to separate out a microbial type from a heterogeneous community and study its activities, removed from complex interactions, in an exacting and reproducible manner. The importance of this advance was monumental and transformed microbiology from a chancy art into an exact science. Many of the pure culture techniques devised by Koch are being used today, more than a hundred years later, without any substantial modification.

Koch's pure culture techniques established a trend in microbiology that has had a profound influence on the approach used by microbiologists: First isolate a pure culture and then see what it does. The terse statement by Oscar Brefeld (1881), "Work with impure cultures yields nothing but nonsense and *Penicillium glaucum,*" summarizes this attitude, and few microbiologists would argue with its wisdom even today. Unfortunately, this approach provides little opportunity for the observation of interactions between microorganisms and their biotic and abiotic surroundings; thus it has limited value in microbial ecology. Interaction is the operative term in defining microbial ecology. We should remember that the inhibition zone around a chance *Penicillium* contaminant on a *Staphylococcus* culture, perceived and correctly interpreted by Sir Alexander Fleming (1929), sparked the line of investigations that eventually yielded penicillin and other lifesaving antibiotics. Microbial ecology depends upon the development of methods for understanding just such interactions.

## Microbial Ecology in the Twentieth Century

The pure culture orientation of microbiologists undoubtedly contributed to the relative neglect of ecological research on microorganisms, but ecological research also had to overcome tremendous methodological difficulties and the views of macroecologists that microorganisms could be treated as if they were nonliving chemical substances. Small size, scarce morphological detail, and low behavioral differentiation of microorganisms are formidable obstacles to conventional ecological observation and research. Treating microorganisms as static elements, however,

overlooks their dynamic activities and important roles in ecological processes.

Although macroecologists tended to ignore microorganisms as critical living elements of ecosystems, work by microbiologists in the nineteenth century began to establish the roles of microbial metabolic activities in global ecological processes. Pasteur's work clearly established the importance of microorganisms in the biodegradation of organic substances. He anticipated but failed to prove transformations of inorganic substances by microorganisms in converting ammonium to nitrate (the nitrification process), but the proof was forthcoming from other investigators. In 1839, Nicolas-Théodore de Saussure reported his observation on the capacity of soil to oxidize hydrogen gas. Because this activity was eliminated by heating, by adding a 25% sodium chloride solution, or by adding a 1% sulfuric acid solution, he correctly concluded that the oxidation was microbial, though hydrogen-oxidizing bacteria were not isolated until the first decade of the twentieth century. Jean Jacques Theophile Schloesing and Achille Müntz (1879) reported that ammonium in sewage was oxidized to nitrate during passage through a sand column. The nitrification activity of the column was eliminated by treatment with chloroform vapors but was restored by inoculation with a soil suspension. Again, microbial nitrifying activity was the only logical explanation for these experimental results, which also pointed to the presence of nitrifying organisms in soil.

All the above early information was obtained without the aid of the pure culture technique, but soon thereafter Sergei Winogradsky (Figure 1.3), a Russian scientist working at various European universities and later at the Pasteur Institute in Paris, successfully isolated nitrifying bacteria (1890). Winogradsky developed a model system for growing anaerobic, photosynthetic, and microaerophilic soil bacteria, now known as the "Winogradsky column." During his long and fruitful career, Winogradsky also described the microbial oxidation of hydrogen sulfide and sulfur (1887) and the oxidation of ferrous iron (1888); he correctly developed the concept of microbial chemoautotrophy—though one of his principal models, *Beggiatoa,* could not be grown as a chemoautotroph in

**Figure 1.3**
Sergei Winogradsky (1856–1953), who established the concept of microbial chemoautotrophy and made major contributions to the development of enrichment culture technique and to soil microbiology. (Source: Waksman Institute of Microbiology, Rutgers University.)

**Figure 1.4**
Martinus Beijerinck (1851–1931), known for his major contributions to the knowledge of nitrogen and sulfur cycling by microorganisms. His works included studies on symbiotic nitrogen fixation. (Source: American Society for Microbiology.)

pure culture until recently. He also described the anaerobic nitrogen-fixing bacteria and contributed to the studies of reduction of nitrate and symbiotic nitrogen fixation. Winogradsky isolated and described the nitrifying bacteria that convert ammonium ions ($NH_4^+$) to nitrite ions ($NO_2^-$) and nitrite ions to nitrate ions ($NO_3^-$). He showed that the nitrifying bacteria are responsible for transforming ammonium ions to nitrate ions in soil, an important process because the change from the positively charged ammonium ion to the negatively charged nitrate ion leads to leaching of nitrate from soil and its loss as a nutrient for plants. He demonstrated that microorganisms can derive energy from inorganic chemical oxidation reactions such as these, while obtaining their carbon from carbon dioxide. He originated the nutritional classification of soil microorganisms into two groups, autochthonous

(humus-utilizing microorganisms that grow on soil organic matter) and zymogenous (opportunistic microorganisms that grow on leaves, other plant matter, and animal wastes that enter soils), and is regarded by many as the founder of soil microbiology (Waksman 1953; Schlegel 1996).

Equally important for the development of soil microbiology and microbial ecology was the work of the Dutch microbiologist Martinus Beijerinck (see Figure 1.4 and the accompanying box) at the University of Delft. In 1905, half a century before the emergence of microbial ecology as an area of specialization, Beijerinck stated, "The way I approach microbiology . . . can be concisely stated as the study of microbial ecology, i.e., of the relation between environmental conditions and the special forms of life corresponding to them" (Van Iterson et al. 1940). Beijerinck isolated the agents of symbiotic (1888) and nonsymbiotic aerobic (1901) nitrogen fixation and also isolated sulfate reducers. His reports on nitrogen fixation by bacteria showed the process by which atmospheric nitrogen is combined with other elements to make this essential nutrient available to plants, animals, and other microorganisms. He also isolated sulfate-reducing bacteria, which are important in the cycling of sulfur compounds in soil and sediment. All of these reactions form the basis of important transformations and movements of elements in soil ecosystems and determine the fertility of soil. The works of Beijerinck contributed greatly to our understanding of the role of microbial transformations, biogeochemical cycling reactions, and the critical role of microorganisms in transforming elements on a global scale. Along with Winogradsky's work, the studies of Beijerinck showed that microbially mediated cycling reactions are essential for maintaining environmental quality and are necessary for supporting life on Earth as we know it.

As a consequence of his numerous studies, Beijerinck recognized the near ubiquity of most micro-

## Martinus Beijerinck: Personality and Science

According to an enduring stereotype, a career in scientific research attracts people who are uncomfortable in dealing with other people. Few have conformed to this stereotype more than Martinus W. Beijerinck (1851–1931). Withdrawn and nervous from childhood, Beijerinck developed an early passion for botany. Having studied at the Universities of Delft and Leyden, he earned his doctorate with a dissertation on plant galls in 1877. After a brief teaching career at an agricultural high school, in 1885 he was hired by the Netherlands Yeast and Alcohol Works as a research scientist. In preparation for this post he traveled to visit the laboratories of the eminent microbiologists DeBary, Hansen, and Koch, but ill at ease and claiming they had little to teach him, he cut short his journey.

For the next 10 years, Beijerinck had a successful career as an industrial microbiologist, yet his self-doubts caused him once to resign his position. He was reassured and kept on by his employers. He buried himself in his laboratory and although he was well paid and respected, he failed to marry or form any close attachments. After his publications earned him a considerable scientific reputation, he was offered a professorial chair at the Technical University of Delft. As a condition of acceptance, he demanded a new building that would house both his laboratories and living quarters. The university complied with his wishes, and in this building Beijerinck worked and lived until his reluctant retirement at the age of 70. His two unmarried sisters lived with him and kept house for him. He had no hobbies and a minimum of social contacts. His devotion to research was single-minded.

Beijerinck was a difficult man with whom to work as he often was contemptuous or antagonistic to colleagues. To his students, he was cold and sometimes insulting. He gave credit reluctantly and was harsh in his criticism. No matter how great his scientific reputation, few assistants were able to bear the atmosphere of his laboratory. As Beijerinck's scientific reputation grew, he managed to convince himself that his painful isolation was a necessary price for scientific success. Told about the marriage plans of one of his assistants,

bial forms and the selective influence of the environment that favors the development of certain types of microorganisms. Based on his principle that "everything is everywhere, the environment selects," Beijerinck, with contributions from Winogradsky, developed the immensely useful and adaptable technique of enrichment culture. Tailoring culture conditions to favor microbes with a particular metabolic ability usually leads to the rapid enrichment and isolation of the desired organism, even if its original numbers were very low in the sample (Van Iterson et al. 1940). With

additional reports on nitrate reduction (Deherain 1897), methanogenesis and methanotrophy (Söhngen 1906), and the isolation of hydrogen bacteria (Kaserer 1906), the microbial contributions to geochemical cycling processes emerged (Doetsch 1960; Brock 1961; Doelle 1974).

The fundamental discoveries pertaining to the role of microorganisms in cycling of materials were initially accomplished by relatively few microbiologists who had an interest in unusual metabolic patterns. Further understanding of the microbial role in cycling

---

Beijerinck's comment was "A man of science does not marry!" To last in Beijerinck's laboratory, an assistant had to be exceptionally able and willing to put up with near-impossible demands in an intimidating atmosphere. The ones who were willing to do so profited greatly from his scientific brilliance and became prominent themselves, but they were few.

Beijerinck's scientific achievements are admirable; his views on the personal life of a scientist are not. It may be more than a coincidence that the successor selected for Beijerinck at the now world-famous Delft School of Microbiology was the similarly talented but exceptionally outgoing and pleasant Albert J. Kluyver (1888–1956). Beijerinck succeeded in spite of and not because of his personal views on life. His success as a scientist can be measured by the impact he had on soil microbiology—his enrichment technique is still widely used in microbial ecology—

and by the succession of scientists who trace their professional lineage to both Beijerinck and the Delft School (see figure A).

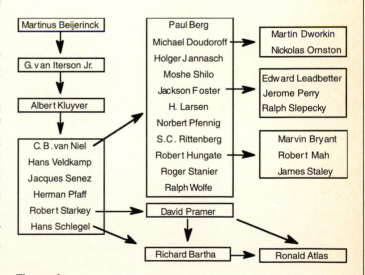

**Figure A**

In marking the 100th anniversary of Martinus Beijerinck becoming a professor, the Delft School of Microbiology undertook a family tree project showing Beijerinck's professional descendants. This illustration shows a few of those scientists who share this heritage.

**Figure 1.5**
Albert Jan Kluyver (1888–1956), who emphasized the unifying features of microbial metabolism. (Source: Waksman Institute of Microbiology, Rutgers University.)

processes and the unifying metabolic features among micro- and macroorganisms emerged from the work of Albert Jan Kluyver, Cornelius Bernardus van Niel, and Roger Stanier; these microbiologists were notable for the breadth, comparativeness, and ecological implications of their work in microbial physiology. Kluyver (Figure 1.5) succeeded Beijerinck as the leading microbiologist at the University of Delft in the hometown of Leeuwenhoek. He took a broad interest in microbial physiology and with his students and coworkers studied a variety of oxidative, fermentative, and chemoautotrophic microorganisms, including unusual metabolic types. His greatest contribution was perhaps his comparative approach, which stressed the unifying metabolic features within the diverse microbial world (Kamp et al. 1959).

A student of Kluyver's, C. B. van Niel (Figure 1.6), came from the same famous school of Delft microbiologists (Bennett and Phaff 1993). After settling in the United States early in his career (1929), he was instrumental in transplanting his school's tradition of comparative and ecologically oriented microbial physiology to his new country. Among his many contributions, his investigations on bacterial phototrophy have special importance. He pointed out the striking similarity of hydrogen sulfide ($H_2S$) and water ($H_2O$) in the photoprocesses of photosynthetic sulfur bacteria and green plants, respectively (Pfennig 1987). Roger Stanier, a student of van Niels, continued the tradition of unraveling the role of microbial metabolism in ecological processes; his work with *Pseudomonas,* for example, showed the tremendous versatility of aerobic microorganisms in degrading complex organic compounds. Van Niel taught a world-famous laboratory course that emphasized the study of microorganisms from nature. The annual summer microbial ecology course now taught at Woods Hole Oceanographic Institute, Woods Hole, Massachusetts, follows the approach established by van Niel. Robert Hungate, who took van Niel's course, further expanded the study of microbial metabolism in the environment by developing methods for culturing strict anaerobes; he also pioneered our understanding of the complex interactions of microbial populations through his studies on microorganisms in the rumen of cows and the guts of termites (Hungate 1979). Today the course at Woods Hole continues the exploration of microbial diversity and unusual ecosystems. Besides helping to expand the scope of the Woods Hole course, Hungate served as president of the American Society for Microbiology (ASM), and in 1970 appointed an ASM Committee on Environmental Microbiology. That same year the International Association of Microbiological Societies established an International Commission on Microbial Ecology (ICME) and appointed Martin Alexander as chairperson.

Thus in 1970 the importance of the role of microorganisms in nature received recognition, and the coherent discipline of microbial ecology was formally recognized. Soon thereafter, another milestone in the development of microbial ecology occurred, the 1972 International Symposium on Modern Methods in Microbial Ecology in Uppsala, Sweden, sponsored by the International Commission on Microbial Ecology. This was followed by regular symposia on microbial ecology and the annual publication of *Advances in Microbial Ecology* under the auspices of the International Commission on Microbial Ecology. Since 1977, international symposia on microbial ecology have been convened every three years (I in Dunedin, New Zealand, 1977; II in Coventry, England, 1980; III in East Lansing, Michigan, 1983; IV in Ljubljana, Yugoslavia, 1986; V in Kyoto, Japan, 1989; VI in Barcelona, Spain, 1992; VII in Santos, Brazil, 1995; VIII in Halifax, Canada, 1998). At these symposia, hundreds of microbial ecologists gather to exchange the latest results of their studies and to discuss their growing understanding of the roles microorganisms play in nature.

The 1970s also marked an era of pragmatism when scientists coupled a basic understanding of the natural roles of microorganisms in the environment with efforts to harness these microbial activities for the maintenance and restoration of environmental quality. Major environmental applications of microorganisms, such as bioremediation, emerged as a means of using microbial activities to eliminate pollutants. Agricultural practices were modified so that microorganisms could be used to improve soil fertility and to protect crops against pests that cause significant economic losses. Industrial manufacturing practices were modified to reduce releases of pollutants that are resistant to microbial attack. New biodegradable substances were developed so as to permit their mineralization and recycling.

Genetically modified microorganisms also were created to deal with persistent environmental problems. The potential for a deliberate environmental release of genetically modified microorganisms sparked debates about the safety of introducing novel DNA sequences. Concerns about the safety of recombinant DNA technology fostered basic studies of interactions among microbial populations and the fate of introduced microorganisms. Thus the last few decades of the twentieth century were marked by fervent interest in both the fundamental and applied aspects of microbial ecology.

**Figure 1.6**
Cornelius Bernardus van Niel (1897–1985), who furthered the study of microorganisms in nature and established a model course for the study of microbial ecology. (Source: Hopkins Marine Station, Stanford University.)

## RELATION OF MICROBIAL ECOLOGY TO GENERAL ECOLOGY AND THE ENVIRONMENTAL SCIENCES

Commonly, ecologists have had prior training in one of the classic biological disciplines such as botany, zoology, or microbiology. This often led to their specialization in either the ecology of plants and animals (microecology) or the ecology of microorganisms (microbial ecology), but the study of ecosystems and global processes requires a more integrated approach. In textbooks, plant and animal ecology are now integrated in a satisfactory manner, but the treatment of microbial processes tends to be rudimentary, if included at all. The decomposition of organic matter and the cycling of mineral nutrients are all too often taken for granted and treated as "black box" processes. In contrast to primary production, their importance and measurement are rarely covered. Considering that nutrient recycling can constrain primary productivity, this neglect is unjustified.

Eventually, microbial ecology will become more integrated with general ecology, but this process will take considerable time. Currently, macroecology consists largely of phenomena in search of mechanistic explanations, whereas microbial ecology principally consists of experimentation in search of theory (Andrews 1991). Although the fields of study of the ecologies of macroorganisms and microorganisms have developed as separate, disjointed disciplines, Andrews points out in his *Comparative Ecology of Microorganisms and Macroorganisms* that the ecologies of microorganisms and macroorganisms are similarly shaped by evolution, operating through differential reproductive success. He compares the genetics, nutrition, size, growth, and responses to the environment of representative bacteria, fungi, and macroorganisms, describing the roles of resource acquisition, growth, and survival in the evolution of life cycles. Similar efforts to compare microorganisms and macroorganisms will gradually diminish the discipline-created barriers within general ecology.

One reason for the historical separation of macroecology and microbial ecology is the basic difference in their methods. Macroecologists use field observation and quantitative surveys of species composition and diversity as their most common investigative approaches. The laboratory is used for data analysis and auxiliary chemical determinations only. In contrast, the microbial ecologist often can do little in the field beyond sample collections; the real work is conducted in the laboratory. Microcosms are preferred to field plots, radioisotopes and sophisticated instrumental analyses are used in place of visual observation. Few investigators are equally skilled at approaches to both microbial ecology and macroecology but, increasingly, teamwork on comprehensive projects fosters communication between microbial and macroecologists. This is evidenced in research teams working together at long-term ecological research (LTER) sites.

Although microorganisms are often overlooked by classical ecologists because of their small size and short generation time, microorganisms have potential advantages for studies in population dynamics. However, observational difficulties have discouraged their use in such investigations. Notable exceptions were the classic experiments of George Francis Gause (1934) on populations of the ciliate protozoa *Paramecium caudatum* and *Didinium nasutum,* the latter preying on the former species. These and similar experiments with *Schizosaccharomyces pombe* (yeast), which is preyed upon by *Paramecium bursaria* (ciliate protozoan), revealed the same out-of-phase cyclic oscillations that were observed in some mammalian predator-prey interactions. At that time, these ecologically oriented, mixed culture experiments elicited little response among microbiologists, while they sparked a great deal of additional research and lively debate among zoologists and ecologists.

Among the few techniques developed for the *in situ* observation of microorganisms in the first half of this century, the contact slide (Cholodny 1930; Rossi et al. 1936) deserves mention. In this method, microscope slides buried in soil or sediment provide a surface not unlike that of soil particles for microbial growth. Careful removal and microscopic observation of these slides provides an opportunity to observe microorganisms as they grow and interact in their natural environment.

Later, scanning electron microscopy with its great focal depth and high resolution allowed the often stunning *in situ* imaging of microbial forms. This method for microscopic observation has been surpassed in microbial ecology by fluorescence microscopy and in particular by the development of confocal scanning laser microscopy and fluorescent probes to reveal the spatial relationships of microorganisms within the environment (Caldwell et al. 1992). Fluorescent probes permit the identification of specific types of microorganisms within complex microbial communities. Confocal scanning laser microscopy permits the observation of microorganisms in three dimensions so that the biofilms and other multilayered microbial communities can be studied.

Although microscopic observations clearly contribute to the understanding of microbial ecology, other methods such as radiotracer and microanalytic techniques were probably more important for the rapid upswing in the pace and range of ecologically oriented microbiological research that occurred in the early 1960s. Much of this research was prompted by the noticeable and troublesome presence in the environment of synthetic pollutants that were not, or not rapidly enough, degraded by microorganisms, and by eutrophication problems caused by detergent fillers and fertilizer runoff.

Microorganisms had often been considered to be infallible biological incinerators. The recognition by Martin Alexander that some compounds produced by humans are recalcitrant, that is, totally resistant to microbial attack, led to increased research on the biodegradability of pollutants (Alexander 1981; Leisinger et al. 1982). In the late 1960s, Ronald Atlas and Richard Bartha began studies on the stimulated biodegradation of petroleum pollutants in the sea, pioneering the field of bioremediation, which uses the metabolic activity of microorganisms to remove environmental contaminants (Atlas and Bartha 1992). Concern also arose about the effects of radiation and pollutants on microbial cycling activities in soil and natural waters. The biomagnification of DDT, PCBs, mercury, and other pollutants called attention to food web interrelations and to the key position of microbial forms as primary producers in aquatic food webs. The nitrogen fertilizer shortage that developed in the wake of the energy crisis of the early 1970s resulted in renewed and intense interest in symbiotic and non-symbiotic nitrogen-fixation processes. The energy crisis also called for research on fuel generation from renewable resources such as organic wastes and plant biomass, with microorganisms as obvious candidates to effect such conversions.

Space exploration was a great stimulus to microbial ecology. The possibility of soft-landing instruments on remote planets prompted the development of methods and instrument packages for detecting extraterrestrial microbial life. The testing of these methods and instruments, in turn, stimulated interest in the microbial communities of extremely harsh terrestrial environments, such as the cold, dry valleys of Antarctica (Cameron 1971). Microorganisms living in very high temperature environments, such as hot springs, were intensively studied by Thomas Brock (1978). Holger Jannasch further expanded our knowledge of life in extreme environments by his studies on the microorganisms living in proximity to deep-sea thermal vents (Jannasch and Mottl 1985).

The recent introduction of molecular techniques into microbial ecology has opened up exciting new possibilities (Akkermans et al. 1995; Pace 1996). Using these tools, the diversity of a microbial community may be assessed by the heterogeneity of its RNA or DNA. Reassociation plots of DNA extracted directly from soil or other ecosystems and melted after appropriate purification (Torsvik et al. 1990) offer a new and promising approach to the determination of the diversity of microbial communities. The presence and abundance of individual microbial strains or of certain community segments may be determined by targeted molecular probes. Rare or unculturable microorganisms may be detected by amplification of their DNA through the polymerase chain reaction (PCR), followed by their characterization using a range of molecular probes. Probes can be designed to detect broad segments of a community, e.g., Bacteria versus Archaea, or they can be made specific down to the species level. Conjugated with fluorescent markers, molecular probes are also suitable for the *in situ* detection and identification of bacterial species. Such measurements confirm the suspicion that the biodiversity of microorganisms is much greater than revealed by the cultural approach. We are familiar with only 1–10% of all existing microbial species. Perhaps the greatest challenge to contemporary microbial ecologists is the exploration of the structure, function, and potential biotechnological uses of the remaining 90–99%.

Long before microbial ecology emerged as a distinct area of specialization, fundamental knowledge about microbe-environment interactions accumulated in several microbial subdisciplines. As described earlier, the microbiology of soil, with its important agricultural implications, attracted the attention and talent of such distinguished investigators as Sergei

Winogradsky and Martinus Beijerinck. Plant pathology, with its related practical implications, also received early attention. As in medical microbiology, the pure culture technique led rapidly to the isolation and characterization of various fungi and bacteria that cause diseases of plants. Beijerinck also made a crucial contribution to this field with his investigation of plant diseases caused by submicroscopic, filterable principles. Continuation of Beijerinck's unfinished work by others led to the startling discovery of a crystallizable plant pathogenic principle: the tobacco mosaic virus.

Freshwater microbiology, with its ties to safe drinking water and acceptable sewage disposal practices, became an early concern of microbiologists and sanitary engineers. A great deal of information on total microbial and coliform counts in fresh water was amassed and used primarily as an indication of water quality. Nevertheless, the survival of nonindigenous coliforms in natural waters and the factors influencing such survival again led to general ecological insights. Marine microbiology, largely devoid of similar sanitary concerns, developed substantially later and largely due to the lifelong work of Claude ZoBell at the Scripps Institute of Oceanography in La Jolla, California. Not only did ZoBell and his coworkers collect an impressive body of data on the occurrence and function of microorganisms in marine waters and sediments, but ZoBell also wrote the first comprehensive text on marine microbiology (1946) and is regarded by many to be the founder of this important field. The ecological implications of his work are many and of foremost importance.

Humans have used microorganisms in the processing of food since prehistoric times and, conversely, have striven to prevent the microbial spoilage of stored food by drying, salting, and other methods. In the early years, of course, this was done without any understanding of the microbial nature of these processes. The insights of the nineteenth century into the microbial nature of spoilage and fermentation sparked the rapid development of the subdiscipline of food microbiology. Their applied nature notwithstanding, studies on fermentations and spoilage processes yielded a great deal of fundamental ecological information on the influence of environmental parameters on microorganisms, on survival under adverse conditions, and on microbial succession.

The 1960s were apparently the right time to consolidate the knowledge that had accumulated in related fields and to identify it as a distinct area of specialization. Recognition that many ecological problems cut across arbitrary environmental boundaries and affect the global ecosystem, rather than only the soil or the aquatic environment, may have speeded the evolution of microbial ecology.

## SOURCES OF INFORMATION FOR THE MICROBIAL ECOLOGIST

To our knowledge, no book or periodical appeared prior to 1957 with *Microbial Ecology* or something comparable as its title, but impressive numbers of such books and periodicals have appeared thereafter (Tables 1.2 and 1.3), attesting to the current vitality of microbial ecology. Publications of interest to microbial ecologists are not limited to the listed periodicals. Many are scattered in a multitude of general science and specialty journals. To list all relevant journals would be tedious, if not impossible. Instead, Table 1.4 on page 22 lists subject areas with some representative examples. Today, access to information on microbial ecology is available through the World Wide Web. Some web sites are devoted to microbial ecology; for example, the Digital Learning Center for Microbial Ecology (http://commtechlab.msu.edu/CTLProjects/dlc-me/) offers a great expanse of information on microbial diversity and environmental aspects of microbial ecology. It also includes a microbial zoo that shows the interactions of microorganisms, and a section on microbial resources that provides updates on where to find information on microbial ecology. The Web provides numerous resources and updated information for microbial ecologists.

Given that microbial ecologists study interactions among various microorganisms, interactions of microorganisms with their abiotic environment, and interactions of microorganisms with plants and animals, the field of microbial ecology cuts across the lines of several established disciplines. To be effective, the microbial ecologist requires a broad background in the physicochemical and biological sciences. Specifically, the microbiology student planning to specialize in this area should take care to acquire a good foundation in physics, chemistry, general biology, molecular biology, and microbiology, including its biochemical aspects. Molecular biological methods have become increasingly important in all fields of biology, including microbial ecology. In addition to these basics, it is desirable for a microbial ecologist to have some degree of familiarity with all or at least some of the subjects of botany (especially phytoplankton and plant physiology) and zoology (especially zooplankton and animal physiology), and with aspects of soil science, limnology (the study of freshwater environments), oceanography, geochemistry, and climatology that are relevant as environmental determinants of microbial life. A background in statistics is essential for designing appropriate sampling schedules and for evaluating the significance of acquired data. It may not be realistic for each student to acquire equal competence in all of the listed areas, and the chosen research subject dictates training priorities. Bear in mind, however, that research trends and opportunities shift rapidly. A broad and flexible background is the best insurance against premature scientific obsolescence.

Professional opportunities for the microbial ecologist currently exist in academic, governmental, industrial, and consulting organizations. During recent academic retrenchments, microbial ecology fared reasonably well, and both faculty and grant-supported research positions have expanded in this area. Government agencies, such as the United States Environmental Protection Agency (EPA) and the United States Department of Agriculture (USDA), provide employment opportunities in their research institutions and also on the administrative-regulatory level. Industrial research laboratories, voluntarily or under regulatory pressure, are conducting a rapidly increasing volume of research on the environmental effects of their products, wastes, and operational procedures. Private consulting firms contract with governmental or industrial organizations to perform similar environmental impact studies. Genetic engineering and the consequent accidental or intentional release of novel microorganisms confront the microbial ecologist with a new set of challenges related to biotechnology (Tiedje et al. 1989). The survival of engineered microorganisms after their release, their ecological interaction and genetic recombination with natural populations, and the resulting effects on the environment are unsolved questions that are not only scientifically intriguing but of potentially vital significance (Alexander 1985).

**Table 1.2**
Periodicals on microbial ecology

| Journal | Description |
| --- | --- |
| *Advances in Microbial Ecology.* 1977–. Plenum Press, New York. | Review series on basic and applied aspects of microbial ecology. |
| *Applied and Environmental Microbiology.* 1976–. American Society for Microbiology, Washington, D.C. | Formerly *Applied Microbiology,* the title was modified to recognize and publish papers on applied and general microbial ecology. |
| *FEMS Microbial Ecology.* 1985–. Federation of European Microbiological Societies, Elsevier Science Publishers, Amsterdam, The Netherlands. | Scope similar to *Microbial Ecology.* Created as a publication outlet for European scientists working in this field. |
| *Microbial Ecology.* 1974–. Springer-Verlag, New York. | Research reports on all aspects of microbial ecology. |

**Table 1.3**
Text and reference books on microbial ecology

| Book | Description |
| --- | --- |
| Aaronson, A. 1970. *Experimental Microbial Ecology*. Academic Press, New York. | A useful compendium of isolation techniques for various types of microorganisms. |
| Alet, K., and P. Nannipieri (eds.). 1995. *Methods in Applied Soil Microbiology and Biochemistry*. Academic Press, London. | Edited volume, excellent collection of techniques useful in microbial ecology research conducted in soil. |
| Alexander, M. 1971. *Microbial Ecology*. Wiley, New York. | Text written in essay style. Useful mainly at the graduate level. |
| Alexander, M. 1977. *Introduction to Soil Microbiology*. Wiley, New York. | Text describes the ecology of soil microorganisms. |
| Alexander, M. (ed.). 1984. *Biological Nitrogen Fixation: Ecology, Terminology and Physiology*. Plenum Press, New York. | A series of papers on the conversion of molecular nitrogen by nitrogen-fixing bacteria. |
| Allsopp, D., D. L. Hawksworth, and R. R. Colwell (eds.). 1995. *Microbial Diversity and Ecosystem Function*. CAB International, Wallingford, Great Britain. | Covers the breadth of microbial diversity and its importance in ecological functioning. |
| Andrews, J. H. 1991. *Comparative Ecology of Microorganisms and Macroorganisms*. Springer-Verlag, New York. | Compares the ecology of macroorganisms and microorganisms, providing a thorough foundation of common ecological principles. |
| Blakeman, J. P. (ed.). 1981. *Microbial Ecology of the Phylloplane*. Academic Press, London. | Collected papers on microorganisms living on the surfaces of above-ground plant structures. |
| Brock, T. D. 1966. *Principles of Microbial Ecology*. Prentice Hall, Englewood Cliffs, NJ. | First textbook on microbial ecology. Advanced undergraduate level. Out of print. |
| Brock, T. D. 1978. *Thermophilic Microorganisms and Life at High Temperatures*. Springer-Verlag, New York. | A comprehensive work on the microorganisms that live at very high temperatures. Written by an authority in the field. |
| Bull, A. T., and J. H. Slater (eds.). 1982. *Microbial Interactions and Communities*. Academic Press, London. | A collection of articles describing the basis for interactions between microbial populations. |
| Burns, R. G., and J. H. Slater (eds.). 1982. *Experimental Microbial Ecology*. Blackwell Scientific Publications, Oxford, England. | An excellent collection of methodological approaches used in microbial ecology, indicating the applicability and limitations of each. |
| Campbell, R. E. 1983. *Microbial Ecology*. Blackwell Scientific Publications, Oxford, England. | Introductory text stressing the role of microorganisms in biogeochemical cycles and food webs. |
| Codd, G. A. 1984. *Aspects of Microbial Metabolism and Ecology*. Academic Press, London. | A series of papers on the ecological aspects of microbial metabolism and energetics. |
| Colwell, R. R., and R. Morita (eds.). 1974. *Effect of the Ocean Environment on Microbial Activities*. University Park Press, Baltimore. | A collection of articles on marine microorganisms. |
| Colwell, R. R., R. K. Sizemore, J. F. Cooney, J. D. Nelson, Jr., R. Y. Morita, S. D. Van Valkenburg, and R. T. Wright. 1975. *Marine and Estuarine Microbiology Laboratory Manual*. University Park Press, Baltimore. | A good selection of exercises on microbial ecology of saltwater environments. |

| Book | Description |
| --- | --- |
| Dix, N. J., and J. Webster. 1995. *Fungal Ecology*. Chapman and Hall, New York. | Coverage of the ecology of fungi. |
| Dixon, B. 1994. *Power Unseen: How Microbes Rule the World*. Freeman/Spectrum, Oxford. | The key role of microbes in maintaining the biosphere, presented at a nontechnical level. |
| Doetsch, R. N., and T. M. Cook. 1973. *Introduction to Bacteria and Their Ecobiology*. University Park Press, Baltimore. | Undergraduate-level text with strong physiological emphasis. |
| Edmonds, P. 1978. *Microbiology—An Environmental Perspective*. Macmillan, New York. | Introductory microbiology text with ecological-environmental emphasis. |
| Edwards, C. (ed.). 1990. *Microbiology of Extreme Environments*. McGraw-Hill, New York. | Edited book with fine chapters on adaptations of thermophiles, acidophiles, alkalophiles, oligotrophs, halophiles, and metal-tolerant microorganisms. |
| Ehrlich, H. L. 1981. *Geomicrobiology*. Marcel Dekker, New York. | Review of the actions of microorganisms in geochemical transformations. |
| Ellwood, D. C., J. N. Hedger, M. J. Latham, J. M. Lynch, and J. H. Slater (eds.). 1980. *Contemporary Microbial Ecology*. Academic Press, London. | Proceedings of the Second International Symposium on Microbial Ecology in 1980 in Coventry, England. |
| Fenchel, T., and T. H. Blackburn. 1979. *Bacteria and Mineral Cycling*. Academic Press, London. | Review of the activities of microorganisms that transform inorganic substances and establish biogeochemical cycles. |
| Fletcher, M., and G. D. Floodgate (eds.). 1985. *Bacteria in Their Natural Environments*. Academic Press, London. | A series of papers on the ecological adaptations of microorganisms and their critical metabolic activities in the environment. |
| Ford, T. E. (ed.). 1993. *Aquatic Microbiology: An Ecological Approach*. Blackwell, Boston. | Perspective on the ecology of aquatic microorganisms and their roles in freshwater ecosystems. |
| Gaudy, A. and E. Gaudy. 1980. *Microbiology for Environmental Science Engineers*. McGraw-Hill, New York. | A general review of the environmental aspects of microbiology with emphasis on the practical engineering implications. |
| Girgorova, R., and J. R. Norris (eds.). 1990. *Techniques in Microbial Ecology, Methods in Microbiology*. Academic Press, London. | Describes many methods used to study microbial ecology. |
| Gorden, R. W. 1972. *Field and Laboratory Microbial Ecology*. WC Brown, Dubuque, Iowa. | Laboratory manual with a good selection of exercises, but lack of detail demands a lot of initiative by the instructor. |
| Gould, G. W., and J.E.L. Corry (eds.). 1980. *Microbial Growth and Survival in Extremes of Environment*. Academic Press, New York. | A series of papers on the adaptations of microorganisms that permit growth and survival under extreme conditions. |
| Goyal, S. M., C. P. Gerba, and G. Bitton (eds.). 1987. *Phage Ecology*. Wiley, New York. | A concise compilation of the literature on the distribution and behavior of phage in the environment. |
| Gray, T.R.G., and D. Parkinson (eds.). 1968. *The Ecology of Soil Bacteria*. University of Toronto Press, Toronto, Canada. | Collection of articles on the ecology of soil microorganisms. |

*(continued)*

**Table 1.3** *(continued)*

| Book | Description |
|---|---|
| Gregory, P. H. 1973. *The Microbiology of the Atmosphere.* Wiley, New York. | Excellent work about the microorganisms of the air. |
| Hattori, T., Y. Ishida, Y. Maruyama, R. Y. Morita, and A. Uchida (eds.). 1989. *Recent Advances in Microbial Ecology.* Japan Scientific Societies Press, Tokyo. | Proceedings of the Fifth International Symposium on Microbial Ecology in 1989 in Kyoto, Japan. |
| Hurst, C. J., G. R. Knudsen, M. J. McInerney, L. D. Stetzenbach, and M. V. Walter. 1997. *Manual of Environmental Microbiology.* ASM Press, Washington, DC. | State-of-the art compendium of methods for environmental microbiology. |
| Kemp, P. F., B. F. Sherr, E. B. Sherr, and J. Cole (eds.). 1993. *Aquatic Microbial Ecology.* Lewis Publishers, Boca Raton, Fl. | Edited volume, very useful collection of contemporary methods employed in aquatic microbial ecology. |
| Klug, M. J., and C. A. Redy. 1984. *Current Perspectives in Microbial Ecology.* American Society for Microbiology, Washington, DC. | Proceedings of the Third International Symposium on Microbial Ecology in 1983 in East Lansing, Michigan. |
| Krumbein, C.W.E. (ed.). 1983. *Microbial Geochemistry.* Blackwell, Oxford, England. | A series of papers on the biogeochemical activities of microorganisms. |
| Kuznetzov, S. I. 1970. *The Microflora of Lakes and Its Geochemical Activity.* University of Texas Press, Austin, TX. | Classic Russian work on the microbiology of freshwater lakes. |
| Laskin, A. H., and H. Lechevalier (eds.). 1974. *Microbial Ecology.* CRC Press, Cleveland, OH. | Collection of reviews on biodegradation of pesticides and on population dynamics in soil and mixed cultures. |
| Levin, M. A., R. J. Seidler, and M. Rogul (eds.). 1992. *Microbial Ecology: Principles, Methods, and Applications.* McGraw-Hill, New York. | An extensive collection of papers describing modern approaches to the study of microbial ecology. |
| Loutit, M., and J.A.R. Miles (eds.). 1979. *Microbial Ecology.* Springer-Verlag, Berlin. | Proceedings of the First International Symposium on Microbial Ecology in 1977 in Dunedin, New Zealand. Papers cover a wide range of subjects. |
| Lynch, J. M., and N. J. Poole (eds.). 1979. *Microbial Ecology—A Conceptual Approach.* Blackwell, Oxford, England. | Good text for advanced students covering the major areas studied by microbial ecologists. |
| Marshall, K. C. 1976. *Interfaces in Microbial Ecology.* Harvard University Press, Cambridge, MA. | Important work on the occurrence and activities of microorganisms at interfaces, such as between air and water. |
| Megusar, F., and M. Gantar. 1986. *Perspectives in Microbial Ecology.* Slovene Society for Microbiology, Ljubljana, Yugoslavia. | Proceedings of the Fourth International Symposium on Microbial Ecology in 1986 in Ljubljana, Yugoslavia. |
| Metting, F. B., Jr. (ed.). 1993. *Soil Microbial Ecology.* Marcel Dekker, New York. | Edited volume emphasizing applications in agricultural and environmental management. |
| Mitchell, R. 1974. *Introduction to Environmental Microbiology.* Prentice Hall, Englewood Cliffs, NJ. | Elementary microbiology text relevant to the environmental sciences, such as sanitary engineering. |

| Book | Description |
| --- | --- |
| Mitchell, R. 1992. *Environmental Microbiology*. Wiley, New York. | In-depth examination of environmental microbiology emphasizing new approaches for investigating the roles of microorganisms in environmental deterioration and restoration. |
| Odom, J. M., and R. Singleton, Jr. (eds.). 1994. *The Sulfate-Reducing Bacteria: Contemporary Perspectives*. Springer-Verlag, New York. | Edited volume that summarizes recent advances concerning sulfidogens. |
| Pickup, R. W., and J. R. Saunders (eds.). 1996. *Molecular Approaches to Environmental Microbiology*. Ellis Horwood, London. | Series of in-depth reviews on bacterial ecology. |
| Postgate, J. 1982. *Fundamentals of Nitrogen Fixation*. Cambridge University Press, New York. | A concise discussion of microbial fixation of molecular nitrogen. |
| Postgate, J. 1984. *The Sulphate-Reducing Bacteria*. Cambridge University Press, New York. | A thorough discussion of the bacteria that reduce sulfate. |
| Postgate, J. 1994. *The Outer Reaches of Life*. Cambridge University Press, Cambridge, England. | Microbial life and ecology under extreme conditions, presented at a nontechnical level. |
| Rheinheimer, G. 1986. *Aquatic Microbiology*. Wiley, New York. | Excellent work describing the ecology of microorganisms in freshwater habitats. |
| Richards, B. N. 1987. *The Microbiology of Terrestrial Ecosystems*. Longman/Wiley, New York. | Undergraduate-graduate-level text that emphasizes systems approach and plant-microbe interactions. |
| Rosswall, T. (ed.). 1972. *Modern Methods in the Study of Microbial Ecology*. Ecological Research Committee, NFR Swedish National Science Research Council, Uppsala, Sweden. | Proceedings of the first international meeting on microbial ecology. Useful collection of method descriptions. |
| Sieburth, J. McN. 1979. *Sea Microbes*. Oxford University Press, New York. | Magnificent collection of micrographs showing microorganisms in marine environments. |
| Slater, J. H., R. Whittenbury, and J.W.T. Wimpenny. 1983. *Microbes in Their Natural Environment*. Society for General Microbiology, Symposium Series #34. Cambridge University Press, Cambridge, England. | Proceedings of a symposium at the University of Warwick in 1983. Articles emphasize metabolic activities of microorganisms in natural habitats. |
| Stolp, H. 1988. *Microbial Ecology: Organisms, Habitats, Activities*. Cambridge University Press, Cambridge, England. | Concise text at undergraduate level aimed at microbiology and nonmicrobiology majors. |
| Williams, R.E.O., and C. C. Spices (eds.). 1957. *Microbial Ecology*. Cambridge University Press, Cambridge, England. | Now mainly of historical interest, this is the proceedings of the first symposium on microbial ecology held at the Seventh Symposium of the Society of General Microbiology in April 1957 in London. |
| Wood, E.J.F. 1965. *Marine Microbial Ecology*. Chapman and Hall, London. | Introductory-level text that assumes the reader has some background in microbiology but none in oceanography. |
| ZoBell, C. E. 1946. *Marine Microbiology*. Chronica Botanica, Waltham, MA. | Classic work that describes microorganisms in the oceans. |

**Table 1.4**
General science and specialty journals containing reports of interest to the microbial ecologist

| Subject area | Journal |
| --- | --- |
| General science | *BioScience* |
| | *Nature* (London) |
| | *Science* (AAAS) |
| General microbiology | *Archives for Microbiology (Archiv für Microbiologie)* |
| | *CRC Critical Reviews in Microbiology* |
| | *Current Biology* |
| | *FEMS Microbiology Letters* |
| | *Journal of Bacteriology* |
| | *Journal of General and Applied Microbiology* |
| | *Journal of Industrial Microbiology* |
| | *Microbiological Reviews* |
| Aquatic environment | *Experimental Marine Biology and Ecology* |
| | *Hydrobiologia* |
| | *Journal of Freshwater Biology* |
| | *Journal of Plankton Research* |
| | *Limnology and Oceanography* |
| Soil environment | *Soil Biology and Biochemistry* |
| | *Soil Science* |
| | *Soil Science Society of America Journal* |
| Extreme environments | *Extremophiles* |
| Molecular biology | *Biotechniques* |
| | *Microbial Releases* |
| | *Molecular Ecology* |
| | *PCR: Methods and Applications* |
| Environment and pollution | *Bulletin of Environmental Contamination and Toxicology* |
| | *Environmental Pollution* |
| | *Environmental Science and Technology* |
| | *Marine Pollution Bulletin* |

# CHAPTER SUMMARY

Microbial ecology is the field of science that examines the relationships between microorganisms and their biotic and abiotic environments. Historically, the earliest studies in microbial ecology were conducted by Sergei Winogradsky and Martinus Beijerinck. These microbiologists examined the microbial transformations of inorganic nitrogen and sulfur compounds in soils. They showed the roles of microorganisms in converting molecular nitrogen into fixed forms that could be used by plants and animals and the microbial transformations of ammonium, nitrite, and nitrate ions. They elucidated global biogeochemical cycling reactions and the contributions of microorganisms to soil fertility. Beijerinck also developed enrichment culture methods for the isolation of microorganisms from soil that had specific metabolic capabilities.

The scientific discipline of microbial ecology as a cohesive branch of science blossomed in the 1960s during an era of public concern with environmental quality and the ecological impact of industrial pollution. Since the early 1960s, environmental problems have focused attention on the essential cycling processes. By 1970, microbial ecology emerged as a field of specialization, and it has experienced dramatic growth in terms of research and publication volume. Judging from the range and magnitude of unsolved environmental problems, microbial ecology should continue to be a challenging field of specialization for microbiologists with broad training and interests.

The development of microbial ecology has been and continues to be highly dependent on methodological advances. Early methods developed by Robert Koch and Louis Pasteur restricted studies to pure microbial cultures and slowed the advancement of the field of microbial ecology, which depends upon examining interactions among diverse microorganisms, macroorganisms, and abiotic environmental factors. Newer methodological approaches, such as confocal laser microscopy and fluorescent gene probes that permit the observation of microbial populations in complex communities, and radiotracers and chemical analytical approaches that permit the measurement of metabolic activities of naturally occurring microbial populations, have proven essential for the emergence of contemporary microbial ecology. Methods that permit *in situ* observations of microorganisms and microbial activities have been especially important in the development of our understanding of the roles of microorganisms in nature. The use of molecular tools, such as gene probes and the polymerase chain reaction, are increasingly important in furthering scientific advances in microbial ecology.

Throughout the development of microbial ecology, there have been attempts to understand the fundamental ecology of microorganisms and the applied environmental consequences of microbial activities. Microorganisms, for example, have been used as models for understanding population interactions such as predation (see Chapter 3). The search for microorganisms in nature and the elucidation of their functional metabolic activities in ecosystems is fundamental to the new scientific interest in exploring biodiversity. Microorganisms are also relied upon to maintain environmental quality and are employed in waste treatment and for cleanup of environmental pollutants (see Chapters 12 and 13). Microorganisms are essential in global processes that contribute to the state of human health and environmental quality, making microbial ecology an extraordinarily relevant field of scientific study.

## STUDY QUESTIONS

1. What role can studies with pure cultures play in microbial ecology? What other approaches can be employed in ecological studies on microorganisms that will permit experimental repetition and verification of scientific findings?

2. How can molecular methods, such as gene probes, be used in microbial ecology?

3. How can radiotracers, such as carbon-14 radiolabeled organic compounds, be used to determine the metabolic activities of microorganisms in natural ecosystems?

4. What contributions did Sergei Winogradsky make to the development of microbial ecology?

5. What contributions did Martinus Beijerinck make to the development of microbial ecology?

6. Why is the microbial contribution to biogeochemical cycling important?

7. How do microorganisms contribute to the maintenance of environmental quality?

8. What sources of information are available about the ecological activities of microorganisms?

9. How does the observation of microorganisms in nature differ from the observation of macroorganisms in their natural habitats?

10. How does determining the functional roles of microorganisms in nature differ from determining the functional roles of macroorganisms?

## REFERENCES AND SUGGESTED READINGS

Akkermans, A. D., J. D. Van Elsas, and F. J. De Bruijn (eds.). 1995. *Molecular Microbial Ecology Manual.* Kluwer Academic Publishers, Norwell, MA.

Alexander, M. 1981. Biodegradation of chemicals of environmental concern. *Science* 211:132–138.

Alexander, M. 1984. *Biological Nitrogen Fixation: Ecology, Technology and Physiology.* Plenum Press, New York.

Alexander, M. 1985. Ecological consequences: Reducing the uncertainties. *Issues in Science and Technology* 1:57–68.

Andrews, J. H. 1991. *Comparative Ecology of Microorganisms and Macroorganisms.* Springer-Verlag, New York.

Atlas, R., and R. Bartha. 1992. Hydrocarbon biodegradation and oil spill bioremediation. *Advances in Microbial Ecology* 12:287–338.

Beijerinck, M. W. 1888. The root-nodule bacteria. *Botanische Zeitung* 46:725–804 (in German). English translation in T. D. Brock. *Milestones in Microbiology,* pp. 220–224.

Beijerinck, M. W. 1901. On oligonitrophilic microorganisms. *Zentralblatt für Bakteriologie,* Part II 7:561–582 (in German). English translation in T. D. Brock. *Milestones in Microbiology,* pp. 237–239.

Bennett, J. W., and H. J. Phaff. 1993. Early biotechnology: The Delft connection. *ASM News* 59:401–404.

Brefeld, O. 1881. *Botanische Untersuchungen über Schimmelpilze: Culturmethoden.* Leipzig.

Brock, T. D. 1961. *Milestones in Microbiology.* Prentice Hall, Englewood Cliffs, NJ.

Brock, T. D. 1978. *Thermophilic Microorganisms and Life at High Temperatures.* Springer-Verlag, New York.

Bulloch, W. 1938. *The History of Bacteriology.* Oxford University Press, London.

Cagniard-Latour, C. 1838. Report on the fermentation of wine. *Annales de Chimie et de Physique* 68:206–207, 220–222 (in French). English translation in H. W. Doelle. *Microbial Metabolism,* pp. 26–32.

Caldwell, D. E., D. R. Korber, and J. R. Lawrence. 1992. Confocal laser microscopy and computer image analysis in microbial ecology. *Advances in Microbial Ecology* 12:1–68.

Cameron, R. E. 1971. Antarctic soil microbial and ecological investigations. In L. O. Quam (ed.). *Research in the Antarctic.* American Association for the Advancement of Science, Washington, DC, pp. 137–189.

Cholodny, N. 1930. Über eine neue Methode zur Untersuchung der Bodenmikroflora. *Archiv für Mikrobiologie* 1:620–652.

Cohn, F. 1876. Studies on the biology of bacilli. *Beiträge zur Biologie der Pflanzen* 2:249–276 (in German). English translation in T. D. Brock. *Milestones in Microbiology,* pp. 49–56.

Deherain, P. P. 1897. The reduction of nitrate in arable soil. *Comptes Rendus Academie des Sciences* 124:269–273 (in French). English translation in H. W. Doelle. *Microbial Metabolism,* pp. 233–236.

Dobell, C. 1932. *Antony van Leeuwenhoek and His Little Animals.* Russell and Russell, New York.

Doelle, H. W. 1974. *Microbial Metabolism.* Benchmark Papers in Microbiology. Dowden, Hutchinson and Ross, Stroudsburg, PA.

Doetsch, R. N. (ed.). 1960. *Microbiology—Historical Contributions from 1766 to 1908.* Rutgers University Press, New Brunswick, NJ.

Fleming, A. 1929. On the antibacterial action of cultures of a *Penicillium,* with special reference to their use in the isolation of *B. influenzae. British Journal of Experimental Pathology* 10:226–236.

Gause, G. F. 1934. *The Struggle for Existence.* Williams & Wilkins, Baltimore.

Grainger, T. H., Jr. 1958. *A Guide to the History of Bacteriology.* Ronald Press, New York.

Häeckel, E. 1866. *Generelle Morphologie der Organismen.* Reimer, Berlin.

Hooke, R. 1665. *Micrographia.* Royal Society, London. (1961. Dover Publications, New York.)

Hungate, R. E. 1979. Evolution of a microbial ecologist. *Annual Reviews of Microbiology* 33:1–20.

Jannasch, H. W., and M. J. Mottl. 1985. Geomicrobiology of deep-sea hydrothermal vents. *Science* 229:717–725.

Kamp, A. F., J.W.M. La Riviere, and W. Verhoeven. 1959. *A. J. Kluyver, His Life and Work.* North Holland Publishers, Amsterdam, The Netherlands.

Kaserer, H. 1906. Die Oxydation des Wasserstoffs durch Mikroorganismen. *Zentralblatt für Bakteriologie,* Part II 16:681–696, 769–815.

Koch, R. 1883. The new methods for studying the microcosm of soil, air and water. *Deutsches Arztblatt* 137:244–250 (in German). English translation in R. N. Doetsch (ed.). *Microbiology—Historical Contributions from 1776 to 1908,* pp. 122–131.

Kruif, P. de. 1926. *Microbe Hunters.* Harcourt Brace Co., New York.

Kützing, F. 1837. Mikroskopische Untersuchungen über die Hefe and Essigmutter nebst mehreren anderen dazu gehörigen vegetabilischen Gebilden. *Journal für Praktische Chemie* 11:385–409.

Lechevalier, H. A., and M. Solotorovsky. 1965. *Three Centuries of Microbiology.* McGraw-Hill, New York.

Leeuwenhoek, A. van. 1683. Letters 39. *Philosophical Transactions of the Royal Society of London,* September 17.

Leisinger, T., A. M. Cook, R. Hütter, and J. Nuesch. 1982. *Microbial Degradation of Xenobiotics and Recalcitrant Compounds.* Academic Press, New York.

Liebig, J. 1839. About the occurrence of fermentation, putrefaction and decay, and their causes. *Annales de Chimie et de Physique* 48:120–122, 130–136, 142–144 (in German). English translation in H. W. Doelle. *Microbial Metabolism,* pp. 434–439.

Pace, N. R. 1996. New perspective on the natural microbial world: Molecular microbial ecology. *ASM News* 62:463–470.

Pasteur, L. 1861. On the organized bodies which exist in the atmosphere; examination of the doctrine of spontaneous generation. *Annales des Sciences Naturelles,* 4th ser. 16:5–98 (in French). English translation in T. D. Brock. *Milestones in Microbiology,* pp. 43–48.

Pfennig, N. 1987. Van Niel remembered. *ASM News* 53:75–77.

Rossi, G., S. Riccardo, G. Gesue, M. Stanganelli, and T. K. Wang. 1936. Direct microscopic and bacteriological investigations of the soil. *Soil Science* 41:53–66.

Saussure, N. de. 1839. *Memoires Société de Physique et Histoire Naturelle de Geneve* 8:136.

Schlegel, H. G. 1996. Winogradsky discovered a new *modus vivendi. Anaerobe* 2:129–136.

Schloesing, J.J.T., and A. Müntz. 1879. On nitrification by organized ferments. *Comptes Rendus Académie des Sciences* 84:301–303 (in French). English translation in R. N. Doetsch (ed.). *Microbiology—Historical Contributions from 1776 to 1908,* pp. 103–107.

Schwann, T. 1837. A preliminary report concerning experiments on the fermentation of wine and putrefaction. *Annales de Chimie et de Physique* 11:184–193. English translation in H. W. Doelle. *Microbial Metabolism,* pp. 19–23.

Söhngen, N. L. 1906. *Het Onstaan en Verdwijnen Von Waterstof En Methaan Onder den Invloed von het Organische Leven*. Dissertation, University of Delft, The Netherlands.

Tiedje, J. M., R. K. Colwell, Y. L. Grossman, R. E. Hodson, R. E. Lenski, R. N. Mack, and P. J. Regal. 1989. The planned introduction of genetically engineered organisms: Ecological considerations and recommendations. *Ecology* 70:298–315.

Torsvik, V., J. Goksøyr, and F. L. Daae. 1990. High diversity in DNA of soil bacteria. *Applied and Environmental Microbiology* 56:782–787.

Tyndall, J. 1877. Further researches on the deportment and vital persistence of putrefactive and infective organisms from a physical point of view. *Philosophical Transactions of the Royal Society of London* 167:149–206. Reprinted in T. D. Brock. *Milestones in Microbiology,* pp. 56–58.

Van Iterson, G., Jr., L. E. Den Dooren de Jong, and A. J. Kluyver. 1940. *Martinus Willem Beijerinck, His Life and Work*. M. Nijhoff, The Hague, The Netherlands.

Waksman, S. A. 1953. *Sergei N. Winogradsky—His Life and Work*. Rutgers University Press, New Brunswick, NJ.

Winogradsky, S. N. 1887. Concerning sulfur bacteria. *Botanische Zeitung* 45:489–507 (in German). English translation in R. N. Doetsch (ed.). *Microbiology— Historical Contributions from 1776 to 1908,* pp. 134–145.

Winogradsky, S. N. 1890. Investigations on nitrifying organisms. *Annales de Institute Pasteur* 4:213–231 (in French). English translation in R. N. Doetsch (ed.). *Microbiology—Historical Contributions from 1776 to 1908,* pp. 146–154.

ZoBell, C. E. 1946. *Marine Microbiology*. Chronica Botanica, Waltham, MA.

# MICROBIAL EVOLUTION AND BIODIVERSITY

*Microorganisms were the first live organisms on Earth. Isotopic ratios and microfossils indicate that chemical evolution led to primitive forms of procaryotic life less than 1 billion years after the formation of planet Earth, which is 4.5 billion years old. Only microbial life existed for the next 3 billion years; the oldest fossils of macroorganisms appeared just 0.7–0.6 billion years ago. The fossil record is sparse, but recent studies of macro-molecular (rRNA) homologies reveal a fascinating story of microbial evolution and diversification along three distinct lines: Archaea, Bacteria, and Eucarya. The ecology of microorganisms has changed dynamically during this evolutionary process with a great radiation of biodiversity. As microorganisms evolved they also radically changed Earth's environment.*

## THE ORIGINS OF LIFE

Until the first half of this century, the prevailing scientific view held that our planet was lifeless during the greater part of its long history. This was based on radioisotopic dating (mainly uranium-to-lead decay) associated with fossils. The oldest macrofossils of plants and animals are only 0.6–0.7 billion years old.

If these were the remains of the original living organisms, the planet would have been lifeless for almost 4 billion years. However, we now have credible evidence that microbial life existed more than 3.85 billion years ago (Mojzsis et al. 1996), that is, less than 1 billion years after the formation of our planet and almost 3 billion years before the appearance of macroscopic plants and animals (Nisbet 1980). Microscopic fossils of procaryotic cells (primitive microorganisms) have been identified in 3.5-billion-year-old rocks (Figure 2.1). Additionally, rocks that are 3.85 billion years old have been found to contain organic matter rich in $^{12}C$; organisms incorporate $^{12}C$ into their biomass more readily than $^{13}C$, thereby obtaining a higher proportion of $^{12}C$ than that found in the atmosphere (Mojzsis et al. 1996). This geochemical evidence indicates that living organisms were assimilating carbon into organic molecules from atmospheric methane and carbon dioxide. Data also suggest that this process was changing the chemical composition of Earth within 1 billion years of Earth's formation. It thus appears that life has been present on Earth throughout most of its history, and that microorganisms had a profound influence in shaping its currently prevailing physicochemical conditions.

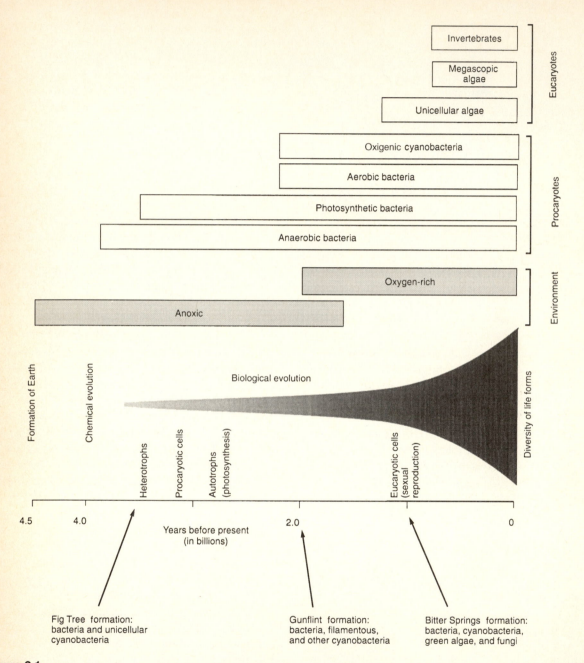

**Figure 2.1**
Time scale of evolutionary events discussed in the text. The most important fossil evidence is shown in relation to the presently accepted scientific interpretation of the major evolutionary events and appearance of organisms. (Source: Schopf 1978.)

Given the great wealth of biodiversity, it is apparent that Earth today provides a favorable environment for the proliferation of life. However, this was not always the case. Initially, life could not have existed on Earth because of the elevated temperatures and lack of liquid water. It probably took millions of years after formation of Earth for conditions to develop that permitted life to evolve and survive. It would not be entirely accurate, though, to conclude that life developed and survived on our planet because conditions were relatively mild and permissive as compared to other planets. It is true that Earth was favored by a sufficient mass and gravitational pull to retain most atmospheric gases and by a distance from the sun that allowed most of its water to remain in the liquid state. However, many other conditions that we consider favorable did not predate life, but rather were shaped by life during its long evolution on our planet. The role of life in forming the physicochemical environment of our planet and its profound importance in maintaining the environment in its current state were emphasized by the Gaia hypothesis (named for the Greek Earth goddess Gaia) formulated by James Lovelock (1979). The Gaia hypothesis states that Earth acts like a superorganism and that through the biochemical activities of its biota, its physicochemical properties are self-regulated so that they are maintained in a favorable range for life. If Lovelock's hypothesis is correct, Gaia exercises her powers principally through microbial processes. As an example,

the sun's temperature has increased by 30% during the past 4–5 billion years. Given the ability of Earth's original carbon dioxide–rich atmosphere to trap heat, the average surface temperature of a lifeless Earth today would be 290°C ± 50°C. By changing the original atmosphere to the present oxidizing atmosphere with low carbon dioxide, life has maintained the average surface temperature of our planet at a favorable 13°C (Table 2.1).

## Chemical Evolution

Our current understanding of conditions on prebiotic Earth and the idea of a gradual chemical evolution toward life were first proposed between 1925 and 1930 independently by the Russian scientist Alexander Ivanovich Oparin and the British scientist John B. S. Haldane (Haldane 1932; Oparin 1938, 1968; Dickerson 1978). According to their views, primitive prebiotic Earth had an anaerobic atmosphere consisting largely of carbon dioxide, nitrogen, hydrogen, and water vapor, with smaller amounts of ammonia, carbon monoxide, and hydrogen sulfide. In such a chemical mixture, organic compounds would have formed with relatively small inputs of energy. Oxygen was absent or present only in trace amounts. Consequently, the lack of an ozone shield allowed high fluxes of ultraviolet light to reach Earth's surface. Temperature extremes, both geographical and seasonal, were probably greater than today. Large amounts of abiotically

**Table 2.1**
Comparison of atmospheric and temperature conditions

| Condition | Mars | Venus | Earth without life | Earth with life |
|---|---|---|---|---|
| Atmosphere | | | | |
| Carbon dioxide ($CO_2$) | 95% | 98% | 98% | 0.03% |
| Nitrogen ($N_2$) | 2.7% | 1.9% | 1.9% | 79% |
| Oxygen ($O_2$) | 0.13% | trace | trace | 21% |
| Surface temperature (°C) | −53 | 477 | 290 ± 50 | 13 |

Source: Lovelock 1979.

formed organic matter were apparently present, mainly in dissolved or suspended forms, from which life could evolve. Radiant, geothermal, electric-discharge, and radioactive-decay energy fueled the slow chemical evolution of this organic matter toward ever more complex and polymeric forms.

The resulting macromolecules were endowed with an inherent tendency to aggregate and form membranelike interfaces toward the surrounding liquid, foreshadowing a cellular organization. In an environment free of oxygen and microbial decomposers, this chemical evolution could proceed uninterrupted for millions of years. This scenario, based largely on theoretical considerations, received experimental support in the 1950s from the work of Stanley L. Miller and Harold C. Urey (Miller 1957; Miller and Urey 1959; Miller and Orgel 1974). Using a relatively simple apparatus containing water and reducing gas mixtures and receiving energy input as heat, electric discharges, or UV radiation (Figure 2.2), they were able to produce a surprising array of organic molecules, including

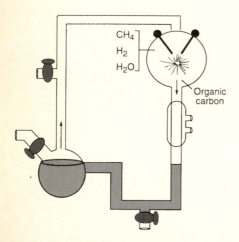

CH$_4$
H$_2$
H$_2$O

Organic carbon

**Figure 2.2**
Apparatus used by Stanley L. Miller and Harold C. Urey to demonstrate the biotic synthesis of organic compounds, including amino acids and nucleotides, under conditions prevalent on the prebiotic planet Earth. The apparatus is filled with reducing gas mixtures. Water vapor is created in a boiling flask and is condensed at another part of the apparatus. In the setup shown, electric discharges between electrodes serve as the principal energy input for organic synthesis.

most of the essential amino acids and nucleic acid bases. In the Miller-Urey experiments, formaldehyde and hydrogen cyanide formed first from the breakdown of methane. These compounds subsequently combined to form urea and formic acid. Later, amino acids were produced, including glycine, alanine, glutamic acid, valine, proline, and aspartic acid.

In an aqueous environment, equilibrium conditions do not favor extensive polymerization, which requires both input of energy and removal of water. Suspended clay particles, however, consist of closely packed silicate and alumina sheets with both negative and positive charges that could provide an absorbing and ordering matrix with primitive catalytic reaction centers. Energy-rich organic molecules, such as amino acid adenylates, were demonstrated to polymerize into proteinlike polypeptide chains on such clay matrices (Katchalsky 1973). Proteins and nucleic acids could have formed in this manner in the reducing atmosphere of early Earth.

In support of an alternative theory, Sidney W. Fox demonstrated the spontaneous formation of "thermal proteinoids" by the moderate heating of amino acid mixtures in the dry state (Fox 1965). Thermal proteinoids exhibit a self-ordering tendency, spontaneously aggregating into microspheres (Fox 1965; Fox and Dose 1977). Some abiotically formed proteinoids and other polymers show rudimentary catalytic activity, suggesting they could have functioned like enzymes. Some of the abiotically formed proteinoids also may have served as templates that allowed their duplication, either by outside chemical forces or by the primitive enzymelike action of other proteinoids.

The updated Oparin-Haldane theory of chemical evolution is the best known and accepted one. This theory suggests that life began on Earth's surface in areas where organic chemicals accumulated. An alternative hypothesis is that life on Earth began at deep ocean thermal vents. There, hot, mineral-rich water emerged through pyrite (iron sulfide)–containing rock. This environment could have provided the mixture of chemicals and catalysts needed for the formation of life. Such an alternative theory for the evolution of the first living organisms based on surface catalysis has been forcefully proposed by the German scientist Günther Wächtershäuser (1988). This theory relies much less on abiotically formed organic matter than does the Oparin-Haldane theory of chemical evolution. The first form of "life" visualized by this theory is an acellular organic film, which is anionically attached to positively charged mineral surfaces and grows chemoautotrophically in an anaerobic thermal environment. Specifically, Wächtershäuser invokes the attachment of simple organic molecules such as glyceraldehyde phosphate and dihydroxyacetone phosphate through their negatively charged phosphate groups to positively charged pyrite ($FeS_2$) surfaces. The monomers, oriented and activated through their surface adsorption, cross-link to form polyhemiacetal structures that remain polyanionically bonded to the pyrite surface. This polymeric film incorporates nitrogen and even carbon dioxide, undergoes complex rearrangements, and eventually forms surface-bonded coenzymes capable of autocatalytic reactions.

Wächtershäuser hypothesizes that the energy for chemical evolution and differentiation was supplied by the reaction of ferrous iron ($Fe^{2+}$) with hydrogen sulfide ($H_2S$), resulting in the formation of pyrite. The organic surface film both catalyzes this reaction and couples its energy yield to $CO_2$ fixation and other endothermic reactions. The precipitating pyrite creates new surfaces for the essentially chemoautotrophic growth of the organic film. A favorable environment for this type of chemical evolution would be the deep-sea geothermal vents rich in reduced minerals including $Fe^{2+}$ and $H_2S$. (These vents will be further described in Chapter 11.) A transition from the two-dimensional organic surface film to cell-like entities might occur either by a partial detachment ("bubble" formation) of the film, or by formation of a surface film surrounding small mineral particles.

Wächtershäuser's theory has some attractive features and proposes thermodynamically feasible mechanisms for otherwise problematic events. However, it is a highly abstract theory based on thermodynamic considerations and proposed chemical reactions. To date it has not been tested with experimental models that could prove or disprove its feasibility to less theoretically oriented biologists.

Regardless of how macromolecules first formed, life emerged only after self-replicating molecules appeared (Orgel 1992, 1994). Initially, RNA formed the basis for living systems. As the RNA system evolved, proteins became the main workers in cells, and DNA became the prime depository of genetic information.

## Cellular Evolution

In addition to his theoretical work on chemical evolution, Oparin and his coworkers performed some fascinating studies on the properties of microspheres that form spontaneously in the colloidal solution of two different polymeric substances, such as gum arabic and histone (Dickerson 1978). These microspheres, which Oparin called coacervates, develop spontaneously when the two polymers are added to water. Coacervates form an outer boundary that resembles the membranes that surround all living cells, having two layers. Coacervates grow by accumulating additional polymers from the surrounding medium; they pinch off projections to form independent new coacervates, much like the division of some living cells; chemical reactions can occur within the cavities of coacervates. Coacervates behave as semipermeable membranes and vacuoles; they are capable of selective uptake of substances from their environment; and they mimic the growth and division of cells. The incorporation of enzymes, electron carriers, or chlorophyll into these coacervate droplets allows the modeling of some anabolic and catabolic processes, electron transport, and light energy utilization that we normally associate only with living cells. Admittedly, these model systems demonstrate only the surprising self-organizing capacity of polymeric molecules; it is not suggested that coacervates were the actual intermediates in the chemical evolution process.

More directly relevant are the microspheres formed by thermal proteinoids and their limited catalytic and self-replicating capabilities demonstrated by Fox (Fox 1965; Fox and Dose 1977). It is conceivable that similar self-replicating proteinaceous microspheres, as yet without nucleic acids, represented the first step toward cellular organization. These postulated primitive cell-like structures are referred to as progenotes or protobionts.

## Did Life Evolve Extraterrestrially?

Did life ever exist on Mars? Did terrestrial life originate somewhere else in the solar system? These questions are often the topics of nonscientific speculations and have also been the subject of recent scientific investigations. The Mars *Viking* lander in 1976 searched for contemporary microbial life on Mars. The results gave what appears to be a false positive indication of life. The kinetics of carbon dioxide fixation were indicative of chemical catalysis rather than biological activity. Most scientists concluded that the results did not show evidence of microbial metabolic activity and the consensus conclusion was that life did not exist in the soils that were sampled. Some scientists, however, reached the opposite conclusion and continue to interpret the results as having indicated that life currently exists on Mars. The *Viking* mission clearly did not end speculation that life might exist on Mars or that life once existed on that planet. The first of several new space probes to explore Mars landed in 1997, but these are not yet designed to continue the search for microbial life on that planet.

Interest in a further search for life on Mars has been heightened by several scientific reports indicating that life once existed on Mars. These reports are based on chemical and microscopic analyses of meteorites transported to Earth from Mars by cosmic impacts. One such meteorite, ALH84001, was found in Antarctica in 1984. Radiometric dating shows that ALH84001 congealed from magma to become part of the original Martian crust 4.5 billion years ago, just 100 million years after the planet formed. It is the oldest rock known from any planet. Still early in Martian history, a meteorite impact shattered the rock, leaving fractures where minerals—including the putative traces of life—formed perhaps 3.6 billion years ago. Much later, another impact launched the rock into space. Radioactive nuclei created by deep-space radiation show that it traveled in space for 16 million years before landing on the Antarctic ice cap.

Using sophisticated laser techniques to lift and separate intact organic molecules from rock surfaces, analytical chemists Simon Clemett and Richard Zare of Stanford University and their colleagues found relatively abundant polycyclic aromatic hydrocarbons (PAHs) on fracture surfaces inside the meteorite (McKay et al. 1996). They interpreted the PAHs as representing decomposition products that might have come from the organic molecules of living organisms. Based on the distribution of the PAHs within the meteorite, they concluded that the PAHs were indigenous to the meteorite rather than earthly contaminants. They also found carbonate globules of about 50 μm in diameter that resemble those formed by bacterial action in freshwater ponds. The larger globules had manganese-containing cores and concentric rings of iron carbonate and iron sulfides, implying that the chemical environment changed as the globules were deposited, perhaps because of bacterial metabolism. High-resolution scanning electron microscopy also revealed structures resembling fossils of micro-organisms (see the accompanying figure). These apparent microfossils were 20–100 nm long, which makes them a hundredth the size of the smallest microfossils of ancient bacteria ever found on Earth. Whether these are microfossils of Martian microorganisms remains unproven and highly controversial.

In a separate report British researchers Monica Grady, Ian Wright, and Colin Pillinger found that carbonate globules in a Martian meteorite had ratios of $^{12}C$ to $^{13}C$, about half those of most terrestrial organic matter (Grady et al. 1996). On Earth, the only known source of such light carbon enrichment would be from biological metabolism such as methanogenesis, implying that this sample indeed holds traces of ancient life. If these findings hold true, life may have existed on Mars over much of its history.

Reports that life may have once existed on Mars have fueled speculation that living organisms could have been transported to Earth from an extraterrestrial source. This possibility was heightened by the finding that life with highly evolved metabolic capabilities may have existed on Earth 3.85 billion years ago (Mojzsis et al. 1996; Holland 1997). As the date for the appearance of life on Earth gets closer to the time the planet formed and conditions cooled to where life could survive, there is less and less time for life to have evolved and hence greater speculation that life was transported to Earth. It is presumed that millions of years would

have been necessary for life to have evolved from simple organic molecules to a living organism with autotrophic metabolism that can selectively enrich light isotopes of carbon. Hence, either life evolved very rapidly on Earth or it came from somewhere else. This same argument can be made for life on Mars, assuming the interpretations of the chemical analyses of Martian meteorites are accurate. Only further scientific investigations can help resolve the paradox of how life appeared on Earth so soon after formation of the planet and whether there are extraterrestrial forms of life.

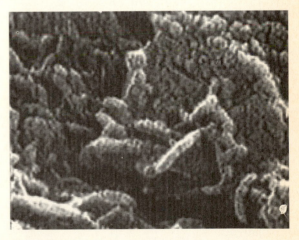

**Figure A**
Electron micrograph of a fractured section of a meteorite from Mars showing "microfossils" that may represent the remains of Martian microorganisms. (Source: NASA.)

A further advance toward cellular organization was probably the acquisition and use of nucleic acids, first probably RNA and later both DNA and RNA, as templates for protein synthesis (Darnell and Doolittle 1986; Orgel 1992, 1994). Along with further development of enzymatic capabilities and membrane organization, this led to the development of eugenotes, primitive versions of the procaryotic cell. Fossil evidence for the existence of such cells was discovered in sedimentary rock dated as approximately 3.5 billion years old (Knoll and Awromile 1983; Schopf 1993).

The scarcity of morphological detail in procaryotes and the poor geological preservation of subcellular features make the fossil record of microbial evolution pitifully incomplete, but the molecular record of evolution can to some extent compensate. If all living forms had a common ancestor that already possessed the basic macromolecules of life, such as RNA, DNA, and protein, one may assume that those organisms with very similar macromolecular sequences were closely related, and those with very different ones diverged early and evolved independently. Comparisons were attempted using protein and DNA sequences, but comparisons of ribosomal RNA

sequences seem to be the most relevant and technically feasible.

By examining the phylogeny (evolutionary history and physiologies) of microorganisms, one can discern the underlying forces that have driven evolution toward the great biodiversity of contemporary ecosystems (Woese 1985). Analyses of ribosomal RNA (rRNA) and other conserved molecules help to trace the natural history of microorganisms; they are the true unit upon which evolutionary systematics can be based (Woese et al. 1990; Pace 1997). A detailed evolutionary tree for procaryotes has been developed based on analyses of 16S ribosomal RNA (Fox et al. 1980; Woese et al. 1990; Winker and Woese 1991). The evolutionary tree of life (Figure 2.3), based on 16S ribosomal RNA homologies, indicates that three evolutionary lines (domains) diverged from a common ancestral state to form the Archaea (archaebacteria), Bacteria (eubacteria), and Eucarya (eucaryotes) (Woese et al. 1990). These analyses place the origin of life on a branch within the Bacterial domain as opposed to the branch leading to the Archaeal and Eucaryal domains (Olsen et al. 1994). The hypothetical "Urcaryote," ancestor of the eucaryotes, received

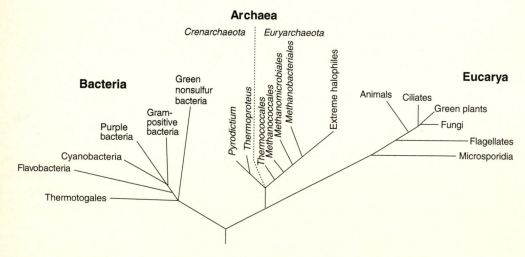

**Figure 2.3**
The tree of life showing the evolutionary descent of the Bacteria, Archaea (archaebacteria)—including the Crenarchaeota and the Euryarchaeota—and the Eucarya. (Source: Woese et al. 1990.)

inputs from both the Archaea and Bacteria (Figure 2.4). Analysis of ribosomal RNAs has also confirmed that the eucaryotic cell is a phylogenetic chimera (composed of two or more genetically distinct cell lines—named after a mythological monster constructed from diverse animal parts) in which several procaryotic evolutionary lines have fused. Chloroplasts and mitochondria of eucaryotic organisms can be traced to the bacterial line of descent, and at least one ribosomal protein is traceable to the Archaea (Zillig et al. 1982). The origin of the cell nucleus in eucaryotes is uncertain and may itself be chimeric. From the Eucaryal line descend the microbial groups protozoa, algae, and fungi, as well as the plant and animal kingdoms.

Divergence into the Bacterial, Archaeal, and Eucaryal domains of life appears to have occurred early in evolutionary history, with Archaea diverging between Bacteria and Eucarya, closer to the eucaryotes (Woese et al. 1990; Olsen et al. 1994). The eucaryotic lineage of cells that contain nuclei separated from the procaryotic Bacterial and Archaeal lineages at a time when cells and genomes were still very primitive. Prior to the divergence of the three domains of life, certain fundamental life functions must have become established in the cells of progenitor organisms including the basis for heredity, gene expression, material transfers, and cellular energetics. Though there is evidence that RNA initially served as the hereditary molecule of primitive cells, DNA evolved as a more stable chemical molecule to pass hereditary information from generation to generation. It also must have been established that gene expression would be based on a flow of information from DNA to RNA to proteins. Furthermore, ATP and protonmotive force are fundamental to the cellular energetics in all organisms and surely evolved in the cells of progenitor organisms. Likewise, the central metabolic pathways of glycolysis and the tricarboxylic acid cycle must have evolved prior to the divergence of the three cellular domains.

Evolutionary divergence into the three domains appears to have begun while the structure of the cytoplasmic membrane was still variable and undergoing natural selection. Apparently a mixture of glycerol ester-linked phospholipids and glycerol ethers were in

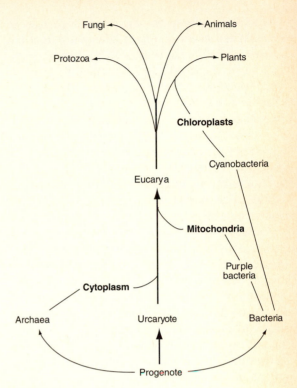

**Figure 2.4**
The evolution of the Eucarya, involving acquisition of cytoplasm and organelles from Bacteria and Archaea (Source: Woese et al. 1990.)

the cytoplasmic membranes of progenitor cells (Figure 2.5). Some bacteria such as *Aquifex,* which seem to be descendants of deep-rooted divergences, still retain that mixture of ether and ester glycerol-based lipids in their cytoplasmic membranes. High temperatures would have favored the natural selection of the ether linkages, and these became the basis for the cytoplasmic membranes of archaea. Extremely thermophilic archaea have cytoplasmic membranes with glycerol diethers or diglycerol tetraethers, which are adaptive for survival at high temperatures. In microorganisms living at lower temperatures, including the eucaryotes and most bacteria, natural selection favored cytoplasmic membranes based on phospholipids with long-chain fatty acids linked by ester bonds to glycerol. Such phospholipids function adaptively under highly varying physiological conditions.

Evolutionary distances—the extent of changes in nucleotide sequences that have occurred during the 3.8 billion years life has been evolving—vary considerably between the Archaea, Bacteria, and Eucarya (Fox et al. 1980; Olsen et al. 1994). The Archaea appear to be less highly evolved than either the Bacteria or Eucarya (Woese 1993). Contemporary archaeal species more closely resemble the primitive archaea from which they descended than do bacteria or eucaryotes. Differences in evolutionary distance observed between Archaea, Bacteria, and Eucarya may reflect the mechanisms of genetic exchange and recombination that have evolved in the three domains. The Archaea appear to have relatively limited mechanisms of genetic exchange that lead to recombination compared to bacteria and eucaryotes. Mating has been observed in only a few extreme halophiles and only limited transformation could occur given that Archaea rarely form biofilms or other cellular aggregates. In contrast to the Archaea, Eucarya exhibit extensive mechanisms of sexual reproduction, which foster genetic recombination. Bacteria represent an intermediary position between Archaea and Eucarya with respect to the rates at which changes have occurred in molecules like rRNAs and also in the mechanisms of genetic exchange and recombination. Although Bacteria principally reproduce asexually by binary fission, they also exhibit transformation, transduction, and mating, which lead to genetic recombination. Thus, extensive diversity has evolved among the Bacteria.

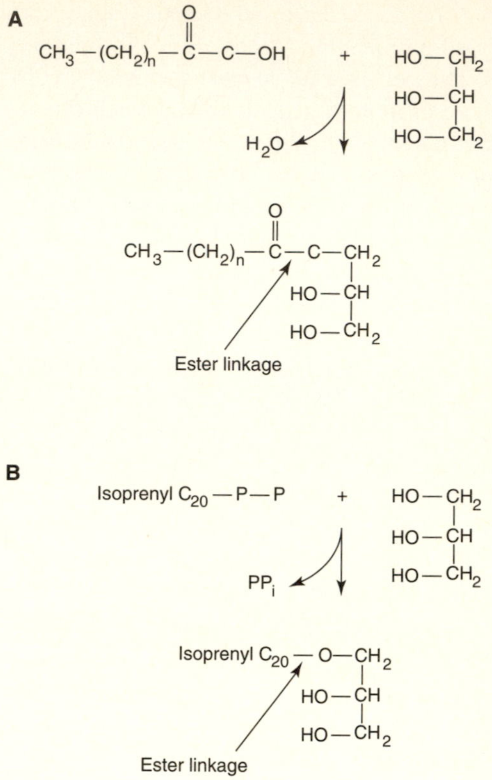

## Evolution of Organelles

The eucaryotic cell is a complex entity containing several types of specialized structures that fulfill functions in a manner analogous to the organs in multicellular forms of life. These specialized structures are therefore designated as organelles. Conspicuous among the organelles are mitochondria (the sites of electron transport and oxidative phosphorylation) and chloroplasts (the sites of photosynthesis). Both are membranous structures that are well delineated from the surrounding cytoplasm. It is possible to visualize these structures as invaginations of the outer cell membrane that eventually became detached organelles embedded in the cyto-

**Figure 2.5**
There is a fundamental difference in the chemistry of Archaeal membranes from those of other living organisms. Membranes of Bacterial and Eucaryal cells have ester linkages, whereas those of Archaeal cells have ether linkages. (A) Formation of the ester linkage involves the reaction of an acid and an alcohol, such as a fatty acid and glycerol. (B) Formation of an ether linkage involves the reaction of a hydrocarbon with an alcohol, such as an isoprenoid hydrocarbon with glycerol.

plasm. However, the facts that both of these organelles contain nucleic acids with sequences differing from those in the nucleus, that they have their own ribosomes that differ from cytoplasmic ribosomes and, finally, that they are never synthesized in the cytoplasm *de novo* but always arise by division of existing mitochondria or chloroplasts suggest a different explanation.

The theory of serial symbiosis (endosymbiosis), advocated most vigorously by Lynn Margulis (1971, 1981), visualized these and perhaps some other

## Ribosomal RNA Analyses for Tracing Microbial Evolution

Ribosomal RNAs (rRNAs) are among the evolutionarily most conserved macromolecules in all living systems. Their functional roles in information processing systems must have been well established in the earliest common ancestors of the Bacteria, Archaea, and Eucarya. Ribosomal RNA genes in all contemporary organisms share a common ancestry, and they do not appear to undergo lateral gene transfer between species. Because of functional constraints, large portions of rRNA genes are well conserved and their sequences can be used to measure phylogenetic distances between even the most distantly related organisms. In essence, changes in rRNA nucleotide sequences are indices of evolutionary change.

The comparison of rRNA molecules isolated from different organisms is useful for determining the evolutionary relationships of all living things (Fox et al. 1980; Schleifer and Stackebrandt 1983; Woese et al. 1990). There are many possible nucleotide sequences of rRNA molecules. Any similarity in two nucleotide sequences suggests some phylogenetic relationship between these nucleotide sequences and the organisms that contain them. In particular, the 16S rRNA of bacteria and archaea is used to determine the phylogenetic relationships among these microorganisms. For eucaryotes, 18S rRNA is analyzed. (The "S" stands for "Svedberg unit." During centrifugation the 16S and 18S ribosomal subunits, characteristic for procaryotes and eucaryotes, respectively, settle at rates proportional to their size and density.) The advantages of using 16S and 18S rRNAs is that they are found in all organisms, are large enough molecules to provide a significant number of nucleotides to compare sequences, and yet they are small enough to conveniently analyze. This is why Carl Woese, who had begun phylogenetic studies with 5S rRNA that has

only 120 nucleotides, switched his studies to the larger 16S rRNA that has 1500 nucleotides. He argued that 16S and 18S rRNAs make excellent molecular chronometers because they (1) occur universally in all organisms, (2) have long, highly conserved regions useful for looking for distant phylogenetic relationships, (3) have sufficient variable regions to assess close relationships; and (4) are not prone to rapid sequence change due to selection because of their central function in gene expression.

Comparisons of nucleotide sequences of 16S rRNA allow the calculation of evolutionary distances and the construction of phylogenetic trees that show relative evolutionary positions and relationships (see Figure A). The resultant phylogeny based on 16S rRNA analyses revealed the separate domains of the Bacteria, Archaea, and Eucarya. When Carl Woese first declared that the Archaea represented a third domain of life, many microbiologists doubted the proposal, viewing it as heresy to break the procaryotic-eucaryotic paradigm. Now that microbiologists almost universally accept that there are three evolutionary domains, it remains for other biologists to embrace this conceptual framework of evolutionary history. Molecular phylogenetic studies provide a view of evolution on a grand scale. When viewed in this manner, the importance of microorganisms in the evolutionary history of life on Earth cannot be ignored.

Several methods can be used to analyze these rRNA molecules (see Figure B on page 39). In the original analytical approach, cells were grown in the presence of the radioactive isotope $^{32}$P so that the radiolabeled phosphate was incorporated into the nucleic acids, including rRNAs. The rRNA was recovered from cells in high quantities and then digested with $T_1$ ribonuclease. This enzyme cut the

*(continued)*

rRNA so that every oligonucleotide it produced ended with a guanine residue at the 3′-OH position. Typically, the oligonucleotides produced by this procedure had up to 20 nucleotides. These oligonucleotides were separated by gel electrophoresis and their nucleotide sequences were determined. Oligonucleotides with 6 or more nucleotides were cataloged for comparison with those obtained from the rRNAs of other microorganisms. Oligonucleotides of this size were chosen because each is likely to occur only once in a 16S rRNA and yet about 25 such sequences generally appear, providing a sufficient basis for comparison. The catalogs of oligonucleotides from different organisms were compared using a mathematical index of similarity $S_{AB}$ that compares the similarity of the sequences from microorganism A with those from microorganism B. $S_{AB} = 2N_{AB}/(N_A + N_B)$ where $N_A$ and $N_B$ are the total number of oligonucleotides in the sequence catalogs from microorganisms A and B, respectively,

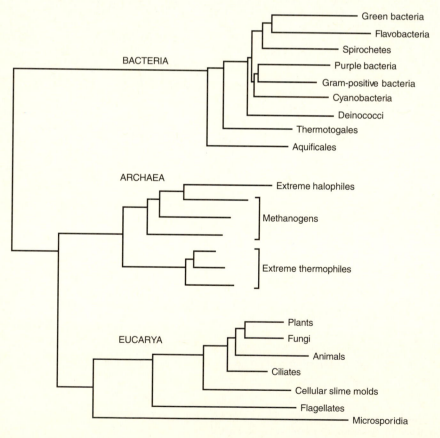

**Figure A**
The three domains of life (Bacteria, Archaea, and Eucarya) and the major evolutionary lines of descent within those domains. (Source: Based on Woese et al. 1992.)

and $N_{AB}$ is the total number of identical oligonucleotide sequences in the catalogs.

Another approach for analyzing rRNA sequences is to extract the rRNA from cells and analyze it directly or use the rRNA as a template for making copy DNA (cDNA) and then use the polymerase chain reaction (PCR) to produce sufficient DNA for analysis. Typically, if rRNA is to be captured for analysis, cells are ruptured in the presence of DNase to degrade all DNA. The RNA is then extracted with aqueous phenol. Large RNA molecules are separated in the aqueous phase. After precipitation of the RNA with alcohol and salt, a DNA primer that is complementary to a conserved region of the 16S rRNA is added. Reverse transcriptase can then be used to generate cDNAs. The cDNAs can be amplified using PCR and the complete sequences of nucleotides in the cDNAs

determined so that the nucleotide sequences in the rRNAs can be deduced from these analyses. The polymerase chain reaction also can be used to amplify the DNA encoding the rRNA genes. This procedure uses synthetically produced primers that are complementary to conserved sequences in rRNA as PCR templates. Use of PCR amplification of the DNA coding for rRNA requires fewer cells than direct rRNA sequencing. It is also faster and more convenient for large-scale studies. Eight primers are now routinely used to obtain virtually complete bacterial 16S rRNA sequences; only about 30 nucleotides from the 3′-OH terminus cannot be sequenced using these primers. Sequencing of 16S rRNAs in this manner—over 5000 have already been done—reveals characteristic signature sequences that can define members of the Bacterial, Archaeal, and Eucaryal domains.

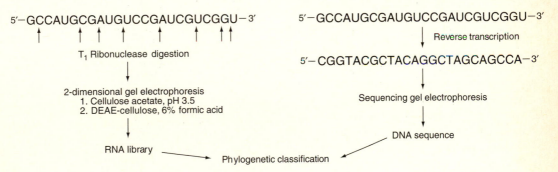

**Figure B**
The descent of bacteria, archaea, and eucaryotic organisms based on homologies of ribosomal RNA (rRNA) sequences. There are two methods for the analysis of rRNA sequences. In one method, the rRNA is cut with $T_1$ ribonuclease to form small oligoribonucleotides, which are then separated by two-dimensional gel electrophoresis. The separation results in clusters of oligoribonucleotides with equal numbers of uracil residues. Each oligoribonucleotide has only one guanine residue, which is located at the 3′-OH position. The pattern of spots within a cluster reveals the positions and numbers of the adenine and cytosine residues. The sequences determined in this manner are used to form an rRNA library. The rRNA library is further analyzed for homology with rRNA libraries from other organisms. Based upon similarities, a phylogenetic classification is made. In a second method, a cDNA (copy DNA or complementary DNA) is made from the rRNA sequence using reverse transcriptase. Sequencing gel electrophoresis is then used to determine the deoxyribonucleotide sequence in the cDNA. This deoxyribonucleotide sequence is aligned and compared with the deoxyribonucleotide sequences from other organisms to determine phylogenetic relationships.

organelles as procaryotes that became permanent symbionts of a eucaryotic cell. Thus, mitochondria were
originally aerobic procaryotic cells resembling bacteria that became symbionts of eucaryotic fermentative
cells and endowed them with a more efficient aerobic
utilization system for organic substrates. Similarly,
cyanobacteria or perhaps the phycobilin-free photosynthetic bacteria, the chloroxybacteria, were the
ancestors of the chloroplast; this symbiotic association
endowed heterotrophic eucaryotic cells with the capacity to live photosynthetically. The fact that numerous
unicellular and multicellular organisms form intracellular associations with bacteria or cyanobacteria adds
further credibility to this explanation. It is assumed that
during their prolonged symbiotic association with the
eucaryote, the ancestors of mitochondria and chloroplasts lost some but not all of their genetic material and
biosynthetic capabilities to their hosts and became
incapable of independent existence. Ultrastructural
evidence indicates that some eucaryotes picked up
cyanobacterial chloroplasts and, in turn, became
endosymbionts of other eucaryotes, with the consequent loss of their cellular independence and functions.
The complex outer membrane structure and pigment
composition of some chloroplasts preserve the record
of such a multistage symbiotic evolution (Wilcox and
Wedemayer 1985; Gray 1994).

The case for the symbiotic derivation of eucaryotic flagella and cilia is weaker. These are clearly different from bacterial flagella; they are much thicker,
have a complex "9 + 2" structure (nine peripheral
fibers wound around two central ones), and are powered by ATP rather than by protonmotive force. They
do not, however, have nucleic acid or ribosomes of
their own and they do not multiply by division. The
possibility of their bacterial symbiotic origin is hinted
at by a curious association of some protozoa with
spirochetes (bacterial cells). The best-studied example
is *Mixotricha paradoxa,* a flagellated protozoan living
in the hindgut of some termites and involved in cellulose digestion. The flagella of *Mixotricha* are inactive,
but it is mobile with what at first appeared to be cilia;
on closer examination, these cilia turn out to be rows
of spirochetes attached to the surface of *Mixotricha* by
bracketlike basal bodies (Cleveland and Grimstone

1964). Their coordinated motion propels *Mixotricha.*
Nonmotile, short, rod-shaped bacteria of unknown
function are also attached to the surface of *Mixotricha*
at regular intervals (Figure 2.6).

Proponents of the serial symbiosis theory believe
that the spirochetes attached in this manner may have
lost their independent metabolic and genetic identity
and become flagella or cilia (Margulis and McMenamin 1990). The thought is intriguing, but because of
the lack of supportive molecular evidence, it is not as
widely accepted as the symbiotic origin of mitochondria and chloroplasts. The endosymbiotic theory predicts a high similarity between tectinlike proteins of

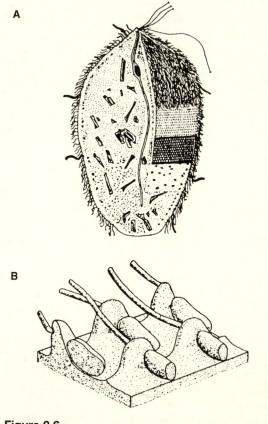

**Figure 2.6**
(A) *Mixotricha paradoxa,* apparently a ciliated flagellate.
(B) The fine structure, revealing brackets and attached
spirochetes. Rod-shaped bacteria of unknown function are
also present. (Source: Cleveland and Grimstone 1964.)

spirochetes such as *Spirochaeta halophila* and the axonemal proteins (tektin, centrin, and calmodulin) associated with motility in eucaryotic cells (Barth et al. 1991). Only one tektinlike protein, however, has been identified in *Spirochaeta,* giving very limited molecular support for spirochetes as the origin of eucaryotic flagella and cilia.

Even more speculative is the origin of the cell nucleus. As cells in the Eucaryal evolutionary lineage diversified and increased in biochemical and morphological complexity, a genome of increased size was needed to code for these traits and functions. The replication of this larger genome during cell division became more complex. It is conceivable that an endosymbiotic bacterial or archaeal cell consolidated its own genome with the genome of its host urcaryal cell, lost its cytoplasm and vegetative functions, and became the nucleus of the new primitive eucaryotic cell. However, a nuclear membrane that compartmentalized the genome of the early eucaryote also could have evolved by invagination of the outer cell membrane or from membranes around vacuoles. More detailed molecular studies are needed to resolve the origins of the nucleus and the early evolutionary history of eucaryotes.

## GENETIC BASIS FOR EVOLUTION

Cells in the Bacterial, Archaeal, and Eucaryal domains continued to evolve based on genetic changes that enhanced their metabolic activities and capacities to survive and to compete for available energy resources. As proposed by Charles Darwin (1860), those organisms best adapted to survive in a given environment have a selective advantage, a principle known as natural selection or survival of the fittest. The introduction of diversity into the gene pools of microbial populations established the basis for selection and evolution (Clarke 1984). Mutations introduce variability into the genomes of microorganisms, resulting in changes in the enzymes the organism synthesizes. Variations in the genome are passed from one generation to another and are disseminated throughout the population. Because of their relatively short genera-

tion times compared to higher organisms, changes in the genetic information of microorganisms can be widely and rapidly disseminated.

In most cases the modification of the genome is harmful to the organism, some mutations being lethal or conditionally lethal, but sometimes a mutation changes genetic information in a favorable way. Favorable mutations introduce information into the gene pool that can make an organism more fit for surviving in its environment and for competing with other microorganisms for available resources. Over many generations, natural selective pressures may result in the elimination of unfit variants and the continued survival of organisms possessing favorable genetic information.

An interesting and important example of natural selection involves the responses of microorganisms to antimicrobics used in medical practice. The excessive use of antimicrobics leads to the natural selection of strains, including those with R plasmids, that are resistant to multiple antibiotics. Medical practitioners have learned that there are limits to the successful uses of antibiotics, leading the American Medical Association to issue frequent warnings to physicians to use antibiotics only when appropriate, and the Centers for Disease Control and Prevention to express concern about the emergence of antibiotic-resistant microorganisms. In Hungary and Romania, where antimicrobics were once used excessively, the incidence of antibiotic-resistant clinical isolates of *Streptococcus pneumoniae* rose to over 60% as a result of the selective pressure (Marton 1992; Hryniewicz 1994). Interestingly, even when the use of antibiotics was greatly curtailed, the incidence of antibiotic resistance among clinical isolates in Hungary has remained high—years after reducing the use of antibiotics, about 40% of the clinical isolates in Hungary are still antibiotic resistant. Equally interesting is the recent evolution of a vancomycin-resistant *Enterococcus* species that actually requires vancomycin for growth. Curing patients infected with this bacterium rests on eliminating the administration of vancomycin rather than increasing the dosage. These examples indicate the speed at which selection of mutant strains can occur in environments with strong selective pressures. They also indicate that once established in a community, selected physiological traits can remain unless there is strong selective pressure against them.

Although mutation is the basis for introducing variability into the genetic information of a cell, genetic exchange and recombination play the critical roles in redistributing genetic information (Hall 1984; Slater 1984). Recombination creates new allelic combinations that may be adaptive. Altering the organization of genetic information within populations provides a basis for evolutionary change. The exchange of genetic information can produce individuals with multiple attributes that favor the survival of that microbial population. The long-term stability of a population depends on its ability to incorporate adaptive genetic information into its chromosomes. Mutation and general recombination provide the raw material for the natural selection of adaptive features. Reciprocal recombination produces evolutionary links between closely related organisms; nonreciprocal recombination provides a mechanism for rapid qualitative evolutionary changes. The fact that unrelated genomes can recombine suggests that different lines of evolution can suddenly converge.

The evolution of biochemical pathways is driven by the basic Darwinian concepts of random mutation and natural selection, but the complexity and multistep nature of biosynthetic pathways makes it difficult to conceptualize how, for example, the ability to synthesize an essential amino acid from a sugar arose by this mechanism. The concept of the backward evolution of biochemical pathways formulated by Norman Horowitz (1965) makes this easier to understand. Generally speaking, a contemporary microorganism that needs compound A as a cell constituent has the ability to synthesize this compound from the very different compound E. Prior to the evolution of the pathways, the primitive microorganism took up compound A directly from its environment. As compound A became scarce, a mutant that possessed the capacity for the one-step conversion of the closely related and abundant compound B to compound A gained selective advantage and became dominant. As compound B in turn became scarce, the mutant that could convert compound C to compound B gained an advantage

because it already had the mechanism to convert compound B to the required compound A. This backward evolutionary sequence can be continued until the very different compound E can be converted to the essential compound A. Transfer and recombination of genetic information, especially if the pathway is coded on highly mobile plasmids or located on transposons, can greatly speed the evolution and diversification of biochemical capabilities.

Natural selection applies to microbial populations and determines which populations can successfully establish themselves within communities. As an extension of Darwinian natural selection, Martinus Beijerinck set forth the principle for microorganisms that "everything is everywhere, the environment selects" (Van Iterson et al. 1983). Some microorganisms possess features that make them better adapted for survival in a particular ecosystem. Microorganisms with features that make them poorly fitted for survival under changing conditions are soon eliminated by natural selection. Overspecialization in the gene pool can lead to temporary success of a population under a single set of conditions, but it will ultimately render the population nonadaptive. Genetic variability within populations and communities is necessary because the habitat of a microbial population is not static. Adaptive features within populations contribute to both change and stability within biological communities.

The role of genetic exchange in bacterial evolution has recently been reviewed by Cohan (1996). He points out that genetic exchange has very different consequences for bacteria and archaea because of their low recombination rates and predominantly asexual means of reproduction than it does for eucaryotic organisms such as plants and animals. Frequent recombination in animal and plant populations efficiently transfers an adaptive mutation throughout the population. Natural selection has little effect on the overall genetic diversity within such sexually reproducing populations because of the high rates of recombination. In contrast, every adaptive mutation in asexually reproducing populations has the potential to result in lowered overall diversity in that population, a process known as periodic selection. Assuming recombination rates of about $10^{-7}$ for bacteria, a periodic selection event can eliminate 99% of the bacterial population's total genetic heterogeneity. In this manner a salt-resistant mutant cell *Bacillus subtilis* could replace all other cells of the population. Because the entire genome originally associated with the adaptive mutant cell remains intact as it crowds out the other cells, the population loses its genetic diversity (Cohan 1994, 1996). This process of selection favors the evolution of ecologically distinct populations of bacteria and archaea in specific habitats.

Given the diversity of habitats, however, the overall diversity of distinct bacterial populations remains high despite this periodic selection process. Although genetic exchange in bacteria is rare, the frequency is sufficient to produce genetic heterogeneity. If the rate of recombination exceeds the rate of mutation by a factor of 10, recombination can totally redistribute genetic alleles within the population (Maynard Smith et al. 1993). In at least some bacterial species, recombination is sufficient to foster adaptive evolution by bringing together adaptive combinations of alleles at different loci. An adaptive allele may be passed from one bacterial species to another, either by homologous recombination or by plasmid transfer. Genetic exchange can create new adaptive combinations of alleles already present in a population and can transfer general adaptations across taxa. However, according to Cohan (1996), genetic exchange in bacteria appears to be too rare to protect genetic variation within a population from the diversity-purging effect of natural periodic selection; genetic exchange also seems to be too rare to prevent adaptive divergence among bacterial populations.

# EVOLUTION OF PHYSIOLOGICAL DIVERSITY

When life evolved on Earth, organic compounds that had formed abiotically served as initial substrates for growth. Cells developed the abilities to degrade these compounds and to derive energy from them for cell growth and maintenance. Methanogenic archaea may have also used hydrogen and carbon dioxide in the reducing atmosphere to generate cellular energy. The central molecule of biological energy transformations became ATP, still employed today by cells as their principal carrier of energy. A number of steps led to the metabolic and genetic diversity of contemporary microorganisms; potential scenarios for this evolutionary process have been reviewed by Trevors (1997a, 1997b).

Gradually, organized sequences of enzymatically catalyzed degradation reactions (catabolic pathways) evolved that permitted cells to use the chemical energy of organic substrates to generate ATP more efficiently. The conversion of carbohydrates to pyruvate via glycolysis became such an ATP-generating pathway central to the energy transfers of many cells. Glycolysis appears to have evolved early and not to have changed in more than 3 billion years. Heterotrophic metabolism using glycolysis led to the formation of various organic end products, including alcohols and acids. These pathways were fermentative; they did not require external electron acceptors and occurred under strict anaerobic conditions. Relatively low amounts of ATP were generated per molecule of substrate so that large amounts of organic substrates had to be transformed to support cellular energy requirements.

In the evolution of archaeal metabolism, methanogenesis evolved as a unique form of metabolism within one evolutionary branch of the Archaea (Euryarchaeota). Other archaea developed modifications of the Entner-Doudoroff pathway, as seen in both halophilic and thermophilic archaea. The Embden-Meyerhof sequence appears to be used in halophiles and methanogens in a gluconeogenic direction. It appears that the Embden-Meyerhof pathway initially evolved for anabolism and remained so in the archaea. Archaea did not evolve ATP-phosphofructokinase as occurred in bacteria and eucaryotes, so the Embden-Meyerhof pathway does not operate in a catabolic fashion in archaea.

Early bacterial and archaeal cells developed the ability to utilize sulfur compounds. Archaeal cells appear to have evolved an early form of anaerobic respiration using sulfate and forming hydrogen sulfide. Rocks that are 2.7 billion years old show evidence of enrichment for the light isotope of sulfur ($^{32}$S). Living organisms use $^{32}$S in preference to $^{34}$S, causing the observed isotopic enrichment. Most of the hyperthermophilic archaea and bacteria are obligate or facultative autotrophs that use molecular hydrogen and reduce elemental sulfur, carbon dioxide, or oxygen. None of the thermophilic archaea exhibit photosynthetic metabolism, suggesting that chemoautotrophy predated photoautotrophy. Unlike the majority of the autotrophic bacteria, the hyperthermophilic archaea do not use the Calvin cycle for $CO_2$ assimilation. Instead, they use modifications of the reductive citric acid cycle or of the reductive acetyl-CoA pathway, which are the exclusive pathways for carbon assimilation used by the autotrophic archaea.

The abiotically formed organic compounds provided only a limited pool of nutritional resources. Therefore, there was selective pressure for more direct utilization of the radiant sun energy to fuel life processes. Cells evolved with the ability to use solar energy to generate ATP. They used hydrogen sulfide, which was present in the oceans, as a source of electrons for the reduction of carbon dioxide. Early photosynthesis was most likely of the anoxygenic (non-oxygen-producing) type found today in the Rhodospirillaceae, Chromatiaceae, and Chlorobiaceae, the anaerobic photosynthetic bacteria. These microorganisms lack photosystem II and are unable to use the hydrogen in water for the reduction of carbon dioxide; instead, reducing power is obtained from organic compounds, molecular hydrogen, or reduced sulfur compounds such as hydrogen sulfide. Early cyanobacteria (formerly known as blue-green algae) probably did not possess photosystem II either and used the same electron donors, which can be split with less energy than that needed for water. Under anoxic, $H_2$S-rich conditions, some contemporary cyanobacteria revert to anoxygenic photosynthesis and use only their photosystem I (Cohen et al. 1986). The use of chemiosmosis for ATP generation in the development of photosynthetic metabolism marked an important evolutionary step because it improved the efficiency of generating ATP.

The oldest assemblage of microfossils in the sedimentary rock of the 3.5-billion-year-old Figtree formation in Africa consists of archaea and/or bacteria.

Carbon isotope ratios suggest that the microfossils resembling cyanobacteria were photosynthetic but that the more advanced oxygenic photosynthesis of cyanobacteria evolved only about 1 billion years later (Schopf 1978, 1993). The interim period was dominated by bacterial mats, as evidenced by stromatolites, which are layered limestone pillars containing organic matter deposits. The recent discovery of living stromatolites in some warm and hypersaline environments, such as the shallow waters of Shark Bay, Australia, greatly aided the interpretation of these stromatolite fossils. It is now clear that they were deposited by filamentous and other bacteria, predominantly cyanobacteria.

The evolution of oxygenic (oxygen-producing) photosynthesis in cyanobacteria is evidenced by the appearance of heterocyst-like structures and banded iron formations approximately 2.0–2.5 billion years ago. Heterocysts produced by cyanobacteria have the function of separating the oxygen-sensitive nitrogen-fixation system from oxygen-evolving photosynthesis and would have been superfluous in cyanobacteria with only anoxygenic photosynthesis. The dating of the development of oxygen-producing metabolism is based upon the observation that about 2.5 billion years ago virtually all iron disappeared from the oceans. Over a very short period—a few million years—oxidized iron was deposited in sediments. Prior to this period, all iron deposits were reduced. Subsequent iron deposits are consistently oxidized unless formed in reducing sediment environments. This record indicates that about 2 billion years ago the originally reducing atmosphere of our planet changed to an oxidizing one. Oxygen produced by living organisms accumulated in the atmosphere.

The evolution of photosynthetic organisms provided a mechanism for carbon recycling and a plentiful source of energy. Eventually, another abundant element in biomass—nitrogen—became a limiting factor for growth. Molecular nitrogen was abundant in the atmosphere, but cells could not directly utilize that form of nitrogen. Cells were dependent on organic nitrogen compounds or reduced inorganic forms of nitrogen. Under the reducing atmosphere, some cells developed the capacity of nitrogen fixation, enabling them to convert molecular nitrogen from the atmosphere to forms that could be used in cellular metabolism.

The geologic evidence suggests that just over 2 billion years ago photosynthetic microorganisms developed the ability to produce oxygen. Some of these also evolved the capacity to fix atmospheric nitrogen. Oxygen accumulation in the atmosphere halted abiotic generation of organic compounds, which occurs only under strictly anaerobic conditions. Ozone formed from molecular oxygen reduced the influx of ultraviolet radiation. Ultraviolet light, particularly of wavelengths less than 200 nm, was probably the major energy source driving the abiotic formation of organic matter prior to the biological introduction of oxygen into the atmosphere.

The evolution of photosystem II in cyanobacteria made available an almost inexhaustible source of reducing power in the form of water, although at the cost of a lower quantum efficiency in the utilization of sunlight. More solar energy is required to split the strong H–O–H bonds of water than to split the weaker H–S–H bonds of hydrogen sulfide. The oxygen evolved in this type of photosynthesis was undoubtedly toxic to most existing forms of anaerobic life; these either became extinct or were restricted to the specific environments that still harbor obligately anaerobic microorganisms. Furthermore, nitrogen-fixing cells had to develop adaptations to protect nitrogenase, the enzyme involved in nitrogen fixation, because oxygen poisons this enzyme.

For the heterotrophic forms that were capable of adapting to the oxidizing atmospheric conditions, new and much more efficient modes of substrate utilization opened up, allowing great physiological diversification. Some cells developed chemoautotrophic metabolic capabilities in which inorganic molecules are used to generate ATP. Others developed respiratory metabolism that increased the efficiency of ATP generation from organic substrates. Respiratory metabolism is based on the chemiosmotic generation of ATP. More efficient metabolic pathways and the need to store genetic information for an ever-increasing array of metabolic, regulatory, morphological, and behavioral traits probably favored the evolutionary diversification of the eucaryotic cell.

## MICROBIAL BIODIVERSITY

New species of microorganisms evolved through the interactions of their genomes with the environment giving rise to great microbial diversity and altered ecosystem functions (Allsopp et al. 1995). The 3 billion years of microbial evolution involved very limited changes in size and morphology. Compared to the evolutionary time scale of multicellular organisms, the pace of microbial evolution was excruciatingly slow. One is tempted to speculate that this long and seemingly uneventful period conceals a gradual evolution of biochemical pathways and regulatory mechanisms that are poorly documented by the geological record but that laid the groundwork for the subsequent explosive morphological diversification of multicellular life forms.

In accordance with Darwinian principles, mutations, genetic recombination, and natural selection all played roles in the evolution of new microbial species. Genetic variations and natural selection favored the proliferation of some kinds of microorganisms and the extinction of others. As evolution proceeded, new kinds of microorganisms appeared so that the diversity of the microbial world increased. Some of the new and diverse microorganisms represented new species (*species* is derived from the Latin word *spec* meaning "look or behold the kind, appearance, or form of something"). The forces governing the evolution of microbial diversity were the same as those driving the appearance of new species of macroorganisms. The biodiversification of microorganisms, however, has been occurring for over 3.85 billion years compared to only 600 million years for macroorganisms. Thus, there has been substantially more time for the evolution of numerous diverse microbial species. The great biodiversity of the microbial world has yet to be discovered.

### Bacterial Biodiversity

The Aquificales (*Aquifex* and *Hydrogenobacter* lineage) represent the most deeply rooted bacterial species, that is, the oldest evolutionary branch within the Bacterial domain. Examining the properties of *Aquifex* and *Hydrogenobacter* gives useful insight into early bacterial ecology and physiology. *Aquifex* species use $H_2$, $S_2O_3^{2-}$ (thiosulfate), and $S^0$ (sulfur) as electron donors to reduce oxygen to water (hence the name *aquifex* meaning "water maker"). In this way, they transfer energy from the electron donors to cellular chemicals, most notably ATP. Water effectively is a metabolic waste product of this energy transfer. *Aquifex pyrophilus* is an extreme thermophile that was isolated from a hydrothermal vent in Iceland. It has a temperature optimum of 85°C but can grow at temperatures as high as 95°C. These physiological properties suggest that the ancestral bacterial progenitor was thermophilic and fixed carbon chemoautotrophically (Achenbach-Richter et al. 1987). Because *Aquifex* and *Hydrogenobacter* depend on free $O_2$, they appear to represent the later stages of evolutionary adaptation of the Aquificales to an aerobic environment. They resemble the facultative aerobic archaeal genera *Acidianus* and *Desulfurolobus,* which grow chemoautotrophically either by the metabolic coupling of elemental sulfur and molecular oxygen (similar to modern bacterial metabolism) or by the coupling of molecular hydrogen and elemental sulfur (characteristic of older archaeal-like metabolism).

The Thermotogales are another deeply rooted evolutionary branch within the Bacterial domain. Like *Aquifex* species, the cytoplasmic membranes of *Thermotoga* species have lipids with ether and ester linkages. This indicates a similarity to the archaea, which all have ether linkages in their cytoplasmic membranes, and to other bacteria that have cytoplasmic membrane lipids with ester linkages. *Thermotoga* has a classical Embden-Meyerhof pathway of glycolysis, which is characteristic of the bacteria but lacking in the archaea. The Thermotogales are extremely thermophilic microorganisms, which supports the hypothesis that the earliest microorganisms were able to grow at very high temperatures that characterized Earth when life first evolved on the planet. Many *Thermotoga* and *Thermosipho* species have been isolated from sulfur hot springs, indicating that sulfur metabolism was also an early characteristic of bacterial physiology.

Besides these early evolutionary branches, the Bacterial domain contains many branches exhibiting diverse physiological properties (Balows et al. 1992). The ancestral bacteria gave rise to the rest of the

contemporary bacteria (Figure 2.7). As the Earth cooled, bacteria evolved that grow at low temperatures, including the low temperatures that characterize most of the oceans and the near-freezing temperatures of many soils. Bacterial species evolved the capacity to utilize the vast and diverse energy resources that became available. Some carry out photosynthesis converting light energy into cellular energy, some are chemolithotrophs that use inorganic compounds as energy sources, and others carry out chemoorganotrophic metabolism—obtaining energy from organic compounds. Notable in the evolution of bacteria is the relative antiquity of the anaerobic photosynthetic forms, including early cyanobacteria. In contrast to contemporary ones, ancestral cyanobacteria probably had only photosystem I and did not evolve oxygen. The spirochetes and gram-positive bacteria also represent evolutionary lines that diverged early. Interestingly, the gram-negative heterotrophic bacteria appear to be descendants of photosynthetic purple bacteria.

## Archaeal Biodiversity

The Archaea differ from other living organisms; they clearly represent a separate evolutionary domain distinct from the Bacterial and Eucaryal domains (Woese 1993). Archaea have distinct physiological properties, many of which appear to relate to their early evolutionary history, when Earth was hot and anaerobic (Heathcock et al. 1985; Zillig 1991; Danson et al. 1992; Kates et al. 1993). Among these distinctive properties, Achaea have cytoplasmic membranes that are chemically distinct, possessing branched hydrocarbons and ether linkages compared to the straight-chain fatty acids and ester linkages found in the membranes of all other organisms; some form tetraethers and have monolayer membranes instead of the typical bilipids. Instead of the peptidoglycan that is typical for Bacteria, their cell walls consist of proteins and glycoproteins; some contain pseudomurein. The metabolic cofactors of the Archaea also differ from those of Bacteria and Eucarya; cofactors of Archaea include coenzyme M (involved in $C_1$ metabolism), factor $F_{420}$ (involved in electron transport), 7-mercaptoheptanoylthreonine phosphate (involved in methanogenesis), tetrahydromethanopterin (instead of folate), methanofuran, and retinal.

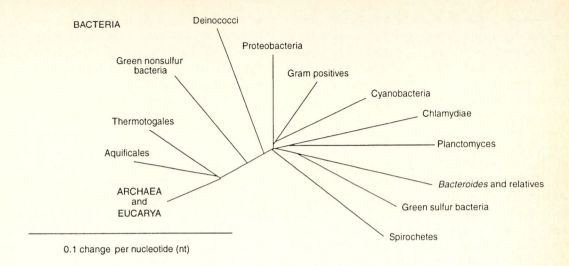

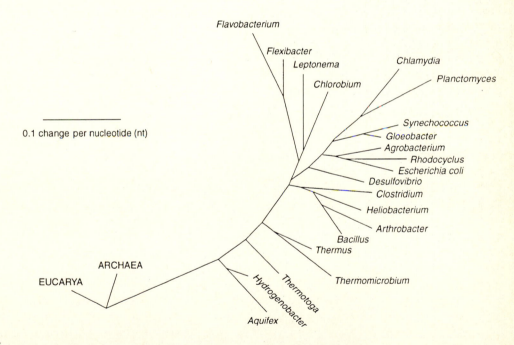

## Figure 2.7

The evolution of the Bacteria (eubacteria) gave rise to at least 12 lineages (kingdoms) of diverse photosynthetic, chemoautotrophic, and heterotrophic forms. (A) There are at least 12 lineages (kingdoms) of bacteria that represent distinct evolutionary branches within the Bacterial domain. The deepest rooted branches (Aquificales and Thermotogales) indicate a thermophilic origin for Bacteria. This was followed by the evolution of photosynthetic anaerobic bacteria that used low molecular weight organic compounds as electron donors (green nonsulfur bacteria). This was followed by the Deinococci, which exhibit high resistance to radiation. Gram-positive bacteria, proteobacteria, oxygen-producing cyanobacteria, and aerobic heterotrophs all evolved later to produce the great diversity of contemporary bacteria. (B) Numerous species, some examples of which are shown here, evolved within the 12 kingdoms. (Source: (A) Angert 1996; (B) Barns et al. 1996.)

The Archaeal domain seems to have arisen from thermophilic ancestry, giving rise to a small but diverse collection of phenotypes, including methanogens, extreme halophiles, extreme thermophiles with sulfur-dependent metabolism, and thermophilic sulfate-reducing species. The Archaeal phylogenetic tree has two major branches, designated as the kingdoms Crenarchaeota and Euryarchaeota; it also has a third deeply rooted branch which is proposed as the kingdom Korarchaeota (Figure 2.8). Crenarchaeota comprises a group of extreme thermophiles that represent the oldest recorded evolutionary branch; these microbes most resemble the ancestral phenotype of the Archaea. Most crenarchaeal isolates are thermophilic and many are hyperthermophiles. They exhibit great diversity in habitats such as thermal springs (Barns et al. 1994). The Euryarchaeota branch of the ancestral Archaea gave rise to contemporary methanogens,

halobacteria, and thermoacidophiles, such as *Sulfolobus*. The physiological adaptations of these archaeans permit some to grow at high temperatures and under strict anaerobic conditions. Many transform elemental sulfur, and there is a common theme of sulfur metabolism; some also tolerate the highly acidic and saline conditions postulated to have characterized early Earth. The discovery of abundant archaea in temperate marine ecosystems (DeLong 1992) represents the newest discovery in the evolutionary history of the Archaea. It has been proposed that these archaea, which have yet to be cultured, represent a third Archaeal evolutionary lineage—the Korarchaeota. Loss of thermophily led to the evolution of the Korarchaeota, which are marine archaea found in low-temperature coastal waters. The archaea thus may be far more abundant and ecologically diverse than originally thought.

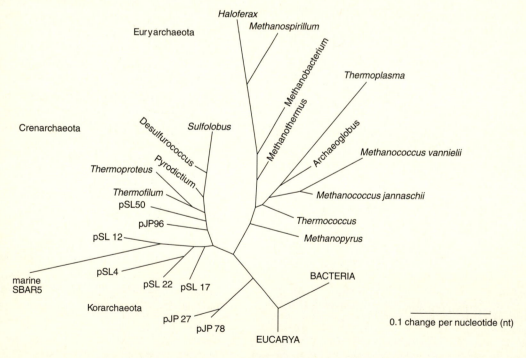

**Figure 2.8**
The evolution of the Archaea (archaebacteria), based upon rRNA analyses, gave rise to three kingdoms—Crenarchaeota, Euryarchaeota, and Korarchaeota. (Source: Barns et al. 1996.)

# Eucaryal Biodiversity

Fossils of eucaryotic forms resembling green algae and perhaps fungi are abundant in the 1-billion-year-old Bitter Springs formation in Australia. The period during which such fossil eucaryotes appear coincides with a decline in stromatolites deposited by bacterial mats. The advent of the nucleated eucaryotic cell, and presumably sexual reproduction, greatly hastened the pace of evolution. About 0.6 billion years ago, the first multicellular macrofossils of plants and animals appeared and the conventional Paleozoic geological age began. Until that time, evolution of life was synonymous with microbial evolution. By the time multicellular plants and invertebrates appeared, microorganisms had changed the atmosphere of Earth and adjusted most of its physicochemical parameters to their present state.

Although the fossil record might indicate that the Eucarya are only about 1.3–1.4 billion years old, rRNA analyses reveal that eukaryotes evolved much earlier, shortly after the evolution of the Archaea. The most primitive evolutionary lineages that have been identified in the Eucaryal domain are unicellular, anaerobic mesophilic organisms. More primitive eucaryotes should have been thermophilic, as has been found in the primitive lineages of the Archaeal and Bacterial domains. A great deal of yet unidentified evolutionary change must have occurred at the cellular level prior to endosymbiotic acquisition of organelles. Even greater diversification of eucaryotes occurred after the acquisition of mitochondria and chloroplasts through endosymbiosis. Independent analyses of cytochromes, ferredoxins, and rRNA molecules indicate that mitochondria originated from the proteobacteria (purple bacteria) and that chloroplasts came from cyanobacteria. The development of sexual reproduction within the eucaryotes, which ensured a high frequency of new genetic combination, clearly led to rapid evolution of new organisms. Particularly within the last 150 million years, there has been a great radiation of diverse eucaryotes, including the evolution of the fungi, plants, and animals at the top of the canopy of the evolutionary tree of life.

The Archeozoa, which until recently have been considered primitive protozoa, represent the earliest evolutionary divergences that have been detected so far within the Eucaryal domain; they are the base of the Eucaryal branch of the evolutionary tree (Cavalier-Smith 1993) (Figure 2.9). The Archeozoa represent the descendants of early eucaryotes that evolved prior to the endosymbiotic acquisition of mitochondria. Archeozoa include the Metamonada (Diplomonads), such as *Giardia* and *Hexamita;* the Microsporidia, such as *Enterocytozoon* and *Vairimorpha;* and the Parabasilia, such as *Trichomonas.* These organisms appear to be primitive forms of eucaryotic cells which had already evolved a nucleus, endoplasmic reticulum, rudimentary cytoskeleton, and the 9 + 2 organization of flagella. However, they lack mitochondria. Moreover, the Metamonada, Microsporidia, and Parabasilia have 70S ribosomes—like those of bacterial and archaeal cells—which distinguishes them from all other contemporary eucaryotes, which have 80S ribosomes. The Metamonada and Microsporidia also lack hydrogenosomes, which are organelles present in some anaerobic protozoa that are involved with energy transformation, and they lack a Golgi apparatus, which is involved in export of materials by exocytosis. The cells of these organisms do not appear to be unions of different evolutionary lineages as has occurred in other contemporary eucaryotic cells that contain organelles acquired by endocytosis (Kabnick and Peattie 1991).

Both *Giardia* and *Hexamita* are primitive eucaryotes that lack many of the normal structures of contemporary eucaryotic cells. *G. lamblia* is a human parasite that attaches to the mucosa of the intestine and reproduces there, causing giardiasis. It carries out anaerobic metabolism. This archeozoan has two nuclei and eight flagella; it lacks mitochondria, endoplasmic reticulum, and Golgi apparatus. *Giardia* has 70S ribosomes with 16S rRNA containing only 1453 nucleotides in the small 30S subunit. *Giardia* also has only a rudimentary cytoskeleton, lacks sexual reproduction, and has a very small genome. All of these features (absence of membrane-bound organelles, 70S ribosome, organization of rRNA coding region, simple cytoskeleton, and lack of sexual reproduction) point to the primitive nature of *Giardia.* Most likely, the progenitor cells for all three evolutionary domains of life had similar characteristics. Interestingly, *Giardia* and other surviving organisms of deeply rooted eucaryotic evolutionary lineages are animal parasites. The earliest free-living forms of eucaryotes have yet to be discovered, leaving gaps in our knowledge of early evolutionary events within the Eucaryal domain.

Protozoa were the next evolutionary line to develop within the Eucaryal domain after the Archeozoa. They have 80S ribosomes and organelles (mitochondria and in some cases chloroplasts) that they acquired through endosymbiosis (Cavalier-Smith 1993). These eucaryotes demonstrate primarily phagotrophic modes of nutrient acquisition. It is not

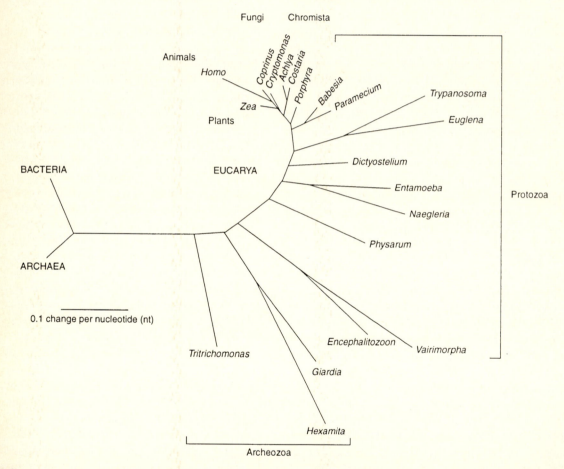

**Figure 2.9**

The evolution of the Eucarya. There is a long evolutionary distance between the divergence of the Eucarya from the Archaea and the first known evolutionary branch within the Archeozoa. The Archeozoa, which have nuclei but still share various structural characteristics with bacteria and archaea such as 70S ribosomes and lack of mitochondria, represent the deepest evolutionary branch within the Eucaryal domain. The Protozoa, which include a wide variety of groups including the slime molds, represent the next evolutionary branches. The ciliate protozoa were the most recent groups of protozoa to evolve. Next comes the evolution of the Chromista, which include the diatoms and red algae. Then the fungi, plants, and animals emerge at the crown of the evolutionary tree. (Source: Barns et al. 1996.)

surprising that some of the bacterial cells they engulfed survived within the eucaryotic cells and lived there symbiotically, eventually losing their independent reproductive capacity and becoming mitochondria and chloroplasts. Acquisition of mitochondria changed the metabolism of eucaryotes from anaerobic fermentation to aerobic respiration.

The kinetoplastid protozoa, such as *Trypanosoma brucei,* and euglenoid protozoa, such as *Euglena gracilis,* represent lineages that branched relatively early in the evolutionary history of the protozoa. These protozoa have flagella with the characteristic 9 + 2 microtubule arrangement that is characteristic of eucaryotes. The branching of *E. gracilis* and *T. brucei* was followed by the relatively early divergences of two independent lineages leading to the cellular slime molds, such as *Dictyostelium discoideum,* and the apicomplexans, such as *Plasmodium berghei.* These protozoa have tubular mitochondrial cristae, although other protozoa that appear to have evolved subsequently have lamellar cristae. The nature of the mitochondrial cristae appears to reflect the progression of evolution of mitochondrial structure throughout the Protozoa. The Entamoebidae appear to have developed at about the same time as the slime molds through the loss of their mitochondria.

As protozoa evolved, they developed more elaborate genetic organizations. Ciliate protozoa emerged as an evolutionary group more than one billion years ago. By that time, meiosis and fertilization had been established in eucaryotes, and modern ciliates share these functions with other contemporary eucaryotes. The major classes of ciliates have a single common ancestor, but there are deep branches within this lineage, so that there are great evolutionary distances among the ciliate protozoa. This deep branching pattern among the ciliates is consistent with the divergence in several independent lineages soon after their common ancestor separated from other eucaryotes.

Late in the evolution of the protozoa, at about the same time the ciliates evolved, there was nearly simultaneous branching of the animals, fungi, chlorophyte algae, plants, and chromophyte algae. The precise branching order of these lineages is uncertain. The great radiation of lineages represents changes in

rRNA molecules of less than 1%; therefore the calculated evolutionary distances cannot be statistically differentiated. One can only speculate as to why there was such a sudden and simultaneous radiation of eucaryotic lineages within a span of only 50–100 million years. It almost certainly reflects a major change in natural selective pressure, perhaps corresponding to the adaptation of aerobic metabolism in an oxidizing environment.

Although algae were originally considered along with protozoa to compose the protists, phylogenetic analyses have indicated that there are several evolutionary lineages of photosynthetic eucaryotes. Chloroplasts in diatoms and brown algae occur in the lumen of the rough endoplasmic reticulum and are surrounded by a unique periplastic membrane. As such, diatoms and brown algae are classified as Chromista (Cavalier-Smith 1993). The unique membrane surrounding the chloroplasts of Chromista arose from the cytoplasmic membrane of the photosynthetic protozoan that was engulfed. Thus, the evolution of diatoms and brown algae involved two stages of endosymbiosis. The phagocytized photosynthetic protozoan entered the rough endoplasmic reticulum by fusion of the phagosome membrane with the nuclear envelope. Some chromists lack ribosomes on the membrane that surrounds the periplastic membrane. This smooth endoplasmic reticulum probably represents the original phagosomal membrane which, unlike other chromists, never fused with the rough endoplasmic reticulum.

Analyses of 18S rRNAs indicate that the water molds (oomycetes) and net slime molds (labyrinthula) are closely related to the photosynthetic diatoms and brown algae. The oomycetes are unlike the true fungi in that they have tubular mitochondrial cristae and generally have cellulosic cell walls. They are like the chrysophytes in having flagellated stages and similar spindle apparatuses.

The kingdom Plantae comprises two distinct evolutionary lineages—one that includes the green algae (Charophyta and Chlorophyta) along with the higher green plants that have embryonic developmental stages, and another that includes the red algae (Rhodophyta). The green algae, red algae, and plants evolved from a phagotrophic protozoan by the symbiotic acquisition of chloroplasts from photosynthetic bacteria, almost certainly cyanobacteria. The evolutionary lineage of chlorophyte algae and plants is distinct from the lineage leading to diatoms and brown algae in the chromists. It is also distinct from the evolutionary branches of dinoflagellates and euglenoids, which occur within the protozoa. Unlike protozoa, the green algae and higher plants do not feed by phagocytosis, which is the dominant nutritional mode of even the photosynthetic euglenoid protozoa. Analyses of rRNAs clearly show that the dinoflagellates and euglenoids are entirely distinct from the evolution of the green or red algae; dinoflagellates are much closer phylogenetically to the ciliate protozoa than to the algae and plants.

The evolution of the fungi from the protozoa, which occurred about 400 million years ago, involved the acquisition of rigid chitinous cell walls that eliminated the phagotrophic mode of nutrition. The origin of the cell wall is a clear evolutionary demarcation between the fungi and protozoa. Fungi obtain their nutrients by absorption and are never phagotrophic. Almost all contemporary fungi have chitinous cell walls. They also always have platelike cristae and lack undulopodia (cilia or flagella) at all stages of their life cycles. Fungi evolved diverse reproductive strategies and mechanisms for resisting desiccation while growing on the surfaces of plants and when being dispersed through the atmosphere. Early fungi were unicellular yeasts that reproduced by binary fission. Later evolutionary lineages of yeasts developed budding as a mode of reproduction, which produced smaller daughter cells from a mother cell. Many fungi developed an asexual mode of growth and reproduction by apical extension of cells and septation to form long filaments called hyphae that become entwined into integrated structures called mycelia—these are the filamentous fungi or molds. Fungi also developed diverse survival and reproductive strategies involving the production of spores. Ascomycete and basidiomycete fungi evolved the capability of sexual reproduction involving specialized spores—the mode of sexual spore production distinguishes these major evolutionary lineages of the fungi. Ascomycetes are a major group of

fungi that form sexual spores (ascospores) within a specialized sac (ascus). The earliest evolutionary lines of ascus-producing fungi were yeasts that reproduced by fission. Subsequently, yeasts evolved that reproduce by budding, and the filamentous ascomycetes also evolved. The budding ascomycetous yeasts are monophyletic and represent a separate lineage from the filamentous ascomycetes, but one that is closely related. Later the more complex basidiomycetes evolved. The basidiomycetes form sexual spores (basidiospores) on specialized cells (basidia) borne on fruiting bodies (basidiocarps) that are usually macroscopic structures such as mushrooms. Basidia have complex structures that approach levels of organizational complexity comparable to some plants and animals. These fungi represent the pinnacle of evolution among microorganisms.

## CHAPTER SUMMARY

Chemical evidence based on ratios of $^{12}$C and $^{13}$C indicate that microbial life evolved about 3.85 million years ago, i.e., only 1 billion years after the formation of our planet. The earliest fossil evidence of microorganisms appeared about 3.5 billion years ago. The first fossils of macroorganisms are 600 million years old, supporting the concept that through most of evolutionary history, microorganisms were the sole forms of life. The great morphological diversification of macroscopic life occurred relatively recently.

The chemical evolution that led up to the first living microorganisms occurred in a reducing environment, but many details of this chemical evolution remain controversial. There are several hypotheses as to how the first living cells evolved on Earth. Experimental evidence has demonstrated that simple organic chemicals could have formed abiotically with energy from electrical (lightning) discharges. It also has been demonstrated that certain chemicals aggregate to form coacervates, which have the fundamental structural organization of a membrane-bounded cell. It is hypothesized that such reactions could have occurred on the surface of Earth, leading to the formation of the first living cells. An alternate hypothesis is that life on

Earth began at deep ocean thermal vents as a result of hot, mineral-rich water emerging through pyrite (iron sulfide)–containing rocks. The first living cells that were capable of self-reproduction and other characteristics of living systems probably used RNA as their informational macromolecule. Gradually, DNA replaced RNA as the hereditary macromolecule of all living organisms.

Three lines of cellular evolution occurred, leading to the Bacteria, Archaea, and Eucarya. These three domains have been revealed by molecular analyses of ribosomal RNA (rRNA) molecules, which has permitted the reconstruction of the evolutionary path (phylogeny) of life. The morphological diversification of the ancestral Bacterial, Archaeal, and Eucaryal cells initially was slow. As life evolved, the interactions of genes and environment through the process of natural selection led to the continued diversification of life on Earth. During this evolutionary process, living organisms developed that changed the reducing atmosphere to an oxidizing one and, through feedback mechanisms, kept conditions such as temperature in a favorable range for life. Initially, living organisms were anaerobes that used organic compounds as energy sources; many also used sulfur compounds for generating cellular energy. Additionally, they were thermophiles that were adapted to growth at elevated temperatures. Photosynthesis developed relatively early, probably more than 3 billion years ago, but was based initially only on photosystem I and occurred anaerobically (photosynthesis initially did not evolve oxygen). The evolution of photosystem II, which splits water and produces oxygen, came much later. The oxidizing atmosphere was toxic to many anaerobes, but it enabled aerobes to evolve a much greater metabolic diversity and gain much more energy from catabolic processes.

New species of Bacteria, Archaea, and Eucarya evolved through the interactions of their genomes with the environment, giving rise to great microbial diversity. The first lineages of bacteria (Aquificales and Thermotogales) appear to have been thermophiles that shared some physiological characteristics with Archaea, such as the presence of ether-containing lipids within their cytoplasmic membranes. The Archaea evolved several important groups that could grow in hostile environments such as highly saline lakes and hot sulfuric pools. The first eucaryotes lacked organelles, as still seen in the Archeozoa. Subsequently, protozoa acquired organelles through endosymbiosis. The cellular organelles of the Eucarya, mitochondria and plastids, were originally independent bacteria, and it is possible that the eucaryotic flagella and cilia were derived in the same manner. Thus, eucaryotes are chimeric. The Eucarya also evolved the capacity for sexual reproduction, allowing genetic recombination that produced an explosive diversification of species, including the relatively recent evolution of fungi, plants, and animals. As a result of the evolutionary process there is enormous contemporary biodiversity among the bacteria, archaea, and eucaryotic microorganisms, much of which has yet to be explored.

## STUDY QUESTIONS

1. When did life appear on Earth? How do we know the approximate date for the earliest living organisms?

2. How could organic compounds needed to support life have first formed on Earth? How does this differ from the way in which organic compounds form on Earth today?

3. Assuming that life originally formed spontaneously on Earth, why is the doctrine of spontaneous generation not applicable for contemporary formation of living organisms?

4. What is a coacervate? How does a coacervate form? How are coacervate related to the evolution of living cells?

5. How are we able to trace the evolutionary history of Bacteria and Archaea?

6. How has the discovery of the Archaea altered our view of evolutionary history?

7. What is the relationship of ecology to evolution?

8. What are stromatolites? How are they formed?

9. What physiological characteristics appear to have been characteristic of the earliest microorganisms?

10. What is meant by the term *endosymbiotic evolution*? How does it explain the origin of organelles in eucaryotic cells? What is the specific ancestry of the mitochondrion? Of the chloroplast?

11. What is the genetic basis for evolution? What is the relationship of Darwin's theory of selection of the fittest to genetic variability based upon mutation and recombination?

12. When did the metabolic capacity for oxygenic photosynthesis develop? How did the biological production of oxygen alter the course of evolution?

13. How have molecular methods contributed to our understanding of microbial biodiversity?

## REFERENCES AND SUGGESTED READINGS

Achenbach-Richter, L., R. Gupta, K. O. Stetter, and C. R. Woese. 1987. Were the original eubacteria thermophiles? *Systematic and Applied Microbiology* 9:34–39.

Allsopp, D., D. L. Hawksworth, and R. R. Colwell (eds.). 1995. *Microbial Diversity and Ecosystem Function.* CAB International, Wallingford, Great Britain.

Amann, R. I., W. Ludwig, and K-H. Schleifer. 1995. Phylogenetic identification and *in situ* detection of individual microbial cells without cultivation. *Microbiological Reviews* 59:143–169.

Angert, E. R. 1996. Phylogenetic analysis of *Metabacterium polyspora:* Clues to the evolutionary origin of daughter cell production in *Epulopiscium* species, the largest bacteria. *Journal of Bacteriology* 178:1451–1456.

Balows, A., H. G. Truper, M. Dworkin, W. Harder, and K-H. Schleifer. 1992. *The Prokaryotes: A Handbook on the Biology of Bacteria—Ecophysiology, Isolation, Identification, Applications,* ed. 2. Springer-Verlag, New York.

Barns, S. M., R. E. Rundyga, M. W. Jeffries, and N. R. Pace. 1994. Remarkable archaeal diversity detected in a Yellowstone National Park hot spring environment. *Proceedings of the National Academy of Sciences of the USA* 91:1609–1613.

Barns, S. M., C. F. Delwiche, J. D. Palmer, and N. R. Pace. 1996. Perspectives on archaeal diversity, thermophily, and monophyly from environmental rRNA sequences. *Proceedings of the National Academy of Sciences of the USA* 93:9188–9193.

Barth, A. L., J. A. Stricker, and L. Margulis. 1991. Search for eukaryotic motility proteins in spirochetes: Immunological detection of a tektin-like protein in *Spirochaeta halophila. Biosystems* 24:313–319.

Carlisle, M. J., J. F. Collins, and B.E.B. Moseley (eds.). 1981. *Molecular and Cellular Aspects of Microbial Evolution.* Cambridge University Press, London.

Cavalier-Smith, T. 1987. The origin of eukaryotic and archaebacterial cells. *Annals of the New York Academy of Science* 503:17–54.

Cavalier-Smith, T. 1993. Kingdom Protozoa and its 18 phyla. *Microbiological Reviews* 57:953–994.

Clarke, P. H. 1984. Evolution of new phenotypes. In M. J. Klug and C. A. Reddy (eds.). *Current Perspectives in Microbial Ecology.* American Society for Microbiology, Washington, DC, pp. 71–78.

Cleveland, L. R., and A. V. Grimstone. 1964. The fine structure of the flagellate *Mixotricha paradoxa* and its associated micro-organisms. *Proceedings of the Royal Society* (London), Series B 159:668–686.

Cohan, F. M. 1994. Genetic exchange and evolutionary divergence in prokaryotes. *Trends in Ecology and Evolution* 9:175–180.

Cohan, F. M. 1996. The role of genetic exchange in bacterial evolution. *ASM News* 62:631–636.

Cohen, Y., B. B. Jørgensen, N. P. Revsbeck, and R. Poplawski. 1986. Adaptation to hydrogen sulfide of oxygenic and anoxigenic photosynthesis among cyanobacteria. *Applied and Environmental Microbiology* 51:398–407.

Corliss, J. O. 1984. The kingdom Protista and its 45 phyla. *Biosystems* 17:87–126.

Crawford, I. P. 1989. Evolution of a biosynthetic pathway: The tryptophan paradigm. *Annual Reviews of Microbiology* 43:567–600.

Danson, M. J., D. W. Hough, and G. G. Lunt (eds.). 1992. *The Archaebacteria: Biochemistry and Biotechnology.* Portland Press, London.

Darnell, J. E., and W. F. Doolittle. 1986. Speculations on the early course of evolution. *Proceedings of the National Academy of Science USA* 83:1271–1275.

Darwin, C. 1860. *On the Origin of Species by Means of Natural Selection, or the Preservation of Favoured Races in the Struggle for Life.* D. Appleton, New York.

Davis, B. D. 1989. Evolutionary principles and the regulation of engineered bacteria. *Genome* 31:864–869.

DeLong, E. F. 1992. Archaea in coastal marine environments. *Proceedings of the National Academy of Sciences* 89:5685–5689.

Dickerson, R. 1978. Chemical evolution and the origin of life. *Scientific American* 239:70–86.

Doolittle, W. F. 1987. The evolutionary significance of the archaebacteria. *Annals of the New York Academy of Science* 503:72–77.

Doolittle, W. F. 1988. Bacterial evolution. *Canadian Journal of Microbiology* 34:547–551.

Eberhard, W. G. 1990. Evolution in bacterial plasmids and levels of selection. *Quarterly Review of Biology* 65:3–22.

Fox, G. E., E. Stackebrandt, R. B. Hespell, J. Gibson, J. Maniloff, T. A. Dyer, R. S. Wolfe, W. E. Balch, R. S. Tanner, L. Magrum, L. Zablen, R. Blakemore, R. Gupta, L. Bonen, B. J. Lewis, D. A. Stahl, K. R. Luehrsen, K. N. Chen, and C. R. Woese. 1980. The phylogeny of prokaryotes. *Science* 209:457–463.

Fox, S. W., 1965. *The Origins of Prebiological Systems and Their Molecular Matrices.* Academic Press, New York.

Fox, S. W., and K. Dose. 1977. *Molecular Evolution and the Origin of Life.* Marcel Dekker, New York.

Freter, R. 1984. Factors affecting conjugal transfer in natural bacterial communities. In M. J. Klug and C. A. Reddy (eds.). *Current Perspectives in Microbial Ecology.* American Society for Microbiology, Washington, DC, pp. 105–114.

Grady, M., I. Wright, and C. Pillinger. 1996. Opening a martian can of worms? (Evidence of life on Mars). *Nature* 382:575–582.

Gray, M., and F. Doolittle. 1982. Has the endosymbiont hypothesis been proven? *Microbiological Reviews* 46:1–42.

Gray, M. W. 1994. One plus one equals one: The making of a cryptomonad alga. *ASM News* 60:423–427.

Haldane, J.B.S. 1932. *The Causes of Evolution.* Harper & Row, New York.

Hall, B. G. 1984. Adaptation by acquisition of novel enzyme activities in the laboratory. In M. J. Klug and C. A. Reddy (eds.). *Current Perspectives in Microbial Ecology.* American Society for Microbiology, Washington, DC, pp. 79–86.

Heathcock, C. H., B. L. Finkelstein, T. Aoki, and C. D. Poulter. 1985. Stereostructure of the archaebacterial $C_{40}$ diol. *Science* 229:862–864.

Heinrich, M. R. (ed.). 1976. *Extreme Environments: Mechanisms of Microbial Adaptation.* Academic Press, New York.

Holland, H. D. 1997. Evidence for life on Earth more than 3850 million years ago. *Science* 275:38–39.

Horowitz, N. H. 1965. The evolution of biochemical synthesis—Retrospect and prospect. In V. Bryson and H. J. Vogel (eds.). *Evolving Genes and Proteins.* Academic Press, New York, pp. 15–23.

Hryniewicz, W. 1994. Bacterial resistance in eastern Europe—selected problems. *Scandinavian Journal of Infectious Diseases—Supplementum* 93:33–39.

Jensen, R. A. 1985. Biochemical pathways in prokaryotes can be traced backward through evolutionary time. *Molecular Biology and Evolution* 2:13–34.

Kabnick, K. S., and D. A. Peattie. 1991. *Giardia:* A missing link between prokaryotes and eukaryotes. *American Scientist* 79:34–43.

Katchalsky, A. 1973. Probiotic synthesis of biopolymers on inorganic templates. *Naturwissenschaften* 60:215–220.

Kates, M., D. J. Kushner, and A. T. Matherson (eds.). 1993. *The Biochemistry of Archaea (Archaebacteria).* Elsevier Science, Amsterdam.

Knoll, A. H. 1985. The distribution and evolution of microbial life in the late Proterozoic era. *Annual Reviews of Microbiology* 39:391–417.

Knoll, A. H., and S. M. Awromile. 1983. Ancient microbial ecosystems. In W. E. Krumbein (ed.). *Microbial Geochemistry.* Blackwell, Oxford, England, pp. 287–315.

Lake, J. A. 1985. Evolving ribosome structure: Domains in Archaebacteria, Eubacteria, Eocytes and Eukaryotes. *Annual Reviews in Biochemistry* 54:237–271.

Lovelock, J. E. 1979. *Gaia: A New Look at Life on Earth.* Oxford University Press, New York.

Lovelock, J. E. 1988. *The Ages of Gaia: A Biography of Our Living Earth.* Norton, New York.

Margulis, L. 1970. *Origin of Eukaryotic Cells.* Yale University Press, New Haven, CT.

Margulis, L. 1971. The origin of plant and animal cells. *American Scientist* 59:230–235.

Margulis, L. 1981. *Symbiosis in Cell Evolution.* Freeman, San Francisco.

Margulis, L., and M. McMenamin. 1990. Marriage of convenience: The motility of the modern cell may reflect an ancient symbiotic union. *The Sciences* 30:30–37.

Marton, A. 1992. Pneumococcal antimicrobial resistance: The problem in Hungary. *Clinical Infectious Diseases* 15:106–111.

Maynard Smith, J., N. H. Smith, M. O'Rourke, and B. G. Spratt. 1993. How clonal are bacteria? *Proceedings of the National Academy of Sciences of the USA* 90:4384–4388.

McKay, D. S., E. K. Gibson Jr., K. L. Thomas-Keprta, H. Vali, C. S. Romanek, S. J. Clemett, X.D.F. Chillier, C. R. Maechling, and R. N. Zare. 1996. Search for past life on Mars: Possible relic biogenic activity in Martian meteorite ALH84001. *Science* 273:924–930.

Miller, S. L. 1957. The formation of organic compounds on the primitive Earth. *Annals of the New York Academy of Science* 69:260–275.

Miller, S. L., and L. E. Orgel. 1974. *The Origins of Life on Earth.* Prentice Hall, Englewood Cliffs, NJ.

Miller, S. L., and H. C. Urey. 1959. Organic compound synthesis on the primitive Earth. *Science* 130:245–251.

Mojzsis, S. J., G. Arrhenius, K. D. McKeegan, T. M. Harrison, A. P. Nutman, and C.R.L. Friend. 1996. Evidence for life on Earth before 3,800 million years ago. *Nature* 382:55–59.

Nisbet, E. G. 1980. Archean stromatolites and the search for the earliest life. *Nature* 284:395–396.

Olsen, G. J., D. J. Lane, S. J. Giovannoni, N. R. Pace, and D. A. Stahl. 1986. Microbial ecology and evolution: A ribosomal RNA approach. *Annual Reviews of Microbiology* 40:337–365.

Olsen, G. J., C. R. Woese, and R. Overbeek. 1994. The winds of (evolutionary) change: Breathing new life into microbiology. *Journal of Bacteriology* 176:1–6.

Oparin, A. I. 1938. *The Origin of Life.* Dover, New York.

Oparin, A. I. 1968. *Genesis and Evolutionary Development of Life.* Academic Press, New York.

Orgel, L. E. 1992. Molecular replication: Origin of life. *Nature* 358:203–209.

Orgel, L. E. 1994. The origin of life on Earth. *Scientific American* 271:76–83.

Pace, N. R. 1997. A molecular view of microbial diversity and the biosphere. *Science* 276:734–740.

Pace, N. R., D. A. Stahl, D. J. Lane, and G. J. Olsen. 1985. Analyzing natural microbial populations by rRNA sequences. *ASM News* 51:4–12.

Schleifer, K. H., and E. Stackebrandt. 1983. Molecular systematics of prokaryotes. *Annual Review of Microbiology* 37:143–187.

Schopf, J. W. 1978. The evolution of the earliest cells. *Scientific American* 239:110–138.

Schopf, J. W. 1993. Microfossils of the early Archean apex chart: New evidence of the antiquity of life. *Science* 260:640–646.

Slater, J. H. 1984. Genetic interactions in microbial communities. In M. J. Klug and C. A. Reddy (eds.). *Current Perspectives in Microbial Ecology.* American Society for Microbiology, Washington, DC, pp. 87–93.

Sukhodolets, V. V. 1988. Organization and evolution of the bacterial genome. *Microbiological Sciences* 5:202–206.

Thayer, D. W. (ed.). 1975. *Microbial Interaction with the Physical Environment.* Dowden Hutchinson and Ross, Stroudsburg, PA.

Trevors, J. T. 1997a. Bacterial evolution and metabolism. *Antonie van Leeuwenhoek* 71:257–263.

Trevors, J. T. 1997b. Evolution of bacterial genomes. *Antonie van Leeuwenhoek* 71:265–270.

Van Iterson, G., Jr., L. E. Den Dooren de Jong, and J. J. Kluyer. 1983. *Martinus Wilem Beijerinck: His Life and His Work.* Science Tech, Madison, WI, pp. 106–132.

Vidal, G. 1984. The oldest eukaryotic cells. *Scientific American* 250:48–57.

Wächtershäuser, G. 1988. Before enzymes and templates: Theory of surface metabolism. *Microbiological Reviews* 52:452–484.

Wilcox, C. E., and G. E. Wedemayer. 1985. Dinoflagellates with blue-green chloroplasts derived from an endosymbiotic eukaryote. *Science* 227:192–194.

Winker, S., and C. R. Woese. 1991. A definition of the domains Archaea, Bacteria, and Eucarya in terms of small subunit ribosomal RNA characteristics. *Systematic and Applied Microbiology* 14:305–310.

Woese, C. R. 1985. Why study evolutionary relationships among bacteria? In K. H. Schleifer and E. Stackebrandt (eds.). *Evolution of Prokaryotes.* FEMS Symposium 29, Academic Press, London, pp. 1–30.

Woese, C. R. 1987. Bacterial evolution. *Microbiological Reviews* 51:181–192.

Woese, C. R. 1992. Prokaryote systematics: The evolution of a science. In A. Balows, H. G. Trüper, M. Dworkin, W. Harder, and K. H Schleifer (eds.). *The Prokaryotes.* Springer-Verlag, New York, pp. 1–18.

Woese, C. R. 1993. The Archaea: Their history and significance. In M. Kates, D. J. Kushner, and A. T. Matherson (eds.). *The Biochemistry of Archaea (Archaebacteria).* Elsevier, Amsterdam, pp. vii–xxix.

Woese, C. R., O. Kandler, and M. L. Wheelis. 1990. Towards a natural system of organisms: Proposal for the domains Archaea, Bacteria, and Eucarya. *Proceedings of the National Academy of Science* 87:4576–4579.

Zillig, W. 1987. Eukaryotic traits in Archaebacteria: Could the eukaryotic cytoplasm have arisen from Archaebacterial origin? *Annals of the New York Academy of Science* 503:78–82.

Zillig, W. 1991. Comparative biochemistry of Archaea and Bacteria. *Current Opinions in Genetics and Development* 1:544–551.

Zillig, W., R. Schnabel, and K. O. Slatter. 1985. Archaebacteria and the origin of the eukaryotic cytoplasm. *Current Topics in Microbiology and Immunology* 114:1–18.

Zillig, W., R. Schnabel, and J. Tu. 1982. The phylogeny of Archaebacteria, including novel anaerobic thermoacidophiles, in the light of RNA polymerase structure. *Naturwissenschaften* 69:197–204.

# part two

## POPULATION INTERACTIONS

# 3

# INTERACTIONS AMONG MICROBIAL POPULATIONS

*Microbes commonly interact in positive and negative ways; neutralism is a rare and perhaps only theoretical phenomenon. Within a single population, microbes cooperate at low and compete at high cell densities. One population may benefit another one in a one-sided commensal way, or two different populations may interact synergistically. Such beneficial interactions are facilitated by close physical proximity, as in biofilms and flocs. Mutualism is a strong, specific, beneficial interaction essential for the survival of both partners. Competition between diverse populations for resources is keen in nature and may be sharpened by amensalism. Parasitism and predation benefit their perpetrators while damaging or destroying the host or prey, respectively. Within a community, positive interactions tend to optimize the utilization of the available resources, and negative interactions act as feedback controls and prevent a complete exhaustion of resources and consequent population crashes.*

## INTERACTIONS WITHIN A SINGLE MICROBIAL POPULATION

According to Allee's principle, both positive and negative interactions may occur even within a single population (Allee et al. 1949). Such interactions, originally observed in animals and plants, are interrelated and are population-density dependent. Subsequent examples will show that Allee's principle is highly suitable for explaining the density-dependent interactions that occur within microbial populations. Generally speaking, positive interactions increase the growth rate of a population, whereas negative interactions have the opposite effect (Figure 3.1). With increasing population density, positive interactions theoretically increase the growth rate to some asymptotic limit. In contrast, negative interactions decrease growth rate as the population density increases.

Commonly, positive interactions (cooperation) predominate at low population densities and negative

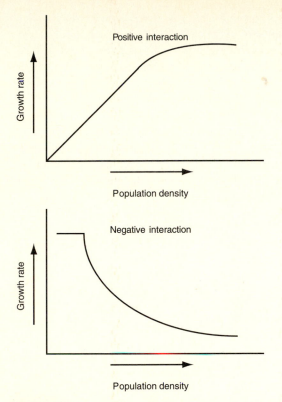

**Figure 3.1**
Effects of independent positive and negative interactions on growth rate within a single population with increasing population density.

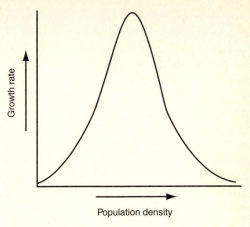

**Figure 3.2**
Combined effect of positive and negative interactions within a single population. The growth rate indicates an optimal population density. At low population densities, positive interactions predominate; at high population densities, negative interactions are dominant.

ones (competition) at high population densities. As a result, there is an optimal population density for maximal growth rate (Figure 3.2). Growth rates below the optimal density are strongly affected by positive interactions; growth rates above the optimal population density are strongly influenced by negative interactions.

## Positive Interactions

Positive interactions within a population are called *cooperation*. Cooperation within a single microbial population is evidenced by an extended lag period or a complete failure of growth when a very small inoculum is used in routine culture transfer procedures. This is especially true for fastidious microorganisms (those having complex physiological requirements for growth)

and is a major obstacle to all isolation procedures that require the growth of single microbial cells into colonies. Populations of intermediate density are generally more successful than individual organisms in the colonization of natural habitats. A well-studied example of this is the "minimum infectious dose" of pathogenic microbial populations. Usually thousands of pathogens are required to cause disease, as a single pathogen is rarely able to overcome host defenses. Cooperation occurs within the population because the semipermeable cell membranes of microorganisms are imperfect and tend to "leak" low-molecular-weight metabolic intermediates that are essential for biosynthesis and growth. In a population, a significant extracellular concentration of these metabolites is established that counteracts further loss and facilitates reabsorption. For a single cell or a very low density population, however, losses may exceed replacement rates and prevent growth. A substantial inoculum, that is, a sufficiently large population, is able to adjust to an initially unfavorable culture medium redox potential, whereas a single cell or very small population may be unable to do so. Such isolation difficulties can be remedied by preparing a sterile filtrate of spent enrichment culture medium and including this filtrate as a major constituent of the new medium on which single cells of fastidious microorganisms are to be isolated.

Colony formation by microbial populations is probably an adaptation based on cooperative interactions within a population. Even motile bacteria that could move away from each other often remain in colonies. Microcolonies, rather than individual microorganisms, are normally observed adhering to particles in nature. The association of a population within a colony allows for more efficient utilization of available resources. Some bacterial colonies even exhibit mass movement, occasionally rotating in place or migrating in a spiral path; such coordinated migration probably obtains beneficial results for the microorganisms within the colony as they seek new sources of nutrients.

Elaborate cooperative interactions within a population are evident in the case of the slime mold *Dictyostelium* (Clark and Steck 1979) (Figure 3.3). When food sources become limiting, the amoeboid cells of *Dictyostelium* swarm together to a central organism.

This swarming action is in response to the chemical stimulus of cyclic AMP being released, and it occurs in a pulsating wave motion as the stimulus to synthesize AMP is transmitted from proximal to distal cells. The cells unite to form a fruiting body and spores that subsequently disperse. Frequently, some spores reach habitats with a more abundant food supply via this mechanism, germinate, and resume an amoeboid life stage. Communication among members of this microbial population allows for cooperative searching and utilization of resources in the habitat. Similar cooperative interactions have been described for populations of myxobacteria (Shimkets 1990; Shapiro 1991; Dworkin 1996).

Cooperative interactions within populations can be particularly important when the population is using insoluble substrates such as lignin and cellulose. The production of extracellular enzymes by individual members of the population makes such substrates available for all members of the population. At low population densities, the soluble products liberated by such enzymes would be rapidly lost from the population by dilution, whereas at higher population densities, the resulting soluble products can be utilized with higher efficiency. As an example, myxobacteria feed predominantly on insoluble substrates, and they use their exoenzymes in a communal manner to solubilize these substrates. Density-dependent growth of *Myxococcus xanthus* on insoluble casein was demonstrated in laboratory experiments (Rosenberg et al. 1977). No growth occurred on casein at cell densities lower than $10^3$/mL, and the growth rate increased with increasing cell densities. This was not observed on prehydrolyzed casein. In addition to cooperative solubilization of substrates, organic acids produced by individuals within a population also can solubilize inorganic elements in certain habitats, such as soils or rock surfaces, making essential elements available for all members of a population.

Cooperation in a population can also function as a protective mechanism against hostile environmental factors. It is commonly observed in the laboratory that a given concentration of a metabolic inhibitor has less effect on a dense cell suspension than on a dilute one. Microbial populations within biofilms are

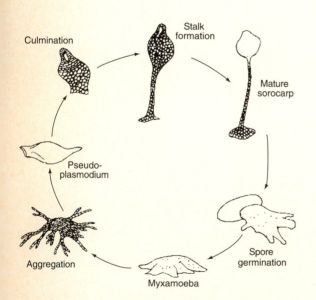

**Figure 3.3**
Life cycle of the slime mold *Dictyostelium* during which individual cells migrate together and form a single structure that aids in the survival of the population.

orders of magnitude more resistant to antimicrobial agents than suspended cells of the same organisms (Nickel et al. 1985; Shapiro 1991). In natural environments, with their exposures to ultraviolet light, high densities of populations probably shield some members from direct exposure, protecting them and allowing continued growth of the population. At high population densities, microorganisms are able to depress the freezing point of water, allowing for continued growth at temperatures that otherwise would preclude availability of liquid water.

Genetic exchange is another cooperative interaction that occurs within a population. Resistance to antibiotics and heavy metals and the ability to utilize unusual organic substrates are often genetically transmitted to other members of the population (Hardy 1981). This phenomenon allows the adaptive information that has arisen in one microorganism to be disseminated through a population. Genetic exchange is important in preventing overspecialization within a microbial population. Many exchange methods have evolved to permit this cooperative effort. These mechanisms include transformation, transduction, conjugation, and sexual spore formation. Even though such genetic exchange events occur only between two members of the population, they usually require high population densities. Bacterial populations, for example, generally require densities of greater than $10^5$/mL for a genetic exchange by conjugation; at lower population densities, the probability of a successful genetic exchange is very low, and the process generally is not significant. Sometimes, however, aggregate formation at low population densities may facilitate genetic exchange. Recipient cells of *Enterococcus faecalis* produce pheromones that induce plasmid-bearing donor cells to synthesize agglutinins and thus to form mating aggregates with recipient cells (Shapiro 1991).

## Negative Interactions

Negative interactions within a microbial population are called *competition*. Because members of a microbial population all use the same substrates and occupy the same ecological niche, if an individual within the population metabolizes a substrate molecule, then that molecule is not available for other members of the population. In natural habitats with low concentrations of available substrates, increased population densities cause increased competition for available resources. Within populations of predatory microorganisms competition occurs for available prey; within populations of parasitic microorganisms competition occurs for available host cells. Infection of a host cell by a member of a population effectively precludes further infection of that cell by other members of the population.

In addition to the direct vying for good sources of food, competition in its broad sense includes actual competition for available substrates, as well as other negative interactions, such as those that result from the accumulation of toxic substances produced by members of the population. Within a high-density population, metabolic products may accumulate to an inhibitory level. As discussed previously, the presence of "leaked" metabolic intermediates may represent a form of cooperation. However, the accumulation of such metabolic products as low-molecular-weight fatty acids and hydrogen sulfide ($H_2S$) constitutes a negative feedback mechanism; the accumulation may effectively limit further growth of some microbial populations even when substrate is still available. As examples of this type of competitive interaction, excessive $H_2S$ accumulation can limit further sulfate reduction; accumulation of lactic acid and other fatty acids can halt the activity of *Lactobacillus;* and the accumulation of ethanol stops further fermentation by *Saccharomyces.* Fatty acid accumulation during hydrocarbon biodegradation similarly can block further microbial metabolism of the hydrocarbon substrates (Atlas and Bartha 1973), and the accumulation of dichloroaniline from 3,4-dichloropropionanilide (propanil) catabolism can stop further growth of *Penicillium piscarium* (Bordeleau and Bartha 1971).

An interesting genetic basis for negative interactions is the occurrence of genes that code for peptides or proteins that have lethal functions (Figure 3.4) (Gerdes et al. 1986a, 1986b). Strains of *Escherichia coli,* for example, have the *hok* (host-killing) gene, which codes for a peptide (Hok) that damages trans-

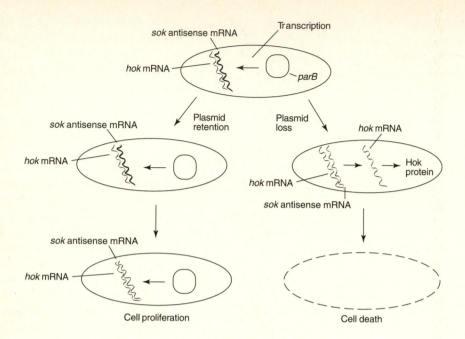

**Figure 3.4**

The *parB* locus of a plasmid in *E. coli* acts as both a suicide and antidote gene, so the plasmid must be maintained for the cell to survive. One strand of the DNA has the *hok* gene that encodes a polypeptide that kills the cell; if *hok* is expressed the cell dies. The other strand of the DNA has the *sok* gene, which produces an antisense mRNA. If the *sok* RNA binds to the *hok* mRNA, the Hok polypeptide is not produced. If *sok* RNA is not there, *hok* is translated. Because the *sok* mRNA has a shorter half-life than the *hok* mRNA, if the plasmid with *parB* is lost, Hok polypeptide is produced and the cell dies. As long as the cell maintains the plasmid with *parB*, production of *sok* RNA blocks the translation of *hok* mRNA and cell proliferation occurs.

membrane potential and leads to death of cells when *hok* is expressed. To prevent *hok* expression, these *E. coli* contain a gene called *sok* (suppression of killing) that codes for an antisense mRNA that blocks the expression of *hok*. As long as the cell is making the mRNA encoded by *sok,* the cell is protected. However, if the cell ceases to make the more labile *sok*-encoded mRNA, the more stable *hok* mRNA is expressed and the cell is killed. Both *hok* and *sok* are encoded on the same plasmids, so as long as the plasmids are retained, the cells of that population survive. If the plasmids are lost, however, the cells of that population self-destruct. This mechanism ensures that the surviving cells retain the plasmids, that is, it is a mechanism for plasmid survival. This may be impor-

tant for the overall long-term benefit of the population since these plasmids also contain genes for antibiotic resistance that otherwise might be lost, but in the short term the population density is limited because some cells (those that lose the plasmids with *hok* and *sok*) kill themselves.

Several other mechanisms of plasmid retention have also been reported (Yarmolinsky 1995). In one of these, the plasmid codes for both a DNA-cutting restriction enzyme and a DNA methylase that prevents this cutting by methylating the sensitive DNA site. The restriction enzyme is more stable than the DNA methylase. Upon loss of the plasmid, the DNA methylase decays and the unprotected DNA is cut by the restriction enzyme, leading to cell death. Beyond plasmid retention, the described "suicide mechanisms" present in a portion of a genetically heterogeneous population seem to benefit the population as a whole under starvation conditions. The starvation-induced "self-sacrifice" and autolysis of one part of the population aids the survival of the remaining cells. In streptomycetes and myxobacteria, the formation of aerial spores and fruiting bodies, respectively, appear to be subsidized by the programmed death, lysis, and utilization of the remaining vegetative cells.

## INTERACTIONS BETWEEN DIVERSE MICROBIAL POPULATIONS

Distinct microbial populations frequently interact with each other. The term *symbiosis* is used to denote any intimate relationship between two populations. In a global context all symbiotic relationships can be viewed as beneficial because they act to maintain ecological balance. Interactions among specific populations, however, are often viewed in a less generic sense. The categories used to describe these interactions represent a conceptual classification system; many specific cases are difficult to classify without ambiguity. Possible interactions between microbial populations can be recognized as negative interactions (competition and amensalism); positive interactions (commensalism, synergism, and mutualism); or interactions that are positive for one but negative for the other population (parasitism and predation). Table 3.1 summarizes the effects.

In simple communities, one or more of these interactions can be observed and studied. Within a complex natural biological community, all these possible interactions will probably occur between different populations. In established communities, positive interactions among autochthonous (indigenous) populations are likely to be more developed than in newer communities. Invaders of established communities are likely to encounter severe negative interactions with autochthonous populations. The negative interactions between populations act as feedback mechanisms that limit population densities. Positive interactions enhance the abilities of some populations to survive as part of the community within a particular habitat.

**Table 3.1**
Types of interactions between microbial populations

| Name of interaction | Effect of interaction | |
|---|---|---|
| | Population A | Population B |
| Neutralism | 0 | 0 |
| Commensalism | 0 | + |
| Synergism (protocooperation) | + | + |
| Mutualism (symbiosis) | + | + |
| Competition | − | − |
| Amensalism | 0 or + | − |
| Predation | + | − |
| Parasitism | + | − |

0 = no effect
+ = positive effect
− = negative effect

The development of positive interactions permits microorganisms to use available resources more efficiently and to occupy habitats that otherwise could not be inhabited. Mutualistic relationships between microbial populations create essentially new organisms capable of occupying niches that could not be occupied by either organism alone. Positive interactions between microbial populations are based on combined physical and metabolic capabilities that enhance growth and/or survival rates. Interactions between microbial populations also tend to dampen environmental stress. The negative interactions represent self-regulation mechanisms that limit population densities. In the long run, such negative interactions benefit the species by preventing overpopulation, destruction of the habitat, and extinction of those species (Bull and Slater 1982).

## Populations Within Biofilms

Biofilms form when microbial populations are enclosed within a matrix that facilitates adherence of cells to each other and/or to surfaces (Costerton et al. 1994, 1995; Denyer et al. 1993). Biofilms are important in the colonization of surfaces and are typically observed at such interfaces (Lawrence et al. 1995). In nature, biofilms contribute to the formation of mats of microorganisms with complex interacting communities (Stal 1994). During the process of adhesion, microbial cells alter their phenotypes in response to the proximity of a surface (Costerton et al. 1994, 1995). Microorganisms exhibit specific responses to the surface environment, including morphological changes and altered gene expression (Lawrence et al. 1995). Microbial interactions within biofilms include the complete range of potential positive and negative interactions that typically are defined in terms of substrate utilization.

In natural habitats biofilm populations are in constant flux. Populations are moving within the biofilm and new populations often displace the original ones so that there is a succession of surface-colonizing species. The succession is based on a sequence of physical and biological events, starting with the adsorption of organic films and closely followed by surface colonization by bacteria. In a process called *epibiosis,* the initial colonizing species are replaced as other organisms with evolutionarily defined requirements become involved with the surface consortium.

The initial attachment of bacteria to surfaces is a two-phase process that includes a reversible attachment phase and an irreversible attachment phase (Lawrence et al. 1995). Reversible attachment is exhibited by cells that attach to surfaces by a portion of the cell or flagellum while continuing to revolve. Specialized flagellar systems have evolved for colonization of different surface environments. Vibrios, for example, possess lateral flagella that provide a mechanism for attachment to surfaces and dispersal in high-viscosity environments, as well as polar flagella that are active in low-viscosity environments. Mixed flagellation provides vibrios with specific flagellar structures for both adherence and transport in a wide range of environments from open ocean to mucosal surfaces.

The development of multicellular biofilm communities involves specific cell-cell interactions, allowing microbial populations to coexist in environments where the individual populations otherwise would not. Different biofilm microorganisms respond to their specific microenvironmental conditions with different growth patterns, and a structurally complex mature biofilm gradually develops. Physiological cooperation is a major factor in shaping the structure and in establishing the eventual spatial relationships that make mature biofilms very efficient microbial communities adherent to surfaces. Within a biofilm the formation of chemically suitable microhabitats and the spatial positioning of syntrophic partners permit the interpopulation cooperation that results in metabolic activities beyond those performed by the individual populations. Various genes are derepressed within biofilms by adhesion to the surface, by conditions at the surface, or by growth in the biofilm mode. The biofilm matrix, which is typically composed of polysaccharides that may contain one or more anionic uronic acids, is densely concentrated around the microcolonies of cells that have produced these polymers and less densely distributed in the extensive spaces between these microcolonies.

Existence of microbial populations within a biofilm makes sustained metabolic cooperation possible. Individual cells within a mature multi-species biofilm typically live in a unique microenvironment where nutrients are provided by neighboring cells and by diffusion, where products are removed by the same processes, and where antagonists may be kept at a distance by diffusion barriers. Organisms first gaining access to newly exposed surfaces may physically exclude a potential competitor organism, and by virtue of such factors as site blocking may benefit from positioning and utilization of adsorbed nutrients. Within the biofilm, microorganisms produce and maintain chemical conditions that favor the growth of specific populations that otherwise might not survive. Chemical variations within the biofilm, such as pH and oxygen gradients, facilitate the survival of diverse fastidious bacteria, each with a unique range of metabolic capabilities (Wimpenny 1992). For example, anaerobic microorganisms, including methanogenic archaea and strictly anaerobic bacteria that are killed by exposure to molecular oxygen, can coexist in biofilms with obligately aerobic microorganisms. Algal-bacterial associations within biofilm communities are commonplace, with algae representing both sites of attachment and sources of nutrients. The heterotrophic bacteria utilize extracellular algal products.

Interactions between populations are a driving force in the evolution of community structure. In the following sections, we shall consider in more detail the types of interactions that can occur between microbial populations. The examples given are representative of the different types of interactions that take place between populations interacting in natural environments. Obviously, in natural environments where multiple populations coexist, the complexities of the interactions are much greater.

## Neutralism

The concept of neutralism implies a lack of interaction between two microbial populations. Neutralism cannot occur between populations having the same or overlapping functional roles within a community and is more likely between microbial populations with extremely different metabolic capabilities than between populations with similar capabilities. Because it is a negative proposition, it is difficult to demonstrate experimentally a total lack of interaction between two populations. Thus, examples for neutralism describe cases where interactions, if any, are of minimal importance.

Neutralism occurs between microbial populations that are spatially distant from each other. It is likely at low population densities where one microbial population does not sense the presence of another. Neutralism between microbial populations occurs in marine habitats and oligotrophic (low-nutrient) lake habitats where population densities are extremely low. In sediment or soil, it occurs when microbial populations occupy separate locations (microhabitats) on soil or sediment particles. Physical separation alone, however, does not ensure a relationship of neutralism. For example, a pathogenic microorganism may invade a plant root, resulting in the death of that plant and the destruction of the habitat of other microbial populations on the leaves of that plant. Even though there has been no direct contact between the two populations, the destruction of the leaf habitat by the root pathogen precludes a relationship of neutralism between the two populations.

Environmental conditions that do not permit active microbial growth favor neutralism. For example, microorganisms frozen in an ice matrix, such as in frozen food products, polar sea ice, or frozen freshwater lakes, are typically in a relationship of neutralism. Environmental conditions that favor the growth of microbial populations decrease or preclude the likelihood of neutralism. Neutralism often occurs between two microbial populations when both populations are outside their natural habitats and in environments where they cannot grow. For example, neutralism is probably the most common relationship between microbial populations in the atmosphere since all atmospheric microorganisms are allochthonous (nonindigenous) and do not naturally grow there.

Resting stages of microorganisms are more likely to exhibit a relationship of neutralism with other microbial populations than are actively growing vegetative cells. The low metabolic rates required for the maintenance of such resting structures do not force these organisms into competitive relationships for available resources with other microorganisms in the community. Production of spores, cysts, and similar resting bodies during periods of environmental stress, such as elevated temperature or drought, allows microbial populations to enter relationships of neutralism. In such situations, the only significant interaction is that with the environmental stress. The strategy for survival is to avoid interpopulation interactions during these times. When environmental conditions become favorable, the resting stages of these organisms can germinate, forming vegetative cells that can then engage in positive or negative relationships.

Resting stages of some microbial populations allow for temporal and spatial niches within a habitat, where temporary coexistence of otherwise competitive populations may occur. Some of these populations would be eliminated by competitive exclusion if such mechanisms did not exist. The formation of resting bodies does not, however, ensure neutralism with other microbial populations. Some microbial populations produce enzymes that can degrade the resting stages of other microbial populations. Many resting microbial stages, though, are resistant to negative interactions with other microorganisms. The complex outer layers of endospores are resistant to enzymatic attack by most microorganisms, as are fungal spore walls with high melanin contents. Such resistant structures allow resting stages to persist within habitats for long periods without being affected by negative interactions with other microorganisms.

## Commensalism

In a commensal relationship, one population benefits while the other remains unaffected. The term *commensalism* is derived from the Latin word *mensa* (table) and describes a relationship in which one organism lives off the "table scraps" of another one. Although commensal relationships are common between microbial populations, they are usually not obligatory. Commensalism is a unidirectional relationship between two populations; the unaffected population, by definition, does not benefit from, nor is it negatively affected by, the actions of the second population. The recipient population may need the benefit provided by the unaffected population, but it may also be able to receive the necessary assistance from other populations with comparable metabolic capabilities.

There are a number of physical and chemical bases for relationships of commensalism. Commensalism often results when the unaffected population, in the course of its normal growth and metabolism, modifies the habitat in such a way that another population benefits because the modified habitat is more suitable to its needs. For example, when a population of facultative anaerobes uses oxygen and lowers the oxygen tension, it creates a habitat suitable for the growth of obligate anaerobes. In such a habitat, the obligate anaerobes benefit from the metabolic activities of the facultative organisms. The facultative organisms remain unaffected by the relationship as long as the two populations do not compete for the same substrates. The occurrence of obligate anaerobes within microenvironments of predominantly aerobic habitats is dependent on such commensal relationships.

Production of growth factors forms the basis for many commensal relationships between microbial populations (Bell et al. 1974). Some microbial populations produce and excrete growth factors, such as vitamins and amino acids, that can be used by other microbial populations. For example, *Flavobacterium brevis* excretes cysteine, which *Legionella pneumophila* can use in aquatic habitats. In soil habitats, many bacteria depend upon the production of vitamins by other microbial populations. As long as the growth factors are produced in excess and excreted from the neutral organism in the relationship, the two populations can have a commensal relationship. The production of growth factors and their excretion into the environment allow fastidious microbial populations to develop in natural habitats.

The transformation of insoluble compounds to soluble compounds and the conversion of soluble compounds to gaseous compounds can also form the basis for a commensal relationship. The changes of state from solid to liquid and liquid to gas mobilize compounds so that they are moved to other habitats where they can benefit other microbial populations. For example, methane produced by bacterial populations in sediment can benefit methane-oxidizing populations in the overlying water column. Methanogenesis may result from a commensal relationship for some populations (Cappenberg 1975). Under certain conditions, *Desulfovibrio* can supply *Methanobacterium* with acetate and hydrogen from anaerobic respiration and fermentation, using sulfate and lactate to generate these products; *Methanobacterium* can then use the products from *Desulfovibrio* to reduce carbon dioxide to methane. Other examples include the production of hydrogen sulfide in buried sediment layers that can be used by photoautotrophic sulfur bacteria on the sediment surface or within a water column, and the transformation of soil-bound ammonia to nitrate by one bacterial population that allows the nitrogen to leach into the underlying soil column, where other soil microbial populations can then get their required nitrogen.

The activities of one microbial population can also make a compound available to another population without actually transforming the particular compound. For example, acids produced by one microbial population may release compounds that are bound or inaccessible to the second population. Such desorption processes are probably common in soil, where many compounds can be bonded to mineral particles or humic materials.

Another basis for commensalism between populations is the conversion of organic molecules by one population into substrates for other populations. Some fungi, for example, produce extracellular enzymes that convert complex polymeric compounds, such as cellulose, into simpler compounds, such as glucose. The simpler compounds can be used by populations of other microorganisms that do not possess the enzymes needed to utilize the complex organic molecules. In some cases, a competitive relationship develops for the available simpler substrates. In other cases, the relationship may be truly commensal. If excess solubilized substrates would be lost for the first population by dilution in the environment, their use by a second population is not detrimental to the first one.

Cometabolism, whereby an organism growing on a particular substrate gratuitously oxidizes a second substrate that it is unable to use as nutrient and energy source, is the basis for various commensal relationships. According to a strict definition of cometabolism, the second substrate is not assimilated by the primary organism, but the oxidation products are available for use by other microbial populations. For example, *Mycobacterium vaccae* is able to cometabolize cyclohexane while growing on propane; the cyclohexane is oxidized to cyclohexanol, which other bacterial populations can utilize (Beam and Perry 1974) (Figure 3.5). These bacterial populations benefit because they themselves are unable to metabolize intact cyclohexane; the *Mycobacterium* is unaffected since it does not assimilate the cyclohexane.

Yet another basis for commensal relationships is the removal or neutralization of a toxic material. The ability to destroy toxic factors is widespread in microbial communities. The oxidation of hydrogen sulfide by *Beggiatoa* is an example of detoxification that benefits H₂S-sensitive aerobic microbial populations. *Beggiatoa* is not known to benefit from its

relationship with the second population. Precipitation of heavy metals, such as mercury, by sulfate reducers provides an additional example of detoxification. Production of volatile mercuric compounds by bacterial populations in aquatic habitats removes this toxic metal from the habitat (Jeffries 1982).

Some microbial populations are able to detoxify compounds by immobilization. As an example of such a commensal relationship, *Leptothrix* reduces manganese concentrations in some habitats, permitting the growth of other microbial populations to which the higher manganese concentrations would be toxic.

In some cases, a microorganism may itself provide the suitable habitat that benefits a commensal partner. Bacteria are often observed on algal surfaces (Sieburth 1975) (Figure 3.6). Not only may the bacteria benefit from the metabolic activities of the algae, but their association with a surface enhances intrapopulation cooperation. In the particular example shown in Figure 3.6, the relationship may also be considered synergistic since this alga fails to grow normally in bacteria-free situations.

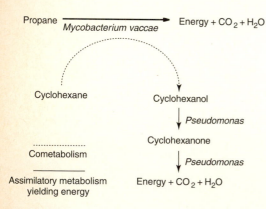

**Figure 3.5**

An example of commensalism based on cometabolism. Cyclohexane is cometabolized in the presence of propane by *Mycobacterium*, allowing for commensal growth of *Pseudomonas* on cyclohexane. (Source: Beam and Perry 1974.)

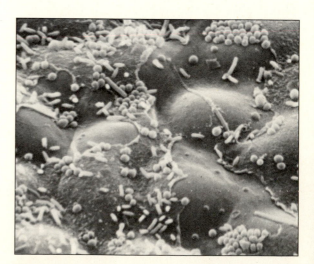

**Figure 3.6**

Epiphytic bacteria on the surface of *Ulva lactuca*. Such a relationship may be commensal with either population benefiting or synergistic with both populations benefiting. (Courtesy of P. W. Johnson and J. M. Sieburth. Source: Sieburth 1975, reprinted by permission, copyright University Park Press.)

## Synergism (Protocooperation)

A relationship of synergism between two microbial populations indicates that both populations benefit from the relationship, but unlike mutualism, to be described in the next section, the association is not an obligatory one. Both populations are capable of surviving in their natural environment on their own, although when initially formed, the association offers some mutual advantages. Synergistic relationships are also loose in the sense that one member population is often easily replaced by another. In some cases, it is difficult to determine whether one of the populations is indeed benefiting, and thus whether the relationship should be considered commensal or synergistic. In other cases, it is difficult to determine whether the relationship is obligatory and thus should be considered one of mutualism.

The term *syntrophism* is applied to the interaction of two or more populations that supply each other's nutritional needs. Figure 3.7 shows a theoretical example of cross-feeding, an example of syntrophism. Population 1 is able to metabolize compound A, forming compound B, but cannot go beyond this point without the cooperation of another population because it lacks the enzymes needed to bring about the next transformation in the pathway. Population 2 is unable to utilize compound A, but it can utilize compound B, forming compound C. Both populations 1 and 2 are able to carry out the metabolic steps subsequent to the formation of compound C, producing needed energy and end products that neither population could produce alone.

Syntrophism may allow microbial populations to perform activities, such as the synthesis of a product, that neither population could perform alone. The synergistic activities of two microbial populations may allow completion of a metabolic pathway that otherwise could not be completed. A classic example of such syntrophism is exhibited by *Enterococcus faecalis* and *Escherichia coli* (Gale 1940) (Figure 3.8). Neither organism alone is able to convert arginine to putrescine. *E. faecalis* is able to convert arginine to ornithine, which can then be utilized by the *E. coli* population to produce putrescine; *E. coli* alone is able

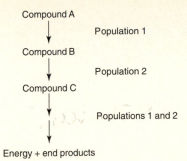

**Figure 3.7**
Synergistic relationship shown in cross-feeding.

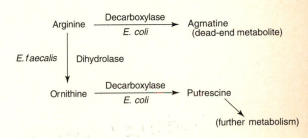

**Figure 3.8**
Classical example of synergistic relationship between *Enterococcus faecalis* and *Escherichia coli* that allows for production of putrescine from arginine. (Source: Gale 1940.)

to utilize arginine, producing agmatine, but cannot produce putrescine without assistance. Once putrescine is produced, both *E. coli* and *E. faecalis* can use it.

Relationships of syntrophism are frequently based on the ability of one population to supply growth factors for another population. In a minimal medium, *Lactobacillus arabinosus* and *E. faecalis* are able to grow together but not alone (Nurmikko 1956) (Figure 3.9). The synergistic relationship is based on the fact that *E. faecalis* requires folic acid, which is produced by *Lactobacillus,* and *Lactobacillus* requires phenylalanine, which is produced by *Enterococcus.* Together the organisms grow quite well. Similarly, cyclohexane can be degraded by a mixed population of a *Nocardia* species and a *Pseudomonas* species, but not by either population alone (Figure 3.10) (Slater 1978). The relationship is based on the ability of the

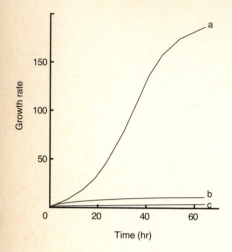

**Figure 3.9**
Synergistic growth of *Lactobacillus arabinosus* and *Enterococcus faecalis* in a medium lacking phenylalanine and folic acid. (a) Combined culture of *L. arabinosus* and *E. faecalis*. (b) *E. faecalis*, which requires folic acid, alone in culture. (c) *L. arabinosus*, which requires phenylalanine, alone in the culture. The two organisms mutually supply each other with required growth factors. (Source: Nurmikko 1956. Reprinted by permission of Birkhauser Verlag.)

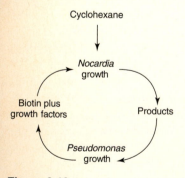

**Figure 3.10**
Synergistic degradation of cyclohexane by a *Nocardia* and a *Pseudomonas*. *Nocardia* supplies cyclohexane degradation products to *Pseudomonas*, which supplies *Nocardia* with biotin. (Source: Slater 1978. Reprinted by permission of Institute of Petroleum, London.)

*Nocardia* to metabolize cyclohexane, forming products that feed the *Pseudomonas* species. The *Pseudomonas* species produces biotin and growth factors required for the growth of the *Nocardia* species.

Other interesting examples of synergism are based on the abilities of *Chlorobium* species to fix carbon dioxide and to oxidize hydrogen sulfide (Figure 3.11) (Wolfe and Pfennig 1977). If there is an available source of hydrogen sulfide and carbon dioxide, *Chlorobium* is able to utilize light energy, producing organic matter. Given a supply of elemental sulfur and formate, *Spirillum* is able to produce hydrogen sulfide and carbon dioxide. Together, *Chlorobium* and *Spirillum* are able to supply each other's nutritional needs. The conversion of hydrogen sulfide to elemental sulfur by the *Chlorobium* species is a detoxifying step, as the hydrogen sulfide concentrations would otherwise kill the *Spirillum* species.

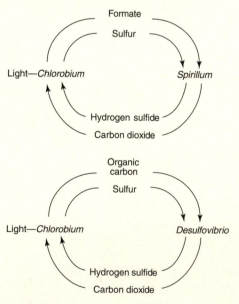

**Figure 3.11**
Synergistic relationships between *Chlorobium* and *Spirillum* (top) and *Chlorobium* and *Desulfovibrio* (bottom). The relationships are based on the cycling of C and S. *Chlorobium* reduces $CO_2$ and oxidizes $H_2S$; *Desulfovibrio* and *Spirillum* oxidize organic C and reduce sulfur to $H_2S$. (Source: Wolfe and Pfennig 1977. Reprinted by permission of American Society for Microbiology.)

*Chlorobium* and *Desulfovibrio* populations also exhibit such a relationship (Wolfe and Pfennig 1977). The *Desulfovibrio* population is able to supply *Chlorobium* with hydrogen sulfide and carbon dioxide; the *Chlorobium* population is able to supply *Desulfovibrio* with sulfate and organic matter required for metabolism by the *Desulfovibrio* and to remove toxic concentrations of hydrogen sulfide. A similar relationship should occur between sulfate-reducing and green sulfur bacteria. The cycling of carbon and sulfur from oxidized to reduced states by these organisms forms a closed loop and allows both organisms to metabolize vigorously in habitats where, on their own, they would be subject to substrate limitation and product inhibition.

There are similar synergistic relationships between bacterial populations involved in the cycling of nitrogen. For example, heterotrophic pseudomonads are chemotactically attracted to organic excretions formed by the heterocysts of *Anabaena spiroides* and related species (Pearl 1987; Pearl and Gallucci 1985) (Figure 3.12). They form dense aggregates around the heterocyst, while few bacteria are associated with the photosynthetic cells of the filament. The pseudomonads oxidize the excreted organics and at the same time

stimulate nitrogenase activity. The most likely mechanism for this stimulation is the lowering of oxygen concentration around the oxygen-sensitive nitrogenase. Such relationships are important in global biogeochemical cycling.

Chemotaxis can play an important role in the association of algae and bacteria in aquatic habitats (Chet and Mitchell 1976; Jones 1982). Like the heterocysts of cyanobacteria, algae excrete organic compounds, some of which attract bacterial populations. The bacteria produce vitamins that are used by the algae. Extracellular products of algae have been shown to stimulate, selectively, certain populations of marine bacteria, enabling algae to attract and form associations with specific bacterial populations. Epiphytic bacteria are often observed on the surfaces of algae. The relationship between epiphytic bacteria and algae may be based on the ability of the alga to utilize light and produce organic compounds and oxygen for the aerobic heterotrophic metabolism of the bacteria (Figure 3.13). The bacteria, in turn, mineralize excreted organic matter, supplying the algae with carbon dioxide and, sometimes, growth factors needed for phototrophic assimilation. Bacteria can also improve algal growth by removing oxygen (Mouget et al. 1995).

Some relationships of synergism are based on the ability of a second population to accelerate the growth rate of the first one. For example, some *Pseudomonas* species can grow on orcinol but show a higher affinity for this substrate and grow more rapidly in the presence of other bacterial populations (Slater 1978) (Figure 3.14). The secondary populations, which cannot

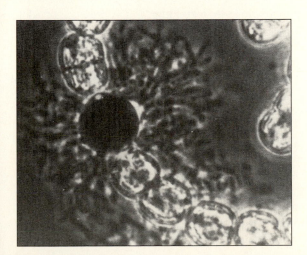

**Figure 3.12**
*Anabaena spiroides* heterocyst (dark cell) surrounded by attached heterotrophic bacteria. (Source: Pearl 1987, reprinted by permission of Springer-Verlag.)

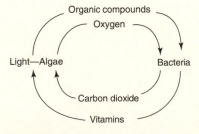

**Figure 3.13**
Synergistic relationship between algae and epiphytic bacteria based on carbon and oxygen cycling.

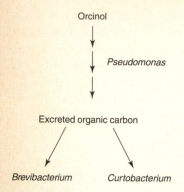

**Figure 3.14**
Synergistic relationship between an orcinol-utilizing
*Pseudomonas* population and two secondary populations,
based on acceleration of the growth rate of the primary
population by the secondary ones. (Source: Slater 1978.
Reprinted by permission of Institute of Petroleum, London.)

utilize orcinol alone, benefit because they are able to
use the excreted organic compounds produced by the
*Pseudomonas.* The *Pseudomonas* species benefits
because its growth rate is accelerated, presumably by
the removal of the excreted organic compounds that
otherwise would act through a negative feedback
mechanism to repress catabolic activity.

Some synergistic relationships allow microorganisms to produce enzymes that are not produced by
either population alone. For example, populations of
closely related *Pseudomonas* have been found to
produce lecithinase when grown together, whereas
neither strain produces lecithinase when it is growing
alone (Bates and Liu 1963). The production of
lecithinase allows both populations to benefit from
the utilization of lecithin. Similarly, some mixed
microbial populations produce cellulase, whereas the
individual populations are unable to attack cellulose.

Several important degradation pathways of agricultural pesticides involve synergistic relationships.
*Arthrobacter* and *Streptomyces* strains isolated from
soil are capable of completely degrading the
organophosphate insecticide diazinon and can grow
on this compound as the only source of carbon and
energy (Gunner and Zuckerman 1968). This is
accomplished by synergistic attack; alone neither culture can mineralize the pyrimidinyl ring of diazinon

or grow on this compound. In a chemostat enrichment culture, *Pseudomonas stutzeri* is capable of
cleaving the organophosphate insecticide parathion to
*p*-nitrophenol and diethylthiophosphate, but it is not
capable of utilizing either of the resulting moieties
(Munnecke and Hsieh 1976). *Pseudomonas aeruginosa* can mineralize the *p*-nitrophenol but is incapable of attacking intact parathion. Synergistically,
the two-component enrichment degrades parathion
with high efficiency, *P. stutzeri* apparently utilizing
products excreted by *P. aeruginosa.*

More complex examples of synergism are based
on the simultaneous removal of toxic factors and production of usable substrates. Two soil fungi, *Penicillium piscarium* and *Geotrichum candidum,* are capable of synergistically degrading and detoxifying the
agricultural herbicide propanil (Bordeleau and Bartha
1971) (Figure 3.15). *P. piscarium* cleaves propanil to
propionic acid and 3,4-dichloroaniline. It uses propionic acid as a carbon and energy source, but is unable
to process the toxic 3,4-dichloroaniline product any
further. *G. candidum,* while unable to attack propanil,
detoxifies 3,4-dichloroaniline by peroxidatic condensation to 3,3′,4,4′-tetrachloroazobenzene and other
azo products. These end products are less toxic to
these soil fungi than either 3,4-dichloroaniline or the
parent herbicide, permitting, in the presence of additional carbon sources, increased growth yields for
both fungal populations. Such mutual synergistic
growth stimulation occurs only in the presence of the
herbicide. In the absence of the herbicide, the two
fungi compete for available nutrient resources and
consequently decrease each other's growth yield.

Archaeal populations involved in methane production (methanogens) have interesting synergistic relationships with bacterial and other microbial populations
(Zeikus 1977; Ferry 1993) (Figure 3.16). The names of
these bacterial genera indicate their syntrophic relationships with $H_2$-consuming methanogenic archaea. *Syntrophomonas* species oxidize butyric acid and caproic
acid to acetate and $H_2$; members of this genus also oxidize valeric acid and enanthic acid to acetate, $CO_2$, and
$H_2$. *Syntrophobacter* oxidizes propionic acid to acetate,
$CO_2$, and $H_2$. The acetate and $H_2$ produced by these
bacteria are used by methanogenic archaea to produce

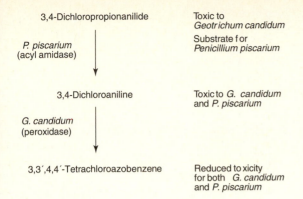

3,4-Dichloropropionanilide — Toxic to *Geotrichum candidum*

Substrate for *Penicillium piscarium*

*P. piscarium* (acyl amidase)

3,4-Dichloroaniline — Toxic to *G. candidum* and *P. piscarium*

*G. candidum* (peroxidase)

3,3′,4,4′-Tetrachloroazobenzene — Reduced toxicity for both *G. candidum* and *P. piscarium*

**Figure 3.15**
Synergistic degradation and detoxification of the herbicide 3,4-dichloropropionanilide (propanil) by two soil fungi. (Source: Bordeleau and Bartha 1971.)

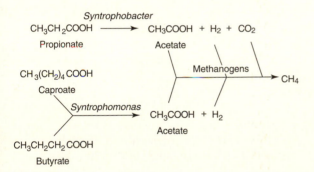

**Figure 3.16**
Metabolism of low-molecular-weight fatty acids, such as propionate by *Syntrophobacter* and caproate and butyrate by *Syntrophomonas,* produces acetate, hydrogen, and carbon dioxide, which are used by methanogenic archaea. The result of this syntrophic relationship is the overall conversion of fatty acids to methane.

methane. Methanogens have novel coenzymes and pathways that use hydrogen to reduce carbon dioxide or in some cases acetate to form methane (Deppenmeier et al. 1996). The $H_2$ heterodisulfide oxidoreductase, the $F_{420}$:$H_2$ heterodisulfide oxidoreductase, and the CO:heterodisulfide oxidoreductase are novel systems that generate a protonmotive force by redox-potential-driven $H^+$ translocation. The methytetrahydromethanopterin:coenzyme M methyltransferase is a unique, reversible sodium ion pump that couples methyl transfer with the transport of $Na^+$ across the cytoplasmic membrane. Formylmethanofuran dehydrogenase is a reversible ion pump that catalyzes formylation and deformylation of methanofuran. The pathways are coupled to the generation of an electrochemical sodium ion gradient and an electrochemical proton gradient that are used directly for ATP synthesis via membrane-integral ATP synthases. The metabolism of the methanogens maintains very low concentrations of $H_2$. The removal of the $H_2$ end product draws the equilibrium of fatty acid fermentation toward additional $H_2$ production, increasing the growth rates of *Syntrophomonas* and *Syntrophobacter* species. It takes special hydrogen removal measures to cultivate these fermenters in the absence of methanogens (Stams et al. 1993).

Although they mediate the ultimate anaerobic decomposition of cellulosic plant residues in lake sediments, swamps, bogs, and in the digestive tracts of various animals, the substrate range of methanogenic archaea is extremely limited. The principal metabolic reaction is the reduction of $CO_2$ with $H_2$ to $CH_4$. The $CO_2$ and $H_2$ are produced in fermentation reactions. The $CH_4$ and residual $CO_2$ are evolved as "biogas" or "marsh gas." Only CO, formate, methylamines, methanol, and acetate are used as additional carbon sources by some methanogens. Because of this narrow substrate range, methanogens rely on anaerobic cellulose degraders to form glucose and other fermentable carbohydrates and on mixed acid fermenters to form a range of short-chain fatty acids. These are fermented further to $H_2$, $CO_2$, and other products by bacteria very closely syntrophic with methanogens. *Methanobacterium bryantii* (formerly *M. omelianskii*) was kept in culture collection for 26 years after its original description in 1941 before it was recognized as the syntrophic association of the methanogen proper and a fermentative "S" organism (Wolin and Miller 1982). This and similar syntrophic fermenters produce $H_2$, oxidized fatty acid, and/or $CO_2$ (Figure 3.17) but are able to do this only if the evolved hydrogen is removed efficiently and does not accumulate to inhibitory concentrations. By reducing $CO_2$ to $CH_4$, the methanogen fulfills this function. The "S" organism and similar syntrophic fermenters

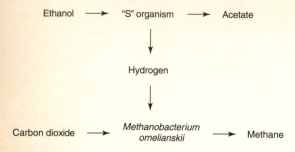

**Figure 3.17**
Mutualism based on hydrogen transfer in methanogens. (Source: Slater 1978. Reprinted by permission of Institute of Petroleum, London.)

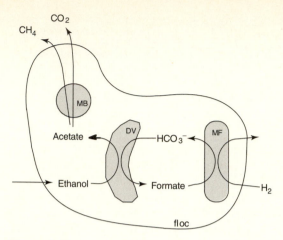

**Figure 3.18**
Model of a three-membered syntrophic association involved in the anaerobic digestion of a whey effluent to methane and carbon dioxide. Within the floc, *Desulfovibrio vulgaris* (DV) converts ethanol to acetate, coupled to the reduction of bicarbonate to formate. The formate is transferred to *Methanobacterium formicicum* (MF), which releases methane. The acetate generated during ethanol oxidation is metabolized by an acetoclastic methanogen, such as *Mesthanosarcina barkeri* (MB), to methane and carbon dioxide. (Source: Thiele and Zeikus 1988.)

were later classified as the *Syntrophomonas* and *Syntrophobacter* genera. Both of these bacteria are hydrogen producers and require the presence of the methanogen as hydrogen removers (Balows et al. 1992; Ferry 1993).

Syntrophic reactions are facilitated by bacterial aggregate (floc) formations that bring the participants into intimate contact with each other. In the anaerobic digestion of a whey effluent, lactate and ethanol were converted to methane by a three-membered syntrophic association (Thiele and Zeikus 1988). As shown in Figure 3.18, in the floc, the bacterium *Desulfovibrio vulgaris* generates acetate and formate from ethanol and bicarbonate. The formate serves as an interspecies electron and hydrogen transfer agent to the archaean *M. formicicum* that evolves methane, shuttling back bicarbonate to *D. vulgaris* for reduction to formate. The acetate generated in the ethanol oxidation process is cleaved by acetoclastic methanogens to methane and $CO_2$. In this system, the cleavage of formate to $CO_2$ and $H_2$ plays only a negligible role and is performed by bacteria not associated with the floc.

## Mutualism

Mutualistic relationships between populations can be considered extended synergism. Mutualism is an obligatory relationship between two populations that benefits both populations. A mutualistic relationship is highly specific—one member of the association

ordinarily cannot be replaced by another related species. Historically mutualism also has been called *symbiosis,* and the term is still used to describe some instances of a mutualistic relationship. For example, the relationship between nitrogen-fixing bacteria and certain plants has been called *nitrogen-fixing symbiosis* rather than *nitrogen-fixing mutualism.* The latter would be a more precise contemporary term as ecologists now use *symbiosis* to indicate any sustained interpopulation interaction.

Mutualism requires close physical proximity between the interacting populations. Relationships of mutualism allow organisms to exist in habitats that could not be occupied by either population alone. This does not exclude the possibility that the populations may exist separately in other habitats. The metabolic activities and physiological tolerances of populations involved in mutualistic relationships are normally quite different from those of either population by itself. Mutualistic relationships between microorganisms allow the microorganisms to act as if they were a single organism with a unique identity. According to the theory of serial symbiosis, some mutualistic endosymbiotic relationships had key roles in the evolution of higher organisms (Margulis 1971).

**Lichens**   The relationships between certain algae or cyanobacteria and fungi that result in the formation of lichens are probably the most outstanding examples of mutualistic, intermicrobial relationships (Lamb 1959; Ahmadjian 1963, 1967, 1993; Hale 1974) (Figure 3.19). Morphologically, there are three major types of lichens. Crustose lichens adhere closely to their substrate; foliose lichens are leafy in form and are attached to their substrate more loosely; fruticose lichens often consist of hollow upright stalks and are the least attached to their substrates.

Lichens are composed of a primary producer (the phycobiont) and a consumer (the mycobiont). The phycobiont uses light energy and produces organic compounds that are used by the mycobiont. The mycobiont provides a form of protection and mineral nutrient transport for the phycobiont. In some cases, the mycobiont also makes growth factors available to the phycobiont. The algal and fungal members of the lichen form distinct layers that function as primitive tissues. The phycobiont may be a member of the cyanobacteria, the Chlorophycophyta, or the Xanthophycophyta; the green alga *Trebouxia* and the cyanobacterium *Nostoc* are very common phycobionts

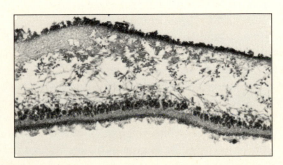

**Figure 3.19**
Photomicrograph of a lichen thallus showing outer fungal layers and inner algal layers. (Courtesy of Carolina Biological Supply Co.)

in lichens. The mycobiont is typically an ascomycete or a basidiomycete, but a few zygomycetes also form lichen associations. An analysis of DNA homologies among lichen-forming fungi indicates that they fall into at least five separate groups (Gargas et al. 1995). This makes it likely that lichen associations have at least five separate evolutionary origins. In contemporary lichens, a specificity in partner selection is evident but not absolute; a given algal species may be able to form a lichen association with any of several compatible fungal species and vice versa, and in some lichens multiple phycobiont and/or mycobiont populations may be present.

Although the lichen represents a tight association between phycobiont and mycobiont, it is possible to dissociate and, in some cases, to reassociate the mutualistic populations. During reassociation of the lichen, which must be carried out under carefully controlled conditions, the flattened portions of the fungal hyphae (appressoria) make contact with the algal cells; if the reassociation is successful, all the structures typical of the lichen thallus are reestablished, including fruiting bodies and soredia, which are algal cells surrounded by mycelial filaments and which act as "spores" of the lichen association (Ahmadjian et al. 1978). Studies on lichen association suggest that the lichen symbiosis is actually a case of controlled parasitism in which the alga has developed a degree of resistance to the parasitic fungus, such that the percentage of algal cells killed is balanced by the production of new cells (Ahmadjian 1982).

Lichens grow very slowly but are able to colonize habitats that do not permit the growth of other microorganisms (Ahmadjian 1993). Most lichens are resistant to extremes of temperature and drying, enabling them to grow in hostile habitats such as on rock surfaces. Lichens also produce organic acids that solubilize rock minerals, aiding their growth on rocks. Lichens have been found growing in such inhospitable habitats as within rocks in the Antarctic dry valleys (Friedmann 1982; Nienow and Friedmann 1993).

Some lichens are able to fix atmospheric nitrogen, and in some habitats they are an important source of combined nitrogen. For example, in tundra soils the lichen *Peltigera*, containing the cyanobacterium *Nostoc,* provides a major source of fixed nitrogen for the biological community. Nitrogen-fixing lichens growing in the forest canopy provide fixed forms of nitrogen for the underlying vegetation; during rainstorms the fixed forms of nitrogen are leached from the lichens and washed to the forest floor, where the nitrogen is taken up by plant roots (Denison 1973).

The mutualistic association in a lichen is very delicately balanced and can be disrupted by environmental changes (Gilbert 1969). Although lichens are able to occupy some hostile habitats, they are particularly sensitive to industrial air pollutants and have been disappearing from industrialized areas (Figure 3.20). It appears that the sulfur dioxide in the atmosphere is inhibitory to the lichens, probably because it inhibits the phycobiont. The reduced efficiency of photosynthetic activity of the phycobiont allows the mycobiont to overgrow it and leads to the elimination of the mutualistic relationship. Following destruction of the phycobiont, the fungus is unable to survive alone and is also eliminated from the habitat.

**Endosymbionts of Protozoa**    As with lichens, interesting mutualistic relationships exist between populations of algae and protozoa. *Paramecium* can host numerous cells of the alga *Chlorella* within its cytoplasm (Ball 1969). The alga provides the protozoan with organic carbon and oxygen, and the protozoan

presumably provides the alga with protection, motility, carbon dioxide, and perhaps other growth factors. The presence of the *Chlorella* within the ciliate allows the protozoan to move into anaerobic habitats as long as there is sufficient light; without the alga the protozoan could not enter and survive in such habitats. Similarly, some foraminiferans enter into mutualistic relationships with Pyrrophycophyta or Chrysophycophyta; the presence of the algae confers a red color on the protozoa (Taylor 1982). Presumably, the mutualistic relationship is based on the ability of the alga to supply oxygen and photosynthate and on the ability of the foraminiferan to protect the algal partner from grazers. Under normal environmental conditions, such mutualistic relationships between algae and protozoa persist; but if stressed, for instance by a prolonged absence of light, the protozoan population may digest the algal population.

Many other protozoa are hosts to endosymbiotic algae and cyanobacteria. Each protozoan can contain 50–100 algal cells. The algae found within freshwater protozoa normally belong to the Chlorophycophyta and are called zoochlorellae. The endosymbiotic algae of marine protozoa are most frequently dinoflagellates (Pyrrophycophyta) but can be Chrysophycophyta; these endozoic marine algae are called zooxanthellae. Endozoic cyanobacteria, which occur in both freshwater and marine protozoa, are called cyanellae.

The bacterial nature of many of the endosymbionts of protozoans has been established by electron microscopic examination, but many of the observable bacteria have yet to be isolated and cultured (Preer and Preer 1984). Some multiply within the nucleus of the protozoan, others within the cytoplasm. The bacterial endosymbiont appears to contribute to the nutritional requirements of the protozoan. In the case of the flagellate protozoans *Blastocrithidia* and *Crithidia,* the bacterial endosymbiont provides hemin and other growth factors to the protozoa; populations of these protozoa lacking endosymbiotic bacteria require external sources of these growth factors (Chang and Trager 1974).

One of the most interesting mutualistic relationships between a protozoan and a bacterium is between *Paramecium aurelia* and a *Caedibacter* endosym-

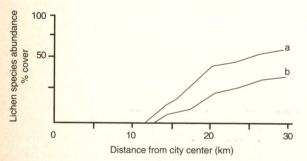

**Figure 3.20**
Disappearance of lichens from cities due to air pollution, showing changes in the lichen cover of ash trees moving away from Newcastle upon Tyne, England, to the west. (a) Combined cover of all sensitive lichens. (b) Cover of a single dominant lichen species. (Source: Gilbert 1969. Reprinted by permission of Centre for Agricultural Publications and Documentation, Wageningen, The Netherlands.)

biont, formerly known as a kappa particle (Sonneborn 1959; Preer 1981). *P. aurelia* populations occur in two forms: killers and sensitives. Killer *P. aurelia* populations contain endosymbionts; the sensitive strains lack the endosymbionts. The nature of the toxic substance associated with killer strains and the mechanisms by which the presence of the endosymbiont confers immunity are not fully known. All *Caedibacter* endosymbionts that confer the killer trait exhibit a strongly refractile inclusion body, known as an R body. The genetic information for the R body is coded on a *Caedibacter* plasmid. Although the R body itself does not appear to be the toxin, evidence indicates that the R body and the toxin are specified by the same coding region of the plasmid; it also appears that the R body is essential for the expression of the killer trait (Dilts and Quackenbush 1986). The presence of *Caedibacter* endosymbionts gives an advantage to killer strains in competition with sensitive strains. The obligately endosymbiotic *Caedibacter* strains are nutritionally dependent on their protozoan host.

Endosymbiotic methanogens have been found in anaerobic ciliate protozoa living within the rumen. These mutualistic methanogenic archaea have been identified by gene probe detection of specific rRNA nucleotide sequences and shown to be *Methanobacterium*, *Methanocorpusculum*, and *Methanoplanus* species that are different from free-living methanogens (Heckmann and Görtz 1992; Van Bruggen et al. 1986). In these relationships, intracellular methanogens appear to be much more numerous than those attached to the external cell surfaces of ciliate protozoa (Figure 3.21). It is likely that endosymbiotic methanogens can directly use molecular hydrogen produced by the ciliate protozoan—many anaerobic protozoa have organelles that generate hydrogen as part of the protozoan cellular energy-generating metabolism. There appear to be morphological interactions between the endosymbiotic methanogens and the protozoa that facilitate material exchange.

**Other Mutualistic Relationships**    The interaction of temperate phage and bacterial populations that establish a state of lysogeny is another relationship that can be viewed as mutualism. The genetic information

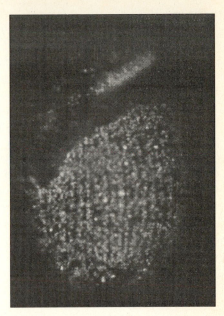

**Figure 3.21**
Micrograph showing fluorescing methanogens within a ciliate protozoan. The symbiotic methanogenic archaea are arranged in parallel lines along the cilia of the protozoan. (Source: Heckmann and Görtz 1992.)

of the phage is incorporated into the genome of the bacterial population. This provides a mechanism of survival for the phage in a dormant state over a long period. Temperate or defective phage do not result in the lysis of the host bacterial populations under normal conditions. The presence of DNA from a lysogenic phage can be difficult to detect in a host population. The addition of the phage DNA to the bacterial genome adds genetic information and capability to the bacterial population. Bacteria harboring lysogenic phage sometimes exhibit greater virulence (infectivity) or produce enzymes that are absent in uninfected bacterial populations. The relationship between temperate phage and bacteria also provides a mechanism for genetic exchange of bacterial DNA via transduction. Bacterial populations harboring lysogenic phage may acquire a competitive advantage over other bacterial populations if the harbored phage acts toward these in a lytic manner. Survival of both the phage and the lysogenized bacterium is enhanced by the relationship.

## Competition

In contrast to positive interactions, competition represents a negative relationship between two populations in which both populations are adversely affected with respect to their survival and growth (Veldkamp et al. 1984). The populations may achieve lower maximal densities or lower growth rates than they would have in the absence of competition. Competition occurs when two populations use the same resource, whether space or a limiting nutrient. In this section, only competition for a resource will be discussed. Interference or inhibition via chemical substances will be discussed separately under amensalism. Competition may occur for any growth-limiting resource. Available sources of carbon, nitrogen, phosphate, oxygen, iron growth factors, water, and so on are all resources for which microbial populations may compete.

Competition tends to bring about ecological separation of closely related populations. This is known as the competitive exclusion principle (Gause 1934, 1935; Fredrickson and Stephanopoulos 1981). Competitive exclusion precludes two populations from occupying exactly the same niche, because one will win the competition and the other will be eliminated; populations may coexist, however, if the populations can avoid absolute direct competition by using different resources at different times.

Gause (1934) showed a classic example of competitive exclusion experimentally by using populations of two closely related ciliated protozoans, *Paramecium caudatum* and *P. aurelia* (Figure 3.22). Individually, with an adequate supply of bacterial prey, both protozoan populations were able to grow and maintain a constant population level. When the protozoans were placed together, however, *P. aurelia* alone survived after 16 days. Neither organism attacked the other or secreted toxic substances; rather, *P. aurelia* exhibited the more rapid growth rate and thus outcompeted *P. caudatum* for available food. In contrast, a mixture of *P. caudatum* and *P. bursaria* were able to survive and reach a stable equilibrium even when grown together. They competed for the same food source, but the two populations occupied different regions of the culture flask. Thus, the

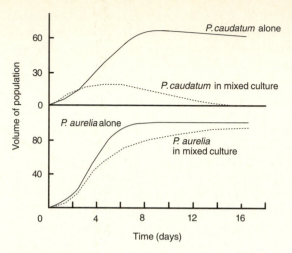

**Figure 3.22**
Competition between two protozoa that inhabit similar niches. In mixed culture *Paramecium aurelia* displaces *P. caudatum*. (Source: Gause 1934. Reprinted by permission, copyright 1934 Williams & Wilkins.)

habitats of *P. caudatum* and *P. bursaria* were sufficiently different to allow the two species to coexist although they had overlapping niches based on their common food source. The ability to occupy different habitats provided a mechanism that minimized competition and prevented extinction of one of the species. This experiment is a prime example of how microorganisms have been used to demonstrate an ecological principle—namely the principle of competitive exclusion.

Experiments in which microorganisms are grown in flow-through growth chambers called chemostats also have been used to demonstrate the principle of competitive exclusion (Veldkamp et al. 1984). Under limiting conditions, a single bacterial population will survive in a chemostat, and other populations competing for the primary resource will be excluded from the system. The population with the highest intrinsic growth rate under the experimental conditions is the one that survives, and populations with lower intrinsic growth rates become extinct. This does not occur, however, if there is a wall effect allowing a population to adhere to the experimental chamber, preventing it from being washed out of the system, or if synergistic or mutualistic interactions supersede competition.

Intrinsic growth rates of competing populations vary under different environmental conditions, explaining the coexistence of populations in the same habitat competing for the same resources. For example, in marine habitats, populations of psychrophilic and psychrotrophic bacteria are found together even though both populations may be competing for the same low concentrations of organic nutrients (Harder and Veldkamp 1971). At low temperatures, the psychrophilic populations exhibit higher intrinsic growth rates, and given sufficient time they would exclude the psychrotrophic populations. At higher temperatures, however, the psychrotrophic populations exhibit the higher intrinsic growth rate and the psychrophilic populations would be excluded. In habitats of varying temperature regimes, the advantage shifts back and forth, leading to seasonal shifts in proportions of psychrotrophic and psychrophilic populations within natural aquatic habitats. In some instances, bacterial populations are excluded from the habitat during periods when temperature or other environmental factors do not allow them to compete successfully with other populations because of their lower intrinsic growth rates. Under different environmental conditions, these same bacterial populations may compete successfully and even become dominant.

Studies indicate that under varying environmental conditions, anoxyphotobacteria competing for the same substrates coexist (Table 3.2) (van Gemerden 1974). *Chromatium vinosum* was shown to outcompete and lead to the exclusion of *C. weissei* when growing in continuous light with sulfide as the growth-rate-limiting substrate. The specific growth rate of *C. vinosum* exceeded that of *C. weissei* regardless of the sulfide concentrations. However, with intermittent illumination, the organisms showed balanced coexistence when grown in continuous culture. The relative proportion of *C. vinosum* was found to be positively correlated to the length of the light period, and the relative proportion of the *C. weissei* was positively correlated to the length of the dark period. The coexistence is explained by the fact that during the light period both strains grow with most of the sulfide being oxidized by the *C. vinosum;* during the dark period, sulfide accumulates, and upon illumination the *C. weissei* oxidizes the greater portion of the accumulated sulfide. The alternation of light and dark periods thus oscillates the balance between the

**Table 3.2**
Relative abundance of *Chromatium vinosum* and *Chromatium weissei* during steady-state coexistence in relation to the light regime

| Illumination regime | Organism | Relative abundance (%) | |
|---|---|---|---|
| | | Inoculum | During steady state |
| Continuous light | *C. vinosum* | 10 | 100 |
| Continuous light | *C. weissei* | 90 | 0 |
| 18 hr light | *C. vinosum* | 30 | 100 |
| 6 hr dark | *C. weissei* | 70 | 0 |
| 6 hr light | *C. vinosum* | 20 | 63 |
| 6 hr dark | *C. weissei* | 80 | 37 |
| 4 hr light | *C. vinosum* | 60 | 30 |
| 8 hr dark | *C. weissei* | 40 | 70 |

Source: van Gemerden 1974.

two populations, allowing them to coexist. Similarly, the daily and seasonal variations in environmental conditions of a habitat lead to temporal oscillations in the success or displacement of competing populations. As long as competitive displacement does not go to completion, these fluctuations can continue.

Competition within natural habitats is complex as organisms are competing for different resources, some of which may be essential and others of which may enhance growth rates. Tilman (1982) developed a mechanistic resource-ratio theory of competition to help understand the outcome of such complex competitive interactions. The applicability of resource-ratio theory to microorganisms has been reviewed by Smith (1993). Resource-ratio theory recognizes that organisms require resources for their growth and reproduction; that different species, as well as different phenotypic strains within a given species, frequently differ significantly in their efficiency of uptake and utilization of potentially growth-limiting resources; and that when such physiological differences exist, they can result in variations in competitive ability among the organisms sharing these resources (Smith 1993). When the quantitative requirements for resources and the mortality rates are known for each species, resource-ratio theory provides a framework that can be used to predict the outcome of competitive interactions between them. Resource competition theory suggests that the outcome of microbial competition can be predicted from $R^*$, the steady-state concentration of growth-limiting resource at which per capita growth rate ($\mu$) of the bacteria of the bacterial population just balances its per capita mortality rate ($m$) according to the equation

$$R^* = \frac{mK_s}{(\mu_{max} - m)}$$

where $R$ is the concentration of a growth-limiting resource, $\mu_{max}$ is the maximum per capita growth rate under conditions of resource saturation, and $Ks$ is the resource concentration at which growth occurs at half the maximum rate.

Studies with algae have supported the resource-based competition theory (Tilman 1976; Smith 1993). The ability of the $R^*$ criterion to predict the outcome

of resource competition has been well-demonstrated experimentally (Smith 1993). For example, the dependence of competitive outcome on $R^*$ is evident in the results of Harder and Veldkamp (1971), who examined competition for lactate between an obligate psychrophilic *Pseudomonas* species and a facultative psychrophilic (psychrotrophic) *Spirillum* species at two dilution rates. In experiments carried out at 16°C, the *Spirillum* species was the superior competitor at both dilution rates because of its consistently lower $R^*$ for lactate. As predicted by resource-ratio theory, this example shows that simple competition between two or more bacteria for one limiting resource—such as light, inorganic compounds, or organic growth substrates—results in the survival of only the competitively dominant species.

Other outcomes of ecological competition, including stable coexistence, have been observed in other laboratory studies employing two species of freshwater diatoms that were potentially limited by phosphate and silicate (Tilman 1976). The relative abundances of these nutrients determined the outcome of competition; coexistence occurred only when the growth rates of both species were limited by different resources. If only one nutrient was limiting, competitive displacement occurred, with the population best able to acquire and utilize the limiting resource displacing the competing species. The algae used in these studies were the diatoms *Asterionella formosa* and *Cyclotella meneghiniana*. If both species were limited by phosphate, *A. formosa* displaced *C. meneghiniana*. Under conditions of silicate limitation, the *C. meneghiniana* population displaced *A. formosa*. Competition of two suspension-feeding protozoan populations for growing bacterial populations in continuous culture can result in coexistence if one population grows faster than the second in one range of resource density and the opposite occurs in another range of resource density (Baltzis and Fredrickson 1984).

The development of dominant populations represents a case of competitive displacement. Abiotic parameters, such as temperature, pH, and oxygen, greatly influence the intrinsic growth rates of microbial populations and the outcome of a competitive struggle. For example, at high substrate concentrations, competition between a marine *Spirillum* and *E. coli* results in the competitive exclusion of the *Spirillum,* whereas at low concentrations the reverse occurs and the *E. coli* is excluded (Jannasch 1968). Dominant microbial populations in sewage, which has a high organic substrate content, are rapidly displaced in competition with the autochthonous microbial populations of receiving streams and rivers, where the concentration of organic matter diminishes in the course of mineralization and dilution.

Competitive advantage need not be based solely on ability to utilize a substrate more rapidly. Tolerance to environmental stress also may be an important factor in determining the outcome of competition between microbial populations. For example, under conditions of drought, populations that can best tolerate and survive desiccation can displace less tolerant populations. Similarly, under other stress conditions such as high temperatures or high salt concentrations, the population with the greatest tolerance to that factor may have the edge in the competition. These cases represent competition for survival during nongrowth conditions. During active growth conditions, the competitive advantage returns to the population with the highest growth rate under those conditions.

Because different species may have distinct resource requirements, competition for multiple resources between two or more microbial species may involve competition for similar types of resources (for example, two essential resources), or competition for differing types of resources (for example, essential and perfectly substitutable resources). Shifts in dominance in experimental microbial communities containing procaryotes were demonstrated by Holm and Armstrong (1981) in their study of the effects of resource supply ratios on competition between the diatom *Asterionella formosa* and the cyanobacterium *Microcystis aeruginosa.* In this study, the outcome of competition between *Microcystis,* which utilizes phosphorus as an essential resource but does not require silicon, and *Asterionella,* which has an absolute requirement for both phosphorus and silicon, differed under conditions of varying silicon/phosphorus supply ratios. The proportion of *Microcystis* decreased linearly with an increase in the Si/P supply ratio and was

reduced to insignificant proportions at supply ratios exceeding the optional Si/P ratio for *Asterionella.* These changes in microbial species competition are consistent with the resource-ratio theory.

## Amensalism (Antagonism)

Microorganisms that produce substances toxic to competing populations will naturally have a competitive advantage (Fredrickson and Stephanopoulos 1981). When one microbial population produces a substance that is inhibitory to other populations, the interpopulation relationship is called *amensalism.* The first population may be unaffected by the inhibitory substance or may gain a competitive edge that is beneficial. The terms *antibiosis* and *allelopathy* have been used to describe such cases of chemical inhibition. There are cases of complex amensalism between populations in natural habitats, for example, virucidal (virus-killing) factors in seawater and fungistatic (fungi-inhibiting) factors in soil (Lockwood 1964). The basis of these relationships is believed to be amensalism, since sterilization eliminates the inhibitory factors, but the chemical background of these complex antimicrobial activities remains to be explored.

Amensalism may lead to the preemptive colonization of a habitat. Once an organism establishes itself within a habitat it may prevent other populations from surviving in that habitat. The production of lactic acid or similar low-molecular-weight fatty acids is inhibitory to many bacterial populations (Pohunek 1961; Wolin 1969). Populations able to produce and tolerate high concentrations of lactic acid, for example, are able to modify the habitat so as to preclude the growth of other bacterial populations. *E. coli* is unable to grow in the rumen, probably because of the presence of volatile fatty acids produced there by anaerobic heterotrophic microbial populations (Wolin 1969). Fatty acids produced by microorganisms on skin surfaces are believed to prevent the colonization of these habitats by other microorganisms. Populations of yeasts on skin surfaces are maintained in low numbers by microbial populations producing fatty acids. Acids produced by microbial populations in the vaginal tract are probably responsible for preventing infection by pathogens such as *Candida albicans* (Pohunek 1961).

The oxidation of sulfur by *Thiobacillus thiooxidans* produces sulfuric acid. In aquatic habitats, this results in greatly lowered pH values. Growth of *T. thiooxidans* often occurs on reduced sulfur compounds associated with coal deposits; the resulting leaching of sulfuric acid produces acid mine drainage (Higgins and Burns 1975). The pH values of approximately 1 to 2 in streams receiving acid mine drainage preclude the growth of most microorganisms in the affected habitats. *T. thiooxidans* is not known to benefit from this amensal relationship with the populations of microorganisms inhibited by the acid mine drainage.

Consumption or production of oxygen may alter the habitat in ways detrimental to microbial populations. The production of oxygen by algae precludes the growth of obligate anaerobes. Few obligate anaerobes are found in habitats where there is a significant production of oxygen by algal populations. Production of ammonium by some microbial populations is deleterious to other populations (Stojanovic and Alexander 1958). Ammonium is produced during the decomposition of proteins and amino acids at concentrations inhibitory to nitrite-oxidizing populations of *Nitrobacter.*

Some microbial populations produce alcohols. Low-molecular-weight alcohols, such as ethanol, are inhibitory to many microbial populations. The production of ethanol by yeasts prevents the growth of most bacterial populations in habitats where the ethanol can accumulate. Thus, few bacterial populations can grow in a habitat of fermenting grapes (wine). Ethanol production does not, however, eliminate all bacterial populations. *Acetobacter* is able to convert ethanol to acetic acid (vinegar) when oxygen is available. The acetic acid produced is also inhibitory to many bacterial populations. The presence in food products of such inhibitory compounds as lactic and propionic acids in cheese and acetic acid in vinegar impedes the growth of spoilage-causing microbial populations.

Inhibitory substances produced by microorganisms may also act as preservatives for organic compounds in natural habitats. For example, during the decomposition of cellulose in soil, organic acids are produced that prevent further breakdown of cellulose metabolites in subsurface soil.

Some microorganisms produce antibiotics. An antibiotic is a substance produced by one microorganism that, in low concentrations, kills or inhibits the growth of other microorganisms. The use of antibiotics in medicine has had a great influence on our ability to control disease and the distribution of some microbial populations. Although under favorable laboratory conditions antibiotics are produced by some microorganisms in high concentrations and can be demonstrated to be potent inhibitors of other microbial populations, their role in natural habitats is subject to debate.

Conditions that favor the production of antibiotics are not normally found in natural habitats. Antibiotics are secondary metabolites and are usually produced when excess substrate concentrations are available to promote high levels of microbial growth. The normal condition of most soil and aquatic habitats is one of limiting organic substrates; antibiotics are not found to accumulate in natural habitats. Many microbial populations are tolerant to antibiotics and/or are capable of degrading them. In aquatic habitats, antibiotics probably are rapidly diluted to ineffective concentration levels. Antibiotics produced in soil may be bound to clay minerals or other particulates and thus be inactivated. Abundant *Streptomyces* and *Bacillus* populations occur in soils, but there is little evidence that they produce significant amounts of antibiotics there. Antibiotic-producing microorganisms usually do not dominate in aquatic habitats. Proportions of antibiotic-resistant strains are not exceptionally high in soils even though antibiotic-producing populations are found in soil habitats. However, if antibiotics were of no use in nature, they probably would not have been selected during evolutionary processes and would not be as widespread as they are.

Production of antibiotics probably has a significant function in establishing amensal relationships within microenvironments and under certain environmental conditions (Park 1967). Opportunistic microorganisms, such as the zymogenous populations in soil habitats, grow under conditions of localized high concentrations of organic matter. These conditions may permit production of antibiotics. Microbial populations growing in such microhabitats have a distinct advantage if they can discourage competition for the available substrates by other populations through an amensal relationship involving antibiotic production. Antibiotic production may aid the initial colonization of a substrate, after which antibiotic production may no longer be required.

Although it is difficult to prove, antibiotic production by microbial populations associated with plant residues—where there is adequate energy to support rapid microbial growth and subsequent production of secondary metabolites—seems to play a role in interpopulation relationships. *Cephalosporium gramineum* is a pathogen of wheat that survives in dead wheat tissues between crops and is capable of secreting antifungal substances, which appear to exclude other fungal populations endeavoring to colonize the dead tissues. Populations of *C. gramineum* that do not produce antibiotics are less able to prevent colonization of dead wheat tissues by other fungal populations and thus are less able to survive in this habitat (Bruehl et al. 1969).

Another interesting relationship occurs on the skin of the New Zealand hedgehog (Smith and Marples 1964). *Trichophyton mentagrophytes* produces the antibiotic penicillin in its natural habitat on the skin of hedgehogs. Populations of *Staphylococcus* found in the same habitat are penicillin resistant. The production of penicillin by the *Trichophyton* population allows it to enter into amensal relationships with non-penicillin-resistant populations that attempt to colonize the skin of the hedgehog. The penicillin-resistant *Staphylococcus* has developed an adaptation that allows it to neutralize the amensal influence of the penicillin-producing *Trichophyton*. Adaptation here could reflect coevolution of the coexisting microbial populations.

Bacteriocins are similar to antibiotics in that they are produced by microorganisms and are active against microorganisms in low concentrations, but they differ in that their action is restricted to microbes very closely related to the producer. Structurally, they are all peptides or low-molecular-weight proteins, and their production is almost always coded for on plasmids or transposons. The mode of action of bacteriocins is to integrate into the membrane of closely related bacterial strains and to destabilize their membrane functions, leading to death and lysis. Bacteriocins were most extensively studied in the gram-negative coliforms (Fredericq 1948); they have also been referred to as colicins for this reason (Fredericq 1957; James et al. 1992). Their production has also been reported in gram-positive bacteria (Hamon and Peron 1963), especially lactobacteria (Jack et al. 1995). Because of their very restricted activity spectrum, bacteriocins received much less attention from microbiologists than antibiotics, although one of the *Lactobacillus* bacteriocins, nisin, is being considered for extending the shelf life of some dairy products. The ecological significance of bacteriocins, however, may be as great as or greater than that of the antibiotics. Microbial strains that produce bacteriocins gain a competitive advantage over precisely the strains that compete for the same ecological niche and that would be most likely to competitively eliminate the bacteriocin producer in the absence of its chemical weaponry.

## Parasitism

In a relationship of parasitism, the population that benefits, the parasite, derives its nutritional requirements from the host, which is harmed. The host-parasite relationship is characterized by a relatively long period of contact, which may be directly physical or metabolic. Usually, but not always, the parasite is smaller than the host. Some parasites remain outside the cells of the host population and are called *ectoparasites;* other parasites penetrate the host cell and are called *endoparasites.*

Normally, the parasite-host relationship is quite specific. The available habitats for obligately parasitic populations are limited to available hosts. In some cases, host specificity depends on surface properties of the organisms that allow physical attachment of the parasite to the host cells.

Viruses are obligate intracellular parasites that exhibit great host cell specificity. There are viral parasites of bacterial, fungal, algal, and protozoan populations (Anderson 1957; Lemke and Nash 1974; van

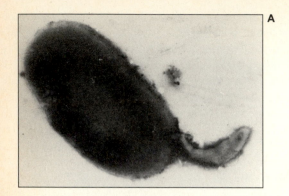

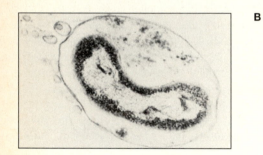

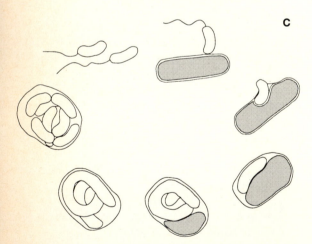

**Figure 3.23**
(A) Electron micrograph showing attachment of the parasitic bacterium *Bdellovibrio* to host cell. (Source: Marbach et al. 1976. Reprinted by permission of Springer-Verlag.) (B) Electron micrograph of thin cross section showing *Bdellovibrio* within host cell. (Source: Marbach et al. 1976. Reprinted by permission of Springer-Verlag.) (C) Life cycle of *Bdellovibrio bacteriovorus*.

Etten et al. 1983). In some habitats, viruses are suspected of being responsible for the decline and disappearance of bacterial populations. Parasitism may contribute to the disappearance of other fecal organisms in sewage that enters aquatic habitats.

The viruses attacking bacteria are called *bacteriophage*. Their most studied representatives attack *E. coli* and are referred to as *coliphage*. Typically a virulent (lytic) coliphage attaches to a susceptible *E. coli* strain and injects its DNA into the host cell, while the empty protein coat or "ghost" of the phage remains outside the bacterial cell. Once inside, the phage DNA redirects the metabolism of the host bacterium to synthesize first copies of the phage DNA and then its protein coat and finally to package the DNA into new phage particles. In a period of 20 minutes the infected bacterial cell bursts, releasing up to 300 new phage particles that are infectious and can resume the lytic cycle. Being obligate parasites, all phage require live and actively metabolizing bacterial hosts for their reproduction.

The described interactions between bacteriophage and their host bacteria are subject to environmental modification (Roper and Marshall 1974). Host bacteria and phage may be adsorbed onto clay particles in sediment. In saline sediments, fecal bacteria such as *E. coli* are protected from phage attack by sorption to clay particles. At lower salinities, *E. coli* and phage are desorbed from the particle, and the parasitic phage can attack and eliminate the host bacterial population. Protection of host populations by sorption onto particles provides an important mechanism for escape from parasitism.

Like bacteriophage, the bacterium *Bdellovibrio* is parasitic on gram-negative bacterial populations (Stolp and Starr 1963, 1965; Starr and Seidler 1971; Rittenberg 1983) (Figure 3.23). *Bdellovibrio* is highly motile, attaining speeds up to 100 cell lengths per second compared to only 10 lengths per second for *E. coli,* a potential host species. The encounter between parasite and prey appears to be random; no clear evidence has been found for chemotactic attraction. Only a small percentage of cell contacts result in permanent attachment of *Bdellovibrio* to the outer cell membrane of its gram-negative host. Subsequently, *Bdellovibrio* penetrates the outer cell membrane of its host and enters the periplasmic space but not the cell proper; hence *Bdellovibrio* is considered an ectoparasite. The parasitic interaction spans approximately 1 hour, during which *Bdellovibrio* modifies the cell envelope of its host in both degradative and synthetic manners. The host cell loses its original shape and becomes spherical (bdelloplast), yet it retains the cell contents for use by the parasite. The cell contents of the host are partially degraded and are used by *Bdellovibrio* with high efficiency. When it enters the periplasmic space, *Bdellovibrio* loses its flagellum and grows into a filament without cell division. When the cell contents of the host are exhausted, the filament divides into individual cells, which develop flagella. The bdelloplast lyses and releases the progeny. The burst size (number of progeny per host cell) depends on the size of the host cell and may range from about 4 in *E. coli* to about 20 in the much larger *Spirillum serpens*. Wild strains of *Bdellovibrio* are obligately parasitic, but in contrast to bacteriophage they have complete sets of catabolic, anabolic, and energy-generating enzymes. Mutants have been obtained that grow on heat-killed host cells and even on rich synthetic media. Although *Bdellovibrio* is capable of eradicating its host in a laboratory setting, the impact of this parasitic interaction in natural environments is strongly attenuated and of limited significance. The interaction of *Bdellovibrio* and host *E. coli* has been observed to be partially inhibited by the presence of montmorillonite clays (Roper and Marshall 1978) (Figure 3.24). The clay particles appear to form an envelope around the *E. coli* and inhibit the ability of the parasitic *Bdellovibrio* to reach the host cells.

Other ectoparasitic microorganisms can cause lysis without direct contact. Myxobacteria, for example, can cause lysis of susceptible microbial strains at some distance, apparently with the aid of exoenzymes. The myxobacteria derive their nutrition from material released by the lysed microorganisms. Soil myxobacteria are able to lyse gram-negative and gram-positive bacterial populations. *Cytophaga* populations produce enzymes that cause lysis of susceptible algae (Stewart and Brown 1969). Some bacterial populations produce chitinase, an enzyme that causes

lysis of chitin-containing fungal cell walls. Other bacterial populations produce laminarinase or cellulase enzymes that similarly attack the cell wall structures of some algal and fungal populations. In all of these cases ectoparasitic populations cause the lysis of host cells, releasing nutrients that can be utilized by the ectoparasites, even though many of these ectoparasites are not obligate parasites and can derive nutrition by other means. Some microbial populations are more resistant to lysis than others. Microbial populations may produce resting stages, such as cysts and spores, that are more resistant to lytic activities of ectoparasites than the vegetative cells. This mechanism for escaping the pressures of ectoparasitism allows the host populations to persist.

Protozoan populations are subject to parasitism by a large number of fungi, bacteria, and other protozoa. The ability of the opportunistic human pathogen *Legionella pneumophila* to parasitize protozoa may play an important role in its distribution and survival in aquatic environments (Fields et al. 1984). Some fungal populations are parasites of protozoa (Madelin

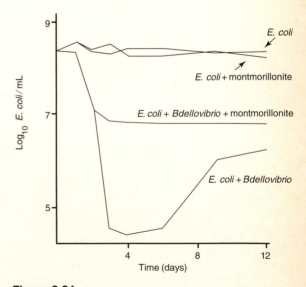

**Figure 3.24**
Effect of clay particles on the interaction of *Bdellovibrio* and *E. coli*. The presence of clay particles (montmorillonite) attenuates the parasitism of *Bdellovibrio*. (Source: Roper and Marshall 1978. Reprinted by permission, copyright Springer-Verlag.)

1968). These may be endo or ectoparasites. In some cases, endoparasites are maintained for long periods within the host protozoan cells. In such cases, the line between endoparasitism and mutualism is often blurred. Algae, too, are attacked by fungi; the chitrids are notable examples. Uniflagellate chitrids are normally ectoparasites, and biflagellate chitrids are normally endoparasites of algal populations. Chitrids frequently infect freshwater algae, leading to decimation of susceptible populations. Some fungal populations are parasitized by other fungal populations (Barnett 1963). Basidiomycetes, such as *Agaricus,* are frequently attacked by other fungi, such as *Trichoderma.* Such infections create difficulties in the commercial cultivation of mushrooms.

Microorganisms that are themselves parasites may also serve as host cells for other parasitic populations. This phenomenon is known as hyperparasitism. For example, *Bdellovibrio,* a bacterial parasite, may serve as a host cell for appropriate phage populations. Fungal populations that are parasitic on algae are themselves subject to bacterial and viral parasitism. Some rust fungi are parasitized by lytic bacteria.

Parasitism has benefits beyond the immediate ones derived by the parasites themselves. Parasitic interactions provide a mechanism for population control. Because the intensity of parasitism is population-density dependent, parasites can thrive only as long as there are abundant host populations.

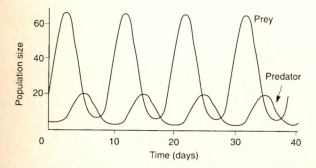

**Figure 3.25**
Theoretical predator-prey fluctuations. (Source: Krebs 1972. Reprinted by permission of Harper and Row; copyright 1972 Charles Krebs.)

Parasitism results in a reduction of host population density that then allows for the accumulation and renewal of the environmental resources being utilized by the hosts. When host populations decline, the resources available for the parasites also diminish, leading to a decrease of the parasite population. As long as it has escaped complete extinction by the parasites, the host population can then recover. Without negative feedback control by mechanisms such as parasitism, host populations might continue to grow unchecked until all the resources needed for their growth were exhausted, which, in turn, would lead to a crash in the populations of both the host and parasite organisms and their possible extinctions.

## Predation

In the microbial world, the distinction between parasitism and predation is not sharp. For example, the interaction between *Bdellovibrio* and susceptible gram-negative bacteria is regarded by some as parasitism, by others as predation. Predation typically occurs when one organism, the predator, engulfs and digests another organism, the prey. Normally, predator-prey interactions are of short duration and the predator is larger than the prey (Slobodkin 1968).

Early theoretical considerations of predator-prey relationships (Lotka 1925; Volterra 1926) led to the prediction that interactions of predator and prey species have regular cyclic fluctuations of the two populations (Figure 3.25). In each cycle, as the prey population increases, the predator population follows, overtakes, and overcomes it, producing a decline in the prey. The predator population then follows the declining prey supply downward until the predators reach such a low level that the prey population begins to rise again, whereupon the predator again follows it upward. Assuming that the environment is constant, the amplitude of the cycle is determined by the initial population density and remains the same. Theoretically, such predator-prey populations could cycle forever.

According to the Lotka-Volterra model, the prey population adds individuals according to its intrinsic rate of increase $(r_1)$ times its density $(N_1)$ and loses individuals at a rate proportional to encounters of predator and prey individuals, hence to the product of prey density $(N_1)$ and predator density $(N_2)$. Thus, the rate of change for the prey population is expressed mathematically as Equation 1.

$$(1) \qquad dN_1/dt = r_1N_1 - PN_1N_2$$

$P$ is a coefficient of predation that relates predator births to prey consumed.

The predator adds individuals at a rate proportional to this same product of densities $(N_1N_2)$ and loses individuals according to a mortality rate $(m)$ times its own density, which mathematically is expressed as Equation 2.

$$(2) \qquad dN_2/dt = PN_1N_2 - m_2N_2$$

The equations describe a cyclic fluctuation that is stable unless disturbed.

Experimental models, however, have rarely supported the Lotka-Volterra model. In a classic series of experiments, Gause (1934) showed that when *Didinium nasutum* is introduced with *Paramecium caudatum,* it preys on the *Paramecium* until the *Paramecium* population becomes extinct. Lacking a food source, the *Didinium* population also becomes extinct (Figure 3.26). If a few members of the *Paramecium* population are able to hide and escape predation by the *Didinium,* then the *Paramecium* population can recover following extinction of the *Didinium.* Only by periodically introducing *Paramecium* and *Didinium* populations was Gause able to produce a sustained interaction with marked fluctuations in population numbers. Gause (1934) also was able to establish periodic oscillations using *P. bursaria* as a predatory species and the yeast *Schizosaccharomyces pombe* as a prey species, but was unable to establish sustained oscillations. In this heterotrophic, nutrient-limited system, the amplitude of the oscillations decreased, leading to extinction of both species. The preceding experiments indicate that intense predator-prey relations may lead to the extinction of both the predator and the prey populations.

The failure of experimental models to reveal persistent population oscillations has forced a reevaluation of the underlying assumptions of the Lotka-Volterra model. The error appears to be the invalidity

of the inherent assumption that predatory encounter is random in time and space and, like a bimolecular collision, is proportional to the product of predator and prey populations (Williams 1980). Experimental evidence (Curds and Bazin 1977; Bazin and Saunders 1978; Boraas 1980) indicates that predator-prey populations establish nonoscillatory steady-state conditions or cycles that become limiting, such that the magnitude of the oscillation progressively decreases. Theoretical models based on saturation kinetics and prey refuge are, for the most part, able to explain these observations (Whittaker 1975; Williams 1980).

Although predation destroys individuals, the prey population as a whole may benefit from accelerated

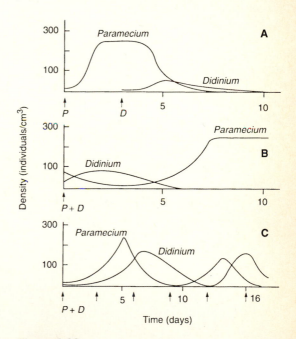

**Figure 3.26**
Predator-prey interactions between *Paramecium* and *Didinium.* (A) *Didinium* introduced at high *Paramecium* levels with no refuge site. Intense predation eliminates *Paramecium,* and *Didinium* subsequently starves. (B) *Didinium* introduced at low *Paramecium* levels with sediment refuge site. *Didinium* starves, and *Paramecium* that escape predation multiply after elimination of *Didinium.* (C) *Paramecium* and *Didinium* introduced every three days, preventing permanent extinction and producing predator-prey cycles. Arrows indicate times of protozoan introduction. (Source: Gause 1934. Reprinted by permission, copyright 1934 Williams and Wilkins.)

nutrient recycling. The increase in phytoplankton growth rates due to nitrogen regeneration by predaceous zooplankton has been found to fully compensate for the mortality of the individual phytoplankton caused by the zooplankton (Sterner 1986). Moderate predatory pressure keeps prey populations from exhausting the carrying capacity of their environment and maintains the prey population in a dynamic state of growth.

It is important to recognize that the interactive nature of predator-prey relations is adaptive. There is an organizational control through negative feedback that regulates the population sizes of the predator and prey. If either the predator or the prey were completely eliminated, populations of the other would be deleteriously affected. In studies with *Tetrahymena pyriformis,* a predator protozoan, and *Klebsiella pneumoniae,* a prey bacterium, van den Ende (1973) found that a stable predator-prey relationship could be established at a level that ensured the survival of both species (Figure 3.27). In the relationship between *Tetrahymena* and *Klebsiella,* natural selection within the predator-prey system increases the efficiency of

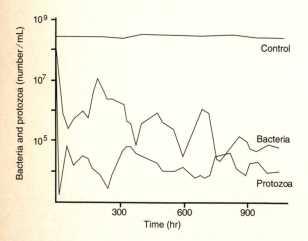

**Figure 3.27**
Predator-prey interactions between *Tetrahymena* and *Klebsiella* in sucrose-limited continuous culture showing out-of-phase cyclic oscillation of predator and prey populations. The control curve shows bacterial numbers in the absence of the predator. (Source: van den Ende 1973. Reprinted from *Science* by permission, copyright 1973 American Association for the Advancement of Science.)

the predator in finding and engulfing its prey but also favors those individual prey that escape predation.

Under conditions of starvation, only the smallest predators survive; that is, as the prey population is consumed, there is selection for small predators. Bacterial populations under strong predatory pressure cease to produce capsules, enabling the bacterial populations to grow more rapidly and to adhere more readily to solid surfaces. In the case of *Tetrahymena* and *Klebsiella,* coexistence is dependent on the ability of the prey to find refuge. This demonstrates that coexistence of a predator and its prey can result from environmental heterogeneity, with the coexisting species being partially separated by their abilities to occupy separate niches, that is, by niche diversification. The diversity of real-world habitats may permit persistent population oscillations and coexistence.

Interactions with clay particles have been shown to provide a protection mechanism for prey bacteria from predatory populations. Montmorillonite clay provided a physical separation of predator and prey that slowed the rate of engulfment of *E. coli* by *Vexillifera* (Roper and Marshall 1978) (Figure 3.28). This again shows that physical structures within natural habitats provide mechanisms for lessening the pressure of predation on prey populations, allowing coexistence. The ability to escape predation by finding refuge enables the microbial community in Lake Cisó to maintain a large biomass with a slow growth rate; this is different from most pelagic microbial communities, where limited biomass is maintained by active predation on very fast growing populations of algae and bacteria (Pedrós-Alió and Guerrero 1993).

In microbial predation, it is common to find great size differences between a predator and its prey. Populations of ciliate, flagellate, and amoeboid protozoa are predatory on bacterial populations. The nondiscriminatory consumption of bacterial populations by such protozoan predators is called *grazing.* The protozoan populations engulf the bacteria by phagocytosis, and the prey species are digested and degraded by lytic enzymes following ingestion (Hirsch 1965). Predation by flagellate protozoa may be responsible for maintaining relatively stable populations of bacteria in aquatic systems. This grazing activity retains carbon within the

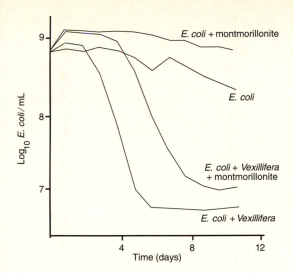

**Figure 3.28**
Effect of montmorillonite clay particles on the predation of *Vexillifera* on *E. coli*. Montmorillonite reduces intensity of interaction. (Source: Roper and Marshall 1978. Reprinted by permission, copyright Springer-Verlag.)

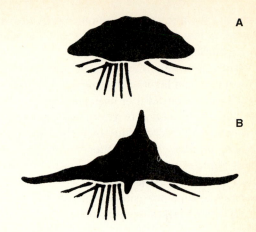

**Figure 3.29**
Normal shape (A) of *Eupotes octocarinatus* and its response (B) to predation by *Lembladion lucens*. The change in prey morphology prevents its engulfment by the predator. (Source: Kuhlman and Heckmann 1985.)

food web (Fenchel and Jørgensen 1977; Fenchel 1980; Sherr et al. 1983; Wright and Coffin 1984). Ciliate protozoa, such as *Paramecium, Vorticella,* and *Stentor,* have a cell mass $10^3$ to $10^4$ times larger than the average prey bacterium, such as *Enterobacter aerogenes.* Such relatively large predatory protozoa often employ a strategy of filter feeding so that they do not consume all their energy chasing small, low-calorie prey. Filter feeding works at an energy deficit when the prey density becomes too low. The strategy of many filter-feeding protozoa appears to be to stop filter feeding in such situations and thus conserve energy. This seems to occur when the homogeneously suspended bacterial prey density falls to between $10^5$ and $10^6$ per mL. Such a shutdown of filter feeding gives the prey population a good opportunity to recover.

Some microbial structures are resistant to predators. For example, soil amoebae engulf and consume vegetative cells of *Bacillus* species, but endospores of *Bacillus* are less subject to predation. The protozoan *Entodinium caudatum* is subject to predation by the larger protozoan *E. vorax*. *E. caudatum* produces spineless and spined cells; *E. vorax* preferentially con-sumes the spineless populations, leading to the extinction of the spineless forms while the spiny populations of *E. caudatum* escape and reproduce. The ciliate protozoan *Euplotes octocarinatus* reacts to predation by *Lembladion lucens* and other ciliate protozoans that engulf their prey by changing its cell shape in a manner that interferes with engulfment (Kuhlman and Heckmann 1985) (Figure 3.29). This defense is so efficient that in axenic culture it leads to the starvation of *L. lucens*. In nature, this defense would induce the predator to engulf alternate prey species.

## CHAPTER SUMMARY

Within a single population, cooperation is usually the predominant interaction at low population densities. Cooperation favors aggregation of individuals, resulting in spatial incongruities as evidenced by the distribution of microcolonies within natural habitats. At higher population densities, competition predominates, leading to dispersal.

Two different populations can exhibit a variety of interactions (see Table 3.1). Neutralism can exist when the populations do not have the opportunity to interact. This can be accomplished by physical separation or by temporal separation of activities and is favored by low population densities and low levels of metabolic activities.

Commensal relationships, which are neutral to one population and favor another population, are frequently based on physical or chemical modifications of the habitat. Production of growth factors, production of substrates, mobilization of growth factors or substrates, and removal of inhibitory substances form the basis for many commensal relationships. Cometabolism is an important basis for commensalism. Other bases include provision of surfaces for growth and provision of transport mechanisms that enhance dispersal.

Synergism benefits both interacting populations; it allows for new or accelerated activities by microbial populations acting together, permitting microorganisms to combine their metabolic activities to perform transformations of substrates that could not be carried out by the individual populations. Synergistic relationships can result in the establishment of elemental cycling reactions and are an important basis for the development of community structure.

Mutualism is an extension of synergism that allows populations to join in an obligate relationship, forming a single unit population that can occupy habitats that would be restrictive for the individual populations. Over evolutionary time it may become impossible to recognize the individual identities of populations that unite in mutualistic relationships.

Competition is a negative interaction between microbial populations. Competition is greatest between microbial populations attempting to occupy the same or overlapping niches. During growth conditions, competitive success is based on the highest intrinsic growth rate under the given environmental parameters. Under nongrowth conditions, competitive success is based on tolerance and survival capabilities. Under constant environmental conditions, competition often will result in the establishment of dominant populations and the exclusion of populations of unsuccessful competitors. Exclusion may result in a spatial or temporal displacement that lessens the competitive interaction for available resources. Varying environmental parameters create conditions that allow for the coexistence of competing populations.

Amensal relationships have a negative impact on one of the populations based on the metabolic activities of the other populations. Microbial populations can enter into amensal relationships with other populations by modifying the habitat and by producing toxic chemicals. Some amensal relationships result from the alteration of concentrations of inorganic compounds such as oxygen, ammonia, mineral acids, and hydrogen sulfide. In other cases, the amensal relationship is based on production of low-molecular-weight organic compounds such as fatty acids or alcohols. In most natural habitats, the role of antibiotics in amensal relationships is difficult to demonstrate, but this does not preclude the possibility that under conditions that exist in some natural habitats, antibiotics may play a significant role in the establishment of amensal relationships.

Parasitism exerts a negative influence on susceptible host populations and benefits the parasite. The parasite population may be entirely dependent on the host for its nutritional requirements (an obligate parasite) or may have alternative mechanisms for meeting its nutritional needs. In an overall sense, parasitism is a mechanism for controlling population densities that provides long-range benefits to host populations and ecosystems alike.

Predation, like parasitism, is a mechanism of population control that dampens population explosions and prevents exhaustion of nutritional resources of the habitat that would lead to severe population crashes. Coexistence of predator and prey species can occur with periodic population oscillations if the prey species can temporarily escape predation pressure and recover. The grazing pressure of predation places a stress on prey populations, which acts through natural selection to encourage evolution of features in prey species that provide mechanisms for escape. Such adaptations include the abilities to reproduce rapidly, to develop resistant resting stages such as endospores, and to acquire surface structures, such as spines, that discourage predators.

## STUDY QUESTIONS

1. How do population interactions explain the relatively high numbers of pathogens required to establish an infection in a susceptible animal?

2. Why does inoculation of an agar plate with a single cell of a bacterium often fail to result in growth and formation of a colony? When they do form, why are the sizes of bacterial colonies limited?

3. Describe the cooperative interactions exhibited by populations of the slime mold *Dictyostelium*.

4. Why is neutralism the predominant or only interpopulation interaction in the atmosphere?

5. What is cometabolism? How can cometabolism serve as a basis for commensalism?

6. What is the difference between synergism and mutualism?

7. What evidence would you consider critical for demonstrating the role antibiotics play in nature? How would you design an experiment, series of experiments, and/or field observations to obtain that evidence?

8. What is meant by the balance of nature? How do interpopulation interactions explain how a balance of nature can be maintained?

9. What is a lichen? Why can lichens grow on rocks and tree bark?

10. What is the difference between predation and parasitism? What ecological functions are served by predation and parasitism?

11. Why don't predators normally totally eliminate their prey populations?

12. What is competitive exclusion? How does it explain which populations colonize specific habitats such as the human intestine?

13. How can populations that compete for the same resources coexist? How does resource-ratio theory explain the coexistence of some competing populations?

14. Why are populations of archaean methanogens dependent on interactions with bacterial populations? What is the physiological basis of this dependence?

15. What is a biofilm? Describe the interpopulation interactions that occur among diverse microbial populations in a biofilm.

## REFERENCES AND SUGGESTED READINGS

Ahmadjian, V. 1963. The fungi of lichens. *Scientific American* 208:122–132.

Ahmadjian, V. 1967. *The Lichen Symbiosis*. Blaisdell, Waltham, MA.

Ahmadjian, V. 1982. The nature of lichens. *Natural History* 91:31–37.

Ahmadjian, V. 1993. *The Lichen Symbiosis*. Wiley, New York.

Ahmadjian, V., J. B. Jacobs, and L. A. Russel. 1978. Scanning electron microscope study of early lichen synthesis. *Science* 200:1062–1064.

Alexander, M. 1971. *Microbial Ecology*. Wiley, New York.

Allee, W. C., A. E. Emerson, O. Park, T. Park, and K. P. Schmidt. 1949. *Principles of Animal Ecology*. Saunders, Philadelphia.

Anderson, E. S. 1957. The relations of bacteriophages to bacterial ecology. In R.E.O. Williams and C. C. Spicer (eds.). *Microbial Ecology*. Cambridge University Press, Cambridge, England, pp. 189–217.

Atlas, R. M., and R. Bartha. 1973. Fatty acid inhibition of petroleum biodegradation. *Antonie van Leeuwenhoek* 39:257–271.

Ball, G. H. 1969. Organisms living on and in protozoa. In T. T. Chen (ed.). *Research in Protozoology.* Pergamon Press, Oxford, England, pp. 565–718.

Balows A., H. G. Trüper, M. Dworkin, W. Harder, and K. H. Schleifer. 1992. *The Prokaryotes: A Handbook on the Biology of Bacteria—Ecophysiology, Isolation, Identification, Applications,* ed. 2. Springer-Verlag, New York.

Baltzis, B. C., and A. G. Fredrickson. 1984. Competition of two suspension-feeding protozoan populations for a growing bacterial population. *Microbial Ecology* 10:61–68.

Barnett, H. L. 1963. The nature of mycoparasitism by fungi. *Annual Review of Microbiology* 17:1–14.

Bates, J. L., and P. V. Liu. 1963. Complementation of lecithinase activities in closely related pseudomonads: Its taxonomic implication. *Journal of Bacteriology* 86:585–592.

Bazin, M. J., and P. T. Saunders. 1978. Determination of critical variables in a microbial predator-prey system by catastrophe theory. *Nature* 275:52–54.

Beam, H. W., and J. J. Perry. 1974. Microbial degradation of cycloparaffinic hydrocarbons via cometabolism and commensalism. *Journal of General Microbiology* 82:163–169.

Bell, W. H., J. M. Lang, and R. Mitchell. 1974. Selective stimulation of marine bacteria by algal extracellular products. *Limnology and Oceanography* 19:833–839.

Boraas, M. E. 1980. A chemostat system for the study of rotifer-algal-nitrate interactions. In W. E. Kerfoot (ed.). American Society for Limnology and Oceanography Special Symposium III: *The Evolution and Ecology of Zooplankton Communities.* University Press of New England, Hanover, NH.

Bordeleau, L. M., and R. Bartha. 1971. Ecology of a pesticide transformation: Synergism of two soil fungi. *Soil Biology and Biochemistry* 3:281–284.

Brock, T. D. 1966. *Principles of Microbial Ecology.* Prentice Hall, Englewood Cliffs, NJ.

Bruehl, G. W., R. L. Miller, and B. Cunfer. 1969. Significance of antibiotic production by *Cephalosporium gramineum* to its saprophytic survival. *Canadian Journal of Plant Science* 49:235–246.

Bull, A. T., and J. H. Slater. 1982. Microbial interactions and community structure. In A. T. Bull and J. H. Slater (eds.). *Microbial Interactions and Communities.* Academic Press, London, pp. 13–44.

Bungay, H. R., and M. L. Bungay. 1968. Microbial interactions in continuous culture. *Advances in Applied Microbiology* 1:269–290.

Cappenberg, T. E. 1975. A study of mixed continuous cultures of sulfate-reducing and methane-producing bacteria. *Microbial Ecology* 2:60–72.

Cappenberg, T. E., E. Jonejan, and J. Kaper. 1978. Anaerobic breakdown processes of organic matter in freshwater sediments. In M. W. Loutit and J.A.R. Miles (eds.). *Microbial Ecology.* Springer-Verlag, Berlin, pp. 91–99.

Chang, K. P., and W. Trager. 1974. Nutritional significance of symbiotic bacteria in two species of hemoflagellates. *Science* 183:351–352.

Chet, I., and R. Mitchell. 1976. Ecological aspects of microbial chemotactic behavior. *Annual Reviews of Microbiology* 30:221–239.

Clark, R. J., and T. L. Steck. 1979. Morphogenesis in *Dictyostelium:* An orbital hypothesis. *Science* 204:1163–1168.

Costerton, J. W., Z. Lewandowski, D. DeBeer, D. Caldwell, D. Korber, and G. James. 1994. Biofilms: The customized microniche. *Journal of Bacteriology* 176:2137–2147.

Costerton, J. W., Z. Lewandowski, D. E. Caldwell, D. R. Korber, and H. M. Lappin-Scott. 1995. Microbial biofilms. *Annual Review of Microbiology* 49:711–746.

Curds, C. R., and M. J. Bazin. 1977. Protozoan predation in batch and continuous culture. *Advances in Aquatic Microbiology* 1:115–176.

DeFreitas, M. J., and G. Frederickson. 1978. Inhibition as a factor in the maintenance of the diversity of microbial ecosystems. *Journal of General Microbiology* 106:307–320.

Denison, W. D. 1973. Life in tall trees. *Scientific American* 228:75–80.

Denyer, S. P., S. P. Gorman, and M. Sussman (eds.). 1993. *Microbial Biofilms: Formation and Control.* Blackwell, Oxford, Great Britain.

Deppenmeier, U., V. Mueller, and G. Gottschalk. 1996. Pathways of energy conservation in methanogenic archaea. *Archives of Microbiology* 165:149–163.

Devay, J. E. 1956. Mutual relationships in fungi. *Annual Reviews of Microbiology* 10:115–140.

Dilts, J. A., and R. L. Quackenbush. 1986. A mutation in the R body sequence destroys expression of the killer trait in *P. tetraaurelia*. *Science* 232:641–643.

Dworkin, M. 1996. Recent advances in the social and developmental biology of the myxobacteria. *Microbiological Reviews* 60:70–102.

Fenchel, T. 1980. Suspension-feeding in ciliated protozoa: Functional response and particle eye selection. *Microbial Ecology* 6:1–11.

Fenchel, T. 1982. Ecology of heterotrophic microflagellates: Adaptations to heterogenous environments. *Marine Ecology Progress Series* 9:25–33.

Fenchel, T. M., and B. B. Jørgensen. 1977. Detritus food chains of aquatic ecosystems: The role of bacteria. *Advances in Microbial Ecology* 1:1–58.

Ferry, B. W. 1982. Lichens. In R. G. Burns and J. H. Slater (eds.). *Experimental Microbial Ecology*. Blackwell, London, pp. 291–319.

Ferry, J. G. 1993. *Methanogenesis; Ecology, Physiology, Biochemistry and Genetics*. Chapman and Hall, New York.

Fields, B. S., E. B. Shotts, Jr., J. C. Feeley, G. W. Gorman, and W. T. Martin. 1984. Proliferation of *Legionella pneumophila* as an intracellular parasite of the ciliated protozoan *Tetrahymena pyriformis*. *Applied and Environmental Microbiology* 47:467–471.

Fredericq, P. 1948. Actions antibiotiques reciproques chez les Enterobacteriaceae. *Belge de Pathologie et Medecine Experimentale* 19(supp. IV):1–107.

Fredericq, P. 1957. Colicins. *Annual Review of Microbiology* 11:7–22.

Fredrickson, A. G. 1977. Behavior of mixed cultures of microorganisms. *Annual Review of Microbiology* 31:63–89.

Fredrickson, A. G., and G. Stephanopoulos. 1981. Microbial competition. *Science* 213:972–979.

Friedmann, E. I. 1982. Endolithic microorganisms in the Antarctic cold desert. *Science* 215:1045–1053.

Gale, E. F. 1940. The production of amines by bacteria. III. The production of putrescine from arginine by *Bacterium coli* in symbiosis with *Streptococcus faecalis*. *Journal of Biochemistry* 34:853–857.

Gargas, A., P. T. DePriest, M. Grube, and A. Tehler. 1995. Multiple origins of lichen symbioses in fungi suggested by SSU rDNA phylogeny. *Science* 268:1492–1495.

Gause, G. F. 1934. *The Struggle for Existence*. Williams & Wilkins, Baltimore.

Gause, G. F. 1935. Experimental demonstration of Volterra's periodic oscillation in the numbers of annuals. *Journal of Experimental Biology* 12:44–48.

Gerdes, K., F. W. Bech, S. T. Jorgensen, A. Lobner-Olesen, P. B. Rasmussen, T. Atlung, L. Boe, O. Karlstrom, S. Molin, and K. von Meyenburg. 1986a. Mechanism of postsegregational killing by the *hok* gene product of the *par*B system of plasmid R1 and its homology with the *rel*F gene product of the *E. coli rel*B operon. *EMBO Journal* 5:2023–2029.

Gerdes, K., P. B. Rasmussen, and S. Molin. 1986b. Unique type of plasmid maintenance function: Postsegregational killing of plasmid-free cells. *Proceedings of the National Academy of Sciences USA* 83:3116–3120.

Gilbert, O. L. 1969. The effect of $SO_2$ on lichens and bryophytes around Newcastle upon Tyne. In *European Symposium on the Influences of Air Pollution on Plants and Animals*. Centre for Agricultural Publishing and Documentation, Wageningen, The Netherlands, pp. 223–235.

Gooday, G. W., and S. A. Doonan. 1980. The ecology of algal–invertebrate symbioses. In D. C. Ellwood, J. N. Hedger, M. J. Latham, J. M. Lynch, and J. H. Slater (eds.). *Contemporary Microbial Ecology*. Academic Press, London, pp. 377–390.

Gunner, H. B., and B. M. Zuckerman. 1968. Degradation of diazinon by synergistic microbial action. *Nature* (London) 217:1183–1184.

Hale, M. E. 1974. *The Biology of Lichens*. Edward Arnold, London.

Hamon, Y., and Y. Peron. 1963. Quelques remarques sur les bacteriocines produites par les microbes gram positifs. *Compte Rendues Seances de l'Academie des Sciences* 104:55–65.

Harder, W., and H. Veldkamp. 1971. Competition of marine psychrophilic bacteria at low temperatures. *Antonie van Leeuwenhoek* 37:51–63.

Hardy, K. 1981. *Bacterial Plasmids. Aspects of Microbiology*, Series No. 4. American Society for Microbiology, Washington, DC.

Heckmann, K., and H.-D. Görtz. 1992. Prokaryotic symbionts of ciliates. In A. Balows, H. G. Trüper, M. Dworkin, W. Harder, and K. H. Schleifer (eds.). *The Prokaryotes*. Springer-Verlag, New York, 3865–3890.

Higgins, I. J., and R. G. Burns. 1975. *The Chemistry and Microbiology of Pollution*. Academic Press, London, pp. 218–223.

Hirsch, J. G. 1965. Phagocytosis. *Annual Reviews of Microbiology* 19:339–350.

Holm, N. P., and D. E. Armstrong. 1981. Role of nutrient limitation and competition in controlling the populations of *Asterionella formosa* and *Microcystis aeruginosa* in semicontinuous culture. *Limnology and Oceanography* 26:622–634.

Jack, R. W., J. R. Tagg, and B. Ray. 1995. Bacteriocins of gram-positive bacteria. *Microbiological Reviews* 59:171–200.

James, R., C. Lazdunski, and F. Pattus (eds.). 1992. *Bacteriocins, Microcins, and Lantibiotics*. Springer-Verlag, New York.

Jannasch, H. W. 1968. Competitive elimination of Enterobacteriaceae from seawater. *Applied Microbiology* 16:1616–1618.

Jannasch, H. W., and R. I. Mateles. 1974. Experimental bacterial ecology studied in continuous culture. *Advances in Microbial Physiology* 11:165–212.

Jeffries, T. W. 1982. The microbiology of mercury. *Progress in Industrial Microbiology* 16:23–75.

Jones, A. K. 1982. The interactions of algae and bacteria. In A. T. Bull and J. H. Slater (eds.). *Microbial Interactions and Communities*. Academic Press, London, pp. 189–248.

Kelly, D. P. 1978. Microbial ecology. In K.W.A. Chater and H. J. Somerville (eds.). *The Oil Industry and Microbial Ecosystems*. Heyden and Son, London, pp. 12–27.

Krebs, C. J. 1972. *Ecology: The Experimental Analysis of Distribution and Abundance*. Harper & Row, New York.

Kuenen, J. G., and W. Harder. 1982. Microbial competition in continuous culture. In R. G. Burns and J. H. Slater (eds.). *Experimental Microbial Ecology*. Blackwell, London, pp. 342–367.

Kuenen, J. G., L. A. Robertson, and H. van Germerden. 1985. Microbial interactions among aerobic and anaerobic sulfur-oxidizing bacteria. *Advances in Microbial Ecology* 8:1–59.

Kuhlman, H. W., and K. Heckmann. 1985. Interspecific morphogens regulating prey-predator relationship in protozoa. *Science* 227:1347–1349.

Lamb, I. M. 1959. Lichens. *Scientific American* 201:144–156.

Lawrence, J. W., D. R. Korber, G. M. Wolfaardt, and D. E. Caldwell. 1995. Behavioral strategies of surface-colonizing bacteria. *Advances in Microbial Ecology* 14:1–76.

Lemke, P. A., and C. H. Nash. 1974. Fungal virus. *Bacteriological Reviews* 38:29–56.

Lockhead, A. G. 1958. Soil bacteria and growth-promoting substances. *Bacteriological Reviews* 22:145–153.

Lockwood, J. C. 1964. Soil fungistasis. *Annual Reviews of Phytopathology* 2:341–362.

Lotka, A. J. 1925. *Elements of Physical Biology*. Williams & Wilkins, Baltimore.

Madelin, M. F. 1968. Fungi parasitic on other fungi and lichens. In G. C. Ainsworth and A. S. Sussman (eds.). *The Fungi*. Vol. 3. Academic Press, New York, pp. 253–269.

Marbach, A., M. Varon, and M. Shilo. 1976. Properties of marine Bdellovibrios. *Microbial Ecology* 2:284–295.

Margulis, L. 1971. The origin of plant and animal cells. *American Scientist* 59:230–235.

Mitchell, K., and M. Alexander. 1962. Microbiological changes in flooded soil. *Soil Science* 93:413–419.

Mitchell, R. 1968. Factors affecting the decline of non-marine microorganisms in seawater. *Water Research* 2:535–543.

Mitchell, R. 1971. Role of predators in the reversal of imbalances in microbial ecosystems. *Nature* 230:257–258.

Mouget, J. L., A. Dakhama, M. C. Lavoie, and J. de la Noue. 1995. Algal growth enhancement by bacteria: Is consumption of photosynthetic oxygen involved? *FEMS Microbiology Ecology* 18:34–43.

Munnecke, D. M., and D.P.H. Hsieh. 1976. Pathway of microbial metabolism of parathion. *Applied and Environmental Microbiology* 31:63–69.

Nickel, J. C., J. B. Wright, I. Ruseka, T. J. Marrie, C. Whitfield, and J. W. Costerton. 1985. Antibiotic resistance of *Pseudomonas aeruginosa* cells growing as a biofilm on urinary catheter material. *Antimicrobial Chemotherapy* 27:619–624.

Nienow, J. A., and E. I. Friedmann. 1993. Terrestrial lithophytic (rock) communities. In E. I. Friedmann (ed.). *Antarctic Microbiology*. Wiley-Liss, New York, pp. 343–412.

Nurmikko, V. 1956. Biochemical factors affecting symbiosis among bacteria. *Experientia* 12:245–249.

Odum, E. P. 1971. *Fundamentals of Ecology.* Saunders, Philadelphia.

Orenski, S. W. 1966. Intermicrobial symbiosis. In S. M. Henry (ed.). *Symbiosis.* Academic Press, New York, pp. 1–33.

Park, D. 1967. The importance of antibiotics and inhibiting substances. In A. Burges and F. Raw (eds.). *Soil Biology.* Academic Press, New York, pp. 435–447.

Pearl, H. W. 1987. Role of heterotrophic bacteria in promoting $N_2$-fixation by *Anabaena* in aquatic habitats. *Microbial Ecology* 4:215–231.

Pearl, H. W., and K. K. Gallucci. 1985. Role of chemotaxis in establishing a specific nitrogen-fixing cyanobacterial association. *Science* 227:647–649.

Pedrós-Alió, C., and R. Guerrero. 1993. Microbial ecology of Lake Cisó. *Advances in Microbial Ecology* 13:155–210.

Pohunek, M. 1961. Streptococci antagonizing the vaginal *Lactobacillus. Journal of Hygiene, Epidemiology, Microbiology, and Immunology* (Prague) 5:267–270.

Preer, J. R., and L. B. Preer. 1984. Endosymbionts. In N. R. Krieg and J. G. Holt (eds.). *Bergey's Manual of Systematic Bacteriology.* Williams & Wilkins, Baltimore.

Preer, L. B. 1981. Prokaryotic symbionts of *Paramecium.* In M. P. Starr, H. Stolp, H. G. Truper, A. Balows, and H. G. Schlegel (eds.). *The Prokaryotes.* Springer-Verlag, Berlin, pp. 2127–2136.

Rittenberg, S. C. 1983. *Bdellovibrio:* Attack, penetration and growth on its prey. *ASM News* 49:435–439.

Roper, M. M., and K. C. Marshall. 1974. Modification of interaction between *Escherichia coli* and bacteriophage in saline sediment. *Microbial Ecology* 1:1–14.

Roper, M. M., and K. C. Marshall. 1978. Effects of a clay mineral on microbial predation and parasitism on *Escherichia. Microbial Ecology* 4:279–290.

Rosenberg, E., K. H. Keller, and M. Dworkin. 1977. Cell-density dependent growth of *Myxococcus xanthus* on casein. *Journal of Bacteriology* 129:770–777.

Seaward, M.R.D. 1977. *Lichen Ecology.* Academic Press, London.

Shapiro, J. A. 1991. Multicellular behavior of bacteria. *ASM News* 57:247–253.

Sherr, B. F., E. B. Sherr, and T. Berman. 1983. Grazing, growth, and ammonium excretion rates of a heterotrophic microflagellate fed with four species of bacteria. *Applied and Environmental Microbiology* 45:1196–1201.

Shimkets, L. J. 1990. Social and developmental biology of the myxobacteria. *Microbiological Reviews* 54:473–501.

Sieburth, J. M. 1975. *Microbial Seascapes.* University Park Press, Baltimore.

Slater, J. H. 1978. Microbial communities in the natural environment. In K.W.A. Chater and H. S. Somerville (eds.). *The Oil Industry and Microbial Ecosystems.* Heyden and Sons, London, pp. 137–154.

Slater, J. H., and A. T. Bull. 1978. Interactions between microbial populations. In A. T. Bull and P. M. Meadow (eds.). *Companion to Microbiology.* Longman, London, pp. 181–206.

Slobodkin, L. B. 1968. How to be a predator. *American Zoologist* 8:43–51.

Smith, J.M.B., and M. J. Marples. 1964. A natural reservoir of penicillin resistant strains of *Staphylococcus aureus. Nature* 201:844.

Smith, V. H. 1993. Implications of resource-ratio theory for microbial ecology. *Advances in Microbial Ecology* 13:1–37.

Society for Experimental Biology. 1975. *Symbiosis.* Cambridge University Press, Cambridge, England.

Sonneborn, T. M. 1959. Kappa and related particles in *Paramecium. Advances in Virus Research* 6:229–356.

Stal, L. J. 1994. *Microbial Mats: Structure, Development and Environmental Significance.* Springer-Verlag, New York.

Stams, A.J.M., J. B. Van Dijk, C. Dijkema, and C. M. Plugge. 1993. Growth of syntrophic propionate oxidizing bacteria with fumarate in the absence of methanogenic bacteria. *Applied and Environmental Microbiology* 59:1114–1119.

Starr, M. P., and R. J. Seidler. 1971. The Bdellovibrios. *Annual Reviews of Microbiology* 25:649–675.

Sterner, R. W. 1986. Herbivores' direct and indirect effect on algal populations. *Science* 231:605–607.

Stewart, J. R., and R. M. Brown, Jr. 1969. *Cytophaga* that kills or lyses algae. *Science* 164:1523–1524.

Stojanovic, B. J., and M. Alexander. 1958. Effect of inorganic nitrogen on nitrification. *Soil Science* 86:208–215.

Stolp, H., and M. P. Starr. 1963. *Bdellovibrio bacteriovorous* gen. et sp. n., a predatory ectoparasitic and bacteriolytic microorganism. *Antonie van Leeuwenhoek* 29:217–248.

Stolp, H., and M. P. Starr. 1965. Bacteriolysis. *Annual Reviews of Microbiology* 19:79–104.

Strelkoff, A., and G. Poliansky. 1937. On natural selection in some infusoria entodiniomorpha. *Zoological Journal* (Moscow) 16:77–84.

Taylor, F.J.R. 1982. Symbioses in marine microplankton. *Annals of the Institute of Oceanography* (Paris) 58:61–90.

Thiele, J. H., and G. Zeikus. 1988. Control of interspecies electron flow during anaerobic digestion: Significance of formate transfer versus hydrogen transfer during syntrophic methanogenesis in flocs. *Applied and Environmental Microbiology* 54:20–29.

Tilman, D. 1976. Ecological competition between algae: Experimental confirmation of resource-based competition theory. *Science* 192:463–465.

Tilman, D. 1982. *Resource Competition and Community Structure.* Princeton University Press, Princeton, NJ.

Van Bruggen, J.J.A., K. B. Zwart, J.G.F. Hermans, E. M. Van Hove, C. K. Stumm, and G. D. Vogels. 1986. Isolation and characterization of *Methanoplanus endosymbiosus* sp. nov., an endosymbiont of the marine sapropelic ciliate *Metopus contortus* Quennerstedt. *Archives of Microbiology* 144:367–374.

van den Ende, P. 1973. Predator-prey interactions in continuous culture. *Science* 181:562–564.

van Etten, J. L., D. E. Burbank, D. Kutzmarski, and R. H. Meints. 1983. Virus infection of culturable *Chlorella*-like algae and development of a plaque assay. *Science* 219:994–996.

van Gemerden, H. 1974. Coexistence of organisms competing for the same substrate: An example among the purple sulfur bacteria. *Microbial Ecology* 1:104–119.

Veldkamp, H., H. van Gemerden, W. Harder, and H. J. Laanbroek. 1984. Competition among bacteria: An overview. In A. J. Klug and C. A. Reddy (eds.). *Current Perspectives in Microbial Ecology.* American Society for Microbiology, Washington, DC, pp. 279–280.

Volterra, V. 1926. Variazioni e fluttuazioni del numero d'individui in specie animali conviventi. *Memorie/Academia Nazionale dei Rome Italy Lincei* (Rome) 2:31–113.

Waksman, S. A. 1961. The role of antibiotics in nature. *Perspectives of Biological Medicine* 4:271–287.

Weis, D. S. 1982. Protozoal symbionts. In R. G. Burns and J. H. Slater (eds.). *Experimental Microbial Ecology.* Blackwell, London, pp. 320–341.

Wessenberg, H., and G. Antipa. 1970. Capture and ingestion of *Paramecium* by *Didinium nasutum. Journal of Protozoology* 17:250–270.

Whittaker, R. H. 1975. *Communities and Ecosystems.* Macmillan, New York.

Williams, F. M. 1980. On understanding predator–prey interactions. In D. C. Ellwood, J. N. Hedger, M. J. Latham, J. M. Lynch, and J. H. Slater (eds.). *Contemporary Microbial Ecology.* Academic Press, London, pp. 349–375.

Wimpenny, J.W.T. 1992. Microbial systems: Patterns in time and space. *Advances in Microbial Ecology* 12:469–522.

Wireman, J. W., and M. Dworkin. 1975. Morphogenesis and developmental interactions in myxobacteria. *Science* 189:516–522.

Wolfe, R. S., and N. Pfennig. 1977. Reduction of sulfur by *Spirillum* 5175 and syntrophism with *Chlorobium. Applied and Environmental Microbiology* 33:427–433.

Wolin, M. J. 1969. Volatile fatty acids and the inhibition of *Escherichia coli* growth by rumen fluid. *Applied Microbiology* 17:83–87.

Wolin, M. J., and T. L. Miller. 1982. Interspecies hydrogen transfer: 15 years later. *ASM News* 48:561–565.

Wright, R. T., and R. B. Coffin. 1984. Measuring microzooplankton grazing on planktonic marine bacteria by its impact on bacterial production. *Microbial Ecology* 10:137–149.

Yarmolinsky, M. B. 1995. Programmed cell death in bacterial populations. *Science* 267:836–837.

Zeikus, J. G. 1977. The biology of methanogenic bacteria. *Bacteriological Reviews* 41:514–541.

# Interactions Between Microorganisms and Plants

*Positive and negative interactions take place not only between microbes but also between microbes and plants. The rhizosphere is a zone of predominantly commensal and mutualistic interactions between plants and microbes. Ecto- and endomycorrhizal fungi provide plants with mineral nutrients and water, receiving photosynthate in return. Under harsh conditions, this mutualistic association can be essential for plant survival. The associations of dinitrogen-fixing bacteria with certain plants provide essential combined nitrogen for crops and ecosystems. The aerial surfaces of plants provide habitats for largely commensal microbes. On the negative side, certain viruses, bacteria, and fungi cause plant diseases that can result in great economic losses and even severe food shortages.*

## INTERACTIONS WITH PLANT ROOTS

Plant roots provide such suitable habitats for the growth of microorganisms that high numbers of many different microbial populations are found on and surrounding plant roots. Interactions between soil microorganisms and plant roots satisfy important nutritional requirements for both the plant and the associated microorganisms (Brown 1974, 1975; Bowen and Rovira 1976; Lynch 1976, 1982a, 1982b; Balandreau and Knowles 1978; Dommergues and Krupa 1978; Newman 1978; Harley and Russell 1979; Bowen 1980). This is apparent by the large numbers of microorganisms found in the rhizoplane (Figure 4.1), which is defined as the actual surface of the plant roots, and within the rhizosphere, which includes the rhizoplane and is defined as the region of soil directly influenced by the plant roots (Campbell and Rovira 1973; Rovira and Campbell 1974; Bowen and Rovira 1976).

## The Rhizosphere

The rhizosphere soil is the thin layer of soil adhering to a root system after shaking has removed the loose soil (Figure 4.2). The size of the rhizosphere depends on the particular plant root structure, but generally the contact area with soil is very large. Per total plant biomass, the fibrous root structure of grassy plants provides a larger surface area than root systems characterized by a taproot. For example, the root system of a single wheat plant can be more than 200 meters in length. Assuming an average root diameter of 0.1 mm,

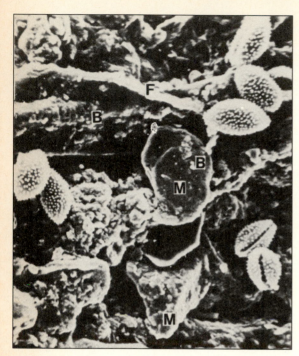

**Figure 4.1**
Scanning electron micrograph of rye grass root showing
complexity of root surface and the rhizosphere. B = bacteria;
F = fungal mycelia; M = mineral grains. Oval structures with
granular surface appear to be fungal spores. (Source:
Campbell and Rovira 1973. Reprinted by permission of
Pergamon Press.)

**Figure 4.2**
Photograph of plant root system showing root hairs and soil
particles attached to the rhizoplane.

we may calculate a root surface area in excess of
6 square meters. Only 4%–10% of the actual rhizoplane, however, is in direct physical contact with
micro-organisms; most microorganisms associated
with roots occur in the surrounding rhizosphere
(Bowen 1980).

An interesting and as yet insufficiently explored
modification of the rhizosphere is the rhizosheath,
characterized as a relatively thick soil cylinder that
adheres to the plant roots (Figure 4.3). The formation
of rhizosheaths is typical of some desert grasses but
also occurs in some grass species that grow under less
extreme conditions (Wullstein et al. 1979; Duell and
Peacock 1985). The sand grains in the rhizosheath are
cemented together by an extracellular mucigel, apparently excreted by the root cells. The rhizosheath

appears to be an adaptation for moisture conservation,
but it undoubtedly also provides an environment for
extensive root-microbe interactions. Increased nitrogen-
fixation activity has been measured in rhizosheath soil.

**Plant Root Effects on Microbial Population**    The
structure of the plant root system contributes to the
establishment of the rhizosphere microbial population
(Nye and Tinker 1977; Russell 1977; Bowen 1980;
Lynch 1982a). The interactions of plant roots and rhizosphere microorganisms are based largely on interactive modification of the soil environment by processes
such as water uptake by the plant, release of organic
chemicals to the soil by the roots, microbial production of plant growth factors, and microbially mediated
availability of mineral nutrients. Within the rhizosphere, plant roots have a direct influence on the composition and density of the soil microbial community,
known as the rhizosphere effect. The rhizosphere
effect can be seen by looking at the ratio of the
number of microorganisms in the rhizosphere soil (R)
to the number of corresponding microorganisms in

**Figure 4.3**
Rhizosheath on cereal rye *(Secale cereale).* The diameter of
the soil cylinders in about 8 mm. Rhizosheaths represent an
adaptation for moisture conservation and also provide an
extended environment for plant-microbe interactions.
(Source: R. W. Duell, Rutgers University, New Brunswick,
New Jersey.)

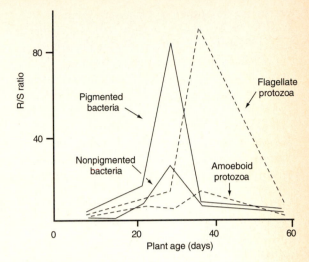

**Figure 4.4**
R/S ratios indicating rise and fall of bacterial and protozoan
populations within the rhizosphere during development of
*Sinapsis alba.* (Source: Campbell, 1977; based on Dar-
byshire and Greaves, 1967. Reprinted by permission of
National Research Council of Canada.)

soil remote from roots (S) (the R/S ratio). Generally
R/S ratios range from 5 to 20, but it is common to find
an R/S ratio of 100, that is, microbial populations
100 times higher in the rhizosphere than in the surrounding root-free soil (Gray and Parkinson 1968;
Woldendorp 1978). The actual extent of the rhizosphere effect depends on the particular plant and its
physiological maturity (Darbyshire and Greaves 1967)
(Figure 4.4).

There is a higher proportion of gram-negative,
rod-shaped bacteria and a lower proportion of gram-
positive rods, cocci, and pleomorphic forms in the rhizosphere than in root-free soil (Rovira and Campbell
1974; Woldendorp 1978; Campbell 1985). There is
also a relatively higher proportion of motile, rapidly
growing bacteria, such as *Pseudomonas,* in the rhizosphere than elsewhere in soil. In many cases this
increase represents a direct influence of plant root
exudates on soil microorganisms, which favor

microorganisms with high intrinsic growth rates.
Organic materials released from roots include amino
acids, keto acids, vitamins, sugars, tannins, alkaloids,
phosphatides, and other unidentified substances
(Rovira 1969). Roots surrounded by microorganisms
excrete many times as much organic material as sterile
roots. Although a few of these materials inhibit
microorganisms, most stimulate microbial growth.
The influence of materials released by the plant into
the soil is evidenced by the observation that bacterial
populations within the rhizosphere have markedly different nutritional properties than bacteria in root-free
soil. Many rhizosphere bacteria require amino acids
for maximal growth, and it is likely that root exudates
supply these acids.

Microorganisms in the rhizosphere may undergo
successional changes as the plant grows from seed
germination to maturity. During plant development, a
distinct rhizosphere succession results in rapidly
growing, growth-factor-requiring, opportunistic microbial populations. These successional changes correspond to changes in the materials released by the plant

roots to the rhizosphere during plant maturation. Initially, carbohydrate exudates and mucilaginous materials support the growth of large populations of microorganisms within the grooves of the epidermal plant cells, on the root surface, and within mucilaginous layers surrounding the roots. As the plant matures, autolysis of some of the root material takes place as part of normal root development and simple sugars and amino acids are released into the soil, stimulating the growth of *Pseudomonas* and other bacteria with high intrinsic growth rates. R/S ratios usually decline when plants stop growing and become senescent.

The microaerophilic *Azospirillum* (formerly *Spirillum lipoferum*) and the aerobic *Azotobacter paspali* are nitrogen-fixing soil bacteria regularly associated with the rhizosphere of certain tropical grasses of the *Digitaria, Panicum,* and *Paspalum* genera. These bacteria use root exudates as the energy source to support significant nitrogen fixation. In field trials, this rhizospheric nitrogen fixation replaced up to 40 kg of nitrogen per hectare per year (Smith et al. 1976). *Azospirillum* was found also in the rhizosphere of some temperate zone grasses and corn *(Zea mays)* (Lamm and Neyra 1981), but the rates of nitrogen fixation in these cases appear to have little practical significance. However, rhizospheric nitrogen fixation helps in meeting the nitrogen demand of rice crops (Swaminathan 1982). A side effect of biochemical nitrogen fixation is the evolution of hydrogen. Only some *Rhizobium* and *Bradyrhizobium* strains have the hydrogenase enzyme to utilize this side product; others wastefully evolve hydrogen gas. Nodulated root systems evolving hydrogen were found to be colonized by hydrogen-oxidizing *Acinetobacter* strains that utilized this resource not commonly available in aerobic environments (Wong et al. 1986).

*Zostera marina* (eel grass) and *Thalassia testudinum* (turtle grass) cover shallow coastal seafloor areas of temperate and tropical regions, respectively. The rhizosphere of these plants in the anaerobic marine sediments is the site of high nitrogen-fixation activity by *Desulfovibrio, Clostridium,* and other anaerobes (Patriquin and Knowles 1972; Capone and Taylor 1980; Smith 1980). Because of the projection of short-term measurements, the reported rates are controver-

sial. Substantial nitrogen-fixation rates were also reported for the rhizosphere of the dominant semisubmerged salt-marsh grass *Spartina alterniflora* (Hanson 1977; Patriquin and McClung 1978), but little is known about the microorganisms involved. There is little doubt, however, that the reported rhizospheric nitrogen-fixation activities constitute significant combined nitrogen inputs for the coastal marine environment.

**Effects of Rhizosphere Microbial Populations on Plants** Just as plant roots have a direct effect on the surrounding microbial populations, microorganisms in the rhizosphere have a marked influence on the growth of plants. In the absence of appropriate microbial populations in the rhizosphere, plant growth may be impaired (Lynch 1976; Dommergues and Krupa 1978; Campbell 1985). Microbial populations in the rhizosphere may benefit the plant in a variety of ways, including increased recycling and solubilization of mineral nutrients; synthesis of vitamins, amino acids, auxins, cytokinins, and gibberellins, which stimulate plant growth; and antagonism with potential plant pathogens through competition and development of amensal relationships based on production of antibiotics (Nieto and Frankenberger 1989; Alvarez et al. 1995).

Plants that grow in flooded sediments and soils have evolved adaptations for conducting oxygen from the shoot to the roots (Raskin and Kende 1985), but in such anaerobic environments the roots also have to cope with the toxic hydrogen sulfide generated by sulfate reduction (Drew and Lynch 1980). Rice, and perhaps other partially submerged plants, are protected against the toxic effect of hydrogen sulfide by a mutualistic association with *Beggiatoa* (Joshi and Hollis 1977). This microaerophilic, catalase-negative, sulfide-oxidizing, filamentous bacterium benefits from the oxygen and catalase enzyme provided by the rice roots, and in turn, *Beggiatoa* aids the rice plant by oxidizing the toxic hydrogen sulfide to harmless sulfur or sulfate, thus protecting the cytochrome system of the rice roots.

Organisms in the rhizosphere produce organic compounds that affect the proliferation of the plant root system (Lynch 1976). Microorganisms synthesize auxins and gibberellin-like compounds, and these compounds increase the rate of seed germination and the development of root hairs that aid plant growth (Brown 1974). *Arthrobacter, Pseudomonas,* and *Agrobacterium* populations found in the rhizosphere have been reported to be capable of producing organic chemicals that stimulate growth of plants. The rhizosphere of wheat seedlings, for example, contains a significant proportion of bacteria that produce indoleacetic acid (IAA), a plant growth hormone that can increase root growth. In older wheat plants, a lower proportion of microorganisms in the rhizosphere is capable of producing IAA. This may be in response to a decline in root exudate production, but it also beneficially corresponds to a decreased need for the growth hormone by the plant.

Allelopathic (antagonistic) substances released by microorganisms in the rhizosphere may allow plants to enter amensal relationships with other plants. Such allelopathic substances surrounding some plants can prevent invasion of that habitat by other plants, and this may represent a synergistic relationship between a plant and its rhizosphere microbial community. Bacterial populations in the rhizosphere of young wheat plants have been shown to inhibit the growth of pea and lettuce plants. As a wheat plant matures, the proportion of these bacteria decreases and they are replaced by a higher proportion of microorganisms capable of producing growth-promoting substances similar to gibberellic acid.

Microorganisms in the rhizosphere influence the availability of mineral nutrients to the plants, sometimes using limiting concentrations of inorganic nutrients before they can reach plant roots, and in other cases increasing the availability of inorganic nutrients to the plant (Barber 1978). Rhizosphere microorganisms increase the availability of phosphate through solubilization of materials that would otherwise be unavailable to plants. Plants have been shown to exhibit higher rates of phosphate uptake when associated with rhizosphere microorganisms than in sterile soils (Campbell 1985). The principal mechanism of increasing phosphate availability is the microbial production of acids that dissolve apatite (a common mineral group including calcium fluophosphate), releasing soluble forms of phosphorus. Iron and manganese

may be more available to plants because of rhizosphere microorganisms that produce organic chelating agents, thus increasing the solubility of iron and manganese compounds. It has also been shown that microorganisms on roots significantly increase the uptake rates of calcium by the roots. This increase may be due to high concentrations in the rhizosphere of carbon dioxide produced by microorganisms, which increase the solubility and thus the availability of calcium. Translocation of various radiolabeled organic compounds and heavy metals along mycelial filaments has also been demonstrated (Grossbard 1971; Campbell 1985).

Although increased uptake of minerals due to rhizosphere microorganisms is beneficial, the abundant microbial populations in the rhizosphere can sometimes create a deficiency of required minerals for the plants (Agrios 1978). For example, bacterial immobilization of zinc and oxidation of manganese cause the plant diseases "little leaf" of fruit trees and "gray speck" of oats, respectively. Microorganisms in the rhizosphere may immobilize limiting nitrogen, making it unavailable for the plant (Campbell 1985). The immobilization of nitrogen by microorganisms in the rhizosphere accounts for an appreciable loss of added nitrogen fertilizer intended for plant use. Part of the nitrogen is immobilized in the form of microbial protein, but some may also be lost to the atmosphere by denitrification.

Although diverse and complex, the majority of interactions in the rhizosphere are mutually beneficial to both plants and microorganisms and are synergistic in character. A further exploration and optimization of these interactions may lead to significant improvements in crop production.

## Mycorrhizae

Some fungi enter into a mutualistic relationship with plant roots called *mycorrhizae* (literally, "fungus root") in which the fungi actually become integrated into the physical structure of the roots (Hartley 1965; Cooke 1977; Dommergues and Krupa 1978; Powell 1982; Campbell 1985; Allen 1991). The fungus derives nutritional benefits from the plant roots, contributes to plant nutrition, and does not cause plant disease. Mycorrhizal associations differ from other rhizosphere associations between plants and microorganisms by the greater specificity and organization of the plant-fungus relationship. The mycorrhizal association involves the integration of plant roots and fungal mycelia, forming integrated morphological units. The widespread existence of mycorrhizal associations between fungi and plant roots attests to the importance of this interaction.

Mycorrhizal associations exist for prolonged periods with the maintenance of a healthy physiological interaction between the plant and the fungus. The mycorrhizal associations of fungi and plant roots represent a diverse relationship—in terms of both structure and physiological function—that leads to a nutrient exchange favorable to both partners. Enhanced uptake of water and mineral nutrients, particularly phosphorus and nitrogen, has been noted in many mycorrhizal associations; plants with mycorrhizal fungi are therefore able to occupy habitats they otherwise could not (Smith and Daft 1978).

There are two basic types of mycorrhizal associations: ectomycorrhizae (Marks and Kozlowski 1973; Marx and Krupa 1978) and endomycorrhizae (Sanders et al. 1975; Hayman 1978). In ectomycorrhizae, the fungus (an ascomycete or basidiomycete) forms an external pseudoparenchymatous sheath more than 40 µm thick and constituting up to 40% of the dry weight of the combined root-fungus structure (Hartley 1965) (Figure 4.5). The fungal hyphae penetrate the intercellular spaces of the epidermis and of the cortical region of the root but do not invade the living cells. The morphology of the root is altered, forming shorter, dichotomously branching clusters with reduced meristematic regions.

In contrast to the predominantly exogenous ectomycorrhizae, endomycorrhizae invade the living cells of the root, which become filled with mycelial clusters (Hartley 1965) (Figure 4.6). Of the various microorganisms colonizing the rhizosphere, mycorrhizal fungi occupy the unique ecological position of being partly inside and partly outside the host. The part of the fungus within the root does not encounter competition with other soil microorganisms. In a widespread form

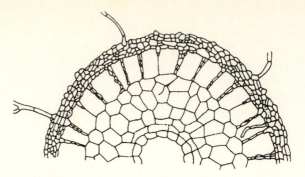

**Figure 4.5**
Cross section of ectotrophic mycorrhizal rootlet showing fungal sheath and intercellular penetration. (Source: Hartley 1965. Reprinted by permission, copyright University of California Press, Berkeley, California.)

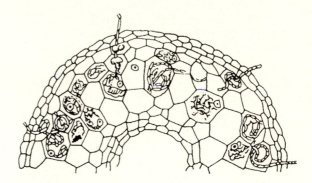

**Figure 4.6**
Cross section of endotrophic mycorrhizal rootlet showing intracellular penetration of hyphae. (Source: Hartley 1965. Reprinted by permission; copyright University of California Press, Berkeley, California.)

of endomycorrhizae, the microscopic appearance of intracellular hyphal clusters causes these to be called vesicular-arbuscular (VA) mycorrhizae (Hartley 1965) (Figure 4.7). In some cases, endo- and ectomycorrhizae may be combined, and are referred to as an ectendomycorrhizae.

**Ectomycorrhizae**    Ectomycorrhizae are common in gymnosperms and angiosperms, including most oak, beech, birch, and coniferous trees (Marks and Kozlowski 1973). Most trees in temperate forest regions have ectomycorrhizal associations. Many fungi can enter

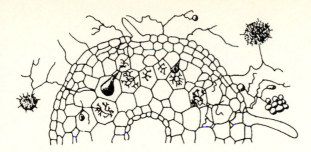

**Figure 4.7**
Cross section of rootlet with vesicular-arbuscular mycorrhiza showing penetrating hyphae and "tree-like" and "vesicle-like" hyphal structures. (Source: Hartley 1965. Reprinted by permission, copyright University of California Press, Berkeley, California.)

into ectomycorrhizal associations, including ascomycetes, such as truffles, and basidiomycetes, such as *Boletus* and *Amanita*. Ectomycorrhizal fungi generally have optimal growth temperatures of 15–30°C and are acidophilic with optimal growth at pH 4.0–6.0 or even as low as pH 3.0 (Hartley 1965). Most ectomycorrhizal fungi grow well on simple carbohydrates such as disaccharides and sugar alcohols. They generally utilize complex organic sources of nitrogen, amino acids, and ammonium salts; many require vitamins such as thiamine and biotin and are able to produce a variety of metabolites that they release to the plant, including auxins, gibberellins, cytokinins, vitamins, antibiotics, and fatty acids (Frankenberger and Poth 1987). Some ectomycorrhizal fungi are capable of producing enzymes such as cellulase, but such activity is normally suppressed within the host plant and, therefore, the fungi do not digest the plant roots.

The plant probably derives several benefits from its association with ectomycorrhizal fungi, including longevity of feeder roots; increased rates of nutrient absorption from soil; selective absorption of certain ions from soils; resistance to plant pathogens; increased tolerance to toxins; and increased tolerance ranges to environmental parameters, such as temperature, drought, and pH (Marks and Kozlowski 1973; Harley and Smith 1983). The ectomycorrhizal fungi receive photosynthesis products from the host plant and thus escape intense competition for organic substrates with

other soil microorganisms. The nutritional benefit to the fungus is demonstrated by the fact that many mycorrhizal fungi fail to form fruiting bodies outside of a mycorrhizal association with a plant, even though vegetative saprophytic growth is usually possible under these circumstances.

An ectomycorrhizal infection has a morphogenetic effect that leads to characteristic dichotomous branching and prolonged growth and survival of plant rootlets, probably due to production of growth hormones by the ectomycorrhizal fungi (Frankenberger and Poth 1987). Formation of root hairs is suppressed, and fungal hyphae overtake their function, thus greatly increasing the radius of nutrient availability for the plant. Ectomycorrhizal roots take up ions, such as phosphate and potassium, in excess of the rates displayed by uninfected roots. The mechanisms of uptake are dependent on fungal metabolic activity. There may be a primary accumulation of phosphate within the fungal sheath followed by transfer to the plant root. Nitrogen-containing compounds and calcium have also been found to be absorbed into the fungal mycelial sheath, followed by transfer to the plant root. Interdependence of the plant root and the ectomycorrhizal fungus is thus based in large part on their ability to supply each other with major and minor nutrients.

Plants with ectomycorrhizae also are able to resist pathogens that otherwise would attack the plant roots. The sheaths produced by ectomycorrhizal fungi present an effective physical barrier to penetration by plant root pathogens, and many basidiomycetes that are ectomycorrhizal have been shown to produce antibiotics. Plants with ectomycorrhizal fungi survive in soils inoculated with pathogens that enter through plant roots; for example, inoculation of nursery soils with fungi that can enter into ectomycorrhizal associations has produced a marked decrease in the mortality of host trees such as Douglas firs (Neal and Bollen 1964). Ectomycorrhizal roots also produce a variety of volatile organic acids that have fungistatic effects. The increased production of such compounds by host cells infected with ectomycorrhizal fungi maintains a balance with the mutualistic fungus and deters infection by pathogenic fungi. Most plants appear to respond to mycorrhizal infection by producing inhibitors that also contribute to the resistance of the ectomycorrhizal roots to pathogenic infection.

**Endomycorrhizae** Endomycorrhizal associations in which the fungus penetrates into the plant root cells, which are not of the vesicular-arbuscular (VA) type, occur in a few orders of plants, such as the Ericales, which include heath, arbutus, azalea, rhododendron, and American laurel (Sanders et al. 1975). The endomycorrhizae of the plant genera belonging to the Ericales are characterized by nonpathogenic penetration of the root cortex by septate fungal hyphae that often form intracellular coils. Although the fungi do not fix atmospheric nitrogen, the endomycorrhizal association may increase plant access to combined nitrogen in soil as demonstrated by better nitrogen nutrition in mycorrhizal as compared to nonmycorrhizal plants. There is greater phosphatase activity in mycorrhizal roots than in nonmycorrhizal roots, and the mycorrhizal fungi can transfer phosphate from external sources to the host plant. The association of endomycorrhizae in Ericales appears to improve the growth of the host plant in nutrient-deficient soils, and the widespread occurrence of endomycorrhizal infections in Ericales indicates that these plant root tissues provide a good ecological niche for these fungi.

Virtually all orchid roots are internally infected and attacked by fungal hyphae, which pass through surface cells into cortical cells to form mycorrhizae. The fungi form coils within the cells of the outer cortex, and later the hyphae lose their integrity and much of their contents passes into the host cell. Orchids are obligately mycorrhizal under natural conditions, often forming associations with the fungi *Armillaria mellea* and *Rhizoctonia solani.* These endomycorrhizal associations enhance the ability of orchid seeds to germinate, but the fungi can also be parasitic to the host plant. This fact and, conversely, the digestion of some fungal mycelium by the plant give this association the character of a precariously balanced mutual parasitism. It may also be that the association of orchids, which are pollinated at night, and the bioluminescent fungus *A. mellea* is based on light production, which would attract nocturnal insects and could aid in the sexual reproduction of the orchids.

Arbuscular mycorrhiza probably evolved with the Devonian land flora (Bagyaraj and Varma 1995). They are formed by most angiosperms, gymnosperms, ferns, and bryophytes. Of the 2.6 million known plant species, 240,000 are estimated to have the potential to form mycorrhizal associations with 6000 fungal species. Ribosomal DNA genes have been sequenced from 12 species of arbuscular mycorrhizal fungi; their phylogenetic analysis confirms the existence of three families: Glomaceae, Acaulosporaceae, and Gigasporaceae. Estimates place the origin of arbuscular mycorrhizal fungi at 383–462 million years ago. This is consistent with the hypothesis that endomycorrhizal fungi were instrumental in the colonization of land masses by ancient plants. Glomaceae appeared first, followed by Acaulosporaceae and Gigasporaceae. The three groups have continued to diverge from each other since the late Paleozoic era 250 million years ago.

The VA type of endomycorrhizal association, which frequently goes unnoticed because it does not have a macroscopic effect on root morphology, occurs in more plant species than all other types of endo- and ectomycorrhizae combined (Mosse 1973; Sanders et al. 1975; Bowen 1984). VA mycorrhizae occur in wheat, maize, potatoes, beans, soybeans, tomatoes, strawberries, apples, oranges, grapes, cotton, tobacco, tea, coffee, cacao, sugarcane, sugar maple, rubber trees, ash trees, hazel shrubs, honeysuckle, and various herbaceous plants. They also occur in angiosperms, gymnosperms, pteridophytes, and bryophytes and in most major agricultural crop plants. VA endomycorrhizal fungi have not as yet been grown in pure culture. Lacking regular septa, VA fungi have traditionally been assigned to the single genus *Endogone,* but this genus has now been subdivided into several genera.

The chief diagnostic feature of VA mycorrhizae is the presence of vesicles and arbuscules in the root cortex (Hartley 1965) (Figure 4.7). Inter- and intracellular hyphae are present in the cortex, and the infection inside the root is directly linked to an external mycelium that spreads into the soil. In general, the mycelium forms a loose network in the soil around the VA mycorrhizal root. These mycorrhizal fungi have the largest known resting spores of any fungi, with diameters of 20–400 µm. Reports on the arbuscular-mycorrhizal fungus *Gigaspora margarita* indicate that there are up to 250,000 bacterial endosymbionts per fungal spore (Biancicotto et al. 1996; Holzman 1996). The bacterial endosymbionts of this fungus have been identified by PCR analysis as *Burkholderia* species (group II pseudomonads). The finding of these bacterial endosymbionts has led to speculation that they are the precursors of the mitochondria of eucaryotic cells.

The mycorrhizal mycelium appears to be more resistant than the root itself to abiotic stresses such as drought, metal toxicity, and soil acidity. The fungi increase plant growth through improved uptake of nutrients, especially phosphorus, made possible by the exploration by the external hyphae of the soil beyond the root hair and phosphorus depletion zones. The VA mycorrhizal association results in increased phosphate uptake by the plant and improved uptake of other ions, such as zinc, sulfate, and ammonium from soil (Chiariello et al. 1982).

The VA mycorrhizal associations are thus similar physiologically to the ectomycorrhizae. These mycorrhizal associations enhance the ability of plants to recolonize soils that are barren of vegetation (Tinker 1975; Wills and Cole 1978). Plants with mycorrhizal fungi have an increased ability to take up nutrients from deficient soils, which is often essential for the survival of plants. The beneficial effect of mycorrhizae on plant growth is prominent in phosphorus-deficient soils. Because of the generally low availability of P in tropical soils, the potential for the exploitation of mycorrhizae in tropical agriculture seems to be much greater than in temperate soils.

The frequent and dismal failure of conventional agriculture on cleared tropical rainforest sites is directly attributable to the failure of farmers to account for phosphorus limitations and the need to use plants with mycorrhizal fungi. The lushness of tropical rainforests is deceiving. They often grow on highly leached and nutrient-deficient soils (Jordan 1982). In temperate forests, litter and soil humus constitute major nutrient reservoirs. Due to high temperatures and humidity, which enhance rapid biodegradation, there is little humus and litter associated with tropical rainforests, and the chief reservoir of nutrients is the living plant biomass. Because of the leaching by

heavy daily rainfall, there are virtually no soluble mineral nutrient salts in the rainforest soil. In this situation, mycorrhizal associations are pivotal to nutrient conservation. Very often mycorrhizal fungus continues to act as a saprophyte and decomposes freshly fallen plant litter at high rates. The liberated inorganic nutrient salts do not enter the soil environment, where they would be rapidly lost by leaching, but are directly transmitted through mycorrhizal hyphae to the plant roots. This "closed circuit nutrient cycling" represents a highly efficient conservation mechanism.

In attempts to use rainforest sites for agricultural production, the natural vegetation is cut down and burned to release the mineral nutrients tied up in the biomass. The nutrients allow the raising of one crop, or at best a few crops, but the soluble nutrients are rapidly leached from the soil. Only substantial input of synthetic fertilizer, usually unavailable or expensive to use, can achieve continued production. The depleted soil becomes barren and often erodes.

At low human population densities, this "slash-and-burn" type of shifting cultivation can be maintained without undue damage because it involves only small patches surrounded by the forest. After two or three crops, the plot is abandoned and a new one is cleared. The abandoned plot gets reseeded and is gradually reclaimed by the forest. Traditionally, this land has been allowed decades for recovery before being used again for raising crops. Increasing population density, however, forces increasingly longer use and shorter recovery cycles, eventually inflicting irreversible damage on the land. Use of cleared tropical rainforest sites for sustainable agriculture with little or no synthetic fertilizer input continues to present a great scientific and agronomic challenge. Most likely any solution to the problem will include the raising of perennial woody crop plants with well-developed mycorrhizal associations. These plants are clearly preferable to annual herbaceous crops, which are unsuitable for continuous closed-circuit mineral nutrient cycling.

A better knowledge and practical use of mycorrhizal associations is also called for in temperate climates, especially in connection with land reclamation. Restoration of clear-cut forests and revegetation of industrial wastelands, such as coal tips (tailings) and strip-mined areas, often depend on using plants with suitable mycorrhizal associations. Preinoculation of seeds of pine trees with a suitable ectomycorrhizal fungus *(Pisolithus tinctorius)* has been shown to enhance the ability of the seedlings to revegetate high-altitude and other unfavorable habitats (Marx et al. 1977; Ruehle and Marx 1979). If high fertilizer application rates are used, the VA-type endomycorrhizae of crop plants provide little or no benefit in terms of yield (Tinker 1975). When little or no fertilizer is added, however, the benefit of the VA mycorrhizae can be clearly demonstrated (Daft and Hacskaylo 1977).

## NITROGEN FIXATION IN NODULES

One of the most important mutualistic relationships between microorganisms and plants involves the invasion of the roots of suitable host plants by nitrogen-fixing bacteria, resulting in formation of a tumorlike growth called a *nodule.* Within the nodule, the nitrogen-fixing bacteria are able to convert atmospheric nitrogen to ammonia, which supplies the nitrogen required for bacterial and plant growth (Dalton and Mortenson 1972; Brill 1975, 1979, 1980; Bergersen 1978; Nutman et al. 1978; Schmidt 1978; Dazzo 1982; Lynch 1982b; Postgate 1982, 1992; Smith 1982; Campbell 1985; Dillworth and Glenn 1991; Evans et al. 1991) (Figure 4.8). The fixation of nitrogen in plant nodules is of extreme importance for the maintenance of soil fertility. In agricultural practices, it is used to increase crop yields.

The fixation of atmospheric nitrogen depends on the nitrogenase enzyme system (Dillworth and Glenn 1991; Stacey et al. 1992; Palacios et al. 1993; Peters et al. 1995). This enzyme system is composed of dinitrogenase (MoFe protein) and dinitrogenase reductase (Fe protein). Dinitrogenase has two dissimilar polypeptides, $\alpha_2\beta_2$. The $\alpha$ polypeptides are encoded by *nifD* and the $\beta$ polypeptides by *nifK* genes. The dinitrogenase protein contains two active metalloclusters: the P cluster containing 8 iron and 7–8 sulfur atoms ($Fe_8S_{7-8}$) and iron-molybdenum cofactor (FeMoco) containing 7 iron, 9 sulfur, 1 molybdenum atom, and 1 molecule of homocitrate ($Fe_7S_9Mo$-homocitrate). The P cluster acts as an intermediate electron acceptor and probably transfers the electron to the FeMoco cluster. The FeMoco cluster functions as the site of nitrogen reduction. The dinitrogenase reductase protein (Fe protein) consists of two identical polypeptides, $\gamma_2$, encoded by the *nifH* gene. Each polypeptide contains two iron atoms. The four Fe atoms are organized into an $Fe_4S_4$ cluster. The main function of the Fe protein is to bind and hydrolyze MgATP and to transfer electrons from the $Fe_4S_4$ cluster to the P cluster of the MoFe protein. Both proteins are folded in such a way as to bring the active centers of each into close proximity.

Nitrogenase is very sensitive to oxygen and is irreversibly inactivated on exposure to even low concentrations. Nitrogen fixation, therefore, often is restricted to habitats in which nitrogenase is protected from exposure to molecular oxygen. In addition to nitrogen reduction, the nitrogenase complex forms one $H_2$ for every $N_2$ reduced and can also reduce other substrates such as acetylene to ethylene. The ability of microorganisms to fix nitrogen is readily detected by the acetylene reduction assay. The assay is based on the fact that the nitrogenase system also catalyzes the reduction of acetylene—which, like molecular nitrogen, has a triple bond. The reduction of acetylene forms ethylene, which is easily detectable by gas chromatography. Only some strains of *Rhizobium* and *Bradyrhizobium* have hydrogenase and can utilize the hydrogen; other nitrogen-fixing bacteria wastefully evolve hydrogen gas.

### Nitrogen-Fixing Associations Between Rhizobia and Legumes

The nitrogen-fixing (diazotrophic) associations of rhizobia with leguminous plants are of great importance both in global nitrogen cycling and in agriculture (Evans et al. 1991; Postgate 1992; Somasegaran and Hoben 1994). Until recently, all nodulating and nitrogen-fixing bacteria associated with leguminous plants were placed into a single genus, *Rhizobium.* Now two additional genera, *Azorhizobium* and *Bradyrhizobium,* are recognized, and additional genera may be added as the numerous species of the legume family are investigated

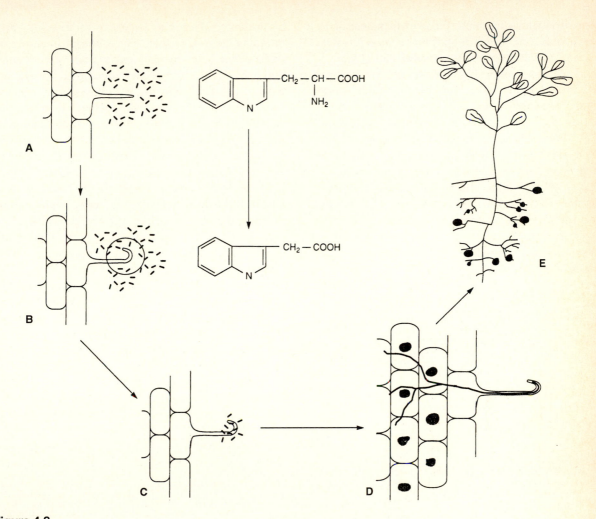

**Figure 4.8**

Interactions between rhizobia and leguminous plant roots leading to infection and nodule formation. (A) Rhizobia are chemotactically attracted to root hair. Mediated by lectins, some attach to the root hair cell wall. Tryptophan is a component of the root hair exudate. (B) Tryptophan is transformed by the rhizobia to indoleacetic acid (IAA). This plant growth hormone causes the root hair to curl or branch around the attached rhizobia. Polygalacturonase, secreted by the rhizobia or possibly by the plant, depolymerizes and softens the root hair cell wall. (C) Rhizobia gain entry into the root hair cell. The root hair cell nucleus directs the development of the infection thread. (D) The infection thread, a tube consisting of cell membrane and surrounding cellulosic wall, grows into the root cortex and infects some tetraploid cells that proliferate and form nodule tissue. The rhizobia are released from the infection thread, lose their rod shape, become irregularly formed bacteroids, and commence nitrogen fixation. (E) Nodulated leguminous plant.

for their nodulating bacteria. Table 4.1 lists some of the characteristics of each of *Rhizobium, Bradyrhizobium,* and *Azorhizobium* (Sprent and Sprent 1990).

*Rhizobium* species are fast-growing whereas *Bradyrhizobium* species grow slowly (*brady* means "slow"). *Bradyrhizobium* species nodulate soybeans, lupines, cowpeas, and various tropical leguminous plants. *Rhizobium* species nodulate alfalfa, peas, clover, and a wide variety of other leguminous plants. *Azorhizobium* is a unique member of the group that forms stem nodules on tropical leguminous trees *(Sesbania rostrata)*. In contrast to members of the two other genera, *Azorhizobium* is capable of growing with atmospheric nitrogen in its free-living state (*azo* refers to nitrogen). *Rhizobium* and *Bradyrhizobium* are not capable of doing so, although some nitrogen fixation by free-living bacteria can be demonstrated at reduced oxygen tension. Besides its slow growth rate, *Bradyrhizobium* differs from *Rhizobium* in several characteristics listed in Table 4.1. However, the infection and nodulation processes are similar for both genera. Unless noted otherwise, information provided for rhizobia pertains to both *Rhizobium* and *Bradyrhizobium.*

Although rhizobia occur as free-living heterotrophs in soil, they are not dominant members of soil microbial communities and do not fix atmospheric nitrogen in this state. Under appropriate conditions, however, rhizobia can invade root hairs, initiate the formation of a nodule, and develop nitrogen-fixing activity. The association between rhizobia and plant roots is specific, with mutual recognition between the two compatible partners based on chemotactic response and specific binding to the root hair prior to invasion and establishment of the root nodule. The legume plant root recognizes the right population of rhizobia, which in turn recognizes the right kind of leguminous root. Within the rhizosphere, plant roots supply the rhizobia with compounds that are transformed by them to substances involved in the initiation of the infection process and subsequent nodule development (Fahrareus and Ljunggren 1968). Establishment of an adequate rhizosphere population of rhizobia is an absolute prerequisite for infection.

Soil conditions have a marked effect on rhizobia in terms of their survival and ability to infect root hairs (Dixon 1969; Alexander 1985). Rhizobia are

**Table 4.1**
Characteristics of the genera *Rhizobium, Bradyrhizobium,* and *Azorhizobium*

| Feature | *Rhizobium* | *Bradyrhizobium* | *Azorhizobium* |
|---|---|---|---|
| Flagella on | | | |
| liquid medium | None | None | One lateral |
| solid medium | Peritrichous | One polar or subpolar | Peritrichous |
| Growth on $N_2$ fixed outside of plants | None | None | All strains |
| Growth rate in culture | Usually fast | Usually slow | Fast |
| Location of *nod* and *nif* genes | Mainly plasmid | Mainly chromosomal | Probably chromosomal |
| Host specificity range | Usually narrow | Often broad | Only one species so far identified |
| Agricultural significance | Most leguminous grain and forage crops | Soybeans | None |

Source: Sprent and Sprent 1990.

mesophilic, but some exhibit tolerance to low temperatures, down to 5°C, and others tolerate temperatures up to 40°C. Some rhizobia are sensitive to low pH and cannot establish root hair infections in acidic soils; nitrate and nitrite ions also inhibit nodule formations at relatively low concentrations.

The process of nodule formation is the result of a complex sequence of interactions between rhizobia and plant roots (Solheim 1984; Brewin 1991) (Figure 4.9). Flavonoids or isoflavonoids secreted by the host plants induce the expression of a number of nodulation *(nod)* genes in the cognate rhizobial bacteria. The products of *nod* genes are enzymes involved in the biosynthesis of species-specific, substituted lipooligosaccharides, called Nod factors. These signal compounds, which are released by induced rhizobial cells, elicit the curling of plant root hairs and division of meristematic cells eventually leading to the formation of root nodules. Rhizobia respond by positive chemotaxis to plant root exudates and move toward

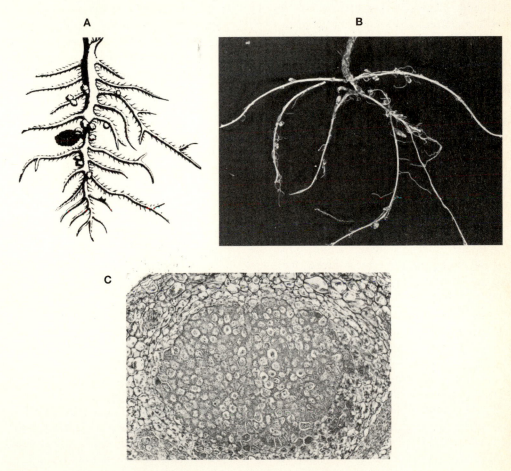

**Figure 4.9**
Root nodule: (A) Drawing showing root nodules, by Marcello Malpighi, 1679. (B) Photograph of roots of clover showing nodulation. (C) Photomicrograph of root nodule cross section showing inner core plant cells densely packed with *Rhizobium*. (Source: Carolina Biological Supply Co.)

localized sites on the legume roots. Both *Bradyrhizobium* and *Rhizobium* species are attracted by amino acids and dicarboxylic acids present in root exudates, as well as by very low concentrations of excreted compounds, such as flavonoids. Lectins, plant proteins with high affinity to carbohydrate moieties on the surface of appropriate rhizobial cells, have been identified as specific mediators of the attachment of rhizobia to susceptible root hairs (Dazzo and Hubbell 1975; Dazzo and Brill 1979; Hubbell 1981). During the nodulation process, tryptophan secreted by the plant roots is metabolized to indoleacetic acid (IAA) by the rhizobia, and the IAA, together with unknown cofactors probably arising from the host plant roots, initiates hair curling or branching. The root hairs grow around the bacterial cells. Polygalacturonase, secreted by the rhizobia or possibly by the plant roots, depolymerizes the cell wall and allows bacteria to invade the softened plant root tissues (Hubbell 1981; Ridge and Rolfe 1985).

After penetration of the primary root hair wall, the infection proceeds by the development of an infection tube ("thread") that is surrounded by the cell membrane and a cellulosic wall. It contains *Rhizobium* cells lying end-to-end in a polysaccharide matrix. The infection thread penetrates through and between root cortex cells. As the infection thread grows, the cell's enlarged nucleus moves and directs the development of the infection thread. The first cells of the developing nodule contain twice the normal number of chromosomes. These tetraploid cells give rise to the central nodule cells in which the rhizobia develop to produce nitrogen-fixing tissue. Associated cells of normal ploidy give rise to uninfected supporting tissues that connect the nodule to the root vascular system.

Within the infected tissue, rhizobia multiply, forming unusually shaped and sometimes grossly enlarged cells called *bacteroids*. Interspersed with the bacteroid-filled cells of the nodule are uninfected vacuolated cells that may be involved in the transfer of metabolites between the plant and microbe tissues. During transformation of normal rhizobial cells into bacteroids, the bacterial chromosomes degenerate, eliminating the bacteroids' capacity for independent multiplication. The bacteroid cells produce and contain active nitrogenase, but host-plant tissues appear to play a role in the initiation and control of nitrogenase synthesis. The bacteroid within the nodule carries out the fixation of atmospheric nitrogen. Under normal conditions, neither free-living rhizobia nor uninfected leguminous plants are able to bring about the fixation of atmospheric nitrogen.

For active nitrogen fixation, the plant-rhizobium association requires various organic and inorganic compounds. The trace element molybdenum is required and forms an important part of the nitrogenase enzyme. Nitrogenase also contains high amounts of sulfur and iron, which thus are requirements for active nitrogen fixation by nodules; cobalt and copper are also required in lower amounts.

Nodules have a characteristic red-brown color owing to the presence of leghemoglobin, which is a constant and prominent feature in the central tissue of all nitrogen-fixing leguminous nodules. The leghemoglobin serves as an electron carrier, supplying oxygen to the bacteroids for the production of ATP and at the same time protecting the oxygen-sensitive nitrogenase system. The heme portion of the leghemoglobin is coded for by the rhizobia and the globin portion by the plant. Leghemoglobins are unique for legume root nodules and occur nowhere else in the plant kingdom.

Specific expression of plant and bacterial genes accompanies the development of the rhizobial-plant symbiosis (Long 1989a, 1989b; Martinez et al. 1990; Nap and Bisseling 1990; Brewin 1991; Stacey et al. 1992; Fischer 1994; Van Rhijn and Vanderleyden 1995). The genes involved in root nodule formation, which are collectively called *nodulin genes,* encode a series of Nod proteins that serve specific functions in the establishment of nodules that permit symbiotic nitrogen fixation (Table 4.2). Nodulin genes essential for infection of the plant root and nodule formation by symbiotic nitrogen-fixing bacteria are divided into two classes. The first class includes genes that specify the biochemical composition of the bacterial cell surface, such as genes determining the synthesis of exopolysaccharides (*exo* genes), lipopolysaccharides (*lps* genes), capsular polysaccharides or K antigens, and ß-1,2-glucans (*ndv* genes). The *exo* and *lps* genes may play a role in determining host specificity, but this has yet to be firmly established. The second class of genes consists of the nodulation (*nod* or *nol*) genes. Inactivation of the nodulation genes can result in various plant phenotypes, such as the absence of nodulation (Nod⁻), a delayed but effective nodulation (Nod$^d$ Fix⁺), or changes in the host range. Some of the *nod* genes appear to be interchangeable for nodulation function between different species and biovars (variants) and are therefore designated as common *nod* genes. Other *nod* genes are involved in the nodulation of a particular host and are hence called host-specific *nod (hsn)* genes.

In the fast-growing *Rhizobium* species, most of the nodulin genes are located on large *Sym* plasmids, whereas the slow-growing *Bradyrhizobium* species carries the late nodulin genes on the bacterial chromosome. Within the gene cluster essential for the process of nitrogen fixation are *nif* and *fix*, which include the structural genes for the nitrogenase enzyme. The rhizobial genes required for nodule formation and nodulin gene expression include the nodulation *(nod)* genes, several groups of genes concerned with the structure of the outer surface of the bacterium (the *exo, lps,* and *ndv* genes), and a number of less well-defined genes. The host-specific *nod* genes determine the specificity of nodulation on a particular host.

The *nod* gene clusters coding for the infection and nodulation process are generally located on the *Sym* plasmids, which also carry specificity genes. It is possible to transfer the *Sym* plasmids between rhizobial strains and thus to alter the range of host legumes they can infect. *Sym* plasmids may even be transferred to *Agrobacterium* and other related bacteria, which then acquire the ability to nodulate the specified plants. However, such associations usually do not fix nitrogen. The *nif* genes that code for the biochemical nitrogen-fixing mechanism may or may not be plasmid-associated in various rhizobial strains (Postgate 1982; Sprent and Sprent 1990).

Besides the *nod* genes, the *Sym* plasmids carry the *nif* and *fix* nitrogen-fixing gene clusters (Table 4.3). The *nif* and *fix* clusters include the structural genes for nitrogenase. In *Rhizobium loti* and in *Bradyrhizobium* and *Azorhizobium* species, the symbiosis-related genes are localized on the bacterial chromosome.

Most *Rhizobium nod* genes are not expressed in cultured cells but are induced in the presence of the plant. This induction requires flavonoids secreted by the plant and also the transcriptional-activator protein NodD. The *nodD* gene is the only *nod* gene that is constitutively expressed in both the free-living and symbiotic states of *Rhizobium*. In combination with flavonoids excreted by plant roots, the NodD protein

**Table 4.2**
Some features of *nod* gene products

| Nod protein | Sequence homology |
|---|---|
| NodA | Unknown |
| NodB | Deacetylase |
| NodC | Chitin synthases |
| NodD | Transcription activator, LysR family |
| NodE | ß-Ketoacyl synthase |
| NodF | Acyl carrier protein |
| NodG | Alcohol dehydrogenase, ß-ketoacyl reductase |
| NodH | Sulfotransferase |
| NodJ | Capsular polysaccharide secretion proteins |
| NodK | Unknown |
| NodL | Acetyltransferase |
| NodM | D-Glucosamine synthase |
| NodN | Unknown |
| NodO | Hemolysin |
| NodP | ATP-sulfurylase |
| NodQ | ATP-sulfurylase and APS kinase |
| NodS | Methyltransferase |
| NodT | Transit sequences |
| NodU | Unknown |
| NodV | Sensor two-component regulatory family |
| NodW | Regulator, two-component regulatory family |
| NodX | Acidic exopolysaccharide encoded by *exoZ* |
| NodY | Unknown |
| NodZ | Unknown |

probably acts as a transcriptional activator for all other *nod* genes, and along with the *nodABC* genes is essential for nodulation. A major function of the *nod* genes is to ensure signal exchange between the two symbiotic partners. The NodD protein binds to conserved DNA sequences upstream of the inducible *nod* operons, called *nod* boxes. In the second step, the bacterium, by means of the structural *nod* genes, produces lipooligosaccharide signals (Nod factors) that induce various root responses.

**Table 4.3**
Functions associated with rhizobia genes for nitrogen fixation

| Gene | Sequence homology |
|------|-------------------|
| *nifH* | Fe protein of nitrogenase |
| *nifD* | α subunit of MoFe protein of nitrogenase |
| *nifK* | β subunit of MoFe protein of nitrogenase |
| *nifE* | Involved in FeMo cofactor biosynthesis |
| *nifN* | Involved in FeMo cofactor biosynthesis |
| *nifB* | Involved in FeMo cofactor biosynthesis |
| *nifS* | Cysteine desulfurase |
| *nifW* | Function unknown; required for full activity of FeMo protein |
| *nif X* | Function unknown |
| *nifA* | Positive regulator of *nif, fix,* and other genes |
| *fixABCX* | Function unknown; required for nitrogenase activity; FixX shows similarity of ferredoxins |
| *fixNOQP* | Membrane-bound cytochrome oxidase |
| *fixGHIS* | Redox process-coupled cation pump |
| *fixLJ* | Oxygen-responsive two-component regulatory system involved in positive control of *fixK* (Rm, Bj, Ac) and *nifA* (Rm) |
| *fixK/fixK2* | Positive regulator of *fixNOQP* (Rm, Bj, Ac), *nifA* (Ac), *rpoN1*, and "nitrate respiration" (Bj); negative regulator of *nifA* and *fixK* (Rm) |
| Rm*fixK'* | Reiterated, functional copy of *fixK* |
| Bj*fixK₁* | Function unknown |
| *fixR* | Function unknown |
| *nrfA* | Regulation of *nifA* |

Nodule-inducing molecules have been purified from plant exudates and identified as flavonoids, three-ring aromatic compounds derived from phenylpropanoid metabolism (Long 1989a). The NodD protein of a particular *Rhizobium* species proves most responsive to the flavonoids excreted by its homologous host. Rhizobia grown in the presence of root exudate or *nod* gene–inducing flavonoids contain factors that cause root hair deformation. In alfalfa and clover, the most active inducers are flavones, such as luteolin (3´,4´,5,7-tetrahydroxyflavone) (Long 1989a). The alfalfa symbiont *R. meliloti* excretes a sulfated β-1,4-tetrasaccharide of D-glucosamine, in which three amino groups are acetylated and one is acylated with an unsaturated $C_{16}$ fatty acid chain. In addition to the *nod* genes, rhizobia have genes that are required for normal nodule development, including the genes involved in the production of bacterial outer surface components such as exopolysaccharides (*exo* genes), lipopolysaccharides (*lps* genes) and (cyclic) glucans (*ndv* genes), in addition to genes related to drug resistance, auxotrophy, and carbohydrate metabolism.

The *nif* and *fix* genes of *R. meliloti, B. japonicum,* and *A. caulinodans* are arranged in distinct patterns. The structure and clustering of these genes are unique to each species (Van Rhijn and Vanderleyden 1995). The *nif* and *fix* gene clusters of the rhizobia are not as tightly regulated as those in *Klebsiella pneumoniae*. *R. meliloti* carries two extremely large plasmids (megaplasmids) of about 1400 kilobase pairs (kb) of DNA (pSym-a or megaplasmid 1) and 1700 kb (pSym-b or megaplasmid 2). Both cluster I (*nidHDKE, nifN, fixABCX nifA nifB frdX*) and cluster II (*fixLJ, fixK, fixNOQP, fixGHIS*) are located on megaplasmid 1. The cluster II genes map at about 220 kb downstream of the *nifHDKE* operon and are transcribed in opposite orientation to it. A functional duplication of the region spanning *fixK* and *fixNOQP* is about 40 kb upstream of *nifHDKE*. A cluster of *nod* genes including the common *nod* genes (*nodABC*) is located in the 30-kb region between *nifE* and *nifN*. Additional genes required for symbiosis are located on megaplasmid 2 and on the chromosome.

Control of the genes for nitrogenase and accessory functions necessary for nitrogen fixation involve a specialized promoter type (with conserved sequences at −24 and −12 [−24/−12 promoter]); an RNA polymerase containing a unique σ factor ($\sigma^{54}$); and an activator protein (NifA) (Stacey et al. 1992). NifA is important in controlling expression of the nitrogenase structural genes and genes encoding accessory functions. A variety of mechanisms have evolved to regulate *nifA* transcription with respect to the cellular oxygen conditions. In *R. meliloti* and *A. caulinodans* this control involves the FixLJ two-component regulatory system, whereas in *B. japonicum nifA* expression is stimulated under low-oxygen conditions by autoactivation. As a consequence, in *R. meliloti* and *A. caulinodans* oxygen control of nitrogen fixation genes is exerted at two levels (FixL, FixJ, and NifA), whereas in *B. japonicum* it is limited to one (NifA). The FixL and FixJ proteins are members of the ubiquitous two-component regulatory systems that enable bacteria to respond to environmental or cytoplasmic signals with specific cellular activities. Typically, signal sensing and transduction include autophosphorylation at a conserved histidine residue in the C-terminal domain of the sensor protein and transfer of the phosphate to an aspartate residue in the N-terminal region of the response regulator protein.

As indicated earlier, a side reaction of the $N_2$-reduction process is the evolution of hydrogen gas. The evolution of $H_2$ wastes photosynthetic energy and leads to lowered yields. Some *Sym* plasmids also carry *hup* genes coding for hydrogenase activity. The hydrogenase oxidizes $H_2$ to water and recovers energy by chemiosmotic coupling with ATP synthesis. This beneficial process saves photosynthetic energy that would otherwise go to waste (Albrecht et al. 1979). The genetic manipulation of the association of rhizobia with legumes is likely to increase both the range and the efficiency of the system. The economic incentives for such research are strong. Important leguminous grain crops include soybeans *(Glycine max)*, peanuts *(Arachis hypogaea)*, and many bean *(Phaseolus, Vigna)*, pea *(Pisum, Cajanus, Cicer)*, and lentil *(Lens)* varieties. Important leguminous forage crops include alfalfa *(Medicago)* and clover *(Trifolium)* varieties. Leguminous trees are critical components of many tropical and subtropical ecosystems ranging from semidesert acacias to important hardwoods of the rainforest (Sprent and Sprent 1990). Other legumes, such as mesquite (Mojave Desert) are important in desert soils that are low in available nitrogen; these legumes have served as important foods for southwestern Native Americans.

## Nonleguminous Nitrogen-Fixing Mutualistic Relationships

In addition to the mutualistic relationship between *Rhizobium* and leguminous plants, other symbiotic relationships between bacteria and nonleguminous plants result in the formation of root nodules and the ability to fix atmospheric nitrogen (Evans and Barber 1977; Akkermans 1978). The formation of root-nodule symbiosis in nonleguminous plants occurs with *Rhizobium* populations, cyanobacteria, and actinomycetes. *Rhizobium,* for example, can fix nitrogen in association with *Trema,* a tree found in tropical and subtropical regions. Likewise, the actinomycete *Frankia alni* infects the roots of trees, leading to the formation of nodules (Benson and Silvester 1993). *Frankia* species are actinomycetes (filamentous bacteria) which form septated hyphae and numerous nonmotile spores; *Frankia* species form associations with various nonleguminous plants including various woody shrubs and small trees. Such an actinomycete-type nitrogen-fixing symbiosis is especially important with angiosperms. The productivity of many forests depends on such nitrogen-fixing symbioses. In *Frankia,* a part of the hyphae becomes differentiated into specialized nitrogen-fixing cells called *vesicles. Frankia* is also capable of forming differentiated vesicles and fixing nitrogen when it is living free of a plant.

Actinomycete *(Frankia)* symbioses are more frequent in temperate and circumpolar regions, whereas cyanobacteria and rhizobial symbioses are more common in tropical and subtropical regions (Benson and Silvester 1993). Actinomycete symbioses occur in angiosperms and characteristically are found in species of *Alnus* (such as alder), *Myrica* (such as bayberry), *Hippophae, Comptonia, Casuarina,* and *Dryas,* among others. Much of the soil nitrogen in high latitudes, as in Scandinavia, probably originates from the root-nodule symbiosis of actinomycetes in non-legumes, particularly *Alnus* plants, and to a lesser extent in *Dryas, Myrica,* and *Hippophae* plants. *Casuarina* inhabits subtropical coastal sand dunes and semidesert environments (Morris et al. 1974; Callahan et al. 1978; Sprent and Sprent 1990).

When the hyphae of suitable actinomycetes penetrate the root, cortical cells are stimulated to divide (Berry 1984). The hyphae penetrate the dividing cells, forming clusters within the host, and vesicles form at the periphery of the infected hyphal tips. In the neighborhood of the primary infected tissue, a root primordium is initiated that grows into the cortex. The endophytic actinomycete invades the meristem cells of the primordium, and factors produced by the actinomycetes stimulate the development of the root primordium. The dichotomous division of the top meristem results in the formation of a cluster of lobes called a *rhizothamnion,* which is typical of all actinomycete nodules. Within the nodule, actinomycetes produce nitrogenase and fix atmospheric nitrogen.

Some liverworts, mosses, pteridophytes, gymnosperms, and angiosperms are able to establish mutualistic relationships with nitrogen-fixing cyanobacteria of the genera *Nostoc* or *Anabaena.* The gymnosperm *Cycas* has specialized root structures, called *coralloid roots,* that exhibit nodule-like structures even before invasion by the cyanobacteria. The angiosperm *Gunnera* has stem nodules. In these symbiotic relationships, the cyanobacteria are restricted to heterotrophic metabolism; the plant supplies suitable organic compounds through its photosynthetic activity, and the cyanobacteria within the underground roots produce fixed forms of nitrogen. There is a relatively high rate of exudation of nitrogenous compounds by the cyanobacteria within the plant roots as compared to free-living cyanobacteria (Postgate 1982; Sprent and Sprent 1990).

## INTERACTIONS WITH AERIAL PLANT STRUCTURES

Stems, leaves, and fruits of plants provide suitable habitats for microbial populations called *epiphytic microorganisms.* Heterotrophic and photosynthetic bacteria, fungi (particularly yeasts), lichens, and some algae regularly occur on these aerial plant surfaces (Preece and Dickinson 1971; Collins 1976; Dennis 1976; Dickinson 1976, 1982; Dickinson and Preece 1976; Blakeman 1981; Morris et al. 1996). The habitat adjacent to the plant leaf surface is known as the phyllosphere, and the habitat directly on the surface of the leaf is the phylloplane. Various bacterial and fungal populations occupy the phylloplane and phyllosphere habitats. The numbers of microorganisms on leaf surfaces depend on the season and age of the leaf.

Numerical taxonomic studies have been used to identify the bacteria in the phyllosphere (Goodfellow et al. 1976a, 1976b, 1978). The principal populations in the phyllosphere of the green needles of some pine trees are *Pseudomonas* species, including *P. fluorescens.* Populations from the phylloplane of pine trees are relatively proficient in utilizing sugars and alcohols as carbon sources compared to bacterial populations in the litter layer underlying these trees, which exhibit more lipolytic and proteolytic activity. Bacterial populations in the phylloplane of rye exhibit seasonal changes: xanthomonads and pink chromogens have high populations in May, xanthomonads and pseudomonads in July, xanthomonads in September, and listeriae and staphylococci in October.

Yeasts frequently inhabit the leaves of plants (Davenport 1976; Dickinson 1976, 1982). Populations of *Sporobolomyces roseus, Rhodotorula glutinis, R. mucilaginosa, Cryptococcus laurentii, Torulopsis ingeniosa,* and *Aureobasidium pullulans* are normal inhabitants of the phyllosphere. There is an abundance of pigmented populations of yeasts and bacteria on leaf surfaces. The pigments of these microbial populations probably afford protection against exposure to direct sunlight on the leaf surface. *Sporobolomyces* is perhaps the most successful fungus that develops in the phyllosphere; it produces ballistospores that it can shoot from one leaf to another, facilitating its dispersal. Many other fungi, including Ascomycota, Basidiomycota, and Deuteromycota, have been isolated from the phyllosphere. Some of these are undoubtedly allochthonous populations; some are associated with plant disease. Populations of *Alternaria, Epicoccum,* and *Stemphylium* have been found to be phylloplane invaders that grow extensively only under favorable conditions. Populations of *Ascochytula, Leptosphaeria, Pleospora,* and *Phoma* found in the phyllosphere are primarily saprophytes that are unable to grow extensively until the onset of senescence. Allochthonous fungal populations frequently found in the phyllosphere include *Cryptococcus, Myrothecium, Pilobolus,* and various other fungal populations whose normal habitat is the soil.

Epiphytic microorganisms on plant surfaces are directly exposed to climatic changes. These populations must withstand direct sunlight, periods of desiccation, and periods of high and low temperatures. Most successful epiphytes are pigmented and have specialized protective cell walls, adaptive features for withstanding these adverse environmental conditions. Epiphytic microorganisms also exhibit various spore discharge mechanisms that allow them to move from one plant surface to another. Insects play an important role in the dissemination of microorganisms on fruit surfaces. Fruit flies carry yeasts between fruit surfaces. Sometimes there is a close synergistic relationship among microorganisms, insects, and plants, such as among figs, yeasts, and fig wasps.

Flowers form a group of short-lived habitats for epiphytic microorganisms (Dickinson 1976, 1982). *Candida reukaufii* and *C. pulcherrima* are found in flower habitats. The high sugar content of the flower nectar makes the flower a suitable habitat for these yeast populations. Many other yeast populations, including other *Candida* species, *Torulopsis, Kloeckera,* and *Rhodotorula,* have been found within flowers. More yeasts have also been found to inhabit stamens and stigmas than the corollas and calyxes of flowers. Following fertilization of flowers and during the ripening into mature fruits, the environmental conditions of this habitat change and populations of microorganisms undergo a succession, with populations of *Saccharomyces* sometimes becoming dominant.

There are positive and negative interactions between the microbial populations found on plant surfaces. The growth of osmophilic yeasts lowers the sugar concentration, making the habitat suitable for invasion by other microbial populations. Unsaturated fatty acids produced by yeasts may inhibit development of gram-positive bacteria on fruit surfaces.

Bacterial populations that develop on fruit surfaces are dependent on growth factors, such as thiamine and nicotinic acid, that are produced by yeasts. Yeast populations are also dependent on growth factors produced by bacteria on fruit surfaces.

Microorganisms grow on the bark of trees. Lichens and various fungi, such as bracket and shelf fungi, are conspicuous colonizers of tree bark (Figure 4.10). Myxomycetes, including species of *Licea, Trichia,* and *Fuligo,* form fruiting bodies on tree bark. The fungi *Colletotrichum* and *Taphrina* grow on woody stems and tree bark. Lichens grow in the canopy of the forest within the phyllosphere. Some lichens fix atmospheric nitrogen that can be used by the surrounding vegetation.

There are several mutualistic relationships between microorganisms and plant structures other than roots that result in nitrogen fixation. The aquatic fern *Azolla* and the cyanobacterium *Anabaena* enter into such a relationship (Peters and Mayne 1974; Schardl and Hall 1988) (Figure 4.11). *Azolla* grows on the surface of quiet water in tropical and subtropical zones. On the lower surface of the *Azolla* leaves are mucilage-containing cavities that always contain *Anabaena.*

**Figure 4.10**
Photograph of a lichen growing on a tree trunk. Lichens commonly colonize tree surfaces. (Source: O. K. Miller. Virginia Polytechnic Institute, Blacksburg, VA.)

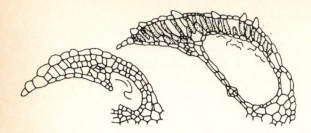

**Figure 4.11**
Drawing illustrating the filaments of the cyanobacterium
*Anabaena azollae* in the leaf cavities of the aquatic fern
*Azolla.* (Source: Smith 1938. Reprinted by permission;
copyright McGraw-Hill.)

During development of the *Azolla* leaf, the cavities
form invaginations around the *Anabaena.* Within
these cavities the *Anabaena* fix large quantities of
atmospheric nitrogen. The relationship is mutualistic,
as the *Azolla* supplies the *Anabaena* with nutrients and
growth factors and the *Anabaena* supplies the *Azolla*
with fixed forms of nitrogen.

Azolla species thrive in subtropical rice paddies,
and under favorable conditions their cyanobacterial
symbionts may fix several kilograms of nitrogen per
hectare per day. This may yield 50–150 kg nitrogen
per hectare per year and is a major factor in the continued fertility of Asian rice fields that receive very little additional nitrogen fertilizer. The *Anabaena-Azolla*
association continues to fix nitrogen even in the presence of added nitrogen fertilizer and is relatively
insensitive to low pH and to salinity. For these reasons, it has great biotechnological potential for replacing scarce synthetic nitrogen fertilizer in developing
countries (Swaminathan 1982).

Nitrogen-fixing bacteria are also found in the phyllosphere of other terrestrial plants, including the phylloplane of conifer trees (Fletcher 1976; Jones 1976).
Some of the nitrogen fixed within the phylloplane is
retained in the canopy and recycled by the microbial
populations, some is leached to the soil, some is taken
up directly by leaves, and some is grazed by herbivores.
Some bacterial species can infect leaves of Myrsinaceae (such as marlberry) and Rubiaceae (such as par-
tridgeberry), forming leaf nodules. Some leaf nodules
are capable of nitrogen fixation. In *Ardisia,* a member

of Myrsinaceae, a symbiotic relationship with bacteria
is associated with the buds. Without the bacterial symbiont, *Ardisia* develops a "cripple" condition. Similar
leaf-nodule associations have been reported in the tropical plants *Paretta* and *Psychotria* with nitrogen-fixing
*Chromobacterium* and *Klebsiella,* respectively (Silver
et al. 1963; Centifanto and Silver 1964).

In several interesting mutualistic associations, fungal endophytes grow intercellularly in wild and cultivated grasses of the Poaceae family and endow them
with protection against herbivores (Johnson et al.
1985; Christensen et al. 1991; Schardl et al. 1991). The
best described are associations of the tall fescue *(Festuca arundinacea)* and the perennial rye grass *(Lolium
perenne)* with the fungi *Acremonium coenophialum*
and *A. lolii,* respectively. The endophytes cause no disease symptoms in the grasses, but while receiving photosynthate from the host plant they synthesize a range
of alkaloids such as ergopeptides, lolines, lolitrems,
and peramines. These act as poisons or feeding deterrents against nematodes, aphids, insects, and mammalian herbivores. The lolitrems are especially potent
mammalian neurotoxins and can cause livestock losses
(rye grass staggers) on heavily infected pastures.

The *Acremonium* species just described have no
free-living stage and are not infectious. They perpetuate themselves through the plant seeds that contain the
endophyte. Experimentally, the seeds can be freed
from the endophyte by high-temperature storage.
*Acremonium* has no sexual stage and is classified with
Deuteromycota, but it also shows strong morphological and biochemical similarities to the ascomycete
*Epichloe typhina* that causes "choke disease" in some
related grasses. *Epichloe typhina* is also an asymptomatic endophyte until the flowering stage of the
infected grass. At that time profuse ectophytic (external) fungal growth with ascospore formation occurs
and halts flower development. It is tempting to speculate that the clearly mutualistic *Acremonium* developed from the moderately parasitic *E. typhina.*

One of the most interesting ecological relationships between bacteria and plants involves the role
of certain phyllosphere bacteria in initiating ice crystal formation that results in frost damage to the plant
(Lindow et al. 1978, 1982a, 1982b; Lindow and

Connell 1984). Some strains of *Pseudomonas syringae* and *Erwinia herbicola* produce a surface protein that can initiate ice crystal formation. Large epiphytic populations of ice-nucleation-active bacteria occur on many plants. Leaf surface populations of these ice-nucleation-active bacteria prevent supercooling in the plant parts on which they reside by initiating damaging ice formation when ambient temperatures reach –2°C to –4°C. The epiphytic bacteria are conditional plant pathogens, causing death due to frost damage only at temperatures that can initiate the freezing process; these bacteria consume the plant after its death, thereby gaining valuable nutritional resources. Laboratory experiments have demonstrated that ice crystals do not form until –7°C to –9°C, when ice-nucleation-active populations are replaced with mutant strains that do not produce the ice-crystal-initiating proteins, thereby limiting frost damage.

The development of genetically engineered strains of ice-minus *P. syringae,* that is, strains that do not form the ice-nucleating surface protein, and the proposal to apply such strains to field crops for frost protection caused great public and scientific concern. Little is known about the importance of the normal role of ice-nucleation bacteria and the possible environmental consequences of modifying the normal ecological relationship between ice-nucleation-active bacteria and the plants upon which they reside. Various government agencies, scientific societies, and institutions of the legal system were involved in the debate over the safety and efficacy of applying ice-minus bacteria to protect agricultural crops against frost damage, and field trials were delayed by the controversy, but eventually both the efficacy and the safety of this frost protection measure were demonstrated (see Chapter 16).

## MICROBIAL DISEASES OF PLANTS— PLANT PATHOGENS

Microbial diseases of plants, whether caused by viruses, bacteria, fungi, or protozoa, are of ecologic and economic importance (Stevens 1974; Wheeler 1975; Robinson 1976; Agrios 1978; Dickinson and Lucas 1982; Strange 1982; Campbell 1985; Fitter 1985). Plant pathology is an extensive field; only an abbreviated discussion of the plant pathogens (called *plant pests* by the U.S. Department of Agriculture) and the resulting plant diseases is possible in this chapter. In a broad sense, microbial diseases of plants cause malfunctions that result in the reduced capability of the plant to survive and maintain its ecological niche. Plant diseases may result in death or may greatly impair the growth yield of the plant. Occasionally, microbial diseases of plants result in famine and hence mass migration of human populations. The potato blight in Ireland in 1845 resulted in mass starvation and widespread emigration from Ireland to North America. Chestnut blight disease destroyed the native North American chestnut trees, which had provided an important cash crop, especially in the Appalachian area. In 1970 a leaf blight of maize caused the destruction of more than 10 million acres of corn crops during that one year.

The development of plant diseases due to microbial pathogens normally follows a pattern of initial contact of the microorganisms with the plant, entry of the pathogen into the plant, growth of the infecting microorganisms, and development of plant disease symptoms. Pathogenic microorganisms may contact the plant in the rhizoplane or the phylloplane. Because most fungal plant pathogens are dispersed through the air as spores, they often contact the leaves or stems of plants. Most viral plant diseases are transmitted by insect vectors; most of these pathogens contact the plant at the phylloplane. Some bacterial and fungal pathogens are also carried by insect vectors (Harris and Maramorosch 1981). Soilborne animals, such as nematodes, transmit some plant pathogens, contacting the plant at the rhizoplane. Motile pathogens in the soil, including plant pathogenic bacteria such as *Pseudomonas* species, and fungi, such as *Oidium,* are attracted to plant roots via chemotaxis and contact the plant in the rhizoplane.

Spores of plant pathogenic fungi distributed by air currents need to attach themselves to leaves or stems of susceptible plants. The conidiospores of the ascomycete *Magnaporthe grisea,* causative agent of the rice blast disease, efficiently attach themselves to hydrophobic surfaces such as the leaf cuticle or a cuticle-simulating Teflon membrane by means of a mucilage stored in the spore tip for this purpose. Moist air or dew causes this mucilage to swell, rupture the spore tip, and glue the spore to the leaf cuticle (Hamer et al. 1988).

The adhesion of the conidiospores of the plant pathogenic fungus *Botrytis cinerea* to surfaces was described as occuring in two distinct phases (Doss et al. 1993, 1995). Hydrated but as yet ungerminated conidiospores adhered to the cuticle of tomato leaves and other surfaces by relatively weak hydrophobic interactions. Hydrophobicity of the surface favored this initial attachment; surfactants inhibited it strongly. The viability of the conidiospores had no influence on this initial attachment. After several hours, the viable conidiospores started to germinate and the germlings secreted close to the germ tube a 25–60-nm-thick ensheathing film that adhered strongly to both hydrophobic and hydrophilic surfaces. This film remained attached to the surface even if the germlings were removed, and it resisted harsh chemical treatments. The film responsible for this strong delayed adhesion had glucose, galactosamine, and protein components, but its exact chemical structure is yet undetermined.

Plant pathogens may enter plants through wounds or natural openings, such as the stomata (Figure 4.12). When entrance is to be gained through the stomata, the hyphae of a germinating spore need a mechanism to locate and recognize such openings. For the germinating uredospores of the rust fungus *Uromyces appendiculatus,* the topographical signal was identified as a ridge approximately 0.5 µm in height, resembling the ridge formed by the stomatal guard cells of the bean plant *(Phaseolus vulgaris)*. When the hyphae encountered such a ridge, even when fabricated from polystyrene for this experiment, they underwent

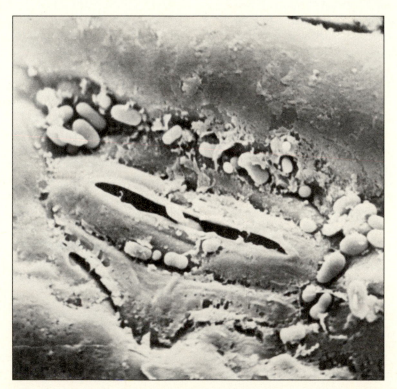

**Figure 4.12**
Scanning electron micrograph of bacteria on leaf surface of *Zea mays* showing penetration through a stoma. (Source: A. Karpoff, University of Louisville.)

morphological differentiation forming appressoria (flattened hyphae) necessary for the penetration of the stomata. Ridges less than 0.25 µm or more than 1.0 µm in height did not elicit such response (Hoch et al. 1987). Many viruses enter plants through wounds caused by the insect vector carrying the virus, although others enter through the roots with the water being taken up by the plant. Some plant pathogens are able to penetrate the cuticle of the plant directly. Such penetration involves attachment of the pathogen to the plant surface, followed by formation of a penetration peg, which passes through the cuticle and the cell wall. When a specific antibody blocked the cutinase of *Fusarium solani,* no infection of the susceptible bean plant took place, although the spore remained viable (Maiti and Kolattukudy 1979). Plant cuticles and tissues are often subjected to enzymatic attack by the pathogen that softens them at the site of penetration. Powdery mildews (*Erysiphe* species), the soft rot pathogen *Botrytis cinerea,* and *F. solani* are examples.

Microbial pathogens that have successfully entered the plant disrupt normal plant function by producing degradative enzymes, toxins, and growth regulators (Friend and Threlfall 1976). Soil plant pathogens produce pectinases, cellulases, and hemicellulases that result in degeneration of the plant structure, producing soft rots and other lesions. Destruction of plant growth regulators by pathogens results in dwarfism, whereas the production of IAA, gibberellins, and cytokinins by some plant pathogens results in gall formation and excessive elongation of plant stems. Toxins produced or induced by pathogenic organisms in plants interfere with the normal metabolic activities of the plant. The toxin produced by *Pseudomonas tabaci,* which causes tobacco wildfire disease, has been characterized as ß-hydroxydiaminopimelic acid; it interferes with the metabolism of methionine.

Some plant pathogenic fungi produce highly selective toxins, including low-molecular-weight cyclic peptides and linear polyketols (Sheffer and Livingston 1984). These appear to interfere with mitochondria and cell membranes. Damage to cell membranes may facilitate the spread of the infection. Tolerance to the toxins is usually associated with resistance to the fun-

gal disease. Resistance to the toxins seems to be based on modified receptor sites.

Plants can develop a variety of morphological or metabolic abnormalities as a result of microbial infections (Table 4.4). Invasion of plant cells by pathogenic microorganisms sometimes results in rapid death of the plant. In other cases, the plant may undergo slower changes. Pathogens that penetrate plants directly often elicit a morphological response by the plant with the formation of structures called *papillae.* This response may be an attempt to block the spread of the pathogens. Cell walls of infected plant tissues are often modified, resulting in swelling or other distortions of the cell. Invasion by plant pathogens may disrupt cell permeability, causing imbalances in water relations that lead to leakage and death of plant cells. Changes in permeability may be caused by pectic enzymes or by toxins produced by the plant pathogens. Bacterial cankers, in diseases such as fire blight of pears and apples caused by *Erwinia amylovora,* involve damage to the water-conducting tissues of plants. Blockage of water transport can also lead to desiccation and symptomatic wilt, as in *Fusarium* wilt of tomatoes caused by a reduction of water flow through the xylem. Various bacterial pathogens

**Table 4.4**
Some symptoms of microbial diseases of plants

| Disease | Symptom |
| --- | --- |
| Necrosis (rot) | Death of plant cells; may appear as spots in localized areas |
| Canker | Localized necrosis resulting in lesion, usually on stem |
| Wilt | Droopiness due to loss of turgor |
| Blight | Loss of foliage |
| Chlorosis | Loss of photosynthetic capability due to bleaching of chlorophyll |
| Hypoplasia | Stunted growth |
| Hyperplasia | Excessive growth |
| Gall | Tumerous growth |

cause wilts by blocking the stomata, which modifies transpiration and water transport in the plant.

Plant pathogens may alter the metabolic activities of the plant. Diseased plants sometimes show changes in respiratory activity, which may be caused by electron transport uncoupling or changes in the glycolytic pathways of carbohydrate metabolism. Plant pathogens may interfere with carbon dioxide fixation. Foliar pathogens sometimes produce chlorosis, which prevents plants from carrying out oxidative photophosphorylation and producing the ATP needed for carbon dioxide fixation. Plant pathogens also may cause

---

## Emerging and Reemerging Diseases of Plants

There are some newly emerging and reemerging plant diseases that pose serious threats to agricultural crops. Thousands of microorganisms, particularly fungi, cause infectious diseases of plants. It is not surprising that ecological changes have resulted in population responses of both beneficial and detrimental microorganisms (Vidaver 1996). Changes in agricultural practices, such as minimum tillage, are conducive to the survival of some pathogens, such as the fungi that cause wheat scab and gray leaf spot of corn. The migration of human populations, their urbanized living patterns, and the air transport of fresh produce have inadvertently but profoundly expanded the global dispersion of plant-associated microorganisms. Exotic fruits and vegetables were imported first to satisfy a demand of recently migrated ethnic groups accustomed to them. Subsequently, much of this produce became popular across ethnic lines. Today, large urban supermarkets sell a range of fresh fruits and vegetables completely unknown in the region just one or two decades earlier. Even more importantly, traditional produce, originally available on a seasonal basis, is now available virtually year-round, being imported from different climate zones or even the same climate zone on the other hemisphere, where the seasons are reversed. Of course, plant-associated microorganisms travel along with the fresh produce, creating dispersion and recombination opportunities that did not exist previously.

More than 150 years after late blight disease devastated potato crops in the United States and Europe and led to the Irish potato famine, this scourge is again creating a major problem worldwide (Fry 1996). Despite decades during which this disease was controlled, recent migrations of exotic strains of *Phytophthora infestans* have caused a worldwide resurgence of late blight disease. The first of the recent migrations probably occurred in the late 1970s and introduced exotic strains into Europe. Additional migrations and secondary migrations have since occurred. In the United States and Canada, the effects of exotic strains were not noticed until 1989, when late blight was severe in the Pacific Northwest. Subsequent migrations affected most potato and tomato production areas by 1995. The speed at which these few clonal lineages of *P. infestans* spread surprised growers and scientists alike. The exotic strains represent a more serious threat than did the previous indigenous strains, which the exotics are displacing. The new strains are especially pathogenic on tomatoes, and some appear to be more aggressive on potatoes than were the previous indigenous strains. The exotic strains are also largely resistant to the systemic fungicide metalaxyl. The reemer-

changes in protein synthesis, resulting in impaired metabolism. Overgrowth and gall formation involve alterations in the nucleic acid function controlling protein synthesis. Changes in protein synthesis may cause alterations of metabolic pathways and activities of the enzymes produced.

Once plants exhibit disease symptoms due to invasion by a primary plant pathogen, they are subject to additional invasion by opportunistic secondary pathogens. Loss of integrity of surface structures and cell walls allows invasion by many opportunistic microorganisms. Zymogenous (opportunistic) soil microorganisms rapidly

---

gence of late blight as a serious disease came as an unwelcome surprise in the United States and Canada. Although fungicide resistance was expected, enhanced pathogenicity was not. In their initial response, many growers have increased their use of fungicides to suppress this disease. For example, in Washington and Oregon in 1995, the cost of managing late blight was estimated at $30 million. Costs over the previous 5 years throughout the United States are estimated at well above $500 million.

Besides potato blight and other fungal plant diseases, for the last decade, geminiviruses transmitted by the whitefly *(Bemisia tabaci)* have been destroying more and more crops in tropical and subtropical regions of the world. In the Old World, geminiviruses cause serious damage to cassava, tomatoes, mung beans, and cotton. By 1987, African cassava mosaic virus was present in all major cassava-growing areas of Africa, and a severe epidemic is occurring in Uganda. In the Middle East, tomato yellow leaf curl virus can quickly wipe out tomato crops. Since 1994, cotton leaf curl virus has caused losses in excess of $2 billion in Pakistan's cotton export trade. In the Western Hemisphere the geminivirus-whitefly complex is affecting several important food crops, including beans and tomatoes. Sometimes entire fields are abandoned because virtually all of the plants are affected. Sev-

eral factors brought about this serious rise in geminivirus-caused epidemics over the last 10 years, including the introduction of the B biotype of the whitefly, which is able to reproduce more effectively than indigenous whiteflies on many different crops; changes in cropping patterns and agricultural practices; the introduction of exotic geminiviruses; difficulties in breeding plants for resistance; the high diversity of geminiviruses and the occurrence of mixed infections; and the development of whiteflies with high tolerance to insecticides.

The infrastructure of plant disease control has not kept up with the increasingly severe challenges due to recent global trade and travel patterns. Funds for inspection and quarantine enforcement have not increased in proportion to trade and travel. Fear of adverse public reaction and consequent economic losses have often delayed the dissemination of important information to growers and consumers about emerging plant diseases. The responses to new outbreaks were often too slow and too limited in scope. On the positive side, there have been numerous scientific advances in diagnostics, in plant breeding for disease resistance, in pesticides, and in biological control. For our continued food supply and economic well-being, it is essential to apply these advances to more effectively control plant diseases.

colonize dead plant material that falls to the soil surface and becomes part of the litter.

Plants under attack by microbial pathogens may react by synthesizing substances called *phytoalexins* (Deacon 1983; Snyder and Nicholson 1990). Phytoalexins comprise a broad range of inducible polyphenolic, flavonoid, or proteinaceous antimicrobial compounds. Their synthesis typically starts in the cells and at the sites that are under direct microbial attack, but their synthesis may spread to adjacent cells and the whole plant. Thus the phytoalexins help to curb the original infection and also protect the plant against subsequent microbial challenges. This phenomenon is called *systemic acquired resistance (SAR)*. A typical additional plant response to microbial infection is the rapid local necrosis (death) and desiccation of the infected cells, which also helps to contain the invading microorganisms.

To viral infections, plants respond typically by synthesis of antiviral proteins. Although the exact mode of action of these antiviral proteins remains to be elucidated, it was found recently that salicylic acid plays a central role in activating the genes coding for them (Malamy et al. 1990; Métraux et al. 1990). Salicylic acid levels in the plants rose rapidly upon virus infection and were correlated with the SAR level of the plant. Also, SAR could be induced without viral infection, merely by treating the plants with salicylic acid. Transgenic plants engineered to express a bacterial salicylic acid hydroxylase were incapable of accumulating salicylic acid and simultaneously lost their ability to acquire SAR. They became highly susceptible to viral, bacterial, and fungal infections, even to some that normally do not affect the plants in question (Gaffney et al. 1993; Delany et al. 1994). Similar and additional mechanisms of SAR will also be discussed in Chapter 16 in the context of biological control.

## Viral Diseases of Plants

Many plant pathogenic viruses are classified according to their ability to cause a particular disease (Table 4.5). Vectors are important in the transport of plant pathogenic viruses that occur in the soil or in diseased plant tissues of susceptible host plants. Various insects, including aphids, leafhoppers, mealybugs, ants, and nematodes, can act as vectors for viral diseases of plants.

A necessary attribute of plant pathogens in general, and viral pathogens of plants in particular, is the

**Table 4.5**
Some plant pathogenic viruses

| DNA viruses |
| --- |
| Caulimovirus group: cauliflower mosaic virus |

| RNA viruses |
| --- |

Rod-shaped viruses
   Tobavirus group: tobacco rattle virus; pea early browning virus
   Tobamovirus group; tobacco mosaic virus

Viruses with flexuous or filamentous particles
   Potexvirus group: potato virus X
   Carlavirus group: carnation latent virus
   Potyvirus group: potato virus
   Beet yellows virus
   Festuca necrosis virus
   Citrus tristeza virus

Isometric viruses
   Cucumovirus group: cucumber mosaic virus
   Tymovirus group: turnip yellow mosaic virus
   Nepovirus group: tobacco ringspot virus
   Bromovirus group: brome mosaic virus
   Tombushvirus group: tomato bushy stunt
   Alfalfa mosaic virus
   Pea enation mosaic virus
   Tobacco necrosis virus
   Wound tumor virus group: wound tumor virus; rice dwarf virus
   Tomato spotted wilt virus

Rhabdoviruses
   Lettuce necrotic yellows virus

ability to survive outside infected host cells until susceptible living plants can be found (Baker and Snyder 1965; Esau 1968; Plumb and Thresh 1983). As obligate intracellular parasites, plant pathogenic viruses are dependent on finding suitable plant cells for their replication. Outside susceptible plant cells—including within vectors—viruses must maintain their integrity in order to retain their infective capability. Persistence of viruses within vectors, where they are not subject to inactivation by soil microbial enzymes as they would be if free in soil, is one means by which viruses may survive in soil. Environmental factors that affect the survival and movement of vector organisms, such as soil texture and moisture, determine in large part the patterns of dissemination of pathogenic viruses. The distribution of viral plant diseases often follows the spatial distribution pattern of the vectors.

Plant pathogenic viruses may also be transmitted within or on infected plant structures. Tobacco rattle virus, for example, is detectable on the pollen of infected petunia plants. Together with pollen, it is disseminated through the air to susceptible plants. Viruses are also transmitted on plant seeds. The spread of viruses on plant structures involved in the reproductive activity of the plant, such as pollen and seeds, ensures that viruses are maintained within the susceptible host plant populations.

Viroids (acellular virus-like microorganisms composed exclusively of RNA) have been implicated as the cause of potato spindle disease, chrysanthemum stunt, and citrus exocortis disease (Diener 1979). It is not clear yet how viroids are successfully transmitted, nor precisely how they code for their own replication.

## Bacterial Diseases of Plants

Plant pathogenic bacterial species occur in the genera *Mycoplasma, Spiroplasma, Corynebacterium, Agrobacterium, Pseudomonas, Xanthomonas, Streptomyces,* and *Erwinia.* These bacteria are widely distributed and cause a number of plant diseases, including hypertrophy, wilts, rots, blights, and galls (Table 4.6).

Because most plant pathogenic bacteria do not form resting stages, they must remain in intimate contact with plant tissues during all stages of their life history.

Many plant pathogenic bacteria can remain viable on plant seeds and in other plant tissues during times of plant dormancy because they are resistant to desiccation. Many are obligate parasites and are unable to compete with saprophytic soil bacteria. Other opportunistic bacterial pathogens of plants are able to reproduce in soil, often causing plant diseases only after sufficient populations have developed in the soil.

Some bacterial pathogens exhibit no significant soil phase. For example, during the winter, *Erwinia amylovora,* which causes fire blight in fruit trees, does not grow but remains dormant within infected tissues of the stems and branches of trees (Figure 4.13). In the spring, rain and insects distribute this organism to new plants.

Some bacterial diseases are caused by pathogens that have a permanent soil phase. For example, some fluorescent *Pseudomonas* species cause soft rots in plants. These organisms, which are abundant and occur as saprophytes in the rhizosphere, infect plants through the roots.

Many plant diseases caused by bacteria are seedborne. These pathogenic bacteria survive on seeds for a transient period in the soil. Bacteria may be carried on seeds as a surface contaminant or in the micropyle. *Pseudomonas phaseolicola,* for example, is carried in the micropyle and causes halo blight of beans, whereas *Xanthomonas malvacearum,* which causes blight of cotton, occurs externally on the cotyledon margins during germination of the seed. As this pathogen is maintained externally, it is subject to considerable influence by soil properties such as texture, moisture, and temperature.

Crown gall is an extremely interesting plant disease that occurs after viable *Agrobacterium tumefaciens* cells enter either through the root or through wounded surfaces of susceptible dicotyledonous plants, usually at the soil-plant stem interface (Lippincott and Lippincott 1975; Nester and Montoya 1979; Kosuge and Nester 1984) (Figure 4.14). Occurring in fruit trees, sugar beets, and other broad-leaved plants, the disease is manifested by formation of a tumor growth, the crown gall. *Agrobacterium tumefaciens* is able to transform host plant cells into tumorous cells. In contrast to normal plant tissues, tumor tissues grow in the absence of added auxin and cytokinin and synthesize either octopine or nopaline, which are amino acid derivatives of arginine. Once established by the initial bacterial infection, the tumor continues to grow and manifest these characteristics even if viable agrobacteria are eliminated. The tumor maintenance principle has been identified as a fragment of a large, tumor-inducing plasmid called the *Ti-plasmid*. A fragment of this bacterial plasmid is transferred to the plant, where it is maintained in the tumor tissue.

Strains of *Agrobacterium* lacking this plasmid fail to induce plant galls. A gene sequence on the *Ti*-plasmid codes for transformation of tryptophan, in two steps, to indole-3-acetamide and indole-3-acetic acid, thus making the transformed plant cells auxin independent (Thomashov et al. 1986).

The same plasmid fragment, which is responsible for tumor induction, also codes for the synthesis of the unusual amino acid derivatives octopine, nopaline, and related products collectively called "opines." The

**Table 4.6**
Some diseases of plants caused by bacteria

| Organism | Disease | Organism | Disease |
|---|---|---|---|
| *Pseudomonas* | | *Erwinia* | |
| *P. tabaci* | Wildfire of tobacco | *E. amylovora* | Fire blight of pears and apples |
| *P. angulata* | Leaf spot of tobacco | *E. tracheiphila* | Wilt of cucurbits |
| *P. phaseolicola* | Halo blight of beans | *E. stewartii* | Wilt of corn |
| *P. pisi* | Blight of peas | *E. carotovora* | Blight of chrysanthemum |
| *P. glycinea* | Blight of soybeans | *Corynebacterium* | |
| *P. syringae* | Blight of lilac | *C. insidiosum* | Wilt of alfalfa |
| *P. solanacearum* | Moko of banana | *C. michiganese* | Wilt of tomato |
| *P. caryophylli* | Wilt of carnation | *C. facians* | Leafy gall of ornamentals |
| *P. marginalis* | Slippery skin of onion | *Agrobacterium* | |
| *P. sevastopol* | Olive knot disease | *A. tumefaciens* | Crown gall of various plants |
| *P. marginata* | Scab of gladiolus | *A. rubi* | Cane gall of raspberries |
| *Xanthomonas* | | *A. rhizogenes* | Hairy root of apple |
| *X. phaseoli* | Blight of beans | *Mycoplasma* | |
| *X. oryzae* | Blight of rice | *M.* sp. | Aster yellows |
| *X. pruni* | Leaf spot of fruits | *M.* sp. | Peach X disease |
| *X. juglandis* | Blight of walnut | *M.* sp. | Peach yellows |
| *X. citri* | Canker of citrus | *M.* sp. | Elm phloem necrosis |
| *X. campestris* | Black rot of crucifers | *Spiroplasma* | |
| *X. vascularum* | Gumming of sugarcane | *S.* sp. | Citrus stubborn disease |
| *Streptomyces* | | *S.* sp. | Bermuda grass witches' broom |
| *S. scabies* | Scab of potato | *S.* sp. | Corn stunt |
| *S. ipomoeae* | Pox of sweet potato | *Burkholderia cepacia* | Sour skin of onion |

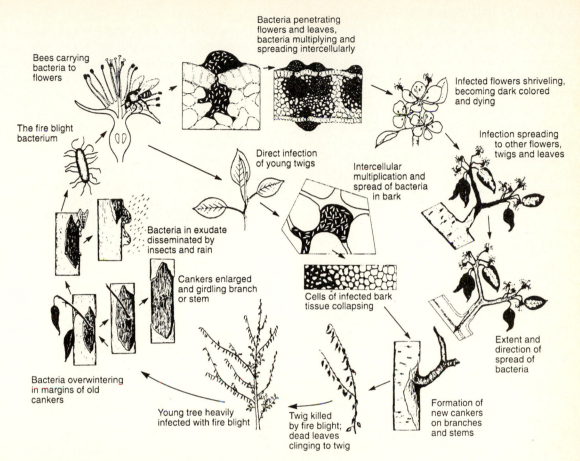

Bacteria penetrating flowers and leaves, bacteria multiplying and spreading intercellularly

Bees carrying bacteria to flowers

Infected flowers shriveling, becoming dark colored and dying

The fire blight bacterium

Infection spreading to other flowers, twigs and leaves

Direct infection of young twigs

Intercellular multiplication and spread of bacteria in bark

Bacteria in exudate disseminated by insects and rain

Cells of infected bark tissue collapsing

Cankers enlarged and girdling branch or stem

Extent and direction of spread of bacteria

Bacteria overwintering in margins of old cankers

Young tree heavily infected with fire blight

Twig killed by fire blight; dead leaves clinging to twig

Formation of new cankers on branches and stems

**Figure 4.13**

Life cycle of *Erwinia amylovora,* causing the fire blight of pears and apples. Note continuous association of the bacterium with plant tissue throughout its life cycle and lack of a free soil phase. (Source: Agrios 1978. Reprinted by permission, copyright Academic Press.)

incorporation of this genetic information into the plant cell diverts some of the plant photosynthate into production of these opines. The inducing *A. tumefaciens* strains have the unusual ability to use the respective opine as their sole source of carbon, energy, and nitrogen. Thus, through genetic recombination, many details of which remain to be elucidated, *A. tumefaciens* creates for itself a highly specific niche in which a constant supply of nutrients is assured. The unusual nature of the opine substrates largely excludes any competitors of *A. tumefaciens* from this niche. As *A. tumefaciens* is closely related to *Rhizobium,* this

natural genetic engineering system is currently under intense investigation for its potential ability to insert useful genetic information, such as nitrogen-fixation capability, into plant genomes.

The *Ti*-plasmid contains *vir* genes, which code for proteins that are required for the transfer of t-DNA (transforming DNA). The *vir* genes are expressed after induction by plant-specified phenolic compounds such as *p*-hydroxybenzoic acid and vanillin. These phenolic inducer molecules are produced by damaged plant tissues. The activities coded for by the *vir* genes lead to the transfer of genetic information contained in the T-region from a bacterial cell to a plant cell. The *virA* gene codes for a protein kinase that uses ATP to phosphorylate the VirG protein. Phosphorylation of the VirG protein converts it to an active state that, in turn, activates other *vir* genes. The VirD protein nicks the *Ti*-plasmid DNA adjacent to the t-DNA. Then the VirE protein, a single-stranded binding protein, complexes to the single-stranded DNA that contains the T-region. The VirE protein–T-region complex is transported into the plant cell via a mechanism similar to bacterial conjugation. The VirB protein acts like a sex pilus and may be involved in the transfer of the single-stranded DNA into the plant cell.

Once inside the plant cell, the T-region-containing DNA is transported into the nucleus and integrates into the plant chromosomes at a number of sites. The t-DNA contains oncogenes that code for the opines that serve as carbon, nitrogen, and energy sources for the infecting bacteria. The expression of these oncogenes also leads to the formation of tumors in the plant.

## Fungal Diseases of Plants

Most plant diseases are caused by pathogenic fungi (Table 4.7). Perhaps the most important economic fungal diseases of plants are caused by the rusts and smuts. These fungi are Basidiomycota and have a complex life cycle. There are more than 20,000 species of

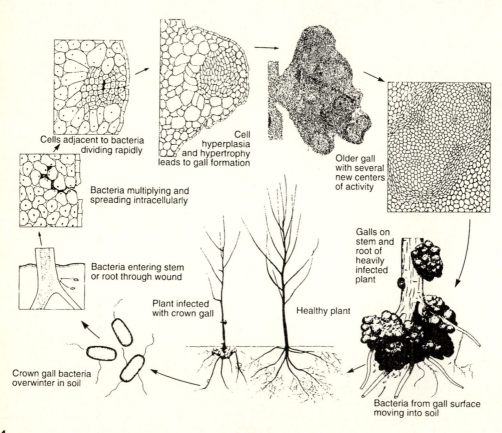

**Figure 4.14**
Life cycle of crown gall caused by *Agrobacterium tumefaciens.* Note tumor-like growth, which is symptomatic of this disease. (Source: Agrios 1978. Reprinted by permission, copyright Academic Press.)

**Table 4.7**
Some diseases of plants caused by fungi

| Organism | Disease | Organism | Disease |
|---|---|---|---|
| Myxomycota | | Basidiomycota | |
| *Plasmodiophora* | Clubfoot of crucifers | *Ustilago* | Smut of corn and wheat |
| *Polymyxa* | Root disease of cereals | *Tilletia* | Stinking smut of wheat |
| *Spongospora* | Powdery scab of potatoes | *Sphacelotheca* | Loose smut of sorghum |
| | | *Urocystis* | Smut of onion |
| Phycomycota | | *Puccinia* | Rust of cereals |
| *Olpidium* | Root disease of various plants | *Cronartium* | Pine blister rust |
| *Synchytrium* | Black wart of potato | *Uromyces* | Rust of beans |
| *Urophlyctis* | Crown wart of alfalfa | *Exobasidium* | Stem galls of ornamentals |
| *Physoderma* | Brown spot of corn | *Fomes* | Heart rot of trees |
| *Pythium* | Seed decay, root rots | *Polyporus* | Blight of turf grasses |
| *Phytophthora* | Blight of potato | *Armillaria* | Root rots of trees |
| *Plasmopara* | Downy mildew of grapes | *Marasmius* | Fairy ring of turf grasses |
| *Rhizopus* | Soft rot of fruits | | |
| | | Deuteromycota | |
| Ascomycota | | *Phoma* | Black leg of crucifers |
| *Taphrina* | Peach leaf curl | *Colletotrichum* | Anthracnose of crops |
| *Erysiphe* | Powdery mildew of grasses | *Cylindrosporium* | Leaf spot of various plants |
| *Microsphaera* | Powdery mildew of lilac | *Alternaria* | Leaf spot and blight of plants |
| *Podosphaera* | Powdery mildew of apple | *Aspergillus* | Rot of seeds |
| *Ceratocystis* | Dutch elm disease | *Botrytis* | Blight of various plants |
| *Diaporthet* | Bean pod blight | *Cladosporium* | Leaf mold of tomato |
| *Endothia* | Chestnut blight | *Fusarium* | Root rot of many plants |
| *Claviceps* | Ergot of rye | *Helminthosporium* | Blight of cereals |
| *Dibotryon* | Black knot of cherries | *Penicillium* | Blue mold rot of fruits |
| *Mycosphaerela* | Leaf spots of trees | *Theilaviopsis* | Black root rot of tobacco |
| *Ophiobolus* | Take all of wheat | *Verticillium* | Wilt of various plants |
| *Venturia* | Apple scab | *Rhizoctonia* | Root rot of various plants |
| *Diplocarpon* | Black spot of roses | | |
| *Lophodermium* | Pine needle blight | | |
| *Sclerotinia* | Soft rot of vegetables | | |

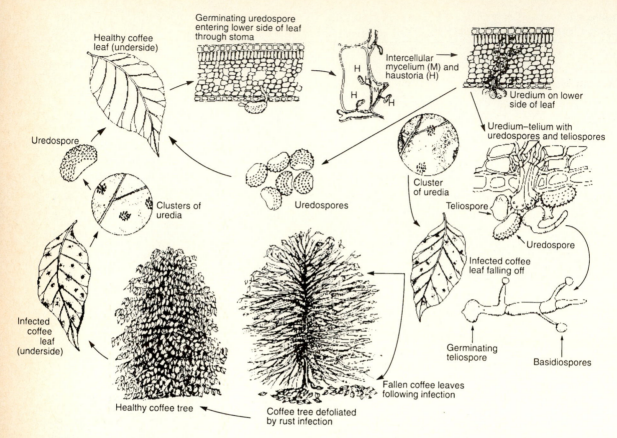

**Figure 4.15**
Life cycle of coffee rust caused by *Hemeleia vastatrix*. (Source: Agrios 1978. Reprinted by permission, copyright Academic Press.)

rust fungi and more than 1000 species of smut fungi. Rust fungi require two unrelated hosts for the completion of their normal life cycle (Figure 4.15). Important diseases caused by smut fungi include loose smut of oats, corn smut, bunt or stinking smut of wheat, and onion smut. Smut and rust fungi cause millions of dollars in crop damage every year.

Many fungi are well-adapted to act as effective plant pathogens. The variety of spores produced by fungi permit aerial transmission between plants, and the production of resting spores allows plant pathogenic fungi to remain viable outside of host plants. Many plant pathogenic fungi exhibit a complicated life cycle, part of which is accomplished during plant infection and part of which is accomplished outside of host plants. Most plant pathogenic fungi spend part of their lives on host plants and part in the soil or on plant debris in the soil (Garrett 1970) (Figure 4.16). Some fungi, such as *Venturia,* pass part of their lives on the host as parasites and part on dead tissues on the ground as saprophytes. These fungi remain in intimate contact with live or dead host tissues.

To invade susceptible plants and cause disease, all plant pathogens require favorable environmental conditions. Survival and infectivity of most plant pathogenic fungi depend on prevailing conditions of temperature and moisture. Germination of mycelia generally occurs only between –5°C and +45°C, with an adequate supply of moisture. Spores, though, can retain viability for long periods under environmental conditions that do not allow for germination.

Changes in environmental conditions may affect the pathogen, the host, or both. Most plant pathogens develop best and cause the most severe disease of plants during the warmer months of the year; during winter many are inactive. Some fungi, however, such as *Typhula* and *Fusarium,* which cause snow mold of cereals and turf grasses, respectively, thrive only in cool seasons or cool regions. In some cases, the optimal temperature for disease development is different than the optimal growth temperature of either the pathogen or the host. For example, the fungus *Thielaviopsis basicola,* which causes black root rot of tobacco, has an optimal growth temperature that is higher than the optimum temperature for the disease; in this case, the host is less able to resist the pathogen at temperatures of 17–23°C. In other cases, such as root rots of wheat and corn caused by the fungus *Gibberella zeae,* the optimum temperature for development of disease is higher than the optimal growth temperatures of both the pathogen and the wheat. Moisture, like temperature, influences the initiation and development of infectious plant diseases. Some plant pathogens are dispersed by rain droplets, initiating contact between the pathogen and the susceptible plant. The distribution of rainfall in some regions is closely correlated with the occurrence of plant diseases. Downy mildew of grapes and fire blight of pears, for example, are more severe when

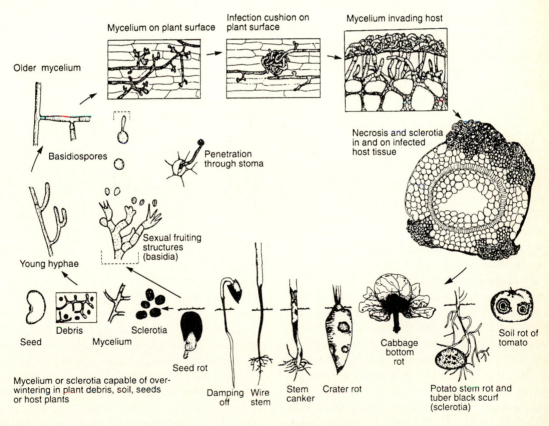

**Figure 4.16**
Life cycle of *Rhizoctonia solani* causing various diseases in plants. Invasion of plant occurs through roots. (Source: Agrios 1978. Reprinted by permission; copyright Academic Press.)

there is high rainfall or high relative humidity during the growing season. Soil pH also has a marked effect on the infectivity of soilborne plant pathogens. For example, *Plasmodiophora brassicae* causes club root of crucifers at a pH value of approximately 5.7, but the disease is completely checked at pH 7.8.

## CHAPTER SUMMARY

Microorganisms interact with plant roots on the actual surface of the root (rhizoplane) and within the region directly influenced by the root (rhizosphere). Interactions of microorganisms and plant roots are especially important in providing nutritional requirements for the plant and its associated microorganisms. The rhizosphere is a complex zone of interactions among microbial populations and between microorganisms and plants. Microorganisms within the rhizosphere are higher in numbers than and physiologically different from those in root-free soil. The differences are due to substances released from plant roots that chemically modify the adjacent soil region. The presence of rhizosphere microorganisms also is important to the plants, enabling some plants to grow better than otherwise would be possible.

In addition to interacting with numerous microorganisms in the rhizosphere, the roots of many plants establish a mutualistic relationship with specific fungi, in which the fungus actually becomes an integral part of the root. Such mutualistic relationships are called *mycorrhizae*. There are ecto- and endomycorrhizae: the vesicular-arbuscular type is a morphologically distinct and widespread form of endomycorrhizae. Mycorrhizae enhance the uptake of mineral nutrients and enable plants to grow in habitats that otherwise might not provide sufficient nutrients.

The establishment of mutualistic relationships of certain plants with nitrogen-fixing bacteria, most notably the relationship between legumes and *Rhizobium,* is extremely important to the ecology of other organisms in the biosphere. Without these nitrogen-fixing activities or human intervention through the introduction of chemical fertilizers, the abilities of all organisms to produce proteins would be highly constrained. Plants capable of forming mutualistic associations for the fixation of atmospheric nitrogen grow well even in nitrogen-deficient soils and leave the soil enriched in nitrogen for the subsequent crop. The relationship of *Rhizobium* and leguminous plants results in the formation of nodules within which the *Rhizobium* cells fix atmospheric nitrogen; the physiology of both the plant root and the *Rhizobium* are drastically altered by this association.

In addition to having root-microbe interactions, some microorganisms colonize the aerial structures of plants. Characteristic microbial populations develop on the phylloplane (leaf surface) of particular plants. Some epiphytic microorganisms may benefit the plant, protecting it against pathogens.

Plants are subject to many diseases caused by microorganisms, and plant pathogens have great ecologic and economic impact. The relationship between some plant pathogens and the host plant is greatly affected by the stationary nature of the plant, the periodicity of plant growth, the protective surfaces of the plant, and the nutritional state of the host plant. Plant pathogens must have either direct or vector-mediated means of dispersal so they can reach plants, they must have some mechanism for survival between finding suitable host plants, and they must have some mechanism for entering the plant. Because obligately plant-pathogenic microorganisms have a limited period of viability outside of host plant tissues, it is possible to control plant pathogens of agricultural crops by appropriate management procedures. These procedures include planting resistant species of crops and using crop rotation procedures. Plants have natural resistance mechanisms to defend against microbial pathogens, and such resistance can be genetically selected. Genetic breeding of crop plants allows for selection of resistant varieties. Planting resistant varieties removes available hosts for plant pathogenic microorganisms. Also, plant pathogens are normally specific for particular host plants. When crops are rotated, suitable plant hosts are periodically removed. Populations of plant pathogens that are high following infection of susceptible crops are greatly reduced due to the absence of suitable plant hosts, allowing for successful reestablishment of susceptible plant crops in successive years.

## STUDY QUESTIONS

1. Define the terms rhizoplane, rhizosphere, and rhizosheath.

2. Compare the microbial populations in the rhizosphere with those in root-free soil.

3. Compare the genera *Rhizobium* and *Bradyrhizobium*.

4. Describe the interactions of *Bradyrhizobium* and a leguminous plant that results in mutualistic nitrogen fixation. What other plant-bacterium nitrogen-fixing associations are known? Describe them.

5. What are mycorrhizae? Compare the three different types of mycorrhizae.

6. What role can mycorrhizal fungi play in restoration of land that has been strip-mined?

7. Why has it been impossible so far for biotechnology to fulfill its promise of producing nitrogen-fixing wheat, corn, or rice plants?

8. How are plant pathogens dispersed?

9. Describe the rust and smut fungi and their economic importance in agriculture.

10. Describe the interactions of *Agrobacterium tumefaciens* with a plant. Why is this plant pathogen potentially useful in biotechnology?

11. What is the overall effect of microorganisms on plant productivity?

## REFERENCES AND SUGGESTED READINGS

Agrios, G. N. 1978. *Plant Pathology*. Academic Press, New York.

Akkermans, A.D.L. 1978. Root nodule symbioses in non-leguminous $N_2$-fixing plants. In Y. R. Dommergues and S. V. Krupa (eds.). *Interactions Between Non-Pathogenic Soil Microorganisms and Plants*. Elsevier, Amsterdam, pp. 335–372.

Albrecht, S. L., R. J. Maier, F. J. Hanns, S. A. Russell, D. W. Emericyh, and H. J. Evans. 1979. Hydrogenase in *Rhizobium japonicum* increases nitrogen fixation by nodulated soybeans. *Science* 203:1255–1257.

Alexander, M. 1985. Ecological constraints on nitrogen fixation in agricultural ecosystems. *Advances in Microbial Ecology* 8:163–183.

Allen, M. F. 1991. *The Ecology of Mycorrhizae*. Cambridge University Press, Cambridge, England.

Alvarez, M.A.B., S. Gagné, and H. Antoun. 1995. Effect of compost on rhizosphere microflora of the tomato and on the incidence of plant growth-promoting rhizobacter. *Applied and Environmental Microbiology* 61:194–199.

Amarger, N. 1984. Evaluation of competition in *Rhizobium* spp. In M. J. Klug and C. A. Reddy (eds.). *Current Perspectives in Microbial Ecology*. American Society for Microbiology, Washington, DC, pp. 300–305.

Bagyaraj, D. J., and A. Varma. 1995. Interaction between arbuscular mycorrhizal fungi and plants. *Advances in Microbial Ecology* 14:119–142.

Baker, K. F., and W. C. Snyder (eds.). 1965. *Ecology of Soil-Borne Plant Pathogens: Prelude to the Biological Control*. University of California Press, Berkeley.

Balandreau, J., and R. Knowles. 1978. The rhizosphere. In Y. R. Dommergues and S. V. Krupa (eds.). *Interactions Between Non-Pathogenic Soil Microorganisms and Plants*. Elsevier, Amsterdam, pp. 243–268.

Barber, D. A. 1978. Nutrient uptake. In Y. R. Dommergues and S. V. Krupa (eds.). *Interactions Between Non-Pathogenic Soil Microorganisms and Plants*. Elsevier, Amsterdam, pp. 131–162.

Barber, D. A., and K. B. Gunn. 1974. The effect of mechanical forces on the exudation of organic substances by the roots of cereal plants grown under sterile conditions. *New Phytologist* 73:39–45.

Barber, D. A., and J. M. Lynch. 1977. Microbial growth in the rhizosphere. *Soil Biology and Biochemistry* 9:305–308.

Bateman, D. F., and R. L. Miller. 1966. Pectic enzymes in tissue degradation. *Annual Review of Phytopathology* 4:119–146.

Benson, D. R., and W. B. Silvester. 1993. Biology of *Frankia* strains, actinomycete symbionts of actinorhizal plants. *Microbiological Reviews* 57: 293–319.

Bergersen, F. J. 1978. Physiology of legume symbiosis. In Y. R. Dommergues and S. V. Krupa (eds.). *Interactions Between Non-Pathogenic Soil Microorganisms and Plants.* Elsevier, Amsterdam, pp. 304–334.

Berry, A. M. 1984. The actinorhizal infection process: Review of recent research. In M. J. Klug and C. A. Reddy (eds.). *Current Perspectives in Microbial Ecology.* American Society for Microbiology, Washington, DC, pp. 222–229.

Biancicotto, V., C. Bandi, D. Minerdi, M. Sironi, H. V. Tichy, and P. Bonfante. 1996. An obligately endosymbiotic mycorrhizal fungus itself harbors obligately intracellular bacteria. *Applied and Environmental Microbiology* 62:3005–3010.

Blakeman, J. P. 1981. *Microbial Ecology of the Phylloplane.* Academic Press, London.

Bowen, G. D. 1980. Misconceptions, concepts and approaches in rhizosphere biology. In D. C. Ellwood, J. N. Hedger, M. J. Lathan, J. M. Lynch, and J. H. Slater (eds.). *Contemporary Microbial Ecology.* Academic Press, London, pp. 283–304.

Bowen, G. D. 1984. Development of vesicular-arbuscular mycorrhizae. In M. J. Klug and C. A. Reddy (eds.). *Current Perspectives in Microbial Ecology.* American Society for Microbiology, Washington, DC, pp. 201–207.

Bowen, G. D., and A. D. Rovira. 1976. Microbial colonization of plant roots. *Annual Review of Phytopathology* 14:121–144.

Brewin, N. J. 1991. Development of the legume root nodule. *Annual Review of Cell Biology* 7:191–226.

Brill, W. J. 1975. Regulation and genetics of bacterial nitrogen fixation. *Annual Review of Microbiology* 29:109–129.

Brill, W. J. 1979. Nitrogen fixation: Basic to applied. *American Scientist* 67:458–466.

Brill, W. J. 1980. Biochemical genetics of nitrogen fixation. *Microbiological Reviews* 44:449–467.

Brill, W. J. 1981. Agricultural microbiology. *Scientific American* 245:198–215.

Brown, M. E. 1974. Seed and root bacterization. *Annual Review of Phytopathology* 12:181–197.

Brown, M. E. 1975. Rhizosphere micro-organisms— Opportunists, bandits or benefactors. In N. Walker (ed.). *Soil Microbiology.* Wiley, New York, pp. 21–38.

Callahan, D., P. D. Tredici, and J. G. Torrey. 1978. Isolation and cultivation *in vitro* of the actinomycete causing root nodulation in *Comptonia. Science* 199:899–902.

Campbell, R. E. 1977. *Microbial Ecology.* Blackwell, Oxford, England.

Campbell, R. 1985. *Plant Microbiology.* Edward Arnold, London.

Campbell, R., and A. D. Rovira. 1973. The study of the rhizosphere by scanning electron microscopy. *Soil Biology and Biochemistry* 5:747–752.

Capone, D. G., and B. F. Taylor. 1980. $N_2$ fixation in the rhizosphere of *Thalassia testudinum. Canadian Journal of Microbiology* 26:998–1005.

Centifanto, Y. M., and W. S. Silver. 1964. Leaf nodule symbiosis. I. Endophyte of *Psychotria bacteriophila. Journal of Bacteriology* 88:776–781.

Chen, T. A., and C. H. Liao. 1975. Corn stunt *Spiroplasma:* Isolation, cultivation and proof of pathogenicity. *Science* 188:1015–1017.

Chiariello, N., J. C. Hickman, and H. A. Mooney. 1982. Endomycorrhizal role for interspecific transfer of phosphorus in a community of annual plants. *Science* 217:941–943.

Christensen, M. J., G.C.M. Latch, and B. A. Tappen. 1991. Variation within isolates of *Acremonium* endophytes from perennial rye grasses. *Mycological Research* 95:918–923.

Collins, M. A. 1976. Colonization of leaves by phylloplane saprophytes and their interactions in this environment. In C. H. Dickinson and T. F. Preece (eds.). *Microbiology of Aerial Plant Surfaces.* Academic Press, London, pp. 401–418.

Cooke, R. 1977. *Biology of Symbiotic Fungi.* Wiley, New York.

Crosse, J. E. 1968. Plant pathogenic bacteria in soil. In T.R.G. Gray and D. Parkinson (eds.). *The Ecology of Soil Bacteria.* University of Toronto Press, Toronto, Canada, pp. 552–572.

Daft, M. J., and E. Hacskaylo. 1977. Growth of endomycorrhizal and nonmycorrhizal red maple seedlings in sand and anthracite soil. *Forest Science* 23:207–216.

Dalton, H., and L. E. Mortenson. 1972. Dinitrogen $(N_2)$ fixation (with a biochemical emphasis). *Bacteriological Reviews* 36:231–260.

Darbyshire, J. F., and M. R. Greaves. 1967. Protozoa and bacteria in the rhizosphere of *Sinapsis alba L., Trifolium repens L.,* and *Lolium perenne L. Canadian Journal of Microbiology* 13:1057–1068.

Darbyshire, J. F., and M. R. Greaves. 1970. An improved method for the study of the interrelationships of soil microorganisms and plant roots. *Journal of Soil Biology Biochemistry* 2:166–171.

Davenport, R. R. 1976. Distribution of yeasts and yeast-like organisms on aerial surfaces of developing apples and grapes. In C. H. Dickinson and T. F. Preece (eds.). *Microbiology of Aerial Plant Surfaces.* Academic Press, London, pp. 325–360.

Dazzo, F. B. 1982. Leguminous root nodules. In R. G. Burns and J. H. Slater (eds.). *Experimental Microbial Ecology.* Blackwell, Oxford, England, pp. 431–436.

Dazzo, F. B., and W. J. Brill. 1979. Bacterial polysaccharide which binds *Rhizobium trifolii* to clover root hairs. *Journal of Bacteriology* 137:1362–1373.

Dazzo, F. B., and D. H. Hubbell. 1975. Cross-reacting antigens and lectin as determinants of host specificity in the *Rhizobium*-clover association. *Applied Microbiology* 30:1017–1033.

Deacon, J. W. 1983. *Microbial Control of Plant Pests and Disease.* Aspects of Microbiology No. 7, American Society for Microbiology, Washington, DC.

Delaney, T. P., S. Uknes, B. Vernooij, L. Friedrich, K. Weymann, D. Negrotto, T. Gaffney, M. Gut-Rella, H. Kessmann, E. Ward, and J. Ryals. 1994. A central role of salicylic acid in plant disease resistance. *Science* 266:1247–1250.

Dennis, C. 1976. The microflora on the surface of soft fruit. In C. H. Dickinson and T. F. Preece (eds.). *Microbiology of Aerial Plant Surfaces.* Academic Press, London, pp. 419–432.

Deverall, B. J. 1977. *Defense Mechanisms of Plants.* Cambridge University Press, Cambridge, England.

Dickinson, C. H. 1976. Fungi on the aerial surfaces of higher plants. In C. H. Dickinson and T. F. Preece (eds.). *Microbiology of Aerial Plant Surfaces.* Academic Press, London, pp. 293–325.

Dickinson, C. H. 1982. The phylloplane and other aerial plant surfaces. In R. G. Burns and J. H. Slater (eds.). *Experimental Microbial Ecology.* Blackwell, Oxford, England, pp. 412–430.

Dickinson, C. H., and J. A. Lucas. 1982. *Plant Pathology and Plant Pathogens.* Blackwell, Oxford, England.

Dickinson, C. H., and T. F. Preece (eds.). 1976. *Microbiology of Aerial Plant Surfaces.* Academic Press, London.

Diener, T. O. 1979. *Viroids and Viroid Diseases.* Wiley-Interscience, New York.

Dillworth, M. J., and A. R. Glenn (eds.). 1991. *Biology and Biochemistry of Nitrogen Fixation.* Elsevier, Amsterdam.

Dixon, R.O.D. 1969. Rhizobia (with particular reference to relationships with host plants). *Annual Reviews of Microbiology* 23:137–158.

Dommergues, Y. R., and S. V. Krupa. 1978. *Interactions Between Non-Pathogenic Soil Microorganisms and Plants.* Elsevier, Amsterdam.

Doss, R. P., S. W. Potter, G. A. Chastagner, and J. K. Christian. 1993. Adhesion of nongerminated *Botrytis cinerea* conidia to several substrata. *Applied and Environmental Microbiology* 59:1786–1791.

Doss, R. P., S. W. Potter, A. H. Soeldner, J. K. Christian, and L. E. Fukunaga. 1995. Adhesion of germlings of *Botrytis cinerea. Applied and Environmental Microbiology* 61:260–265.

Drew, M. C., and J. M. Lynch. 1980. Soil anaerobiosis, microorganisms and root function. *Annual Review of Phytopathology* 18:37–67.

Dreyfus, B. L., D. Alazard, and Y. R. Dommergues. 1984. Stem nodulating rhizobia. In M. J. Klug and C. A. Reddy (eds.). *Current Perspectives in Microbial Ecology.* American Society for Microbiology, Washington, DC, pp. 161–169.

Duell, R. W., and G. R. Peacock. 1985. Rhizosheaths on mesophytic grasses. *Crop Science* 25:880–883.

Esau, K. 1968. *Viruses in Plant Hosts: Form, Distribution, and Pathogenic Effects.* University of Wisconsin Press, Madison, WI.

Evans, H .J., and L. Barber. 1977. Biological nitrogen fixation for food and fiber production. *Science* 197:332–339.

Evans H., G. Stacey, and R. H. Burris. 1991. *Biological Nitrogen Fixation.* Chapman and Hall, New York.

Fahraeus, G., and H. Ljunggren. 1968. Pre-infection phases of the legume symbiosis. In T.R.G. Gray and D. Parkinson (eds.). *The Ecology of Soil Bacteria.* University of Toronto Press, Toronto, Canada, pp. 396–421.

Fischer, H. M. 1994. Genetic regulation of nitrogen fixation in rhizobia. *Microbiological Reviews* 58: 352–386.

Fitter, A. H. 1985. *Ecological Interactions in the Soil Environment: Plants, Microbes and Animals.* Blackwell, Oxford, England.

Fletcher, N. J. 1976. Bacterial symbiosis in the leaf nodules of Myrsinaceae and Rubiaceae. In C. H. Dickinson and T. F. Preece (eds.). *Microbiology of Aerial Plant Surfaces.* Academic Press, London, pp. 465–486.

Frankenberger, W. T., Jr., and M. Poth. 1987. Biosynthesis of indole-3-acetic acid by the pine ectomycorrhizal fungus *Pisolithus tinctorius. Applied and Environmental Microbiology* 53:2908–2913.

Friend, J., and D. R. Threlfall. 1976. *Biochemical Aspects of Plant-Parasite Relationships.* Academic Press, London.

Fry, W. E. 1996. Emerging and reemerging diseases of plants. *ASM News* 62:595–597.

Gaffney, T., L. Friedrich, B. Vernooij, D. Negrotto, G. Nye, S. Uknes, E. Ward, H. Kessmann, and J. Ryals. 1993. Requirement of salicylic acid for the induction of systemic acquired resistance. *Science* 261:754–756.

Garrett, S. D. 1970. *Pathogenic Root-Infecting Fungi.* Cambridge University Press, Cambridge, England.

Goodfellow, M., B. Austin, and D. Dawson. 1976a. Classification and identification of phylloplane bacteria using numerical taxonomy. In C. H. Dickinson and T. F. Preece (eds.). *Microbiology of Aerial Plant Surfaces.* Academic Press, London, pp. 275–292.

Goodfellow, M., B. Austin, and C. H. Dickinson. 1976b. Numerical taxonomy of some yellow-pigmented bacteria isolated from plants. *Journal of General Microbiology* 97:219–233.

Goodfellow, M., B. Austin, and C. H. Dickinson. 1978. Numerical taxonomy of phylloplane bacteria isolated from *Lolium perenne. Journal of General Microbiology* 104:139–155.

Gray, T.R.G., and D. Parkinson (eds.). 1968. *The Ecology of Soil Bacteria.* University of Toronto Press, Toronto, Canada.

Grossbard, E. 1971. The utilization and translocation by micro-organisms of carbon-14 derived from decomposition of plant residues in soil. *Journal of General Microbiology* 60:339–348.

Hamer, J. E., R. J. Howard, F. G. Chumley, and B. Valent. 1988. A mechanism for surface attachment in spores of a plant pathogenic fungus. *Science* 239:288–290.

Hanson, R. B. 1977. Nitrogen fixation (acetylene reduction) in a salt marsh amended with sewage sludge and organic carbon and nitrogen compounds. *Applied and Environmental Microbiology* 33:846–852.

Harley, J. L., and R. S. Russell. 1979. *The Soil-Root Interface.* Academic Press, London.

Harley, J. L., and S. E. Smith. 1983. *Mycorrhizal Symbiosis.* Academic Press, London.

Harris, E., and K. Maramorosch. 1981. *Pathogens, Vectors, and Plant Diseases.* Academic Press, New York.

Hartley, J. L. 1965. Mycorrhiza. In K. F. Baker and W. C. Snyder (eds.). *Ecology of Soil-Borne Plant Pathogens.* University of California Press, Berkeley, pp. 218–229.

Hayman, D. S. 1978. Endomycorrhizae. In Y. R. Dommergues and S. V. Krupa (eds.). *Interactions Between Non-Pathogenic Soil Microorganisms and Plants.* Elsevier, Amsterdam, pp. 401–442.

Henry, S. M. (ed.). 1966. *Symbiosis. Vol. 1: Association of Microorganisms, Plants and Marine Organisms.* Academic Press, New York.

Hoch, H. C., R. C. Staples, B. Whitehead, J. Comeau, and E. D. Wolf. 1987. Signaling for growth orientation and cell differentiation by surface topography in *Uromyces. Science* 235:1639–1662.

Holzman, D. 1996. Bacteria in fungi may be organelle precursors. *ASM News* 62:621–622.

Hubbell, D. H. 1981. Legume infection by *Rhizobium*: A conceptual approach. *BioScience* 31:832–837.

Jensen, H. L., and A. L. Hansen. 1968. Observations on host plant relations in root nodule bacteria on the *Lotus-Anthyllis* and the *Lupinus-Ornithopus* groups. *Acta Agriculturae Scandinavia* (Copenhagen) 18:135–142.

Johnson, M. C., D. L. Dahlman, M. R. Siegel, L. P. Busch, C. M. Latch, D. A. Potter, and D. R. Varney. 1985. Insect-feeding deterrents in endophyte-infected tall fescue. *Applied and Environmental Microbiology* 49:568–571.

Jones, K. 1976. Nitrogen fixing bacteria in the canopy of conifers in a temperate forest. In C. H. Dickinson and T. F. Preece (eds.). *Microbiology of Aerial Plant Surfaces.* Academic Press, London, pp. 451–464.

Jordan, C. F. 1982. Amazon rain forests. *American Scientist* 70:394–401.

Joshi, M. M., and J. P. Hollis. 1977. Interaction of *Beggiatoa* and rice plant: Detoxification of hydrogen sulfide in the rice rhizosphere. *Science* 195:179–180.

Kosuge, T., and E. W. Nester (eds.). 1984. *Plant-Microbe Interactions*. Macmillan, New York.

Kucey, R.M.N. 1987. Increased phosphorus uptake by wheat and field beans inoculated with phosphorus-solubilizing *Penicillium bilaji* strain and with vesicular-arbuscular mycorrhizal fungi. *Applied and Environmental Microbiology* 53:2699–2703.

Lamm, R. B., and C. A. Neyra. 1981. Characterization and cyst production of azospirilla isolated from selected grasses growing in New Jersey and New York. *Canadian Journal of Microbiology* 27:1320–1325.

Last, F. T., and D. Price. 1969. Yeasts associated with living plants and their environs. In A. H. Rose and J. S. Harrison (eds.). *The Yeasts*. Academic Press, New York, pp. 183–218.

Lindow, S. E., D. C. Arny, and C. D. Upper. 1978. Distribution of ice nucleation-active bacteria on plants in nature. *Applied and Environmental Microbiology* 36:831–838.

Lindow, S. E., D. C. Arny, and C. D. Upper. 1982a. Bacterial ice nucleation: A factor in frost injury to plants. *Plant Physiology* 70:1084–1089.

Lindow, S. E., S. S. Hiteno, W. R. Barcket, D. C. Arny, and C. D. Upper. 1982b. Relationship between ice nucleation, frequency of bacteria, and frost injury. *Plant Physiology* 70:1090–1093.

Lindow, S. E., and J. H. Connell. 1984. Reduction of frost injury to almond by control of ice nucleation-active bacteria. *Journal of the American Horticultural Society* 109:48–53.

Lippincott, J. A., and B. Lippincott. 1975. The genus *Agrobacterium* and plant tumorgenesis. *Annual Reviews of Microbiology* 29:377–406.

Lippincott, J. A., B. B. Lippincott, and J. J. Scott. 1984. Adherence and host recognition in *Agrobacterium* infection. In M. J. Klug and C. A. Reddy (eds.). *Current Perspectives in Microbial Ecology*. American Society for Microbiology, Washington, DC, pp. 230–236.

Long, S. R. 1989a. *Rhizobium*-legume nodulation: Life together in the underground. *Cell* 56:203–214.

Long, S. R.1989b. *Rhizobium* genetics. *Annual Review of Genetics* 23:483–506.

Lynch, J. M. 1976. Products of soil microorganisms in relation to plant growth. *CRC Critical Reviews in Microbiology* 5:67–107.

Lynch, J. M. 1982a. The rhizosphere. In R. G. Burns and J. H. Slater (eds.). *Experimental Microbial Ecology*. Blackwell, Oxford, England, pp. 395–411.

Lynch, J. M. 1982b. *Soil Biotechnology: Microbiological Factors in Crop Productivity*. Blackwell, Oxford, England.

Maas Geesteranus, H. P. (ed.). 1972. *Proceedings of the Third International Conference on Plant Pathogenic Bacteria*. University of Toronto Press, Toronto, Canada.

Maiti, I. B., and P. E. Kolattukudy. 1979. Prevention of fungal infection of plants by specific inhibition of cutinase. *Science* 205:507–508.

Malamy, J., J. P. Carr, D. K. Klessig, and I. Raskin. 1990. Salicylic acid: A likely endogenous signal in the resistance response of tobacco to viral infection. *Science* 250:1002–1004.

Marks, G. C., and T. T. Kozlowski. 1973. *Ectomycorrhizae—Their Ecology and Physiology*. Academic Press, New York.

Martinez, E., D. Romero, and R. Palaios. 1990. The *Rhizobium* genome. *CRC Critical Reviews in Plant Science* 9:59–93.

Marx, D. H., and S. V. Krupa. 1978. Ectomycorrhizae. In Y. R. Dommergues and S. V. Krupa (eds.). *Interactions Between Non-Pathogenic Soil Microorganisms and Plants*. Elsevier, Amsterdam, pp. 373–400.

Marx, H. M., W. C. Bryan, and C. E. Cordell. 1977. Survival and growth of pine seedlings with *Pisolithus* ectomycorrhizae after two years on reforestation sites in North Carolina and Florida. *Forest Science* 23:363–373.

Métraux, J. P., H. Signer, J. Ryals, E. Ward, M. Wyss-Benz, J. Gaudin, K. Raschdorf, E. Schmid, W. Blum, and B. Inverardi. 1990. Increase of salicylic acid at the onset of systemic acquired resistance in cucumber. *Science* 250:1004–1006.

Morris, C. E., P. C. Nicot, and C. Nguyen-The. 1996. *Aerial Plant Surface Microbiology*. Plenum, New York.

Morris, M., D. E. Eveleigh, S. C. Riggs, and W. N. Tiffney, Jr. 1974. Nitrogen fixation in the bayberry *(Myrica pennsylvania)* and its role in coastal succession. *American Journal of Botany* 61:867–870.

Mosse, B. 1973. Advances in the study of vesicular-arbuscular mycorrhiza. *Annual Review of Phytopathology* 11:171–196.

Nakas, J. P., and C. Hagedorn (eds.). 1990. *Biotechnology of Plant-Microbe Interactions.* McGraw-Hill, New York.

Nap, J. P., and T. Bisseling. 1990. Developmental biology of a plant-prokaryote symbiosis: The legume root nodule. *Science* 250:948–954.

Neal, J. L., Jr., and W. B. Bollen. 1964. Rhizosphere microflora associated with mycorrhizae of Douglas fir. *Canadian Journal of Microbiology* 10:259–265.

Nester, E. W., and A. Montoya. 1979. Crown gall: A natural case of genetic engineering. *ASM News* 45:283–286.

Newman, E. I . 1978. Root micro-organisms: Their significance in the ecosystem. *Biological Reviews* 53:511–554.

Newman, E. I., and A. Watson. 1977. Microbial abundance in the rhizosphere: A computer model. *Plant and Soil* 48:17–56.

Nieto, K. F., and W. T. Frankenberger, Jr. 1989. Biosynthesis of cytokinins in soil. *Soil Science Society of America Journal* 53:735–740.

Nutman, P. S., M. Dye, and P. E. Davis. 1978. The ecology of *Rhizobium.* In M. W. Loutit and J.A.R. Miles (eds.). *Microbial Ecology.* Springer-Verlag, Berlin, pp. 404–410.

Nye, P. H., and P. B. Tinker. 1977. *Solute Movement in the Soil-Root System.* Blackwell, Oxford, England.

Palacios, R., J. Mora, and W. E. Newton (eds.). 1993. *New Horizons in Nitrogen Fixation.* Kluwer Academic, Dordrecht, Germany.

Patriquin, D., and R. Knowles. 1972. Nitrogen fixation in the rhizosphere of marine angiosperms. *Marine Biology* 16:49–58.

Patriquin, D. G., and C. R. McClung. 1978. Nitrogen accretion, and the nature and possible significance of the N$_2$-fixation (acetylene reduction) in Nova Scotian *Spartina alterniflora* stands. *Marine Biology* 47:227–242.

Peters, G. A., and B. C. Mayne. 1974. The *Azolla, Anabaena azollae* relationship. I. Initial characterization of the association. *Plant Physiology* 53:813–819.

Peters, J. W., K. Fisher, and D. R. Dean. 1995. Nitrogenase structure: A biochemical-genetic perspective. *Annual Review of Microbiology* 49:335–366.

Plumb, R. T., and J. M. Thresh. 1983. *Plant Virus Epidemiology.* Blackwell, Oxford, England.

Postgate, J. R. 1982. *The Fundamentals of Nitrogen Fixation.* Cambridge University Press, Cambridge, England.

Postgate, J. 1992. *Nitrogen Fixation.* Cambridge University Press, New York.

Powell, C. L. 1982. Mycorrhizae. In R. G. Burns and J. H. Slater (eds.). *Experimental Microbial Ecology.* Blackwell, Oxford, England, pp. 447–471.

Preece, T. F., and C. H. Dickinson (eds.). 1971. *Ecology of Leaf Surface Micro-Organisms.* Academic Press, London.

Raskin, I., and H. Kende. 1985. Mechanisms of aeration in rice. *Science* 228:327–329.

Ride, J. P. 1978. The role of cell wall alterations in resistance to fungi. *Annals of Applied Biology* 89:302–306.

Ridge, R. W., and B. G. Rolfe. 1985. *Rhizobium* sp. degradation of legume root hair cell wall at the site of infection thread origin. *Applied and Environmental Microbiology* 50:717–720.

Robinson, R. A. 1976. *Plant Pathosystems.* Springer-Verlag, Berlin.

Rovira, A. D. 1969. Plant root exudates. *Botanical Review* 35:35–57.

Rovira, A. D., and R. Campbell. 1974. Scanning electron microscopy of microorganisms on roots of wheat. *Microbial Ecology* 1:15–23.

Ruehle, J. L., and D. H. Marx. 1979. Fiber, food, fuel and fungal symbionts. *Science* 206:419–422.

Russell, R. S. 1977. *Plant Root Systems: Their Function and Interaction with the Soil.* McGraw-Hill, London.

Sanders, F. E., B. Mosse, and P. B. Tinker. 1975. *Endomycorrhizas.* Academic Press, London.

Schardl, D. J., and D. O. Hall. 1988. The *Azolla-Anabaena* association: Historical perspective, symbiosis and energy metabolism. *Botanical Review* 54:353–386.

Schardl, D. J., J.-S. Liu, J. F. White, Jr., R. A. Finkel, Z. Au, and M. R. Siegel. 1991. Molecular phylogenetic relationships of non-pathogenic grass mycosymbionts and clavicipitaceous plant pathogens. *Plant Systematics and Evolution* 179:27–42.

Schmidt, E. L. 1978. Ecology of the legume root nodule bacteria. In Y. R. Dommergues and S. V. Krupa (eds.).

*Interactions Between Non-Pathogenic Soil Microorganisms and Plants.* Elsevier, Amsterdam, pp. 269–304.

Schmidt, E. L. 1979. Initiation of plant root-microbe interactions. *Annual Reviews of Microbiology* 33:355–378.

Sheffer, R. P., and R. S. Livingston. 1984. Host-selective toxins and their role in plant disease. *Science* 223:17–21.

Silver, W. S., Y. M. Centifanto, and D.J.D. Nicholas. 1963. Nitrogen fixation by the leaf nodule endophyte of *Psychotria bacteriophila. Nature* (London) 199:396–397.

Smith, D.W. 1980. An evaluation of marsh nitrogen fixation. In V. S. Kennedy (ed.). *Estuarine Perspectives.* Academic Press, New York, pp. 135–142.

Smith, D. W. 1982. Nitrogen fixation. In R. G. Burns and J. H. Slater (eds.). *Experimental Microbial Ecology.* Blackwell, Oxford, England, pp. 212–220.

Smith, G. M. 1938. *Cryptogamic Botany. Vol. II, Bryophytes and Pteridophytes.* McGraw-Hill, New York.

Smith, M. S., and J. M. Tiedje. 1979. The effect of roots on soil denitrification. *Journal of Soil Science Society America* 43:951–955.

Smith, R. L., J. H. Bouton, S. C. Schank, K. H. Quesenberry, M. E. Tyler, J. R. Milam, M. H. Gaskins, and R. C. Little. 1976. Nitrogen fixation in grasses inoculated with *Spirillum lipoferum. Science* 193:1003–1005.

Smith, S. E., and M. J. Daft. 1978. The effect of mycorrhizas on the phosphate content, nitrogen fixation and growth of *Medicago sativa.* In M. W. Loutit and J.A.R. Miles (eds.). *Microbial Ecology.* Springer-Verlag, Berlin, pp. 314–319.

Snyder, B. A., and R. L. Nicholson. 1990. Synthesis of phytoalexins in sorghum as a site-specific response to fungal ingress. *Science* 248:1637–1639.

Society for Experimental Biology. 1975. *Symbiosis.* Cambridge University Press, Cambridge, England.

Solheim, B. 1984. Infection process in the *Rhizobium*-legume symbiosis. In M. J. Klug and C. A. Reddy (eds.). *Current Perspectives in Microbial Ecology.* American Society for Microbiology, Washington, DC, pp. 217–221.

Somasegaran, P., and H. J. Hoben. 1994. *Handbook for Rhizobia.* Springer-Verlag, New York.

Sprent, J. I., and P. Sprent. 1990. *Nitrogen Fixing Organisms—Pure and Applied Aspects.* Chapman and Hall, London.

Stacey, G., R. H. Burris, and H. J. Evans (eds.). 1992. *Nitrogen Fixation.* Chapman and Hall, London.

Stevens, R. B. 1974. *Plant Disease.* The Ronald Press Co., New York.

Strange, R. N. 1972. Plants under attack. *Science Progress* (Oxford) 60:365–385.

Strange, R. N. 1982. Pathogenic interactions of microbes with plants. In R. G. Burns and J. H. Slater (eds.). *Experimental Microbial Ecology.* Blackwell, Oxford, England, pp. 472–489.

Strange, R. N. 1984. Molecular basis for the specificity of plant pathogenic microorganisms for their hosts. In M. J. Klug and C. A. Reddy (eds.). *Current Perspectives in Microbial Ecology.* American Society for Microbiology, Washington, DC, pp. 208–216.

Swaminathan, M. S. 1982. Biotechnology research and third world agriculture. *Science* 218:967–972.

Tatum, L. A. 1971. The southern corn leaf blight epidemic. *Science* 171:1113–1116.

Ten Houten, J. G. 1974. Plant pathology: Changing agricultural methods and human society. *Annual Review of Phytopathology* 12:1–11.

Thomashov, M. F., S. Hugly, W. G. Buchholz, and L. S. Thomashov. 1986. Molecular basis for the auxin-independent phenotype of crown gall tumor tissues. *Science* 231:616–618.

Tinker, P.B.H. 1975. Effects of vesicular-arbuscular mycorrhizas on higher plants. In *Symbiosis* (Symposia of the Society for Experimental Biology). Cambridge University Press, Cambridge, England, pp. 325–350.

Vancura, V., and A. Hovaldik. 1965. Root exudates of some vegetables. *Plant and Soil* 22:21–32.

Van Rhijn, P., and J. Vanderleyden. 1995. The *Rhizobium*-plant symbiosis. *Microbiological Reviews* 59:124–142.

Vidaver, A. 1996. Emerging and reemerging infectious diseases: Perspectives on plants, animals, and humans. *ASM News* 62:583–585.

Walker, N. 1975. *Soil Microbiology.* Wiley, New York.

Wallstein, L. H., M. L. Bruening, and W. B. Bollen. 1979. Nitrogen fixation associated with sand grain root sheaths (rhizosheaths) of certain xeric grasses. *Physiologia Plantarum* 46:1–4.

Wheeler, H. 1975. *Plant Pathogenesis.* Springer-Verlag, New York.

Williamson, D. L., and R. F. Whitcomb. 1975. Plant mycoplasmas: A cultivable *Spiroplasma* causes corn stunt disease. *Science* 188:1018–1020.

Wills, B. J., and A.L.J. Cole. 1978. The use of mycorrhizal fungi for improving establishment and growth of *Pinus* species used for high-altitude revegetation. In M. W. Loutit and J.A.R. Miles (eds.). *Microbial Ecology.* Springer-Verlag, Berlin, pp. 320–323.

Woldendorp, J. W. 1978. The rhizosphere as part of the plant-soil system. In *Structure and Functioning of Plant Population.* Verhandeligen der Koninklijke, Neder-landse Akademie van Wetsenschappen, Afdeling Natuurkunde, Twede Reeks, deel 70.

Wong, T.-Y., L. Graham, E. O'Hara, and R. J. Maier. 1986. Enrichment for hydrogen-oxidizing *Acinetobacter* species in the rhizosphere of hydrogen-evolving soybean root nodules. *Applied and Environmental Microbiology* 52:1008–1013.

Wullstein, L. H., M. L. Bruening, and W. B. Bollen. 1979. Nitrogen fixation associated with sand grain root sheaths (rhizosheaths) of certain xeric grasses. *Physiologia Plantarum* 46:1–4.

# 5

# MICROBIAL INTERACTIONS WITH ANIMALS

*Most interactions between microbes and animals are beneficial. The mutualistic relationships of microbial and animal populations involve nutrient exchange and the maintenance of a suitable habitat. External and internal mutualistic associations of microbes with animals help the latter to digest difficult components of their diet, particularly cellulose. Other intestinal symbionts may be commensal or benefit the animal through vitamin production and protection against pathogens. The endozoic algae of coral polyps and other invertebrates supply a major part of the animal's nutritional needs through their photosynthetic activity. Associations with chemoautotrophic bacteria in deep-sea thermal vent environments allow invertebrates to live on geothermal energy independently from photosynthetically produced organic carbon. In a less common mutualistic relationship, endosymbiotic bacteria produce light for some marine invertebrates and fish.*

*Invertebrates that prey on microbes use special strategies such as grazing and filter feeding to overcome their extreme size difference. Predatory relationships also exist in reverse: some fungi prey on nematodes and rotifers. Microbes can also be agents of animal disease either through external toxin produc-*

*tion or by actually infecting the animal host. Disease transmisssion requires pathogen reservoirs, susceptible animals at sufficient density, and often also specific vectors.*

## MICROBIAL CONTRIBUTIONS TO ANIMAL NUTRITION

### Predation on Microorganisms by Animals

Predatory animals are usually unable to survive on disproportionately small prey because they would have to expend more energy capturing such prey than they would derive from their consumption. Nevertheless, many invertebrate animals can satisfy part or all of their food requirements by preying on microorganisms $10^5$ to $10^7$ times smaller in biomass than themselves. This feat is accomplished by two feeding strategies: grazing on microbial aggregations and filter feeding.

**Grazing** A common feeding strategy of aquatic Gastropoda (snails), Echinodermata (sea urchins), and Patellidae (limpets), for example, is to scrape and ingest the microbial crust from submerged surfaces where the microbial populations are able to reach high densities because of the physical absorption of dissolved nutrients on these surfaces (Marshall 1980). Scraping mouth organs, such as the radula of snails and the five-toothed "lantern of Aristotle" of sea urchins, are adaptations for this process. The size difference between predator and prey becomes relatively unimportant in this feeding process, called *grazing,* because the predator pursues coherent masses of millions of microbes rather than individual prey.

The microorganisms associated with fecal pellets are an important source of food for many aquatic and some terrestrial animals (Turner and Ferrante 1979). Digestion of food during passage through the alimentary canal is usually incomplete. Sugars, lipids, and proteins are preferentially digested and absorbed but cellulosic and other fibrous material remains largely intact. The excreted fecal pellets are further decomposed by the remnants of intestinal microorganisms and additional microorganisms from the environment. In this process, recalcitrant plant polymers are solubilized and converted in part to microbial biomass. Reingestion of the fecal pellet by the same animal or other animal populations allows a more complete utilization of the food resource. In addition to converting indigestible plant fiber to more digestible microbial biomass, the microorganisms often supply critical vitamins that otherwise would be absent from the diet.

In the terrestrial environment, various soil microarthropods and certain rodents and lagomorphs, including rabbits, are coprophagous and regularly reingest some of their own fecal material. In aquatic environments, some invertebrates, such as snails, graze on the microbial populations developing on fecal pellets deposited by other animals (Frankenberg and Smith 1967). Various members of the marine meiofauna secrete slime trails, which bacterial, fungal, and algal populations colonize. These slime trails provide nutrients for the growth of the microbial populations. The microorganisms adhere to the slimes, which act as mucous traps. The animals then retrace their tracks and graze on the microbial populations that have grown on and are now entrapped in the mucous slime trails.

Many marine and freshwater invertebrates consume microbial populations growing on detrital particles (Fenchel and Jørgensen 1977; Turner and Ferrante 1979). These animals rely on microorganisms to incorporate mineral nitrogen and to convert plant polymers in detrital particles that have a low N:C ratio into proteinaceous microbial biomass with a high N:C ratio, thereby enhancing the nutritional value of the detritus. Many detritus feeders digest mainly the microbial biomass associated with the detritus particle; microorganisms recolonize the undigested plant polymer, and then detritus feeders reingest the detrital particle with its new microbial biomass. In soil, the earthworm similarly digests mainly the microorganisms associated with ingested soil particles. In one rather unusual example, the desert snail *Euchondrus desertorum* grazes on lichens that grow under the surfaces of the rocks (endolithic lichens). In order to get to the lichens, a local population of snails grinds up approximately 1 metric ton of limestone per hectare per year, contributing substantially to the rock weathering process (Shachak et al. 1987).

Invertebrate grazing can have selective effects on particular microorganisms. The ingestion of *Sphaerocystis* by *Daphnia,* for example, actually enhances the growth of the alga (Porter 1976). Most of the ingested *Sphaerocystis* cells survive passage through the gut of *Daphnia,* whereas other algal species, such as *Chlamydomonas,* are assimilated by *Daphnia* with greater efficiency. The *Sphaerocystis* contributes little to the nutrition of *Daphnia,* but obtains nutrients such as phosphorus from the remains of other algal species within the gut of *Daphnia.* In this case, the digestive activities of the animal enhance the growth of *Sphaerocystis;* in the absence of zooplankton grazers, cyanobacterial populations outcompete the *Sphaerocystis* populations.

**Filter Feeding** Many sessile benthic invertebrates that are permanently attached underwater and planktonic invertebrates that float and move in the water column exhibit a different feeding strategy, called *filter feeding,* to exploit suspended planktonic microbial prey (Jørgensen 1966; Tait and DeSanto 1972; Fenchel and Jørgensen 1977). These animals remain more or less stationary and filter the prey out of suspension; this strategy is energetically advantageous because the prey are minute and in a relatively homogeneous suspension. The animals maintain a flow of water using cilia and/or various modified organs, such as legs, antennae, tentacles, gills, and tails. The microorganisms are filtered from the water through gills, tentacles, and mucous nets. Gills may serve the dual purpose of securing both a food source and an oxygen supply. The filter-feeding activity of the zooplankton is sometimes referred to as grazing, to indicate that most of the prey organisms are primary producers, but secondary producers (bacteria), predators (protozoa), and nonliving detrital particles are also ingested in the process, and therefore it is more accurately called filter feeding.

Benthic filter-feeding invertebrates include the Porifera (sponges), Bryozoa (moss animals), sessile crustacea such as barnacles, tube-building polychaete worms, Lamellibranchiata (bivalves), Brachiopoda (lamp shells or goose barnacles), and Tunicata (sea squirts). These filter feeders ingest planktonic algae, free-swimming microorganisms, and detrital particles with attached microbial biomass. The filter-feeding mechanisms of bivalves and sea squirts are particularly efficient, enabling these animals to capture particles as small as viruses from water at high rates. Important planktonic filter-feeding microcrustacea include Cladocera, which inhabit mainly freshwater environments; Copepoda, which live in both marine and freshwater environments; and Euphausia (krill), found mainly in marine habitats. Rotifers, pelagic snails (Pteropoda), Larvacia (planktonic tunicates), and various invertebrate larval forms (trochophore, nauplius, and zoea larvae) are also planktonic filter feeders, ingesting microalgae as well as protozoa, bacteria, and smaller members of the zooplankton.

## Cultivation of Microorganisms by Animals for Food and Food Processing

Cellulose is the single most abundant plant product, yet most herbivorous animals are unable to digest the cellulosic parts of the plant materials they consume. They rely on the enzymatic capabilities of microor-

ganisms to degrade this material and to produce substances that they can assimilate (McBee 1971). These substances include monomeric biodegradation products of cellulose and microbial biomass. Thus, coprophagy and ingestion of microbe-covered detritus, discussed earlier in this section, can either be viewed as animal predation on microbes or as a loosely organized synergistic effort in food digestion. Other close-knit mutualistic relationships in food digestion can take the form of intestinal symbionts or a directed external cultivation of microbial biomass for subsequent consumption. Several plant-eating insects actually cultivate pure cultures of microorganisms on plant tissues in a mutualistic relationship (Buchner 1960; Brooks 1963; Batra and Batra 1967). The protein-rich microbial biomass is used as the principal food source by the insect population. In turn, the microorganisms are dispersed by the insects and are provided with a habitat in which they can proliferate.

Various leaf-cutting ant populations maintain mutualistic relationships with fungi (Weber 1966, 1972; Batra and Batra 1967) (Figure 5.1). The ants supply leaf tissue for the microorganisms, disperse the microorganisms by inoculating segments of the leaves, and shield the cultivated fungus from competitors, maintaining a virtual monoculture that breaks down rapidly if the cultivating ants are removed. The ability of myrmicine ants to cultivate and maintain a single species of fungi in fungal gardens is essential for the maintenance of the ant population. The cultivation and pruning of fungi within these gardens greatly alters the morphology of the fungi (Figure 5.2). The ant *Acromyrmex disciger* and some *Atta* species cultivate the fungi *Leucocoprinus* or *Agaricus;* the ant *Cyphomyrmex rimoseus* cultivates *Tyridomyces formicarum; Cyphomyrmex costatus* and *Myricocrypta buenzlii* cultivate a *Lepiota* species; and the ant *Apterostigma mayri* maintains a relationship with an *Auricularia* species. The attine ants are important because they are responsible for introducing large amounts of organic matter into the soil in tropical rainforests. The organic matter thus produced forms the basis for food web interactions in which several other animal populations participate.

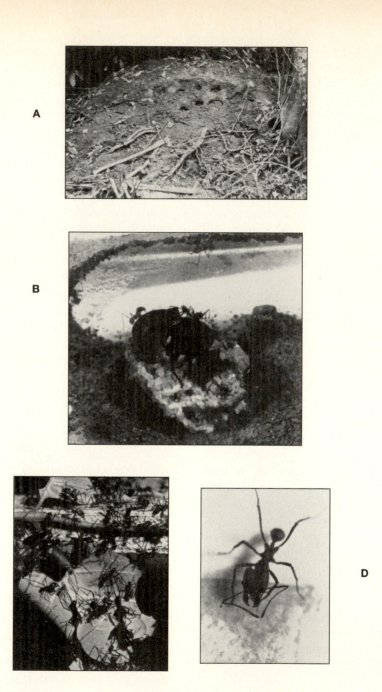

**Figure 5.1**
Cultivation of fungal gardens by ants.
(A) Surface view of an ant colony of the fungus-growing ant *Atta* showing anthill. (B) Tunnel
of fungus-growing ant showing queen and progeny cultivating fungi on leaves. (C) Leaf-
cutting behavior of *Atta*. (D) An ant gathering fungi with mandibles. (Source: Weber 1972.
Reprinted by permission of American Society of Zoologists.)

It is intriguing to consider how the ants maintain these pure fungal cultures. Selective inhibitors produced by ants or by the microbial culture have been suggested but not demonstrated. In the case of the basidiomycete cultivated by *Atta* species, the fungus is deficient in proteases and competes poorly with other fungi if not under cultivation by the ants (Martin 1970). *Atta* chews off sections of green leaves and carries them to a subterranean nest where they are macerated, mixed with saliva and fecal discharge (both of which contain proteases), and inoculated with fungal

mycelia. In this case, complementary enzymatic activity and preemptive colonization maintain the pure culture rather than antibiosis. In populations of ants that are not leaf cutters, woody particles or other plant debris are brought to the ant nest and are inoculated with fungi. Regardless of the means by which the fungi are cultivated, the ants later harvest a part of the fungal biomass and by-products and then ingest them. In addition to gaining the nutritional value of the fungal biomass itself, by feeding on the mycelia and the decomposing cellulosic substrate, the ants also acquire

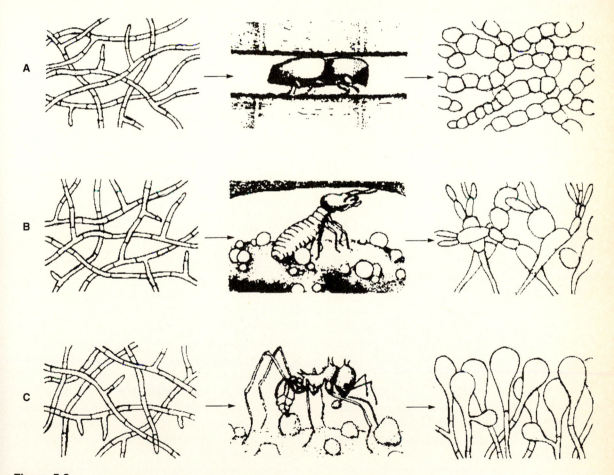

**Figure 5.2**
Appearance of uncultivated (left) and cultivated (right) fungal mycelia and the respective gardening insect (middle): (A) ambrosia beetle, (B) termite, and (C) attine ant *Atta*. (Source: Batra and Batra 1967, *The Fungus Gardens of Insects*. Copyright 1967 Scientific American Inc. All rights reserved.)

cellulase enzymes they are unable to produce themselves. These cellulases continue their depolymerizing activity in the gut of the ant, enabling it to digest cellulose (Martin and Martin 1978; Martin 1979).

The evolutionary history of the fungi acquired by the leaf-cutting ants was investigated by analysis of 28S nuclear ribosomal encoding DNA (rDNA) homologies between the cultivated fungi (Chapela et al. 1994). A simultaneous analysis of ant phylogeny was based on larval morphology characteristics. The leaf-cutting ants were found to be essentially monophyletic (evolutionarily related). Most of the cultivated fungi were found to be of the *Lepiota* genus, but some other basidiomycetes were also represented. The fungus-gardening activity of the ants was estimated to be approximately 50 million years old. The acquisition of fungal strains occurred more than once but was a very rare event. Some current fungal lineages have apparently been propagated by the same ant species as long as 23 million years.

Various wood-inhabiting insects, such as ambrosia beetles, also maintain mutualistic relationships with fungal populations (Baker 1963; Batra and Batra 1967). Each species of ambrosia beetle is normally associated with only one species of ambrosia fungus. Various populations of ambrosia beetles maintain mutualistic relationships with populations of *Monilia, Ceratocystis, Cladosporium, Penicillium, Endomyces, Cephalosporium, Endomycopsis,* and several other fungal genera (Cooke 1977). Many ambrosia fungal species exhibit dimorphism between mycelial and yeastlike forms. The fungi are maintained and protected from desiccation within specialized organs, pocketlike invaginations known as mycangia or mycetangia (Figure 5.3). The mycetangia are present in only one sex of the ambrosia beetle. When an ambrosia beetle tunnels into wood, fungal spores are dislodged from the mycetangia and inoculated onto the wood surface along with secretions that provide nutrients for spore germination.

The growth of the cultivated fungi is highly dependent on temperature and moisture, requiring a wood moisture content in excess of 35%. The ambrosia beetles clean the passages of debris and feces and open and close the entrance to the hole in

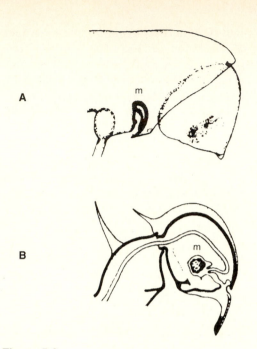

**Figure 5.3**
Mycetangia (m) of (A) the ambrosia beetle and (B) a fungus-growing ant. The ambrosia beetle carries the fungus in the pouch at the base of its front legs. The ant has a pouch in its head to carry the fungus. Both insects are shown in longitudinal sections. (Source: Batra and Batra 1967, *The Fungus Gardens of Insects.* Copyright 1967 Scientific American Inc. All rights reserved.)

response to weather conditions, thereby maintaining favorable growth conditions for the ambrosia fungi. The development of what are essentially monocultures of ambrosia fungi within the tunnels appears to be due to antagonism of the ambrosia fungi toward opportunistic invading microbial populations and to secretions from the ambrosia beetles that may have selective antimicrobial properties. When ambrosia beetles abandon a series of tunnels, many other fungal species rapidly invade the habitat and overgrow the ambrosia fungi.

Ambrosia beetles are not capable of digesting cellulose themselves and depend on the fungi to convert cellulose into protein-rich biomass. Some species, especially in their larval forms, are entirely dependent on ambrosia fungi as their food source. The mutualistic relationship between ambrosia beetles and their associated fungi is required for the survival of the beetle population, as the fungus provides the food required by the insect and its larvae. The fungal population also produces growth factors, such as vitamins, utilized by the beetles. Pupation in ambrosia beetles depends in part on production of ergosterol by the associated fungal population. In turn the beetles supply a suitable habitat for the fungi consisting of wood fragments and fecal material within the humid atmosphere of the excavated tunnels, and they maintain environmental conditions favorable for the growth of the ambrosia fungi.

Similar associations of insect and fungal populations have been found for bark-feeding beetles, ship timber worms, wood wasps, and gall midges (Batra and Batra 1967). In the first three cases, the insects physically excavate passages into wood substances, which they inoculate with fungal spores carried in exterior, pouchlike structures. The fungi grow in the wood structures, degrading plant materials, which then become available for ingestion by the insects. The fungi associated with bark beetles, blue stain fungi, have been shown to degrade sugars, starch, proteins, pectins, and, to a limited extent, cellulose. The larval galleries of the bark beetles are made in the phloem of the tree and usually result in rapid death of the tree. Fungi associated with ship timber worms ferment mainly xylem sap. In each case, the fungal biomass can serve as a food source for the insect populations, especially the larval forms. Some gall midges deposit their eggs, together with fungal spores, in leaves or buds. The fungi grow parasitically on the tissue of the developing gall, while the midge larva feeds, at least in part, on the fungal mycelium.

Various populations of termites maintain mutualistic relationships with external and internal microbial populations (Sands 1969). Some termites cultivate external fungal populations that contribute to their ability to live on wood. Without the associated fungal populations, these termite species are unable to survive on wood alone, and some termites can use only wood that has already been subjected to extensive fungal degradation. As in the case of leaf-cutting ants, the fungal populations appear to contribute enzymes to the guts of the termites. Some cellulase enzymes are produced within the termite gut (as discussed shortly), but others are acquired from the ingestion of fungi growing within the termite nests; that is, the termites acquire digestive enzymes from externally grown fungal populations (Martin and Martin 1978; Martin 1979). Many of the higher termites cultivate species of the basidiomycete *Termitomyces,* much in the manner of the fungus-gardening ants. The termites actively gather and disseminate fungal spores to establish new nests.

Other animal populations exhibit less specific synergistic relationships with external microbial populations that contribute to food digestion. The marine wood-boring invertebrate *Limnoria,* for example, obtains some of its nutrients from marine fungi that grow in the tunnels it creates within wood pilings (Sleeter et al. 1978). The fungi may provide growth factors and other metabolic products to *Limnoria.* Along with some other mollusks, *Limnoria* has been believed to synthesize its own cellulases and thus to be independent of microorganisms in respect to cellulose digestion. This view may need to be revised. Other shipworms of the Teredinae family were found to harbor endosymbiotic proteobacteria in their gill tissue. These proteobacteria produce cellulose-degrading enzymes and, in addition, are capable of nitrogen fixation (Carpenter and Culliney 1975; Distel et al. 1991). Consisting mostly of cellulose, wood is deficient in nitrogen. The described mutualistic endosymbioses are essential for the survival and growth of the marine *Teredo* shipworms. In time similar symbioses may explain the cellulase production by some or all mollusks.

## Commensal and Mutualistic Intestinal Symbionts

Most warm-blooded animals contain extremely complex microbial communities within their gastrointestinal tracts (Figure 5.4). In the lower intestine, each gram of feces contains approximately $10^{11}$ microorganisms, belonging to up to 400 different species (Lee 1985). In the human intestine, the strict anaerobes belonging to the genera *Bacteroides, Fusobacterium,*

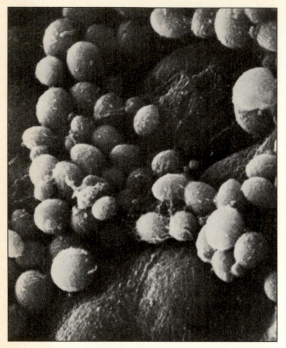

**Figure 5.4**
Scanning electron micrograph showing the yeast *Torulopsis pintolopesii* on the surface of the secreting stomach epithelium in a monoassociated gnotobiotic mouse. *Torulopsis* is an indigenous yeast that colonizes the lining of the stomach of mice and rats following weaning. (Source: Savage 1978. Reprinted by permission, copyright Springer-Verlag.)

*Bifidobacterium,* and *Eubacterium* are the most numerous, but no single species has a dominant role in this highly diverse microbial community. In some animals, such as pigs, the microbial populations of the gastrointestinal tract contribute to the nutrition of the animals by fermenting carbohydrates. There is some evidence that in older pigs microorganisms digest cellulose within the intestinal tract and that the animal can utilize the products of the cellulose degradation (Kenworthy 1973). Other microbial activities within the gastrointestinal tract, such as the degradation of amino acids, may be detrimental to the animal because of competition between the animal and the microbial populations for these nutrients.

In monogastric animals, the main contribution to digestion by intestinal microbial populations appears to be in the production of growth factors rather than in the production of partially degraded substrates. Although animals clearly absorb products derived from the microbial metabolism of ingested foods, it is not always clear whether any of these products are actually required. In some cases, microorganisms supply required vitamins; specific microorganisms synthesize vitamin K, for example, and germfree animals lacking appropriate microbial populations exhibit symptoms of vitamin deficiency (Luckey 1965). Besides their contributions to digestion and nutrition, normal gastrointestinal microbial populations, by their presence and preemptive colonization, constitute an important barrier to attack by intestinal pathogens. The high incidence of severe intestinal infections after prolonged antibiotic therapy and when germfree animals are exposed to normal nonsterilized food demonstrates this protection (Lee 1985).

In the outlined cases, the relationship of the intestinal symbionts to their animal host can be characterized as largely commensal or moderately mutualistic. The animal provides the microbes with a suitable anaerobic habitat and a steady food supply. The intestinal microbes may contribute marginally to food digestion, produce some vitamins for the host, and by their presence help to keep out potentially more harmful microbes. However, when animals derive most or all of their nutrition from compounds that are very difficult to digest, their intestinal symbionts become more specific and the animal's relationship to them shifts from commensal to clearly mutualistic.

Lower termites maintain a mutualistic relationship with internal populations of protozoa, which are responsible for the degradation of cellulose and the production of metabolites that the termite can assimilate (Breznak 1975; Breznak and Pankratz 1977; Yamin 1981) (Figure 5.5). The protozoan and bacterial populations found within the guts of lower termites and wood-eating cockroaches ferment cellulose anaerobically, producing carbon dioxide, hydrogen, and acetate. Some of the hydrogen and carbon dioxide is converted to methane by archaea (Leadbetter and Breznak 1996), but this pathway is largely wasteful for the insect and involves only negligible amounts. Acetogenic bacteria convert most of the $H_2$

and $CO_2$ to acetate (Breznak and Switzer 1986). The acetate is absorbed through the wall of the termite hindgut and is oxidized aerobically, forming carbon dioxide and water.

Some bacterial populations within termite guts also fix atmospheric nitrogen (Benemann 1973). *Enterobacter agglomerans* has been isolated from the guts of some termites and shown to be capable of nitrogen fixation under conditions of reduced oxygen tension (Potrikus and Breznak 1977). The nitrogen-fixing activities of *E. agglomerans* may be important in the nitrogen economy of some termite populations, especially during their developmental stages, because the cellulose-based diet of this termite is deficient in nitrogen.

During their early stages of life, bloodsucking species of insects nearly always feed on microorganisms. Insects that live on such restricted diets also normally develop mutualistic relationships with microbial populations that are essential for their survival (Buchner 1960). The microbial populations, which are often maintained within mycetomes, supplement dietary deficiencies of the animal by producing growth factors. Removal of the microbial populations of mycetomes of lice, for example, results in the animal's failure to reproduce. Reproductive activity and growth can be restored if the animals are supplied with B vitamins and yeast extract.

Some plant-eating birds maintain intestinal populations of bacteria and fungi that produce cellulolytic enzymes (Henry 1967). These microbial populations are able to degrade cellulose within the intestinal tract of the bird, providing it with nutrients. Honey guides, which consume beeswax, contain populations of the bacterium *Micrococcus cerolyticus* and the yeast *Candida albicans* that are able to utilize the beeswax when supplied with cofactors from the bird. Birds can assimilate nutrients produced from the degradation of the beeswax.

Various fish and aquatic invertebrates contain microbial populations within their digestive tracts that contribute to food digestion (Trust et al. 1978; Sochard et al. 1979; Atlas et al. 1982). Amphipods, for example, contain high proportions of chitinase-producing *Vibrio* species; these bacterial populations

partially degrade the chitin ingested by these animals, producing monomers that the animals can absorb and use. Some fish, such as catfish and carp, contain microbial populations that produce cellulase enzymes. The degradation of cellulose by bacterial populations within the fish gut produces metabolic products that the fish absorb.

## Digestion Within the Rumen

Digestion within the rumen is a specific case of animal mutualism with intestinal microbes that deserves more detailed discussion. The contribution of microbial

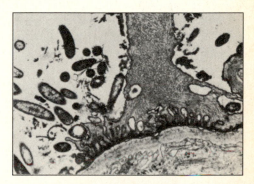

A

B

**Figure 5.5**
Electron micrographs (EM) of microorganisms in a termite gut. (A) Transmission EM of thin section showing presence of protozoa. (B) Scanning EM showing numerous protozoa (P) in the lumen of the gut. (Source: Breznak and Pankratz 1977. Reprinted by permission of American Society for Microbiology.)

populations to food digestion within ruminant animals has been intensively studied (Hungate 1966, 1975). Ruminant animals include deer, moose, antelope, giraffe, caribou, cow, sheep, and goat. These animals consume grasses, leaves, and twigs rich in cellulose. Mammals, including ruminants, do not produce cellulase enzymes themselves but depend on associated microbial populations for degrading cellulosic materials. Ruminants have a specialized chamber known as the rumen that contains large populations of protozoa and bacteria that contribute to food digestion (Figure 5.6). The rumen provides a relatively uniform and stable environment that is anaerobic, is 30–40°C, and has a pH of 5.5–7.0. These conditions, optimal for the associated microorganisms, and the continuous supply of ingested plant material permit the development of very dense ($10^9$–$10^{10}$/mL) communities of microorganisms.

The overall fermentation that occurs within the rumen can be described by Equation 1 (Wolin 1979).

$$(1) \quad 57.5\,(C_6H_{12}O_6) \rightarrow$$
$$65\ \text{acetate} + 20\ \text{propionate} + 15\ \text{butyrate}$$
$$+\ 60\ CO_2 + 35\ CH_4 + 25\ H_2O$$

Carbon flow and energy balances have been determined for the biochemical activities of the microbial populations in the rumen. Microorganisms within the rumen convert cellulose, starch, and other ingested nutrients to carbon dioxide, hydrogen gas, methane, and low-molecular-weight organic acids, such as acetic, propionic, and butyric acids. The organic acids are absorbed into the bloodstream of the animal, where they are oxidized aerobically to produce energy. Ruminants are also able to use protein produced by the associated microbial populations. Fermentatively produced $CO_2$ and methane produced by methanogenic bacteria within the rumen are expelled and do not contribute to the nutrition of the animal.

The anaerobic environment in the rumen ensures that a relatively small percentage of the caloric value

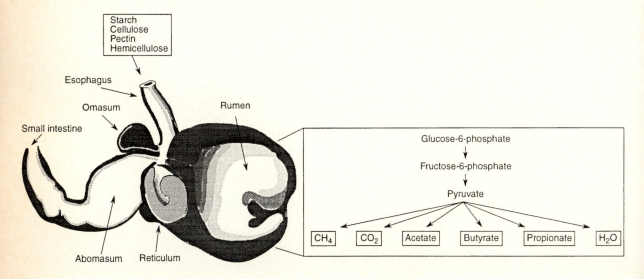

**Figure 5.6**

The rumen is a large anaerobic sac. Cows and other ruminant animals eat grasses and other plants containing cellulose, starch, pectin, and hemicellulose, which are transported to the rumen. Within the rumen, bacterial and archaeal populations convert these complex plant materials to low-molecular-weight fatty acids, carbon dioxide, and methane. The fatty acids, especially acetate, supply the nutritional needs of the animal. The carbon dioxide and methane are lost as waste products.

of food (about 10%) is lost to the animal during the microbial digestion process. Even some of this "lost" energy benefits the animal by helping to maintain its body temperature. Ruminants are excellent utilizers of low-grade, high-cellulose food but relatively inefficient utilizers of the high-grade proteinaceous feed used in feed lots. Cross-linking the proteins in high-grade feed by treatment with formaldehyde, dimethylolurea, and other agents blocks their degradation by rumen microorganisms, ensuring that valuable protein is digested and absorbed in the lower portions of the gastrointestinal tract rather than being fermented to methane (Friedman et al. 1982).

The rumen harbors a great diversity of microorganisms (Hungate 1966, 1975) (Table 5.1). Bacterial populations within the rumen include cellulose digesters, starch digesters, hemicellulose digesters, sugar fermenters, fatty acid utilizers, methanogenic bacteria, proteolytic bacteria, and lipolytic bacteria. These populations include species of *Bacteroides, Ruminococcus, Succinimonas, Methanobacterium, Butyrivibrio, Selenomonas, Succinivibrio, Streptococcus, Eubacterium,* and *Lactobacillus.* Many of these bacterial populations produce acetate, the predominant acid within the rumen. The bacteria also produce propionate, the only fermentation acid that can be converted into carbohydrates by the ruminant. The diverse bacterial community of the rumen possesses the broad enzymatic capabilities required for digesting the various plant components ingested by ruminants. Some nitrogen-fixation activity has also been noted in the rumen, but the amounts (approximately 10 mg of N per head of cattle per day) are too low to make a significant contribution to the nutrition of the

**Table 5.1**
Fermentation products and energy sources of some rumen bacteria

| Organism | Energy sources[*] | Major fermentation products[†] |
|---|---|---|
| *Bacteroides succinogenes* | C, S, G | A, S |
| *Bacteroides amylophilus* | S | A, S, F |
| *Bacteroides ruminicola* | S, X, G | A, S, F |
| *Ruminococcus flavefaciens* | C, X, G | A, S, F, H |
| *Succinivibrio dextrinosolvens* | G | A, S |
| *Succinimonas amylolytica* | S, G | S |
| *Ruminococcus albus* | C, X, G | A, F, H, E |
| *Butyrivibrio fibrisolvens* | C, S, X, G | F, H, B |
| *Eubacterium ruminantium* | X, G | F, B, L |
| *Selenomonas ruminantium* | S, G, L, Y | A, P, L |
| *Veillonella alcalescens* | L | A, P, H |
| *Streptococcus bovis* | S, G | L |
| *Lactobacillus vitulinus* | G | L |
| *Methanobacterium ruminantium* | $H_2 + CO_2$, F | M |

[*]Energy sources: C = cellulose; S = starch; X = xylan; G = glucose; L = lactate; Y = glycerol; F = formate

[†]Fermentation products: A = acetate; S = succinate; F = formate; H = hydrogen; E = ethanol; B = butyrate; P = propionate; L = lactate; M = methane. Many also produce $CO_2$.

Source: Wolin 1979.

animal (Hardy et al. 1968). One reason is that ammonia present in the rumen tends to repress nitrogen fixation. On the other hand, the ammonia in the rumen can be converted by the microbial community to microbial protein, subsequently digested by the ruminant. Theoretically, one could maintain ruminants like cattle on cellulose and ammonium salts alone, but ammonium toxicity precludes this from being a practical approach to raising cattle. However, urea is added as a cheap supplementary nitrogen source to some cattle feed formulae. This nitrogen source is utilized by the animal only indirectly after conversion to microbial biomass.

The rumen contains, in addition to bacteria, large populations of protozoa; most are ciliates, but some flagellates, such as *Eutodinium, Diplodinium,* and *Sarcodina,* are also present. Rumen ciliates are a highly specialized group that grow anaerobically, ferment plant materials for energy, and tolerate the presence of dense bacterial populations. Some protozoan populations within the rumen are capable of digesting cellulose and starch; others ferment dissolved carbohydrates. Some are predators on bacterial populations. The proteins of the rumen protozoa are, in turn, digested by the ruminant's enzymes. Rumen protozoa store large amounts of carbohydrates, which the ruminant digests along with the proteins of the protozoan biomass. The digestion of protozoa occurs in the omasum and abomasum, compartments of the ruminant stomach located adjacent to the rumen. The transfer of carbon from bacteria to protozoa to the ruminant animal constitutes a short and efficient food chain. Protozoa are probably more efficiently digested than bacteria because the latter have resistant cell walls and high nucleic acid contents. Fungi are minor participants in the rumen microbial community, but anaerobic chytrids are present and participate in cellulose depolymerization.

The relationship between the ruminant and the microbial populations of the rumen is mutualistic. Both partners clearly derive benefits from the relationship. Some microbial populations are found only within the specialized environment of the rumen; others also occur in other environments. The microorganisms in the rumen digest plant materials, making low-molecular-weight fatty acids and microbial proteins available to the ruminant. Some bacterial populations in the rumen require growth factors, but others are able to produce vitamins to supply the nutritional requirements of the rumen community and the ruminant.

The rumen provides a suitable environment and a constant supply of substrates for the fermentative activities of these microorganisms. The rumination process (rechewing previously ingested food) grinds the plant material and provides an increased surface area for microbial attack. The animal's saliva also contributes to rendering the ingested plant material susceptible to microbial attack. The movement of the ruminant stomach supplies sufficient mixing for optimal microbial growth and metabolic activities. The removal of low-molecular-weight fatty acids from the rumen by absorption into the animal's bloodstream allows continued prolific growth of the microbial population. An accumulation of these acids would be toxic to the microbes.

The high diversity of microbial populations in the rumen allows the microbial community to respond to changes in the ruminant's diet. Some ingested plant materials contain large amounts of cellulose, others large amounts of hemicellulose materials, and still others, large amounts of starches. The relative proportions of microbial populations within the rumen shift according to the nature of the plant materials ingested. Abrupt changes in diet, such as the change from dry hay in winter to pasture grass in spring, can upset the rumen fermentation system, resulting in excessive production of methane that can distend the rumen, sometimes to the extent that it compresses the lungs, suffocating the animal. This condition is known as bloat of sheep or cattle, and once it has developed, only puncturing the rumen to release excess methane can save the animal.

Other animals that exhibit ruminant-like digestion include colobid monkeys, sloths, hippopotamuses, camels, and macropod marsupials. In each of these animals, microbial populations associated with the foregut are capable of degrading cellulosic and other plant materials. The enzymatic activities of these microorganisms produce volatile fatty acids that the animals can utilize. These microbial populations contribute to partial food digestion. In nonruminant mammals that subsist primarily on plant materials, such as horses, pigs, and rabbits, microbial cellulose digestion occurs in an enlarged cecum with the production of volatile fatty acids. These fatty acids are absorbed through the intestinal lining, enter the bloodstream, and are ultimately oxidized within the animal's cells, producing carbon dioxide and water. Baleen whales that feed on planktonic crustacea (krill) have multi-chambered stomachs and in their forestomach rumen-type fermentation takes place, with abundant fatty acid production. However, here the principal polymer to be digested is chitin, an *N*-acetyl-glucosamine polymer that serves as the exoskeleton of crustacea.

## Mutualistic Associations of Invertebrates with Photosynthetic Microorganisms

Some invertebrate animals enter into mutualistic relationships with photosynthetic microorganisms, including unicellular algae and cyanobacteria (Taylor 1973a, 1973b, 1975; Muscatine et al. 1975). Classically, these microorganisms are called *endozoic algae.* They are described as zooxanthellae if the algal cells are yellow to reddish brown, including the dinoflagellates, which are Pyrrophycophyta; zoochlorellae if the algal cells are pale to bright green; and cyanellae if the dominant pigment is blue-green.

Mutualistic associations with photosynthetic microorganisms have been reported for various species of polychaete worms, platyhelminth worms, molluscs (including bivalves such as the giant clam), tunicates, echinoderms, hydroids, jellyfish, anemones, corals, sea fans, and sponges. The most common occurrence of endozoic algae appears to be in the coelenterates, such as hydra, anemones, and corals. The marine sponges are the most common hosts of cyanobacterial symbionts. Chlorophycophyta are found primarily in freshwater invertebrates. Dinoflagellates are the most frequent algal symbionts of marine invertebrates. Few of the endosymbiotic algae can be cultivated separately from their animal hosts, and consequently their classification is vague. Molecular genetic tools may remedy this situation. In a recent survey of 22 host taxa, closely related zooxan-

thellae were found in taxonomically distant hosts, indicating that associations were established in many independent events rather than in long phylogenetic coevolution between the zooxanthellae and their animal hosts (Rowan and Powers 1991).

The mutualistic relationship between primary-producer microorganisms and consumer animal populations is based on the microorganism's ability to supply the animal with organic nutrients and the animal's ability to provide a physiologically and nutritionally suitable environment for the microorganisms. In some cases, morphological adaptations facilitate close contact between the microbial and animal cells, allowing for efficient materials transfer between microorganisms and animals. The mutualistic relationship between *Convoluta roscoffensis,* a ciliated platyhelminth, and the green alga *Platymonas convolutae* has been extensively examined (Holligan and Gooday 1975). The alga supplies the animal with amino acids, amides, fatty acids, sterols, and oxygen; the animal supplies the alga with carbon dioxide and uric acid (Figure 5.7). The algal-animal association provides for an efficient closed system of mutual nutrient exchange, based on cycling of carbon, nitrogen, phosphorus, and oxygen in chemical forms that one partner can synthesize and another can utilize.

Corals, which are coelenterate animals, establish mutualistic relationships with endozoic dinoflagellates (Yonge 1963). Coral reefs also provide suitable habitats for the growth of external synergistic populations of algae, such as calcareous red algae. The growth of the coral depends on the metabolic activities of the endozoic dinoflagellates living within the tissues of the coral polyp. Reef corals precipitate calcium from seawater mainly during periods of maximal algal photosynthesis. The assimilation of $CO_2$ shifts the equilibrium from the more soluble bicarbonate to the less soluble carbonate. The growing coral polyp benefits from algal production of organic matter and removal of ammonia that builds up within the animal. The mutualistic relationship of endozoic algae and corals appears to be based on the exchange of carbon, nitrogen, phosphorus, and oxygen-containing compounds.

Animals harboring endozoic algae exhibit behavioral characteristics that benefit the algal partner

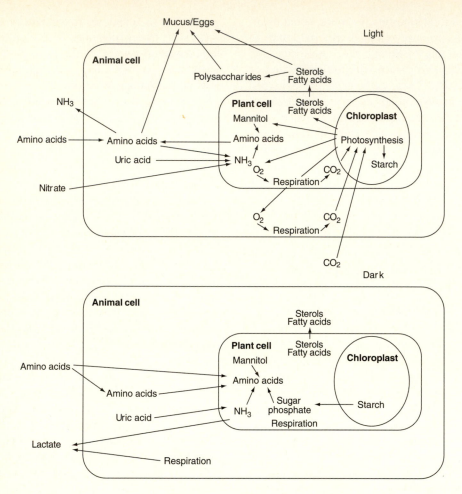

**Figure 5.7**
Metabolic relationship between the alga *Platymonas convolutae* and the flat worm *Convoluta roscoffensis*. The figure shows the shift in this mutualistic relationship between light and dark growth, indicating changes in carbon utilization. The *Platymonas* supplies carbon dioxide and ammonia from uric acid. In the light, the alga produces $O_2$ and organic carbon, which is used by the flat worm. (Source: Holligan and Gooday 1975. Reprinted by permission, copyright Cambridge University Press.)

(McLaughlin and Zahl 1966). Animals with endozoic algae normally exhibit phototactic responses. For example, coral polyps extend toward the light, providing the algae with accessible illumination for photosynthetic activities. Anemones with zooxanthellae also show phototactic responses. Free-swimming animals with endozoic algae move to depths with optimal light penetration for the photosynthetic activities of the endozoic algae.

The mutualistic relationship between photosynthetic microorganisms and animals may be especially beneficial during some periods of the year. *Convoluta,* for example, probably requires an efficient mechanism for retaining and recycling nutrients during winter, when there is less terrestrial runoff to supply nutrients to this coastal organism (Holligan and Gooday 1975).

An interesting seasonal endosymbiotic association has been found between *Euglena* and nymphs of some species of damselfly (Willey et al. 1970). This symbiotic relationship occurs only during the winter, when members of *Euglena* occupy the lower digestive tract of damselfly nymphs. This association allows for the survival of both *Euglena* and damselfly populations during winter, when the lake habitats of these populations are frozen; during summer, the association is interrupted and both populations are independent.

## Mutualistic Associations of Invertebrates with Chemolithotrophic and Methanotrophic Microorganisms

Along midocean ridges, to be described in more detail in Chapter 11, geothermally heated water containing reduced minerals such as $H_2S$ exits deep-sea hydrothermal vents. Chemolithotrophy on these reduced minerals supports communities around these vents that are 500–1000-fold denser than the biomass of the surrounding deep-sea floor (Cavanaugh et al. 1981; Grassle 1985; Jannasch and Mottl 1985; Tunnicliffe 1992). Some of the reduced minerals are oxidized by free-living bacteria that serve as food for various invertebrate grazers and filter feeders, but groups of invertebrates that are mutualistic with chemolithotrophic bacteria also live around the vents. These animals are unique and have not been found in any other marine environments. They are the vestimentiferan tube worms, represented by *Riftia pachyptila,* the vesicomyid clams such as *Vesicomya chordata* and *Calyptogena magnifica,* and the mytilid mussels such as *Bathymodiolus thermophilus.* Each of the three groups has several additional species (Felbeck 1981; Jones 1981; Jannasch and Nelson 1984; Nelson and Fisher 1995).

*R. pachyptila,* the giant tube worm that reaches 1–2 m in length and 10–15 cm in diameter, contains very large populations of endosymbiotic chemolithotrophic bacteria (Figure 5.8). It has a protective tube of chitinaceous-proteinaceous material that is whitish in color. The animal can withdraw in this tube for protection. Emerging from the tube is a striking blood-red plume, the gills of the worm. The adult worm lacks a mouth opening, anal vent, or a digestive tract. Over half of the animal volume consists of tissue harboring endosymbiotic bacteria. This organ is called the *trophosome.* The red color is due to a unique hemoglobin compound capable of transporting $O_2$, $H_2S$, and $CO_2$ between the gills and the trophosome. $H_2S$ attaches irreversibly to the hemoglobin of other animals and renders it unsuitable for oxygen transport. The endosymbiotic bacteria have not yet been cultivated, but their DNA sequences clearly identify them as bacteria. The key enzymes of $H_2S$ oxidation and $CO_2$ fixation have been identified in the trophosome tissue, and there is no doubt that the worm derives its entire food and energy supply from the chemoautotrophic activity of its $H_2S$-oxidizing endosymbionts. The animal protects these bacteria and, through its gills and circulatory system, transports favorable ratios of $H_2S$, $O_2$, and $CO_2$ for their chemolithotrophic activity. The animal, through its respiration, also produces $CO_2$ available for fixation, and its nitrogenous wastes can be utilized by the endosymbiont. Obviously, some combined nitrogen needs to be incorporated from the surrounding seawater, but to date little is known about this process. Tube worms propagate and disperse through free-swimming larval stages, which are believed to filter feed on plankton. The digestive tract disappears after the larva settles. Because the tube worms cannot be cultivated in the laboratory and it is next to impossible to retrieve larval stages from the deep sea, little is known about tube worm development and symbiont acquisition.

The clam *C. magnifica* is large, 30–40 cm long, with blood-red flesh from a hemoglobin similar to the one in the tube worm. The symbionts are located in the fleshy gills of the clam. The clam filter feeds normally and its gill symbionts appear to supplement only its nutrition. A similar association occurs in the mussel *B. thermophylus.* Although none of the endosymbionts could be cultivated, comparison of nucleic acid sequences indicate that each species of animal has its own unique chemolithotrophic endosymbiont, but that these are closely related to each

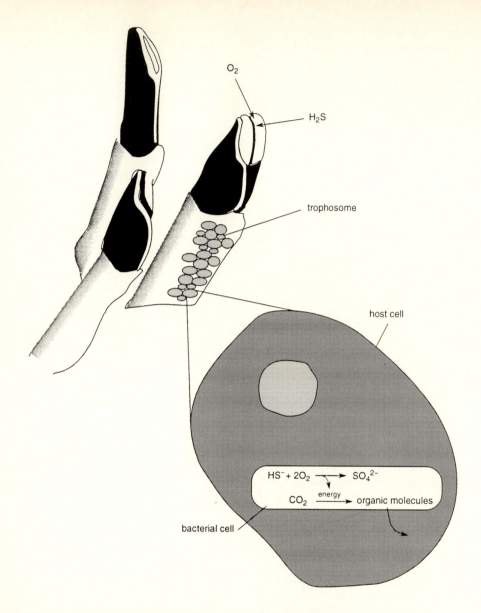

O$_2$

H$_2$S

trophosome

host cell

HS$^-$ + 2O$_2$ $\longrightarrow$ SO$_4^{2-}$

CO$_2$ $\xrightarrow{\text{energy}}$ organic molecules

bacterial cell

**Figure 5.8**

The tube worms of the thermal vents, *Riftia pachyptila,* house extensive endosymbiotic bacterial populations. The bacteria live within specialized tissues. The worm absorbs oxygen, hydrogen sulfide, and carbon dioxide through its gills and transports these compounds to the bacteria. The bacteria, which are chemolithotrophs, convert these inorganic compounds into organic compounds that support the growth of the tube worms. (Source: Tunnicliffe 1992.)

other. All appear to belong to the gamma subgroup of proteobacteria, and the genus *Thiomicrospira* is the closest free-living relative to the chemolithotrophic endosymbionts.

The harboring of chemolithotrophic endosymbionts by animals is clearly reminiscent of the relationships of animals with endozoic algae discussed in the previous section, but the chemolithotrophic relationship is independent of sunlight and, in the case of the geothermal vents, geothermal energy mobilizes the inorganic nutrients that are utilized by the mutualistic association. However, $H_2S$ can also be generated by sulfate reduction in anoxic sediments (see Chapter 11), and the reports on sulfide-oxidizing bacterial symbionts in animals of the deep-sea geothermal vent communities inspired investigations of invertebrates that live in shallow but sulfide-exposed waters. Estuarine sediments evolve high amounts of $H_2S$ caused by sulfate reduction during organic matter degradation in these anoxic sediments. These investigations led to the discovery of sulfide-oxidizing symbiotic bacteria in the gills of several estuarine bivalves, such as the gutless clam *Solemya reidi* and other species of the *Solemya, Lucinoma, Myrtea,* and *Thyasira* genera. Some of the symbionts are intracellular; others are located in separate bacteriocysts between the cuticle and the animal tissue. Some of the bivalves have retained filter-feeding capacity; others rely on their symbionts exclusively (Cavanaugh 1983; Felbeck 1983; Southward 1986). In *S. reidi* the sulfide oxidation is mediated not only by the symbiotic bacteria in the gills but also by the mitochondria of the host clam (Powell and Somero 1986).

Besides the symbiotic associations of chemolithotrophs and animals in deep-sea thermal vent communities, there are some interesting relationships in deep-sea marine environments (for example, the Louisiana Slope, Gulf of Mexico) that are exposed to hydrocarbon seeps, usually in combination with sulfide. Recently discovered mussels of the family Mytilidae living in such environments were found to harbor within their gill tissue symbiotic methanotrophic (methane-oxidizing) bacteria with typical stacked internal membrane structures. The light carbon isotope ratio in both the mussels and their bacterial symbionts indicated that most of the carbon of this symbiotic association originated in fossil methane (Childress et al. 1986; Brooks et al. 1987). Subsequently, these mussels have been grown in the laboratory with methane serving as their only source of carbon and energy (Cary et al. 1988). Of course, methane oxidizers are not chemolithotrophs, but they utilize a highly unusual carbon source that is not available to eucaryotic organisms. In this respect, invertebrate mutualism with methanotrophs is analogous to the invertebrate-chemolithotroph mutualisms. Some mytilids including *B. thermophilus* appear to harbor both chemolithotrophic $H_2S$ oxidizers and methanotrophic endosymbionts (Nelson and Fisher 1995).

## FUNGAL PREDATION ON ANIMALS

### Nematode- and Rotifer-Trapping Fungi

Some fungi prey on nematodes (Figure 5.9) as a source of nutrients (Pramer 1964; Nordbring-Hertz and Jansson 1984; Barron 1992). The most common genera of nematode-trapping fungi are *Arthrobotrys, Dactylaria, Dactylella,* and *Trichothecium.* There are several mechanisms by which these fungi capture nematode prey, including production of networks of adhesive branches, stalked adhesive knobs, adhesive rings, and constrictive rings. When a nematode attempts to move past an adhesive hyphal structure, it sticks to it and is trapped. When it tries to pass through a constricting ring, the fungal ring contracts by a sudden osmotic swelling and traps the nematode. Violent movements and attempts by the nematode to escape generally fail. The fungal hyphae penetrate into the nematode, which is then enzymatically degraded. When growing in the absence of nematodes, some of these fungi fail to produce trap structures. The presence of the prey nematode appears to induce the formation of the morphological structures that trap the nematodes. This is a unique relationship in which the presence of the prey induces the formation of fungal structures that result in its capture and consumption.

Most nematode-trapping fungi, including the ones described above, are Deuteromycota, but a few

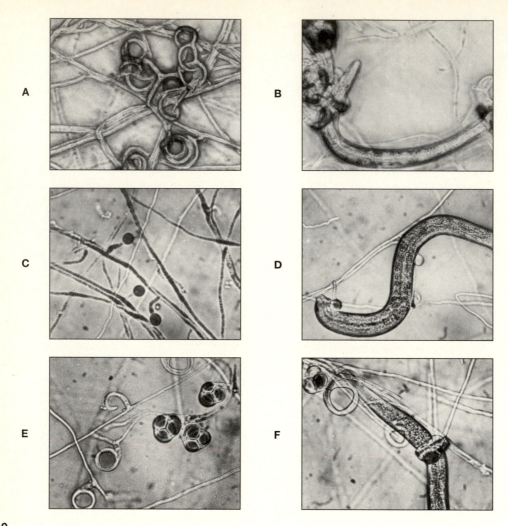

**Figure 5.9**

Photomicrographs slowing examples of nematode-trapping fungi.

(A) *Arthrobotrys conoides* traps consist of adhesive hyphal loops or rings.

(B) *A. conoides* with trapped nematode.

(C) *Dactylella drechslerii* traps are knobs coated with an adhesive.

(D) *D. drechslerii* with trapped nematode.

(E) *A. dactyloides* traps, consisting of rings comprised of three cells each, which capture prey by occlusion. Open traps are shown on left, closed traps on right.

(F) *A. dactyloides* with trapped nematode. (Source: D. Pramer, Rutgers, the State University.)

Basidiomycota also have the ability to attack and digest nematodes. *Hohenbuehelia* and *Resupinatus* species were found to capture nematodes by means of adhesive knobs. The edible oyster mushroom *Pleurotus ostreatus* and related *Pleurotus* species form no trap structures. Instead, by means of some toxin, they rapidly paralyze the nematodes. Subsequently, the hyphae invade and digest the immobilized nematode. The described basidiomycota often grow on decaying wood, a nitrogen-poor substrate. It is suggested that the captured nematodes are a source of supplemental nitrogen for the fungi (Thorn and Barron 1984).

The parasitic oomycete *Haptoglossa mirabilis* attacks rotifer worms. Zoospores of this fungus, after a short swarming period, produce a special cyst that almost immediately germinates in the form of a "gun" cell. The gun cell attached to the cyst resembles a bowling pin in shape. When a rotifer contacts the tip of this structure (the muzzle of the "gun"), within a fraction of a second the gun cell discharges a missile that breaches the cuticle of the rotifer and injects an infectious sporidium. Inside the rotifer, the sporidium grows into a thallus, killing the host. Eventually, new zoospores are released to perpetuate the cycle (Robb and Barron 1982; Barron 1992).

## Fungal–Scale Insect Associations

An interesting relationship exists between scale insects and fungi of the genus *Septobasidium* (Buchner 1960; Brooks 1963; Batra and Batra 1967). Scale insects are plant parasites that extract plant juices with their long sucking tubes (haustorium) (Figure 5.10). Scale insects become infected with fungi when they emerge from the parent scale on a plant; the fungi develop hyphae that surround the maturing scale insects, trapping but not immediately killing all of them. The insects live and produce young within the mass of hyphae covering the parent scale. The fungal hyphae retain the adults while the juvenile scale insects feed on the plant between the hyphae. In this relationship, the fungus affords the scale insects protection from other parasites and predators, and the scale insect provides nutrients utilized by the fungus. The movement of young scale insects from one plant to another ensures dissemination of the fungus. Some mature scale insects live through the winter and produce young before the fungus kills them; fungi invade others before they reach maturity so that they fail to reproduce. The fungus derives nutrients by hyperparasitizing the insect; the insect derives protection from the fungus. The relationship between the scale insect and the fungus allows both populations to survive and reproduce.

Interestingly, *Septobasidium* may also play a role in determining the sex of scale insect offspring. Microorganisms do not occur in association with all scale insect eggs; those eggs that possess symbiotic microorganisms develop into females, whereas eggs lacking microorganisms become males. The mutualistic association appears to prevent loss of the sex chromosome in the female, but the mechanism for this retention is not known.

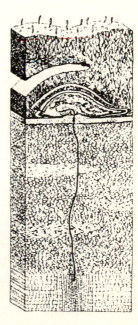

**Figure 5.10**
Scale insect on a leaf, embedded in the mycelium of *Septobasidium* fungus. (Source: Batra and Batra 1967, *The Fungus Gardens of Insects.* Copyright 1967 Scientific American Inc. All rights reserved.)

## OTHER SYMBIOTIC RELATIONSHIPS

### Symbiotic Light Production

Some marine invertebrates and fish establish mutualistic relationships with luminescent bacteria (Buchner 1960; Morin et al. 1975; Hastings and Nealson 1977; McCosker 1977; Nealson and Hastings 1979; Leisman et al. 1980; Nealson et al. 1984). Depending upon the particular species, the organs containing the luminescent bacteria may be localized near the eye, abdomen, rectum, or jaw (Figure 5.11). In squid, for example, luminescent bacteria occur in a pair of glands in the mantle cavity near the ink sac. The luminescent bacteria, *Vibrio* and *Photobacterium* species, are contained within special saclike organs that gener-

ally have external pores that allow the bacteria to enter and provide for exchange with the surrounding seawater. The fish supplies the bacteria with nutrients and protection from competing microorganisms.

Luminescent bacteria generally emit light continuously, but some fish are able to manipulate the organs containing these bacteria so as to emit flashes of light. The flashlight fish *Photoblepharon* is capable of shutting off its light by drawing a dark curtain, like an eyelid, over the light organ. Another small, tropical, light-emitting marine fish, *Anomalops,* has a slightly different mechanism for shutting off its light. Here the light organ, lined on the inside with reflective guanine-containing cells, is rotated like an eyeball, almost 180°. The light, now reflected inward, is obscured. In both *Photoblepharon* and *Anomalops* the light organs

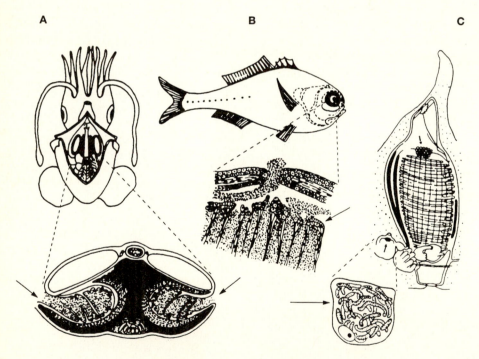

**Figure 5.11**
Symbiotic relationships of luminous bacteria with animals. (A) The cephalopod *Eurymma* with open mantle, showing enlarged section through the organs that contain luminous bacteria (arrows). (B) The flashlight fish *Anomalops,* with luminous organ containing bacteria in its folds (arrow) located under the eye. (C) The tunicate *Pyrosoma* with luminous organs, showing an enlarged mycetocyte with bacterial cells (arrows). (Source: Buchner 1960. Reprinted by permission of Springer-Verlag.)

are situated under the eyes and may be used to some extent as a flashlight or headlamp by these nocturnal fishes. Both *Photoblepharon* and *Anomalops* are gregarious and their light emission is also thought to aid their schooling behavior and perhaps repel predators. The light organs of both fishes are tightly packed with light-emitting bacteria (Figure 5.11B). To date, efforts to culture these bacteria have failed, although these fish are readily accessible in the live state and have also been kept in the laboratory.

Although *Photoblepharon* and *Anomalops* live in shallow waters, most mutualistic associations with luminescent bacteria occur in deep-sea fishes that live below the level of light penetration. The light emitted by the associated luminescent bacteria permits species recognition among these fish. The pattern and location of the luminescent organs on the fish and the fact that they often occur in only one sex indicate that the luminescent bacteria may be critical for mate recognition. Some light organs located near the eyes include a reflective concave mirror of guanine-containing cells and lenslike focusing structures, indicating that some fish use the light as searchlights. Movement of the luminescent organs may also allow these fish to lure prey and to communicate with other fish. Deepwater species cannot be obtained in the live state, making the study of these bacteria-fish associations particularly difficult.

In deep-sea species, it is next to impossible to study the events that lead to the formation of a light organ, but the process was studied in some shallow-water species. In the squid *Euprymna scolopes* the light organ is a saclike structure with an entry pore. In the newly hatched uninfected juvenile squid, the future light organ has elaborate epithelial structure with cilia and microvilli that transfer compatible *Vibrio fischeri* cells into the incipient light organ sac. Upon infection the cilia and microvilli disappear, but they are retained in the uninfected animal (McFall-Ngai and Ruby 1991). Although cultural and colony-hybridization techniques in natural seawater detected only 2 compatible *V. fischeri* cells per milliliter, direct counting techniques detected 200–400 compatible cells per milliliter (Lee and Ruby 1995). The authors concluded that cultural viability tests grossly underes-

timate the numbers of symbiotically infective *V. fischeri* in seawater.

## Novel Procaryotic Endosymbionts

Novel endosymbiotic relationships of bacteria and archaea in invertebrate animals are being described in rapid succession (Bauman et al. 1993). Typically, they are based on microscopic observations in combination with the use of fluorescent oligonucleotide probes specific for procaryotic nucleic acid sequences. If it is possible to eliminate these endosymbionts by antibiotic or other drug treatment, and this leads to an impairment or death of the host, one is justified in suspecting a mutualistic association. However, the specific nature of the interaction often remains to be elucidated. This task is frequently rendered difficult by the inability to grow the endosymbiont outside its host. As one example of such still obscure mutualistic endosymbionts, all aphids have cell clusters that are called *mycetomes* and the individual cells *mycetocytes*. These terms are somewhat misleading because these cells harbor bacteria rather than fungi. Upon the elimination of the endosymbionts by antibiotic treatment, the aphid stops reproducing and eventually dies. Preliminary evidence indicates that the endosymbionts may produce amino acids absent from the plant sap that the aphid feeds on. Illustrating the difficulty of studying these noncultivable endosymbionts, in a recent report the proportional growth of the aphid (*Schizaphis graminum*) and its endosymbiont *Buchnera aphidicola* was demonstrated by correlating the weight increase of the aphid with the number of bacterial gene copies present in the aphid (Baumann and Baumann 1994). The creative use of molecular tools will undoubtedly aid the study of endosymbiotic relationships with endosymbionts that cannot be cultivated outside their host.

A fascinating bacterium because of its huge size, a species of *Epulopiscium* has been identified by molecular probes as an endosymbiont in the intestines of surgeonfish living in the Red Sea (Angert et al. 1993). This bacterium is larger than the ciliate protozoan *Paramecium;* it has a cell size over 1 million times larger than a typical bacterial cell. *Epulopiscium* species have yet to be cultured and so their functional roles are as yet unknown. They are related to clostridia and may play a role in cellulose digestion. *Epulopiscium* is most closely related to the large bacterium *Metabacterium polyspora,* which occurs in the ceca of guinea pigs (Angert et al. 1996). Both *Epulopiscium* and *M. polyspora* produce multiple live offspring instead of quiescent spores.

Besides these associations involving bacteria, a marine crenarchaeota has been discovered living in association with a temperate marine sponge. To date these crenarchaeota have been observed with only one species of sponge, suggesting a specific symbiotic relationship. The sponge-associated crenarchaeota appears to represent a new species distinct from marine planktonic archaea found in temperate waters. The functional relationship between the crenarchaeota and sponge remains to be determined.

## ECOLOGICAL ASPECTS OF ANIMAL DISEASES

Some microorganisms, including various viruses, bacteria, fungi, protozoa, and even algae, cause animal diseases (Dubos and Hirsch 1965; Merchant and Packer 1967; Falconer 1993). We can distinguish two types of disease-causing processes, one in which the microorganism grows on or within the animal, causing an infection that results in a disease condition, and a second in which the microorganism grows outside of the animal, producing toxic substances that cause animal diseases or altering the habitat of the animal so that the animal can no longer survive in a healthy condition.

Microorganisms growing in their natural habitats, such as water or soil, can alter environmental conditions, adversely affecting the animal populations occupying those habitats. Such conditions often arise when there are population imbalances within the microbial community. For example, when eutrophic conditions allow for large algal blooms in lakes, the growth of photoautotrophic populations adds large quantities of organic matter to the lake waters, and the subsequent degradation of this organic matter by het-

erotrophic microorganisms depletes the dissolved oxygen, creating anoxic conditions. This depletion produces disease symptoms and death in the oxygen-requiring animal populations, sometimes causing major fish kills.

Microbial populations may also produce inorganic chemicals or organic toxins that cause diseases in animals. Hydrogen sulfide produced by microbial populations in sediment can accumulate in concentrations toxic to animals burrowing in the sediment. Acid mine drainage, resulting from microbial oxidation of sulfur, can produce highly acidic conditions in drainage streams, causing disease conditions and death of aquatic animals. Toxins produced by microorganisms outside of susceptible host animals often enter the animal during ingestion of food, causing food poisoning (Shilo 1967; Ciegler and Lillehoj 1968; Falconer 1993). Many mushrooms contain toxins that are extremely poisonous to animals that ingest them, resulting in severe disease symptoms and sometimes death. Aflatoxins, produced by some *Aspergillus* species growing on grain products, cause disease in poultry and other populations that consume the toxin-containing food products.

Microbial toxins can remain active even under conditions that do not permit the survival and growth of the population that produced them. Red tides result in disease and death in susceptible animal populations exposed to toxins produced by blooms of dinoflagellates. Some dinoflagellates produce toxins that kill fish, whereas others kill primarily invertebrates. Toxins concentrated by filter-feeding animals can also cause disease in higher members of the food web. Humans acquire paralytic shellfish poisoning by consuming shellfish containing concentrated algal toxins (Falconer 1993).

When considering the ecological aspects of animal diseases caused by toxins, one must examine the conditions under which the toxin-forming microbial populations can grow and produce these substances, the ability of the toxin to remain in an active form in the environment, the concentrations of toxin required to produce disease, and the factors that dilute or concentrate toxins. Toxins are often not produced in sufficient concentrations or are degraded or diluted so that they do not produce diseases in animal populations. Only when conditions permit extensive toxin production by microbial populations do toxins accumulate in concentrations that cause animal diseases. In some cases, toxins produced by microorganisms are concentrated within the food web, producing diseases in higher consumer populations with no apparent effect on lower members of the food web. Environmental conditions that favor the growth of toxin-producing microbial populations increase the possible incidence of toxin-caused animal diseases.

In contrast to animal diseases caused by toxin-producing microorganisms that grow outside the animal, infectious pathogens or parasitic microorganisms must be capable of growing in or on the animal's tissues. Some pathogenic microorganisms are obligate intracellular parasites and are entirely dependent for their existence and survival on their successful invasion and reproduction within susceptible animal cells. Although stable carrier states can occur in which a balance between the pathogen and the host is established, disease-causing infectious microorganisms usually grow for only a limited period within susceptible animals, after which the host animal either dies, resulting in destruction of the habitat for the pathogenic microorganisms, or develops an immune response that precludes further growth of the pathogenic microorganisms. Populations of pathogenic microorganisms, therefore, must be transmitted to new susceptible members of the animal population for continued growth. It is important to consider the routes of transfer, how long the pathogens can survive outside of host animals, the environmental factors that contribute to survival outside the host, and the reservoirs or alternate host populations for the particular pathogenic population.

Infectious microorganisms have a limited number of routes available for entering host animals. Pathogenic microorganisms usually enter animals through normal body openings, such as the respiratory and gastrointestinal tracts. Most pathogens are unable to penetrate the outer skin layers and establish infection, but there are exceptions, including a ciliate *Ichthyophthirius multifilis* that is able to penetrate fish skin surfaces and causes ich, an often fatal disease of tropical fish characterized by the appearance of white spots on the skin, fins, and eyes (Figure 5.12). However, breaks in the protective skin surface caused by wounds or insect bites permit various pathogens to infect animals. Most pathogenic microorganisms are restricted to one portal of entry for establishing disease; entering another part of the body leads to a different relationship between the microbe and the animal. In some cases, a microbial population is nonpathogenic under normal conditions but can become an opportunistic pathogen under particular circumstances. For example, *Escherichia coli* is a normal inhabitant of the human intestine, where it does not produce disease, but if it enters the urinary tract, it causes a urinary tract infection. The limitation of pathogenic microorganisms to a particular portal of entry is caused partly by environmental constraints, such as low pH, which the potential pathogen must tolerate; partly by the immune response system of the host animal, which can recognize and destroy many invading microorganisms before they can establish an infective population level; and partly by the antagonistic activities of the non-disease-causing microorganisms that compose the normal microbiota inhabiting the surfaces of animal tissues.

Although the tissues of healthy animals and humans are sterile, numerous microorganisms colonize their body surfaces. The best-studied example is the human skin (Marples 1969). The sloughing off of epidermal cells and the secretion of sebaceous and sweat glands provide keratin, lipids, and fatty acids as potential growth substrates. However, generally dry conditions, salinity, and inhibitory action of some fatty acids create a somewhat hostile environment that is best tolerated by some gram-positive bacteria and coryneforms and by some yeasts. Most of these microorganisms are harmless commensals, but some of them like *Staphylococcus aureus* and *Candida albicans* have the potential of becoming opportunistic pathogens in debilitated or immunocompromised individuals or if the skin's integrity is disrupted by wounds or burns. Large differences exist in the density and species composition of the microbial populations of various skin areas, caused by variations in the dryness or moistness of different skin areas and in the

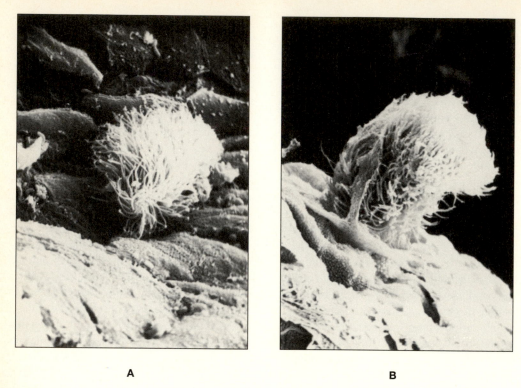

**A**                                              **B**

**Figure 5.12**
Scanning electron micrographs of the ciliate protozoan *Ichthyophthirinus multifiliis*. (A) On a fish fin surface prior to penetration. (B) Penetration into gill tissue. (Source: T. Kozel.)

density of secretory glands. The skin of the forearms and the back are the most sparsely populated "desert" regions of the skin, with only a few hundred to a few thousand microorganisms per square centimeter. On the other hand, the axilla, groin, scalp, and areas between fingers and toes are heavily populated, with $10^5$ to $10^6$ microorganisms per square centimeter. *Staphylococcus* and *Corynebacterium* are the most abundant bacterial genera; gram negatives are restricted to the moister areas of the skin. The most common yeasts are *Pityrosporum ovale* and *C. albicans*. The presence of these microorganisms is not harmful, and by their presence and competitive action they tend to make an invasion by real pathogens more difficult.

The communicability of disease-causing microorganisms depends on the ability of the pathogen to escape from its host animal, to contact a new susceptible animal, and to enter successfully the tissues of that animal. If there is a delay between the time a pathogenic microorganism is released from one host and the time it contacts a new susceptible host, the pathogen must be able to survive this period. Pathogenic microorganisms are normally transmitted by direct contact, through airborne and waterborne dispersal, through ingestion with food, and via biological vectors. Pathogenic microorganisms transmitted via prolonged air travel must be resistant to desiccation, and normally high numbers of microorganisms must be released to ensure successful dissemination to the next susceptible host. Vectors are important in the distribution of pathogenic microorganisms that could not survive for extended periods outside host cells. There is often great specificity between the pathogenic microbes, the vectors, and the susceptible hosts (Table 5.2). The geographic distribution of some infectious diseases reflects the distribution of suitable vector populations. Environmental conditions often determine the distribution of pathogens, affecting host susceptibility, pathogen reproduction, pathogen survival, and possible routes of transmission. Temperature, pH, $E_h$ (redox potential), concentrations of organic nutrients, and concentrations of inorganic nutrients all influence the survival time of pathogens in the environment; these same environmental factors are important in determining the size and distribution of susceptible animal populations and suitable vector populations.

Changes in population balances are involved among causative, reservoir, vector, and host populations for the transmission of various diseases. For example, outbreaks of Legionnaires' disease, caused by *Legionella,* are associated with evaporating water bodies, such as air-conditioning systems, that provide a reservoir for the organism and a mechanism through which the organism can become airborne via aerosol

formation. When considering the ecology of infectious diseases, it is also necessary to recognize the importance of the immune response that renders some animals insusceptible to particular populations of pathogenic microorganisms. The immune system renders these animals unsuitable, for the most part, as habitats for invading microorganisms, and relatively few pathogens succeed in overcoming the immune defense system. Even pathogenic microorganisms that successfully invade and establish an infection within a susceptible animal are normally eliminated from the host animal when the immune response becomes fully activated. If the immune system is impaired, as occurs in AIDS where human T cells have been infected with HIV, the person becomes unprotected against numerous microbial infections and is unable to survive in a nonsterile environment. The physiological state of the host animal often determines in part the effectiveness of the immune system in protecting against microbial invasion. Animals debilitated by poor nutrition or other stresses are extremely susceptible to pathogenic invasion.

**Table 5.2**
Examples of disease-causing microorganisms dispersed by animal vectors

| Etiologic agent | Reservoir | Vector | Disease |
|---|---|---|---|
| *Rickettsia rickettsii* | Rodent | Tick | Rocky Mountain spotted fever |
| *Rickettsia typhi* | Rodent | Flea | Endemic typhus |
| *Rickettsia prowazekii* | Human | Louse | Epidemic typhus |
| *Rhabdovirus* | Rodent, dog | Rodent, dog | Rabies |
| *Togavirus* | Human, monkey | Mosquito (*Aedes aegypti*) | Yellow fever |
| *Arbovirus* | Horse, human, bird | Mosquito | Encephalitis |
| *Trypanosoma cruzi* | Human, various animals | Conebug | Chagas' disease |
| *Yersinia pestis* | Rodent | Flea | Bubonic plague |
| *Trypanosoma gambiense* and other *Trypanosoma* spp. | Human, various animals | Tsetse fly | African sleeping sickness |
| *Leishmania donovani* | Cat, dog, rodent | Sandfly | Dum-dum fever (kala-azar disease) |
| *Borrelia burgdorferi* | Mouse, deer | Deer tick (*Ixodes dammini*) | Lyme disease (borreliosis) |

# Ecology of Emerging Infectious Diseases

Environmental changes appear to be a major cause of the recent emergence of several important infectious human diseases. In a number of cases, changes in human activities have altered the population levels of pathogens or their vectors, resulting in increased likelihood of pathogen transmission to humans. One of the most dramatic indications that humans are disrupting the balance between pathogens and humans came when Brazil built a highway deep into the Amazonian rainforest to its new capital, Brasilia. Soon thereafter, various outbreaks of infectious diseases occurred among highway workers. In 1961, the Oropouche virus was identified as the cause of a flulike epidemic in Brazil that afflicted 11,000 people. This disease outbreak was linked to the highway construction by epidemiologists who showed that midges (minute winged insects) serve as vectors for the Oropouche virus and that midges in Brazil had undergone a huge population explosion due to the disturbance of the rainforest by highway construction. Similar environmental changes may underlie the emergence of the new viruses that cause Ebola hemorrhagic fever, Marburg hemorrhagic fever, and yellow fever, where the viruses probably initially occurred in monkeys; Rift Valley fever, where the viruses probably initially occurred in cattle, sheep, and mosquitoes; and Muerto Canyon fever, where the hantaviruses initially occurred in rodents.

An outbreak of Kyasanur forest disease, a rare disease caused by a virus, provides another example of how populations of pathogenic microorganisms, reservoirs for the pathogens, vectors, and animal hosts are interrelated (Smith 1978). In 1956, there was an outbreak of Kyasanur forest disease associated with the following factors: The infection was naturally maintained within the forest in reservoir populations of birds and mammals with ticks acting as vectors; there was an increase in the human population in the region, which led to extensive cattle grazing in the forest; the presence of the cattle led to an increase in the tick population that was heightened because the adult stage of the tick, which controls the overall tick population, is dependent on large mammals to meet its nutritional requirements; the tick population became infected with the virus, transmitting it to monkeys, thus amplifying it; and, finally, the virus was transmitted to humans.

Another pathogen of current concern that has an interesting ecology is *Borrelia burgdorferi,* a spirochete that causes borreliosis, or Lyme disease, named after the Connecticut community Old Lyme, where the first outbreak in the early 1970s was observed (Miller 1987). Lyme disease is transmitted by the bite of the deer tick *(Ixodes dammini).* Initially, Lyme disease has flulike symptoms with or without a characteristic circular rash around the bite. If recognized and treated early by antibiotics, the infection is relatively easy to cure. When left untreated, the disease may cause severe joint, heart, and central nervous system damage. The young tick feeds on small rodents like the white-footed mouse; the adult feeds mainly on deer. Ticks pick up *Borrelia* from these wild animals that are asymptomatically infected. When the infected tick feeds on humans or some domestic animals, *Borrelia* is transmitted and causes the described disease. The resurgence of the white-tailed deer population near suburban areas appears to be the main cause of increasingly frequent human infections.

# CHAPTER SUMMARY

Microorganisms are important contributors to the nutrition of some animals. Detritus-feeding and coprophagous animals derive a substantial portion of their food from microbial biomass. Grazing and filter feeding on microorganisms by invertebrate animals is a crucial link in aquatic food webs, making the biomass of microbial primary and secondary producers available to higher trophic levels. Many animals lack the enzymes necessary to digest some or all of the food resources available to them and thus require the assistance of microbial populations. Of particular importance is the ability of various microbial populations to produce the extracellular enzymes that degrade complex plant polymers, such as cellulose, which otherwise would be unavailable to the animal. A number of animal populations depend on the microbial conversion of plant polymers to fatty acids that can be used for energy production. Some microbial populations also produce vitamins, which are required but not synthesized by the animal host. The activities of microbial populations in the gastrointestinal tract thus contribute to food digestion, supply vitamins, and provide considerable protection against pathogenic invaders. In most cases, these activities seem essential to the well-being of the animal.

Some microbial and animal populations establish mutualistic relationships, many of which are based on nutrient exchange and maintenance of a suitable habitat. Ants, for example, grow pure cultures of fungi on leaves and use the fungal biomass and metabolic products as their nutrient supply. Termites similarly maintain microbial populations to upgrade the food sources available to them. Various invertebrates contain photosynthetic partners, and there is a mutual exchange of nutrients. Similar relationships exist between invertebrates and chemolithotrophic microorganisms. In some cases, microbes derive their nutrition by preying on animals, as in the case of nematode-trapping fungi. Other animal-microbe interactions have unusual foundations, such as the ability of luminescent bacteria to provide light in the deep ocean.

The spread of disease among animal populations is an ecological process that is dependent on the biological properties of the causative organism, the biological properties of the host organism, and abiotic and biotic factors that affect the transmission of the pathogen between hosts. The relationship between pathogenic microbial populations and host animal populations is important in determining the size and distribution of each population. Animal populations provide suitable reservoirs for the growth and continued existence of successful pathogens, and microbially caused diseases are important in determining the ability of animal populations to compete for and successfully occupy particular niches. Resistance to microbial diseases is a measure of fitness that acts through natural selection to determine the success of particular animal populations. Microbial diseases of animal populations are a selective force that acts to control the animal population, both qualitatively and quantitatively.

# STUDY QUESTIONS

1. What predatory strategies do animals exhibit that allow them to obtain nutrition from microbial populations?

2. What are the differences between grazing and filter feeding? How are they related to the size of the animal and the density of the microbial populations?

3. Describe the relationship between leaf-cutting ants and fungi.

4. How do microorganisms contribute to the nutrition of termites?

5. What roles do microorganisms play in deep-sea thermal vent regions that permit the growth of bivalves and tube worms? What specific

microbial activities are critical in deep-sea thermal vent regions?

6. How do microorganisms contribute to the nutrition of ruminant animals such as cows?

7. What effects do methanogens have on ruminant animals?

8. How do bioluminescent bacteria contribute to the behavior of certain fish populations?

9. How do some fungi obtain nutrients from nematodes?

10. What role do algae play in the growth of corals?

11. What are zoochlorellae, cyanellae, and zooxanthellae? How do they contribute to the survival of animal populations?

12. How are pathogens transmitted through the environment?

13. What role does environmental disturbance by human activities play in the emergence of infectious human diseases?

# REFERENCES AND SUGGESTED READINGS

Angert, E. R., K. D. Clements, and N. R. Pace. 1993. The largest bacterium. *Nature* 362:239–241.

Angert, E. R., A. E. Brooks, and N. R. Pace. 1996. Phylogenetic analysis of *Metabacterium polyspora:* Clues to the evolutionary origin of daughter cell production in *Epulopiscium* species, the largest bacterium. *Journal of Bacteriology* 178:1451–1456.

Atlas, R. M., M. Busdosh, E. J. Krichevsky, and T. Kaneko. 1982. Bacterial populations associated with the Arctic amphipod *Boeckosimus affinis. Canadian Journal of Microbiology* 28:92–99.

Baker, J. M. 1963. Ambrosia beetles and their fungi, with particular reference to *Platypus culindrus* Fab. In P. S. Nutman and B. Mosse (eds.). *Symbiotic Associations.* Cambridge University Press, Cambridge, England, pp. 232–265.

Barron, G. 1992. Jekyll-Hyde mushrooms. *Natural History* 3/92:47–52.

Batra, S.W.T., and L. R. Batra. 1967. The fungus gardens of insects. *Scientific American* 217:112–120.

Baumann, L., and P. Baumann. 1994. Growth kinetics of the endosymbiont *Buchnera aphidicola* in the aphid *Schizaphis graminum. Applied and Environmental Microbiology* 60:3440–3443.

Baumann, P., M. A. Munson, C.-Y. Lai, M. A. Clark, L. Baumann, N. A. Moran, and B. C. Campbell. 1993. Origin and properties of bacterial endosymbionts of aphids, whiteflies, and mealybugs. *ASM News* 59:21–24.

Beck, J. W., and J. E. Davies. 1976. *Medical Parasitology.* Mosby, St. Louis.

Benemann, J. R. 1973. Nitrogen fixation in termites. *Science* 181:164–165.

Bowden, G. H.W., D. C. Ellwood, and I. R. Hamilton. 1979. Microbial ecology of the oral cavity. *Advances in Microbial Ecology* 3:135–218.

Breznak, J. A. 1975. Symbiotic relationships between termites and their intestinal microbiota. In *Symbiosis,* Symposia of the Society for Experimental Biology, No. 29. Cambridge University Press, Cambridge, England, pp. 559–580.

Breznak, J. A., and H. S. Pankratz. 1977. *In situ* morphology of the gut microbiota of wood-eating termites. *Applied and Environmental Microbiology* 33:406–426.

Breznak, J. A., and J. M. Switzer. 1986. Acetate synthesis from $H_2$ plus $CO_2$ by termite gut microbe. *Applied and Environmental Microbiology* 52:623–630.

Brooks, M. A. 1963. Symbiosis and aposymbiosis in arthropods. In *Symbiotic Associations,* Proceedings of the Thirteenth Symposium of the Society for General Microbiology. Cambridge University Press, Cambridge, England, pp. 200–231.

Brooks, J. M., M. C. Kennicutt II, C. R. Fisher, S. A. Macko, K. Cole, J. J. Childress, R. R. Bidigare, and R. D. Vetter. 1987. Deep sea hydrocarbon seep communities: Evidence for energy and nutritional carbon sources. *Science* 187:1138–1142.

Buchner, P. 1960. *Tiere als Mikrobenzüchter.* Springer-Verlag, Heidelberg, Germany.

Carpenter, E. J., and J. L. Culliney. 1975. Nitrogen fixation in marine ship worms. *Science* 187:551–552.

Carr, D. L., and W. R. Kloos. 1977. Temporal study of the Staphylococci and Micrococci of normal infant skin. *Applied and Environmental Microbiology* 34:673–680.

Cary, S. C., C. R. Fisher, and H. Felbeck. 1988. Mussel growth supported by methane as sole carbon and energy source. *Science* 240:78–80.

Cavanaugh, C. M. 1983. Symbiotic chemoautotrophic bacteria in marine invertebrates from sulfide-rich habitats. *Nature* (London) 302:58–61.

Cavanaugh, C. M., S. L. Gardiner, M. L. Jones, H. W. Jannasch, and J. B. Waterbury. 1981. Prokaryotic cells in the hydrothermal vent tube worm *Riftia pachyptila,* Jones: Possible chemoautotrophic symbionts. *Science* 213:340–342.

Chapela, I. H., S. A. Rehner, R. R. Schultz, and U. G. Mueller. 1994. Evolutionary history of the symbiosis between fungus-growing ants and their fungi. *Science* 266:1691–1697.

Childress, J. J., R. C. Fisher, J. M. Brooks, M. C. Kennicutt II, R. Bidigare, and A. E. Anderson. 1986. A methan-otrophic marine molluscan (Bivalvia, Mytilidae) symbiosis: Mussels fueled by gas. *Science* 233:1306–1308.

Ciegler, A., and E. B. Lillehoj. 1968. Mycotoxins. *Advances in Applied Microbiology* 10:155–219.

Clarke, R.T.J., and T. Bauchop (eds.). 1977. *Microbial Ecology of the Gut.* Academic Press, London.

Coleman, G. S. 1975. The role of bacteria in the metabo-lism of rumen entodiniomorphid protozoa. In *Symbiosis,* Symposia of the Society for Experimental Biology, No. 29. Cambridge University Press, Cambridge, England, pp. 533–558.

Cooke, R. 1977. *Biology of Symbiotic Fungi.* Wiley, New York.

Costerton, J. W. 1984. Direct ultrastructural examination of adherent bacterial populations in natural and pathogenic ecosystems. In M. J. Klug and C. A. Reddy (eds.). *Current Perspectives in Microbial Ecology.* American Society for Microbiology, Washington, DC, pp. 115–124.

Distel, D. L., E. F. DeLong, and J. B. Waterbury. 1991. Phylogenetic characterization and *in situ* localization of the bacterial symbiont of shipworms (Teredinidae: Bivalvia) by using 16S rRNA sequence analysis and oligodeoxynucleotide probe hybridization. *Applied and Environmental Microbiology* 60:3440–3443.

Dubos, R. J., and J. G. Hirsch (eds.). 1965. *Bacterial and Mycotic Infections of Man.* Lippincott, Philadelphia.

Falconer, I. R. (ed.). 1993. *Algal Toxins in Seafood and Drinking Water.* Academic Press, New York.

Felbeck, H. 1981. Chemoautotrophic potential of the hydrothermal vent tube worm, *Riftia pachyptila,* Jones (Vestimentifera). *Science* 213:336–338.

Felbeck, H. 1983. Sulfide oxidation and carbon fixation by the gutless clam *Solemya reidi:* An animal-bacteria symbiosis. *Journal of Comparative Physiology* 152:3–11.

Fenchel, T. M., and B. B. Jørgensen. 1977. Detritus food chains of aquatic systems. *Advances in Microbial Ecology* 1:1–58.

Frankenberg, D., and K. L. Smith, Jr. 1967. Coprotrophy in marine animals. *Limnology and Oceanography* 12:443–450.

Friedman, M., M. J. Diamond, and G. A. Bruderick. 1982. Dimethylolurea as a tyrosine reagent and protein protectant against ruminal degradation. *Journal of Agricultural and Food Chemistry* 30:72–77.

Geddes, D.A.M., and G. N. Jenkins. 1974. Intrinsic and extrinsic factors influencing the flora of the mouth. In F. A. Skinner and J. G. Carr (eds.). *The Normal Micro-bial Flora of Man.* Academic Press, London, pp. 85–100.

Gibbons, R. J., and J. van Houte. 1975. Bacterial adherence in oral microbiology. *Annual Reviews of Microbiology* 29:19–44.

Gordon, H. A., and L. Pesti. 1971. The gnotobiotic animal as a tool in the study of host microbial relationships. *Bacteriological Reviews* 35:390–429.

Grassle, J. F. 1985. Hydrothermal vent animals: Distribu-tion and biology. *Science* 229:713–717.

Hardie, J. M., and G. H. Bowden. 1974. The normal microbial flora of the mouth. In F. A. Skinner and J. G. Carr (eds.). *The Normal Microbial Flora of Man.* Academic Press, London, pp. 47–84.

Hardy, R.W.F., R. D. Holsten, E. K. Jackson, and R. C. Burns. 1968. The acetylene-ethylene assay for nitrogen fixation: Laboratory and field evaluation. *Plant Physiol-ogy* 43:1185–1207.

Hastings, J. W., and K. H. Nealson. 1977. Bacterial biolumi-nescence. *Annual Reviews of Microbiology* 31:549–595.

Henry, S. M. (ed.). 1967. *Symbiosis.* Academic Press, New York.

Hoffman, H. 1966. Oral microbiology. *Advances in Applied Microbiology* 8:195–251.

Höfte, H., and H. Whiteley. 1989. Insecticidal crystal proteins of *Bacillus thuringiensis. Microbiological Reviews* 53:242–255.

Holligan, P. M., and G. W. Gooday. 1975. Symbiosis in *Convoluta roscoffensis.* In *Symbiosis,* Symposia of the Society for Experimental Biology, No. 29. Cambridge University Press, Cambridge, England, pp. 205–228.

Hungate, R. E. 1966. *The Rumen and Its Microbes.* Academic Press, New York.

Hungate, R. E. 1975. The rumen microbial ecosystem. *Annual Reviews of Microbiology* 29:39–66.

Hungate, R. E. 1978. Gut microbiology. In M. W. Loutit and J.A.R. Miles (eds.). *Microbial Ecology.* Springer-Verlag, Berlin, pp. 258–264.

Jannasch, H. W., and M. J. Mottl. 1985. Geomicrobiology of deep-sea hydrothermal vents. *Science* 229:717–725.

Jannasch, H. W., and D. C. Nelson. 1984. Recent progress in the microbiology of hydrothermal vents. In M. J. Klug and C. A. Reddy (eds.). *Current Perspectives in Microbial Ecology.* American Society for Microbiology, Washington, DC, pp. 170–176.

Jones, G. W. 1984. Mechanisms of the attachment of bacteria to animal cells. In M. J. Klug and C. A. Reddy (eds.). *Current Perspectives in Microbial Ecology.* American Society for Microbiology, Washington, DC, pp. 136–143.

Jones, M. L. 1981. *Riftia pachyptila* Jones: Observations on the vestimentiferan worm from the Galapagos Rift. *Science* 213:333–336.

Jørgensen, C. B. 1966. *Biology of Suspension Feeding.* Pergamon Press, Oxford, England.

Kenworthy, R. 1973. Intestinal microbial flora of the pig. *Advances in Applied Microbiology* 16:31–54.

Leadbetter, J. R., and J. A. Breznak. 1996. Physiological ecology of *Methanobrevibacter curvatus* sp. nov., isolated from the hindgut of the termite *Reticulothermes flavipes. Applied and Environmental Microbiology* 62:3620–3631.

Lee, A. 1985. Neglected niches: The microbial ecology of the gastrointestinal tract. *Advances in Microbial Ecology* 8:115–162.

Lee, K.-H., and E. G. Ruby. 1995. Symbiotic role of viable but nonculturable state of *Vibrio fischeri* in Hawaiian coastal seawater. *Applied and Environmental Microbiology* 61:278–283.

Leisman, G., D. H. Cohn, and K. H. Nealson. 1980. Bacterial origin of luminescence in marine animals. *Science* 208:1271–1273.

Luckey, T. D. 1965. Effects of microbes on germfree animals. *Advances in Applied Microbiology* 7:169–223.

Marples, M. J. 1969. Life on the human skin. *Scientific American* 220:108–119.

Marples, M. J. 1974. The normal microbial flora of the skin. In F. A. Skinner and J. G. Carr (eds.). *The Normal Microbial Flora of Man.* Academic Press, London, pp. 7–12.

Marshall, K. C. 1980. Reactions of microorganisms, ions and macromolecules at interfaces. In D. C. Ellwood, J. N. Hedger, M. J. Latham, J. M. Lynch, and J. H. Slater (eds.). *Contemporary Microbial Ecology.* Academic Press, London, pp. 93–106.

Martin, J. K. 1979. Biochemical implications of insect mycophagy. *Biological Reviews* 54:1–21.

Martin, M. M. 1970. The biochemical basis of the fungus-attine ant symbiosis. *Science* 169:16–20.

Martin, M. M., and J. S. Martin. 1978. Cellulose digestion in the midgut of the fungus-growing termite *Macrotermes natalensis:* The role of acquired digestive enzymes. *Science* 199:1453–1455.

McBee, R. H. 1971. Significance of intestinal microflora in herbivory. *Annual Reviews of Ecological Systematics* 2:165–176.

McCosker, J. E. 1977. Flashlight fishes. *Scientific American* 236:106–114.

McFall-Ngai, M. J., and E. G. Ruby. 1991. Symbiont recognition and subsequent morphogenesis as early events in an animal-bacterial mutualism. *Science* 254:1491–1494.

McLaughlin, J.J.A., and P. A. Zahl. 1966. Endozoic algae. In S. M. Henry (ed.). *Symbiosis,* Vol. 1. Academic Press, New York, pp. 258–297.

Merchant, I. A., and R. A. Packer. 1967. *Veterinary Bacteriology and Virology.* Iowa State University Press, Ames, IA.

Miller, J. A. 1987. Ecology of a new disease. *BioScience* 37:11–15.

Morin, J. G., A. Harrington, K. Nealson, H. Krieger, T. O. Baldwin, and J. W. Hastings. 1975. Light for all reasons:

Versatility in the behavioral repertoire of the flashlight fish. *Science* 190:74–76.

Mortensen, A. 1984. Importance of microbial nitrogen metabolism in the ceca of birds. In M. J. Klug and C. A. Reddy (eds.). *Current Perspectives in Microbial Ecology.* American Society for Microbiology, Washington, DC, pp. 273–278.

Muscatine, L., C. B. Cook, R. L. Pardy, and R. R. Pool. 1975. Uptake, recognition and maintenance of symbiotic *Chlorella* by *Hydra viridis*. In *Symbiosis,* Symposia of the Society for Experimental Biology, No. 29. Cambridge University Press, Cambridge, England, pp. 175–204.

Nealson, K. H., and J. W. Hastings. 1979. Bacterial bioluminescence: Its control and ecological significance. *Microbiological Reviews* 43:496–518.

Nealson, K. H., M. G. Haygood, B. M. Tebo, M. Roman, E. Miller, and J. E. McCosker. 1984. Contribution by symbiotically luminous fishes to the occurrence and bioluminescence of luminous bacteria in seawater. *Microbial Ecology* 10:69–77.

Nelson, D. C., and C. R. Fisher. 1995. Chemoautotrophic and methanotrophic endosymbiotic bacteria at deep-sea vents and seeps. In D. M. Karl (ed.). *The Microbiology of Deep-Sea Hydrothermal Vents.* CRC Press, Boca Raton, FL, pp. 125–167.

Noble, W.C., and D. G. Pitcher. 1978. Microbial ecology of the human skin. *Advances in Microbial Ecology* 2:245–289.

Nordbring-Hertz, B., and H. Jansson. 1984. Fungal development, predacity, and recognition of prey in nematode destroying fungi. In M. J. Klug and C. A. Reddy (eds.). *Current Perspectives in Microbial Ecology.* American Society for Microbiology, Washington, DC, pp. 327–333.

Porter, K. G. 1976. Enhancement of algal growth and productivity by grazing zooplankton. *Science* 192:1332–1334.

Porter, K. G. 1984. Natural bacteria as food resources for zooplankton. In M. J. Klug and C. A. Reddy (eds.). *Current Perspectives in Microbial Ecology.* American Society for Microbiology, Washington, DC, pp. 340–345.

Potrikus, C. J., and J. A. Breznak. 1977. Nitrogen-fixing *Enterobacter agglomerans* isolated from guts of wood-eating termites. *Applied and Environmental Microbiology* 33:392–399.

Powell, M. A., and G. N. Somero. 1986. Hydrogen sulfide oxidation is coupled to oxidative phosphorylation in mitochondria of *Solemya reidi*. *Science* 233:563–566.

Pramer, D. 1964. Nematode-trapping fungi. *Science* 144:382–388.

Preston, C. M., and E. F. DeLong. 1996. Identification of a sponge-associated Archaeon using fluorescent whole-cell hybridization. *Abstracts of Annual Meeting of American Society for Microbiology* I1.

Rau, G. H. 1981. Hydrothermal vent clam and tube worm $^{13}C/^{12}C$: Further evidence on nonphotosynthetic food sources. *Science* 213:338–340.

Robb, E. J., and G. L. Barron. 1982. Nature's ballistic missile. *Science* 218:1221–1222.

Rosebury, T. 1962. *Microorganisms Indigenous to Man.* McGraw-Hill, New York.

Rowan, R., and D. A. Powers. 1991. A molecular genetic classification of zooxanthellae and the evolution of animal algal symbioses. *Science* 251:1348–1351.

Sands, W. A. 1969. The association of termites and fungi. In K. Krishna and F. M. Wessner (eds.). *Biology of Termites,* Vol. 1. Academic Press, New York, pp. 495–524.

Savage, D. C. 1977. Microbial ecology of the gastrointestinal tract. *Annual Reviews in Microbiology* 31:107–133.

Savage, D. C. 1978. Gastrointestinal microecology: One opinion. In M. W. Loutit and J.A.R. Miles (eds.). *Microbial Ecology.* Springer-Verlag, Berlin, pp. 234–239.

Shachak, M., C. G. Jones, and Y. Cranot. 1987. Herbivory in rocks and the weathering of a desert. *Science* 236:1098–1099.

Shilo, M. 1967. Formation and mode of action of algal toxins. *Bacteriological Reviews* 31:18–193.

Sleeter, T. D., P. J. Boyle, A. M. Cundell, and R. Mitchell. 1978. Relationships between marine microorganisms and the wood-boring isopod *Limnoria tripuncata*. *Marine Biology* 45:329–336.

Smith, C.E.G. 1978. "New" viral zoonoses: Past, present and future. In M. W. Loutit and J.A.R. Miles (eds.). *Microbial Ecology.* Springer-Verlag, Berlin, pp. 170–174.

Smith, H. 1968. Biochemical challenge of microbial pathogenicity. *Bacteriological Reviews* 32:164–184.

Smith, K. M. 1976. *Virus-Insect Relationships.* Longman Group, Cambridge, England.

Sochard, M. R., D. F. Wilson, B. Austin, and R. R. Colwell. 1979. Bacteria associated with the surface and gut of marine copepods. *Applied and Environmental Microbiology* 37:750–759.

Southward, E. C. 1986. Gill symbionts in thiasirids and other bivalve molluscs. *Journal of Marine Biology* 66:889–914.

Tait, R. V., and R. S. DeSanto. 1972. *Elements of Marine Ecology*. Springer-Verlag, New York, pp. 18–33 and 155–169.

Tannock, G. W. 1984. Control of gastrointestinal pathogens by normal flora. In M. J. Klug and C. A. Reddy (eds.). *Current Perspectives in Microbial Ecology*. American Society for Microbiology, Washington, DC, pp. 374–382.

Taylor, D. L. 1973a. Algal symbionts of invertebrates. *Annual Reviews of Microbiology* 27:171–187.

Taylor, D. L. 1973b. The cellular interactions of algal-invertebrate symbiosis. *Advances in Marine Biology* 11:1–56.

Taylor, D. L. 1975. Symbiotic dinoflagellates. In *Symbiosis, Symposium of the Society for Experimental Biology*, No. 29. Cambridge University Press, Cambridge, England, pp. 267–278.

Thorn, R. G., and G. L. Barron. 1984. Carnivorous mushrooms. *Science* 224:76–78.

Trust, T. J., J. I. MacInnes, and K. H. Bartlett. 1978. Variations in the intestinal microflora of salmonid fishes. In M. W. Loutit and J.A.R. Miles (eds.). *Microbial Ecology*. Springer-Verlag, Berlin, pp. 250–254.

Tunnicliffe, V. 1992. Hydrothermal-vent communities of the deep sea. *American Scientist* 80:336–349.

Turner, J. T., and J. G. Ferrante. 1979. Zooplankton fecal pellets in aquatic ecosystems. *BioScience* 29:670–677.

Van Rie, J., W. H. McGaughey, D. E. Johnson, B. D. Barnett, and H. van Mellaert. 1990. Mechanism of insect resistance to the microbial insecticide *Bacillus thuringiensis*. *Science* 247:72–74.

Weber, N. A. 1966. Fungus-growing ants. *Science* 153:587–604.

Weber, N. A. 1972. The fungus-culturing behavior of ants. *American Zoologist* 12:577–587.

Willey, R. L., W. R. Bowen, and E. Durban. 1970. Symbiosis between *Euglena* and damselfly nymphs is seasonal. *Science* 170:80–81.

Wolin, M. J. 1979. The rumen fermentation: A model for interactions in anaerobic ecosystems. *Advances in Microbial Ecology* 3:49–78.

Woodroffe, R.C.S., and D. A. Shaw. 1974. Natural control and ecology of microbial populations on skin and hair. In F. A. Skinner and J. G. Carr (eds.). *The Normal Microbial Flora of Man*. Academic Press, London, pp. 13–34.

Wu, M.M.H., C. S. Wu, M. H. Chiang, and S. F. Chou. 1972. Microbial investigations on the suffocation disease of rice in Taiwan. *Plant and Soil* 37:329–344.

Yamin, M. A. 1981. Cellulose metabolism by the flagellate *Trichonympha* from a termite is independent of endosymbiotic bacteria. *Science* 211:58–59.

Yonge, C. M. 1963. The biology of coral reefs. *Advances in Marine Biology* 1:209–260.

ZoBell, C. E., and C. B. Feltham. 1937. Bacteria as food for certain marine invertebrates. *Journal of Marine Research* 1:312–327.

# part three

## Microbial Communities and Ecosystems

# 6

# Development of
# Microbial Communities

*The ecological hierarchy of microorganisms ranges from individuals to an integrated community within an ecosystem. Populations of microorganisms have functional roles (niches) within communities that permit their survival. Microbial populations exhibit various adaptations for success in diverse communities. These adaptations as well as population interactions contribute to the stability of communities. Communities usually undergo characteristic successional changes that may also lead to greater stability. Disturbances may disrupt the successional process but homeostatic forces act to restore the balance of a community. Stable microbial communities tend to have high diversities. The interactions within the community are often complex; the use of model ecosystems and mathematical models helps to understand population dynamics and ecosystem functioning.*

## Microbial Community Dynamics

The community is the highest biological unit in an ecological hierarchy made up of individuals and populations (Figure 6.1). A microbial community is an integrated assemblage of microbial populations occurring and interacting within a given location called a *habitat.* Studies that examine communities fall in the realm of synecology, which deals with the study of interactions between the various populations. Such studies are in contrast to autecological studies, which examine an individual organism or individual population in relation to its environment, emphasizing the life history and behavior of individual populations as a means of adaptation to their environment. Marshall (1993) indicated that microbial ecology has three important goals with respect to understanding the roles of microorganisms in their natural habitats: (1) to define population dynamics in communities, (2) to define physicochemical characteristics of microenvironments, and (3) to understand the metabolic processes carried out by microorganisms at specific habitats. To achieve these goals, it is essential to determine the roles of individual organisms in the context of functioning communities in the environment (Caldwell 1993).

Populations within a community interact with each other in an integrated manner. They do so at a physical location called a habitat. Each population that functions as a member of the community at that habitat has a specialized functional role called a *niche.* The

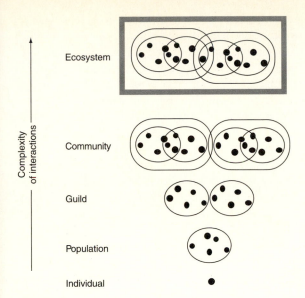

**Figure 6.1**
Levels of ecological organization.

niches within a community are filled by the indigenous populations of that community. Populations compete to occupy the available niches. Each successful population within a community plays a functional role that contributes to the maintenance of that community. Populations within a community that use the same resources—the guild structure of the community—often exhibit intense competition. In some cases the first organisms to arrive and colonize an area have a selective advantage and can retain a niche in the community against competitors. In other cases there is a succession of populations, with better-adapted populations displacing those originally occupying a niche.

The species assemblage that successfully inhabits a delineated volume of resources, such as a leaf, is called a *unit community*. Populations in a unit community tend to interact with each other and not with populations in other unit communities (Swift 1984).

## Population Selection Within Communities: *r* and *K* Strategies

Microorganisms, like higher plants and animals, have evolved strategies that enable them to successfully survive and maintain themselves within communities. One artificial scheme for viewing these strategies classifies organisms along an *r-K* gradient (Andrews 1984). The terms *r* and *K* are derived from the logistic equation for growth of a population (Andrews 1991):

$$\frac{dX}{dt} \cdot \frac{1}{X} = r - \left( \frac{r}{K} \cdot X \right)$$

where

$\frac{dX}{dt} \cdot \frac{1}{X}$ = specific rate of population increase

$r$ = per capita rate of increase of the population

$K$ = carrying capacity of the environment

$X$ = population density as either numbers or biomass

This logistic equation describes population growth in limited environmental conditions. When $X$ is low, the rate of population change is dominated by $r$. When $X$ is high, the growth rate is limited by the carrying capacity of the environment ($K$). The greatest increase in population density occurs at near zero population density (maximum growth rate of $r$); the minimal rate of population density increase occurs at the maximum population density ($K$), when there is no further increase in biomass or numbers of individuals within the population.

The *r-K* scheme assumes a continuum, with evolution favoring either adaptation to high rates of reproduction (*r* strategists) or optimal utilization (conservation) of environmental resources (*K* strategists). The ecological dogma is that organisms optimize either reproductive capacity or conservation of resources, but not both (Andrews 1991). The *r* strategists rely upon high reproductive rates for continued survival within the community. Sergei Winogradsky's zymogenous (opportunistic) soil populations closely correspond to the concept of *r* strategy and his autochthonous (humus-degrading) populations correspond to the concept of *K* strategy (Waksman 1952). Microorganisms initially colonizing a habitat should be *r* strategists with the highest growth rates ($\mu_{max}$), which would favor reproductive success at low population densities (uncrowded conditions) where there is limited competition; conversely, organisms with higher $K$ values should compete better in communities with crowded conditions (Figure 6.2).

Although $r$ strategists have high reproductive rates, they have few other competitive adaptations; they tend to prevail in situations that are not resource limited, that is, where nutrients are not severely limiting, and where high reproduction rates outweigh the advantages of other competitive adaptations. The $r$ strategists should have a high intrinsic growth rate and not depend on contributions from other populations for their survival. An $r$ strategist microorganism would be one that through rapid growth rates takes over and dominates situations in which resources

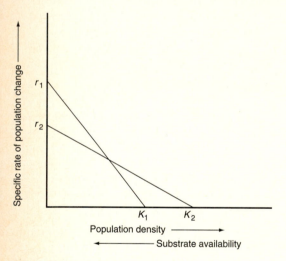

**Figure 6.2**
Comparison of specific rates of increase for two microbial populations at different levels of competition. In comparative terms, population 1 is an $r$ strategist (higher $r$ value and lower $K$ value) and population 2 is a $K$ strategist (higher $K$ value and lower $r$ value). Population 1 outcompetes population 2 when competition is low (low population densities and high substrate availabilities) based on its higher intrinsic growth rate (reproductive capacity). Disturbances that cause environmental fluctuations so that substrate availability remains high and population densities stay low will permit the continued success of population 1. Population 2 will become dominant if the environment remains stable and the population level increases to the point where adaptation to lower substrate availability (carrying capacity) becomes the critical factor determining competitive success. (Source: Andrews 1991)

are temporarily abundant. Selection for $r$ strategists would occur in uncrowded conditions and in unstable environments subject to unpredictable and transitory changes. Populations of $r$ strategists are subject to extreme fluctuations. They tend to prevail in uncrowded communities and devote a large portion of their resources to reproduction. When resources become scarce or conditions turn unfavorable, their populations crash, that is, they experience rapid reduction. Formation of abundant and resistant spores for dispersal and survival during long inactive periods is of great advantage to such microbial $r$ strategists. Fungi, such as *Saccharomyces,* that grow on sugar-rich plant exudates, and bacteria, such as pseudomonads, that rapidly colonize and grow on sugar-rich plant materials fallen onto soil, are $r$ strategists. Archaea growing in the vicinities of deep-sea thermal vents likewise are $r$ strategists that utilize the sulfur compounds emitted from the volcanic plumes. Cyanobacteria and dinoflagellates that respond to phosphate or other mineral nutrient enrichment with an explosive bloom also are $r$ strategists. Similarly, *Aspergillus, Penicillium, Pseudomonas, Bacillus,* and similar heterotrophs are $r$ strategists because they rapidly colonize and degrade easily available high concentrations of organic matter (Andrews and Hall 1986).

Although in comparison to macroorganisms all microorganisms might appear to be $r$ strategists, and microorganisms have generally been viewed in this manner, compared to each other some of them can be considered $K$ strategists. $K$ strategists depend on physiological adaptations to the environmental resources or carrying capacity of the environment. $K$ strategists, which reproduce more slowly than $r$ strategists, tend to be successful in resource-limited situations. Populations of $K$ strategists are usually more stable and permanent members of the community. They prevail under conditions of crowding and devote a smaller portion of their resources to reproduction. Soil streptomycetes that grow slowly on complex soil organic matter exemplify $K$ strategists. Other examples of $K$ strategist microorganisms are desmids in oligotrophic lakes and ponds; marine spirilla and vibrios and freshwater prosthecate bacteria, which are able to use extremely dilute concentrations of organic matter; *Agrobacterium, Corynebacterium,* and similar humus-degrading soil bacteria; and Basidiomycota, which degrade the cellulosic and lignin components of forest litter.

## Succession Within Microbial Communities

The individual populations of a community occupy the niches in that ecosystem. With time, some populations are replaced by other populations that are better adapted to fill a functional role (ecological niche) within the ecosystem; that is, the structure of the community evolves with time. The microbial processes that occur in a particular ecosystem are performed by many populations that interact with each other. Each population performs a specific set of processes that constitutes that population's niche within the ecosystem. Ecosystems vary in terms of their available niches. Some ecosystems have many niches and can support high diversities. Others have fewer niches and will have lower diversities even if all the niches are filled. In some ecosystems not all the niches are filled, which also results in lowered diversities; this occurs, for example, in moderately and severely disturbed ecosystems where there is a lack of populations that are physiologically capable of filling some of the available niches.

The types of interrelationships among populations in a community, as well as adaptations within populations, contribute to the ecological stability of the community. Some interrelationships involving microbial populations are loose associations in which one microbial population can replace another; others are tight associations in which one microbial population cannot replace another.

Development of a more or less stable community usually involves a succession of populations, that is, an orderly sequential change in the populations of the community. Community succession begins with colonization or invasion of a habitat by microbial populations (Golley 1977). If the habitat has not been previously colonized—for example, the gastrointestinal tracts of newborn animals—the process is known as *primary succession.* When succession occurs in a habitat with a previous colonization and succession history, it is called *secondary succession.* Secondary succession is the consequence of some catastrophic event that has disrupted and altered the course of primary succession.

The first colonizers of a virgin environment are called *pioneer organisms.* All pioneer microorganisms must be able to reach the virgin environment, so a common feature of pioneer microorganisms is effective dispersal mechanisms. Beyond this, pioneer characteristics vary with the environment to be colonized. Preemptive colonization occurs when pioneer organisms alter conditions in the habitat in ways that discourage further succession. Preemptive colonization may extend the reign of pioneer organisms, but populations better adapted to the now-colonized and thus altered habitat usually replace the pioneers. As this habitat undergoes additional changes, secondary invaders are also replaced. Succession ends when a relatively stable assemblage of populations, called a *climax community,* is achieved.

It has always been difficult to apply the concept of climax to microbial communities. In some situations, though, regular successional population changes of microorganisms occur, leading to a relatively stable microbial community. The highest sustainable diversities probably occur at levels of intermediary disturbance. According to classical ecological thinking a climax community represents a state of equilibrium; current ecological thinking is that equilibrium and climax communities rarely occur, but rather disturbances randomly disrupt the successional process, preventing the community from ever reaching full equilibrium (Lewin 1983; Wiens 1983).

In some successional processes, microorganisms modify the habitat in a way that permits new populations to develop; for example, the creation of anaerobic conditions by facultative anaerobes allows the growth of obligate anaerobic populations. This is known as *autogenic succession.* In contrast, *allogenic succession* occurs when a habitat is altered by environmental factors, such as seasonal changes. Even when the successional process follows a predictable sequence of population changes, the causative factors responsible for this orderly sequence are often poorly understood.

The rapid generation times of many microorganisms can lead to large population fluctuations, environmental changes may preclude the orderly succession of microbial communities, or initial random events may determine which microorganisms fill the niches of the ecosystem and direct the sequence of successional events that follow; hence, succession to a climax microbial community does not occur in many habitats. Even if an equilibrium in species diversity is attained, this can rarely persist because disturbances intervene. Disturbance alters the interactive equilibrium that has been attained among the populations in the community, promoting the accelerated extinction of some species and facilitating the immigration of new species (Swift 1984).

**Autotrophic-Heterotrophic Succession**  When gross production ($P$) exceeds the rate of community respiration ($R$), organic matter accumulates. (In many ecosystems, production is equivalent to photosynthesis, but in some, such as deep-sea hydrothermal vent communities, production is the result of chemolithotrophic metabolism.) *Autotrophic succession* occurs in cases where $P/R$ is initially greater than 1. As long as $P$ is greater than $R,$ biomass will accumulate during the autotrophic succession. As the $P/R$ ratio approaches 1, succession toward a stable community is occurring. An autotrophic succession of microorganisms occurs in environments largely devoid of organic matter when there is a nonlimiting supply of solar energy. Autotrophic succession occurs in young pioneer communities, such as on newly exposed volcanic rock. In autotrophic succession within a mineral environment, such as on bare rock, the photosynthetic pioneer organisms have minimal nutritional requirements and high tolerance to adverse environmental conditions. The ability to use atmospheric nitrogen is an advantage; terrestrial cyanobacteria and lichens are good examples of pioneers in this type of environment.

As opposed to autotrophic succession, organic matter will disappear when $P/R$ is less than 1 because consumption is greater than production. Succession in such a situation is called *heterotrophic succession.* In heterotrophic succession, the energy flow through the system decreases with time; there is insufficient organic matter input, and the community gradually uses its stored chemical energy. Heterotrophic succession is usually temporary because it culminates in the extinction of the community when the stored energy supply is exhausted. Many microbial communities involved in decompositional processes exhibit such temporary heterotrophic succession. For example, the microbial communities on a fallen log disappear after the log is completely decomposed.

It is possible for heterotrophic succession to lead to a stable community if there is a continuous source of allochthonous organic matter, that is, organic matter from an external source. As an example, heterotrophic succession in the microbial community of the gut leads to a stable climax community as long as there is regular input of food. If the animal stops feeding, however, the microbial community is disrupted and rapidly eliminated. Pioneers in a heterotrophic succession need to have, above all, high metabolic and growth rates in order to stay ahead of secondary invaders.

**Examples of Successional Processes**  An interesting heterotrophic successional process occurs on detrital particles that enter aquatic habitats (Fenchel and Jørgensen 1977) (Figure 6.3 on page 182). Fresh particulate detritus consists mainly of mechanically shredded tissue of dead leaves, roots, stems, or thalli of macrophytes mixed with smaller amounts of debris from other sources. Microbial communities associated with detritus are complex, but predictable population changes occur during succession. If sterilized natural detrital particles are placed in seawater or fresh water inoculated with a small amount of natural detritus, a characteristic succession of organisms occurs. This succession leads to a microbial community closely resembling that of natural detritus. Bacteria occur in small numbers on the particles after 6–8 hours and reach their maximal numbers after 15–150 hours. The bacterial populations then decrease and become relatively stable after about 200 hours. Small zooflagellates appear about 20 hours after inoculation and reach maximal population sizes after 100–200 hours. Ciliates appear after about 100 hours and reach maximal numbers at 200–300 hours. Other groups of microorganisms, including rhizopods and diatoms, usually appear late in the succession.

Environmental factors, such as temperature, influence the time sequence of succession. The individual populations of the microbial community associated with detrital particles interact as a predator-prey system: the bacteria are the prey and the protozoa are the primary predators. The overall result of the microbial succession on detrital particles is the decomposition of some of the nitrogen-poor plant polymers and their partial replacement with nitrogen-rich microbial biomass. For most detritus-feeding invertebrates and vertebrates, this microbial upgrading of the detritus is essential. Few comparable examples for the succession of bacterial populations on plant material that

enters the soil are known. The succession of fungal populations on leaf litter, however, has been studied (Kendrick and Burges 1962) (Figure 6.4 on page 182). A parallel succession of bacterial populations probably occurs simultaneously and may affect the observed fungal succession.

An interesting observation about community succession in soil is that nitrification (the conversion of ammonium to nitrate) is inhibited in many climax ecosystems (Rice and Pancholy 1972). Populations of nitrifying bacteria decrease or disappear in forest and grassland ecosystems during succession to a climax community, resulting in the accumulation of ammonium nitrogen. This successional process appears to have adaptive value to plants and non-nitrifying

---

## Succession Within Biofilm Communities

Biofilms are complex microbial communities that undergo successional development beginning with colonization of a surface (Lawrence et al. 1995). Adherent populations in natural habitats are in constant flux (Characklis et al. 1990). Following immersion of clean surfaces in natural waters a sequence of surface-fouling events occurs, resulting in a succession of surface-colonizing species that dominate at various times. In a process called *epibiosis,* the initial colonizing species are replaced before other organisms with evolutionarily defined requirements become involved with the surface consortium (Wahl 1989). The succession is based on a sequence of physical and biological events, starting with the adsorption of organic films and closely followed by surface colonization by bacterial species.

As illustrated in the figure on page 181, biofilm development starts when a solid surface is immersed in an aqueous environment and organic molecules adsorb, forming a macromolecular con-

ditioning film (Lawrence et al. 1995). Attachment of a variety of bacteria to the surface occurs rapidly. The time frame for the initial phases of surface colonization are relatively short, with the molecular film forming over a period of minutes and with significant bacterial colonization occurring within 24 hours. Motility is critical for the success of many different bacteria during colonization of surfaces; for example, Stanley (1983) demonstrated that adsorption of *Pseudomonas aeruginosa* cells decreased by 90% following mechanical removal of their flagella.

Microorganisms first gaining access to newly exposed surfaces may physically exclude a potential competitor organism, and by virtue of factors such as site blocking they may enjoy significant advantages with respect to positioning and utilization of adsorbed nutrients. Surfaces are heterogeneous, and spatial competition for favorable microsites may occur even when only a small part of the total surface is actually colonized by

*(continued)*

microorganisms. The colonizing bacteria often form microcolonies or cell aggregates from individual points of bacterial colonization. Extensive layers of bacterial cells develop. Surface overcrowding results in nutrient depletion, cessation of growth, and induction of a starvation-survival phase of *Vibrio* species (Kjelleberg et al. 1982; Marshall 1989). While bacterial populations continue to adsorb to exposed surfaces, larger fouling organisms—including amoeba, flagellates, ciliates, diatoms, and larvae—colonize the surface over a period of days (for predatory eucaryotes and diatoms) or weeks (for larval and spore deposition) (Wahl 1989; Decho 1990). This successional pattern of surface colonization has been observed during long-term observation of immersed surfaces in flowing or static systems. Rod-shaped bacteria are often the primary colonizers following exposure of clean surfaces to natural aqueous systems (Marshall et al. 1971; Marszalek et al. 1979), followed by stalked bacteria such as *Caulobacter* species. (Dempsey 1981). Subsequent colonization by filamentous algae, diatoms, and larvae has been observed in stream, river, and oceanic environments, with eventual attraction of predators that feed on the biofilm (Marszalek et al. 1979; Baier 1985; Wahl 1989; Rittle et al. 1990). Various microbial populations within biofilms form associations called *consortia* within which member populations are able to pool their resources, for example, each contributing enzymes to bring about a complete metabolic pathway. Algal-bacterial associations in biofilm communities are commonplace, with algae representing both sites of attachment and sources of nutrients (Bowen et al. 1993).

Some of the microbial populations colonizing the surface produce exopolymers during their growth. The production of extracellular polymers is pivotal to community development on surfaces because it provides an interface between the cell and the external environment, influencing rates of chemical exchange and availability of nutrients and facilitating the creation of microniches. In addition, the presence of exopolymers influences the susceptibility of bacteria to stress and facilitates cell-cell interaction. Biofilm organisms, which frequently represent a range of physiological and functional groups, may benefit from the attached mode of growth through protection provided by the polymeric matrix against outside perturbations (Fletcher 1984). Competition and predatory interactions between bacterial species play a significant role in community development (Byrd et al. 1985; Casida 1992).

The ambient conditions associated with clean surfaces are temporally and spatially modified by the colonization, growth, and activity of bacteria. Microbial consumption of nutrients, production of wastes, and synthesis of cellular and extracellular materials all act in concert to define physicochemically the microenvironmental conditions (Hamilton 1987). Biofilm communities typically are characterized by steep, continuously shifting physicochemical gradients within the biofilm. Within a newly formed biofilm, rapid use of available nutrients leads to an increase in microbial biomass with a concurrent increase in the demand for oxygen. Anaerobic zones form due to metabolic oxygen depletion and diffusion limitation, potentially allowing proliferation of anaerobic microorganisms while limiting the success of aerobes. Heterotrophic aerobic and facultatively anaerobic bacteria associated with aggregates of the cyanobacteria *Aphanizomenon* and *Anabaena* are capable of forming reduced microzones in $O_2$-saturated waters. The site-selective colonization of heterocysts and adjoining cells appears to enhance $N_2$-fixation by these cyanobacteria (Paerl 1980).

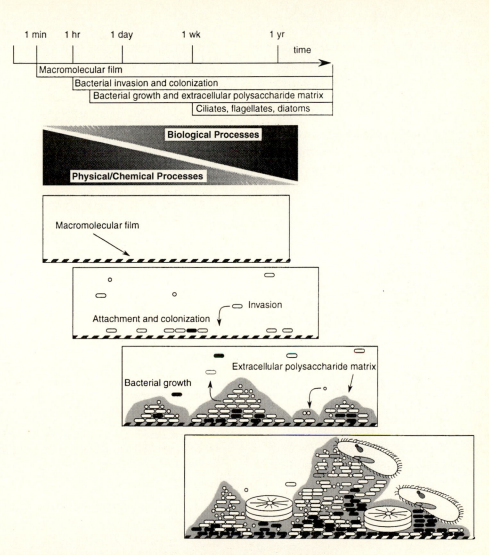

The formation of a biofilm occurs as a successional process. The first step is the physical conditioning of the surface with the deposition of substances that attract bacteria and permit their adherence and growth. Next, populations invade, attaching to the surface and colonizing it. These bacteria initially form a monolayer. As they reproduce to form a thicker layer, new bacteria invade to establish a community with multiple populations. These bacterial populations excrete extracellular polysaccharides that form a matrix within which the biofilm's bacterial populations adhere. Eucaryotic microorganisms, including algae and protozoa, then invade the biofilm, continuing the successional process to form a complex biofilm community that is highly resistant to outside disturbance. (Source: Lawrence et al. 1995)

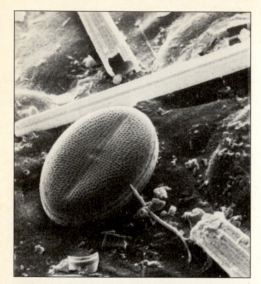

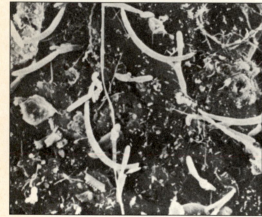

A

B

**Figure 6.3**
Scanning electron micrographs of detrital microorganisms on submerged surfaces: (A) Diatoms on leaf surface. (Courtesy of C. Versfeld) (B) Large curved cells of the fungal species *Lunulospora curvala* on oak leaf litter in a woodland stream. (Source: Suberkropp and Klug 1974. Reprinted by permission, copyright Springer-Verlag.)

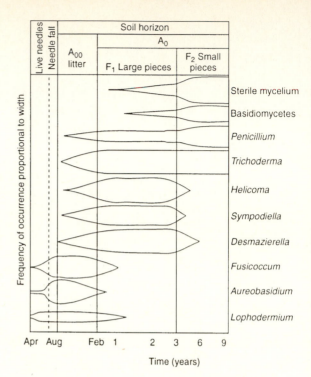

**Figure 6.4**
Succession of fungal populations on pine-needle litter from the initial populations on the live needles (lower left) to the small decomposed pieces in the $A_0$ layer (upper right). The vertical width of the bar indicates the frequency of occurrence for observed portions of pine needles of the same size; the wider the bar, the greater the frequency. (Source: Kendrick and Burges 1962. Reprinted by permission of Braunschweig Verlag von J. Cramer.)

microorganisms because ammonium ions are less readily leached from soil than nitrate ions.

Successions of microbial communities are also associated with animal tissues (Marples 1965; Skinner and Carr 1974; Noble and Pitcher 1978). The sterile intestinal and skin tissues of newborn animals permit observation of community succession from the time of initial colonization. The population levels and types of microbes in climax communities in the gastrointestinal ecosystems are regulated by several processes. Some of the regulatory forces in these processes are exerted by the animal hosts, some by the microbes, some by diet, and some by the environment. Within the gastrointestinal tract are many niches filled by various microbial populations. The succession of bacterial populations in humans and other nonruminant mammals normally begins with colonization of the gastrointestinal tract by *Bifidobacterium* and *Lactobacillus* species. This is followed by a succession of facultative anaerobes, such as *Escherichia coli* and

*Streptococcus faecalis.* Populations of strictly anaerobic bacteria, such as *Bacteroides,* appear late in the succession, after the beginning of solid food ingestion. These populations of obligate anaerobes become dominant. Climax microbial communities in gastrointestinal tracts are generally reached by the time of weaning.

As a specific example, the intestinal microbial community of mice initially is composed of lactic acid bacteria, *Flavobacterium,* and enterococci (Schaedler et al. 1965) (Figure 6.5). Populations of *Flavobacterium* increase for about 8 days, after which they disappear from the intestinal microbial community. Populations of enterococci and coliforms increase dramatically with the disappearance of *Flavobacterium* but decrease to lower population levels several days later. Lactic acid bacteria increase regularly for 10 days, after which their numbers remain relatively constant. Populations of obligately anaerobic *Bacteroides* are absent or present in very low numbers in the initial colonizing microbial community. After 18 days, however, there is a dramatic increase in the population of *Bacteroides,* which becomes the dominant population in the climax community.

In ruminants, succession leads to the development of a complex obligately anaerobic microbial community (Hungate 1975). Included in the climax community of the rumen are populations of cellulose-degrading bacteria, such as *Bacteroides* and *Ruminococcus;* starch-degrading bacteria, such as *Selenomonas;* methanogenic bacteria, such as *Methanobacterium;* cellulose- and pectin-degrading protozoa, such as *Polyplastron;* and other populations. Methanogens are the largest $H_2$-utilizing populations in rumen samples from sheep, cattle, buffaloes, deer, and llamas and in cecal samples from horses. There is a strong correlation between numbers of methanogens and of cellulolytic microorganisms in these animals. Predator-prey relations between the bacterial and protozoan populations are also important. The protozoan populations, predominantly ciliates, appear late in the succession, following the development of the complex bacterial community. The pioneer bacterial community modifies the environment with the production of various volatile acids and the removal of oxygen, allowing succession to proceed to the climax community.

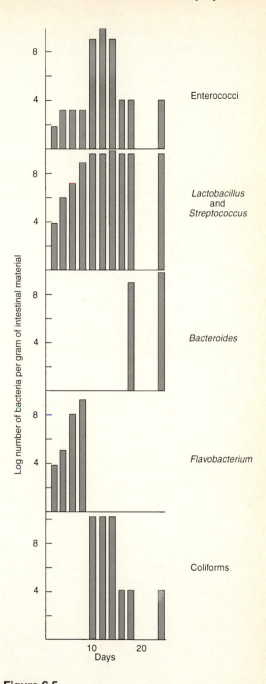

**Figure 6.5**
Succession of microbial populations in the large intestine of mice following birth. The data are expressed as log number per gram of large intestine homogenate. (Source: Schaedler et al. 1965)

**Homeostasis and Secondary Succession** Many established communities have a high degree of stability, that is, they are resistant to change. Part of this apparent stability is based on homeostasis, a compensating mechanism that acts to maintain steady-state conditions and, by a variety of control mechanisms, to counteract perturbations that would upset this steady state. The concept of a stable community does not imply static conditions. Individual populations are subject to regular and irregular fluctuations. These fluctuations occur in response to internal or external conditions and contribute to the maintenance of overall ecosystem stability. As an example, an accumulation of nitrite or hydrogen sulfide in the ecosystem temporarily increases the populations that use these metabolic intermediates; in turn, these increased populations lower the concentrations of materials that otherwise would accumulate to toxic levels. Population shifts may also occur in response to overall environmental conditions, such as seasonal light and temperature changes. A metabolic niche filled by a mesophilic population during the summer season may be occupied by a psychrophilic population during the winter, but the metabolic function that may be vital for the ecosystem is performed in either case. Such seasonal shifts in populations are known to occur on a regular basis.

Some microbial populations exhibit annual rhythms. For example, *Vibrio parahaemolyticus* exhibits an annual cycle in estuaries (Kaneko and Colwell 1975). In temperate zones, this organism occurs in the water column during the spring and summer months but disappears during the winter. The cycle is based in part on low winter water temperatures. Some members of this bacterial population survive in sediment during the winter, allowing for continuance of the cycle.

The occurrence of regularly timed population fluctuations raises the concept of a temporal niche; microorganisms may occupy a niche in a habitat at one particular time but not at another. Various algal populations in many aquatic habitats, for example, exhibit seasonal succession (Stockner 1968) (Figure 6.6). Under the various temperature and light regimes that occur during each season, different populations fill the

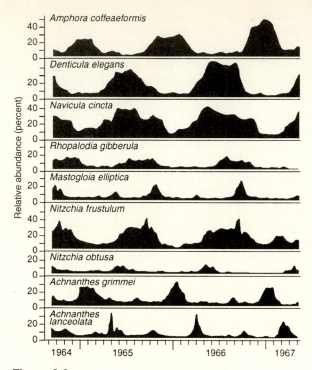

**Figure 6.6**
Fluctuations of diatom populations in a thermal spring showing regularity of seasonal diatom population change, that is, annual succession. (Source: Stockner 1968. Reprinted by permission of British Phycology Society.)

niches of the ecosystem. In some cases, the existence of temporal niches may act to diminish direct competition between populations, allowing the coexistence of some populations that appear to compete for identical resources within spatially overlapping habitats.

Some seasonal population fluctuations can be viewed as repetitive successions toward a stable community that is repeatedly upset by the abrupt environmental changes associated with the change of seasons. An example of such a succession occurs annually in the nearshore regions of the Arctic Ocean (Kaneko et al. 1977). Each spring, there are large blooms of algae on the underside of the sea ice; the blooms occur at the same time each year and represent a regular seasonal successional event (Horner and Alexander 1972). Bacterial populations, predominantly *Flavobacterium* and *Microcyclus* species, flourish after the algal bloom under the ice (Kaneko et al. 1979). As the ice melts, the habitat is removed, ending community succession. The algal populations released into the water column diminish and are consumed by predators or subjected to bacterial decomposition. During the winter, the pigmented bacterial populations also disappear from the surface waters, but some algal and pigmented bacterial populations survive in the sediment. When winter ice forms again, it establishes a suitable habitat for the recurrence of this seasonal succession. With the return of sufficient sunlight in the spring, algae colonize under the ice and the process repeats itself.

Occasionally, severe or catastrophic environmental changes may overwhelm the ecosystem's homeostatic controls, destroying or severely disrupting the existing community and initiating a new successional process. The introduction of pollutants into aquatic or terrestrial ecosystems, applications of fungicide to soils and plants, and many other disturbances initiate secondary successional processes. Catastrophic events, such as volcanic eruptions, can sterilize habitats and create new habitats that then undergo colonization and primary succession.

After a disturbance, homeostasis acts to restore the disrupted community, and once the disrupting factor is removed, usually there is a secondary succession back to the original community. For example, washing the skin disrupts the microbial community of that habitat. Washing normally does not result in a new climax community but rather initiates a succession back to the original microbial community (Marples 1974) (Figure 6.7). Similarly, the microbial community in an agricultural soil returns to its original composition following tillage.

Homeostasis also acts to restore the initial community when alien or allochthonous microorganisms enter the habitat. For example, many of the microorganisms that enter the gastrointestinal tract on food particles are quickly eliminated, and even after the ingestion of microorganisms that cause disease, the climax microbial community of the gastrointestinal tract eventually returns to normal. Similarly, allochthonous microorganisms that enter soil and aquatic habitats are transient members of the microbial community, and antagonistic interactions (negative feedback)

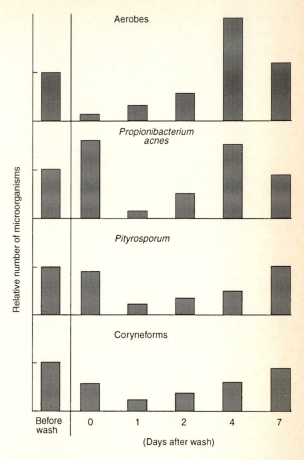

**Figure 6.7**

Succession of microorganisms on the human scalp following shampooing. The graph demonstrates the rapid recovery that occurs following this disturbance. (Source: Marples 1974. Reprinted by permission of Academic Press, London.)

act to remove the alien microbial populations, thereby restoring the original composition of the community.

Population interactions that lead to the establishment of a defined community are most likely based on physiological interactions between the various populations. The functional roles of specific populations within the communities of certain ecosystems have been defined; the interspecies population relationships within the rumen ecosystem, for example, have been characterized, leading to a relatively complete understanding of community structure and ecosystem function (Hungate 1975). Work using chemostats has elucidated some of the interactions between microbial populations that lead to the establishment of stable community structures in aquatic ecosystems (Slater 1978, 1980). In chemostat studies, stability often occurs when several interacting populations cooperate to best exploit the available resources. In some cases two species can constitute a stable community structure, whereas in other experiments additional member populations are needed before community stability is achieved.

Assuming stable environmental conditions, organisms that do not successfully fill a niche or functional role tend to be eliminated from a community (MacArthur and Wilson 1967; Whittaker 1975; May 1976). Competition between two populations tends to eliminate one of the populations from the common habitat, especially when competition is focused on a single resource and when the populations do not otherwise interact; however, a number of factors mitigate the severity of competition, and thus competitors often coexist (Fredrickson and Stephanopoulos 1981; Lewin 1983). Changing conditions, such as seasonal and diurnal fluctuations (time-varying inputs), multiplicity of resources, spatial heterogeneity of habitats, regulation by predators, dormancy, and various other factors can preclude competitive exclusion and permit coexistence of populations apparently occupying the identical niche. Kemp and Mitsch (1979) developed a model to explain the *paradox of the plankton,* a term first introduced by Hutchinson (1961) to describe the fact that diverse phytoplankton species apparently occupy the same niches in many aquatic habitats. Kemp and Mitsch found that turbulence prevented exclusion of competing populations; the underlying principle is that discontinuities in the environment permit the development of diverse stable phytoplankton communities with overlapping niches.

## Genetic Exchange in Microbial Communities

When adaptive features are introduced into the gene pool, the rapid reproductive rates of microorganisms—generation times may be as short as 15–20 minutes although a few hours may be more typical in most

environments—allow for the quick and widespread expression of the features. The rapid spread of antibiotic resistance in bacteria is a good example of the action of natural selection. Antibiotic resistance arose by spontaneous mutation or recombination before the medical use of these substances, but during this period there was no great selective advantage for pathogenic microorganisms to possess the characteristic of antibiotic resistance. Since antibiotic use became prevalent in the 1950s, microorganisms capable of continued growth—that is, infection—in an individual receiving antibiotics acquired a particular selective advantage. Within habitats receiving frequent dosages of antibiotics, such as hospitals, resistance to antibiotics has become widespread and an increasingly common characteristic of disease-causing microorganisms (Martin et al. 1970) (Figure 6.8). Transferable drug resistance has also been demonstrated in sediments beneath fish farms receiving oxytetracycline (Sandaa et al. 1992). Thus gene transfer appears to be widespread in nature whenever there is extensive selective pressure.

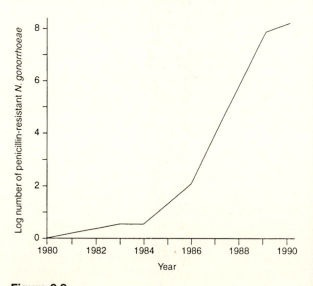

**Figure 6.8**
Development of antibiotic (penicillin) resistance in gonococcal populations during the period 1980–1990. The resistant populations of *Neisseria gonorrhoeae* produce penicillinase. The increasing occurrence of resistant strains coincides with the increased use of antibiotics and reflects selective pressure.

A critical factor in determining the persistence of any population within a community is its genetic fitness, that is, the contribution of one or more gene alleles of the population to succeeding generations (Lenski 1992). Stability of a community depends on the totality of the genes within the individual populations. Genes can be transferred to new populations within the community to form new allelic combinations with differing degrees of fitness (Levy and Miller 1989; Drahos and Barry 1992). Differences in fitness between alleles or genotypes reflect systematic differences in either mortality or reproduction, which in turn reflect systematic differences in ecological properties such as the ability to compete for limiting resources, susceptibility to predation, and so on. Processes that bring about a systematic change in the frequency of alleles include mutation, recombination, and genetic drift (a random change in the frequencies of alleles within a population) (Lenski 1992). Genetic drift differs from selection in that changes in the frequencies of alleles are due to chance events rather than to systematic differences in ecological properties such as competitive ability. Genetic drift may cause some change in the relative frequency of two selectively neutral strains, including even the extinction of one or the other.

Three principal mechanisms of genetic transfer and recombination lead to new combinations of alleles among bacteria: conjugation, a process that involves direct contact between donor and recipient cells; transduction, a process that involves bacteriophage-mediated transfer of DNA from donor to recipient bacterial cell; and transformation, a process that involves absorption of free DNA by a competent recipient cell. There is a relatively high potential for gene transfer by these mechanisms in the environment, particularly when population densities are high, but there are also significant restrictions to potential recombination (Freter 1984; Stotzky 1989; Fry and Day 1990; Lorenz and Wackernagel 1994; Miller 1992; Saye and O'Morchoe 1992; Stewart 1992; Trevors 1996; Veal et al. 1992). Restriction enzymes have the capability to degrade foreign DNA that is not protected by specific methylation of DNA nucleotides (Figure 6.9). It has been demonstrated, however, that

DNA bound to clay particles is protected against digestion by restriction endonucleases and that such bound DNA can still actively transform bacteria (Gallori et al. 1994). The greatest adsorption of DNA from *Bacillus subtilis* to clay occurred at pH 1.0 (Khanna and Stotzky 1992). This adsorbed DNA was fully protected against digestion with DNase. However, no transformation occurred at pH 1.0. The transformation frequency increased as the pH was experimentally raised to pH 7.5, indicating that adsorption, desorption, and binding do not alter the transforming capability of DNA. Thus, genes can be transferred in the environment at relatively high rates, and genetic exchange and recombination can act as a major force for the change and evolution of natural populations (Miller 1992).

Plasmids are especially important in the rapid transfer of genes among populations in a microbial community (Beringer and Hirsch 1984; DeFlaun and Levy 1989). Hospital wastes, raw sewage, sewage effluents, fresh and marine water, animal feedlots, plants, and soils have all been shown to contain bacteria that transfer plasmids by conjugation. Antibiotic resistance genes are rapidly disseminated among

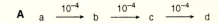

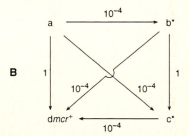

**Figure 6.9**
The effect of methylation and restriction on gene transfer among several bacterial strains. (A) Normal transfer frequencies. (B) Altered frequencies of gene exchange caused by methylation. The asterisk (*) denotes cytosine-methylating host strain; *mcr*+ denotes strain that cleaves C-methylated DNA. Average restricted frequencies of transfer are given as a proportion of the nonrestricted frequency. (Source: Saunders et al. 1990)

bacterial populations, particularly under selective pressure. In a survey of 640 human subjects, a subgroup of 356 persons without recent exposure to antibiotics demonstrated that those with a high prevalence of mercury resistance in their intestinal floras were significantly more likely to also have resistance to two or more antibiotics (Summers et al. 1993). This observation raised the possibility that mercury released from amalgam ("silver") dental restorations might be a selective agent for both mercury- and antibiotic-resistant bacteria in the oral and intestinal floras of primates. Resistances to mercury and to several antibiotics were examined in the oral and intestinal floras of six adult monkeys prior to the installation of amalgam fillings, during the time they were in place, and after replacement of the amalgam fillings with glass ionomer fillings (in four of the monkeys). The monkeys were fed an antibiotic-free diet, and fecal mercury concentrations were monitored. There was a statistically significant increase in the incidence of mercury-resistant bacteria during the 5 weeks following installation of the amalgam fillings and during the 5 weeks immediately following their replacement with glass ionomer fillings. These peaks in incidence of mercury-resistant bacteria correlated with peaks of mercury elimination immediately following amalgam placement and immediately after replacement of the amalgam fillings. Representative mercury-resistant isolates of three selected bacterial families (oral streptococci, members of the family Enterobacteriaceae, and enterococci) were also resistant to one or more antibiotics, including ampicillin, tetracycline, streptomycin, kanamycin, and chloramphenicol. Many of the enterobacterial strains were able to transfer mercury and antibiotic resistances together to laboratory bacterial recipients, suggesting that the loci for these resistances are genetically linked. These findings indicate that mercury released from amalgam fillings can cause an enrichment of mercury resistance plasmids in the normal bacterial floras of primates. Many of these plasmids also carry antibiotic resistance, implicating the exposure to mercury from dental amalgams in an increased incidence of multiple antibiotic resistance plasmids in the normal floras of nonmedicated subjects.

Plasmids with antibiotic resistance genes, as well as those with degradative pathway genes, can be transferred to a wide variety of bacterial species in many genera (Miller 1992). Plasmids can behave dynamically in the environment. Although certain specialized plasmid-borne genes are maintained through many generations, others are rapidly lost (Drahos and Barry 1992). Genes that contribute to the fitness of populations are usually maintained within the community, and those that do not are lost from that community. Nonessential genes should not be maintained, particularly if there is significant competition for an ecological niche, because the expression of a nonessential gene can have a marked inhibition on the relative growth rate of the host cell. Gene transfer, however, can maintain an allele or extrachromosomal element in a population in the face of opposing selection (Stewart and Levin 1977). One strain that is less fit than another can be maintained by recurring mutation or by migration from another source population. One allele that is less fit than another may also be maintained in a population by virtue of its association with a favorable allele elsewhere in the genome (Lenski 1992). Such linkage disequilibrium is prevalent in bacteria because of their asexual reproduction and recombination due to conjugation, transformation, and transduction.

## STRUCTURE OF MICROBIAL COMMUNITIES

### Diversity and Stability of Microbial Communities

Biological communities usually contain a few species with many individuals and many species with few individuals. Although a few dominant species normally account for most of the energy flow within a trophic level, the less abundant species determine in large part the species diversity of that trophic level and the whole community. Diversity generally decreases when one or a few populations attain high densities; high numbers signify successful competition and dominance by a single population.

# Risks of Introducing Genetically Modified Microorganisms

The potential of deliberately releasing genetically modified microorganisms into the environment has sparked a heated debate among the scientific community, regulatory agencies, and environmentalists about the ecological risks associated with such introductions (Sussman et al. 1988; Halvorson et al. 1985; Stewart-Tull and Sussman 1992). A significant component of this debate centers on how long introduced microorganisms and their DNA persist in the environment and whether genes from genetically modified microorganisms will transfer to indigenous microbial populations. Early studies suggested that introduced populations would die off quickly because of intense competition with indigenous populations. It was thought that carrying extra genes introduced by recombinant DNA technology would render genetically modified organisms competitively inferior. One early study on the fate of a 2,4,5-T-degrading pseudomonad initially seemed to confirm this prediction (Kilbane et al. 1983). Using viable plate count procedures, the introduced *Pseudomonas* species population rapidly decreased to undetectable numbers. However, weeks later after addition of 2,4,5-T the population of the genetically modified pseudomonad was again detectable, indicating that it had never totally died out. This and subsequent studies (Steffan and Atlas 1988) indicated that this pseudomonad could persist in soil for prolonged periods. Other studies have similarly shown the persistence of deliberately introduced microorganisms in soils and aquatic ecosystems, perhaps as viable nonculturable cells (Blackburn et al. 1994; Leung et al. 1995).

It was also thought that DNA released from dying organisms would be rapidly degraded by DNase in soils and aquatic habitats. Thus, even if introduced microorganisms persisted, their genes might not readily be transferred by transformation. However, studies have shown that DNA adsorbed to clay particles is resistant to DNase and can persist in soils and sediments and can be transferred by transformation (Gallori et al. 1994). Genes are also transferred by transduction in soils and waters (Levy and Miller 1989). Often the mechanism of gene transfer cannot be determined, as in the case of the appearance of a novel 3-chlorobenzoate-degrading bacterial species over a year after the introduction of a specific strain of *Pseudomonas* into an aquifer (Thiem et al. 1994; England et al. 1995; Zhou and Tiedje 1995). The new strain could be the result of gene exchange between the introduced *Pseudomonas* sp. strain B13 and an indigenous bacterium. This speculation is based on a restriction fragment length polymorphism (RFLP) pattern of ribosome genes that differs from that of *Pseudomonas* sp. strain B13, the fact that identically sized restriction fragments hybridized to the catabolic gene probe, and the absence of any enrichable 3-chlorobenzoate-degrading strains in the aquifer prior to inoculation. Thus, genetic transfer can potentially occur in soil and aquatic ecosystems over a prolonged period. This indicates that introducing genetically engineered microorganisms may alter the gene pool of the community and have an impact on its long-term diversity and stability.

A community that has a complex structure, rich in information as reflected by high species richness (number of different species), needs a lower amount of energy for maintaining such a structure. This lowered energy requirement is reflected in a lower primary production rate per unit biomass while a stable diversity level is maintained. The strong inverse relationship between diversity and productivity is especially pronounced when environmental changes favor rapid microbial growth and the development of complex microbial communities (Margalef 1979; Revelante and Gilmartin 1980).

Species diversity of a community is somewhat like the genetic diversity of a population in that it allows for varied responses within a dynamic ecosystem. If an environment is dominated by a strong unidirectional factor, less flexibility is needed to maintain stability. In such cases, it is adaptive for populations to become stenotolerant (highly specialized) and for communities to be dominated by a few populations (low species diversity). Microbial populations in a salt lake, for example, normally are more stenohaline than populations in an estuary; microbial communities in a hot spring are less diverse than in an unpolluted river.

Species diversity tends to be low in physically controlled ecosystems because adaptations to the prevailing physicochemical stress are of the highest priority and leave little room for the evolution of closely balanced and integrated species interactions. Acid bogs, hot springs, and Antarctic desert habitats are examples of physically controlled habitats where species diversity is relatively low. Species diversity tends to be higher in biologically controlled ecosystems, that is, where the importance of interpopulation interactions outweighs that of abiotic stress. In such biologically accommodated communities the physicochemical environment allows greater interspecies adaptation, resulting in species-rich associations. Microbial diversity in many habitats, such as soil, is normally high; in contrast, under conditions of stress or disturbance, such as in infected plant or animal tissues, diversity is markedly low.

Although stability is associated with high diversity in biologically accommodated microbial communities, there is no established cause-and-effect relationship between diversity and stability. It is clear that no one population is all-important in a community with high diversity, so that even if a population is eliminated the whole community structure will not be disrupted, but it is not clear what level of diversity is necessary to maintain community stability.

The fact that communities with high diversity are able to cope with environmental fluctuations within broad tolerance ranges does not imply that they are able to cope with severe and continued environmental disturbances. The diverse, stable community of activated sludge, for example, can tolerate the influx of low concentrations of many toxic chemicals, but high inputs of some toxic chemicals can cause the community to collapse. As a case in point, an input of hexachloropentadiene and octachloropentene to the municipal sewerage system in Louisville, Kentucky, devastated the microbial community of the treatment plant and caused the cessation of sewage treatment for this municipality for months.

Various investigations on the colonization of substrates by diatoms have examined the premise that the nature of the processes of substrate invasion and succession determines the composition of the community and the diversity of the stable community (Patrick 1963, 1967). The size of the area, the number of species in the pool capable of invading the substrate, and the invasion rate all influence species richness and overall diversity of the diatom community. A reduced invasion rate, with the size, area, and number of species in the species pool remaining the same, lowers the total number of species in the community. Those species that normally are low in numbers within diatom communities are particularly affected, and this decrease in species diversity is seen as lowered species richness. One of the main results of a high invasion rate is that species with relatively low numbers are maintained within the community; thus the presence of rare species is ensured. Such rare species increase diversity and may act to stabilize a community during variable environmental conditions. If environmental conditions change, they may be better adapted to survival than the common species, and species composition of the community, especially relative abundances, might shift. The size of the area available for invasion affects the composition of the community. As species invade the area, the rate of increase of species richness declines, but increasing numbers of species within the community need not alter the biomass of that community. Eventually the number of species reaches a level of stability.

During the early stages of community succession, the number of species tends to increase. Species diversity probably peaks during the early or middle stages of succession and may decline inordinately in the stable climax community. A major question in ecological theory concerns the optimal relationship between diversity and community stability.

Several investigators have used protozoa as experimental organisms to examine the influence of predator-prey interactions on community diversity and stability (Hairston et al. 1968; Luckinbill 1979). The stability of predatory protozoa *(Paramecium)* populations was increased by increasing diversity at the bacterium level, but three species of *Paramecium* were less stable than two-species communities; one pair of *Paramecium* species consistently had greater stability without the third species than with it, indicating that there were significant second-order effects with two species having an interaction that was detrimental to the third species (Hairston et al. 1968). Stability of a predatory protozoa population depends on the characteristics of the species serving as prey and not simply on the diversity of species present (Luckinbill 1979).

## Species Diversity Indices

Several mathematical indices that describe the species richness and apportionment of species within the community, called *species diversity indices,* are used to describe the assemblage of populations within a community (Pielou 1975) (Table 6.1). Species diversity indices have rarely been applied to microbial communities because of the technical difficulties in speciating the large numbers of microorganisms their use requires (Atlas 1984a). Microbial ecologists often use numerical taxonomy to determine the microbial species (taxonomic units) present in a sample (Kaneko et al. 1977; Holder-Franklin et al. 1981; Sørheim et al. 1989; Bascomb and Colwell 1992). In numerical tax-

onomy, a large number of characteristics—often phenotypic—are determined for organisms isolated from a sample, and cluster analyses are performed to establish the similarities of the organisms. Similar organisms are considered to belong to the same species.

Species diversity indices relate the number of species and the relative importance of individual species. The two major components of species diversity are species richness, or variety, and evenness, or equitability. Species richness can be expressed by simple ratios between total species and total numbers. It measures the number of species in the community but not how many individuals of a species are present. Equitability measures the proportion of individuals among the species; this indicates whether there are dominant populations. Assessing the diversity of a community by a single parameter is difficult and subject to various interpretations (Ghilarov 1996), often leading to the question, What does biodiversity mean? For the most part, diversity indices reflect the underlying complexity of community structure.

A widely used measure of diversity is the Shannon-Weaver index (Shannon and Weaver 1963), which is also known as the Shannon-Weiner index or simply the Shannon index. This general diversity index is sensitive to both species richness and relative species abundance. Caution must be used in interpreting the Shannon-Weaver index because it is sensitive to sample size, especially with small samples. Equitability, which is independent of sample size, can be calculated from the Shannon-Weaver index. Another approach, known as rarefaction, is to compare the observed number of species with those predicted by a computer model (Simberloff 1978). This approach has been applied to microbial communities (Mills and Wassel 1980). A problem with these approaches is the similarity level used for defining microbial species. To avoid this problem, Watve and Gangal (1996) suggest using the mean taxonomic distance between all pairs of isolates as a species-less index of bacterial community diversity. According to this measure a bacterial community with a few taxonomically distinct dominant species would have a large mean accompanied by a large variance, whereas a bacterial community with a large number of moderately dissimilar biotypes

**Table 6.1**
Examples of diversity indices

Species richness ($d$)

$$d = \frac{S-1}{\log N}$$   where $S$ = number of species

$N$ = number of individuals

Shannon-Weaver index of diversity ($H$)

$$\overline{H} = \frac{C}{N}\left(N \log N - \sum n_i \log n_i\right)$$

where $C = 2.3$

$N$ = number of individuals

$n_i$ = number of individuals in the $i^{th}$ species

Evenness ($e$)

$$e = \frac{\overline{H}}{\log S}$$   where $\overline{H}$ = Shannon-Weaver diversity index

$S$ = number of species

Equitability ($J$)

$$J = \frac{\overline{H}}{H_{max}}$$   where $\overline{H}$ = Shannon-Weaver diversity index

$H_{max}$ = theoretical maximal Shannon-Weaver diversity index for the population examined—assumes each species has only one member.

would have a large mean accompanied by a small variance.

Theoretically, diversity should increase during succession. This increase in diversity has been observed for the periphyton community of Lake Washington, in the state of Washington, using submerged grids and electron microscopic observations (Jordan and Staley 1976). Diversity, measured with the Shannon-Weaver index, increased during a 10-day period (Table 6.2). During this time, some pioneer populations disappeared, and the relative proportions of biomass shifted from heterotrophic bacteria to algae and cyanobacteria.

Diversity generally is lower in communities under stress (Atlas 1984b; Atlas et al. 1991). For example,

**Table 6.2**
Successional changes in microbial community on submerged grids

| Time (days) | Diversity ($H'$) | Biomass (bacteria/algae) |
|---|---|---|
| 1 | 3.1 | 6.07 |
| 3 | 4.2 | 0.23 |
| 6 | 4.4 | 0.31 |
| 10 | 4.8 | — |

Source: Jordan and Staley 1976.

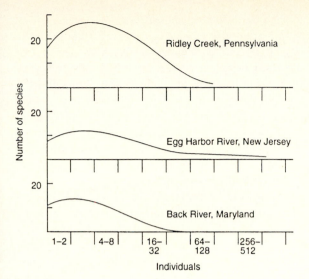

**Figure 6.10**
Effects of pollution on diversity of aquatic diatom popula-
tions. Magnitude of pollution: Ridley Creek < Egg Harbor ≤
Back River. Decreases in diversity are due to pollution
stress. (Source: Patrick 1963. Reprinted by permission of
New York Academy of Sciences.)

**Table 6.3**
Effect of exposure to oil on diversity of bacterial
populations in Arctic seawater

| Time* | Diversity $(H)^{†}$ | Equitability $(J)$ |
|---|---|---|
| 0 | 3.5 | 0.76 |
| 2 | 3.6 | 0.78 |
| 4 | 2.4 | 0.52 |
| 6 | 2.1 | 0.46 |

*Weeks of *in situ* exposure to Prudhoe Bay crude oil.

†Controls not exposed to oil had $\overline{H}$ values (Shannon-Weaver indices)
of 3.4–3.7 and $J$ values of 0.74–0.80 throughout this period.

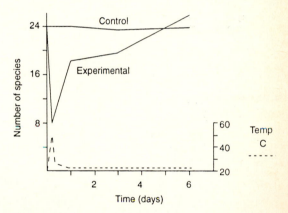

**Figure 6.11**
Effect of thermal shock on species diversity of a protozoan
community. This experiment shows the rapid decrease in
diversity that occurs following thermal shock and subsequent recovery. (Source: Cairns 1969. Reprinted by permission of J. Cairns, Jr.)

diversity calculated with the Shannon-Weaver index is
lower in surface-water bacterial communities in the
Arctic Ocean than in temperate oceans where low
temperatures and ice do not cause the same degree of
physical stress (Kaneko et al. 1977; Atlas 1984a,
1984b). Disturbances, such as the introduction of pollutants into aquatic ecosystems, have been found to
reduce diversity in diatom communities (Patrick
1963) (Figure 6.10) and in bacterial communities
(Sayler et al. 1982, 1983; Atlas 1984a, 1984b; Atlas et
al. 1991; Mills and Mallory 1987; Bej et al. 1991)
(Table 6.3). A rapid decrease in the diversity of protozoan communities was observed after a temporary
thermal shock, followed by a return to diversity levels
of control communities (Cairns 1969) (Figure 6.11).
Diversity of microbial communities is a sensitive
index of pollution. Theoretically, stressed communities with low diversities are less well adapted to deal
with further environmental fluctuations and stress
than biologically accommodated communities with
higher diversities.

## Genetic/Molecular Diversity Indices

The genetic diversity of a microbial community can
be assessed by measuring the heterogeneity of the
DNA from the entire microbial community. To do this,
DNA first must be extracted from the total microbial
community in a sample collected from a given habitat.
The recovered DNA represents the total gene pool of
the community. DNA can be recovered from environmental samples by collecting the microbial cells—

usually by centrifugation—and then lysing the cells, or by directly lysing the cells in the sample and then extracting the DNA (Torsvik 1980; Ogram et al. 1988; Fuhrman et al. 1988; Steffan et al. 1988; Somerville et al. 1989). It is important that impurities be removed from the DNA. Using polyvinylpyrrolidone during the extraction procedure helps remove humic materials that interfere with measurement of the heterogeneity of the DNA. The DNA is further purified using hydroxyapatite column chromatography and/or cesium chloride buoyant density centrifugation. The DNA is then sheared and heated to separate the double-stranded DNA into relatively short single strands. The temperature is lowered, and the rate of reannealing of the DNA to re-form double-stranded DNA is determined by measuring the absorbance at 260 nm.

The rate of DNA reannealing is a measure of DNA heterogeneity (Wetmur and Davidson 1968; Britten et al. 1974) (Figure 6.12). The greater the similarity of DNA fragments (low genetic diversity), the more rapid the rate of DNA reannealing. The greater the heterogeneity of the DNA (high genetic diversity), the slower the rate of DNA reannealing. The initial concentration of DNA multiplied by the time that it takes

for half the DNA to reanneal, a value represented by $C_0t_{1/2}$, is a useful parameter for expressing the diversity of DNA in the population. Dividing the $C_0t_{1/2}$ of the DNA extracted from a microbial community by the mean $C_0t_{1/2}$ value of genomes of bacteria gives the number of totally different bacterial populations in the community. $C_0t$ plots for DNA isolated from bacterial populations take into account both the amount of information and its distribution in the populations.

Torsvik et al. (1990a) compared the phenotypic and genetic diversities of bacterial populations isolated from a soil community. The phenotypic diversity as determined by the Shannon-Weaver index, equitability, rarefaction, and cumulative differences was high but indicated some dominant biotypes. Genetic diversity was measured by reassociation of mixtures of denatured DNA isolated from the bacterial strains ($C_0t$ plots). The observed genetic diversity was high. Reassociation of DNA from all bacterial strains together revealed that the population contained heterologous DNA equivalent to 20 totally different bacterial genomes, that is, genomes without homology. This study showed that reassociation of DNA isolated from a collection of bacteria gave a good estimate of the diversity of the collection and that there was good agreement among different phenotypic diversity measures and in particular the Shannon-Weaver diversity index. $C_0t$ plots, like the Shannon-Weaver index, measure both the number of different populations (different genomes) and the relative proportions of those populations.

Torsvik et al. (1990b) also examined the heterogeneity of DNA extracted directly from soil. They found that a major part of DNA isolated from the bacterial fraction of soil is very heterogeneous. The $C_0t_{1/2}$ of the DNA recovered from the total soil microbial community was approximately 4600, which is equivalent to 4000 completely different genomes of standard soil bacteria. Thus, the soil microbial community appeared to have 4000 different populations based on genetic diversity measurements. These results indicate that the soil microbial community is composed of a large number of genetically distinct bacterial populations. The genetic diversity found was about 200 times higher than measured for isolated strains, indicating

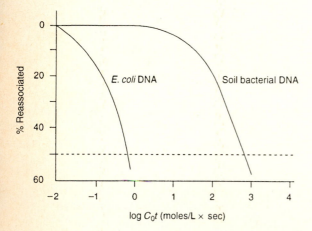

**Figure 6.12**
Reassociation of soil bacterial DNA ($C_0t$ plot). The reassociation of *Escherichia coli* DNA is included for comparison. The abscissa gives the log initial concentration of single-stranded DNA (in mole-nucleotides per liter) multiplied by time in seconds. The ordinate gives the percent of reassociated DNA. (Source: Torsvik et al. 1990a)

that the phenotypically defined populations isolated by standard plating techniques make up only a small fraction of the soil bacterial community. Most of the diversity is located in that part of the microbial community that cannot be isolated and cultured by standard techniques. Nonculturable *K*-selected populations may comprise a large number of different, highly specialized bacterial populations. These results appear to be consistent with a theory that the majority of bacterial populations isolated and grown on agar plates are the *r*-selected bacterial populations that have high growth rates and grow at high nutrient concentrations.

A novel molecular strategy for studying microbiological diversity is based on the restriction digestion of a population of 16S rDNA sequences directly amplified from an environmental sample (Martinez-Murcia et al. 1995). Separate primers are used to amplify bacterial and archaeal ribosomal RNA genes using the polymerase chain reaction (PCR). Digested fragments separated by polyacrylamide electrophoresis generate characteristic profile data for estimation of diversity and overall similarities between the organisms of different environments. The greater the number of restriction bands the greater the diversity. This technique for molecular characterization of the bacterial and archaeal populations appears to be promising as a rapid method for microbial biodiversity fingerprinting, useful to compare several environments and detect major shifts in species composition of the microbial community. Martinez-Murcia et al. (1995) applied this methodology to a set of five ponds in a multi-pond solar saltern covering the salinity gradient from about 6.4% to 30.8%. Bacterial diversity estimated from the complexity of the banding pattern obtained by restriction of the amplicons from the different ponds decreased with increasing salinity, whereas archaeal diversity showed the reverse pattern. Thus, bacterial diversity decreases at higher salinities whereas archaeal diversity increases in habitats with higher salinities.

Muyzer et al. (1993) described a different molecular approach for analyzing the genetic diversity of complex microbial populations. This technique uses denaturing gradient gel electrophoresis (DGGE) to separate PCR-amplified gene fragments, of genes coding for 16S rRNA. This approach may contribute to our understanding of the genetic diversity of uncharacterized microbial populations.

Another approach for assessing diversity at the community level involves analysis of fatty acid methyl ester profiles (FAME analysis). These profiles indicate the presence of specific microbial populations. FAME analyses are used to identify microorganisms isolated from the environment. Ka et al. (1994) used FAME analysis to examine the diversity of populations of 2,4-dichlorophenoxyacetic acid (2,4-D)–degrading bacteria from agricultural plots. The researchers also assessed diversity based on chromosomal patterns obtained by PCR amplification of repetitive extragenic palindromic (REP) sequences, and based on hybridization patterns obtained with probes for the *tfd* genes of plasmid pJP4 and a probe (Spa probe) that detects the specific 2,4-D-degrading species *Sphingomonas paucimobilis* (formerly *Pseudomonas paucmobilis*). A total of 57% of the isolates were identified to the species level by the FAME analysis, and these isolates were strains of *Sphingomonas, Pseudomonas,* or *Alcaligenes* species. Hybridization analysis revealed four groups. Group I strains, which exhibited sequence homology with *tfdA, tfdB, tfdC,* and *tfdD* genes, were rather diverse, as determined by both the FAME analysis and the REP-PCR analysis. Group II, which exhibited homology only with the *tfdA* gene, was a small group and was probably a subset of group I. All group I and II strains had plasmids. Hybridization analysis revealed that the *tfd* genes were located on plasmids in 75% of these strains and on the chromosome or a large plasmid in the other 25% of the strains. One strain exhibited *tfdA* and *tfdB* hybridization associated with a plasmid band, and *tfdC* and *tfdD* hybridized with the chromosomal band area. The group III strains exhibited no detectable homology to *tfd* genes but hybridized to the Spa probe. The members of this group were tightly clustered as determined by both the FAME analysis and the REP-PCR analysis, were distinctly different from group I strains as determined by the FAME analysis, and had very few plasmids; this group contained more of the 47 isolates than any other group. The group III strains were identified as *S. paucimobilis.* The group IV strains, which hybridized to neither the *tfd* gene probe nor the Spa probe, were as diverse as the group I strains as determined by the FAME and REP-PCR analyses; most of the group IV strains could not be identified by the FAME analysis. Strains belonging to groups I and III were more frequently recovered from soils that had greater field exposure to 2,4-D, suggesting they were the better competitors. Members of group I appear to contain mobile catabolic plasmids that have spread among many different organisms. Many of the genes transferred via plasmids have been incorporated into the chromosomes of members of group I and II. The reshuffling of genes and environmental transfer among various species has led to a high degree of diversity among 2,4-D degraders around the world.

## Ecosystems

The community and its abiotic surroundings compose the ecosystem, which is a self-sustaining ecological unit; energy flows through and materials are cycled within the ecosystem by various populations of the community (Odum 1983). The complexity of ecosystems requires that some degree of simplification and some theoretical considerations be applied in order to understand the underlying forces and principles that govern the functioning of ecosystems (Pielou 1969, 1977; Walters 1971; Levin 1974; Smith 1974; May 1976; Hall and Day 1977a, 1977b). The natural environmental fluctuations that occur within ecosystems make this difficult without examining subsystem components and the interrelationships of the subsystems.

### Experimental Ecosystem Models

Experimental models greatly simplify the interactions between microbial populations and between the microbial community and the environment, but each experimental model must be questioned as to how well it mimics the real ecosystem; that is, can the data gathered from the experimental model be extrapolated to the real world? Within experimental models, it is possible to define environmental conditions and biological populations. Models used in laboratory experiments are called *microecosystems* or *microcosms;*

these multicomponent models are needed to understand the interactive relationship of microbial communities and the roles played by microbial populations within ecosystems (Figure 6.13). Microcosms are useful in examining microbial ecological processes (Armstrong 1992; Cripe and Pritchard 1992; Fredrickson et al. 1992; Hagedorn 1992; Hood 1992). When all biological populations are defined or known, the system is said to be axenic or gnotobiotic. The simplest gnotobiotic system is a single pure microbial strain aseptically inoculated into a sterile medium. More complex gnotobiotic systems involve multiple defined microbial populations and sometimes defined plant and/or animal populations.

**Batch Systems** In batch system models, the biological components and a supporting nutritive medium are added to a closed system. Batch systems are self-sustaining when there is a suitable input of radiant energy and when photoautotrophic organisms are present within the enclosed microcosm (Byers 1963, 1964; Pritchard and Bourquin 1984). In such self-sustaining systems, nutrients are recycled within the microecosystem; there is an input of light energy and a loss of heat. In experimental batch systems where there is insufficient input of light energy and/or a lack of photoautotrophs within the microcosm, the system will run downhill and the biological community eventually will be eliminated. Extrapolation of data from heterotrophic batch systems to real ecosystems is often difficult because excess nutrient concentrations are normally added to such systems to permit the continued growth of the enclosed microorganisms for a suitable period of time before the energy is dissipated and the biological community disappears. Batch systems, however, are suitable for modeling ecosystems that receive high inputs of allochthonous organic matter; for example, batch model systems can be used to study the fate of leaf litter in forest soils because the addition of leaves to soils within natural forest habitats occurs within a limited time frame during the fall.

**Flow-Through Systems** Flow-through systems have been developed and used in ecological studies as model systems for aquatic habitats where nutrient concentra-

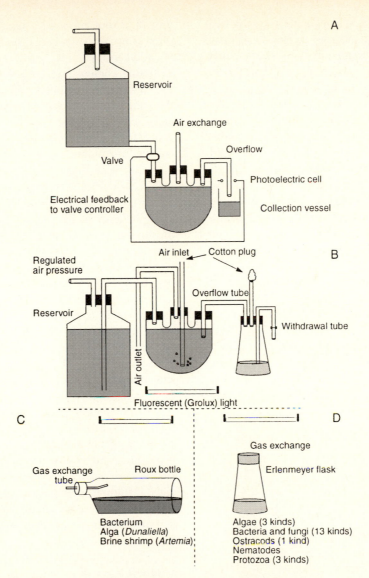

**Figure 6.13**
Examples of flow-through and batch systems: (A) turbidostat, (B) chemostat, and (C and D) batch microcosms. (Sources: Carpenter 1968; Nixon 1969; and Byers 1963. Modified and reprinted with permission of American Society of Limnology and Oceanography.)

tions are often growth-rate limiting. The most commonly used flow-through system for ecological studies is the chemostat (Monod 1950; Jannasch 1965; Tempest 1970; Veldkamp and Kuenen 1973; Jannasch and Mateles 1974; Veldkamp 1977; Veldkamp et al. 1984).

A chemostat permits the continuous flow of growth medium through a chamber containing microbial populations. The growth medium contains some required nutrient in limiting concentrations that determines the specific growth rates of the microbial populations.

The chemostat is a self-regulating system that reaches a steady-state condition. At the steady-state condition, the specific growth rate is equal to the dilution rate, which is the rate of input of the growth medium divided by the volume of the culture chamber. If the growth rate is initially greater or less than the dilution rate, the concentration of microorganisms will change until steady-state conditions are achieved (Monod 1950; Jannasch 1969; Veldkamp 1977; Veldkamp et al. 1984) (Figure 6.14). At steady-state conditions the concentration of biomass and the concentration of growth-limiting substrate within the culture vessel are determined by the concentration of the substrate in the incoming growth medium and by a growth yield coefficient, biomass formed divided by substrate used.

The chemostat is well suited for use as a model system for studies of the interactions of microbial populations in some aquatic habitats. Like all model systems, chemostats have some limitations. Microorganisms that do not actively reproduce will be washed out of chemostats, whereas in nature continuous growth is not required—microorganisms in nature often grow periodically and survive without reproducing at other times.

Using chemostats, it has been demonstrated that the success of microbial populations competing for the same substrate depends on substrate concentration and maximal specific growth rate; at a low substrate concentration one population may outcompete another, whereas at a higher substrate concentration the results of competition may be just the opposite (Veldkamp 1970, 1977; Harder et al. 1977; Kuenen and Harder 1982; Dykhuizen and Hartl 1983; Veldkamp et al. 1984) (Figure 6.15). Phrased another way, some microorganisms are able to sustain higher specific growth rates at lower substrate concentrations than others. Such studies explain why particular microbial populations are more successful than others in ecosystems at particular times. These competition studies have revealed that the diversity within the microbial community can be explained, in part, in terms of selection by substrate concentration (Veldkamp 1977; Veldkamp et al. 1984). Within a constant environment and complete niche overlap, only one population generally will survive within a chemostat; other unsuccessful competitor populations will be washed out. Multiple populations, however, can exist within a chemostat if the environmental conditions are varied in a cyclical manner so that alternate microbial populations periodically have the higher specific growth rates. Multiple populations can also exist within chemostats when the populations are not limited by the same substrate or if they interact positively in utilization of the substrate.

**Microcosms**    More complex interactions can be examined using microcosms that include a variety of microbial, plant, and animal populations and also permit inclusion of multiple habitats and interfaces within one model system—for example, sediment, water, sediment-water interface, and plant and animal surfaces (Byers 1963, 1964; Nixon 1969; Bourquin et al. 1977; Nixon and Kremer 1977; Pritchard and Bourquin 1984; Armstrong 1992; Cripe and Pritchard 1992; Fredrickson et al. 1992; Hagedorn 1992; Hood 1992) (Figure 6.16). Flow-through microcosms per-

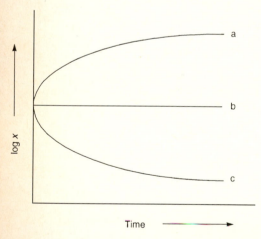

**Figure 6.14**
Relationship between growth rate (μ) and dilution rate (D) in a chemostat showing change of bacterial concentration following inoculation. (a) Initially μ > D; x (biomass) increases and s (concentration of growth-limiting substrate) decreases until μ = D. (b) Steady state is obtained immediately.
(c) Initially μ < D; x decreases and s increases until μ = D.
(Source: Veldkamp 1977, based on Jannasch 1969. Reprinted by permission, copyright Plenum Press.)

**A**

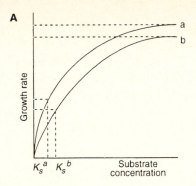

**B**

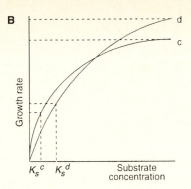

**Figure 6.15**

Growth rate ($\mu$) at different substrate concentrations ($S$) for different organisms (a and b in part A and c and d in part B). As shown, the $\mu$-$S$ relationships for the organisms are in (A) $K_s{}^a < K_s{}^b$ and $\mu_{max}{}^a > \mu_{max}{}^b$ and (B) $K_s{}^c < K_s{}^d$ and $\mu_{max}{}^c < \mu_{max}{}^d$. Bacterium a always grows faster than bacterium b. Bacterium c, however, grows faster than bacterium d only at low substrate concentrations; at higher substrate concentrations bacterium d grows faster than bacterium c because of its higher $\mu_{max}$. (Source: Veldkamp 1970. Reprinted by permission, copyright Academic Press.)

mit studies on the interactions of microbial populations within complex communities and on the flow of energy and materials through the system.

Germfree animals and plants have provided suitable experimental models for investigating their interactions with microorganisms (Phillips and Smith 1959; Hsu and Bartha 1979). Using gnotobiotic systems, that is, systems in which the higher organism as well as all microbial populations are defined, it has been possible to examine the role of microorganisms in nutrition and general health of the animal population. Germfree animals generally have elongated and thinner-walled intestinal tracts as compared to normal controls and may show requirements for additional vitamins normally supplied by the intestinal bacterial community.

Germfree animals provide a direct means of investigating metabolic relationships between known mixtures of microorganisms in their natural habitat, such as the mouth, skin, or intestine. With the use of germfree animals, it has been possible to demonstrate the involvement of particular microbial populations in disease conditions, for example, the involvement of *Lactobacillus* species in the production of dental caries. It has also been possible to demonstrate the necessity of mutually beneficial relationships between

microbial populations for the development of certain diseases in animals.

## Mathematical Models

Examination of experimental model microecosystems and natural ecosystems makes possible the development of conceptual or hypothetical understanding of the functioning of the system that can be expressed by mathematical relationships (Patten 1971; Walters 1971; Williams 1973; May 1976; Pielou 1977; Shoemaker 1977; Christian et al. 1986; Robinson 1986; Wanner 1986). It is possible to express the interrelationships between microbial populations and between microorganisms and their surroundings using various mathematical expressions normally employing linear and/or differential equations. The use of differential equations of the form $dN/dt = f(x)$ permits the expression of a change in parameter $N$, such as microbial biomass, with time, according to some specified relationship $f(x)$, where $f(x)$ may represent various functions of one or more variables. Where ecological relationships follow general laws, such as the preservation of matter and the thermodynamic laws concerning entropy, such relationships can be defined.

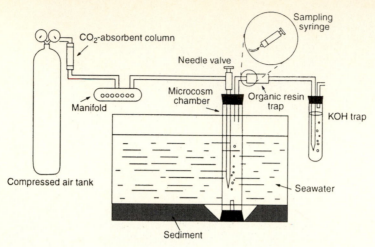

**Figure 6.16**

Microcosm for determining effects and fate of toxicants in a salt marsh. The apparatus contains core chambers implanted into the salt-marsh sediment; $CO_2$ is collected from the exit tube by trapping in KOH; volatile organics are trapped on a resin in the exit tube. (Source: Bourquin et al. 1977. Reprinted by permission; copyright Society of Industrial Microbiology.)

Mathematical models may be based on ecological theory or may be developed to simulate particular ecosystems or subsystems. Some models are developed to describe a particular system, others to predict dynamic change. Theoretical models do not attempt to mimic the details of real ecosystems, but rather to model fundamental or general ecological principles. Simulation models, on the other hand, attempt to accurately reflect the systems being modeled and predict detailed changes within them.

Whenever one constructs a mathematical model, some information about the system must be eliminated to allow increased understanding of the overall system (Hall and Day 1977a). There is an attempt to eliminate "noise," that is, random fluctuations in background data. Just as we do not process all perceptual information available to our brains at all times, models must filter the available data. What can be eliminated depends on the purpose of the model. In some ways, models are analogous to semipermeable membranes; some items are excluded, others retained. Sometimes the wrong information is screened out and eliminated; this is a risk in model building. Like

students studying for an exam, researchers sometimes overlook important information, but other times they glean the right material. Arbitrariness in filtering out information can lead to the development of alternative and conflicting models. The true test is how well the model predicts the actual system, that is, the verification of the model.

A flow diagram illustrating the activities involved in developing a mathematical model is shown in Figure 6.17. This diagram emphasizes the role of feedback in the model-building process. Feedback tends to stabilize both natural and model systems; the outputs from one process influence inputs to that process at a later time.

Within the model there will be state or condition indices, which are measures of particular conditions within the ecosystem, such as bacterial biomass, temperature, and nutrient concentrations. These condition or state indices are interrelated, and hence it is necessary to develop a conceptual model of the component parts and interrelationships between these parts before developing the mathematical model. Because of complex interrelationships between biological populations

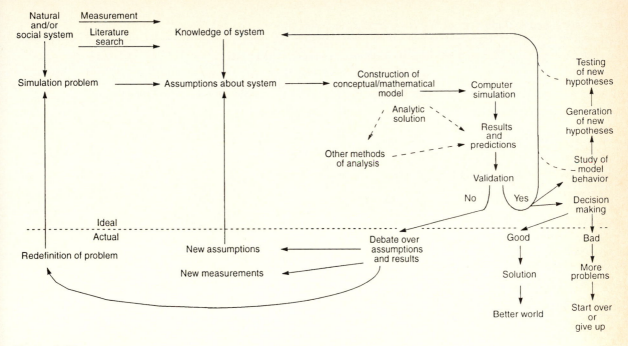

**Figure 6.17**
A diagram illustrating the process of building a mathematical model. (Source: Hall and Day
1977a. Reprinted by permission, copyright John Wiley and Sons.)

and abiotic components of an ecosystem, the development of such a conceptual model is quite difficult. Conceptual models are often constructed in a systems diagram as a first step, after which specific mathematical formulas can be used to express quantitative interrelationships between its components. The components of the model and their relationships are often illustrated by compartmentalized boxes and flow arrows, which represent the flow of energy or materials from one compartment to another.

Mathematical relationships are particularly useful in describing the growth of populations and the interactions between populations (Whittaker 1975). Table 6.4 shows a series of theoretical mathematical relationships describing growth and interactions of microbial populations. Other equations can be used to describe changes in concentrations of nutrients within an ecosystem, rates of enzymatic activities, succession of populations within a community, and so on. These equations can be used to produce graphs of theoretical

or expected results, often called *simulations* (Shoemaker 1977) (Figure 6.18). Sometimes, these equations accurately reflect observed growth interactions within experimental or real ecosystems. In other cases, additional sources of variance must be considered to mimic the real ecosystem. Testing the validity of a model involves determining how well the model explains experimental data. Often statistical tests are used to determine the accuracy of a mathematical model. The least-squares criterion is most often employed (Robinson 1986). A good model should yield the minimal sum of the squared errors for the experimental data about the curve generated by the mathematical model.

Mathematical equations that describe the interrelationships between system components can be used to develop larger models with complex interrelationships between populations (Nixon and Kremer 1977). We shall not consider the mathematics of such complex ecosystem models here, as these require an extensive

## Table 6.4
Mathematical expressions of population growth and interactions

If there are no restricting factors, the growth of a microbial population is described as

$$N_t = N_0 e^{rt}$$

where $N_0$ = initial population density, $r$ = intrinsic rate of growth, and $N_t$ = density after any time period $t$.

If the rate of growth is limited,

$$N_t = \frac{K}{1 + \left[ (K - N_0)/N_0 \right] e^{-rt}}$$

where $K$ = the carrying capacity or limiting density. $e$ = base of natural logarithms, 2.71828.

The growth rates of competing populations are

$$\frac{dN_1}{dt} = r_1 N_1 \frac{(K_1 - N_1 - \alpha_1 N_2)}{K_1} \qquad \frac{dN_2}{dt} = r_2 N_2 \frac{(K_1 - N_1 - \alpha_2 N_1)}{K_2}$$

where the two populations have rates of increase $r_1$ and $r_2$ and competition coefficients $\alpha_1$ and $\alpha_2$.

If $\alpha_1 < K_1/K_2$ and $\alpha_2 > K_2/K_1$, only population 1 survives. If $\alpha_1 > K_1/K_2$ and $\alpha_2 < K_2/K_1$, only population 2 survives.

If $\alpha_1 > K_1/K_2$ and $\alpha_2 > K_2/K_1$, one or the other population survives. If $\alpha_1 < K_1/K_2$ and $\alpha_2 < K_2/K_1$, both populations survive.

The growth of a prey population is

$$\frac{dN_1}{dt} = r_1 N_1 - P N_1 N_2$$

where the prey adds individuals according to its intrinsic rate of growth $(r_1)$ times its density $(N_1)$ and loses individuals at a rate proportional to encounters of predator and prey—prey density times predator density $(N_2)$. The predator adds individuals at a rate proportional to this same product of densities and loses individuals according to death rate $(d_2)$ times its own density:

$$\frac{dN_2}{dt} = a P N_1 N_2 - d_2 N_2$$

where $P$ = a coefficient of predation and a = a coefficient relating predator births to prey consumed. According to this description (Lotka-Volterra equations) there will be cyclic fluctuations of predator and prey populations.

If two populations have a mutually beneficial relationship

$$\frac{dN_1}{dt} = r_1 N_1 \left( \frac{K_1 - N_1 + b N_2}{K_1 + b N_2} \right) \qquad \frac{dN_2}{dt} = r_2 N_2 \left( \frac{K_2 - N_2 + a N_1}{K_2} \right)$$

where $b$ = a coefficient for support of individuals of population 1 by individuals of population 2. a = a coefficient for the effect of population 1 on population 2. If population 1 becomes totally dependent on population 2, $K_1$ approaches zero and the carrying capacity for population 1 is defined by population 2 and the coefficient of support, $b$. Assuming a limit on the benefit per host individual from the interaction with the symbiont, in the form $C = D/(D + N_2)$, a stable mutualism is expressed by

$$\frac{dN_1}{dt} = r_1 N_1 \left( \frac{b N_2 - N}{b N_2} \right) \qquad \frac{dN_2}{dt} = r_2 N_2 \left( \frac{K_2 - N_2 + a N_1 C}{K_2} \right)$$

Source: Whittaker 1975.

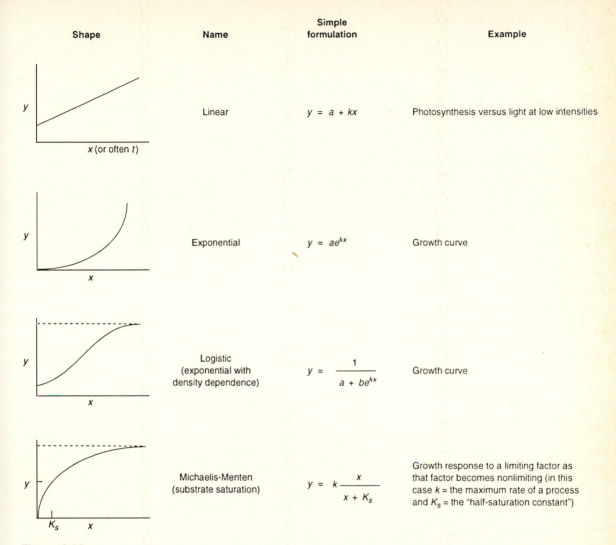

| Shape | Name | Simple formulation | Example |
|---|---|---|---|
| | Linear | $y = a + kx$ | Photosynthesis versus light at low intensities |
| | Exponential | $y = ae^{kx}$ | Growth curve |
| | Logistic (exponential with density dependence) | $y = \dfrac{1}{a + be^{kx}}$ | Growth curve |
| | Michaelis-Menten (substrate saturation) | $y = k\,\dfrac{x}{x + K_s}$ | Growth response to a limiting factor as that factor becomes nonlimiting (in this case $k$ = the maximum rate of a process and $K_s$ = the "half-saturation constant") |

**Figure 6.18**
Mathematical relationships commonly encountered in modeling. $a$, $b$, $k$, and $K_s$ are constants. (Source: Hall and Day 1977a. Reprinted by permission, copyright John Wiley and Sons.)

mathematical background. The suggested readings (Patten 1971; Shoemaker 1977) should be consulted for a detailed examination of the mathematical formulas and the supportive computer programs involved in the development of holistic mathematical ecosystems models. The microbial ecologist, though, should be aware that such mathematical approaches to modeling

exist and make possible the development of models that accurately simulate ecosystems. The development of mathematical models for whole ecosystems has highlighted the fact that microorganisms play important roles within ecosystems and that their functions in mediating the flow of energy and materials through and within ecosystems cannot be ignored.

## MICROBIAL COMMUNITIES IN NATURE

### Microbes Within Macro-communities

Naturalists, ecologists, and plant geographers characterize biological communities by their dominant macrophyte primary producers (Smith 1990). Thus, for example, they designate "tall grass prairie," "oak-hickory forest," and "*Spartina* salt marsh" communities. Obviously, these and similar macrophyte-dominated communities have their inconspicuous but essential microbial components that ensure the biodegradation of organics and the biogeochemical cycling of minerals (see Chapters 11 and 12). In addition, the microbial component of the community interacts with plant and animal life in other important ways (see Chapters 4 and 5). However, the role of microorganisms as primary producers in such environments ranges from negligible to minor (for example, cyanobacterial and algal production in the *Spartina* salt marsh). In the offshore regions of deeper freshwater lakes and of the oceans, which are free of macrophytes, all primary production is due to cyanobacteria and microalgae. It would be logically justified to refer to these as "microbial primary production" communities, but instead, they are designated by tradition as limnetic (freshwater) and pelagic (marine) communities. Of course, their role as primary producers, microorganisms also serve as biodegraders and mineral cyclers in these communities. As zooflagellates and other protozoa, they are amply represented among the first level of consumers. More than 70% of our globe is covered by pelagic and limnetic communities, and we should be aware that the dominant community members in these ecosystems are micro-organisms rather than the more visible fishes and invertebrates.

In terrestrial and shallow-water environments, macrophytes tend to outcompete microorganisms in capturing the radiant energy of the sun. Only when unusually harsh physical conditions restrict the growth of macrophytes can microorganisms dominate or even monopolize primary production. Lichens dominate bare rock face, some hot and cold desert areas, and some types of tundra as primary producers.

Lichens may form thick foliose-fruticose mats amounting to as much as a metric ton of biomass per hectare. Under less favorable conditions, they may adhere as a thin crust to rocks. Under the most hostile conditions, lichens survive endolithically, under the surface of the rocks. In some shallow aquatic environments, the dominance of the microbial community is ensured by anoxic conditions, extremes of temperature, or salinity that excludes macrophytes. Examples of aquatic environments that are unfavorable for growth of primary producers are the anoxic hypolimnions of temporarily or permanently stratified lakes where photosynthesis is primarily controlled by green and purple sulfur and nonsulfur bacteria, alkaline soda lakes with blooms of *Spirulina* and related cyanobacteria, and hypersaline solar salt pans dominated by *Halobacterium* species.

Fossil stromatolites indicate that for more than 2 billion years the predominant communities on our planet were procaryotic microbial mats (see Chapter 2). The development of eucaryotes and multicellular invertebrates brought about the decline of these microbial mats, which appear to be highly vulnerable to invertebrate grazing, but the descendants of the early bacteria continue to exist as cyanobacterial crusts in certain desert environments and as microbial mats in hypersaline bays and evaporation flats (Campbell 1979; Cohen et al. 1984).

### Structure and Function of Some Microbial Communities

Some microbial communities are fairly self-contained with microbe-microbe interactions dominating over the interactions of microbes with plants and animals. Whereas many macro-communities have been studied in great detail and depth, methodological difficulties have until recently prevented similar studies on natural microbial communities. This fact shifted much emphasis to experimental and mathematical models of microbial communities. Although it is still difficult to perform the detailed qualitative and quantitative species inventories used in the characterization of macro-communities on natural microbial communities, it is becoming increasingly clear that diverse microbial communities have their own characteristic and unique composition, dominant species, and population dynamics. On the surface, one may perceive this statement to contradict Martinus Beijerinck's "everything is everywhere" principle (see Chapter 1). In fact, efficient dispersal mechanisms and resistant dormant structures at times result in isolation of microorganisms from uncharacteristic environments (for example, thermophiles from permafrost soils). However, these are not active community members but rather surviving allochthonous species. The active and abundant microbial populations of the community are selected by their habitat and by population interactions within the community. Margulis et al. (1986a, 1986b) have described and pictorially illustrated some examples of such unique microbial communities.

The procaryotic microbial mat shown in Figure 6.19 has been observed on hypersaline "evaporite flats" of tropical seashores. The dominant primary

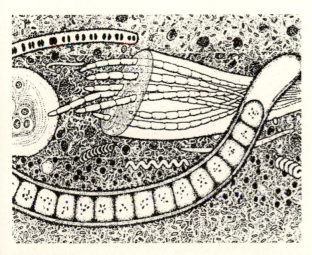

**Figure 6.19**
Drawing of a procaryotic microbial mat from a marine evaporite flat. The mat is dominated by *Microcoleus chthonoplastes* trichromes in a common mucopolysaccharide sheath. Some of these are shown in cross section. A large *Oscillatoria* trichrome has gliding motility, as do the *Microcoleus* trichromes. Other coccoid and filamentous cyano-bacteria, heterotrophs, and sulfate reducers add to the complexity of this microbial mat community. (Source: Margulis et al. 1986a; reprinted by permission of Elsevier.)

producers of the mat are cyanobacteria, particularly the insulated cable-like filaments of *Microcoleus chthonoplastes. Nostoc, Anabaena, Oscillatoria,* and *Spirulina* are also abundant. Below the oxygenic phototrophic cyanobacteria, a layer of purple anoxygenic phototrophic bacteria was observed, and below these a black layer of diverse sulfate reducers. The latter convert photosynthetically produced organic material with seawater sulfate to $H_2S$. Purple sulfur bacteria in turn use the $H_2S$. The cyanobacterial filaments with their extracellular mucopolysaccharide sheaths, in addition to photosynthetic activity, give overall cohesion to the mat and protect it both from disintegration and from drying out during low-tide cycles.

"Desert crusts" (Campbell 1979) are cyanobacterial mats, dominated again by *M. chthonoplastes* and by *M. vaginatus.* Both of these secrete a common mucopolysaccharide sheath for several trichomes. In dry weather, the sheath material forms a brittle film over the desert sand. It protects the cyanobacterial mat and, at the same time, stabilizes the sand. In moist weather, the trichomes slide out of the hydrated sheath, spread, and secrete new sheath material. Associated with the mats are additional cyanobacteria, including *Calothrix, Scytonema, Phormidium, Schizothrix, Gloeocapsa,* and *Nostoc.* Most of these are filamentous and display gliding motility; some have the ability to fix molecular nitrogen. Desert crusts have been described on undisturbed deserts of the southwestern United States. They fulfill an important role in stabilizing desert sand and pave the way for succession by lichens and mosses, but they are fragile and easily destroyed by grazing and trampling. The early Precambrian colonization of dry land was most likely due to similar cyanobacterial crusts.

Lake Cisó in northeastern Spain is fed by underground seepage that passes through gypsum ($CaSO_4 \cdot 2H_2O$) formations and is rich in sulfate. The lake is relatively small, of moderate depth, and protected from wind. These conditions promote stratification. Food webs within Lake Cisó demonstrate the existence of competition based on niche overlap and resource limitation as exemplified by the purple sulfur bacteria (Pedrós-Alió and Guerrero 1993). Niche overlap occurs among the guild of purple sulfur bacteria (Chromatiaceae) because they all use light as the source of energy, sulfide as the source of electrons, and $CO_2$ as the carbon source. These bacteria alter their metabolic activities diurnally and seasonally based on the availability of light and sulfide, which are resources that limit growth of these phototrophic bacteria in Lake Cisó (Figure 6.20). The biomass of purple bacteria increases with light intensity in the spring and decreases in the fall. Competition leads to a favored species composition and the tendency for coexisting species to be as different as possible among themselves. Similar competition for available niches and available resources occurs among other populations and guilds.

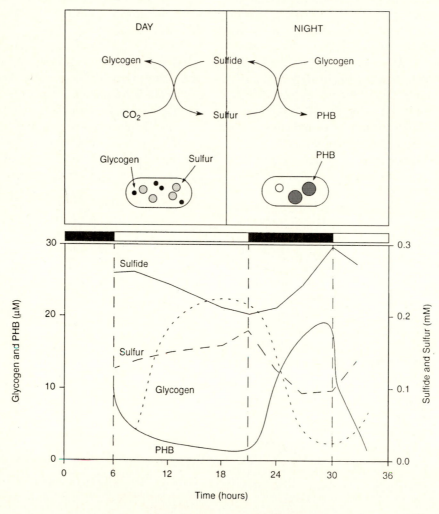

**Figure 6.20**

Changes in the physiology of purple phototrophic bacterial guild through a day-night cycle. The lower panel shows changes in concentrations of sulfide, sulfur, glycogen, and PHB. The upper panel shows the different metabolisms carried out by the bacteria in this guild during the day and night and a schematic drawing of their appearance under the electron microscope. (Source: Pedrós-Alió and Guerrero 1993)

Organic matter from photosynthesis is decomposed at the anaerobic lake bottom predominantly by sulfate reducers such as *Desulfovibrio*. The resulting $H_2S$ rises to the illuminated portion of the water column and is utilized by anaerobic phototrophic purple and green sulfur bacteria, *Chromatium* and *Chlorobium,* respectively. *Chromatium* is less sensitive to oxygen and more sensitive to high $H_2S$ concentrations than *Chlorobium* and stratifies close to the lake surface (Figure 6.21). The green *Chlorobium* layer stratifies underneath, aided also by the fact that it can absorb light of a wavelength that is not efficiently utilized by *Chromatium*. Shifting light and temperature conditions in combination with predation on *Chromatium* by *Vampirococcus* and *Daptobacter* induce bloom and die-off cycles of *Chromatium*. These cycles result in dramatic color changes of the lake from purple to green and back. Eucaryotes (protozoa and algae) in Lake Cisó are normally restricted to the upper few centimeters of oxygenated water. Occasionally, strong winds extend this oxygenated layer,

**Figure 6.21**
Drawing of the *Chromatium* layer of Lake Cisó's anoxic phototrophic community. The large flagellated *Chromatium* cells form a layer close to the surface and above the *Chlorobium* layer, giving the lake water a purple color. (Source: Margulis et al. 1986b; Reprinted by permission of American Institute of Biological Sciences.)

causing algal blooms and additional color changes. Somewhat similar stratification phenomena may develop in eutrophic lakes and fjords during summer if light penetrates into the anoxic portion of the water column below the thermocline.

Some additional characteristic and interesting microbial communities are described in other chapters of this text, including the anaerobic cellulose-digesting microbial communities of the rumen and the termite hindgut (see Chapter 5) and the chemoautotrophic microbial community of deep-sea hydrothermal vents (see Chapters 9 and 11). Attempts to describe the composition and functioning of complex natural microbial communities are relatively recent with much research remaining to be performed.

## CHAPTER SUMMARY

In the ecological organizational hierarchy, numerous interacting microbial populations normally form part of the integrated communities of organisms that occur at specific habitats. Within communities (assemblages of microbial populations occurring and interacting at a given location called a habitat) there are specific functional roles called niches. Autochthonous members of communities occupy the niches of the ecosystem. Allochthonous microorganisms that attempt to invade an ecosystem generally are eliminated because they are not best adapted to fill the niches of the community. Microbial populations within a community compete for available resources. Competition is especially intense among members of the same guild (populations within the community that use the same resources). In some cases microorganisms are eliminated from a community by competitive exclusion, but a number of factors can permit coexistence. Current ecological theories emphasize disturbances and environmental heterogeneity as important factors in permitting coexistence of competitive populations within the same habitat.

Microorganisms have evolved strategies that enable them to successfully survive and maintain themselves within communities. One system for classifying these strategies employs an *r-K* gradient in which organisms are adapted to rapid reproduction (*r* strategists) or the carrying capacity of the environment (*K* strategists). Most microorganisms are viewed as *r* strategists because of their far more rapid reproduction rates compared to higher organisms. However, within microbial communities some microbial populations clearly are better adapted to environmental limitations. Such *K* strategists reproduce more slowly than *r* strategists and tend to be successful in resource-limited situations.

Development of a stable community usually involves a succession of populations, that is, an orderly sequential change in the populations of the community. Community succession begins with colonization or invasion of a habitat by microbial populations. Successional processes occur, sometimes in characteristic patterns. In biofilms, for example, succession involves attachment and colonization of a surface by invading bacteria followed by growth of the initial populations, production of extracellular polysaccharides that form a matrix allowing expansion of the biofilm community, and eventual invasion by eucaryotic microorganisms such as diatoms and ciliate protozoa. In theory, the succession of a community results in a highly evolved and stable climax community. In reality, disturbances often disrupt the orderly development of microbial communities. After a disturbance, homeostasis acts to restore the disrupted community; that is, once the disrupting factor is removed succession tends back to the original community. Homeostasis also acts to restore the initial community when allochthonous microorganisms enter the habitat.

Several patterns characterize the orderly succession of communities. Autotrophic succession occurs in cases where the ratio of photosynthesis (*P*) to respiration (*R*) (*P/R* ratio) is initially greater than 1. Biomass accumulates during the autotrophic succession. Succession toward a stable community involves a shift of the *P/R* ratio toward 1. If the *P/R* ratio is less than 1, biomass disappears from the community. A P/R ratio of less than 1 characterizes heterotrophic succession, such as occurs on detrital particles.

Stability of a community is influenced by the totality of the genes within the individual populations.

Genes can be transferred to new populations within the community to form new allelic combinations with differing degrees of fitness. Plasmids are especially important in the rapid transfer among populations in a microbial community. Genes can be transferred in the environment at relatively high rates, and genetic exchange and recombination can act as a major force for the change and evolution of natural populations.

Communities are usually characterized by a high state of diversity. The diversity of the community is related to the stability of the community. There appears to be an optimal diversity reflecting the available niches of the community. The diversity of the microbial community can be described using diversity indices, including some based on molecular analyses that reveal the genetic heterogeneity of the community. Species diversity tends to be low in physically controlled ecosystems; it tends to be higher in biologically accommodated ecosystems.

The community and its abiotic surroundings compose the ecosystem, which is a self-sustaining ecological unit. Energy flows through an ecosystem and materials are cycled within the ecosystem by various populations of the community. Batch, flow-through, laboratory, and *in situ* model systems permit the microbial ecologist to manipulate both abiotic and biotic parameters in a carefully controlled manner that allows for an understanding of how the components of the ecosystem interact. Substrate concentrations, temperatures, light intensities, and other parameters can be manipulated to mimic particular habitats. In many such model systems, macroorganisms are excluded, permitting examination of the interrelationships between microbial populations. Control of environmental fluctuations greatly simplifies the system, allowing unequivocal interpretation of the results. In some cases, results from these model systems have revealed new bases for interrelationships between microbial populations.

Perhaps the real value of both experimental and mathematical models is that they provide a tool for developing an understanding of ecosystem function and of the factors that control the flow of energy and matter through an ecosystem, thereby allowing for the development of a predictive capability. Both experimental and mathematical models permit the microbial ecologist to test hypotheses concerning the function of microorganisms within the ecosystem and the interactions between diverse microbial populations. The predictive capability developed in such models is especially useful in the proper management of ecosystems. Systems analysis and mathematical models have been applied in the management of waste disposal and control of pathogens. By understanding the function of the overall system, it is possible to predict the consequences of a perturbation to any part of the system. Within the near future, mathematical modeling is likely to have an increased role in microbial ecology, just as it has now in general ecology.

## STUDY QUESTIONS

1. What is a guild? Why should intense competition occur within a guild?

2. What is a niche? How does a niche differ from a habitat?

3. What is a microbial community? How does a community differ from a population?

4. Compare and contrast *r* and *K* microbial strategists.

5. What is preemptive colonization?

6. Describe the succession of a microbial biofilm community.

7. What is a climax community? Do microbial communities ever reach a climax stage?

8. Compare and contrast autotrophic and heterotrophic succession.

9. What is homeostasis? How does homeostasis relate to community stability?

10. How is microbial diversity measured? How does this differ from measurements of the biodiversity of macroorganisms?

11. What is the relationship between ecological diversity and ecosystem stability?

12. How is diversity maintained in microbial communities?

13. What is an ecosystem? What roles do microorganisms play in ecosystems? How can experiments be performed to investigate the functions of microorganisms within ecosystems?

14. Describe some specific examples of communities that are dominated by microorganisms.

## REFERENCES AND SUGGESTED READINGS

Andrews, J. H. 1984. Relevance of *r*- and *K*-theory to the ecology of plant pathogens. In M. J. Klug and C. A. Reddy (eds.). *Current Perspectives in Microbial Ecology.* American Society for Microbiology, Washington, DC, pp. 1–7.

Andrews, J. H. 1991. *Comparative Ecology of Microorganisms and Macroorganisms.* Springer-Verlag, New York.

Andrews, J. H., and R. F. Hall. 1986. *r*- and *K* selection and microbial ecology. *Advances in Microbial Ecology* 9:99–147.

Armstrong, J. L. 1992. Persistence of recombinant bacteria in microcosms. In M. A. Levin, R. J. Seidler, and M. Rogul (eds.). *Microbial Ecology: Principles, Methods, and Applications.* McGraw-Hill, New York, pp. 495–509.

Atlas, R. M. 1984a. Diversity of microbial communities. *Advances in Microbial Ecology* 7:1–47.

Atlas, R. M. 1984b. Use of microbial diversity measurements to assess environmental stress. In M. J. Klug and C. A. Reddy (eds.). *Current Perspectives in Microbial*

*Ecology.* American Society for Microbiology, Washington, DC, pp. 540–545.

Atlas, R. M., A. Horowitz, M. I. Krichevsky, and A. K. Bej. 1991. Response of microbial populations to environmental disturbance. *Microbial Ecology* 22:249–256.

Baier, R. E. 1985. Adhesion in the biologic environment. *Biomaterials, Medical Devices, and Artificial Organs* 12:133–159.

Baross, J. A., J. W. Deming, and R. G. Becker. 1984. Evidence for microbial growth in high-pressure, high temperature environments. In M. J. Klug and C. A. Reddy (eds.). *Current Perspectives in Microbial Ecology.* American Society for Microbiology, Washington, DC, pp. 186–195.

Bascomb, S., and R. R. Colwell. 1992. Application of numerical taxonomy in microbial ecology. In M. A. Levin, R. J. Seidler, and M. Rogul (eds.). *Microbial Ecology: Principles, Methods, and Applications.* McGraw-Hill, New York, pp. 113–137.

Bej, A. K., M. Perlin, and R. M. Atlas. 1991. Effect of introducing genetically engineered microorganisms on soil microbial community diversity. *FEMS Microbiology Ecology* 86:169–176.

Beringer, J. E., and P. R. Hirsch. 1984. The role of plasmids in microbial ecology. In M. J. Klug and C. A. Reddy (eds.). *Current Perspectives in Microbial Ecology.* American Society for Microbiology, Washington, DC, pp. 63–70.

Blackburn, N. T., A. G. Seech, and J. T. Trevors. 1994. Survival and transport of *lac-lux* marked *Pseudomonas fluorescens* strains in uncontaminated and chemically contaminated soils. *Systematic and Applied Microbiology* 17: 574–580.

Bourquin, A. W., M. A. Hood, and R. L. Garnas. 1977. An artificial microbial ecosystem for determining fate and effects of toxicants in a salt marsh environment. *Developments in Industrial Microbiology* 18:185–191.

Bowen, J. D., K. D. Stolzenbach, and S. W. Chrisholm. 1993. Simulating bacterial clustering around phytoplankton cells in a turbulent ocean. *Limnology and Oceanography* 38:36–51.

Britten, R. J., D. E. Graham, and S. R. Neufeld. 1974. Analysis of repeating DNA sequences by reassociation. *Methods in Enzymology* 29:363–418.

Brown, M.R.W., and P. Gilbert. 1993. Sensitivity of biofilms to antimicrobial agents. In L. B. Quesnel,

P. Gilbert, and P. S. Handley (eds.). *Microbial Cell Envelopes: Interactions and Biofilms.* Blackwell, Oxford, England, pp. 87S–97S.

Bunnell, F. 1973. Decomposition: Models and the real world. *Bulletin of the Ecological Research Commission* (Stockholm) 17:407–415.

Byers, R. J. 1963. The metabolism of twelve aquatic laboratory microecosystems. *Ecological Monographs* 33:281–306.

Byers, R. J. 1964. The microcosm approach to ecosystem biology. *American Biology Teacher* 26:491–498.

Byrd, J. J., L. R. Zeph, and L. E. Casida, Jr. 1985. Bacterial control of *Agromyces ramosus* in soil. *Canadian Journal of Microbiology* 31:157–1163.

Cairns, J. C. 1969. Factors affecting the number of species in fresh water protozoan communities. In J. C. Cairns (ed.). *The Structure and Function of Freshwater Microbial Communities.* Virginia Polytechnic Institute and State University, Blacksburg, VA, pp. 219–248.

Caldwell, D. E. 1993. The microstat: Steady-state microenvironments for subculture of steady-state consortia, communities, and microecosystems. In R. Guerrero and C. Pedrós-Alío (eds.). *Trends in Microbial Ecology.* Spanish Society for Microbiology, Barcelona, Spain, pp. 123–128.

Cameron, R. E., R. C. Honour, and F. A. Morelli. 1976. Antarctic microbiology: Preparation for Mars life detection, quarantine and back contamination. In M. R. Heinrich (ed.). *Extreme Environments: Mechanisms of Microbial Adaptation.* Academic Press, New York, pp. 57–82.

Campbell, S. E. 1979. Soil stabilization by a procaryotic desert crust: Implications for Precambrian land biota. *Origins of Life* 9:335–348.

Carpenter, E. J. 1968. A simple, inexpensive algal chemostat. *Limnology and Oceanography* 13:720–721.

Casida, L. E., Jr. 1992. Competitive ability and survival in soil of *Pseudomonas* strain 679-2, a dominant, nonobligate bacterial predator of bacteria. *Applied and Environmental Microbiology* 58:32–37.

Chapman, V. J., and D. J. Chapman. 1973. *The Algae.* Macmillan, London.

Characklis, W. G., G.A . McFeters, and K. C. Marshall. 1990. Physiological ecology in biofilm systems. In W. G. Characklis and K. C. Marshall (eds.). *Biofilms.* Wiley, New York, pp. 341–393.

Christian, R. R., R. Wetzel, S. M. Harlan, and D. W. Stanley. 1986. Growth and decomposition in aquatic microbial systems: Approaches in simple models. In F. Megusar and M. Gantar (eds.). *Perspectives in Microbial Ecology.* Slovene Society for Microbiology, Ljubljana, Yugoslavia, pp. 38–45.

Clarke, P. H. 1984. Evolution of new phenotypes. In M. J. Klug and C. A. Reddy (eds.). *Current Perspectives in Microbial Ecology.* American Society for Microbiology, Washington, DC, pp. 71–78.

Clesceic, L. S., R. A. Park, and J. A. Bloomfield. 1977. General model of microbial growth and decomposition in aquatic ecosystems. *Applied and Environmental Microbiology* 33:1047–1058.

Cleveland, L. R., and A. V. Grimstone. 1964. The fine structure of the flagellate *Mixotricha paradoxa* and its associated micro-organisms. *Proceedings of the Royal Society* (London) Series B 159:668–686.

Cohen, Y., R. W. Castenholz, and H. Halvorson (eds.). 1984. *Microbial Mats: Stromatolites.* Alan R. Liss, New York.

Cohen, Y., and E. Rosenberg. 1989. *Microbial Mats. Physiological Ecology of Benthic Microbial Communities.* American Society for Microbiology, Washington, DC.

Cripe, C. R., and P. H. Pritchard. 1992. Site-specific aquatic microcosms as test systems for fate and effects of microorganisms. In M. A. Levin, R. J. Seidler, and M. Rogul (eds.). *Microbial Ecology: Principles, Methods, and Applications.* McGraw-Hill, New York, pp. 467–493.

Dale, M. B. 1970. Systems analysis and ecology. *Ecology* 51:2–16.

Darnell, J. E., and W. F. Doolittle. 1986. Speculations on the early course of evolution. *Proceedings of the National Academy of Science USA* 83:1271–1275.

Decho, A. W. 1990. Microbial exopolymer secretions in ocean environments: Their role(s) in food webs and marine processes. *Oceanography and Marine Biology Annual Review* 28:73–153.

DeFlaun, M. F., and S. B. Levy. 1989. Genes and their varied hosts. In S. B. Levy and R. V. Miller (eds.). *Gene Transfer in the Environment.* McGraw-Hill, New York, pp. 1–32.

Dempsey, M. J. 1981. Marine bacterial fouling: A scanning electron microscope study. *Marine Biology* 61:305–315.

Dickerson, R. 1978. Chemical evolution and the origin of life. *Scientific American* 239(3):70–86.

Drahos, D. J., and G. F. Barry. 1992. Assessment of genetic stability. In M. A. Levin, R. J. Seidler, and M. Rogul (eds.). *Microbial Ecology: Principles, Methods, and Applications.* McGraw-Hill, New York, pp. 161–181.

Dykhuizen, D. E., and D. L. Hartl. 1983. Selection in chemostats. *Microbiological Reviews* 47:150–168.

England, L. S., H. Lee, and J. T. Trevors. 1995. Recombinant and wild-type *Pseudomonas aureofaciens* strains introduced into soil microcosms: Effect on decomposition of cellulose and straw. *Molecular Ecology* 4:221–230.

Fenchel, T. M., and B.B. Jørgensen. 1977. Detritus food chains of aquatic ecosystems: The role of bacteria. *Advances in Microbial Ecology* 1:1–58.

Fletcher, M. 1984. Comparative physiology of attached and free-living bacteria. In K. C. Marshall (ed.). *Microbial Adhesion and Aggregation.* Springer-Verlag, New York, pp. 223–232.

Fredrickson, A. G., and G. Stephanopoulos. 1981. Microbial competition. *Science* 213:972–979.

Fredrickson, J. K., H. Bolton, Jr., and G. Stotzky. 1992. Methods for evaluating the effects of microorganisms on biogeochemical cycling. In M. A. Levin, R. J. Seidler, and M. Rogul (eds.). *Microbial Ecology: Principles, Methods, and Applications.* McGraw-Hill, New York, pp. 579–606.

Freter, R. 1984. Factors affecting conjugal transfer in natural bacterial communities. In M. J. Klug and C. A. Reddy (eds.). *Current Perspectives in Microbial Ecology.* American Society for Microbiology, Washington, DC, pp. 105–114.

Friedmann, E. I., and R. O. Friedmann. 1984. Endolithic microorganisms in extreme dry environments: Analysis of a lithobiotic microbial habitat. In M. J. Klug and C. A. Reddy (eds.). *Current Perspectives in Microbial Ecology.* American Society for Microbiology, Washington, DC, pp. 177–185.

Fry, J. C., and M. J. Day. 1990. *Bacterial Genetics in Natural Environments.* Chapman and Hall, London.

Fuhrman, J. A., D. E. Comeau, A. Hagstrom, and A. M. Chan. 1988. Extraction from natural planktonic microorganisms of DNA suitable for molecular biological studies. *Applied and Environmental Microbiology* 54:1426–1429.

Gallori, E., M. Bazzicalupo, L. Dal-Canto, R. Fani, P. Nannipieri, C. Vettori, and G. Stotzky. 1994. Transformation of *Bacillus subtilis* by DNA bound on clay in non-sterile soil. *FEMS Microbiology Ecology* 15:119–126.

Ghilarov, A. 1996. What does biodiversity mean—scientific problem or convenient myth? *Trends in Ecology and Evolution* 11:304–306.

Golley, F. B. (ed.). 1977. *Ecological Succession.* Benchmark Papers in Ecology 15. Dowden Hutchinson and Ross, Stroudsburg, PA.

Goodman, M. R. 1974. *Study Notes in System Dynamics.* Wright Allen Press, Cambridge, MA.

Hagedorn, C. 1992. Experimental methods for terrestrial ecosystems. In M. A. Levin, R. J. Seidler, and M. Rogul (eds.). *Microbial Ecology: Principles, Methods, and Applications.* McGraw-Hill, New York, pp. 525–541.

Hairston, N. G., A. D. Allen, R. R. Colwell, D. J. Fustuyma, J. Howell, M. D. Lubin, J. Mahias, and J. H. Vandermeer. 1968. The relationship between species diversity and stability: An experimental approach with protozoa and bacteria. *Ecology* 49:1091–1101.

Hall, B. G. 1984. Adaptation by acquisition of novel enzyme activities in the laboratory. In M. J. Klug and C. A. Reddy (eds.). *Current Perspectives in Microbial Ecology.* American Society for Microbiology, Washington, DC, pp. 79–86.

Hall, C.A.S., and J. W. Day, Jr. (eds.). 1977a. *Ecosystem Modeling in Theory and Practice: An Introduction with Case Histories.* Wiley, New York.

Hall, C.A.S., and J. W. Day, Jr. 1977b. Systems and models: Terms and basic principles. In C.A.S. Hall and J. W. Day (eds.). *Ecosystem Modeling in Theory and Practice.* Wiley, New York, pp. 5–36.

Hall, C.A.S., J. W. Day, Jr., and H. T. Odum. 1977. A circuit language for energy and matter. In C.A.S. Hall and J. W. Day (eds.). *Ecosystem Modeling in Theory and Practice.* Wiley, New York, pp. 37–48.

Halvorson, H. O., D. Pramer, and M. Rogul. 1985. *Engineered Organisms in the Environment: Scientific Issues.* American Society of Microbiology, Washington, DC.

Hamilton, W. A. 1987. Biofilms: Microbial interactions and metabolic activities. In M. Fletcher, T.R.G. Gray, and J. G. Jones (eds.). *Ecology of Microbial Communities.* Cambridge University Press, Cambridge, England, pp. 361–385.

Harder, W., J. G. Kuenen, and A. Martin. 1977. Microbial selection in continuous cultures: A review. *Journal of Applied Bacteriology* 43:1–24.

Heinrich, M. R. (ed.). 1976. *Extreme Environments: Mechanisms of Microbial Adaptation.* Academic Press, New York.

Holder-Franklin, M. A., A. Thorpe, and C. J. Cormier. 1981. Comparison of numerical taxonomy and DNA–DNA hybridization in diurnal studies of river bacteria. *Canadian Journal of Microbiology* 27:1165–1184.

Hood, M. A. 1992. Experimental methods for the study of fate and transport of microorganisms in aquatic systems. In M. A. Levin, R. J. Seidler, and M. Rogul (eds.). *Microbial Ecology: Principles, Methods, and Applications.* McGraw-Hill, New York, pp. 511–523.

Horner, R., and V. Alexander. 1972. Algal populations in Arctic sea ice: An investigation of heterotrophy. *Limnology and Oceanography* 17:454–458.

Horowitz, N. H. 1965. The evolution of biochemical synthesis—Retrospect and prospect. In V. Bryson and H. J. Vogel (eds.). *Evolving Genes and Proteins.* Academic Press, New York, pp. 15–23.

Hsu, T. S., and R. Bartha. 1979. Accelerated mineralization of two-organophosphate insecticides in the rhizosphere. *Applied and Environmental Microbiology* 37:36–41.

Hulbert, E. M. 1963. The diversity of phytoplanktonic populations in oceanic, coastal, and estuarine regions. *Journal of Marine Research* 21:81–93.

Hungate, R. E. 1975. The rumen microbial ecosystem. *Annual Reviews in Microbiology* 29:39–66.

Hurlbert, S. H. 1971. The nonconcept of species diversity: A critique and alternative parameters. *Ecology* 52:577–586.

Hurst, C. J. (ed.). 1991. *Modeling the Environmental Fate of Microorganisms.* American Society for Microbiology Press, Washington, DC.

Hutchinson, G. E. 1961. The paradox of the plankton. *American Naturalist* 95:137–145.

Jannasch, H. W. 1965. Use of the chemostat in ecology. *Laboratory Practice* 14:1162–1167.

Jannasch, H. W. 1969. Estimations of bacterial growth rates in natural waters. *Journal of Bacteriology* 99:156–160.

Jannasch, H. W., and R. I. Mateles. 1974. Experimental bacterial ecology studied in continuous culture. *Advanced Microbial Physiology* 11:165–212.

Jannasch, H. W., and D. C. Nelson. 1984. Recent progress in the microbiology of the hydrothermal vents. In M. J. Klug and C. A. Reddy (eds.). *Current Perspectives in Microbial Ecology*. American Society for Microbiology, Washington, DC, pp. 170–176.

Johnson, C. F., and E. A. Curl. 1972. *Methods for Research on the Ecology of Soil-borne Plant Pathogens*. Burgess, Minneapolis, MN.

Jordan, T. L., and J. T. Staley. 1976. Electron microscopic study of succession in the periphyton community of Lake Washington. *Microbial Ecology* 2:241–276.

Jost, J. L., J. F. Drake, A. G. Frederickson, and H. M. Tsuchiya. 1973. Interactions of *Tetrahymena pyriformis, Escherichia coli, Azotobacter vinelandii*, and glucose in a mineral medium. *Journal of Bacteriology* 113:834–840.

Ka, J. O., W. E. Holben, and J. M. Tiedje. 1994. Genetic and phenotypic diversity of 2,4-dichlorophenoxyacetic acid (2,4-D)-degrading bacteria isolated from 2,4-D-treated field soils. *Applied and Environmental Microbiology* 60:1106–1115.

Kaneko, T., R. M. Atlas, and M. Krichevsky. 1977. Diversity of bacterial populations in the Beaufort Sea. *Nature* 270:596–599.

Kaneko, T., and R. R. Colwell. 1975. Incidence of *Vibrio parahaemolyticus* in Chesapeake Bay. *Applied Microbiology* 30:251–257.

Kaneko, T., M. I. Krichevsky, and R. M. Atlas. 1979. Numerical taxonomy of bacteria from the Beaufort Sea. *Journal of General Microbiology* 110:111–125.

Kemp, W. M., and W. J. Mitsch. 1979. Turbulence and phytoplankton diversity: A general model of the paradox of the plankton. *Ecological Modeling* 7:201–222.

Kendrick, W. B., and A. Burges. 1962. Biological aspects of the decay of *Pinus sylvestris* leaf litter. *Nova Hedwiga* 4:313–344.

Khanna, M., and G. Stotzky. 1992. Transformation of *Bacillus subtilis* by DNA bound on montmorillonite and effect of DNase on the transforming ability of bound DNA. *Applied and Environmental Microbiology* 58:1930–1939.

Kilbane, J. J., D. K. Chatterjee, and A. M. Chakrabarty. 1983. Detoxification of 2,4,5-trichlorophenoxyacetic acid from contaminated soil by *Pseudomonas cepacia*. *Applied and Environmental Microbiology* 45:1697–1700.

Kjelleberg, S., B. A. Humphrey, and K. C. Marshall. 1982. The effect of interfaces on small, starved marine bacteria. *Applied and Environmental Microbiology* 43:1166–1172.

Kuenen, J. G., and W. Harder. 1982. Microbial competition in continuous culture. In R. G. Burns and J. H. Slater (eds.). *Experimental Microbial Ecology*. Blackwell, Oxford, England, pp. 342–367.

Lawrence, J. R., D. R. Korber, G. M. Wolfaardt, and D. E. Caldwell. 1995. Behavioral strategies of surface-colonizing bacteria. *Advances in Microbial Ecology* 14:1–75.

Lenski, R. E. 1992. Relative fitness: Its estimation and its significance for environmental applications of microorganisms. In M. A. Levin, R. J. Seidler, and M. Rogul (eds.). *Microbial Ecology: Principles, Methods, and Applications*. McGraw-Hill, New York, pp. 183–198.

Leung, K., J. T. Trevors, and H. Lee. 1995. Survival of and *lacZ* expression in recombinant *Pseudomonas* strains introduced into river water microcosms. *Canadian Journal of Microbiology* 41:461–469.

Levin, S. A. (ed.). 1974. *Ecosystem Analysis and Prediction*. Proceedings of a Conference on Ecosystems, Alta, Utah, July 1974. Sponsored by SIAMS Institute for Mathematics and Society, and supported by National Science Foundation.

Levy, S. B., and R. V. Miller (eds.). 1989. *Gene Transfer in the Environment*. McGraw-Hill, New York.

Lewin, R. 1983. Santa Rosalia was a goat. *Science* 221:636–639.

Lorenz, M. G., and W. Wackernagel. 1994. Bacterial gene transfer by natural genetic transformation in the environment, *Microbiological Reviews* 58:563–602.

Luckinbill, L. S. 1979. Regulation, stability, and diversity in a model experimental microcosm. *Ecology* 60:1098–1102.

MacArthur, R. H. and E. O. Wilson. 1967. *The Theory of Island Biogeography*. Princeton University Press, Princeton, NJ.

Margalef, R. 1967. *Perspectives in Ecological Theory*. University of Chicago Press, Chicago.

Margalef, R. 1979. Diversity. In A. Sournia (ed.). *Monographs on Oceanographic Methodology*. UNESCO, Paris, pp. 251–260.

Margulis, L., L. L. Baluja, S. M. Awramik, and D. Sagan. 1986a. Community living long before man. *The Science of the Total Environment* 56:379–397.

Margulis, L., D. Chase, and R. Guerrero. 1986b. Microbial communities. *BioScience* 36:160–170.

Marples, M. J. 1965. *The Ecology of the Human Skin.* C. C. Thomas, Springfield, IL.

Marples, R. P. 1974. Effect of germicides on skin flora. In F. A. Skinner and J. G. Carr (eds.). *The Normal Microbial Flora of Man.* Academic Press, London, pp. 35–46.

Marshall, K. C. 1989. Growth of bacteria on surface-bound substrates: Significance on biofilm development. In T. Hattori, Y. Ishida, Y. Maruyama, R. Y. Morita, and A. Uchida (eds.). *Recent Advances in Microbial Ecology.* Japan Scientific Society Press, Tokyo, pp. 146–150.

Marshall, K. C. 1993. Microbial ecology: Whither goest thou? In R. Guerrero and C. Pedrós-Alío (eds.). *Trends in Microbial Ecology.* Spanish Society for Microbiology, Barcelona, Spain, pp. 5–8.

Marshall, K. C., R. Stout, and R. Mitchell. 1971. Mechanisms of the initial events in the sorption of marine bacteria to solid surfaces. *Journal of General Microbiology* 68:337–348.

Marszalek, D. S., S. M. Gerchakov, and L. R. Udey. 1979. Influence of substrate composition on marine microfouling. *Applied and Environmental Microbiology* 38:987–995.

Martin, J. E., A. Lester, E. V. Price, and J. D. Schmale. 1970. Comparative study of gonococcal susceptibility to penicillin in the United States, 1955–1969. *Journal of Infectious Disease* 122:159–161.

Martinez-Murcia, A. J., S. G. Acinas, and F. Rodriguez-Valeria. 1995. Evaluation of prokaryotic diversity by restrictase digestion of 16S rDNA directly amplified from hypersaline environments. *FEMS Microbiology Ecology* 17:247–255.

May, R. M. 1976. *Theoretical Ecology: Principles and Applications.* Saunders, Philadelphia.

Miller, R. V. 1992. Overview: Methods for the evaluation of genetic transport and stability in the environment. In M. A. Levin, R. J. Seidler, and M. Rogul (eds.). *Microbial Ecology: Principles, Methods, and Applications.* McGraw-Hill, New York, pp. 141–159.

Mills, A. L., and L. M. Mallory. 1987. The community structure of sessile heterotrophic bacteria stressed by acid mine drainage. *Microbial Ecology* 14:219–232.

Mills, A. L., and R. A. Wassel. 1980. Aspects of diversity measurement for microbial communities. *Applied and Environmental Microbiology* 40:578–586.

Monod, J. 1950. La technique du culture continue: Theorie et applications. *Annals of the Institute Pasteur* (Paris) 79:390–410.

Morvan, B., F. Bonnemoy, G. Fonty, and P. Gouet. 1996. Quantitative determination of $H_2$-utilizing acetogenic and sulfate-reducing bacteria and methanogenic archaea from digestive tract of different mammals. *Current Microbiology* 32:129–133.

Munson, R. J. 1970. Turbidostats. In J. R. Norris and D. W. Ribbons (eds.). *Methods in Microbiology,* Vol. 2. Academic Press, New York, pp. 349–376.

Muyzer, G., E. C. DeWaal, and A. G. Vitterlinden. 1993. Profiling of complex microbial populations by denaturing gel electrophoresis analysis of polymerase chain reaction-amplified genes encoding for 16S rRNA. *Applied and Environmental Microbiology* 59:695–700.

Nixon, S. W. 1969. A synthetic microcosm. *Limnology and Oceanography* 14:142–145.

Nixon, S. W., and J. N. Kremer. 1977. Narragansett Bay: The development of a composite simulation model for a New England estuary. In C.A.S. Hall and J. W. Day (eds.). *Ecosystem Modeling in Theory and Practice.* Wiley, New York, pp. 621–673.

Noble, W. C., and D. G. Pitcher. 1978. Microbial ecology of the human skin. *Advances in Microbial Ecology* 2:245–290.

Odum, E. P. 1983. *Basic Ecology.* Saunders, Philadelphia, PA, pp. 13–17.

Odum, H. T. 1960. Ecological potential and analogue circuits for the ecosystem. *American Scientist* 48:1–8.

Odum, H. T. 1971. *Environment, Power and Society.* Wiley, New York.

Odum, H. T., S. W. Nixon, and L. H. Disalvo. 1970. Adaptation for photoregenerative cycling. In J. Cairns, Jr. (ed.). *The Structure and Function of Freshwater Microbial Communities.* Research Division Monograph #3. Virginia Polytechnic Institute and State University, Blacksburg, VA, pp. 1–29.

Odum, H. T., and E. Odum. 1978. *Energy Basis of Man and Nature.* McGraw-Hill, New York.

Ogram, A., G. S. Sayler, and T. Barkay. 1988. DNA extraction and purification from sediments. *Journal of Microbiological Methods* 7:57–66.

Overton, W. S. 1977. A strategy of model construction. In C.A.S. Hall and J. W. Day (eds.). *Ecosystem Modeling in Theory and Practice.* Wiley, New York, pp. 49–74.

Pace, N. R., D. A. Stahl, D. J. Lane, and G. J. Olsen. 1985. Analyzing natural microbial populations by rRNA sequences. *ASM News* 51:4–12.

Paerl, H. W. 1980. Attachment of microorganism to living and detrital surfaces in freshwater systems. In G. Bitton and K. C. Marshall (eds.). *Adsorption of Microorganisms to Surfaces.* Wiley, New York, pp. 375–402.

Patrick, R. 1963. The structure of diatom communities under varying ecological conditions. *Annals of the New York Academy of Science* 108:359–365.

Patrick, R. 1967. The effect of invasion rate, species pool, and size of area on the structure of the diatom community. *Proceedings of the National Academy of Sciences USA* 58:1335–1342.

Patrick, R. 1976. The formation and maintenance of benthic diatom communities. *Proceedings of the National Academy of Sciences USA* 120:475–484.

Patten, B. C. 1961. Competitive exclusion. *Science* 134:1599–1601.

Patten, B. C. (ed.). 1971. *Systems Analysis and Simulation in Ecology.* Vols. 1–3. Academic Press, New York.

Pedrós-Alió, C., and R. Guerrero. 1993. Microbial ecology of Lake Cisó. *Advances in Microbial Ecology* 13:155–210.

Phillips, A. W., and J. E. Smith. 1959. Germ-free animal techniques and their applications. *Advances in Applied Microbiology* 1:141–174.

Pielou, E. C. 1969. *An Introduction to Mathematical Ecology.* Wiley, New York.

Pielou, E. C. 1975. *Ecological Diversity.* Wiley, New York.

Pielou, E. C. 1977. *Mathematical Ecology.* Wiley, New York.

Pritchard, O. H., and A. W. Bourquin. 1984. The use of microcosms for evaluation of interactions between pollutants and microorganisms. *Advances in Microbial Ecology* 7:133–215.

Revelante, N., and M. Gilmartin. 1980. Microplankton diversity indices as indicators of eutrophication in the northern Adriatic Sea. *Hydrobiolgia* 70:277–286.

Rice, E. L., and S. K. Pancholy. 1972. Inhibition of nitrification by climax ecosystems. *American Journal of Botany* 59:1033–1040.

Rittle, K. H., C. E. Helmstetter, A. E. Meyer, and R. E. Baier. 1990. *Escherichia coli* retention on solid surfaces as function of substratum surface energy and cell growth phase. *Biofouling* 2:121–130.

Robinson, J. A. 1986. Approaches and limits to modeling microbiological processes. In F. Megusar and M. Gantar (eds.). *Perspectives in Microbial Ecology.* Slovene Society for Microbiology, Ljubljana, Yugoslavia, pp. 20–29.

Sandaa, R.-A., V. D. Torsvik, and J. Goksøyr. 1992. Transferable drug resistance in bacteria from fish-farm sediments. *Canadian Journal of Microbiology* 38:1061–1065.

Saunders, J. R., J. A. Morgan, C. Winstanley, F. C. Raitt, J. P. Carter, R. W. Pickup, J. G. Jones, and V. A. Sanders. 1990. Genetic approaches to the study of gene transfer in microbial communities. In J. C. Fry and M. J. Day (eds.). *Bacterial Genetics in Natural Environments.* Chapman and Hall, New York, pp. 3–21.

Savage, D. C. 1977. Microbial ecology of the gastrointestinal tract. *Annual Reviews of Microbiology* 31:107–134.

Saye, D. J., and S. B. O'Morchoe. 1992. Evaluating the potential for genetic exchange in natural freshwater environments. In M. A. Levin, R. J. Seidler, and M. Rogul (eds.). *Microbial Ecology: Principles, Methods, and Applications.* McGraw-Hill, New York, pp. 283–309.

Sayler, G. S., R. E. Perkins, T. W. Sherrill, B. K. Perkins, M. C. Reid, M. S. Shields, H. L. Kong, and J. W. Davis. 1983. Microcosm and experimental pond evaluation of microbial community response to synthetic oil contamination in freshwater sediments. *Applied and Environmental Microbiology* 46:211–219.

Sayler, G. S., T. W. Sherrill, R. E. Perkins, L. M. Mallory, M. O. Shiaris, and D. Petersen. 1982. Impact of coal-coking effluent on sediment microbial communities: A multivariate approach. *Applied and Environmental Microbiology* 44:1118–1129.

Schaedler, R. W., R. Dubos, and R. Costello. 1965. The development of the bacterial flora in the gastrointestinal tract of mice. *Journal of Experimental Medicine* 122:59–66.

Schieffer, G. E., and D. E. Caldwell. 1982. Synergistic interaction between *Anabaena* and *Zooglea* spp. in carbon dioxide limited continuous cultures. *Applied and Environmental Microbiology* 44:84–87.

Shannon, C. E., and W. Weaver. 1963. *The Mathematical Theory of Communication.* University of Illinois Press, Urbana, IL.

Shoemaker, C. 1977. Mathematical construction of ecological models. In C.A.S. Hall and J. W. Day (eds.). *Ecosystem Modeling in Theory and Practice.* Wiley, New York, pp. 75–114.

Simberloff, D. 1978. Use of rarefaction and related methods in ecology. In K. L. Dickson, J. Cairns, Jr., and R. J. Livingston (eds.). *Biological Data in Water Pollution Assessment: Quantitative and Statistical Analyses.* ASTM STP 652. American Society for Testing and Materials, Philadelphia, PA, pp. 150–165.

Skinner, F. A., and J. G. Carr (eds.). 1974. *The Normal Microbial Flora of Man.* Academic Press, London.

Slater, J. H. 1978. The role of microbial communities in the natural environment. In K.W.A. Chater and H. J. Somerville (eds.). *The Oil Industry and Microbial Ecosystems.* Heyden and Sons, London, pp. 137–154.

Slater, J. H. 1980. Physiological and genetic implications of mixed population and microbial community growth. In D. Schlessinger (ed.). *Microbiology—1980.* American Society for Microbiology, Washington, DC, pp. 314–316.

Slater, J. H. 1984. Genetic interactions in microbial communities. In M. J. Klug and C. A. Reddy (eds.). *Current Perspectives in Microbial Ecology.* American Society for Microbiology, Washington, DC, pp. 87–93.

Smith, J. M. 1974. *Models in Ecology.* Cambridge University Press, Cambridge, England.

Smith, L. 1990. *Ecology and Field Biology.* Ed 4. Harper & Row, New York.

Somerville, C. C., I. T. Knight, W. L. Straube, and R. R. Colwell. 1989. Simple, rapid method for direct isolation of nucleic acids from aquatic environments. *Applied and Environmental Microbiology* 55:548–554.

Sørheim, R., V. L. Torsvik, and J. Goksøyr. 1989. Phenotypic divergences between populations of soil bacteria isolated on different media. *Microbial Ecology* 17:181–192.

Stanley, P. M. 1983. Factors affecting the irreversible attachment of *Pseudomonas aeruginosa* to stainless steel. *Canadian Journal of Microbiology* 29:1493–1499.

Steffan, R. J., and R. M. Atlas. 1988. DNA amplification assay to enhance detection of genetically engineered bacteria in environmental samples. *Applied and Environmental Microbiology* 54:2185–2191.

Steffan, R. J., J. Goksøyr, A. K. Bej, and R. M. Atlas. 1988. Recovery of DNA from soil and sediments. *Applied and Environmental Microbiology* 54:2908–2915.

Stewart, F. M., and B. R. Levin. 1977. The population biology of bacterial plasmids: *A priori* conditions for the existence of conjugationally transmitted factors. *Genetics* 87:209–228.

Stewart, G. J. 1992. Natural transformation and its potential for gene transfer in the environment. In M. A. Levin, R. J. Seidler, and M. Rogul (eds.). *Microbial Ecology: Principles, Methods, and Applications.* McGraw-Hill, New York, pp. 253–282.

Stewart-Tull, D.E.S., and M. Sussman (eds.). 1992. *The Release of Genetically Modified Microorganisms–Regem 2.* Plenum Press, New York and London.

Stockner, J. G. 1968. The ecology of a diatom community in a thermal stream. *British Phycological Bulletin* 3:501–514.

Stotzky, G. 1989. Gene transfer among bacteria in soil. In S. B. Levy and R. V. Miller (eds.). *Gene Transfer in the Environment.* McGraw-Hill, New York, pp. 165–222.

Suberkropp, M. J., and M. J. Klug. 1974. Decomposition of deciduous leaf litter in a woodland stream: A scanning electron microscopic study. *Microbial Ecology* 1:96–103.

Summers, A. O. 1984. Genetic adaptations involving heavy metals. In M. J. Klug and C. A. Reddy (eds.). *Current Perspectives in Microbial Ecology.* American Society for Microbiology, Washington, DC, pp. 94–104.

Summers, A. O., J. Wireman, M. J. Vimy, F. L. Lorscheider, B. Marshall, S. B. Levy, S. Bennett, and L. Billard. 1993. Mercury released from dental "silver" fillings provokes an increase in mercury- and antibiotic-resistant bacteria in oral and intestinal floras of primates. *Antimicrobial Agents and Chemotherapy* 37:825–834.

Sussman, M., C. H. Collins, F. A. Skinner, and D. E. Stewart-Tull (eds.). 1988. *The Release of Genetically-Engineered Micro-organisms.* Academic Press, London.

Swift, M. J. 1984. Microbial diversity and decomposer niches. In M. J. Klug and C. A. Reddy (eds.). *Current Perspectives in Microbial Ecology.* American Society for Microbiology, Washington, DC, pp. 8–16.

Tempest, D. W. 1970. The continuous cultivation of microorganisms. I. Theory of the chemostat. In J. R. Norris and D. W. Ribbons (eds.). *Methods in Microbiology,* Vol. 2. Academic Press, New York, pp. 259–276.

Thayer, D. W. (ed.). 1975. *Microbial Interaction with the Physical Environment.* Dowden Hutchinson and Ross, Stroudsburg, PA.

Thiem, S. M., M. L. Krumme, R. L. Smith, and J. M. Tiedje. 1994. Use of molecular techniques to evaluate the survival of a microorganism injected into an aquifer. *Applied and Environmental Microbiology* 60:1059–1067.

Torsvik, V. L. 1980. Isolation of bacterial DNA from soil. *Soil Biology and Biochemistry* 12:15–21.

Torsvik, V., K. Salte, R. Sørheim, and J. Goksøyr. 1990a. Comparison of phenotypic diversity and DNA heterogeneity in a population of soil bacteria. *Applied and Environmental Microbiology* 56:776–781.

Torsvik, V., J. Goksøyr, and F. L. Daae. 1990b. High diversity in DNA of soil bacteria. *Applied and Environmental Microbiology* 56:782–787.

Trevors, J. T. 1996. Nucleic acids in the environment. *Current Opinion in Biotechnology* 7:331–336.

Veal, D. A., H. W. Stokes, and G. Daggard. 1992. Genetic exchange in natural microbial communities. *Advances in Microbial Ecology* 12:383–430.

Veldkamp, H. 1970. Enrichment cultures of prokaryotic organisms. In J. R. Norris and D. W. Ribbons (eds.). *Methods in Microbiology,* Vol. 3A. Academic Press, New York, pp. 305–361.

Veldkamp, H. 1977. Ecological studies with a chemostat. *Advances in Microbial Ecology* 1:59–94.

Veldkamp, H., and J. G. Kuenen. 1973. The chemostat as a model system for ecological studies. *Bulletin of the Ecological Research Commission* (Stockholm) 17:347–355.

Veldkamp, H., H. van Gemerden, W. Harder, and H. J. Laanbroek. 1984. Competition among bacteria: An overview. In M. J. Klug and C. A. Reddy (eds.). *Current Perspectives in Microbial Ecology.* American Society for Microbiology, Washington, DC, pp. 279–290.

Wahl, M. 1989. Marine epibiosis. I. Fouling and antifouling: Some basic aspects. *Marine Ecological Progress Series* 58:175–189.

Waksman, S. 1952. *Soil Microbiology.* Wiley, New York.

Walters, C. J. 1971. Systems ecology: The systems approach and mathematical models in ecology. In E. P. Odum (ed.). *Fundamentals of Ecology.* Saunders, Philadelphia, PA, pp. 276–292.

Wanner, O. 1986. Analysis of biofilm dynamics. In F. Megusar and M. Gantar (eds.). *Perspectives in Microbial Ecology.* Slovene Society for Microbiology, Ljubljana, Yugoslavia, pp. 30–37.

Watve, M. G., and R. M. Gangal. 1996. Problems in measuring bacterial diversity and a possible solution. *Applied and Environmental Microbiology* 62:4299–4301.

Wetmur, J. G., and N. Davidson. 1968. Kinetics of renaturation of DNA. *Journal of Molecular Biology* 31:349–370.

Whittaker, R. H. 1975. *Communities and Ecosystems.* Macmillan, New York.

Wiens, J. A. 1983. Competition or peaceful coexistence. *Natural History* 92:30–34.

Wilcox, C. E., and G. J. Wedemayer. 1985. Dinoflagellate with blue-green chloroplasts derived from an endosymbiotic eukaryote. *Science* 227:192–194.

Williams, F. M. 1973. Mathematical modeling of microbial populations. *Bulletin of the Ecological Research Commission* (Stockholm) 17:417–426.

Zhou, J. Z., and J. M. Tiedje. 1995. Gene transfer from a bacterium injected into an aquifer to an indigenous bacterium. *Molecular Ecology* 4:13-18.

# 7

# QUANTITATIVE ECOLOGY: NUMBERS, BIOMASS, AND ACTIVITIES

*Understanding the structure and functioning of ecosystems requires more than simply recognizing the interrelationships among populations; it necessitates quantitative information about numbers of organisms, biomass of populations, rates of activity, rates of growth and death, and cycling and transfer rates of materials within ecosystems. Numbers, biomass, and activity represent distinct ecological parameters. Though normally correlated to each other, these parameters should not be used in an interchangeable manner. The nature of the ecological problem dictates which is the most appropriate one to measure. On occasion, technical problems force us to measure a less relevant parameter, such as numbers, and to calculate from this a more relevant parameter, such as biomass. Whenever this is done, it is important to assess critically whether such extrapolation is justified under the circumstances. The methods used in these determinations are critical in defining microbial ecology as a scientific discipline and for understanding the ecology of microorganisms. Employing a quantitative approach, more than anything else, distinguishes ecologists from naturalists.*

## SAMPLE COLLECTION

Numerous methodological approaches have been developed to examine numbers and activities of microbial populations in diverse ecosystems (Hurst et al. 1997). To examine microorganisms in natural systems—in terms of total numbers, numbers of specific populations, or their metabolic activities—representative subsamples are analyzed and the results are projected to the whole community or ecosystem (Board and Lovelock 1973). The term *representative* means that the sample must reflect the diversity and density of organisms in the entirety of the sampled environment. In many environments, the distribution of microorganisms is not homogeneous but patchy. Any single sample is, of necessity, minute as compared to the whole environment being sampled, so it may easily lead to an over- or underestimate of the true abundance. This is particularly true because microorganisms live within microhabitats that are not recognized at the time of sample collection. Processing composite samples, prepared from individual samples collected by the use of a suitable sampling grid, can minimize this error. Confidence limits of extrapolations from samples to the entire environment should be statistically determined. It is important to understand that each determination consists of three phases: sample collection, sample processing, and actual measurement. The manner of sample collection and sample processing can profoundly influence the outcome of the measurements; therefore all three procedures must be considered when the results are interpreted.

Different approaches must be used for sampling microorganisms from such diverse ecosystems as the guts of animals, the surface layer of soils, the waters of a lake, and the sediment of the deep sea. The lack of direct access to some environments requires the use of remote control sampling devices. In some enumeration procedures, sample processing and even counting procedures are coupled with sampling. The method of obtaining samples is determined by the physical and chemical properties of the ecosystem being examined, by the expected abundance of microorganisms, and by the enumeration or measurement procedures to be performed. Different sampling approaches are used for different environments (Table 7.1).

Sampling procedures must ensure that numbers or activities of microorganisms are not altered, either positively or negatively, in a nonquantifiable manner during collection and storage of the sample. Sampling procedures also must ensure that samples are representative and are not contaminated with foreign microorganisms—that is, sampling procedures must ensure that the microorganisms come only from the ecosystem being examined.

## Soil Samples

When collecting soil samples, microbiologists often do not use aseptic technique but pragmatically rely on a shovel and pail because of the abundance of microorganisms in the soil relative to possible contaminants from air or nonsterile containers. When soil must be collected from a particular depth, a soil corer is used. The soil corer, a hand- or motor-driven hollow tube with a sharp cutting edge, is used with or without a liner to hold the core of collected soil. Soil corers are designed to minimize compaction during sample recovery.

The sampling of microorganisms present in soil in relatively low numbers may require the use of attractants or baits. In some cases it is sufficient to provide a surface that will, by absorption, concentrate the naturally occurring dissolved nutrients. The Cholodny-Rossi buried slide technique has been used extensively in the sampling and observation enumeration of microorganisms in soils and sediments (Cholodny 1930; Rossi et al. 1936). In this technique, a glass microscope slide is implanted into the soil or sediment (Figure 7.1). Assuming that the clean glass slide surface is nonselective and acts like the surface of mineral particles in soil, the types and proportions of the organisms that adhere to the slide can be considered representative of the soil community in general. A variation on the buried slide technique is the exposure of electron microscope grids in natural environments (Hirsch and Pankratz 1970). Observation of the retrieved grids with the electron microscope reveals

**Table 7.1**
Comparison of microbial sampling approaches in major natural environments

| Environment | Access | Numbers | Sampling devices | Sample processing |
|---|---|---|---|---|
| Air | Direct | Low | Filters, Andersen samplers | Concentration on filters |
| Water | Direct or remote | High or low | Nets, containers, filters | Dilution or concentration |
| Sediment | Remote | High | Grabs, corers | Serial dilution |
| Soil | Direct | High | Shovels, corers | Serial dilution |

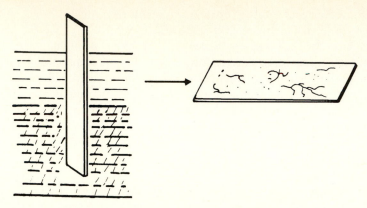

**Figure 7.1**
Schematic representation of buried slide technique for collection and enumeration of microorganisms.

more microbial morphological detail than light microscopy can.

Another variation of the buried slide technique is the replacement of glass slides with flattened glass capillaries, called *pedoscopes* when used in soil and *peloscopes* when used in sediments (Aristovskaya and Parinkina 1961; Perfilev and Gabe 1969; Aristovskaya 1973) (Figure 7.2). The capillaries resemble sediment or soil pore spaces, and microorganisms may enter them freely. The flattened optical surface of the capillaries facilitates microscopic observation and counting after retrieval. The capillaries may also be filled with nutrient solutions to attract microorganisms, in which case the technique resembles an enrichment culture and therefore will not reflect the original composition of the natural microbial community of the environment. Major achievements attributed to the use of capillary techniques in soils include (1) the observation of microbial landscapes of silt deposits, such as the abundance of *Caulobacter,* algae, and flagellate protozoa in wet soils, the development of *Metallogenium* indicative of iron-manganese deposition, and the extensive growth of *Gallionella* when ferrous iron is present; (2) the description of new genera of nonculturable microorganisms with unusual morphological characteristics; and (3) the observation of life-cycle stages in natural habitats.

## Water Samples

Various methods have been used to collect water samples and analyze the microbial populations in them (Kemp et al. 1993; Pepper et al. 1995). Sampling problems are typically greater in aquatic habitats than in soils because remote collection is normally required, and nonindigenous microorganisms could potentially contaminate the relatively low numbers of microorganisms in water samples. Each of the various sampling devices used for collecting water and sediment samples has its advantages and limitations. Many of these devices are designed to ensure that the sample really comes from a particular location—from exactly 100 m of depth, for example.

Water samples collected for enumeration of algae and/or protozoa are often collected with Nansen and VanDorn sampling bottles, but these devices are not suitable for bacteriological sampling because they cannot be sterilized. Planktonic algae and protozoa are often collected in nets towed by a boat, but many microflagellates will not survive this collection method. The planktonic organisms may be funneled into collection bottles, where they are concentrated.

Samplers designed for the collection of bacterial populations from waters include ones consisting of an evacuated chamber that can be opened at a given

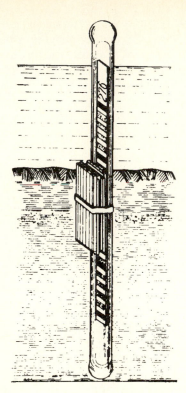

**Figure 7.2**
A peloscope for *in situ* observation of microorganisms in sediment. A pedoscope is a similar device for observation in soil. (Source: Aristovskaya 1973. Reprinted by permission of Swedish National Research Council.)

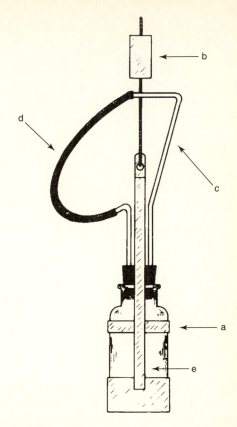

**Figure 7.3**
J-Z sampler for collection of water samples at shallow depths. (a) Bracket. (b) Messenger. (c) Glass tube to be broken by messenger. (d) Rubber inlet tube. (e) Partially evacuated sample bottle.

depth, allowing water to fill the chamber (Bordner and Winter 1978). The J-Z sampler, for example, consists of an evacuated glass bottle or a compressed rubber bulb with a sealed glass tube inlet (Figure 7.3). After the device is lowered to the desired depth, a weighted messenger is sent down the line to break the glass inlet tube, allowing the water to enter the flask or bulb. The Niskin sterile bag water sampler consists of an evacuated polyethylene bag with a sealed rubber tube inlet. The sampling bag is mounted on a spring-loaded holder and lowered to the desired depth. A messenger is then lowered to release a knife blade that cuts the rubber inlet hose, causing springs to spread the sampling bag, thus drawing in a water sample (Figure 7.4). Because the sampling devices are lowered through the water column to reach the desired depth, the collected sample may be contaminated with water from a different depth. Contamination may also originate from the hydrographic wire used to lower the device; more elaborate sampling devices are needed to preclude such contamination (Figure 7.5 on page 223). Specialized sampling devices also are required for collecting water samples from great depths because of decompression problems during recovery; devices have been designed to open at a specific depth, allow a sample to enter, and close again in order to maintain the appropriate pressure during recovery (Jannasch and Wirsen 1977).

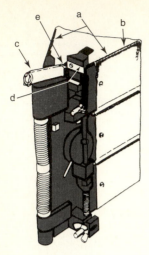

**Figure 7.4**
Sterile Niskin butterfly water collecting bag. (a) Spring-loaded holder. (b) Sterile plastic bag. (c) Rubber inlet tube. (d and e) Knife blade for opening inlet when triggered by messenger.

## Sediment Samples

For collecting sediment samples from marine or freshwater ecosystems there are a variety of grab samplers or corers. Grab samplers have two spring-loaded jaws that are triggered when the sampler reaches bottom or when a messenger is lowered. When triggered, the jaws of the grab sampler snap shut, dig into the sediment, and collect a sample. Most grab samplers do not prevent contamination of the sample by overlying water. Box corers, frequently used by benthic biologists but only rarely by marine microbiologists, recover sediment in a relatively undisturbed state. Core samples are also used for collection of sediments for microbiological analyses. Some caution must be used to prevent compression of the sample so that the vertical stratification of the microbial community can be preserved. Coring devices can have a sterile lining that aids in handling the sample and permits dividing the core sample into vertical sections.

In addition to these remote sampling devices deployed from the surface of the water, divers and submersibles are sometimes used to collect samples for microbiological analyses. These means of collection have the advantage of enabling the collectors to see what they are sampling, to make rational decisions about what to collect, and to describe the samples. Deep-diving submersibles such as the Alvin, which has been used to investigate the deep-ocean thermal vent regions, have been particularly valuable because with their aid some samples can be collected, processed, left *in situ* for incubation, and later recovered for analysis.

## Air Samples

Sampling microorganisms from the air requires that processing be coupled with sample collection. Microbial numbers in air are generally quite low, and it is impractical to collect large volumes of air for later processing. Collection of viable airborne microorganisms requires approaches that minimize sampling stress and capture the particle size of the bioaerosol droplets in which airborne microorganisms typically occur (Stetzenbach 1992). Passive sampling, such as on open petri dishes with agar culture media or glass slides covered with a sticky film, relies on particles settling out of air. Such depositional sampling is useful for enumeration of fungal spores but is inefficient for the collection of airborne bacteria (Buttner et al. 1997). Air samples are most often collected by forcing a measured volume of air through a collection device such as a membrane filter (Gregory 1973; Stetzenbach 1992). The pore size of the membrane filter may vary for the collection of different types of microorganisms. In the Andersen air sampler, air is drawn through a graded series of grids of decreasing pore size (Andersen 1958). An agar plate is placed under each grid to collect microorganisms and other airborne particles that, by their inertia, fall onto the agar surface. Air velocity increases with decreasing grid openings; therefore, increasingly smaller particles land on successive agar plates. Unfortunately, surfaces in such impinger samplers may be overloaded by high concentrations of microorganisms in some aerosols (Stetzenbach 1992).

## Biological Samples

Retrieving microorganisms from plants and animals involves collecting a vital fluid, such as sap or blood;

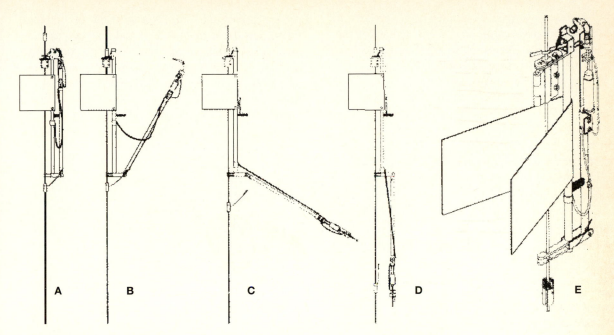

**Figure 7.5**
Microbial water sampling device designed to avoid contamination from the hydrographic wire. (A) Vane maintaining direction into current. (B) Sampling arm swinging out when triggered by a messenger; sterile cover of sample tube pulling away. (C) Syringe plunger retracting to draw in sample. (D) Sampling inlet closing. (E) Detail of sampling apparatus. (Source: Jannasch and Maddux 1967. Reprinted by permission of *Journal of Marine Research.*)

dissecting to recover a particular tissue, such as liver; collecting excreted products, such as fecal matter; or sampling a surface tissue. In cases where the surface is exposed, microorganisms may be scraped or washed from the tissue. Microorganisms can be recovered from plant surfaces by washing with sterile solutions, from the oral cavity by scraping and washing tooth surfaces, and from human skin by swabbing. Such nondestructive sampling requires that the microorganisms not be tightly bonded to the plant or animal, and concern must be given to the efficiency of such recovery methods. In other cases, the tissue or cells may be preserved together with the associated microorganisms. This is especially useful when examination of the anatomical relationship, or enumeration of microbial populations, is required. Such approaches are useful when considering associations between microbial populations, such as between phage and bacteria, as well as when examining associations between plants or animals and microbiota.

## SAMPLE PROCESSING

Only rarely are naturally occurring microbial populations found in concentrations that are convenient for measurements or counting; therefore, the microorganisms in the sample normally must be either concentrated or diluted. Samples with too many microorganisms may be brought to appropriate concentrations by serial dilutions (the successive diluting of the sample with an appropriate diluent), and samples with too few microorganisms can be concentrated by centrifugation or by passage through membrane filters. The process employed affects the eventual numbers of microorganisms counted.

If counts are to reflect accurately the numbers of viable microorganisms present in the sample at the time of collection, then processing must be accomplished quickly because microorganisms reproduce rapidly in collection vessels, yielding artificially elevated counts. This problem, known as the bottle effect, is particularly observed with seawater, which naturally lacks adsorptive surfaces. When seawater is placed into a glass, nutrients adsorb on the wall and become more concentrated and available to microbes, which are then able to reproduce and greatly increase their numbers. Conditions used in processing samples can also kill some of the microorganisms present in the original sample, thus yielding artificially depressed counts.

If samples are to be diluted for viable count procedures, microorganisms must be evenly dispersed in the diluent. This is a difficult task, especially for soil and sediment samples where microorganisms are usually bound to particles. The efficiency of recovery of microorganisms is highly dependent on the chemical composition and osmotic strength of the diluent, the time of mixing, the temperature, the chemical composition of a dispersant if one is used, and the degree of agitation (Tables 7.2 and 7.3). The optimal recovery process varies from sample to sample, precluding an absolute standardization of methodology.

If samples must be concentrated by filtration, appropriate filters must be selected. Filters with pores that are too large fail to collect the microorganisms; filters with pores that are too small clog easily and cannot filter sufficient volumes. In general, polycarbonate filters are considered superior to nitrocellulose filters because of the flatness of the surface and the uniformity of the pores. The particular chemical composition of the filter may also affect the viable counts of microorganisms.

It is obvious that conditions not compatible with the physiological requirements of particular groups of microorganisms will lead to their underestimation because of loss of viability. For example, enumeration of obligate anaerobes requires that diluents be rendered free of oxygen and that all processing be carried out under an oxygen-free atmosphere. The enumeration of obligate psychrophiles requires that the diluent and all glassware, such as pipettes, be prechilled to avoid killing these microorganisms.

When the enumeration procedure is not designed to discriminate between living and dead microorganisms, the samples may be preserved by adding formaldehyde or glutaraldehyde. Such preparations are suitable for direct microscopic observations.

The recovery of viruses from environmental samples requires special processing to concentrate the

**Table 7.2**
Effect of mixing time on viable counts of soil bacteria

| Mixing time in blender | Viable count (#/g) on soil extract agar incubated 12 days at 25°C | |
| --- | --- | --- |
| | Soil 1 | Soil 2 |
| 15 sec | $7.4 \times 10^6$ | $2.9 \times 10^6$ |
| 1 min | $8.1 \times 10^6$ | $4.2 \times 10^6$ |
| 2 min | $*8.7 \times 10^6$ | $3.9 \times 10^6$ |
| 4 min | $8.4 \times 10^6$ | $7.0 \times 10^6$ |
| 8 min | $7.1 \times 10^6$ | $*7.1 \times 10^6$ |

*Optimal mixing time.

Source: Jensen 1968.

**Table 7.3**
Effect of chemical composition of a diluent on viable counts of soil bacteria

| Diluent | Viable count (#/g) on soil extract agar: 8-day incubation at 25°C with 1-min delay between preparation of dilutions and planting |
| --- | --- |
| Tap water | $1.9 \times 10^7$ |
| Pyrophosphate 0.1% | $2.3 \times 10^7$ |
| Ringer's solution | $1.6 \times 10^7$ |
| Winogradsky's solution | $3.0 \times 10^7$ |

Source: Jensen 1968.

viruses (Sobsey 1982; Gerba 1983; Metcalf et al. 1995). Viruses can be concentrated from water by repetitive adsorption and elution processes; in one such procedure, after acidification, viruses in large volumes of water can be adsorbed onto epoxy, fiberglass, or nitrocellulose filters. Adsorbed viruses can then be eluted with an alkaline solution. The sorption and elution process can be repeated, resulting in a many-thousandfold concentration of the viruses. Viruses can also be eluted from particles such as occur in sewage sludge, using flocculating materials and adsorptive filters that maintain the infectivity of viruses during these concentration procedures. Somewhat different procedures are required for recovery of viruses from animal or plant tissues (Figure 7.6).

# DETECTION OF MICROBIAL POPULATIONS

## Phenotypic Detection

The detection of microorganisms based on phenotypic characteristics requires that the microorganisms to be specifically detected must be recovered from environmental samples and that recognizable and distinctive phenotypes must be expressed during *in vitro* culture (Atlas 1992). In some cases, the observation of a single unique characteristic may be sufficient to recognize the specifically targeted microbe. A microorganism with a unique phenotype, such as the failure to produce a peptide that initiates ice crystal formation (ice-minus phenotype), could be selected based on such a single distinguishing characteristic. In other cases, it may be necessary to determine a pattern of multiple characteristics in order to distinguish the specific targeted microbe from all others. The unambiguous detection of a microbe based on phenotype is a difficult task because even distantly related organisms can have similar phenotypes for some characteristics.

The classical approaches for detecting microorganisms are to place viable microbial cells onto a solid medium (plating procedures) or into a liquid broth (enrichment procedures) containing all the nutrients

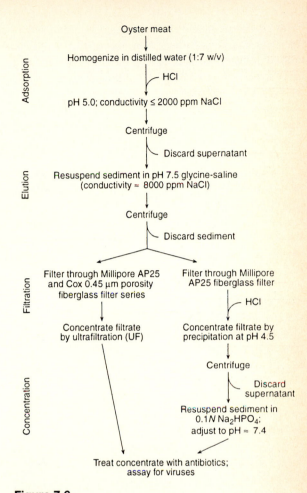

**Figure 7.6**
An example of a viral recovery and concentration method that has been used for examination of shellfish. (Source: Sobsey et al. 1978. Reprinted by permission of American Society for Microbiology.)

essential for the growth of the targeted microorganisms, and to incubate the inoculated cultures under conditions that favor the growth of those microbes so that their phenotypes can be observed.

Plating procedures rely upon the ability to separate microorganisms so that individual microbial cells are deposited at discrete locations on a solid medium; when the deposited microorganisms reproduce, they form discrete colonies that comprise clones of the original microorganisms. Plating procedures accomplish two things. First, they separate individual microbes from the multitude of microorganisms in a natural microbial community so that the phenotypes of individual microbes can be determined, which is the basis of the pure culture methods that are the mainstay of microbiology. Second, they amplify the signal (phenotype) to be observed through cell reproduction. The phenotypic characteristics of the millions of presumably identical cells in a colony can be observed much more readily than those of individual microbial cells.

Plating procedures are effective for detecting a particular microbe when that target microbe constitutes a significant portion of the microbial community, but microorganisms constituting extremely low proportions of a community can be overlooked by plating procedures. In cases where a microbe makes up only a small fraction of a community, growth in liquid cultures under conditions that specifically favor the growth of the target microbe over the growth of other microbes can be used to enrich for the target microbe.

With adjustments for the chemical composition of the growth medium and incubation conditions, plating and enrichment procedures are designed to be differential and/or selective to detect specific microorganisms. Because the ability of a particular microorganism to grow on or in a particular medium is based on its ability to utilize specific organic and inorganic nutrients, a culture medium can be made selective on the basis of its constituents (such as the particular carbon sources, the salt concentration, and so on). The incubation conditions also can be made selective by adjusting the physical growth conditions (such as temperature, oxygen concentration, and so on). The addition of inhibitory compounds to a medium suppresses the development of the majority of microorganisms, enabling the development of the desired species to occur.

Because the phenotype of the microorganism depends on the specific pathways for the metabolism of the nutrients in the medium, specific dyes, redox indicators, and so on can be included in the medium to reflect the metabolism of specific nutrients by different populations and hence the differentiation of target microorganisms. The Biolog microtiter plate assay,

for example, is based on tetrazolium dye reduction as an indicator of sole carbon source utilization (Lee et al. 1995). This method permits determination of the biodegradative activities of pure and mixed cultures; it can be performed on entire communities to avoid artificial selection.

Methods for detecting microorganisms use cultivation media that are usually formulated to take advantage of specific traits of the organism, such as nutritional capabilities and/or resistances to specific antibiotics, so that target microorganisms are favored for growth over other strains. Generally, a visible phenotypic characteristic (such as pigmentation), the ability to use a specific substrate, or resistance to a certain antibiotic or heavy metal is used to differentiate the target microorganism from others.

## Lipid Profile Analyses

Lipids are ubiquitous components of the cytoplasmic membranes that surround all living cells. The lipid compositions of cytoplasmic membranes of diverse microorganisms vary, however; there are six or more classes of lipids, each consisting of individual lipids with six or more structural variations (Tornabene 1985). Each microorganism has a characteristic pattern of lipid composition (proportions of specific lipids) that can be used as a diagnostic characteristic (Lechevalier 1977; Goodfellow and Minnikin 1985; Rattledge and Wilkinson 1988). By examining the profiles of lipids, microbial species can be identified. For example, *Micrococcus* species can be distinguished based on the profiles of branched monoene fatty acids in their membranes ($C_{27}$, $C_{28}$, $C_{29}$ = *M. luteus;* $C_{25}$, $C_{26}$, $C_{27}$ = *M. varians;* $C_{30}$, $C_{31}$, $C_{32}$ = *M. sedentarius*) (Tornabene 1985). Lipids can serve as signatures to define the community structure (White 1995). Profiles of lipid composition in environmental samples can be used for detecting diverse populations and thereby for describing the composition of the microbial community.

Fatty acid methyl ester (FAME) analysis is becoming a frequently used method for the detection of bacterial and eucaryotic microbial species, including those in environmental samples. The full process of FAME analysis consists of the esterification of lipids and the injection, separation, identification, and quantitation of the fatty acid methyl esters by gas chromatography (Eder 1995). Fused silica columns give very good separation of fatty acid methyl esters from biological samples. Fatty acid methyl esters are identified by comparisons of their retention times with those of individual purified standards or well-characterized lipids that have been previously described. Fatty acid methyl esters can be quantitated by peak areas via calibration factors, and absolute concentrations can be determined by including known concentrations of internal standards in the analyses.

Analysis of FAME profiles extracted from soils is a rapid and inexpensive procedure that holds great promise in describing soil microbial community structure without traditional reliance on selective culturing, which seems to severely underestimate community diversity (Cavigelli et al. 1995). Interpretation of FAME profiles from environmental samples, however, can be difficult because many fatty acids are common to different microorganisms and many fatty acids are extracted from each soil sample. Various statistical analytical procedures, including principal component analysis and cluster analyses, are useful for identifying similarities and differences among soil microbial communities described using FAME profiles.

Using FAME analysis, Graham et al. (1995) were able to distinguish five groups of *Bradyrhizobium* species. A number of *Bradyrhizobium* strains isolated from soybean in Korea and northern Thailand had FAME profiles so different from the *B. japonicum* and *B. elkanii* strains as to warrant separation at the species level. A slow-growing isolate from *Lupinus* also had a FAME profile very different from those of the other bradyrhizobia. Franzmann et al. (1996) used FAME analyses to examine the microbial community within a water plume beneath a site at Perth (Australia) that had been contaminated by petroleum hydrocarbons. They found that only a few species dominated the disturbed bacterial community.

Besides FAME analyses, phospholipid-linked fatty acid (PLFA) analyses are used to describe bacterial communities (Bobbie and White 1980; Guckert et al. 1985; White 1983). Using fatty acids specifically

ester-linked to the polar lipid fraction greatly enhances the sensitivity and specificity of detecting specific microbial populations (Baird and White 1985; Dowling et al. 1986; Gillan et al. 1983; Mancuso et al. 1990; Nichols et al. 1986, 1987; White 1988; Kohring et al. 1994). Phospholipid-linked branched fatty acids are characteristic of bacterial origin (Gillan and Hogg 1984). Eucaryotic microorganisms are characterized by polyunsaturated fatty acids, especially 18:2 (Rajendran et al. 1992a, 1992b). The sum of the relative abundances of iso and anteiso isomers of 15:0 phospholipid-linked branched fatty acids represents the bacterial component of the community (Nichols et al. 1987). The ratio of iso and anteiso 15:0 phospholipid-linked branched fatty acids to 16:0 phospholipid-linked branched fatty acids (which are found ubiquitously in bacteria and eucaryotes) provides an index of the proportion of bacterial populations within the community (Mancuso et al. 1990).

Analysis of PLFA profiles provides information not only about the composition and relative abundances of populations within the community but also about the physiological status of those populations (Guckert et al. 1986; Kieft et al. 1994; Peterson and Klug 1994). A ratio greater than 1 of *trans* to *cis* isomers of monounsaturated PLFAs is indicative of starvation or other environmental stress (Guckert et al. 1986; Rajendran et al. 1992a, 1992b; Kieft et al. 1994). Stress also results in increased ratios of saturated to unsaturated fatty acids and increased ratios of cyclopropyl fatty acids to their monoenoic precursors (Kieft et al. 1994). In a study on the effects of soil processing procedures on microbial community composition, Peterson and Klug (1994) observed that stress resulted in increased production of cyclopropyl fatty acids, in a decrease in the degree of fatty acid unsaturation, and in increased ratios of the branched chain fatty acids iso-15:0 and iso-17:0 relative to anteiso-15:0 and anteiso-17:0. They also observed that physical handling of the soil, such as sieving, negatively affected the fungal community as evidenced by decreased concentrations of the 18:2 omega fungal signature fatty acid.

Although PLFA detected some shifts within communities due to stress, such lipid analyses of sulfate-reducing bacterial populations indicated that PLFA patterns do not change as a result of shifts in nutrients or terminal electron acceptors (Kohring et al. 1994). In other cases it was possible to follow changes in microbial communities in response to ecological disturbance and stress and to describe the composition of the community; changes in populations of *Vibrio cholerae,* for example, were followed by Guckert et al. (1985) based on PLFA analyses in response to conditions of nutrient deprivation. Rajendran et al. (1992a, 1992b) found that the microbial communities of Japanese bays reflected the inputs of pollutants. PLFA profiles in bays receiving pollutants showed evidence of bacterial growth in response to inputs of organic pollutants. These analyses indicated that some polluted sites were dominated by anaerobes, particularly sulfate-reducing bacteria. Hendrick et al. (1992) demonstrated the usefulness of PLFA analyses for characterizing the microbial community surrounding a deep-sea hydrothermal vent. They found evidence for a dense archaeal community and possibly thiobacilli on the flange of a black smoker and *Beggiatoa* in the surrounding sediments; they also observed a prevalence of polyenoic fatty acids that are characteristic of barophilic bacteria. These studies illustrate some applications of PLFA analysis in microbial ecology.

## Molecular Detection

Perhaps the greatest advances in microbial ecology in the last few years have come from the application of molecular methods to the detection of microorganisms in environmental samples. The development of molecular methods permits the detection of specific microbial populations and their activities without the need to culture microorganisms. Many of these methods rely on amplification of molecular signature sequences and their detection by hybridization techniques, especially using oligonucleotide probes (Maniatis et al. 1982). Nucleic acid–based methods now provide the main means to track specific microbial populations in the environment (Tiedje et al. 1995). The phylogenetic relationships of bacteria, archaea, and eucaryotic microorganisms can also be determined using gene probes and molecular analyses, giving rise to new perspectives on the natural microbial world (Pace 1996) (Figure 7.7).

**Nucleic Acid Recovery**  To detect specific target genes or ribosomal or messenger RNAs (rRNAs or mRNAs) for ecological studies, it is necessary to recover nucleic acids from environmental samples. This usually involves extensive purification to remove proteins, humic acids, and other compounds that would interfere with analysis of the nucleic acids. A number of specific protocols have been developed for nucleic acid analyses for environmental applications (Atlas 1993). Two approaches have been used to recover DNA and RNA from environmental samples: isolation of microbial cells followed by cell lysis and nucleic acid purification (cell extraction) and direct lysis of microbial cells in the environmental matrix followed by nucleic acid purification (direct extraction) (Steffan et al. 1988). These procedures have employed various methods for releasing nucleic acids from microbial cells and for removing nonnucleic acid compounds found in soils and waters.

For water samples, cells can be collected by filtration and then lysed to isolate their nucleic acids (Bej et al. 1990, 1991a; Fuhrman et al. 1988; Giovannoni et al. 1990; Sommerville et al. 1989). Alternately, filtered cells may first be subjected to enzymatic lysis and/or phenol-chloroform extraction procedures to yield adequate DNA. Sommerville et al. (1989) have demonstrated a simple method for isolating nucleic acids from aquatic samples that allows filtering relatively large volumes of water. Cell collection and lysis are performed in a single filter cartridge, and chromosomal DNA, plasmid DNA, and RNA can be selectively recovered. Paul et al. (1990) reported that with certain algal DNA preparations and with all preparations of environmental DNA, purification by cesium chloride–ethidium bromide ultracentrifugation was required for isolation of purified DNA. In other studies, multiple phenol or phenol-chloroform extractions have produced sufficiently pure DNA from cyanobacteria (Zehr and McReynolds 1989) or planktonic microorganisms (Fuhrman et al. 1988; Lee and Fuhrman 1990). Microgram quantities of rRNA can be recovered from natural microbial communities in

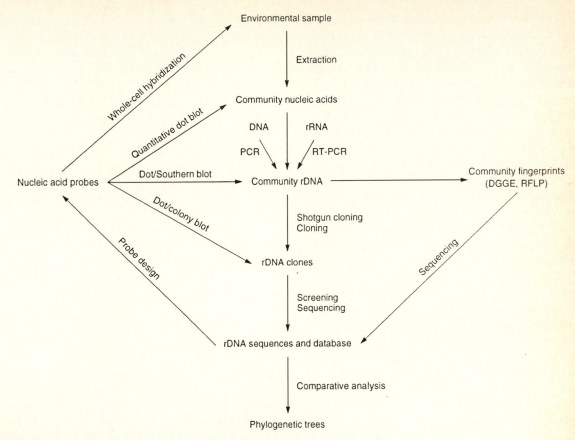

**Figure 7.7**
Phylogenetic relationships of microorganisms in environmental samples can be determined without viable culturing based on nucleic acid analyses. In particular, analysis of
ribosomal RNA genes provides the tools for identifying specific microbial populations.
Reverse transcription (RT) and amplification of DNA using the polymerase chain reaction
(PCR) are useful in obtaining sufficient quantities of target nucleic acid sequences for
analyses. Based on specific diagnostic gene sequences, gene probes can be designed to
detect specific target organisms. In this manner complex microbial communities can be
analyzed. (Note: DGGE = denaturing gradient gel electrophoresis, RFLP = restriction
fragment length polymorphism.) (Source: Pace 1996.)

sediment, soil, and water with a lysozyme–hot phenol
direct extraction method (Moran et al. 1993). Gel filtration with Sephadex G-75 spun columns readily
removed humiclike contaminants without any mea-
surable loss of rRNA and rendered RNA extracts of
sufficient quality for molecular procedures.

Cell extraction methods for soils were developed
by Balkwill et al. (1975) and Goksøyr and colleagues
(Faegri et al. 1977; Torsvik and Goksøyr 1978). A
number of groups have used this approach with some
modification to isolate DNA from soil (Torsvik 1980;
Bakken 1985; Holben et al. 1988; Steffan et al. 1988;
Jansson et al. 1989; Torsvik et al. 1990) or sediment
(Steffan et al. 1988; Steffan and Atlas 1990). One simple but significant improvement of this approach has
been the inclusion of a polyvinylpolypyrollidone

(PVPP) treatment to decrease sample humic content prior to cell lysis (Holben et al. 1988; Steffan et al. 1988), thereby simplifying DNA purification.

Direct extraction of DNA from environmental samples was first described by Ogram et al. (1987). In this method, cells are lysed while still within the soil matrix by incubation with sodium dodecyl sulfate followed by physical disruption with a bead beater. The DNA is then extracted with alkaline phosphate buffer. This method has been successfully used to recover DNA from sediments and soils (Ogram et al. 1987; Steffan et al. 1988). Purification procedures can be any combination of cesium chloride–ethidium bromide ultracentrifugation (Holben et al. 1988; Steffan et al. 1988; Paul et al. 1990), hydroxyapatite or affinity chromatography (Torsvik and Goksøyr 1978; Ogram et al. 1987; Steffan et al. 1988; Paul et al. 1990), phenol-chloroform extractions, ethanol precipitations (Fuhrman et al. 1988), dialysis, or repeated PVPP treatments (Holben et al. 1988; Steffan et al. 1988; Weller and Ward 1989; Paul et al. 1990). Significantly higher yields of DNA are recovered with the direct extraction method than with the cell recovery procedure, but the DNA may contain impurities that can inhibit enzymatic manipulation (Steffan et al. 1988).

A simple, rapid method for bacterial lysis and direct extraction of DNA from soils with minimal shearing was developed by Zhou et al. (1996) to address the risk of chimera formation from small template DNA during subsequent PCR. The method was based on lysis with a high-salt extraction buffer (1.5 M NaCl) and extended heating (2–3 hours) of the soil suspension in the presence of sodium dodecyl sulfate (SDS), hexadecyltrimethylammonium bromide, and proteinase K. The extraction method required 6 hours and was tested on eight soils differing in organic carbon, clay content, and pH, including ones from which DNA extraction is difficult. The DNA fragment size in crude extracts from all soils was greater than 23 kilobase (kb) pairs. Preliminary trials indicated that DNA recovery from two soils seeded with gram-negative bacteria was 92–99%. When the method was tested on all eight unseeded soils, microscopic examination of indigenous bacteria in soil pellets before and after extraction showed variable cell lysis efficiency (26–92%). Crude DNA yields from the eight soils ranged from 2.5 to 26.9 µg per gram of DNA; the yields were positively correlated with the organic carbon content in the soil. DNA yields from gram-positive bacteria from pure cultures were two to six times higher when the high-salt–SDS-heat method was combined with mortar-and-pestle grinding and freeze-thawing, and most DNA recovered was of high molecular weight. Four methods for purifying crude DNA were also evaluated for percentage recovery, fragment size, speed, enzyme restriction, PCR amplification, and DNA-DNA hybridization. In general, all methods produced DNA pure enough for PCR amplification. Given that soil type and microbial community characteristics influence DNA recovery, this study provides guidance for choosing appropriate extraction and purification methods on the basis of experimental goals.

**Gene Probe Detection** Gene probes and nucleic acid hybridization techniques have been employed for the detection of target nucleic acid sequences that are diagnostic of specific microorganisms in environmental samples (Sayler and Layton 1990; Knight et al. 1992). With the use of gene probes, specific microbial populations can be detected in environmental samples. A gene probe is a relatively short nucleotide sequence that can bind (hybridize) to nucleotide sequences with homologous sequences in the target microorganism. Hybridization of the gene probe is diagnostic of the presence of a specific microbial population. Temperature, contacting time, salt concentration, the degree of mismatch between the base pairs, and the length and concentration of the target and probe sequences are factors affecting the hybridization or reassociation of the complementary DNA strands (Berent et al. 1985; Britton and Davidson 1985; Sambrook et al. 1989).

Most hybridization protocols are based on the hybridization of an immobilized target or probe molecule on a solid phase such as a nitrocellulose or nylon filter surface (Figure 7.8). First, single-stranded target nucleic acids are attached to the filter surface. Next, the filters are prehybridized to block nonspecific nucleic acid binding sites. Labeled probe DNA is

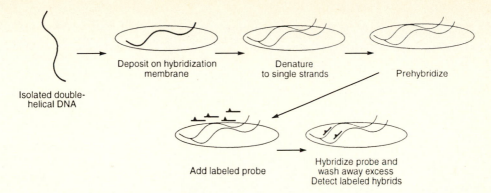

Isolated double-helical DNA

Deposit on hybridization membrane

Denature to single strands

Prehybridize

Add labeled probe

Hybridize probe and wash away excess Detect labeled hybrids

**Figure 7.8**
Illustration of nucleic acid hybridization, which is the basis for gene probe detection.

added to the filters, and the probe is allowed to hybridize. Probes typically are radiolabeled or labeled with fluorescent dyes. The labeled probe establishes a double-stranded molecule with the complementary target sequences. Often, the gene probe is labeled with $^{32}$P, and following hybridization, detection is by autoradiography. $^{32}$P can be incorporated using $^{32}$P-labeled free nucleotides and nick translation or end labeling using T4-polynucleotide kinase to incorporate the $^{32}$P into the gene probe. After hybridization, excess unbound labeled probe is washed off and the hybrid (target-probe) sequences are detected.

**Amplification of DNA—The Polymerase Chain Reaction**    The polymerase chain reaction (PCR) (Mullis et al. 1986; Mullis and Faloona 1987; Mullis 1990) has begun to be applied to environmental detection of microorganisms (Bej et al. 1991c; Steffan and Atlas 1991). It permits the *in vitro* replication of defined sequences of DNA. One application of this technique is to enhance gene probe detection of specific gene sequences. By exponentially amplifying a target sequence, PCR significantly enhances the probability of detecting rare sequences in heterologous mixtures of DNA.

PCR involves melting the DNA to convert double-stranded DNA to single-stranded DNA, annealing primers to the target DNA, and extending the DNA by nucleotide addition from the primers by the action of DNA polymerase (Figure 7.9). The oligonucleotide

primers are designed to hybridize to regions of DNA flanking a desired target gene sequence. The primers are then extended across the target sequence by using Taq DNA polymerase (a heat-stable enzyme derived from the thermophilic bacterium *Thermus aquaticus*) or other thermally stable DNA polymerase in the presence of free deoxyribonucleotide triphosphates, resulting in a duplication of the starting target material. When the product DNA duplexes are melted and the process is repeated many times, an exponential increase in the amount of target DNA results. The essential components of the PCR reaction mixture are Taq DNA polymerase or other thermally stable DNA polymerase, oligomer primers, deoxyribonucleotide (dNTPs), template DNA, and magnesium ions. The temperature cycling for PCR can be achieved using an automated thermal cycler. Annealing temperatures in the range of 55–72°C generally yield the best results. Typical denaturation conditions are 94–95°C for 30–60 seconds. Lower temperatures may result in incomplete denaturation of the target template or the PCR product and failure of the PCR. Too many cycles can increase the amount and complexity of nonspecific background products. Too few cycles give low product yield.

PCR is useful for environmental surveillance (Atlas and Bej 1990). Bej et al. (1990, 1991a) used PCR amplification and radiolabeled gene probe detection to detect coliform bacteria in environmental water samples. The combined methods detected as

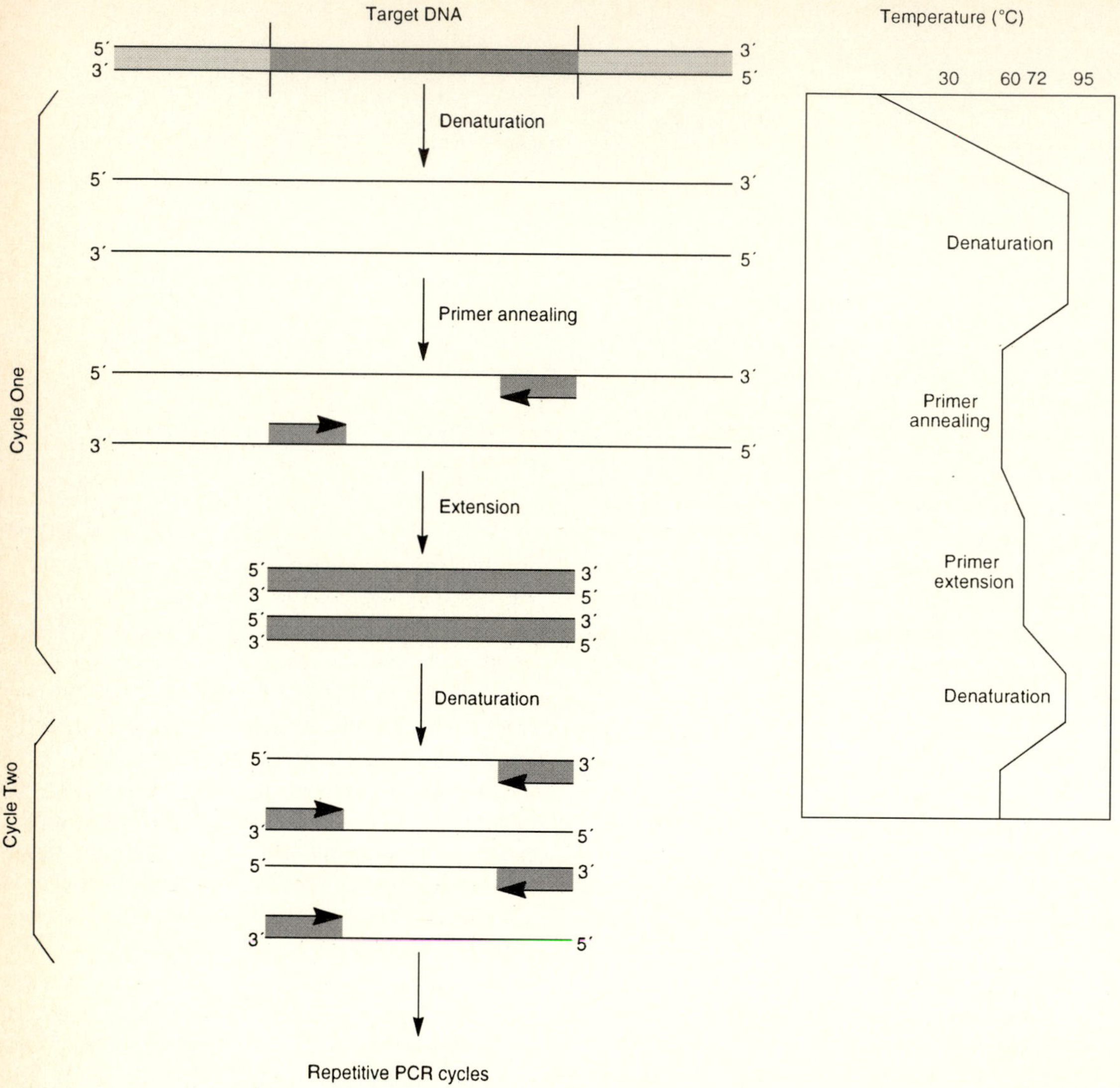

**Figure 7.9**
Illustration of the polymerase chain reaction (PCR) for the amplification of a target gene sequence.

little as 1–10 fg of genomic *E. coli* DNA and as few as one to five viable *E. coli* cells in 100 mL of water, demonstrating the potential use of PCR amplification to detect indicators of fecal contamination of water.

Both viable culturable and viable nonculturable cells of *Legionella pneumophila,* formed during expo-

sure to hypochlorite, showed positive PCR amplification, whereas nonviable cells did not (Bej et al. 1991b). Viable cells of *L. pneumophila* were also specifically detected by using mRNA from the gene that codes for macrophage infectivity potentiator (*mip* mRNA) as the target, reverse transcription to form cDNA, and PCR to amplify the signal. When cells were killed by elevated temperature, only viable culturable cells were detected, and detection of viable culturable cells corresponded precisely with positive PCR amplification.

Steffan and Atlas (1988) used PCR to amplify a 1.0-kb probe-specific region of DNA from the herbicide-degrading bacterium *Burkholderia* (formerly *Pseudomonas*) *cepacia* AC1100 in order to increase the sensitivity of detecting the organism by dot-blot analysis. The 1.0-kb region was an integral portion of a larger 1.3-kb repeat sequence present as fifteen to twenty copies on the *B. cepacia* AC1100 genome. Amplified target DNA was detectable in samples initially containing as little as 0.3 pg of target. The addition of 20 µg of nonspecific DNA isolated from sediment samples did not hinder amplification or detection of the target DNA. The detection of 0.3 pg of target DNA was at least a thousand-fold increase in the sensitivity of detecting gene sequences compared with dot-blot analysis of nonamplified samples. After bacterial DNA was isolated from sediment samples, PCR permitted the detection of as few as 100 cells of *B. cepacia* AC1100 per 100 g of sediment sample against a background of $10^{11}$ diverse nontarget organisms; that is, *B. cepacia* AC1100 was positively detected at a concentration of 1 cell per g of sediment (Figure 7.10). This represented a thousand-fold increase in sensitivity compared with nonamplified samples.

**Genetic Fingerprinting**  The interrelationships of microbial strains from various habitats can be studied by analyzing their DNA to reveal a "genetic fingerprint." This method involves sequencing the DNA and comparing the actual nucleotide sequences for comparable genes. Such analyses of genes for ribosomal RNAs are used to determine phylogenetic relationships (Pace 1996). DNA from different microorganisms can also be compared by cutting with restriction enzymes and comparing the patterns of the resulting fragments and by examining the repetitive sequences within the DNA. Lunge et al. (1994), for example, analyzed genomic DNA from *Bradyrhizobium japonicum* strains by restriction fragment length polymorphism (RFLP) with *nif* and *nod* probes, and by random

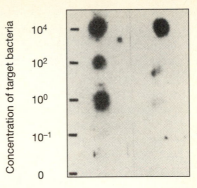

**Figure 7.10**
Dot-blot hybridization following PCR amplification of a gene segment diagnostic of *Pseudomonas cepacia* AC1100 showing increased sensitivity (left) over nonamplified case (right). (Source: Steffan and Atlas 1988. Reprinted by permission.)

amplified polymorphic DNA (RAPD). Polymorphism was observed in both analyses. The RFLP and RAPD banding patterns of different strains were used to calculate genetic divergence and to construct phylogenetic trees, allowing studies of the relationships between the strains. RFLP with *nif* and *nod* probes permitted the separation of the strains into two divergent groups, whereas RAPD separated them into four main groups. RAPD allowed closely related strains to be distinguished. The RAPD method appears to have numerous applications for characterizing such microbial populations (Hadrys et al. 1992).

Separation of 16S rRNA amplified gene fragments by denaturing gradient gel electrophoresis (DGGE) has proved useful for following specific populations of sulfate reducers within biofilms (Muyzer et al. 1993). Amplified ribosomal DNA restriction analysis (ARDRA) has also been found to permit the fingerprinting of specific microbial strains with biofilm communities (Massol-Deyá 1997). ARDRA profiles also allowed the tracking of specific aromatic hydrocarbon degraders in groundwater and bioreactor biofilms (Massol-Deyá 1997). Epidemiological studies also can be conducted by examining RFLP patterns from clinical and environmental samples. Zimmerman et al. (1994), in examining the source of an outbreak of coccidiomycosis in California in 1992, found that most isolates from California and Venezuela exhibited an identical RFLP pattern, but a few isolates from one hospital in the San Joaquin Valley of California yielded a different RFLP pattern; this indicated that most of the strains had come from the same source through a connected chain of transmission but that a few strains at a single location had a totally different origin. To describe the transmission of tuberculosis (TB) at the clonal level in a defined geographic region during a certain period of time, Yang et al. (1994) subjected DNA from all isolates of *Mycobacterium tuberculosis* collected during 1992 from Greenland to RFLP analysis. The RFLP patterns revealed a high degree of similarity among the isolates, indicating a relatively high transmission rate and a close relationship between the individual *M. tuberculosis* clones. The RFLP patterns were compared with those of 245 *M. tuberculosis* strains collected from Denmark during the same period, representing 91% of all new, bacteriologically verified cases of TB in Denmark in 1992. One of the prevalent clusters was traced to a group of immigrants from Greenland living in a small, defined geographical region in Denmark and to a group of Danish citizens either with known contact with these immigrants or, in other cases, with a record of previous travel or work in Greenland.

**Reporter Genes**   Genetic markers, or bioreporters, can be used to track specific microbial populations in the environment (Lindow 1995). A genetic marker is a genetic element that permits the detection of an unrelated biological function. Bioreporter genes are particularly useful because they provide a means of determining gene activity in samples with complex microbial communities (Burlage and Kuo 1994). They can detect microbial activities in natural samples even when there are complex interactions among microbial populations.

The *lacZ* gene, which encodes β-galactosidase, is a useful biomarker. The β-galactosidase enzyme cleaves the disaccharide lactose into glucose and galactose. When the synthetic compound 5-bromo-4-chloro-3-indolyl-β-D-galactoside (X-gal) is substituted, the β-galactosidase is able to cleave the compound, creating an insoluble blue pigment that is very

noticeable on most agar media. The versatility of the *lacZ* system makes it the most widely used reporter gene. It has been used as a reporter of recombinant *Pseudomonas* in studies to determine whether genetically engineered microorganisms will survive and disperse if released at an environmental site (Drahos et al. 1986). *Pseudomonas* strains that incorporate the *lacZY* genes are capable of cleaving the X-gal substrate to produce the characteristic blue color. This trait makes them distinguishable from the nonrecombinant *Pseudomonas* species that are indigenous to the site.

The *xylE* gene of the TOL plasmid, which contains genes for toluene and other low-molecular-weight aromatic hydrocarbon metabolism, has been cloned for use as a transcriptional fusion reporter gene. This gene encodes catechol 2,3-oxygenase (C 2,3 O), and a simple aerosol spray technique has been used to find recombinant colonies. Colonies that turn yellow in the presence of the catechol spray are expressing C 2,3 O and produce 2-hydroxymuconic semialdehyde (Zukowski et al. 1983). Ingram et al. (1989) used the *xylE* reporter gene for a quantitative description of promoters from *Streptomyces*. King et al. (1991) described a similar assay system using the 2,4-dichlorophenoxyacetate mono-oxygenase (*tfdA*) gene. The *tfdA* gene product converts phenoxyacetate to phenol, which then can be reacted with a dye to form a colored compound that can be analyzed spectrophotometrically. Lindgren et al. (1989) isolated the gene for ice nucleation (*inaZ*) and incorporated it into a transposon. This transposon was then used to mutagenize plant pathogenic bacterial strains, and the mutants were tested using a droplet freezing technique. Expression of the *inaZ* gene results in rapid freezing of the droplets at $-9°C$. Dilutions of the cell suspension can be tested in the same way, allowing a sensitivity that is reported to be far greater than that of the *lacZ* system.

The production of visible light (bioluminescence) by various organisms is another unusual trait. It has been studied in great detail in recent years, and its use as a reporter system has increased with genetic and physiological analysis of the *lux* genes, and with the availability of cloning vectors and other genetic constructions (Boivin et al. 1988) that facilitate their use.

Several bacterial species can produce light, including members of *Vibrio, Photobacterium, Alteromonas,* and *Xenorhabdus; Vibrio* has received the most attention. The first practical application of bacterial bioluminescence was in 1985 when Engebrecht et al. (1985) constructed fusions between *E. coli* promoters from the *lac* and *ara* operons and the *lux* genes of *Vibrio fischeri.* A mini-Mu-*lux* vector was used to facilitate these constructions. Induction of the *lac-lux* or *ara-lux* fusion resulted in a significant increase in bioluminescence. This report promoted light measurement as a convenient *in vivo* assay for gene expression.

The *lux* gene constructions have been used to investigate gene expression of plant pathogenic bacteria (Shaw and Kado 1986; Rogowsky et al. 1987). In this work, the induction of gene expression of bacterial virulence genes could be followed in plants by examining light production. Burlage et al. (1990) described a fusion between a promoter *(nah)* for the degradation of naphthalene in *Pseudomonas* and the *lux* genes. Using this plasmid construction, they were able to demonstrate gene expression on a continuous basis, revealing an unexpected pattern.

Environmental analysis using a bioluminescent reporter strain now appears to be a practical technique. King et al. (1990) used a *nah-lux* construction to demonstrate naphthalene degradation in soil slurries. Despite the quenching of bioluminescence that occurs in particulate and contaminated samples, this work was successful in detecting both the presence and bioavailability of specific contaminants in the complex slurry. Rattray et al. (1990) have also described the great sensitivity of this technique in their analysis of bioluminescent *E. coli* cells that were added to soil and liquid media. Their results indicate that bioluminescent bacteria can be detected using a nondestructive assay with a sensitivity matched only by hybridization analysis. These reports support the concept of using bioluminescence as an indicator of presence and activity of bacteria in environmental samples.

In addition to using the *lux* gene as a bioreporter, the green fluorescent protein (GFP) can be used as a biomarker (Chalfie et al. 1994; Chalfie 1995). GFP occurs naturally in the jellyfish *Aequorea victoria* and the sea pansy *Renilla reniformis.* It is not a luciferase but rather an accessory fluorescent protein that serves as the emitter for an associated luminescence system in coelenterates (Hastings 1995). It requires no substrate and can be visualized by its fluorescence in live and dead cells. The protein itself is fluorescent; it is encoded by the biomarker gene and is detected when that gene is expressed. GFP can be expressed in bacterial cells as well as in those of other microorganisms, making it applicable for tracking specific genetically modified microorganisms and following gene expression in those cells (Chalfie et al. 1994). The use of GFP is particularly advantageous because it does not require cofactors for expression so that it can be easily detected with high sensitivity; as a fusion tag, it can be used to follow proteins so that their location and expression can be readily detected (Gerdes and Kaether 1996).

One of the applications of GFP that has been explored is to monitor the survival of genetically engineered bacteria in aquatic environments (Leff and Leff 1996). GFP allows the evaluation of survival of genetically engineered microorganisms by plating to detect viable cells and by direct microscopic observation to detect cells that have lost culturability. A study of *E. coli* survival in stream water showed that GFP did not adversely affect the fitness of the bacterial strain and that *E. coli* survived at higher densities than would have been detected by viable counting (Leff and Leff 1996). Besides its use in tracking genetically engineered microorganisms, GFP has various other applications, including studying host-pathogen interactions (Valdivia et al. 1996) and monitoring the movement of bacterial strains in groundwater (Burlage et al. 1996).

## DETERMINATION OF MICROBIAL NUMBERS

In the case of a pure bacterial culture, the question "How many microorganisms are there?" is relatively simple to answer. When dealing with the mixed communities of environmental samples, however, the problem becomes exceedingly complex and, in most cases, defies a simple and absolute answer. Quantification is possible, but the numbers obtained need to be qualified by the technique used; enumeration techniques need to be chosen with care to ensure that results are relevant to the question being asked.

Microorganisms are extremely diverse, so the methods used to enumerate one group of microorganisms may be inappropriate for another group. The methods used for enumerating viruses (Primrose et al. 1982; Shuval and Katznelson 1972), bacteria (Herbert 1982; Peele and Colwell 1981), fungi (Parkinson 1982), algae (Round 1982), and protozoa (Finlay 1982) are quite different. Special techniques must be used for enumerating specific physiological groups, such as psychrophilic bacteria or obligately anaerobic bacteria (Shapton and Board 1971). Enumeration of such defined groups requires special sampling and processing procedures. Precise differential criteria must be used for enumerating an individual microbial species such as *Escherichia coli,* which is often used as an indicator of sewage contamination.

The enumeration process must begin with a definition of which microorganisms are to be enumerated; all microorganisms, or only certain groups? Are the numbers of microorganisms to be converted to estimates of biomass? What are the characteristics of the habitat being examined? No universal method can be applied to all microorganisms and all habitats; the diversity of microorganisms and their habitats requires the use of a variety of methodological approaches.

The enumeration process can be broken down into three distinct phases: sampling, sample processing, and the actual counting procedure. All phases of the process must be considered when interpreting the results.

Two principal approaches are used for enumerating microorganisms: direct observation (or direct count) procedures and indirect (or viable count) procedures. Occasionally, numbers are also calculated from procedures that measure specific biochemical constituents of microorganisms, though it should be recognized that such procedures actually measure biomass. Each approach has its advantages and limitations (Atlas 1982).

## Direct Count Procedures

**Microscopic Count Methods** Microorganisms can be counted by direct microscopic observations (Jones and Mollison 1948; Frederick 1965; Gray 1967; Gray et al. 1968; Harris et al. 1972; Daley and Hobbie 1975; Byrd and Colwell 1992). Direct count procedures yield the highest estimates of numbers of microorganisms and are occasionally used for the indirect calculation of biomass. There are, however, several major drawbacks to direct observational methods, including the inability to distinguish living from dead microorganisms, the underestimation of microorganisms in samples containing high amounts of background debris, and the inability to perform further studies on the observed microorganisms.

For relatively large microorganisms, such as protozoa, algae, and fungi, direct counts can be conveniently accomplished using a counting chamber (Finlay et al. 1979). A variety of counting chambers that hold specified volumes, such as a hemocytometer or Petroff-Hauser chamber, can be used for counting cells (Parkinson et al. 1971).

A modified agar film technique of Jones and Mollison (1948) is often used for direct observation and enumeration of fungi (Skinner et al. 1952; Thomas et al. 1965; Parkinson 1973). In this technique, the sample is mixed with agar and pipetted onto glass slides, where it forms a thin film. The dried agar film can be stained with phenolic aniline blue, and the slides can then be viewed. The length of mycelia can be estimated by counting intersections with a superimposed grid.

Alternatively, the microscope image can be projected onto a screen and traced. The length can be determined by running a distance-measuring device (map measure) along the traced lines (Table 7.4). If the average width of the mycelial filaments is also measured, the fungal biomass can be calculated (Table 7.5). A problem with this technique is that unless adequate dispersion is achieved, hyphae remain hidden among the soil particles and can be seen only when soil particles are broken (Skinner et al. 1952). This problem can be overcome by establishing the optimum grinding time and using a modern high-speed homogenizer.

The agar film technique for enumeration of fungi can be combined with fluorescence microscopy using fluorescein diacetate as the stain to estimate the biomass of living fungi (Babuik and Paul 1970; Soderstrom 1977). Only metabolically active cells are stained in this procedure because fluorescence occurs only after enzymatic cleavage of the stain molecule; thus, use of fluorescein diacetate stain in conjunction with a vital stain that does not distinguish living from dead fungal hyphae permits the estimation of both living and total fungal biomass. A problem with this procedure is the high background fluorescence that occurs because esterases are released and react with the dye.

Epifluorescence microscopy with stains such as acridine orange (AO), 4´,6-diamidino-2-phenylindole (DAPI), and fluorescein isothiocyanate (FITC) are widely used for direct counting of bacteria (Strugger 1948; Babuik and Paul 1970; Zimmerman and Meyer-Reil 1974; Daley and Hobbie 1975; Russell et al. 1975; Daley 1979; Geesey and Costerton 1979; Coleman 1980; Porter and Feig 1980; Kepner and Pratt

**Table 7.4**
Length of fungal mycelium in tundra soils

| Location | Sites | Mean mycelium length (m/g oven-dry soil) |
|---|---|---|
| Devon Island, Canada | Mesic meadow | 1005 |
| | Raised beach | 199 |
| Moor House, United Kingdom | Blanket bog | 4968 |
| | *Juncus* moor | 1667 |
| | Limestone grass | 826 |
| Signy Island, Antarctica | Hut bank | 6328 |
| | Mountain moss | 2783 |
| | Grassland | 288 |
| | Old moraine | 84 |
| | New moraine | 4 |
| | Marble knolls | 144 |
| | Marble schist soils | 44 |
| Hardangervidda, Norway | Wet meadow | 5000 |
| | Dry meadow | 1000 |
| | Birch wood | 7000 |
| Ireland | Blanket bog | 995 |
| Sweden | Mire | 3260 |
| United Kingdom | Wood | 341 |
| Mt. Allen, Canada | 1900 m elevation | 580 |
| | 2500 m elevation | 801 |
| | 2800 m elevation | 50 |

Source: Dowding and Widden 1974.

**Table 7.5**
Length and biomass of fungal mycelium in soil

| Sample | Length of hyphae (m/g) | Fungal biomass (g/m$^2$) |
|---|---|---|
| Soil 1 | 174 | 0.31 |
| Soil 2 | 619 | 2.69 |
| Soil 3 | 457 | 1.39 |
| Soil 4 | 1602 | 7.66 |

Source: O. K. Miller, Virginia Polytechnic Institute, unpublished data.

**Table 7.6**
Comparison of polycarbonate
and cellulose nitrate filters for direct counts

| | Count (#/mL) | |
|---|---|---|
| Site | Cellulose nitrate (0.2 µm) | Polycarbonate (0.2 µm) |
| Estuary | $8.6 \times 10^5$ | $1.7 \times 10^6$ |
| Reservoir | $4.0 \times 10^5$ | $7.2 \times 10^5$ |
| Pond | $1.7 \times 10^6$ | $4.0 \times 10^6$ |

Source: Hobbie et al. 1977.

1994). Porter and Feig (1980) adapted DAPI for counting aquatic microorganisms and found it to work better than acridine orange for eutrophic and particle-rich water samples. Clays, colloids, and detritus of such samples produce a red-orange background, which impairs acridine-orange counting. Acridine orange and DAPI are comparably efficient in enumerating total organisms in aquatic samples. Porter and Feig (1980) reported that DAPI-stained slide counts remained constant for up to 24 weeks when the stained slides were stored at 4°C in the dark, but that acridine-orange-stained slides yielded decreased counts after storage for a week under the same conditions.

Another useful fluorochrome is Hoechst 33258 (bisbenzimide). Bisbenzimide binds to adenine and thymine-rich regions of the DNA, increasing in fluorescence after binding (Latt and Statten 1976). Hoechst 33258 has been recommended for enumeration of bacteria on surfaces, especially if the surface tends to bind acridine orange (Paul 1982). An advantage of the bisbenzimide stain is that detergent solutions, laboratory salts, or biological materials associated with DNA do not affect it. Fluorescent staining to detect microorganisms in environmental samples by direct microscopy has several applications in microbial ecology.

Use of low-fluorescing immersion oil is important to minimize background autofluorescence. Polycarbonate filters are superior to cellulose filters for direct counting of bacteria because they have uniform pore size and a flat surface that retains all the bacteria on top of the filter (Hobbie et al. 1977) (Table 7.6). The filters can be dyed to create a dark background against

which fluorescing microorganisms can be counted (Jones and Simon 1975). When acridine orange is used as a stain, bacteria and other microorganisms fluoresce orange and green. The green or orange color correlates with the physiological state of the microorganism. Green fluorescence indicates a higher concentration of DNA whereas orange-red fluorescence indicates cells richer in RNA and protein; however, attempts to separate living from dead microorganisms by the color of fluorescence are often misleading and unsatisfactory. Use of DAPI, which stains the DNA of bacterial cells and produces an intense blue fluorescence, has proved superior to use of acridine orange for visualizing small bacterial cells (Coleman 1980).

Counts obtained by direct epifluorescence microscopy are typically two orders of magnitude higher than counts obtained by cultural techniques (Table 7.7). Many small and unusually shaped bacteria are observable and countable with epifluorescence microscopy. These forms are usually impossible to cultivate on laboratory media, however, and it is not clear whether these are "degenerate" nonviable representatives of known bacteria or forms with yet-unknown physiological requirements. In some cases, positive correlation between direct fluorescence microscopic counts and viable plate counts is high (Figure 7.11); in other cases, correlation is low (Table 7.8 on page 240). The differences between direct and plate counts may simply reflect the selectivity of the media and incubation conditions used, the proportion of living and dead or injured bacteria, and the particular species in the sample.

**Table 7.7**
Comparison of direct epifluorescent counts and viable plate counts (number per gram)

| Sample | Soil | | Marine water | |
|---|---|---|---|---|
| | Direct count | Viable count | Direct count | Viable count |
| A | $5.0 \times 10^8$ | $3.1 \times 10^7$ | $2.2 \times 10^3$ | $1.3 \times 10^1$ |
| B | $1.1 \times 10^9$ | $6.2 \times 10^7$ | $8.2 \times 10^4$ | $7.6 \times 10^2$ |
| C | $2.0 \times 10^9$ | $1.7 \times 10^8$ | $1.3 \times 10^6$ | $2.1 \times 10^4$ |

Source: Atlas, unpublished data.

The value of the direct count approach to enumeration using epifluorescence microscopy is that it is applicable to a variety of habitats without the bias inherent in viable plate count procedures. It allows the estimation of numbers of microorganisms in marine, freshwater, and soil habitats despite the great differences in population sizes and physiological types that occur in these various habitats. Direct counts are often directly proportional to biomass and thus can be used to estimate microbial biomass. Image analysis permits converting direct microscopic counts to biomass estimates accurately.

Additionally, if the numbers of dividing cells are counted, it is possible to estimate *in situ* growth rates (Hagstrom et al. 1979). The frequency of dividing cells has been shown to correlate with other measures of microbial growth such as rates of RNA synthesis measured by incorporation of labeled adenine (Christian et al. 1982). This frequency of dividing cells (FDC) method assumes that the time between the initiation of cell constriction and cell separation is constant—an assumption that is not always valid (Staley and Konopka 1985). It is also difficult to recognize dividing cells using light microscopic methods.

The numbers of specific types of microorganisms can be estimated using fluorescent antibody techniques (Hill and Gray 1967; Schmidt 1973; Strayer and Tiedje 1978; Fliermans et al. 1979; Bohlool and Schmidt 1980). The fluorescent antibody technique is extremely specific for an individual microbial species and permits autecological studies, that is, studies of

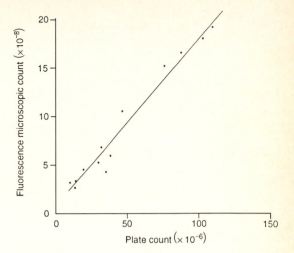

**Figure 7.11**
Correlation between direct microbial counts by fluorescence microscopy and viable plate counts for soil samples. There is a high correlation coefficient (*r*) of 0.97 for the linear regression line described by the equation $y = 900.2 + 15.7 (x - 49.5)$. (Source: Trolldenier 1973. Reprinted by permission of Swedish National Research Council.)

individual microorganisms in their natural environments (Bohlool and Schmidt 1973) (Table 7.9 on page 241). In the FITC method, antibodies are conjugated with a fluorochrome, such as fluorescein isothiocyanate. Problems with the fluorescent antibody technique include nonspecific fluorescence of the background in some samples, the high degree of specificity of the antigen-antibody reaction that may preclude staining of even different strains of the same species, and possible reactivity between different organisms. Fluorescent antibody techniques have been applied to studies on selected microbial species in their natural habitats, including ecologically important organisms (Eren and Pramer 1966); monoclonal antibodies have been used to specifically detect methanogens in environmental samples (Conway de Macario et al. 1981, 1982), and such specific fluorescent dyes are applicable to the enumeration of many other specific populations.

Direct immunofluorescence has been used to detect and enumerate microorganisms in environmental samples (Wright 1992; Kepner and Pratt 1994),

**Table 7.8**
Counts of bacteria (numbers/mL)

| Location | Season/Year | Direct count | Viable count 4°C | Viable count 20°C |
|---|---|---|---|---|
| Beaufort Sea | | | | |
| Ice | Winter 1976 | $9.9 \times 10^4$ | $6.6 \times 10^1$ | $4.5 \times 10^1$ |
| Water | Summer 1975 | $8.2 \times 10^5$ | $9.6 \times 10^3$ | $7.3 \times 10^3$ |
| | Winter 1976 | $1.8 \times 10^5$ | $6.1 \times 10^2$ | $1.1 \times 10^1$ |
| | Summer 1976 | $5.2 \times 10^5$ | $5.0 \times 10^4$ | $2.7 \times 10^4$ |
| NW Gulf of Alaska | | | | |
| Water | Summer 1975 | $3.0 \times 10^5$ | $1.0 \times 10^2$ | $5.2 \times 10^2$ |
| NE Gulf of Alaska | | | | |
| Water | Winter 1976 | $1.4 \times 10^5$ | $1.3 \times 10^2$ | $2.4 \times 10^2$ |

Source: Kaneko et al. 1978.

including in water (Grimes and Colwell 1983), on buried slides, on root surfaces, in nodules, and in soil (Bohlool and Schmidt 1980; Bohlool 1987). This method has also been used to detect viable but noncultrable bacteria (Xu et al. 1982) and hence may be useful for detecting microorganisms in aquatic and marine ecosystems. Distribution of *Vibrio cholerae* in the natural environment of a cholera-endemic region has been studied using immunofluorescence and has been detected in environmental samples when cultural methods were ineffective (Brayton and Colwell 1987). Detection of rhizobia by enzyme-linked immunosorbent assays (ELISA) in peat and in soil has been reported (Nambair and Anjaiah 1985). Fluorescent ELISA results compare with those from the antibiotic-resistance technique when soil populations exceed 104 cells per milliliter (Renwick and Jones 1985). Rhizobial strains in root nodule material can also be identified by ELISA (Wright et al. 1986).

Fluorescent gene probes can also be used for counting specific microbial populations (Amann et al. 1995; Pace 1996; Schramm et al. 1996; Ramsing et al. 1996). Probes for specific diagnostic gene sequences allow detection of microbial species or populations with identical genes. Targeting ribosomal RNAs permit single cell detection. Multiple populations can be counted in the same sample by using several gene probes, each conjugated with a fluorescent dye of a different color. This is especially useful when employed in scanning confocal laser microscopy as it allows the visualization of the relative positions of diverse populations—even within complex communities such as biofilms. The sensitivity of fluorescent gene probe detection can be greatly enhanced by coupling with digital image analysis (Ramsing et al. 1996) and by using confocal laser microscopy (Schramm et al. 1996). These analyses are useful for *in situ* studies on gene structure-function relationships (Harmsen et al. 1996).

Fluorescence-labeled gene probes have been used simultaneously with antibodies for the *in situ* identification of bacteria in mixed cultures, as well as in the rhizosphere of inoculated plants (Aßmus et al. 1997). Counterstaining with DAPI and using scanning confocal laser microscopy or epifluorescence microscopy with a charge-coupled device (CCD) camera permits detection and exact localization of individual cells. A strain-specific monoclonal antibody has been used to detect a specific strain of *Azospirillum brasilense* while fluorescent gene probes were used for other bacteria colonizing the rhizosphere. As an example of

**Table 7.9**
Quantification of *Rhizobium japonicum,* USDA 110, in the rhizosphere of soybean plants grown in the field

| Sample (weeks after planting) | Number *R. japonicum*/g soil* | |
| --- | --- | --- |
| | Uninoculated | Inoculated |
| 2 | $4.1 \times 10^3$ | $6.2 \times 10^6$ |
| 3 | $4.9 \times 10^3$ | $1.9 \times 10^6$ |
| 4 | $4.9 \times 10^3$ | $3.6 \times 10^7$ |
| 5 | NT | $6.4 \times 10^5$ |
| 6 | NT | $1.7 \times 10^6$ |

(NT = not tested)

* = Based on counts of 20 microscopic fields per sample.

Source: Bohlool and Schmidt 1973.

the application of this methodology, in a coinoculation experiment with *A. brasilense* strains Sp7 and Wa3, it was demonstrated by *in situ* identification and quantitative chemoluminescence ELISA that strain Sp7 outcompeted strain Wa3. The combined application of fluorescently labeled antibodies and oligonucleotides appears to be a powerful tool that is generally applicable for monitoring specific bacterial strains, within the background of the same species, in relation to the total microbiota.

Epifluorescence microscopy can be converted to automatic data analysis to relieve the tedium involved in examining a large number of samples. As early as 1952, image analysis was used to count microscopic coal particles (Walton 1952). Pettipher and Rodrigues (1982) applied image analysis to epifluorescence microscopy by counting acridine-orange-stained bacteria in milk. Sieracki et al. (1985) used DAPI stain to detect and enumerate planktonic bacteria. They found that counts done by standard visual analysis and by image analysis gave statistically equal results.

Image analysis can be a powerful technique, but some constraints apply. The results of image analysis will be only as good as the image provided. Staining of each organism must be strong, with little or no background or extraneous fluorescence. This method

has limited application to soil or sediment samples without extreme care to remove particulates (Van Wambeke 1988). Another constraint is that a highly sensitive camera is necessary to detect low levels of light emitted from epifluorescent-stained samples. There is also some question as to the ability of the camera to differentiate between debris and cells when fluorescent counts are recorded. Overall, the expense of the system is compensated for by the reduction in time needed to analyze individual samples and by the increased productivity in analysis.

Fluorescent staining methods can also be used in combination with other procedures to determine numbers of living organisms. By combining the acridine orange direct counting (AODC) method with INT (2-[*p*-iodophenyl]-3[*p*-nitrophenyl]-5-phenyl tetrazolium chloride) staining, for example, it is possible to determine both total numbers of microorganisms and the numbers of microorganisms carrying out respiration (Zimmerman et al. 1978). The method is based on the fact that electron transport systems in respiring microorganisms reduce INT to INT-formazan, so that respiring bacteria accumulate intracellular dark red spots. When applied to Baltic Sea water samples, the method showed 6–12% of the bacteria to be active; in freshwater samples, 5–36% of the bacteria were active (Zimmerman et al. 1978). This method can be difficult to interpret, depending on the size of the bacterial cells and INT grains that develop.

Numbers of actively growing bacteria can also be determined by incubation with nalidixic acid, an antibiotic that inhibits cell division (Kogure et al. 1979). This method is referred to as a direct viability count (DVC). Microscopic observation after fluorescent staining reveals elongated cells (actively growing microbes) and cells of normal size and shape (dormant or dead microbes). The DVC method exploits the finding of Goss et al. (1965) that nalidixic acid is an inhibitor of DNA synthesis, preventing cell division in gram-negative bacteria by suppressing DNA replication. Subsequently, cross-wall formation is obstructed because of lack of replication, so the cells elongate instead of dividing. Kogure and associates (1979) used yeast extract as a nutrient source, and incubation was for 6 hours. This allowed detection of viable bacteria in seawater samples. Incubation of seawater samples beyond 12 hours often allows either growth of gram-negative, nalidixic acid–resistant bacteria (Quinn 1984) or a possible inactivation of nalidixic acid by high salt concentrations. Therefore, it is impossible to quantitate, by extended incubation, slow-metabolizing bacteria in samples, and these may go unnoticed in the 6 hours of incubation usually employed in the DVC procedure.

One can count dormant cells—that is, cells physiologically responsive but not dividing—by DVC, technically a straightforward procedure. The disadvantage of the procedure is the subjective nature of what constitutes an elongated cell. Roszak and Colwell (1987a, 1987b) incorporated the DVC procedure and found that about 90% of those cells counted as responsive in the DVC were metabolically active by microautoradiography.

Obviously, there are various methods to detect viability of bacteria in the environment. Which method is the most accurate has been the subject of debate for many years. Each method measures a different property of the cell, and this should be considered in the method's value. If possible, more than one method should be used to determine viability in environmental samples. However, what should be done in environmental experiments and what actually can be done are often two different things. Methodology for determination of viability is important because many microorganisms that can no longer be cultured by viable plating techniques are now known to remain viable in nature. Nonculturable yet viable microorganisms may regenerate and still cause disease (Roszak and Colwell 1987a).

Another technique for determining bacterial numbers and the spectrum of actively metabolizing cells is autoradiography combined with direct microscopic observation (Brock and Brock 1968; Waid et al. 1973; Ramsay 1974; Fliermans and Schmidt 1975; Hoppe 1976; Faust and Correll 1977; Meyer-Reil 1978). In this method, bacteria incubated with a radiolabeled substrate, such as tritiated glucose, are subsequently collected on a bacteriological filter, which is placed on a glass slide and coated with a photographic emulsion. The actively metabolizing bacteria are radioactive and

can be identified by the dark silver grains surrounding the cell. Applying this method to nearshore water samples indicates that 2.3–56.2% of the total bacteria are metabolically active (Meyer-Reil 1978) (Table 7.10).

Electron microscopy instead of light microscopy can be used for direct counting of microorganisms (Gray 1967; Nikitin 1973; Todd et al. 1973; Bowden 1977; Larsson et al. 1978). Results of enumerations with scanning electron microscopy are comparable to those obtained by epifluorescent microscopy (Bowden 1977) (Table 7.11 on page 244). Caution must be observed in the use of electron microscopic techniques because of the possibility of producing artifacts when specimens are metal-coated to increase contrast for observation and when specimens are placed under high vacuum. As magnification increases, many viewing fields may have to be scanned before a microorganism is observed; therefore, electron microscopic observation has been applied mainly to samples with naturally dense or artificially enriched microbial communities.

**Particle Count Methods** A particle counter, such as a Coulter counter, can also be used to estimate numbers of microorganisms directly (Kubitschek 1969). The Coulter counter electronically measures the number of particles within a fixed size range. Separate estimates of bacteria and protozoa can be obtained by setting appropriate size ranges. The problem with Coulter counter analysis is that small nonliving particles are counted together with microorganisms, which has limited the method's usefulness. However, recent advances in flow cytometry permit the specific recognition of microorganisms in complex samples, and increased usage of cell sorters in the enumeration of microorganisms is expected (Davey and Kell 1996). Wallner et al. (1995), for example, used a combination of flow cytometry and rRNA-targeted fluorescent gene probes to examine the numbers and activities of specific bacterial populations in activated sludge sewage treatment.

### Viable Count Procedures

There are two basic approaches to viable count procedures: (1) the plate count technique and (2) the most

**Table 7.10**
Microbiological variables measured in water samples taken from above sandy
sediments at beaches of the Kiel Fjord and the Kiel Bight (4 to 13 July 1977)

| Station* | Colony-forming units/mL $\times 10^{-3}$ (plate counts) | Total no. of bacteria/mL $\times 10^{-5}$ (direct counts) | Total biomass (mg/mL $\times 10^{-5}$) | Number of active bacteria/mL $\times 10^{-5}$ (autoradiography) | Percent of active bacteria | Actual uptake rate of glucose (g/mL per hr $\times 10^{-3}$) |
|---|---|---|---|---|---|---|
| A  | 261.0 | 41.7 | 50.2 | 19.8 | 47.5 | 18.9 |
| A´ | 188.0 | 57.8 | 65.4 | 32.5 | 56.2 | 23.5 |
| B  | 81.4  | 26.5 | 32.1 | 11.0 | 41.5 | 11.9 |
| B´ | 187.0 | 64.2 | 62.4 | 29.9 | 46.6 | 10.3 |
| C  | 433.0 | 68.8 | 74.2 | 3.1  | 4.5  | 2.6  |
| C´ | 98.2  | 67.2 | 70.9 | 23.8 | 35.4 | 6.6  |
| D  | 3.4   | 52.2 | 58.0 | 1.2  | 2.3  | 1.2  |
| D´ | 3.1   | 51.4 | 40.9 | 6.1  | 11.9 | 7.8  |
| E  | 5.5   | 39.4 | 43.6 | 16.6 | 42.1 | 6.9  |
| E´ | 2.9   | 65.8 | 60.1 | 19.2 | 29.2 | 4.8  |
| F  | 7.4   | 56.1 | 60.8 | 28.3 | 50.5 | 3.8  |
| F´ | 1.7   | 50.0 | 44.7 | 3.9  | 7.8  | 5.2  |

*A to F mark stations at the west side; A´ to F´ are corresponding stations at the east side; Stations A/A´ are located at the inner part, B/B´ at the center part, and C/C´ at the outer part of the Kiel Fjord; Stations D/D´, E/E´, and F/F´ are located at the Kiel Bight.

Source: Meyer-Reil 1978.

probable number (MPN) technique. All viable count procedures require separation of microorganisms into individual reproductive units. All viable count procedures are selective for certain microorganisms; the degree of selectivity varies with the particular viable count procedure. This selectivity is a disadvantage when trying to estimate the total viable microbial biomass within an ecosystem, but it permits the estimation of numbers of particular types of microorganisms. The methods used for the enumeration of microorganisms by viable count procedures must recover live microorganisms from environmental samples, maintain the viability of those microbial populations to be enumerated, and permit their growth in the laboratory so that they can be detected and their numbers quantified. Numerous methodologies are used for the cultivation of diverse microorganisms (Grigorova and Norris 1990); there are thousands of different media formulations for the cultivation of

different bacterial, archaeal, fungal, algal, and protozoan species (Atlas 1995, 1997).

**Plate Count and Related Methods: Selective and Differential Viable Culture Methods**   The agar plate count method has been widely used for the enumeration of viable microorganisms, especially bacteria, but it has been severely criticized (Postgate 1969; Buck 1979). The problems lie in the misuse of the method and the misinterpretation of the results. All too often users fail to recognize that this technique can never be used to achieve "total counts."

Plate count procedures employ various media and incubation conditions. Agar is most often used as the solidifying agent because most bacteria lack the enzymes necessary for depolymerizing agar. Dilutions of samples can be spread on the top of the agar (surface spread method), or the sample suspension can be mixed with the agar just before the plates are poured

**Table 7.11**

Comparison of direct count enumerations of bacterial populations by epifluorescence and scanning electron microscopy (EM) for estuary water samples collected on various types of filters

| | Direct count (number per mL) | | |
|---|---|---|---|
| | | Epifluorescence | |
| Sample | Scanning EM 0.2 µm Polycarbonate | 0.2 µm Polycarbonate | 0.2 µm Cellulose nitrate |
| Estuary 1 | $4.34 \times 10^6$ | $4.81 \times 10^6$ | $2.00 \times 10^6$ |
| Estuary 2 | $3.30 \times 10^6$ | $2.92 \times 10^6$ | $0.78 \times 10^6$ |

Source: Bowden 1977.

(pour plate method). One must consider whether the microorganisms can survive the plating procedure. Some microbes are killed upon exposure to air in the surface spread method; others cannot tolerate the temperature needed to maintain melted agar in the pour plate method. Because the agar used for making media for bacteriological enumeration may contain organic contaminants, it is sometimes replaced with an alternative solidifying agent. When specific nutritional groups of microorganisms are to be enumerated, silica gel may be used for solidification. Because silica gel plates are more difficult to prepare than agar plates, they are used only when unavoidable.

The main considerations for doing plate count procedures are the composition of the medium, the incubation conditions, and the period of incubation. Media for the enumeration of heterotrophs not capable of nitrogen fixation must contain usable sources of carbon, nitrogen, and phosphorus and required cations and anions, such as iron, magnesium, sodium, calcium, chloride, and sulfate. It is not usually clear why a particular medium yields the highest numbers of microorganisms from a particular ecosystem. Clearly, the media must meet nutritional requirements, including growth factors. General-purpose media have nutrient concentrations much higher than those found in the natural ecosystem being studied. Concentrations of nutrients in many of these media

used for total enumerations are high enough to be toxic to at least some microorganisms.

The roll-tube method, used for enumeration of obligate anaerobes, is an extension of the pour plate method (Hungate 1969; Hungate and Macy 1973). The tubes are incubated under specified conditions for a period to allow the bacteria to multiply and form macroscopic colonies, after which the colonies are counted. It is assumed that each colony originated from a single bacterial cell. For this assumption to be valid, the bacteria must be widely dispersed in or on the agar. Tubes with too many colonies cannot be counted accurately because one colony may represent more than one original bacterium. Tubes with too few colonies also must be discarded from the counting procedure for statistical reasons.

The real advantage of viable enumeration procedures is that conditions can be adjusted so that only members of a defined group are enumerated. Plate count media may be designed to be selective or differential. Selective plate count procedures are designed to favor the growth of the desired group of microorganisms. Growth of other groups is precluded by media composition and/or incubation conditions. Differential media do not preclude the growth of other microorganisms but permit detection of the desired group by some distinguishing characteristic.

Media can be designed for the selective enumeration of fungi. The viable plate count technique, though, is generally not the method of choice for enumerating fungi, because this technique favors enumeration of nonfilamentous fungi and spores (Menzies 1965). Plate counts are, however, suitable for enumeration of yeasts. To prevent overgrowth of fungal colonies by bacteria, which are likely to be more numerous than fungi in the sample, bacterial inhibitors are added to the media. The dye rose bengal and the antibiotics streptomycin and neomycin are often added as bacterial inhibitors. A simple technique for suppressing bacteria involves lowering of the pH of the medium to 4.5–5.5. Most fungi are unaffected by this pH, while most bacteria are suppressed.

Media designed to inhibit the growth of one group of organisms while permitting growth of another group are known as selective media. For example,

Sabouraud dextrose agar is used to enumerate fungi based on its low pH and carbohydrate source of carbon. Incorporation of penicillin or methylene blue, which inhibit gram-positive organisms, into a medium is often used to select for gram-negative bacteria. Antibiotic-resistant microorganisms can be enumerated on media with added antibiotics.

Differential media may be designed in a variety of ways. Reagents may be incorporated into the media that permit immediate visual differentiation of the desired bacteria, or reagents may be added after incubation to detect the desired bacteria. The key advantage of differential media is that the procedure permits one to distinguish between the microorganisms being enumerated and others present in the sample.

Eosin methylene blue (EMB) agar and MacConkey's agar are media widely used to determine water quality. These media are both selective and differential. They select for the growth of gram-negative bacteria by incorporating an inhibitor of gram-positive bacteria. They differentiate bacteria capable of utilizing lactose by formation of characteristically colored colonies. On EMB agar, coliform bacteria, which are gram-negative and utilize lactose, form a characteristic colony with a green metallic sheen. Estimates of coliform counts determined in this manner are often used as an indicator of water quality and for quality control in the food industry.

**Colony Hybridization**  Colony hybridization is an application of nucleic acid hybridization that is combined with conventional environmental microbiological sampling and viable plating procedures. Following initial growth, bacterial colonies or phage plaques are transferred from the surfaces of the cultivation media to hybridization filters. The colonies or phage-containing plaques are then lysed by alkaline or enzymatic treatment, after which hybridization is conducted. These methods depend on the ability of the target microorganisms to grow on the primary isolation medium and not to be totally overgrown by nontarget populations. Growth on the isolation medium increases the number of copies of the target gene to a level detectable by a gene probe.

The original protocol developed by Grunstein and Hogness (1975) was shown to be suitable for high-density plate screening for pure cultures (Hanahan and Meselson 1980). In cultures containing both nontarget *E. coli* and target *Pseudomonas putida,* one *P. putida* colony containing a toluene (TOL)-catabolic plasmid in a background of approximately 1 million *E. coli* colonies was detected using a whole TOL plasmid probe (Sayler et al. 1985). In general for this type of environmental assay, the organism of interest must be relatively abundant in the population so that at least one positive colony on an agar plate of 100 to 1000 colonies can be found. Additional sensitivity can be achieved by plating the isolated bacteria onto selective agar before colony hybridization.

In the colony hybridization procedure, bacterial cells growing on a viable culture medium are transferred to a suitable solid support, such as a nitrocellulose filter, and lysed, releasing denatured DNA, which adsorbs to the filter (Figure 7.12 on page 248). The filter membrane with the attached DNA is incubated with a gene probe. The gene probe is prepared by isolating a segment of genetic information and labeling it with either $^{32}P$ or an adduct such as biotin. Hybridization occurs if the base sequence of the lysed cells matches the base sequence of the gene probe and if the formation of the hybrid can be detected by autoradiography for $^{32}P$-labeled probes and by enzymatic development for biotin-labeled probes. In this manner, bacteria with specific genetic properties can be specifically detected. When specific genotypes are in relatively low numbers as compared to other populations, DNA-DNA hybridization techniques should prove particularly useful for the detection of specific populations in environmental samples.

Gene probes can be hybridized with primary isolates from environmental samples (Echeverria et al. 1982; Fitts et al. 1983; Hill et al. 1983a, 1983b; Miliotis et al. 1989) or with secondary cultivation of already described strains (Datta et al. 1988; Falkenstein et al. 1988; Nortermans et al. 1989). The rationales for direct colony hybridization on primary cultivation include (1) avoiding a cultivation bias encountered by subsequent cultivation on selective media, which may underestimate total abundance of a given genotype;

## Detecting Nonculturable Bacteria

Most microorganisms growing in nature have yet to be cultured in the laboratory (Pace 1996). In fact, less than 1% of the microorganisms in natural water and soil samples are cultured in viable count procedures. Also, tens of thousands of microbial species that live as symbionts in plants and animals have yet to be cultured. Even though they are not as yet culturable, and hence have not been characterized by classical microbiological procedures, various techniques are currently employed to study their biodiversity and the ecological distribution. These methods include direct microscopic investigations and a variety of molecular methods, including the use of the polymerase chain reaction to amplify diagnostic gene sequences and the use of analyses of 16S rRNA molecules to identify specific bacteria and archaea.

Instead of isolating microorganisms from their natural environments and culturing them in the laboratory, as discussed elsewhere in this chapter, it is possible to perform direct microscopic examinations on samples collected from nature (Atlas 1982; Bohlool and Schmidt 1980; Byrd and Colwell 1992; Hobbie et al. 1977; Paul 1982; Porter and Feig 1980). Various stains, such as acridine orange and DAPI, permit the enumeration of all microorganisms in a sample. Direct microscopic studies using such stains reveal that culture methods recover less than 1% of the total microorganisms in water and soil samples. Stated another way, over 99% of the microbial cells in soil and water that are observed by direct microscopic observations are nonculturable by current methods.

The observation of so many bacteria and archaea in environmental samples that were not being detected by viable count procedures led to the obvious question of whether these microorganisms were alive or dead. Early studies on soil and water samples using the acridine orange direct counting (AODC) procedure revealed that some cells fluoresce with a green color and others appear orange. This led to an erroneous conclusion that the orange cells were dead and the green cells were alive. The color being observed reflected the physiological state of the cell and not whether it was alive or dead. Fluorescence of acridine-orange-stained cells depends on the ratio of DNA to protein in the cell, so actively reproducing cells tend to appear green and those growing more slowly or not reproducing at the time of staining usually appear orange, even though they may be alive.

Methods were soon developed to distinguish dead from living cells by coupling the direct counting procedures with reagents that reveal metabolic activity (Nybroe 1995). For example, using INT, which deposits red dye in cells that have active dehydrogenases, it is possible to determine which of the observed cells are metabolically active (Zimmerman et al. 1978). A similar respiration assay has been developed based on the reduction of 5-cyano-2,3-ditolyl tetrazolium chloride (CTC) (Nybroe 1995). Membrane-potential-sensitive fluorochromes can distinguish between metabolically active, injured (dying), and dead cells (Lloyd and Hayes 1995). It is also possible to add cell division inhibitors, such as nalidixic acid, to environmental samples; actively growing cells appear elongated after such treatments (Kogure et al. 1979). Using such methods, it appears that most of the cells observed by direct microscopy are alive. Some of these cells may be "injured" and dying. We do not always know the cause of death.

It is also possible that many of the cells observed by direct microscopy have entered into a nonculturable state (Roszak and Colwell 1987a, 1987b). When Rita Colwell first introduced the concept of viable nonculturable cells, it was met with some skepticism. However, she and others have been able to show that some bacteria that cannot be recovered from soils and waters can be observed to be carrying out active metabolism in those samples, and some also retain the ability to cause infections in animals. These experiments clearly showed that viable nonculturable microorganisms exist in nature and that various bacteria, such as *Legionella pneumophila, Salmonella enteritidis, Vibrio cholerae,* and *V. vulnificus* regularly form viable nonculturable cells in nature. Thus direct observational methods are important for the study of microbial ecology and microbial diversity.

Molecular analyses can also be used to study nonculturable microorganisms in nature (Sayler and Layton 1990). Numerous gene probes for diagnostic sequences have been developed so that selected species, genera, or higher level taxonomic groups can be detected. Using gene probes for rRNA sequences, it has been established that marine waters contain vast populations of archaea and bacteria that have yet to be cultured in the laboratory. Oligonucleotide probes of 18–20 nucleotides are proving most useful because they hybridize rapidly to specific DNA sequences of target organisms. These diagnostic gene probes give specific detection of target organisms. They can also reveal closely related organisms or organisms with similar functional capabilities. Especially useful are analyses of rRNA that demonstrate the presence of diverse

microbial populations whose phylogenetic relationships can be ascertained by comparison with rRNA sequences from previously described microorganisms (Amann et al. 1995; Pace 1996). Even low numbers of nonculturable microorganisms in a community can be detected by using PCR amplification of diagnostic DNA sequences (Steffan and Atlas 1991; Bej et al. 1991c). Viable bacterial cells can be identified by targeting specific messenger RNAs that have half lives of less than 1 minute; mRNAs can be detected using reverse transcription PCR (RT-PCR).

Molecular microbial ecologists can infer properties of nonculturable microorganisms in the environment on the basis of homologous properties in cultivated relatives (Pace 1996). Such analyses sometimes reveal that bacteria which appear distant based on phenotypic characteristics may be closely related. For example, based on molecular analyses *Chromatium vinosum,* a hydrogen sulfide–oxidizing photosynthetic bacterium, is closely related to *E. coli,* which derives energy from organic compounds. Because of this close relationship, even though these organisms thrive on very different energy sources, their basic metabolic pathways are expected to be almost identical. Similarly, analyses of rRNA reveal that the sulfur-oxidizing symbionts of *Riftia,* clams, and mussels found at the deep-sea thermal vents are not only close relatives of one another but also representatives of the $\gamma$ group of proteobacteria, which includes other, more extensively studied organisms such as *E. coli* and *Pseudomonas aeruginosa.* Such studies are pioneering in the exploration of the vast and as yet unexplored diversity of microorganisms.

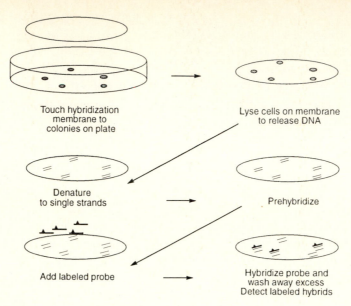

Touch hybridization
membrane to
colonies on plate

Lyse cells on membrane
to release DNA

Denature
to single strands

Prehybridize

Add labeled probe

Hybridize probe and
wash away excess
Detect labeled hybrids

**Figure 7.12**
Colony hybridization procedure.

(2) ensuring that a given genotype is present in the population sampled, even if the genes are poorly expressed or poorly selected; (3) providing optimum permissive growth conditions for stressed organisms that may be unculturable on selective media; and (4) reducing analysis time for cultivation, presumptive quantification, and confirmation of a genotype/phenotype. Colony hybridization on secondary cultivation of pure cultures is usually used to confirm a specific genotype or to test a unique DNA sequence for gene probe development.

The major uses of colony hybridization in environmental studies have been for the detection, enumeration, and isolation of bacteria with specific genotypes and/or phenotypes, and for the development of gene probes. Various microorganisms with specific metabolic activities of ecological importance have been detected using colony hybridization. These have included *Pseudomonas fluorescens* (Festl et al. 1986), 4-chlorobiphenyl degraders (Pettigrew and Sayler 1986), toluene degraders (Jain et al. 1987), naphthalene degraders (Blackburn et al. 1987), and mercury-resistant bacteria (Barkay 1987; Barkay and Olson

1986; Barkay et al. 1985). Jain et al. (1987) used colony hybridization and gene probes to study the maintenance of catabolic and antibiotic-resistance plasmids in groundwater aquifer microcosms, and, using this method, were able to demonstrate that introduced catabolic plasmids or organisms can be maintained in groundwater aquifers without selective pressure. In another study, colony hybridization with a naphthalene gene probe analysis for the catabolic genotype was nearly two orders of magnitude more sensitive than the standard plate assay for naphthalene degradation (Blackburn et al. 1987). Colony hybridization also has been used with environmental samples to enumerate mercury-resistant bacteria in contaminated environments (Barkay et al. 1985; Barkay and Olson 1986).

**Most Probable Number**  The most probable number (MPN) method, an alternative to plate count methods for determination of viable organisms, uses statistical analyses and successive dilution of the sample to reach a point of extinction (Cochran 1950; Alexander 1965; Melchiorri-Santolini 1972; Colwell 1979).

Replicate dilutions, usually 3–10 replicates of each dilution level, are scored as positive or negative, and the pattern of positive and negative scores is used in connection with appropriate statistical analyses to obtain the most probable number of viable microorganisms. Statistical patterns of positive and negative results for 3, 5, and 10 replicates are commonly given in MPN tables, which simplifies converting experimental results to a most probable number of microorganisms. The MPN procedure gives a statistically based estimate of the number of microorganisms in the sample, and when relatively few replicate tubes are used, the confidence intervals are quite large. The MPN method for enumeration of bacteria has the advantage of permitting the use of liquid culture, avoiding the need to add a solidifying agent such as agar with its possible contaminants, but it is more laborious and less precise than the plate count.

It is essential that criteria be established for differentiating positive from negative replicates. In many cases, the MPN test procedures are designed so that increases in turbidity (growth) can be seen and scored as positive. In other procedures, more elaborate tests such as protein or chlorophyll determination are required to score positive tubes. As with plate count procedures, MPN determinations can use selective and differential media.

A modified MPN method designed by Singh (1946) is often used for estimating numbers of protozoa. Multiple glass or polypropylene rings are embedded in sodium chloride agar in petri dishes, forming wells. The agar surface is inoculated with a heavy suspension of a bacterium, such as *Enterobacter aerogenes.* Dilutions of an environmental sample are inoculated into each of the wells, and protozoa present in the sample dilutions feed on the provided bacterial paste, producing a readily recognizable clearing. Clearing of the bacteria within a ring is scored positive, and the lack of clearing is scored negative.

An MPN method can be used for the enumeration of enteric viruses. In this method, serial dilutions of the samples containing viruses are added to tubes of suitable host cells in tissue cultures (Farrah et al. 1977). Following incubation, the tubes are examined for cytopathic effect (CPE), that is, the death of the infected cells. Quantitation can be achieved using MPN tables for tubes scored as CPE-positive. The numbers of viruses may also be quantitated as the $TCID_{50}$ (tissue culture infectious dose—50%), the lowest dilution of the virus suspension that caused CPE in 50% of the tubes.

As in the plate count procedures, media and incubation conditions can be adjusted in the MPN procedure to select for particular groups of microorganisms or to differentiate microorganisms with desired characteristics. Obviously, the combinations of incubation conditions and media that can be used for enumerating specific groups of bacteria are infinite. Each procedure must be carefully selected and tested to permit the correct interpretation of results.

## DETERMINATION OF MICROBIAL BIOMASS

Biomass is an important ecological parameter because, among other things, it represents the quantity of energy being stored in a particular segment of the biological community. Measurement of biomass is used to determine the standing crop of a population and the transfer of energy between trophic levels within an ecosystem. *Biomass* literally means "mass of living material" and can be expressed in units of weight (grams) or units of energy (calories or joules). Unfortunately, the direct measurements of microbial biomass, such as by filtration and dry weight or by centrifugation and packed cell volume measurements as practiced on pure cultures, are rarely applicable to environmental samples. These techniques tend to measure mineral and detritus particles and nonmicrobial biomass along with microorganisms and fail to discriminate between trophic levels, that is, between producers and consumers. Consequently, the determination of microbial biomass is often imprecise.

### Biochemical Assays

The most practical approach to the determination of microbial biomass is to assay for specific biochemicals that indicate the presence of microorganisms. Ideally, all the microbial biomass to be determined should have the same quantity of the biochemical being assayed, so that there is a direct correlation between the amount of the biochemical measured and the biomass of microorganisms. Also, the biochemical being assayed should be present only in the biomass to be determined. These two conditions are rarely, if ever, met, so the results of quantifying a particular biochemical must be extrapolated with caution in order to estimate the biomass of microorganisms that are present.

**ATP and Total Adenylate Nucleotides**  Present in all microorganisms, ATP can be measured with great sensitivity. Though dependent on physiological state, ATP concentrations are fairly uniform relative to cell carbon for many bacteria, algae, and protozoa (Figure 7.13). Because ATP is lost rapidly following the death of cells, a measurement of ATP concentrations can be used to estimate living biomass (Holm-Hansen 1969; Paerl and Williams 1976; Deming et al. 1979; Stevenson et al. 1979). The luciferin-luciferase assay can be used to detect ATP; in this assay, reduced luciferin reacts with oxygen to form oxidized luciferin in the presence of luciferase enzyme, magnesium ions, and ATP. Light is emitted in this reaction in an amount directly proportional to the ATP concentration. High-pressure liquid chromatography can also be used to measure ATP quantitatively. The method used to extract the ATP has a marked effect on the sensitivity and reliability of the assay (Deming et al. 1979; Stevenson et al. 1979). The ATP must be extracted rapidly and in a manner that prevents its conversion to ADP or AMP. A variety of methods are used, including extraction with various organic solvents or hot buffers; the efficiency of a particular procedure depends on the nature of the sample and the microbial community.

Measurements of ATP can be used to estimate microbial biomass. A factor of 250–286 is often used for conversion of ATP to cellular carbon for aquatic samples (Hamilton and Holm-Hansen 1965; Holm-Hansen and Booth 1966; Holm-Hansen 1973a, 1973b; Paerl and Williams 1976); for soil, a factor of 120 is used to convert ATP to biomass carbon (Ausmus 1973; Jenkinson and Oades 1979; Oades and Jenkinson 1979). There are some difficulties, however, in

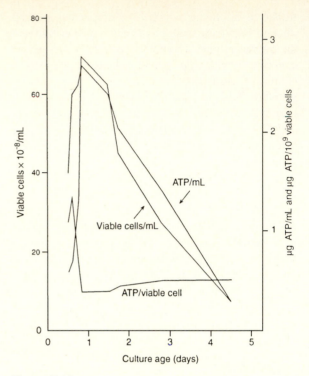

**Figure 7.13**
Correlation of ATP and viable count. In cultures older than 1 day, the ATP content per viable cell remains rather constant even during large changes in population size. (Source: Holm-Hansen 1973. Reprinted by permission, copyright 1973a, University of South Carolina Press.)

accurately estimating microbial biomass based on ATP measurements. Some microorganisms alter their ATP concentrations radically when nutritional or physiological conditions change. Also, in some ecosystems, such as soil, sediment, and nearshore aquatic areas, ATP may be adsorbed on particles (Bancroft et al. 1976; Jenkinson and Oades 1979). The sorption of ATP interferes with its extraction and quantification. In addition, the presence of plant or animal cells, which also contain ATP, limits applicability of this method in some ecosystems. However, improved methods have been developed that improve the recovery of ATP from soils and overcome some of these limitations (Pangburn et al. 1994; Webster et al. 1984).

Perhaps a better measure of microbial biomass, but one that is not universally accepted, is the total adenylate pool ($A_T$). The total adenylate pool (Equation 1) is insensitive to metabolic state:

(1)  $A_T = ATP + ADP + AMP$

The total adenylate pool is determined in order to calculate energy charge and can conveniently be used to simultaneously estimate numbers and biomass of microorganisms. The advantage of using $A_T$ is that it does not vary greatly during changes in metabolic activities of the organisms, whereas ATP is highly dependent on the physiological state of organism. When determinations of the total adenylate pool are used in conjunction with ATP measurements, the energy charge, which is a measure of the physiological state of the organisms within the sample, can be calculated (Wiebe and Bancroft 1975; Karl and Holm-Hansen 1978). The energy charge (EC), which is independent of population size, is calculated as in Equation 2.

(2)  $EC = (ATP + 1/2\ ADP)/(ATP + ADP + AMP)$

Actively growing cells have an EC ratio of 0.8–0.95, cells in stationary growth phase have an EC ratio of about 0.6, and senescent or resting cells have an EC ratio of less than 0.5.

**Cell Wall Components** Most bacteria contain muramic acid in their cell walls, and the specific relationship between murein and bacteria makes quantitation of this cell wall component useful for estimating bacterial biomass (Millar and Casida 1970; Moriarty 1975, 1977, 1978; King and White 1977; White et al. 1979). The assay for muramic acid is based on the release of lactate from muramic acid and either enzymatic analysis (Moriarty 1977) or chemical analysis (King and White 1977) to determine the concentration of lactate.

The conversion of muramic acid (MA) measurements to biomass assumes that all gram-positive bacteria have a ratio of 44 µg MA/mg C and that all gram-negative bacteria have 12 µg MA/mg C. In reality, there is a gradient of concentrations of muramic acid in gram-positive and gram-negative bacteria. To accu-

rately use this method, it is necessary to estimate the proportions of gram-negative and gram-positive bacteria in the sample; erroneous estimates of these proportions will yield inaccurate estimates of biomass.

Gram-negative bacteria contain lipopolysaccharide as part of their cell wall complex. Lipopolysaccharide can be quantitated using the *Limulus* amoebocyte lysate (LPS) method (Watson et al. 1977; Watson and Hobbie 1979). This method uses an aqueous extract from the blood cells of horseshoe crabs *(Limulus polyphemus)* that reacts specifically with lipopolysaccharide to form a turbid solution; the degree of turbidity is directly proportional to the lipopolysaccharide concentration and can be quantitatively assayed. Because lipopolysaccharide occurs only in the cell walls of gram-negative bacteria and occurs in a relatively constant proportion, it is a useful method for estimating numbers of bacteria in ecosystems dominated by gram-negative forms. The LPS method is very sensitive, capable of detecting concentrations as low as 10 cells per milliliter, and correlates well with counts obtained by other measures of biomass (Table 7.12, Figure 7.14).

To estimate fungal biomass, chitin can be measured (Swift 1973; Sharma et al. 1977; Willoughby 1978), because it occurs in the cell walls of many fungi but not in plants or other soil microorganisms. Measurement of chitin can therefore be used to estimate fungal biomass in the presence of other microbial populations

**Table 7.12**
Relative amounts of cell carbon, ATP, and muramic acid in $10^9$ cells of gram-positive and gram-negative bacteria

| Bacteria | Cell C (mg) | ATP (µg) | Muramic acid (µg) |
|---|---|---|---|
| Gram-positive *Bacillus* | 0.09 | 11 | 3 |
| Gram-negative *Pseudomonas* | 0.10 | 0.5 | 0.5 |

Source: Moriarty 1977.

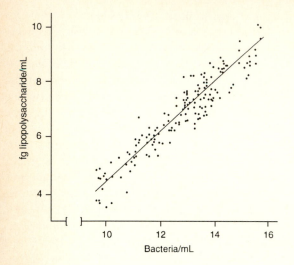

**Figure 7.14**
Correlation of LPS (lipopolysaccharide) and direct counts of bacteria (note: fg of femtogram = $10^{-15}$ g). (Source: Watson et al. 1977. Reprinted by permission of American Society for Microbiology.)

and can be used to determine fungal biomass associated with plants, including plant roots in soil. The presence of microarthropods, though, does interfere with such determinations.

**Chlorophyll and Other Photosynthetic Pigments**
Assuming the absence of plants, it is possible to estimate the biomass of photosynthetic algae and bacteria by measuring chlorophyll or other photosynthetic pigments (Edmondson 1974; Cohen et al. 1977; Holm-Hansen and Riemann 1978). Chlorophyll a, the dominant photosynthetic pigment in algae and cyanobacteria, is a useful measure of the biomass of these photosynthetic microorganisms even though there may not be a constant relationship between biomass and chlorophyll content (Banse 1977). Estimates of the biomass of photosynthetic microorganisms based on chlorophyll determinations have been found to correlate well with such estimates based on ATP determinations (Paerl et al. 1976). Chlorophyll a can be extracted with solvents, such as acetone or methanol, and quantified by measuring absorbance with a spectrophotometer using a wavelength of 665 nm. This

wavelength can be adjusted to the corresponding absorption maxima to measure bacterial chlorophylls; for example, 850 nm is used for determining the biomass of purple photosynthetic bacteria. It is thus possible to estimate the biomass of different photosynthetic microbial populations in the same sample by estimating various chlorophylls that absorb at different wavelengths (Stanier and Smith 1960; Caldwell and Tiedje 1975).

The chlorophyll concentration in the extract can also be determined by spectrofluorometry (Lorenzen 1966; Loftus and Carpenter 1971; Sharabi and Pramer 1973; Caldwell 1977). Chlorophyll a, for example, has an excitation wavelength of approximately 430 nm and a wavelength of maximum fluorescence of approximately 685 nm. The spectrofluorometric determination is more selective than the spectrophotometric method. The double selectivity of excitation and fluorescence maxima tend to reduce interference of nonspecific absorption that may affect spectrophotometric determinations (Sharabi and Pramer 1973).

**DNA** Concentrations of DNA are maintained in relatively constant proportions within microorganisms, and determination of DNA can be used as a measure of microbial biomass (Holm-Hansen et al. 1968; Hobbie et al. 1972; Paul and Meyers 1982; McCoy and Olson 1985). For environmental samples, where sensitivity is critical for accurate DNA determinations, reaction with fluorescent dyes, such as ethidium bromide or Hoechst 33258, and spectrofluorometry are generally employed. Careful purification of the DNA is necessary in these assays to prevent interference, and control for the presence of eucaryotic DNA is also necessary. Estimates of biomass based on DNA determinations and those based on direct counts show significant correlations (McCoy and Olson 1985).

**Protein** Protein is easily quantified (Lowry et al. 1951), and bacterial heme proteins can be specifically detected by chemiluminescence (Oleniacz et al. 1968), but the use of protein measurements for estimating biomass of microorganisms is limited to situations where background protein levels are negligible. Also, different microorganisms contain different amounts of protein; thus, protein determinations are best used for estimation of microbial biomass when only a single population is present. Hence, total protein measurements have only limited applicability to environmental samples.

**Lipid**  In characterizing the microbial community *in situ,* there are advantages to analyzing lipid membranes, because all viable cells are enclosed in lipid membranes containing polar lipids (White 1995). Ergosterol (5,7,22-ergosta-trien-3β-ol) is useful as a biomarker for fungi as it is rare among the major sterols of plants and completely absent in bacteria and archaea. Phospholipid ester-linked fatty acid (PLFA) analyses are commonly employed to simultaneously determine microbial biomass and the relative abundances of specific microbial populations (Baird and White 1985; Balkwill et al. 1988; Gillan and Hogg 1984; White 1983, 1988). The presence of polar lipids can define the viable biomass, as no cell can function without an intact membrane, which contains polar lipids. The activation of endogenous phospholipase activity with cell death can leave traces of the recent lysis in the diglyceride structure. Phospholipid fatty acid methyl ester analysis can be used to estimate microbial numbers. The phospholipid concentration in a sample is determined and approximate bacterial biomass calculated based on equivalents of *E. coli* cells per gram dry weight. For example, based on analyses of phospholipid content, Franzmann et al. (1996) estimated the biomass of bacterial cells in groundwater and sediment samples to be in the range of 0.9–7.8 ng of *E. coli*–equivalent cells per gram of dry weight.

## Physiological Approaches to Biomass Determination

Physiological approaches for estimating microbial biomass have been developed based on respiratory activities. One such approach, which has been used to measure microbial biomass in soil, involves fumigating soil with chloroform and then measuring the $CO_2$ released from the mineralization of the microorganisms killed by the fumigation (Jenkinson 1976;

Jenkinson and Powlson 1976; Anderson and Domsch 1978a). In this procedure, the soil microbes are killed by fumigation with $CHCl_3$ and subjected to mineralization by reinoculation of the soil with a small amount of the original soil; nonchloroform-treated soils incubated under the same conditions act as controls, and the amount of microbial carbon is calculated from the difference between the $CO_2$—C evolved from fumigated and nonfumigated samples. Conversion factors of 0.4–0.5 are recommended based on determinations made with various radiolabeled bacterial and fungal cultures. Average mineralization is 44% for fungi and 33% for bacteria; assuming a bacterial-to-fungal biomass ratio of 1:3 for soil, the combined average mineralization should be 41%. A high correlation has been found between soil ATP and biomass determined by this fumigation method (Oades and Jenkinson 1979) (Table 7.13).

A nonphysiological variation of the chloroform fumigation technique has also been described (Tate et al. 1988; Sparling and West 1988). Instead of relying on the microbial conversion of the killed biomass to $CO_2$, organic carbon in the fumigated soil is extracted by a 0.5 $M$ $K_2SO_4$ solution. The extracted organic carbon in this solution is determined by dichromate oxidation or any other DOC (dissolved organic carbon) analysis. Extracts of umfumigated soil are also analyzed and subtracted as background. This procedure is faster than the previously described one and works better in low-pH soils. Like the mineralization of killed biomass, the $K_2SO_4$ extraction is also incomplete, since cell walls and other insolubles are left behind. In a test on a wide range of soils, on the average 33% of the biomass organic carbon was extracted. Most of the tested soils clustered close to this value, but in some extreme cases the extraction efficiency ranged from 20 to 54%.

Another physiological approach for estimating microbial biomass involves measurement of respiration rates after substrate addition (Anderson and Domsch 1973, 1975, 1978b). The peak respiration rate measured during a short period is assumed to be proportional to the numbers of viable microorganisms in the samples. Microbial inhibitors can be used in the procedure to obtain separate estimates of bacterial and

**Table 7.13**
Comparison of biomass estimated by soil fumigations and ATP in various soils

| Soil sample | $CO_2$-carbon evolved by unfumigated soil in 10 days ($\mu g\ g^{-1}$) | $CO_2$-carbon evolved by fumigated soil in 10 days ($\mu g\ g^{-1}$) | Biomass carbon ($\mu g\ g^{-1}$) | ATP in soil ($\mu g\ g^{-1}$) |
|---|---|---|---|---|
| 1 | 70 | 114 | 88 | 0.75 |
| 2 | 205 | 315 | 220 | 2.07 |
| 3 | 131 | 240 | 218 | 3.14 |
| 4 | 20 | 43 | 48 | 0.64 |
| 5 | 236 | 613 | 754 | 9.03 |
| 6 | 108 | 158 | 99 | 0.90 |
| 7 | 117 | 341 | 448 | 2.97 |
| 8 | 264 | 565 | 603 | 4.56 |
| 9 | 76 | 143 | 135 | 1.37 |
| 10 | 259 | 642 | 766 | 7.00 |
| 11 | 257 | 646 | 778 | 6.55 |
| 12 | 85 | 189 | 208 | 1.32 |
| 13 | 229 | 525 | 591 | 4.20 |

Source: Oades and Jenkinson 1979.

fungal biomass. Good correlation has been reported between this peak respiration rate method and the chloroform fumigation method.

## MEASUREMENT OF MICROBIAL METABOLISM

Recent advances in analytical methodology provide the sensitivity needed to measure natural rates of microbial metabolic activities, but it remains difficult to make such rate measurements that reflect actual activities within natural ecosystems (Christian et al. 1982; Van Es and Meyer-Reil 1982; Staley and Konopka 1985). The difficulty lies in the fact that most methods require manipulation of the system in ways that can alter rates of microbial activity. Even minor manipulations can greatly alter the microenvironmental parameters that determine rates of microbial activity; as examples, simply enclosing a water sample produces a wall effect that can change the

rates of microbial activity, and removal of samples for activity determinations can change various parameters, such as oxygen concentrations, thereby changing the rates of microbial activities being measured.

### Heterotrophic Potential

One approach to measuring natural rates of heterotrophic microbial activity is to measure uptake rates for tracer levels of radiolabeled substrates to determine the heterotrophic potential for the utilization of that substrate (Wright and Hobbie 1965, 1966; Hobbie and Crawford 1969; Wright 1973, 1978). This approach assumes that microorganisms take up solutes from solution according to first-order or saturation kinetics and that the rates of uptake increase with increasing concentrations of the substrate to a maximal uptake rate ($V_{max}$). $V_{max}$ can be calculated by plotting the rates of uptake of [14]C-radiolabeled substrates against their concentrations. The concentrations of substrates used must be low and must approximate their natural concentrations in the environment. In addition to measuring the maximal uptake potential, this method can be used to calculate turnover time for a given substrate and a transport constant that reflects the affinity for the given substrate. Natural turnover time is defined as the number of hours required for the existing heterotrophic population to take up and/or respire a quantity of substrate equal in concentration to the existing *in situ* concentration.

The procedure for determining heterotrophic potential consists of adding various concentrations of radiolabeled substrate to samples and incubating the samples under conditions that simulate the real environment. After incubation, the cells are collected on a filter and the incorporated radioactivity is counted by liquid scintillation. Originally, uptake was only measured by incorporation into cells; however, this method neglected the amount of substrate that had been taken up and metabolized. Therefore, the method was modified so that $^{14}CO_2$ produced during respiration is trapped, and this amount is added to the counts of $^{14}C$ incorporated into the cells (Hobbie and Crawford 1969).

If one assumes that uptake by a heterogeneous heterotrophic population acts like a single enzyme because uptake by different bacteria is functionally equivalent, the results should be comparable to Michaelis-Menten enzyme kinetic analyses. Using the linearized form of the Michaelis-Menten equation (Equation 3):

(3)  $T/F = (K_t + S_n)/V_{max} + A/V_{max}$

where

$T/F$ in hours = time divided by the fraction of added substrate assimilated into the cells or converted into $CO_2$

$A$ = the concentration of substrate added

$K_t + S_n$ = the transport constant plus the natural concentration of that substrate

$V_{max}$ = the maximal rate of substrate uptake

A plot of $T/F$ versus $A$ is linear (Figure 7.15). Using $T/F$ as the $y$ axis and $A$ as the $x$ axis, the slope of the resulting line is equal to $1/V_{max}$; the $y$ intercept is equal to $T_t$ (the turnover time); and the $x$ intercept is equal to $K_t + S_n$. If the *in situ* concentration of the substrate is measured independently, then the transport constant $K_t$ for that substrate can be determined. Conversely, if $K_t$ can be determined independently, the equation may be used to calculate $S_n$, which is frequently too low to be detectable by direct chemical analysis.

The value of measuring $V_{max}$ is that it gives a real estimate of *in situ* heterotrophic activities because the $V_{max}$ value is a function of the existing population. It is sensitive to environmental changes, even when these changes do not affect population size. $V_{max}$ is of great value when comparing seasonal and spatial differences of the metabolic activities of indigenous microorganisms.

The estimation of rates of microbial activity with this method is limited by the substrate(s) used. Using

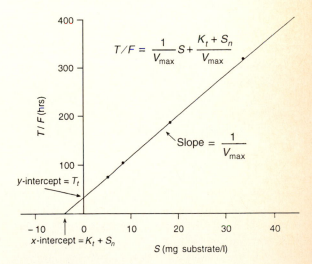

**Figure 7.15**
Measurement of heterotrophic potential showing modified Lineweaver-Burke plot of uptake kinetics. $T_t$ = turnover time, $V_{max}$ = maximal uptake velocity; $k_t + S_n$ = transport constant + natural substrate concentration; $T/F$ = velocity; $S$ = substrate concentration. (Source: Wright and Hobbie 1966. Reprinted by permission, copyright 1966. Ecological Society of America.)

replicate samples, it is possible to determine the relative $V_{max}$ values and turnover times for a variety of substrates. Studies of heterotrophic potentials have utilized acetate, glucose and other carbohydrates, glutamate and other amino acids, or mixed $^{14}C$-labeled photosynthate produced by algae incubated with $^{14}CO_2$ in light.

Some precautions need to be taken in the performance and interpretation of heterotrophic potential measurements. The substrate concentrations added must be within the right range to give a straight line slope that allows for calculation of $V_{max}$, $T_t$, and $K_t + S_n$. This generally requires adding many substrate concentrations, some of which are not utilized in the calculation. Adding too high a concentration of substrate, saturates the system and should yield a rate equal to $V_{max}$. Excessive concentrations of added substrate, however, may be inhibitory. A more refined mathematical treatment is necessary to account for competitive and noncompetitive inhibitory effects. At present, the measurement of heterotrophic potential does not account for competitive inhibition and assumes a unique transport system for each substrate being measured. However, this assumption is not valid, as common transport enzymes carry many substrates.

The measurement of heterotrophic potential also assumes that all members of the microbial population respond in the same way to variations in solute concentration. Again, this need not be true (Vaccaro and Jannasch 1967). In some cases, there is evidence for differential uptake rates by various bacterial populations, and by bacterial versus algal populations. Lower concentrations of added substrate generally give satisfactory slopes for calculation of $V_{max}$ for bacterial populations and higher concentrations of substrates give satisfactory slopes for calculation of $V_{max}$ for algal populations. Although heterotrophic potential measurements correct for $^{14}CO_2$ production, no correction is made for production of other volatile compounds, and this can cause a serious error when methane or volatile fatty acids are major metabolic products.

In addition to measurement of $V_{max}$ and $T_t$, the percentage of respiration ([$^{14}C$ assimilated + $^{14}CO_2$ produced]/$^{14}CO_2$ produced × 100) can be calculated.

The percentage of respiration is indicative of the energy required for maintenance; the greater the percent respiration, the greater the metabolic energy used to maintain the microbial population; the lower the percent respiration (which can never approach zero), the greater the proportion of metabolic energy used for assimilation and growth. In addition to the microorganism and its metabolic pathways, the energy content of the substrate and other environmental conditions (nutrient balance, temperature, etc.) have an effect on the percent respiration, also referred to as metabolic efficiency.

The specificity of the heterotrophic potential measurement is both a problem and an advantage for the substrate being measured. The method gives an estimate for specific heterotrophic activity for a particular substrate; it does not measure overall heterotrophic activity. Measurement of heterotrophic potentials permits studies on the effects of factors such as pollutants on microbial activities.

## Productivity and Decomposition

The use of [$^{14}C$]glucose by Parsons and Strickland (1962) and subsequent development of a method to determine rates of bacterial uptake, respiration, and turnover of organic compounds at natural substrate concentrations provided much data on the decomposition and flow of organic carbon through food webs in a wide range of natural systems (Robarts and Zohary 1993). Because bacteria degrade a large number of organic substrates, the method was modified to use labeled sugars, amino acids, organic acids, lignocellulose, and other dissolved and particulate substrates. These early studies demonstrated that bacteria were actively metabolizing organic matter but did not provide quantitative estimates of growth rates and production.

A limited number of studies on microbial productivity have been conducted using $^{13}C$, which is a stable isotope of carbon (Hama et al. 1993). The stable isotopes $^{13}C$ and $^{15}N$ can be simultaneous analyzed using gas chromatography–mass spectrometry (GC-MS); such analyses provide significant information on the material cycling in aquatic environments. In countries where the use of radioactive substances in natural environments has been severely restricted, such as Japan, the use of the $^{13}$C method is essential to the study of carbon flux in aquatic environments. The $^{13}$C tracer method has some disadvantages compared to the $^{14}$C method; among them are its low sensitivity, which requires larger volumes and longer incubation periods, the difficulties in maintenance and operation of analytical instruments, and the cost of the tracer.

Although the growth of autotrophic bacteria that fix carbon dioxide is routinely measured using $^{14}CO_2$ incorporation, until recently there has not been a reliable method to determine the growth of natural assemblages of heterotrophic bacteria that utilize organic substrates for a carbon source. The three most common methods in use are the incorporation of [$^3$H]adenine into RNA and DNA by bacteria and unicellular algae to give total microbial production, the incorporation of [methyl-$^3$H]thymidine into bacterial DNA, and the incorporation of [$^3$H]leucine into bacterial protein. According to Riemann and Bell (1990), all three methods give complementary results, although there is controversy over whether the [$^3$H]adenine method actually measures total microbial rather than bacterial production. Of the two nucleic acid precursor methods, there are theoretical and procedural advantages in using [$^3$H]-TdR (tritiated thymidine), although it has been criticized, as discussed shortly. Nevertheless, the [$^3$H]-TdR method has been used more frequently over the past 10 years than any other method to determine bacterial production.

**Growth Rate Measurements Based on Nucleotide Incorporation** Because DNA is synthesized in growing cells at a rate proportional to biomass, the rate of DNA synthesis reflects the growth rates of microorganisms (Van Es and Meyer-Reil 1982). Microbial growth rates have been determined in environmental samples by incubating samples with tritiated thymidine and using autoradiography of samples to determine rates of nucleotide incorporation (Brock and Brock 1968; Brock 1969, 1971). Various other analyses have been used to determine the incorporation of radiolabeled nucleotides into RNA and DNA (Karl 1979, 1980, 1981; Fuhrman and Azam 1980;

Fuhrman et al. 1986; Karl et al. 1981a, 1981b; Staley and Konopka 1985).

The incorporation of [$^3$H]-TdR into DNA as a measure of heterotrophic bacterial production in natural environments was first used by Brock (1969) when he used [$^3$H]-TdR in conjunction with autoradiography to calculate the growth rate of the marine epiphyte *Leucothrix mucor*. This technique is only applicable to organisms, such as *Leucothrix* species, that can be recognized microscopically and for which the relation between growth rate and accumulation of radiolabel can be determined independently. Later a relationship between the incorporation rate of [$^3$H]-TdR into trichloroacetic acid (TCA)-insoluble macromolecules by bacterial cultures and growth rate was established by Kunicka-Goldfinger (1976). [$^3$H]-TdR labels the DNA of bacteria only, making it especially useful for studies aimed at examining bacterial productivity (Moriarty 1986).

Fuhrman and Azam (1980, 1982) have used this method extensively for measuring bacterial productivity in aquatic environments. These studies have had the effect of lulling microbial ecologists into believing that it was now an easy process to obtain accurate measures of bacterial production—add a small amount of [$^3$H]-TdR, incubate for a few minutes, extract in ice-cold TCA, collect the material on membrane filters, and convert to cells produced (Robarts and Zohary 1993). Fuhrman and Azam (1980), however, noted that [$^3$H]-TdR incorporation as measured in cold TCA-insoluble material is not necessarily a direct measure of DNA synthesis or production. They made the following assumptions to convert their [$^3$H]-TdR incorporation rates to production estimates: (1) bacteria are the only microorganisms that incorporate [$^3$H]-TdR added at nanomolar concentrations; (2) all growing bacteria utilize [$^3$H]-TdR; (3) labeled DNA composes 80% of the total labeled macromolecules in the cold TCA precipitate; (4) the specific activity of added [$^3$H]-TdR is unaffected by ambient thymidine; (5) total bacterial DNA contains 25 mol% thymidylic acid residues; and (6) the amount of DNA per cell ranges from $7.47 \times 10^{-16}$ to $4.82 \times 10^{-15}$g. The combination of these assumptions yields a conversion factor of $2.0 \times 10^{17}$ to $1.3 \times 10^{18}$ cells produced per mole of [$^3$H]-TdR incorporated.

Although theoretically simple, the measurement of tritiated thymidine to determine bacterial productivity presents several difficulties in practice. Measurement of bacterial rates of DNA synthesis in soils and sediments is complicated because [³H]-TdR adsorbs to humic acids and inorganic components of sediments such as clays and hydrous oxides and DNA is difficult to extract. Macromolecules other than DNA may also be labeled, significant intracellular isotope dilution (and extracellular dilution, especially in sediment or soil samples) may occur, and not all bacteria, notably species of *Pseudomonas,* can incorporate [³H]-TdR into DNA. The significance of the latter is not known because our knowledge of bacterial species in natural populations, and the variance and succession of species within populations, is only rudimentary. Consequently, even when the [³H]-TdR assay is correctly executed, errors in estimates of growth and production rates may still occur. Nonetheless, if the concentrations of RNA and DNA are known, the growth rates of the indigenous microbial community can be determined by this method.

**Photosynthesis** In addition to heterotrophic potential and thymidine incorporation measurements, which assess secondary productivity, rates of primary production (synthesis) can be made using radiotracer and other methods. Both heterotrophic and autotrophic assimilation of $CO_2$ can be measured using radiolabeled bicarbonate by incubating a sample containing the indigenous microbial community with the radiolabeled substrate and then determining the amount of $^{14}CO_2$ assimilated into the cellular organic matter by filtering the cells and counting the $^{14}C$ trapped on the filters (Hubel 1966; Gorden 1972). Washing the filters eliminates any unincorporated $^{14}C$-radiolabeled bicarbonate. The residual $^{14}C$-containing organic compounds can be oxidized with acid dichromate and the released $^{14}CO_2$ trapped and quantitated.

In actual field measurements, photosynthetic and heterotrophic-chemolithotrophic incorporation of $^{14}CO_2$ are differentiated using light and dark bottle sets. In a typical procedure, both clear (light) and opaque or covered (dark) bottles are filled with water samples, radiolabeled bicarbonate is added, and the bottles are incubated *in situ* for several hours or an entire photoperiod. Incorporation results from the dark bottles are subtracted from incorporation results in the light bottles to obtain the net photosynthetic incorporation. Unlabeled $CO_2$ (bicarbonate) in the samples is measured to calculate the actual specific $^{14}CO_2$ activity in the water samples, and with sufficient measurements, rates of productivity for daily or annual periods can be determined.

The time frame of $^{14}CO_2$ incorporation experiments is relevant to the interpretation of the results. Short experimental periods of 1 or 2 hours give values close to the gross primary productivity because there is little chance for the incorporated $^{14}C$ to be mineralized again by respiration. The values obtained for long exposure times will be closer to net primary productivity (photosynthesis minus respiration) because some of the incorporated $^{14}C$ will be mineralized under these conditions.

**Respiration** Radiolabeled carbon dioxide ($^{14}CO_2$) release from labeled substrates can also be used to determine decomposition rates for specific substrates. The complete degradation of a compound to its mineral components in which the organic carbon of the compound is converted to $CO_2$ by respiration is called *mineralization.* Rates of decomposition of both synthetic and natural organic compounds can be determined with this method (Figure 7.16). Measurements of $^{14}CO_2$ release from synthetic organic chemicals, such as pesticides, are essential for evaluating the environmental safety of such compounds because they will accumulate in the environment unless mineralized by microorganisms. In performing such analyses, it is essential to consider the position of the $^{14}C$ label because one portion of a molecule can be degraded while another portion remains intact (Bartha and Pramer 1970).

Various other methods that do not employ radiolabeled substrates can also be used to measure rates of microbial respiration. These methods normally measure either rates of oxygen consumption or rates of carbon dioxide production. As long as aerobic conditions are maintained, $CO_2$ evolution can be used as a measure of microbial respiratory activity with reasonable

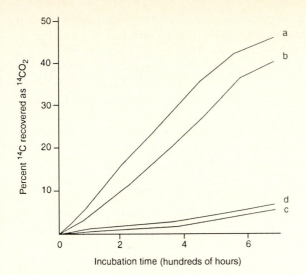

**Figure 7.16**
Decompostion of $^{14}C$-labeled hemlock lignocellulose by soil microorganisms. The use of lignocellulose labeled specifically in different portions of the molecule permits identification of the origin of the $CO_2$. (a) $^{14}C$ cellulose-labeled lignocellulose in soil #1. (b) $^{14}C$ cellulose-labeled lignocellulose in soil #2. (c) $^{14}C$ lignin-labeled lignocellulose in soil #1. (d) $^{14}C$ lignin-labeled lignocellulose in soil #2. (Source: Crawford et al. 1977. Reprinted by permission of American Society for Microbiology.)

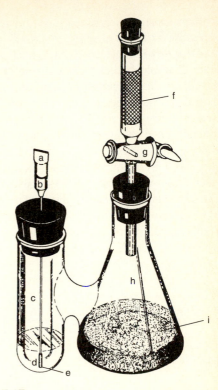

**Figure 7.17**
The biometer flask, a compact, commercially available enclosed unit used for measuring $CO_2$ production from soil. The biometer flask has the advantage that one can withdraw and replace the $CO_2$-absorbing alkali without exposing the system to contamination by atmospheric $CO_2$. (a) Rubber closure. (b) Syringe needle. (c) Sidearm. (d) Alkali. (e) Needle guard. (f) $CO_2$ absorbent (ascarite). (g) Stopcock. (h) Sample compartment. (i) soil. (Source: Bartha and Pramer 1965. Reprinted by permission, copyright Williams and Wilkins, Baltimore.)

accuracy (Pramer and Bartha 1972). For long-term studies, rates of carbon dioxide production are often determined using specially designed enclosed flasks, such as the biometer flask (Bartha and Pramer 1965) (Figure 7.17) or using flow-through incubation systems, such as "gas trains," that pass a stream of $CO_2$-free air through the incubation flask and trap $CO_2$ from the effluent gas stream (Atlas and Bartha 1972). The $CO_2$ that is trapped can be quantitated by titration of the trapping base solution with acid of known concentration to reach a point of neutrality.

Rates of oxygen consumption can also be used as a measure of cellular respiratory activity. Various oxygen electrodes are available, most of them suitable for short-term measurements only. Microprobes can be used for *in situ* measurements (Revsbech 1983; Revsbech et al. 1983). Warburg-type respirometers that monitor either gas or pressure or gas volume changes as measures of oxygen consumption are tedious to use and are not suitable for measurement periods in excess of hours or at most 1 or 2 days. They have been rendered largely obsolete by the more convenient oxygen electrodes, but these are also appropriate for short-term measurements only. Some environmental biodegradation processes are very slow and may necessitate measurements that last several weeks or several months. For such measurements a new generation of accurate, highly automated respirometers has been developed (sapromat, Oxymax, and others). The small volume changes connected with oxygen consumption close or break electric circuits. Either the consumed oxygen is replaced electrolytically or the current actuates solenoid valves that replace the oxygen from a reservoir. The consumption of current or the frequency of valve actuation is accurately recorded and processed by a computer programmed for appropriate data reduction and plotting. The processor can monitor oxygen consumption in multiple chambers, allowing for replication or variation of the experimental conditions. Such respirometers have been used with success to monitor slow processes such as the rate of polluting oil biodegradation in environmental samples (Venosa et al. 1992). These modern respirometers save labor by running virtually unattended for long periods, but their initial cost is high.

## Specific Enzyme Assays

A variety of enzyme assays can also be used for measuring the metabolic activities of indigenous microorganisms. Some, such as measurement of dehydrogenase, esterase, and phosphatase activities, assay general activities of a relatively large portion of the microbial community; others, such as measurement of cellulase, chitinase, nitrogenase, and denitrification enzyme activities, assay the metabolic functions of small but important segments of the microbial com-

**Table 7.14**
Some specific enzyme assays

| Enzyme | Substrate | Description of assay |
| --- | --- | --- |
| Dehydrogenase | Triphenyltetrazolium | Dehydrogenases convert triphenyltetrazolium chloride to triphenylformazan; the triphenylformazan is extracted with methanol and quantitated spectrophotometrically. |
| Phosphatase | $p$-Nitrophenol phosphate | Phosphatases convert the $p$-nitrophenol phosphate to $p$-nitrophenol, which is extracted in aqueous solution and quantitated spectrophotometrically. |
| Protease | Gelatin | Gelatin hydrolysis, as an example of proteolytic activity, can be measured by the determination of residual protein. |
| Amylase | Starch | The amount of residual starch is quantitated spectrophotometrically by the intensity of blue color resulting from its reaction with iodine. |
| Chitinase | Chitin | Production of reducing sugars is measured using anthrone reagent. |
| Cellulase | Cellulose | Production of reducing sugars is measured using anthrone reagent. |
|  | Carboxymethyl cellulose | Cellulases alter the viscosity of carboxymethyl cellulose that can be measured. |
| Nitrogenase | Acetylene | Nitrogenase, besides reducing dinitrogen gas ($N{\equiv}N$) to ammonia ($NH_3$), is also capable of reducing acetylene ($HC{\equiv}CH$) to ethylene ($C_2H_2$); the rate of formation of ethylene can be monitored using a gas chromatograph with flame ionization detector, and the rate of nitrogen fixation can be calculated using an appropriate conversion factor. |
| Nitrate reductase | Nitrate | Dissimilatory nitrate reductase can be assayed by the disappearance of nitrate or by measuring the evolution of denitrification products, such as nitrogen gas and nitrous oxide, from samples using a gas chromatograph; denitrification can be blocked at the nitrous oxide level by the addition of acetylene, permitting a simpler assay procedure. |

munity (Focht 1982; Hsu and Bartha 1979; Prosser and Cox 1982; Skujins 1967, 1973; Sorenson 1978; Yoshinari and Knowles 1976) (Table 7.14). Enzymes involved in biogeochemical cycling are of interest to microbial ecologists; enzymes responsible for carbon and nitrogen cycling are of particular importance in the maintenance of communities and ecosystems. Various assays used to measure specific enzymes, such as the acetylene reduction method for determining nitrogenase activity, are widely employed in microbial ecological studies. Some general assays have also been developed, such as the hydrolysis of fluorescein diacetate to measure the activities of lipases, proteases, and esterases (Federle et al. 1986; Federle 1988). When assaying enzymatic activities, it is important that the microbial community not be altered during the assay procedure if the measurement of enzymatic activity is to reflect *in situ* activities accurately. Caution must be take to maintain *in situ* conditions, particularly with reference to temperature, moisture content, and $E_h$ (redox potential), and incubation periods must be short enough to preclude changes in numbers of microorganisms, which could alter the levels of enzymes present in the sample.

## Chapter Summary

Numbers, biomass, and metabolic activity are the fundamental biotic parameters of microbial ecosystems. Much remains to be done to improve the accuracy and sensitivity in measuring these parameters. Further advances in microanalytical techniques are likely to improve these measurement procedures and reduce interferences. It is equally important to be aware of the true meaning and limitations of each measurement procedure. Knowing that a "total viable count" typically enumerates only about 1% of a microbial community places such data in the proper perspective. Although under some conditions numbers, biomass, and metabolic activity show proportional correlations, under many realistic circumstances they do not. This dictates caution and critical thinking when one parameter is calculated or projected from another directly measured parameter.

It stands to reason that a change in microbial numbers usually correlates to similar changes in biomass and activity. Because such correlations appear to be so self-evident, one needs to be alert to situations when they are either not proportional or entirely absent. Due to life cycles or nutrient availability, the cell size of microorganisms may change. In such situations, biomass may increase or decrease without a corresponding change in microbial numbers. Similarly, in the case of a sporulating fungus or actinomycete, numbers may increase dramatically with little or no change in biomass. Microbial activity will correlate with numbers and biomass only as long as environmental conditions remain constant. Any change in temperature, nutrient availability, or other environmental determinants will alter microbial activity without necessarily changing either numbers or biomass. Unwarranted extrapolations abound in literature; microbial ecologists need to evaluate correlations critically and on a case-by-case basis.

Different approaches are used for sampling microorganisms from diverse ecosystems. Sampling procedures must ensure that numbers or activities of microorganisms are not altered if meaningful ecological information about the microbial populations in those samples is to be obtained. Some procedures, such as buried slides and capillary tubes, are used for the direct recovery of microorganisms. More often, though, plating procedures that recover viable microorganisms or direct observational methods are applied to environmental samples. For water samples, the recovery of microorganisms is complicated by the necessity of collecting remote samples, in marine studies often from great depths, without contaminating the sample or killing the indigenous microorganisms. Recovery of viable organisms requires careful handling of the specimens.

Once recovered, microorganisms can be detected by phenotypic, biochemical, immunological, and molecular analyses. Phenotypic characterization remains the classic approach, especially as it often yields physiological information about the organisms that is useful in understanding their ecological functions. Lipid profiles, such as FAME and PLFA analyses, are important chemotaxonomic approaches that reveal populations within communities and the physiological states of those populations. Molecular analyses, however, are becoming more prevalent as they can be used to detect nonculturable microorganisms, to reveal phylogeny, and even to infer function. Use of the polymerase chain reaction (PCR) and gene probes are especially important for detecting low levels of specific microorganisms in the environment. These analyses rely upon recovery of nucleic acids from soils and waters. Additional analyses of recovered nucleic acids, such as restriction fragment length polymorphism (RFLP) determination, can be used to "fingerprint" microbial populations at the molecular level. This permits following the movement of specific populations through the environment, which is especially useful in epidemiological studies and in tracking genetically modified microorganisms. Reporter genes are also useful in tracking introduced genetically modified microorganisms and in examining the expression of genes in natural environments. The *lacZ* gene and reporter genes based on fluorescence, such as the *lux* genes and the green fluorescent protein genes, are often used for these purposes.

Besides detecting specific microbial populations and monitoring gene expression, microbial ecologists use a variety of classical and molecular methods for determining microbial numbers and biomass in environmental samples. Microorganisms can be enumerated by direct count and viable count procedures. Viable counts using a wide variety of culture media and incubation conditions are employed in many microbial ecology studies. Viable counts, however, appear to severely underestimate microbial populations. Viable but nonculturable microorganisms are not detected by viable count procedures. It is estimated that less than 1% of all living microorganisms in water and soil samples are recovered by viable count procedures. Direct microscopic methods, using stains such as acridine orange and DAPI, are excellent for detecting total numbers of microorganisms in waters. These procedures can be modified to include dyes that respond to metabolic activity so that living macroorganisms, including viable nonculturable cells, can be enumerated.

Microbial biomass can also be estimated based upon biochemical constituents of cells, including ATP, peptidoglycan, nucleic acids, and lipids. Quantitation of all of these chemical constituents of microbial cells has uses in different studies. Phospholipid-linked fatty acid (PLFA) analyses, for example, give valuable and sensitive information about the relative biomass of bacteria, fungi, and specific taxonomic groups of these microorganisms within environmental samples. Such approaches that simultaneously yield information about community composition, physiological state of populations, and quantities of microbial biomass are especially valuable.

A number of metabolic assays are also employed to determine the functional activities of microorganisms in the environment. Some of these assays, such as the heterotrophic potential, are aimed at examining the overall metabolic activity level of the microbial community. Others aim at measuring productivity or decomposition. Often radiotracers or stable isotopes are used for measuring primary and secondary productivity. Tritiated thymidine incorporation is used for measuring bacterial growth rates. Uptake of radiolabeled amino acids is used for determining heterotrophic potential. Specific enzyme assays, such as the acetylene reduction assay for determining rates of nitrogen fixation, are employed to measure ecologically important metabolic activities of microorganisms in the environment.

## STUDY QUESTIONS

1. What factors are critical in collecting environmental samples for the enumeration of microorganisms? What are the differences in collecting samples from air, water, sediment, and soil?

2. How can you collect indigenous marine bacteria from a depth of 100 m?

3. How can you detect all viable individuals of a specific bacterial population in an environmental sample?

4. Why is the plate count procedure highly criticized for use in environmental studies? Why is it still employed?

5. What is the polymerase chain reaction? How can it be used to detect genetically engineered microorganisms in soils?

6. What are reporter genes? How can reporter genes be used to monitor survival of introduced genetically modified microbial populations?

7. Compare the direct count and viable count procedures with regard to sample handling, sample processing, and the ability to discriminate living from dead microorganisms.

8. What is the relationship between cell numbers and biomass? Compare the applicability of cell number and biomass determinations for soil bacteria and fungi.

9. How can $CO_2$ production be used to estimate total microbial biomass?

10. How can specific biochemical compounds be used to determine microbial biomass? Compare the applicability of peptidoglycan, chlorophyll a, ATP, DNA, protein, and organic carbon for determining microbial biomass.

11. What is heterotrophic potential? How is it determined? Why is it a useful measure of microbial activity?

12. Discuss the strengths and limitations of using tritiated thymidine for estimating microbial productivity.

13. Discuss the strengths and limitations of using $^{14}CO_2$ for estimating microbial productivity.

14. How have molecular approaches changed the capability of monitoring microbial populations and their activities in natural ecosystems?

## REFERENCES AND SUGGESTED READINGS

Alexander, M. 1965. Most-probable-number method for microbial populations. In C. A. Black (ed.). *Methods of Soil Analysis. Part 2, Chemical and Microbiological Properties.* American Society of Agronomy, Madison, WI, pp. 1467–1472.

Amann, R. I. 1990. Combination of 16S rRNA-target oligonucleotide probes with flow cytometry for analyzing mixed microbial populations. *Applied and Environmental Microbiology* 56:1919–1925.

Amann, R. I., W. Ludwig, and K. H. Schleifer. 1995. Phylogenetic identification and *in situ* detection of individual microbial cells without cultivation. *Microbiological Reviews* 59:143–169.

Andersen, A. A. 1958. A new sampler for the collection, sizing, and enumeration of the viable airborne bacteria. *Journal of Bacteriology* 76:471–484.

Anderson, J.P.E., and K. H. Domsch. 1973. Quantification of bacterial and fungal contributions to soil respiration. *Archiv für Mikrobiologie* (Berlin) 93:113–127.

Anderson, J.P.E., and K. H. Domsch. 1975. Measurement of bacterial and fungal contributions to respiration of selected agricultural and forest soils. *Canadian Journal of Microbiology* 21:314–322.

Anderson, J.P.E., and K. H. Domsch. 1978a. Mineralization of bacteria and fungi in chloroform-fumigated soils. *Soil Biology and Biochemistry* 10:207–213.

Anderson, J.P.E., and K. H. Domsch. 1978b. A physiological method for the quantitative measurement of microbial biomass in soil. *Soil Biology and Biochemistry* 10:215–221.

Aristovskaya, T. V. 1973. The use of capillary techniques in ecological studies of microorganisms. *Bulletin from the Ecological Research Committee* (Stockholm) 17:47–52.

Aristovskaya, T. V., and O. M. Parinkina. 1961. New methods of studying soil microorganism associations. *Soviet Soil Science* 1:12–20.

Aßmus, B., M. Schloter, G. Kirchhof, P. Hutzler, and A. Hartmann. 1997. Improved *in situ* tracking of rhizosphere bacteria using dual staining with fluorescence-labeled antibodies and rRNA-targeted oligonucleotides. *Microbial Ecology* 33:32–40.

Atlas, R. M. 1982. Enumeration and estimation of microbial biomass. In R. G. Burns and J. H. Slater (eds.). *Experimental Microbial Ecology*. Blackwell, Oxford, England, pp. 84–104.

Atlas, R. M. 1992. Detection and enumeration of microorganisms based upon phenotype. In M. A. Levin, R. J. Seidler, and M. Rogul (eds.). *Microbial Ecology: Principles, Methods, and Applications*. McGraw-Hill, New York, pp. 29–43.

Atlas, R. M. 1993. Environmental monitoring. In G. H. Keller and M. M. Manak (eds.) *DNA Probes*. Stockton Press, New York, pp. 589–616.

Atlas, R. M. 1995. *Handbook of Media for Environmental Microbiology*. CRC Press, Boca Raton, FL.

Atlas, R. M. 1997. *Handbook of Microbiological Media*. CRC Press, Boca Raton, FL.

Atlas, R. M., and R. Bartha. 1972. Degradation and mineralization of petroleum by two bacteria isolated from coastal water. *Biotechnology and Bioengineering* 14:297–308.

Atlas, R. M., and A. K. Bej. 1990. Detecting bacterial pathogens in environmental water samples by using PCR and gene probes. In M. Innis, D. Gelfand, D. Sninsky, and T. White (eds.). *PCR Protocols: A Guide to Methods and Applications*. Academic Press, New York, pp. 399–407.

Atlas, R. M., and J. S. Hubbard. 1974. Applicability of radiotracer methods of measuring $^{14}CO_2$ assimilation for determining microbial activity in soil including a new *in situ* method. *Microbial Ecology* 1:145–163.

Atlas, R. M., D. Pramer, and R. Bartha. 1978. Assessment of pesticide effects on nontarget soil microorganisms. *Soil Biology and Biochemistry* 10:231–239.

Ausmus, B. S. 1973. The use of the ATP assay in terrestrial decomposition studies. *Bulletin from the Ecological Research Committee* (Stockholm) 17:223–234.

Babuik, L. A., and E. A. Paul. 1970. The use of fluorescein isothiocyanate in the determination of the bacterial biomass in grassland soil. *Canadian Journal of Microbiology* 16:57–62.

Baird, B. H., and D. C. White. 1985. Biomass and community structure of the abyssal microbiota determined from the ester-linked phospholipids recovered from Venezuela Basin and Puerto Rico trench sediments. *Marine Geology* 68:217–231.

Bakken, L. R. 1985. Separation and purification of bacteria from soil. *Applied and Environmental Microbiology* 49:1482–1487.

Balderston, W. L., B. Sherr, and W. J. Payne. 1976. Blockage by acetylene of nitrous oxide reduction in *Pseudomonas perfectomarinus*. *Applied and Environmental Microbiology* 31:504–508.

Balkwill, D. L., D. P. Labeda, and L. E. Casida, Jr. 1975. Simplified procedure for releasing and concentrating microorganisms from soil for transmission electron microscopy viewing as thin-section and frozen-etched preparations. *Canadian Journal of Microbiology* 21:252–262.

Balkwill, D. L., F. R. Leach, J. T. Wilson, J. F. McNabb, and D. C. White. 1988. Equivalence of microbial biomass measures based on membrane lipid and cell wall components, adenosine triphosphate, and direct counts in subsurface aquifer sediments. *Microbial Ecology* 16:73–84.

Bancroft, K., E. A. Paul, and W. J. Wiebe. 1976. The extraction and measurement of adenosine triphosphate from marine sediments. *Limnology and Oceanography* 21:473–480.

Banse, K. 1977. Determining the carbon to chlorophyll ratio of natural phytoplankton. *Marine Biology* 41:199–212.

Barkay, T. 1987. Adaptation of aquatic microbial communities to $Hg^{2+}$ stress. *Applied and Environmental Microbiology* 53:2725–2732.

Barkay, T., D. L. Fouts, and B. H. Olson. 1985. The preparation of a DNA gene probe for the detection of mercury resistance genes in Gram-negative communities. *Applied and Environmental Microbiology* 49:686–692.

Barkay, T., and B. H. Olson. 1986. Phenotypic and genotypic adaptation of aerobic heterotrophic sediment bacterial communities to mercury stress. *Applied and Environmental Microbiology* 52:403–406.

Baross, J. A., J. Liston, and R. Y. Morita. 1978. Incidence of *Vibrio parahaemolyticus* bacteriophages and other *Vibrio* bacteriophages in marine samples. *Applied and Environmental Microbiology* 36:492–499.

Bartha, R., and D. Pramer. 1965. Features of a flask for measuring the persistence and biological effects of pesticides. *Soil Science* 100:68–70.

Bartha, R., and D. Pramer. 1970. Metabolism of acylanilide herbicides. *Advances in Applied Microbiology* 13:317–341.

Bej, A. K., R. J. Steffan, J. DiCesare, L. Haff, and R. M. Atlas. 1990. Detection of coliform bacteria in water by polymerase chain reaction and gene probes. *Applied and Environmental Microbiology* 56:307–314.

Bej, A. K., S. C. McCarty, and R. M. Atlas. 1991a. Detection of coliform bacteria and *Escherichia coli* by multiplex polymerase chain reaction: Comparison with defined substrate and plating methods for water quality monitoring. *Applied and Environmental Microbiology* 57:2429–2432.

Bej, A. K., M. H. Mahbubani, and R. M. Atlas. 1991b. Detection of viable *Legionella pneumophila* in water using PCR and gene probe methods. *Applied and Environmental Microbiology* 57:597–600.

Bej, A. K., M. H. Mahbubani, and R. M. Atlas. 1991c. Amplification of nucleic acids by polymerase chain reaction (PCR) and other methods and their applications. *Critical Reviews in Biochemistry and Molecular Biology* 26:301–334.

Berent, S. L., M. Mahmoudi, R. M. Torczynski, P. W. Bragg, and A. P. Bollon. 1985. Comparison of oligonucleotide and long DNA fragments as probes in DNA and RNA dot, southern, northern, colony and plaque hybridizations. *BioTechniques* 3:208–220.

Black, C. A. 1965. *Methods of Soil Analysis.* Part 2, Chemical and Microbiological Properties. American Society of Agronomy, Madison, WI.

Blackburn, J.W., R. L. Jain, and G. S. Sayler. 1987. Molecular microbial ecology of a naphthalene-degrading

genotype in activated sludge. *Environmental Science and Technology* 21:884–890.

Board, R. G., and D. W. Lovelock. 1973. *Sampling—Microbiological Monitoring of Environments.* Academic Press, London.

Bobbie, R. J., and D. C. White. 1980. Characterization of benthic microbial community structure by high resolution gas chromatography of fatty acid methyl esters. *Applied and Environmental Microbiology* 39:1212–1222.

Bohlool, B. B. 1987. Fluorescence methods for study of *Rhizobium* in culture and in situ. In G. H. Elkan (ed.). *Symbiotic Nitrogen Fixation Technology.* Marcel Dekker, New York, pp. 127–155.

Bohlool, B. B., and E. L. Schmidt. 1973. A fluorescent antibody technique for determination of growth rates of bacteria in soil. *Bulletin from the Ecological Research Committee* (Stockholm) 17:336–338.

Bohlool, B. B., and E. L. Schmidt. 1980. The immunofluorescence approach in microbial ecology. *Advances in Microbial Ecology* 4:203–242.

Bohlool, B. B., E. L. Schmidt, and C. Beasley. 1977. Nitrification in the intertidal zone: Influence of effluent type and effect of tannin on nitrifiers. *Applied and Environmental Microbiology* 34:523–528.

Boivin, R., F. Chalifour, and P. Dion. 1988. Construction of a Tn5 derivative encoding bioluminescence and its introduction in *Pseudomonas, Agrobacterium,* and *Rhizobium. Molecular and General Genetics* 213:50–55.

Bordner, R., and J. Winter (eds.). 1978. *Microbiological Methods for Monitoring the Environment.* Part 1, Water and Wastes. Environmental Protection Agency, Cincinnati, OH.

Bowden, W. B. 1977. Comparison of two direct-count techniques for enumerating aquatic bacteria. *Applied and Environmental Microbiology* 33:1229–1232.

Brayton, P. R., and R. R. Colwell. 1987. Fluorescent antibody staining method for enumeration of viable environmental *Vibrio cholerae* O1. *Journal of Microbiological Methods* 6:309–314.

Britton, R. J., and E. H. Davidson. 1985. Hybridization strategy. In B. P. Hames and S. J. Higgins (eds.). *Nucleic Acid Hybridization: A Practical Approach.* IRL Press, New York, pp. 3–15.

Brock, M. L., and T. D. Brock. 1968. The application of micro-autoradiographic techniques to ecological studies. *Mitteilungen der Internationale Vereiningung für Theoretische und Angewandte Limnologie* 15:1–29.

Brock, T. D. 1969. Bacterial growth rate in the sea: Direct analysis by thymidine autoradiography. *Science* 155:81–83.

Brock, T. D. 1971. Microbial growth rates in nature. *Bacteriological Reviews* 35:39–53.

Brown, C. M. 1982. Nitrogen mineralisation in soils and sediments. In R. G. Burns and J. H. Slater (eds.). *Experimental Microbial Ecology*. Blackwell, Oxford, England, pp. 154–163.

Buck, J. D. 1979. The plate count in aquatic microbiology. In J. W. Costerton and R. R. Colwell (eds.). *Native Aquatic Bacteria: Enumeration, Activity and Ecology*. ASTM Special Technical Publication No. 695. American Society for Testing Materials, Philadelphia, pp. 19–28.

Burlage, R. S., and C-T Kuo. 1994. Living biosensors for the management and manipulation of microbial consortia. *Annual Review of Microbiology* 48:291–310.

Burlage, R. S., G. S. Sayler, and F. W. Larimer. 1990. Monitoring of naphthalene catabolism by bioluminescence with *nah-lux* transcriptional fusions. *Journal of Bacteriology* 172:4749–4757.

Burlage, R. S., Z. K. Yang, and T. Mehlhorn. 1996. A transposon for green fluorescent protein transcriptional fusions: Application for bacterial transport experiments. *Gene* 173:53–58.

Buttner, M., P. K. Villeke, and S. A. Grinshpun. 1997. Sampling and analysis of airborne microorganisms. In C. J. Hurst, G. R. Knudden, M. J. McInerney, L. D. Stetzenbach, and M. V. Walters (eds.). *Manual of Environmental Microbiology*. American Society for Microbiology Press, Washington, DC, pp. 629–640.

Byrd, J. J., and R. R. Colwell. 1992. Microscopy applications for analysis of environmental samples. In M. A. Levin, R. J. Seidler, and M. Rogul (eds.). *Microbial Ecology: Principles, Methods, and Applications*. McGraw-Hill, New York, pp. 93–112.

Caldwell, D. E. 1977. Accessory pigment fluorescence for quantitation of photosynthetic microbial populations. *Canadian Journal of Microbiology* 23:1594–1597.

Caldwell, D. E., and J. M. Tiedje. 1975. The structure of anaerobic bacterial communities in the hypolimnia of several Michigan lakes. *Canadian Journal of Microbiology* 21:377–385.

Casida, L. E. 1977. Microbial metabolic activity in soil as measured by dehydrogenase determinations. *Applied and Environmental Microbiology* 34:630–636.

Cavigelli, M. A., G. P. Robertson, and M. J. Klug. 1995. Fatty acid methyl ester (FAME) profiles as measures of soil microbial community structure. *Plant and Soil* 170:99–113.

Chalfie, M. 1995. Green fluorescent protein. *Photochemistry and Photobiology* 62:651–656.

Chalfie, M., Y. Tu, G. Euskirchen, W. W. Ward, and D. C. Parker. 1994. Green fluorescent protein as a marker for gene expression. *Science* 263:802–804.

Cholodny, N. 1930. Über eine neue Methode zur Untersuchung der Bodenmikroflora. *Archiv für Mikrobiologie* (Berlin) 1:650–652.

Christian, R. R., R. B. Hanson, and S. Y. Newell. 1982. Comparison of methods for measurement of bacterial growth rates in mixed batch cultures. *Applied and Environmental Microbiology* 43:1160–1165.

Chrzanowski, T. H., L. H. Stevenson, and B. Kjerfve. 1979. Adenosine 5′-triphosphate flux through the North Inlet marsh system. *Applied and Environmental Microbiology* 37:841–848.

Cochran, W. G. 1950. Estimation of bacterial densities by means of the "most probable number." *Biometrics* 2:105–116.

Cohen, U., W. Krumbein, and M. Shilo. 1977. Solar Lake (Sinai): Bacterial distribution and production. *Limnology and Oceanography* 22:621–634.

Coleman, A. W. 1980. Enhanced detection of bacteria in natural environments by fluorochrome staining of DNA. *Limnology and Oceanography* 25:948–951.

Colwell, R. R. 1979. Enumeration of specific populations by the most-probable-number (MPN) method. In J. W. Costerton and R. R. Colwell (eds.). *Native Aquatic Bacteria: Enumeration, Activity and Ecology*. ASTM Special Technical Publication No. 695. American Society for Testing Materials, Philadelphia, pp. 56–64.

Conway de Macario, E., A.J.L. Macario, and M. J. Wolin. 1982. Specific antisera and immunological procedures for characterization of methanogenic bacteria. *Journal of Bacteriology* 149:320–328.

Conway de Macario, E., M. J. Wolin, and A.J.L. Macario. 1981. Immunology of archaebacteria that produce methane gas. *Science* 214:74–75.

Crawford, C. C., J. E. Hobbie, and K. L. Webb. 1973. Utilization of dissolved organic compounds by microorganisms in an estuary. In L. H. Stevenson and R. R. Colwell (eds.). *Estuarine Microbial Ecology*. University of South Carolina Press, Columbia, pp. 169–180.

Crawford, D. L., R. L. Crawford, and A. L. Pometto III. 1977. Preparation of specifically labelled $^{14}$C-(lignin)- and $^{14}$C-(cellulose)-lignocelluloses and their decomposition by the microflora of soil. *Applied and Environmental Microbiology* 33:1247–1251.

Daley, R. J. 1979. Direct epifluorescence enumeration of native aquatic bacteria: Uses, limitations and comparative accuracy. In J. W. Costerton and R. R. Colwell (eds.). *Native Aquatic Bacteria: Enumeration, Activity and Ecology*. ASTM Special Technical Publication No. 695. American Society for Testing Materials, Philadelphia, pp. 29–45.

Daley, R. J., and J. E. Hobbie. 1975. Direct counts of aquatic bacteria by a modified epifluorescence technique. *Limnology and Oceanography* 20:875–882.

Datta, A. R., B. A.Wentz, D. Shook, and M. W. Trucksess 1988. Synthetic oligodeoxyribonucleotide probes for detection of *Listeria monocytogenes. Applied and Environmental Microbiology* 54:2933–2937.

Davey, H. M., and D. B. Kell. 1996. Flow cytometry and cell sorting of heterogeneous microbial populations: Importance of single-cell analysis. *Microbiological Reviews* 60:641–696.

Dazzo, F. B., and W. J. Brill. 1977. Receptor sites on clover and alfalfa roots for *Rhizobium. Applied and Environmental Microbiology* 33:132–136.

Deming, J. W., G. L. Picciolo, and E. W. Chappelle. 1979. Important factors in adenosine triphosphate determination using firefly luciferase: Applicability of the assay to studies of native aquatic bacteria. In J. W. Costerton and R. R. Colwell (eds.). *Native Aquatic Bacteria: Enumeration, Activity and Ecology*. ASTM Special Technical Publication No. 695. American Society for Testing Materials, Philadelphia, pp. 89–98.

Dowding, P., and P. Widden. 1974. Some relationships between fungi and their environment in tundra regions. In *Soil Organisms and Decomposition in Tundra*. Tundra Biome Steering Committee, Swedish IBP, Stockholm, pp. 123–150.

Dowling, N.J.E., F. Widdel, and D. C. White. 1986. Phospholipid ester-linked fatty acid biomarkers of acetate oxidizing sulphate reducers and other sulphide forming bacteria. *Journal of General Microbiology* 132:1815–1825.

Drahos, D. J., B. C. Hemming, and S. McPherson. 1986. Tracking recombinant organisms in the environment: β-galactosidase as a selectable non-antibiotic marker for fluorescent Pseudomonads. *Bio/Techniques* 4:439–444.

Echeverria, P., J. Seriwatana, O. Chityothin, W. Chaicumpa, and C. Tirapat. 1982. Detection of enterotoxigenic *Escherichia coli* in water by filter hybridization with three enterotoxin gene probes. *Journal of Clinical Microbiology* 16:1086–1090.

Eder, K. 1995. Gas chromatographic analysis of fatty acid methyl esters. *Journal of Chromatography B: Biomedical Applications* 671:113–131.

Edmondson, W. T. 1974. A simplified method for counting phytoplankton. In R. A. Vollenweider (ed.). *A Manual on Methods for Measuring Primary Production in Aquatic Environments*. IBP Handbook No. 12, 2d ed. Blackwell, Oxford, England, pp. 14–16.

Engebrecht, J., M. Simon, and M. Silverman. 1985. Measuring gene expression with light. *Science* 227:1345–1347.

Eren, J., and D. Pramer. 1966. Applications of the immunofluorescent staining to study of the ecology of soil microorganisms. *Soil Science* 101:39–45.

Eriksson, K. E., and S. C. Johnsrud. 1982. Mineralisation of carbon. In R. G. Burns and J. H. Slater (eds.). *Experimental Microbial Ecology*. Blackwell, Oxford, England, pp. 134–153.

Erlich, H. A. (ed.). 1989. *PCR Technology: Principles and Applications for DNA Amplification*. Stockton, New York.

Faegri, A., V. L. Torsvik, and J. Goksøyr. 1977. Bacterial and fungal activities in soil: Separation of bacteria by a rapid centrifugation technique. *Soil Biology Biochemistry* 9:105–112.

Falkenstein, H., P. Bellemann, S. Walter, W. Zeller, and K. Geider. 1988. Identification of *Erwinia amylovora,* the fireblight pathogen, by colony hybridization with DNA from plasmid pEPA29. *Applied and Environmental Microbiology* 54:2798–2802.

Farrah, S. R., S. M. Goyal, C. P. Gerba, C. Wallis, and J. L. Melnick. 1977. Concentration of enteroviruses from estuarine water. *Applied and Environmental Microbiology* 33:1192–1196.

Faust, M. A., and D. L. Correll. 1977. Autoradiographic study to detect metabolically active phytoplankton and bacteria in Rhode River Estuary. *Marine Biology* 41:293–305.

Federle, T. W. 1988. Mineralization of monosubstituted aromatic compounds in unsaturated and saturated subsurface soils. *Canadian Journal of Microbiology* 34:1037–1042.

Federle, T., D. C. Dobbins, J. R. Thornton-Manning, and D. C. Jones. 1986. Microbial biomass, activity, and community structure in subsurface soils. *Ground Water* 24:365–374.

Festl, H., W. Ludwig, and K. H. Schleifer. 1986. DNA hybridization probe for the *Pseudomonas fluorescens* group. *Applied and Environmental Microbiology* 52:1190–1194.

Finlay, B. J. 1982. Procedures for the isolation, cultivation, and identification of bacteria. In R. G. Burns and J. H. Slater (eds.). *Experimental Microbial Ecology*. Blackwell, Oxford, England, pp. 44–65.

Finlay, B. J., J. Laybourn, and I. Strachan. 1979. A technique for the enumeration of benthic ciliated protozoa. *Oecologia* (Berlin) 39:375–377.

Fitts, R., M. Diamond, C. Hamilton, and M. Neri. 1983. DNA–DNA hybridization assay for the detection of *Salmonella* spp. in foods. *Applied and Environmental Microbiology* 46:1146–1151.

Fliermans, C. B., W. D. Cherry, L. H. Orrison, and L. Thacker. 1979. Isolation of *Legionella pneumophila* from nonepidemic-related aquatic habitats. *Applied and Environmental Microbiology* 37:1239–1242.

Fliermans, C. B., and E. L. Schmidt. 1975. Autoradiography and immunofluorescence combined for autecological study of single cell activity with *Nitrobacter* as a model system. *Applied Microbiology* 30:674–677.

Focht, D. D. 1982. Denitrification. In R. G. Burns and J. H. Slater (eds.). *Experimental Microbial Ecology*. Blackwell, Oxford, England, pp. 194–211.

Franzmann, P. D., B. M. Patterson, T. R. Powers, P. D. Nichols, and G. B. Davis. 1996. Microbial biomass in a shallow, urban aquifer contaminated with aromatic hydrocarbons: Analysis by phospholipid fatty acid content and composition. *Journal of Applied Bacteriology* 80:617–625.

Frederick, L. R. 1965. Microbial populations by direct microscopy. In C. A. Black (ed.). *Methods in Soil Analysis*. Part 2, Chemical and Microbiological Properties. American Society of Agronomy, Madison, WI, pp. 1452–1459.

Fuhrman, J. A., and F. Azam. 1980. Bacterioplankton secondary production estimates for coastal waters of British Columbia, Antarctica, and California. *Applied and Environmental Microbiology* 39:1085–1095.

Fuhrman, J. A., and F. Azam. 1982. Thymidine incorporation as a measure of heterotrophic bacterioplankton production in marine surface water: Evaluation and field results. *Marine Biology* 66:109–120.

Fuhrman, J. A., D. E. Comeau, A. Hagstrom, and A. M. Cham. 1988. Extraction from natural planktonic microorganisms of DNA suitable for molecular biological studies. *Applied and Environmental Microbiology* 54:1426–1429.

Fuhrman, J. A., H. Ducklow, D. L. Kirchman, J. Hudak, G. B. McManus, and J. Kramer. 1986. Does adenine incorporation into nucleic acids measure total microbial production? *Limnology and Oceanography* 31:627–636.

Geesey, G. G., and J. W. Costerton. 1979. Bacterial biomass determination in silt-laden river: Comparison of direct count epifluorescence microscopy and extractable adenosine triphosphate techniques. In J. W. Costerton and R. R. Colwell (eds.). *Native Aquatic Bacteria: Enumeration, Activity and Ecology*. ASTM Special Technical Publication No. 695. American Society for Testing Materials, Philadelphia, pp. 117–130.

Gerba, C. P. 1983. Methods for recovering viruses from the water environment. In G. Berg (ed.). *Viral Pollution of the Environment*. CRC Press, Boca Raton, FL, pp. 19–35.

Gerdes, H. H., and C. Kaether. 1996. Green fluorescent protein: Applications in cell biology. *FEMS Letters* 389:44–47.

Gessner, M. O., M. A. Bauchrowitz, and M. Escautier. 1991. Extraction and quantification of ergosterol as a measure of fungal biomass in leaf litter. *Microbial Ecology* 22:285–291.

Gillan, F. T., and R. W. Hogg. 1984. A method for the estimation of bacterial biomass and community structure in mangrove associated sediments. *Journal of Microbiological Methods* 2:275–293.

Gillan, F. T., R. B. Johns, T. V. Verhey, and P. D. Nichols. 1983. Monounsaturated fatty acids as specific bacterial markers in marine sediments. In M. Bjoroy (ed.). *Advances in Organic Geochemistry.* Wiley, New York, pp. 198–206.

Giovannoni, S. J., T. B. Britschgi, C. L. Moyer, and K. G. Field. 1990. Genetic diversity in Sargasso Sea bacterioplankton. *Nature* (London) 345:60–62.

Goodfellow, M., and D. E. Minnikin (eds.). 1985. *Chemical Methods in Bacterial Systematics.* Academic Press, London.

Gorden, R. W. 1972. *Field and Laboratory Microbial Ecology.* WC Brown, Dubuque, IA, pp. 47–50.

Goss, W. A., W. H. Deitz, and T. M. Cook. 1965. Mechanism of action of nalidixic acid on *Escherichia coli*. Part II, Inhibitor of DNA synthesis. *Journal of Bacteriology* 89:1068–1074.

Graham, L. B., A. D. Colburn, and J. C. Burke. 1976. A new, simple method for gently collecting planktonic protozoa. *Limnology and Oceanography* 21:336–341.

Graham, P. H., M. J. Sadowsky, S. W. Tighe, J. A. Thompson, R. A. Data, J. G. Hutchinson, and R. Thomas. 1995. Differences among strains of *Bradyrhizobium* in fatty acid-methyl ester analysis. *Canadian Journal of Microbiology* 41:1038–1042.

Gray, T.R.G. 1967. Stereoscan electron microscopy of soil microorganisms. *Science* 155:1668–1670.

Gray, T.R.G. 1973. The use of the fluorescent-antibody technique to study the ecology of *Bacillus subtilis* in soil. *Bulletin from the Ecological Research Committee* (Stockholm) 17:119–122.

Gray, T.R.G., P. Baxby, I. R. Hall, and M. Goodfellow. 1968. Direct observation of bacteria in soil. In T.R.G. Gray and D. Parkinson (eds.). *The Ecology of Soil Bacteria.* University of Toronto Press, Toronto, Canada, pp. 171–197.

Greenberg, A. E. (ed.). 1995. *Standard Methods for the Examination of Water and Wastewater.* Ed 19. American Public Health Association, New York.

Gregory, P. H. 1973. *The Microbiology of the Atmosphere.* Wiley, New York.

Griffiths, R. P., S. S. Hayasaka, T. M. McNamara, and R. Y. Morita. 1977. Comparison between two methods of assaying relative microbial activity in marine environments. *Applied and Environmental Microbiology* 34:801–805.

Grigorova, R., and J. R. Norris (eds). 1990. *Methods in Microbiology: vol. 22—Techniques in Microbial Ecology.* Academic Press, New York.

Grimes, D. J., and R. R. Colwell. 1983. Survival of pathogenic organisms in the Anacostia and Potomac rivers and the Chesapeake Bay Estuary. *Journal of the Washington Academy of Science* 73:45–50.

Grunstein, M., and D. S. Hogness. 1975. Colony hybridization: A method for the isolation of cloned DNAs that contain a specific gene. *Proceedings of the National Academy of Sciences USA* 72:3961–3965.

Guckert, J. B., C. P. Antworth, P. D. Nichols, and D. C. White. 1985. Phospholipid ester-linked fatty acid profiles as reproducible assays for changes in procaryotic community structure of estuarine sediments. *FEMS Microbial Ecology* 31:147–158.

Guckert, J. B., M. A. Hood, and D. C. White. 1986. Phospholipid ester-linked fatty acid profile changes during nutrient deprivation of *Vibrio cholerae:* Increase in the trans/cis ratio and proportions of cyclopropyl fatty acids. *Applied and Environmental Microbiology* 52:794–801.

Hadrys, H., M. Balick, and B. Schierwater. 1992. Applications of random amplified polymorphic DNA (RAPD) in molecular ecology. *Molecular Ecology* 1:55–63.

Hagstrom, A., V. Larsson, P. Horstedt, and S. Normark. 1979. Frequency of dividing cells, a new approach to the determination of bacterial growth rates in aquatic environments. *Applied and Environmental Microbiology* 37:805–812.

Hama, T., J. Hama, and N. Handa. 1993. $^{13}$C Tracer methodology in microbial ecology with special reference to primary production processes in aquatic environments. *Advances in Microbial Ecology* 13:39–84.

Hamilton, R. D., and O. Holm-Hansen. 1965. Adenosine triphosphate content of marine bacteria. *Limnology and Oceanography* 12:319–324.

Hanahan, D., and M. Meselson. 1980. Plasmid screening at high colony density. *Gene* 10:63–67.

Hanson, R. B. 1977. Nitrogen fixation (acetylene reduction) in a salt marsh amended with sewage sludge and organic carbon and nitrogen compounds. *Applied and Environmental Microbiology* 33:846–852.

Hardy, R.W.F., R. Holsten, E. K. Jackson, and R. C. Burns. 1968. The acetylene-ethylene assay for $N_2$ fixation:

Laboratory and field evaluation. *Plant Physiology* 43:1185–1207.

Harmsen, H.J.M., H.M.P. Kengen, A.D.L. Akkermans, A.J.M. Stoms, and W. W. de Vos. 1996. Detection and localization of syntrophic propionate-oxidizing bacteria in granular sludge by *in situ* hybridization using 16S rRNA-based oligonucleotide probes. *Applied and Environmental Microbiology* 62:1656–1664.

Harris, J. E., T. R. McKee, R. C. Wilson, and U. G. Whitehouse. 1972. Preparation of membrane filter samples for direct examination with an electron microscope. *Limnology and Oceanography* 17:784–787.

Hastings, J. W. 1995. Bioluminescence: Similar chemistries but many different evolutionary patterns. *Photochemistry and Photobiology* 62:599–600.

Hayes, F. R., and E. H. Anthony. 1959. Lake water and sediment. Part VI, The standing crop of bacteria in lake sediments and its place in the classification of lakes. *Limnology and Oceanography* 4:299–315.

Heal, O. W. 1970. Methods of study in soil protozoa. In J. Phillipson (ed.). *Methods of Study in Soil Ecology*. UNESCO, Paris, pp. 119–126.

Hendrick, D. B., R. D. Pledger, D. C. White, and J. A. Baross. 1992. *In situ* microbial ecology of hydrothermal vent sediments. *FEMS Microbial Ecology* 101:1–10.

Herbert, R. A. 1982. Procedures for the isolation, cultivation and identification of bacteria. In R. G. Burns and J. H. Slater (eds.). *Experimental Microbial Ecology*. Blackwell, Oxford, England, pp. 3–21.

Herrero, M., V. DeLorenzo, and K. N. Timmis. 1990. Transposon vectors containing non-antibiotic resistance selection markers for cloning and stable chromosomal insertion of foreign genes in Gram-negative bacteria. *Journal of Bacteriology* 172:6557–6567.

Hill, I. R., and T.R.G. Gray. 1967. Application of the fluorescent antibody technique to an ecological study of bacteria in soil. *Journal of Bacteriology* 93:1888–1896.

Hill, W. E., J. M. Madden, B. A. McCardell, D. B. Shah, J. A. Jagow, W. L. Payne, and B. K. Boutin. 1983a. Foodborne enterotoxigenic *Escherichia coli* detection and enumeration by DNA colony hybridization. *Applied and Environmental Microbiology* 45:1324–1330.

Hill, W. E., W. L. Payne, and C.C.G. Aulisio. 1983b. Detection and enumeration of virulent *Yersinia enterocolitica* in food by DNA colony hybridization. *Applied and Environmental Microbiology* 46:636–641.

Hirsch, P., and S. H. Pankratz. 1970. Study of bacterial populations in natural environments by use of submerged electron microscope grids. *Zeitschrift für Allgemeine Mikrobiologie* (Berlin) 10:589–605.

Hobbie, J. E., and C. C. Crawford. 1969. Respiration corrections for bacterial uptake of dissolved organic compounds in natural waters. *Limnology and Oceanography* 14:528–532.

Hobbie, J. E., O. Holm-Hansen, T. T. Packard, L. R. Pomeroy, R. W. Sheldon, J. P. Thomas, and W. J. Wiebe. 1972. A study of the distribution and activity of microorganisms in ocean water. *Limnology and Oceanography* 17:544–555.

Hobbie, J. E., R. J. Daley, and S. Jasper. 1977. Use of Nuclepore filters for counting bacteria by fluorescence microscopy. *Applied and Environmental Microbiology* 33:1225–1228.

Holben, W. E., J. K. Jansson, B. K. Chelm, and J. M. Tiedje. 1988. DNA probe methods for the detection of specific microorganisms in the soil bacterial community. *Applied and Environmental Microbiology* 54:703–711.

Holm-Hansen, O. 1969. Determination of microbial biomass in ocean profiles. *Limnology and Oceanography* 19:31–34.

Holm-Hansen, O. 1973a. Determination of total microbial biomass by measurement of adenosine triphosphate. In L. H. Stevenson and R. R. Colwell (eds.). *Estuarine Microbial Ecology*. University of South Carolina Press, Columbia, pp. 73–89.

Holm-Hansen, O. 1973b. The use of ATP determinations in ecological studies. *Bulletin from the Ecological Research Committee* (Stockholm) 17:215–222.

Holm-Hansen, O., and C. R. Booth. 1966. The measurement of adenosine triphosphate in the ocean and its ecological significance. *Limnology and Oceanography* 11:510–519.

Holm-Hansen, O., and B. Riemann. 1978. Chlorophyll a determination: Improvement in methodology. *Oikos* 30:438–447.

Holm-Hansen, O., W. H. Sutcliffe, and J. Sharpe. 1968. Measurement of deoxyribonucleic acid in the ocean and its ecological significance. *Limnology and Oceanography* 13:507–514.

Hoppe, H. G. 1976. Determination and properties of actively metabolizing heterotrophic bacteria in the sea, measured by means of microautoradiography. *Marine Biology* 36:291–302.

Hsu, T. S., and R. Bartha. 1979. Accelerated mineralization of two organophosphate insecticides in the rhizosphere. *Applied and Environmental Microbiology* 37:36–41.

Hubel, H. 1966. Die [14]C Methode zur Bestimmung der Primärproduktion des Phytoplanktons. *Limnologica* (Berlin) 4:267–280.

Hungate, R. E. 1969. A roll tube method for cultivation of strict anaerobes. In J. R. Norris and D. W. Ribbons (eds.). *Methods in Microbiology,* Vol. 3B. Academic Press, London, pp. 117–132.

Hungate, R. E., and J. Macy. 1973. The roll-tube method for cultivation of strict anaerobes. *Bulletin from the Ecological Research Committee* (Stockholm) 17:123–125.

Hurst, C. J., S. R. Farrah, C. P. Gerba, and J. L. Melnick. 1978. Development of quantitative methods for the detection of enteroviruses in sewage sludges during activation and following land disposal. *Applied and Environmental Microbiology* 36:81–89.

Hurst, C. J., G. R. Knudsen, M. J. McInerney, L. D. Stetzenbach, and M. V. Watter. 1997. *Manual of Environmental Microbiology.* American Society for Microbiology Press, Washington, DC.

Ingram, C., M. Brawner, P. Youngman, and J. Westpheling. 1989. *xylE* functions as an efficient reporter gene in *Streptomyces* spp.: Use for the study of *galP1,* a catabolite-controlled promoter. *Journal of Bacteriology* 171:6617–6624.

Innis, M., D. Gelfand, D. Sninsky, and T. White (eds.). 1990. *PCR Protocols: A Guide to Methods and Applications.* Academic Press, San Diego.

Jain, R. K., G. S. Sayler, J. T. Wilson, L. Houston, and D. Pacia. 1987. Maintenance and stability of introduced genotypes in groundwater aquifer material. *Applied and Environmental Microbiology* 53:996–1002.

Jannasch, H. W., and G. E. Jones. 1959. Bacterial populations in sea water as determined by different methods of enumeration. *Limnology and Oceanography* 4:128–139.

Jannasch, H. W., and W. S. Maddux. 1967. A note on bacteriological sampling of seawater. *Journal of Marine Research* 25:185–189.

Jannasch, H. W., and C. O. Wirsen. 1977. Retrieval of concentrated and undecompressed microbial populations from the deep sea. *Applied and Environmental Microbiology* 33:642–646.

Jansson, J. K., W. E. Holben, and J. M. Tiedje. 1989. Detection in soil of a deletion in an engineered DNA sequence by using gene probes. *Applied and Environmental Microbiology* 55:3022–3025.

Jenkinson, D. S. 1976. The effects of biocidal treatments on metabolism in soil. Part IV, The decomposition of fumigated organisms in soil. *Soil Biology and Biochemistry* 8:203–208.

Jenkinson, D. S., and J. M. Oades. 1979. A method for measuring adenosine triphosphate in soil. *Soil Biology and Biochemistry* 11:193–199.

Jenkinson, D. S., and D. S. Powlson. 1976. The effects of biocidal treatments on metabolism in soil. Part V, A method for measuring soil biomass. *Soil Biology and Biochemistry* 8:209–213.

Jensen, V. 1968. The plate count technique. In T.R.G. Gray and D. Parkinson (eds.). *The Ecology of Soil Bacteria.* University of Toronto Press, Toronto, Canada, pp. 158–170.

Jones, J. G., and B. M. Simon. 1975. An investigation of errors in direct counts of aquatic bacteria by epifluorescence microscopy, with reference to a new method for dying membrane filters. *Journal of Applied Bacteriology* 39:317–329.

Jones, P.C.T., and J. E. Mollison. 1948. The technique for the quantitative estimation of soil microorganisms. *Journal of General Microbiology* 2:54–69.

Kaneko, T., J. Hauxhurst, M. Krichevsky, and R. M. Atlas. 1978. Numerical taxonomic studies of bacteria isolated from Arctic and subarctic marine environments. In M. W. Loutit and J.A.R. Miles (eds.). *Microbial Ecology.* Springer-Verlag, Berlin, pp. 26–30.

Karl, D. M. 1979. Measurement of microbial activity and growth in the ocean by rates of stable ribonucleic acid synthesis. *Applied and Environmental Microbiology* 38:850–860.

Karl, D. M. 1980. Cellular nucleotide measurements and applications in microbial ecology. *Microbiological Reviews* 44:739–796.

Karl, D. M. 1981. Simultaneous rates of RNA and DNA synthesis for estimating growth and cell division of aquatic microbial communities. *Applied and Environmental Microbiology* 42:802–810.

Karl, D. M., and O. Holm-Hansen. 1978. Methodology and measurement of adenylate energy charge ratios in environmental samples. *Marine Biology* 48:185–197.

Karl, D. M., C. D. Winn, and D.C.L. Wong. 1981a. RNA synthesis as a measure of microbial growth in aquatic environments: Evaluation, verification, and optimization of methods. *Marine Biology* 64:1–12.

Karl, D. M., C. D. Winn, and D.C.L. Wong. 1981b. RNA synthesis as a measure of microbial growth in aquatic environments: Field measurements. *Marine Biology* 64:13–21.

Kemp, P. F., B. F. Sherr, E. B. Sherr, and J. J. Cole. 1993. *Handbook of Methods in Aquatic Microbial Ecology.* Lewis, Boca Raton, FL.

Kepner, R. L., Jr., and J. R. Pratt. 1994. Use of fluorochromes for direct enumeration of total bacteria in environmental samples: past and present. *Microbiological Reviews* 58:603–615.

Kieft, T. L., D. B. Ringelberg, and D. C. White. 1994. Changes in ester-linked phospholipid fatty acid profiles of subsurface bacteria during starvation and desiccation in a porous medium. *Applied and Environmental Microbiology* 60:3292–3299.

King, J. D., and D. C. White. 1977. Muramic acid as a measure of microbial biomass in estuarine and marine samples. *Applied and Environmental Microbiology* 33:777–783.

King, J.M.H., P. M. DiGrazia, B. Applegate, R. Burlage, J. Sanseverino, P. Dunbar, F. Larimer, and G. S. Sayler. 1990. Bioluminescent reporter plasmid for naphthalene exposure and biodegradation. *Science* 249:778–791.

King, R. J., K. A. Short, and R. J. Seidler. 1991. Assay for detection and enumeration of genetically engineered microorganisms which is based on the activity of a deregulated 2,4-dichlorophenoxyacetate monooxygenase. *Applied and Environmental Microbiology* 57:1790–1792.

Knight, I. T., W. E. Holben, J. M. Tiedje, and R. R. Colwell. 1992. Nucleic acid hybridization techniques for detection, identification, and enumeration of microorganisms in the environment. In M. A. Levin, R. J. Seidler, and M. Rogul (eds.). *Microbial Ecology: Principles, Methods, and Applications.* McGraw-Hill, New York, pp. 65–91.

Kogure, K., U. Simidu, and N. Taga. 1979. A tentative direct microscopic method for counting living marine bacteria. *Canadian Journal of Microbiology* 25:415–420.

Kohring, L. L., D. B. Ringelberg, R. Devereux, D. A. Stahl, M. W. Mittelman, and D. C. White. 1994. Comparison of phylogenetic relationships based on phospholipid fatty acid profiles and ribosomal RNA sequence similarities among dissimilatory sulfate-reducing bacteria. *FEMS Microbiology Letters* 119:303–308.

Kubitschek, H. E. 1969. Counting and sizing microorganisms with the Coulter counter. In J. R. Norris and D. W. Ribbons (eds.). *Methods in Microbiology,* Vol. 1. Academic Press, London, pp. 593–610.

Kunicka-Goldfinger, W. 1976. Determination of growth of aquatic bacteria by measurements of incorporation of tritiated thymidine. *Acta Micobiologica Poland* 25:279–286.

Larsson, K., C. Wenbull, and G. Cronberg. 1978. Comparison of light and electron microscopic determinations of the number of bacteria and algae in lake water. *Applied and Environmental Microbiology* 35:397–404.

Latt, S. A., and G. Statten. 1976. Spectral studies on 33258 Hoechst and related bisbenzimadazole dyes useful for fluorescent detection of DNA synthesis. *Journal of Histochemistry and Cytochemistry* 24:24–32.

Lechevalier, M. P. 1977. Lipids in bacterial taxonomy—a taxonomist's view. *CRC Critical Reviews in Microbiology* 5:109–210.

Lee, C., N. J. Russell, and G. F. White. 1995. Rapid screening of bacterial phenotypes capable of biodegrading anionic sulfactants: Development and validation of a microtitre plate method. *Microbiology* 141:2801–2810.

Lee, S., and J. A. Fuhrman. 1990. DNA hybridization to compare species compositions of natural bacterioplankton assemblages. *Applied and Environmental Microbiology* 56:739–746.

Leff, L. G., and A. A. Leff. 1996. Use of green fluorescent protein to monitor survival of genetically engineered bacteria in aquatic environments. *Applied and Environmental Microbiology* 62:3486–3488.

Lindgren, P. B., R. Frederick, A. G. Govindarajan, N. J. Panopoulos, B. J. Staskawicz, and S. E. Lindow. 1989. An ice nucleation reporter gene system: Identification of inducible pathogenicity genes in *Pseudomonas syringae* pv. *phaseolicola. EMBO Journal* 8:1291–1301.

Lindow, S. E. 1995. The use of reporter genes in the study of microbial ecology. *Molecular Ecology* 4:555–566.

Lloyd, A. B. 1973. Estimation of actinomycete spores in air. *Bulletin from the Ecological Research Committee* (Stockholm) 17:168–169.

Lloyd, D., and A. J. Hayes. 1995. Vigour, vitality, and viability of microorganisms. *FEMS Microbiology Letters* 133:1–7.

Loftus, M. E., and J. H. Carpenter. 1971. A fluorometric method for determining chlorophylls a, b and c. *Journal of Marine Research* 29:319–338.

Lorenzen, C. J. 1966. A method for the continuous measurement of *in vivo* chlorophyll concentration. *Deep-Sea Research* 13:223–227.

Lowry, O. H., N. J. Rosebrough, A. L. Farr, and R. J. Randall. 1951. Protein measurement with the Folin phenol reagent. *Journal of Biological Chemistry* 193:265–275.

Lunge, V. R., N. Ikuta, A.S.K. Fonseca, D. Hirigoyen, M. Stoll, and S. Bonatto. 1994. Identification and interrelationship analysis of *Bradyrhizobium japonicum* strains by restriction fragment length polymorphism (RFLP) and random amplified polymorphic DNA (RAPD). *World Journal of Microbiology & Biotechnology* 10:648–652.

Mancuso, C. A., P. D. Franzmann, H. R. Burton, and P. D. Nichols. 1990. Microbial community structure and biomass estimates of a methanogenic Antarctic Lake ecosystem as determined by phospholipid analyses. *Microbial Ecology* 19:73–95.

Maniatis, T., E. F. Fritsch, and J. Sambrook. 1982. *Molecular Cloning: A Laboratory Manual.* Cold Spring Harbor Laboratory, Cold Spring Harbor Press, New York.

Massol-Deyá, A. R. Weller, L. Rias-Hernandez, J.-Z. Zhou, R. F. Hickey, and J. M. Tiedje. 1997. Succession and convergence of biofilm communities in fixed-film reactors treating aromatic hydrocarbons in groundwater. *Applied and Environmental Microbiology* 63:270–276.

McCoy, W. F., and B. H. Olson. 1985. Fluorometric determination of the DNA concentration in municipal drinking water. *Applied and Environmental Microbiology* 49:811–817.

Melchiorri-Santolini, U. 1972. Enumeration of microbial concentration of dilution series (MPN). In Y. I. Sorokin and H. Kadota (eds.). *Techniques for the Assessment of Microbial Production and Decomposition in Fresh Waters.* IBP Handbook No. 23. Blackwell, Oxford, England, pp. 64–70.

Menzies, J. D. 1965. Fungi. In C. A. Black (ed.). *Methods of Soil Analysis.* Part 2, Chemical and Microbiological Properties. American Society of Agronomy, Madison, WI, pp. 1502–1505.

Metcalf, T. G., J. L. Melnick, and M. K. Estes. 1995. Environmental virology: From detection of virus in sewage and water by isolation to identification by molecular biology—a trip of over 50 years. *Annual Review of Microbiology* 49:461–488.

Meyer-Reil, L. A. 1978. Autoradiography and epifluorescent microscopy combined for the determination of number and spectrum of actively metabolizing bacteria in natural waters. *Applied and Environmental Microbiology* 36:506–512.

Miliotis, M. D., J. E. Galen, J. B. Kaper, and J. G. Morris, Jr. 1989. Development and testing of a synthetic oligonucleotide probe for the detection of pathogenic *Yersinia* strains. *Journal of Clinical Microbiology* 27:1667–1670.

Millar, W. N., and L. E. Casida, Jr. 1970. Evidence for muramic acid in soil. *Canadian Journal of Microbiology* 16:299–304.

Moran, M. A., V. L. Torsvik, T. Torsvik, and R. E. Hodson. 1993. Direct extraction and purification of rRNA for ecological studies. *Applied and Environmental Microbiology* 59:915–918.

Moriarty, D.J.W. 1975. A method for estimating the biomass of bacteria in aquatic sediments and its application in trophic studies. *Oecologia* (Berlin) 20:219–229.

Moriarty, D.J.W. 1977. Improved method using muramic acid to estimate biomass of bacteria in sediments. *Oecologia* (Berlin) 26:317–323.

Moriarty, D.J.W. 1978. Estimation of bacterial biomass in water and sediments using muramic acid. In M. W. Loutit and J.A.R. Miles (eds.). *Microbial Ecology.* Springer-Verlag, Berlin, pp. 31–33.

Moriarty, D.J.W. 1986. Measurement of bacterial growth rates in aquatic systems from rates of nucleic acid synthesis. *Advances in Microbial Ecology* 9:246–292.

Morris, I. 1982. Primary production of the oceans. In R. G. Burns and J. H. Slater (eds.). *Experimental Microbial Ecology.* Blackwell, Oxford, England, pp. 239–254.

Mullis, K. B. 1990. The unusual origin of the polymerase chain reaction. *Scientific American* 262(4):56–65.

Mullis, K. B., and F. A. Faloona. 1987. Specific synthesis of DNA in vitro via a polymerase-catalyzed chain reaction. *Methods in Enzymology* 155:335–351.

Mullis, K., F. Faloona, S. Scharf, R. Saiki, G. Horn, and H. Ehrlich. 1986. Specific enzymatic amplification of DNA in vitro: The polymerase chain reaction. *Cold Spring Harbor Symposium on Quantitative Biology* 51:263–273.

Muyzer, G., E. D. deWaal, and A. G. Vitterlinden. 1993. Profiling of complex microbial populations by denaturing gradient gel electrophoresis analysis of polymerase chain reaction amplified genes coding for 16S rRNA. *Applied and Environmental Microbiology* 59:695–700.

Nambair, P.T.C., and V. Anjaiah. 1985. Enumeration of rhizobia by enzyme-linked immunosorbent assay (ELISA). *Journal of Applied Bacteriology* 58:187–193.

Nannipieri, P., R. L. Johnson, and E. A. Paul. 1978. Criteria for measurement of microbial growth in soil. *Soil Biology and Biochemistry* 10:223–229.

Nichols, P. D., J. B. Guckert, and D. C. White. 1986. Determination of monounsaturated fatty acid double bond position and egeometry for microbial monocultures and complex consortia by capillary GC-MS of their dimethyl disulphide adducts. *Journal of Microbiological Methods* 5:49–55.

Nichols, P. D., C. A. Mancuso, and D. C. White. 1987. Measurement of methanotroph and methanogen signature phospholipids for use in assessment of biomass and community structure in model ecosystems. *Organic Geochemistry* 11:451–461.

Nikitin, D. I. 1973. Direct electron microscopic techniques for the observation of microorganisms in soil. *Bulletin from the Ecological Research Committee* (Stockholm) 17:85–92.

Nortermans, S., T. Chakrobarty, M. Leimeister-Wachter, J. Dufrenne, and K. J. Heuvelman. 1989. Specific gene probe for detection of biotyped and serotype *Listeria* strains. *Applied and Environmental Microbiology* 55:902–906.

Nybroe, O. 1995. Assessment of metabolic activity of single bacterial cells and new developments in microcolony and dehydrogenase assays. *FEMS Microbiology Ecology* 17:77–83.

Oades, J. M., and D. S. Jenkinson. 1979. Adenosine triphosphate content of the soil microbial biomass. *Soil Biology and Biochemistry* 11:201–204.

Ogram, A., G. S. Sayler, and T. Barkay. 1987. The extraction and purification of microbial DNA from sediments. *Journal of Microbiological Methods* 7:57–66.

Oleniacz, W. S., M. A. Pisano, M. H. Rosenfeld, and R. L. Elgart. 1968. Chemiluminescent method for detecting micro-organisms in water. *Environmental Science and Technology* 2:1030–1033.

Olson, B. H. 1978. Enhanced accuracy of coliform testing in seawater by a modification of the most probable number method. *Applied and Environmental Microbiology* 36:438–444.

Pace, N. R. 1996. New perspectives on the natural microbial world: molecular microbial ecology. *ASM News* 62:463–470.

Paerl, H. W., M. M. Tilzer, and C. R. Goldman. 1976. Chlorophyll a versus adenosine triphosphate as algal biomass indicators in lakes. *Journal of Phycology* 12:242–246.

Paerl, H. W., and N. J. Williams. 1976. The relation between adenosine triphosphate and microbial biomass in diverse aquatic ecosystems. *Internationale Revue der gesamten Hydrobiologie* 61:659–664.

Pangburn, S. J., M. S. Hall, and F. R. Leach. 1994. Improvements in the extraction of bacterial ATP from soil with field application. *Journal of Microbial Methods* 20:197–209.

Parkinson, D. 1970. Methods for the quantitative study of heterotrophic soil microorganisms. In J. Phillipson (ed.). *Methods of Study in Soil Ecology*. UNESCO, Paris, pp. 101–105.

Parkinson, D. 1973. Techniques for the study of soil fungi. *Bulletin from the Ecological Research Committee* (Stockholm) 17:29–36.

Parkinson, D. 1982. Procedures for the isolation, cultivation and identification of fungi. In R. G. Burns and J. H. Slater (eds.). *Experimental Microbial Ecology*. Blackwell, Oxford, England, pp. 22–30.

Parkinson, D., T.R.G. Gray, and S. T. Williams. 1971. *Methods for Studying the Ecology of Soil Micro-Organisms*. IBP Handbook No. 19. Blackwell, Oxford, England.

Parsons, T. R., and J. D. H. Strickland. 1962. On the production of particulate organic carbon by heterotrophic processes in sea water. *Deep Sea Research* 8:211–222.

Paul, J. H. 1982. Use of Hoechst dyes 33258 and 33342 for enumeration of attached and planktonic bacteria. *Applied and Environmental Microbiology* 43:939–944.

Paul, J. H., L. Cazares, and J. Thurmond. 1990. Amplification of the *rbc*L gene from dissolved and particulate DNA from aquatic environments. *Applied and Environmental Microbiology* 56:1963–1966.

Paul, J. H., and B. Meyers. 1982. Fluorometric determination of DNA in aquatic microorganisms by use of Hoechst 33258. *Applied and Environmental Microbiology* 43:1393–1399.

Peele, E. R., and R. R. Colwell. 1981. Application of a direct microscopic method enumeration of substrate-responsive marine bacteria. *Canadian Journal of Microbiology* 27:1071–1075.

Pepper, I. L., C. P. Gerba, and J. W. Brendecke. 1995. *Environmental Microbiology: A Laboratory Manual.* Academic Press, San Diego.

Perfilev, B. V., and D. R. Gabe. 1969. *Capillary Methods of Investigating Microorganisms.* Oliver and Boyd, Edinburgh, Scotland.

Petersen, S. O., and M. J. Klug. 1994. Effects of sieving, storage, and incubation temperature on the phospholipid fatty acid profile of a soil community. *Applied and Environmental Microbiology* 60:2421–2430.

Pettigrew, C. A., and G. S. Sayler. 1986. The use of DNA:DNA colony hybridization in the rapid isolation of 4-chlorobiphenyl degradative bacterial phenotypes. *Journal of Microbiological Methods* 5:205–213.

Pettipher, G. L., and U. M. Rodrigues. 1982. Semi-automated counting of bacteria and somatic cells in milk using epifluorescence microscopy and television image analysis. *Journal of Applied Bacteriology* 53:323–329.

Porter, K. G., and Y. S. Feig. 1980. The use of DAPI for identifying and counting aquatic microflora. *Limnology and Oceanography* 25:943–948.

Postgate, J. R. 1969. Viable counts and viability. In J. R. Norris and D. W. Ribbons (eds.). *Methods in Microbiology.* Vol. 1. Academic Press, London, pp. 611–628.

Pramer, R., and R. Bartha. 1972. Preparation and processing of soil samples for biodegradation studies. *Environmental Letters* 2:217–224.

Pratt, D., and J. Reynolds. 1972. Selective media for characterizing marine bacterial populations. In R. R. Colwell and R. Y. Morita (eds.). *Effect of the Ocean Environment on Microbial Activities.* University Park Press, Baltimore, pp. 258–267.

Primrose, S. B., N. D. Seeley, and K. B. Logan. 1982. Methods for the study of virus ecology. In R. G. Burns and J. H. Slater (eds.). *Experimental Microbial Ecology.* Blackwell, Oxford, England, pp. 66–83.

Prosser, J. I., and D. J. Cox. 1982. Nitrification. In R. G. Burns and J. H. Slater (eds.). *Experimental Microbial Ecology.* Blackwell, Oxford, England, pp. 178–193.

Quinn, J. P. 1984. The modification and evaluation of some cytochemical techniques for the enumeration of metabolically active heterotrophic bacteria in the aquatic environment. *Journal of Applied Bacteriology* 57:51–57.

Rajendran, N., O. Matsuda, N. Imamura, and Y. Urushigawa. 1992a. Determination of microbial biomass and its community structure from the distribution of phospholipid ester-linked fatty acids in sediments of Hiroshima Bay and its adjacent bays. *Estuarine Coastal and Shelf Science* 34:501–514.

Rajendran, N., Y. Suwa, and Y. Urushigawa. 1992b. Microbial community structure in sediments of a polluted bay as determined by phospholipid ester-linked fatty acids. *Marine Pollution Bulletin* 24:305–309.

Ramsay, A. J. 1974. The use of autoradiography to determine the proportion of bacteria metabolizing in an aquatic habitat. *Journal of General Microbiology* 80:363–373.

Ramsing, N. B., H. Fossing, T. G. Ferdelman, F. Anderson, and B. Thamdrup. 1996. Distribution of bacterial populations in a stratified fjord (Mariager Fjord, Denmark) quantified by *in situ* hybridization and related to chemical gradients in the water column. *Applied and Environmental Microbiology* 62:1391–1405.

Rattledge, C., and S. G. Wilkinson (eds.). 1988. *Microbial Lipids.* Academic Press, London.

Rattray, E.A.S., J. I. Prosser, K. Killham, and L. A. Glover. 1990. Luminescence-based nonextractive technique for *in situ* detection of *E. coli* in soil. *Applied and Environmental Microbiology* 56:3368–3374.

Renwick, A., and D. G. Jones. 1985. A comparison of the fluorescent ELISA and antibiotic resistance identification techniques for use in ecological experiments with *Rhizobium trifolii. Journal of Applied Bacteriology* 58:199–206.

Revsbech, N. P. 1983. *In situ* measurement of oxygen profiles of sediment by use of oxygen microelectrodes. In E. G. Grainger and H. Forstner (eds.). *Polarographic Oxygen Sensors: Aquatic and Physiological Applications.* Springer-Verlag, Heidelberg, Germany, pp. 265–273.

Revsbech, N. P., B. B. Jorgenson, T. H. Blackburn, and Y. Cohen. 1983. Microelectrode studies of the photosynthesis and $O_2$, $H_2S$, and pH profiles of a microbial mat. *Limnology and Oceanography* 28:1062–1074.

Riemann, B., and R. T. Bell. 1990. Advances in estimating bacterial biomass and growth in aquatic systems. *Archive of Hydrobiology* 118:385–402.

Robarts, R. D., and T. Zohary. 1993. Fact or fiction— Bacterial growth rates and production as determined by [methyl-$^3$H]thymidine. *Advances in Microbial Ecology* 13:371–426.

Rogowsky, P. M., T. J. Close, J. A. Chimera, J. J. Shaw, and C. I. Kado. 1987. Regulation of the *vir* genes of *Agrobacterium tumefaciens* plasmid pTi58. *Journal of Bacteriology* 169:5101–5112.

Rossi, G., S. Riccardo, G. Gesue, M. Stanganelli, and T. K. Wang. 1936. Direct microscopic and bacteriological investigations of the soil. *Soil Science* 41:53–66.

Roszak, D. B., and R. R. Colwell. 1987a. Metabolic activity of bacterial cells enumerated by direct viable count. *Applied and Environmental Microbiology* 53:2889–2983.

Roszak, D. B., and R. R. Colwell. 1987b. Survival strategies of bacteria in the natural environment. *Microbiological Reviews* 51:365–379.

Round, F. E. 1982. Procedures for the isolation, cultivation, and identification of algae. In R. G. Burns and J. H. Slater (eds.). *Experimental Microbial Ecology.* Blackwell, Oxford, England, pp. 31–43.

Rowe, R., R. Todd, and J. Waide. 1977. Microtechnique for most-probable-number analysis. *Applied and Environmental Microbiology* 33:675–680.

Russell, W. C., C. Newman, and D. H. Williamson. 1975. A simple cytochemical technique for demonstration of DNA in cells infected with mycoplasmas and viruses. *Nature* (London) 253:461–462.

Sambrook, J., E. F. Fritsch, and T. Maniatis. 1989. In N. Ford, C. Nolan, and M. Feruson (eds.). *Molecular Cloning: A Laboratory Manual,* Vols. I–III. Cold Spring Harbor Laboratory Press, Cold Spring Harbor, New York.

Sayler, G. S., and A. C. Layton. 1990. Environmental application of nucleic acid hybridization. *Annual Review of Microbiology* 44:625–648.

Sayler, G. S., M. S. Shields, E. T. Tedford, A. Breen, S. W. Hooper, K. M. Sirotkin, and J. W. Davis. 1985. Application of DNA-DNA colony hybridization to the detection of catabolic genotypes in environmental samples. *Applied and Environmental Microbiology* 49:1295–1303.

Schmidt, E. L. 1973. Fluorescent antibody techniques for the study of microbial ecology. *Bulletin from the Ecological Research Committee* (Stockholm) 17:67–76.

Schmidt, E. L., R. O. Bankole, and B. B. Bohlool. 1968. Fluorescent-antibody approach to study of rhizobia in soil. *Journal of Bacteriology* 95:1987–1992.

Schramm, A., L. H. Laarsen, N. P. Revsbech, N. B. Ramsing, R. Amann, and K.-H. Schleifer. 1996. Structure and function of a nitrifying biofilm as determined by *in situ* hybridization and the use of microelectrodes. *Applied and Environmental Microbiology* 62:4641–4647.

Shapton, D. A., and R. G. Board (eds.). 1971. *Isolation of Anaerobes.* The Society for Applied Bacteriology Technical Ser. No. 5. Academic Press, London.

Sharabi, E. D., and D. Pramer. 1973. A spectrophotofluorometric method for studying algae in soil. *Bulletin from the Ecological Research Committee* (Stockholm) 17:77–84.

Sharma, P. D., P. J. Fisher, and J. Webster. 1977. Critique of the chitin assay technique for estimation of fungal biomass. *Transactions of the British Mycological Society* 69:479–483.

Shaw, J. J., and C. I. Kado. 1986. Development of a *Vibrio* bioluminescence gene-set to monitor phytopathogenic bacteria during the ongoing disease process in a nondisruptive manner. *Bio/Techniques* 4:560–564.

Shuval, H. I., and E. Katzenelson. 1972. The detection of enteric viruses in the water environment. In R. Mitchell (ed.). *Water Pollution Microbiology.* Wiley, New York, pp. 347–361.

Sieracki, M. E., P. W. Johnson, and J. M. Sieburth. 1985. Detection, enumeration, and sizing of planktonic bacteria by image-analyzed epifluorescence microscopy. *Applied and Environmental Microbiology* 49:799–810.

Simidu, U. 1972. Improvement of media for enumeration and isolation of heterotrophic bacteria in seawater. In R. R. Colwell and R. Y. Morita (eds.). *Effect of the Ocean Environment on Microbial Activities.* University Park Press, Baltimore, pp. 249–257.

Singh, B. N. 1946. A method of estimating the numbers of soil protozoa, especially amoeba, based on their differential feeding on bacteria. *Annals of Applied Biology* 33:112–119.

Skinner, F. A., P.C.T. Jones, and J. E. Mollison. 1952. A comparison of a direct and a plate counting technique for quantitative estimation of soil microorganisms. *Journal of General Microbiology* 6:261–271.

Skujins, J. 1967. Enzymes in soil. In A. D. McLaren and G. H. Peterson (eds.). *Soil Biochemistry.* Vol. 1. Marcel Dekker, New York, pp. 371–414.

Skujins, J. 1973. Dehydrogenase: An indicator of biological activities in arid soils. *Bulletin from the Ecological Research Committee* (Stockholm) 17:235–241.

Smith, D. W. 1982. Nitrogen fixation. In R. G. Burns and J. H. Slater (eds.). *Experimental Microbial Ecology.* Blackwell, Oxford, England, pp. 212–220.

Smith, D. W., C. B. Fliermans, and T. D. Brock. 1972. Technique for measuring $^{14}CO_2$ uptake by soil microorganisms *in situ*. *Applied Microbiology* 23:595–600.

Sobsey, M. D. 1982. Quality of currently available methodology for monitoring viruses in the environment. *Environment International* 7:39–51.

Sobsey, M. D., R. J. Carrick, and H. R. Jensen. 1978. Improved methods for detecting enteric viruses in oysters. *Applied and Environmental Microbiology* 36:121–128.

Soderstrom, D. E. 1977. Vital staining of fungi in pure cultures and in soil with fluorescein diacetate. *Soil Biology and Biochemistry* 9:59–63.

Sommerville, C. C.,T. T. Knight, W. L. Straub, and R. R. Colwell. 1989. Simple, rapid method for direct isolation of nucleic acids from aquatic environments. *Applied and Environmental Microbiology* 55:548–554.

Sorenson, J. 1978. Denitrification rates in a marine sediment as measured by the acetylene inhibition technique. *Applied and Environmental Microbiology* 36:139–143.

Sparling, G. P., and A. W. West. 1988. A direct extraction method to estimate soil microbial C: Calibration *in situ* using microbial respiration and $^{14}C$ labelled cells. *Soil Biology and Biochemistry* 20:337–343.

Staley, J. T., and A. Konopka. 1985. Measurement of *in situ* activities of nonphotosynthetic microorganisms in aquatic and terrestrial habitats. *Annual Review of Microbiology* 39:321–346.

Stanier, R. Y., and J.H.C. Smith. 1960. The chlorophylls of green bacteria. *Biochimica et Biophysica Acta* 41:478–484.

Steffan, R. J., and R. M. Atlas. 1988. DNA amplification to enhance the detection of genetically engineered bacteria in environmental samples. *Applied and Environmental Microbiology* 54:2185–2191.

Steffan, R. J., J. Goksøyr, A. K. Bej, and R. M. Atlas. 1988. Recovery of DNA from soils and sediments. *Applied and Environmental Microbiology* 54:2908–2915.

Steffan, R. J., and R. M. Atlas. 1990. Solution hybridization assay for detecting genetically engineered microorganisms in environmental samples. *Bio/Techniques* 8:316–318.

Steffan, R. J., and R. M. Atlas. 1991. Polymerase chain reaction: Applications in environmental microbiology. *Annual Reviews of Microbiology* 45:137–161.

Stetzenbach, L. D. 1992. Airborne microorganisms. In *Encyclopedia of Microbiology,* vol. 1. Academic Press, New York., pp. 53–65.

Stevenson, L. H., C. E. Millwood, and B. H. Hebeler. 1972. Aerobic, heterotrophic bacterial populations in estuarine water and sediments. In R. R. Colwell and R. Y. Morita (eds.). *Effect of the Ocean Environment on Microbial Activities.* University Park Press, Baltimore, pp. 268–285.

Stevenson, L. H., T. H. Chrazanowski, and C. W. Erkenbrecher. 1979. The adenosine triphosphate assay: Conceptions and misconceptions. In J. W. Costerton and R. R. Colwell (eds.). *Native Aquatic Bacteria: Enumeration, Activity and Ecology.* ASTM Special Technical Publication No. 695, American Society for Testing and Materials, Philadelphia, pp. 99–116.

Strayer, R. F., and J. M. Tiedje. 1978. Application of fluorescent-antibody technique to the study of a methanogenic bacterium in lake sediments. *Applied and Environmental Microbiology* 35:192–198.

Strugger, S. 1948. Fluorescence microscope examination of bacteria. *Canadian Journal of Research,* Ser. C 26:188–193.

Sutcliffe, W. H., Jr., E. A. Orr, and O. Holm-Hansen. 1976. Difficulties with ATP measurements in inshore waters. *Limnology and Oceanography* 21:145–149.

Swift, M. J. 1973. Estimation of mycelial growth during decomposition of plant litter. *Bulletin from the Ecological Research Committee* (Stockholm) 17:323–328.

Tate, K. R., D. J. Ross, and C. W. Feltham. 1988. A direct extraction method soil microbial C: Effect of experimental variables and some different calibration procedures. *Soil Biology Biochemistry* 20:329–335.

Thomas, A., D. P. Nicholoas, and D. Parkinson. 1965. Modification of the agar film technique for assaying lengths of mycelium in soil. *Nature* (London) 205:105.

Tiedje, J. M., S. M. Thiem, A. Massol-Deya, J. O. Ka, and M. R. Fries. 1995. Tracking microbial populations effective in reducing exposure. *Environmental Health Perspectives* 103 Suppl 5:117–120.

Todd, R. L., K. Cromack, Jr., and R. M. Knutson. 1973. Scanning electron microscopy in the study of terrestrial microbial ecology. *Bulletin from the Ecological Research Committee* (Stockholm) 17:109–118.

Tornabene, T. G. 1985. Lipid analysis and the relationship to chemotaxonomy. *Methods in Microbiology* 18:209–234.

Torsvik, V. L. 1980. Isolation of bacterial DNA from soil. *Soil Biology Biochemistry* 12:15–21.

Torsvik, V. L., and J. Goksøyr. 1978. Determination of bacterial DNA in soil. *Soil Biology Biochemistry* 10:7–12.

Torsvik, V. L., J. Goksøyr, and F. I. Daae. 1990. High diversity in DNA of soil bacteria. *Applied and Environmental Microbiology* 56:782–787.

Trolldenier, G. 1973. The use of fluorescence microscopy for counting soil microorganisms. *Bulletin from the Ecological Research Committee* (Stockholm) 17:53–59.

Tsernoglon, D., and E. H. Anthony. 1971. Particle size, water-stable aggregates, and bacterial populations in lake sediments. *Canadian Journal of Microbiology* 17:217–227.

Umbreit, W. W., R. H. Burris, and J. F. Stauffer. 1964. *Manometric Techniques*. Burgess, Minneapolis, MN.

Vaccaro, R. F., and H. W. Jannasch. 1967. Variations in uptake kinetics for glucose by natural populations in seawater. *Limnology and Oceanography* 12:540–542.

Valdivia, R. H., A. E. Hromockyj, D. Monack, L. Ramakrishnan, and S. Falkow. 1996. Applications for green fluorescent protein (GFP) in the study of host-pathogen interactions. *Gene* 173:47–52.

Van Es, F. B., and L. A. Meyer-Reil. 1982. Biomass and metabolic activity of heterotrophic marine bacteria. *Advances in Microbial Ecology* 6:111–170.

Van Wambeke, F. 1988. Numeration et taille des bacteries planctoniques au moyen de l'analyse d'images couplee a l'epifluorescence. *Annales de l'Institut Pasteur—Microbiology* (Amsterdam) 139:261–272.

Venosa, A. D., J. R. Haines, W. Nisamaneepong, R. Govind, S. Pradhan, and B. Siddique. 1992. Efficacy of commercial products in enhancing oil biodegradation in closed laboratory reactors. *Journal of Industrial Microbiology* 10:13–23.

Waid, J. S., K. J. Preston, and P. J. Harris. 1973. Autoradiographic techniques to detect active microbial cells in natural habitats. *Bulletin from the Ecological Research Committee* (Stockholm) 17:317–322.

Wallis, C., J. L. Melnick, and C. P. Gerba. 1979. Concentration of viruses from water by membrane chromatography. *Annual Review of Microbiology* 33:413–438.

Wallner, G., R. Erhart, and R. Amann. 1995. Flow cytometric analysis of activated sludge with rRNA-targeted probes. *Applied and Environmental Microbiology* 61:1859–1867.

Walton, W. H. 1952. Automatic counting of microscopic particles. *Nature* (London) 169:518–520.

Watson, S. W., and J. E. Hobbie. 1979. Measurement of bacterial biomass as lipopolysaccharide. In J. W. Costerton and R. R. Colwell (eds.). *Native Aquatic Bacteria: Enumeration, Activity and Ecology*. ASTM Special Technical Publication No. 695, American Society for Testing and Materials, Philadelphia, pp. 82–88.

Watson, S. W., T. J. Novitsky, H. L. Quinby, and F. W. Valois. 1977. Determination of bacterial number and biomass in the marine environment. *Applied and Environmental Microbiology* 33:940–946.

Weaver, R. W. (ed.). 1994. *Methods of Soil Analysis: Part 2—Microbiological and Biochemical Properties*. Soil Science Society of America, Madison, WI.

Webster, J. J., G. J. Hampton, and F. R. Leach. 1984. ATP in soil: A new extractant and extraction procedure. *Soil Biology and Biochemistry* 16:335–342.

Weller, R., and D. M. Ward. 1989. Selective recovery of 16S rRNA sequences from natural microbial communities in the form of cDNA. *Applied and Environmental Microbiology* 55:1818–1822.

White, D. C. 1983. Analysis of microorganisms in terms of quantity and activity in natural environments. *Society for General Microbiology Symposium* 34:37–66.

White, D. C. 1988. Validation of quantitative analysis for microbial biomass, community structure, and metabolic activity. *Archiv für Hydrobiologie Ergebrisse der Limnogie* 31:1–18.

White, D. C. 1995. Chemical ecology: Possible linkage between macro- and microbial ecology. *Oikos* 74:177–184.

White, D. C., R. J. Bobbie, J. S. Herron, J. D. King, and S. J. Morrison. 1979. Biochemical measurements of microbial mass and activity from environmental samples. In J. W. Costerton and R. R. Colwell (eds.). *Native Aquatic Bacteria: Enumeration, Activity and Ecology.* ASTM Special Technical Publication No. 695, American Society for Testing and Materials, Philadelphia, pp. 69–81.

Wiebe, W. J., and K. Bancroft. 1975. Use of the adenylate energy charge ratio to measure growth state of natural microbial communities. *Proceedings of the National Academy of Science USA* 72:2112–2115.

Willoughby, L. G. 1978. Methods for studying microorganisms on decaying leaves and wood in fresh water. In D. W. Lovelock and R. Davies (eds.). *Techniques for the Study of Mixed Populations.* Academic Press, London, pp. 31–50.

Wolf, H. W. 1972. The coliform count. In R. Mitchell (ed.). *Water Pollution Microbiology.* Wiley, New York, pp. 333–345.

Wright, R. T. 1973. Some difficulties in using [14]C-organic solutes to measure heterotrophic bacterial activity. In L. H. Stevenson and R. R. Colwell (eds.). *Estuarine Microbial Ecology.* University of South Carolina Press, Columbia, pp. 199–217.

Wright, R. T. 1978. Measurement and significance of specific bacteria of natural waters. *Applied and Environmental Microbiology* 36:297–305.

Wright, R. T., and J. E. Hobbie. 1965. The uptake of organic solutes in lake water. *Limnology and Oceanography* 10:23–28.

Wright, R. T., and J. E. Hobbie. 1966. Use of glucose and acetate by bacteria and algae in aquatic ecosystems. *Ecology* 47:447–464.

Wright, S. F. 1992. Immunological techniques for detection, identification, and enumeration of microorganisms in the environment. In M. A. Levin, R. J. Seidler, and M. Rogul (eds.). *Microbial Ecology: Principles, Methods, and Applications.* McGraw-Hill, New York, pp. 45–63.

Wright, S. F., J. G. Foster, and O. L. Bennett. 1986. Production and use of monoclonal antibodies for identification of strains of *Rhizobium trifolii. Applied and Environmental Microbiology* 52:119–123.

Xu, H. S., N. Roberts, F. L. Singleton, R. W. Attwell, D. J. Grimes, and R. R. Colwell. 1982. Survival and viability of nonculturable *Escherichia coli* and *Vibrio cholerae* in the estuarine and marine environment. *Microbial Ecology* 8:313–323.

Yang, Z. H., P.E.W. De Haas, D. Van Soolingen, J.D.A. Van Embden, and A. B. Andersen. 1994. Restriction fragment length polymorphism of *Mycobacterium tuberculosis* strains isolated from Greenland during 1992: Evidence of tuberculosis transmission between Greenland and Denmark. *Journal of Clinical Microbiology* 32:3018-3025.

Yoshinari, T., and R. Knowles. 1976. Acetylene inhibition of nitrous oxide reduction by denitrifying bacteria. *Biochemical and Biophysical Research Communications* 69:705–710.

Zehr, J. P., and L. A. McReynolds. 1989. Use of degenerate oligonucleotides for the amplification of the *nifH* gene from the marine cyanobacterium *Trichodesmium thiebautii. Applied and Environmental Microbiology* 55:2522–2526.

Zhou, J., M. A. Bruns, and J. M. Tiedje. 1996. DNA recovery from soils of diverse composition. *Applied and Environmental Microbiology* 62:316–322.

Zimmerman, C. R., C. J. Snedker, and D. Pappagianis. 1994. Characterization of *Coccidioides immitis* isolates by restriction fragment length polymorphisms. *Journal of Clinical Microbiology* 32:3040–3042.

Zimmerman, R., and L. A. Meyer-Reil. 1974. A new method for fluorescence staining of bacterial populations on membrane filters. *Kieler Wissenschaftliche Meeresforschungen* (Kiel) 30:24–27.

Zimmerman, R., R. Iturriaga, and J. Becker-Birck. 1978. Simultaneous determination of the total number of aquatic bacteria and the number thereof involved in respiration. *Applied and Environmental Microbiology* 36:926–935.

Zukowski, M. M., D. F. Gaffney, D. Speck, M. Kauffmann, A. Findeli, A. Wisecup, and J. P. Lecocq. 1983. Chromogenic identification of genetic regulatory signals in *Bacillus subtilis* based on expression of a cloned *Pseudomonas* gene. *Proceedings of the National Academy of Sciences USA* 80:1101–1105.

# 8

# Physiological Ecology of Microorganisms: Adaptations to Environmental Conditions

*Various abiotic factors strongly influence the ecological distribution and functioning of microbial populations. Autecology considers the influence of environmental parameters on microbial survival and growth. Nutritional constraints and environmental tolerances regulate or exclude the existence of microorganisms in various environments according to Liebig's law of the minimum and Shelford's law of tolerance, respectively. Microorganisms have upper and lower tolerance limits as well as optima in respect to temperature, radiation, pressure, salinity, water activity, pH, and redox potential. Movement and magnetic force also influence some microbes, and requirements for inorganic and organic nutrients need to be satisfied.*

*Microbial ecologists have investigated representatives of the microbial world that show adaptations to the most extreme conditions tolerated by life. Hyperthermophiles grow at 110°C and 500 atm; Deinococcus radiodurans survives 1000 to 10,000 times the dose of ionizing radiation lethal to man. Such "extremophile" microbes are not just curiosities: they give us clues about the possibility of life on other planets and are sources of important biotechnological tools and products.*

## Abiotic Limitations to Microbial Growth

### Liebig's Law of the Minimum

Justus Liebig, a German agricultural chemist active during the middle of the nineteenth century, recognized that like atoms in a molecule, elements in a living organism are present in distinct proportions (Liebig 1840). According to Liebig's law, the total yield or biomass of any organism will be determined by the nutrient present in the lowest (minimum) concentration in relation to the requirements of that organism. To grow, microorganisms must obtain various substances (nutrients) from their environment and use them for the production of energy and for the biosynthesis of cellular macromolecules. Water composes a large part of the cell by weight, about 70–90%, and therefore is an essential nutrient. The remaining solids of the cell are largely composed of hydrogen, oxygen, carbon, nitrogen, phosphorus, and sulfur. Also vital for proper cell functioning, although in substantially smaller amounts, are metal cations of potassium, magnesium, calcium, iron, manganese, cobalt, copper, molybdenum, and zinc, as well as anions such as chloride, and for some microorganisms, growth factors such as vitamins. Each nutrient plays an important role in the overall growth of the cell (Table 8.1).

In any given ecosystem, there will be some limiting nutritional factor. For example, crop yield cannot be increased by the addition of excess phosphorus if the soil is suffering from a shortage of nitrogen. Liebig's law of the minimum applies to microorganisms just as it applies to plants and animals. An increase in the concentration of a particular limiting nutrient allows the affected population to grow or reproduce until another factor becomes limiting. In a given ecosystem, the growth of one microbial population may be limited by concentrations of available phosphorus, and adding nitrogen will not permit additional growth of that population. Within the same ecosystem, however, growth of another microbial population may be limited by concentrations of available

nitrogen, and the addition of nitrogen would permit further growth of those organisms.

## Shelford's Law of Tolerance

The occurrence and abundance of organisms in an environment are determined not only by nutrients but also by various physicochemical factors such as temperature, redox potential, pH, and many others. Shelford's law of tolerance describes how such abiotic parameters control the abundance of organisms in an ecosystem. It states that for survival and growth each organism requires a complex set of conditions (Shelford 1913). In essence Shelford's law says that there are bounds for environmental factors above and below which microorganisms can not grow and survive. For an organism to succeed in a given environment, each of these conditions must remain within the tolerance range of that organism; if any condition,

**Table 8.1**
Principal elements of the cell and their physiological functions

| Element | Percentage of cell dry weight | Physiological functions |
|---|---|---|
| Carbon | 50 | Constituent of all organic cell components |
| Oxygen | 20 | Constituent of cellular water and most organic cell components; molecular oxygen serves as an electron acceptor in aerobic respiration |
| Nitrogen | 14 | Constituent of proteins, nucleic acids, coenzymes |
| Hydrogen | 8 | Constituent of cellular water and organic cell components |
| Phosphorus | 3 | Constituent of nucleic acids, phospholipids, coenzymes |
| Sulfur | 1 | Constituent of some amino acids in proteins and some coenzymes |
| Potassium | 1 | Important inorganic cation and cofactor for some enzymatic reactions |
| Sodium | 1 | One of the principal inorganic cations in eucaryotic cells and important in membrane transport |
| Calcium | 0.5 | Important inorganic cation and cofactor for some enzymatic reactions |
| Magnesium | 0.5 | Important inorganic cation and cofactor for many enzymatic reactions |
| Chlorine | 0.5 | Important inorganic anion |
| Iron | 0.2 | Constituent of cytochromes and some proteins |
| All others | 0.3 | Various functions |

such as temperature, exceeds the minimum or maximum tolerance of the organism, the organism will fail to thrive and will be eliminated. Consequently, psychrophilic microorganisms cannot grow in ecosystems with high temperatures; obligately anaerobic microorganisms cannot survive conditions of high oxygen tension; obligately halophilic microbes cannot grow in freshwater lakes; and so forth. The tolerance ranges of microorganisms and the fluctuations of chemical and physical factors in an ecosystem do not determine which microorganisms are present at any one moment, but rather which microorganisms can be present on a sustained basis in that ecosystem.

In reality, the presence and success of an organism or a group of organisms in an ecosystem depend both on nutrient requirements and on environmental tolerance (Odum 1971). The population levels of most organisms are controlled in an ecosystem by the quantity and diversity of materials for which they have a minimum requirement, by critical physical factors, and by the tolerance limits of the organisms themselves to these and other components of the environment. Tolerance ranges for a given parameter are somewhat interactive with other parameters; thus, a microorganism that is not able to survive at a particular temperature in an ecosystem with a particular hydrogen ion concentration may be able to survive at that same temperature in another ecosystem with a different hydrogen ion concentration. The interactive nature of environmental determinants complicates the task of microbial ecologists in defining precisely the controlling or limiting factors in natural ecosystems. Nevertheless, from a bewildering variety of physicochemical conditions, often a single one can be identified that excludes an organism from a given environment by exceeding the tolerance limit. For microorganisms with complex life cycles, the tolerance of the most sensitive stage is the relevant one.

In classical ecology, the ecology of the individual falls in the realm of autecology, whereas synecology deals with ecological interactions in a population, community, or ecosystem. Microbial ecologists deal with individual populations but not with individual microorganisms. Accordingly, in microbial ecology, autecology studies the interaction of isolated microbial populations with environmental determinants, and synecology considers the interactions of populations with each other. Autecology of individual microbial populations includes the study of environmental determinants, their effect on microbial populations, and the adaptation mechanisms that microorganisms have evolved to cope with them. Our discussion of autecology will include adaptations to environmental extremes and an examination of the environments where these extremes prevail.

The tolerance range to an environmental determinant that emerges from an autecological laboratory study is typically broader than the one that actually exists in nature. It stands to reason that a population existing close to the edge of its upper or lower tolerance limit grows rather slowly under these stressful conditions. In this state, it becomes vulnerable to negative synecological interactions such as competition, parasitism, or predation, factors which are excluded from autecological studies. Synecological interactions may also cause a microbial population to do better under some suboptimal environmental conditions if these effectively exclude its main competitors or predators.

Most measures of environmental determinants record the average condition prevailing in a large sample and fail to consider the existence of microhabitats where microorganisms actually live. As an example, the oral cavity is often considered to be an aerobic environment because of the continuous passage of air through it, but obligate anaerobes survive and grow within anaerobic microhabitats within the oral cavity. One must also consider the fact that interactions among microbial populations can alter the environment in such a way as to allow for or prevent the growth of other microorganisms. For example, a microorganism may produce acidic metabolic products, preventing the survival in that ecosystem of microorganisms that cannot tolerate conditions of low pH; conversely, a microorganism may carry out a metabolic activity, such as nitrogen fixation, whose by-products are required for growth by another microorganism. Microorganisms exhibit tolerances to various toxic chemicals based on both concentration and time of exposure (Figure 8.1).

Another important consideration in examining limiting or tolerance factors is availability. A nutrient may be present in an ecosystem but in a form not available to microorganisms; that is, the microbial populations cannot use it. A microbial ecologist must consider not only the presence of materials but also their availability to the microbes. Toxic compounds, for example, may be bonded to particles such as clay and be unavailable for interaction with microorganisms; microorganisms are protected from the direct effects of the toxic material in such situations and can therefore tolerate higher concentrations of the toxic substance. Reduced availability of required substances can prevent microbial growth. Water or nutrients, for example, may become bound and unavailable for microbial uptake. Lack of availability may also occur because the chemical is in the wrong form. For example, nitrogen gas is present in virtually all ecosystems, but most microorganisms cannot use this form of nitrogen; thus, in many ecosystems, available nitrogen is a limiting factor. Similarly, phosphate is unavailable in environments that have a high pH and high bivalent cation concentrations. Iron in its oxidized form ($Fe^{3+}$) is insoluble and thus unavailable for microbial uptake.

A wide or a narrow tolerance range to an environmental determinant is described by the *eury-* or *steno-* prefixes, respectively. A euryhaline microorganism tolerates wide fluctuations of salt concentrations that typically occur in estuaries and tidal rivers. In contrast, a stenohaline microorganism is confined to a freshwater or a marine habitat. Preference for a particular determinant is expressed by the *-phile* suffix, as in *halophile* or *thermophile*. Microorganisms that have predominantly broad (eury-) tolerance ranges grow in a wide variety of habitats; microorganisms with one or more narrow (steno-) tolerances grow only in a few special environments. Stenothermal psychrophiles or thermophiles will grow only in permanently cold or hot environments, respectively, and will not thrive in environments where the temperatures fluctuate within the mesophilic range.

Some microorganisms are particularly well adapted for survival in extreme habitats where other organisms cannot survive. Their limits of tolerance to

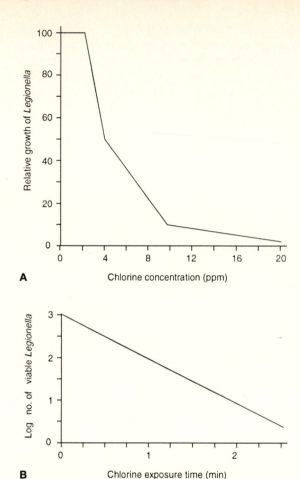

**A**

**B**

**Figure 8.1**
(A) Chlorine kills *Legionella* species and is used for the disinfection of cooling towers to reduce the numbers of this pathogen. (B) Chlorine rapidly kills microorganisms and is widely used for the disinfection of water.

specific stress factors determine, in large part, the inhabitants of extreme environments, such as salt ponds, hot springs, alkaline soda lakes, and desert soils (Table 8.2). Many of these organisms have physiological properties that restrict their growth to extreme habitats. In less severe habitats, the sources of nutrients and the interactions among populations become more important in selecting for the populations that become established within the community.

**Table 8.2**
Some extreme physiological tolerance limits for microbial activity

| Factor | Lower tolerance limit | Upper tolerance limit |
|---|---|---|
| Temperature | −12°C (psychrophilic bacteria) | >110°C (sulfur-reducing bacteria at 1000 atm; sulfur oxidizers in deep-sea thermal vent regions) |
| $E_h$ (redox potential) | −450 mV (methanogenic bacteria) | +850 mV (iron bacteria) |
| pH | 0 (*Thiobacillus thiooxidans*) | 13 (*Plectonema nostocorum*) |
| Hydrostatic pressure | 0 (various microorganisms) | 1400 atm (barophilic bacteria) |
| Salinity | 0 (*Hyphomicrobium*) | Saturated brines (*Dunaliella*, obligate halophilic bacteria) |

## ENVIRONMENTAL DETERMINANTS

Having considered the underlying reasons for examining the physical and chemical properties of an ecosystem, we shall now consider some specific environmental determinants that control microbial growth and activity. The extremes of environmental conditions that microorganisms may have to tolerate include high temperatures approaching that of boiling water, low temperatures approaching freezing, low acidic pH values, high alkaline pH values, high salt concentrations, low water availability, high irradiation levels, low concentrations of usable nutrients, and high concentrations of toxic compounds. Many microorganisms that inhabit extreme environments, including hot springs, salt lakes, and Antarctic desert soils, possess specialized adaptive physiological features that permit them to survive and function within the physicochemical constraints of these ecosystems (Alexander 1976; Kushner 1978, 1980; Gould and Corry 1980; Brock 1985; Edwards 1990). The membranes and enzymes of microorganisms inhabiting extreme environments often have distinct modifications that permit them to function under conditions that would inhibit active transport and metabolic activities in organisms lacking these adaptive features. Diversity in extreme environments generally is low and relatively few microbes possess these adaptations.

Survival and growth under extreme environmental conditions have always intrigued microbial ecologists. In addition to our general fascination with "records," microorganisms that survive and metabolize under extreme conditions have practical importance as spoilage organisms that defy human efforts to kill or inhibit them. More recently, they have also become potential sources of enzymes that can be used as biocatalysts under conditions that would denature most proteins. The key enzyme for the polymerase chain reaction (PCR) that allows the amplification of minute amounts of DNA is derived from a thermophilic bacterium isolated from thermal vents. Its enzyme withstands repeated heating cycles to 80°C.

Space exploration and our ability to soft-land instrument packages on planets like Mars have given additional impetus to research on microbes that can live under extreme environmental conditions. The development of life detection probes in turn sparked interest in the most hostile terrestrial environments, such as the dry valleys of Antarctica, where these devices could be tested.

## Starvation Strategies

Most natural ecosystems are characterized by low concentrations of usable organic matter and other nutrients. Because periods of starvation are probably experienced by most free-living bacteria, starvation survival is important to them. Several survival strategies of starving bacteria in natural environments with low nutrient concentrations have been identified (Roszak and Colwell 1987). Jannasch (1967) indicated that two strategies may be observed: (1) the ability to grow at low substrate concentrations, and (2) the ability to become temporarily inactive but able to survive. The mechanism of low metabolic rate is widespread in soil and marine bacteria (Roszak and Colwell 1987). Brown and Gilbert (1993) noted that cells respond to nutrient deprivation by (1) reducing the requirement for the deficient nutrient by limiting cell components containing the element, by using alternate substrates, or by reorganizing cellular metabolic pathways, (2) altering the cell surface and inducing higher-affinity transport systems, and (3) reducing cellular growth rate. Cano and Borucki (1995) have reported that a dormant bacterial spore from a species most closely related to *Bacillus sphaericus* survived for 25–40 million years within the remnants of the abdominal contents of bees that had been preserved in buried amber.

The phenomenon of multiple divisions leading to the formation of ultramicrobacteria (<0.3 μm diameter) has been reported (Novitsky and Morita, 1976, 1977, 1978; Morita 1982). Ultramicrobacteria appear to be the prevailing dominant bacteria in various marine ecosystems (Button et al. 1993). Under conditions of starvation some bacteria, such as various *Vibrio* species, form very small cells called *minicells*. These cells are not spores but they have very low rates of metabolic activity and are relatively resistant to environmental stresses. These specialized ultramicrobacterial forms have been suggested to be exogenously dormant cells responding to unfavorable environmental conditions (Roszak and Colwell 1987).

Several global regulatory systems play important roles in the ability of bacteria to withstand starvation (see the accompanying table) (Neidhardt et al. 1990). Several of these systems such as the Ntr, Arc, and Pho systems, are two-component signal transduction systems (Hoch and Silhavy 1995). These systems are designed to detect an environmental stimulus and convert this signal to a cellular response. They involve a histidine kinase and phosphorylation of a regulatory protein that controls transcription. Two-component systems are central to much of the cellular physiology that results from alterations in the environment. Starvation for phosphate or nitrogen and adaptation to new sources of nitrogen and carbon are examples of environmental factors that cells overcome with modified cellular physiology mediated by two-component systems.

When they experience a depletion of the amino acid pool (amino acid starvation), some bacteria have a unique mechanism called the *stringent response* (see figure A) for regulating the transcription of specific operons and DNA sequences that code for ribosomal and transfer RNA (rRNA and tRNA) (Neidhardt et al. 1990). This response greatly reduces the rates of protein and other macromolecular synthesis by decreasing the synthesis of rRNA. Using this mechanism of transcription control, the cell has the ability to shut down a number of energy-draining activities as a survival mechanism under poor growth conditions (conditions of starvation). The stringent response involves the

Bacterial starvation regulatory systems

| Starvation factor | System | Microorganism | Genetic control | Description |
|---|---|---|---|---|
| Low concentrations of amino acids | Stringent response | Enterobacteriaceae and other bacteria | *relA* (stringent factor) and *spoT* (ppGpp degradation) | General response to poor growth conditions, triggered by amino acid depletion. Cells decrease rates of rRNA and tRNA synthesis. |
| Low concentrations of ammonia | Ntr system | Enterobacteriaceae | *glnB, glnD, glnG,* and *glnL* (glutamine) | General response to nitrogen starvation, triggered by growth-limiting concentrations of ammonia. Cells synthesize proteins aimed at scavenging very low concentrations of ammonia and obtaining nitrogen from alternate source. |
| Low concentrations of ammonia | Nif system | *Klebsiella aerogenes* and other bacteria | More than 12 nitrogenase regulatory genes | Response of some bacteria to limiting concentrations of ammonia that results in activation of nitrogen fixation enzyme system. |
| Low concentrations of glucose | Catabolite repression | Enterobacteriaceae | *cya* (adenylate cyclase) and *crp* (catabolite repressor protein) | General response to limiting concentrations of readily utilizable organic matter, triggered by low concentrations of glucose. Cells synthesize enzymes for the utilization of other organic carbon sources. |
| Low concentrations of molecular oxygen | Arc system | *Escherichia coli* | *arcA, arcB* (aerobic respiration regulatory genes) | General system in facultative anaerobes that responds to conditions of anoxia (lack of molecular oxygen) and activates metabolic pathways that permit the utilization of alternate terminal electron acceptors for respiratory metabolism so that a shift can occur from aerobic to anaerobic metabolism. |
| Low concentrations of phosphate | Pho system | Enterobacteriaceae | *phoB, phoR, phoU,* and *phoA* (phosphate utilization genes) | General response system to low concentrations of inorganic phosphate. Cells turn on genes for utilization of organic phosphate compounds and for the scavenging of trace amounts of inorganic phosphate. |

Source: Neidhardt et al. 1990                                        *(continued)*

## Starvation Strategies, continued

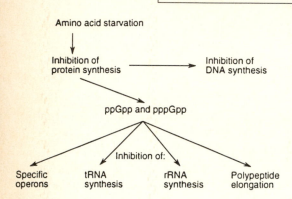

### Figure A

The stringent response occurs when cells encounter conditions of starvation. It is triggered by a depletion of amino acids needed for biosynthesis. During amino acid starvation the *relA* gene product (stringent factor) causes formation of ppGpp and pppGpp, which suppress gene expression. The stringent response results in a decrease in rRNA synthesis so that the number of ribosomes in the cell declines. There also is a major decline in rates of protein, DNA, peptidoglycan, carbohydrate, and nucleotide synthesis. New rounds of DNA synthesis cease. Thus, under growth-limiting conditions—which may be due to amino acid starvation, nitrogen limitation, or a shift to a poorer energy source—this adaptive response restricts growth and halts cell reproduction. (Source: Neidhardt el al. 1990.)

production of two unusual guanosine phosphates, guanosine pentaphosphate (pppGpp) and guanosine tetraphosphate (ppGpp).

Bacteria that exhibit the stringent response produce a protein called *stringent factor* that is a product of the *relA* gene. Stringent factor is normally associated with the bacterial ribosome at a ratio of about 1 molecule per 200 ribosomes. Under conditions of amino acid starvation, uncharged tRNA can enter the aminoacyl site on the ribosome. When this occurs, stringent factor catalyzes the transfer of a pyrophosphate group

from ATP to either guanidine triphosphate or guanidine diphosphate (GTP or GDP), which are involved in protein synthesis. The pyrophosphorylation of GTP (pppG) produces pppGpp and the pyrophosphorylation of GDP (ppG) or dephosphorylation of pppGpp produces ppGpp.

The effector molecule ppGpp may work in several ways. It may specifically bind to promoters of rRNA and tRNA sequences and inhibit their transcription by RNA polymerase. Alternatively, ppGpp causes increased idling or pausing of the translation process and therefore premature termination of specific polypeptides. Some bacterial strains that have mutations in the *relA* gene do not exhibit a stringent response under conditions of amino acid starvation. Such strains are said to be *relaxed strains* and continue to synthesize RNA and protein under nutrient-limiting conditions. These strains have been instrumental in our understanding of *relA* genes.

Within seconds after exposure to starvation conditions, cells shut down RNA, protein, and peptidoglycan biosynthesis. During this period, the rate of proteolysis, or protein turnover, and degradation of RNA increases. Perhaps protein and RNA serve as energy sources to drive critical cell functions. There is a concomitant increase in the synthesis of ppGpp. In the next phase, ppGpp levels fall and macromolecular synthesis increases as cells deplete storage polymers such as poly-β-hydroxybutyric acid or glycogen. Finally, the cells continue to survive for a long period at a low metabolic rate. They synthesize specific proteins that enhance their ability to survive under conditions of starvation and make the cell a more efficient scavenger of the scarce nutrient. The proteins also confer a more stress-tolerant phenotype. In addition, the half-life of mRNA greatly increases.

The number of proteins synthesized depends on the specific nutrient depleted. *E. coli* synthesizes about 30 novel proteins after starvation for a carbon source and 26–32 proteins when deprived of nitrogen. *Bacillus subtilis* produces several new proteins in response to carbon, nitrogen, oxygen, or phosphate limitation. Iron deprivation in gram-negative bacteria leads to the induction of high-affinity iron chelators called *siderophores.* Phosphate deprivation in *E. coli* leads to synthesis of a new porin for membrane transport, PhoE, which has a high affinity for anions such as phosphate. Some of these proteins may be part of a larger global control by which the cell responds to stress. Some marine *Vibrio* species synthesize surface fibers that enhance the aggregation of the cells undergoing starvation.

All of these cellular events lead to the formation of smaller-than-normal cells. There appears to be a correlation between slow growth rate and small cell size (minicells). The unsaturated fatty acids in the cytoplasmic membrane phospholipids of minicells are converted to cyclopropane fatty acids. This renders the lipids more resistant to oxidation. Many gram-positive bacteria normally synthesize phosphorus-rich teichoic acids as cell wall accessory molecules. Under conditions of phosphate limitation, phosphate is more importantly required for DNA, RNA, and ATP; teichoic acids in the cell wall are replaced by phosphorus-free teichuronic acids.

In addition to the stringent response, when concentrations of ammonia become growth-limiting and a bacterium detects a condition of nitrogen starvation, it generally activates the Ntr system that enables the bacterial cell to scavenge the last traces of ammonia (Ninfa et al. 1995). It also activates additional operons, such as the *nac* operon, that are involved in the utilization of organic nitrogen sources. This permits the cell to turn to alternative sources of nitrogen to meet its biosynthetic needs.

When ammonia concentrations become limiting, bacteria are able to turn on the transcription of genes for ammonia production from other nitrogen sources. The transcription of genes for glutamine synthetase is also induced. The glutamine synthetase genes are regulated as part of a multigene system called the *Ntr system* (see figure B). Other genes regulated by the Ntr system code for $NR_{II}$ (a histidine kinase) and $NR_I$ (a response regulator). A two-component regulatory system involving a histidine kinase and a response regulator is a redundant theme in transcriptional regulatory systems. The system is based on phosphorylation of the histidine kinase and transfer of the phosphate to the response regulator that acts as a DNA binding protein to regulate transcription.

The operon controlling the biosynthesis of glutamine synthetase in *Salmonella typhimurium* is *glnA-ntrB-ntrC;* in *E. coli* this operon is *glnA-glnL-glnG; glnA* codes for glutamine synthetase, *glnL* for $NR_{II}$, and *glnG* for $NR_I$. Under nitrogen-limiting conditions these genes are transcribed at high rates because the promoter is controlled by $\sigma^{54}$ rather than the normal $\sigma^{70}$ and because phosphorylation of $NR_I$ stimulates this transcriptional process.

Transcription of the Ntr system genes is inhibited by high concentrations of ammonia (>1 *mM*) and activated at lower ammonia concentrations. High levels of ammonia lead to high $P_{II}$ levels within the cell because glutamine stimulates hydrolysis of

*(continued)*

## Starvation Strategies, continued

Glutamine$<<\alpha$-ketoglutarate

$$P_{II} + 4UTP \xrightarrow[\text{UTase/UR}]{} P_{II}(UMP)_4 + 4PP_i$$

$$NR_I \xrightarrow[\substack{NR_{II} \\ P_{II}(UMP)_4}]{} NR_1\text{-}P \longrightarrow \boxed{\text{activation of } gln \text{ promoter}}$$

Glutamine$>>\alpha$-ketoglutarate

$$NR_1\text{-}P \xrightarrow[\substack{NR_{II} \\ P_{II}}]{} NR_I \longrightarrow \boxed{\text{no activation of } gln \text{ promoter}}$$

$$P_{II}(UMP)_4 \xrightarrow[\text{UTase/UR}]{} P_{II} + 4UMP$$

### Figure B

Low levels of ammonia result in a slowing of the conversion of $\alpha$-ketoglutarate to glutamate and hence the accumulation of $\alpha$-ketoglutarate within the cell. Increased concentrations of $\alpha$-ketoglutarate stimulate the uridylyl-transferase (UTase) activity instead of the uridyl-removing (UR) activity of UR/UTase enzyme, which adds UMP to protein $P_{II}$ to form $P_{II}$-UMP. The decrease in concentration of protein $P_{II}$ stimulates transcription of the Ntr system because $P_{II}$ activates the phosphatase activity of the histidine kinase $NR_{II}$, which in turn inactivates the response regulator $NR_I$. When levels of $P_{II}$ decrease, $NR_{II}$ instead acts as a kinase, phosphorylating $NR_I$, which activates transcription of the glutamine synthetase genes. Glutamine synthetase, which is important for scavenging traces of ammonia, is not synthesized by most bacteria when concentrations of ammonia are high. (Source: Reitzer and Magasanik 1987.)

$P_{II}$-UMP ($P_{II}$-uridinemonophosphate). High levels of $P_{II}$ lead to phosphatase activity of $NR_{II}$, which in turn causes dephosphorylation of phosphorylated $NR_I$ and reduced transcription of the *glnA-glnL-glnG* operon.

A limiting concentration of ammonia leads to a reduction in the ratio of glutamine to $\alpha$-ketoglu-tarate within the cell. This is detected by the UR/UTase protein (uridyl-removing/uridyl-transferase enzyme), leading to phosphorylation of the histidine kinase $NR_{II}$-response regulator $NR_I$ system. As a result, transcription of the genes for glutamine synthetase is activated. These enzymes enable bacteria to assimilate very low levels of ammonia by catalyzing the assimilation into glutamine in an ATP-dependent reaction. Subsequently the amino nitrogen group of glutamine can be transferred to $\alpha$-ketoglutarate to form glutamate, which supplies approximately 85% of the nitrogen that goes into the nitrogen-containing molecules of the cell.

Bacterial cells also have developed an adaptive response for responding to growth-limiting concentrations of phosphate (Wanner 1995). Normally, cells obtain phosphate for incorporation into nucleotides from inorganic phosphates. However, under conditions of inorganic phosphate starvation, the phosphate utilization network (Pho system) is activated, which permits utilization of alternate phosphate sources. Over 100 proteins are synthesized at elevated rates when the Pho system is activated. This system results in production of high concentrations of alkaline phosphatase so that phosphate can be obtained from organic sources. In *E. coli,* alkaline phosphatase can make up to 6% of the cell biomass under conditions of inorganic phosphate starvation, whereas it is usually only a minor protein constituent of cells growing under conditions where inorganic phosphate is not a growth-limiting factor.

**Table 8.3**
Minimal and maximal growth temperatures of representative bacterial and archaeal species

| Microorganism | Minimal growth temperature (°C) | Maximum growth temperature (°C) |
|---|---|---|
| **Bacteria** | | |
| *Micrococcus cryophilus* | −8 | 25 |
| *Vibrio marinus* | −14 | 25 |
| *Xanthomonas pharmicola* | 0 | 40 |
| *Pseudomonas avenae* | 0 | 40 |
| *Xanthomonas rinicola* | −8 | 38 |
| *Escherichia coli* | 7 | 41 |
| *Vibrio cholerae* | 11 | 41 |
| *Staphylococcus aureus* | 15 | 45 |
| *Streptococcus pyogenes* | 20 | 45 |
| *Haemophilus influenzae* | 22 | 40 |
| *Lactobacillus lactis* | 15 | 46 |
| *Bacillus subtilis* | 15 | 50 |
| *Lactbacillus delbrueckii* | 20 | 50 |
| *Bacillus coagulans* | 25 | 65 |
| *Synechococcus lividus* | 30 | 67 |
| *Bacillus stearothermophilus* | 30 | 70 |
| *Thermus aquaticus* | 65 | 102 |
| **Archaea** | | |
| *Halobacterium salinarium* | 20 | 55 |
| *Methanococcus voltae* | 25 | 50 |
| *Methanococcus thermolithotrophicus* | 30 | 75 |
| *Thermoplasma acidophilum* | 40 | 62 |
| *Methanococcus igneus* | 40 | 95 |
| *Methanococcus jannaschii* | 50 | 95 |
| *Pyrodictium occultum* | 60 | 110 |
| *Pyrococcus furiosus* | 70 | 100 |
| *Pyrococcus woesei* | 70 | 105 |

## Temperature

All microorganisms have a characteristic optimal growth temperature at which they exhibit their highest growth and reproduction rates. Microorganisms also have minimal growth temperatures below which they are metabolically inactive and upper temperature limits beyond which they fail to grow. In many ecosystems, temperature fluctuates on a daily and seasonal basis. Measurement of temperature at the time of sample collection does not necessarily reflect the range of temperatures that the organism must tolerate, nor does it indicate whether that single temperature prevails during the entire time of microbial growth and activity. Considering the temperature fluctuations that occur in most habitats and the abilities of most microorganisms to tolerate some fluctuation around their optimal growth temperatures, the recording accuracy for temperature in most cases need only be to the degree centigrade.

Microorganisms exhibit diverse temperature growth ranges—minimal/maximal growth temperatures (Table 8.3)—and optimal growth temperatures. Both the optimal growth temperature and the range of temperatures that a particular microorganism can tolerate determine whether that microorganism will survive and what role it will play in a given ecosystem. Some microorganisms can grow below 0°C; others can grow at over 100°C. Microorganisms are classified as psychrophiles, mesophiles, thermophiles, and hyperthermophiles, respectively, if their optimal growth temperatures are low (<0–<20°C), moderate (20–<40°C), high (40–<80°C), or very high (80–110°C) (Figure 8.2 on page 294). Some hyperthermophiles have been reported with growth temperature optima at 105°C and no growth below 85°C.

Most hyperthermophiles reported to date are archaea (Stetter 1982, 1995; Fischer et al. 1983).

---

## Longevity in Adversity

The life cycle of bacteria stretches from division to division. Death is a consequence of adverse conditions or predation and not part of the normal life cycle. Under optimal culture conditions, the life cycle (doubling time) of many bacteria can be as short as 15–20 minutes, but it can be as long as several hours or even days under the more restrictive conditions common in nature. When conditions for growth deteriorate, most bacteria become dormant. Reducing their metabolic rates and using intracellular reserve materials, they survive for various periods and may profit later from improved environmental conditions. Some aerobic and anaerobic gram-positive bacteria form highly resistant endospores under deteriorating environmental conditions. Typically, these survive much longer and under much harsher conditions than non-spore-forming bacteria.

Viable *Bacillus subtilis* endospores were found in soil crumbs clinging to the roots of plants kept dry as herbarium species for 320 years (Sneath 1962). Abyzov (1993) found viable microorganisms in cores of Antarctic ice 10,000 to 13,000 years old. It may be argued that a permanently frozen state may render microbial survival abnormally long, but viable bacterial endospores were also found in lake sediment samples that were estimated to be 8000–9000 years old (Rothfuss et al. 1997).

Lake Constance, situated on the German-Swiss border, was formed at the end of the last ice age, approximately 13,000 years ago. Its sediments remained undisturbed, and their high clay content prevented water movement within the sediment matrix. In this situation, bacteria remained where they were buried in the sediment, and the time when they were buried can be calculated from their depth in the sediment profile. This sediment was cored and the sediment cores were processed in a manner to prevent sediment disturbance or contamination. Microbial activity and surviving

Many archaea grow at high temperatures, which appears to reflect the fact that the earliest archaea evolved in hot regions or when the entire Earth was still hot (Table 8.4 on page 295). The lowest optimal temperature for archaea that have been cultured is about 30°C, but many archaea have yet to be cultured and may have lower optimal growth temperatures. Some archaea, such as *Methanococcus jannaschii* and *Methanococcus igneus,* are extreme thermophiles with particularly high growth rates and high enzymatic activities at elevated temperatures (Figure 8.3). The differences in optimal growth temperatures and temperature growth ranges among bacteria and archaea result in a spatial separation of these different domains of organisms in nature.

A bacterium can proliferate only when the environmental temperatures are within the temperature growth range of that organism. The ability of a bacterium to compete for survival in a given system is increased when temperatures are near its optimal growth temperature. A typical growth curve for a marine psychrophile (Figure 8.4) indicates that optimal growth occurs at 4°C, that the organism is capable of growth at –1.8°C (the freezing point of seawater), and that the bacterium will not grow at or above 10°C (Morita 1975).

It is of interest to consider the adaptations that allow psychrophilic microorganisms to grow in temperature ranges that are prohibitive to most mesophilic organisms. In most mesophilic organisms, a control

microorganisms were investigated in the sediment profile. Microbial numbers were determined both in unprocessed and in pasteurized sediment samples to differentiate endospores from vegetative bacteria (Rothfuss et al. 1997).

Anaerobic microbial activities such as methanogenesis and nitrate- and sulfate-reduction decreased steeply with sediment depth and were undetectable in sediment below the depth of 50 cm. Viable microorganisms also declined exponentially with sediment depth. Only in the uppermost portions of the cores did the numbers differ prior to and after pasteurization, indicating that in the deeper portions of the cores the only survivors were heat-resistant bacterial endospores. Below a depth of 6–7 m, even bacterial endospores became undetectable, and the age of this sediment layer was estimated to be 8000–9000 years old. The fact that sediment below this depth did not give rise to microbial growth proved the

integrity of the sampling and sample processing procedures.

Studies of this nature are highly sensitive to sample size. In the previously described study, the detectability limit was 5–55 cells per mL. This means that although a 1-mL sample from a 7-m depth remained sterile, a 1-L sample may have contained some viable spores. Negative controls are important in such studies to ensure that microbial contamination was reliably excluded during sampling, storage, and processing. One may conclude from the described study that under the fairly routine conditions of Lake Constance sediment, the bacterial endospores had a low death rate of 0.0013–0.0025 per year (Rothfuss et al. 1997). It is possible that special conditions permit much longer survival of microbial endospores. Cano and Borucki (1995) reported the retrieval of viable microbial endospores from an insect sealed into amber for at least 25 million years!

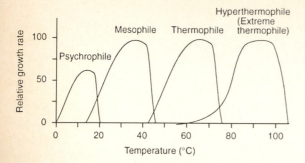

**Figure 8.2**
Temperature classification of microorganisms—psychrophiles, mesophiles, thermophiles, extreme thermophiles. Based on their optimal growth temperatures, microorganisms are classified as psychrophiles (optimal growth <20°C), mesophiles (optimal growth 20°C to 40°C), thermophiles (optimal growth >40°C), and hyperthermophiles (extreme thermophiles) (optimal growth >80°C).

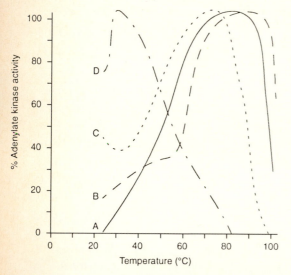

**Figure 8.3**
Comparison of the activities at different temperatures of adenylate cyclase from the thermophilic archaea *Methanococcus voltae* and *Methanococcus thermolithotrophicus* and those of the hyperthermophilic archaea *Methanococcus jannaschii* and *Methanococcus igneus*. Adenylate cyclase from each species shows optimal activities at temperatures corresponding to those of maximal growth rates. A, *Methanococcus igneus;* B, *Methanococcus jannaschii;* C, *Methanococcus thermolithotrophicus;* and D, *Methanococcus voltae*.

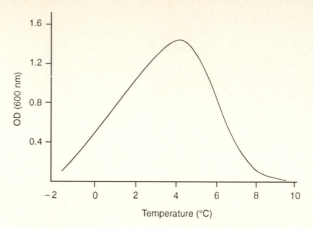

**Figure 8.4**
Biomass attained by an Antarctic psychrophile during 80-hour incubation, measured by optical density (OD), showing low optimal growth temperature and restricted range of temperature tolerance. (Source: Morita 1975. Reprinted by permission of American Society for Microbiology.)

mechanism shuts off protein synthesis if temperatures fall to approximately 5°C or lower; psychrophilic organisms apparently have ways to override these control mechanisms (Inniss and Ingraham 1978). A higher proportion of unsaturated and/or short-chain-length lipids keep the membranes of psychrophiles flexible at low temperatures. It is not known whether there is an absolute low-temperature limit to the metabolic activity of psychrophiles. The practical limit seems to be the freezing temperature of the cell contents and the surrounding water; a liquid phase is essential for metabolic processes. In an Antarctic pond kept from freezing by its high salt content, live microorganisms have been observed at temperatures below –17°C (Simmons et al. 1993). Microorganisms living at these temperatures are probably allochthonous. The salt concentrations required to keep water from freezing at temperatures lower than –10°C appear to prevent microbial growth (Heywood 1984).

**Microbial Growth at High Temperatures** High-temperature adaptations of thermophilic microorganisms include high proportions of saturated lipids in membranes, which prevent melting at high

**Table 8.4**
Optimal growth temperatures of representative archaeal species

| Optimal temperature | Species |
|---|---|
| 50°C | *Methanosarcina thermophila* |
| 55°C | *Methanogenium thermophilicum* |
| 57°C | *Methanogenium frittonii* |
| 60°C | *Methanobacterium wolfei* |
| 65°C | *Methanobacterium thermoaggregans, Methanococcus thermolithotrophicus* |
| 70°C | *Methanobacterium thermoautotrophicum* |
| 75°C | *Thermococcus stetteri* |
| 82°C | *Archaeoglobus profundus* |
| 83°C | *Methanothermus fervidus, Archaeoglobus fulgidus* |
| 85°C | *Desulfurococcus mobilis, Desulfurococcus mucosus, Desulfurococcus saccharovorans, Methanococcus jannaschii* |
| 88°C | *Thermofilum pendens, Methanothermus sociabilis, Thermococcus celer, Thermococcus littoralis, Thermodiscus maritimus, Thermoproteus neutrophilus, Thermoproteus tenax, Desulfurococcus amylolyticus, Methanococcus igneus* |
| 90°C | *Thermoproteus uzoniensis* |
| 91°C | *Caldococcus litoralis* |
| 92°C | *Staphylothermus marinus* |
| 97°C | *Pyrodictium abyssi* |
| 100°C | *Hyperthermus butylicus, Pyrobaculum islandicum, Pyrobaculum organotrophum, Pyrococcus furiosus* |
| 102°C | *Pyrococcus woesei* |
| 105°C | *Pyrodictium brockii, Pyrodictium occultum* |

temperatures (Campbell and Pace 1968; Brock 1978; Castenholz 1979; Edwards 1990). Many thermophilic microorganisms produce enzymes that are not readily denatured at high temperatures (Adams 1993). Sometimes, unusual amino acid sequences occur within the proteins of thermophiles, stabilizing these proteins at elevated temperatures (Zuber 1979). Some thermophiles, when growing at temperatures near the maximal growth temperature, exhibit amino acid and growth factor requirements that are not apparent at the optimal growth temperature. This temperature-dependent auxotrophy is evidence for selective heat inactivation of certain enzymatic pathways. The maximum heat tolerance of vegetative thermophilic cells coincides with the heat stability of their ribosomes. When the maximum growth temperature is exceeded, the ribosomes melt and protein synthesis ceases. Although many thermophiles have relatively high proportions of guanine and cytosine in their DNA that raise the melting point and add stability to the DNA molecules of these organisms, many hyperthermophilic archaea (*Sulfolobus, Acidiana, Desulfurolobus, Methanothermus, Pyrococcus,* and *Staphylothermus*) and thermophilic bacteria (*Clostridium* and *Thermotoga*) have low proportions (<40 mol% G + C) (Rainey et al. 1993; Ravot et al. 1995).

A particular challenge for microorganisms is to maintain the integrity and fluidity of their cell membranes under varying temperature conditions. High temperature can disintegrate the cell membranes, and low temperature can freeze or gel them, interrupting their vital functions. Even in eurythermal microorganisms, the temperature range of their active metabolism rarely exceeds 30–40°C, and this limitation is most likely associated with membrane integrity and fluidity. A cell membrane suitably fluid at low temperature will disintegrate under high-temperature conditions; a membrane stable under high-temperature conditions will freeze up at low temperatures. Mesophilic bacteria have been reported to adjust their membrane composition to some extent to the prevailing growth temperature (Edwards 1990). As growth temperatures increase, the fatty acids in the cell membrane increase in chain length, and their degree of unsaturation decreases (Figure 8.5). It stands to reason that such adjustments have their limits, and life at very high temperatures requires more fundamental changes in cell membrane architecture (Figure 8.6). Eucarya and most Bacteria have normal fatty acid glycerol diester bilayers as the main components of their cell membranes. In contrast, the Archaea have branched isoprenic hydrocarbon chains linked by ether bonds to glycerol. In some Archaea, phytanyl glycerol diether molecules are arranged in bilayer membranes that, except for the ether bonds and the branching of the hydrocarbon chains, strongly resemble the cell membranes of the Eucarya and Bacteria (Gambacorta et al. 1995). The bilayer components are held together by hydrophobic forces only, yet the ether bond and hydrocarbon branching raises the heat resistance of these archaeal membranes.

In hyperthermophilic Archaea, biphytanyl diglycerol tetraether molecules form covalently linked monolayer membranes. Some tetraethers contain pentacyclic rings interspersed with isoprenic hydrocarbon segments. The latter two tetraether structures are highly temperature resistant and, in combination, are the principal membrane components of the hyperthermophiles. Interestingly, the only two hyperthermophilic bacterial genera, *Thermotoga* and *Aquifex*, have cell membranes resembling those of the

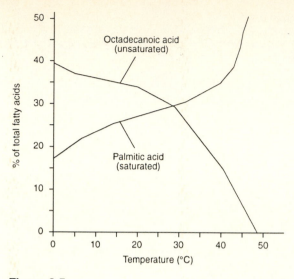

**Figure 8.5**

Effect of temperature on bacterial membrane composition. *Escherichia coli* changes the proportion of saturated and unsaturated fatty acids in the phospholipids of its cytoplasmic membrane. The greater amount of unsaturated fatty acid at lower temperature allows the membrane to remain more fluid at lower temperatures. (Source: Neidhardt et al. 1990.)

hyperthermophilic Archaea. These bacterial genera evolutionarily appear to be close to the branching point of Archaea and Bacteria. Their cell membrane structures may represent an evolutionarily conserved trait rather than a secondary adaptation (Stetter 1995).

At the growth temperature of thermophilic bacteria, the permeability of their cytoplasmic membrane to protons is high as compared to their permeability to sodium ions. In some thermophiles, sodium is the sole energy coupling ion. To test whether sodium is the preferred coupling ion at high temperatures, Van de Vossenberg et al. (1996) determined the proton and sodium permeability in liposomes prepared from lipids isolated from various bacterial and archaeal species that differ in their optimal growth temperature. The proton permeability increased with the temperature and was comparable for most species at their respective growth temperatures. Liposomes prepared from the membranes of thermophilic bacteria are an exception in the sense that the proton permeability is

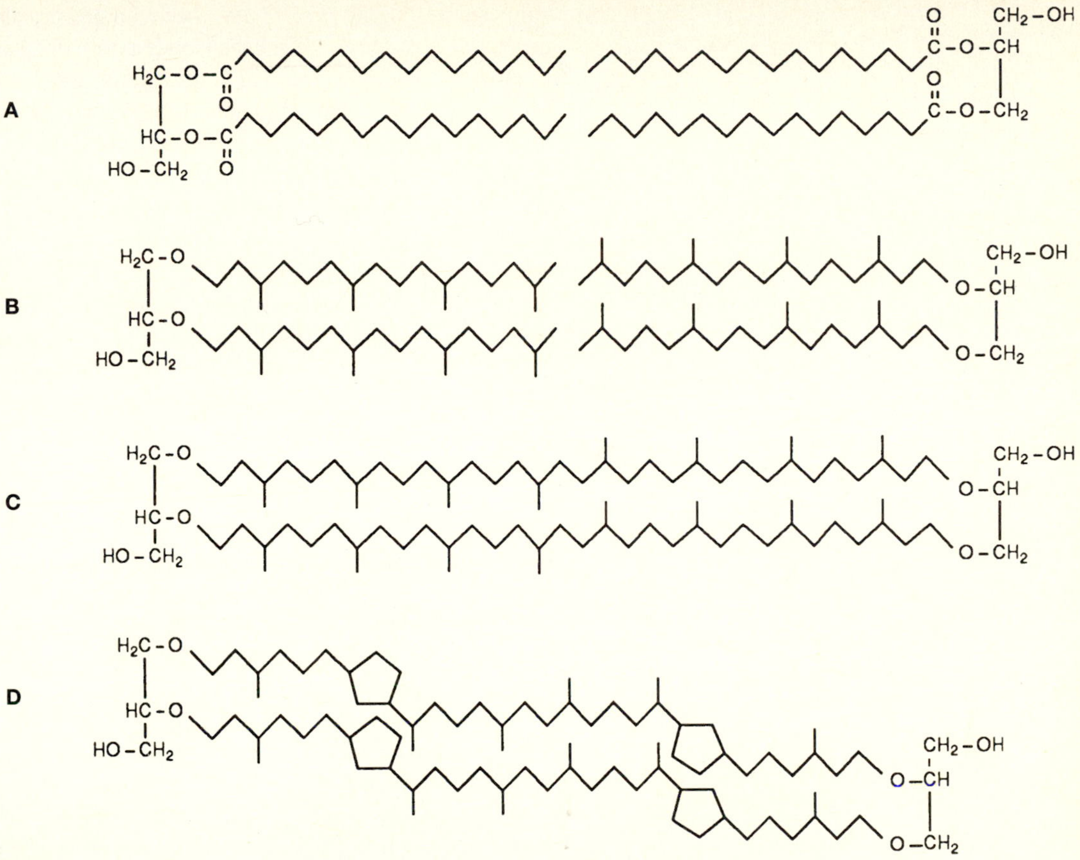

**Figure 8.6**
Type structures of cell membranes. (A) Stearic acid glycerol diester bilayer membrane. The two membrane layers are held together by hydrophobic forces only. The chain length of fatty acids may vary, but this type of structure is typical for the cell membranes of Eucarya and Bacteria. (B) The phytanyl glycerol diether bilayer membrane of some Archaea. The chain length of the hydrocarbons may vary and the ether bonds plus hydrocarbon branching increase heat stability, but the basic bilayer architecture resembles that of Eucarya and Bacteria. (C) The biphytanyl diglycerol tetraether forms a covalently linked monolayer membrane of great heat resistance. (D) A diglycerol tetraether with twin $C_{40}$ hydrocarbon chains that, in addition to isoprenoid segments, incorporate two pentacyclic rings per chain. The latter two monolayer membrane components, often in combination, dominate the cell membranes of the hyperthermophilic Archaea. (Source: White 1995.)

already high at the growth temperature. In all liposomes, the sodium permeability was lower than the proton permeability and increased with the temperature. The results suggest that membrane permeability is a key parameter in determining the maximum growth temperature.

Natural habitats for thermophiles are provided by volcanic activity (Figure 8.7). Steam vents with temperatures up to 500°C occur, but microbial life requires water in the liquid state. Microorganisms inhabit hot springs with temperatures up to the boiling point, but as the temperature rises, diversity generally

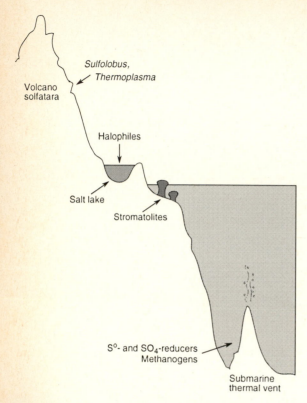

**Figure 8.7**
Thermophilic archaea occur in habitats such as terrestrial and marine thermal vents and solfataras.

decreases. Plants and animals are excluded above 50°C. Eucaryotes (protozoa, fungi, and algae) are excluded above 60°C. Photosynthetic procaryotes (cyanobacteria and anoxyphotobacteria) are excluded above 90°C, but thermophilic Archaea actually increase in diversity between 90°C and 100°C (Brock 1978, 1985) (Figure 8.8). At normal atmospheric pressure, boiling restricts aquatic habitat temperatures to 100°C. However, hydrostatic pressure on the ocean floor raises the boiling point, and water temperatures up to 350°C have been measured in deep-sea hydrothermal vents. Bacterial growth at temperatures up to 250°C by a natural microbial community collected from a hot deep-sea vent has been reported (Baross and Deming 1983; Baross et al. 1984) but was not confirmed and is now considered to have been an experimental artifact (Trent et al. 1984). Growth at

temperatures up to 113°C has been unquestionably measured in the case of Archaea isolated from deep and shallow marine hydrothermal vents (Stetter 1982; Fischer et al. 1983; Jannasch and Mottl 1985; Stetter 1995). In spite of great technical difficulties, these extremely thermophilic Archaea have been intensively studied. These Archaea tend to be anaerobic, and often chemolithotrophic. Some of them use dissolved hydrogen in the hydrothermal fluid to reduce elemental sulfur to $H_2S$ (sulfur respiration) and $CO_2$ as a carbon source. *Pyrodictium, Thermoproteus,* and *Thermodiscus* are examples of Archaea that use this type of metabolism. Other heterotrophic anaerobic Archaea, such as *Desulfurococcus* and *Thermococcus,* use organic compounds as electron donors and elemental sulfur as an electron sink. *Methanothermus fervidus,* an extremely thermophilic methanogenic archaeon found in hydrothermal vents, reduces $CO_2$ with $H_2$ to methane. *Sulfolobus acidocaldarius,* an aerobic thermoacidophilic archaeon, oxidizes $H_2S$ and elemental sulfur to sulfate. In addition to Archaea, a number of novel anaerobic thermophilic bacteria—such as *Clostridium, Thermoanaerobacter, Thermodesulfobacterium,* and *Thermobacteroides* strains—were also isolated from hydrothermal vents. The optimal growth temperatures for these are lower (65–70°C) as compared to those for the hyperthermophilic Archaea. They have either a fermentative or a sulfate-reducing type of heterotrophic metabolism (Brock 1985).

Hyperthermophilic Archaea are characterized by an optimal growth temperature between 80 and 110°C. They are considered to represent the most ancient phenotype of living organisms, and thus their metabolic design might reflect the situation at an early stage of evolution. Enzymes in hyperthermophilic Archaea are very stable at elevated temperatures. The enzyme NADH oxidase isolated from the two thermoacidophilic Archaea—*Sulfolobus acidocaldarius* and *Sulfolobus solfataricus*—displays great stability to heat (Masullo et al. 1996). The half-life of heat inactivation is about 180 minutes at 90°C for *S. acidocaldarius* NADH oxidase and 77 minutes at 98°C for the *S. solfataricus* enzyme.

The modes of metabolism of hyperthermophilic Archaea are diverse and include chemolithoautotrophy and chemoorganoheterotrophy (Schoenheit and Schaefer 1995). No extant phototrophic hyperthermophiles are known. Lithotrophic energy metabolism is mostly anaerobic or microaerophilic and based on the oxidation of $H_2$ or S coupled to the reduction of S, $SO_4^{2-}$, $CO_2$, and $NO_3$ but rarely to $O_2$. The substrates are derived from volcanic activities in hyperthermophilic habitats. The lithotrophic energy metabolism of hyperthermophiles appears to be similar to that of mesophiles. Autotrophic $CO_2$ fixation proceeds via the reductive citric acid cycle, considered to be one of the first metabolic cycles, and via the reductive acetyl-CoA/carbon monoxide dehydrogenase pathway. The Calvin cycle has not been found in hyperthermophiles or any Archaea. Organotrophic metabolism mainly involves peptides and sugars as substrates, which are either oxidized to $CO_2$ by external electron acceptors or fermented to acetate and other products. Sugar catabolism in hyperthermophiles involves nonphosphorylated versions of the Entner-Doudoroff pathway and modified versions of the Embden-Meyerhof pathway. The classical Embden-Meyerhof pathway is present in the hyperthermophilic bacterium *Thermotoga* but not in Archaea. All hyperthermophilic Archaea tested so far utilize pyruvate:ferredoxin oxidoreductase for acetyl-CoA formation from pyruvate. Acetyl-CoA oxidation in anaerobic sulfur-reducers and aerobic hyperthermophiles proceeds via the citric acid cycle; in the hyperthermophilic sulfate-reducer *Archaeoglobus* an oxidative acetyl-CoA/carbon monoxide dehydrogenase pathway is operative. Acetate formation from acetyl-CoA in Archaea, including hyperthermophiles, is catalyzed by acetyl-CoA synthase, a novel enzyme involved in energy conservation. In Bacteria, including the hyperthermophile *Thermotoga,* acetyl-CoA conversion to acetate involves two enzymes, phosphate acetyltransferase and acetate kinase.

In addition to the thermal environments of volcanic origin, domestic and industrial hot water storage tanks provide stable habitats for harmless oligotrophic thermophiles like *Thermus aquaticus* (Brock 1978). The thermophilic spore-former *Bacillus stearothermophilus* is an abundant problem organism for the food canning industry. Composting (see Chapter 12)

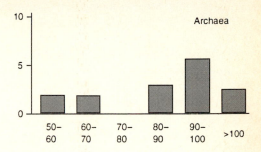

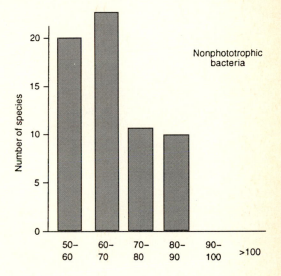

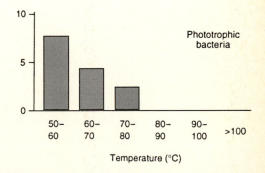

**Figure 8.8**

Effect of temperature on species diversity of procaryotes growing in hot springs. The diversity of Bacteria decreases with increasing temperature, whereas the diversity of Archaea increases up to 100°C. (Source: Brock 1985.)

provides a rich but usually short-lived environment for thermophilic heterotrophic bacteria and fungi.

**Survival and Death of Microorganisms at High and Low Temperatures**    Inability to grow at a particular temperature does not necessarily lead to the death of a microorganism. The temperature tolerance of endospores, cysts, and other resting stages is well known, and even vegetative cells can survive for periods of time at temperatures outside their active growth range. Survival is often greatest at temperatures below the organism's growth range. Thermophiles are frequently isolated from Antarctic soils, for example (Horowitz et al. 1972).

Although microorganisms may survive low temperatures, their growth rates and metabolic activities decline below the optimal temperature. In the microbial ecology of foods, this fact is the basis of preservation and increasing shelf life of products by freezing or refrigeration (Derosier 1970). Many microorganisms in natural soil and aquatic habitats exhibit lower growth rates and metabolic activities during winter when temperatures are low. Temperatures above the growth range of the organism, however, frequently result in death of the organism. Some microorganisms produce resistant resting stages, such as bacterial endospores and sclerotia of fungi, that permit survival at elevated temperatures at which vegetative cells of that organism would not survive. Even such resistant resting stages as the bacterial endospore have upper temperature limits for survival.

The fact that elevated temperatures kill microorganisms is used in the preservation of many food products and the heat sterilization of various items. In the case of food products, the main concern is with the relatively resistant organisms that can cause spoilage and disease (Frazier and Westhoff 1978). The resistance of organisms to elevated temperatures is expressed as the thermal death time (TDT), the time required at a particular temperature to kill a specified number of organisms. Examples of thermal death times for several bacteria, including endospore formers, are listed in Table 8.5. As the TDT is not absolute but depends on the initial numbers of microorganisms present, Table 8.5 and similar TDT tables are based on

a $10^{12}$ (12 log cycle) reduction in numbers. In the practical sense, a $10^{12}$ reduction ensures "no survivors" in the heat-treated sample. The food industry uses TDT numbers to determine the temperature and time period necessary to sterilize food products. Pasteurization is a milder treatment that only reduces the microbial numbers and thus extends the shelf life of food.

The effects of temperature on microorganisms are interactive with other environmental parameters. For example, moisture has a marked influence on the thermal death of microorganisms. Moist heat is more effective in killing microorganisms than dry heat. Whereas fifteen to twenty minutes at 120°C with steam is adequate to sterilize many materials, such as bacteriological media, dry heat at 160–180°C for three to four hours is often needed to achieve similar results. The pH also influences thermal killing; microorganisms tend to be more resistant to high temperatures at neutral pH than at acid or alkaline pH values.

**Effect of Temperature on Microbial Activities**    In addition to affecting survival and growth, temperature influences the metabolic activities of microorganisms. In general, higher temperatures that do not kill microorganisms result in higher metabolic activities. For example, increased $O_2$ consumption occurs as temperature increases (Figure 8.9). The increased respiratory activity reflects the underlying influence of temperature on enzymes up to the temperature where protein denaturation occurs (Hargrave 1969).

**Table 8.5**
Approximate thermal death times for bacteria

| Organisms | Time (min) | Temperature (°C) |
|---|---|---|
| *Escherichia coli* | 20–30 | 57 |
| *Staphylococcus aureus* | 19 | 60 |
| *Bacillus subtilis* (spores) | 50–200 | 100 |
| *Clostridium botulinum* (spores) | 100–330 | 100 |

Source: Frazier and Westhoff 1978.

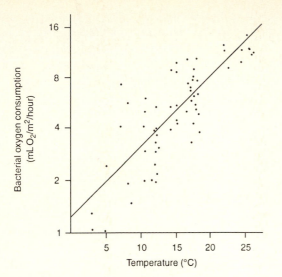

**Figure 8.9**
Relationship of temperature and bacterial respiration in lake sediments. Increased $O_2$ consumption occurs at higher temperatures. (Source: Hargrave 1969. Reprinted by permission of Journal of the Fisheries Research Board of Canada.)

**Table 8.6**
$Q_{10}$ values for some enzymes

| Enzyme | $Q_{10}$ |
|---|---|
| Catalase | 2.2 (10–20°C) |
| Maltase | 1.9 (10–20°C) |
| Maltase | 1.4 (20–30°C) |
| Succinic oxidase | 2.0 (30–40°C) |
| Urease | 1.8 (20–30°C) |

$$Q_{10} = \frac{\text{activity at temp T} + 10°C}{\text{activity at temp T}}$$

The change in enzyme activity caused by a 10°C rise is known as the 10° temperature quotient or $Q_{10}$ value. In general, enzymes have $Q_{10}$ values near 2—that is, an increase in temperature of 10°C within the tolerance range of the enzyme results in a doubling of activity. Table 8.6 shows examples of some $Q_{10}$ values for microbial enzymes. In addition to $Q_{10}$ values for individual enzymes, the ecologist must consider the effects of temperature on the rates of metabolism by certain microbial populations. Populations of sulfate reducers in salt marsh sediment, for example, have been reported to have a $Q_{10}$ of 3.5 for the reduction of sulfate (Abdollahi and Nedwell 1979). Thus sulfate reduction rates appear to be more sensitive to temperature change than most other metabolic processes. It is possible that this is due to changes in membrane fluidity other than a direct effect attributable to the enzyme.

Although biocatalytic reactions run faster at elevated than at mesophilic temperatures, the growth rate (generation time) of thermophilic microorganisms is not faster and often is considerably slower than that of the mesophiles (Brock 1978). The reason for this apparent paradox is the considerable amount of repair a thermophilic microorganism needs to perform in order to replace thermally denatured enzymes and other cell components. For biotechnological use, thermophiles are generally inferior to mesophiles for production of single-cell proteins or antibiotics. They offer advantages, however, if the aim is degradation and bulk reduction, as in composting. It is also advantageous to run depolymerization, fermentation, and methanogenesis reactions using thermophiles. In addition to speeding reaction rates, elevated reaction temperatures reduce cooling costs and contamination problems. Thermophiles are promising sources of heat-resistant enzymes such as proteases and lipases used in laundry detergent formulations, amylases and cellulases used in producing oligomeric sugar substrates for further fermentations, and other thermophilic enzymes used in industry, reagent kits, or scientific research (Brock 1985; Edwards 1990; Ventosa and Nieto 1995).

### Radiation

The spectrum of electromagnetic radiation is continuous from extremely energetic, short-wavelength gamma rays to long-wavelength, low-energy radio waves (Figure 8.10). Portions of this continuous spectrum are defined as ultraviolet, visible, infrared radiation, and so forth. The radiant energy of the sun drives the global ecosystem; photosynthetic interaction with visible light radiation is of profound importance for

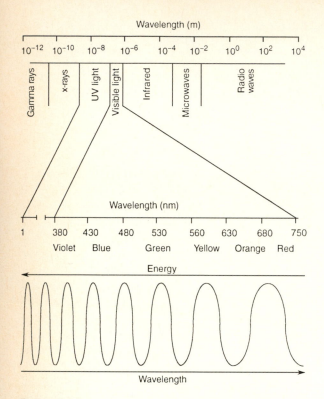

**Figure 8.10**
The continuum of the electromagnetic radiation spectrum. The wavelength scale has been expanded around the range of visible light. The energy content of electromagnetic radiation is inversely correlated with wavelength: The gamma and x-rays, collectively called ionizing radiations, are the most energetic. The unit nm equals $10^{-9}$ m.

terrestrial life. The other portions of the electromagnetic spectrum are also ecologically important and have marked effects on life.

**Ionizing Radiation**   Radiations are designated as ionizing radiations if their interaction with matter produces unstable ions and free radicals that interact with living matter in a destructive manner. Gamma rays and x-rays range in wavelength from $10^{-4}$ nm to 1 nm, with gamma rays at the shorter, more energetic end of the range. Both gamma rays and x-rays are highly penetrating, and their energy levels are destructive to microorganisms. Low-level irradiation may cause mutations, and high-exposure doses destroy both

nucleic acids and enzymes and kill microorganisms. Exposure levels from cosmic and natural radioactive sources are low; nevertheless, these low-level radiations may have contributed to the spontaneous mutations that have formed the material for natural selection over geologic ages.

The resistance of microorganisms to gamma radiation varies. As is true with other environmental extremes, microorganisms tend to be more tolerant of ionizing radiation than macroorganisms. As a practical consequence, it is even necessary to add biocides to the cooling waters of nuclear reactors because the high ionizing radiation levels fail to prevent microbial proliferation.

Bacterial endospores are highly resistant to gamma radiation; it takes 0.3–0.4 million rads (Mrads) to effect a 90% kill, whereas one-tenth of this dose effects the same percentage kill in most vegetative bacteria. Vegetative cells of *Deinococcus radiodurans,* though, display high radiation resistance, tolerating as much as 1 Mrad without a reduction in viable count and some survive even 3 Mrads (Anderson et al. 1956). As a comparison, a human being rarely survives an exposure to 500 rads. Extremely efficient DNA repair mechanisms, rather than any unusual protective substances, are responsible for the radiation resistance of this bacterium.

On our planet, very high exposures to ionizing radiation do not occur naturally. Therefore, the question arises of how and why the extreme radiation resistance of *Deinococcus radiodurans* was selected for. The primary effect of ionizing radiation exposure is an extensive fragmentation of the DNA of the bacterial chromosome. A similar extensive fragmentation of the chromosome occurs in vegetative bacterial cells exposed to desiccation. It seems reasonable to assume that the highly efficient DNA repair mechanism of this non-spore-forming gram-positive coccus developed to repair desiccation damage, and its acquired radiation resistance is merely coincidental (Daly and Minton 1995).

**Ultraviolet Radiation**   Solar radiation includes ultraviolet (UV) light radiation, visible light radiation, and infrared radiation. UV radiation (1–320 nm) is too energetic for photosynthetic use and is destructive to microorganisms (Norman 1954) (Figure 8.11). The most strongly germicidal wavelength (260 nm) coincides with the absorption maximum of DNA, suggesting that damage to DNA is the principal mechanism of the germicidal effect. UV-induced dimerization of thymine bases in DNA strands causes faulty transcription, resulting in defective enzymes. UV-damaged DNA can be repaired enzymatically by excision of the damaged portions, but this process requires time. The survival of the UV-damaged cells is enhanced by conditions that are adverse to rapid growth; optimal growth conditions allow for rapid expression of the UV damage with resulting cell death. Visible light also has a reactivation effect on UV-damaged cells (Rupert 1964; Halldal and Taube 1972). Part of the effect may

be photochemical; blue light tends to break the UV-induced thymine dimers. In addition, visible light triggers a DNA repair mechanism that is, paradoxically, not triggered by the more damaging UV radiation. In nature, microorganisms are exposed to UV radiation only in combination with high visible light intensities, which makes this adaptation understandable.

**Visible Light Radiation**   The visible light spectrum is a relatively narrow band in the total electromagnetic spectrum. It ranges from 320 nm (violet) to the far red end of the spectrum at 800 nm. The quantity of light in a given habitat depends on the obstructions the light beam has to penetrate. Light intensity decreases by the square of the distance from the source. Additional decreases in light intensity occur because of absorption and scattering. The sum of absorption and scattering processes, called *extinction,* is high in ecosystems with many suspended particles. The term *turbidity,* which refers to the cloudiness or number of suspended particles in a volume of water, is often used to describe the resistance of a water body to light penetration.

The intensity of light reaching a particular habitat influences rates of photosynthesis (Halldal 1980). In the absence of light, photosynthesis ceases. Up to some optimal light intensity, rates of photosynthetic activity increase (Steeman-Nielson et al. 1962) (Figure 8.12). As with many other environmental factors, the response of an organism to changes in light intensity will depend on the light intensity to which the organism is adapted. Figure 8.12 clearly shows this by the different response curves of algae that were adapted to 3 kilolux (klx) and those that had been growing at 30 klx. In most cases, organisms can tolerate a wider range of an environmental factor, such as light, if the change is gradual, allowing the organism more time to adapt, than if the change occurs abruptly. Interestingly, some of the cyanobacteria can alternate between oxygen-evolving photosynthesis at high light intensities and anoxygenic photosynthesis, using hydrogen sulfide as the electron donor, at low light intensities (Cohen et al. 1975).

The quality (the color) of light, as well as the intensity of light, influences rates of photosynthesis. Not all wavelengths of light penetrate equally well

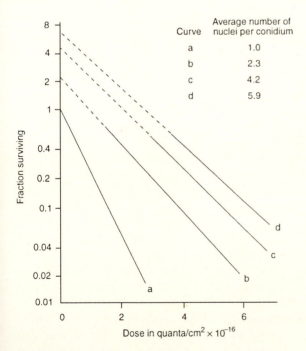

| Curve | Average number of nuclei per conidium |
|-------|---------------------------------------|
| a | 1.0 |
| b | 2.3 |
| c | 4.2 |
| d | 5.9 |

**Figure 8.11**

The inactivation of *Neurospora* conidia by UV radiation. Exposure was at 254 nm. Conidia with higher numbers of nuclei were less susceptible to UV inactivation, probably because UV acts by inactivating DNA segments, and the presence of redundant genes prevents lethal damage. (Source: Norman 1954. Reprinted by permission, copyright Wistar Institute of Biology.)

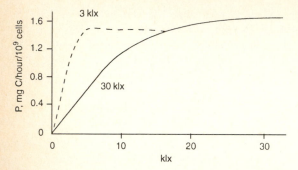

**Figure 8.12**
The rate of photosynthesis per unit cell as a function of light intensity for *Chlorella vulgaris* adapted to high (30 klx) and low (3 klx) light intensities. The graph shows higher rates of photosynthesis at low light intensities by low-light-adapted cells. Maximal rates of photosynthesis (saturation) occur at 5 klx for low-light-adapted cells and at 20–25 klx for high-light-intensity-adapted cells. P = productivity; C = carbon. (Source: Steeman-Nielson et al. 1962. Reprinted by permission of Scandinavian Society of Plant Physiology.)

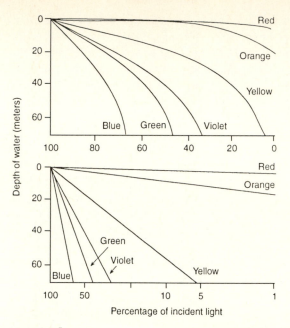

**Figure 8.13**
Penetration of light of varying wavelengths into a water column, generally showing that shorter wavelengths of visible light (such as blue) penetrate to greater depths than lower wavelengths (such as red). Upper graph: arithmetic scale. Lower graph: semilog scale. (Source: Wetzel 1975. Reprinted by permission, copyright W. B. Saunders Co.)

(Figure 8.13). Energy of shorter wavelengths penetrates further than the energy of longer wavelengths. Blue light, for example, can penetrate further into aquatic habitats than red light, a factor that leads to a spatial separation of algae and bacteria with different pigments that can absorb light energy of differing wavelengths.

Some microorganisms exhibit phototactic behavior; they move toward or away from a light source (Carlile 1980; Konopka 1984). This behavior leads to vertical migrations of motile microorganisms that adjust their depth in the water column to that of optimal light intensity. Buoyancy regulation is ecologically important to planktonic cyanobacteria that inhabit thermally stratified lakes (Konopka 1984). In these lakes, the depths at which light energy and inorganic nutrients are most abundant are very different. Cyanobacteria with gas vacuoles, which can migrate between these depths, may have a competitive advantage over other phytoplankton, which are incapable of vertical migration.

Buoyancy in planktonic cyanobacteria is regulated in response to the levels of light energy and inorganic nutrients such as nitrogen and phosphorus. These factors may alter buoyancy as a result of their effects on the rates of energy generation and use. When the growth rate is nutrient-limited, the light intensity at which neutral buoyancy occurs is hypothesized to be directly related to the concentration of the limiting nutrient. Species can mediate this response by either raising cell turgor pressure to collapse some existing gas vesicles or increasing cellular amounts of ballast molecules such as polysaccharide (Konopka 1984).

Light also appears to be a key stimulus in the establishment of circadian rhythms in some eucaryotic microorganisms (Sweeney and Haxo 1961) (Figure 8.14). Thus, light affects not only the growth and survival but also the behavior of microorganisms.

In addition to light energy as a limiting factor for primary production, solar radiation may be considered as a stress factor. Solar radiation contains radiation in

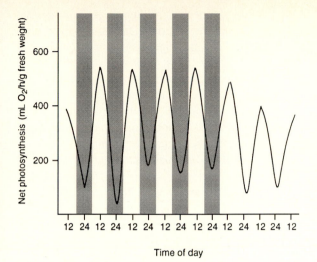

**Figure 8.14**
Circadian rhythms in *Acetabularia.* Shading shows light and dark periods. Periodicity of photosynthesis continues in constant light. (Source: Sweeney and Haxo 1961. Reprinted from *Science* by permission, copyright 1961 by the American Association for the Advancement of Science.)

the UV spectrum, which can cause cell death or mutation. Even excessive intensity of visible light is detrimental, because it causes photooxidative changes. Surface ecosystems—such as the tops of leaves; surfaces of oceans, rocks, soils, and animals; airborne particles; and droplets in clouds—receive high amounts of UV radiation. Microorganisms on snow, on ice, and in brines with crystalline salts receive unusually high UV and visible light exposures because of the reflectivity of their environments. Microorganisms in these environments are selected in part for their tolerance of UV radiation. Pigmentation for shielding the sensitive DNA and efficient repair mechanisms constitute adaptations that provide such tolerance.

## Pressure

**Atmospheric Pressure**   Atmospheric pressure is the pressure exerted by the weight of the air column, which at the surface of the Earth (sea level) is approximately 1 atmosphere (atm) (760 mm mercury or 101.325 kPa). In general, changes in atmospheric pressure do not affect microorganisms. At extremely low atmospheric pressures, such as in the upper atmosphere or in an artificial vacuum, however, water may evaporate, and oxygen becomes limiting, rendering microorganisms metabolically inactive (Gregory 1973).

**Hydrostatic Pressure**   Whereas atmospheric pressure reflects the weight of the air column, hydrostatic pressure is the pressure exerted by the weight of a water column. A 10-m water column over a 1-cm$^2$ area weighs 1 kg (1 l water weighs 1 kg) and exerts about 1 atm pressure, hence hydrostatic pressure increases by approximately 1 atm for every 10 m of depth. Because the atmospheric pressure at sea level is 1 atm, the pressure at 10 m is approximately 2 atm. The precise pressure at a given depth depends on the weight of the water, and hence pressure is greater at a given depth in saline water than at the same depth in fresh water.

Hydrostatic pressure can be calculated by measuring the density and the depth of the water. In routine hydrographic measurements, readings from shielded and unshielded reversing thermometers are compared; hydrostatic pressure compresses the mercury in the unshielded instrument, resulting in a lower reading at a given temperature. Using suitable conversion tables, the difference between the readings indicates the hydrostatic pressure at the point of thermometer reversion.

To study the growth and metabolism of microorganisms under high hydrostatic pressure, simple culture tubes in cylinders can be pressurized by a hydraulic press (ZoBell and Hittle 1967) (Figure 8.15). Precautions must be taken to avoid hyperbaric oxygenation and compression heat. Sudden decompression may rupture microbial cell membranes by releasing gas bubbles, but steady hydrostatic pressure in the range of 1–400 atm has little or no effect on the growth and metabolism of most microorganisms. Higher hydrostatic pressures tend to inhibit or stop the growth of terrestrial and shallow-water organisms, but not that of barotolerant deep-sea organisms, which may be exposed to pressures as high as 1000 atm.

In response to pressures, organisms are either sensitive (they grow optimally at pressures of about 1 atm, and growth rates decline as pressure increases),

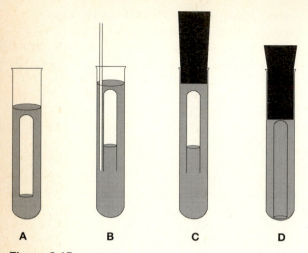

A          B          C          D

**Figure 8.15**
Culture tube for use in pressure cylinders for prevention of hyperbaric oxygenation. A measured amount of oxygen is introduced into an oxygen-free solution prior to pressurization. A rubber stopper, acting as a piston, is forced into the tube by external hydrostatic pressure created by a hydraulic press. (Source: ZoBell and Hittle 1967. Reprinted by permission of National Research Council Canada.)

barotolerant (they tolerate elevated pressures up to given limits without a decline in growth), or barophilic (they grow optimally at elevated pressures and may be completely inhibited or even killed at atmospheric pressure). The existence of obligate barophiles has been a question of prolonged controversy. Sampling and isolation of deep-sea bacteria without loss of *in situ* pressure is required in order to determine the existence of decompression-sensitive strains (Yayanos and Dietz 1983). Early reports about barophilic deep-sea microorganisms (ZoBell 1964) could not be readily confirmed by other laboratories. Barotolerant organisms were found, but not obligate barophiles, probably because deep-sea samples underwent decompression and extensive temperature changes during retrieval.

In 1968, the deep-sea research submersible *Alvin* of the Woods Hole Oceanographic Institution on Cape Cod, Massachusetts, accidentally sank in 1500-m-deep water prior to a mission. The crew escaped, but their lunches, including broth and meat sandwiches,

sank with the submersible. When the *Alvin* was raised 10 months later, the surprisingly unspoiled condition of the food called new attention to microbial metabolic rates under high hydrostatic pressure and prompted Holger Jannasch and associates to investigate the *in situ* activities of deep-sea microorganisms (Jannasch and Wirsen 1977; Jannasch 1979; Jannasch and Nelson 1984). Various microbial media, some containing radiolabeled carbon sources, were incubated *in situ* on the deep-sea floor and in refrigerated incubators at various pressures and temperatures in the laboratory. These tests concluded that low temperatures of 2–4°C only moderately limit the activity of deep-sea microorganisms, but that the combination of low temperature and high hydrostatic pressure imposes a severe limitation on microbial activity. Typically, microbial metabolism at deep-sea pressures was an order of magnitude or more below the activity of the same deep-sea organisms at 1 atm and identical temperature.

When it became possible to retrieve and incubate deep-sea samples without decompression, the majority of isolates recovered using an apparatus that prevented decompression showed barotolerant characteristics, while the remainder (four out of fifteen) exhibited barophilic characteristics (Jannasch et al. 1982).

More extensive investigations based on about one hundred isolates, some of them retrieved from the extreme depth of 10,500 m (Yayanos 1986), indicated that bacteria retrieved from a depth greater than 6000 m are predominately barophilic. Their pressure optimum for growth showed definite correlations with the *in situ* pressure of their collection depth. The deep-sea isolates were also psychrophilic, and their temperature and pressure optima for growth influenced each other in a complex manner. One isolate from about 3600 m deep was clearly barophilic at its *in situ* temperature of 4°C. At its habitat pressure of approximately 360 atm, an increase in temperature up to 12°C increased its growth rate, but the same temperature increase at 1 atm decreased the growth rate drastically. Other isolates showed similar patterns with some quantitative differences. When incubated at *in situ* pressures, most isolates grew better at temperatures somewhat higher than the *in situ* ones. At deep-sea pressures and *in situ* temperature of 2°C in nutrient-rich media, generation times of 7 to 35 hours were measured for barophilic marine bacteria. Under more nutrient-limited conditions, generation times increased up to 200 hours. Although these growth rates are very slow, deep-sea bacteria clearly make significant contributions to biodegradation and to marine food webs.

Considerable difficulty has been experienced in trying to maintain barophilic bacteria in the laboratory. Some of the enrichment cultures from the deep sea lose their viability after two or three transfers to new media, although some barophiles have survived in sediment samples for several months when stored at *in situ* pressures and temperatures. Even at refrigeration temperatures, deep-sea barophiles die off much more rapidly at 1 atm than when compressed to *in situ* pressures. The die-off was accompanied by ultrastructural changes in cell morphology (Chastain and Yayanos 1991). Despite the technical difficulties, many barophilic bacteria have now been cultured. Yayanos (1979) and coworkers have isolated a clearly barophilic deep-sea *Spirillum* that grows at least 15 times faster at pressures between 300 and 600 atm than at 1 atm. At least some of the barophilic bacteria thus far studied have survived decompression during recovery from the deep sea, so temporary decompression may not always cause irreversible damage.

An explanation for the distribution of more-or-less temperature- and pressure-adapted bacteria at intermediate depth zones of the sea might be found in accumulating data on the considerable particle flux from surface waters. Shallow-water bacteria are attached to sinking organic detritus and fecal pellets. Thus, at intermediate depth, bacteria in the sediments and water column may represent in part relatively recent arrivals from areas of low or moderate pressure.

In nonbarophilic microorganisms, high hydrostatic pressure appears to inhibit microbial synthesis of RNA, DNA, and protein, membrane transport functions, and rates of activity of various enzymes (Baross et al. 1972; Hardon and Albright 1974). Enzyme proteins, in order to be active, must be in a proper tertiary configuration. Some researchers have suggested that high hydrostatic pressures distort this configuration, leading to low enzyme activity. In the case of a baro-

tolerant organism, the distortion would be minimal. Most enzymes actually appear to be capable of normal functioning over a wide range of hydrostatic pressures, permitting enzymatic activities even in the deep sea. Theoretically, an obligately barophilic microorganism might have its enzyme in proper tertiary configuration only at elevated hydrostatic pressure and would not function well at lower pressures (Kim and ZoBell 1972) (Figure 8.16).

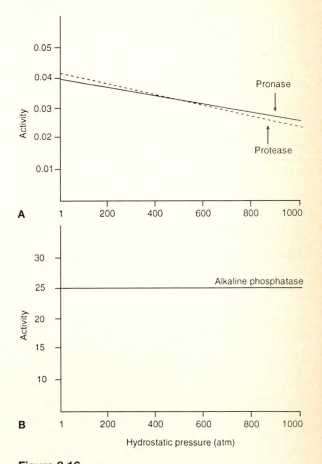

**Figure 8.16**

(A) Slight inhibition of pronase (from *Bacillus subtilis*) and protease (from *Streptomyces griseus*) activity by increased hydrostatic pressure. (B) Lack of inhibition of cell-free alkaline phosphatase activity by elevated hydrostatic pressure. (Source: Kim and ZoBell 1972. Reprinted by permission, copyright University Park Press.)

**Osmotic Pressure** Whereas high hydrostatic pressure is restricted to special habitats, all microorganisms must cope with osmotic pressure, which results from differences in solute concentrations on opposite sides of a semipermeable membrane. In order to equilibrate and equalize solute concentrations, water molecules attempt to move across the membrane in the direction of the higher solute concentration. In some hypotonic habitats, water molecules attempt to move into microbial cells, which could expand and rupture the cells; in hypertonic habitats, water molecules attempt to move out of the cells, which could dehydrate and shrivel the cells.

Microorganisms have evolved adaptive mechanisms that permit them to tolerate osmotic pressure within certain ranges. The rigid cell walls of bacteria and other microorganisms protect these organisms from osmotic shock by preventing the pressure exerted by incoming water molecules from expanding and bursting the cells. The pressure buildup within the cell at equilibrium prevents the entry of additional water. The contractile vacuoles of some protozoa prevent osmotic swelling in hypotonic solution by pumping out excess incoming water.

The majority of microorganisms can withstand the low osmotic pressures that prevail in distilled water, rainwater, and freshwater habitats either by building up intracellular pressure or by actively pumping out excess water from the cell. Fewer microorganisms can withstand the high osmotic pressure of concentrated solutions. In traditional terminology, microorganisms that tolerate or prefer high concentrations of organic solutes (usually sugars) are called *osmotolerant* or *osmophilic,* respectively (Jennings 1990). Honey, sap flows, flower nectar, molasses, and other sugar syrups provide habitats for osmotolerant and osmophilic microorganisms. These may cause spoilage of fruit preserves, syrups, and other food items normally stabilized by their high sugar concentration. *Debaromyces hansenii* and *Zygosaccharomyces rouxii* are osmophilic yeasts; *Aspergillus* and *Penicillium* molds are osmotolerant.

The osmotic pressure of concentrated sugar solutions tends to dehydrate microbial cells. Osmotolerant and osmophilic microorganisms avoid this fate by building up balancing intracellular concentrations of "compatible solutes." These are low-molecular-weight organics such as glycerol, various sugars, glutamate, glycine betaine, and similar compounds. These balance the osmotic pressure and prevent water loss from the cell. The enzymes of osmotolerant and osmophilic microorganisms must be capable of functioning in the presence of these high-solute concentrations. The more adapted osmophiles pay a price for this capability. Their enzymes function suboptimally at low solute concentrations, resulting in optimal growth at water activities below 0.9 (Jennings 1990) (Figure 8.17). Osmotic concentrations tend to change. An osmotolerant or osmophilic microorganism with high intracellular solute concentration might burst when the osmotic pressure of the surrounding medium drops. These microorganisms, however, have the capability of sensing the changes in outside osmotic pressure and reacting by rapidly degrading or polymerizing their intracellular solutes to preserve their osmotic balance.

### Salinity

Microorganisms that tolerate or require high salt concentrations are called *halotolerant* and *halophilic,* respectively (Gilmour 1990). At high salt concentra-

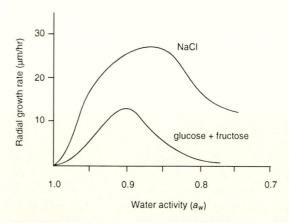

**Figure 8.17**
Effect of water activity and solute on the radial growth of the xerophilic fungus *Basipetospora halophila.* Optimum growth occurs in the range of $a_w$ 0.85–0.90. High water activity inhibits growth. (Source: Jennings 1990.)

tions, the hypertonic environment tends to dehydrate nonhalotolerant microorganisms.

In addition to affecting osmotic pressure, high salt concentrations tend to denature proteins; that is, they disrupt the tertiary protein structure, which is essential for enzymatic activity. Besides denaturing enzymes, high concentrations of salt dehydrate cells. High-salinity habitats include salt lakes, which occur in arid regions where evaporation exceeds freshwater inflow or where a lake is fed by a salt spring. Partially land-locked marine lagoons and tidal evaporation flats can also develop high salt concentrations. Relatively few organisms can grow in highly saline waters, and often the biota of salt lakes are restricted to a few halophilic and halotolerant algal and bacterial species (Kushner 1968, 1980; Post 1977).

Halotolerant and halophilic microorganisms tend to exclude from their cell interiors the high and relatively toxic sodium ion concentrations that usually prevail in their environments. They achieve osmotic balance with their environment by mechanisms similar to those used by the osmophiles. The halophilic unicellular green alga *Dunaliella* that lacks a rigid cell wall builds up high intracellular glycerol concentrations for osmotic balance. The obligately halophilic *Halobacterium*, however, achieves osmotic balance with high intracellular concentrations of potassium chloride. The ribosomes of *Halobacterium* require high concentrations of potassium ions for stability. Its enzymes also require high salt concentrations for maintaining their active configuration and functions and are inactivated at low salinity (Larsen 1962, 1967; Gilmour 1990) (Figure 8.18). *Halobacterium*, a heterotrophic aerobic archaeaon, lacks murein, and its cell wall appears to require sodium ions for stability. Some strains of *Halobacterium* have bacteriorhodopsin bilayer membrane components that serve as light-driven proton pumps. Light energy is used to pump protons out of the cell and thereby generate an electrochemical potential. This, in turn, drives ATP synthesis. The described features make *Halobacterium* superbly adapted to live in highly saline, often saturated brine environments. *Halobacterium* is unable to tolerate low salinities and requires at least 3.0 $M$ NaCl for growth.

Halotolerance is a characteristic of the bacteria *Staphylococcus* and *Halomonas*. Some green algae (*Chlorella, Dunaliella*), some diatoms, and other unicellular algae are also halotolerant. Most algae and bacteria from the marine environments are moderately halophilic. Some marine microbiologists actually define marine bacteria as bacteria that require 3% NaCl for growth. True marine bacteria appear to require sodium for all membrane transport systems, whereas sodium-dependent transport in nonmarine bacteria has so far been shown to occur only in the case of specific and nonessential metabolites (MacLeod 1985). Extreme halophiles are the archaea *Halobacterium, Halococcus, Natronobacterium,* the anoxyphototrophic bacterium *Ectothiorhodospira,* and the green alga *Dunaliella* (Oren 1988; Gilmour 1990).

Great progress has been made in understanding the structure and function of enzymes from extreme halophilic archaea (Eisenberg 1995). These archaea are saturated with salt, and the intracellular electrolyte concentration exceeds that of the extracellular environment. Enzymes and other proteins from extreme halophilic archaea have been purified and studied for many years by biochemical and biophysical methodologies. They are active and stable at multimolar salt concentrations and denature below 2 or 3 $M$ NaCl or KCl. Isocitrate lyase from *Haloferax mediterranei,* for example, has been shown to require high potassium chloride concentrations, optimal activity being found at 1.5–3 $M$ KCl and pH 7.0 (Oren and Gurevich 1995).

A major problem that so far has not been tackled in the study of extreme halophilic archaea is the understanding of protein–nucleic acid interactions, which are essential for the performance of biological function (Eisenberg 1995). Whereas the stability and activity of enzymes and other proteins can be modified to perform at high salt concentrations by use of currently known structural concepts, the existence of meaningful protein–nucleic acid interactions in physiological concentrations of 4–5 $M$ KCl still constitutes an enigma.

## Water Activity

Liquid water is essential for all biochemical processes. For microorganisms, the critical factor is

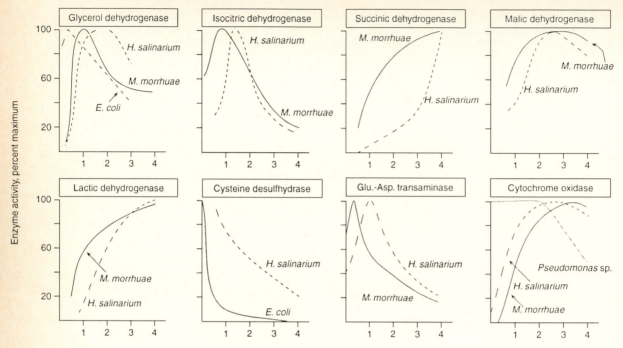

**Figure 8.18**

Effects of sodium chloride concentrations (*M*) on various enzymes of nonhalophilic, halotolerant, and halophilic bacteria. Some of the enzymes of halophilic bacteria (such as succinic dehydrogenase of *Halobacterium salinarium*) require high salt concentrations for maximal activity. Enzyme activities of nonhalotolerant organisms (such as glyceral dehydrogenase of *Escherichia coli* and cytochrome oxidase of *Pseudomonas* sp.) decrease at high salt concentrations. The isocitric dehydrogenase of the halotolerant *Micrococcus morrhuae* shows intermediate behavior. (Source: Larsen 1962. Reprinted by permission, copyright Academic Press.)

the available liquid water rather than the total amount of water present in the environment. The amount of water actually available for microbial use can be expressed as the water activity (*aw*) (Brown 1976; Reid 1980; Griffin 1981). Water availability is also expressed sometimes as water potential (Ψ). *Water potential* is a thermodynamic term and is the chemical potential of the water in the system divided by the partial molar volume. Water potential is related to water activity according to Equation (1).

(1)  $\Psi = RT \ln_e a_w / V$

where $R$ = the gas constant, $T$ = absolute temperature (°K), and $V$ = partial molar volume. Water potential is measured in negative megapascals (−MPa) or bars

(bar = 0.987 atm), expressing the suction pressure necessary to withdraw water from the system. The water potential of pure water is 0. Water potential is frequently used in scientific literature in relation to soil moisture status. Crop plants are unable to withdraw water from soil when its water potential sinks to approximately −15 MPa or −15 bar; therefore, this is their permanent wilting point. This corresponds to approximately 0.90 water activity (Jennings 1990). To avoid confusion, we will consistently use the simpler water activity (*aw*) term in the rest of this text. Soil moisture status will be described in terms of water-holding capacity (WHC) percentage.

Water activity, the index of the water actually available for microbial use, depends on the number of moles of water, the number of moles of solute, and the activity coefficients for water and the particular solute. Water activity can be decreased not only by solutes (osmotic forces) but also by absorption to solid surfaces (matric forces). By definition, *aw* of free distilled water is 1.0. Osmotic and matric forces usually lower *aw* to some fraction of this value. Most microorganisms require *aw* values above 0.96 for active metabolism, but some filamentous fungi and lichens are capable of growth at *aw* values as low as 0.60 (Table 8.7). Such microorganisms are described as *xerotolerant.*

Water availability in soils is traditionally measured in relation to WHC of the soil. A measured amount of dry soil is allowed to soak up water. After excess water is allowed to drain in a humid chamber, the weight increase of the soil sample is recorded. This value is 100% of the WHC. Optimal conditions for activity of aerobic soil microorganisms occur between 50% and 70% WHC, corresponding to 0.98–0.99 *aw*. A higher water content, although not inhibitory by itself, starts to interfere with oxygen availability. The actual water content of a soil can be determined by measuring the wet and dry weights of the soil sample. A sample is weighed and then placed in an oven, usually for 12–14 hours at 105°C, after which the weight is again measured. The difference in weight between the initial (wet weight) and final (dry weight) readings represents the loss of water. The water content of a soil is most meaningfully expressed as a percentage of its total WHC.

In field situations, it is sometimes more convenient to determine water content on a volume basis. This is done by measuring the bulk density (Black 1965). A known volume of soil is collected, the soil dried, and the weight determined. Soil with a high water content will have a low weight per unit volume following drying, assuming that the soil pores were filled with water and not gases.

Microbial activities in the soil fluctuate with the water content, with some microorganisms exhibiting vastly greater tolerance of desiccation than others (Potts 1994). During periods of drought, microbial activities may be severely limited. The water content of soils affects microbial activity not only directly but also indirectly by affecting the diffusion of gases; in waterlogged soils, diffusion of air is limited, generally resulting in anaerobic conditions that may result in a shift from aerobic to anaerobic metabolism.

The water content in the atmosphere is generally low and limiting for microbial growth (Gregory 1973). In some regions, such as in tropical areas, the humidity in the air is sufficiently high to allow microbial growth. In such humid areas, microorganisms may grow on exposed surfaces using water from the air. Lichens tolerate desiccation and grow receiving only intermittent precipitation. A number of fungi and lichens grow on exposed plant surfaces. Various fungi grow on canvas and leather in humid regions. In addition to influencing survival in the atmosphere, water as rainfall causes a flux of microorganisms into and out of the atmosphere. Rainfall washes some organisms out of the atmosphere; raindrops trigger the release to the atmosphere of others (Figure 8.19) (Hirst et al. 1955).

Desert soils, by definition, receive less than 25 cm of rainfall per year. Many deserts are extremely dry and are subject to extreme diurnal variations in temperature

**Table 8.7**
Approximate water activities required for the growth of various microorganisms

| Water activity (*aw*) | Bacteria | Fungi |
|---|---|---|
| 1.00 | *Caulobacter* | |
| | *Spirillum* | |
| 0.90 | *Lactobacillus* | *Fusarium* |
| | *Bacillus* | *Mucor* |
| 0.85 | *Staphylococcus* | *Debaronmyces* |
| 0.80 | | *Penicillium* |
| 0.75 | *Halobacterium* | *Aspergillus* |
| | | *Saccharomyces rouxii* |
| 0.60 | | *Xeromyces bisporus* |

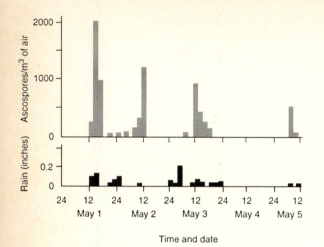

**Figure 8.19**

Concentration of ascospores of *Venturia inaequalis* in air related to rainfall. High numbers of ascospores were found shortly following rainfall. (Source: Hirst et al. 1955. Reprinted by permission of Administration A—Fish, Food, and Plant Pathology—of England and the Controller of Her Britannic Majesty's Stationery Office.)

because of the lack of moisture in the atmosphere overlying them to moderate the loss of heat. Microorganisms living in dry desert soils must be able to tolerate long periods of desiccation (Skujins 1984).

In the dry valleys of Antarctica, microorganisms must also tolerate very low temperatures and, during part of the year, high irradiation levels (Horowitz et al. 1972). In such environments, many microorganisms have developed adaptations that allow them to survive in a dormant state during unfavorable conditions and to grow actively only during those brief periods of time when conditions are favorable, such as after a rainstorm. Many of the bacteria and fungi living in desert soils form spores that allow them to persist, if necessary, for decades between growth periods. When there is adequate moisture the spores germinate, and for a brief period the organisms can actively grow and reproduce.

Most bacteria are unable to form endospores, yet in terrestrial environments they may be exposed to desiccation (air-drying). In vegetative bacterial cells, desiccation may denature proteins that are kept in

their proper tertiary structure by hydration (hydrogen-bonding with water). Desiccation can also fragment nucleic acids, inducing lethal mutations. The combination of these effects may kill susceptible bacteria. Although osmotolerant bacterial species prevent excessive water loss through the synthesis of "compatible solutes," this mechanism seems to offer little protection against desiccation damage (Potts 1994). Many aspects of desiccation tolerance remain to be explored, but the synthesis of the nonreducing sugars trehalose and sucrose appears to be an effective protection. Upon desiccation, these sugars form a noncrystalline "glass" or "gum" phase that is hydrogen-bonded to the proteins and prevents their denaturation upon water removal. In addition, extracellular polysaccharides (EPS) in the form of sheaths, capsules, and slimes provide protection against the destructive effects of desiccation. *Nostoc commune,* a cyanobacterium that commonly grows on exposed rock surfaces and as a constituent of desert crusts, relies on copious amounts of gelatinous EPS as a desiccation protectant.

Rock-inhabiting (lithobiontic) microorganisms colonize rock surfaces, or the rock fabric adjacent to the surface, in a wide variety of climates and environments. Conspicuous among microorganisms on rock surfaces are lichens, which often form brightly colored crusts. These organisms are particularly resistant to desiccation. Lichens are poikilohydrous, meaning that they tend to be in moisture equilibrium with the surrounding air or substrate to which they are attached (Blum 1974). Other microorganisms colonize cracks and fissures within rocks that provide some protection against desiccation and irradiation. These are called *chasmendolithic microorganisms.*

Some microorganisms, called *cryptoendolithic,* also grow within the rock matrix (Friedmann and Ocampo 1976; Friedmann 1982; Friedmann and Ocampo-Friedmann 1984; Wynn-Williams 1990). The morphologies of endolithic colonization in cold and hot deserts are remarkably similar. The uppermost 1–3 mm of rock are free from microorganisms. Colonies are present in the next few millimeters, where the microorganisms adhere to or grow between rock crystals. Endolithic microorganisms in hot deserts and in

Antarctica share a common survival strategy. They are capable of switching their metabolic activities on and off in response to rapid changes in environmental conditions.

There are, however, major differences between the endolithic microorganisms of hot and cold deserts (Friedmann and Ocampo-Friedmann 1984). In hot deserts, all endolithic samples examined to date contained only procaryotic primary producers, which form a narrow green zone a few millimeters below and parallel to the rock crust. They are cyanobacteria, nearly always members of the genus *Chroococcidiopsis*. In hot deserts, a favorable combination of available water and moderate temperature range occurs in early morning after dewfall. Later in the day, the temperature rises and the relative humidity drops drastically. The combination of temperature increase in a hydrated state and the concomitant loss of water imposes a severe environmental stress that eucaryotic algae do not seem to tolerate. This is probably the reason that in hot deserts, endolithic primary producers are exclusively cyanobacteria.

The endolithic microbial communities in polar deserts show a higher level of complexity than those in hot deserts. In most cases, polar endolithic communities contain a number of organisms, including eucaryotes, that are dominant. The fungi and algae together form a symbiotic lichen association of segregated bands within the rock matrix that are very different from the usual integrated thalloid lichen organization. The coherent, protective pseudotissue, termed *plectenchyma,* is missing. Instead, loose filaments and cell clusters grow between rock crystals. In endolithic lichens, the rock matrix prevents the development of and eliminates the need for a coherent plectenchyma. The activity of the cryptoendolithic lichen community results in the mobilization of iron compounds in the rock as well as in a characteristic exfoliative weathering pattern.

Due to a partial dissolution of the rock in the microbially colonized layer, the surface layer peels off, exposing and causing the destruction of the microorganisms. The cryptoendolithic community reestablishes itself below the rock surface, and the process repeats itself with a gradual erosion of the rock over geologic time periods. The growth rate of the Antarctic cryptoendolithic microbial communities appears to be so slow that it strains the imagination. Recent measurements of photosynthetic radiocarbon incorporation at *in situ* temperatures divided by the existing microbial biomass indicated turnover times around 20,000 years (Johnston and Vestal 1991). Even allowing for methodological difficulties and uncertain assumptions, there is little doubt that microbial generation times in such cryptoendolithic microbial communities are on the order of hundreds and perhaps even thousands of years.

## Movement

The movement of air and water aids the passive dispersal of microorganisms. Of equal importance is the role of movement in importing and distributing nutrients for microbial growth and in removing metabolic by-products. Factors such as solubility, diffusion, viscosity, specific gravity, porosity, and the flow characteristics of the ecosystem control the movement of materials in and out of ecosystems.

Some ecosystems are characterized by extensive flow, such as in rivers, or by turbulence, such as in oceans. Other ecosystems are generally quiescent, such as ponds, or static, such as soil. Ecosystems with extensive flow or turbulence have greater mixing capacity. Materials are moved into and out of such ecosystems in part by the movement or mixing of the ecosystem. Even in quiescent and static systems, thermal convection, evapotranspiration, and leaching move materials.

**Diffusion**    In ecosystems that lack extensive mixing, materials may move by diffusion (Koch 1990). Diffusion results in a spreading out of a substance from its source, lowering concentration. Diffusion of materials through ecosystems depends in part on temperature. The molecular weight of the solute and the viscosity (flow characteristics) of the solvent determine in part the ability of a solution to diffuse through an ecosystem. Diffusion is often augmented by mixing due to differences in specific gravity and by thermal convection. Gaseous molecules with low specific gravities, for example, tend to rise, generally moving upward through aquatic ecosystems. In the atmosphere, diffusion of gases is augmented by convection along temperature gradients, with warmer gases rising and cooler gases descending through the atmosphere. The movement of gases along thermal gradients results in turbulence and mixing.

In terrestrial ecosystems, diffusion of materials is a function of porosity. *Porosity* refers to the number and volume of pores in a soil or sediment particle matrix. The pores, sometimes referred to as *interstitial spaces,* may be filled with liquid or gases. Diffusion of materials occurs through the pores, and exchange rates between material in the interstitial spaces and external sources affect diffusion rates and the availability of materials essential for microbial growth and activity.

**Adsorption**    Surface adsorption and tension may restrict movement of materials through an ecosystem. Surface tension may restrict movement of materials into an ecosystem—for example, from the atmosphere into an aquatic ecosystem—resulting in the accumulation of nutrients and pollutants. Adsorption may bind materials to particles, decreasing the availability of those materials within the ecosystem. If the substance is an essential nutrient, this can decrease productivity, but if the substance is toxic, adsorption can increase microbial growth. Because of adsorption, even excessive levels of microbial inhibitors fail to suppress completely microbial activity in soil.

In environments with very dilute nutrient concentrations, the local enrichment of nutrients on adsorptive surfaces increases their utilization by microbes. This phenomenon appears to aid the survival of copiotrophic microorganisms in oligotrophic environments (Kjelleberg 1984). The concentration of organic and inorganic nutrients by adsorption onto particles accounts in part for the preferential growth of many microorganisms on surfaces. The adsorptive properties of an ecosystem depend on available particle surface areas, charged binding sites, hydrophilic binding sites, hydrophobic binding sites, and other factors such as pH. In some cases, adsorption is essential for microbial reproduction. For example, many

microorganisms grow or reproduce only on surfaces such as leaves, skin, teeth, and so on. Some bacterial viruses must adsorb onto specific receptor sites located on pili before penetrating into bacterial cells, where they reproduce.

The mechanisms of adherence of microorganisms to a variety of biotic and abiotic surfaces have been intensively examined (Marshall 1976; Fletcher and Marshall 1982; Costerton 1984; Dazzo 1984; Fletcher and McEldowney 1984; Rosenberg and Kjelleberg 1986). Bacteria growing in a wide variety of environmental and pathogenic situations have been shown to be surrounded by extracellular glycocalyx structures that mediate the attachment process (Costerton 1984); in some cases, proteins known as lectins mediate the specific attachment processes (Dazzo 1984). Charge interactions also bring about adsorption. Adhesion holds the bacterial cell in a suitable habitat, positioning the cell within the surface zone, which is rich in nutrients because organic molecules are attracted to these interfaces. Development of a fibrous, anionic, exopolysaccharide matrix (glycocalyx) acts as an ion-exchange resin, attracting and concentrating charged nutrients. With cell growth, this matrix burgeons into a thick, coherent biofilm. This sessile biofilm mode of growth may protect adherent cells from surfactants, bacteriophages, phagocytic amoebae filter feeders, chemical biocides, antiseptics, antibiotics, disinfectants, antibodies, and phagocytic leukocytes.

## Hydrogen Ion Concentration

Microorganisms generally cannot tolerate extreme pH values. Under highly alkaline or acidic conditions, some microbial cell components may be hydrolyzed or enzymes may be denatured. There are, however, some acidophilic and alkaliphilic bacteria (also called alkalophilic bacteria) that tolerate or even require extreme pH conditions for growth. Table 8.8 shows the optimal pH values and the tolerance of ranges of pH for various bacteria.

The pH affects the dissociation of the amino and carboxyl functional groups on the side chains of protein molecules; in order to perform enzymatic activity, enzymes must be in a particular state of dissociation.

**Table 8.8**
Minimum, optimum, and maximum pH in multiplication of various bacteria

| Organism | pH | | |
|---|---|---|---|
| | Minimum | Optimum | Maximum |
| *Escherichia coli* | 4.4 | 6.0–7.0 | 9.0 |
| *Proteus vulgaris* | 4.4 | 6.0–7.0 | 8.4 |
| *Enterobacter aerogenes* | 4.4 | 6.0–7.0 | 9.0 |
| *Pseudomonas aeruginosa* | 5.6 | 6.6–7.0 | 8.0 |
| *Erwinia carotovora* | 5.6 | 7.1 | 9.3 |
| *Clostridium sporogenes* | 5.5–5.8 | 6.0–7.6 | 8.5–9.0 |
| *Nitrosomonas* spp. | 7.0–7.6 | 8.0–8.8 | 9.4 |
| *Nitrobacter* spp. | 6.6 | 7.6–8.6 | 10.0 |
| *Thiobacillus thiooxidans* | 1.0 | 2.0–2.8 | 6.0 |
| *Lactobacillus acidophilus* | 4.0 | 4.6–5.8 | 6.8 |
| *Bacillus acidocaldarius* | 2.0 | 3.5 | 6.0 |
| *Thermoplasma acidophilus* | 1.0 | 1.5 | 4.0 |
| *Sulfolobus acidocaldarius* | 1.0 | 2.5 | 4.0 |
| *Bacillus alcalophilus* | 8.5 | 9.5 | 11.5 |

Source: Doetch and Cook 1973. Added data from Ingeldew 1990 and Kroll 1990.

Certain pH values will be optimal for activities of specific enzymes. Optimal pH values may depend on other factors, such as salt concentrations (Lieberman and Lanyi 1972) (Figure 8.20). Extreme pH values irreversibly denature most proteins.

The pH of an environment affects microorganisms and microbial enzymes directly and also influences the dissociation and solubility of many molecules that indirectly influence microorganisms. The pH determines in part the solubility of $CO_2$, influencing the rates of photosynthesis; the availability of required nutrients, such as ammonium and phosphate, which limit microbial growth rates in many ecosystems; and the mobility of heavy metals, such as copper, which are toxic to microorganisms.

A common feature of microorganisms that tolerate or even require pH extremes for growth is that their cytoplasm is maintained close to neutrality. Their cell walls and cell membranes need to be adapted to keep their integrity under the pH extremes, maintain the cell interior near neutrality, and perform chemiosmotic ATP synthesis under these unusual conditions. The precise structural and biochemical adaptations remain insufficiently known at this time. Ingledew (1990) and Kroll (1990) discuss the biophysical background to such adaptations for acidophiles and for alkaliphiles, respectively.

Many fungi are acidotolerant, but most bacteria are not. Some acidotolerant bacteria, like *Lactobacillus,* and acidophiles, like *Thiobacillus* and *Sulfolobus* (Table 8.8), create their own low pH environment by producing acids. *Lactobacillus* is a mixed acid fermenter and *Sulfolobus* produces sulfuric acid. *Bacillus acidocaldarius* and *Thermoplasma acidophilus* are heterotrophic thermoacidophiles that live in acidic environments created by chemolithotrophic sulfur oxidizers but do not produce acids themselves. *Thermoplasma* is an archeon that lacks a cell wall and occurs in hot, acidic coal refuse piles. *B. acidocaldarius* occurs in acidic hot springs. *Lactobacillus* has

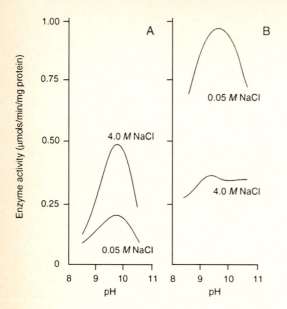

**Figure 8.20**

The pH dependence of threonine deaminase from *Halobacterium cutirubrum* assayed at 0.05 and 4.0 *M* NaCl concentrations in (A) the absence of ADP and (B) the presence of ADP. In the absence of ADP, an increase of the NaCl concentration caused a narrowing of the pH optimum; in the presence of ADP, when the cooperative substrate kinetics were no longer observed, the pH response of the enzyme broadened with increased salt concentration. (Source: Lieberman and Lanyi 1972. Reprinted from *Biochemistry* by permission of American Chemical Society.)

great practical importance in preparation of silage and fermented foods. *Thiobacillus* and *Sulfolobus* are used in bioleaching of low-grade copper and uranium ores (see Chapter 15).

Two species belonging to a novel genus of archaea, designated *Picrophilus oshimae* and *Picrophilus torridus,* have been isolated from two different solfataric locations in northern Japan (Schleper et al. 1996). One habitat harboring both organisms is a dry, extremely acidic soil (pH < 0.5) heated by solfataric gases to about 55°C. In the laboratory both species grew heterotrophically under aerobic conditions at temperatures of 45–65°C; they grew optimally at 60°C. Their pH optimum was 0.7, but growth occurred even around pH 0. Under optimal conditions, the generation

time was about 6 hours, yielding densities of up to $10^{10}$ cells per mL. The cells were surrounded by a highly filigreed regular tetragonal surface protein (S-layer,) and the core lipids of the membrane were mainly biphytanyltetraethers.

Many bacteria and fungi tolerate alkaline pH up to 9.0 (Table 8.8) but have pH optima near neutrality. True alkaliphiles include some *Bacillus* strains such as *B. alcalophilus* and *B. pasteurii.* Also alkalophilic are some cyanobacteria such as *Microcystis aeruginosa, Plectonema nostocorum,* and several species of *Spirulina.* Microorganisms listed earlier as halophilic, such as *Halobacterium, Natronobacterium,* and *Natronococcus,* are also alkalophiles and live in saline lakes with high pH. *Bacillus* strains produce proteases and lipases that are stable at high temperature, at alkaline pH, and in the presence of detergents. These are used in some laundry detergent products to enzymatically remove fat- and protein-based stains (Kroll 1990). *Clostridium paradoxum* has a pH maximum greater than 10 at 55°C and an optimal doubling time of 13 minutes at pH 9.3 (Cook et al. 1996).

## Redox Potential

Many enzymatic reactions are oxidation-reduction reactions in which one compound is oxidized and another compound is reduced. The ability of an organism to carry out oxidation-reduction reactions depends on the oxidation-reduction state of the environment. In a solution, the proportion of oxidized to reduced components constitutes the oxidation-reduction potential or redox potential ($E_h$). Some microorganisms can be active only in oxidizing environments, and others can exist only in reducing environments (Baas-Becking and Wood 1955; Rheinheimer 1974) (Figure 8.21).

The redox potential is a relative value measured against the arbitrary 0 point of the normal hydrogen electrode. Any system or environment that accepts electrons from a normal hydrogen electrode is a half-cell that is defined as having a positive redox potential; any environment that donates electrons to this half-cell is defined as having a negative redox potential. The redox potential is measured in millivolts

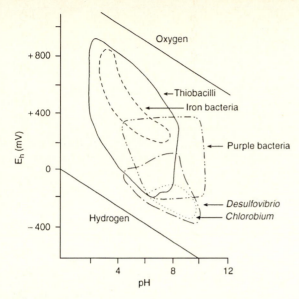

**Figure 8.21**

The pH and $E_h$ tolerance contours of various bacteria involved in several cycling processes. The thiobacilli and iron bacteria are extremely tolerant to highly acidic and aerobic conditions, which are characteristic of their natural habitat. *Chlorobium* and *Desulfovibrio* are restricted to anaerobic and neutral to slightly alkaline pH zones. Note the interaction of pH and $E_h$ as signified by the sloping hydrogen and oxygen potentials. (Source: Rheinheimer 1974. Based on Baas-Becking and Wood 1955. Reprinted by permission of John Wiley and Sons Ltd. and VEB Gustav Fischer Verlag.)

(mV). A high positive $E_h$ value indicates an environment that favors oxidation reactions; a low negative $E_h$ value indicates a strongly reducing environment. Strictly aerobic microorganisms can be metabolically active only at positive redox potentials, whereas strict anaerobes are active only at negative redox potentials. Facultative anaerobes can operate over a wide range of $E_h$ values using oxygen as an electron sink at high redox potentials and fermenting or using alternate electron acceptors, such as ferric iron and nitrate ions, at low redox potentials. The solubility of certain nutrients is strongly influenced by the prevailing redox potential. Chemicals can exist in oxidized or reduced forms at different redox values. At high redox potentials, iron and manganese exist in their trivalent (ferric) and tetravalent (manganic) forms, respectively. These are insoluble and generally unavailable for microbial uptake. The bivalent forms of these metals that exist at low redox potentials are soluble and readily available.

The redox potential is greatly influenced by the presence or absence of molecular oxygen. Environments in equilibrium with atmospheric oxygen have $E_h$ around +800 mV; environments at reduced oxygen tensions have lower redox potentials. Heterotrophic activity keeps the redox potential of aerobic natural waters at 400–500 mV, lower than might be expected for water fully equilibrated with the atmosphere. Below the surface of waterlogged soil and sediment, $E_h$ values are usually negative (Figure 8.22). Low redox potentials may be caused by extensive growth of heterotrophic microorganisms that scavenge all available oxygen. Such is often the case in highly polluted ecosystems where microorganisms utilize the available oxygen for decomposition processes. Sediments rich in organic matter can have $E_h$ values as low as –450 mV. At these low $E_h$ values, sulfate reduction yielding $H_2S$ and $CO_2$ reduction yielding $CH_4$ can readily occur. It should be pointed out that it is difficult to measure $E_h$ in natural habitats, and that heterogeneity is great; the development and use of microelectrodes, however, now makes it possible to measure redox potentials on a scale relevant to microbial microhabitats (Revsbech and Jørgensen 1986). Because of the dynamics at interfaces, a low redox potential can occur in the presence of oxygenated water. Diurnal fluctuations of redox potential due to the prevalence of photosynthetic oxygen release by day and respiratory oxygen consumption by night are common.

## Magnetic Force

The effects of magnetism upon microorganisms have generally been ignored as most bacteria appear to be totally unaffected by changes in magnetic fields. Some bacteria, however, exhibit magnetotaxis, motility directed by a geomagnetic field (Blakemore 1975, 1982; Moench and Konetzka 1978; Spring et al. 1993,

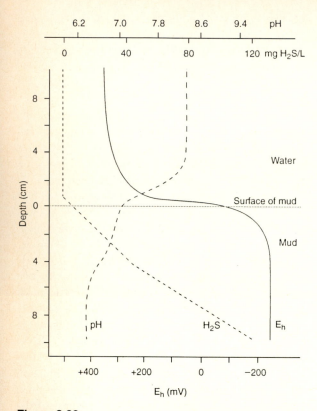

**Figure 8.22**
A sulfur-rich lakeshore habitat showing reduced pH and $E_h$ below the surface of mud. $H_2S$ concentrations were low in water with high $E_h$ (aerobic zone) and high in sediment with low $E_h$ (anaerobic zone). (Source: Rheinheimer 1974. Reprinted by permission John Wiley and Sons Ltd. and VEB Gustav Fischer Verlag.)

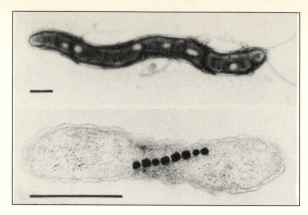

**Figure 8.23**
Electron micrographs of magnetotactic bacteria showing accumulation and regular arrangement of iron-rich inclusions. (Courtesy of R. Blakemore.)

magnetic poles. Initial enrichments of magnetotactic bacteria from sediments were obtained by placing magnets next to the culture flasks and collecting the microorganisms that aggregated near the magnetic poles.

The adaptive value of magnetotactic behavior is as yet unclear. Because the magnetotactic microorganisms that have been described are microaerophilic or anaerobic, it has been suggested that magnetotactic orientation may help these motile organisms to locate deeper, more reduced organic sediments. However, because some of the bacteria move toward the north and others toward the south pole of the magnets, this argument is not very convincing.

Experimentation on a pure culture of magnetotactic bacterium *Aquaspirillum magnetotacticum* (Ricci et al. 1991) revealed that even in a pure culture some bacteria are attracted to the north and others to the south magnetic pole. Pulse magnetization can alter and even reverse the orientation of *A. magnetotacticum* cells. However, the ecological value of magnetic orientation for microorganisms, if any, remains to be determined.

## Organic Compounds

Organic matter in an ecosystem is frequently the limiting factor for growth of heterotrophic microorganisms.

1995). Diverse populations of magnetotactic bacteria have been identified based on rRNA sequence analyses (Spring et al. 1993, 1995). Magnetotactic bacteria contain dense inclusion bodies, which may impart a magnetic moment upon the cell (Figure 8.23). Some of these magnetotactic bacteria contain approximately 4% iron by weight. The magnetic iron is in the form of either magnetite ($Fe_3O_4$) or greigite ($Fe_3S_4$) (Farina et al. 1990; Mann et al. 1990). The magnetic iron is enclosed in membrane-bound magnetosomes. These allow cells to orient themselves in magnetic fields and actively move by flagellar motion toward one of the

Specific organic substrates often favor the growth of particular populations with specific catabolic activities. Some microorganisms require relatively high levels of organic matter, whereas others grow only at relatively low concentrations.

In aquatic ecosystems, the chemical oxygen demand (COD) is often used as an index of the total organic carbon in the sample. The COD is determined by measuring the amount of oxidizing reagent consumed during oxidation of organic matter with dichromate or permanganate. The biological oxygen demand (BOD) yields an estimate of the readily usable concentrations of organic matter. The BOD is determined by allowing microorganisms to consume oxygen in solution during oxidation of the organic matter present in the sample. This measurement is performed in a closed BOD bottle without air space. The bottle contains air-saturated liquid medium, a strongly diluted organic matter sample, and a low microbial inoculum. Dissolved oxygen is determined by an oxygen electrode or by a chemical procedure at time zero and after a suitable (e.g., 5-day) incubation period. A high BOD indicates an abundance of organic substrates that can be used by microorganisms aerobically. When the BOD is high, however, microorganisms often use much of the dissolved oxygen for the degradation of organic matter, creating conditions of oxygen depletion and causing the death of higher organisms, such as fish, that require $O_2$ for survival.

Most natural ecosystems are not characterized by high concentrations of usable organic matter; rather, microorganisms in many ecosystems, such as the oceans, live at very low concentrations of nutrients. Most free-living bacteria probably experience periods of starvation. Starvation survival is important in microbial ecology because it is a mechanism that perpetuates the species, permitting the genome to express itself once the environmental conditions become favorable (Kjelleberg 1984).

There is growing evidence of the existence of bacteria especially suited for the exploitation of low-nutrient flux habitats that can be distinguished from organisms especially suited for high-nutrient flux environments (Poindexter 1981; Button 1985; Fry 1990). As opposed to copiotrophs (bacteria growing on high-nutrient concentrations), whose natural distribution implies that nutrient abundance favors their survival and is an important factor in their competitiveness, oligotrophic (low-nutrient) bacteria possess physiological properties that permit them to efficiently use the limited nutrient resources available to them. Substrate uptake characteristics of oligotrophs must be suitable for acquisition of growth substrates against steep gradients between the cell and its surroundings, and acquired nutrients must be so managed that the cell can maintain its integrity and growth. To achieve a high uptake capacity relative to nutrient-consuming processes, oligotrophs ideally should be small spheres, slender rods, or envelope-appendaged bacteria that have high surface areas and high affinities (low $K_m$) for uptake for a variety of utilizable substrates. Indeed, many oligotrophic microorganisms, such as *Caulobacter* and *Hyphomicrobium,* form appendages for the more efficient transport of the dilute substrates into their cells. The less well known polyprosthecate bacteria appear to represent a similar adaptation to low substrate concentrations (Semenov and Staley 1992). *Prosthecomicrobium* and *Ancalomicrobium* form multiple appendages and resemble irregular sea urchins in appearance. The genera *Stella* and *Labrys* are unique among bacteria in their radial symmetry and resemble starfish. These polyprosthecate bacteria are common in natural waters and in soil but are rarely isolated because of their slow growth and low substrate concentration preference.

Adaptations required for oligotrophs not only make them poor competitors at high substrate concentrations but make high substrate concentrations outright inhibitory. Many obligate oligotrophs that have been isolated cease to grow when substrate concentrations reach 500–1000 mg per liter (0.5–1.0%). Optimal growth occurs around 50–100 mg/l substrate concentration. In contrast, copiotrophs grow optimally around substrate concentrations of 50,000 mg/l (Fry 1990; Semenov and Staley 1992).

Myxobacteria have developed complex life cycles to cope with alternating conditions of sufficient nutritional resources and starvation. These are gliding gram-negative bacteria that can consume bacterial cells, as well as obtain nutrients from dead plants or animals; they commonly grow on rotting plant materials or animal wastes. During growth on the nutrient-rich animal or plant material, vegetative cells divide by binary fission. The cells glide over the surface of the rotting material, growing and consuming nutrients. At a point prior to total consumption of a nutrient source, which would lead to starvation, binary fission ceases and up to a million cells fuse to form a fruiting body. The fruiting body rises up from the surface and myxospores form within it. Myxospores are released from the fruiting body and are disseminated into the surrounding environment. They can survive for prolonged periods. When a myxospore reaches a nutrient-rich environment that is favorable for growth, the myxospore germinates and produces vegetative cells. These vegetative cells reproduce and the process is repeated. This life-cycle strategy permits survival and movement between discrete and widely dispersed sources of nutrients.

Organic compounds can be potential nutrients, but some of them act as inhibitors or poisons. Various metabolic products, such as carboxylic acids, alcohols, and phenolics, are toxic to microbial populations, especially when they accumulate in some anaerobic environments where they are not readily metabolized to less toxic degradation products. Some microorganisms specifically excrete allelopathic substances (allelochemics), which are chemicals (other than food substances) produced by one species that affect growth, health, behavior, or population dynamics of other species (Whittaker and Feeny 1971); production of antibiotics and bacteriocins are prime examples of allelochemics.

## Inorganic Compounds

Many inorganic compounds are essential nutrients for microorganisms (Stotzky and Norman 1964). There are also many inorganic substances that are toxic to microorganisms (Ehrlich 1978). It is generally necessary to consider the chemical form of inorganic compounds when considering such compounds as microbial nutrients or inhibitors. Inorganic compounds of importance in examining the ecology of microorganisms include the gases oxygen, carbon dioxide, carbon monoxide, hydrogen, nitrogen, nitrous oxide, and

hydrogen sulfide; the elemental form of sulfur; the cations ammonium, ferrous iron, ferric iron, magnesium, calcium, sodium, potassium, cobalt, copper, manganese, vanadium, nickel, zinc, mercury, cadmium, and lead; and the anions phosphate, carbonate, bicarbonate, borate, sulfide, sulfate, nitrite, nitrate, chloride, chlorate, bromide, fluoride, silicate, selenite, molybdate, and arsenate.

Of the inorganic ions, the heavy metals deserve special attention. Although some heavy metals are required in trace amounts as nutrients, they become strongly inhibitory for microorganisms at relatively low concentrations (Gadd 1990). A general mechanism of heavy metals' toxicity is their binding to the sulfhydryl (—SH) groups of essential microbial proteins and enzymes. Important factors for heavy metal toxicity are the pH and the organic matter concentration of the environment. Low pH mobilizes heavy metals, and high pH precipitates them and reduces their toxicity. Organic matter tends to bind and chelate heavy metals, also reducing their toxicity.

Seawater is a large natural environment with substantial heavy metal concentrations and low levels of organic matter. Marine microorganisms are under considerable heavy metal stress. Industrial pollution can result in locally high levels of lead, tin, cadmium, mercury, chromium, copper, zinc, nickel, and so on. Microorganisms have evolved a number of defense mechanisms against heavy metal toxicity. These include extracellular precipitation or complexing, impermeability to or reduced transport of the metals across the cell membrane, and intracellular compartmentalization and detoxification. One or more of these defense mechanisms allows some microorganisms to function metabolically in environments highly polluted by heavy metals. A widespread response by microorganisms to heavy metal stress is the synthesis of special metal-binding compounds, the metallothioneins. These are low-molecular-weight cystine-rich proteins that bind and render harmless heavy metals like zinc, cadmium, and copper.

**Oxygen and Its Reactive Forms**   Oxygen exists in several forms with varying degrees of toxicity (Fridovich 1977). Molecular oxygen normally exists as $O_2$ in the atmosphere. Singlet oxygen ($O^*$) has a higher energy and is more toxic to microorganisms. It can be formed both biochemically and chemically. Peroxidase enzyme systems can form singlet oxygen from hydrogen peroxide. The reactivity of singlet oxygen is a key factor in some biological interactions, such as the ability of blood phagocytes to kill invading microorganisms. Singlet oxygen also forms in the upper atmosphere photochemically and reacts with normal molecular oxygen to produce ozone. Ozone ($O_3$) is a strong oxidizing agent that kills microorganisms. Ozone is sometimes used as a sterilizing agent—for example, in some water treatment operations. Another highly reactive oxygen species is the superoxide anion ($O_2^-$). Superoxide anions are generated by reactions of oxygen with many biochemicals such as flavins, quinones, and thiols. The superoxide anion can destroy lipids and other biochemical components of the cell. It is relatively long-lived and may explain the oxygen sensitivity of some obligate anaerobes.

Microorganisms have evolved several enzymes that protect them against the toxic forms of oxygen (Table 8.9). Various obligate anaerobes are not killed by $O_2$ directly but are prevented from growing by the presence of oxygen, apparently because of the production and lack of effective removal of superoxide anions (Morris 1975). The superoxide anion can be converted to hydrogen peroxide plus $O_2$ by the action of the enzyme superoxide dismutase. Peroxide anions, as in hydrogen peroxide, are also quite toxic to microorganisms. Hydrogen peroxide can be decomposed by catalase enzymes to $H_2O + O_2$ or by peroxidase enzymes to $H_2O$ with the coupled oxidation of a broad range of electron donors.

Some facultative anaerobes are able to carry out both aerobic respiration using oxygen as the terminal electron acceptor when molecular oxygen is available and anaerobic respiration using nitrate or other terminal electron acceptors when molecular oxygen levels are depleted. These versatile bacteria adapt to oxygen-limiting conditions by altering their central metabolic pathways. Several regulatory systems are involved in the adaptation to anaerobiosis, including the Arc (anaerobic respiration control) and Fnr (fumarate and nitrate reductase) systems (Iuchi and Lin 1995; Stewart and Rabin 1995).

The Arc system consists of ArcB, a histidine kinase, and ArcA, a response regulator (Figure 8.24) (Iuchi and Lin 1995). Histidine kinases contain a conserved carboxyl terminal sequence in which histidine can be phosphorylated; response regulators contain a conserved amino terminal sequence in which aspartate can be phosphorylated. When concentrations of molecular oxygen become sufficiently low (anaerobiosis—oxygen depletion), ArcB becomes phosphorylated through a coupled reaction with ATP conversion to ADP. Detection of oxygen depletion is probably based on the relative concentrations of reduced and oxidized forms of the electron carriers involved in oxidative

**Table 8.9**
Bacterial enzymes that protect the cell against toxic forms of oxygen

| Microorganism | Catalase | Superoxide dismutase |
|---|---|---|
| Aerobe | + | + |
| Facultative anaerobe | + | + |
| Microaerophile | − | + |
| Obligate anaerobe | − | − |

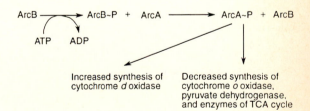

**Figure 8.24**
The Arc system consists of ArcB (a histidine kinase) and ArcA (a response regulator). When concentrations of molecular oxygen become sufficiently low, ArcB becomes phosphorylated through a coupled reaction with ATP conversion to ADP. Phosphorylated ArcB can transfer phosphate to ArcA. Phosphorylated ArcA is responsible for the repression of transcription of genes involved in aerobic growth. (Source: Iuchi and Lin 1995.)

phosphorylation. Phosphorylated ArcB can transfer phosphate to ArcA. ArcA is a DNA-binding protein that can act as a regulator of gene transcription. Phosphorylated ArcA is responsible for the repression of transcription of genes involved in aerobic growth including several dehydrogenases, cytochrome oxidase (cytochrome $o$), several tricarboxylic acid (TCA) cycle enzymes, glyoxylate enzymes, and oxygen-dependent fatty acid oxidation enzymes. Phosphorylated ArcA also induces genes for cobalamin synthesis and cytochrome oxidase (cytochrome $d$) synthesis. The major function of the Arc system appears to be the shutdown of transcription of genes encoding for proteins involved in aerobic respiratory metabolism.

The Fnr system, in contrast, functions primarily to activate genes coding for enzymes involved in anaerobic respiration, including formate dehydrogenase, fumarate reductase, nitrate reductase, and pyruvate formate lyase (Figure 8.25) (Stewart and Rabin 1995). Expression of these genes permits the use of fumarate or nitrate as terminal electron acceptors in respiratory metabolism. These genes are normally repressed when *E. coli* is growing aerobically. The Fnr system also represses genes coding for electron transport carriers needed for aerobic respiration, including cytochrome $d$ and cytochrome $o$.

Additional systems (NarL/NarX/NarQ) further determine which electron acceptors function under anaerobic conditions. These systems stimulate tran-

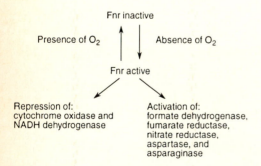

**Figure 8.25**
Fnr is a regulatory protein that is induced during anaerobic growth. It acts as a repressor of aerobically expressed genes and an inducer of anaerobically expressed genes. (Source: Stewart and Rabin 1995.)

scription of nitrate reductase genes and repress genes for other reductases so that nitrate is the preferred electron acceptor in anaerobic respiration. Thus, the combined actions of several regulatory systems facilitate the shift from oxygen to nitrate to fumarate and other compounds as terminal electron acceptors during respiratory metabolism.

**Carbon Dioxide and Monoxide** Carbon dioxide is required for both autotrophic and heterotrophic metabolism. It may be available in solution as carbon dioxide, carbonate, or bicarbonate. At pH 7 about 20% of the total carbon dioxide is found as dissolved $CO_2$ and most of the remainder as bicarbonate. Carbon dioxide consumption is often used as a measure of primary productivity. Production of $CO_2$ is a useful measure of the mineralization of organic matter.

Carbon monoxide is another form of inorganic carbon; it strongly inhibits microbial respiration pathways. Carbon monoxide binds with iron-containing proteins and molecules such as cytochromes, blocking electron transport. Some microorganisms can metabolize CO, but most are inhibited by it.

**Nitrogen** For most microorganisms, nitrogen gas is an inert form of nitrogen. Only a restricted group of nitrogen-fixing bacteria are able to convert gaseous nitrogen into combined forms of nitrogen. The most important inorganic nitrogen-containing nutrients are ammonium, nitrate, and nitrite ions. Nitrogen is required for protein formation. In addition to being required for protein synthesis, ammonium or nitrite is oxidized by some chemolithotrophic microorganisms for generating energy. Some microorganisms use nitrate as the terminal electron acceptor in respiration pathways, resulting in denitrification, which returns nitrogen gas to the atmosphere. The fact that ammonium is a cation and nitrate and nitrite are anions results in differential leaching of these latter nitrogen-containing anions from environments such as soil.

**Phosphorus** Phosphate is required for microbial generation of ATP and for nucleic acid and membrane phospholipid synthesis. High concentrations of phosphate, however, may inhibit microbial growth.

Concentrations of available nitrogen and phosphorus often limit both productivity and decomposition in aquatic habitats. Additions of available nitrogen and phosphorus are often used to increase productivity in aquaculture practices. The elimination of the phosphate limitation is sometimes undesirable, as it can lead to prolific algal or cyanobacterial growth. This growth has occurred following addition of phosphates, in the form of household detergents, to lakes where productivity was phosphate limited. On the other hand, controlled addition of nitrogen and phosphorus can enhance decomposition of polluting organic compounds. For example, the extent of petroleum biodegradation in seawater has been found to be limited by both nitrogen and phosphorus (Figure 8.26); this limitation can be overcome by application of oleophilic nitrogen and phosphorus fertilizer (Atlas and Bartha 1972; Atlas 1977).

**Sulfur**   Microorganisms require inorganic sulfur for formation of proteins and other molecular components. Some oxidized forms of sulfur, such as sulfur dioxide, are toxic to microorganisms and may even be used as disinfecting agents. Some photoautotrophic bacteria use hydrogen sulfide as an electron donor. Hydrogen sulfide is also toxic to many enzyme systems

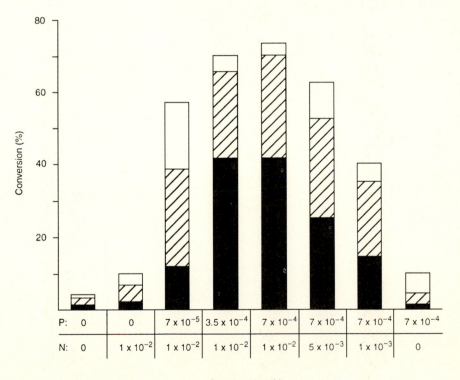

**Figure 8.26**
Limiting effects of nitrogen and phosphorus on the biodegradation of petroleum in seawater. Solid portion of histogram indicates mineralization of oil measured by $CO_2$ evolution. Total height of histogram indicates the biodegradation of oil in 18 days as measured by weight loss. Height of solid plus crosshatched portion indicates biodegradation measured by gas chromatography. Natural levels of available N and P in seawater limit extent of biodegradation of oil spills. (Source: Atlas and Bartha 1972. Reprinted from *Biotechnology and Bioengineering* by permission of John Wiley and Sons.)

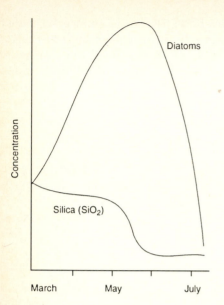

**Figure 8.27**
A graph illustrating that the amount of silica available in a lake can be the limiting factor in the growth of diatoms. Note silica depletion following diatom bloom and subsequent crash in the diatom population. Concentrations of other nutrients were measured, but none showed the type of correlation shown in this graph. (Source: Jensen and Salisbury 1972. Reprinted by permission, copyright Wadsworth Publishing Co., Belmont, Calif.)

that involve heavy metal atoms. Numerous microorganisms produce hydrogen sulfide as a metabolic product of protein metabolism.

**Other Elements**   Iron is required in cytochromes and other iron proteins. The oxidation state of iron depends on the pH and the redox potential. Ferrous and ferric ions demonstrate different degrees of solubility, which affects their availability for biological uptake.

Chloride ions are essential for maintenance of membrane function. Chlorate and hypochlorite ions are strong oxidizing agents and are toxic to microorganisms. Hypochlorite is often used as a disinfectant for drinking water and as a final step in sewage treatment. Thus, it enters ecosystems, such as rivers, as part of the sewage effluent. Measurements of residual chlorine are made on such effluents to determine the concentrations of these toxic compounds.

Diatoms, silicoflagellates, and radiolaria require silicon for building cell wall structures. Figure 8.27 shows an example of the depletion of silicate during blooms of diatoms.

## CHAPTER SUMMARY

A large number of abiotic physical and chemical factors influence the growth, survival, and metabolic activity of microorganisms. A variety of physical measurements and analytical procedures are needed in order to characterize the abiotic factors that govern the microbial inhabitants in a habitat. In some instances, one or a few factors can be identified that regulate the growth and activities of individual microbial populations in a given ecosystem. Often the effect of one abiotic factor on a microbial population is influenced by other abiotic factors. In some cases, microorganisms are limited in their activities by the availability of some essential nutrient (Liebig's law); in other cases, some environmental factor may exceed the maximum or minimum tolerance of a particular microbial population (Shelford's law).

Factors that have major influences on microorganisms include electromagnetic radiation, which in the form of visible light is the principal energy source for the global ecosystem, but which as high-energy ionizing radiation is destructive for life; temperature, which in many cases determines rates of growth and activity as well as the particular microorganisms that occur within an ecosystem and what functions they perform; pressure due to atmospheric, hydrostatic, and osmotic forces, which affects the survival of organisms; redox potential, which affects what forms of microbial metabolism may occur; pH, which influences survival and nutrient supply; availability of liquid water, which is essential for all active life processes; and the concentrations and chemical forms of organic and inorganic compounds, which may be essential nutrients or may act as inhibitors and poisons.

Microorganisms are enormously resilient and versatile in adapting to environmental extremes. New research results keep expanding our notions about the outer limits for active microbial life. Microbial metabolism and growth have been reported in the temperature range of −10°C to 110°C, in the pH range of 1.0 to 11.5, and in the osmotic range of distilled water to saturated brines and syrups. Some microorganisms tolerate and even require a hydrostatic pressure of 1000 atm; others survive at several megarads of ionizing radiation. Even in the most hostile hot and cold deserts, microorganisms form active communities inside porous rocks and leave almost no terrestrial environment uninhabited. Microbial tolerances have informed our search for extraterrestrial life. The enzymes of extremophilic microbes have important biotechnological uses.

## STUDY QUESTIONS

1. What is Liebig's law? How does it explain algal blooms in lakes receiving effluents containing phosphate detergents?

2. What is Shelford's law? How does it differ from Liebig's law?

3. Compare autecology and synecology.

4. How could you determine the factor(s) controlling the growth of specific microbial populations in a soil or water habitat?

5. What are the temperature limits for microbial growth?

6. How have different microbial populations adapted to growth at low and high temperatures?

7. What physiological properties permit yeasts to grow on leaf surfaces?

8. Compare psychrophilic and psychrotrophic bacteria.

9. How do the absorption maxima of photosynthetic pigments relate to the distribution of photosynthetic microorganisms in lakes?

10. How do photosynthetic bacteria respond to light intensity?

11. Compare barophilic and barotolerant microbial populations. How could you collect barophiles and demonstrate that they were true barophiles?

## REFERENCES AND SUGGESTED READINGS

Abdollahi, H., and D. B. Nedwell. 1979. Seasonal temperature as a factor influencing bacterial sulfate reduction in a salt-marsh sediment. *Microbial Ecology* 5:73–79.

Abyzov, S. S. 1993. Microorganisms in Antarctic ice. In E. I. Friedman and A. B. Thistle (eds.). *Antarctic Microbiology*. Wiley, New York, pp. 265–295.

Adams, M.W.W. 1993. Enzymes and proteins from organisms that grow near and above 100°C. *Annual Review of Microbiology* 47:627–658.

Alexander, M. 1976. Natural selection and the ecology of microbial adaptation in a biosphere. In M. R. Heinrich (ed.). *Extreme Environments: Mechanisms of Microbial Adaptation*. Academic Press, New York, pp. 3–25.

Anderson, A. W., H. D. Hordan, R. F. Cain, G. Parrish, and D. Duggan. 1956. Studies on a radio-resistant *Micrococcus*. Part I, Isolation, morphology, cultural characteristics and resistance to gamma irradiation. *Food Technology* 10:575–578.

Atlas, R. M. 1977. Stimulated petroleum biodegradation. *Critical Reviews in Microbiology* 5:371–386.

Atlas, R. M., and R. Bartha. 1972. Degradation and mineralization of petroleum in seawater: Limitation by nitrogen and phosphorus. *Biotechnology and Bioengineering* 14:309–318.

Baas-Becking, L.M.G., and E.J.F. Wood. 1955. Biological processes in the estuarine environment. *Koninkligke*

*Nederlandse Akademie Van Wetenschappen Proceedings B* (Amsterdam) 58:160–181.

Baross, J. A., and J. W. Deming. 1983. Growth of "black smoker" bacteria at temperatures of at least 250°C. *Nature* (London) 303:423–426.

Baross, J. A., J. W. Deming, and R. R. Becker. 1984. Evidence for microbial growth in high-pressure, high-temperature environments. In M. J. Klug and C. A. Reddy (eds.). *Current Perspectives in Microbial Ecology.* American Society for Microbiology, Washington, DC, pp. 186–195.

Baross, J. A., F. J. Hanus, and R. Y. Morita. 1972. Effects of hydrostatic pressure on uracil uptake, ribonucleic acid synthesis, and growth of three obligately psychrophilic marine vibrios, *Vibrio alginolyticus* and *Escherichia coli.* In R. R. Colwell and R. Y. Morita (eds.). *Effects of the Ocean Environment on Microbial Activities.* University Park Press, Baltimore, pp. 180–222.

Black, C. A. (ed.). 1965. *Methods of Soil Analysis: Part 2, Chemicals and Microbiological Properties.* American Society of Agronomy, Madison, WI.

Blakemore, R. 1975. Magnetotactic bacteria. *Science* 190:377–379.

Blakemore, R. P. 1982. Magnetotactic bacteria. *Annual Review of Microbiology* 36:217–238.

Blum, O. B. 1974. Water relations. In V. Ahmadjian and M. Hale (eds.). *The Lichens.* Academic Press, New York, pp. 381–400.

Bott, T. L., and T. D. Brock. 1969. Bacterial growth rates above 90°C in Yellowstone hot springs. *Science* 164:1411–1412.

Brock, T. D. 1978. *Thermophilic Microorganisms and Life at High Temperatures.* Springer-Verlag, New York.

Brock, T. D. 1985. Life at high temperatures. *Science* 230:132–138.

Brock, T. D. 1995. The road to Yellowstone—and beyond. *Annual Review of Microbiology* 49:1–28.

Brown, A. D. 1976. Microbial water stress. *Bacteriological Reviews* 40:803–846.

Brown, M.R.W., and P. Gilbert. 1993. Sensitivity of biofilms to antimicrobial agents. *Journal of Applied Bacteriology* 74:875–975.

Button, D. K. 1985. Kinetics of nutrient-limited transport and microbial growth. *Microbiological Reviews* 49:270–297.

Button, D. K., F. Schut, Q. Pharm, R. Martin, and B. R. Robertson. 1993. Viability and isolation of marine bacteria by dilution culture: Theory, procedures, and initial results. *Applied and Environmental Microbiology* 59:881–891.

Campbell, L. L., and B. Pace. 1968. Physiology of growth at high temperatures. *Journal of Applied Bacteriology* 31:24–35.

Cano, R. J., and M. K. Borucki. 1995. Revival and identification of bacterial spores in 25- to 40-million-year-old Dominican amber. *Science* 268:1060–1064.

Carlile, M. J. 1980. Positioning mechanisms—The role of motility, taxis and tropism in the life of microorganisms. In D. C. Ellwood, M. J. Latham, J. N. Hedger, and J. M. Lynch (eds.). *Contemporary Microbial Ecology.* Academic Press, London, pp. 55–74.

Castenholz, R. W. 1979. Evolution and ecology of thermophilic microorganisms. In M. Shilo (ed.). *Strategies of Microbial Life in Extreme Environments.* Verlag Chemie, Weinheim, NY, pp. 373–392.

Chastain, R. A., and A. A. Yayanos. 1991. Ultra-structural changes in an obligately barophilic marine bacterium after decompression. *Applied and Environmental Microbiology* 57:1489–1497.

Cohen, Y., E. Padan, and M. Shilo. 1975. Facultative anoxygenic photosynthesis in the cyanobacteria, *Oscillatoria limnetica. Journal of Bacteriology* 123:855–861.

Colwell, R. R., and R. Y. Morita (eds.). 1972. *Effect of the Ocean Environment on Microbial Activity.* University Park Press, Baltimore.

Cook, G. M., J. B. Russell, A. Reichert, and J. Wiegal. 1996. The intracellular pH of *Clostridium paradoxum,* an anaerobic, alkaliphilic, and thermophilic bacterium. *Applied and Environmental Microbiology* 62:4576–4579.

Costerton, J. W. 1984. Direct ultrastructural examination of adherent bacterial populations in natural and pathogenic ecosystems. In M. J. Klug and C. A. Reddy (eds.). *Current Perspectives in Microbial Ecology.* American Society for Microbiology, Washington, DC, pp. 115–123.

Daly, M. J., and K. W. Minton. 1995. Resistance to radiation. *Science* 270:1318.

Dazzo, F. B. 1984. Attachment of nitrogen-fixing bacteria to plant roots. *Current Perspectives in Microbial*

*Ecology.* American Society for Microbiology, Washington, DC, pp. 130–135.

Derosier, N. W. 1970. *The Technology of Food Preservation.* AVI, Westport, CT.

Doetch, R. N., and T. M. Cook. 1973. *Introduction to Bacteria and Their Ecobiology.* University Park Press, Baltimore.

Ducklow, H. W. 1984. Geographical ecology of marine bacteria: Physical and biological variability at the Mesoscale. In M. J. Klug and C. A. Reddy (eds.). *Current Perspectives in Microbial Ecology.* American Society for Microbiology, Washington, DC, pp. 22–31.

Edwards, C. 1990. Thermophiles. In C. Edwards (ed.). *Microbiology of Extreme Environments.* McGraw-Hill, New York, pp. 1–32.

Ehrlich, H. L. 1978. How microbes cope with heavy metals, arsenic and antimony in their environments. In D. J. Kushner (ed.). *Microbial Life in Extreme Environments.* Academic Press, London, pp. 381–408.

Eisenberg, H. 1995. Life in unusual environments: Progress in understanding the structure and function of enzymes from extreme halophilic bacteria. *Archives of Biochemistry and Biophysics* 318:1–5.

Farina, M., S. Esquival, and H.G.P.L. deBarros. 1990. Magnetic iron-sulfur crystals from a magnetotactic microorganism. *Nature* (London) 343:256–258.

Fischer, F., W. Zillig, K. D. Stetter, and G. Schreiber. 1983. Chemolithoautotrophic metabolism of anaerobic extremely thermophilic archaebacteria. *Nature* (London) 301:511–513.

Fletcher, M., and K. C. Marshall. 1982. Are solid surfaces of ecological significance to aquatic bacteria? *Advances in Microbial Ecology* 6:199–236.

Fletcher, M., and S. McEldowney. 1984. Microbial attachment to nonbiological surfaces. In M. J. Klug and C. A. Reddy (eds.). *Current Perspectives in Microbial Ecology.* American Society for Microbiology, Washington, DC, pp. 124–129.

Frazier, W. C., and D. C. Westhoff. 1978. *Food Microbiology.* McGraw-Hill, New York.

Fridovich, I. 1977. Oxygen is toxic! *BioScience* 27:462–466.

Friedmann, E. I. 1982. Endolithic microorganisms in the Antarctic cold desert. *Science* 215:1045–1053.

Friedmann, E. I., and R. Ocampo. 1976. Endolithic blue-green algae in the dry valleys: Primary producers in the Antarctic ecosystem. *Science* 193:1247–1249.

Friedmann, E.I., and R. Ocampo-Friedmann. 1984. Endolithic microorganisms in extreme dry environments: Analysis of a lithobiontic microbial habitat. In M. J. Klug and C. A. Reddy (eds.). *Current Perspectives in Microbial Ecology.* American Society for Microbiology, Washington, DC, pp. 177–185.

Fry, J. C. 1990. Oligotrophs. In C. Edwards (ed.). *Microbiology of Extreme Environments.* McGraw-Hill, New York, pp. 93–116.

Gadd, G. M. 1990. Metal tolerance. In C. Edwards (ed.). *Microbiology of Extreme Environments.* McGraw-Hill, New York, pp. 178–210.

Gambacorta, A., A. Gliozzi, and M. De Rosa. 1995. Archaeal lipids and their biotechnological applications. *World Journal of Microbiology and Biotechnology* 11:115–131.

Gilmour, D. 1990. Halotolerant and halophilic microorganisms. In C. Edwards (ed.). *Microbiology of Extreme Environments.* McGraw-Hill, New York, pp. 147–177.

Gould, G. W., and J. E. Corry. 1980. *Microbial Growth and Survival in Extremes of Environment.* Academic Press, New York.

Gray, T.R.G., and J. R. Postgate (eds.). 1976. *The Survival of Vegetative Microbes.* Cambridge University Press, New York.

Gregory, P. H. 1973. *The Microbiology of the Atmosphere.* Wiley, New York.

Griffin, D. M. 1981. Water and microbial stress. *Advances in Microbial Ecology* 5:91–136.

Halldal, P. 1980. Light and microbial activities. In D. C. Ellwood, M. J. Latham, J. N. Hedger, and J. M. Lynch (eds.). *Contemporary Microbial Ecology.* Academic Press, London, pp. 1–14.

Halldal, P., and P. O. Taube. 1972. Ultraviolet action and photoreactivation in algae. In A. C. Giese (ed.). *Photophysiology.* Vol. 7. Academic Press, New York, pp. 163–188.

Hardon, M. J., and L. J. Albright. 1974. Hydrostatic pressure effects on several stages of protein synthesis in *E. coli. Canadian Journal of Microbiology* 20:359–365.

Hargrave, B. T. 1969. Epibenthic algal production and community respiration in the sediments of Marion Lake.

*Journal of the Fisheries Research Board of Canada* 26:2003–2026.

Heywood, R. B. 1984. Antarctic inland waters. In R. M. Laws (ed.). *Antarctic Ecology.* Vol. 1. Academic Press, New York, pp. 279–344.

Hirst, J. M., I. F. Storey, W. C. Wood, and J. J. Wilcox. 1955. The origin of apple scab epidemics in the Wisbeck area in 1953–1954. *Plant Pathology* 4:91–96.

Hoch J. A., and T. J. Silhavy. 1995. *Two-Component Signal Transduction.* American Society for Microbiology Press, Washington, DC.

Horowitz, N. H., R. E. Cameron, and J. S. Hubbard. 1972. Microbiology of the dry valleys of Antarctica. *Science* 176:242–245.

Hugo, W. B. (ed.). 1971. *Inhibition and Destruction of the Microbial Cell.* Academic Press, London.

Ingledew, W. J. 1990. Acidophiles. In C. Edwards (ed.). *Microbiology of Extreme Environments.* McGraw-Hill, New York, pp. 33–54.

Inniss, W. E., and J. L. Ingraham. 1978. Microbial life at low temperatures: Mechanisms and molecular aspects. In D. J. Kushner (ed.). *Microbial Life in Extreme Environments.* Academic Press, London, pp. 73–103.

Iuchi, S., and E.C.C. Lin. 1995. Signal transduction in the Arc system for control of operons encoding aerobic respiratory enzymes. In J. A. Hoch and T. J. Silhavy (eds.). *Two-Component Signal Transduction.* American Society for Microbiology Press, Washington, DC, pp. 223–231.

Jannasch, H. W. 1967. Growth of marine bacteria at limiting concentrations of organic carbon in seawater. *Limnology and Oceanography* 12:264–271.

Jannasch, H. W. 1979. Microbial turnover of organic matter in the deep sea. *BioScience* 29:228–232.

Jannasch, H. W., and M. J. Mottl. 1985. Geomicrobiology of deep-sea hydrothermal vents. *Science* 229:717–725.

Jannasch, H. W., and D. C. Nelson. 1984. Recent progress in the microbiology of hydrothermal vents. In M. J. Klug and C. A. Reddy (eds.). *Current Perspectives in Microbial Ecology.* American Society for Microbiology, Washington, DC, pp. 170–176.

Jannasch, H. W., and C. O. Wirsen. 1977. Microbial life in the deep sea. *Scientific American* 236:42–52.

Jannasch, H. W., C. O. Wirsen, and C. D. Taylor. 1982. Deep-sea bacteria: Isolation in the absence of decompression. *Science* 216:1315–1317.

Jennings, D. H. 1990. Osmophiles. In C. Edwards (ed.). *Microbiology of Extreme Environments.* McGraw-Hill, New York, pp. 117–146.

Jensen, W. A., and F. B. Salisbury. 1972. *Botany: An Ecological Approach.* Wadsworth, Belmont, CA.

Johnston, C. G., and J. R. Vestal. 1991. Photosynthetic carbon incorporation and turnover in Antarctic cryptendolithic microbial communities: Are they the slowest growing communities on Earth? *Applied and Environmental Microbiology* 57:2308–2311.

Kim, J., and C. E. ZoBell. 1972. Occurrence and activities of the cell-free enzymes in oceanic environments. In R. R. Colwell and R. Y. Morita (eds.). *Effects of the Ocean Environment on Microbial Activities.* University Park Press, Baltimore, pp. 365–385.

Kjelleberg, S. 1984. Effects of interfaces on survival mechanisms of copiotrophic bacteria in low-nutrient habitats. In M. J. Klug and C. A. Reddy (eds.). *Current Perspectives in Microbial Ecology.* American Society for Microbiology, Washington, DC, pp. 151–160.

Koch, A. L. 1990. Diffusion: The crucial process in many aspects of the biology of bacteria. *Advances in Microbial Ecology* 11:3770.

Konopka, A. 1984. Effect of light-nutrient interactions on buoyancy regulation by planktonic cyanobacteria. In M. J. Klug and C. A. Reddy (eds.). *Current Perspectives in Microbial Ecology.* American Society for Microbiology, Washington, DC, pp. 41–48.

Kroll, R. G. 1990. Alkalophiles. In C. Edwards (ed.). *Microbiology of Extreme Environments.* McGraw-Hill, New York, pp. 55–92.

Kushner, D. J. 1968. Halophilic bacteria. *Advances in Applied Microbiology* 10:73–97.

Kushner, D. J. (ed.). 1978. *Microbial Life in Extreme Environments.* Academic Press, London.

Kushner, D. J. 1980. Extreme environments. In D. C. Ellwood, M. J. Latham, J. N. Hedger, and J. M. Lynch (eds.). *Contemporary Microbial Ecology.* Academic Press, London, pp. 29–54.

Larsen, H. 1962. Halophilism. In I. C. Gunsalus and R. Y. Stanier (eds.). *The Bacteria: A Treatise on Structure and Function.* Vol. 4, *The Physiology of Growth.* Academic Press, New York, pp. 297–342.

Larsen, H. 1967. Biochemical aspects of extreme halophilism. *Advances in Microbial Physiology* 1:97–132.

Lieberman, M. M., and J. K. Lanyi. 1972. Threonine deaminase from extremely halophilic bacteria: Cooperative substrate kinetics and salt dependence. *Biochemistry* 11:211–216.

Liebig, J. 1840. *Chemistry in Its Application to Agriculture and Physiology.* Taylor and Walton, London.

Lockwood, J. L., and A. B. Filonow. 1981. Responses of fungi to nutrient-limiting conditions and to inhibitory substances in natural habitats. *Advances in Microbial Ecology* 5:1–61.

MacLeod, R. A. 1985. Marine microbiology far from the sea. *Annual Review of Microbiology* 39:1–20.

Mann, S., N.H.C. Sparks, R. B. Frankel, D. A. Bazylinski, and H. Jannasch. 1990. Biomineralization of ferrimagnetic greigite (Fe$_3$S$_4$) and iron pyrite (FeS$_2$) in a magnetotactic bacterium. *Nature* (London) 343:258–261.

Marshall, K. C. 1976. *Interfaces in Microbial Ecology.* Harvard University Press, Cambridge, MA.

Masullo, M., G. Raimo, A. D. Russo, V. Bocchini, and J. V. Bannister. 1996. Purification and characterization of NADH oxidase from the archaea *Sulfolobus acidocaldarius* and *Sulfolobus solfataricus. Biotechnology and Applied Biochemistry* 23:47–54.

Moench, T. T., and W. A. Konetzka. 1978. A novel method for the isolation and study of a magnetotactic bacterium. *Archive für Mikrobiology* (Berlin) 119:203–212.

Morita, R. Y. 1975. Psychrophilic bacteria. *Bacteriological Reviews* 39:144–167.

Morita, R. Y. 1982. Starvation-survival of heterotrophs in the marine environment. *Advances in Microbial Ecology* 6:171–198.

Morris, J. G. 1975. The physiology of obligate anaerobiosis. *Advances in Microbial Physiology* 12:169–246.

Neidhardt, F. C., J. L. Ingraham, and M. Schaechter. 1990. *Physiology of the Bacterial Cell.* Sinnauernderland, MA.

Ninfa, A. J., M. R. Atkinson, E. S. Kamberov, J. Feng, and E. G. Ninfa. 1995. Control of nitrogen assimilation by the NR$_I$-NR$_{II}$ two-component system of enteric bacteria. In J. A. Hoch and T. J. Silhavy (eds.). *Two-Component Signal Transduction.* American Society for Microbiology Press, Washington, DC, pp. 67–88.

Norman, A. 1954. The nuclear role in the ultraviolet inactivation of *Neurospora* conidia. *Journal of Cellular Comparative Physiology* 44:1–10.

Novitsky, J. A., and R. Y. Morita. 1976. Morphological characterization of small cells resulting from nutrient starvation of a psychrophilic marine vibrio. *Applied and Environmental Microbiology* 32:617–622.

Novitsky, J. A., and R. Y. Morita. 1977. Survival of a psychrophilic marine vibrio under long-term nutrient starvation. *Applied and Environmental Microbiology* 33:635–641.

Novitsky, J. A. and R. Y. Morita. 1978. Possible strategy for the survival of marine bacteria under starvation conditions. *Marine Biology* 48:289–295.

Odum, E. P. 1971. *Fundamentals of Ecology.* Saunders, Philadelphia.

Oren, A. 1988. The microbial ecology of the Dead Sea. *Advances in Microbial Ecology* 109:193–229.

Oren, A., and P. Gurevich. 1995. Isocitrate lyase activity in halophilic archaea. *FEMS Microbiology Letters* 130:91–95.

Padan, E. 1984. Adaptation to bacteria to external pH. In M. J. Klug and C. A. Reddy (eds.). *Current Perspectives in Microbial Ecology.* American Society for Microbiology, Washington, DC, pp. 49–55.

Poindexter, J. S. 1981. Oligotrophy: Fast and famine existence. *Advances in Microbial Ecology* 5:63–89.

Poindexter, J. S. 1984. Role of prostheca development in oligotrophic aquatic bacteria. In M. J. Klug and C. A. Reddy (eds.). *Current Perspectives in Microbial Ecology.* American Society for Microbiology, Washington, DC, pp. 33–40.

Post, F. J. 1977. The microbial ecology of the Great Salt Lake. *Microbial Ecology* 3:143–165.

Potts, M. 1994. Desiccation tolerance of prokaryotes. *Microbiological Reviews* 58:755–805.

Rainey, F. A., N. L. Ward, H. W. Morgan, R. Toalster, and E. Stackebrandt. 1993. Phylogenetic analysis of anaerobic thermophilic bacteria: Aid for their reclassification. *Journal of Bacteriology* 175:4772–4779.

Ravot, G., M. Maqot, M. L. Fardeau, B.K.C. Patel, G. Prensier, A. Eqan, J. L. Garcia, and B. Ollivier. 1995. *Thermotoga elfii* sp. nov., a novel thermophilic bacterium from an African oil producing well. *International Journal of Systematic Bacteriology* 45:308–314.

Reid, D. S. 1980. Water activity as the criterion of water availability. In D. C. Ellwood, M. J. Latham, J. N.

Hedger, and J. M. Lynch (eds.). *Contemporary Microbial Ecology.* Academic Press, London, pp. 15–28.

Reitzer, L. J., and B. Magasanik. 1987. Ammonia assimilation and the biosynthesis of glutamine, glutamate, aspartate, asparagine, L-alanine, and D-alanine. In F. C. Neidhardt, J. L. Ingraham, K. B. Low, B. Magasanik, M. Schaechter, and H. E. Umbarger (eds.). Escherichia coli *and* Salmonella typhimurium: *Cellular and Molecular Biology.* American Society for Microbiology Press, Washington, DC.

Revsbech, N. P., and B. B. Jørgensen. 1986. Microelectrodes: Their use in microbial ecology. *Advances in Microbial Ecology* 9:293–352.

Rheinheimer, G. 1974. *Aquatic Microbiology.* Wiley, London.

Ricci, J.C.D., B. J. Woodford, J. L. Kirschvink, and M. R. Hoffmann. 1991. Alteration of the magnetic properties of *Aquaspirillum magnetotacticum* by a pulse magnetization technique. *Applied and Environmental Microbiology* 57:3248–3254.

Rosenberg, M., and S. Kjelleberg. 1986. Hydrophobic interactions: Role in bacterial adhesion. *Advances in Microbial Ecology* 9:353–393.

Roszak, D. B., and R. R. Colwell. 1987. Survival strategies of bacteria in the natural environment. *Microbiological Reviews* 51:365–379.

Rothfuss, F., M. Bender, and R. Conrad. 1997. Survival and activity of bacteria in a deep, aged lake sediment (Lake Constance). *Microbial Ecology* 33:69–77.

Rupert, C. S. 1964. Photoreactivation of ultraviolet damage. In A. C. Giese (ed.). *Photophysiology.* Vol. 2. Academic Press, New York, pp. 283–327.

Schleper, C., G. Peuhler, I. Holz, A. Gambacorta, D. Janekovic, U. Santarius, H. P. Klenk, and W. Zillig. 1996. *Picrophilus* gen. nov., fam. nov.: A novel aerobic, heterotrophic, thermoacidophilic genus and family comprising archaea capable of growth around pH 0. *Journal of Bacteriology* 177:7050–7059.

Schoenheit, P., and T. Schaefer. 1995. Metabolism of hyperthermophiles. World *Journal of Microbiology & Biotechnology* 11:26–57.

Semenov, A., and J. T. Staley. 1992. Ecology of polyprosthecate bacteria. *Advances in Microbial Ecology* 12:339–382.

Shelford, V. E. 1913. *Animal Communities in Temperate America.* University of Chicago Press, Chicago.

Simmons, G. M., J. R. Vestal, and R. A. Wharton. 1993. Environmental regulators of microbial activity in Continental Antarctic lakes. In J. Friedmann (ed.). *Antarctic Microbiology.* Wiley-Liss, New York, pp. 491–541.

Skujins, J. 1984. Microbial ecology of desert soils. *Advances in Microbial Ecology* 7:49–91.

Sneath, P.H.A. 1962. Longevity of microorganisms. *Nature* 195:643–646.

Spring, S., R. Amann, W. Ludwig, K. H. Schleifer, D. Schuler, K. Poralla, and N. Peterson. 1995. Phylogenetic analysis of uncultured magnetotactic bacteria from the alpha-subclass of Proteobacteria. *Systematic and Applied Microbiology* 17:501–508.

Spring, S., R. Amann, K. H. Schleifer, H. van Gemeden, and N. Petersen. 1993. Dominating role of an unusual magnetotactic bacterium in the microanaerobic zone off a freshwater sediment. *Applied and Environmental Microbiology* 59:2397–2403.

Steeman-Nielson, E., V. K. Hansen, and E. G. Jorgensen. 1962. The adaptation to different light intensities in *Chlorella vulgaris* and the time dependence on transfer to a new light intensity. *Physiologia Plantarum* (Copenhagen) 15:505–517.

Stetter, K. O. 1982. Ultrathin mycelia-forming organisms from submarine volcanic areas having an optimum growth temperature of 105°C. *Nature* (London) 300:258–260.

Stetter, K. O. 1995. Microbial life in hyperthermal environments. *ASM News* 61:285–290.

Stewart, V., and R. S. Rabin. 1995. Dual sensors and dual response regulators interact to control nitrate- and nitrite-responsive gene expression in *Escherichia coli.* In J. A. Hoch and T. J. Silhavy (eds.). *Two-Component Signal Transduction.* American Society for Microbiology Press, Washington, DC, pp. 233–252.

Stotzky, G., and A. G. Norman. 1964. Factors limiting microbial activities in soil. Part III. Supplementary substrate additions. *Canadian Journal of Microbiology* 10:143–149.

Sweeney, B. M., and F. T. Haxo. 1961. Persistence of a photosynthetic rhythm in enucleated *Acetabularia. Science* 134:1361–1363.

Trent, J. D., R. A. Chastain, and A. A. Yayanos. 1984. Possible artifactual basis for apparent bacterial growth at 250°C. *Nature* (London) 307:737–740.

Van de Vossenberg, J.L.C.M., T. Ubbink-Kok, M.G.L. Elferink, A.J.M. Driessen, and W. N. Konings. 1996. Ion permeability of the cytoplasmic membrane limits the maximum growth temperature of bacteria and archaea. *Molecular Microbiology* 18:925–932.

Ventosa, A., and J. J. Nieto. 1995. Biotechnological applications and potentialities of halophilic microorganisms. *World Journal of Microbiological Biotechnology* 11:85–94.

Wanner, B. L. 1995. Signal transduction and cross regulation in the *Escherichia coli* phosphate regulon by PhoR, CreC, and acetyl phosphate. In J. A. Hoch and T. J. Silhavy (eds.). *Two-Component Signal Transduction.* American Society for Microbiology Press, Washington, DC, pp. 203–221.

Wetzel, R. G. 1975. *Limnology.* Saunders, Philadelphia.

White, D. 1995. *The Physiology and Biochemistry of Prokaryotes.* Oxford University Press, New York.

Whittaker, R. H., and P. P. Feeny. 1971. Allelochemics: Chemical interaction between species. *Science* 171:757–770.

Wynn-Williams, D. D. 1990. Ecological aspects of Antarctic microbiology. *Advances in Microbial Ecology* 11:71–146.

Yayanos, A. A. 1986. Evolutional and ecological implications of the properties of deep-sea barophilic bacteria. *Proceedings of the National Academy of Science USA* 83:9542–9546.

Yayanos, A., and A. S. Dietz. 1983. Death of a hadal deep-sea bacterium after decompression. *Science* 220:497–498.

Yayanos, A., A. S. Dietz, and R. V. Boxtel. 1979. Isolation of a deep-sea barophilic bacterium and some of its growth characteristics. *Science* 205:808–810.

ZoBell, C. E. 1964. Hydrostatic pressure as a factor affecting the activity of marine microbes. In M. Miyahe and T. Koyama (eds.). *Recent Researches in the Field of Hydrosphere, Atmosphere and Nuclear Geochemistry.* Maruzen, Tokyo, pp. 83–116.

ZoBell, C. E., and L. L. Hittle. 1967. Some effects of hyperbaric oxygenation on bacteria at increased hydrostatic pressures. *Canadian Journal of Microbiology* 13:1311–1319.

Zuber, H. 1979. Structure and function of enzymes from thermophilic microorganisms. In M. Shilo (ed.). *Strategies of Microbial Life in Extreme Environments.* Verlag-Chemie, Weinheim, New York, pp. 393–415.

# 9

# MICROORGANISMS IN THEIR NATURAL HABITATS: AIR, WATER, AND SOIL MICROBIOLOGY

*The ecosphere, or biosphere, constitutes the totality of living organisms on Earth and the abiotic surroundings they inhabit. It can be divided into atmo-, hydro-, and litho-ecospheres to describe the portions of the global expanse inhabited by living things in air, water, and soil environments, respectively. Microorganisms live within the habitats of these ecospheres. Each habitat has a set of physical, chemical, and biological parameters that determine the microbial populations that may thrive there. As a result of natural selection forces, characteristic communities develop within each habitat. In some cases, particularly in extreme habitats such as salt lakes and thermal springs, the indigenous microbial populations exhibit adaptations to their physical and chemical surroundings that permit their survival. In other habitats, intense competition dictates which populations survive and become the autochthonous members of the communities living there.*

## THE HABITAT AND ITS MICROBIAL INHABITANTS

Each of the major divisions of the ecosphere contains numerous habitats. A habitat is the physical location where an organism is found. The habitat is one component of a broader concept known as the *ecological niche*, which includes not only where an organism lives but also what it does there; the niche is the functional role of an organism within an ecosystem. The physical and chemical characteristics of a habitat influence the growth, activities, interactions, and survival of the microorganisms found in it; these parameters determine the niches that microorganisms may occupy at that habitat. For higher organisms, such as animals that range over wide territories, the habitat may be on the scale of a landscape. For microorganisms, in contrast, the habitat often occurs on a microscale. Hence, for microorganisms, one must consider not only the overall characteristics of the general habitat but also the fine features of the microhabitats in which the microorganisms live.

Some microorganisms are *autochthonous* or indigenous within a given habitat. These autochthonous microbes, which are capable of survival, growth, and metabolic activity in that habitat, occupy the environmental niches available to the microbial populations in the given ecosystem. Each autochthonous microorganism must be viewed in terms of its ability to grow, to carry out active metabolism, and to compete successfully with the other autochthonous members of the microbial community. Autochthonous microorganisms generally exhibit adaptive features that make them physiologically compatible with their physical and chemical environment; they must be functional and competitive with the other living organisms present in that habitat.

In contrast to the indigenous members of a microbial community, some microorganisms may be foreign; these organisms are called *allochthonous*. Allochthonous microorganisms are transient members of their habitat and do not occupy the functional niches of that ecosystem. Typically, these microorganisms have grown elsewhere and have been transported into a foreign ecosystem.

Allochthonous microorganisms exhibit great variation in the lengths of time that they can survive in foreign ecosystems; some disappear quite rapidly, as exemplified by *Escherichia coli*, which generally survives less than 24 hours when it enters marine habitats (Mitchell 1968). In contrast, some microorganisms possess adaptations, such as the ability to form spores, that allow them to survive for long periods in foreign habitats. Pertinent points that make organisms autochthonous are the ability to adapt physiologically to the physical and chemical environment, thus enhancing survival, and the ability to escape predation and competition pressures.

Although the definitions of autochthonous and allochthonous microorganisms are mutually exclusive, it is often difficult to determine whether a microorganism found in a particular ecosystem is indeed autochthonous or allochthonous. Ecosystems are dynamic and exhibit continuous change; autochthonous microorganisms may be active during one period but dormant during another. Thus, even when a microorganism found in an ecosystem does not appear to be capable of growth and active metabolism at a given point in time, one must consider whether the environment exhibits cyclic changes that will render it suitable for the growth of that microorganism at some other time. It is also pertinent to know whether the microorganism has the capacity to survive until conditions become favorable. In a few cases, allochthonous microorganisms that enter an ecosystem are able to survive, grow, and carry out active metabolism,

allowing them to fill unoccupied niches and perhaps to become autochthonous microorganisms; this is most likely to occur in ecosystems that are in a state of change due to stress or disturbance.

## ATMO-ECOSPHERE

### Characteristics and Stratification of the Atmosphere

The atmosphere consists of 79% nitrogen, nearly 21% oxygen, 0.034% carbon dioxide, and trace amounts of some other gases. It is saturated with water vapor to varying degrees, and it may contain droplets of liquid water, crystals of ice, and particles of dust. The atmosphere is divided into regions defined by temperature minima and maxima (Rumney 1968) (Figure 9.1). The troposphere, the region nearest the Earth's surface, interfaces with both the hydrosphere and the lithosphere. Above the troposphere is the stratosphere, and above this lies the ionosphere.

For the most part, the chemical and physical parameters of the atmosphere do not favor microbial

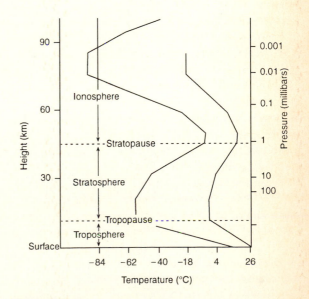

**Figure 9.1**
Divisions of the atmosphere showing temperature and pressure gradients. The two lines indicate seasonal shifts in temperature. (Source: Rumney 1968.)

growth and survival. Temperatures decrease with increasing height in the troposphere. At the top of the troposphere, temperatures are −43°C to −83°C, which are below the minimal growth temperatures for microorganisms. With increasing height in the atmosphere, the atmospheric pressure declines and concentrations of available oxygen decrease to a point that precludes aerobic respiration. The low concentrations of organic carbon are insufficient to support heterotrophic growth; available water is also scarce, limiting even the possibility of autotrophic growth of microorganisms in the atmosphere.

Microorganisms in the atmosphere are exposed to high intensities of light radiation. Exposure to ultraviolet (UV) light, which increases with height as the atmosphere thins and offers less shielding from UV radiation, causes lethal mutations and the death of microorganisms.

The stratosphere contains a layer of high ozone concentration, which acts to absorb UV light, protecting Earth's surface from excessive UV radiation (Thrush 1977). There is a justified concern today that certain human activities, such as flying of supersonic military and commercial jets, excessive use of fluorocarbons, and increased use of fertilizers (which results in increased release of $N_2O$ from microbial denitrification), will decrease concentrations of ozone in the stratosphere, thus allowing increased amounts of UV light to reach Earth's surface. The seasonal development of an Antarctic ozone hole is a clear symptom of the lessening atmospheric concentration of ozone. An increased flux of UV radiation reaching the surface of Earth would be detrimental to the survival of organisms living above ground.

The stratosphere represents a barrier to the transport of living microorganisms to or from the troposphere and is characterized by slow mixing of gases. Organisms in the stratosphere are thus transported slowly and are exposed for prolonged periods to the prevailing concentrations of ozone and high UV light intensities. Only microorganisms shielded from these conditions in the stratosphere—as perhaps within a spacecraft—could survive passage out of Earth's atmosphere. For all practical purposes, the atmoecosphere does not extend above the troposphere.

## The Atmosphere as Habitat and Medium for Microbial Dispersal

Even though the atmosphere is a hostile environment for microorganisms, there are substantial numbers of microorganisms in the lower troposphere, where, because of thermal gradients, there is rapid mixing of air (Gregory 1973). Movement through air represents a major pathway for the dispersal of microorganisms. Some microorganisms have evolved specialized adaptations that favor their survival in and dispersal by the atmosphere. Several viral, bacterial, and fungal diseases are spread through the atmosphere; outbreaks of disease from such microorganisms often follow prevailing winds.

Temporary locations in the troposphere may provide habitats for microorganisms. Clouds possess concentrations of water that permit growth of microorganisms. Light intensities and carbon dioxide concentrations in cloud layers are sufficient to support growth of photoautotrophic microorganisms, and condensation nuclei may supply some mineral nutrients. In industrial areas, there may even be sufficient concentrations of organic chemicals in the atmosphere to permit growth of some heterotrophs. Nevertheless, such "life in the sky" is only a fascinating possibility; conclusive proof is lacking, and the practical importance of such life appears to be negligible.

Although many microorganisms that grow in the hydrosphere or lithosphere can become airborne, there are no known autochthonous atmospheric microorganisms. During dispersal, aquatic and soil microorganisms may enter and pass through the atmosphere before reaching other favorable aquatic or terrestrial ecosystems. Dispersal through the atmosphere ensures continued survival of many microorganisms.

Some microorganisms become airborne as growing vegetative cells, but more commonly, microorganisms in the atmosphere occur as spores. To facilitate discussion, the term *spore* is used here in an extended sense and includes cysts, soredia, and other nonvegetative resistant structures. Spores are metabolically less active than vegetative cells and are generally better adapted to survival in the atmosphere. Spores whose primary function is dispersal are known as *xenospores.* Fungi, algae, some protozoa, some bacteria (especially actinomycetes), and lichens produce spores that occur in the atmosphere. Viruses are metabolically inactive outside of host cells and are transported through the atmosphere as inactive particles that are functionally equivalent to the dormant spores of living microorganisms.

Several properties of spores contribute to their ability to withstand transport through the atmosphere. First, their low metabolic rates mean that they do not require external nutrients and water to generate sufficient energy for maintenance over long periods. This is essential for survival in the atmosphere with its paucity of water and nutrients. Figure 9.2 shows the change in metabolic activities when a resting spore germinates (Sussman 1961). The successful germination of a spore requires a favorable environment for growth. The metabolic activities of vegetative cells that are required for the maintenance of cell integrity cannot be supported for long in the atmosphere. Once the cells' internal reserve materials are used up, vegetative cells in the atmosphere cannot generate enough

energy to maintain vital cellular functions, and the cells die.

Spores are produced in very high numbers; some fungi, for example, produce in excess of $10^{12}$ spores per single fruiting body per year (Ingold 1971). A large percentage of spores do not survive transport through the atmosphere to habitats that favor their germination; the success of only a few spores, however, ensures the survival and dispersion of the microorganism. Various additional adaptations increase the ability of a spore to survive in the atmosphere. Some spores have extremely thick walls, which protect them against severe desiccation. Some spores are pigmented, which adds protection against exposure to damaging UV radiation. The relatively small size and low density of spores permit them to remain airborne for long periods before they sediment from the atmosphere. Usually, spores are relatively light; they may even contain gas vacuoles. They come in a variety of shapes; some are aerodynamically favorable for extended lateral travel through the atmosphere (Gregory 1973) (Table 9.1).

The passive liberation of spores into the atmosphere with air current movements is common among microorganisms that produce dry spores on aerial mycelia (Ingold 1971). Such microorganisms include the actinomycetes and many fungi. Some spores are transmitted upward from microbial fruiting bodies by convection currents; others move both vertically and laterally with wind currents (Figure 9.3). In general,

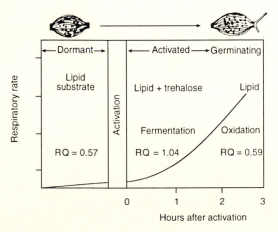

**Figure 9.2**
Metabolic events during germination of *Neurospora* ascospores. The dormant spores exhibit low respiratory rates as compared to germinating spores or vegetative cells. Respiratory quotients (RQs) indicate lipid utilization in the dormant and late germination stages and carbohydrate utilization during the activation period of germination. (Source: Sussman 1961. Reprinted by permission, copyright Burgess Publishing Co.)

**Table 9.1**
Estimated distance traveled by several fungi, calculated from terminal velocities assuming nonturbulent wind moving at 1 m per second

| Fungus | Assumed liberation height | Distance (m) |
|---|---|---|
| *Helminthosporium* | 1 m | 50 |
| *Puccinia* | 1 m | 80 |
| *Agaricus* | 5 cm | 40 |
| *Lycoperdon* | 5 cm | 100 |

Source: Gregory 1973.

the higher the wind speed and the lower the humidity, the greater the movement of spores. Wind-driven spore movement is especially important in the dispersal of microorganisms that occur on plant surfaces; many plant pathogenic fungi spread from one plant to another by this mechanism.

Although some dry spores are readily liberated into the air by wind currents, other spores remain attached even in air currents with high velocities. Some of these spores are liberated when water droplets in the air collide with the spore-bearing bodies (Figure 9.4). Raindrops may liberate spores to the atmosphere by vibrating the structures they are attached to, breaking the adhering forces. The "splash cups" of the bird's-nest fungi are adaptations designed to use the force of landing raindrops to release spores (Brodie 1951).

Spores and even vegetative microorganisms often enter the atmosphere as aerosols. Aerosols may form from a variety of sources, including splash from falling raindrops; spray from breaking waves; rapidly moving water currents striking solid objects, such as rocks in rivers; gas movements through water columns, such as gas bubbles rising from sediment through the water column; forced air streams in sewage treatment

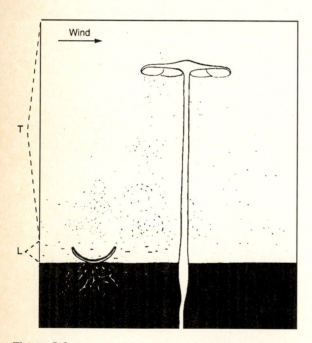

**Figure 9.3**
The discharge of ascospores into the air from a cup fungus and an agaric. Laminar (L) air flow above the ground (horizontal dashes) and turbulent (T) air flow above this (dashes in spirals) are illustrated. The spores of the cup fungus have just been discharged as a puff into the turbulent air zone. The agaric spores are steadily dropping into the turbulent air. (Source: Ingold 1971. Reprinted by permission of Oxford University Press.)

**Figure 9.4**
Splashing of peridiole from a basidiocarp of *Cyathus striatus*. (A and B) Raindrop landing in cup. (C) The peridiole splashing out with hapteron extended. (D) Hapteron sticking to a plant as the peridiole is carried forward by its momentum and the funiculus is extended by a pull. (E) Peridiole jerked backward when the funiculus is extended to its full length. (F) Peridiole swinging around the plant stem as another raindrop falls. (Source: Brodie 1951. Reprinted by permission of National Research Council Canada.)

plants; and so on (Micheli 1729; Teltsch and Katznelson 1978). Some microorganisms are released on droplets by mechanisms such as coughing and sneezing by humans or animals (Figure 9.5). This type of release is especially important in the dispersal through the atmosphere of some pathogenic bacteria and animal viruses (McKissich et al. 1970).

In addition to the passive mechanisms that allow microorganisms to enter the atmosphere, there are a number of adaptive active mechanisms that discharge microbial spores into the atmosphere. In *Pilobolus,* the entire spore cluster is ejected when a vacuole in the sporangium base becomes turgid through an increase in osmotic pressure and then causes the structure to burst and the spores to be carried away in a jet of water (Buller 1909) (Figure 9.6). *Pilobolus* shoots its spore cluster a distance of 1–2 m and orients the release toward the highest light intensity, that is, to an open area where air currents are most likely to cause further dispersal.

In most ascomycetes, the ascospores are actively discharged. Typically, the ascus swells at maturity and bursts at the tip, propelling the spores into the air to a distance ranging from several millimeters to several centimeters. The bursting of the ascus is caused by the change in osmotic pressure when glycogen is converted to soluble sugars. Some ascomycetes exhibit the phenomenon of puffing, that is, the simultaneous breaking of a large number of asci with the release of a visible cloud of spores (Buller 1934) (Figure 9.7). Changes in environmental conditions, such as light, humidity, or temperature, can trigger the puff of spores. In *Sphaerobolus,* a basidiomycete that grows on old dung in succession to *Pilobolus* and ascomycetes, the basidiospores are released when an inner turgid layer of vegetative hyphae flips inside out, propelling the spherical spore mass upward several meters (Figure 9.8).

Having become airborne, both spores and vegetative microbial cells face the problem of survival (Stetzenbach et al. 1992). Most microorganisms can survive a short passage (a few millimeters) through the atmosphere, but relatively few survive long-distance transport because desiccation can cause microorganisms in the atmosphere to lose viability, particularly in the lower layers of the atmosphere during the day. Some microorganisms, though, have adaptations that allow longer exposures to desiccating conditions in the atmosphere (Table 9.2 on page 339).

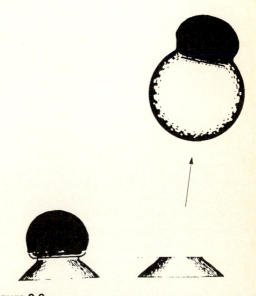

**Figure 9.6**
Release of a spore cluster by *Pilobolus.* The whole sporangium is shot off as a unit. The spore mass, represented by black area, adheres to expelled fluid droplet (light area). (Source: Buller 1909. Reprinted by permission of Hafner Publishing Co.)

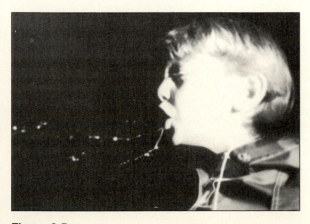

**Figure 9.5**
Moisture droplets released during a violent sneeze, showing aerosol dispersal.

**Figure 9.7**
Spore release by puffing as illustrated (A) by Buller (1934) for *Sarcoscypha protracta;* and (B) by Micheli (1729) for a small cup fungus. (Source: Ingold 1971. Reprinted by permission of Oxford University Press.)

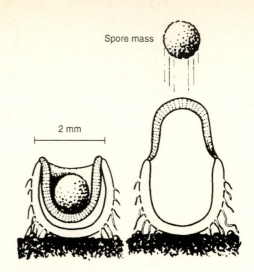

**Figure 9.8**
Spore discharge in *Sphaerobolus.* The spore mass is propelled upward up to 1 m, facilitating dispersal. (Source: Jensen and Salisbury 1972. Reprinted by permission of Wadsworth Publishing Co., Belmont, California.)

Exposure to short-wavelength radiation, such as UV light, is another major cause of loss of viability of microorganisms in the atmosphere. Microorganisms carried through the atmosphere on "rafts," such as dust or soil particles, may be protected from the harmful effects of UV radiation. Some microorganisms are protected from these lethal effects by pigments. Pigmented fungi and bacteria suffer less damage when exposed to UV light than colorless species. Exposure to sunlight in the air is lethal to nonpigmented strains of *Micrococcus luteus,* for example, but not to yellow-pigmented strains (Mathews and Sistrom 1959) (Figure 9.9 on page 340). The presence of the yellow pigment appears to protect these bacteria from exposure to sunlight. Death does not occur in the absence of air, indicating that light-induced killing is a photo-oxidation process that requires oxygen. Similarly, a colorless (carotenoid-free) mutant of *Halobacterium salinarium* was inhibited by high light intensities whereas the pigmented wild type strain was not inhibited (Dundas and Larsen 1962).

## Microorganisms in the Atmo-Ecosphere

There have been attempts to quantitate numbers of individual microbial genera and/or types in the atmosphere (Gregory 1973) (Table 9.3 on page 340). Quantitative sampling of microorganisms in the atmosphere typically employs either a viable plate count procedure or a direct count procedure using a modified contact slide (a slide with a sticky substance passed through the atmosphere by an aircraft). These methodological approaches give very different results. Plate count procedures favor the enumeration of bacteria, yeasts, and some fungal species; contact slide procedures favor the enumeration of fungal spores. In contemporary air samplers, a pump draws a calibrated volume of air through a membrane filter with 0.5 μm or smaller pore size (Andersen 1958). For direct counts, the filter is dissolved or clarified; for viable

**Table 9.2**
Survival times of some bacterial and archaeal species in the air-dried state

| Survival time | Organism |
| --- | --- |
| $10^6$ years | Coryneforms, gram-positive non-spore-forming bacilli, cocci |
| $10^4$–$10^5$ years | Cocci, actinomycetes, gram-negative bacilli, spore-forming bacteria |
| $10^3$ years | *Gloeocapsa, Hormathonema-Gloeocapsa, Chroococcidiopsis* |
| 200 years | *Bacillus* sp., *Clostridium* sp. |
| 140 years | *Nostoc commune* |
| 10–70 years | *Bacillus anthracis* |
| 15 years | *Thermoplasma acidophilum* |
| 3 years | *Listeria monocytogenes* |
| 0.6–1.5 years | *Nocardia asteroides* |
| 1.1 years | *Haloarcula* sp., *Halobacterium* sp., *Sulfolobus* sp., *Halococcus* sp., *Haloferax* sp. |
| 120–200 days | *Streptococcus pyogenes, Mycoplasma mycoides, Corynebacterium diphtheriae, Staphylococcus aureus, Brucella suis, Franciscella tularensis* |
| 60 days | *Mycobacterium avium* |
| 40–50 days | *Coxiella burnetti* |
| 12–40 days | *Campylobacter fetus, Yersinsia pseudotuberculosis, Pasteurella multocida, Proteus morgani* |
| 3.8–10 days | *Serratia marcescens, Mycobacterium tuberculosis, Mycoplasma agalactiae, Moraxella bovis* |
| 12–48 hours | *Streptococcus salivarius, Cowdria ruminatum, Eperythrozoon coccoides, Neisseria gonorrhoeae, Pasteurella multocida, Escherichia coli* |
| 2–4 hours | *Klebsiella pneumoniae, Neisseria meningitidis* |
| 18–40 minutes | *Treponema pallidum, Leptospira interrogans* |
| 6–10 minutes | *Salmonella typhi* |
| 2–6 minutes | *Vibrio cholerae* |

Source: Potts 1994.

counts, the filter is placed on an appropriate solid medium and incubated.

*Cladosporium* is frequently reported to be the major fungal constituent of the atmosphere (Gregory 1973). Typically, concentrations of microorganisms in the atmosphere, up to a height of 3000 m, range from $10^1$ to $10^4$ per cubic meter. The numbers of microorganisms in the atmosphere vary by season. In the Northern Hemisphere, fungi are generally more abundant in June, July, and August than during the rest of the year. On the other hand, bacteria have been reported to be most abundant during spring and autumn (Bovallius et al. 1978) (Figure 9.10 on page 341).

Microorganisms are removed from the atmosphere in a variety of ways. They may settle due to gravitational forces, or they may be removed by rain and other forms of precipitation (Gregory 1973). Following a rainstorm, concentrations of microorganisms in the atmosphere are typically reduced. Despite the factors that tend to remove microorganisms from the atmosphere and reduce their viability during transport, some microorganisms are accomplished air travelers. *Puccinia graminis,* for example, is known to be transported over long distances through the atmosphere while maintaining viability, an important dispersal mechanism for this wheat rust fungus (Bowden et al.

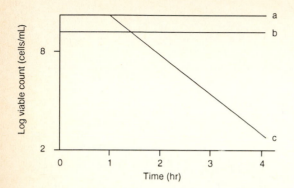

**Figure 9.9**
Exposure to direct sunlight of normal *Micrococcus luteus* (*Sarcina lutea*) (yellow) and pigmentless mutant (white) in air and a nitrogen atmosphere. The yellow wild type (a) is resistant to light both in air and under an atmosphere of nitrogen. The white mutant (b) is resistant to light under nitrogen, but (c) is rapidly killed by exposure to light in the presence of oxygen, demonstrating the protective effect of pigmentation against photooxidation. (Source: Mathews and Sistrom 1959. Reprinted from *Nature* by permission, copyright Macmillan Journals Ltd.)

1971) (Table 9.4). Other microorganisms, including some viruses, bacteria, and fungi, are probably capable of surviving atmospheric transport across oceans (Hirst et al. 1967). The fact that many microorganisms appear to be ubiquitous in nature is largely due to the effectiveness of air transport. Geographical discontinuities in the distribution of some microbial populations are due primarily to the location of suitable habitats for growth.

## HYDRO-ECOSPHERE

The hydrosphere is a more suitable habitat for microbial growth than the atmosphere. By its very definition, the hydrosphere contains water, which is necessary for microbial metabolism. Unlike the atmosphere, the hydrosphere contains autochthonous microbial populations, to which one can ascribe certain limited general characteristics. These microorganisms are able to grow at low nutrient concentrations. Most aquatic microorganisms are motile, by means of either flagella or other mechanisms. Some aquatic bacteria, such as the prosthecates, exhibit unusual shapes that increase the ratio of surface area to volume, allowing for more efficient uptake of the low levels of nutrients available in most freshwater bodies.

**Table 9.3**
Quantitative estimates of microorganisms (%) in the troposphere

| Microorganism | N. Canada 17 m | N. Canada 3000 m | Quebec 3000 m |
| --- | --- | --- | --- |
| **Bacteria** | | | |
| Gram-positive pleomorphic rods | 46 | 24 | 20 |
| Gram-negative rods | 20 | 15 | 4 |
| Spore formers | 18 | 38 | 33 |
| Gram-positive cocci | 15 | 23 | 41 |
| Other bacteria | 1 | 0 | 2 |
| **Fungi** | | | |
| *Cladosporium* | — | 73 | 82 |
| *Alternaria* | — | 7 | 3 |
| *Penicillium* | — | 3 | 2 |

Source: Gregory 1973.

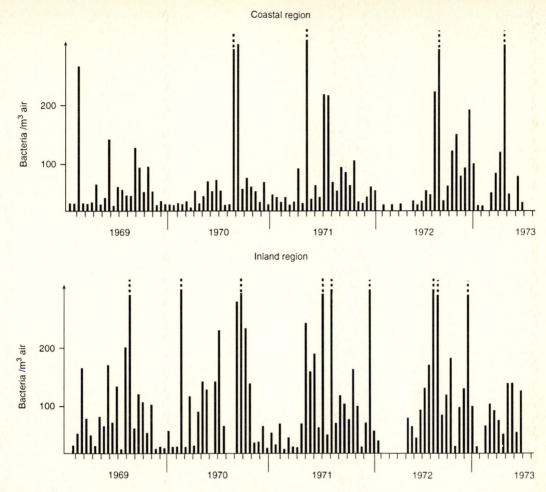

**Figure 9.10**
Bacterial concentration in air showing seasonal variation at two locations in Sweden. Bars with dashed ends in these histograms indicate off-scale readings. Generally, lower concentrations of bacteria occur in coastal regions due to paucity of bacteria in marine air masses. Seasonally low concentrations occur during winter and higher concentrations during summer and fall. (Source: Bovallius et al. 1978. Reprinted by permission of American Society for Microbiology.)

The hydrosphere is divided into freshwater and marine habitats. Freshwater habitats include lakes, ponds, swamps, springs, streams, and rivers. These habitats are collectively designated as *limnetic,* and their study is referred to as *limnology.* Marine habitats are the world's oceans and the estuarine habitats that occur at the interface between freshwater and marine ecosystems.

**Freshwater Habitats**

Freshwater habitats are classified based on their chemical and physical properties. Those with standing water, such as lakes and ponds, are called *lentic habitats;* those with running water are *lotic habitats* (Wetzel 1975).

**Table 9.4**
Dissemination of *Puccinia graminis*

| Distance from source (km) | Concentration relative to source (%) |
|:---:|:---:|
| 0 | 100 |
| 300 | 5 |
| 560 | 6 |
| 840 | 2 |
| 970 | 0.2 |

Source: Stakman and Hamilton 1939.

**The Neuston** The uppermost layer of the hydrosphere, the surface microlayer, represents the interface between the hydrosphere and the atmosphere. It is characterized by high surface tension, a property arising from the interfacing of water with a gas (Marshall 1976). Under quiescent conditions, microorganisms form a surface film known as the *neuston* (Figure 9.11). The neuston layer is a favorable habitat for photoautotrophic microorganisms because primary producers have unrestricted access to carbon dioxide from the atmosphere and to light radiation. Some mineral nutrients and metals become enriched in the surface microlayer. Secondary producers also proliferate here, using nonpolar organic compounds that accumulate in the surface tension layer and the high concentrations of oxygen available from the atmosphere. Microbial numbers in the surface microlayer are often ten- to a hundred-fold higher than in the underlying water column. Bubbles rising through the neuston layer and bursting play an important role in the water-to-air transfer of bacteria and viruses (Blanchard and Syzdek 1970; Baylor et al. 1977). Various devices, including skimmers, touch-on screens, and rotating drums, have been developed for the qualitative and quantitative sampling of the neuston community (Parker and Barsom 1970; Norkrans 1980).

Characteristic autochthonous neuston microbiota include algae, bacteria, fungi, and protozoa (Valkanov 1968). Among the characteristic representative bacterial genera are *Pseudomonas, Caulobacter, Nevskia, Hyphomicrobium, Achromobacter, Flavobacterium,* *Alcaligenes, Brevibacterium, Micrococcus,* and *Leptothrix.* These bacterial genera include gram-positive and gram-negative, pigmented and nonpigmented, motile and nonmotile, rod and coccus, stalked and nonstalked forms. Cyanobacteria also occur in the neuston; typical genera include *Aphanizomenon, Anabaena,* and *Microcystis.* The filamentous fungus *Cladosporium* and various yeasts are frequently associated with the neuston. Algal genera found in the neuston include *Chromulina, Botrydiopsis, Codosiga, Navicula, Nautococcus, Proterospongia, Sphaeroeca,* and *Platychrisis. Nautococcus* has been reported to have adaptive features particularly suited for its existence in the neuston. Protozoa found in the neuston include *Difflugia, Vorticella, Arcella, Acineta, Clathrulina, Stylonychia,* and *Codonosigna.* Some of these same organisms are also found in the underlying water column.

**Wetlands** Wetlands are shallow aquatic environments dominated by emergent plants. Wetlands develop under various climatic conditions in poorly drained shallow basins, often as a result of the gradual filling in of a lake by silt and vegetation. The water surface may be largely obscured by emergent plants that serve as the basis for wetland classification (Brewer 1994). Freshwater marshes are dominated by grassy plants such as reeds *(Phragmites),* cattails *(Typha),* and rushes *(Juncus).* Fens are relatively mineral-rich wetlands with neutral to alkaline pH and are dominated by sedges *(Carex).* Shrub-carrs are covered by dense thickets of willows, dogwoods, and birches. In swamps, full-height coniferous or hardwood trees form a canopy. Characteristically, the productivity of the wetland macrophytes is high, but the biodegradation of plant polymers, especially of lignocellulose, is inhibited by the waterlogged and oxygen-limited conditions. This imbalance leads to the accumulation of partially humified plant residues. When buried and transformed geochemically, these accumulated plant residues form coal deposits. If water levels drop, the accumulations form peat and muck soils (histosols) with low mineral contents.

Bogs are a unique type of wetlands. Bogs develop only in cool, wet climates, usually in shallow rock

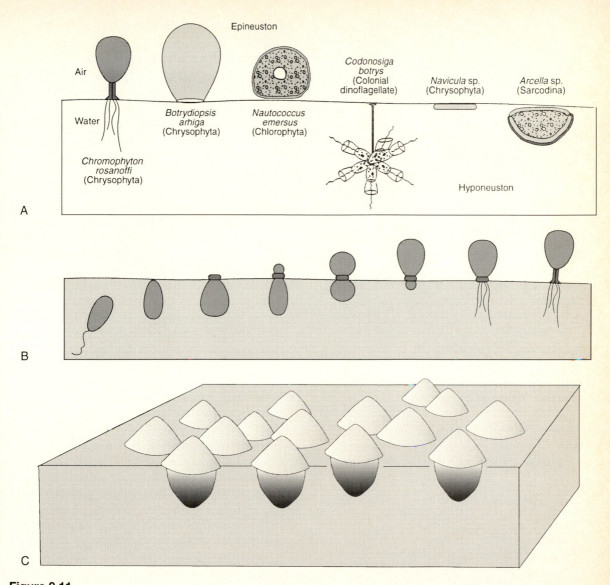

**Figure 9.11**

Illustration of the neuston. (A) The surface tension layer acts as the attachment point for microorganisms that position them-selves either above (epineuston) or below (hyponeuston) this layer. In either case, algae have unlimited access to sunlight and $CO_2$, yet also keep in contact with the water. Heterotrophs benefit from nutrients such as hydrophobic organics enriched in the surface layer and from free access to oxygen. Grazers benefit from the concentrated biomass. (B) The surface tension layer is not only an attachment point but also a barrier that is difficult to cross. The *Chromophyton rosanoffi* life cycle involves a free-swimming flagellated stage. After contacting the surface tension layer, the flagella are lost and a hydrophobic doughnut-shaped droplet is formed. The cell slips through the hole of the "doughnut" and positions itself on the top of it as an epineuston organ-ism. Protoplasmic filaments (rhizids) maintain contact with the water. (C) Microscopic landscape of the water surface with cells of *Chremastochloris conus* (Chlorophyta). Their hydrophobic umbrella is positioned above the surface layer, and the rest of the cell is immersed in the water. (Source: Valkanov 1968.)

pans. The dominant plant in bogs is the *Sphagnum* moss, which forms thick mats. As compared to other wetlands, the productivity of *Sphagnum* bogs is low. The lower portions of the *Sphagnum* mat die off, but anoxic and acidic conditions severely restrict biodegradation and peat accumulates. The *Sphagnum* mat holds water by capillary forces so effectively that the bog can actually grow much higher than the rim of the rock pan. It can be visualized as a water-soaked sponge resting on a shallow plate or bowl. As the bog rises, it can no longer receive nutrients from water running over its surface and is effectively isolated from soil and bedrock through the thick accumulated peat layer. Such a bog depends on nutrients only from the atmosphere and the rain; it becomes ombrotrophic (cloud-nourished).

Wetlands in general, and bogs in particular, are interesting environments because carbon recycling is severely restricted in them. Anoxic and acidic conditions partially explain this restricted recycling. Phenolic and polyphenolic substances from incomplete plant tissue degradation and probably additional, yet-unrecognized factors also contribute to low carbon recycling and to fossil-fuel accumulation.

**Lakes**  Lakes are divided into three zones based on the penetration of light (Figure 9.12). The combined littoral and limnetic zones are known as the *euphotic*

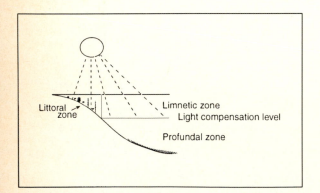

**Figure 9.12**
Zonation of a lake habitat based on light penetration.
(Source: Odum 1971. Reprinted by permission, copyright W. B. Saunders Co., Philadelphia.)

*zone;* here photosynthetic activity can occur. The profundal zone is the area of deeper water beyond the depth of effective light penetration; it does not exist in shallow ponds. In deep lakes the profundal zone extends from the light compensation level to the bottom.

The littoral zone is the region of the lake where light penetrates to the bottom; it is an area of shallow water usually dominated by submerged or partially submerged higher plants and attached filamentous and epiphytic algae. The limnetic zone, where the dominant primary producers are planktonic algae, is an area of open water away from the shore that descends to a level known as the *compensation depth.* The compensation depth is considered to be the lowest level having effective light penetration, where photosynthetic activity balances respiratory activity. Approximately 1% of full sunlight intensity generally penetrates to the compensation depth. Photosynthesis occurs below the compensation depth but at rates that are usually lower than the consumption rates of respiratory activities.

Microorganisms exhibit different absorption spectra determining which wavelengths of light can be utilized for photosynthesis (Stanier and Cohen-Bazire 1957) (Figure 9.13). Green and purple sulfur bacteria normally grow at the sediment-water interface, as within the anoxic portion of the water column, below the layers of short-wavelength-absorbing algal and cyanobacterial growth. They do this by utilizing wavelengths of light not absorbed by the overlying phytoplankton. The purple and green sulfur bacteria obtain reducing electrons from $H_2S$ at lower energy cost than $H_2O$-splitting photoautotrophs and thus require lower light intensities for carrying out photosynthesis.

The bottom of the lake, or benthos, represents the interface between the hydrosphere and the lithosphere. The lithosphere underlying a lake is referred to as *sediment* and is traditionally studied by aquatic microbiologists and geochemists. Conditions in the euphotic zone are favorable for the growth of photoautotrophs. Organisms in the profundal zone are largely secondary producers and are, for the most part, dependent on transport of organic compounds from the overlying zone. The benthic sediment habitat favors proliferation of microorganisms. Particulate nutrients sediment by gravitational forces and concentrate on the surface of the benthic sediment (Fletcher 1979; Marshall 1980; Paerl 1985). Surface sediments may be aerobic, allowing aerobic decomposition of accumulated organic nutrients. Anaerobic decomposition of organic compounds primarily occurs on or under the surface of lake sediments, where oxygen is often depleted. Oxygen can diffuse only very slowly into the water-filled pore spaces of sediments, and the oxidation of organic matter rapidly uses up any available oxygen. For this reason, in organic-rich sediments only the upper few millimeters tend to be oxygenated. In addition, the lower portion of the water

column in many freshwater lakes becomes seasonally anoxic. This is because warm water is less dense than cold water. In spring, as the sun warms the water of the lake, a warm surface layer, the epilimnion, is formed. This layer is separated from the cold deep hypolimnion by the thermocline (Rigler 1964) (Figure 9.14). The epilimnion is the upper zone of water that lies above the thermocline. The thermocline is a zone characterized by rapid decrease in temperature, across which there is little mixing of water. The epilimnion is typically warm and oxygen rich during the summer. Vigorous photosynthetic production tends to deplete mineral nutrients in this layer to the extent that they limit primary production. The hypolimnion is the zone of water below the thermocline, which is generally characterized by low temperatures and low oxygen concentrations—poor light penetration restricts photosynthesis, and respiration depletes existing oxygen. Mineral nutrients tend to be relatively abundant. In the fall, as the epilimnion cools and reaches the temperature of the hypolimnion, the thermocline breaks down; this fall turnover results in a complete mixing of the lake. In this way, the hypolimnion is reoxygenated and mineral nutrients are replenished in the epilimnion.

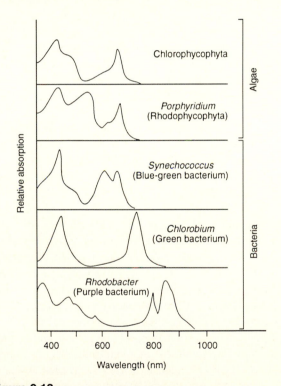

**Figure 9.13**
Absorption spectra of representative photosynthetic microorganisms. Note that *Chlorobium* and *Rhodobacter* can absorb light in the far red part of the spectrum, which is not utilized by algae. Because these bacteria live below the algal layer, this ability offers ecological advantage. (Source: Stanier and Cohen-Bazire 1957. Reprinted by permission, copyright Cambridge University Press.)

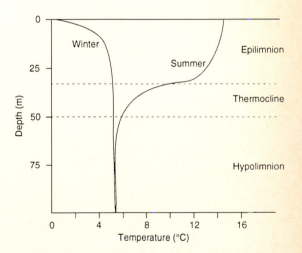

**Figure 9.14**
Typical stratification of a lake in the temperate climate zone during the summer and winter periods, showing the profile of the temperature with depth. During spring and fall, stratification breaks down, resulting in complete mixing (turnover) of the lake water.

Water has the thermal anomaly of being densest at 4°C. Once the whole lake cools to this temperature, water below 4°C does not sink but stays at the surface and freezes. This effectively insulates the lake from further cooling and prevents deeper bodies of water from freezing to their bottom. A weak winter stratification with 0–4°C epilimnion over a 4°C hypolimnion may develop. This stratification breaks down in the spring (spring turnover), followed by development of the summer stratification. Thermal stratification has a strong effect on the seasonal availability of and demand for mineral nutrients. Figure 9.15 shows the effects of stratification on phosphate concentration and turnover time in lake water (Rigler 1964). In some

bodies of water, special hydrographic conditions maintain a permanent rather than a seasonal thermocline. This is often due to a dense saline hypolimnion overlayered by a less saline and less dense epilimnion. A permanent thermocline, often called a *chemocline* to recognize its chemical rather than thermal nature, renders the hypolimnion permanently anaerobic and thus unsuitable for higher forms of life. A prime example of a water body with a chemocline is the Black Sea (Karl 1978). The name given this sea is probably due to its sediments stained dark by anaerobic sulfate reduction.

An ecologically useful classification of lake habitats as oligotrophic or eutrophic is based on productivity and nutrient concentrations (Wetzel and Allen 1970). Oligotrophic lakes have low concentrations of nutrients. Typically, they are deep, have a larger hypolimnion than epilimnion, and have relatively low primary productivity. In contrast, eutrophic lakes have high nutrient concentrations, are usually shallower and warmer than oligotrophic lakes, and have higher rates of primary production. Oxygen concentrations undergo strong diurnal fluctuations in eutrophic lakes because of the extensive aerobic decomposition of organic nutrients during night when there is no sunlight. Many desirable "game fish" species are unable to tolerate the periods of low oxygen concentration and are displaced by hardier species. Oligotrophic lakes do not experience such low-oxygen periods.

A number of important chemical parameters make lakes more or less suitable habitats for microorganisms (Hutchinson 1957). Concentrations of organic nutrients and oxygen, already mentioned, are important factors. Additionally, concentrations of inorganic nutrients, especially those that contain nitrogen and phosphorus, are important in determining the ability of the habitat to support microbial growth and metabolism. Concentrations of such nutrients are often influenced by exchange processes between the surrounding lithosphere and the lake waters. The availability of these essential nutrients is also highly dependent on biological activities that may sequester or mobilize inorganic substances.

The pH is another important factor influencing which microorganisms inhabit a particular lake. Some lakes are alkaline, some neutral, and still others acidic.

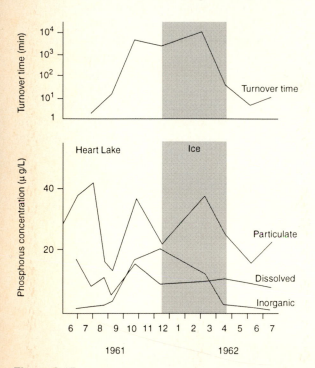

**Figure 9.15**

Seasonal changes in turnover time of inorganic phosphorus and amounts of particulate dissolved and inorganic phosphorus in a lake in Ontario. The turnover times are longer in winter than in summer; during summer, typical turnover times are on the order of minutes. Dissolved phosphorus is available in relatively high concentrations at the beginning of the spring phytoplankton blooms. (Source: Rigler 1964. Reprinted by permission of American Society of Limnology and Oceanography.)

Other conditions being equal, a higher pH favors primary production through higher availability of $CO_2$ in the forms of $HCO_3^-$ and $CO_3^{2-}$.

Salt concentrations also influence the characteristic autochthonous microorganisms of some lakes. Some landlocked lakes have high salt concentrations. The Great Salt Lake in Utah has a salt concentration of almost 28%, eight times higher than that found in oceans. Halophilic archaeal populations develop in saline lakes, such as the Great Salt Lake and the Dead Sea, often turning the color of the water red. Oren and Gurevich (1996) examined a bloom of halophilic archaea and algae in the Dead Sea that developed in the summer of 1992 after dilution of the salinity of the upper water layer by winter rains and floods. High levels of potential heterotrophic activity were associated with the bloom, as measured by the incorporation of labeled organic substrates. After the decline of the algal bloom, archaeal numbers in the lake decreased only slightly, and most of the community was still present a year later. No new algal and archaeal blooms developed after the winter floods of 1992–1993, despite salinity values in the surface layer that were sufficiently low to support a new algal bloom. A remnant of the 1992 *Dunaliella* bloom maintained itself at depths between 7 and 13 m. Its photosynthetic activity was small, and very little stimulation of archaeal growth and activity was associated with this algal community.

**Rivers**    Rivers differ from lakes in several major ways (Hynes 1970). Rivers are characterized by flowing waters; they have zones of rapid water movement and pools with reduced currents. Zones of rapid water movement tend to be shallower than pools. In pool zones, the decreased current velocity allows for deposition of silt. Silt is generally not deposited in zones of high current velocity; therefore, firm, rocky substrates underlie the rapid zones. Rivers have a high degree of interfacing with the lithosphere along the banks of rivers, and there is a great deal of transfer of chemicals from the lithosphere into river waters through rainwater runoff and erosion of river banks.

The upper course of a river is usually characterized by swift flow, a high degree of oxygenation, and low temperature. Shading by forests generally keeps primary production in the upper course low, and organic material input is derived mostly from the surrounding lithosphere. The middle course of a river is characterized by decreasing flow velocity, higher temperature, and less shading, resulting in significant intrinsic primary production. The lower course is subject to high levels of silt deposition; it is also subject to tidal influences resulting in a die-off of stenohaline freshwater microorganisms and their replacement by salt-tolerant estuarine organisms.

Most microbial and many microscopic organisms in rivers are attached to surfaces such as submerged rocks. Dissolved nutrients are rapidly absorbed by these attached organisms and are liberated upon death and decay only to be absorbed again a small distance downstream. As a consequence, nutrients do not move with the speed of the current but exhibit a much slower movement. The cycling of nutrients in a river does not occur in place, but rather nutrient cycling involves some downstream transport before a cycle is completed. The path of a nutrient can be viewed as a spiral rather than a cycle, a phenomenon known as *nutrient spiraling* (Webster and Patten 1979; Newbold et al. 1981) (Figure 9.16).

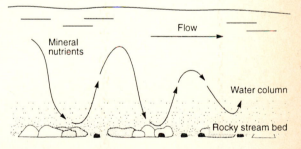

**Figure 9.16**
Spiraling of nutrients in the upper course of a river. The water moves swiftly over the rocky bed, and biota are attached to the rocks as biofilms, or take refuge between and under the rocks. In this situation, essential nutrient elements like phosphorus do not move downstream with the speed of the water because they are taken up by the biomass that is not moving with the water flow. Upon death and mineralization of the biomass (turnover), the nutrients move downstream with the water flow only briefly before their incorporation into biomass is repeated. This spiraling greatly slows the downstream movement of nutrients.

Rivers often receive high amounts of effluents from industries and municipalities. Municipal sewage disposal into rivers introduces high amounts of organic compounds (Figure 9.17). Oxygen concentrations are generally depleted below municipal sewage outfalls because available oxygen is used during microbial decomposition of the organic compounds. Industrial effluents may also introduce toxic chemicals, such as heavy metals, which may adversely affect microbial activities and survival. Rivers may receive high amounts of agricultural chemicals through runoff. Some agricultural chemicals act as toxicants, adversely affecting microbial activities; others, such as fertilizers, may support uncontrolled proliferation of microorganisms.

## Composition and Activity of Freshwater Microbial Communities

The microbial populations of lakes have been much more extensively studied than those of rivers (Hutchinson 1957; Rheinheimer 1991; Cole 1983; Ford 1993). Many similarities exist, but rivers by their nature always contain higher proportions of allochthonous microorganisms. For these reasons, most of the following discussion concerns lakes.

Members of the genera *Achromobacter, Flavobacterium, Brevibacterium, Micrococcus, Bacillus, Pseudomonas, Nocardia, Streptomyces, Micromonospora, Cytophaga, Spirillum,* and *Vibrio* are reported as occurring widely in lake water (Taylor 1942; Rheinheimer 1991). Stalked bacteria, such as *Caulobacter, Hyphomicrobium,* and other genera, are associated with submerged surfaces (Rheinheimer 1991).

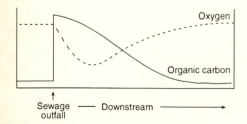

**Figure 9.17**
Relationship of organic carbon and dissolved oxygen in a river above and below a sewage outfall.

Autotrophic bacteria are autochthonous members of the microbiota of lakes and play an important role in nutrient cycling (Caldwell 1977). Photoautotrophic bacteria normally found in lakes include the cyanobacteria and in anoxic zones the purple and green anaerobic photosynthetic bacteria (Rheinheimer 1991). The cyanobacteria *Microcystis, Anabaena,* and *Aphanizomenon* can be dominant plankton in freshwater habitats. Blooms of cyanobacteria, often formed in connection with mineral enrichment due to sewage discharge or fertilizer runoff, can be extensive. The filamentous cyanobacteria may form slimy surface mats buoyed by trapped oxygen bubbles from their photosynthesis. In addition to the general problems of such blooms discussed in connection with eutrophication in Chapter 12, some species of *Anabaena* and *Microcystis* synthesize neurotoxic peptides and alkaloids. Humans are rarely affected from this source, but livestock drinking from lakes and ponds with such cyanobacterial blooms may be poisoned and lost (Falconer 1993). Chemolithotrophic bacteria have important roles in nitrogen, sulfur, and iron cycling within lakes; members of the genera *Nitrosomonas, Nitrobacter,* and *Thiobacillus* are essential members of freshwater microbial communities.

There are important differences in the vertical distribution of bacterial populations within a lake (Rheinheimer 1991) (Figure 9.18). These differences reflect vertical variations in abiotic parameters such as light penetration, temperature, and oxygen concentration. Microorganisms that may be considered autochthonous at the surface of a lake can be considered, in many cases, allochthonous in the benthic regions. For example, cyanobacteria are found typically in high numbers near the surface, where light penetration is adequate to support their photoautotrophic metabolism. Cyanobacteria that settle below the compensation depth are unable to compete; below the compensation depth they are allochthonous microorganisms. Photoautotrophic members of Chlorobiaceae and Chromatiaceae are autochthonous members of freshwater microbial communities at greater depths, where oxygen tensions are reduced and sufficient hydrogen sulfide is present, but where there is still sufficient light penetration. Rhodospirillaceae occupy similar environments but rely on reduced organic electron donors instead of sulfur compounds. Heterotrophic bacterial populations are distributed throughout the vertical water column but usually reach maximum concentrations near the thermocline and near the lake bottom, where concentrations of available organic matter are high.

Microorganisms found in the sediment of freshwater lakes are usually different from those in the overlying waters. In shallow ponds and lakes, anaerobic photoautotrophic bacteria occur on the surface of the sediment, often conferring characteristic colors on these water bodies. Fungi are found on the debris that accumulates on the sediment surface. These fungi include cellulolytic forms. Bacteria capable of anaerobic respiration are important members of sediment microbiota and include *Pseudomonas* species capable of denitrification activities. Within the sediment, obligately anaerobic bacteria occupy important niches. These bacteria include endospore-forming *Clostridium* species, methanogenic bacteria that produce methane gas, and *Desulfovibrio* species that produce hydrogen sulfide.

Lakes vary in terms of the fungal genera that are present; the differences reflect variations in the organic substrates available for fungal utilization and in the biota that can be attacked by fungal parasites (Sparrow 1968). Many fungi in freshwater lakes, rivers, and streams are associated with foreign organic matter and thus should be considered as allochthonous members of such ecosystems. Many ascomycetes and fungi imperfecti are found on wood and dead plant materials in rivers and lakes; when the plant material is degraded, the associated fungi disappear. Replacement occurs when foreign material enters the hydrosphere. Yeasts are found in many freshwater bodies. Weakly fermentative members of *Torulopsis, Candida, Rhodotorula,* and *Cryptococcus* are the yeasts most commonly found in rivers, streams, and lakes.

Algae are clearly important autochthonous members of freshwater ecosystems. In large, deep lakes, phytoplankton contribute most of the organic carbon, which supports the growth of the heterotrophic organisms in freshwater ecosystems. Much information has been gathered on the distribution of freshwater algae;

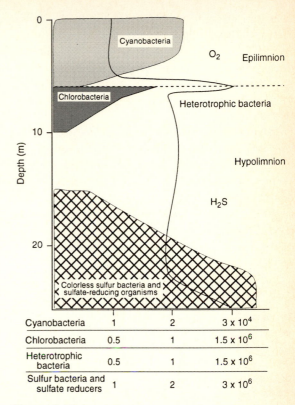

**Figure 9.18**

Vertical distribution of bacteria in a lake. Cyanobacteria are abundant in the epilimnion. Sulfate reducers are abundant in the lower hypolimnion. Maximal concentrations of heterotrophs occur just below the zone of maximal photosynthetic production and at water-sediment interface. (Source: Rheinheimer 1991. Reprinted by permission of John Wiley and Sons Ltd., and VEB Gustav Fischer Verlag.)

many treatises have described the algae of particular water bodies (Prescott 1962). The freshwater algae include members of Chlorophycophyta, Euglenophycophyta, Chrysophycophyta, Cryptophycophyta, and Pyrrhophycophyta. Species of green algae, dinoflagellates, and diatoms dominate in most freshwater ecosystems. Phaephycophyta and Rhodophycophyta are largely marine forms and are poorly represented in freshwater environments.

Protozoa graze on phytoplankton and bacteria in aquatic habitats. The phagotrophic flagellates are especially important grazers of bacterial populations.

Amoeboid, ciliated, and flagellated protozoa are found in streams, rivers, and lakes. Numerous genera of protozoa are found in freshwater habitats, including the common protozoans *Paramecium, Didinium, Vorticella, Stentor,* and *Amoeba.* The flagellate protozoan *Bodo* is common in polluted, low-oxygen waters (Westphal 1976).

In addition to autochthonous microbial populations, many allochthonous terrestrial microorganisms are carried by erosion and runoff from soils into freshwater aquatic ecosystems. Allochthonous microorganisms also enter when leaves from adjacent plants fall into these water bodies and when municipal sewage enters freshwater environments together with high amounts of organic matter. Heterotrophic microbial populations in areas that receive high amounts of organic matter are generally elevated, but as the amounts of imported organic matter decrease, populations of heterotrophic microorganisms also decline (Taylor 1942). The allochthonous microorganisms generally disappear in a relatively short time, being consumed by autochthonous members of the freshwater ecosystem. The numerous sources of input of allochthonous microorganisms, however, mean that microorganisms found in freshwater bodies often closely resemble terrestrial forms.

Microorganisms play a key role in lake productivity and the transformation of organic compounds within a lake (Kuznetsov 1959) (Figure 9.19). Rates of microbial metabolic activities, though, vary greatly

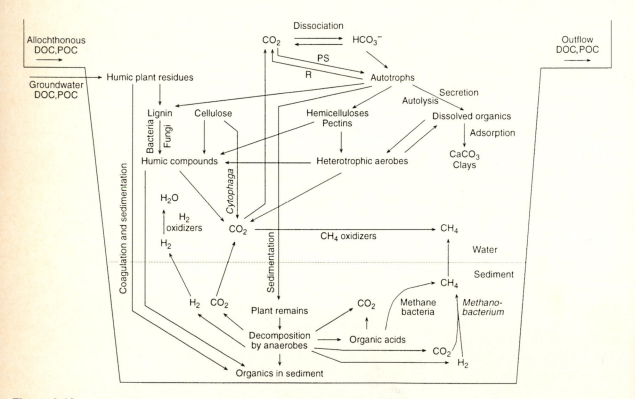

**Figure 9.19**
Carbon cycle of a typical freshwater lake. DOC = dissolved organic carbon; POC = particulate organic carbon; PS = photosynthesis; R = respiration. The figure illustrates the key role of microorganisms in carbon cycling of a lake habitat. (Source: Wetzel 1975. Based on Kuznetsov 1959. Reprinted by permission, copyright W. B. Saunders Co., Philadelphia.)

seasonally and temporally both within individual freshwater bodies and between different freshwater habitats (Overbeck 1966; Wright and Hobbie 1966) (Table 9.5). There is a clear trend of increasing productivity rates from oligotrophic to eutrophic lakes. The annual ranges of rates of nutrient turnover show great variation within lakes and overlap between lakes. Comparison of summer and winter rates, however, shows that rapid nutrient turnover occurs during the summer when productivity is also high. Turnover times are slower during winter when productivity is also reduced.

**Table 9.5**
Some examples of rates of primary
and secondary productivity in freshwater lakes

| Lake[*] | Primary productivity (mg C/m³/day) |
|---|---|
| Schönsee, Germany | 16 |
| Schluensee, Germany | 17 |
| Grosser Plöner See, Germany | 35 |
| Plußsee, Germany | 57 |

| Lake[†] | Turnover $T_1$ (hours) | Secondary productivity (mg C/m³/day) |
|---|---|---|
| Oligotrophic Lawrence, Mich. | 4–300 | 1–80 |
| Mesotrophic Crooked, Ind. | 80–470 | 63–110 |
| Eutrophic Little Crooked, Ind. | 36–232 | 190–205 |
| Lötsjön, Sweden | | |
|   Summer | 0.4–5 | <100 |
|   Winter | 20–300 | <20 |

[*]Source: Overbeck 1966.

[†]Source: Wright and Hobbie 1966.

Substrate = glucose.

The capacity of microorganisms, especially bacteria, to utilize dissolved organic compounds at very low concentrations is important in oligotrophic lakes that have low concentrations of available organic compounds (Kuznetsov et al. 1979; Ormerod 1983). A comparison of rates of algal and bacterial uptake of glucose (Figure 9.20) shows that at low substrate levels bacteria exhibit the greater uptake velocities, and at higher substrate levels algae show the higher uptake rates. Turnover times for carbon at very low substrate concentrations (less than 5 μg C per liter) are much shorter for bacteria than for algae (Wright and Hobbie 1966). The ability of bacteria and some nanoplanktonic flagellate protozoa to utilize low concentrations of organic matter permits introduction of dissolved organic carbon into food webs that support the growth of higher organisms. In the lower trophic range, picoplankton abundance is primarily controlled by the availability of nutrients (Weisse 1993). Low nutrient concentrations generally favor bacterial picoplankton whereas eucaryotic picoplankton becomes increasingly important with higher nutrient load. Low pH

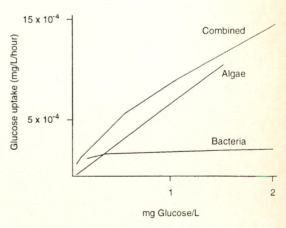

**Figure 9.20**
The velocity of glucose uptake by a bacterium and a green alga. At low substrate concentrations, uptake of glucose is primarily due to bacteria with little algal activity. At high substrate concentrations, bacteria exhibit saturation kinetics and uptake is greater for algae. (Source: Wright and Hobbie 1966. Reprinted by permission, copyright 1966 Ecological Society of America.)

values also selectively favor eucaryotes at the expense of bacterial picoplankton.

Fungi and bacteria in freshwater ecosystems are also largely responsible for the decomposition of allochthonous organic matter (Barnes and Mann 1980; Cole 1983). Microorganisms are the initial colonizers of detrital particles. They initiate a food web that results in the recycling of the organic nutrients of detritus within the ecosystem. Microorganisms mediate the transfer of allochthonous organic carbon into the cell biomass carbon of the autochthonous members of freshwater ecosystems; they also play key roles within freshwater habitats in the transformations and cycling of numerous other elements.

The principal ecological functions of microorganisms in freshwater environments can be summarized as follows: (1) They decompose dead organic matter, liberating mineral nutrients for primary production. (2) They assimilate and reintroduce into the food web dissolved organic matter. (3) They perform mineral cycling activities. (4) They contribute to primary production. (5) They serve as a food source for grazers (Kuznetsov 1970). In large, deep lakes where most of the lake floor is disphotic and devoid of higher plants, planktonic microorganisms are the principal primary producers.

## Marine Habitats

The oceans occupy 71% of Earth's surface, with a volume of $1.46 \times 10^9$ km$^3$, an average depth of 4000 m, and a maximal depth of approximately 11,000 m (Rumney 1968). The huge water masses of the oceans have an important moderating effect on the climate of Earth, being the ultimate reservoir and receptacle of the global water cycle. As much as 50% of the incident sun energy is estimated to be consumed in the evaporation of water from ocean, freshwater, and terrestrial surfaces. The evaporated water eventually precipitates as rain or snow, releasing its stored heat energy in the process (Stewart 1969). The precipitation may enter the oceans directly or indirectly after passing over or through the terrestrial environment as runoff. In the latter process, minerals are leached into the oceans at much higher rates than they can be returned by ocean spray and geological processes to land. Consequently, the oceans are the ultimate sink for all water-soluble minerals and are saline, though not to the same degree as some landlocked lakes in hot, dry climates.

**Estuaries** Freshwater runoff in the form of rivers and groundwater seepage interfaces with marine waters in estuaries. Estuaries are characteristically more productive than either the ocean or the freshwater inflow (Day 1950) because nutrients carried by rapidly flowing rivers are deposited at the river mouths or deltas. They are areas of highly variable environmental parameters in terms of temperature, salinity, pH, organic loading, and other factors. Estuaries are subject to tides and exhibit tidal flushing. Nutrients entering estuaries from rivers oscillate with the tides through the estuary with a net movement to the open sea.

In a typical estuary, there is a salinity gradient from <5 parts per thousand at the upper end to >25 parts per thousand at the mouth (Perkins 1974) (Figure 9.21). The distinction between autochthonous and allochthonous organisms is particularly difficult in such transition zones (Stevenson et al. 1974). Organisms best adapted for continued survival in such habitats must be eurytolerant to many environmental factors. Both true freshwater and true marine organisms are only transitional members of estuaries.

As in freshwater wetlands, productivity in estuaries is high. Photosynthesis in estuaries almost always exceeds respiratory activities (Wood 1967). Large portions of estuaries are overgrown with semisubmerged higher plants; characteristic among these plants are the various grassy *Spartina* species in temperate-zone salt marshes and the mangrove forests in tropical estuaries. Tidal flats are often overgrown with eelgrass *(Zostera)* in the temperate zone and with turtle grass *(Thalassia)* in the tropical zone. Salt-marsh estuaries may receive nutrients through the upwelling of deeper water masses along the continental shelf, but the larger portion of nutrient input usually comes from the adjacent land in the form of runoff. The physical construction of the estuary means that nutrients that enter the estuary or are produced within the

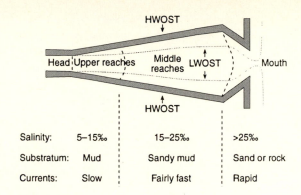

**Figure 9.21**
Principal environmental characteristics of an estuary. An estuary is characterized by a gradient from low salinity near the upper reaches to high salinity near the mouth. HWOST = high water line of spring tide; LWOST = low water line of spring tide. (Source: Perkins 1974. Based on Day 1950. Reprinted by permission, copyright Academic Press Inc. Ltd., London, and Royal Society of South Africa.)

estuary tend to be trapped there. Salt-marsh estuaries tend to recycle nutrients internally with little relative loss to the deeper ocean. Decomposer fungi are extremely important in salt marshes (Newell 1993). The standing crop of living fungal biomass can rise to more than 10% of the total community during the decay of standing plant shoots. Bacterial participation in shoot decay occurs primarily on fallen particles and involves production of lytic enzymes and capture of the dissolved products that are formed by the bacterial populations. The net result of this decomposer system is probably to retain the major portion of the carbon from the decaying-shoot material within the marsh ecosystem as it is converted to microbial and animal biomass.

## Characteristics and Stratification of the Ocean

For the most part, environmental conditions in the marine ecosphere are remarkably uniform (Sverdrup et al. 1942; Stewart 1969; Tait and DeSanto 1972; Anikouchine and Sternberg 1973). This great uniformity is brought about by various mixing mechanisms, including tidal movements, currents, and thermohaline circulation.

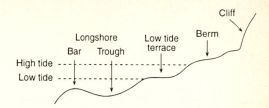

**Figure 9.22**
General characteristics of a beach habitat. The shoreline profile shows the high and low tide lines.

Tidal fluxes of water result in periodic flooding and exposure of shoreline (beach) habitats (Figure 9.22). Tides, which are produced by the gravitational pull of the moon and the sun, have a periodicity of about 12.5 hours; high and low tides occur twice daily in most locations. The differences in high and low tides are greatest every 2 weeks when spring tides occur and the smallest during the alternate weeks when neap tides occur.

Ocean currents arise from the frictional drag of the wind blowing across the surface of the water and the rotation of Earth. The rotational (coriolis) force of Earth and land obstacles results in largely circular current systems. Deep currents arise from variations in temperature and salinity, which create differences in water densities. These water mass densities cause thermohaline currents that mix the water masses vertically.

The oceans contain almost every naturally occurring chemical element, but most are in extremely low concentrations (Table 9.6) (Harvey 1957; Wenk 1969; Ross 1970; Broecker 1974). The major elements in oceans, aside from the hydrogen and oxygen that compose water, are sodium, chlorine, magnesium, sulfate, calcium, and potassium; minor components include carbon, bromine, strontium, boron, silica, and fluorine. Nitrogen, phosphorus, and iron, which are essential for microbial growth, occur in seawater only as trace elements at concentrations of less than 1 ppm.

Salinities of marine habitats are normally in the range of 3.3–3.7 parts per thousand, with an average of 3.5 parts per thousand. The pH of seawater is generally 8.3–8.5. Temperatures below 100 m of depth are usually between 0°C and 5°C; seasonal temperature

**Table 9.6**
Chemical composition of seawater

| Elements in seawater (ppm) | | | | | |
|---|---|---|---|---|---|
| Major | | Minor | | Trace | |
| H | $1.1 \times 10^5$ | Br | $6.5 \times 10^1$ | N | $5.0 \times 10^{-1}$ |
| O | $8.6 \times 10^5$ | C | $2.8 \times 10^1$ | Li | $1.7 \times 10^{-1}$ |
| Cl | $1.9 \times 10^4$ | Sr | $8.0 \times 10^0$ | Ru | $1.2 \times 10^{-1}$ |
| Na | $1.1 \times 10^4$ | B | $4.6 \times 10^0$ | P | $7.0 \times 10^{-2}$ |
| Mg | $1.4 \times 10^3$ | Si | $3.0 \times 10^0$ | I | $6.0 \times 10^{-2}$ |
| $SO_4^{2-}$ | $8.9 \times 10^2$ | F | $1.0 \times 10^0$ | Fe | $1.0 \times 10^{-2}$ |
| Ca | $4.0 \times 10^2$ | | | Zn | $1.0 \times 10^{-2}$ |
| K | $3.8 \times 10^2$ | | | Mo | $1.0 \times 10^{-2}$ |

Source: Ross 1970.

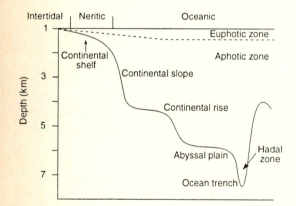

**Figure 9.23**
Major horizontal zonation in an ocean profile. (Source: Odum 1971. Reprinted by permission, copyright W. B. Saunders, Philadelphia.)

fluctuations at any location are usually no more than 20°C, and variations of temperature over all the oceans are within 35°C.

### Vertical and Horizontal Zones of Marine Habitats

Although the environmental conditions of the ocean are highly uniform, definite zones can be recognized (Figure 9.23). The littoral zone, or intertidal zone,

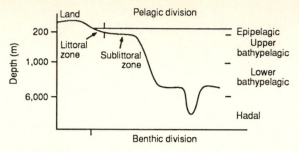

**Figure 9.24**
Major vertical zones of an ocean profile.

occurs at the seashore (Figure 9.24). This zone is subjected to alternate periods of flooding and drying at high and low tides, respectively. The sublittoral zone extends from the low tide mark to the edge of the continental shelf. This region is also known as the neritic, or nearshore, zone. The average depth in the neritic zone is less than 200 m. The oceanic province extends seaward from the edge of the continental shelf. The term *pelagic* is used to designate open water or the high sea and includes portions of the neritic and the entirety of the oceanic provinces. The benthos or benthic region is the bottom, regardless of the overlying zone (Isaacs 1969).

The benthic region begins at the intertidal zone and extends downward. The continental shelf is a gently sloping benthic region that extends away from the land mass. At the continental shelf edge, the slope greatly increases. The continental slope, also known as the bathyl region, drops down to the sea floor. The deep-sea floor is known as the abyssal plain and usually lies at about 4000 m. The ocean floor is not flat but has deep ocean trenches and submarine ridges. The deep ocean trenches are known as the hadal region (from the Greek *Hades,* "underworld"). Ocean trenches extend down to 11,000 m in depth.

As with the freshwater environment, the uppermost layer of the marine ecosphere is the surface tension layer, where the marine ecosphere interfaces with the atmosphere. The seawater-air interface is the habitat for the pleuston, the marine equivalent of the neuston, which includes bacterial and algal inhabitants (Cheng 1975). *Pseudomonas* and various pigmented genera such as *Erythrobacter, Erythromicrobium, Protaminobacter,* and *Roseobacter* are major bacterial populations (Wood 1967; Kaneko et al. 1979). A higher proportion of pleuston bacteria have been reported to utilize carbohydrates than do bacteria in the underlying water. Populations of primary producers, including cyanobacteria *(Trichodesmium),* diatoms *(Rhizosolenia),* and drifting Phaeophycophyta *(Sargassum),* are sometimes found in the pleuston layer.

There does not appear to be a uniquely adapted algal genus in the pleuston that is equivalent to the *Nautococcus* of the neuston. Representatives of fungi and protozoa are occasionally found in the pleuston, along with various macroscopic invertebrates. Light intensities at the surface of tropical seas are often phototoxic for algae, and here the pleuston community is dominated by heterotrophs that live off organic matter, enriched severalfold in the surface tension layer (Sieburth et al. 1977). The pleuston layer also attracts invertebrates that can become conspicuous during periods of extended calm. The lines "Yea, slimy things did crawl with legs upon the slimy sea" in Samuel Coleridge's "Rime of the Ancient Mariner" are a poetic reference to such a condition (David 1965).

The marine ecosphere may also be divided into vertical zones (Figure 9.24). The euphotic zone is the area of effective light penetration to the compensation level. Below the euphotic zone lies the disphotic (aphotic) zone. The pelagic zone can be divided into an epipelagic zone of 0–200 m, which is typically euphotic and warm; a bathypelagic zone, extending from 200 to 6000 m, which is normally disphotic and cold; and a hadal zone, below 6000 m, which is cold and subject to extreme pressure.

Several abiotic factors are important with regard to microbial growth at differing depths in marine habitats. The level of light intensity in the ocean depends largely on turbidity and depth (Figure 9.25). Little light penetrates below 25 m (Figure 9.25). Temperatures usually drop rapidly in the top 50 m of water, and below 50 m they are normally less than 10°C. Due to the concentrations of salt in seawater, normal freezing temperature is −1.8°C. Oxygen

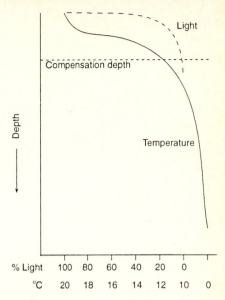

**Figure 9.25**

Vertical distribution of light and temperature in an ocean profile showing the compensation depth. As shown in this figure, there is a thermocline just above the compensation depth. Note that the temperature scale is not linear.

concentrations normally decrease below the surface, reaching a minimum at about 1000 m and then gradually increasing between 1000 and 4000 m to near surface concentrations (Figure 9.26). Phosphorus concentrations reach a maximum at 1000 m and remain in fairly constant concentrations to 4000 m.

Marine sediments exhibit a profile of zonation (Fenchel 1969) (Figure 9.27). The surface sediment has a relatively high $O_2$ concentration, high $NO_3^-$ concentration, high Fe(III) levels, and low $CO_2$ concentration. These parameters change slightly below the surface as the sediment changes from an oxidized zone, through a transitional zone, to a reduced zone. In the reduced zone, $O_2$ concentrations are virtually zero, and there is reduced sulfide as $H_2S$. Levels of Fe(III) decrease and those of Fe(II) increase; $CO_2$ is, in part, replaced by $CH_4$; $NO_3^-$ and $NO_2^-$ are replaced by $NH_4^+$. These chemical changes with depth in the sediment are connected to a change in habitat conditions from aerobic to anaerobic.

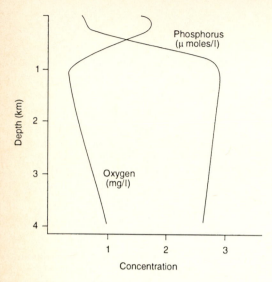

**Figure 9.26**
Vertical distribution of oxygen and phosphorus in an ocean profile.

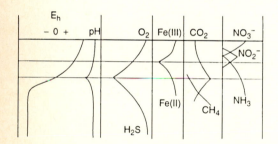

**Figure 9.27**
Profile of a marine sediment showing $E_h$, pH, $O_2/H_2S$, $Fe^{3+}$, $CO_2/CH_4$ and $NO_3^-/NO_2^-/NH_3$ concentrations. In the deeper anaerobic layers, the $E_h$ decreases and reduced forms of minerals replace oxidized forms. (Source: Fenchel 1969. Reprinted by permission of Ophelia.)

Nutrient availability is extremely important in determining microbial productivity in marine habitats (Ducklow and Carlson 1992). Recycling of mineral nutrients is very slow in the pelagic environment. Dead organisms from the euphotic epipelagic zone sink into the great depths of the bathypelagic and

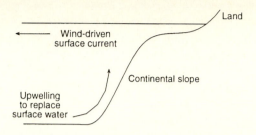

**Figure 9.28**
Upwelling of deep ocean water along continental slope to replace surface waters driven offshore by wind.

ultimately the benthic zone. They carry with them essential nutrients, mainly nitrogen and phosphorus, that are liberated in the perpetual darkness of the deep ocean. From here they are returned to the surface water by upwelling currents at extremely slow rates. It takes several thousand years for the average mineral nutrient molecule to be returned to the warm euphotic surface waters. Consequently, primary production in the euphotic zone of the pelagic environment is severely limited by the lack of mineral nutrients, whereas the nutrient-rich deep waters lack light energy for photosynthetic primary production. As a result, more than 95% of the oceans is characterized by an extremely low rate of productivity, averaging 50 g carbon fixed per square meter per year (Ryther 1969). In addition, most primary producers in the open oceans are extremely small planktonic algae (Round 1984). This condition results in pelagic food chains that are long and inefficient, supporting few sizable fish per water mass.

Virtually all commercial fishing is restricted to less than 5% of the oceans, primarily to coastal regions and specific upwelling zones (Ryther 1969). The nutrient-rich waters in these zones allow higher rates of primary production, the producers tend to be larger planktonic forms, and the food chains tend to be shorter and more efficient. Upwelling phenomena (Figure 9.28) often occur along the continental slope, caused by surface currents running rapidly away from the shore and being replaced by deeper, nutrient-rich water.

Although of limited significance to overall oceanic productivity, coral reefs are islands of strikingly high biomass and productivity, surrounded by the "biological desert" of unproductive tropical oceans. The contrast between the coral reef, teeming with fish and invertebrates, and the emptiness of the surrounding sea impresses even the most casual observer and continues to fascinate naturalists and ecologists. Ideal conditions for formation of coral reefs exist in warm tropical seas where the euphotic zone, at least initially, extends to the ocean floor. Central to the coral reef ecosystem is the association between the various species of coral polyps and their endozoic algae (see Chapter 5). The algae supply photosynthate (organic carbon) and oxygen to the polyp and assist in the calcium carbonate precipitation that builds the reef. The algae receive protection, $CO_2$, and mineral nutrients from the plankton capturing and heterotrophic metabolism of the polyp (Johannes 1967). If the seafloor sinks or the water level rises slowly, the annual growth of the reef keeps it in the euphotic zone. If the growth of the reef cannot keep up and the reef sinks below the euphotic zone, the alga-polyp association is disrupted and the reef dies. If there is no sinking, the reef grows to the ocean surface, and wave erosion balances further growth. A change in light transmission of the water—for example, because of suspended sediment from dredging—can also kill a coral reef by interfering with algal photosynthesis.

In addition to the closed-circuit nutrient cycling between the polyps and algae, the coral reef has additional mechanisms for capturing and retaining crucial mineral nutrients (DiSalvo 1971). Free-living algae and cyanobacteria associated with reef surfaces extract trace levels of nutrients from the seawater even when present at only trace levels. Various invertebrates graze upon them. Fecal pellets and detritus are efficiently retained in the coral reef ecosystem by various filter-feeding invertebrates. The reef acts as a nutrient trap, while in the surrounding sea nutrients are rapidly lost to the disphotic and unproductive bathypelagic zone. This nutrient-capturing ability of the coral reef was tested using radiotracer experiments and found to be highly efficient. The nutritional status of coral reefs is further bolstered by the nitrogen-fixing activity of cyanobacteria, principally *Calothrix crustacea* (Wiebe et al. 1975).

The thermal vent regions are anomalous marine habitats where productivity depends upon chemolithotrophic bacteria rather than photosynthetic microorganisms (Figure 9.29). The warm waters surrounding the thermal vents are rich in reduced sulfur compounds that allow rapid and extensive growth of chemolithotrophic bacterial and archaeal populations that in turn support the growth of unique animal communities (Tunnicliffe 1992). Massive animal communities develop in these habitats, fed by the chemolithotrophic microorganisms. Some of these graze or filter feed on microorganisms; others are directly symbiotic with microorganisms and exhibit chemoautotrophic activity. Microbial mats cover all available surfaces on and near the vents, and high densities of unique clams, mussels, vestimentiferan worms, and other invertebrates cluster in the vicinity. The food webs of the deep-sea thermal vents have sparked great interest in these unusual habitats and their microbial and animal communities. Energetically, the entire vent community is supported by the chemoautotrophic oxidation of reduced sulfur, primarily by *Beggiatoa, Thiomicrospira,* and additional sulfide or sulfur oxidizers of great morphological diversity. Oxidation of $H_2$, $CO$, $NH_4^+$, $NO_2^-$, $Fe^{2+}$, and $Mn^{2+}$ are assumed to contribute to chemoautotrophic production, although measurements of these processes in the vent environment are yet to be accomplished. Methane, derived from reduction of $CO_2$ with geothermally produced hydrogen by extremely thermophilic *Methanococcus* species detected in the anoxic hydrothermal fluid, is also oxidized by methanotrophic bacteria and provides additional carbon and energy input for the vent ecosystem.

## Composition and Activity of Marine Microbial Communities

The pelagic marine habitat is a unique environment for both macro- and microorganisms (Isaacs 1969). It completely lacks higher plants; all primary production is carried out by microscopic algae and bacteria. In the euphotic zone, invertebrates and fishes have no

**Figure 9.29**

Thermal vent communities are unique habitats that occur in oceans where volcanic activity forces hot water and mineral nutrients, including reduced sulfur compounds, into the benthos. Many of these habitats occur in deep-sea regions. Some of the areas of volcanic activity are known as black smokers (right photograph and illustration), so named because of the gray-black plume of material that spews from them. These thermal vents are surrounded by extensive animal communities shown in the illustration. These unusual communities have abundant populations of vestimentiferan tube worms, such as the giant tube worm *Riftia pachytila* (top left photograph), vesicomyid clams such as *Vesicomya chordata* and *Calyptogena magnifica,* and mytilid mussels such as *Bathymodiolus thermophilus.* These animals harbor extensive populations of chemolithotrophic bacteria that utilize reduced sulfur compounds to generate energy and bacterial biomass. The chemolithotrophic bacteria supply the organic compounds needed by the animals for their growth. The surrounding hot aquatic habitat contains vast populations of free-living archaea, such as *Thermococcus* and *Pyrodictium.* There are also large populations of thermophilic bacteria, such as *Thermotoga* species. The surrounding cooler, yet still warm benthic habitat has large populations of chemolithotrophic mesophilic bacteria. Chemolithotrophic bacteria, including filamentous *Thiotrix* species, grow abundantly in this habitat, covering almost all surfaces that are exposed to the $H_2S$-containing plumes from the thermal vents (scanning electron micrograph lower left). Source: Holger Jannasch, Woods Hole Oceanographic Institute.)

opportunity to take refuge in a homogeneous and transparent environment. Glassy transparency and silvery ventral and dark dorsal surfaces offer minimal camouflage. For most fishes, speed is the most important attribute, for escape as well as for predation. Fishes of the epipelagic zone are highly streamlined and powerfully built. Schooling behavior offers some protection and is exhibited by many species. Deep-sea fishes are protected by darkness and are generally not adapted for high-speed swimming. They have to cope with a scarce and unpredictable food supply and often show adaptations for large, infrequent meals (Stockton and DeLaca 1982). Metabolic rates are slow under the prevailing low-temperature, high-pressure conditions (Jannasch and Wirsen 1977; Jannasch 1979).

Microbial numbers are relatively high in nearshore, upwelling, and estuarine waters, but sink as low as 1–100/mL in pelagic waters (ZoBell 1946; Oppenheimer 1963; Kriss et al. 1967; Wood 1967; Colwell and Morita 1972; Litchfield 1976; Simidu et al. 1977; Karl and Holm-Hansen 1978). Here, heterotrophic bacteria tend to be associated with algal surfaces or detrital particles, which offer a nutritional advantage compared to the extremely low concentrations of dissolved organic nutrients in the pelagic seawater. Relatively high numbers of microorganisms occur in the first few centimeters of most marine sediments ($10^7$–$10^8$/g), but the numbers taper off in deeper sediment layers (Karl 1978). The reason seems to be more the depletion of available nutrients than the anaerobic conditions. The highest biomass of microorganisms in marine waters is normally near the surface and decreases with depth (Figure 9.30).

Some microorganisms growing in the surface waters do move downward, often attached to sediment particles. These microorganisms provide food sources to organisms growing in pelagic habitats. Long-term sediment trap studies indicate that high numbers of heterotrophic bacteria (up to $3 \times 10^9$ cells/m²/day) and cyanobacteria (up to $3 \times 10^7$ cells/m²/day) are transported into the deep sea attached to rapidly sedimenting particles (Turley and Mackie 1995). These studies indicate annual bacterial flux is $1.1 \times 10^{12}$ cells/m²/annum, which is equivalent to 56.3 mg bacterial carbon/m²/annum, about 4 mg DNA, 5 mg RNA,

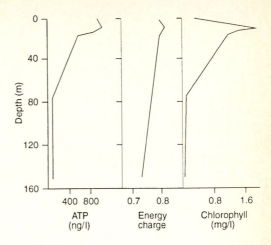

**Figure 9.30**
Distribution of ATP, energy charge, and chlorophyll in a marine profile approximately 5 km offshore in the California bight. Greatest microbial concentrations and potential metabolic activities occur at approximately 10 m of depth. There is a continuous decline in microbial biomass and energy charge below 20 m. (Source: Karl and Holm-Hansen 1978. Reprinted by permission, copyright Springer-Verlag.)

and 27 mg protein/m²/annum, and $27.5 \times 10^{12}$ plasmid-encoded phenotypic genes/m²/annum. Thus the supply of DNA and mechanisms of transfer are potentially available for genetic exchange to occur between populations previously assumed to be genetically isolated: bacteria in the surface waters and those in the deep sea.

**Aspects of Marine Microbial Populations**  The main problem in performing autecological studies on marine bacteria lies in the methods used to obtain viable cultures. Whether the isolates obtained by current culture methods represent the major indigenous populations is unknown. Determining the representative physiological studies that can be performed on the vast numbers of marine bacteria that have yet to be cultured is still a matter of guesswork (Schut et al. 1993).

Nevertheless, one can ascribe certain features to the autochthonous microorganisms of the marine environment (Macleod 1965). Marine microorganisms should exhibit growth at salinities between 20 and 40 parts per thousand. A salt concentration of

33–35 parts per thousand represents the optimal salt concentration for genuine marine microorganisms. By an admittedly arbitrary definition, true marine bacteria will not grow in the absence of sodium chloride. Marine bacteria require the ions in marine waters to maintain proper membrane functions; for example, sodium and chloride are required for active transport. Some marine bacteria have multiple membranes surrounding their cells. Exposure to fresh water disrupts these membrane layers, causing a loss of viability in these bacteria.

Marine bacteria must be capable of growth at the low nutrient concentrations found in the oceans. Many marine bacteria, though, will adsorb onto detrital particles and grow well under localized conditions that are relatively nutrient rich. Typical characteristics of marine bacteria include small size, including ultramicrobacteria with cell volumes less than 0.1 $\mu m^3$ and low DNA content and/or high uptake affinity for substrates; most appear to be obligately oligotrophic—requiring low nutrient concentrations for growth (Schut et al. 1993). Because 90–95% of the marine environment is below 5°C, marine bacteria must be capable of growth at low temperatures. Except in tropical surface waters and in thermal vent communities, most marine bacteria should be psychrophilic or psychrotrophic. Bacteria found in deep-ocean trenches are exposed to great hydrostatic pressures. In such areas, barotolerant and barophilic bacteria are important members of the autochthonous community (Yayanos 1995).

Most marine bacteria are gram-negative and motile (ZoBell 1946). Marine bacteria are generally aerobes or facultative anaerobes; relatively few obligate anaerobes are found in marine waters. There is a relatively high proportion of proteolytic bacteria in marine habitats as compared to freshwater or soil habitats. Many bacterial genera contain marine species. *Pseudomonas* or *Vibrio* species are often found to be the dominant genera in marine environments; *Flavobacterium* species are also found in relatively high numbers. In Chesapeake Bay, for example, Lovelace et al. (1967) found 56% *Vibrio* species, 18% *Pseudomonas* species, and 6% *Flavobacterium* species. *Spirillum, Alcaligenes,*

*Hyphomicrobium, Cytophaga, Microcyclus,* and actinomycetes are also frequently found in marine water samples.

Besides various gram-negative bacteria, some gram-positive bacteria, such as *Bacillus* species, are normally found in marine sediments. Below the surface of marine sediments, anaerobic bacteria compose the autochthonous microorganisms. Marine sediments receive accumulations of organic matter from overlying waters that favor the growth of heterotrophic bacteria. Anaerobic *Desulfovibrio* species are found in marine sediments where these organisms reduce sulfate to hydrogen sulfide. Anaerobic methanogens are normally found in sediment below the layer of available sulfate.

Dilution culture, in which populations are diluted to near extinction prior to cultivation, has proved useful for studying marine bacteria, especially typical small bacteria (ultramicrobacteria) from naturally occurring assemblages (Button et al. 1993; Schut et al. 1993). Over half the marine bacteria isolated from northern marine waters are ultramicrobacteria that initially could be cultured only under low-nutrient conditions (Button et al. 1993). Mean viabilities, determined by comparing cell counts using flow cytometry with recovery of viable bacteria by dilution culture, are between 2 and 60%; viability decreases at organic compound concentrations of greater than 5 mg amino acid carbon per liter. Doubling times are 1 day to 1 week for these oligotrophic ultrabacterial populations.

Important populations of chemolithotrophic bacteria are involved in nitrogen cycling in marine waters (Belser 1979). These include members of genera *Nitrosococcus, Nitrosomonas, Nitrospina, Nitrococcus,* and *Nitrobacter.*

Fungal populations in marine ecosystems have been overlooked in the past, but several major treatises have been compiled in recent decades on the occurrence of fungi in the ocean (Johnson and Sparrow 1961; Hughes 1975). Some fungi found in marine ecosystems require sodium chloride for growth; others are salt tolerant. Yeasts are frequently found in marine waters (Lodder 1971). The most commonly found yeast genera are *Candida, Torulopsis, Cryptococcus,*

*Trichosporon, Saccharomyces,* and *Rhodotorula. Rhodosporidium,* a basidiomycete-related yeast, also has been found in marine habitats. Filamentous basidiomycetes, however, are rarely found in marine ecosystems. Occasionally, blooms of yeasts are encountered in discrete marine water bodies, such as within areas of the North Sea (Phaff et al. 1968).

Marine algae supply an essential input of carbon to the marine ecosystem (Taylor 1957; Boney 1966; Dawes 1974). The marine algae include members of Chlorophycophyta, Euglenophycophyta, Phaeophycophyta, Chrysophycophyta, Cryptophycophyta, Pyrrhophycophyta, and Rhodophycophyta. Most Phaeophycophyta, or brown algae, are marine. There are more than 1500 species of marine brown algae; these algae are a conspicuous intertidal component extending from the upper littoral zone into the sublittoral zone to depths greater than 220 m in clear tropical waters. The marine brown algae include the kelps, such as *Fucus* and *Sargassum.* Members of Chlorophycophyta and Chrysophycophyta are prominent members of plankton. Marine plankton is found in maximal concentrations in the upper regions of the ocean, usually at 0–50 m in depth (ZoBell 1946; Holm-Hansen 1969) (Table 9.7). In very clear tropical waters, because of the high light intensity, the phytoplankton maximum is not found at the surface but at 10–15 m of depth. Green algae are found in greater numbers near the surface, usually disappearing below 30 m. Red algae and golden brown algae occur at somewhat greater depths.

Planktonic diatoms can be described as either holoplanktonic, which are either pelagic or littoral species but live an oceanic existence in the sense that they do not depend on the bottom to complete their life cycle; meroplanktonic, species that are pelagic only a portion of their life cycle and spend the remainder of their existence on the bottom; or tychopelagic, species that actually spend the major portion of their life cycle attached to a fixed substratum but enter the surface layers of the sea when forcefully torn from their usual habitat. Planktonic diatoms exhibit structural and physiological adaptations to the marine environment. Structurally, planktonic diatoms have elaborate projections that enlarge the surface area relative to the volume of the cell, slowing down their sinking.

**Table 9.7**
Concentration of phytoplankton off the coast of southern California

| Depth (m) | Biomass µg C/l | | Diatoms/l |
| | Diatoms | Total phytoplankton | |
|---|---|---|---|
| 0 | 2.1 | 12.1 | 10 |
| 30 | — | — | 500 |
| 50 | 5.5 | 24.4 | 180 |
| 100 | 0.2 | 3.3 | 2 |
| 200 | 0.0 | 0.7 | 0 |

Sources: Holm-Hansen 1969; ZoBell 1946.

Some diatoms selectively adsorb monovalent ions over heavier divalent ions, a physiological adaptation that contributes to buoyancy. Other buoyancy mechanisms used by diatoms and other planktonic organisms are oil storage materials and gas bubbles, such as the gas vacuoles of *Trichodesmium* (Denton 1963).

There are occasional blooms of Pyrrophycophyta in marine waters. Blooms of such dinoflagellates produce the so-called red tides, when concentrations of these algae become so great as to color the ocean red-brown; these blooms occasionally cover several square kilometers. The toxins produced by some of these dinoflagellates kill fish and other marine organisms. The causes of red tide dinoflagellate blooms are not well documented but may be associated with the surfacing of nutrients by the upwelling of deep ocean currents (Round 1984).

Seasonal blooms of dinoflagellates less dramatic than the red tides are harmless to marine life, but the neurotoxins produced by these microalgae accumulate in shellfish that feed on them. When ingested by humans, such tainted seafood can cause paralytic shellfish poisoning (PSP). In mild cases the symptoms are the tingling of lips; higher doses may result in paralysis and death from respiratory arrest. Shellfish beds with a history of such poisoning are closed seasonally to harvest, causing substantial economic losses. Illegal harvest from such areas occasionally causes health problems in faraway cities, but much more prevalent are the poisonings among the local population when individuals choose to ignore the postings and harvest shellfish for their own needs. Several less well known occurrences of seafood-related poisoning are associated with dinoflagellates and certain diatoms (Falconer 1993).

Protozoa are an important component of marine zooplankton (Westphal 1976). Marine protozoa may exhibit adaptations to salt concentrations, sometimes exhibiting tolerances of up to 10% NaCl concentrations. Marine protozoa include flagellates, rhizopods, and ciliates. The flagellate Coccolithophoridae are the smallest planktonic protozoa in the sea and the chief constituent of marine plankton. Species of *Radiolaria* and *Acantharia* are also important components of marine plankton. Most *Radiolaria* species live only as deep as 350 m, but other radiolarians occur at depths down to 4000–5000 m. *Tintinnidium* species are marine ciliates that thrive in the upper layers of the sea. Marine protozoa and microcrustacea graze on bacteria, phytoplankton, and smaller forms of zooplankton. The grazing by zooplankton provides a critical link in the marine food web between the very small primary producers and the higher members of the marine food web.

## Litho-Ecosphere

Lithosphere habitats occur as land masses, consisting of rocks and soil, and as sediments, already discussed in the section on the hydro-ecosphere. The soil, which arises from the weathering of parent rock materials, is by definition capable of acting as a habitat for biological organisms (Brady 1984).

### Rocks

The rocks of Earth's crust are commonly classified as igneous, sedimentary, or metamorphic. Igneous rocks are formed directly by solidification of molten lava and include granite, basalt, and diorite. Quartz and feldspars are the primary minerals of igneous rocks. Sedimentary rocks arise from deposition and consolidation of weathered products of other rocks. For example, sandstone is a sedimentary rock that arises from quartz sands; shale arises from consolidation of

clay. Sedimentary rocks include limestone, dolomite, sandstone, and shale.

Sedimentary rocks differ in their chemical composition based on the parent materials. Like other rocks, sedimentary rocks can undergo weathering, leading to the formation of soil. Metamorphic rocks are formed by the metamorphosis, or change in form, of other rocks. Igneous and sedimentary rocks that have been subjected to high pressure and temperatures change their physical form. Igneous rocks may be converted to coarse-grained crystalline gneisses and schists. Sedimentary rocks may be converted to quartzite from sandstone, slate from shale, or marble from limestone.

Rock surfaces provide a suitable habitat for a limited number of microorganisms. Bacteria, algae, fungi, and lichens colonize many rock surfaces. A high proportion of bacteria and fungi found on terrestrial rock surfaces are able to solubilize silicates and other minerals through production of organic acids and chelating agents (Silverman and Munoz 1970). Bacteria and fungi on terrestrial rock surfaces are often found in crevices, which can retain water.

Along the shores of the oceans, large populations of cyanobacteria and algae inhabit the rocky coasts. These microorganisms occupy the supralittoral, or subaerial, zone. This interface zone between marine and terrestrial habitats is washed by the spray of the sea. Microorganisms that colonize the rock surfaces in this zone include cyanobacteria, such as *Calothrix,* Chlorophycophyta, such as *Enteromorpha,* and the Rhodophycophyta, such as *Porphyra* (Round 1984).

### Soils

Soils form from rocks through a complex process of physical, chemical, and biological forces that reduce rock first to regolith (rock rubble) and then to soil. The five main factors involved in soil formation are parent material, climate, topography, biological activity, and time. Soils contain vastly diverse microbial communities. By definition, soils also support the growth of plants. Microorganisms contribute greatly to soil fertility, that is, the ability of soils to support plant growth (Metting 1993). Plants also have a major influence on the microbial communities in soils. The plant

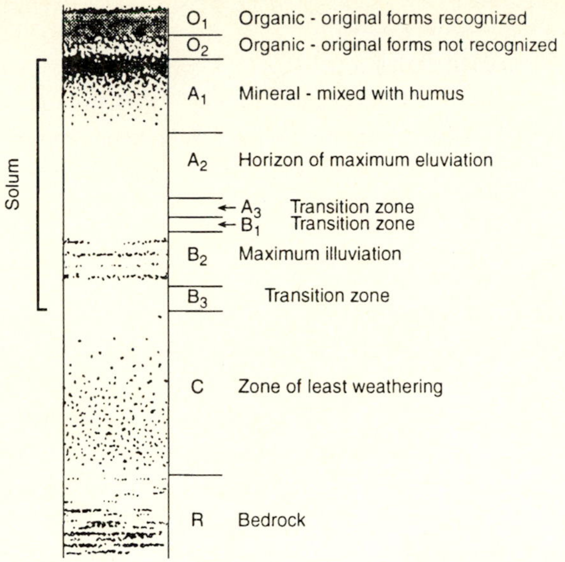


**Figure 9.31**
Vertical soil profile showing soil horizons. (Source: Buckman and Brady 1969. Reprinted by permission, copyright Macmillan Publishing Co.)

cover of the soil is an important factor in determining the types and numbers of microorganisms in that soil. Plant root exudates and senescent parts of plants are important sources of nutrients for soil microorganisms. Rhizosphere and mycorrhizal interactions, as well as plant susceptibility to pathogens, exert selective influences on the soil microbial community.

**Physical Properties** When soil forms from regolith, it typically develops a series of distinct horizons (Figure 9.31) as a result of the weathering process (Brady 1984). The O groups, or organic horizons, develop above the mineral soil and contain the soil organic matter known as humus; these horizons are formed from plant and animal residues deposited on the surface. The O horizon is divided into an $O_1$ horizon, where the original plant and animal forms are recognizable, and an $O_2$ horizon, where the plants and animals have decayed to a point beyond recognition. The A, or eluvial, horizon is a mineral horizon that lies near the soil surface. The A horizon is characterized as a zone of maximal leaching; it is divided into an $A_1$ layer, where mineral soil is mixed with humus, an $A_2$ horizon, with maximal leaching of silicate clays, iron oxides, and aluminum oxides, and an $A_3$ horizon, a transition to the underlying B horizon. The B, or illuvial, horizon is where deposition has taken place and there is the maximal accumulation of materials such as iron oxides, aluminum oxides, and silicate clays. The combined A and B horizons are known as the solum. Biological activities do not greatly affect the C horizon, beneath the solum; the C horizon may contain accumulations of calcium and magnesium carbonates. Beneath the C horizon lie regolith and bedrock.

**Table 9.8**
Comparison of size range, particle number, and surface area per gram of sand, silt, and clay. The calculations assume spherical particles with the maximum diameter within the size range.

| Soil component | Diameter (mm) | No. of particles/g | Surface area ($cm^2$/g) |
|---|---|---|---|
| Sand | 2.00–0.05 | 90 | 11 |
| Silt | 0.05–0.002 | $5.78 \times 10^6$ | 454 |
| Clay | 0.002 | $9.03 \times 10^{10}$ | 8,000,000 |

Regardless of horizons, soils contain varying proportions of clay, silt, and sand particles (Brady 1984). The proportions of these different size particles constitute the texture of the soil. Soil texture is a very important property for the ecology of microorganisms because it describes the surface area that is available as a habitat for the growth of microorganisms. Soils with greater clay compositions have much higher surface areas available for the growth of microorganisms than soils with high sand concentrations, because clays are much smaller particles than sands (Table 9.8). When considering soil particles as habitats for microorganisms, it is also important to consider the nature of the clay particles (Marshall 1980). Clay colloids differ significantly in their physical and chemical properties (Table 9.9, p. 366). These differences influence how many and what types of microorganisms can occupy the particular soil habitat (Hattori and Hattori 1976).

## Deep Subsurface Microbiology

The microbially most active soil is the upper 15-cm-thick "plow layer." Below this, microbial numbers and activity gradually decline with depth. Photosynthetic production is impossible, and the leaching of undegraded but soluble organic matter to deep soil layers is very limited. With the exception of cave habitats, the litho-ecosphere was not considered to extend below the bedrock under the soils.

This view has changed radically since the late 1980s when some systematic explorations of deep subsurface geological formations for microbial life were initiated. Much of this research was sponsored by the U.S. Department of Energy (DOE), interested in the subsurface disposal of hazardous nuclear and chemical wastes (Fredrickson 1992). Similar investigations were conducted in Europe, especially in Sweden. Obviously, microbial activity in subsurface geological formations could influence the fate and mobility of waste materials. The findings were surprising and had significance much beyond subsurface waste disposal.

At least in undisturbed formations, the age of geological layers increases with their depth. Some of the geological layers are water-permeable and constitute aquifers; others are water-impermeable. Aquifers separated from the surface by one or more water-impermeable layers are called "confined" aquifers.

The microbial sampling of deep subsurface formations is technically daunting and expensive. Boreholes need to be drilled to depths often exceeding 1000 m. Drilling techniques used in oil exploration need to be modified to minimize contamination from equipment and drilling fluids. To protect obligate anaerobes, the drill hole may need to be flushed with argon gas. Recovered drill cores need to be stored and processed under special conditions to prevent contamination or deterioration. The cores have to be split aseptically to retrieve uncontaminated rock for microbial investigations. A variety of "tracers" are employed during drilling and processing. Only if these tracers are undetectable in later quality control analysis is the rock sample considered uncontaminated.

The extensive literature on the deep subsurface investigations was reviewed by Pedersen (1993). Microorganisms were found in all deep subsurface geological formations where water was available and the temperature was in a permissible range. The sampled formations included both sedimentary rocks such as dolomitic limestone and igneous rocks such as granite and basalt, as well as unconsolidated deep sediment cores from the Atlantic Coastal Plain of the United States. The deepest samples that yielded bacteria were 3900–4200 m deep and contained thermophilic fermentative bacteria. Anaerobes, sulfate reducers, and methanogens were isolated with much greater frequency than aerobic microorganisms. The diversity of microorganisms from any one location was relatively low, showing the strong selectivity of prevailing conditions. Both diversity and total numbers were highest in the more shallow, unconsolidated sediments of the Atlantic Coastal Plain.

Many deep subsurface samples were taken from confined aquifer water via artesian wells (see the accompanying figure). These are valuable samples because the water gushes out under its own head pressure, allowing extensive flushing prior to the taking of water samples, yielding relatively uncontaminated samples for microbiological investigation. In confined aquifers, the groundwater moves slowly from recharge areas toward distant discharge areas. Thus, aquifer water at different ages may be sampled by artesian wells at increasing distances from the recharge area. Microorganisms were abundant even in aquifer water more than 10,000 years old!

The obvious and as yet incompletely resolved question is what food and energy resources these subsurface bacteria survive on, sometimes at densities up to $10^6$–$10^8$/mL. Most of the bacteria appear to be heterotrophic. Organic carbon in sedimentary rock may become available at a slow rate to support heterotrophic activity. Gaseous and other dissolved organics may enter aquifers from fossil gas, oil, or lignite deposits. In at least one instance, there is evidence that groundwater reacting with reduced basaltic rock evolves hydrogen, and this supports a methanogenic community (Stevens and McKinley 1995).

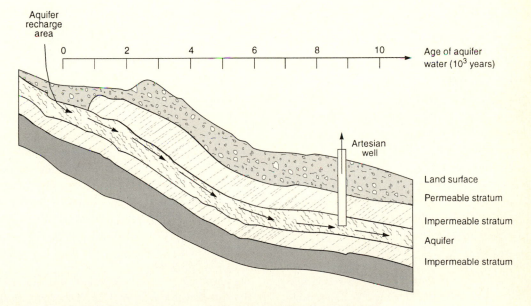

Cross section of a geological formation with water-permeable and water-impermeable strata and a confined aquifer. Deep subsurface bacteria may be sampled in the water of artesian wells. The distance of the wells from the aquifer recharge area correlates with the time the water spends in the aquifer. Bacteria are present and sometimes abundant ($10^6$/mL) in aquifer waters from more than 1000 m deep; these bacteria have spent several thousand years in the aquifer.

**Table 9.9**
Selected properties of major clay colloids

| Property | Montmorillonite | Illite | Kaolinite |
|---|---|---|---|
| Size (µm) | 0.01–1.0 | 0.1–2.0 | 0.1–5.0 |
| Surface (m$^2$/g) | 700–800 | 100–200 | 5–20 |
| Cation exchange capacity (mEq/100g) | 80–100 | 15–40 | 3–15 |

**Chemical Properties**  The chemical properties of soils are important factors for microorganisms (Alexander 1977). The soil organic matter derives from the remains of plants, animals, and microbes (Bear 1964). Humic substances are those portions of the soil organic matter that have undergone sufficient transformation to render the parent material unrecognizable. Humic materials present in mineral soils typically constitute less than 10% by weight of the soil. Humic compounds are random polymers, and at best we can establish only their type structures. The theories on the actual structures in humic materials are controversial and subject to constant revision and refinement. Perhaps the most accepted current theory visualizes an aromatic core consisting of single and condensed aromatic, heterocyclic, and quinoidal rings, linked and cross-linked by carbon-carbon, ether, amino, and azo bonds (Stevenson 1976) (Figure 9.32). The rings bear a variety of functional groups, the more prominent of which are carboxyl, phenolic hydroxyl, and carbonyl groups. Attached to this core are amino acids, peptides, sugars, and phenols, which form further cross linkages. The result is a three-dimensional sponge-like structure that readily absorbs water, ions, and organic molecules in an exchangeable manner and, in addition, may chemically bind suitable compounds to its reactive functional groups. As a consequence, virtually all natural organic compounds and apparently also numerous human-made chemicals can occur in bound or absorbed form in humic substances; even active enzymes have been recovered in humus-bound form.

The genesis of humic material is a two-stage process involving the predominantly microbial degradation of organic polymers to monomeric constituents, such as phenols, quinones, amino acids, and sugars, and the subsequent polymerization of these by spontaneous chemical reactions, autoxidation, and oxidation catalyzed by microbial enzymes such as laccases, polyphenoloxidases, and peroxidases. The aromatic ring structures that serve as the building blocks of the humic acid core may originate from the microbial degradation of lignin or may be synthesized by various microorganisms from other carbon substrates. The humic material is in a dynamic state of equilibrium, its synthesis being compensated for by gradual mineralization of the existing material (Stevenson 1982).

Soils contain vastly differing concentrations and chemical forms of organic carbon, inorganic and organic nitrogen, and available inorganic phosphorus (Brady 1984) (Table 9.10). The composition of the soil atmosphere (atmosphere-lithosphere interface) also varies greatly between soils. The soil atmosphere exists in the porous spaces between soil particles. Bulk density is a measure of packing of soil particles and indicates the extent of space that may be occupied by the soil atmosphere. At times the soil pores are filled with water, which displaces the soil atmosphere. Some soils or soil layers are aerobic, that is, the soil atmosphere contains oxygen, whereas others are anaerobic, that is, there is no free oxygen in the soil atmosphere. Even in aerobic soil layers, there are anoxic regions devoid of free oxygen (Sexstone et al. 1985) (Figure 9.33, p. 370). The oxygen content of the soil atmosphere determines in large part the types of metabolism that can occur and the chemical transformations that the indigenous microorganisms can carry out.

Concentrations of $CO_2$ in the soil atmosphere commonly are one to two orders of magnitude higher than in the above-ground air. The concentrations of both $CO_2$ and $O_2$ in the soil atmosphere are affected by gas diffusion and microbial respiration. Concentrations of $CO_2$ generally increase and $O_2$ concentrations decrease with depth in the soil column. In oxygen-deficient soils, other gases, including $CH_4$ from methanogenesis, and $H_2S$ from anaerobic sulfate reduction, occur in high concentrations in the soil atmosphere.

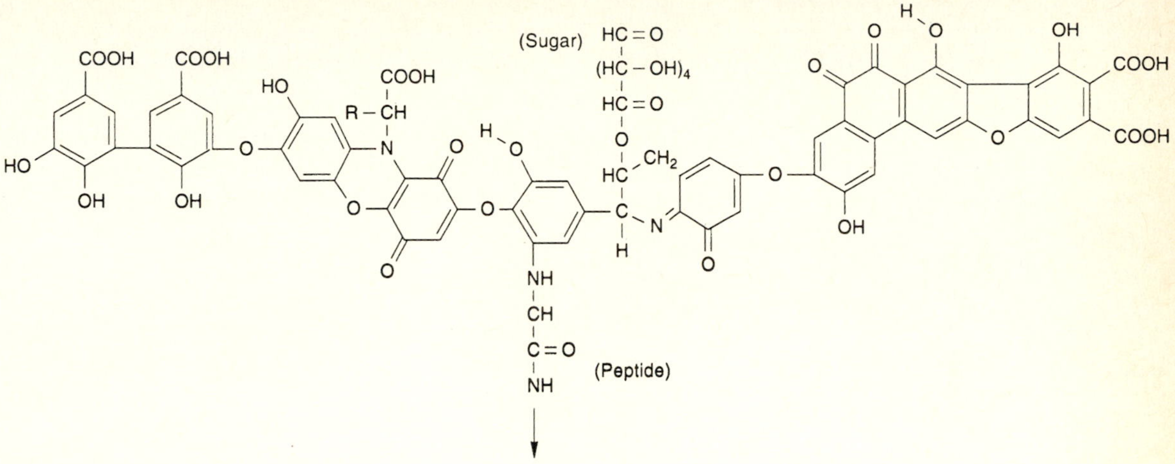

**Figure 9.32**
Proposed typical structure for humic acid. (Source: Stevenson 1976. *Bound and Conjugated Pesticide Residues.* Reprinted by permission, copyright American Chemical Society.)

**Soil Microbial Communities**   Soil is generally a favorable habitat for the proliferation of microorganisms, with microcolonies developing on soil particles (Figure 9.34, p. 370). Numbers of microorganisms in soil habitats (Table 9.11, p. 371) normally are much higher than those found in freshwater or marine habitats (Mishustin 1975). Typically, $10^6$–$10^9$ bacteria per gram are found in soil habitats. Microorganisms found in soil include viruses, bacteria, fungi, algae, and protozoa. Concentrations of organic matter are relatively high in soils, which favor the growth of heterotrophic microorganisms.

Sergei Winogradsky designated as "autochthonous" that part of the soil microbial community capable of utilizing refractory humic substances. Slow but constant activity is characteristic of these organisms, most of which are gram-negative rods and actinomycetes. Winogradsky contrasted zymogenous or opportunistic soil organisms with autochthonous microorganisms. The former generally are not able to utilize humic compounds, but exhibit high levels of activity and rapid growth on easily utilizable substrates that become available in the form of plant litter, animal droppings, and carcasses. Intermittent activity with inactive resting stages is characteristic of such zymogenous organisms. *Pseudomonas, Bacillus, Penicillium, Aspergillus,* and *Mucor* are some of the bacterial and fungal genera of typical zymogenous organisms.

Zymogenous is not, however, synonymous with allochthonous. Although only intermittently active, zymogenous organisms are true indigenous soil forms. The term *allochthonous* should be reserved for those

**Table 9.10**
Amounts of nutrients in temperate surface mineral soils

| Nutrient | Percentage per dry wt of soil |
|---|---|
| Organic matter | 0.40–10.0 |
| Nitrogen | 0.02–0.5 |
| Phosphorus | 0.01–0.2 |
| Potassium | 0.17–3.3 |
| Calcium | 0.07–3.6 |
| Magnesium | 0.12–1.5 |
| Sulfur | 0.01–0.2 |

Source: Brady 1984.

## Determining Soil Texture and Humic Acid Characteristics

Soil texture is important for both plant roots and the soil microbial community. Soils dominated by clay particles have a high water-holding capacity (WHC) and ion exchange capacity (IEC) but have a "heavy" texture. This means they do not drain well and get easily waterlogged and thus become anoxic. On the other extreme, soils dominated by sand have low WHC and IEC, dry out easily and are low in mineral nutrients, but drain well and stay aerobic.

With the aid of a soil triangle, the relative proportions of these particles are used in determining

**Figure A**

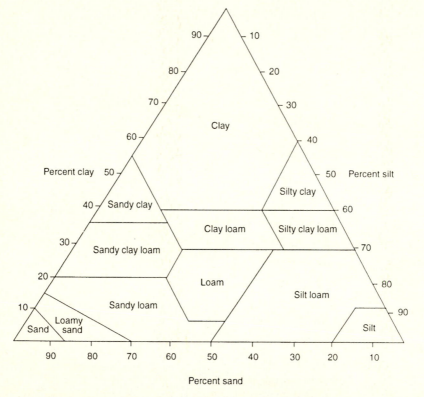

Soil texture triangle showing classes of soil based on proportions of sand, silt, and clay. To determine the class name, one line is drawn from the percent silt of the soil parallel to the percent clay side of the triangle, and another is drawn from the percent clay of the soil parallel to the percent sand side of the triangle. The class is given by the segment in which the two lines intersect. (Source: Alexander 1977. Reprinted by permission of John Wiley and Sons.)

the texture type of the soil (Figure A). Soils that are dominated by one size class of particles are named according to that class, that is, as sand soils, silt soils, or clay soils; soils not dominated by any specific particle size are called loams. Intermediate classes of soil texture are recognized—for example, sandy loam soils. Soils are often described by their texture and location, as in "Lakewood sand," "Nixon sandy loam," or "Georgia clay."

Soil organic matter (SOM) contributes to both WHC and IEC, but it is not considered in terms of texture classification. It is of prime importance to microbial life in soil. It forms a more or less permanent reservoir of organic carbon and chemically bound nutrient elements, including nitrogen and phosphorus. SOM also makes soil less sticky and contributes to good drainage and aeration. Therefore, maintaining soil organic matter is desirable. SOM includes microbial biomass, litter, and humus. Humic substances are nonliving polymerized and quite stable organic material, greatly transformed from the parent material. The turnover (degradation and resynthesis) of humus is slow, 5% or less per year in the temperate zone. Unfortunately, conventional farming practices tend to deplete soil humus, leading to lower fertility and increased soil erosion. Total SOM is usually determined as weight loss on ignition, that is, after converting organic carbon to $CO_2$. This is acceptable for most soils, but carbonates are also converted to oxides, causing additional weight loss. Therefore, this procedure is not suitable for high-carbonate soils.

According to their solubility characteristics, humic substances can be fractionated into fulvic acids, humic acids, and humin (Figure B). None of these fractions can be assigned a definite chemical structure; all three are randomly assembled irregular polymers. The main differences between fulvic and humic acids are that fulvic acids have a lower molecular weight, higher oxygen-to-carbon ratio, and higher ratio of acidic functional groups per weight, but the spectrum is continuous and the dividing line is arbitrary. Molecular weights range from about 700 to about 300,000. Humin is regarded as a strongly bound complex of fulvic and humic acids to mineral material rather than a class of compounds by itself. The alcohol-soluble hymatomelanic acid, a minor fraction, consists of esterified or methylated humic acids.

**Figure B**

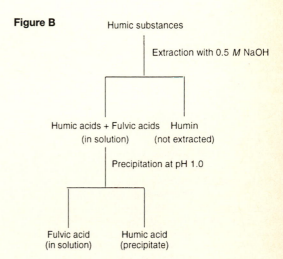

Fractionation of the major humic components of soil according to their solubilities.

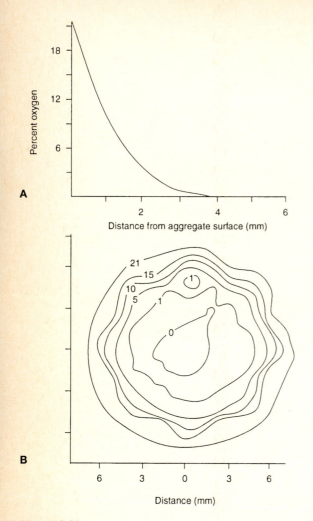

**Figure 9.33**
Oxygen concentrations within soil aggregates. (A) Oxygen profile from a cultivated silt loam soil aggregate showing the rapid decrease in oxygen concentration beneath the surface and the occurrence of an anaerobic zone. (B) Map of oxygen concentration within an aggregate from a cultivated soil. The profile reveals an anaerobic zone near the center of the aggregate. The numbers show percent oxygen contours. (Source: Sexstone et al. 1985.)

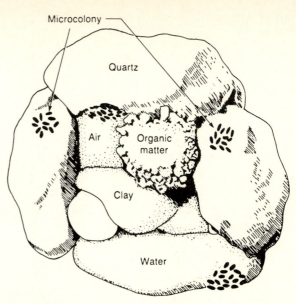

**Figure 9.34**
Soil aggregate showing microhabitats and patchy distribution of bacterial microcolonies. The section also shows the occurrence of water and air within pore spaces. (Source: Brock 1979. Reprinted by permission of Prentice Hall, Englewood Cliffs, NJ.)

may even be several microenvironmental situations that would favor different indigenous populations. In the rich litter horizons of surface soils, indigenous microorganisms tolerate and grow on high concentrations of organic nutrients. Bacteria found in soils may be obligate aerobes, facultative anaerobes, microaerophiles, or obligate anaerobes. Individual soils may favor bacterial populations with a particular type of metabolism. For example, anoxic conditions in flooded soils favor proliferation of facultative and obligate anaerobes.

Although it may not be possible to describe the general features of indigenous soil bacteria, the abiotic parameters of some soils restrict the microbial populations that can develop there. For example, some soils have extremely alkaline pH values, whereas others are extremely acidic. In such soils, the indigenous microbial populations must possess adaptive features that allow them to grow there. Polar soils are frozen much of the year; the indigenous microorganisms in

organisms, such as human and animal pathogens, that do not find suitable growth conditions in soil.

It is difficult to ascribe generalized adaptive features to the indigenous soil microbiota. Soils have many microhabitats, and at a particular location there

**Table 9.11**
The average number in viable counts of major groups of microorganisms in different soil types of the USSR

| Zone | Soils | Total number of microorganisms ($\times 10^6$/g) | Non-spore-forming bacteria (%) | Bacilli (%) | Actinomycetes (%) | Fungi (%) |
|---|---|---|---|---|---|---|
| Tundra and taiga | Tundra-gley and gley-podzolic | 2.1 | 94.9 | 0.7 | 1.5 | 2.9 |
| Forest meadow | Podzols and soddy-podzolic | 1.1 | 77.2 | 12.0 | 8.1 | 2.7 |
| Meadow steppe | Chenozems | 3.6 | 42.4 | 21.4 | 35.4 | 0.8 |
| Dry steppe | Chestnut | 3.5 | 45.4 | 19.4 | 34.6 | 0.6 |
| Desert steppe and desert | Brown and sierozems | 4.5 | 45.7 | 17.7 | 36.1 | 0.5 |

Source: Mishustin 1975.

such soils must be psychrophilic or psychrotrophic. Desert soils are usually hot and arid. Indigenous microorganisms in desert soils must be capable of withstanding long periods of desiccation and high temperatures. There are also cold deserts, such as within the dry valleys of Antarctica. Microorganisms in such dry habitats exhibit adaptations that permit their long-term survival (Friedmann 1993; Wynn-Williams 1990). Bacteria with adaptive features, such as the endospores of *Bacillus* species, are well suited for survival in such desert soils between the sporadic rains that provide sufficient water for growth.

Herman et al. (1995) examined the applicability of the resource island hypothesis to microbial populations in desert soils. According to this hypothesis, soil resources such as nitrogen, phosphorus, and water are distributed relatively evenly in grasslands but have a patchy distribution focused around plants in shrublands. This hypothesis predicts that microbial numbers will follow the available resources and, therefore, will be evenly distributed in grasslands but concentrated around individual plants in shrublands. They will be proportional to plant density when comparing the same vegetation type. Total heterotrophic bacteria and a subset guild of nitrogen-efficient bacteria in three shrublands and grasslands followed the distribution pattern predicted by the resource island

hypothesis. The grasslands samples showed no significant differences in numbers of heterotrophic bacteria or nitrogen-efficient bacteria in at-plant and inter-plant soil samples. Furthermore, populations were generally higher in nutrient-rich grasslands than nutrient-poor grasslands. In contrast, both numbers of heterotrophic bacteria and the guild of nitrogen-efficient bacteria were higher at shrubs than between shrubs in all three shrublands. These results suggest that resource abundance in resource islands predicts the distribution of heterotrophic bacterial numbers in desert soils.

Many bacterial genera occur in soil (Gray and Parkinson 1968). A higher proportion of gram-positive bacteria is found in soil than in marine or freshwater habitats, but in absolute numbers gram negatives predominate also in soil. A higher proportion of indigenous soil bacteria utilize substrates such as carbohydrates than do bacterial populations found in the hydrosphere. Common bacterial genera found in soil include *Acinetobacter, Agrobacterium, Alcaligenes, Arthrobacter, Bacillus, Brevibacterium, Caulobacter, Cellulomonas, Clostridium, Corynebacterium, Flavobacterium, Micrococcus, Mycobacterium, Pseudomonas, Staphylococcus, Streptococcus,* and *Xanthomonas.* There are wide differences in the relative proportions of individual bacterial genera found in particular soils (Alexander 1977) (Table 9.12).

**Table 9.12**
Relative proportions of aerobic, facultatively anaerobic bacterial genera commonly found in soils

| Genus | Percentage |
| --- | --- |
| *Arthrobacter* | 5–60 |
| *Bacillus* | 7–67 |
| *Pseudomonas* | 3–15 |
| *Agrobacterium* | 1–20 |
| *Alcaligenes* | 1–20 |
| *Flavobacterium* | 1–20 |
| *Corynebacterium* | 2–12 |
| *Micrococcus* | 2–10 |
| *Staphylococcus* | <5 |
| *Xanthomonas* | <5 |
| *Mycobacterium* | <5 |

Source: Alexander 1977.

Actinomycetes can compose 10–33% of the bacteria in the soil (Waksman 1961; Hattori and Hattori 1973; Alexander 1977). The genera *Streptomyces* and *Nocardia* are the most abundant. *Micromonospora, Actinomyces,* and many other actinomycetes are indigenous to soils but generally are present in low numbers. Actinomycetes are relatively resistant to desiccation and can survive under conditions of drought in desert soils. They favor alkaline or neutral pH and are sensitive to acidity. Myxobacteria are found in soils and on forest litter. Representative genera of myxobacteria found in soils include *Myxococcus, Chondrococcus, Archangium,* and *Polyangium.*

Important photoautotrophic bacterial populations in soil include the cyanobacterial species *Anabaena, Calothrix, Chroococcus, Cylindrospermum, Lyngbya, Microcoleus, Nodularia, Nostoc, Oscillatoria, Phormidium, Plectonema, Schizothrix, Scytonema,* and *Tolypothrix.* Some of these species, such as *Nostoc,* provide both fixed forms of nitrogen and organic carbon in some soil habitats. Availability of fixed forms of nitrogen is an important limiting factor in soil for microbial activities and growth of higher plants.

Cyanobacteria form surface crusts on soils bare of plant growth and contribute to soil stabilization. *Azotobacter* is an important heterotrophic free-living soil bacterium, capable of converting atmospheric nitrogen to fixed forms of nitrogen. Some anaerobic *Clostridium* species also fix nitrogen in soil; *Rhizobium* and the slower growing *Bradyrhizobium* fix atmospheric nitrogen within the nodules of certain plant roots. Several chemolithotrophic bacteria perform transformations of inorganic compounds that are essential for the maintenance of soil fertility.

Allochthonous microorganisms may reach soil habitats from a variety of sources, entering from the air or the hydrosphere or in association with plant or animal material. For example, some plant pathogens enter with diseased plant tissue. Species of *Agrobacterium, Corynebacterium, Erwinia, Pseudomonas,* and *Xanthomonas* frequently enter the soil together with infected plant material. Some allochthonous microorganisms enter with animal droppings or sewage. Some of these bacteria are pathogens. For example, fecal streptococci and *Salmonella* species are found in soils contaminated with sewage. Normally, allochthonous bacteria are rapidly eliminated from soil, but occasionally they do survive for prolonged periods. Endospores and other resistant forms of microorganisms are able to survive in a dormant state, even in dry soils.

Fungi constitute a high proportion of the microbial biomass in soil (Gilman 1945; Domsch et al. 1980). Most types of fungi can be found in soil, mostly as indigenous and sometimes as allochthonous organisms. Soil fungi may occur as free-living organisms or in mycorrhizal association with plant roots. Fungi are found primarily in the top 10 cm of the soil and are rarely found below 30 cm. They are most abundant in well-aerated and acidic soils.

The most frequently isolated fungi from soils are members of fungi imperfecti, such as species of *Aspergillus, Geotrichum, Penicillium,* and *Trichoderma,* but numerous ascomycetes and basidiomycetes also occur in high numbers (Table 9.13). Some soil fungi, especially those found in association with plant roots, are difficult if not impossible to isolate and identify.

Yeasts are common in most soils. As with the filamentous fungi, most indigenous soil yeasts are fungi imperfecti (Deuteromycota). Species of the genera *Candida, Rhodotorula,* and *Cryptococcus* are probably the most abundant indigenous yeasts in the soil. Species of *Lipomyces, Schwanniomyces, Kluyveromyces, Schizoblastosporion, Hansenula, Candida,* and *Cryptococcus* have been isolated exclusively from soils. The fact that these organisms have been found only in soils implies, but does not prove, that soil is their natural habitat. Many other yeasts are allochthonous organisms in soil, often entering with plant materials.

Most fungi in soil are opportunistic (zymogenous). They grow and carry out active metabolism when conditions are favorable, which implies adequate moisture, adequate aeration, and relatively high concentrations of utilizable substrates. Many soil fungi metabolize carbohydrates, including polysaccharides, and even allochthonous fungi that enter the soil can often grow on the major components of plant residues; relatively few fungal species, though, are able to degrade lignin (Garrett 1981).

Dormancy is a typical condition of soil fungi. Some fungi have been shown to remain dormant but viable for decades. In the absence of available substrates, they are inactive. Numerous fungi occur in soil as specialized dormant structures, which include sporangiospores, conidia, oospores, ascospores, basidiospores, chlamydospores, and sclerotia. Fungal mycelia may also be metabolically inactive in soil.

In soil, widespread inhibitory effects on germination of fungal spores, known as soil fungistasis, are evident (Lockwood 1977; Lockwood and Filonow 1981). Fungistasis occurs in most soils except some deep subsoils, highly acidic soils, and cold-dominated soils. The addition of readily decomposable organic materials reverses soil fungistasis. With the reversal of fungistasis, fungal spores and other propagules germinate, and fungal mycelia resume active growth. Soil fungistasis appears to be associated with microbial activity; sterilization eliminates fungistasis. The nature of the fungistatic agent(s), however, remains to be identified.

The great absorptive capacity of soil and its numerous microhabitats strongly influence interac-

**Table 9.13**
Some representative genera of filamentous soil fungi

| Lower fungi | Fungi imperfecti |
|---|---|
| *Rhizopus* | *Phoma* |
| *Mucor* | *Cephalosporium* |
| *Allomyces* | *Geotrichum* |
| *Saprolegnia* | *Aspergillus* |
| *Pythium* | *Penicillium* |
| | *Aureobasidium* |
| Basidiomycetes | *Cladosporium* |
| *Agaricus* | *Helminthosporium* |
| *Amanita* | *Alternaria* |
| *Coprinus* | *Fusarium* |
| *Rhizoctonia* | *Trichoderma* |
| *Russula* | *Arthrobotrys* |
| *Boletus* | |
| Ascomycetes | |
| *Morchella* | |

tions between soil bacteria and fungi. For example, the presence or absence of montmorillonite-type clay, with its great absorptive and water-holding capacity, was shown to be the decisive factor in the outcome of some survival and competition experiments. Stotzky (1965) devised an ingenious adaptation of the replica-plating technique to study microbial interactions directly in soil. Sterilized soil was enclosed in a petri dish, inoculated at marked points with selected microorganisms, and incubated. Periodically, the soil was sampled by an array of sterile stainless steel needles mounted on a disk to make a brush- or nail-board type of device. This sampling device was subsequently touched to an agar medium, on which a colony pattern developed, replicating the distribution of the microorganisms in the soil. If colony morphology was insufficient to distinguish the interacting microorganisms, agar plates of diagnostic media were used. The spatial and temporal pattern of microbial growth obtained using this technique has revealed numerous positive and negative interactions to be influenced by the soil matrix.

**Table 9.14**
Annual decomposition by fungi and productivity of plants in Alaska

| Site | Decomposition $g/m^2/yr$ | % wt loss cellulose | Measured primary productivity $g/m^2/yr$ | Indicated rate of organic accumulation $g/m^2/yr$ |
|---|---|---|---|---|
| Tundra | 310 | 3.3 | 275 | −35 |
| Taiga | 235 | 3.4 | 203 | −32 |
| Birch forest | 350 | 5.2 | 375 | +25 |
| Spruce forest | 198 | 3.4 | 180 | −18 |

Source: Flanagan 1978.

A number of genera of algae inhabit the soil, living both on the soil surface and within the soil (Trainor 1978). Algae found in soil include members of Chlorophycophyta, Rhodophycophyta, Euglenophycophyta, and Chrysophycophyta. Most soil algae can be found growing on the soil surface or within the top millimeters of the soil, where up to $10^6$ algal cells per gram sometimes are found. Algae that are indigenous at the soil surface may move into the subsurface soil horizons, where they become allochthonous organisms and where other organisms consume them. The majority of soil algae are small and unicellular.

Free-living protozoa are found in most soil samples. Soil protozoa are small in size and low in diversity as compared to those in aquatic environments. Before a protozoan is designated as a soil form, its vegetative stage must be found in the soil; the cysts of non-soil protozoans often enter soil ecosystems. Flagellate protozoa are dominant in terrestrial habitats. Protozoan populations of soils are generally $10^4$–$10^5$ organisms per gram. Protozoa are generally found in greatest abundance near the surface of the soil, within the top 15 cm. Most protozoa require relatively high concentrations of oxygen; this limits their distribution within the soil column. Protozoa are important predators on soil bacteria and algae.

As in aquatic environments, microorganisms in soil are agents of biodegradation and mineral recycling. Important plant polymers such as cellulose and lignin are generally recycled by microbial activity (Flanagan 1978) (Table 9.14). In surface soils where plants are growing, numbers and diversity of heterotrophic microorganisms, especially of bacteria and fungi, are unusually high. Of great importance are nitrogen-fixing and mycorrhizal associations between microorganisms and higher plants. But unlike aquatic environments, in the soil environment higher plants dominate and microorganisms play a very subordinate role in primary production.

## CHAPTER SUMMARY

Habitats are the physical locations where microorganisms live; because of their small size the habitats of many microorganisms occur on a microscale and are viewed as microhabitats. Autochthonous microorganisms fill functional roles called *niches* in their habitats. Other microorganisms are allochthonous, or foreign, to the ecosystem; they may survive for varying periods of time but are viewed as transients that do not fill the ecological niches of that ecosystem.

The ecosphere where organisms live is divided into the atmosphere (air), hydrosphere (water), and lithosphere (soil) environments. The atmosphere is not known to support autochthonous microbial populations, but it serves as a medium for the rapid and global dispersal of many types of microorganisms.

# Extreme Habitats

There are extreme habitats on Earth where conditions of temperature, pH, salinity, pressure, desiccation, and other physical and chemical factors once were thought to prevent life but where we now know some highly specialized microorganisms flourish (Edwards 1990; Horikoshi and Grant 1991; Postgate 1994). Microorganisms growing in such habitats evolved under conditions that permitted their survival and growth. They multiplied in accordance with natural selection. For such adapted microorganisms the conditions of these habitats are not "extreme" but rather the normal physiological conditions for their growth in their natural habitats. The adaptive properties of many of these extremophiles were discussed in Chapter 8. Clearly, microorganisms have adapted to life at high and low temperatures, alkaline and acidic conditions, high salt concentrations, and high pressures. These microorganisms and the habitats in which they live have been extensively studied because they represent the environmental limits to life.

Cold environments prevail in the polar regions and also through most of the world's oceans. Most marine environments are at temperatures less than 5°C, and temperatures of −1.8°C, the freezing point of seawater, are common. In these cold environments, microorganisms typically grow slowly and their populations usually are lower than in temperate regions. The cold benthic regions of the oceans exemplify habitats where microorganisms grow at slow rates with generation times of many hours or even days as opposed to less than half an hour for a typical enteric bacterium living in the gut of a warm-blooded animal. The slow metabolic rates of microorganisms in cold benthic marine habitats

were demonstrated when the deep-diving submarine *Alvin* sank with its hatch open; when recovered a few months later, the meat sandwiches and broth that the crew had packed were still unspoiled. Barophiles and psychrophiles that dominate the very deep cold benthic habitats have slow rates of metabolism.

Interestingly, in polar seas psychrotrophs rather than psychrophiles are the dominant bacterial populations. Physiological versatility, rather than a high degree of specialization, appears to be critical for the long-term survival of microbial populations in these cold habitats. Most of the microorganisms in polar coastal seas are capable of utilizing numerous organic substrates, primarily carbohydrates. During the summer when photosynthetic microorganisms—such as diatoms growing on the subsurface of sea ice—are active during the period of continuous sunlight, carbohydrates serve as primary substrates. Proteins and lipids dominate during the dark winter months from detrital food webs. Pigmented microorganisms dominate the surface layers of snow and ice, presumably because they are protected against ultraviolet radiation of the continuous summer sunlight.

Soil temperatures in polar terrestrial habitats are even colder. Tundra soils are well under 0°C most of the year, with a permafrost layer beneath the soils. Lichens and other microorganisms adapted to slow growth and survival under extreme conditions predominate in these polar habitats. In many Arctic terrestrial habitats, lichens are the main groundcover and serve as the principal food source for caribou and reindeer. The Antarctic dry valleys represent even more extreme habitats that challenge the abilities of microorganisms to survive

*(continued)*

## Extreme Habitats, continued

under cold and dry conditions. In those habitats many microorganisms are endolithic, meaning that they grow within rocks where they are partially protected from the hostile cold and desiccating conditions of those habitats. Yeasts with high lipid concentrations and endospore-forming bacteria are commonly found in polar soils. Endospore-forming bacteria also commonly occur in hot deserts. The ability to remain dormant during prolonged periods of drought allows these bacteria to survive. When water is available, the endospores germinate and the bacteria reproduce.

Thermophilic bacteria and hyperthermophilic archaea also grow in many very hot habitats, including areas of volcanic activity, such as the deep-sea thermal vents, and thermal springs, such as the hot sulfur pools of Yellowstone National Park in the United States and surrounding Rotorua in New Zealand. Temperatures can be well above 100°C in the deep-sea habitats. Extremely thermophilic archaea grow optimally at such high temperatures; some, such as *Pyrodictium brockii* and *Pyrococcus furiosus,* have optimal growth temperatures of 105–110°C. Diverse populations of archaea have been found in hot springs, such as the Obsidian Pool of Yellowstone National Park where the temperatures are 74–93°C (Barns et al. 1996). Some archaea, such as *Sulfolobus* and *Acidianus* species, use inorganic sulfur compounds and chemolithotrophic metabolism to grow in these habitats. Extremely thermophilic bacteria, such as *Thermus aquaticus,* also grow in hot spring pools. Thermophiles grow in the less hot pools with temperatures over 40°C that surround the regions of geothermal activity. *Bacillus stearothermophilus* is often the dominant bacterial species in hot springs in temperature zones of 55–70°C, but many other thermophiles, including thermophilic cyanobacteria and algae, also occur in such hot spring habitats. Cyanobacteria often form dense layers of growth at specific temperature zones within thermal spring habitats.

---

Many microorganisms produce spores that are transported through the atmosphere; their dormant state permits survival during air transport where they must exhibit resistance to desiccation and solar radiation.

Compared to the atmosphere, the hydrosphere is far more suitable for microbial growth. The hydrosphere contains autochthonous microbial populations, most of which are motile and can grow at low nutrient concentrations. Freshwater habitats include lakes, ponds, swamps, springs, streams, and rivers. Large microbial populations typically are found in the neuston, which occurs at the air-water interface. Photosynthetic microorganisms are important members of the neuston and the underlying water column where light penetrates. Algae and cyanobacteria typically occur nearer the surface, and anaerobic photosynthetic bacteria occur at greater depths of lakes. These photosynthetic microorganisms also occur in the sediments of the littoral zone, where light penetrates to the bottom. In deeper waters, decompositional activity dominates below the compensation depth, which is the depth where photosynthetic productivity equals respiratory decomposition. Many lakes are characterized by thermal stratification with vastly different microbial populations inhabiting the epilimnion and hypolimnion above and below the thermocline, respectively.

Many of the sulfur hot springs are also characterized by low pH because of the formation of sulfuric acid from the microbial oxidation of elemental sulfur and reduced sulfur compounds. Some archaea, such as *Sulfolobus acidocaldarius,* grow in acidic habitats with pH less than 2.0. *Picrophilus* species grow in dry, extremely acidic (pH < 0.5) soil habitats of Japan that are heated by solfataric gases to about 55°C; these archaea grow optimally at 60°C and pH 0.7. Acidophilic bacteria, such as *Thiobacillus thiooxidans,* grow in cooler but highly acidic habitats; most thiobacilli exhibit optimal growth at pH 2.0. At the other extreme of pH, there are numerous alkaline lakes with pH values greater than 9.0. Soils with high concentrations of sodium carbonate can also have pH values of 9.0–11.0. Alkaliphilic bacterial and archaeal populations live in such habitats, growing optimally at pH values above 8.5. Some alkaline lakes are also characterized by high salt concentrations. Extremely halophilic and alkaliphilic archaea, such as *Natronobacterium* and *Natronococcus,* grow optimally at pH 10.0 or above. Other nonalkaliphilic archaea, such as *Halobacterium, Halococcus, Haloarcula,* and *Haloferax,* grow in saline lakes and soils at pH values near neutrality. For growth these halophiles require at least 1.5 $M$ NaCl, which is readily found in saline habitats.

Other extreme habitats include those lacking oxygen, those with very low nutrient concentrations, and those with high levels of toxic heavy metals or high-intensity radiation. The environmental conditions of each of these habitats limits the diversity of microbial populations that can survive. Yet in each, some microbial populations have evolved adaptations that permit their growth, so that virtually all habitats on Earth, including the extreme habitats, have their characteristic microbial populations. The announcement of the new journal *Extremophiles* reflects the increasing scientific interest in those microorganisms.

---

Microorganisms play a key role both in lake productivity and in the transformation of organic compounds within a lake. Fungi and bacteria in freshwater ecosystems are also largely responsible for the decomposition of allochthonous organic matter. Members of the genera *Achromobacter, Flavobacterium, Brevibacterium, Micrococcus, Bacillus, Pseudomonas, Nocardia, Streptomyces, Micromonospora, Cytophaga, Spirillum,* and *Vibrio* occur widely in lake water; stalked bacteria, such as *Caulobacter* and *Hyphomicrobium,* are associated with submerged surfaces. The principal ecological functions of microorganisms in freshwater environments include decomposition of dead organic matter, liberating mineral nutrients for primary production; assimilation and reintroduction into the food web of dissolved organic matter; mineral cycling activities; primary productivity; and supplying biomass as a food source for grazers.

The oceans occupy 71% of the Earth's surface, providing vast marine habitats. Microorganisms are the principal producers as well as decomposers in the world's oceans. In marine habitats planktonic microorganisms have a nearly exclusive role in primary production. Higher plants and benthic macroalgae contribute significantly to primary production only in estuaries and littoral areas. Freshwater mixes with marine waters in estuaries, which are characteristically more productive than either the ocean or the freshwater input. Photosynthesis in estuaries almost always exceeds respiratory activities. Estuaries have high populations of semisubmerged higher plants such as grassy *Spartina* species in temperate salt marshes and the mangrove forests in tropical estuaries. Decomposer bacterial and fungal populations are very important in these coastal estuaries.

Whereas conditions within estuaries experience daily tidal fluctuations that radically alter environmental conditions, open ocean environments are characteristically stable: average conditions include salinity of 35 parts per thousand, pH 8.3–8.5, temperatures below the 100-m depth of 0–5°C, and surface water temperature fluctuations of less than 20°C. Within the marine environment, there is a littoral or intertidal zone, a neritic or nearshore zone that extends over the continental shelf, and an oceanic (pelagic) zone that extends outward from the continental shelf; there are epipelagic zones of open water and benthic habitats, some of which occur in trenches at great depths. Each of these represent distinct habitats that harbor characteristic marine microbial populations. Most marine bacteria are gram-negative and motile. In the pelagic zone all primary production is carried out by microscopic algae and bacteria. Rates of productivity are limited by concentrations of phosphates and fixed forms of nitrogen and iron. Chemolithotrophic bacteria are involved in nitrogen cycling in marine waters. Nutrient availability is extremely important in determining microbial productivity in these marine habitats. Marine algae and cyanobacteria supply an essential input of carbon to the marine ecosystem. In many cases, though, heterotrophic marine bacteria live under conditions of near starvation. Hence most autochthonous marine bacteria are capable of growth at very low nutrient concentrations. Exceptions are

the coral reefs, where productivity by endozoic photosynthetic microorganisms provides ample organic resources, and the deep-sea thermal vents, where chemolithotrophic microorganisms convert reduced sulfur compounds into large amounts of biomass.

Soils are heterogeneous habitats where dense and diverse microbial populations grow. Soil is generally a favorable habitat for the proliferation of microorganisms, with microcolonies developing on soil particles. Soils have many microhabitats, and at any particular location there may be multiple microenvironmental situations that favor various different indigenous populations. In soils, microorganisms play a subordinate role to plants as primary producers, but they have a critical role in organic matter decomposition and mineral cycling. Microbial metabolism in soils is essential for maintaining soil fertility for plant growth. Actinomycetes, and other autochthonous microbes, grow slowly in soils, decomposing complex organic compounds (humic substances). Fungi also are critical decomposers in soil habitats. Compared to aquatic habitats, fungal populations are far more important in soils. Many soil fungi are zymogenous (opportunistic) and grow on fresh plant materials that enter the soil. Some fungi form dormant spores that persist in soils for long time periods.

There are some extreme habitats on Earth where condition of temperature, pH, salinity, pressure, desiccation, and other physical and chemical factors challenge the abilities of microorganisms to survive and to grow. Extremophiles have developed adaptive properties that permit their growth in dry desert soils, cold polar regions, saline lakes, deep-sea thermal vent regions, hot springs, alkaline lakes, and other habitats with extreme physical and chemical conditions. These microorganisms and the habitats in which they live have been extensively studied because they represent the environmental limits to life.

## STUDY QUESTIONS

1. What is a habitat? How does a habitat differ from a niche?

2. Describe the atmosphere with reference to the conditions that limit microbial growth in the air.

3. What properties are important for dispersal of microorganisms through the atmosphere?

4. What properties favor survival of microorganisms in the atmosphere?

5. Can microorganisms grow in clouds?

6. Describe the characteristics of freshwater habitats.

7. What ecological functions do microorganisms play in lakes?

8. Where do photosynthetic microorganisms occur in lakes?

9. What are salt marshes? What important ecological roles do microorganisms play in salt marshes?

10. What is an estuary? Why must estuarine microbial populations exhibit dynamic properties with respect to salt and temperature tolerances?

11. How would you define a "true marine bacterium"?

12. Describe the horizontal and vertical zones of the oceans.

13. What is the difference between the neuston and the pleuston?

14. Describe the role of endozoic algae in coral reefs.

15. Describe the roles of chemolithotrophs in deep-sea thermal vent habitats.

16. What limits productivity in the seas? Why are most marine microorganisms in a condition of near starvation?

17. Define *soil* and *soil fertility*. What roles do microorganisms play in determining soil fertility?

18. Compare the roles of fungi in soil and marine habitats.

19. What is a microhabitat? Why are microhabitats important in soils?

20. What is an extreme habitat? Give examples of hot, cold, dry, saline, acidic, and alkaline habitats. How do microorganisms survive in such extreme habitats? What ecological roles do they play in each of these extreme habitats?

## REFERENCES AND SUGGESTED READINGS

Ainsworth, G. C., and A. S. Sussman. 1968. *The Fungi.* Vol. 3, *The Fungal Population.* Academic Press, New York.

Alexander, M. 1977. *Introduction to Soil Microbiology.* Ed 2. Wiley, New York.

Andersen, A. A. 1958. New sampler for the collection, sizing, and enumeration of viable airborne particles. *Journal of Bacteriology* 76:471–484.

Anikouchine, W. A., and R. W. Sternberg. 1973. *The World Ocean.* Prentice Hall, Englewood Cliffs, NJ.

Barnes, R.S.K., and K. H. Mann. 1980. *Fundamentals of Aquatic Ecosystems.* Blackwell, Oxford, England.

Barns, S. M., C. F. Delwiche, J. D. Palmer, and N. R. Pace. 1996. Perspectives on archaeal diversity, thermophily, and monopholy from environmental RNA sequences. *Proceedings of the National Academy of Sciences USA* 93:9188–9193.

Baylor, E. R., V. Peters, and M. B. Baylor. 1977. Water-to-air transfer of virus. *Science* 197:763–764.

Bear, F. E. 1964. *Chemistry of the Soil.* Rheinhold, New York.

Belser, L. W. 1979. Population ecology of nitrifying bacteria. *Annual Review of Microbiology* 33:309–334.

Blanchard, D. C., and L. Syzdek. 1970. Mechanism for the water-to-air transfer and concentration of bacteria. *Science* 170:626–628.

Boney, A. D. 1966. *The Biology of Marine Algae.* Hutchinson Educational, London.

Bovallius, A., B. Bucht, R. Roffey, and P. Anas. 1978. Three-year investigation of the natural airborne bacterial flora at four locations in Sweden. *Applied and Environmental Microbiology* 35:847–852.

Bowden, J., P. H. Gregory, and C. G. Johnson. 1971. Possible wind transport of coffee leaf rust across the Atlantic Ocean. *Nature* (London) 229:500–501.

Brady, N. C. 1984. *The Nature and Properties of Soils.* Macmillan, New York.

Brewer, A. 1994. *The Science of Ecology.* Ed 2. Saunders, Philadelphia, PA, pp. 589–598.

Brock, T. D. 1978. *Thermophilic Microorganisms and Life at High Temperatures.* Springer-Verlag, New York.

Brock, T. D. 1979. *Biology of Microorganisms.* Prentice Hall, Englewood Cliffs, NJ.

Brodie, H. J. 1951. The splash-cup dispersal mechanism in plants. *Canadian Journal of Botany* 29:224–231.

Broecker, W. S. 1974. *Chemical Oceanography.* Harcourt Brace Jovanovich, New York.

Buckman H. O., and N. C. Brady. 1969. *The Nature of Properties of Soils.* Macmillan, New York.

Buller, A.H.R. 1909. *Researches on Fungi.* Vol. I. Longmans, Green, and Co., London.

Buller, A.H.R. 1934. *Researches on Fungi.* Vol. VI. Longmans, Green, and Co., London.

Burns, R. G. 1979. Interaction of microorganisms, their substrates and their products with soil surfaces. In D. C. Ellwood, J. Melling, and P. Rutter (eds.). *Adhesion of Microorganisms to Surfaces.* Academic Press, London, pp. 109–138.

Button, D. K., F. Schut, Q. Pham, R. Martin, and B. R. Robertson. 1993. Viability and isolation of marine bacteria by dilution culture: Theory, procedures, and initial results. *Applied and Environmental Microbiology* 59:881–891.

Cairns, J. (ed.). 1970. *The Structure and Function of Freshwater Microbial Communities.* American Microscopical Society Symposium, Research Division Monograph 3. Virginia Polytech Institute and State University, Blacksburg.

Caldwell, D. E. 1977. The planktonic microflora of lakes. *Critical Reviews in Microbiology* 5:305–370.

Cheng, L. 1975. Marine pleuston: Animals at the sea-air interface. *Annual Reviews in Oceanography and Marine Biology* 13:181–212.

Cole, G. A. 1983. *Textbook of Limnology.* Mosby, St. Louis, MO.

Colwell, R. R., and R. Y. Morita (eds.). 1972. *Effects of the Ocean Environment on Microbial Activities.* University Park Press, Baltimore.

David, P. M. 1965. The surface fauna of the ocean. *Endeavor* 24:95–100.

Dawes, C. J. 1974. *Marine Algae of the West Coast of Florida.* University of Miami Press, Coral Gables, FL.

Day, J. H. 1950. The ecology of South African estuaries. Part 1 of a review of estuaries in general. *Transactions of the Royal Society of South Africa* 33:53–91.

Denton, E. J. 1963. Buoyancy mechanisms of sea creatures. *Endeavour* 22:3–8.

DiSalvo, L. H. 1971. Regenerative functions and microbial ecology of the coral reefs: Labeled bacteria in a coral reef microcosm. *Journal of Experimental Marine Biology and Ecology* 7:123–136.

Domsch, K. H., W. Gams, and T. H. Anderson. 1980. *Compendium of Soil Fungi.* Academic Press, New York.

Ducklow, H. W., and C. A. Carlson. 1992. Oceanic bacterial production. *Advances in Microbial Ecology* 12:113–182.

Dundas, I. D., and H. Larsen. 1962. The physiological role of carotenoid pigments of *Halobacterium salinarium. Archiv für Mikrobiologie* (Berlin) 44:233–239.

Edmonds, R. L. (ed.). 1979. *Aerobiology: The Ecological Systems Approach.* Dowden, Hutchinson and Ross, Stroudsburg, PA.

Edwards, C. 1990. *Microbiology of Extreme Environments.* McGraw-Hill, New York.

Falconer, I. R. (ed.). 1993. *Algal Toxins in Seafood and Drinking Water.* Academic Press, New York.

Fenchel, T. 1969. The ecology of marine microbenthos. Part IV. *Ophelia* 6:1–182.

Flanagan, P. W. 1978. Microbial decomposition in Arctic tundra and subarctic taiga ecosystems. In M. W. Loutit and J.A.R. Miles (eds.). *Microbial Ecology.* Springer-Verlag, New York, pp. 161–169.

Fletcher, M. 1979. The attachment of bacteria to surfaces in aquatic environments. In D. C. Ellwood, J. Melling, and P. Rutter (eds). *Adhesion of Microorganisms to Surfaces.* Academic Press, London, pp. 87–108.

Ford, T. E. (ed.). 1993. *Aquatic Microbiology: An Ecological Approach.* Blackwell, Oxford, England.

Fredrickson, J. K. 1992. DOE explores subsurface biosphere. *ASM News* 58:183.

Friedmann, I. (ed.). 1993. *Antarctic Microbiology,* Wiley-Liss, New York.

Garrett, S. D. 1981. *Soil Fungi and Soil Fertility: An Introduction to Soil Mycology.* Pergamon Press, Elmsford, New York.

Gilman, J. C. 1945. *A Manual of Soil Fungi.* Collegiate Press, Ames, IA.

Gray, T.R.G., and D. Parkinson. 1968. *The Ecology of Soil Bacteria.* University of Toronto Press, Toronto, Canada.

Gregory, P. H. 1973. *The Microbiology of the Atmosphere.* Wiley, New York.

Harvey, H. W. 1957. *The Chemistry and Fertility of Sea Waters.* Cambridge University Press, Cambridge, England.

Hattori, T., and R. Hattori. 1973. *Microbial Life in the Soil: An Introduction.* Marcel Dekker, New York.

Hattori, T., and R. Hattori. 1976. The physical environment in soil microbiology: An attempt to extend principles of microbiology to soil microorganisms. *Critical Reviews in Microbiology* 4:423–462.

Herman, R. P., K. R. Provencio, J. Herrera-Matos, and R. J. Torrez. 1995. Resource island predict the distribution of heterotrophic bacteria in Chihuahua desert soils. *Applied and Environmental Microbiology* 61:1816–1821.

Hirst, J. M., O. J. Stedman, and G. W. Hurst. 1967. Long-distance spore transport: Vertical sections of spore clouds over the sea. *Journal of General Microbiology* 48:357–377.

Holm-Hansen, O. 1969. Determination of microbial biomass in ocean profiles. *Limnology and Oceanography* 14:740–747.

Horikoshi, K., and W. D. Grant. 1991. *Superbugs: Microorganisms in Extreme Environments,* Springer-Verlag, New York.

Hughes, G. C. 1975. Studies on fungi in oceans and estuaries since 1961. Part I. *Lignicolous, Caulicolous, and Foliicolous* species. *Annual Review of Oceanography and Marine Biology* 13:69–180.

Hutchinson, G. E. 1957. *A Treatise on Limnology.* Wiley, New York.

Hynes, H.B.N. 1970. *Ecology of Running Waters.* Liverpool University Press, Liverpool, England.

Ingold, C. T. 1971. *Fungal Spores: Their Liberation and Dispersal.* Clarendon Press, Oxford, England.

Isaacs, J. P. 1969. The nature of oceanic life. *Scientific American* 221:147–162.

Jannasch, H. W. 1979. Microbial turnover of organic matter in the deep sea. *BioScience* 29:228–232.

Jannasch, H. W., and C. O. Wirsen. 1977. Microbial life in the deep sea. *Scientific American* 236(6):42–52.

Jensen, W. A., and F. B. Salisbury. 1972. *Botany: An Ecological Approach.* Wadsworth, Belmont, CA.

Johannes, R. E. 1967. Ecology of organic aggregates in the vicinity of coral reef. *Limnology and Oceanography* 12:189–195.

Johnson, T. W., and F. K. Sparrow, Jr. 1961. *Fungi in Oceans and Estuaries.* Hafner, New York.

Kaneko, T., M. I. Krichevsky, and R. M. Atlas. 1979. Numerical taxonomy of bacteria from the Beaufort Sea. *Journal of General Microbiology* 110:111–125.

Karl, D. M. 1978. Distribution, abundance, and metabolic state of microorganisms in the water column and sediments of the Black Sea. *Limnology and Oceanography* 23:936–949.

Karl, D. M., and O. Holm-Hansen. 1978. Methodology and measurement of adenylate energy charge ratios of environmental samples. *Marine Biology* 48:185–197.

Kriss, A. E., I. E. Mishustina, N. Mitskerich, and E. U. Zemetsora. 1967. *Microbial Population of Oceans and Seas.* Edward Arnold, London.

Kuznetsov, S. I. 1959. *Die Rolle der Mikroorganismen im Stroffkreislauf der Seen.* VEB Deutscher Verlag für die Wissenschaften, Berlin.

Kuznetsov, S. I. 1970. *Microflora of Lakes and Their Geochemical Activity* (in Russian). Izdatel'otro Nauka, Leningrad.

Kuznetsov, S. I., G. A. Dubinina, and N. A. Lapteva. 1979. Biology of oligotrophic bacteria. *Annual Review of Microbiology* 33:377–388.

Litchfield, C. D. 1976. *Marine Microbiology*. Benchmark Papers in Microbiology, Vol. 11. Academic Press, New York.

Lockwood, J. L. 1977. Fungistasis in soils. *Biological Reviews* 52:1–43.

Lockwood, J. L., and A. B. Filonow. 1981. Responses of fungi to nutrient-limiting conditions and to inhibitory substances in natural habitats. *Advances in Microbial Ecology* 5:1–62.

Lodder, J. 1971. *The Yeasts*. North Holland Publishing, Amsterdam.

Lovelace, T. E., H. Tubiash, and R. R. Colwell. 1967. Quantitative and qualitative commensal bacterial flora of *Crassostrea virginica* in Chesapeake Bay. *Proceedings of the National Shellfisheries Association* 58:82–87.

Macleod, R. A. 1965. The question of the existence of specific marine bacteria. *Bacteriological Reviews* 29:9–23.

Marshall, K. C. 1976. *Interfaces in Microbial Ecology*. Harvard University Press, Cambridge, MA.

Marshall, K. C. 1980. Adsorption of microorganisms to soils and sediments. In G. Bitton and K. C. Marshall (eds.). *Adsorption of Microorganisms to Surfaces*. Wiley, New York, pp. 317–329.

Mathews, M. M., and W. R. Sistrom. 1959. Function of carotenoid pigments in non-photosynthetic bacteria. *Nature* (London) 184:1892–1893.

McKissich, G. E., L. G. Wolfe, R. L. Farrell, R. A. Greisemer, and A. Hellman. 1970. Aerosol transmission of oncogenic viruses. In I. H. Silver (ed.). *Aerobiology: Proceedings of the Third International Symposium*. Academic Press, New York, pp. 233–237.

McLean, R. C. 1918. Bacteria of ice and snow in Antarctica. *Nature* (London) 102:35–39.

Meier, F. C. 1935. Microorganisms in the atmosphere of Arctic regions. *Phytopathology* 25:27.

Meredith, D. S. 1962. Spore discharge in *Cordana musae* (Zimm) Hohnel and *Zygosporium oscheoides* Mont. *Annals of Botany* (London), Part II 26:233–241.

Metting, F. B., Jr. 1993. *Soil Microbial Ecology: Applications in Agricultural and Environmental Management*. Marcel Dekker, New York.

Micheli, P. A. 1729. *Novum Plantarum Genera Florentine*. Florence.

Miller, O. K. 1972. *Mushrooms of North America*. Dutton, New York.

Mishustin, E. N. 1975. Microbial associations of soil types. *Microbial Ecology* 2:97–118.

Mitchell, R. 1968. Factors affecting the decline of non-marine microorganisms in seawater. *Water Research* 2:535–543.

Moore-Landecker, E. 1972. *Fundamentals of the Fungi*. Prentice Hall, Englewood Cliffs, NJ.

Newbold, J. D., J. W. Elwood, R. V. O'Neill, and W. van Winkle. 1981. Measuring nutrient spiralling in streams. *Canadian Journal of Aquatic Sciences* 38:860–863.

Newell, S. Y. 1993. Decomposition of shots of a salt-marsh grass: Methodology and dynamics of microbial assemblages. *Advances in Microbial Ecology* 13:301–326.

Norkrans, B. 1980. Surface microlayers in aquatic environments. *Advances in Microbial Ecology* 4:51–85.

Odum, E. P. 1971. *Fundamentals of Ecology*. Saunders, Philadelphia.

Oppenheimer, C. H. 1963. *Symposium on Marine Microbiology*. Thomas, Springfield, IL.

Oren, A., and P. Gurevich. 1996. Dynamics of a bloom of halophilic archaea in the Dead Sea. *Hydrobiologia* 315:149–158.

Ormerod, J. G. 1983. The carbon cycle in aquatic ecosystems. In J. H. Slater, R. Whittenburg, and J.W.T. Wimpenny (eds.). *Microbes in Their Natural Environments*. Thirty-fourth Symposium of the Society for General Microbiology. Cambridge University Press, Cambridge, England, pp. 463–482.

Overbeck, J. 1966. Primärproduktion und Gewässerbakterien. *Naturwissenschaften* (Berlin) 52:145.

Overbeck, J., and H. D. Babenzien. 1964. Bakterien und Phytoplankton eines Kleingewässers im Jahreszyklus. *Journal der Angewandter Mikrobiologie* 4:49–76.

Padan, E. 1979. Impact of facultatively anaerobic metabolism on ecology of cyanobacteria (blue-green algae). *Advances in Microbial Ecology* 3:1–48.

Paerl, H. W. 1985. Influence of attachment on microbial metabolism and growth in aquatic ecosystems. In D. C. Savage and M. Fletcher (eds.). *Bacterial Adhesions: Mechanisms and Physiological Significance*. Plenum Press, New York, pp. 363–400.

Parker, B., and G. Barsom. 1970. Biological and chemical significance of surface microlayers in aquatic ecosystems. *BioScience* 20:87–93.

Pedersen, K. 1993. The deep subterranean biosphere. *Earth Science Reviews* 34:243–260.

Perkins, E. J. 1974. *The Biology of Estuaries and Coastal Waters.* Academic Press, New York.

Pfister, R. M., and P. R. Burkholder. 1965. Numerical taxonomy of some bacteria isolated from Antarctic and tropical seawaters. *Journal of Bacteriology* 90:863–872.

Phaff, H. J., M. W. Miller, and E. M. Mrak. 1968. *The Life of Yeasts.* Harvard University Press, Cambridge, MA.

Polunin, N. 1951. Arctic aerobiology: Pollen grains and other spores observed on sticky slides exposed in 1947. *Nature* (London) 168:718–721.

Postgate, J. R. 1994. *The Outer Reaches of Life.* Cambridge University Press, Cambridge, England.

Potts, M. 1994. Desiccation tolerance of prokaryotes. *Microbiological Reviews* 58:755–805.

Prescott, G. W. 1962. *Algae of the Western Great Lakes Area.* WC Brown, Dubuque, IA.

Reid, G. K. 1961. *Ecology of Inland Waters.* Van Nostrand Rheinhold, New York.

Rheinheimer, G. 1991. *Aquatic Microbiology.* Wiley, New York.

Rigler, F. H. 1964. The phosphorus fractions and the turnover time of inorganic phosphorus in different types of lakes. *Limnology and Oceanography* 9:511–578.

Ross, D. A. 1970. *Introduction to Oceanography.* Appleton-Century-Crofts, New York.

Round, F. E. 1984. *The Ecology of the Algae.* Cambridge University Press, New York.

Rumney, G. R. 1968. *Climatology and the World's Climate.* Macmillan, New York.

Ryther, J. H. 1969. Photosynthesis and fish production in the sea. *Science* 166:72–76.

Schut, F., E. J. de Vreis, J. C. Gottschal, B. R. Robertson, W. Harder, R. Prins, and D. K. Button. 1993. Isolation of typical marine bacteria by dilution culture: Growth, maintenance, and characteristics of isolates under laboratory conditions. *Applied and Environmental Microbiology* 59:2150–2160.

Sexstone, A. J., N. P. Revsbeck, T. B. Parkin, and J. M. Tiedje. 1985. Direct measurement of oxygen profiles and denitrification rates in soil aggregates. *Soil Science Society of America Journal* 49:645–651.

Sieburth, J. M. 1979. *Sea Microbes.* Oxford University Press, New York.

Sieburth, J. M., P. J. Willis, K. M. Johnson, C. M. Burney, D. M. Lavoie, K. R. Hinga, D. A. Caron, F. W. French III, P. W. Johnson, and P. G. Davis. 1977. Dissolved organic matter and heterotrophic microneuston in the surface microlayers of the North Atlantic. *Science* 194:1415–1418.

Silverman, M. P., and E. F. Munoz. 1970. Fungal attack on rock: Solubilization and altered infrared spectra. *Science* 169:985–987.

Simidu, U., T. Kaneko, and N. Taga. 1977. Microbiological studies of Tokyo Bay. *Microbial Ecology* 3:173–191.

Slater, J. H., R. Whittenbury, and J.W.T. Wimpenny. 1983. *Microbes in Their Natural Environments,* Thirty-fourth Symposium of the Society for General Microbiology. Cambridge University Press, Cambridge, England.

Sparrow, F. K. 1968. Ecology of freshwater fungi. In G. C. Ainsworth and A. S. Sussman (eds.). *The Fungi.* Academic Press, New York, pp. 41–93.

Stakman, E. C., and L. M. Hamilton. 1939. Stem rust in 1939. *U.S. Department of Agriculture Plant Disease Reporter Supplement* 117:69–83.

Stanier, R. Y., and G. Cohen-Bazire. 1957. The role of light in the microbial world: Some facts and speculations. In *Microbial Ecology.* Seventh Symposium of the Society for General Microbiology. Cambridge University Press, Cambridge, England, pp. 56–89.

Stetzenbach, L. D., B. Lighthart, R. J. Seidler, and S. C. Hern. 1992. Factors influencing the dispersal and survival of aerosolized microorganisms. In M. A. Levin, R. J. Seidler, and M. Rogul (eds.). *Microbial Ecology: Principles, Methods and Applications.* McGraw-Hill, New York, pp. 455–465.

Stevens, T. O., and J. P. McKinley. 1995. Lithoautotrophic microbial ecosystems in deep basalt aquifers. *Science* 270:450–454.

Stevenson, F. J. 1976. Organic matter reactions involving pesticides in soils. In D. D. Kaufman, G. G. Still, G. D. Paulson, and S. K. Bandal (eds.). *Bound and Conjugated Pesticide Residues.* ACS Symposium Ser. 29. American Chemical Society, Washington, DC, pp. 180–207.

Stevenson, F. J. 1982. *Humus Chemistry.* Wiley-Interscience, New York.

Stevenson, L. H., C. E. Millwood, and B. H. Hebeler. 1974. Aerobic heterotrophic bacterial populations in estuarine water and sediments. In R. R. Colwell and R. Y. Morita (eds.). *Effects of the Ocean Environment on Microbial Activity.* University Park Press, Baltimore, pp. 268–285.

Stewart, R. W. 1969. The atmosphere and the ocean. *Scientific American* 221(3):76–86.

Stockton, W. L., and T. E. DeLaca. 1982. Food falls in the deep sea: Occurrence, quality and significance. *Deep-Sea Research* 29:157–169.

Stotzky, G. 1965. Replica plating technique for studying microbial interactions in soil. *Canadian Journal of Microbiology* 11:629–636.

Sussman, A. S. 1961. The role of endogenous substrates in the dormancy of *Neurospora.* In H. O. Halvorson (ed.). *Spores II.* Burgess, Minneapolis, MN, pp. 198–217.

Sverdrup, H. O., M. W. Johnson, and R. H. Fleming. 1942. *The Oceans.* Prentice Hall, Englewood Cliffs, NJ.

Tait, R. V., and R. S. DeSanto. 1972. *Elements of Marine Ecology.* Springer-Verlag, New York.

Taylor, C. B. 1942. Bacteriology of freshwater. Part III, The types of bacteria present in lakes and streams and their relationship to the bacterial flora of soil. *Hygiene* 42:284–296.

Taylor, W. R. 1957. *Marine Algae of the Northeastern Coast of North America.* University of Michigan Press, Ann Arbor.

Teltsch, B., and E. Katznelson. 1978. Airborne enteric bacteria and viruses from spray irrigation with waste water. *Applied and Environmental Microbiology* 35:290–296.

Thrush, B. A. 1977. The chemistry of the stratosphere and its pollution. *Endeavour* 1:3–6.

Trainor, F. R. 1978. *Introductory Phycology.* Wiley, New York.

Tunnicliffe, V. 1992. Hydrothermal-vent communities of the deep sea. *American Scientist* 80:336–349.

Turley, C. M., and P. J. Mackie. 1995. Bacterial and cyanobacterial flux to the deep NE Atlantic on sedi-menting particles. *Deep-Sea Research Part I Oceanographic Research Papers* 42:1453–1474.

Valkanov, A. 1968. Das Neuston. *Limnologica* (Berlin) 6:381–403.

Waksman, S. A. 1961. *The Actinomycetes.* Williams & Wilkins, Baltimore.

Webster, J. R., and B. C. Patten. 1979. Effects of watershed perturbation on stream potassium and calcium dynamics. *Ecological Monographs* 49:51–72.

Weisse, T. 1993. Dynamics of autotrophic picoplankton in marine and freshwater ecosystems. *Advances in Microbial Ecology* 13:327–370.

Wenk, E., Jr. 1969. The physical resources of the ocean. *Scientific American* 221(3):167–176.

Westphal, A. 1976. *Protozoa.* Blackie, Glasgow, Scotland.

Wetzel, R. G. 1975. *Limnology.* Saunders, Philadelphia, PA.

Wetzel, R. G., and H. L. Allen. 1970. Functions and interactions of dissolved organic matter and the littoral zone in lake metabolism and eutrophication. In Z. Kajak and A. Hillbricht-Ilkowska (eds.). *Productivity Problems of Freshwaters.* PWN Polish Scientific Publishers, Warsaw, pp. 333–347.

Wiebe, W. J., R. E. Johannes, and K. L. Webb. 1975. Nitrogen fixation in a coral reef community. *Science* 188:257–259.

Wolf, F. T. 1943. The microbiology of the upper air. *Bulletin of the Torrey Botanical Club* 70:1–14.

Wood, E.J.F. 1967. *Microbiology of Oceans and Estuaries.* Elsevier, New York.

Wright, R. T., and J. E. Hobbie. 1966. Use of glucose and acetate by bacteria and algae in aquatic ecosystems. *Ecology* 47:447–464.

Wynn-Williams, D. D. 1990. Ecological aspects of Antarctic microbiology. *Advances in Microbial Ecology* 11:71–146.

Yayanos, A. A. 1995. Microbiology to 10,500 meters in the deep sea. *Annual Review of Microbiology* 49:777–806.

ZoBell, C. E. 1946. *Marine Microbiology.* Chronica Botanica, Waltham, MA.

# part four

# BIOGEOCHEMICAL CYCLING

# 10

# Biogeochemical Cycling: Carbon, Hydrogen, and Oxygen

*Biogeochemical cycling of essential nutrient elements occurs both within ecosystems and on a global basis. A chemical form of an element represents a reservoir. The turnover of a reservoir depends on both the intensity of cycling and reservoir size. Small, intensely cycled reservoirs are vulnerable to disturbance. Carbon, hydrogen, and oxygen, all major nutrient elements, are cycled together by the opposing forces of photosynthesis and respiration. The small atmospheric $CO_2$ reservoir is influenced by human activities. Through the "greenhouse effect" this disturbance is warming our global climate. Microorganisms are responding to such increased concentrations of $CO_2$ and may be useful in combatting global pollution problems.*

## Biogeochemical Cycling

Biogeochemical cycling describes the movement and conversion of materials by biochemical activities throughout the atmosphere, hydrosphere, and lithosphere. This cycling occurs on a global scale, profoundly affecting the geology and present environment of our planet. Biogeochemical cycles include physical transformations, such as dissolution, precipitation, volatilization, and fixation; chemical transformations, such as biosynthesis, biodegradation, and oxidoreductive biotransformations; and various combinations of physical and chemical changes. These physical and chemical transformations can cause spatial translocations of materials—from the water column to the sediment, for example, or from the soil to the atmosphere. All living organisms participate in the biogeochemical cycling of materials, but microorganisms, because of their ubiquity, diverse metabolic capabilities, and high enzymatic activity rates, play a major role in biogeochemical cycling (Pomeroy 1974; Jørgensen 1989).

Biogeochemical cycling is driven directly or indirectly by the radiant energy of the sun (Woodwell 1970) or by the energy of reduced minerals. Energy is absorbed, converted, temporarily stored, and eventually dissipated, which is to say that energy flows through ecosystems. This flow of energy is fundamental to ecosystem function. Whereas energy flows through the ecosystem, materials undergo cyclic conversions that tend to retain materials within the ecosystem.

Through the geological ages, biogeochemical activities have altered conditions on Earth in a unidirectional manner. The most crucial of these unidirectional changes were the decomposition of abiotically formed organic matter on primitive Earth by early heterotrophic forms of life and the change of the originally reducing atmospheric conditions to oxidizing ones by the first oxygen-producing phototrophs. Contemporary biogeochemical processes, however, tend to be cyclic. The cyclic nature of material conversions leads to dynamic equilibria between various forms of cycled materials. Without the existence of these equilibria, the present physiological diversity of life could not exist. Not all biogeochemical activities, though, resemble closed cycles. Materials can be imported into or exported from ecosystems, thereby becoming available or inaccessible to microbial activities. Some materials, such as fossil fuel and limestone deposits, may be removed from active microbial cycling for many millions of years. Ecosystems vary greatly in the efficiency with which they retain specific materials, such as essential nutrient elements. Habitats capable of retaining nutrients, such as coral reefs and tropical rainforests, are capable of sustaining high rates of productivity even in generally nutrient-poor surroundings. Habitats that have a low capacity to retain essential nutrients, such as the epipelagic habitats, tend to have low, nutrient-limited primary production rates, even when light and temperature favor high productivity (Odum 1983).

Most elements are subject to some degree of biogeochemical cycling. As may be expected, elements that are essential components of living organisms, the so-called biogenic elements, are most regularly subject to biogeochemical cycling. Because the biogenic elements need to meet definite criteria of atomic weight and chemical reactivity, they are not randomly distributed in the periodic table of elements but form definite groups within the first five periods (Frieden 1972; Mertz 1981) (Table 10.1). This fact made the biogenic significance of certain trace elements, like nickel, predictable even before their requirement and function were experimentally established.

The intensity or rate of biogeochemical cycling for each element roughly correlates to the amount of the element in the chemical composition of biomass. The major elemental components of living organisms (C, H, O, N, P, and S) are cycled most intensely. Minor elements (Mg, K, Na, and halogens) and trace elements (B, Co, Cr, Cu, Mo, Ni, Se, Sn, V, and Zn), which are required in small quantities and not by every form of life, are cycled less intensely. The minor and trace elements Fe, Mn, Ca, and Si are exceptions to this rule. Iron and manganese are cycled extensively in an oxidoreductive manner. Calcium and silicon, though minor components of protoplasm, form important exo- and endoskeletal structures in both micro- and macroorganisms and are consequently cycled on the global scale at the rate of many billions of tons per year. Nonessential and even toxic elements are also cycled to some extent, as evidenced by the bioaccumulation of radioactive strontium and cesium isotopes and by the microbial methylation of mercury, tin, and arsenic (Deevey 1970; Hutchinson 1970; Underwood 1977).

Microorganisms are sources of particular compounds in the ecosphere and sinks for others. Transfer rates between pools vary and generally are enzymatically mediated. The critical enzymatic activities involved in a particular elemental transformation within a habitat may be associated with one particular microbial population or with multiple microbial, plant, and/or animal populations. Some elemental transformations also occur chemically—that is, abiotically—and are not enzymatically mediated.

## Reservoirs and Transfer Rates

In terms of biogeochemical cycling, the various chemical forms of a particular element constitute so-called pools, or reservoirs. When we refer to such reservoirs, we generally mean reservoirs on the global scale. Global reservoirs tend to be stable in the time frame of human history but may undergo shifts during geological ages. Within a particular habitat, elements also occur in reservoirs of a distinct size, and these reservoir sizes can vary greatly from habitat to habitat.

**Table 10.1**
Distribution of biogenic elements within a periodic system

|  | Period number | | | | |
|---|---|---|---|---|---|
|  | 1 | 2 | 3 | 4 | 5 |
|  | 1 H | 3 Li | 11 Na$^*$ | 19 K$^*$ | 37 Rb |
|  |  | 4 Be | 12 Mg$^*$ | 20 Ca$^*$ | 38 Sr |
|  |  |  |  | 21 Sc | 39 Y |
|  |  |  |  | 22 Ti | 40 Zr |
|  |  |  |  | 23 V$^*$ | 41 Nb |
|  |  |  |  | 24 Cr* | 42 Mo* |
|  |  |  |  | 25 Mn$^*$ | 43 Tc |
|  |  |  |  | 26 Fe$^*$ | 44 Ru |
|  |  |  |  | 27 Co$^*$ | 45 Rh |
|  |  |  |  | 28 Ni$^*$ | 46 Pd |
|  |  |  |  | 29 Cu$^*$ | 47 Ag |
|  |  |  |  | 30 Zn$^*$ | 48 Cd |
|  |  | 5 B$^*$ | 13 Al | 31 Ga | 49 In |
|  |  | 6 C | 14 Si$^*$ | 32 Ge | 50 Sn$^*$ |
|  |  | 7 N | 15 P | 33 As | 51 Sb |
|  |  | 8 O | 16 S | 34 Se$^*$ | 52 Te |
|  |  | 9 F* | 17 Cl$^*$ | 35 Br | 53 I$^*$ |
|  | 2 He | 10 Ne | 18 Ar | 36 Kr | 54 Xe |

*(Left axis label: Atomic number and element)*

Major biogenic elements are shown with shading; minor and trace elements are marked with an asterisk.
Most biogenic elements cluster in the first four periods, with only three trace elements falling into the fifth
period. No known biogenic elements occur above atomic weight 53. Therefore, the sixth and seventh
period, the lantanides and actinides, are omitted from this table.

Some chemical forms accumulate within a particular habitat; others are depleted (Odum 1983).

Reservoir size is an extremely important parameter to be considered in connection with possible perturbations of a cycling system. To make this point clear, let us consider a simple cycling system (Figure 10.1) in which water is pumped from the small reservoir $b$ at rate $V_1$ into the large reservoir $a$, from which it returns by gravity flow at rate $V_2$. In equilibrium state, $V_1$ equals $V_2$, and the water levels in each reservoir remain steady. It is easy to see that if the flow equilibrium is disturbed either by slowing the pump speed ($V_1$) or, conversely, by partially closing the outflow valve on reservoir $a$, the effects on the small reservoir ($b$) will be rapid and dramatic. Reservoir $b$ will either overflow or be emptied, while the level of reservoir $a$ will be affected only moderately. Similarly, in biogeochemical cycles, small, actively cycled reservoirs are the most prone to disturbance by either natural or human causes.

Microbiologically mediated portions of biogeochemical cycles are essential for the growth and survival of plant and animal populations. We discussed some of the critical metabolic activities of microorganisms that directly influence plant and animal populations in preceding chapters. It is important to recog-

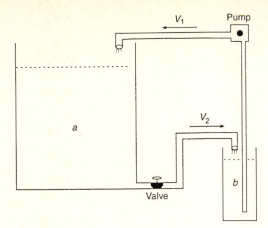

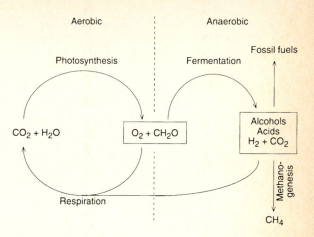

**Figure 10.1**
Mechanical model of reservoirs and biogeochemical cycling.
$a$ = large reservoir of material; $b$ = small reservoir of material;
$V_1$ = transfer rate from $b$ to $a$; $V_2$ = transfer rate from $a$ to $b$.
When $V_1 = V_2$, the system is in equilibrium and the levels in
the two reservoirs remain steady. When $V_1 \neq V_2$ the levels in
the reservoirs will change; this change will occur more
rapidly in the smaller reservoir than in the larger reservoir.
The magnitude of the change will be the same but opposite
in both reservoirs, but the relative changes will be different.

**Figure 10.2**
Interrelation of the biogeochemical cycles of carbon,
hydrogen, and oxygen. The figure shows the involvement
of oxygen and hydrogen in the aerobic and anaerobic
oxidation of organic carbon and in the reduction of $CO_2$.
The formula $CH_2O$ represents organic matter on the oxidation level of carbohydrate.

nize that the biogeochemical cycling activities of
microorganisms determine, in large part, the potential
productivity that can be supported within a habitat.
Alterations in the biogeochemical cycling activities of
microbial populations caused by human activities—
by pollution, for example—can result in changes in
the transfer rates of elements between reservoirs and
in the sizes of reservoirs of elements in particular
chemical forms within habitats. These changes alter
the biochemical characteristics of a habitat and the
populations that can be supported, in both quantitative
and qualitative terms.

In this and the following chapter, we will discuss
the microbially mediated biogeochemical cycling of
various elements, treating each of the elements individually, although the biogeochemical cycles are
interrelated and cannot truly be separated from each
other. This applies especially to the cycling of the first
three major elements, carbon, hydrogen, and oxygen,
all three of which are cycled by the same two oppos-

ing processes of photosynthesis and respiration (Bolin
1970; Cloud and Gibor 1970; Krumbein and Swart
1983). Figure 10.2 makes apparent the degree to
which the cycling of these elements is interwoven.
This figure also illustrates the cycling of carbon
between organic and inorganic forms and the
processes involved in these transformations.

## THE CARBON CYCLE

When examining the biogeochemical cycling of an
individual element, it is useful to consider the global
reservoirs of this element, the size of these reservoirs,
and whether or not these reservoirs are being actively
cycled. The most actively cycled reservoir of carbon
is atmospheric $CO_2$ (0.034% of the atmosphere, or
700 billion ($10^9$) metric tons of carbon). The dissolved
inorganic forms of carbon ($CO_2$, $H_2CO_3$, $HCO_3^-$, and
$CO_3^{2-}$) in surface seawater (500 billion tons of carbon) are in direct equilibrium with atmospheric $CO_2$,
but a much larger portion in the deep sea (34,500 billion metric tons) equilibrates only at the slow rate of

vertical seawater circulation. The living biomass in terrestrial and aquatic environments contains slightly less carbon (450 billion to 500 billion tons) than the atmosphere. Dead (but not fossil) organic matter such as humus and organic sediment contains 3700 billion tons. All of these can be considered actively cycled carbon reservoirs. In comparison, the amounts of carbon in fossil fuels (10,000 billion tons) and carbonaceous sedimentary rock (20,000,000 billion tons) are considerably higher, but the natural turnover rates of these latter reservoirs are minute. The cited numbers (Bolin 1970) are rough estimates, but they illustrate relative reservoir sizes and serve as the basis for calculating carbon turnover rates and humans' influence on them. Carbonaceous rocks, such as limestone and dolomite, may be slowly dissolved by biologically produced acid with the release of $CO_2$ or $HCO_3^-$, but compared to the bulk of carbonaceous rock, this process constitutes a negligible turnover. Some fossil fuels, in the form of coal, petroleum, natural gas, or kerogen, are recycled naturally by the biological degradation of oil and gas seepages; but again, such cycling affects only a small portion of the fossil fuels. However, since the start of the industrial revolution in the early nineteenth century, human activities have reinjected a significant percentage of fossil organic carbon into the atmosphere as $CO_2$ from burnt fuel.

The natural rates of carbon cycling in oceans and on land are close to a steady state; that is, the rates of movement of carbon between the atmosphere and trees or between algae and the dissolved inorganic carbon of the oceans do not change measurably from year to year and tend to balance each other (Hobbie and Melillo 1984). However, human activities have recently introduced changes in the carbon cycle that are large enough to be measured. Today, the global carbon cycling is a mixture of the natural steady-state rates and reservoirs and the changing rates and reservoirs affected by human activities. For example, the flux of carbon from algae into dissolved organic carbon in the open ocean is at steady state because human activities are not great enough to perturb that rate. In contrast, the reservoir of carbon (as $CO_2$) in the atmosphere is no longer in a steady state and is growing from year to year.

**Table 10.2**
Major carbon reservoirs

| Reservoir | Amount (billions of metric tons of carbon) |
|---|---|
| Atmosphere before 1850 | 560–610 |
| Atmosphere in 1978 | 692 |
| Oceans and fresh water | |
|   Inorganic | 35,000 |
|   Dissolved organic | 1,000 |
| Land biota | 600–900 |
|   Soil organic matter | 1,500 |
| Sediments | 10,000,000 |
| Fossil fuels | 10,000 |

Source: Bolin et al. 1979.

Atmospheric $CO_2$, because it is a relatively small carbon pool, has been measurably affected by industrial $CO_2$ release (Bolin et al. 1979) (Table 10.2). Between 1860 and 1980, atmospheric $CO_2$ rose by approximately 70 ppm from a preindustrial 270 ppm to 340 ppm (Houghton et al. 1983; Hobbie and Melillo 1984; La Marche et al. 1984). The increase in atmospheric carbon dioxide is largely due to the burning of fossil fuels, with additional $CO_2$ contributed from forest biomass and soil humus in the course of forest clearing for agricultural land. These inputs should have raised the atmospheric $CO_2$ concentration by substantially more than 70 ppm, but part of the input apparently has been absorbed by the sea as $HCO_3^-$ and/or fixed into a standing crop of biomass.

There is concern today that the continued increase in atmospheric $CO_2$, currently at a rate of about 1 ppm per year, might intensify the "greenhouse effect." $CO_2$ is transparent to visible radiation, but absorbs strongly in the infrared range. Visible sunlight striking Earth is irradiated back as longer-wavelength infrared radiation. An increase in $CO_2$ in the Earth's insulating atmospheric blanket would retain more of this radiation and thus would bring about a warming trend in the climate. The foremost effect of a doubling of the

$CO_2$, perhaps as early as the year 2050, will be on the world climate (Hobbie and Melillo 1984). There will most likely be little direct effect on microbial activity, but if temperature increases and precipitation patterns change, there could be a strong indirect effect. Scientists generally agree that the global temperature will increase, but there is less agreement as to how much and exactly how this will affect air movement and precipitation (National Research Council 1979, 1983, 1991). One computer model predicts a small change in the tropics and a large change at the poles. At 40° to 60° latitude the annual temperature increase will be 4–6°C, and precipitation patterns will also change. This increase in turn could reduce the size of the polar ice caps and substantially raise the level of the oceans—a serious danger for densely populated coastal regions.

Contributing to the greenhouse effect is atmospheric methane, released by human activities such as drilling for oil and natural gas, landfilling of solid waste, and large-scale cattle raising and wetland rice cultivation. Although much lower in amount than the $CO_2$ produced by the burning of fossil fuels, methane traps heat four to five times as effectively as $CO_2$. Thus, even in relatively small amounts, it can contribute to the greenhouse effect significantly.

Although the increase in atmospheric $CO_2$ is well documented and will undoubtedly have some effect on our climate, the prediction of the direction and the magnitude of the effect requires modeling and many assumptions that may or may not be valid and complete. An increase in cloud cover, a possible effect of climate warming, may act as negative feedback and reduce the warming effect. Other pollutants, mainly sulfate from fossil-fuel burning, also contribute to an increased cloud cover and lessen the greenhouse effect (Charlson et al. 1992). Another uncertainty is whether microbial and plant activities will dampen or amplify the effects of increased injection of $CO_2$ into the atmosphere, but microorganisms will probably respond to changes in $CO_2$ concentration and temperature. Increased fixation of $CO_2$ would lessen the effects; increased respiration would heighten them. The described uncertainties along with the painfulness of reducing our fossil-fuel consumption in the absence

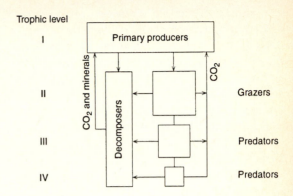

**Figure 10.3**
An idealized food web showing transfers between trophic levels. Organic carbon formed by primary producers is transferred to grazers and predators. Decomposers and respiration of grazers and predators return $CO_2$ to primary producers. The diagram shows that the supportable biomass declines at progressively higher trophic levels.

of adequate alternative energy sources have, to date, delayed meaningful policies to curb a major climate disruption by the greenhouse effect. The necessary international cooperation for an effective global policy would also be difficult to achieve. Yet to delay action until unmistakable signs of a global disaster become manifest is a risky policy because correcting the situation once it develops may prove difficult. Speculative schemes to tie up excess $CO_2$ in terrestrial or oceanic biomass have been advanced, but technical difficulties exist (see the box on pages 394–395) and the monetary, economic, and ecological cost of such solutions may be staggering.

## Carbon Transfer Through Food Webs

The overall involvement of microorganisms with carbon cycling can perhaps best be discussed in the context of a theoretical food web (Figure 10.3). Every food web is based on primary producers. The net fixation of $CO_2$ to form organic compounds is carried out by autotrophic organisms. Among the microorganisms, this includes photosynthetic and chemolithotrophic organisms. The most important groups of microorganisms, in terms of their abilities to convert

$CO_2$ to organic matter, are the algae, the cyanobacteria, and the green and purple photosynthetic bacteria. Chemoautotrophic microorganisms contribute to a lesser extent. The principal metabolic pathway for photosynthetic $CO_2$ fixation is the Calvin cycle. In addition, microorganisms are capable of incorporating $CO_2$ through the phosphoenol pyruvate carboxylase system. In the case of heterotrophic microorganisms, exchange but no net $CO_2$ fixation occurs, but some chemolithotrophic microorganisms use this system either instead of or in addition to the pentose phosphate cycle for net $CO_2$ fixation (Wood 1989). Methanogenic archaea play an important role in the anaerobic reduction of $CO_2$. Only a limited number of microorganisms can utilize the resulting methane (Gottschalk 1979; Haber et al. 1983). These methylotrophs are ecologically important in minimizing methane transfer to the atmosphere.

Carbon dioxide converted to organic carbon by primary producers represents the gross primary production of the community. This process is carried out predominantly by photosynthetic organisms that convert light energy to chemical energy; the chemical energy is stored within the organic compounds that are formed. The conversion of radiant energy to chemical energy in organic compounds is the essence of primary production.

A portion of the gross primary production is converted back to $CO_2$ by the respiration of the primary producers. The remaining organic carbon is the net primary production available to heterotrophic consumers; the heterotrophs complete the carbon cycle, ultimately converting organic compounds formed by primary producers back to $CO_2$ during respiration. The gross primary production and the total community respiration may or may not be in complete balance (Figure 10.4). A net gain in organic matter produced by photosynthesis and not converted back to $CO_2$ is known as the *net community productivity*. A positive net community productivity accumulates organic matter within the ecosystem. If the net community productivity is negative, then there must be an input of allochthonous organic matter or the community will dissipate the available energy and disappear. The standing biomass, or standing crop, in a habitat at

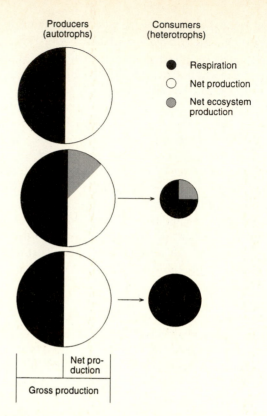

**Figure 10.4**
Balance of primary productivity, respiration, and community productivity. (A) Gross primary production (whole circle) and net production portion (white area) remaining after respiration of primary producers. The net primary production is available for consumers. (B) Situation where there is net ecosystem production because heterotrophs do not consume all the available net primary production, leading to the accumulation of organic matter in the ecosystem. This typically occurs during early successional stages. (C) Situation where consumers use all of the net primary production and total respiration of the community balances total primary production. No organic matter accumulates in the system. This situation is typical of climax ecosystems. (Source: Woodwell 1970, The Energy Cycle of the Biosphere. Reprinted by permission, copyright 1970 Scientific American Inc. All rights reserved.)

any particular point in time should not be confused with productivity. Standing biomass represents stored energy. High biomass in a habitat can be due to high gross primary productivity, low respiration, or net input of organic compounds. During periods of low consumption, standing biomass may accumulate.

The rate of primary productivity can be determined by measuring fluxes of oxygen or carbon dioxide in the light and dark. Using $O_2$ production neglects the contribution to primary production by anaerobic photosynthetic bacteria and by chemolithotrophic bacteria. The amount of oxygen produced in the light can be used as a measure of photosynthetic net primary productivity. Oxygen consumed in the dark can be added to the measured amount of $O_2$ generated in the light to estimate gross primary productivity. The net assimilation of $CO_2$, the net community production, can be assayed by measuring the concentration of $CO_2$ flowing into and out of enclosed chambers containing active biological communities; this approach measures the difference between the carbon fixed from $CO_2$ by primary production and the $CO_2$ produced by respiration. Other methods utilize $^{14}CO_2$ assimilation to measure primary productivity. Short-term $^{14}CO_2$ incorporation in light tends to measure gross photosynthetic productivity; longer incorporation periods measure net productivity (see Chapter 7). The necessity of enclosing a community may alter steady-state conditions, producing inaccurate estimates of primary production (Hubel 1966).

The primary productivity of ecosystems is usually compared on a per square meter per year basis. It may be expressed as grams of carbon fixed, grams of dry organic matter (biomass) formed, or kilojoules (kJ) or (kilocalories (kcal) of energy stored; kcal × 4.2 = kJ. Those values are interconvertible, assuming that 50% of dry organic matter is carbon and on the average 1 g of dry organic biomass corresponds to 5 kcal (21.0 kJ) of energy stored. Table 10.3 compares net primary productivity of several natural ecosystems with agricultural fields. It is important to realize that the agricultural systems (corn, rice, and sugarcane) receive nonrenewable energy subsidies derived from fossil fuels in the form of synthetic fertilizer and labor by fuel-driven farm machinery (Odum 1983). The effi-

**Table 10.3**
Net primary productivity of some natural and agricultural ecosystems

| Description of ecosystem | Net primary productivity (g dry organic matter/m$^2$/year) |
| --- | --- |
| Tundra | 400 |
| Desert | 200 |
| Temperate grassland | up to 1500 |
| Temperate deciduous or evergreen forest | 1200–1600 |
| Tropical rainforest | up to 2800 |
| Cattail swamp | 2500 |
| Freshwater ponds | 950–1500 |
| Open ocean | 100 |
| Coastal seawater | 200 |
| Upwelling area | 600 |
| Coral reef | 4900 |
| Corn field | 1000–6000 |
| Rice paddy | 340–1200 |
| Sugarcane field | up to 9400 |

Source: Woodwell 1970; Heal and Ineson 1984.

ciency of sun-energy use in photosynthesis is low. Less than 0.1% of the sun energy that reaches the surface of Earth is used in photosynthesis, globally producing about 150 billion tons of dry organic matter per year. Even in intensively managed agricultural ecosystems, the efficiency of sun-energy utilization rarely exceeds 1% (Woodwell 1970).

The transfer of energy stored in organic compounds from one organism to another establishes a food chain. The transfer occurs in steps; each step constitutes a trophic level. The interrelationships of food chain steps establish the food web. Individual food chains, such as the detritus food chain, may be based on allochthonous material or on primary producers in the same ecosystem. Without the input of primary producers, however, the food web would decay. Organisms that feed directly on primary producers constitute the trophic level of grazers. Grazers are preyed upon by predators, which may in turn be preyed upon by a trophic level of larger predators. Only 10–15% of the biomass from each trophic level usually is transferred to the next higher trophic level; 85–90% is consumed by respiration or enters the decay portion of the food web. In some extreme cases, however, values considerably higher or lower have been measured. Nevertheless, the higher a trophic level, the smaller its biomass. Many consumers feed on more than one trophic level, some primary producers (phototrophic flagellates) are also consumers (phagotrophic flagellates), and dissolved organic mat-

ter is converted partially to particulate matter (living and dead biomass) by the process of "heterotrophic (secondary) production." The traditional concept of a food web as consisting of unidirectional food chains thus requires conceptual reevaluation. The depicted simple scheme, however, is adequate for our discussion of microbial involvement.

In most terrestrial and shallow-water environments, the predominant primary producers are higher plants, and the dominant grazers are invertebrate or vertebrate herbivores. Microbial primary producers are usually present, but their role is subordinate to that of higher plants. Exceptions are found in some harsh environments—such as exposed rock surfaces,

## Combatting the Greenhouse Effect with Microorganisms

The likelihood of adverse climatic change in response to the human-caused increase in atmospheric $CO_2$ presents an intractable socioeconomic dilemma. Elevated concentrations of $CO_2$ absorb increased amounts of radiation and cause a warming of the Earth's atmosphere called the greenhouse effect (LaMarche et al. 1984; Manabe and Wetherald 1980; Whitman and Rogers 1991). In industrialized countries, our standard of living and our survival at the present high population densities are tied to a high level of energy consumption. All fossil fuels, "clean" or "dirty," generate $CO_2$ emissions. Clean hydropower is in short supply, and we cannot as yet harvest solar energy on a large scale. Nuclear power, though free of $CO_2$ emissions, has serious safety and environmental problems. In the United States, well over 90% of all energy is generated from fossil fuels. Beyond modest conservation, any policy to curb $CO_2$ emissions is believed to spell unemployment and economic disaster for industrial nations. Many developing

nations regard any curbs on their energy use as a ploy to keep them poor and powerless.

Faced with the prospect of continuing $CO_2$ emissions, scientists are trying to develop alternative technologies for reducing atmospheric $CO_2$, especially strategies that involve sequestering rather than decomposition of biomass generated as a result of those technologies. Theoretically, microorganisms could remove enough of this greenhouse gas from the atmosphere that the threat of global warming would be removed. Some microorganisms convert carbon dioxide to various organic compounds, and new strains could be produced that, at least in theory, would do so more efficiently. These improved strains could be produced either by genetic selection from cultures grown in bioreactors or by the use of recombinant DNA technology.

Vast regions of the tropical oceans that are warm and receive abundant sunshine have very low productivity for lack of critical mineral nutri-

polar regions, and high-salinity and thermal environments—that preclude the presence of higher plants and where, therefore, microbial producers predominate. In the limnetic zone of deep lakes and in the pelagic portion of the oceans, however, where no autochthonous higher plants exist, the entire food web is based on microbial primary producers, predominantly unicellular planktonic algae and cyanobacteria. Except in the immediate coastal zone, microorganisms are responsible for most of the ocean's primary production, which is about half of the total photosynthesis of the planet. In these environments, substantial numbers of grazers are also microbial (planktonic protozoa), though they share this role with smaller representatives of the invertebrate zooplankton (Ryther 1969).

Recent investigations indicate that extremely small planktonic forms carry out a major part of primary and secondary productivity as well as respiration in ocean waters (Sherr and Sherr 1984). Nanophytoplankton (<20 µm) composes most of the phytoplankton biomass in seawater, and picophytoplankton (<2 µm) appears to be responsible for a substantial share of the total phytoplankton productivity. The nano- and picophytoplankton are better equipped to cope with the scarcity of critical mineral nutrients in the ocean, and it appears that in most areas of the ocean they are growing at near maximal rates, with

ents. Iron, when it is the limiting mineral nutrient in the sense of Liebig's law, is required in only tiny amounts, and small additions can have large effects on photosynthetic productivity. Much of the produced biomass would be buried in deep-sea sediments and removed from the carbon cycle for millions of years. This scheme for reducing atmospheric concentrations of $CO_2$ was put to a practical test in the equatorial Pacific Ocean, south of the Galapagos Islands. In this region, iron was only 0.03 nanomolar in the seawater and, in bottle experiments, iron additions had a dramatic effect on phytoplankton productivity. In a large-scale experiment, 480 kg of iron sulfate was distributed over an 8-km$^2$ area of the ocean. The test was dubbed IronEx or, jokingly, the "Geritol experiment" from the iron tonic marketed to senior citizens. As confirmed by conventional measurements as well as by satellite monitoring, the iron addition had a marked but short-lived effect (Kerr 1994). In the first 3 days after addition, photosynthetic produc-

tion more than doubled, but it failed to reach the tenfold level predicted by the bottle experiments. The apparent reason was the rapid removal of the iron from the surface seawater by precipitation and sinking. The poor solubility of trivalent (ferric) iron in the alkaline seawater is, of course, the primary reason for iron scarcity in the sea. Though scientifically intriguing, the described approach is not ready to reverse the greenhouse effect.

In the past, wide fluctuations in atmospheric $CO_2$ concentration occurred independently of humankind's activities. In the Cretaceous period, life thrived in an atmosphere believed to be six times richer in $CO_2$ than today (Appenzeller 1993). Aerosol pollution and increases in cloud cover may to some extent mitigate the effects of increased $CO_2$ concentration (Kerr 1992). It is impossible to predict with certainty how disruptive the new greenhouse effect will be, but we seem to be determined to discover it by experience!

primary productivity being severalfold higher than earlier estimates have suggested. A considerable percentage of the organic carbon initially fixed by phytoplankton appears to enter the pelagic food web as dissolved and nonliving particulate organic matter. This nonliving organic material is subsequently incorporated into bacterial cells that are consumed primarily by colorless (heterotrophic) phagotrophic microflagellates. Rough estimates show a ratio of 1 phagotrophic microflagellate to 100 bacteria, and the activity of these microflagellates clears 30–50% of the marine-water column of bacteria per day. The phagotrophic microflagellates have growth rates equal to or greater than the bacteria on which they feed and exert substantial control over their population levels (Fenchel 1986). Surprisingly, even microflagellate members of the freshwater phytoplankton were recently reported to graze on bacteria extensively. They were estimated to consume more bacteria than the total of the various zooplankton organisms (Bird and Kalff 1986). Many colorless heterotrophic microflagellates have close morphological and taxonomic relationships to pigmented phytoflagellates. Surveying the literature, Sanders and Porter (1988) concluded that numerous freshwater and marine phytoflagellates (Euglenophycophyta, Chrysophycophyta, and Pyrrophycophyta) have a potential for mixotrophic growth; that is, they are capable of photosynthesis and phagotrophy at the same time. Under the mineral nutrient limitations of most limnetic and pelagic environments, the ingested bacteria may be more critical as sources of nitrogen and phosphorus than as carbon and energy sources.

Because of the extremely small size of both primary (photosynthetic) and secondary (heterotrophic) producers in the marine environments, the phagotrophic protozoa represent an important link between these tiny producers and the higher trophic levels of the food web. It appears that earlier surveys may have underestimated the abundance and importance of this trophic level (Sherr and Sherr 1984). The motile microflagellates and microciliates are typically distributed in a patchy manner, showing strong spatial and temporal fluctuations. Their abundance in the pleuston and in association with detritus and fecal pellets is greater by several orders of magnitude than

their average distribution in the water column. Pelagic sarcodina (acantharia, amoebae, foraminifera, and radiolaria) also show strong spatial and temporal fluctuations in numbers and, on the average, contribute little to the biomass of planktonic protozoa. Heterotrophic microflagellates, naked and loricate ciliates such as the tintinnids, make up the largest portion of the planktonic protozoa, in terms of both numbers and biomass. They graze on the pico- and nanoplanktonic primary and secondary producers that are too small to be filtered out efficiently by larger forms of zooplankton, such as the microcrustacea. The marine protozoa span a large size range between 2 and 200 μm and are well suited to graze on the smallest forms of primary producers, as well as on bacteria, the only group with some access to the large but extremely dilute dissolved organic material reservoir of the sea. The marine protozoa are of sufficient size to be grazed upon, in turn, by the larger microcrustaceae of the zooplankton, channeling biomass toward larger invertebrates and fish. Because of the number of trophic levels involved, however, the pelagic environment can support few organisms on the higher trophic levels. The length of the food chains contributes to the biological desert character of the open sea.

The decay portion of the food web is dominated by microbial forms in both aquatic and terrestrial environments. The decay portion of the food web involves the degradation of incompletely digested organic matter, such as fecal material or urea, and the decomposition of dead but not consumed plants and animals. The proportion of the biomass recycled by decay rather than by consumption varies greatly within different types of habitats (Figure 10.5), but in forest and salt-marsh habitats, decay may account for 80–90% of the total energy flow. On the other extreme, in pelagic and limnetic habitats, grazers rapidly consume the bulk of primary production, and relatively little biomass is channeled through the decay route (Pomeroy 1984; Sherr and Sherr 1984).

Part of the microbial biomass formed during decomposition is recycled into the food web. Both free-swimming and detritus-attached bacteria in seawater are metabolically active and are significant in the

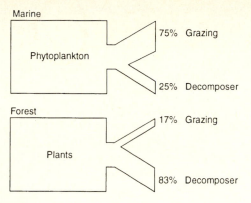

**Figure 10.5**
Relative proportion of energy entering grazing and decomposer food chains in marine and terrestrial habitats. Dominant producers in marine habitat are phytoplankton; in terrestrial habitat they are plants. A higher proportion of energy goes into the grazing food chain in the marine habitat; in the terrestrial habitat a higher proportion enters the decomposer food chain. (Source: Odum 1962. Reprinted courtesy of Ecological Society of Japan.)

utilization of dissolved substrates and the production of biomass. Because they have access to a variety of dissolved and particulate substrates, bacteria are significant producers of biomass in the ocean. Various predators consume microorganisms as a main or supplemental source of carbon and energy. Detritus food chains are based on the consumption of microbial biomass. A crucial contribution of bacteria to food webs is their ability to assimilate dissolved organic carbon from extremely dilute solutions, and thus to convert these nutrients to biomass that can be available to other forms of life not capable of using dissolved nutrients directly. This phenomenon, known as heterotrophic, or secondary, production, is specially important in aquatic habitats with low concentrations of dissolved organic compounds. The detrital food web is intrinsically tied to secondary production including the release of soluble substances from particulates and subsequent cycling through microbial biomass.

## Carbon Cycling Within Habitats

The degradation and recycling of organic matter in most habitats is accomplished by heterotrophic macro- and microorganisms. Microbial activities are crucial in terms of not only the quantity but also the quality of their contributions. Under aerobic conditions, macro- and microorganisms share the ability to biodegrade simple organic nutrients and some biopolymers, such as starch, pectin, proteins, and so on, but microorganisms are unique in their capacity to carry out anaerobic (fermentative) degradation of organic matter. They are also responsible for the recycling of most abundant but difficult-to-digest biopolymers, such as cellulose and lignin. We discussed the importance of digestive associations of microorganisms with macroherbivores in Chapter 5. The ability to degrade humic materials, hydrocarbons, and many human-made synthetics is also virtually unique to microorganisms.

The greatest range of carbon transformations occurs under aerobic conditions. Biodegradation of hydrocarbons and lignin, for example, is very restricted in anoxic environments. On the other hand, certain carbon transformations, such as methanogenesis, occur exclusively under anaerobic conditions. This leads to a biogeochemical zonation of habitats. Some organic compounds can accumulate within particular habitats and be unavailable to the biological community, while in other habitats the same compounds can readily serve as sources of carbon and energy.

Respiratory metabolism yields more energy to cells than fermentative metabolism. Fermentation requires a greater consumption of organic matter to support the same biomass as respiration. Therefore, in aerobic habitats, respiration predominates over fermentation. Complete respiration results in the production of $CO_2$, whereas fermentation, in addition, results in the accumulation of low-molecular-weight organic alcohols and acids. At this point, several possible routes exist for further metabolism. Eventually, the anaerobic conditions may change to aerobic ones, as occurs in flooded soil that drains or dries, and thus the fermentation products are utilized further aerobically. Similarly, fermentation products may diffuse out of the anaerobic environment. As an example, the fatty acids produced in the rumen by anaerobic microorganisms are transferred to the aerobic bloodstream of the ruminant animal, where they are transformed to $CO_2$

by respiration. If conditions remain anaerobic and fermentation products are trapped in this environment, they may be metabolized further with the simultaneous reduction of nitrate or sulfate. In the absence of such secondary electron acceptors, further energy may be extracted from some of the fermentation products by methanogenesis (Large 1983; Zeikus et al. 1985).

## Methanogenesis and Methylotrophy

Methanogens are a unique group of the Archaea (Balch et al. 1979; Ferry 1993). Strictly anaerobic and active at redox potentials between $-350$ and $-450$ mV, they are capable of using $CO_2$ as an electron acceptor. They reduce $CO_2$ using $H_2$ produced in the fermentation process. Because they are capable of using $CO_2$ as their only carbon source, they are considered chemolithotrophic. If $CO_2$ is considered available in carbonate form, the reaction may be represented as in Equation 1 (Gottschalk 1979):

(1) $HCO_3^- + H^+ + 4H_2 \rightarrow CH_4 + 3H_2O$ ($\Delta G'_0$ $= -32.4$ kcal/mol $= -135.6$ kJ/mol)

In Equation 1, $\Delta G'_0$ (Gibbs free energy) indicates the energy yield of the reaction in kilocalories per mole. In exothermic (energy-yielding) reactions, $\Delta G'_0$ is negative.

Carbon dioxide is converted to methane via a pathway that involves several unusual coenzymes. In the first step, $CO_2$ is bound to methanofuran at the formyl reduction level and is further reduced to the methenyl, methylene, methyl, and finally methane levels while successively bound to the coenzymes tetrahydromethanopterin, 2-methylthioethanesulfonic acid, and 2-mercaptoethanesulfonic acid (Jones et al. 1985). The manner of $CO_2$ conversion to cell material in methanogens does not follow the ribulose diphosphate pathway common to other chemolithotrophs, but rather by acetyl-CoA synthase pathway. The methyl group of the acetate is formed by the stepwise reduction of $CO_2$ to methyl via the tetrahydromethanopterin pathway that otherwise leads to methane evolution. This methyl group is then joined to the carbonyl group of acetate that is derived by the reduction of another $CO_2$ to CO by carbon monoxide

dehydrogenase. This same enzyme then catalyzes the synthesis of the methyl group, CO and HS-CoA to acetyl-CoA and, therefore, is also called acetyl-CoA synthase. The acetate is subsequently processed through a reverse tricarboxylic acid cycle to yield pyruvate and other trioses. These can be further condensed to hexoses and other anabolic products (Ferry 1993).

Some methanogens, such as *Methanosarcina barkeri,* are capable of metabolizing methanol, acetate, and methylamines to methane and $CO_2$. Syntrophic associations between methanogens and other anaerobes, such as the short-chain fatty-acid-fermenting *Syntrophobacter* associated with some methanogens, broaden the range of substrates suitable for methanogenesis, even though pure cultures of methanogenic archaea have the narrow substrate range (Bryant et al. 1967). The methanogens depend on the fermentation products of other microbes to serve as their substrates.

In the anoxic water of a deep subsurface confined basaltic aquifer of eastern Washington State, a substantial indigenous microbial community has been detected (Stevens and McKinley 1995). The majority of these microorganisms are chemolithotrophic. Substantial amounts of dissolved hydrogen, methane, and bicarbonate were also detected in the aquifer water. Although the information is preliminary, it appears that the aquifer water reacts with the reduced basaltic rock to produce hydrogen geochemically. The reaction mechanism is as yet unclear, but the microbial biofilm adhering to the basaltic rock may indirectly facilitate the reaction. In the anoxic, bicarbonate-rich aquifer water, the hydrogen is used by methanogens and probably also by sulfate reducers for the chemoautotrophic production of biomass. This chemoautotrophic activity, in turn, also supports populations of anaerobic heterotrophic bacteria. This microbial community is unique in its complete independence of any photosynthetically produced organic carbon, and even of the oxidizing atmosphere created by photosynthesis. The carbon sources, electron donors, and electron sinks for the deep-subsurface microbial community appear to be entirely geochemical.

The gaseous hydrocarbon methane is the ultimately reduced carbon compound and cannot be metabolized further without an appropriate electron sink. The single carbon unit of methane is an unusual substrate, available only to a specialized group of microorganisms, the methylotrophs (Haber et al. 1983). Many of these are obligate methylotrophs, meaning that they are restricted to the utilization of methane, methanol, formate, carbon monoxide, and a few additional reduced single-carbon compounds. Facultative methylotrophs have a broader substrate range. *Methylomonas* (formerly known as *Methanomonas*) species are obligately aerobic microorganisms and utilize methane only in the presence of oxygen. Methylotrophic microorganisms have been reported in sediments at the transition zone between methane production and sulfate reduction (Hanson 1980; Large 1983; Iversen and Jørgensen 1985; Iversen et al. 1987). Some methane escapes to the atmosphere and participates in photochemical processes. The methane concentration of the atmosphere is currently 1.7 ppm and is increasing at 1% per year (Ferry 1993; Conrad 1995).

## Acetogenesis

A group of facultatively chemoautotrophic anaerobes are capable of reducing $CO_2$ with $H_2$ to acetate instead of methane (Drake 1994). *Clostridium thermoaceticum* and *Acetobacterium woodii* carry out this reaction (Equation 2):

$$(2) \quad 2CO_2 + 4H_2 \rightarrow CH_3COOH + 2H_2O \ (\Delta G'_0$$
$$= -25.6 \ \text{kcal/mol} = -107.5 \ \text{kJ/mol})$$

The energy yield of the reaction is less favorable than in methanogenesis. In addition to acetogenesis from $CO_2$ and $H_2$, these organisms also ferment CO, formate, and methanol to acetate and have many metabolic features in common with methanogenic bacteria (Zeikus et al. 1985).

As compared to methanogenesis, the generation of acetate from the same substrates is energetically less efficient. Enrichments on $H_2$ and $CO_2$ tend to yield methanogens rather than acetogens, unless special measures are used for suppressing methanogenesis. It is intriguing to speculate how these two metabolic strategies coexist in nature, without the methanogens outcompeting the acetogens. Although no clear-cut answer is available to this question, the coexistence is likely to be one of an efficient specialist with a less efficient generalist. The methanogens are energetically more efficient, while the facultatively chemolithotrophic acetogens can use a broader range of substrates. Acetogens also have a greater tolerance to low pH than the methanogens. The acetogens are a heterogeneous group of Bacteria, apparently resulting from evolutionary convergence. In contrast, methanogens form a closely related homogeneous group within the Archaea. In nature, acetogens and methanogens may not only compete but also cooperate. Often occurring in the same floc or biofilm, acetate-utilizing methanogens convert the acetate formed by the acetogens to methane, thereby preventing its accumulation to inhibitory concentrations (Drake 1994; Ferry 1993).

## Carbon Monoxide Cycling

We have already discussed the role of microorganisms in the cycling of carbon between the atmosphere and the lithosphere/hydrosphere; the principal carbon form exchanged is $CO_2$, which is removed from the atmosphere during primary production and reintroduced principally during respiration. Microorganisms also are involved in the cycling of carbon monoxide in both a direct and an indirect manner. The global annual production is estimated at 3 billion to 4 billion metric tons per annum (bmta). A major source (1.5 bmta) of this CO is the photochemical oxidation of methane and other hydrocarbons in the atmosphere. Biologically, trace amounts of CO are formed during microbial and animal respiration by the breakdown of heme compounds. Another biological source of CO is an obscure photochemical side reaction in photosynthetic microorganisms and plants. The CO production by this mechanism is proportional to light intensity but is independent of $CO_2$ concentration and photosynthesis rate. Hence, CO production is not an integral part of the photosynthesis process but is part of photooxidation of cell organic carbon. Cyanobacteria and algae, along with photooxidation of dissolved organic matter, make the oceans net producers of CO. The total oceanic production of CO is around 0.1 bmta; plants and soil add another 0.1 bmta (Swinnerton et al. 1970; Weinstock and Niki 1972; Conrad 1988). The anthroprogenic contribution to CO production from the burning of biomass (wood) and fossil fuels is around 1.6 bmta. The atmospheric turnover time of CO is about 0.1–0.4 year.

The destruction of CO occurs in part by photochemical reactions in the atmosphere that convert it to $CO_2$. Microbial processes contribute to the substantial destruction of CO both in the ocean and in soil. Whereas the ocean is a net producer of CO, soil acts as a sink, removing an estimated 0.4 bmta of CO from the atmosphere (Bartholomew and Alexander 1981; Conrad 1988). Carbon monoxide, though highly toxic to most aerobic organisms because of its affinity for cytochromes, can be metabolized both aerobically and anaerobically by specialized microorganisms. Aerobically, the "carboxydobacteria," such as *Pseudomonas carboxidoflava* and *Pseudomonas carboxydohydrogena,* are capable of utilizing CO both as a carbon and as an energy source, although growth under such conditions is slow. The key enzyme, CO-oxidoreductase, catalyzes the reaction in Equation 3:

(3) $CO + H_2O \rightarrow CO_2 + H_2$

In the presence of oxygen, the product $H_2$ is oxidized to water, yielding energy for $CO_2$ fixation. Growth on CO is relatively slow and inefficient; only 4–16% of the CO oxidized is fixed as cell carbon. Hydrogen gas is used preferentially by carboxydobacteria; growth is much more rapid and CO utilization is suppressed when hydrogen is supplied in the gas mixture. Hence, carboxydobacteria can be considered also as hydrogen bacteria that possess CO-oxidoreductase (Meyer 1989).

Anaerobically, CO can be reduced by $H_2$ to $CH_4$ by some methanogens such as *Methanosarcina barkeri* according to the reaction in Equation 4:

(4) $CO + 3H_2 \rightarrow CH_4 + H_2O$

Alternatively, CO can be reduced to acetate by acetogens such as *Clostridium thermoaceticum* (Equation 5) (Zeikus et al. 1985):

(5) $2CO + 2H_2 \rightarrow CH_3COOH$

## Limitations to Microbial Carbon Cycling

Although the enzymatic ability of microorganisms to deal with naturally occurring organic substances is virtually unlimited, adverse environmental conditions, such as lack of oxygen, high acidity, and high concentrations of phenolics and tannins, can prevent the biodegradation of some types of natural substances. Such conditions are evident in muck soils (histosols), peat deposits, and some aquatic sediments. Ultimately, such accumulation of undegraded organic matter leads to fossil-fuel deposits and the removal of carbon from the biogeochemical cycling process.

The formation of humic materials from phenolic intermediates of lignin degradation and other metabolic processes represents an intermediate situation between immediate recycling and fossil-fuel deposition. Humic substances in soil are quite stable, and their average age as determined by $^{14}C$ dating ranges from 20 to 2000 years. Humic compounds in peat and muck deposits persist even longer. Nevertheless, they continue to participate in the cycling process at slow rates.

Molecular structure has a major effect on cycling rates. Some organic compounds are relatively resistant to enzymatic attack; some may even be completely recalcitrant, that is, not subject to enzymatic degradation. Many synthetic chemicals, such as DDT and PCBs, discussed in Chapter 13, are relatively resistant to microbial attack and therefore accumulate within the biosphere, occasionally reaching toxic levels within local habitats (Alexander 1973; 1994).

The activities of microorganisms affect the accessibility of carbon and the energy of organic compounds to the biological community. Some transformations of organic carbon—for example, the production of polymers like humic acids in soil—tend to reduce the rate of cycling or to immobilize that portion of carbon and stored energy. Other transformations, such as the anaerobic degradation of cellulose, mobilize stored carbon and energy by producing simpler organic compounds that can be more readily utilized by the biological community. Transformations that change the physical state, as the production of gaseous compounds such as $CO_2$ or $CH_4$ from liquids or solids, and transformations that alter the solubility, such as the produc-

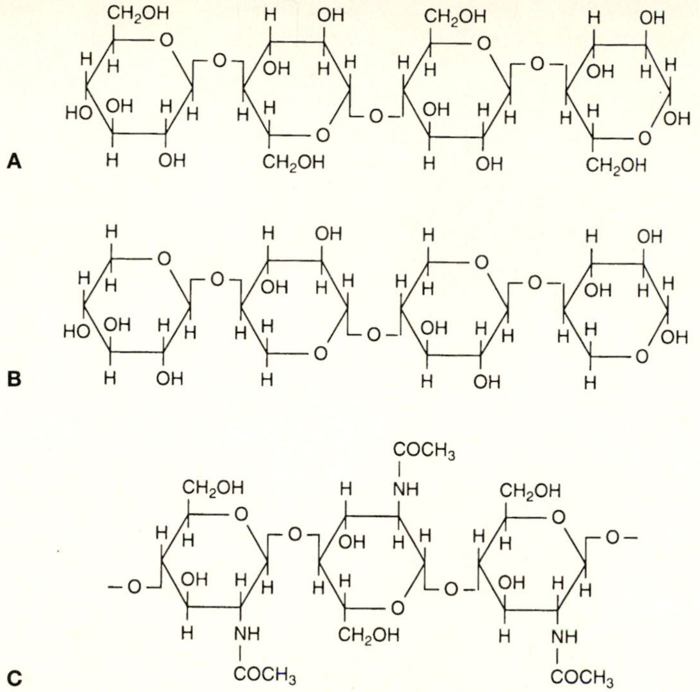

**Figure 10.6**
Composition of some structural polysaccharides. Cellulose (A) consists of β-1,4-linked glucose (hexose) subunits (β-1,4-glucosides). Hemicelluloses are more diverse, often heteropolymeric and branched. The hemicellulose shown (B) is a β-1,4-linked neutral xylan, consisting of xylose (pentose) subunitts. Chitin (C) consists of β-1,4-linked *N*-acetylglucosamine (amino sugar) subunits. Microorganisms play a key role in biodegradation of these structural polymers.

tion of glucose from cellulose, have major effects on the mobility and availability of carbon to the biological community within particular habitats.

## Microbial Degradation of Polysaccharides

An important part of microbial carbon cycling is the biodegradation of plant polymers, a process that is especially critical in terrestrial environments. Plants are responsible for the principal input of organic carbon into soils, and soil microorganisms are largely responsible for the transformation of their structural polymers. As a consequence of their activity, carbon

dioxide is reintroduced to the atmosphere, humic materials are formed, and simpler organic compounds are made available to other populations. Microorganisms within the gastrointestinal tract of herbivorous animals, analogously, play a major role in the degradation of plant polymers, making most of the carbon available to the animal.

Biogenic polymers recycled primarily by microbial degradation in soil include cellulose, hemicelluloses, and chitin (Figure 10.6). Cellulose, the most abundant biopolymer in the world, is a carbohydrate consisting of a linear chain of β-1,4 linked glucose units. In soil, several varieties of fungi, including species of the genera *Aspergillus, Fusarium, Phoma,* and *Trichoderma,* and bacteria, including members of the genera *Cytophaga, Vibrio, Polyangium, Cellulomonas, Streptomyces,* and *Nocardia,* exhibit significant cellulolytic activities (Imshenetsky 1967; Ljungdahl and Eriksson 1985). Various Basidiomycota are prominent cellulose degraders in wood and litter on the soil surface. The soil pH exerts an important influence on which cellulolytic microbial populations are active. Below pH 5.5 filamentous fungi dominate, at pH 5.7–6.2 various fungi and *Cytophaga* species are involved in cellulose degradation, and at neutral-alkaline pH values *Vibrio* species and fungi predominate. Numerous additional bacteria are known to participate in cellulose degradation.

Cellulose degradation occurs under both aerobic and anaerobic conditions. Under aerobic conditions, various fungi, as well as aerobic and facultatively anaerobic bacterial populations, are involved in cellulolytic activities. The main products of cellulose degradation under aerobic conditions are carbon dioxide, water, and cell biomass. Under anaerobic conditions, members of the genus *Clostridium* appear to be the most important cellulose fermenters. Anaerobic fermentation of cellulose results in the production of low-molecular-weight fatty acids as well as carbon dioxide, water, and cell biomass. Fungi generally play a minor role in cellulose degradation under anaerobic conditions. Fermentation yields less energy per unit of substrate consumed than does respiration, so anaerobic cellulose-fermenting bacteria must degrade large quantities of cellulose in order to generate cell biomass. Degradation of cellulose also occurs at elevated temperatures, where it is carried out by thermophilic cellulolytic bacteria, such as *Clostridium thermocellum.* Thermophilic cellulose degradation is important in waste-composting procedures where large amounts of cellulose must be stabilized (see Chapter 12).

The degradation of cellulose is catalyzed by cellulases. The enzyme system actually involves several different cellulases that catalyze various conversions of cellulose. A cellulase system involves three types of enzymes: a $C_1$ enzyme, a $C_x$ or β-1,4-glucanase, and a β-glucosidase. Total degradation of cellulose involves all three enzymes. The $C_1$ enzyme acts on native cellulose and does not appear to exhibit much action against partially degraded cellulose molecules. The $C_x$ enzymes do not hydrolyze native cellulose but instead cleave partially degraded polymers. There are two types of cleavage exhibited by $C_x$ enzymes. *Endo-*β-1,4-glucanases break the chain internally, more or less at random, resulting in the formation of cellobiose and various oligomers. *Exo-*β-1,4-glucanases attack the polymer near the end of the chain, resulting, principally, in the formation of cellobiose. The degradation of cellobiose and other relatively small oligomers is catalyzed by β-glucosidase, resulting in the formation of glucose. In summary, the degradation of cellulose in soil and other habitats involves multiple enzyme systems. Cellulolytic activities are exhibited by various microbial populations; the rates of cellulose degradation and the products formed depend on the species of microorganisms and the environmental conditions within individual habitats.

The second major class of plant constituents that enter soil habitats and that are subject to microbial degradation are the hemicelluloses (Alexander 1977). Hemicelluloses have no structural relationship to cellulose but rather are polysaccharides composed of various arrangements of pentoses such as xylose and arabinose, hexoses such as mannose, glucose and galactose, and/or uronic acids such as glucuronic and galacturonic acids. Examples of hemicellulosic compounds are xylans, mannans, and galactans. Hemicellulosic compounds are subject to degradation by various fungal and bacterial populations. Numerous fungi and bacteria, including actinomycetes and members of the genus *Bacillus,* are capable of degrading xylans. Many enzymes are involved in the degradation of hemicelluloses, including endoenzymes, which cleave bonds within the polymer somewhat at random, and exoenzymes, which normally cleave monomers or dimers from the end of the polymer. The products of hemicellulose degradation include carbon dioxide, water, cell biomass, and a variety of small carbohydrate molecules including monomers and dimers. The complexity of the hemicellulose molecules that enter soil as plant residues leads to a corresponding complexity of microbial degradation products that are formed.

Various other plant components, such as waxes, starch, and pectic substances, are also subject to degradation in various habitats. It is beyond the scope of this discussion to consider all of the molecules in plant residues that enter soil habitats and that are subject to microbial degradation. Suffice it to say that soil microorganisms through their degradative activities are effective in cycling carbon from a wide variety of plant residues, ultimately back to carbon dioxide, which can be used in primary production to complete the carbon cycle.

Chitin is another important polymer subject to microbial degradation in soil habitats. An acetylated amino sugar polymer, it is synthesized by various fungi as part of their cell walls and by various arthropods, including microcrustacea, as part of their skeletal structures. The global production of chitin in the marine and terrestrial environments amounts to many million mta (Gooday 1990), and most of this polymer is recycled by microbial degradation. Chitinases cleave the polymer from the reducing end or in a random way, eventually yielding primarily diacetylchitobiose units. This is hydrolyzed to *N*-acetylglucosamine monomers by acetylglucosaminidases. An alternate way of attack first deacetylates chitin to chitosan, and subsequently depolymerizes this product by chitosanase to chitobiose subunits. Glucosaminidases complete the degradation to glucosamine monomers. The ability to depolymerize and utilize chitin is quite common among bacteria, actinomycetes, and fungi. In contrast to cellulose digestion, many invertebrate and vertebrate animals produce their own chitinolytic enzymes, but in many species intestinal microbiota make substantial contributions to chitin digestion (Kuznetsov 1970; Saunders 1970; Gooday 1990).

Agar, which is produced by numerous marine algae, is decomposed by relatively few species of bacteria of the genera *Agrobacterium, Flavobacterium, Bacillus, Pseudomonas,* and *Vibrio.* Many of these agar-utilizing bacteria occur as algal epiphytes. Because few microorganisms can depolymerize agar, it is especially suitable for the solidification of most microbial media.

## Microbial Degradation of Lignin

Lignin is a structural plant polymer that is almost as abundant in higher plants as cellulose and hemicelluloses. Its unique structure and resistance to degradation justify a separate discussion of this structural plant polymer. In wood and other lignified structures such as grass stems, lignin occurs in intimate association with cellulose and hemicelluloses, adding structural strength and protecting the polysaccharides by its biodegradation-resistant barrier. Lignins have an aromatic structure consisting of phenylpropane subunits, linked together by carbon-carbon (C—C) or ether (C—O—C) bonds into a highly complex three-dimensional structure (Ander and Eriksson 1978; Kirk et al. 1980; Zeikus 1981; Kirk 1984) (Figure 10.7). The biosynthesis of lignin starts from phenylalanine. Deamination, ring hydroxylation, methylation, and carboxyl reduction lead to cinnamyl alcohol precursors, which are oxidatively polymerized. Synthesis of lignin is unusual in that the polymerization does not take place on an enzyme surface. Instead, oxidases and peroxidases produce reactive quinon methid radicals that polymerize spontaneously (Kirk 1984). Lignin and its subunits are, therefore, not optically active, and the randomness of the polymerization process makes subsequent enzymatic degradation of the product much more difficult. In this respect, there is a certain analogy between the biodegradation resistance of lignin and soil humus, although the structure of humus is much more heterogeneous and, consequently, substantially more resistant to biodegradation.

Biodegradation rates for lignin are much lower than for either cellulose or hemicellulose compounds (Kirk 1984). Biodegradation of intact lignin does not occur anaerobically, although aromatic fragments produced by alkaline degradation of lignin can be metabolized anaerobically. Intact wood is attacked first by brown rot and white rot fungi, which are both basidiomycetes. Brown rot fungi, by a mechanism that is not yet clear, bypass the protective lignin barrier and attack the cellulose and hemicellulose components of wood directly. Logs decomposed in this manner fall

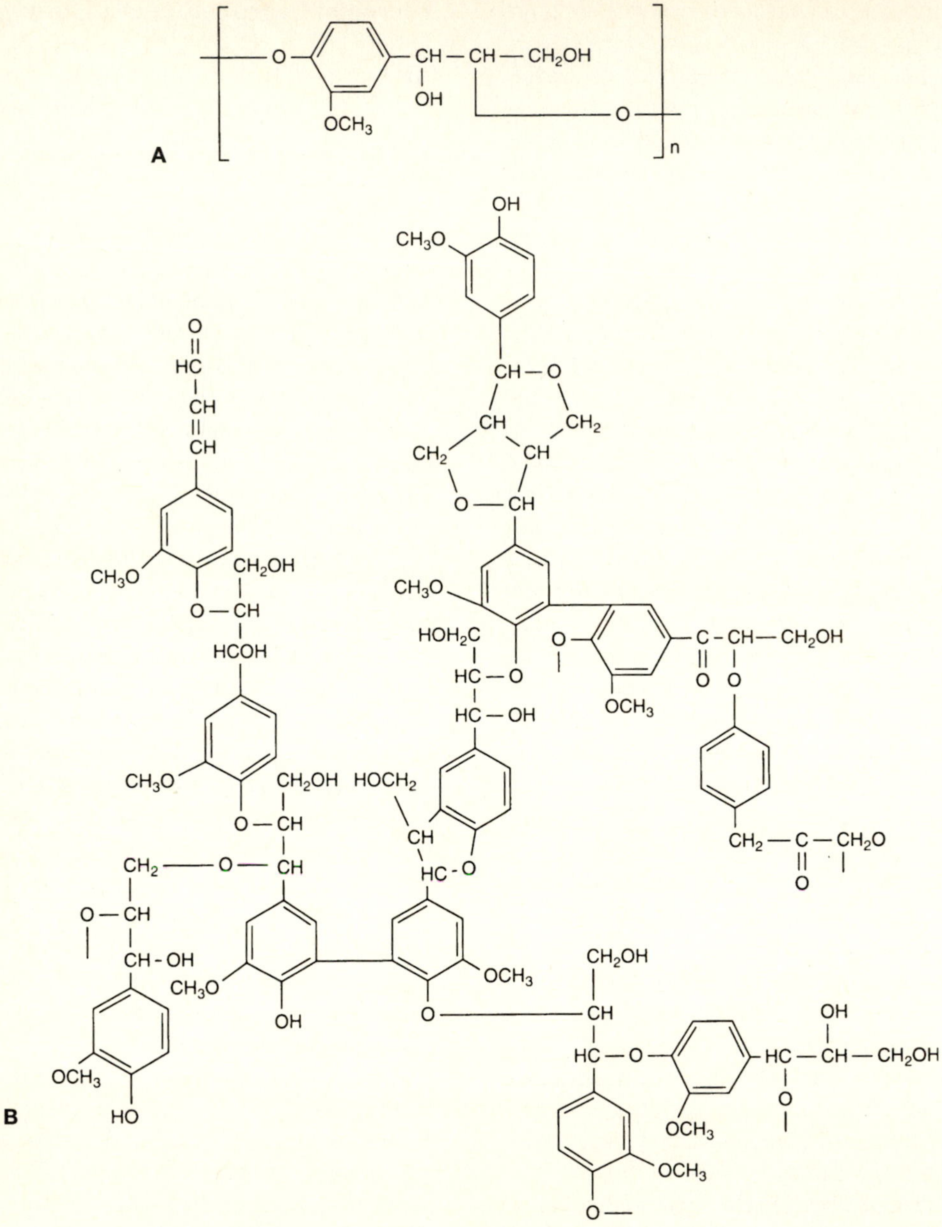

**Figure 10.7**

Chemical composition of the structural plant polymer lignin. The phenylpropane subunit (A) is linked by C—C and C—O—C bonds into (B) a complex three-dimensional structure that is relatively resistant to biodegradation. In the "lignocellulose complex" of wood, it also slows the biodegradation of cellulose.

apart into a brown powder consisting mainly of enzymatically liberated lignin. In contrast, white rot fungi degrade lignin preferentially, leaving a soft, fibrous, cellulosic residue. White rot and brown rot fungi are taxonomically closely related and usually work either sequentially or simultaneously, bringing about the complete biodegradation of wood.

The biodegradation of lignin is a complex oxidative process. Like the formation process for lignin, it is indirect and random. The white rot fungus most intensively studied for its lignin-biodegradation activity, the basidiomycete *Phanerochaete chrysosporium,* appears to produce oxidizing agents such as superoxide anion ($O_2^-$), hydrogen peroxide ($H_2O_2$), hydroxyl radicals (—OH), and singlet oxygen ($^1O_2$). These break the bonds between subunits and bring about a gradual depolymerization of lignin. Tien and Kirk (1983) demonstrated the production of an extracellular, $H_2O_2$-dependent enzyme by *P. chrysosporium* that oxidatively breaks specific bonds in the lignin structure. Lignin does not serve as the sole source of carbon and energy for *P. chrysosporium.* Lignolytic activity is induced at a late growth stage and usually under nitrogen-limiting conditions. Thus, at least with this fungus, lignin biodegradation appears to be a secondary metabolic or idiophasic event.

Other fungi implicated in lignin biodegradation are *Polyporus, Poria, Fomes, Agaricus, Pleurotus, Collybia, Schizophyllum,* and *Fusarium.* Aerobic bacterial genera shown to participate in lignin biodegradation are *Arthrobacter, Flavobacterium, Micrococcus,* and *Pseudomonas.* The depolymerization of lignin results in a variety of phenols, aromatic acids, and aromatic alcohols. Some of these are mineralized to $CO_2$ and $H_2O$, but some of the products, particularly the phenolic biodegradation intermediates, may give rise to humic compounds. This repolymerization is in part a spontaneous oxidative reaction but is also catalyzed by microbial polyphenoloxidases, peroxidases, and laccases. The apparent benefit to the microorganisms that catalyze such reactions is the detoxification of the harmful phenolic intermediates.

Only a portion of soil humus is derived from lignin biodegradation products; numerous other aromatic and nonaromatic organic compounds derived from plants, animals, and microorganisms participate in humus formation. We discussed humus structure and biodegradation in Chapter 9.

## Biodegradation and Heterotrophic Production in Aquatic Environments

Rivers, lakes, and coastal marine environments receive significant amounts of allochthonous plant residues that contain high amounts of structural polymers, such as cellulose and lignin. In contrast to these allochthonous materials, autochthonous organic carbon within aquatic habitats is generally formed through primary productivity of photosynthetic algae and bacteria. The qualitative composition of the organic matter formed in aquatic habitats is somewhat different from the organic compounds formed by terrestrial plants. Both the complexity and the amounts of organic matter present in the water column are generally lower than in soil habitats. Various soluble compounds, including carbohydrates, amino acids, and organic acids, are released into the water column by autochthonous primary producers. In general, this autochthonous material has a higher concentration of available nitrogen than the allochthonous plant residues. Concentrations of organic matter in natural waters are generally quite low; concentrations rarely exceed 1 mg carbon per liter in open seawater. At these low concentrations of organic carbon, the ability of aquatic bacteria to assimilate low concentrations of dissolved organic compounds becomes quite important. There appear to be significant populations of oligocarbophiles (organisms that utilize low nutrient concentrations) in aquatic habitats. We already touched upon the microbial upgrading of detritus in Chapter 5. The ability of most microorganisms to utilize inorganic nitrogen ($NO_3^-$, $NH_4^+$) is crucial to detritivores that cannot survive on nitrogen-deficient plant polymer particles alone. The utilization of both soluble and particulate organic compounds by bacteria in aquatic habitats produces organic matter in a form that can be utilized through a food web and also produces carbon dioxide, normally in the form of bicarbonate, which becomes available for primary producers. Figure 10.8 illustrates an example of the flow of

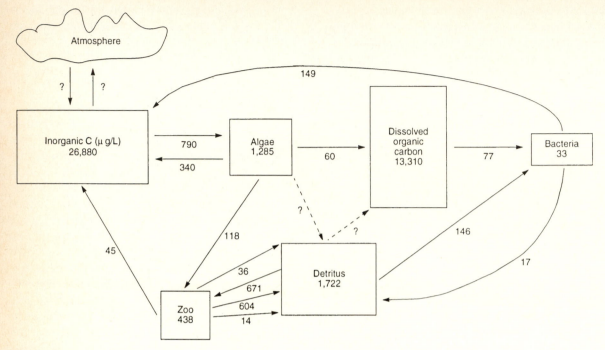

**Figure 10.8**
A flow diagram for carbon transfers in a lake habitat. The numbers associated with boxes indicate reservoirs of carbon; those associated with arrows indicate relative transfer rates. The figure illustrates the roles of algae and bacteria in primary and secondary production, respectively, and in the flow of carbon through aquatic habitats. (Source: Saunders 1970. Reprinted by permissions of J. Cairns, Jr.)

carbon through an aquatic habitat. This figure indicates the pools of soluble organic and inorganic carbon in a lake and the relative transfer rates, showing both production and decomposition processes performed by microbial populations (Hutchinson 1975; Fenchel and Jørgensen 1977).

In addition to the natural input of carbon into soil and aquatic habitats, a large number of organic compounds enter these habitats through human activities. These organic compounds are, for the most part, subject to microbial degradation with the production of carbon dioxide and other compounds that enter the normal carbon cycle. The cycling of organic waste materials, such as garbage and sewage, is discussed in greater detail in Chapter 12; the cycling of human-made organic chemicals, such as pesticides, is discussed in Chapter 13.

## The Hydrogen Cycle

The largest global reservoir of hydrogen is water. This reservoir is actively cycled by photosynthesis and respiration, but because of the large size of the reservoir, the cycling rate is rather slow. Water tied up in crystal lattices of rock is not cycled actively, and the polar ice caps also remove water from active cycling for long periods of time. Substantial inert hydrogen reservoirs are liquid and gaseous fossil hydrocarbons. Living and dead organic material constitute relatively small but actively cycled reservoirs. Free gaseous $H_2$ is produced biologically in anaerobic fermentations and also as a side product of photosynthesis coupled with nitrogen fixation by cyanobacteria and by *Rhizobium*-legume associations (Conrad 1988, 1995). Most of the $H_2$ produced is utilized anaerobically to reduce $NO_3^-$,

$SO_4^{2-}$, $Fe^{3+}$, and $Mn^{4+}$ or to generate $CH_4$ as described earlier. When $H_2$ rises through oxygenated soil or sediment zones, it is metabolized oxidatively to $H_2O$, and only a small part—about 7 million mta—is likely to escape to the atmosphere. Although both evolution and consumption of the $H_2$ occur in the aquatic and the terrestrial environments, the oceans are net producers of an estimated 4 million mta of hydrogen per year, whereas soils serve as net hydrogen sinks. Hydrogen is produced anthropogenically by fossil fuel and biomass burning and as part of the exhaust of internal combustion engines (40 million mta). Hydrogen is also produced in the atmosphere by the photochemical decomposition of methane (40 million mta). The gravitational pull of Earth is not strong enough to prevent the loss of hydrogen to space from the upper atmosphere, where it is also produced by photodissociation of water vapor.

As discussed earlier, the present 21% atmospheric oxygen content was derived primarily by photosynthetic splitting of water, but the question inevitably arises of what happened to the double amount of hydrogen in the water molecules (Cloud and Gibor 1970; Valen 1971). The reduced carbon in living and dead organic matter and in fossil fuels is estimated to contain considerably less hydrogen than could be accounted for from the splitting of water, and there are no other substantial hydrogen sinks. The most plausible explanation appears to be that the missing amount of hydrogen may have been lost to space. Microbial processes that utilize $H_2$ and $CH_4$ and thus prevent their escape to the atmosphere minimize current losses of $H_2$.

The aerobic utilization of $H_2$ is performed by facultatively chemolithotrophic hydrogen bacteria (Schlegel 1989) in the energy-yielding reaction shown in Equation 6:

(6) $H_2 + \frac{1}{2}O_2 \rightarrow H_2O$ ($\Delta G'_0 = -56.7$ kcal/mol $= -238.1$ kJ/mol)

The most efficient hydrogen bacteria belong to the genus *Alcaligenes* (Bowien and Schlegel 1981). In addition to membrane-bound hydrogenases, these bacteria contain a soluble NAD-linked hydrogenase.

A number of bacteria belonging to the genera *Pseudomonas*, *Paracoccus*, *Xanthobacter*, *Nocardia*, and *Azospirillum* contain membrane-bound hydrogenases only, and are capable of growing as hydrogen bacteria at slower rates. Many if not all hydrogen-activating enzymes (hydrogenases) appear to contain the trace metal nickel in their active center (Thauer et al. 1980). The overall equation of hydrogen utilization can be represented as in Equation 7:

(7) $6H_2 + 2O_2 + CO_2 \rightarrow [CH_2O] + 5H_2O$

The formula in brackets represents cell material. Hydrogen bacteria fix carbon dioxide by the same mechanisms as algae and plants, that is, by carboxylation of ribulose 1,5-diphosphate and the regeneration of the above pentose through the Calvin cycle. Hydrogen bacteria can also grow on various organic substrates, or they can grow mixotrophically on a combination of $H_2$ and organic substrates.

The $H_2$ cycling activities discussed so far involve the evolution or utilization of molecular hydrogen. The most important $H_2$ cycling processes, photosynthesis and respiration, do not normally result in $H_2$ evolution or consumption, however. Instead, the electrons from $H_2S$ or some low-molecular-weight organic compounds (anoxyphotobacteria) or from $H_2O$ (all other photosynthetic organisms) are directly utilized in photosynthesis for reduction of $CO_2$. In respiration, the electrons from reduced organic compounds are passed along the respiratory chain, ultimately to reduce oxygen to water. Coupled to this process are phosphorylation reactions that satisfy the energy needs of the cell.

In dinitrogen fixation systems coupled to photosynthesis, that is, for the heterocystous cyanobacteria and the *Rhizobium*-legume symbiosis, the partial or complete uncoupling of the two systems results in the evolution of molecular hydrogen. In cyanobacteria, this seems to occur only under artificial laboratory conditions (Beneman and Weave 1974), but *Rhizobium*-legume associations evolve large amounts of $H_2$ under agricultural field conditions. Improved *Rhizobium* strains are being constructed to eliminate this energetically wasteful process. The improved strains have high hydrogenase activity and are capable of oxidizing $H_2$ with the gain of energy. This energy, in turn, is used in fixation of additional nitrogen (LaFavre and Focht 1983).

A significant aspect of hydrogen cycling is the interspecies transfer of hydrogen between microorganisms with different metabolic capabilities. Interspecies hydrogen transfer, as occurs between the fermentative and methanogenic component of the synthrophic *Methanobacillus omelianskii* association (Bryant et al. 1967), is a mutually beneficial one. We will also discuss interspecies hydrogen transfer that occurs between methanogens and sulfate reducers in Chapter 11.

## THE OXYGEN CYCLE

The establishment of an oxidizing atmosphere was the most profound biogeochemical transformation on our planet. Photosynthesis-derived oxygen not only transformed our atmosphere but oxidized large pools of reduced minerals such as ferrous iron and sulfides. Oxygen deposited in ferric iron and in dissolved and sedimentary sulfates exceeds the oxygen in the atmosphere by severalfold. These mineral reservoirs of oxygen, including the carbonates, participate to some extent in the oxygen cycle, but because of their large mass, their turnover rate is almost negligible. Among the more actively cycled reservoirs, atmospheric and dissolved oxygen, $CO_2$, and $H_2O$ predominate. Nitrate is a small, rapidly cycled oxygen reservoir. The turnover of the much larger sulfate and oxidized iron-manganese reservoirs is much slower. Oxygen in living and dead organic matter constitutes a relatively small but actively cycled reservoir.

The photosynthetic origin of atmospheric oxygen is generally accepted. The geological record clearly indicates that oxidized sediments such as ferric iron deposits were first formed 1.5–1.8 billion years ago. Older sediments are reduced. The oxidoreductive balance of the transition is less clear; the estimates and calculations are by necessity crude. There seems to be a shortage of reduced carbon as compared to atmospheric oxygen and oxidized minerals (Cloud and Gibor 1970; Valen 1971). As mentioned earlier, escape of hydrogen to space is one possible explanation.

Atmospheric oxygen produced in photosynthesis is removed from the atmosphere by respiration, a process that, besides producing $CO_2$, reconstitutes the water cleaved in photosynthesis. The presence or absence of molecular oxygen in a habitat is crucial in determining the type of metabolic activities that can occur in that habitat. Oxygen is inhibitory to strict anaerobes. Facultative anaerobes can gain more energy from organic substrates using oxygen as the terminal electron acceptor than by fermentative metabolism. For example, the aerobic metabolism of glucose yields 686 kcal (2881 kJ) per mole; its fermentation yields only 50 kcal per mole (210 kJ). Metabolic regulatory mechanisms ensure that oxygen is used preferentially as the terminal electron acceptor if it is available. Oxygen serves as the terminal electron acceptor not only in degradation of organic matter but also in the oxidation of reduced inorganic chemicals used as energy sources by chemolithotrophs.

In some habitats, the microbial utilization of oxygen during degradation of organic compounds may produce anoxic conditions. In habitats that are not in equilibrium with the atmosphere and where organic matter is undergoing rapid decomposition, oxygen is normally bound within organic compounds, and molecular oxygen becomes unavailable as an electron acceptor in respiration. Habitats such as marine sediments and flooded soils are normally depleted of molecular oxygen owing to its utilization during decomposition and the slow diffusion of molecular oxygen into these habitats.

The exhaustion of oxygen in an environment initiates the reduction of nitrate, sulfate, ferric iron, and oxidized manganese. If such electron acceptors are unavailable or become exhausted, fermentative metabolism and methanogenesis (reduction of $CO_2$) remain the only metabolic options.

Oxygen can be restored to an anaerobic environment by diffusion, sometimes aided by the bioturbation of worms and other burrowing animals indigenous to sediments and soils, or by photosynthetic activity. Plants, algae, and cyanobacteria produce molecular oxygen during the photosynthetic photoly-

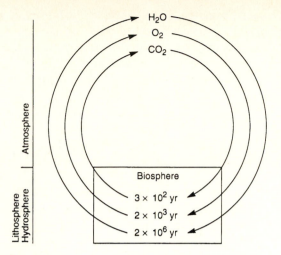

**Figure 10.9**
Turnover rates of $CO_2$, $O_2$, $H_2O$, by biogeochemical cycling showing probability of any given molecule of each being biologically processed. The smaller reservoir of $CO_2$ is more frequently cycled than the larger pools of $O_2$ and $H_2O$. The oceans represent the largest actively cycled $H_2O$ reservoir. Even though all three molecules are used in the same processes of photosynthesis and respiration, their cycling times differ. Perturbation of cycling is most likely to affect the relatively small pool of $CO_2$. (Source: Woodwell 1970, The Energy Cycle of the Biosphere. Reprinted by permission, copyright 1970, Scientific American Inc. All rights reserved.)

sis of water. Oxygen is not produced by the photosynthesis of the anoxyphotobacteria.

The burning of fossil fuels may be expected to have an effect on atmospheric oxygen as well as on $CO_2$ concentrations. Indeed, alarmist articles occasionally appear in the popular press about the potential exhaustion of atmospheric oxygen by human activity. These concerns are groundless because of the sizable oxygen reservoir (21% of the atmosphere); the same processes that perturb the small $CO_2$ reservoir (0.03% of the atmosphere) have negligible effect on the much larger oxygen pool. The burning of all known fossil-fuel reserves would reduce the oxygen supply by only 3% (Broeker 1970).

Figure 10.9 compares the approximate turnover rates of atmospheric $CO_2$, $O_2$, and $H_2O$. All three materials are cycled by the balanced processes of photosynthesis and respiration, yet their differing reservoir sizes result in very different turnover rates. Based on pool sizes and utilization rates, every individual atmospheric $CO_2$ molecule has a chance of being assimilated by photosynthesis every 300 years or less, every atmospheric oxygen molecule will be used in respiration every 2000 years, and every water molecule has a chance to be split by photosynthesis every 2,000,000 years. Thus, a change in the global rates of photosynthesis or respiration would have a more immediate and dramatic effect on atmospheric $CO_2$ concentrations than on either atmospheric $O_2$ or $H_2O$.

In the upper atmosphere, ionizing radiation transforms some of the oxygen from $O_2$ to $O_3$ (ozone). Ozone is not directly subject to biogeochemical cycling. The relatively small ozone pool in the atmosphere, however, is subject to perturbation by human activity and by alterations in the biogeochemical process of denitrification and methanogenesis. The ozone layer is important for its shielding capacity against incoming UV radiation.

## CHAPTER SUMMARY

Biogenic elements cluster in distinct areas of the periodic table and may be subdivided into major, minor, and trace elements. Biogeochemical cycling of elements with several stable valence states tends to be complex and oxidoreductive. Other elements may be cycled without valence changes by solubilization and precipitation only. A chemical form of an element represents a reservoir. Small reservoirs such as atmospheric $CO_2$ are turned over rapidly and are particularly sensitive to disturbances of cycling.

Carbon, hydrogen, and oxygen are cycled primarily by the two opposing processes of photosynthesis and respiration, but because of the differing reservoir sizes, the turnover rates of these three elements differ greatly. In the absence of oxygen, organic carbon may be recycled in fermentative and methanogenic processes. Reduced products of fermentation and methanogenesis often reenter the oxidative cycle. Hydrogen, evolved in some fermentation processes, may combine with various electron acceptors, including $O_2$, CO, and $CO_2$. Atmospheric oxygen is biogenic in origin. It is the preferred electron acceptor for all aerobic and facultatively anaerobic organisms.

All living organisms participate in cycling of C, H, and O. However, microorganisms dominate both the production and catabolic processes in limnetic and pelagic environments. The capability of microbes for uptake of very dilute dissolved organics enables them to engage also in "secondary production." In addition, they dominate the catabolic process in the terrestrial environment because of their unique capacity to degrade complex polymers such as cellulose, lignin, and soil humus.

## STUDY QUESTIONS

1. Why are some elements called biogenic? What is their position in the periodic system?

2. What distinguishes major, minor, and trace biogenic elements?

3. What is the ultimate source of energy for materials cycling?

4. What constitutes a "reservoir" for nutrient elements? How does reservoir size influence turnover rates?

5. Why do human activities have a large impact on atmospheric $CO_2$ concentration?

6. What is the greenhouse effect? How does it work?

7. What are the important, actively cycled carbon reservoirs in addition to atmospheric $CO_2$?

8. What are the two biological processes that drive the cycling of carbon, oxygen, and hydrogen? Why is the cycling of these three elements closely linked?

9. What are the most important and actively cycled reservoirs of oxygen and hydrogen?

10. How is organic material degraded under anoxic conditions? What are methanogens and acetogens?

11. How is the hydrogen and methane generated in anaerobic environments recycled by microorganisms?

12. Why do the turnover times of $CO_2$, $O_2$, and $H_2O$ differ greatly?

## REFERENCES AND SUGGESTED READINGS

Alexander, M. 1973. Nonbiodegradable and other recalcitrant molecules. *Biotechnology and Bioengineering* 15:611–647.

Alexander, M. 1977. *Introduction to Soil Microbiology.* Wiley, New York, pp. 148–202.

Alexander, M. 1994. *Biodegradation and Bioremediation.* Academic Press, San Diego.

Ander, P., and K. E. Eriksson. 1978. Lignin decomposition. *Progress in Industrial Microbiology* 4:1–58.

Appenzeller, T. 1993. Searching for clues to ancient carbon dioxide. *Science* 259:908–909.

Azam, F., T. Fenchel, J. G. Field, J. S. Gray, L. A. Meyer-Reil, and F. Thingstad. 1983. The ecological role of water-column microbes in the sea. *Marine Ecological Progress Series* 10:257–263.

Balch, W. E., G. E. Fox, L. J. Magrum, C. R. Woese, and R. S. Wolfe. 1979. Methanogens: Reevaluation of a unique biological group. *Microbiological Reviews* 43:260–296.

Bartholomew, G. W., and M. Alexander. 1981. Soil as a sink for atmospheric carbon monoxide. *Science* 212:1389–1391.

Beneman, J. R., and N. M. Weave. 1974. Hydrogen evolution by nitrogen-fixing *Anabaena cylindrica* cultures. *Science* 184:174–175.

Bird, D. F., and J. Kalff. 1986. Bacterial grazing by planktonic lake algae. *Science* 231:493–495.

Bolin, B. 1970. The carbon cycle. *Scientific American* 223(3):125–132.

Bolin, B., E. T. Degens, P. Duvigneaud, and S. Kempe. 1979. The global biogeochemical carbon cycle. In B. Bolin, E. T. Degens, S. Kempe, and P. Ketner (eds.). *The Global Carbon Cycle.* Wiley, New York, pp. 1–53.

Bowien, B., and H. G. Schlegel. 1981. Physiology and biochemistry of aerobic hydrogen-oxidizing bacteria. *Annual Reviews of Microbiology* 35:405–452.

Broeker, W. S. 1970. Enough air. *Environment* 12:27–31.

Bryant, M. P., E. A. Wolin, M. J . Wolin, and R. S. Wolfe. 1967. *Methanobacillus omelianskii,* a symbiotic association of two species of bacteria. *Archiv für Mikrobiologie* (Berlin) 59:20–31.

Bull, A. T. 1980. Biodegradation: Some attitudes and strategies of microorganisms and microbiologists. In D. C. Ellwood, J. N. Hedger, M. J. Latham, J. M. Lynch, and J. H. Slater (eds.). *Contemporary Microbial Ecology.* Academic Press, London, pp. 107–136.

Charlson, R. J., S. E. Schwartz, J. M. Hales, R. D. Cess, J. A. Coakley, Jr., J. E. Hansen, and D. J. Hoffman. 1992. Climate forcing by anthropogenic aerosols. *Science* 255:423–430.

Cloud, P., and A. Gibor. 1970. The oxygen cycle. *Scientific American* 223(3):111–123.

Codd, G. A. (ed.). 1984. *Aspects of Microbial Metabolism and Ecology.* Academic Press, London.

Conrad, R. 1988. Biogeochemistry and ecophysiology of atmospheric CO and $H_2$. *Advances in Microbial Ecology* 10:231–283.

Conrad, R. 1995. Soil microbial processes involved in production and consumption of atmospheric trace gases. *Advances in Microbial Ecology* 14:207–250.

Deevey, E. S., Jr. 1970. Mineral cycles. *Scientific American* 223(3):149–158.

Drake, H. L. (ed.). 1994. *Acetogenesis.* Chapman and Hall, New York.

Eriksson, K. E., and S. Christl. 1982. Mineralization of carbon. In R. G. Burns and J. H. Slater (eds.). *Experimental Microbial Ecology.* Blackwell, Oxford, England, pp. 134–153.

Fenchel, T. 1986. The ecology of heterotrophic microflagellates. *Advances in Microbial Ecology* 9:57–97.

Fenchel, T. M., and B. B. Jørgensen. 1977. Detritus food chains of aquatic ecosystems: The role of bacteria. *Advances in Microbial Ecology* 1:1–58.

Ferry, J. G. (ed.). 1993. *Methanogenesis.* Chapman and Hall, New York.

Frieden, E. 1972. The chemical elements of life. *Scientific American* 227(1):52–60.

Gooday, G. W. 1990. The ecology of chitin degradation. *Advances in Microbial Ecology* 11:387–430.

Gottschalk, G. 1979. *Bacterial Metabolism.* Springer-Verlag, New York.

Gottschalk, G. 1989. Bioenergetics of methanogenic and acetogenic bacteria. In H. G. Schlegel and B. Bowien (eds.). *Autotrophic Bacteria.* Springer-Verlag, Berlin, pp. 383–413.

Haber, C. L., L. N. Allen, S. Zhao, and R. Hanson. 1983. Methylotrophic bacteria: Biochemical diversity and genetics. *Science* 221:1147–1153.

Hanson, R. S. 1980. Ecology and diversity of methylotrophic organisms. *Advances in Applied Microbiology* 26:3–39.

Heal, O. W., and P. Ineson. 1984. Carbon and energy flow in terrestrial ecosystems: Relevance to microflora. In M. J. Klug and C. A. Reddy (eds.). *Current Perspectives in Microbial Ecology.* American Society for Microbiology, Washington, DC, pp. 394–404.

Hobbie, J. E., and J. M. Melillo. 1984. Comparative carbon and energy flow in ecosystems. In M. J. Klug and C. A. Reddy (eds.). *Current Perspectives in Microbial Ecology.* American Society for Microbiology, Washington, DC, pp. 389–393.

Houghton, R. A., J. E. Hobbie, J. M. Melillo, B. Moore, B. J. Peterson, G. R. Shaver, and G. M. Woodwell. 1983. Changes in the carbon content of terrestrial biota and soils between 1860 and 1980: A net release of $CO_2$ to the atmosphere. *Ecological Monographs* 53:235–262.

Hubel, H. 1966. Die $^{14}C$ Methode zur Bestimmung der Primärproduktion des Phytoplanktons. *Limnologica* (Berlin) 4:267–280.

Hutchinson, G. E. 1970. The biosphere. *Scientific American* 223(3):45–53.

Hutchinson, G. E. 1975. *A Treatise on Limnology. Vol. I, Geography, Physics and Chemistry.* Part 2, Chemistry of Lakes. Wiley, New York.

Imshenetsky, A. A. 1967. Decomposition of cellulose in the soil. In T.R.G. Gray and D. Parkinson (eds.). *The Ecology of Soil Bacteria.* Liverpool University Press, Liverpool, England, pp. 256–269.

Iversen, N., and B. B. Jørgensen. 1985. Anaerobic methane oxidation rates at the sulfate-methane transition in marine sediments from Kattegat and Skagerrak (Denmark). *Limnology and Oceanography* 30:944–955.

Iversen, N., R. S. Oremland, and M. J. Klug. 1987. Big Soda Lake (Nevada): Pelagic methanogenesis and anaerobic methane oxidation. *Limnology and Oceanography* 32:804–814.

Jones, C. W. 1980. Unity and diversity in bacterial energy conservation. In D. C. Ellwood, J. N. Hedger, M. J. Latham, J. M. Lynch, and J. H. Slater (eds.). *Contemporary Microbial Ecology.* Academic Press, London, pp. 193–214.

Jones, W. J., M. I. Donnelly, and R. S. Wolfe. 1985. Evidence of a common pathway of carbon dioxide reduction to methane in methanogens. *Journal of Bacteriology* 163:126–131.

Jørgensen, B. B. 1980. Mineralization and the bacterial cycling of carbon, nitrogen, and sulphur in marine sediments. In D. C. Ellwood, J. N. Hedger, M. J. Latham, J. M. Lynch, and J. H. Slater (eds.). *Contemporary Microbial Ecology.* Academic Press, London, pp. 239–252.

Jørgensen, B. B. 1989. Biogeochemistry of chemoautotrophic bacteria. In H. G. Schlegel and B. Bowien (eds.). *Autotrophic Bacteria.* Springer-Verlag, Berlin, pp. 117–146.

Kerr, R. A. 1992. Pollutant haze cools the greenhouse. *Science* 255:682–683.

Kerr, R. A. 1994. Iron fertilization: A tonic but no cure for the greenhouse. *Science* 263:1089–1090.

Kirk, T. K. 1984. Degradation of lignin. In D. T. Gibson (ed.). *Microbial Degradation of Organic Compounds.* Marcel Dekker, New York, pp. 399–437.

Kirk, T. K., T. Higuchi, and H. M. Chang. 1980. *Lignin Biodegradation: Microbiology, Chemistry and Potential Applications.* Vols. 1 and 2. CRC Press, Boca Raton, FL.

Kramer, P. 1981. Carbon dioxide concentration, photosynthesis, and dry matter production. *BioScience* 31:29–33.

Krumbein, W. E., and P. K. Swart. 1983. The microbial carbon cycle. In W. E. Krumbein (ed.). *Microbial Geochemistry.* Blackwell, Oxford, England, pp. 5–62.

Kuznetsov, S. I. 1970. *The Microflora of Lakes and Its Geochemical Activity.* University of Texas Press, Austin.

LaFavre, J. S., and D. D. Focht. 1983. Conservation in soil of $H_2$ liberated from $N_2$ fixation by Hup⁻ nodules. *Applied and Environmental Microbiology* 46:304–311.

LaMarche, V. C., Jr., D. A. Greybill, H. C. Fritts, and M. R. Rose. 1984. Increasing atmospheric carbon dioxide: Tree ring evidence for growth enhancement in natural vegetation. *Science* 225:1019–1021.

Large, P. J. 1983. *Methylotrophy and Methanogenesis.* American Society for Microbiology, Washington, DC.

Ljungdahl, L. G., and K. E. Eriksson. 1985. Ecology of microbial cellulose degradation. *Advances in Microbial Ecology* 8:237–299.

Manabe, S., and R. T. Wetherald. 1980. On the distribution of climate change resulting from an increase in $CO_2$ content in the atmosphere. *Journal of Atmospheric Science* 37:99–118.

Mertz, W. 1981. The essential trace elements. *Science* 213:1332–1358.

Meyer, O. 1989. Aerobic carbon monoxide-oxidizing bacteria. In H. G. Schlegel and B. Bowien (eds.). *Autotrophic Bacteria.* Springer-Verlag, Berlin, pp. 331–350.

Morris, I. 1982. Primary production of the oceans. In R. G. Burns and J. H. Slater (eds.). *Experimental Microbial Ecology.* Blackwell, Oxford, England, pp. 239–252.

National Research Council. 1979. *Carbon Dioxide and the Climate: A Scientific Assessment.* National Academy Press, Washington, DC.

National Research Council. 1983. *Changing Climate.* National Academy Press, Washington, DC.

National Research Council. 1991. *Global Environmental Change: The Human Dimensions.* National Academy Press, Washington, DC.

Nedwell, D. B. 1984. The input and mineralization of organic carbon in anaerobic aquatic sediments. *Advances in Microbial Ecology* 7:93–131.

Odum, E. P. 1962. Relationships between structure and function in ecosystems. *Japanese Journal of Ecology* 12:108–118.

Odum, E. P. 1983. *Basic Ecology.* Saunders, Philadelphia.

Pomeroy, L. R. (ed.). 1974. *Cycles of Essential Elements.* Dowden, Hutchinson and Ross, Stroudsburg, PA.

Pomeroy, L. R. 1984. Significance of microorganisms in carbon and energy flow in marine ecosystems. In M. J. Klug and C. A. Reddy (eds.). *Current Perspectives in Microbial Ecology.* American Society for Microbiology, Washington, DC, pp. 405–411.

Ryther, J. H. 1969. Photosynthesis and fish production in the sea. *Science* 166:72–76.

Sanders, R. W., and K. G. Porter. 1988. Phagotrophic phytoflagellates. *Advances in Microbial Ecology* 10:167–192.

Saunders, G. W. 1970. Carbon flow in the aquatic system. In J. Cairns, Jr. (ed.). *The Structure and Function of Freshwater Microbial Communities.* Research Division Monograph 3, Virginia Polytechnic Institute and State University, Blacksburg, pp. 31–46.

Schlegel, H. G. 1989. Aerobic hydrogen-oxidizing (Knallgas) bacteria. In H. G. Schlegel and B. Bowien (eds.). *Autotrophic Bacteria.* Springer-Verlag, Berlin, pp. 305–329.

Sherr, B. F., and E. B. Sherr. 1984. Role of heterotrophic protozoa in carbon and energy flow in aquatic ecosystems. In M. J. Klug and C. A. Reddy (eds.). *Current Perspectives in Microbial Ecology.* American Society for Microbiology, Washington, DC, pp. 412–423.

Stevens, T. O., and J. P. McKinley. 1995. Lithoautotrophic microbial ecosystems in deep basalt aquifers. *Science* 270:450–454.

Swinnerton, J. W., V. J. Linnenbom, and R. A. Lamontague. 1970. The ocean: A natural source of carbon monoxide. *Science* 167:984–986.

Thauer, R. K., G. Diekert, and P. Schönheit. 1980. Biological role of nickel. *Trends in Biochemical Sciences* 5:304–306.

Tien, M., and T. K. Kirk. 1983. Lignin-degrading enzyme from the hymenomycete *Phanerochaete chrysosporium* Bonds. *Science* 221:661–663.

Underwood, E. J. 1977. *Trace Elements in Human and Animal Nutrition.* Academic Press, New York.

Valen, L. V. 1971. The history and stability of atmospheric oxygen. *Science* 171:439–443.

Weinstock, B., and H. Niki. 1972. Carbon monoxide balance in nature. *Science* 176:290–292.

Whitman, W. B., and J. E. Rogers. 1991. *Microbial Production of Greenhouse Gases: Methane, Nitrogen Oxides, and Halomethanes.* American Society for Microbiology, Washington, DC.

Wood, H. G. 1989. Past and present utilization of $CO_2$. In H. G. Schlegel and B. Bowien (eds.). *Autotrophic Bacteria.* Springer-Verlag, Berlin, pp. 33–52.

Woodwell, G. M. 1970. The energy cycle of the biosphere. *Scientific American* 223(3):64–74.

Zeikus, J. G. 1977. The biology of methanogenic bacteria. *Bacteriological Reviews* 41:514–541.

Zeikus, J. G. 1981. Lignin metabolism and the carbon cycle. Polymer biosynthesis, biodegradation and environmental recalcitrance. *Advances in Microbial Ecology* 5:211–243.

Zeikus, J. G., R. Kerby, and J. A. Krzycki. 1985. Single carbon chemistry of acetogenic and methanogenic bacteria. *Science* 227:1167–1173.

# 11

# BIOGEOCHEMICAL CYCLING: NITROGEN, SULFUR, PHOSPHORUS, IRON, AND OTHER ELEMENTS

*The biogenic elements other than carbon, hydrogen, and oxygen are often referred to as mineral nutrients, and their cycles as mineral cycles (Deevey 1970). Mineral nutrients, including nitrogen, sulfur and phosphorus, are usually taken up by autotrophs and prototrophic heterotrophs in the form of mineral salts. Biogenic elements such as nitrogen, sulfur, iron, and manganese exist in the ecosphere in several stable valence states and tend to be cycled in a complex oxidoreductive manner. Elements such as phosphorus, calcium, and silicon exist in only one stable valence state. These elements have relatively simple cycles involving dissolution and incorporation into organic matter, balanced by mineralization and sedimentation.*

## THE NITROGEN CYCLE

Nitrogen, which has stable valence states ranging from −3, as in ammonia ($NH_3$), to +5, as in nitrate ($NO_3^-$), occurs in numerous oxidation states. Nitrogen is a constituent of amino acids, nucleic acids, amino sugars, and their polymers. A large, slowly cycled reservoir for nitrogen ($3.8 \times 10^{15}$ metric tons) is $N_2$ gas of the atmosphere (79%). Large but essentially unavailable reservoirs of nitrogen are present in

igneous ($1.4 \times 10^{16}$ metric tons) and sedimentary ($4.0 \times 10^{15}$ metric tons) rock as bound, nonexchangeable ammonia (Blackburn 1983). Physicochemical and biological weathering releases ammonia from these reservoirs so slowly that it has little influence on yearly cycling models. Geological deposits of more readily available combined nitrogen are rare. Availability of combined nitrogen is an important limiting factor for primary production in many ecosystems. The only natural accumulations of nitrate occur on some islands off the Chilean coast; these nitrate deposits are derived from the decomposition of guano deposited by seabirds. The dry climate of these islands has prevented the leaching of nitrate (Deevey 1970; Delwiche 1970).

The inorganic nitrogen ions, ammonium, nitrite, and nitrate occur as salts that are highly water soluble and consequently are distributed in dilute aqueous solution throughout the ecosphere; they form small, actively cycled reservoirs. Living and dead organic matter also provide relatively small, actively cycled reservoirs of nitrogen. In temperate climates, stabilized soil organic matter, or humus, forms a substantial and relatively stable nitrogen reservoir. The nitrogen of humus becomes available for uptake by living

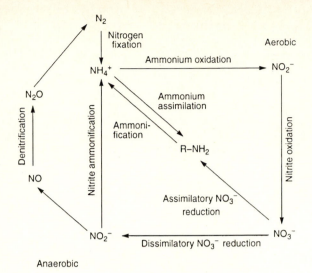

**Figure 11.1**
The nitrogen cycle showing chemical forms and key processes in biogeochemical cycling of nitrogen. The lower left portion of the cycle represents anaerobic, the upper right portion aerobic processes. The critical steps of nitrogen fixation, nitrification, and denitrification are all mediated by bacteria. R—$NH_2$ represents amino groups in cell protein.

organisms only through its slow mineralization, a process measured in decades and centuries. In tropical climates, the temperature and humidity favor the rapid direct mineralization of organic matter, limiting the accumulation of litter and humus.

Plants, animals, and most microorganisms require combined forms of nitrogen for incorporation into cellular biomass (Brown and Johnson 1977), but the ability to fix atmospheric nitrogen is restricted to a limited number of bacteria, archaea, and symbiotic associations. Many habitats depend on plants for a supply of organic carbon that can be used as a source of energy, but all habitats depend either on the bacterial fixation of atmospheric nitrogen or on human intervention through the distribution of nitrogen fertilizers synthesized by the Haber-Bosch process, invented shortly before World War I. Plants could not continue their photosynthetic metabolism without the availability of fixed forms of nitrogen provided by microorganisms or by synthetic fertilizer.

The biogeochemical cycling of the element nitrogen is highly dependent on the activities of microorganisms. Figure 11.1 shows a generalized scheme for the processes involved in the biogeochemical cycling of nitrogen. The various transformations of nitrogen bring about the circulation of nitrogen from the atmosphere through terrestrial and aquatic habitats (Figure 11.2). These movements of nitrogen through the biosphere in large part determine ecological productivity in aquatic and terrestrial habitats. Figure 11.3 on page 417 shows the approximate magnitudes of some critical transfer rates involved in the flow of nitrogen through the biosphere (Burns and Hardy 1975; Soderlund and Svensson 1976). Fixation on land, which includes considerable amounts from agriculturally managed legume crops, amounts to 135 million metric tons per annum. This greatly exceeds $N_2$ fixation in the much larger marine environment (40 million metric tons per annum). Anthropogenic nitrogen inputs in the form of synthetic fertilizer (30 million metric tons per annum), combustion (19 million metric tons per annum), and nitrogen fixation by leguminous and other crops (44 million metric tons per annum) approach the total of nitrogen fixation in grasslands (45 million metric tons per annum), forests (40 million metric tons per annum), other terrestrial areas (10 million metric tons per annum), and the marine environment (40 million metric tons per annum). Synthetic nitrogen fertilizer input is projected to rise further and may reach 100 million metric tons per annum by the year 2000. Volcanic activity, ionizing radiation, and electrical discharges supply additional combined nitrogen to the atmosphere; when washed down with precipitation, this combined nitrogen becomes available to the biosphere, but abiotically fixed nitrogen is estimated to be only 10–20% of the biological fixation. Microorganisms are also responsible for the return of molecular nitrogen to the atmosphere through denitrification and for the transformations that affect the mobility and accessibility of fixed nitrogen to the inhabitants of the litho- and hydro-ecospheres. Prior to human intervention, $N_2$-fixation and denitrification processes appeared to be in balance. With increased anthropogenic inputs, this may no longer be the case.

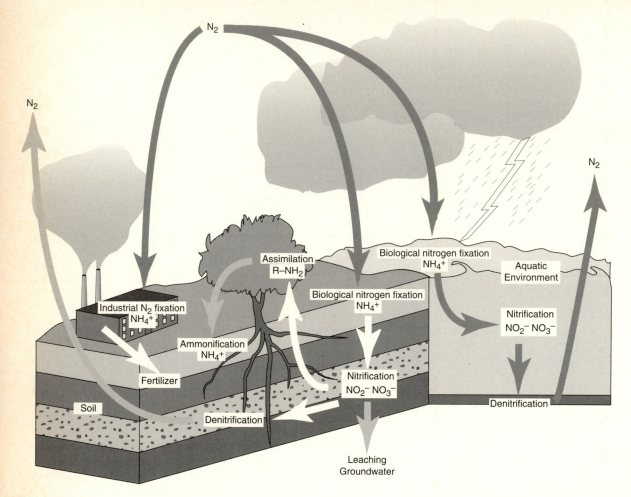

**Figure 11.2**
The individual processes of the nitrogen cycle in different zones within soil and aquatic habitats. Biological nitrogen fixation, anthropogenic inputs of industrially produced nitrogen fertilizer, and nitrogen oxides formed in reactions associated with lightning move nitrogen from the atmosphere to the soil and water. Nitrification alters the ionic charge of the fixed forms of nitrogen so that leaching occurs in soils. Denitrification in anaerobic soils and sediments returns molecular nitrogen to the atmosphere.

## Fixation of Molecular Nitrogen

Nitrogenase is the enzyme complex responsible for nitrogen fixation (Smith 1982; Postgate 1982; Sprent and Sprent 1990; Evans et al. 1991; Postgate 1992). The nitrogenase enzyme system has two coproteins, one containing molybdenum plus iron and the other containing only iron (Figure 11.4 on page 418). Nitrogenase is extremely sensitive to oxygen, requiring low oxygen tensions for activity. The fixation of nitrogen needs not only nitrogenase, but also ATP, reduced ferredoxin, and perhaps other cytochromes and coen-

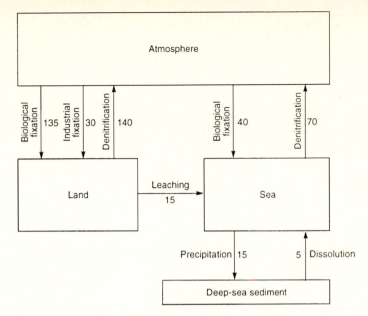

**Figure 11.3**
General scheme for transfer of nitrogen between the atmosphere and marine and terrestrial environments indicating some transfer rates (numbers are millions of metric tons/year) and interconversions within the terrestrial and aquatic reservoirs. As minor transfer processes are omitted, a complete balance is not achieved. (Source: Burns and Hardy 1975. Reprinted by permission, copyright Springer-Verlag.)

zymes. Ammonia is formed as the first detectable product of nitrogen fixation (Equation 1):

(1)  $N_2 + 6e^- \rightarrow 2NH_3$ ($\Delta G'_0$
    $= +150$ kcal/mol $= +630$ kJ/mol)

As indicated by the positive $\Delta G'_0$, the reaction requires high energy input. The ammonia is assimilated into amino acids, which are then polymerized into proteins (Campbell 1977; Brill 1981; Sprent and Sprent 1990).

The biological fixation of molecular nitrogen is carried out by several free-living bacterial genera, some of which may be rhizosphere-associated, and by several bacterial genera that form mutualistic associations with plants as discussed in Chapter 4 (Evans et al. 1991; Postgate 1992; Benson and Silvester 1993). The genes responsible for nitrogen fixation, including the

*nif* genes for nitrogenase production, are under stringent genetic regulation (Evans et al. 1991; Fischer 1994). This is an extremely complex regulatory system that controls the expression of multiple *nif* genes required for the production of active nitrogenase (Figure 11.5 on page 419). The fixation of nitrogen generally occurs in response to low or limiting concentrations of ammonia.

In terrestrial habitats, the symbiotic fixation of nitrogen by rhizobia accounts for the largest contribution of combined nitrogen. The rates of nitrogen fixation by symbiotic rhizobia are often two to three orders of magnitude higher than rates exhibited by free-living nitrogen-fixing bacteria in soil. Rhizobia associated with an alfalfa field may fix up to 300 kg N per hectare per year, compared to a rate of 0.5–2.5 kg N per hectare per year for free-living *Azotobacter* species (Dalton 1974; Burns and Hardy 1975).

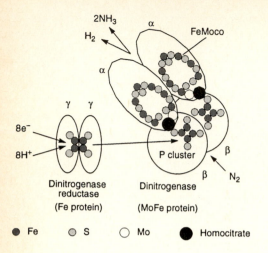

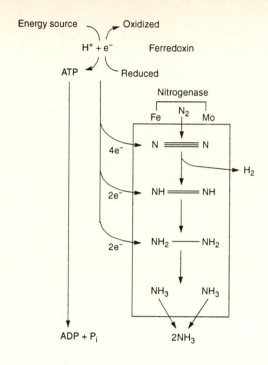

### Figure 11.4

The nitrogenase enzyme system catalyzes the reduction of molecular nitrogen to ammonia. This enzyme system is a complex of dinitrogenase reductase (Fe protein) and dinitrogenase (MoFe protein). Electrons are initially transferred to the dinitrogenase reductase ($Fe_4S_4$ center). They are then transferred to the P clusters ($Fe_4S_4$) of the dinitrogenase protein. The P clusters pass the electrons to the iron-molybdenum cofactors (FeMoco; $Fe_7S_9Mo$-homocitrate) of the dinitrogenase and then on to the $N_2$. $H_2$ is also evolved in this reaction. Nitrogen fixation brought about by nitrogenase-producing bacteria converts atmospheric nitrogen to fixed forms of nitrogen ($NH_3$, which at physiological pH occurs as $NH_4^+$) that can be used by other microorganisms, plants, and animals.

Nitrogen has no radioactive isotope with a convenient half-life; $^{13}N$ decays rapidly and its stable isotope ($^{15}N$) can be analyzed only by expensive and inconvenient mass spectrometry. Studies on the rates of nitrogen fixation were greatly enhanced by development of the acetylene reduction assay (Hardy et al. 1968). This assay is based on the fact that nitrogenase enzymes will reduce acetylene to ethylene. The similarity of the acetylene molecule (HC≡CH) to nitrogen (N≡N) is obvious even from the written structures. The rate of formation of ethylene is a measure of nitrogenase or nitrogen-fixing activity. Ethylene can be conveniently assayed with great sensitivity using a gas chromatograph equipped with a flame ionization detector. For a nitrogenase activity measurement, a small soil core, plant root system, or other environmental sample is placed in a gastight enclosure—for example, a plastic syringe or bag. The enclosure is flushed with acetylene or acetylene-oxygen mixture and incubated for several hours. Because the nitrogenase system has greater affinity to acetylene than to dinitrogen gas, meticulous removal of $N_2$ is not necessary. After incubation, the gas phase is assayed for the amount of ethylene formed by acetylene reduction. Procedures for chemically analyzing the disappearance of nitrogen gas from the atmosphere or the rates

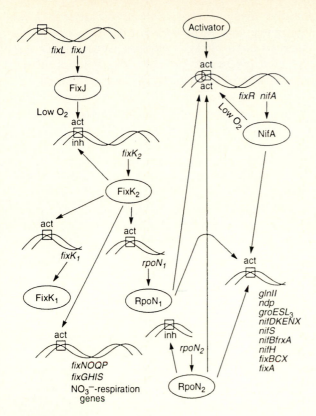

**Figure 11.5**
Diagram showing the genetic regulation of nitrogen-fixation genes in *Bradyrhizobium japonicum.* This regulatory system, like the entire genetic basis for symbiotic nitrogen fixation, is very complex. Changing sigma units that activate promoters between $\sigma^{54}$ and other $\sigma$ factors facilitates switching which genes are turned on and which are turned off through control of the respective promoters. The regulation of the *nif* genes that control and code for the production of nitrogenase, as well as various other genes such as the *fix* genes that appear to help control oxygen levels so that expressed nitrogenase is functional, are especially important. FixJ and NifA are critical in the regulatory system of symbiotic nitrogen fixation. Both *fixJ* and *nifA* are responsive to low concentrations of oxygen. Abbreviations used in this figure include: act = activator; inh = inhibitor; open box = non-$\sigma^{54}$-dependent promoter; open circle = $\sigma^{54}$-dependent promoter. (Source: Fischer 1994.)

of formation of fixed forms of nitrogen are far less sensitive and convenient for routine use. The rate of acetylene reduction, compared with the rate of incorporation of molecular nitrogen into cell biomass, generates roughly a 3:1 conversion factor from moles of ethylene formed to moles of $N_2$ fixed. This conversion factor, though, is not identical in all ecosystems, necessitating a calibration against $^{15}N$-incorporation measurements in each ecosystem.

Acetylene reduction and other quantitative methods, such as measuring growth on nitrogen-free media, have revealed that a number of bacterial species are capable of fixing molecular nitrogen under appropriate environmental conditions. Redox potential is especially important in determining the rates of nitrogen fixation by many bacterial species that are genetically capable of producing nitrogenase enzymes. Many aerobic nitrogen-fixing bacteria have been shown to fix nitrogen more efficiently at oxygen levels below the normal atmospheric concentration (21%). Such conditions are frequently found in subsoil and sediment habitats. In addition to *Azotobacter* and *Beijerinckia,* both well-established genera of free-living nitrogen-fixing soil bacteria, more and more genera have been found over time to fix atmospheric nitrogen. They now include species of *Chromatium, Rhodopseudomonas, Rhodospirillum, Rhodomicrobium, Chlorobium, Azospirillum, Desulfovibrio, Desulfotomaculum, Klebsiella, Bacillus, Clostridium, Azospirillum, Pseudomonas, Vibrio,* and *Thiobacillus* (Stewart 1973; Blackburn 1983). Several members of Actinomycetales have also been shown to fix atmospheric nitrogen, some of which are free-living and others of which fix atmospheric nitrogen in association with compatible plants (see Chapter 4). Overall, the sensitivity of today's methodology has revealed an increasing number of bacterial genera that can fix atmospheric nitrogen when oxygen tensions are appropriate.

Although the rates of nitrogen fixation for free-living soil bacteria are relatively low, these bacteria are widespread in soils. Because of the availability of organic compounds from root exudates, rates of nitrogen fixation by free-living bacteria, such as *Azotobacter* and *Azospirillum,* are higher within the rhizosphere than in soils lacking plant roots, allowing for increased efficiency of nitrogen transfer to photosynthetic organisms (Döbereiner and Day 1974).

In aquatic habitats, cyanobacteria are the principal nitrogen fixers (Paerl 1990). Many of the filamentous nitrogen-fixing cyanobacteria, such as *Anabaena, Aphanizomenon, Nostoc, Gloeotrichia, Cylindrospermum, Calothrix, Scytonema,* and *Tolypothrix* have heterocysts. Heterocysts are thick-walled, less pigmented, and often enlarged cells occurring at more-or-less regular intervals among the regular cells. During their differentiation, heterocysts lose their oxygen-evolving photosystem II but retain their anoxygenic photosystem I. Nitrogen fixation is localized in the heterocysts, where the oxygen-sensitive nitrogenase is protected from inactivation by the photosynthetically produced oxygen. There is an active exchange between the ordinary cells and the heterocysts, the former supplying disaccharides from photosynthesis and the latter supplying fixed nitrogen, mainly as glutamine.

Some nonheterocystous cyanobacteria, such as *Oscillatoria, Trichodesmium, Microcoleus,* and *Lyngbya,* have been shown to fix nitrogen. How these cyanobacteria protect their nitrogenase from oxygen inactivation is less clear, but some mechanisms have been identified that individually or in combination may explain the phenomenon. Some of the nonheterocystous cyanobacteria show a temporal separation between photosynthesis and nitrogenase activity. During daylight hours, photosynthesis and photosynthate storage take place, with little or no nitrogen fixation. During nighttime, in the absence of photosynthesis, nitrogen fixation takes place at the expense of the stored photosynthate. Other nonheterocystous nitrogen fixers form clumps or mats. In these aggregations, the outer cells photosynthesize, whereas the innermost cells, through a combination of shading and respiratory activity, are in a zone of reduced oxygen tension permissive of nitrogenase activity. Nutrient exchange is obviously necessary in such a situation. Apparently, nonheterocystous cyanobacteria possess mechanisms to reactivate or resynthesize their nitrogenases after oxygen exposure.

Rates of nitrogen fixation by cyanobacteria are generally one to two orders of magnitude higher than by free-living nonphotosynthetic soil bacteria. Under favorable conditions, cyanobacteria in a rice paddy may fix up to 150 kg of nitrogen per hectare per year (National Research Council 1979). Nitrogen-fixing cyanobacteria, many of which form heterocysts, are found in both marine and freshwater habitats. Some nitrogen-fixing cyanobacteria form associations with other microorganisms, as in lichens; some form symbiotic associations with plants, such as the *Azolla-Anabaena* association; others are free living.

Bacterial fixation of molecular nitrogen requires a considerable input of energy (150 kcal/mol = 630 kJ/mol) in the form of ATP and reduced coenzymes (Benemann and Valentine 1972; Brill 1981). The energy for carrying out nitrogen fixation may be obtained through the conversion of light energy by photoautotrophs, such as cyanobacteria, or by respiration of heterotrophs, such as *Azotobacter.* In the latter case, nitrogen fixation is limited by the availability of organic substrates, and attempts to increase nitrogen fixation by commercial *Azotobacter* inocula, such as "Nitragin," have been unsuccessful.

Nitrogen fixation within the phyllosphere and rhizosphere is ecologically important because some of the fixed nitrogen is likely to become available to the plants (see Chapter 4). Exudates from the plant may supply some of the energy required for the nitrogen-fixation process. Nitrogen fixation also occurs within the digestive tracts of some animals, such as termites (see Chapter 5). The fixation of nitrogen in organisms consuming primarily nitrogen-free cellulose is especially important for formation of proteins. Substantial nitrogen fixation has been observed in environments characterized by an abundance of carbon sources and a scarcity of nitrogen, such as decomposing logs or oil-contaminated soils (Coty 1967).

*Azotobacter* and *Beijerinckia* can fix nitrogen at normal oxygen tensions and appear to protect their nitrogenases from oxidative inactivation by a combination of compartmentalization and complex biochemical mechanisms. Other free-living nitrogen fixers, such as *Azospirillum,* fix nitrogen only at reduced oxygen tensions. Such environments, especially on the microscale, are not rare in soil and on root surfaces. Oxygen is not a problem for nitrogenases of anoxyphototrophic bacteria such as *Chromatium, Rhodopseudomonas, Rhodospirillum, Rhodomicrobium,* and *Chlorobium,* or for the anaerobic heterotrophs such as *Clostridium, Desulfovibrio,* and *Desulfotomaculum.* The latter are active in anaerobic sediments and in the rhizosphere of plants growing in such sediments (see Chapter 4). As in aerobic nitrogen fixation, carbon-rich, nitrogen-poor substrates such as cellulose favor the process. This has been known to occur indirectly as nitrogen fixers utilized low-molecular-weight products of cellulose fermentation. More recently, direct nitrogen fixation by cellulolytic anaerobes was also documented (Leschine et al. 1988).

## Ammonification

Many plants, animals, and microorganisms are capable of ammonification, a process in which organic nitrogen is converted to ammonia. Nitrogen in living and dead organic matter occurs predominantly in the reduced amino form. Blackburn (1983) emphasized the importance of organic nitrogen mineralization for continued ecosystem productivity. The release of ammonia from a simple nitrogenous organic compound, urea, can be described as follows (Equation 2):

$$(2) \quad NH_2-\overset{\overset{\displaystyle O}{\|}}{C}-NH_2 + H_2O \xrightarrow{urease}$$

$$2NH_3 + CO_2$$

In acidic to neutral aqueous environments, ammonia exists as ammonium ions. Some of the ammonia produced by ammonification is released from alkaline environments to the atmosphere, where it is relatively inaccessible to biological systems. Ammonia and other forms of nitrogen within the atmo-ecosphere are subject to chemical and photochemical transformations and can be returned to the litho- and hydro-ecospheres in precipitation. The amount of ammonium nitrogen in global precipitation has been estimated at 38–85 million metric tons per annum (Soderlund and Svensson 1976).

Ammonium ions can be assimilated by numerous plants and many microorganisms, where they are incorporated into amino acids and other nitrogen-containing biochemicals. The initial incorporation of ammonia into living organic matter is often accomplished either by glutamine synthetase/glutamate synthase reactions or by direct amination of an $\alpha$-keto-carboxylic acid to form an amino acid (Gottschalk 1979). The relative importance of the two assimilation pathways varies among habitats and depends on environmental factors and species composition; for example, at low $NH_4^+$ concentrations, aquatic bacteria primarily utilize the glutamine synthetase/glutamate synthase pathway. The incorporated amino group can be transferred through transamination to form other amino acids. The amino acids can be incorporated into proteins or transformed into other nitrogen-containing compounds that can be utilized as sources of carbon, nitrogen, and energy.

Nitrogen-containing organic compounds produced by one organism can be transferred to and assimilated by others. The transformations of organic nitrogen-containing compounds are not restricted to microorganisms. Animals, for example, produce nitrogenous wastes such as uric acid from the metabolism of nitrogen-containing organic compounds.

## Nitrification

In nitrification, ammonia or ammonium ions are oxidized to nitrite ions (Equation 3) and then to nitrate ions (Equation 4).

$$(3) \quad NH_4^+ + 1\tfrac{1}{2}O_2 \rightarrow$$
$$NO_2^- + 2H^+ + H_2O \ (\Delta G'_0 = -66 \text{ kcal/mol}$$
$$= 277.2 \text{ kJ/mol})$$

$$(4) \quad NO_2^- + \tfrac{1}{2}O_2\,NO_3^- \ (\Delta G'_0 = -17 \text{ kcal/mol}$$
$$= -71.4 \text{ kJ/mol})$$

The process of nitrification appears to be limited for the most part to a restricted number of autotrophic bacteria (Focht and Verstraete 1977; Hooper 1990). Different microbial populations carry out the two steps of nitrification—that is, the formation of nitrite and the formation of nitrate. Normally, however, the two processes are closely coupled and an accumulation of nitrite does not occur. The oxidation of ammonia to nitrite and the oxidation of nitrite to nitrate are both energy-yielding processes. Nitrifying bacteria

**Table 11.1**
Rates of nitrification by some heterotropic and autotropic nitrifiers

| Organism | Substrate | Product | Rate of formation ($\mu$g N/day/g dry cells) | Max. product accumulation ($\mu$g N/mL) |
|---|---|---|---|---|
| *Arthrobacter* (heterotroph) | $NH_4^+$ | Nitrite | 375–9000 | 0.2–1 |
| *Arthrobacter* (heterotroph) | $NH_4^+$ | Nitrate | 250–650 | 2–4.5 |
| *Aspergillus* (heterotroph) | $NH_4^+$ | Nitrate | 1350 | 75 |
| *Nitrosomonas* (autotroph) | $NH_4^+$ | Nitrite | 1–30 million | 2000–4000 |
| *Nitrobacter* (autotroph) | $NO_2^-$ | Nitrate | 5–70 million | 2000–4000 |

Source: Focht and Verstraete 1977.

are chemolithotrophs and utilize the energy derived from nitrification to assimilate $CO_2$. In the first reaction (Equation 3), molecular oxygen is incorporated into the nitrite molecule. The oxidation is a multistep process and involves the generation of hydroxylamine ($NH_2OH$) by ammonia monooxygenase. The single oxygen atom incorporated into hydroxylamine comes from atmospheric oxygen. In the next step, hydroxylamine oxidoreductase produces, from hydroxylamine and water, nitric acid and hydrogen, so the second oxygen atom in nitrite comes from water. The two hydrogens from water are converted back to water by a terminal oxidase using atmospheric oxygen. The production of nitrous acid lowers the pH of the environment where nitrification occurs.

Though oxygen dependent, the second step of nitrification obtains the oxygen for formation of nitrate from a water molecule; the molecular oxygen serves only as an electron acceptor. Both steps of the nitrification process are aerobic. Nitrite oxidation is a single-step process and yields only low amounts of energy. Approximately 100 moles of nitrite must be oxidized for the fixation of 1 mole of $CO_2$, whereas oxidation of 35 moles of ammonia achieves the same end.

In soils, the dominant genus that is capable of oxidizing ammonia to nitrite is *Nitrosomonas,* and the dominant genus capable of oxidizing nitrite to nitrate is *Nitrobacter.* Other bacteria capable of oxidizing

ammonia to nitrite are found in the genera *Nitrosospira, Nitrosococcus, Nitrosolobus,* and *Nitrosovibrio* (Bock et al. 1990). In addition to *Nitrobacter,* members of the genera *Nitrospira, Nitrospina,* and *Nitrococcus* are able to oxidize nitrite to nitrate. *Nitrobacter, Nitrospira, Nitrospina, Nitrococcus, Nitrosomonas,* and *Nitrosococcus* occur in marine habitats. *Nitrobacter, Nitrosomonas, Nitrosospira, Nitrosococcus,* and *Nitrosolobus* are found in soil habitats. Some other microorganisms, including heterotrophic bacteria and fungi, are capable of a limited oxidation of nitrogen compounds, but heterotrophic nitrification does not appear to make a major contribution to the conversion of ammonia to nitrite and nitrate ions (Table 11.1). Relatively few microbial genera are involved in the process of nitrification and environmental stress can severely affect this process. The second step of nitrification is usually the more sensitive one, and under stress conditions some nitrite accumulation may occur (Bollag and Kurek 1980).

The process of nitrification is especially important in soils, because the transformation of ammonium ions to nitrite and nitrate ions results in a change in charge from positive to negative. Positively charged ions tend to be bound by negatively charged clay particles in soil, but negatively charged ions freely migrate in the soil water. The process of nitrification, therefore, must be viewed as a nitrogen mobilization process within soil habitats. Ammonia in soil is normally oxidized rapidly by nitrifying bacteria. Plants readily take up nitrate ions into their roots for assimilation into organic compounds. Nitrate and nitrite ions, however, can also be readily leached from the soil column into the groundwater. This is an undesirable process because it represents a loss of fixed forms of nitrogen from the soil, where plants could utilize them to produce biomass.

## Nitrate Reduction and Denitrification

Nitrate ions can be incorporated by a variety of organisms into organic matter through assimilatory nitrate reduction. A heterogeneous group of microorganisms, including many bacterial, fungal, and algal species, is capable of assimilatory nitrate reduction. The process involves several enzyme systems, including nitrate and nitrite reductases, to form ammonia, which can be subsequently incorporated into amino acids (Gottschalk 1986). The enzyme systems appear to involve soluble metalloproteins and require reduced cofactors, including reduced nicotinamide adenine dinucleotide phosphate (NADPH). Assimilating nitrate enzyme systems that have been examined in bacteria, algae, and fungi are repressed by the presence of ammonia or reduced nitrogenous organic metabolites in the growth environment. Normal atmospheric concentrations of oxygen do not appear to inhibit assimilatory nitrate reductase enzyme systems. Assimilatory nitrate reduction does not result in the accumulation of high concentrations of extracellular ammonium ions, because ammonia is incorporated relatively rapidly into organic nitrogen. Excess ammonium would act through feedback inhibition to shut off nitrate reduction.

In the absence of oxygen, nitrate ions can act as terminal electron acceptors. As reviewed by Focht and Verstraete (1977), the process is known as nitrate respiration, or dissimilatory nitrate reduction. During dissimilatory nitrate reduction, nitrate is converted to a variety of reduced products, while organic matter is simultaneously oxidized. In the absence of oxygen, dissimilatory nitrate reduction allows utilization of organic compounds with a much higher energy yield than fermentation processes.

There are two types of dissimilatory nitrate reduction. A variety of facultatively anaerobic bacteria, including *Alcaligenes, Escherichia, Aeromonas, Enterobacter, Bacillus, Flavobacterium, Nocardia, Spirillum, Staphylococcus,* and *Vibrio,* reduce nitrate under anaerobic conditions to nitrite. The nitrite produced by these species is excreted, or, under appropriate conditions, some of these organisms will reduce nitrite via hydroxylamine to ammonium (nitrate ammonification). These organisms do not produce gaseous nitrogen products, that is, they do not denitrify. Nitrate ammonification plays an important role in stagnant water, sewage plants, and some sediments (Koike and Hattori 1978). Unlike assimilatory nitrate reduction, dissimilatory nitrate reductase is not inhibited by ammonia; thus, ammonium ions can be excreted in relatively high concentrations. As compared to denitrification, however, nitrate ammonification is an environmentally less significant process for the reductive removal of nitrate and nitrite ions; its importance appears to be limited by the number of reducing equivalents that must be consumed in the system.

Denitrifying nitrate reducers such as *Paracoccus denitrificans, Thiobacillus denitrificans,* and various pseudomonads have a more complete reduction pathway, converting nitrate through nitrite to nitric oxide (NO), and nitrous oxide ($N_2O$) to molecular nitrogen. The denitrification sequence is as follows (Equation 5):

$$(5) \quad NO_3^- \rightarrow NO_2^- \rightarrow NO \rightarrow N_2O \rightarrow N_2$$

In soil, the primary denitrifying genera are *Pseudomonas* and *Alcaligenes;* many additional genera, such as *Azospirillum, Rhizobium, Rhodopseudomonas,* and *Propionibacterium,* have also been reported to denitrify under some conditions (Focht 1982). Usually, a mixture of nitrous oxide and nitrogen is evolved, depleting the environment of combined nitrogen. The proportion of the denitrification products is dependent both on the denitrifying microorganisms and on environmental conditions. The lower the pH of the habitat, the greater the proportions of nitrous oxide formed. Formation of molecular nitrogen is favored by an adequate supply or an oversupply of reducing equivalents.

Simultaneously with denitrification, organic matter is oxidized. Utilization of glucose through nitrate reduction by *Pseudomonas denitrificans* can be described as follows (Equation 6):

$$(6) \quad C_6H_{12}O_6 + 4NO_3^- \rightarrow 6CO_2 + 6H_2O + 2N_2$$

The enzymes involved in these processes are the dissimilatory nitrate and nitrite reductase systems. Dissimilatory nitrate reductases are membrane bound, competitively inhibited by oxygen, and not inhibited by ammonia; this is in contrast to assimilatory nitrate reductases, which are soluble, inhibited by ammonia, and not substantially inhibited by oxygen.

Denitrification most often occurs under strictly anaerobic conditions or under conditions of reduced oxygen tension. Some denitrification may occur in generally aerobic environments if these contain anoxic microhabitats (Hutchinson and Mosier 1979). Denitrification is more common in standing waters than in running streams and rivers. Denitrification rates typically are higher in the hypolimnion of eutrophic lakes during summer and winter stratification than during fall and spring turnover.

Nitrification and denitrification in soil often occur in close proximity so that a substantial part of the $NO_3^-$ formed by nitrification afterward diffuses to the anaerobic denitrification zone where it is reduced to $N_2$ (Nielsen et al. 1996). Denitrification activity of some bacteria, such as *Paracoccus denitrificans,* appears to be restricted to anaerobic conditions (Baumann et al. 1996). On a change from aerobic to anaerobic respiration, a culture of *P. denitrificans* enters an unstable transition phase during which the denitrification pathway is induced. The onset of this phase is formed by a 15- to 45-fold increase of the mRNA levels for the individual denitrification enzymes. All mRNAs accumulate during a short period, after which their overall concentration declines to reach a stable value slightly higher than that observed under aerobic steady-state conditions. The first mRNAs to be formed are those for nitrate and nitrous oxide reductase. The nitrite reductase mRNA appears significantly later, suggesting different modes of regulation for the three genes. When the anaerobic cultures switch back to aerobic respiration, denitrification of the cells stops at once, although sufficient nitrite reductase is still present.

In contrast to *P. denitrificans,* several strains of gram-negative bacteria have been shown to be capable of respiring nitrate in the presence of oxygen, although the physiological advantage gained from this process is not entirely clear (Carter et al. 1995). Strains of *Pseudomonas, Aeromonas,* and *Moraxella* express a nitrate reductase and show significant rates of nitrate respiration in the presence of oxygen when assayed with physiological electron donors. Also, a strain of the gram-positive genus *Arthrobacter* is likewise able to respire nitrate in the presence of oxygen but appears to express a different type of nitrate reductase. Thus, it seems likely that the corespiration of nitrate and oxygen may indeed make a significant contribution to the flux of nitrate to nitrite in the environment.

The measurement of denitrification rates was hampered by analytical difficulties mentioned in connection with N fixation. The evolution of nitrogenous oxides can be measured by gas chromatography (Payne 1971, 1973), but the evolution of molecular nitrogen is difficult to quantify against a background of omnipresent atmospheric nitrogen. Consequently, the discovery that denitrification could be arrested at the nitrous oxide level by the acetylene blockage of the $N_2O$ reductase (Balderston et al. 1976; Hallmark and Terry 1985) was an important breakthrough. The addition of acetylene gas at 0.01 atm to the incubation atmosphere allows the gas chromatographic measurement of the denitrification process in the form of a single product, $N_2O$. Measurement of $N_2O$ evolution with time under these conditions gives a good estimate of denitrification rates. The method is applicable to pure cultures as well as to environmental samples and *in situ* measurements, but is limited in sensitivity by the low nitrate availability in many habitats.

Various steps within the nitrogen cycle are subject to repression. For example, ammonium ions normally inhibit the fixation of atmospheric nitrogen. Nitrification occurs readily in neutral, well-drained soils but is inhibited in anaerobic or highly acidic soils. Assimilatory nitrate reductase activity is repressed by ammonia; dissimilatory nitrate reductase is repressed by oxygen.

Because various environmental conditions favor specific nitrogen cycling processes, there is a spatial zonation of cycling processes. Fixation of nitrogen occurs in both surface and subsurface habitats. Nitrification occurs exclusively in aerobic habitats. Denitrification predominates in waterlogged soils and in anaerobic aquatic sediments. The cycling of nitrogen within a given habitat also exhibits seasonal fluctuations; during spring and fall blooms of cyanobacteria, for example, rates of nitrogen fixation in aquatic habitats usually are high, reflecting population fluctuations and availability of needed energy and mineral nutrients for fixation of molecular nitrogen.

# THE SULFUR CYCLE

Sulfur, a reactive element with stable valence states from −2 to +6 (Table 11.2), is among the 10 most abundant elements in the crust of Earth. In living organisms, sulfur occurs mainly as sulfhydryl (—SH) groups in amino acids and their polymers. At an average concentration of 520 ppm, it rarely becomes a limiting nutrient (Ehrlich 1995; Jørgensen 1983). At least some elemental sulfur deposits and some sulfide ores appear to be of biogenic origin (Ivanov 1968). Eruptive and postvolcanic activity continue to introduce additional sulfur into the ecosphere at relatively low rates. With the notable exceptions of ferric and calcium sulfates, most sulfate salts are readily soluble in water. Sulfate is the second most abundant anion in seawater, and the $SO_4^{2-}$ of the marine environment represents a large, slowly cycled sulfur reservoir. Living and dead organic matter compose a smaller, more rapidly cycled sulfur reservoir. Largely inert sulfur reservoirs are metal sulfides in rock, elemental sulfur deposits, and fossil fuels. Human activities, including strip mining and the burning of fossil fuels, have mobilized a part of these inert sulfur reservoirs with destructive pollution consequences. We will discuss some of these consequences later in this chapter.

Plants, algae, and many heterotrophic microorganisms assimilate sulfur in the form of sulfate. For incorporation into cysteine, methionine, and coenzymes in the form of sulfhydryl (—SH) groups, sul-

**Table 11.2**
Oxidation states of sulfur in various compounds

| Form | Example | Oxidation state |
|------|---------|-----------------|
| $S^{2-}$ | Sulfides, mercaptans | −2 |
| $S^0$ | Elemental sulfur | 0 |
| $S_2O_4$ | Hyposulfite | +2 |
| $SO_3^{2-}$ | Sulfite | +4 |
| $SO_4^{2-}$ | Sulfate | +6 |

fate needs to be reduced to the sulfide level by assimilatory sulfate reduction. A direct uptake as sulfide is not feasible for most microorganisms because of the high toxicity of $H_2S$. In assimilatory sulfate reduction, toxicity is avoided by immediately reacting the reduced sulfur with an acceptor—for example, serine—to yield cysteine.

Organosulfur decomposition in soils and sediments yields mercaptans and $H_2S$ (Bremner and Steele 1978). Analogous to ammonification, this process is referred to as desulfuration. Volatile mercaptans and $H_2S$ are the offensive odor components of rotten eggs and cabbage. The action of cysteine desulfhydrase can be described as shown in Equation 7:

$$(7) \quad SH-CH_2-CH-COOH + H_2O \xrightarrow{\text{cysteine desulfhydrase}}$$
$$\qquad\qquad\quad | $$
$$\qquad\qquad\quad NH_2$$
$$OH-CH_2-CH-COOH + H_2S$$
$$\qquad\qquad\quad | $$
$$\qquad\qquad\quad NH_2$$

In the marine environment, a major decomposition product of organosulfur is dimethylsulfide (DMS). This product originates from dimethylsulfoniopropionate (DMSP), a major metabolite of marine algae that may have a role in osmoregulation. Dimethylsulfide is released during zooplankton grazing on phytoplankton and also during decay processes (Dacey and Wakeham 1986). The volatile DMS escapes the oceans; according to some estimates, 90% of the total sulfur flux from the marine environment to the atmosphere occurs in the form of DMS. Another major

## Management of the Nitrogen Cycle in Agriculture

Management of the nitrogen cycle is critical in agricultural areas for maintaining soil fertility to support extensive crop growth and also for maintaining potable water quality in agricultural regions. The natural availability of fixed forms of nitrogen in agricultural soils is determined by the relative balance between the rates of microbial nitrogen fixation and denitrification, application of nitrogen fertilizer, and nitrogen removal with the crop. Both classical and modern agricultural practices rely on management of the microbial cycling of nitrogen. Nitrogen-rich fertilizers are widely applied to soils to support increased crop yields, but proper application of nitrogen fertilizers must consider the solubility and leaching characteristics of the particular chemical form of the fertilizer and the rates of microbial biogeochemical cycling activities. To avoid losses caused by leaching and denitrification, nitrogen fertilizer is commonly applied as an ammonium salt, free ammonia, or urea.

Crop rotation, that is, alternating the types of crops planted in a field, is traditionally used to prevent the exhaustion of soil nitrogen and to reduce the cost of nitrogen fertilizer applications. Leguminous crops such as soybeans often are planted in rotation with other crops because of their symbiotic association with nitrogen-fixing bacteria, which reduce the soil's requirement for expensive nitrogen fertilizer. Leguminous plants accumulate fixed nitrogen, particularly in root nodules. Other plants release nutrients that stimulate free-living nitrogen fixers in the rhizosphere, leading to a similar increase in soil nitrogen. Most of the combined (fixed) nitrogen is released to the soil from decomposition of the crop residues from leguminous plants that are plowed under. Alfalfa can produce 100–280 kg nitrogen fixed per hectare per year; red

clover 75–175 kg, and vetch 60–140 kg. Soybeans, which can produce 60–100 kg nitrogen fixed per hectare per year in the midwestern United States, are often rotated with corn. Corn takes up nitrogen from the soil, substantially decreasing the concentration of soil nitrogen, but during the seasons when soybeans are grown, the level of fixed nitrogen in the soil increases.

In some cases, nitrogen fixation can be enhanced by inoculation of legume seeds with appropriate *Rhizobium* strains. This increases the extent of nodule formation because of the increased numbers of infective rhizobia. Besides increasing the extent of nodule formation, it is possible to take steps to increase the rate of nitrogen fixation within the nodules. In molybdenum-deficient soils, a dramatic improvement in the rate of nitrogen fixation can be achieved by the application of small amounts of molybdenum because this element is a constituent of the nitrogenase enzyme complex that is required for nitrogen-fixing activities. It is important that maximal rates of nitrogen fixation be achieved to successfully replenish soil nitrogen.

Many research groups have been attempting to eliminate the need for adding nitrogen fertilizers or rotating crops by genetically engineering the capacity to fix nitrogen into plants such as wheat, corn, and rice. Forming a genetically engineered nitrogen-fixing crop was considered the greatest promise of biotechnology and, to date, its greatest failure. The complex regulatory system of nitrogen fixation makes the task of expressing *nif* genes in plants very difficult. In one model series of experiments, the genes for nitrogen fixation were first inserted into the genome of a eucaryotic yeast cell; plasmids from *Escherichia coli* and a yeast cell were cleaved and then fused to form a single hybrid plasmid, which could be recognized by the yeast cell and integrated into its chromosomal DNA. In the next step, the genes to be introduced into the yeast were isolated from the chromosome of *Klebsiella pneumoniae,* a nitrogen fixer. The genes, collectively designated *nif,* code for some 17 proteins. Another *E. coli* plasmid was cleaved, and the isolated *nif* genes were introduced to form a second hybrid plasmid. Because of the bacterial DNA already inserted into one of the yeast chromosomes, the yeast cell recognized the hybrid *E. coli* plasmid. The plasmid was then integrated into the yeast chromosome. Although the insertion of the bacterial *nif* genes into the yeast cell demonstrated that genetic material can be transferred between different biological systems, the nitrogen-fixing proteins were not expressed in the yeast. It is increasingly apparent that the ability to engineer organisms, such as eucaryotic plant cells that can fix atmospheric nitrogen, depends on developing a thorough understanding of the molecular biology of gene expression and knowing how to create the environmental conditions for nitrogen-fixing activity. At present agriculture remains dependent on nitrogen fixation by *Rhizobium* and *Bradyrhizobium* species associated with leguminous crops and on adding vast quantities of nitrogen fertilizers.

The addition of large amounts of fertilizers in agricultural areas, such as the corn belt in the central United States, can lead to some serious environmental problems that require further management of the nitrogen cycle. In particular, the problem is that chemolithotrophic nitrifiers transform ammonia from the fertilizers into nitrites and nitrates too fast. These anions leach easily, wasting the fertilizer and also introducing nitrites and nitrates into groundwater. The occurrence of nitrite in groundwater is of serious concern because nitrite can react chemically with amino compounds to form nitrosamines, which are highly carcinogenic. Nitrate in groundwater also constitutes a health hazard. Although nitrate itself is not highly toxic, it may be microbially reduced in the gastrointestinal tract to highly toxic nitrite. The normal stomach acidity of adult humans tends to prevent or minimize such reduction, but infants with lower stomach acidity are highly susceptible. Nitrite combines with the hemoglobin of the blood, causing respiratory distress, the so-called blue baby syndrome. Nitrate reduction to form nitrite may also take place in the rumen of livestock, resulting in animal disease or death.

Nitrate and nitrite in groundwater are problems in agricultural areas receiving heavy concentrations of synthetic nitrogen fertilizer, including the corn belt of the Midwest, the San Joaquin Valley of California, and some areas of Long Island, New York. Wells in such areas need to be closely monitored for nitrate contamination. When nitrification proceeds too quickly, wasteful losses of nitrogen fertilizer and groundwater contamination with nitrate occur. Nitrification of ammonium compounds also yields acid that may need to be neutralized by liming. To control the rate of the microbial transformation of ammonium, nitrification inhibitors such as nitrapyrin are often applied with the fertilizer. The use of nitrification inhibitors can increase crop yields by 10–15% for the same amount of nitrogen fertilizer applied. In addition, by decreasing the rate of nitrification, the problem of groundwater pollution by nitrite and nitrate is reduced.

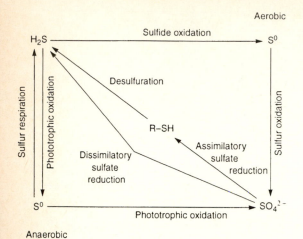

**Figure 11.6**
Representation of the sulfur cycle showing biogeochemical transformations of oxidized and reduced forms of sulfur. R—SH represents sulfhydryl groups of cell protein. Note the similarities between the sulfur cycle and the nitrogen cycle (Figure 11.1).

product is $H_2S$. Once they escape to the atmosphere, DMS, $H_2S$, and mercaptans are subject to photooxidative reactions that ultimately yield sulfate. $H_2S$ also reacts with $O_2$ in the atmosphere.

If $H_2S$ does not escape to the atmosphere, it may be subject to microbial oxidation under aerobic conditions, or it may be phototrophically oxidized under anaerobic conditions. Under anaerobic conditions, sulfate as well as elemental sulfur may serve as electron acceptors, and organic substrates are oxidized. Figure 11.6 summarizes the microbial cycling of sulfur.

## Oxidative Sulfur Transformations

In the presence of oxygen, reduced sulfur compounds are capable of supporting chemolithotrophic microbial metabolism. *Beggiatoa, Thioploca, Thiothrix* (Nelson 1990), and the thermophilic *Thermothrix* (Caldwell et al. 1976), are filamentous, microaerophilic bacteria capable of oxidizing $H_2S$ according to Equation 8.

(8)  $H_2S + \frac{1}{2}O_2 \rightarrow S^0 + H_2O$
   ($\Delta\,G'_0 = -50.1$ kcal/mol $= -210.4$ kJ/mol)

Sulfur globules are deposited within the cells. In the absence of $H_2S$, these globules are slowly oxidized further to sulfate. These typical gradient organisms position themselves on the interface of an anaerobic environment, the sediment, and the partially oxygenated water in contact with the sediment (Jørgensen and Revsbeck 1983).

The large and observable sulfur globules of *Beggiatoa* allowed Sergei Winogradsky to develop the concept of microbial chemolithotrophy almost 100 years ago. Although *Beggiatoa* clearly derived energy from $H_2S$ and $S^0$ oxidation, until recently it was impossible to grow *Beggiatoa* in pure culture under strictly chemolithotrophic conditions, and it was widely assumed that Winogradsky developed the right concept on the wrong microorganism. By a close control of $H_2S$—$O_2$ gradients, however, it was possible to demonstrate clearly that at least some *Beggiatoa* strains are capable of chemolithotrophic metabolism (Nelson and Jannasch 1983; Nelson 1990) (Figure 11.7).

Some species of *Thiobacillus (T. thioparus, T. novellus)* also oxidize $H_2S$ and other reduced sulfur compounds and, because they have a low acid tolerance, deposit elemental sulfur rather than generate sulfuric acid by further oxidation. The filamentous sulfur bacteria and these *Thiobacillus* species are facultatively chemolithotrophic (Kuenen et al. 1985). Other members of the genus *Thiobacillus* species produce sulfate from the oxidation of elemental sulfur and other inorganic sulfur compounds. Elemental sulfur is oxidized according to Equation 9:

(9)  $S^0 + 1\frac{1}{2}O_2 + H_2O \rightarrow H_2SO_4$
   ($\Delta\,G'_0 = -149.8$ kcal/mol $= -629.2$ kJ/mol)

These *Thiobacillus* species are acidophilic, grow well at pH 2–3, and are obligate chemolithotrophs, obtaining their energy exclusively from the oxidation of inorganic sulfur and their carbon from the reduction of carbon dioxide. Most *Thiobacillus* species are obligate aerobes requiring molecular oxygen for the oxidation of the inorganic sulfur compounds. *Thiobacil-*

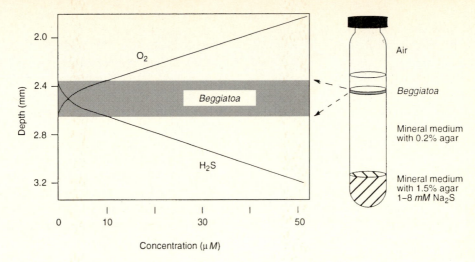

**Figure 11.7**

Chemolithotrophic cultivation of *Beggiatoa,* a typical gradient organism, in a sulfide-oxygen gradient. At right is a culture tube with sulfide agar, overlayered with initially sulfide-free soft mineral agar. The airspace in the closed tube is the source of oxygen. Stab-inoculated *Beggiatoa* grows in a narrowly defined gradient of $H_2S$ and oxygen, as shown. (Source: Nelson 1990.)

*lus denitrificans,* however, can utilize nitrate ions as terminal electron acceptors in the oxidation of inorganic sulfur compounds, as shown for elemental sulfur in Equation 10:

$$(10) \quad 3S^0 + 4NO_3^- \rightarrow 3SO_4^{2-} + 2N_2$$

This organism, though, is not capable of assimilatory nitrate reduction and requires ammonium as a nitrogen source. Members of the archaean genus *Sulfolobus* oxidize elemental sulfur in hot acidic habitats to generate their required energy. Chemoautotrophic sulfur-oxidizing bacteria are widely distributed; they are quite active in soils and aquatic habitats. A variety of other heterotrophic microorganisms oxidize inorganic sulfur to sulfate or thiosulfate but do not appear to derive energy from this transformation.

Sulfur oxidation produces substantial amounts of strong mineral acid. Within soils, this can lead to solubilization and mobilization of phosphorus and other mineral nutrients with a generally beneficial effect on both microorganisms and plants. The activity of *Thiobacillus thiooxidans* may be used for adjusting soil pH. *T. thiooxidans* and *T. ferrooxidans* are used in microbial mining operations. When mining activities, especially strip mining, uncover large amounts of reduced sulfide rock, the activities of the same thiobacilli give rise to acid mine drainage, a destructive pollution phenomenon.

Hydrogen sulfide is also subject to phototrophic oxidation in anaerobic environments (Pfennig 1990; Trüper 1990). Photosynthetic sulfur bacteria, the Chromatiaceae, Ectothiorhodospiraceae, and Chlorobiaceae, are capable of photoreducing $CO_2$ while oxidizing $H_2S$ to $S^0$ (Equation 11), in striking analogy to the photosynthesis of eucaryotes (Equation 12). The formula $[CH_2O]$ symbolizes photosynthate.

$$(11) \quad CO_2 + H_2S \rightarrow [CH_2O] + S$$

$$(12) \quad CO_2 + H_2O \rightarrow [CH_2O] + O_2$$

Chromatiaceae store sulfur globules intracellularly, whereas Ectothiorhodospiraceae and Chlorobiaceae excrete sulfur globules. All have a limited capacity to oxidize sulfur further to sulfate, and they may contribute to biological sulfur deposition. Some cyanobacteria are capable of both oxygenic and anoxygenic photosynthesis; thus, they may participate in the phototrophic oxidation of $H_2S$. Microbial oxidation of reduced sulfur is essential for continued availability of this element in nontoxic forms, but the chemoautotrophic fixation of $CO_2$ connected with this activity contributes only minimally to the carbon cycling in most ecosystems.

Notable exceptions to the above statement are the recently discovered deep-sea hydrothermal vent ecosystems (Karl et al. 1980). Rifts caused by the spreading of the seafloor from midocean ridges allow seawater to percolate deeply into the crust and to react with hot basaltic rock. This hot anoxic hydrothermal fluid, containing geothermally reduced $H_2S$, $S^0$, $H_2$, $NH_4^+$, $NO_2^-$, $Fe^{2+}$, and $Mn^{2+}$, as well as some $CH_4$ and CO, moves upward and through the vents and enters the cold, oxygenated water of the deep sea (Figure 11.8). Depending on the degree of mixing with seawater during upflow, the temperature of the hydrothermal vents ranges from warm (5–23°C) to extremely hot (350–400°C). Because of the prevailing high hydrostatic pressures, the water does not boil at these high temperatures, but on cooling, the precipitation of elemental sulfur and of metal sulfides forms plumes called *white* or *black smokers,* respectively (Jannasch and Mottl 1985).

The vent communities, located at a depth of 800–1000 m or deeper, receive no sunlight and minimal organic nutrient input from the low-productivity surface water above, yet their biomass exceeds that of the surrounding seafloor by orders of magnitude. Microbial mats cover all available surfaces on and near the vents, and high densities of unique clams, mussels, vestimentiferan worms, and other invertebrates cluster in the vicinity (Grassle 1985). Some of these graze or filter feed on microorganisms; others are directly symbiotic with microorganisms and exhibit chemoautotrophic activity. Energetically, the whole vent community is supported by the chemoautotrophic oxidation of reduced sulfur, primarily by *Beggiatoa, Thiomicrospira,* and additional sulfide or sulfur oxidizers of great morphological diversity (Jannasch and Wirsen 1981; Jannasch 1990). Oxidation of $H_2$, CO, $NH_4^+$, $NO_2^-$, $Fe^{2+}$, and $Mn^{2+}$ are

assumed to contribute to chemoautotrophic production (Jannasch and Mottl 1985). Methane, derived from reduction of $CO_2$ with geothermally produced hydrogen by extremely thermophilic *Methanococcus* species and detected in the anoxic hydrothermal fluid, is also oxidized by methanotrophic bacteria and provides additional carbon and energy input for the vent ecosystem.

In environments other than the deep-sea thermal vents, generation of reduced minerals used in chemolithotrophic production is directly tied to oxidation of photosynthetically produced organic matter. Therefore, sustained primary production without input of solar energy is unthinkable even by chemolithotrophs. The described deep-sea hydrothermal vent communities are unique by being independent of solar energy input and by their direct use of geothermal energy instead. It needs to be pointed out, however, that the reduced minerals represent an energy source only in the oxidized environment of the seawater, a condition originally created by oxygenic photosynthesis powered by sun energy.

## Reductive Sulfur Transformations

The analogy between $H_2O$ and $H_2S$ in oxygenic and anaerobic phototrophy, respectively, was pointed out in the preceding section. Elemental sulfur can be used in respiratory processes (Pfennig and Biebl 1981). *Desulfuromonas acetoxidans* grows on acetate, anaerobically reducing stoichiometric amounts of $S^0$ to $H_2S$ (Equation 13).

$$(13) \quad CH_3COOH + 2H_2O + 4S^0 \rightarrow 2CO_2 + 4H_2S$$

The free energy yield ($\Delta G'_0 = -5.7$ kcal/mol = $-23.9$ kJ/mol) of the above reaction is rather low, yet no other sources of carbon and energy are required for growth. *Desulfuromonas* is unable to reduce sulfate or live by fermentative metabolism and uses the substrate acetate. *Desulfuromonas* occurs in anaerobic sediments rich in sulfide and elemental sulfur. It also lives syntrophically with the phototrophic green sulfur bacteria (Chlorobiaceae) that photooxidize $H_2S$ to $S^0$ and excrete elemental sulfur extracellularly. *Desul-*

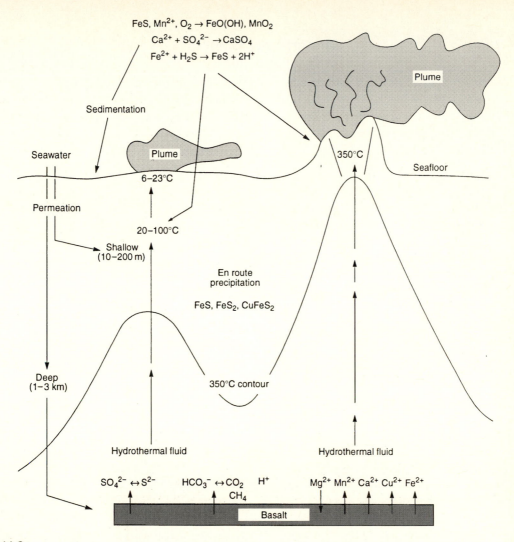

**Figure 11.8**

Schematic diagram showing inorganic chemical processes occurring at warm- and hot-water vent sites. Deeply circulating seawater is heated to 350–400°C and reacts with crustal basalts, leaching various species into solution. The hot water rises, reaching the seafloor directly in some places and mixing first with cold, down-seeping seawater in others. On mixing, iron-copper-zinc sulfide minerals and anhydrite (a form of calcium sulfate) precipitate. (Source: Jannasch and Mottl 1985.)

*furomonas* regenerates $H_2S$ by sulfur respiration, using, at least in part, organic matter leaked by *Chlorobium* cells (Kuenen et al. 1985).

From submarine hydrothermal vent environments, extremely thermophilic anaerobic archaea were iso-lated that are capable of sulfur respiration with hydro-gen gas (Fischer et al. 1983; Stetter and Gaag 1983; Stetter 1990). Several species of *Thermoproteus, Pyrobaculum,* and *Pyrodictium* were described to carry out this chemolithotrophic reaction. *Pyrodictium*

# Winogradsky Column

The Winogradsky column, which is named after the Russian microbiologist Sergei Winogradsky, is a model ecosystem that is used in the study of aquatic and sediment microorganisms (Eveleigh and Davis 1996) (see the accompanying figure). It promotes the development of photosynthetic bacterial populations that use hydrogen sulfide as the electron donor in their photoautotrophic metabolism. A Winogradsky column consists of mud or sediment placed within a glass or clear plastic cylinder. The height of the column allows the development of an aerobic zone at the surface and microaerophilic and anoxic zones below the surface. The column is exposed to light so that various photosynthetic populations develop at differing depths in the column. The mud or sediment contains or is augmented with organic carbon substrates, sulfide, and sulfates. This permits the development of numerous heterotrophic and photoautotrophic populations, including anaerobic photosynthetic sulfur bacteria. Although many variations are possible, a good arrangement is to place mud, carbon substrate such as shredded filter paper, $CaSO_4$, and $CaCO_3$ on the bottom of the column and overlayer it with light-colored sand plus water. This helps to develop a gradient of redox potentials, and pigmented microorganisms show up clearly against the light-colored sand.

Because populations of algae and cyanobacteria (oxygenic photosynthetic microorganisms) grow at the aerobic surface, the upper zone typically appears green. The oxygen produced by these microorganisms maintains an aerobic zone within which heterotrophic aerobic bacterial and fungal populations grow. The water layer just above the sediment has reduced oxygen concentration and receives some $H_2S$ diffusing out of the sediment. This zone is ideal for the microaerophilic sulfide-oxidizers *Beggiatoa* and *Thiothrix,* gradient organisms with white-gray filamentous growth. Non-acid-tolerant thiobacilli such as *Thiobacillus thioparus* also grow in this zone. The uppermost portion of the sand column is reddish-brown from the growth of mainly nonsulfur anaerobic photoheterotrophs (Rhodospirillaceae). Below these, a red-purple zone indicates the growth of purple sulfur bacteria (Chromatiaceae and Ectothiorhodospiraceae). Even lower, a greenish zone indicates the growth of the green sulfur bacteria (Chlorobiaceae). The intensely black zone extending upward from the bottom of the column signifies the activity of the sulfate reducers (*Desulfovibrio, Desulfotomaculum,* etc.). The black color is due to metal sulfides, principally ferrous sulfide (FeS).

The sulfides produced by the metabolism of sulfate reducers are used by anaerobic green and purple photosynthetic sulfur bacterial populations. The green sulfur bacteria are strict anaerobes that carry out photoautotrophic and photoheterotrophic metabolism using sulfide or sulfur as the electron donor. When sulfide is oxidized, elemental sulfur is deposited outside the cell. The green sulfur bacteria include the family Chlorobiaceae with its representative genus *Chlorobium.* These bacteria grow using sulfide or elemental sulfur as the electron donor. The purple sulfur bacteria form a band above the green ones. Though also anaerobic, they are somewhat less sensitive to oxygen and more sensitive to sulfide than the Chlorobiaceae. The purple sulfur bacteria include the family Chromati-

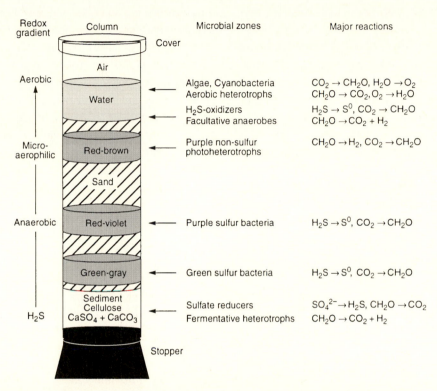

| Redox gradient | Column | Microbial zones | Major reactions |
|---|---|---|---|
| | Cover | | |
| | Air | | |
| Aerobic | Water | Algae, Cyanobacteria<br>Aerobic heterotrophs | $CO_2 \rightarrow CH_2O, H_2O \rightarrow O_2$<br>$CH_2O \rightarrow CO_2, O_2 \rightarrow H_2O$ |
| | | $H_2S$-oxidizers<br>Facultative anaerobes | $H_2S \rightarrow S^0, CO_2 \rightarrow CH_2O$<br>$CH_2O \rightarrow CO_2 + H_2$ |
| Micro-aerophilic | Red-brown | Purple non-sulfur photoheterotrophs | $CH_2O \rightarrow H_2, CO_2 \rightarrow CH_2O$ |
| | Sand | | |
| Anaerobic | Red-violet | Purple sulfur bacteria | $H_2S \rightarrow S^0, CO_2 \rightarrow CH_2O$ |
| | Green-gray | Green sulfur bacteria | $H_2S \rightarrow S^0, CO_2 \rightarrow CH_2O$ |
| $H_2S$ | Sediment<br>Cellulose<br>$CaSO_4 + CaCO_3$ | Sulfate reducers<br>Fermentative heterotrophs | $SO_4^{2-} \rightarrow H_2S, CH_2O \rightarrow CO_2$<br>$CH_2O \rightarrow CO_2 + H_2$ |
| | Stopper | | |

A Winogradsky column, prepared in a glass or clear plastic cylinder. Distinct layers of microorganisms develop that model the spatial distribution of these populations in anoxic water columns. The sulfate reducers, the purple and green sulfur bacteria, and the sulfide oxidizers are all involved in the sulfur cycle.

aceae with its representative genus *Chromatium.* When sulfide is oxidized by *Chromatium,* elemental sulfur is deposited inside the cell. The Ectothiorhodospiraceae deposit sulfur outside the cell. The Rhodospirillaceae use reduced organic compounds rather than sulfur compounds as electron donors. They are photoheterotrophs.

The Winogradsky column is a model ecosystem that mimics the situation in an anaerobic water column that receives light. Similar zonations in natural sediments can develop only on the millimeter scale, as light is unable to penetrate the sediment to any depth. In this respect the Winogradsky column is an artificial sediment system that allows light exposure from the side, through the glass wall. It is possible to prepare largely aquatic Winogradsky columns with only minimal sediment on their bottom. Although these are closer to the nat-

*(continued)*

---

### Winogradsky Column, continued

ural systems, they are less suitable for laboratory demonstrations. Thermal convections in the water column work against the establishment of stable redox gradients essential for a successful Winogradsky column.

One way to examine the biota of a developed Winogradsky column is to draw off, layer by layer, the liquid above the sediment and examine by microscope the algae, protozoa, cyanobacteria,

*Beggiatoa*, and so on associated with these layers. As the described anoxyphotobacteria all have their unique photosynthetic pigment compositions, one may, after incubation, freeze the sediment column, cut apart the colored zones using a hacksaw, with the solvent extract the photosynthetic pigments, and subject them to chromatographic separation. Characteristic pigment bands may be obtained in this manner.

---

*occultum* is the most thermophilic member of the group, having an optimal growth temperature of 105°C and a maximal growth temperature of 110°C. It is probably an advantage for these extreme thermophiles that sulfur is present in hydrothermal vent regions in a molten state, whereas at room temperature it is a hydrophobic solid. Sulfur respiration with molecular hydrogen can be described as shown in Equation 14:

$$(14) \quad H_2 + S^0 \rightarrow H_2S$$

Some of these archaea are facultative chemolithotrophs capable of heterotrophic or mixotrophic growth during sulfur respiration (Parameswaran et al. 1987).

Martinus Beijerinck described the use of sulfate ($SO_4^{2-}$) as terminal electron acceptor in anaerobic respiration much earlier. When obligately anaerobic bacteria carry out dissimilatory sulfate reduction, they are referred to as sulfate reducers or sulfidogens (Postgate 1984; Thauer 1990). The traditional sulfate-reducing genera *Desulfovibrio* and *Desulfotomaculum* were recently joined by several newly described morphological and physiological types, such as *Desulfobacter, Desulfobulbus, Desulfococcus, Desulfonema,* and *Desulfosarcina* (Pfennig et al. 1981). The reduction of sulfate results in production of hydrogen sulfide according to the following equation (Equation 15):

$$(15) \quad 5H_2 + 2SO_2^{2-} \rightarrow 2H_2S + 2H_2O + 2OH^-$$

In addition to anaerobic sulfate-reducing bacteria, some species of *Bacillus, Pseudomonas,* and *Saccharomyces* have been found to liberate hydrogen sulfide from sulfate, but these additional genera do not appear to play a major role in the dissimilatory reduction of sulfate. Sulfate reduction can occur over a wide range of pH, pressure, temperature, and salinity conditions. Only relatively few compounds can serve as electron donors for sulfate reduction. Although hydrogen and sulfate can serve as their only source of energy for growth, most of the bacterial sulfate reducers are not chemolithotrophs. Most lack the enzyme systems to assimilate $CO_2$ and require organic carbon sources. The most common electron donors are pyruvate, lactate, and molecular hydrogen. Though acetate may be utilized to support sulfate reduction (Shannon and White 1996), it generally is not the preferred substrate for sulfate-reducing bacteria (Hines et al. 1994; Uberoi and Bhattacharya 1995). Sulfate reduction is inhibited by the presence of oxygen, nitrate, or ferric ions. The rate of sulfate reduction is often carbon limited. The addition of organic compounds to marine sediments can result in greatly accelerated rates of dissimilatory sulfate reduction.

Although most sulfate-reducing bacteria are not chemolithotrophs, *Desulfobacterium autotrophicum, Desulfomonile tiodjei,* and several other strains were recently shown to grow on $H_2$, $CO_2$, and $SO_4^{2-}$ and to be facultative chemolithotrophs (Hansen 1993). Some *Desulfovibrio* and *Desulfobulbus* strains can grow mixotrophically on acetate, $CO_2$, and $H_2$. In this case, acetyl CoA, $CO_2$, and hydrogen are condensed to pyuvate and all other cell components are synthesized via this compound.

Dissimilatory sulfate and sulfur reduction is carried out by a heterogeneous group of bacteria and archaea also in thermal vent environments at temperatures up to 105°C (Hansen 1995). These microorganisms have the capacity to metabolize a variety of compounds ranging from hydrogen via typical organic fermentation products to hexadecane, toluene, and several types of substituted aromatics. Several of the sulfate-reducing archaea, such as *Archaeoglobus lithotrophicus,* are true chemolithotrophs.

Without exception all sulfate reducers activate sulfate to adenosine-5'-phosphosulfate (APS); the natural electron donor(s) for the ensuing APS reductase reaction is not known. The same is true for the reduction of sulfite; in addition there is still some uncertainty as to whether the pathway to sulfide is a direct six-electron reduction or bisulfite or whether it involves trithionate and thiosulfate as intermediates.

The production of even small amounts of hydrogen sulfide by sulfate reducers can have a marked effect on populations within a habitat. Hydrogen sulfide is extremely toxic to aerobic organisms because it reacts with the heavy metal groups of the cytochrome systems. Production of hydrogen sulfide by *Desulfovibrio* in waterlogged soils can kill nematodes and other animal populations. Hydrogen sulfide also has antimicrobial activity and can adversely affect microbial populations in soil. Heavy metals are extremely reactive with hydrogen sulfide, resulting in the precipitation of metallic sulfides. Black metal sulfides give reduced sediments their characteristic dark color. Hydrogen sulfide is also highly toxic to the cytochrome systems of plant roots and can kill the plants.

In contrast to the specialized dissimilatory sulfate reducers, many organisms are capable of assimilatory sulfate reduction. Assimilatory sulfate reduction produces low concentrations of hydrogen sulfide, which are immediately incorporated into organic compounds. Many microorganisms and plants can utilize sulfate ions as the source of sulfur required for incorporation into proteins and other sulfur-containing biochemicals. Plant roots readily take up sulfate from soils, incorporating it into organic matter.

The assimilation of inorganic sulfate (Ehrlich 1995) involves a series of transfer reactions initiated by the reaction of sulfate with ATP to form APS and pyrophosphate ($PP_i$) (Equation 16). A second reaction between ATP and APS produces 3′-phosphoadenosine-5′-phosphosulfate (PAPS) and ADP (Equation 17).

$$(16) \quad SO_4^{2-} + ATP \xrightarrow[\text{ATP sulfurylase}]{} APS + PP_i$$

$$(17) \quad APS + ATP \xrightarrow[\text{APS kinase}]{} PAPS + ADP$$

The active sulfate of PAPS is subsequently reduced, as shown in Equation 18, to yield sulfite and adenosine 3′,5′-diphosphate (PAP). A second reduction step (Equation 19) yields sulfide that is immediately incorporated into an amino acid (Equation 20).

$$(18) \quad PAPS + 2e^- \xrightarrow[\substack{\text{NADH:PAPS} \\ \text{reductase}}]{} SO_3^{2-} + PAP$$

$$(19) \quad S_2^- + 6H^+ + 6e^- \xrightarrow[\substack{\text{NADH:SO}_3^{2-} \\ \text{reductase}}]{} SO_3^{2-} + PAP$$

$$(20) \quad S^{2-} + \text{O-acetylserine} \longrightarrow \text{cysteine} + H_2O$$

The biochemical mechanism involved in dissimilatory sulfate reduction is similar to the one described above, but the generated $H_2S$ is released to the environment. In sulfate-rich marine environments, most of the $H_2S$ originates from dissimilatory sulfate reductions, but in rich organic sediments, $H_2S$ may accumulate also from the decomposition of organosulfur compounds.

An interesting aspect of the microbial metabolism of sulfur compounds is the ability of microorganisms to fractionate sulfur isotopes. Sulfate-reducing bacteria exhibit a slight preference for $^{32}S$ over $^{34}S$. In contrast, the oxidation of hydrogen sulfide does not exhibit any preferential utilization of sulfur isotopes.

The hydrogen sulfide formed by the action of sulfate-reducing bacteria has a higher proportion of $^{32}$S than the original sulfate. The alteration of the relative abundances of $^{32}$S and $^{34}$S allows the differentiation of biologically generated sulfide and sulfide from strictly geochemical processes (Ivanov 1968). Sulfide readily reacts with heavy metals, and, because of the crustal abundance of iron, it occurs in geological deposits primarily as ferrous sulfide (FeS).

Biological sulfate reduction is probably also involved in the formation of some elemental sulfur deposits. Hydrogen sulfide generated by sulfate reduction may be photooxidized to elemental sulfur under anaerobic conditions by members of the Chromatiaceae, Ectothiorhodospiraceae, or Chlorobiaceae. Under aerobic conditions, especially when oxygen is limiting, hydrogen sulfide may be oxidized to sulfur by the chemical reaction with oxygen or by the activities of the *Beggiatoa-Thiothrix* group. Acid-intolerant thiobacilli *(Thiobacillus thioparus)* may also be involved in the formation of sulfur deposits. Figure 11.9 depicts some scenarios for the biogenic deposition of elemental sulfur in a lake and geological formations.

Present-day sulfur biogenesis has been observed in some Libyan lakes fed by artesian springs containing up to 100 mg per liter of $H_2S$ (Postgate 1984). Members of the Chromatiaceae and Chlorobiaceae photooxidize the $H_2S$ to elemental sulfur. Some $H_2S$ is oxidized to sulfate, but this sulfate is again reduced to $H_2S$ by *Desulfovibrio,* which utilizes the photosynthetically produced biomass. The $H_2S$ produced by *Desulfovibrio* is again available for photooxidation to $S^0$. The elemental sulfur precipitates and is collected on the commercial scale by the local population. It is very likely that the large fossil elemental sulfur deposits in Russia and Texas were formed by similar mechanisms.

Sulfate reduction contributes to the atmospheric cycling of sulfur. Until recently, it was believed that most of the biogenic sulfur transfer to the atmosphere (an estimated 142 million metric tons per annum when calculated as sulfur) takes place in the form of $H_2S$ (Kellog et al. 1972). This was most likely an overestimate, and $H_2S$ represents less than half of a 65–125 metric tons per annum biogenic sulfur transfer to the

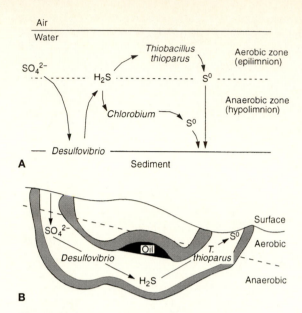

**A**

**B**

**Figure 11.9**

The biological deposition of sulfur (A) in a lake and (B) in geological strata. Sulfate is converted to $H_2S$ in anaerobic zones. The $H_2S$ is oxidized by *Thiobacillus thioparus* in both cases and in the lake habitat also by *Chlorobium,* forming and leading to the deposition of elemental sulfur. In geological strata, oil or gas deposits supply organic matter for sulfate reduction.

atmosphere (Kelly and Smith 1990). The balance of the atmospheric transfer takes place in the form of volatile organosulfur compounds, principally dimethylsulfide (DMS), with minor contributions of carbon disulfide ($CS_2$) and carbonyl sulfide (COS). The major source of all volatile sulfur is the ocean, with minor contributions from swamps and lakes. Although volatile sulfur is produced also in soil, this environment is a net sink rather than a net producer of volatile sulfur. Various thiobacilli rapidly oxidize hydrogen sulfide and other reduced volatile sulfur compounds to sulfate in aerobic soils and sediments. Hydrogen sulfide, dimethylsulfide, and other reduced volatile sulfur compounds, when they reach the atmosphere, are subject to oxidation and photooxidation reactions, ultimately converting them to sulfate.

## Interactions of Sulfur and Iron Cycling

An important practical implication of the sulfur cycle is the anaerobic corrosion of steel and iron structures set in sulfate-containing soils and sediments. This type of corrosion can severely damage or destroy pipes and pilings and has posed an unexpected engineering problem—it was believed that corrosion in anaerobic environments was minimal. The process consists of spontaneous chemical and microbially mediated steps, but the bacterial contribution is essential for driving the whole process (Postgate 1984). The surface of metallic iron spontaneously reacts with water, forming a thin double layer of ferrous hydroxide and hydrogen (Equation 21). The process would tend to stop here except for the activity of *Desulfovibrio desulfuricans,* which removes the protective $H_2$ layer and forms $H_2S$ (Equation 22). The $H_2S$ attacks iron in a spontaneous chemical reaction, forming ferrous sulfide and hydrogen (Equation 23). As the result of the above reactions, metallic iron is rapidly converted to ferrous hydroxide and ferrous sulfide (Equation 24). The reaction steps are:

(21) $\quad Fe^0 + 2H_2O \rightarrow Fe(OH)_2 + H_2$

(22) $\quad 4H_2 + SO_4^{2-} \rightarrow H_2S + 2OH^- + 2H_2O$

(23) $\quad H_2S + Fe^{2+} \rightarrow FeS + H_2$

(24) $\quad 4Fe^0 + SO_4^{2-} + 4H_2O \rightarrow$
$\quad\quad FeS + 3Fe(OH)_2 + 2OH^-$

## THE PHOSPHORUS CYCLE

Phosphorus is an essential element in all living systems. Within biological systems, the most abundant forms of phosphorus are phosphate esters and nucleic acids. Phosphate diester bonds form the links within nucleic acid molecules. Phosphate also forms an essential portion of the ATP molecule. The hydrolysis of phosphate from ATP to ADP forms the basis for most energy transfer reactions within biological systems. Phospholipids, which contain hydrophilic phosphate groups, are essential components of cell membranes. Phosphorus is a constituent of nucleic acids (RNA and DNA), sugar phosphates, and phosphate esters, such as the ATP/ADP/AMP system of cellular energy transfer.

However, phosphorus is not an abundant component of the ecosphere and often limits microbial growth (Cosgrove 1977; Ehrlich 1995). Its availability is restricted by its tendency to precipitate in the presence of bivalent metals ($Ca^{2+}$, $Mg^{2+}$) and ferric ($Fe^{3+}$) ions at neutral to alkaline pH. Large, slowly cycled reservoirs of phosphate occur in marine and other aquatic sediments. Small, actively cycled reservoirs of phosphate are dissolved phosphate in soils and waters and phosphate in living and dead organic matter. A largely inert reservoir has been phosphate rock, such as apatite ($3Ca_3[PO_4]_2 \cdot Ca[FeCl]_2$), but this reservoir is being increasingly tapped by the fertilizer industry. Much of this phosphate is eventually lost to marine sediments, raising concerns about future availability of an important fertilizer. In primary phosphates, such as $NaH_2PO_4$, only one of the three $PO_4^{3-}$ valences is linked to a metal. Primary phosphates have high water solubilities. Secondary and tertiary phosphates have only one or no hydrogen atoms in their molecule, respectively, and their water solubilities are progressively lower. In the manufacture of phosphate fertilizer, the tertiary phosphate of apatite is converted by acid treatment to secondary and primary "superphosphate."

The microbial cycling of phosphorus for the most part does not alter the oxidation state of phosphorus (Stewart and McKercher 1982). Most phosphorus transformations mediated by microorganisms can be viewed as transfers of inorganic to organic phosphate or as transfers of phosphate from insoluble, immobilized forms to soluble or mobile compounds (Figure 11.10). Various microorganisms have evolved transport systems for the regulated acquisition of phosphate from the environment such as the Pst phosphate transport system of *E. coli* (Figure 11.11).

Although phosphate is normally not reduced by microorganisms, it appears that some soil and sediment microorganisms may be capable of utilizing phosphate as a terminal electron acceptor under appropriate environmental conditions. Reliable and recent documentation for this transformation is not

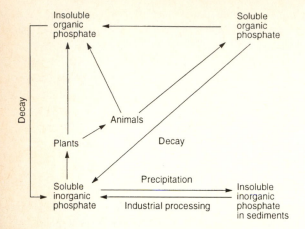

**Figure 11.10**
The phosphorus cycle, showing various transfers, none of
which alters the oxidation state of phosphate.

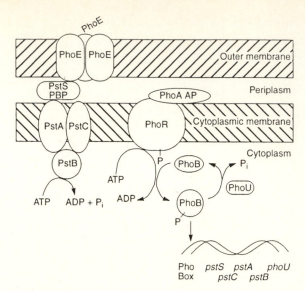

**Figure 11.11**
The Pst phosphate transport system of *E. coli* consists of
the *phoE*-determined outer membrane porin protein, the
periplasmic binding protein (PBP) determined by the *pstS*
gene, and the inner membrane transport system composed
of the PstA, PstB, and PstC polypeptides. The additional
periplasmic enzyme alkaline phosphatase (AP), determined
by the *phoA* gene, releases $P_i$ from organophosphate
compounds so that it can be bound by the PBP. The two
primary regulatory proteins, PhoR and PhoB, undergo an
autophosphorylation-transphosphorylation cycle. The PhoU
protein stimulates dephosphorylation of PhoB. The Pho box
is the DNA binding site for the PhoB regulatory protein.
(Source: Silver and Walderhaug 1992.)

available. Phosphate can possibly serve as a terminal
electron acceptor in the absence of sulfate, nitrate, and
oxygen. The final product of phosphate reduction
would be phosphines ($PH_3$). Phosphines are volatile
and spontaneously ignite on contact with oxygen, producing a green glow. The production of phosphines is
sometimes observed near burial sites and swamps
where there is extensive decomposition of organic
matter. Phosphines can also ignite the methane produced in similar environments, giving rise to
"ghostly" light phenomena. A microbial involvement
in phosphine production is likely but requires experimental confirmation.

Within many habitats, phosphates are combined
with calcium, rendering them insoluble and unavailable to plants and many microorganisms. Some heterotrophic microorganisms are capable of solubilizing
phosphates from such sources. Phosphate is assimilated by these microorganisms, which also solubilize a
large proportion of the insoluble inorganic phosphate,
releasing it for use by other organisms. The mechanism of phosphate solubilization is normally by production of organic acids. Some chemolithotrophic
microorganisms, such as *Nitrosomonas* and *Thiobacillus,* mobilize inorganic phosphates by producing

nitrous and sulfuric acids, respectively (Tiessen and
Stewart 1985).

Within soils, phosphate also exists as insoluble
iron, magnesium, and aluminum salts. The mobilization of insoluble ferric phosphates may occur when
microorganisms reduce ferric ions to ferrous ions
under anaerobic conditions. Flooding of soils enhances
release of phosphate by this mechanism.

Plants and microorganisms can readily take up
soluble forms of inorganic phosphates and assimilate
them into organic phosphates. As an example, inorganic phosphate reacts with ADP to generate ATP

# Smog and Acid Rain

Fossil fuels, especially coal and some heating oils, contain substantial amounts of sulfur. Much of this sulfur is present as pyrite ($FeS_2$) and originates from $H_2S$ produced by sulfate reducers. Some organosulfur is also present (Altschuler et al. 1983). When burned, most of this sulfur is converted to $SO_2$, which combines with atmospheric moisture to form sulfurous acid ($H_2SO_3$) (Kellog et al. 1972). Photooxidation also converts some $SO_2$ to $SO_3$, resulting in sulfuric acid. Atmospheric inversions in urban areas during the winter heating season can lead to the formation of highly irritating and unhealthy acid smog. This condition differs from the urban smog that arises in warmer weather predominantly from automobile exhaust, in which ozone and nitrogen oxides are the main irritants.

On the larger scale, the burning of fossil fuels gives rise to the formation of acid rain. Rainwater, which normally has a pH just below neutrality due to the weak acidity of $H_2CO_3$, becomes quite acidic (pH 3.5–4) from sulfurous and sulfuric acids. Acid rain corrodes buildings and monuments, especially those made of limestone and marble; it may also damage plant leaves. It has little detrimental effect on well-buffered soils and hard waters high in carbonate, but it becomes highly destructive in ecosystems that are not sufficiently buffered—for example, in glacier-scoured portions of Scandinavia, Canada, and New England. These regions have characteristically thin, weakly buffered soils, soft-water lakes, and rivers on hard granite bedrock. Here acid rain causes a substantial decrease in soil and water pH, leading to the elimination of important microbial, plant, and animal species and a general decline in ecosystem diversity and productivity. Strongly industrialized regions are not the only areas affected by acid rain. Wind patterns distribute the air pollutants; much of the acid rain problem in Scandinavia appears to originate from the industrialized regions of England and the German Ruhr Valley. The New England problem seems to originate from the industrialized regions of the Atlantic seaboard and the Great Lakes. The Ohio Valley in the United States contributes to the Canadian problem.

Because of the acid rain problem, air pollution standards limit sulfur dioxide emissions, and there is pressure to further tighten these standards. The option to burn clean fuels, like natural gas and low-sulfur oil, is becoming increasingly expensive. Scrubbing systems, designed to remove $SO_2$ from stack gases when high-sulfur fuels are being used, are expensive and have a variety of operational problems.

Microorganisms show some potential for reducing the acid rain problem by removing sulfur from fossil fuels prior to burning. Various chemical approaches have been considered for the removal of sulfur from coal prior to its use. The activity of sulfur-oxidizing bacteria could theoretically be used for the same purpose and perhaps at lower cost. The physical state of coal, which occurs as large chunks, is not conducive to microbial activities that could remove the sulfur. However, if coal distribution systems are developed in which the coal is ground and transported as a slurry through existing oil pipeline systems, the removal of sulfur from the slurried coal by the activity of the thiobacilli appears to be an option well worth exploring.

when coupled with a sufficiently exothermic reaction. Inorganic phosphate also reacts with carbohydrates, such as glucose at the initiation of glycolysis.

The reverse process, mineralization of organic phosphates, also occurs; this process is catalyzed by phosphatase enzymes. Many microorganisms produce phosphatase enzymes. Some bacteria and fungi produce phytase, which releases soluble inorganic phosphates from inositol hexaphosphate (phytic acid) (Equation 25).

(25)   Inositol hexaphosphate $+ 6H_2O \xrightarrow{\text{phytase}}$
        inositol $+ 6PO_4^{3-}$

Microbial activities may also immobilize phosphorus, rendering it inaccessible to the biological community. The assimilation of phosphorus into microbial cell constituents, such as membranes, removes phosphate from the available pool. In some situations, microorganisms aid plants by mobilizing phosphates; in others, they may compete with plants for available phosphate resources.

Productivity in many habitats is phosphate limited. In aquatic environments, phosphate concentrations exhibit seasonal fluctuations that are associated with algal and cyanobacterial blooms. The precipitation of phosphorus, especially in marine habitats, greatly limits primary productivity. In aquatic habitats, phosphorus may exist in soluble or particulate form. These forms exhibit differential reactivity and availability to the biological community. Phosphate concentrations in freshwater habitats are closely correlated with eutrophication. Phosphate-limited lakes normally are oligotrophic. The addition of phosphates from sources such as detergent fillers causes these lakes to become eutrophic (Chapra and Robertson 1977). The blooms of algae and cyanobacteria associated with eutrophication can greatly increase the concentrations of organic matter in bodies of water. During the subsequent decomposition of this organic matter, the water column can be severely depleted of oxygen, causing major fish kills. The introduction of high concentrations of phosphate from phosphate laundry detergents created such serious eutrophication problems in many water bodies that some municipalities banned their use.

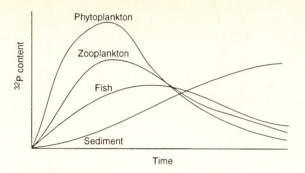

**Figure 11.12**
Idealized uptake and distribution with time of $^{32}PO_4^{3-}$ added to an aquatic ecosystem. The phosphate is taken up directly by the phytoplankton and reaches the higher trophic levels more slowly through feeding. A large portion of the added phosphate is eventually sequestered in the sediment.

Phosphorus, being an essential and often also a limiting mineral nutrient with a convenient radioisotope ($^{32}P$), is particularly suitable for demonstrating the movement and distribution of a nutrient element through food webs. If introduced as $^{32}PO_4^{3-}$ into a natural or model aquatic ecosystem (Figure 11.12), primary producers (phytoplankton) are rapidly labeled. The zooplankton does not take up the phosphate directly, but via ingested phytoplankton, and is therefore labeled more slowly. Higher trophic levels (fish and macro-invertebrates) are labeled even more slowly. In each trophic level, the radiolabeled phosphate concentration goes through a maximum and subsequently declines. There is, however, a steady increase of radiolabel in the sediment. If the experiment is continued long enough, eventually an equilibrium is reached between the precipitated and cycled phosphate. The ratio of the two is determined by water chemistry (high pH and bivalent cations favor precipitation) and hydrological conditions such as stratification that may restrict the free movement of phosphate.

## THE IRON CYCLE

Iron is the fourth most abundant element in the crust of Earth, but only a small portion of this iron is avail-

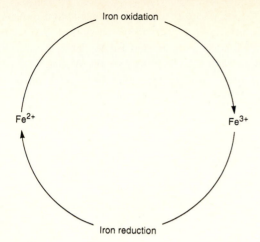

**Figure 11.13**
The iron cycle, showing interconversion of ferrous and ferric iron.

able for biogeochemical cycling (Ehrlich 1995; Nealson 1983a). The cycling of iron consists largely of oxidation-reduction reactions that reduce ferric iron to ferrous iron and oxidize ferrous iron to ferric iron (Figure 11.13). These oxidation-reduction reactions are important in both organic iron-containing compounds and in inorganic iron compounds.

Ferric ($Fe^{3+}$) and ferrous ($Fe^{2+}$) ions have very different solubility properties. Ferric iron precipitates in alkaline environments as ferric hydroxide. Ferric iron may be reduced under anaerobic conditions to the more soluble ferrous form. Under some anaerobic conditions, however, sufficient $H_2S$ may be evolved to precipitate iron as ferrous sulfide. Flooding of soil, which creates anaerobic conditions, favors the accumulation of ferrous iron. In aerobic habitats, such as well-drained soil, most of the iron exists in the ferric state.

In organic compounds, iron is often attached to organic ligands by chelation. Chelated iron can undergo oxidation-reduction transformations, which are utilized in electron transport processes. Cytochromes of electron transport chains contain iron that undergoes oxidation-reduction transformations during the transfer of electrons.

Virtually all microorganisms, with the exception of certain lactobacilli, require iron, employed as a cofactor by many metabolic enzymes and regulatory proteins because of its ability to exist in two stable oxidation states, $Fe^{2+}$ (the ferrous state) and $Fe^{3+}$ (the ferric state). Despite being one of the most abundant elements in the environment, iron is often a limiting factor for bacterial growth as it forms insoluble ferric hydroxide complexes under aerobic conditions and at neutral pH, thus imposing severe restrictions on its availability. Consequently, bacteria have evolved specialized high-affinity transport systems in order to acquire sufficient amounts of this essential element. Most bacteria have the ability to produce and secrete molecules designated *siderophores* (Greek for "iron bearers") to fulfill their iron requirements (Neilands 1981). Siderophores are special iron-chelating agents that facilitate the solubilization and uptake of iron. They are water-soluble low-molecular-weight (500–1500 Da) molecules that bind ferric iron with very high affinity. Many bacteria have also evolved the capacity to exploit iron complexed to siderophores produced by other bacterial and fungal species. The ability to utilize siderophores is associated with the presence of transport systems that can recognize and mediate uptake of the ferric-siderophore complexes into the cell.

Two groups of siderophores have been studied extensively. Phenol-catechol derivatives are synthesized by enterobacteria and have such common names as enterochelin and enterobactin; these systems transport iron into the cell (Figure 11.14). Streptomycetes and some other bacterial groups synthesize derivatives of hydroxamic acids referred to as ferrioxamines. In each case, the ferric iron is chelated by multiple hydroxyl or carbonyl groups as the ferric iron is enclosed in the molecular cage of the chelator. The siderophore receptor shuttles the iron molecule through the membrane and releases the siderophore to chelate additional molecules of ferric iron (Lewin 1984).

The intracellular level of iron is carefully monitored in the bacterial cell. The excretion of siderophores is induced by iron deficiency. A shortage of iron will reduce the growth of bacteria, whereas

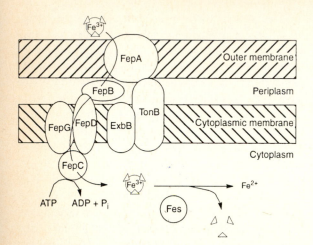

**Figure 11.14**
The Ent enterochelin iron system transports the trimeric catechol enterochelin (triangles). Enterochelin passes through the FepA protein of the outer membrane in a process requiring energy coupling through TonB. The periplasmic FepB protein passes the $Fe^{3+}$ enterochelin to the cytoplasmic membrane proteins FepG and FepD. Passage across the cytoplasmic membrane requires ATP energy through FepC. In the cytoplasm, the Fes enterochelin esterase cleaves enterochelin, allowing the release and subsequent reduction of iron. (Source: Silver and Walder-haug 1992.)

high concentrations of the metal can be toxic. Therefore, the expression of the iron-acquisition systems is regulated in response to iron, being increased under iron limitation. In addition, iron serves as an important environmental signal for the expression of factors unrelated to iron uptake (Litwin and Calderwood 1993).

Iron-dependent regulation has been most extensively studied in *E. coli,* in which the transcription of genes involved in iron acquisition is under the control of a repressor protein called Fur, a cytoplasmic 17-kDa iron-binding protein (Silver and Walderhaug 1992). When complexed to divalent ferrous ions, Fur binds to a specific DNA sequence located in iron-responsive gene promoters and inhibits transcription. At lower iron concentrations, the metal dissociates from the protein and repression is relieved (de Lorenzo et al., 1987).

Siderophore-mediated iron acquisition in pseudomonads has recently been the subject of extensive investigation (Venturi and Koster 1995). Iron assimilation via siderophores is thought to contribute to the plant-growth-promoting potential of many soil pseudomonads as well as to the virulence of pathogenic strains (Litwin and Calderwood 1993; Leong 1986). Pseudomonads have several siderophore-mediated iron-acquisition systems that include the biosynthesis of a siderophore that binds iron which is then transported into the cell and the uptake of heterologous ferric-siderophores in which the siderophore is produced by other microbial species (Venturi and Koster 1995). Several regulators controlling siderophore-mediated gene expression in *Pseudomonas* species have recently been isolated. The regulation of iron acquisition by siderophores employs both positive and negative elements ensuring expression of the relevant genes only when they are absolutely required. Siderophore biosynthesis is induced in response to iron limitation. In contrast, activation of the heterologous transport systems is not only regulated by iron availability but also requires the presence of their cognate ferric siderophores.

In the environment, such as within lake water and sediment, iron forms a variety of oxidized or reduced compounds depending upon the pH and redox potential; this leads to a heterogeneous distribution of various iron-containing compounds (Figure 11.15). Under alkaline to neutral conditions, ferrous iron is inherently unstable in the presence of $O_2$ and is oxidized spontaneously to ferric iron. Under such conditions, microorganisms have little chance to extract energy from the oxidation process. Under acidic reaction conditions in oxygenated environments, however, ferrous iron is relatively stable, and under such conditions, acidophiles such as *Thiobacillus ferrooxidans, Leptospirillum ferrooxidans,* and some strains of *Sulfolobus acidocaldarius* are capable of the chemolithotrophic oxidation of ferrous iron as shown in Equation 26.

(26) $2Fe^{2+} + \frac{1}{2}O_2 + 2H^+ \rightarrow$
$2Fe^{3+} + H_2O\ (\Delta G'_0$
$= -6.5\ \text{kcal/mol} = -27.3\ \text{kJ/mol})$

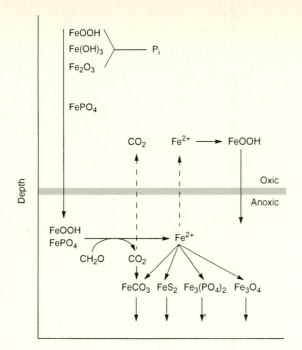

**Figure 11.15**

Diagram illustrating iron transformation reactions in a natural aquatic habitat. Iron precipitates as ferric phosphate and enters the sediment. There metabolic reactions reduce the ferric iron and produce compounds with ferrous iron. Some of the ferrous iron is released back into the oxic water column where metabolic reactions occur that again result in precipitation. (Source: Nealson and Saffarini 1994.)

With the exception of *L. ferrooxidans,* the same microorganisms can also oxidize reduced sulfur compounds.

Interestingly, *T. ferrooxidans,* considered a highly aerobic bacterium, was shown to be capable of anaerobic growth with elemental sulfur as electron donor and ferric iron as electron acceptor (Pronk et al. 1992). Just as sulfide can be oxidized anaerobically by photoautotrophs, the photooxidation of ferrous iron was reported to be mediated by two newly isolated purple bacteria related to *Chlorobium* and *Rhodobacter,* respectively (Ehrenreich and Widdel 1994).

Nonacidophilic iron bacteria, such as the prosthecates *Hyphomicrobium, Pedomicrobium,* and *Planc-*

*tomyces,* and the filamentous *Sphaerotilus* and *Leptothrix,* were at times described as being chemolithotrophs or at least as deriving energy from ferrous iron oxidation. A number of additional "iron bacteria," such as *Gallionella, Metallogenium, Seliberia, Ochrobium, Siderocapsa, Naumanniella,* and *Siderococcus,* were also described from enrichments but were never obtained as stable axenic cultures (Jones 1986; Kuenen and Bos 1990). Although these organisms appear to catalyze ferrous iron oxidation to some extent and become encrusted with the ferric precipitate, the chemolithotrophic or energy-yielding nature of the process has never been demonstrated convincingly. Cell walls may simply act as catalytic surfaces for ferric iron precipitation, or the cells may use ferrous iron oxidation as a sink for harmful excess oxygen.

The activity of iron-oxidizing bacteria can lead to substantial iron deposits. Typically, groundwater seeping through sand formations dissolves ferrous salts. Underground, a lack of oxygen usually prevents iron oxidation. When groundwater seeps to the surface, usually in a swampy area, iron oxidizers convert the ferrous ($Fe^{2+}$) ions to ferric ($Fe^{3+}$), which precipitates as ferric hydroxide and forms bog-iron deposits. Such easily accessible surface deposits were mined extensively and smelted in the early industrial age.

Since oxygenic photosynthesis changed the atmosphere of our planet to an oxidizing one, most iron in the biosphere is kept in the oxidized (ferric) state. Where limited oxygen diffusion and vigorous heterotrophic microbial activity create anaerobic conditions, as occurs in the hypolimnion of stratified lakes, waterlogged soils, and aquatic sediments, ferric iron may act as an electron sink and be reduced to $Fe^{2+}$. A large and heterogeneous group of heterotrophic bacteria, including *Bacillus, Pseudomonas, Proteus, Alcaligenes,* clostridia, and enterobacteria, appear to be involved in iron reduction.

Until recently, the mechanism of iron reduction remained largely unexplored. The subject of dissimilatory iron reduction has been reviewed by Lovley (1993). The fact that nitrate inhibits $Fe^{3+}$ reduction and that nitrate reductase negative mutants lose their ability to reduce $Fe^{3+}$ links iron reduction to the nitrate reductase system, at least in some microorganisms

(Nealson 1983a). Some iron reduction may occur nonenzymatically when reduced products of microbial metabolism, such as formate or $H_2S$, react chemically with $Fe^{3+}$. In soils, iron reduction is linked to a condition called *gleying*. Anoxic conditions due to waterlogging or high clay content give rise to the formation of reduced ferrous iron, which gives the soil a greenish gray color and a sticky consistency. The predominant iron reducers within gleyed soils appear to be *Bacillus* and *Pseudomonas* species.

Recent progress indicates that the form of oxidized iron is critical in respect to its bioavailability. Amorphous ferric oxyhydroxide (FeOOH) was reduced 50 times as fast as hematite ($Fe_2O_2$) (Lovley and Phillips 1986). Microbial ferric iron reduction was documented in a polluted aquifer (Albrechtsen and Christensen 1994). Some pure cultures of iron reducers were isolated and studied (Nealson and Myers 1992). *Shewanella* (formerly *Alteromonas*) *putrefaciens* and a strict anaerobe were grown with various organic substrates with ferric iron or, alternatively, manganic oxide ($MnO_2$) as the only electron acceptors. As electron sinks, FeOOH and $MnO_2$ also supported the conversion of $S^0$ to $SO_4^{2-}$, $H_2S$, and $H^+$ in sediments (Thamdrup et al. 1993). Another obligately anaerobic bacterium, *Geobacter sulfurreducens,* was studied in pure culture by Caccavo et al. (1994). This bacterium could couple the oxidation of acetate or hydrogen to induction of either ferric iron or elemental sulfur. *Geobacter* and *Desulfuromonas* species are important in the biogeochemical cycling of iron. *Desulfuromonas acetoxidans,* for example, grows under anoxic conditions with acetate as the sole electron donor and crystalline Fe(III) as the sole electron acceptor (Roden and Lovley 1993). Magnetite ($Fe_3O_4$) and siderite ($FeCO_3$) are the major end products of Fe(III) reduction. Ethanol, propanol, pyruvate, and butanol also served as electron donors for Fe(III) reduction.

Reduction of ferric iron (Fe(III)) to ferrous iron (Fe(II)) is one of the most important geochemical reactions in anaerobic aquatic sediments because of its many consequences for the organic and inorganic chemistry of these environments (Coleman et al. 1993). In marine environments, sulfate-reducing bacteria produce $H_2S$, which can reduce iron oxyhydroxides to form iron sulfides. The presence of siderite ($FeCO_3$) in marine sediments is anomalous, however, as it is unstable in the presence of $H_2S$. Geochemical and microbiological studies suggest that contemporary formation of siderite in a saltmarsh sediment results from the activity of sulfatereducing bacteria. Some bacteria reduce Fe(III) directly through an enzymatic mechanism, producing siderite rather than iron sulfides. Sulfate-reducing bacteria may thus be important and previously unrecognized agents for Fe(III) reduction in aquatic sediments and groundwaters.

## THE MANGANESE CYCLE

Manganese is an essential trace element for plants, animals, and many microorganisms. It is also cycled by microorganisms between its oxidized and reduced states much like iron, except manganese occurs in the ecosphere either in the reduced manganous ($Mn^{2+}$) or in the oxidized manganic ($Mn^{4+}$) state (Ehrlich 1995; Nealson 1983b; Kuenen and Bos 1990) (Figure 11.16); their stability depends on pH and redox potentials. The manganous ion is stable under aerobic conditions at pH values of less than 5.5, but it is also stable at higher pH values under anaerobic conditions. In the presence of oxygen, at pH values greater than 8, the manganous ion is spontaneously oxidized to the tetravalent manganic ion. The manganic ion forms a dioxide ($MnO_2$) that is insoluble in water. Manganic oxide is not readily assimilated by plants. In some marine and freshwater habitats, the precipitation of manganese forms characteristic manganese nodules (Figure 11.17). The manganese for these nodules originates in anaerobic sediments and is oxidized and precipitated, at least in part with the aid of bacteria, when it enters aerobic habitats, forming the nodules. Manganese is a relatively rare and strategically important metal, and the mining of deep-sea manganese nodules is under consideration.

Various soil and aquatic bacteria and fungi have been reported to catalyze the oxidation of $Mn^{2+}$ to $Mn^{4+}$ as shown in Equation 27.

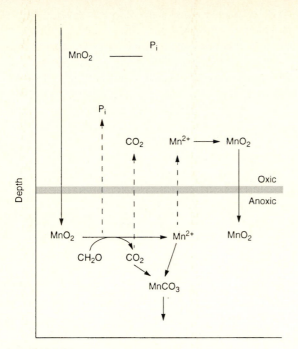

**Figure 11.16**
Diagram illustrating manganese transformation reactions in a natural aquatic habitat. Manganic oxide precipitates into the sediments where reductive reactions produce manganous carbonate. Some manganous ions are released into the oxic water column where oxidation occurs, resulting in the reprecipitation of manganic oxide. These reactions sometimes result in the formation of manganese nodules. (Source: Nealson and Saffarini 1994.)

$$(27) \quad Mn^{2+} + \frac{1}{2}O_2 + H_2O \rightarrow$$
$$MnO_2 + 2H^+ (\Delta G'_0$$
$$= -7.0 \text{ kcal/mol} = -29.4 \text{ kJ/mol})$$

*Gallionella, Metallogenium, Sphaerotilus, Leptothrix, Bacillus, Pseudomonas,* and *Arthrobacter* strains were reported to carry out $Mn^{2+}$ oxidation either in an inducible or in a constitutive manner. Manganese-based chemolithotrophy was repeatedly suggested but was difficult to prove. Manganese oxidation may be catalyzed by oxidases or catalases, and in some instances $Mn^{2+}$ oxidation appeared to be linked to ATP synthesis (Ehrlich 1985). Working with a continuous culture, Kepkay and Nealson (1987) presented

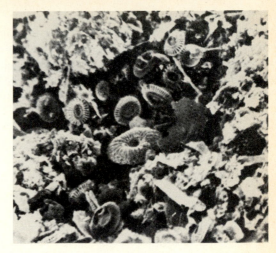

**Figure 11.17**
Scanning electron micrograph showing microorganisms on the surfaces of ferromanganese nodules. (Source: LaRock and Ehrlich 1975. Reprinted by permission, copyright Springer-Verlag.)

solid evidence for chemoautotrophic growth and $CO_2$ fixation of a $Mn^{2+}$-oxidizing marine *Pseudomonas,* but further studies will be needed to confirm and clarify this report. In many previously reported cases, simple surface catalysis on the sheath or cell wall of the bacteria promoted manganese oxidation, without an energy benefit to the microorganism.

Metabolism in anaerobic environments by a broad and heterogeneous group of bacteria results in $Mn^{4+}$ reduction, increasing the solubility and mobility of the resulting $Mn^{2+}$. As in the case of ferric iron, reduced products of microbial metabolism also react chemically with $Mn^{4+}$, reducing it to $Mn^{2+}$. *Shewanella putrefaciens* and a recent anaerobic isolate were documented to be able to use $MnO_2$ as their sole electron acceptor (Myers and Nealson 1988; Nealson and Myers 1992).

In microbial consortia from rapid sand filters, manganese and nitrate transformations appear to be linked (Vandenabeele et al. 1995a). Nitrate appears to have a beneficial effect on the removal of Mn. In aerated batch cultures derived from these consortia, the Mn removal rate was 30% higher in the presence of nitrate and was accompanied by nitrite accumulation. No increase in Mn removal has been observed when ammonium was added instead of nitrate. In microbial flocs originating from two different field sites incubated under anoxic conditions, the presence of $Mn^{2+}$ increased the nitrate-N gradient in the flocs by 35–130%. Nitrate also exerted a stabilizing effect on the removal of Mn: microbial consortia were prevented from reducing $MnO_2$ to $Mn^{2+}$ by the presence of nitrate. In pure cultures of *Nitrosomonas europaea* and *Nitrobacter winogradskyi,* reduction of $MnO_2$ to $Mn^{2+}$ occurs when $NO_2^-$ accumulates (Vandenabeele et al. 1995b). The development of $NO_2^-$ oxidizers is critical in the removal of $Mn^{2+}$. By oxidizing $NO_2^-$ to $NO_3^-$ the negative effect of $NO_2^-$ on the biological oxidation of $Mn^{2+}$ is eliminated.

## CALCIUM CYCLING

As a bivalent cation, calcium is an important solute of the cytoplasmic environment and is required for the activity of numerous enzymes. It also stabilizes structural components of the bacterial cell wall. From the geochemical point of view, however, biological precipitation and dissolution in the form of carbonate ($CaCO_3$) and bicarbonate ($Ca[HCO_3]_2$), respectively, are of the highest significance (Ehrlich 1995). Carbonate precipitation or dissolution may be an incidental consequence of metabolic processes that affect pH. Carbonate precipitation is involved also in formation of exoskeleta of microorganisms and invertebrates. Vertebrate animals deposit carbonates in bones and teeth.

Calcium bicarbonate has a high water solubility, calcium carbonate a much lower one. The equilibrium between $HCO^{3-}$ and $CO_3^{2-}$ is influenced by $CO_2$, which dissolves in water as carbonic acid ($H_2CO_3$). The prevailing pH strongly influences the formation of $H_2CO_3$, a very weak acid, and its salts. Increasing the hydrogen ion concentration encourages dissolution of carbonate; a decrease in hydrogen ion concentration encourages its precipitation.

In well-buffered alkaline to neutral environments rich in $Ca^{2+}$, $CO_2$ from aerobic or anaerobic microbial oxidations precipitates, at least in part, in the form of $CaCO_3$. The processes of ammonification, nitrate reduction, and sulfate reduction increase alkalinity and under appropriate conditions can contribute to $CaCO_3$ precipitation. The most significant process contributing to biological carbonate precipitation, however, is photosynthesis. In seawater, the principal dissolved form of calcium is bicarbonate, which is in equilibrium with carbonate and $CO_2$ (Equation 28).

(28)  $Ca(HCO_3)_2 \rightleftharpoons CaCO_3 + H_2O + CO_2$

If photosynthesis removes $CO_2$ from this equilibrium by assimilation, calcium shifts from the bicarbonate to the carbonate form. The latter, being less soluble, precipitates. Cyanobacterial photosynthesis has contributed to the formation of calcified stromatolites by procaryotic microbial mats (Knoll and Awramik 1983). As endosymbionts, cyanobacteria and algae contribute to exoskeleton formation in Foraminifera and various invertebrate animals, most significantly in corals. Calcium carbonate deposition by corals forms reefs and islands in tropical waters (Figure 11.18). The essential role of the endozoic algae of corals in reef building has been repeatedly emphasized in the scientific literature. Therefore, recent reports that could not confirm a connection between calcification and endozoic algae (Shreeve 1996) in at least some corals were

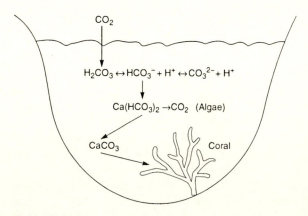

**Figure 11.18**
The reactions of calcium that lead to the formation of corals in seawater.

greeted with surprise and skepticism. Further studies will be needed to clarify this issue. The shells of Foraminifera accumulate and eventually turn into limestone deposits. The famous White Cliffs of Dover on the British channel coast were formed from biologically precipitated calcium carbonate, primarily shells of Foraminifera. Magnesium is a bivalent cation that behaves much like calcium and is abundant in seawater. However, $MgCO_3$ has considerably higher solubility in seawater than $CaCO_3$; therefore, calcium is preferentially used in the exoskeletal structures of marine microorganisms.

Microbial metabolic processes that produce organic acids (fermentation) or inorganic acids (nitrification or sulfur oxidation) contribute to the dissolution and mobilization of carbonates. Calcium readily reacts with phosphate anions, forming insoluble tertiary phosphate, which is unavailable for uptake (Equation 29).

(29)  $3Ca^{2+} + 2PO_4^{3-} \rightarrow Ca_3(PO_4)_2$

Production of organic and inorganic acids by microorganisms solubilizes this precipitated phosphate, a process that effects phosphorus mobilization in soils and sediments.

# SILICON CYCLING

Silicon is the second most abundant element in the crust of Earth, 28% by weight (Ehrlich 1995). It occurs primarily as silicon dioxide ($SiO_2$) and as silicates, the salts of silicic acid ($H_4SiO_4$). Silicon dioxide may be considered as the anhydride of silicic acid. Water solubility of silicic acid is low, ranging in natural waters from a few micrograms per liter to a maximum of 20 µg/l (Krumbein and Werner 1983). Although silicon as an element is closely related to carbon and is capable of polymerization as siloxanes ($HO—Si^{2+}—O—Si^{2+}—O—Si^{2+}—OH$), its biological role appears to be restricted to structural purposes in some microorganisms, many grassy plants, and a few invertebrates, such as siliceous sponges and the radula of some molluscs. In the microbial world, it forms the exoskeleton of important groups such as the diatoms, radiolaria, and silicoflagellates. The form of silicon used for this purpose is amorphous and hydrated silica ($SiO_2 \cdot nH_2O$; opal). In surface waters, the annual precipitation of dissolved silica to form the exoskeleton of diatoms and Radiolaria was estimated to be 6.7 billion metric tons per year. The residence time of the dissolved silica in surface ocean water, in relation to its biological precipitation, was estimated to be around 400 years (Tréguer et al. 1995). However, based on the entire ocean volume, the residence time for silica approaches 15,000 years.

Fungi, cyanobacteria, and lichens living on and within siliceous rocks in harsh environments actively dissolve silica through the excretion of carboxylic acids. In particular, 2-ketogluconic, citric, and oxalic acids have been implicated in dissolution of siliceous rock. The solubilization of siliceous rock by the chelating action of these organic acids contributes to the rock-weathering and soil-formation process.

Diatoms play the most important role in the precipitation of dissolved silica. Up to 90% of the siliceous oozes accumulating as pelagic sediment consist of diatom frustules, with Radiolaria contributing most of the rest. These oozes give rise to geological deposits known as Fuller's Earth, which is used as a filtering aid in the laboratory and in the manufacture of dynamite from nitroglycerine. Dissolved silicic acid is an essential and sometimes limiting nutrient for diatoms and is the major cause of seasonal diatom successions in some lakes (Hurley et al. 1985). The uptake and ordered deposition of silica involves formation of the organic silica complexes having Si—C and Si—O—C type bonds. The silica is deposited in a preformed organic matrix in a highly ordered fashion (Figure 11.19).

Purely chemical precipitation of silica may encrust and preserve microbial cells. Originally calcareous stromatolites become impregnated and preserved by siliceous minerals (Knoll and Awramik 1983). Contemporary siliceous stromatolites are being formed in some hot springs (Walter et al. 1972). The procaryotic mats in these hot springs passively become encrusted with silica as the mineral precipitates during the cooling of the thermal waters. Some fossil siliceous stromatolites may have been formed in a similar fashion.

**A**

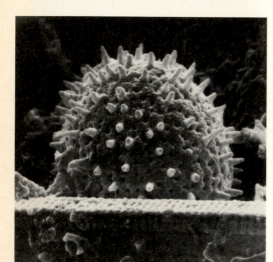

**B**

**Figure 11.19**
Scanning electron micrographs showing silicon-containing structures. (A) The shell of a diatom (*Surirella*) showing the inside of one of the valves. (B) A radiolaria. (Source: C. Versfelt.)

## METAL CYCLING

Various heavy metals exhibit biogeochemical cycles. For example, mercury can exist in a variety of inorganic and organic forms. Some microorganisms are capable of forming methyl mercury and may also form methylated forms of arsenic, selenium, tin, and perhaps lead. We will discuss these methylation processes and the role of microorganisms in concentrating heavy metals and radionuclides in Chapter 13.

## INTERRELATIONS BETWEEN THE CYCLING OF INDIVIDUAL ELEMENTS

In Chapters 10 and 11, we have discussed the cycling of each element separately. It needs to be emphasized, however, that in reality the cycle of each element is dependent on, or at least influenced by, the cycling of other elements. This is true not only for C, H, and O, which are cycled by the same two processes of photosynthesis and respiration, but also for cycles that are driven by different biochemical processes and performed by distinct microorganisms.

The study of biogeochemical cycle interactions is a technically challenging task for the investigator. In a complex natural system with a wide variety of microorganisms, substrates, and electron sinks, it is difficult to determine which group of microorganisms degrades a certain substrate and at what rate. This field of investigation has gained much from the use of selective inhibitors of certain cycling activities (Oremland and Capone 1988). As examples, 2-bromoethanesulfonate can be used to selectively inhibit methanogenesis in sediments, molybdate to suppress sulfate reduction, nitrapyrin to shut down nitrification, and acetylene to block denitrification on the nitrous oxide level. Although the effectivity and selectivity of these inhibitors need to be carefully established case by case, an ability to selectively inhibit a metabolic group within a complex system provides an excellent experimental tool for defining the normal contribution of that group to the system.

The reductive portions of the N, S, Fe, and Mn cycles are driven by chemical energy fixed in organic substances during photosynthesis. The chemolithotrophic reoxidation of N, S, Fe, and perhaps Mn are, in turn, linked to the conversion of $CO_2$ into cell material, again involving the cycling of C, H, and O. Solubilization, uptake, and precipitation of Ca and Si are directly or at least energetically linked to photosynthetic and respiratory cycling of C, H, and O. Acids from nitrification and sulfur oxidation help to mobilize phosphorus; photosynthesis or respiration are required for its uptake and conversion into high-energy phosphates. Sulfur is oxidized with reduction of nitrate by *Thiobacillus denitrificans,* and some extremely thermophilic methanogens can transfer hydrogen not only to $CO_2$ but also to $S^0$. Those are just some of the most obvious examples showing the interdependence of biogeochemical cycles; many other examples could be found. An instructive and ecologically important example of biogeochemical cycle interactions is the sequential use of electron acceptors during the oxidation of organic substrates (Jørgensen 1980; Nedwell 1984).

From the pool of potential electron acceptors, microorganisms within the community use the specific electron acceptor that they are genetically capable of using that yields the maximal energy yield from the available substrate. Each electron acceptor is utilized at different redox potentials (Figure 11.20). This seemingly intelligent decision is in part due to metabolic regulation within a single population, and in part due to the inevitable outcome of competition between populations with diverse metabolic capabilities. Through various regulatory mechanisms, facultatively anaerobic microorganisms shut off their less efficient fermentative or dissimilatory nitrate reduction pathways in the presence of oxygen. In the absence of oxygen, $Fe^{3+}$, and $Mn^{4+}$, $NO_3^-$ is the most oxidizing electron acceptor. From a substrate equally utilizable by nitrate and sulfate reducers, nitrate reducers will obtain the higher energy yield. Therefore, they will obtain the higher biomass per unit substrate utilization. They also outcompete the sulfate reducers because they have lower thresholds for carbon substrates (Cord-Ruwisch et al. 1988). Nitrate and iron, usually scarce in aquatic sediments, are rapidly depleted, leaving sulfate as the most oxidizing electron acceptor. When competing for a common substrate ($H_2$), methanogens have a lower utilization efficiency and a higher threshold for hydrogen uptake than sulfate reducers (Lovley 1985). Consequently, methanogens cannot effectively compete with sulfate reducers until all or most of the sulfate is depleted. In low-sulfate freshwater sediments, this occurs fairly rapidly; in sulfate-rich marine sediments, it occurs much more slowly.

The sequence of electron acceptor utilization can be observed spatially in horizontal layers of increasing

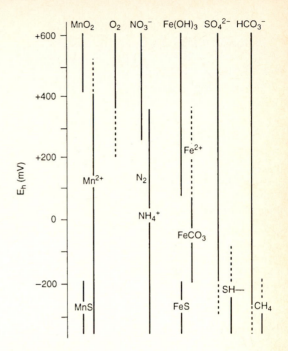

**Figure 11.20**
Redox potential ($E_h$) ranges for microbial utilization of potential electron acceptors. A microbial community will preferentially transfer electrons from an organic substrate to the most oxidizing electron acceptor available in their environment. This "choice" by the community, brought about by a combination of metabolic regulation and competition between populations, maximizes energy yield for the community as a whole. (Source: Nedwell 1984.)

depth in aquatic water columns (Figure 11.21) and sediments (Figure 11.22 on page 451). In a typical littoral marine sediment, only the first few millimeters of the sediment are oxygenated, though bioturbation by invertebrates may extend this oxygenated zone downward. For a few centimeters under the oxygenated zone, nitrate serves as the electron acceptor. Below this, for several meters, sulfate is the principal electron acceptor. Methanogenesis is usually confined to the sulfate-depleted deeper sediment layers, though the generated methane may diffuse upward into the zone of sulfate reduction.

The described classical sequence of electron acceptor utilization is supported by more recently rec-

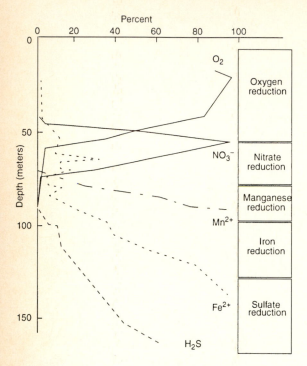

**Figure 11.21**
Sequence of electron acceptor usage in a water column results in zones of oxygen, nitrate, manganese, iron, and sulfate reduction. Oxygen reduction results in formation of water; nitrate reduction releases molecular nitrogen as a gas; manganese reduction results in accumulation of compounds with Mn(II); iron reduction results in accumulation of compounds with ferrous (FeII) iron; sulfate reduction produces hydrogen sulfide. (Source: Nealson and Saffarini 1994.)

ognized patterns of interspecies hydrogen transfer (Wolin and Miller 1982; Thiele and Zeikus 1988). Hydrogenogens, that is, hydrogen-producing fermentative microorganisms, are at a thermodynamical disadvantage if hydrogen accumulates. They live syntrophically with hydrogenotrophs, that is, hydrogen consumers, such as sulfate reducers, methanogens, and acetogens. The syntrophic relationship allows the fermentation to proceed and at the same time supplies the sulfate reducer or methanogen with the hydrogen necessary for $SO_4^{2-}$ or $CO_2$ reduction, respectively. Recent measurements on anaerobic sewage sludge

and lake sediment showed that most of the $H_2$-dependent methanogenesis in these ecosystems occurs via interspecies hydrogen transfer, rather than by the utilization of hydrogen dissolved in water (Conrad et al. 1985). Coculture experiments with a methanogen and a sulfate reducer on the substrates methanol and acetate, not utilizable by the sulfate reducer (Phelps et al. 1985), showed that the sulfate reducer competed effectively for the hydrogen generated by the methanogen from these substrates. The methanogen produced 10 μmol of $H_2$ per liter headspace when growing alone, but $H_2$ was less than 2 μmol per liter headspace when the sulfate reducer was present. The evolution of methane was reduced in coculture. Although the environmental relevance of this coculture experiment remains to be established, it shows that interspecies hydrogen transfer may also be competitive rather than syntrophic, and it confirms the competitive advantage of sulfate reducers over methanogens as long as sulfate is present.

Paradoxically, in some freshwater sediments with very low sulfate concentrations, the numbers and activity potential of sulfate reducers remain high. How do sulfidogens maintain themselves when limited by their specific electron acceptor? It is possible that this may also occur by interspecies electron transfer. Sulfidogens have a broader organic substrate range than methanogens, and are also able to take up hydrogen at lower threshold concentrations than their methanogenic competitors. In the absence of sulfate, sulfidogens may pass electrons acquired either from organic substrates or from hydrogen to methanogens, the latter using them in reducing $CO_2$ (methanogenesis). This scenario has been modeled *in vitro* using pure cultures of sulfidogens and methanogens (Bryant et al. 1985; Pak and Bartha, unpublished results), but its environmental significance remains to be verified.

## CHAPTER SUMMARY

The major elements nitrogen and sulfur are cycled in a complex, oxidoreductive fashion. Their reduced forms support chemolithotrophic metabolism. Their oxidized forms are used as electron sinks in anaerobic

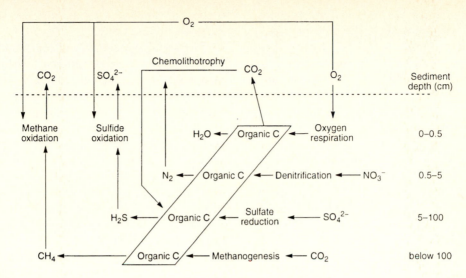

**Figure 11.22**
Utilization of electron acceptors in a marine sediment, showing the strong interactions between biogeochemical cycles and the stratification of electron acceptor use. The dotted line indicates the sediment surface. Sediment depths are approximate and vary with sediment and season. (Based in part on Jørgensen 1980.)

environments. The cycling of nitrogen and sulfur between oxidized and reduced states that is brought about by microbial metabolic activities results in transfers between the atmosphere, hydrosphere, and lithosphere. The importance of these transfers and microbial biogeochemical cycling activities is most evident in the nitrogen cycle.

Virtually all the critical steps of the nitrogen cycle are carried out exclusively by microbial populations. The nitrogen cycle consists of several phases, each mediated by different microbial populations and each having different environmental constraints. In nitrogen fixation, bacteria and archaea convert molecular nitrogen to ammonia. In ammonification, heterotrophic microorganisms convert organic nitrogen to ammonia. In nitrification, a two-step process carried out by different populations of chemolithotrophic bacteria, ammonia is converted to nitrite and nitrite is subsequently converted to nitrate. Denitrification is an anaerobic process that converts nitrate to molecular nitrogen while organic material is being oxidized. Plants, animals, and most microorganisms require

combined forms of nitrogen for incorporation into cellular biomass, but the ability to fix atmospheric nitrogen is restricted to a limited number of bacteria, archaea, and symbiotic associations. Primary productivity is often dependent on bacterial and archaeal fixation and conversion of nitrogen to forms that can be used by plants, animals, fungi, and other microbial populations.

Nitrogenase is the enzyme complex responsible for nitrogen fixation. Nitrogenase activity can be measured using the acetylene reduction assay. This assay has revealed that biological fixation of molecular nitrogen is carried out by several free-living archaeal and bacterial genera, some of which may be rhizosphere-associated, and by several bacterial genera that form mutualistic associations with plants. Nitrogenase is extremely sensitive to oxygen, requiring either low oxygen tensions or physiological protection for activity.

Free-living heterotrophic nitrogen-fixing bacteria, such as *Azotobacter* species, are widely distributed in soils, but the rates of nitrogen fixation by these bacterial populations generally are low. In aquatic habitats, photosynthetic cyanobacteria are the principal nitrogen fixers; many of these cyanobacteria form heterocysts that protect nitrogenase against toxic oxygen. Various bacteria, such as *Rhizobium, Bradyrhizobium,* and *Frankia* species, form mutualistic relationships with plants. Growth within plant nodules protects the nitrogenases of these bacteria and permits extensive nitrogen fixation to occur. Unless expensive nitrogen fertilizers are used, the fertility of agricultural fields is largely dependent on the activities of these bacteria. Traditional crop rotation programs have harnessed mutualistic nitrogen fixation to maintain soil fertility. Inoculation with rhizobia is used to increase the successful nodulation of nitrogen-fixing crops. Attempts have been made to genetically engineer additional nitrogen-fixing crops but, because of the complex genetic regulatory mechanisms that control the expression of nitrogenase, to date these attempts remain unsuccessful.

In nitrification, ammonium ions are oxidized to nitrite and then to nitrate ions by chemolithotrophs. In soils, the dominant genus that is capable of oxidizing ammonia to nitrite is *Nitrosomonas,* and the dominant genus capable of oxidizing nitrite to nitrate is *Nitrobacter.* The process of nitrification is especially important in soils, because the transformation of ammonium ions to nitrite and nitrate results in a charge change increasing nitrogen availability and motility. This may result in fertilizer loss, and the accumulation of nitrate in groundwater creates a human health hazard.

In denitrification, nitrate is converted to molecular nitrogen as a result of dissimilatory nitrate reduction by heterotrophs that utilize nitrate as a terminal electron acceptor during anaerobic respiration. Denitrification occurs under strictly anaerobic conditions or under conditions of reduced oxygen tension. It results in the return of molecular nitrogen to the atmosphere.

Because different environmental conditions favor specific nitrogen cycling processes, there is a spatial zonation of cycling processes. Fixation of nitrogen occurs in both surface and subsurface habitats. Nitrification occurs exclusively in aerobic habitats. Denitri-fication predominates in waterlogged soils and in anaerobic aquatic sediments.

The sulfur cycle involves compounds in which sulfur exhibits several different valences. Sulfur cycling includes sulfate reduction to hydrogen sulfide, and sulfide oxidation to sulfate. In the presence of oxygen, reduced sulfur compounds are capable of supporting chemolithotrophic microbial metabolism. Various *Thiobacillus* species oxidize $H_2S$ and other reduced sulfur compounds, forming sulfate. Plants, algae, and many heterotrophic microorganisms assimilate sulfur in the form of sulfate. In some environments, excessive sulfide oxidation causes acid mine drainage. The thiobacilli responsible for acid mine drainage are acidophilic and grow well at pH 2–3. Hydrogen sulfide is also subject to phototrophic oxidation in anaerobic environments. Photosynthetic sulfur bacteria, the Chromatiaceae, Ectothiorhodospiraceae, and Chlorobiaceae, are capable of photoreducing $CO_2$ while oxidizing $H_2S$ to $S^0$. These bacterial populations grow at the mud-water interfaces of aquatic habitats; their spatial separation can be demonstrated using a Winogradsky column. In hydrothermal vent regions, chemolithotrophs utilize hydrogen sulfide and other reduced sulfur compounds; biomass and metabolic products formed by these organisms feed the microbial and animal communities that grow around the vents. Sulfate-reducing bacteria, such as *Desulfovibrio,* and sulfur-reducing archaea, such as *Pyrodictium,* produce reduced sulfur compounds, such as hydrogen sulfide. Hydrogen sulfide produced by these microorganisms can be toxic to surrounding plants, animals, and other microorganisms. Sulfate reduction also contributes to the atmospheric cycling of sulfur.

Unlike the nitrogen and sulfur cycles, the phosphorus cycle does not involve oxidation-reduction reactions. Rather, it involves the movement of phosphates between soluble and insoluble forms. Most phosphorus transformations mediated by microorganisms can be viewed as transfers of inorganic to organic phosphate or as transfers of phosphate from insoluble, immobilized forms to soluble or mobile compounds. Often the availability of phosphate limits the growth of microorganisms. Within many habitats, phosphates are combined with calcium, rendering them insoluble and unavailable to plants and many microorganisms. Many microorganisms have specialized uptake systems for acquiring this essential nutrient. In aquatic environments, phosphate concentrations exhibit seasonal fluctuations that are associated with algal and cyanobacterial blooms. Productivity in many habitats is phosphate-limited. Excess additions of phosphates to the environment, for example in phosphate detergents, can result in algal blooms, eutrophication of lakes, and fish kills when the excess biomass decomposes and oxygen is depleted.

The cycling of iron consists largely of oxidation-reduction reactions that reduce ferric iron to ferrous iron and oxidize ferrous iron to ferric iron. Ferric iron precipitates in alkaline environments as ferric hydroxide. Ferric iron may be reduced under anaerobic conditions to the more soluble ferrous form. Under some anaerobic conditions, however, sufficient $H_2S$ may be evolved to precipitate iron as ferrous sulfide. Flooding of soil, which creates anaerobic conditions, favors the accumulation of ferrous iron. In aerobic habitats, such as well-drained soil, most of the iron exists in the ferric state. Microbial growth often is limited by the availability of iron. Various bacteria produce siderophores which bind iron and facilitate its cellular uptake. Some

chemolithotrophs oxidize iron to generate cellular energy. These iron-oxidizing bacteria can lead to substantial iron deposits. Like iron, manganese can be cycled between an oxidized and reduced state. In some cases bacterial activities result in precipitation of manganese with the formation of manganese nodules.

Various other elements, including calcium and silicon, are cycled between soluble and insoluble forms by microbial populations. Diatoms that accumulate silicon dioxide in their frustules form deposits of diatomaceous earth. In seawater, the consumption of carbon dioxide by photosynthetic microorganisms shifts the equilibrium away from the soluble bicarbonate to the less soluble carbonate. This results in formation of coral reefs in some marine regions.

Biogeochemical cycles interact with each other extensively in space and time. Under each given set of circumstances, the process that allows for the maximal energy flow is selected. Many of the biogeochemical cycling reactions of individual elements are actually connected by factors such as redox potentials. Individual minerals are oxidized or reduced by microorganisms only at specific redox potentials. This leads to zonations in soil and aquatic environments where minerals accumulate in specific chemical forms and where specific microbial populations proliferate.

## STUDY QUESTIONS

1. Describe the nitrogen cycle. Which microbial populations are associated with each phase of the biogeochemical cycling of nitrogen? What environmental conditions favor each phase of the nitrogen cycle?

2. Compare nitrogen fixation in aquatic and soil habitats.

3. Compare nitrification in soil and aquatic habitats.

4. How do chemolithotrophic nitrifiers affect groundwater quality? Why is nitrate a problem in potable waters?

5. How is the nitrogen cycle managed in agriculture?

6. Describe the sulfur cycle.

7. Describe a Winogradsky column and how it models the spatial distribution of microbial populations in lakes.

8. Describe the importance of sulfur cycling in deep-sea thermal vent habitats.

9. What environmental problems are caused by the activities of *Thiobacillus* species?

10. How could the sulfur cycle be managed to reduce atmospheric sulfur pollutants?

11. How does the phosphorus cycle differ from the nitrogen and sulfur cycles?

12. Describe the role of siderophores in the iron cycle.

13. How are manganese nodules formed?

14. What role does calcium cycling play in the formation of coral reefs? How is calcium cycling related to the metabolic activities of photosynthetic microorganisms?

15. What role is played by microorganisms in the formation of deposits of diatomaceous earth?

16. What is the relationship between the geochemical cycling of minerals and redox potential?

17. Give some examples of how some of the biogeochemical cycles of different elements interact with each other.

18. By what mechanisms do microbial communities select the electron acceptor that under the given circumstances maximizes energy flow?

## REFERENCES AND SUGGESTED READINGS

Albrechtsen, H- J., and T. H. Christensen. 1994. Evidence for microbial iron reduction in a landfill leachate-polluted aquifer (Vejen, Denmark). *Applied and Environmental Microbiology* 60:3920–3925.

Aleem, M.I.H. 1977. Coupling of energy with electron transfer reactions in chemolithotrophic bacteria. In B. A. Haddock and W. A. Hamilton (eds.). *Microbial Energetics.* Cambridge University Press, Cambridge, England, pp. 351–381.

Altschuler, Z. S., M. M. Schneppe, C. C. Silber, and F. O. Simon. 1983. Sulfur diagenesis in Everglades peat and origin of pyrite in coal. *Science* 221:221–227.

Balderston, W. L., B. Sherr, and W. J. Payne. 1976. Blockage by acetylene of nitrous oxide reduction in *Pseudomonas perfectomarinus. Applied and Environmental Microbiology* 31:504–508.

Baumann, B., M. Snozzi, A.J.B. Zehnder, and J. R. van der Meer. 1996. Dynamics of denitrification activity of *Paracoccus denitrificans* in continuous culture during aerobic-anaerobic changes. *Journal of Bacteriology* 178:4367–4374.

Belser, L. W. 1979. Population ecology of nitrifying bacteria. *Annual Reviews of Microbiology* 33:309–333.

Belser, L. W., and E. L. Schmidt. 1978. Nitrification in soils. In D. Schlesinger (ed.). *Microbiology 1978.* American Society for Microbiology, Washington, DC, pp. 348–351.

Benemann, J. R., and R. C. Valentine. 1972. The pathways of nitrogen fixation. *Advances in Microbial Physiology* 8:59–104.

Benson, D. R., and W. B. Silvester. 1993. Biology of *Frankia* strains, actinomycete symbionts of actinorrhizal plants. *Microbiological Reviews* 57:293–319.

Blackburn, T. H. 1983. The microbial nitrogen cycle. In C.W.E. Krumbein (ed.). *Microbial Geochemistry.* Blackwell, Oxford, England, pp. 63–89.

Bock, E., H. P. Koops, and H. Harms. 1990. Nitrifying bacteria. In H. G. Schlegel and B. Bowien (eds.). *Autotrophic Bacteria.* Springer-Verlag, Berlin, pp. 81–96.

Bollag, J. M., and E. J. Kurek. 1980. Nitrite and nitrous oxide accumulation during denitrification in presence of pesticide derivatives. *Applied and Environmental Microbiology* 39:845–849.

Bremner, J. M., and C. G. Steele. 1978. Role of microorganisms in the atmospheric sulfur cycle. *Advances in Microbial Ecology* 2:155–201.

Brill, W. 1975. Regulation and genetics of bacterial nitrogen fixation. *Annual Review of Microbiology* 29:109–129.

Brill, W. 1979. Nitrogen fixation: Basic to applied. *American Scientist* 67:458–466.

Brill, W. 1980. Biochemical genetics of nitrogen fixation. *Microbiological Reviews* 44:449–467.

Brill, W. 1981. Biological nitrogen fixation. *Scientific American* 245:68–81.

Brown, C. M. 1982. Nitrogen mineralization in soils and sediments. In R. G. Burns and J. H. Slater (eds.).

*Experimental Microbial Ecology.* Blackwell, Oxford, England, pp. 154–163.

Brown, C. M., and B. Johnson. 1977. Inorganic nitrogen assimilation in aquatic microorganisms. *Advances in Aquatic Microbiology* 1:49–114.

Bryant, M. P., L. L. Campbell, C. A. Reddy, and M. R. Chabill. 1977. Growth of *Desulfovibrio* in lactate or ethanol media low in sulfate in association with $H_2$-utilizing methanogenic bacteria. *Applied and Environmental Microbiology* 33:1162–1169.

Burns, R. C., and R. F. Hardy. 1975. *Nitrogen Fixation in Bacteria and Higher Plants.* Springer-Verlag, New York.

Caccavo, F., Jr., D. J. Lonengan, D. R. Loveley, M. Davis, J. F. Stolz, and M. J. McFuerney. 1994. *Geobacter sulfurreducens* sp. nov., a hydrogen- and acetate-oxidizing dissimilatory metal-reducing microorganism. *Applied and Environmental Microbiology* 60:3752–3759.

Caldwell, D. E., S. J. Caldwell, and J. P. Laycock. 1976. *Thermothrix thiopara* gen. et sp. nov., a facultatively anaerobic facultative chemolithotroph living at neutral pH and high temperature. *Canadian Journal of Microbiology* 22:1509–1517.

Campbell, R. 1977. *Microbial Ecology.* Blackwell, Oxford, England.

Carter, J. P., Y. H. Hsiao, S. Spiro, and D. J. Richardson. 1995. Soil and sediment bacteria capable of aerobic nitrate respiration. *Applied and Environmental Microbiology* 61:2852–2858.

Chapra, S. C., and A. Robertson. 1977. Great Lakes eutrophication: The effect of point source control on total phosphorus. *Science* 196:1448–1449.

Coleman, M. L., D. Hedrick, D. R. Lovley, D. C. White, and K. Pye. 1993. Reduction of iron-III in sediments by sulphate-reducing bacteria. *Nature* (London) 361:436–438.

Conrad, R., T. J. Phelps, and J. G. Zeikus. 1985. Gas metabolism evidence in support of the juxtaposition of hydrogen-producing and methanogenic bacteria in sewage sludge and lake sediments. *Applied and Environmental Microbiology* 50:595–601.

Cord-Ruwisch, R., H.-J. Seitz, and R. Conrad. 1988. The capacity of hydrogenotrophic anaerobic bacteria to compete for traces of hydrogen depends on the redox potential of the terminal electron acceptor. *Archives for Microbiology* 149:350–357.

Cosgrove, D. J. 1977. Microbial transformations in the phosphorous cycle. *Advances in Microbial Ecology* 1:95–134.

Coty, V. F. 1967. Atmospheric nitrogen fixation by hydrocarbon-oxidizing bacteria. *Biotechnology and Bioengineering* 9:25–32.

Dacey, J.W.H., and S. G. Wakeham. 1986. Oceanic dimethylsulfide: Production during zooplankton grazing on phytoplankton. *Science* 233:1314–1316.

Dalton, H. 1974. Fixation of dinitrogen by free-living microorganisms. *CRC Critical Reviews in Microbiology* 3:183–220.

Dalton, H., and L. E. Mortenson. 1972. Dinitrogen ($N_2$) fixation with a biochemical emphasis. *Biological Reviews* 36:231–260.

Deevey, E. S., Jr. 1970. Mineral cycles. *Scientific American* 223(5):148–158.

de Lorenzo, V., S. Wee, M. Herrero, and J. B. Neilands. 1987. Operator sequences of the aerobactin operon of plasmid ColV-K30 binding the ferric uptake regulation (fur) repressor. *Journal of Bacteriology* 169:2624–2630.

Delwiche, C. C. 1970. The nitrogen cycle. *Scientific American* 223(3):137–146.

Delwiche, C. C., and B. A. Bryan. 1976. Denitrification. *Annual Reviews of Microbiology* 30:241–262.

Döbereiner, J. 1974. Nitrogen-fixing bacteria in the rhizosphere. In A. Quispel (ed.). *The Biology of Nitrogen Fixation.* North-Holland, Amsterdam, pp. 86–120.

Döbereiner, J., and J. M. Day. 1974. Nitrogen fixation in the rhizosphere of tropical grasses. In W.D.P. Stewart (ed.). *Nitrogen Fixation by Free-living Bacteria.* Cambridge University Press, Cambridge, England.

Ehrenreich, A., and F. Widdel. 1994. Anaerobic oxidation of ferrous iron by purple bacteria, a new type of phototrophic metabolism. *Applied and Environmental Microbiology* 60:4517–4526.

Ehrlich, H. L. 1985. Mesophilic manganese oxidizing bacteria from hydrothermal discharge areas at 21° North on the East Pacific Rise. In D. C. Caldwell, J. A. Brierley, and C. L. Brierley (eds.). *Planetary Ecology.* Van Nostrand Reinhold, New York, pp. 186–194.

Ehrlich, H. L. 1995. *Geomicrobiology.* Marcel Dekker, New York.

Evans, H., G. Stacey, and R. H. Burris. 1991. *Biological Nitrogen Fixation.* Chapman and Hall, New York.

Eveleigh, D., and D. Davis. 1996. Whimsical wrinkles with Winogradsky's wonder. *SGM Quarterly* (UK) 23:106–107.

Fenchel, T., and T. H. Blackburn. 1979. *Bacteria and Mineral Cycling.* Academic Press, London.

Fischer, F., W. Zillig, K. O. Stetter, and G. Schreiber. 1983. Chemolithoautotrophic metabolism of anaerobic extremely thermophilic archaebacteria. *Nature* (London) 301:511–513.

Fischer, H-M. 1994. Genetic regulation of nitrogen fixation in rhizobia. *Microbiological Reviews* 58:352–386.

Focht, D. D. 1982. Denitrification. In R. G. Burns and J. H. Slater (eds.). *Experimental Microbial Ecology.* Blackwell, Oxford, England, pp. 194–211.

Focht, D. D., and W. Verstraete. 1977. Biochemical ecology of nitrification and denitrification. *Advances in Microbial Ecology* 1:135–214.

Gersberg, R., K. Krohn, N. Peele, and C. R. Goldman. 1976. Denitrification studies with $^{13}$N-labeled nitrate. *Science* 192:1229–1231.

Gibson, A. H. (ed.). 1977. *A Treatise on Dinitrogen Fixation.* Sec. IV: *Agronomy and Ecology.* Wiley, New York.

Gottschalk, G. 1986. *Bacterial Metabolism.* Springer-Verlag, New York.

Grassle, J. F. 1985. Hydrothermal vent animals: Distribution and biology. *Science* 229:713–716.

Hall, J. B. 1978. Nitrogen-reducing bacteria. In D. Schlesinger (ed.). *Microbiology 1978.* American Society for Microbiology, Washington, DC, pp. 296–298.

Hallmark, S. L., and R. E. Terry. 1985. Field measurement of denitrification in irrigated soils. *Soil Science* 140:35–44.

Halstead, R. L., and R. B. McKercher. 1975. Biochemistry and cycling of phosphorus. In E. A. Paul and A. D. McLaren (eds.). *Soil Biochemistry.* Vol. 4. Marcel Dekker, New York, pp. 31–63.

Hansen, T. A. 1993. Carbon metabolism of sulfate-reducing bacteria. In J. M. Odom and R. Singleton, Jr. (eds.). *The Sulfate-Reducing Bacteria: Contemporary Perspectives.* Springer-Verlag, New York, pp. 21–40.

Hansen, T. A. 1995. Metabolism of sulfate-reducing prokaryotes. *Antonie van Leeuwenhoek* 66:165–185.

Hardy, R.W.F., R. P. Holsten, E. K. Jackson, and R. C. Burns. 1968. The acetylene ethylene assay for N$_2$-fixation: Laboratory and field evaluation. *Plant Physiology* 43:1185–1207.

Hines, M. E., G. T. Banta, A. E. Giblin, and J. E. Hobbie. 1994. Acetate concentrations and oxidation in salt-marsh sediments. *Limnology and Oceanography* 39:140–148.

Hooper, A. B. 1990. Biochemistry of the nitrifying lithoautotrophic bacteria. In H. G. Schlegel and B. Bowien (eds.). *Autotrophic Bacteria.* Springer-Verlag, Berlin, pp. 239–265.

Hurley, J. P., D. E. Armstrong, G. J. Kenoyer, and C. J. Bowser. 1985. Ground water as silica source for diatom production in a precipitation dominated lake. *Science* 227:1576–1578.

Hutchinson, G. L., and A. R. Mosier. 1979. Nitrous oxide emissions from an irrigated cornfield. *Science* 205:1125–1126.

Ingraham, J. L. 1980. Microbiology and genetics of denitrifiers. In C. C. Delwiche (ed.). *Denitrification, Nitrification and Atmospheric Nitrous Oxide.* Wiley, New York, pp. 45–65.

Ivanov, M. V. 1968. *Microbiological Processes in the Formation of Sulfur Deposits.* Translated from Russian. Israel Program of Scientific Translations, Ltd., U.S. Department of Commerce, Springfield, VA.

Jannasch, H. W. 1990. Chemosynthetically sustained ecosystems in the deep sea. In H. G. Schlegel and B. Bowien (eds.). *Autotrophic Bacteria.* Springer-Verlag, Berlin, pp. 147–166.

Jannasch, H. W., and M. J. Mottl. 1985. Geomicrobiology of deep-sea hydrothermal vents. *Science* 229:717–725.

Jannasch, H. W., and C. O. Wirsen. 1981. Morphological survey of microbial mats near deep-sea thermal vents. *Applied and Environmental Microbiology* 41:528–538.

Jones, J. G. 1986. Iron transformations by freshwater bacteria. *Advances in Microbial Ecology* 9:149–185.

Jørgensen, B. B. 1980. Mineralization and the bacterial cycling of carbon, nitrogen and sulphate in marine sediments. In D. C. Ellwood, M. J. Latham, J. N. Hedger, J. M. Lynch, and J. H. Slater (eds.). *Contemporary Microbial Ecology.* Academic Press, New York, pp. 239–251.

Jørgensen, B. B. 1983. The microbial sulfur cycle. In W. E. Krumbein (ed.). *Microbial Geochemistry.* Blackwell, Oxford, England, pp. 91–214.

Jørgensen, B. B., and N. P. Revsbeck. 1983. Colorless sulfur bacteria *Beggiatoa* spp. and *Thiovulum* spp. in $O_2$ and $H_2S$ microgradients. *Applied and Environmental Microbiology* 45:1261–1270.

Karl, D. M., C. O. Wirsen, and H. W. Jannasch. 1980. Deep-sea primary production at the Galapagos hydrothermal vents. *Science* 207:1345–1347.

Kellog, W. W., R. D. Cadle, E. R. Allen, A. L. Lazrus, and E. A. Martell. 1972. The sulfur cycle. *Science* 175:587–596.

Kelly, D. P., and N. A. Smith. 1990. Organic sulfur compounds in the environment, biochemistry, microbiology and ecological aspects. *Advances in Microbial Ecology* 11:345–385.

Kepkay, P. E., and K. H. Nealson. 1987. Growth of a manganese oxidizing *Pseudomonas* sp. in continuous culture. *Archives for Microbiology* 148:63–67.

Knoll, A. H., and S. M. Awramik. 1983. Ancient microbial ecosystems. In W. E. Krumbein (ed.). *Microbial Geochemistry*. Blackwell, Oxford, England, pp. 287–315.

Koike, I., and A. Hattori. 1978. Denitrification and ammonia formation in anaerobic coastal sediments. *Applied and Environmental Microbiology* 35:278–282.

Krumbein, W. E., and D. Werner. 1983. The microbial silica cycle. In W. E. Krumbein (ed.). *Microbial Geochemistry*. Blackwell, Oxford, England, pp. 125–157.

Kuenen, J. G., L. A. Robertson, and H. V. Gemerden. 1985. Microbial interactions among aerobic and anaerobic sulfur-oxidizing bacteria. *Advances in Microbial Ecology* 8:1–59.

Kuenen, J. G., and P. Bos. 1990. Habitats and ecological niches of chemolitho(auto)trophic bacteria. In H. G. Schlegel and B. Bowien (eds.). *Autotrophic Bacteria*. Springer-Verlag, Berlin, pp. 53–80.

LaRock, P. A., and H. L. Ehrlich. 1975. Observations of bacterial microcolonies on the surface of ferromanganese nodules from Blake Plateau by scanning electron microscopy. *Microbial Ecology* 2:84–96.

Leong, J. 1986. Siderophores: Their biochemistry and possible role in the biocontrol of plant pathogens. *Annual Review of Phytopathology* 24:187–209.

Leschine, S. B., K. Howell, and E. Canale-Parola. 1988. Nitrogen fixation by anaerobic cellulolytic bacteria. *Science* 242:1157–1159.

Lewin, R. 1984. How microorganisms transport iron. *Science* 225:401–402.

Litwin, C. M., and S. B. Calderwood. 1993. Role of iron in regulation of virulence genes. *Clinical Microbiology Reviews* 6:137–149.

Lovley, D. R. 1985. Minimum threshold for hydrogen metabolism in methanogenic bacteria. *Applied and Environmental Microbiology* 49:1530–1531.

Lovley, D. R. 1993. Dissimilatory metal reduction. *Annual Review of Microbiology* 47:263–290.

Lovley, D. R., and E.J.P. Phillips. 1986. Organic matter mineralization with reduction of ferric iron in anaerobic sediments. *Applied and Environmental Microbiology* 51:683–689.

Lowenstein, H. A. 1981. Minerals formed by organisms. *Science* 211:1126–1131.

Myers, C. R., and K. H. Nealson. 1988. Bacterial manganese reduction and growth with manganese oxide as the sole electron acceptor. *Science* 240:1319–1321.

National Research Council. 1979. *Microbial Processes: Promising Technologies for Developing Countries*. National Academy of Sciences, Washington DC, pp. 59–79.

Nealson, K. H. 1983a. The microbial iron cycle. In W. E. Krumbein (ed.). *Microbial Geochemistry*. Blackwell, Oxford, England, pp. 159–190.

Nealson, K. H. 1983b. The microbial manganese cycle. In W. E. Krumbein (ed.). *Microbial Geochemistry*. Blackwell, Oxford, England, pp. 191–221.

Nealson, K. H., and C. R. Myers. 1992. Microbial reduction of manganese and iron: New approaches to carbon cycling. *Applied and Environmental Microbiology* 58:439–443.

Nealson, K. H., and D. Saffarini. 1994. Iron and manganese in anaerobic respiration: Environmental significance, physiology, and regulation. *Annual Review of Microbiology* 48:311–343.

Nedwell, D. B. 1984. The input and mineralization of organic carbon in anaerobic aquatic sediments. *Advances in Microbial Ecology* 7:93–131.

Neilands, J. B. 1981. Microbial iron compounds. *Annual Review of Biochemistry* 50:715–731.

Nelson, D. C. 1990. Physiology and biochemistry of filamentous sulfur bacteria. In H. G. Schlegel and

B. Bowien (eds.). *Autotrophic Bacteria,* Springer-Verlag, Berlin, pp. 219–238.

Nelson, D. C., and H. W. Jannasch. 1983. Chemoautotrophic growth of a marine *Beggiatoa* in sulfide gradient cultures. *Archives for Microbiology* 136:262–269.

Nielsen, T. N., L. P. Nielsen, and N. P. Revsbech. 1996. Nitrification and coupled nitrification-denitrification associated with a soil-manure interface. *Soil Science Society of America Journal* 60:1829–1840.

Oremland, R. S., and D. C. Capone. 1988. Use of specific inhibitors in biogeochemistry and microbial ecology. *Advances in Microbial Ecology* 10:285–383.

Paerl, H. W. 1990. Physiological ecology and regulation of $N_2$ fixation in natural waters. *Advances in Microbial Ecology* 11:305–344.

Parameswaran, A. K., C. N. Provan, F. J. Sturmand, and R. M. Kelly. 1987. Sulfur reduction by the extremely thermophilic archaebacterium *Pyrodictium occulatum*. *Applied and Environmental Microbiology* 53:1690–1693.

Payne, W. J. 1971. Gas chromatographic analysis of denitrification by marine organisms. In L. H. Stevenson and R. R. Colwell (eds.). *Estuarine Microbial Ecology*. University of South Carolina Press, Columbia, pp. 53–71.

Payne, W. J. 1973. Reduction of nitrogenous oxides by microorganisms. *Bacteriological Reviews* 37:409–452.

Pfennig, N. 1990. Ecology of phototrophic purple and green sulfur bacteria. In H. G. Schlegel and B. Bowien (eds.). *Autotrophic Bacteria*. Springer-Verlag, Berlin, pp. 97–116.

Pfennig, N., and H. Biebl. 1981. The dissimilatory sulfur-reducing bacteria. In M. P. Starr, H. Stolp, H. G. Trüper, A. Balows, and H. G. Schlegel (eds.). *The Prokaryotes*. Springer-Verlag, Berlin, pp. 941–947.

Pfennig, N., F. Widdel, and H. G. Trüper. 1981. The dissimilatory sulfate-reducing bacteria. In M. P. Starr, H. Stolp, H. G. Trüper, A. Balows, and H. G. Schlegel (eds.). *The Prokaryotes*. Springer-Verlag, Berlin, pp. 926–940.

Phelps, T. J., R. Conrad, and J. G. Zeikus. 1985. Sulfate-dependent interspecies $H_2$ transfer between *Methanosarcina barkeri* and *Desulfovibrio vulgaris* during coculture metabolism of acetate or methanol. *Applied and Environmental Microbiology* 50:589–594.

Pomeroy, L. R. (ed.). 1974. *Cycles of Essential Elements*. Dowden, Hutchinson and Ross, Stroudsburg, PA.

Postgate, J. R. 1982. *The Fundamentals of Nitrogen Fixation*. Cambridge University Press, Cambridge, England.

Postgate, J. R. 1984. *The Sulphate-Reducing Bacteria*. Cambridge University Press, Cambridge, England.

Postgate, J. 1992. *Nitrogen Fixation*. Cambridge University Press, New York.

Pronk, J. T., J. C. de Bruyn, P. Bos, and J. G. Kuenen. 1992. Anaerobic growth of *Thiobacillus ferrooxidans*. *Applied and Environmental Microbiology* 58:2227–2230.

Prosser, J. I., and D. J. Cox. 1982. Nitrification. In R. G. Burns and J. H. Slater (eds.). *Experimental Microbial Ecology*. Blackwell, Oxford, England, pp. 178–193.

Roden, E. E., and D. R. Lovley. 1993. Dissimilatory iron-III reduction by the marine microorganism *Desulfuromonas acetoxidans*. *Applied And Environmental Microbiology* 59:734–742.

Shannon, R. D., and J. R. White. 1996. The effects of spatial and temporal variations in acetate and sulfate on methane cycling in two Michigan peatlands. *Limnology and Oceanography* 41:435–443.

Shreeve, J. 1996. Are algae—not coral—reefs' master builders? *Science* 271:597–598.

Silver, S., and M. Walderhaug. 1992. Gene regulation of plasmid- and chromosome-determined inorganic ion transport in bacteria. *Microbiological Reviews* 56:195–228.

Silverman, M. P., and H. L. Ehrlich. l964. Microbial formation and degradation of minerals. *Advances in Applied Microbiology* 6:153–206.

Smith, D. W. 1982. Nitrogen fixation. In R. G. Burns and J. H. Slater (eds.). *Experimental Microbial Ecology*. Blackwell, Oxford, England, pp. 212–220.

Sorderlund, R., and B. H. Svensson. 1976. The global nitrogen cycle. Scope Report 7, Global Cycles. *Bulletin of the Ecological Research Commission* (Stockholm) 22:23–73.

Sprent, J. I., and P. Sprent. 1990. *Nitrogen Fixing Organisms: Pure and Applied Aspects*. Chapman Hall, London.

Stetter, K. O. 1990. Extremely thermophilic chemolithotrophic archaebacteria. In H. G. Schlegel and

B. Bowien. *Autotrophic Bacteria.* Springer-Verlag, Berlin, pp. 167–176.

Stetter, K. O., and G. Gaag. 1983. Reduction of molecular sulphur by methanogenic bacteria. *Nature* (London) 305:301–310.

Stewart, J.W.B., and R. B. McKercher. 1982. Phosphorus cycle. In R. G. Burns and J. H. Slater (eds.). *Experimental Microbial Ecology.* Blackwell, Oxford, England, pp. 229–238.

Stewart, W.D.P. 1973. Nitrogen fixation by photosynthetic microorganisms. *Annual Reviews of Microbiology* 27:283–316.

Thamdrup, B., K. Finster, J. W. Hansen, and F. Bak. 1993. Bacterial disproportionation of elemental sulfur coupled to chemical reduction of iron and manganese. *Applied and Environmental Microbiology* 59:101–108.

Thauer, R. K. 1990. Energy metabolism of sulfate-reducing bacteria. In H. G. Schlegel and B. Bowien (eds.). *Autotrophic Bacteria.* Springer-Verlag, Berlin, pp. 397–413.

Thiele, J. H., and G. Zeikus. 1988. Control of interspecies electron flow during anaerobic digestion: Significance of formate transfer during syntrophic methanogenesis in flocs. *Applied and Environmental Microbiology* 54:20–29.

Tiessen, H., and J.W.B. Stewart. 1985. The biogeochemistry of soil phosphorus. In D. C. Caldwell, J. A. Brierley, and C. L. Brierley (eds.). *Planetary Ecology.* Van Nostrand Reinhold, New York, pp. 463–472.

Tréguer, P., D. M. Nelson, A. J. Van Bennekom, D. J. DeMaster, A. Leynaert, and B. Quéguiner. 1995. The silica balance in the world ocean: A re-estimate. *Science* 268:375–379.

Trüper, H. G. 1990. Physiology and biochemistry of phototrophic bacteria. In H. G. Schlegel and B. Bowien (eds.). *Autotrophic Bacteria.* Springer-Verlag, Berlin, pp. 267–281.

Uberoi, V., and S. K. Bhattacharya. 1995. Interactions among sulfate reducers, acetogens, and methanogens in anaerobic propionate systems. *Water Environment Research* 67:330–339.

van Berkum, P., and B. B. Bohlool. 1980. Evaluation of nitrogen fixation by bacteria in association with roots of tropical grasses. *Microbiological Reviews* 44:491–517.

Vandenabeele, J., D. De Beer, R. Germonpre, R. Van de Sande, and W. Verstraete. 1995a. Influence of nitrate on manganese removing microbial consortia from sand filters. *Water Research* 29:579–587.

Vandenabeele, J., M. Vande-Woestyne, F. Houwen, R. Germonpre, D. Vandesande, and W. Verstraete. 1995b. Role of autotrophic nitrifiers in biological manganese removal from groundwater containing manganese and ammonium. *Microbial Ecology* 29: 83–98.

Venturi, V., P. Weisbeek, and M. Koster. 1995. Gene regulation of siderophore iron acquisition in *Pseudomonas:* not only the Fur repressor. *Molecular Microbiology* 17:603–610.

Wallace, W., and D.J.D. Nicholas. 1969. The biochemistry of nitrifying organisms. *Biological Reviews* 44:359–391.

Walter, M. R., J. Bauld, and T. D. Brode. 1972. Siliceous algal and bacterial stromatolites in hot spring and geyser effluents of Yellowstone National Park. *Science* 178:402–405.

Winter, H. C., and R. H. Burris. 1976. Nitrogenase. *Annual Review of Biochemistry* 45:409–426.

Wolin, M. J., and T. L. Miller. 1982. Interspecies hydrogen transfer: 15 years later. *ASM News* 48:561–565.

# part five

# BIOTECHNOLOGICAL ASPECTS OF MICROBIAL ECOLOGY

# 12

# ECOLOGICAL ASPECTS OF BIODETERIORATION CONTROL AND SOIL, WASTE, AND WATER MANAGEMENT

*Microbial ecology is a highly relevant scientific discipline with many practical implications and applications. The principles and methods of microbial ecology allow us to understand phenomena that influence our economic well-being, the general public health, and global environmental quality. Preventing the deterioration of foods and materials, maintaining fertile agricultural soils, ensuring the supply of healthful drinking water, and finding acceptable means for the disposal of liquid and solid waste materials are long-standing problems of human society that have solutions through an understanding of microbial ecology and the ability to control microbial growth and activities for the benefit of humankind. An understanding of microbial ecology allows us to reach acceptable solutions to current problems in agriculture, resource recovery, public health, and pollution control by a planned, scientific approach.*

## CONTROL OF BIODETERIORATION

All foods and many traditional materials used by human society are potential substrates for microbial growth. In most cases, their biochemical transformation by microorganisms results in spoilage or deterio-

ration. Food preservation and prevention of biodeterioration are major areas of concern to food and industrial microbiologists and to microbial ecologists. The emphasis of this brief discussion is on principles used to control biodeterioration rather than on procedural details that are available in textbooks (Desrosier 1970; Frazier and Westhoff 1978) and reviews (Hurst and Collins-Thompson 1979). The control methods that are employed represent applications of Liebig's and Shelford's laws, that is, the adjustment of environmental conditions to exceed the growth requirements and tolerance ranges of microbes to prevent potentially destructive microbial growth.

To control undesirable microbial activity, one or more of the following basic approaches are used:

1. All undesirable microorganisms are destroyed or removed by physical or chemical means, and recontamination is prevented by a physical barrier.
2. Food or other materials subject to biodeterioration are kept under environmental conditions that preclude or minimize microbial activity.
3. Food or material is modified, by processing or additives, to reduce its availability as a microbial substrate.

The first approach, sterilization, is used in canning, the preparation of surgical utensils and microbiological media, disposable culture tubes, dishes, and so forth. Initial sterilization is achieved by heat treatment, radiation sterilization, or chemosterilization. We discussed the sensitivity of microorganisms to these factors and the death curves of microbial populations previously. The commonly used physical processes are exposure to wet heat, dry heat, gamma radiation (usually from a $^{60}$Co source), and UV radiation. Because of its low penetration, sterilization by UV radiation is largely restricted to gases or surfaces; it is also used for disinfection in some potable water systems, especially in Europe. Gamma irradiation is used on some heat-sensitive materials, such as sutures and plastics, and some foods. The most frequently used chemosterilants are ethylene oxide, propylene oxide, chlorine, and ozone. Because of residual toxicity and taste problems, chemosterilization is rarely applied to foods, but it is useful for surgical and other medical implements, microbiological plasticware, and so on. Ethylene oxide is commonly used in sterilization of such materials. Chlorine, chloramines, and ozone are employed in the treatment of drinking water. These chemicals are strong oxidizing agents that effectively kill microorganisms.

All of the sterilization treatments tend to affect adversely the material to be preserved, and often only partial sterilization is used in order to minimize damage to the product. Pasteurization of milk and other products, such as beer, is aimed at the destruction of heat-sensitive human pathogens and an overall reduction in microbial numbers; the complete sterilization of milk and beer by heat would render them unpalatable.

In the canning industry, the most dangerous and highly heat-resistant spoilage organism is *Clostridium botulinum*. Minute amounts of the botulin neurotoxin produced by this spore-forming anaerobe can cause rapid fatality by respiratory paralysis. Canned food products that may serve as substrates for *Clostridium* and other endospore-forming bacteria need extensive heat processing to eliminate all viable endospores. Foods that are by nature acidic (fruit preserves, tomatoes, and so on) are satisfactorily preserved with a milder heat process, as *C. botulinum* fails to grow and produce toxin at low pH values. Significantly, when plant-breeding programs developed low-acid tomato varieties, clostridial spoilage problems occurred with several outbreaks of botulism, and the canning process had to be revised.

Indicator microorganisms are used in safety and quality control procedures whenever a potential problem organism cannot be detected with ease and reliability. For safety, an indicator organism should be at least as resistant or persistent as the problem organism. Its presence and survival should indicate the potential presence of viable problem organisms. For easy detection, indicator organisms should be more numerous than the problem organisms, and they should be easy to grow and to identify. In sterilization quality control, each sterilization batch includes at least one sample intentionally contaminated with an organism that is highly resistant to the treatment. These contaminated samples are incubated after the sterilization process under appropriate conditions; lack of growth indicates the success of the sterilization process. Because of the high resistance of its endospores and its easy cultivation, *Bacillus pumilus* serves most frequently as the indicator organism in sterilization procedures. The use of an indicator organism is especially critical in cases where contamination would become obvious only after the appearance of serious health consequences; therefore, it is used with disposable syringes, intravenous tubing, sutures, bandages, and similar medical implements.

Microorganisms can be removed by filtration from solutions or gases that cannot be sterilized by any of the previously discussed approaches. Filtration is used for some beverages, for some pharmaceutical products, and for the sterilization of air. Filtration causes minimal sterilization damage to the product.

Following each of the previously described procedures for killing or removing contaminating microorganisms, the product is physically separated from the environment to prevent recontamination. Generally a barrier, such as a metal can, glass bottle, or plastic-sealed wrapper, is used to block exchange with the nonsterile surroundings. A break in this protective barrier, such as a puncture of a can, allows recontamination and negates the value of the sterilization procedure. If the integrity of the barrier remains intact, however, and the product has been truly sterilized, storage can be at room temperature, and the storage time without biodeterioration (shelf life) can be virtually indefinite.

The second approach, for control of microbial growth, manipulates environmental conditions to restrict microbial activity but does not attempt to eliminate or exclude microorganisms. The environmental parameters most frequently controlled for suppression of microbial activity are water activity and temperature. To reduce water activity, the heat of the sun or fire is used to evaporate water. Meat, fish, vegetables, biscuits, cereals, and so on are preserved from spoilage in this manner. Freeze-drying is a modern modification of this approach that minimizes the deleterious effects of drying on some foods. An alternative way of lowering water activity is by adding high concentrations of salt or sugar.

Salted meat and fish products, candied fruit, and refined sugar and starch products are preserved by their low water activity. Most bacteria will not grow at a water activity below 0.95, although halophilic bacteria occasionally grow on salted fish and meat products. On the other hand, some common fungi will grow at water activities as low as 0.65–0.70, as evidenced by the appearance of molds on various foods stored under damp conditions. Growth of some molds on some grains and nuts stored under damp conditions can result in the synthesis of powerful mycotoxins, even when the overall appearance of the product is only minimally affected. Aflatoxins, produced by certain strains of *Aspergillus flavus,* have high acute toxicity and are also potent carcinogens.

Wood, leather, and cellulosic fibers, such as cotton, hemp, and jute, are natural products quite susceptible to biodeterioration. A general approach to prevent these materials from biodeteriorating is to keep them dry. Addition of preservatives is an alternative that will be discussed later. Wooden structures are built to minimize exposure to moisture by the use of stone or concrete foundations and roofing. The roofs of the picturesque covered bridges served to protect the wooden bridge structure, not its users, from the elements. The primary function of paint, stain, and varnish is to prevent wood from soaking up moisture. In all of these examples, low water activities limit biodeterioration.

Because they affect the quality and taste of food only minimally or not at all, low temperatures (freezing and refrigeration) are popular food preservation methods in developed countries. Freezing arrests biodeterioration (although not chemical deterioration) indefinitely, and at refrigerator temperatures—that is, below 5°C—growth of most spoilage organisms is slow. Before the ready availability of home refrigeration units, this mode of food preservation was seasonally and regionally restricted; it is still unaffordable for the great majority of the world's population.

The third approach, for control of microbial growth, modifies the availability of the substrate to microorganisms through processing or additives. In situations where microorganisms cannot be excluded and environmental parameters (moisture or temperature, for example) cannot be readily controlled, this is the only remaining alternative. Additives designed to suppress microbial activity are not necessarily innocuous to higher organisms. Even traditional additives, such as smoke and nitrate, are controversial because they probably contribute carcinogenic benzpyrenes and nitrosamines, respectively, to the human diet. Nitrite derived from the added nitrate, however, is considered essential for control of *Clostridium botulinum* in sausage-type meat products.

Some common modern spoilage retardants used in food products are acetic, lactic, propionic, citric, and sorbic acids or their salts. Fatty acids have a general antibacterial activity, the mechanism of which is complex and not well understood. Microorganisms exhibit great variations in sensitivity to these agents. Sodium or calcium propionate is extensively used to inhibit the development of molds in bread and other bakery products, but the same agents do not interfere with the activity of yeasts prior to the baking process. Sodium benzoate and the methyl and propyl esters of *p*-hydroxybenzoic acid (methylparaben and propylparaben) are broad-spectrum microbial inhibitors used in various food products. Salicylic acid and salicylates are used as food preservatives in many countries but not in the United States. Benzoates and salicylates interfere with a number of enzymatic processes, but their exact mode of action is not well defined. In sugar manufacturing, molasses and sugar solutions are protected from rapid biodeterioration by osmotolerant bacteria and yeasts by the use of formaldehyde, sodium metabisulfite, or quaternary ammonium compounds.

Ecologically most interesting are the food preservation methods that rely on microbial transformations of one kind to prevent other undesirable microbial transformations. In effect, microorganisms capable of preemptive colonization are used to prevent an ecological succession that would lead to spoiled food products. Lactic acid fermentations often are used in this manner to produce fermented milk products (yogurt, sour milk, and sour cream), various pickles, sauerkraut, and silage for animal feed. In each case, profuse acid production by lactobacilli prevents the activity of other decomposing bacteria. The food product is preserved, at least as long as anaerobic conditions prevail. Somewhat similar stabilization of milk products occurs during the formation of various cheeses by propionibacteria. Acetic acid (vinegar) produced from ethanol by *Acetobacter aceti* is used in stabilizing food products such as pickled herring. Wine, beer, and other alcoholic beverages are preserved by their ethanol content produced by yeasts during the fermentation process.

For some uses, wood and natural fibers cannot be kept from prolonged moisture exposure, and the addition of antibacterial preservatives is needed to prevent rapid biodeterioration. Wood that must be buried for such uses as fence posts, telephone poles, or pilings is commonly impregnated with coal tar or creosote. Both substrates consist of highly condensed and partially oxygenated petroleum fractions. They are antimicrobial, hydrophobic, and highly resistant to decomposition. Other wood preservatives are copper naphthalene and ammoniated or chromated copper arsenate. These products rely on heavy metal toxicity. Tar from the dry distillation of wood or from petroleum is used on rope and sailcloth. Some common modern commercial biocides used on tent canvas, camping gear, and other field equipment are chlorophenols, dithiocarbamates, acrolein, and dibromonitrilopropionamide. Phenylmercury biocides are used

in the pulp industry to retard the development of slime-forming microorganisms. This practice and the dressing of seeds with organomercurials prior to planting have contributed substantially to environmental mercury pollution and are gradually being replaced by other biocides.

The tanning of leather is essentially a stabilizing measure. Tannic acid traditionally was used to establish extensive cross-linkage of protein strands, resulting in substantial resistance to proteolytic enzymes. Chromic salts are used for the same purpose in modern tanning processes.

## MANAGEMENT OF AGRICULTURAL SOILS

Soil management practices vary according to crop and soil characteristics but share certain common features. With the exception of rice grown in paddies, all major crops require aerobic soil conditions. Because the aeration status of soils is controlled principally by their water saturation, it is of prime importance to provide adequate drainage for agricultural land. Prolonged anaerobic soil conditions are injurious to plant roots, not only by direct oxygen deprivation but also because of the microbial use of secondary electron acceptors, such as nitrate, sulfate, and ferric iron. The resulting denitrification causes loss of vital nitrogen; toxic $H_2S$ is produced; and sticky greenish ferrous iron is deposited in gley soils.

The soil pH regulates the solubility of plant nutrients as well as the bioavailability of potentially toxic heavy metals; thus, the management of soil pH is often critical in agricultural production. Biodegradation of plant material and some mineral cycling activities, such as sulfur oxidation and nitrification, result in acid production; in some soils, it is necessary to maintain the pH close to neutrality by liming. On the other hand, the pH may deliberately be lowered for the control of soilborne plant pathogens. Figure 12.1 (p. 468) shows the pH dependence of *Streptomyces scabies* in culture solution and the corresponding occurrence of the potato scab disease in relation to soil pH (Waksman 1952). Because potatoes grow well in acidic soil, it is simple to control this plant disease by

## Fouling Biofilms

The fouling of submerged surfaces, especially in the marine environment, poses a special deterioration problem. Surface fouling is a complex phenomenon initiated by microorganisms but completed by invertebrate animals, such as shipworms *(Teredo)* and other mollusks, barnacles, polychaetes, brachiopods, sponges, and bryozoa. Under euphotic conditions, microalgae and macroalgae also participate in the surface-fouling phenomenon (Sieburth 1975).

Surface fouling results in the direct deterioration of materials such as wood, rubber, many plastics, and insulation materials. Indirect damage occurs from the increased weight and hydrodynamic resistance of cables and other structures, leading to their mechanical failure. Corrosion of ferrous metals is enhanced by damage to the paint coat. Fouling increases the drag of boat and ship hulls, resulting in decreased speed and fuel inefficiency. Surface fouling reduces the efficiency of heat exchangers and is a big problem in cooling systems that use fresh or saltwater.

The ecological succession of surface fouling is initiated by the permanent attachment of heterotrophic marine microorganisms (DiSalvo and Daniels 1975). These microorganisms are attracted even to inert surfaces, such as glass, because the dilute organic nutrients in seawater become concentrated at such interfacial surfaces through physical adsorption. The colonizing microorganisms secrete adhesive mucopolysaccharides and establish a primary surface film (Corpe et al. 1976). Figures A–F show, via scanning electron micrography, examples of microbial primary surface fouling biofilms, which appear to be critical for the subsequent colonization by larvae of various invertebrate animals.

Marine surface fouling can be retarded or prevented by shielding with materials containing toxic substances—for example, substances containing heavy metals, such as copper and lead. Wood is often impregnated with tar, creosote, or other wood preservatives. Submerged metal and other surfaces usually are protected by paint containing toxic heavy metals, such as mercury, lead, tin, chromate, copper, and so on. A disadvantage of the latter approach is that the toxic heavy metals gradually leach into the marine environment and create a pollution problem. A novel approach to surface-fouling control may evolve from recent investigations on microbial chemotaxis. It may be possible to retard surface fouling by the use of specific repellents rather than by using the indiscriminately toxic heavy-metal biocides. Acrylamide, tannic acid, and benzoic acid exhibit promising repellent characteristics, and these or similar substances may be of use in future antifouling paints (Chet and Mitchell 1976).

Fouling of surfaces is also a problem in highly humid terrestrial environments. The walls of shower stalls, bathrooms, indoor pools, cold rooms, basements, and the like may be colonized by microorganisms, especially by molds that are able to grow at low water activities. Paints that incorporate antimicrobial substances and periodic scrubbing with disinfectants are the common remedies to this problem.

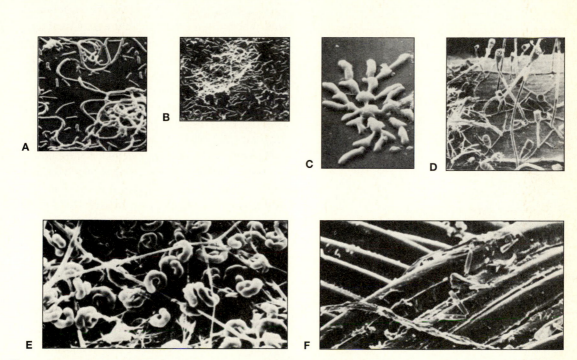

Photomicrographs showing microbial surface fouling. (A) Estuarine bacteria cultured on a clean glass slide for 48 hours in an aquarium containing San Francisco Bay water. (B) Colony and lawn of an estuarine bacterial isolate grown on clean glass slide. (C) Microorganisms attached to a fouling slide immersed in a polluted harbor in the Bahamas for 6 days. (D) Microbial colony developing on a glass slide immersed in San Francisco Bay water for 5 days. (Source A–D: DiSalvo and Daniels 1975. Reprinted by permission, copyright Springer-Verlag.) (E) Fungi on wood surface from Point Judith, Rhode Island, showing mycelia and spores of *Zalerion maritimum*. (F) Microorganisms colonizing nylon fishing line immersed for 4 days at Pigeon Key, Florida, showing attachment of pennate diatoms. (Source E–F: Sieburth 1975. Reprinted by permission, copyright University Park Press.)

acidifying the soil. As it would be dangerous and uneconomic to apply acid directly, soil acidification is conveniently accomplished by applying powdered sulfur to the field. The activity of *Thiobacillus thiooxidans* converts sulfur to $H_2SO_4$, accomplishing the desired acidification.

Before fertilizer application is undertaken, careful consideration must be given to the biogeochemical cycling activities of microorganisms. Solubility and leaching characteristics of the intended fertilizer form need to be considered, too. In order to avoid losses by leaching and denitrification, nitrogen fertilizer is

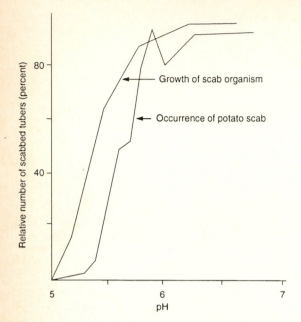

**Figure 12.1**
Growth of *Streptomyces scabies* in culture solution and the occurrence of potato scab disease in the field as related to prevalent pH. Soil acidification is an effective control measure for this plant pathogen. (Source: Waksman 1952. Reprinted by permission of John Wiley and Sons.)

commonly applied as an ammonium salt, free ammonia, or urea, even though most plants prefer nitrogen in the form of nitrate. Nitrification that yields this form of nitrogen may be too fast in some agricultural soils, leading to nitrogen loss and groundwater contamination by nitrate. In such cases, nitrification inhibitors, such as nitrapyrin, are applied along with the nitrogen fertilizer. Nitrification inhibitors can increase crop yield 10–15% for the same amount of nitrogen applied, while decreasing the problem of groundwater pollution by nitrate.

Leguminous crops planted in rotation with others are able, through their symbiotic nitrogen fixation, to reduce the requirement for expensive nitrogen fertilizer. Nitrogen fixation can be improved by inoculation of legume seeds with appropriate *Rhizobium* strains. In some molybdenum-deficient soils, a dramatic improvement in nitrogen fixation can also be achieved by application of small amounts of

molybdenum, an elemental constituent of the nitrogenase enzyme complex.

Organic matter (humus) is an important constituent of soils. It acts as a nutrient reserve, increases ion exchange capacity, and loosens the structure of the soil. When virgin lands are put to agricultural use, their humus content decreases for the next 40–50 years, eventually equilibrating at a much lower value. The probable causes for this phenomenon are increased aeration of the soil through tilling and removal of most of the produced organic matter with the harvest of the crop. Use of heavy farm equipment causes compaction, which reduces aeration and water infiltration in the affected soils. Fields denuded from crop cover are subject to erosion of the topsoil by wind and water, especially if the land is sloping. For the year 1977, the Soil Conservation Service estimated that U.S. farmlands lost 3 billion metric tons of topsoil by erosion. Such losses not only endanger continued agricultural productivity but also constitute a major cause of pollution and silting in waterways and reservoirs.

A relatively novel practice that can provide a solution to the combined problems of humus loss, topsoil erosion, and soil compaction is "no-tillage farming," or "conservation till farming." In this type of soil management, plowing is eliminated or reduced to a minimum. Crop residues are left on the field as mulch cover. Planting is done with drill seeding machines, and herbicides rather than cultivation are used to control weeds. In areas especially vulnerable to erosion, grass or other cover is planted for the winter and then killed with herbicides just before the next year's crop is planted. A 5-year monitoring period demonstrated that on land with a 9% slope, conventional farming resulted in an annual topsoil loss of 1761 kg/ha. On the same land, no-tillage farming reduced topsoil loss to 27 kg/ha. Additional benefits of no-tillage farming are moisture conservation achieved by the accumulating mulch layer, an increased soil humus content, improved soil structure, fuel conservation, and savings on heavy farm equipment. These benefits are balanced in part by an increased need for pesticides and care in management. Nevertheless, in the majority of the agricultural situations, no-tillage farming offers not only soil conservation but also tangible economic advantages in the forms of lower production costs and higher yields. About 15% of the farmland in the United States was under such management in 1980. This figure is expected to reach 45–65% by the year 2000. This management practice holds great promise also for other parts of the world that are threatened by erosion and desertification of agricultural land (Phillips et al. 1980; Gebhardt et al. 1985).

## TREATMENT OF SOLID WASTE

Vast amounts of solid wastes are produced that require safe disposal. Urban solid waste production in the United States is estimated to amount to roughly 150 million tons per year. Part of this material is inert, composed of glass, metals, plastics, and so on, but the rest is decomposable solid organic waste, such as kitchen scraps, paper, and other garbage. Other large sources of waste are sewage sludge derived from treatment of liquid wastes and animal waste from cattle feed lots and large-scale poultry and swine farms.

In traditional small-scale farm operations, most organic solid waste was composted and recycled to the land as manure fertilizer. In societies characterized by urbanization and large-scale agriculture, the disposal of organic waste becomes a difficult and expensive problem. Following is a discussion of the options available for dealing with modern solid waste problems, with an emphasis on the disposal methods that rely on microbial activity.

### Landfills

The simplest way to handle solid waste disposal at the lowest direct cost is in landfills. In this procedure, solid wastes, both organic and inorganic, are deposited in low-lying and hence low-value land. Within the landfill, anaerobic and facultative microorganisms attack the organic compounds in the waste (Senior 1995). There are several problems with waste disposal in landfills. Given adequate moisture and other favorable environmental conditions, the organic content of the landfill undergoes slow, anaerobic decomposition over a period of 30–50 years. During this period, the landfill slowly subsides, and methane is produced.

Exposed waste causes various esthetic and public health problems, attracts insects and rodents, and poses a fire hazard.

Not all materials are biodegraded in landfills. Suflita et al. (1992) recovered nearly intact newspapers and even some food items from the Fresh Kills landfill in New York City decades after their disposal. A lack of water reaching the buried refuse was the critical factor limiting anaerobic decomposition.

In a "sanitary landfill" (Figure 12.2) each day's waste deposit is covered with a layer of soil (U.S. Department of Health, Education and Welfare 1970). This limits the proliferation of pest populations and public health problems. Suflita et al. (1992) found that the disposal of diapers and other materials contaminated with human fecal matter in a landfill did not pose a human health threat. After completion of the landfill, the site becomes usable for recreation and eventually for construction. However, even sanitary landfills have several disadvantages. The limited number of suitable disposal sites available in urban areas are rapidly becoming filled, necessitating longer hauling of the solid waste to more distant sites. Premature construction on the landfill site may result in structural damage to the buildings due to subsidence, and in an explosion hazard due to methane seeping into basements and cellars. Methane seepage may also damage plantings on the disposal site.

The energy shortage of the 1970s prompted some projects to recover the methane gas released from completed landfills. Such recovery requires a sizable investment for collection pipes and a pumping system and for sealing of the landfill to prevent escape of the produced gas (Figure 12.3). Gas collected from landfills contains, along with methane, high amounts of $N_2$, $CO_2$, and $H_2S$ impurities and so requires purification prior to use. Methane production starts several months to a year after construction of the landfill, then goes through a peak period of production, followed by a gradual decline over the next 5–10 years.

In the construction of a landfill, design is important to prevent anaerobic decomposition products, heavy metals, and a variety of hazardous pollutants from seeping out of the landfill site into underground aquifers, polluting much-needed urban water

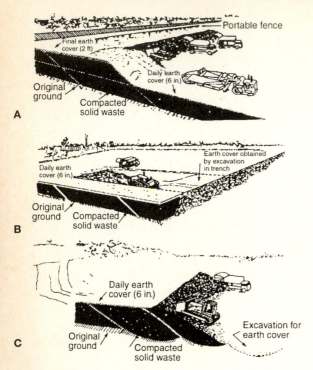

**Figure 12.2**
The sanitary landfill method. (A) The area method. The bulldozer spreads and compacts solid wastes. The scraper (foreground) is used to haul the cover material at the end of the day's operations. Note the portable fence that catches any blowing debris. This is used with any landfill method. (B) The trench method. The waste collection truck deposits its load into the trench, where the bulldozer spreads and compacts it. At the end of the day, the dragline excavates soil from the future trench; this soil is used as the daily cover material. Trenches can also be excavated with a front-end loader, a bulldozer, or a scraper. (C) The ramp variation. Solid wastes are spread and compacted on a slope. The daily cell may be covered with earth scraped from the base of the ramp. This variation is used with either the area or the trench method. (Source: U.S. Department of Health, Education and Welfare 1970.)

resources. Groundwater contamination arising from landfills, leaky gasoline and solvent tanks, and improper industrial and domestic waste disposal practices is a serious problem in the United States (Pye and Patrick 1983). Once pollutants reach an aquifer, their presence is characterized by slow movement and high persistence. Self-purification processes in under-

ground aquifers, in contrast to those in surface waters, are minimal. Low numbers of microorganisms, oxygen and nutrient limitations, and frequently the inherently recalcitrant nature of the pollutants all contribute to the persistence of groundwater contaminants. Once polluted, an aquifer tends to stay that way for many decades. Remedial actions, such as pumping out the aquifer, followed by conventional treatment of the contaminated water or an *in situ* treatment of the aquifer with oxygenated and nutrient-supplemented water, with or without a microbial inoculum, tend to be both inadequate and prohibitively expensive. For these reasons, prevention of groundwater contamination is by far the most effective remedy. Some modern landfills are constructed with liners and drainage systems aimed at minimizing water contamination (Figure 12.4 on page 472). An older but still practical measure is to place an impermeable clay "cap" on the landfill, thus preventing water infiltration and the leaching of pollutants. Some landfill leachates are directed through wetlands where algae and aquatic plants remove heavy metals and other pollutants. Nevertheless, increasing restrictions are being placed on the siting and operation of landfills, and alternatives to the described technique must be found.

## Composting

Composting of organic waste appears to offer an attractive alternative to landfills for the decomposition of solid domestic and agricultural wastes (Diaz et al. 1993; Palmisano and Barlaz 1996). Compared to alternative disposal methods, composting has considerable environmental advantages. It is likely to be practiced in the future on an increased scale. Composting requires some initial sorting of the solid waste into organic and inorganic portions, as only the organics will decompose. This can be accomplished either at the source by the separate collection of garbage (organic waste) and trash (inorganic waste) or at the receiving facility. Many communities have now started "at the source" separation programs for recyclables such as aluminum, glass, metal cans, newspaper, cardboard, and certain plastics. When sorting is done at a receiving facility, ferrous metals can be

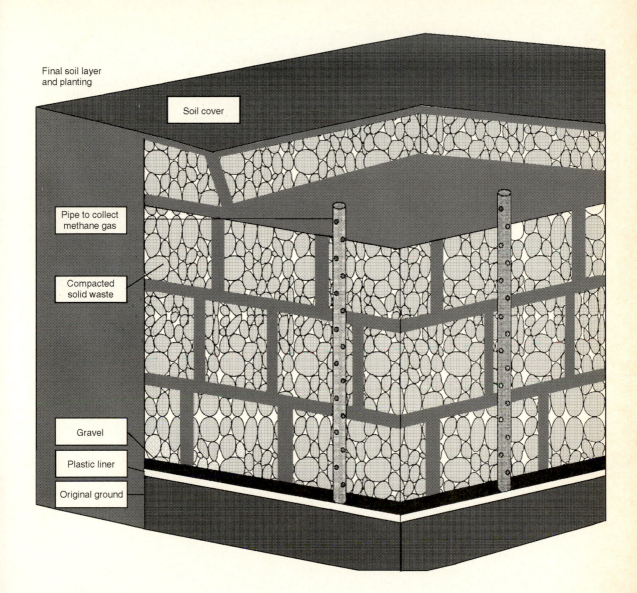

Final soil layer
and planting

Soil cover

Pipe to collect
methane gas

Compacted
solid waste

Gravel

Plastic liner

Original ground

**Figure 12.3**
Some modern landfills are designed to collect the methane produced from anaerobic
microbial decomposition so that it can be used as a fuel. Porous pipes extend into the
landfill to collect the methane gas. A plastic liner and sealed layers prevent diffusion of
methane out of the landfill. The design promotes the efficient collection of methane.

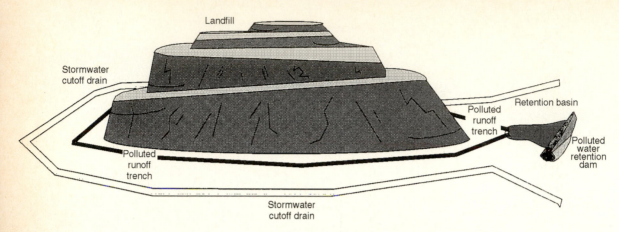

**Figure 12.4**
To avoid the movement of pollutants from landfills into surface and groundwaters, landfills are surrounded by trenches and barriers that limit stormwater drainage and divert polluted waters into a retention basin. The collected water is treated to remove toxicants.

removed by magnetic separators. Mechanical separators based on air flotation or on inertial energy content have been used to sort solid waste with fair success. Glass, aluminum, scrap iron, newspaper, and some plastic materials can be recycled, with some of the sorting expense recovered while the total disposal problem is reduced. The remaining waste, largely organic, can then be ground, mixed with sewage sludge and/or bulking agents such as shredded newspaper or wood chips, and composted (Harteinstein 1981, Diaz et al. 1993).

Composting is a microbial process that converts putrefiable organic waste materials into a stable, sanitary, humuslike product that is reduced in bulk and can be used for soil improvement. Composting is accomplished in static piles (windrows), aerated piles, or continuous feed reactors. The static pile process is simple but relatively slow, typically requiring many months for stabilization. Odor and insect problems can be controlled by covering the piles with a layer of soil, finished compost, or wood chips. Unless turned several times, the finished compost is rather uneven in quality. Under favorable conditions, self-heating in static piles typically raises the temperature inside a compost pile to 55–60°C or above in 2–3 days (Figure 12.5). After a few days at peak temperature, there is a gradual temperature decline.

Oxygen concentrations in the compost are usually five times lower than in ambient air, even when the piles are mechanically turned (Figure 12.6). Some compost piles often are mechanically turned to maintain aerobic conditions (Figure 12.7, p. 474). Turning of a compost pile may cause a secondary temperature rise brought about by the replenishment of the exhausted oxygen supply. Turning also helps to make the compost more uniform, because otherwise the thermophilic processes are restricted to the core of the compost pile. Following the thermophilic phase are several months of "curing" at mesophilic temperatures. During this period, the thermophilic populations decline and are replaced by mesophiles that survived the thermophilic period. Because of the slowness of the composting process, large amounts of land are required, a disadvantage in densely populated urban areas.

The aerated pile process achieves substantially faster composting rates through improved aeration (Epstein et al. 1976; Palmisano and Barlaz 1996) (Figure 12.8, p. 475). The so-called Beltsville process involves suction of air through perforated pipes buried inside the compost pile. This design achieves at least partial oxygenation of the pile, but temperature control is inadequate. Inside the pile, temperatures rise to self-limiting levels of 70–80°C. The improved Rutgers process (Finstein et al. 1983) reverses the airflow

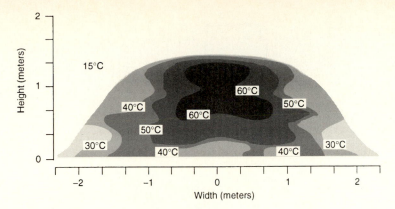

**Figure 12.5**
Temperature profile of a static compost pile. (Source: Diaz et al. 1993.)

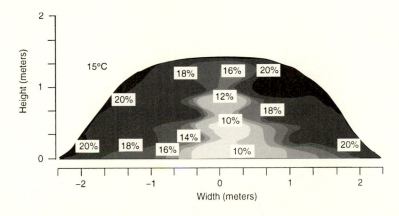

**Figure 12.6**
Concentration of oxygen in a compost pile shown as percent of ambient air at 55°C.
(Source: Diaz et al. 1993.)

from suction to injection. Thermostats placed inside the pile control blower operation, starting when the temperature exceeds 60°C. The injection of air not only oxygenates the pile but cools it sufficiently to avoid a self-limiting rise in the temperature. The heat generated by the biodegradation process is effectively used in evaporating water and results in a dryer and more stable compost. The aerated pile process goes to completion in about 3 weeks. Wood chips, if used as bulking agents, are removed from the final product by screening and are reused. The composting process could be hastened considerably by enriching the input air stream with pure oxygen. Although technically the concept of using pure oxygen seems attractive, it is

highly doubtful that the returns would justify the sharply increased cost (Diaz et al. 1993).

Composting can be accomplished more rapidly using a bioreactor (Figure 12.9). It requires about 20,000 cubic feet of air per ton of organic matter per day for efficient composting (Diaz et al. 1993). This process forms a uniform and stable product, but it also requires a high initial investment. Composting in the reactor is accomplished in 2–4 days. A part or all of the reactor is maintained at thermophilic temperatures, using the heat produced in the composting process. After processing in the reactor, the product requires "curing" for about a month prior to packaging and shipment (Pavoni et al. 1975).

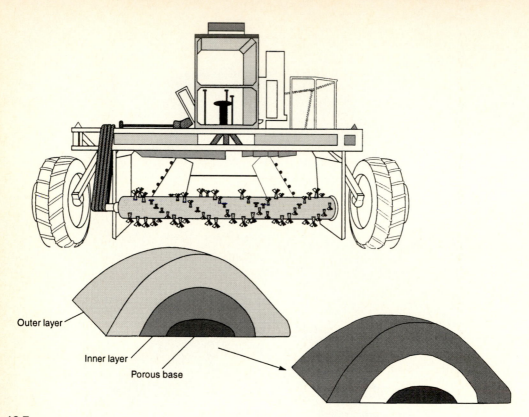

**Figure 12.7**
Specially designed tractors are used to mechanically turn compost piles so that the outer
and inner layers are exchanged to provide better and more even aeration. (Source: Diaz
et al. 1993.)

Regardless of the process design, conducting the composting process in the thermophilic temperature range is desirable because it speeds the process and destroys pathogens that may be present in fecal matter and in sewage sludge. The aerobic oxidation reactions catalyzed by microorganisms produce heat. Under appropriate circumstances, which include sufficient mass and low heat conductivity of the composted material, this self-heating may raise temperatures inside a compost pile to 76–78°C. Temperatures this high are actually inhibitory to biodegradation. Maximal thermophilic activity occurs between 52°C and 63°C. Aeration or turning may be adjusted to prevent excessive self-heating. Periodic water spraying can also reduce the temperature; self-combustion in piles of timber at logging mills is prevented by such periodic spraying. Having sufficiently high temperatures is critical, however, for killing human pathogens because much of the material in compost piles, such as diapers, contains human fecal matter. Inadequate temperatures can lead to human health problems, especially if the piles are mechanically turned and particles become airborne.

The composting process is initiated by mesophilic heterotrophs. As the temperature rises, these are replaced by thermophilic forms. Thermophilic bacteria prominent in the composting process are *Bacillus stearothermophilus*, *Thermomonospora*, *Thermoactinomyces*, and *Clostridium thermocellum*. Important fungi in the thermophilic composting process are *Geotrichum candidum*, *Aspergillus fumigatus*, *Mucor pusillus*, *Chaetomium thermophile*, *Thermoascus auranticus*, and *Torula thermophila* (Finstein and Morris 1975).

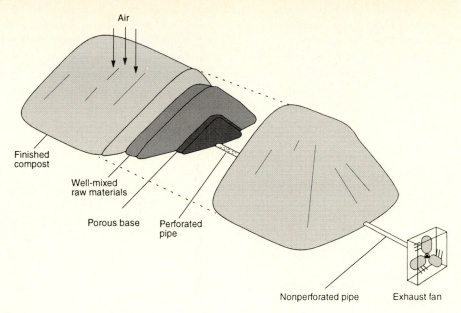

**Figure 12.8**
Diagram of an aerated compost pile in which air is drawn through the pile to ensure
aerobic conditions.

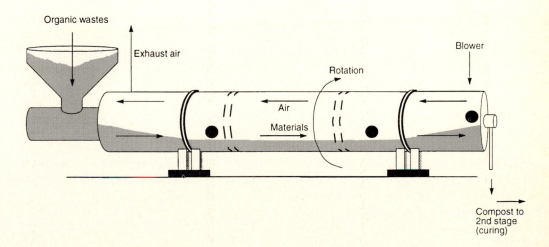

**Figure 12.9**
Diagram of an Eweson rotating drum composter. This system permits the continuous flow
of organic wastes. Forced aeration and rotary mixing ensure aerobic conditions for optimal
rates of organic matter decomposition and the formation of a stable compost product.
(Source: Diaz et al. 1993.)

For optimal composting, several conditions are critical. Adequate moisture (50–60% water content) must be present, but excess moisture (70% or above) should be avoided as it interferes with aeration and lowers self-heating because of its large heat capacity. Carbon-to-nitrogen ratios should not be greater than 40:1. Lower nitrogen content does not permit the formation of a sufficient microbial biomass. Excessive nitrogen (C:N = 25:1 or narrower) leads to volatilization of ammonia, causing odor problems, and lowers the fertilizer value of the resulting compost.

The economic viability of composting is often mistakenly judged only by the sale value of the generated compost. The primary purpose of composting, however, is to dispose of noxious wastes in an environmentally acceptable manner. Any costs recovered from the sale of compost reduce the cost of waste disposal operation but should not be expected to render the waste disposal operation self-supporting. Landfill operations may have lower direct costs than composting, but the long-range environmental costs in terms of groundwater contamination favor the composting process. Because of their water pollution potential, raw or anaerobically digested sewage sludges and other unstable organic wastes are acceptable by federal and state regulations only in a few designated landfill operations. In addition, compost is useful in soil improvement in certain situations.

Compost is a good soil conditioner and supplies some plant nutrients but cannot compete with synthetic fertilizers in agricultural production. If sewage sludge is a major component of the compost mixture, the finished compost may contain relatively high concentrations of potentially toxic heavy metals, such as cadmium and chromium. Little is known about the behavior of these metals in agricultural soils, and because of the possibility that some of these heavy metals may contaminate agricultural products, the large-scale use of sewage sludge or of sewage-sludge-derived compost in agriculture needs careful monitoring. Only low-metal sludges may be used in this manner, and only for limited periods of time. Compost finds unrestricted application in parks and gardens for ornamental plants and in land reclamation, such as for strip-mining reclamation and highway beautification projects.

Although traditional composting is an aerobic process, a relatively new advancement in biological solid waste treatment developed in Belgium is anaerobic composting (Baere et al. 1986; Wilde and Baere 1989). The DRANCO (DRy ANaerobic COnversion) process is carried out at thermophilic temperatures (50–55°C) in specially constructed airtight reactors. The reactor is charged from the top with organic waste (35–40% solids), is preheated to 50°C by steam, and moves passively through the vertical cylinder of the reactor with a residence time of 18–21 days. Gastight loading and extraction systems prevent loss of biogas, and insulation prevents excessive heat loss from the reactor. About 30% of the generated biogas (163 $m^3$ per metric ton of waste) is used in running the process; 70% is used for generating electricity. The discharged and stabilized waste is dewatered on a filter press and dried further using the waste heat of the generator. The stable peat-moss-like end product (70% solids, 300–350 kg per ton of wet waste) is marketed under the trade name Humotex for gardening purposes. The thermophilic nature of the process ensures destruction of pathogens, and the production of electricity and Humotex reduces operating costs, making this a promising system for composting the organic portion of urban solid waste.

A full-scale DRANCO installation with a digestor of 800 $m^3$ treating 10,000 tons of source-separated waste per year has been operational since July 1992 at Brecht in Belgium (Organization for Economic Cooperation and Development 1994). The source-separated waste is vegetable, fruit, garden, and paper waste. After pretreatment, the fraction is introduced into the bioreactor, where it is digested for 3 weeks at a temperature of 55°C. The digested residue is then pressed to produce a dewatered cake of about 55% solids. The organics are finally refined and aerobically composted for about 10 days and sold as a high-quality soil additive, free of pathogens.

## TREATMENT OF LIQUID WASTES

Liquid wastes are produced by everyday human activities (domestic sewage) and by various agricultural and industrial operations. Following drainage patterns or sewers, liquid waste discharges enter natural bodies of surface water, such as rivers, lakes, and oceans. At much slower rates, they may also percolate to the groundwater table, especially if it is high or if fissures are present in the unsaturated (vadose) soil layer. People use these same water bodies in alternative ways: as sources of drinking, household, industrial, and irrigation water; for fish and shellfish production; and for swimming and other recreational activities. Therefore, it is crucial to maintain the quality of these natural waters to the best of our ability. Water quality is a broad concept. Its maintenance means that natural waters cannot be overloaded with organic or inorganic nutrients or with toxic, noxious, or esthetically unacceptable substances. They should not become vehicles of disease transmission from fecal contamination, nor should their oxygenation, temperature, salinity, turbidity, or pH be altered significantly.

Natural waters have an inherent self-purification capacity. Organic nutrients are utilized and mineralized by heterotrophic aquatic microorganisms. Ammonia is nitrified and, along with other inorganic nutrients, utilized and immobilized by algae and higher aquatic plants. Allochthonous populations of enteric and other pathogens are reduced in numbers and eventually eliminated by competition and predation pressures exerted by the autochthonous aquatic populations. Thus, natural waters can accept sufficiently low amounts of raw sewage without significant deterioration of water quality. Dense human populations, community living patterns, and large-scale agricultural and industrial activities typically produce liquid wastes on a scale that overwhelms the homeostasis of aquatic communities and causes unacceptable deterioration of water quality (Dart and Stretton 1977; LaRiviere 1977).

Historically, the first human concern with water quality was prompted by destructive epidemics of cholera, typhoid fever, dysentery, and other diseases spread by waterborne pathogens. Waste treatment, protection of drinking water sources, and disinfection of drinking water and sewage, gradually introduced in the early years of this century, largely eliminated the spread of waterborne epidemics in developed countries; concern remained, however, for the health, environmental, and esthetic problems caused by an overload of organic nutrients in sewage-polluted waters. Even as treatment methods were developed that alle-

viated most of these problems, total sewage volume increased further, and the inorganic nutrient content of sewage started to command additional attention because of "cultural eutrophication" problems caused by the excessive mineral nutrient enrichment of natural waters (National Academy of Sciences 1969; Keeney et al. 1971). Human-made synthetic organic molecules, not readily subject to microbial degradation during sewage treatment, are the subject of additional contemporary concerns.

## Biological Oxygen Demand

In contemporary liquid waste treatment, the usual order of operations is the reduction of the biological oxygen demand (BOD) associated with suspended and dissolved organics, occasionally followed by the removal of inorganic nutrients and recalcitrant organics prior to the discharge of the effluent (Hawkes 1963; Mitchell 1974). Biological oxygen demand is a measure of oxygen consumption required by the microbial oxidation of readily degradable organics and ammonia in sewage. The 5-day BOD expresses the oxygen consumed by a properly diluted sewage sample during 5 days of incubation at 20°C. The sewage sample is diluted in oxygen-saturated water and enclosed without air space in a BOD bottle. After incubation, the decrease in dissolved oxygen is measured, usually by an oxygen electrode. Because some organics are not readily oxidized by microorganisms, and because microbial biomass is also formed, BOD is lower than the chemical oxygen demand (COD) measured using strong chemical oxidants.

Because its solubility is low, dissolved oxygen in natural waters seldom exceeds 8 mg/l, and because of heterotrophic microbial activity, it is often considerably lower than that. Replenishment of dissolved oxygen from the atmosphere (reaeration) and/or by photosynthetic $O_2$ evolution can be considerably slower than the utilization rate of oxygen by heterotrophic microorganisms in the presence of abundant organic substrates. Consequently, the principal impact of sewage overload on natural waters is the lowering or exhaustion of their dissolved oxygen (DO) content. Once oxygen is exhausted, self-purification processes slow drastically. Fermentation products and the reduction of secondary electron sinks, such as nitrate and

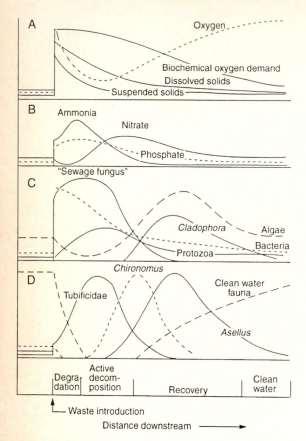

**Figure 12.10**

Diagrammatic presentation of the effects of an organic effluent on a river and the changes as one passes downstream from the outfall. (A and B) Physical and chemical changes. (C) Changes in microorganisms. (D) Changes in invertebrate animals. Sewage fungus is predominantly *Sphaerotilus natans.* (Source: Warren 1971. Based on Hynes 1960. Reprinted by permission of W. B. Saunders Co.)

sulfate, give rise to noxious odors, tastes, and colors; the water becomes anaerobic or septic. Oxygen deprivation kills obligately aerobic organisms, including some microbial forms, fishes, and invertebrate animals. The decomposition of these dead organisms constitutes an additional oxygen demand. Turbidity and toxic metabolic products, such as $H_2S$, also interfere with photosynthetic oxygen regeneration, thus further slowing the recovery process.

Input of a single dose of sewage into a lentic (stagnant, nonflowing) environment causes a septic period of oxygen depletion with an associated reduction in biological diversity (Hynes 1960). After a prolonged septic period, oxygen diffusion eventually reaerates the system and allows the mineralization of the accumulated fermentation products. The mineral nutrients liberated from the degraded organic matter may then give rise to an algal bloom. If there is no further disturbance, secondary succession will eventually restore the aquatic community to its former state. When a lotic (flowing river) environment receives a steady input of raw sewage, the previously described events may be observed as steady-state conditions at various distances downstream from the sewage outfall. Figure 12.10 illustrates the relative changes in some environmental parameters and populations in a river receiving raw sewage. Depending on the rate of sewage discharge, flow rate, water temperature, and other environmental factors, water quality may return close to the original state at distances from a few up to several dozen kilometers downstream from the sewage outfall (Hynes 1960; Warren 1971).

Septic conditions in natural waters, whether they occur temporarily or as a steady state, are clearly undesirable. To avoid these conditions, sewage treatment aims to reduce the BOD of the sewage prior to discharge. Typically, this is achieved in three stages, the first two stages bringing about a more complete reduction of the original BOD. The third stage is usually directed to removal of mineral nutrients and/or recalcitrant organics. These stages are referred to as primary, secondary, and tertiary sewage treatment (Figure 12.11).

Sewage enters the treatment plant through screens, traps, and skimming devices that remove larger objects, grit, floating scum, and grease. Primary sewage treatment removes only suspended solids. This removal is achieved in settling tanks or basins (Figure 12.12 on page 480) where the solids are drawn off from the bottom. They may be subjected to anaerobic digestion and/or composting prior to final disposal in landfills or as soil conditioner. Only a low percentage of the suspended or dissolved organic material is actually mineralized during liquid waste treatment. Most of the

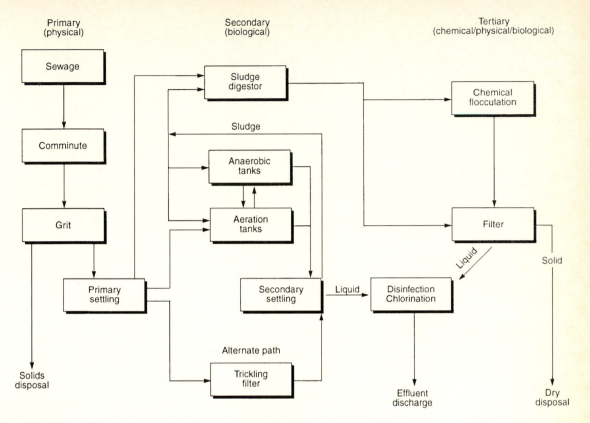

**Figure 12.11**
The three stages of sewage treatment consist of a primary treatment that employs physical methods to remove solids and reduce the BOD, a secondary treatment that employs biological methods (microbial biodegradation) to remove dissolved organics and reduce the BOD, and a tertiary treatment that may involve chemical physical, and/or biological methods to remove other components.

organic material is removed by settling; in a way, the disposal problem is merely displaced to the solid waste area rather than solved by complete recycling. Nevertheless, the fragility of aquatic ecosystems, owing to their low dissolved oxygen content, renders this displacement essential (Warren 1971).

The liquid portion of the sewage containing dissolved organic matter is subjected to further treatment or is discharged after primary treatment only. Liquid wastes vary in composition, and if they contain mainly solids and little dissolved organic matter, primary treatment may remove 70–80% of the BOD and may be considered adequate. For typical domestic sewage (Table 12.1), however, primary treatment

removes only 30–40% of the BOD, and secondary treatment is necessary for acceptable BOD reduction (Schroeder 1977).

In secondary sewage treatment, a smaller portion of the dissolved organic matter is mineralized and a larger portion is converted from a dissolved state to removable solids. The combination of primary and secondary treatments reduces the original BOD of the sewage by 80–90%. The secondary sewage treatment step relies on microbial activity. The treatment may be aerobic or anaerobic and may be conducted in a large variety of devices. In some of these treatments, the microorganisms are associated with surface films; in others, they are homogeneously suspended. A correctly

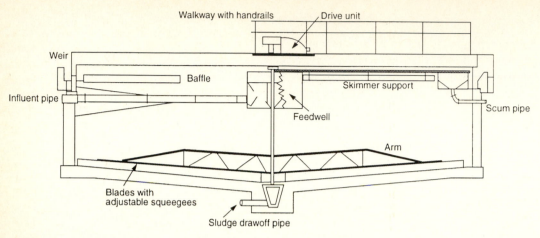

**Figure 12.12**
Typical clarifier cross section of a modern settling tank used for primary treatment of
sewage. Grit and large debris are screened out from the sewage before it enters this
settling tank. (Source: Schroeder 1977. Reprinted by permission, copyright McGraw-Hill.)

designed and operated secondary treatment unit
should produce effluents with BOD and/or suspended
solids of less than 20 mg/l.

## Fixed Film Sewage Treatment Systems

**Trickling Filter System**   A simple and relatively
inexpensive film-flow-type aerobic sewage treatment
installation is the trickling filter (Figure 12.13). The
sewage is distributed by a boom-type sprinkler revolv-
ing over a bed of porous material. It slowly percolates
through this porous bed, and the effluent is collected
at the bottom. Dense, slimy bacterial growth coats the
porous material of the filter bed. *Zooglea ramigera*
and similar bacteria play a principal role in generating
the slime matrix (Figure 12.14, p. 483), which accom-
modates a heterogeneous microbial community
including bacteria, fungi, protozoa, nematodes, and
rotifers (Mack et al. 1975; Hawkes 1977). This microbial community absorbs and mineralizes the dissolved
organic nutrients in the sewage, thus reducing the
BOD of the effluent (Figure 12.15, p. 483). Aeration is
provided passively by the porous nature of the bed. A
food web is established based upon the microbial
biofilm (Figure 12.16, p. 484). Insects, mainly fly larvae, consume the excess microbial biomass generated
but constitute a nuisance to nearby residential areas.

They can be controlled by the continuous rather than
intermittent operation of the trickling filters, because
continuous spreading suppresses the fly larvae, which
successfully feed on the exposed microbial biomass
only when the sprinkling is shut off.

Allowing sloughed-off biomass to settle prior to
discharge further clarifies the effluent from trickling
filters. The sewage may be passed through two or
more trickling filters or recirculated several times
through the same filter. A drawback of this otherwise
simple and inexpensive treatment system is that a
nutrient overload may lead to excess microbial slime,
reducing aeration and percolation rates and necessitating a renewal of the trickling filter bed. Cold winter
temperatures strongly reduce the effectiveness of
these outdoor treatment facilities.

**Rotating Biological Contactor**   An advanced aerobic film-flow-type treatment system is the so-called
rotating biological contactor (RBC) or biodisc system.
Closely spaced discs, usually manufactured from plastic material (Figure 12.17, p. 484), are rotated in a
trough containing the sewage effluent. The partially
submerged discs become coated with a microbial
slime similar to that described in the case of trickling
filters. The continuous rotation keeps the slime well
aerated and in contact with the sewage.

**Table 12.1**
Characteristics of typical municipal wastewater

|  | Concentration, mg/l |
|---|---|
| Solids, total | 700 |
| Dissolved | 500 |
|    Fixed | 300 |
|    Volatile | 200 |
| Suspended | 200 |
|    Fixed | 50 |
|    Volatile | 150 |
| Ultimate biochemical oxygen demand (BOD) | 300 |
| Total organic carbon (TOC) | 200 |
| Chemical oxygen demand (COD) | 400 |
| Nitrogen (as N) | 40 |
|    Organic | 15 |
|    Free ammonia | 25 |
|    Nitrites | 0 |
|    Nitrates | 0 |
| Phosphorus (as P) | 10 |
|    Organic | 3 |
|    Inorganic | 7 |
| Grease | 100 |

Source: Schroeder 1977.

Biofilms developing on an RBC comprise a complex and diverse microbial community of diverse bacterial, protozoan, and metazoan populations (Bitton 1994). Among the filamentous microorganisms are populations of *Sphaerotilus, Beggiatoa, Nocardia,* and *Oscillatoria.* Scanning electron microscopy shows that the RBC biofilm typically has two layers: an outer whitish layer containing *Beggiatoa* filaments and an inner black layer containing *Desulfovibrio.* The black color is due to the precipitation of ferrous sulfide when iron reacts with the hydrogen sulfide produced by sulfate-reducing *Desulfovibrio* species. Figure 12.18 (p. 485) illustrates the relationship between *Desulfovibrio* and *Beggiatoa* within the RBC biofilm community. In the anaerobic zone, fermentative bacteria produce organic acids and alcohols that are used by *Desulfovibrio.* The hydrogen sulfide product of sulfate reduction diffuses into the aerobic zone where it is utilized by *Beggiatoa* as an electron donor. Hydrogen sulfide is oxidized to elemental sulfur, which is deposited within the cells of *Beggiatoa.* The elemental sulfur is subsequently transformed to sulfate, which can be used by *Desulfovibrio* species.

The thickness of the microbial slime layer in all film-flow processes is governed by the diffusion of nutrients through the film. When the film grows to a thickness that prevents nutrients from reaching the innermost microbial cells, these will die, autolyze, and cause the detachment of the slime layer. The sloughed-off microbial biomass can easily be removed by settling (Howell 1977; Schroeder 1977). Biodisc systems require less space than trickling filters, are more efficient and stable in operation, and produce no aerosols, but they require a higher initial investment. They have been used successfully in treatment of both domestic and industrial sewage effluents.

**Submerged Aerobic Filters**   Partially or totally submerging the biological support media significantly improves the efficiency of biological filtration (Organization for Economic Cooperation and Development 1994). In submerged or flooded aerobic filters, effluent flows down through a bed of small natural or plastic media and air is injected into the base of the bed (Figure 12.19, p. 486). This allows the wastewater to be applied at a much higher rate than conventional filters. There may be a second filtration stage below the injection point to remove solids generated in the upper aerobic mixed zone. The solids, which accumulate in the lower filter stage, eventually reach a critical concentration, and the filter is then cleaned by backwashing and air scouring. Repeated backwashings are used until the system is clear and free of solids. The wash water is returned to the front of the treatment plant for settlement.

**Fluidized Bed Reactors**   In fluidized bed reactors the support materials—pumice, sand or plastic—are fluidized by pumping waste water up through the medium (anaerobic) or by injecting air or oxygen (aerobic). In the first instance, the upflow velocity is high

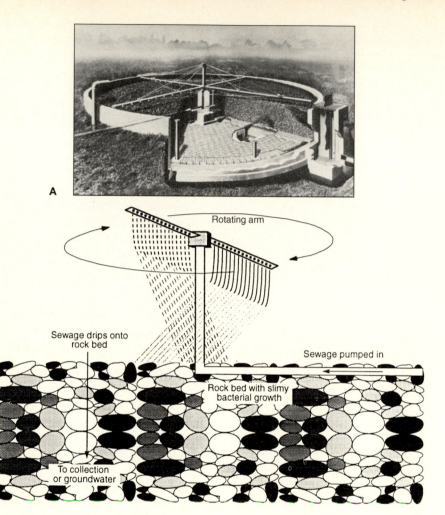

**Figure 12.13**
(A) Trickling filter for the secondary treatment of sewage. (B) Enlarged section shows
construction details of a trickling filter. (Source A: Warren 1971. Reprinted by permission,
copyright W. B. Saunders Co.)

enough to fluidize the support particles so that they are
not in direct contact with each other but not so high as
to shear off the biofilm. The advantage of this system
is that because the particles are not in direct contact
with each other, there is a greater surface area available for biomass support. However, the energy costs
for providing a high enough flow rate, usually involving a high recycle rate to fluidize the bed, are greater.
Fluidization can range from 10–100% of the bed volume when stationary. The term "expanded bed" is

sometimes used for fluidized beds with a low degree
of fluidization.

Other suspended growth systems include "upflow
sludge blanket" reactors, which use "granules" of
anaerobic bacteria on a solid matrix in an upflow reactor. The settling velocities of these granules are high
enough for them to stay in the reactor, with the help of
baffles, while allowing the effluent to exit at the top of
the vessel. High-strength organic wastewaters (BOD
> 1000 mg/l), in particular from food manufacturing,

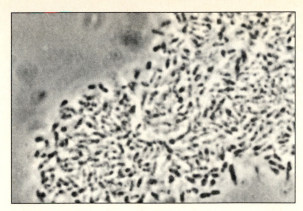

**Figure 12.14**
*Zooglea ramigera,* a sewage bacterium that produces large amounts of extracellular polysaccharide. It plays an important role in surface slime and floc formation during sewage treatment. (Courtesy of P. Dugan, Ohio State University.)

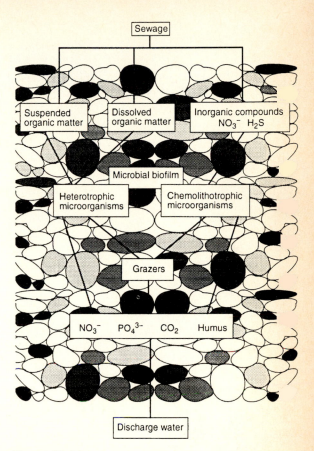

**Figure 12.15**
In a trickling filter system, sewage is sprayed over a porous medium. Heterotrophic and chemolithotrophic microorganisms in a biofilm attack the suspended organic matter, dissolved organic matter, and inorganic compounds. Grazers consume the microbial biomass that is formed. The mineral nutrients and organic humus produced in this process are discharged with the water trickling through the system.

are amenable to treatment in these systems. A further development of this reactor is an upflow fluidized bed reactor where the granular floc is fluidized (without supporting particles). This permits the building of a slender tower reactor. The key to the successful operation of these reactors is that the biomass has a retention time much longer than that of the liquid. Fluidized beds combine the advantages of the percolating filter process with those of activated sludge (discussed shortly). Biological fluidized beds are able to retain about five times the concentration of microorganisms as compared to conventional sewage plants, resulting in significant capital cost savings. They can also be designed for the removal of nitrate as well as the reduction of BOD (Figure 12.20, p. 487).

## Suspended Cell Sewage Treatment Systems

**Oxidation Lagoons**  Oxidation ditches and lagoons are low-cost treatment systems within which microorganisms grow as suspended particles within the water column rather than as biofilms (Bitton 1994) (Figure 12.21, p. 488). Oxidation lagoons tend to be inefficient and require large holding capacities and long retention times. As oxygenation is usually achieved by diffusion and by the photosynthetic activity of algae, these systems need to be shallow. Oxy-

genation is usually incomplete, with consequent odor problems. Performance is strongly influenced by seasonal temperature fluctuations, and usefulness, therefore, is largely restricted to warmer climates.

Most frequently, treated sewage is discharged into surface waters, but in some arid areas, sufficient surface water flow may not exist. In addition, it may be necessary to regenerate the groundwater removed from wells. In such areas, partially treated sewage is used for groundwater recharge. Typically, the sewage

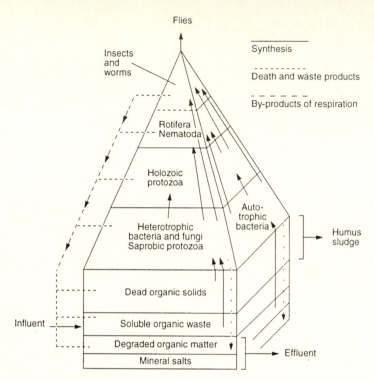

**Figure 12.16**
Main pathways of energy and materials transfer during treatment of dissolved organic wastes by means of trickling filters. Respiration at each level leads to mineralization of organic material and to release of heat energy. (Source: Hawkes 1963. Reprinted by permission of Pergamon Press Ltd.)

**Figure 12.17**
Two views of a rotating biological contactor, or "biodisc unit." (Source: Schroeder 1977. Reprinted by permission, copyright McGraw-Hill.)

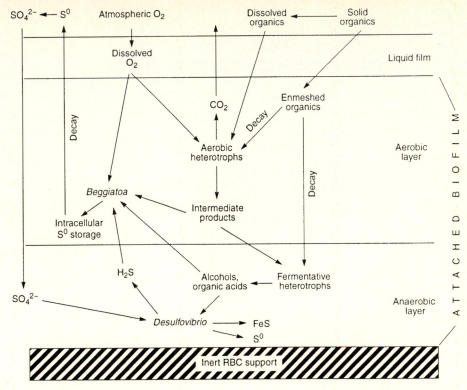

**Figure 12.18**
Relationship between aerobic *Beggiatoa* and anaerobic *Desulfovibrio* species in the biofilm
of a rotating biological contactor. (Source: Bitton 1994.)

is subjected to primary settling and is subsequently channeled through a series of holding ponds. The first holding pond tends to reaerate the oxygen-depleted water. After settling of most of the algal and bacterial biomass, the water is transferred to large, shallow infiltration ponds. From these infiltration ponds, the water flows through natural sand and soil layers and slowly returns to the underground aquifer. Clogging of the infiltration ponds by undegraded microbial polysaccharides and by accumulation of reduced ferrous sulfide is a recurrent problem in groundwater recharge operations. The problem is countered by periodic rest periods for individual infiltration basins. These interruptions allow degradation of the excess polysaccharides and reaerate the sediment of the infil-

tration ponds with the concurrent oxidation of the clogging ferrous sulfide.

**Activated Sludge Process**    A popular suspended growth type of liquid waste treatment system is the activated sludge process (Figure 12.22, p. 489). After primary settling, the sewage, containing dissolved organic compounds, is introduced into an aeration tank (Figure 12.23, p. 489). Aeration is provided by air injection and/or mechanical stirring. Microbial activity is maintained at high levels by reintroduction of most of the settled activated sludge, hence the name of the process. During the holding period in the aeration tank, vigorous development of heterotrophic microorganisms takes place.

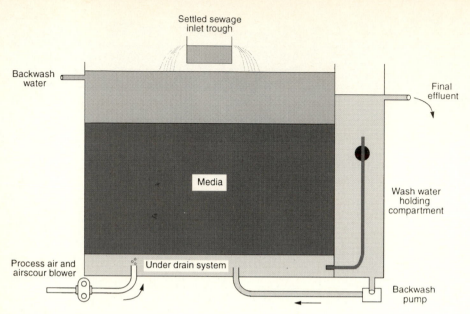

**Figure 12.19**
A biological aerated flooded (BAF) system for the treatment of wastewater.

The heterogeneous nature of the substrate allows the development of diverse heterotrophic bacterial populations. Gram-negative rods predominate, with coliforms *(Escherichia), Enterobacter,* pseudomonads, *Achromobacter, Flavobacterium,* and *Zooglea* being most frequently isolated. *Micrococcus, Arthrobacter,* various coryneforms, and mycobacteria also occur, along with *Sphaerotilus* and other large filamentous bacteria. Filamentous fungi and yeasts normally occur in low numbers and play a subordinate role in the activated sludge process. The protozoa are mainly represented by the ciliates. Along with rotifers, these protozoa are important predators of bacteria. The bacteria occur individually in free suspension and also aggregate as floc. The floc consists predominantly of microbial biomass cemented by bacterial slimes, such as those produced by *Zooglea ramigera* and similar organisms. Most of the ciliate protozoa, such as *Vorticella,* are of the attached filter-feeding type; they adhere to the floc but feed predominantly on the bacteria in suspension. The floc is too large to be ingested by the ciliates and rotifers and thus may be considered a defense mechanism against predation. In the raw sewage, suspended bacteria predominate, but during the holding time in the aeration tank, the numbers of suspended bacteria decrease. At the same time, those associated with floc greatly increase in numbers (Casida 1968; Pike and Curds 1971). The diversity and density of bacteria in activated sewage sludge renders this material a popular inoculum for various enrichment cultures. Table 12.2 (p. 489) shows some typical total and viable bacterial counts at various stages of sewage treatment.

During the holding period in the aeration tank, a portion of the dissolved organic substrates is mineralized. Another portion is converted to microbial biomass. In the advanced stage of aeration, most of the microbial biomass is associated with floc that can be removed from suspension by settling. The settling characteristics of the sewage sludge floc are critical for their efficient removal. Poor settling characteristics are associated with the "bulking" of the sewage sludge, a problem caused by proliferation of filamentous bacteria, such as *Sphaerotilus, Beggiatoa, Thio-*

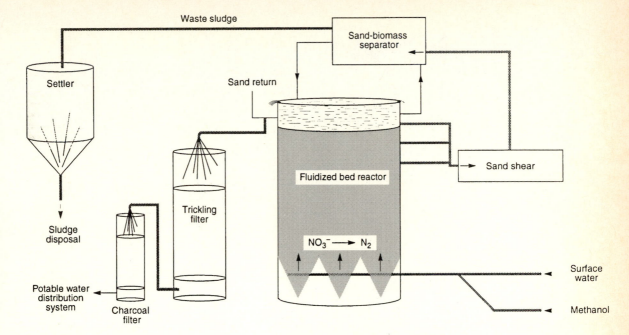

**Figure 12.20**

Combination of anaerobic digestion with denitrification and aerobic treatment for domestic wastewater with minimal production of sludge. A system has been designed to remove nitrogen from wastewater and to produce potable water. The fluidized bed of the bioreactor consists of sand, which becomes covered with the growth of microbial biofilms to a maximum of about 66%. Methanol is added as a carbon source to support heterotrophic denitrification. In a facility operated at Bankhart, Belgium, for the treatment of surface waters, nitrate concentrations are reduced from 75 mg/l to 0 mg/l at 20°C with a flow-through capacity of 750 m$^3$/h. Using methanol as a carbon source minimizes formation of nitrite. Biological nitrate removal is followed by treatment using a trickling filter so as to degrade the methanol and other residual carbon and to reoxygenate the water. The treated effluent is passed through an activated charcoal filter to ensure that the last trace of methanol is removed and that there is no microbial aftergrowth in the distribution system. (Source: Organization for Economic Cooperation and Development 1994.)

*thrix,* and *Bacillus,* and with filamentous fungi, such as *Geotrichum, Cephalosporium, Cladosporium,* and *Penicillium.* The causes for bulking are not always understood, but this condition is frequently associated with high C:N and C:P ratios and/or low dissolved oxygen concentrations.

A portion of the settled sewage sludge is recycled for inoculation of the incoming raw sewage; the excess sludge requires incineration, or additional treatment by anaerobic digestion and/or composting, or disposal in landfills. A past practice of ocean dumping is no longer considered acceptable. Combined with primary settling, the activated sludge process tends to reduce the BOD of the effluent to 5–15% of the raw sewage.

The treatment also drastically reduces the numbers of intestinal pathogens in the sewage, even prior to final disinfection by chlorination. The combined effects of competition, adsorption, predation, and settling accomplish this reduction. Predation by ciliates, rotifers, and *Bdellovibrio* is probably indiscriminate and affects pathogens as well as nonpathogenic

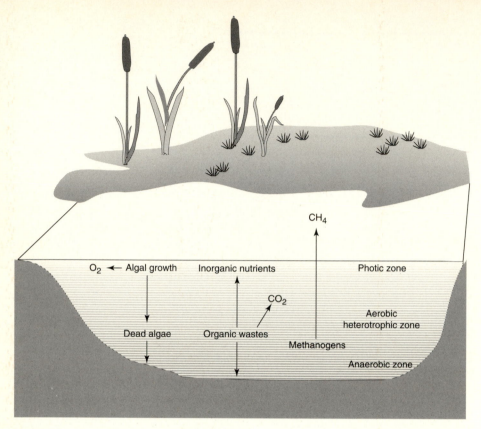

**Figure 12.21**
Illustration of an oxidation lagoon showing various zones that develop and the microbial
activities in these zones.

heterotrophs. Pathogens, however, tend to grow poorly or not at all under the conditions prevailing in the aeration tank, while the nonpathogenic heterotrophs proliferate vigorously. Thus, nonpathogenic heterotrophs are compensating for their removal by predation, but the pathogens are decimated continuously. Settling of the floc removes additional pathogens. Typically, numbers of *Salmonella, Shigella,* and *E. coli* are 90–99% lower in the effluent of the activated sludge treatment process than in the incoming raw sewage. Enteroviruses are removed to a similar degree; here the main removal mechanism appears to be adsorption of the virus particles to the settling sewage sludge floc.

The activated sludge process is essentially a continuous culture process, suitable for mathematical and computer modeling (Pike and Curds 1971). In a steady-state condition, the growth of the sludge bacteria (those associated with floc) must be equal to the sludge wastage (those removed). In Figure 12.24, the steady-state populations of microorganisms are modeled at various dilution and sludge wastage rates. Model A assumes the presence of attached ciliates, a condition that most closely resembles the real-life situation. Simulation B assumes only free-swimming ciliates, and simulation C assumes the absence of ciliates. The role of the attached ciliates in controlling the dispersed bacteria is clearly evident. Thus, the presence of the attached ciliates is critical for removal of the portion of the BOD consisting of dispersed bacteria that would be otherwise discharged with the efflu-

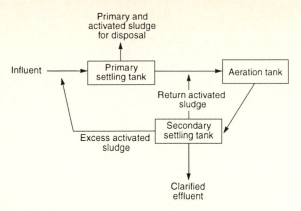

**Figure 12.22**
Flow diagram of an activated sludge secondary sewage treatment system. A portion of the sludge is recycled as inoculum for the incoming sewage. (Source: Imhoff and Fair 1956. Reprinted by permission of John Wiley and Sons.)

**Figure 12.23**
Aeration basin of an activated sludge sewage treatment plant. (Source: Casida 1968. Reprinted by permission, copyright John Wiley and Sons.)

**Table 12.2**
Numbers of total and viable bacteria in samples from different stages of sewage treatment and in the suspended biomass. The low percentage of the "viable" bacteria reflects the inherent selectivity of viable counts.

| | Bacterial count | | | | |
| | In samples (number/mL) | | In biomass (number/g) | | Percent of |
| Stage of treatment | Total | Viable | Total | Viable | bacteria viable |
|---|---|---|---|---|---|
| Settled sewage | $6.8 \times 10^8$ | $1.4 \times 10^7$ | $3.2 \times 10^{12}$ | $6.6 \times 10^{10}$ | 2.0 |
| Activated sludge mixed liquor | $6.6 \times 10^9$ | $5.6 \times 10^7$ | $1.4 \times 10^{12}$ | $1.2 \times 10^{10}$ | 0.85 |
| Filter slimes | $6.2 \times 10^{10}$ | $1.5 \times 10^9$ | $1.3 \times 10^{12}$ | $3.2 \times 10^{10}$ | 2.5 |
| Secondary effluents | $5.2 \times 10^7$ | $5.7 \times 10^5$ | $4.3 \times 10^{12}$ | $4.7 \times 10^{10}$ | 1.1 |
| Tertiary effluents | $3.4 \times 10^7$ | $4.1 \times 10^4$ | $3.4 \times 10^{12}$ | $4.1 \times 10^9$ | 0.12 |

Source: Pike and Curds 1971.

ent. In fact, the types and numbers of protozoa associated with the activated sludge floc can be used as an indicator of sludge condition and, thus, treatment performance. The sludge is in poor condition when few ciliates and many flagellates are observed; ciliates predominate in "good" sludge. The role of the ciliates was also experimentally demonstrated in bench-scale treatment units inoculated with controlled bacterial and protozoan populations, as Table 12.3 shows.

The activated sludge treatment system is efficient and flexible and is able to withstand considerable variations in sewage flow rate and concentration. It is widely used for the treatment of domestic sewage and industrial effluents. It generally produces, however, large volumes of sludge that must be disposed of by other means. Some systems have been designed to minimize the production of excess sludge by combining aerobic and anaerobic stages (Figure 12.25).

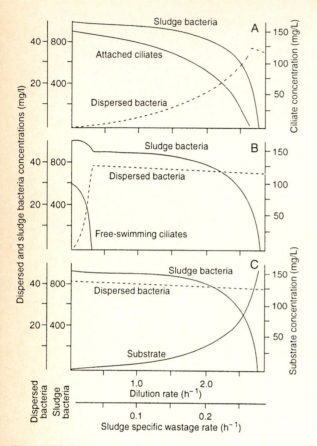

**Figure 12.24**
Steady-state populations of microorganisms at various dilution and sludge wastage rates by computer modeling. (A) Model assuming the presence of attached ciliates. (B) Model assuming the presence of free-swimming ciliates. (C) Model assuming the absence of ciliates. Sludge wastage rate is kept at 1/10 the dilution rate. The substrate concentration curve shown in C is identical for A and B, but is omitted from these plots. The simulations clearly show the strong effect of the attached ciliates on the dispersed bacteria. The reduction of the latter helps to achieve a low BOD discharge. (Source: Pike and Curds 1971. Reprinted by permission, copyright Academic Press, London.)

**Table 12.3**
Effect of ciliated protozoa on the effluent quality of bench-scale, activated sludge plants

| Effluent analysis | Without ciliates | With ciliates |
|---|---|---|
| BOD (mg/l) | 53–70 | 7–24 |
| COD (mg/l) | 198–250 | 124–142 |
| Permanganate value (mg/L) | 83–106 | 52–70 |
| Organic nitrogen (mg/L) | 14–21 | 7–10 |
| Suspended solids (mg/L) | 86–118 | 26–34 |
| Optical density at 620 nm | 0.95–1.42 | 0.23–0.34 |
| Viable bacterial count ($10^6$/mL) | 106–160 | 1–9 |

Source: Pike and Curds 1971.

developed by Union Carbide, uses oxygen instead of air for aeration. Closed tanks and a specially designed stirring system prevent the wastage of oxygen. The deep shaft process developed by the Imperial Chemical Industries (ICI) in England (Figure 12.27) uses air injection and achieves high oxygen dissolution by increasing hydrostatic pressure through an ingenious circulation pattern (Howell 1977).

A number of advanced process designs have been developed more recently that include anaerobic stages in activated sludge sewage treatment systems (Switzenbaum 1983). Some advanced designs make anaerobic digestors efficient and economical for handling relatively dilute wastes, such as primary-treated sewage. The anaerobic activated sludge process closely parallels its aerobic counterpart: Settled biomass is continuously recycled to maximize the rate of digestion per reactor volume. Other designs involve sludge beds, anaerobic filters, or anaerobic expanded fluidized beds. Each design attempts to ensure that the dilute sewage passes through a dense stationary anaerobic biomass. This passage minimizes reactor volume and fluid retention time while maximizing the efficiency of the digestion process. Bacteria involved in the anaerobic digestion process, like their aerobic counterparts, tend to form granules, or aggregates. Complex

Two interesting variations of the activated sludge process have been developed for treatment of high BOD industrial wastes. Both modifications are designed to improve the oxygen transfer rate and thus achieve a higher BOD reduction rate per unit volume of treatment system. The UNOX process (Figure 12.26),

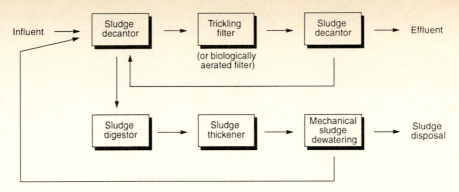

**Figure 12.25**
Combination of anaerobic digestion and aerobic treatment for domestic wastewater with minimal production of sludge. "Decantor" is a type of settling tank.

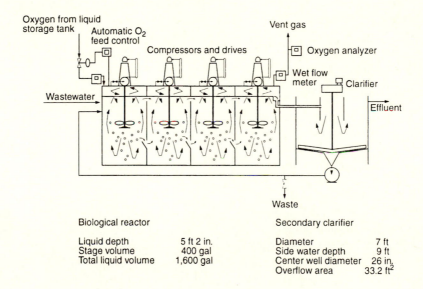

| Biological reactor | | Secondary clarifier | |
|---|---|---|---|
| Liquid depth | 5 ft 2 in. | Diameter | 7 ft |
| Stage volume | 400 gal | Side water depth | 9 ft |
| Total liquid volume | 1,600 gal | Center well diameter | 26 in. |
| | | Overflow area | 33.2 ft$^2$ |

**Figure 12.26**
The UNOX wastewater treatment system, developed by Union Carbide. This system achieves higher biological oxidation rates per volume using oxygen instead of air in its aeration tank. Higher oxygen partial pressures result in more rapid oxygen transfer rates. (Source: Howell 1977. Reprinted by permission, copyright The Institute of Petroleum, London.)

metabolic interactions, including interspecies electron transfer, take place between fermenters, acetogens, sulfate reducers, and methanogens within these granules (Thiele and Zeikus 1988; MacLeod et al. 1990; Wu et al. 1991). The intimate contact between the bacteria within the anaerobic granules appears to be essential for efficient anaerobic digestion.

Besides reducing the BOD, advanced activated sludge sewage treatment systems also remove inorganic nitrogen and phosphate. Concern about nitrogen salts and phosphate in sewage effluents is relatively recent and is connected with the phenomenon of cultural eutrophication of natural waters (Keeney et al. 1971; Godzing 1972). Eutrophication, the process of

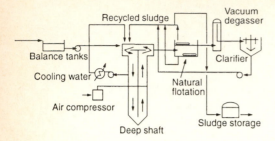

**Figure 12.27**
The ICI deep shaft process for wastewater treatment. This process achieves high oxygen partial pressures and transfer rates through increased hydrostatic pressure. The shaft is 20–30 m deep and is separated by a central divider. Circulation is initially established by air injection into the rising half of the shaft. After circulation is established, air injection is switched to the downcomer side, as shown in the drawing. Air bubbles are retained for a long time period, and the increasing hydrostatic pressure facilitates $O_2$ dissolution. (Source: Howell 1977. Reprinted by permission, copyright The Institute of Petroleum, London.)

becoming rich in nutrients, is a natural sequence in the geological history of lakes and ponds. Initially, deep, cold, nutrient-poor (oligotrophic) waters become shallower, warmer, and more eutrophic as silt settles and organic matter accumulates from biological production. Eventually, the lake is filled in. Cultural eutrophication, frequently referred to only as eutrophication with the same intended meaning, is the result of human activities and causes dramatic changes in lake character within years or decades instead of geological ages. Sudden nutrient enrichment through sewage discharge or agricultural runoff triggers explosive algal blooms. Owing to various known or unknown causes, such as a period of cloudy weather that intensifies mutual shading, exhaustion of micronutrients, toxic products, or disease, the algal population eventually crashes. The decomposition of the dead algal biomass by heterotrophic microorganisms exhausts the dissolved oxygen in the water, precipitating extensive fish kills and septic conditions. Even if eutrophication does not go to this extreme, algal mats, turbidity, discoloration, and shifts of the fish population from valuable species to more tolerant but less valued forms represent undesirable eutrophication changes.

Eutrophication is a complex phenomenon that can be understood in the context of Liebig's law of the minimum. Many natural oligotrophic lakes are limited by phosphorus or by nitrogen, but other nutrient limitation possibilities, such as dissolved $CO_2$ or sulfur, may also exist. If the sewage effluent supplies large amounts of the inorganic nutrient that happens to be limiting in the receiving water body, a eutrophication response is likely to occur. If this is the case and the sewage discharge cannot be stopped or diverted, the obvious remedy is to remove the causative inorganic nutrients from the sewage discharge.

Biological processes for removal of nitrogen have been developed for inclusion in the activated sludge treatment process (Figure 12.28). This typically involves using a series of aerobic and anaerobic treatment stages. In-plant aerobic nitrification can solve the problem of BOD associated with ammonium nitrogen. Vigorous and prolonged aeration is necessary to convert ammonium nitrogen to nitrate by biological nitrification. After conversion to nitrate, it is also possible to remove most of the nitrogen from the effluent by creating anaerobic conditions for denitrification. To achieve this result, aeration is discontinued and organic matter added. The anaerobic oxidation of organic matter converts the nitrate to gaseous denitrification products. Methanol has been used as an additional carbon source, but cost considerations favor the use of the dissolved carbon substrates of the raw sewage itself to drive the denitrification process. This usage can be accomplished by intermittent aeration or by an admixture of raw sewage to extensively aerated and thus nitrified sewage.

The phosphate filler of many detergent formulations, which is added to precipitate bivalent ions such as $Ca^{2+}$ and $Mg^{2+}$ in hard water, is most frequently blamed in eutrophication cases. In Lake Washington, located adjacent to Seattle and surrounding communities, the pattern of eutrophication and the improvement following sewage diversion from Lake Washington to Puget Sound correlated best with phosphate concentrations (Edmondson 1970). Work on Wisconsin lakes indicated that phosphate concentrations exceeding 10 μg P/l at the beginning of the growing season are likely to result in destructive algal blooms.

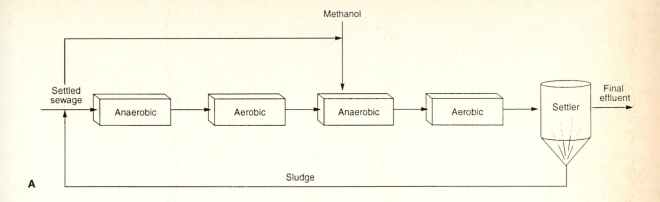

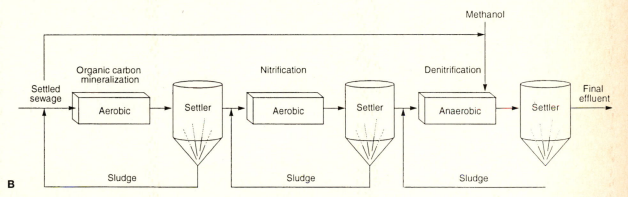

**Figure 12.28**
Variations in the activated sludge process involving aerobic and anaerobic treatments to remove nitrogen as well as to reduce the BOD. (A) A single sludge system with a series of anaerobic (anoxic-oxygen free) and aerobic tanks. (B) A multisludge system using three separate reactors for aerobic decomposition of organic carbon, aerobic nitrification to convert ammonia to nitrate, and anaerobic denitrification to convert nitrate to gaseous molecular nitrogen. (Source: Bitton 1994.)

In these and many other cases, there is little doubt that phosphate has been the main offender, but in the case of nitrogen-limited waters, a treatment to remove phosphate alone is clearly useless. In practice, if eutrophication of the receiving waters is a concern, an effort is made to remove both nitrogen and phosphorus from the effluent (Godzing 1972).

Bacterial uptake and storage of phosphorus in the form of polyphosphates may be encouraged by treatment process modifications (Toerien et al. 1990). Enhanced phosphate removal from sludge appears to

be associated with polyphosphate (poly-P) storage by the *Acinetobacter-Moraxella-Mima* group of bacteria. Under anoxic conditions, these microorganisms incorporate large amounts of fatty acids and store them in the form of poly-β-hydroxybutyrate (PHB). Phosphate is released into soluble form during the anoxic period. When the sewage is subsequently reaerated, the poly-P bacteria rapidly oxidize their intracellular PHB reserves while engaging in "luxury" phosphate uptake, far in excess of their growth requirements. The incorporated phosphate is stored as

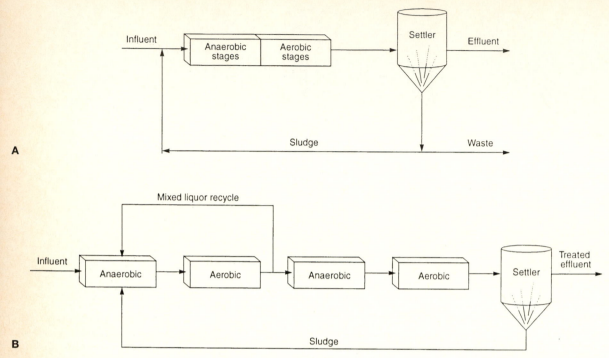

**Figure 12.29**
Modified activated sludge processes for the removal of phosphorus from wastewater.
(A) A/O process. (B) Bardenpho process. (Source: Bitton 1994.)

energy-rich polyphosphate within the cell, thus removing phosphorus from the liquid effluent.

Several biological phosphorus removal systems based on the described mechanisms have been designed and incorporated into the activated sludge treatment system (Bitton 1994) (Figure 12.29). All involve one or more alternate anoxic-oxic (A/O) sewage storage cycles. The A/O process (Figure 12.29A) consists of a modified activated sludge system that includes an anaerobic zone with a retention time of 0.5–1 hour upstream of the conventional aeration tank that has a retention time of 1–3 hours. During the anaerobic phase, inorganic phosphorus is released from the cells as a result of polyphosphate hydrolysis. The energy liberated is used for the uptake of BOD from wastewater. Removal efficiency is high when the BOD-to-phosphorus ratio exceeds 10. During the aerobic phase, soluble phosphorus is taken up by bacteria, which synthesize polyphosphates, using the

energy released from BOD oxidation. The A/O process results in the removal of phosphorus and BOD from effluents and produces a phosphorus-rich sludge. The key features of this process are the relatively low solid retention time and high organic loading rates.

The Bardenpho process (Figure 12.29B), which was developed in South Africa, consists of two aerobic tanks and two anaerobic tanks that are free of molecular oxygen (anoxic) followed by a sludge settling tank. Tank 1 is anoxic and is used for denitrification, with wastewater used as a carbon source. Tank 2 is an aerobic tank utilized for both carbon oxidation and nitrification. The mixed liquor from this tank, which contains nitrate, is returned to Tank 1. The anoxic Tank 3 removes the nitrate remaining in the effluent by denitrification. Finally, Tank 4 is an aerobic tank used to strip the nitrogen gas that results from denitrification, thus improving mixed liquor settling. It is important to have little or no nitrate present during the

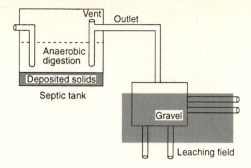

**Figure 12.30**
Diagram of a septic tank. (Source: Mitchell 1974. Reprinted by permission, copyright Prentice Hall.)

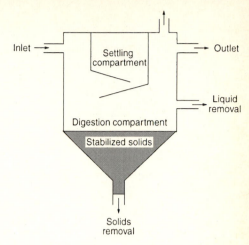

**Figure 12.31**
Diagram of an Imhoff tank. A separate settling compartment is baffled in a way so as to prevent gas bubbles from carrying solids back up into the tank. The flow passes along this baffled compartment perpendicularly to the plane of the drawing. Stabilized solids are removed from the bottom of the tank. Gases are vented and may be utilized as fuel. (Source: Mitchell 1974. Reprinted by permission, copyright Prentice Hall.)

anoxic phase. Nitrate is used as an alternative electron sink by the poly-P bacteria, and its presence would interfere with the PHB storage that primes the poly-P bacteria for their phosphate uptake binge. Biological phosphate removal saves cost and avoids the impact of precipitating chemicals.

Other schemes of biological N and P removal involve the uptake of nitrogen and phosphorus into algal biomass in shallow holding ponds. Problems with harvesting and utilizing the algal biomass, for example, in animal feed, need to be solved before this approach can be practiced on a large scale. Higher aquatic plants, such as water hyacinths and cattails, also have potential for the removal of nitrogen and phosphorus from sewage effluents and might prove to be easier to harvest if appropriate uses for such biomass could be found. One should be aware, however, of the practical difficulty of devoting large land areas to such operations near urban centers.

**Anaerobic Digestors**    Anaerobic wastewater treatment methods are generally slower but save energy compared to processes requiring forced aeration. Some anaerobic treatment systems can also salvage a part of the chemical energy content of the wastewater by generating biogas, a useful fuel (Cillie et al. 1969; Toerien and Hatting 1969; Zinder 1984). The simplest anaerobic treatment system is the septic tank (Figure 12.30), popular in rural areas without sewer systems. The organics in the wastewater undergo limited anaerobic

digestion. Residual solids settle to the bottom of the tank. The clarified effluent is distributed over a leaching field, where dissolved organics undergo oxidative biodegradation. Septic tank treatment does not reliably destroy intestinal pathogens, and it is important that the leaching field not be in the proximity of water wells. The Imhoff tank (Figure 12.31) has an improved design that maintains anaerobic conditions more strictly, produces some utilizable biogas, and facilitates the settling of solids, but requires expert maintenance (Imhoff and Fair 1956; Mitchell 1974).

Large-scale anaerobic digestors (Figure 12.32) are used for further processing of sewage sludge produced by primary and secondary treatments. Although anaerobic digestors can and have been used directly for the treatment of sewage, the economics of the situation favor aerobic processes for such relatively dilute wastes. Large-scale anaerobic digestors, therefore, are used primarily for processing of settled sewage sludge and for treatment of some very high BOD industrial effluents (Wu et al. 1991).

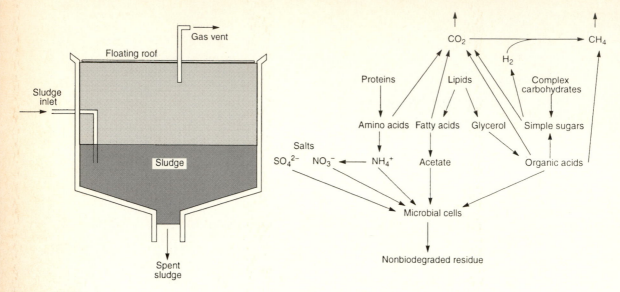

**Figure 12.32**
Greatly simplified diagram of an anaerobic digestor showing the chemical reactions that occur within the reactor. (Source: Mitchell 1974. Reprinted by permission, copyright Prentice Hall.)

Conventional anaerobic digestors are large fermentation tanks designed for continuous operation under anaerobic conditions. Provisions for mechanical mixing, heating, gas collection, sludge addition, and draw off of stabilized sludge are incorporated. The digestor contains high amounts of suspended organic matter; values between 20 and 100 g/l are considered favorable. A considerable part of this suspended material is bacterial biomass, viable counts of which can be as high as $10^9$–$10^{10}$ bacteria per ml. Anaerobic counts are typically two to three orders of magnitude higher than aerobic ones. Fungi and protozoa are present in low numbers only and are not considered to play a significant role in anaerobic digestion.

The anaerobic digestion of wastes can be considered as a two-step process, even though it really is a coupled sequence of microbiological interactions. First, complex organic materials, including microbial biomass, are depolymerized and converted fermentatively to fatty acids, $CO_2$, and $H_2$. A large variety of nonmethanogenic obligately or facultatively anaerobic bacteria participate in these processes. In the next step, methane is generated, either by the direct reduction of methyl groups to methane or by the reduction of $CO_2$ to methane by molecular hydrogen or by other reduced fermentation products, such as fatty acid, methanol, or even carbon monoxide (Balch et al. 1979). Table 12.4 lists some of the methanogenic bacteria and the mechanisms of their methane production.

The operation of anaerobic digestors requires the close control of several parameters, such as retention time, temperature, pH, and C:N and C:P ratios. The reactors are usually heated to 35–37°C for optimal performance. Control is necessary for pH to stay within the 6.0–8.0 values, with pH 7.0 being optimal. Extremes of pH, and the influx of heavy metals, solvents or other toxic materials, can easily upset the operation of the anaerobic digestor. In a "stuck" or "sour" digestor, methane production is interrupted and fatty acids and other fermentation products accumulate. Restoring a stuck digestor to normal operation is difficult. The reactor must usually be cleaned and charged with large volumes of anaerobic sludge or appropriate methanogenic bacteria from an operational unit.

**Table 12.4**
The origin of biogenic methane and some representative methanogenic bacteria

| Source of $CH_4$ carbon | Electron donor | Methanogenic bacteria |
|---|---|---|
| $CO_2$ | $H_2$ | *Methanobacterium bryantii* |
| $CO_2$ | $H_2$ | *Methanobacterium thermoautotrophicum* |
| $CO_2$ | $H_2$ | *Methanomicrobium mobile* |
| $CO_2$ | $H_2$, formate | *Methanococcus vannielii* |
| $CO_2$ | $H_2$, formate | *Methanobrevibacter ruminantium* |
| $CO_2$ | $H_2$, CO, formate | *Methanobacterium formicicum* |
| $CO_2$, methanol, methylamine, di- and trimethylamine, acetate | $H_2$ | *Methanosarcina barkeri* |

A normally operating anaerobic digestor yields a reduced volume of sludge. This material still causes odor and water pollution problems and can be directly disposed of only at a limited number of landfill sites. Aerobic composting further consolidates the sludge and renders it suitable for disposal in any landfill site or for use as a soil conditioner. The biogas produced consists of methane, $CO_2$, small amounts of other gases, such as $N_2$ and $H_2S$, and occasionally traces of $H_2$. This gas either is burned directly in the treatment plant to drive the pumps and maintain the temperature of the digestor at the desired level or, after purification, may be added to municipal gas distribution systems (Finstein and Morris 1979).

Anaerobic digestors are relatively expensive to construct and require expert maintenance, though the production of methane gas offsets some of the cost. The use of anaerobic lagoons as an inexpensive alternative is seldom feasible because of the noxious odors associated with such an operation. A special case in which the anaerobic lagoon performs in a relatively acceptable fashion is in the treatment of meat-packing-plant effluents. Fatty materials and animal stomach contents form a thick, insulating scum layer on the surface of such anaerobic lagoons that substantially reduces the odor problem and renders such facilities acceptable if they are a sufficient distance from residential areas.

## Tertiary Treatments

The previously discussed aerobic and anaerobic biological liquid waste treatment processes are designed to reduce the BOD represented by dissolved, biodegradable organic substrates; in some cases newly designed systems also remove nitrogen and phosphate during this phase of treatment. All are classified as secondary liquid waste treatment.

Tertiary treatment is any practice beyond secondary. Tertiary liquid waste treatments are aimed at the removal of nonbiodegradable organic pollutants and mineral nutrients. The removal of nonbiodegradable organic pollutants, such as chlorophenols, polychlorinated biphenyls, and other synthetic pollutants, is necessary because of the potential toxicity of these compounds. Activated carbon filters are used to remove such materials from secondary-treated industrial effluents. Previous secondary treatment is necessary in order to avoid overloading this expensive treatment stage with biodegradable materials that can be removed in more economic ways.

Phosphate is commonly removed by precipitation as calcium or iron phosphate. This can be accomplished as an integral part of primary or secondary settling or in a separate facility with recycling of the precipitating agent. Nitrogen, present mainly as ammonia, can be removed by "stripping," that is, by volatilization as $NH_3$ at a high pH. Some of the ammonia eliminated from the sewage in this manner, however, may return to the watershed in the form of precipitation and still cause eutrophication problems. An alternative for ammonia nitrogen removal is breakpoint chlorination. Addition of hypochlorous acid in a 1:1 molar ratio results in the formation of monochloramine as in Equation 1:

(1) $HOCl + NH_3 \rightarrow NH_2Cl + H_2O$

Further addition of hypochlorous acid results in the formation of dichloramine (Equation 2):

(2) $HOCl + NH_2Cl \rightarrow NHCl_2 + H_2O$

Breakpoint chlorination occurs at the approximate molar ratio of 2 mol of chlorine to 1 mol of ammonia (7.6 mg Cl to 1 mg ammonium-N) and results in the near-quantitative conversion of ammonia to molecular nitrogen according to the simplified reaction in Equation 3:

(3) $2NHCl_2 + H_2O \rightarrow N_2 + HOCl + 3H^+ + 3Cl^-$

As chlorination of the sewage effluent is commonly practiced for disinfection purposes (discussed in the next section), chlorination to this "breakpoint" can accomplish the removal of ammonium nitrogen in the same process. The removal of ammonium nitrogen also lowers the BOD of the effluent because the nitrification process would consume oxygen dissolved in the receiving water.

The removal of toxic metals during sewage treatment is a process of increasing importance both in the industrially developed and in the newly industrializing countries. The heavy metals that are of the greatest concern with respect to human health are mercury, cadmium, chromium, and lead; the World Health Organization (WHO) guideline values set for these metals are less than 0.001 g, 0.005 g, 0.05 mg, and 0.05 mg per liter, respectively, in drinking water. Heavy metal discharges can result in severe ecotoxicological problems in receiving waters, thereby restricting the effectiveness of natural self-purification mechanisms. Although the uptake of toxic metal ions by microbes in conventional activated sludge treatment processes has been an accepted process feature

for many years, such mechanisms have been subjected to little more than cursory investigation as far as wastewater treatment is concerned. It is also important to remember that, unlike biodegradable pollutants, sorbed metal ions are generally converted into either toxic products or residues that remain associated with the microbe-biopolymer matrix and can either be released during sludge treatment or be remobilized after sludge disposal. The general tendency of bacteria to concentrate heavy metals in their biomass is favorable to effluent quality, but it complicates the disposal of sludges. On an experimental basis, processes similar to microbial mining (see Chapter 15) are being considered to reduce the heavy metal burden of sewage sludges prior to their disposal on agricultural land as soil conditioner. Acid produced by *Thiobacillus* would solubilize the heavy metals and leach them from the sludge. Subsequently, the heavy metals would be chemically precipitated from the leachate and either reprocessed for use or permanently immobilized.

## Disinfection

The final step in sewage treatment is disinfection, designed to kill enteropathogenic bacteria or viruses that were not eliminated during the previous steps of sewage treatment. Disinfection often occurs as the final stage of secondary treatment, but it may also follow tertiary treatment processes. Disinfection is commonly accomplished by chlorination, using either chlorine gas ($Cl_2$) or hypochlorite ($Ca[OCl]_2$ or $NaOCl$). Chlorine gas reacts with water to yield hypochlorous and hydrochloric acids (Equation 4):

(4) $Cl_2 + H_2O \rightarrow HOCl + HCl$

Hypochlorite also reacts with water to form hypochlorous acid (Equation 5):

(5) $Ca(OCl)_2 + 2H_2O \rightarrow 2HOCl + Ca(OH)_2$

or (Equation 6):

(6) $NaOCl + H_2O \rightarrow HOCl + NaOH$

The hypochlorous acid or the hypochlorite ($ClO^-$) ion is the actual disinfectant. The total concentration of hypochlorous acid and hypochlorite is designated as free residual chlorine. Hypochlorite is a strong oxidant, which is the basis of its antibacterial action. As an oxidant, it also reacts with residual dissolved or suspended organic matter, ammonia, reduced iron, manganese, and sulfur compounds. The oxidation of such compounds competes for HOCl and reduces its disinfectant action, making necessary chlorination to a point that these reactions are satisfied with several milligrams per liter of excess free residual chlorine remaining in solution. This process requires high amounts of hypochlorite, resulting in high salt concentrations in the effluent. Therefore, it is desirable to remove nitrogen and other contaminants by alternate means and use chlorination for disinfection only.

A disadvantage of disinfection by chlorination is that more resistant types of organic molecules, including some lipids and hydrocarbons, are not oxidized completely but become, instead, partially chlorinated. Chlorinated hydrocarbons tend to be toxic and are difficult to mineralize (see Chapter 13). However, alternative means of disinfection are more expensive, so chlorination remains the principal means of sewage disinfection.

## Treatment and Safety of Water Supplies

Closely related to the safe disposal of liquid wastes is the problem of safe and healthful water for drinking and other uses. Increasing population densities and urbanization during the eighteenth and nineteenth centuries initially were not accompanied by adequate sanitation practices. This situation created conditions for devastating epidemics caused by enteropathogenic microorganisms such as *Vibrio cholerae* (cholera), *Salmonella typhi* (typhoid fever), various other *Salmonella* and *Shigella* strains (gastrointestinal infections of varying severity), and *Entamoeba histolytica* (amoebic dysentery). The common feature of these diseases is that the infectious organisms are shed in the feces of sick individuals and clinically asymptomatic carriers. Fecal contamination, through untreated or inadequately treated sewage effluents entering lakes, rivers, or groundwaters that in turn serve as municipal water supplies, creates conditions for rapid dissemination of the pathogens. The primary route of infection is ingestion of drinking water, but fruits, vegetables, and eating utensils washed with contaminated water are other possible carriers. The obvious remedy to this situation is to prevent the fecal contamination of water supplies. This is done to a certain degree during sewage treatment, but the adequate treatment of all sewage discharges is by no means assured. A major sanitation effort, therefore, is necessary to treat and safely distribute public water supplies. Such sanitation practices have led to the virtual elimination of waterborne infections in developed countries, but these infections continue to be major causes of sickness and death in undeveloped regions (Sobsey and Olson 1983).

Public water supplies originate from groundwater through wells or from surface waters such as rivers, lakes, or reservoirs. In the case of groundwater, disinfection is often all that is required. Surface waters and some groundwaters have to be treated by settling and filtration. Dissolved ferrous iron and divalent manganese are oxidized prior to settling by addition of permanganate. Filtration is carried out through gravel and fine sand beds. Microbial films on the surface of the bed particles enhance the effectiveness of the filtration. The filter beds have to be backwashed frequently to prevent clogging.

Disinfection of municipal water supplies has traditionally been accomplished by chlorination, as described for the disinfection of sewage discharges (Equations 4–6). This treatment is relatively inexpensive, and the free residual chlorine content of the treated water is a built-in safety factor against pathogens surviving the actual treatment period and against recontamination. The disadvantage of chlorination is the creation of trace amounts of trihalomethane (THM) compounds. The fact that THMs were formed in virtually all municipal water supplies that used chlorination for disinfection linked the formation of these contaminants to the chlorination process. Because some of the THMs are suspected carcinogens, the U.S. Environmental Protection Agency (EPA) established in 1979 a maximal THM limit in drinking water of 100 µg/l. To keep the levels within this limit using traditional chlorine disinfection, organic compounds have to be removed from the water meticulously by sand filtration and other techniques. This method is often both impractical and too expensive. Fortunately, disinfection by monochloramine is effective but produces much lower amounts of THMs. As an example, traditional chlorination of Ohio River water produced 160 μg THM/l, but chloramine treatment produced THM levels consistently below 20 μg/l. Monochloramine may be generated right in the water to be disinfected by adding ammonium prior to or simultaneously with chlorine or hypochlorite. Once hypochlorous acid is formed according to Equations 4–6, it reacts with the added ammonia according to Equation 1, generating monochloramine. The practice of using chloramines as drinking water disinfectants, the least expensive way to reduce THM formation, is spreading rapidly (Wolfe et al. 1984).

Ozone ($O_3$) has been used for water disinfection with good results both in Europe and in the United States. Ozone treatment kills pathogens reliably and does not result in the synthesis of undesirable THM contaminants. Because ozone is an unstable gas, however, water treated with ozone does not have any residual antimicrobial activity and is prone to chance recontamination. Ozone has to be generated from air on site in ozone reactors, using electrical corona discharge. Only about 10% of the electricity actually generates ozone and the rest is lost as heat, making disinfection by ozone considerably more expensive than by chlorination (Mitchell 1974).

## Water Quality Testing

The public health importance of clean drinking water requires an objective test methodology to evaluate the effectiveness of treatment procedures and to establish drinking water safety standards (Bonde 1977; Hoadley and Putka 1977). The detection of actual enteropathogens such as *Salmonella* or *Shigella* in routine monitoring studies would be a difficult and uncertain undertaking. Instead, the bacteriological tests of drinking water simply establish the fact and the degree of fecal contamination of the water sample by demonstrating the presence of so-called indicator organisms. The most frequently used indicator organism for fecal

contamination is the normally nonpathogenic *Escherichia coli*. Positive tests for *E. coli* do not prove the presence of enteropathogenic organisms but establish the possibility of such a presence. Because *E. coli* is plentiful and easier to grow than the enteropathogens, the test has a built-in safety factor for detecting potentially dangerous fecal contamination.

Ideally, an indicator organism should be present whenever the pathogens concerned are present, should be present only when there is a real danger of pathogens being present, must occur in greater numbers than the pathogens to provide a safety margin, must survive in the environment as long as the potential pathogens, and must be easy to detect with a high reliability of correctly identifying the indicator organism regardless of what other organisms are present in the sample. *E. coli* meets many of these criteria, but there are limitations to its use as an indicator organism, and various other species have been proposed as additional or replacement indicators of water safety. There probably is no universal indicator organism for determining water quality. Under different conditions, different populations may be better indicators than others (Wolf 1972).

Prior to 1989, the EPA had certified only two techniques for the detection of coliform bacteria in water: the multiple tube fermentation technique and the membrane filtration test. These procedures take several days to complete. In 1991, the EPA eliminated the requirement for the enumeration of coliform bacteria in water samples, instituting regulations based only on the presence or absence of coliform bacteria. This was done in response to studies that demonstrated that the level of coliform bacteria was not quantitatively related to the potential for an outbreak of waterborne disease, and that the presence or absence of coliform bacteria provided adequate water quality information. Culture-requiring methods for the detection of coliform bacteria, however, are limited in their ability to detect viable but nonculturable bacteria. In oligotrophic situations, like drinking water distribution systems, a proportion of the total population of coliform bacteria may be unrecoverable while in the pseudosenescent state associated with bacteria adapted to low-nutrient situations.

The classic test for the detection of fecal contamination involves, in the first step, inoculation of lactose broth with undiluted or appropriately diluted water samples. Gas formation detected in small inverted test tubes (Durham tubes) gives positive presumptive evidence of contamination by fecal coliforms; this is the presumptive test. Gas formation in lactose broth at elevated incubation temperature is a characteristic of fecal *Salmonella, Shigella,* and *E. coli* strains but also of the nonfecal coliform *Enterobacter aerogenes* and some *Klebsiella* species. In the second stage, the confirmed test, positive lactose broth cultures are streaked out on a lactose-peptone agar medium containing sodium sulfite and basic fuchsin (m-Endo agar). Fecal coliform colonies on this medium acquire a characteristically greenish metallic sheen, but *Enterobacter* forms reddish colonies and nonlactose fermenters form colorless colonies. If a subculture in lactose broth at 35°C yields gas formation, a positive test for fecal coliforms has been completed. In the second test stage of this procedure, the presence of enteric bacteria also can be confirmed by streaking samples from the positive lactose broth cultures onto eosin methylene blue (EMB) agar. Fecal coliform colonies on this medium acquire a characteristically greenish metallic sheen, *Enterobacter* species form reddish colonies, and nonlactose fermenters form colorless colonies, respectively; this is a confirmed test. Alternatively, the confirmed test can be accomplished by using brilliant green lactose-bile broth (BGLB). If BGLB is used, it is then subcultured onto EMB. Subculture colonies showing a green metallic sheen on EMB and incubated in lactose broth at 35°C should produce gas formation, completing a positive test for fecal coliforms; this is called a completed test.

It is possible to simplify this three-stage test. In the Eijkman test, suitable dilutions are incubated in lactose broth at 44.5°C. At this temperature, fecal coliforms still grow, but nonfecal coliforms are inhibited. Gas formation in lactose broth at 44.5°C constitutes a one-step positive test, but precise temperature control is mandatory as temperatures only a few degrees higher inhibit or kill fecal coliforms. Another technique is filtration of known volumes of diluted or undiluted water samples through 0.45-µm-pore

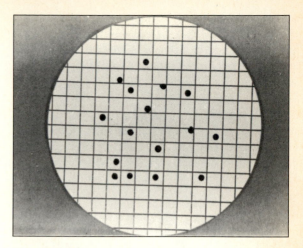

**Figure 12.33**
Filter used in filtration of fecally contaminated water showing typical colonies of *E. coli* after incubation of Endo agar.

Millipore filters and incubation of these filters directly on Endo medium. Colonies of fecal coliforms show up with a characteristic metallic sheen and can be counted (Figure 12.33). The dried filters can be filed for a permanent record.

Several alternative procedures are able to provide the information necessary for determining drinking water quality in the presence-absence test format. These tests can be completed in 24 hours or less. One test protocol uses defined substrate technology to determine enzymatic activities that are diagnostic of coliform bacteria and the fecal coliform *E. coli*. A medium containing isopropyl β-D-thiogalactopyranoside (IPTG) is used to detect β-galactosidase, which is diagnostic of total coliform bacteria, and a medium containing o-nitrophenol-β-D-galactopyranoside-4-methylumbelliferyl-β-D-glucuronide (MUG) is used to detect β-glucuronidase, which is diagnostic of *E. coli*. The defined substrate test requires only a day to complete (Edberg et al. 1988, 1989a, 1989b). Gene probes and other molecular approaches may also be used to detect coliform bacteria and *E. coli*. Bej et al. (1990, 1991a, 1991b) developed a method using the polymerase chain reaction (PCR) to detect total coliform bacteria based on the *lacZ* gene and *E. coli* based on the *uidA* gene; these genes code for the enzymes detected in the defined substrate tests.

The drinking water standard does not absolutely exclude the possibility of ingesting enteropathogens but attempts to reduce this possibility to a statistically tolerable limit. Enteropathogens are likely to be present in much lower numbers than fecal coliforms, and a few infective bacteria are usually unable to overcome body defenses. A minimum infectious dose from several hundred to several thousand bacteria is necessary for various diseases to establish an actual infection. Drinking water supplies that meet the 1/100 ml coliform standard have never been demonstrated to be the source of waterborne bacterial infections (Olson and Nagy 1984).

Fecal coliform counts are also used to establish the safety of water for shellfish harvesting and recreational uses. Shellfish tend to concentrate bacteria and other particles through their filter-feeding activity. Some shellfish are consumed raw and thus can transmit infection by waterborne pathogens. This is reflected by the relatively stringent standard (70/100 ml) for waters in use for shellfishing. Clinical evidence for infection by enteropathogenic coliforms through recreational use of waters for wading or swimming is unconvincing, but as a precaution, beaches are usually closed when fecal coliform counts exceed the recreational standard of 1000/100 mL. Some regional standards require that disinfected sewage discharges not exceed this limit.

We discussed the fate of nonpathogenic and pathogenic fecal coliforms in natural waters earlier in the context of allochthonous organisms and competitive interactions. In general, fecal coliforms are poor competitors at the low substrate concentrations that prevail in natural waters and so tend to be eliminated by competition and predation. Low water temperatures, sediment adsorption, and anoxic conditions occasionally contribute to the prolonged survival of fecal coliforms in natural waters.

Enteroviruses and the cysts of some pathogenic protozoa are somewhat more resistant to disinfection by chlorine chloramine or ozone than bacteria, and occasionally active virus particles or live cysts are recovered from water treated to meet fecal coliform standards (Sobsey and Olson 1983; Olson and Nagy 1984). Thus, water treated according to accepted standards may occasionally become a source of viral or protozoan infection. As many as one hundred different viral types have been demonstrated to be shed in human feces, but practical concern has been mainly with the causative viruses of infectious hepatitis, polio, and viral gastroenteritis. There is evidence that infectious hepatitis was, on occasion, spread by water supplies, though a much more prevalent way of infection is the consumption of raw shellfish from fecally contaminated waters. Spread of polio infection through water supplies and/or recreational use of beaches has been suspected in some cases, but conclusive proof is lacking (Shuval and Katznelson 1972; Vaughan et al. 1979). The situation with viral gastroenteritis is similar. It seems fair to say that though the possibility of the occasional spread of viral infection through drinking water adequately treated by bacteriological standards cannot be excluded, there is no supporting evidence for actual epidemics caused by such water. Similarly, it is unclear whether properly disinfected water has ever spread protozoan pathogens such as the flagellate *Giardia lamblia* or the amoeba *Naegleria fowleri* (Sobsey and Olson 1983). There is ample evidence for destructive epidemics by enteroviruses and protozoa caused by untreated drinking water in various underdeveloped countries.

The considerable uncertainty about the hazards posed by enteroviruses in water supplies and recreational waters is due to the difficulty of detecting and enumerating viruses in such waters. For detection, viruses have to be grown in suitable tissue culture cell lines and/or detected by immunological procedures. Virus concentrations are generally low, 0.1–1 particle per milliliter in treated sewage effluent and as low as 0.1–1 per liter in receiving natural waters. Therefore, the first problem is to concentrate the viruses sufficiently for detection and enumeration. Table 12.5 lists and compares some of the available methods.

The oldest procedure is the gauze pad method. Gauze pads are suspended in water for about 24 hours. They concentrate viruses by absorption. Water expressed from the retrieved gauze pad contains higher numbers of viruses than directly collected water samples. Sample incorporation relies on concentrated

**Table 12.5**
A comparison of various methods for detecting viruses in water

| Method | Sample volume (liters) | Concentration factor | Recovery efficiency (%) |
|---|---|---|---|
| Gauze pad | | 10–50 | 0.5–5 |
| Sample incorporation | 0.06–0.15 | 10–20 | 95 |
| Ultracentrifugation | 1–10 | 30–50 | 20–100 |
| Membrane filter adsorption | 10–1,000 | $10^3$ | 5–38 |
| Soluble ultrafilters | 10 | $10^3$ | 35–100 |
| Hydro-extraction | 1 | $10^2$ | 24–64 |
| Phase separation (two steps) | 5 | $10^3$ | 35–100 |
| Electrophoresis | 0.3 | $10^2$ | 100 |
| Adsorption to particulate materials | | | |
|     calcium phosphate | 3.0 | $10^3$ | 50–100 |
|     cobalt chloride | 1 | $10^3$ | 100 |
|     aluminum hydroxide | 3.8–19 | $10^3$ | 50–100 |
|     ion exchange resins | 0.1 | 50–100 | 20–50 |
|     passive hemagglutination | | | 80–100 |
|     insoluble polyelectrolytes | 1,000 | $10^3$–$10^5$ | 35–80 |

Source: Shuval and Katznelson 1972.

media that allow the introduction of relatively large (10–50 mL) water samples.

Ultracentrifugation concentrates viruses by sedimentation. It requires expensive instrumentation and is time-consuming. Filters do not actually filter out viruses but retain them by adsorption. Subsequently, viruses are eluted from the filter, or the filter is dissolved. Hydro-extraction is actually a dialysis process. Water is extracted through the dialysis tubing by concentrated polyethylene glycol. Virus particles remain with other large molecules in the tubing and are concentrated. Phase separation involves partitioning between two liquid phases. Electrophoresis takes advantage of the negative charge on virus particles. Adsorption to and elution from various particulate materials has also been used with varying success.

Considerable research effort is currently directed at elucidating the duration and mechanisms of enterovirus survival in natural waters. Generalizations are difficult at this time, but enteroviruses appear to be eliminated from natural waters more slowly than fecal coliforms. Adsorption to sediment particles appears to offer considerable protection against inactivation and, under some circumstances, may promote dispersion of the viruses (Smith et al. 1978). Changing environmental conditions, such as pH or salinity, may cause the desorption of the still-infective viral particles. Recent surveys sporadically identified human enteroviruses in both freshwater and saltwater environments, but the numbers of enteroviruses showed little correlation to the number of fecal coliforms. Whether this is due to differential survival or to nonidentical contamination sources is not clear at this time. Virus recovery, cultivation, and enumeration from natural waters clearly needs further scientific progress before standards and routine monitoring processes can be established.

## CHAPTER SUMMARY

Practical applications of microbial ecology are evident in the practices of biodeterioration control and of soil, water, and waste management. Sterilization and

## Safe Drinking Water

Safe drinking water has been one of the proud achievements of developed countries and an important milestone that less developed countries are trying to achieve. According to rough estimates, more than 15 million deaths worldwide result annually from waterborne infections. Diarrheal diseases of small children alone result in more than 2 million deaths annually in developing countries (Young 1996). The outbreak of cholera in South America in 1991–1995 resulted in more than 1 million cases and over 10,000 fatalities.

Cholera, typhoid fever, and amoebic dysentery can easily kill otherwise healthy adults. Milder forms of waterborne infections, spread likewise by fecal contamination of drinking water, normally cause only discomfort and less serious illness in healthy adults, but they can be serious and easily fatal in very young children, in the elderly, and in persons debilitated by other illnesses, especially AIDS.

Providing safe drinking water is a complex problem that goes far beyond a treatment step. In many countries, the quality of the distribution system is so poor that the initially chlorinated water becomes unsafe before it reaches the consumer. The upgrading of the distribution system is a much more complex and expensive problem than the initial treatment of the water. In addition to the physical upgrading of treatment and distribution systems, education, sanitary engineering, and monitoring of water safety are essential elements in upgrading water quality. The education of political leaders and of the public at large is critical. Without it, the necessary resources are unlikely to be devoted to this pressing health problem.

Although most sickness and death due to unsanitary water are confined to developing countries, all is not well even in the developed countries. Groundwater pollution and a certain complacency due to past successes in disease control have created disturbing trends and incidents. In the United States, an alarming portion of the groundwater is becoming chemically polluted (Pye and Patrick

aseptic containment prevent spoilage of food and perishable materials. Alternatively, storage under unfavorable physicochemical conditions or the addition of preservatives is used to retard biodeterioration. Controlling the formation of biofilms on surfaces, such as ship hulls, represents a special problem. Biofouling is often controlled by using paints with toxic antimicrobial agents such as heavy metals.

Agricultural soils are managed to encourage aerobic and discourage anaerobic cycling processes. In addition, fertilizer technology and soil pH control take into account and often utilize microbial cycling activities. Using natural bacterial nitrogen-fixing capabilities and controlling leaching losses that result from nitrification when fertilizers are added are important aspects of maintaining the fertility of agricultural soils. The use of no-tillage farming is important for the conservation of some soils and the prevention of topsoil erosion that is a major cause of soil infertility.

Microorganisms are extensively used in the biological treatment of solid and liquid wastes. The composting of solid waste and the biological treatment of sewage are complex microbial processes that recycle and/or stabilize organic wastes and protect the environment. Landfills represent a simple means of solid waste disposal that relies on anaerobic microbial

1983). In 1993, a combination of spring floods and inadequate water treatment caused 400,000 cases of cryptosporidiosis in Milwaukee, Wisconsin, with more than 100 fatalities (Young 1996). *Cryptosporidium,* a protozoan parasite harbored by cattle and many other mammals, got distributed through the water system of the city. *Cryptosporidium, Giardia, Acanthamoeba, Entamoeba,* and *Naegleria* in their encysted forms are more resistant to chlorination treatment than bacterial pathogens.

Since May 1996, there have been reports of clusters and sporadic cases of infection in the United States with the coccidian protozoon *Cyclospora cayetanensis.* Symptoms of *Cyclospora* infection include prolonged, watery diarrhea, as well as anorexia, weight loss, and tiredness. *Cyclospora* appears to be a newly emerging waterborne pathogen, and outbreaks of *Cyclospora* infection have been linked to contaminated water (Soave and Johnson 1995). *Cyclospora* was detected in water samples taken from the water storage tank that supplied a small military detachment in Pokhara, Nepal, where cases of persistent diarrhea were reported among British soldiers and dependents (Rabold et al. 1994). This outbreak suggests that it is necessary to boil water or use an adequate filtration device to produce potable water in areas where *Cyclospora* is endemic.

Currently no simple routine monitoring techniques for these protozoan parasites exist, and the development of simple, rapid techniques for this purpose remain a challenge. Molecular probes in the form of easy-to-use kits are the likeliest tools to be developed for such monitoring tasks. In a 1995 international colloquium and in its 1996 report, the American Academy of Microbiology issued a strong warning about water safety and urged renewed attention to and action against this serious health threat (Young 1996).

processes to decompose the wastes. In this procedure, solid wastes, both organic and inorganic, are deposited in low-lying and hence low-value land. Sanitary landfills are covered with layers of soil on a regular basis to minimize pest rodent and insect populations. Landfills are not managed to optimize biodegradation, and decomposition in them is slow and uneven. Leachates from landfills contain heavy metals and organic decomposition products that can contaminate aquifers. The management of landfills attempts to minimize this hazard by capping, liners, and leachate collection and treatment. Methane production in landfills may pose an explosion hazard to neighboring houses. In some landfills the methane produced has been collected and used as an energy resource.

Solid wastes can also be stabilized by composting. Composting is a microbial process that converts putrefiable organic waste materials into a stable, sanitary, humuslike product that is reduced in bulk and can be used for soil improvement. Composting is accomplished in static piles (windrows), aerated piles, or continuous feed reactors, each of which maintains favorable thermophilic temperatures, moisture levels (50–60% water), and aerobic conditions that permit the rapid decomposition of organic wastes. Composting can also be accomplished anaerobically using the dry anaerobic conversion (DRANCO) process. This latter process produces methane that can be used as a fuel and a stable material that can be used as a soil conditioner.

Liquid wastes are treated by a variety of sewage treatment processes that are aimed at reducing the biological oxygen demand (BOD) and removing nutrients that could cause eutrophication of receiving waters. Sewage treatment can involve physical removal of solids (primary treatment); biological decomposition of organic compounds (secondary treatment); chemical, physical, or biological removal of other constituents such as heavy metals, nitrogen, and phosphates (tertiary treatment); and disinfection to remove potentially pathogenic microorganisms. A variety of bioreactors are used for secondary treatment of liquid wastes. These include fixed film bioreactors, such as trickling filters and rotating biological contactors in which the microorganisms are attached to solid surfaces. In other types of treatment units, such as activated sludge reactors, the microbial biomass is suspended in the liquid. Each of these systems relies on a diverse microbial community to degrade the organic compounds in the waste. Increasingly, the treatment of liquid wastes involves sequential aerobic and anaerobic degradation processes. Anaerobic conditions within a bioreactor permit denitrification and removal of nitrogen compounds that could cause eutrophication. Sludges collected during primary treatment or the ones that form during secondary sewage treatment can be further decomposed in anaerobic digestors with the formation of a stable solid product that can be used as a soil conditioner. Methane that can be used as a fuel is a useful by-product. Bacteria, algae, and plants can be used in tertiary treatments to remove phosphates and heavy metals that would be harmful if released into receiving waters. The final disinfection step often uses chlorine or hypochlorite to kill enteropathogens.

Disinfection is also used for the treatment of potable water supplies to guard against the spread of waterborne epidemics. Chlorination, chloramination, and ozonation are widely used for the disinfection of potable waters. The effectiveness of such disinfective treatment is monitored through counts of indicator organisms, most notably the coliform bacterium *Escherichia coli*. *E. coli* is an effective indicator of fecal contamination that may harbor the enteropathogenic bacteria *Salmonella* and *Shigella,* but other direct tests may be desirable in the future to protect against protozoa, such as *Giardia* and *Cryptosporidium,* and various enteric viruses that may be present in water and pose a threat to human health.

## STUDY QUESTIONS

1. How is biodeterioration of foods prevented?

2. How is biofouling of ship hulls controlled?

3. How are soil management practices used to maintain soil fertility?

4. Describe the disposal of municipal wastes in landfills including the benefits and problems associated with this waste disposal method. How does a sanitary landfill minimize pest problems?

5. Compare composting and landfills for disposal of municipal wastes.

6. Describe how aeration is maintained in compost piles.

7. Compare traditional aerobic composting with the DRANCO process.

8. What is BOD? Why is it important to reduce the BOD of wastewaters before they are discharged into rivers or lakes?

9. Describe the biological and chemical changes that occur in a river below a sewage outfall.

10. What are primary, secondary, and tertiary treatments of sewage?

11. Describe a trickling filter.

12. Describe a rotating biological contactor.

13. Describe the operation of a conventional activated sludge treatment facility.

14. Describe the microbial populations within an activated sludge tank.

15. Why is it important to remove inorganic nitrogen and phosphate from wastewater?

16. How can a traditional activated sludge treatment facility be modified to remove inorganic nitrogen from wastewater?

17. How can a traditional activated sludge treatment facility be modified to remove phosphate from wastewater?

18. How can a traditional activated sludge treatment facility be modified to remove industrial organic wastes from wastewater?

19. What determines the selection of a specific wastewater treatment process for a community?

20. Describe the operation of a septic tank.

21. How are anaerobic digestors used in wastewater treatment?

22. Describe how wastewaters and potable waters are disinfected.

23. How is the microbiological safety of potable waters assessed?

24. What is an indicator organism? Why are coliforms used as indicator organisms?

25. How are coliform counts performed? What are the limitations of coliform counts for assessing water quality?

# REFERENCES AND SUGGESTED READINGS

Baere, L .D., O. Verdonck, and W. Verstraete. 1986. High rate dry anaerobic composting process for the organic fraction of solid wastes. *Proceedings, Biotechnology and Bioengineering Symposium No. 15.* Wiley, New York, pp. 321–330.

Balch, W. E., G. E. Fox, L. J. Magrum, C. R. Woese, and R. S. Wolfe. 1979. Methanogens: Reevaluation of a unique biological group. *Bacteriological Review* 43:260–296.

Bej, A. K., J. L. DiCesare, L. Haff, and R. M. Atlas. 1991a. Detection of *Escherichia coli* and *Shigella* spp. in water by using polymerase chain reaction (PCR) and gene probes for *uid. Applied and Environmental Microbiology* 57:1013–1017.

Bej, A. K., M. H. Mahbubani, J. L. DiCesare, and R. M. Atlas. 1991b. Polymerase chain reaction-gene probe detection of microorganisms by using filter-concentrated samples. *Applied and Environmental Microbiology* 57:3529–3534.

Bej, A. K., R. J. Steffan, J. L. DiCesare, L. Haff, and R. M. Atlas. 1990. Detection of coliform bacteria in water by using polymerase chain reaction and gene probes. *Applied and Environmental Microbiology* 56:307–314.

Bitton, G. 1994. *Wastewater Microbiology.* Wiley Liss, New York.

Bonde, G. J. 1977. Bacterial indicators of water pollution. *Advances in Aquatic Microbiology* 1:273–364.

Casida, L. E., Jr. 1968. *Industrial Microbiology.* Wiley, New York.

Chet, I., and R. Mitchell. 1976. Control of marine fouling by chemical repellents. In J. M. Sharpley and A. M. Kaplan (eds.). *Proceedings of the Third International Biodegradation Symposium.* Applied Science Publishers, Essex, England, pp. 515–521.

Cillie, G. G., M. R. Henzen, G. J. Stander, and R. D. Baillie. 1969. The application of the process in waste purification. Part IV, Anaerobic digestion. *Water Research* 3:623–643.

Corpe, W. A., L. Matsuuchi, and B. Armbruster. 1976. Secretion of adhesive polymers and attachment of marine bacteria to surfaces. In J. M. Sharpley and A. M. Kaplan (eds.). *Proceedings of the Third International Biodegradation Symposium.* Applied Science Publishers, Essex, England, pp. 433–442.

Dart, R. K., and R. J. Stretton. 1977. *Microbiological Aspects of Pollution Control.* Elsevier, Amsterdam.

Desrosier, N. W. 1970. *The Technology of Food Preservation.* Ed. 3. AVI, Westport, CT.

Diaz, L. F., G. M. Savage, L. L. Eggerth, and C. G. Goleuke. 1993. *Composting and Recycling: Municipal Solid Waste.* CRC Press, Boca Raton, FL.

DiSalvo, L. H., and G. W. Daniels. 1975. Observations on estuarine microfouling using the scanning electron microscope. *Microbial Ecology* 2:234–240.

Edberg, S. C., M. J. Allen, D. B. Smith, and the National Collaborative Study. 1988. Enumeration of total coliforms and *Escherichia coli* from drinking water: Comparison with the standard multiple tube fermentation method. *Applied and Environmental Microbiology* 54:1595–1601.

Edberg, S. C., M. J. Allen, D. B. Smith, and the National Collaborative Study. 1989a. Defined substrate method for the simultaneous detection of total coliforms and *Escherichia coli* from drinking water: Comparison with presence-absence techniques. *Applied and Environmental Microbiology* 55:1003–1008.

Edberg, S. C., M. J. Allen, D. B. Smith, and N. J. Kriz. 1989b. Enumeration of total coliforms and *Escherichia coli* from source water by the defined substrate technology. *Applied and Environmental Microbiology* 56:366–368.

Edmondson, W. T. 1970. Phosphorus, nitrogen and algae in Lake Washington after diversion of sewage. *Science* 169:690–691.

Edwards, J. D. 1995. *Industrial Wastewater Treatment: A Guidebook.* Lewis, Boca Raton, FL.

Epstein, E., G. B. Wilson, W. D. Burge, D. C. Mullen, and N. K. Enkiri. 1976. A forced aeration system for composting wastewater sludge. *Journal (Water Pollution Control Federation)* 48:655–694.

Finstein, M. S., F. C. Miller, P. F. Strom, S. T. MacGregor, and K. M. Psarianos. 1983. Composting ecosystem management for waste treatment. *Biological Technology* 1:347–353.

Finstein, M. S., and M. L. Morris. 1975. Microbiology of municipal solid waste composting. *Advances in Applied Microbiology* 19:113–151.

Finstein, M. S., and M. L. Morris. 1979. Anaerobic digestion and composting: Microbiological alternatives for sewage sludge treatment. *ASM News* 45:43–48.

Flint, K. P. 1982. Microbial ecology of domestic wastes. In R. G. Burns and J. H. Slater (eds.). *Experimental Microbial Ecology.* Blackwell, Oxford, England, pp. 575–590.

Frazier, W. D., and D. C. Westhoff. 1978. *Food Microbiology.* McGraw-Hill, New York.

Gebhardt, M. R., T. C. Daniel, E. E. Schweizer, and R. R. Allmaras. 1985. Conservation tillage. *Science* 230:625–630.

Godzing, T. J. 1972. The role of nitrogen in eutrophication processes. In R. Mitchell (ed.). *Water Pollution Microbiology.* Wiley-Interscience, New York, pp. 43–68.

Harteinstein, R. 1981. Sludge decomposition and stabilization. *Science* 212:743–749.

Hawkes, H. A. 1963. *The Ecology of Waste Water Treatment.* Pergamon Press, Oxford, England.

Hawkes, H. A. 1977. The ecology of activated sludge. In K.W.A. Chater and H. J. Somerville (eds.). *The Oil Industry and Microbial Ecosystems.* Institute of Petroleum, London, pp. 217–233.

Henze, M. 1995. *Wastewater Treatment: Biological and Chemical Processes.* Springer-Verlag, New York.

Hester, R. E., and R. M. Harrison. 1995. *Waste Treatment and Disposal.* CRC Press, Boca Raton, FL.

Hoadley, A. W., and B. J. Putka (eds.). 1977. *Bacterial Indicators/Health Hazards Associated with Water.* ASTM Technical Publication 635. American Society for Testing Materials, Philadelphia.

Howell, J. A. 1977. Alternative approaches to activated sludge and trickling filters. In K.W.A. Chater and J. H. Somerville (eds.). *The Oil Industry and Microbial Ecosystems.* Institute of Petroleum, London, pp. 199–216.

Hurst, A., and D. L. Collins-Thompson. 1979. Food as bacterial habitat. *Advances in Microbial Ecology* 3:79–134.

Hynes, H.B.N. 1960. *The Biology of Polluted Waters.* Liverpool University Press, Liverpool, England.

Imhoff, K., and G. M. Fair. 1956. *Sewage Treatment.* Ed 2. Wiley, New York.

Keeney, D. R., R. A. Herbert, and A. J. Holding. 1971. Microbiological aspects of the pollution of fresh waters with inorganic nutrients. In G. Sykes and F. A. Skinner (eds.). *Microbial Aspects of Pollution.* Academic Press, London, pp. 181–200.

LaRiviere, J.W.M. 1977. Microbial ecology of liquid waste treatment. *Advances in Microbial Ecology* 1:215–259.

Mack, W. N., J. P. Mack, and O. Ackerson. 1975. Microbial film development in a trickling filter. *Microbial Ecology* 2:215–226.

MacLeod, F. A., S. R. Guiot, and J. W. Costerton. 1990. Layered structure of bacterial aggregates produced in an upflow anaerobic sludge bed and filter reactor. *Applied and Environmental Microbiology* 56:1598–1607.

Mitchell, R. 1974. *Introduction to Environmental Microbiology.* Prentice-Hall, Englewood Cliffs, NJ.

National Academy of Sciences. 1969. *Eutrophication: Causes, Consequences, Correctives.* National Academy of Sciences, Washington, DC.

Organization for Economic Cooperation and Development. 1994. *Biotechnology for a Clean Environment.* Organization for Economic Development and Cooperation, Paris.

Olson, B. H. and L. A. Nagy. 1984. Microbiology of potable water. *Advances in Applied Microbiology* 30:73–132.

Palmisano, A. C., and M. A. Barlaz (eds.). 1996. *Microbiology of Solid Waste.* CRC Press, Boca Raton, FL.

Pavoni, J. L., J. E. Heer, Jr., and D. J. Hagerty. 1975. *Handbook of Solid Waste Disposal, Materials, and Energy Recovery.* Van Nostrand Reinhold Co., New York.

Phillips, R. E., R. L. Blevins, G. W. Thomas, W. W. Frye, and S. H. Phillips. 1980. No-tillage agriculture. *Science* 208:1108–1113.

Pike, E. B., and C. R. Curds. 1971. The microbial ecology of the activated sludge process. In G. Sykes and F. A. Skinner (eds.). *Microbial Aspects of Pollution.* Academic Press, London, pp. 123–147.

Pye, V. I., and R. Patrick. 1983. Ground water contamination in the United States. *Science* 221:713–718.

Rabold, J. G., C. W. Hoge, and D. R. Shlim. 1994. *Cyclospora* outbreak associated with chlorinated drinking water. *Lancet* 344:1360–1361.

Schroeder, E. D. 1977. *Water and Wastewater Treatment.* McGraw-Hill, New York.

Senior, E. 1995. *Microbiology of Landfill Sites.* CRC Press, Boca Raton, FL.

Shuval, H. J., and E. Katznelson. 1972. The detection of enteric viruses in the water environment. In R. Mitchell (ed.). *Water Pollution Microbiology.* Wiley-Interscience, New York, pp. 347–361.

Sieburth, J. M. 1975. *Microbial Seascapes.* University Park Press, Baltimore.

Slechta, A. F., and G. L. Culp. 1967. Water reclamation studies at the South Tahoe public utility district. *Journal (Water Pollution Control Federation)* 39:787–814.

Smith, E. M., C. P. Gerba, and J. L. Melnick. 1978. Role of sediment in persistence of enteroviruses in the estuarine environment. *Applied and Environmental Microbiology* 35:685–689.

Soave, R., and W. E. Johnson. 1995. *Cyclospora:* Conquest of an emerging pathogen. *Lancet* 345:667–668.

Sobsey, M. D., and B. H. Olson. 1983. Microbial agents of water-borne disease. In P. S. Berger and Y. Argaman (eds.). *Assessment of Microbiology and Turbidity Standards of Drinking Water.* U.S. Environmental Protection Agency, Washington, DC, pp. 1–69.

Suflita, J. M., C P. Gerba, R. K. Ham, A. C. Palmisano, W. L. Rathje, and J. A. Robinson. 1992. The world's largest landfill: A multidisciplinary investigation. *Environmental Science and Technology* 26:486–495.

Switzenbaum, M. S. 1983. Anaerobic treatment of wastewater: Recent developments. *ASM News* 49:532–536.

Thiele, J. H., and G. Zeikus. 1988. Control of interspecies electron flow during anaerobic digestion: Significance of formate transfer versus hydrogen transfer during syntrophic methanogenesis in flocs. *Applied and Environmental Microbiology* 54:20–29.

Toerien, D. F., A. Gerber, L. H. Hötter, and T. E. Cloete. 1990. Enhanced biological phosphorus removal in activated sludge systems. *Advances in Microbial Ecology* 11:173–230.

Toerien, D. F., and W.H.J. Hatting. 1969. Anaerobic digestion. Part I, The microbiology of anaerobic digestion. *Water Research* 3:385–416.

U.S. Department of Health, Education and Welfare. 1970. *Sanitary Landfill Facts.* SW 41s. Government Printing Office, Washington, DC.

Vaughan, J. M., E. F. Landry, M. Z. Thomas, F. J. Vicale, and W. F. Penello. 1979. Survey of human enterovirus occurrence in fresh and marine surface waters on Long Island. *Applied and Environmental Microbiology* 38:290–296.

Waksman, S. A. 1952. *Soil Microbiology.* Wiley, New York.

Warren, C. E. 1971. *Biology and Water Pollution Control.* Saunders, Philadelphia.

Wilde, D. B., and D. L. Baere. 1989. Experiences on the recycling of municipal solid waste to energy and compost. Paper presented at the Fifth International Conference on Solid Waste Management and Secondary Materials, 5–8 December, Philadelphia.

Wolf, H. W. 1972. The coliform count as a measure of water quality. In R. Mitchell (ed.). *Water Pollution Microbiology.* Wiley-Interscience, New York, pp. 333–345.

Wolfe, R. L., N. R. Ward, and B. H. Olson. 1984. Inorganic chloramines as drinking water disinfectants: A review. *Journal of the American Water Works Association* 76:74–88.

Wu, W. M., R. F. Hickey, and J. G. Zeikus. 1991. Characterization of metabolic performance of methanogenic granules treating brewery wastewater: Role of sulfate-reducing bacteria. *Applied and Environmental Microbiology* 57:3438–3449.

Young, P. 1996. Safe drinking water: A call for global action. *ASM News* 62:349–352.

Zinder, S. H. 1984. Microbiology of anaerobic conversion of organic wastes to methane: Recent developments. *ASM News* 50:294–298.

# Microbial Interactions with Xenobiotic and Inorganic Pollutants

*The unprecedented population increase and industrial development during the twentieth century has not only increased conventional solid and liquid waste pollutants to critical levels but produced a range of previously unknown pollution problems for which society was unprepared. For various purposes, an ingenious chemical industry now manufactures many xenobiotic compounds that greatly differ in their structure from natural organics. Some of these xenobiotic halosubstituted and nitrosubstituted organics such as propellants, refrigerants, solvents, PCBs, plastics, detergents, explosives, and pesticides, are completely resistant (recalcitrant) to biodegradation. Others degrade only slowly in a cometabolic rather than substrate utilization mode, or give rise to bound and polymeric residues of environmental concern. Some of the more recalcitrant xenobiotics are subject to biomagnification in the food web that begins with microorganisms, inflicting serious ecological damage on the most vulnerable top-level carnivores. Petroleum hydrocarbons, although not xenobiotic, by their large-scale use and accidental release have occasionally inflicted serious environmental damage. As xenobiotics may be viewed as substituted hydrocarbons, the common biodegradation pathways of aliphatic, alicyclic, and aromatic hydrocarbons are of interest; how certain substituents block these biodegradation pathways helps explain the structural reasons for recalcitrance of certain xenobiotics.*

*Inorganic compounds can become pollutants due to human activities, and as with xenobiotics the pollution may be biomagnified. Strip mining exposes large amounts of reduced sulfide minerals, which causes acid mine drainage problems. Excessive use of agricultural fertilizers causes atmospheric and groundwater pollution problems and eutrophication of surface waters. Microorganisms methylate and thereby increase the toxicity of certain heavy metals such as mercury and tin. Microorganisms also methylate and thus mobilize arsenic and selenium. Microbial cells have a tendency to accumulate heavy metals and radionuclides, thereby introducing these pollutants into food webs with destructive consequences. A scientific understanding of these complex phenomena, and of the roles microorganisms play in them, is essential for preventing or controlling any ecological damage xenobiotic pollutants may cause.*

## PERSISTENCE AND BIOMAGNIFICATION OF XENOBIOTIC MOLECULES

Given favorable environmental conditions, all natural organic compounds degrade. Although this hypothesis has never been put to a rigorous and exhaustive test, its truth appears self-evident, as there are no large-scale accumulations of natural organic substances. If any organic compound produced in the ecosphere were inherently resistant to recycling, huge deposits of this material would have accumulated throughout the geological ages. This clearly has not been the case; substantial organic deposits, such as of fossil fuels, accumulate only under conditions adverse to biodegradation.

Alexander (1965) formalized this general understanding of the biodegradative capacity of microorganisms as the principle of microbial infallibility, expressing the empirical observation that no natural organic compound is totally resistant to biodegradation provided that environmental conditions are favorable. This should hardly be surprising. The evolution of various biopolymers was slow and gradual, measured in millions and billions of years, allowing time for a parallel evolution of microbial catabolism appropriate for every newly available substrate. In contrast, the explosive development of synthetic organic chemistry during the last century has led to the large-scale production of a bewildering variety of organic compounds that, either by design or by accident, eventually wind up in the environment. Once there, their fates vary. Most synthetic compounds have natural counterparts or are sufficiently similar to naturally occurring compounds to be subject to microbial metabolism (Dagley 1975). Others are xenobiotic, having molecular structures and chemical bond sequences not recognized by existing degradative enzymes. These resist biodegradation or are metabolized incompletely, with the result that some xenobiotic compounds accumulate in the environment. Human ingenuity outpaced microbial evolution, and the fallibility of the taken-for-granted "biological incinerators" was exposed.

One can imagine many reasons for a xenobiotic organic compound proving recalcitrant (totally resistant) to biodegradation (Alexander 1981). Unusual substitutions (as with chlorine and other halogens), unusual bonds or bond sequences (such as in tertiary and quaternary carbon atoms), highly condensed aromatic rings, and excessive molecular size (in the case of polyethylene and other plastics) are some of the common reasons for recalcitrance. Other more subtle reasons include the failure of a compound to induce the synthesis of degrading enzymes, even though it may be susceptible to their action. Failure of the compound to enter the microbial cell for lack of suitable permeases, unavailability of the compound due to insolubility or adsorption phenomena, and excessive toxicity of the parent compound or its metabolic products all could contribute to lack of degradation.

The term *biodegradation* has been used to describe transformations of every type, including those that yield products more complex than the starting material as well as those responsible for the complete oxidation of organic compounds to $CO_2$, $H_2O$, $NO_3^-$, and other inorganic components. On occasion, microbial transformations result in residues that are more stable than the parent compound, yet this phenomenon is sometimes called degradation because the parent compound disappears. This ambiguous terminology has proven confusing to legislators and interested lay people alike, who, for example, would hear one expert testify that the insecticide DDT is degradable, as it is converted in part to DDD, DDE, and other closely related compounds (Wedemeyer 1967) (Figure 13.1). Another expert would insist that DDT is persistent, because the basic carbon skeleton remains unaltered. To preclude misunderstanding, the term *mineralization* has been proposed for describing the ultimate degradation and recycling of an organic molecule to its mineral constituents.

What happens if a persistent organic compound is introduced into the ecosphere? Particle size and solubility characteristics, among other factors, influence its mode and rate of travel, but chances are good that it will be distributed to places far removed from its original application site. The fallout from atmospheric nuclear tests has dramatized the capacity of atmospheric forces to distribute chemicals from point sources globally (Hanson 1967). The experience with

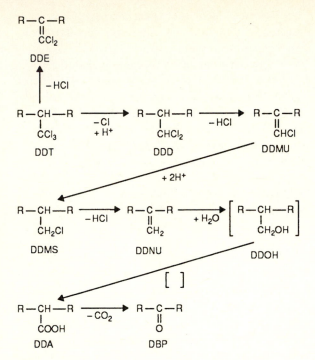

**Figure 13.1**

Transformations of the insecticide DDT by *Enterobacter (Aerobacter) aerogenes.* All transformations are restricted to the $CCl_3$ moiety. Anaerobic conditions favor dechlorination steps. The final product DBP is still recalcitrant and biologically active.

R = a *p*-chlorophenyl moiety;
DDT = 1,1,1-trichloro-2,2-*bis*(*p*-chlorophenyl) ethane;
DDE = 1,1-dichloro-2,2-*bis*(*p*-chlorophenyl) ethylene;
DDD = 1,1-dichloro-2,2-*bis*(*p*-chlorophenyl) ethane;
DDMU = 1-chloro-2,2-*bis*(*p*-chlorophenyl) ethylene;
DDMS = 1-chloro-2,2-*bis*(*p*-chlorophenyl) ethane;
DDNU = *unsym-bis*(*p*-chlorophenyl) ethylene;
DDOH = 2,2-*bis*(*p*-chlorophenyl) ethanol;
DDA = 2,2-*bis*(*p*-chlorophenyl) acetate;
DBP = 4,4′-dichlorobenzophenone.
(Source: Wedemeyer 1967. Reprinted by permission of American Society for Microbiology.)

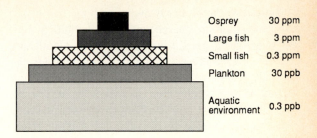

**Figure 13.2**

Biomagnification of DDT. Minute concentrations of dissolved DDT move by physical partitioning into plankton. Further concentration of the pollutant takes place through the shrinkage of biomass between successive trophic levels. DDT concentrations are idealized and although typical, do not represent actual analytical data.

chlorinated hydrocarbon insecticides has been similar; they have been detected in remote and even Arctic regions, thousands of miles removed from the nearest possible application site (Cade et al. 1971). It is important, therefore, to keep in mind that assessing the effect of a persistent organic chemical on the environment to which it is directly applied is insufficient.

The production and release of persistent organic chemicals into the environment has a relatively short history. Their distribution, however, is widespread (National Research Council 1972; Higgins and Burns 1975). Distribution tends to dilute; organochlorines in environments only indirectly exposed often are present in the low parts per billion (ppb) range. Why should such low concentrations still cause concern? Because of a phenomenon called biological magnification, or biomagnification for short. To be subject to this phenomenon, the pollutant must be both persistent and lipophilic (Gosset et al. 1983). Because of their lipophilic character, minute dissolved amounts of these substances are partitioned from the surrounding water into the lipids of both procaryotic and eucaryotic microorganisms (Figure 13.2). Concentrations in their cells, compared to the surrounding medium, may increase by one to three orders of magnitude. Members of the next higher trophic level then ingest the microorganisms. Only 10–15% of the biomass is transferred to the higher trophic level, the rest dissipated in respiration, but the persistent lipophilic pollutant is neither degraded nor excreted to a significant extent, and so is preserved practically without loss in the smaller biomass of the second trophic level. Consequently, its concentration increases by almost an order of magnitude. The same thing occurs at successively higher trophic levels. The top trophic level, composed of birds of prey, mammalian carnivores, and large predatory fish, may carry a body burden of the environmental pollutant that exceeds the environmental concentration by a factor of $10^4$–$10^6$.

If the pollutant is a biologically active substance, such as a pesticide, at such levels it may cause death or serious debilitation of the affected organism. Chlorinated hydrocarbons, including DDT, were implicated in the death or reproductive failure of various birds of prey (Cade et al. 1971). In the case of local application, even a relatively short food chain such as sprayed vegetation → earthworm → robin can be destructive to the bird. We humans derive our food from various trophic levels and are in a less exposed position than a top-level carnivore. Nevertheless, at the time of unrestricted DDT use, the average individual in the United States with no occupational exposure carried a body burden of 4–6 ppm DDT and its derivatives. Although this amount was not considered acutely dangerous, the trend for an increasing contamination of the higher trophic levels of the ecosphere became sufficiently clear and led to the ban on the use of DDT in the United States and most other developed countries for all but emergency situations.

## Recalcitrant Halocarbons

Many xenobiotic pollutants that have proven recalcitrant to microbial attack are halocarbons. The carbon-halogen bond is highly stable. Cleavage of this bond is not exothermic but rather requires a substantial energy input; it is an endothermic reaction. As a consequence, halocarbons are chemically and biologically very stable. Stability is desirable in some of these products, but the same property causes persistence and environmental problems. The energetics of their degradation are such that there is little prospect for microorganisms ever to evolve a capability for utilization of extensively halogenated carbon compounds as growth substrates, though some cometabolism and photodegradation may occur.

Important groups of halocarbons include the $C_1$–$C_2$ haloalkyl propellants, solvents and refrigerants, haloaromatics such as chlorobenzenes, chlorophenols and chlorobenzoates, polychlorinated or polybrominated biphenyls and triphenyls, chlorodibenzodioxins, and chlorodibenzofurans. Some organochlorine insecticides are also highly recalcitrant.

**Haloalkyl Propellants and Solvents** Haloalkyl propellants and solvents are $C_1$–$C_2$ alkanes in which all or nearly all hydrogen atoms have been replaced by fluorine-chlorine combinations. They serve as solvents and aerosol propellants in spray cans for such things as cosmetics, paint, and insecticides and as the working fluid in the condensor units of air conditioners and refrigerators. Most commonly used have been the $CCl_3F$ and $CCl_2F_2$ freons, designated by the codes F-11 and F-12, respectively. Dichloromethane, chloroform, carbon tetrachloride, dichloro-, trichloro- and tetrachloroethenes (or -ethylenes) are important industrial and cleaning solvents. Spilled halocarbon propellants and solvents have seriously contaminated groundwater. Being inert and quite volatile, some of these components rise to the stratosphere upon release, depleting Earth's protective ozone layer by photochemical interactions (Molina and Rowland 1974; National Research Council 1976). Partial destruction of the ozone layer would result in increased UV radiation on the surface of Earth, causing an increased incidence of skin cancer and mutagenesis. Although volatile halocarbons represent only one of several ozone depletion mechanisms, legislation has been enacted in the United States and other developed countries to phase out halocarbons as aerosol propellants. Intensive research efforts are under way to find a suitable substitute for halocarbons as refrigerants, but their use as coolants will continue for some time to come. Some effort is being made to extract and reuse the refrigerant fluids from defunct cooling units.

At the same time, a new generation of refrigerants is gradually replacing the freons in refrigeration and air conditioning units specifically modified to accommodate these new working fluids. These $C_2$-based halocarbons are no more biodegradable than freons, but they contain chlorine rather than fluorine substituents. They are photochemically less destructive for the ozone layer than the classic freons.

Dehalogenation of organic compounds is thermodynamically favored under anaerobic conditions; microorganisms have been found that produce dehalogenases and carry out reductive dehalogenation (Suflita et al. 1982). Sulfate-reducing bacteria transform tetrachloroethene to trichloroethene and *cis*-1,2-dichloroethene by anaerobic dehalogenation (Bagley and Gossett 1990). The fully chlorinated but unsaturated tetrachloroethene (perchloroethene, PCE) is subject to stepwise dechlorination to the toxic product vinyl chloride and eventually ethene (Mohn and Tiedje 1992) (Figure 13.3). Such PCE degradation has been demonstrated in a methanogenic bacterial consortium growing on acetate in an anaerobic reactor (Vogel and McCarty 1985; Galli and McCarty 1989). Aerobically, dichloromethane was shown to serve as the only carbon source for a pseudomonad, and dichloroethane served as substrate for a microbial consortium (Stucki et al. 1981). Extensive aerobic degradation of trichloroethene (TCE), a widely distributed halocarbon pollutant, by a methane-utilizing microbial consortium has been demonstrated (Fogel et al. 1986; Little et al. 1988). The low specificity of methane monooxygenase allows the conversion of TCE to TCE epoxide, which subsequently spontaneously hydrolyzes to polar products (formic, glyoxylic, and dichloroacetic acids) utilizable by microorganisms (Gibson et al. 1995) (Figure 13.4). As a curious side product, small amounts of chloral ($Cl_3C \cdot CHO$) are also formed, requiring a carbon-to-carbon transfer of one of the Cl atoms. TCE is also attached by toluene dioxygenase of *Pseudomonas* (Gibson et al. 1995). An unstable intermediate with two oxygen atoms spontaneously hydrolyzes to formic and glyoxylic acids. The described two mono- and dioxygenase systems fail to cometabolize PCE. *Methylococcus capsulatus* was reported to convert chloro- and bromomethane to formaldehyde, dichloromethane to CO, and trichloromethane to $CO_2$ while growing on methane (Dalton and Stirling 1982). Thus, methanotrophic bacteria show some promise for bioremediation of halocarbon-polluted aquifers.

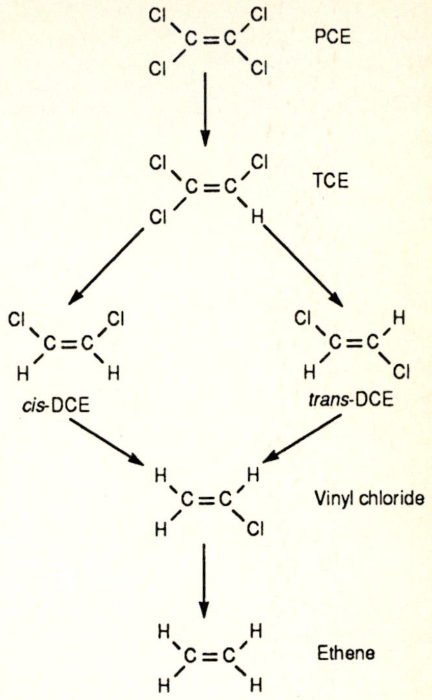

**Figure 13.3**
Sequential anaerobic dechlorination (hydrogenolysis) of perchloroethene (PCE) by methanogenic consortia in the presence of acetate or methanol.

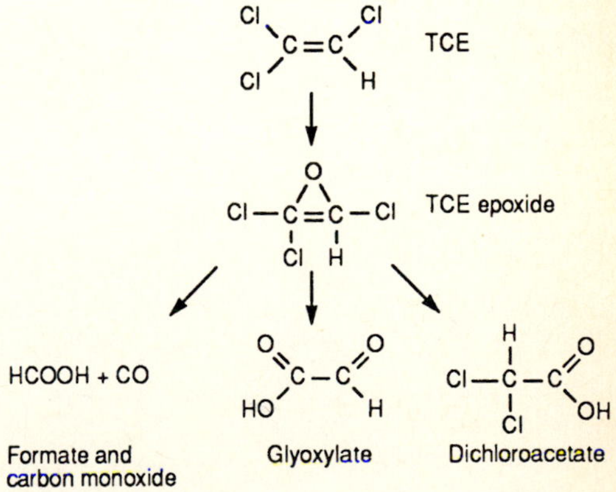

**Figure 13.4**
Aerobic cometabolism of trichloroethene (TCE) by methanotrophic microorganisms. The key reaction is the formation of TCE epoxide by methane monooxygenase. The methanotrophs do not utilize the products but other microbes complete the degradation.

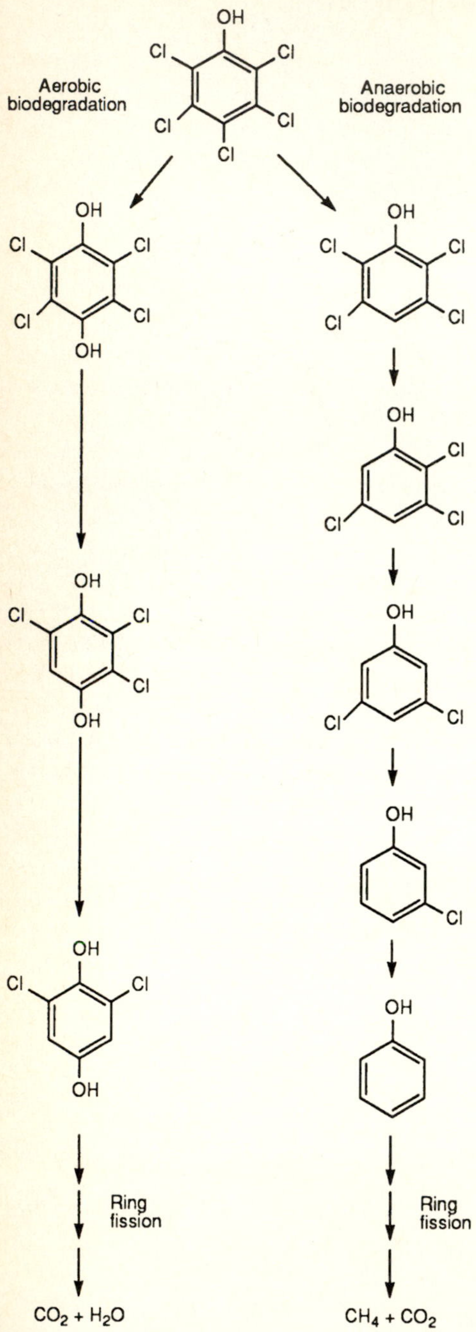

**Figure 13.5**
Aerobic and anaerobic biodegradation of pentachlorophenol (PCP).

**Halobenzenes, Halophenols, and Halobenzoates**
Chlorobenzenes are extensively used as industrial solvents. With chlorobenzenes and other haloaromatics, it is a common trait that their aerobic biodegradability decreases with the number of halosubstituents, but the same extensively halogenated aromatics are dechlorinated under anaerobic conditions with relative ease. As the halosubstituents are sequentially removed, the products are less and less likely to be dehalogenated further, and monochlorobenzene is not dechlorinated anaerobically (Mohn and Tiedje 1992). Hexachlorobenzene is dechlorinated relatively rapidly to 1,3,5-trichlorobenzene in anaerobic sewage sludge, but further dechlorination to 1,4-dichloro- and monochlorobenzenes is slow and incomplete. In contrast, mono- and dichlorobenzenes are degraded aerobically with relative ease by various *Pseudomonas* and *Alcaligenes* strains that use dioxygenases to produce chlorocatechols. The aerobic biodegradation of trichloro- and tetrachlorobenzenes is more difficult, but some *Pseudomonas* strains with such capabilities were isolated (Sander et al. 1991).

Chlorophenols, particularly the highly chlorinated pentachlorophenol (PCP), are used as preservatives for wood and canvas. Other chlorophenols are used in the synthesis of pesticides, resins, dyes, and pharmaceuticals. In addition to being difficult to degrade, these products also have high toxicity to microorganisms, as indicated by their use as preservatives. Nevertheless, in appropriately low concentrations, various microorganisms are capable of degrading chlorophenols under both aerobic and anaerobic conditions (Chaudhry and Chapalamadugu 1991). The early steps of PCP dechlorination are shown in Figure 13.5. Aerobically, PCP is converted by a monooxygenase to tetrachlorohydroquinone through the oxidative elimination of the chlorine *para* to the phenolic hydroxyl. A *Flavobacterium sp.* and *Mycobacterium chlorophenolicum* were described to catalyze this reaction. Stepwise dechlorination to 2,5-dichlorohydroquinone is followed by ring opening. Anaerobically, PCP is reductively dechlorinated stepwise to phenol. Phenol can be metabolized further anaerobically to methane and $CO_2$.

Although both haloalkyl and haloaryl compounds may be reductively dehalogenated under anaerobic conditions, there are notable differences in the two processes. Haloalkanes are dehalogenated by a wide spectrum of anaerobic, facultatively anaerobic, and even microaerophilic microorganisms. The reactions appear to be coincidental, with no obvious benefit to the dehalogenating microorganism. Anaerobic degradations of chlorophenols and chlorobenzoates are usually performed by complex methanogenic or sulfidogenic microbial consortia and in the presence of additional carbon sources, yet the dechlorinations are quite substrate-specific. Recently, it was possible to obtain in pure culture an aryl dehalogenating microorganism *Desulfomonile tiedjei* (Mohn and Tiedje 1992; Suflita and Townsend 1995). The organism is a strictly anaerobic rod-shaped sulfidogen with a peculiar collar structure. It removes chloro substituents from the *meta* position of chlorobenzoates. It also dehalogenates some highly chlorinated phenols and PCE. *D. tiedjei* appears to use the chloro substituents as electron acceptors and derives energy from the dechlorination reactions. Chloro-, bromo-, and iodo- but not fluoro-substituents can also be removed by *D. tiedjei*. Sulfate appears to inhibit the dehalogenation reactions competitively. *D. tiedjei* appears to form complex and as yet incompletely understood syntrophic relationships with methanogens and perhaps other strict anaerobes.

## Recalcitrant Nitroaromatic Compounds

Nitroaromatics are common military explosives, such as trinitrotoluene (TNT), solvents, such as nitrobenzene, and pesticides, such as nitrophenols. Their manufacture and disposal left many sites polluted. The toxicity and mutagenicity of these residues are high. Similar to halogen substituents, nitro-substitution of aromatic rings has a strong negative effect on biodegradability. Both halogen and nitro-substituents are electron-withdrawing and tend to deactivate the aromatic ring. Compounds with several nitro-substituents tend to be recalcitrant (Hallas and Alexander 1983). Whereas oxidative transformations on haloaromatics are not favored thermodynamically (they burn poorly or not at all), nitroaromatics have high chemical energy potentials, exemplified by TNT. However, to date no efficient metabolic pathways have evolved to release this potential energy for microbial growth. The biodegradation of nitroaromatic compounds tends to be slow, and often leads to bound or polymerized residues in soils and sediments. Similarly to chloroaromatics, extensively nitro-substituted aromatics are more easily transformed under reductive than under oxidative conditions. As an example of a mononitroaromatic compound, the oxidative and the reductive pathways of nitrobenzene biodegradation are shown in Figure 13.6 (Spain 1995). In the oxidative pathway, an attack by a dioxygenase converts nitrobenzene to a diol and $NO_2^-$ is spontaneously released during rearrangement to catechol. Subsequently, the catechol ring is opened by *meta*-cleavage (see later in this chapter). The more complicated reductive pathway appears to be energetically more favorable and does not require strict anaerobic conditions to occur. In this more common pathway, the nitro group is stepwise reduced through nitrosobenzene to phenylhydroxylamine. The latter undergoes rearrangement by a mutase to 2-aminophenol. The 2-aminophenol ring is subsequently oxidatively opened and the nitrogen is eliminated as ammonium during conversion to oxalocrotonate. In contrast, for the military explosive TNT there appears to be no efficient microbial biodegradation pathway (Spain 1995). Under anaerobic and microaerophilic conditions, the nitro groups of TNT are reduced one by one to amino groups, but each subsequent reduction is slower and less complete (Figure 13.7). If conditions are shifted to aerobic, instead of ring cleavage, the partially reduced intermediates form very complex and mutagenic azo condensation products.

## Polychlorinated Biphenyls and Dioxins

Polychlorinated biphenyls (PCBs) are mixtures of biphenyls with one to ten chlorine atoms per molecule (Figure 13.8). They are oily fluids with high boiling points, great chemical resistance, low electrical conductivity, and high refractive index. Because of these properties, they have been used as plasticizers in polyvinyl polymers, as insulators-coolants in trans-

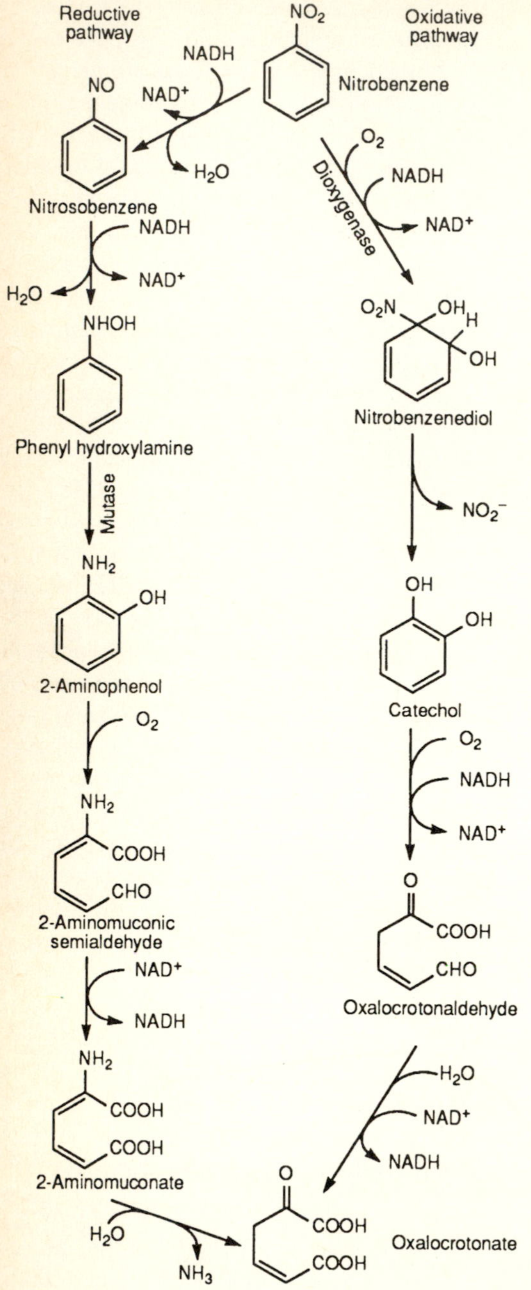

**Figure 13.6**
Oxidative and reductive pathways of nitrobenzene biodegradation, catalyzed by *Comamonas* sp. and *Pseudomonas pseudoalcaligenes,* respectively.

formers, and as heat-exchange fluids in general. Minor uses involve inks, paints, sealants, insulators, flame retardants, and, as microbiologists should know, microscope immersion oils. The chemical inertness of PCBs is paralleled by their great biological stability, which increases with the degree of their chlorination.

The structure of PCBs is similar in some ways to that of DDT, and so is their behavior in the environment in regard to persistence and potential for biological magnification. Whereas most of the enumerated uses of PCBs would not seem to be conducive to widespread environmental contamination, PCB residues have in fact been detected in a large percentage of random environmental samples, and they accumulate in higher-trophic-level animals (Gustafson 1970; National Research Council 1979).

Concentrations of PCB over 1 ppm have been detected in one-third of the sampled U.S. population with no known occupational exposure. In some freshwater habitats, older individuals of predatory fish, such as trout and salmon, accumulate 20–30 ppm of PCBs, and predatory and fish-eating birds were found to contain, on occasion, several hundred ppm of PCBs. In 1968, PCB-contaminated cooking oil, caused by a leaky heat exchanger, poisoned nearly a thousand people in Japan; the main symptoms were liver damage and a severe skin condition called chloracne. In this case, the victims had consumed several grams of the substance (Fujiwara 1975). Low PCB intakes from general environmental contamination are not known to harm humans or most other mammals, but along with chlorinated hydrocarbon insecticides, PCBs were implicated in eggshell thinning and reproductive failure of some predatory and fish-eating birds. Reproductive failure in cultured mink was caused by the approximately 5 ppm PCB content of their fish-based feed, and some species of fish, shrimp, and algae were affected by PCB concentrations in the low ppb range. Besides having acute effects, PCBs—and some other chlorinated hydrocarbons, including DDT—are under suspicion of being potential human carcinogens, although this point is still controversial.

The various degrees of chlorination and the high number of isomers render the positive identification and quantitative measurement of PCBs a difficult ana-

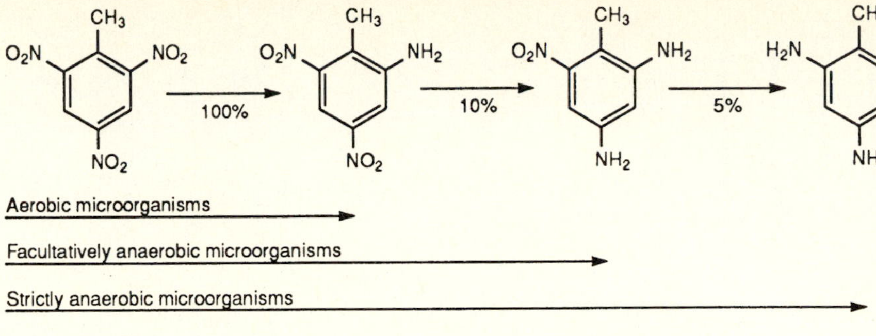

**Figure 13.7**
Reductive transformations of trinitrotoluene (TNT). Each reductive step is less complete than the previous one. The first reduction may be catalyzed even by aerobic microbes, the last one only by strict anaerobes. The reduction sequence does not lead to mineralization but rather to polymerization or binding of the residues. (Source: Spain 1995.)

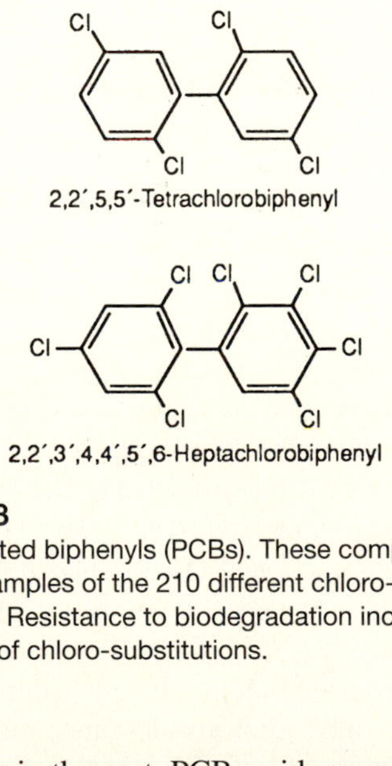

2,2′,5,5′-Tetrachlorobiphenyl

2,2′,3′,4,4′,5′,6-Heptachlorobiphenyl

**Figure 13.8**
Polychlorinated biphenyls (PCBs). These compounds are only two examples of the 210 different chloro-substitution possibilities. Resistance to biodegradation increases with the number of chloro-substitutions.

lytical task; in the past, PCB residues were frequently confused with those of chlorinated hydrocarbon insecticides. Photochemical conversion of DDT to PCBs may contribute to the widespread occurrence of these environmental contaminants (Maugh 1973).

Biphenyl is able to serve some microorganisms as their only source of carbon and energy, and mono-, di-, tri-, and tetrachlorobiphenyls are, to some degree,

subject to biodegradation, as evidenced by formation of hydroxylated metabolites (Ahmed and Focht 1973; Massé et al. 1984; Safe 1984). In the more extensively chlorinated biphenyls, the substituents prevent ring hydroxylation; these highly chlorinated analogs cause the most concern with respect to persistence and environmental contamination. Voluntary curbs by manufacturers coupled with government regulations have removed PCBs from food-processing equipment and food-packaging material. Disposable items using PCBs as plasticizers have been phased out in an effort to reduce the amount of contaminating PCBs. As of 1978, the use and discharge of PCBs in the United States came under a complete government ban. Continuing sources of PCB pollution, however, are previously contaminated sediments, landfills, and older electric transformers.

Although PCBs are relatively resistant to biodegradation, a number of microorganisms have been isolated that transform them (Chaudhry and Chapalamadugu 1991). Aerobic biodegradation of PCBs is carried out by the white rot fungus *Phanerochaete* (Bumpus 1989), by *Acinetobacter* (Adriaens and Focht 1990), and by *Alcaligenes* (Bedard et al. 1987), and anaerobically by reductive dehalogenation (Quensen et al. 1988). Degradation of PCBs typically is by cometabolism and is enhanced by the addition of

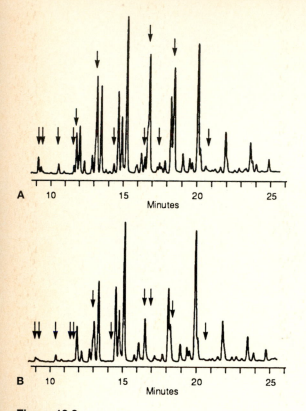

**Figure 13.9**

Biodegradation of arochlor PCBs. (A) undegraded standard; (B) degraded sample. Each peak in the gas chromatographic tracings represents a specific PCB congener. The height of each peak represents the concentration of that congener. The arrows point to congeners that have been biodegraded. (Source: Kohler et al. 1988.)

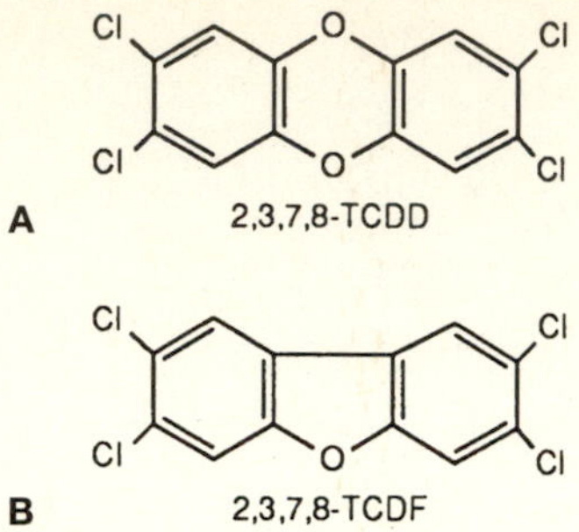

**Figure 13.10**

(A) 2,3,7,8-tetrachlorodibenzodioxin (TCDD), (B) 2,3,7,8-tetrachlorodibenzofuran, contaminants and/or thermal degradation products of PCBs and certain phenoxyalkanoic acid herbicides. These and related chlorodibenzodioxins and chlorodibenzofurans are extremely toxic and highly resistant to biodegradation.

less chlorinated analogs such as dichlorobiphenyl (Adriaens et al. 1989; Novick and Alexander 1985). Extensive degradation of some PCB congeners has been found in soils and aquatic waters and sediments (Bedard et al. 1987; Brown et al. 1987; Novick and Alexander 1985; Bedard and Quensen 1995) (Figure 13.9). The specific congeners are differentially degraded, and various PCB products, according to their composition, exhibit different degrees of susceptibility to biodegradative transformations. Again, the more extensively chlorinated PCBs are more likely to be dechlorinated than the less chlorinated ones. *Meta* and *para* positions are dechlorinated in preference to *ortho* positions. Nevertheless, frustratingly little is yet known about the microorganisms and mechanisms involved in anaerobic PCB dechlorination. Besides providing anaerobic conditions, little can be done to specifically stimulate the PCB dechlorination process, and much basic research remains to be done before more specific bioremediation strategies can be formulated (Bedard and Quensen 1995).

Frequent contaminants of PCBs and of the herbicide 2,4,5-T, to be discussed later in this chapter, are 2,3,7,8-tetrachlorodibenzodioxin (TCDD), related chlorodibenzodioxins, and chlorodibenzofurans (Figure 13.10). Some of these contaminants arise during manufacture, others are formed through thermal degradation of the chlorophenols and chlorobiphenyls. Not only high recalcitrance but also an unusually high degree of acute and chronic toxicity characterize TCDD and related compounds. Contamination as low as in the ppb range is considered hazardous to human health. Human settlements that became contaminated with TCDD and related substances—as occurred in Times Beach, Missouri, in the United States through spreading of contaminated waste oil and in Soveso in Italy by the explosion of a

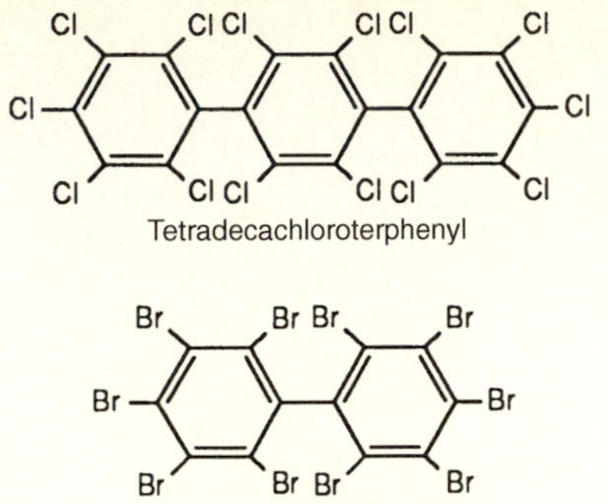

**Figure 13.11**
Examples of polychlorinated terphenyls and polybrominated biphenyls. Commercial mixtures contain numerous partially halogenated homologues. The extensive halogenation of these compounds results in high resistance to biodegradation.

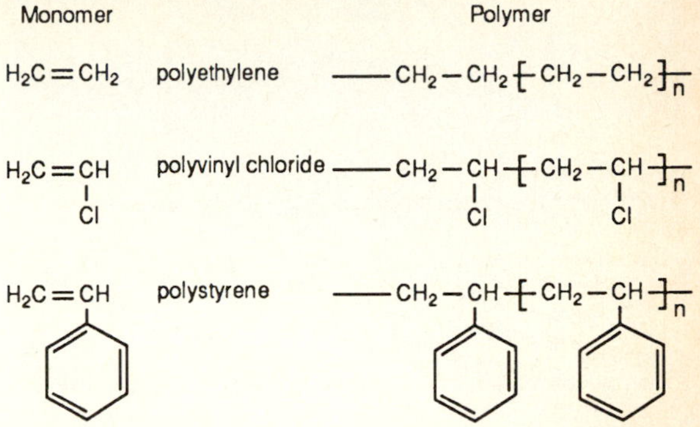

**Figure 13.12**
Chemical structure of some plastic materials of importance in environmental contamination. Left: Monomeric starting material. Right: Polymer chain with repeating unit shown in brackets. Excessive molecular weight and a lack of depolymerizing exoenzymes make these polymers virtually nonbiodegradable. Monomers or short polymer chain fragments of the same materials tend to be biodegradable.

chemical reactor—were evacuated and closed indefinitely (Tucker et al. 1983). Bumpus et al. (1985) reported oxidation of TCDD and some other chlorinated hydrocarbon pollutants by the lignin-degrading basidiomycete *Phanerochaete chrysosporium*. The amounts of $^{14}CO_2$ evolved from the radiolabeled test substrates ranged only between 1% and 4% and may not have been in excess of the radiochemical impurities of the test substances. Therefore, the biodegradability of TCDD continues to be doubtful.

Polybrominated biphenyls (PBBs), which are used as flame retardants, and polychlorinated terphenyls (PCTs), which have three attached phenyl rings and are employed as plasticizers (Figure 13.11), have pollution potentials similar to PCBs. To date, they have been manufactured on a much smaller scale than PCBs. Their behavior as environmental contaminants received little attention until an unfortunate incident in 1976, when, in a chemical plant that manufactured both PBB flame retardants and cattle feed additives, large amounts of cattle feed were inadvertently mixed with PBBs and fed to dairy cows in Michigan. The incident necessitated the destruction of many dairy herds, causing great economic losses. Although no human fatalities could be proven, large numbers of people were contaminated with PBBs through the dairy products before the cause was traced and eliminated. Although the incident was clearly a case of human error, it has served as a reminder of the long residence time and high biomagnification potential of PBBs as environmental pollutants.

## Synthetic Polymers

Synthetic polymers are easily molded into complex shapes, have high chemical resistance, and are more-or-less elastic. Some can be formed into fibers or thin, transparent films. These properties have made them popular in the manufacture of garments, durable and disposable goods, and packaging materials. About 50 million metric tons per year of plastics are produced in the United States (Thayer 1990). Disposable goods and packaging material, about one-third of the total plastic production, have the largest environmental impact. More than 90% of the plastic material in municipal garbage consists of polyethylene, polyvinyl chloride, and polystyrene, in roughly equal proportions (Figure 13.12).

**Figure 13.13**
Photograph of film-mulched agricultural field. (Source: B. L. Pollack; New Jersey Agricultural Experiment Station.)

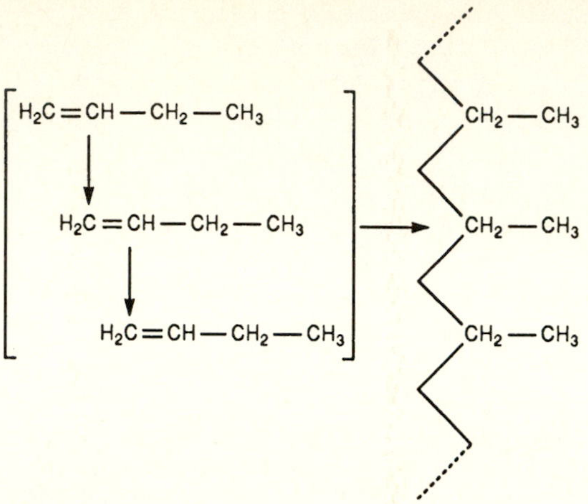

**Figure 13.14**
Chemical structure of a polybutene film-mulch polymer, which is degradable by a combined photodegradation-biodegradation process. Left: Monomeric precursor. Right: Polybutene polymer. Photochemical reactions break the polymer chain at the susceptible tertiary carbon, allowing a subsequent biodegradative attack on the resulting chain fragments. (Source: Reich and Bartha 1977. Reprinted by permission, copyright Williams and Wilkins.)

Typically, these materials have molecular weights ranging from several thousand to 150,000 and appear to resist biodegradation indefinitely. Older reports on plastic biodegradation involve, on closer scrutiny, only the degradation of the plasticizers, the additives designed to render the plastic pliable. Frequently, plasticizers are esters of long-chain fatty acids and alcohols, such as dioctyl adipate, or esters of phthalic acid, such as dioctyl phthalate. Their biodegradation renders the material brittle, but the polymer structure is not affected. The contention that the basic polymer structures are not subject to biodegradation was originally based on relatively crude weight-loss measurements but recently has been confirmed by highly sensitive measurements using $^{14}C$-labeled polymers. Resistance to biodegradation seems to be associated here with excessive molecular size. Biodegradation of long-chain $C_{30}$ and higher $n$-alkanes declines with increasing molecular weight, and $n$-alkanes in excess of a molecular weight of 550–600 become refractory to biodegradation. If the molecular size of polyethylene is reduced to a molecular weight under 500, by pyrolysis, for example, the fragments are susceptible to biodegradation.

Plastic in the environment has been regarded as more of an aesthetic nuisance than a hazard because the material is biologically inert. Reports about large numbers of floating plastic spherules in the ocean and their ingestion by small fish with consequent intestinal blockage, however, indicate that even inert materials are not necessarily innocuous (Carpenter 1972). Remains of plastic nets and ties also ensnare and destroy wildlife.

A new agricultural practice involving plastics, the so-called film-mulching technique (Figure 13.13), lends special urgency to the development of biodegradable plastic film material. This practice involves covering fields with plastic film in order to control weeds and conserve moisture. It is impractical to re-use or even to collect the film at the end of the growing season; a large accumulation of plastic fragments in the field is equally undesirable. Because polyethylene, polybutene, and other polyolefins are susceptible to photochemical degradation, it is possible to devise materials that sustain sufficient photochemical damage during a growing season to become susceptible to subsequent microbial degradation (Reich and Bartha 1977) (Figure 13.14). The resistance of the material to various irradiation levels can be adjusted by appropriate additions of antioxidants.

Tests have shown that the native polymer was resistant to biodegradation, but the irradiated material became susceptible to it.

Responding to pressure from environmental groups and legislators, several manufacturers started to sell products stamped "environmentally friendly" or "degradable." A lack of clear standards and definitions made it difficult to challenge these somewhat misleading claims. Some of these materials contain photosensitizers or pro-oxidants (oxidation catalysts), alone or in combination with 3–15% modified starch (Evans and Sikdar 1990; Thayer 1990). Prolonged sun irradiation (several weeks to several months) causes breaks in the large polymer molecules, resulting in brittleness and disintegration. Extensive photodamage may prepare the molecules for limited microbial degradation (Lee and Levy 1991). Without photodamage, only the accessible starch granules are degraded, leading to some porosity and brittleness but no further degradation (Lee and Levy 1991; Krupp and Jewell 1992; Yabannavar and Bartha 1993, 1994).

Truly biodegradable poly-β-hydroxyalkanoates are produced by *Alcaligenes eutrophus, Bacillus cereus,* and various pseudomonads (Brandl et al. 1988; Ramsay et al. 1990). These intracellular storage products have thermoplastic properties and can be molded. Their properties can be influenced by the substrate fed to the bacteria. A β-hydroxybutyric and β-hydroxyvaleric acid copolymer gives the best properties. Up to 50% of the cell dry weight is β-hydroxyalkanoate under the proper growth conditions. But the price of this product is five to seven times higher than that of petrochemical-based polyethylene, restricting its use to specialty products. Recently, some shampoo bottles and disposable diaper liners were also manufactured from this material. Properly modified, starch and other natural polymers may yet yield useful and biodegradable plastics. The synthetic caprolactone polyester that contains hydrolyzable bonds is also a good candidate as biodegradable plastic.

## Alkyl Benzyl Sulfonates

Alkyl benzyl sulfonates are the major components of anionic detergents. Like other surface active agents, the molecule has a polar (sulfonate) and a nonpolar

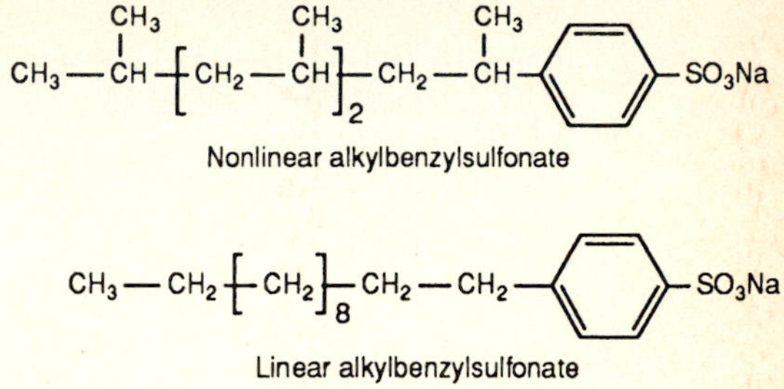

**Figure 13.15**
Chemical structures of some nonlinear alkylbenzyl sulfonates (ABS) and linear alkylbenzyl sulfonates (LAS). The methyl branches in the former group of compounds interfere with rapid biodegradation and cause foaming problems in contaminated water. LAS compounds are free of this problem.

(alkyl) end. Emulsification of fatty substances, and hence cleaning, occurs when these molecules form a monolayer around lipophilic droplets or particles. The molecules orient with their nonpolar end toward the lipophilic substance and their sulfonate end toward the surrounding water. Nonlinear alkylbenzyl sulfonates (ABS) (Figure 13.15) are resistant to biodegradation and cause extensive foaming of rivers that receive ABS-containing wastes. ABS is easier to manufacture and has slightly superior detergent properties, but the methyl branching of the alkyl chain interferes with biodegradation because the tertiary carbon atoms block the normal β-oxidation sequence (Larson 1990). The problem of restricted biodegradation of ABS was largely alleviated when the detergent industry switched to linear alkylbenzyl sulfonates (LAS) that were free of this blockage and consequently more easily biodegraded. The ABS-LAS story is a remarkable one, as it was one of the first instances when a synthetic molecule was redesigned to remove obstacles to biodegradation while essentially preserving the other useful characteristics of the compound (Brenner 1969).

## Petroleum Hydrocarbons

**Petroleum Hydrocarbons as Pollutants** Petroleum is, in one sense, a natural product, resulting from the anaerobic conversion of biomass under high temperature and pressure. It has always entered the biosphere

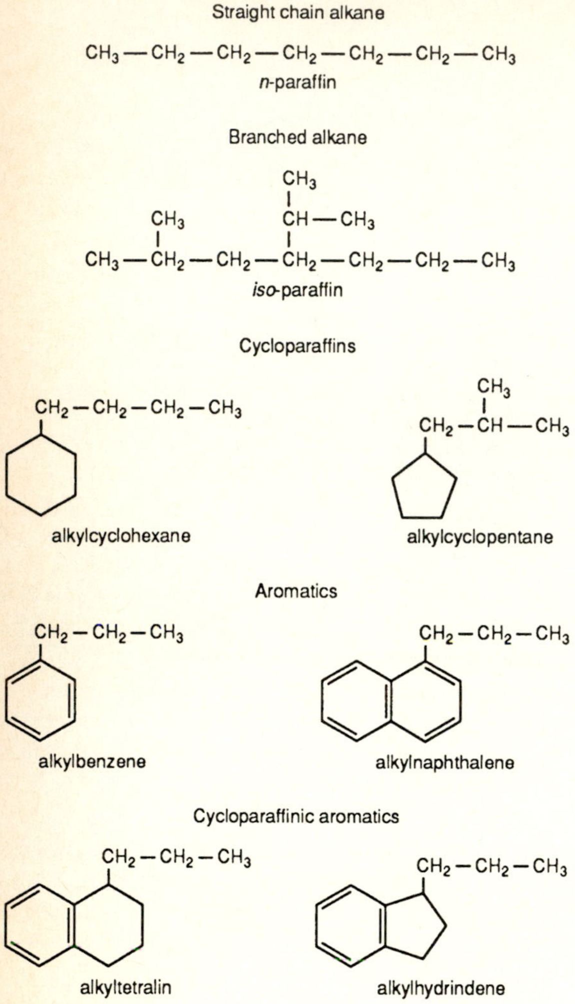

Straight chain alkane

$$CH_3 - CH_2 - CH_2 - CH_2 - CH_2 - CH_2 - CH_3$$

*n*-paraffin

Branched alkane

*iso*-paraffin

Cycloparaffins

alkylcyclohexane

alkylcyclopentane

Aromatics

alkylbenzene

alkylnaphthalene

Cycloparaffinic aromatics

alkyltetralin

alkylhydrindene

**Figure 13.16**
Components of crude oil include aromatic, paraffinic, and cycloparaffinic structures. Homologues, isomers, and combinations result in hundreds of individual hydrocarbon compounds in crude oil samples.

by natural seepage, but at rates much slower than the forced recovery of petroleum by drilling, currently estimated to be about 2 billion metric tons per year. Petroleum, or at least most of its components, are subject to biodegradation, but at relatively slow rates. The production, transportation, refining, and ultimate disposal are introducing, by conservative estimate, 3.2 million metric tons of oil annually into the oceans (National Research Council 1985). This load is heavily concentrated around offshore production sites, major shipping routes, and refineries and frequently exceeds the self-purification capacity of the receiving waters. Oil floating on water is technically difficult to contain and collect. It is destructive to birds and various forms of marine life and, when driven ashore, causes heavy economic and esthetic damage. Cleanup costs are high, often amounting to $10–15 per gallon of spilled oil. Prevailing weather conditions often completely thwart the containment and cleanup of oil slicks. Dispersing of the oil with the use of detergents or sinking the oil with chalk or siliconized sand are essentially cosmetic measures. They remove the oil from the surface but increase the exposure of marine life to the pollutant and are, therefore, best avoided.

In addition to killing birds, fish, shellfish, and other invertebrates, oil pollution appears also to have more subtle effects on marine life. Dissolved aromatic components of petroleum disrupt, even at a low ppb concentration, the chemoreception of some marine organisms. As feeding and mating responses largely depend on chemoreception, such disruption can lead to elimination of many species from the polluted area even when the pollutant concentration is far below the lethal level as defined in the conventional sense. Another disturbing possibility is that some condensed polynuclear components of petroleum that are relatively resistant to biodegradation and are carcinogenic may move up marine food chains and taint fish or shellfish.

Petroleum is a complex mixture of aliphatic, alicyclic (cycloaliphatic saturated ring structures), and aromatic hydrocarbons (Figure 13.16) and a smaller proportion of nonhydrocarbon compounds, such as naphthenic acids, phenols, thiols, heterocyclic nitrogen, and sulfur compounds, as well as metalloporphyrins. There are several hundred individual components in every crude oil, and the composition of each varies with its origin. Most xenobiotic pollutants can be regarded as substituted or modified hydrocarbons; therefore, it is useful to review here briefly the biodegradation pathways of various hydrocarbon compounds.

Susceptibility to biodegradation varies with the type and size of the hydrocarbon molecule (Atlas 1984; National Research Council 1985). *n*-Alkanes of intermediate chain length ($C_{10}$–$C_{24}$) are degraded most rapidly. Short-chain alkanes are toxic to many microorganisms, but they generally evaporate from oil slicks rapidly. Very-long-chain alkanes become increasingly resistant to biodegradation. As the chain length increases and the alkanes exceed a molecular weight of 500, the alkanes cease to serve as carbon sources. Branching, in general, reduces the rate of biodegradation because tertiary and quaternary carbon atoms interfere with degradation mechanisms or block degradation altogether. Aromatic compounds, especially of the condensed polynuclear type, are degraded more slowly than alkanes. Alicyclic compounds are frequently unable to serve as the sole carbon source for microbial growth unless they have a sufficiently long aliphatic side chain, but they can be degraded via cometabolism by two or more cooperating microbial strains with complementary metabolic capabilities (Atlas 1981).

**Principal Pathways of Petroleum Hydrocarbon Biodegradation** The initial attack on alkanes occurs by enzymes that have a strict requirement for molecular oxygen, that is, monooxygenases (mixed function oxidases) or dioxygenases (Britton 1984; Singer and Finnerty 1984). In the first case (Equation 1), one atom of $O_2$ is incorporated into the alkane, yielding a primary alcohol. The other is reduced to $H_2O$, with the reduced form of nicotinamide dinucleotide phosphate ($NADPH_2$) serving as electron donor.

(1) $R-CH_2-CH_3 + O_2 + NADPH_2 \rightarrow$

$\quad R-CH_2-CH_2-OH + NADP + H_2O$

In the second case (Equation 2), both atoms of $O_2$ are transferred to the alkane, yielding a labile hydroperoxide intermediate that is subsequently reduced by $NADPH_2$ to an alcohol and $H_2O$ (Equation 3).

(2) $R-CH_2-CH_3 + O_2 \rightarrow$

$\quad R-CH_2-CH_2-OOH$

(3) $R-CH_2-COOH-OOH + NADPH_2 \rightarrow$

$\quad R-CH_2-CH_2-OH + NADP + H_2O$

Most frequently, the initial attack is directed at the terminal methyl group, forming a primary alcohol that, in turn, is further oxidized to an aldehyde and fatty acid. Occasionally, both terminal methyl groups are oxidized in this manner, resulting in the formation of a dicarboxylic acid. This variation, described as diterminal or ω-oxidation, is one of several ways to bypass a block to β-oxidation due to branching of the carbon chain.

Once a fatty acid is formed, further catabolism occurs by the β-oxidation sequence. The long-chain fatty acid is converted to its acyl coenzyme A form (Equation 4) and is acted upon by a series of enzymes, with the result that an acetyl CoA group is cleaved off and the fatty acid is shortened by a two-carbon unit (Equations 4–9). This sequence is then repeated. The acetyl CoA units are converted to $CO_2$ through the tricarboxylic acid cycle. The end products of hydrocarbon mineralization, thus, are $CO_2$ and $H_2O$.

(4) $R-CH_2-CH_2-CH_2-C\,OOH \xrightarrow[+CoA]{}$

(5) $R-CH_2-CH_2-CH_2-\overset{\overset{\displaystyle O}{\|}}{C}-CoA \xrightarrow[-2H^+]{}$

(6) $R-CH_2-CH=CH-\overset{\overset{\displaystyle O}{\|}}{C}-CoA \xrightarrow[+H_2O]{}$

(7) $R-CH_2-\underset{\underset{\displaystyle OH}{|}}{CH}-CH_2-\overset{\overset{\displaystyle O}{\|}}{C}-CoA \xrightarrow[-2H^+]{}$

(8) $R-CH_2-\underset{\underset{\displaystyle O}{\|}}{C}-CH_2-\overset{\overset{\displaystyle O}{\|}}{C}-CoA \xrightarrow[+CoA]{}$

(9) $R-CH_2-\underset{\underset{\displaystyle O}{\|}}{C}-CoA + CH_3-\overset{\overset{\displaystyle O}{\|}}{C}-CoA$

The β-oxidation sequence does not necessarily require the presence of molecular oxygen, and after the initial oxygenation, fatty acid biodegradation may proceed under anaerobic conditions. A direct dehydrogenation of an intact hydrocarbon (Equation 10)—leading through a 1-alkene (Equation 11), alcohol (Equation 12), and aldehyde (Equation 13) to a fatty acid (Equation 14)—has been suggested as a potential anoxic biodegradation mechanism.

$$(10) \quad R-CH_2-CH_3 \xrightarrow[-2H^+]{}$$

$$(11) \quad R-CH=CH_2 \xrightarrow[+H_2O]{}$$

$$(12) \quad R-\underset{\underset{OH}{|}}{C}H-CH_3 \xrightarrow[-2H^+]{}$$

$$(13) \quad R-CH_2-CHO \xrightarrow[-2H^+, +H_2O]{}$$

$$(14) \quad R-CH_2-COOH$$

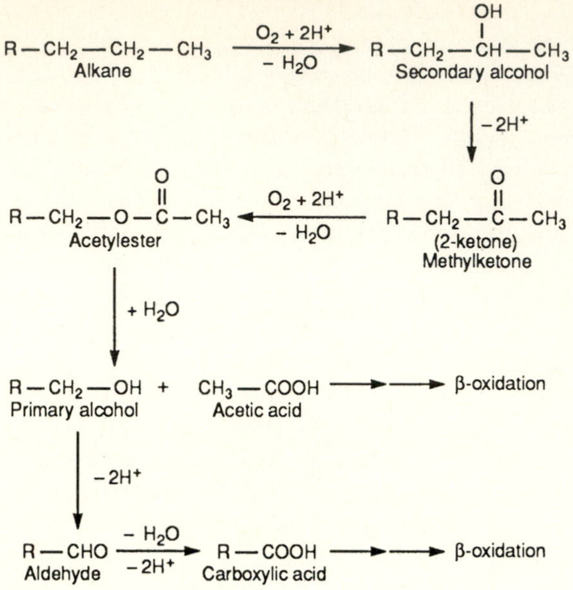

This sequence would allow the anaerobic metabolism of an intact hydrocarbon in the presence of an electron acceptor such as nitrate. The evidence for such a sequence at this time is tenuous, and significant metabolism of intact aliphatic hydrocarbons in a strictly anaerobic environment is yet to be demonstrated. Geologic and environmental experience indicate that in the absence of molecular oxygen, hydrocarbons persist.

Some microorganisms attack alkanes subterminally; that is, oxygen is inserted on a carbon atom within the chain instead of at its end (Figure 13.17). In this manner, a secondary alcohol is formed first, which then is further oxidized to a ketone and finally to an ester. The ester bond is cleaved, yielding a primary alcohol and a fatty acid. The sum of the carbon atoms

**Figure 13.17**
Pathway through which subterminal oxidation of alkanes yields two fatty acid moieties, which are metabolized further by β-oxidation.

in the two fragments is equal to that of the parent hydrocarbon. The alcohol fragment is oxidized through the aldehyde to the fatty acid analog, and both fragments are metabolized further by the β-oxidation sequence (Britton 1984; Singer and Finnerty 1984).

Alicyclic hydrocarbons having no terminal methyl groups are biodegraded by a mechanism similar to the subterminal oxidation shown in Figure 13.17. In the case of cyclohexane (Figure 13.18), hydroxylation by a monooxygenase leads to an alicyclic alcohol. Dehydrogenation leads to the ketone. Further oxidation inserts an oxygen into the ring and a lactone is formed. The hydroxyl group is oxidized, in sequence, to an aldehyde and carboxyl group. The resulting dicarboxylic acid is further metabolized by β-oxidation. Microorganisms have been found that can grow on cyclohexane (Trower at al. 1985) and hence must be

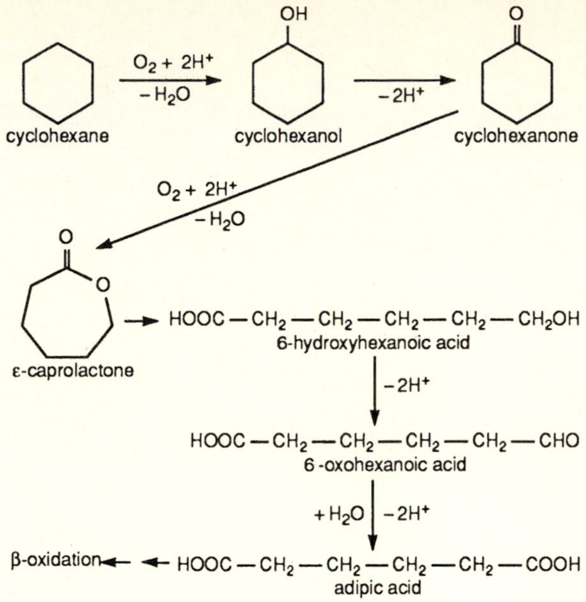

**Figure 13.18**
Microbial oxidation of cyclohexane as an example of metabolism of alicyclic hydrocarbons.

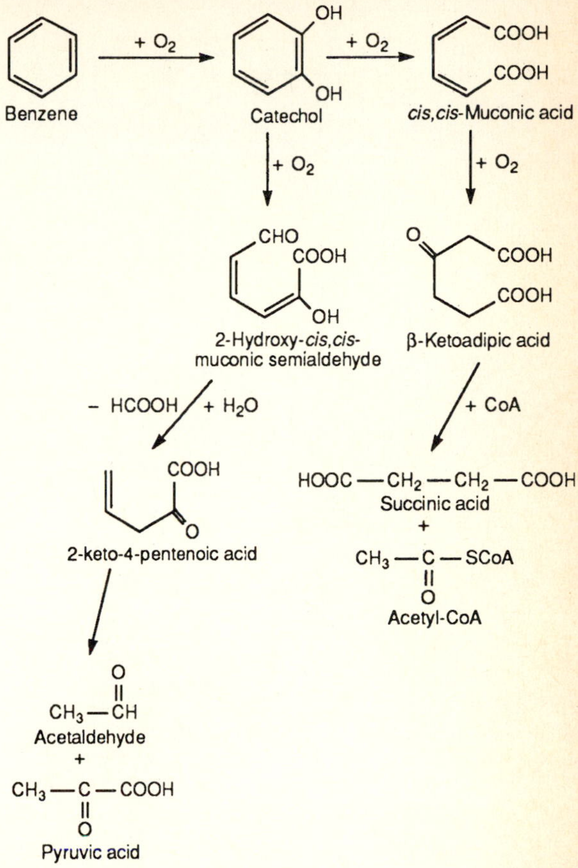

**Figure 13.19**
Microbial metabolism of the aromatic ring (simplified) by *meta* or *ortho* cleavage, as shown for benzene.

capable of carrying out the whole degradation sequence. More frequently, however, organisms capable of converting cyclohexane to cyclohexanone are unable to lactonize and open the ring and vice versa. Consequently, commensalism and cometabolism play an important role in the biodegradation of alicyclic hydrocarbons (Perry 1984; Trudgill 1984).

Aromatic hydrocarbons are oxidized by dioxygenases to labile *cis,cis*-dihydrodiol that spontaneously convert to catechols (Figure 13.19). The dihydroxylated aromatic ring is opened by oxidative "ortho cleavage," resulting in *cis,cis*-muconic acid. This is metabolized further to β-ketoadipic acid, which is oxidatively cleaved to the common tricarboxylic cycle intermediates, succinic acid, and acetyl-CoA. Alternatively, the catechol ring may be opened by *meta* cleavage, adjacent to rather than between the hydroxyl groups, yielding 2-hydroxy*cis,cis*-muconic semialdehyde. Further metabolism leads to formic acid, pyru-

vic acid, and acetaldehyde. Condensed aromatic ring structures, if degradable, are also attacked by dihydroxylation and the opening of one of the rings (Figure 13.20). The opened ring is degraded to pyruvic acid and $CO_2$, and a second ring is attacked in the same fashion. Many condensed polynuclear aromatic compounds, however, are degraded only with difficulty or not at all (Cerniglia 1984; Gibson and Subramanian 1984). One reason for resistance to biodegradation is that induction of the enzymes responsible for polynuclear aromatic hydrocarbon degradation in

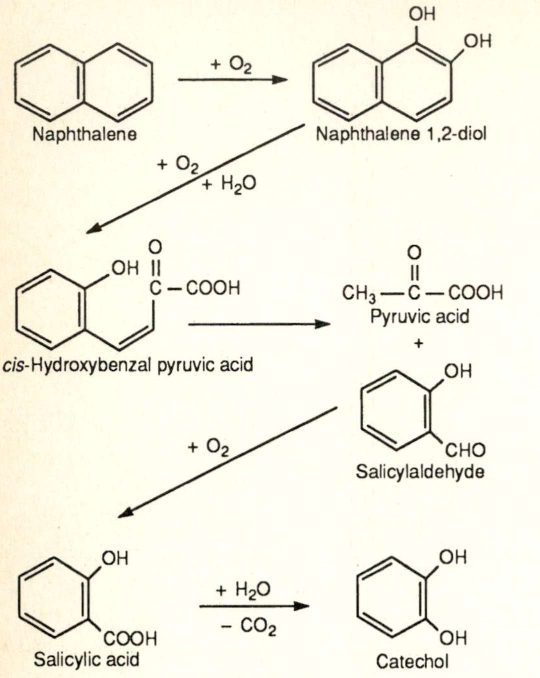

**Figure 13.20**
Microbial metabolism of a condensed aromatic ring structure (simplified) as shown for naphthalene. The resulting catechol is metabolized further by *ortho* or *meta* cleavage, as shown in Figure 13.19.

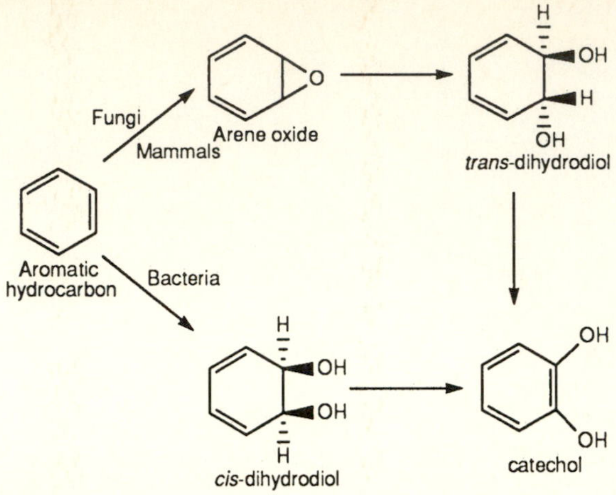

**Figure 13.21**
Fungi and other eucaryotic cells form *trans*-diols, whereas most bacteria form *cis*-diols when they oxidize aromatic hydrocarbons.

some cases depends upon the presence of lower-molecular-weight aromatics (Heitkamp and Cerniglia 1988).

Importantly, eucaryotic microorganisms (fungi and algae)—like mammalian liver systems—produce *trans* diols, whereas most bacteria oxidize aromatic hydrocarbons to *cis* diols (Cerniglia 1984; Gibson and Subramanian 1984) (Figure 13.21). *Trans* diols of various polynuclear aromatic hydrocarbons are carcinogenic, whereas *cis* diols are not. Until recently, it was held that polycyclic aromatic hydrocarbons (PAH) with more than three condensed rings fail to serve as growth substrates and are attacked, if at all, by cometabolism only. Starting around 1990, pure cultures were isolated in several laboratories that grew on four-ring PAHs such as fluoranthene and pyrene as their only source of carbon and energy (Weissenfels et al.

1990; Walter et al. 1991; Boldrin et al. 1993; Cerniglia 1993; Jimenez and Bartha 1996). PAHs of five or more rings are still believed to be subject to cometabolic transformations only by bacteria such as *Beijerinckia* and by white-rot fungi such as *Phanerochaete chrysosporium* (Sutherland et al. 1995). Undoubtedly, one of the major problems in utilization of the multiring PAHs is their extremely low water solubility.

The generally accepted view that hydrocarbons without hydroxyl-, carbonyl-, or carboxyl-substituents are not degraded under strictly anaerobic conditions needed recent revision. Grbic-Galic and Vogel (1987) clearly demonstrated that the simple aromatics benzene and toluene are metabolized under anaerobic methanogenic conditions. The oxygen used in the ring hydroxylation comes from $H_2O$ (Vogel and Grbic-Galic 1986). The evidence for anaerobic degradation of xylenes and of ethylbenzene is as yet less clear-cut, but preliminary work suggests it may occur (Colberg and Young 1995). Although benzene has often been observed to be resistant to microbial degradation under anoxic conditions, a number of recent studies have demonstrated that anaerobic benzene utilization can occur (Coates et al. 1996a, 1996b; Lovley et al.

1994, 1995, 1996). Enrichments capable of toluene degradation under $O_2$-free denitrifying conditions have also been established from agricultural soils, compost, aquifer material, and contaminated soil samples from different geographic regions of the world (Fries et al. 1994). Molybdate, an inhibitor of sulfate reduction, has been shown to inhibit benzene uptake and production of $^{14}CO_2$ from ($^{14}C$) benzene (Lovley et al. 1995). Benzene metabolism stopped when the sediments became sulfate depleted, and benzene uptake resumed when sulfate was added again. The stoichiometry of benzene uptake and sulfate reduction was consistent with the hypothesis that sulfate can serve as the principal electron acceptor for benzene oxidation. Benzene can be oxidized in the absence of $O_2$, with sulfate serving as the electron acceptor; some sulfate reducers are capable of completely oxidizing benzene to carbon dioxide without the production of extracellular intermediates. Even the PAH compounds naphthalene and phenanthrene were reported to be mineralized under sulfate-reducing conditions (Coates et al. 1996a). The alkane n-hexadecane was also found to be subject to slow mineralization under sulfate-reducing conditions (Ackersberg et al. 1991).

Anaerobic benzene oxidation also can be coupled to the reduction of chelated Fe(III) (Lovley et al. 1995). Fe(III) chelated to such compounds as EDTA, N-methyliminodiacetic acid, ethanol diglycine, humic acids, and phosphates stimulated benzene oxidation coupled to Fe(III) reduction in anaerobic sediments from a petroleum-contaminated aquifer as effectively as or more effectively than nitrilotriacetic acid (Lovley et al. 1996). These results indicate that many forms of chelated Fe(III) might be applicable to aquifer remediation.

Anaerobic microbial degradation of benzene has been found in sediments from various geographical locations and range from aquifer sands to fine-grained estuarine muds, under methanogenic, sulfate-reducing, and iron-reducing conditions (Kazumi et al. 1997). In aquifer sediments under methanogenic conditions, benzene loss was concomitant with methane production, and microbial utilization of ($^{14}C$)benzene yielded $^{14}CO_2$ and $^{14}CH_4$. In slurries with estuarine and aquifer sediments under sulfate-reducing condi-

tions, the loss of sulfate in amounts consistent with the stoichiometric degradation of benzene or the conversion of ($^{14}C$)benzene to $^{14}CO_2$ indicates that benzene was mineralized. Benzene loss also occurred in the presence of Fe(III) in sediments from freshwater environments. These results indicate that the potential for the anaerobic degradation of benzene, which was once thought to be resistant to all but oxygenase attack, exists in a variety of aquatic sediments from widely distributed locations. Although the biodegradation of hydrocarbons is definitely much slower under anaerobic conditions than under aerobic ones, the rates of anaerobic toluene and m-xylene biodegradation were considered significant enough for use in aquifer bioremediation (Zeyer et al. 1986, 1990).

**Crude Oil Biodegradation**  Crude oils are composed of complex mixtures of paraffinic, alicyclic, and aromatic hydrocarbons. A marine oil spill left to its natural fate is gradually degraded by the just-described biological and also by some nonbiological mechanisms. Autooxidation in the absence of light plays a minor role because the low temperatures of the marine environment provide no opportunity for activation. Photochemical oxidation, however, may contribute substantially to the self-purification of the marine environment. Laboratory experiments suggest that in eight hours of effective sunshine, as much as 0.2 metric ton of oil per square kilometer may be destroyed by photooxidation, though the actual figures are probably substantially lower. The contribution of photodegradation is made especially important by the fact that this process preferentially attacks the same tertiary carbon atoms that tend to block biodegradation.

Communities exposed to hydrocarbons become adapted, exhibiting selective enrichment and genetic changes resulting in increased proportions of hydrocarbon-degrading bacteria and bacterial plasmids encoding hydrocarbon catabolic genes (Leahy and Colwell 1990). Because adapted microbial communities have higher proportions of hydrocarbon degraders, they can respond to the presence of hydrocarbon pollutants within hours. In the case of the *Amoco Cadiz* and *Tanio* spills along the coast of Brittany, France, for example, the adapted hydrocarbon-degrading populations increased by several orders of magnitude within a day of the spillages, and biodegradation occurred as fast as or faster than evaporation in the days following these spills (Atlas 1981).

The measurement of biodegradation rates under favorable laboratory conditions has led to the estimate that as much as 0.5–60 g of oil per cubic meter of seawater per day may be mineralized to $CO_2$ in this manner, but this estimate is far too optimistic. *In situ* measurements of hydrocarbon biodegradation in seawater using $^{14}C$-labeled hexadecane indicate rates of 1–30 mg of hydrocarbon per cubic meter of seawater per day converted to $CO_2$, depending on temperature and mineral nutrient conditions.

The principal forces limiting the biodegradation of polluting petroleum in the sea are the resistant and toxic components of oil itself; low water temperatures; scarcity of mineral nutrients, especially nitrogen and phosphorus; the exhaustion of dissolved oxygen; and, in previously unpolluted pelagic areas, the scarcity of hydrocarbon-degrading microorganisms (Atlas 1981).

Low winter temperatures can limit rates of hydrocarbon biodegradation, increasing residence time of oil pollutants (Bodennec et al. 1987). In a recent diesel oil spill from the *Bahia Paraiso* in the Antarctic, Kennicutt (1990) reported turnover rates, measured as $^{14}C$-hexadecane mineralization, in excess of 2 years. This was considerably slower than the rates previously measured in Arctic zones.

Microbial degradation of oil has been shown to occur by attack on the aliphatic or light aromatic fractions of the oil. Although some studies have reported their removal at high rates under optimal conditions (Rontani et al. 1985; Shiaris 1989), high-molecular-weight aromatics, resins, and asphaltenes are generally considered to be recalcitrant or exhibit only low rates of biodegradation. In aquatic ecosystems, dispersion and emulsification of oil in slicks appear to be prerequisites for rapid biodegradation; large masses of mousse, tar balls, or high concentrations of oil in quiescent environments tend to persist because of the limited surface areas available for microbial activity. Petroleum spilled on or applied to soil is largely adsorbed to particulate matter, decreasing its toxicity

but possibly also contributing to its persistence. In the short run, petroleum and petroleum fractions containing asphaltic components are not degraded quantitatively. The residues, along with polymerization products formed from reactions of free radical degradation intermediates with each other, form tar globules. The tar, a partially oxygenated high-molecular-weight material, is quite resistant to further degradation, and floating tar globules are encountered in the marine environment in increasing quantities (Butler et al. 1973).

As the water solubility of many solid hydrocarbons is extremely low, transport limitation can cause an apparent recalcitrance of otherwise degradable hydrocarbons. This was demonstrated by packaging highly recalcitrant *n*-hexatriacontane ($C_{36}$) into liposomes (Miller and Bartha 1989). Hexatriacontane transported in this manner into the cells of a *Pseudomonas* strain originally isolated on *n*-octadecane ($C_{18}$) utilized the $C_{36}$ hydrocarbon at the same rate as the water-soluble substrate succinate. Efroymson and Alexander (1991) have also shown that some bacteria can utilize hydrocarbons directly from the nonaqueous phase. Utilization of pyrene by a *Mycobacterium* was greatly stimulated by small amounts of inert solvents (Yimenez and Bartha 1996).

An ability to isolate high numbers of certain oil-degrading microorganisms from an environment is commonly taken as evidence that those microorganisms are the most active oil degraders of that environment. This projection is questionable, but *in situ* measurements of hydrocarbon biodegradation activity are few. Using selective inhibitors, Song et al. (1986) determined that in a field soil with no hydrocarbon spill history, 80% of added hexadecane was degraded by bacteria and only 20% by fungi. In the same soil, bacterial and fungal population segments shared glucose degradation evenly.

Accidental oil spills are generally easier to contain and clean on land than on water, though gasoline and other low-viscosity distillation products may seep into subsoils and persist there because of prevailing anoxic conditions. They may also pollute groundwater and pose an explosion hazard in nearby basements and sewers. Oil spills are destructive to vegetation not only because of contact toxicity, but because hydrocarbon biodegradation in the soil renders plant root zones anoxic. The lack of oxygen and accompanying $H_2S$ evolution kills the roots of most plants, including those of large, well-established trees (Bossert and Bartha 1984).

Natural gas seepages from underground pipe systems or from former landfills have a similar deleterious effect on vegetation. Here, the anoxic conditions are created by a combination of the physical displacement of soil air by natural gas and the activity of *Methylomonas* and other bacteria capable of oxidizing gaseous alkanes. Destruction of ornamental and shade trees occurred on a large scale in some communities that replaced coal-derived generator gas with natural gas. The former is generated by blowing a mixture of steam and air through hot coals, giving rise to a combustible gas mixture containing hydrogen, carbon monoxide, nitrogen, and various impurities. This gas mixture has a high moisture content. When natural gas that consisted mainly of methane and was quite dry was distributed through the same old municipal pipe networks, pipe joint gaskets dried out, shrank, and became leaky. The underground gas seepage caused widespread tree kills through anoxic soil conditions, though the direct toxicity of methane and other gaseous alkanes to plants is quite low (Hoeks 1972).

## Pesticides

Monocultures are inherently unstable ecosystems, and of necessity a large part of any agricultural production effort goes toward the control of competing weeds, destructive insects, and other pests. The cost of manual labor and the increasing scale of agricultural operations in developed countries both have worked in favor of chemical pest control. By 1975, 1170 pesticides were registered for use in the United States—including 425 herbicides, 410 fungicides, and 335 insecticides. The total annual production of synthetic organic pesticides in the same year was 725 million kg. In terms of effectiveness, economy, and quality control, pesticides have been an unqualified success; the dangers inherent in our ignorance of the ultimate fate and unintended side effects of pesticides were

recognized only gradually. Rachel Carson's controversial *Silent Spring* (1962) played a large role in alerting legislators and the general public to the proven and potential dangers of unwise pesticide use. In the subsequent, highly emotional debate, groups with conflicting interests and philosophies made sweeping endorsements or condemnations of pesticides. In reality, a sudden discontinuation of pesticide use would surely precipitate an economic and public health crisis, whereas uncontrolled pesticide use would, in the long term, cause irreversible environmental damage. A responsible pesticide policy clearly demands careful risk-benefit analysis for each compound and its various uses.

**Recalcitrant Halogenated pesticides** The chlorinated pesticides are relatively resistant to microbial attack. In general, the more extensive the chlorine substitution, the more persistent the pesticide (Ghosal et al. 1985; Kennedy et al. 1990; Chaudhry and Chapalamadugu 1991). Mirex ($C_{10}Cl_{12}$) and Kepone ($C_{10}Cl_{10}O$) are extensively chlorinated insecticidal compounds (Figure 13.22). Mirex has been used in the United States in the fire ant control program. Kepone was manufactured principally for export and as a precursor for other pesticides. Kepone came to national attention in the United States when it poisoned a sub-

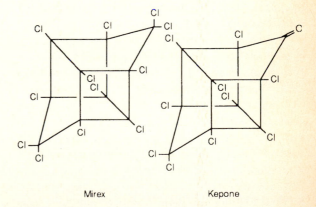

**Figure 13.22**
Structural formulae of the insecticides Mirex and Kepone. Extensive chlorination renders these compounds extremely resistant to biodegradation.

stantial number of workers in a manufacturing plant at Hopewell, Virginia. The subsequent investigation revealed extensive environmental contamination around the plant. The Kepone incident necessitated the prolonged closing for fishing of the contaminated section of the James River. No biological mineralization was demonstrated for either Kepone or Mirex, although both compounds are subject to limited dechlorination by anaerobic microbial consortia (Orndorff and Colwell 1980) and photodegradation (National Research Council 1978b).

The much less extensively chlorinated pesticide DDT is subject to some biochemical transformations both *in vitro* and in the environment, but the basic carbon skeleton persists in nature for excessively long periods. The white-rot fungus *Phanerochaete chrysosporium* is able to attack DDT (Bumpus and Aust 1987). Pfaender and Alexander (1972) succeeded in demonstrating the *in vitro* mineralization of DDT ring carbon by sequentially using cell-free extracts of a hydrogen-oxidizing bacterium, whole cells of *Arthrobacter,* the addition of cosubstrates, and a regimen of alternating anaerobic and aerobic conditions. Nevertheless, they came to the conclusion that biochemical DDT mineralization in the environment either does not occur or occurs at exceedingly slow rates. Other than the unfavorable energetics of the dechlorination steps, no satisfactory explanation could be found for this fact. Chlorinated pesticides, including DDT, are subject to reductive dehalogenation, that is, removal of the chlorine substituents by anaerobic microorganisms (Genthner et al. 1989a, 1989b). A nitrogen-heterocyclic herbicide, for example, has been shown to be attacked by reductive dehalogenation (Adrian and Suflita 1990). Chlorobenzoates and chlorobenzenes are also degraded by this mechanism (Dolfing and Tiedje 1987; Fathepure et al. 1988; Stevens and Tiedje 1988; Stevens et al. 1988; Linkfield et al. 1989; Mohn and Tiedje 1990a, 1990b).

**Biodegradable Pesticides** Most of the currently used organic pesticides are subject to extensive mineralization within the time span of one growing season or less. Biochemical processes, alone or in combination with purely chemical reactions, are responsible for

their disappearance. Synthetic pesticides show a bewildering variety of chemical structures, yet most can be traced to relatively simple hydrocarbon skeletons that bear a variety of substituent groups, such as halogen, amino, nitro, hydroxyl, and others. Aliphatic carbon chains are degraded by the β-oxidation sequence. The resulting $C_2$ fragments are further metabolized via the tricarboxylic acid cycle. Aromatic ring structures are metabolized by dihydroxylation and ring cleavage. Prior to these transformations, chemical groups attached to the aromatic ring are completely or partially removed. Substituent groups uncommon in natural compounds, such as halogens and nitro- and sulfonate groups, if situated so as to impede the oxygenations, will frequently cause recalcitrance, whereas methyl, methoxy, carboxyl, and carbonyl groups can often be removed metabolically from blocking positions. If the dihydroxylation can occur on a substituted aromatic compound, the previously described degradation pathways will be followed with minor modification according to the position and nature of the substituents. Saturated ring systems, such as cyclohexane and decalin, are more refractory than their aromatic analogs. They rarely support growth of any single microorganism, but some are degraded in the presence of other substrates and by the cooperative effort of several microbial strains. This phenomenon is observed also with other difficult-to-degrade compounds and relates to the concept of cometabolism (Horvath 1972).

Cometabolism is the phenomenon that occurs when a compound is transformed by a microorganism, yet the organism is unable to grow on the compound and does not derive energy, carbon, or any other nutrient from the transformation. Cometabolic transformation occurs when an enzyme of a microorganism, growing on compound A, recognizes as substrate compound B and transforms it to a product. The transformation is limited, because the next enzyme of the organism that should attack in sequence has a higher specificity and does not recognize the product of B as a substrate. In the case of a pure culture, cometabolism is a dead-end transformation without benefit to the organism. In a mixed culture or in the environment proper, however, such an initial cometabolic transformation may pave the way for subsequent attack by another organism. In this manner, cometabolic and substrate-utilization synergistic-type transformations may eventually lead to the recycling of relatively recalcitrant compounds that do not support the growth of any microbial culture.

As organic molecules to be degraded become more complex and consist of aliphatic as well as aromatic, alicyclic, or heterocyclic portions, few generalizations can be made about their degradation pattern. If the moieties of the molecule are connected by ester, amide, or ether bonds that can be cleaved by microbial enzymes, the initial attack usually takes this form, and the resulting compounds are subsequently metabolized as outlined before. If such an attack cannot occur, degradation will commonly be initiated at the aliphatic end of the molecule. If this end is blocked by extensive branching or by other substituents, however, the attack may start from the aromatic end. The site and mode of the initial attack is determined not only by molecular structure, but also by the enzymatic capabilities of the microorganisms involved, as well as by the prevailing environmental conditions, such as the redox potential, pH, and ionic environment. These factors will modify not only the rate, but also the pathway and the ultimate products of the degradation (Hill and Wright 1978).

The chemical structures of some biodegradable and some recalcitrant pesticides are compared in Figure 13.23. 2,4-Dichlorophenoxyacetic acid (2,4-D) is biodegraded within days; 2,4,5-trichlorophenoxyacetic acid (2,4,5-T) differs only by one additional chlorine substitution in the *meta*-position, yet this compound persists for many months. The additional substitution interferes with the hydroxylation and cleavage of the aromatic ring. The primary amine group in isopropyl-*N*-phenyl-carbamate (propham) is cleaved by microbial amidases so rapidly that for some applications the addition of amidase inhibitors becomes necessary. The secondary amine group of *N*-isopropyl-2-chloroacetanilide (propachlor) is not subject to attack by such amidases, and this compound persists considerably longer. 1-Naphthyl-*N*-methyl-carbamate (carbaryl) is biodegraded quite rapidly, whereas hexachlorooctahydro-dimethanonaphthalene

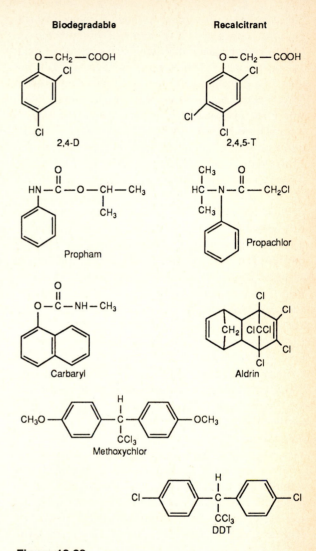

**Figure 13.23**

Molecular structures of some biodegradable and some recalcitrant pesticides. The upper four compounds are herbicides, the lower four insecticides. The *biodegradable* and *recalcitrant* are used here in a relative sense and imply neither instant biodegradation nor indefinite resistance. The pairs of compounds (left and right) were selected for overall structural similarity in order to help pinpoint molecular features that render the compounds in the right column recalcitrant. These features are the 5-chloro-substitution in the case of 2,4,5-T, the *N*-alkyl-substitution in the case of propachlor, the multiple chloro-substitutions in the case of aldrin, and the two *p*-chloro-substitutions in the case of DDT.

(aldrin) persists or undergoes only a minor change by epoxidation. 1,1,1-Trichloro-2,2-*bis*(*p*-methoxy-phenyl)-ethane (methoxychlor) is less persistent than 1,1,1-trichloro*bis*(*p*-chlorophenyl)-ethane (DDT) because the *p*-methoxy groups are subject to dealkylation, whereas the *p*-chloro-substitution endows DDT with great biological and chemical stability.

Trichlorophenoxyacetic acid (2,4,5-T) is relatively resistant to biodegradation. Chakrabarty and coworkers (Kellogg et al. 1981; Chatterjee et al. 1982; Kilbane et al. 1982) were able to isolate a recombinant 2,4,5-T-degrading *Bunkholderia cepacia* only following molecular breeding in which a mixture of plasmid-bearing strains were maintained in a chemostat in the presence of 2,4,5-T. In contrast to 2,4,5-T, dichlorophenoxyacetic acid (2,4-D) is readily degraded by many aerobic soil microorganisms. The genes involved in the 2,4-D degradation pathway have been identified, and most have been cloned (Harker et al. 1989) (see the accompanying box).

In some cases, one portion of the pesticide molecule is susceptible to degradation and the other is recalcitrant. Some acylanilide herbicides are cleaved by microbial amidases, and the aliphatic moiety of the molecule is mineralized. The aromatic moiety, being stabilized by chlorine substitutions, resists mineralization, but the reactive primary amino group may participate in various biochemical and chemical reactions leading to polymers and complexes that render the fate of such herbicide residues extremely complex. Figure 13.24 shows some of the transformations of *N*-(3,4-dichlorophenyl)-propionamide (propanil) (Bartha and Pramer 1970). Microbial acylamidases cleave the propionate moiety, which is subsequently mineralized. A portion of the released 3,4-dichloroaniline (DCA) is acted upon by microbial oxidases and peroxidases, with the result that they dimerize and polymerize to form highly stable residues such as 3,3′,4,4′tetrachloroazobenzene (TCAB) and related azo compounds. *p*-Bromoaniline, liberated during the biodegradation of the phenylurea herbicide 3-(*p*-bromophenyl)-1-methoxy-1-methylurea (bromuron), under-goes acetylation by soil fungi (Figure 13.25).

The reasons for such transformations are still somewhat obscure. They may occur by chance when a

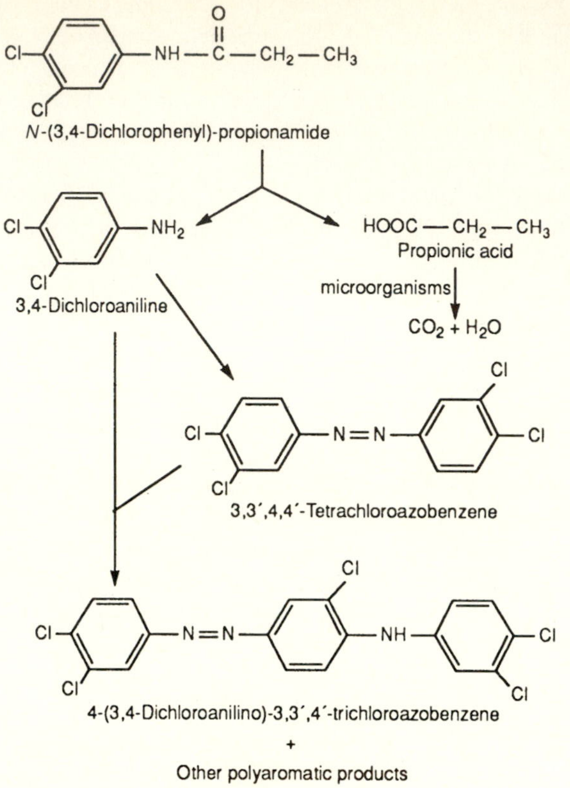

**Figure 13.24**
Microbial metabolism of the herbicide *N*-(3,4-dichlorophenyl)-propionamide (propanil). The aliphatic portion of the molecule is degraded, but the aromatic portion is dimerized and polymerized to persistent residues.

microbial enzyme having another synthetic function recognizes and acts on the human-made residue. In some cases, the reaction seems to detoxify the residue from the microbe's point of view, but the overall persistence and environmental impact of the pesticide is increased by such synthetic transformations (Bartha and Pramer 1970).

Only a small portion of the total halogenated aniline residues derived from the degradation of various phenylurea, phenylcarbamate and acylanilide herbicides, and some other pesticide compounds undergoes transformation as previously described. The bulk of

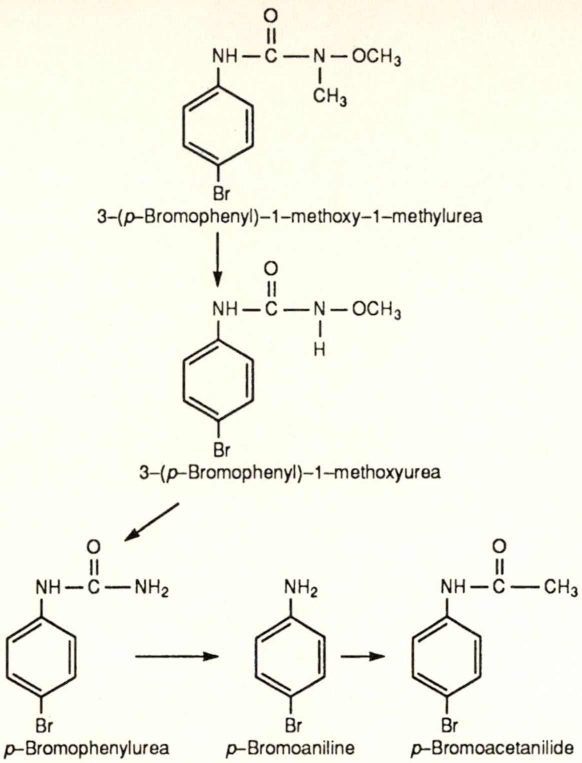

**Figure 13.25**
Metabolism of the phenylurea herbicide 3-(p-bromophenyl)-1-methoxy-1-methylurea by stepwise dealkylation and conversion to p-bromoaniline. Instead of further biodegradation, p-bromoaniline is acetylated to p-bromoacetanilide.

the liberated anilines disappears, that is, becomes unextractable, without evidence of rapid conversion to $CO_2$. The major mechanism of this phenomenon is the chemical attachment of the anilines to humic substances present in both soils and surface waters (Bartha 1980; Bartha et al. 1983). There is increasing evidence that residues of other pesticides may become similarly attached to humic compounds (Kaufman et al. 1976; Sjoblad and Bollag 1977). Humification is part of the natural carbon cycle, and it should not have been unexpected that aromatic residues of pesticides may be subject to it. At least some pesticide residues preserve their xenobiotic character when bound to

humus and when subsequently liberated by the biodegradation of the surrounding humic matrix (Figure 13.26). Thus, humus-bound pesticide residues may contaminate crops and biota that were never directly exposed to the pesticide (Still et al. 1980). Humus-bound residues explain some puzzling instances of low-level crop contamination by a "wrong" pesticide, but the levels involved are so low that any concerns about human health and effects on soil fertility seem unjustified (Bartha 1980).

## MICROBIAL INTERACTIONS WITH SOME INORGANIC POLLUTANTS

The pollution problems discussed thus far in this chapter mostly arise from the inability of microorganisms to mineralize certain organic molecules efficiently. In contrast, the pollution problems to be discussed in the following section are a consequence of the normal biogeochemical cycling activities of microorganisms. Pollution problems arise when the activities of industrialized societies inadvertently increase the pool of an inorganic material subject to microbial cycling. The original material may be relatively innocuous, but its microbial conversion products may not be so. To foresee the full environmental impact of various agricultural and industrial activities requires a knowledge of the microbial cycling processes relevant to those activities.

### Acid Mine Drainage

Coal and various metal ores are enclosed in geological formations of a reduced nature. Coal, in particular, is often associated with pyrite ($FeS_2$). When mining activities expose this material to atmospheric oxygen, a combination of autoxidation and microbial iron and sulfur oxidation produces large amounts of acid. The iron-rich acidic mine drainage kills aquatic life and renders the contaminated stream unsuitable as a water supply or for recreational use. At present, approximately 10,000 miles of U.S. waterways are affected in this manner, predominantly in the states of Pennsylvania, Virginia, Ohio, Kentucky, and Indiana.

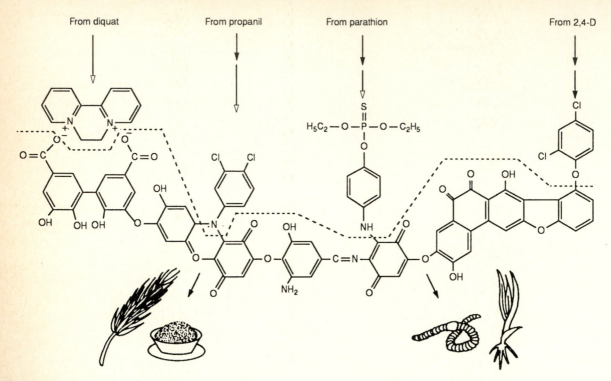

**Figure 13.26**
Some attachment mechanisms of pesticide residues to humus. Subsequent microbial mobilization of the residues may result in contamination of organisms and agricultural products. White arrows represent chemical processes; black arrows represent enzymatic processes. The xenobiotic residues are separated from the type structure of natural humus with a dashed line.

Some acid mine drainage originates from subsurface mining because of water flowing through the mine itself and runoff from mounds of mine tailings or gob piles, rock and low-grade coal separated from the high-grade coal before shipment. This problem is limited and relatively easily controlled. In subsurface mining, as coal is removed, the empty seam is either filled in with tailings or allowed to collapse. In this procedure, only a limited amount of rock is exposed to oxidative action at any one time. In contrast, strip mining removes the overburden and leaves it with the tailings as porous rubble, exposed to oxygen and percolating water. As a result of iron and sulfur oxidation, the pH drops rapidly and prevents the establishment of vege-

tation and a stable soil cover that would, eventually, seal the rubble from oxygen. The strip-mined region continues to give rise to acid mine drainage until most of the sulfide is oxidized and leached out. The recovery of the land may take from 50 to 150 years.

The mechanism of pyrite oxidation is complex. At a neutral pH, oxidation by atmospheric oxygen occurs spontaneously and quite rapidly, but below pH 4.5, autoxidation slows down drastically. In the pH range of 3.5 to 4.5 the stalked iron bacterium *Metallogenium* catalyzes the reaction. As the pH drops below 3.5, the acidophilic bacteria of the genus *Thiobacillus* take over. At this stage, the rate of the microbially catalyzed oxidation is several hundred times higher than

## Biochemistry and Genetics of 2,4-D Biodegradation

The biochemistry and genetics of the biodegradation of the herbicide 2,4-dichlorophenoxyacetic acid (TFD or 2,4-D) have been extensively studied. Biodegradation of 2,4-D occurs via a modified *ortho* cleavage pathway (see the accompanying figure). This biodegradation pathway for 2,4-D is similar to other chlorinated aromatics, such as 3-chlorobenzoate (3CBA) (Perkins et al. 1990). In this pathway, chlorinated aromatic compounds are degraded via a chloro-substituted catechol, which is always *ortho* cleaved by a chlorocatechol 1,2-dioxygenase. The enzymes involved in the mineralization of chlorocatechols have wider substrate specificities than the ordinary *ortho* cleavage pathway enzymes, which is why it is called a modified *ortho* cleavage pathway (van der Meer et al. 1992). The genes for the modified *ortho* cleavage pathways are generally located on catabolic plasmids;

Biochemical pathway of 2,4-dichlorophenoxyacetic acid (2,4-D) biodegradation and the genetic organization of the *tfd* genes that encode metabolism of 2,4-D in *A. eutrophus* JMP134(pJP4). The plasmid-encoded gene products (Tfd enzmes) and the reactions they catalyze are indicated in the biochemical pathway. The final metabolic steps are encoded by chromosomal genes. The *tfdA* gene that catalyzes the initial reaction is separated from the remaining plasmid-encoded genes. The *tfdX* gene is assigned to an open reading frame that showed homology to *tfdS* and *tcbR* but that was only partially sequenced; *tfdA_{II}* and *tfdC_{I}* depict the locations of the presumed duplicated gene copies of *tfdA* and *tfdC,* respectively.

*(continued)*

## Biochemistry and Genetics of 2,4-D Biodegradation, continued

their organization into operon structures differs substantially from that of the chromosomally encoded genes of the normal *ortho* cleavage pathway.

One of the best-studied plasmids for the degradation of chlorinated aromatics is pJP4 of *Alcaligenes eutrophus* JMP134. Plasmid pJP4 is an 80-kilobase, IncP1, broad-host-range conjugative plasmid encoding most of the degradation pathways for 2,4-dichlorophenoxyacetic acid, 2-methyl-4-chlorophenoxyacetic acid, and 3-CBA and for resistance to mercuric chloride and phenylmercuric acetate (Perkins et al. 1990). By using transposon mutagenesis, deletion analysis, gene cloning, and restriction analysis, a genetic and biophysical map of pJP4 was constructed (Don and Pemberton 1985). This plasmid contains a series of genes designated *tfd* genes (abbreviation for two-four-D genes) that encode the enzymes needed for the initial steps in the biodegradative pathway of 2,4-D; the organization of these genes is illustrated in the preceding figure along with the biochemical pathway of 2,4-D biodegradation.

Six genes on pJP4 that encode enzymes involved in the degradation of 2,4-D are known (Perkins et al. 1990). Three of these, *tfdA, tfdC,* and *tfdD,* begin with a GTG translational start. However, *tfdB, tfdE,* and *tfdF* begin with ATG. As noted previously, the final four bases of *tfdC* coincide with the initial four bases of *tfdD,* creating an overlap in reading frames. A nearly identical reading frame overlap occurs between *tfdE* and *tfdF,* with an ATG rather than GTG translational start. The promoters of *tfdBCDEF* and *tfdA* have a region between -33 and -86, relative to the transcriptional start, resembling a conserved operator region. The expression

of *tfdA* and *tfdCDEF* is constitutive in the absence of *tfdR.* A fourth gene in the chlorocatechol oxidative operon of pJP4, *tfdF,* is essential for 3,5-dichlorocatechol catabolism but is not involved in the catabolism of 3-chlorocatechol. *tfdf* has been tentatively identified as a *trans*chlorodienelactone isomerase.

*A. eutrophus* JMP134 catalyzes the conversion of 2,4-D to 2,4-dichlorophenol (2,4-DCP) by the action of the product of *tfdA.* Although TfdA catalyzes a hydroxylation reaction and has repeatedly been reported to be a monoxygenase, in fact it is not (Hausinger and Fukumori 1995). Rather, TfdA is an Fe(II) and alpha-ketoglutarate-dependent dioxygenase that metabolizes the latter cosubstrate to succinate and carbon dioxide. A variety of other phenoxyacetates and alpha-ketoacids can be used by the enzyme, but the greatest catalytic efficiencies were found using 2,4-D and α-ketoglutarate. The enzyme possesses multiple essential histidine residues, whereas catalytically essential cysteine and lysine groups do not appear to be present. Growth of *A. eutrophus* JMP134 on 2,4-D requires a 2,4-dichlorophenol hydroxylase encoded by gene *tfdB,* which hydroxylates 2,4-DCP to form 3,5-dichlorocatechol. The *tfdA* and *tfdB* gene products are apparently unique to the TFD pathway (Harker et al. 1989). These two gene products also convert chlorophenoxyacetic acid to chlorocatechol.

3,5-Chlorocatechol is oxidized via a series of steps to 2-chloromaleyl acetate by enzymes encoded by the *tfdCDEF* operon of pJP4. The chloromaleyl acetate is then catabolized by chromosomally encoded enzymes. Enzymes involved in this transformation are chlorocatechol 1,2-dioxy-

## Biochemistry and Genetics of 2,4-D Biodegradation, continued

genase (catechol 1,2-dioxygenase II or pyrocate-chase II; EC 1.13.11.1), encoded by *tfdC* of pJP4; chloromuconate cycloisomerase (EC 5.5.1.1), encoded by *tfdD* of pJP4; chloromuconate cyclo-isomerase, encoded by *tfdD,* is specified by an open reading frame of 1113 bases; and dienelac-tone (4-carboxymethylenebut-2-en-4-olide) hydro-lase (EC 3.1.1.45) is encoded by *tfdE* of pJP4. In *A. eutrophus* JMP134(pJP4), 3,5-dichlorocatechol is catabolized by the same pathway as 3-chlorocate-chol with one exception: a fourth gene is required for growth on 2,4-D but not 3CBA. This gene, *tfdF,* encodes a putative *trans*-chlorodienelactone (*trans*-2-chloro-4-carboxymethylenebut-2-en-4-olide) isomerase. The amino acid sequence of TfdF predicted from the nucleotide sequence shows 30% identity with those of iron-containing alcohol dehydrogenases (van der Meer et al. 1992). This suggests that it is responsible for the NADH-con-suming activity that occurs when chloromaleyl-acetate is converted to oxoadipate in cell extracts of *A. eutrophus* JMP134.

Dichloromuconic acids are not completely dechlorinated by cycloisomerization and dienelac-tone hydrolysis. In *A. eutrophus* JMP134, 2-chloro-maleylacetate can be dehalogenated reductively by a maleylacetate reductase that also converts maleylacetate to 3-oxoadipate (Jannsen et al. 1994). The protein is a dimeric enzyme of 35 kDa. The sequence of this protein is not known, but the N-terminal part of the reductase is similar to that of the polypeptides encoded by the *tfdF* and *tcbF* genes of catabolic plasmids pPJ4 and PP51, respectively. These genes reside in regions encod-ing the lower part of haloaromatic metabolism and thus may specify maleylacetate reductases as well.

NADH is the preferred cofactor of the *A. eutrophus* maleylacetate reductase. The predicted polypep-tides of the *tfdF* and *tcbF* genes indeed contain an adenine nucleotide cofactor-binding motif. They also share sequence homology to alcohol dehy-drogenases.

Transposon mutagenesis has localized *tfdB* and *tfdCDEF* to *Eco*RI fragment B of plasmid pJP4 (Perkins et al. 1990). The complete nucleotide sequence of *tfdB* and *tfdCDEF* is contained within a 7954-base-pair *Hind*III-*Sst*I fragment from *Eco*RI fragment B. Sequence and expression analysis of *tfdB* in *Escherichia coli* suggests that 2,4-dichlorophenol hydroxylase consists of a single subunit of 65 kDa. The amino acid sequences of proteins encoded by *tfdD* and *tfdE* have been found to be 63 and 53% identical to those of func-tionally similar enzymes encoded by *clcB* and *clcD,* respectively, from plasmid pAC27 of *Pseudomonas putida. P. putida*(pAC27) can utilize 3-chlorocate-chol but not dichlorocatechols. A region of DNA adjacent to *clcD* in pA27 is 47% identical in amino acid sequence to *tfdF,* a gene important in catabo-lizing dichlorocatechols.

Interestingly, gene *tfdA* is located at a distance of 13 kb from the gene cluster encoding the hydroxylation and cleavage of 2,4-dichlorophenol (Harker et al. 1989). A similar separation of cata-bolic genes into upper and lower pathway gene clusters has also been observed on the NAH (naphthalene degradation) and the TOL (toluene degradation) plasmids. This finding provides addi-tional support for the "module" theory, which pos-tulates an evolution of degradative pathways by sequential assembly of distinct parts of the path-way (Streber et al. 1987). Another trait that gene

*(continued)*

## Biochemistry and Genetics of 2,4-D Biodegradation, continued

*tfdA* has in common with other catabolic genes is the broad substrate specificity of the encoded enzyme. It is able to use 2,4-D, 2-methylchlorophenoxyacetic acid, 4-chlorophenoxyacetic acid, and phenoxyacetic acid as substrates.

Hybridization of total community DNA from vadose soils has shown that the 2,4-D degrading populations have diverse genes and that pJP4-like *tfd* genes (*tfdA* and *tfdB*) are not harbored by a significant percentage of the community (Xia et al. 1995). A survey of 2,4-D degrading bacteria shows diverse patterns of *tfd* genes, supporting the concept that these bacteria contain mosaics of catabolic genes (Fulthorpe et al. 1995). Most strains showed combinations of *tfdA-, B-,* and *C-*like elements that exhibited various degrees of homology

to the genes of *A. eutrophus* JMP134. Members of the beta subdivision of the Proteobacteria class, specifically *Alcaligenes, Burkholderia,* and *Rhodoferax* species, carried DNA fragments with 60% or more sequence similarity to *tfdA* of pJP4, and most carried fragments showing at least 60% homology to *tfdB*. However, many strains did not hybridize with *tfdC*, although they exhibited chlorocatechol dioxygenase activity. Members of the alpha subdivision of the Proteobacteria class, mostly of the genus *Sphingomonas,* did not hybridize to either *tfdA* or *tfdC,* but some hybridized at low stringency to *tfdB*. The data suggest that extensive interspecies transfer of a variety of homologous degradative genes has been involved in the evolution of 2,4-D-degrading bacteria.

---

the spontaneous oxidation. Therefore, although pyrite oxidation starts spontaneously, microorganisms have a decisive role in its maintenance at high rates.

Both *Thiobacillus thiooxidans* and autoxidation produce sulfate and hydrogen ions from pyrite in the first step (Equation 15):

$$(15)\quad 2FeS_2 + 7O_2 + 2H_2O \rightarrow$$
$$2Fe^{2+} + 4SO_4^{2-} + 4H^+$$

The solubilized ferrous iron ($Fe^{2+}$) is oxidized by *Thiobacillus ferrooxidans* to ferric iron ($Fe^{3+}$) (Equation 16):

$$(16)\quad 2Fe^{2+} + \tfrac{1}{2}O_2 + 2H^+ \rightarrow 2Fe^{3+} + H_2O$$

The second reaction (Equation 16) is the rate-limiting and, therefore, most critical step in the oxidation sequence. The ferric iron produced is able to oxidize the remaining sulfide to sulfate in a nonbiological reaction (Equation 17).

$$(17)\quad 8Fe^{3+} + S^{2-} + 4H_2O \rightarrow$$
$$8Fe^{2+} + SO_4^{2-} + 8H^+$$

As seen in Equation 17, the ferric iron is reduced back to ferrous iron, which is available again for oxidation in the reaction of Equation 16. Alternatively, the ferric iron produced in reaction (16) may precipitate as ferric hydroxide (Equation 18), releasing the hydrogen ions consumed in reaction (16) plus four additional hydrogen ions.

$$(18)\quad 2Fe^{3+} + 6H_2O \rightarrow 2Fe(OH)_3 + 6H^+$$

The overall reaction for the oxidation of pyrite can be summarized as shown in Equation 19:

$$(19)\quad 2FeS_2 + 7\tfrac{1}{2}O_2 + 7H_2O \rightarrow$$
$$2Fe(OH)_3 + 4H_2SO_4$$

The sulfuric acid produced accounts for the high acidity and the precipitated ferric hydroxide for the deep brown color of the effluent.

Conventional water treatment techniques were designed for organic pollution and are ineffective against pollution by acid mine drainage. The best way to deal with the problem is to prevent it at the source. It is often feasible to seal abandoned subsurface mines, thus preventing or restricting the availability of oxygen for pyrite oxidation. In the case of strip mining, acid mine drainage can be effectively controlled by prompt reclamation of the land. This involves spreading topsoil over the rubble and establishing a vegetation cover. The same technique is effective on mounds of mine tailings. Of course, this involves extra cost, but after prolonged controversy, federal laws were enacted in the United States that require the prompt and complete reclamation of strip-mined land areas.

If the sealing off of pyritic material from oxygen cannot be accomplished, acid mine drainage can still be curbed, at least in theory, by suppressing the activity of the iron- and sulfur-oxidizing bacteria. Broad-spectrum antimicrobial agents would be dangerous pollutants themselves and so cannot be considered for this purpose. In the laboratory, good control of iron and sulfur oxidizers has been achieved with low concentrations of some carboxylic and alpha-keto acids. These compounds are not known to be hazardous to other organisms.

The feasibility of a novel treatment technique for acid mine effluents using the activity of *Desulfovibrio* and *Desulfotomaculum* was demonstrated on the laboratory scale. The mine effluent is combined with large amounts of organic waste materials, such as sawdust. The activity of aerobic and facultatively anaerobic cellulolytic microorganisms lowers the redox potential and produces degradation intermediates that can be utilized by the sulfate reducers. The hydrogen sulfide generated first reduces the ferric iron to ferrous and precipitates the latter as FeS. The process restores neutral pH and removes the iron and sulfur from the effluent, but the economic and environmental feasibility of the proposed process is yet to be explored (Higgins and Burns 1975).

## Microbial Conversions of Nitrate

Nitrate reduction and denitrification are normal parts of the nitrogen cycle and balance the nitrification and nitrogen-fixation processes, respectively. Heavy use of nitrogen fertilizers in agriculture can greatly increase the nitrate pool. Nitrate itself is relatively innocuous, but its reductive microbial conversion products cause both local and global pollution problems. For this reason, nitrate in drinking water should not exceed 10 ppm. Nitrate can be reduced to nitrite in anaerobic soils, sediments, and aquatic environments.

Nitrate reduction in foods and feeds is of special concern. Production of nitrite in damp forage, which is high in nitrate, has caused poisoning incidents in cattle. Spoilage of high-nitrate vegetable foods, such as spinach, may cause similar nitrite poisoning in humans. Cured meat products are preserved, in part, by addition of nitrate or nitrite. In the former case, some of the added nitrate is converted by microbial action to nitrite, which is the active preserving and curing agent. Nitrite, through its reaction with myoglobin, lends a pleasing red color to cured meat. Unfortunately, the same affinity to hemoglobin causes its toxicity, and residual nitrite in cured meat is limited to 200 mg/kg. Nitrite, by a still obscure mechanism, inhibits *Clostridium botulinum,* the most dangerous food-poisoning agent. Therefore, even though there is valid concern about the safety of nitrate and nitrite in food products, an abrupt phaseout of this curing agent would probably have grave health consequences.

Besides its direct toxicity, nitrite may react in the environment or in foods with secondary amines to form N-nitrosamines. This reaction may occur spontaneously in some cases or may be mediated by microbial enzymes. For instance, *N*-nitrosodimethylamine ($[CH_3]_2N—NO$) has been reported in various food products. *N*-nitrosamines are potent carcinogens, and their ingestion in food and water has proven to be a health hazard. Whether *N*-nitrosamine-forming reactions can proceed to a significant extent in the intestinal tract of a healthy individual is uncertain at this time. *N*-nitrosamines are relatively labile compounds and are subject to chemical as well as microbial degradation. Nevertheless, because of their high carcinogenic potential, even low and occasional exposure may be hazardous. Considerable research effort was devoted to a better understanding of the formation and effects of these pollutants (Wolff and Wasserman 1972).

Further microbial reduction of nitrite in anaerobic soils and sediments leads either to ammonium ($NH_4^+$) or, through nitric oxide (NO), to nitrous oxide ($N_2O$) and/or to elemental nitrogen. Nitrous oxide and $N_2$ are both products of denitrification, and at a low pH, their release predominates. Nitrous oxide may rise to the stratosphere and through its photodecomposition contribute to the depletion of the protective ozone layer of the atmosphere. In this manner, excessive denitrification, resulting from an elevated nitrate pool caused by synthetic fertilizer input, becomes a global pollution problem.

Ozone formation in the stratosphere is initiated by photodissociation when light energy (hv) hits molecular oxygen as seen in Equation 20:

(20) $O_2 + hv \rightarrow O + O$

Some of the singlet oxygen reacts with molecular oxygen to form ozone (Equation 21):

(21) $O + O_2 \rightarrow O_3$

In reality, the reactions are more complex, some of them contributing to ozone formation, others depleting it. The equilibrium concentration of ozone strongly depends on the concentration of singlet oxygen.

Ozone is an effective absorber of UV radiation. Without a protective ozone layer, high amounts of UV radiation would reach the surface of Earth with deleterious consequences for living organisms. Even a modest depletion of the ozone layer would be expected to increase the incidence of skin cancer.

Nitrous oxide depletes ozone through a series of photochemical and chemical reactions. The photodissociation of $N_2O$ (Equation 22) produces $N_2$ and singlet-state oxygen in which one of the electrons has been raised to an excited state ($O^*$). The excited singlet oxygen then may react with additional $N_2O$ to form NO (Equation 23).

(22) $N_2O + hv \rightarrow N_2 + O^*$

(23) $N_2O + O^* \rightarrow 2NO$

Nitric oxide (NO) reacts with ozone according to Equations 24 and 25.

(24) $NO + O_3 \rightarrow NO_2 + O_2$

(25) $NO_2 + O \rightarrow NO + O_2$

The pair of catalytic reactions (Equations 24 and 25) deplete the stratospheric ozone and also the singlet oxygen that is involved in the formation of ozone, without changing the concentrations of either NO or $NO_2$. This is a highly efficient catalytic sequence for the conversion of $O_3 + O$ to $O_2$. Figure 13.27 shows a summary of the natural ozone production and removal processes.

As to the extent and rate of ozone depletion by the above mechanism, calculations and predictions contain many speculative elements and vary widely. There is little doubt, however, that increased denitrification caused by intensive nitrogen fertilizer use contributes to ozone depletion. The fact that fluorocarbons and oxides of nitrogen from internal combustion and jet engines also contribute to ozone depletion makes the problem even more acute. More prudent and modest use of nitrogen fertilizer could control the problem, but this would also result in decreased agricultural yields. An increased reliance on symbiotic nitrogen fixation would also diminish the problem. An interesting alternative approach is the use of selective nitrification inhibitors. If the fertilizer is applied as ammonia or urea, denitrification cannot occur until the fertilizer is oxidized to nitrate. Very low concentrations of nitrification inhibitors, such as nitrapyrin (Figure 13.28), inhibit the activity of the nitrifying bacteria of the *Nitrosomonas* group. This leads to better plant utilization of the nitrogen fertilizer and a decreased nitrate pool. The latter, in turn, decreases the problems connected with nitrate in groundwater and the deleterious effects of nitrate reduction denitrification products (Huber et al. 1977). Better timing of fertilizer addition and altered tillage practices can also reduce the problem of nitrate leaching.

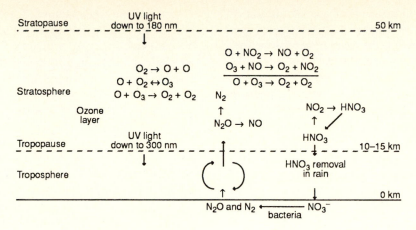

**Figure 13.27**

A summary of natural ozone production and removal processes in the atmosphere. (Source: National Research Council 1976.)

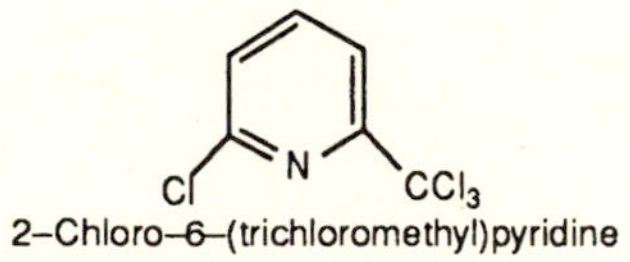

**Figure 13.28**

2-Chloro-6-(trichloromethyl)-pyridine (nitrapyrin), a highly effective nitrification inhibitor. When added to ammonium fertilizer, it ensures better fertilizer utilization by crop plants and decreases nitrate contamination of groundwater.

## Microbial Methylations

Microorganisms are capable of transferring methyl groups onto various heavy metals and some metalloids, such as selenium and arsenic. Methylation processes result in increased toxicity and biomagnification of these elements. Modern technology uses heavy metals extensively, in both their elemental and combined forms. Microbial interactions with some of these heavy metals result in the mobilization and potentiation of heavy metals as environmental toxicants. Mercury, which has perhaps received the most attention in recent years as a heavy-metal pollutant,

serves well to illustrate a process that is not restricted to this metal alone (Summers and Silver 1978).

Metallic mercury is extensively used in the electrical industry, instrument manufacturing, electrolytic processes, and chemical catalysis. Mercury salts and phenylmercury compounds show strong antimicrobial activity and find applications as fungicides, disinfectants, and spoilage retardants. The worldwide annual production and use of mercury is estimated to be 10,000 metric tons. Only a small portion of this material is recycled; most of it winds up as environmental pollutant. The burning of fossil fuels is estimated to release an additional 3000 metric tons of mercury. The natural input of mercury from rock by weathering is only a fraction of the amount that is released through human activities (National Research Council 1978a).

Mercury salts and phenylmercury compounds, though fairly toxic, are excreted efficiently; therefore, environmental contamination by trace amounts of such compounds were initially not regarded with alarm. A tragic occurrence in Japan dramatized the danger of mercury in the environment and called attention to an insidious microbial process—the methylation of mercury in anaerobic sediments.

In the early 1950s, many inhabitants of a small fishing village at Minamata Bay came down with severe disturbances of the central nervous system (Nomura 1968; Sakamoto et al. 1991). These included tremors and impairment of vision, speech, and coordination. Eventually, 2200 cases with 750 fatalities were recorded. Most severely affected were the families that consumed, as a major part of their diet, fish and shellfish taken from the bay. Effluents of a chemical plant containing various mercury compounds, including some methylmercury, were discharged into the same bay. Methylmercury is lipophilic and highly neurotoxic. It was taken up directly, as well as via the food chain by the fish and shellfish in the bay. The inorganic mercury wastes, once incorporated into the anaerobic sediment of the bay, may have been methylated by microorganisms and may have added to the methylmercury contamination, though the contribution of biological methylation versus direct methylmercury discharge was not quantified, and the contribution from microbial methylation probably was minor in this incident.

In contrast to the inorganic and phenylmercury compounds, alkyl mercury is excreted in humans very slowly, with a half-life of thirty days. Consequently, methylmercury concentrations built up in persons consuming tainted seafood that contained as much as 50 ppm of the pollutant, causing the described symptoms, now often referred to as Minamata disease. A similar incident occurred at another Japanese fishing village at Niiagata Bay (D'Itri 1972).

Fortunately, environmentally mediated methylmercury poisoning on a similar scale did not occur elsewhere, but methylmercury did build up to alarming levels in lakes and freshwater fish in Scandinavia because of the use of organomercury fungicides on seeds. A hazardous situation also developed in some of the Great Lakes in the United States, caused by industrial discharges, which forced large areas to be closed to fishing. Even more disturbing are recent reports about elevated mercury levels in fish from pristine freshwater lakes in the northern part of the U.S. Midwest and in Canada (Watras et al. 1995). These lakes have received no point-source mercury inputs, and their only known source of mercury input is atmospheric precipitation. Typically, mercury in lake water is in the low parts per trillion (ppt) range; nevertheless, in larger predatory fish, such as pike, pickerel, and bass, it exceeds the current EPA action level of 1 ppm. For reasons that are not entirely clear as yet, in sediments of acidic freshwater lakes the methylation of mercury is particularly efficient and results in disproportionate bioaccumulation in fish. The closing of these scenic lakes to sports fishing causes large economic losses to the tourist industry (Winfrey and Rudd 1990). Ocean fish of higher trophic levels and older age such as tuna and swordfish contain lower but significant amounts of mercury, and occasionally some catches had to be condemned. There is no evidence that the mercury in pelagic fish is a consequence of industrial pollution; comparable amounts have been found in museum specimens dating back as far as 100 years. The phenomenon illustrates the general tendency of aquatic food chains to accumulate heavy metals and indicates that the margin of safety for increasing the mercury concentration of the marine environment is narrow indeed.

The environmental methylation of mercury and some other heavy metals was attributed to the system responsible for the anaerobic generation of methane (Wood 1971; Ridley et al. 1977; Oremland et al. 1991). Methylcobalamine (methyl-vitamin $B_{12}$) is able to transfer its methyl group to $Hg^{2+}$ ions, yielding reduced vitamin $B_{12}$ ($B_{12}$-r). The process may be enzymatically mediated, but it also proceeds spontaneously. Under environmental conditions, the predominant product is monomethylmercury ($Hg^+CH_3$), but in a second step, smaller amounts of dimethylmercury ($CH_3HgCH_3$) may also be formed (Figure 13.29). The biomethylation of mercury may be inci-

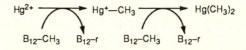

**Figure 13.29**
Methylation of mercuric ions to monomethyl- and dimethylmercury. The donor of the methyl groups here is methylcobalamine (the methylated form of vitamin $B_{12}$). (Source: Wood 1971.)

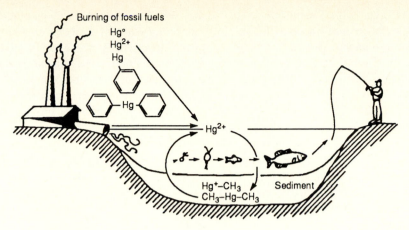

**Figure 13.30**
The cycling of mercury and the biological magnification of methylmercury in the aquatic food chain.

dental or may represent a detoxification mechanism for the microbe. The synthesis and persistence of methylmercury is favored under anaerobic conditions, whereas a high redox potential promotes the microbial degradation of methylmercury (Olson and Cooper 1974, 1976; Compeau and Bartha 1984). There appears to be a dynamic equilibrium between generation of methylmercury in anaerobic sediments and its oxidation in aerated water layers. The resulting minute methylmercury concentrations in the water are sufficient to contaminate aquatic food chains (Figure 13.30).

Phenylmercury compounds are also subject to microbial degradation, and the liberated inorganic mercury, if incorporated into the anaerobic sediment, may be converted to methylmercury. Dimethylmercury is highly volatile and tends to escape to the atmosphere. It is also chemically unstable and decomposes to monomethylmercury under low pH conditions. These factors combine with its low synthesis rate to render dimethylmercury relatively unimportant as an environmental pollutant. The main concern is with monomethylmercury, taken up by fish and shellfish directly through the gills, as well as through the food chain. Additional mercury methylation may result from the activity of anaerobic microorganisms in the intestinal tract.

The involvement of methanogens and some other bacteria in the environmental mercury methylation process was inferred from *in vitro* experiments using isolated microorganisms and laboratory media (Robinson and Tuovinen 1984). Use of selective inhibitors of methanogenesis and sulfate reduction (Oremland and Capone 1988) directly in anaerobic aquatic sediments yielded the surprising result that more than 95% of mercury methylation in these sediments was performed by sulfate-reducing bacteria, a group not previously suspected to be involved in the biomethylation process (Compeau and Bartha 1985). In a mercury-methylating *Desulfovibrio desulfuricans* strain, the methyl group transferred to mercury originated from $C_3$ of serine. The methyl transfer agent was found to be vitamin $B_{12}$, a cobalt corrinoid (Berman et al. 1990; Choi and Bartha 1993).

Our knowledge of the microbial cycling of other heavy metals and metalloids in nature is rudimentary. Extracts of *Veillonella alcaligenes (Micrococcus lactilyticus)* were shown to perform reductive transformations of many metal and metalloid compounds, including selenium, lead, tin, cobalt, and thallium, but we know little about the rate or the significance of these transformations in nature.

Selenium is an essential micronutrient for animals and bacteria that in other than minute concentrations becomes highly toxic (Doran 1982). Chemically, it is closely related to sulfur. Its reduced form, selenide ($Se^{2-}$), is oxidized by microorganisms to $Se^0$, $SeO_3^{2-}$ and $SeO_4^{2-}$, possibly supporting chemolithotrophic growth, though the evidence on this point is yet inadequate. Like sulfate, oxidized forms of selenium serve as electron acceptors under anaerobic conditions for oxidation of hydrogen or organic hydrogen donors. In addition, inorganic selenium can be methylated primarily to dimethylselenide, a volatile product. In contrast to mercury, methylation of selenium decreases rather than increases its toxicity and probably represents a detoxification reaction that occurs readily in aerobic soils and sediments. Under anaerobic conditions, methylation of inorganic selenium was low, but dimethylselenide was released from organoselenium compounds. For methylation of inorganic selenium, both methylcobalamine and $S$-adenosylmethionine function as methyl donors.

Arsenic is a highly toxic, nonbiogenic element. Its toxicity is at least in part due to the fact that arsenate

may replace phosphate in biochemical reactions, thus interfering with the synthesis of essential high-energy phosphate esters. Arsenate can be methylated by some filamentous fungi such as *Scopulariopsis brevicaulis* to mono- and dimethylarsines (Figure 13.31). The methyl group is donated here by either $S$-adenosylmethionine or methylcobalamine. The products are volatile and highly toxic compounds. Some poisonings occurred when fungi growing on damp wallpaper converted and volatilized arsenate in paint in this manner and the residents inhaled the resulting methylarsines.

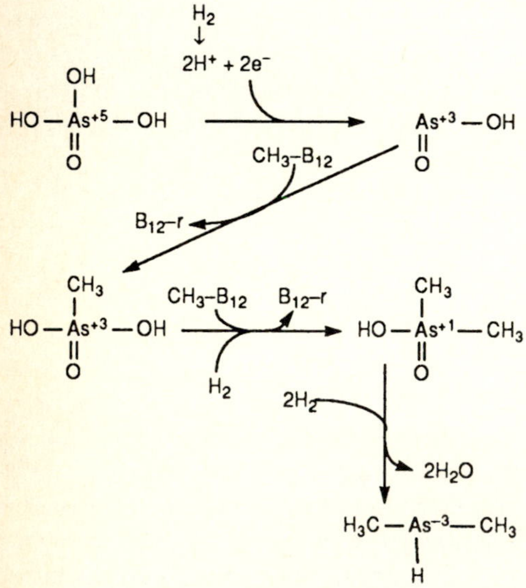

## Microbial Accumulation of Heavy Metals and Radionuclides

Various heavy metals other than mercury, including tin, cobalt, chromium, nickel, cadmium, and thallium, are used in metal alloys or as catalysts. Their mining, smelting, and ultimate disposal cause heavy-metal pollution problems. All these metals are substantially toxic to plants, animals, and many microorganisms.

Radionuclides as environmental pollutants originate from atmospheric testing of thermonuclear weapons, uranium mining and processing, disposal of nuclear wastes, the routine operation of nuclear power plants, and accidents at such installations. To date, atmospheric nuclear testing has been the most significant radionuclide pollution source, but the accumulation of radioactive wastes poses an increasing and not yet satisfactorily solved problem.

Microorganisms, owing to their large surface-to-volume ratio and high metabolic activity, are important vectors in introducing heavy metal and radionuclide pollutants into food webs. At neutral to alkaline pH, heavy metals in soils and sediments tend to be immobilized by precipitation and/or adsorption to cation exchange sites of clay minerals. Microbial production of acid and chelating agents can reverse this adsorption and mobilize the toxic metals. Microbial metabolic products that can chelate metals include dicarboxylic and tricarboxylic acids, pyrocatechol, aromatic hydroxy acids, polyols, and some specific chelators such as the enterochelins and ferrioxamines (see Chapter 11).

**Figure 13.31**
The methylation of arsenic to mono- and dimethyl arsines by filamentous fungi. (Source: Wood 1971. Reprinted by permission, copyright John Wiley and Sons.)

Mobilization is often followed by uptake and intracellular accumulation of the heavy metals, both by microorganisms and by plant roots. It is not entirely clear why some of these toxic metals are taken up and stored by microorganisms, but intracellular sequestering seems to confer heavy-metal resistance on at least some bacteria. Filamentous fungi were shown to transport heavy metals and radionuclides along their hyphae. This has some implications for the potential role of mycorrhizal fungi in transmitting such pollutants into higher plants. Direct root uptake of heavy metals mobilized by microbial acid production or chelation is an alternative possibility.

The heavy metal cadmium is of special concern in this respect. Cadmium is highly toxic and tends to accumulate with even very low exposures because it is excreted extremely slowly. Its approximate half-life in humans is ten years. Cadmium in humans causes, at low chronic exposure, hypertension and kidney damage. Higher exposures in Japan through rice grown on industrially contaminated fields have caused the painful and crippling itai-itai (ouch-ouch) bone-and-joint disease. Unfortunately, cadmium occurs in low concentrations in some phosphate rocks and thus is present also in phosphate fertilizer spread on agricultural fields. Another potential source of cadmium and other heavy metals is sewage sludge. Such sludge is being considered for use as soil conditioner. As a substantial portion of sewage sludge is derived from microbial biomass, the relatively high concentration of heavy metals in this material also reflects the ability of microorganisms to concentrate these pollutants. Obviously, the overall mobility of heavy metals in agricultural soils, their uptake by crop plants, and the role of soil microorganisms in these processes should be clarified prior to any large-scale use of sewage sludge on agricultural fields.

Microbial accumulation of radionuclides, with clear human health implications, has been demonstrated in some Arctic areas (Hanson 1967). Lichens are extremely effective in concentrating the radionuclides such as $^{90}$Sr and $^{137}$Cs from atmospheric fallout (Figure 13.32). During periods of snow cover, when the lichens are shielded from direct fallout, concentrations of radionuclides in the lichens decrease. During

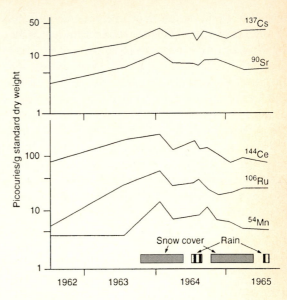

**Figure 13.32**
Concentrations of $^{54}$Mn, $^{90}$Sr, $^{106}$Ru, $^{137}$Cs, and $^{144}$Ce in *Cladonia letiaria* lichens in Anaktuvud Pass, Alaska, during 1962–1965. (Source: Hanson 1967. Reprinted by permission, copyright Pergamon Press Ltd.)

periods of rain, concentrations of radionuclides increase. Because lichens serve as the primary producers in a food chain of lichen → caribou → humans, there can be an efficient transfer of such concentrated elements to the highest member of the food chain. These radionuclides, being deposited in bone tissue, may affect blood cell synthesis in the bone marrow and cause leukemia.

## Chapter Summary

Industrialized societies and those with mechanized agricultural production are now beset by a number of pollution problems that were largely unknown prior to World War II. Prominent among these problems is environmental pollution by xenobiotic synthetic chemicals that fail to be recycled by microorganisms and may be biomagnified with destructive effects. Some xenobiotic organics are thermodynamically unsuitable as substrates. In other cases, microbes may yet need to evolve suitable catabolic pathways as they did in the case of natural products over several billion years. The structural reasons for recalcitrance often involve carbon-halogen bonds, nitro-substituents, tertiary and quaternary carbon atoms, and excessive molecular size. Other xenobiotics undergo partial or even synthetic transformations to compounds with altered biological activity. Our understanding of the molecular, biochemical, and environmental factors that determine the fate of xenobiotics is increasing but is still far from complete. Biogeochemical cycling by microbes interacts with the mining, agricultural, and industrial activities of humans, resulting in local and global pollution problems. Acid mine drainage originates from strip-mining regions and involves the activity of sulfide- and iron-oxidizing bacteria. Excessive use of nitrogen fertilizer may result in global ozone depletion due to the activity of nitrate reducers. Microbial methylation of some heavy metals, accumulation of the same, and additional metals and radionuclides in microorganisms facilitate the entry of these pollutants into food webs and, ultimately, into the human diet.

## STUDY QUESTIONS

1. Why do we call some synthetic organic compounds "xenobiotic"?

2. Name some structural features characteristic of xenobiotic compounds.

3. What is biomagnification?

4. What are the two characteristics shared by all pollutants subject to biomagnification?

5. What are freons? Why are they a threat to the ozone layer?

6. Which xenobiotic compounds are more readily attacked under anaerobic than aerobic conditions?

7. What are chlorobenzodioxins and chlorobenzofurans? What processes create them?

8. What makes synthetic polymers (plastics) resistant to biodegradation?

9. Name a truly biodegradable thermoplastic. How is it produced?

10. Why are linear alkylbenzylsulfonates (LABSs) biodegraded more easily than normal alkylbenzylsulfonates (ABSs)?

11. What are the first biodegradation steps in case of a normal alkane? How does the biodegradation continue?

12. What are the initial biodegradation steps for a cycloalkane? Why is it difficult to isolate cycloalkane-degrading pure cultures?

13. What are the two patterns of benzene ring degradation?

14. Why do many genes associated with biodegradation of xenobiotics reside on plasmids?

15. What is acid mine drainage? How can it be prevented?

16. Why is nitrate dangerous in drinking water?

17. What is the biological activity of nitrosamines? How are nitrosamines formed?

18. How do products of denitrification interact with ozone?

19. How can one minimize denitrification?

20. Why is the methylation of mercury in anaerobic sediments a dangerous process?

21. What is the "Minamata disease"?

22. Where does the property of bacteria to accumulate heavy metals create a problem?

23. How do radionuclides enter the food chain?

# References and Suggested Readings

Ackersberg, F., F. Bole, and F. Widdel. 1991. Anaerobic oxidation of a saturated hydrocarbon to $CO_2$ by a new type of sulfate-reducing bacterium. *Archives for Microbiology* 156:5–14.

Adriaens, P,. and D. D. Focht. 1990. Continuous coculture degradation of selected polychlorinated biphenyl congeners by *Acinetobacter* spp. in an aerobic reactor system. *Environmental Science and Technology* 24:1042–1049.

Adriaens, P. H., P. E. Kohler, and D. Kohler-Staub. 1989. Bacterial dehalogenation of chlorobenzoates and coculture biodegradation of 4,4′–dichlorobiphenyl. *Applied and Environmental Microbiology* 55:887–892.

Adrian, N. R., and J. M. Suflita. 1990. Reductive dehalogenation of a nitrogen heterocyclic herbicide in anoxic aquifer slurries. *Applied and Environmental Microbiology* 56:292–294.

Ahmed, M., and D. D. Focht. 1973. Degradation of polychlorinated biphenyls by two species of *Achromobacter. Canadian Journal of Microbiology* 19:47–52.

Alexander, M. 1965. Biodegradation: Problems of molecular recalcitrance and microbial fallibility. *Advances in Applied Microbiology* 7:35–80.

Alexander, M. 1981. Biodegradation of chemicals of environmental concern. *Science* 211:132–138.

Atlas, R. M. 1981. Microbial degradation of petroleum hydrocarbons: An environmental perspective. *Microbiological Reviews* 45:180–209.

Atlas, R. M. (ed.). 1984. *Petroleum Microbiology*. Macmillan, New York.

Bagley, D. M., and J. M. Gossett. 1990. Tetrachloroethene transformation to trichloroethene and *cis*-1, 2-dichloroethene by sulfate-reducing enrichment cultures. *Applied and Environmental Microbiology* 56:2511–2516.

Bartha, R. 1980. Pesticide residues in humus. *ASM News* 46:356–360.

Bartha, R., and D. Pramer. 1970. Metabolism of acylanilide herbicides. *Advances in Applied Microbiology* 13:317–341.

Bartha, R., I.-S. Yon, and A. Saxena. 1983. Humus-bound residues of phenylamide herbicides and their nature and monitoring. In J. Mijamoto and P. C. Kearney (eds.).

*Pesticide Chemistry Human Welfare and the Environment Vol. 3.* Pergamon Press, Oxford, pp. 345–350.

Bedard, D. L., and J. F. Quensen, III. 1995. Microbial reductive dechlorination of polychlorinated byphenyls. In L. Y. Young and C. E. Cerniglia (eds.). *Microbial Transformation and Degradation of Toxic Organic Chemicals.* Wiley-Liss, New York, pp. 127–216.

Bedard, D. L., R. E. Wagner, and M. J. Brennan. 1987. Extensive degradation of arochlors and environmentally transformed polychlorinated biphenyls by *Alcaligenes eutrophus* H850. *Applied and Environmental Microbiology* 53:1094–1102.

Berman, M., T. Chase, Jr., and R. Bartha. 1990. Carbon flow in mercury biomethylation by *Desulfovibrio desulfuricans. Applied and Environmental Microbiology* 56:298–300.

Bodennec, G. J., P. Desmarquest, B. Jensen, and R. Kantin. 1987. Evolution of hydrocarbons and the activity of bacteria in marine sediments contaminated with discharges of petroleum. *International Journal of Environmental and Analytical Chemistry* 29:153–178.

Boldrin, B., A. Thiem, and C. Fritzske. 1993. Degradation of phenanthrene, fluorene, fluoranthene and pyrene by a *Mycobacterium* sp. *Applied and Environmental Microbiology* 59:1927–1930.

Bossert, I., and R. Bartha. 1984. The fate of petroleum in soil ecosystems. In R. M. Atlas (ed.). *Petroleum Microbiology.* Macmillan, New York, pp. 435–473.

Brandl, H., R. A. Gross, and R. W. Lenz. 1988. *Pseudomonas oleovorans* as a source of poly (β–hydroxyalkanoates) for potential applications as biodegradable polyesters. *Applied and Environmental Microbiology* 54:1977–1982.

Brenner, T. E. 1969. Biodegradable detergents and water pollution. *Advances in Environmental Science Technology* 1:147–196.

Britton, L. N. 1984. Microbial degradation of aliphatic hydrocarbons. In D. T. Gibson (ed.). *Microbial Degradation of Organic Compounds.* Marcel Dekker, New York, pp. 89–129.

Brown, J. F., D. L. Bedard, and M. J. Brennan. 1987. Polychlorinated biphenyl dechlorination in aquatic sediments (river sediments). *Science* 236:709–712.

Bumpus, J. A. 1989. Biodegradation of polycyclic aromatic hydrocarbons by *Phanerochaete chrysosporium.* *Applied and Environmental Microbiology* 55:154–158.

Bumpus, J. A., and S. D. Aust. 1987. Biodegradation of DDT [1,1,1-trichloro-2,2-bis(4-chlorophenyl) ethane] by the white rot fungus *Phanerochaete chrysosporium.* *Applied and Environmental Microbiology* 53:2001–2028.

Bumpus, J. A., M. Tien, D. Wright, and S. D. Aust. 1985. Oxidation of persistent environmental pollutants by a white rot fungus. *Science* 228:1434–1436.

Butler, J. N., B. F. Morris, and J. Sass. 1973. Pelagic tar from Bermuda and the Sargasso Sea. *Bermuda Biological Station Special Publication No. 10.* Bermuda.

Cade, T. J., J. L. Lincer, C. M. White, D. G. Roseneau, and L. G. Swartz. 1971. DDE residues and eggshell changes in Alaskan falcons and hawks. *Science* 172:955–957.

Carpenter, E. J. 1972. Polystyrene spherules in coastal waters. *Science* 178:749–750.

Carson, R. 1962. *Silent Spring.* Houghton-Mifflin, New York.

Cerniglia, C. E. 1984. Microbial transformation of aromatic hydrocarbons. In R. M. Atlas (ed.). *Petroleum Microbiology.* Macmillan, New York, pp. 99–128.

Cerniglia, C. E. 1993. Biodegradation of polycyclic aromatic hydrocarbons. *Biodegradation* 3:351–368.

Chatterjee, D. K., J. J. Kilbane, and A. M. Chakrabarty. 1982. Biodegradation of 2,4,5-trichlorophenoxyacetic acid in soil by a pure culture of *Pseudomonas cepacia.* *Applied and Environmental Microbiology* 44:514–516.

Chaudhry, G. R., and S. Chapalamadugu. 1991. Biodegradation of halogenated organic compounds. *Microbiological Reviews* 55:59–79.

Choi, S. C., and R. Bartha. 1993. Cobalamin-mediated mercury methylation by *Desultovibrio desulfuricans.* LS. *Applied and Environmental Microbiology* 59:290–295.

Coates, J. D., R. T. Anderson, and D. R. Lovley. 1996a. Oxidation of polycyclic aromatic hydrocarbons under sulfate-reducing conditions. *Applied and Environmental Microbiology* 62:1099–1101.

Coates, J. D., R. T. Anderson, J. C. Woodward, E. J .P. Phillips, and D. R. Lovley. 1996b. Anaerobic hydrocarbon degradation in petroleum-contaminated harbor sediments under sulfate-reducing and artificially imposed iron-reducing conditions. *Environmental Science and Technology* 30:2784–2789.

Colberg, P. J .S., and L. Y. Young. 1995. Anaerobic degradation of nonhalogenated homocyclic aromatic compounds coupled with nitrate, iron or sulfate reduction. In L. Y. Young and C. E. Cerniglia (eds.). *Microbial Transformation and Degradation of Toxic Organic Chemicals.* Wiley-Liss, New York, pp. 307–330.

Colwell, E. B. (ed.). 1971. *The Ecological Effects of Oil Pollution on Littoral Communities.* Applied Science Publishers, London.

Compeau, G., and R. Bartha. 1984. Methylation and demethylation of mercury under controlled redox, pH and salinity conditions. *Applied and Environmental Microbiology* 48:1203–1207.

Compeau, G., and R. Bartha. 1985. Sulfate-reducing bacteria: Principal methylators of mercury in anoxic estuarine sediment. *Applied and Environmental Microbiology* 50:498–502.

Dagley, S. 1975. A biochemical approach to some problems of environmental pollution. In P. N. Campbell and W. N. Aldridge (eds.). *Essays in Biochemistry.* Vol. 2. Academic Press, London, pp. 81–130.

Dalton, H., and D. I. Stirling. 1982. Co-metabolism. *Philosophical Transactions of the Royal Society* (London), Ser. B 297:481–491.

D'Itri, F. M. 1972. *The Environmental Mercury Problem.* CRC Press, Cleveland, OH.

Dolfing, J., and J. M. Tiedje. 1987. Growth yield increase linked to reductive dechlorination in a defined 3-chlorobenzoate degrading methanogenic coculture. *Archives of Microbiology* 149:102–105.

Don, R. H., and J. M. Pemberton. 1985. Genetic and physical map of the 2,4-dichlorophenoxyacetic acid degradative plasmid pJP4. *Journal of Bacteriology* 161:466–467.

Doran, J. W. 1982. Microorganisms and the biological cycling of selenium. *Advances in Microbial Ecology* 6:1–32.

Drinkwine, A., S. Spurlin, J. Van Emon, and V. Lopez-Avila. 1991. Immuno-based personal exposure monitors. In *Field Screening Methods for Hazardous Wastes and Toxic Chemicals.* U.S. Environmental Protection Agency and U.S. Army Toxic and Hazardous Materials Agency, Las Vegas, NV, pp. 449–459.

Efroymson, R. A., and M. Alexander. 1991. Biodegradation by an *Arthrobacter* species of hydrocarbons partitioned into an organic solvent. *Applied and Environmental Microbiology* 57:1441–1447.

Evans, J. D., and S. K. Sikdar. 1990. Biodegradable plastics: An idea whose time has come. *Chemtech* 20:38–42.

Fathepure, B. Z., J. M. Tiedje, and S. A. Boyd. 1988. Reductive dechlorination of hexachlorobenzene to tri- and dichlorobenzenes in anaerobic sewage sludge. *Applied and Environmental Microbiology* 54:327–330.

Fogel, M. M., A. R. Taddeo, and S. Fogel. 1986. Biodegradation of chlorinated ethanes by a methane-utilizing mixed culture. *Applied and Environmental Microbiology* 51:720–724.

Fries, M., J. Zhou, J. Chee-Sanford, and J. M. Tiedje. 1994. Isolation, characterization, and distribution of denitrifying toluene degraders from a variety of habitats. *Applied and Environmental Microbiology* 60:2802–2810.

Fujiwara, K. 1975. Environmental and food contamination with PCBs in Japan. *Science of the Total Environment* 4:219–247.

Fulthorpe, R. R., C. McGowan, O. V. Maltseva, W. E. Holben, and J. M. Tiedje. 1995. 2,4-Dichlorophenoxy-acetic acid-degrading bacteria contain mosaics of catabolic genes. *Applied and Environmental Microbiology* 61:3274–3281.

Galli, R., and P. L. McCarty. 1989. Biotransformation of 1,1,1-trichloroethane, trichloromethane, and tetra-chloromethane by a *Clostridium* sp. *Applied and Environmental Microbiology* 55:837–844.

Genthner, B. R .S., W. A. Price, and P. H. Pritchard. 1989a. Anaerobic degradation of chloroaromatic compounds in aquatic sediments under a variety of enrichment conditions. *Applied and Environmental Microbiology* 55:1466–1471.

Genthner, B. R .S., W. A. Price, and P. H. Pritchard. 1989b. Characterization of anaerobic dechlorinating consortia derived from aquatic sediments. *Applied and Environmental Microbiology* 55:1472–1476.

Ghosal, D., I. S. You., D. K. Chatterjee, and A. M. Chakrabarty. 1985. Microbial degradation of halogenated compounds. *Science* 228:135–142.

Gibson, D. T., and V. Subramanian. 1984. Microbial degradation of aromatic hydrocarbons. In D. T. Gibson (ed.). *Microbial Degradation of Organic Compounds.* Plenum Press, New York, pp. 181–252.

Gibson, D. T., S. M. Resnick, K. Lee, J. M. Brand, D. S. Torok, L. P. Wackett, M. J. Schocken, and B. E. Haigler. 1995. Desaturation, dioxygenation, and monooxygenation reactions catalyzed by naphthalene dioxygenase from *Pseudomonas* sp. strain 9816-4. *Journal of Bacteriology* 177:2615–2621.

Gosset, R. W., D. A. Brown, and D. R. Young. 1983. Predicting the bioaccumulation of organic compounds in marine organisms using octanol/water partition coefficients. *Marine Pollution Bulletin* 14:387–392.

Grbic-Galic, D., and T. M. Vogel. 1987. Transformation of toluene and benzene by mixed methanogenic cultures. *Applied and Environmental Microbiology* 53:254–260.

Greaves, M. P., H. A. Davies, J. A .P. Marsh, and G. I. Wingfield. 1977. Herbicides and soil microorganisms. *CRC Critical Reviews of Microbiology* 5:1–38.

Gustafson, C. G. 1970. PCBs: Prevalent and persistent. *Environmental Science and Technology* 4:814–819.

Hallas, L. E., and M. Alexander. 1983. Microbial transformation of nitroaromatic compounds in sewage effluent. *Applied and Environmental Microbiology* 45:1234–1241.

Hanson, W. C. 1967. Cesium-137 in Alaskan lichens, caribou and Eskimos. *Health Physics* 13:383–389.

Harker, A. R., R. H. Olsen, and R. J. Seidler. 1989. Phenoxyacetic acid degradation by the 2,4-dichlorophenoxyacetic acid (TFD) pathway of plasmid pJP4: Mapping and characterization of the TFD regulatory gene, *tfdR. Journal of Bacteriology* 171:314–320.

Harker, A. R., and Y. Kim. 1990. Trichloroethylene degradation by two independent aromatic-degrading pathways in *Alcaligenes eutrophus* JMP134. *Applied and Environmental Microbiology* 56:1179–1181.

Hausinger, R. P., and F. Fukumori. 1995. Characterization of the first enzyme in 2,4-dichlorophenoxyacetic acid metabolism. *Environmental Health Perspectives* 103:37–39.

Heitkamp, M. A., and C. E. Cerniglia. 1988. Mineralization of polycyclic aromatic hydrocarbons by a bacterium isolated from sediment below an oil field. *Applied and Environmental Microbiology* 54:1612–1614.

Higgins, I. J., and R. G. Burns. 1975. *The Chemistry and Microbiology of Pollution.* Academic Press, London.

Hill, I. R., and S.J.L. Wright (eds.). 1978. *Pesticide Microbiology.* Academic Press, London.

Hoeks, J. 1972. Changes in composition of soil near air leaks in natural gas mains. *Soil Science* 113:46–54.

Horvath, R. S. 1972. Microbial co-metabolism and the degradation of organic compounds in nature. *Bacteriological Reviews* 36:146–155.

Huber, D. M., H. L. Warren, D. W. Nelson, and C. Y. Tsai. 1977. Nitrification inhibitors—New tools for food production. *BioScience* 27:523–529.

Janssen, D. B., F. Pries, and J. R. van der Ploeg. 1994. Genetics and biochemistry of dehalogenating enzymes. *Annual Reviews of Microbiology* 48:163–191.

Jimenez, I. Y., and R. Bartha. 1996. Solvent-augmented mineralization of pyrene by a *Mycobacterium* sp. *Applied and Environmental Microbiology* 62:2311–2316.

Johnson, L. M., C. S. McDowell, and M. Krupha. 1985. Microbiology in pollution control: From bugs to biotechnology. *Developments in Industrial Microbiology* 26:365–376.

Kaufman, D. D., G. G. Still, G. D. Paulson, and S. K. Bandal (eds.). 1976. *Bound and Conjugated Pesticide Residues.* ACS Symposium Series No. 29, American Chemical Society, Washington, DC.

Kazumi, J., M. E. Caldwell, J. M. Suflita, D. R. Lovley, and L. Y. Young. 1997. Anaerobic degradation of benzene in diverse anoxic environments. *Environmental Science and Technology* 31:813–818.

Kellogg, S. T., D. K. Chatterjee, and A. M. Chakrabarty. 1981. Plasmid assisted molecular breeding—New technique for enhanced biodegradation of persistent toxic chemicals. *Science* 214:1133–1135.

Kennedy, D. W., S. D. Aust, and J. A. Bumpus. 1990. Comparative biodegradation of alkyl halide insecticides by the white rot fungus, *Phanerochaete chrysosporium* (BKM–F–1767). *Applied and Environmental Microbiology* 56:2347–2353.

Kennicutt, M. C. 1990. Oil spillage in Antarctica. *Environmental Science and Technology* 24:620–624.

Kilbane, J. J., D .K. Chatterjee, J. S. Karns, S. T. Kellog, and A. M. Chakrabarty. 1982. Biodegradation of 2,4,5-trichlorophenoxyacetic acid by a pure culture of *Pseudomonas cepacia. Applied and Environmental Microbiology* 44:72–78.

Kohler, H.-P. E., D. Kohler-Staub, and D. D. Focht. 1988. Cometabolism of polychlorinated biphenyls: Enhanced transformation of Aroclor 1254 by growing bacterial cells. *Applied and Environmental Microbiology* 54:1940–1945.

Krupp, L. R., and W. J. Jewell. 1992. Biodegradability of modified plastic films in controlled biological environments. *Environmental Science and Technology* 26:193–198.

Larson, R. J. 1990. Structure-activity relationships for biodegradation of linear alkylbenzenesulfonates. *Environmental Science and Technology* 24:1241–1246.

Leahy, J. G., and R. R. Colwell. 1990. Microbial degradation of hydrocarbons in the environment. *Microbiological Reviews* 54:305–315 .

Lee, K., and E. M. Levy. 1991. Bioremediation: Waxy crude oils stranded on low-energy shorelines. In *Proceedings of the 1991 International Oil Spill Conference. American Petroleum Institute,* Washington, DC, pp. 541–547.

Linkfield, T. G., J. M. Suflita, and J. M. Tiedje.1989. Characterization of the acclimation period before anaerobic dehalogenation of halobenzoates. *Applied and Environmental Microbiology* 55:2773–2778.

Little, C. D., A. V. Palumbo, and S. E. Herbes. 1988. Trichloroethylene biodegradation by a methane-oxidizing bacterium. *Applied and Environmental Microbiology* 54:951–956.

Lovley, D. R., J. C. Woodward, and F. H. Chapelle. 1994. Stimulated anoxic biodegradation of aromatic hydrocarbons using Fe(III) ligands. *Nature* 370:128–131.

Lovley, D. R., J. D. Coates, J. C. Woodward, and E.J.P. Phillips. 1995. Benzene oxidation coupled to sulfate reduction. *Applied and Environmental Microbiology* 61:953–958.

Lovley, D. R., J. C. Woodward, and F. H. Chapelle. 1996. Rapid anaerobic benzene oxidation with a variety of chelated Fe(III) forms. *Applied and Environmental Microbiology* 62:288–291.

Massé, R., F. Messier, L. Peloquin, C. Ayotte, and M. Sylvestre. 1984. Microbial degradation of 4-chlorobiphenyl, a model compound of chlorinated biphenyls. *Applied and Environmental Microbiology* 47:947–951.

Maugh, T. H. 1973. DDT: An unrecognized source of polychlorinated biphenyls. *Science* 180:578–579.

Miller, R. M., and R. Bartha. 1989. Evidence from liposome encapsulation for transport-limited microbial metabolism of solid alkanes. *Applied and Environmental Microbiology* 55:269–274.

Mohn, W. M., and J. M. Tiedje. 1990a. Catabolite thiosulfate disproportionation and carbon dioxide reduction in strain DCB-1, a reductively dechlorinating anaerobe. *Journal of Bacteriology* 172:2065–2070.

Mohn, W. M., and J. M. Tiedje. 1990b. Strain DCB-1 conserves energy for growth from reductive dechlorination coupled to formate oxidation. *Archives of Microbiology* 153:267–271.

Mohn, W. M., and J. M Tiedje. 1992. Microbial reductive dehalogenation. *Microbiological Reviews* 56:482–507.

Molina, M. J., and F. S. Rowland. 1974. Stratospheric sink for chlorofluoromethanes—chlorine atom-catalysed destruction of ozone. *Nature* (London) 249:810–812.

National Research Council. 1972. *Degradation of Synthetic Organic Molecules in the Biosphere.* National Academy of Sciences, Washington, DC.

National Research Council. 1976. *Halocarbons: Effects on Stratospheric Ozone.* National Academy of Sciences, Washington, DC.

National Research Council. 1978a. *An Assessment of Mercury in the Environment.* National Academy of Sciences, Washington, DC.

National Research Council. 1978b. *Kepone, Mirex, Hexachlorocyclopentadiene: An Environmental Assessment.* National Academy of Sciences, Washington, DC.

National Research Council. 1979. *Polychlorinated Biphenyls.* National Academy of Sciences, Washington, DC.

National Research Council. 1985. *Oil in the Sea: Inputs, Fates and Effects.* National Academy Press, Washington, DC.

Nomura, S. 1968. Epidemiology of Minamata disease. In M. Kutsura (ed.). *Minamata Disease.* Kunamoto University, Kunamoto, Japan, pp. 5–36.

Novick, N. J., and M. Alexander. 1985. Cometabolism of low concentrations of propachlor, alachlor, and cycloate in sewage and lake water. *Applied and Environmental Microbiology* 49:737–743.

Olson, B. H., and R. C. Cooper. 1974. *In situ* methylation of mercury in estuarine sediment. *Nature* (London) 252:682–683.

Olson, B. H., and R. C. Cooper. 1976. Comparison of aerobic and anaerobic methylation of mercuric chloride in San Francisco Bay sediments. *Water Research* 10:113–116.

Oremland, R. S., and D. G. Capone. 1988. Use of "specific" inhibitors in biogeochemistry and microbial ecology. *Advances in Microbial Ecology* 10:285–383.

Oremland, R. S., C. W. Culbertson, and M. R. Winfrey. 1991. Methylmercury decomposition in sediments and bacterial cultures: Involvement of methanogens and sulfate reducers in oxidative demethylation. *Applied and Environmental Microbiology* 57:130–137.

Orndorff, S. A., and R. R. Colwell. 1980. Microbial transformation of Kepone. *Applied and Environmental Microbiology* 39:398–406.

Perkins, E. J., M. P. Gordon, O. Caceres, and P. F. Lurquin. 1990. Organization and sequence analysis of the 2,4-dichlorophenol hydroxylase and dichlorocatechol oxidative operons of plasmid pJP4. *Journal of Bacteriology* 172:2351–2359.

Perry, J. J. 1984. Microbial metabolism of cyclic alkanes. In R. M. Atlas (ed.). *Petroleum Microbiology.* Macmillan, New York, pp. 61–97.

Pfaender, F. K., and M. Alexander. 1972. Extensive microbial degradation of DDT *in vitro* and DDT metabolism by natural communities. *Journal of Agricultural Food Chemistry* 20:842–846.

Quensen, J. F., J. M. Tiedje, and S. A. Boyd. 1988. Reductive dechlorination of polychlorinated biphenyls by anaerobic microorganisms from sediments. *Science* 242:752–754.

Ramsey, B. A., K. Lomaliza, C. Chavarie, B. Dube, P. Bataille, and J. Ramsay. 1990. Production of poly-(β-hydroxybutyric-co-β-hydroxyvaleric) acids. *Applied and Environmental Microbiology* 56:2093–2098.

Reich, M., and R. Bartha. 1977. Degradation and mineralization of a polybutene film-mulch by the synergistic action of sunlight and soil microbes. *Soil Science* 124:177–180.

Ridley, W. P., L. J. Dizikes, and J. M. Wood. 1977. Biomethylation of toxic elements in the environment. *Science* 197:329–332.

Robinson, J. B., and O. H. Tuovinen. 1984. Mechanism of microbial resistance and detoxification of mercury and organomercury compounds: Physiological, biochemical and genetic analyses. *Microbiological Reviews* 48:95–124.

Rontani, J. F., F. Bosser-Joulak, E. Rambeloarisoa, J. E. Bertrand, G. Giusti, and R. Faure. 1985. Analytical study of Asthart crude oil asphaltenes biodegradation. *Chemosphere* 14:1413–1422.

Safe, S. H. 1984. Microbial degradation of polychlorinated biphenyls. In D.T. Gibson (ed.). *Microbial Degradation of Organic Compounds.* Marcel Dekker, New York, pp. 361–369.

Sakamoto, M., A. Nakano, Y. Kinjo, H. Higashi, and M. Futatsuka. 1991. Present mercury levels in red blood cells of nearby inhabitants about 30 years after the outbreak of Minamata disease. *Ecotoxicology and Environmental Safety* 22:58–66.

Sander, P., R. M. Wittich, P. Fortnagel, H. Wilkes, and W. Franke. 1991. Degradation of 1,2,4-trichloro- and 1,2,4,5-tetrachlorobenzene by *Pseudomonas* strains. *Applied and Environmental Microbiology* 57:1430–1440.

Shiaris, M. P. 1989. Seasonal biotransformation of naphthalene, phenanthrene, and benzo[a]pyrene in surficial estuarine sediments. *Applied and Environmental Microbiology* 55:1391–1399.

Singer, M. E., and W. R. Finnerty. 1984. Microbial metabolism of straight-chain and branched alkanes. In R. M. Atlas (ed.). *Petroleum Microbiology.* Macmillan, New York, pp. 1–59.

Sjoblad, R. D., and J. M. Bollag. 1977. Oxidative coupling of aromatic pesticide intermediates by a fungal phenol oxidase. *Applied and Environmental Microbiology* 33:908–910.

Song, H. G., T. A. Pedersen, and R. Bartha. 1986. Hydrocarbon mineralization in soil: Relative bacterial and fungal contribution. *Soil Biology Biochemistry* 18:109–111.

Spain, J. C. (ed.). 1995. *Biodegradation of Nitroaromatic Compounds.* Plenum Press, New York.

Stevens, T. O., and J. M. Tiedje. 1988. Carbon dioxide fixation and mixotrophic metabolism by strain DCB-1, a dehalogenating anaerobic bacterium. *Applied and Environmental Microbiology* 54:2944–2948.

Stevens, T. O., T. G. Linkfield, and J. M. Tiedje. 1988. Physiological characterization of strain DCB-1, a unique dehalogenating sulfidogenic bacterium. *Applied and Environmental Microbiology* 54:2938–2943.

Still, C. C., T.-S. Hsu, and R. Bartha. 1980. Soil-bound 3,4-dichloroanilines: Source of contamination in rice grain. *Bulletin of Environmental Contamination and Toxicology* 24:550–554.

Streber, W. R., K. N. Timmis, and M. H. Zenk. 1987. Analysis, cloning, and high-level expression of 2,4-dichlorophenoxyacetate monooxygenase gene *tfdA* of *Alcaligenes eutrophus* JMP134. *Journal of Bacteriology* 169:2950–2955.

Stucki, G., W. Brunner, D. Staub, and T. Leisinger. 1981. Microbial degradation of chlorinated $C_1$ and $C_2$ hydrocarbons. In T. Leisinger, A. M. Cook, R. Hütter, and J. Nüesch (eds.). *Microbial Degradation of Xenobiotics and Recalcitrant Compounds.* Academic Press, London, pp. 131–137.

Suflita, J. M., A. Horowitz, D. R. Shelton, and J. M. Tiedje. 1982. Dehalogenation: A novel pathway for the anaerobic biodegradation of haloaromatic compounds. *Science* 214:1115–1117.

Suflita, J. M., and G. T. Townsend. 1995. The microbial ecology and physiology of aryl dehalogenation reactions and implication for bioremediation. In L. Y. Young and C. E. Cerniglia (eds.). *Microbial Transformation and Degradation of Toxic Organic Chemicals.* Wiley-Liss, New York, pp. 243–268.

Summers, A. O., and S. Silver. 1978. Microbial transformations of metals. *Annual Reviews of Microbiology* 32:637–672.

Sutherland, J. B., F. Rafi, A. A. Khan, and C. E. Cerniglia. 1995. Mechanisms of polycyclic aromatic hydrocarbon degradation. In L. Y. Young and C. E. Cerniglia (eds.). *Microbial Transformation and Degradation of Toxic Organic Chemicals.* Wiley-Liss, New York, pp. 269–306.

Thayer, A. M. 1990. Degradable plastics create controversy in solid waste issues. *Chemical Engineering News* 68:7–14.

Trower, M. K., R. M. Buckland, R. Higgins, and M. Griffin. 1985. Isolation and characterization of a cyclohexane metabolizing *Xanthobacter* sp. *Applied and Environmental Microbiology* 49:1282–1289.

Trudgill, P. W. 1984. Microbial degradation of the alicyclic ring. In D. T. Gibson (ed.). *Microbial Degradation of Organic Compounds.* Marcel Dekker, New York, pp. 131–180.

Tucker, R. E., A. L. Young, and A. P. Gray (eds.). 1983. *Human and Environmental Risks of Chlorinated Dioxins and Related Compounds.* Plenum Press, New York.

van der Meer, J. R., W. M. de Vos, S. Harayama, and A.J.B. Zehnder. 1992. Molecular mechanisms of genetic adaptation to xenobiotic compounds. *Microbiological Reviews* 56:677–694.

Vogel, T. M., and D. Grbic-Galic. 1986. Incorporation of oxygen from water into toluene and benzene during anaerobic fermentative transformation. *Applied and Environmental Microbiology* 52:200–202.

Vogel, T. M., and P. L. McCarty. 1985. Biotransformation of tetrachloroethylene to trichloroethylene, dichloroethylene, vinyl chloride and carbon dioxide under methanogenic conditions. *Applied and Environmental Microbiology* 49:1080–1083.

Walter, U., M. Beyer, J. Klein, and H. J. Rehm. 1991. Degradation of pyrene by *Rhodococcus* sp. UW1. *Applied Microbiology and Biotechnology* 34:671–676.

Watras, C. J., K. A. Morrison, J. S. Host, and N. S. Bloom. 1995. Concentration of mercury species in relationship to other site-specific factors in the surface waters of northern Wisconsin lakes. *Limnology and Oceanography* 40:556–565.

Wedemeyer, G. 1967. Dechlorination of l,l,l-trichloro-2,2,-bis (*p*-chlorophenyl) ethane by *Aerobacter aerogenes*. *Applied Microbiology* 15:569–574.

Weissenfels, W. D., M. Beyer, and J. Klein. 1990. Degradation of phenanthrene, fluorene and fluoranthene by pure bacterial cultures. *Applied Microbiology and Biotechnology* 32:479–484.

Winfrey, M. R., and J.W.M. Rudd. 1990. Environmental factors affecting the formation of methylmercury in low pH lakes. *Environmental Toxicology and Chemistry* 9:853–869.

Wolff, I. A., and A. E. Wasserman. 1972. Nitrates, nitrites and nitrosamines. *Science* 177:15–19.

Wood, J. M. 1971. Environmental pollution by mercury. *Advances in Environmental Science Technology* 2:39–56.

Xia, X., J. Bollinger, and A. Ogram. 1995. Molecular genetic analysis of the response of three soil microbial communities to the application of 2,4-D. *Molecular Ecology* 4:17–28.

Yabannavar, A., and R. Bartha. 1993. Biodegradability of some food packaging material in soil. *Soil Biology and Biochemistry* 25:1469–1475.

Yabannavar, A., and R. Bartha. 1994. Methods for assessment of biodegradability of plastic films in soil. *Applied and Environmental Microbiology* 60:3608–3614.

Zeyer, J., P. Eicher, J. Dolfing, and P. R. Schwarzenbach. 1990. Anaerobic degradation of aromatic hydrocarbons. In D. Kamely, A. Chakrabarty, and G. S. Omenn (eds.). *Biotechnology and Biodegradation*. Gulf Pub. Co., Houston, TX, pp. 33–40.

Zeyer, J., E. P. Kuhn, and R. P. Schwarzenbach. 1986. Rapid microbial mineralization of toluene and 1,3-dimethylbenzene in the absence of molecular oxygen. *Applied and Environmental Microbiology* 52:944–947.

# BIODEGRADABILITY TESTING AND MONITORING THE BIOREMEDIATION OF XENOBIOTIC POLLUTANTS

*Both legislation and technology aimed at cleaning up and preventing further damage to the environment have been prominent developments in the late twentieth century and have supported the birth of bioremediation technology. Legislation regulating environmental releases of toxic xenobiotic compounds includes the Toxic Substances Control Act (TSCA) of 1976 to establish requirements for premanufacture testing and review of potentially toxic novel chemicals. The Resource Conservation and Recovery Act (RCRA) of 1976 and the Comprehensive Environmental Response, Compensation, and Liability Act (CERCLA) of 1980, along with subsequent amendments such as the Superfund Amendments and Reauthorization Act of 1986, established the regulatory framework for the disposal of hazardous wastes and the cleanup (remediation) of sites that had been polluted during an era when many industrial chemicals were carelessly released into the environment. Technologies using microorganisms with extensive biodegradative capacities have been developed for use in both pollution prevention and site remediation. Bioremediation (technology employing living organisms for removal of pollutants from the environment) is one of several technologies that may be applied. For bioremediation*

*to be effective, the pollutant must be subject to microbial attack (metabolic transformation), the metabolic products must be safe, and the process must not cause adverse ecological side effects. Environmental conditions must permit in situ growth of the microorganism capable of bioremediation or the extraction of the pollutant from the environment so that it can be biodegraded ex situ in bioreactors. When bioremediation is applicable, it is often a cost-effective means of restoring environmental quality. Although not the panacea for all pollution problems, in many cases bioremediation can biodegrade, detoxify, or immobilize hazardous pollutants and is becoming a widely used technology for environmental cleanup.*

## BIODEGRADABILITY AND ECOLOGICAL SIDE EFFECT TESTING

### Testing for Biodegradability and Biomagnification

Microorganisms have an extensive but finite capacity to recycle synthetic organic molecules. Because recalcitrance of an organic substance introduced into the biosphere on a large scale may cause problems, regulatory bodies have increasingly demanded experimental proof from manufacturers that their products will be recycled to harmless compounds when those products enter the environment. In practice, this usually requires proof of biodegradation within a reasonable period of time and, in addition, a demonstration that essential processes in the environment are not disrupted. Such procedures add substantially to the development costs of new products, and the consumer eventually bears these costs. In the long run, however, the haphazard introduction of new materials into the biosphere would prove even costlier.

The U.S. government's authority to regulate the manufacture and distribution of potentially dangerous chemicals was vastly broadened by the Toxic Substances Control Act (TSCA). This legislation requires the producer to show that a newly introduced chemical will not have undue toxic environmental side effects. Permits for the large-scale manufacture and sale of new chemicals are contingent on the outcome of tests. The legislation is based on the experience that, regardless of intended use, any recalcitrant and toxic chemical manufactured on a large scale is likely to cause environmental pollution problems, as occurred with DDT, PCBs, and similar compounds. Test procedures must be reasonably representative, accurate, and broadly comparable, yet simple and routine enough not to impose unacceptable delays and financial burdens on the introduction of new products.

In the United States, biodegradability and environmental safety testing are the responsibility of the Environmental Protection Agency (USEPA) and, to a lesser degree, of the Food and Drug Administration. Other countries have similar regulatory agencies. However, it was recognized that international trade could be seriously disrupted by a web of fragmented or contradictory environmental regulation and test procedures. A product could be rejected by an importing country solely because it has stricter or simply different environmental regulations than the exporting countries. To prevent this type of trade gridlock, the international Organization for Economic Cooperation and Development (OECD) has taken the lead in coordinating environmental regulations and test procedures (OECD 1981). The United States and other industrially advanced countries have made major contributions to the OECD regulations and test procedures and, consequently, they strongly resemble USEPA and European Economic Community (EEC) policies. Although designed to achieve standardization, the test procedures are not static. They are continuously revised and evaluated by international committees of scientists to keep up with scientific advances. After thorough review, the modified procedures become incorporated in updated regulations and test protocols.

To avoid unnecessary expense and complexity, biodegradability tests are organized in tiers. Compounds that prove readily biodegradable in first-tier screening tests and have chemical structures that are not associated with toxicity, recalcitrance, or biomagnification may be approved for manufacture at that point. Compounds that are not biodegraded readily and are suspected of being environmentally hazardous based on their chemical structures have to satisfy more detailed and more stringent tests prior to their approval for manufacture.

First-tier environmental safety screening tests for novel chemicals attempt to determine their "ready" or "inherent" biodegradability in wastewater or soil environments using $CO_2$ evolution. $O_2$ consumption and dissolved organic carbon (DOC) decrease measurements. Ready or inherent biodegradability tests are conducted under generally optimized conditions in respect to moisture, temperature, mineral nutrients, microbial inoculum, and aeration, if the test is an aerobic one. Tests that indicate a 50–60% conversion to $CO_2$ within a specified period of days or weeks, depending on the specific test, indicate that under the appropriate conditions the compound will be degraded by microorganisms. A great source of variability in all of these tests is the sewage sludge inoculum in the case of wastewater test systems and the soil sample in the case of soil tests. Though certain guidelines exist, satisfactory standardization has not been achieved. Some of the test procedures provide for gradual preconditioning of the inoculum with the test compounds; others use no such preconditioning. To minimize variability, tests need to include positive and negative controls. As positive controls, compounds with known biodegradability (glucose, benzoate, acetate, or aniline) are included. A lack of degradation in the case of the positive controls signifies problems with the inoculum or with test conditions. Degradation in uninoculated negative controls may indicate autoxidation or other nonbiological degradation processes.

A compound that passes ready biodegradability or inherent biodegradability tests may need to be tested further for biodegradation rates under specific conditions that resemble their typical disposal situation. Will a detergent molecule degrade during sewage treatment fast enough to prevent a foaming problem in receiving rivers? More generally, will the biodegradation of the compound be sufficiently rapid so that it will not unduly add to the biological and chemical oxygen demands (BOD/COD) burden of the sewage plant effluent? Such questions require kinetic studies under conditions that closely resemble standard wastewater treatment practices. Increasingly there is a focus on biodegradation kinetics in regulatory decision making (Hales et al. 1977).

To date, most biodegradability testing has been conducted under aerobic conditions. In some situations, it is valid to ask what the fate will be of the test compound under anaerobic conditions, such as anaerobic sewage treatment plants, aquatic sediments, or anaerobic aquifers. Generally, under aerobic conditions a broader range of chemicals can be degraded and at faster rates than under anaerobic conditions. However, reductive dechlorination and reductive nitrosubstituent removal from some aromatic compounds can actually be stimulated under anaerobic treatment conditions.

Even first-tier tests are much more definitive and sensitive when conducted with radiolabeled materials, and this type of testing is strongly recommended (U.S. Food and Drug Administration 1987; Code of Federal Regulations 1992). Radiolabeling is even more essential when detailed studies on environmental biodegradation become necessary.

Conversion of the bulk of the test substance to $^{14}CO_2$ is the most clear-cut proof of mineralization. The $^{14}C$ label, if it is not uniform, must be carefully placed. Biodegradation may affect only a few carbon

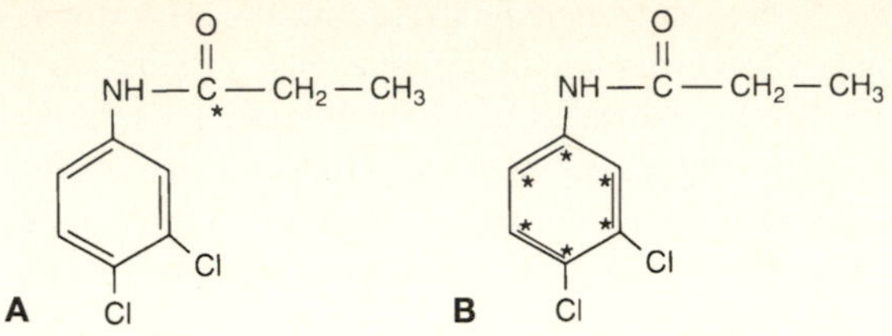

**Figure 14.1**
Significance of the position of $^{14}C$ label in biodegradation tests. Asterisks indicate label positions in the herbicide N-(3,4-dichlorophenyl)-propionamide (propanil). Tests with propanil labeled in the acyl moiety (A) indicated more than 90% mineralization in two weeks. Labeling in the 3,4-dichloroaniline ring (B) resulted in less than 5% mineralization during the same time period.

atoms in the molecule of the test substance, but if these happen to be the labeled ones, the mistaken conclusion would be that the whole molecule was mineralized (Figure 14.1). If the $^{14}C$ label is uniform or is placed in the difficult-to-degrade portion of the molecule, it can be of great help in the identification of degradation products. These may have biological activity substantially different from the parent substance. The custom labeling of test substances involves considerable expense, yet current test procedures rely on it heavily. In some cases, however, $^{14}C$ labeling is not feasible and both first-tier and more detailed tests need to be performed without the aid of this technique. Whether or not radiolabeled, the metabolic intermediates and final products of biodegradation are separated and analyzed with advanced microanalytical techniques. These include gas-liquid chromatography (GC) with various detector systems such as flame ionization (FID), electron capture (EC), and other more specific detector systems. Thin layer chromatography (TLC) and high-performance liquid chromatography (HPLC) serve to separate metabolites that are not volatile enough for GC. Mass spectrometry (MS) is used for identification of the separated metabolites along with various spectrometric (UV, visible, and IR) techniques. Nuclear magnetic resonance (NMR) and electron spin resonance (ESR) are used for the resolution of fine structural details.

A great advantage of radiolabeling the test substance is that it facilitates the calculating of mass balances during testing. Early tests often monitored only the disappearance of the test substance. Of course, compounds never disappear, they are only transformed. The nature of the products is important. If the main product is $^{14}CO_2$, this indicates that the biodegradation is complete. Of course, even highly biodegradable compounds are not quantitatively transformed to $^{14}CO_2$. Some of the radiocarbon remains in microbial biomass, some may be humidified and become part of the soil organic matter. Most products of incomplete biodegradation can be extracted, quantified, and their nature determined. At the end of the test, close to 100% of the added radiocarbon needs to be accounted for in the form of various products or at least in compartments such as "biomass" or "humus." A failure to close the mass balance indicates that transformation products were missed, and these may not be innocuous. A serious gap in mass balance necessitates the rejection and repetition of a test.

Biodegradation experiments in environmental samples incubated under controlled laboratory conditions are probably the best routine tests for degradability. But though they are certainly superior to experiments with pure cultures or even mixed enrichments, they do not duplicate certain field conditions. Photodegradation, evaporation, and leaching are excluded or restricted in these laboratory experiments. Some cometabolic pesticide transformations seem to be greatly stimulated in the plant rhizosphere by the presence of root exudates (Hsu and Bartha 1979), yet to test for such effects on a routine basis appears to be too laborious. Laboratory tests require final verification by field experience.

If biodegradation tests indicate a high degree of recalcitrance to biodegradation and the residue has a strongly lipophilic character, there is a good chance that the substance will be subject to biomagnification. The lipophilic character and, hence, the potential for biomagnification can be predicted to some degree from the partition coefficient of the pollutant between water and a less polar solvent—*n*-octanol, for example (Gosset et al. 1983). The stronger the lipophilic character, the greater the potential for biomagnifica-

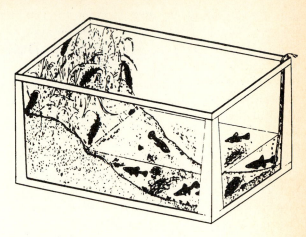

**Figure 14.2**
Model ecosystem developed by Metcalf and associates for testing the biomagnification tendency of pesticides. (Source: Metcalf et al. 1971, *Environmental Science and Technology*. Reprinted by permission, copyright American Chemical Society.)

tion. However, this simple partitioning test fails to predict changes that render the pollutant more polar and facilitate its excretion.

To use the environment as the testing laboratory, as occurred with DDT, PCBs, and other persistent pollutants, is too costly in terms of ecological damage. Metcalf and associates (1971) designed a useful model ecosystem for testing biomagnification potential (Figure 14.2). The model ecosystem is in a small aquarium that contains a sand slope and is partially filled with water. Sorghum is planted on the sand slope, and the radiolabeled test compound, such as DDT or an analog, is applied in a small volume of acetone to the plant leaves. Salt-marsh caterpillar *(Estigmene)* larvae are introduced and feed on the sorghum leaves. Their droppings enter the aquatic environment containing a mixed bacterial and planktonic inoculum from a pond. Other added organisms are a filamentous green alga *(Oedogonium),* an aquatic snail *(Physa),* mosquito larvae *(Culex),* and the mosquito fish *(Gambusia).* The ecosystem is maintained for 30 days after introduction of the radiolabeled test compound. After this time, the macroscopic organisms are sorted, the planktonic organisms

## Biosensor Detection of Pollutants

Traditionally, the monitoring of environmental pollutants and the contaminants they produce has involved physicochemical analytical techniques. Spectrometry (UV, visible, IR) and chromatography (GC, TLC, HPLC) represent increasingly powerful analytical tools that are capable of detecting, quantifying, and identifying xenobiotic pollutants in parts per million (ppm) and even parts per billion (ppb). These powerful analytical techniques are now being supplemented by biosensors, which are biological systems based on reporter genes or immunoassays that can detect specific pollutants. Biosensors are just beginning to be commercialized for a few chemicals; for the most part though, they are still in experimental development for environmental monitoring (Van Emon 1989; Van Emon et al. 1989, 1991).

Reporter genes can be readily detected when they are expressed. These genes can be joined through recombinant DNA technology to the genes that code for specific metabolic pathways that are inducible. When the pathway is induced, so is the reporter gene. Thus, a reporter gene that codes for production of light, such as the *lux* gene that codes for luminescence, can be coupled with various inducible genes. If light is emitted, the pathway has been induced, indicating the presence of a specific inducer substance. If that inducer is a pollutant, the reporter gene can be used as a sensitive indicator of that pollutant. Biosensors based on the *lux* gene have been genetically engineered to detect naphthalene; in the presence of naphthalene, light is emitted at an intensity proportional to the concentration of naphthalene (Burlage et al. 1990).

Immunoasssay biosensors have been developed to detect a variety of organic molecules, including benzopyrene and parathion (Vanderlaan et al. 1988; Van Emon et al. 1989; Reynolds and

*(continued)*

are filtered out, and radioactivity is determined in each group of organisms and also in the sand and water. A compound like DDT typically shows $10^5$- to $10^6$-fold biomagnification in *Gambusia,* which represents the highest trophic level in this model ecosystem. Less persistent and/or more polar compounds show proportionally less biomagnification. This model ecosystem is a flexible one and can be modified with relative ease to model other food chains. Improvements on the system include an enclosed atmosphere and appropriate scrubbers to account for evolution of $^{14}CO_2$ and other volatiles. The predictive value of tests in such model systems appears to be good, and their cost is not excessive.

Related test systems for the evaluation of pollutant behavior are microcosms (Pritchard and Bourquin 1984). These differ from model ecosystems in that they are not synthetic but attempt to bring a minimally disturbed subsample of the real environment into the laboratory. Such systems are of value because they give not only qualitative but also reasonably good quantitative results about the behavior of a pollutant in the sampled environment. Biodegradation of a pollutant in an appropriate microcosm closely resembles the rate measured in the corresponding environment. A simple microcosm is the "eco-core," which models estuarine and other shallow-water environments. A sediment core is placed in a glass column of corresponding diameter and overlayered with a simultaneously collected water sample. The water column is aerated, but the anaerobic sediment is left undisturbed. The effluent air is scrubbed through an alkali trap, and

## Biosensor Detection of Pollutants, continued

Yacynych 1991; Schultz 1991). These assays are based on the specificities of immunological reactions. Because antibodies react only with specific antigens, immunoassays can be used to detect substances that are both pollutants and antigenic, that is, capable of reacting with a specific diagnostic antibody. Monoclonal antibodies, which react only with a single specific antigen, are particularly useful as diagnostic biosensors for the immunological detection of environmental pollutants.

Although still a novel application of this technology, immunoassays of various types have been developed for environmental pollutants (Lukens et al. 1977; Chamerlik-Cooper et al. 1991; Dohrman 1991). These immunoassays use different labels for detection, including radioactive labels in radioimmunoassays (RIAs), enzymatic reactions that produce colored products in enzyme-linked immunosorbent assays (ELISAs), and fluorescent dyes in fluorescent immunoassays (FIAs). Radioimmunoassays have been developed for detection of dieldrin, aldrin, warfarin, benomyl, and parathion; ELISAs for molinate, metalaxyl, chlorsulfuron, paraquat, triadimefon, diflubenzuron, and terbutryn; and FIAs for diclofop methyl. Portable, field-test immunoassay kits for polychlorinated biphenyls (PCBs) and pentachlorophenol (PCP) are now commercially available. Field-test kits have also been developed for the toxic aromatic hydrocarbons benzene, toluene, and xylene.

Present research in immunochemical biosensors is moving toward the development of innovative assays for air samples (Drinkwine et al. l991; Stopa et al. 1991). Efforts in this area of environmental detection, previously thought incompatible with immunological techniques, are evidence of the growing realization of the potential value of these methods in environmental measurements.

the $^{14}CO_2$ evolution rate from radiolabeled pollutants is monitored. Periodic analysis of replicate eco-cores for nonvolatile residues complements $^{14}CO_2$ analysis.

## Testing for Effects on Microorganisms

In the case of biologically active substances that are introduced into the environment in large quantities, such as pesticides, it should be ascertained that nontarget organisms are not unduly affected. Such testing may involve toxicity tests for wildlife or fish, but as applied to the natural microbiological activity in aquatic systems and in soil, it should be demonstrated that essential microbial processes are not seriously disrupted. For example, it is essential that biologically active compounds not disrupt aerobic or anaerobic sewage treatment, and specific tests are conducted in bench-scale treatment units at various concentrations to exclude the possibility of interference with wastewater treatment. Anaerobic treatment systems are particularly sensitive and methanogenesis can be inhibited at very low concentrations of organochlorine solvent residues. It is also important that pesticides and agrochemicals should not interfere with nontarget soil microorganisms in a manner that may be detrimental to soil fertility (Greaves et al. 1977). Barnhart and Vestal (1983) examined the effects of heavy metals, detergents, and pesticides such as diquat on the metabolic activities of microbial communities. As compared to wastewater treatment, test procedures are less standardized in this area. Of various possible approaches the most sound and relevant ones appear to be those that measure direct effects on biogeochemical cycling in environmental samples (Johnen and Drew 1977; Atlas et al. 1978). For example, the effect of a pesticide on the aerobic and anaerobic mineralization of a model plant constituent, such as cellulose, may be measured at field application and at 10 times the suggested concentration levels. Similarly, the effect of the pesticide on nitrogen fixation, nitrification, sulfur oxidation, and perhaps phosphatase activity may be tested.

Measurements of effects on microbial numbers appear to be less useful, but effects on ATP or on the adenylate energy charge may prove to be relevant toxicity indicators. Least useful are tests of pesticide toxicity *in vitro* on a selected microbial strain, such as *Azotobacter* or *Nitrobacter*. Such tests ignore the diversity and homeostasis of natural microbial communities as well as the detoxification of the pesticide in the natural environment by soil absorption and microbial degradation. No valid extrapolations are possible from such *in vitro* pure culture experiments to effects on biogeochemical cycling in the environment, and there seems to be little scientific or practical justification for such tests.

One xenobiotic may influence the biodegradation of another; for example, some carbamate insecticides inhibit acylamidases that cleave acylanilide and phenylcarbamate herbicides. The great diversity of xenobiotics seems to preclude routine testing for such possible interactions. At best, the effect of a newly developed xenobiotic might be tested on the mineralization of some other radiolabeled compounds selected to represent some prominent classes of xenobiotic compounds.

# BIOREMEDIATION

Bioremediation involves the use of microorganisms to remove pollutants (Atlas and Pramer 1990). For bioremediation to be considered as an applicable technology for the cleanup of a specific pollutant, it is necessary to show that a specific chemical or chemical mixture is biodegradable and that the process of bioremediation will not result in untoward ecological side effects. The biodegradation of pollutants in the environment is a complex process whose quantitative and qualitative aspects depend on the nature and amount of the pollutant present, the ambient and seasonal environmental conditions, and the composition of the indigenous microbial community (Atlas 1981; Leahy and Colwell 1990; Hinchee and Olfenbuttel 1991a, 1991b). Bioremediation can be applied to sites contaminated with a variety of chemical pollutants (Table 14.1). Careful site characterization is needed to identify the pollutants and their concentrations (Shineldecker 1992; LeGrega et al. 1994). When carefully managed, this biotechnological approach can reduce the risk of adverse impacts of toxic and hazardous chemicals in the environment (Norris et al. 1988).

Although in practice the separation of causes is often difficult, in theory one may assume that the failure of biodegradation in case of a chemical waste may be due to unfavorable environmental conditions, the absence of appropriate catabolic pathways, or both. Established or emerging biotechnological approaches can correct such situations and protect the environment from xenobiotic pollutants. With the recognition that rates of pollutant biodegradation are often limited by environmental constraints or more rarely by the lack of suitable microbial populations, it is possible to carry out bioremediation programs to overcome these limitations (Bluestone 1986; Zitrides 1990).

There have been a number of review articles and books published in the last few years describing the scientific underpinnings and engineering aspects of bioremediation (Alexander 1994; Atlas 1995a; Baker and Herson 1994; Borden et al. 1994; Boulding 1995; Cookson 1995; Flathman et al. 1994; Gibson and Saylor 1992; Hinchee and Olfenbuttel 1991a, 1991b; Hinchee et al. 1994a, 1994b; Levin and Gealt 1993; Means and Hinchee 1994; National Research Council 1993; Riser-Roberts 1992; Rosenberg 1993; Stoner 1994). These works include extensive descriptions of actual cases in which bioremediation has been employed as well as the experimental background for more far-reaching applications. They highlight the utility and limitations of various approaches to bioremediation and the need to consider bioremediation

**Table 14.1**
Chemicals potentially suitable for bioremediation

| Class | Example | Aerobic process | Anaerobic process |
|---|---|---|---|
| Monochlorinated aromatic compounds | Chlorobenzene | + | + |
| Monoaramatic hydrocarbons | Benzene, toluene, xylene | + | + |
| Non-halogenated phenolics and cresols | 2-Methylphenol | + | + |
| Polynuclear aromatic hydrocarbons | Creosote | + | − |
| Alkanes and alkenes | Fuel oil | + | − |
| Polychlorinated biphenyls | Trichlorobiphenyl | + | − |
| Chlorophenols | Pentachlorophenol | + | + |
| Nitrogen heterocyclics | Pyridine | + | + |
| Chlorinated alkanes | Chloroform | + | + |
| Chlorinated alkenes | Trichloroethylene | + | + |

Source: Organization for Economic Cooperation and Development, 1994.

within the broader context of environmental cleanup technologies.

The two general approaches to bioremediation are environmental modification, such as through nutrient application and aeration, and the addition of appropriate xenobiotic degraders by seeding. The end products of effective bioremediation, such as water and carbon dioxide, are nontoxic and can be accommodated without harm to the environment and living organisms. Using bioremediation to remove pollutants is inexpensive compared to physical methods for decontaminating the environment, which can be extraordinarily expensive. Whereas conventional technologies call for moving large quantities of toxic waste–contaminated soil to incinerators, bioremediation typically can be performed on-site and requires only simple equipment. Bioremediation, though, is not the solution for all environmental pollution problems. Like other technologies, it is limited in the materials it can treat, by conditions at the treatment site, and by the time available for treatment. Bioremediation has great potential for destroying environmental pollutants, especially in cases of fuel or creosote-contaminated soil (Mueller et al. 1989, 1991; Song et al. 1990). Several hundred contaminated sites have been identified where

bioremediation is being tested as a possible cleanup technology. Petroleum and creosote are most often the pollutants of concern, comprising about 60% of the sites where bioremediation is being used in field demonstrations or for full-scale operations (Hinchee and Olfenbuttel 1991a, 1991b).

## Bioremediation Efficacy Testing

To demonstrate that a bioremediation technology is potentially useful, it is important to document enhanced biodegradation of the pollutant under controlled conditions. This generally cannot be accomplished *in situ* and thus must be accomplished in laboratory experiments. Laboratory experiments demonstrate the potential a particular treatment may have to stimulate the removal of a xenobiotic from a contaminated site (Bailey et al. 1973). Laboratory experiments that closely model real environmental conditions are most likely to produce relevant results (Bertrand et al. 1983). In many cases, this involves using samples collected in the field that contain indigenous microbial populations. In such experiments, it is important to include appropriate abiotic controls to separate the effects of evaporation or weathering of the pollutant from actual biodegradation. Such experiments do not replace the need for field demonstrations, but are critical for establishing the scientific credibility of specific bioremediation strategies. They are also useful for the screening of potential bioremediation treatments.

The parameters typically measured in laboratory tests of bioremediation efficacy include enumeration of microbial populations (Song and Bartha 1990), measurement of rates of microbial respiration (oxygen consumption or carbon dioxide production), and determination of degradation rates (disappearance of individual or total pollutants) as compared to untreated controls. The methodologies employed in these measurements are critical.

Undoubtedly, the most direct measure of bioremediation efficacy is the monitoring of disappearance rates of the pollutant. When using this approach, the appropriate controls and the proper choice of analytical techniques become especially critical. The "disappearance" of pollutants may occur not only by biodegradation but also by evaporation, photodegradation, and leaching.

In order to promote biotechnology and bioremediation, the EPA and the University of Pittsburgh Trust have entered into a multiyear cooperative agreement to establish the National Environmental Technology Applications Corporation (NETAC). The purpose of NETAC is to facilitate the commercialization of technologies being developed by the government and the private sector that will positively affect the nation's most pressing environmental problems. The corporation's efforts encompass encouraging new technologies with promising commercial potential, as well as innovations aimed solely at modifying and improving existing technologies or processes (USEPA 1990). Under the agreement with the EPA, NETAC convenes a panel of experts to review proposals for products that have been developed for use as bioremediation. The panel recommends those products that offer the most promise for success in the field. The recommended products are subjected to laboratory testing at the EPA laboratory in Cincinnati, Ohio. The objective of the laboratory protocol is to determine if commercial bioremediation products can enhance the biodegradation of a pollutant to a degree significantly

better than that achievable by simple environmental modification. The laboratory tests consist of electrolytic respirometers set up to measure oxygen uptake over time and shake flask microcosms to measure degradation and microbial growth (Venosa et al. 1991). Pollutant constituents remaining are analyzed. Products that demonstrate potential efficacy are screened for toxicities, and products passing the toxicity tests are then considered for field testing.

The evaluation of pollutant biodegradation *in situ* is far more difficult than in laboratory studies. Analyses that require enclosure, such as respiration measurements, typically are precluded from field evaluations. Field evaluations, therefore, have relied upon the enumeration of pollutant-degrading microorganisms and the recovery and analysis of residual pollutants. This is especially complicated because the distribution of pollutants in the environment typically is patchy; therefore, a high number of replicate samples must be obtained for results to be statistically valid.

## Side Effects Testing

In addition to demonstrating efficacy, bioremediation treatments must not produce any untoward ecological effects (Colwell 1971; O'Brien and Dixon 1976; Doe and Wells 1978). The focus of ecological effects testing of bioremediation has been on the direct toxicity of chemical additives, such as fertilizers, to indigenous organisms. Standardized toxicological tests are used to determine the acute toxicities of chemicals. Chronic toxicities and sublethal effects may also be determined. Generally, toxicity tests are run using the microcrustacean *Daphnia,* bivalves (such as oyster larvae), and fish (such as rainbow trout). Sometimes regionally important species, such as salmon or herring, are included. Additionally, tests are run to determine effects on algal growth rates. These tests are aimed at determining levels of fertilizer application that will stimulate biodegradation without causing eutrophication.

To exclude the possibility that some unsuspected toxic or mutagenic residue of pollutant degradation remains undetected, it is sometimes desirable to complement residue analysis with bioassays. As a rapid and convenient measure of acute toxicity, the reduction of light emission by *Photobacterium phosphoreum* (Microtox assay) has been used in the verification of land treatment efficacy for fuel-contaminated soil (Wang and Bartha 1990; Wang et al. 1990). These measurements showed that the moderate acute toxicity of the intact fuel increased in the early phase of biodegradation, but upon completion of the biodegradation process, it returned to the background level of uncontaminated soil. Bioremediation accelerated both the transient increase and the ultimate disappearance of toxicity. The Microtox assay has been used also to determine treatability, such as a need to dilute the soil prior to bioremediation when high concentrations of toxic residues interfere with biodegradation activity (Matthews and Hastings 1987).

Mutagenic residues, especially those of polycyclic aromatic hydrocarbons, are assayed for by the Ames test (Maron and Ames 1983). In the case of a soil contaminated by diesel fuel, the initially moderate mutagenic activity of the residue increased sharply with the onset of microbial degradation, especially when the assay was run without activating microsomal enzymes (S-9 mix). However, as biodegradation progressed, the mutagenic activity returned to the background level of uncontaminated soil (Wang et al. 1990). Rudd et al. (1996) also found that fungal biodegradation of crude oils resulted in reduced mutagenicity as determined using the Ames assay.

In contrast to such studies that show reduced mutagenicity after using the Ames assay, Wyman et al. (1979) found that picric acid (10 μg per plate) produced by reduction of 2,4,6-trinitrophenol (picric acid) by a strain of *Pseudomonas aeruginosa* demonstrated mutagenicity (both frame shift and base substitution-type mutations) only after activation with a rat liver homogenate preparation. Picramic acid (1 microgram per plate) induced both base pair substitution and frame shift–type mutations without activation by the rat liver preparation. Kitamori (1996) also found that the biodegradation of the several mutagenicities of three diphenyl ether–derived herbicides, chlomitrofen (CNP), nitrofen, and chlormethoxynil, and their amino derivatives were assayed by the Ames test

using TA98, TA100, and YG strains. Chlomitrofen was weakly mutagenic in YG1029, nitrofen was weakly mutagenic in YG1029 and highly mutagenic in YG1026. But neither of three herbicides were mutagenic using TA98 and TA100. All of their amino derivatives were mutagenic especially in YG1024 and YG1029, acetyltransferase-rich mutants of TA98 or TA100. In YG1029, the mutagenic potency of the amino derivatives was relatively high compared with that of each parent compound. Concerning biodegradation products of chlomitrofen, amino-chlomitrofen was highly mutagenic and acetylamin-chlomitrofen was moderately mutagenic in YG1026, but others were nonmutagenic. In river water, chlomitrofen was degraded rapidly and converted to amino-chlomitrofen. Change in mutagenicity of river water to which chlomitrofen was added seemed to reflect changes in amino-chlomitrofen concentration in river water. Therefore, when assessing the health impact of chemicals released in the natural environment, their degradation products must be considered along with parent compounds.

In the case of soil contaminated by oily sludge or fuel spills, the progress of bioremediation and the decrease in toxicity was sometimes documented also by seed germination and plant growth bioassays (Dibble and Bartha 1979c; Bossert and Bartha 1985; Wang and Bartha 1990). As compared to microbial tests, seed and plant bioassays have moderate sensitivities and usually show effects only above 1.0% hydrocarbon of the soil dry weight. Their main function is to determine when the revegetation of an oil-inundated site can be attempted.

The fungal degradation of polyaromatic hydrocarbons (PAH) in a contaminated soil from a hazardous waste site was evaluated in a pilot-scale study by Baud-Grassert et al. (1993). As some PAH are known to be mutagens, the *Tradescantia*-micronucleus test (TRAD-MCN) was selected to evaluate the genotoxicity of the soil before and after fungal treatment. The genotoxicity test was conducted with *Tradescantia* clone 4430. Cuttings were exposed for 30 hours to different dilutions of soil extracts from the PAH-contaminated soil before and after fungal treatment. Soil extracts before fungal treatment exhibited a relatively strong genotoxic effect in the meiotic pollen mother cells even at a 1% concentration, and the highest concentration without significant effect was 0.25%. After fungal treatment, the depletion of selected PAH was associated with a reduction of the soil genotoxicity. The 2% concentration of the extract from the fungal-treated soil showed genotoxic effects comparable to the 1% soil extract without fungal treatment. These results indicated that the RAD-MCN test has a potential utility for evaluating the efficiency of bioremediation of genotoxic soil contaminants.

## APPROACHES TO BIOREMEDIATION

### Environmental Modification for Bioremediation

Some common environmental limitations to biodegradation of hazardous chemical wastes are excessively high waste concentrations, lack of oxygen, unfavorable pH, lack of mineral nutrients, lack of moisture, and unfavorable temperature. Once the limitations by environmental conditions are corrected, the ubiquitous distribution of microorganisms allows, in most cases, for a spontaneous enrichment of the appropriate microorganisms. In the great majority of cases, an inoculation with specific microorganisms is neither necessary nor useful. Exceptions exist when the biodegrading microorganisms are poor competitors and fail to maintain themselves in the environment or when the chemical waste is only cometabolized and thus fails to provide a selective advantage to the catabolic organism(s). A massive accidental spill of a toxic chemical in a previously unexposed environment constitutes another situation where inoculation with preadapted microbial cultures may hasten biodegradative cleanup. However, inoculation should always be combined with efforts to provide the inoculum with reasonable growth conditions in the polluted environment. As a minimum, suitable growth temperature, adequate water potential, suitable pH, suitable nutrient balance, and, for aerobic processes, adequate oxygen supply need to be ensured. If the pollutant to be eliminated does not support microbial growth, the addition of a suitable growth substrate and/or repeated massive inoculations is necessary. Inoculation in absence of the appropriate ecological considerations rarely attains the desired improvement in biodegradation.

An approach originally developed for the isolation of cometabolizing microorganisms shows promise for promoting the biodegradation of some recalcitrant chemical wastes. If a xenobiotic organochlorine compound fails to support microbial growth, a microorganism may be enriched for on a nonchlorinated or less chlorinated structural analog. If the organism has sufficiently broad-spectrum enzymes, it may cometabolize the xenobiotic chemical even though the organism cannot grow on the chemical. It stands to reason that soil contaminated with a recalcitrant organochlorine compound may be detoxified if a biodegradable structural analog is provided. This was in fact demonstrated in the case of PCBs and 3,4-dichloroaniline. In the former case, biphenyl was used as the stimulating substrate; in the latter, aniline was used (You and Bartha 1982; Brunner et al. 1985). The disappearance of the xenobiotics was accelerated with this approach by an order of one magnitude or more.

The availability of oxygen in soils, sediments, and aquifers is often limiting and dependent on the type of soil and on whether the soil is waterlogged (Jamison et al. 1975; Huddleston and Cresswell 1976; Bossert and Bartha 1984; von Wedel et al. 1988; Lee and Levy 1991). The microbial degradation of petroleum contaminants in some groundwater and soil environments is severely limited by oxygen availability. In surface soil and in on-site bioremediation, oxygenation is best ensured by providing adequate drainage. Air-filled pore spaces in the soil facilitate diffusion of oxygen to hydrocarbon-utilizing microorganisms, whereas in waterlogged soil, oxygen diffusion is extremely slow and cannot keep up with the demand of heterotrophic decomposition processes. Substantial concentrations of decomposable hydrocarbons create a high oxygen demand in soil, and the rate of diffusion is inadequate to satisfy it even in well-drained and light-textured soils. Cultivation (ploughing and rototilling, for example) has been used to turn the soil and ensure its maximal access to atmospheric oxygen. *In situ* bioremediation based largely on the injection of oxygen is being extensively used in wastewater and groundwater

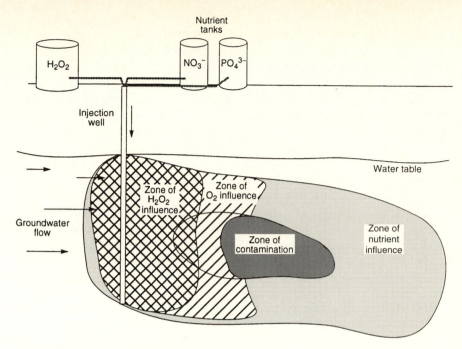

**Figure 14.3**

*In situ* bioremediation of hydrocarbon-contaminated aquifer by injection of hydrogen peroxide to provide a source of molecular oxygen and nitrate and phosphate to provide nutrients for the growth of hydrocarbon degraders. As shown in this illustration, the zone of nutrient influence is much greater than the aerobic zone of oxygen influence. (Source: Cookson 1995.)

treatment and to remove biodegradable organic wastes in industrial sites (Brubaker 1995; Hinchee 1994).

In many cases, hydrocarbons have contaminated soil and groundwater from leaking underground storage tanks (Dowd 1984). Microorganisms in such subsurface environments degrade hydrocarbons and other xenobiotics only extremely slowly, but these rates can be substantially enhanced (Johnson et al. 1985; Aelion et al. 1987; Aelion and Bradley 1991; Frederickson et al. 1991). If digging up and surface spreading of the contaminated soil (on-site bioremediation) is not feasible, *in situ* treatment of the undisturbed soil is performed. Intrinsic or *in situ* bioremediation is increasingly becoming a popular alternative to other cleanup methods because it is cheaper, but it requires careful monitoring to ensure safe and effective performance (Hart 1996). *In situ* treatment of contaminated

aquifers involves oxygen and mineral nutrient supplementation of the pollutant plume for a prolonged period. More rarely, microbial seed cultures and/or other supplements are also added through appropriate injection walls.

The most troublesome problem facing *in situ* bioremediation often is the oxygen limitation, especially in groundwater and in deep soil layers contaminated by hydrocarbons. Because oxygen solubility in water is low, this can best be achieved by pumping down dilute solutions of hydrogen peroxide in appropriate and stabilized formulations (Brown et al. 1984, 1985; Yaniga and Smith 1984; American Petroleum Institute 1987; Thomas et al. 1987; Berwanger and Barker 1988). The decomposition of hydrogen peroxide releases oxygen, which can support aerobic microbial metabolism (Figure 14.3). To avoid formation of gas pockets and microbial toxicity, the practical concentration of hydrogen peroxide in injected water is kept around 100 ppm (Brown et al. 1984; Yaniga and Smith 1984). As an example, Berwanger and Barker (1988) investigated *in situ* bioremediation of aromatic hydrocarbons in an originally anaerobic, methane-saturated groundwater situation using hydrogen peroxide as an oxygen source. Batch biodegradation experiments were conducted with groundwater and core samples obtained from a Canadian landfill. Hydrogen peroxide, added at a nontoxic level, provided oxygen, which promoted the rapid biodegradation of benzene, toluene, ethyl benzene, and *o-, m-,* and *p-*xylene.

Although oxygen availability can severely limit the biodegradation of hydrocarbons, other compounds are more rapidly degraded under anaerobic conditions than when molecular oxygen is available. Thermodynamic considerations, as well as practical experience, indicate that dechlorination of halocarbon compounds is favored under anaerobic conditions (Suflita et al. 1982). Unfortunately, these same conditions usually prevent the oxidative cleavage of aromatic rings. One would expect, however, that sequential anaerobic-aerobic conditions would promote the biodegradation of halocarbons. Fogel et al. (1983) demonstrated this for the insecticide methoxychlor in soil. As measured by $^{14}CO_2$ evolution from radiolabeled methoxychlor, the insecticide was mineralized slowly under continuous aerobic conditions, and no $^{14}CO_2$ evolved during anaerobic incubation. When anaerobic incubations were switched to aerobic, however, a rapid burst of $^{14}CO_2$ evolution was observed. Redox potential can be easily manipulated in waste streams, and the same can be accomplished in contaminated soils through periodic flooding. Anaerobic bioreactor systems have been utilized to establish the mechanism of the microbial biodegradation of polychlorinated biphenyls (PCBs). Spiking the PCB mixture Aroclor 1248 with a sanitary landfill leachate as a novel nutrient, carbon and microbial source resulted in an 11% decrease in total chlorine and a 23% decrease in concentration of biphenyl within 13 weeks (Pagano et al. 1995). These results show that the use of an anaerobic bioreactor system is a promising technology for environmental bioremediation.

For the bioremediation of highly chlorinated compounds, sequential anaerobic and aerobic treatment may well be the best practical solution (Abramowicz 1990) (Figure 14.4). During an initial anaerobic phase the higher-molecular-weight PCB congeners are dehalogenated to form lower-molecular-weight compounds with fewer chlorines. Subsequently, under aerobic conditions the lower-molecular-weight congeners are degraded to carbon dioxide, water, and chloride ions. This approach has been demonstrated for the bioremediation of PCB-contaminated sediments of the Hudson River in New York and in the Sheboygan River in Wisconsin (Jones et al. 1993). In these studies, large steel casings were driven into contaminated sediments. The cylinders were sealed and nutrients added to support anaerobic dehalogenation of the PCBs. Analyses of samples collected from the enclosures showed conversion to lower-molecular-weight PCB congeners. Then agitation of the sediments and forced aeration were used to create aerobic conditions. The lower-molecular-weight PCB congeners were biodegraded under these conditions. Thus biodegradation of both the higher- and lower-weight PCB congeners was achieved by sequential anaerobic and aerobic bioremediation.

Besides oxygen availability and redox potential, biodegradation rates can be limited by the available concentrations of various nutrients. Several major oil spills have focused attention on the problem of hydrocarbon contamination in marine and estuarine environments and the potential use of bioremediation through nutrient addition to remove petroleum pollutants. Because microorganisms require nitrogen and phosphorus for incorporation into biomass, the availability of these nutrients within the same area as the hydrocarbons is critical. Under conditions where nutrient deficiencies limit the rate of petroleum biodegradation, the beneficial effect of fertilization with nitrogen and phosphorus has been conclusively demonstrated and offers great promise as a countermeasure for combating oil spills (Pritchard and Costa 1991). Atlas and Bartha (1973) developed an oleophilic nitrogen and phosphorus fertilizer that places the nitrogen and phosphorus at the oil-water interface, the site of active oil biodegradation. Because the

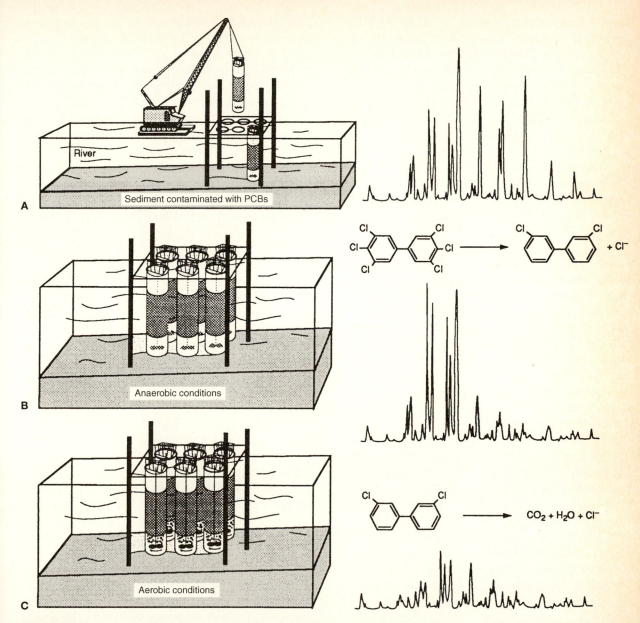

**Figure 14.4**

Bioremediation of PCB-contaminated river sediments. (A) Placement of steel caissons into
sediments; chromatographic tracing showing full range of contaminating PCB congeners.
(B) Nutrients added to sealed caissons lead to creation of anaerobic conditions: anaerobic
dehalogenation converts higher-molecular-weight congeners to ones with fewer chlorines;
chromatographic tracing shows disappearance of higher-molecular-weight congeners
with 4–6 chlorines and increased concentrations of lower-molecular-weight PCBs with
2–3 chlorines. (C) Forced aeration and stirring create aerobic conditions; biodegradation
of lower-molecular-weight congeners leads to cleaner sediments.

fertilizer is oleophilic, it remains with the oil and is not rapidly diluted from the site where it is effective. In the aftermath of the *Amoco Cadiz* oil spill of 1978 in France, a commercial oleophilic fertilizer was developed by Elf Aquitaine (Tramier and Sirvins 1983; LaDousse et al. 1987; Sveum and LaDousse 1989; LaDousse and Tramier 1991). The product, called Inipol EAP 22, is a microemulsion that contains urea as a nitrogen source, lauryl phosphate as a phosphate source, and oleic acid as a carbon source to boost the populations of hydrocarbon-degrading microorganisms. Inipol EAP22 was used extensively for the treatment of the 1989 *Exxon Valdez* spill in Prince William Sound, Alaska.

For the bioremediation of pollutants in surface soils it is generally easy to add nutrients as agricultural fertilizers. However, getting nutrients to subsurface soil and groundwater populations is more complex. One method that has been explored is the use of electrical currents to help move the nutrients to the pollutants. This approach to *in situ* remediation utilizing low-level direct-current electric potential differences to transport ionic nutrients has been used for enhancing the biodegradation process to clean radioactively contaminated soils (Acar et al. 1996). A remediation technology using hydraulic soil fracturing to form channels and electric currents to drive nutrients through the soil, called the lasagna process, has been developed to improve the treatment of contaminated soils and groundwater (Ho et al. 1995). The approach, which integrates electrokinetics with sorption and degradation in treatment zones of the contaminated soil, could treat contamination due to organic and inorganic compounds and mixed wastes. Testing results have shown that the process is an effective alternative for treating contamination in low-permeability soils.

## Microbial Seeding and Bioengineering Approaches to the Bioremediation of Pollutants

Microbial pollution control products, including dried or liquid microbial inocula with or without nutrient additives, currently have annual sales of $7 million to $10 million, and the potential market may be as high as $200 million. Johnson et al. (1985) describe several successful examples of pollution abatement by specifically designed microbial agents. An inoculation program with hydrocarbon-degrading bacteria significantly improved the performance of a petrochemical waste-treatment system. The removal of tertiary butyl alcohol from a waste stream was improved by inoculation with specifically adapted microorganisms, and a large accidental formaldehyde spill was successfully cleaned up by biodecontamination. Unfortunately, rigorous controls are not available in such case studies, and it is often difficult to determine how much of the improvement can be ascribed to bioremediation treatment.

Because bioremediation relies upon the biodegradation capacity of the microorganisms in contact with the pollutants, some have proposed seeding with pollutant-degrading bacteria. This approach is called bioaugmentation because it augments the metabolic capabilities of the indigenous microbial populations. Bioaugmentation involves the introduction of microorganisms into the natural environment for the purpose of increasing the rate or extent, or both, of biodegradation of pollutants. The rationale for this approach is that indigenous microbial populations may not be capable of degrading xenobiotics or the wide range of potential substrates present in complex pollutant mixtures. Several commercial enterprises have begun to market microorganism preparations for removing petroleum pollutants. Commercial mixtures of microorganisms are being marketed for use in degrading oil in pollutants in contained treatment bioreactors as well as for *in situ* applications (Applied Biotreatment Association 1989, 1990).

The feasibility of using straw compost and remediated soil as inocula for bioremediation of pentachlorophenol (PCP)-contaminated soil has been studied under field-simulating conditions (Laine and Jørgensen 1996). Results indicate that straw compost and remediated soil can effectively mineralize PCP with trace amounts of chloroanisoles as the only biotransformation products. The use of these inoculants does not cause any harmful side reactions.

Many different microorganisms are being marketed or considered for future bioremediation applications. Pure cultures as well as undefined mixtures of microorganisms are used for bioremediation. *Pseudomonas* species are often selected because of their ability to degrade a wide range of pollutants, including the low-molecular-weight hydrocarbons associated with many fuel spills. Bioaugmentation with certain specific microbial strains has been shown to increase the rates of removal of the pollutant trichloroethylene (TCE) from groundwater (Munakata-Marr et al. 1996). These bacterial cultures can promote transformation of TCE in the absence of inducing compounds such as phenol or toluene. A bacterial strain that has been tested to work effectively in bioaugmentation is *Burkholderia (Pseudomonas) cepacia* G4; in comparison to conventional bioremediation techniques for groundwater that employ indigenous microorganisms and addition of cosubstrates, the use of *B. cepacia* cultures removes twice the amount of TCE from groundwater.

The white rot fungus *Phanerochaete,* which has extensive biodegradative capabilities, has been proposed for bioremediation of many more complex pollutant compounds (Bumpus et al. 1985). *Phanerochaete chrysosporium* produces laccases and peroxidases that normally are involved in the degradation of lignin, which is a complex polyaromatic substance. These enzymes are also able to attack a diverse range of compounds, and *Phanerochaete* has been shown to biodegrade pesticides such as DDT (Bumpus and Aust 1987); munitions, such as TNT (Fernando et al. 1990); high-molecular-weight polynuclear aromatics, such as benzo(a)pyrene (Bumpus 1989); and plastics, such as polyethylene (Lee et al. 1991). *Phanerochaete chrysosporium* shows a high level of transcription of three manganese peroxidase (MnP) genes during growth on soil containing polycyclic aromatic hydrocarbons (PAHs) (Bogan et al. 1996). After a brief lag period, the high *mnp* gene transcription is followed by a high level of MnP enzyme activity. The expression of *mnp* and activities of MnP correlate with the degradation of fluorene and chrysene. This indicates that MnP-dependent pathways can degrade high-ionization-potential polynuclear aromatic hydrocarbons (PAHs).

The absence of a catabolic pathway for a xenobiotic compound appears to be the ultimate obstacle to its biodegradative cleanup. But this obstacle is no longer an absolute one. Biochemical pathways are under constant evolution, and plasmid-mediated genetic information exchange between microbial strains can greatly accelerate this process. In each case, selective pressure is applied to evolve the desired characteristic, such as utilization of a recalcitrant xenobiotic compound. Typically, an enrichment culture is started in a chemostat that is fed small concentrations of the xenobiotic compound and higher concentrations of a related but utilizable substrate. During the enrichment procedure, which may take weeks or even months, the concentration of the utilizable substrate is gradually decreased while the concentration of the xenobiotic compound is increased. Spontaneous mutants with increased ability to utilize the xenobiotic compound are selected for under these circumstances. Spontaneous mutation may be supplemented by treating a part or all of the chemostat culture with UV light or chemical mutagens. Recombinant DNA technology holds great promise for developing microbial strains that can aid in the environmental removal of toxic chemicals (Kilbane 1986; Mongkolsuk et al. 1992).

One approach for providing the enzymatic capability to degrade diverse pollutants is to use genetic engineering to create microorganisms with the capacity to degrade a wide range of hydrocarbons. A hydrocarbon-degrading pseudomonad engineered by Chakrabarty was the first organism that the Supreme Court of the United States ruled, in a landmark decision, could be patented. However, considerable controversy surrounds the release of such genetically engineered microorganisms into the environment, and field testing of these organisms must be delayed until the issues of safety, containment, and potential for ecological damage are resolved (Sussman et al. 1988). Given the current regulatory framework for the deliberate release of specifically genetically engineered microorganisms, it is unlikely that any would gain the necessary regulatory approval in time to be of much use in treating the oil spill for which it was created.

Advances in the directed evolution of microorganisms have been aided by the recognition that many genes coding for the biodegradation of xenobiotics are located on transposable chromosomal elements (transposons) or on plasmids (Eaton and Timmis 1984). Evidence indicates that the transfer and recombination of such movable genetic elements play important roles in the evolution of antibiotic and heavy-metal resistance and utilization of novel substrates in natural environments (Hardy 1981). It is possible to augment the evolution of new degradative pathways by feeding into a chemostat enrichment microorganisms known to harbor plasmids, coding for portions of the desired biodegradative pathway. Exchange, recombination, and amplification of genetic information under selective pressure, along with spontaneous and induced mutation, can greatly accelerate an evolutionary process. Combinations of the described techniques yielded specially constructed *Pseudomonas* strains capable of degrading a wide array of chlorobenzoates and chlorophenols (Hartmann et al. 1979; Reineke and Knackmuss 1979). After the introduction of these strains into the waste stream of a chemical manufacturing plant, the removal of haloaromatic xenobiotics was greatly improved (Knackmuss 1983, 1984). Plasmid-assisted molecular breeding also produced a *Burkholderia (Pseudomonas) cepacia* strain with the capacity to grow on the herbicide 2,4,5-T, though no 2,4,5-T-degrading microorganism could be isolated previously from the environment (Kellogg et al. 1981). Subsequently, it was demonstrated that the treatment of a heavily contaminated soil sample with this engineered *B. cepacia* effectively eliminated the 2,4,5-T contaminant while growing on it (Ghosal et al. 1985) (Figure 14.5). The soil detoxified in this manner was subsequently able to support the growth of herbicide-sensitive plants.

The introduction of genetically engineered microorganisms into the environment, for whatever purpose, has its own hazards. It requires scientific forethought and governmental regulation (Halvorson et al. 1985). It can be argued, however, that the procedures previously described simply speed up evolutionary processes that would eventually take place naturally. They do not involve *in vitro* splicing and manipulation of DNA. Therefore, the environmental release of *in vivo* engineered organisms for cleanup of xenobiotic residues is not expected to be highly controversial.

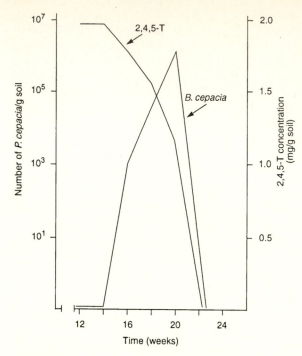

**Figure 14.5**

Disappearance of 2,4,5-T and simultaneous growth of *Burkholderia cepacia* AC1100 in soil. (Source: Kellogg et al. 1981.)

Microbial exoenzymes have been demonstrated to be effective in detoxifying pesticide residues in soils, in used pesticide containers, and in manufacturing wastes (Munnecke 1981). The lignin-degrading enzyme complex of the basidiomycete *Phanerochaete chrysosporium* was effective in oxidizing and immobilizing a number of highly recalcitrant halocarbon xenobiotics, including DDT and TCDD (Bumpus et al. 1985).

Finally, microbial treatment methods may complement other disposal techniques. As an example, photodegradation is quite effective in dehalogenating halocarbon compounds and hydroxylating condensed polycyclic aromatics, but the complete photodegradative destruction of these compounds would be technically difficult and prohibitively expensive. On the other hand, a short photodegradative treatment can be sufficient to prime a recalcitrant halocarbon for biodegradation. A moderate dose of UV radiation was demonstrated to prime the biodegradation of such problem xenobiotics as 2,4-dichlorophenol, 2,4,5-trichlorophenol, and benzo(a)pyrene (Miller et al. 1988a, 1988b). Wastewater containing such recalcitrant compounds could be subjected briefly to UV radiation prior to mixing with other effluents. Conventional secondary sewage treatment would then be able to degrade these otherwise recalcitrant molecules.

# Bioremediation of Various Ecosystems

## Bioremediation of Contaminated Soils and Aquifers

Bioremediation is being used at sites contaminated with hydrocarbons from leaking underground storage tanks. In some cases, treatment is *in situ* or on site; in others, the contaminated material is treated in bioreactors. Treatments range from addition of microbial cultures to nutrient addition and oxygenation.

Hundreds of thousands of leaking underground storage tanks in the United States have contaminated soil and groundwater with low-molecular-weight aromatic hydrocarbons that can threaten human health, particularly if these hydrocarbons get into drinking water supplies. These contaminants can be bioremediated using either *in situ* or *ex situ* systems (Figure 14.6). Bioremediation has certain advantages for cleaning up groundwater. The cleanup of pollutants from leaking underground storage tanks at a bus maintenance and fueling facility in Denver is an example of such treatment. Gasoline, diesel fuel, and possibly lubricating oil contaminated the soil and underlying groundwater near the leaking tanks. Beginning in 1993, the polluting hydrocarbons were removed by air sparging (physical transfer to the atmosphere) and the "pump and treat" technique in which the contaminated water was pumped to the surface, treated, and reinjected. Oxygen and mineral nutrients introduced into the water by this process supported the biodegradative metabolism of indigenous microorganisms. The dissolved oxygen

concentration in the petroleum-contaminated groundwater was as high as 2.8 mg per liter with an average concentration of 0.7 mg per l. The measurements showed that the native bacteria were capable of consuming fuel residues at a rate of about 4.2 g of hydrocarbon per liter of water per year.

Effluent treatment by refineries and petrochemical plants generates large amounts of oily sludges, including gravity (API) separator sludges, air flotation sludges, centrifugation residues, filter cakes, and biotreatment sludges. Tank bottoms, sludges from cleaning operations, and, occasionally, used lubricating and crankcase oils that are considered nonrecyclable are additional sources of oily wastes (CONCAWE 1980; Bartha and Bossert 1984). From the available disposal alternatives, the use of soil bioremediation is the most economical. The process is referred to as "landtreatment" or "landfarming" and constitutes a deliberate disposal process in which place, time, and rates can be controlled. Rates of biodegradation may be slower using on-site landfarming than using bioreactor treatment (Figure 14.7), but it is much more cost effective. In landtreatment, the chosen site has to meet certain criteria and needs to undergo preparation to assure that floods, runoff, and leaching will not spread the hydrocarbon contamination in an uncontrolled manner (Bartha and Bossert 1984). Oily sludges are applied to soil at rates to achieve approximately 5% hydrocarbon concentration in the upper 15- to 20-cm layer of soil. Hydrocarbon concentrations above 10% definitely inhibit the biodegradation process. This limit translates to approximately 100,000 liters of hydrocarbon per ha, usually in three to four times as high sludge volume (Dibble and Bartha 1979a). The soil pH is adjusted to a value between 7 and 8 or to the nearest practical value, using agricultural limestone. Nitrogen and phosphorus fertilizers are applied in ratios of hydrocarbon:N = 200:1 and hydrocarbon:P = 800:1. Adequate drainage is essential, but irrigation is necessary only in very arid and hot climates.

Undegraded hydrocarbons do not leach readily into the groundwater from landtreatment sites (Dibble and Bartha 1979b), and the environmental impact of properly operated sites appears to be minimal (Arora et al. 1982). Currently, open-air land treatment is

**Figure 14.6**
(A) Diagram showing leakage from an underground storage tank. The contaminated soil and groundwater can be bioremediated *in situ* or *ex situ*. (B) Diagram of *in situ* bioremediation of subsurface hydrocarbon-contaminated soil and groundwater. (C) Diagram of *ex situ* bioremediation of subsurface soil and groundwater contaminated by hydrocarbons.

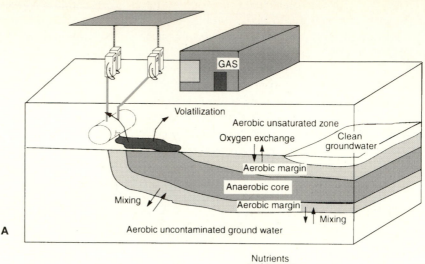

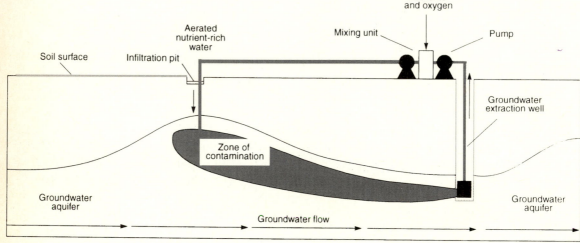

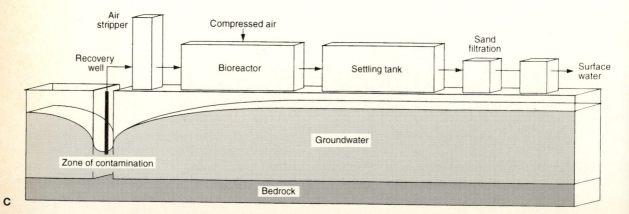

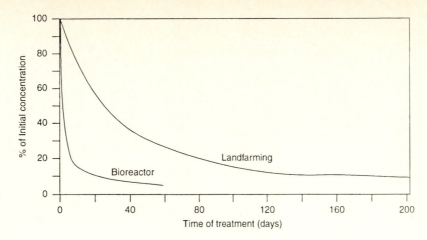

**Figure 14.7**
Comparison of the relative rates of biodegradation of oily wastes in an on-site
landfarming operation and using a bioreactor at a test site in the Netherlands.
Source: Organization for Economic Cooperation and Development 1994.

practiced in the United States (American Petroleum Institute 1980; Arora et al. 1982), in various European countries (CONCAWE 1980; Shailubhai 1986), in Brazil (Amaral 1987; Tesan and Barbosa 1987), and most likely in many other countries. As some volatiles are inevitably lost to the atmosphere in this type of treatment, a variation of the procedure may be performed in a temporary plastic foil enclosure with treatment of the exhaust air. Typically, a portion of the waste organic chemical is mineralized during treatment; another portion is, after partial biodegradation, incorporated into soil humus, bringing about a high degree of detoxification and immobilization. In some cases, ascertaining that such bound residues will not be remobilized at a later time is necessary.

Essentially the same process as landtreatment has been used for bioremediation of surface soils contaminated by crude oil or by refined hydrocarbon fuels due to accidental spills and leaks. Because of their accidental nature, the location and rate of these contamination events cannot be controlled, but it is important to know whether or not biodegradation can be applied as an effective cleanup measure at such sites and how to optimize the process. Extensive site characterization is needed to establish the levels of

contaminants and the direction of subsurface movement of any pollutant plumes (Figure 14.8).

If fuel and site characteristics are favorable, the decision for on-site bioremediation is economically and environmentally sound. The contaminated soil is dug out and spread out in a 15- to 20-cm-thick layer. Although bioremediation may be slow and has its limitations, the alternatives are more expensive and often are environmentally inferior (Jones and Greenfield 1991). In a controlled pilot study (Shen and Bartha 1994), soil contaminated with No. 2 fuel oil due to a leaky underground tank was bioremediated on site. In 500 days (2 growing seasons) the initial 10,200-ppm hydrocarbon concentration was reduced to 250 ppm. The initial soil toxicity, as measured by the Microtox technique, was $EC_{50} = 44$ µg soil. After a transient increase during biodegradation, by day 400 the toxicity declined to the level of the uncontaminated soil control (220 µg). The Microtox technique measures the decrease in light emission by luminescent bacteria such as *Photobacterium* under the influence of the pollutant. The pollutant concentration that decreases light emission by 50% ($EC_{50}$) is analogous to the $LD_{50}$ (dose that is lethal to 50% of the test animals) value in toxicology.

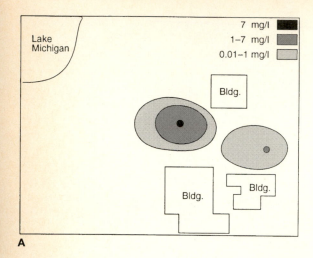

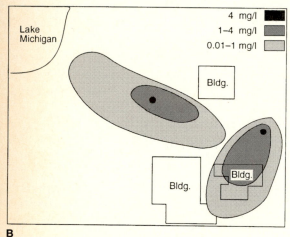

**Figure 14.8**
Site characterization following a pollutant spill, showing the plume of contaminants. (A) Trichloroethylene. (B) Vinyl chloride. (Source: McCarty et al. 1991.)

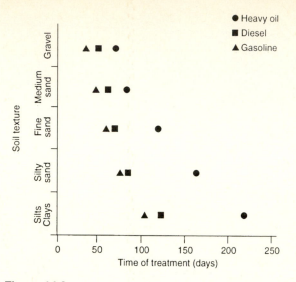

**Figure 14.9**
Biodegradation rates as a function of hydrocarbon source and soil type. As shown in this illustration, rates of biodegradation are lower for heavy fuels than for gasoline and hydrocarbon biodegradation rates are slower in fine-grained soils than in coarse soils. As such, it is more difficult to bioremediate a heavy oil spill in a silt clay than a gasoline spill in gravel. (Source: Cookson 1995.)

Investigating the bioremediation potential of common fuels, Song et al. (1990) concluded that the process is most suitable for the medium fuel distillates such as jet fuel, diesel oil, and No. 2 fuel oil. Whereas gasoline responds to bioremediation, in surface soils biodegradation cannot keep up with evaporation rates, and most of the product is lost to the atmosphere. In laboratory experiments, Song et al. (1990) had limited success with No. 6 (residual) fuel oil. However, Jones and Greenfield (1991) reported quite promising results in an on-site bioremediation effort in Florida. Soil contaminated by an average of 10,000 ppm of No. 6 fuel oil was treated with fertilizer and a commercial microbial inoculum. The soil was turned, cultivated, and kept moist. In three hundred days, about 90% of the contaminant was eliminated, leaving approximately 1000 ppm residue, which included multi-ring PAHs. The inoculum without fertilizer was ineffective, but in combination with fertilizer it significantly improved degradation rates. Climate factors and photodegradation may have contributed to the relative success of their bioremediation effort with a difficult product. Figure 14.9 shows the combined influences of hydrocarbon pollutant type and soil fixture on the time periods required for bioremediation. When other parameters are equal, time requirements increase with the "heaviness" (boiling point) of the hydrocarbon and fineness of the soil texture (Cookson 1995).

Aromatic solvents such as benzene, toluene, ethyl-benzene, and xylene (BTEX), chlorinated aromatics, and haloethanes and halomethanes leak into aquifers from landfills and manufacturing and waste storage sites (Kuhn et al. 1985; Wilson et al. 1986; Berwanger and Barker 1988). The common feature in these pollution incidents has been that the contaminated soil, because of its depth or because of surface structures, was inaccessible to excavation, yet the continued pollution of the aquifers was not tolerable and required intervention.

*In situ* bioremediation techniques for hydrocarbon-contaminated subsurface systems have been reviewed and evaluated in several reports (Vanlooke et al. 1975; Raymond et al. 1976; Brown et al. 1985; Wilson et al. 1986; Lee et al. 1987; Thomas et al. 1987; Wilson and Ward 1987). Aquifer bioremediation depends strongly on local geological and hydrological conditions, and the engineering aspects of the process are beyond the scope of this text. In broad outline, an attempt is usually made to isolate the contamination plume from wells and other sensitive areas. This may be accomplished by using physical barriers, such as cement, bentonite, or grout injection, or dynamically by pumping the polluted portion of the aquifer. In the latter case, groundwater flow is redirected toward rather than away from the contaminated plume, thus preventing the spreading of contamination.

Besides containment, the pumping process recovers free-flowing hydrocarbon and contaminants dissolved in water. In theory, prolonged pumping could eventually flush out all the contaminant, but the solubility characteristics of hydrocarbons make reliance on physical flushing alone prohibitively slow and expensive. Hydrocarbons have much higher affinities than water to soil particles (Verstraete et al. 1976). To clean an aquifer by simple water flushing may take 15–20 years and several thousand times the volume of water in the contaminated portion of the aquifer. Physical flushing may be facilitated by the addition of dispersants and emulsifiers through injection wells around the periphery of the contamination plume, while water is continuously withdrawn from the center of the plume. However, the use of combined biodegradation and emulsification by hydrocarbon-utilizing microorganisms is usually more efficient and economic (Brown et al. 1985; Thomas et al. 1987; Beraud et al. 1989). This may be accomplished by a pump and treat system such as the one shown in Figure 14.6B. In a common modification, the pumped-up contaminated groundwater may be aerobically treated for several hours prior to returning it to the aquifer replenished with oxygen and, if necessary, with mineral nutrients.

Volatile pollutants that are nonmiscible with water may be removed from vadose (water-unsaturated) soils by air stripping or venting. Air is pumped underground, volatilizing and removing the pollutant. In its most primitive form, the treatment simply transfers the pollutant to the atmosphere where it might be eventually photodegraded. In more sophisticated treatment, the pollutant is removed from the effluent air by activated carbon and/or biofilters. In bioventing, the air injection is managed in a way such that the contaminated air stream passes through layers of uncontaminated soil. During this passage, the soil acts as biofilter and removes, by biodegradation, some or most of the pollutant. Some filtration after treatment may still be necessary. As an example, in 1993, the U.S. Air Force completed a full-scale soil bioventing project to clean up a 27,000 gal jet-fuel spill at Hill Air Force Base in Utah. During the 18-month project, jet-fuel residues in soil were reduced from an average total petroleum hydrocarbon concentration of about 900 mg per kg to less than 10 mg per kg. In this bioventing operation, 60% of the hydrocarbons removed from the soil volatilized directly into the atmosphere, and the remaining 40% was biodegraded to carbon dioxide and water.

As discussed in more detail by Alexander (1994), a general problem related to the bioremediation of certain xenobiotic pollutants in soils and sediments is bioavailability. It is a common experience that a pollutant is degraded rapidly when it freshly enters the soil, but the biodegradation levels off and stops with some percentage of the pollutant still present in the soil and conditions still favorable for degradation. Extraction and chemical analysis can detect these pollutants; that is, they have not become bound residues, yet microorganisms no longer appear to have access to them. In the case of old spills, remediated years after the pollution event, much of the pollutant may be in non-bioavailable form, rendering bioremediation efforts futile or at best incomplete. The nature of the pollutant, the nature of the soil, other pollutants, and the time elapsed since the spill all have an influence on bioavailability.

The reasons for restricted bioavailability are not entirely clear yet, but some probable mechanisms are emerging (Alexander 1994). Pollutants may be absorbed and sequestered into clay lattices and inside humic aggregates where microorganisms have no access to them. In addition, they may be partitioned into other pollutants that form a separate hydrophobic phase. These nonaqueous phase liquids (NAPLs) can also sequester and render otherwise biodegradable pollutants unavailable. Phthalate esters, polycyclic aromatic hydrocarbons (PAHs), and numerous other pollutants with low water solubility can behave in this manner. Eventually, it may become possible to overcome these problems of restricted bioavailability by surfactants and/or other solubilizing agents, but at this time the low bioavailability of some residual pollutants is a major obstacle in bioremediation technology.

Bioremediation of aquifers contaminated with halogenated aromatics, haloethanes, and halomethanes presents additional complex problems (Kuhn et al. 1985; Wilson et al. 1986; Berwanger and Barker 1988). Although some of these materials are dehalogenated anaerobically, others cannot serve as substrates under either aerobic or anaerobic conditions and are attacked only cometabolically in the presence of methane or toluene, and only under oxidative conditions.

McCarty and collaborators at Stanford University have demonstrated that cometabolism can degrade TCE and tetrachloroethylene (McCarty et al. 1991). They found that a consortium of bacteria growing under methanogenic conditions can degrade these chlorinated solvents under strictly anaerobic conditions. McCarty also found that a methane-, phenol-, and toluene-utilizing microbial consortium could degrade TCE aerobically in contaminated groundwater when the respective cosubstrates are added. By supplying methane and air in a bioventing configuration, this consortium could be stimulated to bioreme-

diate the TCE-contaminated groundwater (Figure 14.10). The bacteria in this consortium ordinarily oxidize the cosubstrates through the action of monooxygenase enzymes. These monooxygenases can also convert TCE to TCE epoxide, which subsequently breaks down chemically to form other compounds, such as formic acid and glyoxylic acid. These are further metabolized by other microorganisms. However, the effects of cosubstrates on microorganisms are complex, making the results of *in situ* treatment by use of cometabolism unpredictable. Adding a cosubstrate to induce monooxygenase activity in soil microorganisms sometimes produced extensive TCE degradation in field tests. For as yet unknown reasons, in some other cases the identical treatment didn't perform adequately.

Because methylotrophs, through their production of methane monooxygenase (MMO), are able to degrade trichloroethene (TCE), dichloroethene (DCE), and vinyl chloride by cometabolism (Fogel et al. 1986), several investigators have considered using methylotrophs for the bioremediation of sites contaminated with these halogenated compounds. A field test to determine the validity of *in situ* bioremediation has shown a 98% reduction of TCE concentrations in groundwater (Duba et al. 1996). McCarty et al. (1991) found that they could stimulate indigenous methylotrophic populations. They developed a model *in situ* bioremediation treatment that would require 5200 kg of methane and 19,200 kg of oxygen in order to convert 1375 kg of chlorinated hydrocarbons from an aquifer of 480,000 m$^3$ containing a total contaminant load of 1617 kg of halogenated compounds. Palumbo et al. (1991) found, however, that the presence of perchloroethene (PCE) inhibited the methylotrophs and suggested that anaerobic PCE removal would be necessary prior to stimulating methylotrophs to remove TCE. Semprini et al. (1991) found that carbon tetrachloride-, trichloroethane-, and freon-contaminated sites could be bioremediated by stimulating indigenous denitrifying populations through the addition of acetate. Bioremediation by indigenous microorganisms of anaerobic aquifer systems contaminated with the highly toxic and carcinogenic compound vinyl chloride has been proposed; this approach to bioreme-

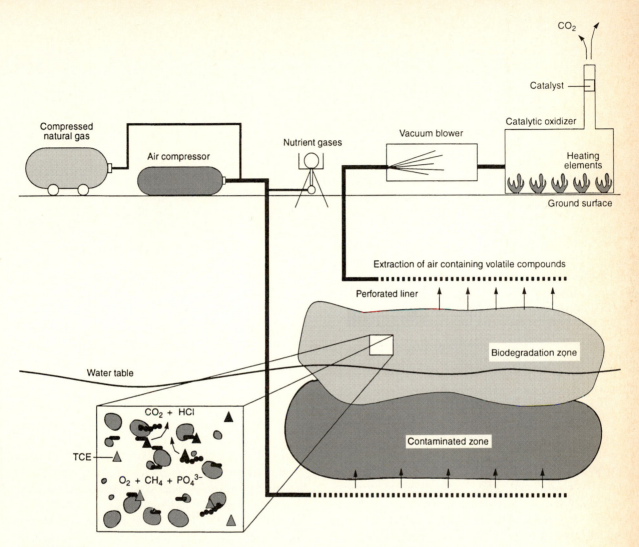

**Figure 14.10**

Bioventing system for treating TCE-contaminated groundwater based on injection of air and the cosubstrate methane to stimulate a bacterial consortium that can utilize methane and cometabolize TCE. Much of the TCE is biodegraded in the treatment zone. Residues in the extracted air are destroyed in a catalytic oxidizer.

diation of such contaminated aquifers involves establishing iron(III)-reducing conditions to promote anaerobic oxidation of the vinyl chloride (Bradley and Chapelle 1996).

Bioremediation has also been shown to be useful for detoxification of nitroaromatics from soil, includ-

ing 2,4,6-trinitrotoluene (TNT) (Bruns-Nagel et al. 1996). TNT was converted into aminodinitrotoluene, diaminonitrotoluene, and acetyldiaminonitrotoluene by the activity of microorganisms. Percolation of soil columns with a glucose-containing phosphate solution resulted in the removal of 90% of the extractable

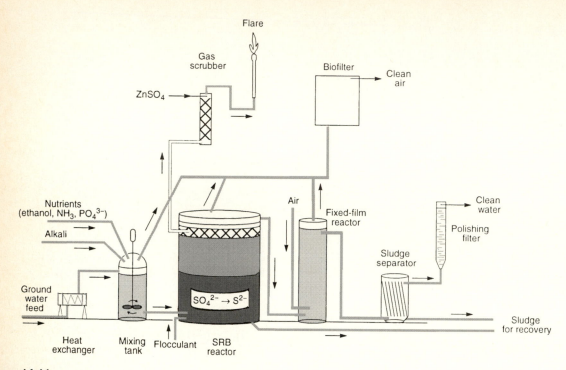

**Figure 14.11**
Diagram showing the system employing sulfate-reducing bacteria to immobilize metals that is used by Shell in the Netherlands.

nitroaromatics in a TNT-contaminated soil within 19 days. TNT was totally removed from the percolation solution. The acute toxicity and the genotoxicity of the treated soil decreased substantially. However, the mechanism of bioremediation in this case was probably a binding to soil organic matter through the amino groups rather than mineralization of the TNT. Bioremediation by a similar mechanism has been shown to be effective for the detoxification of the herbicide Dinoseb (2-*sec*-butyl-3,4-dinitro-*o*-cresol), which commonly is found along with TNT in soil at facilities where munitions are produced and disposed of (Roberts et al. 1996). Adding an external carbon source to the soil, such as acetate, soluble starch, and glucose, favors the formation of anaerobic conditions that allow the initial metabolic steps in the biodegradation of these compounds.

Besides its use for attacking organic compounds, bioremediation can be used to treat sites contaminated with heavy metals or radionuclides (Organization for Economic Cooperation and Development 1994). In one example, Royal Dutch Shell uses sulfate-reducing bacteria (SRB) to immobilize metals at an old zinc refining site at Budelco in the Netherlands (Figure 14.11). The groundwater at that site was contaminated with heavy metals and now contains high concentrations of zinc and cadmium as well as sulfate from the original refining operations. As part of the remediation operation, groundwater is pumped through a bioreactor to which ethanol, ammonia, and phosphate are added to support the growth of sulfate-reducing bacteria. These sulfate-reducing bacteria convert the sulfate in the groundwater to hydrogen sulfide, which reacts with the heavy metals to form insoluble metal sulfides such as zinc sulfide and cadmium sulfide. The microbial process is operated under nonsterile, neutral conditions using ethanol as the growth and energy substrate. Ammonia and phosphate are added as nutrients to a mixing tank that is fed into an SRB reactor. Sulfate concentration in the reactor's aqueous effluent is controlled by the ethanol-to-sulfate ratio in the process feed. An oxidation potential lower than –300 mV is needed to maintain maximum methanogen activity so that the small amount of acetate produced (an SRB by-product) is converted into carbon dioxide and methane, ensuring that the effluent has a low biological oxygen demand. A flocculant is added to the reactor to maximize retention of the very small particles of metal sulfides. A flocculant ensures retention of the precipitated metal sulfides. Effluent controls ensure the retention of the precipitated metal sulfides. The effluent waters contain only a few parts per billion of heavy metals and about 100 ppm sulfate, levels that are environmentally acceptable. The effluent, containing soluble sulfides, passes through a fixed-film bioreactor where aerobic micro-organisms remove hydrogen sulfide from the gaseous stream before the methane is flared. The sludge stream, which contains the metal sulfides, can be recycled to the zinc refinery roaster.

## Bioremediation of Marine Oil Pollutants

Marine oil spills are major pollution events that can have a dramatic impact on coastal ecosystems. A number of technologies, including bioremediation, have been developed to mitigate the effects of marine oil spills. Few studies have been conducted in open waters and the effectiveness of bioremediation in such cases remains unproven (Swannell et al. 1996). Nutrient supplementation in coastal regimes has been shown to be an effective means of stimulating microbial hydrocarbon biodegradation, thereby reducing the impact of marine oil pollutants (Atlas 1995b, 1996; Bragg et al. 1994; Prince 1993; Swannell et al. 1996). In some cases, such as the *Amoco Cadiz* spill, there are sufficient inputs of inorganic nitrogen and phosphates to support extensive biodegradation and it is possible to rely upon intrinsic bioremediation (Gundlach et al.

1983). Intrinsic bioremediation is the use of natural biodegradative activities without further stimulation. When the indigenous rates of hydrocarbon biodegradation are high enough, this approach to bioremediation simply employs monitoring to follow the natural microbial removal of the petroleum pollutants.

In other cases the rate of petroleum biodegradation in coastal marine environments is severely limited by the available concentrations of fixed forms of nitrogen and phosphate. In these cases, fertilizer addition is effective for stimulating the hydrocarbon biodegradative activities of the indigenous microbial populations (Atlas 1996; Prince 1993; Swannell et al. 1996). In particular, oleophilic fertilizers have been shown to be effective, because they are retained with the oil and not diluted by tidal fluxes to levels that would not support extensive petroleum biodegradation. The most widely used oleophilic fertilizer is Inipol EAP 22, a microemulsion of urea in brine encapsulated in oleic acid and lauryl phosphate that is produced by Elf Aquitaine in France (Tramier and Sirvins 1983; Sirvins and Angles 1986). It was one of the fertilizers extensively used in the cleanup of the 1989 *Exxon Valdez* Alaskan oil spill (see the accompanying box). This fertilizer formulation is effective on rocky shorelines, but has not worked well on some oil-polluted fine-grain sand beaches (Swannell et al. 1996).

The problem with many of the studies on bioremediation of marine oil spills is that they take place following real tanker accidents when the emphasis is on emergency response and not scientific study. Planning and proper controls are often limited so that interpretation of data typically is ambiguous. Especially controversial is whether seeding with hydrocarbon-degrading microbial cultures is a useful adjunct to nutrient addition. To answer some of the lingering questions about the effectiveness of bioremediation for treating marine oil spills, an experimental oil spill study was conducted along the shoreline of Delaware Bay to determine if bioremediation with inorganic mineral nutrients and/or microbial inoculation enhanced the removal of crude oil contaminating a sandy beach and to calculate intrinsic and enhanced biodegradation rates (Venosa et al. 1996). This study showed that significant hydrocarbon biodegradation

## Bioremediation of the *Exxon Valdez* Alaskan Oil Spill

The *Exxon Valdez* supertanker ran aground in March 1989, resulting in the spillage of about 11 million gallons of crude oil into Prince William Sound in Alaska. Over 1000 miles of Alaskan shorelines were contaminated with oil. This was the worst oil spill in the United States and threatened fish, birds, and marine mammals as well as the overall quality of the beautiful, pristine Alaskan environment. Exxon initially responded by physically trying to wash the oil from the rocks of the sound using water washing and other physical means. More than $1 million a day was spent in an only partially successful attempt to clean the oiled rocks this way.

Because of the limited effectiveness of physical washing of shorelines, bioremediation was considered as a method to augment other cleanup procedures. The EPA and Exxon entered into an agreement to jointly explore the feasibility of using bioremediation. The project focused on determining whether nutrient augmentation could stimulate rates of biodegradation by the indigenous natural populations (Pritchard and Costa 1991; Bragg et al. 1992). Numerous laboratory tests were included, but the crux of the program involved field demonstrations to establish the efficacy of bioremediation under real-world conditions.

One of the early field demonstrations consisted of applying various fertilizers to plots on oiled beaches. Fertilizers tested included various water-soluble, slow-release, and oleophilic formulations. The application of the oleophilic fertilizer produced dramatic results, stimulating biodegradation so that the surfaces of the oil-blackened rocks on the shoreline turned white and were essentially oil free

within 10 days after treatment (Pritchard and Costa 1991) (Figure A). The striking results strongly supported the idea that oil degradation in Prince William Sound was limited by the amounts of available nutrients and that fertilizer application was a useful bioremediation strategy. The dramatic positive results focused interest on using bioremediation to treat the *Exxon Valdez* spill (Beardsley 1989). Toxicity and ecological effects testing showed that oleophilic and slow-release fertilizer could be safely applied in concentrations that would at least double the rates of oil biodegradation. The use of Inipol and a slow-release fertilizer was approved for shoreline treatment in 1989 and became a major part of the cleanup effort.

Despite the dramatic visual results of fertilizer applications and the decision for its widespread application, doubts remained about the efficacy of oleophilic fertilizer and the scientific proof that bioremediation was effective. Although monitoring demonstrated that fertilizer application sustained higher numbers of oil-degrading microorganisms in oiled shorelines and that potential rates of biodegradation were enhanced in samples collected from fertilizer-treated field sites, analyses of residual hydrocarbons recovered from samples of fertilizer-treated and untreated control plots were not significantly different (Prince et al. 1990; Chianelli et al. 1991). The problem was the high degree of variability brought about by the very patchy distribution of oil in both experimental and control plots. An oiled rocky shoreline is extraordinarily heterogeneous, and some statisticians even suggested releasing more oil to increase the evenness of oiling, a suggestion that was quickly rejected.

## Bioremediation of the *Exxon Valdez* Alaskan Oil Spill, continued

A

**Figure A**
Photograph showing results of Inipol application to a shoreline in Prince William
Sound, Alaska. The "white window" square in the photograph was treated with the
oleophilic fertilizer 10 days earlier. While the surrounding untreated area remained
black and oil covered, the treated area was relatively free of oil. Tests indicated that
simple physical removal was not responsible and that biological degradation of oil
was occurring. (Source: Russ Chianelli, EXXON Corporate Research, Annandale, NJ.)

Therefore, another set of field demonstrations
were conducted the following year in an attempt to
establish the scientific credibility of fertilizer-
enhanced hydrocarbon biodegradation and to gain
authority for continuing bioremediation of the remaining oiled Alaskan shorelines (Bragg et al.
1992, 1994). These tests included sampling wells
for monitoring oxygen and nutrient concentrations
in the pore waters. They also included more extensive chemical analyses of residual oils, including

*(continued)*

## Bioremediation of the *Exxon Valdez* Alaskan Oil Spill, continued

determining the concentrations of hopanes by GC-MS techniques. Hopanes are $C_{27}$ alicyclic hydrocarbons that do not appear to be biodegraded. Because they are preserved in oiled sediments, hopanes can serve as internal standards and the concentrations of other residual hydrocarbons can be normalized to the hopane concentrations. This reduces the variability between samples due to patchy oil distribution and permits more meaningful statistical analyses. Using hopane-normalized chemical data and sophisticated statistical regression models, it was possible to establish definitively that bioremediation was an effective treatment for reducing the hydrocarbon concentrations of oiled Alaskan shorelines. Rates of biodegradation were a function of how much nitrogen from the fertilizer was retained in the sediments (Figure B). Rates of hydrocarbon biodegradation were stimulated three to five times when fertilizer was applied at rates of 4–8 kg per 10 m² of contaminated shoreline. These studies showed that fertilizer application stimulated subsurface biodegradation as well as oil removal from the surfaces of the oiled shorelines. Although higher rates of oil biodegradation could have been achieved, these application rates were chosen to remain well below those which could have caused adverse ecological effects and well below the ammonia toxicity levels to salmon.

Owing to its effectiveness, bioremediation became the major treatment method for removing oil pollutants from the impacted shorelines of

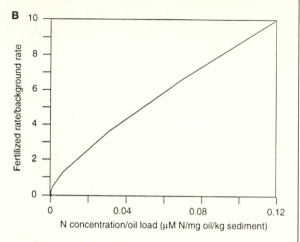

**Figure B**
Relative increase in biodegradation rate of total hydrocarbons in oiled sediments predicted by regression model derived from field tests. The relative success of bioremediation is a function of how much nitrogen was retained in the sediments relative to the concentration of oil in the sediments. According to these results, bioremediation could have been stimulated up to 10 times. In reality, nitrogen loads of 0.03–0.05 µM N per mg oil per kg sediment were applied so that rates of oil biodegradation in treated shorelines were three to five times higher than in untreated ones. (Source: Bragg et al. 1992.)

Prince William Sound. The application of fertilizers reduced the time for removal of biodegradable and toxic hydrocarbons from the predicted 10–20 years to 2–3 years at most impacted sites. The success of bioremediation for treating the *Exxon Valdez* spill also raised the visibility of this technology and stimulated research and development of bioremediation technologies for other applications.

occurred also in untreated plots. However, significant differences were observed in the biodegradation rates of total alkane and total aromatic hydrocarbons between treated and untreated plots. There were no significant differences between plots treated with nutrients alone and plots treated with nutrients and the indigenous inoculum. First-order rate constants for the disappearance of alkanes and PAHs showed loss patterns typical of biodegradation. Thus, nutrient addition was the critical factor in stimulating hydrocarbon biodegradation and the seeding with nonindigenous bacterial cultures was not necessary for bioremediation of the oil pollutants. The general consensus is that indigenous populations of hydrocarbon-degrading microbial populations are adequate and that the critical aspect of bioremediation is overcoming the environmental factors limiting the growth and activity of these populations.

A novel approach to supplying fertilizers that does require seeding with nonindigenous cultures has been developed in Israel (Rosenberg et al. 1992). In this approach the fertilizer, which is a proprietary polymeric formulation, cannot be used by most microorganisms. Thus the nitrogen and phosphate nutrients in the fertilizer are not available to the indigenous microbial populations and cannot be used alone for bioremediation. A hydrocarbon-utilizing bacterium that can also attack the polymeric fertilizer and utilize the nitrogen and phosphate it contains has been isolated. This bacterium is added along with the polymeric fertilizer to oil-contaminated shorelines. This approach gives a selective advantage to the seed bacteria because they are the only ones that can gain direct access to the nutrients. By avoiding competition for the nutrients in the fertilizer, the hydrocarbon biodegradative activities of the seed bacteria are greatly favored and more effective bioremediation can be achieved. This bioremediation treatment has been shown to be effective in the removal of oil pollutants from sand beaches along the Mediterranean Sea.

## Bioremediation of Air Pollutants

Air emissions from various industrial or waste-treatment processes release into the atmosphere substances that may be noxious or hazardous to humans and may contribute to smog formation or to depletion of the atmospheric ozone layer. Air emissions are controlled by various physicochemical means, such as chemical scrubbing or washing, condensation, filtration, adsorption, and flaring (incineration). All of these processes tend to be cumbersome and costly. Most volatile organic emissions tend to be potential microbial substrates, and the use of microorganisms for air pollution control in some cases represents a more cost-effective alternative. Microorganisms are used for air emission control in three types of devices: biofilters, trickling biofilters, and bioscrubbers (Ottengraf 1986; Leson and Winer 1991; Dragt and van Ham 1992). In biofilters and biotrickling filters, multiple microbial communities grow on solid surfaces to produce multilayered complexes called *biofilms*. When gas streams containing organic pollutants are passed through these systems, the pollutants are degraded. Several companies in the Netherlands and Germany have taken the lead in developing such biological air treatment systems.

In bioscrubbers, air moves countercurrent to a fine spray of microbial suspension that washes out water-soluble vapors from the air. The actual degradation takes place in a stirred reactor into which the collected spray is channeled. This device contains no solid phase. It is effective only for highly water-soluble volatile organic chemicals (VOCs). The use of microorganisms for control of air emissions is a relatively new technique. Nevertheless, in Europe, some large units with 75,000 m$^3$ per hour capacity are operating with good results, and this biotechnology is likely to evolve further (Leson and Winer 1991).

Biofilters have been used to control odors and VOCs in contaminated air (Ottengraf and Van den Oever 1983; Leson and Winer 1991). Compost beds and soil beds have been used at sewage treatment plants to control odors associated with hydrogen sulfide, terpenes, mercaptans, and other compounds. The odor-forming compounds are sorbed onto a biofilm and transformed by the microorganisms in that biofilm to their mineral constituents. The operation of such biofilters for the treatment of contaminated air is analogous to wastewater treatment in biofilm-bearing

**Table 14.2**
Removal of pollutants from air by biofilters

| Substance | Percent removed |
| --- | --- |
| Hydrogen sulfide | >99 |
| Dimethyl sulfide | >91 |
| Terpene | >98 |
| Organo-sulfur gases | >95 |
| Ethylbenzene | >92 |
| Tetrachloroethylene | >86 |
| Chlorobenzene | >69 |
| Nitrobenzene | >95 |
| BTX (Benzene, toluene, xylene) | >95 |
| Methanol | >98 |
| Styrene | >90 |
| Formaldehyde | >95 |

devices. In both applications, bacteria are immobilized on a solid support as a biofilm and the microorganisms form products that are less toxic and generally environmentally acceptable. The classical biofilter technology uses peat, compost, bark, or soils as filter media and includes initial addition of nutrients and buffers. During operation, only lost moisture is replenished. Table 14.2 gives a summary for the removal of specific odor compounds.

Air treatment bioreactors are in use in the Netherlands to remove formaldehyde from air released from plywood production facilities and phenols from resin producers (Dragt and van Ham 1992). Similar biofiltration systems are being tested to remove solvents from indoor air at paint production facilities. Biofiltration has been used since 1989 to treat gases given off by soybean toasters in Hengelo in the Netherlands (Organization for Economic Cooperation and Development 1994). The gases pass through a column packed with a proprietary solid support. A biofilm growing on this support biodegrades more than 95% of the organic compounds in the gases. This biofilter, which covers an area of 240 m$^3$, can process 300 m$^3$ of gas per m$^3$ of packing per hour. A cattle feed extru-

sion plant in Zwolle, the Netherlands, also uses biofiltration to remove more than 99% of the odorous gases from its emissions. This facility handles 600 m$^3$ of gas per m$^3$ of packing per hour. Another example of the use of biofiltration in Europe is a German animal rendering plant that treats 214,000 m$^3$ of gas per hour using a biofilter filled with peat and heather that has a volume of 3240 m$^3$. Odors are reduced 94–99% (Organization for Economic Cooperation and Development 1994). A ceramics factory in southern Germany uses biofiltration to remove more than 99% of the ethanol and isopropyl alcohol released into the air from the drying ceramics. The alcohols (90% ethanol and 10% isopropyl alcohol) are released at a concentration of 230 ppm organic carbon and a flow rate of 30,000 m$^3$ per hour. A simple biofilter with a volume of 200 m$^3$ removes them.

Limitations exist in the current biofilter technology. Key limitations are that residual biomass accumulates in the filter media and that acids produced from the degradation of chlorinated organics and sulfur compounds consume the buffering capacity of the bed. Thus the process, at high organic loadings in air, experiences increasing pressure drop across the media and decreasing pH. The time of operation before media replacement depends on the pollutant loadings in the air. Low pollutant loadings result in process runs of more than one year. In trickling-filter-type devices, the biofilm is associated with a porous solid, like in the case of a biofilter, but in addition to air that moves through this medium, liquid is also circulated, either in the same direction or countercurrent to the air. This type of device offers more process control, as the circulating liquid can be periodically amended with nutrients, neutralized, or diluted if salts accumulate. This type of device is essential if VOC metabolism produces acidity, alkalinity, or salts, as for instance in the case of chlorinated or nitro-substituted solvent vapors.

The diagram of a laboratory-scale trickling air biofilter that was used for the removal of monochlorobenzene, dichlorobenzene, chlorobenzene mixtures, and also nitrobenzene is shown in Figure 14.12 (Oh and Bartha 1994, 1997). The hydrochloric acid generated during chlorobenzene degradation and the

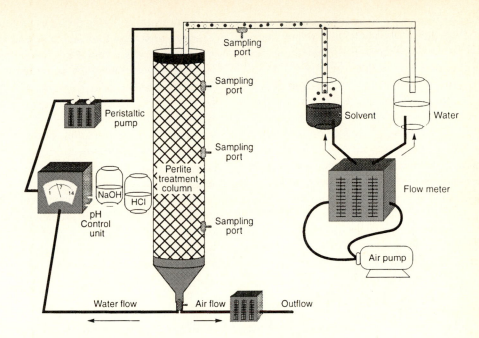

**Figure 14.12**
Diagram of a laboratory-scale trickling air biofilter used for removal of chlorobenzenes and nitrobenzene from air. A glass column, packed with a highly porous inert mineral (perlite) serves as support for the appropriate microbial biofilms. Both air and liquid medium pass through the column in the downflow mode. At the bottom of the column, air and liquid are separated. The liquid is recirculated to the top of the column through a pH control unit that automatically neutralizes the medium. The air, after passing a flowmeter and a sampling port, is discharged. For this experimental device, "polluted air" is created by directing separate streams of air through a solvent and a water trap. This allows the total air flow and the pollutant concentrations in air to be varied independently. Pollutant concentrations in the air are determined by taking, through sampling ports, air samples by a gastight syringe and injecting these into a gas chromatograph. From the pollutant concentrations prior to and after the column, and from the airflow rates, the pollutant removal rates are calculated.

ammonium hydroxide generated from nitrobenzene metabolism were automatically neutralized by a pH-stat unit of the type used in fermentors. Without pH control, chlorobenzene biofiltration activity was lost within a week due to pH drop, but with pH control, chlorobenzene removal was steady in experiments of several months in duration. Because of salt buildup, the recirculating liquid needed to be exchanged when NaCl reached 200 m$M$ concentration. This occurred approximately weekly. The described biotrickling filter could remove on a sustained basis 200 g chlorobenzene or chlorobenzene mixtures per m$^3$ of

filter volume per hour from air. The air residence time in the filter column was 30–40 seconds.

From nitrobenzene, the released nitrite was quickly reduced on the column to ammonia, raising the pH to 8.7. Liquid recirculation was necessary to maintain biofiltration activity but, because of the broad pH optimum of the microorganisms, pH control was found to be unnecessary. At the alkaline pH, excess ammonia was stripped by the airstream, making neutralization unnecessary and avoiding a salt buildup.

For alcohols, ketones, and other common products of microbial metabolism, a special inoculum for biofilters is usually unnecessary. However, for more recalcitrant xenobiotic compounds, such as previously described chloro- and nitrobenzenes, the columns had to be inoculated with appropriate enrichments developed specifically for each compound. Mixed enrichments consistently performed better than pure cultures.

In all the cases described, the VOC compounds were capable of supporting growth of a properly adapted microbial consortium. It may be possible to remove biologically some nonsubstrate type of compounds like trichloroethylene (TCE) cometabolically, but in such cases, low amounts of an appropriate and growth-inducing substrate such as methane or toluene need to be added to the airstream. Biomass buildup can also become a problem in trickling air filters, especially at high loadings. In the EPA's Risk Reduction Engineering Laboratory in Cincinnati, Ohio, high pollutant loadings (greater than 200 ppm) of organic compounds in air were fed to a trickling-filter-type biotower. The biotower removed essentially all of the organic pollutants from the air in 2 minutes of retention time but exhibited relatively rapid accumulation of residual biomass and tower flooding in several months. Biomass buildup can be controlled if the filter is not in continuous use. A slow clean airstream, as between work shifts, will induce starvation conditions and "burn off" excess biomass.

## CHAPTER SUMMARY

Pollution problems caused by xenobiotics have necessitated an elaborate environmental safety testing program for newly introduced chemicals. Remedies to existing pollution problems by xenobiotics include redesigning the molecules of synthetic products, testing the fate and effects of newly introduced chemicals in model ecosystems and microcosms, optimizing environmental conditions for biodegradation, and engineering new microorganisms with broader biodegradative abilities. The destruction of the stratospheric ozone layer, acid mine drainage, heavy-metal and metalloid biomethylation, and radionuclide pollution are all processes that are either mediated or exacerbated by microbial processes. Amelioration of these

environmental pollution problems depends, in part, on a better understanding and eventual control of the microbial processes involved.

A new biotechnological solution to pollution problems—bioremediation—has emerged. Bioremediation involves the use of microorganisms to remove pollutants. Using bioremediation to remove pollutants is inexpensive compared to physical methods for decontaminating the environment. Site characterization that shows the concentrations of specific pollutants is critical in evaluating which remediation technologies can be used. In addition to routine toxicity tests, evaluations of biodegradability, biomagnification, and environmental fate are performed in microcosms prior to licensing and release. The environmental monitoring of xenobiotic pollutants relies on sophisticated analytical instrumentation and, increasingly, also on microbial biosensors.

To demonstrate that a bioremediation technology is potentially useful, it is important to document enhanced biodegradation of the pollutant under controlled conditions. Testing the biodegradability of substances and potential environmental side effects are critical for determining the appropriateness of bioremediation. The classical approach to demonstrating the presence of microorganisms capable of carrying out pollutant biodegradation has been the enrichment culture method, with the test substance serving as substrate. Respirometry, including radiorespirometric measurements, are often used to show actual rates of biodegradation. Placement of the radiolabel is critical for the proper interpretation of such tests. Model ecosystems that take into account the important environmental parameters are also essential for studying the fate of pollutants and the applicability of bioremediation. In evaluating specific bioremediation treatments it is important to include appropriate controls to permit identifying the specific effects of bioremediation treatment on pollutant biodegradation. The most direct measure of bioremediation efficacy is the monitoring of disappearance rates of the pollutant, but in many cases other measures, such as oxygen consumption, are employed.

The two general approaches to bioremediation are environmental modification, such as through nutrient application and aeration, and the addition of appropriate xenobiotic degraders by seeding. If the indigenous population is capable of biodegrading the pollutant, often there is no need to add microbial cultures. In those cases bioremediation relies upon modifying environmental conditions to favor biodegradative metabolism. Often it is critical to supply oxygen or use other methods such as soil tilling so as to ensure aerobic conditions. This is especially important for the bioremediation of petroleum hydrocarbons, which are rapidly biodegraded only under aerobic conditions. In other cases anaerobic conditions favor the needed biodegradative metabolism. Reductive dehalogenation, for example, occurs most rapidly under anaerobic conditions. Bioremediation of some pollutants, such as PCBs, requires sequential anaerobic and aerobic conditions to achieve maximal biodegradation of the various isomers found in complex pollutant mixtures.

Besides regulating oxygen, mineral nutrients, notably nitrogen and phosphorus, are necessary to support the growth of microorganisms on pollutants such as petroleum hydrocarbons. Various fertilizer formulations, including slow-release and oleophilic fertilizers, are used in different applications of bioremediation to contaminated soils and waters. Getting nutrients to subsurface soils and groundwaters can be complex and various specialized methods, including the use of electrical currents, are used to drive the nutrients to the pollutants. Some pollutants, such as TCE, are not readily attacked by primary metabolism and are degraded via cometabolism only. Cosubstrates, such as methane and toluene, can be added to stimulate biodegradation but cometabolic transformations are difficult to manage and the successes of such treatments vary.

In cases where the indigenous microbial populations are not capable of degrading pollutants even under favorable environmental conditions, it is possible to add microorganisms with specific metabolic capabilities. Seeding with microorganisms, called *bioaugmentation,* is particularly effective for the bioremediation of xenobiotic compounds with multiple chlorine substituents. Recombinant DNA technology has been used to genetically engineer bacteria with specific biodegradative metabolic capabilities which are potentially useful for bioremediation. Uncertainties about the consequences of deliberately releasing genetically modified microorganisms into the environment have so far precluded the wide use of such microorganisms.

The uses of bioremediation are expanding. The leakages of gasoline from many underground storage tanks into soils and groundwaters are being treated by bioremediation. Some of these treatments are conducted *in situ* and involve ensuring aerobic conditions and adding nitrogen- and phosphate-containing fertilizers. Other treatments are conducted *ex situ* and involve pumping contaminated water into a bioreactor where microbial cultures are supplied with oxygen and nutrients to biodegrade the pollutants. Marine oil spills are also treated by bioremediation involving either intrinsic bioremediation or the application of fertilizers, including ones such as the oleophilic fertilizer Inipol EAP 22. Successful bioremediation of petroleum spillages produces harmless carbon dioxide and water, greatly reducing the environmental impact of such pollution events.

Bioremediation also is used for the treatment of various air pollutants. Biofilters, biotrickling filters, and bioscrubbers are used to remove odor-causing compounds from air near farms, sewage treatment facilities, and various industrial operations. These bioreactors have biofilms of microorganisms that can remove over 99% of volatile pollutants from air. Toxic compounds, such as toluene, hydrogen sulfide, and chloro- and nitrobenzenes, also can be removed in this manner. Thus, the uses of bioremediation continue to expand.

## STUDY QUESTIONS

1. What is a biosensor? How can biosensors be used in site monitoring?

2. What is bioremediation? Why is it an attractive alternative to incineration and other physical/chemical means of environmental cleanup?

3. What factors must be taken into account in determining whether bioremediation is applicable to a specific polluted site?

4. How can the feasibility and safety of bioremediation be determined?

5. Describe the general approaches used for bioremediation.

6. Describe how bioremediation can be used for the treatment of hydrocarbons leaking from an underground storage tank.

7. Describe how bioremediation can be used for the treatment of river sediments contaminated with PCBs from electrical transformers.

8. Describe how bioremediation can be used for the treatment of coastal ecosystems contaminated by a major oil spill.

9. Describe how bioremediation can be used for the treatment of an aquifer contaminated with TCE.

10. What properties could be incorporated into a genetically engineered bacterium for TCE biodegradation? Why would such bacteria potentially be very useful for the bioremediation of TCE?

11. Why is the use of genetically engineered bacteria in bioremediation controversial?

12. Compare the advantages and limitations of *in situ* and *ex situ* bioremediation for contaminated soils and groundwater.

## REFERENCES AND SUGGESTED READINGS

Abramowicz, D. A. 1990. Aerobic and anaerobic biodegradation of PCBs: A review. *Critical Reviews in Biotechnology* 10:241–251.

Acar, Y. B., E. E. Ozsu, A. N. Alshawabkeh, M. F. Rabbi, and R. J. Gale. 1996. Enhance soil bioremediation with electric fields. *Chemtech* 26:40–45.

Aelion, C. M., and P. M. Bradley. 1991. Aerobic biodegradation potential of subsurface microorganisms from a jet fuel–contaminated aquifer. *Applied and Environmental Microbiology* 57:57–63.

Aelion, C. M., C. M. Swindoll, and F. K. Pfaender. 1987. Adaptation to and biodegradation of xenobiotic compounds by microbial communities from a pristine aquifer. *Applied and Environmental Microbiology* 53:2212–2217.

Alexander, M. 1994. *Biodegradation and Bioremediation.* Academic Press, San Diego.

Amaral, S. P. 1987. Landfarming of oily wastes: Design and operation. *Water Science Technology* 19:75–86.

American Petroleum Institute. 1980. *Manual on Disposal of Petroleum Wastes.* American Petroleum Institute, Washington, DC.

American Petroleum Institute. 1987. *Field Study of Enhanced Subsurface Biodegradation of Hydrocarbons Using Hydrogen Peroxide as an Oxygen Source.* American Petroleum Institute Pub. 4448. American Petroleum Institute, Washington, DC.

Applied Biotreatment Association. 1989. *Case History Compendium.* Applied Biotreatment Association, Washington, DC.

Applied Biotreatment Association. 1990. *The Role of Biotreatment of Oil Spills.* Applied Biotreatment Association, Washington, DC.

Arora, H. S., R. R. Cantor, and J. C. Nemeth. 1982. Land treatment: A viable and successful method of treating petroleum industry wastes. *Environment International* 7:285–292.

Atlas, R. M. 1981. Microbial degradation of petroleum hydrocarbons: An environmental perspective. *Microbiological Reviews* 45:180–209.

Atlas, R. 1995a. Bioremediation. *Chemical & Engineering News* April 3:32–42.

Atlas, R. 1995b. Bioremediation of petroleum pollutants. *International Biodeterioration and Biodegradation* 1995:317–327.

Atlas, R. 1996. Slick solutions. *Chemistry in Britain* 32:42–45.

Atlas, R. M., and R. Bartha. 1973. Stimulated biodegradation of oil slicks using oleophilic fertilizers. *Environmental Science and Technology* 7:538–541.

Atlas, R. M., and R. Bartha. 1992. Hydrocarbon biodegradation and oil spill bioremediation. *Advances in Microbial Ecology* 12:287–338.

Atlas, R. M., and D. Pramer. 1990. Focus on bioremediation. *ASM News* 56:7.

Atlas, R. M., D. Pramer, and R. Bartha. 1978. Assessment of pesticide effects on nontarget soil microorganisms. *Soil Biology Biochemistry* 10:231–239.

Bailey, N.J.L., A. M. Jobson, and M. A. Rogers. 1973. Bacterial degradation of crude oil: Comparison of field and experimental data. *Chemical Geology* 11:203–221.

Baker, K. H., and D. S. Herson. 1994. *Bioremediation*. McGraw-Hill, New York.

Barnhardt, C. H., and J. R. Vestal. 1983. Effects of environmental toxicants on metabolic activity of natural microbial communities. *Applied and Environmental Microbiology* 46:970–977.

Bartha, R. 1986. Biotechnology of petroleum pollutant biodegradation. *Microbial Ecology* 12:155–172.

Bartha, R., and I. Bossert. 1984. The treatment and disposal of petroleum wastes. In R. M. Atlas (ed.). *Petroleum Microbiology*. Macmillan, New York, pp. 553–577.

Baud-Grasset, S., F. Baud-Grasset, J. M. Bifulco, J. R. Meier, and T. H. Ma. 1993. Reduction of genotoxicity of a creosote-contaminated soil after fungal treatment determined by the *Tradescantia*-micronucleus test. *Mutation Research* 303:77–82.

Beardsley, T. 1989. No slick fix: Oil spill research is suddenly back in favor. *Scientific American* 261(3):43.

Beraud, J. F., J. D. Ducreux, and C. Gatellier. 1989. Use of soil-aquifer treatment in oil pollution control of underground waters. In *Proceedings of the 1989 Oil Spill Conference*. American Petroleum Institute, Washington, DC, pp. 53–59.

Bertrand, J. C., E. Rambeloarisoa, J. F. Rontani, G. Giusti, and G. Mattei. 1983. Microbial degradation of crude oil in sea water in continuous culture. *Biotechnology Letters* 5:567–572.

Berwanger, D. J., and J. F. Barker. 1988. Aerobic biodegradation of aromatic and chlorinated hydrocarbons commonly detected in landfill leachate. *Water Pollution Research Journal of Canada* 23:460–475.

Bluestone, M. 1986. Microbes to the rescue. *Chemical Week* 139:34–35.

Bogan, B. W., B. Schoenike, R. T. Lamar, and D. Cullen. 1996. Manganese peroxidase mRNA and enzyme activity levels during bioremediation of polycyclic aromatic hydrocarbon-contaminated soil with *Phanerochaete chrysosporium*. *Applied and Environmental Microbiology* 62:2381–2387.

Borden, R. C., T. M. Vogel, J. M. Thomas, and C. H. Ward. 1994. *Handbook of Bioremediation*. Lewis Publishers, Boca Raton, FL.

Bossert, I., and R. Bartha. 1984. The fate of petroleum in soil ecosystems. In R. M. Atlas (ed.). *Petroleum Microbiology*. Macmillan, New York, pp. 435–473.

Bossert, I., and R. Bartha. 1985. Plant growth in soils with a history of oily sludge disposal. *Soil Science* 140:75–77.

Bossert, I., W. M. Kachel, and R. Bartha. 1984. Fate of hydrocarbons during oily sludge disposal in soil. *Applied and Environmental Microbiology* 47:763–767.

Boulding, J. R. 1995. *Practical Handbook of Soil, Vadose Zone, and Ground-water Contamination: Assessment, Prevention, and Remediation*. Lewis Publishers, Boca Raton, FL.

Bradley, P. M., and F. H. Chapelle. 1996. Anaerobic mineralization of vinyl chloride in Fe(III)-reducing, aquifer sediments. *Environmental Science and Technology* 30:2084–2087.

Bragg, J. R., R. C. Prince, E. J. Harner, and R. M. Atlas. 1994. Effectiveness of bioremediation for the Exxon Valdez oil spill. *Nature* 368:413–418.

Bragg, J. R., R. C. Prince, J. B. Wilkinson, and R. M. Atlas. 1992. *Bioremediation for Shoreline Cleanup Following the 1989 Alaskan Oil Spill*. Exxon Co., Houston, TX.

Brown, R. A., R. D. Norris, and R. L. Raymond. 1984. Oxygen transport in contaminated aquifers. In *Proceedings of the Conference on Petroleum Hydrocarbons and Organic Chemicals in Ground Water—Prevention, Detection, and Restoration.* National Water Well Association, Worthington, OH, pp. 441–450.

Brown, R. A., R. D. Norris, and G. R. Brubaker. 1985. Aquifer restoration with enhanced bioreclamation. *Pollution Engineering* 17:25–28.

Brubaker, G. R. 1995. The boom in *in situ* bioremediation. *Civil Engineering* 65:38–42.

Brunner, W., S. H. Southerland, and D. D. Focht. 1985. Enhanced biodegradation of polychlorinated biphenyls in soil by analog enrichment and bacterial inoculation. *Journal of Environmental Quality* 14:324–328.

Bruns-Nagel, D., J. Breitung, E. von Low, K. Steinbach, T. Gorontzy, M. Kahl, K.-H. Blotevogel, and D. Gemsa. 1996. Microbial transformation of 2,4,6-trinitrotoluene in aerobic soil columns. *Applied and Environmental Microbiology* 62:2651–2657.

Bull, A. T. 1980. Biodegradation: Some attitudes and strategies of microorganisms and microbiologists. In D. C. Ellwood, J. N. Hedger, M. J. Latham, and J. M. Lynch (eds.). *Contemporary Microbial Ecology.* Academic Press, New York, pp. 107–136.

Bull, A. T., C. R. Ratledge, and D. C. Ellwood (eds.). 1979. *Microbial Technology: Current State and Future Prospects, Twenty-Ninth Symposium of the Society for General Microbiology.* Cambridge University Press, Cambridge, England.

Bumpus, J. A. 1989. Biodegradation of polycyclic aromatic hydrocarbons by *Phanerochaete chrysosporium. Applied and Environmental Microbiology* 55:154–158.

Bumpus, J. A., and S. D. Aust. 1987. Biodegradation of DDT [1,1,1–trichloro–2,2–bis(4–chlorophenyl) ethane] by the white rot fungus *Phanerochaete chrysosporium. Applied and Environmental Microbiology* 53:2001–2028.

Bumpus, J. A., M. Tien, D. Wright, and S. D. Aust. 1985. Oxidation of persistent environmental pollutants by a white rot fungus. *Science* 228:1434–1436.

Burlage, R. S., G. S. Sayler, and F. Larimer. 1990. Monitoring of naphthalene catabolism by bioluminescence with *nah–lux* transcriptional fusions. *Journal of Bacteriology* 172:4749–4757.

Chamerlik-Cooper, M., R. E. Carlson, and R. O. Harrison. 1991. Determination of PCBs by enzyme immunoassay. In *Field Screening Methods for Hazardous Wastes and Toxic Chemicals.* U.S. Environmental Protection Agency and U.S. Army Toxic and Hazardous Materials Agency, Las Vegas, NV, pp. 625–628.

Chianelli, R. R., T. Aczel, R. E. Bare, G. N. George, M. W. Genowitz, M. J. Grossman, C. E. Haith, F. J. Kaiser, R. R. Lessard, R. Liotta, R. L. Mastracchio, V. Minak–Bernero, R. C. Prince, W. K. Robbins, E. I. Stiefel, J. B. Wilkinson, S. M. Hinton, J. R. Bragg, S. J. McMillan, and R. M. Atlas. 1991. Bioremediation technology development and application to the Alaskan spill. In *Proceedings of the 1991 International Oil Spill Conference.* American Petroleum Institute, Washington DC, pp. 549–558.

Code of Federal Regulations. 1992. Inherent biodegradability in soil. *CFR* 40:796.3400 pp. 224–229. U.S. Government Printing Office, Washington DC.

Colwell, E. B. (ed.). 1971. *The Ecological Effects of Oil Pollution on Littoral Communities.* Applied Science Publishers, London.

CONCAWE. 1980. *Sludge Farming: A Technique for the Disposal of Oily Refinery Wastes.* Rep. 3/80. CONCAWE, The Hague, Netherlands.

Cookson, J. T., Jr. 1995. *Bioremediation Engineering: Design and application.* McGraw-Hill, New York.

Dibble, J. T., and R. Bartha. 1979a. Effect of environmental parameters on the biodegradation of oil sludge. *Applied and Environmental Microbiology* 37:729–739.

Dibble, J. T., and R. Bartha. 1979b. Leaching aspects of oil sludge biodegradation in soil. *Soil Science* 127:365–370.

Dibble, J., and R. Bartha. 1979c. Rehabilitation of oil-inundated agricultural land: A case history. *Soil Science* 128:56–60.

Doe, K. G., and P. G. Wells. 1978. Acute toxicity and dispersing effectiveness of oil spill dispersants: Results of a Canadian oil dispersant testing program (1973 to 1977). In L. T. McCarthy, Jr., G. P. Lindblom, and H. F. Walter (eds.). *Chemical Dispersants for the Control of Oil Spills.* American Society for Testing and Materials, Philadelphia, pp. 50–65.

Dohrman, L. 1991. Immunoassays for rapid environmental contaminant monitoring. *American Laboratory* Oct:29–30.

Dowd, R. M. 1984. Leaking underground storage tanks. *Environmental Science and Technology* 18:309–312.

Dragt, A. J., and J. van Ham (eds.). 1992. *Biotechniques for Air Pollution Abatement and Odour Control Policies: Proceedings of an International Symposium.* Elsevier, Amsterdam.

Drinkwine, A., S. Spurlin, J. Van Emon, and V. Lopez-Avila. 1991. Immuno-based personal exposure monitors. In *Field Screening Methods for Hazardous Wastes and Toxic Chemicals.* U.S. Environmental Protection Agency and U.S. Army Toxic and Hazardous Materials Agency, Las Vegas, NV, pp. 449–459.

Duba, A. G., K. J. Jackson, M. C. Jovanovich, R. B. Knapp, and R. T. Taylor. 1996. TCE remediation using in situ, resting-state bioaugmentation. *Environmental Science and Technology* 30:1982–1990.

Eaton, R. W., and K. N. Timmis. 1984. Genetics of xenobiotic degradation. In M. J. Klug and C. A. Reddy (eds.). *Current Perspectives in Microbial Ecology.* American Society for Microbiology, Washington, DC, pp. 694–703.

Fernando, T., J. A. Bumpus, and S. D. Aust. 1990. Biodegradation of TNT (2,4,6–trinitrotoluene) by *Phanerochaete chrysosporium. Applied and Environmental Microbiology* 56:1666–1671.

Flathman, P. E., D. E. Jerger, and J. H. Exner. 1994. *Bioremediation-field Experience.* Lewis Publishers, Boca Raton, FL.

Fogel, M. M., A. R. Taddeo, and S. Fogel. 1986. Biodegradation of chlorinated ethanes by a methane-utilizing mixed culture. *Applied and Environmental Microbiology* 51:720–724.

Fogel, S., R. L. Lancione, and A. E. Sewal. 1982. Enhanced biodegradation of methoxychlor in soil under sequential environmental conditions. *Applied and Environmental Microbiology* 44:113–120.

Frankenberger, W. T., Jr., K. D. Emerson, and D. W. Turner. 1989. *In situ* bioremediation of an underground diesel fuel spill: A case history. *Environment Management* 13:325–332.

Fredrickson, J. K., F. Brockman, and D. Workman. 1991. Isolation and characterization of a subsurface bacterium capable of growth on toluene, naphthalene, and other aromatic compounds. *Applied and Environmental Microbiology* 57:796–803.

Ghosal, D., I. S. You, D. K. Chatterjee, and A. M. Chakrabarty. 1985. Microbial degradation of halogenated compounds. *Science* 228:135–142.

Gibson, D. T., and G. S. Sayler. 1992. *Scientific Foundations of Bioremediation: Current Status and Future Needs.* American Academy of Microbiology, Washington, DC.

Gosset, R. W., D. A. Brown, and D. R. Young. 1983. Predicting the bioaccumulation of organic compounds in marine organisms using octanol/water partition coefficients. *Marine Pollution Bulletin* 14:387–392.

Greaves, M. P., H. A. Davies, J.A.P. Marsh, and G. I. Wingfield. 1977. Herbicides and soil microorganisms. *CRC Critical Reviews of Microbiology* 5:1–38.

Gundlach, E. R., P. D. Boehm, M. Marchand, R. M. Atlas, D. M. Ward, and D. A. Wolfe. 1983. The fate of *Amoco Cadiz* oil. *Science* 221:122–129.

Hales, S. G., T. Feijtel, H. Kin, K. Fox, and W. Verstraete (eds.). 1997. *Biodegradation Kinetics: Generation and Use of Data for Regulatory Decision Making.* SETAC Europe Press, Sheffield, England.

Halvorson, H. O., D. Pramer, and M. Rogul (eds.). 1985. *Engineered Organisms in the Environment: Scientific Issues.* American Society for Microbiology, Washington, DC.

Hardy, K. 1981. *Bacterial Plasmids.* Aspects of Microbiology Series, No. 4. American Society for Microbiology, Washington, DC.

Hart, S. 1996. *In situ* bioremediation: Defining the limits. *Environmental Science and Technology* 30:398–401.

Hartmann, J., W. Reineke, and H. J. Knackmuss. 1979. Metabolism of 3-chloro, 4-chloro-, and 3,5-dichlorobenzoate by a pseudomonad. *Applied and Environmental Microbiology* 37:421–428.

Hinchee, R. E. (ed.). 1994. *Air Sparging for Site Remediation.* Lewis Publishers, Boca Raton, FL.

Hinchee, R. E., and R. F. Olfenbuttel (eds.). 1991a. In Situ *Bioreclamation: Applications and Investigations for Hydrocarbon and Contaminated Site Remediation.* Butterworth-Heinemann, Boston.

Hinchee, R.E., and R. F. Olfenbuttel (eds.). 1991b. *On-Site Bioreclamation: Processes for Xenobiotic and Hydrocarbon Treatment.* Butterworth-Heinemann, Boston.

Hinchee, R. E., D. B. Anderson, F. B. Metting, Jr., and G. D. Sayles (eds.). 1994a. *Applied Biotechnology for Site Remediation.* Lewis Publishers, Boca Raton, FL.

Hinchee, R. E., B. C. Alleman, R. E. Hoeppel, and R. N. Miller. 1994b. *Hydrocarbon Bioremediation.* Lewis Publishers, Boca Raton, FL.

Ho, S. V., P. W. Sheridan, C. J. Athmer, M. A. Heitkamp, J. M. Brackin, D. Weber, and P. H. Brodsky. 1995. Integrated *in situ* soil remediation technology: The lasagna process. *Environmental Science and Technology* 29:2528–2534.

Hsu, T. S., and R. Bartha. 1979. Accelerated mineralization of two organophosphate insecticides in the rhizosphere. *Applied and Environmental Microbiology* 37:36–41.

Huddleston, R. L., and L. W. Cresswell. 1976. Environmental and nutritional constraints of microbial hydrocarbon utilization in the soil. In *Proceedings of the 1975 Engineering Foundation Conference: The Role of Microorganisms in the Recovery of Oil.* NSF/RANN, Washington, DC, pp. 71–72.

Jain, R. K., and G. S. Sayler. 1987. Problems and potential for *in situ* treatment of environmental pollutants by engineered microorganisms. *Microbiological Sciences* 4:59–63.

Jamison, V. M., R. L. Raymond, and J. O. Hudson, Jr. 1975. Biodegradation of high-octane gasoline in groundwater. *Developments in Industrial Microbiology* 16:305–312.

Johnen, B. G., and E. A. Drew. 1977. Ecological effects of pesticides on soil microorganisms. *Soil Science* 123:319–324.

Johnson, L. M., C. S. McDowell, and M. Krupha. 1985. Microbiology in pollution control: From bugs to biotechnology. *Developments in Industrial Microbiology* 26:365–376.

Jones, M., and J. H. Greenfield. 1991. *In situ* comparison of bioremediation methods for a Number 6 residual fuel oil spill in Lee County, FL. In *Proceedings of the 1991 International Oil Spill Conference.* American Petroleum Institute, Washington, DC, pp. 533–540.

Jones, J., J. Rogers, M. Nolina, R. Araujo, D. Wubah, B. Nummer, R. Adams, and A. Tai. 1993. Strategies for enhancement of bioremediation of contaminated sediments: Laboratory and field studies. *36th Conference of the International Association for Great Lakes Research,* De Pere, WI, p. 104.

Kellogg, S. T., D. K. Chatterjee, and A. M. Chakrabarty. 1981. Plasmid assisted molecular breeding—new technique for enhanced biodegradation of persistent toxic chemicals. *Science* 214:1133–1135.

Kilbane, J. J. 1986. Genetic aspects of toxic chemical degradation. *Microbial Ecology* 12:135–146.

Kilbane, J. J., D. K. Chatterjee, and A. M. Chakrabarty. 1983. Detoxification of 2,4,5-trichlorophenoxyacetic acid from contaminated soil by *Pseudomonas cepacia.* *Applied and Environmental Microbiology* 45:1697–1700.

Kitamori, S. 1996. Biodegradation of herbicide chlornitrofen (CNP) and mutagenicity of its degradation products. *Fukuoka Igaku Zasshi-Fukuoka Acata Medica* 87:142–150.

Knackmuss, H. J. 1983. Xenobiotic degradation in industrial sewage: Haloaromatics as target substances. In C. F. Phelps and P. H. Clarke (eds.). *Biotechnology.* The Biochemical Society, London, pp. 173–190.

Knackmuss, H. J. 1984. Biochemistry and practical implications of organohalide degradation. In M. J. Klug and C. A. Reddy (eds.). *Current Perspectives in Microbial Ecology.* American Society for Microbiology, Washington, DC, pp. 687–693.

Kuhn, E. P., P. J. Colberg, J. L. Schnoor, O. Wanner, A.J.B. Zehnder, and R. P. Schwartzenbach. 1985. Microbial transformations of substituted benzenes during infiltration of river water to groundwater: Laboratory column studies. *Environmental Science and Technology* 19:961–968.

LaDousse, A., C. Tallec, and B. Tramier. 1987. Progress in enhanced oil degradation. In *Proceedings of the 1987 Oil Spill Conference.* American Petroleum Institute, Washington, DC, Abstract 142.

LaDousse, A., and B. Tramier. 1991. Results of 12 years of research in spilled oil bioremediation: Inipol EAP 22. In *Proceedings of the 1991 International Oil Spill Conference.* American Petroleum Institute, Washington, DC, pp. 577–581.

Laine, M. M., and K. S. Jørgensen. 1996. Straw compost and bioremediated soil as inocula for the bioremediation of chlorophenol-contaminated soil. *Applied and Environmental Microbiology* 62:1507–1514.

Leahy, J. G., and R. R. Colwell. 1990. Microbial degradation of hydrocarbons in the environment. *Microbiological Reviews* 54:305–315.

Lee, B., A. L. Pometto, and A. Fratzke. 1991. Biodegradation of degradable plastic polyethylene by *Phanerochaete* and *Streptomyces* species. *Applied and Environmental Microbiology* 57:678–685.

Lee, K., and E. M. Levy. 1991. Bioremediation: Waxy crude oils stranded on low-energy shorelines. In *Proceedings of the 1991 International Oil Spill Conference.* American Petroleum Institute, Washington, DC, pp. 541–547.

Lee, M. D., J. T. Wilson, and C. H. Ward. 1987. *In situ* restoration techniques for aquifers contaminated with hazardous wastes. *Journal of Hazardous Material* 14:71–82.

LeGrega, M. D., P. L. Buckingham, and J. C. Evans. 1994. *Hazardous Waste Management.* McGraw-Hill, New York.

Leson, G., and A. M. Winer. 1991. Biofiltration: An innovative air pollution control technology for VOC emissions. *Journal of Air and Waste Management Association* 41:1045–1054.

Levin, M. A., and M. A. Gealt. 1993. *Biotreatment of Industrial and Hazardous Waste.* McGraw-Hill, New York.

Lukens, H. R., C. B. Williams, S. A. Levinson, W. B. Dandliker, D. Murayama, and R. L. Baron. 1977. Fluorescence immunoassay technique for detecting organic environmental contaminants. *Environmental Science and Technology* 11:292–297.

Maron, D. M., and B. N. Ames. 1983. Revised methods for the *Salmonella* mutagenicity test. *Mutation Research* 113:173–215.

Matthews, E., and L. Hastings. 1987. Evaluation of toxicity test procedure for screening treatability potential of waste in soil. *Toxicity Assessment* 2:265–281.

McCarty, P. L., L. Semprini, M. E. Dolan, T. C. Harmon, C. Tiedeman, and S. M. Gorelick. 1991. *In situ* methanotrophic bioremediation for contaminated groundwater at St. Joseph, MI. In R. E. Hinchee and R. F. Olfenbuttel (eds.). *On-site Bioreclamation: Processes for Xenobiotic and Hydrocarbon Treatment.* Butterworth-Heinemann, Boston, pp. 16–40.

Means, A. J. 1991. *Observations of an Oil Spill Bioremediation Activity in Galveston Bay,* TX. U.S. Dept. of Commerce, National Oceanic and Atmospheric Administration, National Ocean Service, Seattle, WA.

Means, J., and R. E. Hinchee. 1994. *Emerging Technology for Bioremediation of Metals.* Lewis Publishers, Boca Raton, FL.

Metcalf, R. L., G. K. Sangha, and I.P. Kapoor. 1971. Model ecosystems for evaluation of pesticide biodegradability and ecological magnification. *Environmental Science and Technology* 5:709–713.

Miller, R., G. M. Singer, J. D. Rosen, and R. Bartha. 1988a. Photolysis primes the biodegradation of benzo(a)pyrene. *Applied and Environmental Microbiology* 54:1724–1730.

Miller, R., G. M. Singer, J. D. Rosen, and R. Bartha. 1988b. Sequential degradation of chlorophenols by photolytic and microbial treatment. *Environmental Science and Technology* 22:1215–1219.

Mongkolsuk, S., P. S. Lovett, and J. E. Trempy. 1992. *Biotechnology and Environmental Science: Molecular Approaches.* Plenum Press, New York.

Moore, A. T., A. Vira, and S. Fogel. 1989. Biodegradation of trans-1,2-dichloroethylene by methane-utilizing bacteria in an aquifer simulator. *Environmental Science and Technology* 23:403–406.

Morgan, P., and R. J. Watkinson. 1989. Hydrocarbon biodegradation in soils and methods for soil biotreatment. *CRC Critical Reviews in Biotechnology* 8:305–333.

Mueller, J. G., P. J. Chapman, and P. H. Pritchard. 1989. Creosote-contaminated sites: Their potential for bioremediation. *Environmental Science and Technology* 23:1197–1201.

Mueller, J. G., D. P. Middaugh, and S. E. Lantz. 1991. Biodegradation of creosote and pentachlorophenol in contaminated groundwater: Chemical and biological assessment. *Applied and Environmental Microbiology* 57:1277–1285.

Munakata-Marr, J., P. L. McCarty, M. S. Shields, M. Reagin, and S. C. Francesconi. 1996. Enhancement of trichloroethylene degradation in aquifer microcosms bioaugmented with wild type and genetically altered *Burkholderia (Pseudomonas) cepacia* G4 and PR1. *Environmental Science and Technology* 30:2045–2053.

Munnecke, D. M. 1981. The use of microbial enzymes for pesticide detoxification. In T. Leisinger, A. M. Cook, R. Huffer, and J. Nüesch (eds.). *Microbial Degradation of Xenobiotics and Recalcitrant Compounds.* Academic Press, New York, pp. 251–270.

National Research Council. 1993. In Situ *Bioremediation.* National Academy Press, Washington, DC.

Norris, R. D., R. E. Hinchee, R. Brown, P. L. McCarty, L. Semprini, J. T. Wilson, D. H. Kampbell, M. Reinhard, E. J. Bouwer, and Omenn, G. S. (ed.). 1988. *Environmental Biotechnology: Reducing Risks from Environmental Chemicals through Biotechnology.* Plenum Press, New York.

O'Brien, P. Y., and P. S. Dixon. 1976. The effects of oil and oil components on algae: A review. *British Phycology Journal* 11:115–142.

Office of Technology Assessment. 1991. *Bioremediation for Marine Oil Spill.* U.S. Congress, Washington, DC.

Oh, Y.-S., and R. Bartha. 1997. Removal of nitrobenzene vapors by a trickling air biofilter. *Journal of Industrial Microbiology* 17: in press.

Oh, Y.-S., and R. Bartha. 1994. Design and performance of a trickling air biofilter for chlorobenzene and o-dichlorobenzene vapors. *Applied and Environmental Microbiology* 60:2717–2722.

Organization for Economic Cooperation and Development. 1981. *Guidelines for Testing Chemicals.* Organization for Economic Development and Cooperation, Paris.

Organization for Economic Cooperation and Development. 1994. *Biotechnology for a Clean Environment.* Organization for Economic Development and Cooperation, Paris.

Ottengraf, S.P.P. 1986. Exhaust gas purification. In W. Schønborn (ed.). *Biotechnology.* Vol. 8. VHC Verlagsgellschaft, Weinheim, Germany, pp. 425–452.

Ottengraf, S.P.P., and A.H.C. Van den Oever. 1983. Kinetics of organic compound removal from waste gases with a biological filter. *Biotechnology and Bioengineering* 25:3089–3102.

Pagano, J. J., R. J. Scrudato, R. N. Roberts, and J. C. Bemis. 1995. Reductive dechlorination of PCB-contaminated sediments in an anaerobic bioreactor system. *Environmental Science and Technology* 29:2584–2590.

Palumbo, A. V., W. Eng, P. A. Boerman, G. W. Strandberg, T. L. Donaldson, and S. E. Herbes. 1991. Effects of diverse organic contaminants on trichloroethylene degradation by methanotrophic bacteria and methane-utilizing consortia. In R. E. Hinchee and R. F. Olfenbuttel (eds.). *On-site Bioreclamation: Processes for Xenobiotic and Hydrocarbon Treatment.* Butterworth-Heinemann, Boston, pp. 77–91.

Pramer, D., and R. Bartha. 1972. Preparation and processing of soil samples for biodegradation studies. *Environmental Letters* 2:217–224.

Prince, R. C. 1993. Petroleum spill bioremediation in marine environments. *Critical Reviews in Microbiology* 19:217–242.

Prince, R., J. R. Clark, and J. E. Lindstrom. 1990. *Bioremediation Monitoring Program.* Joint Report of EXXON, the U.S. Environmental Protection Agency, and the Alaskan Department of Environmental Conservation, Anchorage, AK.

Pritchard, P. H., and A. W. Bourquin. 1984. The use of microcosms for evaluation of interactions between pollutants and microorganisms. *Advances in Microbial Ecology* 7:133–215.

Pritchard, P. H., and C. F. Costa. 1991. EPA's Alaska oil spill bioremediation project. *Environmental Science and Technology* 25:372–379.

Raymond, R. L., V. W. Jamison, and J. O. Hudson. 1976. Beneficial stimulation of bacterial activity in ground waters containing petroleum products. In *Water—1976.* American Institute of Chemical Engineers, New York, pp. 319–327.

Reineke, W., and H. J. Knackmuss. 1979. Construction of haloaromatic utilizing bacteria. *Nature* (London) 277:385–386.

Reynolds, E. R., and A. M. Yacynych. 1991. Miniaturized electrochemical biosensors. *American Laboratory* March:19–28.

Riser-Roberts, E. 1992. *Bioremediation of Petroleum Contaminated Sites.* CRC Press, Boca Raton, FL.

Roberts, D. J., F. Ahmad, and S. Pendharkar. 1996. Optimization of an aerobic polishing stage to complete the anaerobic treatment of munitions-contaminated soils. *Environmental Science and Technology* 30:2021–2027.

Rosenberg, E. (ed.). 1993. *Microorganisms to Combat Pollution.* Kluwer Academic Publishers, Dordrecht.

Rosenberg, E., R. Legmann, A. Kushmaro, R. Taube, E. Adler, and E. Z. Ron. 1992. Petroleum bioremediation—a multiphase problem. *Biodegradation* 3:337–350.

Rudd, L. E., J. J. Perry, V. S. Houk, R. W. Williams, and L. D. Claxton. 1996. Changes in mutagenicity during crude oil degradation by fungi. *Biodegradation* 7:335–343.

Schultz, J. S. 1991. Biosensors. *Scientific American* 265(2):64–69.

Semprini, L., G. D. Hopkins, P. V. Roberts, and P. L. McCarty. 1991. *In situ* biotransformation of carbon tetrachloride, Freon-113, Freon-11 and 1,1,1-TCA under anoxic conditions. In R. E. Hinchee and R. F. Olfenbuttel (eds.). *On-site Bioreclamation: Processes for Xenobiotic and Hydrocarbon Treatment.* Butterworth-Heinemann, Boston, pp. 41–58.

Shailubhai, K. 1986. Treatment of petroleum industry oil sludge in soil. *Trends in Biotechnology* 4:202–206.

Shen, J., and R. Bartha. 1994. On-site bioremediation of soil contaminated by No. 2 fuel oil. *International Biodeterioration and Biodegradation* 33:61–72.

Shineldecker, C. L. 1992. *Handbook of Environmental Contaminants: A Guide for Site Assessment.* Lewis Publishers, Boca Raton, FL.

Sirvins, A., and M. Angles. 1986. Development and effects on marine environment of a nutrient formula to control pollution by petroleum hydrocarbons. *NATO ASI Series* G9:357–404.

Song, H. G., and R. Bartha. 1990. Effect of jet fuel spills on the microbial community of soil. *Applied and Environmental Microbiology* 56:641–651.

Song, H. G., X. Wang, and R. Bartha. 1990. Bioremediation potential of terrestrial fuel spills. *Applied and Environmental Microbiology* 56:652–656.

Stoner, D. L. 1994. *Biotechnology for the Treatment of Hazardous Waste.* Lewis Publishers, Boca Raton, FL.

Stopa, P. J., M. T. Goode, A. W. Zulich, D. W. Sickenberger, E. W. Sarver, and R. A. Mackay. 1991. Real time detection of biological aerosols. In *Field Screening Methods for Hazardous Wastes and Toxic Chemicals.* U.S. Environmental Protection Agency and U.S. Army Toxic and Hazardous Materials Agency, Las Vegas, NV, pp. 793–795.

Suflita, J. M., A. Horowitz, D. R. Shelton, and J. M. Tiedje. 1983. Dehalogenation: A novel pathway for the anaerobic biodegradation of haloaromatic compounds. *Science* 214:1115–1117.

Sussman, M., C. H. Collins, F. A. Skinner, and D. E. Stewart-Tull (eds.). 1988. *Release of Genetically-engineered Microorganisms.* Academic Press, London.

Sutherland, J. B. 1992. Detoxification of polycyclic aromatic hydrocarbons by fungi. *Journal of Industrial Microbiology* 9:53–61.

Sveum, P., and A. LaDousse. 1989. Biodegradation of oil in the Arctic: Enhancement by oil-soluble fertilizer application. In *Proceedings of the 1989 Oil Spill Conference.* American Petroleum Institute, Washington, DC, pp. 439–446.

Swannell, R.P.J., K. Lee, and M. McDonagh. 1996. Field evaluations of marine oil spill bioremediation. *Microbiological Reviews* 60:342–365.

Tesan, G., and D. Barbosa. 1987. Degradation of oil by land disposal. *Water Science Technology* 19:99–106.

Thomas, J. M., M. D. Lee, P. B. Bedient, R. C. Borden, L. W. Carter, and C. H. Ward. 1987. *Leaking Underground Storage Tanks: Remediation with Emphasis on in situ Bioreclamation.* EPA/600/S2–87/008. U.S. Environmental Protection Agency, Ada, OK.

Tramier, B., and A. Sirvins. 1983. Enhanced oil biodegradation: A new operational tool to control oil spills. In *Proceedings of the 1983 Oil Spill Conference.* American Petroleum Institute, Washington, DC, pp. 115–119.

United States Environmental Protection Agency. 1990. *ORD/NETAC: Bringing Innovative Technologies to the Market, EPA Alaskan Oil Spill Bioremediation Project Update.* Office of Research and Development, Washington DC.

United States Food and Drug Administration. 1987. Aerobic biodegradation in soil. In *Environmental Assessment Technical Assistance Handbook.* USFDA, Washington, DC. pp. 159–178.

Vanderlaan, M., E. B. Watkins, and L. Stanker. 1988. Environmental monitoring by immunoassay. *Environmental Science and Technology* 22:247–288.

Van Emon, J. M. 1989. Selected references addressing the development and utilization of immunoassay. In U. M. Cowgill and L. R. Williams (eds.). *Aquatic Toxicology and Hazard Assessment.* ASTM STP 1027. American Society for Testing and Materials, Philadelphia, pp. 427–431.

Van Emon, J. M., R. W. Gerlach, R. J. White, and M. E. Silverstein. 1991. U.S. EPA evaluation of two pentachlorophenol immunoassay systems. In *Field Screening Methods for Hazardous Wastes and Toxic Chemicals.* U.S. Environmental Protection Agency and U.S. Army Toxic and Hazardous Materials Agency, Las Vegas, NV, pp. 815–818.

Van Emon, J. M., J. N. Seiber, and B. D. Hammock. 1989. Immunoassay techniques for pesticide analysis. In

G. Zweig (ed.). *Analytical Methods for Pesticides and Plant Growth Regulators,* Vol. XVII. Academic Press, New York, pp. 217–263.

Vanloocke, R., R. DeBorger, J. P. Voets, and W. Verstraete. 1975. Soil and groundwater contamination by oil spills: Problems and remedies. *International Journal of Environmental Studies* 8:99–111.

Venosa, A. D., J. R. Haines, W. Nisamaneepong, R. Goving, S. Pradhan, and B. Siddique. 1991. Screening of commercial inocula for efficacy in enhancing oil biodegradation in closed laboratory system. *Journal of Hazardous Materials* 28:131–144.

Venosa, A. D., M. T. Suidan, B. A. Wrenn, K. L. Strohmeier, J. R. Haines, B. L. Eberhart, D. King, and E. Holder. 1996. Bioremediation of an experimental oil spill on the shoreline of Delaware Bay. *Environmental Science & Technology* 30:1764–1776.

Verstraete, W., R. Vanlooke, R. deBorger, and A. Verlinde. 1976. Modeling of the breakdown and the mobilization of hydrocarbons in unsaturated soil layers. In J. M. Sharpley and A. M. Kaplan (eds.). *Proceedings of the Third International Biodegradation Symposium.* Applied Science Publishers, London, pp. 98–112.

von Wedel, R. J., J. F. Mosquera, C. D. Goldsmith, G. R. Hater, A. Wong, T. A. Fox, W. T. Hunt, M. S. Paules, J. M. Quiros, and J. W. Wiegand. 1988. Bacterial biodegradation and bioreclamation with enrichment isolates in California. *Water Science Technology* 20:501–503.

Wang, X., and R. Bartha. 1990. Effects of bioremediation on residues: Activity and toxicity in soil contaminated by fuel spills. *Soil Biology and Biochemistry* 22:501–506.

Wang, X., X. Yu, and R. Bartha. 1990. Effect of bioremediation on polycyclic aromatic hydrocarbon residues in soil. *Environmental Science and Technology* 24:1086–1089.

Wilson, B. H., G. B. Smith, and J. F. Rees. 1986. Biotransformations of selected alkylbenzenes and halogenated aliphatic hydrocarbons in methanogenic aquifer material: A microcosm study. *Environmental Science and Technology* 20:997–1002.

Wilson, J. 1991. Performance evaluations of *in situ* bioreclamation of fuel spills at Traverse City, Michigan. In *Proceedings of the In Situ and On-Site Bioreclamation: An International Symposium.* Butterworth, Stoneham, MA.

Wilson, J. T., and C. H. Ward. 1987. Opportunities for bioreclamation of aquifers contaminated with petroleum hydrocarbons. *Developments in Industrial Microbiology* 27:109–116.

Wyman, J. F., H. E. Guard, W. D. Won, and J. H. Quay. 1979. Conversion of 2,4,6 trinitrophenol to a mutagen by *Pseudomonas aeruginosa. Applied and Environmental Microbiology* 37:222–226.

Yaniga, P. M., and W. Smith. 1984. Aquifer restoration via accelerated *in situ* biodegradation of organic contaminants. In *Proceedings of the Conference on Petroleum Hydrocarbons and Organic Chemicals in Ground Water—Prevention, Detection, and Restoration.* National Water Well Association, Worthington, OH, pp. 451–470.

You, I. S., and R. Bartha. 1982. Stimulation of 3,4-dichloroaniline mineralization by aniline. *Applied and Environmental Microbiology* 44:678–681.

Zitrides, T. G. 1990. Bioremediation comes of age. *Pollution Engineering* 12:59–60

# MICROORGANISMS IN MINERAL AND ENERGY RECOVERY AND FUEL AND BIOMASS PRODUCTION

*The metabolic capabilities of microorganisms are being harnessed to improve the recovery of metals and petroleum from the environment. Sulfur-oxidizing thiobacilli are commercially employed in bioleaching opera-tions for the recovery of copper and uranium. Surfactants (xylan gums) produced by* Xanthomonas campestris *are widely used in petroleum recovery operations.*

*Besides aiding in mineral and fuel recovery, microorganisms are being used to produce biomass, for human and animal food, and fuels. Biofuels, such as methane and ethanol, are supplementing fossil fuels, and hydrogen may become a clean-burning biofuel in the future. Biomass and biofuels are renewable resources that will become increasingly important in sustainable global development that supports human population, fosters economic development, and maintains environmental quality.*

## RECOVERY OF METALS

As the high-grade deposits of petroleum and metal ions are depleted, there is a need to find innovative and economical procedures to recover oil and metals from low-grade deposits that, for technical or eco-nomic reasons, have been beyond the reach of current recovery techniques. Ores with low metal content are not suitable for direct smelting but, at least in the case of some sulfide or sulfide-containing ores, it is possible to extract metal from such low-grade ores economically using the activity of sulfur-oxidizing bacteria, especially *Thiobacillus ferrooxidans* (Zimmerley et al. 1958; Kuznetsov et al. 1963; Beck 1967; Tuovinen and Kelly 1974; Kelly 1976; Karavaiko et al. 1977; Torma 1977; Brierley 1978, 1982; Murr et al. 1978; Kelly et al. 1979; Lundgren and Silver 1980; Norris and Kelly 1982; Karavaiko 1985; Ehrlich and Brierley 1990; Agate 1996). This microbial recovery of metals is sometimes referred to as microbial mining, or biohydrometallurgy (Mersou 1992).

The process is currently applied on a commercial scale to low-grade copper and uranium ores (Brierley 1978, 1982). Laboratory-scale experiments indicate that the process also has promise for recovering nickel, zinc, cobalt, tin, cadmium, molybdenum, lead, antimony, arsenic, and selenium from low-grade sulfide-containing ores. The general metal recovery process can be represented by Equation 1:

$$(1) \quad MS + 2O_2 \xrightarrow[\text{\textit{T. ferrooxidans}}]{} MSO_4$$

**Figure 15.1**
Heap leaching of low-grade ore. The ore is mined, crushed, and heaped in the form of a truncated cone on a suitable asphalt pad. The leaching liquor is pumped to the top of the heap and percolates through the ore. The leachate is collected, processed, and recycled. (Source: Zajic 1969. Reprinted by permission, copyright Academic Press.)

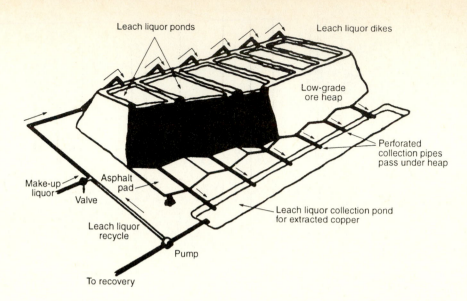

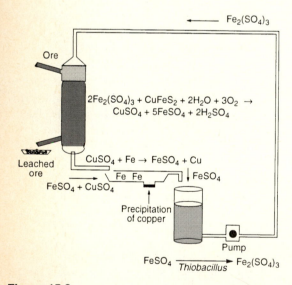

**Figure 15.2**
Diagram of apparatus for extracting copper from low-grade ore by a continuous leaching process. The oxidation of sulfide and ferrous iron is carried out by *Thiobacillus ferrooxidans,* generating the acid for leaching. Copper is precipitated by exchange, using scrap iron. This process was the basis of U.S. patent No. 2,829,964, assigned to Kennecott Copper Co. (Source: Zimmerley et al. 1958.)

where M represents a bivalent metal that is insoluble as a sulfide but soluble, and thus leachable, as a sulfate. *T. ferrooxidans* is a chemolithotrophic bacterium that derives energy through the oxidation of either a reduced sulfur compound or ferrous iron. It exerts its bioleaching action directly by oxidizing the metal sulfide and/or indirectly by oxidizing the ferrous iron content of the ore to ferric iron; the ferric iron, in turn, chemically oxidizes the metal to be recovered by leaching.

When microbes are employed to bioleach metals from low-grade ores, it is usually necessary to mine and break up the ore and heap it in piles on a water-impermeable formation or on a specially constructed apron (Brierley 1982) (Figure 15.1). Water is then pumped to the top of the ore heap and allowed to trickle down through the ore to the apron. Figure 15.2 shows a continuous reactor-type leaching operation for recovery of copper from low-grade sulfide ore. The leachate is collected and processed for the recovery of the metal. Most commonly, the leached metal is partitioned into an organic solvent and subsequently recovered by "stripping" (evaporating) the solvent.

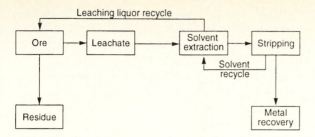

**Figure 15.3**
Flowchart of metal recovery from low-grade ores by bioleaching using the activity of *T. ferrooxidans.* (Source: Torma 1977.)

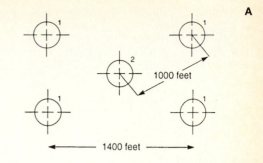

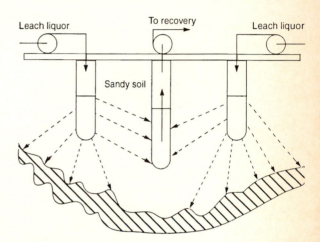

**Figure 15.4**
Hole-to-hole leaching of low-grade ores, an *in situ* process for metal recovery by bioleaching using the activity of thiobacilli. The process may be practiced in relatively porous ore overlying impermeable bedrock. Leaching is from injection wells to a collection well. (A) Overhead view of layout of wells. 1 = leach liquor shafts; 2 = recovery shaft. (B) Side view of wells. (Source: Zajic 1969. Reprinted by permission, copyright Academic Press.)

Both the leaching liquor and the solvent are recycled. Figure 15.3 shows the flowchart of a typical operation.

Geological formations play a key role in determining the suitability of ore deposits for recovery by *in situ* bioleaching. Rarely, under favorable geological conditions, microorganisms may be induced to release the metals into solution without any mechanical mining of the metal-bearing rocks. If the ore formation is sufficiently porous and overlies water-impermeable strata, a suitable pattern of boreholes is established. Some of the holes are utilized for the injection of the leaching liquor; others are used for the recovery of the leachate (Figure 15.4).

The mineralogy of the ore is significant in determining its susceptibility to bioleaching. In some cases, the chemical form of the element within the ore is resistant to microbial attack. In other cases, microorganisms can attack the ore initially, but toxic products preclude further bioleaching (Tuttle and Dugan 1976). In still other cases, the ore minerals exist in chemical forms that are readily subject to bioleaching. The size of mineral particles to be leached is critical in determining the rate of leaching; increasing the surface area, which can be achieved by crushing or grinding, greatly enhances the rate of bioleaching.

A variety of ecological factors affect the efficiency of bioleaching. Factors that influence the activities of the most important leaching bacterium, *T. ferrooxidans,* include temperature, generally considered optimal between 30°C and 50°C; acidity, optimally at pH 2.3–2.5; iron supply, optimally 2–4 g/l of leach liquor; oxygen; and the availability of other nutrients required

for growth (Brierley 1978; Summers and Silver 1978). *T. ferrooxidans* is generally unable to initiate growth on ferrous iron above pH 3.0. Ammonium nitrogen, phosphorus, sulfate, and magnesium are essential for the growth of *T. ferrooxidans.* These nutrients may be limiting in some leaching operations and need to be added. Availability of sufficient water can also be an important consideration in bioleaching processes. In open-air leaching operations, light has an inhibitory

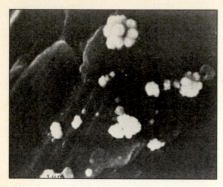

**Figure 15.5**
Scanning electron micrograph of thermophilic, acidophilic, and chemoautotrophic bacteria capable of oxidizing reduced iron and sulfur compounds. The bacteria are adhering to ore particles. They appear to be related to *Sulfolobus* and are potentially useful for leaching low-grade chalcopyrite and molybdenite ores. (Source: Brierley and Murr 1972. Reprinted from *Science*, copyright American Association for the Advancement of Science.)

effect on some species of *Thiobacillus,* with the greatest inhibition occurring at the shorter wavelengths. Suspended particles of ferric iron offer a degree of protection against inhibitory light intensities.

Temperatures in some mineral deposits can be significantly increased by the oxidative activities of the thiobacilli and may exceed the tolerance limits of a *Thiobacillus* species, leading to decreased bioleaching activity. Because of the high temperatures associated with some leaching operations, thermophilic sulfur-oxidizing microorganisms may play an important role in the bioleaching process (Brierley and Murr 1972; Brierley and Lockwood 1977; Brierley and Brierley 1978; Brock 1978). Members of the genus *Sulfolobus* are obligate thermophilic Archaea that oxidize ferrous iron and sulfur in a manner similar to the members of the genus *Thiobacillus*. Thermophilic *Thiobacillus* species have also been isolated from various hot sulfur-rich environments. The abilities of these acid-tolerant thermophilic bacteria to oxidize inorganic substrates make them likely candidates for use in bioleaching metal sulfides. *Sulfolobus* has been used

especially in the bioleaching of molybdenite (molybdenum sulfide) (Figure 15.5). *Thiobacillus* species are unable to leach molybdenite efficiently because of the toxicity of molybdenum to this bacterium; *Sulfolobus* is less sensitive to molybdenum. Still other microorganisms, perhaps in mixed populations, are potential candidates for use in bioleaching processes (Norris and Kelly 1982).

Several molecular approaches have been developed to help monitor microbial populations involved in bioleaching so that the processes can be optimized. In one such system, a nonradioactive immunobinding assay helps detect and estimate the population sizes of the moderate thermophile *Thiobacillus caldus* and *Sulfolobus acidocaldarius* by incorporating the DNA extracted from cells in the samples into a nitrocellulose membrane in the form of a dot or slot (Amaro et al. 1994). The use of enhanced chemiluminescence and peroxidase-conjugated antibodies help detect bound immunoglobulins. Immunological assays help identify thermophilic bioleaching microorganisms involved in bioleaching systems. In another system, analysis of DNA from ores, leaching systems, or laboratory cultures indicates the predominance of different bacteria populations depending on the growth conditions (Pizarro et al. 1996). Polymerase chain reaction (PCR) amplification and characterization of the spacer regions between the 16 and 23S genes in the rRNA genetic loci indicates that *Thiobacillus ferrooxidans* predominates at high ferrous iron concentrations and that *T. thiooxidans* and *Leptospirillum ferrooxidans* predominate at low ferrous iron levels.

## Microbial Assimilation of Metals

Microorganisms have been considered not only for use in bioleaching of metals but also as accumulators of metals from dilute solutions (Charley and Bull 1979; Norris and Kelly 1979, 1982; Brierley 1982; Ehrlich and Brierley 1990). Large numbers of bacteria, yeasts, and algae are capable of accumulating metal ions in their cells to concentrations several orders of magnitude higher than the background concentration of these metals. The mechanism of accumulation may involve intracellular uptake and storage via active cation transport systems, surface binding, or some undefined mechanisms. These processes have a potential use in extracting rare metals from dilute solution or removing toxic metals from industrial effluents. The selectivity and gradient of accumulation in general do not, however, compete favorably with conventional chemical extraction and partition processes, and it is doubtful whether such microbial accumulations will ever form the basis of a technological process. Bioaccumulation of toxic heavy metals has a definite practical significance, however, in terms of an increased but undesirable introduction of these pollutants into food webs.

## Bioleaching of Copper and Gold

Bioleaching with thiobacilli and related iron-oxidizing bacteria contributes to the commercially important recovery of copper (Groudev and Genchev 1978; Rangachari et al. 1978; Groudev 1979). Copper is generally in short supply but is in high demand in the electrical industry and for various metal alloys. In the bioleaching of copper, the action of *Thiobacillus* involves both the direct oxidation of CuS and the indirect oxidation of CuS via generation of ferric ($Fe^{3+}$) ions from ferrous sulfide (Tuovinen 1990) (Table 15.1; Figure 15.6). Ferrous sulfide is present in the economically most important copper ores, such as chalcopyrite ($CuFeS_2$); a typical low-grade ore contains 0.1–0.4% copper.

Copper is recovered from the leaching solution either by solvent partitioning or by the use of scrap iron; in the latter method, copper replaces iron according to Equation 2:

(2) $CuSO_4 + Fe^0 \rightarrow Cu^0 + FeSO_4$

**Table 15.1**
Reactions involved in microbial bioleaching of copper

---

Direct oxidation of monovalent copper in chalcocite ($Cu_2S$) by *Thiobacillus ferrooxidans*:

$$2Cu_2S + O_2 + 4H^+ \rightarrow 2CuS + 2Cu^{2+} + 2H_2O$$

$$\text{Chalcocite} \rightarrow \text{Covellite}$$

$$(4Cu^+ \rightarrow 4Cu^{2+} + 4e^-)$$

No change in valence of sulfur. Electrons from $Cu^+$ oxidation probably used as energy source by the bacteria.

Indirect oxidation of covellite by *T. ferrooxidans* via elemental sulfur:

$$CuS + \tfrac{1}{2}O_2 + 2H^+ \rightarrow Cu^{2+} + H_2O + S^0 \text{ (spontaneous)}$$

Accumulation of a film of elemental sulfur on the mineral causes the reaction to cease.

$$S^0 + 1\tfrac{1}{2}O_2 + H_2O \rightarrow 2H^+ + SO_4^{2-} \text{ (bacterial)}$$

Removal of protective film by bacteria keeps the reaction going:

$$\text{Overall: } CuS + 2O_2 \rightarrow Cu^{2+} + SO_4^{2-}$$

Indirect oxidation of covellite (also other ores) with ferric iron ($Fe^{3+}$) and regeneration of ferric iron from ferrous by bacterial oxidation:

$$CuS + 8Fe^{3+} + 4H_2O \rightarrow Cu^{2+} + 8Fe^{2+} + SO_4^{2-} + 8H^+ \text{ (chemical)}$$

$$8Fe^{2+} + 2O_2 + 8H^+ \rightarrow 8Fe^{3+} + 4H_2O \text{ (bacterial)}$$

$$\text{Overall: } CuS + 2O_2 \rightarrow Cu^{2+} + SO_4^{2-}$$

Recovery of elemental copper from copper ions by reaction with scrap iron:

$$Cu^{2+} + Fe^0 \rightarrow Fe^{2+} + Cu^0 \text{ (chemical)}$$

---

Sources: Brock and Gustafson 1976; Torma 1976; Brock 1978; Summers and Silver 1978.

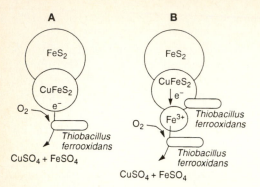

**Figure 15.6**
Two biological leaching mechanisms for deriving copper from pyrite ($FeS_2$)/chalcopyrite ($CuFeS_2$). (A) Direct leaching with transfer of electron ($e^-$) to molecular oxygen. (B) Indirect leaching with $Fe^{3+}$ as the primary electron acceptor. (Source: Tuovinen 1990.)

The latter method is more advantageous for copper recovery in the bioleaching process. When solvent partitioning is used, residues in the leaching liquor, unless carefully removed by activated carbon, may inhibit the activity of *T. ferrooxidans*. In laboratory studies, as much as 97% of the copper in low-grade ores has been recovered by bioleaching, but such high yields are seldom achieved in actual biomining operations. Nevertheless, even a 50–70% recovery of copper by bioleaching from an ore that would otherwise be useless is an important achievement. In the case of low-grade ores, bioleaching costs only one-half to one-third as much as direct smelting (Merson 1992). The principal disadvantage of bioleaching is the relative slowness of the process. It may take decades to recover metals from a deposit by bioleaching that could be exploited by mining and smelting in only a few years.

To date, gold has been mined principally from alluvial deposits or from shallow oxidized ores. In these cases, the recovery of the metallic gold is relatively simple. As these deposits are becoming depleted, gold is increasingly mined from deeper reduced geological strata, where it occurs intermixed with and enclosed by chalcopyrite ($CaFeS_2$) and pyrite ($FeS_2$). From these low-grade sulfidic ores, gold cannot be extracted by the usual sodium cyanide leaching process that converts gold to a soluble cyanide complex according to Equation 3.

$$(3)\ 4Au + 8NaCN + O_2 + 2H_2O \rightarrow$$
$$4NaAu(CN)_2 + 4NaOH$$

Sulfidic gold ores need to be pretreated by roasting or by pressure-oxidation to free the gold from the enclosing sulfides prior to cyanide leaching, and these pretreatments are costly in the case of low-grade ores. Substantial savings are realized by substituting bioleaching in reactors for roasting or pressure-oxidation. Bioleaching, as described for copper, converts the copper and iron to sulfates and leaves behind in the now porous ore the exposed gold for cyanide leaching. After this pretreatment, 70–95% of the gold in the ore can be recovered by the usual cyanide leaching process (Moffat 1994). This process was introduced in South Africa on a pilot scale in 1986 and became a full-scale commercial operation in 1990. Similar bioleaching plants for sulfidic gold ores are being constructed in Ghana and Australia. In the United States, very low grade sulfidic gold ores are being processed at a Nevada mine by the heap leaching process. Because both the reactor and the heap leaching processes generate heat that can inhibit *T. ferrooxidans* activity, thermophilic archaea such as *Sulfolobus* are being substituted for, or are used in combination with, *T. ferrooxidans*.

## Uranium Bioleaching

Uranium is another metal that can be recovered by microbial leaching (Brierley 1982; McCready and Gould 1990). Uranium is used as a fuel in nuclear power generation, and the microbial recovery of uranium from otherwise useless low-grade ores can be considered a contribution to energy production. Bioleaching can have a direct bearing on the economics of nuclear facilities by providing a mechanism for commercial utilization of low-grade uranium deposits and for the recovery of uranium from low-grade nuclear wastes.

Tetravalent uranium oxide ($UO_2$) occurs in low-grade ores and is insoluble. It can be converted to the

**Table 15.2**
Reactions involved in microbial bioleaching of uranium

Indirect oxidation of uranium ore with ferric iron:

$UO_2^{2-}$ tetravalent uranium, insoluble oxide

$UO_2So_4^{2-}$ hexavalent uranium (uranyl ion, $UO_2^{2-}$), soluble sulfate

$$UO_2 + 2Fe^{3+} + SO_4^{2-} \rightarrow UO_2SO_4 + 2Fe^{2+}$$

$$(U^{4+} + 2Fe^{3+} \rightarrow U^{6+} + 2Fe^{2+})$$

$Fe^{2+}$ is reoxidized by *T. ferrooxidans*.

---

leachable form by oxidation with ferric ($Fe^{3+}$) ions. Carbonate-rich uranium deposits are leached with alkaline bicarbonate-carbonate solutions. Pyrite-containing uranium deposits are leached with dilute sulfuric acid solutions. The ferrous ions ($Fe^{2+}$) produced during uranium oxidation are converted back to $Fe^{3+}$ by chemical oxidants such as chlorate ($ClO_3^-$), manganese dioxide ($MnO_2$), or hydrogen peroxide ($H_2O_2$). The chemical oxidants add substantial cost to the leaching process, but in pyrite-containing uranium ores, the $Fe^{3+}$ oxidant may be produced and regenerated at lower cost by the action of *T. ferrooxidans* (Guay et al. 1977; Torma 1985). *T. ferrooxidans* oxidizes the ferrous iron in pyrite (FeS), which often accompanies uranium ores, to ferric iron, which in turn acts as an oxidant to convert $UO_2$ chemically to the leachable $UO_2SO_4$ (Table 15.2).

The feasibility of using *Thiobacillus* for the recovery of uranium depends primarily on the composition of the mineral deposit (Tomizuka and Yagisawa 1978). Pyritic uranium oxide ores, for example, are suitable for bioleaching, but uranium ores that lack iron-containing minerals or are high in carbonates are not. In general, bacterial leaching of uranium is feasible in geological strata where the ore is in the tetravalent state and is associated with reduced sulfur and iron minerals. In an acidic medium, those energy sources provide a suitable environment for the growth of *T. ferrooxidans*.

## Phosphate Recovery

After nitrogen, phosphate fertilizer is the agricultural chemical used worldwide in the second largest volume. Phosphate is mined as the insoluble tertiary phosphate apatite, and is converted to soluble "superphosphate" by treatment with sulfuric acid. The process leaves huge amounts of low-grade gypsum ($CaSO_4$) waste. An early microbial process, now of historic interest only, was developed at the New Jersey Agricultural Experiment Station by Lipman et al. (1916). They mixed insoluble phosphate with elemental sulfur and compost and relied on sulfuric acid production by *Thiobacillus thiooxidans* to convert and solubilize the tertiary phosphate.

Currently, a microbial process for solubilizing tertiary phosphate under mild conditions and with less waste production is under development at the Idaho National Engineering Laboratory (Goldstein et al. 1993). Selected strains of *Burkholderia cepacia* and *Erwinia herbicola* are used for converting glucose and glucose-containing wastes into gluconic and 2-ketogluconic acids. These organic acids solubilize the tertiary phosphate. It is expected that the process will be ready for commercial use prior to the year 2000.

## RECOVERY OF PETROLEUM

Petroleum and natural gas are relatively clean and convenient energy sources, and the United States relies on these fuels for about 70% of its energy needs. Domestic production supplies less than two-thirds of the U.S. oil demand. High petroleum imports and unpredictable supplies from politically volatile countries have led to an unfavorable trade balance and economic vulnerability. Limited prospects exist for finding new high-quality oil reserves, but microbial processes—called *microbially enhanced oil recovery (MEOR)*—may contribute to improved petroleum recovery from existing old wells, as well as from formations that for technical or economic reasons have not been tapped to date (Geffen 1976; Forbes 1980; Matthews 1982; Moses and Springham 1982; Finnerty and Singer 1983; Hitzman 1983; Singer et al. 1983; Westlake 1984; McInerney and Westlake 1990).

Under ideal circumstances, petroleum will gush spontaneously from a drill hole. Spontaneous flow and pumping when needed recover on the average only about one-third of the total petroleum deposit. Gas pressurizing, water flooding, miscible flooding, and thermal methods, considered to be secondary recovery techniques, have been used for additional recovery of petroleum. Gas pressurizing and water flooding involve the deliberate injection of gas or water into drill holes in order to dislodge and push petroleum toward producing wells. Injected under high pressure, carbon dioxide in its supercritical state becomes an effective lipophilic solvent that decreases the viscosity of heavy crude oils but separates from the petroleum spontaneously after the reduction of pressure. For these reasons, miscible flooding with pressurized $CO_2$ is an especially promising technique. Thermal methods involve steam injection or controlled underground combustion designed to increase the flow of heavy, viscous petroleum. Tertiary oil recovery techniques, which include the use of solvents, surfactants, and polymers designed to dislodge oil from geological formations, have the potential for recovering an additional 60 billion to 120 billion barrels (8.5 billion to 17 billion metric tons) of petroleum from U.S. deposits alone (Figure 15.7). Some promising surfactants and polymers, such as the xanthan gums (Figure 15.8), are

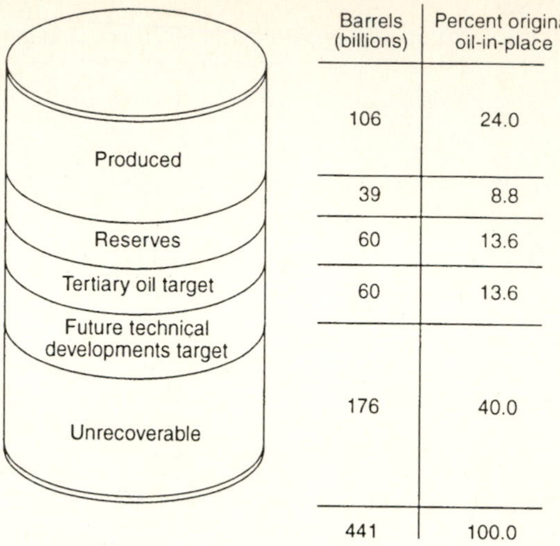

| | Barrels (billions) | Percent original oil-in-place |
|---|---|---|
| Produced | 106 | 24.0 |
| | 39 | 8.8 |
| Reserves | 60 | 13.6 |
| Tertiary oil target | 60 | 13.6 |
| Future technical developments target | | |
| Unrecoverable | 176 | 40.0 |
| | 441 | 100.0 |

**Figure 15.7**
The U.S. crude oil "barrel" as of 1975, showing target of tertiary oil recovery. The oil shortage and world energy crisis beginning in the late 1970s made secondary and tertiary processes for the recovery of oil essential and economical. (Source: Geffen 1976.)

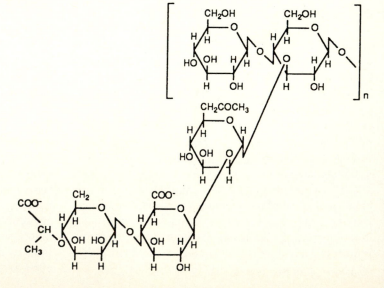

**Figure 15.8**
Structure of xanthan gum produced by *Xanthomonas campestris.* The gum is used in the tertiary recovery of oil. As a additive in water flooding operations, it helps to push crude oil toward production wells. (Source: Sutherland and Ellwood 1979. Reprinted by permission; copyright Cambridge University Press.)

produced by the bacterium *Xanthomonas campestris* (Sandvik and Maerker 1977; Cooper and Zajic 1980; Cooper 1983; Gutnick et al. 1983; Westlake 1984; Zajic and Mahomedy 1984). The critical characteristic of these polymers is their substantial viscosity combined with flow characteristics that allow them to pass through small pore spaces. These materials are produced by conventional fermentation processes and are injected as additives in water-flooding operations.

Another possible though less promising approach involves the use of microorganisms *in situ* for dislodging oil (Moses and Springham 1982; Finnerty and Singer 1983). Claude E. ZoBell (1947) first promoted this idea. Microbial growth on rock pore surfaces dislodges oil directly by physical displacement or indirectly by synthesis of surface active metabolites and gases such as $H_2$, $CO_2$, $CH_4$, and $H_2S$. In addition, the viscosity of the oil may be altered by partial microbial degradation. ZoBell (1947) considered *Desulfovibrio* strains as promising microbial agents for increasing petroleum recovery by *in situ* action, and La Riviere (1955a, 1955b) experimentally demonstrated enhanced oil release by microbial action in the laboratory.

In *in situ* tests, microbial suspensions injected in combination with a carbon source such as molasses or milk whey into an oil formation were shown to enhance oil recovery from wells with previously low rates of production (Finnerty and Singer 1983). In these tests, the wells were sealed and time was allowed for microbial action, after which production was resumed; oil flow was increased when the wells were reopened. In spite of these preliminary results, difficulties with the *in situ* approach are numerous, and the practicality of this approach remains in doubt. Growth conditions, salinity, pH, temperature, and redox potential are quite unfavorable; anaerobic utilization of petroleum is marginal at best; introduction of air can cause undesirable changes in petroleum quality; and, perhaps most importantly, microbial growth may actually close pore spaces and thus decrease the flow of oil (Updegraff 1983).

In addition to oil wells, tar sands and oil shales form extensive fossil hydrocarbon reserves. Tar sands contain mainly bitumen, a highly viscous hydrocarbon

mixture soluble in aromatic solvents; oil shales are impermeable, fine-grained, sedimentary rock formations that contain some bitumen and considerable amounts of kerogen, a highly cross-linked and condensed hydrocarbon complex that is insoluble in benzene. Tar sands and oil shales may contain as much as 50–60% hydrocarbon material, but 20–30% is a more common figure for deposits of economic importance. The current technology of oil production from tar sands and oil shales uses heat treatment to recover and process the hydrocarbons into a usable product. The costs of processing these oil reserves are too high at the present time, and technologies using microorganisms are being considered to improve the economics of recovering oil from these reserves (Westlake 1984).

Biosurfactants may be useful for releasing oil from tar sands (Zajic and Gerson 1978; Singer et al. 1983; Westlake 1984). In the case of oil shales that occur in association with substantial amounts of carbonates and some pyrite, the carbonates can be dissolved by acid, increasing porosity and reducing the bulk of the shale so that the oil can be more efficiently recovered (Figure 15.9). The acid can be produced most economically by using the thiobacilli as in metal recovery (Meyer and Yen 1976; Yen 1976a, 1976b; Westlake 1984). In laboratory experiments, bioleaching of oil shale has increased oil yield approximately four times (Figure 15.10).

## PRODUCTION OF FUELS

Microorganisms used in enhanced oil recovery have the potential of contributing to fuel production in several additional ways. Microorganisms may be used to convert waste products, plants, or microbial biomass into liquid or gaseous fuels (Schlegel and Barnea 1976; Keenan 1979; National Research Council 1979; Bungay 1981) and can also be used to convert solar energy into biomass that can be fermented to yield fuels (Bennemann and Weissman 1976). The governments of some Organization for Economic Cooperation and Development (OECD) countries have been studying the possibility of encouraging the production of liquid biofuels from agricultural surpluses

**Figure 15.9**
Flowchart of bioleaching of oil shale with recycling of sulfur. Kerogen is liberated from the leached shale and is converted subsequently to refinery stock by hydrogenation. The leaching process uses the activity of thiobacilli; sulfur is recycled using *Desulfovibrio* and organic wastes as substrates. (Source: Yen 1976a.)

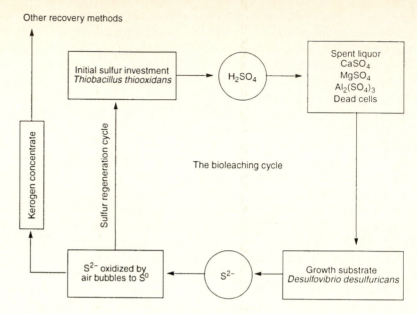

**Figure 15.10**
Effect of bioleaching on oil shale. Oxidizability of the kerogen by permanganate is used as a measure of liberation from the shale showing accessibility of hydrocarbon. Raw unleached shale uses little permanganate; bioleached shale shows permanganate use about four times as high, indicating the effectiveness of bioleaching. (Source: Yen 1976a.)

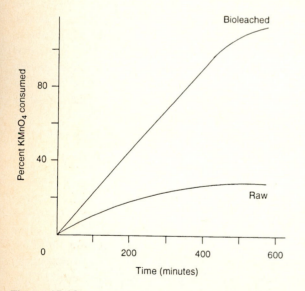

(Michaelis 1994). Attention is particularly focused on ethanol made from corn, wheat, and sugar crops. The OECD concluded that a cost-effective strategy could be based on the production of liquid biofuels from fast-growing trees and grasses planted expressly for liquid biofuel production. Meanwhile a directive has been proposed within the European Community to increase microbial production of fuels (Rose 1994). The EC's Biofuels Directive was proposed with the aim of solving two great problems, those of agricultural overproduction and high carbon dioxide emissions levels. Under the directive, alternative fuels such as ethanol and methanol may be obtained via fermentation of agricultural products such as sugarcane, wheat, wood, and agricultural wastes.

## Ethanol

The ability of microorganisms, especially yeasts, to produce ethanol by the fermentation of carbohydrate-containing materials is well known. The microbial formation of ethanol is used in the production of many beverages; ethanol can also serve as a valuable fuel resource (National Research Council 1979; Venkatasubramanian and Keim 1981; Eveleigh 1984). The addition of ethanol to gasoline can greatly extend this petroleum-based fuel (Anderson 1978). Gasoline-ethanol mixtures are commonly known as gasohol. The normal ratio of gasoline to ethanol is 9:1. Gasohol can be used directly in present internal combustion automobile engines without any engineering modifications. Gasohol is an efficient fuel, lowering the release of atmospheric hydrocarbon pollutants compared to petroleum. Brazil, which has suitable land and climate for large-scale growing of sugarcane that can be fermented to ethanol, has embarked on an ambitious and generally successful program to replace gasoline with ethanol (Jackson 1976; Lindeman and Rocchiccioli 1979).

The extensive production of ethanol requires a large supply of carbohydrate substrates. The production of substrates suitable for conversion to fuels such as ethanol and methane involves the conversion of solar energy to plant or microbial biomass and/or the utilization of organic wastes. The use of photosynthetic activities for the production of suitable fermentation substrates raises some conflict with the agricultural production of food supplies, which are also becoming limiting because of population growth. It is necessary to seek increasingly efficient processes for the primary conversion of solar energy to cellular biomass and to utilize the energy stored in biomass. Fortunately, many agricultural wastes such as stems and leaves of fruit-bearing plants are, in theory, suitable candidates as substrates for microbial fuel production. These sources of biomass are normally plowed back into the soil, where microorganisms degrade them. The stored energy is lost as heat, and the fixed carbon is returned to the atmosphere. The materials recycling is desirable, but this process can be combined with a recovery of chemical energy.

In situations where ethanol is considered as a potential energy source, the chemical composition of the substrate is critical in determining whether it can be converted to ethanol efficiently. Ethanol is normally produced from simple carbohydrates by yeasts. The yeasts used in commercial production are unable to attack complex polymers, and it is usually necessary initially to degrade plant polymers with enzymes

produced by the plant itself or by microorganisms other than yeasts. In the brewing industry, for example, the starches in the grain substrates are initially subjected to amylase attack, producing simple carbohydrates from starches. The coculture of an amylolytic *Aspergillus niger* strain with *Saccharomyces cerevisiae* was demonstrated to convert potato starch wastes to ethanol, yielding in 2 days up to 96% of the theoretical maximum (Agouzied and Reddy 1986). Similarly, if cellulosic materials are considered for the production of ethanol, it will be necessary initially to catalyze the breakdown of this polymer to simple carbohydrates before yeasts or genetically engineered microorganisms with the necessary enzymes can be utilized for ethanol production. Because of their heat tolerance and rapid metabolism, several thermophilic microorganisms appear to be promising prospects for future ethanol production from cellulosic wastes (Eveleigh 1984).

The production of agricultural crops, both as food sources and as potential substrates for microbial fuel production, is limited by a number of factors, including the availability of arable land and the availability of fixed forms of the nitrogen required for plant and microbial growth. Attempts to establish additional nitrogen-fixing symbiotic relationships between plants and bacteria, through genetic manipulation, may have an important influence on whether sufficient plant material can be grown cheaply as a substrate for fuel production.

Although microorganisms may be capable of alleviating the scarcity of fixed forms of nitrogen for plant production, it is still likely that land resource availability will severely limit the expansion of conventional agricultural practices. Therefore, novel approaches to terrestrial biomass production from solar energy conversion may have to be considered for adequate production of substrates that can be converted to usable forms of chemical energy, such as ethanol. Forest biomass represents a largely unused resource that could be tapped for fuel production. Biomass production in terrestrial ecosystems ranges from less than 1 to more than 700 tons per hectare per year. Although much of the biomass produced in forest ecosystems will not be available for microbial fuel production because it is inaccessible or dedicated to other uses, forest residuals such as branches, wood chips, and sawdust are good potential substrates (Steinbeck 1976). Intensive forest management can greatly increase the production of plant biomass for microbial conversion, but the slow metabolism of lignocellulosic material is a technical obstacle to the use of forest biomass. A novel "steam explosion" technology, which first exposes wood to high-pressure steam and subsequently explosively releases the pressure, shredding the wood and achieving partial breakdown of the lignocellulose complexes, may overcome this difficulty and convert wood into a fermentable substrate. This, together with recent progress in understanding the biochemistry and genetics of lignin biodegradation (Paterson et al. 1984), may make the microbial conversion of lignocellulosic material into a liquid fuel a technical and economic reality.

Algae, cyanobacteria, and submerged or semi-submerged higher plants growing in aquatic, marine, and freshwater habitats can make a major contribution to the production of biomass through the conversion of solar energy. At present, these habitats are not intensively managed for the production of biomass. There are several advantages to considering aquatic habitats in the production of substrates for microbial energy production. Algae and cyanobacteria are not grown on a large scale as food resources, thus eliminating the conflict of resource utilization between food production and production of substrates for energy. The rapid growth rates of algae and cyanobacteria permit efficient substrate production. Microalgae may reach actual yields of 55 tons per hectare per year. Compared to higher plants, however, microalgae and cyanobacteria are difficult to harvest. Productivity in aquatic habitats is also naturally limited by the availability of nitrogen and phosphorus. Cyanobacteria are potentially attractive sources of substrates for microbial energy production because many cyanobacteria are capable of nitrogen fixation. In enclosed basins, it is possible to add fertilizers and maintain effective nutrient recycling within the system to promote biomass production. In open ocean systems, it might become possible to take advantage of natural nutrient upwellings or to create artificial upwellings and thus enhance biomass production for conversion to fuel (Roels et al. 1976; Soeder 1976).

## Methane

Methane, produced through methanogenesis by bacteria, is an extremely important potential fuel source (Pfeffer 1976; National Academy of Sciences 1977; National Research Council 1979). Methane can be used in the generation of mechanical, electrical, and heat energy. It can be used as a fuel source for homes and industry by transmission through natural gas pipelines and converted by microbial action or chemical means to methanol, which can be used as fuel in internal combustion engines.

Large amounts of methane are produced during the anaerobic decomposition of organic materials, but this energy resource normally is reoxidized, as in many aquatic habitats, or lost to the atmosphere, as in most terrestrial habitats. Methane production can be based on the decomposition of waste materials or on the conversion of biomass produced as a step in the conversion of solar energy to usable chemical energy. The production and utilization of methane as an energy source can close an important loop in the biogeochemical cycling of carbon, allowing for a recycling of energy that is initially trapped in organic compounds through the conversion of solar energy.

Methane can be produced from the biomass of primary producers, such as marine seaweeds. The growth of marine algae for the production of methane by methanogenic bacteria is an attractive way of coupling solar energy with the production of a gaseous hydrocarbon. Anaerobic photoorganotrophic bacteria can be grown on animal wastes in the presence of light to produce high-protein biomass and various fatty acids (Ensign 1976). The use of such photoheterotrophic bacterial populations permits the direct coupling of solar energy conversion and recycling of organic wastes to produce a higher-grade product that can be used either as an animal feed or in the generation of methane.

One of the most promising ways of producing methane is through the bioconversion of waste materials (Figure 15.11; Table 15.3). Anaerobic digestors

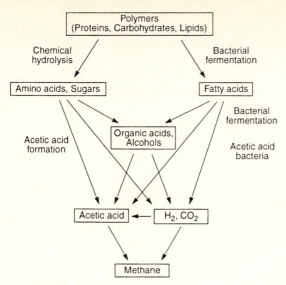

**Figure 15.11**
Processes used by Siemens Company in Germany to generate methane as a fuel from polymeric waste materials. (Source: Organization for Economic Cooperation and Development 1994.)

**Table 15.3**
Gas yields from anaerobic digestion of wastes

| Nature of solid waste | Total gas yield ($m^3$/kg) |
|---|---|
| Municipal sewage sludge | 0.43 |
| Municipal garbage only | 0.61 |
| Municipal paper only | 0.23 |
| Municipal refuse combined | 0.28 |
| Dairy wastes, sludge | 0.98 |
| Yeast wastes, sludge | 0.49 |
| Brewery wastes, hops | 0.43 |
| Stable manure, with straw | 0.29 |
| Horse manure | 0.40 |
| Cattle manure | 0.24 |
| Pig manure | 0.26 |
| Beet leaves | 0.46 |
| Maize tops | 0.49 |
| Grass | 0.50 |

Source: Imhoff et al. 1971.

can be used for the production of methane, and indeed, methane is a normal by-product of anaerobic sewage treatment facilities. In some sewage treatment plants, the methane generated in anaerobic digestors is used as an energy source to power the plant. The energy generated by sewage treatment facilities is also used to supply power for some small municipalities. Landfills containing organic wastes generate methane for years; pilot projects have been conducted to trap and use this gas. It is theoretically possible to place anaerobic digestors in private residences and small industries to permit the recycling of available energy resources with maximal retention and utilization within closed systems. Municipal and agricultural wastes could be supplied to central facilities for the large-scale production of methane.

Unlike the production of ethanol, which is carried out by pure cultures of yeasts, the production of methane is carried out by a mixed microbial community. Some microbial populations are involved in the breakdown of various organic materials, including complex polymers and simple fatty acids, hydrogen, carbon dioxide, and alcohols. Methanogenic bacteria utilize these fermentation products for the production of methane. Methanogenesis is commonly carried out by microbial populations involved in synergistic or mutualistic relationships. The microorganisms responsible for the conversion of organic matter to methane represent a balanced microbial community. This mixture presents some problems for bioengineers, who design fermentors for industrial applications that optimize conditions for defined microbial populations. Effective designs for the conversion of organic matter to methane require relatively compact fermentors for the ready trapping of gaseous methane (Switzenbaum 1983).

The evolution of methane from anaerobic digestors and other bioconversion processes occurs simultaneously with the evolution of carbon dioxide. The ratios of methane to carbon dioxide depend on the chemical composition of the substrate and the environmental conditions under which the bioconversion is carried out. Biotechnological processes can, and must, be adjusted to maximize the proportions of methane in the evolved gases. The methane must be trapped and separated from other gases to be a useful energy resource that can supplement or replace natural gas as a fuel.

## Hydrocarbons Other Than Methane

To date, little consideration has been given to the development of processes for the microbial production of hydrocarbons other than methane. Microorganisms are believed to play a role in the formation of petroleum deposits. The formation of petroleum, however, appears to be the result of physicochemical as well as microbial processes and occurs over long periods of time. Some microorganisms are known to produce hydrocarbons. Hydrocarbon biosynthesis occurs in various algae, fungi, and bacteria, such as the bacterium *Micrococcus luteus* (Tornabene 1976).

Some bacteria, fungi, and algae synthesize significant levels of hydrocarbons, suggesting the possibility that microorganisms that could produce hydrocarbons on a commercial scale could be found. Studies have shown that a tenfold increase in hydrocarbon production can be achieved with *Micrococcus* through genetic transformation. Obtaining a useful level of hydrocarbon production by microorganisms apparently may depend on their genetic modification and selection of efficient hydrocarbon-producing strains. In theory, the algae and cyanobacteria that produce hydrocarbons may permit the conversion of solar energy to chemical forms of energy that could power conventional combustion engines. This possibility deserves further consideration but, at this time, faces considerable technical and economic obstacles.

## Hydrogen

Hydrogen, not presently a major fuel, can be produced by various microorganisms and could become an important fuel resource (Reeves et al. 1976; National Research Council 1979). Hydrogen is produced as an end product from the fermentation of carbohydrates by bacteria that carry out a mixed acid fermentation. Rapid hydrogen removal favors the fermentation

process. The theoretical efficiency of the conversion of carbohydrates to energy stored in hydrogen is approximately 33%, compared to 85% for methane formation from organic matter. It is evident, therefore, that methane formation from organic compounds, rather than hydrogen formation, should be considered as the preferred process for microbial energy production via fermentation.

In contrast to hydrogen production from fermentation processes, phototrophic microorganisms may be capable of producing significant amounts of molecular hydrogen (Bennemann and Weissman 1976). Various microorganisms are capable of biophotolysis, that is, the production of hydrogen from water, using solar energy. Hydrogen production occurs in various photosynthetic bacteria, including purple and green sulfur bacteria, and in some cyanobacteria. The photosystems of cyanobacteria, algae, and plants are all capable of splitting water, releasing free oxygen and using the hydrogen to reduce carbon dioxide to carbohydrate. Theoretically, it should be possible to uncouple the process from $CO_2$ reduction and directly evolve hydrogen gas as the result of photosynthesis. In reality, the photoproduction of hydrogen has substantial obstacles. Algae rarely possess the enzyme hydrogenase needed for hydrogen release; this enzyme must be added to algal chloroplast preparations from bacterial sources. These hydrogenases are extremely sensitive to oxygen, yet the photolysis of water inevitably produces this gas. Photoproduction of hydrogen by biological systems is an intriguing and important concept, but at present technical difficulties stand in the way of its practical use.

Several bacteria are being investigated for their potential to produce hydrogen. These include *Desulfovibrio gigas,* which has a hydrogenase that functions as a catalyst for hydrogen production and consumption (Cammack 1995). Various cyanobacteria are also receiving extensive study for their abilities to simultaneously produce molecular hydrogen and remove excess amounts of atmospheric carbon dioxide. One study has focused on the cyanobacterium *Anabaena variabilis,* which converts fructose to $H_2$ and $CO_2$ in a light-dependent reaction when incubated in the presence of an inert gas such as argon (Reddy et al. 1996).

## Biotechnological Production of Hydrogen to Reverse Global Warming

Japanese academic, industrial, and government research, which is tightly coordinated by the government's Ministry of International Trade and Industry (MITI), is attempting to develop biotechnological methods that would combat global warming and also generate new fuel industries for Japan. Algae have been isolated at the Marine Biotechnology Laboratory at Kamaishi, Japan, that convert carbon dioxide to carbohydrates 10 times faster at 40°C than terrestrial green plants can. In theory, such algae could be grown in bioreactors near power plants where they would remove carbon dioxide from the atmosphere as it was released by fossil fuel burning at the power plant. However, these algae convert the carbon dioxide into organic compounds that would subsequently be biodegraded to carbon dioxide and water, releasing the carbon dioxide back into the atmosphere. A successful process will depend on finding microorganisms that produce lignins or other polymeric compounds that are as resistant to biodegradation as the original fossil fuels were. Such conversions would immobilize the carbon, reducing the buildup of carbon dioxide in the atmosphere.

Alternatively, microorganisms, particularly marine organisms called foraminifera, can convert carbon from carbon dioxide into calcium carbonate. This process, which also occurs in coral reef formation, removes carbon from the normal biogeochemical carbon cycle that circulates carbon between organic compounds and carbon dioxide. Such treatment, however, would consume enormous quantities of calcium, creating its own impact on the environment.

The Japanese research teams are not only searching for means of using microorganisms to remove $CO_2$ from the atmosphere, they are also trying to find strains of photosynthetic microorganisms that will simultaneously produce molecular hydrogen. The idea is to biologically produce enough hydrogen to serve as a transportation fuel, replacing in large part the current use of petroleum. Combustion of hydrogen does not produce gases that alter the atmosphere; hence, it is a clean fuel that would reduce atmospheric pollution and the greenhouse effect. Already Japan has introduced into California prototype hydrogen-fueled automobiles and an experimental service station that supplies the hydrogen fuel. The research project, however, has not solved the problem of producing sufficient quantities of hydrogen to meet worldwide fuel needs. Despite the technical and conceptual difficulties with this project, this research effort may succeed in attacking global pollution problems.

These Japanese strategies, if developed, would raise the need for international understanding of the uses of this technology. If successful, Japanese efforts to reduce global warming by removing excess carbon dioxide from the atmosphere will have far-reaching effects. Japanese programs to replace petroleum with biologically produced hydrogen and to replace gasoline-powered automobiles with cars that burn hydrogen would reduce future buildup of carbon dioxide. A conversion to hydrogen fuel produced by microorganisms would be a major new use of microorganisms for pollution prevention that would revolutionize not only the petrochemical and automotive industries but the worldwide economy.

Hydrogen production depends on the availability of fructose and heterocyst. The production of $H_2$ increases proportionately with fructose concentration.

Various environmental conditions affect the rates of evolution of hydrogen gas through biophotolysis. In some nitrogen-fixing cyanobacteria, it is possible to release hydrogen effectively through biophotolysis when the organisms are nitrogen starved. Photoheterotrophic bacteria, such as *Rhodospirillum* or *Rhodopseudomonas,* can be used for hydrogen production from waste materials. As with other potential sources of future energy supplies, technological and economic considerations play a large part in determining which fuel resources are developed and used. A lack of knowledge about many areas of biophotolysis prevents assessment of the prospects for producing and using hydrogen generated by microorganisms on a large scale. It can be expected, however, that efforts will be made in the future to determine the feasibility of using photosynthetic microorganisms in the conversion of solar energy to hydrogen gas.

# PRODUCTION OF
# MICROBIAL BIOMASS

## Single-Cell Protein Production

Microbial biomass may be produced not only as a starting material for fuel production but also for human and animal consumption as food or feed (Mateles and Tannenbaum 1968; Gaden and Humphrey 1977; Litchfield 1977; Rose 1979; Bhattacharjee 1980; Linton and Drozd 1982; Shennan 1984). Microbial biomass is a potentially attractive food additive because it usually contains a large percentage of high-grade protein. Microbial biomass production for food or feed is frequently referred to as single-cell protein production. Human diets in many underdeveloped and developing countries are essentially grain-based and deficient in protein in general, and in some essential amino acids in particular. As an example, corn-based diets are deficient in lysine, and such deficiencies can lead to malnutrition and deficiency diseases, especially in children, even if caloric intake is otherwise adequate.

Because microorganisms can convert relatively inexpensive materials, such as molasses and possibly even cellulosic wastes, into protein with high efficiency, the protein supplement from microbial sources should be more affordable in countries with low per capita income than other protein-rich food products, such as fish, meat, milk, and eggs. To illustrate this point, the conversion of 100 kg of carbohydrate can yield up to 65 kg of yeast, but only 10–20 kg of meat products.

The disadvantages of single-cell protein production include the high nucleic acid content and the digestion-resistant cell walls of some microorganisms, as well as the need for the industrial facilities and technical sophistication required to safely and efficiently produce single-cell protein. The main barriers to the use of single-cell protein as a food supplement, however, are sociological rather than technical. Food habits are deeply ingrained in cultural and ethnic heritages and are not easily modified. The general public gives little consideration to the fact that microbes are present in some traditional food products, such as lactobacilli in yogurt, yet most people consider a microbial source of protein to be a distasteful or disquieting notion. The acute food shortages in Europe during and following World War II prompted some experimentation with microbial biomass in human nutrition. For instance, a highly nutritious and reasonably palatable liverwurst substitute was concocted from a combination of compressed bakers' yeast, *Saccharomyces cerevisiae,* and soybean meal, but this and similar substitutes were promptly discontinued when traditional food products became plentiful. It is somewhat paradoxical that industrialized societies, capable of producing and perhaps more ready to accept microbial food products, normally have no need for them, whereas undernourished societies that lack manufacturing and distribution capabilities are also culturally less ready to accept novel food products. Consequently, for the time being, the major nutritional role of microbial biomass is in animal feed supplements.

An objective rather than cultural-sociological problem with microbial single-cell protein is the high DNA-RNA content of bacterial and yeast cells. The metabolism of nucleic acids yields excessive amounts of uric acid that can cause kidney stones and gout. Two grams of nucleic acids per day from microbial single-cell supplements appears to be the upper limit for human consumption. If, therefore, such microbial single-cell proteins should become a major part of the human diet, efforts will have to be made to reduce the nucleic acid content of the microbial biomass. This reduction can be accomplished with acid precipitation, with acid or alkaline hydrolysis, or by nuclease enzymes, but the treatment increases the cost of the single-cell protein product. Digestibility of microbial cell walls varies, and in some cases, pretreatment to increase digestibility will be necessary. Some bacterial strains produce toxic or indigestible by-products. Poly-β-hydroxybutyric acid, a common microbial storage product, though not toxic, is apparently not digestible by mammals. Mice fed on biomass of the hydrogen-oxidizing microorganisms develop intestinal blockages due to this storage product. Selection of appropriate microbial strains or mutants, however, can eliminate this type of problem (Schlegel and Oeding 1971).

The group of microorganisms most extensively grown for single-cell protein (SCP) are yeasts (Rose 1979). Their high nutritional value (50–60% protein), easy cultivation, and lack of toxic by-products all contribute to their usefulness. A common substrate for cultivation of various *Saccharomyces* species is molasses from sugar refining. An interesting and novel process grows yeast biomass on starch in a single step, employing a mixed culture of the amylase-producing yeast *Endomycopsis fibuliger* and *Candida utilis* (Figure 15.12); the former organism overproduces amylase, and the bulk of the sugar produced from the starch is utilized by *C. utilis,* which constitutes 85–90% of the final yeast biomass (Skogman 1976).

Prior to 1970, when petroleum was considered inexpensive, hydrocarbons were thought to be suitable substrates for single-cell protein production, and several commercial processes were developed (De Pontanel 1972; Shennan 1984). Some yeasts, such as *Candida lipolytica,* that readily utilize normal alkanes of intermediate chain length ($C_{12}$–$C_{16}$) were grown as feed yeast by the British Petroleum Company and various other commercial enterprises. When the price of

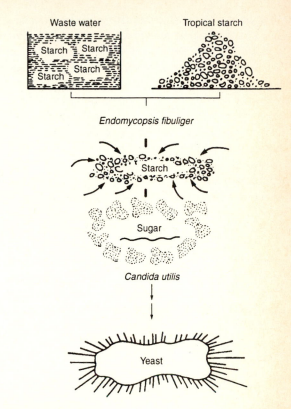

**Figure 15.12**
One-step production of yeast biomass from starch-containing wastewaters of food processing plants or from starch especially produced for this purpose, such as from cassava. *Endomycopsis fibuliger* produces amylase, an uncommon metabolic feature in yeasts, and supplies sugar for the more rapidly growing *Candida utilis.* The final yeast biomass consists of 85–90% *C. utilis* and 10–15% *E. fibuliger.* (Source: Skogman 1976. Reprinted by permission of Applied Science Publications, Inc.)

petroleum increased, however, these commercial operations became uneconomic. Changing organisms and substrates to natural gas-derived methanol, for example, may make single-cell protein production economically viable once again.

From the point of view of cost, the use of waste materials for single-cell protein production seems particularly attractive (Bellamy 1974; Birch et al. 1976; Skogman 1976; Litchfield 1977). Various schemes have been proposed to convert animal waste from cattle feed lots or hog farms into feed protein. Technical and sanitary difficulties have thus far thwarted the use of animal waste in this manner, but the approach has merits because it not only creates an important commodity but also provides partial solution to a waste disposal problem. The waste sulfite liquor from wood-pulp processing has been used commercially with good success for production of yeasts for animal feed.

Algae and cyanobacteria have the advantages as potential sources of single-cell protein; only inorganic nutrients and sunlight are required for their production (Bennemann et al. 1976, 1977). The cyanobacterium *Spirulina,* which forms large surface blooms on Lake Chad, Africa, has traditionally been used as a food supplement by the local population and has high potential as a food or feed supplement. The historic record indicates that a similar use of *Spirulina* was traditional in Mexico at the time of the Spanish conquest (Ciferri 1983). The cyanobacterial bloom that floats to the surface is simply scooped up and usually dried for storage and distribution. It is eaten raw or added to various dishes. Of the dry weight, 60–70% is high-grade protein. Total nucleic acids are less than 5%, which is considerably less than in most bacteria and yeasts. *Spirulina maxima* is commercially produced at Lake Texcoco, Mexico, at a rate approaching 2 metric tons per day. The *Spirulina maxima* biomass is currently used as animal feed, and uses in human food are under consideration. The *Spirulina* biomass is a by-product of a large solar evaporator for production of soda lime. Spirulina is harvested from the external portion of the helical evaporator, where the brine is most dilute. Harvest is by filtration. After homogenization and pasteurization, the product is spray-dried (Ciferri and Tiboni 1985).

In some Pacific islands, certain species of marine macroalgae are traditional dietary supplements. *Ulva, Caulerpa* (Chlorophycophyta), *Laminaria* (Phaeophycophyta), and *Porphyra* (Rhodophycophyta) are used in this manner. They are consumed fresh as salad, dried as a snack, or are added as supplements to other dishes. These algae add important vitamins and minerals to the rice- and fish-based diets of these regions. The unicellular freshwater alga *Chlorella* can be grown in simple media and has good potential as a food supplement. In Japan, cultivated *Chlorella* has been used as a protein and vitamin supplement in yogurt, ice cream, bread, and other food products. The acceptability problem of microbial biomass as food can be solved by its conversion to fish or shellfish protein as practiced in aquaculture. Food value is lost in the process, but easier harvestability and better palatability of the product compensate for this. According to one scheme, atolls surrounded by deep ocean could be used in combined energy and biomass production (Pinchot 1970; Othmer and Roels 1973). The heat energy of warm tropical surface seawater (25–30°C) could be used to evaporate a low-boiling working fluid and to drive low-pressure turbines. The vapors are condensed by piping to the surface cold seawater (5–6°C) from the depth of 900–1000 m. After its use for cooling, the nutrient-rich and now-warm deep seawater is piped into the shallow lagoon of the atoll and used in production of algal biomass. The latter supports the production of fish, shrimp, or shellfish. Serious technical problems remain to be surmounted, especially in respect to marine surface fouling of the bulky heat exchangers, but the soundness of the concept has been verified in small-scale demonstration projects.

## Mushroom Production

The discussion of microbial biomass as food would not be complete without mentioning mushroom cultivation, although mushrooms are grown more for their flavor than for their nutritional value (Gray 1970; Chang and Hayes 1978; National Research Council 1979). The Basidiomycota cultivated in this manner are grown essentially on waste materials, and their fruiting bodies are marketed fresh, dried, or canned. *Agaricus bisporus* has been the mushroom commercially grown in Europe and in the United States. Composted horse manure is used as the growth substrate; cultivation takes place in caves, cellars, or specially constructed mushroom houses. The substrate is placed in trays or beds and is inoculated with spawn, a mycelial mass grown from spores under controlled and sterile conditions. Temperature and humidity conditions are carefully controlled during the next

15–30 days of mycelial proliferation. At the end of this period, the compost is covered with a thin layer of soil or sand casing. Ventilation needs to be carefully controlled in the following period because elevated $CO_2$ concentrations inhibit fruiting body formation. One to three months after application of the casing, the mushroom caps appear and are harvested. Production continues in periodic cycles, called *breaks.* Commonly the compost is replaced after four breaks, allowing two 6-month production cycles per year. The annual production of mushrooms in the United States for 1995–1996 was 355,000 metric tons at $758 million wholesale and well over a billion-dollar retail value (American Mushroom Institute, Washington, D.C.).

In various countries of Indochina, the straw mushroom *Volvariella volvacea* is cultivated on a commercial scale. Rice straw, tied in bundles and soaked in water, is made into beds approximately 3 by 1 m and placed either in open fields or in sheds. Occasionally, small supplements of rice bran and distillery residues are added. Inoculation is from spent straw beds. Mushrooms are produced 3–4 weeks after inoculation, and production continues in about 10-day intervals for several cycles. By this simple cultivation process, *V. volvacea* is grown by farmers for home use and local markets, and also by large-scale operators for canning.

The shiitake mushroom *Lentinula edodes* is commercially cultivated in Japan on deciduous logs, mainly oak. The wood used for this purpose, boles 10–30 cm in diameter, has little or no commercial value. The logs are soaked, the bark is pounded and lacerated, and the sapwood is inoculated with a spore suspension of *L. edodes.* The logs are placed for 5–8 months in near-horizontal position in shady outdoor "laying yards," where mycelial proliferation takes place. At the end of this period the logs are transferred to a vertical position and a lower-humidity environment in "raising yards," where the mushroom caps develop. Logs continue to produce for 3–6 years and, aside from occasional watering and harvesting, require little care.

In addition to the three species discussed above, in recent years the production of a number of "specialty mushrooms" has become economically significant in the United States. A shift to higher-priced fresh *Agaricus bisporus* and to specialty mushrooms has occurred in part due to a strong competition for the more common varieties from import, primarily canned mushrooms from countries with cheaper labor. *Pleurotus ostreatus* (oyster mushroom), other *Pleurotus* species like the trumpet-shaped domatake, *Grifola frondosa* (chicken of the woods), *A. bisporus* portabella strain, and the previously mentioned *Lentinula edodes* (shiitake) have been commercial successes, and growers experiment with many other species.

The specialty mushrooms are grown in the United States on sawdust, milled corncobs, and other lignocellulosic waste material. The sawdust is blended with nutrient supplements (bran, molasses, etc.), placed in bags of 5–6 l, and either sterilized or pasteurized. The bags are inoculated with aseptically grown spawn. The mycelium grows throughout the sawdust substrate and solidifies it into "logs," which are subsequently taken out of the bags and placed on shelves in climate-controlled mushroom houses. Fruiting body formation is induced by a temperature and humidity regimen that differs according to species. The fruiting bodies are picked off by hand. The logs are usually soaked in water to replenish moisture and induced to form a new break, up to five or six times per log. Thereafter, the spent log is discarded and the cycle repeated. The mushroom houses have sophisticated temperature and humidity controls, and the air is filtered to control mold spores and diseases. Large numbers of mushroom growers are located around the town of Kennett Square, Pennsylvania. The operations are highly efficient, producing up to 100 kg of fresh mushrooms per square meter per month.

## CHAPTER SUMMARY

Microbial activities can be used to aid in the recovery of metals from low-grade ores. *Thiobacillus* and other iron- and sulfur-oxidizing bacteria are currently employed in some mining operations to increase the rate of recovery of copper and uranium. Bioleaching with thiobacilli and related iron-oxidizing bacteria contributes significantly to the commercially important recovery of copper. The recovery process generally is based on the transformation of iron sulfide (pyrite) associated with the mineral resource. By either direct or indirect microbial oxidation, the insoluble metal sulfide is transformed to water-soluble metal sulfate, which can be leached from the mineral deposit and recovered. The use of bioleaching for mineral recovery is governed by the economics of the process and the value of the recovered mineral resource. Bioaccumulation of metals by microorganisms may provide another mechanism for enhanced metal recovery.

Microorganisms are also important in the recovery of petroleum. Microbially enhanced oil recovery (MEOR) can contribute to improved petroleum recovery from existing old wells, as well as from formations that for technical or economic reasons have not been tapped to date. Xanthan gums produced by *Xanthomonas campestris* are used as surfactants to increase the yields of petroleum from oil-bearing formations. Biosurfactants are also used to release oil from tar sands. Future prospects for MEOR include *in situ* production of gas to force petroleum out of reservoirs.

Microbial fuel production can contribute to meeting world energy requirements. Microorganisms can produce various gaseous and liquid fuels. In many communities, gasoline is routinely supplemented with ethanol produced by microbial fermentations. Many waste treatment plants and landfills capture methane produced by methanogenic archaea and use the methane to generate electricity. Hydrogen production is being developed as a potential automotive fuel that would alleviate global warming due to $CO_2$ production.

The brightest prospects for employing microorganisms in the production of renewable and sustainable fuel resources involve a conversion of solar energy to biomass and the subsequent formation of alcohols, hydrogen, and hydrocarbons, particularly methane, by the microbial fermentation of this biomass. Obviously, the described solar energy conversion schemes will need to compete with the more direct photovoltaic use of sun energy. However, the periodicity of sunlight and the difficulty of storing electricity for vehicular propulsion favor production of conventional fuels by solar energy. Several microbially produced fuels could partially replace petroleum and natural gas as energy sources in conventional engines. In addition to being used for the production of conventional fuels, microorganisms can be used in bioleaching processes to enhance the recovery of petroleum hydrocarbons and nuclear fuels, such as uranium. Microbial recovery processes can extend our available energy resources. The production of energy will undoubtedly be a major concern of scientists, including microbial ecologists, until ways are found to convert solar energy to usable fuels that are safe and that can be produced on a scale that will permit a high worldwide standard of living.

Traditional uses of microbial biomass for human food are limited to yeasts, mushrooms, and certain algae. An expanded future use of microbial biomass for human food or animal feed requires suitable and inexpensive substrates that will make the process economical and provide a nutritious product acceptable to consumers. Hydrocarbons were once considered as prime substrates for single-cell protein production, but the increased cost of petroleum made these processes uneconomic. New processes are being developed based on natural-gas-derived methanol and on the utilization of cellulose and various waste materials.

---

# Study Questions

1. What is bioleaching? Why are thiobacilli important for bioleaching?

2. Why is bioleaching especially useful for the recovery of copper? What chemical reactions are involved in the bioleaching of copper? Which of these are mediated by microorganisms?

3. How is bioleaching used for the recovery of uranium? What chemical reactions are involved in the bioleaching of uranium? Which of these are mediated by microorganisms?

4. Discuss the prospects for using biotechnology to recover precious metals. What experiments would you conduct to determine the feasibility of using microorganisms for the recovery of gold from mine tailings?

5. What is MEOR? How is it currently used for increasing the world supply of usable petroleum?

6. What *in situ* processes can be employed for the microbially enhanced recovery of petroleum?

7. How can microorganisms be used to increase the world supply of fuels? How can microbial production of fuels be made sustainable?

8. How can production of biofuels be coupled with improving the environmental quality of air, water, and soil?

9. Describe the potential benefits and limitations for the production of each of the following fuels: ethanol, methane, gasoline, and hydrogen.

10. How can microorganisms be used to increase the world's food supply?

11. What is single-cell protein (SCP)? Discuss whether you would eat SCP.

## REFERENCES AND SUGGESTED READINGS

Abouzied, M. M., and A. Reddy. 1986. Direct fermentation of potato starch to ethanol by cocultures of *Aspergillus niger* and *Saccharomyces cerevisiae*. *Applied and Environmental Microbiology* 52:1055–1059.

Agate, A. D. 1996. Recent advances in microbial mining. *World Journal of Microbiology and Biotechnology* 12:487–495.

Amaro, A. M., K. B. Hallberg, E. B. Lindstrom, and C. A. Jerez. 1994. An immunological assay for detection and enumeration of thermophilic biomining microorganisms. *Applied and Environmental Microbiology* 60:3470–3474.

Anderson, E. V. 1978. Gasohol: Energy mountain or molehill? *Chemical and Engineering News* 56:8–15.

Beck, J. V. 1967. The role of bacteria in copper mining operations. *Biotechnology and Bioengineering* 9:487–497.

Bellamy, W. D. 1974. Single cell proteins from cellulosic wastes. *Biotechnology and Bioengineering* 16:869–890.

Bennemann, J. R., B. Koopman, J. Weissman, and W. J. Oswald. 1976. Biomass production and waste recycling with blue-green algae. In H. C. Schlegel and J. Barnea (eds.). *Microbial Energy Conversion*. Report of the UNITAR/BMFT Göttingen Seminar. Pergamon Press, New York, pp. 399–412.

Bennemann, J. R., B. Koopman, J. Weissman, and W. J. Oswald. 1977. Energy production by microbial photosynthesis. *Nature* (London) 268:19–23.

Bennemann, J. R., and J. C. Weissman. 1976. Biophotolysis: Problems and prospects. In H. C. Schlegel and J. Barnea (eds.). *Microbial Energy Conversion*. Report of the UNITAR/BMFT Göttingen Seminar. Pergamon Press, New York, pp. 413–426.

Bhattacharjee, J. K. 1980. Microorganisms as potential sources of food. *Advances in Applied Microbiology* 13:139–161.

Birch, G. G., K. J. Parker, and J. T. Morgan (eds.). 1976. *Food from Waste*. Applied Science Publishers, London.

Brierley, C. L. 1978. Bacterial leaching. *CRC Critical Reviews in Microbiology* 6:207–262.

Brierley, C. L. 1982. Microbiological mining. *Scientific American* 247(2):44–53.

Brierley, C. L. 1990. Metal immobilization using bacteria. In H. L. Ehrlich and C. L. Brierley (eds.). *Microbial Mineral Recovery*. McGraw-Hill, New York, pp. 303–324.

Brierley, C. L., and L. E. Murr. 1972. Leaching: Use of a thermophilic and chemoautotrophic microbe. *Science* 179:488–489.

Brierley, J. A., and S. J. Lockwood. 1977. The occurrence of thermophilic iron-oxidizing bacteria in a copper leaching system. *FEMS Microbiology Letters* 2:163–165.

Brierley, J. A., and C. L. Brierley. 1978. Microbial leaching of copper at ambient and elevated temperatures. In L. E. Murr, A. E. Torma, and J. A. Brierley (eds.). *Metallurgical Applications of Bacterial Leaching and Related*

*Microbiological Phenomena.* Academic Press, New York, pp. 477–490.

Brock, T. D. 1978. *Thermophilic Microorganisms and Life at High Temperatures.* Springer-Verlag, New York.

Brock, T. D., and J. Gustafson. 1976. Ferric iron reduction by sulfur- and iron-oxidizing bacteria. *Applied and Environmental Microbiology* 32:567–571.

Bungay, H. R. 1981. *Energy, the Biomass Options.* Wiley, New York.

Cammack, R. 1995. Splitting molecular hydrogen. *Nature* 373:556–558.

Chang, S. T., and W. A. Hayes. 1978. *The Biology and Cultivation of Edible Mushrooms.* Academic Press, New York.

Charley, R. C., and A. T. Bull. 1979. Bioaccumulation of silver by a multi-species community of bacteria. *Archives of Microbiology* 123:239–244.

Ciferri, O., 1983. *Spirulina,* the edible microorganism. *Microbiological Reviews* 47:551–578.

Ciferri, O., and O. Tiboni. 1985. The biochemistry and industrial potential of *Spirulina. Annual Review of Microbiology* 39:503–526.

Cooper, D. G. 1983. Biosurfactants and enhanced oil recovery. In S. B. Clark and E. S. Donaldson (eds.). *Proceedings of 1982 International Conference on the Microbial Enhancement of Oil Recovery.* Technology Transfer Branch, Bartlesville Technology Center, Bartlesville, OK, pp. 112–114.

Cooper, D. G., and J. E. Zajic. 1980. Surface active compounds from microorganisms. *Advances in Applied Microbiology* 26:229–253.

De Pontanel, H. G. (ed.). 1972. *Proteins from Hydrocarbons.* Proceedings of Symposium Aix-en-Provence. Academic Press, London.

Ehrlich, H. L., and C. L. Brierley (eds.). 1990. *Microbial Mineral Recovery.* McGraw-Hill, New York.

Ensign, J. C. 1976. Biomass production from animal wastes by photosynthetic bacteria. In H. G. Schlegel and J. Barnea (eds.). *Microbial Energy Conversion.* Report of the UNITAR/BMFT Göttingen Seminar. Pergamon Press, New York, pp. 455–482.

Eveleigh, D. E. 1984. Biofuels and oxychemicals from natural polymers: A perspective. In M. J. Klug and C. A. Reddy (eds.). *Current Perspectives in Microbial Ecol-*

*ogy.* American Society for Microbiology, Washington, DC, pp. 553–557.

Finnerty, W. R., and M. E. Singer. 1983. Microbial enhancement of oil recovery. *Biotechnology* 1:47–54.

Forbes, A. D. 1980. Microorganisms in oil recovery. In D.E.F. Harrison, I. J. Higgins, and R. Watkinson (eds.). *Hydrocarbons in Biotechnology.* Heyden and Son, London, pp. 169–180.

Gaden, E. L., and A. E. Humphrey. 1977. Single cell protein from renewable and nonrenewable resources. *Biotechnology and Bioengineering Symposium 7.* Wiley, New York.

Geffen, T. M. 1976. Present technology for oil recovery. In *The Role of Microorganisms in the Recovery of Oil.* Proceedings of 1976 Engineering Foundation Conferences, NSF/RA-770201. Government Printing Office, Washington, DC, pp. 23–32.

Goldstein, A. H., R. D. Rogers, and G. Mead. 1993. Mining by microbe. *Biotechnology* 11:1250.

Gray, W. D. 1970. *The Use of Fungi as Food and in Food Processing.* CRC Press, Cleveland, OH.

Groudev, S. 1979. Mechanism of bacterial oxidation of pyrite. *Mikrobiologija Acta Biologica Iugoslavica* (Belgrade) 16:75–87.

Groudev, S. N., and F. N. Genchev. 1978. Mechanisms of bacterial oxidation of chalcopyrite. *Mikrobiologija Acta Biologica Iugoslavica* (Belgrade) 15:139–152.

Guay, R., M. Silver, and A. E. Torma. 1977. Ferrous iron oxidation and uranium extraction by *Thiobacillus ferrooxidans. Biotechnology and Bioengineering* 19:727–740.

Gutnick, D. L., Z. Zosim, and E. Rosenberg. 1983. The interaction of emulsan with hydrocarbons. In S. B. Clark and E. S. Donaldson (eds.). *Proceedings of 1982 International Conference on the Microbial Enhancement of Oil Recovery.* Technology Transfer Branch, Bartlesville Energy Technology Center, Bartlesville, OK, pp. 6–11.

Hitzman, D. O. 1983. Petroleum microbiology and the history of its role in enhanced oil recovery. In S. B. Clark and E. S. Donaldson (eds.). *Proceedings of 1982 International Conference on the Microbial Enhancement of Oil Recovery.* Technology Transfer Branch, Bartlesville Energy Technology Center, Bartlesville, OK, pp. 162–218.

Imhoff, K., W. J. Müller, and D.K.B. Thistlethwayte. 1971. *Disposal of Sewage and Other Water-borne Wastes.* Ann Arbor Science Publishers, Ann Arbor, MI.

Jackson, E. A. 1976. Brazil's national alcohol program. *Process Biochemistry* 11:29–30.

Jernelov, A., and A. L. Martin. 1975. Ecological implications of metal metabolism by microorganisms. *Annual Reviews of Microbiology* 29:61–78.

Karavaiko, G. I. 1985. *Microbiological Processes for the Leaching of Metals from Ores.* UNEP, Center of International Projects GKNT, Moscow.

Karavaiko, G. I., S. I. Kuznetsov, and A. I. Golomzik. 1977. *The Bacterial Leaching of Metals from Ores.* Technicopy, Stonehouse, England.

Keenan, J. D. 1979. Review of biomass to fuels. *Process Biochemistry* 5:9–15.

Kelly, D. P. 1976. Extraction of metals from ores by bacterial leaching: Present status and future prospects. In J. Barnea and H. G. Schlegel (eds.). *Microbial Energy Conversion.* Report of the UNITAR/BMFT Göttingen Seminar. Pergamon Press, New York, pp. 329–338.

Kelly, D. P., P. R. Norris, and C. L. Brierley. 1979. Microbiological methods for the extraction and recovery of metals. In A. T. Bull, D. C. Ellwood, and C. Ratledge (eds.). *Microbial Technology: Current State, Future Prospects.* Cambridge University Press, Cambridge, England, pp. 263–308.

Kuznetsov, S. I., M. V. Ivanov, and N. N. Lyalikova. 1963. *Introduction to Geological Microbiology.* McGraw-Hill, New York.

La Riviere, J.W.M. 1955a. The production of surface-active compounds by microorganisms and its possible significance in oil recovery. Part I. Some general observations on the change of surface tension in microbial cultures. *Antonie van Leeuwenhoek* 21:1–8.

La Riviere, J.W.M. 1955b. The production of surface-active compounds by microorganisms and its possible significance in oil recovery. Part II. On the release of oil from oil-sand mixtures with the aid of sulfate reducing bacteria. *Antonie van Leeuwenhoek* 21:8–27.

Lindeman, L. R., and C. Rocchiccioli. 1979. Ethanol in Brazil: Brief summary of the state of industry in 1977. *Biotechnology and Bioengineering* 21:1107–1119.

Linton, J. D., and J. W. Drozd. 1982. Microbial interactions and communities in biotechnology. In A. T. Bull and J. H. Slater (eds.). *Microbial Interactions and Communities.* Academic Press, London, pp. 357–406.

Lipman, J. G., H. C. McLean, and H. C. Lint. 1916. The oxidation of sulfur in soils as a means of increasing the availability of mineral phosphates. *Soil Science* 1:533–539.

Litchfield, J. H. 1977. Comparative technical and economic aspects of single-cell protein processes. *Advances in Applied Microbiology* 22:267–305.

Lundgren, D. G., and M. Silver. 1980. Ore leaching by bacteria. *Annual Review of Microbiology* 34:263–283.

McCready, R.G.L., and W. D. Gould. 1990. Bioleaching of uranium. In H. L. Ehrlich and C. L. Brierley (eds.). *Microbial Mineral Recovery.* McGraw-Hill, New York, pp. 107–126.

McInerney, M. J., and D. W. Westlake. 1990. Microbial enhanced oil recovery. In H. L. Ehrlich and C. L. Brierley (eds.). *Microbial Mineral Recovery.* McGraw-Hill, New York, pp. 409–445.

Mateles, R. I., and S. R. Tannenbaum. 1968. *Single Cell Protein.* MIT Press, Cambridge, MA.

Matthews, D. 1982. Here's how enhanced oil recovery works. *EXXON USA* 21:16–23.

Mersou, J. 1992. Mining with microbes. *New Scientist* 133:17–19.

Meyer, W. C., and T. F. Yen. 1976. Enhanced dissolution of shale oil by bioleaching with *Thiobacilli. Applied and Environmental Microbiology* 32:310–316.

Michaelis, L. 1994. The real costs of liquid biofuels. *OECD Observer* 190:23–27.

Moffat, A. S. 1994. Microbial mining boosts the environment, bottom line. *Science* 264:778–779.

Moses, V., and D. G. Springham. 1982. *Bacteria and the Enhancement of Oil Recovery.* Applied Science Publishers, London.

Murr, L. E., A. E. Torma, and J. A. Brierley (eds.). 1978. *Metallurgical Applications of Bacterial Leaching and Related Microbiological Phenomena.* Academic Press, London.

National Academy of Sciences. 1977. *Methane Generation from Human, Animal, and Agricultural Wastes.* National Academy of Sciences, Washington, DC.

National Research Council. 1979. *Microbial Processes: Promising Technologies for Developing Countries.* National Academy of Sciences, Washington, DC.

Norris, P. R., and D. P. Kelly. 1979. Accumulation of metals by bacteria and yeasts. *Developments in Industrial Microbiology* 20:299–308.

Norris, P. R., and D. P. Kelly. 1982. The use of mixed microbial cultures in metal recovery. In A. T. Bull and J. H. Slater (eds.). *Microbial Interactions and Communities.* Academic Press, London, pp. 443–474.

Organization for Economic Cooperation and Development. 1994. *Biotechnology for a Clean Environment.* Organization for Economic Cooperation and Development, Paris.

Othmer, D. F., and O. A. Roels. 1973. Power, freshwater, and food from cold deep seawater. *Science* 182:121–125.

Paterson, A., A. J. McCarthy, and P. Broda. 1984. The application of molecular biology to lignin degradation. In J. M. Graingor and J. M. Lynch (eds.). *Microbiological Methods for Environmental Biotechnology.* Academic Press, New York, pp. 33–68.

Pfeffer, J. T. 1976. Methane from urban wastes: Process requirements. In H. C. Schlegel and J. Barnea (eds.). *Microbial Energy Conversion.* Report of the UNITAR/BMFT Göttingen Seminar. Pergamon Press, New York, pp. 139–156.

Pinchot, G. F. 1970. Marine farming. *Scientific American* 223(6):14–21.

Pizarro, J., E. Jedlicki, O. Orellana, J. Romero, and R. T. Espejo. 1996. Bacterial populations in samples of bioleached copper ore as revealed by analysis of DNA obtained before and after cultivation. *Applied and Environmental Microbiology* 62:1323–1329.

Rangachari, P. N., V. S. Krishnamachar, S. G. Pail, M. N. Sainani, and H. Balakrishnan. 1978. Bacterial leaching of copper sulfide ores. In L. E. Murr, A. E. Torma, and J. A. Brierley (eds.). *Metallurgical Applications of Bacterial Leaching and Related Microbiological Phenomena.* Academic Press, London, pp. 427–439.

Reddy, P. M., H. Spiller, S. L. Albrecht, and K. T. Shanmugam. 1996. Photodissimilation of fructose to $H_2$ and $CO_2$ by a dinitrogen-fixing cyanobacterium, *Anabaena variabilis. Applied and Environmental Microbiology* 62:1220–1227.

Reeves, S. G., K. K. Rao, L. Rosa, and D. D. Hall. 1976. Biocatalytic production of hydrogen. In H. G. Schlegel and J. Barnea (eds.). *Microbial Energy Conversion.* Report of the UNITAR/BMFT Göttingen Seminar. Pergamon Press, New York, pp. 235–243.

Roels, O. A., S. Laurence, M. W. Farmer, and L. van Hemelryck. 1976. Organic production potential at artificial upwelling marine culture. In H. G. Schlegel and J. Barnea (eds.). *Microbial Energy Conversion.* Report of the UNITAR/BMFT Göttingen Seminar. Pergamon Press, New York, pp. 69–81.

Rose, A. H. (ed.). 1979. *Microbial Biomass. Economic Microbiology.* Vol. 4. Academic Press, London.

Rose, J. 1994. Biofuel benefits questioned. *Environmental Science and Technology* 28:63A.

Sandvik, E. I., and J. M. Maerker. 1977. Application of xanthan gum for enhanced oil-recovery. In R. F. Gould (ed.). *Extracellular Polysaccharides.* American Chemical Society Symposium Ser. 48, Washington, DC, pp. 242–264.

Schlegel, H. G., and J. Barnea (eds.). 1976. *Microbial Energy Conversion.* Report of the UNITAR/BMFT Göttingen Seminar. Pergamon Press, New York.

Schlegel, H. G., and V. Oeding. 1971. Selection of mutants not accumulating storage materials. In *Radiation and Radioisotopes for Industrial Microorganisms.* International Atomic Energy Agency, Vienna, Austria, pp. 223–231.

Shennan, J. L. 1984. Hydrocarbons as substrates in industrial fermentation. In R. M. Atlas (ed.). *Petroleum Microbiology.* Macmillan, New York pp. 643–683.

Singer, M. E., W. R. Finnerty, P. Bolden, and A. D. King. 1983. Microbial processes in the recovery of heavy petroleum. In S. B. Clark and E. S. Donaldson (eds.). *Proceedings of 1982 International Conference on the Microbial Enhancement of Oil Recovery.* Technology Transfer Branch, Bartlesville Energy Technology Center, Bartlesville, OK, pp. 94–101.

Skogman, H. 1976. Production of symba-yeast from potato wastes. In G. G. Bach, K. J. Parker, and J. T. Woregan (eds.). *Food from Waste.* Applied Science Publishers, Essex, England, pp. 167–176.

Soeder, C. J. 1976. Primary production of biomass in fresh water with respect to microbial energy conversion. In H. G. Schlegel and J. Barnea (eds.). *Microbial Energy Conversion.* Report of the UNITAR/BMFT Göttingen Seminar. Pergamon Press, New York, pp. 59–68.

Steinbeck, K. 1976. Biomass production of intensively managed forest ecosystems. In H. G. Schlegel and J. Barnea (eds.). *Microbial Energy Conversion.* Report of the UNITAR/BMFT Göttingen Seminar. Pergamon Press, New York, pp. 35–44.

Summers, A. O., and S. Silver. 1978. Microbial transformations of metals. *Annual Review of Microbiology* 32:637–672.

Sutherland, I. W., and D. C. Ellwood. 1979. Microbial exopolysaccharides-industrial polymers of current and future potential. In A. T. Bull, D. C. Ellwood, and C. Ratledge (eds.). *Microbial Technology: Current State, Future Prospects.* Cambridge University Press, Cambridge, England, pp. 107–150.

Switzenbaum, M. S. 1983. Anaerobic treatment of wastewater: Recent developments. *ASM News* 49:532–536.

Tomizuka, N., and M. Yagisawa. 1978. Optimum conditions for leaching of uranium and oxidation of lead sulfide with *Thiobacillus ferrooxidans* and recovery of metals from bacterial leaching solution with sulfate-reducing bacteria. In L. E. Murr, A. E. Torma, and J. A. Brierley (eds.). *Metallurgical Applications of Bacterial Leaching and Related Microbiological Phenomena.* Academic Press, London, pp. 321–344.

Torma, A. E. 1976. Biodegradation of chalcopyrite. In J. M. Sharpley and A. M. Kaplan (eds.). *Proceedings of the 3rd International Biodegradation Symposium.* Applied Science Publishers, Essex, England, pp. 937–946.

Torma, A. E. 1977. The role of *Thiobacillus ferrooxidans* in hydrometallurgical processes. In N. Blakebrough, A. Fiechter, and T. K. Ghose (eds.). *Advances in Biochemical Engineering.* Vol. 6. Springer-Verlag, Berlin, pp. 1–37.

Torma, A. E. 1985. Scientific fundamentals of technology of tank leaching of uranium. In G. I. Karavaiko and S. N. Groudev (eds.). *Biotechnology of Metals.* UNEP, Centre of International Projects GKNT, Moscow, pp. 266–274.

Tornabene, T. G. 1976. Microbial formation of hydrocarbons. In H. G. Schlegel and J. Barnea (eds.). *Microbial Energy Conversion.* Report of the UNITAR/BMFT Göttingen Seminar. Pergamon Press, New York, pp. 281–299.

Tuovinen, O. H. 1990. Biological fundamentals of mineral leaching processes. In H. L. Ehrlich and C. L. Brierley (eds.). *Microbial Mineral Recovery.* McGraw-Hill, New York, pp. 55–78.

Tuovinen, O. H., and D. P. Kelly. 1974. Use of microorganisms for the recovery of metals. *International Metallurgical Reviews* 19:21–71.

Tuttle, J. H., and P. R. Dugan. 1976. Inhibition of growth, iron and sulfur oxidation in *Thiobacillus ferrooxidans* by simple organic compounds. *Canadian Journal of Microbiology* 22:719–730.

Updegraff, D. M. 1983. Plugging and penetration of petroleum reservoir rock by microorganisms. In S. B. Clark and E. S. Donaldson (eds.). *Proceedings of 1982 International Conference on the Microbial Enhancement of Oil Recovery.* Technology Transfer Branch, Bartlesville Energy Technology Center, Bartlesville, OK, pp. 81–85.

Venkatasubramanian, K., and C. R. Keim. 1981. Gasohol: A commercial perspective. *Proceedings of the New York Academy of Sciences* 369:187–204.

Westlake, D.W.S. 1984. Heavy crude oils and oil shales: Tertiary recovery of petroleum from oil-bearing formations. In R. M. Atlas (ed.). *Petroleum Microbiology.* Macmillan, New York, pp. 537–552.

Yen, T. F. 1976a. Current status of microbial shale oil recovery. In *The Role of Microorganisms in the Recovery of Oil.* Proceedings of 1976 Engineering Foundation Conferences. NSF/RA-770201. Government Printing Office, Washington, DC, pp. 81–115.

Yen, T. F. 1976b. Recovery of hydrocarbons from microbial attack on oil-bearing shales. In *The Genesis of Petroleum and Microbiological Means for Its Recovery.* Institute of Petroleum, London, pp. 22–46.

Zajic, J. E. 1969. *Microbial Biogeochemistry.* Academic Press, New York.

Zajic, J. E., and D. F. Gerson. 1978. Microbial extraction of bitumen from Athabasca oil sand. In E. V. Lown and O. P. Strausz (eds.). *Oil Sands and Oil Shale Chemistry.* Verlag-Chemie, Weinheim, Germany, pp. 145–161.

Zajic, J. E., and A. Y. Mahomedy. 1984. Biosurfactants: Intermediates in the biosynthesis of amphipathic molecules in microbes. In R. M. Atlas (ed.). *Petroleum Microbiology.* Macmillan, New York, pp. 221–297.

Zimmerley, S., D. Wilson, and J. Prater. 1958. *Cyclic Leaching Process Employing Iron-oxidizing Bacteria.* USA Patent No. 2,829,964, assigned to Kennecott Copper Corp.

ZoBell, C. E. 1947. Bacterial release of oil from oil-bearing materials. Vols. I, II. *World Oil* 126:36–44:127:35–40.

# MICROBIAL CONTROL OF PESTS AND DISEASE-CAUSING POPULATIONS

*A fascinating and economically important area of applied microbial ecology is the biological control of pests and disease-causing agents using microorganisms. Biological control using microorganisms to initiate disease in pest populations has the potential of reducing agricultural reliance on chemical pesticides. The negative interactions (amensalism, predation, and parasitism) among microbial populations and between microbes and higher organisms have always formed a natural basis for the biological control of pests and pathogens, and biological control methods take advantage of those relationships. Biological methods to control populations of disease-causing organisms and pests are based on modification of host and/or vector populations, modification of reservoirs of pathogens, and the direct use of microbial pathogens and predators. Biotechnology may improve approaches for controlling pest and disease-causing populations.*

As environmental contamination by toxic chemicals, including pesticides and herbicides, has increased, alternative approaches for controlling pest populations have become research priorities. These have included biological or ecological control methods for limiting the destructive impacts of pest populations, especially on agriculture (National Academy of Sciences 1968; Wilson 1969; Baker and Cook 1974; Woods 1974; Henis and Chet 1975; Huffaker and Messenger 1976; Simmonds et al. 1976; Coppel and Mertins 1977; Burges 1981; Batra 1982; Arntzen and Ryan 1987; Chet 1987, 1993; Hedrin et al. 1988; Harman and Lumsden 1990; Nakas and Hagedorn 1990; Canaday 1995; Hokkanen and Lynch 1995). Biological control methods take advantage of existing amensal, predatory, and parasitic relationships that normally control pest populations and often involve the intentional release of pathogens or toxins aimed at specific pest populations.

The use of biological insect control agents is likely to increase as farmers search for alternatives to chemical pesticides (Federici and Maddox 1996). In determining the efficacy of using biological control, a risk analysis is advisable. The uses of microbial biopesticides are governed by several factors, including host specificity, microbial habitat, extent of control of the pest or pathogen, and susceptibility to environmental variables (Kloepper 1996). Indirect interactions can result in species competition and extinction so that examining host specificity of biological control agents is a primary criterion in evaluating and weighing risks of host expansion and host switching (Secord and Kareiva 1996). The use of insect parasitoids and predators as biological control agents is limited by potential damage to nontarget organisms. The host ranges of all potential biocontrol agents need to be known precisely and population ecology studies need to be included in all such risk assessment evaluations (Onstad and McManus 1996). The determination of host specificity of insect predators and parasitoids used as biological control agents is guided by relevant information on the evolution, environmental relations, and the initiation of the host-parasite relationship (Strand and Obrycki 1996). All this information is essential for determining the risk of a control plan prior to field application (McEvoy 1996).

## MODIFICATION OF HOST POPULATIONS

Several important methods for controlling pests and pathogens are based on modifying host populations. Host populations have natural defense mechanisms against infection by pathogens and attack by pests, and it is possible to enhance these mechanisms to control disease. In agriculture, selective breeding has been extensively used to develop plant populations that are genetically resistant to disease-causing pathogens. Many new plant strains have been developed on this basis. Selective breeding is successful because of the specificity of host-pathogen interactions. Unfortunately, pest populations are subject to evolution, selection, and geographical spreading. Thus, there is a need in agriculture for a continuous breeding program in order to develop new strains of resistant plants and to replace strains of plants that are, or are becoming, susceptible to diseases caused by pathogens and pests (Beck and Maxwell 1976).

Resistance to disease is the inherent capacity of a plant that enables it to prevent or restrict the entry or subsequent activities of a pathogen to which the plant is exposed under conditions that could lead to disease. The basis for resistance in plant populations may be anatomical or biochemical. Insects or nematodes, some of which are vectors for pathogens, may be unable to penetrate plants with thicker cuticles or cork layers. For example, the resistance of some species of barberry to penetration by basidiospores of *Puccinia graminis* has been attributed to the thickness of the cuticle on the epidermis of the leaves. Strains of plants capable of closing their stomata when conditions are favorable for infection also possess a mechanism for disease resistance (Snyder et al. 1976). Infected plants may respond with morphological and/or biochemical changes that render the plant more resistant to the pathogen.

Agricultural management practices are frequently directed at avoiding plant disease (National Academy of Sciences 1968; Batra 1982). Because many plant pathogens are transmitted from one infected individual to another, increasing the spacing between individual plants decreases the likelihood that a pathogenic microorganism will be successfully transmitted from infected to uninfected plants. In cases where pathogens are not spread from plant to plant, high-density planting produces good crops with only minor losses due to disease. For example, dense seeding of cotton reduces losses due to *Verticillium* wilt. In contrast, dense plantings in hemlock result in increased losses due to twig rust, because this pathogen spreads from plant to plant. Density of host plant populations also results in environmental modifications that affect the development of plant pathogens. Dense planting of tomatoes, for example, results in retention of humidity, which favors development of blight due to *Botrytis*.

Environmental conditions at the time of planting are important in controlling pathogenic infections of plants. At suboptimal temperatures, plants often increase the exudation of amino acids and carbohydrates by roots. Such exudates act as nutrients that favor the rapid development of microbial populations in the vicinity of the plant. Development of *Pythium* and *Rhizoctonia* populations on exudates often results in fungal infection of the developing seedlings. Other suboptimal abiotic factors, such as lack of oxygen because of excessive moisture content, also result in increased production of exudates by plants, which in turn favors the development of pathogenic microbial populations.

Considerations analogous to those discussed for plant populations can also be applied to domesticated animal populations. Management of domesticated animals includes practices that decrease the probability of widespread disease among the animal population. Some animal populations have been bred specifically for their resistance to disease (Davis et al. 1975).

## Immunization

In vertebrate animals, including humans, disease control is often based on the immune response, in which exposure to antigens results in the establishment of a resistant state. An antigen can be any biochemical that elicits the immune response. One portion of the immune response involves the production of antibodies in response to antigen exposure. Antibodies are blood serum proteins. Antibodies react with antigens, and if the antigens are toxins, these reactions can neutralize the toxins and prevent the onset of disease. If the antigens are on the surface of a pathogenic microorganism, reaction with antibodies can result in agglutination and loss of infectivity. Reaction with antibodies can also result in the lysis of infectious microorganisms. In addition to forming antibodies, the immune response involves the appearance of specifically altered lymphoid cells, such as lymphocytes and macrophages, that phagocytize infecting microorganisms.

The stimulation of antibody formation by intentional exposure to antigens occurs as a result of vaccination (also called immunization). When a vertebrate animal is exposed to a foreign antigen for the first time, there is a primary immune response. The primary immune response is characterized by a relatively long lag period before the onset of antibody formation and by a relatively low production of antibody. Subsequent exposure to the same antigen results in a secondary, or memory, response, characterized by a much shorter lag period, a much higher level of antibodies, and greater specificity of the antigen-antibody reaction. The secondary response normally is triggered by a lower threshold dose of antigen than the primary response. The capacity to produce a secondary response can provide long-lasting immunity against infection.

The introduction of a pathogen with its associated antigens into an immune animal results in the rapid production of antibodies that react with the antigens to prevent the onset of disease. The ability to produce a secondary response varies with the particular antigens and with the physiological state of the host animal. Some antigens, such as the toxin produced by *Clostridium tetani,* evoke secondary responses even decades after primary exposure. Under conditions of physiological and metabolic stress, the immune response capability of the animal may be impaired, allowing invasion by pathogens and the development of disease.

Vaccination is used as a preventive measure against several human diseases including smallpox, diphtheria, tetanus, polio, measles, mumps, German measles, yellow fever, typhus fever, typhoid fever, paratyphoid fever, cholera, plague, influenza, pertussis, and tuberculosis. It is used also to prevent animal diseases, including rabies and distemper in dogs and cholera in hogs. Vaccines normally contain antigens as killed noninfectious pathogens or as live pathogens of attenuated virulence. Vaccination results in a modification of the host population by establishing the capability of the secondary or memory immune response, greatly increasing the resistance to the particular disease-causing microorganisms. If the pathogen has a narrow host range and all potentially exposed hosts can be rendered disease resistant by vaccination, the disease can be effectively eradicated. A well-coordinated campaign by the World Health Organization succeeded in the worldwide eradication of smallpox, eliminating the need for continued immunization.

In response to infecting pathogens, plants produce a variety of polycyclic and polyaromatic compounds, called *phytoalexins,* that have antimicrobial activities. Plants that have previously been exposed to invading microorganisms and have survived the infection retain such chemicals for a time, during which the plants have an increased resistance to infection by pathogenic microorganisms. Exposure to attenuated pathogens that cause only mild symptoms of disease can also induce such acquired systemic resistance (Deacon 1983).

In plants, a more specific resistance mechanism against infection by closely related viruses is cross protection. A plant systemically infected by one type of virus will not develop additional disease symptoms when challenged with a closely related second virus. This protection is always reciprocal among two related viruses. The phenomenon allows plant protection against some virulent viruses by an approach reminiscent of immunization, although the mechanism of protection differs from the animal immune response. Tobacco mosaic virus (TMV) causes, on the average, 15% loss of greenhouse-grown tomatoes. Deliberate infection of the tomato seedlings with an attenuated TMV mutant that causes an essentially symptomless infection provides protection against attack by virulent TMV. The inoculation process is fairly simple. Tomato plants infected with the mild TMV mutant are ground up, and the virus is enriched with differential centrifugation and sprayed in water suspension on the tomato seedlings. The spray also contains carborundum particles as an abrasive agent, inflicting on the leaves small wounds through which the virus can enter.

A similarly successful protection of citrus trees against the tristeza virus has been instituted in Brazil and Peru (Bettiol 1996). The citrus trees were inoculated with an attenuated virus mutant that arose naturally and was isolated from healthy-looking trees in badly affected orchards. The virus is systemic and easily transmitted through the grafting propagation of the infected trees. It provides satisfactory protection even in environments where wild strains of the tristeza virus and their aphid vectors pose a severe challenge.

The described successes have sparked additional research on cross protection of plants against viral infections. The mechanism of cross protection is not yet fully understood. A probable theory is that the single-stranded RNA genome of TMV and similar viruses acts in the early infection stage as messenger RNA and is the template for production of a replicase subunit. This replicase subunit combines with a host protein to form a functional replicase. The specificity of replicases makes it likely that the replicase produced by the mild virus will attach to the RNA of the infecting wild strain because of the similarity of the

two binding sites. However, the mutant-specific replicase is unable to replicate the wild-type virus RNA, thus aborting the infection process (Deacon 1983). Other theories on the mechanism of cross protection assume some type of interaction between the plant and coat proteins of the inducing and the pathogenic viruses. This theory gains experimental support from the fact that tobacco plants transformed to incorporate genetic information encoding for the coat protein of TMV acquired at least partial resistance against infection with virulent TMV (Abel et al. 1986). This type of genetic manipulation may become a powerful tool of plant protection against viral diseases.

## MODIFICATION
## OF RESERVOIRS OF PATHOGENS

Various control measures are used to eliminate or diminish reservoirs of pathogenic microorganisms. Many such procedures can be called sanitation practices and include sewage treatment and disinfection of drinking water supplies. These procedures reduce the reservoir populations of potential animal pathogens. Many practices involved in food processing and preparation are carried out to reduce the pathogens in food products. These practices include heat and filter sterilization and pasteurization. Disinfection of utensils used in food processing also removes a potential reservoir of pathogens. Similarly, instruments and materials used in medical and dental procedures are normally sterilized to remove possible pathogenic microorganisms. In horticultural practices, soils are sometimes fumigated or heat-sterilized to remove plant pathogens. Because many plant pathogens contaminate plant seeds, disinfection of seeds by chemical or hot-water treatments can greatly reduce the incidence of disease within a plant population.

Removal of infected plant or animal tissues is also used to control the spread of disease because it effectively reduces the reservoir of pathogens. In agricultural practice, this is often accomplished by crop rotation. The removal of the infected crop also removes the pathogens contained in infected tissues. The specificity of host-pathogen interactions precludes the establishment of infection by that pathogen in other crops used in a system of rotation. Given sufficient time, the infected tissues are eliminated from the soil and the pathogen population is greatly reduced. The reintroduction of the original plant species can then be accomplished without undue loss. When the reservoir of pathogens increases, the crops are again rotated (Batra 1982). Sometimes infested animal populations are killed. During the early 1990s, many cattle in Britain were killed in an attempt to control the spread of bovine spongioform encepholopathy (BSE).

For some diseases, control is achieved by eliminating the populations of animals or plants that act as alternate hosts for the pathogens. To this end, rodent control programs are aimed at reducing the reservoir of human pathogens associated with rodent populations. Elimination of rat populations by means as drastic as burning whole villages has been used historically to control outbreaks of bubonic plague, for which the rat population acts as a reservoir. The apparent association of histoplasmosis with infected bird roosts has been used as justification for blackbird eradication campaigns. Other control methods include the vaccination and population control of canines that may harbor the rabies virus transmittable to humans. Elimination of alternate hosts can also be used to control plant diseases. The economically important rust fungus, *Puccinia graminis,* which infects wheat, uses the barberry shrub, *Berberis vulgaris,* as an alternate host. Eliminating or reducing the population size of this alternate host can curtail the transmission of disease caused by this rust fungus (Moore-Landecker 1972).

Another procedure for controlling reservoirs of pathogenic microbial populations is the containment or elimination of infected organisms. Hobbyists who maintain tropical fish aquariums, as well as commercial plant and animal breeders, know well that infected organisms must be separated lest the pathogens or parasites spread from infected individuals to other members of the population. Quarantine regulations for human travelers, as well as for plant and animal shipments, are designed to prevent the unwitting introduction of pathogens and pests into areas that are normally free from such organisms.

## MODIFICATION OF VECTOR POPULATIONS

Programs designed to eliminate or reduce animal (usually insect) populations that transmit microbial pathogens are often used to control diseases that are spread in this manner (Laird 1978). A number of human diseases are transmitted by mosquito vectors; by controlling the population levels of mosquitoes, the incidence of these diseases can be greatly reduced. Mosquito populations can be controlled by using chemical insecticides, by biological control methods, and by habitat destruction. The tsetse fly, vector for the sleeping sickness caused by the flagellate *Trypanosoma,* requires moist jungle soil for larval development. Deforestation is an extreme but effective measure for controlling this vector. Less drastic actions, such as the elimination of stagnant water bodies required by mosquito larvae or the introduction of larva-eating fish species, decrease the reproduction and thus the population density of mosquito vectors.

Control of fleas and ticks is often achieved simultaneously with the control of animal reservoirs of pathogenic microbial populations. For example, elimination of rat populations also eliminates or greatly reduces populations of rat fleas. Some animals, such as monkeys, have developed grooming behavior that reduces the populations of tick and flea vectors of microbial pathogens. Humans use appropriate sanitary procedures to eliminate populations of body lice, which also may act as vectors for pathogenic microorganisms.

Insects and nematodes act as vectors for viral, bacterial, and fungal plant pathogens. Outbreaks of plant diseases that are transmitted by vectors can be avoided by appropriate vector control. Control of aphids is especially important because these organisms often act as vectors for various viral plant diseases.

## MICROBIAL AMENSALISM AND PARASITISM TO CONTROL MICROBIAL PATHOGENS

Attempts to utilize antagonistic relationships between microbial populations have been considered mainly to control plant pathogens. Although many plant diseases are caused by fungal and bacterial populations, microbial plant pathogens constitute only a small proportion of the microbes growing in the vicinity of plants. Many saprophytic microorganisms that occur in the rhizosphere and phyllosphere protect plants against pathogens, and this phenomenon may be used in plant protection. A variety of products have been developed, especially from *Streptomyces* species, that have amensal effects and that are useful in agricultural pest control (Table 16.1). These include antibiotics, such as streptomycin, that are effective against bacterial pathogens, and other substances, such as bilanafos, that are active against weeds. Bilanafos (bialaphos) has strong herbicidal activity against a wide range of weeds when foliage is treated (Duke et al. 1996; Yamaguchi 1996). The application rates are 1–3 kg per hectare, depending on the growth stage of the weeds and whether they are annuals or perennials. Bilanafos works by inhibiting the glutamine synthetase system in weeds, resulting in a deficiency of glutamine in the plant cells, as well as an abnormal accumulation of ammonia, known to be a strong uncoupler of photophosphorylation. It exerts potent herbicidal activity by foliage application but shows very weak phytotoxic activity toward vegetables when it is present in soils.

Microbial antagonism toward animal pathogens has been clearly demonstrated but does not offer the same possibilities for disease control as with plants. Autochthonous microbial populations on the skin surface and in the gastrointestinal tract are responsible for preventing infections by many potential pathogens. Germfree animals are much more susceptible to infectious disease than are animals with associated indigenous microbial populations. The

**Table 16.1**
Microbial agents produced by *Streptomyces* species and used in agriculture in Japan

| Substances | Source | Effective against |
| --- | --- | --- |
| **Antifungal** | | |
| Basticidin S | *Streptomyces griseochromogenes* | Rice blast |
| Kasugamycin | *Streptomyces kasugaensis* | Rice blast |
| Polyoxins | *Streptomyces cacaoi* var *asonensis* | Rice sheath blight, fungal diseases of fruit trees |
| Validamycin A | *Streptomyces hygroscopicus* | Rice sheath blight, fungal diseases of vegetables |
| Mildiomycin | *Streptomyces rimofaciens* | Powdery mildew of rose and crape myrtle |
| **Antibacterial** | | |
| Streptomycin | *Streptomyces griseus* | Bacterial diseases of fruit trees and vegetables |
| Dihydrostreptomycin | *Streptomyces griseus* | Bacterial diseases of fruit trees and vegetables |
| Oxytetracyclin | *Streptomyces rimosus* | Bacterial diseases of fruit trees and vegetables |
| **Insecticidal** | | |
| Polyactins | *Streptomyces aureus* | Mites of fruit trees and tea plants |
| Milbemectins | *Streptomyces hygroscopicus* | Mites of fruit trees and tea plants |
| **Herbicidal** | | |
| Bilanafos | *Streptomyces hygroscopicus* | Weeds in orchards and mulberry fields |

Source: Yamaguchi 1996.

widespread use of antibiotics in disease treatment threatens to diminish this natural antagonism of indigenous microorganisms against invading populations, including pathogens. Disruption of the normal microbiota can increase the host's susceptibility to invasion by opportunistic pathogens. Ensuring the maintenance of the normal indigenous microbial populations can reduce the opportunity for infection.

## Antifungal Amensalism and Parasitism

Amensalism is used to control plant pathogenic fungi. As an example, papaya *(Carica papaya)* grown in Hawaii, mainly on lava rock, is highly susceptible to root rot by *Phytophthora palmivora,* particularly in its seedling state. The porous and practically humus-free volcanic rubble has a rudimentary microbial community that offers no hindrance to the spread of *P. palmivora.* Losses from the root rot can be effectively controlled, however, by drilling small depressions, filling these with microbe-rich topsoil, and planting papaya seeds in the depressions. Antagonistic and competitive effects of the established microbial community toward *P. palmivora* slow down the spread of the pathogen and allow the seedlings to become established and disease resistant (Schroth and Hancock 1981). By stimulating the saprophytic segment of the microbial community, organic supplements added to the rhizosphere or to the soil in general often suppress the spread and infectivity of fungal plant pathogens. In so-called disease-suppressive soils, a poorly understood combination of physicochemical and biological factors limits the survival, spread, and infectivity of soilborne fungal plant pathogens (Baker 1980; Schroth and Hancock 1982). Soil fungistasis (see Chapter 9) is believed to be one of the many factors that contribute to the suppression of plant pathogens in some soils (Lockwood 1979).

Some bacterial species produce antifungal substances. Addition of some *Bacillus* and *Streptomyces* strains to soil or seeds has been shown to control plant disease caused by the fungus *Rhizoctonia solani,* which causes damping off disease, and several other plant diseases in cucumbers, peas, and lettuce. *Bacillus*

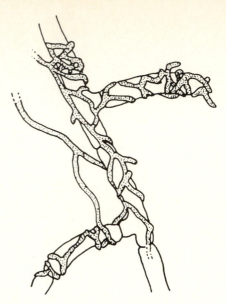

**Figure 16.1**
*Trichoderma* can coil its hyphae around the wider hyphae of the pathogenic fungus *Rhizoctonia solani*. (Source: Deacon 1983.)

*subtilis* also has been found to control stem rot and wilt of carnations caused by a *Fusarium* species (Schroth and Hancock 1981; Schroth et al. 1984).

Mycoparasitism of *Trichoderma harzianum* and *T. hamatum* on the soilborne plant pathogens *Botrytis cinerea, Sclerotium rolfsii,* and *Rhizoctonia solani* offers a possibility to control several economically important plant diseases caused by the latter fungi. The mycelium of *Trichoderma* winds around the mycelial strands of the plant pathogen (Figure 16.1) and, by lytic action, penetrates their cell wall. The cell contents of the plant pathogens are lysed and utilized by *Trichoderma.* It seems, however, that *Trichoderma* does not attack young, vigorously growing hyphae of the pathogens, but only stressed or senescent ones. This fact limits the effectiveness of the biological control (Henis 1983; Dubos 1984). Additional mycoparasitic relationships are being investigated for biological control of plant pathogens. Several strains of the fungus *Trichoderma* have been demonstrated to be effective biocontrol agents of various soilborne plant pathogenic fungi under greenhouse and field

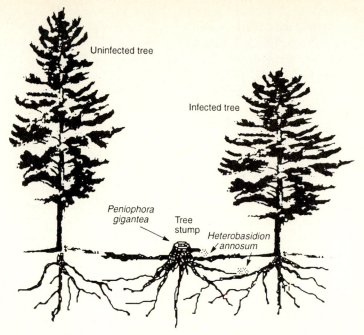

**Figure 16.2**

*Peniophora gigantea* prevents airborne spores of the pathogen *Heterobasidion annosum* from colonizing stumps of trees and traveling into the root zone. Once a population of *Peniophora* is established in the tree stump, it can restrict the spread of the pathogen from the stump to uninfected roots of adjacent trees. (Source: Deacon 1983.)

conditions (Chet and Inbar 1994; Bettiol 1996). Biochemical and molecular biology studies carried out to explore the mechanisms involved in biological control revealed that *Trichoderma* is a rather specific mycoparasite. Lectins were found to be involved in the recognition between *Trichoderma* and its host fungi, whereas chitinase is involved in the degradation of the host cell wall. Genetic engineering techniques were employed to increase the effectiveness, stability, and biocontrol capacity of *Trichoderma* species as well as other biocontrol agents, such as *Pseudomonas* species and *Rhizobium* species.

The basidiomycete *Laetisaria arvalis* shows control potential against the plant diseases caused by *Pythium ultimum* and *R. solani* (Schroth and Hancock 1981). The mechanism of control was identified as the production of 8-hydroxylinoleic acid (laetisaric acid) by *L. arvalis* (Bowers et al. 1986). By a mechanism not yet clearly identified, this compound induces rapid

lysis of *P. ultimum, R. solani, Fusarium solani,* and several additional plant pathogenic fungi. The simple chemical structure of this antibiotic lends itself to synthetic production and structural optimization for maximal potency.

*Heterobasidion annosum* (formerly *Fomes annosus*) is a basidiomycete that causes serious damage to managed forests, especially to pine trees, by causing butt and root rot (Deacon 1983). The infection occurs on the stumps of cut trees (Figure 16.2). Treatment of stumps with chemical agents did not succeed in eliminating the problem. *Peniophora gigantea,* a mildly parasitic basidiomycete, sometimes colonizes pine stumps naturally, and in such cases excludes *H. annosum.* This antagonistic action has been used to control *H. annosum* infection with spectacular success. A *P. gigantea* spore suspension, which is readily preserved in a concentrated sucrose solution, is painted on stumps of cut trees. It rapidly colonizes the cut stump and excludes *H. annosum. Peniophora gigantea* is not an aggressive pathogen and does not spread to the roots of healthy standing trees. The control measure is elegant, highly effective, and very economic. The mechanism of *H. annosum* exclusion by *P. gigantea* is termed *hyphal interference.* On making contact with *P. gigantea* hyphae, *H. annosum* stops growing, shows impaired membrane integrity, and degenerates. The effect is strictly localized to contact areas, and its biochemical basis is yet unknown.

Pruning of fruit trees often creates a portal of entry for fungal plant pathogens. Canker of apple trees, caused by *Nectria galligena,* and silver leaf disease of plum and other fruit trees, caused by *Stereum purpureum,* can be controlled by painting the pruning wounds with a spore suspension of *Trichoderma viride,* a highly antagonistic saprophyte. The dieback and gummosis disease of apricots, caused by the fungus *Eutypa armeniaceae,* can be controlled by painting pruning wounds with *Fusarium lateritium* spores. These control techniques are in various stages of development and have not yet been practiced extensively (Deacon 1983).

## Antibacterial Amensalism and Parasitism

Amensalism also plays a role in protecting plants against bacterial diseases. Agrocins, highly specific antibiotic-like substances with a killing effect on *Agrobacterium* strains closely related to the agrocin producer, are highly effective in controlling crown gall infections (Kerr and Tate 1984; Whipps and Lynch 1986). Agrocin 84 is a plasmid-encoded adenine nucleotide antimetabolite produced by certain strains of *A. radiobacter.* It selectively kills the pathogenic strains of *A. tumefaciens.* Its highly selective action depends on a permease encoded on the same *Ti* plasmid that is responsible for the pathogenic property of *A. tumefaciens.* Nearly 100% biological control of crown gall infection can be achieved by simply dipping seeds, cuttings, or roots of young plants into a suspension of an Agrocin 84-producing strain of *A. radiobacter.* Agrocin 84 is effective only against certain strains of *A. tumefaciens,* but fortunately the controlled strains are the most frequent pathogens. Other types of agrocins with different specificities have been found and are under investigation. Fluorescent pseudomonads produce fluorescent siderophores and antibiotics that inhibit the growth of plant root pathogens, making them potential biocontrol agents (O'Sullivan and O'Gara 1992).

## MICROBIAL PATHOGENS AND PREDATORS FOR CONTROLLING PEST POPULATIONS OF PLANTS AND ANIMALS

Populations of pathogenic or predatory microorganisms that are antagonistic toward particular pest populations provide a natural means of controlling population levels of pest animals and weeds. Preparations of antagonistic microbial populations are called *microbial pesticides.* The ideal microbial pesticide should not be subject to attack by hyperparasites; should be virulent, causing disease in the pest population when applied at the recommended concentration; should not be sensitive to moderate environmental variations; should survive following application until infection within the pest population has been established; should rapidly establish disease in the pest populations so as to minimize destruction by the pest population; should be rather specific for the pest population so as not to cause disease in nontarget populations.

The most spectacular successes in biological control of pests have been achieved when a pest has been accidentally introduced to a new environment—for example, a new continent (Batra 1982). In such accidental introductions, pests have frequently been separated from their parasite or predator control agents. In the new environment devoid of such control agents, their effect is often devastating. Identifying the control agents that kept them in balance at their place of origin and intentionally introducing those agents to the problem area often achieves a quick and economic solution to the pest problem. Several examples of such successes will be presented.

The biological control of a pest that is not a recent introduction and that has evolved in balance with its own parasites and predators is considerably more difficult. Such organisms become intolerable pests not because of an absolute absence of parasites or predators but because of environmental changes introduced by man. Changes such as monoculture may favor the pest and, at the same time, put its parasites and predators at a disadvantage. In such cases, one needs to modify the environmental conditions and agricultural production techniques rather than simply identify and introduce a biological control agent. Another important consideration in biological control is timing. Natural biological control mechanisms often eliminate pest populations only after they have reached very high densities and have inflicted unacceptable crop damage. The aim may be to activate biological control at a lower pest population level by hastening the outbreak of a disease before extensive damage to the crop occurs (Batra 1982).

## Microbial Control of Insect Pests

Microbial control methods have been developed for the suppression of arthropod pests, especially insects (Falcon 1971; Lipa 1971; McLaughlin 1971; Stairs 1971; David 1975; Weiser et al. 1976; Ferron 1978; Longworth and Kalmakoff 1978; Deacon 1983; Aronson et al. 1986). Several commercial microbial insecticides have been developed and marketed. Microbial suppression of insect populations is aimed at those that cause crop and other plant damage and at those that act as vectors of disease-causing microorganisms. Potentially, many viral, bacterial, fungal, and protozoan populations can be used in the control of insect pests and vectors.

**Viral Pesticides** Insect pathogenic viruses have the potential to become useful pesticidal agents (Krieg 1971; Stairs 1971; David 1975; Tinsley 1979; Deacon 1983). More than 450 viruses have been described from approximately 500 arthropod species. Insect pathogenic viruses frequently cause natural epizootics, the analog of epidemics applied to animals. Viruses pathogenic for insects are found in the families Baculoviridae, Poxviridae, Reoviridae, Iridoviridae, Parvoviridae, Picornaviridae, and Rhabdoviridae. Some of these are nuclear polyhedrosis viruses (NPV), cytoplasmic polyhedrosis viruses (CPV), and granulosis viruses (GV). Nuclear polyhedrosis viruses develop in the host cell nuclei; the virions are occluded singly or in groups in polyhedral inclusion bodies. Cytoplasmic polyhedrosis viruses develop only in the cytoplasm of host midgut epithelial cells; the virions are occluded singly in polyhedral inclusion bodies. Granulosis viruses develop in either the nucleus or the cytoplasm of host fat, tracheal, or epidermal cells; the virions are occluded singly or, rarely, in pairs in small occlusion bodies called *capsules.*

Baculoviruses are perhaps the most studied insect viruses. They include nuclear polyhedrosis and granulosis viruses. Pathogenic baculoviruses have been found principally for Lepidoptera, Hymenoptera, and Diptera. Infection is often transmitted by ingestion of contaminated food. Cell invasion probably begins in the midgut. Several nuclear polyhedrosis viruses are being produced on a large scale in the United States for control of insect pests. Lepidoptera and Hymenoptera larvae that feed on plant leaves are important pests that cause great economic loss. Inoculation of leaves with polyhedrosis viruses can initiate epizootics, resulting in decreases in pest populations. Many nuclear polyhedrosis viruses kill host larvae, releasing the polyhedra over the plant. The polyhedra remain infective for a long time. Nuclear polyhedrosis viruses have been used extensively in controlling pests of forest trees (Stairs 1972). Gypsy moths, tent caterpillars, and spruce budworms are subject to epizootics caused by nuclear polyhedrosis viruses.

Nuclear polyhedrosis viruses cause disease in sawflies. The accidental introduction of the European spruce sawfly *(Gilpinia hercyniae)* into North America in the twentieth century threatened the spruce forests of North America. Introduction of nuclear polyhedrosis viruses into the European spruce sawfly population caused a spectacular epizootic that reduced the sawfly populations and saved many spruce forests. Similarly, the European pine sawfly *(Neodiprion sertifer),* which was causing serious damage to pines in New Jersey, Ohio, and Michigan, has been controlled by introducing insects containing nuclear polyhedrosis viruses into the population, resulting in epizootics. Other sawfly populations have been subjected to similar controls.

The use of nuclear polyhedrosis viruses for biological control can be optimized by using bioreporters (Yu-Chan et al. 1996). The green fluorescent protein (GFP) introduced into the *Autographa californica* multiple nuclear polyhedrosis virus is useful for the biological control of lepidopterous pests. The baculovirus causes larval death, and the green fluorescence produced by GFP on excitation with light is used for the early detection of infected individuals among healthy larvae. GFP eliminates the need for molecular analysis to detect the presence of viruses in the larvae. Baculovirus containing similar GFPs can be used to predict the dispersal and presence of a virus that adversely affects the environment.

Virally induced infertility was proposed as a potential control measure against the economically important corn earworm *(Helicoverpa zea)* pest (Raina and Adams 1995). Infection by a newly described gonad-specific virus (GSV) resulted in sterile, agonadal (AG) adult moths of the corn earworm that failed to reproduce. The virus did not invade other body cells and did not kill either the larval or moth stages of the corn earworm. The virus appears to infect immature eggs in the female. Mature eggs are not infected, and the infection of larvae or adults becomes manifest only in their offspring. The release of infected but otherwise normal adults could be used to spread infertility in corn earworm populations, thus controlling their numbers. This technique has yet to be field-tested.

Viruses have been used in attempts to control outbreaks of a variety of pests, including gypsy moths, Douglas fir tussock moths, pine processionary caterpillars, red-banded leaf rollers (pest of apples, walnuts, and other deciduous fruits), Great Basin tent caterpillars, alfalfa caterpillars, white butterflies, cabbage loopers, cotton bollworms, corn earworms, tobacco budworms, tomato worms, army worms, wattle bagworms, and others. A few viruses cause diseases in mites (Lipa 1971; David 1975) (Figure 16.3). Mites cause extensive crop damage, for example, to European citrus fruits; control of these mite populations is of great economic importance (Gustafsson 1971).

**Bacterial Pesticides**   There are several bacterial pathogens of insects that currently are used as insecticides or that have potential for such use in the future (Aronson et al. 1986). They include *Rickettsiella popiliae, Bacillus popiliae, B. thuringiensis, B. lentimorbus, B. sphaericus, Clostridium malacosome, Pseudomonas aeruginosa,* and *Xenorhabdus nematophilus. B. thuringiensis* has many subspecies that

**Figure 16.3**
Photograph of a mite infected with a virus showing characteristic crystal inclusions (white spots). The crystals apparently result from metabolic disturbance and indicate the presence of infecting virus. (Source: Lipa 1971. Reprinted by permission, copyright Academic Press Ltd., London.)

differ in the number and type of plasmids they contain. The genetic information coding for the insecticidal toxins of these strains is borne on these plasmids.

*B. thuringiensis,* or BT as it is commonly known, is an important biological control agent used since the late 1960s for the control of lepidopteran target pests (Aronson et al. 1986; Porter et al. 1993). The insecticidal action of *B. thuringiensis* was first observed as the cause of the sotto disease in the silkworm *Bombyx mori* in 1901 and in the pupae of the flour moth *Anagasta kuehniella* in 1911 (Adams et al. 1996). The name *B. thuringiensis* comes from the German province Thüringen in which it was discovered. In 1957 Thuricide (a preparation of *B. thuringiensis*) was commercialized by Pacific Yeast Products as a biological control agent. The interest in biological control as an effective "green" technology for pest

**A**

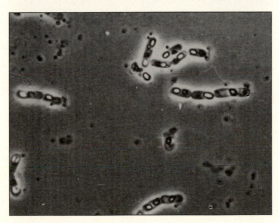

**B**

**Figure 16.4**

(A) Various commercial products containing *Bacillus thuringiensis*. (B) A micrograph of *B. thuringiensis* showing spores and parasporal inclusions of this broadly used, toxin-producing microbial pesticide. (Source A: Courtesy of Sandoz, Inc., San Diego. Source B: Courtesy of B. N. Herbert, Shell Research Ltd., Kent, England.)

control has led to a variety of research programs aimed at finding new strains of *B. thuringiensis* with different insecticidal activities. The worldwide market for BT insecticides was $60 million in 1991, and is estimated to reach $375 million a year by the year 2001. However, the current BT market is only 1% of the total insecticide market (Adams et al. 1996).

*B. thuringiensis* is called a crystalliferous bacterium because, in addition to endospores, it produces discrete parasporal bodies within the cell (Figure 16.4). Several toxic substances have been isolated from *B. thuringiensis* and are designated as either exotoxins

or endotoxins, the latter being responsible for most of the insecticidal activity (Aronson et al. 1986; Hurley et al. 1987; Hofte and Whiteley 1989; Porter et al. 1993). The endotoxins comprise the paracrystalline inclusion body. In most cases, this is located outside the exosporium; in a few strains, it is associated with the exosporium. The proteinaceous parasporal crystal is the toxic factor. Four separate toxic substances are produced by *B. thuringiensis*.

The main components of the paracrystalline inclusions are polypeptides 130 to 140 kilodaltons (kDa) in size. These molecules are termed *protoxins*. They are solubilized in the alkaline midgut of susceptible insect larvae, releasing an active toxin estimated to have a size of 30–80 kDa. The activation process is complex and necessary to bring about toxicity. Activated toxin binds to the convoluted brush border membranes of the columnar cells of the insect midgut epithelium. Binding of BT toxin affects osmoregulation and specifically alters the flux of potassium ions across the epithelium of the midgut. The $\omega$-endotoxins are a family of polypeptides showing some conserved (identical) and some variable portions. The variations determine specific activity against particular insect species. BT $\delta$-endotoxins are activated within the midgut of the insect by the action of alkaline proteases that cleave the protoxin to form the active toxic protein. The BT $\delta$-endotoxin is potently insecticidal, as demonstrated by effective $LC_{50}$s (the concentrations lethal to 50% of susceptible larvae) that are often as low as a fraction of a microgram per milliliter (less than 1 part per million) (Adams et al. 1996). Insects that consume BT $\delta$-endotoxins usually die within 3–5 days.

Since the introduction of *B. thuringiensis* as a biological control agent, there have been many investigations of the basis for toxicity and for strains that may have better biological control agents (Adams et al. 1996). Using *B. thuringiensis* is especially attractive for pest control in developing nations, particularly when it can be locally produced to avoid the economic drain of hard currency (Capalbo 1995). There is growing recognition that different strains of *B. thuringiensis* have different insecticidal activities toward a given insect pest. A standard BT preparation, called E-61, prepared from *B. thuringiensis* subspecies *thuringiensis* E-61 by the Pasteur Institute in Paris is used for

**Table 16.2**
Some registered uses for *Bacillus thuringiensis* products in the United States

| Pest | Plant |
| --- | --- |
| Alfalfa caterpillar *(Colias eurytheme)* | Alfalfa |
| Artichoke plume moth *(Platyptilia carduidactyla)* | Artichokes |
| Bollworm *(Heliothis zea)* | Cotton |
| Cabbage looper *(Trichoplusia ni)* | Beans, broccoli, cabbage, cauliflower, celery, collards, cotton, cucumbers, kale, lettuce, melons, potatoes, spinach, tobacco |
| Diamondback moth *(Plutella maculipennis)* | Cabbage |
| European corn borer *(Ostrinia nubilalis)* | Sweet corn |
| Imported cabbageworn *(Picris rapae)* | Broccoli, cabbage, cauliflower, collards, kale |
| Tobacco budworm *(Heliothis virescens)* | Tobacco |
| Tobacco hornworm *(Manduca sexta)* | Tobacco |
| Tomato hornworm *(Manduca quinquemaculata)* | Tomatoes |
| Fruit tree leaf roller *(Archips argyrospilus)* | Oranges |
| Orange dog *(Papilio cresphontes)* | Oranges |
| Grape leaf folder *(Desmia funeralis)* | Grapes |
| Great Basin tent caterpillar *(Malacosoma fragile)* | Apples |
| California oakworm *(Phryganidia californica)* | Oaks |
| Fall webworm *(Hyphantria cunea)* | Ailanthus, ash, roses, wisteria |
| Fall cankerworm *(Alsophila pometaria)* | Maple, elm |
| Gypsy moth *(Lymantria [Porthetria] dispar)* | Pine |
| Linden looper *(Erannis tiliaria)* | Linden |
| Spring cankerworm *(Paleacrita vernata)* | Maple, elm |

comparisons. In this way *B. thuringiensis* subspecies *kurstaki* has been found to have 200-fold better insecticidal activity against the cabbage looper *Trichoplusia ni,* the tobacco budworm *Heliothis virescens,* and the pink bollworm *Pectinophora gossypiella* than E-61. In 1970, Abbott Laboratories introduced Dipel, based on the subspecies *kurstaki.* This strain has been important for caterpillar control in the forestry and agricultural markets. Other commercially important variants of *B. thuringiensis* include the subspecies *israelensis,* which has activity against mosquitoes and black flies, and *tenebrionis,* which is active against beetle larvae. Several other subspecies of *B. thuringiensis* have been discovered with activity toward nematodes, ants, and fruit flies.

At least 12 manufacturers in five countries have commercially produced *B. thuringiensis* preparations for control of pest insects. These include Abbott, Ciba-Geigy, Ecogen, Mycogen, Novo Nordisk, Plant Genetic Systems, Sandoz, and Toa Gosei. There are currently 410 preparations of *B. thuringiensis* registered in the United States for use on many agricultural crops, forest trees, and ornamentals for control of various insect pests (Table 16.2), and it has been tested successfully against more than 140 insect species, primarily members of Lepidoptera and Diptera. Recent novel *B. thuringiensis* isolates have extended its utility to include the control of certain dipteran and coleopteran pest species. For the control of caterpillar larvae, the spore/toxin preparations of *B. thuringiensis*

**Table 16.3**
Commercial *Bacillus thuringiensis* (BT) products

| BT strain | Product | Target insect |
|---|---|---|
| *Bacillus thuringiensis* var. *aizawai* | Certan | Wax moth larvae |
| *Bacillus thuringiensis* var. *israelensis* | Vectobac-AS<br>Skeetal<br>Teknar | Mosquito and blackfly larvae |
| *Bacillus thuringiensis* var. *kurstaki* | Dipel<br>Bactospeine<br>Thuricide<br>Javelin | Lepidopteran larvae |
| *Bacillus thuringiensis* var. *san diego* | M-One | Colorado potato beetle larvae |

generally are applied at concentrations of 30–50 g per acre (Porter et al. 1993). The potency is about 300 times higher than synthetic pyrethroid chemical pesticides. The BT toxins are degraded within a few days and the spores of *B. thuringiensis* do not appear to have adverse effects on nontarget organisms.

As mentioned earlier, molecular genetic analyses of insecticidal activity have shown that the genes encoding *B. thuringiensis* insecticidal crystal proteins are most often carried by plasmids, certain of which have the ability to transfer via conjugation. Many toxin genes have been isolated and characterized with respect to their DNA sequence. These analyses have yielded important information regarding the diversity of *B. thuringiensis* toxin genes and set the stage for future gene structure and function studies.

Various commercial preparations of *B. thuringiensis* bring about acceptable suppression of various insect parasites of plants (Table 16.3). Additional targets of *B. thuringiensis* include cabbage worms and cabbage loopers, which damage vegetable crops, and tent caterpillars, bagworms, and cankerworms, which are pests of forest trees. Suppression of gypsy moths and spruce budworm can be achieved, but only when high application rates are used and uniform foliage coverage is achieved. The BT subspecies *kurstaki* and *israelensis* as well as *B. sphaericus* produce endotoxins that are effective against mosquitoes, including some that are malaria vectors. As the resistance of malaria vectors against conventional insecticides is

rapidly rising, an alternative strategy to control these mosquitoes is urgently needed.

Attempts are under way to improve *B. thuringiensis*-based bioinsecticides by changing the conventional formulation of *B. thuringiensis* crystal protein (Rowe and Margaritis 1987; Currier and Gawron-Burke 1990). This strategy involves altering the active ingredient, either the *B. thuringiensis* strain or the crystal protein, and/or changing aspects of the formulation itself. The ability to improve *B. thuringiensis* strains has been greatly aided by molecular genetics used to alter the genes responsible for insecticidal activity. The diversity of *B. thuringiensis*-toxin-encoding genes, especially as related to differences in insecticidal activity, coupled with the ability of certain toxin-encoding plasmids to conjugally transfer, provides the basis for the directed development of *B. thuringiensis* strains. Novel combinations of δ-endotoxin genes can be derived without the use of recombinant DNA techniques via selective plasmid curing and conjugal transfer. Selective plasmid curing to remove plasmids carrying toxin genes of low activity can yield strains that can be used as recipients in conjugal transfer. Conjugal transfer of toxin plasmids into partially cured derivatives can produce *B. thuringiensis* strains with elevated activities against specific insect pests as well as strains with a broader spectrum of insecticidal activity.

The other strategy is to use recombinant DNA technology to incorporate the genes encoding the toxins of *B. thuringiensis* directly into plant species or

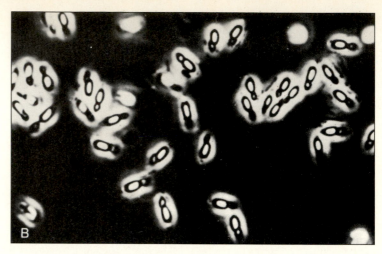

**Figure 16.5**
(A) A can of Doom. (B) A micrograph of *Bacillus popilliae,* one of the two active components in this microbial pesticide that is effective in controlling Japanese beetles. (Source A: Fairfax Laboratories, Clinton Corners, NY. Source B: Michael Klein, U.S. Department of Agriculture, Wooster, Ohio.)

rhizosphere microorganisms to afford them protection against insect parasites (Moffat 1991).

*Bacillus popilliae* and *B. lentimorbus* control Coleoptera such as the scarabid Japanese beetles, causing the "milky disease" of their larvae. The Japanese beetle feeds voraciously on some 300 species of plants and has been responsible for large economic losses. In Japan, the beetle encounters natural antagonists and is only a minor pest. In the United States, where the beetle does not have antagonists, good success in suppressing this pest has been obtained using bacteria that produce milky disease. For many years, spore dust containing *B. popilliae* and *B. lentimorbus* has been marketed under the trade name Doom (Figure 16.5). *B. lentimorbus* does not produce a parasporal body and infects mainly first- and second-instar grubs. Some strains of *B. popilliae* produce parasporal bodies and infect third-instar grubs. The use of these *Bacillus* species to produce milky disease in these grubs has been largely responsible for the control of Japanese beetle populations. Whereas in the past there have been major infestations of Japanese beetles in the United States, today there are relatively few. *B. popilliae* fails to form spores on artificial media; for production of spore powders, infected insects have to be ground up. Obtaining grubs, inoculating them, and subsequently

processing the infected grubs is a cumbersome and expensive process. However, *B. popilliae* spores survive in soil for years and provide long-lasting control. *B. popilliae* is ineffective against the adult beetle; thus, in severe infestations, short-term control of adults by chemical insecticides needs to be combined with long-term biological control of the larvae.

Among the nonsporulating bacterial pathogens of insects, *Pseudomonas aeruginosa* has received consideration, but problems have been associated with its use as an insecticide because it is an opportunistic pathogen capable of producing disease in humans. It also tends to infect only stressed or injured insects, has a very limited shelf life, and has only a short survival on exposed dry surfaces such as leaves and stems of plants. Other bacterial pathogens of arthropods occur among the Rickettsiae; rickettsial infections cause diseases in Coleoptera, Diptera, and Orthoptera, cause the blue disease of Japanese beetles, and cause diseases of grubs of the European chafer. Problems similar to those discussed in connection with *P. aeruginosa* have prevented their use in biological control.

**Protozoan Pesticides** Many protozoa are pathogens of arthropods, but for the most part, protozoa are not suited for use as short-term, quick-acting microbial

**Figure 16.6**
Scanning electron micrographs showing interaction of *Beauveria bassiana* and corn earworm. (A) First-instar corn earworm larva *(Heliothis zea)* with many setae (1) and spiracles (2). (B) Hyphae of poorly pathogenic mutant of *B. bassiana* growing errantly over the larval surface with little or no penetration of the larval integument. (C) Germinating conidia (c) and germ tubes (g) of *B. bassiana* penetrating the integument of a corn earworm larva. With highly pathogenic mutants, penetration occurs soon after germination. (D) Enzymatic degradation (arrow) of the larval integument by a penetrating germ tube of *B. bassiana*. (Source: E. Grula.)

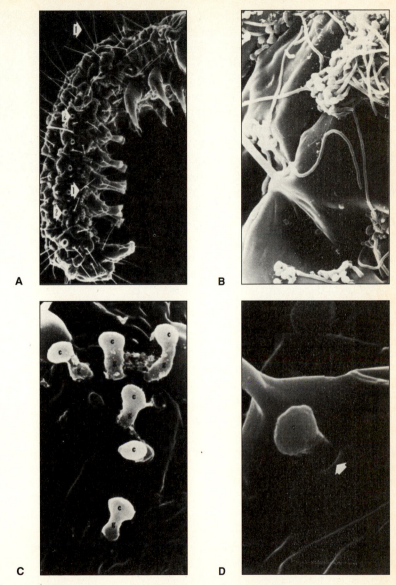

A    B

C    D

insecticides; few act with sufficient speed to prevent severe crop damage. Protozoa must be applied before outbreaks of disease to effect proper control. The relatively slow development of protozoan infections of pest animal populations—and difficulties with storage and environmental stability—limit the prospects of their use in biological control.

Few attempts have been made to use protozoa as a practical measure of pest suppression. There does appear to be some potential for use of protozoa on grasshoppers, mosquitoes, and boll weevils to augment other methods of controlling these pest populations. Some attempts have also been made to control lepidopteran pests of fruit trees using sporozoan protozoa (Pramer and Al-Rabiai 1973).

**Fungal Pesticides** Fungi are potentially important in the control of pest populations (Roberts and Yendol

1971; Ferron 1978; Deacon 1983; Howe 1990). Most studies on entomogenous fungi (fungi that live on insects) have been concerned with members of the fungal genera *Beauveria, Metarrhizium, Entomophthora,* and *Coelomomyces. Beauveria bassiana* was used extensively in the Soviet Union to control the eastward spread of the Colorado beetle and to control the codling moth. It also infects the corn earworm, a major pest in the United States (Figure 16.6).

There were several attempts to use the fungus *Entomophaga maimaiga* for the control of the gypsy moth, with mixed results (Carrington 1993). Early (1910–1911) attempts in Massachusetts seemed completely ineffective, yet many years later spectacular epizootics were caused by this fungus in the original release area. More recent (1989–1991) introductions in Michigan were partially successful. The degree of control seems to depend strongly on the weather. The successful sporulation and spread of the pathogen requires periods of 100% humidity.

Fungi of the genus *Aschersonia* were used to control pests of citrus trees in the Soviet Union near the Black Sea. In Florida, *Hirsutella* has been used against the citrus rust mite. The fungus *Metarrhizium* is used in Brazil to control populations of leaf hoppers and frog hoppers. Members of the genus *Entomophthora* show promise as pathogens of aphids. Some members of the genus *Coelomomyces* are pathogenic to the larvae of the mosquito populations of *Anopheles, Opifex,* and *Aedes.* Because these mosquitoes are important vectors for microbial pathogens of humans, control of these pests by fungal pathogens could become an important contribution to disease control. Similarly, several fungal species have been shown to produce diseases in mites, which also are important vectors for microbial diseases of humans.

## Microbial Control of Other Animal Pests

Microbial control of invertebrate animal populations other than insects has received less attention to date but may become important in the future. Some aquatic snails, for example, harbor important human pathogens, such as the causative agent of schistosomiasis. Some bacterial and protozoan populations are parasites of mollusks and may provide a mechanism for controlling these invertebrates (Steinhaus 1965).

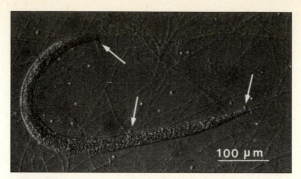

**Figure 16.7**
Nomarski interference micrograph of the nematode-trapping fungus *Dactylaria candida* showing the nematode captured by several adhesive knobs of the fungus, indicated by arrows. (Courtesy of S. Olson and B. Norbring-Herz, University of Lund.)

Predaceous nematode-trapping fungi have been suggested for the control of pest nematode populations in soils and animals (Pramer 1964; Pramer and Al-Rabiai 1973; Eren and Pramer 1978; Gronvold et al. 1993) (Figure 16.7). In Denmark two series of experiments have been performed to study the interactions between larvae of bovine gastrointestinal nematode parasites and nematode-trapping fungi (Gronvold et al. 1993). Laboratory tests with the fungus *Arthrobotrys oligospora* showed that motile free-dwelling larvae of a wide range of animal-parasitic nematodes and some soil-living nematodes effectively induce the formation of traps. Larvae of all parasitic nematodes are rapidly captured in these traps. The induction of traps was influenced by temperature, number of larvae, atmosphere, light, and media composition. Captured first- and second-stage larvae were quickly penetrated and killed, but third-stage larvae were killed more slowly, perhaps because they are partially protected by an outer sheath. Laboratory and field studies showed that when *A. oligospora* material was directly mixed into dung, a significant reduction in the number of infective parasite larvae in the dung and in the surrounding plants occurs. This reduction was also reflected in the acquired worm burden of calves grazing on the pasture treated by the fungus. However, the *A. oligospora* strain under study did not survive passage through the alimentary tract of cattle. This prompted a second series of experiments to isolate

## Biological Control of Rabbits

Microorganisms have been used in several attempts to control pest populations of rabbits. The beginnings of this idea can be traced to Louis Pasteur, who demonstrated that *Pasteurella multocida* was capable of killing wild rabbits when they ate contaminated cut alfalfa. After European rabbits *(Oryctolagus cuniculus)* were introduced into Australia in 1859, they rapidly became serious pests because they lacked natural enemies and proliferated without control. Pasteur sent *P. multocida* to Australia to be used in a campaign to control rabbit populations, but the program was never initiated. Rabbits were also significant agricultural pests in some regions of Europe.

After a chance observation in Uruguay that imported European rabbits were wiped out by a disease caused by the myxoma virus (Poxviridae), to which the native South American rabbit *(Sylvilagus brasiliensis)* was resistant due to coevolution, the disease was deliberately imported to a walled estate in France. In spite of precautions, the disease escaped containment and in a few years swept through Europe, severely decimating rabbit populations. Transmission of the virus depends on insect vectors; in Europe, the rabbit flea served as the principal vector. By the late 1950s, however, the evolution of attenuated virus strains and increasing immunity allowed a gradual recovery of the rabbit population in Europe.

Because of the severity of the rabbit problem in Australia, myxomatosis was deliberately introduced there in the early 1950s. In Australia the disease was spread primarily by mosquito vectors, and the initial mortality of infected rabbits was 99.4–99.8%. Because of lower genetic heterogeneity or other, unknown reasons, control in

Australia was more persistent than in Europe, and in 1970 the rabbit population was only 1 percent of the 1950 level (Deacon 1983). The virulence of the myxoma virus for the surviving rabbits, however, subsequently declined. The survivors of the initial epidemics had been selected for their resistance to the virus. The resistance of the rabbits is innate and is not due to an immunological defense system. Thus, within a few decades, an equilibrium was achieved between the virus and the Australian rabbits. Myxomatosis was effective in lowering the Australian rabbit population to about 20% of its level before the introduction of the virus. However, the introduction of the myxoma virus did not completely eliminate the rabbits, as was originally envisioned. Rather, after killing 99% of the rabbits in Australia, some rabbits developed resistance. Later the virus mutated into a less virulent form and the mortality rate from infection dropped to 40%; the rabbit population rebounded (Morell 1993).

Other means of biological control using genetically engineered myxoma viruses have been explored to further reduce the rabbit populations of Australia. Myxoma viruses have been genetically engineered that will reduce the fertility of rabbits without killing them (Morell 1993; Holland and Jackson 1994; Robinson and Holland 1995). Such an approach is likely to exert less selective pressure for resistance in the rabbits and at the same time has great potential for limiting rabbit population size in Australia. Such deliberate releases of genetically engineered microorganisms are controversial. There are some who fear that once released, the genetically engineered virus cannot be contained and that it might reach Europe, where it could devastate the rabbit populations. The

*(continued)*

## Biological Control of Rabbits, continued

genetically engineered virus proposed for controlling the Australian rabbits was formed by inserting a gene for a rabbit sperm protein into the virus. Replication of the genetically engineered virus within a female rabbit would release sperm protein so that the female rabbit would develop "immunity" to male sperm. The female rabbit would produce antibodies against the male sperm protein. The antibodies of an "immune" female rabbit would attack male sperm so that reproduction could not occur. It would also work on foxes, another major problem in Australia. In essence the genetically engineered virus would act as a contraceptive. This is a novel means of biological control with a genetically engineered microorganism and represents an interesting means of achieving biological control.

Yet another approach for controlling the Australian rabbit population involves a rabbit calcivirus (rabbit hemorrhagic virus) from China. This virus kills rabbits within 40 hours of infection. The rabbits hemorrhage and die from heart and lung failure. The virulence of this virus led scientists to postulate that it would be more effective at reducing the rabbit population than myxoma virus. Experiments were being conducted on Wardang Island off the coast of Australia to determine the efficacy and to evaluate the safety of using calcivirus to control Australian rabbits (Drollette 1996; Masod 1995). The experiment began in March 1995 and involved introducing the rabbit calcivirus into the rabbits on the island. Great precautions were taken to ensure that the virus was restricted to the island. However, shortly after many rabbits died of rabbit hemorrhagic fever in September 1995, winds blew bushflies from the island to the mainland. Some of the bushflies carried the rabbit calcivirus to the mainland by October 1995; the bushflies had apparently acquired them by feeding on the rabbits that had died of rabbit hemorrhagic fever. Almost immediately, tens of thousands of rabbits on the mainland started dying, including those that were being reared for commercial purposes. Well over 1 million rabbits had died by the beginning of 1996. Amid controversy, the Australian government has announced plans to release additional calciviruses on the mainland to increase the epidemic and to control the rabbit population that currently is causing $100 million per year in losses to the wool and meat industries and is bringing about the erosion of millions of acres of topsoil.

---

fungi that could survive the passage through the gut of cattle. Different soil and compost samples were screened by an *in vitro* stress selection technique. This simulated certain important stress factors that occur during passage through the alimentary tract of ruminants. Rumen exposure was found to be a major limiting factor, but some *Arthrobotrys* and *Duddingtonia* strains survived submersion in rumen fluid. In a subsequent *in vivo* experiment, some of these survivors were fed to calves, and it was demonstrated that isolates of *Arthrobotrys* and *Duddingtonia* were able to survive passage through calves and significantly reduce the number of developing preparasitic larvae in the dung of those calves. In a controlled field experiment, isolates of *Duddingtonia* reduced the level of infective third-stage larvae in the pasture by 74–85%.

Nematode-trapping fungi have been used in attempts to control root knot disease of pineapples in Hawaii. Successful control was achieved, but it depended on supplementing the soil with organic matter. It is not clear whether control of the nematodes was due to the predaceous fungi or to an alteration in food web relationships caused by the addition of organic supplements. Subsequent attempts to demonstrate that nematode-trapping fungi rather than soil supplements were primarily responsible for controlling nematode populations in soil had ambiguous results. Under appropriate conditions, nematode-trapping fungi, together with supplemental organic matter, appear to have the potential for diminishing the effects of nematodes on susceptible plant populations. Other possibilities for controlling pest nematodes include infection with parasitic fungi, protozoa, bacteria, and viruses.

## Microbial Control of Weeds and Cyanobacterial Blooms

Although much of the work concerning the use of microorganisms as pesticides has been aimed at insect and other animal pest populations, some studies have been aimed at the potential use of plant pathogenic microorganisms to control weeds (Charudattan 1975; Andres et al. 1976). Such pathogenic microbial populations can be called *microbial herbicides*. Studies to develop microbial herbicides for important agricultural weeds have lagged behind studies on microbial insecticides. In part, this may have been due to the experiences of plant pathologists with the accidental introduction of pathogens that destroyed important crops, such as the chestnut blight in the United States and the potato blight in Ireland. There have been understandable safety concerns and a reluctance on the part of investigators to develop microbial herbicides lest they introduce pathogens that might cause catastrophic economical or ecological losses.

There are, however, some precedents in which the accidental or intentional introduction of microbial pathogens resulted in the biological control of terrestrial weeds. In Australia, bathurst burr was successfully attacked by *Colletotrichum xanthii*. Crofton weed, also in Australia, has been attacked by a leaf spot disease. It appears that the pathogen *Cercospora eupatorii* was accidentally introduced with a gallfly imported from Hawaii for the control of this weed. Crofton weed is now held in check by the leaf spot disease and by a native beetle. The rust fungus *Puccinia chondrillina* has been introduced into Australia to control brush skeleton weed; the fungus has spread rapidly and appears to have been effective (Hasan 1974). The choice of *P. chondrillina* was based on the observation that in the western Mediterranean this fungus is more effective in reducing skeleton weed than associated arthropod grazers. Similar studies have demonstrated that powdery mildews can also be used to control skeleton weed. In the Soviet Union, *Alternaria cuscutacidae* was used to control weeds in alfalfa fields. In Europe, *Uromyces rumicis* has been used to control curly dock. On the experimental scale, the indigenous rust fungus *P. caniculata* has been shown to effectively control the yellow nutsedge, which causes a serious weed problem in the United States (Phatak et al. 1983). The control system has good potential for herbicidal use but needs further development and safety testing. Several aquatic weeds, such as water hyacinth, hydrilla, alligator weed, and water milfoil, pose important problems in the southeastern United States by choking waterways and irrigation canals. These weeds are subject to infections by pathogenic microorganisms. Various fungal, bacterial, and viral populations have been examined for their abilities to control aquatic weeds (Wilson 1969; Zettler and Freeman 1972).

In freshwater ponds and lakes, cyanobacteria are frequently the dominant component of destructive algal blooms. In addition to their basic sequence of bloom, die-off, and oxygen depletion, which results in septic odors and fish kills, some cyanobacteria, such as *Anabaena flos-aquae,* form potent neurotoxins (Carmichael et al. 1975; Falconer 1993). These may cause respiratory arrest and rapid death in livestock and waterfowl that drink the water during the cyanobacterial bloom. Cyanobacteria are subject to viral and fungal infections and also to bacterial lysis; cyanophages are similar to other bacteriophages both in their morphology and in their life cycle and are believed to be an important factor in the natural control of cyanobacterial population densities. Various chitrids (Phycomycetes) are parasitic on cyanobacteria; aquatic myxobacteria are also capable of lysing cyanobacteria. All microbial antagonists to cyanobacteria, especially the cyanophages, are receiving considerable attention as potential control agents of cyanobacterial blooms (Stewart and Daff 1977).

## Bacterial Control of Dutch Elm Disease

Dutch elm disease has had devastating effects on millions of elm trees in Europe and North America. It is caused by the fungus *Ceratocystis ulmi* and transmitted by beetle vectors. Transmission of the disease is directly related to the distribution of the beetle vectors. Control of Dutch elm disease may be achieved by quarantine and by eliminating the beetle vectors. It may also be controlled by the bacterium *Pseudomonas syringae* (Strobel and Lanier 1981). So far thousands of trees across the United States and Canada have been treated with *P. syringae*.

In one set of experiments, cultures of *P. syringae* were administered to elm seedlings and after 2 weeks the trees were inoculated with a pathogenic culture of *C. ulmi.* When the trees were examined 8 weeks later, none of the trees treated with the bacteria showed symptoms of Dutch elm disease. Control trees exposed to the fungus alone or treated with bacteria that do not produce antimycotics all exhibited symptoms of the disease. The effectiveness of *P. syringae* in disease control seems to be related to the ability of the bacterium to make antimycotics, because a mutant that does not synthesize them was completely ineffective in controlling the disease.

The biological treatment of mature diseased trees in the field has also shown some promise. In one experiment, 22 diseased trees were treated with the bacteria and an equal number of diseased trees were left untreated as controls. All the control trees but one either died or declined drastically in the course of two growing seasons. In the treated group, seven of the eight trees that were lightly infected and were treated early in the growing season survived with little or no sign of decline over two growing seasons. The other treated trees that either were treated later in the season or were more heavily infected died or declined. The treatment is most successful if it is done early in the season during the time of maximum sap flow in the tree. Three of the treated trees had apparently made a complete recovery, as shown by the fact that it was not possible to reisolate *C. ulmi* from them.

## GENETIC ENGINEERING IN BIOLOGICAL CONTROL

Genetics has always played an important role in biological control, but the deliberate release of genetically engineered microorganisms is scientifically controversial because of possible undesirable ecological effects (Halvorson et al. 1985; Wilson and Lindow 1993; Hokkanen and Lynch 1995). Plants and animals have been bred and selected for disease resistance, pathogenic viruses have been mutated to obtain attenuated strains for cross protection or immunization, and biological control agents have been mutated and selected for enhanced virulence and toxin production. Examples of such manipulations were presented in the preceding sections. *In vitro* genetic engineering has broadened the possibilities for custom-designing biological control agents but has also unleashed unprecedented controversy over whether these possibilities should be utilized (Maramorosch 1991; Hokkanen and Lynch 1995). Advances in the genetic engineering of plants have allowed the development of agronomically important traits, such as herbicide, insect, and viral resistances (Copping 1996). These have occurred

**Table 16.4**
Genetic basis for resistance to microbial pathogens and pests in transgenic plants

| Plant species | Cloned genes | Defense mechanism |
|---|---|---|
| *Phaseolus* (bean) | Phenylalanine ammonia lyase | Phenylopropenoid phytoalexin biosynthesis |
| | Chalcone synthase | Phenylopropenoid phytoalexin biosynthesis |
| | Chalcone isomerase | Phenylopropenoid phytoalexin biosynthesis |
| | Chitinase | Hydrolytic enzyme that degrades cell walls of fungal pathogens |
| | Cinnamyl alcohol dehydrogenase | Increases synthesis of plant cell walls to create a thicker layer through which a pathogen or pest must penetrate to cause plant disease |
| *Petroselinum* | Phenylalanine ammonia lyase | Phenylopropenoid phytoalexin biosynthesis |
| | Coummarate CoA lyase | Phenylopropenoid phytoalexin biosynthesis |
| | Chalcone synthase | Phenylopropenoid phytoalexin biosynthesis |
| *Arachis* | Reversatrol synthase | Phenylopropenoid phytoalexin biosynthesis |
| *Lycopersicon* | 3-Hydroxy-3-methylglutaryl CoA reductase | Terpenoid phytoalexin biosynthesis |
| *Ricinus* | Casbene synthetase | Terpenoid phytoalexin biosynthesis |
| *Nicotiana* | Lignin-forming peroxidase | Increases synthesis of plant cell walls to create a thicker layer through which a pathogen or pest must penetrate to cause plant disease |
| | Gluconase | Hydrolytic enzyme that degrades cell walls of fungal pathogens |
| | Chitinase | Hydrolytic enzyme that degrades cell walls of fungal pathogens |

by the transfer of single dominant genes into plants. Such strategies could be applied to achieve plant protection against bacterial and fungal diseases.

Transgenic plants have been engineered to increase their defenses against microbial pests and pathogens (Hokkanen and Lynch 1995) (Table 16.4). For example, the genes for phytoalexins, which are produced by varieties of soybean, pea, and tomato in response to microbial infections, have been introduced into transgenic plants to protect them against various fungal infections. Agricultural use of such transgenic plants could reduce reliance on chemical fungicides for control of fungal pathogens. Some of the genes that have been introduced into transgenic plants code for hydrolytic enzymes that attack the cell walls of microbial pathogens. For example, chitinases cloned into plants are protective against various fungal infections because many fungi contain chitin in their cell walls. In other cases, protection of the plant against disease or pest damage is based on the thickness of the cell wall. Some plants produce calluses that are too thick for pests or pathogens to penetrate. Genes coding for synthesis of additional cell wall components have been introduced into some transgenic plants, making them more resistant to disease. Other defenses, collectively called *pathogen-related defenses,* are based on the production of proteins whose functions have yet to be determined. In some cases these proteins probably block biosynthetic or other essential metabolic activities that are necessary for a pathogen or pest to cause plant damage or disease.

Some of the genes that have been introduced into transgenic plants make them more resistant to viral, fungal, and bacterial infections. Transgenic tobacco and tomato plants with viral resistance have been engineered in this manner by incorporating genes for viral coats into the plant chromosome; the mechanism by which expression of viral coat protein protects against viral infections is not known. Resistant transgenic plants have also been created by introducing genes in inverted orientations so that they produce antisense mRNAs, that is, RNAs that have a sequence the reverse of the normal mRNA for a specific gene necessary for the pathogenicity of a plant virus or the deleterious effect of other plant pests. Transgenic tobacco and tomato plants have been created that have increased resistance to insects based on the introduction of a toxin gene from the bacterium *Bacillus thuringiensis* or a proteinase inhibitor from a cowpea plant. Expression of these genes protects the plants against various insect pests.

There are legitimate ecological concerns about unforeseen and perhaps unforeseeable side effects the environmental release of such organisms might cause (Halvorson et al. 1985). Some groups have also raised objections to genetic engineering and the release of engineered organisms on philosophical, ethical, and religious grounds, but, for broader appeal, these are often presented in the context of safety concerns. It is important to differentiate in this debate legitimate ecological concerns from deliberate obstructionism. Following are some examples of engineered biological control agents that were tested only after prolonged controversy. Others, except for the described controversy, would be ready now for field testing. The EPA and other regulatory authorities have implemented extensive review processes to ensure the safety of deliberate releases of recombinant microorganisms (Milewski 1990).

## Frost Protection

Freezing weather in spring and fall can cause extensive damage to nonhardy agricultural crops. Damage is not from the low temperature per se but from formation of ice crystals that disrupt cell membranes. In the absence of ice-nucleating agents, water can be cooled several degrees below 0°C without freezing. The most important ice-nucleating agents on leaf surfaces are cells of *Pseudomonas syringae,* a pseudomonad pathogenic to lilacs but a harmless commensal epiphyte for most other plants, except for its ice-nucleating activity in freezing weather (Lindow 1983, 1988a). The ice-nucleating factor in this bacterium appears to be a membrane-bound proteinaceous substance. The DNA sequences coding for the ice-nucleating agent have been identified and partially characterized by cloning procedures. Deletion (*ice⁻*) mutants were prepared by site-directed *in vitro* excision and ligation of the DNA (Lindow 1985). They appear to correspond in every respect to the wild strain, except for a lack of ice-nucleating activity.

A biological control strategy has been developed for reducing frost damage. This strategy is based on competition between populations that help initiate ice nucleation and those that do not (Figure 16.8). Treating leaves to reduce the population sizes of ice-nucleating bacteria reduces the incidence of frost injury to plants (Lindow 1985, 1987, 1988b, 1990). Bactericides that reduce population sizes of *P. syringae* enhance protection against frost damage. Non-ice-nucleating bacteria also reduce the incidence of freezing injury (Lindow 1990). A strain of naturally occurring *Pseudomonas fluorescens,* for example, has been registered commercially as Frostban B for the protection of pear trees (Wilson and Lindow 1993). Non-ice-nucleating bacteria (*ice⁻* bacteria) can act as biological control agents to prevent frost injury to plants. The *ice⁻* bacteria prevent the growth of wild *P. syringae* strains on plants but do not kill or displace these strains once they are established on plants. Competitive exclusion of *ice⁺ P. syringae* strains has been reported on plants only when the population size of *ice⁻* strains was at least $10^5$ cells per gram of plant (Lindow 1990).

It has been shown in laboratory and greenhouse-scale experiments that spraying young plants with suspensions of the *ice⁻ P. syringae* mutant preempts subsequent colonization by the wild strain, preventing ice

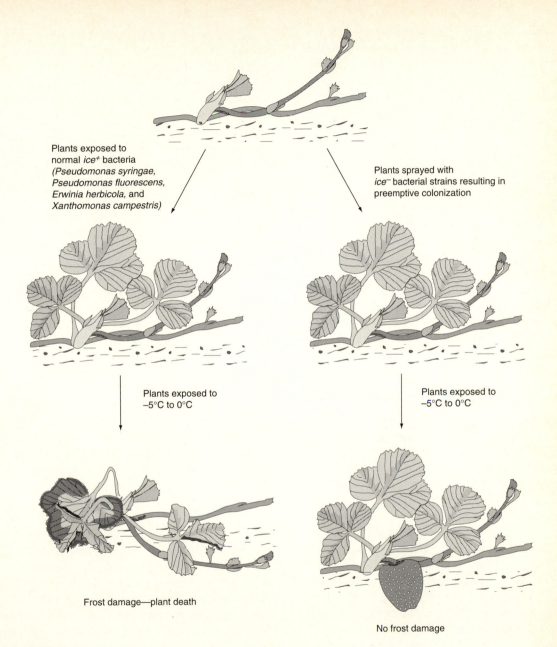

Plants exposed to normal *ice⁺* bacteria (*Pseudomonas syringae, Pseudomonas fluorescens, Erwinia herbicola*, and *Xanthomonas campestris*)

Plants sprayed with *ice⁻* bacterial strains resulting in preemptive colonization

Plants exposed to −5°C to 0°C

Plants exposed to −5°C to 0°C

Frost damage—plant death

No frost damage

### Figure 16.8

Preemptive colonization of the leaves of strawberries and other plants with ice-minus strains of *Pseudomonas syringae* can lead to protection against frost damage. The colonization of the phylloplane by the ice-minus bacteria prevents invasion by bacteria that produce peptides involved in ice nucleation at low temperatures. This biological control can protect against frost damage at temperatures 5°C lower than those tolerated by untreated plants

nucleation and crop damage in subfreezing weather. The mutant shows no detectable differences from the wild strain except for its lack of ice-nucleating activity. After great controversy and repeated delays, field trials using this engineered microorganism were finally approved.

Initial field trials of *ice⁻ P. syringae* strains applied to strawberries and potatoes were carefully designed and intensively monitored to restrict and to detect the dissemination of recombinant strains. Limited dispersal of recombinant *ice⁻ P. syringae* strains was detected in field trials (Lindow and Panopoulos 1988). *Ice⁻ P. syringae* strains inoculated onto potato plants were a significant part of the total epiphytic microflora for 4–6 weeks. The population size of *ice⁺ P. syringae* strains on plants colonized by *ice⁻ P. syringae* strains was significantly decreased compared to that on uninoculated control plants (Lindow 1990). The incidence of frost injury was significantly lower to potato plants inoculated with *ice⁻ P. syringae* strains than to uninoculated control plants in several natural field frost events that occurred in the field in a northern California test site.

## *Bacillus thuringiensis* Pesticides

The potency of δ-endotoxin in *Bacillus thuringiensis* (BT) against lepidopteran insects was described earlier. *B. thuringiensis* toxin genes have been introduced via recombinant DNA technology into the genome of plants or plant-associated microorganisms (Adang et al. 1987; Currier and Gawron-Burke 1990). When specific promoters are used that allow toxin gene expression in the plant or plant-associated microorganism, insect control can be achieved in laboratory tests. *B. thuringiensis* toxin genes have been introduced into tobacco plants, tomato plants, cotton plants, and a rhizosphere-colonizing pseudomonad.

A group of scientists at Monsanto Agricultural Products Company in St. Louis, Missouri, undertook to transfer the genetic information coding for δ-endotoxin formation from *B. thuringiensis* variety *kurstaki* to a bacterium that would readily colonize the rhizosphere and could be used as seed inoculant (Watrud et al. 1985). Microbial transformation for agricultural

use involves introducing the *cryIAc* genes of *B. thuringiensis* (Adams et al. 1996). (The *cry* designation refers to the specific gene that actually encodes the crystal protein possessing insecticidal activity.) If expressed, the δ-endotoxin would confer resistance of the crop plants against lepidopteran pests. By *in vitro* genetic engineering techniques, the portion of the *B. thuringiensis* plasmid coding for formation of δ-endotoxin was first ligated into an *Escherichia coli* plasmid. Subsequently, the δ-endotoxin genes were transferred to *Pseudomonas fluorescens,* which commonly inhabits the rhizosphere of corn. The genes were expressed, and δ-endotoxin was formed. In feeding trials, the efficacy and action spectrum of the δ-endotoxin formed by the engineered *P. fluorescens* was identical to that of *B. thuringiensis* subspecies *kurstaki*. Growth chamber and greenhouse experiments demonstrated the capacity of the engineered *P. fluorescens* to protect, as seed inoculant, the plants from lepidopteran target pests with no side effects on nontarget insects such as bees.

Mycogen optimized the process further in a patented system called CellCap, which was the first genetically engineered microorganism for agricultural use to receive registration in the United States (Adams et al. 1996). In this process, the *P. fluorescens* host expressing the BT gene is treated with cross-linking agents to fortify the bacterial cell wall. In field trials, the encapsulation process reportedly lengthened the residual activity of the crystals contained within the cells. Another interesting delivery method is the introduction of the BT gene into the bacterial endophyte *Clavibacter xyli* that can be inoculated into a wild-type corn plant. The corn plant is protected from insects in much the same way as if it had been transformed directly with genes from *B. thuringiensis*.

Plant transformation with genes from *B. thuringiensis* has been a much more difficult process, requiring the ability to regenerate whole plants from single cell transformants (Adams et al. 1996). This technology was first reported in 1985 and is widely used today by a number of companies including Agrigenetics, Calgene, Ciba-Geigy, Zeneca, Monsanto, Pioneer Seed, Plant Genetics Systems, and others. Expression of the toxin in plants and field efficacy have been greatly improved by tailoring of the bacterial genetic codons to ones resembling those preferred by the plant.

Various concerns have been raised about the persistence of the toxin and the potential transfer of the genes to nontarget organisms. Tapp and Stotzky (1995a) reported that the release of transgenic plants and microorganisms expressing truncated genes from various subspecies of *B. thuringiensis* that encode active insecticidal toxins rather than inactive protoxins can result in the accumulation of those active proteins in soil, especially when bound on clays and other soil particles. They showed that toxins from two *B. thuringiensis* subspecies *kurstaki* and *tenebrionis,* either free or adsorbed on the clay fraction of soil, were toxic to larvae of the tobacco hornworm *Manduca sexta* and the Colorado potato beetle *Leptinotarsa decemlineata*. The 50% lethal concentrations ($LC_{50}$) of free toxins from *B. thuringiensis* subspecies *kurstaki* were higher than those of their adsorbed complexes on clays, indicating that adsorption of these toxins on clays increases their toxicity in diet bioassays. Clay and the strength of the binding were of influence, but surprisingly, the results indicated that the insecticidal activity of these toxins is retained and sometimes enhanced by adsorption and binding on clays.

To monitor the fate of bound BT toxins in soil, Tapp and Stotzky (1995b) used a dot blot enzyme-linked immunosorbent assay (ELISA) that detected free and particle-bound toxins from *B. thuringiensis* subspecies *kurstaki* and *tenebrionis*. The toxins that were added to sterile and nonsterile soil were detected on the clay-particle-size fraction of the soil after various periods of incubation, but no toxins were detected on the silt- and sand-particle-size fractions. The toxins were still detectable on the clay-particle-size fraction of nonsterile soil after 40 days. This agreed with preliminary results of other studies in this laboratory that when these toxins bind on clay minerals, they become resistant to utilization by microorganisms.

Bacteria of the *Xenorhabdus* and *Photorhadbus* genera associate with the entomopathogenic (insect-pathogenic) nematode *Steinerma* and *Heterorhabditis* species, respectively, in a complex symbiotic manner (Forst and Nealson 1996). This association has poten-

tial for the biological control of various soilborne insect pest larvae (Gaugler and Kaya 1990). *Steinerma* carries *Xenorhabdus* in special vesicles, and *Heterorhabditis* harbors *Photorhabdus* in its gut. The entomopathogenic nematodes enter the digestive tract of various susceptible insect larvae, penetrate the wall of the gut, and enter the hemocele (circulatory system) of the larvae. Here they release the harbored bacteria into the hemolymph (blood) of the insect. The bacteria proliferate rapidly, and by releasing toxic proteins and lytic enzymes they quickly kill the insect larvae. Both the bacteria and the nematodes digest the larval tissues, but the nematodes also feed on the bacteria and digest many of them. The bacteria produce a range of antibiotics that prevent other microorganisms from participating in degradation of the larval carcass. After the digestion of the larva is completed, the nematodes stop feeding on *Xenorhabdus* and *Photorhabdus* and reassociate with these bacteria, forming a new infective stage. A new larva is infected and the cycle repeats. The relationship of the nematodes with the bacteria is largely mutualistic: The nematodes serve as vectors to infect the insect larvae with the bacteria, and the nematodes benefit from the bacteria killing and digesting the insect larva because they feed on both the insect tissue and the bacteria proliferating in it. Together, the nematodes and bacteria form a parasitic-predatory association highly destructive for soilborne insect larvae. These symbiotic-pathogenic associations have been described since the early 1980s, and much remains to be learned about them.

## Other Applications

In addition to the examples described so far, genetic engineering could make other useful contributions to biological control. There is little doubt that genetically engineered biocontrol systems will contribute substantially to the protection of human health, crops, and livestock and will decrease our overdependence on chemical pesticides. Attempts are being made to control mosquito populations, including those that serve as vectors for diseases like malaria. In one set of model experiments, *Ancylobacter aquaticus* was transformed with a plasmid containing genes that confer considerable toxicity to mosquito larvae (Yap et al. 1994). The mosquitocidal activity range of the recombinant indicates that it may be useful for the biological control of mosquitoes. Similarly, experiments are being conducted with recombinant viruses in efforts to control pest insect populations. Recombinant virus vaccines may be more effective, more easily produced, and more easily applied than traditional ones (Moss and Butler 1985).

Biological control has also been considered for preventing chestnut blight by using the phenomenon of transmissible hypovirulence in the chestnut blight fungus, *Cryphonectria parasitica* (Nuss 1992). The hypovirulence occurs when the fungal pathogen's virulence is attenuated by an endogenous viral RNA genetic element. Recent progress in the molecular characterization of a hypovirulence-associated viral RNA has provided an emerging view of the genetic organization and basic expression strategy of this class of genetic elements. Several lines of evidence now suggest that specific hypovirulence-associated virus-encoded gene products selectively modulate the expression of subsets of fungal genes and the activity of specific regulatory pathways. The construction of an infectious cDNA clone of a hypovirulence-associated viral RNA represents a major advancement that provides exciting new opportunities for examining the molecular basis of transmissible hypovirulence and for engineering hypovirulent strains for improved biocontrol.

Genetic engineering may also be able to move microbial genes coding for the biodegradation of a herbicide into a crop plant to make the plant resistant to a herbicide (Goodman and Newell 1985). In this way, an inherently nonselective herbicide could be made into a selective one.

# ADDITIONAL PRACTICAL
# CONSIDERATIONS

It should be pointed out that the development and use of microorganisms in controlling pest populations requires considerations that go well beyond simply finding a pathogen for a particular weed or animal pest population (Falcon 1976). There are questions of economics, production, quality control, application, side effects, and safety. In many cases, the economics of developing, producing, and applying microbial pesticides would not permit the commercial development of an otherwise promising biological control system. Many pathogens known to produce epizootics cannot presently be grown in the laboratory or do not produce infective stages when grown outside of host populations. Many protozoa, for example, do not produce infective spores or cysts when cultured on artificial media.

Large, stable batches of potential microbial pesticides must be produced and stockpiled for field application. Quality control must ensure that different batches of microbial pesticides have the same virulence, so that standard application rates may be used. The microorganisms must remain viable long enough to contact and establish widespread disease within the pest population. This is most readily accomplished using resistant stages, such as spores or cysts.

The effectiveness of the microbial pathogens must be carefully evaluated. It is difficult to achieve repeatable results with some candidate microbial pathogens. Environmental conditions must be taken into account, as these affect the virulence of microbial pesticides. Persistence must also be considered. Some candidate microorganisms have short survival times, whereas others persist for long periods. Persistence is required for long-term control of pest populations. Also, resistance of the target organism may develop. Coevolution can lead to avirulence depending on host density and the virulence of the pathogen (Knoll 1989).

Ideally, microbial pesticides should exhibit a high degree of host specificity. They should not cause diseases in nontarget populations. The host specificity, though, should not be so narrow as to preclude effectiveness against genetic variations within a pest population. In many cases, it is difficult to predict whether a microbial pesticide could establish disease in nontarget populations. It is impossible to test infectivity against all possible nontarget populations. Clearly, microbial pesticides should be harmless to humans and valued plant and animal populations (Kurstak 1978). Microbial pesticides are probably best used in an integrated program that employs management practices for agricultural crops and domestic animals that minimize opportunities for infection or interaction, along with limited applications of chemical pesticides, carefully timed for maximum effect (Worthy 1973). The use of chemical insecticides can be further minimized and their action can be made more specific when used in combination with insect pheromones. Pheromones are highly specific intraspecies chemical attractants that can be used to attract the target insect to the insecticide rather than to blanket the environment with the insecticidal compound (Silverstein 1981). Integrated pest control programs incorporate the described features and combine maximum effectiveness with minimal environmental disruption. The use of this approach is on the increase. Biological control systems of the traditional and of the genetically engineered types will undoubtedly play major roles in integrated pest control programs (Batra 1982).

## CHAPTER SUMMARY

The use of living organisms to control plant and animal diseases is called *biological control*. Biological control methods can augment the use of chemical pesticides in controlling pest populations. Biological control methods take advantage of amensal, predatory, and parasitic relationships that act to control populations in nature. Microorganisms, including viruses, bacteria, and fungi, have great potential for use in controlling populations of pest animals and weeds.

Host populations have natural defense mechanisms that defend against infection by pathogens and attack by pests, and it is possible to enhance these natural defense mechanisms to control disease. Plant and animal populations can be bred for resistance or rendered more resistant to infection by previous exposure to killed or attenuated microbial pathogens. Both cases represent an ecological change in that the ability of a pathogenic population to establish an antagonistic relationship with host populations is reduced.

Some outbreaks of plant and animal diseases can be controlled by reducing or removing the reservoirs of pathogenic microorganisms. Plants can be spaced farther apart to reduce the risk of transmitting infectious agents. Many animal populations are immunized to reduce the susceptible populations; by achieving herd immunity major epizootics can be avoided. A variety of disinfection and isolation procedures are used to reduce the reservoirs of pathogenic microorganisms. Control of vector populations can often prevent the transmission of pathogenic microbial populations to susceptible hosts. For some diseases, control is achieved by eliminating the populations of animals or plants that act as alternate hosts for the pathogens. Quarantine procedures are employed to limit the geographic distribution of pathogens and pests. These practices all are aimed at reducing the probability that healthy individuals will contact disease-causing microorganisms.

Amensalism is used to control various plant pathogenic fungi. Various bacteria and bacterial metabolites are used to control fungal pathogens of plants. Bacterial populations also can be controlled by amensalism. For example, agrocins, highly specific antibiotic-like substances, are used to control populations of *Agrobacterium* that cause crown gall. Parasitism is similarly used to control serious plant pathogenic fungi and other plant pests. Microbial pesticides are formulations of live microorganisms or microbial toxins that can kill pest populations. The ideal microbial pesticide should not be subject to attack by hyperparasites; should be virulent, causing disease in the pest population when applied at the recommended concentration; should not be sensitive to moderate environmental variations; should survive following application until infection within the pest population has been established; should rapidly establish disease in the pest populations so as to minimize destruction by the pest populations; should be rather specific for the pest population; and should not cause disease in nontarget populations.

A variety of microorganisms have been used or considered for use as microbial pesticides. Baculoviruses are perhaps the most studied insect viruses in this regard. Nuclear polyhedrosis viruses have been used for controlling various insect populations such as sawflies. A mixture of *Bacillus popilliae* and *B. lentimorbus* is used to control Japanese beetles. *Bacillus thuringiensis,* or BT, is probably the most widely used microbial pesticide. BT produces crystal toxins that are effective in killing a variety of pests, especially caterpillars that eat plants; gypsy moth control also has relied on BT as a microbial pesticide. Other potential microbial pesticides include the nematode-trapping fungi, which have been considered for control of a variety of pest nematodes, and various viruses that have been used to control rabbit populations.

Biotechnology has permitted the genetic engineering of new microbial pesticides, increasing the potential commercial applications of microbial pesticides.

Frost damage to plants can be prevented using genetically engineered ice-minus strains of *Pseudomonas syringae.* Molecular biology has permitted the introduction of the toxin genes from *B. thuringiensis* into other organisms, including plants and rhizosphere bacteria. Transgenic plants are being genetically engineered with increased resistances to plant pests. Care must be taken to maximize effectiveness and minimize undesirable side effects of such control measures. Additional research is needed to further advance the practical application of biological control of pests. Clearly, though, biotechnology and biological control will find appropriate safe and effective applications in integrated pest management programs.

---

# STUDY QUESTIONS

1. What is biological control? Describe its relationship to natural predation and parasitism. Describe its relationship to natural plant and animal diseases.

2. Why is biological control often preferable to the use of chemical pesticides?

3. What factors influence the use of microbial amensalism to control plant pests?

4. Describe some examples of how plant pathogenic fungi are controlled using amensalism.

5. Describe the uses of baculoviruses for controlling insect pests.

6. Describe the basis for using *Bacillus thuringiensis* as a biocontrol agent. What are the major limitations for using BT as a biological control agent?

7. How can genetic engineering be used to enhance the use of *Bacillus thuringiensis* and BT toxins in biological control?

8. How can nematode-trapping fungi be used for biological control? What limits their uses as biological control agents?

9. What is a microbial pesticide? Describe how Japanese beetles can be controlled using microbial pesticides.

10. How can frost damage to plants be controlled with *Pseudomonas syringae*? Why was the introduction of genetically engineered ice-minus strains of *P. syringae* controversial?

---

# REFERENCES AND SUGGESTED READINGS

Abel, P. P., R. S. Nelson, B. De, N. Hoffmann, S. G. Rogers, R. T. Fraley, and R. N. Beachy. 1986. Delay of disease development in transgenic plants that express the tobacco mosaic virus coat protein gene. *Science* 232:738–743.

Adams, L. F., C-L Liu, S. C. MacIntosh, and R. L. Starnes. 1996. Diversity and biological activity of *Bacillus thuringiensis*. In L. G. Copping (ed.). *Crop Protection Agents from Nature: Natural Products and Analogues.* SCI Royal Society of Chemistry, Cambridge, England, pp. 360–388.

Adang, M. J., E. Firoozabady, J. Klein, D. DeBaker, V. Sekar, J. D. Kemp, E. Murray, T. A. Rocheleau, K. Rashka, G. Staffeld, C. Stock, D. Sutton, and D. J . Merlo. 1987. Expression of a *Bacillus thuringiensis* insecticidal crystal protein gene in tobacco plants. In C.J. Arntzen and C. Ryan (eds.). *Molecular Strategies for Crop Protection.* Alan R. Liss, New York, pp. 345–353.

Andres, L. A., C. J. Davis, P. Harris, and A. J. Wapsphere. 1976. Biological control of weeds. In C. B. Huffaker and P. S. Messenger (eds.). *Theory and Practice of Biological Control.* Academic Press, New York, pp. 481–500.

Arntzen, C. J., and C. Ryan (eds.). 1987. *Molecular Strategies for Crop Protection.* Alan R. Liss, New York.

Aronson, A. I., W. Beckman, and P. Dunn. 1986. *Bacillus thuringiensis* and related insect pathogens. *Microbiological Reviews* 50:1–24.

Baker, K. F. 1980. Microbial antagonism: The potential for biological control. In D. C. Ellwood, J. N. Hedger, M. J. Latham, J. M. Lynch, and J. H. Slater (eds.). *Contemporary Microbial Ecology.* Academic Press, New York, pp. 327–347.

Baker, K. F., and R. J. Cook. 1974. *Biological Control of Plant Pathogens.* Freeman, San Francisco.

Batra, S.W.T. 1982. Biological control in agroecosystems. *Science* 215:134–139.

Beck, S. D., and F. G. Maxwell. 1976. Use of plant resistance. In C. B. Huffaker and P. S. Messenger (eds.). *Theory and Practice of Biological Control.* Academic Press, New York, pp. 615–636.

Bettiol, W. 1996. Biological control of plant pathogens in Brazil. *World Journal of Microbiology and Biotechnology* 12:505–510.

Bowers, W. S., H. C. Hock, P. H. Evans, and M. Katayama. 1986. Thallophytic allelopathy: Isolation and identification of laetisaric acid. *Science* 232:105–106.

Burges, H. D. (ed.). 1981. *Microbial Control of Pests and Plant Diseases 1970–1980.* Academic Press, New York.

Canaday, C. H. 1995. *Biological and Cultural Tests for Control of Plant Diseases.* American Phytopathological Society, St. Paul, MN.

Capalbo, D. M. 1995. *Bacillus thuringiensis:* Fermentation process and risk assessment. *Memorias do Instituto Oswaldo Cruz* 90:135–138.

Carlton, C. B. 1988. Development of genetically improved strains of *Bacillus thuringiensis.* In P. A. Hedrin, J. J. Menn, and R. Hollingworth (eds.). *Biotechnology of Plant Protection.* American Chemical Society, Washington, DC, pp. 261–279.

Carmichael, W. W., D. F. Biggs, and P. R. Gorham. 1975. Toxicology and pharmacological action of *Anabaena flos-aquae* toxin. *Science* 187:542–544.

Carrington, P. 1993. The gypsy, the fungus and the rain. *Natural Science* 8:18–21.

Charudattan, R. 1975. Use of plant pathogens for control of aquatic weeds. In A. W. Bourquin, D. G. Ahearn, and S. P. Myers (eds.). *Impact of the Use of Microorganisms on the Aquatic Environment.* EPA 660-3-75-001. U.S. Environmental Protection Agency, Corvallis, OR, pp. 127–146.

Chet, I. (ed.). 1987. *Innovative Approaches to Plant Disease Control.* Wiley, New York.

Chet, I. (ed.). 1993. *Biotechnology in Plant Disease Control.* Wiley-Liss, New York.

Chet, I., and J. Inbar. 1994. Biological control of fungal pathogens. *Applied Biochemistry and Biotechnology* 48:37–43.

Coppel, H. C., and J. W. Mertins. 1977. *Biological Insect Pest Suppression.* Springer-Verlag, Berlin.

Copping, L. G. (ed.). 1996. *Crop Protection Agents from Nature: Natural Products and Analogues.* SCI Royal Society of Chemistry, Cambridge, England.

Currier, T. C., and C. Gawron-Burke. 1990. Commercial development of *Bacillus thuringiensis* bioinsecticide products. In J. P. Nakas and C. Hagedorn (eds.). *Biotechnology of Plant-Microbe Interactions.* McGraw-Hill, New York, pp. 111–143.

David, W.A.L. 1975. The status of viruses pathogenic for insects and mites. *Annual Reviews of Entomology* 20:97–117.

Davis, D. E., K. Myers, and J. B. Hoy. 1975. Biological control among vertebrates. In C. B. Huffaker and P. S. Messenger (eds.). *Theory and Practice of Biological Control.* Academic Press, New York, pp. 501–520.

Deacon, J. W. 1983. *Microbial Control of Plant Pests and Disease.* Aspects of Microbiology No. 7. American Society for Microbiology, Washington, DC.

Drollette, D. 1996. Australia fends off critic of plan to eradicate rabbits. *Science* 272:191–192.

Dubos, B. 1984. Biocontrol of *Botrytis cinerea* on grapevines by an antagonist strain of *Trichoderma harzianum*. In M. J. Klug and C. A. Reddy (eds.). *Current Perspectives in Microbial Ecology.* American Society for Microbiology, Washington, DC, pp. 370–373.

Duke, S. O., H. K. Abbas, T. Amagasa, and T. Tanaka. 1996. Phytotoxins of microbial origin with potential for use as herbicides. In L. G. Copping (ed.). *Crop Protection Agents from Nature: Natural Products and Analogues.* SCI Royal Society of Chemistry, Cambridge, England, pp. 82–113.

Eren, J., and D. Pramer. 1978. Growth and activity of the nematode-trapping fungus *Arthrobotrys conoides* in soil. In M. W. Loutit and J.A.R. Miles (eds.). *Microbial Ecology.* Springer-Verlag, Berlin, pp. 121–127.

Falcon, L. A. 1971. Use of bacteria for microbial control of insects. In H. D. Burges and N. W. Hussey (eds.). *Microbial Control of Insects and Mites.* Academic Press, London, pp. 67–96.

Falcon, L. A. 1976. Problems associated with the use of arthropod viruses in pest control. *Annual Reviews of Entomology* 21:305–324.

Federici, B. A., and J. V. Maddox. 1996. Host specificity in microbe-insect interactions. *BioScience* 46:410–421.

Ferron, P. 1978. Biological control of insect pests by entomogenous fungi. *Annual Reviews of Entomology* 23:409–442.

Forst, S., and K. Nealson. 1996. Molecular biology of the symbiotic-pathogenic bacteria *Xenorhabdus* spp. and *Photorhabdus* spp. *Microbiological Reviews* 60:21–43.

Gaugler, R. R., and H. K. Kaya (eds.). 1990. *Entomopathogenic Neuratodes in Biological Control.* CRC Press, Boca Raton, FL.

Goodman, R. M., and N. Newell. 1985. Genetic engineering of plants for herbicide resistance: Status and prospects. In H. O. Halvorson, D. Pramer, and M. Rogul (eds.). *Engineered Organisms in the Environment: Scientific Issues.* American Society for Microbiology, Washington, DC, pp. 47–53.

Gronvold, J., J. Wolstrup, P. Nansen, S. A. Henriksen, M. Larsen, and J. Bresciani. 1993. Biological control of nematode parasites in cattle with nematode-trapping fungi: A survey of Danish studies. *Veterinary Parasitology* 48:311–325.

Gustafsson, M. 1971. Microbial control of aphids and scale insects. In H. D. Burges and N. W. Hussey (eds.). *Microbial Control of Insects and Mites.* Academic Press, London, pp. 375–384.

Halvorson, H. O., D. Pramer, and M. Rogul (eds.). 1985. *Engineered Organisms in the Environment: Scientific Issues.* American Society for Microbiology, Washington, DC.

Harman, G. E., and R. D. Lumsden. 1990. Biological disease control. In J. M. Lynch (ed.). *The Rhizosphere.* Wiley, New York, pp. 259–280.

Hasan, S. 1974. First introduction of a rust fungus in Australia for the biological control of skeleton weed. *Phytopathology* 64:253–254.

Hedrin, P. A., J. J. Menn, and R. M. Hollingworth (eds.). 1988. *Biotechnology of Plant Protection.* American Chemical Society, Washington, DC.

Henis, Y. 1983. Ecological principles of biocontrol of soilborne plant pathogens: *Trichoderma* model. In M. J. Klug and C. A. Reddy (eds.). *Current Perspectives in Microbial Ecology.* American Society for Microbiology, Washington, DC, pp. 353–361.

Henis, Y., and I. Chet. 1975. Microbial control of plant pathogens. *Advances in Applied Microbiology* 19:85–111.

Hofte, H., and H. Whiteley. 1989. Insecticidal crystal proteins of *Bacillus thuringiensis. Microbiological Reviews* 53:242–255.

Hokkanen, H.M.T., and J. M. Lynch. 1995. *Biological Control: Benefits and Risks.* Cambridge University Press, New York.

Holland, M. K., and R. J. Jackson. 1994. Virus-vectored immunocontraception for control of wild rabbits: Identification of target antigens and construction of recombinant viruses. *Reproduction, Fertility, and Development* 6:631–642.

Howell, C. R. 1990. Fungi as biological control agents. In J. P. Nakas and C. Hagedorn (eds.). *Biotechnology of Plant-Microbe Interactions.* McGraw-Hill, New York, pp. 257–317.

Huffaker, C. B., and P. S. Messenger (eds.). 1976. *Theory and Practice of Biological Control.* Academic Press, New York.

Hurley, J. M., L. A. Bulla, Jr., and R. E. Andrews, Jr. 1987. Purification of the mosquitocidal and cytolytic proteins of *Bacillus thuringiensis* subsp. *israelensis. Applied and Environmental Microbiology* 53:1316–1321.

Kerr, A., and M. E. Tate. 1984. Agrocins and the biological control of crown gall. *Microbiological Sciences* 1:1–4.

Kloepper, J. W. 1996. Host specificity in microbe-microbe interactions. *BioScience* 46:406–409.

Knolle, H. 1989. Host density and the evolution of parasite virulence. *Journal of Theoretical Biology* 136:199–207.

Krieg, A. 1971. Possible use of Rickettsiae for microbial control of insects. In H. D. Burges and N. W. Hussey (eds.). *Microbial Control of Insects and Mites.* Academic Press, London, pp. 173–180.

Kurstak, E. 1978. Viral and bacterial insecticides: Safety considerations. In M. W. Loutit and J.A.R. Miles (eds.). *Microbial Ecology.* Springer-Verlag, Berlin, pp. 265–268.

Laird, M. 1978. Microbial and integrated control of vectors of medical importance. In M. W. Loutit and J.A.R. Miles (eds.). *Microbial Ecology.* Springer-Verlag, Berlin, pp. 272–277.

Lindemann, J., and T. V. Suslow. 1987. Competition between ice nucleation active wild-type and ice nucleation deficient deletion mutant strains of *Pseudomonas syringae* and *P. fluorescens* biovar I and biological control of frost injury on strawberry blossoms. *Phytopathology* 77:882–886.

Lindow, S. E. 1983. The role of bacterial ice nucleation in frost injury to plants. *Annual Reviews of Phytopathology* 21:363–384.

Lindow, S. E. 1985. Ecology of *Pseudomonas syringae* relevant to the field use of Ice⁻ deletion mutants constructed *in vitro* for plant frost control. In H. O. Halvorson, D. Pramer, and M. Rogul (eds.). *Engineered Organisms in the Environment: Scientific Issues.* American Society for Microbiology, Washington, DC, pp. 23–35.

Lindow, S. E. 1987. Competitive exclusion of epiphytic bacteria by Ice⁻ mutants of *Pseudomonas syringae. Applied and Environmental Microbiology* 53:2520–2527.

Lindow, S. E. 1988a. Construction of isogenic Ice⁻ strains of *Pseudomonas syringae* for evaluation of specificity of competition on leaf surfaces. In F. Megusar and M. Gantar (eds.). *Microbial Ecology.* Slovene Society for Microbiology, Ljuvljana, Yugoslavia, pp. 509–515.

Lindow, S. 1988b. Lack of correlation of antibiosis in antagonism of ice nucleation active bacteria on leaf surfaces by non-ice nucleation active bacteria. *Phytopathology* 78:445–450.

Lindow, S. E. 1990. Use of genetically altered bacteria to achieve plant frost control. In J. P. Nakas and C. Hagedorn (eds.). *Biotechnology of Plant-Microbe Interactions.* McGraw-Hill, New York, pp. 85–110.

Lindow, S. E., and N. J. Panopoulos. 1988. Field tests of recombinant Ice⁻ *Pseudomonas syringae* for biological frost control in potato. In M. Sussman, C. H. Collins, and F. A. Skinner (eds.). *Proceedings of the First International Conference on Release of Genetically Engineered Microorganisms.* Academic Press, London, pp. 121–138.

Lipa, J. J. 1971. Microbial control of mites and ticks. In H. S. Burges and N. W. Hussey (eds.). *Microbial Control of Insects and Mites.* Academic Press, London, pp. 357–373.

Lockwood, J. L. 1979. Soil mycostasis: Concluding remarks. In B. Schippers and W. Gams (eds.). *Soilborne Plant Pathogens.* Academic Press, London, pp. 121–129.

Longworth, J. F., and J. Kalmakoff. 1978. An ecological approach to the use of insect pathogens for pest control. In M. W. Loutit and J.A.R. Miles (eds.). *Microbial Ecology.* Springer-Verlag, Berlin, pp. 269–271.

Maramorosch, K. 1991. *Biotechnology for Biological Control of Pests and Vectors.* CRC Press, Boca Raton, FL.

Masood, E. 1995. Rabbit virus threatens ecology after leaping the fence. *Nature* 378:531.

McEvoy, P. B. 1996. Host specificity and biological pest control. *BioScience* 46:401–405.

McLaughlin, R. E. 1971. Use of protozoans for microbial control of insects. In H. D. Burges and N. W. Hussey (eds.). *Microbial Control of Insects and Mites.* Academic Press, London, pp. 151–172.

Milewski, E. 1990. EPA regulations governing release of genetically engineered microorganisms. In J. P. Nakas and C. Hagedorn (eds.). *Biotechnology of Plant-Microbe Interactions.* McGraw-Hill, New York, pp. 319–340.

Moffat, A. S. 1991. Research on biological pest control moves ahead. *Science* 252:211–212.

Moore-Landecker, E. 1972. *Fundamentals of the Fungi.* Prentice Hall, Englewood Cliffs, NJ, pp. 103–105.

Morell, V. 1993. Australian pest control by virus causes concern. *Science* 261:683–684.

Moss, B., and M. L. Butler. 1985. *Vaccinia* virus vectors: Potential use as live recombinant virus vaccines. In H. O. Halvorson, D. Pramer, and M. Rogul (eds.). *Engineered Organisms in the Environment: Scientific Issues.* American Society for Microbiology, Washington, DC, pp. 36–39.

Nakas, J. P., and C. Hagedorn (eds.). 1990. *Biotechnology of Plant-Microbe Interactions.* McGraw-Hill, New York.

National Academy of Sciences. 1968. Plant-disease development and control. *Principles of Plant and Animal Pest Control.* Vol. I, Publication 1596. National Academy of Sciences, Washington, DC.

Nuss, D. L. 1992. Biological control of chestnut blight: An example of virus-mediated attenuation of fungal pathogenesis. *Microbiological Reviews* 56:561–576.

Onstad, D. W., and M. L. McManus. 1996. Risks of host range expansion by parasites of insects. *BioScience* 46:430–435.

O'Sullivan, D. J., and F. O'Gara. 1992. Traits of fluorescent *Pseudomonas* spp. involved in suppression of plant root pathogens. *Microbiological Reviews* 56:662–676.

Phatak, S. C., D. R. Sumner, H. D. Wells, D. K. Bell, and N. C. Glaze. 1983. Biological control of yellow nutsedge with the indigenous rust fungus *Puccinea caniculata. Science* 219:1446–1447.

Porter, A. G., E. W. Davidson, and J. W. Liu. 1993. Mosquitocidal toxins of bacilli and their genetic manipulation for effective biological control of mosquitoes. *Microbiological Reviews* 57:838–861.

Pramer, D. 1964. Nematode-trapping fungi. *Science* 144:382–388.

Pramer, D., and S. Al-Rabiai. 1973. Regulation of insect populations by protozoa and nematodes. *Annals of the New York Academy of Sciences* 217:85–92.

Raina, A. K., and J. R. Adams. 1995. Gonad-specific virus of corn earworm. *Nature* 374:770.

Roberts, D. W., and W. G. Yendol. 1971. Use of fungi for microbial control of insects. In H. D. Burges and N. W. Hussey (eds.). *Microbial Control of Insects and Mites.* Academic Press, London, pp. 125–150.

Robinson, A. J., and M. K. Holland. 1995. Testing the concept of virally vectored immunosterilisation for the control of wild rabbit and fox populations in Australia. *Australian Veterinary Journal* 72:65–68.

Rowe, G. E., and A. Margaritis. 1987. Bioprocess developments in the production of bioinsecticides of *Bacillus thuringiensis. CRC Critical Reviews in Biotechnology* 6:87–127.

Schroth, M. N., and J. G. Hancock. 1981. Selected topics in biological control. *Annual Reviews of Microbiology* 35:453–476.

Schroth, M. N., and J. G. Hancock. 1982. Disease suppressive soil and root-colonizing bacteria. *Science* 216:1376–1381.

Schroth, M. N., J. E. Loper, and D. C. Hildebrand. 1984. Bacteria as biocontrol agents of plant disease. In M. J. Klug and C. A. Reddy (eds.). *Current Perspectives in Microbial Ecology.* American Society for Microbiology, Washington, DC, pp. 362–369.

Secord, D., and P. Kareiva. 1996. Perils and pitfalls in the host specificity paradigm. *BioScience* 46:448–453.

Silverstein, R. M. 1981. Pheromones: Background and potential for use in insect pest control. *Science* 213:1326–1332.

Simmonds, F. J., J. M. Franz, and R. I. Sailer. 1976. History of biological control. In C. B. Huffaker and P. S. Messenger (eds.). *Theory and Practice of Biological Control.* Academic Press, New York, pp. 17–41.

Snyder, W. C., G. W. Wallis, and S. N. Smith. 1976. Biological control of plant pathogens. In C. B. Huffaker and P. S. Messenger (eds.). *Theory and Practice of Biological Control.* Academic Press, New York, pp. 521–542.

Stairs, G. R. 1971. Use of viruses for microbial control of insects. In H. D. Burges and N. W. Hussey (eds.). *Microbial Control of Insects and Mites.* Academic Press, London, pp. 97–124.

Stairs, G. R. 1972. Pathogenic microorganisms in the regulation of forest insect populations. *Annual Reviews of Entomology* 17:355–372.

Steinhaus, E. A. 1965. Diseases of invertebrates other than insects. *Bacteriological Reviews* 29:388–396.

Stewart, W.D.P., and M. J. Daft. 1977. Microbial pathogens of cyanophycean blooms. *Advances in Aquatic Microbiology* 1:177–218.

Strand, M. R., and J. J. Obrycki. 1996. Host specificity of insect parasitoids and predators. *BioScience* 46:422–429.

Strobel, G. A., and G. N. Lanier. 1981. Dutch elm disease. *Scientific American* 245(2):56–66.

Tapp, H., and G. Stotzky. 1995a. Insecticidal activity of the toxins from *Bacillus thuringiensis* subspecies *kurstaki* and *tenebrionis* adsorbed and bound on pure and soil clays. *Applied and Environmental Microbiology* 61:1786–1790.

Tapp, H., and G. Stotzky. 1995b. Dot blot enzyme-linked immunosorbent assay for monitoring the fate of insecticidal toxins from *Bacillus thuringiensis* in soil. *Applied and Environmental Microbiology* 61:602–609.

Tinsley, T. W. 1979. The potential of insect pathogenic viruses as pesticidal agents. *Annual Reviews of Entomology* 24:63–87.

Watrud, L. S., F. J. Perlak, M. T. Tran, K. Kusano, E. J. Mayer, M. A. Miller-Wiedeman, M. G. Obukowicz, D. R. Nelson, J. P. Kreitinger, and R. J. Kaufman. 1985. Cloning of *Bacillus thuringiensis* subsp. *kurstaki* delta endotoxin gene into *Pseudomonas fluorescens:* Molecular biology and ecology of an engineered microbial pesticide. In H. O. Halvorson, D. Pramer, and M. Rogul (eds.). *Engineered Organisms in the Environment: Scientific Issues.* American Society for Microbiology, Washington, DC, pp. 40–46.

Weiser, J., G. E. Bucher, and G. O. Poinas, Jr. 1976. Host relationships and utility of pathogens. In C. B. Huffaker and P. S. Messenger (eds.). *Theory and Practices of Biological Control.* Academic Press, New York, pp. 169–188.

Whipps, J. M., and J. M. Lynch. 1986. The influence of the rhizosphere on crop productivity. *Advances in Microbial Ecology* 9:187–244.

Wilson, C. L. 1969. Use of plant pathogens in weed control. *Annual Reviews of Phytopathology* 7:411–434.

Wilson, M., and S. E. Lindow. 1993. Release of recombinant microorganisms. *Annual Review of Microbiology* 47:913–944.

Woods, A. 1974. *Pest Control: A Survey.* Wiley, New York.

Worthy, W. 1973. Integrated insect control may alter pesticide use patterns. *Chemical Engineering News* 51:13–19.

Yamaguchi, I. 1996. Pesticides of microbial origin and applications of molecular biology. In L. G. Copping (ed.). *Crop Protection Agents from Nature: Natural Products and Analogues.* SCI Royal Society of Chemistry, Cambridge, England, pp. 20–49.

Yap, W. H., T. Thanabalu, and A. G. Porter. 1994. Expression of mosquitocidal toxin genes in a gas-vacuolated strain of *Ancylobacter acquaticus. Applied and Environmental Microbiology* 60:4199–4203.

Yu-Chan, C., S. L. Chen, and C-F. Li. 1996. Pest control by fluorescence. *Nature* 380:396.

Zettler, F. W., and T. E. Freeman. 1972. Plant pathogens as biocontrols of aquatic weeds. *Annual Reviews of Phytopathology* 10:455–470.

# GLOSSARY

**A horizon**   the uppermost layer of soil; topsoil.

**Abiotic**   the absence of living organisms.

**Absorption**   the uptaking, drinking in, or imbibing of a substance; the movement of substances into a cell; the transfer of substances from one medium to another, e.g., the dissolution of a gas in a liquid; the transfer of energy from electromagnetic waves to chemical bond and/or kinetic energy, e.g., the transfer of light energy to chlorophyll.

**Accessory pigments**   pigments including carote-noids and chlorophylls that harvest light energy and transfer it to the primary photosynthetic reaction centers; these pigments allow capture of light at different wavelengths.

**Acellular**   lacking cellular organization; not having a delimiting cytoplasmic membrane; organizational description of viruses, viroids, and prions.

**Acetylene reduction assay**   method for measuring rates of nitrogen fixation based on the conversion of acetylene to ethylene by nitrogenase, the enzyme responsible for nitrogen fixation.

**Acid mine drainage**   consequence of the metabolism of sulfur- and iron-oxidizing bacteria when coal mining exposes pyrite to atmospheric oxygen and the combination of autoxidation and microbial sulfur and iron oxidation produces large amounts of sulfuric acid, which kills aquatic life and contaminates water.

**Acidic**   a compound that releases hydrogen ($H^+$) ions when dissolved in water; a compound that yields positive ions upon dissolution; a solution with a pH value less than 7.0.

**Acidophiles**   microorganisms that show a preference for growth at low pH, e.g., bacteria that grow only at very low pH values, ca. 2.0.

**Acrasin**   a substance (3′,5′-cyclic AMP) secreted by a slime mold that initiates aggregation to form a fruiting body.

**Acridine orange direct count (AODC)**   a direct count method using the fluorescent dye acridine orange to stain bacterial cells; it detects total numbers of cells, both living and dead.

**Actinomycetes**   members of an order of bacteria in which species are characterized by the formation of branching and/or true filaments.

**Activated sludge process**   an aerobic secondary sewage treatment process using sewage sludge containing active complex populations of aerobic microorganisms to break down organic matter in sewage.

**Adaptation**   a structure or behavior that enhances survival and reproductive potential of an organism in an environment.

**Adhesins**   substances involved in the attachment or adherence of microorganisms to solid surfaces; factors that increase adsorption.

**Adhesion factors**   substances involved in the attachment of microorganisms to solid surfaces; factors that increase adsorption.

**Adsorption**   a surface phenomenon involving the retention of solid, liquid, or gaseous molecules at an interface.

**Aerated pile method**   method of composting for the decomposition of organic waste material where the wastes are heaped in piles and forced aeration provides oxygen.

**Aerobes**   microorganisms whose growth requires the presence of air or free oxygen.

**Aerobic**   having molecular oxygen present; growing in the presence of air.

**Aerosol**   a fine suspension of particles or liquid droplets sprayed into the air.

**Algae**   a heterogeneous group of eucaryotic, photosynthetic organisms, unicellular or multicellular but lacking true tissue differentiation.

**Algicides**   chemical agents that kill algae.

**Alkaline**   a condition in which hydroxyl ($OH^-$) ions are in abundance; solutions with a pH of greater than 7.0; basic.

**Allochthonous**   an organism or substance foreign to a given ecosystem.

**Amensalism**   an interactive association between two populations that is detrimental to one and does not adversely affect the other.

**Ammonification**   the release of ammonia from nitrogenous organic matter by microbial action.

**Anaerobes**   organisms that grow in the absence of air or oxygen; organisms that do not use molecular oxygen in respiration.

**Anaerobic**   the absence of oxygen; able to live or grow in the absence of free oxygen.

**Anaerobic digestor**   a secondary sewage treatment facility used for the degradation of sludge and solid waste.

**Anions**   negatively charged ions.

**Anoxic**   absence of oxygen; anaerobic.

**Anoxygenic photosynthesis**   photosynthesis that takes place in the absence of oxygen and during which oxygen is not produced; photosynthesis that does not split water and evolve oxygen.

**Anoxyphotobacteria (anaerobic photosynthetic bacteria)**   bacteria that have only photosystem I and do not evolve oxygen in the course of their photosynthesis. They live in anaerobic aquatic habitats that receive some light.

**Antagonism**   the inhibition, injury, or killing of one species of microorganism by another; an interpopulation relationship in which one population has a deleterious (negative) effect on another.

**Aquatic**   growing, living in, or frequenting water; a habitat composed primarily of water.

**Aquifer**   a geological formation containing water, such as subsurface water bodies that supply the water for wells and springs; a permeable layer of rock or soil that holds and transmits water.

**Arbuscules**   specialized inclusions in root cortex cells in the vesicular-arbuscular type of mycorrhizal association.

**Archaea (archaebacteria)**   procaryotes with cell walls that lack murein, having ether bonds in their membrane phospholipids; analysis of rRNA indicates that the Archaea represent a primary biological domain distinct from both Bacteria and Eucarya.

**Archaeal domain**   phylogenetic domain of microorganisms lacking a membrane-bounded nucleus (procaryotes) that have cytoplasmic membranes containing lipids with ether linkages and ribosomal RNAs distinct from organisms in other domains.

**Ascomycetes**   members of a class of fungi distinguished by the presence of an ascus, a saclike structure containing sexually produced ascospores.

**Asexual reproduction**   reproduction without union of gametes; formation of new individuals from a single individual.

**Assimilation**   the incorporation of nutrients into the biomass of an organism.

**Atmo-ecosphere**   that portion of the atmosphere in which living organisms are found and which is chemically transformed through the metabolism of organisms.

**Atmosphere (atm)**   the whole mass of air surrounding Earth; a unit of pressure approximating $1 \times 10^6$ dynes/cm$^2$.

**Autecology**   branch of ecology that examines individual organisms in relation to their environment, emphasizing the "self-properties" of an organism's physiological attributes.

**Autochthonous**   microorganisms and/or substances indigenous to a given ecosystem; the true inhabitants of an ecosystem; referring to the common microbiota of the body or soil microorganisms that tend to remain constant despite fluctuations in the quantity of fermentable organic matter.

**Autotrophs**   organisms whose growth and reproduction are independent of external sources of organic compounds, the required cellular carbon being supplied by the reduction of $CO_2$ and the needed cellular energy being supplied by the conversion of light energy to ATP or the oxidation of inorganic compounds to provide the free energy for the formation of ATP.

**Autoxidation**   the oxidation of a substance upon exposure to air.

**B horizon**   the soil layer beneath the A horizon, consisting of weathered material and minerals leached from the overlying soil.

**Bacteria**   members of a group of diverse and ubiquitous procaryotic, single-celled organisms; organisms with procaryotic cells, i.e., cells lacking a nucleus.

**Bacterial domain**   phylogenetic domain of microorganisms lacking a membrane-bounded nucleus (procaryotes) that have cytoplasmic membranes containing phospholipids and ribosomal RNAs distinct from organisms in other domains.

**Bactericidal**   any physical or chemical agent able to kill some types of bacteria.

**Bacteriochlorophyll (bacterialchlorophyll)**   photosynthetic pigment of green and purple anaerobic photosynthetic bacteria.

**Bacteriophage**   a virus whose host is a bacterium; a virus that replicates within bacterial cells.

**Bacteriostatic**   an agent that inhibits the growth and reproduction of some types of bacteria but need not kill the bacteria.

**Bacteroids**   irregularly shaped (pleomorphic) forms that some bacteria can assume under certain conditions, e.g., morphological forms of rhizobia found in root nodules.

**Barophiles**   organisms that grow best or grow only under conditions of high pressure, e.g., in the ocean's depths.

**Barotolerant**   organisms that can grow under conditions of high pressure but do not exhibit a preference for growth under such conditions.

**Basidiomycetes**   a group of fungi distinguished by the formation of sexual basidiospores on a basidium.

**Benthos**   the bottom region of aquatic habitats; collective term for the organisms living at the bottom of oceans and lakes.

**Beta-oxidation (β-oxidation)**   metabolic pathway for the oxidation of fatty acids resulting in the formation of acetate and a new fatty acid that is two carbon atoms shorter than the parent fatty acid.

**Biocide**   an agent that kills microorganisms.

**Biodegradable**   a substance that can be broken down into smaller molecules by microorganisms.

**Biodegradation**   the process of chemical breakdown of a substance to smaller molecules caused by microorganisms or their enzymes.

**Biodeterioration**   the chemical or physical alteration of a product that decreases the usefulness of that product for its intended purpose.

**Biodisc system**   a secondary sewage treatment system employing a film of active microorganisms rotated on a disc through sewage.

**Biofilm**   a microbial community occurring on a surface as a microlayer.

**Biofilter**   a device used for the bioremediation of air pollutants consisting of an immobilized microbial community as a biofilm through which air is passed to detoxify contaminants.

**Biogas**   gas produced by anaerobic microorganisms, primarily methane.

**Biogenic element**   an element that is incorporated into the biomass of living organisms.

**Biogeochemical cycling**   the biologically mediated transformations of elements that result in their global cycling, including transfer between the atmosphere, hydrosphere, and lithosphere.

**Bioleaching**   the use of microorganisms to transform elements so that the elements can be extracted from a material when water is filtered through it.

**Biological control**   the deliberate use of one species of organism to control or eliminate populations of other organisms; used in the control of pest populations.

**Biological oxygen demand (BOD)**   the amount of dissolved oxygen required by aerobic and facultative microorganisms to stabilize organic matter in sewage or water; also known as biochemical oxygen demand.

**Bioluminescence**   the generation of light by certain microorganisms; proteins called luciferins are converted in the presence of oxygen to oxyluciferins by luciferase with the liberation of light.

**Biomagnification**   an increase in the concentration of a chemical substance, such as a pesticide, as the substance is passed to higher members of a food chain.

**Biomass**   the dry weight, volume, or other quantitative estimation of organisms; the total mass of living organisms in an ecosystem.

**Bioremediation**   the use of biological agents to reclaim soils and waters polluted by substances hazardous to human health and/or the environment; it is an extension of biological treatment processes that have traditionally been used to treat wastes in which microorganisms typically are used to biodegrade environmental pollutants.

**Bioscrubber**   a device in which air moves through a fine spray or a microbial suspension in order to remove pollutants from the air.

**Biosensor**   an immunological or genetic method of detecting chemicals or microbial activities, e.g., based on the emission of light or electrical detection.

**Biosphere**   the part of Earth in which life can exist; all living things together with their environment.

**Biosurfactant**   a surface active agent produced by microorganisms.

**Biotic**   of or relating to living organisms, caused by living things.

**Biotower**   a device similar to a trickling filter that employs a biofilm through which air is passed to remove pollutants.

**Bioturbation** mixing caused by movement of living organisms, responsible in part for the aeration of soils and sediments.

**Black smoker** a geothermal eruption occurring in deep-sea regions that emits metal- and sulfide-rich waters that form black metal precipitates.

**Blight** any plant disease or injury that results in general withering and death of the plant without rotting.

**Bloom** a visible abundance of microorganisms, generally referring to the excessive growth of algae or cyanobacteria at the surface of a body of water.

**Bottle effect** growth of microorganisms within a collection vessel that results in artificially elevated microbial counts.

**Breakpoint chlorination** procedure for the removal and oxidation of ammonia from sewage to molecular nitrogen by the addition of hypochlorous acid.

**$C_0t_{1/2}$** a measure of genetic diversity given as the initial concentration of single-stranded DNA multiplied by the time it takes for half of the single-stranded DNA to reanneal to form double-stranded DNA.

**C horizon** the soil layer beneath the B horizon consisting of the broken or partially decomposed underlying bedrock.

**Calvin cycle** the primary pathway for carbon dioxide fixation (conversion of carbon dioxide to organic matter) in photoautotrophs and chemolithotrophs.

**Cankers** plant diseases, or conditions of those diseases, that interfere with the translocation of water and minerals to the crown of the plant.

**Carbon cycle** the biogeochemical cycling of carbon through oxidized and reduced forms, primarily between organic compounds and inorganic carbon dioxide.

**Carrying capacity** the largest population that a habitat can support.

**Catabolic pathway** a degradative metabolic pathway; a metabolic pathway in which large molecules are broken down into smaller ones.

**Cations** positively charged ions.

**Cellulase** an extracellular enzyme that hydrolyzes cellulose.

**Cellulose** a linear polysaccharide of $\beta$-D-glucose.

**Chelator** a substance that binds metallic ions.

**Chemical oxygen demand (COD)** the amount of oxygen required to oxidize completely the organic matter in a water sample.

**Chemoautotrophs** microorganisms that obtain energy from the oxidation of inorganic compounds and carbon from inorganic carbon dioxide; organisms that obtain energy through chemical oxidation and use inorganic compounds as electron donors; also known as chemolithotrophs.

**Chemocline** a boundary layer in an aquatic habitat formed by a difference in chemical composition, such as a halocline formed in the oceans by differing salt concentrations.

**Chemolithotrophs** microorganisms that obtain energy through chemical oxidation and use inorganic compounds as electron donors and cellular carbon through the reduction of carbon dioxide; also known as chemoautotrophs.

**Chemoorganotrophs** organisms that obtain energy from the oxidation of organic compounds and cellular carbon from preformed organic compounds.

**Chemostat** an apparatus used for continuous-flow culture to maintain bacterial cultures in a selected phase of growth, based on maintaining a continuous supply of a solution containing a nutrient in limiting quantities that controls the growth rate of the culture.

**Chemotaxis** a locomotive response in which the stimulus is a chemical concentration gradient; movement of microorganisms toward or away from a chemical stimulus.

**Chitin** a polysaccharide composed of repeating *N*-acetylglucosamine residues that is abundant in arthropod exoskeletons and fungal cell walls.

**Chloramination** the use of chloramines to disinfect water.

**Chlorination** the process of treating with chlorine, as in disinfecting drinking water or sewage.

**Chlorophycophyta** green algae; may be unicellular, colonial, or filamentous; most cells are uninucleate; some form coenocytic filaments, contain contractile vacuoles, or store starch as reserve material; their cell walls are composed of cellulose, mannans, xylans, or protein.

**Chlorophyll** the green pigment responsible for photosynthesis in plants; the primary photosynthetic pigment of algae and cyanobacteria.

**Chlorosis** the yellowing of leaves and/or plant components due to the bleaching of chlorophyll, often symptomatic of microbial disease.

**Chytrids** members of the Chytridiales, which are mainly aquatic fungi that produce zoospores with a single posterior flagellum.

**Ciliophora** members of one subphylum of protozoa that possess simple to compound ciliary organelles in at least one stage of their life cycle; these protozoa are motile by means of cilia.

**Circadian rhythms** daily cyclical changes that occur in an organism even when it is isolated from the natural daily fluctuations of the environment.

**Climax community** the organisms present at the end-point of an ecological succession series.

**Coliforms** gram-negative, lactose-fermenting, enteric rods, e.g., *Escherichia coli.*

**Colonization** the establishment of a site of microbial reproduction on a material, animal, or person without necessarily resulting in tissue invasion or damage.

**Colony** the macroscopically visible growth of microorganisms on a solid culture medium.

**Colony-forming units (CFUs)** number of microbes that can replicate to form colonies, as determined by the number of colonies that develop.

**Colony hybridization** hybridization that is combined with conventional plating procedures in which bacterial colonies or phage plaques are transferred directly onto hybridization filters; the colonies or phage containing plaques are then lysed by alkaline or enzymatic treatment, after which hybridization is conducted.

**Cometabolism** the gratuitous metabolic transformation of a substance by a microorganism growing on another substrate; the cometabolized substance is not incorporated into an organism's biomass, and the organism does not derive energy from the transformation of that substance.

**Commensalism** an interactive association between two populations of different species living together in which one population benefits from the association, and the other is not affected.

**Community** highest biological unit in an ecological hierarchy composed of interacting populations.

**Compensation depth** the depth of an aquatic habitat at which photosynthetic activity balances respiratory activity; in lakes, the depth of effective light penetration, separating the limnetic and profundal zones.

**Competition** an interactive association between two species, both of which need some limited environmental factor for growth and thus grow at suboptimal rates because they must share the growth-limiting resource.

**Competitive exclusion principle** the statement that competitive interactions tend to bring about the ecological separation of closely related populations and preclude two populations from occupying the same ecological niche.

**Competitive inhibition** the inhibition of enzyme activity caused by the competition of an inhibitor with a substrate for the active (catalytic) site on the enzyme; impairment of the function of an enzyme due to its reaction with a substance chemically related to its normal substrate.

**Composting** the decomposition of organic matter in a heap by microorganisms; a method of solid waste disposal.

**Concentration gradient** condition established by the difference in concentration on opposite sides of a membrane.

**Consortium** an interactive association between microorganisms that generally results in combined metabolic activities.

**Coprophagous** capable of growth on fecal matter; feeding on dung or excrement.

**Corrosion** the eating away of a metal resulting from changes in the oxidative state.

**Crenarchaeota** kingdom of archaea consisting of extreme thermophiles.

**Crop rotation** the alternation of the types of crops planted in a field.

**Cross-feeding** the phenomenon that occurs when two organisms mutually complement each other in terms of nutritional factors or catabolic enzymes related to substrate utilizations; also termed syntrophism.

**Crown gall** plant disease caused by *Agrobacterium tumefaciens,* which infects fruit trees, sugar beets, and other broad-leafed plants, manifested by the formation of a tumor growth.

**Culture** to encourage the growth of particular microorganisms under controlled conditions; the growth of particular types of microorganisms on or within a medium as a result of inoculation and incubation.

**Cyanobacteria** procaryotic, photosynthetic organisms containing chlorophyll a, capable of producing oxygen by splitting water; formerly known as blue-green algae.

**Cyst** a dormant form assumed by some microorganisms during specific stages in their life cycles, or assumed as a response to particular environmental conditions in which the organism becomes enclosed in a thin- or thick-walled membranous structure, the function of which is either protective or reproductive.

**Decomposers** organisms, often bacteria or fungi, in a community that convert dead organic matter into inorganic nutrients.

**Dendrograms** graphic representations of taxonomic analyses, showing the relationships between the organisms examined.

**Denitrification** the formation of gaseous nitrogen or gaseous nitrogen oxides from nitrate or nitrite by microorganisms.

**Desert** a region of low rainfall; a dry region; a region of low biological productivity.

**Desiccation** removal of water; drying.

**Desulfurization** removal of sulfur from organic compounds.

**Detergent** a synthetic cleaning agent containing surface-active agents that do not precipitate in hard water; a surface-active agent having a hydrophilic and a hydrophobic portion.

**Detrital food chain** a food chain based on the biomass of decomposers rather than on that of primary producers.

**Detritivore** an organism that feeds on detritus; an organism that feeds on organic wastes and dead organisms.

**Detritus** waste matter and biomass produced from decompositional processes.

**Diatomaceous earth** a silicaceous material composed largely of fossil diatoms, used in microbiological filters and industrial processes.

**Diatoms** unicellular algae having a cell wall composed of silica, the skeleton of which persists after the death of the organism.

**Dinoflagellates** algae of the class Pyrrhophyta, primarily unicellular marine organisms, possessing two unequal flagella.

**Direct counting procedures** methods for the enumeration of bacteria and other microbes that do not require the growth of cells in culture but rather rely upon direct observation or other detection methods by which the undivided microbial cells can be counted.

**Direct viability count** a direct microscopic assay that determines whether or not microorganisms are metabolically active, i.e., viable.

**Diversity** the heterogeneity of a system; the variety of different types of organisms occurring together in a biological community.

**Diversity index** a mathematical measure that describes the species richness and apportionment of species within the community.

**Domestic sewage** household liquid wastes.

**Dormant** an organism or a spore that exhibits minimal physical and chemical change over an extended period of time but remains alive.

**Dot blot** a hybridization technique in which a small amount of DNA (dot of DNA) is transferred to a solid support (blotted on the support) and then detected using a labeled probe.

**Dwarfism** plant condition resulting from degradation or inactivation of plant growth substances by microorganisms.

**Ecological balance** the totality of the interactions of organisms within an ecosystem that describes the stable relationships among populations and environmental quality.

**Ecological niche** the functional role of an organism within an ecosystem; the combined description of the physical habitat, functional role, and interactions of the microorganisms occurring at a given location.

**Ecological succession** a sequence in which one ecosystem is replaced by another within a habitat until an ecosystem that is best adapted is established.

**Ecology** the study of the interrelationships between organisms and their environments.

**Ecosystem** a functional self-supporting system that includes the organisms in a natural community and their environment.

**Ectomycorrhizae** a stable, mutually beneficial (symbiotic) association between a fungus and the root of a plant where the fungal hyphae occur outside the root and between the cortical cells of the root.

**Effluent** the liquid discharge from sewage treatment and industrial plants.

**$E_h$ (redox potential)** measure of the tendency of a given system to donate electrons (i.e., to act as a reducing agent) or to accept electrons (i.e., to act as an oxidizing agent); the $E_h$ of a given system (measured as volts) may be determined by measuring the electrical potential difference between that system and a standard hydrogen electrode whose potential is, by convention, arbitrarily taken to be zero volts.

**Endomycorrhizae** mycorrhizal association in which there is fungal penetration of plant root cells.

**Endophytic** a photosynthetic organism living within another organism.

**Endospores** thick-walled spores formed within a parent cell; in bacteria, heat-resistant spores.

**Endosymbiotic** a symbiotic (mutually dependent) association in which one organism penetrates and lives within the cells or tissues of another organism.

**Endosymbiotic evolution** theory that bacteria living as endosymbionts within eucaryotic cells gradually evolved into organelle structures.

**Enrichment culture** any form of culture in a liquid medium that results in an increase in a given type of organism while minimizing the growth of any other organism present.

**Enteric bacteria** bacteria that live within the intestinal tract of mammals.

**Entomogenous fungi** fungi living on insects; fungal pathogens of insects.

**Enumeration** determination of the number of microorganisms.

**Enzyme-linked immunosorbent assay (ELISA)** a technique used for detecting and quantifying specific serum antibodies based on tagging the antigen-antibody complex with a substrate that can be enzymatically converted to a readily quantifiable product by a specific enzyme.

**Epilimnion** the warm layer of an aquatic environment above the thermocline.

**Epiphytes** organisms growing on the surface of a photosynthetic organism, e.g., bacteria growing on the surface of an algal cell.

**Epizootic** an epidemic outbreak of infectious disease among animals other than humans.

**Equitability** the measure of the proportion of individuals among the species present.

**Erosion** breakdown of material from the earth's crust by various physical and chemical processes.

**Estuary** a water passage where the ocean tide meets a river current; an arm of the sea at the lower end of a river.

**Eubacteria** procaryotes other than archaebacteria.

**Eucaryal domain** phylogenetic domain containing organisms having a unit membrane-bound (true) nucleus and usually other organelles.

**Eucaryotes** cellular organisms having a membrane-bound nucleus within which the genome of the cell is stored as chromosomes composed of DNA; eucaryotic organisms include algae, fungi, protozoa, plants, and animals.

**Euglenophycophyta** unicellular division of algae that contain chlorophylls a and b and appear green, lack a cell wall, and are surrounded by a pellicle; they store paramylon as reserve material and reproduce by longitudinal division; they are widely distributed in aquatic and soil habitats.

**Euphotic** the top layer of water, through which sufficient light penetrates to support the growth of photosynthetic organisms.

**Eurythermal** microorganisms that grow over a wide range of temperatures.

**Eutrophic** containing high nutrient concentrations, such as a eutrophic lake with a high phosphate concentration that will support excessive algal blooms.

**Eutrophication** the enrichment of natural waters with inorganic materials, especially nitrogen and phosphorus compounds, that support the excessive growth of photosynthetic organisms.

**Evenness** a description of the distribution of microbial populations within a community based on the apportionment of individuals and species.

**Evolution** the directional process of change of organisms by which descendants become distinct in form and/or function from their ancestors.

**Extreme environments** environments characterized by extremes in growth conditions, including temperature, salinity, pH, and water availability, among others.

**Extreme thermophiles** organisms having an optimum growth temperature above 80°C.

**Fastidious** an organism with stringent physiological requirements for growth and survival; an organism difficult to isolate or culture on ordinary media because of its need for special nutritional factors.

**Floc** a mass of microorganisms cemented together in a slime produced by certain bacteria, usually found in waste treatment plants.

**Flocculate** to aggregate or clump together individual, tiny particles into small clumps or clusters.

**Food web** an interrelationship among organisms in which energy is transferred from one organism to another; each organism consumes the preceding one and in turn is eaten by the next higher member in the sequence.

**Freshwater habitats** lakes, ponds, swamps, springs, streams, and rivers.

**Fruiting bodies** specialized microbial structures that bear sexually or asexually derived spores.

**Frustules** the silicaceous cell walls of a diatom.

**Fungal gardens** fungi grown in pure culture by insects.

**Fungi** a group of diverse, unicellular and multicellular eucaryotic organisms, lacking chlorophyll, often filamentous and spore-producing.

**Fungicides** agents that kill fungi.

**Fungistasis** the active prevention or hindrance of fungal growth by a chemical or physical agent.

**Galls** abnormal plant structures formed in response to parasitic attack by certain insects or microorganisms; tumorlike growths on plants in response to an infection.

**Genetic engineering** the deliberate modification of the genetic properties of an organism by the application of recombinant DNA technology.

**Germ-free animal** an animal without microbiota; all of its surfaces and tissues are sterile, and it is maintained in that condition by being housed and fed in a sterile environment.

**Gnotobiotic** culture or environment containing only defined forms of life.

**Grazers** organisms that prey upon primary producers; protozoan predators that consume bacteria indiscriminately; filter-feeding zooplankton.

**Greenhouse effect** rise in the concentration of atmospheric $CO_2$ and a resulting warming of global temperatures.

**Gross primary production**   total amount of organic matter produced in an ecosystem.

**Groundwater**   subsurface water in terrestrial environments.

**Growth rate**   increase in the number of microorganisms per unit of time.

**Guild**   populations within a community which use the same resources.

**Habitat**   a location where living organisms occur.

**Halophiles**   organisms requiring NaCl for growth; extreme halophiles grow in concentrated brines.

**Herbicides**   chemicals used to kill weeds.

**Heterocysts**   cells that occur in the trichomes of some filamentous cyanobacteria that are the sites of nitrogen fixation.

**Heterotrophs**   organisms requiring organic compounds for growth and reproduction; the organic compounds serve as sources of carbon and energy.

**Holdfast**   a structure that allows certain algae and bacteria to remain attached to the substratum.

**Host**   a cell or an organism that acts as the habitat for the growth of another organism; the cell or organism upon or in which parasitic organisms live.

**Hot springs**   thermal springs with a temperature greater than 37°C.

**Humic acids**   high-molecular-weight irregular organic polymers with acidic character; the portion of soil organic matter soluble in alkali but not in acid.

**Humus**   the organic portion of the soil remaining after microbial decomposition.

**Hydrosphere**   the aqueous envelope of Earth, including bodies of water and aqueous vapor in the atmosphere.

**Hydrostatic pressure**   pressure exerted by the weight of a water column; it increases approximately 1 atm with every 10 m in depth.

**Hyperparasite**   a parasite of a parasite.

**Hyperthermophiles**   organisms having an optimum growth temperature above 80°C; some grow best at 110°C.

**Hypolimnion**   the deeper, colder layer of an aquatic environment; the water layer below the thermocline.

**Immobilization**   the binding of a substance so that it is no longer reactive or able to circulate freely.

*In situ*   in the natural location or environment.

*In vitro*   in glass; a process or reaction carried out in a culture dish or test tube.

*In vivo*   within the living organism.

**Indicator organism**   an organism used to identify a particular condition, such as *Escherichia coli* as an indicator of fecal contamination.

**Indigenous**   native to a particular habitat.

**Insecticides**   substances destructive to insects; chemicals used to control insect populations.

**Ionizing radiation**   radiation, such as gamma and X-radiation, that forms toxic free radicals disruptive to the biochemical organization of cells.

**Kelp**   brown algae with vegetative structures consisting of a holdfast, stem, and blade that form large macroscopic structures.

**Landfarming (landtreatment)**   the application of toxic organic wastes to soils for the purpose of biodegradation.

**Landfill**   a site where solid waste is dumped and allowed to decompose; a process in which solid waste containing both organic and inorganic material is deposited and covered with soil.

**Landtreatment (landfarming)**   the application of toxic organic wastes to soils for the purpose of biodegradation.

**Leach**   to wash or extract soluble constituents from insoluble materials.

**Leguminous crop**   plants belonging to the *Leguminosae* which have a seed pod divided into two parts or valves.

**Lichens**   a large group of composite organisms consisting of a fungus in symbiotic association with an alga or a cyanobacterium.

**Lignin**   a class of complex polymers in the woody material of higher plants, second in abundance only to cellulose.

**Limnetic zone**   in lakes, the portion of the water column excluding the littoral zone where primary productivity exceeds respiration.

**Liquid wastes**   waste material in liquid form, the result of agricultural, industrial, and all other human activities.

**Lithosphere**   the solid part of Earth.

**Lithotrophs**   microorganisms that live in and obtain energy from the oxidation of inorganic matter; chemoautotrophs.

**Littoral**   situated or growing on or near the shore; the region between the high and low tide marks.

**Magnetotaxis**   motility directed by a geomagnetic field.

**Manganese nodules**   nodules (round, irregular mineral masses) produced in part by microbial oxidation of bivalent manganese oxides.

**Marine**   of or relating to the oceans.

**Mesophiles**   organisms whose optimum growth is in the temperature range of 20–45°C.

**Methanogens**   methane-producing procaryotes; a group of archaea capable of reducing carbon dioxide or low-molecular-weight fatty acids to produce methane.

**Methylation**   the process of substituting a methyl group for a hydrogen atom.

**Microbial ecology**   the field of study that examines the interactions of microorganisms with their biotic and abiotic surroundings.

**Microbial mining**   a mineral recovery method that uses bioleaching to recover metals from ores not suitable for direct smelting.

**Microbial pesticides**   preparations of pathogenic or predatory microorganisms that are antagonistic toward a particular pest population.

**Microbiology**   the study of microorganisms and their activities.

**Microbiota**   the totality of microorganisms associated with a given environment.

**Microorganisms**   microscopic organisms, including algae, bacteria, fungi, protozoa, and viruses.

**Mildew**   any of a variety of plant diseases in which the mycelium of the parasitic fungus is visible on the affected plant; biodeterioration of food or fabric due to fungal growth.

**Mineralization**   the microbial breakdown of organic materials into inorganic materials brought about mainly by microorganisms.

**Mixotrophs**   organisms capable of utilizing both autotrophic and heterotrophic metabolic processes, e.g., the concomitant use of organic compounds as sources of carbon and light as a source of energy.

**Most probable number (MPN)**   a method for determination of viable organisms using statistical analyses and successive dilution of the sample to reach a point of extinction.

**Mutualism**   a stable condition in which two organisms of different species live in close physical association, each organism deriving some benefit from the association; symbiosis.

**Mycangia**   see mycetangia.

**Mycelia**   the interwoven mass of discrete fungal hyphae.

**Mycetangia**   specialized pocketlike invaginations of fungus-cultivating insects for storage of mycelial inoculum.

**Mycobiont**   the fungal partner in a lichen.

**Mycorrhizae**   a stable, symbiotic association between a fungus and the root of a plant; the term also refers to the root-fungus structure itself.

**Necrosis**   the pathological death of a cell or group of cells in contact with living cells.

**Net primary production**   amount of organic carbon in the form of biomass and soluble metabolites available for heterotrophic consumers in terrestrial and aquatic habitats.

**Neuston**   the layer of organisms growing at the interface between air and water.

**Neutralism**   the relationship between two different microbial populations characterized by the lack of any recognizable interaction.

**Niche**   the functional role of an organism within an ecosystem; the combined description of the physical habitat, functional role, and interactions of the microorganisms occurring at a given location.

**Nitrification**   the process in which ammonia is oxidized to nitrite and nitrite to nitrate; a process primarily carried out by the strictly aerobic, chemolithotrophic bacteria of the family Nitrobacteraceae.

**Nitrifying bacteria**   Nitrobacteraceae; gram-negative, obligately aerobic, chemolithotrophic bacteria occurring in aquatic environments and in soil that oxidize ammonia to nitrite or nitrite to nitrate.

**Nitrite ammonification**   reduction of nitrite to ammonium ions by bacteria; does not remove nitrogen from the soil.

**Nitrogen fixation**   the reduction of gaseous nitrogen to ammonia, carried out by certain procaryotes.

**Nitrogenase**   the enzyme that catalyzes biological nitrogen fixation.

**Nodules**   tumorlike growths formed by plants in response to infections with specific bacteria within which the infecting bacteria fix atmospheric nitrogen; a rounded, irregularly shaped mineral mass.

**No tillage farming**   a type of soil management involving elimination of plowing, retention of crop residues as mulch cover, and planting done with drill seeding machines.

**Numerical taxonomy**   a system that uses overall degrees of similarity and large numbers of characteristics to determine the taxonomic position of an organism; allows organisms of unknown affiliation to be identified as members of established taxa.

**O horizon**   the organic layer of soil, consisting of humic substances.

**Obligate aerobes**   organisms that grow only under aerobic conditions, i.e., in the presence of air or oxygen.

**Obligate anaerobes**   organisms that cannot use molecular oxygen; organisms that grow only under anaerobic conditions, i.e., in the absence of air or oxygen; organisms that cannot carry out respiratory metabolism.

**Obligate intracellular parasites**   organisms that can live and reproduce only within the cells of other organisms, such as viruses, all of which must find suitable host cells for their replication.

**Obligate thermophiles**   organisms restricted to growth at high temperatures.

**Oligotrophic**   lakes and other bodies of water that are poor in those nutrients that support the growth of aerobic, photosynthetic organisms; microorganisms that grow at very low nutrient concentrations.

**Optimal growth temperature**   the temperature at which microbes exhibit the maximal growth rate.

**Optimal oxygen concentration**   the oxygen concentration at which microbes exhibit the maximal growth rate with maximal product yield.

**Osmophiles**   organisms that grow best or only in or on media of relatively high osmotic pressure.

**Osmotic pressure**   the force resulting from differences in solute concentrations on opposite sides of a semipermeable membrane.

**Osmotolerant**   organisms that can withstand high osmotic pressures and grow in solutions of high solute concentrations.

**Oxidation pond**   a method of aerobic waste disposal employing biodegradation by aerobic and facultative microorganisms growing in a standing water body.

**Oxidation-reduction potential**   a measure of the tendency of a given oxidation-reduction system to donate electrons, i.e., to behave as a reducing agent, or to accept electrons, i.e., to act as an oxidizing agent; determined by measuring the electrical potential difference between the given system and a standard reference system.

**Oxygen tension**   concentration of oxygen in water.

**Ozonation**   the killing of microorganisms by exposure to ozone.

**P/R ratio**   the relationship between gross photosynthesis and rate of community respiration.

**Paralytic shellfish**   poisoning caused by toxins produced by the dinoflagellate *Gonyaulax,* which concentrates in shellfish such as oysters and clams.

**Parasites**   organisms that live on or in the tissues of another living organism, the host, from which they derive their nutrients.

**Parasitism**   an interactive relationship between two organisms or populations in which one is harmed and the other benefits; generally, the population that benefits, the parasite, is smaller than the population that is harmed.

**Pathogens**   organisms capable of causing disease in animals, plants, or microorganisms.

**Pelagic zone**   the portion of the marine environment beyond the edge of the continental shelf, comprising the entire water column but excluding the sea floor.

**Pest**   a population that is an annoyance for economic, health, or aesthetic reasons.

**Pesticides**   substances destructive to pests, especially insects.

**pH**   the symbol used to express the hydrogen ion concentration, signifying the logarithm to the base 10 of the reciprocal of the hydrogen ion concentration.

**Photoautotrophs**   organisms whose source of energy is light and whose source of carbon is carbon dioxide; characteristic of plants, algae, and some procaryotes.

**Photoheterotrophs**   organisms that obtain energy from light but require exogenous organic compounds for growth.

**Photolysis**   liberation of oxygen by splitting of water during photosynthesis.

**Photosynthesis**   the process in which radiant (light) energy is absorbed by specialized pigments of a cell and is subsequently converted to chemical energy; the ATP formed in the light reactions is used to drive the fixation of carbon dioxide, with the production of organic matter.

**Photosynthetic membranes**   specialized membranes in photosynthetic bacteria that are the anatomical sites where light energy is converted to chemical energy in the form of ATP during photosynthesis.

**Photosystem I**   cyclic photophosphorylation; photosynthetic system for generating a protonmotive force which does not require an external electron donor and does not generate reduced coenzyme.

**Photosystem II**   noncyclic photophosphorylation; photosynthetic system for generating a protonmotive force which requires an external electron donor and generates reduced coenzyme.

**Phototaxis**   the ability of bacteria to detect and respond to differences in light intensity, moving toward or away from light.

**Phototrophs**   organisms whose sole or principal primary source of energy is light; organisms capable of photophosphorylation.

**Phycobiont**   the algal partner of a lichen.

**Phytoplankton** passively floating or weakly motile photosynthetic aquatic organisms, primarily cyanobacteria and algae.

**Phytoplankton food chain** a food chain in aquatic habitats based on the consumption of primary producers.

**Plankton** collectively, all microorganisms and invertebrates that passively drift in lakes and oceans.

**Plasmid** an independent self-replicating DNA molecule, which compared to a bacterial chromosome carries relatively few genes which are not essential for survival under nonselective growth conditions.

**Plate counting** method of estimating numbers of microorganisms by diluting samples, culturing on solid media, and counting the colonies that develop to estimate the number of viable microorganisms in the sample.

**Pollutants** materials that contaminate air, soil, or water; substances—often harmful—that foul water or soil, reducing their purity and usefulness.

**Predation** a mode of life in which food is primarily obtained by killing and consuming animals; an interaction between organisms in which one benefits and one is harmed, based on the ingestion of the smaller organism, the prey, by the larger organism, the predator.

**Predators** organisms that practice predation.

**Preemptive colonization** alteration of environmental conditions by pioneer organisms in a way that discourages further succession.

**Prey** an animal taken by a predator for food.

**Primary producers** organisms capable of converting carbon dioxide to organic carbon, including photoautotrophs and chemoautotrophs.

**Primary sewage treatment** the removal of suspended solids from sewage by physical settling in tanks or basins.

**Prions** infectious proteins; substances that are infectious and reproduce within living systems but appear to be proteinaceous, based on degradation by proteases, and to lack nucleic acids based on resistance to digestion by nucleases.

**Profundal zone** in lakes, the portion of the water column where respiration exceeds primary productivity.

**Proto-cooperation** synergism; a nonobligatory relationship between two microbial populations in which both populations benefit.

**Protonmotive force** potential chemical energy in a gradient of protons and electrical energy across the membrane.

**Protozoa** diverse eucaryotic, typically unicellular, nonphotosynthetic microorganisms generally lacking a rigid cell wall.

**Psychrophile** an organism that has an optimum growth temperature below 20°C.

**Psychrotroph** a mesophile that can grow at low temperatures.

**Pure culture** a culture that contains cells of one kind; the progeny of a single cell.

**Putrefaction** the microbial breakdown of protein under anaerobic conditions.

**Pyrite** a common mineral containing iron disulfite.

**Recalcitrant** a chemical that is totally resistant to microbial attack.

**Red tides** aquatic phenomenon caused by toxic blooms of *Gonyaulax* and other dinoflagellates that color the water and kill invertebrate organisms; the toxins concentrate in the tissues of filter-feeding molluscs, causing food poisoning.

**Reporter gene** a gene whose expression is easily detected and that can be used to track the transcription of other genes, e.g., the *lux* gene that codes for light production and can be used to detect the expression of other genes.

**Resistant crop varieties** species of agricultural plants that are not susceptible to particular plant pathogens.

**Rhizosphere** an ecological niche that comprises the surfaces of plant roots and the region of the surrounding soil in which the microbial populations are affected by the presence of the roots.

**Rhizosphere effect** evidence of the direct influence of plant roots on bacteria, demonstrated by the fact that microbial populations usually are higher within the rhizosphere (the region directly influenced by plant roots) than in root-free soil.

**Rotating biological contactor** see biodisc system.

**Rots** plant diseases characterized by the breakdown of tissue caused by any of a variety of fungi or bacteria.

**Rusts** plant diseases caused by fungi of the order Uredinales, so called because of the rust-colored spores formed by many of the causal agents on the surfaces of the infected plants.

**Salt lake** a landlocked water body with a high salt concentration often approaching saturation.

**Sanitary landfill** a method for disposal of solid wastes in low-lying areas; the deposited wastes are covered with a layer of soil each day.

**Sarcodina** a major taxonomic group of protozoa characterized by the formation of pseudopodia.

**Secondary sewage treatment** the treatment of the liquid portion of sewage containing dissolved organic matter, using microorganisms to degrade the organic matter that is mineralized or converted to removable solids.

**Self-purification**    inherent capability of natural waters to cleanse themselves of pollutants based on biogeochemical cycling activities and interpopulation relationships of indigenous microbial populations.

**Septic tank**    a simple anaerobic treatment system for waste water where residual solids settle to the bottom of the tank and the clarified effluent is distributed over a leaching field.

**Seston**    all material, both organic and inorganic, suspended in a waterway; all the fine particulate matter which drifts passively in lakes, seas and other bodies of water, including living organisms.

**Sewage**    the refuse liquids or waste matter carried by sewers.

**Sewage treatment**    the treatment of sewage to reduce its biological oxygen demand and to inactivate the pathogenic microorganisms present.

**Sludge**    the solid portion of sewage.

**Smuts**    plant diseases caused by fungi of the order Ustilaginales; typically involve the formation of masses of dark-colored teliospores on or within the tissues of the host plant.

**Soil horizon**    a layer of soil distinguished from layers above and below by characteristic physical and chemical properties.

**Solfatara**    hot, sulfur-rich environment; a volcanic area or vent which yields sulphur vapors, steam, and the like.

**Solid waste**    refuse; waste material composed of both inert materials—glass, plastic, and metal—and decomposable organic wastes, including paper and kitchen scraps.

**Southern blot**    a hybridization technique, named after Edward Southern, who invented the process in order to analyze fragments of DNA in which DNA fragments that have been separated by electrophoresis are transferred to nitrocellulose sheets for detection with labeled gene probes.

**Sparge**    to pass a gas through a solution.

**Stenohaline**    organism unable to withstand wide variation in salinity and which is restricted to growth at a specific salt concentration.

**Stenothermophiles**    microorganisms that grow only at temperatures near their optimal growth temperature.

**Stenotolerant**    highly specialized and therefore having a narrow tolerance for a specific growth factor.

**Succession**    the replacement of populations by other populations better adapted to fill the ecological niche.

**Sulfur cycle**    biogeochemical cycle mediated by microorganisms that changes the oxidation state of sulfur within various compounds.

**Symbiosis**    an obligatory interactive association between members of two populations, producing a stable condition in which the two organisms live together in close physical proximity to their mutual advantage.

**Symbiotic nitrogen fixation**    fixation of atmospheric nitrogen by bacteria living in mutually dependent associations with plants.

**Synergism**    in antibiotic action, when two or more antibiotics are acting together, the production of inhibitory effects on a given organism that are greater than the additive effects of those antibiotics acting independently; an interactive but nonobligatory association between two populations in which each population benefits.

**Syntrophism**    the phenomenon that occurs when two organisms mutually complement each other in terms of nutritional factors or catabolic enzymes related to substrate utilization; also termed cross-feeding.

**Temperature growth range**    the range between the maximum and minimum temperatures at which a microorganism can grow.

**Tertiary recovery of petroleum**    the use of biological and chemical means to enhance oil recovery.

**Tertiary sewage treatment**    a sewage treatment process that follows a secondary process, aimed at removing non-biodegradable organic pollutants and mineral nutrients.

**Thermal stratification**    division of temperate lakes into an epilimnion, thermocline, and hypolimnion, subject to seasonal change; zonation of lakes based on temperature where warm and cold water masses do not mix.

**Thermal vents**    hot areas located at depths of 800–1000 m on the sea floor, where spreading allows seawater to percolate deeply into the crust and react with hot core materials; life around the vents is supported energetically by the chemoautotrophic oxidation of reduced sulfur.

**Thermocline**    zone of water characterized by a rapid decrease in temperature, with little mixing of water across it.

**Thermophiles**    organisms having an optimum growth temperature above 40°C.

**Tolerance range**    the range of a parameter, such as temperature, over which microorganisms survive.

**Transposons**    translocatable genetic elements; genetic elements that move from one locus to another by non-homologous recombination, allowing them to move around a genome.

**Trickling filter system** a simple, film-flow aerobic sewage treatment system; the sewage is distributed over a porous bed coated with bacterial growth that mineralizes the dissolved organic nutrients.

**Trophic level** the position of an organism or population within a food web: primary producer, grazer, predator, etc.

**Trophic structure** the collection of steps in the transfer of energy stored in organic compounds from one to another.

**Trophozoite** a vegetative or feeding stage in the life cycle of certain protozoa.

**Turbidity** cloudiness or opacity of a suspension.

**Turbidostat** a system in which an optical sensing device measures the turbidity of the culture in a growth vessel and generates an electrical signal that regulates the flow of fresh medium into the vessel and the release of spent medium and cells.

**Ultraviolet light (UV)** short wavelength electromagnetic radiation in the range 100–400 nm.

**Vectors** organisms that act as carriers of pathogens and are involved in the spread of disease from one individual to another.

**Vesicular-arbuscular mycorrhizae** a common type of mycorrhizae characterized by the formation of vesicles and arbuscules.

**Viable nonculturable microorganism** microorganisms that do not grow in viable culture methods, but which are still metabolically active and capable of causing infections in animals and plants.

**Viable plate count** method for the enumeration of bacteria whereby serial dilutions of a suspension of bacteria are plated onto a suitable solid growth medium, the plates are incubated, and the number of colony-forming units is counted.

**Viroids** the causal agents of certain diseases, resembling viruses in many ways but differing in their apparent lack of a virus-like structural organization and their resistance to a wide variety of treatments to which viruses are sensitive; naked infective RNA.

**Virus** a noncellular entity that consists minimally of protein and nucleic acid and that can replicate only after entry into specific types of living cells; it has no intrinsic metabolism, and its replication is dependent on the direction of cellular metabolism by the viral genome; within the host cell, viral components are synthesized separately and are assembled intracellularly to form mature, infectious viruses.

**Visible light** radiation in the wavelength range of 400–800 nm that is required for photosynthesis but can be lethal to some nonphotosynthetic microorganisms.

**Volatile organic chemical (VOC)** organic compound that vaporizes into the atmosphere.

**Water activity ($a_w$)** a measure of the amount of reactive water available, equivalent to the relative humidity; the percentage of water saturation of the atmosphere.

**Wilts** plant diseases characterized by a reduction in host tissue turgidity, commonly affecting the vascular system.

**Windrow method** a slow composting process that requires turning and covering with soil or compost.

**Xenobiotic** a synthetic product not formed by natural biosynthetic processes; a foreign substance or poison.

**Xerotolerant** able to withstand dryness; an organism capable of growth at low water activity.

**Yeasts** a category of fungi defined in terms of morphological and physiological criteria; typically, unicellular, saprophytic organisms that characteristically ferment a range of carbohydrates and in which asexual reproduction occurs by budding.

**Zymogenous** term used to describe opportunistic soil microorganisms that grow rapidly on exogenous substrates.

# INDEX